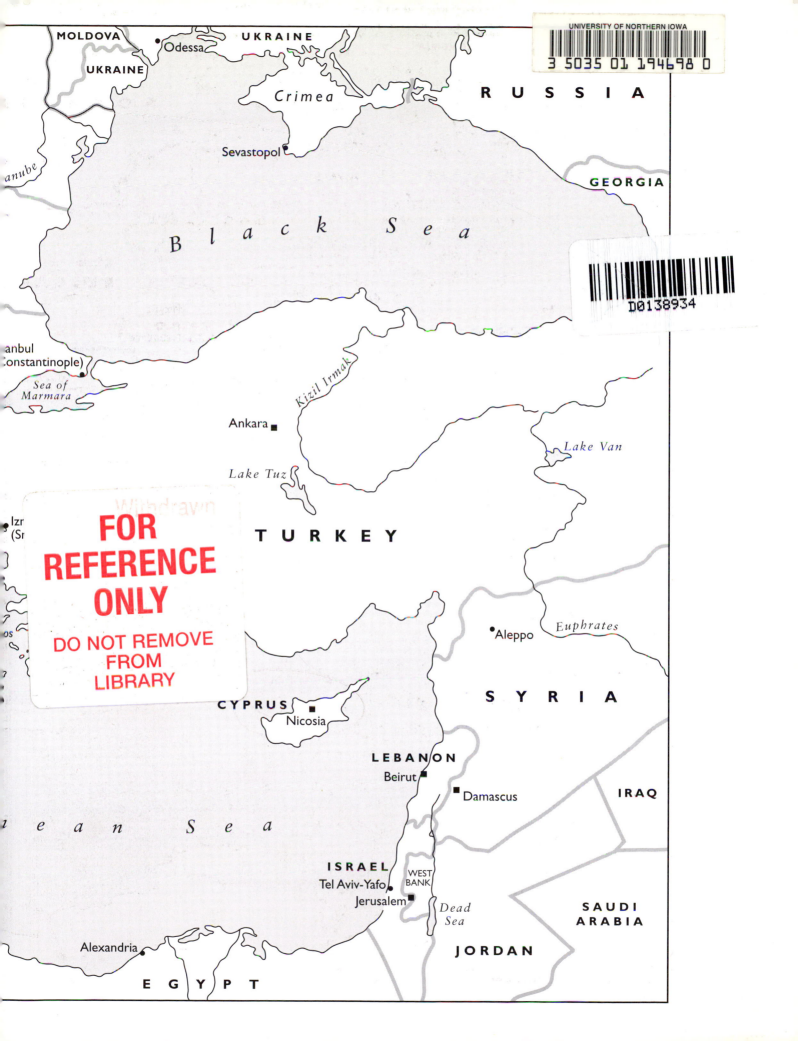

MOLDOVA

UKRAINE

Odessa

UKRAINE

Crimea

RUSSIA

Sevastopol

GEORGIA

Danube

B l a c k   S e a

Istanbul
(Constantinople)

*Sea of
Marmara*

Kizil Irmak

Ankara

Lake Van

Lake Tuz

Izmir
(Smyrna)

T U R K E Y

Euphrates

Aleppo

CYPRUS

Nicosia

S Y R I A

ean Sea

LEBANON

Beirut

Damascus

IRAQ

ISRAEL

WEST
BANK

Tel Aviv-Yafo

Jerusalem

*Dead
Sea*

SAUDI
ARABIA

Alexandria

JORDAN

E G Y P T

ENCYCLOPEDIA OF
GREECE
AND THE
HELLENIC
TRADITION

Volume I

ENCYCLOPEDIA OF
GREECE
AND THE
HELLENIC
TRADITION

Volume 1
A–K

Editor
GRAHAM SPEAKE

FITZROY DEARBORN PUBLISHERS
LONDON • CHICAGO

Copyright © 2000 by
FITZROY DEARBORN PUBLISHERS

FITZROY DEARBORN PUBLISHERS
919 North Michigan Avenue, Suite 760
Chicago, Illinois 60611
USA

or

310 Regent Street
London W1B 3AX
England

British Library and Library of Congress Cataloguing in Publication Data are available

ISBN 1–57958–141–2

First published in the USA and UK 2000

Typeset by Lorraine Hodghton, Radlett, Herts, UK
Printed and bound by Butler and Tanner Ltd, Frome and London

Cover design by Philip Lewis

Cover illustrations:
vol. 1: Alexander the Great: portrait bust in marble, sculptor unknown,
        Graeco–Roman Museum, Alexandria.
vol. 2: Alexander the Great: mural by Theophilos (1868–1934),
        Museum of Greek Folk Art, Athens, reproduced by permission of
        the Greek Ministry of Culture Archaeological Receipts Fund.

CONTENTS

MAPS AND SITE PLANS

EDITOR'S NOTE

This is first and foremost a book about Greece. But what do we mean by Greece? Is it that remote fairyland of myth and legend ruled by unruly demigods such as Theseus and Agamemnon? Or is it the (much closer to home) source of democracy, reason, fair play, and all the values that we think of today as forming the basis of "our" so-called Western civilization? Do we mean the homeland of Alexander the Great, that most successful general and most romantic hero of all time, who extended his conquests as far as Central Asia? Or is it rather the fatherland of Aristotle Onassis, doyen of 20th-century shipowners, who was born in Asia Minor and was a man of the world if ever there was one? Do we regard Greece as the heart of an empire that touched most of the shores of the Mediterranean and beyond, or as one of the less conspicuous members of NATO or the European Union? Does it put us in mind of dreaming columns in the sunset at Sunium, or of icons and incense on Mount Athos, of *Zorba the Greek*, or the gay clubs of Mykonos? Greece is all these things, and more. They are all the subject-matter of this book.

Secondly it is a book about the Greeks. But who are the Greeks? This question has been debated by scholars for centuries, and the debate continues to this day. For the purposes of this book, we take the Greeks to be all those who speak or spoke the Greek language.

Thirdly, and just as important, it is a book about the Hellenic tradition. We are all of us, whether we like it or not, participants in a tradition, or more likely several traditions. The Hellenic tradition is the cultural tradition in which all Greeks, all Greek-speaking people, participate. Its manifestations are legion and they take different forms at different times. Some of these exhibit a clear thread of continuity throughout the three and a half millennia of Greek history; others, perhaps the majority, come and go, shining brightly for a while before disappearing, but later perhaps resurfacing. The most obvious vehicles of cultural transmission are language and (at least for the last two millennia) religion; but this book will demonstrate that there have been many others, less conspicuous but equally effective, at work in the process.

It will have become clear already that this is not a book about the Hellenic tradition in global terms. It is not about the influence that Hellenism has exerted on other cultures and other peoples. It is restricted to the history and culture of the Greeks themselves, though such restrictions do not preclude (indeed they demand) a global dimension: the Hellenic tradition today is spread far and wide and is just as vibrant in Toronto and Melbourne, and in London and Johannesburg, as it is in Corfu and Nicosia. Even Constantinople, once the queen of cities and Greek-speaking hub of a multi-ethnic empire, later the ultimate but ultimately unattainable goal of the Great Idea, now the home of a tiny and ever-dwindling minority, is still the seat of the Ecumenical Patriarchate to which all Eastern Orthodox Churches owe allegiance.

These then are the cultural boundaries of the book: Greece and the Greeks for the 3500 years of their recorded history. But the syllabus would not be comprehensive without the inclusion of certain extramural topics. Thus there are articles on many of the peoples who have impinged on Greek history and have made significant contributions to the development of Greek culture. In each case the article focuses on the nature of that contribution and the period of that people's interaction with the Greeks, not on the history of the people as a whole. Similarly, articles concerned with places outside the Greek heartlands concentrate primarily on the time during which they were relevant to Greek culture, not their entire history. And there are a few (very few actually) articles about individuals who were not Greeks at all but who are remembered for the contribution that they themselves made to Greece (Hadrian, Mehmet II, Byron, to name but three). In all categories hard decisions had to be made about selection. The result is inevitably a compromise, but we hope at least a representative one.

In addition to the articles on people and places there are thematic articles which attempt to trace the manifestations of the theme concerned throughout the span of Greek history. Again there will be exceptions, because certain themes apply only to particular periods in time; but wherever practicable, the attempt has been made to demonstrate the continuities in Greek culture across the centuries.

Finally there are two extended series of articles. Those devoted to the political history of Greece are easily found because they follow on sequentially under "Political History". These articles are, for reasons of convenience and practicality, divided into the normally recognized periods (though elsewhere in the book there is a conscious effort to avoid periodization). Complementing them is a second series of articles devoted to the cultural history of those same periods; but these are scattered through the book according to the name by which they are most usually known. Thus, after articles on Prehistory, Minoans, and Mycenaeans, there follow Dark Age, Geometric, Archaic, Classical, Hellenistic, Roman, Byzantine (Early, Middle, and Late), Latin Empire, Venetokratia, Ottoman, and Modern Period.

Every article is equipped with a number of suggestions for further reading on the subject. Wherever possible, these are easily accessible sources in major European languages. Cross-referencing between articles has been kept to a minimum in view of the lists of articles at the start of the book and the index at the end; but in general it operates in the direction from the particular to the general.

Acknowledgements

This book was my idea; but a great many people have devoted time and expertise to making it happen. On the academic side, the headword list was compiled with the generous assistance of a distinguished panel of advisers who are listed on p.ix. A vast army of expert contributors from every continent responded with enthusiasm and scholarly acumen to a challenging brief. It has been an enormous privilege for me to work with them. If this book fills a gap in the reference library, it does so only because of their willingness to participate in it. Their efforts fill me in equal measure with gratitude and humility.

On the practical side, maps were compiled by Olive Pearson and site plans by Tom Willcockson, and pictures were researched by Linda Proud. Editorial management and a sense of order were imposed by Carol Jones and, in the final year of the project, by Jonathan Dore, who worked with great dedication to see it through to completion. Delia Gaze, Kara Hattersley-Smith, and Lucilla Watson edited the manuscript; David Edmonds read the proofs; and Christine Headley made the index. I am more grateful than I can say to all of them. But my greatest public debt is to Daniel Kirkpatrick, Managing Director of Fitzroy Dearborn, who was bold enough to commission the project in the first place and has been the most hard-working and the most unassuming member of the team ever since.

This is no place to acknowledge my private debts. The people involved already know who they are, though only I know just how much I owe them. This book is for them. But it is also for all other Hellenists, Hellenes, and Philhellenes everywhere. What has impressed me more than anything about Greece in compiling this book is its astonishing capacity for survival and regeneration. No matter how devastating the catastrophe – from whatever it was that destroyed the civilizations of the Bronze Age to the Asia Minor disaster of 1922 – Greece will always rise again. The tradition is unsinkable. There is something inspiring about that.

GRAHAM SPEAKE
Feast of St Gregory Palamas
26 March 2000

ADVISERS

Sir John Boardman
Anthony Bryer
David Buckton
Dimitri Conomos
John Haldon
Elizabeth Jeffreys

Bishop Kallistos of Diokleia
Paschalis Kitromilides
Robert Parker
James Pettifer
Malcolm Wagstaff
Nigel Wilson

CONTRIBUTORS

Maria Anastasopoulou
Michael J. Anderson
Dimiter G. Angelov
Roxane Argyropoulos
I.N. Arnaoutoglou
Rhiannon Ash
David Asheri
Gabriella-Evangelia Aspraki
Nina Athanassoglou-Kallmyer
Michel Austin
Ivars Avotins
Balbina Bäbler
Robin L.N. Barber
John W. Barker
Eleni Bastéa
Lesley A. Beaumont
Hans Beck
Peter Bien
Scott Blanchette
E. Kerr Borthwick
Emmanuel C. Bourbouhakis
Steven B. Bowman
Julian M.C. Bowsher
Michael J. Boyd
David Braund
Sebastian Brock
Maria Brosius

C.G. Brown
Christopher G. Brown
Anthony A.M. Bryer
John Buckler
David Buckton
Stephanie Lynn Budin
J.K. Campbell
Costa Carras
Jeffrey Carson
Craige Champion
Catheryn Cheal
Peter D. Chimbos
Charalampos Chotzakoglou
Paul Christesen
John Chryssavgis
Diskin Clay
Thomas M. Conley
David Connolly
Dimitri Conomos
Stephanos Constantinides
Maria Constantoudaki
Robin Cormack
Mark A. Coumounduros
Nigel B. Crowther
Mary B. Cunningham
Virginia M. da Costa
Andrew Dalby

Ken Dark
Lila de Chaves-Chronopoulos
Kyriacos Demetriou
Eleanor Dickey
Gert-Jan van Dijk
John Dillery
Kenneth Dover
Nektarios Drosos
D.J. Edmonds
Mark Edwards
Michael J. Edwards
Constantinos Ehaliotis
Rennos Ehaliotis
Sarah Ekdawi
Andrew W. Erskine
J.D.G. Evans
James Allan Evans
Don Evely
Nicholas Fennell
Eugénie Fernandes
Barbara Fiedler
Elizabeth A. Fisher
K.E. Fleming
A. Foley
Clive Foss
Elizabeth French
William H.C. Frend
Chrysanthi Gallou
George K. Gantzias
Katerina Gardikas
Robert Garland
Martin Garrett
Zaga Gavrilović
Ioannis Georganas
David W.J. Gill
Michael Given
Dimitrios Gkamas
Erik Goldstein
René Gothóni
Basil C. Gounaris
Daniel W. Graham
Mark W. Graham
G.B. Greatrex
Molly Greene
Richard P.H. Greenfield
Maarten J. Grond
Michael Grünbart
Jonathan M. Hall
Wendy C. Hamblet
Victor Davis Hanson
Lorna Hardwick
Gelina Harlaftis
Anthea Harris
Jonathan Harris
Thomas Harrison
J.F.W. Hendrikx
Martin Henig
Paul Hetherington
Thomas Hidber
Michael D. Higgins

Martin Hinterberger
C.A. Hoffman
Gail Holst-Warhaft
David Holton
Katerina Ierodiakonou
Johannes Irmscher
Elizabeth M. Jeffreys
Michael Jeffreys
Fred W. Jenkins
Edward Johnson
Jane Jurgens
Walter E. Kaegi
Dimitris A. Kalogeras
Demetris I. Kamaras
Lambros Kamperidis
Celia Kapsomera
Vassos Karageorghis
George E. Karamanolis
Andromache Karanika-Dimarogona
Patricia Karlin-Hayter
Manolis Kartsonakis
Aglaia Kasdagli
George Kazamias
Antony G. Keen
Georgia Kefalas
Frangiska Kefallonitou
Jennifer Y.T. Kennedy
Ewald Kislinger
Kenneth F. Kitchell
Cynthia K. Kosso
Katerina Krikos-Davis
Eric Kyllo
Michael Lambrou
Kenneth D.S. Lapatin
Kostas A. Lavdas
George Lemos
Jon van Leuven
J.H.W.G. Liebeschuetz
Alexander Lingas
A.R. Littlewood
Dimitrios Livanios
Michael Llewellyn Smith
Peter Lock
Andrew Louth
John Lowden
Marianne McDonald
Roger T. Macfarlane
John A. McGuckin
Vasilios Makrides
Chryssa A. Maltezou
Evangelos Mantzaris
M.E. Martin
Hugh J. Mason
Richard A.E. Mason
Elaine Matthews
Kenneth Mayer
Theano Michailidou
Sophie Mills
Valsamis Mitsilegas
Nicoletta Momigliano

J.R. Morgan
M. James Moscovich
Konstantinos P. Moustakas
Charles L. Murison
Heinz-Günther Nesselrath
Ann M. Nicgorski
Efthymios Nicolaidis
Ioanna A. Nicolaidou
Steven M. Oberhelman
Graham Oliver
T.G. Otte
Neni Panourgiá
Charalambos K. Papastathis
Robert Shannan Peckham
Robert J. Penella
Jacqueline Petropoulos
Nicholas Petsalis-Diomidis
James Pettifer
Irene Philippaki-Warburton
Marcus Plested
Anthony J. Podlecki
Judith Powell
Panayiota Pyla
Oliver Rackham
Claudia Rapp
Steve Reece
E.E. Rice
John M. Riddle
Maria Roumbalou
T.T.B. Ryder
Yanis Saitas
Daniel C. Scavone
Albert Schachter
Ulf Scharrer
Constantina Scourtis
John F. Shean
Andrew N. Sherwood
Kathleen Donahue Sherwood
Franziska E. Shlosser
David Sider
James L. Siebach
Lucas Siorvanes
John E. Sisko
Andrew Smith
Dion C. Smythe
Eleni Sotiriu
Christina Souyoudzoglou-Haywood
Graham Speake

Susan Spencer
Efrossini Spentzou
Konstantinos Staikos
Astrid Steiner-Weber
Paul Stephenson
Charles Stewart
P.J. Stylianou
D.A. Sykes
Anestis T. Symeonides
Barbara Syrrakos
Anna Tabaki
Veronica Tatton-Brown
John E. Thorburn
Lara G. Tohme
R.A. Tomlinson
Shaun Tougher
Sevasti Trubeta
Gocha R. Tsetskhladze
Despina Tsourka-Papastathi
David R. Turner
Matthew R.H. Uttley
Thanos M. Veremis
Susannah Verney
George N. Vlahakis
Heinrich von Staden
Cornelis de Waal
Peter Walcot
Richard Wallace
Kallistos Ware
A.J.L. Waskey, Jr
Alexandra-Kyriaki Wassiliou
Pamela A. Webb
D.P.M. Weerakkody
Linda Welters
Stephanie West
Mary Whitby
Katherine V. Wills
Nigel Wilson
David Winfield
T.J. Winnifrith
Timothy F. Winters
Roger D. Woodard
Hugh Wybrew
Naoko Yamagata
Stelios Zachariou
Barbara Zeitler
Eleni Zim

ALPHABETICAL LIST OF ENTRIES

THEMATIC LIST OF ENTRIES

Entries by Category

EVENTS

*c.*1270 BC	Trojan War	1878	Berlin, Treaty of
499–479 BC	Persian Wars	1897	Graeco-Turkish War
490 BC	Marathon, Battle of	1912–13	Balkan Wars
431–404 BC	Peloponnesian War	1914–18	World War I
338 BC	Chaeronea, Battle of	1920	Sèvres, Treaty of
168 BC	Pydna	1922	Asia Minor Campaign and Disaster
146 BC	Corinth, Sack of		
636	Yarmuk, Battle of	1923	Lausanne, Treaty of
1071	Manzikert, Battle of	1939–45	World War II
1204	Constantinople, Sack of	1945–49	Civil War
1259	Pelagonia, Battle of	1967–74	Junta
1453	Constantinople, Fall of	1981	European Community and European Union
1669	Candia, Fall of		
1821–32	Independence, War of		

PERIODS

Prehistory
Minoans
Mycenaeans
Dark Age
Geometric Period
Archaic Period

Classical Period
Hellenistic Period
Roman Period
Byzantine Period, Early
Byzantine Period, Middle
Latin Empire

Venetokratia
Byzantine Period, Late
Ottoman Period
   (Tourkokratia)
Modern Period

CITIES, ISLANDS, LAKES, MONASTIC FOUNDATIONS, MOUNTAINS

Acragas
Adrianople
Aegae
Aegina
Alexandria
Amalfi
Ambelakia
Amphipolis
Ani
Antioch
Aphrodisias
Argos
Arta
Athens
Athos, Mount
Beirut
Carthage
Catana
Chalcis
Chersonesus
Chios
Constantinople
Copais, Lake
Corfu
Corinth
Cos
Crete
Cyclades
Cyprus

Cyrene
Cythera
Delos
Delphi
Dodecanese
Dodona
Dyrrachium
Eleusis
Ephesus
Epidaurus
Eretria
Euboea
Florina
Gaza
Gortyn
Halicarnassus
Hydra
Ioannina
Ionian Islands
Jerusalem
Kalamata
Kastoria
Kavalla
Knossos
Larissa
Laurium
Lebadea
Lemnos
Lesbos

Mallia
Mar Saba
Massilia
Megalopolis
Megara
Melos
Messene
Meteora
Miletus
Missolonghi
Mistra
Monemvasia
Mycenae
Naucratis
Naupactus
Nauplia
Naxos
Nicaea
Nicopolis
Odessa
Ohrid
Olbia
Olympia
Olympus, Mount
Olynthus
Orchomenus
Paestum
Palmyra
Paphos

Patmos
Patras
Pella
Pergamum
Petra
Phaestus
Piraeus
Plataea
Prespa, Lake
Priene
Pylos
Ravenna
Rhodes
Rome

St Catherine's Monastery, Sinai
Salamis (city)
Salamis (island)
Samos
Samothrace
Santorini
Serres
Sicily
Sinope
Skopje
Smyrna
Sparta
Sporades
Symi

Syracuse
Tarentum
Thasos
Thebes
Thessalonica
Tinos
Tiryns
Trebizond
Trikkala
Tripolis
Venice
Verroia
Volos
Xanthus

REGIONS

Acarnania
Achaea
Aetolia
Africa, North
Albania
Anatolia
Apulia
Arabia
Arcadia
Argolid
Armenia
Athos, Mount
Attica
Australia
Bactria
Bithynia
Black Sea
Boeotia
Bosnia
Britain
Bulgaria
Byzantium
Calabria

Canada
Cappadocia
Caucasus
Chalcidice
Chersonese, Thracian
Cilicia
Crimea
Croatia
Cyrenaica
Dalmatia
Egypt
Epirus
France
Georgia
Italy
Laconia
Lycia
Macedonia
Magna Graecia
Mani
Messenia
Moldavia
Montenegro

Palestine
Pamphylia
Pelion, Mount
Peloponnese
Persia
Pindus
Pontus
Romania
Rumeli
Russia
Serbia
South Africa
Spain
Souli
Syria
Thessaly
Thrace
Turkey
Ukraine
USA
Wallachia
Zagori

ETHNIC GROUPS

Aeolians
Arabs
Bulgars
Byzantines
Catalans
Copts
Dorians
Etruscans
Genoese
Goths
Gypsies
Hellenes
Illyrians

Ionians
Jews
Karamanlides
Laz
Mardaïtes
Minoans
Muslims
Mycenaeans
Normans
Ottomans
Parthians
Paulicians
Persians

Phoenicians
Pomaks
Romans
Sarakatsans
Sassanians
Seljuks
Serbs
Slavs
Tsakonians
Venetians
Vlachs

THEMES

Social History

Abortion
Adoption
Adultery
Ancestor Worship
Anthropology
Antiquity, Reception of
Antisemitism
Aristocracy
Baptism
Birth
Burial Practices
Celibacy
Children
Cities
City State
Contraception
Corruption
Death
Demography
Diaspora
Divorce

Dowry
Dreams
Dress
Emigration
Eunuchs
Fairs and Markets
Family
Food and Drink
Foreigners
Freedom
Games and Sports
Gender
Guilds
Health
Hippodrome
Homosexuality
Honour and Shame
Hospitality
Imperialism
Inheritance
Kafeneion

Karamanlides
Kinship
Land Tenure
Literacy
Marriage
Men
Metics
Minorities
Onomastics
Patronage
Prostitution
Refugees
Slavery
Symposium
Town Planning
Transhumance
Travel
Urbanization
Village Society
Women

Cultural History

Acropolis of Athens
Aesthetics
Agora of Athens
Alphabet
Anthology, Greek
Archaeological Service
Anti-westernism
Archaic Period
Architecture
Archives
Biography and
    Autobiography
Books and Readers
Byzantine Period, Early
Byzantine Period, Middle
Byzantine Period, Late
Censorship
Ceremony, Byzantine
Chronicles
Cinema
Classical Period
Comedy
Commonwealth, Byzantine
Coronation
Dance
Dark Age
Dialects
Dithyramb
Dress
Education

Enamel
Enlightenment
Epigram
Epistolography
Fable
Folklore
Furniture
Gardens
Gems and Seals
Geometric Period
Glass
Gold
Grammar
Great Idea
Great Palace
Hellenism and Neohellenism
    in the Greek tradition
Hellenism as viewed by
    visiting artists
Hellenistic Period
Hellenization
Hippodrome
Historiography
Humanism
Identity
Instruments, Musical
Ivory
Jewellery
Kafeneion
Karaghiozis

Language
Latin Empire
Libraries
Linear B
Literacy
Manuscripts
Marble and other decorative
    stones
Media
Metalwork
Minoans
Modern Period
Monasticism
Mosaic
Museum of Alexandria
Museums
Music
Mycenaeans
Neoclassicism
Novel
Olympic Games
Opera and Operetta
Oral Tradition
Orthodoxy and Hellenism
Orthodoxy and Nationalism
Ottoman Period (Tourkokratia)
Painting
Papyrus, parchment, and paper
Patronage
Photography

Poetry, Epic
Poetry, Lyric
Portraiture
Pottery
Prehistory
Printing
Purple
Renaissance, Palaiologan
Renaissance, Veneto-Cretan
Rhetoric

Roman Period
Romance, Byzantine
Romanticism
Satyr Play
Scholarship, History of
Schools and Universities
Sculpture
Second Sophistic
Shrines, Wayside
Silk

Silver and Lead
Song
Syllabary, Cypriot
Symposium
Theatres
Tragedy
Translation from Greek
Translation into Greek
Venetokratia
Woodworking

Political and Military History

Armatoloi
Army
Asia Minor Campaign and
    Disaster
Balkan Wars
Berlin, Treaty of
Brigandage
Bureaucracy
Candia, Fall of
Chaeronea, Battle of
City State
Civil War
Colonization
Communist Party
Constantinople, Fall of
Constantinople, Sack of
Constitution
Corinth, Sack of
Corruption
Crusades
Delian League
Democracy
Diplomacy
Eagle, Double-Headed
EAM and ELAS
Enosis
European Community and
    European Union

Exile and Detention
Fascism
Federal States
Fire, Greek
Graeco-Turkish War
Great Idea
Hetairists
Hospitaller Knights of St
    John
Imperialism
Independence, War of
Inscriptions
Janissaries
Judicial Procedure
Junta
Kodjabashis
Lausanne, Treaty of
Law
Magistrates
Manzikert, Battle of
Marathon, Battle of
Military League
Monarchy
Nationalism
NATO
Navy
Oligarchy
Ostracism

Pelagonia, Battle of
Peloponnesian War
Persian Wars
Phanariots
Philhellenes
Political History to 490 BC
Political History 490–323 BC
Political History 323–31 BC
Political History 31 BC–AD 330
Political History 330–802
Political History 802–1204
Political History 1204–1261
Political History 1261–1453
Political History 1453–1832
Political History since 1832
Pydna
Republic
Sèvres, Treaty of
Siegecraft
Sublime Porte
Theme System
Trojan War
Tyranny
Warfare
World War I
World War II
Yarmuk, Battle of

Religious History

Afterlife
Altars
Ancestor Worship
Antisemitism
Apophthegmata Patrum
Apostasy
Atheism
Baptism
Bishops
Burial Practices
Canonization
Canon Law
Celibacy

Christianity
Church-State Relations
Conversion to Islam
Councils, Ecumenical
Cult
Dead, cult of the
Demons and Spirits
Diocese
Divination
Ecumenism
Evil Eye
Fasts
Fate

Festivals
Fundamentalism, Orthodox
Games and Sports
Gnostics
Gods and Goddesses
Hades
Hagia Sophia
Hagiography
Healing Cults
Heresy
Heroes and Heroines
Hesychasm
Hymnography

Science, Medicine, Philosophy

Economic History

Geography

INDIVIDUALS AND FAMILIES

Antiquity

Orators
Aeschines
Demosthenes
Isocrates
Lysias

Poets, Scholars, Prose Writers
Achilles Tatius
Aeschylus
Aesop
Apollonius Rhodius
Aratus
Archilochus
Aristarchus of Samothrace
Aristides, Aelius
Aristophanes
Aristoxenus
Athenaeus
Babrius
Bacchylides
Callimachus
Crates of Mallus
Dio Cocceianus
Dionysius of Halicarnassus
Euripides
Hecataeus of Miletus
Heliodorus
Herodas
Herodes Atticus
Hesiod
Homer
Longus
Lucian
Lycophron
Menander
Nicander
Pausanias
Philodemus
Pindar
Sappho
Simonides
Sophocles
Strabo
Theocritus

Rulers, Politicians, Warriors, Lawgivers
Agesilaus II
Alcibiades
Alexander III the Great
Antigonids
Antiochus III the Great
Attalids
Cimon
Cleisthenes
Cleomenes III

Cleopatra
Dionysius I
Epaminondas
Evagoras
Hadrian
Hieron I
Julian the Apostate
Leonidas
Lysander
Mausolus
Nero
Pericles
Philip II
Philip V
Philopoemen
Pisistratus
Ptolemies
Pyrrhus
Seleucids
Solon
Themistocles
Zenobiao

Philosophers, Scientists, Mathematicians
Anaxagoras
Anaximander
Apollonius of Perge
Aratus
Archimedes
Aristides, Aelius
Aristotle
Aristoxenus
Carneades
Dio Cocceianus
Diogenes of Sinope
Dioscurides
Empedocles
Epicurus
Erasistratus
Eratosthenes
Euclid
Eudoxus
Galen
Heraclitus
Herodes Atticus
Heron
Herophilus
Hipparchus
Hippocrates
Hypatia
Parmenides
Philo
Philodemus
Plato
Plotinus

Plutarch
Porphyry
Ptolemy
Pyrrho
Pythagoras
Socrates
Theophrastus
Zeno of Citium

Historians and Biographers
Appian
Arrian
Cassius Dio
Diodorus Siculus
Diogenes Laertius
Dionysius of Halicarnassus
Ephorus
Hecataeus of Miletus
Herodotus
Hieronymus of Cardia
Josephus, Flavius
Plutarch
Polybius
Posidonius
Strabo
Theopompus
Thucydides
Timaeus
Xenophon

Religious
Apologists, Greek
Clement of Alexandria, St
Ephraim the Syrian, St
Evagrius of Pontus
Ignatius, St
Irenaeus
Isaac the Syrian, St
Justin Martyr, St
Macarius (pseudo-)
Mary, Blessed Virgin
Nemesius
Origen
Paul, St
Philo

Artists
Amasis
Apelles
Execias
Lysippus
Phidias
Polygnotus
Praxiteles
Scopas

Byzantium

Scholars and Teachers
Arethas of Caesarea
Argyropoulos, John
Blemmydes, Nikephoros
Choricius of Gaza
Chrysoloras, Manuel
Eusebius
Eustathios
Gaza, Theodore
George of Trebizond
Gregoras, Nikephoros
Kabasilas, Nicholas
Leo the Mathematician
Libanius
Metochites, Theodore
Michael of Ephesus
Philoponus, John
Photios
Planudes, Maximos
Plethon, George Gemistos
Proclus
Procopius of Gaza
Simplicius
Synesius
Themistius
Triklinios, Dimitrios
Tzetzes, John

Rulers and Politicians
Alexios I Komnenos
Andronikos I Komnenos
Andronikos II Palaiologos
Basil I
Basil II
Constantine I the Great
Constantine V
Constantine VII
Constantine IX Monomachos
Constantine XI Palaiologos
Doukas family
Herakleios
Irene
John I Tzimiskes
John II Komnenos
John III Vatatzes
John VI Kantakouzenos
John VIII Palaiologos

Justinian I
Kantakouzenos family
Komnenos family
Laskaris family
Leo III
Leo V
Leo VI
Manuel I Komnenos
Manuel II Palaiologos
Metochites, Theodore
Michael VIII Palaiologos
Palaiologos family
Romanos I Lekapenos
Stephan IV Dushan
Theodora (497–548)
Theodora (d. 867)
Theophilos
Zoe

Historians and Prose Writers
Akropolites, George
Doukas family
Eusebius
Gregoras, Nikephoros
Komnene, Anna
Kritoboulos, Michael
Procopius of Caesarea
Psellos, Michael
Simokattes, Theophylaktos
Sphrantzes, George
Symeon the Logothete
Theophanes the Confessor, St
Zonaras, John

Religious and Theologians
Akindynos, Gregory
Anastasios of Sinai, St
Andrew of Crete, St
Arethas of Caesarea
Athanasios of Athos, St
Athanasius of Alexandria, St
Barlaam of Calabria
Basil the Great, St
Bessarion
Cyril, St
Cyril of Alexandria, St
Demetrius, St

Dionysius the Areopagite,
    pseudo-
Epiphanius of Salamis, St
Eusebius
Eustathios
Germanos I
Gregory of Nazianzus, St
Gregory of Nyssa, St
Gregory Palamas, St
Helena, St
Italos, John
John Chrysostom, St
John Klimakos, St
John of Damascus, St
Kabasilas, Nicholas
Maximos the Confessor, St
Methodios, St
Neophytos Enkleistos
Nestorius
Philoponus, John
Photios
Procopius of Gaza
Symeon of Thessalonica, St
Symeon the New Theologian,
    St
Synesius
Theodore of Stoudios, St
Theodoret
Theophanes the Confessor, St
Tzetzes, John
Zonaras, John

Poets, Musicians, Artists
Andrew of Crete, St
Apseudes, Theodore
Chrysaphes, Manuel
Digenis Akritis
Geometres, John
George of Pisidia
Joseph the Hymnographer, St
Kassia
Koukouzeles, St John
Nonnus
Panselinos, Manuel
Prodromos, Theodore
Romanos the Melodist, St

Tourkokratia/Frangokratia

Scholars and Teachers
Corydalleus, Theophilos
Dionysios of Phourna
Korais, Adamantios
Maximos the Greek, St
Moisiodax, Josephos
Theotokis, Nikiphoros

Voulgaris, Evgenios

Writers
Byron, George Gordon, Lord
Chortatsis, Georgios
Kalvos, Andreas
Kornaros, Vitsentzos

Makriyannis, Yannis
Velestinlis, Rigas

Rulers, Warriors, Politicians
Ali Pasha of Ioannina
Botsaris, Markos
Bouboulina, Laskarina

Kapodistria, Count Ioannis
Karaiskakis, Georgios
Kolokotronis, Theodore
Makriyannis, Yannis
Mavrokordatos family
Mavromichalis family
Mehmet II
Miaoulis, Andreas
Soutsos, Mikhail
Velestinlis, Rigas

Ypsilantis family

Religious and Theologians
Argenti, Eustratios
Cyril I Lukaris
Gennadios II Scholarios
Gregory V
Jeremias II Tranos
Kosmas the Aetolian, St
Maximos the Greek, St

Paisy Velichkovsky, St

Artists
Damaskinos, Michael
Dionysios of Phourna
Klontzas, Georgios
Theophanes of Crete
Theotokopoulos, Domenikos
 (El Greco)
Tzanes, Emmanuel

Modern

Writers, Artists, Musicians, Film Directors
Andronikos, Manolis
Angelopoulos, Thodoros
Cacoyannis, Michalis
Callas, Maria
Cavafy, Constantine
Chatzidakis, Georgios N.
Chatzimichail, Theophilos
Dimaras, K.T.
Doxiadis, Constantinos
 Apostolou
Elytis, Odysseus
Gatsos, Nikos
Ghika
Gyzis, Nikolaos
Hadjidakis, Manos
Kaftantzoglou, Lysandros
Kazantzakis, Nikos
Kontoglou, Photis
Lytras, Nikephoros
Myrivilis, Stratis
Palamas, Kostis
Pallis, Alexandros
Papadiamantis, Alexandros
Paparrigopoulos, Konstantinos

Parren, Callirrhoe
Pikionis, Dimitris
Politis, Nikolaos
Prevelakis, Pantelis
Psycharis, Yannis
Ritsos, Yiannis
Roidis, Emmanouil
Sakellarides, John Theophrastos
Seferis, George
Sikelianos, Angelos
Skalkotttas, Nikolaos
Solomos, Dionysios
Theodorakis, Mikis
Tsarouchis, Ioannis
Varnalis, Kostas
Vizyinos, Georgios
Xenakis, Iannis

Rulers, Warriors, Politicians
Constantine I
Deliyannis, Theodoros
George I
George II
Kanaris, Constantine
Karamanlis, Constantine
Kolettis, John

Makarios III, Archbishop
Melas, Pavlos
Metaxas, Ioannis
Otho
Papadopoulos, George
Papagos, Alexandros
Papanastasiou, Alexandros
Papandreou family
Plastiras, Nikolaos
Theotokis, George
Trikoupis, Charilaos
Velouchiotis, Ares
Venizelos, Eleftherios
Zervas, Napoleon

Industrialists
Chandris, Antony
Livanos, George P.
Niarchos, Stavros
Onassis, Aristotle

Religious
Athenagoras
Nektarios of Aegina, St
Makarios III, Archbishop

CHRONOLOGICAL
LIST OF INDIVIDUALS

fl.8th or 7th century BC	Hesiod
fl.8th or 7th century BC	Homer
fl.7th century BC	Archilochus
c.640–c.560 BC	Solon
b. c.630 BC	Sappho
fl.6th century BC	Aesop
fl.6th century BC	Amasis
fl.6th century BC	Execias
fl.6th century BC	Pythagoras
b. c.557/56 BC	Simonides
d. c.547 BC	Anaximander
c.530–480 BC	Leonidas
d. c.528 BC	Pisistratus
fl.525–505 BC	Cleisthenes
c.525–456 BC	Aeschylus
c.525–459 BC	Themistocles
c.518–c.438 BC	Pindar
c.515–c.440 BC	Parmenides
b. c.510 BC	Bacchylides
c.510–c.450 BC	Cimon
fl.6th–5th centuries BC	Hecataeus of Miletus
fl. c.500 BC	Heraclitus
fl.5th century BC	Polygnotus
c.500–428 BC	Anaxagoras
c.496–406 BC	Sophocles
c.492–429 BC	Pericles
c.492–432 BC	Empedocles
c.490–420s BC	Phidias
484–c.425 BC	Herodotus
c.480–c.407/06 BC	Euripides
fl.478–466 BC	Hieron I
470–399 BC	Socrates
c.460–c.370 BC	Hippocrates
c.459/58–c.375 BC	Lysias
451/50–404/03 BC	Alcibiades
c.445–374/73 BC	Evagoras
c.444–359 BC	Agesilaus II
c.436–338 BC	Isocrates
c.430–367 BC	Dionysius I
c.430–c.353 BC	Xenophon
429–347 BC	Plato
fl.4th century BC	Praxiteles
c.400–c.320s BC	Ephorus
d. c.395 BC	Thucydides
d.395 BC	Lysander
b. c.390 BC	Lysippus
c.390–c.340 BC	Eudoxus
d. c.386 BC	Aristophanes
384–322 BC	Aristotle
384–322 BC	Demosthenes
383/82–336 BC	Philip II
378/77–c.320 BC	Theopompus
c.371–c.287 BC	Theophrastus
b. c.370 BC	Apelles
b. c.370 BC	Aristoxenus
c.365–275 BC	Pyrrho
c.364–?260 BC	Hieronymus of Cardia
d.362 BC	Epaminondas
fl.360–335 BC	Scopas
356–323 BC	Alexander III the Great
d.353 BC	Mausolus
342–292 BC	Menander
341–270 BC	Epicurus
335–263 BC	Zeno of Citium
c.330–c.260 BC	Herophilus
d. 320s BC	Diogenes of Sinope
c.320–c.240 BC	Callimachus
319–272 BC	Pyrrhus
c.315–c.240 BC	Erasistratus
fl.4th–3rd centuries BC	Euclid
fl.3rd century BC	Apollonius of Perge
fl.3rd century BC	Herodas
fl.3rd century BC	Theocritus
c.295–215 BC	Apollonius Rhodius
c.287–212/11 BC	Archimedes
d. c.260 BC	Timaeus
260–219 BC	Cleomenes III
c.252–182 BC	Philopoemen
c.242–187 BC	Antiochus III the Great
d. c.240 BC	Aratus
238–179 BC	Philip V
b. c.215 BC	Crates of Mallus
c.215–c.143 BC	Aristarchus of Samothrace
214/13–129/28 BC	Carneades
d. c.200 BC	Eratosthenes
fl.3rd or 2nd century BC	Lycophron
fl. c.2nd century BC	Nicander
fl.2nd century BC	Hipparchus
c.200–c.118 BC	Polybius
c.135–c.51 BC	Posidonius
c.110–40 BC	Philodemus
fl.1st century BC	Dionysius of Halicarnassus

*fl.*1st century BC	Diodorus Siculus
69–30 BC	Cleopatra
*c.*64 BC–*c.*AD 19	Strabo
*c.*20 BC–*c.*AD 50	Mary, Blessed Virgin
*fl.*1st century AD	Philo
*c.*AD 30–107	Ignatius, St
37–68	Nero
37–after 93	Josephus, Flavius
*c.*40–112	Dio Cocceianus
*fl. c.*45–75	Dioscurides
*c.*50–120	Plutarch
d. *c.*64	Paul, St
76–138	Hadrian
*c.*90–160	Arrian
*c.*95–160s	Appian
*fl.*1st or 2nd century	Babrius
*fl.*1st or 2nd century	Heron
*fl.*2nd century	Achilles Tatius
*fl.*2nd century	Ptolemy
*c.*100–*c.*165	Justin Martyr, St
*c.*101/03–177	Herodes Atticus
*c.*115–180	Pausanias
117–*c.*180	Aristides, Aelius
*c.*120–180	Lucian
129–?208/16	Galen
*c.*130–*c.*202	Irenaeus
b. *c.*150	Athenaeus
*c.*150–*c.*215	Clement of Alexandria, St
*c.*164–after 229	Cassius Dio
184/85–254/55	Origen
*fl.*2nd or 3rd century	Diogenes Laertius
*fl.*2nd or 3rd century	Longus
*fl.*3rd century	Zenobia
205–269/70	Plotinus
234–*c.*305	Porphyry
*c.*255–*c.*330	Helena, St
*c.*260–339	Eusebius
273/74–337	Constantine I the Great
d. *c.*300	Demetrius, St
*fl.*4th century	Heliodorus
*fl.*4th century	Macarius (pseudo-)
*fl.*4th century	Nemesius
*c.*300–373	Athanasius of Alexandria, St
*c.*306–373	Ephraim the Syrian, St
314–*c.*393	Libanius
*c.*317–*c.*388	Themistius
*c.*329–*c.*390	Gregory of Nazianzus, St
*c.*330–379	Basil the Great, St
*c.*330–*c.*395	Gregory of Nyssa, St
331/32–363	Julian the Apostate
*c.*345–399	Evagrius of Pontus
*c.*347–407	John Chrysostom, St
370–413	Synesius
*c.*370–415	Hypatia
*c.*378–444	Cyril of Alexandria, St
*c.*381–*c.*451	Nestorius
*c.*393–*c.*466	Theodoret
d.403	Epiphanius of Salamis, St
*fl.*5th century	Nonnus
410/11–485	Proclus
*c.*475–*c.*538	Procopius of Gaza
*c.*482–565	Justinian I
*c.*490–570s	Philoponus, John
*c.*497–548	Theodora
*fl. c.*500	Dionysius the Areopagite, pseudo-
*fl.*6th century	Choricius of Gaza
*fl.*6th century	Simplicius
d. after 555	Romanos the Melodist, St
d. *c.*560	Procopius of Caesarea
*c.*575–641	Herakleios
*c.*575–*c.*649	John Klimakos, St
580–662	Maximos the Confessor, St
*fl.*7th century	Anastasios of Sinai, St
*fl.*7th century	George of Pisidia
*fl.*7th century	Isaac the Syrian, St
*fl.*7th century	Simokattes, Theophylaktos
*c.*660–740	Andrew of Crete, St
*c.*685–741	Leo III
*fl.*7th–8th century	Germanos I
718–775	Constantine V
d. *c.*750	John of Damascus, St
*c.*752–803	Irene
759–826	Theodore of Stoudios, St
*c.*760–818	Theophanes the Confessor, St
*c.*780–820	Leo V
*c.*790–after 869	Leo the Mathematician
*fl.*9th century	Kassia
*c.*810–*c.*893	Photios
812/13–842	Theophilos
812/18–*c.*886	Joseph the Hymnnographer, St
*c.*815–885	Methodios, St
826/27–869	Cyril, St
*c.*830–886	Basil I
866–912	Leo VI
d.867	Theodora
*c.*870–948	Romanos I Lekapenos
*fl.*10th century	Geometres, John
*fl.*10th century	Symeon the Logothete
905–959	Constantine VII
*c.*925–976	John I Tzimiskes
*c.*927/30–*c.*997	Athanasios of Athos, St
d. after 932	Arethas of Caesarea
949–1022	Symeon the New Theologian, St
958–1025	Basil II
*c.*978–1050	Zoe
*c.*1000–1055	Constantine IX Monomachos
1018–after 1081	Psellos, Michael
b. *c.*1025	Italos, John
*c.*1057–1118	Alexios I Komnenos
1083–*c.*1153/54	Komnene, Anna
1087–1143	John II Komnenos
*fl.*12th century	Apseudes, Theodore
*fl.*12th century	Michael of Ephesus
*fl.*12th century	Prodromos, Theodore
*fl.*12th century	Zonaras, John
*c.*1110–after 1165	Tzetzes, John
*c.*1115–*c.*1195	Eustathios
1118–1180	Manuel I Komnenos
*c.*1118/20–1185	Andronikos I Komnenos
1134–1219	Neophytos Enkleistos
*c.*1192–1254	John III Vatatzes
1197–1272	Blemmydes, Nikephoros
1217–1282	Akropolites, George
*c.*1225–1282	Michael VIII Palaiologos
*c.*1255–*c.*1305	Planudes, Maximos
1259/60–1328	Andronikos II Palaiologos
1270–1332	Metochites, Theodore
*c.*1280–*c.*1340	Triklinios, Dimitrios

c.1290–1348	Barlaam of Calabria
1290/94–1358/61	Gregoras, Nikephoros
c.1295–1383	John VI Kantakouzenos
1296–1359	Gregory Palamas, St
fl. c.1300	Panselinos, Manuel
fl.13th–14th centuries	Koukouzeles, St John
c.1300–c.1348	Akindynos, Gregory
c.1319–c.1391	Kabasilas, Nicholas
c.1350–1415	Chrysoloras, Manuel
1350–1425	Manuel II Palaiologos
d. 1355	Stephan IV Dushan
c.1360–1452	Plethon, George Gemistos
1392–1448	John VIII Palaiologos
1395–1472/73 or c.1484	George of Trebizond
fl.15th century	Chrysaphes, Manuel
fl.15th century	Kritoboulos, Michael
c.1400–1472	Bessarion
c.1400–1475/76	Gaza, Theodore
1401–1477/78	Sphrantzes, George
1405–1453	Constantine XI Palaiologos
c.1405–c.1472	Gennadios II Scholarios
c.1415–1487	Argyropoulos, John
d.1429	Symeon of Thessalonica, St
1432–1481	Mehmet II
c.1470–1556	Maximos the Greek, St
c.1490–1559	Theophanes of Crete
fl.16th century	Chortatsis, Georgios
c.1530–c.1592	Damaskinos, Michael
c.1530–1595	Jeremias II Tranos
c.1535–1608	Klontzas, Georgios
c.1541–1614	Theotokopoulos, Domenikos (El Greco)
1553–c.1614	Kornaros, Vitsentzos
1570–1638	Cyril I Lukaris
c.1574–1646	Corydalleus, Theophilos
c.1610–1690	Tzanes, Emmanuel
c.1670–after 1744	Dionysios of Phourna
c.1687–c.1757	Argenti, Eustratios
1714–1779	Kosmas the Aetolian, St
1716–1806	Voulgaris, Evgenios
1722–1794	Paisy Velichkovsky, St
c.1725–1800	Moisiodax, Josephos
1731–1800	Theotokis, Nikiphoros
1745–1821	Gregory V
1748–1833	Korais, Adamantios
1750–1822	Ali Pasha of Ioannina
c.1757–1798	Velestinlis, Rigas
1769–1835	Miaoulis, Andreas
c.1770–1825	Bouboulina, Laskarina
1770–1843	Kolokotronis, Theodore
1774–1847	Kolettis, John
1776–1831	Kapodistria, Count Ioannis
1778–1864	Soutsos, Mikhail
1782–1827	Karaiskakis, Georgios
1788–1824	Byron, George Gordon, Lord
1790–1823	Botsaris, Markos
1792–1869	Kalvos, Andreas
1795–1877	Kanaris, Constantine
1797–1864	Makriyannis, Yannis
1798–1857	Solomos, Dionysios
1811–1885	Kaftantzoglou, Lysandros
1815–1867	Otho
1815–1891	Paparrigopoulos, Konstantinos
1826–1905	Deliyannis, Theodoros
1832–1896	Trikoupis, Charilaos
1832–1904	Lytras, Nikephoros
1836–1904	Roidis, Emmanouil
1842–1901	Gyzis, Nikolaos
1844–1916	Theotokis, George
1845–1913	George I
1846–1920	Nektarios of Aegina, St
1848–1941	Chatzidakis, Georgios N.
1849–1896	Vizyinos, Georgios
1851–1911	Papadiamantis, Alexandros
1851–1935	Pallis, Alexandros
1852–1921	Politis, Nikolaos
c.1853–1938	Sakellarides, John Theophrastos
1854–1929	Psycharis, Yannis
1859–1940	Parren, Callirrhoe
1859–1943	Palamas, Kostis
1863–1933	Cavafy, Constantine
1864–1936	Venizelos, Eleftherios
1868–1922	Constantine I
1870–1904	Melas, Pavlos
1871–1941	Metaxas, Ioannis
1873–1934	Chatzimichail, Theophilos
1876/79–1936	Papanastasiou, Alexandros
1883–1953	Plastiras, Nikolaos
1883–1955	Papagos, Alexandros
1883–1957	Kazantzakis, Nikos
1884–1951	Sikelianos, Angelos
1884–1974	Varnalis, Kostas
1886–1972	Athenagoras
1887–1968	Pikionis, Dimitris
1890–1947	George II
1891–1957	Zervas, Napoleon
1892–1969	Myrivilis, Stratis
c.1895–1965	Kontoglou, Photis
1900–1971	Seferis, George
1900 (or 1906)–1975	Onassis, Aristotle
1904–1949	Skalkottas, Nikolaos
1904–1992	Dimaras, K.T.
1905–1945	Velouchiotis, Ares
1906–1994	Ghika
1907–1998	Karamanlis, Constantine
1909–1986	Prevelakis, Pantelis
1909–1990	Ritsos, Yiannis
1909–1996	Niarchos, Stavros
1910–1989	Tsarouchis, Ioannis
1911–1996	Elytis, Odysseus
1913–1975	Doxiadis, Constantinos Apostolou
1913–1977	Makarios III, Archbishop
1916–1995	Gatsos, Nikos
1919–1992	Andronikos, Manolis
1919–1999	Papadopoulos, George
1922–	Xenakis, Iannis
1922–	Cacoyannis, Michalis
1923–1977	Callas, Maria
1924–1984	Chandris, Antony
1925–	Theodorakis, Mikis
1925–1994	Hadjidakis, Manos
1926–1997	Livanos, George P.
1935–	Angelopoulos, Thodoros

NOTE ON TRANSLITERATION

Transliteration is always a problem when dealing with a non-Roman alphabet across such a vast span of time and space, and it is as impossible to please everybody as it is to be consistent within the rules one has set. But, on the principle that good transliteration like good writing is by definition inconspicuous, the aim throughout has been to present the reader with the form of any word which is likely to be the most familiar and least jarring. In general, ancient names have been presented in their "Latin" form (e.g. Thucydides), but medieval and modern names in their "Greek" form (e.g. Alexios I Komnenos). Since a point in time had to be chosen for the switch from "Latin" to "Greek" forms, that (entirely arbitrary) moment is taken to be the death of Justinian I (14 November, 565) who was probably the last Byzantine emperor to speak Latin. Greek is always transliterated into the Roman alphabet. Here again the more usual "ancient" system (e.g. *basileus*) is employed until (simply because a date had to be chosen) 1453 when the switch is made to the "modern" system (e.g. *vasilefs*). Places that have a standard ancient (or English) form (such as Thessalonica or Athens) retain that form throughout. Nevertheless inconsistencies and infelicities are inevitable and we can only crave the reader's indulgence where they occur.

GRAHAM SPEAKE

The Greek Alphabet

Capital	Lower Case	Name		Transliteration (pre-1453/post-1453)
A	α	Alpha	=	*a*
B	β	Beta	=	*b/v*
Γ	γ	Gamma	=	*g* (hard, as in "good")
Δ	δ	Delta	=	*d*
E	ε	Epsilon	=	*e* (as e in "net")
Z	ζ	Zeta	=	*z*
H	η	Eta	=	*e* (as ee in "meet")
Θ	θ	Theta	=	*th*
I	ι	Iota	=	*i*
K	κ	Kappa	=	*k*
Λ	λ	Lambda	=	*l*
M	μ	Mu	=	*m*
N	ν	Nu	=	*n*
Ξ	ξ	Xi	=	*x*
O	o	Omicron	=	*o* (as o in "spot")
Π	π	Pi	=	*p*
P	ρ	Rho	=	*rh, r*
Σ	σ ς	Sigma	=	*s* (ς when final letter)
T	τ	Tau	=	*t*
Y	υ	Upsilon	=	*u/f* after *a* and *e*
Φ	φ	Phi	=	*ph*
X	χ	Chi	=	*ch* (hard, as in "chord")
Ψ	ψ	Psi	=	*ps*
Ω	ω	Omega	=	*o* (as o in "lone")

BYZANTINE EMPERORS

Constantine I the Great	324–337	Romanos I Lekapenos	920–944
Constantine II	337–340	Stephen and Constantine Lekapenos	944–945
Constans I	337–350	Constantine VII	945–959
Constantius II	337–361	Romanos II	959–963
Julian	361–363	Nikephoros II Phokas	963–969
Jovian	363–364	John I Tzimiskes	969–976
Valens	364–378	Basil II	976–1025
Theodosius I	379–395	Constantine VIII	1025–1028
Arcadius	395–408	Romanos III Argyros	1028–1034
Theodosius II	408–450	Michael IV Paphlagon	1034–1041
Marcian	450–457	Michael V Kalaphates	1041–1042
Leo I	457–474	Zoe and Theodora	1042
Leo II	473–474	Constantine IX Monomachos	1042–1055
Zeno	474–491	Theodora	1055–1056
Basiliscus	475–476	Michael VI Stratiotikos	1056–1057
Anastasius I	491–518	Isaac I Komnenos	1057–1059
Justin I	518–527	Constantine X Doukas	1059–1067
Justinian I	527–565	Romanos IV Diogenes	1068–1071
Justin II	565–578	Michael VII Doukas	1071–1078
Tiberios I	578–582	Nikephoros III Botaneiates	1078–1081
Maurice	582–602	Alexios I Komnenos	1081–1118
Phokas	602–610	John II Komnenos	1118–1143
Herakleios	610–641	Manuel I Komnenos	1143–1180
Herakleios Constantine and Heraklonas	641	Alexios II Komnenos	1180–1183
Constans II	641–668	Andronikos I Komnenos	1183–1185
Constantine IV*	668–685	Isaac II Angelos	1185–1195
Justinian II	685–695	Alexios III Angelos	1195–1203
Leontios	695–698	Isaac II and Alexios IV Angelos	1203–1204
Tiberios II	698–705	Alexios V Doukas	1204
Justinian II (second reign)	705–711	Theodore I Laskaris	1205–1222
Philippikos	711–713	John III Vatatzes	1222–1254
Anastasios II	713–715	Theodore II Laskaris	1254–1258
Theodosios III	715–717	John IV Laskaris	1259–1261
Leo III	717–741	Michael VIII Palaiologos	1259–1282
Constantine V	741–775	Andronikos II Palaiologos	1282–1328
Leo IV	775–780	Michael IX Palaiologos	1294–1320
Constantine VI	780–797	Andronikos III Palaiologos	1328–1341
Irene	797–802	John V Palaiologos	1341–1391
Nikephoros I	802–811	John VI Kantakouzenos	1347–1354
Staurakios	811	Andronikos IV Palaiologos	1376–1379
Michael I Rangabe	811–813	John VII Palaiologos	1390
Leo V	813–820	Manuel II Palaiologos	1391–1425
Michael II	820–829	John VIII Palaiologos	1425–1448
Theophilos	829–842	Constantine XI Palaiologos	1449–1453
Michael III	842–867		
Basil I	867–886		
Leo VI	886–912		
Alexander	912–913		
Regency for Constantine VII	913–920		

Constantine III was a usurper emperor in the western empire, 407–411

A

Abortion

Like other ethnic groups in the ancient Mediterranean area, the Greeks afforded the community's protection of law after a child was accepted by the father in a naming ceremony called the *amphidromia*. At any time prior to that event the foetus or child could be killed with impunity and usually without adverse moral judgement.

Abortion was practised through both chemical and surgical procedures. The latter was considered more dangerous and, consequently, most of the anecdotal and medical data refer to drugs, usually taken orally. Only after Christianity was established did this cultural pattern change and even then not dramatically. In pre-Christian Hellenic and Hellenistic societies abortion was regarded as a normal exercise of a woman. The exception was the moral and sometimes legal obligation to bear a child in wedlock when the father wanted the progeny. In Christian Greek- and Latin-speaking communities a woman was free to terminate what we regard as an early pregnancy, but not after she declared herself pregnant or when the foetal development made pregnancy obvious.

Contraception, abortion, and infanticide (provided it was before the ceremonial acceptance into the family) were means to limit family sizes as well as to dispose of unwanted, illegitimate, or deformed children. Exposed babies could be given or sold to slave traders. Hesiod (*fl. c.*700 BC) warns families not to have more than one son. Socrates said that midwives – his own mother was one – knew the drugs to "cause miscarriages if they think them desirable" (Plato, *Theaetetus*, 149d). Aristotle spoke of unspecified drugs to prevent children "before sense and life have begun in the embryo" (*Politics*, 7. 14. 10/1335b). In much the same way Plato voiced the same sentiments for public policy in the ideal state to limit unneeded children. A later report that the lawgivers of Athens and Sparta, Solon and Lycurgus, prohibited abortions is not regarded as authentic. Instead it was merely a reflection of sentiments in the 2nd century AD when Galen made the claim.

The medical writings beginning with those attributed to Hippocrates have prescriptions for causing an abortion. Sometimes they were not explicitly stated for an abortion but for stimulation of the onset of menstruation, although the function was to terminate, in our vocabulary, an early pregnancy. Such plants as the rue, pennyroyal, myrrh, juniper, and birthwort (*Aristolochae*) were among those commonly employed. Birthwort was considered suitable for late-term abortions or, similarly, to initiate labour for delayed childbirth.

The modern question of "when does life begin" was not formulated in ancient Greek society with the meaning we give to it. Plutarch said that Plato regarded the foetus as a living being, but nevertheless Plato recommended abortions for women over 40. Aristotle's biological observations on foetal development, mostly observed with birds' eggs, influenced later Christian theological thinking. Knowing that an accident or Caesarian birth can result in a live birth, Aristotle asked when the foetus developed independent life. Although he did not consistently answer the question in the same way, one of his answers heavily influenced later philosophical and religious attitudes towards abortion. When the foetus had all of its form, Aristotle said that it had *psyche*, meaning "life". The Stoics developed the notion of "soul" for which they employed the word *psyche*. The Christians, when reading Aristotle, thought that his question was not when independent life was expected but ensoulment. The only explicit reference to abortion in the Bible or Torah occurs in Exodus 21: 23 in answer to a question about the fault of a person assaulting a pregnant woman with a miscarriage resulting. The answer was "life is for life". The Hebrew word for life, *nefesh*, was translated by the Septuagint as *psyche*, thus the implication in late, Classical Greek to give a "soul for a soul" as punishment for the act. Most of the Church Fathers adapted Aristotle's views and believed that ensoulment came at that point in a pregnancy when there was foetal movement. They envisioned the soul to have come from God, not the parents, and the divine act came when the foetus was formed. Prior to ensoulment a woman was free to terminate her fertility by returning to her menstrual cycle.

Not all pre-Christian or pagan Greeks subscribed to faultless abortion. For example, a Greek inscription above a sanctuary in Lydia (north Africa) prohibits entry to those who commit contraception, abortion, or infanticide. In its early version the Hippocratic Oath forbade a physician from prescribing an abortive pessary. The 2nd-century AD gynaecology writer Soranus explained that pessaries were more dangerous than oral-route drugs, and thus to be avoided. By late Hellenistic and Roman periods, however, some versions of the oath excised the word for pessary, thereby alleging that a physician was prohibited from the administration of any kind of abortion. Probably no version of the oath was actually taken by physicians in ancient or Byzantine times, but physicians were no doubt aware of the ethical values espoused.

The Stoics asserted that life began with the taking in of the first breath of cold air, but some Stoics argued that the foetus had the potential for life. No writings of Greek Stoics speak directly on abortion, but later Stoics asserted that intercourse should only be for procreation. Writing in the late 3rd century, Porphyry discussed the question of when the soul enters the new being and answered that it may be as early as when the sperm enters the womb. Porphyry's answer (among others he proposed) was not accepted in Greek culture until the latter part of the 19th century.

In the Hellenistic and Byzantine periods some modifications were made to the ancient formula regarding abortion after foetal formation. The Gnostics regarded intercourse of any kind under any circumstances as wrong. The hateful *pharmakia* ("drugs") in biblical and early Christian works (e.g. Galatians 5: 20 and *Didache*, 5. 1) are oblique references to abortifacients.

Generally the Greek Church Fathers took a stronger position against the termination of pregnancy at any time than did the Latin Fathers. Gregory of Nyssa (d. *c.*395) followed the Latin approach in saying that an unformed (i.e. prequickening) foetus could not be considered a human being. His elder brother Basil (d. *c.*379) spoke harshly against women who "destroyed a foetus ... whether ... formed or unformed". A feticide is the same as homicide; but he mitigated the punishment and recommended compassion and a lesser repentance if circumstances merited it. Essentially the Eastern Orthodox Church adopted as canonical the pronouncement by Basil. Arethas of Caesarea (9th–10th century) and Michael Psellos (11th century) held similar views. Since the Renaissance the Greek Orthodox Church has had a more consistent position compared with the Roman Catholic Church regarding birth control. Essentially the Greek Church rejects any artificial intervention in procreation. In the 20th century, however, it has modified its position on contraception but not on abortion.

Discontinuity existed between Greek medieval religious doctrine and practices, if medical works and legal codes are to be accepted as reflecting actual practice. Those medical works that were based on Classical, Byzantine, and borrowed Arabic authorities all continue prescriptions for abortifacients, most of which were effective. Some were disguised as menstrual stimulators, ostensibly to return to menstruation, but they caused an abortion should pregnancy have been the reason for delay. Procopius, writing in the 6th century, spoke of the empress Theodora employing abortifacients. Justinian's *Digest* protected a male's right to have a child sired in wedlock. Later Byzantine law inflicted capital punishment for widows who killed foetuses for money. Gradually the tolerance for abortion became more restrictive in Greek as well as Latin lands. The 14th-century *Hexabilos* identified suppliers of abortion drugs as murderers. A famous case in 1370 found guilty the father (in this case, a monk) of an unborn child for administering an abortion and sent into exile the physician who supplied the drugs.

JOHN M. RIDDLE

See also Birth, Contraception

Further Reading

Feen, Richard, "Abortion and Exposure in Ancient Greece: Assessing the Status of the Fetus and 'Newborn' from Classical Sources" in *Abortion and the Status of the Fetus*, edited by William B. Bondeson *et al.*, Dordrecht: Reidel, 1983

Nardi, Enzo, *Procurato aborto nel mondo greco romano*, Milan: Giuffré, 1971 (an essential guide to ancient references)

Poulakou-Rembelakou, E., J. Lascaratos, and S.G. Marketos, "Abortions in Byzantine Times, 325–1453 AD", *Vesalius: Acta Internationalia Historiae Medicinae*, 2/1 (1996): pp. 19–25

Riddle, John M., *Contraception and Abortion from the Ancient World to the Renaissance*, Cambridge, Massachusetts: Harvard University Press, 1992

Riddle, John M., *Eve's Herbs: A History of Contraception and Abortion in the West*, Cambridge, Massachusetts: Harvard University Press, 1997

Academy of Athens

Philosophical school founded by Plato

The Academy was a public gymnasium in Athens, sacred to the hero Academus. It was located northwest of Athens, near the Dipylon gate. Plato founded his school there about 388/87 BC when he returned to Athens from his travels in Sicily. He acquired a house with a garden where Mithridates later set up a statue of him and where Speusippus, Plato's nephew and successor, erected statues of the Muses. We do not know much about the organization and legal status of the Academy. Although Plato was not the first to found a school of secondary education in Athens, his school had certain distinctive characteristics. Membership of the Academy was not the exclusive privilege of the few; nor did it presuppose adherence to certain doctrines. Plato did not charge his students – who included women – a fee. Mainly responsible for the teaching was the scholarch, but other senior members could lecture too. Subjects taught, apart from philosophy, included mathematics, astronomy, and natural science. An insight into the activity of the Academy is offered by a fragment of the comic writer Epicrates (4th century).

Unlike the founders of other schools (Socratics, sophists), Plato made provision for the continuation of the school after his death (347 BC), by appointing Speusippus as his successor. His school was maintained until the 1st century BC, enjoying an unbroken line of elected successors. Already the ancients distinguished two main phases in the history of the Academy: (1) the Old Academy from Speusippus to Crantor, and (2) the New Academy from Arcesilaus to Philo of Larissa. Later, doxographers make further divisions, often distinguishing four or five phases. The first phase is that of doctrinal Platonism, whereas with Arcesilaus (316–240 BC) the Academy enters a period of scepticism which gradually became less radical. Unfortunately not a single extant work survives from Plato's successors. Thus our knowledge of the development of Platonic philosophy is often shadowy. Figures who were regarded as crucial for later developments such as Polemo (scholarch 314–276 BC) remain entirely obscure to us. Yet our knowledge of the succession is firm thanks to a variety of ancient sources, notably a papyrus from Herculaneum (*Index Academicus*).

Speusippus had a strong interest in logic and mathematics. He elaborated Plato's theory of division and developed a theory of definition. Speusippus argued for the separate existence of numbers as immutable and eternal objects of knowledge preferable to Plato's ideas. He admitted two opposite principles: the One and the multiplicity. Yet these principles are not universal for the several kinds of substances, but each of them has its own principles. In Aristotle's view this lack of ultimate principles deprives the world of internal order and fails to account for a final cause. As regards ethics, Speusippus maintained that both pleasure and pain should be avoided as they are disturbances. Xenocrates (scholarch 339–314 BC), as we can infer from his list of writings, had a strong interest in moral philosophy, while he was also interested in giving a systematic account of the nature of gods and demons and their relation to heavenly bodies. With Polemo the interest in moral questions predominates. Crates and Crantor apparently continued Polemo's line. Crantor became renowned for his treatise "On Grief" and for composing the first commentary on a Platonic dialogue, namely the *Timaeus*.

The term "New Academy" bears a critical overtone. It was first coined by Antiochus of Ascalon (1st century BC) in order to criticize the sceptical Academy as diverging from a dogmatic Plato. Arcesilaus introduced scepticism into the Academy appealing to Socrates' aporetic method. The aim now was to challenge dogmatic doctrines dialectically. Neither Arcesilaus nor his most important successor Carneades (c.214–129 BC) wrote anything; their positions were expounded by their successors, Lacydes and Clitomachus respectively. Arcesilaus questioned Stoic claims that firm knowledge is attainable through sense impressions, arguing that no sense impression is such that it cannot be false. Arcesilaus' alternative to holding mere beliefs was to postulate suspension of judgement as the safest way to avoid error. Carneades systematically questioned dogmatic arguments, insisting on the impossibility of distinguishing cognitive from non-cognitive impressions. He maintained that suspension of judgement still allows for action; we can follow plausible impressions, but we do not have to assent to them.

Philo of Larissa was to be the last scholarch of the Academy. He succeeded Clitomachus around 110 BC, but with the occupation of Athens by Sulla in 89/88 BC he fled to Rome where he continued to teach for about a decade until his death. Philo started as a faithful follower of Carneadian scepticism, but later he reinterpeted it as allowing for formation of philosophical judgements. He maintained that things are actually knowable but we lack a criterion of truth such as the Stoic one, and he argued that this position was being held in the Academy all along, thus presenting the early Academic scepticism of Arcesilaus and his followers as being a reaction to Stoic dogmatism. Antiochus, Philo's disciple, found Philo's new position infuriating. He withdrew from the Academy, reproaching the "New" (i.e. sceptical) Academy as an aberration of Plato's philosophy. He himself propounded the revival of the "Old" Academy, claiming adherence to the ancients. Interestingly Antiochus included among the ancients Aristotle and the early Peripatetics, and argued for an essential agreement between the Academy and the early Peripatos. He also thought that the Stoics were in many respects in accord with the ancients exactly because they borrowed so much from them, only modifying their terminology. Yet Antiochus failed to restore the Old Academy. His philosophical outlook was heavily Stoic; his epistemology was essentially Stoic and his ethics more Peripatetic than Stoic. Antiochus never became scholarch of the Academy; he taught in his own school in the Ptolemaion gymnasium in Athens, while the Academy was abandoned after Sulla's sack of Athens. Antiochus' own school did not last long either.

There is no evidence of any philosophical activity in the Academy in the subsequent centuries. The term "Academic" now meant "sceptic", contrasted to "Platonic" which first applied to Thrasyllus (1st century AD), the editor of Plato's works in tetralogies. Plutarch, however, tried to restore the original meaning of the term "Academic" and defended the aporetic character of Plato's thought. A formal institution of Platonism no longer existed and there were no successors of Plato. Individual Platonists taught their students in their own schools, located either in a gymnasium or in their own house. This was the case with Ammonius and his disciple Plutarch (1st century AD) and also with Taurus (2nd century). In AD 176 the Roman emperor Marcus Aurelius set up chairs for teachers of philosophy in Athens, and Atticus was probably the first incumbent of the Platonist chair. Plotinus (3rd century AD) taught in Rome in an establishment provided by a rich patron, while later Neoplatonists taught in Alexandria, Syria, and Athens. The Athenian school of Neoplatonism established successions. Proclus (5th century) claimed descent from Plato; and Damascius (6th century) argued for an unbroken "Golden Chain" of successors from the time to Plato to himself. But this was a historical illusion propagated by the Athenian Neoplatonists to lend authority to their own school, which was not located in the gymnasium of the Academy. The closure of the Academy by Emperor Justinian in 529 did not stop all philosophical activity. Simplicius and Olympiodorus wrote most of their works after that date.

GEORGE E. KARAMANOLIS

See also Neoplatonism, Plato

Summary

Philosophical school in Athens founded by Plato c.388/87 BC. Subjects taught included mathematics, astronomy, and natural science as well as philosophy. Known as the "Old" Academy from Speusippus to Crantor (c.269 BC) and the "New" from Arcesilaus to Philo of Larissa (in the latter phase dogmatic Platonism was abandoned in favour of scepticism), the school was deserted after Sulla's sack of Athens in 88 BC.

Texts

Heinze, Richard, *Xenokrates: Darstellung der Lehre und Sammlung der Fragmente*, Leipzig: Teubner, 1892

Mette, H.-J., "Zwei Akademiker heute: Krantor von Soloi und Arkesilaos von Pitane", *Lustrum*, 26 (1984): pp. 7–94

Mette, H.-J., "Weitere Akademiker heute: Von Lakydes bis zu Kleitomachos", *Lustrum*, 27 (1985): pp. 39–148

Mette, H.-J., "Philon von Larisa und Antiochus von Askalon", *Lustrum*, 28/9 (1986–87): pp. 9–63

Philodemus, *Storia dei filosofi: Platone e l'Academia*, edited and translated into Italian by Tiziano Dorandi, Naples: Bibliopolis, 1991

Plato, *Opera* (texts in Greek), edited by John Burnet, 5 vols, Oxford: Clarendon Press, 1900–07

Plato, *The Dialogues*, translated by Benjamin Jowett, 4 vols, Oxford: Clarendon Press, and New York: Scribner, 1868–71; new edition, edited by D.J. Allan and H.E. Dale, 4 vols, Clarendon Press, 1953

Plato, *Dialogues*, translated by H.N. Fowler *et al.*, 15 vols, London: Heinemann, and Cambridge, Massachusetts: Harvard University Press, 1914–35 (Loeb edition; many reprints)

Tarán, Leonardo, *Speusippus of Athens: A Critical Study with a Collection of the Related Texts and Commentary*, Leiden: Brill, 1981

Further Reading

Cameron, Alan, "The Last Days of the Academy at Athens", *Proceedings of the Cambridge Philological Society*, new series 15 (1969): pp. 7–29

Cherniss, Harold F., *The Riddle of the Early Academy*, Berkeley: University of California Press, 1945

Dillon, J.M., "The Academy in the Middle Platonic Period", *Dionysius*, 3 (1979): pp. 63–77

Glucker, John, *Antiochus and the Late Academy*, Göttingen: Vandenhoeck & Ruprecht, 1978

Long, A.A., *Hellenistic Philosophy: Stoics, Epicureans, Sceptics*, 2nd edition, London: Duckworth, and Berkeley: University of California Press, 1986

Lynch, John Patrick, *Aristotle's School: A Study of a Greek Educational Institution*, Berkeley: University of California Press, 1972

Acarnania

Region in western Greece

The Ambracian gulf and the Ionian sea formed Acarnania's northern and western borders, while its border with Aetolia, to the east and south, was less stable. Mount Thyamus and the Achelous river, however, are usually considered the limits of the ancient Acarnanian state. Its most populous region was the plain of the Achelous, commanded by the town of Stratus. The increased excavation activity in Acarnania contributes to a more precise definition of its historical outline. However, issues concerning the provenance of its earliest inhabitants, the role they played in Greek history, and the development of its political institutions are still insufficiently understood due to the small number of comprehensive studies dealing with the region.

Little is known about Acarnania before its colonization by the Corinthians in the 7th century BC; in epic poetry there are references to the region, though without mentioning its name, as the kingdom of the cruel king Echetos. Information on the prehistoric inhabitants of Acarnania, the Taphians, Teleboans, Leleges, and Kouretes, is also vague. It seems that the region was not heavily populated in the Bronze Age; all the sites of this period are located in the region of Astacus, while there is a remarkable absence of Bronze Age sites along the coast.

The Acarnanians of the early historical period moved into the region at the time of, or a little after, the Dorian migration and spoke a northwest Greek dialect, characteristics of which have been traced to Illyria and Epirus. Before the arrival of Corinthian colonists, there was a settlement at Oeniadae. According to a myth narrated by Thucydides, an oracle directed Alcmaeon, Amphiaraus' son, to establish it after his act of matricide. Thus Alcmaeon became the first ruler of this area and his son Acarnan gave his name to the people. The Corinthians colonized primarily the northwest of the territory (Leucas, Anactorium, Sollium) despite native opposition. Consequently, Corinthian artistic influence has been observed in Acarnania during the Archaic period.

Although Acarnania as a whole did not play an active role in the events of the Greek world, at least until the 4th century BC, it was involved in many wars because of its strategic position along the western sailing route to Italy. It was only the Corinthian colonies, Leucas, Anactorium, and Ambracia, which participated in the Persian Wars, sending contingents to Salamis and Plataea. In the middle of the 5th century BC contacts between Acarnania and Athens were developed, as the latter began to expand its sphere of influence in the west of Greece. With the aid of Athens the Acarnanians managed to subdue the Corinthian colonies on their coast. Being in alliance with Athens, they became involved in the Peloponnesian War and sent forces to Sicily in aid of Demosthenes.

By the mid-5th century BC the notion of *ethnos* (nation) existed among the Acarnanians as is demonstrated by the common defence of towns in cases of external attack. The individual poleis were organized into a federal state, the Acarnanian *koinon*, but they retained their autonomy. Each of them contributed troops for the defence of Acarnania, while an official body was located at Stratus from the 4th century BC. The earliest coins of the federal state were issued around 350 BC. The economy of the region was still agriculturally based in the 5th century BC; the production of grapes, olives, wheat, and barley and the keeping of livestock served local consumption, while there are no indications of interstate trade on a regular basis. The strong commercial presence of Corinth is reflected in the adoption of Corinthian coinage from the end of the 6th to the 3rd century BC.

In the Corinthian war (395 BC) Acarnania sided with Athens and its allies against the Lacedaemonians. In 390 BC the Spartan king Agesilaus II attacked Acarnania, which consequently allied with Sparta. Under the threat posed by Philip II of Macedon, the Acarnanians joined the second Athenian Confederacy and fought against him at Chaeronea (338 BC). Macedonia, however, soon replaced Athens as the Acarnanians' ally and protector, especially against Aetolia.

An Acarnanian–Macedonian alliance was encouraged by Cassander in 324 BC, in order to prevent Antigonus' activity in Aetolia which threatened the Macedonian ruler. In 314 BC the Acarnanian communities near the Aetolian border agreed to concentrate in the larger cities. In 294 BC Alexander IV ceded some rights over Acarnania to Pyrrhus in return for military assistance. During the years of Pyrrhus' rule Acarnania was prosperous because of the flow of trade from Greece to south Italy and Sicily and the temporary peace with Aetolia. This peace did not last long and frontier disputes with the Aetolians resulted in the dissolution of the Acarnanian *koinon* and the partition of Acarnania between them and the Epirotes around 252–250 BC.

In 231 BC, after the end of the war between Aetolia and Macedonia (239–234 BC), the Acarnanians managed to regain control of their territory and a year later to reestablish their league. They acquired from Epirus the island of Leucas which became their capital. The main target of the new federation's policy was the liberation of the Acarnanian communities under Aetolian control. Antigonus Doson and Philip V supported the league. In 219 BC Philip campaigned along the

Acarnania: looking east from Stratos across the valley of the river Archelous

Aetolian–Acarnanian border and recovered Phoetiae and Oeniadae. At the end of the summer in 217 BC peace was agreed between Philip and the Aetolians at Naupactus.

The Acarnanians sided with Philip against Rome (200 BC) and as a result Leucas was separated from the *koinon* and Thyrreion became the new capital. The Acarnanian confederacy survived until 31–29 BC, but the coastal cities suffered from pirate raids and the whole region from the Roman civil wars. Following the battle of Actium (31 BC) the country was ravaged by Octavian, and its inhabitants settled in Nicopolis (founded 30 BC.)

From Byzantine to modern times Acarnania and Aetolia have shared a common history and development. The region became part of the theme of Nicopolis and then of the despotate of Epirus. Their ancient names, however, were occasionally in use until the 6th century AD. Acarnania took a prominent part in the national uprising of 1821 against Turkish domination and since 1833 has been joined with Aetolia as a nome.

ELENI ZIMI

See also Aetolia

Summary

Region of western Greece colonized by the Corinthians in the 7th century BC. With the aid of Athens the Acarnanians expelled the Corinthians in the 5th century BC and formed a federal state or

koinon. Allied in turn with Athens, Sparta, Athens again, and Macedonia, Acarnania suffered constant friction with neighbouring Aetolia. The confederacy survived until 29 BC when the region was laid waste by Octavian.

Further Reading

Archaiologiko kai Istoriko Synedrio Aitoloakarnanias: Mnimiaki klironomia kai Istoria tis Aitoloacarnanias, Agrinio 21–23 Octovriou 1988 [Monumental Heritage and History of Aitoloacarnania: Congress on Archaeology and History of Aitoloacarnania, Agrinio, 21–23 October 1988], Agrinio, 1988

Berktold, Percy, Jürgen Schmidt and Christian Wacker (editors), *Akarnanien: Eine Landschaft im antiken Griechenland*, Würzburg: Ergon, 1996 (see illustrations, p. 231)

Domingo-Forasté, Douglas, "A History of Northern Coastal Akarnania to 167 BC: Alyzeia, Leukas, Anaktorion and Argos Amphilochikon" (dissertation), Santa Barbara: University of California, 1988

Ferentinos, Georgios A., *Istoria tis Akarnanias apo Archaiotaton Chronon methri tis Epochis tou Christou* [Acarnanian History from Ancient to Christian Times], Athens, 1988

Katopodis, Gerasimos S., *Archaia Akarnania* [Ancient Acarnania], Agrinio, 1988

Larsen, J.A.O., *Greek Federal States: Their Institutions and History*, Oxford: Clarendon Press, 1968

Murray, William Michael, "The Coastal Sites of Western Acarnania: A Topographical and Historical Survey" (dissertation), Philadelphia: University of Pennsylvania, 1982

Nerantzis, I.G., *Epigraphes kai Archaiologika evrymata Archaias Akarnanias sto Mouseio Thyrreiou Akarnanias* [Inscriptions and

Archaeological Finds from Ancient Acarnania in the Thyrreion Museum], Agrinio, 1994

Nerantzis, I.G., *I archaia Stratiki Akarnanias: Mnimiaki Topographia, Epigraphis kai Archaiologika evrimata* [Ancient Stratos of Acarnania: Topography, Inscriptions and Archaeological Finds], Agrinio, 1997

Oost, Stewart Irvin, *Roman Policy in Epirus and Acarnania in the Age of the Roman Conquest of Greece*, Dallas: Southern Methodist University Press, 1954

Paliouras, Athanasios, *I Aitoloakarnania sti Byzantini Epochi* [Aitoloacarnania in Byzantine Times], Athens, 1985

Schoch, Marcel, *Beiträge zur Topographie Akarnaniens in klassischer und hellenistischer Zeit*, Würzburg: Ergon, 1997

Schweighart, Benedikt, *Bibliographie über Akarnanien und angrenzende Gebiete in der Antike*, Munich: Oberhummer, 1993

Achaea

Region in the Peloponnese

Achaea is located in the northwest of the Peloponnese, between Elis and Sicyon, in the restricted land space between the Corinthian Gulf and the mountains. The region is relatively well watered and wooded, especially in its southern portion. Its three highest peaks, Panahaiko, Erimanthos, and Aroaneia, all located in the south, are dotted with numerous attractive villages. Coastal towns in the north are separated by small bays.

Evidence for early settlement in the region includes material remains from the Neolithic, Middle Helladic, and Late Helladic eras. Vestiges of Mycenaean occupation are found in both textual accounts and archaeological data. According to Homer (*Iliad*, 2. 574) Aigion, east of Patras, was part of Agamemnon's territory. And, indeed, archaeological discoveries at Aigion include a fairly extensive Late Helladic necropolis. Pausanias reported a variety of stories connecting the region with ancient Mycenaean, Dorian, and Ionian traditions. According to his description of the upheaval following the decline of the Mycenaean centres, the local "Ionians" moved from Achaea to Attica while "Dorians" from Argos and Sparta moved into the area. Originally named "Aigialea", the region received its Classical name Achaea after the arrival of the Dorian settlers. Herodotus (1. 145) gives us the names of the twelve main parts, *merea*, or cities in Achaea: Aegae, Aigion, Aegira, Bura, Dyme, Helike, Olenus, Patras, Pellene, Phareae, Rhype, and Tritaeae. These cities (or regions) formed a religious and military alliance known as the First Achaean League, which lasted until the late 4th century BC. Of these cities, several gained particular importance: first Helike, then Aigion, was the meeting place of the Achaean League; and Patras (named after Patreas, chief of the Achaeans) very early on became and remained a vital economic centre.

Achaea did not play a leading political role for most of Archaic and Classical antiquity, but it did play an important part in colonial settlement in south Italy, where Achaeans founded several cities including Sybaris and Croton. Achaea also maintained political ties with other Peloponnesian states and was occasionally considered by these neighbours as a means to increase their own power. Hence, in an effort to strengthen their influence in the Peloponnese, the Spartans transferred the bones of Teisamenos (a pre-Dorian hero and son of Orestes) to Sparta. Though the Delphic oracle had reportedly ordered the transfer, the move did not ultimately strengthen the ties between the two states.

Achaean involvement in some of the greatest events in Classical Greek history seems to have been limited. Achaeans did not participate in the Persian Wars (at least neither the Spartan nor the Athenian ally lists mention the Achaeans). And while the region became strategically important during the Peloponnesian War, it only occasionally played an active role in it, as in the Athenian and Achaean battle against the Corinthians in the harbour of Patras in 429 BC.

During the 4th and 3rd centuries Greece was politically unsettled and so Achaea's importance grew, since Achaean cities had largely maintained their democratic institutions (only Pellene had ever been ruled by a dictator or tyrant) and maintained strong league alliances. Except for the earthquake that destroyed Helike in 373 BC, the Achaeans experienced relative stability after the Peloponnesian War. Treaties with the Achaean League, therefore, became an important part of the foreign policy of several states. Epaminondas of Thebes (in 366 BC), for instance, led troops into the Peloponnese and entered Achaea hoping to make an alliance and thereby check Arcadia's political strength. He easily won an alliance there, but it did not last because the Thebans unwisely decided to overturn the local governments. Resistance and revolt resulted, causing the Thebans to lose Achaea, and drawing Sparta and Achaea into a short-lived, but close, association. As Macedonian influence grew, the Achaean League responded with policies opposed to Philip II, but with little longterm effect. Philip and his superior troops changed Greek politics for ever. Macedonians would remain dominant in Greece and Achaea until the coming of the Romans. Indeed, even after the death of Philip's son, Alexander the Great, the Antigonids (the dynasty founded by Antigonus I) took control of the region and in 303 BC parts of Achaea were held by Demetrius Poliorcetes (son of Antigonus I).

Twenty years after the Macedonians dissolved the First Achaean League, the Second Achaean League was created (280 BC). The new league was much more inclusive than its earlier version, and by the mid-3rd century it was led by Aratus of Sicyon. Aratus continued the anti-Macedonian tradition – keeping Achaea out of the Roman–Macedonian wars. This course initially benefited league members in their relations with the increasingly powerful Romans. Thus, as a result of these policies, the Romans brought most of the Peloponnese under the control of Achaea. Nevertheless, close Roman–Achaean ties were soon disturbed due to Roman interference in league affairs and their insistence that Sparta be released from the league. The Spartans had grown opposed to Achaean League power and, when forced to join the confederation, resented league treatment of them. (The Achaeans had torn down the walls of Sparta and disrupted traditional educational practices.) Sparta appealed to the Roman Senate for aid in their conflict with the league. Attempts at arbitration, influenced by a series of misunderstandings, favoured Sparta, resulting in the Achaean war (146 BC), the temporary dissolution of the league, the destruction of Corinth and Patras, and a permanent Roman presence in the region. By 31 BC Octavian made Achaea just another part of the Roman province of Achaea.

There is abundant evidence for vital religious traditions in Achaea throughout its history. Numerous temples, shrines, and sanctuaries dot the landscape. Achaean coins bear the likeness of Poseidon and Athena. In Pellene Pausanias saw a statue to Athena reportedly created by Phidias. He also mentioned an "infallible" oracle for the sick, located at a spring near Patras. The church of St Andrew was later built at the same site, and the waters there were considered to have miraculous powers well into the 19th century. Inhabitants of the region embraced Christianity somewhat earlier than the rest of Greece, in part, perhaps, because St Andrew preached in Patras and was martyred there. Early Christian conversion was accompanied by the urge to build churches, chapels, and monasteries. Not surprisingly, therefore, many early Christian sites can be found in Achaea. One of the region's oldest intact Christian buildings is the monastery of Makellaria, where an inscription claims that the structure was built by Belisarius (d. 565), general of Justinian I.

During the Slav migrations, Achaea received a new influx of Christianized people, particularly from the 6th to the 9th centuries. Over time these Slavic people quietly assimilated Greek culture and language while Achaea again sank into relative political insignificance. However, like other regions in Greece, there was a quickening of political and economic activity during the 9th century and soon thereafter Achaea would become a prize to be won during western Europe's crusading years. In 1205 the region again occupied centre stage with the founding of the principality of Achaea by the Franks (which included the region of Achaea and most of the Peloponnese or "Morea"). By the end of the 13th century parts of central Greece were once again in Byzantine hands, but the principality of Achaea remained under the control of the Franks. Later it passed into the hands of the Palaiologos family, then to the Turks in 1460. Between 1687 and 1715 the area was part of a Venetian colony. On 21 March 1821 Germanos the archbishop of Patras called for "freedom or death" from the monastery of Hagia Lavra, originally constructed in AD 961. A revolutionary banner was raised in the monastery garden and, after fierce fighting, the region was finally liberated in 1828. Nowadays the small coastal and mountain villages in Achaea are popular among tourists for their picturesque qualities and their ancient and medieval monuments, while Patras is the largest city in the Peloponnese, the capital of the region, and is again among the most important transportation centres in Greece.

CYNTHIA K. KOSSO

See also Peloponnese

Summary

Region in northwestern Peloponnese. Achaea was settled in the Neolithic period and has fairly extensive Mycenaean remains. Its cities formed a federal state which became politically significant during the Peloponnesian War and remained so until the Roman period. Its principal town Patras was the centre of a Frankish principality of Achaea for two centuries after 1205.

Further Reading

Adshead, K., *Politics of the Archaic Peloponnese: The Transition from Archaic to Classical Politics*, Amersham, Buckinghamshire: Avebury, 1986

Andrews, Kevin, *Castles of the Morea*, Amsterdam: Hakkert, 1978

Aymard, André, *Les Premiers Rapports de Rome et de la Confédération Achaienne*, Bordeaux: Féret, 1938

Cook, Robert and Kathleen Cook, *Southern Greece, An Archaeological Guide: Attica, Delphi and the Peloponnese*, New York: Praeger, and London: Faber, 1968

Green, Peter, *Alexander to Actium: An Essay on the Historical Evolution of the Hellenistic Age*, Berkeley: University of California Press, and London: Thames and Hudson, 1990

Hamilton, Charles D., *Sparta's Bitter Victories: Politics and Diplomacy in the Corinthian War*, Ithaca, New York: Cornell University Press, 1979

Kallet-Marx, Robert Morstein, *Hegemony to Empire: The Development of the Roman Imperium in the East from 148 to 62 BC*, Berkeley: University of California Press, 1995

Larse, J.A.O., *Greek Federal States: Their Institutions and History*, Oxford: Clarendon Press, 1968

Papadopoulos, Thanasis J., *Mycenaean Achaea*, 2 vols, Gothenburg: Åströms, 1978–79

Schmitt, John (editor), *The Chronicle of Morea: A History in Political Verse, Relating the Establishment of Feudalism in Greece by the Franks in the Thirteenth Century*, London: Methuen, 1904

Tritle, Laurence A. (editor), *The Greek World in the Fourth Century: From the Fall of the Athenian Empire to the Successors of Alexander*, London and New York: Routledge, 1997

Achilles Tatius

Novelist of the 2nd century AD

Achilles Tatius wrote the novel *Cleitophon and Leucippe*, probably in the 2nd century AD. The *Suda* credits him also with works on etymology, on remarkable people, and on astronomy; but the third of these works, entitled *On the Sphere*, may belong to a different Achilles. Photios, Eustathios, and the *Suda* refer to him as an Alexandrian. The report in the *Suda* that he became a Christian bishop is doubtful, and nothing certain is known of his life.

The eight books of his novel set forth the romantic adventures of a young Greek couple, a youth from Tyre and a maiden from Byzantium. The historical setting appears to be the Hellenistic age, but no precise dates are indicated. The narrator of the tale is the hero himself. The tone fluctuates considerably, as passion and drama alternate with wit and farce. The first portion of the novel describes how Cleitophon woos Leucippe while she and her mother are residing as guests in his father's house. To escape the suspicions of Leucippe's mother, the lovers run away and set sail for Alexandria. When a storm destroys the ship, Cleitophon and Leucippe land together on the coast of Egypt and are captured by an army of bandits, who plan to sacrifice Leucippe; but the hero and heroine are soon rescued. They travel to Alexandria and then Pharos, where Leucippe is abducted by a zealous admirer and a gang of brigands, who dupe their pursuers into believing that Leucippe is dead. Several months later Cleitophon reluctantly agrees to marry Melite, a young widow who has fallen deeply in love with him. They journey to her home in Ephesus to be wed, and there Cleitophon discovers that Leucippe is still alive and working as a slave on Melite's estate. Melite's husband Thersander, previously presumed dead, now returns to Ephesus. Incited by the wicked servant Sosthenes, he imprisons Cleitophon on a charge of adultery and develops a passionate lust for Leucippe, but his schemes are eventually foiled. Leucippe and Cleitophon return home to be married.

Like the other ancient Greek novels, Achilles Tatius' work is written in Atticist prose, that is, with vocabulary and syntax imitating those of Athenian prose authors of the 5th and 4th centuries BC. Substantial portions are highly artificial in style, reflecting the literary tastes of the Second Sophistic: for example, strings of two- and three-word phrases often interrupt the regular flow of the prose; adjacent sentences may reflect one another syntactically and rhythmically.

Achilles employs several dramatic and rhetorical elements common to the Greek novels. In addition to engaging in frequent, often witty dialogue, the characters delight in making speeches. Cleitophon and his friend Clinias debate at length the relative merits of love for boys and love for women (2. 35–38); Melite pleads passionately and eloquently when attempting to seduce Cleitophon (5. 25–26). The artificial language is concentrated in such passages, the argumentation elaborate and sometimes facetious. Achilles also exercises his rhetorical skills in copiously detailed descriptions of events and physical objects: a ship wrecked by a storm (3. 1–4), a hippopotamus (4. 2) and an elephant (4. 4), the city of Alexandria (5. 1). Particularly striking are the several descriptions of works of art, or *ekphraseis* (cf. Philostratus' *Imagines*), the most celebrated of which features a painting of Europa and the bull; situated at the opening of the novel, the lavish visual description of the maiden's abduction announces love and travel as major themes of the ensuing narrative. Other notable rhetorical elements include Achilles' theoretical discourses on the physical mechanisms and psychological effects of emotions and sensations: how kisses give pleasure (2. 8), how rage and anger may vie for control over the soul (6. 19).

Unique among the ancient Greek novels is Achilles' use of a first-person narrator, a technique that offers the reader an intimate and emotionally charged account of events and enhances the characterization of the hero. Like the first-person narrators of the pseudo-Lucianic *Ass* and Apuleius' *Metamorphoses*, Achilles' narrator sometimes appears naive, sentimental, or comic. He occasionally presents himself as an object for mild mockery, as when he is duped into thinking Leucippe dead and pitiably laments her loss (3. 16, 5. 7, and 7. 5), and when he dresses in Melite's clothing to escape Thersander (6. 1–5).

Like his fellow novelists, Achilles attaches considerable importance to the heroine's chastity. Leucippe is instructed by Artemis in a dream to preserve her virginity (4. 1), and in the final book a magical test at the temple of Artemis at Ephesus gives public proof of it (8. 6, 8. 13–14). Achilles' other characters, however, are not subject to the same scrutiny.

Achilles makes liberal use of the mythological and literary tradition. The narrator and other characters, for example, introduce myths as subjects of *ekphraseis* and as exempla in argumentation. Melite playfully likens Cleitophon dressed in women's clothing to Achilles in disguise at the palace of Lycomedes. The characters also quote and allude to a range of authors from the Archaic, Classical, and Hellenistic periods, including Homer, Hesiod, Aristophanes, Plato, Herodotus, Demosthenes, and Theocritus. While portraying the characters as educated and urbane, such references also suggest that Achilles wrote for a sophisticated reading public.

Several papyrus fragments of the novel attest to its popularity from the 2nd to the 4th centuries AD. Achilles was again read and admired in Byzantine times. Photios and Michael Psellos comment on his faults and his merits. Achilles was a major influence on the 12th-century novelists, particularly on Eustathios Makrembolites, whose *Hysmine and Hysminias* borrows many features of Achilles' plot, including the flight of hero and heroine from home, the shipwreck, and the chastity test. Makrembolites also adopts Achilles' first-person narrative and shows a similar fondness for visual description and the analysis of emotions.

MICHAEL J. ANDERSON

See also Novel, Romance

Biography
Novelist of the 2nd century AD, author of *Cleitophon and Leucippe*, a romantic adventure story. Achilles was a major influence on the novels of the 12th century, notably the *Hysmine and Hysminias* of Eustathios Makrembolites.

Writings
Leukippe und Kleitophon, edited and translated into German by Karl Plepelits, Stuttgart: Hiersemann, 1980
Leucippe and Clitophon, translated by John J. Winkler, in *Collected Ancient Greek Novels*, edited by B.P. Reardon, Berkeley: University of California Press, 1989

Further Reading
Bartsch, Shadi, *Decoding the Ancient Novel: The Reader and the Role of Description in Heliodorus and Achilles Tatius*, Princeton, New Jersey: Princeton University Press, 1989
Hägg, Tomas, *The Novel in Antiquity*, Oxford: Blackwell, and Berkeley: University of California Press, 1983
Vilborg, Ebbe (editor), *Leucippe and Clitophon: A Commentary*, Stockholm: Almqvist & Wiksell, 1955

Acragas
City in Sicily

Acragas (Agrigentum in Latin, Girgenti in Italian, then renamed Agrigento after its Latin name by Mussolini; today a provincial capital with about 55,000 inhabitants) was founded four km inland from the southwest coast of Sicily about 582/81 BC by the city of Gela and its Greek mother city Rhodes; the site, steeply rising on three sides, provided a natural fortress. Called "the most beautiful of cities" by Pindar (*Pythian* 12. 1), Acragas' importance already in the 6th century BC is confirmed by the legends about the tyrant Phalaris (560 BC), who built a fortification and widened the city's sphere of influence. At the beginning of the 5th century BC another tyrant, Theron, seized power and made Acragas the second most important city of Sicily; together with his son-in-law Gelon of Syracuse, he defeated the Carthaginians at the Himera river in 480 BC. The rich booty (including 25,000 prisoners of war) provided the means for an enormous building programme, the impressive remains of which can still be seen in the so-called "Valley of temples".

Acragas: the Temple of Concordia, built *c.*430 BC

This term for what is a unique archaeological site is some-what misleading, as most of the temples are standing on the hilltops along the town wall, so as to be seen clearly from the sea. Similarly, most of the modern names of the temples are not backed up by ancient evidence. The easternmost "Temple of Juno Lacinia" (a peripteros of 6 × 14 columns) was built in the middle of the 5th century BC; it measures 38.10 × 16.91 m, which is relatively small in comparison with other Sicilian temples. It was restored several times in the Roman era, but fell into decay afterwards and was rebuilt in 1785, from then on inspiring numerous paintings and engravings (e.g. by Caspar David Friedrich). The "Temple of Concordia" (named after a Roman inscription found nearby but unconnected with the building) was built about 430 BC. It is one of the best-preserved Greek temples anywhere, because in the 6th century AD it was transformed into a Christian church; most of the Christian refurbishments were removed during the restoration of 1785. Like most of the Classical temples in Sicily it is rather small (39.42 × 16.92 m) and has a peristyle of 6 × 13 columns. A third temple, dedicated to Heracles (this is confirmed by Cicero's description), lies further west along the town wall. Measuring 67 × 25 m, it is the largest and earliest Doric peripteral temple at Acragas, constructed at the beginning of the 5th century BC during Theron's reign, on the site of a previous temple, as excavations have shown. Its architecture shows

the transition from Archaic to Classical times: the cella has a pronaos, inner sanctuary, and open opisthodomos, and for the first time the closed adytum that was in use in the region before is lacking. According to Cicero the temple contained a bronze cult statue by the Athenian sculptor Myron (5th century BC) and a painting of Heracles killing the snakes by the famous painter Zeuxis of Heraclea (end of the 5th century). North and west from this temple was the site of the ancient city with its agora (only slight traces remain) and the main gate; beyond the city wall are large necropoleis, and at some distance the ruins of a temple of Asclepius (middle of the 5th century BC).

To the west of the city gates lie the impressive ruins of the Temple of Olympian Zeus, a unique example in Greek architectural history. This Olympieion of gigantic size (56.30 × 113.50 m) was put up by the Carthaginians taken prisoner in 480 BC (though never finished). Unlike other temples, it had no freestanding peristyle, but closed walls, on the outward side of which there were 7 × 14 half-columns (about 20 m high), and between them colossal Atlas figures apparently weighed down by the upper part of the temple – an eloquent symbol of the defeat suffered by the Carthaginians. Inside was an immense hall of pillars consisting of three aisles, the middle of which was open to the sky; these peculiar architectural features were taken over from the Phoenician-Carthaginian world and in this way symbolically "imprisoned" within Greek architecture.

To the west of the Olympieion lies the sanctuary of the Chthonian gods, originally of the 6th century, but greatly enlarged during the 5th; it contained several small buildings and numerous altars, the purposes of which are not yet entirely clear. Another two Doric temples were built next to it in the 5th century. Standing in the northwest corner is the so-called "Temple of the Dioscuri", today one of the landmarks of Acragas. It was heavily restored in the 19th century according to people's imagination of how it should look and by mixing remains of the 5th-century BC structure with those of its first restoration in Hellenistic times. Next to it is "Temple L", slightly larger (17.20 × 38.80 m) and today almost completely destroyed. On the western side of this precinct a large artificial lake (probably constructed under Theron) once formed the water reservoir of the city, but is now a steeply descending valley; beyond are the ruins of the Temple of Hephaestus, the last one built by the city (probably at the end of the 5th century) and unfinished.

After the fall of the tyrants in the early 460s BC, Acragas had a kind of democratic government, in which the city's most prominent son, the philosopher Empedocles, seems to have played a role. A massive Carthaginian offensive at the instigation of Segesta (from 409 BC onwards) brought an end to Acragas' might and prosperity; in 406/05 BC the cities of Selinus, Himera, and Acragas fell before this onslaught. In Acragas the revengeful Carthaginians totally destroyed the Temple of Olympian Zeus; furthermore, the city had to demolish its walls and to pay heavy reparations; it never again fully recovered from this blow. In the 4th century BC Timoleon led a new colony to the almost deserted place and Acragas enjoyed a brief revival under the tyranny of Phintias (286–280 BC). In the Punic wars, however, the city again suffered heavily: it was taken successively by the Romans (261) and the Carthaginians (255), and when it fell in 210 BC as the last Carthaginian outpost in Sicily, the whole population was enslaved by the Romans (who soon, however, brought in Sicani as colonists). In the 1st century BC the city regained some importance because of its agricultural production, and accordingly it suffered under Verres' plundering of Sicily (73–71 BC). In Byzantine times it dwindled to a small village, which after the Arab conquest of 827 grew again and – now being called Kerkent/Gergent – became the centre of the Arab population in Sicily. Today's Agrigento covers only the acropolis of the much larger Greek city.

BALBINA BÄBLER

See also Sicily

Summary
A city in Sicily, founded in 582/81 BC by the city of Gela and its mother city Rhodes. Acragas flourished in the 5th century BC and was the home of the philosopher Empedocles. It is famous today for its sequence of well-preserved Doric temples.

Further Reading
Braccesi, Lorenzo and Ernesto De Miro (editors), *Agrigento e la Sicilia greca*, Rome: Bretschneider, 1992
Finley, M.I., *Ancient Sicily*, revised edition, London: Chatto and Windus, and Totowa, New Jersey: Rowman and Littlefield, 1979
Gabba, Emilio and Georges Vallet, *La Sicilia antica*, Naples: Storia di Napoli e della Sicilia, 1980
Holloway, R. Ross, *The Archaeology of Ancient Sicily*, London and New York: Routledge, 1991
Manni, Eugenio, *Geografia fisica e politica della Sicilia Antica*, Rome: Bretschneider, 1981
Wilson, R.J.A., *Sicily under the Roman Empire: The Archaeology of a Roman Province, 36 BC–AD 535*, Warminster: Aris and Phillips, 1990

Acropolis of Athens

The Acropolis is the heart of the ancient city of Athens. It was the focus of habitation from the earliest days of known settlement; its limestone rock, relatively sheer-sided, provided a place of refuge, and it has abundant springs of water round its lower slopes, particularly on the north side. In course of time it became the Late Bronze Age citadel, strengthened with massive fortification walls similar to those at Mycenae and Tiryns, with a palace-type structure within. Sections of the wall survive and are still visible: there is an important stretch at the west end of the rock, while more is concealed behind later walls. The principal entrance was at the west end. It was obliterated at the end of the 6th century BC, and there has been much discussion of the form it took, but it must have had an outer courtyard, edged to the south by a projecting bastion based on the natural rock, and a dog-leg passage through a gateway at the northeast. Of the palace no real traces survive, but it was presumably situated towards the summit of the rock, at its approximate centre. A curiosity is a well, sunk down the side of the rock on the north, within the line of the walls, which gave access to a good water supply even when the Acropolis was under siege. The eventual fate of the citadel at the end of the Late Bronze Age is uncertain. Obviously, it was prepared for attack: the Athenian tradition (which deserves respect) is that the attack on the city was repulsed, and that its history was unbroken.

Certainly the citadel continued to be the focus through the early years of the first millennium BC. Whether it continued as a place of residence for kings is uncertain, but changing circumstances meant that it became rather the chief place of a cult, dedicated to Athena, the protectress of the city (Polias). Her altar was at the summit of the rock, and probably by the end of the 8th century BC a simple temple was situated near to it. The fortification walls remained, and the rock was still defensible, the entrance being as yet unchanged from its Mycenaean form. A curious survival is found at the well. This had partly collapsed and was filled in after only a short period of use, but the opening and the first few steps down remained, and were used for an annual ritual in which young girls chosen as priestesses descended as far as they could with mysterious bundles that they deposited at the bottom, perhaps an unconscious reenactment of collecting water when the well had functioned.

Development of the site was centred on the provision of improved structures for the cult of Athena. The temple in front of the altar (generally referred to as the "Old Temple") was steadily improved. A substantial foundation wall for its north side was constructed in the 7th century BC, and is still visible. Eventually, perhaps at the end of the 7th or in the 6th century

Acropolis of Athens: from the southwest with the odeum of Herodes Atticus in the foreground

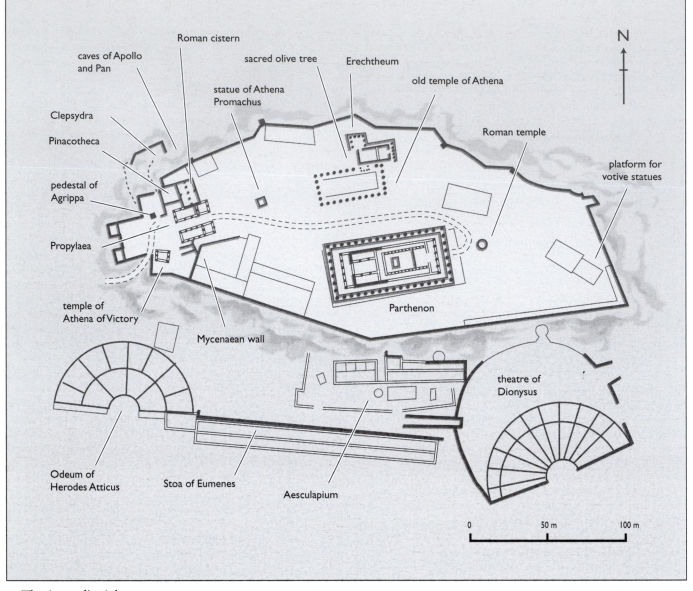

caves of Apollo
and Pan

Roman cistern

sacred olive tree

Erechtheum

old temple of Athena

statue of Athena
Promachus

Roman temple

Clepsydra

Pinacotheca

platform for
votive statues

pedestal of
Agrippa

Propylaea

N

temple of
Athena of Victory

Mycenaean wall

Parthenon

Odeum of
Herodes Atticus

Stoa of Eumenes

Aesculapium

theatre of
Dionysus

0   50 m   100 m

1. The Acropolis, Athens

BC (the date is disputed), the temple became peripteral. It had a complex cella, double ended, the main room facing east to the altar, the west divided into two chambers side by side and with an antechamber. The whole building was surrounded by an outer Doric colonnade, behind which at each end inner rows of four columns stood in front of the porches (prostyle porches). The temple was decorated with sculpture, great pediment groups of heraldic felines, which were removed during later repairs and buried on the Acropolis, where they were found in the 19th century. They are now in the Acropolis Museum. The final rebuilding came towards the end of the 6th century BC, at the end of the period in which Pisistratus, and afterwards his son Hippias, ruled Athens as autocrats (tyrants in the Greek sense), and supposedly had a palace on the Acropolis. In its final form the temple was given a new external limestone colonnade, with metope panels of Parian marble, and new Parian marble pediment groups in the latest style, a battle of gods and giants, which included a striding Athena

killing a giant, much of which survives in the museum. This temple contained the venerable and original cult statue, which was a simple image carved from olive wood. For it, the maiden priestesses of Athena wove, once every four years, a new dress or *peplos*, which was brought to the statue in a sacred procession. By the 6th century BC this procession of the Panathenaic Festival, held once a year, with a particularly important one for the bringing of the *peplos* every fourth year, was the main event in Athens' religious calendar, and resulted in a gathering of the majority of the citizens.

Less clear are the other structures on the Acropolis at this time. There is evidence for another large temple to the south of the Old Temple, which by the end of the 6th century BC seems also to have had marble metopes; and fragments of the superstructure of several small buildings, often highly decorated, for which no foundations survive. What is certain, though, is that the religious usages, the shrines, and the sacred spots on the Acropolis rock established during the early centuries of the first millennium BC formed the basis of its continuing function throughout the Classical period.

Improvements began to be made at the end of the 6th and early in the 5th century BC. The Acropolis was last defended, in a minor skirmish, by the Spartan king Cleomenes I in an abortive intervention following the downfall of the tyrants; but it was then essentially demilitarized, the city being defended, presumably, by an outer circuit of walls. The old Mycenaean gateway was therefore torn down, though the forecourt, presumably an important point in the passage of the procession on to the rock, was retained. A new marble gateway with a colonnaded façade was eventually constructed. More importantly, after the victory of Marathon in 490 BC, the southern temple was pulled down and work started on a new, large, and magnificent Doric temple, in marble quarried on Mount Pentelicus, for which the first requirement was deep foundations, 20 courses of limestone, along its south side so that it could be extended in that direction. This work must have caused severe damage to the Mycenaean walls, which were here in a state of collapse.

The work stopped abruptly in the late 480s BC, when the threat of a new Persian invasion probably meant that all available funds were diverted to the building of warships. Athens was abandoned to the invader. The wooden cult statue, together with the women and children, was evacuated, and the walls of the Acropolis hastily patched up and a forlorn defence mounted, not perhaps in opposition to the policy of evacuation and naval defence but because the Athenians felt an obligation to defend the goddess's property. The Acropolis fell and was sacked. The innumerable statues set up as offerings to Athena (many on behalf of the priestesses when their period of office ended) were vandalized, and the partly built new temple, in its scaffolding, and hardly risen above platform level, was burned. The centre of resistance was probably at the gateway building, which would have been fiercely defended. This was severely damaged. The Old Temple was also burned.

When the Persians were driven out, the Athenians returned to tidy up the Acropolis, but not, as yet, to rebuild. The broken statues were gathered up, and, as the property of Athena, buried on the rock itself. The damaged outer colonnade of the Old Temple was dismantled, and part of its entablature built into new walls surrounding the Acropolis, near where the temple stood, on the north side, presumably as a war memorial. It is still visible there. The gateway building was repaired, using secondhand material. Some sort of simple shrine was built at the side of the Old Temple to house the wooden statue, returned from evacuation. The west cella of the Old Temple was patched, to serve perhaps as a repository for sacred objects rather than as a temple. And nothing else: either the resources of Athens were devoted rather to the prosecution of the continuing war against Persia, or the Athenians felt bound by an oath sworn by their army before the battle of Plataea, not to rebuild the vandalized buildings but to leave them in a ruined state as a memorial to the barbarians' sacrilege.

The revival finally got underway in 451 BC. Athens's prestige as a leader of the Greek world demanded splendid buildings on the Acropolis. Control of what was now in effect an empire provided funds, and the war against the Persians had reached some form of satisfactory conclusion. The rebuilding is essentially associated with Athens's greatest politician,

Pericles, though he did not live to see it completed. Work began with the south temple, known as the Parthenon, the temple to Athena the virgin goddess (though her cult title was still Protectress of the City). Material left undamaged from the unfinished predecessor was used, including the massive south foundation, but the temple was slightly larger and certainly more magnificent, with eight rather than six columns forming its façade. It was built of Pentelic marble; the architects are named as Callicrates and Ictinus. The lavish sculptural decoration was designed by Phidias, though a whole gang of craftsmen would have been employed to execute the work. All the metopes are carved, and a tremendous continuous frieze ran across the inner porches and over the side walls of the cella. The pediments depicted the contest of Athena and Poseidon for the patronage of Athens, and the birth of Athena. The cult statue was a masterpiece in gold and ivory. The whole was completed in 436 BC.

The second building to be replaced was the gateway, the Propylaea, elaborated to include not only the gateway itself, with Doric porches, but also adjacent rooms, one, at least, to the northwest side being used for ritual feasting and decorated with paintings. Work started in 436 BC, to the design of Mnesicles, but, with war against Sparta looming, the plan was truncated, the inner rooms being abandoned. The structure was brought to a hurried completion just before the war broke out, in 431 BC. The abandoned rooms were never built, though indications of their position can still be seen.

Other building was resumed in the years of peace that began in 421 BC. A small temple of Victory (Nike) in the Ionic order was constructed on the bastion of the entrance. Shortly after, the replacement for the Old Temple was started on a new site to the north: the remains of the Old Temple were eventually removed, leaving only the foundations, which are still visible. The new building (popularly called the Erechtheum, after the legendary king Erechtheus, but more officially "The Temple in which is the Old Image") is built to a most unconventional plan. It has a rectangular cella, on two levels, higher at the east, lower at the west, with an internal arrangement recalling the Old Temple. The eastern room housed the cult statue, and had a façade of six Ionic columns. There is another Ionic porch at the west end of the north side, Ionic columns on the west end (but with bases at the higher, eastern floor level), and on the south, a small projecting porch whose roof and entablature rest on the heads of six incongruous draped female statues, recalling the earlier statues of the priestesses, which were now buried nearby. This building is more than a temple, rather a decorative embellishment to a number of sacred spots and shrines. It gives access, through a subsidiary door in the north porch, to the shrine of Pandrosos and the sacred olive tree, the gift of Athena herself when she contested the patronage with Poseidon. In the north porch is Poseidon's effort, a pool of salt water, which appeared when he struck the Acropolis with his trident. Building the Erechtheum dragged on. Completion was delayed by a fire, and it was finished only in 406 BC, just before the Athenians were finally defeated by the Spartans.

After that, Athens no longer had the money for lavish buildings. Statues and other offerings were dedicated in abundance over the years, one of the earliest and certainly the largest being the colossal bronze statue of Athena the Champion by

Phidias, which stood between the Propylaea and the temples. In the years after the death of Alexander the Great in 323 BC the successor king Demetrius Poliorcetes took up residence on the Acropolis as befitted a king (the stories of his orgies with prostitutes there may well be a calumny). In the 1st century BC the Erechtheum was again damaged by fire, but was carefully repaired, the new workmanship being of the same high standard as the original. The same craftsmen were employed, to judge from the details of the work, to build a small circular shrine dedicated to Rome and Augustus, placed in front of the Parthenon. After that little changed, though the Parthenon was severely damaged by fire in the 4th century AD and needed repair. The Acropolis had become a classic monument to Athens's days of glory; its fame, and the reputation of its buildings, was universal, even when other places were built more lavishly, and on a larger scale.

Change, naturally, came in the Middle Ages. The Parthenon retained a religious significance until the 1830s: it was converted, with the construction of an apse in its east porch, into a Christian church dedicated to the Holy Wisdom (which of course recalls its original dedication). Under the Franks in 1204 it became a Roman Catholic cathedral. With the Turkish conquest in 1456 it became a mosque, and the bell tower of the church that had been built into the western porch was converted into a minaret. In 1687 it was used by the Turks as a gunpowder magazine during the siege of Athens by the Venetians, in the expectation, a vain one, that it would be respected by the besiegers. The resulting explosion blew out the walls of the cella and took off the later roof that then covered it. Later a small mosque was built on the ruins. The Erechtheum became a residence for the Turkish governor and his harem; the Propylaea was adapted as a castle, with a massive tower built on its southwestern wing. Like the Parthenon it was damaged by the explosion of a gunpowder store. Above all, the Acropolis had reverted to its original function as a stronghold: it held a Turkish garrison. It was seized and held by the Greek insurgents against Turkish attack in the War of Independence in the 1820s.

After the freeing of Greece from Turkish rule the last Turkish garrison marched out through the later fortifications and gateway that had been built in front of the Propylaea. For Greece, the Acropolis was now a symbol of the renewal of the old Hellenic spirit and tradition, and the later accretions had to be removed. The Turkish houses and cisterns on it were quickly taken down. The gun position built by the Turks on the Nike bastion was demolished, revealing the dismembered marble of the original temple, well enough preserved for Ludwig Ross to reconstruct it. The "Frankish" tower on the Propylaea was removed at the expense of Heinrich Schliemann in 1874. All the Classical buildings were consolidated and, as far as possible, repaired. At present the Acropolis and its buildings are undergoing another crisis, caused by the vast number of tourists, the atmospheric pollution of the modern city, and the poor quality of some of the earlier repairs. A new and astronomically expensive programme of conservation demonstrates the continuing importance of the Acropolis to the Hellenic tradition.

R.A. TOMLINSON

Summary

Rocky outcrop that was always the focus of the ancient city of Athens. In the Bronze Age it became a citadel encompassing a palace. Later it became the centre of the cult of Athena and temples were built from the end of the 8th century BC. Sacked by the Persians in 480, the temples were rebuilt (451–436 BC) in grand style by Pericles. Later a church and then a mosque, the Parthenon and other buildings stand as a symbol of the survival of the Hellenic tradition.

Further Reading

Economakis, Richard (editor), *Acropolis Restoration: The CCAM Interventions*, London: Academy Editions, 1994

Hopper, R.J., *The Acropolis*, London: Weidenfeld and Nicolson, and New York: Macmillan, 1971

Korres, M., *From Pentelicon to the Parthenon: The Ancient Quarries and the Story of a Half-Worked Column Capital of the First Marble Parthenon*, Athens: Melissa, 1995

Tournikiotis, Panayotis (editor), *The Parthenon and Its Impact in Modern Times*, Athens: Melissa, 1994

Adoption

The major preoccupation of modern legislation on adoption is the welfare of the adopted child. In ancient Greek cities adoption was used mainly as a succession strategy for childless people. It also entailed duties of a religious character for the adopted person. Adoption has always had a public dimension, expressed either with a declaration in the marketplace or in a civic ceremony or, as in Hellenistic Egypt and Byzantium, with the written instrument or, as happens today, with a court decree.

The laws of Gortyn regulate in detail the process of adoption (called anpansis). Only male adults had the right to adopt. The adoption took place in public, in the agora. The declaration was followed by a ceremony in the political association (*hetaireia*) of the adopter and a sacrifice. The existence of natural children was not an impediment to adopting other children. Legal implications related mainly to inheritance. In particular, if the adopter died without natural heirs, then the adopted inherited his property as well as the obligation to perform religious rites. If the adopter had natural sons (or daughters), then the adopted received a portion equal to that of the natural heiresses. If the adopted died without natural children, the property he inherited was transferred to the next of kin (*epiballontes*) of the adopter. The adoption was cancelled in public and the adopter had to pay 10 staters to the judge, who in his turn gave this amount to the adopted.

In Athens adoption (*(eis)poiesis*) was geared towards the establishment of an heir to the adopter's property and the continuation of his *oikos* (family). Adoptions could be performed in one of three ways: during the lifetime of the adopter (*inter vivos*), by will (testamentary), and posthumously. Only men could adopt, and it was more likely that adult men rather than boys would be adopted. The adopted was able to inherit the property of the adopter like a natural son, without any previous legal formalities. Testamentary adoption was introduced by Solon at the beginning of the 6th century BC. It allowed a man without sons to adopt by testament an adult male, who would inherit from him. If there was a natural daughter, the adopted son would either marry her himself or provide her with a dowry equal to half of the paternal property. Elderly people were safeguarded from being manipulated by a law annulling an adoption if the adopter was very old or suffered from a mental or physical illness or was under the influence of drugs or was threatened. Finally and most curiously, a posthumous adoption could be performed by the family in the context of a mutually acceptable settlement.

As for other Greek cities we know that in Sparta an adoption took place in front of the kings while in Thebes there was a connection between adoption and grants of land. Adoptions are attested in a large number of inscriptions, especially from Rhodes.

Adoption in the early Byzantine period presents similarities with adoption in Greco-Roman Egypt, where adoption ceased to be oral and took written form. Both parents of the adopted had to consent. In the 6th century Justinian I introduced two kinds of adoption: *adoptio plena* when somebody was adopted by a natural forbear, and *adoptio minus plena* for all other adoptions. In the latter case, the adopted retained the property and succession rights of his natural family.

In the 10th century Leo VI the Wise reformed the system of adoption by granting the right to adopt to women and eunuchs and by banning marriage between a natural and an adopted child. In practice, adoptions were concluded in writing. Adoption agreements did not in themselves constitute the adoption. However, these agreements expounded the rights and duties of the contracting parties; the adopters had to provide the material necessities and a dowry while the adopted was expected to serve and honour his adopted parents. The right to inherit was not automatically granted but had to be explicitly stated. Otherwise, the adopted had a claim to intestate inheritance.

Adoption was used in the imperial court by childless emperors to provide a successor to the throne or by ambitious pretenders anxious to get nearer to the centre stage.

In modern Greek law adoption is allowed if the adopters do not have children of their own. A court decision is required when there are exceptional circumstances. Adults can be adopted by a person older than 50, while a minor can be adopted by anyone older than 30. In any case there should be a difference of 18 years between the adopted and the adopter. The consent of the adopted is required; but if he is a minor, parental consent is needed. Adoption results in the adopted having the same rights and duties as a natural child; however the adopted person retains the rights and duties towards his natural family unless otherwise stated. The adoption is cancelled either by recognition of the adopted as the parent's own child or with marriage between the adopted and the adopter or by court decree.

I.N. Arnaoutoglou

See also Children, Family, Inheritance

Further Reading

Gaudemet, J., "Formes et fonctions de l'adoption dans le monde antique", in his *Droit et société aux derniers siècles de l'Empire romain*, Naples: Jovene, 1992

Kurylowicz, M., "Adoption on the Evidence of Papyri", *Journal of Juristic Papyrology*, 19 (1983): pp. 61–75

Kurylowicz, M., "Die justinianische Adoption", in *Sodalitas: Scritti in onore di Antonio Guarino*, vol. 7, Naples: Jovene, 1984, pp. 3305–16

Macrides, R., "Kinship by Arrangement: The Case of Adoption", *Dumbarton Oaks Papers*, 44 (1990): pp. 109–18

Rice, E.E., "Adoption in Rhodian Society" in *Archaeology in the Dodecanese*, edited by Søren Diezt and Ioannis Papachristodoulou, Copenhagen: National Museum of Denmark, 1988

Rubinstein, Lene, *Adoption in IV. Century Athens*, Copenhagen: Museum Tusculanum Press, 1993

Adrianople

City in Thrace

Adrianople (modern Edirne) is located on the middle Hebrus (Maritsa/Euros/Meric) river where it is joined by two other rivers, the Arda and the Tunca (Tundzha). These rivers and their valleys provide access through the Macedonian mountains to the west, the major access from Bulgaria to the northwest, and the route to the Black Sea to the north. Adrianople's strategic location at the western end of an extensive plain which had the city of Constantinople at the eastern end meant that it was used to help safeguard Constantinople from invasions from the north and made it a focal point of military activity.

The original settlement, Orestias, was refounded as Hadrianopolis c.AD 126 by the emperor Hadrian, who perhaps was following Trajan's failed attempt to increase urbanization in Thrace. Adrianople itself rarely receives mention as an administrative centre and its importance as a bishopric, known since the end of the 4th century, declined from 27th position in the 7th century to 40th in the 10th century. Instead, more than a dozen battles and sieges in and around the city lend it its significance.

On 3 July 324 Constantine the Great engaged and defeated the forces of the eastern emperor, Licinius, setting the stage for Constantine's ultimate victory and consolidation of the empire under his sole rule. On 9 August 378 the Goths defeated the eastern emperor, Valens, just to the northwest of the city (see below). The city's defences proved strong enough to resist several attacks, in 378 by the Goths, in 583 by the Avars, and later in the 9th and 10th centuries by the Bulgarians, when the city was used as a strong point against them. It was successfully defended in subsequent centuries many times but fell and changed hands frequently during conflicts between Constantinople and its opponents in the 13th and 14th centuries. The city eventually became the Ottomans' capital until their capture of Constantinople in 1453.

The most important of these conflicts was the complete defeat of the Roman forces at the hands of a Gothic-Hunnic force in 378. Earlier in the 360s, Valens had pursued and defeated Gothic bands, forcing them to accept disadvantageous terms and to recognize the Danube as the boundary between the two peoples. By the mid-370s, however, internal dissension and pressures exerted upon the Goths and other Germanic tribes by the Huns, who were sweeping westward across the steppes of Central Asia, began to cause considerable difficulties. The Goths were being squeezed between two very powerful groups, the Huns and the Romans.

In 376, led by Fritigern and Alavivus, perhaps as many as 70,000 to 80,000 (ancient sources say 200,000) Tervingian Goths were given permission by Valens to cross the Danube and to enter Roman territory, upon the condition of surrendering weapons and young males as hostages. No doubt Valens thought he would have new recruits for his armies. The situation was desperate for the refugees, who had suffered supply problems even on the left bank of the river. Roman officials either did not realize how many Goths were crossing and were unable to deal with the flood of refugees, or they exploited the starving masses by exchanging dog meat for children, who were enslaved. During this chaos a second group of Goths (Greuthungians) sought permission to cross the Danube along with some Alanic and Hunnic refugees and their mounts. They were refused but crossed anyway during the confused circumstances caused by the ill treatment of the Tervingi, whom they joined.

In what may have been an attempt to resolve the explosive situation, the Roman commander of Thrace, Lupicinus, invited Fritigern and Alavivus to a dinner in Marianopolis (Shumla). Here he either tried to assassinate the leaders, or he seized them and killed their bodyguard after a riot began when other Goths were denied access to the city. After the escape of Fritigern, the Goths laid waste the Thracian countryside.

More Alans and Huns had joined Fritigern by 378 and he had come to some sort of agreement with the Franks and Alemanni on the Rhine, who kept the western emperor Gratian from aiding his uncle Valens, who had settled his Persian affairs and moved his court from Antioch to Constantinople. Valens' general Sebastianus quickly brought the Goths and their allies to a standstill about 14 km northwest of the city. The Goths, probably about 20,000 warriors in a large group of 90,000 to 100,000, remained behind their wagon laager (war wagons assembled into a defensive circle). Valens rejected the advice of his general to await the reinforcements from Gratian and moved his army to Adrianople.

Receiving intelligence reports of a Gothic force of only 10,000 infantry and no cavalry, Valens followed the advice of Sebastianus and his staff against the dissenting voice of his general Victor and decided to attack, despite Richomeres' arrival with the information that Gratian's army was only a few days away. On the morning of 9 August, having deposited his baggage train and treasury in the city, Valens moved to engage the enemy.

He marched his 20,000 to 35,000 men (ancient sources give 60,000), of which one third was light and heavy cavalry, through 14 km of dusty, fired terrain under a soon-to-be scorching sun. Proper supplies and, it seems, reconnaissance were abandoned since, when the Roman force suddenly came upon the Goths, they were deployed without having had rest or a meal.

Fritigern, expecting the arrival of his cavalry at any moment, opted for delay by sending ambassadors to Valens seeking a truce. The talks came to nothing and, as often happens, the battle began by accident when Roman guards fired upon the Gothic camp without orders. Within minutes the battle was joined and the Roman line, still forming, was under attack. At the same time the Gothic/Alan cavalry returned and struck the Roman cavalry on the right. The Roman horse held its ground until the Roman centre was separated from the left flank, which had moved partially round the circle of wagons. At this point Fritigern moved to isolate the Roman cavalry on the left, driving them from the field. The Goths now were able to flank the Roman centre, pushing it against the laager and the Roman cavalry on the right. Under the pressure of heavy archery fire, the Roman horse on the right broke and fled the field, leaving the infantry to deal with both Gothic cavalry and infantry. In an ever-decreasing amount of space that hindered their defence, the Romans were overwhelmed and slaughtered when the Gothic reserve charged forth from the laager.

The devastation suffered by the Romans was tremendous: 14,000 to 25,000 casualties, and much of the command structure of both the infantry and cavalry including Sebastianus and other top commanders, 35 military tribunes, and the emperor himself. If the higher estimates are believed, not since Cannae had the Romans suffered such losses of manpower and commanders. These losses, coupled with the presence of a very considerable and hostile Gothic force, created a desperate situation for the eastern empire.

The Goths tried to follow up their victory on the battlefield by assaulting Adrianople and Constantinople but failed. Much more serious were their unhindered attacks upon smaller settlements and the damage suffered throughout the rest of Thrace. The threat they represented had important consequences for the future of the empire: the appointment of Theodosius as emperor, his enrolment of barbarian recruits into the army, and the settlement of Goths as federates within the empire with special privileges.

The battle of Adrianople has often been regarded as a turning point in history and in the history of western warfare. Yet in many ways this is not so. Simple mistakes and miscalculations gave the Goths the victory. Had Valens acted immediately upon his intelligence or waited for Gratian's forces the result would probably have been different. Nor did the role of the Gothic cavalry drastically alter warfare as has been argued. By far the most important results were Roman accommodation of their barbarian neighbours and the growth and use of barbarians in Roman military ventures.

ANDREW N. SHERWOOD

Summary

City in Thrace whose strategic location made it the site of numerous battles and sieges, most notably the battle of AD 378 in which the Roman army was routed by a combined force of Goths and Huns. A direct consequence of that battle was the greater use of barbarians in the Roman army. Briefly the Ottoman capital, Adrianople was renamed Edirne in modern Turkey.

Further Reading

Arvites, J.A., "The Military Campaigns of Adrianople", *History Today*, 31 (1981): pp. 30–35

Austin, N.J.E., *Ammianus on Warfare: An Investigation into Ammianus' Military Knowledge*, Brussels: Latomus, 1979

Austin, N.J.E. and N.B. Rankov, *Exploratio: Military and Political Intelligence in the Roman World from the Second Punic War to the Battle of Adrianople*, London and New York: Routledge, 1995

Burns, Thomas S., "The Battle of Adrianople: A Reconsideration", *Historia*, 22 (1973): pp. 335–45

Burns, Thomas S., *Barbarians within the Gates of Rome: A Study of Roman Military Policy and the Barbarians, c.375–425 AD*, Bloomington: Indiana University Press, 1994

Crump, Gary A., *Ammianus Marcellinus as a Military Historian*, Wiesbaden: Steiner, 1975

Elton, Hugh, *Warfare in Roman Europe, AD 350–425*, Oxford: Clarendon Press, and New York: Oxford University Press, 1996

Ferrill, Arthur, *The Fall of the Roman Empire: The Military Explanation*, London and New York: Thames and Hudson, 1986

Gabriel, Richard A. and Donald W. Boose Jr, *The Great Battles of Antiquity: A Strategic and Tactical Guide to Great Battles That Shaped the Development of War*, Westport, Connecticut: Greenwood Press, 1994

Grant, Michael, *The Fall of the Roman Empire*, 2nd edition, London: Weidenfeld and Nicolson, and New York: Collier, 1990

Jones, A.H.M., *The Later Roman Empire, 284–602: A Social, Economic and Administrative Survey*, 3 vols, Oxford: Blackwell, and Norman: University of Oklahoma Press, 1964

Pavan, M., "La battaglia di Adrianopli (378) e il problema gotica nell'impero romano", *Studi Romani*, 27 (1979): pp. 153–65

Wolfram, H., "Die Schlacht von Adrianopel", *Anzeiger der Österreichischen Akademie des Wissenschaften (Wien), Philosophisch-Historische Klasse*, 114 (1977): pp. 228–45

Zachariadou, E.A., "The Conquest of Adrianople by the Turks", *Studi Veneziani*, 12 (1970): pp. 211–17

Adultery

Hellenic culture has exhibited an almost obsessive concern with female chastity since the time of Homer; Helen's elopement with Paris led to the Trojan War, while Aegisthus' seduction of Clytemnestra destroyed her husband and endangered his house. One key to this concern is the legitimacy of children; a man can never be absolutely sure of his own paternity and that of his children, and even Telemachus, son of the super-chaste Penelope, admits that it is a wise child who knows his own father (*Odyssey*, 1. 215–16). Equally important is the impact of female unchastity on social relationships between men. These relationships are informed by concepts of honour, shame, and public reputation, ideas crucial to an understanding of the sexual mores not only of Greek antiquity but also of modern Hellenic society.

With regard to adultery (*moicheia*) in ancient Greece, it was the married or marriageable status of the woman involved that was the crucial point, not the status of the man. *Moicheia* comprised sex between any man, for whom marital status was irrelevant and marital fidelity unnecessary, and a female under a male citizen's protection (that is, the wife, daughter, sister, or mother of a citizen); for a man, married or unmarried, sex with a slave or a prostitute, male or female, did not constitute adultery.

Concerns about adultery in antiquity were informed by particular political and inheritance systems. In Classical Athens, where the male line was a critical factor in the transmission of property and citizen status, the avoidance of adulterine bastardy was accorded a corresponding importance; where patrilineal inheritance pertains, all property depends upon the chastity of women.

Extreme penalties were attached to adultery in Athens. A Draconian law of 621 BC allowed the summary execution of an adulterer caught in flagrante, while Plutarch attributes to Solon a law that allowed a father to sell into slavery an unmarried daughter caught with her seducer (*Solon*, 23. 2), an unparalleled treatment of a free person in Attic law and an indication that the ruined girl no longer had any civic status to violate. These uncompromising penalties had fallen into disuse by the Classical period, but still adultery was criminalized as an act of hubris (disrespect, outrage) against both the individual (that is, the citizen in charge of the ruined woman) and the community. Adultery was regarded as an anti-democratic offence, an act of political as well as sexual subversion, and, accordingly, the social and legal consequences could be severe. Adultery could be used as a justification for homicide if the adulterer (*moichos*) was caught in the act, but the penalty attaching to the charge of adultery (*graphe moicheias*) was more usually a fine or public humiliation. However, there is no firm extant example of the use of the *graphe moicheias* and a prosecution for hubris (*graphe hubreos*) may have been preferred. There was no legal procedure available against the woman taken in adultery, but her punishment was severe also; she was compulsorily divorced and prohibited from participating in public sacrifice ([Demosthenes], 59. 87; Aeschines, 1. 183–84). However, the shame attaching to the cuckold and the compulsion to return both wife and dowry may have induced some husbands to keep the matter quiet and out of the public arena (Euripides, *Hippolytus*, 462–63; Aeschines, 1. 107), and there is evidence to suggest that others manipulated the situation to extort money from adulterers ([Demosthenes], 59. 64–70).

Despite the potential consequences, adultery provided an opportunity for erotic and romantic attachments in a society where arranged marriages were the norm. Many may have thought it a risk worth taking, and several texts imply such behaviour may not have been uncommon (for example, Aristotle claims that it is easy to commit adultery with the wife of a friend or neighbour: *Ethica Nichomachea*, 1137a5). Nevertheless, adultery was regarded as such a severe dereliction of social and civic duty that it could be described as a crime worse than rape (Lysias, 1. 32–33), perhaps because seduction involves the desire and complicity of the woman, and her deception may extend to passing off a lover's children as a husband's. Thus the adulterer and his offspring could take over the household and its legitimate line of descent.

For democratic Athens the civic consequences of adultery were incorporated in the political notion of hubris, but the personal and social dishonour that attaches to the man who cannot guard the women of his household or avenge their disgrace is a transhistorical concept for Hellenic culture which has persisted into 20th-century Greek society. A man's honour (*time*, a term used in both ancient and modern Greek), that is to say, the social recognition of his worth, is defined largely through the chastity of his women. If the chastity of a man's mother is compromised, his own legitimacy is at stake; if his wife is suspected of adultery, the implication is that his children may be bastards, while the idea that a man is not man enough to control his women is a slur on his masculinity (*andrismos*, a modern Greek term). Conversely, the adulterer, while condemned as socially disruptive and a threat to family stability, may enhance his reputation for virility through his behaviour. The cuckold, however, is a shamed, emasculated, and stigmatized figure. Women are expected to safeguard their own and their families' reputations by cultivating the appearance of sexual modesty (*dropi*, again a modern Greek term). In the 5th century BC Pericles proclaimed that a woman's greatest glory was not to be talked about (Thucydides, 2. 45), and the public demonstration of female chastity is crucial still – women must not only be chaste, they must be seen to be chaste. Social reputation and gossip are particularly significant in face-to-face societies, not only in those of the ancient world such as Athens but in any close-knit Hellenic community in or outside Greece, and perhaps especially important in village life.

These common social attitudes towards adultery are supported by the Church's attempts to regulate sexual behaviour. Adultery has been marked out for especial censure throughout the Christian tradition, which condemns fornication, a notion that embraces any extramarital sex, either premarital or adulterous, and which threatens the Christian ideal of the "pure" marriage. Indeed, later canon law prescribed death for the adulterer, the strong proscription being based on Matthew 5: 32, which proclaimed that "whoever looks at a woman to lust after her commits adultery with her already in his heart", a pertinent illustration of the Christian principle that sexual fidelity is expected of husbands as well as wives, a marked contrast to the ancient world. However, it is the adultery of wives, not husbands, that provides the only valid grounds for divorce in the Orthodox Church, at least technically, referring to the authority of Matthew 19: 9, which states that if a man remarries, having divorced his wife for any cause other than adultery, he himself commits adultery. For Christian Greeks in particular the marital status of men as well as women is relevant to the definition of adultery, but from antiquity to the present, in both social and religious terms, the unchastity of wives has been the greater concern.

EUGÉNIE FERNANDES

See also Divorce, Family, Honour and Shame, Marriage

Further Reading

Brandes, S., "Reflections of Honor and Shame in the Mediterranean" in *Honor and Shame and the Unity of the Mediterranean*, edited by David Gilmore, Washington, D.C.: American Anthropological Association, 1987

Cairns, D.L., "Hybris, Dishonour and Thinking Big", *Journal of Hellenic Studies*, 116 (1996): pp. 1–32

Campbell, J.K., *Honour, Family and Patronage: A Study of Institutions and Moral Values in a Greek Mountain Community*, Oxford: Clarendon Press, 1964

Cartledge, P., "Spartan Wives: Liberation or Licence?", *Classical Quarterly*, 31/1 (1981): pp. 84–105

Cohen, David, "The Social Context of Adultery at Athens" in *Nomos: Essays in Athenian Law, Politics and Society*, edited by Paul Cartledge, Paul Millett and Stephen C. Todd, Cambridge and New York: Cambridge University Press, 1990, pp. 147–65

Cohen, David, *Law, Sexuality and Society: The Enforcement of Morals in Classical Athens*, Cambridge and New York: Cambridge University Press, 1991

Dubisch, Jill (editor), *Gender and Power in Rural Greece*, Princeton, New Jersey: Princeton University Press, 1986

Du Boulay, Juliet, *Portrait of a Greek Mountain Village*, Oxford: Clarendon Press, 1974

Du Boulay, Juliet, "Lies, Mockery and Family Integrity" in *Mediterranean Family Structures*, edited by J.G. Peristiany, Cambridge and New York: Cambridge University Press, 1976

Fisher, N.R.E., *Hybris: A Study in the Values of Honour and Shame in Ancient Greece*, Warminster: Aris and Phillips, 1992

Gagarin, Michael, *Drakon and Early Athenian Homicide Law*, New Haven, Connecticut: Yale University Press, 1981

Giovannini, M., "Female Chastity Codes in the Circum-Mediterranean" in *Honor and Shame and the Unity of the Mediterranean*, edited by David Gilmore, Washington, D.C.: American Anthropological Association, 1987

Goria, Fausto, *Studi sul matrimonio dell'adultera nel diritto giustiniano e byzantino*, Turin: Giappichelli, 1975

Harris, E.M., "Did the Athenians Regard Seduction as a Worse Crime than Rape?", *Classical Quarterly*, 40/2 (1990): pp. 370–77

Herzfeld, M., "Semantic Slippage and Moral Fall: The Rhetoric of Chastity in Rural Greek Society", *Journal of Modern Greek Studies*, 1 (1983): pp. 161–72

Ogden, Daniel, *Greek Bastardy in the Classical and Hellenistic Periods*, Oxford: Clarendon Press, and New York: Oxford University Press, 1996

Patterson, C.B., "Those Athenian Bastards!", *Classical Antiquity*, 9/1 (1990): pp. 40–73

Pitt-Rivers, J., "Honour and Social Status" in *Mediterranean Family Structures*, edited by J.G. Peristiany, Cambridge and New York: Cambridge University Press, 1976

Roy, J., "Traditional Jokes about the Punishment of Adulterers in Ancient Greek Literature", *Liverpool Classical Monthly*, 16 (1990): pp. 73–76

Todd, S.C., *The Shape of Athenian Law*, Oxford: Clarendon Press, 1993

Aegae

City in Macedonia

The Macedonian city of Aegae (more properly Aegeae) is situated in the northern foothills of the mountain range of Olympus, by the modern village of Vergina, overlooking the river Haliacmon and what is now a rich extent of flat cultivated plain but in antiquity was more likely, at best, marshland. The ancient road to northern Greece, followed by an Athenian army in 432 BC, ran from the coastal towns of Pydna and Methone westwards past Aegae before turning north at the next locality, Beroea. This area formed the Macedonian heartland, and from it successive Macedonian kings extended their rule west and north, until by the 5th century BC the whole region round and beyond the Axios (which flows down from the central Balkans) was part of the Macedonian state.

The city itself is still largely unexcavated. Traces of its fortifications and a city gate, enclosing an acropolis-type hill, can be made out, but archaeological work has concentrated on the areas below this, where important discoveries have been made. The existence of important remains was first noticed by the French archaeologists L. Heuzey and H. Daumet in the 1860s, though they did not identify the site as the ancient Aegae. Following an ambiguous passage in the Roman historian Justinus (7. 1. 7) it was believed that Aegae was situated at Edessa, where there were also ancient remains; but in an important paper given at the First International Symposion on Ancient Macedonia in 1967 N.G.L. Hammond pointed out that this was a misinterpretation, and that Aegae was located elsewhere: because of its archaeological remains, and other literary evidence, particularly Theophrastus, *De Ventis*, 27, he suggested Vergina. Subsequent discoveries there have more than confirmed this.

Outside the town, on the flat ground, is an extensive cemetery of pit graves covered with low tumuli dating from the early Iron Age (the turn of the 2nd and 1st millennia BC) into the Classical period. The contents of the earlier tombs show connections with regions further to the north, and they are therefore to be identified as the graves of the original Macedonian settlers. There is no good archaeological evidence for the adjacent settlement at this time, and it hardly merits being called a city. Its importance is demonstrated rather by the large number of graves. Aegae is thus the traditional Macedonian centre, and remained so, particularly in terms of its religious function, even when a new city was created at Pella. It should have been a place of residence for the Macedonian kings, but although the 5th-century king Perdiccas was encountered there by the Athenian army in 432 BC, there is no trace of an actual royal residence until the end of the 4th century BC when a substantial palace was built, measuring overall 104.5 by 88.5 m. This consists of a central courtyard 44.5 m square with a peristyle of 16 Doric columns on each side. To the east and north are open verandahs (a most unusual feature for Greek residences, which are invariably closed and inward looking) commanding extensive views over the Haliacmon. Most of its rooms are equipped as formal dining rooms, appropriately graded to accommodate the different ranks of the Macedonian court; the palace seems to have been designed primarily for ceremonial or religious functions rather than as a conventional administrative building.

Below the palace is the theatre, which had wooden seats arranged on the earth slopes, apart from the first row which was limestone. It was here that the great Philip II was murdered in 336 BC, watching a procession in celebration of the marriage of his daughter Cleopatra. Nearby is a small temple, dedicated to the goddess Eucleia by Philip's mother Eurydice. But the most convincing evidence that Vergina is the ancient Aegae is the Great Tumulus, excavated by Manolis Andronikos. Aegae was known from literature (Plutarch, *Pyrrhus*, 26. 6–7) to have been the burial place of the Macedonian kings. Hammond suggested that a built vaulted tomb, of the type categorized as Macedonian and excavated by K. Rhomaios in the 1930s, decorated in the same form of the Ionic order as the monument of Philip at Olympia, might be where he was buried after his assassination. Andronikos's excavation of the largest of the tumuli uncovered more "Macedonian" tombs, including one that was unrobbed, containing the remains of the cremated dead (a man and a woman) in chests of gold together with a vast array of other objects, gold, silver, ivory, and an iron breastplate similar to that worn by Philip's son Alexander in the mosaic which depicts him at the battle of Issus. The remains of the dead man were not completely reduced to ashes, and enough of the bone structure remained to indicate that he was of Philip's age when he died, and that, like Philip, he had been blinded in one eye by an arrow which had entered the skull from above; in all there is ample evidence to confirm the identity of the great Macedonian king and the locality at Vergina as the city of Aegae.

The subsequent history of Aegae is uncertain, and there is no secure archaeological evidence later than the Hellenistic palace. During the troubled years which followed the death in 297 BC of king Cassander (who may have been responsible for the palace) the royal tombs were plundered by Gallic mercenary soldiers employed by the king of Epirus, Pyrrhus, during his invasion of Macedonia in 288 BC. Somehow, Philip's tomb escaped, and it was after this that Antigonus Gonatas, when he secured the kingship of Macedon for himself in 277/76 BC, heaped over it and another unplundered royal tomb the great mound which preserved it intact.

After the final Roman conquest of Macedon following the battle of Pydna in 167 BC, Aegae disappears from history. It is not one of the capitals of the four separate regions into which the Romans divided the former kingdom. Too closely associated with the traditions of the Macedonian people and monarchy, it had no place in the Roman system of things. If not deliberately destroyed, it was defortified and, probably, allowed to dwindle away, its place as the leading city of this area being taken over by Beroea.

R.A. TOMLINSON

Summary

Ancient city in Macedonia near the modern village of Vergina. It was the religious centre of Macedonia and the burial place of its kings. Following a suggestion made by N.G.L. Hammond in 1967, Manolis Andronikos excavated an unrobbed tomb containing spectacular grave goods which can be safely identified as that of Philip II.

Further Reading

Andronikos, Manolis, *Vergina*, vol. 1: *To Necrotapheion Ton Tymvon* [The Tymbon Cemetery], Athens, 1969
Andronikos, Manolis, *Vergina: The Royal Tombs and the Ancient City*, Athens: Ekdotike Athenon, 1984, reprinted 1992
Hammond, N.G.L., "The Archaeological Background to the Macedonian Kingdom", *Ancient Macedonia*, 1 (1970): pp. 53ff.
Heuzey, L. and H. Daumet, *Mission archéologique de la Macédoine*, Paris: Firmin-Didot, 1876

Aegina

Island in the Saronic gulf

The island of Aegina lies centrally in the Saronic gulf, some 20 km southwest of Piraeus and the same distance from the Argolid peninsula; it has an area of 83 sq km. The location of the island so close to Attica resulted in a greater involvement with the events and developments of mainland Greece throughout its history than any other island of the Aegean. It has always benefited from a fine natural harbour on the west coast, beside which the town of Aegina grew up and flourished. Its climate is more sheltered than most of the Aegean islands, and its land produces major crops of pistachio nuts as well as olive oil, grapes, almonds, and figs.

Colonized in the 3rd millennium BC, by the 2nd millennium BC Aegina had already become an important trading post. During the 10th century BC (according to Herodotus) the island was colonized by Dorians from Epidaurus, having previously undergone Mycenaean occupation; since then it has

Aegina: the temple of Aphaea, built in the late 6th or early 5th century BC

played at various points an active, and sometimes vital, part in Greek history. The Aeginetan navy was a force of paramount importance from the 7th to the 5th centuries BC, and played a major role in the defeat of the Persians at Salamis (480 BC). Also flourishing during these centuries were the skills of its potters and bronze-founders, and modern products of the former are still sold widely today. But the outstanding survival from this period is the temple dedicated to Aphaea, built in the late 6th or early 5th century BC on a hill in the northeast of the island and looking out over the Saronic gulf towards Attica. Although considerably damaged, it still retains 24 of its 32 original columns, and of particular interest are surviving traces of pigmentation on the floors of the pronaos and cella; originally the columns, of local limestone, were stuccoed and then coloured. Figures from the pediments, carved in Parian marble by the famous Aeginetan sculptor Onatas, were taken to Munich after their discovery in 1811. The individuality of Onatas' artistic style is suggested by the comment of Pausanias (5. 25) that his figures, "even though they are in the Aeginetan style, I would not assess as inferior to those of the Attic school of sculptors". Another sculptor from Aegina called Smilis, the son of Euclides must have been one of the more famous sculptors of his day, since the cult image of Hera in the huge temple on Samos was, according to Pausanias, made by him (7. 4). Later, the inhabitants of Aegina were expelled at the start of

the Peloponnesian War, but were able to return by 400 BC. For the rest of the pre-Christian period the history of the island was closely linked to that of Athens.

Several early Christian basilicas have been excavated within the area of the town of Aegina, indicating a continuing prosperity into the 6th century AD. To the north of the town the hill of Colonna was fortified by this time, and a unique survival is the 4th-century floor mosaic of a synagogue, of which the inscription gives its cost; the building was converted to a church after the 7th century. Around AD 580 the island became a place of refuge for the inhabitants of Corinth, fleeing the Slavic invasions of the Peloponnese, and during the 9th century, like many other of the islands and coastal sites, Aegina suffered from Arab raids.

In the Deed of Partition of 1204, after the Fourth Crusade, Aegina was one of the two Aegean islands awarded unambiguously to Venice, but its position meant that in reality it was ruled first by the dukes of Athens, and then, from the early 14th century, by the Catalan dynasty of the Fadrique (they styled themselves "Lords of Aegina" and sometimes "of Aegina and Salamis"). On the death of Antonello de Caupena in 1451 without heirs, the island was bequeathed to Venice, who appointed a governor responsible to their administration in Nauplia. The Venetians were to hold Aegina until its devastation by Khaireddin Barbarossa, the much-feared admiral of

Suleiman the Magnificent, in 1537. His massacre of the male population and the abduction of all the women and children left the island largely depopulated for the first time since the 10th century BC, and the later revival of its economy must have been due in part to Albanians who were subsequently introduced by Barbarossa.

It was probably during the Arab attacks that the first settlement was made on the hill towards the northwest of the island now called Palaiochora. With the growing insecurity and increase in danger from piracy that marked the 11th and 12th centuries, inland sites such as this grew in importance, and Palaiochora was to develop into a major ecclesiastical and administrative centre. During the period of Catalan and Venetian domination of the island it was the de facto capital and the seat of the Orthodox metropolitan; there are still 35 churches to be seen on this hilltop site, most built in the 14th–16th centuries; inscriptions survive here recording the restoration of individual buildings in 1533, 1610, 1619, and 1674, and so carried out during the Tourkokratia. This remains the largest and best-preserved source for knowledge of church building in this part of the Aegean during these centuries. Further rebuilding must have followed an attack in 1654 by the Venetian admiral Morosini, who succeeded in re-occupying the island for the Republic for more than half a century. At the Treaty of Karlovitz of 1699 Venice was specifically permitted to retain Aegina, and the island was ceded to the sultan only in 1718 at the Conference of Passarovitz.

The vigour of the Aeginetan economy is indicated by the population figures, which by the 1820s were said to be around 8,500; visitors to Palaiochora reported its population to be between 3,000 and 4,000 in the town alone, which had some 400 houses. It must have been this relative prosperity that, combined with its favourable location, caused the island to play a final brief but significant part on the stage of Greek political life. In 1826 Aegina became the seat of the Greek National Assembly during the period of instability that followed the War of Independence, and in 1829 the first coins of the modern Greek state were minted on Aegina under Ioannis Kapodistria. The monetary unit was named appropriately as the silver *phoenix*, with subdivisions of 100 *lepta*, and was renamed as the *drachma* only in 1833.

More recently Aegina has become the resting place of the embalmed body of St Nektarios (1846–1920) who as metropolitan of Pentapolis founded the Convent of the Holy Trinity there in 1904; in 1961 he became the first saint to be canonized by the Greek Orthodox Church in modern times.

Over many centuries and in a variety of ways Aegina can be seen to have contributed more to the Hellenic tradition than almost any other Aegean island.

PAUL HETHERINGTON

See also Nektarios

Summary

Located in the Saronic gulf some 20 km southwest of Piraeus, Aegina has been closely involved in the history of mainland Greece. It had a famous navy in the 7th–5th centuries BC which fought at Salamis. It was ceded to Venice in 1204 and taken for the Ottomans by Barbarossa in 1537. In 1826 it was the seat of the Greek National Assembly.

Further Reading

Miller, William, *The Latins in the Levant: A History of Frankish Greece, 1204–1566*, London: John Murray, and New York: Dutton, 1908; reprinted Cambridge: Speculum Historiale, and New York: Barnes and Noble, 1964

Miller, William, *Essays on the Latin Orient*, Cambridge: Cambridge University Press, 1921, reprinted New York: AMS Press, 1983

Moutsopoulos, N., *I Paleachora tis Aiginis* [Palaeochora on Aegina], Athens, 1952

Woodhouse, C.M., *Modern Greece: A Short History*, 5th edition, London and Boston: Faber, 1991

Aeolians

Ancient ethnic group

Of all the major ethnic groups of ancient Greece the Aeolians are the most indistinct. In modern scholarship the term is generally applied to the populations of Thessaly, Boeotia, the eastern Aegean islands of Lesbos and Tenedos, and the northwestern littoral of Asia Minor north of the Hermus valley – largely on the basis of the structural similarities between the dialects of these areas (although the Boeotian dialect displays several "Northwest Greek" characteristics while the Aeolic dialects of the eastern Aegean are marked by "Ionicizing" features almost certainly due to regular contact with neighbouring Ionian settlements).

In antiquity, however, the term "Aeolians" was applied more indiscriminately. The 1st-century BC geographer Strabo (8. 1. 2) says not only that all the populations north of the Corinthian isthmus (with the exception of the Athenians, Megarians, and Dorians "around Parnassus") were Aeolian, but that the Dorians of northern Greece were themselves originally Aeolians whose speech and customs eventually became distinct as a result of their isolation from their neighbours. He claims further that Aeolians had inhabited the Peloponnese prior to the arrival of the Dorians but that most had assimilated with the Dorian invaders save for the Achaeans, the Eleans, and the Arcadians. It should nevertheless be noted that the West Greek dialects of Achaea and Elis and the Arcado-Cypriot dialect of Arcadia appear to demonstrate little or no similarity with the Aeolic dialect group. The lack of coincidence between claims of ethnic origin and the linguistic situation marks a striking contrast with the case of the Ionians and Dorians, and it has been suggested that the etymology of the term "Aeolians" indicates a group of mixed origins.

According to tradition, Thessaly had originally been called Aeolis (Herodotus, 7. 176. 4), though the 5th-century BC historian Thucydides (3. 102. 5) believed that ancient Aeolis was the area surrounding the Aetolian towns of Calydon and Pleuron. Sixty years after the Trojan War, the Aeolian Boeoti who had formerly been settling Thessaly were expelled and occupied Boeotia to the south (Thucydides, 1. 12. 3; Pausanias, 10. 8. 4). Immediately after settling Boeotia, some of the Boeoti accompanied Penthilus, son of Orestes, in his expedition to colonize the island of Lesbos and Aeolis in Asia Minor (Thucydides, 7. 57. 5; Strabo, 9. 2. 5). There were, however, variant versions – the 2nd-century AD traveller Pausanias (3. 2. 1) says that Penthilus colonized Lesbos and his grandson Gras settled Aeolis, but Strabo (13. 1. 3) reports that it was Gras who settled Lesbos, while the city of Cyme on the coast of Asia Minor was founded by two other descendants of Agamemnon, Kleues and Malaus – and it is generally believed that the tradition of the Aeolian migration was a relatively late compilation that is unlikely to predate the 5th century BC. In particular, the idea that the Aeolian Boeotians were led by the ethnically unrelated Penthilus parallels the tradition of the Dorians returning to the Peloponnese under the leadership of the descendants of Heracles and was almost certainly coined to justify the claims of the Penthilidai, the ruling family in the Lesbian city of Mytilene (Aristotle, *Politics*, 5. 10).

In fact, it is more than likely that a sense of Aeolian identity first emerged among the cities that were founded in the eastern Aegean c.1000 BC. At the beginning of the 7th century BC Hesiod (*Works and Days*, 636) described how his father had left "Aeolian Cyme" for Boeotia; a century later the poetess Sappho evokes "the Muse in Aeolian Eresus" (a city on Lesbos), while a tribe named "Aeolis" is attested in the Lesbian city of Methymna. It is telling that the only Aeolian city which participated in the foundation of the 6th-century Hellenion sanctuary at Naucratis was the Lesbian city of Mytilene (Herodotus, 2. 178. 2). The principal vehicle for the expression of this identity was without doubt the league of 12 cities in Asia Minor which is described in the 5th century BC by Herodotus (1. 149) and which was originally thought to include Smyrna, Cyme, Larissa, Neon Teichos, Temnos, Cilla, Notion, Aegiroessa, Pitane, Aegaeae, Myrina, and Gryneia. Herodotus goes on to report how Smyrna was captured by the Colophonians and transferred to the Ionian Dodecapolis. It has been suggested that the league should predate the 8th century BC since from this time the archaeological evidence at Old Smyrna appears to display no qualitative differences from other Ionian settlements. On the other hand, there is no evidence that ethnic affiliations in ancient Greece were necessarily expressed through distinctive repertoires of material culture, and it is far more likely that the league emerged in the course of the archaic period (possibly the early 6th century) as a direct response to the foundation of the Ionian Dodecapolis. On the basis of perceived ties with central Greece (perhaps historical as well as invented), a sense of Aeolian affiliation may have spread from the eastern Aegean to the regions of Boeotia and Thessaly.

Towards the end of the 6th century BC the compiler of the pseudo-Hesiodic *Catalogue of Women* attempted to systematize and harmonize the variant genealogical traditions of different Greek cities so as to anchor local mythologies within a broader panhellenic context. Besides accounting for relationships between various local heroes, the *Catalogue* articulated in genealogical form the relationship between various Greek ethnic groups by deriving filiation of their eponymous ancestors (Aeolus, Dorus, Ion, Achaeus) from the original ancestor of the Greeks, Hellen (Hesiod, fr. 9, 10a). But whereas Dorus, Ion, and Achaeus are relatively faceless figures whose only function would appear to be to express relationships between Greek population groups, Aeolus stands at the head of a developed genealogical tradition that includes a host of heroes from various localities throughout Greece. It is highly likely that the Aeolus who acts as the ethnic eponym for the Aeolians has here been assimilated with an older homonymous figure and

that Strabo's extensive application of the term "Aeolians" stems from the widespread distribution of local heroes belonging to this Aeolid lineage.

From the end of the 5th century BC Aeolian identity ceases to operate in any meaningful way. It is possible that it was its indiscriminate application that militated against any solid criteria for collective consciousness, but the political situation on both sides of the Aegean sea also played a role. In the east the Aeolian cities – like their Ionian neighbours – succumbed to the successive domination of Lydia, Persia, the Athenian empire, Persia again, the Seleucids, the Attalids, and finally Rome, though even prior to their incorporation within the Lydian empire they had, with the exception of the cities on Lesbos and Tenedos, accepted the leadership of the Ionians (Herodotus, 1. 151. 3). On the Greek mainland, Thessaly became increasingly riven by internal disputes while the Boeotian city of Thebes concentrated on promoting a pan-Boeotian federation over which it claimed hegemony; but any sentiment of ethnic affinity between the two regions was counteracted by their siding with opposing alliances during the Peloponnesian War and by the construction of an ethnicizing rhetoric between Dorians and Ionians in which the Aeolians found no voice.

JONATHAN M. HALL

See also Dialects, Hellenes

Summary
Shadowy ethnic group of ancient Greece now identified on linguistic grounds with the populations of Thessaly, Boeotia, Lesbos, Tenedos, and the northwest coast of Asia Minor. All trace of their separate identity disappears at the end of the 5th century BC.

Further Reading
Bérard, Jean, "La Migration éolienne", *Revue Archéologique* (1959): pp. 1–28
Cook, John M., "Greek Settlement in the Eastern Aegean and Asia Minor" in *History of the Middle East and the Aegean Region, c.1380–1000 BC*, edited by I.E.S. Edwards, N.G.L. Hammond, and E. Sollberger, Cambridge: Cambridge University Press, 1975 (*The Cambridge Ancient History*, vol. 2, part 2, 3rd edition)
García-Ramón, José L., *Les Origines postmycéniennes du groupe dialectal éolien*, Salamanca: University of Salamanca Press, 1975
Meyer, Eduard, Aioles entry in *Real-Encyclopädie der klassischen Altertumswissenschaft*, edited by August Pauly et al., vol. 1.1, 1030–31
Vanschoonwinkel, Jacques, *L'Egée et la Méditerranée orientale à la fin du deuxième millénaire: Témoignages archéologiques et sources écrites*, Louvain: Université Catholique de Louvain, 1991

Aeschines *c.390–c.322* BC

Orator

Aeschines came from an Athenian family that was impoverished by the Peloponnesian War. He was forced to earn a living, and his various early occupations included working as the secretary to the assembly and as a tragic actor. These, and military service for which he was decorated, would stand him in good stead in his political career, which took off after the destruction of Olynthus by Philip II of Macedon in 348 BC. Aeschines was sent to Arcadia as an ambassador to promote Eubulus' proposed Greek congress, which would discuss resistance to Philip, but in the event in 346 BC he was one of the negotiators of the short-lived Peace of Philocrates. One of his fellow ambassadors was the staunchly anti-Macedonian Demosthenes, and the two men, who had fallen out when serving on the council in 347/46 BC, became sworn enemies. Aeschines may have been duped by Philip, who appeared friendly towards Athens, but Demosthenes accused him of accepting bribes. Demosthenes soon received more ammunition for this charge, as Philip invaded Phocis; Aeschines was sent to plead for fair treatment of the defeated Phocians, and Philip held a feast attended by Aeschines and his fellow envoys. On Aeschines' return to Athens Demosthenes began proceedings against him for treason (346/45 BC), but acted through the notorious rake Timarchus. Aeschines successfully countered with his *Against Timarchus*, in which he prosecuted Timarchus for addressing the assembly when forbidden to do so because of his immorality, and it was not until 343 BC that the mood in Athens was right for Demosthenes to bring the case himself. Aeschines delivered his *On the False Embassy* speech and was narrowly acquitted, but his credibility was undermined. Nevertheless, in 339 BC he was sent as an Athenian representative to the Amphictionic Council at Delphi; but at a time when Greek unity against the threat of Philip was essential, Aeschines managed to stir up a Sacred War against Amphissa. As a result Philip had the excuse he needed to intervene in central Greece, and Athens and Thebes were compelled to oppose him at the disastrous battle of Chaeronea. With his background of friendly relations with Philip and hostility towards Demosthenes, Aeschines was sent on the embassy to negotiate peace terms, after which he largely withdrew from the political arena.

Two opportunities subsequently presented themselves for Aeschines to return to the limelight and attack Demosthenes. In 336 BC Ctesiphon proposed that Demosthenes should be crowned for his services to Athens in the theatre at the Great Dionysia, and this gave Aeschines the chance to prosecute Ctesiphon for making an illegal proposal. Philip's murder, however, meant that the trial was delayed, and it was not until 330 BC, after the failure of Agis III's revolt and with Athens firmly under Macedonian control, that the second occasion presented itself. Aeschines delivered his *Against Ctesiphon*, in which he raised probably valid technical reasons for the illegality of Ctesiphon's proposal, but also attempted to show that Demosthenes' career made him unworthy of such an honour. Demosthenes replied with his superlative *On the Crown* speech, and Aeschines failed to secure one-fifth of the votes. He was thus fined heavily, but it was his humiliation that led him to retire to Rhodes, where he probably spent the rest of his life teaching rhetoric and giving public declamations.

Aeschines was not a professional speech writer, and there is no firm evidence that he studied rhetoric, even if he did become a teacher. His speeches are primarily important for their subject matter, but as with his political career, estimation of Aeschines' literary merits has suffered unduly in ancient and modern times by comparison with Demosthenes. Aeschines writes clear, vivid narrative, sometimes with lengthy sentences but regularly in shorter periods, and with an avoidance of hiatus that is evidence for careful composition. He employs ordinary Attic vocabulary, interspersed with poetic and rare words; and his actor's training leads him to frequent quotations of poetry, which are often long and largely irrelevant. He is prone to using exaggerated language (one of his favourite words is *deinos*, "terrible"), with accumulations of synonyms and appeals to the gods, and he has a range of vivid metaphors at his disposal. Aeschines has an innate wit, which is particularly noticeable when he is attacking Demosthenes, and these attacks can, in the fashion of the time, become extremely abusive. But generally Aeschines' Greek has a dignified tone, as befits a dignified man who deplored the use of extravagant gestures while speaking.

Only the three speeches mentioned above survive, and this was the case also in the Roman period, when Caecilius of Caleacte pronounced a fourth speech concerning Delos spurious. All three are forensic, though delivered in connection with wider public issues. Aeschines, however, tends to avoid these issues and to concentrate on the legalities of the case, but at the same time his talent lies in narrative rather than argument. Hence in *On the Embassy*, Aeschines' best speech, he does not attempt to explain his policies, but offers an amusing and lucid narrative of Demosthenes' totally losing his nerve in the presence of Philip on the first embassy sent to discuss the Peace of Philocrates. When it came to *Against Ctesiphon* Aeschines could not avoid discussing the wider issues, but he concentrates on the results of Demosthenes' policy, not the policy itself. Demosthenes' response was to emphasize the patriotism that underlay his opposition to Philip, and Aeschines later could not help but admire the speech that ruined him.

If Demosthenes' victory in the *Crown* trial undermined Aeschines' subsequent political and literary reputation, some of his merits were, nevertheless, praised by the ancient literary critics, in particular his powerful voice and delivery. The activities of his last years in Rhodes were recognized in the 3rd century AD by the sophist Philostratus of Lemnos, who included Aeschines in his *Lives of the Sophists* and credited him with being the first in a new generation of declamatory sophists, the founder of the so-called "Second Sophistic", which flourished in the 1st and 2nd centuries AD. Aeschines, like other members of the canon of ten Attic orators that had been firmly established by the 2nd century AD, served as a model of Classical Attic oratory, and the sophistic tradition continued in the schools of rhetoric through late antiquity and the Byzantine period down to the Renaissance. The speeches of the *Crown* trial continued to be the focus of attention, and if this was to the greater glory of Demosthenes, it helped to keep Aeschines in the forefront of study. The sophist Himerius, who taught rhetoric in Constantinople (AD 343–52) and Athens (AD 352–61), wrote a speech in the person of Demosthenes against Aeschines; George Chrysokokkes, the Byzantine schoolmaster, copied the manuscripts of Aeschines in the period 1420–28 for his Italian patron Aurispa; and the Cretan Demetrios Doukas assisted in the preparation of the first printed edition of Aldus Manutius in 1513. One final indicator of the continuing study of Aeschines is the collection of scholia to Demosthenes and Aeschines in the monastery of St John on Patmos.

MICHAEL J. EDWARDS

See also Rhetoric

Biography

Born in Athens *c*.390 BC, Aeschines scratched a living as an actor and soldier until 348 BC when he was sent on an embassy to Arcadia. On another in 346 he incurred the enmity of Demosthenes, who charged him with treason. Aeschines successfully counterattacked with a speech *Against Timarchus*, and in 343 was acquitted after delivering his speech *On the False Embassy*. When Demosthenes was offered a crown by Ctesiphon, Aeschines attacked again with his speech *Against Ctesiphon*. Demosthenes successfully defended himself and Aeschines went into exile in Rhodes where he died *c*.322 BC.

Writings

The Speeches, translated by Charles Darwin Adams, London: Heinemann, and New York: Putnam, 1919 (Loeb edition; many reprints)

Further Reading

Harris, Edward M., *Aeschines and Athenian Politics*, New York: Oxford University Press, 1995

Kennedy, George Alexander, *The Art of Persuasion in Greece*, Princeton, New Jersey: Princeton University Press, 1963, pp. 236–45

Kindstrand, Jan Fredrik, *The Stylistic Evaluation of Aeschines in Antiquity*, Uppsala: Acta Universitatis Upsaliensis, 1982

Lane Fox, R., "Aeschines" in *Ritual, Finance, Politics*, edited by Robin Osborne and Simon Hornblower, Oxford: Clarendon Press, 1994

Aeschylus *c*.525–456 BC

Tragedian

Aeschylus saw Athens victorious over the Persians in 490 BC and again in 480–479 BC. His tomb at Gela tells us that he fought at Marathon, but nothing about his drama. Supposedly he came from a distinguished family. He was invited by Hieron I to visit Syracuse in Sicily, and he wrote his *Women of Aetna* on the occasion of Hieron's founding of the city of Aetna. His plays were esteemed for their inspirational and educational value. In Aristophanes' *Frogs* (405 BC) the god Dionysus brings Aeschylus back from the dead so that the Athenians can enjoy good drama once more; Aeschylus claims that his *Seven Against Thebes* is "full of Ares" and that whoever sees it is anxious to become a warrior (*Frogs*, 1021–22).

Seven of Aeschylus' plays survive: *Persians* (472 BC), *Seven against Thebes* (467 BC), *Suppliant Women* (*c*.466 BC), the *Oresteia* trilogy comprising *Agamemnon*, *Choephoroe*, and *Eumenides* (458 BC), and possibly *Prometheus Bound*, though authorship of this play has been disputed. He is said to have written some 80 plays, and he won victories with about 13 of them. Legend has it that, after beginning to compete in 499 BC, he won his first victory in 484 BC and that he was triumphant on every subsequent occasion that he competed. Fragments exist of many of the missing tragedies, rarely extensive, except in a few cases (*Myrmidones*, *Niobe*, *Prometheus Unbound*). His satyr plays were highly regarded and the more substantial of his fragments are in fact from these (*Netfishers*, and *Theoroi*, also known as *Spectators at the Isthmian Games*).

Aeschylus generally wrote his plays in the form of a thematically connected trilogy, and the only trilogy from any of the ancient tragic playwrights that survives is his. This form allows the development of a theme, as in the *Oresteia*, with its admonition that the perpetrators of crime will be punished. This is called a violent grace, accorded by the gods to man to teach him to be wise, to learn through suffering (*Agamemnon*, 176–83). A family curse shows man's dependence on fate for generation after generation, and yet the responsibility for wrongdoing remains his. The lesson is an important one, and Aeschylus charts the transition from personal blood feud and murderous vengeance to the public law court. This trilogy was written two years after the democratic reforms limited the Council of the Areopagus to murder trials. Aeschylus shows respect for the Areopagus, but also seems to espouse the development towards democracy.

Aeschylus' plays include many exchanges between a single actor and the chorus. As much as one half of a play can be choral, and his choruses are particularly dramatic. It is easy to imagine the Persians appearing in their lavish costumes, and the demonic arrival of the Erinyes, or Furies, whose appearance we are told caused women to miscarry. Aristotle tells us that Aeschylus introduced a second actor and his later extant plays show more dialogue between two actors, and, after Sophocles introduced the third actor, sometimes three.

Of the three playwrights from 5th-century BC Athens whose works survive, Aeschylus' language is perhaps the most poetic, with his abstract usage, invented and rare words coupled with bold metaphors. He is certainly the most difficult to translate. He often takes an image and carries it throughout the play, or trilogy, as, for instance, in the *Oresteia* with the related images of net, hunt, blood, fertility, sacrifice, and war: public pursuits that lead to private disaster.

Alone of the three great tragedians, Aeschylus deals with a historical subject, the *Persians*, less than a decade after their defeat. He showed sympathy for the enemy, a useful quality for rising statesmen in the new democracy. In this work he also extolled the merits of democracy by comparison with the Persians, who were governed by a tyrant.

When Aeschylus died, a state decree was issued allowing his plays to be entered at the tragic festivals in competition with living playwrights. Aristophanes' *Frogs* shows us that he was still held in high repute after his death, since he is shown victorious over Euripides. Soon, however, Euripides became more popular. There are few quotations from Aeschylus in writings of the 4th century BC, and Aristotle says little about him. Around 330 BC the Athenian politician Lycurgus prescribed that copies of the texts of the plays should be deposited in the official archives, and that future performances should conform to these texts. The purpose was to safeguard the plays from adaptation and interpolation by actors and producers, of a kind to which they had already become vulnerable. These copies were lent to the Egyptian king, Ptolemy Euergetes I, and would have passed into the library at Alexandria, to form the basis of the critical edition made by the librarian Aristophanes of Byzantium (*c*.257–180 BC). Aristophanes divided the lyrics (previously written as continuous prose) into metrical cola. He also added brief introductory comments, probably making use of Aristotle's lost *Didaskaliai* (production records). Part of these comments survive in the *hypotheses* (plot summaries) that were prefixed to the plays by later scholars in the Roman period. The composition of commentaries (or scholia) on the plays was begun in the Hellenistic period (by scholars such as Aristarchus of Samothrace, c.217–145 BC, and Didymus, ?80–10 BC). Further scholia were added in the Byzantine period.

Greek plays were popular in Rome. Quintus Ennius (238–169 BC) wrote a play called *Eumenides* that used characters from the *Oresteia*. Lucius Accius (170–?86 BC), in addition to plays based on characters from the *Oresteia*, also wrote *Persian Women*, *Prometheus*, and *Myrmidones*. For these Roman plays we have only the titles or a few fragments. In the imperial period Seneca (?AD 1–65) reworked the Greek tragedies in his ten extant plays. His *Agamemnon* and *Thyestes* are both derived in part from Aeschylus' *Oresteia*.

The selection of the seven plays by Aeschylus that we possess was probably made in the 2nd or 3rd century AD, and scholia were included for school use. After parchment gradually replaced papyrus (around the 4th century AD) the unselected plays gradually passed out of use. After the Athenian Academy was closed in 529, the classical texts disappeared from sight for several centuries and did not reemerge until the revival of learning in the middle Byzantine period, when they were copied from the uncial into the new minuscule script. Among the scholars who wrote commentaries and handled the texts of the plays the most important are Thomas Magister (late 13th century), Manuel Moschopoulos (*fl.*1300), and Demetrios Triklinios (early 14th century). Triklinios brought a new metrical awareness to the amendment of the text, in particular the lyrics. The plays that were most preferred by the Byzantines were *Persians*, *Prometheus*, and *Seven against Thebes*. Giovanni Aurispa brought the "Medicean" manuscript, written about 1000, from Constantinople to Italy around 1453. This included the seven plays that survive; it is our only source for *Suppliant Women* and *Choephoroe*. The *Agamemnon* is more fully preserved in two manuscripts from the 14th century and an autograph edition by Triklinios.

Texts of Aeschylus were available in Europe from the early 16th century (six of his plays were published in 1518) but he was not a favourite at this time. For the next 400 years interest in these texts was restricted to western Europe. Opera was founded at the end of the 16th century as a revival of Greek tragedy; in the 17th century Corneille and Racine both reworked Greek tragedy. Further interest followed in the 18th century with Goethe, Lessing, and Schiller, followed by Nietzsche and Kleist in the 19th century, and other reworkings throughout Europe and America.

In 1927 Eva Sikelianos revived performances of Greek tragedy at Delphi, beginning with *Prometheus Bound*. *Suppliant Women* was performed there in 1930. This tradition still continues at Delphi. Tadashi Suzuki took his *Clytemnestra* there, after it was performed in Toga, Japan, in 1983. That same year he did *The Tragedy* (*The Fall of the House of Atreus*) in Tokyo. The National Theatre in Greece regularly performs the ancient plays at Epidaurus, the odeum of Herodes Atticus in Athens, and elsewhere. Tony Harrison's and Peter Hall's *Oresteia* was performed in London in 1981 and at Epidaurus in 1982, the first imported production in that theatre.

In 1954 Dimitris Rondiris, a pupil of Reinhardt, established two festivals to revive ancient Greek drama on a yearly basis, one at Epidaurus, the other at the Herodes Atticus theatre in Athens. In 1980 Karolos Koun directed a fine production of the *Oresteia* in which Melina Mercouri starred as Clytemnestra. Earlier, in 1965, he had done an outstanding production of the *Persians*, which was also performed in London. In 2000, Katie Mitchell directed Ted Hughes's translation of the *Oresteia* in London. Spiro Evangelatos produced an *Oresteia* in 1990 with music by Theodorakis. This play has been performed in Greece since 1903, *Prometheus Bound* since 1917, and *Seven against Thebes* since 1925. *Prometheus Bound* was performed again at Delphi in 1995, ably directed by Theodoros Terzopoulos (he had previously done the *Persians* in 1990). Karolos Koun mounted a splendid production in 1975, and Giannis Tsarouchis a particularly artistic version in 1982. *The Persians* has also been popular and has been regularly performed in Greece since 1889, with an outstanding production by Terzopoulos in 1990 which emphasized the cruel suffering that revolutionary and idealistic defiance can entail. Yearly festivals that revive ancient Greek drama in addition to the ones listed above have occurred at Syracuse in Sicily since 1914 and at Delphi in Greece since 1981.

There have also been several films made of plays by Aeschylus, such as *Prometheus in Chains* (Greece, 1927) by Costas and Demetrios Gaziadis, and *Prometheus Second Person Singular* (Greece, 1975) by Costas Ferris, *Les Perses* (France, 1961) by Jean Prat, and *Notes for an African Oresteia* (Italy, 1970) by Pier Paolo Pasolini.

MARIANNE MCDONALD

See also Tragedy

Biography

Born at Eleusis *c.*525 BC, Aeschylus is the father of Greek tragedy. Seven plays survive. His drama is characterized by large issues and the splendour of his choruses. His trilogies showed divine justice acting over generations. He utilized spectacle to advantage, coupling it with equally spectacular poetic words. His plays have a particular appeal for contemporary audiences. He died at Gela in Sicily in 456 BC.

Writings (in translation)

Plays, translated by Frederic Raphael and Kenneth McLeish, 2 vols, London: Methuen, 1991, reprinted 1998

The Complete Greek Tragedies (Centennial Edition), edited by David Grene and Richmond Lattimore, vol. 1: *Aeschylus*, Chicago: University of Chicago Press, 1992

Oresteia, translated by Hugh Lloyd-Jones, London: Duckworth, 1979

The Oresteia, edited and translated by Michael Ewans, London: Dent, 1995

Suppliants and Other Dramas, edited and translated by Michael Lewis, London: Dent, 1996

Texts and Commentaries

Denniston, John Dewar, and Denys Page (editors), *Agamemnon*, Oxford: Clarendon Press, 1957

Diggle, James (editor), *Tragicorum Graecorum Fragmenta Selecta*, Oxford: Clarendon Press, 1998

Fraenkel, Eduard (editor), *Agamemnon*, 3 vols, Oxford: Clarendon Press, 1950

Garvie, A.F. (editor), *Choephori*, Oxford: Clarendon Press, and New York: Oxford University Press, 1986

Griffith, Mark (editor), *Prometheus Bound*, Cambridge and New York: Cambridge University Press, 1983

Hall, Edith (editor), *Persians*, Warminster: Aris and Phillips, 1996

Hutchinson, G.O. (editor), *Septem contra Thebas*, Oxford: Clarendon Press, 1985

Johansen, H. Friis and Edward W. Whittle (editors), *The Suppliants*, Copenhagen: Gyldendalske, 1980

Page, Denys (editor), *Septem Quae Supersunt Tragoedias*, Oxford: Clarendon Press, 1972

Radt, Stefan (editor), *Tragicorum Graecorum Fragmenta*, vol. 3: *Aeschylus*, Göttingen: Vandenhoeck & Ruprecht, 1985

Sommerstein, Alan H. (editor), *Eumenides*, Cambridge and New York: Cambridge University Press, 1989

West, M.L. (editor), *Aeschyli Tragodiae cum incerti poetae Prometheo*, Stuttgart: Teubner, 1990

Further Reading

Albini, Umberto, *Viaggio nel teatro classico*, Florence: Monnier, 1987

Albini, Umberto, *Nel Nome di Dioniso: Vita teatrale nell'Atene classica*, Milan: Garzanti, 1991

Easterling, P.E. (editor), *The Cambridge Companion to Greek Tragedy*, Cambridge: Cambridge University Press, 1997

Ewans, Michael, *Wagner and Aeschylus: The Ring and the Oresteia*, London: Faber, 1982

Flashar, Hellmut, *Inszenierung der Antike: Das griechische Drama auf der Bühne der Neuzeit, 1585–1990*, Munich: Beck, 1991

Flashar, Hellmut (editor), *Tragödie: Idee und Transformation*, Stuttgart: Teubner, 1997

Herington, John, *Aeschylus*, New Haven, Connecticut: Yale University Press, 1986

Italie, G. (editor), *Index Aeschyleus*, Leiden: Brill, 1964

McDonald, Marianne, *Ancient Sun, Modern Light: Greek Drama on the Modern Stage*, New York: Columbia University Press, 1992

MacKinnon, Kenneth, *Greek Tragedy into Film*, London: Croom Helm, and Rutherford, New Jersey: Fairleigh Dickinson University Press, 1986

Pfeiffer, Rudolf, *History of Classical Scholarship*, 2 vols, Oxford: Clarendon Press, 1968–76

Reynolds, L.D. and N.G. Wilson, *Scribes and Scholars: A Guide to the Transmission of Greek and Latin Literature*, 3rd edition, Oxford: Clarendon Press, and New York: Oxford University Press, 1991

Rosenmeyer, Thomas G., *The Masks of Tragedy: Essays on Six Greek Dramas*, Austin: University of Texas Press, 1963

Rosenmeyer, Thomas G., *The Art of Aeschylus*, Berkeley: University of California Press, 1982

Walton, J. Michael, *Living Greek Theatre: A Handbook of Classical Performance and Modern Production*, New York: Greenwood Press, 1987

West, M.L., *Studies in Aeschylus*, Stuttgart: Teubner, 1990

Winnington-Ingram, R.P., *Studies in Aeschylus*, Cambridge and New York: Cambridge University Press, 1983

Zeitlin, Froma I., *Playing the Other: Gender and Society in Classical Greek Literature*, Chicago: University of Chicago Press, 1996

Aesop

Legendary fabulist

Although Aesop's very existence has sometimes been considered to be a fable, the many ancient and Byzantine statements about him may contain a historical nucleus, though this is hard to determine. The earliest reference to him is a brief passage from Herodotus (2. 134), which contains the following information: Aesop was a slave of one Iadmon from Samos; he was a fellow slave of Rhodopis, a *hetaira* (courtesan) living in the time of the Pharaoh Amasis (570–525 BC); and urged by an oracle, the Delphians paid compensation to atone for Aesop's death, which was received by Iadmon's homonymous grandson.

These data can be compared and combined with other testimonies. The indications of the place of Aesop's origin and activity vary; some locate him on Samos, others in Lydia, but most in either Thrace or Phrygia. Strikingly enough, all of these are peripheral regions of the ancient Greek world. This may tentatively be connected with the provenance of the fable genre from abroad (Mesopotamia). However this may be, Maximos Planudes' derivation of "Aesop" from "Aethiopian" is at any rate etymologically incorrect.

Instead of Iadmon, Aristotle (fr. 573 Rose) names one Xanthos as Aesop's master. More important than the latter's identity is Aesop's alleged social status: the emperor Julian (*Orations*, 7. 3) plausibly observes that Aesop, as a slave, could not speak out but had subtly to disguise his counsels in fables.

If Aesop really existed, he probably belonged to the 6th century BC. Eusebius of Caesarea even dates his death to 564 BC precisely. Herodotus implicitly connects him with Sappho, since he reports that it was her brother who redeemed Rhodopis. An inscription of the 1st century AD (*Inscriptiones Graecae*, 14. 1297) makes Aesop a contemporary of Pisistratus, whereas Plutarch (in his *Symposium*) has him converse not only with the equally legendary Seven Sages but also with Solon, and states that Croesus, the last king of Lydia, sent him as an envoy to Delphi.

This mission was allegedly to be his death, as is already implied by the passage from Herodotus discussed above. Aristophanes (*Wasps*, 1446f.) refers to a story in which Aesop was accused by the Delphians of the theft of a bowl dedicated to Apollo. Later testimonies explain that Aesop incurred the anger of the Delphians because he exposed their habit of greedily misappropriating gifts to the oracle; whereupon they falsely accused him of sacrilege, and put him to death by stoning and/or throwing him from the rocks (*Oxyrhynchus Papyrus* 1800, 2nd century AD; Plutarch; Lucian, Himerius, 4th century AD). He was, however, avenged by Apollo. This legend, which may reflect the ritual expulsion of a scapegoat, must have been well known by as early as the 5th century BC, as indicated by the very brevity of Aristophanes' and Herodotus' allusions. The story's popularity is also indicated by the application of the proverb "Aesop's blood" to persons involved in crimes difficult to expiate (Zenobius, 1. 47, 2nd century AD; Apostolius, 1. 73, 15th century).

Aristophanes (*Wasps*, 1448) adds that Aesop told the Delphians a fable about a dung beetle. Again, the conciseness of the passage shows that the playwright presupposed that the audience would be acquainted with the full story. An ancient commentator explains that Aesop (vainly) tried to prevent his execution by telling the Delphians a story about a tiny scarab who took a terrible revenge on the mighty eagle.

From the 5th century BC it became customary to connect fables with the name of Aesop. This was done in various ways: either Aesop was presented as the narrator of a fable on some occasion of his life, or he figured as a fable character, or the

Aesop: Venetian woodcut, 1491

fable was simply labelled as "Aesop's" or "Aesopic". All these ways of ascribing fables to Aesop occur for the first time in Aristophanes' *Wasps*. By the end of the 5th century BC Aesop's fables must already have enjoyed great popularity, as is clear from passages from Aristophanes and Plato. The former (*Birds*, 471) considers unfamiliarity with Aesop's fables to be a serious lack of cultivation, whereas the latter (*Phaedo*, 60) reports that they were versified by Socrates (who was unjustly condemned to death like Aesop). It is a matter of dispute whether or not these passages imply the circulation of a text-book with Aesop's fables in Classical Athens.

The popularity of Aesop's fables is also evident from archaeology. It is generally assumed that a red-figure *kylix* (drinking cup, *c.*450 BC; now in the Vatican Museum) depicting a hunch-back speaking to a fox represents the fabulist in conversation with his favourite fable character. Later testimonies refer to statues of Aesop by Lysippus and Aristodemus and describe an allegorical painting of Aesop and his fables (Tatian, 2nd century AD; Philostratus' *Imagines*, *c.* AD 200; Agathias, 6th century AD). The fabulist was honoured also by literary monuments: apart from various biographical notes (in the *Suda* lexicon and prologues of fable collections) and a fictionalized *Life*, which will be discussed below, we have one fragment of an *Aesop* staged by the comedian Alexis (4th century BC; extant in Athenaeus, 10. 431).

The ascription of fables to Aesop soon became a standard practice, which lasted throughout antiquity. Fables somehow connected with Aesop's name occur in the works of writers from the Classical (Democritus, Aristotle), Hellenistic (Callimachus), and imperial periods of Greek literature (e.g. Galen, Dio of Prusa, Dionysius of Halicarnassus, Plutarch, Lucian, Diogenes Laertius, Libanius, Themistius), as well as in early Christian Greek (St Irenaeus, St Basil the Great).

The first to compose a fable collection (Demetrius of Phalerum, *c.*300 BC) also used Aesop's name as a kind of generic label. This was done by other ancient fabulists (Babrius and Phaedrus, his Latin *collega proximus*) as well, and has become customary ever since, as is clear from the habit of Byzantine authors of quoting from "Aesop's fables" (Michael Psellos, John Tzetzes, Eustathios of Thessalonica, Nikephoros Gregoras). Hence it has naturally, but mistakenly, been believed by some that the ancient so-called Aesopic fable collections, which are extant in many Byzantine manuscripts, were by the genre's founding father himself. This myth was, however, definitively unmasked by Sir Richard Bentley (1699), who mainly on internal linguistic evidence convincingly proved that the prose fables cannot have been composed before the Christian era; their author must remain anonymous.

Aesop's renown (according to some perhaps rivalling that of Homer) may be especially based upon the fables ascribed to him, but throughout antiquity and the Byzantine period his name is also connected with apophthegms and proverbs (in John Georgides, *c.*10th century; *codex Mosquensis*, 239, 14th century). His fame was further enhanced by the anonymous *Life of Aesop*, a biographical romance from the imperial Roman period that creatively combines traditional stories about the legendary fabulist with heterogeneous elements derived from various other sources, notably anecdotes about the Seven Sages and the Assyrian book of Ahiqar. Aesop is portrayed as a typical anti-hero, physically and socially inferior but mentally the master of his superiors, and as the champion of popular wisdom, problem-solving, and fable-telling. The text's structure is tripartite; the setting shifts from Samos via the Near East to Delphi. Part 1 relates how Aesop, dumb from birth and enslaved, is granted first the power of speech by the goddess Isis and then freedom by his master Xanthos because, respectively, of his faithfulness and cleverness, and how he reconciles his fellow citizens with their powerful enemy, King Croesus of Lydia. In part 2 Aesop, as a counsellor of King Lycurgus of Babylon, manages to escape a plot set up against him by his adoptive son Ainos ("Fable") and to win an enigmatic battle for his master against the Egyptian pharaoh Nectanebo. Part 3 is about Aesop's tragic end in Delphi (see above). He is, however, with divine approval, avenged by allied Graeco-Babylonian forces.

Of this highly original and at times scabrous text three different versions are extant, viz. the ancient G and W, and the Byzantine *Pl*, named respectively after the place where the manuscript was originally kept (Grottaferrata; also containing fables of Babrius), after its first editor (Westermann; Braunschweig, 1845), and after Maximos Planudes, who made a somewhat abbreviated version *ad usum delphini* which was to become an early printing bestseller, translated into Latin, German, French, English, Dutch, Spanish, and other European languages. Modern Greek versions are the anonymous *Life of Aesop the Phrygian* (Venice, 1783) and Andreas Moustoxidis's *Life of Aesop* (Corfu, 1857).

In antiquity and in Byzantine times it was told (Photios and the *Suda* lexicon) that Aesop rose from the dead and was reincarnated more than once. Even if one does not believe in metempsychosis, the story of Aesop redivivus aptly symbolizes the eternal resurrection of the creation of Hellas's famous fabulist.

GERT-JAN VAN DIJK

See also Fable

Biography

The eponymous father of Greek fable. Little is known of his life, and indeed his very existence is in doubt. If he existed, it was probably in the 6th century BC. He was by tradition a slave, perhaps on Samos. Fables continued to be ascribed to Aesop throughout antiquity and have been popular ever since.

Writings

Fabulae Romanenses Graece Conscriptae ex Recensione et cum Adnotationibus, edited by Alfred Eberhard, Leipzig: Teubner, 1872

Aesopica: A Series of Texts Relating to Aesop or Ascribed to Him or Closely Connected with the Literary Tradition That Bears His Name, edited by Ben Edwin Perry, vol. 1, Urbana: University of Illinois Press, 1952, reprinted: New York: Arno Press 1980, pp. 79–292

Aesop without Morals: The Famous Fables, and a Life of Aesop, translated by Lloyd W. Daly, New York: Yoseloff, 1961

Further Reading

Beschorner, A. and N. Holzberg, "A Bibliography of the Aesop Romance" in *Der Äsop-Roman: Motivgeschichte und Erzählstruktur*, edited by Niklas Holzberg, Tübingen: Narr, 1992

Birch, C.M., "Traditions of the Life of Aesop" (dissertation), St Louis: Washington University, 1955

Daly, Lloyd W. (translator), *Aesop without Morals: The Famous Fables, and a Life of Aesop*, New York: Yoseloff, 1961, pp. 31–90

Dijk, J.G.M. van, "The Fables in the Greek *Life of Aesop*", *Reinardus*, 8 (1995): pp. 131–50

Dimitriades-Touphexis, E., "Index Verborum Vitae Aesopi Perryanae", *Epistemonike epeterida tes filosofikes scholes tou Aristoteliou panepistemiou Thessalonikes*, 20 (1981): pp. 69–153

Holzberg, Niklas (editor), *Der Äsop-Roman: Motivgeschichte und Erzählstruktur*, Tübingen: Narr, 1992

Hostetter, Winifred Hager, "A Linguistic Study of the Vulgar Greek *Life of Aesop*" (dissertation), Urbana: University of Illinois, 1955

Jedrkiewicz, Stefano, *Sapere e paradosso nell'antichità: Esopo e la favola*, Rome: Ateneo, 1989

Papademetriou, J.T. *Aesop as an Archetypal Hero*, Athens, 1997 (in Greek)

Papathomopoulos, Manolis, *Aesopus revisitatus: Recherches sur le texte des vies ésopiques*, Ioannina, 1989

Papathomopoulos, Manolis (editor), *O Bios tou Aisopou: H Parallag G* [The Life of Aesop: H and G in Parallel Text], Ioannina, 1990

Perry, Ben Edwin, *Studies in the Text History of the Life and Fables of Aesop*, Haverford, Pennsylvania: American Philological Association, 1936

Sarkady, J., "Aisopos der Samier: Ein Beitrag zur archaischen Geschichte Samos", *Acta Classica Universitatis Scientiarum Debreceniensis*, 4 (1968) pp. 7–12

Tallmadge, E.R., "A Grammatical Study of the Greek *Life of Aesop*" (dissertation), Urbana: University of Illinois, 1938

West, M.L., "The Ascription of Fables to Aesop in Archaic and Classical Greece" in *La Fable*, edited by Francisco R. Adrados, Geneva: Hardt, 1984, pp. 105–36

Wiechers, Anton, *Aesop in Delphi*, Meisenheim am Glan: Hain, 1961

Zeitz, Heinrich, "Die Fragmente des Äsopromans in Papyrushandschriften" (dissertation), Giessen, 1935

Aesthetics

Although the word "aesthetics" is itself derived from the Greek word *aisthanomai* ("I perceive"), it was not coined until 1753, by the German philosopher Alexander Gottlieb Baumgarten. Since then it has gradually come to embrace philosophies of both art and beauty (whether natural or created). This is not to say that the ancients did not have a tradition of what we understand by aesthetics, i.e. a philosophy concerned with the essence and perception of beauty and ugliness.

Apart from the evidence that is implied in their creative works, we are able to form some idea of the views on art and beauty held by the Greeks from at least four types of writing: literary criticism, art criticism, philosophy, and rhetoric. One general idea that emerges from this evidence is that to the Greeks art was a representation (*mimesis*) of life. This is evident from the description of Achilles' shield in *Iliad* 18 where the artist's depiction is praised for its faithfulness to life. This was true not only of the visual arts and works of literature, but even of instrumental music. However, what the Greek thinkers understood by *mimesis* was something much broader than mere copying. It could encompass a wide range of modes of depiction and symbolism that ranged from imitative realism to imaginative idealism and embraced different accounts of the artists' relations to their creations, circling around the polarities of nature and craft, inspiration and technique. Accordingly, ancient attitudes to the representative arts include many distinctive configurations of emphasis. As Aristotle says in the 26th chapter of his *Poetics*, the artist could represent men as they are, as they ought to be, or as they are thought to be.

According to Xenophon, Socrates regarded the beautiful as coincident with the good, while both of them are resolvable into the useful. We call something beautiful when it serves some rational end, be it human gratification or human security. He seems to have emphasized the power of a beautiful object to further the more necessary ends of life rather than the immediate gratification it afforded to perception and contemplation. For him, beauty was a relative thing. Unlike Plato, he did not recognize a "beauty itself" existing absolutely without any relation to a percipient mind. The *Memorabilia* (3. 10) records a conversation with the sculptor Parrhesius in which Socrates introduces two qualifications to the idea of representation: the sculptor can combine into one statue features that in real life belong to many people; and the artist represents not only physical features but also the soul.

The earliest aesthetic theory of any scope is that of Plato. According to him, reality consisted of forms or archetypes that were themselves imperceptible to the senses but were perceptible to the soul in its purest essence. But they were the patterns on which all objects of sense perception were modelled. Thus phenomena imitate the forms or participate in them. From the objects of sense perception the philosopher reasons to the pure forms of which they are mere imitations. But the artist merely copies the objects of sense experience without possessing a knowledge of their forms. What he produces is, thus, an imitation of an imitation. Because he did not possess the philosopher's knowledge of reality, the artist had no claim to be the teacher of men. Plato also believed that certain types of artistic production, such as those that portrayed the character and actions of base people, were harmful to the moral and emotional integrity of their audiences. Even certain musical modes could induce laziness or incite people to intemperate actions. Accordingly, in formulating an ideal state, Plato, in the *Republic*, recommends rigorous censorship (or even expulsion) of the existing breed of poets and painters in favour of an ideal race of artist-philosophers whose creations should provide moral and political training.

Although Plato was inclined to the conception of an absolute beauty that took its place within his scheme of self-existing forms or ideas, it is not easy to determine exactly what he meant by beauty. Various definitions are rejected in his dialogues by the Platonic Socrates as being inadequate. The only notion of a common element in beautiful objects that we come across in his dialogues is proportion, harmony, or unity among their parts. According to the *Symposium*, true beauty is not something that one can find as an attribute in this or that beautiful thing. For beautiful things, although they partake of beauty, are not themselves "beauty itself". Eros or love causes aspiration towards the pure idea of beauty that Plato also identifies with goodness and truth. According to the *Phaedo*, the soul's knowledge of beauty itself results from recollection of its prenatal existence.

In several of his works Aristotle attempts to defend the claims of representative art as the basis of moral education, the origin of catharsis, and the instrument of character formation. He attempts to develop certain principles of beauty and art by scientific analysis. For Aristotle, just as for Plato, aesthetics was inseparable from morality and politics. In his *Politics* (8. 5) he dwells on the power of art to influence human character, and hence the social order. In the *Metaphysics* he tries to make a distinction between the good and the beautiful: the good is always found in action, whereas beauty may exist in motionless things as well. The good may also be called beautiful under certain circumstances, although essentially they are two different things. Beauty is also different from what is fitting, and is above the useful and the necessary. The pleasure it provides is of the purest kind. The universal elements of beauty are order, symmetry, and definiteness or determinateness (*Metaphysics*) as well as a certain magnitude (*Poetics*); an object should not be so large as to prevent a synoptic view of the whole, or so small as to prevent a clear perception of the articulation of the parts.

The more mystical writings of Plato, the *Timaeus* in particular, suggest a different approach to aesthetics based on the Pythagorean theory of the cosmos or ordered universe. This exerted a decisive influence on the Neoplatonists. Among them Plotinus (born *c*.AD 205) accorded far greater significance to art than did Plato. The essence of his philosophy is the desire to escape from the material world. According to him, *nous* or objective reason, which is self-moving, invests form on inanimate matter, thereby turning it into a *logos* or notion whose beauty lay in its form. Objects that have not been acted upon by reason are formless, and therefore ugly. The creative reason is absolute beauty, which Plotinus calls the more-than-beautiful. Beauty manifests itself in three stages: the highest is human reason; next comes the human soul, which is less perfect because of its links with the material body; lowest of all are the "real" objects. In other words, he explains the universe by a hierarchy rising from matter to soul, soul to reason, and reason

to God, the final abstraction, without form or matter, i.e. pure existence. Only the spiritual world contemplated by reason is real, the phenomenal world being a creation of the soul and, hence, a thing without real existence, while matter is only a receptacle for forms imposed on it by the soul. Unlike Aristotle, he believed that a single thing indivisible into parts might be beautiful through its unity and simplicity. He accorded a high place to the beauty of colours in which material darkness is overpowered by light and warmth. According to him, art reveals the form of an object more clearly than ordinary experience does, and it raises the soul to contemplation of the universal. When the artist contemplates notions as models of his creations, such creations may attain to greater beauty than the products of nature. For Plotinus, the highest moments of life were mystical, and by this he meant that in the world of forms the soul was united with the divine or the "one". Since one loses oneself in contemplating an aesthetic object, aesthetic experience comes closest to mystical experience.

The influence of Plato is also manifest in the rhetorical treatise known as Longinus' *On the Sublime* (? 1st century AD). According to this author, "sublimity consists in a certain excellence and distinction in expression" and "it is from this source alone that the greatest poets and historians have acquired their preeminence and won for themselves an eternity of fame." According to him, the sublime not merely persuades but transports the audience out of themselves. It is thus a mystic experience, an ecstasy, which is why its effect is different from that of all merely technical skills. In the 7th chapter he says: "for by some innate power the true sublime uplifts our souls; we are filled with a proud exaltation and a sense of vaunting joy, just as though we had ourselves produced what we had heard." For him, the sublimity of a work is proved by its ability to stand repeated hearings and its unanimous recognition or universal appeal. In chapter 9 he describes the sublime as the echo of a noble mind. The sources of sublimity are: (1) the ability to form grand conceptions; (2) the stimulus of powerful and inspired emotions; (3) figures of speech and thought; (4) diction; and (5) composition. Although he makes several references to the visual arts, his prime concern is literature.

Among the Greeks, examples of art criticism are found in literary works, mostly from the later periods, which contain descriptions of works of art. One such work is Pausanias' *Guide to Greece* (2nd century AD); another is the *Eikones* by one of the Philostrati of Lemnos who appear to have lived in the 2nd–3rd centuries AD. The latter consists of two sets of descriptions in prose of pictures that the author professes to have seen.

There was a strong tendency among the ancient Greeks to connect both art and beauty to more general considerations of human needs and values, so that their aesthetics, so far from being isolated, was involved with the psycho-sociological aspects of culture. In considering questions concerning the origin, subject-matter, form, style, and effect of the arts, several Greek writers adopted a comparative approach. The elder Simonides described poetry as vocal painting and painting as silent poetry. Aristotle, in his *Poetics*, also makes frequent references to the visual arts; and so do the later authors of rhetorical treatises, even though their analogies are often misleading.

Christianity at first regarded the depiction of religious images as idolatrous because of the Old Testament's prohibition against graven images (Exodus 20: 1–5). This reservation was, however, overcome and a pictorial tradition was established by the 3rd century AD. It is in relation to this early condemnation of pagan idolatry and the consequent reluctance to depict sacred Christian figures and stories that early Byzantine art must be understood. Although many notable exceptions exist, figural scenes were usually avoided and were presented in an allusive symbolic mode or were embedded in complex programmes that rendered the veneration of single images practically impossible. From about AD 550 such restraint weakened, and in 7th-century church decorations small isolated panels depicting single figures begin to appear at or near eye level.

The representational theory of art was retained through the Byzantine period as well, and even hagiography emphasized the resemblance of the icon to the original. This naturalistic approach was, however, contradicted by the concept of bodily beauty as a reflection of the absolute beauty of God. The artists aimed at representing what was eternal, rather than what was ephemeral, and they therefore concentrated on the "spiritual" elements of the human body, the face and especially the eyes. The figures are frontal and stable, the opposite qualities being the marks of devils, barbarians, and the enemy in general. Being didactic in purpose, Byzantine art sought to convey its message through a symbolic language. Along with its historical place and time, each event depicted had its place in the ever-repeating cycle of the divine plan, thus conferring upon it a profound significance.

D.P.M. WEERAKKODY

Further Reading

Beardsley, Monroe C., *Aesthetics from Classical Greece to the Present: A Short History*, New York: Macmillan, 1966

Beardsley, Monroe C., *Aesthetics: Problems in the Philosophy of Criticism*, 2nd edition, Indianapolis, Indiana: Hackett, 1981

Cooper, David E. (editor), *A Companion to Aesthetics*, Oxford and Cambridge, Massachusetts: Blackwell, 1992

Gardner, Percy, *The Principles of Greek Art*, New York: Macmillan, 1914

Maguire, Henry, *Art and Eloquence in Byzantium*, Princeton, New Jersey: Princeton University Press, 1981

Mathew, Gervase, *Byzantine Aesthetics*, London: John Murray, 1963; New York: Viking, 1964

Micheles, P.A., *An Aesthetic Approach to Byzantine Art*, London: Batsford, 1955

Tatarkiewicz, Władysław, *History of Aesthetics*, 3 vols, The Hague: Mouton, 1970–74

Aetolia

Region in central Greece

Aetolia is a region in north central Greece whose southern border is the coastline along the Gulf of Corinth. Its western border is formed by the Acheloüs river, which separates modern-day Greece from Albania and in Classical antiquity marked the division between Aetolia and Acarnania. In the 5th century BC an uneven line running from the area just west of

Thermopylae in the north to Naupactus on the Corinthian Gulf in the south formed Aetolia's eastern boundary; its northern border abutted the kingdoms of Macedonia and Thrace. At present Aetolia and Acarnania, as the conglomerate Aitolakarnania, comprise the most westerly nome of central Greece; this nome lies between the Gulf of Patras and Epirus. Throughout the centuries the territorial boundaries of Aetolia have dramatically expanded or contracted in accordance with the ebb and flow of the Aetolians' political fortunes.

From the 1st-century-BC geographer Strabo we learn that in antiquity Aetolia fell into two divisions: Old Aetolia and New or Acquired (*Epiktetos*) Aetolia. The area between the Acheloüs and Euenus rivers is known as Old Aetolia. Its most striking geographical features are the complex series of lagoons of the Aetolian plains and Lake Trichonis. Old Aetolia included the city of Calydon, of great mythological significance as the scene of the tragic story of Meleager, Atalanta, and the Calydonian boar hunt. Moreover, Aetolian cities gained undying fame in the catalogue of ships in Book 2 of Homer's *Iliad* (lines 638–44); the poet reports that Thoas, son of Andraimon, led an Aetolian contingent of 40 black ships in the expedition against Troy. New Aetolia extended from the Euenus river eastwards to the land of the Ozolian Locrians. This region did not have the sort of prestige which Greek mythology bestowed upon Old Aetolia; indeed, the 5th-century BC Athenian historian Thucydides (3. 94) remarks that its rude inhabitants spoke a nearly unintelligible form of Greek and ate raw flesh.

Aetolia's period of greatest power and prosperity fell between the years 338 BC, when the victory of Philip II of Macedon over a coalition of Greek city states led by Athens and Thebes changed for ever the configurations of inter-state power relations in Greece, and 189 BC, when Rome imposed a harsh settlement upon the Aetolians in the aftermath of the Roman victory over Aetolia and its ally the Seleucid king Antiochus III. The Aetolian Confederacy (or *koinon*) held regular representative meetings in which federal magistrates were elected, had a pan-Aetolian sanctuary at Thermon, and conducted a common foreign policy.

Sometime around 300 BC Aetolia gained control of the venerable sanctuary of Apollo at Delphi. Aetolia's territorial extent in this period may be calculated on the basis of the number of votes which the Aetolians controlled in the Delphic Amphictionic Council. In antiquity Aetolia's claim to fame lay in the defence of the sanctuary in 279 BC against a Gallic attack. Although it is clear that the Phocians also played a significant role in the repulse of this Gallic incursion, the Aetolians claimed sole responsibility. Some 30 years after the invasion they reorganized the Delphic festival of thanksgiving on a grander scale and represented themselves as the heroic defenders of Hellenism against a barbarian menace. This propaganda apparently was effective: the 2nd-century AD traveller Pausanias (*Description of Greece*, 10. 19. 5) states that the Gallic attack of 279 BC was the gravest peril in all of Greek history. The historian Polybius (*Histories*, 2. 35. 7), writing in the mid-2nd century BC, reluctantly pairs the event with the great 5th-century BC Persian invasions of Greece (although he refuses to name the Aetolians as the authors of the sanctuary's preservation). Throughout its ancient history Aetolia had an uneasy relationship with the Macedonian monarchy, alternately being its ally and its enemy. In the so-called Social War (220–217 BC) the Macedonian king Philip V stunned the confederation by striking deep into its heart with his sack of the federal sanctuary at Thermon.

Aetolia is a rugged land. The lack of geographical and climatic amenities enjoyed by other parts of Greece may give some help towards understanding the Aetolian Confederacy of the 3rd and 2nd centuries BC. The Aetolian economy was based on the annual conduct of war and raiding expeditions; in some cases Aetolia granted other Greek states immunity from its marauding expeditions through treaties of inviolability, or *asylia*. The Aetolian Confederacy was essentially a nation of corsairs and mercenaries. We have already noted the negative assessment of Thucydides. The Aetolians' propaganda centred on their exploits at Delphi in 279 BC must in part be viewed as an attempt to counteract their negative international reputation. In the 2nd century BC, Polybius, as a citizen of the arch-enemy of Aetolia, the Achaean Confederacy, delivered in his *Histories* the most scathing indictment of Aetolia in the literary tradition (see especially the opening of book 4).

Aetolia struck up an alliance with Rome in 211 BC against Macedonia. This act hardly enhanced Aetolia's international image, as many Greeks at this time viewed the Romans as uncouth barbarians. At the conclusion of the Second Macedonian War (200–196 BC) Romano-Aetolian relations broke down as a result of a disagreement over the terms of the treaty. Aetolia was deprived of cities which it believed rightfully belonged to it; and the disgruntled Aetolians called in the Syrian king Antiochus III against Rome, which led to the aforementioned defeat and harsh settlement of 189 BC. Aetolia would never regain its former international position.

Yet in its subsequent history Aetolia takes a conspicuous place in the Hellenic fight against foreign oppression. Early in the 13th century AD Aetolia was a bastion of Greek resistance against the coming of the Franks. Michael Doukas (Despot of Epirus 1204–15) wrested the western seaboard from Naupactus to Dyrrhachium, including much of Old Aetolia, from the Latin Boniface, Marquis of Montferrat. In the 18th century St Kosmas the Aetolian (1714–79) established schools throughout Greek-speaking lands in his fight for Greek Orthodoxy and the Greek language; he was eventually executed by the Ottomans and became one of the so-called Neomartyrs. Finally, mention must be made of Aetolia's part in the Greek War of Independence (1821–32), as well as in the tragic fate of the Romantic poet and philhellene George Gordon, Lord Byron. The Aetolians defeated the Turks at Karpenisi, and under the leadership of Markos Botsaris, Missolonghi heroically withstood several sieges. Byron committed his material and spiritual resources to the moderate prince Alexander Mavrokordatos and the Greek cause. But his frail constitution buckled under the cold Aetolian winter and he died at Missolonghi on 19 April 1824. Yet he soon became a Greek national hero and an inspirational force behind the defeat of the Turko-Egyptian fleet at Navarino in 1827, which assured the end of the Tourkokratia.

Much of Aetolia has remained untouched by modernization. The plains produce olives, currants, and some tobacco, while the mountain eparchies rely upon forest produce, much as did their ancient forbears. The region is for the most part rugged and forbidding; only the hardiest tourist with the stamina of Aetolia's intrepid 19th-century topographers Bazin, Leake, and Woodhouse is likely to penetrate its depths.

CRAIGE CHAMPION

See also Acarnania

Summary

Region of north central Greece which became a federal state in the 4th century BC. Best known for its defence of Delphi against a Gallic attack in 279 BC. Aetolia was a centre of resistance to the Franks in the 13th century and to the Turks in the War of Independence. It remains largely untouched by modernization.

Further Reading

Ager, Shiela L., *Interstate Arbitrations in the Greek World, 337–90 BC*, Berkeley: University of California Press, 1996

Antonetti, Claudia, *Les Etoliens: image et religion*, Paris: Belles Lettres, 1990

Bommeljé, Sebastiaan *et al.* (editors), *Aetolia and the Aetolians: Towards an Interdisciplinary Study of a Greek Region*, Utrecht: Parnassus Press, 1987

Champion, Craige, "The *Soteria* at Delphi: Aetolian Propaganda in the Epigraphical Record", *American Journal of Philology*, 116 (1995): pp. 213–20

Champion, Craige, "Polybius, Aetolia, and the Gallic Attack on Delphi", *Historia*, 45 (1996): pp. 315–28

Cheetham, Nicolas, *Mediaeval Greece*, New Haven, Connecticut and London: Yale University Press, 1981

Clogg, Richard, *A Concise History of Greece*, Cambridge and New York: Cambridge University Press, 1992

Flacelière, Robert, *Les Aitoliens à Delphes*, Paris: Boccard, 1937

Larsen, J.A.O., *Greek Federal States: Their Institutions and History*, Oxford: Clarendon Press, 1968

Mendels, Doron, "Did Polybius Have 'Another' View of the Aetolian League?", *Ancient Society*, 15–17 (1984–86): pp. 63–73

Nachtergael, Georges, *Les Galates en Grèce et les Sôtéria de Delphes*, Brussels: Palais de Académies, 1977

Rigsby, Kent J., *Asylia: Territorial Inviolability in the Hellenistic World*, Berkeley: University of California Press, 1996

Scholten, Joseph, *The Politics of Plunder: The Aitolians and Their Koinon in the Early Hellenistic Era, 279–217 BC*, Berkeley: University of California Press, 2000

Walbank, F.W., *The Hellenistic World*, revised edition, London: Fontana, and Cambridge, Massachusetts: Harvard University Press, 1992

Woodhouse, W.J., *Aetolia: Its Geography, Topography, and Antiquities*, Oxford: Clarendon Press, 1897, reprinted New York: Arno Press, 1973

Africa, North

Ancient Greeks called Africa "Libya", after the name of a tribe in Cyrenaica. The term Africa is a Latin one, initially used by the Romans, especially for the region around Carthage. Libya, however, remained the preferred term in high-style Greek literary texts throughout the Byzantine period. The Greeks believed Libya to be a continent that stretched from the Red Sea and Sinai or Nile to the Pillars of Hercules, or straits of Gibraltar. Although Egypt was in a strict sense considered to be part of the continent of Libya, the Greeks did not normally include Egypt and Egyptians in the terminology for Libya and Libyans.

Although the ancient Greeks knew something of the vicinity of the upper Nile, and were familiar with an ethnic group known as the Ethiopians already in the time of Homer, their knowledge of the African interior remained limited. Greeks from Thera colonized Cyrene c.630 BC. Elites in its vicinity, including those in the nearby towns of Apollonia, Barka, and Ptolemais, continued to speak Greek and use Greek for written records at least until the Islamic conquest in the 640s AD, although the indigenous people, who presumably were the majority, continued to speak their own languages. A lively trade with peoples in the interior developed. Greeks normally confined themselves to coastal regions and traded ceramics, wine, and other goods for raw African materials, such as the highly prized plant called silphium that once existed in Cyrenaica. Some cities along the coast west of Cyrenaica, such as Oea, Sabratha and Leptis Magna, also received enduring Greek names, as in Tripoli, although they probably had Phoenician origins. Because of the nature of winds and currents, most shipping between the Levant or Greek mainland and Africa took a northern route, via the Sicilian coast, although navigation did cross from the Greek mainland to Cyrenaica via Crete, or to Egypt via Cyprus. West of Cyrenaica along the African coast, a few traders or seamen may have used Greek, but after the Roman conquest in the 2nd century BC elites and townspeople spoke Latin and some local dialects. A lively Greek Christian culture was still thriving in Cyrenaica at the end of the 4th century AD, however, as the writings and correspondence of Synesius of Cyrene, bishop of Ptolemais, attest.

The Vandal conquest of Africa ruptured the continuity of Roman control in the third decade of the 5th century AD, although their failure to seize Cyrenaica reinforced the cultural and linguistic separation of Cyrenaica (which remained Hellenic, as did Alexandria, in Egypt) from the Latin-speaking coastal areas further west. It immediately became a priority for Byzantine emperors to recover Africa, for reasons of strategy, economics, and prestige. In 468 the Byzantine emperor Leo I unsuccessfully sought to reconquer Africa from the Vandals by authorizing a disastrous and costly naval expedition. Vandal naval raids against the Greek mainland and islands were an annoyance but had only a limited effect in the late 5th century. African refugees in Constantinople lobbied intensively for another military expedition. The Arian theology and clergy of the Vandals, who intermittently persecuted orthodox Christians, added an important ecclesiastical motive for a Byzantine reconquest. In the 6th century internal Vandal strife and a diplomatic peace with the Persians allowed Emperor Justinian I to shift resources westward. He appointed the extremely capable commander Belisarius to lead a naval expedition in September 533, which, in the following months, swiftly overwhelmed the Vandals, whose males were deported and whose government, church, and society were eradicated. Byzantine Africa continued to exist until its final conquest by the Muslims at the end of the 7th century.

Byzantine reoccupation brought part of Africa, especially the provinces of Africa Proconsularis and Byzacena, into a closer relationship with the Greek east than ever before. Although the language of the Church remained Latin, a number of Greek-speaking ecclesiastics and monks from the east settled or took up temporary residence or asylum or were exiled there by the imperial government. Greek-speaking officials and soldiers from the east added to this Hellenic element. Nevertheless, west of Cyrenaica, the littoral remained Latin-speaking and the inhabitants of the countryside probably continued to speak various Berber dialects. There was no mass migration of Greek-speakers to Africa in the wake of the Byzantine reconquest, although a few inscriptions attest to the presence of Greek-speakers. In addition to Africa Proconsularis and Byzacena, the Byzantine army reasserted control over much of Numidia, but only over fragments of Mauretania Caesariensis, and the tip of Mauretania Tingitana, part of what is now Morocco. Ties were also resumed with the bishops of Sicily, Italy, and Sardinia. For Justinian I and his contemporaries the reconquest of Africa was a sign of divine favour and an encouragement to additional territorial expansion in the central and western Mediterranean.

The Byzantine empire, however, lacked the financial and military resources to restore Roman Africa to its dimensions and prosperity of the 2nd and 3rd centuries AD. After the initial reconquest by Belisarius, the government failed to send its best generals and troops to garrison the region. From as early as 536, the slow and inadequate payment and provisioning of the soldiers led to serious military rebellions, in which some Berber elements joined. Berber raids spread insecurity and devastation, so compelling the government and inhabitants to devote extensive resources to the construction and upkeep of town fortifications and watchtowers. Justinian I and his successors also encountered difficulties with implementing their Christological policies in Africa. The African Church had strong local traditions of autonomy and adherence to its own strict policies, and preferred to look more to Rome than to Constantinople for cues in ecclesiastical matters.

By the late 6th century Berber raids had led the imperial government to create a new official, a kind of governor-general, the Exarch of Africa, with combined civilian and military powers. His seat was at Carthage and, although there was no conscious Byzantine effort to Hellenize Africa, the region did acquire a stronger Hellenic imprint. It was also a significant source of revenue, second only to Egypt, in its contribution to imperial funds.

Between 608 and 610 the African exarch Herakleios and his son Herakleios successfully rebelled against the usurper-emperor Phokas, using Africa as the springboard for their seizure of the imperial throne. For the first time in many years, the empire had an emperor whose spouse was from Africa, and although Herakleios' African wife Fabia/Eudocia soon died, ties between Africa and Constantinople remained close, if bittersweet, throughout the life of the Herakleian dynasty (AD 610–95).

The pattern of Muslim conquest in Africa between 643 and 698 was similar but not identical to that of western Asia and Egypt. It occurred in the midst of fiscal, political, ecclesiastical, and theological discord even more acrimonious than that which existed further east. Contemporaries found it easy to blame religious disputes for the problems in Africa, but no one could find a satisfactory way out of the difficult situation that still preserved personal property and integrity.

During the 7th century north Africa loomed larger than ever in the Byzantine worldview, but at a high price. Emperor Herakleios (610–41) had spent ten years of his life there and had married an African landowner's daughter. He and his ruthless treasurer Philagrios, who was briefly exiled to Africa, became familiar with Africa's fiscal potential, which they and their successors utilized to full advantage. Given the very pressing financial needs for defending the Byzantine empire against the Persians and then the Muslims, the Herakleian dynasty naturally turned to Africa for tax revenues. The loss of Egypt in 642–46 meant that African revenues became even more important to the empire. The coming and going of exiles to and from Africa further alerted officials in Constantinople to the region's wealth. By squeezing north Africa for maximal fiscal revenues, the Byzantine authorities exacerbated the already acrimonious theological disputes and hindered the development of an effective defence against the encroaching Muslims. Byzantine policy aimed to spend the seized precious metals, coin, other portable wealth from local churches to fight the enemies of the empire, whether Persians or Muslims. Resistance to such policies from north African landowners and the Church took a number of forms, including the dissemination of hagiographic accounts as well as grumbling and open clashes with the secular authorities. What was Africa getting in return for the ever greater demands for revenue from the central Byzantine imperial authorities?

Byzantine relations with the Berbers had not been good in the 6th century. Memories of Byzantine trickery and the murder of Berber leaders poisoned, or at least complicated, the atmosphere in the 7th century. Yet no possibility existed for raising large numbers of Byzantine troops for the defence of Africa without using Berbers. There were not enough local Latin inhabitants for recruitment into the army, nor could they be drawn away from the empire's threatened borders in the Balkans, Anatolia, and Italy. Berber resistance against the Muslims was not cohesive or well coordinated and it too eventually failed.

At a time when there was the most urgent need for unity and commitment in Africa, Byzantine Africa was rent by political and ecclesiastical divisiveness. The Byzantine monk Maximos the Confessor devoted more time to resisting imperial theology on Christology than to raising popular resistance against the Muslims. By the 650s the Byzantine government was already conceding the loss or virtual loss of Africa to the Muslims, although Byzantine resistance would persist for another four decades. The finger-pointing had already begun as to who was responsible for the debacle, and individuals and factions were interested in making points rather than solving the problem.

A number of incentives motivated the Muslims to conquer Africa, eject the Byzantines, and neutralize or take the region's wealth. The Muslims had probably heard of a failed imperial plan to move troops from Numidia to help Egypt in 633 and may have wished to forestall any repetition or improved version of such an effort. They also did not want the Byzantines in Constantinople to draw on the revenues of Africa to finance their resistance to Islam in Asia Minor, or to use Africa as a base for naval attacks against Muslim-controlled Egypt or other coastal areas. By forcing the Byzantines to pay tribute or even just to defend Africa, the Muslims were depriving them of funds that would otherwise be used in the fight against Islam.

Byzantine Africa did not fall quickly to the Muslims, in contrast to Syria, Mesopotamia, and Egypt. Byzantine resistance continued for many reasons, including financial and strategic ones. The Byzantines, from the perspective of Constantinople, did not want the valuable African resources to fall into Muslim hands. Old Africa Proconsularis (modern Tunisia) was the only place where the Byzantines had any hope of stopping the Muslim advance; logistical problems and lack of Byzantine manpower made it impracticable to consider serious resistance west of Carthage. In this region, however, the Byzantines could still use their fleet and their proximity to Sicily and Malta to advantage. For the Byzantines, holding on to Africa was closely bound up with the prestige of the Herakleian dynasty.

The Muslim conquest of Africa was also more violent than that of Syria, Palestine, Mesopotamia, or Egypt. According to Muslim narrators, the conquest involved more slaughter in combat, more massacres and more mass captivity of civilians, and consequently, more terror and terror-induced flight. Although this may be a case of mere historiographical exaggeration, it may also reflect a greater degree of local resistance, and the fact that Constantinople tried to prevent local officials from making arrangements with the Muslims that might have drained imperial funds and infringed Byzantine sovereignty.

The Muslim conquest of Africa benefited from the momentum, prestige, and confidence that came from so many earlier conquests. The greatest technological assets the Byzantines had were their naval knowledge and fleet, neither of which was used to full advantage. No navy could save the north African interior from the Muslims. Growing apocalypticism may also have contributed to Muslim successes, while Christian apocalypticism probably reduced the strength of Christian resistance, spreading terror and even inducing resigned acquiescence. Only very rarely did the Muslims find willing cooperation from Graeco-Latin leaders in Byzantine Africa, who were willing to give up their localities and accept Muslim rule.

The Christian inhabitants of north Africa left no records of their experiences in those years. There are no reports of martyrdoms, in a land that had previously been replete with Christian martyrs. The absence of such records is also consistent with what happened in Syria and Palestine. The Latin and Greek Christian population of Africa did not welcome and was not indifferent to the Muslims. Their reaction was one of resistance or at least fear, and they made any accommodation with Muslims under duress. The Muslim conquest occurred at a moment of great Hellenic religious ferment in Africa, as Greek works such as the *Doctrina Jacobi nuper Baptizati* and the correspondence of Maximos the Confessor attest. Only a few echoes of that period, however, survive in the *Synaxarion* (church calendar of daily commemoration) of Constantinople.

The Greek-speaking population of Africa had never been large, and disappeared after the Muslim conquest, perhaps because it became indistinguishable from the remaining Latins, all of whom were called *Rum*. Many fled from Africa to Europe (to Spain, Italy, Sicily, or Malta), such as the young man who later became the renowned Hadrian of Canterbury in England; some perished, others assimilated. Africa was to become the staging-ground for Muslim assaults on Byzantine

Sicily and southern Italy between the 7th and 11th centuries. Although the Byzantines made a few raids against Muslim-controlled Africa, and later engaged in important diplomacy with the local Muslim rulers, for example in the 10th century, they never had the resources to consider a serious recovery of Africa after its loss in 698. North Africa was too large and too populous to yield to any deep process of Hellenization.

WALTER E. KAEGI

See also Cyrenaica, Egypt

Summary

North Africa was called Libya by the ancient Greeks and Africa by the Romans. They and the Byzantines regarded all the land between the Red Sea and the Straits of Gibraltar as Africa, though Egypt was usually excluded from the designation. The first Greek settlements were made in the 7th century BC. Most of north Africa was Latinized by the Roman conquest, but the coastal towns of Libya were Greek-speaking until the Muslim conquest in the 7th century AD.

Further Reading

Cameron, Averil, "Gelimer's Laughter: The Case of Byzantine Africa", "Byzantine Africa: The Literary Evidence", and "The Byzantine Reconquest of North Africa and the Impact of Greek Culture", all in her *Changing Cultures in Early Byzantium*, Aldershot, Hampshire: Variorum, 1996

Diehl, Charles, *L'Afrique byzantine: histoire de la domination byzantine en Afrique, 533–709*, Paris: Leroux, 1896

Kaegi, Walter, "Byzantium and the Trans-Saharan Gold Trade: A Cautionary Note", *Graeco-Arabica*, 3 (1984): pp. 95–100

Pringle, Denys, *The Defence of Byzantine Africa from Justinian to the Arab Conquest: An Account of the Military History and Archaeology of the African Provinces in the Sixth and Seventh Centuries*, Oxford: BAR, 1981

Afterlife

Greek beliefs in the afterlife were complex and contradictory, even no doubt within the same individual. We can only speculate about those that were current in the prehistoric period. Marine motifs painted on the surfaces of terracotta Minoan coffins known as *larnakes* have sometimes been fancifully interpreted as evidence that the Minoans believed in an afterlife that lay across the water. The fact that the Mycenaeans were prepared to clear away previous burials in so-called tholos (or beehive) tombs to make way for a new interment has been taken as evidence by some archaeologists that the Mycenaean corpse was believed to be sentient as long as the flesh remained on the bones. Conversely it has been suggested that the plentiful use of gold in Mycenaean royal burials may have been intended to preserve the body from physical decay, judged to be a necessary precondition for a healthy afterlife. The belief that the dead have need of their possessions in the world to come might account for the ritual slaughtering of animals at the time of burial – a practice for which there is evidence in protogeometric as well as Mycenaean times. Myths such as that of the sacrifice of Polyxena at the grave of Achilles have been taken to suggest knowledge of human sacrifice, conceivably practised with a similar object in mind.

It is only when we have written evidence to supplement the archaeological record, however, that we can begin to identify with some degree of certainty the beliefs about the afterlife that underlay funerary ritual. Undoubtedly the most prevalent, and one, moreover, that has persisted into modern times, has to do with Hades, the subterranean kingdom where the bloodless dead lead a cheerless and monotonous existence punctuated only by the appearance of new arrivals. In the earliest surviving description of the region as provided by Homer in book 11 of the *Odyssey*, every human being with one exception ultimately enters this kingdom, irrespective of their qualities. That exception is Menelaus, who is destined to live out eternity in a favoured region known as Elysium, which is situated at the ends of the earth (4. 561ff.). It is not his virtue that has earned Menelaus his privileged status, however, but merely the fact that he happens to be Zeus' son-in-law. Homeric Hades is therefore a place of equal misery for all and contains no trace of a system of punishments and rewards that are meted out to ordinary mortals, though a few who have sinned on a truly grand scale, such as Ixion, Sisyphus, and Tartarus, are condemned to suffer never-ending torment. The rest of the dead tend to confine themselves to sententious moralizing about their past. Greek tragedy occasionally intimates that kings preserve the same status in Hades as they did in life (e.g. Aeschylus, *Persians*, 691). Judging from depictions of the handshake motif in funerary art, a popular belief in Classical Athens was that upon arrival in the underworld a reunion took place between the recently deceased and their previously dead relatives.

Though belief in Hades probably remained dominant throughout antiquity, from the 6th century BC onwards it had to compete with more nebulous philosophical ideas about the afterlife. Orphism and Pythagoreanism, for instance, taught that the soul or *psyche* experiences incarceration in the body in this world and is released from its earthly constraints into its own element at the moment of death. Precisely what the *psyche* signified to these sects is unclear but it was without doubt a more personalized entity than a Homeric shade. The Pythagoreans also taught that the soul migrated to another body at the moment of death, since it is on a journey that will ideally lead it to a state of moral perfection. Attaining that state of perfection might therefore be expected to take several incarnations. The belief in transmigration (*metempsychosis*) seems to have been confined to philosophical circles. It is advanced in a number of Plato's dialogues, including the *Phaedrus*.

Mystery religions, of which the most important were the Eleusinian mysteries, so named because they were celebrated at Eleusis in Attica, held out the promise of a better afterlife in the case of those who underwent initation. So far as we know, however, the promise was not conditional upon a person's conduct in this life – a circumstance that outraged Diogenes the Cynic, who poured scorn on a belief system that maintained that ethical considerations play no part in determining a person's destiny in the afterlife. The only group that was excluded from initiation were murderers, but this may have been more on ritualistic than moral grounds since the shedding of human blood caused pollution.

Alcestis (centre left) is rescued from Thanatos (death, far left) by Hermes Psychopompus (the soul carrier) on the instructions of Persephone (far right) from the temple of Artemis at Ephesus, British Museum, London

From elsewhere, however, there is evidence to suggest that some Greeks at least came to believe that those guilty of serious crimes would be punished in the afterlife. A notable example is Pausanias' description of a painting by Polygnotus that depicted, among other things, a man who had mistreated his father being throttled by him in the underworld (10. 28. 5). In apparent reference to Orphic belief Aristophanes in *Frogs* (145ff.) comically suggests that "anyone who has stolen from a child, thrashed his mother, struck his father or sworn falsely" will be consigned to "everlasting mud". There are also a few references in tragedy to a post-mortem judgement (e.g. Aeschylus, *Suppliants*, 230f. and *Eumenides*, 269ff.; Euripides, *Helen*, 1013ff.). Though belief in a dualistic afterlife never became universal, it made significant inroads into the Homeric picture of an undifferentiated afterlife.

At no period did the Greeks trouble themselves to formulate a clear image of the rewards that lie ahead in the afterlife for those who manage to escape the fate reserved for the rest of mankind. Very likely they merely envisioned a world whose delights in general terms were identical to the best that is on offer in this one. Such seems to have been the idea behind Elysium, otherwise known as the Isles of the Blest, described by Homer as a place where life is easiest for men and where a gentle breeze always blows. A series of Classical grave reliefs depict the dead reclining, enjoying the pleasures of the symposium. Likewise Plato mocks the Pythagoreans for envisaging an afterlife consisting of "eternal drunkenness" (*Republic*, 2.

363c). The *Homeric Hymn to Demeter*, which incorporates the founding charter of the Eleusinian mysteries, merely states in vague terms that initiates will become "prosperous" (*olbioi*, lines 480–82). From the 5th century BC onwards a small minority of funerary inscriptions also refer to a celestial as opposed to a subterranean afterlife for the *psyche* located in the *aither*, i.e. the upper air. There is no suggestion that the dead retain any individuality or even consciousness once they have merged with this element, however. A few dead, notably Castor and Pollux, were transformed into stars, but again it is uncertain what existence they enjoyed as such.

Despite all their attempts to locate the dead above or below the earth, the Greeks found it difficult to envisage their dead as wholly incorporeal. In Classical Athens there is evidence of increasing concern with the physical well-being of the dead, deemed to be dependent upon offerings of food and drink that were placed on the tomb by their relatives, irrespective of whether the dead had been inhumed or cremated. Little can be deduced about eschatological beliefs from the method of disposing of the dead.

In rural Greece to this day beliefs about the afterlife constitute an amalgam of Orthodox Christian teaching alongside notions that have survived from antiquity. In particular the belief that the soul, though disembodied, continues to be dependent upon the living for the necessities of life remains widespread. Hence, food, drink, and clothing are frequently placed on the grave. Likewise candles and lamps are lit in churchyards in accordance with the belief that the other world (*allos kosmos*), like its Classical forebear, is a place of darkness. The dead can only reach Paradise, their ultimate goal, once the flesh has decomposed and the bones have become white and clean. In the preceding, liminal period memorial services are performed on their behalf to assist the deceased on their journey.

ROBERT GARLAND

See also Burial Practices, Death, Hades

Further Reading

Bremmer, Jan, *The Early Greek Concept of the Soul*, Princeton, New Jersey: Princeton University Press, 1983

Danforth, Loring M., *The Death Rituals of Rural Greece*, Princeton, New Jersey: Princeton University Press, 1982

Garland, Robert, *The Greek Way of Death*, London: Duckworth, and Ithaca, New York: Cornell University Press, 1985

Lawson, John Cuthbert, *Modern Greek Folklore and Ancient Greek Religion: A Study in Survivals*, Cambridge: Cambridge University Press, 1910

Agesilaus II *c.*444–359 BC

King of Sparta

Agesilaus was born to a life of controversy. The younger son of king Archidamus II, he was not expected to ascend the throne. He also suffered from a lame leg, a birth defect for which he tried to compensate throughout his life. He received the ordinary rigorous training of the Spartiates, which inculcated in him a sense of duty to superiors and the law. Extremely ambitious, he harboured an arrogance that he unsuccessfully disguised under a diaphanous cloak of humility. His elder brother, king Agis II, died in 400 BC, which ignited an ugly contest for the throne. Agis' son Leotychides was accused of being illegitimate and, despite his handicap, Agesilaus advanced himself as Archidamus' true son. The furore was fuelled by Diopeithes, an expounder of oracles, who declared that the divine will rejected a lame king, for he would bring "unexpected afflictions and whirling man-killing wars". The result of this unsavoury contest was the recognition of Agesilaus as king.

Agesilaus owed his first important military command to his lover Lysander, the famous war hero. Agesilaus' first assignment was to free the Greek cities of Asia Minor from Persian rule. Accompanied by Lysander, he sailed in 396 BC. His first landfall, at Aulis in Boeotia, was in imitation of Agamemnon, who had sacrificed Iphigeneia there before continuing to Troy. When Agesilaus offered a sacrifice, contrary to native custom, Boeotian officials abruptly disrupted the ceremony. Agesilaus left for Asia Minor with feelings of foreboding and a fierce anger against Thebes.

Agesilaus accomplished comparatively little against the Persians. In 395 BC he unsuccessfully attacked Sardis, the principal city of Lydia, but in all he engaged in desultory operations that inflicted little damage on the Persians. He obviously had no strategic concept of how to defeat such a powerful enemy over such a large expanse of terrain. In any case, events in Greece put an end to his ambitious and unrealistic dream of conquering Persia. Thebes, Athens, Argos, and Corinth banded together to crush Sparta, and in response Sparta promptly recalled Agesilaus to meet the challenge. The Corinthian War (395–386 BC), as the ensuing conflict is known, severely strained Agesilaus' abilities and Sparta's resources.

Hurrying back to Greece, Agesilaus marched overland through the north until he reached Coronea in Boeotia. In August 394 BC he encountered a Theban and allied army, and in a furious battle made a tactical blunder that cost him dearly: he received several wounds, and his troops suffered many casualties. Despite this tactical and strategic defeat, in 391 BC he led a successful invasion of Argos and Corinth, in which he inflicted serious damage. In the following year he campaigned very effectively in Perachora immediately to the north of Corinth but again without decisive results. He fared better in 389 BC, when he defended Sparta's Achaean allies from their neighbour Acarnania.

Victory for Sparta, however, came from diplomacy not from warfare. In 386 BC the Spartan ambassador Antalcidas negotiated the King's Peace that ended the war between Persia and the Greeks. Yet those hoping that this treaty would bring peace were promptly disappointed.

As in 386 BC, Sparta resorted to diplomacy to win the peace. In 371 BC Sparta, Athens, and other Greeks renewed the common peace, but Agesilaus expelled Thebes from it. The irony of this diplomatic victory is that it led to military defeat on the field of Leuctra, which resulted in the downfall of Sparta. In the Peloponnese pent-up anger quickly vented itself: in 370 BC Elis, Arcadia, and Argos allied with Thebes to cripple Sparta as the surest guarantee of their mutual safety. Epaminondas led them into Laconia, where they spread devastation and liberated helots and others. He next led them to the liberation of Messenia, which broke the back of the Spartan economy while raising an implacable foe on Sparta's doorstep. Agesilaus rallied his countrymen through the ordeal, but could not undo the harm for which he was solely responsible. In the following years Sparta declined and Agesilaus languished. His last encounter with Epaminondas was at the battle of Mantinea in 362 BC, a Theban victory but in which the Theban leader was killed. Agesilaus spent his declining years as a mercenary in Egypt, dying in 359 BC on his way back to Sparta.

For all his military fame, Agesilaus never won a major battle. His diplomatic policies almost uniformly led to unnecessary disaster. When he assumed the throne in 400 BC he reigned over a Sparta supreme in Greece; at his death, owing largely to his failures, Sparta was beaten and isolated. His fame survived him, but his mark on history was scarcely stellar. Diopeithes' interpretation of the warning against a lame king had come true.

JOHN BUCKLER

See also Sparta

Biography

Born *c*.444 BC the younger son of king Archidamus II of Sparta, Agesilaus was not brought up to be king. But on the death of his elder brother, King Agis II, in 400 BC, Agis' son was accused of being illegitimate and Agesilaus successfully negotiated for the throne. He had some military success against the Persians but never won a major battle and presided over Spartan decline. He died in Cyrenaica in 359 BC.

Further Reading

Cartledge, Paul, *Agesilaos and the Crisis of Sparta*, Baltimore: Johns Hopkins University Press, and London: Duckworth, 1987

Cawkwell, G.L., "Agesilaus and Sparta", *Classical Quarterly*, 70 (1976): pp. 62–84

Hamilton, Charles D., *Sparta's Bitter Victories: Politics and Diplomacy in the Corinthian War*, Ithaca, New York: Cornell University Press, 1979

Shipley, D.R., *A Commentary on Plutarch's Life of Agesilaos: Response to Sources in the Presentation of Character*, Oxford: Clarendon Press, and New York: Oxford University Press, 1997

Smith, R.E., "The Opposition to Agesilaus' Foreign Policy, 394–371 BC", *Historia*, 2 (1953–54): pp. 274–88

Agora of Athens

Marketplace of ancient Athens

The Agora was located to the northwest of the Acropolis. It was traversed by the Panathenaic Way and formed a large open square serving various public functions. Laid out early in the 6th century BC, it remained the focal point for Athenian commerce, culture, and politics for many centuries. It originally consisted of a square space defined by boundary stones (*horoi*). The first public buildings were erected on the west side and seem to have served the needs of the Council. When Pisistratus was in power at Athens, in the second half of the 6th century BC (566–510 BC), limited building activity took place in the Agora, which expanded gradually to the east and south. A large house-like building preceded the Tholos at the southwest corner of the Agora, but its use has not been defined with certainty; it was probably built as the palace of the tyrants and later served the domestic needs of the Council. A fountain house, supplied by a terracotta aqueduct, appeared at the southeast corner of the square, while an altar of the Twelve Gods was established at the north. The street of the Panathenaia passed diagonally through the square, as it ran from the Dipylon gate to the Acropolis. Although the line of the road goes back to the Iron Age, when it led to the cemetery of Kerameikos, it was incorporated in the Agora during the 6th century BC.

The constitutional reforms of Cleisthenes at the end of the 6th century BC (508/07 BC) were followed by considerable building activity in the Agora. Several buildings accommodated the new government, including the Heliaea (the principal law court) along the south side of the square, and the Bouleuterion (Senate House), and the Royal Stoa (or Stoa Basileios) – headquarters of the king archon, where the laws were also put on public display – along the west side. Furthermore, shrines to the Mother of Gods, Zeus, and Apollo were built along the west side of the Agora. The Assembly of the citizens (*Ekklesia*), which used to meet in the Agora, found a new gathering place on the Pnyx Hill. The Persian attack in 480/79 BC left all these buildings in ruins, as was also the case on the Acropolis. Repair works, however, took place at the Bouleuterion, the Heliaea, and the Royal Stoa, which were shortly in use again.

After the Persian invasions and during Cimon's time, the architectural development of the Agora was remarkable. Cimon is also reported to have adorned the area with trees. From 479 BC to the middle of the 5th century BC, besides the reconstruction of the buildings destroyed by the Persians, the Painted (or Poikile) Stoa, the Tholos – a round building, functioning as the headquarters of the *prytaneis* ("standing committtee") of the Boule, where they also dined – the Herms, and the aqueduct to the Academy were built. The Painted Stoa is among the most famous buildings in the Athenian Agora. It was first known as Peisianaktios, after the man responsible for its construction, and was decorated with painted wooden panels by the outstanding painters of Athens, such as Polygnotus, Micon, and Panaenus.

The Periclean building programme in the middle of the 5th century BC did not include extensive activity in the Agora, because there was a shift of attention to the Acropolis and Attica. The work was therefore concentrated on repairs to sanctuaries and shrines, such as the altar of the Twelve Gods, the altar of Aphrodite, and the Crossroads Enclosure. Among the first new buildings were the temple of Hephaestus, which was not completed before the Peace of Nicias (421–415 BC), and the Strategeion, the headquarters of the generals.

Although the Peloponnesian War had affected the Periclean building programme leaving several monuments unfinished, a burst of building activity occurred in the Agora during the last 30 years of the 5th century BC, indicating an interest in civic structures. The new Bouleuterion was built immediately to the west of the old one; the Stoa of Zeus Eleutherios was a religious building and an informal meeting place of the Athenians; the South Stoa I, a public market building, also housed the officials responsible for the administration of the commercial life of Athens as well as the official weights, measures, and

standards; the Mint was the public foundry that produced not only bronze coins but other material in bronze required by the state, such as weights and measures. These constructions were erected with limestone and brick, demonstrating the extent of Athenian resources even in times of war. The old Bouleuterion, known as the Metroon, did not go out of use, but housed the official archives of the city and the cult of Rhea, the Mother of Gods. The construction of the South Stoa and the Mint on the south side of the Agora made this area the official commercial centre, just as the west served administrative needs.

Besides the public buildings, excavations have brought to light many establishments for private industry and commerce, especially on the southwest of the Agora, such as the pottery and metalwork workshops, as well as sculptors' and marble workers' ateliers and shoemakers' shops. These workshops were in most cases attached to the private dwellings of the artisans and tradesmen. Moreover, wine shops and tavernas were found close to the east side of the Agora.

Construction works in the Agora were abandoned during the first half of the 4th century BC, because Athens was recovering from the Peloponnesian War. In the second half of the 4th century BC, when the city's economy improved, partly because of renewed activity at the Laurium mines, a new fountain house was built at the southwest corner, as well as a water clock, and the monument of the Eponymous Heroes was located in front of the Bouleuterion, the latter used for the posting of civic announcements. On the west side of the Agora was the shrine of Zeus Phratrios and Athena Phratria and the temple of Apollo Patroos. The square peristyle at the northeast corner of the Agora housed the law courts, as indicated by the finds of scattered bronze discs, which are identified as public ballots. Associated with the law courts is the state prison, recognized in a building located outside the southwest corner of the square, which dates from the middle of the 5th century BC.

The prosperity of Athens in the 2nd century BC and the benefactions of the eastern monarchs revived building activity in the Agora. The erection of the Middle Stoa, the East Building, and the South Stoa II created a complex, the South Square, which cut off the south half of the square from the north, changing the plan of the Agora. The most likely suggestion about the function of the complex is that it was a commercial centre, the two stoas serving as market buildings. Moreover, a two-storey colonnade, the gift of Attalus II, king of Pergamum (159–138 BC), housed stores and closed the east side of the main square. Also built at this time was the new Metroon on the west side of the square. The remodelling of the 2nd century BC gave a different appearance to the Agora, which it retained for the rest of antiquity. Its area was 50,000 square metres; all sides were now enclosed by colonnades; and the open central square became smaller, divided into two unequal halves by the Middle Stoa.

In 88 BC the Athenians sided with King Mithridates of Pontus in his revolt against Rome. For this reason Athens was besieged in 86 BC by Sulla, and several monuments of the Agora were damaged. Among them the Tholos, the southwest fountain house, the Heliaea, South Stoa II, and the East Building seem to have been destroyed; the Tholos was the only monument soon to be repaired. The south side of the Agora was later reoccupied by private industrial activities, such as

Agora: the Athenian Agora from the southeast with the temple of Hephaestus in the background to the left

iron foundries, potters' kilns, and marble-workers' workshops. In the time of Hadrian this area was cleaned up and restored to public use.

An important development in the Agora during Roman times was the construction of a marketplace to the east, in the form of a large open courtyard surrounded by colonnades. The construction, which started with Julius Caesar and was completed by Augustus around 11–9 BC, affected the plan of the old Agora. Thus it was no longer thought necessary to maintain the central open square, which was soon covered by the Odeum of Agrippa, housing musical performances, and the temple of Ares; the latter was a 5th-century building standing somewhere in Attica which was dismantled and re-erected in the Agora.

Limited construction works took place in the Athenian Agora during the 1st century AD. The southwest and the southeast temples were erected from reused materials and the civic offices were built at the southwest corner of the square. Additions were also made to already existing buildings, such as an annex behind the stoa of Zeus, probably to house the imperial cult, a columnar porch to the Tholos, and a Doric propylon to the entrance of the Strategeion.

During the reign of Trajan Athens went through a period of prosperity. The earliest building in the Agora, dating to the 2nd century AD and situated along the Panathenaic Way just south of the Stoa of Attalus, was a public library, built by Pantaenus, the son of Flavius Menander. South of the library, a complex of shops was built in the middle of the 2nd century AD. An Ionic porch fronted the shops and was aligned with a similar one in front of the library, so as to create a fashionable street colonnade. Around the same time, during the reign of Trajan, the basilica at the northeast corner of the square was built. It was a three-aisled hall, which served as a law court, but also for commercial and administrative needs. Another 2nd-century addition to the Agora was a Nymphaeum, an elaborate fountain house, built west of the Panathenaic Way. It was begun during the reign of Hadrian, and completed in AD 140 under Antoninus Pius. A round building in front of the Stoa of Attalus, probably built to shelter a statue, dates to the Antonine period. At about this time the Odeum of Agrippa was rebuilt. Lastly, a library was erected by the emperor Hadrian (AD 117–38) to the east of the stoa of Attalus. Throughout the 2nd century AD the Agora flourished as a commercial and cultural centre.

The Athenian Agora was seriously damaged by the Herulians, a tribe who invaded Greece from the north in AD 267. They sacked and burned many cities, including Athens. The temple of Hephaestus survived, and excavations in the surrounding area indicate that several civic buildings on the west and north sides of the Agora, such as the Tholos, the

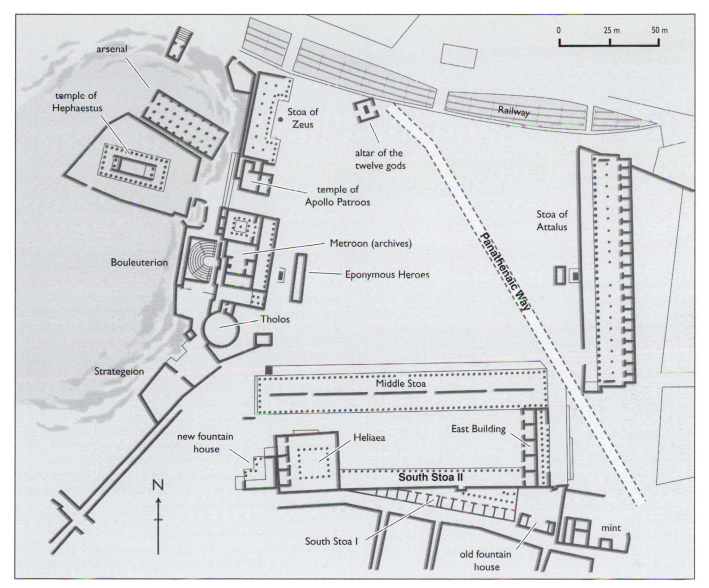

2. The Agora, Athens

temple of Apollo, the stoa of Zeus, the Royal stoa, and the Painted Stoa, continued to stand, though they were perhaps damaged.

Although the 4th century AD was a period of decline, limited reconstruction work took place: in the Agora the Metroon was restored, the wall of the Tholos was strengthened, and many of the houses were reoccupied. Towards the end of the century, in AD 395, Alaric and the Visigoths reached the walls of Athens; the literary sources disagree about the damage caused to the city, but excavations indicate that such buildings as the Tholos, the temple of Apollo, and the Stoa of Zeus, which survived the Herulians, were destroyed and abandoned.

After the departure of the Visigoths there was a new burst of building activity in the area of the old Agora. A large part of the square was taken up with a gymnasium complex and a porch, the so-called Porch of the Giants. Moreover, the eastern stoa of the library of Pantaenus was rebuilt with a second storey and served as a façade to a new public complex built on two levels.

The area of the Agora suffered again in the attacks of the Slavs who arrived from the north and destroyed the city in AD 582/83. There is scant evidence of reoccupation in the ruins of the Agora from the 7th until the 10th century AD when the town extended again to this area. The temple of Hephaestus was converted to a Christian church early in the 7th century AD, the building was reoriented, and an apse was added.

In later Byzantine, Frankish, and Turkish times the area of the Agora became a residential district. During the Greek War of Independence (1821–28) most of the houses in the area were destroyed; these were again rebuilt after 1834, when Athens became the capital of the modern Greek state.

ELENI ZIMI

Summary
The marketplace of ancient Athens to the northwest of the Acropolis. The Agora was first laid out in the early 6th century BC and remained the centre of the city's commercial, cultural, and political life

throughout antiquity. In later Byzantine, Frankish, and Turkish times it became a residential district.

Further Reading

Camp, John M., *The Athenian Agora: Excavations in the Heart of Classical Athens*, London and New York: Thames and Hudson, 1986, revised 1992

Camp, John, M., *The Athenian Agora: A Guide to the Excavation and the Museum*, 4th edition, Athens: American School of Classical Studies at Athens, 1990

Wycherley, R.E., *The Athenian Agora*, vol. 3: *Literary and Epigraphic Testimonia*, Princeton, New Jersey: American School of Classical Studies at Athens, 1957

Agriculture

In many regions of the Mediterranean agriculture underwent little change between antiquity and the modern age. The socioeconomic and technological developments that have affected the ancient traditions of agriculture have been relatively recent. Ethnographers have found a number of similarities between the cultivation techniques of today and those described by early Greek poets such as Homer and Hesiod.

Ancient and traditional agriculture in Greece has two major factors broadly in common: climate and terrain. The continuing impact of these factors, combined with the extensive survival of cultivating cereals, vines, and olives, has ensured that many techniques of ancient agriculture have survived for thousands of years. The pioneering work of Paul Halstead has revealed a great deal about the traditional agricultural techniques that have survived among the Greek peoples of the Mediterranean.

The recommendations of ancient authors on agriculture sometimes amount to little more than aphorisms or ethical guidelines. In some respects, practice may have differed from such advice. Ancient authors advocate that fields should be left fallow for a year so that the soil could be rested. But pressures on subsistence farms may have required the cultivation of land that otherwise might have been left temporarily idle. A compromise may have been found by planting different crops on land sown previously with, for example, cereals.

Some leases outlining the obligations for the cultivation of land have survived from antiquity. An example from Piraeus allows land to be ploughed for the nine years of the agreement, but in the tenth it was to be left fallow (*Inscriptiones Graecae*, ii^2, 2498). Such strictures indicate the importance attached to leaving land fallow. The need for such guidelines also suggests that farmers may well have avoided leaving fields fallow for a year.

The cultivation of cereals, vines, and olives has remained central to Greek agriculture from antiquity. The climate – broadly speaking, low annual rainfall, dry summers, mild winters – is typical of the Mediterranean. Some regions had superior soil, others more favourable microclimates. A rich, ruddy, fertile soil was a distinctive feature of Boeotia; Thessaly enjoyed extensive tracts of land ideal for the cultivation of cereals. Some regions were famous for specific types of produce: honey in Attica from Classical to Roman times, wine from Chios, Cos, and Thasos, and olive oil on Samos.

Although it is dangerous to generalize, it is clear that the spread of olive, grain, and vine cultivation throughout the Mediterranean world and the location of Greek colonies from the archaic period were not mutually exclusive. It is no coincidence that those areas colonized were seldom unable to support these three crops, and in particular the olive.

The olive was grown by most Greek communities. Highly resistant to low rainfall, but cultivable only at relatively low altitudes, olive trees were long lasting and required little maintenance. Olives could be harvested every other year, but the trees would take 10 to 15 years to reach fruit-bearing maturity. Harvesting took place in autumn or early winter, but the particular timing would have varied from region to region. Olives provided not only foodstuff but also oil, which in turn was used as a base for perfumes and medicines, as fuel for lighting, and for athletics and bathing. The relatively simple cultivation and harvesting of the olives was a less complex task than the production of the oil itself. Processing oil required crushing, pressing, and separation of the olive. Beam presses and rotary mills were the most common devices for crushing and pressing. The study of ancient olive presses has been informed by the examination of presses still used today, where the beam press has remained little changed from antiquity.

Vines were altogether a far more labour-intensive crop to cultivate, maintain, and harvest. The spread of viticulture into southern Spain and the Black Sea cannot be separated from the diffusion of Phocaean and Greek settlers respectively. Vine growing and so wine consumption was a major feature of Hellenic civilization, and the legacy continues today. The ancient symposium was centred around the drinking of wine, albeit diluted with water. The great festival in honour of Dionysus, the Anthesteria, celebrated in late February the new wine, and the wine storage vessels were symbolically opened on the first day of the ceremonies.

The centrality of agriculture to ancient Greek life is nowhere more apparent than in the cultivation of cereals. The two most important crops, barley and wheat, were usually sown in autumn. Of the different types of wheat, the best bread-making, light wheat (hexaploid) was grown in the Black Sea region where the cooler climate and higher rainfall were more suitable for this very popular but less hardy variety. Although wheat is generally more vulnerable to extremes in climate than barley, it is more nutritious and has a much higher yield. It was therefore widely preferred. But the higher-quality bread wheats were not as well suited to the climate in most regions of Greece, especially those in the south. In the second half of the 19th century wheat was far more widely cultivated than barley, on a ratio of 3:1. The evidence from Classical Greece indicates that barley was the more common of the two crops. The high population densities, patterns of land-ownership, and farm size may have affected the selection of barley as the preferred crop. Even the best breads in antiquity were more coarse than many of those today, while barley was a main ingredient for the large variety of "cakes" eaten in antiquity.

The selection of crops for cultivation was probably driven to some extent by expected yields. The vulnerability of cereals to frost when the crop was young and green, to shortfalls in rain when ripening, and to too much rain before harvest were far greater problems for wheat than for barley. An inscription

Agriculture: agricultural implements on sale at Elassona in Thessaly

from Eleusis recording the contribution in 329–328 BC of first fruits from Attica and the Athenian-controlled territories of Lemnos and Imbros suggests that more barley than wheat was dedicated at Eleusis. It is likely that the figures reveal that there was a poor harvest in Attica that year, and that wheat yields would have suffered more seriously than barley.

Agriculture in Greece rarely concentrated on any one of the three main crops. It is almost certain that most domestic Greek farms would have practised polyculture. Farmsteads devoted to the intensive production of one crop are known but exceptional; a large number of industrial "farms" are known at Chersonesus in the Crimea where estates were exporting their produce, probably wine. Legumes, pulses, and figs could have been grown in many areas. A variety of crops were probably grown on a typical farmstead. Intercropping, the planting of cereals, trees, vines, and pulses on one plot of land, was a likely feature of the Greek farm.

Archaeology cannot always confirm the nature of occupation in some rural establishments. A considerable amount of evidence indicates more permanent installations, some of which we might describe as farms. The Greek farm probably took many forms. People may have worked land close to their settlement, walking out to their fields daily or living in temporary shelters. Ancient and traditional Greek agriculture has generally centred around nucleated settlements, villages, or towns. Patterns of land tenure, the nature of agriculturally

productive land, and sometimes issues of security have all influenced the location of settlement. It is now believed that a typical Greek household in antiquity would have had sufficient land to provide for its members. In some communities this may have been more an ideal than a reasonable ambition. Archaeological survey is suggesting that many ancient communities would have been of a size that could be sustained from local agricultural produce.

Excavation and archaeological survey in the rural landscape over the last 30 years have advanced considerably our knowledge of settlement in the countryside. Farms can be difficult to identify. Buildings with or without agricultural functions are often indistinguishable. But ancillary constructions such as threshing floors, olive presses, and field walls – all of which have changed little since antiquity – usually confirm the agricultural concerns of the building. Buildings with towers are a familiar type of rural building often used as a farm and are found throughout the Greek countryside. Aerial photography has revealed the extensive use of retaining walls in the Greek countryside and illustrates the extent to which more marginal land was exploited throughout history. However, it is very difficult, perhaps almost impossible, to date accurately such retaining or field walls.

The margins of survival for the subsistence farm may have been slim; a sequence of bad years would have had a severe impact on the household. Household size would have fluctuated as children matured, moved away, or stayed at home and married, as children were born, and their grandparents died, as slaves were bought or sold.

The intensification of agricultural production by purchasing slaves or using animals for ploughing or transporting may have been too much of a burden for the small farm. Cooperation between neighbours or members of the extended family may have allowed resources to be used within rural communities. Smaller farms were probably unable to support extensive animal farming. Larger herds would have been tended on more mountainous or marginal lands, and there is plenty of direct and indirect evidence for the extensive use of such land in the Classical period.

Storing agricultural produce was one method of protecting against shortfalls in harvests, but such methods could provide only limited amounts. A number of farmsteads in the Greek countryside consisted of a house with a tower-like structure. Such features have survived in the Mediterranean from antiquity. It is almost certain that the tower structure on such farmsteads was used for storing produce and property and on occasion for security.

Human interference was probably the greatest threat to agricultural security, in both real and conceptual terms. The interruption of agricultural activities by warfare is a major feature in Greek history: perhaps most famously, the Spartans and their allies timed their invasions of Attica during the Archidamian War (431–421 BC) to coincide with the harvest period, a critical moment for those who were required to gather the crops. Such interruptions in the agricultural year, at their most extreme the cutting off of cities from the surrounding countryside by siege, presented the most common need for food supplies to be brought in from outside a Greek community.

The connections between life in ancient Greece and agriculture are difficult to separate; the Athenians found it difficult to move from the countryside into the city during the Peloponnesian War (Thucydides, 2. 16. 2). All communities in ancient Greece were dependent on agricultural produce for supplies of food (Plato, *Republic*, 369d, 371c, 372c–d); those communites that could grow all their own grain had considerable advantages over those who needed to import food supplies (see Thucydides, 6. 20. 4).

Self-sufficiency (*autarkeia*) was an ideal that features in many ancient Greek authors when assessing structures such as the household or the polis (Plato, *Laws*, 5. 744b–e). There are few extant works that treat explicitly the art of agriculture: Xenophon's *Oikonomikos* has a great deal to say about agriculture; Theophrastus heralds a higher level of scientific understanding of botanical observation (*Research on Plants and Plant Explanations*) in the later 4th century BC. But common to almost all Greek literature is the primacy of agriculture: the shield of Achilles (Homer, *Iliad*, 18. 541ff.) includes a rural scene of ploughmen wheeling their teams of draught animals; the Linear B tablets are full of ideograms and logograms that allow the scribes to maintain the palace accounts of agricultural produce.

The continuing importance of agriculture to Greek life is seen most clearly in the work of archaeological surveys carried out in a variety of locations such as Messenia, the southern Argolid, Nemea, Methana, Boeotia, Aetolia, Ceos, Melos, Crete, and Lesbos. Common to these studies is the observation of the human impact on the Greek landscape over a long period of time. The surveys present findings from geological prospecting to the results of research on recent land use. The collation of statistics, anecdotes, and records of agricultural activities and settlement during the 19th and 20th centuries has produced important information for both comparative and quantitative studies of Greek agriculture.

In many respects the continuities in practices and pressures can be seen stretching from antiquity to the present day. In the Byzantine period polyculture continued, dominated by grain and vine cultivation. In addition, specialist crops appeared such as flax and cotton; in some areas, such as the Peloponnese, silk was produced. There were few technological developments: horses were used in ploughing from the 10th century and windmills started to flourish in the 13th. Increased production still depended largely on extending the area of land under cultivation. Some areas of Greece, particularly the Peloponnese, enjoyed considerable agricultural prosperity in this period.

The main differences between the preindustrial and modern eras of Greece are the more recent technological developments – mechanization and advances in irrigation – and the new socioeconomic factors. On one level, these are the increasing demands of regional markets, and the wider economic context provided by the European Union. In antiquity the farmers of Greece generally operated to provide sufficient produce for their household. Few areas would have been devoted to providing produce for export. But the high quality of produce such as figs, honey, olives, and wine has been a consistent feature of Greek culture throughout history.

GRAHAM OLIVER

See also Geology, Olive, Transhumance, Vine

Further Reading

Alcock, S.E., J. Cherry, and J.L. Davis, "Intensive Survey, Agricultural Practice and the Classical Landscape of Greece" in *Classical Greece: Ancient Histories and Modern Archaeologies*, edited by Ian Morris, Cambridge and New York: Cambridge University Press, 1994

Boserup, Ester, *The Conditions of Agricultural Growth: The Economics of Agrarian Change under Population Pressure*, London: Allen and Unwin, and New York: Aldine, 1965, reprinted London: Earthscan, 1993

Bradford, John, "Fieldwork on Aerial Discoveries in Attica and Rhodes", *Antiquity*, 36 (1956): pp. 172–80

Bradford, John, *Ancient Landscapes: Studies in Field Archaeology*, London: Bell, 1957

Cooper, A.B., "The Family Farm in Greece", *Classical Journal*, 73 (1977–78): pp. 162–75

de Ste Croix, G.E.M., "The Estate of Phaenippus (Ps.-Dem. xliii)" in *Ancient Society and Institutions: Studies Presented to Victor Ehrenberg*, edited by E. Badian, Oxford: Blackwell, 1966; New York: Barnes and Noble, 1967

Dufkova, M. and J. Pecrika, "Excavations of Farms and Farmhouses in the Chora of Chersonesos in the Crimea", *Eirene*, 8 (1970): pp. 123–74

Foxhall, L. and H. Forbes, "Sitometreia: The Role of Grain as a Staple Food in Classical Antiquity", *Chiron*, 12 (1982): pp. 41–90

Gallant, Thomas W., *Risk and Survival in Ancient Greece: Reconstructing the Rural Domestic Economy*, Stanford,

California: Stanford University Press, and Cambridge: Polity Press, 1991

Garnsey, Peter, "Grain for Athens" in *Crux: Essays Presented to G.E.M. de Ste Croix on His 75th Birthday*, edited by Paul Cartledge and F.D. Harvey, Exeter: Imprint Academic, 1985

Garnsey, Peter, *Famine and Food Supply in the Graeco–Roman World: Responses to Risk and Crisis*, Cambridge and New York: Cambridge University Press, 1988

Halstead, P., "Traditional and Ancient Rural Economy in Mediterranean Europe: Plus ça Change", *Journal of Hellenic Studies*, 107 (1987): pp. 77–87

Halstead, P. and G. Jones, "Agrarian Ecology in the Greek Islands: Time Stress, Scale and Risk", *Journal of Hellenic Studies*, 109 (1989): pp. 41–55

Hanson, V.D., *Warfare and Agriculture in Classical Greece*, Pisa: Giardini, 1983; revised edition Berkeley: University of California Press, 1998

Hodkinson, S., "Animal Husbandry in the Greek Polis" in *Pastoral Economies in Classical Antiquity*, edited by C.R. Whittaker, Cambridge: Cambridge Philological Society, 1988

Hughes, J. Donald, *Pan's Travail: Environmental Problems of the Ancient Greeks and Romans*, Baltimore: Johns Hopkins University Press, 1994

Isager, Signe and J.E. Skydsgaard, *Ancient Greek Agriculture: An Introduction*, London and New York: Routledge, 1992

Jameson, Michael H., Curtis N. Runnels and Tjeerd Van Andel, *A Greek Countryside: The Southern Argolid from Prehistory to the Present Day*, Stanford, California: Stanford University Press, 1994

Jones, J.E., L.H. Sackett and A.J. Graham, "The Dema House in Attica", *Annual of the British School at Athens*, 57 (1962): pp. 75–114

Jones, J.E., L.H. Sackett and A.J. Graham, "An Attic Country House: Below the Cave of Pan at Vari", *Annual of the British School at Athens*, 68 (1973): pp. 355–452

Jones, J.E., "Town and Country Houses of Attica in Classical Times" in *Thorikos and the Laurion in Archaic and Classical Times*, edited by H. Mussche, Paule Spitaels, and F. Goemaere-de Poerck, Ghent: Belgian Archaeological Mission in Greece, 1975

Osborne, Robin, *Classical Landscape with Figures: The Ancient Greek City and Its Countryside*, London: George Philip, and Dobbs Ferry, New York: Sheridan House, 1987

Pecirka, J., "Homestead Farms in Classical and Hellenistic Hellas" in *Problèmes de la terre en Grèce ancienne*, edited by M.I. Finley, Paris: Mouton, 1973

Sallares, Robert, *The Ecology of the Ancient Greek World*, London: Duckworth, and Ithaca, New York: Cornell University Press, 1991

Salmon, John and Graham Shipley, *Human Landscapes in Classical Antiquity: Environment and Culture*, London and New York: Routledge, 1996

Wells, Berit (editor), *Agriculture in Ancient Greece*, Stockholm: Swedish Institute at Athens, 1992

Akindynos, Gregory *c.1300–c.1348*

Theologian

A native of Prilapon (modern Prilep) in Macedonia, Gregory Akindynos received his formative experiences in Pelagonia (modern Bitola) on the Via Egnatia. He then proceeded to Thessalonica, where he studied under Thomas Magistros and the archdeacon Bryennios. He may have met Barlaam in Thessalonica in 1326/27. Akindynos then became a professor of grammar and tutor in Beroea. There he came into contact with St Gregory Palamas, who from 1326 to 1331 lived in a nearby hermitage. In 1330 Palamas gave Akindynos a copy of Nikephoros Gregoras's treatise on astronomy. In 1332, possibly at Palamas's instigation, he visited Mount Athos. He does not appear to have liked the intellectual atmosphere, or lack of it, on the Holy Mountain, but, unlike Barlaam, never spoke against the monks of Athos. In 1336 he received from Palamas a letter criticizing the anti-Latin treatises of Barlaam. At about this time he settled in Constantinople.

Up to 1341 Akindynos acted as a mediator between Barlaam and Palamas. He strongly advised Barlaam to desist from his attacks on the hesychast monks, though his advice was ignored. A letter from Palamas began to raise doubts in his mind, but he continued to support Palamas's cause, arranging for Palamas's summons to Constantinople to be reworded as an invitation. Palamas stayed with Akindynos on his arrival in the capital in December 1340–January 1341. Akindynos gave his full support to Palamas at the synod of June 1341, on the condition that Palamas would withdraw certain expressions in his work that Akindynos found unsound. Palamas appears to have suggested that he would indeed retract these expressions. He did not, however, compromise, and in fact forced the convocation of another synod in July 1341. Akindynos found himself de facto leader of the anti-Palamite cause.

The debate rapidly escalated into a full-blown controversy, fought with ferocious zeal. Akindynos survived at least one assassination attempt, thanks to the second thoughts of the would-be assassin. Akindynos undertook a prodigious campaign against the "new theology" of Palamas, and did so openly from June 1342. Palamas was arrested and imprisoned in September of that year. Akindynos was ordained in late 1344, being groomed, it seems, for the metropolitan see of Thessalonica. Akindynos was vindicated by the Constantinopolitan synod of October 1345, a decision that was upheld by the patriarch John Kalekas against both the wishes of the regent, Anne of Savoy, and widespread monastic pressure. The positions of Akindynos and Palamas were, however, reversed with the ascendancy of the emperor John VI Kantakouzenos, who finally took the city on the night of the 2–3 February 1347. Palamite theology was canonized by the synods of February 1347 and May 1351, and that of Akindynos condemned. Akindynos died before May 1348.

Akindynos's works are not abundant, and are restricted largely to polemic. He composed refutations of both Barlaam and Palamas. He couched some of anti-Palamite theology in poetic form, as in his *509 Iambics*. We are now in a position to assess an important part of his work following the publication of his *Two Refutations of the Work of Gregory Palamas Entitled "A Dialogue between an Orthodox and a Barlaamite"*. The main thrust of Akindynos's argument is that Palamas's assertion of a real difference between the divine essence and the divine energies or operations is inconsistent with the patristic witness. Akindynos's method is very straightforward; he tackles Palamas point by point, producing a host of patristic testimonies at every opportunity. Akindynos's work is heavy and repetitive, frequently digressing into areas the pertinence of which is obscure. He emphasizes the point that between God and the world there is no *tertium quid*, no *metaxi*. On grace, for example, he argues that there is hypostatic, uncreated grace which is the Son and the Holy Spirit, and created, non-hypostatic grace, and nothing more. He characterizes Palamas's distinction between the essence and energies of God as a lapse into polytheism and an impious denigration of the divine unity. Furthermore, on Akindynos's reading, Palamas teaches that man participates not in God himself, but in some inferior divinity. There is, however, little real development in Akindynos's thought. His principal objection is quite simply that Palamite theology is new, and therefore inadmissible.

Akindynos was not a scholar of the stature of Barlaam, or indeed of Palamas, as he himself admits. His polemical works are more of an assembly of patristic texts than a sustained theological argument. This may be due to their quasi-official character, being prepared as they were at the request of the patriarch John Kalekas. Akindynos was without doubt sincere in his attacks on Palamite theology, deeming it unsound, dangerous, and innovative. The best rebuttal of that theology was, as he saw it, a demonstration of its inconsistency with the patristic witness. His condemnation at the Palamite councils of 1347 and 1351 has meant that his influence has been virtually nil, being perceptible perhaps only in the far more thorough-going defence of the divine unity found in the Byzantine Thomist Demetrios Kydones. Akindynos's innate conservatism and suspicion of change have, however, been shared by many representatives of the Byzantine and post-Byzantine tradition.

MARCUS PLESTED

See also Hesychasm

Biography
Born at Prilep in Macedonia, probably in 1300, Akindynos studied in Thessalonica where he mixed with both Barlaam and St Gregory Palamas. For a while he acted as mediator between them, but from 1342 was openly hostile to Palamas. With the accession of John Kantakouzenos as emperor in 1347 Akindynos lost favour and he died the next year.

Writings
Letters, translated by Angela Constantinides Hero, Washington, D.C.: Dumbarton Oaks, 1983

Further Reading
Canellas, J.N. (editor), *Refutationes duae Operis Gregorii Palamae cui titulus Dialogus inter orthodoxum et Barlaamitam*, Turnhout: Brepols, 1995 (Corpus Christianorum, Series Graeca, 31; excellent introductory section)

Akropolites, George 1217–1282

Statesman, historian, and teacher

George Akropolites was born into an aristocratic family that had remained in Constantinople after its fall to the Latins in 1204. The numerous autobiographical digressions in his chronicle provide our main source for his life and career. At a young age he left Constantinople in secret for the court of the Nicaean emperor John III Vatatzes (1221–54), under whom the revived Byzantine empire in exile reached its political and cultural apogee. In Nicaea he studied with the most learned teachers of the time; he was taught rhetoric by Theodoros Hexapterygos and the famous Nikephoros Blemmydes introduced him to philosophy. Akropolites was later to become a teacher himself of philosophy and mathematics. His most famous students included John III Vatatzes's son and successor Theodore II Laskaris (1254–58) and the patriarch Gregory II of Cyprus (1283–89), both of whom praised his erudition.

An aristocratic origin and a superb education ensured a rapid career in the imperial service, which culminated in Akropolites's appointment as Grand Logothete or imperial chancellor of the empire, first in Nicaea and then in Constantinople. In the 1240s and 1250s he headed important diplomatic missions to Bulgaria and to the Greek despotate of Epirus, Nicaea's main ideological rival. An unfortunate accident during a surveillance mission in Macedonia led to his capture by the Epirots and a two-year confinement (1257–59) in Arta at the court of the despot Michael II (c.1231–71). A political opportunist, after his release from captivity Akropolites was quick to side with the usurper Michael VIII Palaiologos (1259–82) and supported the blinding of the legitimate child-emperor John IV Laskaris (1258–61). After the recapture of Constantinople in July 1261, Akropolites composed prayers of thanksgiving that were publicly read during Michael VIII's triumphal entry into the old imperial capital on 15 August. Michael VIII seems to have trusted Akropolites not only because of his administrative and diplomatic experience, but also on account of his kinship with the Palaiologan family. As a Grand Logothete, Akropolites led the Byzantine embassy that concluded the doomed Union of Lyons (1274) subjecting the Orthodox Church to the papacy. He personally took a solemn oath on behalf of Michael VIII, recognizing the primacy of the Roman curia in matters of both doctrine and administration. He died in 1282 after an embassy to Trebizond that he had led in the same year.

George Akropolites's renown lies less in his activities as a teacher and a diplomat than in his authorship of an important chronicle covering the period from 1203 to 1261. The chronicle is written in a classicizing, yet simple, concise, and unencumbered style. In this respect he stands in stark contrast to subsequent Palaiologan historians such as, for example, Nikephoros Gregoras and John Kantakouzenos, who closely followed Classical models. His chronicle is the main source for the history of the Byzantine splinter states of Nicaea and Epirus in the period between the fall of Constantinople to the Latins in 1204 and its recapture in 1261. Despite his claims for historical objectivity, Akropolites was far from a dispassionate observer of his times. The time and circumstances of the chronicle's composition (between 1261 and 1267) influenced strongly the historian's verdict on the main political figures of the period. His point of view is always pro-Nicaean, pro-aristocratic, and pro-Palaiologan. He consistently played down the imperial claims of the rival despots of Epirus and mistrusted the Bulgarians and Serbians. He praised John III Vatatzes as a consummate diplomat and military commander, but his son and heir, Theodore II Laskaris, is the anti-hero of the chronicle. The historian deeply disliked his anti-aristocratic policies, his autocratic tendencies, and his irascible and suspicious temper. He left a vivid description of how Theodore II punished him with 24 lashes after a disagreement. The emperor's negative characteristics make Michael VIII Palaiologos and his new regime appear in the best possible light. The chronicle ends with a reference to a lost oration written by Akropolites and exhorting the emperor to declare his firstborn son, Andronikos II, co-ruler.

In addition to the chronicle, George Akropolites wrote rhetorical and theological works. He composed a funeral oration for John III Vatatzes's wife Irene Laskaris in 1239 and for the death of the Nicaean emperor himself in 1254. During the period of his captivity in Epirus he wrote two seemingly anti-Latin theological tracts on the procession of the Holy Spirit. Although these treatises repeat many of the traditional anti-Latin arguments, Akropolites made an effort to accommodate the opposing views. In particular, he pointed out the fact that both Greeks and Latins were united by the common name *Romaioi*, or Romans. His son, Constantine Akropolites, also rose to the rank of Grand Logothete and wrote numerous lives of saints and other works.

DIMITER G. ANGELOV

Biography

Born in Constantinople in 1217, George Akropolites studied in Nicaea under Theodoros Hexapterygos and Nikephoros Blemmydes. He himself became a teacher of philosophy and mathematics but then switched to the imperial service, becoming Grand Logothete and a senior diplomat. Author of an important chronicle of the years 1203–61. He died in Constantinople in 1282.

Writings

Chronicon Constantinopolitanum: *Die Chronik*, edited and translated into German by Wilhelm Blum, Stuttgart: Hiersemann, 1989
Macrides, Ruth, "A Translation and Historical Commentary of George Akropolites' *History*" (dissertation), London: King's College, 1978

Further Reading

Angold, Michael, *A Byzantine Government in Exile: Government and Society under the Laskarids of Nicaea, 1204–1261*, Oxford: Oxford University Press, 1975
Hunger, Herbert, *Die hochsprachliche profane Literatur der Byzantiner*, vol. 1, Munich: Beck, 1978, pp. 442–47
Richter, G. "Des Georgios Akropolites Gedanken über Theologie, Kirche und Kircheneinheit", *Byzantion*, 54 (1984): pp. 276–99
Zhavoronkov, P. "Nekotorije aspektji mirovozrenija Georgija Akropolita", *Vizantiiskii Vremennik*, 47 (1986): pp. 125–33

Albania

The modern Albanian state came into existence in 1913 in the final stages of the dissolution of the Ottoman empire. The territory has always been subject to Greek influences, and there has always been a Greek-speaking minority in the country. The history of Greek settlement in the region is very controversial and has been dogged by political factors, mostly about the relative degrees of Greek and Illyrian influence in southern Albania and the nature of the tribes that lived there. The geographer Strabo noted that many of these tribes were Epirote and could probably speak some Greek. These people have generally lived in the south of what became modern Albania, in the territory known to Greeks as *Voreio Ipeiros*, northern Epirus. They are probably descended from bilingual ancient tribes who inhab-

ited the area in later antiquity, with additional influences from Greek-speaking labourers settled there by the Ottoman Turks, remnants of ancient Greek coastal colonization, mostly from Corfu, and some emigration of Greek communists and their families after the end of the Greek Civil War in 1949. Greek speakers can also be found in Berat, Tirana, and a number of other Albanian towns. The traditional Greek community in Korça, known to the Greeks as Koritsa, has gone into rapid decline since World War II, but a strong Greek presence remains in many rural areas in the southeast of the country.

In Ottoman times Greek was widely used as the language of business and government in Albania, but it never had much popular presence north of the Shkumbini river in the traditional Albanian heartland. Under the monarchical regime of King Zog in the 1930s Greek-language education was repressed, though the designation of Greek-minority areas recognized by the communist regime of Enver Hoxha at first offered some hope of improvement. But although a few ethnic Greeks rose to high positions under communism, particularly in the defence ministry and secret police, the majority of Orthodox rural villagers were subject to discrimination on grounds of race and religion. This process accelerated in the last years of the communist regime, when, in the pro-atheism campaigns, the Orthodox Church in the south was attacked and many church buildings were closed or desecrated.

With the end of communism in 1991, the position of the Greek minority improved somewhat, and a human rights association, OMONIA, won freedom of religion and of political assembly from the disintegrating one-party state. But the political turmoil in the Balkans that everywhere accompanied the end of communism also affected southern Albania, and the Greek minority began to leave for Greece in a process of mass emigration as soon as they were able to do so. This has resulted in depopulation of a number of traditional Greek centres, particularly the coastal strip between Sarande and Himara. Many ethnic Greeks from Albania have settled in cities in Greece, and Greek-language newspapers have started for them in Athens and Thessalonica. At the same time, there has been steady Greek business investment in Albania, mostly in the food, construction, and tobacco industries. Greek education has developed on a private basis in Albania since 1991, but there are still difficulties with the provision of public education. The position of the Church has much improved, with Greek-speaking priests in post in many places, although many controversial issues still remain, mostly connected with what Albanians see as excessive "Greek" dominance of the hierarchy. Many church buildings have been well restored, and some new churches are under construction. Priests have returned to most parishes. In the uprising in spring 1997 that overthrew the government of Dr Sali Berisha ethnic Greeks played an important part. There are many people with some Greek blood or connections in the governing coalition that came to power at that time.

JAMES PETTIFER

Further Reading

Pettifer, James and Miranda Vickers, *Albania: From Anarchy to a Balkan Identity*, London: Hurst, and New York: New York University Press, 1997

Vickers, Miranda, *The Albanians: A Modern History*, London and New York: Tauris, 1995

Alchemy

Despite its Arabic prefix, the word "alchemy", like "chemistry", appears to be derived from the Greek root *cheo*, meaning "I pour", and its ostensible purpose is the transmutation of metals. As Jung and his followers have shown, however, the process was often treated by its more erudite exponents as a symbol of therapeutic operations on the soul. Mircea Eliade has demonstrated that in many ancient cultures the artisan enjoyed the reputation of a sorcerer, and was credited with skills beyond human science. Thus in Greek mythology Prometheus, the discoverer of fire, is the creator of human beings, while two smiths, the mortal Daedalus and the god Hephaestus, were said to have fashioned animated creatures. It is striking that all suffered injury as a consequence of their follies or misdemeanours; Zeus reserved the severest retribution for the Titans, who invented iron weapons in their war against the gods. The literary tradition pays little honour to the Cyclopes who stoked the fires of Aetna, or to the Telchines who combined the arts of witchcraft and metallurgy in Rhodes. In Israel, where all images were forbidden, there could hardly be such a thing as a pious craftsman: in the apocryphal Book of Enoch the use of stones and metals was traced back to the fallen angels, while in Genesis 4 all brass and iron artifacts, as well as musical instruments, were invented by the posterity of Cain.

The first Greek to display the classic features of the alchemist is Empedocles (*fl.* 480 BC), whose theory that every natural kind is formed by a specific combination of the four elements appears to have been the basis of his pharmaceutic remedies for disorders of the soul. The story that he died by leaping into the crater of Aetna, leaving only a golden sandal, is consistent with his magian character. Nevertheless, the first alchemical literature is attributed to the atomist Democritus and his school. He himself is credited with four treatises on the tincture, or immersion, of gold, silver, stones, and "purple", while fragments survive of a fifth on *Physical and Mystical Matters*. These overlap with the *Baphika*, or *Tinctures*, which has survived under the name of his pupil Bolus, though certain parts at least must date from the early Christian era. This maintains that every natural substance can be produced by the application of a tincture (*baphe*) to iron, copper, tin, or lead. Tincture is the addition of a solvent to a metal, which precipitates new substances according to a fixed succession of colours (black, white, yellow, and red). These correspond to the four elementary metals, but even these are reducible to lead, which, when converted to its liquid state by blackening, or *melansis*, is the prime matter of all the elements and the basis of all ensuing transformations. To know what one is making, one needs to be acquainted with the combinative properties of the reagents, or, as Bolus says, their sympathies and aversions. Sulphur, which is said to evince an extraordinary affinity with metals, is the most potent of the additives, but the ingredients of the process also include a golden alloy, Pontic rhubarb, and Italian wine.

This religious and anthropomorphic imagery, so alien to the style of the real Democritus, is justified by an appeal to books allegedly deposited in a temple by the Persian sage Ostanes. Despite this, the majority of relevant documents are papyri from Egypt, and they leave little doubt that the poetry of the Greek alchemists originated there. The esoteric lore of Ptolemaic and Roman Egypt was collected in the *Hermetika*, so called because its contents were attributed to Hermes Trismegistus; it was he, or rather his Latin equivalent Mercury, who gave his name to the liquid essence that later alchemists used as the catalyst in their experiments. The most remarkable symbol of transformation in the philosophical portions of the *Hermetika* (often arbitrarily separated from the esoteric writings) is the *krater*, or cup, of Treatise 4, which conflates the alchemist's crucible with the mixing bowl of Plato's Demiurge (the creator of the universe). It is possible that the Egyptian name Poimandres, given to the self-transforming Mind who imparts the initial revelation in Treatise 1, commended itself to the Greeks because of its likeness to the word *poimandria* ("cauldron"). Though nothing survives in extenso under Hermes' name, he is mentioned in extant treatises as the writer of authoritative works.

The Hellenization of Egyptian literature was partly the work of Jews, and thus one is not surprised to find a papyrus which conflates the wisdom of the pharaoh Kufu with that of the Hebrew Sabaoth. No doubt it was under Jewish influence that the goddess Isis, in another alchemical papyrus, becomes a pupil of the angel Amnael and gives instruction to Horus in the role of a prophetess. Since Jewish writers generally saw cunning as a property of women, they attributed the invention of the chief alchemical instruments to Maria, another prophetess and a pupil of Ostanes. Her devices included the alembic for distillation, the conical pot, or *phanos*, for sublimation, and another vessel, the *kerotakion*, for change of colours. Sulphur again is the element to which these new refinements are applied. Since the Democritean corpus does not allude to Mary, we may assume that she is a later figment; the readiness with which this alien woman was admitted into the canon is an indication that alchemy had already become a syncretistic faith.

Most of our information about Mary comes from the pagan Zosimus of Panopolis (*fl.* AD 300) in Egypt, whose works are both the most copious and the most interesting vestiges of the ancient practice. The scholarly Neoplatonist Olympiodorus in the late 4th century thought them worthy of a philosophical commentary. Yet Zosimus, for all his pretensions, offers no philosophy in the strict sense, but rhetorical accounts of private visions, which leave us doubting whether they are remembered or imagined, and whether he is recounting a chain of episodes or describing one event in different ways. The usual polarity between the dense substrate and the fluid solvent is presented in such a manner as to make the first analogous to the body and the second to the soul. The self, which is both the subject and the goal of transformation, is represented as a man of various metals, who stands beside the crucible as a priest before an altar, then assumes the role of victim by dismembering and devouring his own flesh. This figure (the homunculus of Goethe and Paracelsus) is identified with Adam, who, with a clear allusion to the book of Genesis, is styled the virgin earth in Zosimus' *Treatise on the Omega*, where the experiment culminates in an (uninterpreted) vision of the Son of God. We may assume that mercury (or honey, as it is also called) is the object seen with the outward eyes, but of course this is merely the symbol of a mental revelation, which enables the philosopher to return to his proper dwelling place, escaping the fatal influence of the stars. Though Jung may be right to understand these visions as a manifestation of archetypal images, their content is (as one would expect) determined by the literary traditions that were available to a mystic of that era. With the Jewish and Christian vocabulary are mingled the names of Enoch, Zoroaster, and Ostanes, but the stories of Jewish captivity under Nebuchadnezzar (the statue of diverse metals, the blazing furnace, the degradation of the king) are surely the most important prototype.

Zosimus, like the Gnostics of the 3rd century AD, relied on a lost compilation by Nicotheus, "the Hidden One", and alchemy appears to be entwined with the very roots of the Christian heresy (*Omega*, 11; cf. Porphyry, *Life of Plotinus*, 16). The (Phrygian) Naassenes of the 2nd century derived both matter and spirit from a "single blessed substance", and maintained that the soul is in constant oscillation between the two. The first man (whose ethnic character is disputed, as in Zosimus) is called Adam because he is present in every one of us as a living stone of adamant. Hermes is the spiritual demiurge who effects our liberation, while the mutilated deities Attis, Osiris, and Dionysus offer symbols of rebirth. The last named should remind us of the notorious Greek myth in which the Titans tear apart and eat the infant Dionysus, son of Zeus. After Zeus destroys them with a thunderbolt, humanity is created from their ashes, owing its divine spirit to Dionysus and its vices to the intractable Titanic residue.

Alchemy became the guiding principle of a universal science, which allotted the names and colours of different metals to the four humours, the seven ages, and the planets, which were thought to influence both. In addition, the alchemist was required to be a skilled herbalist and an expert in the medical and prophylactic properties of gems. Affinities were easily discerned between alchemical symbolism and the New Testament, where Christ is both the apex and the foundation of a temple which is identical with the body and yet made up of "living stones". Synesius of Cyrene (*fl.* AD 400) wrote a commentary on the Democritean corpus, while the notion of a single blessed substance that "becomes all things" was adapted to meditation on the Trinity by Evagrius (*Epistle* 29). Yet a discipline that purported to derive its code from nature could transcend not only the bounds of race and Church, but those of orthodoxy and heresy. Book 9 of the 13th-century epic *Parzival* by Wolfram von Eschenbach alludes to a legend cherished by the Cathars, and therefore perhaps of eastern (Bogomil) origin, according to which the Holy Grail was a stone cast out of heaven and assigned to the custody of fallen angels. Being thus an emblem of both Christ and Adam, it is able, when the proper question is put to it, to heal the bodily ailments which result from the transgression of the soul.

The ideal of Renaissance alchemy, the union of the personality through the "conjunction of opposites", is derived from Arabic sources such as the Tabula Smaragdina. These in turn look back to a fabulous epoch of Byzantium, giving the name of the emperor Heracleios to the tutelary power of the planet Mercury, and also to a king whose impotent son begets an heir by arcane devices. In fact it is unlikely that the Christian emperors would have looked on alchemy with any more favour than did their pagan predecessor Diocletian, who attempted to burn the manuals of the art in the time of Zosimus. Most of the Byzantine writings on the subject are contained in a single collection of the 9th or early 10th century and dedicated to a certain Theodore. It includes poems under the names of Hierotheos, Heliodoros, and Archelaos, but the most important item is Stephen of Byzantium's treatise *On the Making of Gold*. Like the later volume of the same name by the polymath Michael Psellos, this treats the extraction of precious metals as its principal enterprise. It was another scholar, Gemistos Plethon, who drew the attention of the Western humanists to the *Hermetica*; but he, like Psellos, was chiefly a compiler of other men's doctrines, and the great tradition of alchemy was indebted to Byzantine authors more for what they copied than what they wrote.

MARK EDWARDS

Further Reading

Berthelot, M., *Les Origines de l'alchimie*, Paris: Steinheil, 1885
Berthelot, M., *Collection des anciens alchimistes grecs*, 3 vols, Paris: Steinheil, 1887–88
Eliade, Mircea, *The Forge and the Crucible*, 2nd edition, Chicago: University of Chicago Press, 1978 (1st French edition, 1956)
Festugière, A.-J., *La Révélation d'Hermès Trismégiste*, vol. 1, Paris: Lecoffre, 1944
Fowden, Garth, *The Egyptian Hermes: A Historical Approach to the Late Pagan Mind*, Cambridge and New York: Cambridge University Press, 1986
Hopkins, Arthur John, *Alchemy: Child of Greek Philosophy*, New York: Columbia University Press, 1934
Jung, C.G., *Alchemical Studies*, Princeton, New Jersey: Princeton University Press, 1967
Kingsley, Peter, *Ancient Philosophy, Mystery, and Magic: Empedocles and Pythagorean Tradition*, Oxford: Clarendon Press, and New York: Oxford University Press, 1995
Lindsay, Jack, *The Origins of Alchemy in Graeco–Roman Egypt*, London: Muller, 1970
Scott, Walter, *Hermetica: The Ancient Greek and Latin Writings which Contain Religious or Philosophic Teachings Ascribed to Hermes Trismegistus*, vol. 4, Oxford: Clarendon Press, 1925
Silberer, Herbert, *Hidden Symbolism of Alchemy and the Occult Arts*, reprinted New York: Dover, 1971 (first published 1917)

Alcibiades 451/50–404/03 BC

Athenian general and politician

Born into a wealthy family, Alcibiades became the ward of Pericles and his brother Ariphron after his father Cleinias was killed at the battle of Coronea in 447 BC. Although he had fought at Potidaea in 432 BC, where he was wounded and his life saved by Socrates, his first datable political activity was in 420 BC in the immediate aftermath of the Peace of Nicias, which had ended the first phase of the Peloponnesian War (Thucydides, 5. 43). While Nicias advocated that diplomatic pressure should be exerted on the Spartans to persuade their allies to conform to the treaty by carrying out agreed concessions to the Athenians, Alcibiades sought to exploit the

Spartans' difficulties with their allies, even at the expense of the peace. He won the argument and an alliance was made with the Argives and two of Sparta's renegade allies, Mantinea and Elis, but he was unable to obtain sufficient votes to secure the necessary resources to support his policy: only 1300 Athenian troops fought at the battle of Mantinea in 418 BC, when victory enabled the Spartans to recover their lost allies and restore their domination of the Peloponnese.

Thucydides comments on Alcibiades' youth in 420 BC; he reports that Nicias referred to him as "a young man in a hurry" in the debate on whether to send an expedition to Sicily in the spring of 415 BC (Thucydides, 6. 12). Alcibiades was handsome and eloquent, and his charisma had been enhanced by his success in the Olympic festival of 416 BC, when three of his seven entries in the chariot race were placed first, second, and fourth. His advocacy of the Sicilian expedition clearly contributed to the atmosphere of great enthusiasm and high expectations; Thucydides reports that in the end those opposed to the scheme did not dare to vote against it (6. 24). Nevertheless, his flamboyance and palpable personal ambition created mistrust, helped by the deviousness he had shown in an ostracism campaign, probably in 416 BC, when he had agreed with Nicias that they should protect one another by directing their supporters to vote against Hyperbolus (who was then ostracized) and then by a highly unusual proposal to appoint Alcibiades sole commander of the expedition (which was rejected in favour of his sharing responsibility with Nicias and Lamachus); and in the public hysteria that followed the sacrilegious mutilation of the many busts of Hermes on the streets of Athens, his enemies were able to link him with rumours of revolutionary plots to establish oligarchy or tyranny.

When the expedition reached Sicily and Nicias favoured a concentration on limited objectives, Alcibiades failed to support Lamachus' proposal of a direct attack on Syracuse, the chief threat to Athenian interests, which might well have succeeded. Instead he forced Lamachus to back his own plan first to secure more allies, despite their having failed to receive the expected help from Thurii, Rhegium, and Segesta. Alcibiades' policy was adopted with limited success, Naxos and Catane being won over, but Messana and Camarina refusing. At this point he was recalled to stand trial, but, knowing that his enemies at home had been poisoning minds against him since his departure, he eluded his escort at Thurii and fled to the Peloponnese, the Athenians sentencing him to death in his absence.

It is debatable how far Alcibiades' recall affected the Athenian forces, because Nicias now supported Lamachus' plan; after twice defeating the Syracusans outside their city, in the early summer of 414 BC he was completing a series of blockade walls around the town and had high hopes of its surrender. Alcibiades, however, had gone to Sparta and urged the Spartans to send help to Syracuse, emphasizing the extent of Athenian ambitions and their threat to the Peloponnese, and suggesting that the Spartans should at least send a competent general to organize its defence (Thucydides, 6. 91). The Spartans were persuaded and sent Gylippus, whose leadership of the Syracusans was a major factor in the disastrous defeat of the Athenians in 413 BC.

In 412 BC Alcibiades was influential in persuading the Spartans to send ships to the eastern Aegean in order to foment revolts among Athens' allies; he himself helped to win over Chios and Miletus. Meanwhile, king Agis, whose wife he had seduced, persuaded the Spartans that he was unreliable and should be eliminated, but he took refuge with Tissaphernes, satrap of the Anatolian coastal provinces, whom he sought to turn against the Spartans, also hoping thereby to facilitate his own recall to Athens. He then tried to promote a sympathetic regime there by promising that the removal of democracy would secure Persian help; and, although negotiations between Tissaphernes and the Athenian envoys failed and the Persians made a treaty with Sparta, the move against democracy, which had started, succeeded, and a short-lived oligarchy was set up in summer 411 BC.

Ironically, Alcibiades' exile was now cancelled by the commanders of the Athenian fleet at Samos, who refused to accept the oligarchy's authority. On joining them he played important roles first in preventing them abandoning their position in the eastern Aegean to attack Athens, and then in victories over the Spartans in the Hellespont (autumn 411 BC) and off Cyzicus (spring 410 BC). This must have been the period in Thucydides' mind when he said that "his conduct of the war was excellent" (6. 15), and he went on to recover Byzantium in 408 BC.

At this point (407 BC) Alcibiades thought that it was safe to return to Athens. There he received a warm welcome, his exile was officially rescinded, and he enhanced his popularity by organizing the annual procession to the festival at Eleusis to go by land for the first time since the Spartan occupation of Decelea in north Attica in 413 BC. There was still, however, according to Xenophon (Hellenica, 1. 4. 17), underlying mistrust of his ambitions and, when he briefly left the fleet in charge of his helmsman Antiochus, who was rashly provoked by Lysander and lost 22 ships, he was relieved of his command and prudently retired into exile. About a year and a half later Aristophanes in his Frogs had Dionysus say about him that the city "longs for and hates him and wishes to have him" (line 1425). But he was still in exile near the Hellespont in the late summer of 405 BC, when his warning to the Athenian generals of their folly in beaching their fleet at Aegospotami was disregarded and a surprise Spartan attack took all but eight ships almost without a fight and effectively won the war. After Athens' surrender in 404 BC Alcibiades crossed to Asia, where he was soon killed, probably on the orders of Pharnabazus, satrap of Phrygia, at Lysander's request.

Tradition held that Alcibiades was both the object of Socrates' passion and his pupil, and this association, it seems, was much in the mind of Socrates' accusers when they charged him with corrupting the city's youth. Plato had him figuring prominently with Socrates in his Symposium and Alcibiades I (Alcibiades II is almost certainly not Platonic). Paired by Plutarch in his Parallel Lives with the Roman Coriolanus, he was taken up, like Coriolanus, by Shakespeare, who used him in his historically inaccurate Timon of Athens. He has continued to fascinate the modern world, notably as the central character of Peter Green's novel Achilles His Armour (1955).

T.T.B. RYDER

See also Peloponnesian War

Biography

Born in Athens in 451 or 450 BC, Alcibiades was brought up by his guardian Pericles and was a pupil of Socrates. As a politician he was flamboyant but inconsistent, supporting first Athens, as one of the leaders of the disastrous Sicilian expedition, then Sparta. Losing the confidence of both, he fled to Persia but was subsequently recalled to direct operations of the Athenian fleet. Exiled again, he crossed to Asia after the defeat of Athens in the Peloponnesian War and was murdered in Phrygia in 404/03 BC.

Further Reading

Ellis, Walter M., *Alcibiades*, London and New York: Routledge, 1989

Kagan, Donald, *The Peace of Nicias and the Sicilian Expedition*, Ithaca, New York: Cornell University Press, 1981

Kagan, Donald, *The Fall of the Athenian Empire,* Ithaca, New York: Cornell University Press, 1987

Lewis, D.M. *et al.* (editors), *The Fifth Century BC*, Cambridge: Cambridge University Press, 1992 (*The Cambridge Ancient History*, vol.5, 2nd edition)

Plutarch, *Plutarch's Lives*, translated by Bernadotte Perrin, 11 vols, London: Heinemann, and New York: Macmillan, 1914–26 (Loeb edition; vol. 4)

Plutarch, *The Rise and Fall of Athens: Nine Greek Lives*, translated by Ian Scott-Kilvert, Harmondsworth: Penguin, 1960, reprinted 1975

Thucydides, *Thucydides*, translated by C. Forster Smith, revised edition, 4 vols, Cambridge, Massachusetts: Harvard University Press, 1928–30 (Loeb edition; many reprints)

Thucydides, *History of the Peloponnesian War*, translated by Rex Warner, revised edition, Harmondsworth and Baltimore: Penguin, 1972

Xenophon, *Hellenica*, translated by Carleton L. Brownson, London: Heinemann, and New York: Putnam, 1918 (Loeb edition; many reprints)

Xenophon, *A History of My Times*, translated by Rex Warner, revised edition, Harmondsworth and New York: Penguin, 1978

Alexander III the Great 356–323 BC

King of Macedon

After the assassination of his father king Philip II of Macedon, at Aegae (modern Vergina) in 336 BC, the 20-year-old prince Alexander acceded to the throne as Alexander III. The vast kingdom of Macedonia that he inherited extended eastward at this time to Thrace and the Black Sea, south to Thessaly, west into modern Albania, and north into the former Yugoslav republics and parts of Bulgaria. As a kingdom, it was politically distinct from the city states of the Greek mainland, although there had been contact between Macedon and Greece for hundreds of years. To give a few examples: an ancestor of Alexander III of the 5th century BC, king Alexander I, was known as "the philhellene" because of his alleged secret help to the Greeks during the Persian Wars, and Greek cities founded along the east coast of Macedonia and in Chalcidice certainly had been in contact with the Macedonians for centuries. Most importantly, recent archaeological investigations in Macedonia have shown beyond doubt that there were close links between aristocratic Macedonian society and the culture of mainland Greece: Attic pottery was imported to Macedonia by the end of the 6th century BC (found in cist graves at Sindos); the city of Pella (developed as the new capital at the end of the 5th century BC) has revealed the best extant pebble mosaics, impressive small finds from the agora, and the recently excavated royal palace, besides being the place where the great Athenian tragedian Euripides ended his life in exile; and the spectacular gold and silver vessels, armour, and jewellery from the 4th-century BC royal tombs at Vergina prove beyond doubt that the Macedonian court class was a rich, cultivated, and sophisticated society completely familiar with the culture of Greece. None the less, there was a deep-seated ethnic rivalry between Macedonian and Greek that the troubled political situation of the 4th century BC intensified. Throughout his life Alexander appears to have regarded the Greeks with suspicion, and never trusted them in political terms.

Alexander's father Philip II had become the political leader of mainland Greece after his defeat of the Greek forces at the battle of Chaeronea in Boeotia in 338 BC. He controlled the city states by enrolling them in an unequal alliance with him known as the League of Corinth (where the first meeting was held), and enlisted his Greek "allies" in a war of revenge against the Persian empire, ostensibly to free the Greek cities of Asia Minor from Persian rule, but in all probability to extend Macedonian control into Asia Minor. The young Alexander inherited control both of the League of Corinth and of the war to win the "freedom of the Greeks of Asia". It is on this basis that he undertook his famous expedition to the east, which has immortalized him as one of the greatest conquerors of all time, worthy of the epithet "the Great". Alexander's military campaigns, his defeat of the Great King of Persia and assumption of that title and position, his further expedition to the Indus river system in the Punjab, his return to the west after a troop mutiny, and his untimely death at Babylon in June 323 BC are all well known and described in an ever-expanding bibliography. His extraordinary military exploits and invincibility inspired later generals (Pompey, Caesar, Augustus, Trajan, and even Napoleon) to emulate him, and his early death at the pinnacle of his fame ensured his elevation to heroic legendary status and his position as a quintessentially romantic, fascinating historical figure.

Alexander the Great's contribution to the Hellenic tradition must be assessed in various ways. Merely to assert that he was the greatest and most famous figure in Greek history whose allure has lasted to modern times is not enough; although this claim alone may justify Alexander's place in posterity, it is a simplistic view based on our admiration for his achievements and fascination with such an enigmatic man. Various issues emerge from the study of Alexander, however, that are relevant to our appreciation of him in the context of Hellenic tradition. These embrace fields as diverse as art history, political developments, religion, and literature.

During his lifetime Alexander was responsible for an innovation that had important consequences for the history of Greek art. Up to the end of the 4th century BC the medium of portraiture was confined to "generic" portraits (a suitable type depicting a noble statesman, a general, etc.) and "imaginary" portraits (e.g. a hypothetical depiction of Homer; if a poet called Homer had indeed existed in the 8th century BC, certainly no one hundreds of years later could have known

Alexander: portrait bust in marble, sculptor unknown, Graeco-Roman Museum, Alexandria

what he looked like) (see G.M.A. Richter [rev. by R.R.R. Smith], *The Portraits of the Greeks*, Oxford: Phaidon, 1984). Although the beginnings of individualistic portraiture may be traced to Persian kings and satraps of the 4th century BC, Alexander seems to have been the first ruler in the Greek world to control the production of his own image. The ancient sources tell us that he had a court sculptor, a court painter, and a court gem engraver whom alone he trusted to depict him in the approved manner. The surviving portraits of Alexander show that he was represented in a highly idealized way that was immediately identifiable (see J.J. Pollitt, *Art in the Hellenistic Age*, Cambridge: Cambridge University Press, 1986, pp.19–25). It could be argued that it was desirable for the peoples of his vast empire to have a recognizable depiction of their king, but such a conscious manipulation of one's image was quite new in Greek art, whether it stemmed from deliberate calculation on Alexander's part or merely excessive vanity. The canonical image of Alexander was taken over by his successors for propaganda purposes (see below), and the art of portraiture developed in the Hellenistic age into a major artistic genre, because the kings of the new Greek empires immediately appreciated the ways in which images of themselves could prove beneficial (see R.R.R. Smith, *Hellenistic Royal Portraits*, Oxford: Clarendon Press, 1988).

The personal empire that Alexander created in Asia was not the same as the Macedonian state. At the age of 20 the king

had left his homeland under the control of the regent Antipater, with whom he had only sporadic contact for the next 11 years, and he died unexpectedly – never having returned home or secured the Macedonian succession with an heir – with only interim administrative arrangements in place for the vast eastern territories he had conquered. By the end, Alexander's entourage consisted not of an inner circle of nobles who had traditionally advised the king according to Macedonian custom, but of a group of self-made, ambitious generals whose position depended on their personal loyalty to Alexander himself. These men (the so-called "successors") were suddenly left leaderless in Babylon, and some 20 years of chaos ensued before the emergence of three relatively stable new empires, which form the focus of the "Hellenistic" history of the next three centuries.

It soon became clear that Alexander's empire could not survive intact under a single successor. Alexander's posthumous infant son Alexander and his half-witted half-brother Philip Arrhidaeus were declared joint kings, Alexander IV and Philip III. Their regent Antipater, who had been a general under Philip II, firmly resolved to take the kings home to Macedonia, thereby returning Macedon to its origins as a Balkan kingdom. This might have allowed the royal Argead dynasty of Macedonian kings (the family to which both Philip II and Alexander the Great belonged) to continue to rule in an unbroken bloodline in their European homeland, but both kings were soon murdered in the power struggles among the successors, as were, eventually, all the immediate members of Alexander the Great's family. This signalled the extinction of the Argead line of Macedonian kings. Paradoxically, the political and personal influence of Alexander, the absent king, in his Macedonian homeland was far less important than that of his father Philip II had been, and it pales into insignificance when compared to his posthumous reputation and influence in the Asia he had opened up to the Greeks.

Since the sole uniting feature of Alexander's empire had been the king himself, various successors, who were eager to establish their own power in areas of Asia, sought to cloak themselves with the aura of Alexander's legacy in an effort to gain political legitimacy. Although none actually claimed to be Alexander's sole successor, attempts at "identification" with the late king proved a forceful propaganda tool in establishing the validity of their respective political power. Much of this imitation was achieved by the manipulation of royal iconography and the use of Alexander's image. For example, although Alexander himself never minted coins with his own portrait on them, shortly after his death some successors issued coinage with a highly idealized, almost divinized, head of Alexander adorned with subtly emotive attributes: the horns of Zeus Ammon (the oracular god whose shrine in the Egyptian desert Alexander had visited and with whom he felt a particular affinity for the rest of his life), the elephant-scalp headdress (which refers to his victories in India where he faced elephants in battle), and the royal diadem. These early portrait coins of Alexander clearly illustrate the potency of his image, but also directly influence the coinage of all his royal Hellenistic successors, which contains the head of the particular ruler and a selection of themes with propaganda value pertinent to the royal house in question (see Norman Davis and Colin M.

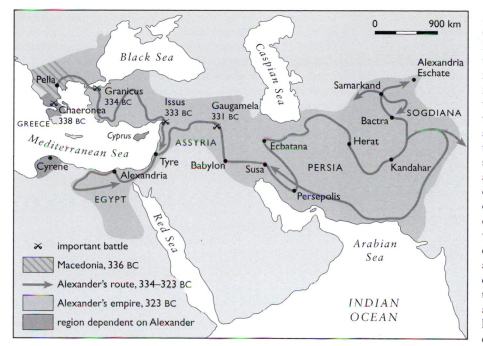

3. The empire of Alexander the Great in 323 BC

Kraay, *The Hellenistic Kingdoms: Portrait Coins and History*, London: Thames and Hudson, 1973, plates 1–9) .

The strength of Alexander's posthumous reputation as a tool of royal propaganda is seen most clearly in the kingdom of Ptolemaic Egypt (ruled by Alexander's former Macedonian general Ptolemy who subsequently declared himself king and founded a dynasty that ruled Egypt until the suicide of Cleopatra VII in 31 BC). Ptolemy hijacked the funeral cortège of Alexander while it was en route from Babylon, and brought his body to Egypt, eventually burying it in a magnificent tomb in his capital, Alexandria. By this devious act, Ptolemy became the guardian of the body of Alexander, which elevated his importance even as it linked him inextricably with the late king. The remains of Alexander and his magic belonged to Ptolemy. The tomb became the focus for the worship of Alexander (in Alexandria he was worshipped as the "founder God") and, later, of the royal cult of the Ptolemies themselves (see below). The continuing importance of the tie of the Ptolemaic royal family with Alexander was graphically illustrated in a procession staged in Alexandria by Ptolemy I's son and heir, Ptolemy II Philadelphus. A major part of this procession honoured the Greek god Dionysus (from whom the Ptolemies claimed descent), and one important pageant depicted Dionysus as the returning conqueror of India. The parallel between the Indian victories of Dionysus and Alexander (who also features in the procession) was made explicit in the context of the procession, and the Ptolemies shared in the splendour of the eastern triumph as the heirs of Alexander and Dionysus (see E.E. Rice, *The Grand Procession of Ptolemy Philadelphus*, Oxford: Oxford University Press, 1983, pp.84–86). In Egypt Alexander's image and posthumous reputation were deliberately used as powerful symbols of invincibility, divine connections, and the legitimate transfer of political power to the Ptolemaic royal house.

Alexander's views about his own divinity remain unclear because there is little evidence as to what he himself thought about it. He was not the first mortal to receive honours of a superhuman nature, but it appears that he was voted certain divine honours and welcomed them, even if he did not actually demand them. However this may be, the worship of Alexander was widespread in many parts of Greece and Asia after his death, as various cults, priests, dedications, etc., attested. This worship of Alexander clearly influenced the development of the ruler cults of the various Hellenistic monarchies, the deification of monarchs during their lifetime, and the civic cults established by Greek cities in honour of various kings, once the boundary between gods and men, and the honours appropriate to each, had become blurred. When the Romans came to dominate the Greek east, the establishment of the imperial Roman cult in this area can be seen as a natural progression of the acceptance of the worship of a human being (see S.R.F. Price, *Rituals and Power: The Roman Imperial Cult in Asia Minor*, Cambridge: Cambridge University Press, 1984).

A far more difficult issue is the question of Alexander's role in the Hellenization of the east. How far was Alexander himself responsible for the fact that, over the following several centuries, vast areas of Asia (comprising the Middle East, modern Turkey, Iran, Iraq, and parts of Afghanistan and Pakistan as far as India) became urbanized, populated by Greeks living in harmony with native peoples and remaining largely Greek-speaking, even after many of these territories were incorporated into the Roman empire? Alexander is often regarded as one of the greatest city-founders of all times. His cities were mostly named "Alexandreia" (the transliterated form of the name in Greek), and stretched from Alexandria in Egypt at the southwest tip of his empire to Alexandria Eschate ("the Furthest") on the Jaxartes river (modern Syr Darya) in Central Asia in the extreme northeast of it. It has often been claimed that these Alexander-foundations were responsible for spreading the light of Greek civilization throughout barbarian Asia, but the truth is impossible to ascertain. The ancient sources differ widely about the number (from very few to very many) and locations of his city foundations, as well as their nature. Some, we are told, were cities in the proper sense: permanent settlements with civic institutions and buildings in the Greek style. Others appear to have been fortified military settlements sited at strategic geographical points, and yet others outlying guard posts established as needed to control the surrounding area. There is no evidence for Alexander's reasons for founding cities – if indeed he had a well-thought-out policy in so doing beyond a general preference for civic life – although the rationale behind those that had a military or strategic importance seems obvious enough. In the few cases where we are told of its composition, the population was a mixture of time-expired Macedonian veterans, Greek mercenaries, and local inhabitants who volunteered to settle there. It is no coincidence that very few Alexandrias known from literary sources have been identified on the ground. In the first place, the pattern of life in Central Asia was essentially nomadic, not accustomed to urbanization. Furthermore, the artificially gathered population was an unhappy mix of peoples (many of them thousands of miles from home and probably longing to return) who had no natural affinity with each other. Many Alexandrias probably soon died out from lack of interest, starvation, internal warfare due to ethnic tensions, or migratory invasions from outside, leaving no identifiable archaeological remains. Other Alexandrias may have been refounded and renamed by Alexander's successors, leaving no clue as to their original foundation.

Given the above considerations, the conclusion must be that Alexander's ephemeral cities themselves can have hardly caused the east to be Hellenized as it was to become in the Seleucid and Graeco-Roman period. The sense in which Alexander can indeed be said to be ultimately responsible for the spread of Hellenic culture in this region is that it was he who opened up the east geographically to the west and created the possibility of Graeco-Macedonian domination there, even though he did not live long enough himself to see it permanently pacified and administered by a ruling class of his creation. The eventual results of Alexander's actions, therefore, must not be confused with his irrecoverable intentions at the time, since it was left to his successors to carry out their own schemes of urbanization and Hellenization.

Finally, Alexander's achievements and extraordinary fame contributed in an unexpected way to the development of ancient Greek literature and, through it, to the development of medieval and modern literature. Many histories of Alexander were written in antiquity, from contemporary eyewitness accounts of the campaigns to works by writers who lived hundreds of years later. The former survive only by title or in quotation by the latter, who drew upon these first-hand accounts as well as on a large body of popular tales that quickly grew up about a figure as world-famous as the great Macedonian conqueror. None the less, these serious histories of Alexander – however important they undoubtedly are to our understanding of Greek historiography – share the stage with a work of a type that has more in common with the ancient novel, namely the romance, a genre of Greek literature that was increasingly popular in the Hellenistic and Graeco-Roman periods.

The so-called *Alexander Romance* is a fascinating "pseudo-historical" source for Alexander the Great. It is a fictitious account of Alexander's exploits based loosely on the historical record, combining several different sources into the main Greek version which has come down to us (it was falsely assigned to Alexander's official historian Callisthenes – hence its frequent attribution in modern literature to pseudo-Callisthenes). Scholars have argued that the *Alexander Romance* dates in its present form from the 3rd century AD (although it incorporates older elements), and that various identifiable strands in it include a fictitious biography of Alexander, an epistolary novel of Alexander's supposed letters, and set-piece descriptions of marvels (see Tomas Hägg, *The Novel in Antiquity*, Oxford: Blackwell, 1983, pp.125ff.).

However this may be, the *Alexander Romance* was a hugely popular and influential work, and the vehicle by which a version of Alexander's deeds passed into several different cultures. There was a Byzantine metrical version of the *Romance*, and it was translated in the Middle Ages into some 35 different languages, among them Latin, Syriac, Arabic, Armenian, Hebrew, Ethiopic, and Hungarian. The Alexander of the *Romance* and his amazing exploits became one of the most popular heroes in the medieval Ottoman Karagöz shadow-puppet theatre, and can still be seen today in its modern Greek equivalent, the Karaghiozis puppet theatre.

E.E. RICE

See also Alexandria, Antigonids, Imperial Cult, Karaghiozis, Macedonia, Philip II, Ptolemies, Seleucids

Biography
Born in 356 BC, the son of Philip II and Olympias, Alexander was a pupil of Aristotle. He fought at Chaeronea in 338 and succeeded to the throne of Macedon on his father's death in 336. Having established himself a master of the Greek world, he crossed the Hellespont in 334 with a huge army to conquer the Persian empire. He died on his return, at Babylon in 323 BC. His military exploits and early death ensured his immortality in the Hellenic tradition.

Further Reading
Bieber, Margarete, *Alexander the Great in Greek and Roman Art*, Chicago: Argonaut, 1964
Bosworth, A.B., *Conquest and Empire: The Reign of Alexander the Great*, Cambridge and New York: Cambridge University Press, 1988
Briant, Pierre, *Alexander the Great*, London: Thames and Hudson, and New York: Abrams, 1996
Engels, Donald W., *Alexander the Great and the Logistics of the Macedonian Army*, Berkeley: University of California Press, 1978
Green, Peter, *Alexander of Macedon, 356–323 BC: A Historical Biography*, revised edition, Berkeley: University of California Press, 1991
Hamilton, J.R., *Alexander the Great*, London: Hutchinson, 1973
Hammond, N.G.L. and F.W. Walbank, *A History of Macedonia*, vol. 3: 336–167 BC, Oxford: Clarendon Press, 1988
Hammond, N.G.L., *Alexander the Great: King, Commander and Statesman*, 3rd edition, London: Bristol Classical Press, 1994
Hammond, N.G.L., *The Genius of Alexander the Great*, London: Duckworth, and Chapel Hill: University of North Carolina Press, 1997
Lane Fox, Robin, *Alexander the Great*, London: Allen Lane, 1973; New York: Dial Press, 1974
Lane Fox, Robin, *The Search for Alexander*, London: Allen Lane, and Boston: Little Brown, 1980
Lewis, D.M. *et al.* (editors), *The Fourth Century BC*, Cambridge: Cambridge University Press, 1994 (*The Cambridge Ancient History*, vol. 6, 2nd edition), chapters 14–17
Milns, R.D., *Alexander the Great*, London: Hale, 1968; New York: Pegasus, 1969
Pseudo-Callisthenes, *The Greek Alexander Romance*, translated by Richard Stoneman, London and New York: Penguin, 1991
Rice, E.E., *Alexander the Great*, Stroud: Sutton, 1997
Sekunda, Nick, *The Army of Alexander the Great*, London: Osprey, 1984
Stewart, Andrew, *Faces of Power: Alexander's Image and Hellenistic Politics*, Berkeley: University of California Press, 1993
Stoneman, Richard (editor and translator), *Legends of Alexander the Great*, London: Dent, and Rutland, Vermont: Tuttle, 1994

Alexandria

City in Egypt

At the time of Alexander the Great's invasion of Asia, Egypt had been, intermittently, a remote part of the Persian empire since 526/25 BC when the Great King Cambyses invaded and conquered the country. Persian rule appears to have been harsh during the 4th century, with the result that Alexander was welcomed by the Egyptian populace to whom another foreign conqueror was welcome if it meant the end of hated Persian rule. Alexander entered Egypt from Gaza, and paid his respects at the inland dynastic capital Memphis (south of Cairo) before sailing north along the Nile via the western branch of its delta to the Mediterranean coast, to a small native town called Rhakotis.

There, in 331 BC, Alexander made the first, and indisputably the greatest, of his city foundations, and named it "Alexandreia" (in Greek) after himself. The ancient literary sources give us a romantic picture of the young Alexander appreciating the suitability of the site and taking a personal interest in the design of the city, pacing out the line of the city walls and marking the location for various structures inside. However this may be, the coastal site of Alexandria was a magnificent choice for a city, facing on to the Mediterranean, endowed with good natural harbours, and with easy access to the interior of Egypt through the river system. It may be that local Greek traders in the region (Greeks had been settled at the inland delta city of Naucratis since the 7th century BC) persuaded Alexander of the site's potential, or perhaps Alexander – with a view to his posterity – just acted upon a suggestion that was attractively presented to him. The actual design of the new city was left to Deinocrates, a Macedonian town planner/architect in Alexander's entourage.

Alexander left Egypt and continued his expedition to the east, leaving Alexandria under the control of an appointed financial administrator, Cleomenes of Naucratis. Alexandria seems to have functioned as a Greek polis from shortly after its foundation. When Alexander died in 323 BC, the territory which he had conquered was divided up among his successors for the purposes of administration. The satrapy of Egypt was assigned to Ptolemy son of Lagus, a Macedonian boyhood friend of Alexander who served as a general during the eastern expedition, and it remained firmly in his hands throughout all the struggles of the successors. Cleomenes had proved to be notoriously corrupt in his dealings with the grain trade. After Ptolemy arrived in Alexandria, he made Cleomenes subordinate to him and eventually had him killed. When, in line with the other successors, Ptolemy declared himself a "king" in 305/04 BC, Alexandria became the capital city of his new kingdom, and it remained the capital of the Ptolemaic empire throughout the course of its existence.

During the reigns of Ptolemy I and his son Ptolemy II Philadelphus, Alexandria developed into a great city which became the jewel of the Mediterranean, taking over from Athens as the commercial and cultural capital of the Greek world. Immigrants were recruited from all over the Greek world to settle in the new city, and soon there evolved a mixed population of Greeks, native Egyptians, Jews, and other ethnic groups. To the first Ptolemies must be attributed the developed layout of the city (based on a grid plan around two main intersecting thoroughfares running the length of the ancient city) and the construction of its most famous features. (The best ancient description of the city is found in book 17 of the geographer Strabo, who visited Alexandria in 24 BC.) Knowledge of ancient Alexandria is limited both because the ancient city has been continuously inhabited and built over, and because the shoreline has sunk several metres since antiquity, submerging large areas of the original city.

The great Pharos, or Lighthouse, of Alexandria was constructed in the eastern harbour, perhaps on the site of an earlier beacon, on the small offshore island of Pharos (whence the lighthouse takes its name) which in antiquity was connected to the mainland by a causeway. The site is occupied today by the 15th-century fort of the Sultan Qait Bey. The Pharos is described by many ancient authors and is depicted on coins of the Roman period. It was the latest construction to be reckoned as one of the seven wonders of the ancient world. An inscription attests the involvement of Sostratus of Cnidus, but whether as architect or dedicator is unknown. Recent underwater excavations near the fort have revealed major remains from the structure.

The main royal complex of the Ptolemies was a huge area known as "the palaces", comprising several major buildings. Its location was thought to be in the area of the Lochias promontory, approximately the site of the smaller modern headland Silsileh on the eastern side of the east harbour, and this has been confirmed by exciting new underwater excavations west of Silsileh. Finds apparently from the palaces have been recovered but they are still being studied. The royal residences of the Ptolemies would undoubtedly have been grand and luxurious, reflecting their acclaimed wealth, but the palaces contained other structures which housed institutions credited with the preservation and dissemination of Greek culture.

The Museum (in Greek *Mouseion* – Shrine of the Muses) was founded probably by Ptolemy I as a complex of residential blocks and study facilities for scholars. Attached to it was the famous Library of Alexandria, founded originally in imitation of the library in Athens but soon eclipsing it in size and fame (ancient sources mention some 490,000 papyrus rolls). The librarian was appointed directly by the king and held the post for life. The library was responsible for the codification, copying, and therefore preservation of much of Greek literature, and attached to the museum and library were some of the greatest Greek scholars and writers of their day from all over the Greek world, many specially invited to Alexandria by the king: the 3rd-century BC poets Callimachus, Theocritus, Lycophron, and Apollonius Rhodius, the mathematician Euclid, the astronomer and geographer Eratosthenes of Cyrene, the grammarian Aristophanes of Byzantium, the 2nd-century AD geographer Claudius Ptolemy, to name but a few. It was an irreparable loss that the library was accidentally burnt in 48 BC during Julius Caesar's "Alexandrian War". A second large library was attached to the temple of Sarapis (or "Sarapeum") in the southern part of ancient Alexandria.

The Greek translation of the Hebrew Old Testament, the so-called Septuagint, was made at Alexandria. Tradition maintains that King Ptolemy II summoned the greatest Jewish scholars of the day to his city, and entertained them while the

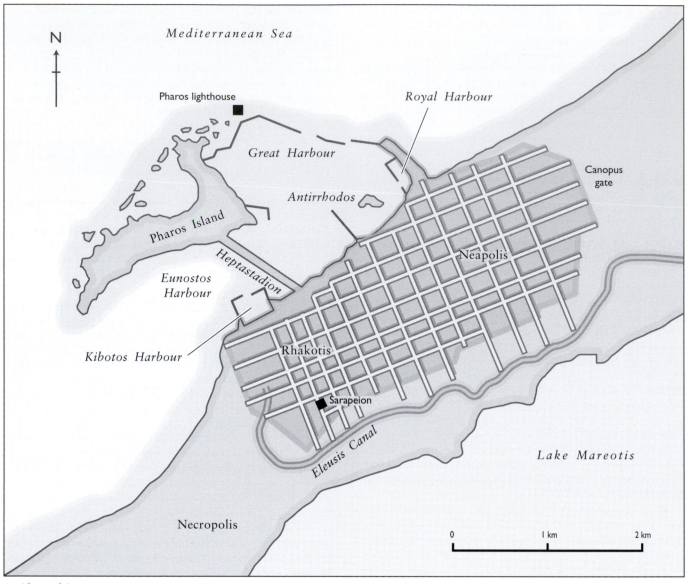

4. Alexandria

translation was made. It may rather have been at the behest of the Hellenized Jewish community whose knowledge of Hebrew was decreasing to the point that they could no longer read their holy books in their original language.

Alexandria's fame was furthermore ensured by the burial there of Alexander the Great. His funeral cortege from Babylon was diverted by Ptolemy I to Egypt, and his body first buried in the dynastic capital Memphis before being transferred to a grand tomb (in Greek the "Sema" or "Soma") in or near the palaces area in Alexandria. The various chronological stages of construction for this tomb are uncertain due to varying literary tradition, but, in time, the Ptolemies themselves were buried there and the Sema became the focus of the cult of Alexander and the ruler cult of the Ptolemies. The original gold sarcophagus is said to have been replaced later by an alabaster one, and it is attested that the 3rd-century AD Roman emperor Caracalla gazed upon the embalmed Alexander.

Throughout the centuries of Ptolemaic rule in Egypt,

Alexandria remained their capital, and, so far as we can tell, primarily a Greek city, although Egyptian architectural and decorative elements can be seen, especially in the extensive necropolis areas with their rock-cut chamber tombs designed for multiple burials. In common with the other Hellenistic kingdoms, Alexandria came to the attention of Rome, and by the 1st century BC became involved in the Roman civil wars. It is well known that the last Ptolemaic queen, Cleopatra, had a liaison with Julius Caesar, and a renowned love affair with Mark Antony. Their naval defeat at Actium at the hands of Octavian (later the emperor Augustus) led to the suicides of both Antony and Cleopatra.

After the death of Queen Cleopatra VII in 31 BC the Ptolemaic dynasty came to an end and Egypt became a province of the Roman empire. Alexandria continued to flourish due to its advantageous location for east–west trade, and became the second largest city of the empire. For the first three centuries AD massive freighters carrying the Egyptian grain which fed the population of Rome set out on their journeys from Alexandria every spring. Alexandria continued as a centre of learning. It was the home of the Neoplatonist school of philosophy, whose most influential member was the 3rd-century AD scholar Plotinus, who studied in Alexandria for a time. The school remained active until the 6th century AD, and influenced later Byzantine Greek thought, among much else. A great corpus of commentaries on the famous 4th-century BC Greek philosopher Aristotle was produced by the Alexandrian school.

This pagan tradition existed alongside Christianity, which came early to Alexandria. The evangelist St Mark is reputed to have come to Alexandria in the 1st century AD, to have been its first bishop, and to have been martyred there. Alexandria became one of the main centres of the Christian Church in the first centuries of its existence. A group of influential Greek Christian writers lived and worked in Alexandria in the 2nd and 3rd centuries AD, among them St Clement of Alexandria and Origen. In the 4th century AD Alexandria became the focus for the Arian heresy (named after its promulgator Arius), which was condemned by Athanasius, soon to become the bishop of Alexandria and a champion of orthodox Christianity, at the Council of Nicaea in AD 325. The learned pagan scholar Hypatia, a teacher of Neoplatonic philosophy, was murdered by a Christian mob in Alexandria in 415. The 5th-century bishop Cyril of Alexandria vigorously refuted the pagan writings of Julian the Apostate. Alexandria, a city gleaming with marble according to an Arab source, fell to the Arabs in 642, thereby ending its existence as a Greek city, although Greeks continued to live there.

In the 19th century the renewed maritime prowess of Alexandria made it the second city of Egypt (after Cairo). The city attracted thousands of immigrant merchants and craftsmen from all over Europe and the Mediterranean who founded foreign enclaves; among these was a large Greek population, many of whose descendants remained in Alexandria for generations. This exotic, levantine, cosmopolitan city is memorably evoked in the pages of Lawrence Durrell's four novels which form *The Alexandria Quartet*. Probably the most famous Greek resident of Alexandria in the late 19th and early 20th centuries was the poet Constantine Cavafy (1863–1933), who spent most of his life in the city.

E.E. RICE

See also Alexander, Egypt, Jews, Libraries, Museum of Alexandria, Ptolemies, Septuagint

Summary

City in Egypt founded by Alexander the Great in 331 BC. After Alexander's death in 323 Egypt became the kingdom of Ptolemy. Alexandria remained the capital of Ptolemaic Egypt until the fall of the dynasty in 31 BC. It succeeded Athens as the centre of Greek culture and was famous for its lighthouse, palaces, museum, and library. Later it was an important Christian centre. It fell to the Arabs in 642.

Further Reading

Bell, H. Idris, *Egypt, from Alexander the Great to the Arab Conquest: A Study in the Diffusion and Decay of Hellenism*, Oxford: Clarendon Press, 1948

Bowman, A.K., *Egypt after the Pharaohs, 332 BC–AD 642: From Alexander to the Arab Conquest*, 2nd edition, London: British Museum Press, and Berkeley: University of California Press, 1996

Butler, Alfred, J., *The Arab Conquest of Egypt and the Last Thirty Years of the Roman Dominion*, 2nd edition, edited by P.M. Fraser, Oxford: Clarendon Press, 1978

Clayton, Peter A. and Martin J. Price, *The Seven Wonders of the Ancient World*, London and New York: Routledge, 1988, chapter 7

Durrell, Lawrence, *The Alexandria Quartet*, London: Faber, and New York: Dutton, 1957–60

Ellis, Walter M., *Ptolemy of Egypt*, London and New York: Routledge, 1994

Forster, E.M., *Alexandria: A History and a Guide*, revised edition, London, Haag, 1982 (first published 1922)

Fraser, P.M., *Ptolemaic Alexandria*, 3 vols, Oxford: Clarendon Press, 1972

Haas, Christopher, *Alexandria in Late Antiquity: Topography and Social Conflict*, Baltimore: Johns Hopkins University Press, 1997

La Riche, William, *Alexandria: The Sunken City*, London: Weidenfeld and Nicolson, 1996

Rice, E.E., *The Grand Procession of Ptolemy Philadelphus*, Oxford and New York: Oxford University Press, 1983

Seton-Williams, Veronica and Peter Stocks, *Egypt*, 2nd edition, London: A. & C. Black, and New York: Norton, 1988 (*Blue Guide* series)

Tomlinson, Richard, *From Mycenae to Constantinople: The Evolution of the Ancient City*, London and New York: Routledge, 1992, chapter 7

True, Marion, and Kenneth Hamma (editors), *Alexandria and Alexandrianism*, Malibu: Getty Museum, 1996

Alexios I Komnenos c.1057–1118

Emperor

Alexios I Komnenos (1081–1118), the third son of John Komnenos and Anna Dalassene, was born around 1057, the same year that his uncle, Isaac I Komnenos, ascended the imperial throne. He died on 15 August 1118. His life and reign were the subject of the *Alexiad*, a historical work that his daughter, Anna Komnene, completed a generation after his death. A contemporary, often highly critical account is contained in the *Epitomi Historion* of John Zonaras. The divergence between these two principal sources has been perpetuated in modern scholarship, where Alexios is considered either a paragon "who saved his empire from the rocks on which it seemed likely to founder before 1081" (Nicol, 1991), or as an arch-reactionary who ruthlessly crushed the enlightened "New Society" that had emerged in the mid-11th century (Lemerle, 1977). By all accounts it is clear that Alexios's early diplomatic and military successes set the seal on the triumph of provincial aristocratic values over those of civilian intellectuals and bureaucrats, and allowed his own extended family to dominate Byzantine political life throughout the 12th century. The triumph of kin is paramount: unlike any emperor of the 11th century, Alexios was succeeded by his son (John II), grandson (Manuel I), and great-grandson (Alexios II).

Alexios came to prominence as a ruthless and effective general. As Grand Domestic after 1078 he defeated the imperial pretenders Nikephoros Bryennios and Nikephoros Basilakes, thus securing Nikephoros III Botaneiates's tenuous hold on power. This was ended by his own successful coup: Alexios's troops entered and looted Constantinople on 1 April 1081. Thereafter, he consolidated his position in the capital through ties of kinship. He entrusted general administration to his mother and elder brother Isaac, and forged an association with the Doukas family, marrying Irene Doukaina, and betrothing his infant daughter Anna to the *porphyrogennetos* ("born to the purple") Constantine Doukas (son of Michael VII Doukas). Alexios was thus free to remain in the field, where for the next decade he campaigned against both the Normans under Robert Guiscard, and the nomadic Pechenegs. To defeat the Normans he required the support of the Venetians, to whom he granted extraordinary trading privileges throughout the empire. The first phase of his reign ended with the crushing victory over the Pechenegs at Levunium on 29 April 1091, about which, Anna reports, it was sung thereafter: "All because of one day the Scythians never saw May." Consequently, Alexios was able to disinherit Constantine Doukas in favour of his own infant son John.

Alexios wished to recover imperial territory in Anatolia from the Seljuk Turks, and appealed to pope Urban II for fellow Christian warriors to aid in his *reconquista*. The response provoked by Urban's preaching, the First Crusade, was a shock and a challenge for Alexios, who succeeded to a large extent in turning the crusaders' energies to his advantage, recovering the western and southern littorals of Asia Minor. Nevertheless, the tensions between East and West that resulted from this grand encounter, and the establishment of the Latin crusader states free from Byzantine suzerainty, set the agenda for future Byzantine foreign policy. It is not surprising that Anna, writing after the Second Crusade (1147–48), suppressed her father's role as a catalyst for the first armed pilgrimage, and we must rely on references in a few Latin accounts, and the testimony of a 13th-century chronicler, the so-called Theodore Skoutariotes, for details of his actions before 1096.

An immediate consequence of soured relations between Alexios and certain Latins was the threat of a second crusade aimed at capturing Constantinople, which was promoted throughout Latin Christendom by the Norman, Bohemond of Taranto. Although this greater menace was averted by Alexios's diplomacy, a second phase of Byzantine–Norman wars in the western Balkans ensued. The treaty of Devol, which brought these to an end in 1108, sealed Alexios's last major foreign-policy success, but to a great extent revealed how hollow were his achievements in that sphere. The stipulation that the Normans must return Antioch to imperial control upon Bohemond's death could not be enforced, and consequently Alexios's successors were committed to long and arduous campaigns and diplomatic entanglements in the Holy Land. Moreover, Alexios failed to drive the Seljuk Turks from Anatolia, and his last campaign of 1116 reinforced this failure: he created a frontier zone around Bithynian Olympus, and evacuated as many of the native population of the interior as would follow him.

Alexios's domestic policy was not truly his own: "He had little interest in (or perhaps aptitude for) the running of government" (Angold, 1996), and entrusted such matters to a series of powerful individuals. First, as we have seen, were his mother and brother; later, after 1112, Alexios entrusted affairs to his wife, and not his son, which precipitated a succession crisis upon his death. Alexios's administrators presided over a major monetary reform around 1092. Gold coin, which had been debased dramatically, was restored in fineness, and fractional denominations were introduced in electrum, billon, and copper. This facilitated a reform in taxation practices, the *Nea Logarike*. After 1102 a new imperial officer, the Logothete of the Sekreta, seems to have had overall control of fiscal administration; the office was held only by the emperor's close relatives. A second significant innovation was the foundation of the Orphanotropheion, a charitable complex in Constantinople. Based around the church of St Paul, it was "like a city within a city" (Magdalino, 1996), which housed, fed, and treated the old and infirm, and educated the children of the poor and orphans. The Orphanotropheion served as a powerful symbol of Alexios's personal piety, a characteristic that he promoted as a counterweight to his persecution of certain individuals whom he tried and condemned as heretics. The most notorious trials were those of the intellectuals John Italos, Eustratios of Nicaea, and Basil the Bogomil.

Alexios's last years were plagued by illness, and one of the most powerful scenes in the *Alexiad* describes his death, surrounded by his kin. His father's death also moved John II, who had a series of panels commissioned that celebrated Alexios's exploits, but also featured his death. Clearly, Alexios's image was created and recreated after his death as a means to legitimate the competing imperial claims of his children. In this context we might better understand the *Mousai*, a work attributed to Alexios, and supposedly intended as advice to his son, which now appears more likely to be another posthumous creation. In the absence of further contemporary evidence Alexios will remain something of an enigma, and the historical appraisal of his life and achievements ambiguous.

PAUL STEPHENSON

See also Komnenos family

Biography

Born *c.*1057 the son of John Komnenos and Anna Dalassene, Alexios served as a general under Michael VII and Nikephoros III. He came to the throne in 1081 with the support of the military aristocracy. He shared power with his mother and brother Isaac. He campaigned against the Normans and Pechenegs. With the help of the First Crusade (1096–99) he recovered the coast of Asia Minor from the Turks. He died in Constantinople in 1118.

Further Reading

Angold, Michael, "Alexios I Komnenos: An Afterword" in *Alexios I Komnenos*, edited by Margaret Mullet and Dion Smythe, Belfast: Belfast Byzantine Enterprises, 1996

Angold, Michael, *The Byzantine Empire, 1025–1204: A Political History*, 2nd edition, London and New York: Longman, 1997

Chalandon, Ferdinand, *Essai sur le règne d'Alexis Ier Comnène*, Paris: Picard, 1900, reprinted New York: Franklin, 1971

Lemerle, Paul, *Cinq études sur le XIe siècle byzantin*, Paris: CNRS, 1977

Lilie, Ralph-Johannes, *Byzantium and the Crusader States, 1096–1204*, Oxford: Clarendon Press, and New York: Oxford University Press, 1993

Magdalino, Paul, "Innovations in Government" in *Alexios I Komnenos*, edited by Margaret Mullet and Dion Smythe, Belfast: Belfast Byzantine Enterprises, 1996

Mullet, Margaret and Dion Smythe (editors), *Alexios I Komnenos*, Belfast: Belfast Byzantine Enterprises, 1996

Nicol, Donald, *A Biographical Dictionary of the Byzantine Empire*, London: Seaby, 1991

Shepard, Jonathan, "When Greek Meets Greek: Alexius Comnenus and Bohemond in 1097–98", *Byzantine and Modern Greek Studies*, 12 (1988): pp. 185–277

Ali Pasha of Ioannina 1750–1822

Governor of Epirus

Ali Pasha of Ioannina was the Ottoman-appointed governor of Epirus in northern Greece during the critical decades leading up to the first outbreak of the Greek War of Independence in 1821. At the peak of his power, Ali or members of his immediate family controlled the whole of the Peloponnese and the Greek mainland, with the sole exception of the southernmost portions of Attica.

Thought to have been born in 1750 in the southern Albanian village of Tebelen, Ali was a member of a low-ranking noble Albanian Muslim family. By the time of his birth, however, all that remained of his family's nobility was its title – Ali's early biographers all report that his family was virtually destitute in the mid-18th century. It is this poverty that is often used to explain Ali's activities as a brigand and bandit, activities which paved the way for his rise through the Ottoman bureaucracy. Before the age of 20, Ali and his band of Albanian scipetars – the warriors who made up Albanian brigand groups – held de facto control over much of southern Albania and Epirus. The Ottoman state recognized Ali's domination of and familiarity with these territories and in 1778 attempted to coopt his power and influence by appointing him to his first position in the Ottoman hierarchy, that of *kahya* (deputy) to the *derbendler başbuğu*, or chief of police of the mountain defiles, a position which dated from Byzantine times and which had been adopted in turn by the Ottomans. In this new capacity Ali was able further to consolidate his power and simultaneously to please his Ottoman masters by eradicating all brigand activity for which he himself was not responsible. He did not, however, cease himself to be a brigand, but rather gave his brigand activity a pseudo-official quality, instituting regional tariffs, demanding tribute from the citizenry, and charging fees for safe passage through the rugged mountain passes of the region.

Thus it is that early on the Ottoman state established what was to be the pattern for its relationship with Ali throughout his life. Recognizing his formidable power and their own minimal ability to subvert it (Ali's territories were among the westernmost of the Ottoman empire, difficult for the distant Istanbul bureaucracy to control), the Ottomans sought instead to make it appear that Ali's powers were the product of Ottoman choosing rather than of Ali's own doing. So it is that Ali was subsequently appointed to a series of increasingly prestigious Ottoman positions. In 1787 Ali himself became *derbendler baùbuXu* and was appointed *mutassarif* (chief administrator) of Ioannina that same year, becoming vizier in 1798.

As pasha of Ioannina – the date of his appointment as pasha (governor) is contested – Ali was in control of an overwhelmingly Greek population, and the policies he instituted within his pashalik exerted a strong influence over the social, economic, and intellectual conditions of Greece in the 18th and early 19th centuries.

In the 18th century Ioannina was established as Greece's premier city of learning, and housed a number of educational institutions. Many of these existed through the endowments of Ioannina's wealthy community of merchants, who in the 17th and 18th centuries had established far-flung trade networks throughout the Balkans, in the Black Sea area, and in the Italian city-states, particularly Venice. Such wealthy Ioanninite families as the Zosimades founded schools that added to the traditional, religiously based curriculum the western European emphasis on and interest in Hellenism, the pre-Byzantine past, and Classical philology. In addition to such "modernized" institutions, Ioannina also had long-established ecclesiastical centres of Greek education. While Ali did not directly promote these institutions, he unwittingly was influenced by them and in some ways furthered their aims. He was the first major ruler of the Balkans, for instance, to use demotic Greek as the language of his courtly affairs. This emphasis on the vernacular for official business helped lay the groundwork for the demoticist point of view in the early years of the modern Greek state, when intellectuals and reformers debated whether to use Classical or demotic Greek as the official state language.

Although a native speaker of Albanian, Ali was fluent in Greek, and the vast majority of his courtiers, secretaries, and physicians were Greek. It seems that Ali's knowledge of Turkish was minimal, at best. The Ottoman landowners of the region, too, overwhelmingly used Greek. Such travellers as the Englishman William Martin Leake wrote in their travel journals of the "high quality" and "clarity" of the Greek used in Ali's territories, and commented on the number and variety of institutions of learning based in Ioannina.

Just as Ali Pasha's influence on Hellenism was great but largely unwitting, so too was his impact on the Greek political affairs of the period. By the beginning of the 19th century, the Ottoman state was no longer prepared to pursue its policy of toleration towards Ali's accumulation of power, illegal activities, and treason against the empire. Ali had, by the turn of the century, become increasingly overt in his claims to exercise power and privilege in his own right, not simply as a representative of the Ottoman government. He had, for instance, entered into secret negotiations with both the French and the English, even while those powers were not recognized as Ottoman allies. His almost entirely Albanian army had grown huge, and it was becoming increasingly clear that these troops were just as likely to be deployed against the Ottoman army as against Ottoman enemies. Finally, in 1820, Ali declared himself independent, and as a result Ottoman troops were deployed against him.

All of these events were occurring at the same time as the Greek populations of the Ottoman empire were actively planning a revolution against their Turkish rulers. Ali provided a much-needed diversion for the revolutionary Greeks, who wisely timed the outbreak of the War of Independence to coincide with the battle between Ali's forces and the Ottomans. It is likely that without this intra-Ottoman conflict – a conflict which taxed Ottoman military and economic resources – the initial stages of the War of Independence would not have succeeded. For his part too, Ali recognized the significance and potential usefulness of the Greek revolutionaries, and in an unsuccessful last-minute bid to augment his own resources against the Ottoman army, he tried to convince the Greek leadership that his cause and theirs were one and the same. Ali lived to see only the first phases of the Greek revolutionary movement, and was killed in 1822 by Ottoman representatives.

Ali remains a somewhat double-edged figure in the modern history of Hellenism. Reviled by Greek folk tradition as a cruel and despotic ruler, the oppressor of Orthodoxy, and a tyrant of epic proportions, he nevertheless played an important albeit indirect role in the development of Greek language, culture, and politics.

K.E. FLEMING

See also Epirus, Ioannina

Biography
Born at Tebelen in Albania in 1750 into a noble but poor Muslim family, Ali attempted to overcome poverty by brigandage. As he gained control over much of Albania and Epirus, the Ottoman state sought to regularize his position by giving him a series of official posts. As pasha of Ioannina, he ruled most of mainland Greece and declared himself independent in 1820, thus diverting Ottoman attention away from the incipient Greek revolution. He was killed by Ottoman agents in 1822.

Further Reading
Byron, Lord, *Childe Harold's Pilgrimage*, London: John Murray, 1812; complete edition, 2 vols, 1819

Davenport, R.A., *The Life of Ali Pasha of Tepeleni, Vizier of Epirus, Surnamed Aslan, or the Lion*, London: Tegg, 1837

Fleming, Katherine, *The Muslim Bonaparte: Diplomacy and Orientalism in Ali Pasha's Greece*, Princeton, New Jersey: Princeton University Press, 1999

Hobhouse, John Cam, *Travels in Albania and Other Provinces of Turkey in 1809 and 1810*, London: John Murray, 1855

Minta, Stephen, *On a Voiceless Shore: Byron in Greece*, New York: Holt, 1998

Plomer, William, *The Diamond of Jannina: Ali Pasha, 1741–1822*, London: Cape, and New York: Taplinger, 1970

Alphabet

The ancient Greeks can be credited with providing humankind with the first fully alphabetic writing system – an intellectual achievement and technological leap of no mean significance. As is almost universally the case with such advances, the Greek alphabet was built upon a previously existing model – in this case, the consonantal script of speakers of a west Semitic language. Herodotus gives the credit to Cadmus and his fellow Phoenicians who had come to Greece in search of the abducted princess Europa:

> And these Phoenicians who had come with Cadmus ... and settled this country brought to the Greeks, among many other arts, the letters – which, I believe, were not previously known to the Greeks. Eventually they changed the sound and the shape of the letters. In this time, it was mostly Ionian Greeks living around the Phoenicians, who, having learned the letters from them, used these, making a few changes in their shape. The Greeks still called the letters "Phoenician", as was right, since the Phoenicians had brought them to Greece

(Herodotus, 5. 58–61)

Modern scholarship has been almost unanimous in its agreement with Herodotus regarding the Phoenician source of the alphabet.

Herodotus was probably also accurate in envisioning that the Greek adaptation of the Semitic consonantal script took place in a setting in which Greeks and Phoenicians lived in close proximity to one another. Beyond that, the Greek alphabet may have made its first appearance in the Aegean among the West Ionic speakers of Euboea, bordering upon the region of Boeotia in which Cadmus is reported to have settled. The actual Greek acquisition of the Phoenician script, however, probably took place in some other locale and somewhat later than the date in the 2nd millennium BC in which Herodotus' Cadmus would have arrived in Greece.

Prominent among those places that have been proposed for the Greek adaptation of the Semitic writing system are Crete, Rhodes, Al Mina, and Cyprus. Of these, the most compelling candidate (on both linguistic and non-linguistic grounds) appears to be Cyprus, where literate Greeks writing with a syllabic script (the Cypriot Syllabary) lived side-by-side with Phoenicians using their consonantal script. The probable date of adaptation is the early 8th century BC (or possibly even the late 9th century BC).

The Phoenician script, like other West Semitic writing systems of antiquity, consists only of characters for consonants; vowels are not directly represented in Phoenician orthography. Since the Phoenician language possesses several consonants not occurring in Greek, the Greek adapters of the Phoenician script had at their disposal several superfluous consonantal symbols. These they converted to vowel characters: Phoenician *aleph*, representing a glottal stop, was adopted as a symbol for the vowel *a*, that is *alpha* (A); Phoenician *he*, the symbol for *h*, became Greek *epsilon* (E), spelling *e*; *'ayin*, symbol for the Phoenician voiced pharyngeal fricative, was taken over as *omicron* (O), representing Greek *o*; *yod*, the character for *y*, became Greek *iota* (I), used to spell *i*; and Phoenician *waw*, *w*, came to be used for spelling the Greek vowel *u* – the letter *upsilon* (Υ, as well as being used for the consonantal character called *digamma* (F), representing *w*). In this way, those Greeks who adapted the Phoenician script for their own use created the first writing system to represent systematically both individual consonant and vowel sounds.

In time, two additional vowel characters appeared in the Greek alphabet. The Phoenician letter *het*, representing a voiceless pharyngeal fricative, was first used for Greek *h*. The consonant *h* did not, however, occur in certain dialects of Greek (such as Cretan and East Ionic); in these, the Greek symbol derived from *het*, that is *eta* (H), came to be used to represent a long vowel *ē*. In parallel fashion an additional vowel character was created (being derived from the symbol *omicron*) in order to represent the distinct long vowel *ō* – the character *omega* (Ω) – and was appended to the very end of the alphabet. Prior to these developments, *epsilon* and *omicron* had been used for representing both short and long *e* and *o* respectively.

The Greek adapters of the Phoenician script included in their alphabet two different characters representing *s*- sounds. One of these stands in the alphabetic position of the Phoenician letter *ṣade* (representing a so-called emphatic fricative or affricate, a consonantal sound characteristic of Semitic languages), the other in the position of Phoenician *shan* (Hebrew *shin*, symbol for *sh*). The former of these corresponds to the Greek letter commonly called *san* (M), the latter to that called *sigma* (Σ). The inclusion of both in the early Greek alphabet suggests that the Greek dialect of the adapters was one in which two distinct *s*-type sounds occurred – a picture consistent with a Cypriot origin of the alphabet. Most Greek dialects had only a single *s*-sound, however, so that the various local, or epichoric, varieties of the Greek alphabet that developed as the script spread across the Greek-speaking regions retained only one of these two symbols.

The name of the character *sigma* is certainly secondary, not continuing a Phoenician letter name (though the contrary claim has been made), and was derived from the Greek root *sig-*, seen in the verb *sizo* ("I hiss"), having an earlier stem *sig-yo-*. Herodotus (1.139) writes that among some Greeks the character *sigma* is itself given the name *san*, and this is also the name by which the latter is commonly denoted in Greek poetry. In all likelihood, *san* was the early Greek name of the *sigma*-character (Σ) and simply continues the name of the corresponding Phoenician letter, *shan*. The original Greek name of that non-*sigma* *s*- character, the one more commonly called *san* (M, corresponding to Phoenician *ṣade*) is thus unknown, the name *san* having become affiliated with it in those epichoric alphabets from which the *sigma*-character was excised.

Also noteworthy is the inclusion in the early Greek alphabet of two double-consonant characters (i.e. letters that represent a sequence of two individual consonants). The letters in question are Greek *zeta* (Z) and *xi* (Ξ). *Zeta* represents the sequence *zd* (having become *z* in modern Greek) and corresponds to the Phoenician letter *zayin* (symbol for *z*); while *xi* was assigned the value of *ks* by the Greek adapters, and is derived from the Phoenician symbol *samek* (representing *s*, though perhaps earlier with a value such as *kʸ*). The presence of these symbols in the early Greek alphabet is a curious matter, given that they are completely redundant; in other words, the consonant sequences that they represent could have been written using two individual consonant letters. Thus, the sound sequence of *zeta*, for instance, could have been spelt *sd* (sigma (Σ) + *delta* (Δ); in accordance with Greek phonetic structure, in this context *sigma* would automatically have the voiced value *z*); and, similarly, the sound sequence of *xi* could have been spelt *ks* (kappa (K) + *sigma* (Σ)). The incorporation of these characters in the alphabet again points to Cyprus as the place of adaptation, where similar biconsonantal symbols are properly accounted for within the structure of the Cypriot Syllabary.

In addition to the Greek letters that the adapters derived from corresponding Phoenician characters, and to the vowel letter *omega*, added to the end of the alphabet, certain of the local Greek alphabets are characterized by the presence of three additional letters, immediately preceding *omega*. These are the so-called "supplementals", having no formal Phoenician counterparts. One of these supplementals is the letter *phi*, representing an aspirated stop *ph* (which later becomes the fricative *f*). The second is *chi*, spelling an aspirated velar stop *kh* (later a velar fricative, often transcribed *ch*). The third is yet another biconsonantal character; in this case one representing the sequence *ps*, namely *psi*. As will be seen below, however, different values are in some places attached to these two last-named letters.

The numerous regional forms of the alphabet that developed among the ancient Greeks can be subdivided into three fundamental types on the basis of these supplemental characters. To begin with, there are some epichoric alphabets that lack the supplementals. These are the so-called "primitive" scripts of Crete, Thera, and Melos (also called the "green" scripts, after the colour-coded map of Greek alphabets which was included in Kirchhoff, 1867, most recently republished in 1973). In those alphabets that do include the supplemental characters, the letter *phi* (Φ) appears everywhere with the value *ph*. Differences occur, however, in regard to the remaining two supplementals.

In the "blue" alphabets (again, so called after Kirchhoff's map) *chi* appears as C, representing *kh*; and *psi* (Ψ) has the value *ps*. Among a subset of blue alphabets, however, the supplemental *psi* does not occur (and *ps* is spelt with two letters: *phi* + *sigma*; in the same way these alphabets lack the Phoenician-based biconsonantal letter *xi* (Ξ), and spell *ks* as *chi* + *sigma*). The blue alphabets lacking *psi* have been dubbed "light blue", the remainder "dark blue". Light blue alphabets were used, for example, in Attica and on some of the Aegean Ionic islands; Corinth, Mycenae, and the Ionic cities of Asia Minor, among other places, used the dark blue alphabet.

A large number of regional alphabets show yet a different configuration with regard to the supplemental characters; these are the so-called "red" alphabets. Here the symbol X (blue *chi*) represents not *kh*, but the sequence *ks* (and the Phoenician-based Ξ, representing *ks* in dark blue alphabets, does not occur). Moreover, the symbol Ψ in the red alphabets does not spell *ps*, as in the dark blue alphabets, but is used to represent *kh* (and there is no single symbol for *ps*). The order of the supplementals in the red alphabets is X (*ks*), Φ (*ph*), Ψ (*kh*), versus dark blue Φ (*ph*), X (*kh*), Ψ (*ps*). Among those places using red alphabets were Euboea (and its colonies), Boeotia, and Thessaly.

In 403 BC the Ionic alphabet (a dark blue script) was adopted by Athens as its official alphabet. Within a few decades, this Attic alphabet had spread throughout the Greek-speaking world and replaced most of the regional varieties. Beyond being the ancestor of the modern Greek alphabet, this script would have great influence on the development of writing in Europe, and beyond.

St Cyril and St Methodios, accompanied by other Greek missionaries, set out in the 9th century AD to bring Christianity to the Slavs. As a part of their evangelistic efforts, and on the basis of their own Greek alphabet, the saints developed two alphabetic writing systems with which the Bible could be translated and recorded in the Slavic language of their converts (Old Church Slavonic). One of the scripts, Glagolitic, would survive only in limited usage, but the other, Cyrillic, would give rise to the writing systems of numerous different Slavic peoples – Russian, Ukrainian, Serbian, Bulgarian. The Russian Cyrillic alphabet would in turn be adapted for writing various non-Slavic languages of Eurasia. The alphabetic scripts which, by tradition, St Mesrop designed for writing Armenian and Georgian (5th century AD), though perhaps of mixed heritage, were also clearly fundamentally based on the Greek alphabet.

It was a Greek alphabet of Magna Graecia, of the red variety, that was acquired by the Etruscans in the 7th century BC. This in turn was transmitted to various peoples of the Italian peninsula, most significantly to the Romans. The Roman alphabet probably inspired the development of the Runic scripts of the Germanic peoples of Europe (and perhaps the curious Celtic Ogham script as well), but, more importantly, was spread to Europe itself, both by Roman armies and, in time, by the Roman Catholic Church. Acquired as the writing system of English and other languages of Europe, it would be spread around the globe. In the final analysis, all alphabetic writing systems in use today have their origin in the Greek alphabet, with the exception of the Han'gul script of Korean.

ROGER D. WOODARD

See also Phoenicians, Syllabary

Further Reading

Carpenter, Rhys, "The Antiquity of the Greek Alphabet", *American Journal of Archaeology*, 37 (1933): pp. 8–29

Carpenter, Rhys, "The Greek Alphabet Again", *American Journal of Archaeology*, 42 (1938): pp. 58–69

Cook, B., "Greek Inscriptions" in *Reading the Past*, introduced by J.T. Hooker, London: British Museum Press, and Berkeley: University of California Press, 1990

Guarducci, M., "La culla dell'alfabeto greco", *Rendiconti dell'Accademia nazionale dei Lincei*, 33 (1978): pp. 381–88

Immerwahr, Henry, *Attic Script: A Survey*, Oxford: Clarendon Press, and New York: Oxford University Press, 1990

Jeffery, Lilian, *The Local Scripts of Archaic Greece*, revised edition, Oxford: Clarendon Press, and New York: Oxford University Press, 1990

Kirchhoff, Adolf, *Studien zur Geschichte des griechischen Alphabets*, Berlin: Dümmler, 1867, reprinted Hildesheim: Olms, 1973

McCarter, Kyle, *The Antiquity of the Greek Alphabet and the Early Phoenician Scripts*, Missoula, Montana: Scholars Press, 1975

Robb, Kevin, *Literacy and Paideia in Ancient Greece*, Oxford and New York: Oxford University Press, 1994

Threatte, Leslie, "The Greek Alphabet" in *The World's Writing Systems*, edited by Peter Daniels and William Bright, Oxford and New York: Oxford University Press, 1996

Woodard, Roger, "Writing Systems" in *Atlas of Languages*, edited by Bernard Comrie, Stephen Matthews and Maria Polinsky, London: Quarto, and New York: Facts on File, 1996

Woodard, Roger, *Greek Writing from Knossos to Homer*, Oxford and New York: Oxford University Press, 1997

Woolley, Leonard, "Excavations at Al Mina, Sueidia", *Journal of Hellenic Studies*, 58 (1938): pp. 1–30, 133–70

Altars

Altars of one kind or another have been employed continuously from a very early period in Greek history, but the two contrasting dictionary definitions, a "flat-topped block for sacrifice or offerings to a deity" and a "communion table" point to significant discontinuity.

Prehistoric altars could be portable ("tables of offering") or permanent. The latter include rough stones (Mycenae), bench altars (Knossos, Mycenae, Kea, Phylakopi, Tiryns), and some freestanding structures. Of the last, one, apparently used for human sacrifice, comes from Middle Minoan Crete (Anemospilia, Archanes), another stands in the central court at Phaestus, and a further example is represented in the frescos of Xeste 3 at Akrotiri on Thera. In Early Bronze Age Crete stone-built altars are associated with tombs. Sometimes (sanctuary of Apollo Maleatas, Epidaurus, prehistoric phase) altars were formed of the gradually accumulated debris of offerings, whether of sacrificial animals or material gifts, deposited on a sacred spot. By the Archaic period altars were often regular in shape, frequently made of ashlar masonry and with some architectural decoration (e.g. volutes, mouldings, friezes: Cape Monodendri, Miletus).

The most prominent altar type of later antiquity (including the Classical period) was the built *bomos* (platform altar), sometimes an isolated structure, but normally associated with a temple and standing outside its eastern front. On this sacrificial victims were burned. Altars were still sometimes (altar of Zeus at Olympia) composed of debris. From the Hellenistic period some public altars were enclosed by huge, monumental structures and bore extensive sculptural decoration (Great Altar of Zeus at Pergamum). Heroes and chthonic deities, as distinct from the Olympian gods, had a ground altar (*eschara*) which allowed wine and blood to soak into the earth, their natural home.

Smaller private altars, domestic or funerary in function, and of various shapes, are also found. Funerary altars, often round and decorated with garlands and bucrania (the decoration refers to the garlanding of sacrificial animals) are common only in later periods, especially the Roman. Not all offerings were sacrificial: wine, cakes, etc. might be appropriate, according to the occasion, and were more commonly offered on the smaller altars.

In Christian practice the altar originally connoted the table (*iera trapeza*, "holy table") of the Last Supper and was the location of its ritual re-enactment in the liturgy. Later it acquired a variety of symbolic connotations (e.g. Christ's tomb). The first Christian altars (up to the 4th century AD) were mostly small, wooden, and portable. One later type is simply a translation of this into stone. The solid rectangular stone form that became most common may be derived from the tombs of the martyrs, where it was customary to celebrate the Eucharist, in commemoration of their sacrifice. Also connected with this custom was the practice of containing relics of the martyrs within the altar, or in a crypt beneath.

In Christian times the altar continued to be closely associated with the chief sacred building – the church – though now it was situated inside. The interior location allowed it to be adorned with coverings, and to carry symbols permanently (crosses, candlesticks, etc.), although this development did not occur before the 10th century AD. Often an elaborate canopy (ciborium) was raised over the altar.

In spite of the evidence for some degree of overlap between the pagan and Christian traditions (e.g. in the use of sanctuary sites, iconography), and the possibility that pagan altar structures had some influence on Christian types, there is no evidence for either material or ideological continuity in the case of altars. The former, in any case, would surely have been offensive to Christians. Nevertheless, as the idea of sacrifice inherent in the death of Christ and commemorated in the liturgy became more prominent in Christian thought, there was some convergence of the two traditions, although in Christian practice the sacrifice at the altar is symbolic.

ROBIN L.N. BARBER

See also Christianity, Religion

Further Reading

Braun, Joseph, *Der christliche Altar in seiner geschichtlichen Entwicklung*, Munich: Koch, 1924

Burkert, Walter, *Greek Religion: Archaic and Classical*, Oxford: Blackwell, and Cambridge, Massachusetts: Harvard University Press, 1985

Fraser, P.M., *Rhodian Funerary Monuments*, Oxford: Clarendon Press, and New York: Oxford University Press, 1977

Leclercq, Henri, Autel entry in *Dictionnaire d'archéologie chrétienne et de liturgie*, edited by Fernand Cabrol, Paris: Letouzey & Ané, 1907

Mylonas, George E., *Mycenaean Religion: Temples, Altars and Temenea*, Athens: Academy of Athens, 1977

Nilsson, Martin P., *The Minoan-Mycenaean Religion and Its Survival in Greek Religion*, 2nd edition, Lund: Gleerup, 1950

Turner, Jane (editor), *The Dictionary of Art*, London and New York: Grove, 1996 (Altar entry)

Yavis, C.G., *Greek Altars: Origins and Typology*, St Louis: St Louis University Press, 1949

Amalfi

Port on the west coast of Italy

Amalfi is a seaport in Campania, 50 km south of Naples on the rocky estuary of the Dragone on the north side of the Gulf of Salerno. First mentioned in AD 596 by pope Gregory the Great and frequently mentioned by Constantine VII Porphyrogennetos (913–59) in *De Administrando Imperio*, virtually nothing is known of Amalfi's early history beyond its importance with Naples as a Byzantine naval base. This was signalled in 664 when it was visited by Constans II (641–68) during what proved to be the last visit of any eastern emperor to his possessions in Italy. At the close of the 9th century it formed part of the Byzantine duchy of Naples, from which it became separated by the Lombards. Nominally subject to the emperor in Constantinople, it exploited this status to become, with the Venetians, one of the principal carriers in the east–west trade. Bishop Liutprand of Cremona mentioned the merchants of Amalfi as the suppliers of purple silk to Italian prostitutes and monks; presumably churches and royal courts should be numbered among their customers too, since Liutprand's comments had been occasioned by the confiscation of his own purchases of purple silk by the Byzantine customs authorities. Although there is no surviving record of an Amalfitan colony at Constantinople before the 11th century, it is possible that there were Amalfitan and Venetian commercial colonies in the capital by the middle of the 10th century, since Liutprand mentions "Venetici et Amalphitani" in the army of Nikephoros II Phokas (963–69) and these were presumably men settled in Constantinople. Amalfitan connections at the imperial court secured permission to found a Benedictine monastery on Mount Athos sometime after 985.

During the 1050s the rulers of Amalfi tried to organize resistance to the Normans in southern Italy. In this they failed and in 1073 the city passed under the control of the Norman Robert Guiscard and became part of his duchy of Apulia. The position and privileges of the Amalfitans in Constantinople were to suffer as a consequence. In 1082 it was merchants from Amalfi settled in Durazzo who opened the gates of that town to Guiscard, eight months after a Venetian flotilla had secured the town for the Byzantines. In the same year their trading privileges in Constantinople were subordinated to those of Venice. Again in 1147, when Roger of Sicily attacked the cities of Corinth and Thebes, the Amalfitan commercial quarter was closed down. Nevertheless, although no longer pre-eminent in the Italy–Constantinople trade, there were still Amalfitan merchants living in Constantinople in their quarter clustered around the church of S. Maria de Latina in 1204, since it was one of the quarters attacked by the Greek populace in that year. If after 1073 Amalfitan trade in the Aegean was to be eclipsed by that of Venice and it was in many ways to become a trading centre of the second rank, the port was to remain a wealthy one, with links to Antioch, Acre, and Alexandria, with a reputation for trading voyages and links with Arabs, Sicilians, and Africans.

The cathedral church of St Andrew in Amalfi still has the bronze doors made in Constantinople by a certain Simeon sometime around 1065 and commissioned by the rich Amalfitan merchant Maurus, son of Panteleon, whose family owned property in Constantinople. The doors were much copied by other ecclesiastical establishments in Italy in the 11th century, most notably by abbot Desiderius of Montecassino who sent the measurements of the door to Constantinople to have a set of bronze doors manufactured. The money for this additional set of doors was raised by the same Maurus.

PETER LOCK

Summary

A port on the coast of Italy 50 km south of Naples, Amalfi was originally founded as a Byzantine naval base, probably in the 6th century. By the 10th century it had become a major trading centre. An Amalfitan monastery was founded on Mount Athos in the late 10th century. By the 11th century there was an Amalfitan colony in Constantinople.

Further Reading

Balard, M., "Amalfi et Byzance (X–XII siècles)", *Travaux et Memoires*, 6 (1976): pp. 85–95

Belting, H., "Byzantine Art in Southern Italy", *Dumbarton Oaks Papers*, 28 (1974) pp. 3–29

Citarella, A., "Patterns in Medieval Trade: The Commerce of Amalfi before the Crusades", *Journal of Economic History*, 28 (1968): pp. 531–55

Frazer, M., "Church Doors and the Gates of Paradise: Byzantine Bronze Doors in Italy", *Dumbarton Oaks Papers*, 27 (1973): pp. 145–62

Galasso, G., "Il commercio amalfitano nel periodo normanno" in
Studi in Onore di Riccardo Filangieri, vol. 1, Naples: L'Arte, 1959
Schwarz, Ulrich, *Amalfi im frühen Mittelalter*, Tübingen: Niemeyer,
1978

Amasis

Potter and painter of the 6th century BC

The potter Amasis first became known when a vase (560 BC) signed with his name *Amasis me poiesen*, ("Amasis made me") was found at Vulci in 1828. In all, eight black-figure vases bearing his signature are known, and their decoration has often been attributed to a single painter known as the Amasis Painter. Amasis' other work as a potter consists of two vases for Lydos and a cup decorated by a red-figure painter. His earliest signature as a painter occurs on a fragmentary band-cup of around 550 BC.

The name Amasis is a Hellenized form of the common Egyptian name A-ahmes. This has resulted in much scholarly debate as to the potter's origins. It has been suggested either that Amasis was an Athenian named after the Egyptian king Amasis (Ahmosis) or that he was not Athenian by birth and that his name was adopted in Ionia or after he came to Athens. Those who support the former hypothesis argue that the potter and the painter are different men; according to the latter view, the potter and painter are identified as the same person.

The Amasis Painter decorated a wide range of shapes – such as belly- and neck-amphorae, *oinochoae* (wine jugs), cups, *lekythoi* (oil flasks), an *alabastron* (perfume vase), an *aryballos* (oil flask), and a tripod *pyxis* (box), as well as small and large plaques. He did not, however, restrict himself to standard types of vases, but explored different variations of certain shapes, as, for example, the cups and the neck amphorae.

The style of the Amasis Painter is usually considered conservative because, even when he adopted new conventions, he did not abandon established forms. The precision of drawing and the ability to work on different scales seem the main characteristics of his work. He also paid attention to the harmony between the shape of the vase and its decoration, as seen on the panel amphorae he decorated.

In the early stages of his career his style reflected the work of the Heidelberg Painter and of the Siana cup painters. From the former he adopted stately processions, garments with fringes, and certain conventions for the rendering of anatomical details, while the latter probably inspired him to adapt a procession of horsemen to panel-amphorae. Moreover, the influence of Cleitias may be seen in his miniature style. The Amasis Painter also shared a number of features with Lydos, such as the preference for symmetry in his compositions as well as certain details in drawing. Although he used the common black-figure floral ornaments above the panels of his scenes, he reinforced the frames by more than one glaze lines, and a vertical band of meander or chevrons. He used bands of upright buds or palmette and lotus to decorate the area above the panels on amphorae.

In the late phase of his career, instead of foldless drapery, he painted flat, angular folds, and women's flesh was drawn in outline, not white on black, the standard convention of his time. Other characteristics of his work include a change in the ornament framing his compositions – the lotuses lose their central leaf – and the occasional omission of the ground line for his figures. The Amasis Painter demonstrated a great interest in the representation of jewellery and armour, especially of shield devices, as well as of architectural elements (fountain houses, column shafts, and a distyle *in antis*), which offered opportunities to represent spatial depths. He often used stippling for the hairy bodies of the satyrs, figures who had features in common with those drawn by Lydos, and for head-hair and beards. The growing understanding of the human body was reflected in his figures, which gesticulated expressively.

The Amasis Painter decorated vases with a wide repertoire of scenes that extend from the Olympian gods and heroes to daily life in Athens and the Attic countryside. Although several of his figures are labelled with painted inscriptions, the scenes are not always easily recognizable. He prefers to fill out his scenes with figures that either participate in the action or act as mere spectators; only occasionally did he concentrate on just the essential elements of the subject. Dionysus is one of his favourite characters, standing between satyrs, maenads, and mortals or supervising the vintage; the hero Heracles is represented being received on Mount Olympus after his death. His mythological scenes are well composed but rarely show the originality of his representation of the divine stables. The Amasis Painter was one of the first to introduce complex everyday scenes on vases – such as a wedding procession, the fullest early pictorial account of an Attic wedding – women at various stages of wool working and weaving, a hunter's return, and a cavalcade. He also demonstrated a consistent inclination to blur the lines between the realms of mortals and immortals or to combine the two.

The vases decorated by the Amasis Painter were widely distributed in the ancient world, as is also the case with other Attic potters and painters: in south Russia (Berezan), Italy and Sicily (Cumae, Capua, Gravisca, Vulci, Orvieto, Chiusi, Cerveteri, and Selinus), North Africa (Naucratis, Cyrene), Cyprus, and Greece (Athens, Eleusis, Tanagra, Perachora, Kavalla, Rhodes, Samos, Delos). Surviving signed works are now held in various museums around the world, including the Museo Gregoriano Etrusco in the Vatican, the Museum of Fine Arts in Boston, the British Museum in London, the Louvre and the Cabinet des Medailles of the Bibliothèque Nationale in Paris, the Martin von Wagner Museum at Würzburg University, and the Getty Museum in Malibu.

ELENI ZIMI

See also Painting, Pottery

Biography

Name of a potter and painter of the 6th century BC. He may have been an Athenian named after the Egyptian king Ahmosis; or he may have come to Athens from elsewhere and acquired the name in Ionia. If the former, potter and painter are assumed to be two different men; if the latter, they are one. As potter Amasis signed eight black-figure vases, two other vases, and a cup. The Amasis Painter painted a wide range of scenes on a wide variety of vase shapes.

Further Reading

Beazley, J.D., *The Development of Attic Black-Figure*, Berkeley: University of California Press, 1986, pp. 52–57

Boardman, John, *Athenian Black-Figure Vases: A Handbook*, London: Thames and Hudson, 1974, pp. 54–56

Karouzou, Semne, *The Amasis Painter*, Oxford: Clarendon Press, 1956

Mommsen, H., "Amasis Mepoiesen: Beobachtungen zum Töpfer Amasis" in *Athenian Potters and Painters*, edited by John H. Oakley, William D.E. Coulson and Olga Palagia, Oxford: Oxbow, 1997

Papers on the Amasis Painter and His World, Malibu, California: Getty Museum, 1987

von Bothmer, Dietrich, *The Amasis Painter and His World: Vase-painting in Sixth-Century BC Athens*, Malibu, California: Getty Museum, and London: Thames and Hudson, 1985

Ambelakia

Town in Thessaly

The village of Ambelakia is situated in the prefecture of Larissa in Thessaly, on the northwest slopes of Mount Ossa (Kissavos), at a height of 390 m. Although it is now only a village with fewer than 500 inhabitants, it was prosperous during the Ottoman period (Tourkokratia) and it made an important contribution to modern Greek culture. It was particularly famous for its commercial development in the late 18th and early 19th centuries. As the name Ambelakia suggests, the surrounding region produces wine.

The establishment of the village of Ambelakia is generally dated to the beginning of the 16th century. There has been much debate, however, about whether the site was inhabited in ancient times, since according to 17th-century sources ancient coins and bronze statues of Heracles were found in the area. In the late 18th century a bronze statue of Heracles was given to Gregorios Konstantas, who was the director of Ambelakia's renowned school. In Byzantine times the region of Ambelakia may have belonged to the monastery of St Demetrios, ruins of which survive today on the eastern slopes of Mount Ossa. Ambelakia was never inhabited by Turks, and, until Thessaly was annexed to the modern Greek state in 1881, the population was exclusively Christian, although there were many Turkish inhabitants in the surrounding region. G. Kordatos maintains that during the Ottoman period Ambelakia, like many villages in Pelion and Epirus, belonged to the administrative category of *waqf* (pious endowment), and was not suppressed by the Ottomans. N. Vees and A. Vakalopoulos have argued that the first inhabitants of Ambelakia came from the village of Lykostomio when it was occupied by the Turks in the 14th century and that the people decided to move further up the mountain. A scholar from Ambelakia,

Ambelakia: the Schwartz house, built in 1787, now a museum

Leonardos, has suggested that there was a village even further north than Ambelakia, in the area of Paliochori.

The school of Greek letters, the Hellenomouseion, was established after 1723. In 1873 Diamantes Maniares contributed generously towards the construction of the famous Maniareios Scholi, which was equipped with the most modern science laboratories, gardens, and accommodation for the school's teachers. The building itself was remarkable for its architecture, but unfortunately collapsed in 1928. World War II dealt the final blow to the vivid intellectual and commercial life of the town, and what now remains is just a small village.

The first agricultural cooperative in Greece was established in Ambelakia, and thus the town became famous for its economic activity and for its role in European economic and social history. The French scholar Boulanger thought that the cooperative at Ambelakia was the first one in Europe and that the spirit of financial cooperation and the idea of building a strong capital economy out of the work of many was first born in Ambelakia. Marxist Greek scholars such as Kordatos have argued vehemently against this view. What is certain is that the cooperative organization between merchants, craftsmen, workers, and farmers established in Ambelakia proved beneficial for the town's cotton industry and intellectual life in the 18th and 19th centuries. Well-endowed libraries were built and the best scholars of the day were invited to teach at the local schools. Many eminent intellectuals of the Greek Enlightenment period – scholars such as Evgenios Voulgaris, Konstantinos Koumas, Gregorios Konstantas, Spyridon Asanes, Georgios Trikalinos, and even Rigas Velestinlis – were associated with the intellectual life of Ambelakia. At least two major works of the Greek Enlightenment were published with a generous subsidy from Ambelakia, *Geographia Neoteriki* (*Modern Geography*, 1791) by Daniel Philippides and Gregorios Konstantas, and *Lexikon tis Ellinikas Glossas* (*Dictionary of the Greek Language*, 3 vols, 1809–16) by Anthimos Gazes.

The town became well known abroad for its textile industry and had close trading contacts with businessmen in the great commercial centres of Europe. Its most important monuments are the church of St George with frescos and decorations carved in wood, and the Schwartz mansion. Georgios Mavros Schwartz was the president of the Ambelakia agricultural cooperative and his house was its headquarters. It was built in 1787 and was decorated with wall paintings and carved wooden ornamentation which are important examples of folk art. The mansion was purchased by the Greek state in the 1960s and now functions as a local folk museum open to the public. The inhabitants of Ambelakia also built the church of Hagia Paraskevi in Tempe in 1651.

ANDROMACHE KARANIKA-DIMAROGONA

Summary

A town in Thessaly on the northwest slopes of Mount Ossa, Ambelakia was probably founded in the 16th century and flourished during the Tourkokratia on the strength of its cotton industry. It was the first town in Greece to have an agricultural cooperative. It was also an intellectual centre for scholars of the Greek Enlightenment. It is now a small village.

Further Reading

Avramopoulos, M., *Ta Thessalika Ampelakia* [Thessalian Ambelakia], Thessalonica, 1961

Boulanger, François, *Ambélakia: ou, Les Associations et les municipalités helléniques, avec documents confirmatifs*, Paris, 1875; reprinted Athens, 1970

Kordatos, Gianes, *T'ampelakia ki o mythos gia to synetairismo tous* [Ambelakia and the Story of its Cooperative], Athens, 1973

Nikolopoulos, E., *Domes kai Thesmoi sten Tourkokratia: ta Ampelakia kai o koinonoikonomikos metaschematismos tou helladikou chorou* [Structures and Institutions under the Turkish Yoke: Changes in the Community Economy of the Greek Countryside], Athens, 1988

Prokovas, G., *Ampelakia: To likno tou sunetairismou* [Ambelakia: The Cradle of the Cooperative Movement], Athens, 1982

Amphipolis

City in Thrace

The Athenians and their allies under the general Hagnon, son of Nicias, founded Amphipolis in 437/36 BC on the site of the earlier Thracian city of Ennea Odoi ("Nine Ways"). According to Thucydides (4. 102) Hagnon named it Amphipolis because the river Strymon flowed on each side of the city. It was inhabited by a mixed Greek population, including many Ionian settlers from neighbouring cities, and controlled the rich Strymon basin and its hinterland.

Early in the Peloponnesian War (424 BC) it surrendered to the Spartan general Brasidas; two years later Cleon's unsuccessful expedition to recover it ended with his own death as well as Brasidas' in the battle of Amphipolis (422 BC). Although in the Peace of Nicias (421 BC) there was a special provision for Amphipolis's restoration to Athens, Athenian operations in the region, which did not cease until the time of Philip II of Macedon, indicate that the city was not totally under Athenian control.

The economy of Amphipolis did not depend solely on the rural population which cultivated the Strymon valley, but also on merchants and craftsmen. The city's prosperity is reflected in a lavish series of coins after the Peace of Nicias. Inscriptions provide information about the administrative organization of the city, and the ways in which it controlled trade and protected the life and property of its citizens through its institutions and special officials.

In 357 BC Philip II conquered Amphipolis and established a Macedonian garrison. The city became a royal mint as well as the base for Macedonian operations to the east of the Strymon. In 334 BC the fleet of Alexander the Great set sail on its Asiatic campaign from the harbour of Amphipolis. Moreover, the importance of the city at this period is indicated by Alexander's decision to make Amphipolis one of the six major cult centres of his empire – the others being Delos, Delphi, Dodona, Dion, and Kyrros – and to build a magnificent temple of Artemis Tauropolos, a plan which was never realized.

After Alexander's death his mother Olympias issued a decree by which the garrison of Amphipolis was given to Cassander. It was here that Alexander's wife Roxane and his son and heir Alexander IV were exiled. The strategic location of the city, commanding the bridge over the Strymon, and its

Amphipolis: the Lion monument, on the west side of river Strymon, dating from the 4th century BC

hinterland, rich in agricultural products, precious metals (gold and silver), and timber, ensured its prosperity into Hellenistic and Roman times and it became a strong military, economic, and cosmopolitan centre.

Although archaeological surveys in the area of Amphipolis were undertaken in the 19th century, it was not until 1956 that systematic excavations commenced, bringing important finds to light. A large part of the Classical city wall was revealed. Seven gates provided access to the city, while round towers in elevated positions along the wall controlled all movements on both the east and west banks of the river. The largest and strongest gate was the so-called Bridge Gate, mentioned by Thucydides (4. 103, 108) in connection with the battle between Cleon and Brasidas in 422 BC. The fortifications of the city underwent repeated repairs in Roman and Byzantine times.

In addition to the city walls, an inner fortification wall encircled the acropolis of Amphipolis, which was located on a hill at the most prominent part of the site. At the west end of the acropolis and inside its Classical enceinte, a house of the 4th century BC was excavated, indicating the existence of a Classical suburb in this area, which continued to be inhabited

in the Hellenistic period. Moreover, a Hellenistic house of the 2nd century BC with painted walls recalling the First Pompeian style was found in the south sector of Amphipolis.

The first large public building to be identified from epigraphic evidence was the gymnasium. It was located in the southeast sector of the city, between the inner and the outer walls, and next to a narrow water channel, indispensable to the function of the building. It was built by the Hellenistic period and remained in use until the early imperial period, when it was probably destroyed by a fire. An important inscription of the 1st century BC provides information about the education of youths, the society of Amphipolis, and its topography, mentioning an agora, workshops, a road network, and a theatre.

The cult of the king of Thrace, Rhesus, son of Eion and Cleio, already attested in Homer, is the earliest known cult at Amphipolis. In addition, there are sanctuaries of the muse Clio (first half of 4th century BC), of Attis, and a Thesmophorion or Nymphaeum (5th century BC) outside the north city wall, and an open-air structure with niches for the cult of Attis and Cybele, which became popular in Hellenistic and Roman times.

Classical and Hellenistic cemeteries have been discovered outside the city walls. Numerous graves of various types have yielded a vast quantity of grave offerings, such as gold jewellery, terracotta figurines, pottery, bronze objects, and grave stelae. An impressive example of burial sculpture of the 4th century BC is the Monument of the Lion, on the west side of the river Strymon. It was set up in honour of an Amphipolitan citizen, probably Laomedon, one of Alexander's admirals. Today it stands restored on a high podium at the spot where it was found.

After the battle of Pydna (168 BC) Amphipolis became the capital of one of the four administrative districts (*merides*) into which Macedonia was divided by the Romans in order to achieve the break-up of its political unity. Although in the mid-1st century BC Amphipolis suffered invasions by Thracian tribes, which resulted in the destruction of its buildings, both the ancient literary sources and the archaeological evidence reveal that the city flourished as a commercial and artistic centre as well as a mint down to the final years of the Roman empire. With the support of Roman emperors, especially Augustus and Hadrian, Amphipolis remained one of the most important urban centres in Macedonia, as is reflected in its monumental buildings with mosaic floors and mural paintings.

The importance and prosperity of Amphipolis, through which St Paul passed on his journey from Philippi to Thessalonica (AD 49/50), continued in early Christian times, largely because the Via Egnatia ran through the city. Amphipolis became the seat of a bishop and remained as such until AD 692. The discovery of a number of early Christian monuments on the ancient acropolis of Amphipolis – four basilicas with impressive polychrome mosaic floors, a large rectangular building, often identified as an episcopal palace, and a hexagonal church – demonstrates the importance of the city as an urban and religious centre in the early Christian period. The total area covered by Amphipolis in this period is not known with certainty, but the arrival of plague and the raids of the Slavs in the 7th century contributed to the city's decline, gradually resulting in its demise as an urban centre.

It is likely that the city was destroyed by the Slavs' attacks in the 8th or 9th century AD and many of its inhabitants resettled at the mouth of the river Strymon very close to the ancient Eion, where they established a new city on the harbour, named Chrysopolis. Large parts of the Byzantine fortification of the city, a small church, and other scattered structures are preserved. The name Amphipolis continued to be used by Byzantine authors. Furthermore, the site of the ancient city, known at this time as Popolia, retained its strategic importance until the end of the Byzantine empire, as is demonstrated by the fortifications and other activities in the region during the late Byzantine times. Two towers were built on either side of the Strymon, one of them erected in 1367 by two generals, the brothers Alexios and Ioannis, who were also the founders of the monastery of Pantocrator on Mount Athos. Both towers at Amphipolis were owned by the monasteries of Athos, and were probably used to store the agricultural produce of the monastic properties (*metochia*) in the area.

ELENI ZIMI

Summary

City in Thrace, first founded by the Athenians and their allies in 437/36 BC. Its strategic position, commanding the crossing of the Strymon, and its rich hinterland ensured its prosperity throughout antiquity. Its size and prosperity may have been reduced by the Slav invasions of the 7th century, but it remained the seat of a bishop until 692. The city was probably destroyed in the 8th or 9th century when its population was resettled near the mouth of the Strymon.

Further Reading

Broneer, Oscar, *The Lion Monument at Amphipholis*, Cambridge, Massachusetts: Harvard University Press, 1941

Lazaride, Kalliope, "To Gymnasio tis Amphipolis" [The Gymnasium of Amphipolis] in *Mnimi D. Lazaridi: Polis kai Chora stin Archaia Macedonia kai Thraki* [In Memory of D. Lazarides: City and Countryside in Ancient Macedonia and Thrace], Thessalonica, 1990

Lazarides, Dimitrios, *Amphipolis kai Argilos* [Amphipolis and Argilos], Athens, 1972

Lazarides, Dimitrios, "Les Fortifications d'Amphipolis" in *La Fortification dans l'histoire du monde grec*, Paris: CNRS, 1986

Lazarides, Dimitrios, *Amphipolis*, translated by David Hardy, Athens: Ministry of Culture Archaeological Research Fund, 1997

Zikos, Nikolaos, *Early Christian and Byzantine Amphipolis*, translated by William Phelps, Athens: Ministry of Culture Archaeological Research Fund, 1989

Anastasios of Sinai, St

Theologian of the 7th century

The life of this priest-monk is virtually unknown, but he lived in turbulent times. His writings give us a fascinating insight into the world of the Christian Near East at a time when the Monophysite and Monothelite controversies were still raging, and when it had recently been subject to the traumas of the Islamic conquest.

Anastasios travelled widely in Egypt and Syria to refute Monophysites of various types; he was attacking them in Alexandria before 642. His arguments were crystallized in his *Hodegos* or *Guide*. His stance is resolutely Chalcedonian but

also exhibits great tact and diplomacy, for example in his recommendation that only pre-Chalcedonian authorities should be used in discussions with the Monophysites. He claims to detect the source of Monophysitism in the categories of Aristotle. Other works include *Two Sermons on the "According to the Image"*, against the Monophysites; a work *Against the Monothelites*; a work *On the Holy Synaxis*; a treatise on the *Hexaemeron*, of which only the last book of 12 survives, and the famous *Questions and Answers*.

The *Questions and Answers*, in the form in which we have them, are certainly not the work of Anastasios. The substance is definitely Anastasian, but has been added to and reworked with great liberty by a later writer, or writers. The work of disengaging the Anastasian from the pseudo-Anastasian content is still in progress. This summary therefore can be only tentative. The question–answer format has a long pedigree: it is found, for instance, in St Basil the Great, the pseudo-Macarius, and in the monks of Gaza, Barsanuphios and John. Anastasios shows a keen understanding of the difficulties of Christian life under Islamic occupation, allowing, for example, that in the absence of an ordained confessor an act of contrition will suffice. He declares: "Each man's conscience is the norm for the reception of the holy mysteries." The difficulties of the post-conquest established Church may have led him to stress the inner life of the Christian. Speaking of the indwelling of God, he asserts that when the soul has become a temple and a dwelling place of God, it loses all desire for churches that have been built, and for the sacraments performed in them – a very audacious statement, but perhaps encouraging for those unable to attend church. His *On the Holy Synaxis* shows that he had no antipathy against the established Church as such, but was appalled by the slovenly attitude of the congregations. He is particularly critical of those who turn up just in time for communion! He also deals with a host of other questions, concerning mixed marriages, money matters, and many other basic pastoral issues: can one, for example, take communion after accidentally swallowing water?

Anastasios was an original, lively, and highly engaging thinker; this becomes increasingly clear as the later accretions to his work are cleared away. He discusses the nature of the soul, the question of chance, the utility of prayer for the dead, the fate of children who die unbaptized, and the salvation of non-Christians. He stresses the common monotheism of Christians and Muslims, but was horrified at the desolation caused by the Islamic conquest. He has no time for the argument that the conquest occurred at the command of God: how could God, Anastasios asks, have urged the profanation of his own body and blood?

In the *Questions and Answers* frequent appeal is made to scripture and patristic witnesses, with citations from, for example, St Basil the Great, St Gregory of Nyssa, St Cyril of Jerusalem, St John Chrysostom, Mark the Monk, and St Maximos the Confessor. His edited dogmatic works reveal a staggeringly extensive range of sources. They confirm the impression given in the *Questions and Answers* that Anastasios was both an original and a deeply traditional thinker. Besides an almost exhaustive appeal to the Fathers, he also demonstrates a familiarity with the works of Aristotle and the Platonic tradition. While continuing to enjoy great authority in the Church, the works of Anastasios deserve to be far better known than they are at present. Among his works is a story that perfectly sums up his own generous attitude to the Hellenic tradition. A certain scholar was constantly cursing Plato, until one night Plato himself appeared to him in a dream saying: "Man, stop cursing me: for you are only hurting yourself. I do not deny that I was a sinful man: but when the Christ came down into hell, truly no one believed in him before I did."

MARCUS PLESTED

Biography

Almost nothing is known of the life of this 7th-century theologian. He attacked the Monophysites of Alexandria around 640 and was a monk of Sinai by 700. His works include the *Hodegos* (*Guide*) and *Two Sermons on the "According to the Image"*, both against Monophysitism; *Against the Monothelites*; *On the Holy Synaxis*; a treatise on the *Hexaemeron*; and the *Questions and Answers*.

Writings

Hodegos/Guide: *Viae Dux*, edited by Karl-Heinz Uthemann, Turnhout: Brepols, 1981 (Corpus Christianorum, Series Graeca 8)
Two Sermons: *Sermones duo in constitutionem hominis secundum imaginem Dei*, edited by Karl-Heinz Uthemann, Turnhout: Brepols, 1985 (Corpus Christianorum, Series Graeca 12)
Questions and Answers, edited by M. Richard and J.A. Munitiz, Turnhout: Brepols, forthcoming (Corpus Christianorum, Series Graeca)

Anatolia

In geographical terms Anatolia (otherwise Asia Minor) occupies the territory of Turkey between the Aegean Sea and the Euphrates river. The western and southern coastal areas were part of the Mediterranean world. In the Graeco-Roman period several regions existed within Anatolia, corresponding to separate languages, cultures, and religious beliefs: Bithynia, Cilicia, Cappadocia, Galatia, Paphlagonia, and Pontus.

Anatolia has always been a crossroads of different peoples and cultures, and it was dominated at different times by different political and cultural entities. The Hittite empire was the major power in Anatolia in the Late Bronze Age but its collapse in c.1200 BC allowed new cultures to rise. At the beginning of the Iron Age neo-Hittite states were established in the southeast, and at the turn of the 9th century BC the Urartians emerged as a leading power in the east and northeast of the region. Both the Hittites and Urartians frequently clashed with their Assyrian neighbours. However, political difficulties in Anatolia never prevented close cultural contacts and the exchange of artistic ideas.

Greeks from mainland Greece started to settle the western shores of Anatolia and the offshore islands from about the 11th century BC onwards. Aeolians founded cities between the Troad and the gulf of Smyrna; the Dorians established six major cities in Caria and on the islands of Rhodes and Cos. The Ionians, who arrived in much greater numbers than either of these, established themselves between the two. The culture created together by these three peoples is known as East Greek. The 12 Ionian cities – Chios, Samos, Phocaea, Clazomenae, Erythrae, Teos, Lebedos, Colophon, Ephesus, Priene, Myus,

and Miletus – were much the most advanced. Smyrna, in the north of Ionia, was in origin an Aeolian town, but at an early date it was captured by Ionians from Colophon.

In the 8th century BC the situation in Anatolia changed once again. The Phrygians emerged as a major political power, with their capital at Gordion. Relations between Phrygians and Greeks were close. Already in the 8th century BC the Phrygian king Midas was married to the daughter of Agamemnon, the king of Aeolian Cyme. This Midas was most probably the same one who sent a dedication (a throne) to the Greek sanctuary in Delphi. Decoration on some Greek pottery, bronze fibulae, cauldrons, bronze belts, etc. demonstrates Phrygian influence on Greek culture as early as the 8th century BC. Phrygia lost its dominant position after the Cimmerian raids of c.696 BC and became part of the Lydian empire, the dominant power from the mid-7th century BC having its capital at Sardis. The Ionian contribution to the creation of Lydian culture is witnessed in dress and in architecture (columns and relief panels). In Lydia and Phrygia buildings were decorated and protected by clay relief revetments, often decorated in a Greek style and depicting Greek mythological scenes. At the same time, Greeks took to worshipping the Anatolian goddess whom they knew as Cybele. Lydian rulers were hostile to Ionian and other cities. Alyattes destroyed Smyrna; Croesus subdued others but sent gifts to the temples in Delphi and Ephesus. This was a time when very close cultural links were forged between Lydia and the Ionians, bringing Graeco-Lydian art into existence. Lydian court life was more Greek than oriental in its physical aspects.

The Lydians were conquered by the Persians in 547/46 BC. For the next two centuries, until the conquests of Alexander the Great in 334 BC, this new Persian empire held mastery over Anatolia and the whole of the Near East, including the Greek cities of Anatolia. Many Ionians fled Persian conquest to establish colonies in the west and the east (around the Black Sea). Indeed the creation of Ionian colonies was already under way from the second half of the 7th century BC when Lydian pressure started to make itself felt.

Achaemenid art is a unique phenomenon. Monarchs started to create a court culture, bringing together artists from all corners of their huge domains. These artists, architects, and masons were employed by the king and executed work according to his tastes and wishes. During the construction of the palace in Susa, Darius recorded details of the programme of work: the ornamentation of the walls was brought from Ionia; the captives who worked the stone were Ionians and Sardians; Sardians and Egyptians collaborated on the woodwork; Babylonians on the brickwork; Medes and Egyptians on the decoration of walls and on goldsmiths' work. The sources of the materials used are also given: gold came from Sardis and Bactria; lapis lazuli and cornelian from Sogdiana; turquoise from Chorasmia; silver, ebony, and copper from Egypt; ivory from Ethiopia, India, and Arachosia; cedars of Lebanon were carried to Babylon by Assyrians, and thence to Susa by Carians and Ionians. The Ionian contribution to Achaemenid royal culture was considerable. Although Persian buildings, designed more for effect and ceremonial than for living, were inspired by Mesopotamia, masons were brought from Ionia and Lydia. Greek architectural orders and techniques were introduced to Persia. Nearly all the buildings at Pasargadae were built by

Ionians. Persian sculpture reveals Greek influence and practice in the treatment of drapery; seals show Greek craftsmanship, as do the wall paintings from Gordion. The tomb monuments at Xanthus are decorated with stone reliefs executed in Ionian style.

The Persian empire was divided into provinces (satrapies). Usually, each conquered country formed a separate satrapy, sometimes with a local family as nominal rulers. The provincial capitals housed a Persian civil service and garrison. The king introduced a system of gift-giving and *tributari*.

The Ionian Greeks were supported by Athenians in their revolt of 499 BC. This led to Persian–Athenian conflict. In 492 BC Darius sent a force against northern Greece and in 490 BC to central Greece. Ten years later Xerxes marched against Greece and sacked Athens. By the mid-5th century BC the Greek cities of the eastern Aegean were free, under the hegemony of Athens. After the Persian Wars many Persian ideas filtered through to Athens. Persian metalwork had considerable influence on Athenian pottery – rhyton (drinking-horn) cups are an example. The same can be seen in Greek seals, where the Graeco-Persian style flourished in Anatolia, reaching mainland Greece and spreading throughout the Greek colonial world.

Alexander the Great put an end to the Achaemenid empire. He burned Persepolis and liberated Greeks, including artists and intellectuals who had been persecuted by the Persians. The establishment of Hellenistic kingdoms on the ruins of the Persian empire opened the way to further penetration by and of Greek culture. Greeks followed Alexander the Great to Anatolia and the Near East, establishing new cities and new cultural centres, but at the same time absorbing features of local cultures to create new and cosmopolitan traditions.

The Hellenistic period in Anatolia brought fresh military difficulties. In 302 BC Lysimachus, a Macedonian from Pella, invaded Asia Minor, fought against Antigonus, and secured victory for Seleucus in the battle of Ipsus (301 BC). Most of Asia Minor passed to him, and he proved a financially rapacious ruler until his defeat by Seleucus in 281 BC. Thereafter the region was in the hands of the Seleucids who, from the outset, continued Achaemenid institutional practice in the army and administration and in their colonizing policies. One of their capitals was at Sardis. By the peace of Apamea, negotiated between Antiochus III and Rome in 188 BC, the Seleucids relinquished their possessions north of the Taurus mountains, retaining Pamphylia and Cilicia.

The Mithridates family ruled Pontus from 302 BC. Mithridates IV established good relations with Cappadocia and Rome (whose ally, Pergamum, he helped in a war against Bithynia). His successor invaded Phrygia and Cappadocia, maintained friendly relations with Greece, and was honoured as a benefactor of Athens and Delos. Mithridates VI Eupator was the most famous king of Pontus, and Rome's most dangerous enemy in the 1st century BC. He conquered the whole of the Black Sea and annexed Bithynia and Cappadocia. During the First Mithridatic War against Rome (89–85 BC) in Asia his army swept all before it, and he ordered the massacre of Romans and Italians living there. He was welcomed in Athens and won over most of Greece, but the Roman response under Sulla (87 BC) brought him defeat; Athens was captured,

and the war taken to Asia. Peace was arranged and Mithridates lived to fight another day: to further defeat in the Third Mithridatic War in 63 BC and an assisted suicide at the sword of a bodyguard when his son revolted against him prior to further alleged foreign exploits.

The culture of Hellenistic Anatolia flourished. Troy IX was a Hellenistic city furnished with temples, theatre, odeum, *bouleuterion* (council chamber) etc. Pergamum was a very important city, to the safety of whose fortress Alexander the Great's successor Lysimachus entrusted part of his treasure – 9000 talents. During the reign of Attalus I Pergamum became a wealthy and powerful state and the city a worthy royal capital. Its ruler could indulge in patronage of the arts, literature, and philosophy, and gain prestige and pleasure with his horses and chariots at Olympia and other Greek centres. Under Eumenes II the city achieved architectural eminence: the defended area of the acropolis was enlarged so as to contain a further large gymnasium and a second agora, the acropolis itself was built up on a series of grand arched terraces, and an advanced high-pressure water system put in place. The best possible use was made of the natural shape of the land to provide a dazzling backcloth to the expanding city below. The royal palace, barracks, and arsenal crowned the summit; lower down a library, second only to Alexandria's, overlooked the temple of Athena; on a lower level stood an altar to Zeus, 12 m high, which provided a rich opportunity for the local school of sculpture to portray the fight of the gods against the giants; still lower were the agora, and then a great terrace on arches, built into the rock, from which the theatre climbed up the hillside. In 130 BC the last member of the Attalid dynasty bequeathed this prosperous state to Rome and it became part of the province of Asia.

Ephesus and Miletus reverted to being centres of Hellenic culture in Asia Minor once they had recovered from Persian rule. Alexander the Great rebuilt Miletus. The temple of Artemis at Ephesus and the new marble temple of Apollo in Didyma were among the most impressive buildings anywhere in the Greek world.

Roman Asia, the jewel of the empire, comprised the territories of Mysia, Lydia, Pisidia, and Phrygia (Rhodes was added subsequently) along the western coast of Asia Minor. It was stable (the borders remained largely unchanged until the late 3rd century AD) and prosperous, and Hellenic influence remained strong. From 27 BC the province was under the authority of the Senate, administered by a proconsul based in either Pergamum or Ephesus. Administration varied from area to area, and many of the cities that had enjoyed a fair measure of autonomy under the Attalids retained it, despite their inclusion in the province. The province's economic strength was due mainly to its position astride the east–west trade routes, and that strength attracted migrants. Ports such as Smyrna, Miletus, and Rhodes flourished on the trade of foreign vessels passing through, and the cities invested their wealth in their own beautification. Greek notions of self-determination persisted in the cities, an echo of the polis. Schools of philosophy, education, and medicine functioned in Smyrna, Ephesus, and Pergamum; and Pergamum emerged as a centre for eastern deities such as Asclepius. The acceptance of older eastern gods and the toleration of newer ones was another visible link to the absorbent nature of Greek civilization. This was the Roman province in which Christianity (initially, another cultural import assimilated from the east) and the early Church prospered.

With the foundation of Constantinople in AD 330, the division of the Roman empire, and the mutation of the eastern empire into the Byzantine, Anatolia became a cornerstone of this new Greek, Christian polity. As Byzantine power waxed and waned, so did the extent of its control over Anatolia (in opposition to Arabs and, subsequently and fatally, Turks). The Seljuk Turks' crushing defeat of the Byzantine army in Armenia in 1071 paved the way for the loss of control over most of Asia Minor. The Latin west was called to aid the Greek east, and the Crusades provided temporary relief for the Byzantines. Alas it was to be the Fourth Crusade of 1204 which captured and sacked Constantinople, splintered the Byzantine empire, and created a pale Latin imitation in its place (for less than 60 years in a portion of its territory). The reintegrated but reduced Byzantine empire had soon to face the Ottoman Turks, who captured Bithynia in 1339 and seized Adrianople in 1362. Constantinople itself fell, finally, in 1453. The Greek empire of Trebizond, far to the east on the Black Sea, one of the splinters resulting from the events of 1204, and ruled by the Grand Komnenoi, remnants of the penultimate Byzantine dynasty, fell a mere eight years later.

The Byzantine empire was the centre of Greek Orthodox culture for a millennium, and that culture permeated throughout all its regions and beyond. Christian ideology and norms, as well as church architecture, painting, illuminated writings, etc., created in Constantinople, were adopted, copied, and adapted throughout the Orthodox world. Hagia Sophia formed the great inspiration for architects. One of the finest examples of Byzantine church architecture was St John's in Seljuk, on the Aegean coast of Turkey: it is built to a cruciform plan, with a broad nave, chancel, and transepts, many cupolas, marble facings to the wall, and richly carved capitals. Above it rises the citadel, on the site of a Byzantine fort. Halicarnassus was a bishopric of Byzantine Caria. The southern shore of Turkey is particularly rich in Byzantine churches. Patara and its bishopric have been important since the 6th century. Recent excavation at Sinope has yielded remains of another Byzantine church with fine mosaics. In Trebizond stand the 14th-century church of St Eugenius, the coronation church of the Panagia Chrysokephalos, and its own, rich Hagia Sophia, noted for its murals; within 50 km, amid fortresses, churches, and deserted villages, are three spectacular cave-monasteries – the Panagia Soumela, St George Peristera, and St John the Forerunner Vazelon. The well-known monastery of Soumela continued to flourish under the Ottomans. Many churches – including the basilica in Dag Pazari – contain impressive mosaics, and many rock churches contain murals.

GOCHA R. TSETSKHLADZE

Summary

Geographically Anatolia is the land between the Aegean and the Euphrates river, comprising most of modern-day Turkey. Greeks settled on its western shores from the 11th century BC. From the mid-6th to the mid-4th centuries BC it was part of the Persian empire. It was conquered by Alexander in 334 BC and flourished. Called Asia

by the Romans, it remained culturally Greek and formed the heart of the Byzantine empire until lost to the Turks between the 11th and 15th centuries.

Further Reading

Akurgal, Ekrem, *Ancient Civilizations and Ruins of Turkey*, 7th edition, Istanbul: NET Turistik Yayinlar, 1990

Boardman, John, *The Diffusion of Classical Art in Antiquity*, London: Thames and Hudson, and Princeton, New Jersey: Princeton University Press, 1994

Boardman, John, *The Greeks Overseas: Their Early Colonies and Trade*, 4th edition, London and New York: Thames and Hudson, 1999

Brewster, Harry, *Classical Anatolia: The Glory of Hellenism*, London and New York: Tauris, 1993

Bryer, Anthony and David Winfield, *The Byzantine Monuments and Topography of the Pontos*, Washington, D.C.: Dumbarton Oaks, 1985

Burn, A.R., *Persia and the Greeks: The Defence of the West, c.546–478 BC*, 2nd edition, London: Duckworth, and Stanford, California: Stanford University Press, 1984

Cohen, Getzel, *The Hellenistic Settlements in Europe, the Islands, and Asia Minor*, Berkeley: University of California Press, 1995

Cook, J.M., *The Greeks in Ionia and the East*, London: Thames and Hudson, 1962; New York: Praeger, 1963

Cook, J.M., *The Persian Empire*, London: Dent, and New York: Schocken, 1983

Foss, Clive, *History and Archaeology of Byzantine Asia Minor*, Aldershot, Hampshire: Variorum, 1990

Jones, A.H.M., *The Cities of the Eastern Roman Provinces*, Oxford: Clarendon Press, 1937; revised by Michael Avi-Yonah *et al.*, 1971

Lloyd, Seton, *Ancient Turkey: A Traveller's History of Anatolia*, Berkeley: University of California Press, 1989

McGing, B.C., *The Foreign Policy of Mithridates VI Eupator, King of Pontus*, Leiden: Brill, 1986

Matthews, R. (editor), *Ancient Anatolia*, Ankara: British Institute of Archaeology at Ankara, 1998

Mitchell, Stephen, *Anatolia: Land, Men, and Gods in Asia Minor*, 2 vols, Oxford: Clarendon Press, and New York: Oxford University Press, 1993

Olmstead, A.T., *History of the Persian Empire: Achaemenid Period*, Chicago: University of Chicago Press, 1948

Porada, Edith, *The Art of Ancient Iran: Pre-Islamic Cultures*, New York: Crown, 1965

Syme, Ronald, *Anatolica: Studies in Strabo*, Oxford: Clarendon Press, 1995

Anatomy and Physiology

Repeated observations of human victims of warfare and accidents, and likewise of animal victims of hunting and sacrifice, probably underlie the remarkable familiarity with gross anatomy displayed in Greek literature from the *Iliad* to the early 5th century BC. Many Homeric descriptions of woundings bear witness to a precise knowledge of vulnerable points in the torso, notably of the anatomical disposition of the principal organs and bones, and of the likely consequences of lesions to each.

Only with the systematic use of dissection did Greek anatomical knowledge advance substantially beyond the level reflected in Homeric epic. A controversial passage in a 4th-century AD commentary on Plato's *Timaeus* claims that Alcmaeon of Croton (5th century BC) first dared to cut out the eye and discovered its communication with the brain. Along with reports that Alcmaeon knew of the nasal passages and of certain features of the vascular system, this has led some modern scholars to conclude that Alcmaeon was the first to dissect animals for scientific purposes. Similar claims have been made for Democritus. There is, however, no conclusive evidence to support such inferences. Although several Presocratics displayed a keen interest in anatomical structures and in physiological processes such as perception, respiration, and reproduction, they clearly lacked close familiarity with the physical appearance and configuration of the internal structures they describe. According to Diogenes of Apollonia's extensive description (preserved by Aristotle) of the vascular system, for example, two independent networks of vessels (*phlebes*) are distributed throughout the body, one originating in the liver and serving the right side of the body, the other originating in the spleen and serving the left. The bilateral symmetry displayed by the external structure of the body here is apparently assumed to have an internal counterpart.

Hippocratic writings offer many anatomical observations (e.g. *On Places in a Human Being*, *On Fleshes*, *On Fractures*, *On Joints*, *Epidemics*, the pastiche known as *On the Nature of Bones*, and the Hellenistic treatise *On the Heart*). But no systematic Hippocratic treatment of anatomy as such is extant; a 27-line work of disputed date, *On Anatomy* – the shortest text in the vast Hippocratic Corpus – merely enumerates major internal parts of the human torso and summarizes their configuration. Diocles of Carystus, to whom Galen attributes the earliest treatise on anatomy, may have observed the womb in dissected mules, but there is no convincing evidence that he dissected human cadavers.

Aristotle, who occasionally refers to his lost work *Dissections* (*Anatomai*), dissected and vivisected various animals in the course of extensive zoological investigations that covered the lives, reproductive activities, and structures of well over 500 genera. He frequently referred to the human body, too, providing detailed observations on the vascular system and the internal topography of the body, particularly in his *History of Animals*. He acknowledged, however, that he relied on animal anatomy to make inferences about human anatomy and physiology (e.g. *History of Animals*, 1. 16. 494b21–4) and, like Empedocles and others, he made the heart, not the head or the brain, the centre of cognitive activity (whereas Alcmaeon, Democritus, Diogenes, the Hippocratic author of *On Sacred Disease*, and Plato had recognized the central role of the brain).

Spectacular advances in anatomical knowledge were made in the early 3rd century BC, when Herophilus and Erasistratus became the first – and apparently the last – ancient physicians to conduct systematic dissections of human cadavers. According to credible ancient sources they also performed vivisectory experiments on humans, probably on condemned criminals handed over to them by kings in the name of future benefits for all of humanity (Celsus, *Medicina*, proem. 23–26). Their discovery of the nerves, the four coats of the eye, the ventricles of the brain, the ventricles of the heart, the heart valves, the ovaries, numerous vascular structures, etc. had an enduring impact on the history of European anatomy and physiology. Herophilus and Erasistratus attempted not only to describe parts of the body but also to account for their func-

tions on the basis of dissection and vivisectory experiments. They diligently explored respiration, digestion, the pulse, reproduction, and sensory and muscular activity.

Not all ancient physicians agreed, however, that physiological explanations, even if discovered or confirmed by dissections, are necessary to clinical efficacy. The Hellenistic Empiricist "school" by and large rejected physiological investigation and systematic dissection, claiming that the accumulation and transmission of clinical observations, notably of observed instances of successful treatments (even when the success remained unexplained) generally sufficed. Numerous later rival physiological and anatomical treatises, some known mainly through Galen, bear witness, however, to the continuing importance of anatomy and physiology. Though advocating divergent doctrines, Asclepiades of Bithynia, Archigenes, Soranus, and Rufus of Ephesus presented wide-ranging physiological theories based on anatomical beliefs. Furthermore, extensive dissections of animals were conducted in the 2nd century by Marinus, Quintus of Rome, Satyrus, Numisianus, Pelops, and Galen.

Ancient Greek anatomy and physiology culminated in Galen, whose authority went virtually unchallenged for more than a millennium. Aware of the remarkable scientific results which Herophilus and Erasistratus had achieved by means of human dissection, Galen at times wistfully conceded that their access to human cadavers had enabled them to make observations which eluded him, even though his repeated, meticulous dissections of – and vivisectory experiments on – apes, monkeys, pigs, goats, oxen, sheep, mules, horses, donkeys, mice, and other animals allowed him to correct the accounts of many predecessors. To some extent Galen's anatomy is characterized by the superimposition of the soft parts of apes upon the human skeleton, despite his frequent insistence that a dissecting physician should try to choose animals that most closely resemble human beings. He presented his anatomy most fully in his monumental *On Anatomical Procedures* 1–15 (of which more than six books are extant only in a 9th-century Arabic translation). Several shorter anatomical treatises also survive (e.g. *Anatomy of the Womb*, *Anatomy of the Nerves*, *Anatomy of Arteries and Veins*, and *Anatomy of Muscles*).

Galen insisted that anatomy is a prelude not only to surgery but also to physiology. His comprehensive commitment to a teleological explanation of every structure, part, activity, and susceptibility of the body is visible throughout his voluminous anatomical and physiological writings. He fused his expropriations of the theories of several precursors into a coherent teleological model, in which all major physiological activities – respiration, digestion, heartbeat and pulsation, sensation and perception, voluntary and involuntary movement, locomotion, reproduction – are interdependent and interactive. He adapted the four-humour theory of the Hippocratic author of *On the Nature of a Human Being*, introducing more systematic, elaborate correlations between the primary qualities (hot, cold, wet, dry), the elements (earth, air, fire, water), the humours, the four seasons, character types or "constitutions", and stages of life. Inspired by the Platonic theory of a tripartite soul, Galen argued that there are three souls ruling yet serving the body, each manifesting itself through a distinctive faculty (*dynamis*, i.e. a power to act or to be acted upon). In the brain resides the "psychic faculty" which, presiding over reason and thought, renders sensation, perception, and voluntary motion possible. In the heart resides the "vital faculty", responsible *inter alia* for our emotions. And in the liver dwells the "natural faculty" responsible for nutrition. In *On Natural Faculties*, which Galen recommended to his readers as a sequel to *On Anatomical Procedures*, he added subsidiary faculties, including the "attractive faculty" (e.g. to explain how all parts of the body "attract" nutriment from the blood), the "retentive faculty" to explain how substances can remain in any given place within the body, the "alterative faculty" (e.g. to account for the conversion of food into blood), the "expulsive faculty" to explain secretions and excretions, etc.

A further central feature of Galen's physiology is his theory of innate heat. A flame of life inside the body, innate heat needs air to sustain itself while being tempered continuously by cooler, freshly inhaled air. Some Hippocratics (e.g. *On Fleshes*, 2) and Plato had recognized that bodily heat is essential to life, but for this feature of his physiology Galen seems most indebted to Aristotle. Against those who claimed that the body upon birth acquires heat from without (e.g. Praxagoras, Erasistratus), Galen endorsed the view of Aristotle and the Pneumatists, arguing that we are born with this natural heat, which is the first instrument of the soul. He further agreed with Aristotle that the innate heat is purest and most intense in the heart, and he added that the arteries distribute heat (along with blood and *pneuma* (breath), as Herophilus had claimed) throughout the body.

From Herophilus, Galen also took over the distinction between sensory and motor nerves, and from Erasistratus – against whom Galen wrote more than one fiercely polemical treatise – the influential distinction between "psychic *pneuma*" (in the nerves) and "vital *pneuma*" (in the arteries). According to Galen, the spongy flesh of the lungs acts upon the air we inhale, converting it into a subtler product, *pneuma*. This refined breath passes through very fine "pores" into branches of the pulmonary vein (or "venous artery", in Galen's conception) and thence is "attracted", with blood, by the attractive faculty into the left ventricle of the heart, where it encounters more hot blood and becomes metamorphosed into life-giving, i.e. "vital" *pneuma*. When this cardiac ventricle contracts, blood charged with vital *pneuma* is "attracted" into the aorta and thence into the entire arterial network. After the carotid arteries have distributed vital *pneuma* to the brain, the brain transforms it into "psychic *pneuma*", in part by using air drawn into the cerebral ventricles by way of the nostrils and channels extended into the olfactory bulbs. From the brain psychic *pneuma* – subdivided into sensory and kinetic *pneuma* – flows through imperceptible ducts inside the sensory and motor nerves, enabling sensation and voluntary muscle movements. Medieval Galenists described a third kind of *pneuma*: "natural *pneuma*" produced in the liver, transported through the veins, and functioning as the instrument of the "vegetative" soul. In the vast corpus of Galen's extant texts there is, however, only a single, hypothetical allusion to "natural pneuma" (*Method of Healing*, 12. 5).

Perhaps nowhere is Galen's commitment to teleology expressed more emphatically than in his discussion of reproduction in his major physiological treatise *On the Usefulness of the Parts* (books 14–15), in which he once again fuses the views of many predecessors, even as he criticizes them. With "astonishing skill" Nature has done all she could to make her mortal work – the human body – immortal through reproduction, endowing humans with perfect anatomical instruments for conception, a faculty joined to these instruments to produce pleasure, and a "vegetative soul" that has an irrepressible desire to use the instruments of conception. Being essential to human reproduction, gender-specific anatomical features display Nature's amazing providence: the uterus is bicameral, its hotter right chamber being for the conception and gestation of males, and the colder left chamber for female offspring. To traditional polarities used at least since the Presocratics and Hippocratics to distinguish between female and male – left–right, colder–hotter, weaker–stronger, less perfect and more perfect – Galen added the influential polarity introverted–extroverted: because the female foetus develops in the colder left womb, her generative parts remain inside her body, whereas the male, developing more fully in the hotter right uterus, has extroverted reproductive parts. In support of these in part archaic polarities Galen mustered the formidable weaponry of his meticulous dissections, of his elaborate physiological system, and of his all-encompassing teleology, thereby rendering the old anatomy and physiology scientifically rejuvenated.

Many currents of pre-Galenic anatomy and physiology thus were appropriated and selectively transformed by Galen into an authoritative new medical system which, by and large, was not superseded in Europe and the Near East until the early modern period. Byzantine writers excerpted, paraphrased, and adapted his works on anatomy and physiology, while scholars in Baghdad translated them into Syriac and Arabic, especially in the 9th century, thus ensuring that Galen's views became the almost undisputed norm until systematic human dissection was resumed in the early Renaissance.

HEINRICH VON STADEN

See also Health, Medicine

Further Reading

Craik, E.M., "The Hippocratic Treatise *On Anatomy*", *Classical Quarterly*, New Series 48 (1998): pp. 135–67

Cunningham, Andrew, *The Anatomical Renaissance: The Resurrection of the Anatomical Projects of the Ancients*, Aldershot, Hampshire: Scolar Press, 1997

Edelstein, Ludwig, *Ancient Medicine: Selected Papers of Ludwig Edelstein*, edited by Owsei Temkin and C. Lilian Temkin, Baltimore: Johns Hopkins University Press, 1967, pp. 247–301

Galen, *On the Natural Faculties*, translated by Arthur John Brock, Cambridge, Massachusetts: Harvard University Press, and London: Heinemann, 1916 (Loeb edition)

Galen, *On Anatomical Procedures*, translated by Charles Singer, London and New York: Oxford University Press, 1956 (books 1–9)

Galen, *On Anatomical Procedures: The Later Books*, translated by W.C.H. Duckworth, edited by M.C. Lyons and B. Towers, Cambridge: Cambridge University Press, 1962 (books 9–15)

Galen, *On the Usefulness of the Parts of the Body*, edited and translated by Margaret Tallmadge May, 2 vols, Ithaca, New York: Cornell University Press, 1968

Galen, *On Respiration and the Arteries*, edited and translated by David J. Furley and J.S. Wilkie, Princeton, New Jersey: Princeton University Press, 1984 (four shorter physiological treatises)

Galen, *Selected Works*, translated and edited by P.N. Singer, Oxford and New York: Oxford University Press, 1997 (15 treatises, several on physiology)

Harris, C.R.S., *The Heart and the Vascular System in Ancient Greek Medicine, from Alcmaeon to Galen*, Oxford: Clarendon Press, 1973

Laser, Siegfried, *Medizin und Körperpflege*, Göttingen: Vandenhoeck & Ruprecht, 1983 (excellent analysis of Homeric "anatomical" and "physiological" views, especially pp. 2–62)

Lloyd, G.E.R. (editor), *Hippocratic Writings*, Harmondsworth and New York: Penguin, 1978 (17 Hippocratic treatises)

Lloyd, G.E.R., *Science, Folklore and Ideology: Studies in the Life Sciences in Ancient Greece*, Cambridge and New York: Cambridge University Press, 1983, especially parts 2 and 3.4–5

Lloyd, G.E.R., *Methods and Problems in Greek Science*, Cambridge and New York: Cambridge University Press, 1991, chapters 8 and 10

Onians, Richard Broxton, *The Origins of European Thought about the Body, the Mind, the Soul, the World, Time and Fate*, 2nd edition, Cambridge: Cambridge University Press, 1954

Temkin, Owsei, *Galenism: Rise and Decline of a Medical Philosophy*, Ithaca, New York: Cornell University Press, 1973

von Staden, Heinrich, *Herophilus: The Art of Medicine in Early Alexandria*, Cambridge and New York: Cambridge University Press, 1989, especially chapters 6–7

von Staden, Heinrich, "Anatomy as Rhetoric: Galen on Dissection and Persuasion", *Journal of the History of Medicine and Allied Sciences*, 50 (1995): pp. 47–66

von Staden, Heinrich, "Teleology and Mechanism: Aristotelian Biology and Early Hellenistic Medicine" in *Aristotelische Biologie*, edited by Wolfgang Kullmann and Sabine Föllinger, Stuttgart: Steiner, 1997

Anaxagoras *c.*500–428 BC

Philosopher

Anaxagoras was born in the Ionian city of Clazomenae. After establishing himself as a philosopher there, perhaps by giving lectures or classes, he seems to have come to the attention of Themistocles, who invited him to Athens, where he lived from some time after 470 BC until he was exiled in the late 430s BC. His expulsion was due partly to his friendship with Pericles, and partly to his scientific views, which took no account of the traditional gods in explaining the nature of the heavens. He spent his last few years in Lampsacus.

Although several works are ascribed to him, he probably wrote only one, but it may well have undergone revisions during the course of his stay in Athens. The fame of this book was guaranteed by the reference to it in Plato's *Apology*, where Socrates says that it can be bought in the Agora for a drachma. Elsewhere in Plato's dialogues, most notably in the *Phaedo*, Socrates says that he was disappointed when he read it because Anaxagoras explains everything, including the nature of man, with a reference to what today we would call its chemical make-up, which in turn is governed by *nous*. This is the force that first set the universe in motion and which still determines the mechanism of our changing universe, from the large-scale phenomena of the heavens to (borrowing a term from modern physics that derives from the atomists contemporary with Anaxagoras) the subatomic arrangement of every object; *nous* is often translated as "mind" or "intelligence", and reasonably

so, given Plato's punning on the "mindlessness" of Anaxagoras' use of this word. As is clear from Socrates' several attempts to distance himself from Anaxagoras, as well as from Aristophanes' broad satire of Socrates in the *Clouds*, Anaxagoras' contemporaries understood his *nous* either as a new divinity to rival Zeus in his stewardship of the heavens or as a mechanistic (and hence atheistic) cosmic principle. Since Anaxagoras thought that *nous* was present only in some things, presumably animals and plants, the true nature of his *nous* lies somewhere between the anthropomorphic (and somewhat unpredictable) Zeus and what we might call the Laws of Nature.

Although it is tempting to think of *nous* as non-corporeal, Anaxagoras' own words of description are merely that it is the "lightest and purest of all things", and is the only thing capable of existing in a pure form, with no admixture of normal matter. As such, it is not only self-ruling, it also rules all else. In the universe as a whole it works largely by setting things into a vortex that separates heavier objects from lighter ones, pushing the former into the centre, much as a whirlpool can drive pebbles into its middle. Thus the "Socrates" in the *Clouds*, in fact an amalgam of several sophists and Presocratics, presents as a new divinity a pot called *dinos* in Greek, which puns on Zeus/Dios and *dine*, the vortex responsible for the formation of all the heavenly bodies in Anaxagoras' theory.

Just as the vortex stirs things up so that like objects have the opportunity to unite with each other, so too does the breakdown of food during digestion allow like to join with like. (The attraction of like to like was a common belief raised to a scientific principle by many Presocratics.) Anaxagoras, that is, thought that the building blocks of animals (blood, flesh, bone, hair, etc.) were contained within the food they consumed, for, as he says, "how could hair come from not-hair and flesh from not-flesh?"

Much of the first part of his book was devoted to explaining the microscopic nature of matter. Since nothing can come from nothing, there must be some basic unchanging material. And since visible matter takes many forms, few if any of which are permanent, this bedrock of matter must itself come in different, but at this level unchanging, forms, which Anaxagoras metaphorically called "seeds". Thus far, Anaxagoras may be compared to the first atomists Leucippus and Democritus; but his explanation of seeds differed markedly from their atoms. Each seed is indestructible, with fixed shape, colour, and savour. Also fixed is the ration of *dynameis* (roughly "powers" or "qualities") contained within each seed, which tend to exist in polar pairs. These *dynameis* are of an unknown number, but the chief ones named by Anaxagoras are hot/cold, dark/light, heavy/light, and moist/dry. Since each seed contains a fixed amount of *dynameis*, its nature is determined by the combination of the various ratios. Thus, a stone has more heavy than light (both imagined to exist in the same seed simultaneously) and more dry than moist. The facts of nutrition can accordingly be explained by, for example, bread's containing seeds too small to be seen of flesh, bone, hair, etc. The scientific principle at work here – of comprehending the unseen by means of appearances – was expressed by Anaxagoras himself in the form "phenomena are a view of the unseen".

Since, roughly speaking, any object in the cosmos is a mixture just as is the cosmos itself, and since one thing (that is, an object characterized by a certain ratio of qualities) can break down and "become" another, Anaxagoras also deduced that "everything is in everything". For these and similarly scientific attempts to explain matter, change, and causation, Anaxagoras was compared by Aristotle to a sober man among stammerers. He and Democritus were credited by Aristotle and others with elegant and comprehensive theories that could explain both large- and small-scale phenomena.

DAVID SIDER

Biography

Born in Clazomenae c.500 BC, Anaxagoras moved to Athens after 470 and remained there until exiled in the 430s. He died in Lampsacus in 428 BC. He wrote (probably) just one book, of which substantial fragments are preserved by Simplicius. It is largely concerned with the nature of matter, which he sees as being governed by a promordial *nous*.

Writings

Testimonianze e frammenti, edited and translated into Italian by Diego Lanza, Florence: Nuova Italia, 1966 (the best collection of Greek texts)
The Fragments, edited by David Sider, Meisenheim: Hain, 1981

Further Reading

Gershenson, Daniel E. and Daniel A. Greenberg, *Anaxagoras and the Birth of Physics*, New York: Blaisdell, 1964 (the most complete collection of ancient sources, in English translation)
Graham, D.W., "The Postulates of Anaxagoras", *Apeiron*, 27 (1994): pp. 77–121
Kerferd, G.B., "Anaxagoras and the Concept of Matter before Aristotle", *Bulletin of the John Rylands Library*, 52 (1969): pp. 129–43
Laks, A., "Mind's Crisis: On Anaxagoras' *Nous*", *Southern Journal of Philosophy*, 31 (1993), supplement: pp. 19–38
Schofield, Malcolm, *An Essay on Anaxagoras*, Cambridge and New York: Cambridge University Press, 1980
Woodbury, L., "Anaxagoras and Athens", *Phoenix*, 35 (1981): pp. 295–315

Anaximander

Philosopher of the 6th century BC

Anaximander of Miletus was active in the first half of the 6th century BC (the date of his death is given by Diogenes Laertius as 547/46 BC). He was said to have been a pupil and kinsman of Thales of Miletus, and is included by ancient historians of philosophy among the group of early thinkers who tried to explain the world on the basis of a single material substance. No work of his survives. For our knowledge of his ideas we rely entirely on reports given by later writers from Aristotle onwards; most of the available information comes from authors writing in the 1st century AD or later, and in these cases it is likely that they are relying on general histories of philosophy and encyclopaedias that go back ultimately to the work of Aristotle's successors (especially Theophrastus).

According to Anaximander, the originative substance was the *apeiron*, a term whose precise meaning is not entirely clear; it might mean either infinite or indeterminate, though since Anaximander believed that his originative substance had both of these qualities the uncertainty does not affect the interpretation of his ideas. The creation of the cosmos came about by the separating out of the opposites from the *apeiron*, in such a way as to achieve an overall balance; the details of this process are obscured by the tendency of our sources to assimilate Anaximander's system to one of the cosmological views of their own time (so making the *apeiron* a mixture or an intermediate substance). The *apeiron* surrounds and controls the cosmos, and is eternal, unageing, and perhaps divine. Anaximander apparently produced something like a complete cosmology. He believed that the earth was cylindrical, its depth a third of its width, and that it was supported by nothing, but stayed where it was because it was equidistant from everything else. The heavenly bodies, he believed, were rings of fire, enclosed except at points where there were holes through which the fire showed through. He claimed that the ring of the sun was 27 times, and the ring of the moon 18 times, the size of the earth. Eclipses were caused when the holes were blocked up (though we are not told what causes the holes to get blocked up). He explained rain as arising from moisture that evaporates under the influence of the sun, and thunder as the wind, enclosed within clouds, breaking out. He seems to have believed also that the earth was drying out (perhaps impressed by the receding coastline in Ionia). Reports of his views on the origins of life are intriguing, though enigmatic. He apparently believed that life originated in moisture, and that the first creatures came into being enclosed in a bark-like shell, which they subsequently shed. In the case of human beings, he argued that, since the human infant is incapable of looking after itself for some years, the first people must have come to maturity under the protection of some other creature; they grew to puberty, he claimed, within fish-like animals, from which they emerged in adulthood when they were old enough to be self-sufficient.

It is, however, his production of the first known Greek map that most interests the ancient sources. Maps had, of course, been known to the ancient societies of Mesopotamia for centuries, and it is not surprising that it was in a trading city like Miletus that the concept was first introduced to Greece. There is another intriguing report that Anaximander invented the gnomon (a kind of simple sundial), which he used to mark solstices and equinoxes, and that he set one up in Sparta. He did not invent the gnomon, in fact, because it already had a long history (indeed, Herodotus attributes its invention to the Babylonians), and this may be another case of Anaximander's introducing foreign ideas to Greece. He was the first known Greek to attempt to produce a complete, comprehensive, and rational account of the world and its development, including the early history of the human race.

Anaximander is also the first recorded writer of Greek prose. He is said to have written a number of books, and an account of his cosmology given by Simplicius (writing in the 6th century AD) in his commentary on Aristotle's *Physics* (24. 13) may contain a quotation from one of them: "that from which existing things have their coming-into-being is also that into which they are destroyed according to necessity; for they pay penalty and retribution to one another for their injustice, according to the assessment of time" (as he puts it in these rather poetic words). Unfortunately, it is impossible to say for certain where the quotation begins and where it ends, but it is probable that in this passage is contained the earliest surviving piece of Greek prose.

RICHARD WALLACE

See also Cartography, Cosmology

Biography
Active in the first half of the 6th century BC, Anaximander of Miletus is said to have been a pupil of Thales of Miletus. None of his writings survive; but we learn from later writers that he tried to account for the world on the basis of a single material substance which he called the *apeiron* (the infinite or indeterminate). He also was the first known Greek to draw a map. He died *c*.547 BC.

Further Reading

Barnes, Jonathan, *The Presocratic Philosophers*, vol. 1, London and Boston: Routledge and Kegan Paul, 1979

Guthrie, W.K.C., *A History of Greek Philosophy*, vol. 1, Cambridge: Cambridge University Press, 1962, reprinted 1971

Kahn, Charles H., *Anaximander and the Origins of Greek Cosmology*, New York: Columbia University Press, 1960, reprinted Indianapolis: Hackett, 1994

Kirk, Geoffrey Stephen, John Earle Raven and Malcolm Schofield, *The Presocratic Philosophers: A Critical History with a Selection of Texts*, Cambridge: Cambridge University Press, 1957, reprinted 1983

Ancestor Worship

The tendency has been noted (Antonaccio, 1995, p. 268; cf. Humphreys and King 1981, p. 267) that, where political power is fluid and personal, the focus, on occasions of death, impels towards the intense interaction of the living; on the other hand, where the base of power is more stable, resting with a historically grounded social group, care of the dead becomes the focus. There is evidence of both with the Greeks, reflecting the belief in the power of the dead over the living and the inconstancy of political structures.

Mycenaean burial sites, where the norm was collective burial in chamber tombs or tholoi, suggest that certain tombs were singled out for special treatment, but that the dead were not worshipped. The evidence indicates instead that veneration of the deceased was not practised, since tombs were often re-entered, and earlier relics and grave goods swept aside or removed. Those ancestors who drew continued interest and with whom claims of connection were maintained were usually claimed as "heroes" and their personal histories and the status or power ascribed to them after death tended to be reinterpreted according to the needs of the descendants. There is no consistency in the accounts of the births, lives, or ends of these glorified ancestors (heroes sometimes disappear rather than die), but they were believed to have lived mortal, if extraordinary, lives.

Conviction held that ancestors reigned over present events. Patrons and guardians to their progeny, they could grant success in diverse endeavours or curse them with disaster – barrenness, disease, pestilence, or military failure. Thus the dead were rarely ignored, even where not worshipped. They were remembered, feared, and invoked by the living through prayer, votive dedication, animal (and in some cases even human) sacrifice, and commemorated in poetry, in song, and at athletic events. The variety of "heroic" ancestry grew over time until, by the late Classical period, athletes, founders of colonies, and even ordinary folk came to be "heroized" as supermortal.

Links with the ancestral past tended to be broken on the mainland during the Dark Ages except in the colonies where Homeric tradition was preserved, and later reintroduced to the mainland during the "renaissance" of the late 8th century BC. The close of the Dark Ages was accompanied by a revival of enthusiasm for the past, born partly of the nostalgia for lost ancestral links, but also as a matter of expedience, as heroic personifications were adopted to lend legitimacy and historical grounding and to provide patronage for the newly founded city or polis. Ancestral claims could also be strategically deployed to reinforce the power of an elite now threatened by the emergent polis and the levelling tendencies of democracy. The "ancestral yearning" (Snodgrass, 1971, pp. 195–96) of this period is witnessed in art, literature, and ceremonial ritual. Formal hero cult was intense during this period. Tomb cult, one of its manifestations, is connected to the loss of stability in social structures and the struggle for the control of land during the transition from pastoralism to an agricultural society. Noteworthy ancestry could aid in the project of legitimizing and stabilizing the power of certain families, connecting them with an epoch of excellence and lending authenticity to claims of landownership. Tomb cult offerings, though largely private and unofficial, also provided a personal connection with the ancient inhabitants of a place, securing the protection and the favour of ancestral powers and appeasing the anonymous hostile forces thought to dwell therein. Tomb cult peaked in the 8th century BC and continued into the Classical period.

During the late Iron Age trade and prosperity intensified, creating greater social and cultural complexity. Where the region favoured social interaction among the elites, claims of ancestry remained a matter of prestige and burial custom stayed competitive. Teams of asses or horses, armour and weaponry, and a variety of luxury imports were buried with the deceased and there is evidence, at the grave site, of intense ceremonial activity among the living. However, as configurations of power tended towards the personal and fluid, claims of archaic ancestry declined, as did extravagance of burial custom once sanctuaries came to be employed as the arena for communal and regional competitions. In the more isolated regions, however, the ancestral claims of older families were probably maintained.

The well-established polis continued the practice of corporate worship of the ancestral spirits. This provided a unity to its worshipping community, though it could also have a divisive effect since it tended to serve the power of the aristocrats. Some tomb cults were ongoing, monuments being claimed by later generations, but generally they were of short duration and limited scope. As political power came to depend on the redistribution of wealth and on the charismatic draw of individuals, kinship claims were no longer the necessary base of power. During this period there is evidence of a continuing concern for the ancestral past. The dead continue to be related to one another, graves being connected by mounds or tumuli and enclosed within walls for protection against encroachment by expanding settlement.

Scholars generally agree that the antiquity of the Greek clan or extended family (*genos*) over centuries is a myth without foundation (Cavanaugh, 1991, pp. 100, 103; Antonaccio, 1995, pp. 252–53, 264). Even the most prominent families had no extensive pedigree. In Attica there is no evidence of long-term use of a common lot at any time from the Mycaenaean to the Classical period. Nor is there any sign of the continual tending of graves or consistent cult worship. Ancestral links seem to have been maintained over four generations or less, whether oral or written records helped to keep genealogical memory alive.

On the whole, times of instability and social disruption tended to favour a nostalgia for the past, impelling towards reaffirmations of heroic ancestry, renewed family-based claims of political legitimacy, and increased belief in the power of the dead, evidenced by greater care of the burial sites. With increased stability and prosperity, less emphasis was placed upon ancestral heritage, and there was a return to corporate burial. In the latter case, vigorous interaction between the living tended to be the focus rather than care of the dead.

In the early centuries of the Christian era, the Roman empire's contact with the east brought a blaze of interest in Near Eastern, Egyptian, and Oriental mystery religions, eclipsing for a time the glories of its Greek heritage. As Rome began to crumble, eastern influences triumphed over Classical tradition, not so much because of the superior splendour of the oriental, but because its mystical bent was more suited to the needs of the decaying empire. Its secret ritual practices, its pomp and ceremony, but also the sense of discipline and fellowship it promoted, brought consolation to the world-weary spirit in this era of decline. By the 3rd century Mithraism had spread throughout the empire, embracing the bulk of the army. Though the disillusioned were no longer drawn by the pagan insights of the sheer joy of life, characteristic of the Greeks, eastern mystery cults did promote the belief in the continuance of the soul and the cycle of rebirth, which continued the demand for reverence for the ancestors.

Upon the rubble of decaying Rome the emperor Constantine erected a new empire, Byzantium, committed to Christianity. To complete the transformation of the new empire, he established a second capital city, Constantinople, dedicated in AD 330. This site embraced all the elements of the reformed empire – Greek, Roman, and Christian – but, since it was set on the Greek-speaking coasts around an old Greek city, it was the Hellenistic past of the new empire that was highlighted. Constantine did all that he could to promote that historical connection, making the city a centre of education and the arts, stocking its libraries with Greek manuscripts and its museums with Greek treasures, and beautifying its streets and squares with Greek works. An obsession with its Hellenistic past flared throughout the empire. Even in the 12th century aristocrats were said to boast that their ancestors had arrived with Constantine (Runciman, 1933, p. 28).

Every corner of the Western world to some degree or other owes to its Greek heritage a cultural and political debt. During the national revival of the early 19th century, the Greeks, at least within the intelligentsia, bore the consciousness of being the heirs of a heritage universally revered. An obsession with past glories, *progonoplexia* ("ancestor weaving": Clogg, 1992, p. 2), characterized much of the country's cultural life, yielding movements of purification of the language and nostalgia for ancient ideals. Early Greek nationalists looked only to the Classical past for its inspiration, rejecting the glories of the Byzantine era. But in the mid-19th century Konstantinos Paparrigopoulos, a professor of history at the University of Athens, reinterpreted Greek history as a single continuum linking ancient, medieval, and modern periods.

It is central to the historical experience of the Greeks that their "Greekness" was understood, not so much with reference to a specific place, as to a way of being in the world. Due to its wealth of overseas communities, Greece had always included a large population of those who dwelt beyond the mainland, sojourners in foreign lands. This fact must have raised acutely and continuously the question of what constitutes the Greek identity. Language and religion could in no definitive way answer this question. Ancestry is the only inalienable link that accompanies people wherever they may go. This may explain the continued emphasis on ancestral heritage within the Greek world.

WENDY C. HAMBLET

See also Dead

Further Reading

Alcock, Susan E., "Tomb Cult and the Post-Classical Polis", *American Journal of Archaeology*, 95 (1991): pp. 447–67

Alcock, Susan E. and Robin Osborne (editors), *Placing the Gods: Sanctuaries and Sacred Space in Ancient Greece*, Oxford: Clarendon Press, and New York: Oxford University Press, 1994

Antonaccio, Carla, *An Archaeology of Ancestors: Tomb Cult and Hero Cult in Early Greece*, Lanham, Maryland: Rowman and Littlefield, 1995

Barrett, J.C., "The Living, the Dead and the Ancestors: Neolithic and Early Bronze Age Mortuary Practices" in *The Archaeology of Context in the Neolithic and Bronze Age: Recent Trends*, edited by J.C. Barrett and I.A. Kinnes, Sheffield: University of Sheffield Department of Archaeology and Prehistory, 1988

Bloch, M., "The Past and the Present in the Present", *Man*, 12 (1977): pp. 278–92

Burkert, Walter, *Greek Religion: Archaic and Classical*, Oxford: Blackwell, and Cambridge, Massachusetts: Harvard University Press, 1985

Cavanaugh, W., "Surveys, Cities and Synoecism" in *City and Country in the Ancient World*, edited by John Rich and Andrew Wallace-Hadrill, London and New York: Routledge, 1991

Clogg, Richard, *A Concise History of Greece*, Cambridge and New York: Cambridge University Press, 1992

Desborough, V.R.d'A., *The Greek Dark Ages*, London: Benn, and New York: St Martin's Press, 1972

Dougherty, Carl and Leslie Kurke (editors), *Cultural Poetics in Archaic Greece: Cult, Performance, Politics*, Cambridge and New York: Cambridge University Press, 1993

Drews, Robert, *Basileus: The Evidence for Kingship in Geometric Greece*, New Haven, Connecticut: Yale University Press, 1983

Farnell, Lewis Richard, *The Cults of the Greek States*, 5 vols, Oxford: Clarendon Press, 1896–1909

Farnell, Lewis Richard, *Greek Hero Cults and Ideas of Immortality*, Oxford: Clarendon Press, 1921

Fleming, A., "Social Boundaries and Land Boundaries" in *Ranking, Resource and Exchange: Aspects of the Archaeology of Early European Society*, edited by Colin Renfrew and Stephen Shennan, Cambridge and New York: Cambridge University Press, 1982

Fustel de Coulanges, Numa, *The Ancient City: A Study on the Religion, Laws and Institutions of Greece and Rome*, Boston: Lee and Shepard, 1874, reprinted Baltimore: Johns Hopkins University Press, 1980

Garland, Robert, *The Greek Way of Death*, London: Duckworth, and Ithaca, New York: Cornell University Press, 1985

Hägg, Robin and Nanno Marinatos (editors), *Sanctuaries and Cults in the Aegean Bronze Age*, Stockholm: Svenska Instituti Athen, 1981

Hägg, Robin, Nanno Marinatos, and Güllog Nordquist (editors), *Early Greek Cult Practice*, Stockholm: Svenska Instituti Athen, 1988

Hughes, Dennis, *Human Sacrifice in Ancient Greece*, London and New York: Routledge, 1991

Humphreys, S.C. and Helen King (editors), *Mortality and Immortality: The Anthropology and Archaeology of Death*, London and New York: Academic Press, 1981

Kurtz, Donna and John Boardman, *Greek Burial Customs*, London: Thames and Hudson, and Ithaca, New York: Cornell University Press, 1971

Morris, Ian, *Burial and Ancient Society: The Rise of the Greek City-State*, Cambridge and New York: Cambridge University Press, 1987

Morris, Ian, *Death-Ritual and Social Structure in Classical Antiquity*, Cambridge and New York: Cambridge University Press, 1992

Mylonas, G., "Homeric and Mycaenean Burial Customs", *American Journal of Archaeology*, 52 (1948): pp. 56–81

Nagy, Gregory, *The Best of the Achaeans: Concepts of the Hero in Archaic Greek Poetry*, Baltimore: Johns Hopkins University Press, 1979, revised edition 1999

O'Shea, John M., *Mortuary Variability: An Archaeological Investigation*, Orlando, Florida: Academic Press, 1984

Rohde, Erwin, *Psyche: The Cult of Souls and Belief in Immortality among the Greeks*, London: Kegan Paul Trench Trubner, and New York: Harcourt Brace, 1925 (German edition, 1894)

Runciman, Steven, *Byzantine Civilisation*, London: Arnold, and New York: Longman, 1933

Snodgrass, Anthony, *The Dark Age of Greece*, Edinburgh: Edinburgh University Press, 1971

Thomas, Rosalind, *Oral Tradition and Written Record in Classical Athens*, Cambridge and New York: Cambridge University Press, 1989

Vermeule, Emily, *Aspects of Death in Early Greek Art and Poetry*, Berkeley: University of California Press, 1979

Andrew of Crete, St *c.660–740*

Hymnographer and preacher

St Andrew of Crete was one of the most famous Byzantine writers of hymns and homilies. He lived at a period when the Byzantine empire was besieged by Arabs and invaders from the north and when literary production consequently declined. He is perhaps best known for his invention of a new hymnographic form, the canon; whether or not he was really the inventor of this form is disputed by scholars, but his authorship of the best-known example of this genre, *The Great Canon*, is well attested. His homilies, while evidently well loved by contemporary and later medieval audiences, judging by the large number of manuscripts in which they are transmitted, are not suited to modern delivery, being highly rhetorical and employing a fairly recherché vocabulary.

According to an anonymous, but probably early, *Life* written by one Niketas, Patrician and Quaestor, Andrew of Crete was born around 660 in Damascus, Syria. Judging by his own writings, which display a secure command of Attic Greek and the late antique rules of rhetoric, he received a good education in the schools of the Arab-ruled Near East. At the age of fourteen or fifteen he was received as a monastic novice at the church of the Resurrection in Jerusalem. In 685 Andrew was sent to Constantinople in order to convey the agreement of the patriarchate of Jerusalem to the acts of the Sixth Ecumenical Council, held in 680–81. He remained in the imperial city, serving first as a deacon in the Great Church and later as the head of an orphanage and an almshouse in the city. The exact date of his ordination as archbishop of Crete is unknown, owing to the lack of literary sources for the period. However, the ordination must have taken place between 692, when a metropolitan of Gortyn named Basil signed the Acts of the Council in Trullo, and 711, when Andrew, in that capacity himself, signed the decree of a conciliabule ordered by Philippikos Bardanes that temporarily overturned the decisions of the Sixth Ecumenical Council and restored Monothelite doctrine. It is generally assumed, although difficult to prove, that most of Andrew's hymns and homilies were composed when he was serving as archbishop of Crete. A few of the homilies may be dated precisely on the basis of internal evidence, but the majority provide no clues concerning the circumstances of their delivery. It is clear from a few references in the homilies that Andrew lived well into the first period of iconoclasm (730–787) and the date of his death can therefore be placed in 740. Since he refers only rarely to the theological dispute over holy images, however, it can be inferred that he did not play an active part in the controversy. His authorship of a fragment of a text in defence of icons has been disputed, but he does deplore the imperial stance against images in his homily *In Circumcisionem et in S. Basilium* (*Clavis Patrum Graecorum* 8175). Andrew died on the island of Lesbos on his return journey to Crete after a visit to Constantinople, where he had sought imperial aid for his Cretan flock, which had been devastated not only by the Arab invasions but also by plague and famine. He was buried in the church of the holy martyr Anastasia.

Fifty-eight homilies have been attributed to Andrew, but a number of these, which remain unedited, may in fact belong to other authors. It is likely that between 30 and 35 homilies will prove to be his, but all of these texts await detailed stylistic and theological analysis. Most of Andrew's homilies are festal; that is, they belong to a genre that was intended for formal delivery in the context of the liturgical celebrations for particular feast days. Cycles of three or four sermons in honour of the Theotokos, or Mary the "God-bearer", survive that were probably preached in succession during the all-night vigils that preceded her feasts. These homilies reveal the strong influence of earlier marian literature, including especially the *Akathistos* Hymn. Repetitive and highly poetic in style, they celebrate the Virgin with typological and other theological images. Several homilies were written in honour of dominical feasts, including the Raising of Lazarus, Palm Sunday, and the Transfiguration, and a number of panegyrical sermons also survive, honouring both local Cretan saints and martyrs and more universal heroes such as St George and St Nicholas. It should be noted, however, that Andrew's authorship of the last works has been called into question by scholars. The two panegyrics on St

George differ so much in their accounts of the saint's ordeals and martyrdom that it is likely that they were based on two different sources. The encomium on St Nicholas, although transmitted in many manuscripts that attribute the text to Andrew, depends largely on a text that may have been written in the 9th century (cf. Anrich, 1917, pp. 346–56). All of these encomia, as well as an account of the miracles of St Therapon, await detailed analysis before they can be attributed securely to Andrew of Crete. The literary influences on Andrew's homilies lie both in hymnography and in homiletics. His choice of images and poetic word play sometimes echoes those of Romanos the Melodist, a hymnographer of the 6th century, while his prose style reflects most closely that of Gregory of Nazianzus.

The surviving hymns of Andrew of Crete, like his homilies, await detailed study. His Great Canon, which is sung during the fifth week of Lent, is extremely long, with 250 strophes. What is chiefly striking about this hymn is its penitential and personal tone. Andrew speaks in the first person but also on behalf of every Christian, both repenting of his sins and seeking God's forgiveness. He also wrote canons in honour of feasts including the Birth of the Virgin Mary, the Conception of St Anna, her mother, and the Raising of Lazarus. A number of hymns still await critical editions, and for all of them a detailed literary and musical analysis would be desirable. As one of the first, if not the first, writers of canons, Andrew introduced into Greek theological literature a penitential, at times mystical, tone that had previously been absent. Both his hymns and his homilies influenced subsequent hymnographers and preachers in Byzantium. The inclusion of Andrew's homilies in liturgical collections, in which they featured as readings for individual feast days, and the use of his canons in the service of *orthros* (matins), allowed these works to serve as literary models until the end of the Byzantine period.

MARY B. CUNNINGHAM

See also Hymnography

Biography

Born in Damascus *c*.AD 660, Andrew was educated in the Near East but moved to Constantinople in 685 where he served as a deacon and later as head of an orphanage. Between 692 and 711 he was ordained archbishop of Crete. He died on Lesbos in 740. He wrote numerous homilies, mostly for particular feast days, and hymns, including the Great Canon for the fifth week of Lent.

Writings

In *Patrologia Graeca*, edited by J.-P. Migne, vol. 97, 805–1444

Further Reading

Anrich, Gustav, *Hagios Nikolaos: Der heilige Nikolaos in der griechischen kirche*, vol. 2, Leipzig and Berlin, 1917
Auzépy, M.-F., "La Carrière d'André de Crète", *Byzantinische Zeitschrift*, 88/1 (1995): pp. 1–12
Eustratiades, S., "Andreas ho Kretes ho Ierosolumites", *Nea Sion*, 29 (1934): pp. 673–88 (in Greek)
Cunningham, Mary B., "Andrew of Crete: A High-Style Preacher of the Eighth Century" in *Preacher and Audience: Studies in Early Christian and Byzantine Homiletics*, edited by Cunningham and Pauline Allen, Leiden: Brill, 1998
Vailhé, S., "Saint André de Crète", *Echos d'Orient*, 5 (1902): pp. 378–87

Andronikos I Komnenos *c.*1118/20–1185

Emperor

Andronikos I Komnenos (1183–85) was one of the most controversial personalities on the Byzantine throne. The son of Isaac Komnenos and Eirene, and thus the nephew of Emperor John II Komnenos (1118–43), he grew up with Manuel I Komnenos (1143–80). The two cousins had some characteristics in common, such as chivalrous audacity and lasciviousness, but the desire they shared for exclusive leadership made them rivals. Manuel sought in vain to integrate Andronikos into the power network that the imperial family had built up with other aristocratic clans. Highly talented and able to impress and fascinate both men and women alike, Andronikos handled the tasks entrusted to him carelessly. He even conspired against the emperor, was imprisoned, and twice managed to escape. During a decade (*c.*1167–79) of exile in the Arab world, Georgia, and the crusader states he acquired a critical attitude to his country's situation. Although he was not xenophobic himself, he was unscrupulous in his exploitation of anti-Latin resentment, and in 1182 tolerated a massacre at Constantinople in order to take over the regency for the minor Alexios II, whom he suppressed and killed within a year.

In foreign policy the costly, but hardly effective, support of the crusader states was now definitely abandoned. An understanding was reached between Byzantium and the Muslim sultan Saladin concerning their respective spheres of influence in Asia Minor, Syria, and Palestine. The political programme of Andronikos was mainly oriented towards internal affairs in order to regain absolute control: too much power had shifted to the regional magnates, who managed the adminstrative apparatus in the provinces at will. Harsh measures against the salvage of cargo or the exploitation of peasants, for example, were not intended to favour special groups or social strata, but were aimed at creating an efficient and uncorrupt bureaucracy. The old ruling class, seeing its positions endangered, either impeded the imperial reforms or even rose in revolt, which Andronikos and his collaborators (many of them unqualified newcomers) suppressed with cruelty. Increasingly noblemen fell victim to a reign of terror on mere suspicion or denunciation of disloyalty.

Neighbouring countries such as Hungary tried to profit from the unstable situation and, incited by refugees, invaded Byzantine territories, but they were driven back. We may assume that Andronikos would have also succeeded in beating off an unexpected Norman attack from Italy. After the loss of Thessalonica (August 1185) the Byzantine army had already split up the invaders and slowed down their advance eastwards. Nevertheless tension and fear prevailed in the capital, which was inflamed when the mediocre aristocrat Isaac Angelos, stricken with panic, killed an imperial official who had come to arrest him. Seeking asylum in Hagia Sophia, Isaac unwillingly became the champion of a popular uprising and was crowned emperor on 12 September 1185. Andronikos fled, was imprisoned, mutilated, and finally butchered by the mob. His death brought to an end the drastic and often inhuman measures intended to restructure a state in economic and political decline. Two decades later, in 1204,

Constantinople and nearly the whole empire fell an easy prey to the so-called Fourth Crusade.

EWALD KISLINGER

See also Political History 802–1204

Biography
Born c.1118/20, Andronikos fought his way to the Byzantine throne in 1183, but was himself murdered two years later in Constantinople. He was the last ruler of the Komnenian dynasty, with a brilliant mind, but a lascivious temper. He inaugurated reforms against corruption and to strengthen the central power against regional magnates, but their resistance caused a reign of terror which culminated in the emperor's murder.

Main Sources
Choniates, Nicetas, *Historia*, edited by Jan Louis van Dieten, Berlin: de Gruyter, 1975

Eustathios of Thessalonica, *Syngraphe Haloseos* [Account of the Capture], edited by E. Kyriakides, translated into Italian by V. Rotolo, Palermo, 1961

Eustathios of Thessalonica, *The Capture of Thessaloniki*, translated by John R. Jones, Canberra: Australian Association for Byzantine Studies, 1988

Further Reading
Brand, Charles M., *Byzantium Confronts the West, 1180–1204*, Cambridge, Massachusetts: Harvard University Press, 1968, pp. 31–75

Cheynet, Jean-Claude, *Pouvoir et contestations à Byzance (963–1210)*, Paris: Publications de la Sorbonne, 1990, especially pp. 110–19 and pp. 427–40

Eastmond, Anthony, "An Intentional Error? Imperial Art and "Mis"-Interpretation under Andronikos I Komnenos", *Art Bulletin*, 76 (1994): pp. 502–10

Hecht, Winfried, *Die byzantinische Aussenpolitik zur Zeit der letzten Komnenenkaiser (1180–1185)*, Neustadt: Schmidt, 1967, pp. 30–86

Jurewicz, Oktawiusz, *Andronikos I. Komnenos*, Amsterdam: Hakkert, 1970 (contains various errors; use with caution)

Kislinger, Ewald, "Zur Chronologie der byzantinischen Thronwechsel, 1180–1185", *Jahrbuch der österreichischen Byzantinistik*, 47 (1997): pp. 195–98

Varzos, Konstantinos, *I genealogia ton Kominon* [The Genealogy of the Komnenoi], vol. 1, Thessalonica, 1984, pp. 493–638

Andronikos II Palaiologos 1259 or 1260–1328
Emperor

The long reign of Andronikos II Palaiologos (1282–1328) was marked by the beginning of the Ottoman advance in Asia Minor, religious dissensions, and a civil war, but it also witnessed the last efflorescence of Byzantine art and culture. Born in 1259 or 1260, Andronikos was proclaimed co-emperor in 1274 by his father Michael VIII Palaiologos (1259–82), who wished to ensure a smooth transition of power and to strengthen the position of the Palaiologan dynasty, which had ousted the Laskarids of Nicaea in 1261. Andronikos II had, however, a personality and a political credo very different from those of his father. Michael VIII had ruled the empire with an iron hand, subordinating through the Union of Lyons (1274) the Byzantine Church to the papacy in order to ward off western ambitions for the reconquest of Constantinople. Immediately after his accession, Andronikos II Palaiologos repudiated the unpopular Union of Lyons and restored Orthodoxy. Another internal split within the Byzantine Church, the "Arsenite schism", was not healed until 1310. The Arsenites were followers of the patriarch Arsenios (1255–60 and 1261–67), who had supported the dynastic claims of the Laskarid dynasty and of its last representative, the child-emperor John IV Laskaris (1258–61) who had been blinded by Michael VIII's order. The end of the Arsenite schism was also a belated recognition of the legitimacy of the Palaiologan dynasty.

Andronikos II Palaiologos was a devout and staunchly Orthodox emperor. During his rule the influence of the Church in late Byzantine society grew steadily. He included churchmen as judges in the supreme imperial court as reformed in 1296 (the so-called "General Judges of the Romaioi"). In 1312 he transferred the administration of the monasteries of Mount Athos from his own jurisdiction to that of the patriarch. The episcopal dioceses and their order of precedence were also reorganized during his reign. The strong-willed patriarch Athanasios I (1289–93 and 1303–11), writer of numerous letters and sermons, protected the poor inhabitants of Constantinople from the abuses of merchants and imperial officials, and took to heart the plight of the Greek refugees from the Turkish advance in Asia Minor in the early years of the 14th century. Under his guidance, in 1304 the synod issued a new law, which was confirmed by the emperor in 1306; it covered such topics as inheritance, the opening hours of taverns and bath houses, prostitution, adultery, etc.

The Turkish expansion in Asia Minor became the nemesis of the Byzantines during the reign of Andronikos II. Michael VIII Palaiologos had withdrawn troops from the empire's eastern frontier, which now collapsed under the pressure of successive waves of Turkoman tribes fleeing the Mongol menace. Unlike Michael VIII, who had been preoccupied with the Latin west, however, Andronikos II made efforts to remedy the situation by personally leading an army in Asia Minor; and, for a short time in 1294, the campaigns of the great general Alexios Philanthropenos raised hopes. But he was opposed by powerful landlords in the area, pushed into an unsuccessful rebellion, and his successes were short-lived. Asia Minor rapidly fell to the Turks after the Byzantine defeat at the battle of Bapheus near Nikomedeia (1302) by the forces of Osman, the eponymous founder of the Ottoman state. The Ottomans took Bursa in 1326 and made it their capital. Further south, in the first decade of the 14th century, Ephesus, Smyrna, Miletus, and Sardis fell to the Seljuk emirates. In an unsuccessful effort to turn the tide of Turkish conquests, in 1303 Andronikos II hired a group of undisciplined Catalan mercenaries. After an initial success in the capture of Philadelphia in 1304, the so-called Grand Catalan Company turned against its Byzantine masters, laying waste Thrace and Mount Athos and settling first in the Cassandra peninsula and later in Thessaly. In 1311 the Catalans moved further south to Attica, expelled the ruling Frankish lords, and founded the Catalan principality of Athens and Thebes (1311–88).

Another source of trouble for Andronikos was the aggressive plans for the revival of the Latin kingdom of

Constantinople led in the early 14th century by Charles of Valois, brother of the French king Philip IV the Fair (1285–1314) and husband of the heiress to the Latin kingdom, Catherine de Courtenay. Fortunately for Andronikos, in 1314 Charles of Valois gave up his intentions, which had found support even among some Byzantine aristocrats. The reign of Andronikos II also saw the beginning of the Serbian expansion, which would culminate in the great conquests of Stephan IV Dushan (1331–55). In 1282 the Serbs occupied Byzantine-held northern Macedonia, capturing the strategic city of Skopje. Andronikos had to acknowledge the Serbian conquests; in 1299 the Serbian king Stephan II Milutin (1282–1321) married his five-year-old daughter Simonis and received as a dowry the lands north of the Ochrida–Prilep–Shtip line in Macedonia.

The internal collapse of the late Byzantine state began in the last years of Andronikos II's reign, when a civil war broke out between the ageing emperor and his grandson Andronikos III (1321/28–41). Having started as a private quarrel provoked by the emperor's decision in 1321 to exclude his grandson from the succession, the civil war became an outlet for social tensions and dragged on intermittently for seven years. High taxation and official corruption had plagued Andronikos II's reign. The younger Andronikos tried to lure aristocratic supporters through lavish tax exemptions, which in the long run damaged the imperial fisc and led to the devaluation of the Byzantine golden coin (hyperpyron). In 1328 the young Andronikos finally managed to oust his grandfather without any bloodshed, and Andronikos II was confined to the imperial palace. Two years later the supporters of Andronikos III forced the old emperor to enter a monastery, where he died on 13 February 1332.

The reign of Andronikos II saw not only troubling political developments, but also some remarkable cultural achievements. The philologists Maximos Planudes, Thomas Magister, and Manuel Moschopoulos commented on and systematized works of Classical authors. The numerous Byzantine intellectuals and literati of the period were associated, in one way or another, with the court of Andronikos II. Two of the greatest Byzantine encyclopedic scholars, Nikephoros Choumnos (died 1327) and Theodore Metochites (1270–1332), served in the imperial administration and rose to the rank of mesazon, or prime minister. Both were of relatively modest social origin but managed to connect their families with the ruling Palaiologan dynasty through marriage. Theodore Metochites became notorious for his corruption and was sacked by the young Andronikos III in 1328. Nikephoros Choumnos, Theodore Metochites, and Nikephoros Gregoras all composed panegyrics in honour of Andronikos II.

DIMITER G. ANGELOV

See also Renaissance (Palaiologan)

Biography

Born in 1259 or 1260, Andronikos II reigned for 46 years from 1282 to 1328. He died a monk in Constantinople in 1332. His reign was marred by Ottoman advances in Asia Minor, by religious controversy, and by civil war. It also witnessed the final flourishing of Byzantine art and culture, the so-called Palaiologan Renaissance. Andronikos was deposed in 1328 by the supporters of his grandson Andronikos III.

Further Reading
Boojamra, John Lawrence, *Church Reform in the Late Byzantine Empire*, Thessalonica, 1982
Laiou, Angeliki E., *Constantinople and the Latins: The Foreign Policy of Andronicus II, 1282–1328*, Cambridge, Massachusetts: Harvard University Press, 1972
Nicol, Donald M., *The Last Centuries of Byzantium, 1261–1453*, 2nd edition, Cambridge and New York: Cambridge University Press, 1993
Runciman, Steven, *The Last Byzantine Renaissance*, Cambridge: Cambridge University Press, 1970

Andronikos, Manolis 1919–1992

Archaeologist

Manolis Andronikos was one of the foremost Greek archaeologists of the 20th century, well known for his devotion to, and promotion of, archaeological investigation in Macedonia. He was born in Prousa (Bursa) of a Samian family, which moved to Thessalonica in 1922 as part of the population exchange with the Turks. This family history may have influenced his subsequent career.

Thessalonica remained the centre of his life, except for a short period of time which he spent at Oxford University on a scholarship, studying under the direction of Sir John Beazley, a well-known British scholar of Greek archaeology. Upon his return to Greece, Andronikos joined the ranks of the Greek Archaeological Service, and began a teaching career at the Aristotelian University of Thessalonica. He was very active in the field, excavating sites in Macedonia and Chalcidice, including Verroia, Naousa, Kilkis, Dion, and Thessalonica. One of his early publications, *Vergina*, vol. 1: *To Necrotapheion Ton Tymvon* [The Tymbon Cemetery], summarizing his excavation work on Iron Age graves in the vicinity of Vergina, made a fundamental contribution to our understanding of Iron Age chronology in central Macedonia.

Andronikos first began excavating in the Hellenistic palace at Vergina under the direction of K.A. Rhomaios in the 1930s. He remained especially devoted to the area and the site, and with George Bakalakis later resumed and expanded the excavations at the Hellenistic palace. The tumulus at Vergina also fascinated Andronikos, but the mound was too expensive to excavate and the foreign schools of archaeology were uninterested in such a project at that time. It was not until he received the support of Constantine Karamanlis, prime minister of Greece and a Macedonian by birth, that his goal was realized. Work at Vergina began in 1976, and a year later he announced that he had discovered a *heroon* (hero shrine), an unlooted 4th-century BC chamber tomb, and an unusually large cist tomb, which had already been stripped of its contents but was still decorated with magnificent wall paintings. Andronikos claimed that the chamber tomb contained the burials of King Philip II of Macedon, father of Alexander the Great, and his wife.

At the time of his discovery he maintained that the archaeological evidence confirmed the site of Vergina as ancient Aegae – the Macedonian royal burial ground and early capital. This evidence consisted of lavishly appointed tombs with

Manolis Andronikos among the ruins of Vergina, which he excavated

splendid wall paintings, clearly dated to the second half of the 4th century BC. The skeletal remains, wrapped in purple, and individual items found in the main chamber and antechamber of the chamber tomb, such as a gold *larnax* (or casket), the lid of which was decorated with the Macedonian star, and elaborate armour, also appeared to support a royal identification. Andronikos found a second chamber in 1978, also unlooted, which he considered to belong to Alexander IV, the son of Alexander the Great and the Bactrian princess Roxane. While most scholars agree with the latter designation, the identification of the remains in the first chamber tomb is still debated. In 1987 he uncovered the tomb of Eurydice, the mother of Philip, which is the earliest and the largest of the Macedonian tombs, containing a magnificent marble throne covered with painted and relief decorations. These finds stimulated great interest and controversy in the field of Greek archaeology, focusing the attention of the Greeks and the rest of the world on Macedonia, and gave new impetus to archaeological excavation in the area.

Andronikos directed excavations at the site of Vergina, revealing the city plan, including a theatre, an agora, the circuit walls, and the acropolis. The seminal publication of his work there, *Vergina: The Royal Tombs and the Ancient City*, appeared in 1984. He also discovered and excavated a number of 4th-century BC tombs at the nearby village of Palatitsa. His

frequent, dramatic lecture presentations and the publication of numerous monographs and articles continued to focus attention on Vergina and the archaeology of the region even after the excitement and controversy of his initial discoveries had died down.

As a result of his efforts on behalf of Macedonian archaeology Andronikos gained worldwide renown. He was the recipient of many international professional honours, notably the Hergen award in Austria, and was affiliated with a number of foreign institutions and archaeological schools in Greece, such as the German Archaeological Institute. In addition, he was given the Grand Phoenix Cross, the highest civilian award bestowed by the Greek government.

Andronikos's international prominence benefited Macedonian archaeology by focusing the attention of the world on that region, and maintaining a high level of interest in subsequent work. Excavations continue in a number of locations, including the palaces at Vergina and Pella, and urban sites such as Dion, the religious capital of Macedonia, and Amphipolis, an Athenian colony established in 437 BC. In addition, cemeteries containing burials of the common people have yielded a wealth of information about culture and funerary customs in the Archaic and early Classical periods. His finds at Vergina made new and important contributions to the understanding of 4th-century art and architecture, particularly in the areas of work in precious metals, tomb architecture, and painting. Andronikos in the course of his career trained a new generation of Greek archaeologists to carry on his work, not only to conduct in-depth research and publication of some of his finds, but to continue excavation work in the area, maintaining the hard-won attention of the community of scholars working in the field of Greek archaeology. Perhaps most important of all for the Greek people, he assumed the role of a national hero as his countrymen used the finds from his excavations as evidence that there were strong ethnic and cultural ties between the ancient Macedonians and the Greek city states to the south, promoting the idea that the Macedonians were above all a Greek tribe.

KATHLEEN DONAHUE SHERWOOD

See also Aegae, Macedonia

Biography

Born in 1919 at Bursa in Asia Minor, Andronikos and his family moved to Thessalonica in 1922 in the exchange of populations and remained based there for the rest of his life. Andronikos became professor of archaeology at the Aristotelian University in 1964. He concentrated on sites in Macedonia and achieved renown as the excavator of the royal tombs (including that of Philip II) at Vergina from 1976. He died in 1992.

Writings

Vergina: The Prehistoric Necropolis and the Hellenistic Palace, Lund: Bloms, 1964

Vergina, vol. 1: To Necrotapheion Ton Tymvon [The Tymbon Cemetery], Athens, 1969

The Royal Graves at Vergina, Athens: Archaeological Receipts Fund, 1980

Vergina: The Royal Tombs and the Ancient City, Athens: Ekdotike Athenon, 1984, reprinted 1992

Further Reading

Borza, Eugene, obituary in American Journal of Archaeology, 96 (1992): pp. 57–58

De Grummond, Nancy Thomson, An Encyclopedia of the History of Classical Archaeology, Westport, Connecticut: Greenwood Press, and London: Fitzroy Dearborn, 1996, vol. 1, p. 47

Demand, Nancy, A History of Ancient Greece, New York: McGraw Hill, 1996, pp. 299–302

Ginouvès, René (editor), Macedonia: From Philip II to the Roman Conquest, Princeton, New Jersey: Princeton University Press, 1994

Sakellariou, M.B. (editor), Macedonia: 4000 Years of Greek History and Civilization, Athens: Ekdotike Athenon, 1983

Angelopoulos, Thodoros 1935–

Director, scriptwriter, producer, and critic

Theo Angelopoulos is the most celebrated contemporary film maker working in Greece and a film stylist of striking originality who makes frequent use of extended long shots in his work. His Aioniotita kai Mia Mera (Eternity and a Day) won the Palme d'Or at the Cannes Film Festival in 1998, while Ulysses' Gaze, starring Harvey Keitel, was winner of the 1995 Festival's Grand Prize. A major Angelopoulos retrospective took place at the Museum of Modern Art in New York in 1990

and, more recently, a special Angelopoulos season was held at the Riverside Studios in London (1998).

Angelopoulos was born in Athens on 27 April 1935 and studied law at the University of Athens (1953–57). After finishing his military service he left for Paris where he enrolled at the Sorbonne, attending lectures by the anthropologist Claude Lévi-Strauss. He also studied at the Institut des Hautes Etudes Cinématographiques, although he left the IDHEC, ostensibly because of disagreements with the staff, and found a mentor in Jean Rouch, the ethnographer and director, at the Musée de l'Homme. In 1964 Angelopoulos returned to Athens were he worked as a film critic for the left-wing newspaper Dimokratiki Allayi and for Synchronos Kinimatographos, the first serious Greek film magazine, which was founded in 1969 as a Greek equivalent to the influential French film journal, Cahiers du Cinéma.

Angelopoulos's first film was a black-and-white short of 23 minutes entitled The Broadcast (1968), which won the Critics' Prize at the Thessalonica Film Festival. This was made in collaboration with the cinematographer Yorgos Arvanitis and initiated a long and successful partnership. In total, Angelopoulos has made 11 features. Anaparastasi (Reconstruction, 1970), his first feature film, was made during the Colonels' regime and won the coveted Prix Georges Sadoul (1971). It is generally regarded, together with Evdokia (1971) by Alexis Damianos (1919–), as inaugurating the New Greek Cinema. Shot on a low budget and using non-professional actors, Anaparastasi stands out conspicuously from the mainstream commercial cinema of the 1960s which was dominated by light comedy and melodramas that pandered to the audience's desires for social mobility. On one level it tells the story of the death of the village in late 20th-century Greece and explores the break-up of a traditional rural community under the pressures of urbanization. The action, which is based on a true incident reported in the Greek newspapers, takes place in a mountain village in Epirus where Kostas Gousis (Michalis Photopoulos) returns after years spent in Germany as a guest worker. On his homecoming he is murdered by his wife Eleni (Toula Stathopoulou) with the help of her lover, Christos Grikakas (Yannis Totsikas). The dark, brooding landscape of northern Greece anticipates Angelopoulos's subsequent films which, for the most part, evoke a dilapidated provincial Greece of crumbling façades, far removed from the clichés of sunny Attica. The unity of place in Anaparastasi is juxtaposed with disconcerting chronological leaps since the film focuses on the attempts by the police to reconstruct the scene of the crime. Angelopoulos himself plays a cameo role as an investigative journalist. While there are strong documentary aspects to the film, Anaparastasi foreshadows many of the technical strategies and thematic preoccupations of Angelopoulos's later work.

The motif of the journey, for example, runs through all of Angelopoulos's films from Anaparastasi to Aioniotita kai Mia Mera which describes the wanderings of an elderly writer, Alexandros (Bruno Ganz), through Greece. Similarly, the theme of the journey figures strongly in O Thiasos (The Thiasus, 1975, distributed in the UK as The Travelling Players), in Taxidi sta Kythira (Voyage to Cythera, 1984), where the old communist Spyros (Manos Katrakis) returns to Greece from exile in the Soviet Union, and in O Melissokomos (The Beekeeper, 1986), where the middle-aged schoolteacher

(Marcello Mastroianni) leaves his wife and job to follow the pollen route. Finally, the two children Voula (Tania Palaiologou) and Alexandros (Michalis Zeke) in *Topio stin Omichli* (Landscape in the Mist, 1988) voyage like Telemachus in search of their lost father whom they have never known and who may be a figment of their imaginations.

In *Anaparastasi* notions of homecoming are frequently bound up with a mythic structure; Kostas Gousis's repatriation is linked to Aeschylus' *Oresteia*, and more particularly to Clytemnestra's murder of Agamemnon. In other films, such as *O Thiasos*, the actors bear the names of protagonists in the *Oresteia* cycle and perhaps most obviously, in *Ulysses' Gaze*, the peripatetic film maker is dramatized as a Homeric hero in search of his lost homeland. Angelopoulos's work is pervaded with allusions, both visual and verbal, to Classical Greece, and echoes from the work of Angelopoulos's favourite poet George Seferis, notably from the sequence *Mythistorema* (1935), recur in the films.

Much of Angelopoulos's work is concerned with history and the director has designated a collection of his early films the "Historical Trilogy"; this includes *Meres tou '36* (Days of '36, 1970), *O Thiasos*, and *I Kynigoi* (The Hunters, 1977), three films which did much to establish the director's international stature. The first is set around the time of the Metaxas dictatorship and focuses on a political prisoner called Sofianos (Kostas Pavlou) who holds a politician hostage, with dire consequences. The second, which was made shortly before the fall of the military Junta, is a four-hour film that explores the conflicts of the Civil War as seen through the eyes of a troupe of actors whose performances are continually and tragically interrupted. This is undoubtedly one of Angelopoulos's most ambitious films which moves chronologically from the 1930s to the 1950s, encompassing the Metaxas dictatorship, the Italian invasion of Greece, the German occupation, and the Nazi defeat. The final film in the trilogy, *I Kynigoi*, begins in the 1970s with the discovery by hunters of the body of a partisan killed in 1949.

While Angelopoulos's films engage with the turbulence of Greek history and explore real historical moments, on another level they probe the meanings of history itself. As one critic has aptly observed, they should perhaps be regarded as "reflections on history, rather than historical films". As in *I Kynigoi*, they shed light on the ways in which history, embodied in the dead partisan, is continually and unexpectedly resurfacing to trouble the present. Similarly, in *Megalexandros* (1980), the director both celebrates and undermines notions of a grand historical narrative, in a manner that recalls the panoramic sweep of Bernardo Bertolucci's *1900* (1976). The film was shot in a remote village near Grevena in Greek Macedonia and, like Bertolucci's film, takes place in 1900. It relates the story of a heroic Greek bandit (Omero Antonutti) who has ambitions to become a modern Alexander the Great. Escaping from prison with a band of his followers, the bandit kidnaps a group of Englishmen and women and seizes a village in northern Greece which has established an egalitarian way of life based on the abolition of property and the equality of rights. The narrative charts the destruction of the Utopian community, however, as the hostages are murdered and Alexander changes from a hero into a ruthless tyrant. Eventually he is murdered by the villagers and the village itself is secured by government forces.

Following the so-called "trilogy of silence" which included *Taxidi sta Kythira*, *O Melissokomos*, and *Topio stin Omichli*, Angelopoulos produced two films which reflect upon the significance of borders and identity. In *To Meteoro Vima tou Pelargou* (The Suspended Step of the Stork, 1991) a young TV journalist (Gregory Karr) attempts to unearth the secret of a politician's (Marcello Mastroianni) disappearance on the Greek-Albanian border, while the narrative of *Ulysses' Gaze* centres on a film maker's (Keitel) journey to Sarajevo across the borders of a war-torn southeastern Europe in search of three missing reels of the first film footage ever shot in the Balkans. The emotional power of both films is enhanced by Eleni Karaindrou's haunting musical score.

ROBERT SHANNAN PECKHAM

See also Cinema

Biography
Born in Athens in 1935, Angelopoulos studied law at the University of Athens and anthropology at the Sorbonne. Returning to Athens in 1964, he became a film critic. He directed his first film, a short, in 1968, and since then he has directed more than a dozen feature films as well as TV work. His films have won numerous awards.

Further Reading
Canosa, Fabiano, George Kaloyeropoulos and Gerald O'Grady (editors), *Theo Angelopoulos*, New York: Museum of Modern Art, 1990

Horton, Andrew, "Th. Angelopoulos and the New Greek Cinema", *Film Criticism*, 6/1 (Fall 1981): pp. 10–20

Horton, Andrew, "Theodore Angelopoulos, The New Greek Cinema and Byzantine Iconology", *Modern Greek Studies Yearbook*, vol. 2 (1986)

Horton, Andrew, "The New Greek Cinema and Theodore Angelopoulos' Melissokomos", *Modern Greek Studies Yearbook*, vol. 13 (1987)

Horton, Andrew (editor) *The Last Modernist: The Films of Theo Angelopoulos*, Trowbridge, Wiltshire: Flicks, and Westport, Connecticut: Greenwood Press, 1997

Horton, Andrew, *The Films of Theo Angelopoulos: A Cinema of Contemplation*, Princeton, New Jersey: Princeton University Press, 1997

Kolovos, Nikos, *Thodoros Angelopoulos*, Athens, 1990 (in Greek)

Ani

Capital of medieval Armenia

Ani lies 45 km east of Kars in northeastern Anatolia. Its stunning position, a naturally strategic triangular site with eventually walled sides, each about 2 km long, overlooks a gorge of the Arpa Çay (Ahurean river) which is today the border between Turkey and Armenia, and could not escape early defences. In the 5th century AD the Kamsarakan dynasty held a fortress on the citadel at the southern point. From the 8th to the 10th centuries the area (Armenian Shirak) was in Arab hands, but the Armenian Bagratids made Kars their capital. In 961 Ashot III (952–77) moved his capital from Kars to Ani, initiating immense public works. Under Smbat II (977–89) the cathedral was begun and the outline of the great city walls, punctuated by semicircular towers, was completed. Under

Gagik I (989–1020) the cathedral was completed and Ani became the seat of the *katholikos* (patriarch) of Armenia, whose synod hall and regal sepulchral churches lie around the monastery of Horomos, 15 km north of Ani, on the serpentine border which has both divided and preserved them.

The building boom in cut redstone which lasted at Ani from 961 to the early 11th century also included the construction of cisterns, baths, palaces, caravansarays, and churches – variously put by Armenians at 1001 churches and by Ibn al-Athir at a more credible 500. The most delightful surviving church is St Gregory Abugamrents, a 10th-century cylinder with conical dome. But the architect of the three most striking churches is named by inscription as Trdat, a genius who looked back to varied early Armenian examples. For Smbat II and Katranidze, wife of Gagik I, Trdat built the cathedral (989–1001): a vast domed basilica, the largest upstanding building in Ani, which to Westerners who have not seen St Gayane at Vagharshapat looks Romanesque; the ruined circular church of St Gregory of Gagik (1001) is based on Zvartznots; and the immense church of the Redeemer, which Trdat built in 1036 for a merchant prince, is an octafoil carrying an inscription of market regulations and a very large dome, which is falling in stages.

Following Basil II's Byzantine expansion into northeastern Anatolia, the Armenian *katholikos* Peter Getadarts surrendered Ani to the Byzantines in 1045, which then served as capital of the short-lived theme of Iberia until it was taken by the Seljuks in 1064. There seems to be no building activity attributable to this period. After the battle of Manzikert in 1071, the Seljuks sold Ani to the Kurdish Shaddadid emirs whence it passed to the Zakarids, but the place remained a strategic and polyglot commercial centre after the arrival of the Mongols of the Ilkhans of Iran. For example, in 1215 a merchant prince, Tigranes Honents, financed a beautiful church overlooking the gorge above the now broken bridge between Turkey and Armenia. Dedicated to St Gregory the Illuminator of Armenia, his miracle cycle was painted by Georgian artists – Greek work has also been claimed. It was only with the Timurid Mongol conquest of the early 15th century that Ani lost its importance. When it was in Russian hands in the 19th century and Turkish in the 20th century, it was examined by many archaeologists, but the border has preserved it for further study.

ANTHONY A.M. BRYER

See also Armenia

Summary
Situated in northeast Anatolia, the city of Ani lies on the modern border between Turkey and Armenia. After two centuries of Arab rule, the area became Armenian again and Ashot III (952–77) moved his capital from Kars to Ani. Grand buildings were constructed. From 1045 Ani was the capital of Byzantine Iberia but it was taken by the Seljuks in 1064. Ani lost its importance after the Mongol conquest in the 15th century.

Further Reading
Lynch, H.F.B., *Armenia*, vol. 1: *The Russian Provinces*, London: Longman, 1901, pp. 316–408
Sinclair, T.A., *Eastern Turkey: An Architectural and Archaeological Survey*, vol. 1, London: Pindar, 1987, pp. 349–84

Animals

In Hellenic society animals have been essential with regard to the practicalities of farm work and food production, transport and war, hunting and sacrifice. Yet for the Greeks the cultural significance of animals goes beyond the practical. Greek myth in words and pictures represents real and imagined animals to explore culture, and uses them as conceptual tools. The Greeks not only used animals for practical purposes, they also used animals to think with.

In Greek society, predominantly rural, animal husbandry has always been important and in the late 20th century nearly one-third of the Greek population works in agriculture, although many farm animals are now reared indoors, often by intensive methods. The imagery of farming has informed Greek expression from Homeric epic on, where "towards evening'" is rendered as "the time for unyoking oxen" (*boulytonde*, as in the *Iliad*, 16. 779 and the *Odyssey*, 9. 58), while the early system of writing left to right and back again was described in terms of oxen ploughing (*boustrophedon*). Even the Greek gods were herdsmen (Apollo in the *Homeric Hymn to Hermes*; Helios in the *Odyssey*) and Zeus, Poseidon, and Dionysus have special taurine associations. Sheep and goats were indispensable for their wool as well as their milk and meat (Theocritus' goatherd and shepherd argue about whose fleeces are best, *Idyll* 5) and feature often in the mythic imagination. Pan is the goat god and the song that accompanied the sacrifice of a billy goat (*tragos*) is linked to the development of tragedy, while the shepherd tending his flock is a common literary theme; Polyphemus and Paris on Ida are early examples, while the Hellenistic pastoral of Theocritus and Longus romanticized shepherds as figures of past innocence, and Christian iconography represents Christ as a shepherd caring for his flock.

Animals were the objects of scientific enquiry for scholars such as Aristotle (*History of Animals*) and the 14th-century writer of the Byzantine *Diegesis ton Tetrapodon Zoon* [Descriptions of Four-Legged Animals]. Foreign fauna interested travellers such as Herodotus and Kosmas Indikopleustes and the Byzantines exhibited exotic creatures such as lions, leopards, crocodiles, bears, antelopes, and ostriches in the hippodrome and in zoos – in the 11th century Constantine IX Monomachos set up a menagerie in Constantinople (Attaleiates, 48–50). Wild animals provided entertainment by fighting (*theriomachountes*), each other or humans; animal–human combat is documented by Justinian I (*Novellae*, 105. 1) and features in Christian martyrology and hagiography.

Horses were valued highly for their service in battle and equestrian competition. The Homeric heroes in their horsehair-crested helmets fight from horsedrawn chariots and many, in particular Hector, are epithetically tamers of horses. Several war horses have their names recorded (unusual for animals): Alexander's Bucephalas was famous (Plutarch, *Alexander*, 61, Strabo, 698) while Achilles' horses, including Xanthus who prophesied Achilles' death (*Iliad*, 19. 478–94), mourned Patroclus (*Iliad*, 17. 443–47). At Athens the citizen class of cavalrymen, said to have been instituted by Solon, consisted of men from wealthy families – the cavalry provided their own horses. Equestrianism was associated with the rich; in

Aristophanes' *Clouds* Strepsiades complains that his son is bankrupting him with his mania for horses and racing. At the Panathenaic games competitors rode bareback or drove four-horse chariots around the race course (*hippodromos*). Pindar in an epinician ode records the victory of a successful race-horse, Pherenicus (*Olympian*, 1. 18), and many of the prize vases presented to the victors depict races. However, Church Fathers such as John Chrysostom were less enthusiastic about horse-racing (*Patrologiae Cursus, Series Graeca*, 59. 519. 33–34).

Animals are often anthropomorphized; writers from Aesop to Aristotle (*Historia Animalium*, 488b13–24) ascribed to animals human characteristics, while Aristophanic comedies such as *Birds* and *Wasps* and the political verse of 14th-century Byzantium such as Theodore Prodromos's *Katomyomachia* and the anonymous *Porikologos* and *Opsarologos* used animals to satirize contemporary society. Human beings are often described in animal terms – greedy people are like wolves, timid people are like deer, and, according to Semonides' poem of the 7th century BC which categorizes women according to animal type, chaste women are like bees (fr. 7 Diehl). The animal skins worn by maenads and the lion slayer Heracles represent an immediate association with the natural and the wild, yet too intimate an affinity with the bestial collapses the radical distinction between humans and other animals, an important predicate of Greek thought in antiquity and the Christian era, although the theory of reincarnation associated with the Pythagoreans which envisaged the transmigration of human souls into animals' bodies blurred this boundary. Hesiod separated man from animal on the grounds that men possess justice and do not eat one another (*Works and Days*, 276ff.); the Homeric hero should display the ferocity that wild creatures embody (Achilles entering battle is a ravening lion, *Iliad*, 20. 164–73) but should not become too beastly (Achilles' desire to eat Hector raw, *Iliad*, 22. 345–46)); the wild carnage and desire to eat raw flesh assimilates the bestialized man to the non-human, a wild animal or a monster like the uncivilized, cannibalistic Cyclops.

Greek myth transforms human beings into animals typically as a punishment: the witch Circe turns Odysseus' crew into pigs (*Odyssey*, 10. 233–43); Artemis makes Callisto a bear and Actaeon a stag; Lycaon, who sacrificed his child to Zeus, became a wolf (and was associated with the werewolf cult). Myth produced a variety of species hybrids like the hippocampus (horse–fish) and chimaera (lion–snake–goat) but Greek myth was interested particularly in animal–human mixtures such as satyrs (donkey–men) and centaurs (horse–men), anomalous creatures which, in blurring the human–animal boundary, draw attention to its importance. The wildness of drunken satyrs, played in satyr drama and painted on sympotic pottery, suggested the dangerous pleasures of bestializing Dionysiac excess; the centauromachy of the Parthenon in which the savage centaurs who disrupt the wedding feast are defeated by the Lapiths signifies the victory of civilization over wildness. Animal imagery is important too in Christian myth and iconography; in the Byzantine period the *Physiologos* and *Hexaemeron* used animals to symbolize virtues and vices and throughout the Christian era the devil has been represented as a snake. Dragons too were identified with evil and with enemies of the Church such as the emperor Julian (361–63);

saints such as George and Elisabeth were portrayed defeating dragons.

Artemis, associated iconographically with the stag, was mistress of wild animals (*Iliad*, 21. 470) and she protected them, although as the huntress she killed beasts. Similes of hunting and wild predators are common in Homer and scenes of horses and hounds were popular with artists, who depicted the killing of deer, boar, hares, and lions. In the Byzantine period scenes of animal–human combat were added to this repertoire, as were illustrations of falconry, a popular pastime. A portion of the hunted animal was offered to the gods, yet wild animals were seldom thought to be the proper objects of sacrifice (one exception is the cult of Artemis at Patras: Pausanias, 7. 18. 12). The ritual slaughter of domestic beasts, however, was ubiquitous, although the vegetable offerings and vegetarianism of Orphic and Pythagorean cult ran counter to this principle. The best sacrifice was a bull; also of value were cows, sheep (rams were better than ewes), pigs, and poultry. Pigs were slaughtered in purification rituals. Fish and smaller animals were rarely offered to the gods, although Pausanias mentions puppy sacrifice (3. 14. 8).

The choice of sacrificial victim sometimes mirrored a religious iconography that frequently associated gods with specific animals: at Athens Athena, who carries a goatskin aegis, was honoured with goat sacrifices, while more generally bulls were connected with Zeus and Dionysus, cattle with Hera, doves with Aphrodite, and horses with Poseidon, mythically the ultimate ancestor of the horse. Typically sacrifice entailed the ritual cutting of the animal's throat, but at Argos horses were drowned for Poseidon (Pausanias, 8. 7. 2). Christianity rejected the tradition of animal sacrifice but pagan magic continued to use animals.

Animals were important in prophecy; seers inspected the entrails of sacrificial victims and augurs inferred the future from watching birds in flight and, less commonly, fish swimming. Birds of prey were particularly significant: the eagle was Zeus' bird, and Hesiod's tale of the hawk and the nightingale is a fable of kingly power (*Works and Days*, 202–12). Snakes, thought to be intermediaries between this world and the next, were associated with oracles, with the dead, and with chthonic deities such as Aeschylus' snaky-haired Erinyes. Indeed, several autochthonous myths have serpentine nuances; Cecrops, the first earthborn king of Athens, was a serpent from the waist down, while the foundation of Thebes was marked by the birth of the Spartoi, sprung from the dragon's teeth.

Traditionally the Greeks have kept animals for their usefulness, but in modern Greece cats and dogs, caged birds, and fish are popular pets and even in the ancient world some animals lived indoors; Telemachus' dogs follow him around the house (*Odyssey*, 2. 11, 17. 62), Theocritus' housewife orders her slave to let the dog in and keep the cats out of the knitting basket, although the cats here – *galeai* – may have been pole cats (*Idyll*, 15. 44 and 28), and the Byzantines kept animals as companions. Homer in particular describes human affection for animals: Polyphemus' doting care for his flock is his one redeeming characteristic (*Odyssey*, 9. 446–60) and Odysseus weeps when his old dog Argos dies (*Odyssey*, 17. 290–327).

EUGÉNIE FERNANDES

See also Divination, Hunting, Mythology, Satyr Play, Spells, Zoology

Further Reading

Anderson, John Kinloch, *Ancient Greek Horsemanship*, Berkeley: University of California Press, 1961

Bowie, A.M., "Greek Sacrifice: Forms and Functions" in *The Greek World*, edited by Anton Powell, London and New York: Routledge, 1995

Burkert, Walter, *Homo Necans: The Anthropology of Ancient Greek Sacrificial Ritual and Myth*, Berkeley: University of California Press, 1983

Burkert, Walter, *Greek Religion: Archaic and Classical*, Oxford: Blackwell, and Cambridge, Massachusetts: Harvard University Press, 1985

Buxton, Richard, *Imaginary Greece: The Contexts of Mythology*, Cambridge and New York: Cambridge University Press, 1994

Detienne, Marcel, *The Gardens of Adonis*, Hassocks, East Sussex: Harvester Press, and Atlantic Highlands, New Jersey: Humanities Press, 1977, reprinted Princeton, New Jersey: Princeton University Press, 1994

Detienne, Marcel and Jean-Pierre Vernant, *The Cuisine of Sacrifice among the Greeks*, translated by Paula Wissing, Chicago: University of Chicago Press, 1989

Dowden, Ken, *The Uses of Greek Mythology*, London and New York: Routledge, 1992

DuBois, Page, *Centaurs and Amazons: Women and the Prehistory of the Great Chain of Being*, Ann Arbor: University of Michigan Press, 1982

Isager, Signe and Jens Erik Skydsgaard, *Ancient Greek Agriculture: An Introduction*, London and New York: Routledge, 1992

Lissarrague, F., "Why Satyrs Are Good to Represent" in *Nothing to Do with Dionysos? Athenian Drama in Its Social Context*, edited by John J. Winkler and Froma I. Zeitlin, Princeton, New Jersey: Princeton University Press, 1990

Lissarrague, F., "On the Wildness of Satyrs" in *Masks of Dionysus*, edited by Daniel E. Anderson, Albany: State University of New York Press, 1993

Lloyd, G.E.R., *Science, Folklore and Ideology: Studies in the Life Sciences in Ancient Greece*, Cambridge and New York: Cambridge University Press, 1983

Loraux, Nicole, *The Children of Athena: Athenian Ideas about Citizenship and the Division between the Sexes*, Princeton, New Jersey: Princeton University Press, 1993

Murray, Oswyn (editor), *Sympotica: A Symposium on the Symposion*, Oxford: Clarendon Press, and New York: Oxford University Press, 1990

Onians, Richard Broxton, *The Origins of European Thought about the Body, the Mind, the Soul, the World, Time and Fate*, 2nd edition, Cambridge: Cambridge University Press, 1954

Redfield, James M., *Nature and Culture in the Iliad: The Tragedy of Hector*, Chicago: University of Chicago Press, 1975, expanded edition Durham, North Carolina: Duke University Press, 1994

Renenhan, R., "The Greek Anthropocentric View of Man", *Harvard Studies in Classical Philology*, 85 (1981): pp. 239–59

Seaford, R., "The Origins of Satyric Drama", *Maia*, 28 (1976): pp. 209–21

Sourvinou-Inwood, Christiane, *"Reading" Greek Culture*, Oxford: Clarendon Press, and New York: Oxford University Press, 1991

Talbot Rice, T., "Animal Combat Scenes in Byzantine Art" in *Studies in Memory of David Talbot Rice*, edited by Giles Robertson and George Henderson, Edinburgh: Edinburgh University Press, 1975

Tambiah, S.J., "Animals are Good to Think and Good to Prohibit", *Ethnology*, 8 (1969): pp 423–59

Théodoridès, J., "Les Animaux des jeux de l'Hippodrome", *Byzantine Studies*, 19 (1958): pp. 73–84

Thompson, D'Arcy Wentworth, *A Glossary of Greek Birds*, Oxford: Clarendon Press, 1895, reprinted Hildesheim: Olms, 1966

Thompson, D'Arcy Wentworth, *A Glossary of Greek Fishes*, London: Oxford University Press, 1947

Veyne, Paul, *Did the Greeks Believe in Their Myths? An Essay on the Constitutive Imagination*, Chicago: University of Chicago Press, 1988

Vidal-Naquet, Pierre, *The Black Hunter: Forms of Thought and Forms of Society in the Greek World*, Baltimore: Johns Hopkins University Press, 1986

Anthology, Greek

Collection of epigrams from the 7th century BC to the 10th century AD

The present *Greek Anthology* is the culmination of a process of anthologizing which began in the 3rd century BC. It properly consists of two collections of epigrams written mainly in the elegiac metre. The *Palatine Anthology* is a compilation from the 10th century AD of 3765 poems, so called from a manuscript once in Rome and now divided between Heidelberg (Universitätsbibliothek, Palat. gr. 23) and Paris (Bibliothèque Nationale, suppl. gr. 384). The *Planudean Anthology* is a 13th- or 14th-century compilation of approximately 2,400 poems, of which 388 do not appear in the *Palatine Anthology*. It was this shorter collection, first published in 1494 by the Byzantine émigré John Laskaris, that was long known in the West as the *Greek Anthology*. The *Palatine Anthology* was not published until the early 19th century, by Friedrich Jacobs (Leipzig, 1813–17).

It was common practice for individual poets of the Hellenistic period to collect their own short poems into an individual book, and the *Soros* [Heap] may have been a joint edition of the epigrammatists Asclepiades, Posidippus, and Hedylus in the early 3rd century BC. True anthologies of poems by different authors were much rarer, although there is some scanty evidence for them from the end of the 4th century BC. The earliest extensive such compilation known today appears to be the *Stephanos* [Garland] of Meleager of Gadara in Syria, which was put together around 100 BC. This is an artistically arranged selection of poems from the previous two centuries, to which Meleager added a preface in which he named all the poets and attributed to each the name of a flower. His collection included graceful poems of his own composition, mainly erotic and addressed to both boys and girls. A second *Garland*, arranged alphabetically by the first word of each poem, was compiled, probably during the reign of Nero, by Philip of Thessalonica. His choice was more eclectic than Meleager's with less emphasis on love and more on rhetorical description (his personal contribution comprises 80 such poems). The first compilation to be called an "anthology", literally a "gathering of flowers", is that of Diogenianus of Heraclea during the time of Hadrian, although the title may be a lexicographer's description and not Diogenianus' own. *Cycle* was the name selected by the lawyer and historian Agathias of Myrina for a further anthology published probably shortly after AD 560. This contains classicizing epigrams by his Constantinopolitan friends and about 100 from his own hand.

The first really comprehensive anthology was that of Constantine Kephalas, who was possibly a palace chaplain mentioned by chroniclers as active in 917. It comprised the poems gathered by Meleager, Philip, Diogenianus (probably from a 4th-century abridgement), Agathias, and other anthologists and in further individual collections such as the pederastic *Musa Puerilis* of the 2nd-century AD poet Straton of Sardis and the often humorous and satiric poems of the 4th-century AD Alexandrian schoolmaster Palladas. Remarkably, it also included poetic inscriptions on Byzantine churches copied down by a contemporary, the *magistros* Gregory of Kampsa (in Macedonia), during his travels in Greece, Macedonia, and Asia Minor. Although Kephalas's anthology is lost, it formed the bulk of the surviving *Palatine Anthology*. This huge compilation included additional Christian and rhetorically descriptive epigrams. Its compiler is unknown, but it may have been the early 10th-century poet Constantine of Rhodes, three of whose poems it includes.

The *Palatine Anthology* is divided thematically into 15 books of widely differing lengths. Their contents are: (1) 123 Christian epigrams that are mainly copies of inscriptions on Byzantine churches; (2) 65 descriptions in hexameters by the 5th- to 6th -century Egyptian poet Christodoros of Koptos (known also as of Thebes) of the statues of Classical mythological and historical figures in the baths of Zeuxippos in Constantinople; (3) 19 epigrams on filial mythological themes inscribed by two brothers on the columns of a temple at Cyzicus in honour of their mother; (4) the four prefaces to their anthologies of Meleager, Philippos, and Agathias (2); (5) 309 amatory epigrams; (6) 358 dedicatory epigrams; (7) 748 epitaphs; (8) 254 epigrams of St Gregory of Nazianzus; (9) 827 declamatory and descriptive epigrams; (10) 126 hortatory epigrams; (11) 64 convivial and 378 satiric epigrams; (12) 258 erotic and usually pederastic epigrams attributed, probably not always correctly, to Straton; (13) 31 miscellaneous poems in 30 different metres or combinations; (14) 150 arithmetical problems (perhaps all by Metrodoros), riddles, and oracles; (15) 51 miscellaneous poems including six *technopaegnia* (jeux d'esprit), the shapes of whose lines resemble panpipes, an axe, a pair of wings, an altar (two poems), and an egg.

Around 1300 Maximos Planudes, a scribe in the imperial palace and translator of Latin texts, made his own anthology of epigrams. For this he used three now lost manuscripts, two of collections similar to the *Palatine Anthology* and a third of an abridged version of Kephalas's collection. Planudes both rejected many poems and, making skilful use of his metrical knowledge, "emended" others to reflect contemporary propriety. The *Planudean Anthology* is divided into seven books – epideictic, satiric, funerary, ekphrastic epigrams, the hexameters of Christodoros, votive, and amatory epigrams. Each book is subdivided, poems on each theme being arranged alphabetically. Planudes' autograph manuscript (Venice, Biblioteca Nazionale Marciana, Marc. gr. 481) is dated 1301 (or 1299) and there survive also a preliminary and an incomplete final revision done under the compiler's supervision. The 388 poems unique to this compilation, usually collectively called the *Planudean Appendix* or, incorrectly, book 16 of the *Palatine Anthology*, are mainly epigrams about or imaginarily inscribed upon statues and paintings.

The *Anthology* has had a decisive influence on the literatures of modern European languages, especially during the Renaissance. In Greece itself, however, it was largely unknown to the vernacular poets, and the writers in the "purified" language (katharevousa) turned rather to French and Italian models. The main exception is Cavafy, an Alexandrian like many of the poets in the *Anthology*. Many of his poems are on Hellenistic themes, while the homoerotic ones are often inspired by or even based upon the *Anthology*'s epigrams of death and love. Unlike their predecessors, however, they are not pederastic, and, despite being less explicit, are generally more sensuous and anguished as a result of both his own personality and the contemporary attitude towards homo-sexuality.

The *Greek Anthology* is a garden with possibly more weeds than flowers, but it shows in an incomparable way the development of the genre of the epigram over more than one and a half millennia. It contains some of the most exquisite poems ever written in Greek: the world would be immeasurably the poorer were it not for its survival.

A.R. LITTLEWOOD

See also Epigram

Summary

The *Greek Anthology* is a collection of Greek epigrams dating from the 7th century BC to the 10th century AD. It consists of two collections – the *Palatine Anthology* (3765 poems) compiled in the 10th century and the *Planudean Anthology* (which contains 388 additional poems in its total of about 2400) compiled in the 13th–14th centuries. It demonstrates the evolution of the Greek epigram as a genre over more than 1500 years.

Text

The Greek Anthology with an English Translation, translated by W.R. Paton, 5 vols, London: Heinemann, and New York: Putnam, 1916–18 (Loeb edition; frequently reprinted)

Further Reading

Caires, V.A., "Originality and Eroticism: Constantine Cavafy and the Alexandrian Epigram", *Byzantine and Modern Greek Studies*, 6 (1980): pp. 131–55

Cameron, Alan, *The Greek Anthology: From Meleager to Planudes*, Oxford: Clarendon Press, and New York: Oxford University Press, 1993

Fowler, Barbara Hughes, *The Hellenistic Aesthetic*, Madison: University of Wisconsin Press, and Bristol: Bristol Classical Press, 1989

Anthropology, Social

Social anthropology (*anthropos*: Greek for "human being") involves the study of societies, particularly the cultural values and institutions such as religion, law, or politics that organize relations between people. Anthropologists attempt to understand how people in various communities perceive and inhabit their worlds. The focus below will be on social anthropological studies of Greece as well as anthropological studies done by Greeks.

Herodotus is generally viewed as the father of anthropology. He travelled extremely widely for a man of his time, from the Black Sea to Aswan in Upper Egypt, and from Sicily to Cyprus. His *Histories* mention more than 50 different tribes or "nations", including lengthy descriptions of the Egyptians and the Scythians. He did not stay long in these various places; he was more like a tourist than an ethnographic fieldworker. What distinguished him from earlier historians and mythographers was his application of a rationalist approach, which he called *historia*, literally "research, inquiry" – the very same term the early philosophers used to describe their investigations of nature. He would compare accounts and reject the less likely, or register his own scepticism. As he demurs at one point, "For myself, my duty is to report all that is said, but I am not obliged to believe it all."

Herodotus approached the study of society with distinct categories and questions in mind. He operated according to an implicit social theory that led him to scrutinize descent, language, and religion as the criteria that distinguished one group from another. In his accounts of specific groups he tended to emphasize marriage customs, religious rites, burial practices, and food habits – categories that would shape subsequent ethnographic thought throughout the Middle Ages. The pole of comparison of these various forms of life was, of course, the 5th-century Greek world. In kinship and marriage, for example, the Greeks were patriarchal and patrilineal, and this made for comparative interest in the Lycians who reckoned descent matrilineally, or in the Massagetae who were promiscuous, or the Issedonians who ate their dead parents, but treated their wives as equals.

Herodotus' rational historical method tended to break down in the description of peoples inhabiting the limits of the known world such as the Issedonians. His report that in India there was a tribe "that will not take life in any form; they sow no seed, and have no houses and live on a vegetable diet" apparently contained a kernel of truth. Yet in other passages he wrote of people with feet like goats and others who slept half the year. The Roman imperial historian Pliny continued this exoticizing of peripheral peoples, expanding Herodotus' inventory of ethnological curiosities to include the Gamphastes who went naked and practised non-violence, and the headless Blemmyae whose eyes and mouths were set in their chests. These and other fantastic stories found their way on to medieval maps and influenced the perception of the world until the age of exploration.

The 16th and 17th centuries not only brought Europe into contact with hitherto unexplored parts of the world, it was also the period of the rebirth of humanistic interest in ancient Greece. One result of this historical coincidence of philological and geographical exploration was the appearance of books comparing the institutions and values of the ancients with those of contemporary "savages" in the newly colonized world. The French missionary Joseph-François Lafitau's 1724 volume comparing native North Americans to the Greeks and Romans was just one example of this trend. In addition to his primary interest in religion, Lafitau collected correspondences in domains such as government, family organization, education, and the gendered division of labour. The general conclusion that Lafitau and his contemporaries drew from this kind of research was that native Americans and the people of Classical antiquity must have sprung from one and the same source.

The chronological and evolutionary specifics of the relationship between contemporary inhabitants of small-scale societies and the ancients were further worked out in the 19th century. The view of high Victorian anthropology drew heavily on the ideas of evolution and progress. For E.B. Tylor, who became the world's first professional anthropologist upon assuming a readership at Oxford in 1884, all humans possessed the same mental equipment but some had developed faster and further than others. He divided humanity into three stages: savagery, barbarism, and civilization. The Britain of his day exemplified the last stage, and he and his countrymen could look at small-scale societies in places like Africa and Melanesia, or ancient societies in Greece or Rome, to see what they had once been like. Savagery was characterized by "animism" – the idea that spirits and supernatural beings animated and controlled the natural and human worlds. Homeric descriptions of the souls of warriors departing through their mouths at death could be compared with similar beliefs among peoples of the Malay archipelago. Tylor also considered that isolated elements from earlier stages of humanity could filter through to civilized societies as "survivals" – little irrationalities and superstitions like saying "Bless you!" when someone sneezed.

One of the goals of Tylor's follower, Sir James Frazer, was to identify and extirpate these survivals, thereby paving the road to progress. Frazer's multivolume work *The Golden Bough* (1890–1915) exhaustively catalogued and compared beliefs in fertility, death, and resurrection held by ancient societies, contemporary "primitive" societies, and even European peasants who, it was thought, had not been touched by "civilization". Frazer was an accomplished Classical scholar and his cross-cultural ethnographic learning also found its way into his six-volume commentary on the Greek traveller Pausanias. His influence touched the turn-of-the-century "Cambridge Ritualist" school of Jane Harrison, F.M. Cornford, and others, who made ample use of cross-cultural materials in presenting their arguments about the priority of ritual to myth in ancient Greek society.

Beginning with Bronislaw Malinowski in the 1920s, fieldwork, involving a residence of a year or more among the people under study, became the standard method of data collection in anthropology. During this time the anthropologist was expected to learn the language of the group under study and attempt, through the method of "participant observation", to capture "the native's point of view". Malinowski eschewed the hypothetical historicism of his Victorian predecessors. Societies were to be explained by his functional theory that emphasized how institutions enabled people to adapt to their environment and maintain social harmony in the present.

Malinowski's revolution spelled the end of the comparative, evolutionary, anthropological interest in ancient Greece that had flourished since the Renaissance, and it was not until after World War II that a variety of new approaches began to emerge. In 1955 Claude Lévi-Strauss published his essay on "The Structural Study of Myth" in which he applied his structuralist method to the myth of Oedipus. This called for a solid ethnographic knowledge of the society and the region whose myths were being considered. Lévi-Strauss was no specialist on ancient Greek culture and he even admitted in the course of his essay that Oedipus was "an arbitrary example, treated in an arbitrary manner". His structuralist method, however, was later to prove fruitful in the hands of the French Classical scholars Jean-Pierre Vernant and Marcel Detienne who produced stunning analyses of the cult of Hestia and the myth of Adonis respectively. These analyses depended upon detailed knowledge of Greek domestic space arrangements, ideas about gender, sexuality, and the symbolic associations of herbs and spices, to name just a few cultural categories.

Another postwar development was the general application of anthropological theories to illuminate Classical Greek values and institutions. The classicist E.R. Dodds (*The Greeks and the Irrational*, 1951) borrowed the American anthropologist Ruth Benedict's distinction between shame and guilt cultures to differentiate the Homeric world, where public appearances counted most, from the world depicted by the Classical tragedians, where actors were riven by internalized dilemmas. In another novel departure the ancient historian M.I. Finley applied the economic anthropological theories of Mauss and Polanyi to the understanding of ancient Greek gift giving, friendship, and trade (*The World of Odysseus*, 1954). From this point onwards anthropological theories and comparative examples have featured prominently and regularly in major works such as Walter Burkert's study of Greek sacrifice (*Homo Necans*, 1983) or James Redfield's study of social values in Homeric epic (*Nature and Culture in the Iliad*, 1975).

The study of modern Greek societies through ethnographic field research represented another important mid-20th-century departure. Up until this moment modern Greek village life and traditonal beliefs had been the province of folklorists and travellers from the 19th century and earlier. Scholars such as John Cuthbert Lawson and Nikolaos Politis were primarily interested in discovering survivals of ancient culture in modern Greece. Although roughly contemporary with the British Victorian anthropologists mentioned above, these folklorists took an entirely different view of survivals. In their view survivals added to knowledge about the revered ancients while also furnishing documentary evidence that the modern Greeks really were valid descendants of the ancients. This was an important national issue for the Greek state after nearly 400 years of Ottoman domination.

The new generation of anthropologists were not concerned with these issues, but rather with Malinowski's programme of rendering a holistic account of the community under immediate study. The American anthropologist Ernestine Friedl presented a monograph (1962) describing life in a Boeotian farming village that considered issues of tradition and modernity. And John Campbell published an account (1964) of the Sarakatsani, a transhumant group of pastoralists in Epirus. Campbell's study was the first full-length exploration of a cognatic kindred, a system where descent is reckoned through both parents. More theoretical focus was given to early anthropological research in Greece by John Peristiany, arguably the first Greek anthropologist to emerge after Herodotus. Peristiany conducted fieldwork in his native Cyprus and edited an influential volume entitled *Honour and Shame: The Values of Mediterranean Society* (1966) that drew together studies documenting a pan-Mediterranean set of complementary values. Men in these societies were held to possess "honour" – the ability to protect one's immediate kin, property, and good name. Women, on the other hand, possessed "shame" – the obligation to conduct themselves with modesty.

Once thought to be the key to understanding Greece, and all Mediterranean societies, the honour and shame complex has been criticized as too rigid. Current research in Greece has moved on to consider the fundamental duality in modern Greek social identity between Classical/western and Ottoman/eastern alternatives – between Hellenism and *Romiosyni*. Among themselves, contemporary Greeks may acknowledge the Ottoman influences on their culture and speak in affectionate, expressive terms that contain numerous Turkish-derived words. For purposes of self-presentation to outsiders these features are downplayed and links with the ancients are emphasized. In such situations more vocabulary may be selected from the katharevousa register, a version of modern Greek invented in the 19th century and designed to purge the spoken language of Turkish and Balkan elements. The performance of Greek identity thus involves constant code-switching between Hellenic and Romaic registers.

One consequence of the florescence of anthropological research on contemporary Greece and Cyprus is that Classical historians may now draw on these data to inform their reconstructions of earlier communities in the very same regions. Archaeologists have exploited this situation to make advances in the area of ethnoarchaeology. In order to further their understanding of ancient Greek subsistence and seasonal work patterns, for example, they may conduct field research among contemporary farmers and shepherds to gain an idea of how much grain a hectare of land normally yields, or how much milk a flock of sheep and goats can provide.

The orientation of this research is paralleled in the work of historians such as David Cohen who argue that the honour and shame complex identified through anthropological research in Greece may deepen the understanding of public morals in Classical Athens. Since independence in 1832 the Greek state, supported by folklorists and foreign travellers, has asserted that it continues the rational and sophisticated traditions of the ancients. Lying, vendettas, and the practices of remote agriculturalists probably did not figure in the state's initial vision of claimable survivals. An unintended consequence of this new research is that the ancient Hellenes now resemble *Romii avant la lettre* and contemporary practices hitherto disparaged as Romaic can now be confidently claimed as Hellenic.

The anthropology of Greece has come full circle in one other respect. Anthropological practice underwent critical re-examination in the 1980s resulting in greater sensitivity to the issues of representation and reflexivity. In principle this meant that more space should be given to representing the unmediated statements and opinions of the people under study, even to the point of making them co-authors of the ethnography. Reflexivity called for the anthropologists to include more information on their personal experiences and feelings in the field. These theoretical developments coincided with the establishment of social anthropology as an academic discipline in Greek universities. Increasing numbers of Greek anthropologists are now undertaking extensive field research in Greece. This rise of an indigenous anthropology offered one solution to the "crisis of representation". Greek anthropologists such as Neni Panourgiá, Nadia Seremetakis, Evthymios Papataxiarchis, and Vassos Argyrou have been able to utilize their total linguistic competence and relative insider status to offer striking accounts of death as experienced within an Athenian family, funeral lamentation in Mani, patterns of drinking and friendship on the island of Lesbos, and champagne as opposed to "traditional" weddings in Cyprus respectively. Public debates have centred on whether these indigenous anthropologists can render more valid accounts of Greek society. The preliminary verdict seems to be "no"; there are likely to be as many different anthropological accounts of a given society as there are anthropologists.

CHARLES STEWART

See also Folklore, Honour and Shame, Identity

Further Reading

Argyrou, Vassos, *Tradition and Modernity in the Mediterranean: The Wedding as Symbolic Struggle*, Cambridge and New York: Cambridge University Press, 1996

Campbell, J.K., *Honour, Family and Patronage: A Study of Institutions and Moral Values in a Greek Mountain Community*, Oxford: Clarendon Press, 1964

Cohen, David, *Law, Sexuality and Society: The Enforcement of Morals in Classical Athens*, Cambridge and New York: Cambridge University Press, 1991

Dodds, E.R., *The Greeks and the Irrational*, Berkeley: University of California Press, 1951

Friedl, Ernestine, *Vasilika: A Village in Modern Greece*, New York: Holt Rinehart, 1962

Herzfeld, Michael, *Anthropology through the Looking-Glass: Critical Ethnography in the Margins of Europe*, Cambridge and New York: Cambridge University Press, 1987

Hodgen, Margaret Trabue, *Early Anthropology in the Sixteenth and Seventeenth Centuries*, Philadelphia: University of Pennsylvania Press, 1964

Humphreys, S.C., *Anthropology and the Greeks*, London and Boston: Routledge, 1978

Jameson, Michael H., Curtis N. Runnels and Tjeerd H. van Andel (editors), *A Greek Countryside: The Southern Argolid from Prehistory to the Present Day*, Stanford, California: Stanford University Press, 1994

Kardulias, P. Nick (editor), *Beyond the Site: Regional Studies in the Aegean Area*, Lanham, Maryland: University Press of America, 1994

Loizos, Peter and Evthymios Papataxiarchis (editors), *Contested Identities: Gender and Kinship in Modern Greece*, Princeton, New Jersey: Princeton University Press, 1991

Panourgiá, Neni, *Fragments of Death, Fables of Identity: An Athenian Anthropography*, Madison: University of Wisconsin Press, 1995

Seremetakis, C. Nadia, *The Last Word: Women, Death and Divination in Inner Mani*, Chicago: University of Chicago Press, 1991

Antigonids

Dynasty of Macedonian kings

With the death of Alexander the Great in 323 BC and the murder of all the members of his immediate family within the following 30 years, the Argead dynasty of Macedonian kings (of which Alexander was a member) was extinguished. The throne of Macedonia was vacant and briefly occupied by various contenders, creating a political situation of great turmoil and instability. Only when Antigonus Gonatas secured

the throne around 277 BC, held it for nearly 30 years, and sired a son who inherited it, can we speak meaningfully of the Antigonid dynasty of kings of Macedonia, but their roots in Macedonian history go back for more than half a century.

The grandfather of Gonatas was Antigonus Monophthalmus (the "One-Eyed"), who was a general throughout the Asian expedition of Alexander the Great. After Alexander's death, he was declared "general" (in Greek *strategos*) – essentially supreme commander – of all Asia, which gave him great power and control over a vast territory. Throughout the next 20 years Antigonus fought to consolidate his position and extend his power at the expense of the other successors of Alexander. At the period of his greatest successes, it might be argued that he came closest to recreating Alexander's kingdom. After some notable military victories, he declared himself and his son Demetrius "kings" in 306 BC. Although they were "kings" without a kingdom in geographical terms, this joint claim suggests that Antigonus intended to establish a hereditary line of rulers.

Antigonus Monophthalmus died on the battlefield of Ipsus in 301 BC, facing a coalition of the other successors. His son Demetrius Poliorcetes ("the Besieger"), who had already acted as Antigonus' roving general throughout Greece and Asia, inherited his father's ambitions. He interfered in the politics of mainland Greece, subdued Athens for a time, and was briefly declared king of Macedonia. In 293 BC Demetrius founded by synoecism a new city, Demetrias, near the site of Classical Pagasae (in turn near the site of Bronze Age Iolcus, from where the legendary Jason set forth on his journey to find the Golden Fleece) in the Gulf of Volos, a few kilometres from the modern city of Volos. In 285 BC, in the course of attempting to recover his father's Asian possessions, Demetrius was captured by Seleucus I of Syria and died in captivity two years later.

Antigonus Gonatas, the son of Demetrius and his wife Phila (the daughter of Antipater, the regent of Macedonia during Alexander the Great's absence), immediately took the title of king and entered the fray for the throne of Macedon. He finally secured it around 277 BC. His long reign saw the Chremonidean war in the 260s BC, when Athens and Sparta tried unsuccessfully to overthrow Macedonian control, and naval victories over the Ptolemies at the battles of Cos and Andros (usually placed in the context of the Chremonidean war). Gonatas died in 239 BC, having outlived all his royal contemporaries. Although his control over mainland Greece was insecure and he had been threatened in Macedonia, he reestablished Macedonia as a nation and made it a kingdom to be ruled by his descendants. On the cultural side, Antigonus had been a pupil of the philosophers Menedemus of Euboea and Zeno of Citium, and his court at Pella was a centre for writers and scholars, among them the historian Hieronymus of Cardia (author of the most reliable account of the decades after the death of Alexander the Great), and the poets Aratus of Soli and Alexander Aetolus.

Gonatas' son Demetrius II had probably been acting as the king's general during much of his father's long rule, but his defence of Macedonia against an Epirot attack at the time of the Chremonidean war is his only known action. He fought a war against Aetolia and the anti-Macedonian Achaeans around 238 BC, and was killed fighting the Illyrian Dardani tribe on the Macedonian frontier in 229 BC, leaving an eight-year-old son, Philip, to face the barbarian threat and the consequences in Greece of a weakened Macedonia.

The boy king Philip V was placed in the care of a regent, Antigonus Doson, a grandson of Demetrius Poliorcetes from one of his minor marriages. Antigonus proved a blessing to the threatened Macedonia, and his loyalty to the young Philip remained unshaken even after he was himself granted the throne around 227/26 BC (thereby becoming Antigonus III). Doson defeated the warlike Dardani tribe, and turned his attention to the south and east. He defeated the Aetolians and Thessalians in 228 BC, and made an expedition to Caria in 227 BC (the circumstances, cause, and purpose of this adventure remain obscure). His chance to re-establish Macedonian influence in mainland Greece came at the surprising request of the usually anti-Macedonian Aratus of Sicyon (the head of the Achaean League) for help in the Peloponnese against the aggressions of Sparta and Aetolia. Doson readily agreed, and was formally offered the citadel of Acrocorinth (which dominated the Isthmus of Corinth) in return for his military support in 225–24 BC. Corinth was occupied by a Macedonian military garrison, and Doson pushed back the threatening Spartan king.

One of the most important acts of Doson's reign was the foundation in 224 BC of the so-called Hellenic League, an alliance of existing Greek federations under Macedonian hegemony. The various federations were to be internally autonomous but interdependent with respect to foreign policy. The foundation of the Hellenic League was potentially significant because Greece was shortly to face the power of Rome, and it is a landmark in the history of federalism. Unfortunately, Doson's premature death prevented the fruition of his plans having real effect. After recovering Arcadia in 223 BC and defeating the Spartan king Cleomenes III at the battle of Sellasia (just north of Sparta) in 222 BC, he returned to Macedonia to face another Illyrian invasion. A burst blood-vessel in his lungs worsened his already weak health, and he died some months later in 221 BC, having provided for the education of his charge Philip V by sending him to Aratus of Sicyon, Macedonia's recent ally, to learn about Greek affairs.

The accession of Philip V as an independent monarch marks the beginning of the end for an independent Macedon, due to its involvement with a now very powerful Rome. Philip was still a teenager when his regent Doson died, but he was immediately plunged into the so-called Social War in which he and the newly founded Hellenic League faced Aetolia and its allies. The war lasted from 220 to 217 BC, and marked Philip's growth into a mature king. He gradually turned away from his new mentor Aratus and towards the camp of an Illyrian dynast named Demetrius of Pharos (the island of Hvar in modern Croatia) in the Adriatic Sea. Rome had rewarded Demetrius with the rule of this petty state when he delivered Corcyra (modern Corfu) into Roman hands, but his various aggressions in the Aegean caused Rome to expel him in 219 BC, and he escaped to Philip in Macedonia nursing a major grievance. Demetrius encouraged Philip's alienation from Aratus and the Achaean League and continually incited him against Rome, in the first instance against the Romans in Illyria. Furthermore, Philip's treaty with the Carthaginian general Hannibal was the death-knell of any hope of friendship with Rome.

The First Macedonian War between Macedonia and Rome began in 214 BC, and soon Rome forged an alliance with Aetolia against Philip. The war began inauspiciously for Philip, with various disasters in the Peloponnese, an ultimate break with Aratus, and the forced burning of his fleet, but his superior forces on land, combined with Roman inaction at critical periods, forced terms on Aetolia in 206 BC. The First Macedonian War was ended by the Peace of Phoenice (a city in Epirus, now in modern Albania), proposed by Rome in 205 BC and favourable to Philip.

Philip turned his attentions eastward, colluding in 203/202 BC with Antiochus III to divide Egypt and experiencing a naval defeat off the island of Chios in 201 BC at the hands of the combined Rhodian and Pergamene fleets. Fearing Philip's intentions, Rome declared the Second Macedonian War in 200 BC. Campaigns were fought in Greece, Thrace, Macedonia, and Thessaly, sometimes with notable successes for Philip, until in desperation Rome appointed Titus Quinctius Flamininus to the command in 198 BC. Under his leadership, in 197 BC the Romans decisively defeated Philip's forces at the battle of Cynoscephalae in Thessaly. Harsh military and financial terms were imposed upon Macedon, and Philip's elder son Demetrius was taken as a hostage to Rome.

Confined to Macedonia as part of the peace terms, Philip concentrated on rebuilding his country. He was now perforce an ally of Rome, albeit an uneasy one, and he had to be seen to support it – which he did against the usurper Nabis of Sparta, Antiochus III, and Aetolia. Rome remained suspicious of Philip, rightly so in view of his aggressive policy in the Balkans after 185 BC (defeating various Thracian tribes, resettling some, and making alliances with others). Philip, probably with the connivance if not the encouragement of his younger son Perseus, engineered the death of his pro-Roman son Demetrius after he was freed from his Roman sojourn, and secured the succession for Perseus, who shared his imperialist tendencies. On a tour of his kingdom in 179 BC, Philip V died of sickness at Amphipolis.

Upon his accession to the throne, Perseus renewed his treaty of friendship with Rome, but carried on his father's policy of consolidating Macedonia. He furthermore made a convenient dynastic marriage to Princess Laodice, daughter of Seleucus IV of Syria. Complaints by Eumenes II of Pergamum in the Roman Senate about Perseus' growing power led to the declaration of the Third Macedonian War in 171 BC. Macedonian advantages in the early years of the war were ended by the appointment of the Roman general Lucius Aemilius Paullus to the command in 168 BC. The Roman forces utterly defeated Perseus at the battle of Pydna (on the east coast of Macedonia south of Thessalonica) in 168 BC. Perseus fled to Samothrace but finally surrendered to the Romans. He and his children were taken captive to Rome, paraded in chains in Paullus' triumph, and the king – the last of the Antigonids – died in a Roman prison shortly thereafter. Macedonia was sacked of all of its wealth and its people were treated harshly. The royal kingdom was abolished, and the country was divided into four republics with elected officials who operated under Roman supervision. A pretender to the throne, Andriscus from Adramyttium in the Troad, claimed to be the son of Perseus, and raised some support for his cause. He had some military successes c.153–148 BC but was defeated by the Roman general

Q. Caecilius Metellus Macedonicus, captured, paraded in triumph at Rome, and executed. Macedonia became a full province of Rome in 146 BC.

The Antigonids re-established Macedonia as a nation after the years of Alexander the Great's absence, the decades of chaos after his death, and the extinction of the Argead dynasty. Under their rule, the country gradually regained its prosperity after the severe depletion of manpower occasioned by the removal of some 40,000 men in their prime to accompany and reinforce the expedition of Alexander the Great. The wealth of Macedonia could not perhaps compete with that of the Ptolemaic and Seleucid empires, but the amount that was removed by the Romans (attested in literary sources) shows that the Antigonid kings could hold their own among other Greek monarchs. However, it was the serious mistakes in judgement by the later Antigonid kings regarding the level of Rome's interest in the Greek east and its ability to carry out its policy that led Macedonia to lose its independence and became the first of the Hellenistic empires to fall under Roman control.

E.E. RICE

See also Macedonia

Further Reading

Astin, A.E. *et al.* (editors), *Rome and the Mediterranean to 133 BC*, Cambridge: Cambridge University Press, 1989 (*The Cambridge Ancient History*, vol. 8, 2nd edition), chapters 4, 8, and 9

Billows, Richard A., *Antigonos the One-Eyed and the Creation of the Hellenistic State*, Berkeley: University of California Press, 1990

Brisco, J., "The Antigonids and the Greek States, 276–196 BC" in *Imperialism in the Ancient World*, edited by P.D.A. Garnsey and C.R. Whittaker, Cambridge and New York: Cambridge University Press, 1978

Errington, R. Malcolm, *A History of Macedonia*, Berkeley: University of California Press, 1990

Gabbert, Janice J., *Antigonus II Gonatas: A Political Biography*, London and New York: Routledge, 1997

Ginouvès, René (editor), *Macedonia: From Philip II to the Roman Conquest*, Princeton, New Jersey: Princeton University Press, 1994

Gruen, Erich S., *The Hellenistic World and the Coming of Rome*, Berkeley: University of California Press, 1984

Hammond, N.G.L. and F.W. Walbank, *A History of Macedonia*, vol. 3: *336–167 BC*, Oxford: Clarendon Press, 1988

Hammond, N.G.L., *The Macedonian State: Origins, Institutions and History*, Oxford: Clarendon Press, and New York: Oxford University Press, 1989

Le Bohec, Sylvie, *Antigone Dôsôn roi de Macédoine*, Nancy: Presses Universitaires de Nancy, 1993

Manni, Eugenio, *Demetrio Poliorcete*, Rome: Signorelli, 1951

Müller, Olaf, *Antigonos Monophthalmos und "das Jahr der Könige"*, Bonn: Habelt, 1973

Price, Martin, *Coins of the Macedonians*, London: British Museum, 1974

Sakellariou, M.B. (editor), *Macedonia: 4000 Years of Greek History and Civilization*, Athens: Ekdotike Athenon, 1983

Tarn, W.W., *Antigonos Gonatas*, Oxford: Clarendon Press, 1913

Walbank, F.W., *Philip V of Macedon*, Cambridge: Cambridge University Press, 1940

Walbank, F.W. *et al.* (editors), *The Hellenistic World*, Cambridge: Cambridge University Press, 1984 (*The Cambridge Ancient History*, vol. 7, part 1, 2nd edition), chapters 7 and 12

Wehrli, Claude, *Antigone et Démétrios*, Geneva: Droz, 1968

Antioch

City in the Roman province of Syria

Antioch (now Antakya in Turkey) was founded by Seleucus I in 300 BC on the left bank of the Orontes, *c.*24 km from the sea, by transfer of 5300 Athenian and Macedonian settlers. The city became the capital of the Seleucid empire, and subsequently of the Roman province of Syria. In addition to being a great centre of administration the city benefited from being on the trade route from Asia to the Mediterranean. Its population, which in the 4th century AD reached around 250,000, was matched in the east only by that of Alexandria, and later that of Constantinople. At that time the city was a splendid sight with an imperial palace, an octagonal cathedral, churches, colonnaded streets, baths and theatres, and mansions with beautiful mosaic floors at the residential suburb of Daphne. The inhabitants were of mixed origins, but the city was Greek in political institutions, culture, and language, and from it Greek language and civilization spread into the villages and towns of northern Syria.

The most important Antiochene secular writers, both of the 4th century AD, were Ammianus Marcellinus, who adapted the tradition of Greek historiography to compose a Latin history of the Roman empire, and Libanius, the most famous orator of his time, a pagan whose pupils included St John Chrysostom and probably St Basil of Caesarea. Antioch had a large Jewish community, and Christianity came there very early. It was the starting point of Paul's mission to the cities of the Greek east, and it was here that Christians were first called by that name. The Antiochene school of biblical exegesis, in contrast to that of Alexandria, emphasized the importance of the literal as against the allegorical meaning of the text. Influential exponents were Diodorus of Tarsus, John Chrysostom, Theodore of Mopsuestia, and Theoderet of Cyrrhus. Antiochene exegesis became associated with Nestorianism, and was forced out of the empire after the Second Council of Ephesus (449). Its traditions continued in the Nestorian school at Nisibis, where much Greek philosophy and theology was translated into Syriac.

The patriarch of Antioch was the leader of all bishops between the Taurus and the Egyptian border, though his authority was weakened during most of the 4th century by divisions in the Antiochene Church. In the Christological controversies of the 5th and 6th centuries supporters of Chalcedon were generally in the majority at Antioch. But Severus, patriarch 512–18, was a principal Monophysite theologian. He wrote in Greek, though his works survive only in Syriac. The hinterland of Antioch became Monophysite and developed a liturgy and literature in Syriac. Later a separate Monophysite patriarchate was established, but its bishop usually resided in a monastery outside the city.

Antioch was devastated by an earthquake in 528 (others struck in 551, 557, 587, 588). It was captured and burnt by the Persians and many of its inhabitants deported in 540. In 542 Antioch suffered the first of a series of visitations of plague. In the early 6th century the city was rebuilt by Justinian I, but the island quarter – the location of the palace, the cathedral, and the hippodrome – was left outside the walls. From 511 to 528 the city was occupied by the Persians, and in 638 it was captured by the Arabs, apparently without much resistance.

Some inhabitants left, and land was assigned to Muslims from Baalbek and Homs. The Chalcedonian (Melkite) community survived at Antioch and after 742 chose a local man as patriarch. The Melkite Church adopted an Arabic liturgy and survives to the present day.

Antioch under the Muslims was a frontier city of an inland empire. Its built-up area seems to have shrunk, particularly after the end of the Umayyad dynasty (750). But the walls remained intact, as did at least two churches and the Roman water supply. In 969 the city was reconquered by the Byzantines who held it until 1089 when it was captured by the Seljuk Turks. In 1098 Antioch was captured by the crusaders after a long siege and became the centre of a Frankish principality which managed to survive, with the help, and sometimes under the suzerainty, of the Byzantine empire. Antioch was once more a large and prosperous city, but in 1268 it was captured and destroyed by the Mamluks. Ever since Antioch has been a small but neat country town, which to the present day preserves considerable traces of its Classical street plan.

J.H.W.G. LIEBESCHUETZ

Summary

City in (ancient) Syria, now Antakya in Turkey. Founded in 300 BC by Seleucus I, it became the capital of the Seleucid empire, and later of the Roman province of Syria. Its people were of mixed origins, but Antioch was Greek in political institutions, culture, and language. Captured by the Arabs in 638, it was Byzantine again from 969 to 1089. Taken by the crusaders in 1098, it was finally destroyed by the Mamluks in 1268.

Further Reading

Devreesse, Robert, *Le Patriarcat d'Antioche*, Paris: Gabalda, 1945

Downey, Glanville, *The History of Antioch in Syria: From Seleucus to the Arab Conquest*, Princeton, New Jersey: Princeton University Press, 1961

Festugière, A.J., *Antioche païenne et chrétienne*, Paris: Boccard, 1959

Karalevskij, C., Antioche entry in *Dictionnaire d'histoire et de géographie ecclésiastique*, vol. 3, Paris: Letouzey & Ané, 1924, pp. 563–703

Kennedy, H., "Antioch: From Byzantium to Islam and Back Again" in *The City in Late Antiquity*, edited by John Rich, London and New York: Routledge, 1992

Lassus, Jean, *Les Portiques d'Antioche*, Princeton, New Jersey: Princeton University Press, 1972

Levi, Doro, *Antioch Mosaic Pavements*, Princeton, New Jersey: Princeton University Press, 1947

Liebeschuetz, J.H.W.G., *Antioch: City and Imperial Administration in the Later Roman Empire*, Oxford: Clarendon Press, 1972

Paverd, Frans van de, *Zur Geschichte der Messliturgie in Antiocheia und Konstantinopel gegen Ende des vierten Jahrhunderts*, Rome: Pontificale Institutum Orientalium Studiorum, 1970

Antiochus III the Great *c.*242–187 BC

Seleucid king

Antiochus III the Great was the sixth king (223–187 BC)in the Seleucid dynasty and the greatest ruler in the dynasty since Seleucus I (*c.*355–281 BC), the founder of the empire. Son of Seleucus II, he succeeded his elder brother Seleucus III on his

assassination in 223 BC. The epithet "great" (*megas*) was probably taken by the king around 204 BC as the result of his eastern expedition of 212–205 BC, though it was subsequently dropped in favour of the title "great king Antiochus" (*basileus megas Antiochos*) that he assumed in 200 BC after his conquest of Coele Syria from Ptolemy V. The title asserted Antiochus' claims over the rule of Asia, following the Persian kings and Alexander the Great, and his superiority over his rivals the Ptolemies, who had claimed the title for themselves.

The best ancient account of Antiochus' reign is that of Polybius, but it is fully preserved only down to 217 BC and is fragmentary thereafter. Polybius must have drawn his information from one or more writers contemporary with the king, though who these were is uncertain. For the story of Antiochus' conflict with the Romans in the 190s BC down to the Treaty of Apamea in 188 BC reliance must be placed on Appian (*Syriake*, 1–44) and Livy (33–38); though derived in part from Polybius, these accounts are written from a Roman, not a Seleucid, perspective, and may not reproduce fully the Polybian original. In addition a large number of Greek inscriptions, chiefly from Asia Minor, provide important information on Antiochus' relations with the Greek communities there.

Antiochus came to power at a young age and in difficult circumstances, but he gradually asserted himself and went on to restore and extend the Seleucid empire as no previous king since Seleucus I had done. A rebellion in the eastern provinces led by Molon, the satrap of Media, who took the royal title, had to be put down (222–220 BC). Achaeus, a relative of the king in charge of Asia Minor from his capital at Sardis, proclaimed his independence and took on the royal title (220 BC), and was not eliminated until 213 BC. A war against Ptolemy IV of Egypt (219–217 BC) resulted in defeat at the battle of Raphia in Palestine, though Antiochus regained control of Seleucia in Pieria. From 212 to 205 BC Antiochus undertook a grandiose expedition to the east (the *anabasis*), perhaps in emulation of Alexander the Great, in which he brought Commagene and Armenia under control, sought to restore Seleucid dominance over Parthia and Bactria (though he was unable to dislodge the ruling king Euthydemus, with whom he made an alliance), and renewed links with India. On his return he made an expedition to the Persian Gulf, though he had to accept the continued independence of the trading city of Gerrha. After an incursion into Asia Minor (204/03 BC) he turned his attention to the successful conquest of Coele Syria, Palestine, and Judaea from Ptolemy V (*c.*202–198 BC). He then moved into Asia Minor to restore Seleucid rule over the Greek cities there, and into Thrace with the object of rebuilding Lysimachea, previously under Seleucid control (197/96 BC). His advance led him into contact with the Romans, who had defeated Philip V of Macedon at Cynoscephalae (197 BC) and had proclaimed the "freedom of the Greeks" at the Isthmian festival (196 BC). Misunderstandings and suspicions developed between both parties as to their respective intentions, and it is not easy to determine the responsibilities for the conflict that eventually broke out when Antiochus landed on the mainland of Greece posing as a champion of Greek freedom against the Romans (192 BC). Expelled by the Romans from Greece (191 BC), Antiochus was then defeated by them at the battle of Magnesia in Lydia (190/89 BC). By the Treaty of Apamea (188 BC) he was forced to evacuate all lands to the north of the

Taurus, reduce his military forces, pay heavy war indemnities, and provide hostages. Significantly reduced, the Seleucid empire remained nevertheless powerful and wealthy. Antiochus himself was killed soon after on an eastern expedition (187 BC) while pillaging a temple of Bel in Elymais.

Antiochus' reputation in the extant sources is very mixed. Polybius found fault in the king's early years when the young ruler lacked authority and experience, though he praised his conduct and achievements in the eastern expedition. He denounced the secret pact that Antiochus allegedly made in 203/02 BC with Philip V to partition the possessions of Ptolemy V. He accused the king of failing in his later years to live up to the promises of his early reign, and thought he had mishandled the campaign against the Romans. The presentation in Livy and Appian of Antiochus' role in the war against Rome is negative. The king is credited with aggressive intentions against Rome, and with mismanaging the war. Roman propaganda also presented him in the guise of an "oriental despot", a second Xerxes invading Greece who was repulsed and defeated by the Romans.

Little is known of the personality of Antiochus (the same is true of most of the kings in the dynasty), though many of his known actions suggest a ruler of exceptional ambition. At some time in his reign (before 193 BC) he instituted a divine cult of himself and his ancestors which was organized on an empire-wide basis, and to which he added (193 BC) a similar cult of his first wife, the Pontic princess Laodice whom he had married in 222 BC. No previous or subsequent Seleucid ruler is known to have done this. He made extensive use of dynastic marriages in his imperial designs, and it is to his reign that belongs the only recorded instance of brother-sister marriage in the dynasty (his eldest son Antiochus was married to his daughter Laodice). On the other hand Antiochus was not a great city founder, unlike Seleucus I and his son Antiochus I, and this affected his subsequent memory. His inglorious end after defeat at the hands of the Romans obscured the memory of his earlier achievements and leaves the historian with an unresolved enigma.

MICHEL AUSTIN

See also Seleucids

Biography

Born *c.*242 BC, Antiochus succeeded his elder brother Seleucus III in 223. He assumed the title "great" probably in 204, but dropped it in 200 in favour of "great king Antiochus" asserting his claims over Asia. He considerably expanded the territory of the Seleucid empire, but was defeated by the Romans at Magnesia in 190/89 BC. He died fighting in 187 BC.

Further Reading

Austin, M.M., "War and Culture in the Seleucid Empire", forthcoming; German translation published as "Krieg und Kultur im Seleukidenreich" in *Zwischen West und Ost: Studien zur Geschichte des Seleukidenreichs*, edited by Kai Brodersen, Hamburg: Kovac, 1999

Bevan, E.R., *The House of Seleucus*, 2 vols, London: Arnold, 1902; reprinted London: Routledge and Kegan Paul, and New York: Barnes and Noble, 1966

Bikerman, Elins Joseph, *Institutions des Séleucides*, Paris: Geuthner, 1938

Bilde, Per *et al.* (editors), *Religion and Religious Practice in the Seleucid Kingdom*, Aarhus: Aarhus University Press, 1990

Bouché-Leclercq, A., *Histoire des Séleucides, 323–64 avant J.-C.*, 2 vols, Paris: Leroux, 1913–14

Brodersen, Kai, *Appians Abriss der Seleukidengeschichte (Syriake 45, 232–70, 369)* and *Appians Antiochike (Syriake 1, 1–44, 232)*, 2 vols, Munich: Maris, 1989–91 (text and commentary)

Edson, C.F., "Imperium Macedonicum: The Seleucid Empire and the Literary Evidence", *Classical Philology*, 53 (1958), pp. 153–70

Habicht, C., "Athen und die Seleukiden", *Chiron*, 19 (1989): pp. 7–26

Grainger, John D., *The Cities of Seleukid, Syria*, Oxford: Clarendon Press, and New York: Oxford University Press, 1990

Grainger, John D., *A Seleukid Prosopography and Gazetteer*, Leiden and New York: Brill, 1997

Musti, Domenico, "Lo stato dei Seleucidi: Dinastia popoli città da Seleuco I ad Antioco III", *Studi classici e orientali*, 15 (1966) pp. 61–200

Schmitt, Hatto H., *Untersuchungen zur Geschichte Antiochos' des Grossen und seiner Zeit*, Wiesbaden: Steiner, 1964

Sherwin-White, Susan and Amélie Kuhrt, *From Samarkhand to Sardis: A New Approach to the Seleucid Empire*, London: Duckworth, and Berkeley: University of California Press, 1993

TOPOI: Orient-Occident vol. 4.2, Lyon: Maison de l'Orient Méditerranéen, 1994 (collected articles commenting on Sherwin-White & Kuhrt 1993)

Anti-westernism

Anti-westernism is a worldwide phenomenon concerning the reaction of native populations in various continents to the political, economic, and cultural imperialism of western Europeans in the wake of their colonization and expansionist policies in modern times. Anti-westernism has been expressed in various forms, including the nativistic and revitalization movements that try to perpetuate indigenous traditions to face the threatening influx of imported elements and to reverse the process of westernization. The term "West" nowadays is not limited to western Europe, but includes other cultural and political units too, especially the US.

The roots of a particular form of anti-westernism that can be observed in Greece as well as in eastern Europe (e.g. in Russia) must be sought especially in the Byzantine period and in the endemic tension between eastern and western Romans for religious and socio-political reasons alike. The Byzantines, due to the geographical position of their empire, mostly used the term "Occident" for Europe and "Orient" for Asia. The west signified for them the *pars occidentalis* of the Roman empire, which by AD 476 had been subjected to the barbarians. Progressively, the Byzantines considered the west as a separate entity, alienated from them, especially after the rise of the Franks and the coronation of Charlemagne as "emperor of the Romans" in 800. The religious tension between the two worlds culminated in the definitive schism of 1054 and was of paramount importance for their continuing estrangement. The consequences of the schism were manifold as far as the Byzantine attitude towards the West was concerned. The foreign occupation of Constantinople from 1204 to 1261 in the wake of the Fourth Crusade as well as theological differences (e.g. the hesychast controversy in the 14th century) deepened the chasm between the two worlds. As a result, the Latin west came to signify for the Orthodox east a geographical place out of which nothing but dangers and problems had originated. The attempted union of the Churches did not achieve any results, even when the Byzantines faced the threat of Ottoman expansion. The Byzantine preference for the "Turkish turban" rather than for the "Latin tiara" is indicative of the pronounced anti-western sentiments of the day. Even when the traditional notion of Byzantine superiority over other peoples had vanished and western progress was seen as worth imitating, anti-westernism still prevailed as a pattern of orientation on a large scale.

During the Tourkokratia (1453–1821) the schism between East and West intensified in a number of ways. The Greek world was not considered to be a part of Europe, which had been fully identified with the West. The patriarchate of Constantinople was entrusted with the task of safeguarding the Orthodox identity of its members from Islam and from Roman Catholic propaganda. The Orthodox opposition to the Latins was accentuated in this period, as various published and unpublished texts clearly demonstrate. At the cultural level, the impressive development of western Europe in many domains (science, technology, philosophy, economy, and politics) created a serious feeling of inferiority in the East. This was more conspicuous during the 18th century when "the enlightened Europe" was promoted by many Greeks as the best model to be imitated. Such an adoration of the West and its progress met with the declared opposition of many Orthodox, who severely criticized the developments in the fallen and heretical West and tried to compensate for Greece's multiple deficits. Two main anti-western strategies put the emphases on the accomplishments of the ancient Greeks and on the possession of Orthodoxy, i.e. the sole true faith in the entire world. Anti-western views reached their peak when several Orthodox circles tried to legitimize the Ottoman rule with religious arguments, claiming that God intended in this way to protect Orthodoxy from potential submission to the Latin West. Greece's closer contacts with the West and their allegedly fatal consequences for Orthodoxy were thus strictly criticized.

Anti-western attitudes have also been evident since the foundation of the Greek state. In the reign of the Bavarian king Otho (1833–62) there was a systematic attempt to westernize the country in all domains, including the religious one, through the Church's subjection to the state. This enforced process of westernization signified a serious rupture in the Greek historical consciousness and caused a deep cultural schism. There were several indigenous reactions to the dependence on the West, which were manifest both in the thought of individuals (e.g. Y. Makriyannis) and in various socio-religious movements (e.g. of Papoulakos, c.1770–1861). In the 19th and 20th centuries this identity crisis also led many Greeks to propose various alternative ways of modernization on the basis of their own heritage (e.g. Eastern Orthodox communalism vs. western individualism). This was a reaction against the wholesale adoption of western patterns of orientation and the constant intervention of western powers in Greek politics. These anti-western efforts were mostly unsuccessful, since Greece still oscillates between tradition and modernity. This lack of equilibrium is the principal cause of various contradictory phenomena in modern Greece, including those of xenomania and xenophobia.

Despite Greece's membership of the European Union, anti-western and even anti-European sentiments are still common in the country in various open and disguised forms. These may be observed in the political arena, for example among the Communists for ideological reasons or among the Socialists of PASOK under A. Papandreou (1981–89), who promised Greeks an independent and nationally dignified foreign policy, away from western European and American interference. Papandreou was also very critical of Greece's membership of NATO and the EU. There exists also a religious anti-westernism, usually among Orthodox fundamentalists, who use the incomparable superiority of Orthodoxy as a defensive mechanism against the heretical West. Anti-western feelings have also been evident among Greek intellectuals of various persuasions (e.g. the generation of the 1930s, the Neo-orthodox current, several leftist groups), who tried to recover Greece's own heritage from the adulterating western influences and to construct a feasible Greek identity in the modern competitive international environment. There exists finally a popular, wide, and diffuse anti-westernism among various population strata for many reasons (e.g. social, psychological, political). However, because the entire Greek society is deeply permeated by western ideas, lifestyles, and consumerist spirit, the Greek public shows a simultaneous love and dislike for these multifaceted influences. This attests to the profound orientation problems that characterize modern Greek society and its ambivalent attitude towards the West.

In Huntington's schema Greece can be described as a "torn country". Its political and economic elites are pro-western, but its history, culture, religion, and tradition are essentially non-western. Its enforced westernization has not so far produced the anticipated results but created additional structural problems that are still evident. However, if Greece redefines its cultural identity, it will modernize itself without rejecting the central elements of its indigenous culture. Such a road to an autonomous, syncretic modernity may mitigate to a considerable degree anti-western sentiments and attitudes and finally lead to a healthier relationship with the West.

VASILIOS MAKRIDES

See also Foreigners, Identity

Further Reading

Argyriou, Astérios, "Les Courants idéologiques au sein de l'Hellénisme et de l'Orthodoxie à l'époque de la domination turque", *Contacts*, 36 (1984): pp. 285–305

Carabott, Philip (editor), *Greece and Europe in the Modern Period: Aspects of a Troubled Relationship*, London: Centre for Hellenic Studies, King's College, 1995

Clogg, Richard, "The 'Dhidhaskalia Patriki' (1798): An Orthodox Reaction to French Revolutionary Propaganda", *Middle Eastern Studies*, 5 (1969): pp. 87–115

Daskalov, Roumen, "Ideas about, and Reactions to Modernization in the Balkans", *East European Quarterly*, 31 (1997): pp. 141–80

Dimaras, Konstantinos, "I photismeni Evropi" [Enlightened Europe], *Nea Estia*, 51 (1952): pp. 225–30; pp. 306–11

Dimitras, Panayote, "L'Anti-occidentalisme grec", *Esprit*, 8/6 (June 1984): pp. 123–30

Dölger, Franz, *Byzanz und die europäische Staatenwelt*, Ettal: Buch-Kunstverlag, 1953

Engels, Odilo and Peter Schreiner (editors), *Die Begegnung des Westens mit dem Osten*, Sigmaringen: Thorbecke, 1993

Evert-Kappesowa, H., "La Tiare ou le turban", *Byzantinoslavica*, 14 (1953): pp. 245–57

Fouyas, Methodios G., *Ellines kai Latinoi* [Greeks and Latins], Athens, 1990

Geanakoplos, Deno John, "A Byzantine Looks at the Renaissance: The Attitude of Michael Apostolis toward the Rise of Italy to Cultural Eminence", *Greek and Byzantine Studies*, 1 (1958): pp. 157–62

Geanakoplos, Deno John, *Byzantine East and Latin West: Two Worlds of Christendom in Middle Ages and Renaissance*, Oxford: Blackwell, and New York: Harper and Row, 1966

Geanakoplos, Deno John, *Interaction of the "Sibling" Byzantine and Western Cultures in the Middle Ages and Italian Renaissance, 330–1600*, New Haven, Connecticut: Yale University Press, 1976

Hunger, Herbert, *Phänomen Byzanz: Aus europäischer Sicht*, Munich: Bayerische Akademie der Wissenschaften, 1984

Hunger, Herbert, *Graeculus perfidus – Italos itamos: Il senso dell' alterità nei rapporti Greco–Romani ed Italo–Bizantini*, Rome: Istituti di Archeologia, Storia e Storia dell'arte, 1987

Huntington, Samuel P., *The Clash of Civilizations and the Remaking of World Order*, New York: Simon and Schuster, 1996

Jelavich, Barbara, *History of the Balkans: Eighteenth and Nineteenth Centuries*, vol. 1, Cambridge and New York: Cambridge University Press, 1983, pp. 45–50

Keller, A.G., "A Byzantine Admirer of 'Western' Progress: Cardinal Bessarion", *Cambridge Historical Journal*, 11 (1955): pp. 343–48

Kolia-Dermitzaki, Athina, "Die Kreuzfahrer und die Kreuzzüge im Sprachgebrauch der Byzantiner", *Jahrbuch der Österreichischen Byzantinistik*, 41 (1991): pp. 163–88

Makrides, Vasilios, "Le Rôle de l'Orthodoxie dans la formation de l'antieuropéanisme et l'antioccidentalisme grecs" in *Religions et transformations de l'Europe*, edited by Gilbert Vincent and Jean-Paul Willaime, Strasbourg: Presses Universitaires de Strasbourg, 1993

Metallinos, George, "Das Problem der deutschen Einflüsse auf die griechische akademische Theologie in der Gründungsphase der Athener Universität", *Orthodoxes Forum*, 3 (1989): pp. 83–91

Nicol, Donald M., "The Byzantine View of Western Europe", *Greek, Roman and Byzantine Studies*, 8 (1967): pp. 315–39

Noutsos, Panayotis, "Anatoli–Dysi: Metamorphoseis enos ideologimatos" [East–West: Transformations of an Ideology], *Dodoni*, 12 (1983): pp. 81–92

"Orient–Occident: La signification profonde du schisme, Un entretien avec Christos Yannaras", *Service Orthodoxe de Presse*, 150 (1990): pp. 29–35

Roth, Klaus, "Wie 'europäisch' ist Südosteuropa? Zum Problem des kulturellen Wandels auf der Balkanhalbinsel" in *Wandel der Volkskultur in Europa: Festschrift für Günter Wiegelmann*, edited by Nils-Arvid Bringéus et al., vol. 1, Münster: Coppenrath, 1988

Savramis, Demosthenes, "Die nichttheologischen Faktoren der Perpetuierung der Trennung zwischen der orthodoxen und der römisch-katholischen Kirche", *Kyrios*, new series 14 (1974): pp. 139–56

Ševčenko, Ihor, "The Decline of Byzantium Seen through the Eyes of Its Intellectuals", *Dumbarton Oaks Papers*, 15 (1961): pp. 167–86

Shepard, J., "Aspects of Byzantine Attitudes and Policy towards the West in the Tenth and Eleventh Centuries", *Byzantinische Forschungen*, 13 (1988): pp. 67–118

Stathopoulou, Theoni, "To kinima tou Papoulakou: Oi politikes, koinonikes kai thriskevtikes diastaseis tou" [The Papavoulakos Movement: Its Political, Social, and Educational Controversies] (dissertation), Athens: Panteion University, 1991

Wenturis, Nikolaus, *Griechenland und die Europäische Gemeinschaft: Die soziopolitischen Rahmenbedingungen griechischer Europapolitiken*, Tübingen: Francke, 1990, pp. 176–94

Yannaras, Christos, "Orthodoxy and the West", *Greek Orthodox Theological Review*, 17 (1972): pp. 115–31

Yannaras, Christos, *Orthodoxia kai Dysi sti Neoteri Ellada* [Orthodoxy and the West in Modern Greece], Athens, 1992

Antiquity, Reception of

Hellenic culture is the product of a complex and sometimes problematic relationship with its ancient past, cultural and linguistic. From late antiquity to the modern era an emphasis on continuity with the Classical tradition has been seen as a way of maintaining and expressing ideals of Hellenic identity and unity, marked particularly when these ideals have been perceived as being under threat from "alien" hegemonies – the Roman empire, the Tourkokratia – and in times of national reunification and reinvention.

In antiquity itself the Greeks cherished and derived inspiration from their cultural heritage and sought to gain prestige through establishing ancestral connections, communal and personal, with the gods and heroes of myth. It was the Greek writers and scholars of the Hellenistic world and the early Roman empire, however, who laid the foundations for subsequent attitudes to antiquity in the Greek-speaking world. The intensive scholarly enterprise of the Hellenistic age, focused around the great libraries – particularly that of Alexandria where the gathering and editing of ancient texts and fragments were prioritized as the proper object of academic energy – not only preserved the culture of high antiquity for the future but also provided a model of activity for later scholars. This retrospection extended to the Alexandrian literati who displayed their erudition in sophisticated treatments of esoteric myth and a familiarity with earlier genres, dialects, and metres; following the Hellenistic model, the notion that the literature and language of earlier antiquity were the proper exemplars became a standard for later writers.

The Greeks of the early Roman empire exhibited a more pronounced nostalgia for the past; the literary renaissance of the 2nd and early 3rd centuries AD, dubbed the Second Sophistic by Philostratus, was informed heavily by the culture of Classical Athens (designated as the First Sophistic). The orators Herodes Atticus and Aelius Aristides took Classical rhetoric as their model; the travel writer Pausanias sought to describe Greek culture before the Roman conquest; while Phrynicus produced a lexicon of "correct" vocabulary predicated on Classical usage and the notion of ancient Greek as a linguistic and cultural ideal. This "Atticism", a Classicizing and archaizing written style distinct from the developing spoken Greek language, became a marker of the educated elite and a potent ideological symbol of the continuity between past and present which persisted through the Byzantine period and into the 20th century.

The Greek language which had become the koine of the Hellenistic world remained the lingua franca of the Byzantine empire, an important factor in the reception of antiquity by Byzantine writers and scholars, for whom the literary tradition of ancient Greece was central. Writers of the 5th and 6th centuries AD were well acquainted with the literature of antiquity and this familiarity informed their own work: Homer and Aristotle were particularly important exemplars, while Procopius in the early 6th century was influenced by Thucydides and Herodotus and wrote in the language of his Classical models. The problematic 7th and 8th centuries represented a hiatus in Byzantine literary enterprise, but from the late 8th century the focus of scholarly interest was the reaccumulation and re-editing of the ancient texts and fragments that had been lost in the preceding period; the 9th and 10th centuries saw the production of the *Suda* and Photios's *Bibliotheca*. In the 7th–11th centuries Roman rather than Hellenic antiquity provided the literary model for Byzantine writers, although the copying of Classical texts and scholia continued. In the mid-11th century, however, there was a renaissance of interest in the culture of ancient Greece during the reign of Constantine IX Monomachos. Classical Greek texts were revered particularly, and the Classical revival was marked by a resumption of scholastic endeavour. Noted Classical scholars such as Michael Psellos and John Italos in the 11th century and John Tzetzes and Eustathios of Thessalonica in the 12th did not confine themselves to the copying and editing of ancient manuscripts but became the self-appointed exegetes of the Classical tradition, writing essays and commentaries in a broadly "Classical" style, albeit from a Byzantine perspective, and using ancient texts to reflect upon contemporary and often ecclesiastical issues. During the Palaiologan period (13th century on) there was a revival in Classical philology and many Greek texts owe their survival to the efforts of Planudes in the 13th century and Triklinios in the 14th. Yet antiquity did not have a monopoly of influence upon the Byzantine literati; the histories of Anna Komnene demonstrate a high Attic style but take the Second Sophistic and late antiquity as models as well as the Classical period, while in the Palaiologan period Byzantium was influenced too by the literature of the medieval West, and much of the religious literature of the empire – in particular the hagiographies and hymnographies – owed nothing to the ancient tradition.

There existed within the Church an equivocal attitude towards the culture of antiquity. From the time of Constantine the term Hellenic (*Hellenikos*) was equated with paganism and was construed as a rival to Christianity; the Church preferred the plainer koine to the "pagan" high Classical style of secular literature and repudiated the polytheism and "immoral" gods of ancient mythology. Indeed in the 10th and 11th centuries any involvement with the myth and philosophy of antiquity invited the charge of anti-Christian behaviour; long ago Justinian had tried to suppress the philosophical schools at Athens, and in the mid-11th century the Platonic and Neoplatonic researches of John Italos were denounced as heretical. Yet paganism proved difficult to eradicate: the cult of Dionysus in particular gathered strength in the period of late antiquity, as evidenced by Nonnus' epic *Dionysiaca* of the mid-5th century, while Christian converts used the mythical iconography of ancient Greece in their churches and incorporated elements of the outlawed pagan worship into the new religion. Furthermore, the literature, philosophy, and rhetoric of Greek antiquity were integral to Christian thought and education: the distinction between the repudiation of Hellenism as paganism and a reverence for the secular literature of Hellenic antiquity was an uneasy one.

The 19th century saw the coincidence of two factors that were highly significant with regard to the reception of the Classical tradition – the revival of Classical scholarship in Europe and the emergence of an independent Greece. The influence of European interest in Greece and the many important archaeological finds impressed upon the Greeks the value, artistic, historical, and commercial, of their past. A series of measures that aimed to preserve the Greek heritage were taken in the first half of the 19th century: in 1826 the provisional government issued a decree for the protection of antiquities, and three years later the fourth National Assembly at Argos prohibited their export, and the first archaeological museum in Greece was founded at Aegina. However, many important artefacts had been taken already, for example the friezes from the Parthenon and Bassae, still in London, and the sculptures from the temple of Aphaea on Aegina, now in Munich. The recovery of antiquities is still a political issue in Greece and a focus of national pride.

When the seat of the new government was moved to Athens the city was rebuilt in the Neoclassical style, and between 1834 and 1837 the Acropolis was "cleansed" in an attempt to restore the purity of the Classical past. Indeed, an emphasis on cultural continuity and "purity" became the keynote for a Greek nation that had survived Ottoman domination and its concomitant cultural and linguistic "contamination": Greek identity was to be reconstructed on the foundations of ancient Hellenism and the image of a new philhellenic Greece entering a new Periclean age. The literature of the period is indicative of this classicizing enterprise: Konstantinos Paparrigopoulos's *History of the Greek Nation* (1860–72) stressed the continuity of Greece from antiquity to the modern era; Adamantios Korais (1748–1833) edited a series of Classical texts, and Philippos Ioannou composed verse in Classical metres – the emphasis was on the perpetuation of the Classical tradition and an archaizing purity of language. Classical studies became the basis of education (as indeed was the case throughout Europe); the University of Athens, founded in 1837, emerged as a bastion of linguistic archaism while the syllabus laid down for the "demotic" schools in 1883 concentrated on the rote learning of Classical texts and the study of ancient Greek.

One primary educational and political concern was the question of a national language; the members of the new Greek state spoke a variety of dialects and languages, including Turkish, and the notion of the standardization of Greek and what form it might take occupied thinkers and politicians for much of the 19th and 20th centuries. One school of thought held that the national language should reflect the tradition of ancient Greece and Byzantium and that Greeks should speak the language of antiquity or at least a "corrected" form of contemporary Greek. In the view of such "archaizers" a knowledge of ancient Greek would give the people access to their cultural inheritance and the translation of ancient texts into the vernacular represented a degradation of the past. Contrarily, others argued that the national language should reflect contemporary Greek linguistic practice and culture. For these "demoticizers" ancient Greek was incomprehensible to ordinary people and its study was available only to the privileged few; thus the prioritization of the learned Greek of antiquity over the modern, demotic language was an elitist anachronism, a socially divisive programme that would separate the people from their heritage. The translation of ancient texts and the performance of ancient drama in demotic Greek was supported in particular by Kostis Palamas (1859–1943); however, feelings regarding the "bastardization" of ancient culture ran so high that a performance in 1903 of Aeschylus' *Oresteia* in a vernacular translation resulted in a riot. The "language question" has informed the political ideology of both left and right and has persisted well into the 20th century; while the Venizelos government introduced the teaching in schools of demotic Greek in 1917, it was not until the Education Act of 1976 that it was decided that the language of education should be modern Greek.

Many modern writers have felt that an artificial "corrected" form of Attic Greek and a "fossilizing" approach to ancient culture are not only reactionary but also a bar to poetic creativity – Dionysios Solomos (1798–1857) in particular was a champion of demoticism, and the vernacular is now the literary as well as the spoken norm. However, much modern Greek poetry is informed and inspired by antiquity: Solomos, while imbued by the Italian tradition, was influenced by Platonism, as was Palamas. Angelos Sikelianos (1884–1951) too was interested in Plato and in ancient mystery religions, while the "historical" poems of Constantine Cavafy (1863–1933) are set in Hellenistic Alexandria and Byzantium. Yet perhaps the cultural genre of antiquity that appeals most to the contemporary cultural imagination is 5th-century BC drama. There have been many European productions of Greek tragedies from the 16th century on throughout Europe (see Burian, 1997), nearly all of them in languages other than Greek, but during the 20th century in particular there has been a revival of interest in the drama of antiquity in Greece itself and a reintroduction of the ancient notion of the dramatic festival: in the 1920s Sikelianos instituted a cultural festival at Delphi, staging Aeschylus' *Prometheus Bound* and *Suppliant Women*, and in the mid-1950s festivals of ancient drama were instituted at Epidaurus and at the Odeum of Herodes Atticus in Athens. Some modern productions have aimed at authenticity; Sikelianos derived the costumes and movements of the chorus from ancient vase paintings for his staging of Aeschylus, while the film maker Michalis Cacoyannis's *Trojan Trilogy* (1961–76) used ancient sites and costumes. However, tragic performances by Karolos Koun's Theatro Technis are informed by modern Greek rituals and there have been several modern treatments of ancient drama that not only use contemporary settings but also use the narratives of antiquity to explore contemporary issues. Jules Dassin's screen adaptation of Euripides' *Hippolytus* (1961) is a critique of Greek high society – Theseus is transformed into a shipping magnate; Hippolytus dies not in a chariot but in an Aston Martin; and Phaedra, played by Melina Mercouri, overdoses on sleeping pills. More recently the fratricide and divided loyalties of Sophocles' *Antigone* were staged by Nikos Koundouros in the no man's land between northern Greece and the former Republic of Yugoslavia.

Translations of ancient texts into modern Greek and new media such as film have engaged a wider audience. Poets, theatre directors, and film makers have taken antiquity out of the museum and classroom and into a wider public arena, reinstating ancient literature and thought as part of the living tradition of Greece and as an integral part of contemporary Hellenic culture. Yet while an engagement with antiquity may be a source of inspiration to its inheritors, the achievements of the past may also provoke what has been called the "anxiety of influence": in the Palaiologan period the scholar Theodore Metochites complained that there was nothing left to say – the ancients had said it all; in the 20th century George Seferis, for whom Greece's ancient ruins signified the sterility of the modern imagination, intimated that the sheer weight of a glori-

ous cultural inheritance could be a burden as well as an inspiration: "I awoke with this marble head in my hands" (*Mythistorema*, 3).

EUGÉNIE FERNANDES

See also Identity, Language, Tragedy

Further Reading

Anderson, Graham, *The Second Sophistic*, London and New York: Routledge, 1993

Beaton, Roderick, *An Introduction to Modern Greek Literature*, 2nd edition, Oxford: Clarendon Press, 1999

Bowersock, G.W., *Hellenism in Late Antiquity*, Cambridge: Cambridge University Press, and Ann Arbor: University of Michigan Press, 1990

Brixhe, Claude (editor), *La Koiné grecque antique*, Nancy, 1993

Brown, Peter, *The World of Late Antiquity*, London: Thames and Hudson, and New York: Harcourt Brace, 1971, reprinted New York: Norton, 1989

Burian P., "Tragedy Adapted for Stages and Screens: The Renaissance to the Present" in *The Cambridge Companion to Greek Tragedy*, edited by P.E. Easterling, Cambridge and New York: Cambridge University Press, 1997

Cameron, Averil, *Procopius and the Sixth Century*, London: Duckworth, and Berkeley: University of California Press, 1985

Coutelle, Louis, *Formation poétique de Solomos, 1815–1833*, Athens: Hermes, 1977

Fletcher, R., "Cultural and Intellectual Developments 1821–1911" in *Greece in Transition: Essays in the History of Modern Greece, 1821–1974*, edited by John T.A. Koumoulides, London: Zeno, 1977

Goldhill, Simon, "The Paradigms of Epic: Apollonius Rhodius and the Example of the Past" in *The Poet's Voice: Essays on Poetics and Greek Literature*, edited by Goldhill, Cambridge and New York: Cambridge University Press, 1991

Horrocks, Geoffrey, *Greek: A History of the Language and its Speakers*, London and New York: Longman, 1997

Kazhdan, A.P. and Simon Franklin, *Studies in Byzantine Literature of the Eleventh and Twelfth Centuries*, Cambridge and New York: Cambridge University Press, 1984

Keeley, Edmund, *Cavafy's Alexandria: A Study of Myth in Progress*, Cambridge, Massachusetts: Harvard University Press, 1976; London: Hogarth Press, 1977

Komnene, Anna, *The Alexiad*, translated by E.R.A. Sewter, Harmondsworth and Baltimore: Penguin, 1969

McDonald, Marianne, *Euripides in Cinema: The Heart Made Visible*, Philadelphia: Centrum, 1983

Macintosh, F., "Tragedy in Performance: Nineteenth- and Twentieth-Century Productions" in *The Cambridge Companion to Greek Tragedy*, edited by P.E. Easterling, Cambridge and New York: Cambridge University Press, 1997

Mackridge, Peter, "Brussels and the Greek Poetry Mountain: Some Thoughts on Greek Culture" in *Greece in the 1980s*, edited by Richard Clogg, London: Macmillan, and New York: St Martin's Press, 1983

Sarafis, Marion and Martin Eve (editors), *Background to Contemporary Greece*, vol. 1, London: Merlin Press, and Savage, Maryland: Barnes and Noble, 1990

Trypanis, C.A. *Greek Poetry: From Homer to Seferis*. Chicago: University of Chicago Press, and London: Faber, 1981

Wilson, N.G., *Scholars of Byzantium*, revised edition, London: Duckworth, and Cambridge, Massachusetts: Medieval Academy of America, 1996

Woolf, G., "Becoming Roman, Staying Greek: Culture, Identity and the Civilizing Process", *Proceedings of the Cambridge Philological Society*, 40 (1994): pp. 116–43

Antisemitism

The modern-day equation of Greekness with Orthodox Christianity is one that is often assumed by Greeks and non-Greeks, by government and Church officials alike. We would be well advised, however, to bear in mind that long before there were Greek Christians, there were Greek Jews, for despite present constitutional guarantees regarding freedom of religion, and the legal separation of Church and state, in the modern era it has been very easy to assume that Orthodoxy is essential to Greekness, and Greekness somehow essential to Orthodoxy. Obviously, such an assumption is not tantamount to outright antisemitism, but the close relationship between Orthodoxy and Greekness has at many times in the modern period borne undertones of antisemitism, and has provided a potentially alienating and dangerous environment for Greek Jews.

Although this equation of Orthodoxy and Greekness is now pervasive and established, if one considers the historical sweep of the Hellenic tradition, it is also a relatively late development. Judaism first became a feature of the Greek world during the Hellenistic period. The relationship between Hellenism and Judaism was both consolidated by, and reflected in, the translation of the Jewish scriptures into Greek (270 BC). With the accession of the Seleucid king Antiochus Epiphanes in 176 BC an aggressive policy of Hellenization of Jerusalem and the surrounding regions furthered the development of a strongly Hellenized Jewish population. When revolt broke out in Judaea, Antiochus imposed a number of policies designed specifically to control and subdue the Jews. Circumcision was forbidden, worship of the Judaean God outlawed, and the Temple desecrated.

Thus there were already tensions early on in the history of Graeco-Jewish relations. To characterize them, however, as simply reflective of Greek antisemitism would be both anachronistic and lacking in interpretive subtlety. For although it is in the Hellenistic period that we find the first clash between Greekness and Jewishness, far more important is the fact that it is then that we also see the union, in many significant ways, of these two cultural concepts, and the expansion of both as a result of this union.

Thus it is that long before the advent of Christianity, Hellenism and Judaism came in contact with one another, became to some extent syncretized, and developed a familiar, if at times uneasy, coexistence. The rise of Christianity, a form of which has since come to be regarded as almost synonymous with "Greekness", long postdated this symbiosis between the two traditions, and had to negotiate its way between them.

In order to talk with any real accuracy of something specifically designated as "antisemitism in the Hellenic tradition", one needs to jump far ahead, to the Tourkokratia, if not modernity. For even during the Byzantine period, when the union among imperium, Orthodoxy, and the Hellenic linguistic and philosophical traditions was at its height, the fundamental assumption was nevertheless of a culture that was religiously and ethnically heterogeneous. It would still in this period be grossly anachronistic and heavy-handed to speak of antisemitism as a distinctly Greek phenomenon. The Jews of Byzantium, like those of western Europe in the period, were certainly subject to persecution, invasions, and various other hardships, but such events were a sad product of the general antisemitism so prevalent throughout the Christian world in the medieval period. In comparison to those in western Europe, the Jews of Byzantium fared relatively well.

While during the Byzantine era Greek Jews constituted a minority community within an empire that defined itself as Greek and Orthodox, during the Tourkokratia all Greeks, Jewish and Orthodox alike, were the minority subjects of a potentially hostile empire. It is therefore not surprising that it is during the Tourkokratia, when the Greek community had self-consciously to consolidate, preserve, and propagate its distinct cultural identity, that we find the first clear articulations of Greekness (as an ethnic category) and Orthodoxy as being somehow fused inseparably together. As the dominant Greek "minority" community (albeit a very sizeable and influential one), the Greek Orthodox polity came to bear sole responsibility, and ultimately establish hegemony, as the propagator of Hellenism. The period of Turkish rule gave rise, through the influential role granted to the Orthodox Church by the Ottoman regime, to a form of Greekness that was suffused with Orthodox Christianity. Thus it is that during the Tourkoratia we also first find the origins of what might with some accuracy be identified as a tradition of Greek antisemitism. The rise of an assumed cultural ideology whereby the Orthodox Church was the primary, indeed virtually the only, transmitter and repository of Hellenic tradition came to bear strongly antisemitic undertones.

Outside the most heavily Jewish Ottoman territories, such as Thessalonica, Greekness was articulated primarily through the vocabulary of Orthodoxy. The Greek language and the Greek educational, legal, and fiscal systems were all under the jurisdiction of the Orthodox Church. As a result of this fusion between religious and political and other secular functions, Judaism came to be regarded as inimical to true Greekness. The articulation of a form of Greekness that did not strive to accommodate or include Judaism is clearly a form of Greek antisemitism, one that was strengthened with the establishment of the Greek nation state, and furthered during the modern period.

With the creation of the kingdom of Greece in 1834, following the protracted battle for Greek independence, Jews in Greek lands found themselves in an environment potentially far more alienating than the Ottoman empire had been. The new Greek state articulated itself as strongly Orthodox in character, despite the fact that the Orthodox Church itself was placed under a significant degree of governmental control. The result was that Jews were regarded as not being truly Greek. This contributed significantly to the increasing isolation of Greek Jews from broader Greek society, an isolation both cultural and geographic that made them all-too-easy targets when the Holocaust spread to Greece. Paradoxically, however, in the decades immediately prior to the Holocaust, the overall status of Greek Jews had been gradually improving.

When in October 1940 Greece was brought into World War II, a new and hideous set of tensions was brought to bear on the Greek Jewish communities. On the eve of the war it is estimated that there were some 75,000 Jews living in Greece; at the end of the war, following repatriation, there were fewer than 10,000. The role played by antisemitism in this process is all too evident. It is far more difficult to address the question of the possible role of a distinctly Greek antisemitism in the eradication of Greek Jewry. As is well known, the Greek chief of police Angelos Evert provided Greek Jews with false identification papers in an effort to protect them from the Holocaust, and archbishop Damaskinos made repeated interventions with both the Greek government and the German authorities on their behalf.

The official Church position regarding Judaism has always condemned antisemitism, and Judaism's vital contribution to Christianity is respected and recognized. Nevertheless, over the years many Church officials have published or publicly spoken on strongly antisemitic themes. Such antisemitism often takes the form of a conflation of Zionism with Judaism, and in fact what in many instances is referred to as Greek antisemitism is much more appropriately referred to as Greek anti-Zionism. Much Greek antisemitic rhetoric assumes Zionism and Judaism to be one and the same thing, and accuses Jews of being anti-Greek or dangerous to the Greek state because of the supposed support of all Jews for the Zionist cause. In its most hysterical and hyperbolic form, such rhetoric argues that all Jews have loyalty only to a "world Zionist state" (that is, Israel), and is based on the belief that Israel has world domination as its goal. Such formulations are dangerous in the extreme, for they both discredit legitimate political positions (by making them seem specifically anti-Jewish) and syllogistically and inaccurately convert all Jews into Zionists. That Greece's stance on the Palestinian problem has been distinctly anti-Israeli is certainly not evidence that Greece is in some fundamental way antisemitic. Nor is the fact that some Greeks are Jews any sort of evidence whatsoever that they consider themselves to be anything other than Greek, or that their "true" loyalty is to the state of Israel.

Not surprisingly, the routine equation of Zionism and Judaism has led to outbreaks of anti-Jewish propaganda and activity that correspond to political events in the Middle East. Following the Israeli invasion of Lebanon in 1982, for example, articles in the mainstream Greek press referred to Israelis as "Nazis", and the "descendants of Hitler". The reception of such statements in Greece, where little care has been taken to distinguish between Israel, Judaism, and Zionism, has been one that has helped to sustain and perpetuate various forms of antisemitism. The recent strengthening of diplomatic and military ties between Turkey and Israel has contributed to the lack of subtlety in distinguishing between the various issues, although the situation has improved somewhat since prime minister Mitsotakis recognized Israel in 1990.

Perhaps most troublingly, such sweepingly inaccurate rhetoric distracts attention from the other, far less overt forms of antisemitism that are still present in a society that has for hundreds of years in many ways equated Greekness with Orthodox Christianity. The Greek educational system still places a heavy emphasis on Christian education, little effort is made to explore and teach the history of Greek Jews, and Greece's numerous if small extreme right-wing organizations, publications, and political parties have for the most part been dealt with leniently by the Greek legal system. Some acts of antisemitic violence have been reported, although in comparison to other European nations they are relatively few. In 1987 a Volos synagogue and several Jewish-owned stores were vandalized; two years later a Jewish memorial at the Lianokladi railway station in Thessaly commemorating victims of the Holocaust was smashed; routinely at international sporting events Israeli teams are jeered at in neo-Nazi rhetoric.

A survey of 1988 reported, depressingly, that fully 71 per cent of Greeks report holding a "somewhat or strongly unfavourable" view of Jews. This fact notwithstanding, the Greek government for the most part is exceedingly hesitant to acknowledge antisemitism as a real problem in Greek society. To some extent this is the intentional turning of a blind eye, but to a large degree it can been seen as the response of a society that is dramatically homogeneous in its ethnic makeup and thus unskilled at dealing with the pressing issues of pluralism and tolerance. The very things that have historically given rise to Greek antisemitism – the linkage between Hellenism and Orthodoxy, and the ethnic homogeneity of Greek society – have, alas, also been the very things that have made Greece ill-equipped to deal with it.

K.E. FLEMING

See also Jews, Septuagint

Further Reading

Bowman, Steven B., *The Jews of Byzantium, 1204–1453*, University: University of Alabama Press, 1985

Kitroeff, Alexander, *The Jews of Modern Greece: A Bibliography*, East Hampton, New York: Modern Greek Society, 1986

Mazower, Mark, *Inside Hitler's Greece: The Experience of Occupation, 1941–44*, New Haven, Connecticut and London: Yale University Press, 1993

Perdurant, Daniel, *Antisemitism in Contemporary Greek Society*, Jerusalem: Hebrew University, 1995

Pierron, Bernard, *Juifs et chrétiens de la Grèce moderne: histoire des relations intercommunautaires de 1821 à 1945*, Paris: Harmattan, 1996

Plaut, Joshua Eli, *Greek Jewry in the Twentieth Century, 1913–1983: Patterns of Jewish Survival in the Greek Provinces before and after the Holocaust*, Cranbury, New Jersey: Associated University Presses, 1996

Sciaky, Leon, *Farewell to Salonica: Portrait of an Era*, New York: Wyn, and London: W.H. Allen, 1946

Stavroulakis, Nicholas, *The Jews of Greece: An Essay*, Athens: Talos Press, 1990

Apelles

Painter of the 4th/3rd century BC

Apelles was the most celebrated and the most written-about painter in antiquity, yet we know neither his date of birth nor his date of death. However, his likeable and colourful personality, his rivalries with others, and his special relationships with the most powerful men of his day have generated many anecdotes about the man, the artist, and his works. He attained remarkably high social and economic status, and wrote treatises about his painting. Unfortunately, neither his writings nor his famous creations survive. All we have are anecdotes, the mention of more than 30 titles of his works, perhaps a few very vague and suspect reminiscences in Roman paintings, and a few elaborate literary descriptions, the last of which formed the basis for attempted recreations of his works by Renaissance artists.

Born sometime around 370 BC, in either Cos or Colophon, Apelles first trained in the Ionic school under Ephorus of Ephesus. He then moved to the Greek mainland, paying a large sum for the privilege of becoming the student of Pamphilus, the master of the Sicyonian school. Combining the grace of the Ionic style with the thoroughness of the Sicyonian school, Apelles attained a reputation that by c.340 BC was sufficiently prominent to gain him entry to the court of Philip II in Macedonia, where he painted portraits of the ruler and his court. During the reign of Alexander the Great, Apelles' affable nature and abilities as a painter advanced him to the point where the ruler made him his official portraitist. Apelles joined the ranks of the sculptor Lysippus and the engraver Pyrgoteles as the only artists officially allowed to depict Alexander. The latter was attempting, it seems, to develop his official portraiture, and to control the quality, and messages conveyed by, his images.

Apelles' easy relationship with Alexander and his associations with other powerful rulers and commanders made the artist's reputation. His works fetched extraordinary prices and were avidly collected. His portrait of *Alexander as Zeus Keraunophoros* [the Thunder-Bearer] for the temple of Artemis at Ephesus fetched 20 talents; his *Aphrodite Anadyomene* [Rising from the Sea], intended for the temple of Asclepius at Cos, was eventually taken by the emperor Augustus in exchange for remission of a 100-talent debt.

Apelles' works included a variety of subjects: historical portraits of Philip, Alexander, Menander (satrap of Caria), and Antigonus Monophthalmus; such figures as philosophers, men of letters, actors, and priests; elaborate allegories; personifications; and naturalistic renditions of animals. He even painted a self-portrait, perhaps the first of antiquity. The most famous portraits were those of Alexander. Whereas it was Lysippus who appears to have been chiefly responsible for the development of a heroic image of Alexander, Apelles (and perhaps also Pyrgoteles) created a superhuman image and divine personality which were more suited to the needs of an Alexander who was the ruler of a great and unified empire. *Alexander as Zeus Keraunophoros* had obvious religious and political overtones for the new empire. Some details of the painting are recorded (see below) though even the subject's basic pose is not described: perhaps Alexander was seated on a throne following Phidias' *Olympian Zeus*. The painting of Alexander in the house of the Vettii at Pompeii may reflect some of Apelles' influence.

Of Apelles' numerous portraits of Alexander, two others are notable for conveying the elevated status of the ruler: *Alexander in the company of Nike and the Dioscuri*, and *Alexander in a Triumphal Chariot* with the personification of War (Polemos) with bound hands. Such overt imagery was useful to later rulers, accounting for the prominent display of both paintings in the Forum of Augustus in Rome. Associations with that ruler were made even more directly when Claudius had Alexander's features replaced by those of Augustus. By creating such portraits of Alexander, Apelles breached the divide separating the human from the divine, making the deification of mortals much easier for later artists and rulers.

Of Apelles' allegorical paintings, his *Calumny*, created after he had been slandered and subsequently cleared at Ptolemy's court in Alexandria, is the most famous. Lucian (*Calumny*, 4) provides both the context and description for the work, which has been cited as the only known example of painted satire in antiquity. Several Renaissance artists (among them Dürer and Botticelli) attempted to capture the essence of the lost work using only Lucian's words.

The *Aphrodite Anadyomene*, Apelles' most famous painting, also inspired Renaissance artists. According to one tradition, Apelles had fallen in love with Alexander's mistress while painting her portrait. When he realized what had happened, the king gave her to Apelles, who then used her as the model for the *Anadyomene*. The story fits well with other information about his relationship with Alexander and with his reputation as a naturalistic painter of great talent. The painting was eventually displayed by Augustus in the temple of Julius Caesar, where it would remind viewers of Caesar's claim of descent from Venus-Aphrodite.

Some of Apelles' more elaborate concepts of abstract personifications included depictions of *Thunder* (*Bronte*), *Lightning* (*Astrape*), and the *Thunderbolt* (*Keraunobolia*). All probably were examples of his experimentation with lighting effects, which are recorded or surmised for other paintings. Lucian states that studied gradations in colours were used in the faces of the *Calumny* to distinguish its personifications. Lighting technique may also account for the three-dimensional effect of the fingers holding the sparkling bolt of lightning in the *Keraunophoros*. The suggestion that Apelles increased the brightness of the bolt to make it stand forth by darkening the figure of Alexander provides a hint of what his experimentation might have accomplished.

He is praised continually for the amazing realism of his works. His portraits were said to be so perfect that a physiognomist was able to determine the subject's age and how much longer he had to live. As with earlier painters, stories developed in which animals became judges of paintings, and were unable to distinguish between painted images and reality. When Apelles, entered in a contest to paint horses, realized that a conspiracy had already decided the outcome, he had real horses brought in to prove his skill by their neighing only at his work. As a general attribute of great artists, such comments about naturalistic renditions tell us little about the painters, but often allow other deductions.

The stories about Apelles seem to indicate that he concentrated on human and animal subjects rather than scenery and incidental detail. Nor does he seem to have been much concerned with elaborate perspective, although some of his works imply an interest in foreshortening. He painted an oblique portrait of Antigonus Monophthalmus, so that only his good eye would be visible, and a Heracles seen from behind.

Anecdotes about his friendly rivalry with Protogenes, another important painter, reveal some of Apelles' other techniques and interests. The two painters probably refined the skiagraphic technique (shadow painting), raising it to a new level. The contest in which they vied with one another in drawing a finer, steadier line reveals the importance of manual dexterity and control, which, in conjunction with the daily drawing practice of Apelles, serves to emphasize his probable belief that these skills were the foundations of his success. Naturalistic illusion through fineness of line seems to have been the key to Apelles' approach to painting.

His skill also was reflected by his use of only four colours. The technique had been in use for some time, but was probably brought to its acme by Apelles, whose fame inspired Renaissance artists to attempt to emulate his success with the restricted palette. The use of few colours and his eschewing of elaborate perspective and scenery made his simplicity of design, his beauty of line, and his charm of expression his chief merits.

In addition to his advances in artistic style and technique, Apelles also developed some sort of transparent varnish, a dark glaze (atramentum) that preserved the paintings and softened the colours, perhaps adding to the naturalism of the subject. Attempts to rediscover this substance have failed.

Unlike most other artists, Apelles was unusually receptive to criticism from all quarters, though he was also quick to counter undeserved criticism, whether from a ruler of Alexander's stature or a common cobbler. The story of him hiding to hear criticisms of his works from people in the street, and then altering his paintings accordingly, fits well with his acknowledgements of other painters' abilities: Melanthius spaced his figures better, Asclepiodorus had better symmetry and proportions. Apelles believed himself the painter who excelled all in grace or charm (charis). His peers, his clients, and Roman emperors and nobles not only agreed, but regarded him as the best painter of antiquity. Scholars and artists since the Renaissance, intrigued by his reputation and descriptions of his paintings and techniques, have tried in vain to recover his genius.

ANDREW N. SHERWOOD

See also Painting

Biography

Born c.370 BC in either Cos or Colophon, Apelles studied first at Ephesus under Ephorus and later at Sicyon under Pamphilus. He gained entry to the court of Philip II of Macedon. He alone was permitted to paint Alexander. He painted historical portraits, types, personifications, and animals. He achieved fame in his lifetime and became the most celebrated painter in antiquity, though none of his works now survives.

Further Reading

Benezit, E. (editor), Dictionnaire critique et documentaire des peintres, sculpteurs, dessinateurs, et graveurs de tous les temps et de tous les pays, new edition, Paris: Gründ, 1976

Benndorf, O., "Bermerkungen zur griechischen Kunst-geschichte: Die Anadyomene des Apelles", Mitteilungen des Deutschen Archäologischen Instituts (Athenische Abteilung), 1 (1876): pp. 50–66

Berger, Ernst, Die Wachsmalerei des Apelles und seiner Zeit, Munich: Callway, 1917

Bruno, Vincent J., Form and Color in Greek Painting, New York: Norton, 1977

Cast, David, The Calumny of Apelles: A Study in the Humanist Tradition, New Haven and London: Yale University Press, 1981

Charlton, W. and A. Saville, "The Art of Apelles", Proceedings of the Aristotelian Society, London, 53 (1979): pp. 167–206

Daut, Raimund, "Belli facies et Triumphus", Mitteilungen des Deutschen Archäologischen Instituts (Römische Abteilung), 91 (1984): pp. 115–23

Gage, J., "A Locus Classicus of Colour Theory: The Fortunes of Apelles", Journal of the Warburg and Courtauld Institutes, 44 (1981): pp. 1–26

Gombrich, E.H., The Heritage of Apelles: Studies in the Art of the Renaissance, Oxford: Phaidon, and Ithaca, New York: Cornell University Press, 1976

Lepik-Kopaczynska, Wilhelmina, Apelles: Der Berühmteste Maler der Antike, Berlin: Akademie, 1962

Maas, E., "Apelles und Protogenes", Jahreshefte des Österreichischen Archäologischen Instituts in Wien, 11 (1908): pp. 29–47

Massing, Jean-Michel, La Calomnie d'Apelle et son iconographie: du texte à l'image, Strasbourg: Presses Universitaires de Strasbourg, 1990

Meissner, Günter (editor), Allgemeines Künstler-Lexikon, new edition, vol. 3, Leipzig: Seemann, 1990 (Apelles entry, pp. 694–95)

Overbeck, Johannes, Die antiken Schriftquellen zur Geschichte der bildenden Künste bei den Griechen, Hildesheim: Olms, 1959 (originally published 1868)

Pfuhl, Ernst, Malerei und Zeichnung der Griechen, vol. 2, Rome: Bretschneider, 1969

Pliny the Elder, The Elder Pliny's Chapters on the History of Art, edited by E. Sellers and translated by K. Jex-Blake, Chicago: Ares, 1976

Robertson, Martin, A History of Greek Art, London: Cambridge University Press, 1975

Robertson, Martin, Greek Painting, Geneva: Skira, 1959; New York: Rizzoli, 1979

Rumpf, Andreas, Malerei und Zeichnung der klassischen Antike, Munich: Beck, 1953

Thieme, Ulrich and Felix Becker (editors), Allgemeines Lexikon der bildenden Künstler von der Antike bis zur Gegenwart, Leipzig: Engelmann, 1908

Aphrodisias

City in Asia Minor

Aphrodisias, an ancient city of Caria in Asia Minor (now Geyre in Turkey), is located about 240 km southeast of Izmir (formerly Smyrna) in a fertile plain with a good supply of spring water. The site was inhabited by the late Neolithic period; in the 4th millennium BC a prominent settlement was established and continued to exist there throughout the Bronze Age. Already in prehistoric times a fertility goddess was venerated at the site. As the fame of the local goddess, called Ninoe, gradually spread, a settlement with a sanctuary and a surrounding area under its protection was founded in the 1st millennium BC. Although a vigorous community developed during the Archaic period, one cannot speak of the existence of a city at this time.

Until the Hellenistic period Aphrodisias remained a sacred site with a sanctuary, associated, perhaps from the 3rd century BC, with the Greek goddess Aphrodite, after whom it was named, as indicated by coin inscriptions of the late 2nd and early 1st centuries BC. Its transformation into a city seems to be connected with the establishment of Roman power in western Asia. Although excavations on the site were undertaken at the beginning of the 20th century, it was not until 1961 that Aphrodisias began to be systematically excavated. The site is notable for its extensive and well-preserved monuments.

With the arrival of the Romans in Anatolia Aphrodisias flourished, largely because of its close relationship with Rome

Aphrodisias: an ancient city in western Asia Minor recently brought to life by the excavations of Kenan Erim

and especially with the family of Caesar. Thus Aphrodisias resisted Mithridates VI in 88 BC and the "Liberators" – Brutus and Cassius – after Caesar's death. In 40 BC Labienus, one of their supporters, attacked Aphrodisias and both the city and the sanctuary were plundered before Antony defeated him (39 BC). Thereafter Aphrodisias lay in Antony's sphere of influence. At this time the name of Aphrodisias appeared on coins together with that of the neighbouring city of Plarasa. In 39 and 35 BC Antony sent a senatorial decree to Aphrodisias, in which the Plarasians and Aphrodisians were addressed as citizens of the city, which presumably resulted in the unification of the two cities. The decree guaranteed Aphrodisias its freedom as well as certain special privileges, such as a non-taxable status and asylum rights to the sanctuary of Aphrodite. During the Roman empire the population reached 50,000, and the city enjoyed a long period of prosperity and was transformed into an important cultural, religious, and artistic centre.

The city was laid out according to the Hippodamian town planning system and in the second half of the 3rd century AD a fortification wall, *c*.3.5 km long, was built around it against the threat of Gothic invasions. Elaborate buildings, such as the theatre, the tetrastoon, the agora, the baths of Hadrian, the Sebasteion, the odeum, the temple of Aphrodite, and the stadium (which could seat almost 30,000 spectators) were erected in Aphrodisias during Roman times. Traces of a gymnasium complex and a sculptor's workshop have also been recovered.

The theatre of Aphrodisias, one of the best preserved in Turkey, was built in the second half of the 1st century BC. It remained in use during the early Byzantine period and could hold around 8000 spectators. The wall of the north parodos was discovered to be lined with inscriptions and was thereafter referred to as the "archive wall". These documents – mostly letters – form a unique record for the history of Aphrodisias and of Roman Asia Minor.

To the southwest of the temple of Aphrodite stood a residential complex of the 3rd century AD. The building consisted of several rooms and halls and a peristyle court decorated with blue marble columns. Originally this may have been a private dwelling of a high Roman official, but in the Byzantine period it was the bishop's palace. A similar building, constructed in the 3rd century AD to the north of the temple of Aphrodite, is identified as a school of philosophy, which in the 6th century AD was used as a residence.

Aphrodisias became famous as a centre for medicine and philosophy. Xenocrates composed his medical treatises here, while the philosophers Alexander (one of the best commentators on Aristotle) and Adrastus originated from Aphrodisias. Statues, reliefs, and sarcophagi were produced in the sculpture workshops of Aphrodisias for local use and export. Local sculptors gained fame, and their signatures are found in many regions of the Mediterranean; their craftsmanship was appreciated even in Rome, and a school of sculpture was founded which lasted to the end of the 5th century AD. The sculptors managed to give new meanings to Classical models and did not limit themselves to mere reproduction of well-known works of Classical art. The marble quarries in the vicinity of Aphrodisias were a source of white and dark marbles. Sculpture competitions were also held in the city.

In the 3rd century AD changes in the administration of the Roman empire affected the privileged status of Aphrodisias, which was considered part of the province of Asia. After the formation of a new province of Caria and Phrygia in the 250s, Aphrodisias probably became its administrative centre. Under Diocletian (284–305), it was the capital of the separate province of Caria.

With the spread of Christianity Aphrodisias became the seat of an archbishop in the 4th century and the temple of Aphrodite was transformed into a triple-naved basilica. The earliest known Aphrodisian bishop is Ammonius, who participated in the Council of Nicaea in 325. Palaces with audience halls flanked the church. The agora to the south was abandoned after an earthquake in the 4th century, and many public buildings were rebuilt at that time.

In the course of the 5th and 6th centuries several bishops of Aphrodisias became involved in the theological disputes concerning the nature of Christ. Paganism was vigorous in the city throughout the 5th century, but there was also an important Monophysite church. Both pagans and Christians made generous benefactions to the city. The city's name was changed to Stavroupolis [City of the Cross] in the 7th century, but by the 12th century it was commonly known by the name of the province, Caria. An earthquake in the reign of Herakleios (610–41) destroyed many buildings in the city, such as the theatre, the odeum, and the agora gate, which were never repaired. The mound of the theatre was then surrounded by walls and transformed into a citadel, where the population could take refuge in times of danger. The city was sacked by Theodore Mankapas in 1188 and by the Seljuks in 1197. It became Turkish in the late 13th century. Gradually the size of the city decreased until it was no more than a village, called Geyre, a name deriving from Caria and mentioned by 17th-century travellers.

ELENI ZIMI

Summary

City in Asia Minor, known as Geyre today. The site was inhabited in prehistoric times and was the centre of a local cult, perhaps associated with Aphrodite. But Aphrodisias did not flourish as a city until Roman times, when it was granted special privileges. A large number of well-preserved monuments survive and the city became an important cultural, religious, and artistic centre. In the 4th century it became the seat of an archibishop and the temple of Aphrodite was turned into a basilica.

Further Reading

Alföldi, Andreas *et al.*, *Aion in Merida und Aphrodisias*, Mainz: Zabern, 1979

Erim, Kenan T., *Aphrodisias: City of Venus Aphrodite*, London: Muller Blond and White, 1986

Erim, Kenan T., *Aphrodisias: A Guide to the Site and its Museum*, 3rd edition, Istanbul: NET Turistik Yayinlar, 1992

Joukowski Sharp, Martha, *Prehistoric Aphrodisias: An Account of the Excavations and Artifact Studies*, Providence, Rhode Island: Brown University Center for Old World Archaeology and Art, 1986

La Genière, Juliette de and Kenan T. Erim (editors), *Aphrodisias de Carie: colloque du Centre de Recherches Archéologiques de l'Université de Lille III, 13 novembre 1985*, Paris: Editions Recherche sur les Civilisations, 1987

MacDonald, David, *The Coinage of Aphrodisias*, London: Royal Numismatic Society, 1992

Reynolds, Joyce, *Aphrodisias and Rome: Documents from the Excavation of the Theatre at Aphrodisias Conducted by Professor Kenan T. Erim, together with some Related Texts*, London: London Society for the Promotion of Roman Studies, 1982

Roueché, Charlotte, *Aphrodisias in Late Antiquity: The Late Roman and Byzantine Inscriptions, Including Texts from Excavations at Aphrodisias Conducted by Kenan T. Erim*, London: London Society for the Promotion of Roman Studies, 1989

Roueché, Charlotte, and Kenan T. Erim (editors), *Aphrodisias Papers, 1: Recent Work on Architecture and Sculpture*, Ann Arbor, Michigan: Journal of Roman Archaeology, 1990

Roueché, Charlotte, and R.R.R. Smith, *Aphrodisias Papers, 3: The Setting and Quarries, Mythological and Other Sculptural Decoration, Architectural Development, Portico of Tiberius, and Tetrapylon*, Ann Arbor, Michigan: Journal of Roman Archaeology, 1996

Smith, R.R.R. and Kenan T. Erim (editors), *Aphrodisias Papers, 2: The Theatre, a Sculptor's Workshop, Philosophers, and Coin-types*, Ann Arbor, Michigan: Journal of Roman Archaeology, 1991

Smith, R.R.R., *Aphrodisias 1: Results of the Excavations at Aphrodisias in Caria Conducted by New York University: The Monument of C. Julius Zoilos*, Mainz: Zabern, 1993

Smith, R.R.R. and Christopher Ratté, "Archaeological Research at Aphrodisias in Caria", *American Journal of Archaeology*, 99–102 (1995–98)

Apollonius of Perge

Mathematician and astronomer of the 3rd century BC

The work of Apollonius of Perge, who was active in the late 3rd century BC, marks the end of the great creative period of Greek geometry. He was the author of a number of mathematical works, including *On the Cutting off of a Ratio* (which survives in an Arabic translation), and we are told by Ptolemy (who quotes one of his theorems) that he did important work on the mathematics of astronomy. His status as one of the great mathematicians of antiquity, however, rests on his *Conica*, a treatise in eight books on the geometry of the ellipse, the parabola, and the hyperbola. The first four books, the only ones to survive in Greek, are described by Apollonius in his preface as an "elementary introduction", and deal with the construction of the figures, their fundamental properties, and a series of theorems on a variety of mathematical relationships; they are modelled, both in their method of presentation and in their organization, on the *Elements* of Euclid. Of the remaining four books, three survive only in Arabic translation, and the fourth is completely lost. They deal with a number of separate additional problems, with little attempt to bring them together into a single system of argument; the quality of mathematical thought in these books (and especially book 5) is very high.

Apollonius himself makes little claim to originality, and it is certainly true that when he wrote his treatise Greek geometers had already been working on conic sections for some time. The first to do so was probably Menaechmus, in the 4th century BC, as part of his attempt at a solution to the problem of duplicating the cube. Later Euclid wrote a work on conics (now lost), and Archimedes also deals with them, particularly the parabola. Apollonius, however, in suggesting that he is simply compiling and systematizing the work of his predecessors, seriously understates his achievement. Earlier Greek geometers had treated these curves as sections of different kinds of cone, cut by a line perpendicular to one of the sides of the cone. Cutting an acute-angled cone produces an ellipse, a right-angled cone a parabola, and an obtuse-angled cone a hyperbola. What Apollonius did was to show how all of these curves could be generated from sections of a single type of cone, the double oblique cone, thus achieving a much greater degree of generality. He deals with most of the features of conics familiar to modern mathematicians, and where he omits some (as, for example, the focus of the parabola) it is more likely that the reason is that he was trying to write an elementary treatise, rather than that he was unaware of them.

The *Conica* established itself as a sort of supplement to Euclid, and one of the basic texts of Greek mathematics, at a very early date. It was still being studied in the 4th and 5th centuries AD, when it was the subject of commentaries by, among others, Serenus, Hypatia, and Eutocius. The oldest surviving manuscripts date from the 9th century, a period when interest in mathematics was being revived in the Byzantine empire, which perhaps indicates that the *Conica* was still being regarded at that period as a fundamental text.

The 3rd-century AD mathematician Pappus gives brief descriptions of five other works by Apollonius which are now completely lost: *On the Cutting off of an Area, On Determinate Sections, On Tangencies, Plane Loci,* and *Vergings.* Pappus also preserves an extract of a description of a method of expressing and manipulating very large numbers, using 10,000 as base. Other works that are credited to Apollonius are a *Comparison of the Dodecahedron with the* Eicosahedron, a *General Treatise* (on the fundamental principles of geometry), *On the Cylindrical Helix,* a work on unordered irrationals, and the *Quick Delivery,* in which he calculated the value of π to a high degree of accuracy.

RICHARD WALLACE

See also Mathematics

Biography

Active in the late 3rd century BC, Apollonius of Perge is best known for his work on *Conics* (of its eight books, four survive in Greek, three in Arabic, and one is lost). His only other surviving work is *On the Cutting off of a Ratio* which is preserved in an Arabic translation. Ptolemy says he also worked on the mathematics of astronomy.

Writings

Treatise on Conic Sections, edited by Sir Thomas Little Heath, Cambridge: Cambridge University Press, 1896; reprinted Cambridge: Heffer, and New York: Barnes and Noble, 1961

Further Reading

Heath, Sir Thomas Little, *A History of Greek Mathematics,* 2 vols, Oxford: Clarendon Press, 1921, reprinted New York: Dover, 1981

Apollonius Rhodius *c.*295–215 BC

Epic poet and scholar

Apollonius was born at Alexandria (cf. Strabo, 14. 655) or, less probably, at Naucratis (Athenaeus, 7 p. 283; Aelian, *De Natura Animalium,* 15. 23). However, he is generally called the Rhodian on account of his retirement in Rhodes, where he is said to have revised his epic after its supposed initial failure to impress the Alexandrian audience, and, through his poem and his work as a rhetorician, to have won the recognition of the Rhodians and even the citizenship of Rhodes. There is probably an element of fiction in this account, which may have been suggested by the existence of some variants quoted in the scholia, which seem to point to an earlier text. According to his two anonymous biographies (contained in the Laurentian manuscript of the *Argonautica* and probably incorporating material derived from the late 1st century BC) and the *Suda,* he was a pupil of Callimachus, with whom he is said to have quarrelled over the merits of long traditional epics over short and highly finished poems. The supposed existence of such an enmity — a supposition based on rather flimsy evidence — is, however, rendered improbable by the many striking parallels in the work of the two poets. According to Oxyrhynchus papyrus no. 1241 (late 2nd century AD), Apollonius followed Zenodotus as director of the library in Alexandria (270–247 BC) and was succeeded by Eratosthenes. The *Suda* puts him after Eratosthenes, no doubt due to a confusion with Apollonius the Eidograph, who is mentioned in the papyrus as the successor to Eratosthenes.

Apollonius' lost works include prose tracts on Hesiod (in which he apparently rejected the *Ornithomanteia* but accepted the *Shield of Heracles* as genuine), Archilochus, Antimachus, and a monograph on Homer entitled *Against Zenodotus* (cf. the Venetian scholia on Homer, *Iliad,* 13. 657), a choliambic poem on Egyptian legends entitled *Canobus,* and *ktiseis* or poems on the origin or foundation of cities (a genre fashionable at the time and reflecting Alexandrian enthusiasm for local history and cult) such as Alexandria, Naucratis, Caunus, Cnidus, Rhodes, and possibly Lesbos. The only surviving example of his epigrams (if the attribution is reliable) is an attack on Callimachus (*Anthologia Palatina,* 11. 275).

He was the first ancient writer to divide his own work into books, and in their number as well as in their length, the four books of his epic follow Aristotle's advice in the *Poetics* (chapter 23) that ideally an epic should be as long as the series of three tragedies and one satyr play presented by each poet at a dramatic competition. The *Argonautica* (which runs to 5,835 lines) narrates how Jason and his followers sailed to Colchis by the Propontis and Black Sea (books 1–2), how he won the Golden Fleece with Medea's help (book 3), and how the ship returned home (book 4).

Among the poet's major literary antecedents may be mentioned the fourth Pythian Ode of Pindar, with its account of the Argonautic expedition, and the *Medea* of Euripides. However, Apollonius' main inspiration is Homer, and this influence permeates almost every aspect of his creation, and is most evident in set scenes. Thus the catalogue of the Argonauts (1. 23–233) corresponds to Homer's catalogue of ships in *Iliad* 2, while the description of Jason's cloak (1. 721–67) has been suggested by the shield of Achilles in *Iliad* 18. These scenes serve to bring out by contrast the significant differences in Apollonius' poem. The same is also true of individual characters in relation to their Homeric prototypes: compare Jason with Odysseus or Medea with Nausicaa and Circe.

The Hellenistic period was an age of scientific and scholarly achievement, and the Hellenistic poets considered this knowledge as part of their artistic material. In keeping with contemporary trends, therefore, Apollonius brings his scholarship to bear on his composition by explaining the causes (*aitia*) of names, cults, relics, customs, and natural phenomena. The scholia record many of the sources that he so diligently consulted. His learning stresses the significance of the Argonautic expedition as a voyage of acculturation, establishing Greek tradition. It has been suggested that the repeatedly positive evaluation of Greek culture (including cult and mythology) should be connected with the Ptolemaic context of the work, since the Ptolemies promoted themselves as the true heirs and champions of Classical Greek culture (Hunter, 1993, chapter 6).

Apollonius was also the first Greek poet to place love in the foreground of the action in an epic and to study its psychology, thereby creating a new trend in western literature. Although he is dealing with a heroic legend, its central theme is not war but love. The capacity he shows for sympathetic analysis in his account of Medea's love for Jason is something not found in earlier Greek literature, with the possible exception of Sappho, whose work, however, has survived only in fragments. His descriptive power is revealed in the many charming *ekphraseis* (descriptions) with which he adorns his poem, once more in keeping with Hellenistic tradition. He also introduces a number of striking and suggestive similes. These descriptions and similes, as well as his fresh treatment of old episodes, serve to attract the reader.

The principal defect of the poem, according to some modern critics, is its lack of structural unity. In their view, Apollonius fails to organize into a whole his abundant array of erudite material, and too often the narrative breaks into long, disjointed passages. It has been pointed out, however, that discontinuity is Apollonius' principle of composition, and that this principle operates in the organization of the narrative both within the book and between books. Although constructed with great care, especially in its versification, its uniform mediocrity often makes the poem positively tedious. He has also been criticized for weak characterization. His Jason lacks the energy expected of a heroic leader, and lacks sufficient development to attract the reader's interest. In each of the two last books where she appears, Medea, as impressionable virgin and dangerous sorceress respectively, is inconsistent (when seen against Aristotle's requirement of consistency for the dramatic character), though she is beautifully drawn and the gradual growth of her love for Jason is described with a truly artistic moderation.

His hexameters generally follow the Homeric pattern, and so does his vocabulary. However, in keeping with the usage of Alexandrian authors, he continually varies and "interprets" the Homeric words and phrases. His greatest stylistic achievement is in fact the subtle adaptation of the Homeric language to express the romantic sentiments of his own age, but its brevity and conciseness are in marked contrast to the natural and easy flow of the Homeric poems.

The *Argonautica* appears to have enjoyed considerable popularity even during Apollonius' own lifetime, for we hear that contemporaries, such as Charon, wrote commentaries on it. Our present scholia are abridged from the commentaries of Lucillus of Tarrha, Sophocles, and Theon, all of whom apparently belong to the pre-Christian era. There are 52 known manuscripts, and numerous papyri testify to the poem's popularity in later antiquity. There are two sets of scholia: the Florentine and the Parisian. The former were published in the edition by J. Lascaris (Florence, 1496), and the latter were first published in Schaefer's edition (2 volumes, Leipzig, 1810–13) and consist mainly of verbal explanations and criticisms. The scholia also speak of one Eirenaius as the author of a critical and exegetical commentary. During the reign of the Byzantine emperor Anastasius I (AD 491–518), one Marianus paraphrased the *Argonautica* in 5608 iambics. In recent times the *Argonautica* has attracted the serious attention of scholars. Surprisingly, there were no English translations of the *Argonautica* until those of E.P. Coleridge (1889), R.C. Seaton (1912), and E.V. Rieu (1959). However, Between 1990 and 1997, three new translations appeared, by Barbara Hughes Fowler (1990), Richard L. Hunter (1993), and Peter Green (1997).

D.P.M. WEERAKKODY

See also Poetry (Epic)

Biography

Born *c*.295 BC probably in Alexandria, Apollonius is called the Rhodian because he retired to Rhodes, apparently to revise his epic poem, the *Argonautica*, after its poor reception in Alexandria. A pupil of Callimachus, he was director of the Alexandria library after Zenodotus and before Eratosthenes. Lost works include prose tracts on other poets and poems on the foundation of cities. He died in 215 BC.

Writings

Argonautica

The Argonautica, translated by Edward P. Coleridge, London: Bell, 1889, reprinted New York: Heritage Press, 1960
The Argonautica, translated by R.C. Seaton, London: Heinemann, and New York: Macmillan, 1912 (Loeb edition; many reprints)
The Voyage of Argo: The Argonautica, translated by E.V. Rieu, 2nd edition, Harmondsworth and Baltimore: Penguin, 1971
In *Hellenistic Poetry: An Anthology*, edited and translated by Barbara Hughes Fowler, Madison: University of Wisconsin Press, 1990
Jason and the Golden Fleece: The Argonautica, translated by Richard Hunter, Oxford: Clarendon Press, and New York: Oxford University Press, 1993
The Argonautika, translated by Peter Green, Berkeley: University of California Press, 1997

Further Reading

Albis, Robert V., *Poet and Audience in the Argonautica of Apollonius*, Lanham, Maryland: Rowman and Littlefield, 1996
Beye, Charles Rowan, *Epic and Romance in the Argonautica of Apollonius*, Carbondale: Southern Illinois University Press, 1982
Campbell, Malcolm, *Echoes and Imitations of Early Epic in Apollonius Rhodius*, Leiden: Brill, 1981
DeForest, Mary Margolies, *Apollonius' Argonautica: A Callimachean Epic*, Leiden and New York: Brill, 1994
Feeney, D.C., *The Gods in Epic: Poets and Critics of the Classical*

Tradition, Oxford: Clarendon Press, and New York: Oxford University Press, 1991

Hunter, Richard, *The Argonautica of Apollonius: Literary Studies*, Cambridge and New York: Cambridge University Press, 1993

Hutchinson, G.O., *Hellenistic Poetry*, Oxford: Clarendon Press, 1988

Apologists, Greek

The precise identification of the individuals who came to be known collectively as the Greek Apologists has been a matter of debate. An average list would contain as many as 12 names: Quadratus, Aristides of Athens, Aristo of Pella, St Justin Martyr, Tatian the Syrian, Miltiades, Apollinaris of Hierapolis, Athenagoras of Athens, Theophilus of Antioch, Melito of Sardis, the author of the *Epistle of Diognetus*, and Hermias. Of these, some are represented by little surviving text, while others may be read at fair length. The *Epistle of Diognetus*, it may be argued, is best treated separately.

As the name implies, these were Christian writers who wrote in defence of their faith, their apologetic directed in the first instance against what were seen as dangerous misunderstandings and calumnies that might affect the treatment of Christians within the empire at large and within local society. Some were supposedly addressed to emperors, though there is no evidence of response. It was seen as essential that Christian communities should be treated not as potentially dissident, but as loyal citizens of the empire, people whose form of worship, though distinctive, posed no threat to private morality or public order. The Christian Eucharist, with its reference to eating a body and drinking blood, was no crude cannibalism but a deeply spiritual expression of unity. Of more lasting significance are those parts of their work in which these writers attempt to face the intellectual criticism, often scorn, that they met or might expect to meet from their educated counterparts. Though they may not emerge as deeply original thinkers, they show some acquaintance with current thought patterns as they had been traditionally developed, and they are able to engage with ideas that might either be demonstrated to have affinities with Christian teachings or to be inimical to them. They saw their task as setting out as clearly as they could, in debate with Jews or pagans, lines of continuity, while preserving what they regarded as the inalienable uniqueness of their belief. The Apologists try to isolate fundamental points of monotheistic faith or philosophical tenets that tend in their direction, particularly where there is a Platonic angle to be examined. A writer such as Justin, who feels committed to fighting on two fronts, hoping to win acceptance in the philosophical schools through which he claims to have successively passed and equally among people of the Jewish faith from which Christianity had emerged, engaged in a formidable undertaking. While there are tedious and ill-considered tracts in, say, Tatian, there are also fascinating insights into skills of communication. Whatever success, or lack of it, we are to attribute to the Greek Apologists in their own time, we cannot doubt the influence they had on later Christian writers, setting a pattern of reasoned debate, rather than wilful isolation.

Of Quadratus only a fragment survives, quoted by Eusebius, dated around 124. If we accept the statement of that same historian, we would take Aristides to be the earliest whose *Apology* survives, and, indeed, the Syrian and Armenian texts on which our knowledge is based are prefaced by the statement that it is addressed to Hadrian (emperor 117–38). It is, however, more likely to be later, written during the reign of his successor, Antoninus Pius, perhaps c.140. If so, it would retain its place as the earliest surviving apology. Aristides attempts to preserve a cool tone. While maintaining the uniqueness of Christians, in that they alone have attained a true knowledge of God, he wishes to place them in the context of Greek philosophical speculation about the nature of deity, writing in terms that would be familiar to the Stoics and indeed to anyone who had done a little serious reading on the being of God (or god) and the nature of the created order. Biblical references are sparse and the Christological section, of interest as a summary of tradition, makes no attempt at exposition.

All this changes when we pass to Justin. He is the outstanding centre point of the group (as such, he is treated in a separate article). In summary, Justin tries to bring together his philosophical background and his biblical convictions, rooted in Hebrew prophecy, to enunciate distinctively Christian tenets in outline Trinitarian form. The *Logos* communicates God's truth to the world, all humanity sharing in affinity with the *Logos* through rational (*logikos*) creation.

Tatian, a pupil of Justin in Rome, resembles him in some ways. They both came from a pagan background, exploring philosophy on their way to conversion. Yet Tatian can take on an arrogant, dismissive tone, unlike Justin's, in referring to Greek philosophy; nor would he have had Justin's support in his lapses into extreme asceticism, though the question of his link with Gnosticism is best left open. Again, his emphasis on divine transcendence is not balanced by any whole-hearted exposition of the Incarnation and work of the *Logos* (never called "Christ"). On the other hand, he did bring out the *Diatessaron*, a setting out of the four gospels in continuous form that kept before generations of readers the central narratives that must be woven into any future Christology.

In Athenagoras we again meet a man with aspirations to be taken seriously in philosophy. (Indeed, his *Legatio* describes itself as "by Athenagoras the Athenian: Philosopher and Christian".) He shows his claim to the title by a more serious appreciation than Tatian's. His writing has more claim to elegance than anything seen so far and could well have impressed open-minded contemporaries. What Athenagoras conveyed in the *Legatio* or *Supplication* (Greek *Presbeia*) around 177 (the year of the martyrdoms, in the reign of Marcus Aurelius, in Gaul at Lyons and Vienne) was not the expected rebuttal of false reports on Christian behaviour but a balanced account of the nature of the faith. Beginning and remaining a strict monotheist, he goes on to assert the divine unity in the context of a Spirit who speaks through the prophets and is integral to the Godhead, fitting into a form of Trinitarian expression that points forward.

Towards the end of the 2nd century Theophilus exhibits similarities and individual features. Eusebius calls him the sixth bishop of Antioch. He had however grown up a pagan. By the time he came to write *Ad Autolycum*, probably c.180, he had taken up a strongly monotheistic position, opposed alike to polytheism and to Marcion with his two gods, the Demiurge and the good God, Father of Christ. Unlike Tatian, Theophilus came to have some repute as an anti-heretical writer. He maintains a philosophical stance, drawing largely on Middle Platonism for concepts and terminology, and it is through the development of philosophical notions that he reaches a distinctive doctrine of *Logos*. He turns more to Stoicism, contrasting the "innate" (*endiathetos*) with the "external" or "expressed" (*prophorikos*) *Logos*. While looking for philosophical underpinning, Theophilus stays in close sympathy with Hellenistic Jewish monotheism, yet being the first Christian writer to use the term "Trinity" (*Trias*). Again, his Christian position is characterized by the breadth of his New Testament quotations.

A group of "mixed ability", the Greek Apologists have in common an awareness of the world outside the Church, Jewish and pagan, and the pressing need for communication with that world. At the same time, their concentration on undeveloped Christian beliefs begins to point a way forward to later thinkers as diverse in outlook and varying in quality as Irenaeus, Tertullian, Novatian, Methodius, Lactantius, and Eusebius.

D.A. SYKES

See also Justin Martyr

Summary

A group of perhaps 12 writers of the 2nd and 3rd centuries AD who wrote in defence of the Christian faith: Quadratus, Aristides of Athens, Aristo of Pella, St Justin Martyr, Tatian the Syrian, Miltiades, Apollinaris of Hierapolis, Athenagoras of Athens, Theophilus of Antioch, Melito of Sardis, the author of the *Epistle of Diognetus*, and Hermias. Their writings are important for the history of Christian dogma.

Further Reading

Aristides, *The Apology*, translated by D.M. Kay, Edinburgh: Clark, 1897
Athenagoras, *Legatio and De Resurrectione*, edited and translated by William R. Schoedel, Oxford: Clarendon Press, 1972
Cross, F.L. (editor), *The Oxford Dictionary of the Christian Church*, 3rd edition, Oxford and New York: Oxford University Press, 1997
Edwards, Mark *et al.*, *Apologetics in the Roman Empire: Pagans, Jews, and Christians*, Oxford: Clarendon Press, 1999
Goodspeed, Edgar J., *Die ältesten Apologeten*, Göttingen: Vandenhoeck & Ruprecht, 1914
Grant, Robert M., *Greek Apologists of the Second Century*, Philadelphia: Westminster Press, 1988
Quasten, Johannes, *Patrology*, vol. 1: *The Beginnings of Patristic Literature*, Utrecht: Spectrum, and Westminster, Maryland: Newman Press, 1950
Tatian, *Oratio ad Graecos and Fragments*, edited and translated by Molly Whittaker, Oxford and New York: Clarendon Press, 1982
Theophilus of Antioch, *Ad Autolycum*, edited and translated by Robert M. Grant, Oxford: Clarendon Press, 1970

Apophthegmata Patrum

Religious compilation of the 5th and 6th centuries

The *Apophthegmata Patrum*, or *Sayings of the Desert Fathers*, represent the single most important source for the history and spiritual teachings of early Egyptian monasticism. The *Sayings* give us an invaluable picture of monastic life in all its complexity and richness from the pioneering days of St Antony the Great to the monastic diaspora of the 5th century. Dealing with every aspect of the ascetic life, from day-to-day concerns to the highest states of prayer, the *Sayings* have had an enormous influence on the Christian tradition, and continue to provide nourishment in our own age.

The *Sayings* are centred on the semi-eremitic form of monasticism that flourished in the descent of Scetis, with many pieces coming also from Nitria and Kellia. References to the fully developed coenobia of the Pachomian type are rare, and often gently critical. Elements deriving from the Palestinian diaspora forced by the barbarian incursions of the early 5th century refer back most especially to the Scetiote tradition.

The *Sayings* as we have them were compiled over the 5th and 6th centuries from the words of instruction spoken by the elders of Egypt, which had initially been preserved by oral transmission. The preface to the Greek alphabetical collection speaks of the redactor's desire to gather together the diffused words of the initiators and masters of the monastic way of life, and to order them alphabetically for the sake of clarity. The fact that the *logoi* of the Desert Fathers were so well known and remembered precluded any significant reworking of the texts. What we have is therefore very much the raw matter of the Desert Fathers' teachings. The main differences in the manuscript traditions are of arrangement, not so much of content. The most familiar arrangement is the alphabetical collection. The anonymous collection, grouped more or less haphazardly, originally, it seems, formed a sequel to the alphabetical collection. Lastly, we have the systematic collection, grouped according to subject matter. The complexities surrounding the genesis of these different arrangements are far from being unravelled.

There is no artificial unity to the *Sayings*. A great many different perspectives are represented. There is, however, a certain unity arising from the common goal and common struggle of the monks whose counsels are preserved. An ideal of monastic perfection is held up, but allowance is made for human frailty. As Amma Syncletica puts it: "lack of proportion always corrupts". We do get occasional glimpses into the highest reaches of mystical experience, as, for example, the vision of Abba Arsenius "entirely like a flame". These glimpses are, precisely, glimpses; the sayings witness to a certain reticence about delving too deeply into such advanced states. Miracles do occur, but are often treated with caution. The ecclesiastical hierarchy is regarded with enormous, but not automatic, respect. Relations within the monastic community form a kind of leitmotif. Laymen are occasionally held up as being of superior virtue to even the greatest of monks: a nice stimulus to monastic modesty. References to the decline in monastic virtue and prowess are frequent. These stem largely from the diaspora element to which we have referred. Most importantly, perhaps, the *Sayings* preserve a record of the living relationships between elder and disciple: they give us an insight into the means by which the wisdom of the desert was passed on from generation to generation.

The attitude of the *Apophthegmata* to outer learning is not unremittingly hostile. While the possession of books is often frowned upon, and philosopher-monks such as Evagrius of Pontus are gently but firmly chastised, the prevailing opinion is that secular learning is not wrong in itself, but rather inadequate for the intensely practical business of the ascetic life. This is wittily illustrated in two of the apophthegms of Abba Arsenius, formerly tutor in the household of the emperor

Theodosius I (379–95). Arsenius is asked by an anonymous interlocutor: "How is it that we get nowhere, while the Egyptian peasants acquire so many virtues?" Arsenius replies: "We indeed get nothing from our secular education, but the Egyptian peasants acquire the virtues by hard work." Again, speaking of an old Egyptian monk he had consulted, Arsenius comments: "I indeed have been taught Latin and Greek, but I do not even know the alphabet of this peasant."

The genre of the *Sayings* has certain precedents in Classical literature. Cato, for example, composed a collection of the apophthegms of Socrates. Peter Brown (1978, p. 82) has characterized the *Sayings* as "the last and one of the greatest products of the Wisdom Literature of the ancient Near East". The *Sayings*, in their various forms, rapidly became the staple diet of the monastic movement wherever it spread. The *Dialogismoi* of Abba Zosimus already quote, in early 6th-century Palestine, from the *Sayings*. They continued to be, and still are, essential reading for monastics of all traditions. They remain an extremely rich source of a form of spirituality that is both profound and intensely practical.

MARCUS PLESTED

Summary

The *Sayings of the Desert Fathers*, compiled in the 5th and 6th centuries from oral tradition passed down by the elders of early Egyptian monasticism. They deal with all aspects of the ascetic life and provide a valuable insight into monastic life from the time of St Antony the Great to the 5th-century monastic diaspora.

Text

The Sayings of the Desert Fathers: The Alphabetical Collection, translated by Benedicta Ward, London: Mowbray, and Kalamazoo, Michigan: Cistercian, 1975, revised edition, 1984

Further Reading

Brown, Peter, *The Making of Late Antiquity*, Cambridge, Massachusetts: Harvard University Press, 1978
Burton-Christie, D., *The Word in the Desert: Scripture and the Quest for Holiness in Early Christian Monasticism*, Oxford and New York: Oxford University Press, 1993
Chitty, Derwas J., *The Desert a City: An Introduction to the Study of Egyptian and Palestinian Monasticism under the Christian Empire*, Oxford: Blackwell, and Crestwood, New York: St Vladimir's Seminary Press, 1966, reprinted 1995
Gould, Graham, *The Desert Fathers on Monastic Community*, Oxford: Clarendon Press, and New York: Oxford University Press, 1993
Rubenson, Samuel, *The Letters of St Antony: Monasticism and the Making of a Saint*, Minneapolis: Fortress Press, 1995

Apostasy

Apostasy, the abandonment of Christianity, was an offence under both canon and Byzantine secular law. Whether it is realized by accession to another religion, to atheism, or to non-religiosity is irrelevant. The acceptance of another Christian confession – according to the prevalent opinion – is not considered apostasy, but heresy. In order to commit apostasy, one must already be a regular member of the Church. The offence is committed either voluntarily or involuntarily, and it can be manifested either expressly or tacitly.

The Church had to deal with apostasy relatively early on, because of the persecutions, when a number of Christians grew fearful of remaining in the flock. An immediate consequence of the offence is that the apostate no longer belongs to the Christian community. The sources of canon law of the unified Church of the first centuries very often make special reference to apostasy in relation to the treatment of those who have repented and wish to revert to Christianity. Relevant canons were set forth by the First Ecumenical Council (11 and 12), the Synod in Ankara (1–9), St Basil the Great (73 and 81), St Gregory of Nyssa (2), and St Peter of Alexandria (1–14); there is also canon 62 by the Holy Apostles. Most of these canons are occasional; they dealt with apostates in the time of the persecutions. These canons obviously lack significance today, because they refer to an offence that was committed prior to their enactment. Similarly, there are canons of general validity, such as canon 62 of the Holy Apostles, which determines that any cleric who denies Christ out of fear of non-Christians should be expelled from the Church. But – it continues – if he simply rejects the role of cleric, then he should be unfrocked. If he repents, he may come back to the Church as a layman. In any case, the type of penalty depended on the time at which the offence was committed – that is, on whether it was committed in a time of persecution or in one of peace. Thus, canon 73 of Basil the Great and canon 2 of Gregory of Nyssa, which refer to a time of peace, establish that those who have voluntarily apostatized and have later repented should be subject to a life-long penalty. Only in the last moments of their lives may they be deemed worthy of receiving Holy Communion. By contrast, the treatment of those who committed apostasy during periods of persecution was more lenient. For those who became apostates involuntarily, the prescribed penalty was a nine-year deprivation of Holy Communion. Although clergymen would preserve their priesthood, they remained in suspension for the remainder of their lives: they were not allowed even to preach (canons 1 and 2 of the Synod of Ankara; 10 of Peter of Alexandria).

Byzantine secular law initially punished apostasy with fines (*Codex Theodosianus*, 16. 8. 7). Later the legislation of Justinian prescribed the death penalty (*Codex*, 1. 11. 10pr.). The *Ecloga* (17. 6) enacted particular measures for prisoners of war who were forced to deny their Christian faith. On their return to Byzantium, they were subjected only to ecclesiastical penalties. The same treatment was adopted by the *Zakon Soudnyj Ljudem*, the legal collection that the Thessalonian missionary Methodios drafted and introduced to Great Moravia. Evidently, the reason that the *Ecloga* introduced this lenient measure, was so that prisoners should not be hesitant about repatriating. As for the rest, all the other statutes of Byzantine legislation maintained their validity, as is demonstrated by the Appendix to the *Ecloga* (3. 12. 16–17). The statutes on captives in the *Ecloga* were repeated in the *Ecloga Privata Aucta* (17. 35–36) and in the *Eclogadium* (17. 27). By contrast, the *Procheiros Nomos* (39. 33) and the *Eisagoge* (= *Epanagoga*; 40. 35) do not contain this statute, but only a general one on the elimination of the death penalty, presumably because apostasy under conditions of coercion no longer interested the state, only the Church (according to Troianos, p.

47). The *Basilica* repeated the statutes of Justinian. By way of the *Basilica*, these were incorporated in the *Syntagma* of Matthaios Vlastaris, in the *Hexabiblos* of Constantinos Harmenopoulos, and in the *Nomokanon* of Manouil Malaxos. Furthermore, the secular law provided for concurrent penalties. The apostate was unable to bear witness, to make a will, or to inherit. Other penalties included confiscation of his property and exclusion from civil and military offices.

During the period of Ottoman rule, large numbers of Christians (and Jews) converted to Islam, voluntarily or involuntarily. Because of the restrictions imposed by the Ottomans, the Church was unable to take any of these measures against them. However, Islamic converts who reverted to Christianity received the death penalty from the Turkish authorities; this was the penalty prescribed by Muslim religious law (the *Sharia*) for apostates from Islam. The latter constituted the body of "neomartyrs" in the Orthodox Church.

In more recent and contemporary Greek secular law, apostasy no longer constitutes a criminal offence. On the basis of the principles and the constitutional statutes on religious freedom, accession to another religion is a matter of personal freedom. Its penal treatment is confined to canon law only: laymen may be excommunicated and clergymen unfrocked (and subsequently excommunicated). The excommunication is imposed under the Synod of the Hierarchy (article 4, §9 of Law 590/1977 = Charter of the Church of Greece). Although the consequences of excommunication are ecclesiastical in nature, excommunication undoubtedly also affects the social status of the person subjected to it.

CHARALAMBOS K. PAPASTATHIS

See also Canon Law, Neomartyrs

Further Reading

Kotsonis, Ieronymos, Apostasy entry in *Thriskeftiki kai Ithiki Encyclopedia* [Encyclopedia of Religion and Ethics], vol. 2, Athens, 1963, pp. 1158–60

L'Huillier, Peter, *The Church of the Ancient Councils: The Disciplinary Work of the First Four Councils*, Crestwood, New York: St Vladimir's Seminary Press, 1996, pp. 64–65, 69

Nikodim, Milaš, *Pravila Pravoslavnoj Cerkvi s' Tolkovanijami*, vols 1–2, St Petersburg, 1911–12

Panayotakos, P., *Ecclesiastical Law as it is Applied in Greece*, vol. 3: *The Penal Law of the Church*, Athens, 1962, pp. 352–64 (in Greek)

Rallis, C.M., *Penal Law of the Eastern Orthodox Church*, Athens, 1907, pp. 322–23 (in Greek)

Troianos, Spyros N., *O Poinalios tou Eclogadiou* [The Penal Law of the Eklogadium], Frankfurt: Klostermann, 1980, pp. 45–48

Appian *c.*AD 95–160s

Historian

Appian was a Romanized Greek, who was born in the dynamic but turbulent city of Alexandria in Egypt. Josephus refers to the "constant strife between the natives and the Jewish colony" (*Jewish War*, 2. 487) that had existed ever since Alexander the Great had given the Jews permission to reside in the city with the same rights as the Greeks. One dramatic fragment of

Appian's lost autobiography relates his narrow escape from an angry group of Jews during the Jewish revolt (AD 115–17). This personal experience of civil unrest may help to explain why Appian devotes such a large proportion of his historical narrative to the Roman civil wars of the 1st century BC. Subsequently, he left Alexandria and moved to the more secure environment of Rome, where he became an advocate and was eventually awarded a procuratorship. We have a letter from Fronto to Antoninus Pius (emperor AD 138–61) requesting this position for his friend.

Appian's most important achievement is his historical work, the *Romaica* (written between *c.*AD 148 and 161), which narrates the rise of Rome and its progressive conquests of different nations "in order to understand the weaknesses or endurance of peoples, as well as the virtues or good fortune of their conquerors, or any other factor which contributed to the result" (preface, 12). This focus recalls the pragmatic historiography of Polybius (*c.*200–*c.*118 BC), who in the *Histories* likewise seeks to explain the growth of Roman power. Yet where Polybius analyses a 53-year period in 40 books, Appian's chronological scope is broader, moving from the kings of Rome to Trajan's war in Arabia in 24 books. The *Romaica* are structured along geographical and ethnic lines, with each book usually devoted to a particular people, although book 8 (Hannibal) and book 12 (Mithridates VI) break the pattern by focusing on individual enemies of Rome.

We do not have Appian's whole work, but what survives is impressive and revealing. Appian was writing for a cultured Greek-speaking readership, who wanted to understand more about Roman history and institutions. Consequently, the narrative is punctuated with practical explanations, which frequently remind us that Appian is looking at Rome from the viewpoint of the provincial outsider. So, the military eagle is described as "the symbol held in the highest regard by the Romans" (*Civil War*, 2. 61. 256). Not only does Appian offer explanations of potentially unfamiliar terms, but his Greek prose is accessible and sometimes even includes transliterated Latin words. The 9th-century Byzantine scholar Photios approvingly characterized Appian's Greek as "plain and unadorned". The discovery of a papyrus at Dura Europos containing fragments from Appian and Herodotus suggests that the Alexandrian historian was indeed popular. Some modern critics suggest that Appian's main significance lies in his preservation of crucial material from lost historians such as Asinius Pollio, but this is to undervalue the *Romaica*. Appian in his own right made Roman history accessible to an inquisitive Greek-speaking audience, who were themselves increasingly involved in government and administration within the empire. That there was an appetite for historical texts about Rome among this mobile, Greek-speaking elite is suggested by Zenobius' translation of Sallust's works into Greek under Hadrian. Of course, Greek speakers could always turn to the universal histories of Nicolaus of Damascus or Diodorus Siculus, but these were almost too comprehensive (144 and 40 books respectively), and both narratives stopped in the 1st century BC. The expansion of the Roman empire between the reigns of Augustus and Trajan called for an updated history, which Appian provided.

Although the *Romaica* helped to orientate Greek-speaking readers in the Roman world, Appian could still criticize

Roman methods and shortcomings. So Appian narrates the proscriptions with particular disgust (*Civil War*, 4. 16), and outlines the sufferings of the people of Gomphi, including one incident where 20 distinguished elders, who had poisoned themselves, were discovered lying on the floor "as if they had succumbed to drunkenness" (*Civil War*, 2. 64. 268). Poignantly, Appian juxtaposes the genuine inebriation of Caesar's callous soldiers with the apparent drunkenness of these desperate citizens. It is at such moments that Appian's background as a provincial offers us some uncompromising perspectives of Rome.

Appian's *Romaica* survived, albeit in a fragmented state, largely thanks to the efforts of the excerptors who worked for the emperor Constantine VII Porphyrogennetos (913–59). The first printed edition (Venice, 1477) was a Latin translation by Pier Candido which had been commissioned by Pope Nicholas V. The popularity of this edition prompted first an Italian translation (Rome, 1502) by Alessandro Braccio on the foreign wars, and a French translation (Lyons, 1544) by Claude de Seysell dedicated to King Louis XII of France. Seysell's translation inspired several baroque dramatists, including Pierre Corneille, who took material from Appian for his tragedy *Rodogune* (Paris, 1647). Yet no printed text of Appian in Greek appeared until Carolus Stephanus' edition (Paris, 1551). The first English translation (London, 1578), by William Barker, was grandly entitled *An Auncient Historie and Exquisite Chronicle of the Roman Warres, with a Continuation from the Death of Sextus Pompeius till the Overthrow of Antonie and Cleopatra* and praised Appian as a "noble orator and historiographer". Since Appian's narrative of the civil wars ends with the death of Sextus Pompey, Barker decided to supplement the account with material from Plutarch. Subsequently, William Shakespeare used Barker's Appian when writing *Antony and Cleopatra* and especially *Julius Caesar*. Appian's work remained popular, although not everybody had to rely on translations. In a letter to Engels, Karl Marx wrote: "As a relaxation in the evenings I have been reading Appian on the Roman civil wars in the original Greek. A very valuable book. The chap is an Egyptian by birth. Schlosser says that he has 'no soul', probably because he goes to the roots of the material basis for these civil wars." So, from the late 15th century onwards, Appian has continued to appeal to notable dramatists and intellectuals seeking to gain access to the Roman world through a lucid and accessible historian, who originally wrote to inform a predominantly non-Roman audience.

RHIANNON ASH

Biography

Born in Alexandria *c.*AD 95, Appian experienced the Jewish revolt of 115–17 before moving to Rome where he became an advocate and later a procurator. He died in the 160s. He wrote a history of Rome in 24 books for a Greek-speaking readership. Beginning with the kings of Rome, it is organized on geographical and ethnic principles, and ends with Trajan's war in Arabia. Not all of it survives.

Writings

Roman History, translated by Horace White, 4 vols, London: Heinemann, and New York: Macmillan, 1912–13 (Loeb edition; several reprints)

The Civil Wars, translated by John Carter, London and New York: Penguin, 1996

Further Reading

Alonso-Núñez, J.M., "Appian and the World Empires", *Athenaeum*, 62 (1984): pp. 640–44

Brodersen, Kai, "Appian und sein Werk" in *Aufstieg und Niedergang der römischen Welt*, edited by Hildegard Temporini et al., 2. 34. 1, Berlin: de Gruyter, 1993, 339–63

Brunner, T.F., "Two Papyri of Appian from Dura-Europus", *Greek, Roman and Byzantine Studies*, 25 (1984): pp. 171–75

Cuff, P.J., "Appian's *Romaica*: A Note", *Athenaeum*, 61 (1983): pp. 148–64

Gowing, Alain M., *The Triumviral Narratives of Appian and Cassius Dio*, Ann Arbor: University of Michigan Press, 1992

Reinhold, M., "Roman Attitudes towards Egyptians", *Ancient World*, 3 (1980): pp. 97–103

Schanzer, Ernest (editor), *Shakespeare's Appian: A Selection from the Tudor Translation of Appian's Civil Wars*, Liverpool: Liverpool University Press, 1956

Swain, Simon, *Hellenism and Empire: Language, Classicism and Power in the Greek World, AD 50–250*, Oxford: Clarendon Press, and New York: Oxford University Press, 1996

Apseudes, Theodore
Painter of the late 12th century

The signature of this master painter is to be found at the Enkleistra of St Neophytos near Paphos in Cyprus. The inscription, which is in a shallow cavity below the *Deesis* (Supplication) panel on the north wall, and below the prostrated figure of the donor, St Neophytos, reads: "The Enkleistra was painted by the hand of me, Theodore Apseudes, in the year 6691 [1183]". Another inscription in the adjoining church tells us that "The most venerable church of the life-giving Cross was hewn out, built and painted by the contribution and great toil of our holy and divinely inspired father, Neophytos, in the year 6704 [1196]". The problem is that between the two dates there are perhaps five periods of painting, most of which are very close in style, and it is not clear to which (if not to all) of the paintings Apseudes is referring. For the moment, therefore, it is best to regard Apseudes as an important master in a school of painting. The style of most of the work in the Enkleistra relates to the well-known late 12th-century development of elaborate linear patterning in Byzantine painting.

St Neophytos carved his tomb in the cell where he first lived, and on the ceiling of it are small paintings of the *Crucifixion* and the *Anastasis* (Resurrection). The Byzantine Anastasis combines the two scenes of the Descent into Hell and the Resurrection, and Apseudes' version is full of movement and powerful emotion, which are intensified by the linear patterns of the clothing. The *Crucifixion* depicts the relatively new type of Christ wearing only a loincloth, with his body hanging in a curving shape indicative of resignation and suffering. The figure of St John is in a style similar to the St John of a second *Crucifixion* scene painted on the partition between the cell and the bema. The linear elaboration of St John's garments is less marked than elsewhere in the Enkleistra. The most striking feature is the head, which is bowed in grief and supported by the right arm and hand. The face is realistically cupped in the hand with the little finger just below the eye socket, as if wiping away a tear. The eyebrows and the lines below the eye are contorted as if in sorrow. The overwhelming effect of grief constitutes a new achievement in medieval painting. The depiction of a recognizable human emotion was to become a standard feature in Byzantine painting and it was later adopted by 13th-century Italian painters under Franciscan patronage. The other feature that these small paintings have in common is the sense of monumentality. Their size, as with any great work of art, is irrelevant and they are as effective if projected on to a large screen as they are in the original small scale of the Enkleistra. Among the larger paintings in the cell, the *Deesis* is notable for a technical innovation in the use of fresh plaster patches for the heads of the figures. In some of the cell and bema paintings this is combined with the practice of reworking the plaster to bring moisture to the surface before completing heads and hands at the finishing stages of a painting.

These technical innovations, together with the stylistic feature of wind-blown draperies, link the school of Apseudes with the important paintings at Lagoudera in Cyprus, dated to 1192. The church at Lagoudera is high in the Pitsillian region of the Troodos mountains and its remoteness has no doubt contributed to the fine state of preservation of its paintings. The church is small and the painter chose to depict only a few scenes from the life of Christ, and two from the life of the Mother of God, all on a grand, monumental scale. Similarities in small painterly details such as highlights and linear patterns between the two churches make it quite clear that the paintings come from the Apseudes school. They also share the rarely observed technical similarity of fresh plaster patching a century before this practice appears in Italy. Similar stylistic links appear in a single grand painting of *St George* in the south bay of the narthex of the church at Asinou, and in some of the paintings at the church of the Archangel at Kato Levkara. There are therefore enough stylistic and technical affinities between these paintings to link these four churches to the Apseudes school. There are also icons that can be linked to the same school.

The salient characteristic of the school is the windblown draperies which can be found in an icon of the Annunciation at the monastery of St Catherine on Mount Sinai and in churches at Nerezi and at Kurbinova in Macedonia. The influence of this style can be detected further afield in some of the mosaics of the Sicilian churches, and in St Mark's, Venice. The wider influence of the Hellenic tradition can be detected in the undoubted affinities of these windblown draperies to the Classical sculptures of ancient Greece. It is not necessary to suppose any direct observation of ancient sculpture on the part of painters, so much as to suggest that a long-standing cultural influence was at work here.

DAVID WINFIELD

See also Painting

Biography

Master painter active in Cyprus in the late 12th century. Nothing is known of his life. His paintings are notable for the introduction of human emotion and a sense of monumentality to Byzantine painting.

The use of wind-blown draperies links his work with earlier examples in Sinai and Macedonia and with the Classical sculpture of ancient Greece.

Further Reading

Mango, Cyril and E. Hawkins, "The Hermitage of St Neophytos and its Wall Paintings", *Dumbarton Oaks Papers*, 20 (1966): pp. 119–206

Papageorghiou, Athanasius, *Icons of Cyprus*, translated by James Hogarth, New York: Cowles, 1970

Papageorghiou, Athanasius, *Hiera Metropolis Paphou: Historia kai Techne* [The Bishopric of Paphos: History and Art], Nicosia, 1996

Stylianou, Andreas and Judith A. Stylianou, *The Painted Churches of Cyprus: Treasures of Byzantine Art*, London: Trigraph, 1985

Wharton, Annabel Jane, *Art of Empire: Painting and Architecture of the Byzantine Periphery: A Comparative Study of Four Provinces*, University Park: Pennsylvania State University Press, 1988, pp. 79–90

Winfield, David, "Dumbarton Oaks' Work at Haghios Neophytos, Monagri, Perachorio, and Lagoudera, 1971–73" in *Report of the Department of Antiquities*, Nicosia, 1978, pp. 279–87

Winfield, David, *The Church of the Panaghia tou Arakos, Lagoudhera, Cyprus, and its Painterly Significance*, Washington, D.C.: Dumbarton Oaks, 2000

Apulia

Region of southeast Italy

Apulia (modern Puglia) has been associated with Greek culture since antiquity. The region has Messapian or Greek foundation legends, mentioned already in the writings of Herodotus (7. 170). The name Iapygia is used by Greek writers to denote the same region, although it also refers to the region of Calabria. Many places in Apulia were colonized by Greek cities by the end of the 8th century BC, but that was just the climax of a long history of contacts between the Greeks and the autochthonous population of Italy. One of the most important cities of the area, Tarentum (ancient Greek Taras, modern Taranto), was supposed to have been founded around 706 BC by Spartans as their only colony. The gulf of Taranto had already been colonized by Achaeans from the Peloponnese, who first established Sybaris in 721 BC and then Croton and Metapontium. Taras, the only Dorian colony, was founded after the First Messenian War (traditionally in 706 BC), an example of the tensions in Greece that led to colonization. The founders came from Amyclae, an ancient sacred town of the Spartan state, and according to Strabo (6. 3. 2f.) were linked to Spartans by the maternal side only; they were thought to be illegitimate children of unmarried women, thus they had the name *partheniai* ("sons of concubines"). It is possible that they were of pre-Dorian origin. They were guided by an oracle to establish a colony in the west, and this is typical of the role of religion, and oracles in particular, in sanctioning new settlements. One of the first things that the colonists would do was to establish their religion.

The Greek colonies in Apulia flourished thanks to the craftsmanship and trade that soon developed. Taras, in particular, owed its prosperity to the textile and pottery industries that were soon supplying the rest of Italy. Taras was also famous for its jewellery, as the exquisite collection of the modern archaeological museum bears witness today. Many of the most important archaeological finds were made only as a result of bombings in World War II. Sybaris was proverbial for its wealth and luxury (Herodotus, 6. 126) and had developed commercial relations with Miletus in Asia Minor. After the initial colonization, many of the cities were able to found further colonies; thus Sybaris founded Poseidonia (the Latin Paestum) on the west coast of Italy. Metapontium, Sybaris, Croton, Siris, and Paestum are known as the "Achaean" area, a term that refers not only to the origin of many of the colonists but also to the artistic styles that were developed there. The artistic currents of Magna Graecia combine many elements.

Sybaris was destroyed by Croton in 510 BC, and the city of Thurii was founded on its site, at the initiative of Pericles, in 444 BC. The famous city planner Hippodamus of Miletus designed the city and was himself one of the leading colonists. This was a part of the ambitious strategy of Pericles to make Athens the centre of a greater Greece. The geographical situation that gave all these cities immediate access to the sea and a fertile hinterland was a significant factor for their later development. This economic growth was soon to be followed by cultural development. Apulia, together with Calabria and Sicily, constituted the region of Magna Graecia. The region of Apulia drew the attention of Rome at the end of the 4th century BC and the Tarentines invited king Pyrrhus of Epirus to assist them in 280 BC. During the Hannibalic and Social Wars there were serious revolts against Rome, which were followed by the destruction of many Apulian cities. After it was annexed to the Roman empire, the region experienced troubled times. Under Diocletian Apulia and Calabria formed a single province. Christianity reshaped the cultural history of the region.

In Byzantine times Apulia suffered material damage in the wars of Justinian I against the Goths, and was later conquered by the Lombards. In the 8th century the Arabs, the Byzantines, and the Lombards laid claims to the area. Apulia was reconquered by the emperor Basil I (876–86) and it stayed under Byzantine rule until the 11th century when the Normans captured it. In 1480, having completed the conquest of continental Greece, Mehmet II managed to occupy the harbour city of Otranto, then considered the most important centre of Greek culture. Several Byzantine churches still survive in Apulia, one of the most famous being the 11th-century church of San Pietro at Otranto, which has several layers of painting. In the southern part of the peninsula the city of Callipoli was founded as a colony of Taras. The Spartan Leucippus soon made it a free city; it was an important commercial settlement in Byzantine times, and there were many monasteries in the area. It was occupied by the Normans in 1071 and later by the Turks in 1481. A minority Greek population survived until the 20th century, consisting mainly of merchants and sailors.

A Greek dialect is still spoken today in the area of Salento, and particularly in the area of Lecce. The villages or towns that preserve some form of that dialect, referred to by the locals as *griko* or *grigo*, are Calimera, Sternatia, Soleto, Martignano, Castrignano, Melpignano, Galatina, and Zollino. There is debate among scholars as to the origin of the dialect, whether it originates from the ancient Greek of Magna Graecia, or is derived from later Byzantine dialects. There is a rich Hellenic tradition that has shrunk significantly in modern times. In some places, such as Calimera and Sternatia, an attempt has been made to preserve an otherwise dying culture and language.

ANDROMACHE KARANIKA-DIMAROGONA

See also Magna Graecia

Summary

The heel of Italy, Apulia has had Greek connections since antiquity. There were many Greek colonies by the end of the 8th century BC. Taras (modern Taranto) was founded by Sparta c.706 BC. Apulia prospered by trade and by developing textile and pottery industries. It formed a single province with Calabria under Diocletian. It was disputed between Arabs, Lombards, and Byzantines until the 11th century when it was taken by the Normans. A Greek dialect is still spoken in some villages.

Further Reading

Aprile, Rocco, *Grecia salentina: origini e storia*, Calimera, 1994
Karanastase, Anastasius, *Historikon Lexikon ton Hellenikon Idiomaton tes Kato Italias* [Historical Dictionary of the Greek Dialects of Southern Italy], Athens, 1984
Lepore, Ettore, *Colonie greche dell'Occidente antico*, Roma: Nuova Italia Scientifica, 1989
Marchese, Nicola Gerardo, *La civiltà della Magna Grecia*, Rome: Consiglio Nazionale delle Ricerche, 1992
Pugliese Carratelli, Giovanni (editor), *The Western Greeks: Classical Civilization in the Western Mediterranean*, London: Thames and Hudson, 1996; as *The Greek World: Art and Civilization in Magna Graecia and Sicily*, New York: Rizzoli, 1996
Rohlfs, Gerhard, *Historische Grammatik der Unteritalienischen Gräzität*, Munich: Bayerischen Akademie der Wissenschaften, 1950
Vranopoulos, Epameinondas, *Odoiporiko ste Megale Hellada* [Guide to Magna Graecia], Athens, 1989

Arabia

The geographic term "Arabia" is applied to the Arabian peninsula (*Shibh al-Jazirah al-'Arabiyah* in Arabic), which is located in the extreme southwestern corner of Asia and encompasses the modernday countries of Kuwait, Qatar, the United Arab Emirates, the Sultanate of Oman, Yemen, and the Kingdom of Saudi Arabia. The Arabian peninsula is bordered by the Red Sea on the west and the southwest, and the Gulf of Aden on the south, the Arabian Sea on the south and southeast, and the Gulf of Oman and the Persian Gulf (also called the Arabian Gulf) on the northeast. Geographically, the peninsula and the Syrian desert merge in the north. The peninsula's total area is about 2,590,000 sq km. The length bordering the Red Sea is approximately 1900 km and the maximum breadth is approximately 2000 km.

The ancient Greeks, who coined the term "Arabia", derived it from the name of a pastoral people, the Arabs, whose presence in the northern Arabian and Syrian desert is well attested to by Assyrian records dating from the 7th century BC which refer to them as *Aribu* or *Aribi*. When the Greeks first reached the shores of the Arabian peninsula, sometime between the 6th and 5th centuries BC, they gave the name Arabia first to the northern desert area, and then by extension to the whole peninsula to the south. In time there developed a distinction between a Desert Arabia (*Arabia Deserta* in Latin) in the northern part of the peninsula; a Rocky Arabia (*Arabia Petraea* in Latin) on the western fringes of the desert; and a Fertile Arabia (*Arabia Eudaimon* in Greek; *Arabia Felix* in Latin) in the south. None of these three regions was strictly defined, and they were for the most part unexplored.

In antiquity, and until the 7th century AD, trade was the main link between Arabia and the Greek-speaking world. Trade through Arabia also involved items from Ethiopia (Axum), India, and China. The importance of this region to the Byzantine world lay in its strategic proximity to Iran (Byzantium's imperial rival) and its control of the route to India. Most Arabian cities were founded along the caravan trade route that ran along the western edge of the desert, and it was in these cities that interactions between Arabs and Greeks took place.

Knowledge of the history of Arabia comes from records of early travellers and historians, such as Herodotus (*c*.430 BC), Strabo (*c*.AD 22), and Pliny (*c*.AD 23). Most of these accounts concentrate on south Arabia, whence the trade goods originated. In marked contrast with the arid wastes of northern and central Arabia, southern Arabia was a fertile, sedentary, and civilized region. South Arabia was famous for its wealth in spices, minerals, and fruits, as well as for its various kingdoms. In fact, the Greek writer Eratosthenes (writing in the 3rd century BC) described southern Arabia as inhabited by four major peoples, and it is on the basis of his nomenclature that scholars today speak of the south Arabian kingdoms of the Minaeans, the Sabaeans, the Qatabanians, and the Hadramites.

Between the 3rd and 6th centuries AD several Byzantine imperial and ecclesiastical missions were sent to the western and southern parts of the peninsula, and a few cities were converted to Christianity. However, Mecca, the pilgrimage centre of Arabia and the city where Muhammad (the Prophet of Islam) appeared in the first decade of the 7th century, was not converted. Muhammad's mission quickly and fundamentally altered the face of Arabia and its relationship to its Greek-speaking neighbour, the Byzantine world. Arabia became the base of operations against Byzantium. After the Prophet's death in 632, the Arabs wrested the Levant, Egypt, and the rest of North Africa from the Byzantines. By the advent of the Umayyad dynasty in 660, attacks against the Byzantines were conducted from the Umayyad capital, Damascus in Syria, and thus Arabia virtually lost its relevance to the Greek world.

LARA G. TOHME

Summary

Arabia was the Greek name for the peninsula between the Red Sea and the Persian Gulf. Greeks first visited Arabia in the 6th century BC and traded with it until the 7th century AD. Southern Arabia in particular was famous for its spices, minerals, and fruits. The rise of Islam put an end to relations between Arabia and the Greek world.

Further Reading

Crone, Patricia, *Meccan Trade and the Rise of Islam*, Princeton, New Jersey: Princeton University Press, and Oxford: Blackwell, 1987

Salibi, Kamal, *A History of Arabia*, Delmar, New York: Caravan, 1980

Shahid, Irfan, *Byzantium and the Arabs in the Fourth Century*, Washington, D.C.: Dumbarton Oaks, 1984

Shahid, Irfan, *Byzantium and the Semitic Orient before the Rise of Islam*, London: Variorum, 1988

Shahid, Irfan, *Byzantium and the Arabs in the Fifth Century*, Washington, D.C.: Dumbarton Oaks, 1989

Arabs

According to modern usage, Arabs are any of the Arabic-speaking peoples living in the vast region extending from Mauritania on the Atlantic coast of Africa, to southwestern Iran, including the entire Maghrib of North Africa, Egypt and the Sudan, the Arabian peninsula, Syria, and Iraq. In antiquity this term usually referred to the largely nomadic and pastoral Semitic tribes and peoples who lived in and around the modern Arabian peninsula. However, Neo-Assyrian and biblical references dating back to the 9th–7th centuries BC do not relate Arabs particularly with the country of Arabia, but refer to tribes in the Sinai, in Jordan and Syria, and even along the banks of the Euphrates. The term is believed to be absent from inscriptions of Yemen prior to the 2nd century BC. In this article the term is used in a somewhat broad sense, denoting not solely people of Arab blood but including all those who were politically under Arab rule, who spoke the Arab language, and who, since the birth of Islam, have followed that religion. More important than political, racial, or religious unity is the Arabs' common cultural history and their participation in the scientific heritage derived from the Hellenistic world.

Arabic-speaking peoples are mostly Caucasoids of the Mediterranean physical type, although considerable regional variations exist, with admixtures of Negroids of Africa and Mongoloids of Asia. The early inhabitants of the Arabian peninsula reared sheep, goats, and camels in their harsh desert environment, while those settled in the oases cultivated dates and cereals. These oases also served as centres of the caravan trade. From around the 5th century BC Arab families or tribes began to found small states, often at centres of the overland caravan trade. Of these, Petra in present-day Jordan became the capital of the Nabataeans; in AD 106 it was conquered by the Romans, who allowed it to flourish well into the 3rd century. The Syrian desert town of Palmyra came under Roman domination around AD 160 and reached its height in the mid-3rd century.

Herodotus was familiar with the Arabs of southern Palestine and the Sinai as well as those of the frankincense-producing region. According to him the Arabs were among the nations that paid tribute to Darius I of Persia (Hderodotus, 7. 69, 3. 97). But it was the expeditions of Alexander the Great in the region of the Red Sea that brought greater knowledge of the Arabs to the Greeks, as reflected, for example, in the partially preserved work of Agatharchides, the source of Diodorus Siculus' description. According to Arrian (*Anabasis*, 7. 19. 5), Alexander's last plans included the conquest of the eastern Arabian coast, and in preparation for this he dispatched naval expeditions to both the Persian Gulf and the

Red Sea. The presence of Hellenistic Greeks in Bahrain and especially in Failaka, and Antiochus III's expedition to Gerrha in the Saudi interior, reflect early interest in Arabian and Indian trade on the part of the Seleucids. Ariston explored southwards as far as Babel-Mandeb for Ptolemy, who punished the hostile Nabataeans of Petra by tapping the incense route to the south of the city through a trade arrangement with the Lihyanites of Dedan. During Hellenistic times the northern territories as far as the Negev and Transjordan were inhabited by the Nabataean Arabs, who developed their land through skilful water conservation. The southern kingdoms were Minaea on the Red Sea, Katabania at the straits of Hormuz, and Sabaea, the Hadramaut, and Mhra along the south coast. Minaea had ceased to exist by the 2nd century BC and Yemen was dominated by a confederacy of Sabaeans and Homerites. Apart from these petty kingdoms of the south and the north, and to a large extent within them, the political organization of pre-Islamic Arabia was a primitive kinship structure united in clans and tribes which were named after a supposed common ancestor. As a political unit, pre-Islamic Arabia existed only in the careless nomenclature of the Greeks, who used the name Sarakenoi (apparently from the Arabic *Sharqinun*, "easterners") to denote all the population of the peninsula.

For his accounts of the Arabs of Mesopotamia (along the Euphrates), Egypt (Sinai and the Red Sea), southern Jordan (the Nabataeans), the steppe, and eastern Arabia (Gerrha), Strabo depended on Hellenistic sources as well as the Arabian campaign of Aelius Gallus under Augustus. Although this expedition ended in failure, Roman naval predominance in the Red Sea was secured, and the movement of Roman merchantmen between Egypt and India was facilitated by the reduction of Aden, whoever may have been responsible for it (*Peripl. M.E.* 26).

For the Greeks and the Macedonians, Arabia was important chiefly for its incense and spices as well as for gold and gems. They also depended on the Arabs as middlemen for their Indian trade. However, the importance of this role diminished after Hippalus discovered the use of the monsoons for annual direct voyages to India. It is sometimes claimed that this practice was already known to the Arabs for centuries and that the Greeks merely learned from them; but one has to question whether Arab ships of the time were capable of such voyages even if the Arabs knew the "secret" of the monsoons. For both Classical and biblical authors, the defining characteristics of the Arabs were nomadism, pastoralism, and the camel-based caravan trade. However, their military strength is already mentioned in early (Assyrian) sources, and becomes prominent in Roman times. The organization of the southern sector of the *limes* shows that the Romans of the empire took account of their historical role, their steady pressure on the settled lands of the north, and their infiltration into the Syrian end of the Arabian peninsula. The evolution of this military frontier-in-depth from the Euphrates to the Red Sea involved absorption of the client Nabataeans into the Roman provincial system. This was achieved by Trajan in AD 106 through the expedition of Cornelius Palma. The resulting province of Arabia expanded slightly to the north under Septimius, and was divided by Diocletian into Arabia and Palaestina Salutaris, the latter subsequently incorporated into Palestine around AD 358. During the 4th and 5th centuries the *limes* was strengthened in

response to the Saracen threat; but by the 6th century it had fallen into decay, so that the Muslim Arab invasions of the early 7th century found it no obstacle. The Arab *foederati* who (with the Phylarch as their chief) shared with the *limes* the defence of the Roman east, included the Tanukhids of the 4th century, the Salihids of the 5th, and the Ghassanids of the 6th.

The birth and spread of Islam in the 7th century led to the unification of the Arab tribes, and during the centuries following the death of the prophet Muhammad in AD 632, the new religion spread throughout most of the present-day Arabic-speaking world and beyond into Central Asia, the Iberian peninsula, Sicily, sub-Saharan Africa, Madagascar, the Indian subcontinent, and the Malay peninsula. Consequent upon the rapid establishment of Islamic supremacy Arabic, the language of the Holy Qu'ran, was adopted throughout much of the Middle East and North Africa.

Although Arab relations with the Byzantine empire consisted largely of invasions and conquests, there were also significant economic and cultural exchanges. Arabs (and Syrians) came as merchants not only to Constantinople, but even as far as Athens, where an Arab colony appears to have existed during the 10th and 11th centuries according to archaeological evidence. Close contact with certain Byzantine circles is suggested by Abbasid attempts to support insurgents from Thomas the Slav to Andronikos Doukas. People of mixed Arab and Greek parentage were so common in the eastern provinces that one of them became the hero of the epic *Digenis Akritas*. There were Christian communities and monasteries within the Abbasid caliphate in which Greek literature flourished during the 8th century and probably later. The caliphs encouraged scholarly contact and tried to invite to Baghdad Byzantine scholars, such as Leo the Mathematician, while Photios went there on an embassy.

Byzantine art and architecture imbibed a considerable amount of Islamic influence. Emperor Theophilos's palace in Constantinople, with its wild animals, automata in the shape of birds or lions, and garden of artificial trees made of precious metals, is said to have been built on Arab models, being similar to Abbasid palaces in Baghdad. Ruins of a palace on the Asian side of the Bosporos with a domed audience hall are thought to relate to a series of earlier Islamic palaces. Early Islam may also have had some impact on the changes in coinage introduced by Justinian II and on iconoclasm. Objects with Islamic motifs appear more abundantly during the Macedonian and Komnenian periods, and in fact down to the Latin conquest of 1204. Roundels with animals or hunting scenes typical of Islamic and early Iranian designs appear on textiles, and silks in particular, while official or expensive costumes tend to adopt eastern cuts and motifs. Ceramic vessels and decorative tiles adopt several motifs and techniques developed in the Muslim world. The crown of Constantine IX and the Pala d'Oro in Venice incorporate enamels with dancers and hunters typical of Islamic art. Islamic features are also evident in what have been interpreted as Byzantine silver objects from central Russia. Imitation of the angular Kufic style of Arabic writing produced the "pseudo-Kufic" motifs which decorated Greek churches. The treasury of St Mark's church in Venice contains a glass cup with an imitation of an Arabic inscription so well executed as to seem legible, placed next to beautifully copied antique motifs. Traces of Islamic influence are evident in

Byzantium from the 9th century, yet Byzantine art was less consistently affected by Islam than the art of other Christian groups in western Asia who came under Islamic political domination, such as Armenians, Georgians, Syrians, and Copts. Religious art rarely reflects Islamic influences, and never in style and expression, the formal means by which Byzantine art differentiates itself from other medieval traditions. On the other hand, it is in the secular art of emperors and in many aspects of material culture that Islamic themes are most evident. This is not surprising since it was an emphasis on representations of pleasure (dancing, singing, music, and hunting) as an expression of power and wealth that Muslim princes introduced into the language of imperial art.

In science the Arabs preserved and developed Greek mathematics, physics, chemistry, astronomy, and medicine, and transmitted to Europe this Greek heritage, after enriching it considerably. Arabic scientific terms still lie embedded in European speech. Islam appeared at a time when the Greek mind, which had earlier attained such heights of learning and wisdom, had come to a point of virtual stagnation. Muslim scholars lost no time in picking up the threads of Greek science. They not only procured and translated Greek texts, but they critically analysed them, collating, correcting, and even substantially supplementing the Greek contributions to science and philosophy. In the field of science the Arabs did not merely transmit to posterity what they received from the Greeks, but gave it a new lease of life and a fresh development in the Arab environment. In mathematics and astronomy they coordinated the work of Greek and Indian scientists and thence made a very real advance. They developed both algebra and plane and spherical trigonometry. They diligently made and recorded astronomical observations which not only extended their Hellenistic inheritance, but also checked and corrected older records. The new astronomy of the 13th century was in a way a futile attempt to correct what the Arabs had perceived as defects in the Ptolemaic cosmology, something that was not achieved until Copernicus. Al-Khwarizmi (780–850) improved on Ptolemy's latitudes and longitudes and reduced his overstatements of size, e.g. of the Mediterranean. He also added many place names which had originated after the Islamic conquests, and were therefore unknown to Ptolemy. By the mid-9th century Arab scientists were able to consolidate what knowledge they had inherited from the Persians and Greeks, and to assimilate it to their own scientific knowledge. Through the Nestorians most of the Greek scientific and philosophical classics had been translated into Syriac and, through Syriac as well as independently, into Arabic. Most significant in this respect was the knowledge which they obtained concerning Hippocrates, Plato, and Galen. This last writer, in particular, came to be criticized by Arab anatomists: e.g. by Abd al-Latif al-Baghdadi (11th century) for asserting that the lower jaw is composed of one bone only; and by Ali Ibn Abbas for suggesting that there were three layers in the walls of blood vessels. Moreover, whereas Galen held that there were only seven bones in the human skull, Muslim anatomists believed that there were eight.

The survival of scientific medicine in the west during the dark ages was due chiefly to three factors: the activities of Jewish physicians who circulated Graeco-Arabic medical knowledge in Christendom; the Byzantine culture of southern Italy; the rendering into Latin of Greek and Arabic medical treatises. The school of Salerno was probably best situated and best prepared to take advantage of these influences. Those who taught and studied there included Greek, Latin, Muslim, and Jewish physicians, and until the 12th century Salerno remained the leading medical institution in Latin Europe.

It is interesting to note that although many Greek texts were translated into Arabic and thence into Latin, few Arabic texts are known to have been translated into Greek. These few are primarily scientific texts, especially on astronomy and, to a lesser extent, on medicine and pharmacology. Among the eastern texts that penetrated Greek literature in the 11th century were the *Stephanites* and *Ichnelates*, translated from Arabic by Symeon Seth. In other fields such as fables, stories, games, numbering system, and music, the Arab contribution is widely accepted as one of transmission from lands further east than one of origination.

D.P.M. WEERAKKODY

Summary

"Arabs" here includes all those of Arab blood and politically under Arab rule. The Arab world was first made manifest to the Greeks by Alexander the Great. Arabia was important as a source of incense and spices, gold and gems. Relations between Arabs and Byzantines were characterized not only by invasions and conquests but also by economic and cultural exchanges.

Further Reading

Bowersock, G.W., *Roman Arabia*, Cambridge, Massachusetts: Harvard University Press, 1983

Eph'al, Israel, *The Ancient Arabs: Nomads on the Borders of the Fertile Crescent*, Jerusalem: Magnes Press, 1982

Millar, Fergus, *The Roman Near East: 31 BC–AD 337*, Cambridge, Massachusetts: Harvard University Press, 1993

Mirza, Mohammad R. and Muhammad Iqbal Siddiqi (editors), *Muslim Contribution to Science*, Lahore: Kazi, 1986

O'Leary, De Lacy, *How Greek Science Passed to the Arabs*, London: Routledge and Kegan Paul, 1949

Potts, D.T., *The Arabian Gulf in Antiquity*, Oxford: Clarendon Press, and New York: Oxford University Press, 1990

Rice, Michael, *The Archaeology of the Arabian Gulf*, London and New York: Routledge, 1994

Shahid, Irfan, *Byzantium and the Semitic Orient before the Rise of Islam*, London: Variorum, 1988

Aratus

Author of astronomical poetry of the 3rd century BC

Aratus, the author of *Phaenomena*, the most influential poem in ancient Greek after the Homeric epics, flourished in the first half of the 3rd century BC. Four ancient *Lives* and the entry in the *Suda* combined show that he was born in Soli in Cilicia, that he studied in Athens, where he associated with Callimachus and the philosophers Timon of Phlius and Menedemus of Eretria, and that he was taught Stoicism by Zeno. The only sure date in his biography is 277/76 BC, when king Antigonus Gonatas brought him into the royal Macedonian court at Pella. After a time in residence at the court of the Syrian king Antiochus, Aratus returned to Pella, where he predeceased Antigonus (d. 240 BC).

Aratus composed many works, including a scholarly commentary on Homer's *Odyssey*, a hymn to Pan that celebrated Antigonus' defeat of the Celts in 277 BC, epigrams (two survive), other elegiac poems, funeral dirges, a hexameter poem called *Iatrica* ("Medical Healing"), a poem about the harmony of the spheres called the *Canon* ("Table"), and *Astrica* ("On Stars") in at least five books. This list may include a collection called *To Kata Lepton* ("Works Slenderly Composed", from which the collection in the *Appendix Vergiliana* derived its title), or that descriptive may apply to Aratus' poetic style generally. His only surviving work is the *Phaenomena*, a didactic epic poem in the style of Hesiod that deals with the astronomical constellations and with weather prognostication. The poem consists of 1154 hexameters: a Stoic proem to Zeus, whose influence pervades the poem (1–18); the constitution of individual constellations in the northern and southern skies (19–453); the planets (454–61); the measurement of time and how to mark nocturnal time by simultaneous risings and settings (462–757); weather signs (758–1141); and a conclusion (1142–54).

The first *Life* explains that Antigonus commissioned the *Phaenomena* by asking Aratus to versify the prose treatise on astronomy by Eudoxus of Cnidus (*fl.*340 BC). The extant commentary by Hipparchus details the relationship between Aratus' poem and Eudoxus' source material. Although Aratus' astronomical inaccuracies disturbed Hipparchus, the poem enjoyed immediate recognition and lasting success among readers who were taken by its poetic achievement. The *Phaenomena* masterfully proceeds in an epic style calculated to emulate Hesiod, whose reputation flourished in the early 3rd century BC, the golden age of Hellenistic poetry. Aratus' literary accomplishment was not lost on contemporaries. The great Hellenistic poets Callimachus (*Epigrammata*, 27) and Leonidas of Tarentum (*Anthologia Palatina*, 9. 25) praised Aratus' refinement – each using the adjective *leptos* (subtle) particularly – and Ptolemy Philadelphus stated in an epigram (*Supplementum Hellenisticum*, 712) that the *leptologos* (subtle-tongued) Aratus deserved to wield the sceptre among poets on astronomical topics. This terminology suggests that the poet's intended audience was an elite readership with interests in literary esoterica.

That some 20 subsequent authors wrote commentaries on Aratus or composed *Aratea* demonstrates the breadth of the poem's influence. It is among a handful of Greek poems to have been translated anciently into Arabic. And its influence on Roman poetry is of tremendous importance. The influence is manifest in the great didactic hexameter poems written by Lucretius and Virgil (*Georgics*) in the 1st century BC, both clearly having been influenced by Aratus' style. Latin poets exhibited a "strong urge to win Aratus for Latin" as part of a patriotic move to "absorb the three great poets [i.e. Callimachus, Theocritus, and Aratus] of the classic Hellenistic generation" (Courtney, 1993). This urge was made manifest among the new poets by Cinna, who brought a copy of *Aratus* back from Bithynia; by Varro of Atax, whose *Ephemeris* closely recalls Aratus in its extant fragments; and by a youthful Cicero himself, whose *Aratea* consists of 480 continuous lines and some 70 additional lines called the *Prognostica*.

Virgil mines Aratus for material in a remarkable passage of the *Georgics* (1. 351–460). Although Ovid's *Phaenomena* survives in only two fragments, both bear strong resemblance to Aratus. Germanicus modernized Aratus, fitting the whole into 725 lines, of which 200 are not based on Aratus, and correcting some errors. Avienus (*fl.* mid-4th century AD) composed a version expanded by more than 700 lines over what Aratus himself had written: *Aratea Phaenomena* (1325 hexameters) and *Aratea Prognostica* (552 hexameters). This interest propelled Aratus into western literature with immense influence (Böker), which is still working today.

ROGER T. MACFARLANE

Biography

Born in the late 4th century BC in Soli in Cilicia, Aratus studied in Athens where he was taught Stoicism by Zeno and associated with Callimachus, Timon of Phlius, and Menedemus of Eretria. In 277/76 BC he was introduced to the Macedonian royal court at Pella by Antigonus Gonatas. He composed much poetry but only the *Phaenomena* survives, a didactic poem on astronomy. He died before 240 BC.

Writings

Phaenomena, translated by G.R. Mair, in *Callimachus, Lycophron, Aratus*, London: Heinemann, and New York: Putnam, 1921 (Loeb edition)
Phaenomena, edited and translated into French by Jean Martin, Florence: Nuova Italia, 1956
Phaenomena, edited and translated by Douglas Kidd, Cambridge and New York: Cambridge University Press, 1997

Further Reading

Courtney, Edward (editor), *The Fragmentary Latin Poets*, Oxford: Clarendon Press, and New York: Oxford University Press, 1993
Erren, Manfred, *Die Phainomena des Aratos von Soloi*, Wiesbaden: Steiner, 1967
Ludwig, Walter, "Die *Phainomena* Arats als Hellenistische Dichtung", *Hermes*, 91 (1963): pp. 425–48
Ludwig, Walter, Aratus (6) entry in *Real-Encyclopädie der klassischen Altertumswissenschaft*, edited by August Pauly *et al.*, supplement 10, 1965, 26–39
Martin, Jean (editor), *Scholia in Aratum Vetera*, Teubner: Stuttgart, 1974
Toomer, G.T., Aratus (2) entry in *The Oxford Classical Dictionary*, 3rd edition, edited by Simon Hornblower and Antony Spawforth, Oxford and New York: Oxford University Press, 1996

Arcadia

Region of the central Peloponnese

Arcadia is a mountainous region in the centre of the Peloponnese rising to heights of more than 2000 m. It did not gain political independence until late in the Classical period when in 366 BC Megalopolis, the "great city", was founded. But in 234 the poleis of Arcadia joined the Achaean League which became subject to the Romans. After the defeat of the Macedonians at the Battle of Pydna in 168 BC, the Romans took 10,000 Arcadian nobles as hostages to Italy; among them was Polybius, who was later to become an admirer of Roman

Arcadia: the 5th-century BC temple of Apollo at Bassae, high in the mountains of southwest Arcadia

imperialism. The destruction of Corinth in 146 BC also resulted in the end of Arcadian liberty.

Arcadia was not only a physical landscape; it became also a mental landscape ("geistige Landschaft"; as described by Bruno Snell in *Die Entdeckung des Geistes*), representing a cultural idea on which certain ideals were based. Poets of the Hellenistic period made Arcadia the scene of a charming but unrealistic poetry of shepherds and other herdsmen, chief among whom was Pan, the lewd god of the herdsmen, with the legs of a billygoat, who was always playing the panpipes. The bucolic genre, however, did not arise in Arcadia, but in Sicily (Theocritus, the Greek representative of bucolic poetry, was born in Syracuse).

It was the Roman Virgil (70–19 BC) who combined Arcadia and bucolic poetry. He knew the historical work of Polybius with its warm description of the inhabitants of old Arcadia, and he wrote the *Bucolica*. Thus Virgil founded a special genre for all European literatures.

The Italian Renaissance marked a rebirth of Arcadism, beginning with the poetry of Francesco Petrarch (1304–75), the Italian patriot and forerunner of European humanism. Influenced by Virgil, Petrarch wrote poems of minor aesthetic value, which were published posthumously under the title *Bucolicum Carmen*. But the real originator of modern Arcadism was Jacopo Sannazaro (1458–1530) from Naples,

with his romance *Arcadia* (c.1480). Sannazaro took motifs from Virgil and other Classical writers and imagined an Arcadian golden age, in which life was full of merriment and love, far removed from the realities of rural life and Christian asceticism.

The personality of Sannazaro and his achievement had an enormous effect. In 1590 in Italy Giovanni Battista Guarini (1538–1612), a nobleman, diplomat, and professor of literature, published his *Pastor Fido*, a tragicomic pastoral drama which includes a portrait of Arcadia with strict morals and little licence, and only in the final part do we find a description of the golden age. In the territories dominated by the Venetians, such as Crete and Zakynthos, the *Pastor Fido* was issued in modern Greek. In Spain, Guarini was followed by Garcilaso de la Vega (1503–36), a soldier and writer who cultivated the Italian style in his eclogues; by the great adventurous poet Felix Lope de Vega Carpio (1562–1635), who wrote a pastoral romance *Arcadia* (1598); and by the famous Miguel de Cervantes Saavedra (1547–1616), who in 1585 published – without much acclaim – the bucolic romance *Galatea*. In France, Rémy Belleau (1528–77), a younger member of the Pléiade, published his *Bergerie* (1565), a collection of occasional poems in which personalities from public life appeared in the guise of shepherds in order to hold allegorical conversations about problems of the court and of the state – a masterly travesty of Arcadism. In the Netherlands, Johan van Heemskerck (1597–1656), a member of the High Council of Amsterdam, wrote his often imitated *Batavische Arcadia* (1637) in order to entertain his political friends with historical and folkloric episodes. In England, Sir Philip Sidney (1554–86), a favourite of the royal court, an Oxford scholar, and a diplomat who was wounded as an officer fighting against the Spanish, wrote his romance *Arcadia* (published posthumously in 1590). He was said to be a successor of Sannazaro and included in his work (in which poetical intermezzi were introduced) the political and moral opinions of the Renaissance ruling class. In Silesia, Valentinus Theokritus translated Sidney's *Arcadia* into German (1629), and Martin Opitz (1597–1639), the famous German critic of language and literature, revised this translation which was printed posthumously in 1642.

In 17th-century Germany a form of Arcadism developed which was fed by both the Classical and the humanistic traditions. The striving for harmony, balance, peace, and quietness was an understandable reaction to the unnatural culture of feudalism. Friedrich Spee (von Langenfeld) (1591–1635) SJ was a follower of this kind of Arcadism; in his collection of poems called *Trutznachtigall*, published posthumously in 1639, he combined spiritual content with bucolic forms. The middle-class intellectuals of the town of Nuremberg made different use of the Arcadian idea. They founded a literary society named Pegnitzorden (the community of the river Pegnitz) which sought to inculcate social graces by distancing themselves from the mastersingers surrounding Hans Sachs. Their protagonist was the lawyer Georg Philipp Harsdörffer (1607–43).

Apart from literary Arcadism, which flourished in most European countries, forms of Arcadism are also found in the figurative arts. This development began in the Renaissance and was at first connected with Rome. The new feeling for nature stimulated artistic production in two ways. The first way can be described as heroic; its roots were the mythology and the architecture of antiquity. The second way was determined by literary Arcadism in all its manifestations. Landscape painting corresponded with this idea and was an ideal medium in which to display gods and nymphs, herds and herdsmen, singing and playing. A forerunner of this style was Giovanni Bellini (c.1430–1516) from Venice. For preference he painted biblical scenes with detailed treatment of flora and fauna. The Arcadian style was continued by Giorgio Giorgione (c.1477–1510) with his *Tempesta* in the Accademia of Venice and his *Slumbering Venus* in the Dresden Gallery. The acme of this artistic Arcadism was represented by the Frenchman Nicolas Poussin (1594–1665) who from 1624 lived permanently in Rome. He painted a landscape showing a tombstone with the inscription "Et in Arcadia ego" (*Les Bergers d'Arcadie*, Louvre). This motif, which demonstrates that even in Utopian Arcadia death is always present, was first treated by Bartolommeo Schedoni (c.1570–1614); the inscription was used in a different sense by Friedrich Schiller (1759–1805) ("I too was born in Arcadia") and Johann Wolfgang Goethe (1749–1832). The Arcadian style of painting was continued, occasionally with a Christian context, by Claude Lorrain (1615–75), Poussin's brother-in-law, and by others. But all these paintings rendered an ideal Arcadia without the benefit of the artists' inspection. Only at the beginning of the 19th century did travel to the Peloponnese become possible and regular.

It was not only writers and artists who were fascinated by the Arcadian idea. The queen of Sweden, Christina (1626–89), assembled writers, poets, and scholars at her palace in Rome in order to discuss their new works. After the death of the queen this circle became the Accademia degli Arcadi, and Canon Giovanni Mario Crescimbeni (1663–1728) its spokesman. The main purpose of the academy was to revive Italian poetry which had been subjected to barbarism in the past; its declared enemy was baroque Marinism, the form of poetry invented by Giambattista Marini (1569–1625). The members of the academy belonged to the upper classes, but women also were admitted. They had to read their poems, but "mala carmina et famosa, obscoena, superstitiosa, impia" (poems that were "evil, scandalous, obscene, superstitious, or impious") were excluded. In 1711 the academy had 1195 members and was supported by Pope Clement XI. In 1795 King John V of Portugal built the academy on the Janiculum. The academy published valuable collections of poems which influenced the aesthetics of an epoch and propagated a formal classicism. In the second half of the 18th century the academy lost much of its prestige, but it survived and still exists today as the Accademia Letteraria Italiana dell'Arcadia.

In Greece the Arcadian ideal has been cultivated for some decades by local societies and the (private) Arcadian Academy in Athens. The old ideals of combining nature and art are being revisited by the modern movement for the protection of nature and the environment.

JOHANNES IRMSCHER

Summary

The central region of the Peloponnese, Arcadia played little part in political history. Its chief city, Megalopolis, was founded in 366 BC. It succumbed to Roman rule after the destruction of Corinth in 146 BC. Its bucolic landscape however has inspired poets from Virgil to Goethe with an ideal of idyllic life, of love, and of peace.

Further Reading

Bertana, Emilio, *In Arcadia: saggi e profili*, Naples: Perrella, 1909

Irmscher, Johannes, "Arkadismus und Revolutionarismus", *Rivista Storica dell'Antichità*, 22/23 (1992): pp. 267–74

Praktika A' Synedriou gia tin Anaviosi tou Arkadikou ideodous [Acts of the First Conference for the Revival of the Arcadian Ideal], Athens 1984

Snell, Bruno, "Arkadien: die Entdeckung einer geistigen Landschaft", *Antike und Abendland*, 1 (1945): pp. 26ff.

Archaeological Service

The centuries preceding the creation of the modern Hellenic state in 1830 witnessed the destruction and removal from Greek soil of many ancient monuments and artefacts. Many antiquities suffered severe damage in times of battle, as foreign powers fought each other for the ownership of Greece, and in the more peaceful interludes, particularly during the 18th and early 19th centuries, foreign antiquarians and travellers carried home with them many prized and admired pieces of ancient

Greek sculpture and architecture. By the early 19th century, however, Hellenism and the longing to be free of the ruling hand of the Ottoman Turk were gathering momentum, and these growing feelings of national identity came to express themselves in part in a new-found pride and respect for the monuments of Hellas's great and Classical past. In 1813 the Philomousoi, a society of Greek and foreign lovers of arts and letters, was founded in Athens and when in 1821 the Greeks rose against the Ottoman Turks in the War of Independence, the Philomousoi attempted to protect antiquities from suffering any further damage and destruction.

The speed with which matters now progressed is indicative of the important place that the ancient Greek past occupied in the consciousness of the proud, new, and independent state of Hellas. By 1829 the statesman Ioannis Kapodistria had founded on the island of Aegina the first national museum, under the direction of Andreas Moustoxydis. In 1833 the Ministry of Education was established by royal decree and was charged, among other things, with the excavation, preservation, and protection of antiquities. A year later the first archaeological law entered the statute books: its aim was to maintain the Greek national heritage by preventing the illegal excavation and export of antiquities. By this law was created the nucleus of the Greek Archaeological Service, the body that has acted until the present day as guardian of antiquities. Its first general director was the German A. Weissenburg, and under him were three regional directors (L. Ross, K. Pittakis, and I. Kokkonis) who were, respectively, allocated responsibility for the Peloponnese, central Greece, and the islands. By the end of 1834 the newly formed Archaeological Service had already started work on the Athenian Acropolis to clear the site of modern houses and to raise the fallen columns of the Parthenon.

In 1837, furthermore, three years after the creation of the state Archaeological Service, the Athenian Archaeological Society was founded, a private body that also still exists. Since that time, the society has published the results of its archaeological excavations and research in its annual *Praktika* (or *Proceedings*) and *Ephimeris* (*Journal*) publications, and also since 1954 in the annual *Ergon* (or *Work*) of the society. Also by 1837 conditions were sufficiently settled to move the contents of the Aegina museum to Athens; at first they were housed in temporary quarters, including the ancient Theseum or temple of Athena and Hephaestus above the Athenian Agora. Plans, meanwhile, were made to erect a great National Archaeological Museum in the capital. The designs were drawn up shortly after the middle of the 19th century by the German architect Ludwig Lange, and its construction followed shortly thereafter, making it one of the great early European museum foundations.

As the years passed, the work of the Archaeological Service increased dramatically as the Greek national borders expanded: gradually the Ionian islands (1864), Thessaly (1880–81), and Chios, Crete, Epirus, Lesbos, Macedonia, Samos, and Thrace (1912–13) were all absorbed into Greek territory. Finally, in 1948 the Dodecanese too came under Greek sovereignty. Reflecting this expansion of geographical responsibility, archaeological law was passed in 1910 to reorganize and expand the Archaeological Service: the service was now recognized as a department of the Ministry of Education and was to be headed by a Director of Antiquities, to whom an increased number of regional officers were to report. An Archaeological Council was also created to discuss and decide matters of particular importance. For the first time, too, the significance of Greece's Byzantine heritage was officially acclaimed by the appointment of an inspector of Christian and medieval antiquities: this was quickly followed in 1914 by the foundation in Athens of a national Byzantine museum. The archaeological law of 1910, and another of 1932, still serve to protect and preserve antiquities in Greece.

Throughout both the Graeco-Turkish war of 1920–22 and World War II, the Archaeological Service continued to fulfil its role as the guardian of Hellenic cultural heritage. During the hostilities in Asia Minor it oversaw the transfer of antiquities to Smyrna for safe keeping from abandoned archaeological sites in the surrounding region, and also conducted the excavation of sites such as Nysa on the Maeander and of the Byzantine church of St John at Ephesus. At the time of the German occupation of Greece, the contents of Greek museums were saved from damage and looting by the passionate dedication of the archaeologists, who emptied their exhibition galleries and hid the antiquities with great ingenuity. Following World War II, much was done to reorganize the national and, by now, numerous regional museums, and from 1950 the archaeological laws were extended to protect monuments and works of art post-dating 1830.

As it exists today, the Archaeological Service forms a major department of the Greek Ministry of Culture. The investigation, care, and presentation of sites and areas of archaeological and historical importance, and of the antiquities and works of art housed in the Greek museums, are divided between three main divisions of the service: Prehistoric and Classical Antiquities, Byzantine and Postbyzantine Antiquities, and Modern (post-1830) Monuments. These three main departments are subdivided into regional units, responsible for archaeology and museums in their particular locale. The Central Archaeological Council in Athens, nevertheless, has ultimate control. A special branch of the service also deals with conservation and restoration matters, and additional departments oversee underwater archaeology, caves and palaeoanthropology, private collections, and the archaeological fieldwork activities of Greek universities and of the foreign archaeological schools and institutes based in Athens. One of the main tasks that falls to the regional units of the Archaeological Service is the oversight of all development and construction work in their districts, which may either uncover ancient remains or affect listed buildings: areas found to be of archaeological importance during, for example, the course of digging new building foundations must, by law, be subjected to rescue excavation by the Archaeological Service. If the antiquities are found to be of particular significance, the modern development work may be completely and permanently halted, the area declared an "archaeological zone", and the land expropriated for state ownership.

Greece is richly strewn with the debris of its past, a factor that today is both a source of great national pride and a valued asset in its development of cultural tourism. However, the demands of antiquity on the present are considerable: the conservation and partial restoration of the major standing monuments, such as those of the Athenian Acropolis, and the development and construction of new museums for the ever-expanding treasury of excavated antiquities require longterm planning and the commitment of national finances. Furthermore, the sheer weight of archaeological finds and discoveries loads the archaeologists with a heavy burden and backlog of material to be studied and published: the Archaeological Service's annual publications, *Archaiologikon Deltion* (*Archaeological Bulletin*) and *Archaiologika Analekta ex Athinon* (*Athens Annals of Archaeology*), therefore announce recently discovered material in summary form until it can be published in full. But, for all the difficulties of management that Greece's past poses for its present, the soul of modernday Hellas is, nevertheless, entwined inextricably with its past: incidences of the repatriation to Greece of antiquities removed at some earlier date are, for example, often occasions for national rejoicing. As this article is written, a new, comprehensive, and updated archaeological law is in preparation. Its provisions aim to ensure that, as Greece moves forward into the new millennium, the nation's rich cultural heritage will be well protected, investigated, and managed on behalf of present and future generations.

LESLEY A. BEAUMONT

See also Archaeology, Museums

Further Reading

Archaiologia, 46 (March 1993), special issue

Bracken, C.P., *Antiquities Acquired: The Spoliation of Greece*, Newton Abbot, Devon: David and Charles, 1975

Gratziou, O., P. Papangeli, and E. Spathari (editors), *Ergo kai Leitourgia mias Yperesias gia ten Prostasia ton Mnemeion Semera* [The Task and Functioning of an Organization for the Protection of Monuments Today], Athens, 1987

Kokkou, Angelike, *E merimna gia tis archaiotetes sten Hellada kai ta prota mouseia* [Concern for Antiquities in Greece and the First Museums], Athens, 1977

Petrakos, Vasileios C., *Dokimio gia tin Archaiologiki Nomothesia* [Essay on Archaeological Legislation], Athens, 1982

Petrakou, Vasileios C., *He peripeteia tes Hellenikes archaiologias ston vio tou Chrestou Karouzou* [The Experience of Greek Archaeology in the Life of Chrestos Karouzos], Athens, 1995

Zois, A., *I Archaiologia stin Ellada: Pragmatikotites kai Prooptikes* [Archaeology in Greece: Actuality and Prospects], Athens, 1990

Archaeology

Our knowledge of Greek culture was originally derived from written documents, historical texts, and other literature, transmitted through the Middle Ages and the schools of Constantinople. It was largely the dispersal of Byzantine manuscripts to the west that led to the revival of interest in ancient Greece and its achievements, and the development of Classical Greek studies as a fundamental part of western education. At the same time, the conquest of Greece by the Ottoman Turks made Greece difficult of access, and Greek remained essentially a matter of book learning. Travellers such as Cyriac of Ancona, who visited and recorded surviving monuments in the mid-15th century, were most exceptional.

During the 18th century there was a considerable development of interest in the physical remains of antiquity, particularly in Italy. Antiquities were collected by wealthy aristocrats making the Grand Tour, and excavation was carried out at ancient sites, above all Pompeii. The Greek remains in southern Italy, especially the temples at Paestum, came to be known, appreciated, and even copied (e.g. the columns in Joseph Bonomi's church of St James at Great Packington in Warwickshire, of 1789–90). More crucially, in 1751 the aristocratic Society of Dilettanti sent James Stuart and Nicholas Revett to Greece itself, to produce accurate measured drawings of the ancient Greek buildings in Athens and elsewhere, as exemplars for Greek Revival architecture. This was a real stimulus to antiquarian interest in the material remains of ancient Greece, even if there was in all this much of the approach that can be summarized as "Fair Greece, sad relic". From this time there was a steady stream of artists and architects visiting Greece to record the monuments.

All this was transformed, if slowly, by the War of Independence and the freeing of at least part of Greece. The recovery of the material evidence for ancient Greek culture now became a fundamental aspect of the national heritage, and even as Karl Friedrich Schinkel was producing plans for his "dream palace" to house the Bavarian king Otho on the Acropolis of Athens, Kyriakos Pittakis (the brother-in-law of Theresa Makri, Byron's Maid of Athens) was struggling to recover and preserve the fallen and scattered fragments of Classical buildings and sculpture as the Turkish structures there were demolished. The new Greek state passed its law of 10/22 May 1834 that concerned the uncovering and conservation of antiquities. Already, in 1829, Kapodistria had established the Archaeological Service, and in 1833 Adolf Weissenberg had been put in charge of "the conservation, discovery and collection of the archaeological treasures of the Kingdom", with Pittakis responsible for northern Greece, J. Kokkonis for the islands of the Aegean, and Ludwig Ross for the Peloponnese. In 1837 came the foundation of the Archaeological Society of Athens.

Their work was undoubtedly hampered by the poverty of the newly independent state. At first there were very few purpose-built museums (that on Aegina was one of them). At Athens antiquities were stored in the Theseum (temple of Hephaestus), in the Propylaea, in a Turkish cistern in front of the west end of the Parthenon, and in a Turkish house behind the Erechtheum. Conservation work was often crude; although the temple of Nike was resurrected from the Turkish gun bastion into which it had been incorporated, the patching of the Erechtheum was elementary, while the north wall of the Parthenon was supported by a rough and intrusive structure of brickwork.

Into this context came the foundation of the foreign schools, beginning with the French in 1847, which brought much greater resources to the development of Greek archaeology, whether state-supported or funded by wealthy individuals. There was increasingly a new approach, the transformation from collection and antiquarianism to scientific archaeology. Already in the 1850s Charles Newton was emphasizing, in his proposals to excavate the Mausoleum at Halicarnassus, the need for a proper archaeological approach (which he achieved with the recording of his work, including the use of photography), even though, by digging in what was still the Ottoman empire rather than Greece, his main purpose was to acquire material for the collections at the British Museum. At the same time, significantly, he was stressing the need for archaeology to be recognized as an essential element in the study of Greek civilization.

From this time, archaeology has transformed our knowledge of Greek culture. In many ways, the most significant single development has been the discovery and ongoing interpretation of Greek prehistory. Excavations at the major prehistoric sites, on the mainland at Mycenae, Tiryns, Pylos, and a whole host of other places, together with those on the island of Crete, have revealed a complete new world of Greece before the Classical Greeks. The discovery at Knossos, Pylos, and elsewhere (most recently, under the streets of modern Thebes) of the Linear B tablets, and their brilliant decipherment in the 1950s by Michael Ventris, has brought us knowledge of the Greek language at a stage more than 500 years earlier than Homer, and with this an understanding of Greek society in a different form, centuries before the evolution of the Classical city states. It has shown us, too, the pre-Greek world of Crete, on top of which the prehistoric Greeks developed, and has enabled us to trace its formative elements from Egypt, the Near East, and Asia Minor. None of this was known before the excavations of Heinrich Schliemann, Arthur Evans, Carl Blegen, and many others.

Turning to the Classical period, archaeology has broadened immensely our knowledge of the Greek world at that time. In Athens we can now see the Agora, not just read about its involvement in the affairs of the city. We no longer have to rely on Thucydides' assurances to understand the physical contrast between the cities of Athens and Sparta. Even things of little significance in themselves make our understanding of the Classical world more real and vivid: we can now actually see the gash made in the forehead of Philip of Macedon by the arrow that removed the sight of one of his eyes at his siege of Methone; but more significantly, in the material that was buried with him in his vaulted tomb at Aegae/Vergina we can see something of the luxurious wealth that characterized his royal existence in the palace at Pella (whose plan itself has been revealed in recent excavations). Beyond the Classical period, archaeology traces (more clearly than the broken written record) the essential continuity of the Greek world; more attention than previously is paid to post-Classical remains, for example, in the excavations at Corinth.

The contribution of archaeology to our understanding of Greek culture can be divided into two broad categories: first, the recovery of actual material from the earth, and secondly its interpretation. Recovery is not confined to excavation. Surveys of extended areas, the study of the distribution of artefacts over the ground, give information about settlement patterns outside the obvious city sites, and their variation at different periods of Greek history, down to the present day. The study of surface evidence, as well as that from excavation, has given us the street plans of innumerable Greek cities. We can now see not only the great temples of the major religious sanctuaries, but also places of lesser, or even completely minor cults, and thereby understand more of the place that these cults had in the lives of the ancient Greeks. It is possible to see more of the workings of the cults, the objects deposited as offerings, the buildings associated with religious practice, often specialized such as those provided – for a select minority – for the ritual feasting that was an essential element of Greek religion. Archaeology has extended our documentary evidence for Greek civilization, above all the discovery and recording, already started by Cyriac of Ancona in the 15th century, of inscriptions. The range of these is immense: they include major historical events, such as the evacuation of Athens at the onset of Xerxes' invasion (though this inscription is later than the event, and raises problems of interpretation). From inscriptions we have the oath sworn by the founders of Thera's colony at Cyrene, records for building the temples at Athens, and of the development of the sanctuary of Asclepius (and thus the Asclepius cult) at Epidaurus. We can assess the tribute paid by the dependent states of Athens' empire, and read the lists of property confiscated from those who mutilated the hermae on the departure of Athens' doomed expedition to Syracuse. Excavation in Egypt, whether organized or, to use a euphemism, commercial, has produced the texts of literary works that did not survive the rigorous exclusions of Byzantine copying, but also more personal documents, bills, receipts, even the private letters of the Greeks in Hellenistic and Roman Egypt. The list is never-ending.

In short, archaeology has shown the complete context in which Greek civilization developed and flourished, as well as its periods of decline. It has given us a first-hand knowledge, not easily recoverable from other sources of information, of Greek art and architecture (which is Classical archaeology in its original meaning). Though much has been lost, discoveries are still accumulating. Without archaeology we would have no visual knowledge of the sculptures that decorated the temple of Zeus at Olympia, or of the marble masterpieces dedicated on the Acropolis of Athens in the 6th century BC and buried after their desecration at the hands of Xerxes' soldiers in 480 BC. Even if chance finds have given us the powerful bronze god (surely Zeus) fished up off Cape Artemisium, or the Riace warriors, plausibly if not with certainty attributed to Phidias himself, it is the techniques developed for the conservation of antiquities that have restored and stabilized them. The literary sources – such as Pausanias – tell us of important paintings, and tantalize us with their descriptions of lost masterpieces; archaeology has restored to us at least the masterpieces painted on the walls of the royal tombs at Vergina, revealed in the late 1970s by Manolis Andronikos, their colours as fresh as the day they were painted, their style compared by their discoverer with that of the old masters. These same graves, and others elsewhere, both in and beyond the Greek world, have produced for us splendid examples of Greek metalworking, in gold and silver as well as bronze, of which there are otherwise only the dimmest echoes in the ancient written sources.

Archaeology has also recovered much of the everyday aspects of Greek civilization. We now have examples of the houses in which the Greeks lived, generally reduced to foundations and footings, but with some better preserved, and certainly with more evidence to show what they were like when they were intact, ranging in date from the prehistoric to the present day, and from all levels of society. Archaeology has uncovered much of the paraphernalia of everyday life, or at least that which was not made of perishable materials (in rare circumstances, even this has survived). The painted vases, too, illustrate not only legends and mythology, but also scenes from everyday life – in the house, at school, at the workplace, at the bottom of the mines, in the exercise grounds of the gymnasia. They show us the drinking parties, as well as the fun and games that went on there. But they also help to fill out our knowledge of contemporary houses, for they illustrate the furniture – couches, chairs, chests – and the way that objects were hung on the walls of the feasting rooms.

More specialized aspects of archaeology give us further information. Underwater research has been particularly rewarding, starting with the finds dredged up, like the Artemisium *Zeus*, by fishing nets, but more recently developing, thanks to advances in diving technology, into a branch of scientific research that not only locates wrecks but investigates and records them in every detail. The identification of such wrecks, and their cargoes, of all periods, has produced much information on patterns of trade in Greek waters, and wider afield in the Mediterranean. It has even led to the recovery of the remains of ancient ships, particularly the 4th-century BC Kyrenia wreck, which has given us information about the relative longevity of ordinary small trading vessels, and, most invaluably, about the technique of ship construction.

With archaeology go the scientific techniques developed to assist in interpretation. Analysis of pollen, seeds and other vegetable remains in soils and in rubbish pits tells us about crops and diet. Analysis of pottery fabrics tells us where they were made, including the plain wares that were, with their contents, an important part of the export trade of Greece. If our understanding of the Greek world, from the beginning to the present day, is so much wider now than it was a century ago, or compared with the time when the texts were our only source of information, it is archaeology that has made the difference.

R.A. TOMLINSON

See also Archaeological Service, Inscriptions, Linear B, Pottery

Further Reading

Archaiologikon Deltion (in Greek: describes the work of the Greek Archaeological Service)

Bulletin de Correspondance Hellénique, 120 (1995) (describes work of the French school)

Bulletin de Correspondance Hellénique (other full reports, in French)

MacKendrick, Paul, *The Greek Stones Speak: History of Archaeology in Greek Lands*, 2nd edition, New York: Norton, 1981

Petrakos, B.C., *E en Athenais Archaiologike Hetaireia: E Istoria ton 150 Chronontes, 1837–1987* [The Athens Archaeological Society: The History of 150 Years, 1837–1987], Athens, 1987

Stoneman, Richard, *Land of Lost Gods: The Search for Classical Greece*, London: Hutchinson, and Norman: University of Oklahoma Press, 1987

Tsigakou, Fani-Maria, *The Rediscovery of Greece: Travellers and Painters of the Romantic Era*, London: Thames and Hudson, and New Rochelle, New York: Caratzas, 1981

Waterhouse, Helen, *The British School at Athens: The First Hundred Years*, London: British School at Athens, 1986

Reports of archaeological work in English are given each year in *Archaeological Reports* published by the Society for the Promotion of Hellenic Studies and the British School at Athens.

Archaic Period *c.*700–479 BC

The Archaic period of Greece, which follows the Geometric and precedes the Classical period, is traditionally dated *c.*700–479 BC, for the Geometric style of pottery decoration ends and Orientalizing styles appear around 700 BC, while the end of the Persian Wars in 479 BC marks a significant turning point in Greek history. Some, however, especially archaeologists, like to distinguish the first 100 years of this span (*c.*700–600 BC) as the Orientalizing period, and others prefer to start the Archaic as early as *c.*750 BC so that its beginning coincides with the Greek renaissance. Some recent scholars would also like to end the Archaic period *c.*500 BC, somewhat earlier than the traditional date of 479.

The Archaic period is marked by some of the greatest achievements of the Greeks, visible in such diverse areas as pottery and sculpture, the architecture of the great temples and sanctuaries, lyric poetry, philosophical speculation, and the shift to new forms of political organization. In most respects these achievements were the direct result of developments begun at the time of the Greek renaissance from *c.*750 BC on. The great colonization movement that had begun then continued during this period. Most of the Greek colonies had been established in the west by 650 BC and in southern Italy and Sicily later became known as Magna Graecia because of the large number of newly established Greek settlements there. The Greeks, however, also went further afield, into France and Spain, North Africa and the Near East, and, in fact, the colonization movement did not end until about the middle of the 6th century BC.

This was an era of great thinkers and writers. In Ionia Greek philosophy was born. Thales, Anaximander, and Anaximenes, all from Miletus, sought answers to profound philosophical questions, but elsewhere other schools evolved, each with its own ideas and followers, and significant advances were made in science and mathematics. In literature lyric poetry replaced epic poetry; instead of sweeping accounts of gods and heroes as in Homer's *Iliad* and *Odyssey*, this was personal, often very poignant poetry, filled with the range of human emotions. Archilochus, Alcman, Mimnermus, and Sappho all wrote at this time.

The shift in poetic style can be seen as a symptom of this new age, which was a time of political and social transformation. The poleis – the city states – were now consolidated, but the era was one of turmoil and revolution, as well as of greater individualism, as the work of the lyric poets demonstrates. At the beginning of the 7th century BC city states were typically ruled by aristocracies that were generally quite conservative in outlook and, in some respects, greedy and corrupt. Time had come for change, however, and in many city states this meant the adoption of tyranny. The first tyranny on the Greek mainland was in Corinth, where Cypselus took power from the noble Bacchiad family in the 650s BC, and most of the other major states followed suit, with the notable exceptions of Sparta, where two royal families continued to rule, and Athens, where tyranny came relatively late – in the mid-6th century BC.

The 7th century BC also represents a time of significant change in artistic style. This was the so-called Orientalizing period, when Greece accepted much influence from its eastern neighbours. It was the heyday of Corinth and it was there that the Geometric style first came to an end (c.720 BC) to be replaced by a new Orientalizing ware known as Protocorinthian. Both incision and polychromy were used to great effect and new motifs, generally inspired by the east, made their appearance on the pottery: floral motifs were employed, as were representations of real and imagined creatures such as lions, sphinxes, and griffins. Corinthian artists are especially known for their miniature pots; exquisitely decorated and filled with oils and perfumes, these were bound for export not only within Greece itself but also to the colonies, and they attest the pre-eminent economic position enjoyed by Corinth at this time. By the later part of the 7th century BC, however, Protocorinthian pottery became mass produced, a victim of its own success, and with this a noticeable change, not to say decline, set in. By the time that the so-called Corinthian ware (the successor of Protocorinthian) had established itself towards the end of the 7th century BC, Corinth's position of wealth and economic dominance was waning and would soon be eclipsed by Athens, whose fortunes were on the rise.

The Orientalizing period also saw the appearance of the type of sculpture known as Daedalic. The eastern, particularly Egyptian, characteristics of such sculpture are obvious in the very stiff frontal pose of the figures, depicted with arms at their sides and heads with triangular faces, low foreheads, and stylized hair. These statues were the forerunners of the famous *kouroi* (male) and *korai* (female) statues of the 6th century BC.

Sculptures are often associated with sanctuaries that themselves grew and prospered throughout the 7th and 6th centuries BC. An emphasis on public religion had begun in the geometric period, but it was in the 7th century BC that the temple became the religious focus of poleis all over the Greek world. Essentially a home for the deity, the temples, which had started life as wood or mud-brick constructions, some as early as the 8th century BC, were now built of stone and followed newly defined rules of architecture – the Doric and Ionic canons. The typical Greek temple comprised three rooms and had a colonnaded porch that surrounded the building. Besides the individual temples built in the poleis there were also the great Panhellenic sanctuaries that received worshippers from all over the Greek world and which were also venues for various types of competitions, particularly athletic and musical ones. The most famous of these sanctuaries were Delphi and Olympia, but others, such as Isthmia, Nemea, Delos, and Dodona, also enjoyed widespread renown. Delphi was known particularly for its oracle of Apollo and it acquired great prestige with visitors coming from all over Greece to receive advice and offer dedications there. Dedications, such as large bronze tripod cauldrons and figurines, demonstrate the popularity already enjoyed by Olympia in the later part of the Geometric period. As the home of the Olympic Games, the first celebration of which is traditionally dated to 776 BC, Olympia came to achieve a very prestigious position in the Archaic period. Treasuries as well as various other buildings, both religious and secular, were erected throughout the Archaic period at both sanctuaries.

In sculpture the 6th century BC was the time of the *kouroi* and *korai* which may, in general, be described as idealized portraits of young adults, the *kouroi* being nude males and the

Archaic Period: marble horseman from the Acropolis at Athens, possibly representing a victor in the Pythian Games.

korai clothed females. Normally the *kouroi* stand stiffly, one leg slightly forward and their arms held tightly at their sides and, on their faces, the famous Archaic smile. These stone statues, many of which acted as grave markers, are often life-size or larger, but their features are not sufficiently distinct to be intended as individual portraits of the deceased; these are men shown in the prime of life – an idealization of manhood. With the *korai* the situation is somewhat different: many appear in sanctuaries as dedications and, while identification remains problematic, it is felt that some may represent votaries. The *korai*, which also show the Archaic smile, are normally clothed, and various colours are used to highlight clothing, hair, jewellery, etc. While these statues are very stiff and block-like when they first appear, the sculptors gradually develop a softer approach in their work and, by the Classical period, have achieved a great degree of naturalism.

One of the major developments of the 6th century BC was the re-emergence of Athens as the leading state after having lost its pre-eminence to Corinth for about a century. This dominance is seen archaeologically in the appearance of Attic black-figure pottery which succeeded the proto-Attic style of the 7th century BC, itself characterized by Orientalizing motifs and an abandonment of Geometric conventions. The Athenian black-figure ware of the 6th century BC managed to surpass the Corinthian ware of that period and became as popular and widely exported as the Protocorinthian had been in the 7th century BC. Incision was used with such exactness and delicacy that finely detailed paintings were possible. Quite apart from the technical excellence of the pottery, the scenes that the painters chose have been an enormous and valuable source of information about all aspects of life, for Athenians are shown engaged in various everyday pursuits. Grape and olive picking are depicted, for instance, as are pottery making, sculpting, feasting, taking part in the Panathenaic Games (horse racing, wrestling, javelin throwing, etc.), going to school, and so on. Moreover these scenes have afforded glimpses of clothing and furnishing styles, of architectural details, and much more. Mythological scenes were also very popular and feature exploits of a number of heroes and deities such as Achilles, Ajax, Heracles, Athena, Poseidon, Dionysus, and the like. Signatures on the pottery help to identify individual potters and/or painters; among the most famous are Exekias and Amasis, both of whom were active in the 6th century BC.

Politically, too, Athens underwent great changes in the 6th century BC as the aristocrats were challenged, and although attempts at reform were undertaken, most notably by Solon in 594 BC, tyranny was established by Pisistratus in the late 560s BC. After twice being expelled, Pisistratus was able to take over power and command Athens until his death in 528/27 BC. Under his rule Athens flourished and, like his earlier Corinthian counterparts, he also patronized the arts and literature and did much to foster Athenian trade, commerce, and industry. The Acropolis became the centrepiece of Athens as the temple of Athena, the predecessor of the Parthenon, was begun. In general Pisistratus' reign was thus a time of peace and prosperity, but when his two sons took over power in 527 BC the character of the tyranny changed and became oppressive after one of them was murdered. The tyranny was finally overthrown in 510 BC and, two years later, in 508 BC, the Athenians developed a new type of political system, democracy, under the leadership of Cleisthenes. This gave the Athenian citizen a direct say in running the state. It should be noted, however, that women were excluded from this process. The polis system, and in Athens democracy itself, was male-dominated and women were segregated and confined to specific gender-related and socially acceptable roles. The rules governing the role of women varied, however, according to class and status as well as from place to place; in Sparta, for instance, women enjoyed a much freer lifestyle as a result of Sparta's particular social system.

The end of the Archaic period is marked by the onset of the Persian Wars (490–479 BC), caused by the expansionist policies of the Persians. In these wars the two great Persian kings, Darius and then Xerxes, were defeated by a coalition of Greeks, although the brunt of the offensive was borne by Athens and Sparta. After the extraordinary naval victory of the Athenians at Salamis in 480 BC, the battles of Plataea and Mycale the following year mark the end of the Persian threat in Greece.

A. FOLEY

See also Colonization, Philosophy, Poetry (Lyric), Pottery, Sanctuaries, Sculpture, Tyranny

Summary

Dated c.700–479 BC, the Archaic period follows the Geometric and precedes the Classical. It is marked by developments in pottery and sculpture, the architecture of temples and sanctuaries, lyric poetry, philosophical speculation, and the shift to new forms of political organization. It ends with the final defeat of Persia at the naval Battle of Mycale in 479 BC.

Further Reading

Bergquist, Birgitta, *The Archaic Greek Temenos: A Study of Structure and Function*, Lund: Gleerup, 1967

Boardman, John, *Athenian Black Figure Vases*, London: Thames and Hudson, 1974

Boardman, John, *Greek Sculpture: The Archaic Period*, London: Thames and Hudson, and New York: Oxford University Press, 1978

Boardman, John, *The Greeks Overseas: Their Early Colonies and Trade*, 4th edition, London and New York: Thames and Hudson, 1999

Bowra, C.M., *Greek Lyric Poetry from Alcman to Simonides*, 2nd edition, Oxford: Clarendon Press, 1961

Burn, A.R., *The Lyric Age of Greece*, 2nd edition, London: Arnold, 1967; New York: Minerva Press, 1968

Charbonneaux, Jean, Roland Martin and François Villard, *Archaic Greek Art, 620–480 BC*, London: Thames and Hudson, and New York: Braziller, 1971

Donohue, A.A., *Xoana and the Origins of Greek Sculpture*, Atlanta: Scholars Press, 1988

Dougherty, Carol and Leslie Kurke (editors), *Cultural Poetics in Archaic Greece: Cult, Performance, Politics*, Cambridge and New York: Cambridge University Press, 1993

Gruben, Gottfried and Helmut Berve, *Greek Temples, Theatres, and Shrines*, New York: Abrams, 1963

Homann-Wedeking, E., *Archaic Greece*, London: Methuen, 1968

Hurwit, Jeffrey M., *The Art and Culture of Early Greece, 1100–480 BC*, Ithaca, New York: Cornell University Press, 1985

Jeffery, L.H., *Archaic Greece: The City States, c.700–500 BC*, London: Benn, and New York: St Martin's Press, 1976

Johnston, Alan, *The Emergence of Greece*, Oxford: Elsevier Phaidon, 1976

Lawrence, A.W., *Greek Architecture*, 5th edition revised by R.A. Tomlinson, New Haven, Connecticut: Yale University Press, 1996

Morris, Ian, *Burial and Ancient Society: The Rise of the Greek City-State*, Cambridge and New York: Cambridge University Press, 1987

Murray, Oswyn, *Early Greece*, Brighton: Harvester Press, and Atlantic Highlands, New Jersey: Humanities Press, 1980

Payne, Humfry, *Necrocorinthia: A Study of Corinthian Art in the Archaic Period*, Oxford: Clarendon Press, 1931

Payne, Humfry and Gerard Mackworth-Young, *Archaic Marble Sculpture from the Acropolis: A Photographic Catalogue*, 2nd edition, London: Cresset Press, 1950

Polignac, François de, *Cults, Territory, and the Origins of the Greek City-State*, Chicago: University of Chicago Press, 1995

Richter, Gisela M.A., *Korai: Archaic Greek Maidens: A Study of the Development of the Kore Type in Greek Sculpture*, London: Phaidon, 1968; New York: Hacker, 1988

Richter, Gisela M.A., *Kouroi: Archaic Greek Youths: A Study of the Development of the Kouros Type in Greek Sculpture*, 3rd edition, London and New York: Phaidon, 1970

Snodgrass, Anthony, *Archaic Greece: The Age of Experiment*, London: Dent, 1980

Starr, Chester G., *The Economic and Social Growth of Early Greece, 800–500 BC*, New York: Oxford University Press, 1977

Tomlinson, R.A., *Greek Sanctuaries*, London: Elek, 1976

Archilochus

Lyric poet of the 7th century BC

Archilochus was born to an aristocratic family on Paros in the early 7th century BC, and his career and poetry exemplify trends in the Greek world during a period of great change in traditional social structures and attitudes. This was the era of Greek colonization and exploration in the Mediterranean and beyond, and Archilochus was a soldier and a wanderer, politically active, and involved in the later stages of the colonization of Thasos begun under his father, c.680 BC. Like Hesiod and the early lyric poets, his poetry moves away from the impersonal tone of Homer to one in which the individual is more prominent. The poetic persona that emerges from surviving fragments is consistently passionate, tough, practical, and impatient with pretension and traditional values: he appears as a devotee of war, poetry, women, drink, and, above all, survival.

Much of Archilochus' style and language is Homeric: no early poet could escape the influence of Homeric formulaic language, although Archilochus himself probably composed in writing rather than orally. Different from Homer is much of its subject matter and tone. The world of proud heroes and elevated expression gives way to one where the humbler details of subsistence in a harsh environment, quite absent from Homer, are given as much attention as loftier themes. One notorious poem records the loss of the poet's shield in combat with barbarians: the poem seems unbothered by what should have been a shameful loss – "let it go, I'll get another one just as good." Later sources allege that Archilochus' works were banned from Sparta because of such unsuitable content. Far away is the Iliadic view of death as a worthy end in itself: Archilochus' view is more that of an adventurer who fights for survival, not for glory and death. While such poems strike a new and un-Iliadic note, their atmosphere is not utterly dissimilar to that of the *Odyssey*, and Archilochus' persona resembles Thersites' in some respects. Very Odyssean is one poem in which he encourages his heart "neither to rejoice too much in delights nor be too vexed in troubles, knowing what sort of rhythm possesses man". His attacks on grandiosity and pretension are sometimes thought to reflect a newer, more egalitarian spirit in the newly founded city states of the Archaic age.

Ancient critics consistently link Archilochus with two great predecessors, Homer and Hesiod. His literary power is said to resemble Homer's; his attitudes and subjects are closer to Hesiod's, though he takes his individualism to a greater extreme. He is also the earliest Greek poet to write specifically about sexuality, sometimes using obscenities that are entirely missing from Homer or Hesiod. He was especially famous in antiquity for an abusive iambic poetry whose forerunner was the apotropaic ritual abuse associated with the rites of Demeter, with whom iambic verse itself seems to have had a particular connection. Paros had an old Demeter cult with which Archilochus' family may have been connected. Such traditions also influenced mock-epics such as the *Margites*, and Aristotle makes iambic verse the antecedent of comedy. The obscenities in Archilochus can be remarkably mingled with tender romanticism, and this uniquely dual tone has made him very popular with moderns. In none of his poems is this duality more noticeable than in an unusually long fragment (Page, *Supplementum Lyricis Graecis*, 5478) in which an unidentifiable speaker tries gently to persuade a young woman to make love with him – when she suggests that her sister Neobule is more suitable for him, he abuses Neobule, calling her oversexed and past her prime.

The poem was a particularly important discovery, because of the most famous tradition about Archilochus. According to later sources, he was engaged to be married to Neobule, but when her father Lycambes broke the engagement off, he assailed the family with verses so vicious that they eventually hanged themselves. Nothing specific about the betrothal is found before Horace, but evidence from fragmentary comedy (Cratinus) suggests that the story was well known in 5th-century BC Athens. While some suspect that the story is fictional and derives from misunderstood ritual abuse, the names Lycambes and Neobule do appear in the fragments, and archaeological evidence has proved the reality of some others of Archilochus' addressees. Parian inscriptions indicate that both Archilochus and Lycambes were from leading families, and thus a proposed alliance between the two is plausible. Some of the Lycambes poems were expressed as beast fables, a form derived from Asia Minor that first appears in Greek literature in Hesiod, and later in Aesop. In these, Archilochus could give full rein to his anger while appearing detached and sardonic.

Archilochus' reputation abroad was that of a dangerous, angry man, but within Paros he posthumously acquired an almost heroic status. An inscription of the 3rd century BC describes an Apolline command to honour Archilochus along with the Muses, Apollo, Dionysus, and others, in a place dedicated to his memory. While it admits that the Parians banished him for his abuse, it also mentions the mass attack of impotence sent on them by Dionysus as a punishment for the banishment, and portrays Archilochus as a poet under divine patronage, whose immortality was prophesied to his father by the Delphic oracle. A later inscription, a biography of Archilochus by Demeas (a Parian historian of the 4th century BC), records his death in battle against the Naxians. Such inscriptional evidence tells of participation in embassies and battles, and the Parians apparently remembered him as more community-minded than his fiercely individualistic reputation would suggest: only a few fragments of songs with a community emphasis now remain.

The brilliant violence of his verses brought him admiration for his talent and condemnation for his subject matter in equal measure. Pindar condemns Archilochus' anger as unattractive and unproductive, but he was popular in 5th-century BC Athenian comedy: his apparent rejection of establishment values and pretension made him attractive to the democracy. Plato mentions him in the company of Homer and Hesiod, but does not recommend his writing as edifying. He was the subject of treatises by Heraclides of Pontus and Aristotle, and the Alexandrians included him in their canon of iambic poets along with Semonides and Hipponax. Apollonius Rhodius wrote a book about him, and while Callimachus mentions his ferocity with apparent disapproval, his own iambics were a kind of Archilochean revival. Aristophanes of Byzantium and Aristarchus of Samothrace wrote commentaries on the poems, but unsurprisingly they were omitted from the educational syllabus of later antiquity because of their tone and subjects. Archilochean papyri date from the mid-3rd century BC to the 3rd century AD. The early Church Fathers preserve some references and quotations: for them, Archilochus was undeniably great but a thoroughly bad character, all too typical of pagan behaviour. The emperor Julian forbade priests to read his work. It is probable that his poetry survived plentifully at least to the 5th century AD, but after Eusebius little is heard of him for the next few centuries. It is hard to know how much survived as far as Byzantium: such quotations as we have may well derive only from anthologies. The first Renaissance edition of his poems is Henri Estienne's *Carmina Poetarum Novem Fragmenta* (Paris, 1560).

SOPHIE MILLS

Biography

Born on Paros in the early 7th century BC to an aristocratic family, Archilochus left in disgrace for Thasos where he became a mercenary, eventually dying in battle against the Naxians. Probably the first major literate poet of the Greek world, he was ranked with Homer and Hesiod by ancient critics; but there is far more passion in his verses than in those of his predecessors.

Writings

Elegy and Iambus ... with the Anacreontea, translated by J.M. Edmonds, vol. 2, London: Heinemann, and New York: Putnam, 1931 (Loeb edition; several reprints)
In *Die Fragmente der Griechischen Historiker*, edited by Felix Jacoby, 3b, Leiden: Brill, 1950, pp. 479–80
Fragmenta, edited by Giovanni Tarditi, Rome: Athenaei, 1968
In *Iambi et Elegi Graeci ante Alexandrum Cantati*, edited by M.L. West, vol. 1, 2nd edition, Oxford and New York: Oxford University Press, 1989

Further Reading

Burnett, Anne Pippin, *Three Archaic Poets: Archilochus, Alcaeus, Sappho*, Cambridge, Massachusetts: Harvard University Press, and London: Duckworth, 1983
Lefkowitz, Mary R., *The Lives of the Greek Poets*, Baltimore: Johns Hopkins University Press, 1981
Pouilloux, J. *et al.*, *Archiloque: sept exposés et discussions*, Geneva: Hardt, 1964
Rankin, H.D., *Archilochus of Paros*, Park Ridge, New Jersey: Noyes Press, 1977
Russo, Joseph, "The Inner Man in Archilochus and the Odyssey", *Greek, Roman and Byzantine Studies*, 15 (1974): pp. 139–52
West, M.L., *Studies in Greek Elegy and Iambus*, Berlin and New York: de Gruyter, 1974
Will, Frederic, *Archilochos*, New York: Twayne, 1969

Archimedes *c*.287–212/11 BC

Mathematician and inventor

Archimedes was killed in the Roman sack of Syracuse in 212 or 211 BC, which gives us one of the few firm dates in the history of ancient science; if, as a 12th-century Byzantine author reports, he was 75 years old at the time of his death, he would have been born around 287 BC. His father, Phidias, was an astronomer, so that for Archimedes science was the family trade. He came from Syracuse, and did most of his work there,

at the court of king Hieron II (and at least some of his writings were originally composed in the Doric dialect spoken in Syracuse); he also seems to have spent some time in Alexandria, and corresponded with the mathematicians Conon, Eratosthenes, and Dositheus, who were based there.

Both in antiquity and in the modern world Archimedes has principally been famous for two reasons: because of the ingenious mechanical devices he is alleged to have discovered; and through anecdotes representing him as the archetype of the scientist so absorbed in his work that he forgets about ordinary life. So it is reported that he would forget to bathe, and when his friends persuaded him to do so he would draw geometrical diagrams in the oil on his body; his death in the sack of Syracuse is said to have been brought about because he was so preoccupied with a geometrical problem that he spoke rudely to the soldier who came to capture him; most famously, while in the bath he reached a solution to the problem of how to find out whether gold that had been given to a craftsman to make a crown had been adulterated with silver, and was so excited that he forgot himself and ran naked through the street shouting "I have found it!" He is credited with the invention of a number of ingenious engineering devices. He is said to have supervised the construction of a massive 4,200-ton ship for Hieron II, and, when it was finished and no one knew how to launch such a large vessel, he supposedly devised a system of pulleys by means of which he was able to move it single-handed; this is of course impossible, because real pulleys (as opposed to mathematical concepts) waste energy through friction, and the whole story is perhaps a fiction designed to illustrate his work on mechanics, and particularly his saying "Give me somewhere to stand and I will move the world." Better attested is his construction of a number of moving models of the celestial sphere. He was also reputed to have invented the Archimedean screw (a device for raising water) and a hydraulic organ. The difficulty that the Romans had in capturing Syracuse was explained by the formidable defence put up by the war-engines devised by Archimedes. In itself this is quite plausible, since in the Hellenistic and Roman periods mathematicians were involved in the construction and use of such machines as catapults. The account was, however, embroidered as time went on, and by the 2nd century AD we are told (by Galen) that he used burning mirrors to set on fire the Roman ships. The story became a favourite one for Byzantine writers, and indeed we are told that in AD 514 the philosopher Proclus used exactly the same technique to drive the fleet of Vitalian away from Constantinople. Though the report is not plausible, and is surely based on inferences from Archimedes' work on the geometry of optics, repeated attempts have been made to show that the device could work (most recently by a Greek journalist, whose practical demonstration, though spectacular, failed to convince sceptical historians that a burning mirror could be made into a practical weapon of war).

Archimedes' interesting eccentricities, and his engineering achievements, tended to obscure the importance of his mathematical work. So when the Roman Cicero, as quaestor in Sicily in 75 BC, rediscovered the tomb of Archimedes overgrown with thickets outside Syracuse, he reported that it carried on it a representation of a sphere and a cylinder. He seems, however, to have had no idea that this represents Archimedes' discovery of the ratio of the volume of a cylinder to that of a sphere inscribed within it (*On the Sphere and Cylinder*, 1. 34). Archimedes, in fact, was not only a great mathematician, he is also the only one of the truly creative mathematicians of antiquity whose work survives to any extent (since the surviving writings of Euclid and Apollonius of Perge are largely systematizations of the work of their predecessors). In pure mathematics, his greatest work is probably *On the Sphere and Cylinder*, on the volume and surface area of spheres and segments of spheres. Other works in the same field are: *On Conoids and Spheroids*, which deals with the solids created by the revolution of conic sections; *The Quadrature of the Parabola*, which is on the area of parabolas; *On Spirals*, dealing with the geometry of the so-called Archimedean spiral; and *The Measurement of the Circle*, which calculates upper and lower limits for the value of p. In these works Archimedes uses the methods of his predecessors, and especially Eudoxus' "method of exhaustion" with great ingenuity, and sets out his results in traditional Euclidean form. Another surviving treatise, *The Sand-Reckoner*, purports to be a calculation of how many grains of sand it would take to fill the universe, but is actually a demonstration of a method of writing very large numbers using base 100,000,000. He extended the scope of mathematical method by applying it to statics in *On the Equilibrium of Planes* (on centres of gravity and the theory of the lever) and to hydraulics (a subject he seems to have invented) in *On Floating Bodies* (known only in Latin translation until a Greek text was discovered in 1899).

Archimedes' account of his work in the prefaces to his treatises makes it clear that the discovery of a mathematical proposition, and the method by which it was discovered, was quite separate from the presentation and publication of the proof in Euclidean form. In 1906 a previously unknown work of Archimedes, *The Method*, was discovered in Constantinople on a parchment of the 10th century, which had been partially erased so that a Euchologium could be written over it. In this work Archimedes shows how he originally discovered a number of the propositions that are set out in Euclidean form in his other works. He treats figures as combinations of infinitely thin strips, to which the methods of mechanics can be applied, and to some extent anticipates the methods used by the discoverers of calculus in the 17th century. Archimedes himself regarded the method as insufficiently rigorous (and so published proofs in more traditional form). The discovery of this work gives us a rare opportunity to see one of the greatest creative minds of antiquity in action.

Some time in late antiquity (probably in the 6th century AD) the more elementary of Archimedes' works (and in particular *On the Sphere and Cylinder* and the *Measurement of the Circle*) were translated from Doric into Attic Greek, presumably to make them more accessible to readers. This development may be associated with the school of Isidore of Miletus (one of the architects of Hagia Sophia in Constantinople), and is evidence of the continued use of at least some works of Archimedes in education. It was, however, not until the 9th-century revival of the study of mathematics in Constantinople that a proper collection of his works was made, which is the basis of the texts we have today.

RICHARD WALLACE

See also Mathematics, Technology

Biography

Born *c.*287 BC in Syracuse, Archimedes was the son of an astronomer. He worked mostly in Syracuse at the court of Hieron II, but he also visited Alexandria. He is best remembered for the many engineering devices he is said to have invented, but he was also one of the most creative mathematicians of antiquity. He died in the Roman sack of Syracuse in 212 or 211 BC.

Further Reading

Dijksterhuis, Edward Jan, *Archimedes*, Copenhagen: Munksgaard, 1956, reprinted Princeton, New Jersey: Princeton University Press, 1987
Heath, Sir Thomas Little, *A History of Greek Mathematics*, 2 vols, Oxford: Clarendon Press, 1921, reprinted New York: Dover, 1981

Architecture

Domestic

Domestic architecture describes the space in which people live as private individuals and, generally, as part of a nuclear or extended family. Houses, often the least documented buildings in history, are part of an organic architectural fabric that over time continuously changes and adapts to the inhabitants' ever-evolving needs and desires. Houses are also primarily the domain of women, since women usually decide the arrangement of domestic spaces, keep them in good order, and tend the animals and garden that might form part of a household. Furthermore, beyond providing shelter and a space for familial gathering, houses may also accommodate religious, commercial, manufacturing, or agricultural activities that involve the extended family. In some cases, groups of families and individuals live together in multi-family buildings, thus blurring the line between private and public spheres. A review of domestic architecture through time elucidates not only the conditions of daily and family life, but also the broader context of historical, technological, and economic change. The stylistic details of a house reveal cultural alliances and influences, both within the community and in a broader geographical context. At the same time, however, domestic architecture is markedly conservative and resistant to change. Building methods and the arrangement of space both exhibit a tenacious attachment to traditional materials, techniques, and practices, which are primarily dependent on local resources and climatic conditions. Dramatic changes in building practices are invariably the outcome of major economic, political, and demographic restructuring.

Our knowledge of Classical Greek houses is derived primarily from the 1930s excavations of Olynthus, a town in Chalcidice that was founded in 432 BC according to the Hippodamian manner. While the orthogonal street grid resulted in the erection of buildings in blocks of equal size, housing lots varied slightly in size, undoubtedly the result of individual agreements among landowners. The ground space of a typical residential block was roughly a square measuring 17.2 metres per side. Larger houses had five to seven rooms, smaller houses had one or two. All had a small, interior, south-

Architecture (Domestic): view over Mykonos town where the island house type prevails

facing courtyard, where many of the daily activities took place, notably cooking and often weaving. Several of the courtyards also had permanent altars, commonly dedicated to Zeus Herkeios. The houses were constructed of unbaked bricks, on a foundation of rubble. Pillars were mostly wooden, while the sloping roofs were covered with tiles. Water was supplied from the city cisterns or occasionally by a private cistern.

Athenian houses of the 5th and 4th centuries BC bore an affinity with those of Olynthus both in arrangement and in materials. Due to the irregular street pattern of Athens, however, both the houses and the rooms themselves were irregular in size and shape. The rooms of Athenian houses were arranged around a small, usually south-facing courtyard that could be reached either directly from the street, or through a narrow passage. In fact, the courtyard pattern is characteristic of most ancient Greek houses. Some courtyards had a porch supported by columns, on one or more sides. They were later paved with pebbles set in cement, while most floors were made of hard earth topped with clay. The walls of the principal rooms were covered with plaster and painted with a light colour wash. Literary sources frequently refer to the second storey of houses, though none has survived.

Despite the number of passing literary references to the different spaces, and their uses, within the ancient Athenian house, it is still impossible to match these descriptions to archaeological findings. For example, while texts make references to separate men's quarters (*andron* or *andronitis*) and women's quarters (*gynaikonitis*), archaeologists have been unable to identify such specific locations as little evidence exists of the character of individual rooms. This may also indicate a certain versatility of function among the rooms, depending on the season or on the special needs of the household. Another clear social distinction, that between free and slave inhabitants, is also absent from the physical remains of Athenian houses. Presumably, all men slept in the men's quarters and all women in the women's.

Women's work was confined to the house and included the care of children, the cleaning of the house and its contents, the preparation of meals and the processing of food for storage, as well as spinning and weaving to make clothing and bedding. Many professional men also used their house as a place of business. Marble cutting, pottery making, or metalworking often took place in the courtyard. Rooms that opened directly on to the street were used as offices, workshops, retail shops, taverns, or warehouses. Wealthier and poorer housing quarters were not necessarily mutually distinct. Finally, the majority of Greek towns, including, to an extent, Athens, were home to farmers who worked the surrounding countryside. Wealthier city dwellers maintained handsome residences in the countryside as well. These were not only more spacious than most of the town houses, but also more regular in plan, as the space occupied by town dwellings was restricted by the irregular street pattern.

New socio-economic conditions during the Hellenistic period brought about the creation of a new urban class of merchants, manufacturers, retired soldiers, and civil servants who prospered in the unified Hellenistic world of the Mediterranean basin and who were able to afford larger and luxurious villas. Architects experimented with new building methods and artistic trends, creating impressive domestic complexes. The layout of Hellenistic houses is similar to that of the houses at Olynthus, but larger and more elaborate. The finest surviving examples of the period are found on the island of Delos, a major mercantile centre at the time. Rooms were arranged around an interior courtyard, usually a complete peristyle with elongated Doric columns. The courtyard and the floor of the principal room often featured mosaic decorations. In the Roman period many of the houses also had an atrium, in addition to the peristyle court. As the Greek and Roman cultures infiltrated each other, their domestic worlds also grew more similar.

In the cities of the late Roman empire the apartment house (*insula*) was a more common housing type than the individual dwelling (*domus*). Two *insula*-type buildings have been unearthed in Ephesus. Constructed in the 1st century AD, they underwent several remodellings until the 7th century. There were vaulted shops on the ground floor and modest rectangular rooms on the upper floor, while a two-storey mansion formed a component of one of the *insulae*. Literary sources also confirm the existence of *insulae* in Constantinople. In fact, residents of a five-storey *insula* complained when some of their neighbours kept pigs in the upper storeys. The individual dwelling (*domus*) continued to be based on the central peristyle courtyard surrounded by rooms and other service areas. These included a bath, kitchen, latrines, plumbing and heating systems, and storage rooms.

Building laws regulated the construction of new houses or the remodelling of existing ones (*Codex Justinianus*, 8. 10. 12). A distance of at least 12 Greek feet had to be maintained between houses. Repairs to old houses were allowed, provided the original plan was not altered. New buildings had to respect neighbours' access to daylight and, especially in Constantinople, view of the sea. Balconies could only be built on streets that were over 12 feet wide, and exterior staircases from the street to the balcony were not permitted, as they could obstruct traffic and pose fire hazards.

Byzantine houses built after 1000 were of several building types. A common plan for a private residence, found in Corinth, Athens, Thebes, and Pergamum, consisted of a rectangular building with a central open space without a peristyle. Storerooms for agricultural produce, workshops, and stables were situated on the ground floor, while the living quarters were upstairs. The quality of the construction was usually poor, with rooms small and irregular and houses built on narrow alleys. New buildings were often raised against existing ancient structures, while architectural elements of demolished ancient buildings (*spolia*) were routinely incorporated into new ones. The private mansion of Attaleiates in Constantinople, described in his foundation charter of 1077, consisted of several two-storey buildings connected by a common courtyard. The mansion also included a separate three-storey dwelling with a donkey-driven mill on the ground floor and a family chapel. By the 12th century chapels and churches had become quite common in the residences of the wealthy. Adorned with paintings, marble, and lamps, these private chapels blurred the distinction between domestic and religious architecture. Similarly, the elaborate architecture of the private mansions is reflected in the middle Byzantine churches which shrank to almost domestic proportions.

In the Ottoman period travellers were often unable to distinguish between the houses of Christian and Muslim inhabitants. Stylistic differences in domestic architecture represented social rather than religious or ethnic distinctions. Travelling building groups (*bouloukia* or *tsourma*) were responsible for the most complicated structures, regardless of whether the patron was Greek or Muslim. As they travelled widely, they adapted their building vocabulary to regional practices. Some groups also disseminated the style of the major cities to the rest of the empire. Members of building groups usually came from the same village, and several groups developed secret dialects, which ensured them privacy while carrying out their work. These building groups were usually the architects of the imposing and elaborate mansions (*archontika*), which in turn provided architectural paradigms to local builders.

While, under Ottoman rule, the Greek population generally avoided the exhibition of wealth in order to escape heavy taxation, certain regions flourished as the result of foreign trade: they were notably some of the islands, and on the mainland around centres of local manufacturing. This new urban class was able to display its wealth by building impressive private mansions in Constantinople and Kastoria, in Ambelakia and Kozani, in Makrinistsa and Tyrnavos, and on the islands of Chios and Hydra, Spetsae and Psara, among other urban centres. The designs of these mansions reflect the unique architectural character of each region, and, by extension, the decentralized nature of political, economic, and cultural activity under the Ottomans.

Despite significant regional differences, there were also common characteristics that distinguished island from mainland architecture. The island house was based on a one-storey, single-space nucleus covered with a flat, stone roof. Its dimensions depended on the construction material, essentially the size of the wooden beams. The houses on the island of Santorini, with their barrel-vaulted roofs built in volcanic stone, constitute the notable exception to the general pattern. In some cases we also find two-storey houses, with storage rooms on the ground floor and living quarters upstairs. As in antiquity, most daily activities continued to take place in the courtyard. In the countryside there were also agricultural buildings for shepherds' quarters, the storage of produce, threshing, preparation of wine, and the keeping of animals. In some cases people and animals were housed in the same building (common practice in many parts of the world), the people sleeping on a higher platform. Finally, important influences in the domestic architecture of the islands between the 15th and 19th centuries came from the Venetian urban houses in Crete, the Genoese houses in Chios, and the Italianate mansions of Zakynthos and Corfu. By introducing elements of Classical and Renaissance architecture in the Greek lands, these mansions prepared the stylistic ground for the subsequent introduction of Neoclassicism in the 19th century.

While island architecture displayed distinct western influences, mainland architecture remained closer to eastern models. The two-storey middle-class house that was common in the Peloponnese, western Roumeli, and northern Greece was built to an elongated plan, with an external wooden or stone staircase leading to the *hayiati*, the covered second-storey interior balcony. Animals were kept on the ground floor, which was also used for storage and sometimes for the loom. Living space was divided into three areas: the *gonia*, with the fireplace where cooking took place and where the inhabitants slept during the winter; a small room over the entrance; and the *sala*, a formal reception area. The *archontika*, rather than being aggregate of humbler farming units, were influenced by the architecture of other urban centres and, possibly, by the local defensive towers that preceded them. As in the islands, wealthy landowners and merchants who travelled abroad often brought back western furnishings, design ideas, and even craftsmen to work on their mansions. The Greek architectural landscape thus continued to reflect the confluence of both local and external political and economic forces. After the War of Independence (1821–32) the construction of the palace, the university, the academy, and other prominent public and private buildings in Athens helped anchor northern European Neoclassicism in Greece. The first Neoclassical houses were built by wealthy residents who had lived in Europe and who often employed foreign architects and builders. Their elements were quickly copied and adapted by local builders who followed the capital's political and cultural lead.

The most dramatic changes in domestic architecture began in the years between World Wars I and II and escalated after the 1960s. In that period Athens and all other major cities were transformed into giant worksites, as each one- and two-storey house was demolished and replaced by a multi-family apartment building (*polykatoikia*). At first glance, the ubiquitous apartment building may signal the modernization of the country, giving Greek cities that elusive "European" image. It is true that a few of these apartment buildings were designed by professional architects who sought innovative ways to cater for the needs of an urbanized nation without sacrificing aesthetic and cultural precepts. The vast majority of them, however, are the work of engineers and developers whose purpose was the purely practical maximizing of buildable area and, therefore, of private profits. While this little-regulated urban building made private ownership (of individual flats) affordable to the majority of the population, it came at considerable public cost. Public spaces, parks, sports facilities, community buildings, and protected nature areas are sorely absent from Greek cities today. Architects and planners are therefore confronted with the formidable tasks of accommodating a growing population, modifying ageing apartment buildings for contemporary needs, providing open spaces in cities, and creating new areas of affordable housing, while remaining sensitive to the inhabitants' needs and to the natural environment.

ELENI BASTÉA

See also Family, Neoclassicism, Town Planning, Women

Further Reading

Bakalakis, Georgios and Iris Douskou, "Private Architecture and Palaces" (in Greek) in *Historia tou Hellenikou Ethnous* [History of the Greek Nation] vol. 5, Athens, 1974, p. 438

Bastéa, Eleni, "The Sweet Deceit of Tradition: National Ideology and Greek Architecture", *Art and Culture*, 1/2 (Spring 1990): pp. 84–99

Biers, William, R., *The Archaeology of Greece: An Introduction*, Ithaca, New York: Cornell University Press, 1980

Jameson, Michael, "Private Space and the Greek City" in *The Greek City from Homer to Alexander*, edited by Oswyn Murray and Simon Price, Oxford: Clarendon Press, and New York: Oxford University Press, 1990

Kazhdan, A.P. (editor), *The Oxford Dictionary of Byzantium*, New York and Oxford: Oxford University Press, 1991 (Houses entry, vol. 2, pp. 953–54)

Mathews, Thomas F. and Annie-Christine Daskalakis Mathews, "Islamic-Style Mansions in Byzantine Cappadocia and the Development of the Inverted T-Plan", *Journal of the Society of Architectural Historians*, 56/3 (September 1997): pp. 294–315

Philippides, Dimitri (editor), *Greek Traditional Architecture*, translated by David Hardy and Philip Ramp, 2 vols, Athens: Melissa, 1983–90

Philippides, Dimitri, *Neohellenike architektonike* [Modern Greek Architecture], Athens, 1984

Travlos, John, "Poleodomia" [Town Planning] in *Historia tou Hellenikou Ethnous* [History of the Greek Nation], vol. 3b, Athens, 1972

Tsakirgis, Barbara, "Houses and Households", *American Journal of Archaeology*, 100/4 (October 1996): pp. 777–81

Wycherley, R.E., *How the Greeks Built Cities*: 2nd edition, London: Macmillan, and New York: Norton, 1962

Wycherley, R.E., *The Stones of Athens*, Princeton, New Jersey: Princeton University Press, 1978

Fortifications

Over the centuries in the Greek world the art of fortification struggled to keep pace with methods of attack; in the long term the attacker prevailed. At times the consequent catastrophes were overwhelming, and the systems being defended collapsed, resulting in a complete regression before the process started again. Therefore no constant line of development and improvement can be traced. In addition, these aspects of warfare did not occur in isolation; external developments, new ideas brought from outside the Greek world, affected the systems employed in Greece.

The Minoan world appears to have eschewed the use of fortifications. There are no walls around the Cretan cities, implying a surprising degree of stability and peacefulness among the various communities on the island. By contrast, the mainland citadels of the Late Bronze Age were fortified, and with the passing of time these fortifications were steadily strengthened. The walls enhance the strength of places already chosen for their steep sides and difficulty of approach. Generally, they are built of massive, irregularly shaped blocks of stone that rely on their sheer weight to keep them in place and the walls intact; this may imply that attack using battering rams was anticipated, and in any case there is no doubt that the massiveness was designed to impress and so deter any would-be attacker. The systems grew up more or less fully fledged, indicating that their origin is to be sought elsewhere – without doubt the even more massive defences of the major Hittite sites, such as Boğazköy in central Anatolia. Gateways were strongly defended, projecting bastions being used to

Architecture (Fortifications): the 4th-century BC fort at Eleutherae, northwest of Athens

provide flanking protection to the actual gate, which, at Mycenae in particular, was given massive jambs and a lintel surmounted by the famous sculptured slab depicting heraldic lions facing a pillar.

Repaired where necessary (and invariably with less massive masonry), these walls served for centuries the communities that emerged from the collapse of Late Bronze Age civilization. New fortifications were rare during the early centuries of the 1st millennium BC. The best example is the walls of Smyrna, in which a high footing of carefully fitted stone surmounted by a thick superstructure of mud brick protected the city from landward attack. This dates from the late 9th or early 8th century BC, and was renewed and replaced until the end of the 7th century BC, when it had to defend the city against an attack by Alyattes, king of Lydia, who brought with him the techniques of siegecraft developed by the Assyrians, particularly overtopping the walls by constructing against them a huge siege mound. Against this the fortifications were helpless, and the same is true a little over a century later, when the Persians used a similar mound against the Cypriot Greek city of Paphos, despite strenuous attempts by the Paphians to undermine the mound by tunnelling.

Within Greece itself this siegecraft was not developed. During the 5th century BC city walls were sufficient to keep out attacks by other Greek forces. In particular, the heavily armoured infantry (hoplites) were too unwieldy, and the risk of losing citizen lives too great. Many cities therefore defended

themselves with walls, using stone footings (generally with inner and outer faces only, and a rubble and clay fill) and a superstructure of mud brick. The only practical method of attacking such a wall was to surround it and starve the defenders into submission. This was circumvented by Athens, which linked the city walls with those of its harbour, Piraeus, by means of long walls running the full 7 km between the two places, and then using its command of the sea to import food, protecting the inhabitants from starvation.

Important developments took place in the 4th century BC. Techniques of siegecraft were improved, partly by the introduction of Near Eastern methods, partly by the increased use of specialized non-citizen troops. Siege engines began to be employed, and in consequence the fortification systems had to be strengthened. A crucial development resulted from the victory of the Boeotians over the Spartans in 371 BC. Messenia was liberated, and the Boeotian leader hurriedly created a new strongly defended city at Messene. A huge circuit of more than 6 km was completed within months, allotted section by section to a multitude of constructors. The wall is made throughout of stone, with outer faces of strong rusticated masonry and rubble fill. The most significant development is the addition of towers at regular intervals, to carry missile-throwing engines and archers who could prevent an enemy reaching the curtain wall itself. Gateways were particularly strong; a good example is the Arcadian gate, flanked by towers, an outer gateway giving access only to an inner circular forecourt in which an attacker would be surrounded before being able to reach a second inner gate. Such systems began to be found in other places. In Boeotia itself there is a smaller version at Siphae which is backed by a system of free-standing watchtowers of similar construction.

Some experimentation can be seen in the methods used to build the walls. With the likelihood of direct assault on the fabric of the walls, it was found that a rubble fill might contribute to total collapse if the outer face was dislodged. Different fills, such as packed mud brick, and dividing the interior of the wall into compartments by using through stones binding the inner and outer faces together at intervals, were tried. At the same time, siege engines improved. Philip of Macedon and, especially, Alexander the Great had formidable arsenals of such weapons. Alexander's engines were thwarted only by the walls of Phoenician Tyre, of extra large blocks and gypsum mortar, until he found a weak spot that he could attack by sea. By the end of the 4th century BC systems were extremely sophisticated, but even the walls of Rhodes, strengthened by internal arcaded buttressing, were breached by the elaborate siege engines of Demetrius, and only a desperate defence saved the city. Demetrius' siege engines included a massive mobile tower called the Helepolis, the Taker of Cities, which earned him the nickname of the Besieger; Rhodes was his only failure.

Thus the final phase of Hellenistic Greek fortification had to be designed to keep the siege engines at bay; once they reached the wall, it was virtually doomed to collapse. This was done by providing taller towers that held whole batteries of counter-siege engines, enfilading the wall as well as firing outwards, and by constructing outer systems (proteichismata) of secondary walls with deep ditches in front to prevent the heavy and cumbersome engines of the attacker getting close enough to the walls. Parts of the *proteichisma* of Athens, recently excavated, have in front a sheer-sided ditch 6 m in depth. The strongest and most elaborate of these systems was built late in the 3rd century BC at Syracuse in Sicily, designed by the great scientist Archimedes, but even this failed, after a bloody siege by the Romans.

Despite this, most Hellenistic cities were surrounded by fortification systems so extensive that many of them are well preserved. There are excellent examples at the Greek or Hellenized cities of Asia Minor. Heracleia by Mount Latmos, close to Miletus, is a good example. Miletus itself must have had similar walls, and one of the largest circuits is that at Ephesus. Both Heracleia (a small city) and Ephesus have walls that, like those a century or so earlier at Messene, include a much vaster area than needed for developed habitation, either anticipating expansion or, more likely, leaving room to receive people evacuated from the surrounding countryside in time of war. The walls of Ephesus certainly, and probably also Heracleia, were built for the Successor king Lysimachus, who took over the region after the battle of Ipsus in 301 BC. The walls are of good ashlar, built on the compartment system. Where they run up hillsides, the rock is carefully trimmed in steps to receive the blocks. Towers are generally square, but there are some circular ones, including at Ephesus a massive tower towards the seaward end of the wall. Such walls serve a variety of functions, even if it must have been accepted that they were bound to succumb to a protracted siege vigorously maintained. They certainly gave routine security against brigandage and small-scale attack, but, most important, they gave their possesors a sense of pride. At some places, such as Perge in Pamphylia, one gets the feeling that the walls, and especially the main gate, were intended as much to look impressive as to be militarily effective.

With the development of Roman authority, military needs changed. The Romans learned their siegecraft from the Hellenistic Greek specialists. The engineers who developed the siege engines worked in a Hellenistic context. Vitruvius, who was Julius Caesar's engineer, certainly knew the engines invented and described in treatises by his Hellenistic predecessors, to whom he refers in his own *De Architectura*. Methods of fortification were vastly improved by the development of concrete construction techniques, which at last made the fill so permanent and durable that any outer facing employed was for decorative purposes only. Moreover, the extension of the empire and the creation of the Pax Romana removed the need for fortifications from the cities of the Greek world. Where walls were retained they were obviously for secondary purposes only, local security, and local pride. The real defence was on the frontiers of the empire.

The incursion of invading peoples into the Aegean area in the 3rd century AD brought a sudden reversal of this situation. Many places were to all intents and purposes undefended. Athens was attacked and sacked by the Heruli in AD 267. A new system of defence was necessary. This had to take account of the fact that a Greek city like Athens no longer had a significant army of its own, or Roman troops to help. It would have to rely on its own limited resources, and this meant that it could no longer hope to defend a circuit as long as that which had surrounded the Classical city, and which, though ruined, survived in part. A new circuit was therefore created, consid-

erably reducing the length of wall and the area defended. This can be seen most clearly in the Agora, most of which was now outside the wall – generally referred to as the "Valerian" wall, after the contemporary emperor at Rome – but this in no way implies that it was an official imperial creation. The wall itself is plainly makeshift. It was made from reused elements of demolished Classical buildings, forming a line of solid but unmortared masonry. At sections, it includes actual buildings; the stoa of Attalus, at the eastern edge of the Agora, survived relatively well preserved because its main structure was incorporated into the new defences. The Agora itself was razed almost completely, not by the Heruli but to create an open zone devoid of cover for an enemy in front of the wall. Beyond this area, the temple of Hephaestus remained intact. The wall ran up to the entrance of the Acropolis. No attempt was made to refortify the Classical Propylaea; instead, a new gate with a small opening and flanking bastions was created, again from reused material, a little below. Everything looks makeshift. It is not constructed according to the latest systems of military works, and, except in so far as it reuses material, it is not a revival of older Classical systems. The city soon redeveloped to include areas outside this wall, but sections of it, particularly on the Acropolis, remained to be incorporated into later medieval fortifications.

Athens in the 3rd century AD is an example of what a Greek city was able to achieve relying entirely on its own resources. Constantine's city of New Rome, Constantinople, represents the opposite extreme, fortified with the full resources of the imperial authorities. The main landward wall, the Theodosian, was laid out in the early part of the 5th century AD. It was built largely of mortared stonework, with regular stringcourses of brick, in the manner that had evolved for Roman concrete construction at the time of the early empire; the obvious comparison is the walls built in the 3rd century AD by Aurelian at Rome. It incorporates larger blocks of stone, for decorative effect rather then necessity, and where a special effect was felt appropriate, there are elements completely faced in good squared masonry; this was particularly so at the Porta Aurea, the great Golden Gate. Such masonry here was a direct revival of the appearance, at least, of the Classical and Hellenistic walls. The wall itself had a regular series of tall towers, placed at intervals of 50 or 60 m. Most were square, some were octagonal, mostly occasionally but near the Golden Gate alternating with the square examples. In front of the wall was a *proteichisma*, lower, but like the main wall, battlemented. It also had towers, but these were not much higher than the wall itself. In front of this was a deep ditch, vertical sided, the sides being supported where necessary by masonry. This was a strong system. Maintained, but not essentially altered in character, it survived as the main defences of the city, and sufficed for resistance to all attacks, perhaps the longest survival of a defensive system, until the Turks set about it with cannon and gunpowder in 1453. Yet, apart from the use of mortar in its construction, it was little modified from the Hellenistic walls of the 3rd and 2nd centuries BC. All the elements in its layout are found in the walls of Hellenistic Athens, and, particularly, in Archimedes' great defences at Syracuse. It is an important example of a continuing military tradition.

Other Byzantine walls may be less spectacular. Many of the cities in the Byzantine empire were already important in the

Hellenistic age. Here the fortifications are often merely the earlier walls repaired and altered as necessary with mortared rubble. Such walls are found on Acrocorinth, for instance, incorporating sections of the gateway of the fortress built by Demetrius the Beseiger. Even with the coming of the Turks and gunpowder, such walls were frequently maintained and defended by garrisons as late as the War of Independence.

R.A. TOMLINSON

See also Siegecraft, Technology, Warfare

Further Reading

Adam, Jean-Pierre, *L'Architecture militaire grecque*, Paris: Picard, 1982

Lawrence, A.W., *Greek Aims in Fortification*, Oxford: Clarendon Press, and New York: Oxford University Press, 1979

Lawrence, A.W., "A Skeletal History of Byzantine Fortification", *Annual of the British School at Athens*, 78 (1983): pp. 171–227

Müller-Wiener, Wolfgang, *Bildlexikon zur Topographie Istanbuls*, Tübingen: Wasmuth, 1977 (Landmauer and Porta Aurea entries)

Winter, F.E., *Greek Fortifications*, London: Routledge, 1971

Military, and Masonry Developments

Military architecture from the ancient world survives in the form of city walls and citadels, and linear walls with towers. The main features of ancient fortification can best be seen in Greek wall building.

City fortification is probably as old as the formation of the city itself. Herodotus tells us that the seven walls of Ecbatana, built in the 9th century BC, were concentric, and towers can be seen on Assyrian reliefs depicting military sieges. A well-preserved early example of city walling is at the Hittite capital of Hattusas, Boğazköy in Asia Minor. It has an earth glacis or berm lined with stone at the base of the wall. On the top was either wooden palisading or mud-brick walling. The warring Greek city states improved on these examples, adding their own innovations.

The Lion Gate at Hattusas has a straight principal entry, like the Lion Gate at Mycenae, and both these gates were strengthened spiritually by the presence of the religious sculptural decoration. The idea of a spiritual aid to defence continues into the Byzantine period, when gates were dedicated to Christ or the Mother of God or to a saint. The gates or guardian towers often had a chapel incorporated in them, usually on the first floor.

The Lion Gate at Mycenae testifies to the importance attached to the defence of city gates. It was placed at an angle in the walls so that attackers approaching the gate on the road beneath were subject to flanking fire before they actually reached it and, in addition, it has a defensive bastion on the opposite side to the city wall. The obvious importance of the gate to any fortification is echoed by literary tradition which describes how each of the seven leaders in the Theban war was in command of the attack on one of the seven gates of the city, and that six of them were killed. At Troy a legend has it that Achilles was wounded by an arrow in the heel while attacking the Scaean Gate, which suggests defensive fire from a flanking bastion. By the 4th century BC the more developed form of a gate flanked by two defending towers can be seen at Messene. This type became the standard defence to the principal gate of many cities in the Greek, Roman, and Byzantine periods, since such towers offset the weakness of the gate itself. At the same time they provided protection for an orderly sortie of counter-attacking cavalry or infantry. In times of peace, such a gate was also used for important fêtes and processional purposes. Two other forms of gateway appear in Greece from the 5th century onwards. The bent gate forces an enemy to turn a corner between heavily defended walls before he reaches the gate. A development of the bent gate in Byzantine and crusader times provided for a second or even a third bend inside the principal gate so that, if the besiegers broke it down, they still lacked clear access to the town or citadel that they were attacking. The postern gate served the defenders as a secretive means of communication with the outside world and as a means for covert counter-attack. A postern gate appears at Hattusas, Boğazköy, and was not an invention of the Greeks, but it became a regular element in Greek, Roman, Byzantine, and Frankish fortification.

Walls and towers antedate ancient Greece, but from the Bronze Age onwards the Greeks made great developments in wall construction. Early Cyclopean masonry can be seen at Tiryns and Mycenae. It is typified by the use of huge blocks of irregular masonry shored up by smaller stones and backed by earth and rubble. From the 5th century BC onwards there was a rapid development of masonry types. For their strength these mainly rely on the masonry surfaces of the wall, which were backed up by a core of earth and rubble and could absorb the shock of a missile or the impact of a ram. The surface blocks were made of regular ashlars fitted closely together. The setting pattern for these blocks developed in the Classical period. Instead of regular blocks laid in horizontal courses with the long side outwards, a pattern of headers and stretchers was developed that greatly strengthened the wall. The headers went deep into the earth and rubble core and gave much greater stability. This type of walling, known as casemate walling, probably derives from timber bonding, which was used in mud and masonry walls from the time of the Old Testament onwards (1 Kings 6: 36). A second development was the use of embossed masonry, which can be seen in the 4th-century BC fortifications of Aegosthena and Messene. Whereas ashlar blocks had a smooth surface, the embossed block had smooth margins at the edges while the rest of the surface was rough hewn and irregular. It was designed to dull or deflect the impact of missiles. Its efficacy is reflected in its long history that ends only with the decorative use of it as rusticated masonry in the Baroque period in western Europe.

The early historical development of masonry that makes use of lime mortar as opposed to earth has yet to be charted. It is of vital importance not only to military building but to all architecture since lime mortar transformed the wall into a single strong structural component; earlier, it had consisted of the two elements of fitted surface blocks with an interior core of earth and rubble filler. Vitruvius names an early type of lime mortared walling – *opus incertum*. He remarks that this walling is much stronger than *opus reticulatum* and attributes it to the Greeks, and says that it is not to be made light of. Philo of Byzantium, writing in the 2nd century BC, refers to mortars and to the use of *gypsos*, which may be gypsum rather than lime. However that may be, his lack of emphasis on the use of lime suggests that he did not fully understand its potential. It was the Roman military engineers and builders who made the greatest advances in the use of lime mortars and lime concrete, and their technical advances were in turn made use of by the Greeks in the Byzantine period. The massive Slav invasions of Greece from the 5th century onwards and the Persian invasions of Asia Minor in the 5th and 6th centuries AD followed by the Arab invasions in the 7th to 9th centuries, saw the transformation, and often the virtual destruction, of the great Greek and Roman cities of the plains. There was a need for rapidly built and efficient defensive walling, and the type of masonry favoured by Byzantine military engineers was the Vitruvian *opus incertum* or mortared rubble wall, with a bonding system of either brick or timber. This could be constructed under the supervision of a military engineer with the use of unskilled labour, most probably the soldiers themselves with the help of forced levies of the local population to bring in stones. It did not require a large force of skilled masons to perform the slow task of shaping ashlars for the smooth surface of a wall. Nor did it require stone suitable for cutting and shaping, since any shape or size of stone could be firmly bedded into the wall mortar with its smoothest face to the outer surface. The outer surface of the wall was protected from water penetration by a shelter coat of lime plaster. In the Byzantine period from the 6th to the 15th century there are numerous examples of *opus incertum* military walling scattered throughout Greece, the Balkans, and Asia Minor. Unlike ashlar walling, *opus incertum* does not look elegant or impressive, and it is difficult to date unless it incorporates inscriptions, brick bonding courses, or decorative features. It has not attracted much attention from Classical scholars because it is not aesthetically pleasing, but its legacy was of fundamental importance not only in military architecture but in all workaday building in the medieval and modern world until Portland cement replaced lime mortar.

The two main categories of military architecture lie in the defence of cities and the defence of frontiers. In the siting and defence of cities the Greeks carried on an ancient tradition of using naturally defended sites: either around a hilltop as at Mycenae, or in the case of ports by using natural ravines. Such natural defences could be improved by rock clearance or ditching. The Greeks concentrated on the development of hilltop citadels such as Aegosthena or Acrocorinth to serve as a final stronghold if the walls of the city were to fall. A Greek city in the plains such as Mantinea was an exception that only became the rule after the Roman conquest; it was not until the 3rd century AD, with the Gothic invasions, that there was an enemy of consequence. In the Byzantine period cities often reverted to Hellenistic hilltop sites and it is not uncommon to find a city with the original Greek ashlar masonry at the base of the wall and Byzantine mortared rubble masonry in the higher courses.

Linear fortifications were used at Athens to link the city with its port and at Acrocorinth to link city and citadel, but they were more suited to frontiers or to the creation of walled mountain refuges that sheltered the whole population of an area with its livestock. Thus the walls of Messene enclose not just a city but a whole landscape. During the Peloponnesian War a defensive wall across the base of the peninsula was planned. Another example is the Byzantine long wall of Thrace.

In both city walls and linear fortifications towers were a regular feature. But once again it was the Greeks of the ancient world who seem to have made the most significant developments in the construction of towers. Early towers seem to have been an integral part of wall construction. They were conceived as vantage points, higher than the adjoining wall, and by projecting a little they acted as buttresses from which flanking fire could be directed upon the attackers. By 304 BC towers that were structurally independent of the walls had been developed. At Rhodes Demetrius Poliorcetes destroyed the curtain wall to either side of a tower, but he was unable to take the tower itself. The text of Philo of Byzantium on the subject of towers is ambiguous, but he does appear to suggest that some towers were structurally independent of the walls, and that they were heightened by the addition of a smaller turret on the top level. The archaeological evidence for the upper work of towers is lacking since none survives intact, but in the 6th century AD Procopius describes independent tower keeps that were forerunners of the medieval keep. No Byzantine examples survive, but their existence is suggested by 16th-century Ottoman examples, such as the White Tower at Thessalonica, and the three great towers of Rumeli Hisar outside Constantinople. In the individual forms of towers and in the traces of walls the ancient Greeks were also innovators. They built towers that were rectangular, round, and U-shaped. Philo of Byzantium seems to recommend the pentagonal, prow-shaped tower. Its pointed shape served well to deflect missiles, and it was a favourite choice in Byzantine fortifications. A version even survived to form a part of artillery fortifications from the 16th century onwards. Philo of Byzantium also describes a wall traced on the pattern of saw teeth. A good example is the 9th-century walls of the Byzantine city of Ankara.

The modern visitor to Greece will be struck by the many medieval castles that are labelled Frankish. Mistra is one example, said to have been built by Villehardouin. The fact that there is a Byzantine chapel in the citadel and that the wall construction is basically Byzantine suggests that Mistra and many other Greek medieval sites were of Byzantine construction but occupied and repaired by the Franks. Another prominent feature of the Greek landscape is the massive artillery fortifications built by the Venetians and the Turks in the 17th and 18th centuries. These fall outside the Hellenic tradition; they owe their radically new design to Italian military engineers, although the continuity of Hellenistic design may be detected in the modified shape of the prow tower.

The surviving evidence of military architecture thus shows that the ancient Greeks and the Byzantines were important developers in this field, and sometimes skilled innovators.

DAVID WINFIELD

See also Siegecraft, Technology

Further Reading

Andrews, Kevin, *Castles of the Morea*, Princeton, New Jersey: American School of Classical Studies at Athens, 1953

Bon, Antoine, "Les Forteresses médiévales de la Grèce centrale", *Bulletin de la Corréspondence Hellénique*, 61 (1969): pp. 136–208

Bon, Antoine, *La Morée franque: recherches historiques, topographiques et archéologiques sur la principauté d'Achaïe, 1205–1430*, Paris: Boccard, 1969

Foss, Clive and David Winfield, *Byzantine Fortifications: An Introduction*, Pretoria: University of South Africa, 1986

Lawrence, A.W., *Greek Aims in Fortification*, Oxford: Clarendon Press, and New York: Oxford University Press, 1979

Philo of Byzantium, Greek text in *Recherches de poliorcétique grècque*, edited by Yvon Garlan, 1974; English translation in Lawrence, 1979

Vitruvius, *On Architecture*, translated by Frank Granger, 2 vols, London: Heinemann, and New York: Putnam, 1931–34 (Loeb edition; many reprints)

Winter, F.E., *Greek Fortifications*, London: Routledge, 1971

Palaces

If palaces are defined as buildings that served as a residence and place for fulfilling the administrative duties of a ruler, it is obvious that they will not form a significant element in the architecture of Classical Greece, since at that time monarchy was not a normal political system. At other periods, before and after, the picture is different. The prehistoric societies of Greece, in their developed forms, depended on a complex, centralized administration which, presumably, was under the supreme control of individuals, though, apart from the palaces themselves, the only evidence for this is in later legend, with all the dangers of distortion that implies. There are two main types of palace found in the Bronze Age communities of Greece, the Cretan (Minoan, in the archaeological terminology invented by Sir Arthur Evans, who excavated the greatest of them, at Knossos) and the mainland (Mycenaean). Since we have no written record of how these presumably monarchical states functioned, other than references to authority in the Linear B tablets, interpretation of their palace architecture has to be based on the buildings themselves.

The palace at Knossos comprises areas that can be assigned with some certainty to residential purposes and others that functioned as storerooms, workshops, record office, and thus administrative functions; and others, less easily understood, that were probably designed to accommodate some, at least, of the religious functions of a monarch. The structure developed over a protracted period of time, punctuated by natural disruptions, particularly earthquake, before final destruction some time in the 14th century BC. The placing of the various elements round a central courtyard (a regular feature of the Minoan palaces) gives a superficial appearance of unity; in fact, it is clear from the archaeological evidence that the palace was rather the result of piecemeal development. There is no simple unity to the plan: the different sections have their own organization, and, generally, their own separate routes of access, a feature that is normal in Minoan architecture. The residential areas are on the eastern side of the courtyard. They presented two storeys to the court, though there were also basements taking advantage of the slope down from the courtyard and overlooking a river valley. Grand, wide staircases surrounding a light well led up and down. The individual rooms are spacious and well decorated. (Evans's attempt to assign occupiers to some of them, such as the "Queen's Megaron", are entirely fanciful.) A distinctive feature is the division of a room from a shaft by means of a set of folding doors set between piers. This must have been designed to control and modify the ventilation, to allow free circulation of air during the hot summers, to restrict it in the cooler winters. The religious function seems to have been served by at least one room on the opposite, western side of the court, one of the oldest parts of the palace: a lavishly decorated room, containing a solitary stone "throne", and with basins sunk in the floor, for water and possibly some purification ritual. The courtyard itself, it is suggested, may have been the location for the bull-jumping ritual depicted in Minoan art. The storage and workshop areas comprise long passages, with magazines and other rooms leading off. They are much vaster than would be required to meet the consumption of the residents in the palace: the materials stored and produced would be intended for trade, in a system of economy that would be managed and controlled by the centralized palace authority.

The Mycenaean palaces developed later, after the apparent collapse of Minoan Crete, and were obviously influenced by their Minoan predecessors, whose centralized political and economic systems they probably imitated. There is, however, a significant architectural difference. The central element is a rectangular hall building, divided into an open porch, with two columns, and a square room, sometimes separated from the porch by an antechamber. This was the formal area of the palace. It contained a large central hearth, too big and too magnificent to be merely for heating, and which presumably had some ritual significance. The room may have functioned as an audience chamber, or perhaps the place where the monarch consulted some form of council. It is generally assumed that it corresponds to the room where the kings of the Homeric poems carried out such functions, and the term given to it by Homer, the megaron, is normally applied to its Mycenaean predecessor. In addition, there were often subordinate rooms of similar plan, and, as on Crete, archive and storerooms for a similarly centralized administrative and economic system.

After the collapse of these complex systems, the divided Greek communities may still have been ruled by individuals; a monarchical system, dualized, survived at Sparta throughout its independence, and there were kings even in the Classical period in more backward areas, such as Epirus and Macedon. The houses of these kings may have been somewhat bigger than ordinary dwellings, or placed in particularly prominent locations – a good example is that at Emporio on Chios – but they were of no architectural pretensions, and it would be misleading to call them palaces. Under the non-monarchical regimes of the classical cities, such buildings would only exist under tyrant administrations, but there is no archaeological evidence for the form these took (the palace at Vouni in Cyprus of the 5th-century BC seems to be non-Greek in origin).

Palace architecture becomes important again with the rise of Macedon. Traditionally the Macedonian kings resided at Aegae, but the palace found there in the 19th century dates only from the end of the 4th century BC. Before then, at the end of the 5th century BC, king Archelaus transferred his administrative centre to Pella and built a palace there. This remained the palace of Philip II, and it was there that Alexander the Great was born. It was situated at the top of an acropolis hill, overlooking the city. It is currently being excavated by the Greek Archaeological Service, but it had been very thoroughly destroyed at the end of Macedonian independence and little more than its foundations survive. Its principal feature is that

Architecture (Palaces): the so-called Palace of Porphyrogennetos, now known as the Tekfur Saray, built in Constantinople in the 13th century

it incorporates five distinct courtyards, not all built at the same time, and certainly separating official from residential areas. The residential section probably dates back to the 4th century BC. We know that important artists, such as the painter Apelles, were recruited by Archelaus to decorate and embellish it, but, inevitably, nothing of this survives.

The palace at Aegae, probably built by the successor king Cassander, who wanted to revert to the older Macedonian tradition, is better preserved. It consists of two parts, a smaller courtyard structure at the back, added at a later date, and a large formal courtyard in front, overlooking the plain of the Haliacmon river. This measures 44.50 m square, and was surrounded by Doric columns, 16 on each side and made of local limestone. The entrance is at the centre of the east side, into which it is incorporated. It is marked by two marble piers, each fronted with engaged Ionic half columns, and gives a degree of formality and axiality that is not found in ordinary Greek houses. To the left of the entrance, and entered from the court, is a circular room containing a throne, probably religious in function, dedicated to Heracles Patroos. As far as can be seen from the remains (not all are well preserved), the other rooms that surround the court were all designed for formal feasting. Those on the south side were particularly splendid, two being entered from a vestibule with marble half columns recalling those of the porch. Their floors had magnificent mosaic decoration. Those on the west had space on the

surrounding plinths for 30 dining couches. Despite their dimensions, 16.74 by 17.66 m, they were roofed and tiled, with the largest unsupported spans known in Greek architecture, an indication of the superior quality of Macedonian timberwork. The graduation of size and splendour (the floors of the largest rooms were paved with broken fragments of marble only) suggests the hierarchy of the Macedonian court. The whole concept, which was probably anticipated at Pella, was influenced by the Macedonian tradition of erecting large (100-couch) temporary dining pavilions or tents in sanctuaries for particular religious occasions. Such a pavilion was taken by Alexander on his campaign of conquest.

These Macedonian palaces must have influenced the palaces of the successor kings who established themselves in the different fragments of Alexander's empire, though little archaeological evidence survives for them. At the same time the Persian royal tradition was also influential. At Pergamum, which became the capital of an independent kingdom in the second half of the 3rd century BC, there survives on the top of the hill on which the city was built a group of houses that would have served the royal family. They have good-quality mosaic floors, but apart from their select position have nothing special about them to distinguish them from the better-quality Hellenistic houses.

More important was the palace of the Ptolemies at Alexandria. There are no surviving archaeological traces of this, though evidence for its position has been confirmed by recent underwater research in the adjoining harbour area. Literary evidence gives us some idea of its arrangement and what it comprised. The city had been founded by Alexander as a place in which he could gather the existing Greek settlers in Egypt. He may have intended a palace, though whether he would have regarded it in any sense as his capital in Egypt is unclear. Rather, the palace was developed by his successor Ptolemy I Soter (305–282 BC) and his descendants. An area by the sea and in the northeast part of the city was designated as the royal area (Basileia). It had two main parts. The outer, which was accessible to the public, contained sanctuaries and buildings such as the Museum with its great library, and the theatre. It seems to have been an open space of parkland – it included a zoo – within the city, with the buildings spread out. There was still room in the 1st century BC for Cleopatra to build a shrine-sanctuary dedicated to her lover, Julius Caesar. The inner area, on the promontory Lochias that formed the eastern side of the Grand Harbour, was occupied by the private quarters of the royal family. Even here there seems to have been open space, and the building of which we have the fullest description was a typical Macedonian dining pavilion with 100 couches, lavishly decorated and carpeted. It was built by Ptolemy II Philadelphus (282–246 BC); we have no idea if it was anything more than a temporary structure, though the description we have, by the late author Athenaeus (*fl.* AD 200), derives from the near-contemporary Callixinus, and refers to a structure then long since disappeared.

Much more remote, and part of a very different tradition, was the palace at a Greek settlement known only by its modern name of Ai Khanum in Afghanistan. Here a large area to the west of the main road through the city was devoted to the palace. It dates from the foundation of the place in the early 3rd century BC, with a final phase of about 150 BC. It was vast, covering an area of 87,500 sq m. It was entered by way of a monumental propylaea building, and then a second propylon after the road turned through 90 degrees. This led to a large courtyard surrounded with Corinthian columns, at the back of which was an oriental-type open audience hall, with a wide room behind. Behind all this was the residential area. There are distinct Mesopotamian elements in this, though it undoubtedly belonged to a Greek ruler.

The word "palace" is itself derived from the name of the Palatine Hill in Rome, where the emperors lived. At first their residences were almost entirely in the non-Hellenic tradition of the Roman atrium house. The intention was to play down the concept of monarchy, now equated with the Hellenistic rulers, but as the imperial system came more and more to incorporate elements of the Hellenistic monarchies over whose territories it now ruled, aspects of Hellenistic palace architecture were adopted by the Romans, for example in Nero's Golden House and Domitian's palace on the Palatine.

As a result, later palaces in the Greek area echo rather the Roman type; this can be seen in the palace of Galerius at Thessalonica with its adjacent hippodrome. The same is true of the Great Palace at Constantinople, though this has suffered badly in successive destruction and rebuilding. As with the earlier imperial palaces it comprised an official, administrative area to the east, and a residential one to the west. The entrance to the official section was at the gate called Chalke, south of Hagia Sophia. Within were audience chambers, quarters for the imperial bodyguard, a church, and a 19-couch dining hall. Terraces faced southeast, overlooking the sea, while to the northwest was the Hippodrome, corresponding in its relationship to the palace with the Circus Maximus in Rome. Little of all this remains visible, though the monuments decorating the central line of the racecourse, including the serpent column taken from Delphi, survive. Written descriptions of the sumptuous decoration within give a general idea of its magnificence; excavation has revealed mosaic floors of the highest quality.

In form, this was in complete contrast to a much later building, probably of the 13th century AD, long after the Great Palace had been abandoned. This is the so-called Palace of Porphyrogennetos (Tekfur Saray), which seems much more Western in style except for the decoration of the façade. It comprises a simple rectangular plan with three floors, the first supported on vaults, the second on wooden beams. The ground floor is entered through open arcading, and there are rows of arched windows for the upper floors. Very similar, and of the same approximate date, is the palace of the Despots at Mistra. This too includes a rectangular hall on three floors, together with a more confused wing at right angles. It is now in the process of extensive restoration.

The next Greek palace follows the liberation of Greece from the Turks, and was built for the first king, Otho of Bavaria, between 1837 and 1841, to the designs of Friedrich von Gartner, when it was by far the largest building in the still small city of Athens. It is rather plain, but has good Classical detail to the windows, and a porch of ten Doric columns, as though to emphasize that it is a Greek building rather than a German *Residenz*. It now serves as the Boule, the parliament building.

R.A. TOMLINSON

See also Great Palace, Minoans, Mycenaeans

Further Reading

Blegen, Carl W. and Marion Rawson (editors), *The Palace of Nestor at Pylos in Western Messenia*, 3 vols, Princeton, New Jersey: Princeton University Press, 1966–73

Evans, Arthur, *The Palace of Minos: A Comparative Account of the Successive Stages of the Early Cretan Civilization as Illustrated by the Discoveries at Knossos*, London: Macmillan, 1921–35; New York: Biblo and Tannen, 1964

Graham, J. Walter, *The Palaces of Crete*, Princeton, New Jersey: Princeton University Press, 1987

Hood, Sinclair and William Taylor, *The Bronze Age Palace at Knossos: Plans and Sections*, Athens: British School at Athens, and London: Thames and Hudson, 1981

Müller-Wiener, Wolfgang, *Bildlexikon zur Topographie Istanbuls*, Tübingen: Wasmuth, 1977 (Grosser Palast entry)

Nielsen, Inge, *Hellenistic Palaces: Tradition and Renewal*, Aarhus: Aarhus University Press, 1994

Rice, David Talbot, *The Great Palace of the Byzantine Emperors: Second Report*, Edinburgh: Edinburgh University Press, 1958

Public Works

While domestic architecture provides shelter to individuals and families, public architecture exists primarily for the benefit of the health, safety, and wellbeing of the larger community. Public architecture caters, among other things, for the provi-

Architecture (Public): the ancient theatre at Palmyra, dating from the 2nd or 3rd century AD

sion of water, removal of waste, facilities for personal hygiene, street paving and other civic utilities, and defensive works. Public architecture, in the form of harbours and lighthouses, roads and bridges, markets, and, more recently, railways and telecommunication systems, also facilitates and encourages commerce and other exchange. Finally, public works, such as poorhouses and hospitals, schools and orphanages, police headquarters and prisons, are associated with social welfare and public order. Depending on the historical period and on the particular administration, responsibility for the undertaking and maintenance of these projects rested variously on private individuals, the city state, the Church, the local or central administration, and national or international commercial concerns. A review of representative public works provides an insight into the daily life of an average citizen, with its attendant inconveniences and occasional luxuries, and reveals the major preoccupations and priorities of various administrations.

In the cities of Classical, 5th-century BC Greece civic buildings and public works were commissioned and financed by the citizens themselves. They included roads and fortifications, temples and theatres, stoas and gymnasia, water fountains and reservoirs. In the pre-Classical period these were financed by kings and tyrants, while in the subsequent Hellenistic and

Roman eras they were often commissioned by wealthy donors and, in some cases, by the emperors themselves. Provision of water and removal of waste formed the core of most public works projects.

Although there were elaborate bathing facilities in the palaces of Crete and Mycenae, and simpler ceramic bathtubs (similar in shape to our own) in Olynthus, most people in antiquity bathed in public baths. These had separate spaces for men and women and were often located at the entrance of cities for the convenience of travellers. Public baths gained widespread popularity in Roman times, becoming large and impressive social spaces that were adorned with marble, mosaics, and statues. Public latrines, built also by the city states, similarly provided for the needs of both travellers and residents, since most houses did not have private latrines. In the Roman Agora of Athens an elegant public latrine building accommodated up to 64 customers in a generous, roughly square room. Lavatory seats, carved out of marble, were arranged around the walls. Running water continuously flushed the latrines, while an opening in the centre of the roof allowed for ventilation.

Drinking water for people and animals was supplied by wells, fountains, aqueducts, and reservoirs. In the 6th century BC the tyrant Pisistratus erected the Enneakrounos (nine-spouted) fountain in the Agora of Athens on the site of the simple spring called Kallirrhoe (fair-flowing). It became famous both for its architectural elegance and for its cool water, which was used in wedding ceremonies for the bathing of the bride. Several other fountains and wells in the Agora and the rest of the city provided water for residents and travellers, their animals and plants. In the Agora of Athens alone 400 wells were opened up throughout a 1000-year period, as indicated by pottery shards found in excavations. In Athens the supervisors of the fountains – *epimeletes krenon*, as Aristotle called them – were elected by the citizens to serve four-year terms, while less important municipal posts were assigned by lot. Care and maintenance of the water supply have always remained an upmost priority for each administration, as it directly affects the life and health of the whole population.

In the islands and other places with little rainfall, residents built private cisterns in their courtyards and occasionally public ones, like the large cistern on the island of Delos (measuring 15.5 × 6.3 m) that gathered rainwater falling in the theatre. A famous water reservoir, built in the island of Samos during the rule of tyrant Polycrates in the 6th century BC, remained in use for 1000 years. According to Herodotus, it was the work of the architect Eupalinus from Megara.

The swelling population of cities and the widespread institution of public baths increased the demand for additional water. New aqueducts transported water from the nearby mountains to central reservoirs in the cities. From there, a network of clay pipes directed the water to baths and fountains. The most elaborate fountains, called nymphaia, were monumental in size and shape, embellished with the statue of the emperor or donor and with numerous sculptures of water nymphs, satyrs, and river gods. Among the most celebrated fountain buildings in the Greek world were the nymphaeum of Herodes Atticus in Olympia and the three-storey nymphaeum of Miletus, both dating from the 2nd century AD. The Roman emperor Hadrian, who embellished Athens with several new structures, also addressed its water supply. He built an aqueduct system that collected water from the nearby mountains of Parnes and Penteli and brought it to a great reservoir in Athens, on the southeast slope of Lycabettus. The reservoir, which can still be seen today, was cleaned up and used again in 1857 and in 1925–26. Waste water along with the rainwater of the Athenian Agora was collected in a closed conduit that led to the Eridanos river. The sewer, which survives almost intact, is still in use today.

In Archaic and Classical cities roads were usually narrow and meandering. One of the most famous roads of antiquity was the Sacred Way that started from the Sacred Gate of Athens and ended 20 km away at the temple of Demeter in Eleusis. The road was 5 m wide, defined on either side by two courses of rough stones and paved with small stones and packed earth. The road was punctuated by stone markers denoting the distance from Athens. Unlike their predecessors, Hellenistic cities were laid out with generous and regular streets. Alexandria, in Egypt, featured an orthogonal street pattern with seven parallel avenues, the central one of which was 31 m wide. Each avenue was bisected by a tree-planted island 1 m wide. One side was paved and intended for people on horses, while the other side was covered with packed earth and pebbles for carriages and chariots.

The construction of harbours was also an important undertaking in ancient Greece, since most of the commercial and military activities relied on sea routes. Harbour entrances were usually wide enough for only one ship to pass through and could be closed with a chain in case of danger. Dock buildings (*neosoikoi*) housed the boats during the winter, while the boats' movable parts – sails, anchors, ropes, chains, etc. – were stored in separate buildings called tool chests (*skeuothekai*). *Neosoikoi* could be found in the Piraeus, Sunium, and other towns by the sea, while the most famous *skeuotheke*, that of Philon in Piraeus, took its name from the architect who designed it.

The Pharos of Alexandria, one of the seven wonders of the ancient world, was the most famous lighthouse in antiquity. It was built on a little island called Pharos for Ptolemy II of Egypt *c.*280 BC. It is said to have been more than 110 m high, with a light that could be seen from a distance of about 300 stadia (about 55 km) at night, while its smoke could be seen from even further away in the daytime. A broad spiral interior ramp allowed the mules to carry wood for the fire that burned at the top. The outside of the lighthouse was made of white stone and decorated with marble and bronze designs. An inscription recorded the name of the architect, who was also known for other works he completed: "Sostratos, the son of Dexiphanos, dedicates this to the gods, saviours of those who travel." Continuously repaired, the Pharos was still standing in the 12th century.

Defensive walls were often one of the most costly public works of a town. They usually enclosed all of a city's area and were expanded as a city grew. Athens, for instance, built first the Mycenaean walls (1240–1220 BC) and the Pelasgic walls, followed by the Themistoclean (479/78 BC) and the post-Herulian walls of the 3rd century AD. Ruined parts of earlier buildings including stones, unbaked bricks, and tiles were commonly incorporated into the walls, which were often built in haste. In case of danger, they provided refuge not only for a town's residents, but also for the inhabitants of the surrounding countryside.

The extensive public works established by the Romans continued to be used and maintained by the Byzantine emperors and administrators. Constantinople drew its main water supply from about 15 km northwest of the city, through an aqueduct built by Hadrian and later restored by Valens. The masonry arches which carried it a distance of 970 m still stand today. A new network of aqueducts was constructed in the late 4th century to accommodate the needs of the growing population. Additional water was supplied by large cisterns, which became the main source of water after the aqueducts fell into disuse around the 7th century. Cisterns supplied water to public baths, monasteries, and churches. The city of Constantinople, whose daily water consumption was about 10,000 cubic m, had a number of open cisterns, with approximate capacity of 900,000 cubic m, and more than 80 covered cisterns, with a capacity of 160,000 cu m. Most houses in the cities and the countryside had no plumbing. Even three-storey houses in Constantinople were often built without sewer drains. Residents obtained water from cisterns and wells and used latrines located outside the main buildings. The large public Roman latrines remained in use until about the 7th century, but apparently not beyond. Building codes regulated the construction of new latrines and other plumbing installations, such as gutters, sewers, and water pipes.

Public baths continued to play an important social role in the late Roman and early Byzantine periods. There were as many as nine public and 153 private baths in 5th-century Constantinople, with elaborately decorated interiors, featuring statues and other marble decorations. Although clergy and monks also used public baths, the Church regarded baths as centres of immorality, prohibiting mixed bathing and condemning frequent visits there by the clergy. Population decline, coupled with their high maintenance cost and the Church's disapproval, caused the gradual abandonment of public baths after the 6th century. While few remained in use in the subsequent centuries, most buildings were converted to other uses. By the 11th and 12th centuries monastic guidelines prescribed bathing from twice a month to three times a year, with the norm being once a month. The Church promoted the healing nature of bathing and allowed patients in monastic hospitals frequent or even unlimited baths. Monastic baths continued to be built throughout the Byzantine era.

The Byzantine state supported a host of public welfare institutions that tended to the sick, the poor, and the orphans: the hospital (*xenon* or *nosokomeion*), the hospice (*xenodocheion*), the old-age home (*gerokomeion*), the poorhouse (*ptochotropheion*), the orphanage, and the ecclesiastical welfare centre (*diakonia*). Byzantine philanthropy had, of course, antecedents in the pre-Christian era. What made its character unique, however, was the emphasis on spiritual salvation both for the giver and for the beneficiary and the designation of all philanthropic institutions as ecclesiastical units. Although the Church played a prominent role in public charity, some of the welfare institutions were lay sponsored, while others were directly dependent on the emperor. After the 10th century all new charitable institutions were affiliated to monastic communities.

The Ottoman empire perpetuated the tradition of public welfare with the establishment of the *waqf*, a philanthropic, income-producing foundation that expended this income on charitable purposes. *Awqaf* supported mosques, colleges, hospices, fountains, bridges, dervish convents, etc. They generated income for the support of these institutions by building and managing stable establishments that secured a steady rent: Turkish baths, bazaars, shops, bakeries, oil presses, mills, slaughterhouses, tanneries, etc. While in principle *awqaf* were established to support charitable institutions pleasing to God, in practice they also benefited individuals and contributed to the economic life of cities. The few Ottoman structures that still survive in Greece today – baths, covered markets, inns, bridges, fountains – bespeak of an extensive and well-organized network of public works for the cities and the countryside that built upon the legacies of Rome and Byzantium.

After the War of Independence (1821–32) feverish building activity signalled the new state's extensive reconstruction efforts. Initiated by prime minister Charilaos Trikoupis, public works projects between 1882 and 1895 included the construction of a 2640 km road network, 894 km of railway lines, and 6,500 km of telegraph lines. Of the extensive works carried out in harbours, bridges, and lighthouses, two clearly stand out: the draining of Lake Copais, begun in 1882 by a French company, and the opening of the Corinth Canal in 1893, an 11-year project directed by a Hungarian engineer. The belief that technological and economic progress would help Greece gain entry into the family of western Europe began to shift the country's focus from the Classical culture of antiquity to the technological culture of the present and the future. Recent efforts have improved the transport infrastructure – harbours, highways, railways, and airports – in order to encourage both the import–export market and the growing demands of the travel industry. Finally, public works have also focused on environmental projects that include the treatment of waste water dumped in the sea, reforestation and fire protection, pollution control and recycling. Greece has to balance the often competing demands of a growing economy and raised standard of living with their attendant impact on the environment and the ecosystem.

ELENI BASTÉA

See also Harbours, Railways, Theatres, Water Management

Further Reading

Clogg, Richard, *A Short History of Modern Greece*, 2nd edition, Cambridge and New York: Cambridge University Press, 1986

Demetriades, Vasiles, *Topographia tes Thessalonikes kata ten epoche tes Tourkokratias, 1430–1912* [Topography of Thessalonica during Ottoman Rule, 1430–1912], 1983 (with English summary)

Foka, Ioanna and Panos Valavanes, *Architektonike kai Poleodomia* [Architecture and Urbanism], 1992

Inalcik, Halil, "Capital Formation in the Ottoman Empire", *Journal of Economic History*, 29/1 (March 1969): pp. 97–140

Karidis, Dimitris N., "Poleodomika ton Athenon tes Tourkokratias" [Urban Issues in Athens during Ottoman Rule] (dissertation), Athens: National Technical University, 1981

Wycherley, R.E., *The Stones of Athens*, Princeton, New Jersey: Princeton University Press, 1978

Religious

In the prehistoric period the practices of religion were partly associated with the palaces, in which rooms or areas were set aside for cult purposes. In addition, there were shrines at localities that had some particular religious significance; on mountain peaks, for instance, in Minoan Crete, or in caves. There is an obvious shrine building below the citadel at Mycenae, but its religious character is attested by its contents – terracotta cult figures and frescos – rather than the architecture, which is nondescript.

Classical religious architecture begins with the revival of the Greek world following the collapse of the Bronze Age communities and its aftermath. There is undoubtedly some continuity of religious belief, though the movements of peoples may bring different cults with them, and there may have been some association of religious practice or beliefs with the ruins of abandoned structures surviving the collapse, but by and large religion was at first devoid of monumental structures, and cults might well be performed at nothing more than an open-air altar. Yet the gods were identified as persons, and inevitably could be represented, whether or not realistically, by images. References in late literary sources (especially Pausanias) to wooden cult images of great antiquity, similar to the one that survived at Athens, suggest that these were frequent, and needed to be protected from the weather. There are a number of early, simple, square buildings at Kommos, in Crete, of the early 1st millennium BC, which probably housed such images.

Architecture (Religious): Temple of Athena Nike, on the Acropolis at Athens, dating from 427–424 BC

From these simple origins there developed a regular system for the architectural requirements of Greek religion. The central act was the sacrifice, performed at an altar. Some altars were non-architectural (the altar of Zeus at Olympia was no more than a pile of ash), but normally they were built of stone, rectangular in shape, and decorated with the conventional architectural mouldings or other features (triglyph and metope systems, for example, in districts associated with Corinth). In the most elaborate examples, generally Hellenistic, the actual altar of sacrifice might be included in an elaborate architectural frame, as at the temple of Athena at Priene, or, most famously, the great altar of Zeus at Pergamum. The general rule, however, was simplicity.

The sacrifices would be attended, not only by human worshippers, but by the god, in the form of the cult image, and the greatest scope for architectural embellishment was the provision of housing for the image. This is the temple, which is literally the home of the god. Its basic form is the rectangular box, a room for the image, with a porch in front. In the simplest sanctuaries, even the porch may be lacking, but very often the temple was elaborated far beyond this. The starting point was the house as a hut. Very early temples, such as that of Apollo at Eretria, were little, if at all, distinguishable from contemporary hut houses. From this point, architectural development diverges. Houses become more complex in plan, with a multiplicity of rooms arranged round a courtyard. Temples retain the simple hut plan, but embellish it, particularly externally. The original forms use simple materials, timber, wattle, mud brick, thatch, and the only durable element is often a rough footing of field stones. During the 7th century BC the development of quarrying and stone-carving techniques led to the construction of temples built of local stone, generally a form of limestone. The decorative systems become more elaborate, with recognized standard regional forms, of the column, of the entablature the columns supported, and the embellishment of the roof. These constitute the "orders" of Greek architecture, Doric in the mainland and, generally, the west, Ionic in the islands of the Aegean and the east Greek areas. Marble is used where it is locally available (the Cyclades), while the temple of Artemis at Ephesus, supported by king Croesus of Lydia, took advantage of neighbouring quarries of marble to become the first colossal building in that material. Size was a matter of prestige and cost. Temples might increase the dimensions of their basic room, the cella, but this required internal supports (the temple of Artemis at Ephesus was unroofed). Size could also be made more impressive by the addition of external colonnades. The platforms on which these stood were stepped, but as size increased it is noticeable that often, particularly with Doric temples, it was essentially a matter of scaling up the smaller buildings: where these took three steps of reasonable dimensions to give access to the platform, the larger temples retained three steps as a convention, even though as a result they became too large to be of practical use, and special provision for access, a ramp or additional steps, would be needed at the front of the building. The 7th century BC was one of great innovation, but thereafter the forms of temple architecture were essentially static, development being restricted merely to the refinement of detail. Thus in basic appearance there is no real difference between the limestone temple of Artemis at Corcyra (Corfu), of the early 6th century BC, and

the Parthenon at Athens, built between 447 and 436 BC. Both have eight-column Doric façades. The difference lies in the proportions of the columns and the Doric order in general, the proportions of the whole building, the refinement of its lines, and the quality and style of the carved decoration applied, as well as the difference of material that makes all this possible. Similarly, there would have been little significant difference between the temple of Artemis at Ephesus of the 6th century BC and its successor, built on the same foundations after the earlier building was destroyed by fire in 356 BC.

There are relatively few colossal buildings. The average important temple seems to have been about 30 m in length and less than 15 m in width. Within this width, the cella would be reduced to around 6 m wide, giving a reasonable room for the cult statue and the deposition of sacred objects, utensils, and valuable offerings, allowing individuals to admire the interior, but certainly not affording room for anything resembling a congregation. The worshippers gathered outside, and were not accommodated in buildings. Thus it was possible for many temples – probably the majority – to be much smaller, and certainly far less elaborate. The conventional view of a Greek temple as a peripteral building, that is, surrounded on its exterior with a colonnade, is misleading.

Other buildings in sanctuaries were ancillary, aimed at providing shelter for a variety of purposes. The most frequent takes the concept of the colonnade, with the orders invented for the temples, and applies them as façades for long, open-roofed porticoes, or stoas. They might provide shelter for worshippers, or for objects deposited in the sanctuary that could not go into the temple. They were useful for defining lines, and so, often, the boundaries of the sanctuary. They would not be so solidly built as temples, and thus are not so durable. Other buildings were more specialized. The core of the cult practices in most sanctuaries was the ritual consumption of the sacrificial victims, the meat being roasted and shared among the worshippers. Mostly it would be consumed alfresco – inevitably, given the thousands who would attend the major festivals – but in many sanctuaries buildings were provided to accommodate the couches on which a privileged few might recline. These often have a porch, with rooms accommodating 11 couches round their walls. Some provide more accommodation. The great banqueting building at Epidaurus had six 11-couch rooms, but also two large halls each holding more than 100. Such buildings were invariably arranged round a courtyard, and this principle, adapted from the now normal form of the Greek house, could serve a variety of other purposes, particularly the enclosed exercise ground. Other specialized buildings are found attached to sanctuaries, perhaps in an area away from the temple/altar complex, such as the open-air theatres and music buildings (odeia), and the stadium for athletic contests. Where a cult placed particular significance on performance, the theatre might well be architecturally dominant, with only an insignificant temple, as in the sanctuary of Dionysus at Athens. The entrance to the sanctuary on occasions (but not always) might be given an elaborate gateway building or propylon, two colonnaded porches placed in front and behind a wall with the actual door openings. The coherence of all these structures within the sanctuary would normally depend on the repetitive use of the architectural order; though use of the orders soon spread outside the sanctuaries, they originated specifically in the religious context.

Some sanctuaries might require special buildings. Major sanctuaries, like Olympia or Delphi, which were international in character, were often given buildings as offerings by individual cities to the presiding deity; these "treasuries" generally took the form of miniature temples. Others had particular cult requirements, the most important being those cults where the ritual involved the performance of secret procedures seen only by people who had been initiated into the cult. Foremost was the cult of Demeter and Kore at Eleusis, where a large enclosed and roofed building was put up (following earlier and smaller structures) in the 5th century BC; eventually, this too was given a colonnaded porch.

Such sanctuaries continued to be built and used during the Roman period; the Roman form of temple was similar, but generally stood on an elevated podium, approached only from one end. There are surprisingly few specifically Roman-form (as opposed to chronologically Roman) temples in the Greek world, except at places such as Corinth, which had now become actual Roman colonies. Generally, Greek religion remained loyal to the Greek type of temple.

The acceptance by the Greek world of Christianity brought about a profound change. The new religion was both initiatory and congregational; it required closed buildings in which the ritual could be performed, but large enough to accommodate the congregation. The model for this therefore was not the pagan sanctuary with its outdoor altar and sacrifices, but the Roman basilica, a building form that had developed in the 2nd century BC, almost certainly from Hellenistic royal origins (hence its name), but used by the Romans essentially for secular purposes: legal actions, political gatherings, commercial transactions. It would normally be one of the buildings attached to the forum of a Roman city, and comprised a rectangular hall with a platform for a presiding magistrate or judge, usually at one end, and formed by an apse projecting from the main hall. To support the roof, it was divided along its length by two rows of columns supporting a clerestory, with the roof itself carried on wooden beams. Because of developments in Roman woodworking technique it was now possible for the central nave to be reasonably wide; together with the aisles to either side it could hold a congregation easily. In secular Roman architecture the form of the building remains conservative for most of its history. The columns bear a horizontal architrave, and the roof supports remain wooden.

Such a building required virtually no modification to serve as a church. The apsidal tribunal, filled with semicircular tiers of seats, accommodated the priests. Privacy was maintained during services by the construction of a closed porch across the front of the building, the narthex, to which the catechumens, those seeking to become members of the church, would be admitted and from which they could glimpse the proceedings. Outside this, and in major examples, an enclosed colonnaded court provided additional privacy. Such Christian basilicas were built at Rome (Old St Peter's, San Paolo fuori le Mura) and at Constantinople, as well as in the older Greek cities. There was a particularly large and splendid basilical church at Lechaion, the harbour town of Corinth.

An alternative form of church developed in the Greek areas. It seems to have originated with a special type of building

devised to embellish burial places, particularly of people designated saints; a most important example was the church covering the Holy Sepulchre in Jerusalem. For this an alternative Roman form of construction, the dome, was adopted. In the first instance it came over circular buildings, and is obviously related to a whole range of Roman secular structures. At the same time, there were large roofed halls in other structures, where the roofs were not supported by wooden beams, but formed by concrete vaults, particularly the great cross-vaulted cold rooms, the frigidaria, of Roman imperial bath buildings. One secular basilica, that of Maxentius and Constantine at Rome, had already employed this system in a freestanding building. The new development was to combine the domed structure with the vaulted hall, using the device of pendentives to transfer the circle of the dome to a square of massive piers linked by arches. In front of this, the nave and aisles would be vaulted over piers linked by arcades; behind, the projecting apse, as in colonnaded basilicas, was covered with a semidome. Subsidiary domes might replace the vaults in the body of the church. Such construction culminates in the great churches of St John at Ephesus, and Hagia Sophia at Constantinople. Although there is no hard and fast rule, later churches in the Greek east tend to the domed form, those in the west the basilical. Thus it was the Orthodox domed church that influenced the Islamic architecture of the Ottoman empire, while in the west the basilica led to the medieval cathedral.

The subsequent influences of Greek religious architecture are varied. The form of the Classical temple, or rather of its colonnaded porch, can be adapted to a range of buildings, and this was done particularly when direct knowledge of ancient Greek architecture was reacquired in the 18th century; through Roman architecture, similar porches in the Corinthian order were already added to churches. Perhaps the oddest example of a revival of ancient Greek forms is the church of St Pancras in London, which incorporates, most incongruously, the decorative forms, including the porch of the Maidens, originally used at the Erechtheum at Athens. That this was unsuitable for church architecture was noted almost immediately.

R.A. TOMLINSON

See also Altars, Hagia Sophia, Sanctuaries

Further Reading

Berve, Helmut and Gottfried Gruben, *Greek Temples, Theatres, and Shrines*, New York: Abrams, and London: Thames and Hudson, 1963

Dinsmoor, William Bell, *The Architecture of Ancient Greece: An Account of its Historic Development*, 3rd edition, London: Batsford, 1950

Krautheimer, Richard and Slobodan Ćurčić, *Early Christian and Byzantine Architecture*, 4th edition, New Haven, Connecticut and London: Yale University Press, 1986

Lawrence, A.W., *Greek Architecture*, 5th edition, revised by R.A. Tomlinson, New Haven and London: Yale University Press, 1996

Milburn, Robert, *Early Christian Art and Architecture*, Aldershot, Hampshire: Scolar, 1988

Tomlinson, R.A., *Greek Sanctuaries*, London: Elek, and New York: St Martin's Press, 1976

Archives

Antiquity

Archives, in the modern sense of the term, were slow to appear in ancient Greece and even then never really corresponded to their modern counterparts in form or function. Oral tradition remained paramount at least until the 5th century BC. Written documents were not necessarily viewed as authoritative or considered important in and of themselves until relatively late in the Classical era. While the Mycenaeans certainly created written records, as witnessed by the many surviving tablets in Linear B, little can be said about their retention and organization. Record-keeping remained sporadic and unsystematic throughout the Archaic period. Cities often recorded important public documents, such as laws, lists of officials, and treaties, on stone. These inscriptions might be found in a variety of locations and in no way constituted a single collection of public records, although groupings of inscriptions are sometimes referred to as archives. Both individuals and cities often used temples as repositories for documents; Heraclitus, for example, allegedly deposited a copy of his writings in a temple of Artemis. Records not deemed worthy of stone were consigned to less durable media, such as wooden tablets (*pinakes*), whitened boards (*leukomata*), and papyrus.

Athens instituted a central archive, the Metroon, in the late 5th century BC (probably between 409 and 405 BC). This was placed in the old council house (Bouleuterion), when a new council house was built on an adjacent site. The building served as a shrine to Demeter as well as the archive, hence the name Metroon. The archives were under the jurisdiction of the Council (Boule) and were staffed by public slaves. It is likely that the contents originally consisted largely of council documents: decrees, correspondence, treaties, etc. As in the past, the keeping of administrative records usually remained in the hands of the individual officials. Many of these officials failed to keep records or treated them as temporary mnemonic devices to be destroyed once their purpose was served. Later in the 4th century BC other documents, such as laws, came to be placed in the central archives. Individuals began depositing personal documents in the public archives at some point in the late 4th century BC. Epicurus deposited his will (Diogenes Laertius, 10. 16) and probably copies of many of his writings in the Metroon.

By the later 4th century BC the use of written documents was increasing. Greek cities of the 4th century BC and Hellenistic period usually had an archive or record office. These served as depositories for the original copies of public records, usually on papyrus or parchment. Private documents, such as contracts and wills, were also frequently deposited in city archives (Aristotle, *Politics*, 1321b). Important public documents might be inscribed on stone in a public place as well; these have sometimes survived. The contents of these "stone archives" tended to be selective and focused on a particular theme. The documents often concerned the rights and privileges of the city. At Priene a small archive on stone preserved decrees and letters of Alexander the Great and Lysimachus that apparently granted various rights to the Prienians. Similarly at Aphrodisias a number of inscriptions document relations between the city and Rome from the late Republic to the time of Septimius Severus with the aim of establishing grants of autonomy and immunity to the city by Rome. Local cults and festivals also figure prominently in Hellenistic inscriptional archives. An example is an archive from the agora of Magnesia-on-Maeander, which concerns the Panhellenic festival of Artemis Leukophyrene.

The best-known and most developed Greek archives are those found in Ptolemaic and Roman Egypt. These tended to be more elaborate than those found elsewhere in the Greek world, reflecting the highly bureaucratic nature of Egyptian society. In addition to the central archive in Alexandria, each district (*nome*) had its own archive, which kept records of many private transactions as well as official ones. Many larger villages had their own record offices (*grapheia*) which kept local records and sent copies or summaries of these to the *nome* archives. The workings of the *grapheion* in the village of Tebtunis during the 1st century AD are particularly well understood thanks to the many surviving documents. In the Roman period the *nome* archives also sent summary records to the central archive in Alexandria. Many private archives of Graeco-Roman Egypt also survive in part. While some of these represent accidental groupings of related papers, others indeed represent conscious record keeping by individuals or families. Some of the better known archives of this type include those of Zenon (3rd century BC), Nemesion (1st century AD), Heroninus (3rd century AD), Aurelius Isidorus (4th century AD), Abinnaeus (4th century AD), and Dioscouros of Aphrodito (6th century AD).

FRED W. JENKINS

See also Inscriptions

Further Reading

Bagnall, Roger S., *Reading Papyri, Writing Ancient History*, London and New York: Routledge, 1995

Boegehold, Alan L., "The Establishment of a Central Archive at Athens", *American Journal of Archaeology*, 76/1 (January 1972): pp. 23–30

Clay, Diskin, "Epicurus in the Archives of Athens", *Hesperia*, supplement 19 (1982): pp. 17–25

Harris, William V., *Ancient Literacy*, Cambridge, Massachusetts: Harvard University Press, 1989

Posner, Ernst, *Archives in the Ancient World*, Cambridge, Massachusetts: Harvard University Press, 1972

Sherwin White, S.M., "Ancient Archives: The Edict of Alexander to Priene: A Reappraisal", *Journal of Hellenic Studies*, 105 (1985): pp. 69–89

Thomas, Rosalind, *Oral Tradition and Written Record in Classical Athens*, Cambridge and New York: Cambridge University Press, 1989

Byzantium

There can be no doubt that documentary archives were compiled and carefully maintained in Byzantium. The survival of over 40,000 Byzantine lead seals is firm evidence for the production of large numbers of documents, which would have needed to be preserved, whether by secular or ecclesiastical officials, monasteries, cathedrals, or private individuals. The imperial archives in Constantinople appear to have been extensive and very well organized. According to the 6th-century writer John Lydos, the legal records of the Praetorian

Prefecture of the East were kept in vaults beneath the seating area of the hippodrome, and stretched for some 300 m. Byzantine historians often had access to the imperial archives and quoted relevant documents in their works (e.g. Anna Komnene, *Alexiad*, 3. 6. 156).

Sadly, the administrative archives maintained by the Byzantine government have now completely disappeared, those in Constantinople probably having been destroyed in 1204 or 1453. The only exception are the records of the exarchate of Ravenna, the capital of Byzantine Italy from about 568 until 751, which date from 445 onwards, and which are preserved in the State Archives and the Archiepiscopal Archives in Ravenna. The 6th- and 7th-century papyri are particularly informative about the Byzantine administration of the exarchate and the activities of soldiers and officials. Otherwise such Byzantine imperial documents that do survive have done so by chance and are preserved as isolated examples in libraries and archives all over the world. The British Library in London, for example, has a letter of the emperor Manuel II Palaiologos, dated 3 February 1401, with part of the seal still attached. Written in Latin, it thanks the king of England (Henry IV) for a gift of 3000 marks towards the defence of Constantinople (Nero, B. xi, f. 174). The work of Franz Dölger and others has done something to replace what has been lost, by compiling a chronological survey of imperial acts drawn from these isolated survivals and from references in literary works. A similar task has been carried out by B. Hendrickx for the period of Latin rule in Constantinople, 1204–61.

Much the same has to be said about ecclesiastical records as about imperial documents. The existence of the office of *chartophylax*, or Guardian of the Documents, in Hagia Sophia suggests the existence of a patriarchal archive in Constantinople, but again nothing has survived. The acts of the patriarchate of Constantinople which are recorded in literary sources have since been gathered and published by V. Grumel and others.

Yet, although the great imperial and ecclesiastical archives of Constantinople have not come down to us, some collections of documents compiled in the Byzantine period by monastic communities are still intact. Of these the most important are to be found in the monasteries of Mount Athos, which contain numerous charters of the Byzantine period, surviving either in their original form or as copies. The richest collection is that of the monastery of Vatopedi, which has about 250 Byzantine documents. The Great Lavra possesses 172 charters and acts from before 1453, the oldest being a deed of sale dated 897. The monastery of Iviron has some 150 Byzantine documents, including the will of Kale Pakouriane (1090), which gives a detailed description of the lands, icons, and liturgical vessels which she bequeathed. The Serbian monastery of Hilandar has over 300 Greek and Serbian documents from the medieval period.

Other monasteries on Mount Athos, notably Dionysiou, Docheiariou, Esphigmenou, Koutloumousiou, Pantokrator, St Panteleimon, Xenophontos, Xeropotamou, and Zographou, have smaller collections of Byzantine documents, concerned mainly with land transactions or property disputes. Karyes, the administrative centre of Athos, has 13 documents from the period 883–1406, which are primarily regulations concerning

all the Athonite monasteries. They include the famous foundation charter of the emperor John I Tzimiskes, dating from between 970 and 972 and known as the *tragos*, or "goat", because it was written on a large piece of goatskin, and that of Constantine IX Monomachos (1045). These archives are of vital importance to the Byzantinist not only for the light which they throw on the practice of monasticism, but also for the information which they provide on agrarian conditions, ethnic composition, literacy, and economic development. Since 1937 a systematic survey and publication of the documents from Athos has been in progress in Paris.

Monasteries other than those on Athos have preserved collections of documents from the Byzantine period, and what follows is by no means an exhaustive list. St John the Theologian on Patmos has a rich archive containing imperial privileges, land surveys, and private acts, and the Theotokos Eleousa in Stroumitza in Macedonia has a chrysobull of Alexios I Komnenos dated July 1085, along with numerous other documents. The Nea Mone of Chios preserves chrysobulls and charters of a number of emperors from Constantine IX to Andronikos II Palaiologos which are informative about land ownership, the status of the peasantry, and taxation of the Jews. Several monasteries in southern Italy, an area which was part of the Byzantine empire from the mid-6th century until 1071, have preserved relevant documents. The monastery of St Elias and St Anastasius of Carbone in Calabria, for example, still has eight Greek documents, including a number of wills, from the period 1007–61, in spite of two damaging fires in 1174 and 1432. For the later period, the monastery of St John the Forerunner on Mount Menoikeion near Serres has important Byzantine, Serbian, and Ottoman documents from the 13th century onwards.

Finally, a number of archives in western Europe, although not Byzantine in origin, contain much information about the Greek world in the period 1204–1453. The archives of the Order of St John, held in the National Archive of Malta, throw light on the condition of the Greek population of Rhodes under the rule of the Knights Hospitallers up to 1522. The administrative records preserved by the Italian maritime republics, especially Venice and Genoa, contain a vast amount of documentary information about Byzantium in the later period. Of particular importance are the records of the deliberations of the Venetian senate on matters of policy towards Byzantium in the years 1293–1453, which often include a detailed discussion of events which are not mentioned in the literary sources. The deliberations have been summarized by F. Thiriet, while J. Chrysostomides has recently published a collection of documents from Venice and elsewhere which concern Latin-ruled Greece. However, the Venetian State Archives also contain a great deal of relevant material which has yet to be systematically explored.

JONATHAN HARRIS

Further Reading

Brown, T.S., *Gentlemen and Officers: Imperial Administration and Aristocratic Power in Byzantine Italy*, AD 554–800, London: British School at Rome, 1984, pp. 224–25

Chrysostomides, J. (editor), *Monumenta Peloponnesiaca: Documents for the History of the Peloponnese in the 14th and 15th Centuries*, Camberley: Porphyrogenitus, 1995

Dölger, Franz and Peter Wirth (editors), *Regesten der Kaiserkunden des oströmischen Reichs von 565–1453*, Munich and Berlin: Oldenbourg/Beck, 1924–65

Grumel, V., A.A. Darrouzès, and V. Laurent (editors), *Les Régestes des actes du Patriarcat de Constantinople*, vol. 1: *Les Actes des patriarches*, Paris: Institut Français d'Etudes Byzantines, 1972

Guillou, André, *Les Archives de Saint-Jean-Prodrome sur le Mont Ménécée*, Paris: Presses Universitaires de France, 1955

Hendrickx, B., "Régestes des empereurs latins de Constantinople, 1204–1261/72", *Byzantina*, 14 (1988): pp. 7–221

Lemerle, Paul *et al.* (editors), *Archives d'Athos*, Paris: CNRS and Académie d'Athènes, 1937–

Lemerle, Paul *et al.*, *The Agrarian History of Byzantium from the Origins to the Twelfth Century: The Sources and Problems*, Galway: Galway University Press, 1979, pp. 156–92

Morris, Rosemary, "Dispute Settlement in the Byzantine Provinces in the Tenth Century" in *The Settlement of Disputes in Early Medieval Europe*, edited by Wendy Davies and Paul Fouracre, Cambridge and New York: Cambridge University Press, 1986

Morris, Rosemary, *Monks and Laymen in Byzantium, 843–1118*, Cambridge and New York: Cambridge University Press, 1995

Robinson, Gertrude, *The History and Cartulary of the Greek Monastery of St Elias and St Anastasius of Carbone*, 3 vols, Rome: Pontificio Istituto Orientale, 1928–30

Thiriet, F. (editor), *Régestes des délibérations du Sénat de Venise concernant la Romanie*, 3 vols, Paris: Mouton, 1958–61

Whittow, Mark, *The Making of Orthodox Byzantium, 600–1025*, Basingstoke: Macmillan, 1996, pp. 1–3

Modern

For the greater part of its history, and until the War of Independence (1821–27), the official archive material relating to modern Greece originated chiefly from foreign administrations, notably Latin and Ottoman, which ruled the Greeks until they attained independence. With the fall of the Byzantine empire in the 15th century, the state bureaucratic record-keeping tradition of the Byzantines continued principally in the Venetian-ruled Greek lands. Venetians were renowned for their habit of meticulously maintaining extensive records in the places they administered; in fact, such importance did they place on records that they would negotiate with the Turks their safe return to Venice when they pulled out of a dominion. The Venetian archives, preserved nearly in their entirety to the present day, provide a valuable source for the history of Latin rule in the east (Crete, the Ionian islands, the Peloponnese, and Cyprus). In the Ottoman-ruled lands of Hellenism, sultanic bureaucracy and religious law favoured a regional archival policy, centred around the responsible *qadi* (Muslim religious judge), who was expected to enter every decree of the central government in his codices before it took effect in the province. In parallel, the decentralized administrative and taxation system, in cooperation with the Orthodox Church and local communities, allowed the preservation of records to be an activity largely shared with independent and private bodies. Accordingly, apart from the archives of the Turkish authorities and the old repositories of the monastic complexes at Meteora and on Mount Athos, archives were kept at the time by church authorities, communities, schools, notaries, guilds, and subconsulates. More specifically, given the lay jurisdiction with which the Church was vested during the Ottoman rule, church archives became depositories of collected material of broader interest pertinent to all walks of life of the Orthodox subjects. In addition, important and multifarious material was left by

scholars, ecclesiastical figures, merchants, teachers, and other individuals in collections of private documents, letters, commercial registers, notes, etc. Lastly, on the fringe of and outside the empire, namely in the Danubian principalities and in Europe, Greek communities kept their own archives illuminating in detail the activities and the organization of the Hellenism of the diaspora (16th–19th centuries). By the end of War of Independence, a great deal of material from the archives of the Ottoman lands had been destroyed and continued to be destroyed in the Greek-inhabited lands of Turkey which were later incorporated into Greece. Still, enough of it survived the turmoils to reach the independent state, providing an invaluable source of historical knowledge.

It was from the outbreak of the Greek revolution onwards that the first Greek official documents were issued by the insurgent Greeks in their struggle to establish a rudimentary state structure. The rapid proliferation of these documents pointed to the need for their proper preservation, so that, at the time of Ioannis Kapodistria (1828–32), the first head of independent Greece, a public service was set up for this purpose. This was suppressed later on, at the time of the Bavarian regency (1833–35), and the preservation of historical state papers was entrusted to the Court of Audit (*Elenktiko Synedrio*). By the end of the 19th century, however, much of the material had been auctioned off, while further volumes of documents lay forgotten in public basements. In the 19th century Romanticism, in its quest for the national past, gave Greek historical studies and archive research a boost; but, despite the fresh preoccupation with the past, emphasizing the need for collecting and arranging primary historical material, the new intellectual trend failed to translate into a public record-keeping policy. Only diplomatic records attracted state protection from the beginning, for since 1832 King Otho had assigned their preservation to the newly established Secretariat of State of the Royal House and External Relations (the foreign ministry's predecessor). Provisionally, the Historical and Ethnological Society of Greece, since its foundation in 1882, made up for state inertia by saving much archival material, notably relating to the War of Independence.

To the complications in the formation of a structured record-keeping policy in Greece was added the piecemeal unification of the country; the state found itself provided with the well-organized archive services of the annexed regions (Ionian republic, 1864; Cretan republic and Samos principality, 1913) before it established a principal state record office. This was set up only in 1914, under the Venizelos government, with the foundation of the General State Archives (*Genika Archeia tou Kratous*). Their housing for decades in a wing of the Athens Academy building proved highly inappropriate for the preservation of the material.

Even nowadays the state of the historical archives in Greece is far from being a cause of national pride by modern standards. This situation reflects the chronic failure of the country to include research in its public priorities, and, culturally, is related to a national reluctance to address questions of historical self-awareness. Sadly, voluminous records of modern Greek history still moulder in public warehouses – a massive testimony to the need for a fully fledged state record office, the process of the completion of the new building for which has been under way since 1976. In parallel, the principal old-established public archives make no secret of their difficulties. Poor in funds and in research facilities, understaffed, and the victims of official apathy, they can prove a test to the unsuspecting scholar's stamina. Moreover, it is only lately that the state archives are being staffed at last with graduate archivists. Lastly, relics of a lingering attitude of national secrecy over archival records may cause additional frustration, particularly to scholars exploring 20th-century issues touching on current national sensitivities (minorities, Macedonia, Thrace, matters relating to current Graeco-Turkish frictions, contemporary politics, etc.).

Nevertheless, the policy of numerous institutions, societies, and organizations, as a rule loosely associated with the state, has shown a fresh outlook. They have set up and enthusiastically arranged their archives, and encouraged access to records which had long remained unknown to the general researcher. This serves also as a verification that the national long-term project of compiling the definitive corpus of the Greek archival collections throughout the country has some prospect of one day attaining its objectives. As regards Greek historians, archival and research institutes and societies have to their credit popularized over the last 20 years a new pattern of openness and expertise in the management of historical records, breaking free from the "research-unfriendly" tradition. Moreover, the introduction of fresh matters within the scope of historical research, in parallel with the traditional ones of political and diplomatic history, has encouraged the creation of steadily growing archive units. There now follows a rough outline of the available archives of interest to the student of modern Greek history.

The General State Archives, ever since they were founded, have constituted the largest and principal archival repository for all aspects of modern Greece. They have authority over state historical records (excluding those of the foreign ministry), and de jure collect material from all the ministries and state directories (the 50-year rule applies). The main sources span the period from the War of Independence (or Greek revolution, 1821–27) onwards, but the material after 1863 remains unclassified. They are divided into four categories: Revolution archive (1821–27); Kapodistrian archive (1828–32); archive of Otho's reign (1833–62); and archive of George I's reign (1863–1913). Other records include the Yannis Vlachogiannis (first director of the archives) collection (mostly on the Greek revolution); the dossier of the Mixed Commission on Ottoman Estates (1829–77); and the Mavrokordatos papers (1833–80). Of the 20th-century archives, most significant are the Population Exchange Files on Asia Minor Hellenism; that of Kapetan T. Vardas (1905–30), fighter of the Macedonian struggle; and the papers of the premiers I. Metaxas and, in part, E. Tsouderos.

Regional records are preserved with the archive services organized on a prefecture basis under the aegis of the General State Archives. Apart from the fact that the irregular integration of Greek territories into the Greek state gave extra emphasis to the study of regional history as a field in its own right, some of these archive services (namely those of Crete, Samos, and especially the Ionian islands) amassed particularly valuable material from the structured archives kept under foreign administrations. Thus, Cretan history, for example, from 1669

onwards is traced through the Historical Archives of Crete in Chania and Heraklion (containing records ranging from the material of the Turkish archives and the archives of the Translation Offices and the ecclesiastical court, up to the 19th-century collections of the Cretan revolts and the Cretan principality). Similarly, the records from the Archives of Corfu and Levkas (Santa Maura) provide valuable sources for Ionian history during Venetian rule (16th–18th centuries); the Historical Archive of Samos contains a mass of material spanning the entire history of the island (1725–1950), especially as a principality (1834–1912). This is also illustrated by the preservation of the contemporaneous Italian occupation archive (1912–45) with the archive of the Dodecanese, on Rhodes, annexed only after World War II to Greece. Lastly, among regional archives, the Archive of Macedonia in Thessalonica merits a reference for its hundreds of manuscripts (18th–19th centuries).

The Historical Archive of the Greek Ministry of Foreign Affairs, where the country's diplomatic records are kept, is the other principal state archive. Dating from 1822, but chiefly from 1833 with the establishment of Greece as a modern kingdom, the records of the archive still reflect the 1833 classification (general correspondence, legations and consulates, official royal correspondence, treaty papers, treaties, and miscellaneous). The archives open to research today are divided into three sections: (1) General correspondence containing the ministry's drafts of dispatches to its envoys abroad, and their reports to foreign governments. This arrangement is increasingly interspersed with files on particular topics, such as the Cretan revolution (1866–69), the annexation of Thessaly (1881), and the peace conference (1919) (2) Embassy and consular records (from 1834), containing *inter alia* the Greek consuls' reports from the Ottoman empire, a multifarious source on various aspects of its Greek-inhabited provinces. (3) Miscellaneous papers including separate dossiers on such varied and significant subjects as brigandage, taxation, commerce, and landed property. Here, too, much of the material held in the archive awaits classification before it can be accessible to scholars (recently, as a result of a policy of openness to research, the 30-year rule was adopted). Post-World War II records referring to Greece's accession to the European institutions are in the possession not of the Historical Archive but of the General State Archives of the ministry.

The National Library (founded 1866) holds records relating to local history at the time of Ottoman rule, but sources mostly concern the War of Independence (fighters' archive). Later 19th-century collections held give information on various matters concerning the economy, justice, welfare, administration, and education. Here also is deposited the G. Georgiadis archive (1913–40) on the Italian occupation of the island of Rhodes.

The Library of Parliament (founded 1845) houses documents relating generally to the War of Independence (fighters' archive and correspondence of the revolutionary governing bodies), along with documents relating to parliamentary history (from 1844) and a few private collections of papers. *The Benaki Library* annexe (founded 1928) holds a collection of some 3600 newspaper titles (1789–1970), the second largest in the country after that of the National Library.

The Gennadius Library (founded 1926), named after its founder Ioannis Gennadius, a devoted bibliophile, is much used by scholars in Athens. Ottoman-ruled and modern Hellenism (especially the Greek Enlightenment, War of Independence, travellers' literature, and the Eastern Question) are very well represented in its comprehensive bibliographical and documentary holdings. Archival collections contain the documents of Ali Pasha of Ioannina; Ioannis Gennadius's personal archive; the correspondence of K. Mousouris (Turkish ambassador to Athens in the 1840s); the archives of the Dragoumis family, which achieved distinction in society and politics (1840 to present); A. Souliotis-Nikolaidis papers on the Macedonian struggle; part of E. Tsouderos' papers (World War II); and also manuscripts and papers of personalities such as the poets G. Seferis and O. Elytis and the conductor D. Mitropoulos.

The Benaki Museum (founded 1930) provides rich primary material for the study of the period 1814–1974. It holds 550 archival units, or about 500,000 unbound documents, partly sorted. More specifically, its records bear on the *Philiki Hetaireia* (Friendly Society); the Greek revolution; the Kapodistrian and Othonian periods (notably the D. Kallergis papers); the Cretan question 1866–1905 (*inter alia*, the archive of the provisional administration and the papers of Colonel T. Vassos and Prince George); the Macedonian struggle and the Balkan Wars. Greek politics (1900–25) is illuminated by the Benaki and Venizelos family archives and the papers of important Venizelists (N. Plastiras, G. Ventiris, I. Politis, P. Danglis). In addition, collections of outstanding literary figures (Angelos and Eva Sikelianos, C. Cavafy, P. Nirvanas, K. Palamas, and others); contemporaneous files on national resistance (1941–44); and the premier A. Korizis papers (d. 1941) are held. There is also a well-stocked archive of some 4000 photographs.

The Historical and Ethnological Society of Greece contains an archive relating to the period of the Greek revolution. The society is based at the National Historical Museum (formerly the old parliament building), and since its foundation in 1882 has collected important material on the entire Hellenism of the east. Records include particular dossiers on the Cretan revolution of 1866–69 and the Macedonian struggle.

The Greek Literary and Historical Archive (ELIA), a private archival society founded in the mid-1960s, is today a privileged source for research for the student of modern Greek history. Especially strong in family archives spanning periods from a few decades to 150 years, ELIA boasts a particularly broad variety of records to meet the wide-ranging interests of the scholar of political, social, economic, intellectual, and cultural history. Its historical archive consists of hundreds of collections of papers from the revolutionary period up to the time of the German occupation (1941–44) and the Greek civil war (1945–49). These include papers of fighters in the War of Independence; families eminent in public and intellectual life (Valaoritis, Gerulanos, Romas, Eftaxias, Streit, Bountouris, etc.); the papers of Trikoupis covering *inter alia* his correspondence with King George I on foreign policy; the papers of Venizelos (1910–20) and some of his associates; and collections of papers shedding light on contemporary history (Metaxas regime, occupation, and resistance). Also at ELIA are a specialized library of 14,000 titles of rare 19th-century

printed books and pamphlets; a collection of 300,000 photographs (from 1860 onwards); a rich map collection of Greece (1830–1950); and the archive of the Greek colony in Egypt (c.1850–1950).

The Institute of Neohellenic Research of the National Hellenic Research Foundation, which deserves credit for the dissemination of a fresh attitude to archival research in public life, itself possesses a small number of collections: the A. Louriotis papers (1809–35); A. Pallis papers (1912–64); A. Karatheodoris papers (1816–1906); K. Schinas and P. Argyropoulos papers (1823–80); the Gerousis Trade House archive (1823–1925); and microfilm collections including that of modern Greek portraiture (7000 photographs of distinguished personalities, 15th–20th centuries).

The British School of Archaeology holds among its archives the historian George Finlay's collection of papers concerning the Greek revolution and the period of Otho's monarchy.

For the study of Asia Minor Hellenism until its exodus in 1922, *the Centre for Asia Minor Studies,* a private research centre, holds an oral history archive, unique of its kind, of 150,000 pages, arranged by communities and regions, along with manuscripts (1856–1924), a photographic archive (5000 items), and a specialized library. Other historical societies dealing with specific regions, such as *the Thracian, Epirot, Peloponnesian Studies Societies,* and others, keep significant archive material.

On the study of the Greek civil war and the communist movement (1918 to the present day) the *ASKI Archives* (Contemporary Social History Archives) accommodate part of the Greek Communist Party archives (1918–68), left-wing resistance organizations archives, archive collections and records of political refugees, far-left parties' and organizations' material, etc.

Among the plethora of scattered ecclesiastical archives, the Archives of the Catholic Bishoprics of Tinos and Naxos in the Cyclades deserve special mention for material relating to the early modern period of the area, as does the archive of the Thessalonica Metropolis, a significant source for Macedonian history from the mid-18th century onwards. As to monastic archives, the repositories of the monasteries of Mount Athos, along with the records at the monasteries of Patmos and Kalavryta (16th–18th centuries), are unparalleled.

Of numerous private historical archives in the possession of individuals, *the Pavlos A. Zannas archive* deserves mention as a rich source of documents, correspondence, and reminiscences from the late 19th century onwards. It consists of four archives covering themes from the Graeco-Turkish War (1897) and the Macedonian struggle to the Greek army's Asia Minor expedition (1919–22) and the Axis occupation (1941–44).

On military history, the archive of the *War Museum* holds collections of military papers and documents (1822–1949). The earlier ones include the D. Plapoutas–T. Kolokotronis correspondence (1822–24), General D. Deligiorgopoulos's documents (1828–41), and the Notaras–Petropoulakis archive (1832–67). The bulk of the material concerns archives of high-ranking officers in the wartime periods of 20th-century Greece (from World War I to the Greek Civil War). Likewise, the *Naval Museum* preserves material from naval operations, still in the process of arrangement. Also, the *Army History Directorate* keeps full records of Greek army operations

(Graeco-Turkish War, 1897; Balkan Wars, 1912–13; Asia Minor operations, 1919–22; Italian invasion, 1940–41; and the Korean War, 1950–53), including personal archives.

On the economic history of the country (19th–20th centuries), the *Historical Archive of the National Bank of Greece* provides a most valuable record of the economic development of modern Greece. Similarly, the *Agricultural Bank* has established its own historical archive illustrating the development of Greek agriculture; and other banks, too, have followed this line by arranging their archives for historical research.

Different aspects of modern Greek history and society can be traced through other archives held by various organizations, institutions, and societies. Thus, for example, the organization of higher education and the impact of the national university on Greek culture and ideology are illuminated by the archive of *Athens University* (founded 1837). Also, the course of archaeological excavations in Greece from 1837 to the present day is chronicled through the archive of the *Archaeological Society*, supplemented by the archives of the foreign archaeological schools. For the study of Greek folklore, *the Greek Folklore Research Centre of Athens Academy* keeps some 4200 manuscripts of folklore interest (19th–20th centuries) and large audio collections of folk music. In addition, the archive of *the Greek Folklore Society* provides primary folklore material from the early 1900s, including the collection of G. Megas, a university professor of folklore.

Moreover, a multitude of private societies and unions have opened their archives to scholarly research, a fact reflecting the broadening of the historical field achieved in our time in understanding modern Greek society. Already knowledge of the history of the Greek workers' and trade union movement has been advanced considerably by the research into archives of workers' centres and trade union organizations. Now there is further interest in the archives of industrial enterprises such as that of the French Mining Company at Laurium (1876–1980). The study of medical care and epidemics is served by the archive of the *Evangelismos Infirmary* (from 1884), made up of patients' files, medical reports, and administrative documents. Of learned and literary societies, *Parnassos* (founded 1865), which achieved early prestige among the scholarly coteries of Athens, preserves the archive of N. Levidis (minister and historian, 1848–1942), as well as miscellaneous material from the political and cultural elite of the time. On Greek women's studies, there is the archive of the *National Council of Greek Women*, dating from 1908, which keeps the council's correspondence with the European Department of the International Women's Council (CECIF). Lastly, *the Historical Archive of Greek Youth*, albeit not an archive literally speaking, focuses on material relating to the history of Greek youth, commissioning research projects on young people's involvement in all public and social activities (19th–20th centuries).

Modern Greek history cannot be studied on the basis of records held in Greece alone. However, even an incomplete listing of archival sources of Greek interest abroad, such as the official archives of the Great Powers and those of the Greek communities of the diaspora scattered from France to Russia – to speak only of European sources – would lead us far beyond the purposes of this article. Suffice it to allure the reader with the idea that the mosaic of the ecumenical tradition of Hellenism would be reflected in a lively manner in this enthralling research journey: from the diplomatic records of the British Foreign Office and the Quai d' Orsay, through the archives of Vienna and the records of the Italian cities and the Vatican, northward to the state archives of St Petersburg, and eastward to the Istanbul Bachve-Kalet and the codices of the Orthodox patriarchates.

RENNOS EHALIOTIS

Further Reading

Archive Management

Bannan, Alfred J. and Achilles Edelenyi, *A Documentary History of Eastern Europe*, New York: Twayne, 1970

Jenkinson, Hilary, *A Manual of Archive Administration*, 2nd edition, London: Lund Humphries, 1965

Schellenberg, T.R., *Modern Archives: Principles and Techniques*, Chicago: University of Chicago Press, 1956

Schellenberg, T.R., *The Management of Archives*, New York: Columbia University Press, 1965

Modern Greek Archives

oConstantinidis, C.G., "Les Archives de Grèce", *Archives, Bibliothèques, Collections, Documents*, 5 (Jan.–Feb. 1952): pp. 123–27

Diamantis, K.A. (editor), *Ta Periechomena ton Genikon Archeion tou Kratous* [The Contents of the General State Archives], 5 vols, Athens, 1972–76

Dontas, Domna, Greek section in *The Times Survey of Foreign Ministries of the World*, edited by Zara Steiner, London: Times Books, and Westport, Connecticut: Meckler, 1982, pp. 259–73

"Elliniko Logotechniko kai Istoriko Archeio" [Greek Literary and Historical Archive, ELIA], *Epta Imeres/Kathimerini*, Athens (21 April 1996)

Guide to the Archives of the Ministries of Foreign Affairs of the Member States of the European Communities and the European Political Cooperation, Luxembourg: Office for Official Publications, 1989 (Greece entry, pp. 28–31)

Hussey, J.M., *The Finlay Papers: A Catalogue*, London: Thames and Hudson, 1973

Institute of Neohellenic Research of the National Hellenic Research Foundation, *Report 1981–1991*, Athens: INR/NHPF, 1991

Kokkinis, S., *Vivliothikes kai Archeia stin Ellada* [Libraries and Archives in Greece], 2nd edition, Athens, 1970

Liata, Evtychia, *Geniko Evretirio tou Istorikou Archeiou tis Ethnikis Trapezis* [General Index of the Historical Archive of the National Bank], Athens, 1980

Loukos, Despoina (editor), *Ellinika Archeia: Ta Periechomena 100 Archeiakon Syllogon* [Greek Archives: The Contents of 100 Archive Collections], Athens, 1988

Mazower, Mark, *Inside Hitler's Greece: The Experience of Occupation, 1941–44*, New Haven and London: Yale University Press, 1993 (note on sources: pp. 423–28)

Miller, William, "Modern Greek History in the Gennadeion", *Journal of Modern History*, 2 (1930): pp. 612–28

Miller, William, "Additions to Modern Greek History in the Gennadeion", *Journal of Modern History*, 9 (1937): pp. 56–63

Nicolopoulos, J.A., *Inventaire du fonds grec au Quai d'Orsay: correspondance politique 1707–1833: mémoirs et documents, 1821–1862*, Athens: Centre for Neohellenic Research of the National Research Foundation of Greece, 1975

Panagiotopoulos, V.P., "Archeio Monis Ioannou Theologou Patmou" [The Archive of St John the Theologian Monastery on Patmos], *Eranistis*, 15/16 (1965): pp. 145–56

Patrinelis, C., *Vivliothikes kai Archeia ton Monon tou Agiou Orous* [Libraries and Archives of the Mount Athos Monasteries], Athens, 1963

Ploumidis, Georgios S., *Diagramma tou Archeiakon Pigon tis Neoellinikis Istorias* [Chart of Archival Sources for Modern Greek History], 3rd edition, Athens, 1983

Prevelakis, E., *Ta Vretanika Koinovoulevtika Engrafa kai i Neoteri Elliniki Istoria, 1801–1860* [British Parliamentary Documents and Modern Greek History, 1801–1860], Thessalonica, 1960

Richter, H., "The German Federal Archives – Military Archives – and the History of Greece, 1941–1944", *Modern Greek Society: A Newsletter*, 4 (May 1975): pp. 45–50

Sakellariou, M.V., "Piges tis Neas Ellinikis Istorias" [Sources for Modern Greek History], *Nea Estia*, 39 (1946)

Svoronos, Nikos G., *Salonique et Cavalla, 1686–1792: inventaire de correspondances de Consuls de France au Levant*, Paris: Maisonneuve, 1951

"Oi Thisavroi tou Mouseiou Benaki" [The Treasures of the Benaki Museum], *Epta Imeres / Kathimerini*, Athens (20 February 1994)

Tomadakis, N.B., "Peri Archeion en Elladi kai tis Archeiakis Ypiresias" [On Archives in Greece and the Archival Service] and "Ekthesis peri Archeion Kerkyras" [Report on the Archives of Corfu], *Deltion Istorikis kai Ethnologikis Etaireias tis Ellados* [Bulletin of the Historical and Ethnological Society of Greece], 11 (1956): pp. 1–42

Topping, Peter, "The Public Archives of Greece", *American Archivist*, 15 (1952): pp. 249–57

Topping, Peter, "La Bibliothèque 'Gennadeion': son histoire et ses collections", *L' Hellènisme Contemporain*, 9/2–3 (1955): pp. 121–48

Vardas, Christina, "Ta Archeia tis Gennadeiou Vivliothikis" [The Gennadius Library Archives], *Mnimon*, 12 (1989): pp. 217–24

Vardas, Christina (editor), *Ta Archeia tis Gennadeiou Vivliothikis: Synoptiki Anagrafi* [The Gennadius Library Archives: Concise Catalogue], Athens, 1991

Vasdravellis, I.K., *Istorika Archeia Makedonias* [Historical Archives of Macedonia], 3 vols, Thessalonica, 1952–55

"Vivliothiki (1)" [The Library], *Epta Imeres / Kathimerini*, Athens (24 November 1996)

Vizvizi-Dontas, Domna, "Greece: History of the Foreign Ministry Archives" in *The New Guide to the Diplomatic Archives of Western Europe*, 2nd edition, edited by Daniel H. Thomas and Lynn M. Case, Philadelphia: University of Pennsylvania Press, 1975

Vranousis, L., Archeia [Archives] entry in *Megali Elliniki Enkyclopedia* [Great Greek Encyclopedia], supplement vol. 1, pp. 736–38

Zakythinos, D.A., "Ta Istorika kai Monastiriaka Archeia tis Kritis" [The Historical and Monastic Archives of Crete], *Epetiris Etaireias Kritikon Spoudon* [Yearbook of the Society of Cretan Studies], 2 (1939): pp. 505–26

Arethas of Caesarea

Scholar and politician of the 9th to 10th centuries

Arethas was born in Patras. Nothing is known of the circumstances of his coming to Constantinople or of his studies. The Euclid in the Bodleian that he had copied in 888 terms him simply "Arethas of Patras"; he was then still a layman. By 895 he was a deacon with a role at the imperial court; in 902 or 903 he was made *protothronos* or metropolitan bishop (archbishop) of Caesaraea of Cappadocia, the first ranking among the sees subject to Constantinople. It has been suggested that he remained permanently in Constantinople, where his political activity took place. But although only Constantinople is named in his historical texts, his sermons point to residence in Caesaraea, and there is no reason to assume that he did not conform to the canonical requirements.

Arethas led the opposition to the fourth marriage of the emperor Leo VI (the "Tetragamy"). After burying three wives, in 905 Leo at last had a son by his mistress, Zoe Carbonopsina. Legitimizing this heir to the throne was paramount. Theodore of Stoudios's writings show that third and fourth marriages were quite frequent and allowed by law, but they were forbidden under canon law, which an emperor might find harder to circumvent than one of his subjects. The patriarch, Nicholas I (whose involvement in a plot to overthrow the emperor had been discovered), was eager to satisfy Leo. But although he managed to obtain an imperial baptism for the infant, he dared not disregard the opposition of the synod, led by Arethas and Epiphanios, metropolitan bishop of Laodicaea, to Leo's marriage. Leo had Arethas tried on a trumped-up charge and exiled, compelled Nicholas to abdicate, under threat of prosecution for high treason, and appealed to Rome. The pope sanctioned the marriage; a new patriarch was elected; Arethas and Leo were reconciled. Arethas's speeches and letters, as well as the scholia to a canonical corpus that he jotted down during the affair, supplement the other documentation. Like iconoclasm, the Tetragamy has received disproportionate attention because of the abundance of surviving sources.

Arethas had an enormous library for the days before printing, as attested by surviving manuscripts, by later ones with notes showing that they were copied from ones in his possession, and by marginal notes in various other manuscripts. His familiarity with Classical literature points in the same direction. Surviving manuscripts include: two volumes of Plato (one in fragmentary condition; when complete, the two manuscripts probably constituted an "Arethas edition" of Plato); Aristotle, poorly represented by the *Categories* and *De Virtutibus et Vitiis* (Arethas certainly owned more, for he describes himself as a "fiery enthusiast for Aristotle, and enquirer into his writings", and he quotes widely from him in the *Scripta Minora*); the oldest surviving manuscript of Euclid (mathematics was still part of philosophy, and hence of theology); an Aelius Aristides; the *Codex Apologetarum* with works by Clement of Alexandria, Eusebius, Justin, and Athenagoras (the manuscript formerly also included Tatian); and a copy of Lucian. He also mentions in a letter a Marcus Aurelius that he has just had copied; a Pausanias in Paris (Bibliothèque Nationale, gr. 1410) is a copy of a manuscript, now lost, that belonged to him; notes and scholia show that he probably also owned the *Orphica*, the *Life of Apollonius of Tyana*, the *Onomastikon* of Pollux, and he may also have owned a more complete Pindar than the one that survives today.

He quotes frequently from Homer (of the *Iliad*, all but three books, but only nine of the *Odyssey*), sometimes several lines, either literally or adapting the text to what he has to say. One of his letters begins: "I have often wondered, reading Homer, what could possess such a sage to have made his poetry from anything so bizarre as myths. If you ask me these should not be seen as myths but as allegories." This remark echoes Plutarch in *How Poetry Should Be Understood* (19e). The significance of the behaviour of the gods is one of the oldest themes in Greek literature, taking very diverse forms, and although the word "allegory" did not appear until later, the idea is recognizable in Aristotle: "the ancients transmitted, in the form of myths, [the fact] that these things are gods" (*Metaphysics*, 8. 1074b). Arethas was also familiar with Hesiod, Thucydides, Aristophanes (to whom he devotes a page of high praise), Gorgias, and many others. His commentary on The Book of Revelation is almost entirely derived from Andrew of Crete.

His scholia range from "*Or(aio)*" ("Good"), through notes on current affairs (dynastic, local, wars with Bulgars), topographical information, differences between spoken and Classical Greek, lexicology, archaeology, passing tussles with the author, etc., to full-scale "refutations" of the work in question.

Arethas's texts may be divided into those where profane quotations abound – both aggressively when he is responding to a personal attack, and urbanely in letters to friends – and those where there are none: sermons, dogmatic letters, the defence of his action before the synod (although quotations from Aristotle are occasionally present; he was not considered a "profane" author, but a professional source for theologians). A number of other Byzantine writings dealing exclusively with religion (including the *Corpus Dionysiacum*) lack profane quotations; it has been suggested that their authors were following the same policy.

Arethas's address to a Jewish public was apparently a serious attempt to convince them of the truth of Christianity from their own scriptures. His "Letter to the Vizir" (or "Emir"), which includes references to the Qur'an, is aggressive in tone throughout.

PATRICIA KARLIN-HAYTER

Biography

Born in Patras in the mid-9th century, Arethas made his way to Constantinople where he was ordained a deacon before 895 and archbishop of Caesarea in 902 or 903. He led the synod's opposition to the fourth marriage of Emperor Leo VI. Surviving manuscripts suggest that he had a large library and he was well read in Classical literature. He died after 932.

Writings

Scripta Minora, edited by W.G. Westerink, 2 vols, Leipzig: Teubner, 1968–72 (Greek text, Latin summaries and commentary)

Further Reading

Byzantine Books and Bookmen, Washington, D.C.: Dumbarton Oaks, 1975

Karlin-Hayter, P., "Studies in Byzantine Political History", no. 7, *Byzantion*, 34 (1964): pp. 613–17; and no. 9, *Byzantion*, 35 (1965): pp. 455–81

Koster, W.J.W., "Aristophane dans la tradition byzantine", *Revue des Etudes Grecques*, 76 (1963): pp. 381–96

Kougeas, S.B., *O Kaisareias Arethas kai to ergon autou* [Arethas of Caesarea and his Work], Athens, 1913

Lemerle, Paul, *Byzantine Humanism: The First Phase*, Canberra: Australian Association for Byzantine Studies, 1986, chapter 8

Wilson, N.G., *Scholars of Byzantium*, revised edition, London: Duckworth, and Cambridge, Massachusetts: Medieval Academy of America, 1996

Argenti, Eustratios *c.1687–c.1757*

Theologian

Little is known about Eustratios Argenti's life. He was a native of Chios, where the Argentis had long been one of the leading families. After graduating from the Patriarchal Academy in Constantinople, he spent about ten years in the west, visiting Venice, Leghorn, Innsbruck, and probably Halle, and perhaps studying at Padua. During his time in Italy and Germany he acquired a good knowledge of both medicine and theology. Around 1720 he returned to Chios where he practised as a doctor. He married, but almost nothing is known of his wife Leonou or of his two children; one of his grandsons, Eustratios Argenti the Younger, was a close associate of Rigas Velestinlis, and the two died together as *ethnomartyres* [martyrs for their nation] at Belgrade in 1798.

From 1748 to 1751 the elder Eustratios was resident in Egypt, where he is known to have engaged in public debates with Roman Catholic missionaries. In a letter of 1751 he describes the precarious state of the Greek Orthodox patriarchate of Alexandria, in imminent danger of being taken over by Rome. In general he takes a pessimistic view of the situation of Orthodoxy throughout the Near East. The Orthodox, he writes, "will lose this second throne as well as the first throne of Rome; the other two, Antioch and Jerusalem, have almost been destroyed; and we shall be as the Armenians and the Maronites, the Copts and the Syrians, with only one Patriarch, of Constantinople, whom the Papists will afterwards expel root and branch with little trouble, when he is left alone and without his brethren" (in K.A. Uspensky, *The Patriarchate of Alexandria* [in Russian], vol. 1, St Petersburg, 1898, p. 346).

Back in Chios in the early 1750s, Argenti continued his anti-Catholic activities, and in particular during the rebaptism controversy he provided valuable theological support for patriarch Cyril V of Constantinople. The extent of his influence in his native island is evident from a report made in 1756 by the French viceconsul in Chios, who wrote: "One of the most effective ways of restoring tranquillity in this country would be to seize … the doctor *Strati Argenti*, and to have [him] hanged." According to the viceconsul Argenti and two others, all of them "sworn enemies of Catholicism", were in control of the island, and "it is only by their downfall that it will be possible to avoid that of our religion" (in P.P. Argenti, *Diplomatic Archive of Chios 1577–1841*, Cambridge, 1954, pp.1010–11). As far as is known, the threat of hanging was not carried out. Although Argenti had certainly died before 1760, there is no reason to suspect that his end was anything but natural.

Argenti's published works are entirely theological, and they are all polemical treatises against Roman Catholicism. The most ambitious of his writings, the *Treatise against Unleavened Bread* (Leipzig, 1760; 2nd edition, Navplion, 1845), was written with the encouragement of the patriarch Matthew of Alexandria. Its scope is wider than the title suggests, and it is in fact a comprehensive discussion of all the main points on which Orthodox and Catholics differ in Eucharistic practice. Of the three parts of the *Treatise*, the first is directed against the Latin use of *azymes*, or unleavened bread, which Argenti sees as an unjustified innovation, conflicting with the apostolic and early Christian usage. The second and longest section insists upon the need for an *epiklesis*, or invocation of the Holy Spirit, in the Eucharistic prayer of consecration. The third and final part attacks the Latin practice of withholding the chalice from the laity and of denying communion to young children. In the *Treatise* Argenti, following patriarch Dositheos and the Council of Jerusalem (1672), employs the term "transubstantiation" (*metousiosis*); but, unlike them, he refrains from applying to the Eucharist the distinction between "substance" and "accidents". The *Treatise* is not a work of great originality, but it is well documented and clearly argued; there is no other Greek work published on the subject in the period of the Tourkokratia that is comparable in its detail and thoroughness.

Argenti's *Manual Concerning Baptism* (Constantinople, 1756; 2nd edition, Leipzig, 1757) is much shorter than the *Treatise against Unleavened Bread* but has greater originality. Until the middle of the 18th century it was normal for Roman Catholic converts to the Orthodox Church to be received by anointing with the holy chrism. Cyril V, ecumenical patriarch from 1748 to 1751 and from 1752 to 1757, insisted that they should be henceforward admitted through the sacrament of baptism. This provoked a sharp controversy, but eventually Cyril's viewpoint was confirmed in 1755 by a synodical decree signed by himself and the patriarchs of Alexandria and Jerusalem. The practice of receiving Roman Catholics by rebaptism remained the norm in Greek-speaking churches until the late 19th century; since then it has been customary to receive them by chrismation, but rebaptism is still required in certain places, most notably Mount Athos.

In his *Manual Concerning Baptism* Argenti endorses Cyril V's standpoint. Immersion, he claims, is an essential element in the administration of baptism, symbolizing as it does the true significance of the sacrament as burial and resurrection with Christ; it can be omitted only in situations of emergency. The Latin practice of usually administering the sacrament by affusion (pouring water over the candidate's forehead) renders their baptism null and void. Another book advocating the rebaptism of Latins, *Sprinkling Pilloried* (Constantinople, 1756), often attributed to Argenti, is almost certainly not his work; the author is probably Christopher the Aetolian.

Argenti also wrote a *Short Treatise against the Purgatorial Fire of the Papists*, edited by Michael Constantinides (Athens, 1939). Here he allows for a middle state between heaven and hell, where the souls of the faithful departed are "neither honoured nor punished"; but this middle state is in his view altogether different from the Latin purgatory, since the souls there do not undergo "expiatory chastisement and torment". Argenti's treatises on papal infallibility and on the identification of the pope with the Antichrist survive in manuscript but remain unpublished.

In his anti-Latin polemic Argenti says relatively little about the *filioque* clause. An interesting passage in the *Treatise against Unleavened Bread* singles out the rationalism of Latin scholasticism, with its excessive dependence upon Aristotelian philosophy, as the basic cause of the schism between East and West (1st edition, pp. 171–72). Although trained in the terminology of western theology, Argenti himself is neither a Latinizer like Dositheos of Jerusalem nor a Protestantizer like Cyril Lukaris, but he stands apart from both of the westernizing "schools" of 17th-century Orthodoxy. In contrast to his younger contemporary Evgenios Voulgaris, he shows little sympathy for the world of the western Enlightenment. Essentially a conservative, he has more in common with Nikodemos of the Holy Mountain and the Kollyvades; but, unlike them, he makes no use of the tradition upheld by Gregory Palamas and the Hesychasts.

KALLISTOS WARE

Biography

Born in Chios *c*.1687, Argenti was educated at the Patriarchal Academy in Constantinople and spent ten years in western Europe, acquiring a good knowledge of both medicine and theology. Returning to Chios *c*.1720 he practised as a doctor and married. In 1748–51 he lived in Egypt and debated with Roman Catholic missionaries. He wrote a number of polemical treatises against Catholicism. He died *c*.1757.

Further Reading

Papadopoullos, Theodore H., *Studies and Documents Relating to the History of the Greek Church and People under Turkish Domination*, Brussels, 1952 [n.p.]; New York: AMS Press, 1973, especially pp. 409–18

Sarou, Aimilia K., *Bios Eustratio Argente tou Iheologou* [Life of Eustratios Argenti, the Theologian], Athens, 1938

Ware, Timothy, *Eustratios Argenti: A Study of the Greek Church under Turkish Rule*, Oxford: Clarendon Press, 1964

Argolid

Region in southern Greece

The Argolid is most simply defined as the territory of Argos when it was a city state, but simple definitions are never complete. Argos came to control the entire plain which it dominates geographically from the west, but beyond that there are other areas which in a broad sense constitute part of the Argolid, but which were not part of Argos. Often the term Argolid is taken to include the whole of the area between the Saronic Gulf to the north and the Gulf of Argos to the south, but it is best restricted to the plain and its surrounding mountains, for within the wider area the plain of Argos is distinct from the mountainous and more broken region to the east. All the important communities are positioned in or around the plain; of those beyond, Epidaurus, though claimed by Argos, was rarely under Argive control, while the more distant cities of Troezen and Hermione were always completely separate entities. It is the Argive plain that matters.

Along the plain's southern edge is an extensive sweep of beach; though the ancient coastline was inland from this, it must have been similar. The plain extends northwards to form a roughly triangular area. Argos is almost at the southwestern corner; at the southeastern corner is Nauplia (modern Navplion), and, a little to the west, Tiryns. Mycenae is, more or less, at the northern apex. Today the best harbour and most important town are at Navplion. In antiquity Tiryns probably had little more than an open beach and probably used Nauplia's harbour. Argos is further away from the sea, but evidence for overseas trade is clear for the Archaic period, and some form of maritime outlet is certain.

Otherwise communication and access are by land. Until recently the main route, followed by road and railway alike, entered the plain from the north, from the territory of Corinth and its neighbour Phlious down past Mycenae. It left Argos heading south, where, near Lerna, the mountains come closer to the sea; it then went across a smaller plain, into the hills that took it up to Arcadia, the centre of the Peloponnese, or along the coast into yet another plain, the Thyreatis, the possession of which was long disputed between Argos and Sparta. The Argive plain was therefore of some strategic significance, coming between the central and southern Peloponnese and the north, but it was not as strategic as Corinth, which could block the passage from south to north absolutely. There were alternative routes past the Argive plain through the hills and mountains to the west, from Arcadia, past Tegea and Mantinea, across to Phlious, and down to Sicyon and the gulf of Corinth. The modern motorway follows part of this route past Mantinea and over to Phlious, although this is only achieved with the help of a substantial tunnel. Nevertheless, the pass over the mountains at this point was always feasible, and this was the route preferred by the Spartan armies.

The Argive plain is potentially fertile. Though no great river flows through it, the surrounding limestone hills retain the water, and there are abundant springs round its edge. It is here that the communities grew up, and there is much evidence for settlement already in the Neolithic period. By the Early Bronze Age there were important communities around the plain, especially on the site of Argos itself, but the period of greatest significance was undoubtedly the Late Bronze Age, generally termed the Mycenaean Age to give emphasis to the apparent predominance of that state. This is based partly on archaeological evidence, and partly on an interpretation of the Homeric poems, which give supreme authority to Agamemnon, king of Mycenae, over an alliance of the whole of mainland Greece. How far this reflected political reality is impossible to say, but in so far as there is evidence of a common standard of material existence and wealth in mainland Greece, the importance of Mycenae is certain, though it is an importance shared with the other communities of the Argolid.

How this wealth was acquired is unclear. Today the plain produces a mixture of crops, including citrus fruit, but in antiquity much of it was probably used for corn. Horse-rearing also seems to have been significant, particularly in the Late Bronze Age, and remains of horses have been found deliberately buried, presumably with their owners, in Late Bronze Age graves. Homer often mentions horse rearing and describes Mycenae specifically as "rich in gold", though this would have come from elsewhere. Mycenae, with its heavily fortified citadel, is often compared to a robbers' lair, but this is over-dramatizing the situation: the fortifications are repeated at Tiryns and elsewhere in this period, and are essentially defensive. Control of the sea may have involved overseas raiding – the genesis of the story of the siege of Troy may lie in a memory of such activity – but trade and exchange, however it was conducted, is the likeliest explanation for the Argolid's wealth.

Argos seems to have been less important in the Late Bronze Age than in the succeeding Classical period, and this can lead to some confusion, since Athenians in the 5th century BC were liable to attribute the Homeric stories to the kings of Argos rather than Mycenae, which by the 5th century BC barely existed. More significant is the existence of a whole string of communities along the eastern side of the Argive plain, starting with Mycenae in the north. Not all their ancient names are known. Next to Mycenae is the locality known as the Argive Heraion, where the most important of the Classical sanctuaries developed. Graves indicate that there was a prehistoric settlement here. A short, dry gorge leads northeast to the small plain of Berbati, with hills all round except at the point of entry: again, a place of Late Bronze Age settlement. Further south are Dendra, with important graves, and Midea, with its long fortification wall leading to a remote hilltop site. Finally, at the southern end of this string of communities is Tiryns.

There is a pattern to these places. There is a reasonable degree of separation between them, so that they could function independently. They are all situated at springs, or where springs once existed, another clue to their existence. Whether they actually were independent, or whether they were all placed under the control of one authority, is not known. Mycenae and Tiryns were both equipped with structures suitable for a ruler and his needs. Their fortifications were very extensive, with spectacular and well-defended entrances. Inside the fortifications of both places was a rectangular building, with a porch at one end and a ceremonial hearth within. These buildings have been identified as palaces and would seem to have been where rulers could perform their official duties. Both buildings have storage space and have yielded evidence of imported goods from overseas. Mycenae, more than Tiryns, has massive cemeteries with different types of graves. The earlier shaft graves, which were excavated in the 19th century by Heinrich Schliemann, contained the fabulous gold treasures and other objects now in the National Museum at Athens. The later graves include the tremendous tholos tombs with their high corbel-domed chambers which, though mostly robbed centuries ago, still impress with their structural competence and scale. More ordinary graves, particularly rockcut chamber tombs, which are related in form to the tholoi, have been found at all the Late Bronze Age sites. Although these tombs probably belonged to people of lesser rank, they often contained offerings of value. Taking all this into account, and comparing it with other regions of Greece of the same period, it is clear that in the Late Bronze Age the Argolid was the wealthiest and the most important area of mainland Greece, and that it had taken over from the earlier supremacy of Minoan Knossos in Crete.

In the 11th century BC all this collapsed, despite the construction of massive fortifications in the principal centres. What eventually emerged in the 8th century BC was rather different. Some of the Late Bronze Age centres continued as communities, such as Mycenae, Tiryns, and Asine, near Nauplia. They may, like Mycenae, have patched up their stupendous fortifications. Mycenae's connection with the heroes of the Homeric poems was accepted, and the hero worship of Agamemnon was established in the greatest of the tholoi, which was identified as his tomb (or, alternatively, as the treasure chamber of his father, Atreus). Tiryns also continued to be inhabited, but, like Mycenae, seems to have had a much-reduced population. According to Herodotus, at the time of the Persian invasions in the early 5th century Mycenae and Tiryns, unlike Argos, sided with the anti-Persian alliance and between them could only field an army of 400 men. The Argive Heraion was now a sanctuary, rather than a settlement. The lead undoubtedly had passed to Argos. Behind this development lies the arrival, into a depopulated region, of Dorian settlers who established themselves at Argos rather than the eastern sites, which perhaps overawed them with their massive remains. At Argos they settled on the lower ground below the citadel, just as at Sparta they chose a new, low-lying site across the river from the Bronze Age settlement. The eastern Argolid communities may have continued to be descended from the earlier population. The Argive Heraion, to judge from the objects deposited in it, at first belonged to its eastern geographical neighbours.

In the 7th and 6th centuries BC this changed as Argos took political control of the entire area. The Heraion now became the principal sanctuary for the whole of the Argolid. It was this that made Argos one of the major cities of Classical Greece, though its control was briefly broken as a consequence of the Battle of Sepeia in about 494 BC when it was defeated by Sparta, and Mycenae and Tiryns regained their independence. It was not long, however, before Argos recovered and reunited the Argolid under its control. But the Argolid never regained the preeminence it had enjoyed in the Late Bronze Age. The overseas trade, and the benefits of that trade, moved from the gulf of Argos to the Saronic gulf and Athens. All this is reflected at the Argive Heraion. The sanctuary is an important one. It contains the remains of one of the earliest peripteral temples in Greece which, although its columns were of wood, is likely to have been a forerunner of the Doric order. Destroyed by fire in 416 BC, it was replaced with a more up-to-date stone temple. Little of this replacement remains, apart from its foundations, but the sculpture, including the cult statue, was attributed to the greatest of the Argive sculptors, Polyclitus. Even so, and although in its design it shows Athenian influence, this temple nowhere approaches the Athenian buildings in quality or magnificence.

The later history of the Argolid is relatively uneventful, and is essentially that of the city of Argos. During the Roman empire the Argolid continued as a prosperous backwater, with most of the population probably living in the city. There is a Roman bath building at the Argive Heraion, which was excavated in the early 20th century, and which has partly eroded away. Otherwise there is little Roman construction outside the city. There are some good examples of late mosaic floors, now in the Argos museum, which indicate continued prosperity into the 5th century AD. Later still, scattered over the Argolid, and often incorporating the remains of Classical buildings, are a number of delightful but small Byzantine churches which suggest a population living in villages, most noticeably on the eastern side of the plain, and continuing a traditional pattern of life.

R.A. TOMLINSON

Summary

The Argolid is the plain that extends south from Mycenae to Argos, Nauplia, and the sea coast. Though it has no great rivers, it is potentially fertile and by the Late Bronze Age was the focus of an important group of sites, notably Mycenae and Tiryns, where spectacular archaeological finds have been made. Argos only emerged in the 7th and 6th centuries BC to dominate the region.

Further Reading

Dietz, Søren, *The Argolid at the Transition to the Mycenaean Age: Studies in the Chronology and Cultural Development in the Shaft Grave Period*, Copenhagen: National Museum of Denmark, 1991

Ecole Français d'Athènes, *Etudes Argiennes*, Paris: Boccard, 1980

Foley, Anne, *The Argolid, 800–600 BC: An Archaeological Survey*, Göteborg: Aström, 1988

Roux, Georges, *L'Architecture de l'Argolide aux IVe et IIIe siècles avant J.-C.*, Paris: Boccard, 1961

Zangger, Eberhard, *The Geoarchaeology of the Argolid*, Berlin: Mann, 1993

Argos

City in southern Greece

The city of Argos has a continuous history from the Neolithic period to the present day. It centres on two hills, the high acropolis, called the Larisa, to the south, and the lower, rounder Aspis to the north. The main area of settlement is on the eastern side of these two hills. Of the earliest occupation only traces remain, but of the Middle Bronze Age there is more substantial evidence, particularly on the Aspis. By the Late Bronze Age the hills were fortified. They look across the plain towards Tiryns, on the coast, and Mycenae, further inland. The relationship between the three communities during this period is imprecisely known; Argos may have been the least significant of the three, and as such perhaps the least likely to survive during their decline at the end of the Late Bronze Age. Whatever the reason, it was occupied by new settlers, of Dorian origin, who seem to have assimilated the descendants of the original population. By the 8th century BC Argos was again a flourishing city and a leading community in the Greek world as it emerged from the obscurity that followed the collapse of the Late Bronze Age states. It produced an abundant sequence of pottery decorated in the Geometric style, less refined than that of Athens, but equally vigorous. Much survives from local burials, indicating a degree of prosperity in the community. Even more significant is the suit of bronze armour – comprising a helmet, breastplate, and shield – that was found in one of the graves at Argos, named the "Panoply Grave" after this discovery. The bronze from which this armour was fashioned would have been imported, a sign of revival at Argos, and it probably indicates the first stages in the development of the form of warfare which led to the heavily armoured infantryman, the hoplite, of Classical history.

There is a tradition that at this time Argos controlled a wide area of the Peloponnese, but this was still a long time before true historical record began, and it may be an anachronism, either a reflection of the larger territorial states of the Late Bronze Age or the predominance of another city, Sparta, in the Classical period. It is unlikely that in the 8th century BC Argos controlled even the eastern side of the Argive plain.

During the 7th century BC Argos underwent changes. The city's pottery industry seems to have collapsed, or, at least, ceased producing vases to be deposited in graves. Political resurgence brought a certain Pheidon to power. He is described by Aristotle as a king (meaning, perhaps, that he exercised traditional religious and military power) who became an authoritarian ruler (a tyrant, in the Greek sense) seizing control of the Olympic Games on the other side of the Peloponnese and engaging in war with the Spartans as well as with more closely neighbouring cities. He is also said to have introduced a standard of coinage, an anachronism for the 7th century BC and possibly again a misinterpretation. Whatever the truth of all this, Argos was by that time clearly becoming a major city, powerful enough to challenge Spartan supremacy in the Peloponnese, though not to prevail. At the battle of Sepeia (494 BC?) the Argive army was crushed by the Spartans, and Argos forced into a submissive peace. Subsequently Argos was invited by Athens and Sparta to join their resistance to Persia, but Argos tactfully set impossible conditions, so justifying its refusal and doubtless hoping to play the Persians against the Spartans. When the peace between Argos and Sparta expired after 30 years, the Argives, this time in alliance with the Athenians, challenged the Spartans but again were crushed. Nevertheless the city flourished. On the lower ground below the Larisa the agora was developed at this time, its edges being delimited in part at least by extended porticoes (stoas) of a thoroughly up-to-date form. A further attempt at victory over the Spartans, again in alliance with the Athenians, ended in defeat for the Argives at the Battle of Mantinea in 416 BC. In the years that followed Argos rallied support from other Peloponnesian cities who had turned against Spartan authoritarianism. This led to the so-called Corinthian War, during which an interesting political experiment, a union between Argos and Corinth, gave much alarm to the Spartans, who duly suppressed it.

A revival in the city's fortune came about fortuitously when the Macedonian kings, whose family name was Argeadae, claimed descent from the legendary kings of Argos, apparently on the dubious basis of the similarity of name and the invention of a fictitious genealogy. This meant, after the Macedonian victory of Chaeronea, that the Argives were in favour. Even after the death of Alexander the Great and the confusion which followed, Argos remained loyal to its Macedonian connection, and eventually to Antigonus Gonatas who ruled Macedon for much of the first half of the 3rd century BC. His enemy Pyrrhus tried to take Argos by surprise, but lost the initiative when one of his battle elephants (previously used spectacularly in his fruitless war with the Romans) got stuck under a city gate. Pyrrhus himself broke into the town, only to meet an ignominious death when an old woman dropped a heavy rooftile on his head. For much of the 3rd century BC Argos was ruled by pro-Macedonian tyrants, who were derided for their subservience by Greeks opposed to Macedonian supremacy, but who were perfectly acceptable to the citizens of Argos, who prospered as a result.

With the Roman conquest of Greece, Argos lost what prominence it had, and under the Roman empire was far less important than Corinth. It became a typical Roman provincial town, its prosperity signalled by public buildings, particularly a substantial bath complex of the 2nd century AD, the most extensive ancient ruin in Argos apart from the theatre, which cut into the slope of the Larisa and was certainly in existence early in the 4th century BC. Argos also retained in the Roman period the fortifications on the Larisa, large portions of which date from the 5th century BC. These were refurbished in the Byzantine period, when Argos continued as a small town, and

resisted a long Frankish siege in the 13th century. The city's key position, on one of the routes from the north into the southern Peloponnese, ensured both its continuation and the maintenance and improvement (finally, during the Turkish occupation) of its fortifications.

The major contribution of Argos to the Classical tradition in the arts lay undoubtedly in the field of sculpture. The early Argives' skills in bronze working produced in the 7th century BC a series of decorated shields, primarily for dedication in the sanctuary at Olympia and probably reflecting the Argive involvement there. With the development of the lost-wax technique of hollow casting, these bronze-working skills were later applied to freestanding sculpture. The pioneer in this, Ageladas, is no more than a name. He is eclipsed by the 5th-century sculptor Polyclitus, perhaps a pupil, though the chronology is uncertain. Only copies of Polyclitus' works survive. One in particular, called the *Doryphoros* (spear-bearer), seems to have been produced as the sculptor's ideal of masculine human beauty. The form, as well as the style, influenced sculptors of the succeeding century, and in the Roman period Polyclitus was regarded as the supreme exponent of his art, so that Polyclitan forms are used, for instance, for portrait statues of the Roman emperors, such as the Prima Porta *Augustus*; others, incongruously, go even further and depict emperors in Polyclitan nudity.

R.A. TOMLINSON

Summary

City in southern Greece with a continuous history from the Neolithic period to the present day. After the Bronze Age, when it was overshadowed by neighbouring Mycenae and Tiryns, it was occupied by Dorian settlers and the city flourished during the Classical period, when it was noted for its sculpture.

Further Reading

Aupert, P., "Argos aux VIII–VII siècles", *Annuario della Scuola Italiana di Atene*, 60: p. 21ff.

Excavation reports of the French School in *Bulletin de Correspondance Hellénique* from 1970 onwards

Kelly, Thomas, *A History of Argos to 500 BC*, Minneapolis: University of Minnesota Press, 1976

Tomlinson, R.A., *Argos and the Argolid: From the End of the Bronze Age to the Roman Occupation*, London: Routledge, and Ithaca, New York: Cornell University Press, 1972

Argyropoulos, John c.1415–1487

Scholar

John Argyropoulos was one of the most prominent of the Byzantine émigré scholars who took up residence in Italy after the capture of Constantinople by the Ottoman Turks in 1453. In his teaching at the University of Florence he won adulation rivalled only by that accorded to Manuel Chrysoloras, and his students included some of the foremost Italian humanists of the next generation.

In the years before the fall of Constantinople, Argyropoulos had belonged to the narrow circle of Byzantine intellectuals. He had taught rhetoric at the Katholikon Mouseion, or higher

IOANNES ARGYROPYLVS
PHILOSOPHVS.

Magnus Ariftoteles loquitur quòd in orbe Latinè:

John Argyropoulos, from a 16th-century engraving

school, and had written a number of rhetorical works in traditional style in praise of the emperors John VIII (1421/25–48)
and Constantine XI (1449–53) Palaiologos. His reputation
outside Byzantium began to grow from 1438, when he accompanied John VIII to the Council of Florence as part of the
Byzantine delegation and became a supporter of the union of
the Churches proclaimed there. He appears to have remained
in Italy until about 1443, giving private lessons in Greek and
studying Latin at the University of Padua. The knowledge of
Latin that he obtained in this period undoubtedly stood him in
good stead in the future, as did the contacts he made with such
prominent Florentines as Palla Strozzi. He was once more in
Italy in August 1454 as a refugee following the fall of
Constantinople, and after a period in Greece at the court of the
despot Thomas Palaiologos at Patras, he returned to western
Europe in 1456 as an ambassador to the papal, French, and
English courts.

It was while he was in Italy on this mission in October 1456
that Argyropoulos received an invitation from the Florentine
statesman Cosimo de' Medici to take up the chair of Greek at
the University of Florence, with a substantial yearly stipend of
400 florins. His teaching in Florence proved to be immensely
popular, and served to revive the interest in Greek studies that
had languished since the departure of Manuel Chrysoloras in
1400. His public lectures on Aristotle, given in the mornings,
were thronged by eager listeners from all over Europe. In the
afternoons he gave private lessons to some of the most prominent Florentine intellectuals, including Pallas Strozzi, the child
prodigy Angelo Poliziano, Alamanno Rinuccini, Donato
Acciaiuoli, the bookseller Vespasiano da Bisticci, and Cosimo's
grandson, Lorenzo de' Medici, "the Magnificent". He came to
enjoy something approaching celebrity status, becoming a
leading member of the Accademia Fiorentina, a literary club
that met in Rinuccini's house, and receiving a house in the Via
Larga and Florentine citizenship in 1466.

Argyropoulos's popularity was probably due, at least in
part, to two aspects of his teaching method. The first was the
importance that he attached to speculative philosophy as an
essential part of the curriculum, rather than adhering solely to
rhetoric, the traditional mainstay of humanist education. In an
introductory lecture given in November 1458 to his course on
Aristotle's *Physics*, Argyropoulos, like Theodore Gaza before
him, extolled the usefulness of Greek philosophy as a training
for effective participation in political life. His lectures therefore
covered ethics, logic, physics, and metaphysics, as well as
rhetoric and the Greek language itself. Secondly, there was his
choice of philosopher. Although personally an Aristotelian
who accepted the traditional, scholastic interpretations of
Aristotle's philosophy, in his private teaching Argyropoulos
gave instruction in the works of Plato. His exposition of Plato
proved to be so effective that many of his students, particularly
Acciaiuoli and Rinuccini, transferred their interest from
rhetoric to Plato's metaphysical philosophy, with important
long-term consequences for the development of Florentine
political thought.

As well as teaching, Argyropoulos was active as a translator
of Greek texts into Latin. He prepared versions of a number of
Aristotle's works, including the *Nicomachean Ethics*, the
Physics, and the *Metaphysics*, all of which he dedicated to
members of the Medici family. Unlike Manuel Chrysoloras and
Theodore Gaza, however, he preferred a literal translation,
distrusting literary elegance, which he considered likely to
obscure meaning. This may explain why his translations were
never as widely used as those of Theodore Gaza and cardinal
Bessarion.

In spite of the high reputation he had obtained during his 15
years in Florence, in 1471 Argyropoulos moved to Rome for
reasons that are not entirely clear. He may have been moved to
leave Florence by the death of his patron, Cosimo's son, Piero
de' Medici, in 1469, and by hopes of obtaining the favour of
the Greek cardinal Bessarion. He had also found a new patron
in pope Sixtus IV, Francesco della Rovere, whom he may well
have met earlier at Padua in the 1440s. Argyropoulos remained
in Rome for the rest of his life – apart from a short period in
Florence in the years 1477–81 – giving public lectures in the
Vatican on Greek philosophy and literature. His most prominent student in this last period of his life was the German
humanist Johannes Reuchlin. He continued to translate Greek
texts, notably St Basil's *Hexaemeron*. He died on 26 June
1487, allegedly from an over-indulgence in watermelon, but
one tangible reminder of his time in Rome can still be seen
today: his portrait appears in the frescos by Domenico
Ghirlandaio on the walls of the Sistine chapel.

JONATHAN HARRIS

Biography

Born in Constantinople c.1415, Argyropoulos accompanied John VIII to the Council of Florence in 1438 and remained in Italy until c.1443. After the fall of Constantinople he returned to Italy and in 1456 was invited by Cosimo de' Medici to take the chair of Greek at the University of Florence. In 1471 he moved to Rome where he died in 1487.

Further Reading

Brown, Alison M., "Platonism in Fifteenth-Century Florence and its Contribution to Early Modern Political Thought", *Journal of Modern History*, 58 (1986): pp. 383–413

Brown, V., "Giovanni Argiropulo on the Agent Intellect: An Edition of Magliabechi V 42 (ff. 224–228v)" in *Essays in Honour of Anton Charles Pegis*, edited by J. Reginald O'Donnell, Toronto: Pontifical Institute of Mediaeval Studies, 1974

Cammelli, Giuseppe, *I dotti bizantini e le origini dell'umanesimo*, vol. 2: *Giovanni Argiropulo*, Florence: Monnier, 1941

Geanakoplos, Deno John, *Greek Scholars in Venice: Studies in the Dissemination of Greek Learning from Byzantium to Western Europe*, Cambridge, Massachusetts: Harvard University Press, 1962; as *Byzantium and the Renaissance*, Hamden, Connecticut: Archon, 1973

Geanakoplos, Deno John, "The Career of the Byzantine Humanist Professor John Argyropoulos in Florence and Rome: The Turn to Metaphysics" in his *Constantinople and the West*, Madison: University of Wisconsin Press, 1989

Harris, Jonathan, *Greek Emigres in the West, 1400–1520*, Camberley, Surrey: Porphyrogenitus, 1995

Kraye, Jill, "Philosophers and Philologists" in *The Cambridge Companion to Renaissance Humanism*, edited by Kraye, Cambridge and New York: Cambridge University Press, 1996

Lee, Egmont, *Sixtus IV and Men of Letters*, Rome: Storia e Letteratura, 1978, pp. 171–73

Siegel, J., "The Teaching of Argyropoulos and the Rhetoric of the First Humanists" in *Action and Conviction in Early Modern Europe: Essays in Memory of E.H. Harbison*, edited by Theodore K. Rabb and Jerrold E. Siegel, Princeton, New Jersey: Princeton University Press, 1969

Wilson, N.G., *From Byzantium to Italy: Greek Studies in the Italian Renaissance*, London: Duckworth, and Baltimore: Johns Hopkins University Press, 1992

Aristarchus of Samothrace c.215–c.143 BC

Librarian and scholar

Aristarchus was born in Samothrace c.215 BC and died at the age of 72 (we are told) c.143 BC in Cyprus. Most of his adult life, however, was spent in Alexandria, first as tutor to several young royals of the house of Ptolemy and then as one of a distinguished line of librarians at the most famous centre of learning in the Greek world, the Museum. His predecessors were Zenodotus, Apollonius of Rhodes, Eratosthenes, and Aristophanes. Although nowadays we tend to think of librarians primarily as cataloguers and maintainers of the texts in their collections, those at Alexandria were also scholars and occasionally, most notably in the cases of Apollonius and Eratosthenes, poets as well. (Callimachus, however, the most famous of Hellenistic poets and the compiler of the *Pinakes*, a list of authors and their works so complete that it could serve as library catalogue, never served as a librarian.)

Aristarchus has his detractors as well as fans, but despite the frequent difficulty in distinguishing his contribution from the vast amount of scholiastic material in the margin of extant Greek texts, especially the scholia of Homer, the overall nature of his contributions is clear. Like his predecessors, and much like any modern editor and commentator, Aristarchus was responsible for establishing the standard text and explaining his choice of readings and the meanings of puzzling words, expressions, character motivation, and overall meaning. Prose works, arriving in the library in fewer copies with fewer textual variants, required (or at any rate received) little work of this sort, although Aristarchus did write a commentary on Herodotus, some traces of which survive. Poetry, however, written in all the dialects ever spoken in Greece, to say nothing of the artificial forms that Homer and others felt free to create, and showing up – "published" is too narrow a term – in varying lengths for the same work and with a variety of lexical and morphological forms, required a battery of methodological skills. Homer and Hesiod, therefore, along with the more difficult lyric (notably Alcman and Pindar) and tragic poets, received the greatest attention from the Alexandrian poet-scholars.

The first task, as suggested above, was to establish a standard text, which in large part was derived from what was thought to be the best readings of preexisting manuscripts; but to a lesser extent, when the manuscripts were deemed unsatisfactory, editorial intervention was brought to bear. The gentlest instance of the latter was the use of marginal signs designed to alert the reader to questionable lines, which would be allowed to stand in the text. Aristarchus, for example, kept many lines which Zenodotus had expunged from his official text of Homer. A stronger measure would excise one or more lines or alter individual words.

Of all the poets treated by Aristarchus – Homer, Hesiod, Archilochus, Alcaeus, Pindar, Aeschylus, Sophocles, Euripides (very likely), and the comic poet Aristophanes – it is the author of the *Iliad* and *Odyssey*, thanks to the vast amount of carefully attributed scholia surviving in medieval manuscripts, who provides us with the best picture of Aristarchus' activities as both editor and commentator. In hundreds of places the scholia on Homer name Aristarchus as their source; in others a suggestion that is anonymous in the scholia is attributed to Aristarchus elsewhere, which strongly suggests that many other anonymous scholia owe their origin to him. We even on occasion learn his earlier views along with his later thoughts, as expressed in his second commentary on Homer. Some of the characteristics of Aristarchan scholarship are:

(1) Removing narrative inconsistencies. For example, to avoid inconsistency between Odysseus' account to Alcinous in book 7 of the *Odyssey* and Homer's narrative of the same event in book 6, Aristarchus altered a sunset in the earlier book to late afternoon, although, even if this was an inconsistency, rather than the result of yet one more bending of the truth on Odysseus' part, it would be Homer's and not that of a scribe; it would deserve not textual emendation so much as notice (with or without censure). In fact Aristarchus himself did this on other occasions in his separately published commentaries, as when he pointed out, without demanding alteration or excision, that the emissaries to Achilles in *Iliad* 9 ate two dinners on the same day (as what soldier could not?).

(2) Excising "improper" passages. Homer had been criticized for describing gods impiously as early as Xenophanes and most notably by Plato, but although the editorial vice of actually removing such passages is associated chiefly with Zenodotus, Aristarchus too is guilty of this. It is, for example, only thanks to Plutarch that we know the lines spoken by Phoenix in *Iliad* 9, where he says that he considered killing his own father, which were ejected from the text by Aristarchus and from all subsequent copies. But these lines are part of a long speech in which Phoenix artfully develops a parallel between his younger self and Achilles, who had threatened *his* superior, Agamemnon.

(3) "Explaining Homer from Homer". The idea behind this well-known phrase is an excellent starting point for any commentator, but Aristarchus could carry it too far, occasionally misinterpreting a Homeric word, when even a text so close in time to Homer as an early Homeric hymn would explain and defend Homer's usage. Since excesses of this sort were largely limited to his commentaries, they did not affect the text. Some close readings of the text, moreover, such as Aristarchus' attempts to understand the point of individual similes, can still stand.

Many of Aristarchus' readings were adopted by later editors and still appear in current editions. More important than any tabulation of his presence in later texts, however, is the example that he and his fellow Alexandrian editors left for their successors. For all that their methodology has been tempered with a greater understanding of Greek historical linguistics and the nature of poetry, their diligence and desire to explain all puzzling passages on rational principles remain the core of modern editorial practice. Their philology is our philology.

DAVID SIDER

See also Scholarship

Biography

Born in Samothrace *c*.215 BC, Aristarchus spent most of his career at Alexandria. He was tutor to the Egyptian royal family. He succeeded Apollonius as head librarian of the Museum and was also a scholar and critic. He produced critical editions of Homer, Hesiod, Archilochus, Alcaeus, Anacreon, and Pindar. He wrote commentaries on Homer, Hesiod, Archilochus, Alcman, Pindar, Aeschylus, Sophocles, Aristophanes, Herodotus, and perhaps Euripides. He died in Cyprus *c*.143 BC.

Further Reading

Fraser, P.M., *Ptolemaic Alexandria*, vol. 1, Oxford: Clarendon Press, 1972, pp. 461–67

Janko, Richard, *The Iliad: A Commentary*, vol. 4: *Books 13–16*, Cambridge and New York: Cambridge University Press, 1992, pp. 25–29

Montanari, F., "Zenodotus, Aristarchus, and the *Ekdosis* of Homer" in *Editing Texts – Texte Edieren*, edited by Glen W. Most, Göttingen: Vandenhoeck & Ruprecht, 1998

Pfeiffer, Rudolf, *History of Classical Scholarship from the Beginnings to the End of the Hellenistic Age*, Oxford: Clarendon Press, 1968, pp. 210–33

Valk, Marchinus van der, *Textual Criticism of the Odyssey*, Leiden: Sijthoff, 1949

Aristides, Aelius AD 117–*c*.180

Writer and orator

In many respects Aristides is a typical representative of the cultural tendencies of his age, the so-called Second Sophistic, while in others he cuts a rather peculiar figure. Born into a well-to-do family of the little town of Hadriani in Mysia, he acquired a thorough rhetorical education based on the great texts of the Greek classics and soon began to pursue the career of a professional speaker (a "sophist" in the parlance of the time) for the multifarious public occasions that the cultural life of his times provided. A long-lasting illness, however, with symptoms of physical as well as psychic distress, which broke out soon after he had returned from an educational journey to Egypt, forced him to curtail public appearances and to spend long periods within the precinct of the healing god Asclepius at Pergamum. Aristides himself documented these periods in his *Hieroi Logoi* (Sacred Discourses), relating how the god appeared in his dreams and gave him various (and sometimes quite strange) commands to fulfil, but also encouraged him to carry on with his rhetorical studies, promising that he might even surpass the great Demosthenes. The *Hieroi Logoi* thus reveal not only the workings of an overanxious and selfcentred mind, but also a singular determination to rival and outdo the best of the Classical authors he had been taught to emulate.

It was apparently in the AD 150s that Aristides was able to put his illness behind him and publicly perform some of his great speeches, among them the famous *Encomium to Rome*; in this he celebrated (not without some exaggeration) the civilizing power of the Roman empire that had given the Mediterranean and especially the Greek world a stable frame within which to survive and prosper (Aristides was a Roman citizen, a distinction probably inherited from his father). Like other Greek intellectuals of his time, however, he looked back even more to the glorious days of Classical Greece and wrote an even longer speech (the *Panathenaikos*, its title not fortuitously evoking its great predecessor written by Isocrates) extolling the cultural and political achievements of Athens in its most illustrious days. In a similar vein, his *Meletai* ("declamations", i.e. speeches conceived as if pronounced by some great historical figure in a certain historical situation) tried to bring back to life some of the most decisive moments of Classical history (e.g. the situation on the eve of the Battle of Leuctra in 371 BC; the Athenians deliberating about reinforcements to their troops fighting against Syracuse in 414 BC); and a number of hymns in prose – a genre of which Aristides even claimed to be the inventor – praised the gods of Classical religion. Still, at least some part of his rhetorical activity was also directed to the present. Like Dio Chrysostom, he addressed various cities and exhorted them to put aside their internal differences and rivalries with each other. His most remarkable achievement in this domain is the speeches on Smyrna, which he addressed to the Roman emperors Marcus Aurelius and Commodus after the city had been levelled by a disastrous earthquake in AD 177 or 178; these speeches actually moved the Roman authorities to contribute decisively to Smyrna's resurrection.

Some of Aristides' most elaborate works were probably never performed, but were disseminated in written form and soon proved to be influential. In three long essays he intervened in an intellectual struggle of already long standing, that between rhetoric and philosophy, both of which claimed to be the most important subject of a higher education. Since Plato had carried out his formidable attacks on rhetoric in the *Gorgias*, that struggle had never ceased, and now Aristides came down emphatically on the side of rhetoric. A long double essay *On Rhetoric* proclaimed the pre-eminent worth of its subject against philosophy, and the equally long *In Defence of the Four* aimed to rehabilitate the achievements of the four great Athenian statesmen and generals Miltiades, Themistocles, Cimon, and Pericles, which had been ferociously taken apart in the *Gorgias*. Later on, the Neoplatonists took these attacks on their founding father seriously enough to react to them: in the latter part of the 3rd century AD Porphyry wrote *Against Aristides* in seven books, and in the 5th century Olympiodorus and Proclus still felt obliged to take note of Aristides' essays.

It was, however, in the field of rhetoric itself that Aristides proved most influential. He was one of the foremost exponents of literary Atticism in his age, and his efforts to make his style conform as much as possible to the way Attic authors had expressed themselves some 500 years earlier were astonishingly successful. He had no gift for extemporizing speeches (an ability that was very much sought after in his time), but rather preferred to polish his texts as meticulously as possible in his study. This may in fact have assured their survival; Aristides is one of the very few typical authors of the Second Sophistic whose work was preserved beyond the end of antiquity, and he even belongs to the small number of Greek writers whose works survive almost in their entirety. For centuries after his death (which probably occurred around AD 180) Aristides very nearly attained the goal he had so fervently pursued: to surpass Demosthenes. Already in the 3rd century AD the rhetorician Longinus regarded him as the defender of Atticism against the dissoluteness of so-called Asianic oratory (characterized by bombast and emotion); at about the same time the rhetorical treatises of Menander of Laodicea (who also wrote the first commentary on him) cite Aristides as often as Isocrates and Plato and considerably more frequently than Demosthenes and Lysias. In the 4th century AD Libanius and Himerius show his influence: Libanius wrote set pieces against declamations that Aristides had worked out (e.g. his *Embassy Speech to Achilles*) and the *Hieroi Logoi* provided inspiration for his autobiography, while Himerius' *Polemarchikos* drew on Aristides' *Panathenaikos*. At about the same time Sopater of Apamea provided an *Introduction* to Aristides' work and commentaries, which – together with the exegetical notes of other authors – later became a part of the extensive scholia (explanatory notes) that were added in the margins of the manuscripts.

After the dark centuries of early Byzantium we find Aristides holding an important place in higher education. Photios in his *Bibliotheca* (cod. 246–48) provided excerpts of the *Panathenaikos* and the long anti-Platonic speeches on rhetoric; in the 10th century archbishop Arethas ordered the writing of what today is the most important Aristides manuscript (A, Oxford, Bodleian Library, MS E.D. Clarke 39) and added notes to it. In the 11th century Theodora (daughter of the emperor Constantine VIII and later an empress herself) copied a text of Aristides in her own hand, and Michael Psellos

commended studying him – besides such classics as Demosthenes, Isocrates, and others – as a necessary means for attaining mastery of style. The Palaiologan renaissance preserved Aristides' influence; two speeches *On Exemption from Public Burdens* (also called the "Leptinean orations") by Thomas Magistros (who also excerpted Aristides for his lexicon) even found their way into the Aristidean corpus. In the 14th century Theodore Metochites not only modelled his *Byzantios* on Aristides' encomium on Rome, but also wrote an essay comparing Aristides and Demosthenes, and in the 15th century the *Hieroi Logoi* still provided inspiration for John Chortasmenos's reports on his own sickness. The fall of Byzantium finally put an end to Aristides' long importance as a model for elaborate rhetorical writing.

HEINZ-GÜNTHER NESSELRATH

Biography

Born in AD 117 at Hadriani in Mysia, Aristides was educated in Athens and Pergamum and travelled widely (to Egypt, Cyzicus, and Rome) before settling at Smyrna. Chronic illness forced his (temporary) retirement and enabled him to pursue his rhetorical studies. He became a great exponent of literary Atticism for which he was much admired by posterity. He died *c*.180.

Writings

Aristides, vol. 1: *Panathenaic Oration and In Defence of Oratory*, translated by C.A. Behr, Cambridge, Massachusetts: Harvard University Press, and London: Heinemann, 1973 (Loeb edition)

The Complete Works, translated by C.A. Behr, 2 vols, Leiden: Brill, 1981–86

Discorsi sacri, translated into Italian by Salvatore Nicosia, Milan: Adelphi, 1984

Further Reading

Behr, C.A., *Aelius Aristides and the Sacred Tales*, Amsterdam: Hakkert, 1968

Behr, C.A., "Studies in the Biography of Aelius Aristides" in *Aufstieg und Niedergang der römischen Welt*, edited by Hildegard Temporini et al., 2.34.2, Berlin: de Gruyter 1994, 1140–1233

Karadimas, Dimitrios, *Sextus Empiricus against Aelius Aristides: The Conflict between Philosophy and Rhetoric in the Second Century AD*, Lund: Lund University Press, 1996

Lenz, Friedrich Walter, *The Aristeides Prolegomena*, Leiden: Brill, 1959

Moreschini, Claudio, "Elio Aristide tra retorica e filosofia" in *Aufstieg und Niedergang der römischen Welt*, edited by Hildegard Temporini et al., 2.34.2, Berlin: de Gruyter 1994, 1234–47

Oliver, James H., "The Ruling Power: A Study of the Roman Empire in the 2nd Century after Christ Through the Roman Oration of Aelius Aristides", *Transactions of the American Philosophical Society*, new series, 43/4, (1953): pp. 871–1003

Oliver, James H., *The Civilizing Power: A Study of the Panathenaic Discourse of Aelius Aristides against the Background of Literature and Cultural Conflict*, Philadelphia: American Philosophical Society, 1968 (includes translation)

Swain, Simon, *Hellenism and Empire: Language, Classicism, and Power in the Greek World, AD 50–250*, Oxford: Clarendon Press, and New York: Oxford University Press, 1996

Treadgold, Warren (editor), *Renaissances before the Renaissance: Cultural Revivals of Late Antiquity and the Middle Ages*, Stanford, California: Stanford University Press, 1984

Aristocracy

Rule by the "best"

Aristocracy (*aristokratia*), a form of government based on the principle that the "best" should rule, is a compound of the Greek words for the best (*ariston*) and rule (*kratos*). Aristocracy may appear similar to rule by the rich (plutocracy), or by the few (oligarchy), or by honour (timocracy), but it is distinguished by the exercise of power by a hereditary minority, usually a relatively small landed class. Aristocrats claim to be the best because they are the possessors of some superiority by blood, lineage, rank, talent, virtue, or wisdom, which becomes a legitimizing principle. A variety of socio-political practices and political arguments have been used to justify the resulting privileges. Aristocracies develop traditions to set themselves apart from the common mass of people. By adopting distinctive styles of behaviour, dress, habits, speech, interests, education, and even sexual practices, aristocrats are marked as qualitatively different from ordinary people. These cultural distinctions are inculcated into all members of the aristocratic families. Aristocrats seek to maintain themselves by the principle of purity of blood so that only a noble may marry a noble. They usually maintain control of the principal sources of wealth, military training, and the institutions of religion. By means of these controls power can be held for generations. Aristocracies degenerate in several ways. Excessive inbreeding can eliminate the vigour needed to rule. Intermarriage with the *nouveaux riches*, or with powerful oligarchs, to renew ebbing fortunes violates the genetic principle and puts the aristocracy up for sale. Or they may simply fail to cope with changing times.

In Homer "the best" usually means the best warriors. By the Archaic period the Homeric military elite of merit had changed to a nobility of birth. When combined with the advantages that family traditions and wealth provide, aristocracy can produce those who are the apparent "natural leaders" of society. Greek aristocratic families claimed that descent from a heroic or mythical person set them apart from and above others in every generation. The aristocrats were the eupatrids, or those born to "good fathers".

In the 8th century BC when the Greek city states were emerging from the Dark Ages, the kings of earlier times had all but vanished, except at a few places such as Argos and Sparta. Elsewhere kings were replaced by or dominated by aristocrats. For the next few centuries the aristocrats ruled or dominated their respective city states, usually through a council (*boule*). Often the ruling class came from only one clan.

By the end of the 6th century BC socioeconomic and military changes brought challenges to aristocratic power. Growing population pressures and economic difficulties impoverished small farmers. Lenders, often aristocrats, sold indebted fellow citizens into slavery. These conditions and practices led to socioeconomic tensions which were aggravated by the revolutionary changes in warfare. In the heroic age aristocrats had been the most powerful warriors. Riding to battle on a horse or in a chariot, they often fought only their social equals. Now the hoplite, a heavily armed, middle-class soldier, fighting as part of a unit called a phalanx, became the core of the city state's army. The new middle class, who could afford the armour but not the horse, demanded a share of the political power. When the aristocrats refused to accept reforms, the ensuing conflict with the lower classes turned into class warfare.

In some cases of civil strife in the city states a disgruntled aristocrat would lead the people in revolt against the aristocracy. These "class traitors" eventually acquired the name *tyrannos* (tyrant). Cypselus became tyrant of Corinth after the aristocratic family, the Bacchiadae, were overthrown. The 5th century BC was virtually the age of tyrants in Greece, a time when the old aristocratic system was breaking down, to be replaced by oligarchies, or democracies. The civil strife ended in some city states, such as at Athens, with a democratic form of government. Elsewhere it produced oligarchies. In Sparta, however, the regime was successful in suppressing any democratic tendencies that threatened the prevailing aristocracy.

Athenian aristocratic families included the Alcmaeonidae, Philaedae, Eumolpidae, Phytalidae, Eteoboutadae, and Lycomidae. Individual Athenian aristocrats included Draco, Solon, Hippias, Cleisthenes, Pericles, and Alcibiades. Individual Spartan aristocrats included Lycurgus and Leonidas. The Presocratic philosopher Heraclitus of Ephesus was an aristocrat, as were many other philosophers, including Plato. The rise of democracy reduced the power of aristocrats, yet they often provided the leadership in many fields.

Plato in his *Republic* advocates rule by an aristocracy of intellect. Generally, aristocrats have avoided intellect as a criterion of membership in the aristocracy because there is no guarantee that remarkable aristocrats will have anything other than ordinary children. Aware of this, Plato rejected physical succession in his Utopia in favour of a system of recruitment that sought the best and brightest, even if born into the lower orders. Aristotle's theory of aristocracy, as developed in the *Politics*, has been used over the centuries to support aristocratic aspirations. He argues that aristocracy is the good form of rule by the few because they are the best from virtue, and that such a regime itself cultivates virtue in the city state.

In the Hellenistic age a few aristocratic families continued their traditions, but for the most part the Hellenistic kings ruled through bureaucracies, as did the Romans. By the time of the emperor Justinian (527–65) a system of military districts called "themes" arose. The theme system encouraged ownership by many small landholders who could easily serve as soldiers. By the reign of Basil II (976–1025) large landowners had emerged from the military aristocracy. Their efforts to create large estates led to civil war. Although they were defeated, they eventually took over from within, and emperors were drawn from aristocratic families. Consolidation of landownership ruined the theme system, which had been the source of military strength for the empire.

After the fall of Constantinople in 1453, moneyed aristocrats eventually emerged among the Greeks living in the Ottoman empire. Composed of Greek and Hellenized Albanian and Romanian families, they were called the Phanariots after the lighthouse quarter in Constantinople.

A.J.L. WASKEY, JR

Further Reading

Andrewes, Antony, *The Greek Tyrants*, London: Hutchinson, 1956; New York: Harper and Row, 1963

Aristotle, *The Politics*, edited and translated by Ernest Barker, Oxford: Clarendon Press, 1948; New York: Oxford University Press, 1962

Arnheim, M.T.W., *Aristocracy in Greek Society*, London: Thames and Hudson, and Boulder, Colorado: Westview Press, 1977

Forrest, W.G., *A History of Sparta, 950–192 BC*, 2nd edition, London: Duckworth, 1980

MacKendrick, Paul, *The Athenian Aristocracy, 399–31 BC*, Cambridge, Massachusetts: Harvard University Press, 1969

Mosca, Gaetano, *The Ruling Class*, New York: McGraw Hill, 1939

Ostrogorsky, George, *History of the Byzantine State*, revised edition, Oxford: Blackwell, 1968; New Brunswick, New Jersey: Rutgers University Press, 1969

Plato, *The Republic*, translated by Francis MacDonald Cornford, Oxford: Clarendon Press, 1941; New York: Oxford University Press, 1945

Plutarch, *Lives of the Noble Greeks*, edited by Edmund Fuller, New York: Dell, 1959

Pomeroy, Sarah B., *Families in Classical and Hellenistic Greece: Representations and Realities*, Oxford: Clarendon Press, and New York: Oxford University Press, 1997

Starr, Chester G., *The Aristocratic Temper of Greek Civilization*, Oxford and New York: Oxford University Press, 1992

Willetts, R.F., *Aristocratic Society in Ancient Crete*, Westport, Connecticut: Greenwood Press, 1980

Aristophanes

Athenian comic dramatist of the 5th–4th centuries BC

Aristophanes composed 40 comedies, 11 of which have survived, the earliest of these being datable to 425 BC and the last to 388. In the course of the Classical period comedy underwent great changes in character and structure. Aristophanes is a representative of Old Comedy – its supreme representative, in the judgement of late antiquity, and therefore the only one whose works have survived.

Nothing quite like Old Comedy exists in the modern theatre; it comprises elements of farce, but includes much that we associate with pantomime, situation comedy, savage political satire, and animated cartoons. Its dramatic time is always the present, and its topicality constitutes one of its essential differences from the universality of "New Comedy", which held the stage two generations after Aristophanes' death. The characters in some of his comedies were living people known to the audience, such as Euripides (in *Acharnians*) and Socrates (in *Clouds*). The plot sometimes turns upon an issue which was a real political issue at the time of performance.

By no means all Aristophanes' plays are political, and whether they are or not, the resolution of the plot entails unlimited fantasy. In *Birds*, for example, a plausible Athenian persuades the (Greek-speaking) birds to build a city in the sky and lay siege to the gods; and in *Frogs* the god Dionysus travels to the underworld and presides over a poetical contest between the ghosts of Aeschylus and Euripides. The operation of cause and effect in the world as we know it is suspended to whatever extent the poet wishes, and the audience is not expected to say "But how could...?" or "But surely...!" because consistency is readily sacrificed. In *Lysistrata*, for instance, an Athenian woman organizes the citizens' wives of the belligerent states to go on a sex strike until negotiations for peace are opened. The plot envisages that while the younger wives stay at home, tantalizing and frustrating their husbands, the older women occupy the Acropolis; but then we find that *all* the wives have shut themselves away on the Acropolis.

Whereas there is some evidence that some of Aristophanes' plays were performed in the Greek cities of southern Italy and Sicily for a while after his death, that seems not to have been the case in Athens, where popular taste in comedy changed rapidly and fundamentally. In the 3rd century BC, however, scholars were attracted to the reading and study (though not the performance) of Aristophanes, and successive commentaries on his texts were composed. By about AD 900, when interest in ancient pagan literature revived at Byzantium after a long lapse, manuscripts of 11 out of the original 40 plays could still be found, and within those 11 a canon of three took shape: *Wealth* (*Plutus*), *Clouds*, and *Frogs*. *Wealth*, far in the lead in respect of the number of medieval manuscripts which contain it, owed its popularity and educational utility to the universality of its theme – the "injustice" which everywhere rewards the dishonest and impoverishes the righteous – and to the consequent paucity of references which demand antiquarian knowledge. Its comparative avoidance of outright obscenity and of difficult passages in elaborate poetic language no doubt contributed to its high status.

Aristophanes became known to western European scholars in the 15th century; the first printed edition of his plays appeared in 1498, and many Latin translations followed (there was even an Italian translation in 1545). When an individual play appeared in a modern language, it was usually *Wealth*, for the Byzantine evaluation, inherited by the Renaissance, prevailed for nearly three centuries. After the beginning of the 19th century school editions of all the plays, together with translations for the educated public, proliferated. The editions were often ruthlessly bowdlerized by excision, which obscured the point of jokes, as did evasive paraphrase in translations.

According to an ancient anecdote, Plato told the Syracusan tyrant Dionysius that for a proper understanding of Athenian democracy a thorough reading of Aristophanes was essential. That advice was not taken (and probably not known) by the protagonists of the Hellenic cultural revival which from small beginnings in the 17th century increasingly came to engage Greek intellectuals at the end of the 18th century. While school pupils in the west were becoming well acquainted with Aristophanes, he had no place in the 30 volumes of Korais' *Hellenic Library*, and first found a modern Greek editor (Neophytos Doukas) in 1845. Doukas, rather like the Byzantine scholars, valued Aristophanes above all as an exponent of the Classical Attic language, whereas Korais and other participants in the Greek revival were aiming at moral and intellectual regeneration, an end to which a poet so often frivolous, cynical, and obscene did not seem to make a contribution of value. Within living memory, students at Greek universities heard no lectures on Aristophanes. There exists, however, in Greece a long and rich tradition of obscene, satirical, anti-establishment popular song, together (in some regions) with touring market-square comic performances, and it is noteworthy that the first translations of Aristophanes into demotic Greek (by Rangavis) coincided with the introduction in 1860 of shadow-plays whose stock characters always included an ingenious and imaginative rogue of Aristophanic type (karaghiozis). During the last 50 years performances of

Aristophanes, son of Philippos, father of Greek comedy

Aristophanes in demotic translation have come to be one of the most striking achievements of the modern Greek theatre.

In a typical Aristophanic play a substantial part is played by a chorus, sometimes representing animals, birds, insects, or personified abstractions. That is a tradition which Aristophanes inherited, for a vase painting dating from long before his time depicts men dressed as birds dancing in line. The chorus of *Wasps*, pitiless old jurymen, is a metaphor realized in the flesh. Except in his last two plays, *Women in the Assembly* (*Ecclesiazusae*) and *Wealth*, where we see the start of the process which soon led to the limitation of the chorus's role to song-and-dance intermezzi for which the poet did not write the songs himself, the chorus at a central point in the play steps wholly, partly, or minimally out of its role in the plot and addresses the audience directly. It may speak for the poet, as "he" or (as part of the time in *Clouds*) "I", denigrating the poets who were his rivals for prizes at dramatic festivals; it may criticize, often with a light and humorous touch, political behaviour of the citizen body; or it may (as in *Birds*) exploit with jocular imagination ideas which emerge from the plot of the play. This direct address to the audience, usually preceded and followed by lyric hymns addressed to deities, is the "parabasis" of the play, and it raises the question: when it seems to us to be serious, is it really serious?

On one occasion at least it is hard to avoid saying "yes". In *Frogs* the parabasis urges the restoration of citizen rights to the men who had been disfranchised for their involvement in an oligarchic revolt six years earlier. That was a practicable step (even if unwise), and a step actually taken some months later after disastrous defeat at sea. But it is not just in the parabasis that the question arises; it is raised also by the purposes which the "hero" of the play (there is not always one) realizes triumphantly. We can be certain that the audience of *Acharnians* contained some people who shared the view that going to war against Sparta had been a mistake and that there was now an opportunity to stop it, because we know that not everyone had favoured war at the start and that in its second year, under the impact of the plague, the assembly had seriously contemplated negotiation for peace. It is wrong, though, to think of Aristophanes as a pacifist in the modern sense; between the belief that killing is always a sin and the recognition that there are times when peace is more advantageous there is a considerable gap. Perhaps, diffidently, he was a feminist, who in *Lysistrata* and *Women at the Thesmophoria* gives a powerful voice to the dissatisfactions of women, though to his audience the idea that women (or sheep, or sharks) could organize themselves like men would have been intrinsically funny, and *Women in the Assembly* treats women as preoccupied with food, drink, and sex.

While his parodies of tragedy can be acquitted of malice, his uninhibited attacks on named individuals can hardly be dismissed as harmless fun, seeing that at the end of *Clouds* Socrates and his disciples, driven out of the school by fire and pelted with stones, suffer the fate of traitors whose crimes were judged so monstrous as to deprive them of the law's protection. Plato blamed Aristophanes for creating popular prejudice against Socrates; and there were a few critical occasions on which vilification of named individuals on the comic stage was temporarily forbidden by law. Perhaps humorous periodicals which are frequently sued for libel are the nearest modern equivalent to Aristophanes.

KENNETH DOVER

See also Comedy, Karaghiozis

Biography
Born probably in the 450s BC, Aristophanes was the greatest exponent of Old Attic Comedy but little is known of his life. Of 40 plays written by him, 11 have survived, ranging in date from 425 to 388 BC. They are now popular on the modern Greek stage. Aristophanes died *c*.386 BC.

Writings (in translation)
The Frogs and Other Plays, translated by David Barrett, Harmondsworth and Baltimore: Penguin, 1964 (contains *The Wasps, The Poet and the Women* [*Thesmophoriazusae*], *The Frogs*)
The Archanians, The Clouds, Lysistrata, translated by Alan H. Sommerstein, Harmondsworth: Penguin, 1973
The Knights, Peace, The Birds, The Assembly-women, Wealth, translated by David Barrett and Alan H. Sommerstein, Harmondsworth and New York: Penguin, 1978
Clouds, Women in Power, Knights, translated by Kenneth McLeish, Cambridge and New York: Cambridge University Press, 1979
The Comedies, edited and translated by Alan H. Sommerstein, Warminster: Aris and Phillips, 1980–

Three Plays by Aristophanes: Staging Women, edited and translated by Jeffrey Henderson, New York and London: Routledge, 1996 (contains *Lysistrata*, *Women at the Thesmophoria*, *Assemblywomen*)

Birds, Lysistrata, Assembly-women, Wealth, translated by Stephen Halliwell, Oxford: Clarendon Press, and New York: Oxford University Press, 1997 (2 more vols in preparation)

Further Reading

Anonymous, *Summary of a Comparison of Aristophanes with Menander in Plutarch's Moralia*, vol. 10, translated by H.N. Fowler, London: Heinemann, and Cambridge, Massachusetts: Harvard University Press, 1936 (Loeb edition)

Cartledge, Paul, *Aristophanes and His Theatre of the Absurd*, Bristol: Bristol Classical Press, 1990

Dover, K.J., *Aristophanic Comedy*, London: Batsford, and Berkeley: University of California Press, 1972

Harriott, Rosemary M., *Aristophanes, Poet and Dramatist*, London: Croom Helm, and Baltimore: Johns Hopkins University Press, 1986

MacDowell, Douglas M., *Aristophanes and Athens: An Introduction to the Plays*, Oxford and New York: Oxford University Press, 1995

McLeish, Kenneth, *The Theatre of Aristophanes*, London: Thames and Hudson, and New York: Taplinger, 1980

Russo, Carlo Ferdinando, *Aristophanes: An Author for the Stage*, London and New York: Routledge, 1994

Süss, Wilhelm, *Aristophanes und die Nachwelt*, 2nd edition, Leipzig: Dieterich, 1911

Van Steen, Gonda, "Aristophanes and the Modern Greek Stage", *Dialogus: Hellenic Studies Review*, 2 (1995): pp. 71–90

Van Steen, Gonda, *Venom in Verse: Aristophanes in Modern Greece*, Princeton, New Jersey: Princeton University Press, 2000

Aristotelianism

It is not possible to understand "Aristotelianism" properly without understanding the complex reception of Aristotle's works. It is true that there are concepts one immediately associates with Aristotle's teachings – the four causes, the doctrine of the mean, and the like – but Aristotle meant many things to many readers over time. As is well known, Aristotle's writings were not in circulation for more than two centuries after his death. It is not entirely clear who was responsible for recovering them, but copies of his works were evidently available in Rome in the 1st century BC. Aristotle's ideas had little detectable influence, however, except in the fields of rhetoric and cosmology. It was not until the 3rd and 4th centuries AD that Aristotle was the subject of lectures and commentary activity in the schools of philosophy at Alexandria and Athens, notably by the Neoplatonists, Porphyry and Alexander of Aphrodisias, both of whom concentrated mainly on the works comprising the *Organon*. Porphyry's *Eisagoge* (Introduction) to Aristotle's *Categories* was enormously influential through the Greek and, later, the Latin Middle Ages, as was Alexander's commentary on the *Topics*. These Alexandrian and Athenian exegetes, however, were concerned above all to reconcile Aristotle with Plato, on the assumption that in the works of both one could find the truths of philosophy, but expressed differently. By comparison with Plato, they found Aristotle notoriously obscure – intentionally, these commentators explain. In the 6th century significant commentary activity was carried on by John Philoponus and Simplicius, both students of the Neoplatonist Ammonius Hermeiou in Alexandria. In Ravenna, then the capital of the western Roman empire, Boethius produced a translation of the *Topics* into Latin and commentaries (now lost) on the *Analytics*. The Boethian version of the *Topics*, along with his *De Differentiis Topicis*, formed the core of the "Old Logic" that was to persist well into the Latin Middle Ages.

As early as the 4th century Aristotle was being translated in Edessa into Syriac. These Syriac versions formed the base for translations into Judaeo-Arabic and, in 10th-century Baghdad, into Arabic. These aroused keen interest among Muslim scholars both in Baghdad and, in the two succeeding centuries, in Moorish Spain. Among the most influential of those scholars were al-Farabi (d. 950), Ibn Sina (Avicenna) (d. 1137), and Ibn Rushd (Averroes) (d. 1198), all of whom produced editions, with commentaries (often collating Greek manuscripts checked against the Syriac), of Aristotle's major works with the exception of the *Politics*, the *Eudemian Ethics*, and the *Magna Moralia*. Like their Greek Neoplatonist predecessors, whose prolegomena and commentaries they also translated and studied, Arabic exegetes understood Aristotle as the author of a closed system and supposed him to be in complete agreement with Plato.

Aristotelianism in the Middle Ages must, of course, be differentiated, for there were two separate traditions, the Byzantine and that of the Latin west. In Byzantium Aristotle was looked upon with some suspicion, as a pagan thinker who believed, for instance, that matter was eternal and that, if there is a divinity, it is physically represented by the ether that fills the void in the universe. In the 9th and 10th centuries there was a surge in interest in Aristotle and the production of some important manuscripts of his works – some of them possibly obtained from libraries in Baghdad and Basra. By far the most widely circulated were the books that make up the *Organon*, with the treatises on natural history running a distant second. In the 11th century Michael Psellos and his student John Italos lectured on Aristotle, mainly on dialectic. One of Italos's students, Eustratios, composed a commentary on book 6 of the *Nicomachean Ethics*. Italos and Eustratios, however, found it hard to stay safe from persecution, as Italos was twice condemned by Orthodox theologians and Eustratios, in 1117, was condemned for, among other things, claiming that Christ reasoned in Aristotelian syllogisms. In the decades that followed, members of a scholarly circle sponsored by the secluded Anna Komnene, chiefly Michael of Ephesus and Stephanos Skylitzes, produced commentaries on many of Aristotle's works for which there was no commentary tradition in Greek. One of the commentaries that may have come out of the activity sponsored by Anna is that on *Nicomachean Ethics* 6 by Eustratios, which begins with a dedication praising her piety and learning and addressed to a young reader by an old writer. Eustratios also composed a commentary on *Nicomachean Ethics* 1, one on book 2 of the *Posterior Analytics*, and a short piece based on Aristotle's *Meteorology*. Michael of Ephesus produced a much larger number of works than did Eustratios. It is generally agreed that he composed scholia and/or commentaries on *Nicomachean Ethics* 5, 9, and 10; the *Parva Naturalia*, the biological treatises; *Metaphysics* E–N; *The Generation of Animals*; *Topics* (lost); *Physics* (lost);

De Interpretatione (lost); *Prior Analytics*, book 2; *Sophistic Refutations*; and the *Rhetoric*. Even allowing for the fact that Michael obviously depended on earlier commentaries on these works, his output was nothing short of amazing – the extant material alone filling more than 1100 printed pages. At the end of the 13th and during the 14th century, there was another "renaissance" of interest in Aristotle in the synoptic works of Nikephoros Blemmydes (d. 1272), who composed epitomes of both the *Organon* and the *Physics*. Even in the 14th century writers such as Theodore Metochites complained about the "labyrinthine" obscurity of Aristotle's style. Aristotle's philosophy, on the whole, never played an important part in Byzantine thinking.

In the Latin west, Aristotle arrived in the mid-13th century via Latin translations by Gerard of Cremona and William of Moerbeke of Arabic versions of his works. His influence, channelled partly through the commentaries of Ibn Rushd and Maimonides, was enormous on the works of Aquinas and such thinkers as Siger de Brabant. In spite of the strenuous opposition of the Catholic hierarchy, Aristotle made significant inroads into medieval thinking. Indeed, he was universally known as "The Philosopher". This was, once again, primarily in the field of logic; but his influence is also apparent in discussions on the nature of an "art" and a "science", in the need to discuss all subjects in terms of the four causes, and in the fact that Aristotelian (Latin) technical vocabulary became the virtual lingua franca of all the disciplines, not least theology. Theological discussions were controlled by Aristotelian principles of valid deduction to such a degree that Byzantine theologians had difficulty both in following and in countering western arguments in their encounters in the 14th and 15th centuries. As a consequence, Gennadios Scholarios produced translations into Greek of parts of Aquinas' *Summa contra Gentiles* and his *De Ente et Essentia*, the *Summulae Logicales* of Peter of Spain, and the commentary on Aristotle's *Categories* by Gilbert de la Porrée.

During the 15th and 16th centuries in Europe there was a huge growth in interest in Aristotle's works. This was due in part to the proliferation of printing presses after 1470 or so and the consequent publication, by 1600, of over 3000 editions of *Aristotelica*. With the fall of Constantinople to the Turks in 1453, large numbers of codices containing the works of Aristotle and his Greek commentators arrived in the west as did a number of Greek scholars who brought instruction in Greek to western universities. These were critical factors in the Renaissance recovery of Aristotle, and although Byzantine teachers had been active in Italy well before 1453, the second half of the 15th century witnessed activity of a different order. Scholars such as Demetrios Chalkondyles and Leonikos Thomaios lectured on Aristotle at the University of Padua, where a chair of Greek letters was established in 1463. In 1497 a chair of Aristotelian philosophy was established at Padua, where Aristotle's works were read by students in virtually every discipline, including medicine. In 1542 a chair of Greek and Latin philosophy was established at the Collège Royal, and Francesco Vimercato was invited from Milan to lecture on Aristotle's *De Anima*. The first printed edition of the Greek text of Aristotle's works (minus the *Rhetoric*) had been published by Aldus Manutius in Venice in 1498. This enormous project could not have been realized without the assistance of the indefatigable Markos Moussouros, who himself was responsible for the publication of Alexander of Aphrodisias's *Commentary on the Topics* (1514) – highly influential on Renaissance study of Aristotle.

The University of Padua became perhaps the most influential centre of Aristotle studies in Europe at a time when there was enormous interest in Aristotle. (As the eminent scholar Charles Lohr has observed, there was more commentary activity during this period than in the whole millennium between Boethius and Pietro Pomponazzi.) At Padua Aristotle was combined with Scholastic methods and principles to produce a kind of neo-Aristotelianism that was to inspire a new enthusiasm for philosophy. Greek scholars such as Michael Sophianos and Daniel Fourlanos joined with Jacopo Zabarella (d. 1589) in lecturing on Aristotle's *Poetics*, the *De Anima*, and the *Parts of Animals*; and Fourlanos produced Latin versions of *Parts* and of *De Anima* in 1574. That same year Maximos Margounios (1549–1602) published a Latin translation of Psellos on book 2 of the *Posterior Analytics*.

The following generation of Aristotle scholars at Padua included such teachers as Joannes Kottounios (1577–1658), a Macedonian from Ohrid who would succeed the famous Cesare Cremonini as professor of philosophy – chiefly Aristotle's works on natural philosophy. In his lectures on Aristotle's *De Caelo* and *Meteorologia* Kottounios sided with Cremonini, who had become famous as the man who would not look through Galileo's telescope. Unlike his "Aristotelian" predecessor Zabarella, Cremonini had little use for direct observation – which should remind us of the important fact that Renaissance "Aristotelians" were extremely eclectic. Some Renaissance "Aristotelians" took up Aristotle's logic without paying attention to anything else; others adopted his moral philosophy without the natural philosophy; some revered his natural philosophy without his *Metaphysics*; and some, indeed, continued to read Aristotle in Neoplatonic fashion, looking for traces of the *prisca scientia* contained in the works of writers like Hermes Trismegistos.

In 1613 another of Cremonini's students, Theophilos Corydalleus, (1570–1646) successfully completed disputations on medical questions as well as on Aristorte's *De Anima* and the question of how odours are perceived according to the *Physics* , and was granted a double doctorate in medicine and philosophy. Corydalleus, who would be an important influence on Greek education until the end of the 18th century, spent the rest of his life propagating the Paduan version of Aristotle throughout the Balkans, spending time teaching in Cephalonia, Zakynthos, his native Athens, and Constantinople. At Constantinople in 1625 he was appointed dragoman of the Patriarchate and *didaskalos* in the Patriarchal Academy, which he promptly reorganized along "Italian" lines. Three years later he would depart for Zakynthos to teach there again; but he returned to Constantinople in 1636. Corydalleus wrote extensively on various Aristotelian treatises, but only his *Rhetoric*, a synthesis of Aristotle and the still dominant Ciceronian doctrine, was published in his lifetime – in London, by Nikodemos Metaxas, in 1625. All of the rest exist only in manuscripts, the sheer number and distribution of which make it clear how pervasive his influence was. These include commentaries on the *Metaphysics*, *De Anima*, and *De Caelo*; notes on the *Physics* and *On Generation and Corruption*; and his *Commentary and Questions Concerning Aristotle's Logic as a Whole*. These were used in schools in the Ionian islands, Bucharest, Jassy, and Constantinople well into the 18th century, towards the end of which printed editions of some began to appear. It is notable that Corydalleus wrote his treatises in Attic Greek, possibly because modern Greek had not yet stabilized, but certainly because he thought it best to write about Aristotle in Aristotle's language.

The generation after Corydalleus saw continued interest in Aristotle's works, most notably, perhaps, in the activities of the Phanariot Alexander Mavrokordatos (1641–1709). Mavrokordatos had been educated in Rome, Padua, and Bologna, where he studied medicine. Mavrokordatos eventually went to Constantinople, where he taught at the Patriarchal Academy, and later (in 1673) was appointed to the office of Grand Dragoman by the Sublime Porte. Amid all his various duties, he found time to write a number of books on a wide range of subjects, including a commentary on and synopsis of Aristotle's *Rhetoric*. One of Mavrokordatos's students, Sebastos Kyminitis, is recorded as having lectured on *On Vices and Virtues* at the Greek Academy in Bucharest in 1689.

Interest in Aristotle's philosophy was beginning to wane, however, among teachers of philosophy, many of whom were educated in Italy and Germany and were consequently (and increasingly) drawn to the "new" philosophy as propounded by the likes of Descartes, Leibniz, and Locke. Thus, on the one hand, George Sougdouris taught Aristotelian logic and poetics in the Corydalleus tradition in Ioannina between 1682 and 1715; but on the other, his student, Methodios Anthrakistes (b. c.1662), was condemned by a patriarchal synod in 1723 for not adhering to the Peripatetic school. This action represents a major readjustment within the Orthodox Church (recall Eustratios), which in reaction to the new philosophies of the west had adopted the Paduan version of Aristotle as its philosophical framework.

Padua continued to be a centre for Aristotle studies well into the 18th century. Some traditional branches of philosophy – chiefly physics – no longer looked to Aristotle's teachings, but ethics, metaphysics, logic, and rhetoric at Padua retained a strongly Aristotelian character. This was particularly evident in the teaching and writing of Vikentios Damodos (1700–52). Damodos was yet another Greek who studied in Italy, but returned to his homeland to teach. Born in Cephalonia, he studied first at the Flanginian Academy, founded in 1626 and sponsored by the metropolitan of Venice, and then went to Padua, where he took a double *Juris Doctor* degree in 1721. He returned shortly after to Cephalonia, first to practise law, but before long to teach in his native village, Chavriata. He wrote on a large number of subjects, most often from an Aristotelian standpoint, as in his *Metaphysics*, a synopsis of the *Nicomachean Ethics*, an *Epitome of Aristotelian Logic*, and two treatises on rhetoric strongly influenced by Aristotle's *Rhetoric*. None of his works was published in his lifetime, although his *Epitome of Aristotelian Logic* and his *Art of Rhetoric* were well enough known to be published in Venice in 1759.

At this juncture, evidence for interest in Aristotle becomes thin and widely dispersed. Such interest seems to have narrowed to his logical works and, to a somewhat lesser degree, to the *Ethics*. Thus, for instance, the *Introduction to Aristotle's Logic* by Georgios Sougdouris (d. 1740) came out in a 1792 edition in Venice. Manasse Eliades (d. 1785), who did not consider himself an Aristotelian, lectured on the *Categories* at the Academy in Bucharest. Neophytos Kavsokalyvytis (d. 1780) produced scholia on the *Ethics* for his students in Chios. In general, however, Greek philosophers were more interested in translating into Greek such authors as Malebranche and Condillac than in continuing the Aristotelian tradition. Occasionally Aristotle was pressed into service for arguments about other matters. Adamantios Korais, for instance, produced in his Hellenic Library editions of the *Politics* (1822) and the *Ethics* (1825), suggesting in the prefaces to those editions that they might be of assistance in constitutional decisions that had to be made after the War of Independence. That suggestion, it seems, foreshadowed similar determinations in England and Germany 20 years later, during the years of political liberalization, when there was a similar ripple of interest in Aristotle. Since then, it is fair to say, interest in Aristotle has been limited largely to philological circles in Greece, as it has been in the countries of western Europe.

THOMAS M. CONLEY

See also Aristotle, Philosophy

Further Reading
Henderson, G.P., *The Revival of Greek Thought, 1620–1830*, Albany: State University of New York Press, 1970
Knös, Börje, *L'Histoire de la littérature néo-grecque: la période jusqu'en 1821*, Stockholm: Almqvist & Wiksell, 1962
Moraux, Paul, *Der Aristotelismus bei den Griechen: Von Andronikos bis Alexander von Aphrodisias*, 2 vols, Berlin: de Gruyter, 1973–84
Peters, F.E., *Aristoteles Arabus: The Oriental Translations and Commentaries of the Aristotelian Corpus*, Leiden: Brill, 1968
Schmitt, Charles B., *Aristotle and the Renaissance*, Cambridge, Massachusetts: Harvard University Press, 1983
Steenberghen, Fernand van, *Aristotle in the West: The Origins of Latin Aristotelianism*, 2nd edition, Louvain: Nauwelaerts, and New York: Humanities Press, 1955

Aristotle 384–322 BC

Philosopher

Aristotle was born at Stagira in Chalcidice; his father, Nicomachus, was court physician to the Macedonian king Amyntas III. At the age of 17 he went to Athens to study at Plato's Academy, remaining a member for 20 years (first as a student and later as a teacher). Shortly after Plato's death in 347 BC, he left Athens for the court of Hermias at Atarneus in Asia Minor. He lived for two years on the island of Lesbos, where he engaged in some zoological researches and met Theophrastus, who was to become his student. In 343 BC he went to the court of the Macedonian king Philip II at Pella and there served as tutor to Philip's son, Alexander. In 335 BC, when Athens had come under Macedonian rule, Aristotle returned and founded his own school, in the Lyceum (a sanctuary located outside the eastern section of the ancient wall). There was a *peripatos* – a colonnaded walk – in the building, from which the school acquired its name – the Peripatetic school. On the death of Alexander in 323 BC there was an eruption of anti-Macedonian sentiment in Athens, and Aristotle himself was charged with impiety. He fled and came to reside on a family estate at Chalcis on the island of Euboea. One report has him stating that he fled "so that Athens might not commit another crime against philosophy" (in 399 BC Socrates had been charged with impiety, found guilty, and sentenced to death.) He died at Chalcis a year later, perhaps of a stomach ailment.

Aristotle was a student of Plato, but his own writings clearly show that he was by no means a Platonist. (Some of his early works, of which only a few fragments survive, contain Platonist elements, but these may have been propagandist writings for the Academy.) Plato's grand theory was that of the Forms. He held that certain unitary, unchanging, and perfect realities exist in a realm beyond perception. Among these realities are the Good Itself and the Beautiful Itself. The theory of the Forms has both ontological and epistemological aspects. The Forms are basic realities and so the existence of all other things (within our own changeable and imperfect realm of perception) is dependent upon them. Further knowledge, for Plato, is a cognitive grasp of the Forms. Knowledge is gained, not through a process of justification (in which experience or belief is built up into knowledge through argument or investigation), but through a process of discovery. To come to know the Forms is to turn the mind's eye towards these self-justifying realities.

Aristotle explicitly rejects the theory of the Forms. His ontology and epistemology are profoundly anti-Platonist. For Aristotle, individual substances – such as "this man here" and "this horse here" – are ontologically basic. (It has been suggested that Aristotle's emphasis on biological individuals, in contrast to Plato's emphasis on quasi-mathematical individuals – the Forms – is due to the influence of the profession of Aristotle's father.) All else is dependent upon these primary substances: particular quantities and qualities would not exist if primary substances did not exist. Further, the universals that range above individual substances – universals such as man, horse, and animal – are substances only in a derivative sense. These indicate the character of a plurality of primary substances, but they do not exist as unitary basic realities. Thus, Aristotle reverses the Platonic model: he takes what is changeable to be ontologically basic and he denies that universals are substantial unities.

Scientific knowledge, according to Aristotle, is a cognitive grasp of the cause of a thing together with an understanding that the cause could not be otherwise. Aristotle thought of the sciences as axiomatic deductive systems. (Here Plato's fascination with mathematics may have been of some influence.) According to his view, one has scientific knowledge when one can demonstrate the cause of a thing from first principles. These first principles are better known and prior to the conclusion of a scientific demonstration. Thus, for Aristotle, knowledge of, say, why snakes have a larynx but no epiglottis is akin to knowledge of why two triangles with the same base and height are equal in area. In each case, knowledge is secured through demonstration from the first principles of the relevant science. First principles, however, cannot be demonstrated. These must be grasped by some other means. Aristotle holds that our perceptual experience provides the ultimate justifica-

tion of first principles. Our nature is such that we store perceptions within the soul. Owing to memory we come to have experience (a grasp of concepts based on particulars) and owing to experience we come to entertain the principles of science (concepts involving the grasp of strict universals). For example, Aristotle asserts that it is from perceptual experience that we grasp the truth that an eclipse is a certain loss of light on the moon. This, however, is not knowledge of the cause of an eclipse. Knowledge of the cause – obstruction of the sun's light by the Earth – is secured through a process of inference to the best explanation. Other candidate explanations (say, rotation of the moon) fail the test of perceptual experience (our familiarity with the precise pattern of loss of light on the moon during an eclipse suggests that the rotation of the moon is not a suitable explanation). Reason tests candidate explanations against our perceptual experience and so it is this experience that provides the ultimate justification of first principles. Aristotle's empiricism, thus, lies in stark contrast to Plato's rationalism.

Aristotle was the first philosopher to develop a theory of formal logic. His theory of deductive inference is that of the categorical syllogism. By first establishing the validity of four "perfect" (axiomatic) syllogistic forms, he was able to show which remaining standard syllogistic forms are valid. (Out of 256 standard syllogistic forms, only 24 are valid.) Aristotelian logic was for two millennia treated as the whole of logic. The logical writings constitute a singular and unparalleled achievement and Aristotle was himself aware of this. In a rare self-congratulatory passage he lauds his own achievements in logic as being entirely without precedent among Greek philosophers.

In areas where his predecessors had expounded theories, Aristotle would often begin his own studies by setting out, analysing, and comparing their views. He would then explore what is common among such theories, mark differences, and locate areas in which such theories stand at odds (with one another, with the perceived phenomena, or within themselves). He would then guide his own positive investigation in the light of the results of this inquiry. In such inquiries Aristotle sought to preserve what is true in earlier theories and to understand better the difficulties within a given field. (He claimed that it is impossible for one to untie a knot that one does not know.) Inquiry of this sort occupies the philosophical branch of Aristotle's dialectical method, a method of arguing from the opinions of others.

Dialectical inquiry is most evident in the works on natural science. In these works, among other things, Aristotle sets out and studies the theories of the Presocratic philosophers. We owe practically all that we know of the Presocratics to Aristotle; for a majority of the extant fragments come from his own writings, the writings of his student Theophrastus, and the writings of his Greek commentators (such as Simplicius). Within the works on natural science we find many of the distinctive conceptual advances that mark Aristotle's thought as superior to that of his predecessors. One such advance can be found in his treatment of causality. While many of the Presocratic philosophers had attempted to account for natural phenomena through an analysis of matter, Aristotle argues that a complete treatment of such phenomena must take into account not only material causes, but formal, final, and efficient ones as well. Just as a complete account of a sculpture will make reference to its matter (bronze), its form (shape or organization), its efficient cause (the sculptor who initiated the shaping of the bronze), and the purpose for which it was made, a complete account of the genesis of a living thing, or of the organic functioning of a living thing, will make reference to four causes.

Aristotle utilizes the doctrine of the four causes within both his psychological and his biological works. In his main psychological work, the *De Anima*, he argues that soul is not a body, and yet it is also not an immaterial substance that might exist in separation from the body. Soul is the form of the living body: it is the organization-for-the-sake-of-functioning of the living thing. This theory – hylomorphism – avoids the pitfalls of both elemental materialism (which fails to give an account of purposes or goals in nature) and Platonic dualism (which, when conjoined with the doctrine of the transmigration of soul, fails to give an account of how different kinds of bodies might prove to be suitable hosts for some one kind of soul). The theory of hylomorphism is, perhaps, compromised within Aristotle's account of intellect. He suggests that intellect may be separable from the body. (This move towards dualism is, perhaps, an anomaly within his writings, an anomaly that may betray a Platonist influence.)

The doctrine of the four causes shapes Aristotle's biological investigations. (The writings on biology take up more than one-fourth of the extant corpus.) His view of nature is teleological. Thus, taking the fully developed and flourishing member of the species to be the end towards which the species itself aims, he holds that the biologist must focus his studies on healthy mature adults within a given species. The variety and depth of Aristotle's investigations into the anatomy, development, and habits of animals are dazzling. While a summary of his work in zoology cannot be attempted here, it should be noted that even into the 19th century naturalists were (re)discovering certain anatomical features of species that Aristotle had already noted in his own researches.

The central concept of Aristotle's ethics is flourishing (*eudaimonia*). The concept is also central to his political writings, for he asserts that the main function of government is to promote *eudaimonia* among its citizens. He thinks that, since humans differ from other animals in so far as they are rational, flourishing for a human must be living a certain life of active reason. We are rational, however, in two ways: part of us exercises reason and part of us is obedient to reason. Out of this distinction – a distinction between intellect and passion – Aristotle generates a theory of human excellence that treats both rational excellence and moral excellence. The moral excellences (such as courage and temperance) are means between extremes. To be temperate, for example, is to have an intermediate disposition in respect to bodily pleasures. These excellences are acquired through habituation. One becomes courageous, for example, by doing courageous things (even if at first one does not do courageous things courageously). The intellectual excellences (such as wisdom and prudence) are not means between extremes. These excellences are not acquired through habituation, rather they are taught. In his discussion of the best life, Aristotle places special emphasis on the intellectual activity of contemplation. He maintains that the life of contemplation is the best life: it is the best life in so far as it involves the activity of some divine element within us.

Aristotle's conception of God is linked to his cosmological theory. He holds that the earth is the centre of a finite spherical cosmos and that the heavens are constituted by a set of nesting concentric spheres that move eternally in perfect circles. The motion of the spheres has a first cause. This cause is an unmoved mover: it is an immaterial god. The unmoved mover (the highest sort of being) engages eternally in thought (the highest sort of activity). It is not the generative cause of the cosmos. Rather, it lives an exalted life of contemplation. The unmoved mover is eternally self-thinking thought.

After Aristotle's death Theophrastus became the second head of the Peripatetic school. Under his leadership the school thrived. He was a talented empirical scientist and a vigorous thinker intensely interested in the study of Aristotle's works. After his death the Peripatetic school fell into decline. His successors were either highly specialized thinkers (like Strato) or markedly unoriginal thinkers (like Lyco). It is probable that the Peripatetic school in Athens did not survive into the 1st century BC. Aristotle's thought, however, did not perish in the Lyceum. A considerable number of his writings have survived. In the 1st century BC Andronicus of Rhodes produced an edition of Aristotle's works and from the time of this edition there has been a continuous history of the transmission of Aristotle's texts within the Greek tradition. (The corpus as we now have it contains, perhaps, one third of what Aristotle had written.) Texts survived, but in addition Aristotle's thought did not go the way of dead dogma: his works were studied in the Neoplatonic schools of Athens, Constantinople, and Alexandria. Some of his doctrines found their way into Neoplatonism itself. (For example, the doctrine of the unmoved mover as self-thinking thought clearly reemerges in the writings of Plotinus.) These schools established a tradition of writing commentaries on Aristotle's works and in so doing they secured his legacy within Hellenic culture.

JOHN E. SISKO

See also Aristotelianism, Cosmology, Ethics, Dialectic, Government, Logic, Lyceum, Plato, Zoology

Biography
Born at Stagira in Chalcidice in 384 BC, Aristotle studied at Plato's Academy in Athens and remained there until soon after Plato's death (347 BC), when he moved first to Asia Minor and then Lesbos. On Lesbos he met Theophrastus, who became his pupil. In 343 he moved to Pella in Macedonia as tutor to the son of Philip II, Alexander. In 335 he returned to Athens and founded the Peripatetic school in the Lyceum. After Alexander's death he was charged with impiety and fled to Euboea where he died in 322 BC.

Writings
The Complete Works: The Revised Oxford Translation, edited by Jonathan Barnes, 2 vols, Princeton, New Jersey: Princeton University Press, 1984

Further Reading
Barnes, Jonathan, Malcolm Schofield and Richard Sorabji (editors), *Articles on Aristotle*, 4 vols, London: Duckworth, and New York: St Martin's Press, 1975–79

Barnes, Jonathan, *Aristotle*, Oxford and New York: Oxford University Press, 1982

Barnes, Jonathan (editor), *The Cambridge Companion to Aristotle*, Cambridge and New York: Cambridge University Press, 1995

Broadie, Sarah, *Ethics with Aristotle*, Oxford and New York: Oxford University Press, 1991

Cooper, John M., *Reason and Human Good in Aristotle*, Cambridge, Massachusetts: Harvard University Press, 1975

Furley, David J. and Alexander Nehamas (editors), *Aristotle's Rhetoric: Philosophical Essays*, Princeton, New Jersey: Princeton University Press, 1994

Gotthelf, Allan and James G. Lennox (editors), *Philosophical Issues in Aristotle's Biology*, Cambridge and New York: Cambridge University Press, 1987

Hardie, W.F.R., *Aristotle's Ethical Theory*, 2nd edition, Oxford: Clarendon Press, and New York: Oxford University Press, 1980

Irwin, Terence (editor), *Classical Philosophy: Collected Papers*, vols 5–6, New York: Garland, 1995

Judson, Lindsay (editor), *Aristotle's Physics: A Collection of Essays*, Oxford: Clarendon Press, and New York: Oxford University Press, 1991

Keyt, David and Fred Miller (editors), *A Companion to Aristotle's Politics*, Oxford and Cambridge, Massachusetts: Blackwell, 1991

Kraut, Richard, *Aristotle on the Human Good*, Princeton, New Jersey: Princeton University Press, 1989

Lear, Jonathan, *Aristotle: The Desire to Understand*, Cambridge and New York: Cambridge University Press, 1988

Nussbaum, Martha C. and Amélie Oksenberg Rorty (editors), *Essays on Aristotle's De Anima*, Oxford: Clarendon Press, and New York: Oxford University Press, 1992

Patzig, Günther, *Aristotle's Theory of the Syllogism: A Logicophilological Study of Book A of the Prior Analytics*, Dordrecht: Reidel, 1969

Robinson, Timothy A., *Aristotle in Outline*, Indianapolis: Hackett, 1995

Rorty, Amélie Oksenberg (editor), *Essays on Aristotle's Ethics*, Berkeley: University of California Press, 1980

Rorty, Amélie Oksenberg (editor), *Essays on Aristotle's Poetics*, Princeton, New Jersey: Princeton University Press, 1992

Waterlow (Broadie), Sarah, *Nature, Change, and Agency in Aristotle's Physics: A Philosophical Study*, Oxford: Clarendon Press, and New York: Oxford University Press, 1982

Aristoxenus

Writer on music in the 4th century BC

Born around 370 BC in Taras (Latin Tarentum; modern Taranto), Aristoxenus grew up when this town was ruled by Archytas the Pythagorean. His first instructor was his father Mnesias, a musician, and it is by this title, *musicus*, that Aristoxenus was persistently called, although in his case this term must be understood to refer primarily to his theoretical writings on music rather than to the skill he had in singing and in playing instruments. (That he had such abilities is demonstrated by his basing his theory of harmonics on aesthetic principles at variance with the purely mathematical views of more orthodox Pythagoreans.) His later teachers included the obscure Lampros of Erythrae (perhaps while still in Taras), then the Pythagorean Xenophilus, and finally Aristotle. His reputation in the Lyceum was such that he expected to be head of the school after Aristotle's death. That the headship fell instead to Theophrastus, whose interests were as wide-ranging as Aristotle's (including some technical works on music), should have come as no surprise.

Aristoxenus, for all his 453 books (as tallied by the *Suda*) on various philosophical, biographical, and historical topics, seems to have concentrated his best efforts on music. Indeed, we now know very little of his straightforward philosophical works, not even how large a proportion of the whole they formed. His comments on the nature of the soul owe little if anything to Aristotle's *De Anima* but have more to do with Pythagorean ideas of harmony in the soul such as are found in Plato's *Phaedo* and *Timaeus*. Since our sources (chiefly Cicero and Lactantius) associate these ideas with musical harmony, Aristoxenus may well have introduced them in his musical writings rather than in a separate work on the nature of the soul. Some sources refer to his *Hypomnemata* (Memorabilia), but this is a catch-all title that says nothing about the work's subject matter; other sources add the word *Miscellaneous* to the title. Here too Aristoxenus is said to have discussed musical matters, although perhaps not as technically as in his treatises devoted to the subject. Even his biographies may have been chosen because of his interest in music. This is obviously so in the case of his comprehensive work entitled *On Tragic Poets* and a separate life of Telestes the dithyrambic poet but, even in his biographies of Plato, Socrates, Archytas, and, of course, Pythagoras, he would have had much to say about their views of music as well as more usual matters, such as Socrates' two wives and Plato's travels. The quality of his biographical writings was praised by none other than the master of the genre, Plutarch, comparing the great and unalloyed pleasure they provide to that obtained by reading Herodotus or Homer.

We also hear of works entitled *Rules of Education* (in at least ten books), *Political Laws* (in at least eight books), *Mantinean Character*, and (if different from the last) *Praise of Mantineans*. Most of these fragments have nothing to do with music: they discuss the difference between two words having to do with shame, the fact that one educates one's son best by making him a citizen of a well-governed city, that Lycurgus died in Crete; but even here (in *Political Laws*), Aristoxenus has something to say about the composition of pseudo-Epicharmic verses by Chrysogonus the *aulos* player.

Aristoxenus truly deserves his title of *musicus*, then. In addition to some of the pertinent works named above, we hear of and learn a little about the following: *On Music*, *Course on Music* (these may be two titles for the same work), *On Music in Lyric Poetry*, and *Praxidamantea* (presumably on the views of the musical theorist Praxidamas). Significant portions, however, are extant of works entitled *Elementa Rhythmica* and *Elementa Harmonica* (in three books), although the latter seems rather to be selections from two distinct works. These actual words of Aristoxenus can be further supplemented by passages in later writers who drew freely from Aristoxenus: Porphyry, Michael Psellos, and two anonymous works.

Much of these two works is concerned with the technical details of notes, tempi, modes, scales, intervals, etc., but it is plain that Aristoxenus considered himself to be an innovator in the writing of musical theory. Arguing against those who, although ignorant of the true nature of music, nonetheless denied it any significance, Aristoxenus also distinguished himself from the extreme intellectualism of the Pythagoreans (see above), although he accepted some of their views on the relationship between music and ethical behaviour. He could not, however, bind himself to a rigidly mathematical scheme that failed to take into account the slight but inherent disparities that are as much a part of music as (his example) the deviations from straight lines that woodworkers and other craftsmen in visual arts incorporate into their products. These deviations can be perceived, and then described, only by someone skilled in music.

Later writers on music theory made frequent reference to the theories expounded by Aristoxenus (even when they do not name him), some going so far as to ally themselves specifically with him in opposition to Pythagorean views.

DAVID SIDER

See also Music

Biography

Born *c*.370 BC in Taras (now Taranto) the son of a musician, Aristoxenus was taught first by his father, then by Lampros of Erythrae. Probably in Athens he was a pupil of Xenophilus and then joined Aristotle's Lyceum. He wrote copiously – 453 books according to the *Suda* – and mostly on music. He failed to succeed Aristotle as head of the Lyceum. His date of death is unknown.

Writings

Aristoxenou Harmonika Stoicheia: The Harmonics of Aristoxenus, edited and translated by Henry S. Macan, Oxford: Clarendon Press, 1902

Die Schule des Aristoteles: Texte und Kommentare, vol. 2: *Aristexonos*, edited by Fritz Wehrli, Basel: Schwabe, 1967 (the fragments in Greek with commentary in German)

In *Greek Musical Writings*, vol. 2: *Harmonic and Acoustic Theory*, translated by Andrew Barker, Cambridge and New York: Cambridge University Press, 1989 (translations of *Elementa Harmonica* and *Elementa Rhythmica*, with notes)

Elementa Rhythmica: The Fragment of Book II and the Additional Evidence for Aristoxenean Rhythmic Theory, edited and translated by Lionel Pearson, Oxford: Clarendon Press, and New York: Oxford University Press, 1990 (translations and commentary)

Armatoloi

Licensed militias

Literally "men at arms", the *armatoloi* (singular *armatolos*) made up the quasi-official local militias that patrolled the numerous mountain passes of the northern mainland of Greece from the Byzantine period onwards. They were particularly dominant from the 15th to the 18th centuries, and were also present throughout the mountainous Balkan territories of the Ottoman empire, in Albania, Bosnia, Bulgaria, and Macedonia. During the Ottoman period, Balkan territories were divided into administrative subdistricts known as *armatoliks*, each of which had appended to it an *armatoloi* militia.

In addition to preventing brigand activity, the *armatoloi* were in some instances responsible also for rounding up enemies of the Ottoman government, guarding strategically critical areas, and serving as bodyguards for visiting travellers. For performing these functions, the *armatoloi* were paid by the local populations of the areas in which they served (in the form of a fee charged by the Ottoman government), and in some instances enjoyed also the revenue gathered in the form of tolls or passage taxes charged to those passing through the mountains or over the bridges which they often guarded.

Initially established as part of the administrative structure of the Byzantine empire, these militias were subsequently adopted by both the Venetian and Ottoman provincial administrations, and thus provide a clear example of the numerous cases of political and cultural continuity, syncretism, and cooption linking the Byzantine, Ottoman, and modern Greek era. In the Peloponnese a rough equivalent of the *armatoloi* were of the *kapoi* (singular *kapos*), whose role was also to guard against brigands. During the Ottoman period, however, the *armatoloi* were in the direct employ of the Ottoman state, whereas the *kapoi* were employed by the wealthy Greek landholding class known as the Primates. Although technically under the control of the Ottoman government, the *armatoloi* in many instances acted wholly independently, and for this reason came increasingly to be regarded by the Ottoman state as untrustworthy and possibly treasonous.

The primary target of the *armatoloi* were, in theory, the klephts, a generic and fairly loosely applied term used to designate the numerous brigands of the mountainous areas of Greece, brigands whose ranks were constantly replenished by an ample surplus male population fleeing the chronic regional problems of poverty and famine. In many instances, however, the boundary between klephts and *armatoloi* was fluid, and many *armatoloi* were, prior to their recruitment, active klephts. Indeed, in some instances individuals acted in both capacities simultaneously. The relationship between the two groups, then, was often one of collusion rather than hostility. This was most markedly the case during the late 18th and early 19th centuries, when Greek revolutionary activity relied heavily on both groups for its success.

The fluidity between the groups was also marked in specific territories where local Ottoman governors attempted to replace an old Greek *armatoloi* establishment with new hand-picked *armatoloi* of their own choosing. The most dramatic example of this is seen in the Epirot lands of Ali Pasha of Ioannina, who in the latter half of the18th century made the region's *armatoloi* almost exclusively Albanian. Deposed Greek *armatoloi* in such areas became klephts instead, and understood their subsequent anti-*armatoloi* behaviour to constitute not just a form of brigandry, but also a sort of resistance to Ottoman domination. Just as many *armatoloi* had earlier been klephts, so too were many klephts former *armatoloi*. Indeed, the French folklorist Claude Fauriel has argued that "the titles of Armatole and Klepht might be used almost interchangeably for either".

In Greek regions of the Ottoman empire the *armatoloi* were drawn largely from the Greek Orthodox population, a fact which was to have significant implications for the long process of Greek liberation, for in the revolutionary period the military and social power enjoyed by the *armatoloi* came to be equated with Greek revolutionary activity. In other regions, such as Bosnia and Albania, the *armatoloi* were drawn from the local Muslim populations. Both the klephts and *armatoloi* came in effect to be groups of well-trained guerrillas, trained over a lifetime of living in the mountains off pillage and forage, and were very important for their minute knowledge of Greece's mountainous terrain, their stamina, and their ruthlessness during the first phases of the Greek War of Independence.

The *armatoloi* as an official force of the Ottoman state were disbanded by firman (imperial decree) in 1721, a full century before the first outbreak of the Greek War of Independence, but they continued throughout the 18th century to exist in practice if not in theory. During this period the Ottoman fear of Russian influence in the region, coupled with an increasing distrust of Greek *armatoloi*, led to the dismissal of most Greek *armatoloi* and their replacement with Albanian Muslims. The Greek former *armatoloi* became almost without exception klephts.

The importance of the *armatoloi* to both the Greek independence movement and to Greek historical tradition in general is amply testified to by Greek folk tradition. A common theme of Greek folksong is the narration of the exciting and dangerous lives of famous *armatoloi*, who are usually depicted not so much as the employees of the Turks as their antagonists. Other important sources for information regarding the *armatoloi* include the military memoirs of various participants in the Greek War of Independence, such as Nikolaos Kasomoulis, whose *Military Recollections* (*Stratiotika Enthymemata*) demonstrates their importance to the success of the Greek revolutionaries. The *armatoloi*, then, while marginal members of Greek society from a legalistic and political standpoint, were critical players in the early stages of the establishment of the new Greek state; and the success of the Greek War of Independence owes as much to them as to the intellectual elites who spread revolutionary rhetoric among the Ottoman Greek populations.

K.E. FLEMING

See also Brigandage

Summary

Armatoloi (literally "men at arms") were semi-official local militias which patrolled the mountainous Balkan territories of the Ottoman empire. They were intended to prevent brigandage, round up enemies of the state, and protect visiting travellers. They enjoyed a good measure of independence and were increasingly regarded as untrustworthy by the Ottoman government. Although officially disbanded in 1721, they continued to exist throughout the 18th century.

Further Reading

Campbell, John and Philip Sherrard, *Modern Greece*, London: Benn, and New York: Praeger, 1968

Clogg, Richard (editor and translator), *The Movement for Greek Independence, 1770–1821: A Collection of Documents*, London: Macmillan, 1976

Dakin, Douglas, *The Greek Struggle for Independence, 1821–1833*, London: Batsford, and Berkeley: University of California Press, 1973

Kolokotronis, Theodore, *Kolokotrones: The Klepht and the Warrior*, London: Unwin, and New York: Macmillan, 1892; as *Memoirs from the War of Greek Independence, 1821–1833*, edited by E.M. Edmonds, Chicago: Argonaut, 1969

Leake, William Martin, *An Historical Outline of the Greek Revolution, with a Few Remarks on the Present State of Affairs in That Country*, London: John Murray, 1825

Makriyannis, I., *The Memoirs of General Makriyannis, 1797–1864*, edited and translated by H.A. Lidderdale, London: Oxford University Press, 1966

Woodhouse, C.M., *The Greek War of Independence: Its Historical Setting*, London: Hutchinson, 1952, reprinted New York: Russell, 1975

Zakythinos, D.A., *The Making of Modern Greece: From Byzantium to Independence*, Oxford: Blackwell, 1976

Armenia

In the Classical and Byzantine periods Armenia covered roughly the rugged upland plateau southeast of the Black Sea, south of Iberia (Georgia), and southwest of Caucasian Albania (Azerbaijan) and the Caspian Sea and also the more fertile lands of the upper Tigris valley; but its boundaries fluctuated greatly and it was frequently fragmented. Its early history is largely dependent upon foreign sources since the Armenian alphabet was not devised until *c*.AD 400 (although governmental documents and other texts were written in Iranian in Aramaic characters, Greek or, for some ecclesiastical documents, Syriac), and even for a few centuries after that most native histories were ecclesiastical and with little interest in secular matters.

The origin of the Armenians is mysterious. Although their language is the sole member of an Indo-European subgroup, they were probably of ancient Anatolian stock akin to the Hurrians and entered the failing kingdom of Urartu, with its capital at Van, from the west around 600 BC. The area's subsequent status as a satrapy of the Achaemenid Persian empire earned it brief mention by Herodotus (e.g. 3. 93), but the first substantial documented contact between Armenians and Greeks is given by Xenophon, who led the Greek mercenaries safely home from Mesopotamia through Armenian territory in 401–400 BC (*Anabasis*, 4. 4–5). After his victory at Gaugamela in 331 over Darius III, for whom Armenia had furnished 40,000 infantry and 7000 cavalry, Alexander appointed Mithranes, the turncoat son of the last Persian satrap, as its governor. Although the Seleucids never exerted direct control over the principalities of a usually fragmented Armenia, Greek influence grew rapidly and can be seen most vividly today in seven inscriptions cut into a rockface at Armavir in the Araxes valley around 200 BC, one of which refers to Hesiod while another is a compilation of extracts from Greek dramas. Seleucid overlordship ended when Antiochus III was defeated at Magnesia in 190 BC by the Romans, who allowed his two Armenian satraps Artashes (Artaxias) and Zareh (Zariadris) to establish themselves as kings of Greater Armenia and Tsophk (Sophene) respectively.

Greek acculturation increased, notably in the 1st century BC during the reign of Tigran II who, before being forced in 66 BC to cede many of his conquests and accept Roman suzerainty, briefly, in alliance with his father-in-law Mithridates VI Eupator of Pontus and chiefly at the expense of Parthia, made Armenia an important empire stretching from the Caspian to the Mediterranean. He built in the Hellenistic style his new capital Tigranakert (Tigranocerta, possibly the later Byzantine Martyropolis), to which he removed many thousands of Greeks. His philhellene inclinations continued under his son Artavazd II, who maintained a theatre and is reputed to have himself written tragedies and other forms of literature in

Greek. For much of the Roman period Armenia was a buffer state (and often the site of warfare) between the Roman and the Parthian or, later, the Sassanian empire, although the Romans did annex a small portion west of the Euphrates (Armenia Minor) and briefly under Trajan the whole area (Greater Armenia). Latin, however, made no headway and the elite continued to use Greek (and Iranian) in addition to their native tongue. The correspondence of Libanius, the celebrated rhetorician of Antioch in the 4th century AD, indicates that he taught at least 20 Armenian students. Owing to the swift and thorough conversion of the Armenians to Christianity (which became the official religion in 314) by the Parthian missionary Gregory the Illuminator, little Graeco-Armenian art survives and, owing to their scrupulous adherence to the commandment prohibiting the making of graven images, almost no sculpture. The sole surviving temple is a magnificent grey basalt peripteral Ionic structure erected by the Arsacid Trdat (Tiridates) I in the second half of the 1st century AD and preserved only through its conversion into a royal summer residence (though ruined by an earthquake in 1679 it has been reerected). Once housing a statue of Mithras, it still displays a luxuriantly carved frieze of Armenian and Hellenistic motifs. In the neighbouring Roman bath-house a mythological mosaic of Ocean and Sea offers the curious Greek inscription "we worked without reward".

A 50-year power struggle between the Sassanians and the Byzantines, in which the heavily involved Armenians attempted to assert some measure of independence, ended in 387 with a peace treaty in accordance with which the much larger eastern part of the territory (Persarmenia) became a Sassanian and the western a Byzantine vassal state (later divided by Justinian I into four small provinces, Armenia I–IV, and considerably enlarged at Sassanian expense by the emperor Maurice in 591). Arsacid rule died out in both halves, the Sassanian *marzpan* (margrave) respecting the rights of the ever-quarrelling *nakharas* (local barons), the Byzantine authorities trying to destroy the feudal system and impose imperial institutions and customs. The Byzantines made another tactical error in their efforts to force the Chalcedonian formulation (451) of Christ's two natures unconfusedly, inseparably, and immutably within one hypostasis upon the Armenians, who charged the Byzantines with Nestorianizing and developed their own Church, formally severing their relations with the Constantinopolitan patriarchate at the second Council of Dvin (554). This, in combination with Sassanian attempts to convert them to Zoroastrianism, both encouraged a sense of nationalism, which was zealously fostered by the Armenian *katholikos* (archbishop), and in the 7th century to some extent facilitated conquest by the Arabs, who offered religious tolerance. Byzantium thus temporarily lost its share of Armenia.

The caliphate, while incorporating Iberia and Albania to create the huge province of Arminiya, established a military zone in the west, but the Byzantine crises of the early 8th century soon drew the Arabs still further west. The ensuing consolidation of Arab control of Armenia begat growing revolts from the *nakharas*, who were largely eliminated as numerous Muslim emirates were set up. In the 9th century, however, the resurgence of Byzantine power and its eastward expansion, coupled with the decline of the Abbasid caliphate, enabled the Armenians slowly to regain control of their affairs.

The Bagratid dynasty was established in the major portion of the country with the coronation of Ašot I in 884, while in 908 the Artsrunid Gagik became king of Vaspurakan, which lay in the south between lakes Van and Urmia. Caliph and emperor vied with each in granting recognition and honorific titles to Armenian sovereigns.

The Byzantines were themselves responsible for the destruction of this bulwark against their Muslim foes. Although in 974 the attempt by John I Tzimiskes (himself of Armenian origin) to expand Byzantine territory was rebuffed so effectively by Ašot III that the emperor was induced to declare him an ally and "spiritual son", Taron in the southwest had already been taken over under his predecessor Nikephoros II Phokas, while his successor Basil II annexed Armenian Tayk in the northwest. Even more seriously, Vaspurakan was ceded to the Byzantines in 1021–22 and Ani, the royal capital founded by Ašot III east of Kars, was surrendered in 1045. Thus by the middle of the 11th century most of Armenia was divided into Byzantine themes and its nobility had fled abroad. The first Seljuk raid into Armenia was ordered by the sultan Tughrul in 1048, Ani fell to Alp-Arslan 16 years later (prompting a futile cession of Kars to the Byzantines), and when Romanos IV Diogenes lost the Battle of Manzikert in 1071 there were no Armenian leaders left to prevent the Seljuks from sweeping through the rest of their territory and into Anatolia and thereby depriving the Byzantines permanently of most of their Asiatic possessions. Armenia itself enjoyed a brief respite, with Georgian protection, under the rule of the Christianized Kurdish Zakarids before falling into the hands of the Mongols in 1236.

The Seljuk conquest created an Armenian diaspora. Many Armenians fled north to Georgia or the Crimea and thence to southern Russia and Poland, while others moved southwest into Cilicia. This was the mountainous area between the Taurus and Anti-Taurus ranges, but included too the fertile lowlands around the Gulf of Alexandretta and the crucial Cilician Gates (the easiest pass through the Taurus from Anatolia and thence to the eastern littoral of the Mediterranean). Some Armenians were already there, since, after Nikephoros II Phokas had wrested a largely depopulated Cilicia from the Arabs in 965, the Byzantines had appointed local Armenians as governors and later had ceded them tracts of land, thus making possible the establishment of independent enclaves only nominally obedient to Constantinople. After a short-lived unification under an Armenian adventurer known to the Byzantines as Philaretos Brachamios (Varazhnuni), local Armenian chieftains slowly extended their domains at imperial expense, despite briefly successful campaigns by John II Komnenos and Manuel I Komnenos in 1137–38 and 1158 respectively, and from 1199 Cilicia was an independent kingdom under the Armenian Rubenid and Hetumid and latterly the Latin Lusignan dynasties until it fell to the Mamluks in 1375. Its position on a major east–west mercantile route enabled Cilicia to prosper for a while, especially while it enjoyed the Mongols' protection in the second half of the 13th century before the latter's conversion to Islam. Contact with the Latins began in 1097 with the First Crusade and, partly through intermarriage, the Armenians became increasingly influenced by westerners rather than Byzantines, a development which even led to highly divisive and ultimately aborted attempts at ecclesiastical union with Rome.

After Mesrop Maštoc, with the aid of the Greek calligrapher Rufinus, had devised an Armenian alphabet, there was an immediate surge of Armenian translations, produced largely in important Christian cities, notably Constantinople and Edessa and, a little later, Jerusalem. At first these translations, starting with the Old Testament's Proverbs, were almost exclusively religious. Lives of eastern martyrs, Syrian patristic texts, and Eusebius' *Ecclesiastical History* were translated from Syriac, Eusebius' *Chronicle* and works by the Cappadocian Fathers, Athanasius of Alexandria, and others from Greek. Many Greek works, including *Questions and Answers on Genesis and Exodus* by Philo Judaeus and some by John Chrysostom, are known only from Armenian translations. After that initial burst of energy religious translations were sporadic, although activity revived around 700 when Stephen of Siwnik translated *inter alia* the corpus of pseudo-Dionysius the Areopagite, and again in the Cilician period, especially by Nerses of Lambron, who sought out rare Greek (and Latin) texts. Owing to theological disagreement very few post-Chalcedonian Byzantine works were translated into Armenian, George of Pisidia's *Hexaemeron* being a rare exception (as, significantly, are the polemical treatises of the monophysite patriarch of Alexandria Timothy Ailouros).

In secular literature the most influential translation was of the *Art of Grammar* by Dionysius Thrax, which spawned extensive Armenian commentaries, followed by redactions of the rhetorical works of, among others, Theon and Aphthon. In philosophy translations were made of Aristotle, Porphyry, and the 6th-century Alexandrians Olympiodorus, Elias, and David (wrongly claimed by Armenians as a pupil of Mesrop Ma_toc), thereby showing an interest particularly in logic. Other works appeared in redactions to accommodate Christian beliefs (e.g. the *Alexander Romance*) or Armenian interests (e.g. the Syriac *Chronicle* of the late 12th-century Jacobite patriarch of Antioch, Michael I). Original Armenian theological writing is largely defensive in respect to Byzantium. Historical compositions show little interest in Byzantium as such, but are often important in supplying information on the empire's eastern borders: Matthew of Edessa's *Chronicle* is of particular value for information on imperial involvement in Cilicia. Byzantine interest in Armenian literature is minimal, although there are Greek translations of the establishment of Christianity in Armenia by the pseudonymous Agathangelos and a pro-Chalcedonian anonymous account of Armenio-Byzantine ecclesiastical relations (now known as the *Narratio de Rebus Armeniae*) written c.700 and, significantly, lost in the Armenian original.

The Byzantine contribution to Armenian architecture is immediately evident, but styles of other circumjacent states (especially Syria) left their marks too. In the other direction, despite the wild exaggeration in the famous claims of Joseph Strzygowski for the Armenians' adaptation of Central Asian styles learned through Sassanian intermediaries and passed on by them to the whole of Christendom, Armenian architects did indeed develop great expertise which was not without effect upon Byzantium. Notably it was the Armenian master builder Trdat who was deemed most capable of repairing the damage caused by an earthquake in 989 to Constantinople's principal

church, Hagia Sophia. Materials available dictated that virtually all churches were constructed of a rubble conglomerate faced with large blocks of yellow, red, or grey tufa. Simple single-aisled basilicas, some according to historical accounts adapted from Hellenistic temples and all small except for a remarkable example of c.500 at Ereruk, gave way in the 6th century to domed (usually cross-domed) buildings, with squinches or (less often) pendentives. This experimentation with centralized plans is almost certainly due to Byzantine influence. During the period of Armenian independence in the late 9th to early 11th centuries, drums and domes grew taller and were often distinctively polygonal (the latter usually also conical or pyramidal), while some Islamic features such as *muqarnas* (stalactitic squinches) appear. Cilician churches were largely traditional.

Figural sculpture became far more widespread, dominant, and exuberant than in Byzantine architecture, the outstanding, though somewhat idiosyncratic, example being the early 10th-century figures and biblical scenes on the exterior of the church of the Holy Cross on the island of Aghtamar in Lake Van, where Graeco-Roman and Arab elements jostle with Byzantine. The few surviving examples of interior fresco decoration largely follow Byzantine models, but interestingly at Aghtamar there is an Old Testament (Genesis) cycle (long abandoned in the Byzantine world) and at Tatev western artists are reputed to have been employed in the early 10th-century church of SS Peter and Paul. Manuscript illumination is usually iconographically and stylistically Byzantine, but in both respects (and sometimes even as late as the 12th century) harks back to the pre-iconoclastic period, while some 11th-century pmanuscripts exhibit the stark naivety of painters striving to reduce art to its essentials. Cilician Armenian painting is often highly individualistic. While some of its manuscript illuminations are again naive, others show a consummate intimacy with Byzantine work but yet have an expressiveness of their own; this is especially so in the work of the outstanding late 13th-century painter Toros Roslin, who worked mainly at Hromkla, whither the patriarchal see had been transferred in 1151. In the 14th century his namesake Taron was prominent in a group which deliberately opposed Byzantium in developing anti-Chalcedonian imagery.

As a result of forced eviction and voluntary migration, Armenians constituted a substantial minority of the Byzantine population, even when Armenia itself was not in imperial hands. Their military valour induced emperors, beginning on a small scale with Justinian I, to transplant them to threatened border regions. In the late 6th century the emperor Maurice proposed to the Sassanian monarch that Armenians on either side of their line of partition through the country should be deported, and for his part moved a vast number to Thrace (then including much of modern Bulgaria, which still has a sizeable Armenian minority). Thousands more were moved there later by Constantine V and to neighbouring Macedonia by Basil II. Tiberius II forced possibly as many as 10,000 to migrate to Cyprus in 578, Nikephoros I used them to resettle Sparta in the early 9th century, and Nikephoros II to resettle Crete after his conquest of the island in 961, while others were sent to Sicily and southern Italy in the 8th and 9th centuries. Religious belief was the cause of another Byzantine resettlement in an attempt under Basil I in 878 to extirpate the virulently iconoclastic Armenian Paulicians who had established their own state around Tephrike (Divriği) in Cappadocia. (It is still unclear if they were Adoptionists or Manichaean dualists believing in a docetic Christology. Despite their expulsion they spawned the communities of the Tondrakites, which continued to cause Byzantium problems into the 11th century.) Foreign invasion, and especially the Arab seizure of much of their territory, also forced or encouraged many thousands of Armenians to migrate to the Byzantine theme of Armeniakon and elsewhere in Asia Minor, Constantinople itself, and Bulgaria. In times of relative quiet, military enlistment and possibilities for economic advancement, especially through trade, induced many others to leave their homeland for the empire (and the caliphate).

The Byzantine attitude towards Armenians was generally, though not uniformly, unfavourable. In writing to his Sassanian counterpart, Maurice (the tradition of his own Armenian origin is most probably apocryphal) called them "a knavish and indocile nation" and claimed that whether they killed or were killed in Thrace enemies would have died. The patriarch Joseph I Galesiotes pronounced them "morbid and rebellious" and the patriarch Athanasios I classed them with Jews as defiling to Christians. Doubtless the majority's rejection of Chalcedonian dyophysitism, the internecine turbulence of their country whether under foreign rule or not, their stubborn adherence to their own culture, and their usually rustic manners were distasteful to the educated city dwellers who constitute most Byzantine literary sources. Moreover, what little evidence there is suggests that this contempt may have been shared by the lower classes. Nevertheless Armenians played a prominent role in Byzantine history.

Procopius claims that emperors had traditionally chosen Armenians for their bodyguard and names no fewer than 17 Armenian generals who were employed by Justinian: of these one, the aged eunuch Narses, was given supreme command of Byzantine forces in Italy and crushed the Ostrogothic forces of Totila in 552. From the late 6th century until the Arab invasion of the mid-7th Byzantine military recruitment was largely Armenian, since Avaro-Slavic incursions into the Balkans severely restricted possibilities there. It has been estimated that even after that, until the loss of Anatolia to the Seljuks, Armenians drawn from Byzantine-controlled territory predominated in the Byzantine army. Some, and most who achieved high rank, were, however, of Chalcedonian persuasion. Several emperors of the 9th and 10th centuries were of Armenian origin: Leo V, a fine and honest soldier responsible for the restoration of iconoclasm; Basil I, born into a family transplanted to Macedonia and founder of the "Macedonian" dynasty; Romanos I Lekapenos, a highly successful emperor and the only navy officer to attain that position; and John I Tzimiskes, another militarily competent emperor. In addition Theodora, wife of Theophilos and later regent for their son Michael III, was of Armenian origin, and other emperors had Armenian connections. Generals, loyal, and especially traitorous (Kazhdan finds 25 mutinies under Armenian leadership, or at least with Armenian participation, between 976 and 1204), were often of Armenian stock. Among good servants of the empire were Melias, the Armenian prince Mleh who founded the *kleisoura* (small administrative unit) of Lykandos in the Anti-Taurus mountains, and John Kourkouas, who recovered

the holy Mandylion of Edessa: both played an important part in Byzantine expansion eastwards. Armenians were less likely to be courtiers (at least until the Komnenian period), but even here there were influential figures like Stylianos Zaoutzes, at one time father-in-law of Leo VI. At least two 12th-century patriarchs were of Armenian stock: Michael II, of the Kourkouas family and, on his father's side, Theodosios Boradiotes. While there were no specifically Armenian monasteries on Mount Athos, there were Armenian monks there, one of whom, Theoktistos, abbot of Esphigmenou, rose to be *protos* (head) of the whole community in the 1030s. The annexation of Armenian territory in the late 10th and first half of the 11th century hugely increased the number of Armenians in the empire, and it has been estimated that in the latter century 10 to 15 per cent of the Byzantine aristocracy were Armenian. Nevertheless, in the Komnenian and Palaiologan periods they appear to have filled far fewer positions of authority, and with the creation of an Armenian state in Cilicia the arrival of newcomers came to an end.

A.R. LITTLEWOOD

See also Cilicia

Further Reading

Adontz, Nicholas, *Etudes arméno-byzantines*, Lisbon, 1965

Adontz, Nicholas, *Armenia in the Period of Justinian: The Political Conditions Based on the Naxarar System*, translated by Nina G. Garsoïan, Lisbon: Gulbenkian Foundation, 1970

Atiya, Aziz S., *A History of Eastern Christianity*, London: Methuen, 1968, pp. 303–56

Bauer, Elisabeth, *Die Armenier im byzantinischen Reich und ihr Einfluss auf Politik, Wirtschaft und Kultur*, Yerevan: Academy of Sciences of the Armenian SSR, 1978

Burney, Charles and David Marshall Lang, *The Peoples of the Hills: Ancient Ararat and Caucasus*, London: Weidenfeld and Nicolson, 1971; New York: Praeger, 1972

Chahin, M., *The Kingdom of Armenia*, London: Croom Helm, 1987

Charanis, P., *The Armenians in the Byzantine Empire*, Lisbon, 1963

Edwards, Robert W., *The Fortifications of Armenian Cilicia*, Washington, D.C.: Dumbarton Oaks, 1987

Garsoïan, Nina G., Thomas F. Mathews, and Robert W. Thomson, *East of Byzantium: Syria and Armenia in the Formative Period*, Washington D.C.: Dumbarton Oaks, 1982

Garsoïan, Nina G., *Armenia between Byzantium and the Sasanians*, London: Variorum, 1985

Kazhdan, A.P., "The Armenians in the Byzantine Ruling Class Predominantly in the Ninth through Twelfth Centuries" in *Medieval Armenian Culture*, edited by Thomas J. Samuelin and Michael E. Stone, Chico, California: Scholars Press, 1984, pp. 439–51

Lang, David Marshall, *Armenia: Cradle of Civilization*, 3rd edition, London and Boston: Allen and Unwin, 1980

Manandian, Hakob A., *The Trade and Cities of Armenia in Relation to Ancient World Trade*, translated by Nina G. Garsoïan, Lisbon, 1965 (includes Byzantine relations)

Narkiss, Bezalel and Michael E. Stone (editors), *Armenian Art Treasures of Jerusalem*, New Rochelle, New York: Caratzas, 1979

Nersessian, Sirarpie der, *Armenia and the Byzantine Empire: A Brief Study of Armenian Art and Civilization*, Cambridge, Massachusetts: Harvard University Press, 1945

Nersessian, Sirarpie der, *The Armenians*, London: Thames and Hudson, 1969; New York: Praeger, 1970

Nersessian, Sirarpie der, *Armenian Art*, London: Thames and Hudson, 1978

Sarkissian, Karekin, *The Council of Chalcedon and the Armenian Church*, London: SPCK, 1965; 2nd edition, New York: Armenian Church Prelacy, 1975

Thierry, Jean-Michel, *Armenian Art*, New York: Abrams, 1989

Tourmanoff, C., "Armenia and Georgia" in *The Byzantine Empire*, edited by J.M. Hussey, Cambridge: Cambridge University Press, 1966 (*The Cambridge Medieval History*, vol. 4, part 1, 2nd edition), pp. 593–637

Vryonis, S., "Byzantine Images of the Armenians" in *The Armenian Image in History and Literature*, edited by Richard G. Hovannisian, Malibu, California: Undena, 1981

Army

Armies and war making were the focus of one of the landmarks of early Greek culture, Homer's *Iliad*. The epic poems of the 8th century BC looked back to the battles and warriors of the Bronze Age, so vividly depicted in the *Iliad*, with awe and fascination. War making played a key role in the Mycenaean heroic age and its aftermath, after 1100 BC, when the Dorians, Iron Age warriors who invaded and eventually settled in Greece, changed the political and social landscape. The dearth of historical and archaeological information on the post-Mycenaean years, the so-called Greek Dark Age between 1100 BC and 800 BC, makes it difficult to ascertain the exact causes and consequences of the decline of the Mycenaeans. It appears, however, that the decline of Mycenae had begun before the advent of the Dorians. It appears also that a series of invasions by the armies of the migrating Sea Peoples (who overran the Hittite empire, and sought to conquer Egypt, and one of whose tribes, the Philistines, settled in Palestine) were among the factors leading to the general exhaustion that marked the Mycenaean world even before 1100 BC. After 1000 BC Greek society was reduced to small local communities, from which there gradually emerged the city state (polis).

Military conflict between the city states of mainland Greece was not rare even at a later period, between the 8th century BC and the beginning of the Persian Wars in the early 5th century BC. Yet, with the exception of Sparta, the city states sought to avoid the maintenance of a standing army. By the time of the first Persian War (490 BC) most city states used cavalry, but its extensive use was confined to the Thessalian League. For the rest, their military strength was represented by the organization of the infantry. The hoplites, the armed citizen-soldiers, fought on foot and were organized in companies (*lochoi*) and platoons (*enomotiai*). In the ten years between the first and the second Persian War (480–479 BC), Athens concentrated on strengthening its sea power by building a large trireme fleet. After the Persians' devastating defeat in 479 BC, which ended the Persian threat to the Greek world, Athenian hegemony was established gradually in mainland Greece and, with the help of the Delian League, throughout the Aegean, from Thasos to Rhodes.

Armies in Classical antiquity represented the organized mobilization of citizenry in case of war. Therefore, while military conflict was not uncommon, it implied the temporary militarization of life – again with the exception of Sparta, the only city state in which a militaristic structure and way of life defined all other social and political activity. In Athens the relaxed quality of civic life in the polis during the Periclean age is contrasted by Thucydides to the poisonous atmosphere brought about through war, militarization, and the suspension of many features of the Athenian democracy. The Peloponnesian Wars (460–445, 431–404 BC), caused by a complex series of perceived threats and counter-threats, manifested the consequences of the imperial expansionism of the Athenian League and the commitment by Sparta and the Peloponnesian League to total victory and the destruction of the power of Athens. In particular the second, so-called Great, Peloponnesian War displayed a succession of intense clashes and a relentless crusade towards total supremacy. It was the dominance of that mentality in both camps that explains the Sicilian expedition in the final years of the war, a colossal undertaking by Athens aimed at conquering Sparta's allies in Sicily. The defeat of Athens left Sparta in the position of a dominant player. But the inward-looking character of the Spartan regime, combined with the fragmentation of the Greek city states and the efforts by the Persians to influence political developments in Athens and elsewhere, resulted in political complications which moderated the significance of the Spartan victory.

The rise of Macedon in the 4th century BC, which soon put an end to Spartan supremacy, owed much to the military innovations introduced and perfected by Philip and his son Alexander the Great. These were the development of siege weaponry to obviate the need for lengthy blockades, and the perfection of infantry/cavalry tactics based on new models for the organization of the deep phalanx, which enabled complex manoeuvres and combined infantry/cavalry deployment (Connolly, 1977 and Humble, 1980). In the invasion of Asia Alexander led an army in which not only Macedonians but all Greeks participated, with the exception of the Spartans. After Alexander's death (323 BC) the Macedonian empire suffered the wars of the generals, which introduced the war elephant to the battlefield. The fragmentation of the Hellenistic world, the result of intense conflict between Alexander's successors, prepared the ground for the gradual absorption of large segments of that world into the emerging Roman empire.

Throughout the Roman and early Byzantine periods, inhabitants of the Greek peninsula often served in the auxiliary cohorts of the army, which was a professional long-service force. Discharged veterans received a pension from a public fund and/or a small estate. In the Byzantine period the administrative structure of the empire was dependent on the spatial organization of the military command in politico-military units (themes) led by generals. The theme was a combined administrative and military unit established by the emperor Herakleios in the 7th century AD and, despite subsequent changes and reforms in other aspects of the army, this basic structure was preserved. By contrast, there was considerable temporal variation concerning military duties and conscription. At some point, all adult male subjects under the age of 40 had to be available for military service. Foreign mercenaries were used extensively on various occasions, particularly (but not exclusively) after the 10th century. The imperial guard had only foreign soldiers, mainly from northern Europe and Scandinavia (the Varangian Guard). During the years of Ottoman rule, war making and the army were in the hands of the Muslims, while trade and economic activities were left to the non-Muslim subjects, usually Greeks and Jews. Yet the Ottomans also had licensed bands of Christian irregulars (the *armatoloi*) in mainland Greece in order to use them against the brigands (the klephts) who often dominated the mountainous districts of the region.

The Greek War of Independence was fought against the Ottomans mainly by Christian irregulars and brigands, bands of philhellenes, and, on a couple of occasions, regular European armies. In the War of Independence and in subsequent political developments an important role was played by the *armatoloi* and the klephts, a "distinctive military class" (Koliopoulos, 1987) which was the product of the years of Ottoman rule combined with the geographical (a mountainous terrain) and social particularities of the Greek peninsula. These groups continued to play key roles after 1830, when the modern Greek nation state came into being. The territorial settlement of 1830 was seen by many as provisional; Greek irredentism was a formidable force between 1830 and 1922, when the irredentist drive came to an abrupt end with defeat at the hands of the emerging Turkish secular state. The irregulars of the War of Independence followed two paths after 1830. Some joined the Greek army, which was gradually developed along Western lines. The regular army soon became an important mechanism, along with the educational establishments, for the social and often also the linguistic Hellenization of its recruits (Kitromilides, 1989). Others remained outside the regular army. In the latter category, most joined irredentist bands which became the protagonists of nationalist mobilizations in the mid-1850s, in 1877–79, in 1897, and in the struggle for Macedonia in the early years of the 20th century (1903–08).

Despite early efforts, particularly by the Trikoupis governments, to perfect the regular army, it was only in 1912 that the Greek state was in a position to use a well-organized and equipped professional army. From the beginning of the 20th century to the mid-1970s the army played key roles in political development, starting with the coup in 1909 which, apart from its corporatist aspects linked to the officers' professional concerns, appeared to favour liberal politicians. In this sense the 1909 coup presaged and favoured a bourgeois outcome. The new regime after 1909 did much to increase military professionalization. In turn, Greek gains in the Balkan Wars (1912–13) did much to increase the domestic prestige and role of the army.

But the domestic role of the army soon became so entangled in political strife that it was difficult in the interwar period to distinguish between interventions by the military as an institution and the use being made by segments of the political elite of different groups of military officers. Pronunciamentos, coup attempts, and other forms of intervention by royalist officers against a liberal government and by liberal officers against a royalist government became common, resulting in considerable politicization of the army. The Civil War of the 1940s reinforced internal security as a major task for the army, and the controlled and limited democracy which ensued in the 1950s saw the army assume the position of an arbiter of the regime. Still, despite its militaristic features, the regime of controlled democracy reintroduced the aforementioned intra-military fragmentation along political lines. This is evident in the coup of 1967, which was meant to block the possibility of

a centre-left government emerging from the planned elections of that year. The fierce anti-communism of the junta should not be taken very seriously as the main explanation for the coup. The politicization of the army being a critical background factor, the authoritarian regime of 1967–74 reflected to an extent the efforts by middle-ranking officers to reassert the role of the army as an arbiter. In fact, the royalist generals had been preparing a coup on behalf of the king in 1967, when the junta took over and neutralized both the centre-left and the royalist factions in the officer corps. The officers who led the coup in 1967 had been members in the 1940s of a far right military fraternity known by the initials IDEA (Holy Band of Greek Officers). The group had been founded among Greek officers in the Middle East during the German occupation of Greece.

The breakdown of the authoritarian regime in 1974 amid foreign policy crises and domestic upheaval marked a crucial change in the army's position in the political system. The Karamanlis government, angered by apparent US and NATO passivity and tolerance of the Turkish intervention in Cyprus, decided to withdraw from the military section of NATO. The withdrawal had two aims. First, it wanted to give the Greek government complete control over the armed forces in case of a direct Greek–Turkish clash. Second, it was a symbolic act indicating Greece's determination to defend its national interest and search for appropriate alliances in the process rather than the other way round (the structure of alliances determining the course of action). Greece's NATO withdrawal was a tactical mistake. First, it left Athens with no ability to influence the NATO Council during subsequent developments. Second, it gave a mixed signal to the West, complicated by the fact that French influence in Athens, which was on the increase, particularly irritated the USA. Third, the Greek military establishment was cut off from its NATO links, even if only temporarily. This was a mixed blessing for the new regime in Athens. On the one hand, to the extent that the military regime had any clear US or NATO backing, this move could perhaps have facilitated the democratization process. On the other hand, the move underlined the extent to which the post-junta role and legitimacy of the Greek military became dependent on Greek–Turkish rivalry. Last but not least, the fourth implication of Greece's withdrawal was that when Athens decided to return to the military section of NATO a few years later the Turkish side was able to negotiate, along with the other partners, the conditions for Greece's reintegration.

The crisis in relations with Turkey over Cyprus in 1974 left the impression in Greece that the Greek army was inadequately prepared and that its domestic preoccupations had undermined its credibility as a military force abroad. After 1974 the army went through a process of reorientation from its traditional role (internal security plus commitment to defend the northern borders against NATO enemies) to a new one (protection of national interests against perceived Turkish expansionism). The professionalization of the officer corps has increased since the return to democracy in 1974 and has been combined more recently with modern curricula at the Military Academy, regular exchanges in western Europe and the USA, and efforts to better integrate new officers within a democratic context. Developments in international relations in southeastern Europe since 1989 have added a new dimension to the role of the Greek army, in view of the fact that the defence orientation towards the eastern borders against a background of relative stability in the north cannot now be taken for granted.

Bearing in mind the peculiarities of the country as well as the analytical issues posed by the comparative examination of the role of the army in newly consolidated democracies, it can be argued that the role of the Greek army in the 1990s was defined by four main parameters. First, Greece maintained a very substantial level of defence spending, one of the highest in NATO. Second, there were waverings (inherited from the early, populist years of PASOK in government in the 1980s) between a clearly defined role for the professional army and a rather confused notion of popular defence (*pallaiki amyna*) whose original conception in the 1980s had borrowed freely from both the Israeli and the late Yugoslav models. What enabled the continuation of this debate was the third of these parameters, namely, the evolution of Greek–Turkish rivalry over Cyprus and certain issues which concerned the Aegean, coupled with the weighty role of the military establishment in Turkish politics. Finally, developments on the EU front were crucial in two respects. On the one hand, the agreement over Economic and Monetary Union put increased pressure on Greece to adjust its economy in order to be able to participate in the Euro zone after 2001. There are crucial budgetary dilemmas ahead, and military expenditure cannot avoid becoming embroiled in the debates at some point. On the other hand, the steps towards strengthening the Western European Union (WEU) created the opportunity for Greek military integration in WEU mechanisms and operations. The Yugoslav conflict and subsequent peace-keeping operations in the area offered the opportunity for involvement by the Greek army in new roles in a combined UN-NATO-WEU structure.

Unlike comparable processes in Spain and Portugal, Greece's change of regime and democratic consolidation after the mid-1970s had to address the issue of the new role and legitimacy of the army with reference to a major external factor. It remains to be seen whether Greek political elites will now endeavour to shift the reference point for the legitimacy of the post-authoritarian role of the Greek army from Greek–Turkish rivalry to common European security. This is, of course, an interactive process, and depends also on developments on the Turkish side. The Europeanization of Turkey will increase the likelihood of cooperation in Greek–Turkish relations, while regression to militarist nationalism or a shift towards Islamic fundamentalism, the other possible paths for the future of the Turkish state, may favour conflict. Despite oscillations, the general trend in Greece since 1974 has favoured high military spending legitimized through the precipitate embrace of a mentality of *vis pacem, para bellum*. As the challenges of European convergence and Europeanization require the mobilization of energies and resources towards a new direction, old maxims and inherited "common wisdom" need to be re-examined.

KOSTAS A. LAVDAS

See also Junta, Warfare

Further Reading

Agüero, Felipe, "Democratic Consolidation and the Military in Southern Europe and South America" in *The Politics of Democratic Consolidation: Southern Europe in Comparative Perspective*, edited by Richard Günther, P. Nikiforos Diamandouros and Hans-Jürgen Puhle, Baltimore: Johns Hopkins University Press, 1995

Blinkhorn, Martin and Thanos Veremis (editors), "Modern Greece: Nationalism and Nationality", special issue of *European History Quarterly*, 19 (1989)

Charalambis, Dimitris, *Stratos kai Politiki Exousia: I Domi tis Exousias stin Metemphilaki Ellada* [The Military and Political Power: The Structure of Power in Postwar Greece], Athens: Exantas, 1985

Connolly, Peter, *The Greek Armies*, London: Macdonald, 1977

Connor, W. Robert, *Thucydides*, Princeton, New Jersey: Princeton University Press, 1984

Coutogeorgis, Georgios (editor), *Koinonikes kai Politikes Dynameis stiin Ellada* [Social and Political Forces in Greece], Athens: Exantas, 1977

Dakin, Douglas, *The Unification of Greece, 1770–1923*, London: Benn, and New York: St Martin's Press, 1972

Dertilis, George, *Koinonikos Metaschimatismos kai Stratiotiki Epemvasi: 1880–1909* [Social Transformation and Military Intervention, 1880–1909], Athens: Exantas, 1977

Humble, Richard, *Warfare in the Ancient World*, London: Cassell, 1980

Hussey, J.M. (editor), *The Byzantine Empire*, Cambridge: Cambridge University Press, 1966–67 (*The Cambridge Medieval History*, vol. 4, parts 1–2, 2nd edition)

Kitromilides, Paschalis M., "'Imagined Communities' and the Origins of the National Question in the Balkans", special issue of *European History Quarterly*, 19 (1989)

Koliopoulos, John S., *Brigands with a Cause: Brigandage and Irredentism in Modern Greece, 1821–1912*, Oxford: Clarendon Press, and New York: Oxford University Press, 1987

Lavdas, Kostas, "The European Union and the Yugoslav Conflict", *Journal of Political and Military Sociology*, 24 (1996)

McDonald, Robert, "The Colonels' Dictatorship, 1967–74" in *Background to Contemporary Greece*, edited by Marion Sarafis and Martin Eve, London: Merlin, and Savage, Maryland: Barnes and Noble, 1990

Mavrogordatos, George T., *Stillborn Republic: Social Coalitions and Party Strategies in Greece 1922–1936*, Berkeley: University of California Press, 1983

Papacosma, S. Victor, *The Military in Greek Politics: The 1909 Coup d'Etat*, Kent, Ohio: Kent State University Press, 1977

Papageorgiou, Stephanos, "The Army as an Instrument for Territorial Expansion and for Repression by the State: The Capodistrian Case", *Journal of the Hellenic Diaspora*, 12 (1985)

Petropulos, John A., *Politics and Statecraft in the Kingdom of Greece, 1833–1843*, Princeton, New Jersey: Princeton University Press, 1968

Richter, Heinz, "The Greek–Turkish Conflict" in *Background to Contemporary Greece*, edited by Marion Sarafis and Martin Eve, London: Merlin, and Savage, Maryland: Barnes and Noble, 1990

Stavrou, Nicolaos, *Symmachiki Politiki kai Stratiotikes Epemvaseis* [Allied Politics and Military Interventions: The Political Role of the Greek Military], Athens: Papazisis, 1976

Veremis, Thanos, "The Officer Corps in Greece, 1912–1936", *Byzantine and Modern Greek Studies*, 2 (1976)

Veremis, Thanos, *The Military in Greek Politics: From Independence to Democracy*, London: Hurst, 1997; Buffalo, New York: Black Rose, 1998

Arrian *c.*AD 90–160

Historian

In his preface to the *Anabasis of Alexander* Arrian declares that wherever Ptolemy and Aristobulus, the Alexander historians, "have both given the same accounts of Alexander the son of Philip, it is my practice to record what they say as completely true, but when they differ, to select the version I regard as more trustworthy and also more telling". He has chosen these two authors because both of them took part in Alexander's expedition and both wrote after his death, thus not being "under any constraint or hope of gain", particularly Ptolemy, who became king. Other accounts Arrian intends to record only as "tales" told of Alexander (Praefatio, 1–3). In this unique statement on principles of selection and use of sources Arrian sweepingly disqualifies the bulk of his predecessors, including Callisthenes (mentioned only as a historical figure in the *Anabasis of Alexander*), Clitarchus, Diodorus, and Plutarch, names that never appear in Arrian's extant works. In the so-called "second preface" to the same *Anabasis* Arrian even boasts that before him Alexander's exploits were never properly recorded, and that he, at last, "will make Alexander's deeds known to men" (1. 12. 2–5). He also displays a similar attitude elsewhere. In the *Indica* (2. 9) he singles out Eratosthenes as "more trustworthy than any other writer", and Nearchus and Megasthenes since both are "remarkable men" (17. 6); in the opening chapter of the *Tactica* he enumerates tactical writers, including Pyrrhus, Polybius, and Posidonius, only to declare them all useless.

Predecessors and sources are not necessarily models. Arrian's ideal was Xenophon – his career as a soldier and, later in life, as a retired gentleman-writer (*Cynegeticus*, 1). He called himself "Xenophon", and was nicknamed the "new Xenophon" by later biographers. Arrian was indeed as prolific and versatile a writer as Xenophon. Like Xenophon, who started his intellectual career as a disciple of Socrates, Arrian began his as a disciple of Epictetus, turning thereafter to other subjects. Yet, he did not write contemporary history as Xenophon had done. All his historical work bears upon the past: the *Antiquities of Bithynia*, the monographs on Dion and Timoleon, the *Anabasis of Alexander*, the *Events after Alexander*. Actually, he must have had more than one model. Herodotus, for example, is quoted and used several times. Arrian's works bristle with Herodotean reminiscences in content, in vocabulary, and in style. In true Herodotean fashion he reports versions that he does not credit, has reservations about his sources, and leaves it to others to judge or explain. In the *Indica* he even adopts the Ionic style. Sometimes he feels compelled to find a compromise between Herodotus and his avowed model Xenophon. A case in point is his belief in the existence of Amazons in mythical times, as attested by Herodotus and by Athenian funeral orators, while disbelieving their survival in historical times, as Xenophon's silence would suggest (*Anabasis*, 7. 13. 5–6). Arrian's debt to Thucydides and Theopompus (never mentioned by name) should perhaps remain a matter of speculation, but the influence of Atthidography on his local chronicle of Bithynia (*Bithyniaca*) is quite evident. His presumably continuous survey of Bithynian antiquities from mythical times to 74 BC, as well as

his self-identification as a priest of Demeter and Core, the tutelary goddesses of Nicomedia, echo a topos already exploited by Cleidemus and Philochorus in the 4th century BC.

Having predecessors, and even being influenced by them, does not necessarily imply slavish imitation. Arrian read and absorbed his sources, but though sometimes he followed them passively, he developed a style of his own. His historical work is a mixture of the "pragmatic" school of Thucydides, Xenophon, and Polybius, and of the encomiastic trend of Alexander-historians such as Callisthenes and the "vulgate" tradition. And, of course, Arrian was a child of his times. The very project of compiling a laudatory monograph on Alexander cannot be dissociated from the impact of the Parthian wars of Trajan on Greek intellectuals, or from the reminiscences and propaganda about the Persian wars emanating in the 2nd century from Hadrian's Panhellenion in Athens.

Arrian's reputation among his younger contemporaries and later, as having an exemplary career as a philosopher, a historian, or a master of style, is well attested. For Lucian, Arrian was "a disciple of Epictetus, a Roman of the highest distinction, and a life-long devotee of letters", a man who did not disdain writing the life even of the brigand Tilliborus (a work otherwise unknown). Aulus Gellius was acquainted with Arrian's edition of Epictetus' *Discourses*. Cassius Dio wrote a "Life of Arrian the Philosopher" (not extant) and in his *Roman History* he mentioned Arrian's role in the war against the Alani. Dexippus apparently used and followed closely Arrian's history of the Diadochi without mentioning his name. In the 4th century AD Eusebius put Arrian's *floruit* in AD 149/50 and Themistius pronounced him a famous example of a philosopher engaged in public life. In the 5th century Malalas called Arrian a "most wise chronographer" and used his *Parthica* for Trajan's wars. His contemporary Johannes Lydus quoted him on the antiquities of the Parthians. Procopius quotes him on Kytaia, the Colchian city of Medea, and the Neoplatonist Simplicius mentions a *Life of Epictetus* written by Arrian. In the 6th century Stephanus of Byzantium used Arrian extensively, consulting particularly the *Bithyniaca* and the *Parthica* for his own purposes and quoting verbatim several passages.

Photios's encomium of Arrian, appended to the epitome of the *Events after Alexander*, is one of the longest in the *Bibliotheca*. To Photios, Arrian was "inferior to no one of the best writers of history", a true imitator of Xenophon, a writer worthy of praise for his clarity, composition, and style, as well as for his lack of out-of-place digressions and parentheses, and for his traditional choice of words. Photios abridged Arrian's historical works and knew of his edition of Epictetus' teachings. Arrian's reputation for composition is also attested in Byzantine times by the anonymous author of a treatise *On Syntax*.

The *Suda* lexicon has an entry on Arrian and refers to him repeatedly, particularly to the *Parthica*, from which many substantial passages are quoted. A 10th-century collection of *excerpta* includes passages from Arrian's *Anabasis of Alexander*, and a passage from this same work on the statues of Harmodius and Aristogiton at Athens is quoted in the scholia to Proclus' commentary on Plato's *Timaeus*. In the 12th century Tzetzes and the *Etymologicum Magnum* used Arrian's *Bithyniaca*, and Eustathios drew heavily on both the

Bithyniaca and the *Anabasis of Alexander* for his commentaries on Homer and Dionysius Periegetes, preserving sizeable passages quoted verbatim. Finally, around 1200 the Codex Vindobonensis (Vienna, Nationalbibliothek, hist. gr. 4) was copied, from which all the extant manuscripts of the *Anabasis of Alexander* are descended.

DAVID ASHERI

Biography

Born in Nicomedia in Bithynia *c.*AD 90, Arrian studied under the Stoic Epictetus before moving to Greece (108–12) and a career in the civil service under Hadrian. He served as legate of Cappadocia (131–37) and then retired to Athens where he died *c.*160. Arrian wrote on a wide range of subjects including geography, hunting, military tactics, and local history, but is best known for his *Anabasis*, a history of the campaigns of Alexander the Great.

Writings

[Works] edited by A.G. Roos, revised by G. Wirth, 2 vols, Leipzig: Teubner, 1967
In *Die Fragmente der Griechischen Historiker*, edited by Felix Jacoby, 2b, Leiden: Brill, 1962
History of Alexander and Indica, translated by P.A. Brunt, 2 vols, Cambridge, Massachusetts: Harvard University Press, and London: Heinemann, 1976–83 (Loeb edition)
"Arrian's *Events after Alexander*: Summary of Photius and Selected Fragments", edited and translated by W.J. Gozalski, in *Aufstieg und Niedergang der römischen Welt*, edited by Hildegard Temporini *et al.*, 19, Berlin: de Gruyter 1989, 81–108
Gli eventi dopo Alessandro, edited and translated into Italian by A. Simonetti Agostinetti, Rome: Bretschneider, 1993
Tactical Handbook and The Expedition against the Alans, edited and translated by James G. DeVoto, Chicago: Ares, 1993

Further Reading

Bosworth, A.B., *A Historical Commentary on Arrian's History of Alexander*, vols 1–2, Oxford: Clarendon Press, and New York: Oxford University Press, 1980–95 (vol. 3 in preparation)
Bosworth, A.B., *From Arrian to Alexander: Studies in Historical Interpretation*, Oxford: Clarendon Press, and New York: Oxford University Press, 1988
Bosworth, A.B., "Arrian and Rome: The Minor Works" in *Aufstieg und Niedergang der römischen Welt*, edited by Hildegard Temporini *et al.*, 2. 34. 1, Berlin: de Gruyter, 1994, 226 ff.
Bosworth, A.B., Arrian entry in *The Oxford Classical Dictionary*, 3rd edition, edited by Simon Hornblower and Anthony Spawforth, Oxford and New York: Oxford University Press, 1996
Devine, A.M., "Arrian's *Tactica*" in *Aufstieg und Niedergang der römischen Welt*, edited by Hildegard Temporini *et al.*, 2. 34. 1, Berlin: de Gruyter, 1994, 312 ff.
Gray, V.J., "The Moral Interpretation of the 'Second Preface' to Arrian's Anabasis", *Journal of Hellenic Studies*, 110 (1990): pp. 180 ff.
Hammond, N.G.L., *Sources for Alexander the Great: An Analysis of Plutarch's Life and Arrian's Anabasis Alexandrou*, Cambridge and New York: Cambridge University Press, 1993
Marincola, J.M., "Some Suggestions on the Proem and the '2nd Preface' of Arrian's Anabasis", *Journal of Hellenic Studies*, 109 (1989): pp. 186–89
Marincola, J.M., *Authority and Tradition in Ancient Historiography*, Cambridge and New York: Cambridge University Press, 1997
Moles, J.L., "The Interpretation of the 'Second Preface' in Arrian's Anabasis", *Journal of Hellenic Studies*, 105 (1985): pp. 162 ff.
Schwartz, E., Arrianos entry in *Real-Encyclopädie der klassischen Altertumswissenschaft*, edited by August Pauly *et al.*, 2. 1 (1895), 1230 ff.
Silberman, A., "Arrien, 'Périple du Pont Euxin': Essai d'interprétation et d'évaluation des données historiques et géographiques" in *Aufstieg und Niedergang der römischen Welt*, edited by Hildegard Temporini *et al.*, 2. 34. 1, Berlin: de Gruyter, 1994, pp. 276 ff.
Stadter, Philip A., "Flavius Arrianus: The New Xenophon", *Greek, Roman and Byzantine Studies*, 8 (1967): pp. 155 ff.
Stadter, Philip A., *Arrian of Nicomedia*, Chapel Hill: University of North Carolina Press, 1980
Stadter, Philip A., "Arrian's Extended Preface", *Illinois Classical Studies*, 6 (1981): pp. 157 ff.
Tonnet, Henry, *Recherches sur Arrien: sa personnalité et ses écrits atticistes*, 2 vols, Amsterdam: Hakkert, 1988

Arta

Town in Epirus

The town of Arta lies some 14 km north of the Ambracian Gulf, in a bend of the Arachthus river where it winds down from the Xerovouni mountains to the west coast of Greece. It has always been the principal coastal town of the district of Epirus, and was known in antiquity as Ambracia. Its situation close to the estuary of the Arachthus allowed its inhabitants to reap the agricultural benefits of the flat, fertile, and well-watered surrounding land.

The area was first colonized by Corinth in the late 7th century BC, and a century later had become fully established. Pyrrhus, the king of Epirus, the son of Aeacides and Phthia, consolidated his position by settling there in 295 BC, and was the first ruler to make the town into a substantial capital, erecting many public buildings and sculptures. These were largely removed by the Romans when they took the town in 189 BC, and the inhabitants were moved to populate the new city of Nicopolis.

During the medieval period Arta became an important Venetian trading post, and by the mid-12th century was the seat of an archbishopric. However, the geographical remoteness of Epirus from the main centres of power in Greece meant that it was never given any great significance in imperial Byzantine policy. This remoteness was turned to advantage after 1204, when the dismemberment of the Byzantine empire after the Fourth Crusade allowed Michael I Angelos to establish an autonomous Byzantine state with its capital at Arta, thus initiating the most brilliant and (for the Greek world) influential period of the town's history. He adopted the title of despot, and so the despotate of Epirus became an independent state that was to persist under various governments until long after Turkish rule had been established in the rest of Greece.

The surviving monuments of Arta provide a vivid demonstration of the individuality that was established during its years as capital of a Byzantine despotate. Although acknowledging Byzantine traditions, the town is much closer to Italy than to Thessalonica or Constantinople, and western influences clearly formed part of its cultural input. The fortress on the town's low acropolis has visible Classical foundations, and its walls, now much restored, contain reused Classical *spolia*, although they now have little to show of their medieval past. But it is the large metropolitan church of the Panagia Parigoritissa ("Virgin of Consolation") which conveys most graphically the meeting of Constantinopolitan and western

Arta: bridge on the Arachthus river at Arta, celebrated in legend and song

sources that was such an authentic feature of the despotate. Built between 1283 and 1296 to a square plan, its west, south, and exterior walls are pierced by two rows of double-arcaded windows, and appear to have more in common with the forms of a central Italian *palazzo* than with any Byzantine tradition, but the five apses and six cupolas all show the Greek origins of the despotate. Further acknowledgement of Byzantine origins can be found within the spacious interior of the church, where a relief of a double-headed eagle is set into the floor and mosaics can just be seen high up in the large central cupola.

Two other churches in Arta itself broaden this impression: that of St Basil, a wooden-roofed basilica of the second half of the 13th century, of which the most prominent feature is an outstandingly rich and colourful exterior at its east end, formed partly from glazed polychrome tiles; and that of St Theodora of 1246–67, of which the dedication is due to the pious Theodora of the family Petraliphas, the wife of the despot Michael II (1246–67), whose tomb is located here. She appears in the graphically expressive relief carving of the tomb with beside her the second of her six children, the despot Nikiphoros I (1267–96).

Among other churches that exemplify the vitality of the despotate in the surroundings of Arta, that of Pangia tou Vlacherna, in the village of Vlacherna, demonstrates the inven-

tiveness of local builders who, under the despot Michael II, added three cupolas to what was originally a 12th-century three-aisled basilica. The smaller, domed, 13th-century church of St Nicholas tes Rhodias, built on an inscribed cross plan, is distinguished by a broad Greek meander pattern, set in thin bricks and running right round its exterior; this gesture to antiquity is balanced by some unusual 13th- to 14th-century frescos on its interior walls.

The prosperity of Epirus and the major town of Arta meant that they were coveted by a succession of powers under various leaders. Both before and after the restoration of Greek rule in Constantinople in 1261 attempts had been made to regain control of Arta by successive emperors, but a long period was to ensue when its rulers were principally non-Greeks. For almost 20 years until 1338 it had been occupied by the Orsini family, who were then ruling in the Adriatic as counts of Cephalonia. Andronikos III recovered Arta for the Byzantine empire in that year, but by 1348 it had fallen to Stephan IV Dushan, the powerful and ambitious *kral* of Serbia. In 1359 his successor, Symeon Uroš, decided to divide his growing territory in northern Greece, and placed Arta under the care of an Albanian lord, Peter Losha, giving him the title of despot of Arta and Rogoi. This despotate survived until 1384, when Italians from the Adriatic restored hegemony, and the fortunes of Arta became linked to the counts of Cephalonia, with their islands of Ithaca and Zakynthos and mainland holdings in western Greece.

Albanians again became involved in the fortunes of the town when Muriki and Yaqub Spata became lords of Arta between 1399 and 1416, until another Italian, Carlo Tocco, entering Arta in 1416, declared himself despot. The growing Turkish power meant that for much of the 15th century Venice was to assume, in order that its many possessions should be protected, an increasing power and responsibility in the area, and the last nominal despot of Arta, Leonardo III Tocco, was left to rule by the agreement of the republic. When he died in 1479, all of Epirus, including Arta, was under full Turkish control.

During the centuries of Ottoman domination Arta was to share the fate of the rest of Greece, and even so was only to achieve its desired status as fully Greek territory quite late in the struggle for Greek independence. Its geographical position was again to become important when, in 1832, the Arta–Volos line was established as the northern limit of the new kingdom of Greece. In spite of this, the town of Arta with its immediate surrounding territory was only to emerge again as a fully Greek possession in 1881; in that year the reconvened frontier commission came to an agreement that granted Arta, with its surrounding area, and Thessaly to Greece, but allowed Turkey to retain both Ioannina to the north and Preveza a short distance to the southwest. This anomalous arrangement was finally resolved only in 1912.

Thus it can be said that the two periods of Arta's most notable contribution to the Hellenic tradition occurred initially under Pyrrhus, who first made the town his capital in the 3rd–2nd century BC, and later, as an independent Byzantine despotate, when it was able to express a vigorous individualism which was reflected in the outstanding range of buildings that can still be seen today.

PAUL HETHERINGTON

See also Epirus

Summary
The chief coastal town of Epirus, Arta was known as Ambracia in antiquity. The area was colonized by Corinth in the 7th century BC. Arta was the capital of Pyrrhus, king of Epirus in the 3rd–2nd centuries BC. In the Middle Ages it was an important Venetian trading post. From 1204 to 1479 it was the capital of the Despotate of Epirus.

Further Reading
Finlay, George, *A History of Greece from Its Conquest by the Romans to the Present Time, BC 146 to AD 1864*, revised by H.F. Tozer, 7 vols, Oxford: Clarendon Press, 1877, reprinted New York: AMS Press, 1970
Hussey, J.M. (editor), *The Byzantine Empire*, Cambridge: Cambridge University Press, 1966 (*The Cambridge Medieval History*, vol. 4, part 1, 2nd edition), chapter 7
Nicol, Donald M., *The Despotate of Epiros*, Oxford: Blackwell, 1957
Nicol, Donald M., *The Despotate of Epiros, 1267–1479: A Contribution to the History of Greece in the Middle Ages*, Cambridge and New York: Cambridge University Press, 1984
Woodhouse, C.M. *Modern Greece: A Short History*, 5th edition, London and Boston: Faber, 1991

Asia Minor Campaign and Disaster

1919–1922

The Asia Minor campaign and its culmination, the disaster of 1922, were the dramatic climaxes in the pursuit of the Great Idea (the reconstruction of the Byzantine empire), and important landmarks in the history of modern Greece. Their effects were far reaching: the centuries-old Greek populations of Asia Minor were uprooted, with horrific loss of life and property. The destitute refugees flooded into Greece and the word *katastrophi* (disaster) became synonymous with the Asia Minor affair.

In 1919, after the conclusion of the European war, the situation for Greece and the Greeks had appeared auspicious. Greece was sitting at the Peace Conference on the side of the victors; a general consensus appeared to exist among the victorious powers that the Ottoman empire (along with the German and Austro-Hungarian empires) would be dismembered or, at least, divided into spheres of influence; even more importantly, Greece had ethnographic grounds to support its own claims, grounds that were at the core of the Allied wartime declarations, including Woodrow Wilson's "Fourteen Points"; all this could only augur well for the Greek populations and for the realization of the Great Idea, the core of Greek policy over the previous 80 years. A further advantage for Greece was that it bordered the regions it claimed, a geographical advantage that no other power possessed.

The head of the Greek government was Eleftherios Venizelos, a statesman of international repute; but in 1919 the country was still deeply divided by the National Schism, and its constitutional order was irregular: Venizelos had come to power following an intervention of the Entente powers, and, as his opponents were saying, "by foreign bayonets"; king Constantine had left the country in 1917 without abdicating, appointing in his place his second son, Alexander; and Venizelos was ruling by means of a "resurrected" parliament elected in 1915, in which his supporters had a majority. On 29 March 1919 the Italians began to occupy the area of Adalia in southern Anatolia and to advance northwest towards Smyrna. Alarmed by this development, on 7 May the British prime minister Lloyd George, the American president Wilson, and the French premier Clémenceau, in the absence of the Italian delegation, authorized Greece to occupy the city of Smyrna and its hinterland, to protect the Christian populations of that city. The landing took place on 15 May, under the protection of Allied warships. The Greek occupation was not uneventful: the Greek troops were fired on by Turkish irregulars on arrival at the quays of Smyrna and Turkish guerrillas began raids on the Greek-occupied area. With atrocities occurring on both sides, military considerations made a speedy occupation of the Greek zone imperative.

By the autumn of 1919, the Greeks were well established, militarily and administratively, in Smryna and its vicinity, even though Turkish nationalist irregulars were harassing the Greek forces and the Christian inhabitants of the area. However, given the weakness of their opponents, the attacks were easily repulsed. The most difficult problem was the geographical boundaries in which the Greek army could operate, these being no more than 3 km outside the Greek zone. Within this limited

Asia Minor Disaster: Greek refugees fleeing before the advancing Turkish army, 1922

area, mopping-up operations continued throughout the rest of 1919 and during the first half of 1920. After the nationalist attack on the British garrison at Izmit in June 1920, however, the ban on operations was lifted (initially with the blessing of the Allied High Command in Constantinople) and the Greek army was allowed not only to pursue the attacking forces, but also to extend its zone of occupation inland.

The Greek territorial claims and the occupation of Smyrna were formalized in the Treaty of Sèvres, signed on 10 August 1920; it confirmed the Greek mandate for the Smyrna area from the Gulf of Adramyttio to Scala Nuova; the Greek zone was contiguous with a British occupation zone (to the north) and an Italian one to the south; the French were in Cilicia. The treaty was draconian for Turkey, which was limited to a small kernel in central Asia Minor; yet despite a comprehensive list of obligations, the open question was how Turkey would be compelled to accept and fulfil the terms of the treaty. Almost immediately it became clear that the Turks were not going to accept them; and that the Entente was collectively unwilling and even unable to enforce them militarily. The one power that was prepared to intervene militarily to enforce the treaty was Greece; however, its own resources, even if strained to the limit, were numerically insufficient for the task

The Greek landing in Smyrna and the Treaty of Sèvres caused considerable upheaval and reactions among the Turkish populations. Mustafa Kemal (later Atatürk) became the focus and organizer of resistance to the treaty. From central Asia Minor he organized two conferences of Turkish nationalists (in July and September 1919), both of which affirmed the rejection of the Sèvres treaty. The new Ottoman parliament, elected in November 1919, had a majority of nationalist deputies and was openly against the Treaty of Sèvres; the Allies dissolved it, but Kemal reconvened it in Ankara in April 1920, renamed as the Grand National Assembly. This became the supreme power for the Turkish nationalists, and soon the only power in Turkey.

In November 1920, following the death of king Alexander, Venizelos held elections in Greece; he was defeated decisively and left the country. This led to a series of resignations and the replacement of Venizelist officers from commands of units on the Asia Minor front. These included the replacement of general Paraskevopoulos, commander of the army in Smyrna, with general Papoulas. More importantly, the change in government resulted in a change in the Entente stance towards Greece: on 21 November 1920 the Entente issued a common declaration informing Greece that the return of Constantine to the throne would result in the immediate cessation of financial aid and that the Allies would no longer assume any responsibility towards Greece. The restoration of Constantine gave the French and Italians the pretext they needed to distance themselves from their already shaky support of Greece and allowed them to effect a rapprochement with Mustafa Kemal's nationalists. Further adverse developments were also taking place: on 13 November 1920, in London, the French had suggested to the Allies the return of Smyrna to Turkey; on 20 November 1920 the Armenians capitulated and agreed to renounce their gains from the Treaty of Sèvres; while a rapprochement between the Turkish nationalists and the Soviets led to the signing of a treaty of friendship between the two on 3 March 1921. By the summer of 1921 the French and Italian military forces had begun evacuating the regions they were occupying, while their governments were vying with each other over supplying the nationalists; Mustafa Kemal had received large amounts of financial aid from the Soviets; and the British government had declared that it would remain neutral in the conflict. Despite these developments the Greek government and high command decided on a further push eastwards, which would later take the Greek army just short of Ankara, the capital of the nationalists. The campaign, which lasted until the end of August 1921, was only partly successful: the Turkish forces were generally pushed back and often defeated with many casualties and loss of equipment, but the Greeks failed to inflict a decisive defeat; long lines of communication and some war-weariness were also taking their toll. By September 1921 it was obvious that the front could not be held as it was; the Greek forces retreated westwards to a defensive line between Eskişehir and Afyonkarahisar. A military stalemate ensued with the front remaining stable until August 1922.

On the diplomatic front the Entente had attempted to find a solution to the stalemate in the summer of 1921, with little success. In February and March 1922 a further attempt was made, again with no success; both the Ottoman and the nationalist Turkish delegations insisted on the evacuation by the Greeks of both Asia Minor and Thrace before any further discussion could take place. The Greeks rejected this condition. The conference ended with the Entente proposals (modifications of the treaty of Sèvres and an autonomous status for Smyrna) given to the belligerents, but neither really accepting them. More importantly, Lloyd George, in meetings with the Greek delegation, encouraged the Greeks to seek a military solution to the issue. This was particularly welcome to the Greek government and in line with the Greek staff's confidence in the capability of the Greek army; the result was the Greek offensive of the spring and summer of 1921.

In October 1921 the French government signed the Franklin–Bouillon pact that recognized de facto the nationalists as the legitimate government of Turkey; the remaining French troops were withdrawn from Cilicia and arms and munitions (including 10 war planes) handed over.

In March 1922 the Entente made another attempt to find a solution to the stalemate; the proposals were more far-reaching than before, including changes in the demilitarized zone of the straits, evacuation of Constantinople by the Allied troops, a national homeland for the Armenians in Cilicia, and a League of Nations mandate for Smyrna; but the Greeks reserved their

5. Asia Minor campaign, 1919–22

reply to the proposals and the Turks rejected them, insisting once more on an unconditional withdrawal of the Greeks. All along, while Britain (particularly Curzon, the foreign secretary) was trying to find a solution, the other two members of the Entente, France and Italy, continued to supply Kemal's nationalists. In July the Greeks (in a veiled threat) asked for permission to enter Constantinople; they were refused and they did not move.

In the meantime Kemal's army was becoming stronger; and while the Greeks were not in any way inferior, general Hadjanestis, appointed in May 1922 as the new commander of the troops in Asia Minor, changed the organization of the Greek forces, centralizing command; his own headquarters were in Smyrna. Given the length of the front and the difficulties in communication, this was to prove a fatal mistake. On 26 August 1922 Kemal, from his headquarters a few kilometres behind the front line, launched a massive offensive and broke the Greek front between Afyonkarahisar and Savran. The Greek retreat was badly mismanaged and ended in several divisions being surrounded and having to surrender. By 8 September Smyrna was evacuated by the Greek troops; Turkish cavalry entered the city the next day. The evacuation of the Greek army from the Asia Minor seaboard was completed by 16 September 1922.

In Smyrna the departure of the Greek forces was to open a tragic page in Greek history. A wholesale massacre of Armenians and Greeks by regular and irregular Turkish troops was followed by the organized and systematic burning of the Armenian, Greek, and European quarters of the city. The toll was more than 25,000 dead. More than 200,000 destitute and panic-stricken people, mostly women and children, flocked to the shore, in a desperate attempt to find some means to leave.

Further atrocities took place there, in front of the foreign warships that were anchored in the Smyrna harbour. Among the dead was Chrysostomos, the Greek metropolitan of Smyrna, who was cut to pieces by the Turkish mob in front of a French marines patrol. A few days later, Nureddin, the Turkish military commander, issued a proclamation by which all Greek and Armenian men aged between 18 and 45 were rounded up and taken inland, to work in the notorious *amele taburu* (work battalions); most did not return. The remaining Greeks and Armenians were given until 30 September to leave; if they did not, the proclamation continued, they would "be considered suspect of threatening the security of the army and public order" and deported. Similar scenes of looting, destruction, massacre, and deportation were repeated in other towns and villages of the coast where Greek populations were living.

British intervention (which France grudgingly agreed to support) resulted in an armistice signed in Moudania on 11 October 1922. Greece had to evacuate eastern Thrace and withdraw west of the Mariza (Evros) river. Following this decision, the Greek population of eastern Thrace abandoned their homes and followed the Greek army into Greece. The region was handed over to the British authorities who, in turn, handed it to the Turkish nationalist representatives on the same day.

The results of the Asia Minor campaign were confirmed with the Lausanne treaty, which finalized the end of the Greek dreams, killing with them the Great Idea. As a result of the disaster and the Treaty of Lausanne, 1.5 million Greeks left Turkey for Greece, exchanged for 350,000 Muslims who left Greece for Turkey. The compulsory exchange of populations made Asia Minor, along with eastern Thrace, Pontus, and later Imbros and Tenedos, part of what became known in Greek as the *chamenes patrides* (lost homelands).

GEORGE KAZAMIAS

See also Great Idea, Lausanne, Refugees, Sèvres, Smyrna

Further Reading

Aktsoglou, I.Z., *Chroniko Mikrasiatikou Polemou, 1919–1922* [Chronicle of the War in Asia Minor, 1919–1922], Athens, 1998

Directorate of Military History — Greek General Staff, *I Ekstrateia eis tin Mikran Asian* [The Asia Minor Campaign], 10 vols, 1957–65

Horton, George, *The Blight of Asia: An Account of the Systematic Extermination of Christian Populations by Mohammedans and the Culpability of Certain Great Powers, with a True Story of the Burning of Smyrna*, Indianapolis: Bobbs Merrill, 1926

Houspian, Marjorie, *The Smyrna Affair*, New York: Harcourt Brace, 1971

Llewellyn Smith, Michael, *Ionian Vision: Greece in Asia Minor, 1919–1922*, London: Allen Lane, and New York: St Martin's Press, 1973, reprinted with a new introduction Ann Arbor: University of Michigan Press, 1998

Markezinis, S., *Politiki Istoria tis Neoteras Ellados* [Political History of Modern Greece], vol. 3: *I Megali Exormisis, 1900–1922* [The Great Campaign, 1900–1922], Athens, 1968

Pallis, A.A., "Racial Migrations in the Balkans during the Years 1912–1924", *Geographical Journal*, 66/4 (October 1925)

Pallis, A.A., *Greece's Anatolian Venture — and After: A Survey of the Diplomatic and Political Aspects of the Greek Expedition to Asia Minor, 1915–1922*, London: Methuen, 1937

Pentzopoulos, Dimitri, *The Balkan Exchange of Minorities and Its Impact upon Greece*, Paris: Mouton, 1962

Psomiades, Harry J., *The Eastern Question: The Last Phase*, Thessalonica: Institute for Balkan Studies, 1968

Reinhardt, Richard, *The Ashes of Smyrna: A Novel of the Near East*, New York: Harper and Row, 1971; London: Macmillan, 1972

Toynbee, A.J., *The Western Question in Greece and Turkey: A Study in the Contact of Civilisations*, 2nd edition, London: Constable, 1923

Astrology

Astrology is a pseudoscience that uses astronomical phenomena to make mundane predictions. Its origins lie in Mesopotamian astral, planetary, and meteorological omens, which were being catalogued already in the 2nd millennium BC in the cuneiform text *Enu–ma Anu Enlil* (much of its material is to be found in later Greek manuals such as those of Ptolemy, Hephaestion of Thebes, and John the Lydian in the 2nd, 5th, and 6th centuries AD respectively). Although it was not at first true astrology, in so far as there was no suggested relationship of cause and effect, increasingly exact astronomical observations from the 7th century BC encouraged the Babylonians to extend their science to making predictions for individual humans. By the late 5th century this Babylonian protoastrology had penetrated a Greek world made receptive through its divinization of celestial bodies. Greeks are responsible for its complex developments made chiefly in the period c.300 BC – c.AD 300.

Astrology is dependent upon a belief in sympathetic magic, which postulates a link between the macrocosm (universe) and the microcosm (man). It is based upon the supposed characteristics and associations with mundane phenomena of the seven "planets" (Sun, Moon, Saturn, Jupiter, Mars, Venus, and Mercury) and the twelve constellations of the zodiac, the latter being groupings as seen from earth of unrelated stars in a moving band eight or nine degrees each side of the ecliptic (the apparent course of the sun's annual orbit). The attribution of characteristics and associations to celestial bodies has on rare occasions a vestige of reason: thus Saturn, whose orbit is furthest from the sun of the planets known to the ancient world, was considered cold and malign, the cause of freezing weather, pestilences, and scarcity, and in man of dysentery, colic, the bringing up of phlegm, elephantiasis, etc. More typically, however, his lordship over the right ear (like Mercury's over the buttocks) appears quite arbitrary. Other associations depend upon contemporary theories: for instance, Pythagorean mathematics, by classifying all even numbers as female, dictates that Taurus (the Bull), since it is the second sign of the zodiac, should be female.

The "planets" were seen as moving anticlockwise at various speeds against the zodiacal circle, which itself revolved clockwise against an envisaged stationary circle whose four cardinal points were those of the risings and settings on the horizon of the ecliptic and the zenith and the nadir. This second circle was divided into usually 12 segments or "places" (today commonly "houses"). The degree of influence on mundane phenomena of each celestial body was believed dependent upon its position in respect to other bodies (its "aspects") and its "place", but there were so many calculations of often contradictory evidence that failure of predictions could easily be explained away. This was even more possible with the addition of the *dodecatemoria*, the division of each sign of the zodiac into 12 equal parts of two and a half degrees, each assigned to one of the 12 signs of the zodiac and thus allowing a "planet" to be in, say, the *dodecatamorion* of Scorpio in the sign of Gemini. All astrologers tended to base their predictions upon tables rather than observation, despite the accurately calculated discovery by Hipparchus in the late 2nd century BC of the precession of the equinox (the retrograde movement of the equinoctial points along the ecliptic), and thus continued to work on the assumption that the vernal equinox occurred at the first point of Aries rather than at some point in Pisces.

Believers were divided into those who, through acceptance of a purely mechanistic universe, held that the celestial bodies dictated an ineluctable fate and those who believed that astrology merely gave clues to personalities and trends and whose role was therefore that of a guide. The commonest application of astrology was for genethlialogy in which predictions were made about an individual on the basis of celestial positions at the hour of his birth or, far less commonly and of course less accurately calculated, his conception. These predictions could be updated by anniversary horoscopes. Large numbers of often astronomically impossible horoscopes have survived on papyrus, while there is one more "scientifically" reputable ancient collection from *c*.AD 130 in the *Anthologies* of the Antiochian Vettius Valens. Catarchic astrology determined the most favourable moments for commencing various enterprises such as journeys and military campaigns. Largely a subdivision of this was iatromathematics which dictated when certain herbs should be picked for greatest efficacy, predicted the course of illnesses, and gave clues as to treatment. Interrogational astronomy was dependent upon the positions of the celestial bodies at the time of the question.

Philosophical underpinnings to Greek astrology gave it respectability. Thus even the supremely competent astronomer Claudius Ptolemy in the 2nd century AD accepted and, indeed, even wrote a textbook (*Apotelesmatika* or *Tetrabiblos*, Astrology or the Fourfold Book) on the subject. Opposition was largely aimed at quack practitioners and those who threatened the stability of the state by making public predictions of the death of its ruler. Stoics, with the notable exception of Panaetius, were particularly drawn to astrology by their belief in cosmic sympathy, and in the early 1st century AD Manilius wrote a didactic poem (in Latin) on the subject. Epicureans and Cynics, however, scoffed at it. The most detailed surviving refutations are those of the Sceptic Sextus Empiricus in the 2nd century AD and of Plotinus and Origen in the 3rd century AD. Since astrology offended the concept of man's free will, Christian opposition was at times virulent but could not entirely extirpate it owing to belief in the "star" that led the Magi to Bethlehem. The 4th-century Priscillianist heretics in Spain even went so far as to hold that God used the celestial bodies to make manifest his will.

Hellenistic astrology passed through Sanskrit translations (most notably the *Yavanatjataka*, Sphujidhvaja's versification of Yavaneśvara's translation of AD 149/50) to India, where it was modified to accommodate local beliefs. Sassanian Iran learned its astrology from both Greek and Indian sources

and, before it passed it on to the Islamic world, added another type, the political, wherein predictions were made for whole nations.

Knowledge of astronomy almost completely died out in the Latin west through the non-existence there of astronomical tables. It continued, however, in Byzantium, beginning with an iatromathematical treatise on bed-illnesses by Pancharius, but in the period from the 4th to the 7th century it consisted of little other than compendia of Hellenistic material. Translations from Arabic began shortly before the year 1000 and introduced political astronomy. Belief was strongest probably during the 12th century when it was enthusiastically promoted by the emperor Manuel I. Both Arab and Byzantine astrologers were in consultation over the malign conjunction of planets on 16 September 1186, the elaborate attempts to protect the imperial palace from whose threat were mocked by Niketas Choniates. The Palaiologan period saw vast compilations of both Arabic and especially earlier Greek material, the latter of which was sometimes revised.

Knowledge of Greek astrology returned to the west from Islamic Spain by the 12th century. Astronomical discoveries in the 16th and 17th centuries undermined its validity, although most astronomers still retained belief in it and Johannes Kepler attempted to accommodate it to a heliocentric universe. Any intellectual basis for belief was finally eradicated by Newtonian physics (despite his own dabbling with horoscopes). Thereafter one of the most ingenious creations of the Greek mind has retained only a popular following, which has predictably been strongest at periods of crisis and disillusionment with established institutions both religious and political.

A.R. LITTLEWOOD

See also Fate

Further Reading

Barton, Tasmyn, *Ancient Astrology*, London and New York: Routledge, 1994

Barton, Tasmyn, *Power and Knowledge: Astrology, Physiognomics, and Medicine under the Roman Empire*, Ann Arbor: University of Michigan Press, 1994

Boll, Franz, Carl Bezold and Wilhelm Gundel, *Sternglaube und Sterndeutung: Die Geschichte und das Wesen der Astrologie*, 5th edition, Stuttgart: Teubner, 1966

Bouché-Leclercq, A., *L'Astrologie grecque*, Paris: Leroux, 1899

Catalogus Codicum Astrologorum Graecorum, 12 vols, Brussels: Lamertin, 1898–1936

Gundel, Wilhelm and Hans Georg Gundel, *Astrologumena: Die astrologische Literatur in der Antike und ihre Geschichte*, Wiesbaden: Steiner, 1966

Manilius, *Astronomica*, edited and translated by G.P. Goold, Cambridge, Massachusetts: Harvard University Press, 1977 (Loeb edition)

Ptolemy, *Tetrabiblos*, translated by F.E. Robbins, London: Heinemann, and Cambridge, Massachusetts: Harvard University Press, 1940 (Loeb edition; several reprints)

Tester, Jim, *A History of Western Astrology*, Woodbridge, Suffolk: Boydell, 1987

Vettius Valens, *Anthologiarum Libri Novem*, edited by David Pingree, Leipzig: Teubner, 1986

Astronomy

Greek astronomy can be defined as the astronomy of epicycles, an invention of the 3rd century BC. To arrive at this solution for planetary movements, the astronomers of the 3rd century had behind them three centuries of observations and mathematical theories.

Little is known about the mathematical astronomy of the Presocratics. Thales of Miletus (7th–6th century BC) is considered to be the first Greek astronomer. He predicted solar eclipses by studying their periodic recurrences, but with an important factor of error. Anaximander (6th century BC) observed the inclination of the ecliptic. Pythagoras (6th–5th century BC) found the "right" (in the geocentric system) order of the planets (Earth, Moon, Mercury, Venus, Sun, Mars, Jupiter, Saturn, while Aristotle later placed the Sun between the Moon and Mercury). A little more is known about the contemporary of Socrates, Meton, who, observing from the hill of Pnyx about 432 BC, defined the solar–lunar cycle of 19 years.

The observational data (especially those concerning the retrograde planetary motions and Sun and Moon anomalies) were important enough in Plato's time for him to pose the problem of "saving the phenomena" (interpreting celestial bodies' motions by circular orbits with uniform speed). According to Simplicius (6th century AD), it was Eudoxus who produced that system, composed of homocentric spheres. The combination of two spheres rotating with unchanging velocities can effectively represent the retrograde planetary motions. For the motion of the Sun he employed three spheres (one to account for an observation known to have been mistaken), and another three for the Moon.

Eudoxus' system only partially saved the phenomena: in particular it did not take into account the variations in the distance of the heavenly bodies (the variation in the apparent diameter of the Sun or in the brilliance of the planets). This problem was posed during the 3rd century BC. The heliocentric system proposed by Aristarchus of Samos (4th–3rd century) was an adequate response to that problem but, probably for philosophical reasons, it was not followed by the main Greek astronomers. According to a later source, Theon of Smyrna (2nd century AD), a system had been proposed during the 3rd century BC similar to that imagined 19 centuries later by Tycho Brahe. In that system the two "inner" planets, Mercury and Venus, orbit the Sun, while the latter orbits the earth, the centre of the universe. This system resolved far better than that of Eudoxus the motion of Mercury and Venus; it is highly probable that it is the origin of the astronomy of epicycles. Indeed, if the orbit of the Sun is replaced by the deferent cycle of Mercury and Venus, the solution attributed to Apollonius of Perge (born c.244 BC) is reached.

In an effort to respond to the solar anomaly, while respecting the principle of circular uniform motion, 3rd-century Greek astronomers proposed the "eccentric" solution: the Sun travels on an eccentric circle (centred on a point that does not correspond to the earth's centre). This system presented two difficulties: it was not symmetrical and it was contradictory to Aristotelian physics, which could not accept a motion around an imaginary point. It was probably Apollonius who resolved the problem of symmetry, by demonstrating the equivalence of an eccentric to an epicycle travelling around a concentric (deferent circle), while the "Aristotelian" problem has never been resolved. This epicycle plus deferent solution was to characterize all the astronomical systems until the beginning of the 17th century, when Kepler formulated his first planetary law, that of the elliptical orbits.

Between Apollonius and Hipparchus (who was observing at Rhodes c.128 BC), Greek astronomers had developed a complete epicycle plus deferent astronomical theory. By combining the radius and the motions (clockwise or anticlockwise), these astronomers could reproduce the retrograde motion of the planets (but not the fact that the "loops" produced by this motion were not symmetrical) and represent approximately the Sun's and the Moon's motion.

By reversing the "methodological" approach of astronomy, Hipparchus played a decisive role in the development of Greek astronomy. According to available information, which comes mainly from Ptolemy, Hipparchus was the first to give priority to the collection of observations in order to find the empirical laws of the motion. After that, he tried to solve the problem by circular uniform movements. Hipparchus tried to determine the radii of the deferents and the epicycles of the planets and computed a successful theory for the motion of the Sun. He also showed how to calculate the Moon's motion; his work was masterfully completed by Ptolemy.

As for the Sun, Hipparchus determined its eccentricity, resolving thus its principal anomaly, that of the inequality of the seasons' length. It was probably while working on the theory of the Sun that he made his main discovery, that of the precession of the equinoxes. By comparing historical observations, Hipparchus remarked that, in its annual movement, it took the Sun a little more time to reach the same zodiacal point than to reach the equator: the sidereal year would then be different from the solar year. This phenomenon, due to the spinning-top movement of the axis of the earth, was interpreted by Hipparchus as a very slow movement of the sphere of the stars, from west to east (about 1 degree per century, while the true value is 1 degree, 23 minutes, 30 seconds).

As for the Moon, the problem was much more complicated, as the motion of the earth's satellite presents six main anomalies. Although Hipparchus knew only one, he did not succeed in resolving it, but he posed the problem of the parallaxis relating to solar and lunar observations: he said that astronomers must consider the earth as a point only with respect to the fixed stars. He also tried to determine the dimensions and the distances of the heavenly bodies.

The apex of Greek astronomy was the magisterial work of Claudius Ptolemy. His book, the *Great Mathematical Syntaxis of Astronomy*, known as the *Almagest*, finished between AD 142 and 146, included all the astronomical phenomena known at that time. This book constituted a unique advance in the history of science: it was to be the main reference for all astronomers until the work of Tycho Brahe and Kepler, almost 1500 years later. Indeed, all Greek, Islamic, or Roman planetary astronomy until Kepler can be characterized as Ptolemaic.

Ptolemy continued and concluded Hipparchus' work. His method was similar: to collect as many observations as possible; to show up the anomalies of the planetary motions; to find the empirical laws for these anomalies; to combine various circular uniform movements in order to save the phenomena;

to choose the most adequate among the different solutions, and determine the radii and the positions of the circles and the angular speeds; to compute the planetary tables. The coincidence of forecast with observation confirmed the theory.

The main celestial movements according to Ptolemy were the following two: (a) the diurnal motion of the sky from east to west; (b) all other motions, which mainly took place from west to east and close to the ecliptic. Whenever Ptolemy was able to choose from among many solutions, he preferred the simplest. He adopted Hipparchus' solution for the Sun, but for reasons of simplicity he chose the eccentric from the deferent plus epicycle. For all the other heavenly bodies he presented his own solution, which in the case of Venus, Mars, Jupiter, and Saturn involved the famous "equant" (it was given this name during the Middle Ages): the centre of the epicycle does not move with a uniform motion; the circular uniform motion is "transferred" to a point of another circle (the equant). As a consequence, the phenomena were saved (the planets travel faster at their perigee and more slowly at their apogee), but this represented a serious departure from Aristotelian physics and from the principle of uniform circular motion posed by Ptolemy himself. The system was also extremely complicated: Ptolemy even added circles to move the level of the epicycle from that of the deferent!

Ptolemy presented his cosmological speculations (the mechanisms responsible for all the motions of the heavenly bodies) in his book *Planetary Hypotheses*. This work was the precursor of Islamic astronomical theories on the mechanisms of the celestial spheres. Another astronomical work of Ptolemy, the *Handy Tables*, a revised version of the *Almagest*, remained in use throughout the Middle Ages.

The main Greek commentator on Ptolemy was Theon of Alexandria (4th century AD). His commentary on the *Almagest* and two commentaries on the *Handy Tables* were the last important works of ancient Greek astronomy. In the 6th century John Philoponus wrote the first known *Treatise on the Astrolabe* (c.520–50), based on an unknown source. The first Byzantine astronomer of any note is considered to be Stephanus of Alexandria. He wrote a *Commentary on the Handy Tables* (c.610–20) inspired by the *Small Commentary* of Theon, a work designed for students unable to do multiplication and division.

Little is known about astronomy during the iconoclast period (except for some astrological works such as that of a certain Stephanus, written about 775, with previsions for the Muslim dynasties). The 9th century, however, is marked by the personality of Leo the Mathematician, and by the splendid copies made of Ptolemy's and Theon's works. These copies secured the transmission of the great astronomical works of antiquity.

The first indication of the influence of Arab astronomy on Byzantium dates to about 1032: an anonymous marginal commentary comparing Ptolemy's astronomy with that of the "moderns" (i.e. the Arabs, and especially the astronomer al-Alam). About 1072–78 another anonymous treatise introduces pure trigonometric methods in astronomy, inspired by the work of Habash al-Hasib. During the 12th century the works of Ptolemy were translated into Latin in Sicily, from Greek manuscripts offered by the emperor of Byzantium to the king of Sicily.

The great period of Byzantine astronomy began at the end of the 13th century, during the reign of Andronikos II Palaiologos. There were two main streams of thought: that of the renaissance of Ptolemaic astronomy and that of the foreign influences.

Theodore Metochites, "Grand Logothete" (the equivalent of prime minister), finished c.1316 a monumental astronomical work, the *Elements of Astronomy*. His pupil Nikephoros Gregoras (c.1290–1358) introduced Byzantine scholars to the practise of computing eclipses based on Ptolemy's method. Theodore Meliteniotes (fl.1393) wrote the *Astronomical Tribiblos*, a huge treatise restoring Ptolemy's astronomy among others.

At the end of the 13th century the physician Gregory Chioniades travelled from Trebizond to Tabriz to study Persian astronomy (the Maragha was then the world's most famous observatory). He brought back knowledge and manuscripts which, in 1346, were translated into Greek by George Chrysokokkes whose work, *Introduction to the Persian Astronomical Syntaxis*, was one of the most frequently copied Byzantine astronomical texts: more than 40 copies have survived. Maragha's astronomy was transmitted to Europe by means of Greek translations; Copernicus based his astronomical system on the "Al-Tusi couple", which he probably knew from a Greek manuscript. Another foreign influence on Byzantine astronomy was that of the Jews. In 1435 Michael Chrysokokkes translated Immanel ben Jacob Bonfils de Tarascon's tables of eclipses (*Ioudaikon Hexapterygon*). The *Alphonsine Tables* were also translated into Greek, first in Cyprus (c.1340) and then in Constantinople by Demetrios Chrysoloras (c.1360–c.1416), a high-ranking Byzantine official.

The last Byzantine astronomer was the philosopher George Gemistos Plethon (c.1360–1452); his Hellenic patriotism, mysticism, and late contact with the West encouraged him to propose an extremely original calendar reform.

The next important Greek astronomical work was the 16th century adjustment of the tables of *Ioudaikon Hexapterygon* by Damaskinos Stoudites, archbishop of Arta and Lepanto. From the 17th century only very simple manuals presenting the main lines of Ptolemaic astronomy survive. At the end of the century Chrysanthos Notaras (later patriarch of Jerusalem) adapted, probably from Persian, the main astrolabe problems and in 1716 he edited in Paris the first Greek printed book presenting non-Ptolemaic astronomy. As late as 1748 an important text for the history of the astrolabe was printed, "Peri Astrolavou" (On the Astrolabe, in *Odos Mathimatikis*), written by Methodios Anthrakistes some years earlier. This work is considered to be the last text of the Greek tradition concerning the construction of the astrolabe. Newtonian astronomy was introduced in the Greek communities of the Ottoman empire after the second half of the 18th century. Nikiphoros Theotokis was one of the main scholars professing the "new astronomy" in the Greek colleges. Textbooks such as the Lalande's *Astronomy* were published at the very beginning of the 19th century.

Observational astronomy was to revive in Greece in 1842, when Simon Sinas founded the Athens Observatory near the place where Meton had once observed. There Julius Schmidt drew his famous lunar maps. He was the only foreign astronomer, for very soon Greeks, who had previously studied in European observatories, began to run the institution following international standards.

EFTHYMIOS NICOLAIDIS

Further Reading

Dicks, D.R., *Early Greek Astronomy to Aristotle*, London: Thames and Hudson, and Ithaca, New York: Cornell University Press, 1970

Grasshoff, Gerd, *The History of Ptolemy's Star Catalogue*, New York: Springer, 1990

Heath, Sir Thomas Little, *Aristarchus of Samos: The Ancient Copernicus*, Oxford: Clarendon Press, 1913; reprinted New York: Dover, 1981

Heath, Sir Thomas Little, *Apollonius of Perga*, Cambridge: Heffer, 1961

Kirk, G.S., J.E. Raven, and M. Schofield, *The Presocratic Philosophers*, Cambridge and New York: Cambridge University Press, 1983

Maula, Erkka, *Studies in Eudoxus' Homocentric Spheres*, Helsinki: Societas Scientiarum Fenni, 1974

Neugebauer, Otto, *The Exact Sciences in Antiquity*, 2nd edition, Providence, Rhode Island: Brown University Press, 1957, reprinted New York: Dover, 1969

Neugebauer, Otto, *A History of Ancient Mathematical Astronomy*, Berlin, Heidelberg, and New York: Springer, 1975

Tihon, A., "L'Astronomie byzantine (du Ve au Xve siècle)", *Byzantion*, 51 (1981), 603–24

Toomer, G.J., *Ptolemy's Almagest*, London: Duckworth, and New York: Springer, 1984

Athanasios of Athos, St *c.927/30–c.997*

Founder of the first Athonite monastery

St Athanasios, who became known as the Athonite, was born in Trebizond in Asia Minor and was baptized under the name of Avramios. He came from a wealthy family, but having lost both of his parents at an early age, his upbringing was entrusted first to a nun who was a relative of his, and, after her death, to a eunuch who was related to the emperor Romanos I Lekapenos (920–44). He was educated in Constantinople and, after spending some time teaching there, he abandoned the secular world and entered the monastery of Kyminas in Bithynia where the abbot was Michael Maleinos, the uncle of Nikephoros II Phokas (963–69). When Nikephoros marched against the Arabs in Crete, he asked Athanasios to accompany him. Athanasios, who then was a monk on Mount Athos, accepted the invitation and lived in Crete until 961 when the island regained its independence. Nikephoros also gave Athanasios a considerable sum of money in order to build up a monastery, where he himself intended to become a monk at a later date. Thus, Athanasios founded the monastery of the Great Lavra in 963. It was the first monastery to be established in the territory of Mount Athos and today it still holds the leading position in the ranking of Athonite monasteries. It should be pointed out, however, that before Athanasios's time the eremitic type of monasticism, combined with some form of communal life but loosely organized, had already existed on Athos. But Athanasios inaugurated the cenobitic form of monastic life under a central administration, because he real-

ized that the poor sketes could not give a home to a long-lived monastic tradition. With imperial support the Lavra was granted annual revenue and lands and Athanasios initiated large-scale construction.

Quite soon, however, Athanasios faced the condemnation of some Athonite ascetics, who blamed him for abandoning their cherished monastic traditions and the concept of the "poor monastery" and for secularizing Athos. Yet, both the ascetics and emperor John I Tzimiskes (969–76), the successor of Nikephoros, soon came to realize that such innovations were not new inventions, but simply the continuation of the old and well-established tradition of cenobiticism in the east. A consequence of these disputes was the creation of the Typikon (rule) of the Great Lavra, which came to be known by the name of *Tragos* (972). This document, composed by order of Tzimiskes, contained the reforms of Athanasios. Thus for the first time on Athos there existed a book of rules concerning the internal organization of monasteries. In addition, through this Typikon Athos was recognized as an independent monastic polity. In it Athos is referred to not simply as the Mountain, as it used to be called up to that point, but as the Holy Mountain, a name that was officially acknowledged later on by emperor Constantine IX Monomachos (1042–55). From then on, Athanasios became the spiritual leader and reformer of Athonite monasticism. Even today he is regarded as the father and patriarch of all Athonite monks, because his reforms contributed to the establishment of cenobitic monasticism and to the subsequent flourishing of Athos. Consequently, the celebration of the millennium of the foundation of the Great Lavra in 1963 coincided with that of Orthodox monasticism on Athos.

The contribution of St Athanasios to the Greek Orthodox monastic tradition is immense. Although the monastic tradition of lavras no longer existed in Byzantium, he instigated on Athos the creation of a cenobium on which a small number of monastic cells depended. His reforms were endorsed by all subsequently created monasteries on Athos and elsewhere. It is also worth mentioning that Athanasios introduced into his monastery new time-saving devices, such as a machine driven by oxen to prepare dough.

Athanasios died on Athos probably in 997, for his signature appeared in the "Acts of Lavra" for the last time in October 996. The first biographies of Athanasios were composed in the third decade of the 11th century.

FR. NEKTARIOS DROSOS

See also Athos, Monasticism

Biography

Born in Trebizond *c.927/30* to a wealthy family, Athanasios lost his parents early and was brought up first by a nun and then by a relative of the emperor. He was educated in Constantinople and became a teacher before entering a monastery in Bithynia. He lived in Crete until 961 when he moved to Athos. In 963 he founded the first cenobitic monastery on Athos, the Great Lavra. He died on Athos *c.997*.

Further Reading

Anastasievich, Dragutin N., "La Date du typikon de Tzimisces pour le Mont Athos", *Byzantion*, 4 (1927/28): pp. 7–11

Dolger, Franz, "Die Echtheit des Tragos", *Byzantinische Zeitschrift*, 41 (1941): pp. 340–50

Dumont, Pierre, O.S.B., "Vie de Saint Athanase l'Athonite", *Irenikon*, 8 (1931): pp. 457–99, 667–89; 9 (1932): pp. 71–95, 240–64

Galavaris, G., "The Portraits of St Athanasius of Athos", *Byzantine Studies / Etudes Byzantines*, 5 (1978): pp. 96–124

Gedeon, Manouel I., *Athos: Anamneseis – engrapha – semeioseis* [Athos: Recollections – Records – Notes], Athens: Ermis, 1990

Halkin, F., "Eloge inedit de Saint Athanase l'Athonite", *Analecta Bollandiana*, 79 (1961): pp. 26–39

Lemerle, Paul, "La Conversion de Saint Athanase l'Athonite composée au debut du XIe siècle par Athanase de Lavra" in *Le Millénaire du Mont Athos, 963–1963: Etudes et Mélanges*, vol. 1, Chevetogne: Editions de Chevetogne, 1963, pp. 108–22

Leroy, Julien, "Saint Athanase et la Regle de Saint Benoit", *Revue d'Ascetique et de Mystique*, 29 (1953): pp. 108–22

Leroy, Julien, "Les Deux Vies de saint Athanase l'Athonite", *Analecta Bollandiana*, 82 (1964): pp. 409–29

Meyer, Philipp, *Die Haupturkunden für die Geschichte der Athosklöster*, Leipzig: Hinrichs, 1894, pp. 102–22; reprinted Amsterdam: Hakkert, 1965

Noret, Jacques, "La Vie la plus ancienne d' Athanase l'Athonite confrontée d'autres vies de Saints", *Analecta Bollandiana*, 103 (1985): pp. 243–52

Papachrysanthou, Dionysia, *O Athonikos Monachismos* [Athonite Monasticism], Athens, 1992

Petit, Louis A.A., "Vie de saint Athanase l'Athonite, *Analecta*, 25 (1906): pp. 5–89

La Vie de saint Athanase l'Athonite, introduction by Olivier Rousseau, Gembloux: Editions de Chevetogne, 1963

Ware, Kallistos, "St Athanasios the Athonite: Traditionalist or Innovator?" in *Mount Athos and Byzantine Monasticism*, edited by Anthony Bryer and Mary Cunningham, Aldershot, Hampshire: Variorum, 1996

Athanasius of Alexandria, St *c.*300–373

Pope of Alexandria

Athanasius first appears on the scene of history as the deacon of Alexander, the pope of Alexandria, at the First Ecumenical Council of Nicaea in 325. Of his early years we know nothing, though from his writings we can deduce that he was not a product of the formal system of education in late antiquity, but nonetheless had a good command of Greek, and an adequate familiarity with the ideas of the Classical and Hellenistic philosophers: he revered Plato as "that great one among the Greeks [i.e. pagans]". All this is consistent with the suggestion that he received his education among protomonastic ascetic circles in Egypt. As a young man, he must have caught the eye of Alexander and attached himself to his circle. In 328, having barely reached the canonical age of 30, he was elected bishop of Alexandria (or "pope", the traditional title for this post) to succeed his mentor. The election was contested, and perhaps not just because of his age. He continued Alexander's opposition to the Alexandrian priest Arius, who had been condemned at the First Ecumenical Council for denying the unqualified divinity of Christ, and was embroiled in the Meletian schism, a legacy of the great persecution at the beginning of the 4th century. He remained pope of Alexandria until his death in 373, though in the course of his life he was deposed several times and exiled four times. His position in the history of the Christian Church is bound up with his sustained opposition to those bishops in the east, and to the emperors whose support

they secured, especially Constantius II, who were unwilling to endorse the creed (or symbol) of the Council of Nicaea and sought to replace it with a series of creeds all endorsed by conciliar authority, and with the eventual victory of what has come to be called "Nicene orthodoxy", though he did not live to see the Second Ecumenical Council (held at Constantinople in 381), called by the emperor Theodosius to reinstate the authority of Nicaea. He pursued this struggle through his many writings against those he somewhat unfairly dubbed "Arians" or "Ariomaniacs", some of which tell the history of the struggle, others of which assert the authority of bishops, not emperors, to define Christain doctrine and govern the Christian Church. Even within his lifetime Athanasius was regarded by many with awe, and his dominant position is reflected in all the surviving church histories of the 4th century.

Athanasius' importance is found, first of all, in his championing of Nicene orthodoxy, which formally became the religious orthodoxy of the Byzantine empire in 381. Central to this is the confession that the Son of God, who became incarnate in Jesus of Nazareth, is consubstantial (*homoousios*) with the Father, that is, of the same unqualified divinity as the Father. He also, in his latter years, defended the divinity of the Spirit, and therefore the doctrine of the Trinity. But, more generally, in Athanasius' thought we find, perhaps for the first time, the pattern and the essential themes that were to characterize Byzantine theology: the doctrine of a consubstantial and coequal Trinity; the doctrine of the creation of the universe out of nothing through the Word of God, the second person of the Trinity, and of humankind's special role within the cosmos as being created in the image of God; the idea of the fall of humankind, through human disobedience, a fall that has cosmic implications; and the conviction that, through the assumption of a human life, the Word of God has redeemed humanity by conquering death and revealing the risen life through his resurrection, and has not only redeemed humanity, but promises deification (*theopoiesis* or *theosis*, a sharing in the divine nature) to all those who believe and strive to conform their lives to his through ascetic struggle and sacramental grace. All this is stated with amazing conciseness in his early work, *On the Incarnation*. Later Byzantine theology would explore the intricacies of this grand vision, but not alter its broad outline, with its main span reaching from creation to deification. A further dimension to Athanasius' importance is the strong link he forged between his hierarchical office and the emerging monasticism of the 4th century. This is symbolized in the ascription to Athanasius (an ascription that has been questioned in recent times, but is probably still sound) of the *Life of St Antony*, the great Egyptian hermit. The *Life of St Antony* became the pre-eminent model for the saint's *vita*, the most popular form of literature in the Byzantine world. This work, in which Athanasius embraces the characteristic demonology of the Fathers of the Desert (something otherwise rare in his writings), and his other ascetical writings (many of which survive in Coptic, Syriac, or Armenian) make clear the depth of Athanasius' commitment both to the monastic movement and to the more traditional urban and village asceticism that he also took steps to organize.

ANDREW LOUTH

Biography

Born in Alexandria c.AD 300, Athanasius received a good education and had some knowledge of the Classical philosophers. Elected pope of Alexandria at the age of 30, he was five times deposed and exiled. He championed orthodox Christianity against the heresy of Arianism. Other surviving works include a treatise *On the Incarnation* and (of uncertain authorship) the *Life of St Antony*. He died in Alexandria in 373.

Writings

In *Patrologia Graeca*, edited by J.-P. Migne, vols 25–28

Werke, edited by Hans Georg Opitz, Berlin: de Gruyter, 1934–41 (a few historical works only)

Sur l'incarnation du Verbe, edited by Charles Kannengiesser, Paris: Cerf, 1973

In *Nicene and Post-Nicene Fathers*, 2nd series, vol. 4, edited by Philip Schaff and Henry Wace, reprinted Peabody, Massachusetts: Hendrickson, 1994

Further Reading

Anatolios, Khaled, *Athanasius: The Coherence of his Thought*, London and New York: Routledge, 1998

Barnes, Timothy David, *Athanasius and Constantius: Theology and Politics in the Constantinian Empire*, Cambridge, Massachusetts: Harvard University Press, 1993

Brakke, David, *Athanasius and the Politics of Asceticism*, Oxford and New York: Oxford University Press, 1995 (contains translations of several of Athanasius' ascetical works)

Kannengiesser, Charles (editor), *Politique et théologie chez Athanase d'Alexandrie*, Paris: Beauchesne, 1974

Kannengiesser, Charles, *Athanase d'Alexandrie: evêque et écrivain*, Paris: Beauchesne, 1983

Pettersen, Alvyn, *Athanasius*, London: Geoffrey Chapman, and Harrisburg, Pennsylvania: Morehouse, 1995

Roldanus, J., *Le Christ et l'homme dans la théologie d'Athanase d'Alexandrie*, Leiden: Brill, 1968

Atheism

Atheism conventionally refers to a system of belief that denies the existence of a personal divinity. Taken in this sense, it is of fairly recent coinage in Greek intellectual history. In a broader sense, however, atheism, taken to refer to godlessness or, polemically, to the rejection of particular religious beliefs, has a better-documented pedigree.

Atheos is the Greek for "atheist". This is etymologically an adjective of broad application designating most frequently godlessness or the denial of a particular set of divinities. Thus, for example, in the *Eumenides* by the Athenian playwright Aeschylus, Orestes is called *atheos* because contrary to religious convention he had murdered his mother Clytemnestra, although his conversations with Apollo necessitate his belief in the existence of gods. Likewise, in *Oedipus the King* by Sophocles, the chorus protests its loyalty to Oedipus by wishing to be abandoned by friends (*aphilos*) and gods (*atheos*) alike if it wishes any ill towards him.

The number of known atheists in antiquity is very small. Though the historical record is somewhat fragmentary in most instances, during the latter part of the 5th century BC Athens witnessed a small number of piety trials directed against natural philosophers, who were commonly perceived as athe-

ists. These early scientists became objects of legal persecution largely because of their attempts to substitute natural causality for divine intervention. Diagoras of Melos is traditionally known as "the atheist" although the evidence indicates that he did not reject the existence of all gods. Anaxagoras was more clearly atheistic in his outlook since he specifically rejected the divine nature of the sun by referring to it as a piece of "hot stone". Protagoras held a more ambivalent position by proclaiming his uncertainty one way or the other as to the existence of the gods. Most famously, Socrates was tried and executed in 399 BC because he allegedly rejected the state divinities, introduced new gods, and corrupted the youth. The truth of these charges is unknowable, but three aspects of the case are significant. First, Socrates was represented in the *Clouds*, a comic play by Aristophanes, as rejecting the gods in favour of apotheosized natural mechanisms. Second, in Plato's *Apology*, a fictitious representation of his defence speech, Socrates specifically denies the charge of atheism, thereby demonstrating his vulnerability on that very point. Third, he is represented by the relevant witnesses as possessing a personal oracle, known as the *daemonion*, and observing the religious customs of his day, thus leaving him vulnerable to the charge of introducing new gods. Obviously, the atheism of Socrates was not the religious nihilism of the modern era.

Subsequent to Socrates, it is possible to speak of atheistic beliefs within a broader Graeco-Roman context. The Epicurean school of philosophy with its strict materialism and denial of divine intervention in human affairs is chiefly associated with these ideas. The Roman poet Lucretius, writing in the 1st century BC, aimed to popularize this particular outlook with his epic poem *On the Nature of Things*, a spirited challenge to the religious beliefs of his day. Plutarch, who lived during the last half of the 1st century and first half of the 2nd century AD, in his book *On Superstition*, gives atheism a very modern sense, saying that it is a denial of the existence of gods, but adds that it results from spurious reasoning. Doubtless the agnosticism of Marcus Aurelius, the Stoic emperor who reigned AD 161–80, easily falls within the bounds of ancient atheism. Lucian, a contemporary of Marcus Aurelius, describes in his *Icaromenippus* several schools of thought about the nature of the divine, some of which are atheistic, whether in the ancient or the modern sense

Christians, because they rejected the religious norms of their contemporaries and refused to yield in their monotheistic views, were regularly persecuted for their atheism. Lucian relates how Alexander of Abunoteichos, a spiritual mountebank, incited his followers to stone the Christians because they were blaspheming atheists. For their part, Christians enthusiastically labelled non-Christians and various sectarians as atheists. For example, in his Letter to the Ephesians Paul says that before the coming of Christ the gentiles were "without hope and atheists". According to Clement of Alexandria in his *Exhortation to the Greeks*, Diagoras and others who were in his view rightly sceptical about traditional Greek religion were not atheists; rather the true atheists were those who upheld pagan religious norms. The Christian apologist Athanasius refers to those who do not share his views on the relationship between Jesus Christ and God as atheists and non-believers. Polemical allegations of atheism aside, it appears that no evidence for intellectual atheism during the late antique period survives. As one writer has noted of this time, "sceptics and rationalists, if they existed, have left no mark on history and literature" (Jones, 1964, vol. 2, p.957).

Christian polemicists within the Greek Orthodox Church appear to have been just as tendentious in their application of the term "atheist" as their ancient predecessors. *Planosparaktes*, an anonymous 18th-century poem, is an example of this. In it a certain Auxentios, a miracle-working monk murdered in 1752, is called an atheist because of his support for the patriarch Cyril V, whose controversial views on the baptism of former Roman Catholics resulted in his being deposed twice from his see.

The latter part of the 18th and early part of the 19th centuries mark a period when leading intellectuals, influenced by exposure to the Enlightenment in western Europe, began to confront a Church hierarchy that was far too supportive of the Ottomans. In this context appears the *Ellenike Nomarchia*, a sustained and vigorous attack on the Orthodox Church and the Church's condemnation of Beniamin Lesvios in 1804 for teaching that the earth revolved around the sun, to cite two examples of the level of controversy. The *Didaskalia Patriki* of 1798 surely ranks as paramount among Church apologetics directed against the perceived atheistical tendencies of the French Revolution and its intellectual underpinnings. Concerned about the revival of Classical learning and growing interest in Enlightenment thought, the patriarchate reopened its presses to ensure the publication of doctrinally sound material.

The impact of Marxism and its explicitly atheistic outlook must also be noted. During the Civil War of 1946–49 it is said that a sizeable number of Orthodox priests and monks were executed by members of the far left. In the Eastern bloc countries the constraints of Communism were likewise felt. Thus the Orthodox Church in Bulgaria was forced to make certain concessions in order to retain a slightly privileged status under the regime there.

C.A. Hoffman

Further Reading

Burkert, Walter, *Greek Religion: Archaic and Classical*, Oxford: Blackwell, and Cambridge, Massachusetts: Harvard University Press, 1985, pp. 313–17

Clogg, Richard, "The 'Dhidhaskalia Patriki' (1798): An Orthodox Reaction to French Revolutionary Propaganda," *Middle Eastern Studies*, 5/2 (May 1969): pp. 87–115

Clogg, Richard, "Anti-Clericalism in Pre-Independence Greece, c.1750–1821", *Studies in Church History*, 13 (1976): pp. 257–76

Ferguson, John, *The Religions of the Roman Empire*, Ithaca, New York: Cornell University Press, 1981, reprinted 1985, pp. 190–210

Jones, A.H.M., *The Later Roman Empire, 284–602: A Social, Economic and Administrative Survey*, 3 vols, Oxford: Blackwell, and Norman: University of Oklahoma Press, 1964, reprinted Oxford: Blackwell, and Baltimore, Maryland: Johns Hopkins University Press, 1986, pp. 938–85

Lane Fox, Robin, *Pagans and Christians*, London: Viking, 1986; New York: Knopf, 1987

MacDowell, Douglas M., *The Law in Classical Athens*, Ithaca, New York: Cornell University Press, and London: Thames and Hudson, 1978, pp. 200–02

Martin, Luther H., *Hellenistic Religions: An Introduction*, Oxford and New York: Oxford University Press, 1987, pp. 36–40

Papadopoullos, Theodore H., *Studies and Documents Relating to the History of the Greek Church and People under Turkish Domination*, 2nd edition, Aldershot, Hampshire: Variorum, 1990

Parker, Robert, *Athenian Religion: A History*, Oxford: Clarendon Press, and New York: Oxford University Press, 1996, pp. 199–217

Rinvolucri, Mario, *Anatomy of a Church: Greek Orthodoxy Today*, New York: Fordham University Press, and London: Burns and Oates, 1966

Woodbury, Leonard, "The Date and Atheism of Diagoras of Melos", *Phoenix*, 19/3 (1965): pp. 178–211

Athenaeus

Prose writer of the 2nd century AD

Athenaeus was born in Naucratis, a Greek community in Egypt, around AD 150. He was prominent among the Greek scholars of the so-called Second Sophistic, and but one of several produced by Naucratis. These scholars, Athenaeus included, were concerned with the revival of Classical Greek culture in the context of Roman imperial rule. Athenaeus spent time in Rome in the patronage of P. Livius Larensis, a cultured Roman bibliophile with a strong interest in Hellenism. However, there is no evidence for the frequent assertion that he belonged to the circle of Julia Domna, the wife of the Roman emperor Septimius Severus.

His principal work was his *Deipnosophistae*, (Sophists at Dinner). It is divided into 15 books (not 30, as sometimes claimed), of which the opening and closing books are fragmentary: for these, we depend largely upon an epitome. The *Deipnosophistae* forms part of a long Hellenic tradition of sympotic literature, a direct descendant of Plato's *Symposium*, Xenophon's *Symposium*, Plutarch's *Sympotic Questions*, and Lucian's *Symposium*, among other texts. However, it is far longer than these predecessors. The diners, 24 in total with the host Larensis included, discuss both the dinner itself and a bevy of issues that arise from particular dishes or circumstances – cooks (Greek and non-Greek), extraordinary concoctions, outstanding banquets, dances, music, musical instruments, furniture, wines, health, cultivated fruits, gluttony, austerity, luxury, scholarship, and humour.

Each diner receives his own characterization, but some are more strongly drawn than others. They include Ulpianus of Tyre, committed to the purity of Attic Greek and always concerned to raise a pedantic point of grammar (and probably not to be identified with Ulpian the jurist); Kynoulkus, a Cynic who takes pleasure in goading the irascible Ulpian; Galen the physician; Masourius, with pretensions to musical expertise; Ploutarchus, a grammarian; and Myrtilus with his taste for proverbs. How far these characters are real people in Larensis' circle remains a matter of doubt: Athenaeus has been suspected of sly humour in his construction and naming of the diners. Certainly, humour is a pervasive feature of the *Deipnosophistae*, both in the interaction of characters and in the dubious and often overblown learning in which the diners compete. The *Deipnosophistae* is best read as a work of both philosophy and satire, appropriately enough in the sympotic tradition.

Athenaeus' work has most often been used as a source for earlier Greek dining or for lost texts, which are quoted very extensively throughout. Its thematic division (e.g. book 7 on fish; book 13 on courtesans) encourages the former approach, while the sheer density of quotation makes the latter inevitable. In accordance with the humorous tone of the work, quotations from Greek comedy are particularly frequent and constitute an enormous part of our knowledge of the genre. Athenaeus' quotations are drawn from some 1250 authors: they include the titles of some 1000 plays and run to some 10,000 lines of verse. The combination of verse quotation and prose text indicates Athenaeus' debt to the genre of Menippean satire.

However, Athenaeus also quotes heavily from prose works, as well as from verse. For example, the historian Callixinus' lengthy account of the grand procession of Ptolemy II Philadelphus is preserved in the *Deipnosophistae*. Athenaeus displays through his characters a historical sensibility far beyond that of an antiquarian. In particular, although his work focuses especially upon Greek culture in its broadest sense, there is also a recurrent concern with the contemporary historical situation, with Rome and its emperors (8. 361f on Hadrian; 12. 537f on Commodus). Moreover, the most recent scholarship encourages the suspicion that Athenaeus not only preserved quotations, but also inserted his own additions and emendations: in any event, it is often difficult to be sure where quotation ends and Athenaeus' own writing begins. There is also an uncomfortable inconsistency in the details of the setting: the first ten books seem to relate to a single banquet, books 11–14 indicate a second gathering, while the final book 15 contains a third session, the whole covering three successive days, it seems. The dramatic context has been taken to range inconsistently between January (9. 372b), April (8. 361f), and August (3. 99e), whether by authorial error or in consequence of the manuscript tradition. However, although January and August are mentioned in the text, it is only 21 April (the ritual "birthday" of Rome) that is clearly given as the time of the dinner(s).

Athenaeus mentions two further works of his own in the course of the *Deipnosophistae*. Neither survives, but both represent features of the concerns that he displays in the extant work. One may be regarded as a historical work in view of its title, *On the Kings of Syria* (*Deipnosophistae*, 5. 211a). However, the rulers of Syria, who might include not only the Greek Seleucids but even Semiramis, offered ample scope for a wealth of anecdote, humour, and moralistic philosophizing, so that the work may not have been the solid historical text that has often been imagined. Certainly, the short passage quoted in the *Deipnosophistae* suggests that its tone may not have been so very different from that of the extant work. Athenaeus' other work survives only as a title: it was a treatise on Archippus' comedy *Fishes*, produced after 403 BC (*Deipnosophistae*, 7. 329c). This play seems to have centred upon an imaginary treaty between Athens and the fishes, akin to the central conceit in Aristophanes' *Birds*: as with the birds of the latter, the play no doubt raised numerous issues of the identification, terminology, and qualities of a wide range of fish, a matter of keen interest to the author of the *Deipnosophistae*.

The oldest surviving manuscript of the *Deipnosophistae* is dated to the 10th century AD. The work seems to have been much used in the Middle Ages, at least in epitomized form: for his commentary on the Homeric poems, Eustathios draws from the epitome on some 2000 occasions. At present in Greece the term "Deipnosophist" has been resurrected in a series of articles on taste and aesthetics, which appeared in the newspaper *Kathemirini* intermittently from 1989 to 1991 and which have now been collected and published as a book, of which *Deipnosophist* constitutes both the title and its author's nom de plume. The inspiration of Athenaeus is explicitly acknowledged, but the modern work is not a dialogue and does not seek to reproduce the texture or flavour of its ancient forebear.

DAVID BRAUND

See also Symposium

Biography

Born in Naucratis c.AD 150, Athenaeus was a leading figure in the movement known as the Second Sophistic. He spent some time in Rome as the guest of P. Livius Larensis. His principal work is an example of sympotic literature, the *Deipnosophistae*, which contains quotations from many other works that are now lost, notably comedy.

Writings

The Deipnosophists, translated by Charles Burton Gulick, 7 vols, London: Heinemann, and Cambridge, Massachusetts: Harvard University Press, 1927–41 (Loeb edition)

Les Deipnosophistes, books 1–2, edited and translated into French by A.M. Desrousseaux, Paris: Belles Lettres, 1956

Further Reading

Anderson, G., "Athenaeus: The Sophistic Environment" in *Aufstieg und Niedergang der römischen Welt*, 2. 34. 3, edited by Hildegard Temporini *et al.*, Berlin: de Gruyter, 1997, 2173–85

Baldwin, B., "Athenaeus and His Work", *Acta Classica*, 19 (1976): pp. 21–42

Baldwin, B., "The Minor Characters in Athenaeus", *Acta Classica*, 20 (1977): pp. 37–48

Bowersock, G.W., *Greek Sophists in the Roman Empire*, Oxford: Clarendon Press, 1969

Bowie, E.L., "The Greeks and Their Past in the Second Sophistic" in *Studies in Ancient Society*, edited by M.I. Finley, London and Boston: Routledge, 1974

Braund, David and J.M. Wilkins (editors), *Athenaeus and His World: Reading Greek Culture in the Roman Empire*, Exeter: Exeter University Press, 2000

Henry, M.M., "The Edible Woman: Athenaeus' Concept of the Pornographic" in *Pornography and Representation in Greece and Rome*, edited by Amy Richlin, New York: Oxford University Press, 1992

Lukinovich, A., "The Play of Reflections between Literary Form and the Sympotic Theme in the Deipnosophistae of Athenaeus" in *Sympotica: A Symposium on the Symposion*, edited by Oswyn Murray, Oxford: Clarendon Press, and New York: Oxford University Press, 1990

Rice, E.E., *The Grand Procession of Ptolemy Philadelphus*, Oxford and New York: Oxford University Press, 1983

Zecchini, Giuseppe, *La cultura storica di Ateneo*, Milan: Vita e Pensiero, 1989

Athenagoras 1886–1972

Patriarch of Constantinople

Athenagoras was an important ecclesiastical figure of international standing during the 20th century. He was born on 25 March 1886 in the village of Tsaraplana (now Vasilikon) in Epirus and his lay name was Aristoklis (Spyrou). From 1903 to 1910 he studied theology at the school of Chalki, a traditional educational centre of the ecumenical patriarchate of Constantinople, and in March 1910 he was ordained a deacon. He then served in the diocese of Pelagonia (in the area of Monastir), where he undertook the supervision of Greek Orthodox schools and remained during the Balkan Wars and World War I. Following a short stay on Mount Athos in 1918, in March 1919 he was named secretary of the new archbishop of Athens, Meletios Metaxakis, who was very involved in ecumenical contacts. Athenagoras remained in Athens during that turbulent political period and was ordained priest in December 1922. In the same month he was elected bishop of Corfu and Paxoi, where he engaged in wide social, political, and ecclesiastical activities.

Athenagoras showed an early interest in the promotion of interreligious and particularly interdenominational dialogue, a fact that was manifested later in his strong ecumenical engagement. In 1930 he was named secretary of a conference, held at the monastery of Vatopedi on Mount Athos, to prepare for a prospective Panorthodox synod. In the same year he also participated in the Lambeth Conference in Britain to promote the continuation of Orthodox–Anglican dialogue. In August 1930 he was elected archbishop of North and South America by the Patriarchal Synod, a development that would have immense influence on his future ecumenical endeavours. Though not familiar with the conditions in the US, when confronted with the serious frictions in the ecclesiastical body and the Greek communities there, Athenagoras pursued a policy that proved to be very effective. During his 18-year stay in the US (1930–48), he managed, among other things, to bring about the internal unity of the Greek Orthodox Church in America, to provide the structure of the archdiocese with a set of administrative regulations that functioned well, to develop an effective charity system, and to secure its future on a solid basis through the organization of an Orthodox-oriented education system both for lay persons and for the priests of the archdiocese (e.g. the Holy Cross School of Theology in Brookline, Massachusetts). He also contributed to Greek War Relief, which aimed at alleviating the suffering of the Greek people in the wake of World War II. He initiated an approach between the various Orthodox national Churches (e.g. the Russian, the Serbian, and the Romanian) in an attempt to secure Orthodox unity and collaboration in the US. He also had the opportunity to develop further his international ecclesiastical and political contacts (e.g. with president Harry Truman).

Though an American citizen, Athenagoras was elected ecumenical patriarch of Constantinople on 1 November 1948. The Turkish state did not present any obstacles to such an election, but after his death in 1972 it changed its attitude on the matter. Serious criticism of his election came principally from the Soviet Union, which suspected the manipulation of Orthodoxy by the US to increase its influence in Eastern Europe. Such a reaction was fully understandable on the eve of the ensuing Cold War. During his long patriarchal reign Athenagoras transformed the Phanar from an isolated Orthodox centre, laden with spiritual resources and bygone glory, into a religious institution of international prestige and significance. He was also particularly interested in promoting the mutual rapprochement between Greeks and Turks. Such a policy was especially difficult considering the resurgence of nationalist confrontation between the two nations (e.g. the violent acts against the Greek community in Istanbul on 6–7 September 1955) and the Cyprus problem. This resulted in the evident suspicion with which the Turkish state viewed Athenagoras's ecumenical contacts and related activities.

Apart from his great interest in the dioceses of the patriarchate in Europe, America, and Oceania, Athenagoras placed particular emphasis upon inter-Christian reconciliation. In the official celebrations for the millennium of Mount Athos in 1963, he invited the prelates of other Christian confessions to participate alongside the Orthodox hierarchs. He also fostered the continuing dialogue with the Anglicans, the Old Catholics, and the Protestants, and made visits to Canterbury, Rome, and Geneva (to the World Council of Churches). Athenagoras's most important contribution to Christian unity was perhaps his initiation of the dialogue between the Orthodox and the Roman Catholic Churches. Between 1964 and 1967 Athenagoras and pope Paul VI had regular meetings in Jerusalem, Constantinople, and Rome. On 7 December 1965 the mutual anathemas, pronounced by the two Churches following the definitive schism between them in 1054, were withdrawn. This symbolic act of reconciliation and love, which was hailed as a decisive step in the future relations of the two Churches, was severely criticized by Orthodox hardliners and fundamentalists as well as by other Orthodox as a compromise, or worse, as a betrayal of the Orthodox faith due to the still existing theological differences between the two Churches.

Another important challenge that Athenagoras had to face was the disrupting and divisive effects of nationalism in the various Orthodox Churches, which had destroyed to a considerable degree traditional Orthodox unity. He therefore paid visits to the other three Orthodox patriarchates as well as to several other autocephalous Orthodox Churches. The preparation of a great Panorthodox synod to discuss various dogmatic, liturgical, and practical matters of common heritage and interest lay at the heart of his endeavours, as manifested in the Panorthodox conferences on the island of Rhodes in 1961, 1963, and 1964, and in Geneva in 1968. Moreover, the tension between Constantinople and Moscow was mitigated to a certain extent when patriarch Aleksii of Moscow visited the Phanar in 1961 and acknowledged the canonical rights of the patriarchate of Constantinople. Yet the pretensions of Moscow to be the great Orthodox Church were not in accord with the ecumenical vision of Athenagoras and his historic role as primus inter pares among all Orthodox patriarchs and archbishops. Although the results of these early Panorthodox conferences were unimpressive, certain positive steps have been taken in several directions, for example, concerning the non-Chalcedonian (Monophysite) and Nestorian Churches.

Athenagoras's death in 1972 signified a major turning point in Turkish policy vis-à-vis the ecumenical patriarchate. The

Turkish state intended to intervene more actively in the election procedures of the new patriarch, who from now on had to be a Turkish citizen too. The theological division of the school of Chalki was closed in August 1971, a development that seriously affected the patriarchate's capacity to provide its numerous Orthodox dioceses all over the world with the necessary ecclesiastical personnel. In addition, a clear intention of the Turkish state was to undermine the international and ecumenical role of the patriarchate by considering it solely as the religious head of the tiny Greek community in Istanbul. Such a policy, however, is in clear contrast to the heritage left by Athenagoras and his successful efforts in upgrading the patriarchate's international role in the contemporary world.

VASILIOS MAKRIDES

See also Ecumenism, Patriarchate of Constantinople

Biography

Born in Epirus in 1886, Athenagoras was educated at the patriarchal school of Chalki in Constantinople before being ordained a deacon in 1910. In 1919 he became secretary to the archbishop of Athens; and in 1922 he was ordained a priest and bishop of Corfu and Paxoi. After a spell as archbishop of North and South America (1930–48) he was elected ecumenical patriarch of Constantinople in 1948 in which capacity he made major contributions to ecumenical dialogue with other Churches. He died in 1972.

Further Reading

Anastasiou, Ioannis, *Athenagoras I, Oikoumenikos Patriarchis o Ipeirotis* [Athenagoras I, the Ecumenical Patriarch from Epirus], Ioannina, 1975

Clément, Olivier, *Dialogues avec le Patriarche Athénagoras*, Paris: Fayard, 1969

Gheorghiou, Virgil, *La Vie du Patriarche Athénagoras*, Paris: Plon, 1969

Ohse, Bernhard, *Der Patriarch Athenagoras I. von Konstantinopel: Ein ökumenischer Visionär*, Göttingen: Vandenhoeck & Ruprecht, 1968

Panotis, Aristeidis, *Pavlos VI – Athenagoras I: Eirinopoioi* [Paul VI – Athenagoras I: Peacemakers], Athens, 1971

Panotis, Aristeidis, *Les Pacificateurs: Jean XXIII, Athénagoras, Paul VI, Dimitrios*, Athens: Dragan, 1974

Tomos Agapis: Vatican–Phanar, 1958–1970 [The Book of Love: Vatican – Phanar, 1958–1970], Rome and Istanbul, 1971

Tsakonas, Demetrios, *A Man Sent by God: The Life of Patriarch Athenagoras of Constantinople*, Brookline, Massachusetts: Holy Cross Orthodox Press, 1977

Athens

Capital of modern Greece

The modern city of Athens extends across the largest plain of Attica at a distance of 6–7 km from the coast to the south. Apart from this southern edge, which opens to the port of Piraeus and the Saronic Gulf, the city is surrounded by mountains, namely Aigaleo, Penteli, Parnitha, and Hymettos in a clockwise direction.

Archaeological evidence shows that the earliest settlement took place during the late Neolithic period around 4000 BC. The substantial remains of later periods have obscured these prehistoric settlements, but we know that the first nucleus of life in the region developed on the rock of the Acropolis and its cavities, with farms and roughly made huts subsequently spreading to the south. There is evidence of extensive farming, herding, and fishing and of the worship of a goddess of fertility. Subsequently a number of small and independent kingdoms were established around this nucleus, such as those in Kifisia, Brauron, Marathon, and Eleusis; trade links were developed, especially with the Cyclades; arteries to the Peloponnese and mainland Greece to the north were established; and fortifications were built, especially around coastal settlements, but also around the Acropolis in the second half of the 13th century BC. Athens continued to grow amid these independent conglomerations, and by the Late Bronze Age it was undoubtedly considered one of the most prestigious Mycenaean centres, as indicated by wealthy 14th-century BC tombs, the remains of a Mycenaean palace on the Acropolis, and the 13th-century BC fortifications.

It was sometime during the 14th or 13th century BC that all the kingdoms of Attica formed a political union called *Athinai* (in the plural) and centred around the ancient Athini or Kekropia. Even if not entirely peaceful, the unification – widely known as synoecism and assigned to the mythical hero Theseus who thus became the first king of the city state of Athens – was panegyrically celebrated in the Classical period with two major festivals, the Synoecia and the Panathenaea, which took place in the Agora.

The Mycenaean period is inextricably associated with a series of mythical kings, such as Cranaus, Erechtheus, Cecrops, Pandion, Ion, Aegeus, Codrus, and of course Theseus, whose lives nourished the Athenians' collective consciousness in historical times. But the city's prosperity was seriously affected during the collapse of Mycenaean civilization and the Dorian invasion at the end of the 2nd millennium BC. These tumultuous events brought about social changes that eventually led to the abolition of kingship. The Athenians took great pride in the fact that the Dorians never invaded the city, and it is from this period that the myth of autochthony stems. It was also at that time that Athenian refugees moved across to Ionia, in Asia Minor, in what would later be known as the first movement of colonization.

The descent of the Dorians (11th century BC) also marks the beginning of the Geometric period in Greek history, which lasted until the 8th century BC. Even though the period is often called the Dark Age of ancient Greece – mainly because of the general shortage of raw materials, the decline of trade, and the non-existence of writing – Athens steadily increased in size, new settlements were built, and its pottery with the famous geometric designs and the first sketchy outlines of the human body prepared the ground for subsequent artistic achievements.

In the course of the 7th century BC the increasing significance of craftsmanship and handicraft and the revival of trade put under scrutiny the unquestionable hegemony of the aristocracy of titles and land. There is evidence of a failed attempt of Cylon in 636 BC to exploit this general dissatisfaction in order to become a tyrant. Amid continuing struggle Draco codified the hitherto unwritten – mainly criminal – body of laws, but the unrest did not subside until Solon, a man trusted by all, reformed the state and the laws in 594 BC. His reforms

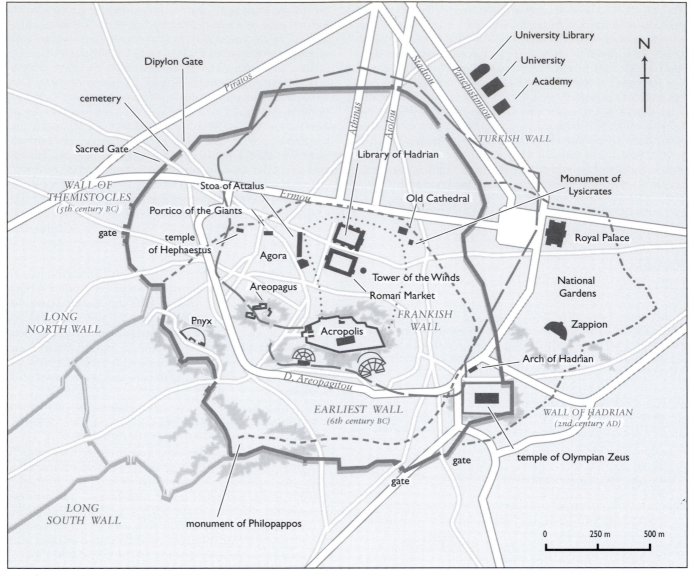

6. Athens

aimed mainly at including the lowest body of Athenians in political decisions, and they are often now considered as the first step towards the realization of democracy, even if they did not manage to elicit general consent.

Encouraged by their newly established political rights, the farmers and cattle breeders kept pressing for an improvement in their position and in 561 BC one of their most able politicians, Pisistratus, took advantage of their unrest and support to set up a tyranny. In spite of his hegemonic spirit, he gave out agrarian loans, boosted trade with other tyrannical states in the Aegean area, and opened the city up to Ionian philosophical and artistic influences. Ancient sources assign to him the first recording of the Homeric epics and the establishment in 566 BC of the Panathenaea, a first major instance of collective religious worship. The tyrannical regime became oppressive during the years of Hippias, who was finally chased away in 510 BC. After two years of renewed political struggle Cleisthenes from the aristocratic family of the Alcmaeonidae enlarged the list of Athenian citizens, divided the population

into ten tribes of mixed origins, and inaugurated the policy of ostracism – enabling the citizens to demand the removal from the city for ten years of any citizen they deemed too influential. The newly established Athenian democracy provoked Persia by supporting the Ionian Revolt and subsequently successfully resisted the Persian assaults at Marathon (490 BC) and Salamis (480 BC).

A more integrated form of democracy is associated with the rule of Ephialtes (who was assassinated by reactionary aristocrats in 461 BC) and Pericles. But Athens' leading role in Greek politics had been formally acknowledged already from 478 BC with the foundation of the Delian League, which brought all subject allies under Athenian control. Led by able politicians and generals such as Aristides, Cimon, and Pericles himself, Athens prospered for 50 years in political, artistic, philosophical, and financial spheres alike; suffice it here to remind ourselves of the Parthenon, the golden-ivory statue of Athena in it, and Athenian tragedy – all products of that famous *pentekontaetia* (50 years) brought to an end in 431 BC by the eruption of the Peloponnesian War, which was the result of Sparta's growing discontent in the face of an increasing Athenian expansionism in the late 430s BC. Lasting 27 years, the unprecedented cruelty of this conflict with Sparta exhausted the city and at the same time let Persia into Greek internal affairs in 407 BC, when the former stepped into the war on the side of Sparta.

The antagonism between the two principal Greek cities continued over the course of the 4th century BC and Persia was once again called upon during the Corinthian War (395–386 BC), this time on the side of Athens. During the short revival of its independent status in the first half of the 4th century BC, Athens pursued an alliance with rising Thebes and made a series of failed attempts, including a second Athenian League, to restore its imperial role. The cultural life was still flourishing but the political prestige and the finances of the city were in steep decline. The emergence of Philip II of Macedon around the middle of the century and his appeal for a Panhellenic alliance that would campaign against the Persians were met with Athenian distrust and hostility, as Demosthenes' well-known and flagrantly rhetorical speeches against the Macedonian king testify. Athens' military power received a heavy blow from the Macedonian army at Chaeronea in 338 BC, but its leaders in the 330s and 320s BC, notably Eubulus and Lycurgus, carried on with policies of retrenchment that stripped the city of its last opportunities for a viable political role in the new order.

Under Cassander of Macedon, Demetrius of Phaleron ruled peacefully but tyrannically so that the arrival of the Antigonid ruler, Demetrius Poliorcetes in 307 BC was enthusiastically welcomed. In spite of the financial adversities that kept on driving the citizens away (mostly to the Asian courts whose armies employed them as mercenaries), Athens in the Hellenistic period established itself as a centre of culture and philosophy of international status. Epicurean and Stoic schools were now added to the Platonic Academy and the Aristotelian Lyceum, while the theatre and the arts thrived. Roman domination in 146 BC had no effect on Athens' intellectual and cultural prestige, which was to last throughout the years of Roman rule as well as the early Byzantine era up to the 5th century AD. The city enjoyed a new economic boom around 100 BC, related to privileges bestowed upon it by the Romans. But the Athenians' support of Mithridates VI in an effort to regain their freedom was severely punished by Sulla in 86 BC.

From the 50s BC Roman nobles and emperors with philhellenic attitudes – notably Hadrian, Herodes Atticus, and Gaius Antiochus Philopappus – became benefactors of the city. During the 1st century AD the altar to the Unknown God and the first Jewish synagogue were erected. The Gothic descent on Europe had its impact on Athens, which was devastated by an invasion of Heruli in AD 267 and of Alaric in AD 396. The city's demographic and financial decline – which had already started by the end of the Peloponnesian War, when Athens is estimated to have had a population of around 36,000 people – was precipitated after the last destructions. At the same time, Christianity started making inroads. Already in the 3rd century AD celebrated Christian philosophers were teaching in new schools on the outskirts of the city.

Throughout the early Byzantine era Athens, together with all the dioceses of the Greek mainland, was placed under the administrative authority of the papal throne in Rome, maintaining at the same time a close relationship with Constantinople. However, in 732 emperor Leo III attached all the Greek dioceses to the patriarchate of Constantinople, as a retaliatory measure against the pope because of his opposition to Leo's own iconoclastic policy.

The attachment of Athens to Constantinople and the favourable presence of Irene the Athenian as consort to emperor Leo IV signified the start of a period of increasing prosperity for Athens. This was the period of the Slavic attacks against the Byzantine empire, which in the 19th century prompted Jakob Fallmerayer's claims about a Slavic prevalence in the Greek south before the 10th century. The current scholarly position maintains, however, that the influence of these Slavic nomadic groups was significantly limited in Attica – as, for example, the rarity of Slavic place names signifies – and that Athens, throughout these attacks, continued its increasingly prosperous existence, which was also reflected in the upgrading of the episcopate of Athens to a diocese in the 9th century, and the visit in 1018 of the Byzantine emperor Basil II Boulgaroktonos (Bulgar Slayer), following his victory over the Bulgarians of Samuel. The city also seems to have been little affected by the raids of Saracen pirates from Crete on the coasts of Attica in the beginning of the 10th century. The only significant disturbances to the prosperity of Athens were certain friction points with Thebes, the administrative centre of the Hellenic theme (i.e. the administrative division with political and military character that was formed during the 8th century AD in response to the Slavic pressure), in relation to tax collections and other decisions concerning Athens.

During the reign of the Komnenos dynasty – 10th–11th centuries – trade, agriculture, and craftsmanship continued to grow and a series of important monuments were built, the churches of Kapnikarea, Agioi Theodoroi, Agios Ioannis Karea, Omorphi Ekklisia, parts of the monastery of Kaisariani, and the monastery of Daphni with its famous mosaics on the west side of the city. However, education and intellectual life remained unresponsive to the cultural renaissance of Constantinople during the Komnenian dynasty. Michael Choniatis, the erudite last bishop of Athens before the Frankish occupation, draws in his writings a bleak picture of the intellectual achievements of the Athenians. This image should be associated especially with the second half of the 12th century, a time of steady decline for the city mainly due to regular pirate raids, the increasingly frequent encroachments of the Normans, and the arbitrary and heavy taxation rates imposed by the tax collectors of the Byzantine empire.

Athens was conquered by the Franks in 1205 and attached to the Frankish kingdom of Thessalonica. Even though under foreign rule, the city enjoyed a prolonged period of economic as well as political prosperity, which was additionally strengthened by its increasingly close relationship with the principality of Achaea. But desire for expansion towards the north brought in the Catalans as a mercenary army, who subsequently turned against the Franks and eventually conquered Athens in 1311. The Catalonian period was particularly painful for the Athenians, whose civil rights severely dwindled and who were reduced to a state of serfdom. Throughout the 14th century Venetian, Sicilian, and Spanish aspirations enfeebled the Catalans until they finally succumbed to the expansionism of the Florentine ruler of Corinth, Nerio Azaggioli, who occupied the Acropolis in 1388.

The Florentines relieved some of the oppression infamously connected with the Catalans. Certain religious freedoms were restored for the Orthodox, and a few Greek representatives were admitted into the local administration. The period before the Turkish occupation in 1458 was one of prolonged turmoil, however, with Venetians, Turks, and Florentines clashing over the dominion of the city. The first half of the 15th century brought some renewed prosperity to Athens mainly due to the tolerant policy of Antonio Azaggioli towards the Greeks. But the economic, political, and social abuse of the westerners and the deep schism between the Orthodox and the Catholics, as underlined by the turbulent council of Ferrara-Florence (1438–39), aggravated the hostility between Latins and Greeks. As a result, when the sultan Mehmet II entered the city in 1458 its few remaining residents received him with feelings of relief.

Excited about this illustrious addition to his empire, Mehmet granted Athens special privileges, including the right to some form of local self-rule. This initial favouritism did not prevent religious oppression, however, which generated neomartyrs such as Philothei Venizelou, or aggression, such as the mass kidnapping of children; whereas the distrust of the local rulers also counteracted on an everyday basis the sultan's flexible attitude.

Driven by the hope that the Turko-Venetian war that had erupted in 1684 would prove useful in their own struggle for liberation, the Athenians entrusted the city to the Venetians on 10 September 1687. The battles that followed caused severe damage to the Parthenon and resulted in a very short-lived Venetian domination. When the Turks reoccupied the Acropolis, the Athenians fled the city en masse and did not start to return for three years, in 1691. The period of relatively liberal rule that followed, and lasted for most of the first half of the 18th century, came to an abrupt end with the friction between Turks and Russians towards the end of the century, when Turks again felt threatened by the Greeks' urge for liberation. Russians and Turks came to a – temporary – agreement in 1774, but the arbitrariness of the sultans and the local *voivode* was not eliminated. It was during the first years of the 19th century that Lord Elgin, having obtained the sultan's permission to collect already detached stones and inscriptions, managed to transfer the Parthenon and Erechtheum marbles to England.

The Revolution of 1821 spread great enthusiasm among the Athenians who became involved at once. Important military men came to the city's succour, among them Androutsos, Makriyannis, Karaiskakis, and later on the French Favière and Derigny. The Turks finally surrendered control of the Acropolis on 31 March 1833 and on 18 September 1834 Athens was declared the capital of the newly founded modern Greek state.

The transference of the capital from Nauplia to Athens transformed the small town of 1500 houses into the first political, economic, and intellectual centre of the new state. This transformation took time, however, and for most of the 19th century the robust, cosmopolitan periphery, with cities such as Ermoupolis and Patras, continued to attract the main financial activities of the new state, even though its political power was concentrated in Athens. From the very beginning, however, and within the narrow space of autonomous expression left to it by the conflicting interests of the supervising European Great Powers, the city struggled to establish a modern Greek identity for the new state. This effort was further undermined due to the mutual antipathies between the indigenous people and the newly arrived emigrants from Europe, as well as the military and the political leaders. Much energy was directed towards urban development, which combined two dominant styles, the more spontaneously romantic, with folk elements, and the Neoclassical. The latter was particularly boosted by the involvement of Classically educated German architects in designing the city and some of its most important public buildings, such as the palace (started 1832), the university (started 1839), and Hotel Grande Bretagne (started 1842). The subsequent years brought more freedom and a predominantly eclectic architectural style, even though the monolithic dependence on Classical antiquity as the prevalent tool for modern Greek self-expression meant that a fair number of Byzantine and later monuments were still being destroyed.

During the last decades of the 19th century Athens' political role continued to expand just as it was actively involved in the republican reformation of 1843, and the turbulent change of dynasty in 1863. Charilaos Trikoupis's premierships (in the 1880s and 1890s) brought further development, and vital work on the infrastructure that was largely missing in this architecturally impressive city was carried out. By the 1890s Athens had already begun to acquire a centrality not unrelated to the urban pull and overconcentration that plague it today. This centrality was boosted by the detachment between the 1880s and the 1920s of several other Greek regions from the ailing Ottoman empire and their attachment to the new state. People and resources from regions such as Thessaly, Epirus, Macedonia, Western Thrace, and Asia Minor, successively, were concentrated in Athens, thus enabling its industrialization at the expense of the periphery. The city has ever since been inextricably connected with all the most highly influential events of modern Greek political life, from the mutinies of royalists and Venizelists of the period 1909–35 through to the resulting dictatorship of Ioannis Metaxas on 4 August 1936 and the clashes of December 1944 between ELAS and British forces (also known as *Dekemvriana*) in the centre of Athens which, it is estimated, left about 800 buildings in ruins. Finally, in 1973, the protests of students at the Athens Law School and Polytechnic, which symbolized the discontent of the country as a whole with the military junta of the colonels, and heralded the fall of their regime a few months later.

From 1950 onwards there has been impressive economic and demographic expansion in the environs of Athens, attracting the greater part of the political, cultural, and administrative activities of the country. It is estimated that it has accommodated almost half of the national industry and produces almost half of the national income. Such a disproportionate growth has resulted in urban anarchy, pollution, and serious infrastructure failures that disfigure this otherwise dynamic city. The state has been aware of these problems and their impact on the socioeconomic development of Greece as a whole, and has been trying to design policies that will redress this imbalance.

EFROSSINI SPENTZOU

See also Acropolis, Agora, Delian League, Piraeus

Summary

Inhabited since the Neolithic period (*c.*4000 BC), Athens was a major Mycenaean centre in the Late Bronze Age. A tyranny was set up Pisistratus in 561 BC, to be followed at the end of the 6th century by the democratic reforms of Cleisthenes. After the Persian Wars Athens emerged as leader of Greece and centre of Hellenic culture. Political hegemony was dissipated by the Peloponnesian War and subsequent struggles with Macedon and Rome; cultural supremacy was retained undimmed until the 5th century AD. Athens was named the capital of the modern Greek state in 1834 and has ever since been the prime focus of political and cultural activity in the country.

Further Reading

Bires, K.E., *Ai Athinai apo tou 190u eis ton 200n aiona* [Athens from the 19th to the 20th Century], Athens, 1995

Carter, L.B. *The Quiet Athenian*, Oxford: Clarendon Press, and New York: Oxford University Press, 1986

Chateaubriand, F.-R., *Travels in Greece, Palestine, Egypt and Barbary during the Years 1806 and 1807*, London: Colburn, 1812 (French edition 1811)

Connolly, Peter, *The Ancient City: Life in Classical Athens and Rome*, Oxford and New York: Oxford University Press, 1998

Fallmerayer, Jakob Philipp, *Welchen Einfluss hatte die Besetzung Griechenlands durch die Slaven auf das Schicksal der Stadt Athen und der Landschaft Attika?*, Stuttgart and Tübingen, 1835

Goff, Barbara (editor), *History, Tragedy, Theory: Dialogues on Athenian Drama*, Austin: University of Texas Press, 1995

Gregorovius, Ferdinand, *Geschichte der Stadt Athen im Mittelalter*, 2 vols, Stuttgart: Cotta, 1889

Hamilton, Richard, *Choes and Anthesteria: Athenian Iconography and Ritual*, Ann Arbor: University of Michigan Press, 1992

Hornblower, Simon and M.C. Greenstock (editors), *The Athenian Empire*, 3rd edition, London: London Association of Classical Teachers, 1984

Mossé, Claude, *Athens in Decline, 404–86 BC*, London and Boston: Routledge, 1973

Osborne, Robin, *Greece in the Making, 1200–479 BC*, London and New York: Routledge, 1996

Panourgiá, Neni, *Fragments of Death, Fables of Identity: An Athenian Anthropography*, Madison: University of Wisconsin Press, 1995

Rhodes, Robin Francis, *Architecture and Meaning on the Athenian Acropolis*, Cambridge and New York: Cambridge University Press, 1995

Sant Cassia, Paul and Constantina Bada, *The Making of the Modern Greek Family: Marriage and Exchange in Nineteenth-Century Athens*, Cambridge and New York: Cambridge University Press, 1992

Sapkidis, Olga, *Kaissariani: un quartier de réfugiés, à Athènes*, Paris: Stahl, 1991

Setton, Kenneth M., *Catalan Domination of Athens, 1311–1388*, Cambridge, Massachusetts: Mediaeval Academy of America, 1948

Setton, Kenneth M., *Athens in the Middle Ages*, London: Variorum, 1975

Simopoulos, Kyriakos, *Xenoi taksidiotes stin Ellada* [Foreign Travellers to Greece], Athens, 1970

Travlos, John, "Architectural Development of Athens", Athens, 1960–61 (unpublished typescript)

Webster, T.B.L. *Everyday Life in Classical Athens*, London: Batsford, and New York: Putnam, 1969

Athos, Mount

Principal centre of Orthodox monasticism

Mount Athos is a peninsula in northern Greece, the most easterly of the three claws that Chalcidice extends into the Aegean Sea. From the isthmus in the northwest to the southeast point the distance is about 56 km, while that from coast to coast is rarely more than 8 km. About 6 km south of the isthmus a wall marks the frontier, and beyond it the ground rises steeply to wooded peaks of 500 and 600 m. South of Karyes, the capital, which stands more or less in the centre of the peninsula, the woods turn to scrub and eventually to bare rock as the contours rise, peaking finally at 2030 m before a sudden drop down to the sea. For more than a thousand years Athos has been the exclusive preserve of Orthodox monks; to this day it remains the principal centre of monasticism for all the Eastern Orthodox Churches. It is dedicated to the glorification of the Virgin Mary (or Theotokos), whose garden by tradition it is. She alone is held to represent her sex there, which is why Athos is closed to women.

In antiquity Athos was already a holy mountain, its peak being sacred to Zeus. In 492 BC the Persian fleet of Mardonius was dashed to pieces on the rocks at the southern point; mindful of this, the next time the Persians invaded Macedonia by sea, in 480 BC, they cut a canal through the isthmus to ensure the safe passage of their ships. Several cities were founded on the peninsula, and in the 4th century BC there was even a bizarre proposal to carve the mountain itself into the image of Alexander the Great; but the king told his architect to concentrate rather on designing the new city of Alexandria, and by the early centuries AD it seems that the place was deserted.

No one knows when the first monks arrived on Athos, but it is unlikely to have been before the 8th century. (Some monasteries claim foundation dates as early as the 3rd or 4th century, but there is no evidence to support them.) The first recorded reference to Athonite monks is at the synod, known as the "Triumph of Orthodoxy", convened by the empress Theodora in 843 to celebrate the end of iconoclasm; and some 9th-century hermits are known by name: Peter the Athonite, who lived in a cave *c.*840–90, and Evthymios of Thessalonica, who founded the first community of ascetics. The first real monastery was established in 963 by St Athanasios of Athos with the support and encouragement of the emperor Nikephoros II Phokas. Still known as the Great Lavra (or Megiste Lavra), it holds first place in the hierarchy of all the monasteries, and the Athonite millennium was duly celebrated there in 1963. The ascetics opposed the introduction of cenobitic (common life) monasticism and, after the murder of Nikephoros in 969, appealed to the new emperor, John I Tzimiskes; but he overruled their objections, and ever since then both traditions – the eremitic and the cenobitic – have coexisted on Athos.

Further monasteries were soon founded, though not all survive today. Of the twenty that do, nine were established in the 10th century, four more in the 11th, one in the 12th, one in the 13th, four in the 14th, and the last in the 16th. These figures reflect the fortunes of the empire at the time. In earlier centuries there were many monastic centres and many holy mountains elsewhere; but after the Turkish conquest of Asia Minor, the Latin occupation of many Byzantine provinces in Europe, and the Slav advances in the Balkans, by the 14th century Athos was the only one to survive. Since then it has always been known as *the* Holy Mountain (*Agion Oros* in Greek).

Athos has always been an international centre, a focus for monasticism and pilgrimage for all the Orthodox Churches. The Bulgarian monastery (Zographou) was founded in the 10th century, as was the Georgian house of Iviron (now Greek); Russians have had a monastery since the 11th century, Serbs since the 12th; Moldavians and Wallachians have long been represented, and there was even a Benedictine monastery for Amalfitans from the 10th century to the 14th. Today seventeen of the twenty monasteries are Greek-speaking; there is one each for Serbs, Bulgarians, and Russians; and two sketes (monastic villages) are reserved for Romanians. All sketes, cells, and hermitages are subordinated to the larger foundations, which is why the latter are called "ruling monasteries". Each of them is a self-governing, independent entity within the monastic federation, and between them they rule the Mountain. Each sends an elected representative to serve for a year in the Holy Community, the parliament of Athos, which meets regularly in Karyes. These arrangements have been in place since an imperial decree of 1046, on the strength of which the monks claim that theirs is the oldest continuing democracy in the world. From the start the Mountain came under the jurisdiction of the emperor, but by the early 13th century the new monasteries had become stavropegic (under the authority of the patriarchate) and in 1312 authority over the whole Mountain was transferred to the patriarch by emperor Andronikos II Palaiologos.

Athos survived the turmoil of the empire's last centuries, but not without a fight. All the monasteries suffered constant assaults by pirates, crusaders, adventurers, and Turks who would stop at nothing to strip them of their treasures. The need for self defence made them look more like castles and fortified towns, which is in many ways what they became. In order to attract wealthy and influential recruits, many monasteries began to depart from the cenobitic system (according to which all wealth is contributed to a common purse) in favour of a more individualistic (or idiorrhythmic) way of life in which personal wealth and profit were accepted. Though frowned upon at first, this alternative system did eventually gain imperial sanction in 1406 and was until recently followed by at least half of the monasteries.

As the chief monastic survivor, Athos was able to take full advantage of the so-called Palaiologan renaissance, the cultural flowering that Byzantium enjoyed while the empire crumbled. Artists such as Manuel Panselinos were employed to decorate the principal churches. Musicians such as St John Koukouzeles, a monk of the Great Lavra, revolutionized the tradition of Byzantine chant. Theologians such as St Gregory Palamas, whose doctrine of hesychasm forms the basis of Athonite spirituality to this day, made Athos an international centre of scholarship. Emperors, anxious to gain the sympathy of the monks, or of the people, or of God, endowed the monasteries with treasures; and some were even tonsured monks themselves. In the late Byzantine period the monasteries were major landowners, and their surviving records are among the most important documentary evidence for Byzantine economic life.

Although the confiscation of monastic estates had begun even before the end of the empire, Athos was still in a strong position when Ottoman occupation began in 1430. The monks lost their remaining estates in Macedonia and Thrace, and they were forced to pay tax to the sultan; but they retained their autonomy, they remained under the spiritual protection of the ecumenical patriarch, and they continued to enjoy a period of prosperity. During the 16th century another monastery (Stavronikita) was founded, library holdings continued to expand, and the Cretan school of painters was active on Athos, creating some of the most glorious examples of their art. While the rural population fell into a state of increasingly profound ignorance, poverty, and despondency, the monasteries, and especially those of the Holy Mountain, upheld the traditions not only of Orthodoxy but also of Byzantium. Indeed it is no exaggeration to say that during the long, dark centuries of the Tourkokratia Athos was one of the principal guardians of Hellenism.

Even in the 17th century, when standards of education and literacy in Greece and Asia Minor had reached a very low ebb, the monasteries continued to acquire books for their libraries. But in the 18th century there was a decline, which the patriarch Cyril V made a determined effort to resist with the foundation in 1753 of an academy near the monastery of Vatopedi. His intention was to restore Athos to its place as a centre of religious culture and learning and to that end he appointed the philosopher Evgenios Voulgaris as director of the school. But the experiment failed: Voulgaris's theories proved too liberal for the monks, within a few years he was removed to Constantinople, and the school was destroyed by fire.

In the late 18th century, while the secularizing spirit of the Enlightenment began to take hold of Western Europe, a conservative reaction to it sprang up on Athos. The members of this movement, known as the Kollyvades, sought to show that Greek national awareness would be regenerated not by adherence to Western notions of secular liberalism but by a return to the spiritual values of true Orthodoxy and patristic theology. Among the leading figures of this "fundamentalist" revival were St Makarios of Corinth (1731–1805) and St Nikodemos of the Holy Mountain (1748–1809), who collaborated to produce an extensive anthology of Athonite spiritual writing known as the *Philokalia* (Venice, 1782), a work that retains its popularity and influence to this day. Salvation through Orthodoxy was also the message of another Athonite monk of the 18th century, St Kosmas the Aetolian (1714–79). He made a number of missionary journeys through the Greek-speaking lands in an attempt to revive the flagging morale of the people, emphasizing the link between Orthodoxy and the Greek language, and founding Greek schools wherever he went. Eventually falling foul of the Ottoman authorities, he was executed and joined the ranks of the so-called Neomartyrs who died for their faith during the Tourkokratia.

Throughout much of the 19th and 20th centuries Athos felt the impact of political events in the outside world. The preference of most elders was to hold aloof from involvement in the War of Independence (1821–32), but many younger monks could not resist showing their sympathy for those fighting for freedom. The Turks quickly snuffed out the revolt and installed

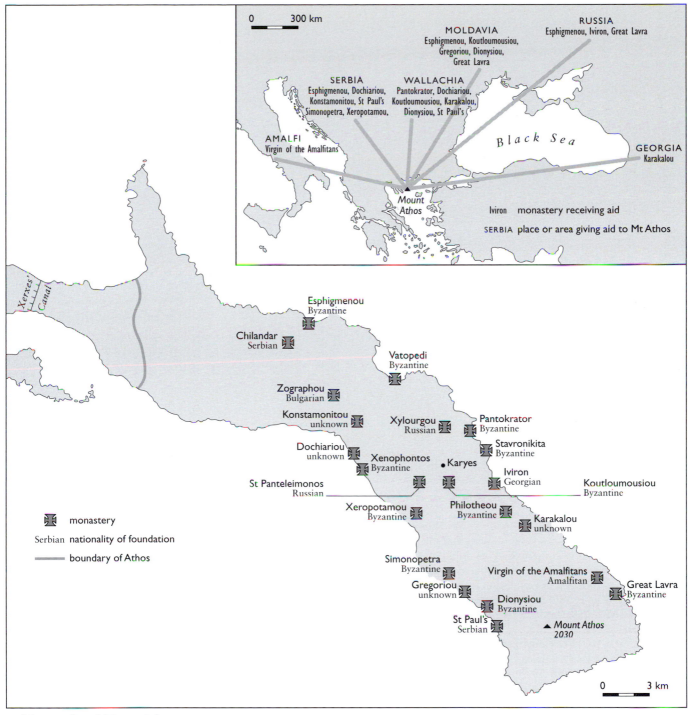

7. Monasteries of Mount Athos

a garrison of 3000 troops on the Mountain. As a result many more monks fled and the population fell to barely a thousand.

After the establishment of an independent Greece in 1832 the fortunes of Mount Athos began to recover, only to be threatened again from another direction. During the latter part of the 19th century the number of Russian monks at the monastery of St Panteleimonos began to increase dramatically. The buildings there and at the Russian sketes were enlarged out of all proportion to accommodate the influx, and there were soon more Slavs than Greeks on the Mountain (5500 out of a total population of 9800 in 1910). The motive for this was perhaps more political than religious, though that is not to say that there were not many pious ascetics among them. Some say that the tsar had set his sights on the throne of Constantinople and saw Athos as a convenient strongpoint from which to dominate the Aegean. But, whatever the motive for it, the attempted Russian takeover failed – for two reasons. First, the Great Powers intervened and refused to ratify the treaty of San Stefano (1878) which would have ceded most of what is now northern Greece to a greater Bulgaria under Russian patron-

Athos: the monastery of Simonopetra dating from the 14th century with the peak of Athos itself behind

age. Second, despite their numbers, the Russians never controlled more than a single monastery; and on Athos what counts is not monks on misericords but ruling monasteries in the Holy Community. Even so, the Russians remained numerically dominant until the Revolution of 1917, after which borders were sealed and there was a rapid decline. Numbers at St Panteleimonos have been falling ever since.

The other event that had a significant impact on the Holy Mountain was the dismemberment of the Ottoman empire. Along with the rest of northern Greece, Athos was liberated in 1912; but it took another 11 years of almost continuous war before any sort of stability returned. Even then, the price paid by the monasteries was the confiscation of their estates in Chalcidice to make way for some of the hundreds of thousands of refugees "returning" to Greece from Asia Minor in 1923 in the compulsory exchange of population. Suddenly, after nearly 500 years of Turkish rule, Athos was stripped of a large part of its raison d'être – as the guardian of Hellenism. Like Cavafy's barbarians, the Turks were "a kind of solution". Even though the Great Idea was in ruins and Greece was overrun by impoverished, starving, and unemployed refugees, the Greeks were a free people with their own land, their own language, their own culture, and their own religion. Finally released from its political-cultural responsibility, the Mountain needed to find a new role to play. It faltered – for half a century – and by the 1960s,

when Athos was celebrating a past of 1000 years, it seemed to many observers to have no future at all, except as a museum of Byzantine art and architecture, and the Greek government was keen to realize its potential as a centre for tourism.

But the spiritual traditions of Athos, which had not died at all, are extremely resilient. While the monasteries, especially the idiorrhythmic ones, became so depleted in numbers that some were even threatened with closure, there was increased activity in the sketes and cells at the remote tip of the peninsula, the so-called desert of Athos. This area had always attracted hermits and ascetics who shunned the monasteries and withdrew entirely from the world. During the 1950s and 1960s a number of such men gained reputations as gifted teachers and acquired groups of disciples, mostly educated young men eager to follow their example. Several monasteries on the brink of collapse turned to these men and invited them in, at the same time accepting the need to revert from the idiorrhythmic to the cenobitic way of life. At first this meant no more than a reshuffling of the existing population; but from the 1970s there was a steady increase in numbers over all, and by the mid-1990s the total was approaching 2000 from a low in 1971 of 1145.

All 20 monasteries now follow the cenobitic rule; standards of spirituality have risen markedly with the influx of better-educated monks; buildings that had fallen into disrepair are being restored; treasures are being properly cared for; libraries are being catalogued and manuscripts conserved; skills such as icon painting, wood carving, and chanting are being revived on traditional lines; there is clear evidence of renewal in nearly every monastery (the exceptions to this are the non-Greek houses). The revival is an entirely traditional one: in no sense is it a reform; even the abolition of the idiorrhythmic system signals a return to the original cenobitic way of life. The downside is that, as monks tend increasingly to come from an urban, educated background instead of a rural, peasant one, some skills such as farming and fishing have to be relearnt; and in order to fund the revival, some monasteries have been tempted to overexploit their forests, resulting in the replacement of mules and mule-tracks by motor vehicles and a network of roads. Furthermore, the determination of the majority of the monasteries to assert their autonomy and their panorthodox traditions has on occasion resulted in friction with both the patriarchate in Constantinople and the government in Athens which are charged respectively with spiritual and civil authority over the Mountain. But the fact is that at last Athos has rediscovered its raison d'être, which is to provide a radical alternative to the ever-increasing secularization of modern society. As a result it has resumed its traditional role and is once again operating as the spiritual heart and voice of Orthodoxy.

GRAHAM SPEAKE

See also Hesychasm, Kollyvades, Monasteries, Monasticism, Philokalia, Pilgrimage, Renaissance (Palaiologan), Zealots

Summary

Principal centre of monasticism for all the Eastern Orthodox Churches. First monastery founded in 963. Expanded rapidly in the 10th and 11th centuries. Flourished in the late Byzantine period as a centre of scholarship and art. Operated as the guardian of Hellenism throughout the Tourkokratia. Declined spiritually in the 19th century and numerically in the 20th. Enjoying revival since the 1970s. Closed to women.

Further Reading

Alexander (Golitzin), Hieromonk (translator), The Living Witness of the Holy Mountain: Contemporary Voices from Mount Athos, South Canaan, Pennsylvania: St Tikhon's Seminary Press, 1996
Amand de Mendieta, Emmanuel, Mount Athos, the Garden of the Panaghia, Berlin: Akademie, 1972
Bryer, Anthony and Mary Cunningham (editors), Mount Athos and Byzantine Monasticism, Aldershot, Hampshire: Variorum, 1996
Byron, Robert, The Station. Athos: Treasures and Men, 2nd edition, London: Duckworth, 1931, New York: Knopf, 1949; reprinted London: Century, 1984
Cavarnos, Constantine, The Holy Mountain, Belmont, Massachusetts: Institute for Byzantine and Modern Greek Studies, 1973
Cavarnos, Constantine, Anchored in God: An Inside Account of Life, Art and Thought on the Holy Mountain of Athos, 2nd edition, Belmont, Massachusetts: Institute for Byzantine and Modern Greek Studies, 1975
Choukas, Michael, Black Angels of Athos, 2nd edition, London: Constable, and Brattleboro, Vermont: Stephen Daye Press, 1935
Dawkins, R.M., The Monks of Athos, London: Allen and Unwin, 1936
Gothóni, René, Paradise within Reach: Monasticism and Pilgrimage on Mount Athos, Helsinki: Helsinki University Press, 1993
Gothóni, René, Tales and Truth: Pilgrimage on Mount Athos Past and Present, Helsinki: Helsinki University Press, 1994
Hasluck, F.W., Athos and Its Monasteries, London: Kegan Paul, Trench and Trubner, and New York: Dutton, 1924
The Holy and Great Monastery of Vatopaidi: Tradition – History – Art, 2 vols, Mount Athos: Monastery of Vatopaidi, 1998
Loch, Sydney, Athos: The Holy Mountain, London: Lutterworth Press, 1957
Le Millénaire du Mont Athos, 963–1963, Etudes et mélanges, 2 vols, Chevetogne: Éditions de Chevetogne, 1963–64
Papadopoulos, Stelios (editor), Simonopetra: Mount Athos, Athens: Hellenic Industrial Development Bank, 1991
Runciman, Steven, The Great Church in Captivity: A Study of the Patriarchate of Constantinople from the Eve of the Turkish Conquest to the Greek War of Independence, London: Cambridge University Press, 1968
Sherrard, Philip, Athos: The Mountain of Silence, London and New York: Oxford University Press, 1960
Sherrard, Philip, Athos: The Holy Mountain, London: Sidgwick and Jackson, 1982; Woodstock, New York: Overlook Press, 1985
Treasures of Mount Athos, 2nd edition, Thessalonica: Ministry of Culture and Museum of Byzantine Culture, 1997 (exhibition catalogue)
Ware, Timothy, The Orthodox Church, 2nd edition, London and New York: Penguin, 1993

Atomism

One of the greatest contributions of ancient Greek philosophical logos to world civilization was the expression of a series of theories on the beginnings and structure of matter. Some were simple; others were more complex. Regardless of whether or not they were correct, they were a significant source of ideas and rationales that eventually played a role in the formation of modern scientific thought, even if they were incomprehensible to some.

The so-called atomic theory played a leading role. It consisted of a characteristic central idea that rejected the notion of an infinite divisibility of matter, as opposed to Aristotelian philosophy. The founder of the ancient theory of atomism is supposed to have been Mochus or Moschus, before the Trojan War. Leucippus, Democritus, and Epicurus, though not the introducers, described it and proved reasonably that atoms are the first principles of bodies. The views of Epicurus are considered by many to be the foundations on which many later Europeans formulated their own theories. As for Leucippus, whose historical existence has on occasion been disputed, we know that he was active in Miletus around the middle of the 5th century BC. According to Aristotle and Theophrastus, the title of his work was the Great World System (Megas Diakosmos). One of his students was Democritus, who was born in Abdera around 460 BC. All the original writings of Democritus are lost but excerpts of his work survive in later writers. Epicurus continued after Democritus.

The basis for adopting the existence of atoms is the acceptance of the existence of a vacuum, which is another distinction from Aristotelian philosophy. The existence of a vacuum, however, contradicts the theory of an infinite divisibility of matter. For this contradiction to be resolved, Leucippus' atom must be free of any vacuum and remain unchanged; a vacuum can exist only in the space between the atoms. Atoms are not born; they are indestructible, unchangeable, simple, and therefore eternal and with specific dimensions. They are not motionless but are in a state of a perpetual spin, which allows similar atoms to come closer together. According to Democritus, bodies are initially formed by the joining and binding of groups of atoms that eventually mould a world or worlds, since atomistic philosophers support the existence of infinite worlds. The perfect atoms move towards the peripheral and form a spherical celestial dome; heavier materials move towards the centre of the sphere and constitute the earth. Based on the atomic theory, Democritus tried to give a convincing interpretation of the subject of colours, maintaining that the four primary colours – white, black, red, and yellow – were the result of the different types and positions of the atoms inside the body.

From the ancient Greek theory of atomism, Newton mainly adopted that of hardness when he expanded his atomic theory in the *Opticks* (Query 23). Many, however, consider that the scientist who brought the atomic theory into the public eye was Pierre Gassendi, who in 1649 published his comments on the 10th book of Diogenes Laertius and the *Syntagma Philosophiae Epicuri*, both of which contained a presentation of Epicurean and Democritean atomization.

This general theory by Western Europeans concerning the atomic structure of bodies was also basically accepted by Greek scholars during the Tourkokratia. Everybody now accepts that atoms are the basic factors of matter. Nikiphoros Theotokis, in the first chapter of his book, *Elements of Physics* (*Stichia Physikis*, 1766–67), wrote characteristically:

> Lucretius, Gassendi, Boerhaave, Desaguliers, and the other modern philosophers suppose atoms to be the principles of every body. These atoms are quite small, hard, moveable, pathetic, impenetrable, impassable. As they are elements of every body, and the basis of bigger bodies, we need to find their properties.

Scholars also accepted Dalton's later theory on atoms formulated in 1805. Dalton's atom was, of course, quite different from the modern atom, but it constituted one more link in the chain of the evolution of scientific thought from antiquity up to today.

GEORGE N. VLAHAKIS

See also Physics

Further Reading

Bergman, Robert, "Leibniz and Atomism", *Nature and System*, 6 (1984): pp. 237–48
Jackson, Kenneth, "Studies in the Epistemology of Ancient Greek Atomism" (dissertation), Princeton, New Jersey: Princeton University, 1982
Karas, Iannis, *Germanikes Epidraseis sti Skepsi tis Neoellinikis Anagenniseos: Stephanos Dougas i "Peri Physikis Philosophias"* [German Influences to the Thought of the Neohellenic Renaissance: Stephanos Dougas or "On Physical Philosophy"], Athens, 1993
Karas, Iannis, *I Ennoia tis Ylis stin Neoelliniki Anagennisi* [The Meaning of Matter in the Neohellenic Renaissance], Athens, 1997
Konstan, David, "Ancient Atomism and its Heritage: Minimal Parts", *Ancient Philosophy*, 2 (1982): pp. 60–75
Psimmenos, Nikos, *I Elliniki Philosophia apo to 1453 eos to 1821* [Greek Philosophy from 1453 to 1821], 2 vols, Athens, 1988–89
Sakkopoulos, Sotirios, "Empirical Foundations of Atomism in Ancient Greek Philosophy", *Science and Education*, 5/3 (July 1996): pp. 293–303
Vlahakis, George N., "Philosophical and Scientific Arguments on the Existence of Vacuum: The Case of the Greek Scholars during the XVIII Century", *Phlogiston*, 6, pp.73–95

Attalids

Ruling dynasty of the Hellenistic kingdom of Pergamum

The Attalids were the ruling family of the kingdom of Pergamum, which flourished under their control in the Hellenistic period from 281 to 133 BC. The dynasty was established by Philetaerus, a general in the army of Lysimachus, one of the successors of Alexander the Great. Lysimachus had gained control of Thrace and northwestern Asia Minor in the struggles after Alexander's death (323 BC), and he kept a large part of his state treasury in the city of Pergamum, which was under Philetaerus' command. In 281 BC Lysimachus was killed in battle, and Philetaerus laid claim both to Pergamum and to the treasury of 9000 talents. The 18 years of Philetaerus' rule (281–263 BC) were dedicated primarily to establishing and extending his control of northwestern Asia Minor and solidifying his family's position as the rulers of Pergamum.

In the early 3rd century BC Pergamum was a small Greek city built on top of a high acropolis whose walls enclosed houses, military barracks, storerooms, water cisterns, an agora (marketplace), and a small temple built of andesite (the locally available stone) honouring Athena (patron deity of the city); near the lower reaches of the citadel, outside the walls, was a temple of Demeter. Food was supplied by farms in the surrounding plain of the fertile Caicus river valley. With his financial wealth, an easily defended acropolis, a fertile farming region, and reliable water sources, Philetaerus' main problem was protecting the outlying parts of Pergamum from the city's enemies. The most insistent of these were the marauding Gauls, a warlike tribe from central Europe that had crossed into Asia Minor in 278 BC and was harassing the cities and towns of northern and western Anatolia. While Philetaerus waged several successful battles against the Gauls between 278 and 276 BC, he often dealt with their threats of attack and plunder in the same manner as other local political leaders – by paying hefty tribute.

Philetaerus, who had no children of his own, adopted his nephew Eumenes, and named him his successor. Eumenes I (263–241 BC) was occupied in much the same manner as his uncle: he defended Pergamum against the more powerful Hellenistic kings, especially the Seleucids, extended the territory under his control, and continued the policy of pacifying the Gauls through payment of onerous tribute. Eumenes I was followed by his cousin Attalus I, who ruled from 241 to 197 BC. Attalus was an astute politician, a brilliant general, and a patron of education and the arts. It was during his reign that Pergamum began its transition from a hilltop fortress to a splendid Hellenistic metropolis. His first major act was to refuse to pay tribute to the ever-menacing Gauls. He led the Pergamene army against them, defeating them solidly. In honour of his achievement, the epithet "Soter" (Saviour) was added to his name, and he was the first of his family to be given the title "king". The victory over the Gauls was followed by a number of military successes, often in alliance with an increasingly powerful Rome, and Pergamum's control and influence in Asia Minor were extended and strengthened.

Two of his sons followed Attalus I as king – Eumenes II (197–159 BC) and Attalus II (159–138 BC). Their reigns brought Pergamum to its zenith as a prominent political and cultural centre in the Hellenistic world. The city's population increased to more than 100,000 people, while the kingdom as a whole covered 172,880 sq km with a population of 5,500,000 comprising five classes of residents: citizens, foreign residents, soldiers, freedmen, and slaves. From the beginning, Pergamum had been governed by the constitution of a Greek city state, although the monarchy had exercised great authority in the political system. During the reign of Eumenes II the military alliance with Rome, which had contributed much to the growing strength of Pergamum, was temporarily broken and Eumenes led his army unassisted in an important battle against the Gauls, who were waging frequent attacks on many of the cities in Asia Minor. This victory, won without the help of his powerful ally, substantially enhanced Eumenes' standing among neighbouring political leaders and greatly increased the power of the Pergamene monarchy.

Attalus II was an elderly man when he ascended the throne upon the death of Eumenes II. During his 21-year reign (159–138 BC) he continued the policies of his brother. He was a competent military leader and diplomat, continued the alliance with Rome, and was a patron of scholars and artists. Attalus II was succeeded by Attalus III, a son of Eumenes II, who ruled for only five years (138–133 BC). Upon his death this last Attalid king bequeathed Pergamum to Rome in his will. This act has never been clearly understood, but his decision may have been based on the knowledge that there was little chance that Pergamum could remain independent much longer. Rome had conquered mainland Greece, and devastated those who stood against it. Because of Attalus III, the citizens of Pergamum were neither plundered nor enslaved, but continued their lives in peace under the new regime. Pergamum became the capital of the Roman province of Asia in 129 BC.

The Attalids, especially from the time of Attalus I, saw themselves as the preservers of Classical civilization in the Hellenistic period. Since the political and military endeavours of Alexander the Great and his successors in the 4th century BC had moved the focus of the Greek world to Asia Minor and the Near East, resulting in the diminishment of mainland Greece, the goal of the dynasty was to make Pergamum the cultural and artistic successor of Athens. Along with the wealth of the original treasury of Lysimachus, the Attalids had a number of sources of income with which to implement their plan. Taxes were paid by the indigenous communities in the surrounding territory; tribute was paid by subject cities; and duties were assessed on items that were transported through territory under Attalid control. Pergamum also had great natural resources. Farms in the Caicus river valley produced wheat, barley, grapes, figs, olives, pomegranates, horses, pigs, cattle, and sheep. Mines and quarries supplied gold, zinc, copper, andesite, and marble. Pergamene factories produced wool, carpets, woven textiles, sewn garments, leather, perfumes, pottery, armour, and parchment. The great wealth of the

kingdom by the 2nd century BC allowed Eumenes II to institute a major building programme that turned Pergamum into a magnificent city of marble monuments that was more than four times its original size.

Along with city planners and architects, Eumenes II welcomed artists and scholars. Pergamum had been known for its school of sculpture since the reign of Attalus I in the 3rd century BC when several famous sculptors came to the city to create a multifigured group to commemorate the king's victory over the Gauls. The epitome of the Pergamene school, and of all Hellenistic sculpture, however, was the reliefs of the spectacular Pergamum Altar (now in the Berlin Staatliche Museen), a monument that honoured the Attalid dynasty, their military victories, and Pergamum's founding hero, Telephus. Dynastic support of a wide range of scholars, especially those connected to the schools of philosophy in Athens, had begun during the reigns of Eumenes I and Attalus I. Attalus' own teacher had been a Peripatetic philosopher from Athens, and his son Attalus II studied at the Academy in Athens. While Pergamum did not develop a professional school comparable to that at Alexandria, the scholarly environment created by the kings attracted a large number of well-respected philosophers, mathematicians, historians, biographers, geographers, astronomers, poets, playwrights, engineers, physicians, and scientists. The Attalids' support was not restricted to the professional class, however, but extended as well to a sophisticated secondary education system in which both boys and girls from Pergamum received instruction.

The scholarly climate was enhanced even further by the creation of the renowned Pergamene library during the reign of Eumenes II in the 2nd century BC. Second only to the library at Alexandria in antiquity, at its height it may have owned as many as 200,000 works. The most significant scholar in Pergamum in that period was Crates of Mallus, a Stoic philosopher, literary critic, grammarian, and geographer, who was also probably director of the library. He created a system of cosmogony in which the earth was round, and while he was not the first person to describe the earth as a sphere, he was the first to construct a three-dimensional geographical globe. Crates seems to have been influential in encouraging the production and export of fine-quality parchment, for which Pergamum became justly famous. The use of parchment not only eventually displaced papyrus as the main writing material in antiquity, but it facilitated the development of the paged book (codex), which had replaced rolled documents by the 4th century AD.

As the power of the Roman empire waned in the 3rd century AD, Pergamum declined in population and contracted in size. The city diminished in standing as a centre of political, commercial, and military activity. Except for the renovation of the temple of the Egyptian gods as a Christian basilica, it also played only a small role in ecclesiastical affairs. The sanctuary of Asclepius was abandoned, as were most other buildings in the plain and on the lower levels of the acropolis. By the late 3rd century AD the city consisted primarily of houses built over earlier structures on the fortified upper acropolis. Pergamum did continue the Attalid tradition of being a centre of intellectual activity, however, playing a prominent role in the scholarship of the 4th century. It was home to the school of Aedesius (d. 355), a Neoplatonist who trained most of the famous teachers of philosophy in western Anatolia, including Maximus of Ephesus (d. 371), one of whose pupils was the future emperor Julian. Oribasius (d. 400), a companion of Julian and a native of Pergamum, was one of the most famous doctors and medical writers of the period; he was especially noted for his compilation of excerpts from the works of earlier Greek and Roman physicians.

While Pergamum continued to be occupied during the Byzantine period, it is little more than a shadow on the page of history. It was captured for brief periods by the Arabs in the 7th and 8th centuries, and refortified by the Byzantine emperors Constans II and Manuel Komnenos in the 7th and 12th centuries, respectively. It came under the authority of the Greek emperor of Nicaea, Theodore Laskaris, in 1214, then Turkish emirs gained control in 1302. By the end of the 14th century Pergamum had been nearly destroyed by invasion and sacking. In the Byzantine period ancient Greek manuscripts and knowledge of Classical culture were preserved in major centres of learning, such as Constantinople, Thessalonica, and southern Italy. How much influence came down to them from the scholarly environment created by the Attalids at Pergamum – through the disbursement of the library's holdings or through the students trained by teachers from Pergamum – remains unclear from the current state of knowledge.

PAMELA A. WEBB

See also Pergamum

Summary

The Attalids were the founders and ruling dynasty of the kingdom of Pergamum in Asia Minor between 281 and 133 BC. They saw themselves as the preservers of Classical civilization and their goal was to make their capital city the successor to Athens as the cultural and artistic centre of the Hellenistic world. To this end they compiled a library of some 200,000 works and supported a large number of scholars in all areas of Greek learning, as well as artists, city planners, and architects, who turned Pergamum into a metropolis of marble monuments.

Further Reading

Foss, Clive, *History and Archaeology of Byzantine Asia Minor*, Aldershot, Hampshire: Variorum, 1990

Geanakoplos, Deno John, *Constantinople and the West: Essays on the Late Byzantine (Palaeologan) and Italian Renaissances and the Byzantine and Roman Churches*, Madison: University of Wisconsin Press, 1989, especially pp. 6–7, 39–42, 61

Hansen, Esther Violet, *The Attalids of Pergamon*, 2nd edition, Ithaca, New York: Cornell University Press, 1971

Pfeiffer, Rudolf, *History of Classical Scholarship from the Beginnings to the End of the Hellenistic Age*, Oxford: Clarendon Press, 1968, pp. 234–51

Vryonis, Speros, Jr, *The Decline of Medieval Hellenism in Asia Minor and the Process of Islamization from the Eleventh through the Fifteenth Century*, Berkeley: University of California Press, 1971

Webb, Pamela A., *Hellenistic Architectural Sculpture: Figural Motifs in Western Anatolia and the Aegean Islands*, Madison: University of Wisconsin Press, 1996, especially pp. 55–71

Webb, Pamela A., "The Functions of the Pergamon Altar and the Sanctuary of Athena" in *Stephanos: Studies in Honor of Brunilde Sismondo Ridgway*, edited by Kim J. Hartswick and Mary C. Sturgeon, Philadelphia: University Museum, University of Pennsylvania, 1998

Attica

Region of central Greece

Ancient Attica was made up the greater part of the modern nome of the same name. A three-sided peninsula which protrudes from central Greece, Attica is surrounded by sea on two sides with Cape Sunium and its famous temple of Poseidon at the southernmost tip. On the landward side Boeotia and Megara lie on the borders. In antiquity Attica covered over 2400 sq km and embraced a variety of mountain ranges and valleys as well as coastal and inland plains. The extent of the territory increased in specific periods, as the disputed areas fought over by Athens and Boeotia or Athens and Megara were added to Attica.

The Parnes mountain range separates Attica from its main northern rival, Boeotia. Here the competing poleis (or city states) fought over the upland plains and near the coast the important centre of Oropus. At the heart of Attica lies the Cephisus plain with the city of Athens at its centre. Enclosing the city and its plain are the mountain ranges of Hymettus on the east and Aegaleus on the west. Beyond Aegaleus stretches the Thriasian plain and the border with Megara. Eleusis lies at the southern edge of this plain. It looks across to the island of Salamis which was part of the Athenian polis in antiquity. To the northeast of Athens lie the Penteli mountains. Both Hymettus and Penteli provided the city with marble for building projects, most famously those on the Athenian Acropolis of the 5th century BC funded by the maritime empire. In southern Attica, the other major upland area, the Laurium hills were famous for silver and lead ores. The silver financed the construction of Athenian ships in the first quarter of the 5th century and continued to provide Athens with a large reserve of wealth on which it built its success. The natural resources of Attica, precious metal and marble, supplemented its agricultural assets, in particular olive oil, honey, and figs. These were the three most important cultivated crops of the region in antiquity.

Attica has been occupied since neolithic times. Evidence for human activity on the Acropolis dates back to about 3000 BC: pits and wells containing late neolithic pottery have been found near the Clepsydra spring on the north slopes. Wells and burials of the Early and Middle Helladic periods (3000–1500 BC) show signs of continued and expanding human settlement in Attica into the Late Bronze Age. In the Mycenaean period (Late Helladic: 1550–1100) the growth in the number and quality of sites and the associated finds in Attica is remarkable. The end of the Mycenaean period sees a drop in the number of sites and quality of burial goods in Attica during the second half of 12th century BC. The Dark Age period, which covers the sub-Mycenaean to the end of the Protogeometric periods (1100 – c.900 BC), is fast becoming a misnomer in the history of Attica. Iron technology spread quickly in this period, and was the dominant metal for swords, knives, axes, daggers, dress pins, and fibulae in the latter half of the 11th and the 10th centuries BC. The number of sites in Attica reaches a nadir in 1100 BC; but c.1050 BC there appears a new style of Attic pottery, the Protogeometric style, and a growing number of settlements on the east coast and inland become identifiable. This steady transformation of occupation after the sub-

Mycenaean period is reflected in changes to burial practices; in addition, at the end of the 10th century, sanctuary offerings start to appear, examples of which are found at the Academy in Athens and on Mount Hymettus.

The Geometric period (c. 900–700 BC) marks a rapid progression of developments in Attica. The number of known sites rises more than threefold between the 9th and the end of the 8th centuries. By 700 BC nearly half of the known Classical deme sites of Attica show signs of occupation. Despite the growth in evidence of monumental sanctuaries in the wider Greek world in the 8th and 7th centuries, Attica betrays fewer signs of such advances until later on. The 8th century is generally thought to be the time when Attica becomes a territory dominated by Athens; the widespread distribution of small settlements in the countryside is reflected by the large number of cemeteries found in the Attic countryside. These numbers fall in the 7th century and cult activity becomes the best indication of rural settlement. The 7th century is considered to be a time of revolutionary political changes in Attica: the mythical synoecism of Attica by Thesus may belong to the Geometric period or before, but the stories of family conflicts, the Cylonian conspiracy (c.630 BC), and the Solonian reforms of the early 6th century mark important periods in the history of Attica.

In the late 7th and 6th centuries political developments were centred on the control of power in Athens, and the reforms enacted there affected the whole of Attica. The unification of Attica as a political entity took place by the 7th century, and its subsequent history revolves around the relationship between the urban centre of Athens and its smaller, often rural communities. The power struggles of the 6th century, which present themselves as factional competition between groups, sometimes related by kinship ties, centre on regions within Attica (Herodotus, 1. 59). The experience of tyranny in Attica in the second half of the 6th century was not harsh. Many developments focused on Athens, but settlements outside the urban centre were improved during this period of growing prosperity and peace: Eleusis was developed with an impressive circuit wall and the Telesterion (the hall of the mysteries) took on the square hypostyle design which existed at the end of antiquity; the early developments of the theatre at Thoricus belong to this period; the temple of Apollo on Cape Zoster at Vouliagmeni dates back to this time.

The fall of the Pisistratids and the reforms of Cleisthenes of 508/07 transformed the political organization of Attica and so shaped the subsequent structure of the region's history. The people of Attica were formally arranged by demes, small village- or town-sized communities. A number of demes were located in Athens, but the majority of the demes were extra-urban. These 139 demes were allocated to 30 regional groupings (trittyes). Attica was divided into three groups of ten trittyes: there were ten trittyes from the coastal areas, ten from the plain or inland area, and ten from the city area. The grouping of demes into these local enclaves allowed some manipulation of territorial control. One trittys from each of the three areas made up a tribe, and there were ten tribes. This political reorganization of Attica ensured that for much of antiquity the history of Athens could not be separated from the history of its surrounding rural territory.

The central role of demes formalized the political standing of rural settlements. The Cleisthenic reforms produced a system of political participation which involved the whole population of Attica in the running of the polis, even if the seat of power was located in the urban centre.

Attica in the Classical period flourished and became one of the most densely populated regions in Greece. Exploitation of the countryside increased rapidly, and the extent of farming and animal tending in the 4th century saw activity on even the most marginal of land.

The major cult centres of Attica at Rhamnous, Sunium, and Eleusis underwent intense contruction work. New temples were also built at Acharnae and at Brauron. The insecurities created by the Peloponnesian War saw the construction of forts in Attica: Thoricus and Sunium were enclosed by defences, fortresses were built at Phyle and Panakton. The war had considerable impact on the Attic countryside. Pericles' defence of Athens during the Archidamian War (431–421) forced those living in the countryside to move into the city on a regular basis. The countryside was not abandoned completely, but there are signs of devastation: the Dema wall house is thought to have fallen into disuse during this period. The relatively brief summer invasions by the Spartan army during these years were less severe than the disruptions which the construction of a Spartan fort on Deceleia achieved between 413 and 403. The role of the harbour town Piraeus and the strategic roles played by Eleusis, Sunium, and Rhamnous were crucial to the security of Attica. Their functions became more formalized by the end of the 4th century and were to remain so for at least the next three centuries.

The archaeological evidence for settlement and activity in Attica peaks in the 4th century: epigraphic evidence for the erection of decrees, funerary material, and religious dedications all climax in this period. The decline of evidence and signs of activity in the 3rd and 2nd centuries is thought to suggest that people withdrew from the countryside and migrated to the city. But the continuing success of Eleusis and Rhamnous throughout the Hellenistic period and the importance of the countryside as a source of food supplies suggest that Attica remained relatively well populated in the 3rd to 1st centuries BC. Clear signs of decline in activity focus on the Laurium mining region which had been heavily populated in the 5th and especially 4th centuries. The exploitation of silver by Athens in this area attracted large numbers of slaves, industry, and farming. The decline of mining in the first half of the 3rd century, and the small level of activity from the late 3rd century onwards, mark a stark contrast with the Classical period. The occupation of Attica in the 3rd and 2nd centuries should not be based on the exceptional patterns of activity seen in Laurium; Heracleides Creticus, writing in the late 3rd century, described Attica as a fertile region with a large number of inns and good road networks, all of which indicates some level of rural occupation.

The Hellenistic period may signify a decline in the intense exploitation of Attica; the real drop in activity belongs to the late Hellenistic and early Roman period in line with many other rural areas in Greece. The virtual disappearance of settlement and activity in and around Panakton in the previously disputed area between Boeotia and Attica from 200 BC to the late Roman period symbolizes the reduced pressure on the countryside in this period. The pattern of exploitation in marginal land in Attica is one way of calibrating the levels of activity in the area.

But the Roman period also sees an increasing revival in prosperity in other parts of Attica concentrated among a much smaller number of individuals. In the early 2nd century AD Herodes Atticus displayed his wealth in Athens but also developed Marathon as a personal estate. In contrast, some areas declined as the urban centre of Athens increasingly became the focus of expenditure: the Augustan period saw the removal of elements from the temple of Poseidon at Sunium into the rebuilt temple of Ares in the Agora at Athens.

In the late Roman period there is a brief intensification of activity in Attica, in line with general signs of revival in Athens. The Herulian sack of Athens in AD 267 and the subsequent decline of activity in Attica mark the gradual drift of the region from the prosperity of the Greek and Roman periods.

Invasions from the end of the 6th to the 8th centuries, however, delayed any revival. Byzantium had reasserted control in Greece by the middle of the 9th century and Attica began to rediscover some prosperity, enjoying greater security from the middle of the 10th century. In 967 Crete was recovered from the Arabs, thereby reducing the threat of raids in Attica. The formal establishment of Christianity in the 5th and 6th centuries AD had seen the construction of churches and the conversion of some ancient temples in Attica, and many new churches in the region date from the 11th to the 13th centuries. The monastery of Kaiasariani on the lower slopes of Mount Hymettus dates back to the 11th century. It escaped the imposition of taxation by the Turks following the conquest of Attica in 1456, and remained independent of Athens until 1716.

The Latin conquest of Constantinople in 1204 brought changes for Athens and Attica. The Burgundian knight Otto de la Roche was given control of Boeotia and Attica by Boniface III. Under Frankish rule Attica prospered for around 100 years. The countryside is still dotted with Frankish towers built during this period.

Frankish control was broken in 1311 and the region was under Catalan control for much of the 14th century. The Venetians wrested Attica from the Catalans in 1386 and remained in power until the Turkish occupation. Attica was annexed to the Ottoman empire in 1456, and stayed under Turkish control until the Greek War of Independence (1821–32). Athens was finally liberated and became the capital of free Greece in 1834.

The population of Athens expanded into Attica during the 1920s following the resettlement and exchange of Greek and Turkish peoples in 1923. During World War II Attica suffered considerably. The German forces occupied the area between April 1941 and October 1944. Koropi was the last village in Attica to be burnt down by the German army as it retreated from the coast. In December 1944 a communist revolution broke out in Athens. On the slopes of Hymettus there was fierce fighting between the British troops and the forces of ELAS.

The history of Attica cannot be separated easily from that of Athens, but its importance for the political development of Athens in antiquity cannot be underestimated. A number of major sites in Attica illustrate the wealth and success of the region. The modern development of Athens and its expansion into Attica confirm the symbiotic relationship which typified the dependence of Athens on Attica in the Classical period.

GRAHAM OLIVER

Summary

Attica, a peninsula protruding from central Greece, is the region surrounding Athens. In antiquity it provided the raw materials that were fundamental to the city's success—marble, silver, and crops. Attica was politically unified by the 7th century BC and reorganized by the reforms of Cleisthenes in 508/07 BC. Its prosperity declined in the late Roman period. It received an influx during the exchange of populations in 1923.

Further Reading

Alcock, Susan E., *Graecia Capta: The Landscapes of Roman Greece*, Cambridge and New York: Cambridge University Press, 1993

Barber, Robin, *Athens and Environs*, 4th edition, London: A. & C. Black, 1999 (*Blue Guide* series)

Coulson, W.D.E. *et al.* (editors), *The Archaeology of Athens and Attica under the Democracy*, Oxford: Oxbow, 1994

Ellis-Jones, J., "The Laurion Silver Mines: A Review of Recent Researches and Results", *Greece and Rome*, 29 (1982): pp. 169–83

Fowden, G., "City and Mountain in Late Roman Attica", *Journal of Hellenic Studies*, 108 (1988): pp. 48–59

Garland, Robert, *The Piraeus: From the Fifth to the First Century* BC, London: Duckworth, and Ithaca, New York: Cornell University Press, 1987

Hoff, Michael C. and Susan I. Rotroff (editors), *The Romanization of Athens*, Oxford: Oxbow, 1997

Iatrides, John O., *Revolt in Athens: The Greek Communist "Second Round", 1944–1945*, Princeton, New Jersey: Princeton University Press, 1972

Lancaster, Osbert, *Classical Landscape with Figures*, London: John Murray, 1947; Boston: Houghton Mifflin, 1949

Lauter, H., "Some Remarks on Fortified Settlements in the Attic Countryside" in *Fortificationes Antiquae*, edited by S. Van de Maele and J.M. Fossey, Amsterdam: Gieben, 1992

Lock, Peter and G.D.R. Sanders (editors), *The Archaeology of Medieval Greece*, Oxford: Oxbow, 1996

Mossé, Claude, *Athens in Decline, 404–86 BC*, London and Boston: Routledge, 1973

Osborne, Robin, *Demos: The Discovery of Classical Attika*, Cambridge and New York: Cambridge University Press, 1985

Setton, Kenneth M., *Athens in the Middle Ages*, London: Variorum, 1975

Travlos, John (editor), *Bildlexikon zur Topographie des antiken Attika*, Tübingen: Wasmuth, 1988

Whitehead, David, *The Demes of Attica 508/7–c.250 BC: A Political and Social Study*, Princeton, New Jersey: Princeton University Press, 1986

Wordsworth, Christopher, *Athens and Attica: Journal of a Residence There*, 2nd edition, London: John Murray, 1837

Australia

There were no Greeks among the first white settlers in Australia who arrived with the First Fleet in 1788. The first mention of Greeks on Australian soil, in 1818, is not a flattering one: a local newspaper in Sydney complained of rubbish being thrown in the streets by Greeks and other foreigners. The earliest Greeks in Australia were perhaps from the island of Cyprus. Most of the first Greeks in the Antipodes were

Australia: procession of Greek Australians celebrating their dual heritage

certainly from the Greek islands: Poros and Hydra, Ithaca and Samos, Rhodes and Euboea, Calymnos and Cos, Cythera and Castellorizo; those from the mainland were from the Peloponnese. At home they had been mostly either people of the sea (sailors, fishermen, and sponge divers) or else people of the land (farmers and shepherds). In Australia they worked on sugar plantations or in the mines; later they moved to the cities, where they managed restaurants or grocery stores. Although many of them were rapidly well established, it was not at all easy for the early immigrants, who worked hard in the hope someday of returning to Greece, a dream that was fulfilled only by a few. World War I and the Italian occupation

of the Dodecanese islands sowed the seeds of an ever-increasing emigration. Almost all of the inhabitants of Castellorizo, for example, migrated overseas, most to Australia. After World War II the wave of migration continued unabated. In comparison to the difficulties faced by the earlier migrants, those who migrated during the 1950s, 1960s, and 1970s left their mark on Australian society, both socially and commercially, in spite of the fact that many of them first worked in factories. Today the Greeks are an integral part of Australia, holding important positions in government and society, and are well known for their contribution to commerce, politics, and education.

From the early 20th century, many of the islanders had

formed their own associations (or brotherhoods) in Australia. And though the first Greeks were unlettered for the most part, one Greek doctor opened a medical practice in Melbourne in 1902. The Greek press also began in Melbourne, in 1913 with the publication of *Afstralia* (the paper was later renamed *Ethnikon Vima*, under which name it still appears today). Other daily newspapers also appeared, such as the *National Herald* and, more recently, *O [Neos] Kosmos*.

The presence of Greeks in Australia, however, is particularly associated with the growth of the Orthodox Church. The early migrants quickly felt the need to build churches and to organize their social and spiritual life with adjacent halls and schools. It is this close connection of the Greek people with their Church that has accounted for the rapid development of educational establishments (on the primary, secondary, and even tertiary levels) and welfare institutions (especially the care of the aged). Any study of the Greeks in Australia is therefore inevitably linked to an understanding of the Greek Orthodox Church, but the close cooperation of the Greek people with their Church has at times been intense and contentious.

The historical development of the Greek Orthodox Church in Australia has been an increasingly significant feature in the life and culture of the Antipodes. Although it is difficult to discover the origins of Hellenism or of Orthodoxy there – there are very few clear references to them – the overall impact of the Eastern Orthodox Church is today easily perceived in a society where pluralism and multiculturism are not abstract humanitarian ideals but already, at least to a certain degree, realities of everyday life. The Greek Orthodox faith and Church, particularly after World War II, are not marginal phenomena in Australia, but have been gradually integrated into society at large. Before 1945 there were only 10,000 Greeks in Australia, while by 1950 there were 75,000, by 1960 there were 160,000, by 1970 about 400,000, and today more than 600,000. The Orthodox population numbers around 1 million, out of a total population of 17 million. Fewer than half of these were born in Australia, while fewer than 5 per cent have both parents born in Australia.

The first Liturgy in Australia – in Sydney, possibly during Bright Week of 1820 – was celebrated by a Russian Orthodox priest called Fr Dionisii, who was the chaplain on a ship that sailed to the Antarctic and round the world in the years 1819–21. But it was not until 1895, when a Greek priest named Archimandrite Dorotheos Bakaliaros arrived in Australia, that regular parish life appears to have begun. He travelled between Sydney and Melbourne, performing services in local town halls, but he had probably left Australia before the completion of the first Orthodox church, which was built in Sydney in 1898 and dedicated to the Holy Trinity.

The canonical jurisdiction and status of the first Orthodox churches are equally unclear. It appears that originally clergy were secured from the patriarchate of Jerusalem, which provided the communities in Sydney and Melbourne with priests during the early years. The first church in Melbourne was constructed in 1900. Two years later, the Church of Greece assumed spiritual responsibility for the churches in Australia, and began to send out priests for the pastoral needs of the Greek-speaking parishes. The earliest parishes served a multilingual congregation, and the clergy from Jerusalem were clearly well qualified for this purpose. In 1922 the ecumenical patriarch in Constantinople, Meletios Metaxakis, claimed jurisdiction over all the Greek Orthodox living abroad, and in 1924 he established the Greek Orthodox metropolis of Australia and New Zealand "for the better organization of the Orthodox Church" in that part of the world. The ecumenical patriarch has exercised spiritual authority over the Greek Orthodox Church in Australia and appointed its canonical archbishop ever since.

The Greek Orthodox Church (promoted to the status of archdiocese in 1959, and separated from New Zealand in 1970, when the latter was formed as its own metropolis) is divided into five archdiocesan districts, with local offices in the federal capitals, and has more than 120 clergymen, and more than 100 organized parishes with their own catechetical and afternoon language classes and community centres. The archbishop (since 1975 His Eminence archbishop Stylianos) is based in Sydney, and has three assistant bishops.

JOHN CHRYSSAVGIS

Further Reading

Chryssavgis, John and Miltiades Chryssavgis, *Persons and Events in Orthodoxy*, Sydney: Greek Orthodox Archdiocese, 1985

Chryssavgis, John, "The Greek Orthodox Clergyman in Australia" in *Religion and Ethnic Identity: An Australian Study*, 3 vols, edited by Abe I. Wade Ata, Richmond, Victoria: Spectrum, 1988–90

Chryssavgis, John, "Orthodoxy and Australia: Retrospect and Prospect", *Ostkirchliche Studien*, 39, 2–3 (1990): pp. 193–205

Chryssavgis, John, "An Old Faith in *Terra Nova* : The Eastern Orthodox Tradition", *Prudentia*, supplement (1994): pp. 329–36

Gilchrist, Hugh, *Australians and Greeks*, vol. 1: *The Early Years*, Sydney: Halstead Press, 1992

Simmons, Harry L.N., "Eastern Orthodoxy in Australia: A Forgotten Chapter", *St Vladimir's Theological Quarterly*, 23 (1979): pp. 181–85

Simmons, Harry L.N., *Orthodoxy in Australia: Parallels and Links with the USA*, Brookline, Massachusetts: Hellenic College Press, 1986

B

Babrius

Writer of fables of the 1st or 2nd century AD

Babrius wrote verse fables, 144 of which are extant in their original metrical form. In addition, two proems (prefaces) remain, which seems to indicate that the fables were originally published in two books. The first proem is dedicated to one "boy Branchus", the second to "king Alexander's son". These two addressees are probably one and the same person. It is, however, unclear with what historical king Alexander prince Branchus' father is to be equated. We do possess external termini ante quem: since Babrius' fables can be shown to have been well known by the early 3rd century AD, the author can safely be assumed to have lived in the 2nd or late 1st century AD; a still earlier date is excluded by the linguistic evidence. Quite unlike his predecessor Phaedrus (early 1st century AD), who was a Greek writing Latin fables, Babrius wrote in Greek, but was in all probability of Roman origin. This is indicated both by his very name, which occurs only in Latin and not in Greek inscriptions, and by a peculiarity of his metrical technique, accentuating each penultimate syllable, which is in accordance with Roman rather than with Greek prosody and stress. Babrius may have lived in the eastern (Greek-speaking) part of the Roman empire, more particularly in or near Syria. This is suggested by the literary and historically surprisingly exact ascription of the genre's origin to the Syrians (i.e. Assyrians) in the second proem. Further clues may be found in the author's professed personal experience with Arabs (57. 12), and in the oriental local colour of no. 8.

Babrius' fables are written in so-called choliambic trimeters (iambic trimeters with a long penultimate syllable). In both proems he selfconfidently states that he has "softened" the stinging iambs, by which he may be taken to mean that he has innovatively tempered the originally satiric connotations of choliambic metre. The fables' length varies considerably: on the one hand, the quatrain form is quite frequent, but the collection also includes a fable of 102 lines (no. 95). Many fables feature metrical epimythia, whose authenticity has sometimes unjustly been disputed. The collection has obviously been preserved incompletely, the alphabetic order in the principal manuscript abruptly ending with omicron.

The fables' subject matter is partly traditional and partly original, including all kinds of variations as well as fabuliza-tions of mythological and other materials. Babrius seems to have drawn from a variety of sources. His narrative elaborations, psychological portrayal of protagonists, and mildly humorous tone are all stylistically idiosyncratic.

Babrius' fables enjoyed immediate popularity. A papyrus fragment dating from the early 3rd century AD (*Oxyrhynchus Papyri*, edited by B.P. Grenfell and A.S. Hunt, 1898–, 10. 1249) contains parts of four Babrius fables dealing with the theme of false judgement, which may be an indication that they were included in some sort of anthology used for moral education. That Babrius did soon become a school author is clear from various testimonies. First, the bilingual Graeco-Roman *Hermeneumata* ("Interpretations") by pseudo-Dositheus, which can be dated exactly to AD 207 and are explicitly composed "for lovers of Latin", contain 17 fables, 3 of which derive from Babrian prototypes. Second, 14 fables, 11 of which are in Babrian choliambs, have been preserved on the so-called Van Assendelft wax tablets (named after their Dutch buyer) from Palmyra (destroyed in AD 272); the many mistakes made in the Greek, as well as the very writing material, show that the fables served as a dictation given by a schoolmaster to a not-too-brilliant pupil. Third, we have a papyrus scrap (*Amherst Papyri*, edited by B.P. Grenfell and A.S. Hunt, 1900–, 2. 26; late 3rd or early 4th century AD) with fragments of three fables by Babrius, whose educational application is again clear from the accompanying Latin verbatim translation. Finally, another papyrus (*Bouriant Papyri*, 1; 4th century AD; edited by P. Collart, Paris: Champion, vol.1), undoubtedly a Greek language teaching method, starting with monosyllabic words, ends with part of the first proem of Babrius' fable collection.

Babrius' fables also found more literate readers. In a Greek letter (*Epistle* 82; AD 362) the Roman emperor Julian explicitly quotes from a book containing fables by Babrius. In addition, Babrius' collection is the principal source for the 42 Latin fables in elegiac distichs by the Roman fabulist Avianus (*c*.AD 400), who pays tribute to his predecessor in the prose preface to his verse collection dedicated to the erudite Macrobius Ambrosius Theodosius, future praetorian prefect of Italy (AD 430).

The fables' popularity lasted throughout the Byzantine period. First of all, the *Suda* lexicon quotes more than 50 times from Babrius to exemplify particular words, and even lists the fabulist under a separate entry – in a way the Byzantine predecessor of this essay. John Georgides included many *epimythia* (concluding morals) from fables by Babrius in his *Gnomologium* (*c.*10th century). Two lexica (the so-called *Etymologicum Genuinum* and *Etymologicum Magnum*, dating from the 9th and 12th centuries respectively) exemplify two rare words (*omphax* and *pepromenon*) by quoting from two fables by Babrius. Two other lexica (Photios and, again, the *Suda*) paraphrase a Babrian fable to illustrate the meaning of a proverb (*tn kheira*). One fable (no. 141) is only (if incompletely) preserved by two rather late testimonies, the Byzantine polyhistor John Tzetzes (12th century) and the neo-Latin Natalis Comes (16th century).

An important witness of the collection's popularity is the large number (148) of prose paraphrases of Babrian fables. Many of these (more than 50) give the outline of fables not preserved in their original metrical form. In addition, Babrius is the primary source of the Byzantine *Tetrastichs*, a collection of 89 fable quatrains in quasi-ancient iambic trimeters or typically Byzantine dodecasyllabic verses, ascribed to Ignatios (Diakonos?; 9th century). Their author(s) may have found inspiration in the frequency of four-liners among Babrius' fables mentioned above. The *Tetrastichs* were widely read in the Middle Ages, as is demonstrated by the great number of manuscripts, many of them falsely proclaiming Babrius as their author, and even misspelling his name as Babrias, Gabrias, or even worse. Their alleged Babrian authorship has been taken for granted more than once; even the famous French fabulist Jean de la Fontaine states that he has used Babrius, whereas it can be shown that he really read the *Tetrastichs*, and that in a Latin translation. Conversely, a scholium on Thucydides (4. 92) quotes as if from Aesop two verses by Babrius, whose proems admittedly do stereotypically mention the legendary fabulist as a source of inspiration.

Three Byzantine manuscripts containing fables by Babrius are extant: A, G, and V, named after the libraries in which they once were, or still are, kept, on Mount Athos, in Grottaferrata, and the Vatican, respectively. The principal manuscript A (now in the British Library, Add. 22087; 10th century) contains 122 fables, which are, like the prose paraphrases and the so-called Aesopic fables, alphabetically ordered by their incipit; the alphabetization of the second proem (under *m*, as it begins with *mythos*) makes it a priori unlikely that this order is the author's. G (now in the Pierpont Morgan Library, New York, Cod. 397; 10th century) has – in addition to an important version of the *Life of Aesop* – 31 fables, 4 of which are preserved only here; V (Cod. Vaticanus Gr. 777; 15th century) has 30 fables, 12 of which are not in A.

Modern times have seen the gradual publication of Babrius' collection. The fables from A and V, as well as the wax tablets, *Hermeneumata*, and prose paraphrases, were first published in the 19th century, whereas G and the papyri reappeared only in the 20th century. The rediscovery of the Athonite manuscript in 1842 by Minoides Mynas and its subsequent first edition (edited by J.F. Boissonade, Paris, 1844) were a first-rate scholarly sensation at the time. The enthusiastic finder was inspired by his success to compose a series of fables in the manner of Babrius; his forgeries did mislead one editor (G.C. Lewis, London, 1846), but the pseudo-Babrius was soon unmasked as a jackdaw strutting with borrowed feathers. This curious little anecdote epitomizes a problematic implication of the fables' popularity. In view of the author's own complaint in his second proem that imitators "sneaked in when I first opened the door", those studying the many fables and paraphrases connected with his name should at least not rule out too easily the possibility that the accepted body of Babrius's work includes some forgeries.

GERT-JAN VAN DIJK

See also Fable

Biography
Babrius lived in the 2nd or late 1st century AD, perhaps in Syria. He was probably of Roman origin but wrote verse fables in Greek, of which 144 survive in their metrical form. Prose paraphrases of more than 50 others survive. He remained popular throughout the Byzantine period.

Writings
In *Babrius*, edited by W.G. Rutherford, London: Macmillan, 1883
In *Babrius and Phaedrus*, translated by Ben Edwin Perry, Cambridge, Massachusetts: Harvard University Press, and London: Heinemann, 1965, reprinted 1990
Mythiambi Aesopei, edited by Maria Jagoda Luzzatto and Antonio La Penna, Leipzig: Teubner, 1986

Further Reading
Adrados, Francisco Rodriguez, *History of the Graeco-Latin Fable*, vol. 2: *The Fable in the Imperial Roman and Medieval Period*, translated by L.A. Ray and revised and updated by the author and Gert-Jan van Dijk, Leiden: Brill, 2000
Christoffersson, Herman, "Studia de fabulis Babrianis", dissertation, Lund: Möller, 1901
Dijk, J.G.M. van, "The (Pseudo-) Ignatius Tetrastichs: Byzantine Fables 'D'une élégance laconique'", *Reinardus*, 9 (1996): pp. 161–78
Dijk, J.G.M. van, *Ignatios Diakonos: Fabelkwatrijnen*, Groningen: Styx, 2000
Getzlaff, Eric, "Quaestiones Babrianae et Pseudo-Dositheanae", dissertation, Marburg, 1907
Giurdanella Fusci, G., *Babrio: Le sue favole e il loro rapporto con le esopiane e con quelle di Fedro e di Aviano*, Modica: Papa, 1901
Hohmann, Ernest, "De indole atque auctoritate epimythiorum Babrianorum", dissertation, Königsberg: Hartung, 1907
Holzberg, Niklas, *Die antike Fabel: eine Einführung*, Darmstadt: Wissenschaftliche Buchgesellschaft, 1993
Nøjgaard, Morten, *La Fable antique*, vol. 2: *Les Grands Fabulistes*, Copenhagen: Busck, 1967
Vaio, J., "Babrius and the Byzantine Fable" in *La Fable*, edited by F.R. Adrados, Geneva: Hardt, 1984
Zachariae, T., "De dictione Babriana", dissertation, Leipzig: Naumann, 1875

Bacchylides
Lyric poet of the 5th century BC

Bacchylides, from Iulis on Ceos, was born around 510 BC and was active until the third quarter of the 5th century BC. A papyrus discovered in 1896 has preserved substantial remains of some 14 of his epinician odes (victory songs) and six dithyrambs (poems on heroic subjects). Bacchylides also composed hymns to the gods, paeans (hymns to Apollo), hyporchemes (songs for dancing), prosodia (processional songs), partheneia (songs for maidens), erotica (songs of love), and possibly enkomia (songs of praise), of which only fragments remain.

Little is known of his life. The poetic talents of the young Bacchylides probably developed under the influence of his uncle Simonides, who composed in a similar range of genres. Like many Greek poets before him, Bacchylides enjoyed the attention of a wealthy prince. Three of his surviving epinician odes are addressed to Hieron, tyrant of Syracuse, and the poet must have spent time in Sicily in the 470s BC. Ancient scholars believed that Bacchylides and his contemporary Pindar rivalled each other at Hieron's court for the favour of the powerful ruler. Bacchylides and his poems were also well received in many other parts of the Greek world. Among the addressees of his victory odes were athletes from Ceos, Aegina, Athens, Thessaly, Phlius, and Metapontum; and his surviving dithyrambs appear to have been performed in Athens, Delos, Delphi, and Sparta.

Bacchylides composed his victory odes for performance in the victor's home town after his return from the games, or, in the case of shorter hymns, to be performed at the athletic festivals. The odes were performed by choruses, which danced or processed while singing the odes to the accompaniment of the aulos and/or the lyre. The poems typically contain a mixture of praise, aphoristic statements, and myth. Since an ode usually records the name of the athlete, the specific contest won (chariot race, wrestling, etc.), and the location of the competition (Olympia, Delphi, etc.), it functions as an announcement and commemoration of the victory. Also included in the poet's praise are the victor's family and city of origin. Scattered gnomic statements, expressing proverbial wisdom or beliefs, enhance and temper the words of praise: "no mortal is blessed in all things" (5. 53–55), "fame follows him whom the gods honour" (5. 193–94). The third typical component of the odes, the often extended narration of heroic myth, serves several purposes. The inclusion of myths is a form of praise for the poems' addressees, as some association is implied between the achievements of the athletes and the exploits of the heroes. In poem 13, for example, the games at Nemea are understood to commemorate the struggle between Heracles and the Nemean lion. Recollections of specific mythic figures sometimes reflect the noble past of a victor's homeland. Poem 1, composed for a Cean victor, tells the story of Dexithea and her son, the Cean hero Euxantius. Myths of the heroic past may also illustrate principles and beliefs. Poem 3 relates the miraculous rescue of the semi-mythological king Croesus as evidence that the gods reward generosity and piety.

The dithyrambs, intended for choral performance at religious festivals and competitions, narrate scenes from heroic myth. Perhaps Bacchylides' most famous dithyramb, ode 17, tells how Theseus, while sailing to Crete with Minos and the contingent of captive Athenian youths and maidens, descended into the sea to the house of his father Poseidon and received gifts from Amphitrite. The poem characterizes the hero as a champion of the Athenians, opposing the aggression of Minos, and the affirmation that Theseus was the son of Poseidon may reflect the growth of Athenian naval power in the Aegean between and after the Persian Wars. The subjects of Bacchylides' other dithyrambs include the embassy of Menelaus and Odysseus to Troy, Heracles' celebration of the capture of Oechalia, the arrival of the young Theseus at Athens, Io's escape from Argus, and the marriage of Idas and Marpessa.

Bacchylides drew upon a range of previous poetry for his mythic material. Prominent among these sources were the early epic poets, from whom Bacchylides adopted legends about Heracles, Menelaus, and Meleager. He quotes one aphorism directly from Hesiod, and other maxims recall Theognis and Solon. It is reasonable to assume that, in regard to style and manner of presentation, Bacchylides was heavily indebted to his uncle Simonides, a pioneer in the development of the victory ode, but the scanty remains of Simonides allow little comparison. Bacchylides shares in common with Pindar the use of myth and maxim, and he seems occasionally to have imitated his older contemporary, but the styles of the two poets differ significantly. Pindar favours daring metaphor and dense imagery, while Bacchylides prefers simpler modes of expressions. Bacchylides also prefers clear, linear narration of myth, as was the practice in epic. His introduction of dialogue into his narration is reminiscent of Homer and was probably influenced by Stesichorus.

Bacchylides found no immediate successor, and the types of choral lyric he composed waned in popularity as the 5th century BC progressed, but his poetry was remembered long after his death. Alexandrian scholars counted Bacchylides among the nine great lyric poets. He is mentioned several times in the scholia of Homer, Hesiod, Pindar, and others. He found an admirer and imitator in the Roman poet Horace. Quotations and references to Bacchylides in such authors as Longinus, Plutarch, Athenaeus, and Stobaeus attest to his enduring appeal, but the manuscript transmission seems to have been broken in the Roman period and his works were lost until the discovery of the papyrus in 1896.

MICHAEL J. ANDERSON

Biography

Born c.510 BC on Ceos, Bacchylides was active at least until 450 BC. He was the nephew of the poet Simonides and was no doubt influenced by him. In the 470s BC he spent time at the court of Hieron I, tyrant of Syracuse, where he may have been a rival of Pindar. Substantial fragments of poems in various genres survive, notably epinician odes and dithyrambs.

Writings

The Poems and Fragments, translated by Richard C. Jebb, Cambridge: Cambridge University Press, 1905; reprinted Hildesheim: Olms, 1967

Complete Poems, translated by Robert Fagles, New Haven, Connecticut: Yale University Press, 1961

Carmina cum Fragmentis, edited by Bruno Snell and Herwig Maehler, Stuttgart and Leipzig: Teubner, 1992

Further Reading

Burnett, Anne Pippin, *The Art of Bacchylides*, Cambridge, Massachusetts: Harvard University Press, 1985

Pfeijffer, Ilja and Simon Slings (editors), *One Hundred Years of Bacchylides*, Amsterdam: V. U. University Press, 1999

Bactria

Region of Central Asia

Annexed to the Persian empire by Cyrus II (Herodotus, l. 153), probably in the 530s BC, Bactria was an important satrapy of the Achaemenids, bordering on the Oxus river in the north, the Pamir mountains in the northeast, and the Hindu Kush in the south. In 522/21 BC the satrap of Bactria, Dadarshish, supported Darius I against the rebellious Armenians and quashed the uprising of neighbouring Margiana. His successor was Artabanus, who probably was satrap between 500 BC and 465 BC. Bactrian infantry and cavalry, equipped with reed bows and short spears, fought under the command of Hystaspes, a brother of Xerxes, in the invasion of Greece in 480/79 BC (Herodotus, 7. 64). Together with the Medes and Saka, the Bactrian contingent wintered in Thessaly in 480/79 BC under the command of Mardonius. In consequence of a palace intrigue Xerxes' brother Masistes, the *hyparchos* (subordinate governor) of Bactria, planned a revolt against the king in Bactria, but was killed on his way there (Herodotus, 9. 113). At the battle of Gaugamela Bactrian and Saka forces faced Alexander and his companions, marking them as the strongest force in the army of the Persian king. After his defeat Darius III tried to escape to Bactria, but he was killed by its satrap Bessus, who was also a relative of the king (Arrian, *Anabasis*, 3. 21. 5, 3. 30. 4). When Bessus assumed the Persian tiara and proclaimed himself king, Alexander immediately moved his army to Bactria to kill Bessus. The Bactrian capital Bactra, modern Balkh, was Alexander's residence in 329/28 BC before he continued his campaign against Sogdiana the following spring. Bactrian rebellion against Alexander in the summer of 329 BC lasted for two years, and when it was finally quashed, Alexander took 30,000 Bactrians and Sogdians as hostages.

Bactria was a wealthy province, profiting undoubtedly from trade between Persia and India, but also benefiting from fertile oases and pasturage. According to Herodotus (3. 92) Bactria paid an annual tribute of 360 talents of silver to the king of Persia. Reliefs at Persepolis show a Bactrian delegation bringing gold and camels as gifts to the king. The fact that several of Bactria's satraps were relatives of the king of Persia reflects the importance of this province for the Persian empire.

In the Seleucid period Bactria-Sogdiana formed a vast satrapy under one satrap, and was recognized as a wealthy province with valuable resources. In the 230s BC, led by the Greek Diodotus, Bactria revolted against the Seleucids and Diodotus proclaimed himself king. In 206 BC, after a two-year siege, Antiochus III was forced to recognize the Bactrian king Euthydemus. The Greek-Bactrian kingdom survived until 140 BC, when the Saka invaded Bactria, only to be expelled by a new power, the Tocharians, who invaded the country in AD 100.

Little evidence exists to elucidate the influence of Bactrian culture on the Greeks. While new foundations and extensive irrigation systems attest to the emergence of a growing Greek population in Bactria, the nature of the relationship between the local population and the new Greek-Bactrian rulers is difficult to establish. This uncertainty is illustrated by Ai Khanoum, a city of Greek foundation, complete with gymnasium and theatre, whose religious architecture, however, is distinctly oriental. Though Greek artists brought to Bactria much of the Greek style in art and architecture, they gradually assimilated new, local forms and styles. Bactrian Greek art was probably produced for the ruling elite, but must have existed alongside local traditions. Among the new species of plants introduced from Bactria to the Hellenistic world were the pistachio tree, which, according to Theophrastus, grew there (*Historia Plantarum*, 4. 4. 7).

MARIA BROSIUS

Summary

A region of Central Asia, Bactria was annexed to the Persian empire in the 530s BC. Bactrians fought alongside Persians in the invasion of Greece in 480/79 BC. After the Battle of Gaugamela Alexander took up residence at Bactra in 329 BC and put down a Bactrian rebellion. The Greek-Bactrian kingdom survived until 140 BC. A Greek city was built at Ai Khanoum.

Further Reading

Bernard, Paul, "L'Asie centrale et l'empire Séleucide", *Topoi*, 4/2 (1994): pp. 473–511

Boardman, John, *The Diffusion of Classical Art in Antiquity*, London: Thames and Hudson, and Princeton, New Jersey: Princeton University Press, 1994

Bosworth, A.B., *Conquest and Empire: The Reign of Alexander the Great*, Cambridge and New York: Cambridge University Press, 1988

Gardin, Jean Claude and P. Gentelle, "Irrigation et peuplement dans la plaine de Aï-Khanoum de l'époque achéménide à l'époque musulmane", *Bulletin de l'École Française de l'Extrême Orient*, 63 (1976): pp. 59–99

Sherwin-White, Susan and Amélie Kuhrt (editors), *Hellenism in the East: Interaction of Greek and Non-Greek Civilizations from Syria to Central Asia after Alexander*, London: Duckworth, and Berkeley: University of California Press, 1987

Sherwin-White, Susan and Amélie Kuhrt, *From Samarkhand to Sardis: A New Approach to the Seleucid Empire*, London: Duckworth, and Berkeley: University of California Press, 1993

Sims-Williams, N., Bactria entry in *Encyclopaedia Iranica*, edited by Ehsan Yarshater, vol. 3 London and Boston: Routledge, 1989, pp. 339–49

Thompson, D., "Agriculture" in *The Hellenistic World*, edited by F.W. Walbank *et al.*, Cambridge: Cambridge University Press, 1984 (*The Cambridge Ancient History*, vol. 7, part 1, 2nd edition)

Balkan Wars 1912–1913

The Balkan Wars were events of momentous importance to Greece. They mark the beginning of a decade of war and expansion, a decade during which Greece would come very close to the realization of the territorial aspect of the Great Idea. However, the Balkan Wars were also the natural culmination of the Macedonian struggle and one of the last phases of the Eastern Question.

The First Balkan War broke out in October 1912 and ended with the Treaty of London in May 1913. It was the natural outcome of the network of treaties concluded (or, in the case of the Graeco-Serbian treaty, discussed) between Bulgaria, Greece, Montenegro, and Serbia during 1912; the initial moves

| boundaries, August 1913 |
| land ceded under Treaty of Bucharest |
| by Turkey |
| by Bulgaria |

8. The outcome of the Balkan Wars, 1912–13

were made as a result of Russian initiatives, but the events soon moved away from Russian control. The result was a military alliance between Bulgaria, Greece, Montenegro, and Serbia, directed against the Ottoman empire.

Hostilities began in October 1912, following a prearranged schedule whereby Montenegro declared war on the Ottoman empire and the other three Balkan states mobilized and followed suit. During the First Balkan War the numerical superiority of the allies was crushing. What resulted was victory for the allied armies. Greece made quick progress, invading Epirus and Macedonia and advancing rapidly on all fronts. On 26 October 1912 the Ottoman commander of Thessalonica surrendered the city to the Greek army. Greek army units also laid siege to Ioannina, the principal city of Epirus. The Greek navy quickly established superiority in the Aegean, stopping the Ottomans from transporting troops by sea from Anatolia and also liberating the islands of the eastern Aegean Sea. Crete once more proclaimed union with Greece. The other Balkan allies were equally successful; by May 1913 the Great Powers put an end to the conflict, forcing the belligerents to sign the Treaty of London. With this the Ottoman empire ceded all territory west of a line between Enos and Media (both points in eastern Thrace) to the victorious Balkan allies.

The problem facing the allies was now the division of the spoils. The territorial clauses of the Serbo-Bulgarian treaty left territory unassigned, while no territorial clauses had been included in the Graeco–Bulgarian treaty. A further complication arose out of the creation (at the insistence of the Great

Powers) of an independent Albanian state, whose territories figured in the aspirations of the allies. Bulgaria, however, was dissatisfied with the outcome of the war: Bulgaria felt it had borne the brunt of the fighting, while its territorial gains were disproportionate to its contribution; clashes had already begun during the war between Bulgarian and Greek units (with fighting breaking out in Thessalonica and elsewhere) as well as with the Serbs. Fear of Bulgaria led to secret discussions between Serbia and Greece, with a secret treaty signed between the two countries in June 1913. It was a very timely action: within the month the Bulgarians attacked both the Greeks and the Serbs in an attempt to break the front and separate the two armies, thus sparking off the Second Balkan War. The attack failed; Serbia and Greece were soon joined in the war against Bulgaria by the Ottoman empire which seized the chance of recovering territory occupied by Bulgaria (including the city of Adrianople); and by Romania, which invaded Bulgaria from the north. Within a month the war was over. With the Treaty of Bucharest, concluded in August 1913, Bulgaria lost territory to Serbia, Greece, Romania, and the Ottoman empire; it lost the city of Kavalla (which had been given to it after the First Balkan War), though it retained an outlet to the Aegean Sea including the city of Dedeagach (Alexandroupolis).

For Greece, the Balkan Wars were highly successful. Greece acquired the whole of the southern Macedonian lands, most of Epirus (with the exception of the northern part) and the islands of the eastern Aegean including Lemnos, Chios, Lesbos, and Samos as well as Crete; the islands of Imbros and Tenedos (whose population was Greek, although occupied by Greece during the First Balkan War), were put at the disposal of the Great Powers, and were eventually given to Turkey. Greece increased its land area by some 70 per cent and its population rose from 2.8 million to almost 4.8 million. The important cities of Thessalonica (the major port of the Balkans), Kavalla, and Ioannina were incorporated in the kingdom, along with rich and fertile lands. The success of Greece in the war also took it considerably closer to the realization of the Great Idea, though there were now obstacles in further expansion (not least the Bulgarian outlet to the Aegean, which blocked potential Greek eastward expansion towards Constantinople). Greece was also faced with the major problem of the integration of the new territories into the kingdom; this was not easy, given that considerable parts of the population of these territories were non-Greek. The task would be delayed by the outbreak of World War I and would only be completed in the aftermath of the Asia Minor disaster in 1922. The conflict between expansionists and those who advocated integration of the newly acquired lands before further territorial expansion would also be one of the causes that gave rise to the national schism. More generally, the Treaty of Bucharest created a lasting resentment in both Bulgaria and the Ottoman empire, a resentment that would decisively influence their choice of allies in World War I and subsequently.

GEORGE KAZAMIAS

Further Reading

Anderson, M.S., *The Eastern Question, 1774–1923: A Study in International Relations*, London: Macmillan, and New York: St Martin's Press, 1966

Carnegie Endowment for International Peace, *International Commission to Inquire into the Causes and Conduct of the Balkan Wars: Report*, Washington, D.C.: Carnegie Endowment, 1914

Clogg, Richard, *A Concise History of Greece*, Cambridge and New York: Cambridge University Press, 1992

Dakin, Douglas, *The Greek Struggle in Macedonia*, Thessalonica: Institute for Balkan Studies, 1966

Dakin, Douglas, *The Unification of Greece, 1770–1923*, London: Benn, and New York: St Martin's Press, 1972

Thaden, Edward C., *Russia and the Balkan Alliance of 1912*, University Park: Pennsylvania State University Press, 1965

Trotskii, L., *The Balkan Wars 1912–13: The War Correspondence of Leon Trotsky*, New York: Monad Press, 1980

Banking

Banking in Greece is, as M. Rostovtzeff remarks, "as ancient as the use of a coinage issued and guaranteed by the state". The earliest bankers (*trapezites*), the money-changers, sat behind their tables (*trapezai*) in the streets and marketplaces of ancient Greece ready to exchange coins of other cities. If the banking business is loosely defined as the storage of valuables and the lending of money at interest to borrowers, then the first primitive banks of Greece can be considered to be the temples. Since they were recipients of the offerings of the devout and because their sacrosanct character made them ordinarily safe from pillage, it is easy to see how this form of business began. Funds deposited in temples remained untouched and cash was lent from the temples' own funds to states, and also apparently – although the evidence is not certain – to individuals. The temple of the goddess Athena at Athens, for example, lent money to the state between 433 and 427 BC at 6 per cent. It must, however, be emphasized that the temples never operated a general banking business; that was left to private individuals.

The earliest mentioned banker in Greece for whom we have proper evidence is one Philostephanus of Corinth, who received a deposit of the considerable sum of 70 talents from Themistocles. In the 4th century BC we know the names of about 20 Athenian bankers. But banking in ancient Athens was a small private concern, never a great international system, organized and carried on in a modern way. The never-ending wars of ancient Greek cities and the great danger that pirates constituted to foreign trade made international banking impossible. Even among towns in the same state there were no banking facilities. The cheque and the bill of exchange were unknown.

The banking operation in Athens, like nearly all other commercial activities, was performed mainly by metics (people not native to the city). For this reason, bankers were sometimes considered marginal to society. The most famous and wealthy ancient Greek banker was Pasion (d. 370/69 BC), a former slave. Although there were rich and famous bankers, yet money-lending and foreign exchange operations were, to a large extent, carried on by usurers. Interest rates of 30 per cent were not uncommon, especially for loans made to merchants and shipmasters for the furtherance of commercial ventures in overseas trade.

In addition to temples and individuals, some city banks existed (in the case of Athens the evidence is not strong). Miletus, for example, known for its financial strength, instead of having recourse to private bankers or temples for its money transactions, created a state bank. A further step was the establishment of a state bank monopoly.

The banking business, despite its local character and the absence of foreign operations, was relatively well developed in the ancient Greek city states, a characteristic that was later inherited by the banks of the Hellenistic world. One of the new principal features of that period was the rapid spread of city as well as temple banks, the best known of which were those of Cos, Ephesus, and Sardis. Although the evidence is not abundant, we know that temples in the Seleucid empire were highly respected at least in the early times of the dynasty. When, because of financial difficulties, some Seleucid emperors required the surrender of temple wealth, the action provoked a fierce reaction from the citizens because the bulk of the money consisted of private deposits.

The Ptolemaic banking system, on the other hand, assumed a peculiar and unique character. Its chief novelty was the centralization of banking by the creation of a state bank in Alexandria. Private banks played a secondary role in the economic life of Egypt. The Ptolemaic central bank was organized on a Greek pattern and in general was not very different from a regular city bank. Because the bank was an institution whose primary business was the custody and investment of the state's money and sometimes the collection of taxes, the interests of private clients were of secondary concern to it. Given the guarantees needed by the state bank to finance private ventures, individuals in need of money almost certainly had recourse to private banks. As a consequence of its good management, citizens preferred to deposit their money in it. The kings were not opposed to this extension of the activities of the bank as it meant an increase in their income and involved very little risk. In addition to these activities, the bank had dealings in corn, since corn in Egypt was almost an equivalent of money. The government's granaries were effectively a network of corn banks with their centre in Alexandria. They were managed by a special staff, who had the same functions as the bankers; namely, they acted as intermediaries for either state or private corn transactions. The Ptolemaic banking system did not disappear with the rule of the Ptolemies. It was retained with some modifications by the Roman administrators of Egypt and it influenced the Roman and Byzantine system of tax and rent collection.

Byzantium did not have a state bank like the Ptolemaic banking system, either because of the financial fragility of the Byzantine state or for religious reasons, since for Christians it was highly unethical to lend money at interest. The treasury, whose main business was the management of state money and the collection of taxes, effectively performed some of the activities of a central bank. The money market was strictly controlled by the government, in particular by means of measures limiting the rate of interest. In the 4th century the legally permitted interest rate was 12.5 per cent, though this did not mean that a higher rate could not be obtained. Short-term loans for foreign trade that involved higher risks could command more than 50 per cent. The law did not recognize this rate, however, and it could not be enforced in a law court.

It appears that bank credit was often used, particularly for covering the cost of military undertakings, and that taxes under collection were used as security. After Justinian's death in 565, his successor had first to cover the banking debts of his predecessor. One way of dealing with such problems was by confiscating the property of political opponents who had to face prosecution after a change of government. Another characteristic of the Byzantine banking system was that all bankers had to belong to a corporation. This was also true for every important business activity in order for the state to control and tax it effectively.

During the last centuries of Byzantium Constantinople was undeniably the financial centre of the empire, while its bankers, not only Greeks but also Italians and Jews, were the most wealthy and famous inhabitants. It was normal to make loans using foreign currency; these consisted of exchange contracts on which the interest was in fact hidden in the exchange rate established. Cheques or promissory notes began gradually to be used. These were commonly employed by the Latin bankers but were also introduced and largely adopted by the Byzantines. The bankers of the late Byzantine empire, especially those with big foreign and domestic operations, had undeniable economic power, but in contrast with the Latin west they never succeeded in creating real public banks. Despite their ability to handle every known type of financial transaction of their time and to engage in spontaneous business ventures that promised to be profitable, they remained private institutions. The same is true even after the fall of the empire to the Ottomans.

In the first years following the Turkish conquest, Greek bankers had no formal operations because of the expulsions and the absence of any commercial activity, although usury never disappeared. Gradually rich Greeks, Jews, and Armenians began to invest their capital in money lending since the velocity of money circulation in the Ottoman empire was slow and credit was the usual method of payment in trade. These bankers had accumulated their wealth through commerce and were engaged in every economic activity deemed profitable, not only money lending.

In Constantinople the Phanariots provided most of the bankers. They were Greek nobles who had many privileges granted to them by the Porte. They were highly educated and became senior officials of the Ottoman state such as secretaries, interpreters, and ambassadors. The Phanariots had very good relations with the Porte and some of them became bankers to the sultan. The main requirement for anyone desiring to be engaged in banking operations was the availability of capital. But sometimes it could be done even without capital, as was occasionally the case with Albanians who borrowed money from Jewish bankers. The Albanians had no difficulty in raising money for their speculations because they had established themselves as being of good character in their financial affairs.

No particular laws regulated the interest rate, which therefore fluctuated greatly according to the creditworthiness of the borrower and the security posted. Loans to the state had a 10 per cent interest rate; those made to European merchants in Smyrna also had a 10 per cent rate. In Greece the rates varied from 10 to 30 per cent according to the creditworthiness of the customer. Maritime loans, being less secure, bore a higher interest rate, between 17 and 50 per cent, depending on the vessel's destination and the season in which the voyage took place. Bankers' profits were not only derived from the rate charged on loans but also from some arbitrary practices of the Turkish authorities, such as the payment of tax prior to the harvest in order to favour money-lenders. The peasants therefore had no alternative but to borrow money until harvest time and usually on the condition that bankers could buy their produce at a price between 2 and 6 per cent lower than its market value.

At the time of the Greek War of Independence (1821) organized banking facilities in Greece operated only in Thessalonica and the islands of Hydra and Spetsae. The preferred way of transferring large amounts of money as well as financing the purchase of merchandise was the bill of exchange. Bankers advanced loans to traders with security for the commodities and received bills payable over a period ranging from one month to two years. Although in Constantinople the cashing of bills was a common operation, in Athens such facilities did not exist until 1817.

Greek banking during the years of Turkish occupation is characterized by the personal nature of the business and by the absence of banks such as existed in western Europe. This situation gradually changed with the establishment of an independent Greek state. The first bank in Greece was established in 1828 under the name National Financial Bank (Ethniki Chrimatistiki Trapeza). It was a state institution issuing securities on behalf of the Greek government and had no other operations, but it failed to gain confidence and ended its operations about six years later. The second serious attempt, a successful one, was the founding in 1841 of the National Bank of Greece (Ethniki Trapeza tis Ellados). Initially the main operations of the bank were the issuing of currency, the trading of debt securities, and the granting of mortgages. By the end of the century the institution had expanded its operations to all types of transactions and activities related to banking and had become the most important Greek bank, a position that it still holds. A large number of banks were founded during this period, but apart from one or two, most were of a regional or personal character. Because of their inadequate capital base and limited revenues, they failed to survive and either ceased operations or were acquired by the big ones. The main reasons for this development were: the absence of government regulation and intervention, and the tendency of the financial institutions to perform indiscriminately every banking activity without being specialized in core operations.

In December 1927 the Central Bank (Trapeza tis Ellados) was established with its main business being the issuing of currency, a task performed until then mainly by the National Bank of Greece among its other activities. Moreover during this period two other specialized financial institutions were founded, the National Mortgage Bank (Ethniki Ktimatiki Trapeza) in 1927, a former subsidiary of the National Bank of Greece, and the Agricultural Bank (Agrotiki Trapeza) in 1929. These two banks specialized in real estate and agricultural credit respectively, operations that had been performed mainly by the National Bank of Greece. After World War II the transformation of the Greek banking industry continued, with a reversal of the tendency to create small banking units of regional character, as well as with the adoption of modern Western banking practices.

DIMITRIOS GKAMAS

See also Finance, Taxation

Further Reading

Angelomatis-Tsougarakis, Helen, *The Eve of the Greek Revival: British Travellers' Perceptions of Early Nineteenth-Century Greece*, London and New York: Routledge, 1990

Austin, M.M. and P. Vidal-Naquet, *Economic and Social History of Ancient Greece: An Introduction*, Berkeley: University of California Press, and London: Batsford, 1977

Bolkenstein, Hendrik, *Economic Life in Greece's Golden Age*, edited by E.J. Jonkers, Leiden: Brill, 1958

Cavallo, Guglielmo (editor), *The Byzantines*, Chicago: University of Chicago Press, 1997

Cohen, Edward E., *Athenian Economy and Society: A Banking Perspective*, Princeton, New Jersey: Princeton University Press, 1992

Finley, M.I., *Studies in Land and Credit in Ancient Athens, 500–200 BC: The Horos Inscriptions*, New Brunswick, New Jersey: Rutgers University Press, 1951

Finley, M.I., *Economy and Society in Ancient Greece*, London: Chatto and Windus, 1981; New York: Viking, 1982

Finley, M.I., *The Ancient Economy*, updated edition, Berkeley: University of California Press, 1999

French, A., *The Growth of the Athenian Economy*, London: Routledge and Kegan Paul, 1964

Haussing, Hans Wilhelm, *A History of Byzantine Civilization*, London: Thames and Hudson, 1971

Kostis, K. and V. Tsokopoulos, *Oi Trapezes stin Ellada* [The Banks in Greece, 1898–1928], Athens, 1988

Meijer, Fik and Onno van Nijf, *Trade, Transport and Society in the Ancient World: A Sourcebook*, London and New York: Routledge, 1992

Michell, H., *The Economics of Ancient Greece*, 2nd edition, Cambridge: Heffer, 1957

Millett, Paul, *Lending and Borrowing in Ancient Athens*, Cambridge and New York: Cambridge University Press, 1991

Rostovtzeff, M. I., *The Social and Economic History of the Hellenistic World*, 3 vols, Oxford: Clarendon Press, 1941; revised 1953

Siamsiaris, K., *He Elliniki Trapeziki Organosi* [The Hellenic Banking Industry], Athens, 1996

Baptism

The literal meaning of the Greek word *baptizo* is "immerse" or "dip in" and it is in this sense that the word occurs from the time of Hippocrates. In antiquity, however, the word is found in a sacral context only occasionally and did not acquire a technically religious meaning. There are some early examples of sacral baths, such as those found in the Eleusinian cults (5th century BC) and in Bacchic consecrations. Yet the underlying motive of sacral washings in Hellenism is that of bathing, washing, or cleansing. Later on, the notion became spiritualized and ritual immersions acquired in Judaism the meaning of purification. St John the Baptist first gave an eschatological orientation to baptism by relating it to penitence and the forgiveness of sins (cf. Mark 1: 4–8). From then on, the belief became common that a ritual absolution that signified a desire for purity of soul and the forgiveness of sins will be effaced by God in the same manner as corporeal dirt, i.e. by the use of water.

In Christianity baptism occupied a place of utmost significance from the very beginning. In the New Testament baptismal immersion was linked to Christ's death, burial, and resurrection (cf. Romans 6: 3–4). This is the reason why baptism in the early Church took place during the Easter vigil, thus emphasizing its final aim, regeneration and eternal life. Moreover, because baptism is connected with Christ's death, who "died to sin once for all" (Romans 6: 10), it is administered only once. Subsequently, the meaning of baptism was enlarged even further to signify incorporation and integration into the Church.

In the early Church there was a lengthy process of initiation for the catechumens for baptism, which lasted up to three years. However, by the middle of the 2nd century, infant baptism became common practice. Yet the baptismal rite retained the final part of the "catechumenate" and incorporated it into the service. Thus the Orthodox rite begins with the exorcism of Satan and the evil spirits of error, wickedness, idolatry, covetousness, the renunciation of evil, and the confession of faith. Previously all these were pronounced by the adult catechumens before baptism. Since infant baptism was established, that part of the service has been fulfilled by a spiritual guardian or godparent who acts on behalf of the infant. It is popular practice in Greece for the godparent to stand for children only of the same sex, since it is believed that children who have the same spiritual guardian are spiritual kinsmen. Such children are regarded therefore as "brothers" and "sisters" and marriage among them is prohibited. Here spiritual unity becomes the binding element between the two persons, thus emphasizing spiritual kinship as superior to biological. From the time of baptism onwards, the child's "religious education" should ideally be carried out by its godparent, its family, and the Church. At the beginning of the service the priest also asks the godparent the name of the infant. In Greece an infant remains unnamed until the actual day of baptism. Usually Greek children are named after one of their grandparents, thus pointing out the continuity of life even after death and the regeneration of generations.

The baptismal sacrament proper begins with the blessing of the water in a long prayer recited by the priest. The surface of the water is signed with sanctified olive oil and the godparent anoints the infant with this oil. Both water and oil are life-giving substances. Their use in baptism signifies the redemption of matter; they are the medium through which communion with God is achieved.

The priest, invoking the name of the Holy Trinity, baptizes the child by three total immersions and emersions. This triple act symbolizes Christ's three-day burial and resurrection. The baptismal font becomes the tomb in which the baptized is immersed or "buried" and from which he or she is immersed or "raised up", so that he or she may walk in newness of life (cf. Romans 6: 4). The baptismal font, however, is also, in the words of the Church Fathers, the "Divine Womb" whence one receives a new birth. Thus, baptism introduces the Orthodox to a new mode of existence, to a regeneration, and to the transcendence of his or her biological "hypostasis" (cf. J. Zizioulas).

Baptism: 5th-century mosaic of the baptism of Christ, Baptistery of the Orthodox, Ravenna

An essential difference between the Orthodox and western liturgical practices is that in the Orthodox rite the sacraments of baptism and chrismation or confirmation are merged together. Chrismation is the sacrament of Pentecost. For the Orthodox it is not a separate sacrament but the fulfilment of baptism, as indeed Pentecost is for Easter. Through chrismation human nature, purified by baptism, receives the gift of the Holy Spirit. The priest anoints the various parts of the infant's body – forehead, eyes, nostrils, lips, ears, breast, hands, and feet – with chrism (*myron* in Greek). Chrismation is considered to be the "ordination of the laity"; through it the baptized infant becomes a full member of the Christian community.

In the early Church baptism and confirmation were not administered in the church but in a separate place called the *baptisterion* (baptistery). Following chrismation, the newly baptized were dressed in white robes, symbolic of the "newness of life", and were led by the clergy for the celebration of the Eucharist, where they received their first Holy Communion. Today also baptism and confirmation are followed by a procession of the priest, accompanied by the godparent holding the newly baptized infant, round the baptismal font. The fulfilment of baptism and chrismation is found in the Eucharist. For three consecutive Sundays the neophyte will receive the sacrament of Holy Communion. In the early Church the neophytes remained in the church for eight days. This "rite of passage" ended on the eighth day with the washing of the holy chrism, the cutting of the hair, and their return into the world.

Although the above description points to the prevalent form of baptism in Orthodoxy, there also exists what is known as "clinical" baptism. When a person is seriously ill and has not been baptized, then baptism may be administered by any baptized Christian either in the air or by affusion. But such a form of baptism, though necessary in certain circumstances, is considered as imperfect and is administered only by the use of "ecclesiastical economy", i.e. concession or dispensation. The Orthodox also regard the Latin baptism as incomplete, because it is not done by immersion but by sprinkling. Since the middle of the 18th century a big debate has been created in the Orthodox Church on whether western converts should be "rebaptized". It was held that sprinkling alone was inadequate for conveying to the baptized person the regeneration achieved through immersion. The debate still continues today. However, the usual practice – since 1932 when archbishop Chrysostomos I introduced into the Euchologion the "Service of Conversion to Orthodoxy from the Latin Church" – is for baptized Christians of other Churches to be received in Orthodoxy by chrismation alone. Finally, it is worth noting that a symbolic "second baptism" is part of the tonsuring ritual of the monastic profession.

ELENI SOTIRIU

Further Reading

Baptême entry in *Dictionnaire de Spiritualité*, vol. 1, Paris: Beauchesne, 1937

Campbell, J.K., *Honour, Family and Patronage: A Study of Institutions and Moral Values in a Greek Mountain Community*, Oxford: Clarendon Press, 1964

Coniaris, Anthony M., *Introducing the Orthodox Church: Its Faith and Life*, Minneapolis: Light and Life, 1982

Cross, Lawrence, *Eastern Christianity: The Byzantine Tradition*, Philadelphia: Dwyer, 1988

French, R.M., *The Eastern Orthodox Church*, London and New York: Hutchinson, 1951

Kittel, Gerhard (editor), *Theological Dictionary of the New Testament*, vol. 1, Grand Rapids, Michigan: Eerdmans, 1964 (entries at bapto, baptizo, baptismos, baptisma, baptistis)

Metallinos, George D., Fr., *I Confess One Baptism*, Holy Mountain of Athos: St Paul's Monastery, 1994

Schmemann, Alexander, *For the Life of the World: Sacraments and Orthodoxy*, 2nd edition, Crestwood, New York: St Vladimir's Seminary Press, 1973

Schmemann, Alexander, *Of Water and the Spirit: A Liturgical Study of Baptism*, Crestwood, New York: St Vladimir's Seminary Press, 1974

Ware, Timothy, *The Orthodox Church*, 2nd edition, London and New York: Penguin, 1993

Zizioulas, John D., *Being as Communion: Studies in Personhood and the Church*, Crestwood, New York: St Vladimir's Seminary Press, 1985

Barlaam of Calabria *c.*1290–1348

Theologian

A native of Seminara in Calabria, Barlaam had his initial formation in a Greek-rite monastery, perhaps at St Elias of Galatro. There he studied Greek and Latin, the philosophy of Plato and Aristotle, and Western scholasticism. He arrived in Constantinople around 1328, seeking a closer knowledge of both the Byzantine Church and the Hellenic philosophical tradition. Court favour won him a chair in theology and patristic exegesis, and his lectures soon attracted a wide audience, including Gregory Akindynos. His success attracted the rivalry of Nikephoros Gregoras. For a time he taught in Thessalonica, where his pupils included Demetrios Cydones.

Barlaam was the only theologian in the empire deemed capable of dealing with the Dominican legates of pope John XXII sent in 1333. To them he gave an able defence of the single procession of the Holy Spirit from the Father, pointing out that the Latin syllogistic arguments were not strictly apodictic, or demonstrative, according to the definition of Aristotle. It was as this time that his disputes with St Gregory Palamas began, Gregory becoming uneasy with Barlaam's theological method. Barlaam, examining the methods of prayer used by the hesychast monks, found their physical method strange and even scandalous. He began to draw attention to the abuses he perceived, notwithstanding the protestations of Akindynos. Forced to withdraw from the capital, he continued his campaign in Thessalonica, provoking Palamas's first *Triad in Defence of the Holy Hesychasts*.

Returning from an abortive mission to gather support in the West for an anti-Turkish crusade in 1339, Barlaam found Palamas's second *Triad* to which he replied with his *Against the Messalians*. This in turn instigated Palamas's third *Triad*. Again ignoring the counsel of Akindynos, Barlaam formally accused the hesychast party at the Constantinopolitan synod of June 1341. He was soon put on the defensive, his accusations against the hesychast monks being deemed groundless and his explanation of the light of the Transfiguration inconsistent with the patristic witness. With the death of Andronikos III, his patron, Barlaam was almost entirely isolated, and left for the West. He was consecrated bishop of Gerace in Calabria in 1342. He returned to Constantinople only once, in 1346, as leader of a fruitless papal mission to Anne of Savoy that was overtaken by events. He died in 1348.

Barlaam was a prolific writer. Against the Latins he produced 18 works on the procession of the Holy Spirit and 3 on papal primacy. One of his works on the Holy Spirit was directed specifically against Thomas Aquinas. His arguments are chiefly based on philosophical reasoning. His anti-Palamite polemic survives only in fragments, with some further information contained in his surviving letters. He was accused of denying that God really differs from his operations and teaching that the light of the Transfiguration was created. After his return to the West, Barlaam also produced Catholic apologetic. His *Reply to Demetrios Cydones*, which is edited, is a good example. Less well known are his philosophical and scientific works. He composed a work on Stoic ethics, and addressed a series of philosophical solutions to George Lapithos, the Cypriot scholar. Lastly we must mention his works on astronomy, his highly regarded works on algebra and arithmetic, and his treatise on the celestial harmonies in music.

Barlaam has been ill-served by posterity. His reputation in the East has been blackened out of recognition. In the West he has been seen as overly vacillating. Palamite sources have characterized him as a Western stooge or fifth columnist. This is unfair. Barlaam was certainly familiar with Western scholasticism, but exhibited no great sympathy for it in his Byzantine period. His treatise against Thomas Aquinas demonstrates this. In fact, up to 1341 he was a more committed anti-Unionist than was Palamas. Barlaam's theological method was greatly influenced by Aristotelian argument. He was also well versed in Plato and the traditions of Neoplatonism. He was particularly indebted to Dionysius the Areopagite.

Barlaam's influence has naturally been restricted by the canonization of Palamite theology. Even the anti-Palamite faction of Akindynos repudiated him. Barlaam did, however, retain a small circle of supporters in Byzantium, the most notable of them being Demetrios Cydones, the Byzantine Thomist. His anti-Latin works may have furnished some material for the anti-Unionist party in the last hundred years of the Byzantine empire. Equally, his Catholic apologetic appears, through Cydones, to have influenced the Unionist party.

MARCUS PLESTED

See also Gregory Palamas, Hesychasm

Biography

Born at Seminara in Calabria *c.*1290, Barlaam became a monk in Italy and studied the ancient philosophers as well as Western scholasticism. He moved to Constantinople *c.*1328 where he became a professor of theology and patristic exegesis. His attacks on hesychasm and St Gregory Palamas divided the Church and Barlaam returned to the West where he became Bishop of Gerace in 1342. He died in 1348, perhaps at Avignon.

Further Reading

Jugie, M., Barlaam de Seminara entry in *Dictionnaire d'histoire et de géographie ecclésiastiques*, Paris: Letouzey & Ané, 1912–

Meyendorff, John, "Un mauvais théologien de l'unité au XIVe siècle: Barlaam le Calabrais" in *L'Église et les églises: neuf siècles de douloureuse séparation entre l'Orient et l'Occident*, edited by Lambert Beauduin, vol. 2, Chevetogne: Éditions de Chevetogne, 1955

Sinkewicz, R.E., "The Doctrine of the Knowledge of God in the Early Writings of Barlaam the Calabrian", *Medieval Studies*, 44 (1982): pp. 181–242

Basil I *c*.830–886

Emperor

The figure of Basil I (867–86) is prominent in Byzantine history because he was the founder of the so-called Macedonian dynasty, which lasted from 867 until the death in 1056 of its last representative, the empress Theodora. Basil had risen to power as a favourite of the emperor Michael III (842–67) of the Amorian dynasty, and seems to have been of humble origin, a fact reflected in both the panegyrical *Vita Basilii* and the hostile Logothete chronicle tradition. As the son of peasants Basil was not the recipient of an elite education, and as emperor he seems to have been intellectually primarily dependent on Photios. On his accession to sole power in 867 Basil had at first removed Photios from the patriarchate and exiled him, only to recall him to the palace and later re-establish him as patriarch in 878, which position Photios still held on Basil's death in 886.

Photios is well known as the explicit source of the crucial cultural monuments of the 9th century, such as the *Bibliotheca*, his letter of advice to the recent Christian convert Boris of Bulgaria, and his own collection of homilies. Photios's hand can also be detected in other endeavours designed with the Macedonian dynasty in mind, such as the illustrated manuscript of the homilies of Gregory of Nazianzus (Paris, Bibliothèque Nationale, gr. 510), which contains portraits of Basil, his wife Eudokia Ingerine, and their sons Leo and Alexander.

Basil's name is, however, attached to the two parainetic texts from his reign, written as if by him to his son and heir Leo VI. Of these two texts the first and earlier is the better known. They are inspired by previous examples of the genre of advice such as Isocrates' *To Nicocles* and *To Demonicus*, but most notably by the 6th-century *Ekthesis* of Agapetus, deacon of Hagia Sophia, which was addressed to the emperor Justinian I (527–65). They probably date from 879 and 886 respectively, the first on Leo's elevation to the position of heir apparent, the second on his restoration as heir apparent following his disgrace and confinement. Given Basil's lack of literary ability it is unlikely that he was the real author of the texts, and Photios's hand again has been suggested, especially for the *First Parainesis*. This text is closest to the model of Agapetus. It is divided into distinct chapters, having 66 compared to the 72 of the *Ekthesis*. The acrostic device used by Agapetus is also used,

spelling out the message *Basil Emperor of the Romans in Christ for His Beloved Son and Co-emperor Leo*. Unlike the work of Agapetus, each chapter is given an individual heading, setting out its theme. The second text is much shorter, has no acrostic, and is not subdivided into topics, but again consists of the typical ideological and moralistic reflections, and exploits in particular the Old Testament Wisdom literature. The texts together reflect the vogue for parainetic and didactic texts, but more particularly for the achievements of the age of Justinian – reflected in the art of the reign (triumphal images of Basil recalling those commemorating the military victories that marked the reign of Justinian) but especially in the interest in, and production of, legislation under Basil.

The main project of Basil's reign was the endeavour to revise and produce the essential version (in Greek) of the Roman *Corpus Juris Civilis*, that is, the collection of legal texts issued under Justinian, namely the *Institutes*, *Digest*, *Codex*, and his own *Novels* (these were issued in Greek from the beginning). This exercise, resulting in 60 books, seems to have been completed under Leo VI (886–912), and became known as the *Basilika*, or the imperial laws. As a preliminary and introductory volume to the *Basilika* there appeared under Basil, Leo, and Alexander (912–13) the *Epanagoge* (or rather *Eisagoge*); here too Photios's hand can be detected, for it seems likely that he contributed the preface and the individual titles on the emperor and the patriarch. The *Procheiron* (a practical law book drawing on the *Institutes* and the *Ecloga* of Leo III (716–41), issued in the names of Basil, Constantine – Basil's eldest son, who predeceased him in 879 – and Leo), has been identified by Schminck as a later reworking of the *Epanagoge* by Leo VI, though some (e.g. Lokin) would still see it as an authentic Basilian text.

Thus, as far as the Hellenic tradition goes, Basil himself was not such an active figure; his virtue is that he provides the opportunity for others. Indeed one could say that Basil's career and circumstances provided the greatest inspiration. He was of low origin, his accession as emperor was not without scandal, and as such he needed much ideological weight thrown behind him. Thus poets, writers, orators, intellectuals, artists, and builders (not just Photios) were inspired to come to his aid and create a very special atmosphere in the 9th and 10th centuries. Basil is the focus of such celebratory works as poems by Photios, the *Epitaphios* of Leo VI, the *Vita Basilii* commissioned by Constantine VII Porphyrogennetos (913–59), and Basil's own important ecclesiastical foundation the Nea Ekklesia ("new church"). This latter was Basil's major ecclesiastical foundation, built within the Great Palace and dedicated in 880. The richly decorated five-domed church had as its divine dedicatees Christ, the prophet Elijah (Basil's particular divine patron it seems), the archangel Michael (perhaps originally Gabriel), the Virgin and St Nicholas. Basil's building projects are recorded most extensively in the *Vita Basilii*. These entailed the repair and restoration of many of the late-Antique churches of Constantinople (including Hagia Sophia, the Holy Apostles, and St Mokios), and also the construction of new structures, especially in the imperial palace itself, which in addition to the Nea Ekklesia included a courtyard with fountains, porticoes enclosing a garden, a polo ground (the Tzykanisterion), and imperial apartments. The most famous of the apartments is the Kainourgion which was decorated with mosaics, including depictions of the emperor and his labours, his generals and their military successes, and the imperial family.

All these projects aspired to present Basil as a God-favoured emperor, whether as a new David or a direct descendant of both Alexander the Great and Constantine the Great. It was the creation and establishment of a new dynasty that provided the impetus for the literary, artistic, architectural, and legal projects of the age, and this is the cultural legacy of Basil I.

SHAUN TOUGHER

Biography

Born of humble stock in Thrace or Macedonia c.830, Basil achieved power as a favourite of Michael III. On Michael's murder in 867 Basil became emperor and founder of the Macedonian dynasty. During his reign his armies campaigned in the east and in Italy, but his main project was the attempt to revise and codify the law. He died in Constantinople in 886 after a hunting accident.

Further Reading

Agapitos, P.A., "I Eikona tou Avtokratora Basileiou A' sti Philomakedoniki Grammateia 867–959" [The Portrait of Emperor Basil I in Pro-Macedonian Literature 867–959], *Hellenika*, 40 (1989): pp. 285–322

Brubaker, Leslie, "Politics, Patronage, and Art in Ninth-Century Byzantium: The *Homilies* of Gregory of Nazianzus in Paris (BN gr. 510)", *Dumbarton Oaks Papers*, 39 (1985): pp. 1–13

Brubaker, Leslie, (editor), *Byzantium in the Ninth Century: Dead or Alive?*, Aldershot, Hampshire: Ashgate, 1998

Bury, J.B., *A History of the Eastern Roman Empire from the Fall of Irene to the Accession of Basil I, AD 802–867*, London: Macmillan, 1912; reprinted New York: Russell, 1965

Lokin, J.H.A., "The Significance of Law and Legislation in the Law Books of the Ninth to Eleventh Centuries" in *Law and Society in Byzantium, 9th–12th Centuries*, edited by Angeliki E. Laiou and Dieter Simon, Washington, D.C.: Dumbarton Oaks, 1994

Magdalino, P., "Observations on the Nea Ekklesia of Basil I", *Jahrbuch der Österreichischen Byzantinistik*, 37 (1987): pp. 51–64

Maguire, H., "The Art of Comparing in Byzantium", *Art Bulletin*, 70/1 (1988): pp. 88–103

Markopoulos, A., "An Anonymous Laudatory Poem in Honor of Basil I", *Dumbarton Oaks Papers*, 46 (1992): pp. 225–32

Moravcsik, G., "Sagen und Legenden über Kaiser Basilius I", *Dumbarton Oaks Papers*, 15 (1961): pp. 59–126

Schminck, Andreas, *Studien zu mittelbyzantinischen Rechtsbüchern*, Frankfurt: Lowenklau, 1986

Schminck, Andreas, "'Frömmigkeit ziere das Werk': Zur Datierung der 60 Bücher Leons VI", *Subseciva Groningana*, 3 (1989): pp. 79–114

Tougher, Shaun, *The Reign of Leo VI, 886–912*, Leiden and New York: Brill, 1997

Vogt, Albert, *Basile Ier empereur de Byzance (867–886) et la civilisation byzantine à la fin du 9e siècle*, Paris: Picard, 1908

Basil II 958–1025

Emperor

Basil II (976–1025) is generally considered the greatest of all the Byzantine emperors. He was a successful military leader whose campaigns brought the empire to its greatest geograph-ical extent. He spent much of his early life under the regency of his mother, the empress Theophano, and a series of military strongmen. Upon the death of John I Tzimiskes (969–76) Basil, now 18, decided to assert his rights to the throne. Bardas Skleros, the former *domestikos* (commander) of the east under John Tzimiskes, rose up to challenge him. By 978 he had seized control of most of Asia Minor. Basil Lekapenos, the grand chamberlain, turned to Bardas Phokas for help against Skleros. At Pankaleia in 979 Phokas defeated first Skleros in a single combat and then his entire army. Despite Basil's success, power continued to be exercised by Lekapenos until his exile in 985, after which the emperor assumed total control of the government. Basil's brother, Constantine VIII, showed little interest in ruling and spent most of his time in extravagant pleasures. Later, in 987, after Basil's defeat by the Bulgarians at Trajan's Gates, the nobility rose up against him, the chief leaders being Bardas Skleros and Bardas Phokas. Both rebels had widespread support among the senior officers of the army and the landed nobility. Originally Phokas and Skleros agreed to share the empire between them, but later Phokas had Skleros arrested and, having brought all of Asia Minor under his control, prepared to attack Constantinople. Basil was only able to defeat Phokas with the help of Vladimir I of Kiev, who sent 6000 troops to support him. These troops would later become the nucleus of the famous Varangian Guard. In return for his timely aid, Basil gave his sister Anna to Vladimir in marriage, an act that also led to the conversion of Russia to Orthodox Christianity.

The revolts of Phokas and Skleros had a lasting impact on Basil and he continued to be suspicious of the military aristocracy. As a result he decided, in 996, to restrict the power of the *dynatoi* by issuing new legislation on the alienation of soldiers' land. He repealed Nikephoros Phokas's earlier legislation which limited monastic landholding, mainly because he felt this law worked more in the interests of the landowning class, and issued new regulations restricting monastic lands. Small houses of eight monks or fewer that stood on peasant land were subordinate to the village community but exempt from paying tribute to the bishop, while larger houses were made subordinate to the bishop but could make no new acquisitions of land. Basil also decreed that all property acquired by the *dynatoi* (notables) from the poor since the time of Romanos I Lekapenos (920–44) should be returned without any compensation. The state claimed a right of eviction on all land that had been under state control as far back as the time of Augustus. Later he made the *dynatoi* responsible for the outstanding tax payments of the peasantry. Despite his efforts the *dynatoi* continued to be powerful and many noble families who figure prominently in later Byzantine history could trace their origins back to Basil's reign.

Basil spent a good part of his reign waging war against Bulgaria, which had become a serious threat again under the leadership of Samuel, who established his capital at Ohrid. At first, Basil was unsuccessful, being defeated by the Bulgarians at Trajan's Gates in 986. He returned in 991, but war with the Fatimids in Syria forced him to turn his attention elsewhere. In 1001, after concluding a peace treaty with the Fatimids, Basil returned again to Bulgaria. One of the most infamous incidents of this war followed his victory at Kleidion in 1014: he had thousands of Bulgarian prisoners of war blinded and then sent

Basil II: frontispiece of an 11th-century psalter showing Basil triumphant over the defeated Bulgarians, Biblioteca Marciana, Venice

them back to their king, Samuel, who purportedly died from the shock of seeing so horrific a sight. The war finally concluded with the capture of Ohrid in 1018. Basil's successful conquest of Bulgaria earned him the title "Bulgaroktonos" (Bulgar Slayer). He next extended Byzantine control over Croatia and Serbia. In the east he organized the kingdom of David of Tayk'/Tao into the theme of Iberia and in 1022 incorporated the kingdom of Vaspurakan into another theme. Basil also offered a marriage alliance to the German emperor Otto III between Otto and Basil's neice Zoe; however, Otto died before the marriage could take place. Basil's future military plans called for the reconquest of Sicily and war with the Western empire, but he did not live to carry out these projects. Because of his preoccupation with warfare, he treated scholars with disdain and consequently his reign witnessed a decline in intellectual and creative activity. Basil never married and died in Constantinople on 15 December 1025. He was succeeded by his brother Constantine VIII.

JOHN F. SHEAN

Biography

Born in 958, Basil succeeded John I Tzimiskes in 976, but until 985 power was exercised by Basil Lekapenos. Having defeated the rebellions of Bardas Phokas and Bardas Skleros, Basil curbed the rights of wealthy landowners. After several campaigns he conquered Bulgaria and earned the nickname "Bulgar Slayer". In the east he defeated the Georgians and planned the (unrealized) reconquest of Sicily. He died in 1025.

Further Reading

Felix, Wolfgang, *Byzanz und die islamische Welt im früheren 11. Jahrhundert*, Vienna: Akademie der Wissenschaften, 1981

Psellos, Michael, *Chronographie*, edited with French translation by Émile Renauld, 2 vols, Paris: Belles Lettres, 1926–28

Schlumberger, Gustave, *L'Épopée byzantine à la fin du dixième siècle*, 3 vols, revised edition, Paris: Boccard, 1925

Scylitzes, John, *Synopsis Historiarum*, edited by J. Thurn, Berlin and New York: de Gruyter, 1973 (*Corpus Fontium Historiae Byzantinae*, vol. 5)

Basil the Great, St c.330–379

Christian writer

The "Cappadocian father" who made the greatest impact in his lifetime, Basil was the younger brother of St Macrina (the younger) and the elder brother of St Gregory of Nyssa. Growing up in a prosperous and cultured Christian family, he benefited from an extensive and extended education that left him with a knowledge not only of Christian writers but also of a range of Classical Greek philosophical and literary figures. Caesarea in his native Cappadocia saw the start of this education, and lengthy study followed in Constantinople and Athens. His university life in Athens was marked by the breadth and depth of his studies and by a somewhat austere regime of work and church attendance. Here he set himself mastery of pagan as well as Christian authors, sharing his enthusiasm with Gregory of Nazianzus, to become a lifelong friend, and also with Julian, later as emperor to abandon Christianity and with it Basil's friendship. Partly under the

influence of the formidable and very talented Macrina, Basil abandoned a promising secular career in rhetoric, turning to monastic seclusion, briefly in Syria and Egypt, before settling to an eremitical life in Neocaesarea in 358. This was not a totally solitary existence, since he was joined by his friend Gregory with whom he undertook preaching expeditions in the surrounding countryside. This pattern was to be broken around 364 when the recognition of a basic talent brought him into active life in Caesarea. Its bishop, Eusebius, felt himself under extreme pressure from the emperor Valens who had taken up a marked Arian stance. Seeing in Basil a man who had not only maintained a firm Nicene orthodoxy but one who possessed outstanding powers of expression and determined character and, as it turned out, clear gifts of leadership, Eusebius summoned him to the defence of his Church against the stringent demands of the emperor. Working closely with his bishop, the newly ordained Basil rapidly made himself indispensable, gaining recognition as the natural successor to the see. Succeed Eusebius he did in 370, beginning a decade of administrative brilliance in a time of theological and ecclesiastical turmoil. The Arian ideas championed by Valens took on new forms in the teachings of Eunomius, while the divinity of the Holy Spirit was attacked by the Pneumatomachian party. Basil's opposition was vigorous in speech and writing. He did not live to see the Council of Constantinople (381), but his contributions to its definitive statements of orthodox belief are manifest.

It was not only unorthodox belief that occupied Basil. When it came to Church affairs he was no less capable of taking a strong line, even when it meant conflict with Rome and Alexandria over the appointment of the bishop of Antioch. Nor was he averse from exerting influence in political affairs. Having begun at the top with his confrontation with Valens, he would tackle provincial governors and imperial administrators on issues that he felt involved social justice or Church autonomy. His social concerns combined with his sense of ecclesiastical power, as he established a whole complex of social services, centred on buildings instituted as hospitals and refuges from poverty, setting up schemes for famine relief and poor relief programmes that would outlive him. A whole new Caesarea grew up, to the disapproval of some who wanted a more church-centred bishop, but strongly defended by others such as Nazianzen who saw here a vital expression of Christian concern, a proper complement to the vigorous sermons preached by Basil. The style might draw on the rhetorical practices of his youth in its telling use of standard figures, but it is saved from formalism by the liveliness of his insights and the pastoral concern evinced for his large and eager congregations. Whether he is expounding, against all comers, the Christian doctrine of creation, as in the *hexaemeron* sermons of 370, preached before he became bishop, or interpreting psalms or events in the liturgical year or again attempting to explain the nature of Christian duty and restraint, Basil emerges as a powerful expositor. He is equally effective in his numerous letters. When collected, they became recognized as literary models, yet content outweighs form, since the letters express deep feeling for friends, consolation for loss, commendation of perceived merit, alongside official correspondence dealing with behaviour in Church affairs and letters, sometimes of treatise length, setting out his understanding of the Nicene faith and its legitimate development in terms of the Holy Spirit and the Trinity. His writing of sermons and letters was in competition for Basil's time not only with his episcopal administrative duties but also with the production of his strictly theological works. His lifelong adhesion to Nicene orthodoxy came out in 360 in his attack on the extreme Arian stance of Eunomius. The work by which he is probably best known is *On the Holy Spirit*, dedicated to his friend Amphilochius of Iconium.

The interest shown in correspondence with contemporaries who were not Christians is echoed in Basil's continued concern with Classical Greek literature. His awareness of his Christian past may be exemplified in the edition of selections of Origen's works that he produced in collaboration with Gregory of Nazianzus under the title *Philokalia*, yet he never lost interest in the writings of the Classical centuries, as he demonstrates in a treatise setting out educational principles on which young Christians may be encouraged to explore certain authors who predate Christianity. Written probably in his final years, this *Address* displays an understandable mixture of openness and caution. His young readers would be encouraged to range over poets from Homer to Euripides and to give thought to the works of Plato. Basil had seen Julian's attempt to place Christians on the cultural sidelines by banning them from teaching the Classics, a move he had passionately opposed. Yet he maintains a certain moral austerity, calling for concentration by his students on examples of excellence of character.

In the midst of this multifarious activity, Basil did not abandon another of his youthful enthusiasms, a yearning for the ascetic life. Amazingly, alongside a life of varied and apparently exhausting activity, he maintained a monastic vocation, having formulated in his early days alongside Nazianzen some 80 rules for right Christian conduct, the *Moralia*, applicable to all Christians prepared to follow ascetic practice within daily life, but especially focusing on the monastery. Later, Basil set out in detail in the *Asceticon*, the "Rule of St Basil", as it is widely known, a comprehensive understanding, in question and answer form, of the fundamentals of monastic life. Strict, without the vitiation of extremes, the Rules point to a life that was to become standard. Limited means, manual work, and study were to be set within a pattern of liturgical practice within a community life that enjoined obedience and chastity. This life, however, was not to be self-regarding. The bishop of social and educational concerns is visible in the monastic injunctions to relieve poverty and take part in training children. His emphasis on worship may also be traced in the "Liturgy of St Basil", partly attributable to him.

Any one of Basil's activities might have seemed sufficient to occupy a full life: their combination is astonishing. His influence continued in theological development, in educational practice through the Byzantine centuries into the Renaissance, and, perhaps most visibly, in the dominance of his Rule both in the East, where it remains central to this day, and in the West where, through the mediation of Rufinus, John Cassian, and most notably St Benedict, it had a profound effect. Basil is visible also in another sense, in that his stature as "the Great" was recognized in portraiture, where he is pictured as an elderly bishop, though he died around the age of 50, or with the attribute of a dove, interesting in a man whose career was far from totally eirenic. Representations of Basil occurred

notably in Constantinople, on Mount Athos, in Sinai, and in Ochrid in Macedonia.

D.A. SYKES

See also Cappadocia, Gregory of Nazianzus, Gregory of Nyssa

Biography

Born *c.*330 at Caesarea in Cappadocia, Basil was the brother of both St Gregory of Nyssa and St Macrina the Younger. Educated in Athens and Constantinople, he became the lifelong friend of St Gregory of Nazianzus. Abandoning rhetoric, he devoted himself to the ascetic life and in 370 became bishop of Caesarea. Surviving works include sermons, letters, a treatise *On the Holy Spirit*, an essay on pagan literature, and the *Asceticon* (his monastic rule). He died probably in 379.

Writings

The Ascetic Works, translated by W.K. Lowther Clarke, London: SPCK, and New York: Macmillan, 1925

The Letters, translated by Roy J. Deferrari, 3 vols, London: Heinemann, and Cambridge, Massachusetts: Harvard University Press, 1926–39 (Loeb edition)

In *Mosaïques: anthologie des Sources Chrêtiennes*, edited by Louis Doutreleau, Paris: Cerf, 1993 (texts and French translations)

Letters and Select Works, translated by B. Jackson, vol. 8 of *Nicene and Post-Nicene Fathers*, 2nd series, edited by Philip Schaff and Henry Wace, reprinted Peabody, Massachusetts: Hendrickson, 1994

Further Reading

Armstrong, A.H. (editor), *Cambridge History of Later Greek and Early Medieval Philosophy*, London: Cambridge University Press, 1967, chapter 29

Callahan, J.F., "Greek Philosophy and the Cappadocian Cosmology", *Dumbarton Oaks Papers*, 12 (1958): pp. 29–57

Campenhausen, Hans von, *The Fathers of the Greek Church*, London: A. & C. Black, 1963, chapter 7

Clarke, W.K. Lowther, *St. Basil the Great: A Study in Monasticism*, Cambridge: Cambridge University Press, 1913

Fedwick, P.J., *The Church and the Charisma of Leadership in Basil of Caesarea*, Toronto: Pontifical Institute of Mediaeval Studies, 1978

Fedwick, P.J. (editor), *Basil of Caesarea: Christian, Humanist, Ascetic: A Sixteen-Hundredth Anniversary Symposium*, 2 vols, Toronto: Pontifical Institute of Mediaeval Studies, 1981

Gregg, Robert C., *Consolation Philosophy: Greek and Christian Paideia in Basil and the Two Gregories*, Cambridge, Massachusetts: Philadelphia Patristic Foundation, 1975

Grillmeier, Aloys, *Christ in Christian Tradition*, vol. 1, 2nd edition, London: Mowbray, and Atlanta: John Knox Press, 1975

Hanson, R.P.C., *The Search for the Christian Doctrine of God: The Arian Controversy, 318–381*, Edinburgh: Clark, 1988

Meredith, Anthony, *The Cappadocians*, London: Geoffrey Chapman, and Crestwood, New York: St Vladimir's Seminary Press, 1995

Morison, E.F., *St. Basil and His Rule: A Study in Early Monasticism*, London and New York: Oxford University Press, 1912

Otis, Brooks, "Cappadocian Thought as a Coherent System", *Dumbarton Oaks Papers*, 12 (1958): pp. 95–124

Pelikan, Jaroslav, *Christianity and Classical Culture: The Metamorphosis of Natural Theology in the Christian Encounter with Hellenism*, New Haven and London: Yale University Press, 1993

Quasten, Johannes, *Patrology*, vol. 3: *The Golden Age of Greek Patristic Literature from the Council of Nicaea to the Council of Chalcedon*, Utrecht: Spectrum, and Westminster, Maryland: Newman Press, 1960

Stead, Christopher, *Philosophy in Christian Antiquity*, Cambridge and New York: Cambridge University Press, 1994

Wilson, Nigel G. (editor), *Saint Basil on the Value of Greek Literature*, London: Duckworth, 1975

Beirut

City in Phoenicia

Archaeological evidence of occupation on the site of Beirut goes back to Neolithic times. The earliest mention of the name occurs in the Amarna letters (1377–1360 BC). After Alexander the Great had conquered the Near East, the city was Hellenized under the rule of the Ptolemaic and Seleucid dynasties. The Roman emperor Augustus settled veterans on the site, and around 14 BC Beirut (Latin Berytus) received the status of a Roman colony. Henceforth it was an island of Latin culture in the Greek Near East.

Beirut owed not a few of the monumental buildings that marked it as a Graeco-Roman city to the patronage of king Herod of Judaea and his descendants. The religion of Beirut had a Graeco-Roman superstructure built on Semitic foundations. Poseidon/Neptune, the principal deity, was probably a Hellenized version of Baal Markod. The patron goddess of the city, Aphrodite/Venus, who was worshipped in a temple of Roman design, was probably Astarte in Graeco-Roman guise.

Beirut was a trading city known for its silk and purple dyeing. Around AD 238 the school of Roman law is mentioned for the first time. Gregory Thaumaturgus, later to be a famous missionary bishop, was a student. In the 4th century many young men who were hoping to make a career in the imperial service or the courts enrolled to study Roman law. At the time the sophist Libanius was worried that the competition of professional studies in Latin and law would replace the traditional rhetorical education based on the study of Greek literature. In the end his fear proved groundless. The latest known public inscription from Beirut written in Latin dates from AD 344. In the 5th century Greek became the language of instruction at the law school. From the prefecture of Cyrus (AD 439–42) praetorian prefects issued their edicts in Greek. In the 5th and early 6th centuries some very well-known jurists taught at Beirut, two of them members of the commission set up by Justinian to compile the *Corpus Iuris Civilis*. With the publication of the Code legal education was restricted to the schools in Constantinople, Rome, and Beirut.

By the 3rd century Christianity was well established at Beirut. Theodosius II gave it the status of an ecclesiastical metropolis, which it retained after the Council of Chalcedon (451), although by then it no longer had any suffragan sees subordinated to it. At this time Beirut, like much of Phoenicia, still had numerous practising pagans. Zacharias of Mytilene has left a vivid account of how sometime around 480 a group of Christian student activists organized a search for manuals of magic among fellow students, including at least one Christian, with a view to forcing their owners to surrender them. The books are said to have been works of Zoroaster, Ostanes, and Manetho, and their magic, though potentially capable of achieving a wide range of wicked purposes, appears to have been employed chiefly to further sexual relations and to find hidden treasure. It was claimed that a human sacrifice was being planned and that ownership of magical literature was much more widespread than had been suspected at first. Leadership of the campaign was taken over by the bishop. A popular rising in defence of the books and their owners was defeated with the help of a band of peasants brought in from the countryside. The books were burnt in the presence of the civil authorities. A pagan professor of law named Leontius was sent into exile until he converted to Christianity.

Beirut suffered a disastrous earthquake in 551 when 300,000 inhabitants are said to have been killed, though archaeological evidence suggests that not all the city was destroyed. According to the contemporary historian Agathias, the teaching of law resumed after the city had been rebuilt, but there are no later references to the law school. After the city was captured by the Arabs in 635, Muslims gradually formed the majority of the population, but the city contined to have Christian communities: Melkites, Monophysites, and, from the late 7th century, Maronites. Beirut was taken and held briefly by the emperor John I Tzimiskes in 975.

J.H.W.G. LIEBESCHUETZ

Summary

Beirut (Latin Berytus) was first Hellenized under the Ptolemaic and Seleucid dynasties. Augustus made it a Roman colony and it remained Latin-speaking until the 4th century. The city was famous for its school of Roman law, established c.AD 238 and still flourishing in the 6th century, and for its silk and purple dyeing. It fell to the Arabs in 635.

Further Reading

Butcher, K. and R. Thorpe, "A Note on Excavations in Central Beirut 1994–96", *Journal of Roman Archaeology*, 10 (1997): pp. 291–306

Collinet, Paul, *Histoire de l'école de droit de Beyrouth*, Paris: Société Anonyme du Recueil Sirey, 1925

Hall, L.J., "Latinitas in the Late Antique Greek East: Cultural Assimilation and Ethnic Distinction" in *Essays in Honor of Anna Lydia Motto and John R. Clark*, edited by F. Byrne and E. Cueva, Wauconda, Illinois: Bolchazy-Carducci, 1999

Jidejian, Nina, *Beirut through the Ages*, Beirut: Dar el-Machreq, 1973

Korolevskij, C., Beyrouth entry in *Dictionaire d'histoire et de géographie écclésiastiques*, vol. 8, Paris: Letouzey & Ané, 1935: pp. 1300–40

Lauffray, J., "Beyrouth, archéologie et histoire, époques gréco-romaines, 1: Période hellénistique et haute-empire romaine" in *Aufstieg und Niedergang der römischen Welt*, edited by Hildegard Temporini *et al.*, 2.8, Berlin: de Gruyter, 1978

Liebeschuetz, W., Berytus entry in *Reallexikon für Antike und Christentum Supplement* (forthcoming)

Zacharias of Mytilene, *Vie de Sevère*, edited and translated by M.A. Kugener, Paris: Firmin Didot, 1903 (Syriac with French translation)

Zacharias of Mytilene, *The Life of Severus*, translated by R.A. Darling Young, in *Ascetic Behavior in Greco-Roman Antiquity: A Sourcebook*, edited by Vincent L. Wimbush, Minneapolis: Fortress Press, 1990

Berlin, Treaty of 1878

The Congress of Berlin, held in Berlin in June 1878, resulted in the treaty of Berlin. The congress and the treaty signalled Europe's readiness to involve itself more deeply in Balkan affairs. The terms of the treaty, while intended to impose a measure of stability on the peninsula, in fact set the stage for the violent conflicts that would devastate the area in the decades to come. For both these reasons, the treaty of Berlin has been called the single most important agreement for the Balkan nations of the 19th century. For Greece the consequences of the treaty were deeply negative. It was forced to accept a new state on its northern border, Bulgaria, that was directly competitive with it in Macedonia. Up to this time Greece had always assumed that it would be the beneficiary of any Ottoman retreat from the Balkans. After the treaty of Berlin this could no longer be taken for granted.

Although the decisions taken by the congress were of the utmost importance to the people of the Balkans, it was very much a meeting of the Great Powers and was intended to serve their interests. None of the Balkan states was allowed to participate fully in the proceedings, and they had to limit themselves to sending representatives who were permitted only to present their arguments. In no case were these arguments able to alter a major decision. The Great Powers – Britain, Russia, Austria-Hungary, and Germany – were concerned first and foremost to restore the European balance of power which had been upset by Russia's backing of a greater Bulgaria. The establishment of the new state of Bulgaria was a direct result of the troubled decade of the 1870s.

After 40 years of relative quiet the Balkans endured a protracted and peninsula-wide upheaval during the 1870s. Beginning with a peasant rebellion in Bosnia and Hercegovina in the summer of 1875 that refused to go away, the Great Powers – particularly Austria-Hungary and Russia – became increasingly concerned that the status quo could no longer be preserved. In the summer of 1876, as Serbian and Montenegrin forces began to invade Bosnia-Hercegovina, Russia and Austria-Hungary agreed to the following: if the Balkan armies were defeated, then Russia and Austria-Hungary would work together to maintain the status quo. Should they be victorious, then together, again, these two powers would partition the Ottoman empire but with the proviso that no great Balkan state should be established.

In the end Russia abandoned this rather hands-off approach. Spurred on by the disastrous performance of the Serbian military as well as the unwillingness of the Ottoman government to allow interference in the affairs of Bosnia-Hercegovina, in April 1877 Russia declared war on the Ottoman empire. Russian willingness to take on the Ottomans would give it extra leverage vis-à-vis the other great powers when the war was over, leverage that it would use to support its new client, Bulgaria. The Russo-Turkish war presented all the Balkan states, Greece among them, with an agonizing choice. Greece was well aware that Russia had plans for a Bulgarian state and it was afraid that, if it fought, the end result might be to wrest territory from the Ottomans only to give it to the Slavs. On the other hand, if it refrained from entering, it could well be left out of a peace settlement. By entering the war at the very last minute in February 1878,

Greece got the worst of both worlds: it angered Britain, who had not wanted it to enter the conflict, but did not give any appreciable help to the Russians, who could thus disregard it.

Taking advantage of its victory over the Ottomans, Russia signed a bilateral treaty with the sultan in March 1878. The treaty of San Stefano, which established a new Bulgarian state, shocked European and Balkan powers alike. If the terms of the treaty had been carried out, Bulgaria would have embraced territory both north and south of the Balkan mountains, Thrace, and most of Macedonia. The state, now the largest in the Balkans, would clearly be under Russian control. For Greece this meant the end of its hopes to extend its boundaries to include Thrace and, especially, Macedonia. Not only that; the territory that Greece coveted was to be awarded to a detested Balkan enemy. For Austria-Hungary and Britain this was a completely unacceptable extension of Russia's influence in the Balkans without any corresponding gain for themselves. Austria-Hungary felt this particularly strongly. As far as it was concerned, Russia had violated their agreement, whereby if Russia extended its influence in the eastern Balkans, then Austria-Hungary had to be compensated with Bosnia-Hercegovina. Tremendous international pressure was brought to bear upon Russia and it eventually agreed to the meeting in Berlin, the express purpose of which was to rewrite the treaty of San Stefano.

If at least one Balkan power – Bulgaria – was satisfied by the terms of the treaty of San Stefano, none was made happy by the treaty of Berlin. Bulgaria was cut down to size, thereby ensuring a permanent sense of grievance on the part of the Bulgarians. The area south of the Balkan mountains was burdened with the tortured status of a semiautonomous province with a Christian governor chosen by an intricate process. This complex arrangement did not last, and in 1886 eastern Rumelia, as the area was known, was won for Bulgaria through force of arms. Unable to decide what should be done with them, the Great Powers handed Macedonia and Thrace back to the Ottoman empire. Every Balkan state interpreted this as a temporary arrangement and this ensured that, over the next 35 years, the area would become a bloodbath as Serbia, Greece, and Bulgaria sought to establish their claims over Macedonia in particular. Greece itself gained no territory at Berlin. Serbia was dismayed to see that its former ally, Russia, was concerned first and foremost to satisfy Austria-Hungary which, as a result of the treaty, received the right to occupy and administer Bosnia and Hercegovina. Thus Serbian ambitions in these areas, which were considerable, were blocked, just as Greece's were in Macedonia. This served only to increase Serbian interest in Macedonia.

By establishing a smaller Bulgarian state and awarding control in Bosnia-Hercegovina to Austria-Hungary, the Great Powers were able to re-establish amicable relations among themselves. But the treaty left every Balkan government feeling aggrieved and thus the arrangements made at Berlin increased, rather than decreased, the possibility of future conflict.

MOLLY GREENE

See also Bulgaria, Macedonia

Further Reading

Anderson, M.S., *The Eastern Question, 1774–1923: A Study in International Relations*, London: Macmillan, and New York: St Martin's Press, 1966

Bridge, F.R., *The Habsburg Monarchy among the Great Powers, 1815–1918*, New York: Berg, 1990

Jelavich, Charles and Barbara Jelavich, *The Establishment of the Balkan National States, 1804–1920*, Seattle: University of Washington Press, 1977

Kent, Marian (editor), *The Great Powers and the End of the Ottoman Empire*, London: Cass, 1996

Kiraly, Bela K. and Gale Stokes (editors), *Insurrections, Wars, and the Eastern Crisis in the 1870s*, Boulder, Colorado: Social Science Monographs, 1985

Medlicott, W.N., *The Congress of Berlin and After: A Diplomatic History of the Near Eastern Settlement, 1878–1880*, London: Methuen, 1938; 2nd edition, London: Cass, and Hamden, Connecticut: Archon, 1963

Stavrianos, L.S., *The Balkans since 1453*, New York: Rinehart, 1958

Sumner, B.H., *Russian and the Balkans, 1870–1880*, Oxford: Clarendon Press, 1937; reprinted Hamden, Connecticut: Archon, 1962

Bessarion *c.*1400–1472

Cardinal and scholar

Bessarion, a Byzantine monk and later cardinal of the Roman Church, was the most prominent of the Byzantine émigrés who took up residence in Italy during the 15th century. His background as a member of the Byzantine educated elite and his status as a powerful and wealthy cardinal of the Roman Church enabled him to assume a unique role both in preserving the Hellenic literary tradition of Byzantium and of the ancient world, and in disseminating that tradition throughout Italy and Western Europe. Above all he helped to stimulate the revival of the study of Plato during the Italian Renaissance.

In Constantinople in the early years of the 15th century Bessarion followed the traditional Byzantine higher education syllabus, studying under John Chortesmenos and George Chrysokokkes. He later spent time at Mistra with George Gemistos Plethon, the champion of Platonic studies, before being appointed metropolitan of Nicaea in 1437. The following year he accompanied the Byzantine emperor John VIII Palaiologos to the Council of Ferrara-Florence, where he emerged as one of the most prominent supporters of union with the Roman Church among the Byzantine clergy. His *Dogmatic Discourse on the Union*, addressed to the Byzantine delegation, urged them to accept union with the Latin Church, the authority of the pope, and the "Western creed with its controversial addition of the word *filioque* ("and the son"), in the hope that military aid against the Turks would follow. When agreement was finally reached, Bessarion was accorded the honour of reading out the decretal of union in Greek in the cathedral of Florence on 6 July 1439. The union of the Churches, however, was not well received by the people of Constantinople, and from about 1442 Bessarion was living permanently in Rome. He was made a cardinal and was even considered for the papacy on two occasions.

Although many Byzantines saw Bessarion's conversion as treachery, he remained deeply concerned for his country and compatriots. He used his personal wealth and influence to assist his fellow Byzantines in exile, paying the ransoms of many of those taken prisoner after the fall of Constantinople in 1453. He also played an active role in the efforts to organize a crusade to retake the city. In 1471 he published his *Oration to the Leaders of Italy Regarding the Imminent Perils* in which he urged them to unite against the common enemy of all Christians.

Yet it was not only the military threat posed by the Turks to Italy that worried Bessarion, but the realization that their capture of Constantinople might finally extinguish the inheritance of Greek Classical literature that had been preserved for so long under the Byzantine empire. According to his own account, after 1453 he embarked on a systematic rescue mission, collecting manuscripts of the Greek Classics to preserve them for posterity. His servants were sent as far afield as Constantinople and Trebizond to purchase Greek manuscripts, and a small army of scribes was employed to make copies of these works, both in Italy and in the Venetian colony of Crete. Bessarion himself contributed to the process both by copying manuscripts and by scouring Italian monastic libraries in search of long-forgotten codices. He is alleged to have scored a notable success in the monastery of San Niccolò di Casole near Otranto, where he discovered the texts of works by Colluthus and Quintus Smyrnaeus.

Bessarion also promoted the translation of Greek texts into Latin, as a way of bringing them to a wider, non-Greek readership. He himself prepared Latin versions of Xenophon's *Memorabilia*, the metaphysical essay of Theophrastus, and Aristotle's *Metaphysics*, the last remaining the standard Latin translation until well into the 19th century. He also encouraged similar work by his protégés George of Trebizond and Theodore Gaza.

As a result of these activities, Bessarion expended the enormous sum of 30,000 florins and built up a vast collection of some 800 books. In 1468, having decided that the Venetian republic was the most stable of the Italian states and so most likely to be able to preserve the Hellenic inheritance, he donated the entire collection to the church of St Mark in Venice, where it is still preserved in the Marciana Library. It included some of the most important manuscripts of Classical literature, such as the famous Codex Venetus of Aristophanes (Marc. gr. 474). They were a major reason why, in the 1490s, the publisher Aldus Manutius chose Venice as the site for his Greek printing press, which before 1515 produced editions of nearly all the works of the major Greek authors of antiquity.

Apart from the collection, reproduction, and translation of manuscripts of Classical Greek texts, Bessarion also played an important role in promoting discussion and debate as to their value and meaning. His residence next to the church of the Holy Apostles in Rome became a meeting place for scholars, an "Academy" where prominent Italian humanists such as Flavio Biondo, Lorenzo Valla, and Poggio Bracciolini could discuss Hellenic philosophy and literature with the many Greek expatriates, including George of Trebizond, Theodore Gaza, and Andronikos Kallistos, who lived under Bessarion's protection.

Bessarion and his circle were at the centre of the debate on the merits of the works of Plato, which were only now once more becoming available in the West. While the philosophy of

Beſſarion.

Bessarion: 16th-century engraving of Bessarion in his cardinal's hat

Aristotle had long ago come to be regarded as compatible with Christian doctrine, aspects of Plato's thought, such as the concept of metempsychosis, or the transmigration of souls, were much more difficult to reconcile with traditional theology. The debate had begun in 1438 when Bessarion's teacher, George Gemistos Plethon, had circulated his treatise *On the Differences of Plato and Aristotle* at the Council of Florence, and the whole question had become much more heated when George of Trebizond had published his *Comparisons of Plato and Aristotle*, a strongly worded attack on both Plato and Plethon. In 1469 Bessarion produced his *Against the Calumniator of Plato*, in both Latin and Greek, as a reply to the attacks of George of Trebizond. Bessarion sought to defend Plato by stressing those areas of his thought that were reconcilable with Christianity, and by relegating the "celestial republic", with its communal sharing of property and wives, to the status of an ideal, unattainable in a fallen world. His championship of Plato proved to be much more successful than Plethon's had been: by expounding Plato's thought in Latin, *Against the Calumniator* made it accessible to a much wider readership, and by stressing the points of agreement both with Aristotle and with Christian doctrine, it helped to make its study respectable.

JONATHAN HARRIS

Biography

Born around 1400 at Trebizond, Bessarion was educated in Constantinople and Mistra. He became a monk in 1423 and was appointed Metropolitan of Nicaea in 1437. In 1438 he attended the Council of Florence as a leader of the unionists. In 1439 he converted to Roman Catholicism and became a cardinal. He devoted himself to

rescuing manuscripts of Greek Classical literature and bringing them to Italy. On his death in 1472 he left his library of some 800 books to Venice.

Further Reading

Geanakoplos, Deno John, *Greek Scholars in Venice: Studies in the Dissemination of Greek Learning from Byzantium to Western Europe*, Cambridge, Massachusetts: Harvard University Press, 1962

Gill, Joseph, *The Council of Florence*, Cambridge: Cambridge University Press, 1959

Harris, Jonathan, *Greek Emigres in the West, 1400–1520*, Camberley: Porphyrogenitus, 1995

Keller, A., "A Byzantine Admirer of 'Western' Progress: Cardinal Bessarion", *Cambridge Historical Journal*, 11 (1953–5): pp. 343–48

Labowsky, Lotte, *Bessarion's Library and the Biblioteca Marciana: Six Early Inventories*, Rome: Storia e Letteratura, 1979

Mohler, Ludwig, *Kardinal Bessarion als Theologe, Humanist und Staatsmann*, 3 vols, Paderborn: Schöningh, 1923–67

Monfasani, John, *Byzantine Scholars in Renaissance Italy: Cardinal Bessarion and Other Emigrés*, Aldershot, Hampshire: Variorum, 1995

Reynolds, L.D. and Nigel G. Wilson, *Scribes and Scholars: A Guide to the Transmission of Greek and Latin Literature*, 3rd edition, Oxford: Clarendon Press, and New York: Oxford University Press, 1991

Setton, Kenneth M. "The Byzantine Background to the Italian Renaissance", *Transactions and Proceedings of the American Philosophical Society*, 100 (1956): pp. 1–76

Taylor, John Wilson, "Bessarion the Mediator", *Transactions and Proceedings of the American Philosophical Society*, 55 (1924): pp. 120–27

Wilson, Nigel G., *From Byzantium to Italy: Greek Studies in the Italian Renaissance*, London: Duckworth, and Baltimore: Johns Hopkins University Press, 1992

Biography and Autobiography

The genre of biography, if it can indeed be called a genre before the advent of the saint's *Life*, was one of extreme fluidity, some examples being categorized in antiquity rather under other genres such as the encomium and the funeral speech. The format too varied greatly: Satyrus' *Life of Euripides*, for instance, a work of the 3rd century BC, was even written as a dialogue. The term "biography" itself does not appear before the 5th century AD (in fragments of Damascius' *Life of Isidorus*), although *bios* (life) occurs for some varieties of biography from the 4th century BC, when it was even used collectively for Dicaearchus' cultural *Life of Greece*. The word "autobiography" is not ancient at all, but appears to have been coined by an anonymous English reviewer in 1797, and rejected by its author as pedantic.

The germ of biography is evident in the earliest Greek literature. In each of the Homeric epics an interest in the doings of individuals is signalled in the opening line. The *Iliad* deals centrally with the wrath of Achilles in his quarrel with Agamemnon and adds excursus on the prowess of a host of other noble warriors in preference to detailing the progress of a campaign; the *Odyssey* focuses on the adventures over a ten-year period of its eponymous hero. Personal revelations are made by Hesiod in his *Works and Days* and also, although there is much modern scholarly argument over their veracity, by the lyric poets of the Archaic age. An interest in genealogy too is attested towards the end of this period.

True biography and autobiography, however, began only in the 5th and 4th centuries BC. According to Momigliano, the first occurred largely in Greek Asia Minor, and he plausibly attributes it to eastern influence, and the second in mariners' accounts of their voyages, but the scanty evidence precludes any certainty in either case. From the beginning, however, as far as can be perceived, and throughout the history of surviving Classical and Byzantine biographical writing, one feature was consistently maintained: in the case especially of political and military figures, to a far greater extent than in the modern world, a distinction was drawn between histories containing biographical information and works centred upon an individual. The former generally restrict themselves to adult activities, detail the individual's publicly important actions, and strive for a high standard of truth; the latter include information on childhood, emphasize the personality, and often twist the strict truth for the sake of the work's overall purpose (the loci classici are Polybius, 10. 24 and Plutarch, *Life of Alexander*, 1. 2).

Commonly cited as the earliest of all Greek biographies, and dating from the first third of the 5th century BC, is *Matters Concerning Heraclides, King of Mylasa* by Scylax of Caryanda. However, only the title is preserved (and that only in a Byzantine compilation of the 10th century AD), there is no indication whatsoever of the nature of the work, and its attribution to this rather than the later Scylax of Halicarnassus or even to a third Scylax is open to question. Quotations direct and indirect from *On Themistocles, Thucydides and Pericles* by Stesimbrotus of Thasos (c.470–425 BC) clearly indicate a decided bibliographic interest, but even here the exact nature of the work is unclear. Possibly groundbreaking is the roughly contemporary prose *Epidemiai* by the poet Ion of Chios in which he describes, with obvious autobiographical elements, his visits to and impressions of notable men both political and literary (e.g. the tragedians Aeschylus and Sophocles), while fragments indicate that he mentioned philosophers too, including Socrates (without proving in this case any personal acquaintance).

In the earliest surviving Greek history Herodotus shows overt biographical interest in eastern rulers, whereas his Greeks generally appear as individuals more covertly through their actions, the latter a tendency even more pronounced in Thucydides. This may simply be explicable on the ground of familiarity to their audiences, but may reflect oriental practice in monarchies in contrast to the more communal emphasis in the Greek city states. The oldest surviving Greek works actually centred upon an individual date from the first half of the 4th century BC and take notably different forms. First there are "apologies" (legal defences), especially of Socrates, for whom both Plato and Xenophon initiated a series of ever more imaginary material which continued until the sophist Libanius' declamation in the 4th century AD. Plato's became increasingly regarded as the standard biography of the historical Socrates, while Xenophon supplemented his with a collection of reminiscences (*Memorabilia*) of the philosopher's conversations, most, if not all, garnered from other sources. In imitation

Isocrates, in 353 BC at the age of 82, after an unsuccessful law suit, felt compelled to write an imaginary forensic defence of his own life's work (*Antidosis*). Demosthenes' *De Corona*, on the other hand, is a real and spirited defence of the author's political career delivered personally in court in 330 BC but dealing with the period before Athens' submission to Macedon. Fully fledged encomia too appeared in the first half of the 5th century BC. Isocrates asserts in his *Evagoras* (king of Salamis in Cyprus who was assassinated in 374 BC) that he is the first to "praise a man's virtues in prose", presumably meaning in an extended single work. The dramatic, though fictional, setting is a funeral oration, which in a democracy was usually reserved for citizens collectively lost in battle. His uncritical laudatory example was followed by Xenophon, whose *Agesilaus* similarly describes its subject's actions and virtues, but may have been inspired by adverse criticism of the Spartan king (died 359 BC). Two further works of Xenophon demonstrate the extended range of biographical writing. The *Anabasis* vigorously and memorably describes his own role in leading home from Mesopotamia the Greek mercenaries after the battle of Cunaxa in 401 BC. The *Cyropaedia* is extraordinarily difficult to classify, since it deals only briefly with its ostensible subject (the education of Cyrus the Great), and is closer to a very lengthy dissertation on ideal kingship. It has been described as both a philosophical novel and the precursor of the love-romance. Moreover, whereas in the *Anabasis* historical veracity is occasionally subordinated to a self-advertisement necessitated by (lost) rival accounts, the *Cyropaedia* is so cavalier with truth as, among numerous flagrantly fictitious assertions, to have its hero die in bed rather than battle.

Aristotle encouraged a continuing Peripatetic biographical interest in other directions. The only surviving work is Theophrastus' *Characters*, a series of 30 sketches of unpleasant types of personality. His contemporary Clearchus of Soli attempted descriptions of different peoples. Others, not all Peripatetics, wrote on real individual figures (Theophrastus himself on Aristotle's nephew Callisthenes of Olynthus, a historian of Alexander the Great executed by the king) and especially philosophers. Aristoxenus' *Lives* were anecdotal and waspish; Antigonus of Carystus raised the subject to a higher level of scholarly accuracy in the mid-3rd century BC; and in the early 2nd century BC Sotion tried in his 13-book *Succession of the Philosophers* to establish an intellectual lineage from teacher to student, a serial form of philosophical biography best known today in Diogenes Laertius' work of the 3rd (?) century AD. Poets were not forgotten, and with older figures (beginning with Homer) ignorance was often not permitted to vitiate a full account: Chamaeleon, for instance, in the late 4th or early 3rd century BC, inferred biographical facts from the writers' own compositions, a practice that could lead to ludicrous inaccuracies and (a far more serious problem) to numerous suspect assertions not demonstrably false. Through a love of sensationalism, in the 3rd century BC Hermippus of Smyrna was deliberately fraudulent in his biographies of philosophers, poets, and lawgivers, of whom some were mythical.

Political biography from the Hellenistic period has also perished. Nevertheless, scattered fragments and allusions point to an increasing interest in individual rulers which was inspired by the charismatic career of Alexander the Great and continued under the numerous subsequent monarchies. Some of these works naturally veered towards panegyric, such as *How Alexander was Brought Up* by the king's helmsman Onesicritus, who probably modelled his work on Xenophon's *Cyropaedia*. Adversely critical moral judgements, however, are suggested by monographs on types of public figures such as the Peripatetic Phaenias' *On the Tyrants of Sicily* and *The Slaying of Tyrants for Revenge*, Idomeneus' *On* [Athenian] *Demagogues* and Hermippus' *Lives of Those who Passed from Philosophy to Tyranny and Despotic Rule*. Nepos' surviving Latin biographies (including some of Greeks) from the 1st century AD, which have both an encomiastic and an ethical purpose, probably reflect a trend in most lost Hellenistic productions. Apologetic memoirs too by public figures continued, including the influential work of Aratus, the Sicyonian statesman of the 3rd century BC.

It is only from the imperial Roman age that true Greek biography and autobiography survive in substantial quantity, and even then not until the 1st and 2nd centuries AD. A largely new aspect of autobiographical works is their composition by intellectuals. Unfortunately only fragments remain of *On My Own Life and Education* by Nicolaus of Damascus, a Peripatetic aristocrat, tutor of the children of Mark Antony and adviser to Herod the Great (who wrote also a now fragmentary biography of Augustus which was based upon the emperor's own autobiography), but the Hellenized aristocratic Jewish priest Josephus saw fit to include intellectual matters in his surviving *Life*, which is chiefly intended as a defence of his command of Galilee during the first Jewish revolt (AD 66–70). The *To Himself* (*Meditations*) of the Roman emperor Marcus Aurelius, a unique work from antiquity consisting of very private self-exploratory musings on human existence whose subsequent publication is a complete mystery, also reflects (although it may not be categorized as a true autobiography) this trend, as does more clearly the physician Galen's philosophical *On My Own Opinions*. Notable later examples are the autobiography of the Antiochene rhetorician Libanius, written over nearly 20 years and in the form of a sophistic discourse, and most especially Synesius of Cyrene's *Dion*, in which he defends his attachment to Classical culture against both monkish asceticism and excessive pagan superstition.

Biographies of public figures reached their acme with Plutarch, whose *Parallel Lives* (in which he paired Greeks and Romans with usually a concluding comparison) was already an educational text by the early Byzantine period. Unlike many Greek biographies, they are of genuine literary merit and, despite some problems, real historical value; and they deal with the entire lives of their subject. Nevertheless, their primary aim was moral education through examples of virtuous and vicious behaviour. Their psychological observations are on occasion subtly perceptive. Historical monographs (rather than true biographies), centred upon an individual and usually verging on the encomium, also continued to be written, such as Arrian's *Anabasis of Alexander* and the somewhat earlier second book of Maccabees (an epitome of a lost work by a certain Jason of Cyrene).

Biographies of philosophers are still to be found in the imperial age, but, in reflection of current literary interests, sophists replace poets. Modern knowledge of the Second Sophistic is largely dependent upon the 3rd-century *Lives of the Sophists* by Lucius Flavius Philostratus ("the Athenian"), a collection of brief and at times tendentious sketches. Diogenes Laertius' compendium of the lives and tenets of ancient philosophers, derived from similar earlier compilations, is a work of industry but little critical acumen and is chiefly valuable today for its quotation of three compositions by Epicurus. Generally more scholarly, though laudatory, biographies are those of the Neoplatonists Plotinus and Proclus by their pupils Porphyry and Marinus respectively, while biographies of Pythagoras by Porphyry and Iamblichus claim him as the source of Plato's philosophy.

In the imperial (and Byzantine) age, far more than before, contemporary rulers were subject to epideictic oratory, which contained many biographical details, albeit highly encomiastic and selective. The late 3rd-century rhetorician Menander, in laying down their formulaic contents, shows the types into which these addresses were divided: they included the encomiastic imperial oration and the address to local governors, speeches of welcome and valediction, speeches at weddings, birthdays, and funerals, the ambassador's speech, and many more. Most surviving examples are Byzantine, the emperor expecting one every year at Epiphany, and the ecumenical patriarch on Lazarus Saturday.

Biography of the Hellenistic and imperial ages had similarities with and probably influence on the anecdotal style of the synoptic gospels, a feature that persisted into the Lives of martyrs and saints. It is unclear to what extent the rise of Christianity or simply the common culture of late antiquity may have prompted the empress Julia Domna (d. 217) to bid Philostratus write a biography of the neo-Pythagorean holy man Apollonius of Tyana, a fictionalized amalgam of exotic travel, miracles, exorcisms, sage advice, religious asceticism, and nonconformity unique in pagan biography. At least it elicited a comparison between Apollonius and Jesus, which in turn provoked a refutation by Eusebius in the early 4th century. Lives of Christian saints most probably induced Eunapius to follow Philostratus in producing similar, though inferior and idealized, sketches of 4th-century pagan philosophers, rhetoricians, and iatrosophists.

By far the most important form of biography in the Byzantine period is hagiography (see the separate entry under that title), an edifying and often exciting recital of an individual's struggle for union with God. Saints themselves, though frequently vouchsafing much personal information in their letters and other writings, rarely wrote overt autobiographies. That by Gregory of Nazianzus is made doubly remarkable by his preference for verse over prose. In the 11th century St Christodoulos of Patmos attached an autobiography to the Typikon (charter) of his monastery, a practice followed also by the historian Michael Attaleiates and later by Michael VIII Palaiologos (1259–82).

Byzantine historians were often eyewitnesses of or participants in what they describe, and Michael Psellos in his 11th-century *Chronographia* was especially and notoriously unable to forget the importance of his own involvement. Nevertheless, although Nikephoros Basilakes discusses his education and teaching in an introduction to a collection of his works which he made around 1160, true autobiography does not reappear until the Palaiologan period, when it appealed to a variety of men. The most interesting examples are those of the teacher and scholar Nikephoros Blemmydes (an apologia of his life), the cultured Constantinopolitan patriarch Gregory II, the scholarly statesman Theodore Metochites, and the philo-Latin Roman convert to Roman Catholicism Demetrios Kydones. Perhaps classifiable also as autobiography are the *Histories* of the usurping emperor John VI Kantakouzenos, written after he became a monk in 1354, who with the sedulously fostered guise of objectivity sought to defend his political career.

Byzantine secular biographies are even less common, although a few imperial figures such as Theodora the wife of Theophilos (829–42), and John III Vatatzes (1221–54) received them in hagiographic form. They are nearly all encomiastic, more critical appraisals being reserved for histories (although hagiography could take the form of hostile biography as in Niketas David Paphlagon's *Life* of Ignatios, which becomes an attack on the rival patriarch Photios). The biography of Basil I, written or at least commissioned by Constantine VII Porphyrogennetos (913–59), is indeed embedded within a history (the so-called *Theophanes Continuatus*) and was designed to validate the position of Constantine. The *Alexiad* stands on its own and is a far more ambitious defence of her father by the princess Anna Komnene, while the five-book history by Michael Kritoboulos of Imbros is to a considerable extent a eulogy of the conqueror of Constantinople, Mehmet II Fatih, to whom it is dedicated. In complete contrast, except that they too seemingly veer from the strict truth, are a few biographical invectives. Noteworthy in this connection are two from the 12th century. The anonymous *Anacharsis or Ananias* belabours an aristocratic failure at soldiering, riding, hunting, musicianship, calligraphy, and astrology, whose second marriage was to a Jewess whom even baptism could not save from being called a frog. Nikephoros Basilakes' target is a certain Bagoas, an educated catamite of humble birth who feigned piety to insinuate himself into the palace.

During the period of foreign occupation after the fall of Constantinople in 1453 various eyewitness accounts of specific calamitous events contain personal details. Autobiographical writing proper was rare and usually restricted to descriptions of journeys or captivity, such as that of "Christopher Angell [Angelos], a Grecian, who tasted of many stripes and torments inflicted by the Turkes for the faith which he had in Christ Iesus", as the English version proclaims. He used Classical Greek for his work, published in 1617 at Oxford where he taught his native language, whereas his near contemporary Georgios Mosketes, professor of Greek at Pisa, chose Italian for an account of his travels in the Levant, imprisonment by the Turks, and subsequent ransom. Memoirs became more common in the second half of the 18th century (including some by the Constantinopolitan patriarch Meletios II in the high language) and reached their climax during the War of Independence, most notably in the vivid and idiosyncratic vernacular reminiscences of General Makriyannis.

Biographies before the late 18th century are rare and at first rather chronicles of a series of rulers or patriarchs. However, the increasing involvement of Russia in Greek affairs encouraged in 1736 a lengthy *Life of Peter the Great* in Italian by Antonios Katephoros, which was later translated into vernacular Greek. Growing patriotism in anticipation of escape from Turkish rule spawned biographies of ancient heroes: an adaptation of the pseudo-Callisthenic *Alexander Romance* (1800) is attributed to Demetrios Gobdelas, professor and rector of the Greek school at Jassy, while Athanasios of Stagira used western sources for his *Lives* of Themistocles (1816) and Miltiades (1818); and whereas a certain Spyridon Kaphireus wrote on the *Virtues and Deeds of Demosthenes* (1820), the Athenian patriot in the struggle against the Macedonians, Georgios Bentotes, was inspired by Marmontel's *Bélisaire* to translate that imaginative reconstruction of the romantic Byzantine general's latter days (1783). Far more useful, however, is *The New Greece* (published posthumously in 1872) by Georgios Zabiras (1744–1804), which presents biographies of 517 Greek savants of the Tourkokratia. An interest in personality types reappeared too during this period, inspired by Theophrastus' *Characters*: Adamantios Korais edited this work and translated it into French (1799), Demetrios Darbaris produced a Greek translation with a few additional characters of his own (1795), and Charisios Megdanes composed imitations under the title *Lychnos tou Diogenous* [Lantern of Diogenes] (1818).

Later 19th- and 20th-century Greek biography and autobiography largely followed, generally without any great distinction, the styles of other European literatures. Three works, however, stand out. In his *To Taxidi Mou* [My Journey] of 1888 Ioannis Psycharis chose semi-fictional autobiographical travels around the Greek world to make his clamant demand for official recognition of the demotic language; Ilias Venezis's *Noumero 31328* [Number 31328] is a graphic description of his time as a prisoner of the Turks (1922–23); Nikos Kazantzakis's last, and posthumously published, work, *Anaphora ston Greko* [Report to Greco] (1957), is a highly fictionalized autobiography in which he seeks to give a spiritual and philosophical coherence to his journey through life.

A.R. LITTLEWOOD

See also Hagiography, Historiography, Rhetoric

Further Reading

Austin, N.J., "Autobiography and History: Some Later Roman Historians and Their Veracity" in *History and Historians in Late Antiquity*, edited by Brian Croke and Alanna M. Emmett, Oxford and New York: Pergamon Press, 1983

Cox, Patricia, *Biography in Late Antiquity: A Quest for the Holy Man*, Berkeley: University of California Press, 1983

Edwards, M.J. and Simon Swain (editors), *Portraits: Biographical Representation in the Greek and Latin Literature of the Roman Empire*, Oxford: Clarendon Press, 1997

Geiger, Joseph, *Cornelius Nepos and Ancient Political Biography*, Wiesbaden: Steiner, 1985

Gentili, Bruno and Giovanni Cerri, *History and Biography in Ancient Thought*, Amsterdam: Gieben, 1988

Hinterberger, Martin, *Autobiographische Tradition in Byzanz*, Vienna: Akademie der Wissenschaften, 1999

Hunger, Herbert, *Die hochsprachliche profane Literatur der Byzantiner*, vol. 1, Munich: Beck, 1978, pp. 165–70

Jacoby, Felix, *Die Fragmente der griechischen Historiker Continued*, part 4a: *Biography*, edited by G. Schepens, Leiden: Brill, 1998–

Knös, Börje, *L'Histoire de la littérature néo-grecque: la période jusqu'en 1821*, Stockholm, Almqvist & Wiksell, 1962

Lewis, R.G., "Suetonius' 'Caesares' and Their Literary Antecedents" in *Aufstieg und Niedergang der römischen Welt*, edited by Hildegard Temporini *et al.*, 2. 33. 5, Berlin: de Gruyter, 1991, 3623–74

Lewis, R.G., "Imperial Autobiography, Augustus to Hadrian" in *Aufstieg und Niedergang der römischen Welt*, edited by Hildegard

Temporini *et al.*, vol. 2. 34. 1, Berlin: de Gruyter, 1993, 629–706 (both articles by Lewis, though primarily on Latin literature, are useful for Greek biographic and autobiographic material in the early imperial age)

Menander, *Menander Rhetor*, edited and translated by D.A. Russell and N.G. Wilson, Oxford: Clarendon Press, and New York: Oxford University Press, 1981

Misch, Georg, *A History of Autobiography in Antiquity*, 2 vols, London: Routledge, and Cambridge, Massachusetts: Harvard University Press, 1950

Momigliano, Arnaldo, *The Development of Greek Biography*, Cambridge, Massachusetts: Harvard University Press, 1971; reprinted 1993

Stuart, Duane Reed, *Epochs of Greek and Roman Biography*, Berkeley: University of California Press, 1928; reprinted New York: Biblo and Tannen, 1967

Birth

Birth is a crucial feature of the life cycle. In the Greek cultural milieu, childbearing and family continuity are of paramount importance, with marriage and children considered to be life's highest attainment. The procreative purpose of female sexuality is emphasized, the role of the mother is glorified, and there is an apparent tendency to chide those who are either unable to achieve such a state within marriage or in some way rebel against it. The birth of a child is seen as ensuring the regeneration of life within the family and the community. It is regarded as a way of defeating death and securing personal immortality, since Greek children often bear their grandparents' names. In antiquity the Greeks were also dependent on their offspring for the perpetuity of their families (*oikoi*), for support in old age, and for the tending of their tombs after death.

Until recently birth was primarily the concern of women. Its social history points to similarities in the experience and status of Greek women in all historical periods. The principal role of all Greek women was that of bearers and nurturers of legitimate children and, indeed, continuance of the race. Although we cannot speak of Greek women in antiquity as a unified group, legal and historical sources attest to the exclusion of women throughout Greece from the public domain, and to their devotion solely to reproduction. Indeed, even Spartan women – who were considered to be different and more visible than other Greek women in the public sphere because of their involvement in many athletic events – engaged in such activities with the main goal of bracing their bodies for delivering children for the city. Thus infertility in antiquity was viewed as a calamity; conversely, the birth of a child brought about a great change in the bride's position through full admission into the conjugal family, denied to her up to then.

Conception and childbirth were also seen as beneficial for female health and were prescribed as cures for a number of gynaecological conditions. Labour and delivery, however, could be difficult and in some cases could even lead to death. A high rate of both maternal and infant mortality is often assumed by researchers who report on the use of various herbal drinks, induced sneezing, or the tying of a pumice or a dead cyclamen root on a woman's thigh as a means of easing a difficult delivery. There was also a belief that delivery would be impeded if things were tied on or around the mother, for example, her hair or a belt. Because of the dangers involved in childbirth, women often invoked the help of certain deities who were believed to protect them on delivery, such as Artemis (Lochia), Athena, Eileithyia, and Genetyllis (in Attica).

Women gave birth at home with the assistance of female relatives and neighbours and/or a midwife. Male doctors were expected to assist only in cases of prolonged and hazardous labour. The role of the midwife was notable both in antiquity and in the recent past, and in some cases she shared the same status as a doctor. At birth it was the midwife who announced the sex of the child, cut and tied the umbilical cord, and judged its fitness to live. Yet, the expertise of the midwife was not limited to the process of delivery and to the birth itself. She was able to treat many female complaints that had to do with the uterus as well as postnatal problems, such as puerperal fever. In fact, a competent midwife possessed a wide knowledge of such diverse fields as dietetics, pharmacology, surgery (meaning the "work of hands"), and magic.

The use of a wet-nurse or dry-nurse was also common in Greek antiquity, but the mother was regarded as the infant's prime caretaker. However, children belonged to their fathers, not to their mothers, and Greek law codes asserted that in the event of the father's death the newborn should be offered to its father's family. Male infants were favoured and the male foetus was believed to be more active than the female. Women who carried a male child were thought to be healthier with a better complexion, as well as having an easier pregnancy and delivery. Many ethnographic data refer to the use of figurines to increase fertility. Women who desired to have a child made an effigy of themselves as pregnant or an effigy of their prospective child as an adult and carried it as a talisman. Some researchers believe that the large number of female idols found in the Aegean and dating from the early Neolithic period may reveal an earlier preference for the birth of girls, since fertility was crucial for the survival of the group and pregnancy as well as maternity may even have granted special symbolic value to women. However, data on infanticide and the exposure of infants in Hellenistic Greece reveal that, if such a preference existed in early antiquity, it must have ceased later on because girls formed the group that was most highly at risk from such practices. Both infanticide and abortion were regarded as acceptable forms of family planning, with the former being preferable to the latter from the point of view of the mother's health.

Childbirth was considered unclean both in antiquity and in the present day, because it is coloured by natural, profane blood and thus ritually pollutes all those concerned, especially the mother. In antiquity the mother was considered impure until her postnatal bleeding had stopped. For that period of time contact with the sacred was avoided and women were excluded from the temples. A 40-day purification period was also followed by women after an abortion.

During the Byzantine era birth was institutionalized with the establishment of some lying-in hospitals, but the majority of women continued to give birth at home with the help of a midwife. Although evidence is lacking concerning the size of families and the frequency of births in this period, there was still a high rate of maternal and infant mortality. In this regard, A. Laiou estimates the net birth rate in the 14th century as 22 per 1000. Christianity, however, changed attitudes towards marriage and procreation, which were now viewed as subordinate to celibacy. At the same time the prestige of the woman as wife and mother grew due to her association with the greatest archetype of Christian cosmology, the Mother of God. The birth of boys was still favoured over that of girls since girls had to be endowed with dowries, and infertility was still a source of tremendous shame. In Byzantium many pre-Christian beliefs concerning childbearing persisted despite their condemnation by the Church. In the absence of medical expertise midwives often employed a mixture of medical folklore practices and outright witchcraft to facilitate birth. Midwives were thus often associated with heretical beliefs and rituals. Women used various religious objects in order to gain divine assistance during delivery. The use of pagan amulets was also widespread, and was responsible for women commonly being accused of superstitious practices.

Christian writers condemned contraception and abortion, at any stage of pregnancy, as even worse than murder since they claimed that the victim lost the chance to become a human being. Nevertheless, Byzantine women used several means to prevent continuous pregnancies, the most common being toxic herbal medicines and long periods of breast-feeding, which reduced the risk of pregnancy, as well as postnatal taboos on sexual intercourse. Sexual intercourse was also prohibited on Sundays and fasting days, and there was a belief that women who conceived on such days would give birth to lepers and epileptics. In the absence of effective contraception the only option that remained open to parents, especially those living in extreme poverty, was the abandonment of infants. Many children were abandoned at the entrance of churches or wealthy households, and the Christian emperors could do little in such cases. Constantine I, in a law of 329, permitted the sale of children in cases of extreme poverty. The creation of orphanages represented an attempt by the Church and the state to relieve such problems.

Under Ottoman rule the desire of Greeks for male children became more palpable than ever, for boys were equated with weapons and thus increased the hope of liberation. Birth continued to take place at home, as in earlier periods. It is worth noting, however, that during the Tourkokratia the custom of breastfeeding became established throughout Greece, since it was closely related to the survival of infants, and thus of the Greek people in general. Greek mothers considered breastfeeding to be the "eighth sacrament" of the Church, thus making it a sacred act. Moreover, evidence shows that the socialization of girls into motherhood and breastfeeding practices started at 3 years of age when the child was given her first doll. Maternal mortality during this period was more than 35 per cent – 20 times greater than it is today – and the wet nurses (vizastres) were therefore honoured by the people and the Church. They were the first to receive the consecrated host (antidoron) from the priest in church, and those who had nursed many children were automatically granted absolution. The patron saint of wet nurses was St Marina, and the woman who nursed nine children was called "St Marina and Mistress". The importance attached to breastfeeding is also attested by the fact that children who were nursed by the same woman were considered to be siblings, and were therefore forbidden to marry one another.

In the rural areas of modern Greece such practices continued – and still continue in some areas even today with minor variations. The wealth of folk traditions and rituals regarding pregnancy, childbirth, the first weeks of life of the infant, and the transitional period faced by the mother persisted in modern Greece until the 1960s, and some persist today. In some cases, the incorporation of ancient traditions and rituals into Orthodox Christianity is obvious. Today the saints who are most often invoked by pregnant women are St Elevtherios – his name derives from the word elevtheria (freedom) and he helps women in delivery – and St Marina. It is notable that in Athens the churches devoted to these particular saints are built on the ruins of temples of Eileithyia, the deity who was connected with labour and delivery in antiquity.

It is not necessary to delve very far into the past to find the belief that during pregnancy and the postnatal period women were considered open to demonic attack and were protected by certain prohibitions, such as the 40-day taboo, the avoidance of crossing over ravines, the constant censing of the house, and the fear of darkness. The infant, too, was considered to be particularly susceptible to the "evil eye", and for 40 days was kept inside the house. The end of that period was, and still is, marked by an act of purification where mother and child receive the blessing of the priest at church (sarantisma). There is also a widespread belief that on the first, third, or seventh day after birth – depending on the area – the infant is visited by the Fates (Moires), known also as "old women" (gries), which predetermines his or her luck and the events of the whole of his or her life. Special measures had to be taken for the reception of the Fates. The dogs of the house had to be tied up, so as not to scare the Fates into leaving; the furniture of the house was moved so as not to obstruct their way; and a table with honey, bread, wine, and sweets had to be laid out. The mother, however, was not left alone because the Fates were old and envious and might harm her. Other customs that have endured include the use of certain herbs to induce fertility, and formulas followed during the rite of marriage, conception, pregnancy, and childbirth to increase the chance of the birth of male infants (arrenogonia). Finally, the belief that pregnant women crave certain foods is very much alive, as is the belief that, if they do not eat them, they will either lose the baby or their baby will have a birthmark.

Up to the 1960s the midwife was an important figure in village communities, and in some areas of northern Greece is still honoured on 8 January, on what is known as the "day of the midwife". From the 1950s, however, childbirth has been increasingly institutionalized and the magico-religious practices surrounding it have gradually disappeared. Women now give birth in hospitals or private clinics under the care of obstetricians who are mostly males. Breastfeeding is no longer widespread, and since maternal and infant mortality is greatly reduced, couples have fewer children than in the past. Indeed, the recent decline in the birth rate is one of the greatest problems of Greece. Between 1975 and 1995 the birthrate decreased to about 40 to 60 per cent; the average number of children in 1995 was estimated to be between 1.25 and 1.49. Infertility, however, is still regarded as a social and personal defect, for which women are held responsible, though increasingly medical science persuades men to bear responsibility as well.

Compared to other life-cycle rituals, such as marriage and death, birth was and still is less publicly ritualized. Moreover, in all historical periods the father does not really figure in the process, because in Greece a second, superior "social" birth exists that usually negates the part played by women and transfers control to men. In antiquity children were incorporated into society in a celebration held five or ten days after their birth (*amphidromia*) in which they were given a name and were publicly acknowledged as family members. In the context of Greek Orthodoxy children receive a second, superior birth with baptism and become full members of the Christian community; it is during baptism that they receive their name and hence become persons. Finally, one of the ways in which infertility was confronted, both in antiquity and at present, was through adoption. In certain areas of modern Greece, the father would pass the adopted child through a wide sleeve that was stitched on to his shirt, in a symbolic act of birth known as *arrenolocheia* (couvade).

ELENI SOTIRIU

See also Abortion, Children, Women

Further Reading

Ballas, K.N., "I Kyisi, o Toketos, i Locheia kai to Neogno sto Laiko Politismo ton Neoellinon" [Pregnancy, Childbirth, Lying-In, and the Neonate in Popular Modern Greek Culture], *Materia Medica Greca*, 8/5 (October 1980): pp. 544–48

Brouskou, Aigli, "Enfants vendus, enfants promis", *L'Homme*, 105 (1988) pp. 76–87

Brouskou, Aigli, "Anthropologia tis gennisis" [Anthropology of Childbirth], *Archeia Ellinikis Iatrikis* [Archives of Greek Medicine], 8/4 (July–August 1991) pp. 252–56

Cameron, Averil and Amélie Kuhrt (editors), *Images of Women in Antiquity*, London: Croom Helm, 1983 (see especially articles by J. Herrin, "In Search of Byzantine Women: Three Avenues of Approach", and by S.B. Pomeroy, "Infanticide in Hellenistic Greece"), revised edition London: Routledge, and Detroit: Wayne State University Press, 1993

Cantarella, Eva, *L'ambiguo malanno: condizione e immagine della donna nell'antichità greca e romana*, 2nd edition, Rome: Riuniti, 1985

Chrysanthopoulou-Farrington, Vas., "An Analysis of Rituals Surrounding Birth in Modern Greece", dissertation, Oxford University, 1984

Clark, Gillian, *Women in Late Antiquity: Pagan and Christian Lifestyles*, Oxford: Clarendon Press, and New York: Oxford University Press, 1993

Handman, Marie-Elisabeth, *Via kai Poniria: Andres kai Gynaikes s'ena Elliniko Chorio* [Violence and Deceit: Men and Women in a Greek Village], 2nd edition, Athens, 1990, pp. 182–93

Hornblower, Simon and Antony Sprawforth (editors), *The Oxford Classical Dictionary*, 3rd edition, Oxford and New York: Oxford University Press, 1996 (entries on Abortion, Birthday, Childbirth, Embryology, Gynaecology, Infanticide, Motherhood, Pollution, Women)

Kokkinidou, Dimitra and M. Nikolaidou, *I Archaiologia kai i Koinoniki Tavtotita tou Phylou: Prosengiseis stin Aigiaki Proistoria* [Archaeology and the Common Identity of the Tribe: Towards a Prehistory of Aegi], Thessalonica, 1993

Koukoules, Phaidon I., *Vyzantinon vios kai politismos* [Life and Culture of the Byzantines], vol. 4, Athens, 1951, pp. 9–69

Loukatos, Dimitrios S., "O syzygos eis ta kata tin Gennisin Ethima kai Laographikai Endeixeis peri Arrenolocheias" [The Husband in Childbirth Customs and Traces of Couvade in Folklore], *Epetiris tou Laographikou Archeiou tis Akadimias Athinon*, 8 (1953/54): pp. 124–68

Loukatos, Dimitrios S., "Patir tikton" [The Father who Gives Birth], *Epetiris tou Laographikou Archeiou tis Akadimias Athinon* [Yearbook of the Folklore Archive of Athens University], 11–12 (1958/59): pp. 27–42

Meinardus, O.F.A., "Fertility and Healing Cult Survivals in Athens: Haghia Marina", *Zeitschrift für Ethnologie*, 99 (1974): pp. 270–76

Moffatt, A., "The Byzantine Child", *Social Research*, 53/4 (1986): pp. 705–23

Oikonomopoulos, Christos, "O thilasmos stin Ellada kata tin Tourkokratia" [Breast-Feeding in Greece during the Turkish Rule], *Deltio I. Paidiatrikis Klinikis tou Panepistimiou Athinon* [Bulletin of the Paediatric Clinic of Athens University], 29/6 (November–December 1982): pp. 420–42

Oikonomopoulos, Christos, "I arrenogonia kai i thilygonia stin elliniki laiki paradosi" [Descent by Male and Female Line in Greek Popular Tradition], *Themata Maievtikis Gynaikologias* [Topics in Obstetric Gynaecology], 12 (January–March 1998): pp. 59–75

Papamichael, Anna J., *Birth and Plant Symbolism: Symbolic and Magical Uses of Plants in Connection with Birth in Modern Greece*, Athens, 1975

Politis, Nikolaos G., "Ta kata tin gennisin" [Childbirth Matters], *Neoellinika Analekta* [Modern Greek Miscellany], 1 (1872)

Spyridakis, Georgios K., "Ta kata tin gennisin, tin vaptisin kai ton gamon ethima ton Vyzantinon ek ton agiologikon pigon" [Byzantine Customs at Childbirth, Baptism, and Marriage Gathered from Hagiographic Sources], *Epetiris tou Laographikou Archeiou tis Akadimias Athinon* [Yearbook of the Folklore Archive of Athens University], 7 (1952): pp. 102–47

Bishops

The Greek word *episkopos*, the Latinized form of which (*episcopus*) is the root of the word "bishop", literally means "overseer". In the Christian Church it has come to denote the highest ministry, after those of deacon and priest.

In Classical antiquity and in the apostolic age the noun referred to a function or an activity, namely that of being a supervisor. In ancient Greece *episkopoi* are attested as supervisors and business managers in both a secular and a religious context, as state or city officials or as officers of pagan cults. There are only six passages in the New Testament – none of them in the gospels – that use the word and its cognates to refer either to Christ as the shepherd and guardian of souls (1 Peter 2: 25) or to those who occupy a supervisory role within the communities (Acts 1: 20; Acts 20: 28; Philippians 1: 1; 1 Timothy 3: 1–7; Titus 1: 7–9). It is significant that these passages allow for the possibility of several *episkopoi* within a congregation and that they do not specify the need for every congregation to appoint *episkopoi*. In fact, before the 4th century, Christian writers often fail to make a clear distinction between the episcopate and the presbyterate.

Paul's First Letter to Timothy (1 Timothy 3: 2–7) provides the earliest description of the ideal character of an *episkopos*, inspiring all later writing on the subject. He has to be well respected, irreproachable in his lifestyle, of sound character, not a recent convert, and a gifted teacher. He also has to be an able manager of his own household – thus proving his potential to hold authority in the congregation – and may not be married more than once.

The monarchic episcopate, where there is only one bishop for a community, is first attested in the epistles of Ignatius of Antioch (died c.107). The word *episkopos* now acquired the additional sense of a specific office in the Christian Church. Ignatius regards the monarchic episcopate simultaneously as a reflection of the One God and as a guarantor for the doctrinal unity of the Church. The bishop represents God while the presbyters represent the Apostles. At the same time he is the first among equals within the presbyterate. To his congregation he is the spiritual model due to his exemplary conduct and the sacral centre due to his liturgical functions.

By the 4th century the episcopal office had acquired clearer contours, and traditions regarding episcopal appointment had been established that would remain valid, with certain variations, to the present day. A minimum age of 30 years is required for ordination to the priesthood in the Orthodox Church, and by extension also for the episcopate. The bishop's character must be above reproach. He may not be a neophyte and he must have the higher education essential to his duty as a teacher. The celibacy of bishops that has become customary today was demanded in the legislation of the emperor Justinian (527–65), but it was not consistently enforced. Still in 692 the Council in Trullo (Quinisext Council) stipulated that, if a bishop-elect was married, his wife had to enter a monastery at some distance from his residence. Eventually, the problem was eliminated by recruiting bishops from monasteries. Another concern was simony, i.e. the purchase of ecclesiastical office. Contested episcopal elections between ambitious candidates could easily turn into riots and lead to bloodshed, as John Chrysostom reports for the city of Antioch. Church councils repeatedly inveigh against this practice, which undermined the honour of the episcopal office.

The concrete circumstances of the election of a bishop vary over time and in different regions. The general guidelines were set down by the Council of Nicaea (325) which repeats in essence the *Apostolic Tradition* of Hippolytus of Rome: a new bishop must be elected by the inhabitants and the clergy of the city where his see is located, as well as by all the other bishops in the relevant diocese, either at a synod or by letter. Once the candidate is confirmed by the metropolitan, his ordination is performed by three, or at least two, bishops from neighbouring sees through the laying on of hands, in a demonstration of the principle of collegiality. A bishop may not leave his diocese for prolonged periods of time, nor may he seek a lateral transfer to another episcopal see.

In the early Church only the bishops were allowed to preach and to perform baptisms, but these functions were eventually extended to priests. However, the ordination of priests and deacons as well as the consecration of church altars remains the exclusive domain of bishops to the present day. The bishop is assisted by one or more deacons in his liturgical functions, and by an *oikonomos* (manager) and a *chartophylax* (document keeper) in the financial and administrative governance of his diocese. The most prominent manifestation of the bishops' role in clarifying Christian doctrine, and of the principle of collegiality among them, is their participation in synods and councils. Once or twice a year the bishops of a province gather for a synod under the presidency of their metropolitan. As

participants in ecumenical councils, they stand for the universal Church in its entirety.

The bishops acquired public prominence when the emperor Constantine ended the great persecution and extended his imperial patronage to the Christian Church. In convening the Council of Nicaea, he not only bestowed official recognition on the bishops as representatives of the Church, but also accorded them the privilege of imperial officials to travel by the imperial post. The council was attended by some 300 bishops, most from the eastern regions of the Roman empire. It solidified the shape of the ecclesiastical organization that had developed in analogy to the administrative and territorial structure of the Roman empire. Corresponding to the provinces of the empire were the dioceses of the Church. The largest city within such a territory (the metropolis) was the seat of provincial government and also became the seat of the metropolitan bishop, who presided over the bishops of the lesser cities within his diocese. Responsible for vast stretches of rural hinterland were *chorepiskopoi* (literally: "country bishops"). They were subordinate to their bishop, with whose approval they could ordain deacons and priests. This custom was prevalent especially in Asia Minor in the early Byzantine period, but lost importance by the 8th century, and had become obsolete by the 12th.

As a result of Constantine's advocacy of Christianity, Church and empire became coterminous. This also affected the role of the bishops. They were increasingly called upon by the imperial legislation to take an active role in the administration of their cities, to administer justice even in civil matters, to monitor the performance of imperial provincial officers, and to report abuses. The emperor Justinian, for example, stipulated in 530 that bishops had to collaborate with the city council in the supervision of public building works, road construction, and the maintenance of aqueducts and public baths.

At times of crisis, bishops often became the focal point of authority in their cities. During the periods of severe famine in the 6th century, they saw to the distribution of food and regulated the grain supply. In the course of the Persian and Arab invasions of the 7th century, they organized the relief efforts for the population and even became involved in the military defence of their cities. In subsequent centuries, as the properties of the Church increased, so did the power of the bishops. In addition to the city with its religious structures – churches, monasteries and convents, hospitals and orphanages – they were often in charge of a large territory with towns and villages. After the Council of Chalcedon (451) the bishops also held the authority over the monasteries in their diocese.

The letters and sermons by bishops of the Byzantine period give us a vivid picture of the concrete circumstances of their lives (Basil of Caesarea, John Chrysostom, Severus of Antioch, Leo of Synada). More formal treatises that deal with the various aspects of the episcopate were composed by the Church Fathers Gregory of Nazianzus (*On his Flight*), John Chrysostom (*On the Priesthood*), and pseudo-Dionysius the Areopagite (*The Ecclesiastical Hierarchy*). Many saints' *Lives* celebrate the deeds of holy bishops, such as the *Life of John the Almsgiver* and the *Life of the Patriarch Eutychius*.

Under the Tourkokratia, since adherence to Orthodox Christianity shaped the identity of the inhabitants of the former Byzantine empire, the bishops were important figures of leadership, especially in fostering education by maintaining schools and institutions of higher learning.

Today, in the autocephalous Orthodox Church of Greece, bishops continue to play an important role in ministering to the pastoral and spiritual needs of their dioceses. In 1922 all episcopal sees were declared to have the rank of metropolitans. There are 81 dioceses, with an additional number of titular metropolitans and bishops with special missions. They convene once a year for the Holy Synod, presided over by the metropolitan of Athens.

CLAUDIA RAPP

See also Orthodox Church

Further Reading

Ferguson, Everett, Bishop entry in *Encyclopedia of Early Christianity*, 2nd edition, edited by E. Ferguson, 2 vols, New York: Garland, 1997, pp. 182–85

Hussey, J.M., *The Orthodox Church in the Byzantine Empire*, Oxford: Clarendon Press, 1986

Runciman, Steven, *The Great Church in Captivity: A Study of the Patriarchate of Constantinople from the Eve of the Turkish Conquest to the Greek War of Independence*, London: Cambridge University Press, 1968

Telfer, W., *The Office of a Bishop*, London: Darton Longman and Todd, 1962

Ware, Timothy, *The Orthodox Church*, 2nd edition, London and New York: Penguin, 1993

Bithynia

Region of northwest Asia Minor

Bordering the Sea of Marmara, the straits of the Bosporus, and the southern shores of the Black Sea, and situated opposite Constantinople (Istanbul), Bithynia is today part of Turkey, and well known for its Byzantine fortifications and churches. Although originally confined to the peninsula of Chalcedon, it gradually extended eastwards to Heraclea and Paphlagonia and southwards across the Propontis to Mysian Olympus, a well-known Byzantine monastic centre during the iconoclastic period. Though mountainous and densely forested, it was one of the most prosperous regions of Asia Minor. Not only did it contain good pastureland, but it also produced fine timber and all kinds of fruits and grains. It was blessed with fine harbours, fertile valleys, and supplies of marble. The principal routes to the Anatolian plateau and to Pontus ran across it. However, its chief channel of communication was the Sangarius river which, with its tributaries, watered its fertile agricultural lands. As a corridor between Europe and inner Anatolia, Bithynia was situated in a strategic yet vulnerable position between east and west.

Bithynia was named after the Bithyni, one of the warlike Indo-European tribes that had emigrated from Thrace during the latter part of the 2nd millennium BC. In 560 BC the land was conquered by king Croesus of Lydia, but it fell into the hands of the Persians when the latter conquered Lydia four years later. However, foreign rule had very little effect on Bithynia, which

retained its ethnic identity and survived into Hellenistic times under the rule of a local dynasty. It often waged war with the Greek colonies of the coast, and the warlike nature of its inhabitants saved it from complete domination by the Persians after the 6th century BC. It was occupied by Alexander the Great in 334 BC, although the warlike tribes did not fully submit to his conquest. After Alexander's death in 323 BC, Antigonus I ruled the land nominally for some time and founded Nicaea (modern Iznik), which subsequently became a prominent city of Bithynia. But the Bithynians regained their independence under Zipoetes in the early 3rd century BC. His son Nicomedes I established the first dynasty of Bithynian kings and ruled from 278 to 250 BC. In 264 BC he founded Nicomedia (modern Izmit) and made it his capital. He made an unsuccessful offer to pay the heavy public debt of the Cnidians in return for the *Venus* of Praxiteles. In order to protect themselves against the Seleucids and their rival Heraclea, the kings adopted a policy of both aggression and judicious alliance. As a result their power spread to inner Paphlagonia, to the fertile basins round Nicaea and Prusa, and eventually over the cities of the coast. Nicomedes invited into Anatolia as mercenary allies the warlike Celts who were subsequently settled in Galatia. This led to turbulent conditions in the land for many years thereafter. The country, however, prospered under his successors, stabilizing itself internally while shifting alliances and waging wars with powerful neighbours such as Pergamum to which, however, it lost some territory during the 2nd century BC. These kings founded cities and promoted Greek culture.

The kingdom reached the height of its power in the early 2nd century BC, but this was followed by a century of rapid decline under incompetent leadership. Its notable rulers were Prusias I (237–192 BC), Prusias II (192–148 BC), Nicomedes II (142–91 BC), and Nicomedes III (91–74 BC). The last mentioned was a close ally of the Romans, being little more than a Roman puppet, and on his death he bequeathed his kingdom to Rome. This led to the Third Mithridatic War (74–63 BC) when Mithridates VI of Pontus tried without success to prevent the Romans from annexing Bithynia. During 65–63 BC Pompey organized Bithynia and Pontus into a single Roman province for purposes of administration. Its capital was Nicomedia which, nearly three centuries later, became the imperial seat of Diocletian. To facilitate the maintenance of order and the collection of taxes, Pompey divided the territory among 11 cities. Much of the land was split up into large estates, especially in the region of Nicaea. Although this area was heavily exploited by the Publicani (tax-farmers) during the 1st century BC, and in consequence much land was transferred to Italian owners, under the empire it became very prosperous. The rapid recovery of these cities from the ravages of war speaks well for Roman rule.

At first, the new province was governed by proconsuls. However, under the Julio-Claudian emperors imperial procurators assumed greater responsibilities owing to the importance of the highways to the eastern frontiers and Syria as well as the maritime connections with the Black Sea. Under Trajan and Hadrian the proconsuls were replaced by special imperial legates, and this agreement became permanent from the time of Marcus Aurelius. Pliny the Younger was sent as propraetor to Bithynia to restore the solvency of some cities there, particularly Nicaea and Nicomedia, which so rivalled one another in building as to risk bankruptcy. His correspondence with Trajan well reflects the conditions of Bithynian city life in the early 2nd century AD, while the speeches of Dio Cocceianus show symptoms of a booming but uncontrolled civic prosperity, as reflected in embezzlement by magistrates, lavish building programmes, bitter feuds between cities, and popular discontent.

Bithynia was the home of some well-known scientists and writers such as Hipparchus of Nicaea and Arrian of Nicomedia. It was also the temporary residence of the Latin authors Catullus and Suetonius, as well as the younger Pliny. Helena, the mother of the emperor Constantine, came from Bithynia. The *octophorus*, or eight-man litter, was particularly associated with the Bithynian kings. Bithynia became a separate province in the early 4th century AD, and continued to exist into the 8th century when Slav captives were settled there.

Under the Byzantine empire the territory of Bithynia was restricted to an area west of the Sangarius, and constituted a province in the diocese of Pontus. Although the growth of Constantinople eclipsed its cities, Bithynia prospered as a result of its position on the military and commercial routes between Constantinople and Anatolia. In the 7th century it became part of the Opsikion theme and was subsequently divided between that theme and the Optimatoi. Ecclesiastically, after 451 Bithynia was divided into the three provinces of Nicomedia, Nicaea, and Chalcedon. It was overrun by the Turks under Osman in 1298, and thereafter formed an integral part of the Ottoman empire.

D.P.M. WEERAKKODY

Summary

A region of northwestern Asia Minor, Bithynia was named after the tribe of the Bithyni which had emigrated from Thrace. It was taken by the Persians in 556 BC and by Alexander the Great in 334 BC, but it was never fully subdued. A successful dynasty of Bithynian kings ruled from 278 to 74 BC. In 65–63 BC Pompey organized Bithynia and Pontus into a single province. It was later part of the Byzantine Opsikion theme and was overrun by the Ottomans in 1298.

Further Reading

Jones, A.H.M., *The Cities of the Eastern Roman Provinces*, Oxford: Clarendon Press, 1937, revised by Michael Avi-Yonah *et al.*, 1971

Magie, David, *Roman Rule in Asia Minor, to the End of the Third Century after Christ*, 2 vols, Princeton, New Jersey: Princeton University Press, 1950; reprinted New York: Arno Press, 1975

Black Sea

The Greek *Pontos Euxeinos* or *Axeinos,* Arabic *Bahr al-Nitash*, medieval Latin *Mare Majus*, Slavonic *Chernoye More*, and Turkish *Kara Deniz,* is called the Black Sea in most languages, probably in apposition to oriental concepts of geography by colour – e.g. the Yellow Sea and the Mongol Golden Horde were somewhere east or north, and for medieval Greeks (and modern Turks) the White Sea was the Aegean, while the Red Sea was also thought to embrace the Indian Ocean. Classical Greek explanations that the "hospitable" Euxine replaced the "inhospitable" Axine may mask an Iranian origin in variants of "black" *afshin*. Certainly non-classicizing Greeks call it so as the *Mavri Thalassa*.

The Black Sea is a vast basin, in shape a figure of 8 on its side, 1180 km in width from Thrace to Colchis (where the Argonauts sought the Golden Fleece) but only 263 km at its waist from the Crimea to Anatolia. This basin is filled by great rivers: clockwise from the Thracian Bosporus are the Classical Panysos (Bulgarian Kamcija), the Istros (Danube, the single greatest river, with many mouths), the Tyras (Slavonic Dnestr), the Hypanis (Slavonic Bug), and the Borosthenes (Slavonic Dnepr). The Tanais (Slavonic Don) percolates across the Sea of Maiotis (Azov), through the Cimmerian Bosporus, into the Black Sea proper. The Phasis (Rioni) runs down from the Caucasus to the most humid corner of the Black Sea. Indeed Batumi, known to French sailors as "Le pissoir de la Mer Noire", sustains a staggering annual rainfall of almost 2500 mm, while the western lobe of the sea attracts from 350 mm in the Crimea to 500 mm in Istanbul. From Anatolia on the south coast the Iris (Kizil) and Halys (Yeşil), the Red and Green rivers of Turkey, debouch through broad deltas.

The Euxine basin is tilted south, from floating weeds at the mouths of the Dnestr and Dnepr and the 8-metre shallows of the Sea of Azov below the Don, to a depth of 2245 m just north of Sinope. At some stage, still disputed by geologists, this great accumulation of fresh river water burst out through the Thracian Bosporus above Byzantium into the progressively more salty waters of the Mediterranean and, eventually, of the Atlantic. Yet this Bosporus is a mere pinhole. The result is that the Black Sea is sulphurous and lifeless below about 150 m. Through a double current, it has been estimated that the Bosporus can recycle the surface waters within 140 years, but the stagnant depths take up to 2500 years to renew. Nevertheless the Black Sea harbours some 180 kinds of fish, including an anchovy (*engroulis encrasicolus*, Aristotle's *amias*, Turkish *hamsi*) and Maiotic sturgeon, the produce of which, including varieties of caviare, were preserved for Lenten austerity in medieval Constantinople. But preservation requires salt, of which the sea itself is short. As Strabo observed, the fish which most attracted Greeks into it was the Greek *palamida* (Latin *pelamys sarda*, Turkish *palamut*, or English bonito), which gyrates clockwise round the sea, against its sluggish prevailing current. The palamida starts off life in the Danube delta in spring, and skirts the northern coast of Anatolia from Trebizond to Sinope where fishermen, with long rods, cluster to catch it in late summer. In autumn the palamida plunges down the Bosporus, returning from the Aegean in winter. Among other products, grain from the Balkans and northern steppe was first in bulk and significance. It was important to ancient Greece and medieval Italy and essential to Constantinople after Egypt was lost to Islam. There was Vlach cheese and Crimean wine, Scythian and Caucasian slaves – including Mamluks for Egypt. The 10th-century Varangian route down the Dnepr rapids brought products of the north, such as furs, wax, honey, amber, and pilgrims, to Constantinople in *monoxyla* (dugout canoes), and in turn gave the Mediterranean a back door to the Baltic where, unlike the Anglo-Saxons, the Vikings knew what a sponge was. Anatolia and the Caucasus exported minerals (silver, copper, tin, iron, alum, naptha); Trebizond wine, oil, and hazelnuts (once

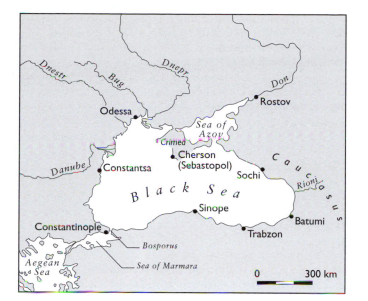

9. Black Sea

tended to turn their backs on their hinterland. External interest was in three stages. In the first the significance of the Greek colonies established from the 7th to the 5th century BC was largely cultural – the encounter of peoples of the interior with Classical Hellenism – and then strategic – the concern of Rome and Byzantium with how to deal with successive waves of steppe peoples from the 3rd to the 13th century AD, by acculturization, evangelization, or simply summer warfare. The pattern of ancient Greek colonization, from Megara but mostly Milesian, was strikingly replicated in a second stage from 1261 to 1475, by Italian stations from Venice (but mostly Genoese, and sometimes both). These were more miniature Hong Kongs than colonies, but opened a European window on the east to merchants such as Marco Polo and Franciscan missionaries throughout the Mongol empire. But such is the continuity of settlement in the first two stages that they may be taken together.

The *periplus* or circuit of major Greek settlement in the first two stages may be taken clockwise from and to the Bosporus, with the run of the palamida. On the west coast lay Mesembria (medieval Mesembre, modern Nesebur); Tomis (modern Constanţa, where Ovid was exiled); and Histria, whose shrunken walls were built against against 3rd-century Gothic and 7th-century Avar attack; its function was replaced by the medieval settlement of Vicina, up the Danube. The major Greek colony of the Crimea was Cherson, replaced as an entrepôt by Theodosia (medieval Caffa, modern Feodosiya), and finally, as a naval arsenal, by Sebastopol. Around Rostov at the mouth of the Don lay the shifting and most remote of ancient Greek and medieval Venetian colonies: Tanais (medieval Tana). The Cimmerian Bosporus was flanked on the west by settlements around Pantikapaion (medieval Vospro, modern Kerch) and, on the eastern Taman spit of the often autonomous Bosporus, by Tmutorokan (medieval Matrega). On the east coast lay Georgippa (modern Anapa), another integrated site of local and Greek peoples from the 5th century BC, and Pityous (medieval Pezonda, modern Pitsunda), whence St John Chrysostom was on his way to exile when he died in AD 407. The "deep harbour" of Bathys Limen (medieval Lovati, modern Batumi) may have been the best in the Black Sea, but led nowhere. Trapezous (medieval Trebizond, modern Trabzon) was not really a harbour, but led everywhere in Central Asia. Other Anatolian Greek settlements, concluding the circuit west, followed the same pattern: Kerasous (modern Giresun); Amisos (medieval Simisso, modern Samsun), which during the 19th century sprang from being a small Turkish village to the largest Greek city of the sea, controlling the Ottoman tobacco trade); Sinope; Amastris (modern Amasra); and Pontic Herakleia (medieval Puntarachia, modern Ereğli).

From 1475 to 1793 the Black Sea became an Ottoman lake, crossed by monks of Trebizond to the Danubian principalities, khans of Crim-Tatary, or pilgrim patriarchs of Antioch, all Ottoman subjects or tributaries. The third Greek phase of its history began with the Russian conquest of the north from 1793. Within reach of Constantinople and the warm sea of the Mediterranean, the Russians named Odessa with antiquarian zeal after the ancient Greek colony of Odessos, near Varna, changing its sex on the way, and the Orthodox Church found that St Andrew, the first-called Apostle, had put in there in 9th-century tradition on his anticlockwise *periplus* of the Black Sea

known from Novgorod to the Nile); and Paphlagonia timber and livestock (which was brought to Constantinople either on the hoof or as bacon).

Such products of its hinterland might have brought Greek colonists earlier into the Black Sea were it not so inhospitable to shipping. Any Argonaut from the Aegean (the tale is only exemplary) faced a climb against the surface current up the straits of the Dardanelles, through the prosperous Sea of Marmara (where Proconnesus provided the white marble of Constantinople), and then a dash through the sphincter of the Bosporus, whence the Clashing Rocks spewed him into the further alarms of the Black Sea. It is not surprising that, while ancient Troy was a haven for porterage to the south, 7th-century BC Byzantium was a late-comer to the north. The tideless sea has few natural harbours. Typically, local boats are double-ended and hug the shore, up on to which they are winched. Oared craft, like the *Argo*, are hazardous and do not carry much. Along with portolan maps and double-entry book-keeping, the Italians introduced larger cargo ships from the 13th century, but few exceeded 500 tons and a 900-ton ship launched from Sinope in 1461 was a wonder of its day. The northern, shallower parts are liable to ice during three winter months and to sudden storms, which can snap masts in two as late as March. The Anatolian coast is free of fog for only three summer months. This means that ancient and medieval shipping from the south tended to transhibernate, which encouraged colonization on the alien shores. Nevertheless Euxine transport by sea was still more economical than by land (where the price of grain might double every 50 km), and allowed Constantinople the luxury of a double cuisine – based on both olive oil and animal grease. Depending on the weather, the sea was about two weeks' sail from end to end (by which route Georgians reached Mount Athos and Armenians Bulgaria) and, if lucky, just two days at its waist from the Crimea to Sinope: but many travellers hung around for months – a rhythm broken only when steam replaced sail.

Apart from grain, and perhaps wine and salt fish, most Euxine commerce was internal. Except for exploiting it, ports

which began with Byzantium. Nevertheless Odessa attracted Greek settlers, and a revolutionary brotherhood, the *Philike Hetaireia,* was founded there in 1814, now memorialized in an excellent museum. After the Greek War of Independence and further Russian intervention, the Treaty of Adrianople of 1829 allowed southern access to the Black Sea again, when Greeks eagerly reinvigorated the old pattern, now largely commercial. In 1853 a Russian squadron sank a Turkish flotilla in the harbour of Sinope, precipitating the Crimean War. But the greater revolution thereafter was of steam over sail, in which Greek entrepreneurs participated. Septinsular Greeks (from Ithaca especially) cornered the Danube shipping trade. Sinope itself, the historic hub of the Black Sea, enjoyed a final period of prosperity as a coaling station. The 20th century brought a sequence of changes which has come near to concluding the third stage of Greek involvement in the Black Sea. In Sinope today a giant radar establishment faces an equivalent station in the Crimea, both now dormant. Ottoman Greek palamida fishers were replaced by Turks from Greece after 1923, but with the end of steam, they can only look at international shipping that has no call on Sinope, even for its fish, which struggle for survival in the now poisonous waters brought down by the rivers into the Black Sea.

ANTHONY A.M. BRYER

Further Reading

Ascherson, Neal, *Black Sea*, London: Cape, and New York: Hill and Wang, 1995

H.M. Admiralty, *The Black Sea Pilot*, London, 1855–1942

Koromela, Marianna L., *Oi Hellines sti Mavri Thalassa: apo ten Epochi tou Chalkou os tis Arches tou 20ou Aiona* [Greeks at the Black Sea: From the Bronze Age to the Start of the Twentieth Century], Athens, 1992

"The Black Sea" (symposium), *Archeion Pontou*, 35, Athens, 1979

Blemmydes, Nikephoros 1197–1272

Scholar and teacher

Nikephoros Blemmydes was born in Constantinople, the son of a physician. After the Latin occupation of the capital in 1204 he moved with his parents to Nicaea, where he studied medicine, mathematics, philosophy, and theology. His subsequent career in the Church was initiated by the patriarch Germanos II, who ordained him *anagnostes* (reader), deacon, and *logothetes* (patriarchal official). In 1235 he took monastic vows and was appointed *hegoumenos* of the monastery of Gregory Thaumatourgos in Ephesus. During the years 1239–40 he travelled to Mount Athos, Thessalonica, Larissa, and Ohrid in search of books, which were not available in Nicaea or Ephesus. In 1241 he founded his own monastery near Ephesus, but he did not manage to ensure its independence, so it finally became a *metochion* (dependency) of the Galesios monastery. In 1254 he was offered the patriarchal throne, but refused it and chose to remain a monk. He died in his monastery in 1272.

Blemmydes was one of the most learned and influential scholars of his time. He was also renowned as a devoted teacher, and among his students were George Akropolites and

the emperor of Nicaea Theodore II Laskaris (1254–58). He left two versions of a remarkable autobiography, the *Curriculum Vitae et Carmina* (1264) and the *Autographia sive Curriculum Vitae* (1265). It has elements of a hagiographical work as well as some vivid passages with valuable information about his education and intellectual development. The arrogance and the exaggerations that this work contains in places give us a good idea of Blemmydes' difficult character.

Around 1260 he wrote an introductory *Compendium* in two books, the first summarizing logic and the second physics. The introduction to logic, which was written at the suggestion of the emperor, opens with the statement that logic is very helpful in understanding scripture. It gives in 40 chapters the contents of Porphyry's *Isagoge* and Aristotle's *Categoriae, De Interpretatione, Analytica Priora,* and *Sophistici Elenchi,* using the logical works of the ancient commentators as well as of earlier Byzantine scholars such as Michael Psellos. The introduction to physics contains 32 chapters, which briefly summarize Aristotle's *Physica, De Generatione et Corruptione, De Caelo,* and *Meteorologica,* following Olympiodorus, Simplicius, and Philoponus. In this work Blemmydes discusses with particular interest the notions of time and place and Aristotle's doctrine of the fifth element, i.e. aether, which in fact is the only point where he disagrees with Aristotle. Both introductions are quite brief and clear, especially suitable for teaching purposes. Although they are undoubtedly compilations from Aristotle and the previous commentators, they also show that Blemmydes was no mere copyist. He did include his own ideas on different occasions, and he rephrased the passages he borrowed from his sources in a way that proves he understood them. Even if they are not particularly original, these introductions were extremely influential both in the East and in the West, up to the 17th and 18th centuries – a fact that is clearly attested by the great number of manuscripts that contain them and which can be found in major libraries all over Europe.

In addition to his compendium, Blemmydes wrote two treatises on geography. The more concise of them is very similar to chapters 28 and 29 of his introduction to physics; the other is a guide to geography which turns out to be nothing more than a prose paraphrase of the poem by Dionysius Periegetes.

In his theological writings Blemmydes tried to harmonize Plato and Aristotle with Christian doctrine. He wrote treatises on the procession of the Holy Spirit, on faith (595–606), on virtue and its exercise as well as ascetic works and fragments of a Typikon. His other works include letters, medical treatises, verses, and the *Imperial Statue,* which belongs to the genre of the Mirror of Princes (which offers advice to a ruler) and in which Blemmydes gives ethical and practical advice to his student Theodore II Laskaris. It was paraphrased in the 14th century by George Galesiotes and George Oinaiotes in order to be more accessible to the layman.

KATERINA IERODIAKONOU

Biography

Born in Constantinople in 1197 the son of a doctor, Blemmydes moved with his family to Nicaea after 1204 where he studied medicine, mathematics, philosophy, and theology. Tonsured in 1235, he became abbot of a monastery at Ephesus. In 1254 he declined the offer to become patriarch of Constantinople. He was a learned and influential scholar and teacher. He died in 1272.

Writings

In *Scriptorum Veterum Nova Collectio*, edited by Angelo Mai, 10 vols, Rome, 1825–38

In *Scriptorum Graeciae Orthodoxae Biblioteca Selecta*, vol. 1, edited by H. Laemmer, Freiburg, 1864, pp. 96–186

In *Patrologia Graeca*, edited by J.-P. Migne, vol. 142, 675–1004 and 1005–1320

Curriculum Vitae et Carmina, edited by August Heisenberg, Leipzig: Teubner, 1896

Autographia, sive Curriculum Vitae, edited by Joseph A. Munitiz, Turnhout: Brepols, 1984

Further Reading

Hunger, H. and Ihor Ševčenko (editors), "Imperial Statue", *Wiener Byzantinistische Studien*, 18 (1986)

Lackner, W., "Zum Lehrbuch der Physik des Nikephoros Blemmydes", *Byzantinische Forschungen*, 4 (1972): pp. 157–69

Munitiz, Joseph A. (editor), "Typikon", *Revue des Études Byzantines*, 44 (1986): pp. 199–207

Munitiz, Joseph A. (translator and editor), *Nikephoros Blemmydes: A Partial Account*, Louvain: Spicilegium Sacrum Louvaniense, 1988

Ševčenko, Ihor, "A New Manuscript of Nicephorus Blemmydes, *Imperial Statue*, and of Some Patriarchal Letters", *Byzantine Studies*, 5 (1978): pp. 222–31

Ševčenko, Ihor, "Nicéphore Blemmydes: autobiographies (1264 et 1265)" in *La Civiltà bizantina dal XII al XV secolo: aspetti e problemi*, Rome: Bretschneider, 1982

Tsouyopoulos, N., "Das Ätherproblem und die Physik-Abhandlung des Nikephoros Blemmydes" in *Rechenpfennige: Aufsätze zur Wissenschaftsgeschichte*, Munich: Deutschen Museums, 1968

Verhelst, M., "La Tradition manuscrite de Nicephore Blemmyde: A propos du ms. Paris. Gr. 1999", *Bulletin de Philosophie Médiévale*, 8–9 (1966–67): pp. 111–18

Boeotia

Region of central Greece

The land of Boeotia is hemmed in by mountains on all sides. Along the Corinthian gulf the high mass of Mount Helicon and the lower pine-clad heights of Mount Cithaeron form the southern links in the great chain of mountains starting with Pindus in the north and continuing with Parnassus in Phocis. Parnassus in turn sends a spur eastwards to meet a spur of Cnemis, the two leaving only a gap of some 400 m for the course of the Cephissus river. This line forms the boundary between Boeotia and Phocis. From Oeta in Thessaly another chain advances until it meets Parnes, which stretches westwards towards Cithaeron, thereby separating Boeotia from Attica.

Within these mountains Boeotia lay split into two great basins, that of Orchomenus in the west and that of Thebes in the east, each of them quite distinct and separated from the other by the ridge of Onchestus. Copais, the largest lake in Greece for most of history, further served to divide Boeotia. Reaching from Mount Ptoos in the east to Helicon in the west, the lake left only a narrow ribbon of land to carry the road between Orchomenus and Thebes. Apart from the mountains

Lake Copais, drained in the late 19th century, was the most conspicuous feature of the landscape, covering an area of some 360 sq. km.

The western basin of Boeotia is a patchwork of small plains and valleys separated from one another by bare, rugged hills, and watered by numerous springs and rivulets. The region was thickly settled, with Chaeronea, Lebadea, Coronea, and Haliartus each commanding the resources of level ground, and Orchomenus dominating the entire area. The eastern basin was marked by more and larger plains that supported numerous cities. The combination of good land and an ample, steady supply of water ensured prosperous farming. The openness of the terrain also permitted easy communication among cities. This region possessed the only good road to the sea. Its many cities included Thisbe, Thespiae, Plataea, Acraephia, Tanagra, and Aulis. Within the basin the centrally located city of Thebes was predominant. From the outset of the Persian Wars until the *pax Romana* Boeotia was the "dancing floor of Ares", the scene of countless battles, an epithet equally applicable to later ages.

Within the western basin the plain of Chaeronea, onto which ran the high road from northern Greece, formed the threshold to Boeotia. Commanding a fertile plain some 20 km in length and 3 km in breadth, the walled city of Chaeronea stood at the foot of the hills on the southern side of the plain. Its scanty remains include the theatre and the lion monument that marks the site of the battle there in 338 BC between Philip of Macedon and the Greeks. Sulla defeated the army of the Hellenistic king Mithridates there in 86 BC. From Chaeronea a main road led northeastwards to Orchomenus, the principal city of the western basin. The city stood at the southern foot of Mount Acontium immediately above Lake Copais. Connecting the city with its fortified citadel runs a long line of magnificent walls. Its most notable architectural remains include the tholos, or beehive tomb, and the remains of a palace, both of which testify to the greatness of Orchomenus during the Mycenaean period (c.1600–1250 BC). From the Classical period comes the newly found theatre, and from the Byzantine period dates the church of Koimesis tis Theotokou (the Falling Asleep of the Mother of God), built in the Bulgar architectural tradition. Orchomenus was also the site of the battle of Lake Copais in 1311, when soldiers of the Catalan Grand Company smashed the defenders of Frankish Greece.

South of Orchomenus lay Lebadea, overlooking a fertile plain that stretched from Mount Helicon to the Copaic basin. The city itself was always strategically significant owing to its location on the main road between the western and eastern basins. Its prominence in antiquity was due to the famous oracle of Trophonius, which functioned from the 6th century BC until the 3rd century AD. Lebadea flourished during the Middle Ages. The extant Frankish fortifications testify to its prosperity and military importance. During the 14th century it was fought over by the Catalans, Franks, and Navarrese, only to fall to the Turks in 1394. It was the second city in Greece from the time of the Turks until the War of Independence. Its magnificent 18th-century watchtower is still conspicuous evidence of its prominence. The route westwards from Lebadea to Thebes passed the valley of Coronea, at the entrance of which sat the city on a twin-peaked summit. Remains of the city are few, but in its neighbourhood stood the renowned sanctuaries of Itonian Athena and Athena Alalcomenae. Coronea was additionally important because of its communications up the Phalarus valley to a highland route over Mount Helicon. Its topographical position meant that Coronea was the scene of several major battles. At the eastward end of the road stood Haliartus, one of the strongest points between Lake Copais and Mount Helicon. Situated on a low hill and surrounded by stout circuit-walls, Haliartus commanded a narrow pass that could not be outflanked, wherefore it too often became a battlefield. Haliartus possessed a small, but fertile, plain, and its low, fortified acropolis contained a temple and several other public buildings. Onchestus, to the east of Haliartus, occupied a low ridge between Copais and the Theban plain. Its significance was religious, political, and symbolic in nature. In the 6th century BC it was the seat of an amphictyonic league composed of several major Boeotian cities. There the Boeotians celebrated their unity by a common festival dedicated to Poseidon. Onchestus reached its acme in history as the political capital of the re-established Boeotian Confederacy of the Hellenistic period.

East of Onchestus lay Thebes, the principal city of the eastern basin and the capital of Boeotia. It controlled the large, fruitful Aonian plain in the north, and lay near both the Asopus valley to the south and the Teneric plain to the west. Its rich and open land, combined with ample and constant supplies of water, nurtured a thriving agricultural economy. The acropolis of Thebes was the low plateau of Cadmea, which has been the primary seat of inhabitation from prehistory to today. Remains of the city, however, are few. Nonetheless, Thebes played a distinguished role in Greek affairs throughout history, and at one point in the 4th century BC it was the greatest power in Greece.

Emanating north of Thebes was a road leading to Acraephia of which little remains, and a much more important route passed to the northeast of Acraephia to Aulis and Chalcis. Aulis was the best harbour in Boeotia. It was the point where Agamemnon sacrificed Iphigeneia before sailing to Troy, and from it Hesiod sailed to Euboea. It was the chief harbour of Epaminondas' naval programme of 364 BC, and served as a port for two large Hellenistic fleets. Its most famous monument was the temple of Artemis and its adjacent buildings. Almost due east of Thebes is Tanagra, situated in the eastern part of the plain of the Asopus river. It is Homer's "Graia by the sea". Little is left of the city except for fragments of the circuit-wall and the foundations of a few buildings.

Plataea was located south of Thebes at the foot of the major passes over Mount Cithaeron from Megara and Attica. As the portal of southern Boeotia, Plataea was the perfect base from which to guard the passes. Though not large, its plain was capable of sustaining a city of ample size. Plataea was most famous for the decisive victory won there by the Greeks over the Persians in 479 BC. After the battle the Greeks erected the altar of Zeus Eleutherios (Zeus the Free). Thereafter, it became insignificant apart from its Panhellenic festivals, which were still celebrated as late as the 3rd century AD. Southwest of Thebes in the eastern basin, Thespiae overlooked a small region of rich river valleys beneath low hills. It had access to the Corinthian Gulf by way of Creusis and farther west by Thisbe, both separated from Thespiae by mountains. Thespiae boasts only a few ruins, for in the 19th century French archae-ologists destroyed much of its walls in search of inscriptions. It survived into the time of the Roman empire as a religious centre, owing to its Panhellenic festivals of Eros and the Muses.

Boeotia was prominent throughout history, but its grandest moments came during the Classical period. It survived the Persian Wars to emerge as a united people and government. In 447 BC it created a confederacy that introduced the first effective federal body in Greek history. Having helped to defeat Athens in the Peloponnesian War, Boeotia rose to ascendancy in Greece during the Theban hegemony. In the Hellenistic period Boeotia suffered decline, but rose again during the Roman empire. The Middle Ages saw the spread of Christianity through the region and economic prosperity that even innumerable wars never entirely destroyed. Only with the coming of the Turks did Boeotia again decline. In the 19th and 20th centuries Boeotia yet again enjoyed a prosperity that endures today.

JOHN BUCKLER

Summary

A region of central Greece, Boeotia is surrounded by mountains. In the 5th century its cities formed a confederacy which helped to defeat Athens in the Peloponnesian War. After the war Boeotia briefly dominated Greece during the so-called Theban hegemony. It declined during the Hellenistic period but rose again under the Romans. During the Byzantine period it was prosperous but declined again under the Ottomans. Its prosperity returned in the 19th century.

Further Reading

Buck, Robert J., *A History of Boeotia*, Edmonton: University of Alberta Press, 1979
Buck, Robert J., *Boiotia and the Boiotian League, 423–371 BC*, Edmonton: University of Alberta Press, 1994
Buckler, John, *The Theban Hegemony, 371–362 BC*, Cambridge, Massachusetts: Harvard University Press, 1980
Fossey, John M., *Topography and Population of Ancient Boiotia*, Chicago: Ares, 1988
Pausanias, *Description of Greece*, edited by J.G. Frazer, vol. 5, London and New York: Macmillan, 1898, pp. 1–212
Roesch, Paul, *Etudes béotiennes*, Paris: Boccard, 1982

Books and Readers

The two main pre-alphabetic scripts in use in the Bronze Age, Linear A (used c.1800–1450 BC in Minoan Crete) and Linear B (attested in Mycenaean inscriptions from the 13th century BC), seem to have been exclusively employed for administrative recording. Writing and reading were confined to professional scribes.

In the early 8th century BC the alphabetic script was adopted in the Greek world from the east (the first examples date from c.740 BC). The absence of writing for many centuries had encouraged the oral mode of literary production, which the Homeric epics seem to reflect. Although writing and communication with written messages were known, Archaic Greece was predominantly a society of oral traditions (law, religion, history). Poetry (epic or lyric), whether orally composed or written down, was meant to be heard and was orally performed. Yet we hear of editions of the poems of Sappho and

Alcaeus arranged in a certain order, and we assume that there were books of them owned by the performers and by the poets themselves, who appear to have known each other's work. From the 7th century BC papyrus was used for writing purposes, becoming the main writing material around 500 BC. The Greek word for "book" (*biblion*) means papyrus strip, thus suggesting the primacy of the papyrus roll as a book form. Other writing materials included leather, and Herodotus (5. 8) mentions that the Ionians used leather rolls. Books were scarce, afforded only by magistrates such as the tyrants Polycrates of Samos and Pisistratus of Athens, who are said to have owned collections of books (Athenaeus, 1. 3a).

The papyrus plant grew mainly in Lower Egypt, especially the Nile valley, and from a very early date it served writing purposes in Pharaonic Egypt. Its manufacture involved cutting the stem into short segments, slicing the white pith into thin strips, and placing them vertically parallel to each other; over this layer a second layer of strips was placed horizontally; the two layers were compressed so as to become one, and the sheet was then smoothed with a stone. Afterwards dried sheets were glued together to form a roll, usually 6–8 m long; rollers often protected the outer sheets. The scribes normally used for a writing surface the inside of the roll, where the fibres are horizontal, allowing the pen to run smoothly along them. The text was arranged in columns (*selides*) of varying height and length. The writing was in majuscule script without word division, punctuation, accents, or breathings. Titles, mostly later inventions, and authors' names usually came at the end of the roll. The lack of a law of copyright made forgeries common. Divisions into books largely reflect divisions into rolls and are artificial for all Greek writers before the 4th century BC. The reader held the roll with both hands, rolling up and unrolling so that the required portion of text was in front of him. Reading in antiquity amounted to reading aloud. It was difficult to make references or to quote with precision. Hence ancient readers usually quote from memory.

In the Classical period the use of books (i.e. rolls) became widespread, as the testimony of a number of Attic vases clearly shows. Intellectuals wrote down their treatises and published them by reading them aloud or having them read out (*ekdosis*) by a literate slave (*anagnostes*). Socrates in the *Phaedo* (97b–98b) says that he heard read a book of Anaxagoras and subsequently procured it to read it by himself. Protagoras also published his *On the Gods* by having it read aloud. There is evidence for an organized book market, and we learn that Anaxagoras' works were available for a drachma (*Apology*, 26d). The plays of Aeschylus, Sophocles, and Euripides were also available in book form. Dionysus in the *Frogs* (52f.) reads Euripides' *Andromeda*, and Aristophanes' audience is able to consult books (*Frogs*, 1114). The dissemination of book culture in the 4th century BC made a teacher of writing and reading indispensable for the education of children (*Protagoras*, 325d–e). Although literacy levels varied, the habit of reading now became widespread, especially in higher social classes. Socrates praises a young man who spends money on books, and Aristotle was nicknamed "reader", since he used to study his books in solitude. The earliest surviving papyri with Greek texts (Timotheos, *Persai*, and the Derveni Papyrus) date from the end of the 4th century BC.

Until the end of the Classical period there were only private collections of books, often owned by an erudite individual such as Speusippus, Aristotle, and Arcesilaus or by a private institution such as the Academy and the Lyceum. In the 3rd century BC public libraries were built by the Attalids and the Ptolemies, in Pergamum and in Alexandria respectively. In the Museum in Alexandria the foundations were now laid for the editing of Classical texts. Such scholars as Zenodotus, Aristophanes of Byzantium, and Aristarchus showed critical acumen in their editions of Homer, Hesiod, and the lyric and dramatic poets. They invented critical signs to indicate spurious verses and repetitions; they marked the metrical cola; and they devised aids to the reader (e.g. punctuation, change of speaker). Their work led to a general rise in the standards of book production. Division and arrangement of the contents into books were now employed by the authors themselves. Greek books circulated widely in the Roman world, featuring in private libraries of intellectuals such as Cicero and Atticus. The Bible was now translated into Greek for the Greek-speaking Jews.

Book culture flourished in late antiquity and most surviving papyri come from this period. The availability of books encouraged the making of anthologies, miscellanies, and encyclopedic works. Scholars such as Galen, Aulus Gellius, and later Origen and Eusebius, hired secretaries to help them in compiling their books. Parchment now became available as a more durable alternative to papyrus. But the appearance of the codex, the ancestor of the modern book, as an alternative book form was the most important event in book culture. A codex consists of a number of wide sheets folded vertically in half and then stitched together so that a single sheet forms two leaves. The earliest codices date from the late 2nd century AD. For some time rolls and codices coexisted (3rd–4th centuries AD), but soon the codex prevailed and became the usual book form. Initially there were codices of both papyrus and parchment, but parchment soon became dominant. The establishment of the codex form was presumably due to its adoption by Christians. Early codices contained almost exclusively Christian texts. Systematic translation from rolls to codices took place in the 4th–5th centuries AD. The earliest extant codices are the famous Codex Sinaiticus and Codex Vaticanus of the Bible (4th century). Christians developed their own literature, and Christian centres of learning were established (Caesarea, Alexandria). Important collected editions appeared, such as Andronicus' edition of Aristotle, Thrasyllus' arrangement of Plato's dialogues, Porphyry's edition of Plotinus' treatises, and textbooks with selections of Classical authors for school use.

The codex was the usual book form in the Byzantine period, but the roll survived in the transmission of liturgical texts and in the imperial chancery. The dominant Christian culture affected book production. Prayer books, bibles, and psalters enjoyed the widest readership. The lower classes tended to read hagiographic literature, collections of patristic sayings, and popular stories (e.g. *Physiologus*), while the middle classes may have also read chronicles, history (e.g. the *Patria Constantinopolis*), and novels. Books of practical use, for example medicine, astrology, and of course school books, circulated widely. The Byzantine intellectual elite was largely preoccupied with Classical texts, thus ensuring their preservation for posterity. Ancient treatises were the models for the

Byzantines – from science to literature. Books were expensive, and, at least until the introduction of paper, only the affluent could afford them. Shortages of writing materials account for the use of palimpsests, i.e. manuscripts where the original was erased and a new text written over it.

The Byzantine renaissance of the 9th–10th centuries brought a revival in book culture. The first significant change in book production was the adoption of minuscule script in the 9th century and the transcription of majuscule manuscripts into minuscule. Most of our earliest manuscripts come from this period. Majuscule manuscripts of the years 600–800 have not survived. Photios in his *Bibliotheca* gives us an idea of the books that were available at that time. Some texts were already extremely hard to find – e.g. the historians Theopompus and Ctesias, available to Photios, were no longer available to Arethas a few decades later. Arethas's recensions included division of the text into chapters and paragraphs, as well as the addition of marginal comments, lists of contents, and bibliographical notes. Many monasteries housed important scriptoria, where monks with growing professionalism prepared copies of (mostly) ecclesiastical and (some) secular authors. Luxury manuscripts might include illumination and cover decoration. This flourishing book culture ceased abruptly with the sack of Constantinople by the Fourth Crusade in 1204. The stream of humanists in the 13th and 14th centuries very successfully carried out the task of preserving such Classical literature as then survived, so that few texts that the Byzantines had in 1261 have failed to reach us. The introduction of paper, a material originally invented in China and adopted by the Arabs in the 9th century, marks an important change in book production. By the 14th century parchment had been largely replaced by paper, much of it now produced in western Europe.

The fall of Constantinople in 1453 increased the flow of Greek intellectuals to Italy, where the Renaissance was blossoming. The demand for Classical texts was great, and Greek and western scholars organized missions to procure manuscripts of Classical authors from Constantinople. Many of them owned impressive collections of Greek manuscripts. The most important event regarding book production was the invention of printing in 1452. The grammar of Constantine Laskaris was the first Greek printed book, in 1476. In the 1490s Aldus Manutius set up a publishing house in Venice dedicated to the production of Greek Classical texts. In mainland Greece under Turkish rule almost 4500 separate publications are recorded between the 1500s and the 1820s, many of them reissues of existing works. Books with religious content predominate, principally printed by Greek printers in Venice. But in the 18th century the number of books with secular content rose considerably, and by the beginning of the 19th century they outnumbered books with religious content. This shift highlights the effect of the Greek Enlightenment. The Greeks became increasingly aware of the important scientific and cultural events taking place in Europe, such as new scientific discoveries, the French Enlightenment, and modern European philosophy, and the emergent Greek intelligentsia tried to transplant the new ideas into Greece. Intellectuals such as Moisiodax, Kodrikas, Doukas, and Korais draw heavily on western philosophical and scientific treatises. Books by prominent European intellectuals (Voltaire, Locke, Newton, Beccaria) now appeared in translation. Literature played a

minimal role in this revival. Greek books were now being printed within the confines of the Ottoman empire, in Iasi, Bucharest, and in Constantinople, where a patriarchal press was set up in 1798. The first Greek newspaper (*Ephimeris*) appeared in 1797 and periodicals such as *Logios Ermis* (1811–21) were published. Levels of literacy were low among the Greek lower classes; those who could read preferred religious texts or popular literature such as the life of Alexander the Great, Aesop's *Fables*, *Bertoldos*, the *Story of Sosanna*, 17th-century Cretan literature, and translations of western romances. Some of this literature, notably the Cretan, was meant to be recited aloud rather than read silently.

The establishment of the modern Greek state in the 1830s brought a revival in the printing of books, newspapers, and journals. The language question divided book culture for a long time. The official language of the Greek state was the purified, archaizing katharevousa, which displaced the spoken demotic. Greek literature, strongly influenced by French culture, was mostly cultivated by an intellectual elite (the Phanariots). But around 1880 an intellectual change took place: talented prose writers appeared (Papadiamantis, Karkavitsas), and demotic started to gain ground. In the 20th century there was a considerable increase in the production of literature, but also an expansion of readership. In the last decades there has been an upsurge of book production. There are now more than 580 individual publishers as well as 40 to 50 institutions with publishing activity. Most are located in Athens (90.5 per cent) and in Thessalonica (8.1 per cent). In 1997 more than 5000 new titles came out (plus 3000 reprints). Literature (Greek, translated, and children's) enjoys the widest readership, with books of history, essays, technology, and classics coming next.

GEORGE E. KARAMANOLIS

See also Libraries, Literacy, Media, Papyrus, Printing, Scholarship

Further Reading

Antiquity

Dain, Alphonse, *Les Manuscrits*, Paris: Belles Lettres, 1949

Gamble, Harry Y., *Books and Readers in the Early Church*, New Haven and London: Yale University Press, 1995

Hunger, Herbert *et al.*, *Geschichte der Textüberlieferung der antiken und mittelalterlichen Literatur*, vol. 1, Zurich: Atlantis, 1961

Kenyon, Frederic E., *Books and Readers in Ancient Greece and Rome*, 2nd edition, Oxford: Clarendon Press, 1951, reprinted Chicago: Ares, 1980

Roberts, Colin H. and T.C. Skeat, *The Birth of the Codex*, London and New York: Oxford University Press, 1983

Turner, E.G., *Greek Manuscripts of the Ancient World*, 2nd edition, revised by P. J. Parsons, London: Institute of Classical Studies, 1987

Turner, E.G., *Greek Papyri: An Introduction*, Oxford: Clarendon Press, and Princeton, New Jersey: Princeton University Press, 1968, reprinted Oxford: Clarendon Press, 1998

Byzantium

Hunger, Herbert, *Schreiben und Lesen in Byzanz*, Munich: Beck, 1989

Kougeas, S., *O Kaisareias Arethas kai to Ergon autou* [Arethas of Caesarea and his Work], Athens, 1913

Reynolds, L.D. and N.G. Wilson, *Scribes and Scholars: A Guide to the Transmission of Greek and Latin Literature*, 3rd edition, Oxford: Clarendon Press, and New York: Oxford University Press, 1991

Postbyzantine / Modern Greece

Clogg, Richard, "Elite and Popular Culture in Greece under Turkish Rule" in his *Anatolica: Studies in the Greek East in the 18th and 19th Centuries*, Aldershot, Hampshire: Variorum, 1996

Dimaras, K.T., *O Neoellinikos Diafotismos* [The Modern Greek Enlightenment], Athens, 1977

Gedeon, M., *I Pneumatiki Kinisis tou Genous ton 18o kai 19o aiona* [The National Intellectual Movement of the 19th and 20th Centuries], Athens, 1976

Ichneutis, monthly journal devoted to the production and circulation of Greek books

Le Livre dans les sociétés pré-industrielles, Athens: Centre de Recherches Néoelléniques, 1982

Politis, Linos, *A History of Modern Greek Literature*, Oxford: Clarendon Press, 1973

Skiadas, N.E., *Chroniko tis Ellinikis tipografias* [Account of Greek Printing], vols 1–3, Athens, 1981–82

Wilson, N.G., *From Byzantium to Italy*, London: Duckworth, and Baltimore: Johns Hopkins University Press, 1992

Bosnia

Part of Roman Dalmatia

The earliest mention of Bosnia occurs in *De Administrando Imperio* by the Byzantine emperor Constantine VII Porphyrogennetos (913–59). At first limited to the valley of the river Bosna, the name was later applied to a wider area. Once part of the Roman province of Dalmatia, Bosnia was originally inhabited by Illyrian tribes. Archaeological evidence shows an influence of the Greek colonies in the eastern Adriatic, including Narona, at the mouth of the Neretva. The long period of Roman rule left a stronger imprint. With the exploitation of mines and a new system of communications, the economy developed and urban settlements were created.

A proconsular province since Justinian's time, Byzantine Dalmatia suffered Avaro-Slav attacks and was finally colonized by two Slavonic tribes, the Croats and the Serbs, during the reign of Herakleios (610–41). By the 10th century Croats had settled between Istria and the rivers Cetina and Pliva, while Serbs occupied territory east of that line, bordering the Bulgarian state and the Byzantine theme of Dyrrachium.

As Christianity spread from the coastal cities, a bishopric was established in Bistue Nova (modern Vitez). The most important remains of early Christian architecture are at Blagaj, Breza, Dabravine, and Zenica. In the late 9th century the Old Church Slavonic liturgy was introduced by the followers of Saints Cyril and Methodius. Although the area was under the jurisdiction of the Roman archbishopric of Salona and later of Dubrovnik and Kalosca, liturgy in Old Church Slavonic was retained; the Cyrillic script eventually replaced the Glagolitic.

Bosnia was part of the Serbian state of Prince Časlav until 950. In the following period its local rulers (*bans*) had to confront the attacks of the Croatian king Krešimir and the Bulgarian tsar Samuel. When Basil II reconquered the Balkans for Byzantium (after 1014), Bosnian *bans* became his vassals. In the 12th century Bosnia accepted the supremacy of Hungary, but rejoined the Byzantine empire under Manuel I, who mentioned it in his imperial title. After Manuel's death in 1180, Hungary's suzerainty was restored. In the late 12th century a dualist heresy (Bogomilism) reached Bosnia. *Ban*

Kulin (1180–1204) had to withstand accusations from Rome and Hungary: this was the beginning of a long struggle against the "Bosnian Church" in which Rome, the Hungarian kings, and the Dominican and Franciscan orders took a leading part. Kulin was a relation of Stefan Nemanja, a well-known opponent of the heresy in Serbia. An inscription found near Visoko mentions Kulin's portrait above the entrance to one of his churches. His charter to Dubrovnik, dated 1189, giving privileges to its traders, is one of the oldest preserved official documents in Serbian-Slavonic and in Cyrillic.

The region of Hum, comprising the valley of Neretva and the hinterland of Dubrovnik, came into the possession of the Bosnian rulers in the 14th century. These were parts of the Serbian state, with a bishopric established there by St Sava (after 1219). Other Orthodox centres of western Serbia were joined to the Bosnian state during the reign of Tvrtko I (1353–91). As the Serbian state disintegrated after the death of Tsar Stephan IV Dushan (1331–55), Tvrtko assumed the role of an heir to the Nemanjić kings to whom he was related. Referring to them as "my ancestors", he was crowned "King of the Serbs, Bosnia, the Littoral and the Western parts" by the Serbian Metropolitan at Mileševa, the burial church of St Sava. The coronation took place on the feast of St Demetrius in 1377 and was approved by Tvrtko's suzerain, King Lajos I of Hungary. Having added to his own the name Stephan, the traditional name of the Serbian kings, Tvrtko founded a new city near Kotor, which he put under the patronage of St Stephen (later Herceg Novi). On the western border, parts of Croatian Catholic lands were also joined to Bosnia. As the mining industry developed, Bosnian cities became prosperous centres of trade.

From Tvrtko's reign onwards, Bosnian history reflects the diversity of political and cultural influences which met on its territory. Religion continued to be an important factor. Catholicism was strong in the cities where miners from Saxony and foreign merchants had their colonies. Orthodoxy prevailed in the eastern parts of the country, while the "Bosnian Church" had its supporters (*patarens*) among the feudal lords. Among the most powerful was Stephan Vukčić Kosača, ruler of Hum, who in 1448 assumed the title of "Herceg of St Sava". His lands became known as Herzegovina. Vukčić's diplomacy, involving dealings with Rome, Venice, Dubrovnik, the kingdom of Naples, Hungary, the despotate of Serbia, and the Turks, illustrates the precarious position of the central Balkans in his time. Originally a *pataren*, he later favoured the Orthodox Church. In 1454 Patriarch Gennadios Scholarios reassured the monks of the Sinai monastery of St Catherine about donations received from Vukčić and advised them to pray for him. The churches of St George at Goračde and of Saints Sergius and Bacchus at Podi were Vukčić's foundations and his Orthodoxy is confirmed by the mention of icons and holy relics in his will.

By 1463 the greater part of Bosnia fell to the Turks who advanced also into Croatia and Slavonia. Although not imposed, Islamization gradually took place. Migrations, either spontaneous or forced, resulting from constant wars and devastation throughout Serbia and Bosnia-Herzegovina, became a feature in the following periods. Settlers in the border regions (Krajine), encouraged by the Habsburg emperors to continue fighting the Turks, were granted important privileges.

The pre-Ottoman cultural heritage of Bosnia-Herzegovina includes both Catholic and Orthodox churches and monasteries (with some monumental painting still extant) and many fortresses. Book illumination was practised in monastic and princely scriptoria. Of particular interest are the sepulchral stone monuments (*steći*) with carved decoration, especially at Radimlja, Olovo, and Vlasenica.

The Orthodox churches, monasteries, and schools were governed by the Serbian patriarchate of Peć until it was abolished by the Turks in 1766 and the jurisdiction transferred to the Ecumenical patriarchate (until 1920). Many churches were rebuilt and received new fresco decoration in the 16th and 17th centuries, including Papraća, Lomnica, Ozren, Žitomislić, and Zavala. Icon painting and work in precious metal were renowned. In this activity much support was provided by the contacts with the Serbian monastery of Hilandar on Mount Athos.

Under Ottoman rule Islamic arts flourished. Patrons were Ottoman dignitaries who were often Islamized members of the local families. The best monuments were planned by Mimar Sinan and his contemporaries: mosques in Sarajevo, Banja Luka, and Foča; bridges at Višegrad, Mostar, and Trebinje.

With the decline of the Ottoman empire, revolts against the Turks became more frequent, culminating in the Serbian uprising of 1875 in Herzegovina. As Austria's political drive towards the east coincided with the emergence of a united South-Slav state concept, dreaded by the Habsburgs, the geopolitical role of Bosnia-Herzegovina became crucial. Occupied by Austria after the Congress of Berlin in 1878, it was annexed to the Austro-Hungarian empire in 1908. Austria promoted industry and trade and allocated lavish funds for the urbanization of Sarajevo. However, the agrarian problems were left unattended, as Ottoman feudalism remained unchanged. The new regime was based on Austrian bureaucracy and legislature, and the use of German language.

According to the 1910 Austrian census, the population of Bosnia-Herzegovina was 1,898,044, with Serbs (Orthodox) accounting for 43.49 per cent, the Muslims 32.25 per cent, and the Croats (Catholics) 22.87 per cent. Habsburg policies exacerbated friction between these groups. Initiated in that period and later fostered by Nazi ideology, a genocidal programme against the Orthodox Serbs and their culture was implemented by the Ustaše in the "Independent State of Croatia" (which included Bosnia-Herzegovina) during World War II. The Western Powers' disregard for the delicate nature of Bosnia-Herzegovina's history had tragic repercussions in most recent times.

ZAGA GAVRILOVIĆ

Further Reading

Andrić, Ivo, *Bosnian Story*, translated by Kenneth Johnstone, London: Lincoln-Prager, 1958, reprinted 1961

Andrić, Ivo, *The Bridge on the Drina*, translated by Lovett Edwards, London: Allen and Unwin, and New York: Macmillan, 1959, reprinted Chicago: University of Chicago Press, 1977

Cvijić, Jovan, *The Annexation of Bosnia and Herzegovina and the Serb Problem*, London: Cox, 1909

Evans, Arthur, *Through Bosnia and Herzegovina on Foot during the Insurrection, August and September 1875*, 2nd edition, London: Longman, 1877

Evans, Arthur, *Illyrian Letters: A Revised Selection of Correspondence from the Illyrian Provinces of Bosnia, Herzegovina, Montenegro, Albania, Dalmatia, Croatia and Slavonia, Addressed to the "Manchester Guardian" during the Year 1877*, London: Longman, 1878

Jelavich, Barbara, *History of the Balkans*, vol. 1: *Eighteenth and Nineteenth Centuries*, Cambridge and New York: Cambridge University Press, 1983

Mackenzie, G. Muir and A.P. Irby, *Travels in the Slavonic Provinces of Turkey-in-Europe*, 2 vols, 3rd edition, London: Daldy Isbister, 1877

Malcolm, Noel, *Bosnia: A Short History*, London: Macmillan, and New York: New York University Press, 1994

Terzić, Slavenko (editor), *Bosnia and Herzegovina from the Middle Ages to the Present Time*, Belgrade, 1995

Botany

Ancient Greek literary writers often mentioned plant names, but without revealing whether these meant much to their audience. Theocritus and Sappho decorated their verses with pretty names of plants, and a famous fragment of a play by Eupolis has a chorus of goats declaiming a (very inaccurate) list of the plants that they were supposed to eat. There is nothing to show whether ancient Greek countryfolk had a profound knowledge of edible and medicinal wild plants.

Theophrastus (c.371–c.287 BC), colleague and successor of Aristotle, and the author of the *History of Plants* and *Explanations of Plants*, is regarded as the father of botany. He was a busy teacher at the Lyceum with many other interests, who probably had little time for botanical research. He seems to have known (at first or second hand) some 300 out of the 6000 species of wild plants that can today be found in modern Greece.

To judge by the *History of Plants*, Greek botanists were interested in five aspects of botany: (1) the structure and physiology of plants – for example, whether roots and shoots grow simultaneously; (2) the cultivation and propagation of field, orchard, and garden crops; (3) the occurrence and uses of wild trees; (4) drugs and medicinal herbs; (5) the occurrence of plants in particular localities.

On drug plants Theophrastus overlaps with the contemporary or earlier corpus of works associated with Hippocrates, later to be developed by Dioscorides and Galen, the great physicians of the early Roman empire. Herbs, gathered by professional herbalists, were evidently articles of commerce; Crete, with its many endemic species, was a special source.

Theophrastus does not stand alone: he mentions earlier botanists whose works do not survive. Many of his known successors were Roman rather than Greek. The technology of cultivation was taken up with greater success by Columella, Pliny the Elder, and Palladius Rutilius.

Ancient Greek botany laboured under many difficulties, beginning with that of identification and taxonomy. Botanists need to know which species of plant they are talking about. Writing a workable description of a plant, one from which someone else can recognize that plant, was a skill not far advanced in ancient times. Theophrastus mentioned brief points of difference between two or three similar species, but rarely, if ever, gave enough information to identify an unknown plant. Dioscorides attempted the systematic description of plants; in an early Byzantine manuscript his descriptions are accompanied by illustrations copied from a lost work by Crateuas; fewer than half of these actually describe or depict a recognizable plant. Botanical illustration was a skill known to the ancient Greeks, but illustrations were not accurately reproduced until the invention of woodblock printing in the Middle Ages. Without the means of identifying plants and explaining that identification to others, the science of botany could not get far. The ancient physician often did not know what exactly he was prescribing for his patient.

Even worse was the ancient Greek vice of theorizing from small amounts of data. Although this led to some success in astronomy, it could not cope with the complexities and irregularities of plant life. *The Explanation of Plants* poses such vaguely physiological questions as "Why are not all plants more fragrant in hot countries?" Its "answers" lead into a morass of abstraction and generality, Aristotelian logic at its worst, having virtually no contact with actual plants. There is no sign of the patient collection, verification, and comparison of data from which real insights might have been gained; nor of the procedure of producing a theory from existing material and then seeking fresh data with which to test it.

Theophrastus collected information about tropical plants from remote parts of the world. But he valued information not for its own sake but in order to illustrate whatever theory he was writing about. Not much of a traveller, he relied on what others told him, and displayed little interest in verifying his data. He put into circulation some misinformation that is still current: for example, the notion that ivy destroys the tree on which it grows, which he could have disproved without leaving Athens.

However, he has some genuine insights into the behaviour of plants, noticing, for example, that firs like shade and pines like sun. At one point he attempted an ecological account of an actual place, the seasonal lake of Copais, with its unique reeds, and special craft of musical-instrument-making.

Evidence suggests that the ancient Hebrews and Romans were better botanists than the Greeks: much of Theophrastus' material comes from Italy, where he had never been. This conclusion, however, depends on surviving writings, which are presumably only a small fraction of the literature that once there was. (In other fields, such as engineering and shipbuilding, the Greeks' achievements were far greater than we would suspect from the written evidence.)

By way of the Romans, the Byzantine *Geoponika* of the 10th century AD, and the Arabs, Theophrastus' legacy regarding cultivated plants was carried forward to initiate modern agricultural writing, in the form of the works of Alonso de Herrera in the 16th century. Ancient herbalism continued into Byzantine times, as shown by the attention paid to Dioscurides and his illustrations. This is the source of the post-medieval western tradition of herbals, which developed into modern botany. It was also an impetus to the development of modern plant taxonomy, as early modern botanists visited Greece and other countries to try to identify and recover Dioscurides' drug plants. The herbalistic tradition continues in Greece to this day: *Votanotheriapeutiki*, a herbal by I.K. Prinea and A.M. Sphakianaki published in Athens in 1980, is explicitly in the Dioscuridean tradition.

In some parts of modern Greece there is a precise and far-reaching vernacular knowledge of medicinal and edible wild plants. Many Cretan countryfolk are fully familiar with their island's wealth of endemic plants, and are able to give the name of each one, together with their virutes.

OLIVER RACKHAM

See also Plants

Further Reading
Baumann, Hellmut, *Greek Wild Flowers and Plant Lore in Ancient Greece*, London: Herbert Press, 1993 (an optimistic assessment of Theophrastus, passing over some of the difficulties)
Rackham, Oliver, "Ecology and Pseudo-Ecology: The Example of Ancient Greece", in *Human Landscapes in Classical Antiquity: Environment and Culture*, edited by Graham Shipley and John Salmon, London and New York: Routledge, 1996

Botsaris, Markos 1790–1823

Souliot hero in the War of Independence

Markos Botsaris, an important Souliot leader in the Greek War of Independence, became an icon for the courage of the Souliot warrior. Like many other great Greek warriors before him, he possessed such admirable personal qualities as bravery, endurance, a strong attachment to his native land and people, and above all a fierce devotion to freedom.

When Ali Pasha took over Souli in 1803, he abandoned all the favouritism that he had shown the Botsaris family while Markos's grandfather, George, and later his father, Kitsos, were in his employment. The pasha's persecution of the Botsaris family was as vigorous and savage as it was of all the Souliots. Many of their close relatives and friends were killed by the pasha's army. The surviving members of the clan, including Markos's father, were exiled to the Ionian island of Corfu where they came under the protectorate of the British. It was here that Markos and his father joined foreign armies, as was customary for Greek warriors in exile, Markos serving in an Albanian regiment under French command.

By the age of 10, Markos had begun his training in the use of arms. Like the great Spartan warriors of antiquity, the Souliots were taught to fight from an early age. They learned to move quickly and to take cover when and where they could. The Souliot warriors were renowned throughout the country for the fierceness with which they fought their battles, their ability to endure great deprivation, and the perseverance with which they strove to win their freedom.

Markos's education had begun early in Souli and probably continued during his exile on Corfu. In an attempt to help spread the Greek language, in 1809 he wrote a simple Greek–Albanian dictionary, which is in part preserved in the French Bibliothèque Nationale. In 1980 Tito Giohalas added it to the series of publications of the Academy of Athens.

The passionate love of his home finally brought Markos back to Epirus in 1819. Soon after his return from exile, he conducted negotiations with Ali Pasha which provided for the return of Souli to the Souliots in exchange for their assistance in opposing the sultan's forces. It was at this time, through his successes on the battlefield, that Botsaris gained the respect and admiration of his fellow Souliots, and renown among the leaders of Greece. He became the commander-in-chief to the Souliot forces after the demotion of Georgios Varnakiotis, who was suspected by the parliamentary authorities of striking an bargain with the Turks. Such changes of allegiance were not uncommon among the Greek and Turkish warriors of the Greek War of Independence. Botsaris himself had fought at one time against Ali Pasha's Albanian army, while at another he had fought alongside the pasha against the sultan's beleaguering forces. The ultimate goal of freedom, however, remained constant.

In July 1822, with a force of 300 warriors, Botsaris joined the Greek army at Komboti. The first battles at Plaka were successful, but later the Turkish forces took the advantage. With his remaining 32 men, Botsaris left at once for Peta, but this proved to be another disappointing defeat.

Not dissuaded by such defeats, Botsaris continued to harass the Turkish army at every turn. As winter approached in 1822, he went to assist Alexander Mavrokordatos in his defence of Missolonghi, helping to fortify the city and prepare for the advancing Turkish forces. He was also to prove himself a very capable diplomat in the Greek attempts to sow the seeds of dissension among the Turks. In a ploy to gain the time needed to receive supplies and reinforcements, Markos met the Turkish military leaders, Omer Vrionis, Mehmed Reshid, and Yusuf Pasha, with various false proposals for capitulation. At great risk to himself, he carried out this and other cunning deceptions until the government, persuaded by Mavrokordatos as to the importance of a stronghold at Missolonghi, sent reinforcements. Garrisons led by Mavromichalis, Zaimis, and Londos were included among the new arrivals.

In recognition of his abilities, the government gave Markos Botsaris the title of general, which sparked some dissension among the other chieftains of western Greece. But Markos impressed upon them the important role that unity would play in the successful liberation of Greece from the Turkish yoke. He pointed out that generals are made on the battlefield and, with this, kissed the diploma (which he had received along with the title of general) out of respect for his country, and then tore it into small pieces. This powerful demonstration won the confidence of his fellow chieftains, who all agreed to work together in earnest.

Perhaps the most famous of Markos's battles was his final one. Following the successful defence of the first siege of Missolonghi, Markos and his Souliot warriors, some 1000 men, went to Karpenisi where the Turkish-Albanian forces were ten times that number. Botsaris and his men attacked at night, taking their opponents completely by surprise, and succeeded in killing nearly 800 Turkish-Albanians. After only a short period of fighting, in an attempt to reach the tent of the pasha whom he wished to kill personally, Botsaris was hit by a stray bullet in his right eye and was able only to call out: "I've been hit, brothers!" In order to conceal his death so that the other soldiers would not lose heart, the Souliots covered his body with a coat. Later, his body was carried off the battlefield over his cousin's shoulder to be taken back to Missolonghi, where he was given a hero's burial. Unfortunately, the sense of victory after this battle fell short of its true advantage. Having

lost their commanding chief, the Souliot soldiers were to become once again the undisciplined clan that they had been before Botsaris's leadership.

Markos Botsaris's heroism has been honoured in the works of such great Greek poets as Solomos, Kalvos, Palamas, and Balaorites. His bravery has been applauded in plays by Zampelios, Soutsos, and Alkeos. A statue of him resides in the Plateia Botsaris in Missolonghi, at the Museum of the Revolution. His tragic death is depicted in four of Iatridis's ink drawings. His courage and fierce patriotism have been the subject of many klephtic ballads. One such heart-rending ballad describes the agony with which the loss of this great hero was mourned by his fellow Souliots, as well as by the whole of Greece.

JACQUELINE PETROPOULOS

Biography

Born in 1790 in Souli, Botsaris was exiled with his father to Corfu. There he served in an Albanian regiment under French command. Returning to Epirus in 1819, he became commander-in-chief of the Souliot forces. During the War of Independence he was revered for his bravery and dedication to the cause of Greek freedom and given the rank of general. He died in battle at Karpenisi in 1823.

Further Reading

Baggally, John W., Greek Historical Folksongs: The Klephtic Ballads in Relation to Greek History 1715–1821, Chicago: Argonaut, 1968

Clogg, Richard (editor), The Struggle for Greek Independence: Essays to Mark the 150th Anniversary of the Greek War of Independence, London: Macmillan, and Hamden, Connecticut: Archon, 1973

Clogg, Richard, A Short History of Modern Greece, 2nd edition, Cambridge and New York: Cambridge University Press, 1986

Dakin, Douglas, The Unification of Greece, 1770–1923, London: Benn, and New York: St Martin's Press, 1972

Dakin, Douglas, The Greek Struggle for Independence, 1821–1833, London: Batsford, and Berkeley: University of California Press, 1973

Diamandoures, Nikiforos P. (editor), Hellenism and the First War of Liberation, 1821–1830: Continuity and Change, Thessalonica: Institute for Balkan Studies, 1976

Holm, Adolf, The History of Greece from its Commencement to the Close of the Independence of the Greek Nation, 4 vols, London and New York: Macmillan, 1894–98

Howarth, David, The Greek Adventure: Lord Byron and the Other Eccentrics in the War of Independence, New York: Atheneum, and London: Collins, 1976

Kanellopoulou, Haris and Kalliopi Kyriakopoulou, 21 apo to '21 [21 from '21], Athens, 1998

Kolokotrones, Theodoros, Kolokotrones: The Klepht and the Warrior, London: Unwin, and New York: Macmillan, 1892; as Memoirs from the War of Greek Independence, 1821–1833, edited by E.M. Edmonds, Chicago: Argonaut, 1969

Lappa, Takis, Leukoma Agoniston 1821 [Album of the Combatants of 1821], Athens

St. Clair, William, That Greece Might Still be Free: The Philhellenes in the War of Independence, London and New York: Oxford University Press, 1972

Stratikis, Potis, To Athanato 1821 [The Immortal 1821], Athens, 1990

Woodhouse, C.M., Capodistria: The Founder of Greek Independence, London: Oxford University Press, 1973

Woodhouse, C.M., Modern Greece: A Short History, 5th edition, London and Boston: Faber, 1991

Bouboulina, Laskarina, *c*.1770–1825

Heroine of the War of Independence

Laskarina Bouboulina was born in Constantinople, where her father Stavrianos Pinotsis was imprisoned for his participation in the Orlov revolution of 1770. After Pinotsis's death in Heptapyrgeio prison his wife Skevo emigrated from her native Hydra to Spetses, where she married Demetrios Lazarou, a prosperous sea captain. Both islands had been settled in the early 18th century by Albanians whose maritime activities were exempt from the fiscal administration of the Porte; together with the Greek islands of Psara and Kasos, which enjoyed similar exemptions, these islands were to contribute the greatest number of ships to the Greek cause during the War of Independence.

Waxing tall, dark, and athletic, Laskarina married Demetrios Yannouzas, a sea captain, probably in 1788. She bore him three children before his death at sea in 1797. The eponym by which she is universally known derives from the name of her second husband, Demetrios Bouboulis, a wealthy Spetsiot shipowner and captain, to whom she bore three more children. On his death in 1811 Bouboulina was a wealthy woman. When the Porte sought to confiscate her inheritance on the grounds of Bouboulis's participation in the Russo-Turkish War she sought the protection of the Russian ambassador Stroganoff; by contriving an audience with the mother of the sultan she won protection for her property.

Bouboulina was apparently initiated into the *Philiki Hetaireia* during a stay in Constantinople. On her return to Spetses she undertook to build several ships. At 48 cubits and 18 cannon the frigate *Agamemnon* surpassed the prescribed limits for private vessels; Bouboulina is said to have bribed the *kapitan* Hussein Pasha into permitting its use.

During the Napoleonic wars Spetses and Hydra had profited from western European demand for imported grain. This prosperity abated when grain prices fell after the peace of 1815 and again after the good European harvest of 1820. The *Hetaireia* found the inactive sailors and merchants of the islands receptive to promises of Russian support for an insurrection. Spetses was the first island to declare independence, in late March or early April 1821.

On 4 April 1821 Greek forces besieged Nauplia; on the same day Bouboulina and the *Agamemnon* arrived in the Gulf of Argos together with the ship of the Spetsiot notable Gikas Botasis. Bouboulina obtained several more ships from Spetses, and a blockade of Nauplia was effected. On 10 April, Easter Sunday, the Turks broke the land siege. Bouboulina disembarked at the Mills of Argos (Myloi), and on the fourth day after Easter she rode into Argos to a grand reception. According to Philemon, the people of Argos saw her as another Telesilla, the Argive poetess who armed the women of Argos after its defeat by Cleomenes of Sparta (Plutarch, *Moralia*, 245 c–f). Bouboulina and Botasis provided money, munitions, and a boost to Greek morale which made possible the resumption of the siege of Nauplia. On 25 April her son Yannis Yannouzas was killed in the defence of Argos. Bouboulina is said to have reported to the administration of Spetses: "My son is dead but Argos is still ours." In May she left her brother in charge of the blockade at Nauplia, and sailed with the *Agamemnon* to assist at the blockade of Monemvasia. The impregnable fortress was starved into submission on 5 August 1821. By mid-September Bouboulina left the Mills of Argos to be present for the anticipated fall of Tripolitsa. Kolokotronis and Petrobey Mavromichalis allowed her to enter the city in order to persuade the harem of Khurshid Pasha to give up their money and jewels in return for safety. As the Greek army became aware that the six-month siege was being prolonged by such private negotiations designed to reserve the booty for their chiefs, their indignation was such that they contrived to storm the city without their leaders on 5 October 1821. The anarchic sack of Tripolitsa, during which perhaps 8000 Turks were killed, was a blow to the authority of Kolokotronis. Shortly thereafter Bouboulina's daughter Eleni was engaged to Kolokotronis's eldest son, Panos.

Bouboulina then returned to the siege of Nauplia; when the city fell in December, she was again accused of intriguing with Kolokotronis for the wealth of the Ottoman women. Frantzis reports that on being sent to scout the Ottoman ladies Bouboulina concealed many valuables in her bosom, few of which were declared to the state commission. Panos Kolokotronis and Eleni Boubouli were married with pomp at Nauplia. Panos was named the garrison commander and Bouboulina was installed as the leading figure of the city.

It was Bouboulina's kinsmen from Hydra and Spetses who would oust her. The approval of a British loan to Greece in the amount of £300,000 became the occasion for a civil war which pitted the party of Kolokotronis, including Bouboulina, against the government of the Spetsiot Botasis and the Hydriot notable Konduriottes, who as president was designated recipient of the loan. This "war of Kolokotronis" was resolved in June 1824 when Panos Kolokotronis agreed to surrender Nauplia in return for a share of the money. Konduriottes in turn refused to enter the city until Bouboulina was evacuated.

Bouboulina returned to Spetses where the travellers Emerson and Pecchio met her in May 1825. They report her response at the news of Kolokotronis's imminent release: "If it's true, I'll return to the army with him to fight the Turks." In the event, she was killed on 22 May by Yannos Koutsis, in revenge for his sister's elopement with Bouboulina's son.

Of the many women associated with the Greek revolution, such as Mado Mavrogenous, with whom she might be compared, Laskarina Bouboulina – an Arvanitissa and native Albanian speaker – retains the greatest hold on the Greek imagination. She has been celebrated in verse by Soutsos and others; novels and a tragedy have been composed about her. Her sculpture can be seen on Tinos and Spetses, and her home in Spetses is open to the public.

C.G. BROWN

Biography

A native Albanian speaker, Bouboulina was born in Constantinople *c*.1770. Returning to Hydra with her mother, she moved to Spetses and in 1788 married Demetrios Lazarou, a ship's captain. After his death in 1797, she married Demetrios Bouboulis, a wealthy shipowner. He died in 1811. She joined the *Philiki Hetaireia* and agreed to supply ships to the war effort, notably for the siege of Nauplia in 1821. She was murdered in 1825.

Further Reading

Bastias, Kostis, *I Bouboulina*, Athens, 1943

Finlay, George, *A History of Greece from its Conquest by the Romans to the Present Time, BC 146 to AD 1864*, 7 vols, Oxford: Clarendon Press, 1877, reprinted New York: AMS Press, 1970

Grèce, Michel de [Prince Michael of Greece], *La Bouboulina*, Paris, 1993

Kathareios, Alexandros, *I Bouboulina: Tragodia* [Bouboulina: A Tragedy], Athens, 1907

Papathanasopoulos, Elias, *Bouboulina*, Athens, 1973

Xyraki, Koula, *Gynaikes tou '21* [Women of '21], Athens, 1995

Brigandage

Brigandage was endemic in the mountains of continental Greece throughout the period of Ottoman administration. The Greeks who engaged in this activity were generally young bachelors belonging to the mountain villages and transhumant shepherd communities in the area where they operated. They shared with the inhabitants of the mountains, who were also their principal victims, the same social values predicated on notions of honour, pride, and shame, and the same social institutions which protected the material interests and social reputation of the family. Before the War of Independence brigands were known as "klephts", a term which in one sense simply means "thief", but carried more complex associations in patriotic claims to heroism and sometimes countercharges of brutality. Klephts were generally shepherds or villagers who through debt, sheep theft, homicide, or other troubles had fallen foul of the Ottoman Turkish authorities and taken to the hills. They lived by levying protection money from villagers or by looting their houses. Captives were also held to ransom, and normally decapitated if the stipulated sum was not paid. To combat these breaches of order the Ottoman authorities recruited bodies of local militia known as *armatoloi*, who were similarly men-at-arms, very often former klephts who had regained respectability through amnesty.

Klephts and *armatoloi* together formed a complementary security system that cost the Ottoman Turks very little. A captain of *armatoloi* granted the klephts in his district a certain tolerance since only their existence justified his own employment. Klephts aimed to cause just sufficient disorder to encourage the authorities to give them, in turn, amnesty and employment as *armatoloi*. The victims were, of course, the villagers, taxed by the *armatoloi* and raided by the klephts.

The fate of this klephtic tradition in the new state of modern Greece was ambiguous. It was hardly satisfactory to have to admit that many of the glorious heroes of the War of Independence had previously been brigands, and that during the course of the war some klephts had even re-entered Turkish service. The klephts now had to be portrayed as patriots resisting Turkish rule. This indeed, in a sense, was true, but it was incidental to the other purposes of the klephts already described. A heroic pastoral existence that included killing Turks, tossing the boulder, and Homeric feasting was attributed to them by folklorists and historians (not always Greek), a romantic construction far removed from the reality of klephtic life, which was generally short and often brutal, for both the klepht and his victims.

After the war many of the irregulars found it impossible to return to the unprestigious and unrewarding toil of peasant farming. If they could not find service in the Greek government's own irregular contingents, they turned again to brigandage, though they were no longer officially known as klephts. That term was too closely linked to the heroes of the War of Independence to be sullied by association with common brigandage. They had now become *listes*, common thieves and freebooters. Yet circumstances would again conspire to call on these men to join their illegal activities to a more patriotic cause.

The frontier of the new Greece, set up by the European powers, ran between Arta and Volos, excluding from the nation state more Hellenes than it included. Greece was inexorably drawn into repeated attempts to liberate Greeks still living under Ottoman rule. Its small regular army, essentially intended for internal security and ceremonial, could not hope to match the Turkish forces; nor was Great Britain prepared to allow Greece (always vulnerable to naval blockade) to contribute towards any further weakening of the Ottoman empire. In this pattern of relations brigands found their place. Whenever domestic difficulties or irredentist pressures dictated, the Greek government encouraged the formation of irregular bands to cross the frontier and foment revolt among the Christian population. The operations of irregulars could not be attributed to the Greek government with the same certainty as invasion by regular forces; and they had the added advantage that they exported the depredations of brigands to Turkish territory.

It was almost the end of the 19th century before these tactics were abandoned, partly because the revolts that they provoked regularly failed, partly because brigandage itself lost its local support with the gradual restriction of the transhumant pastoral economy in the mountains. (Many brigands were shepherds.) Moreover the political patrons of leading brigands who in the past had protected them from prosecution and used them to exert pressure at elections, or create disorder to embarrass the government, increasingly found such clients a political liability in the gradually developing state.

Klephts organized themselves in bands generally numbering between 20 and 30 men, about the number which a leader without the support of hierarchical discipline could reasonably dominate by the force of his personality. Bodies of klephts consisting of as many as 400 men were invariably temporary confederations of smaller bands which did not surrender their identities. The leader of a band was known as the *kapetanios* (captain) or *protoklephtis* (the first klepht), and his followers as *pallikaria*. The term *pallikari* emphasizes the parallel between its use in describing the duties of the young unmarried son or brother who guards the family honour, and its application in marking the role of the klephtic hero, also as a rule unmarried. The band in some respects resembled, and was modelled on, an extended family without the presence of women, the same kinship basis as that of the typical transhumant shepherd group, the *tselingato*, from which many klephts were drawn. In such bands there was generally a nucleus of two or three brothers, cousins, or kinsmen, who provided the leader with unquestioning support. Between these men and the other unrelated klephts a network of ritual relations was created through blood brotherhood. In a society where unrelated men were mutually hostile and untrusting, the *vlamides* or *bratimoi* ("blood brothers") owed each other the trust and straight dealing on which their survival depended – in the same measure as brothers.

A band of klephts operated in an area known to the captain and his closest associates. Kinsmen in villages and shepherd encampments provided intelligence and food (meat, flour, and salt), without which they could not survive or plan rational operations. In their mountain wilderness, the klephts created what order they could, establishing a number of *limeria* (camps) in inaccessible positions, between which they circulated to avoid surprise. As far as they were able, they paid great attention to their clothing and their arms, on which the leaders especially were prepared to spend extravagantly. In common with *armatoloi* and Albanian soldiers, they wore the white fustanella kilt, elaborately decorated waistcoats with silver buttons, and silver knee-plates when they could be afforded. Personal cleanliness was not a concern and it was a matter of professional pride that their kilts had become grey with encrusted dirt and grease. They armed themselves with long guns, curved swords with a fine cutting edge, and daggers, all of which could be very elaborately decorated. This concern with the display of pride, of appearing above others, was a form of visual boast, which also had the effect of discouraging their opponents.

J.K. CAMPBELL

See also Armatoloi

Further Reading

Koliopoulos, John S., *Brigands with a Cause: Brigandage and Irredentism in Modern Greece, 1821–1912*, Oxford: Clarendon Press, 1987 (the only reliable analysis of the subject, it includes an exhaustive bibliography)

Britain

Britain has felt the strong influence of Hellenism in literature, education, political and social ideas, and the visual arts, notably architecture. The country has served as a refuge for the persecuted and exiled, providing social and economic conditions that allowed Greek enterprise to flourish. Thus in the 19th century England became a centre of Greek commercial and maritime enterprise, and in the 20th century a home for a large Cypriot community. Today Britain is host every year to many thousands of students from Greece and Cyprus. In the other direction Britain has been important to the Hellenic world as a source of political and social ideas, an inspiration in literature, and a Great Power that played a determining role in the political evolution of the modern Greek state.

Greek seamen had penetrated to Britain by the 5th century BC and the traveller Pytheas of Marseilles who circumnavigated the British Isles in the late 4th century BC left a good account of this journey, which is reproduced by Strabo. In the Christian era there were contacts between England and Byzantium by way of the Carolingian courts. The Greek scholar and teacher Theodore of Tarsus occupied the see of Canterbury in the 7th century AD. Fine Byzantine silver artifacts were found in the Sutton Hoo ship burial (7th century), and the influence of Byzantium can be seen in Anglo-Saxon arts of the 10th and 11th centuries.

In the dark period after the fall of Constantinople, when Greece was lost to western European knowledge, a number of Greek scholars and mercenaries found their way to Britain. From the 16th century British trade in the Levant, conducted largely with Greeks, led to renewed interest in the Greek Orthodox Church and in the state of affairs in Greek lands. The contacts of Cyril Lukaris, the "Calvinist patriarch" (died 1638), with England contributed to this: it was at Cyril's initiative that the printing press set up for the London Greek commercial community by Nicodemus Metaxas of Cephalonia was brought to Constantinople and began to publish theological works in Greek. A Greek theologian, Nathaniel Conopius, later archbishop of Smyrna, incidentally introduced coffee to Oxford and London in the mid-17th century. By 1677 there was a sufficient community of Greek businessmen in London for them to found a (short-lived) Greek church in Soho.

Alongside these commercial and theological links, which extended to an abortive exploration of union between the Orthodox and the Anglican Churches, British 17th-century travellers and patrons helped to foster a new interest in the artistic heritage and the present state of Hellenism. John Milton was an early representative of what came to be called Philhellenism. English collectors began to take an acquisitive interest in Greek antiquities. The publication of Stuart and Revett's *Antiquities of Athens* in 1762 on behalf of the Society of Dilettanti was a turning point in the diffusion of knowledge of the Hellenic heritage. British travellers and philhellenes made a major contribution to the "rediscovery" of Greece, and to creating the climate of opinion in which the independence of the Greek state became feasible. Byron's contribution to awakening the conscience of Europe to the Greek cause was such that he is still revered by all Greeks.

The influence of British political and social ideas and administrative practice can be traced in Greek thought from the late 17th century, and was felt directly in the Ionian islands during the British protectorate from 1814 to 1864. But the primary external influence in the consolidation of the institutions of the modern Greek state was German, exercised through the Bavarian monarchy of king Otho. British liberal and free-trading ideas were attractive to the rising Greek bourgeoisie represented in the early 20th century by Eleftherios Venizelos, whose close understanding with Lloyd George and belief in the need to align Greece with the dominant maritime power in the Mediterranean led to the national schism in Greece in World War I and thence to the catastrophe at Smyrna and the uprooting of Hellenism from Asia Minor.

The main interaction of the two countries and traditions in the 19th and 20th centuries has been strategic and maritime, Greece playing an important role in Britain's approach to, control of, and influence in the eastern Mediterranean region, and Britain being seen in Greece as a key strategic factor (and at crucial times an ally) from the time of independence until after World War II. In the case of Cyprus, briefly occupied by Richard I in 1191 (and then sold), occupied again by Britain in 1878, and later a crown colony until the establishment in 1960 of the independent Republic of Cyprus, the strategic interest is still evident in the presence of British sovereign base areas on the island.

The Hellenic presence in Britain today consists of an economically dynamic business community centred on shipping and working in the City of London; a transient population of more than 20,000 students, undergraduate and post-graduate, at British universities; and a large permanent population of Greek Cypriots concentrated mainly in north London. A small Greek commercial community has been present in London since the 17th century; but the rapid growth in importance of the community dates from the late 18th century, when merchants mainly from Chios began to establish trading houses with networks extending from southern Russia to Constantinople and Smyrna to Livorno, Marseilles, and London. This emigration was given an enormous boost by the tragic effects of the Turkish massacre of Chios in 1822, which pushed members of the prominent Chiot trading families into emigration. The largest of the great Greek trading houses, Rallis Bros, first established its London office in 1818.

This community of Greeks, drawing on their widespread family networks and applying their commercial acumen in the British liberal free-trading environment at a time of expanding European trade, established their offices and homes in the City of London around Finsbury Circus, and from modest beginnings grew mightily between 1820 and the middle of the 19th century. Their trade was the import of grains from Russia through Odessa, and the export of textiles and manufactured goods. From the middle of the century on, some firms extended their commerce to India, where a great part of the Rallis activity and fortune was made. The prominent families, Rallis, Argentis, Schilizzis, and others, governed the affairs of their community through a committee or brotherhood. Their houses, their churches, first in London Wall, then the St Sophia cathedral in Bayswater, consecrated in 1876, and their funereal monuments at the Greek cemetery in West Norwood, are witness to a solidly prosperous community, characterized by intermarriage between prominent families. Greek traders from Chios played a major part in the development of the Baltic Exchange. As their prosperity grew, the prominent families moved out of the City westwards to Paddington, Bayswater, Notting Hill, and Holland Park. Towards the end of the 19th century they tended to assimilate themselves more and more with the British middle, and in some cases upper, classes. With the passing of time, education in British public schools distanced the younger generation from their Greek roots.

Shipowning developed side-by-side with commerce in the second half of the 19th century. The maritime connection has endured until the present day, though the nature of Greek commercial activities has changed and new families have come to prominence in the community. In the later 19th century a network of shipowner-traders from the Ionian islands (mainly Cephalonia and Ithaca) active in the Danube grain trade displaced the Chiots from their preeminent position. The leading new figure was Panaghis Vaglianos, a shipowner and trader who also played a central role in financing the development of the Greek merchant fleet. In the 20th century London maintained its position as a new generation from Chios, Andros, Kassos, and Oinoussai came to the fore and as the Greek fleet developed into the world's largest, specializing in dry bulk cargoes and, after World War II, in oil tankers also.

The Greek shipowning community has endured and prospered because of the perceived benefits to Greek owners of keeping their offices or agencies in London, which include tax advantages and synergy with the City of London's services. Since 1936 it has been represented by the Greek Shipping Cooperation Committee, of which the president has been seen as the doyen of the Greek community, while the metropolitan archbishop of Thyateira and Great Britain is its spiritual leader.

A substantial community of Cypriots has also developed in Britain. From a modest number early in the 20th century, this grew rapidly through successive waves of emigration after World War II, in the early 1960s when Cyprus became a republic, and after the Turkish occupation of Northern Cyprus in 1974. The Greek Cypriot community, which may now number between 100,000 and 200,000, is mainly concentrated in north London, and is present also in Birmingham, Bristol, Manchester, Liverpool, and other British cities. It is active in the restaurant and clothing trades, in services, and in the professions.

MICHAEL LLEWELLYN SMITH

Further Reading

Calvocoressi, Peter, *Threading my Way*, London: Duckworth, 1994

Casson, Stanley, *Greece and Britain*, London: Collins, 1943

Catsiyannis, Timotheos, *The Greek Community of London*, London: Nikos Smyrnis, 1993

Clogg, Richard (editor), *The Greek Diaspora in the Twentieth Century*, London: Macmillan, and New York: St Martin's Press, 1999

Harlaftis, Gelina, *Greek Shipowners and Greece, 1945–1975: From Separate Development to Mutual Interdependence*, London: Athlone, 1993

Harlaftis, Gelina, *A History of Greek-owned Shipping: The Making of an International Tramp Fleet, 1830 to the Present Day*, London and New York: Routledge, 1996

Pallis, Alexandros Anastasios, *Xenitimenoi Hellines* [Greek Expatriates], Athens, 1953

Runciman, Steven, *The Great Church in Captivity: A Study of the Patriarchate of Constantinople from the Eve of the Turkish Conquest to the Greek War of Independence*, London: Cambridge University Press, 1968

Spencer, Terence, *Fair Greece! Sad Relic: Literary Philhellenism from Shakespeare to Byron*, London: Weidenfeld and Nicolson, 1954; reprinted New York: Octagon, 1973, Bath: Chivers, 1974

Vikelas, D., *My Life*, Athens, 1908

Bulgaria

Greek colonization of the Bulgarian coast, part of the region known in antiquity as Thrace, began in the 7th century BC with Miletus leading the way. The main sites were Apollonia (modern Sozopolis), Odrysos (modern Varna), Anchialos (Pomorie), Krounoi (Balchik), Naulochus (Ozbar), and Mesembria (Nesebar). These cities led an unexciting if prosperous existence, trading wine and salt in exchange for grain and livestock. Philip of Macedon conquered the interior of Bulgaria and founded Philippopolis (modern Plovdiv) in 342 BC. Only his more powerful successors kept control of this area, and only some stubborn campaigning in 28 and 29 BC by Marcus Licinius Crassus, son of the triumvir, brought the

Roman frontier as far as the Danube. Thrace remained a client kingdom until the reign of the emperor Claudius (AD 41–54) when it was incorporated into the Roman empire. For the next 150 years the south-eastern part of Europe prospered. More cities were founded in the interior, and it is clear from the evidence of inscriptions that Greek rather than Latin was the lingua franca in most of Bulgaria except for the Danube frontier. Ovid, although actually writing about Tomis in Romania, gives a fair picture of the hybrid culture of the Roman era, well preserved in Bulgarian archaeological museums.

10. **Bulgaria**

Barbarian pressure on the Danube frontier began towards the end of the 2nd century AD in the reign of the emperor Marcus Aurelius (AD 161–80), although at the beginning of the century Trajan had advanced Roman power across the Danube into Dacia. From AD 200 to 600 there was endless pressure on this frontier. Many barbarians passed into the Roman empire. On the other hand Greek influence spread to new cities of the interior such as Marcianopolis, Diocletianopolis, Nicopolis ad Istrum, and Nicopolis ad Nestum. A fair portrait of life in some of these cities and Greek cities on the coast is given by the 4th-century historian Ammianus Marcellinus and the author of the *Historia Augusta*. In the 6th century the western Balkans were devastated by barbarian invasion, but imperial armies were still active in Bulgarian territory in close proximity to Constantinople.

Finally the Danube frontier collapsed in 602. This did little to affect the coastal cities, but the fragile Graeco-Roman culture in the interior collapsed. Serdica and Philippopolis held out until the 9th century, but then Sofia became a Bulgarian city, and Plovdiv went into a period of decline. After the attacks of tsar Simeon at the beginning of the 10th century even the Black Sea ports passed briefly under Bulgarian control, until the Byzantine revival at the end of the century brought the whole of the Balkans under imperial sway. Greek influence, however, remained largely confined to the coast. It was a commonplace of Greek ecclesiastical writers to complain of the primitive conditions in the interior, and Western travellers during the Crusades agreed on this point.

The rise of the second Bulgarian empire and the Fourth Crusade (1204) meant that Byzantium lost control of the Bulgarian interior for ever, and the coastal cities for a temporary period. Michael VIII Palaiologos recovered the latter during an extensive campaign in 1262, and curiously, in spite of temporary losses in Bulgarian, Greek, and Turkish raids, they remained as part of the empire until 1453. Under Ottoman rule the seaports continued to prosper. Great Byzantine names appear in the records of these towns. Michael Kantakouzenos's wealth is noted in the 16th century, although eventually he was executed by the sultan. Cossack raids in the 17th century damaged the towns, and the great monasteries of Sozopol were destroyed in 1629. Greek priests and merchants were a powerful force of Hellenism in the interior, although they never really penetrated the countryside. Plovdiv was settled extensively by Greek merchants, whose houses can still be seen, and in the south Melnik and Nevrokop, now Goce Delčev, were centres of Hellenism. At the beginning of the 19th century we find some collaboration between Bulgarian bands under such leaders as Dimitris Vakiotis and the Greek movement for independence. Since Greek schools were the only schools to provide education, even nationalist Bulgarian intellectuals derived inspiration from Greek models. The work of Dimitrios Darvaris (1751–1823) was influential in education and literature. Soon, however, Bulgarians began demanding their own schools, Church (gained in 1870), and an independent state (virtually gained in 1878 although full independence was not granted until 1908). Greek cities survived, either because, like Melnik, they were not even in 1878 a part of Bulgaria, or because, like the coastal ports, they were in a part of Bulgaria that involved a strange mixture of races, as for instance the Gagauz, Turkish-speaking Christians who often allied with the Greeks.

The Balkan Wars and World War I led to the hardening of frontiers. Greece and Bulgaria were on different sides in two of these wars, and the position of Greek speakers in Bulgaria became difficult. Accordingly in a series of well-documented population exchanges most of the Greek speakers left centres where Greek had been spoken for 2500 years in exchange for homes in Macedonia and western Thrace previously inhabited by Bulgarians. Some of the poorer inhabitants remained behind, and fairly rapidly became assimilated. It is still possible to find old people in Nesebar speaking Greek among themselves, and Nesebar, Goce Delčev, and Melnik look like Greek towns. In the census of 1965 there were more than 8000 inhabitants of Bulgaria speaking Greek, but the collapse of Communism has meant that many of these, like the 4500 Karakatchans also speaking Greek, emigrated to Greece.

T.J. WINNIFRITH

Bulgaria: the port building of Zographon, the Bulgarian monastery on Mount Athos

Further Reading

Horak, Stephan M., *Eastern European National Minorities, 1919–1980: A Handbook*, Littleton, Colorado: Libraries Unlimited, 1985

Ladas, Stephen P., *The Exchange of Minorities: Bulgaria, Greece and Turkey*, New York: Macmillan, 1932

Sugar, Peter F., *Southeastern Europe under Ottoman Rule, 1354–1804*, Seattle: University of Washington Press, 1977

Velkov, Velizar, *Cities in Thrace and Dacia in Late Antiquity*, 2nd edition, Amsterdam: Hakkert, 1977

Whitby, Michael, *The Emperor Maurice and His Historian: Theophylact Simocatta on Persian and Balkan Warfare*, Oxford: Clarendon Press, and New York: Oxford University Press, 1980

Bulgars

The Bulgars were a non-Indo-European people originating in southern Russia. Under khan Asparuch (*c.*AD 650–*c.*700), one of many semi-legendary leaders of Bulgaria, they reached and crossed the Danube. In AD 681 the emperor Constantine IV was forced to recognize a Bulgarian kingdom north of the Haemus mountains. By this time most of the Balkans had been penetrated by the Slavs, and in the next 100 years Bulgaria took control of these Slav settlements, depriving them of their non-Indo-European identity in the process. A Byzantine revival in the 9th century was halted by khan Krum, who in 811 defeated and slew the emperor Nikephoros I. By this time the Bulgarian realm stretched over much of northern Greece and threatened Constantinople, which Krum attacked.

Krum's successor, Omurtag, made peace with Byzantium. He was the last ruler with a non-Slavonic name. His grandson Boris was converted to Christianity, but Bulgaria still remained a thorn in the side of the Byzantine empire. Boris's son Simeon, although or because he had been brought up in Constantinople, harboured ambitions to succeed to the Byzantine throne. He was known as "the half-Greek", and introduced Greek culture to Bulgaria. He defeated the Byzantines decisively in 917, but his successors Peter and Boris II were faced with internal dissension, threats from Russia, and a renascent Byzantium which under John I Tzimiskes (969–76) overran the eastern half of Bulgaria. In west Bulgaria there was a last Bulgarian revival under tsar Samuel, who kept the Byzantines at bay until 1014 when he was decisively defeated by them under the appropriately named Basil Bulgaroktonos (Bulgar Slayer).

The centre of Samuel's empire was around lakes Ohrid and Prespa, but he had at times ruled as far west as the Adriatic and as far south as Thessaly. His racial origins are obscure, and it has been claimed that he was Macedonian rather than Bulgarian. All that he ruled passed under Byzantine control and remained so for more than 150 years, although there were sporadic revolts. In 1185 two local chieftains in the Haemus mountains rose up in protest against extortionate taxes. The enfeebled Byzantine empire was in no position to suppress this revolt, and Asen's brother Kalojan was able to take advantage of the Fourth Crusade (1204) to establish a strong Bulgarian state that was never again to acknowledge Byzantine rule. Tsar Asen II from 1218 to 1241 ruled over a kingdom that stretched from the Black Sea to the Adriatic, a kingdom almost as large as that of Samuel. As with Samuel there is some doubt about the racial origin of the Asenids, since Byzantine sources frequently refer to them as Vlachs. The narrow chauvinism of modern historians cannot obscure the fact that both Bulgarian empires were multi-ethnic states.

After a brief period when it was the principal power in the Balkans the second Bulgarian empire rapidly declined. There was an invasion by the Tatars, internal dissension, and a revival of Byzantine power under the Palaiologoi. The Bulgarians were no match for the growing power of the Serbs, who defeated them decisively at Kyustendil in 1341, and an enfeebled and divided kingdom rapidly fell a victim to the Ottomans who were to rule over Bulgaria for 500 years. Oddly, the disastrous 14th century saw a revival in Bulgarian art and literature, inspired by Byzantine models.

There were some spasmodic revolts against Turkish authority, but on the whole Bulgarian resistance was tame. A number of Bulgarians were converted to Islam; a number of Turks settled in Bulgaria. The Bulgarian Church was subordinated to the patriarchate at Constantinople, and Greek priests discouraged Bulgarian patriotism and the use of the Bulgarian language. By the 1840s, however, Bulgarian schools were being founded and Russian support fostered Bulgarian nationalism. Surprisingly many early Bulgarian leaders received their education in Greece. Relations between Bulgaria and Greece deteriorated sharply in 1870 when the Turkish authorities allowed a separate Bulgarian Church, known as the Exarchate. For the next 50 years Patriarchists supporting the Greek Church and Exarchists supporting the Bulgarian Church fought with each other, sometimes literally, for the allegiance of the inhabitants of the central Balkans, while simultaneously fighting for independence from the Turks. In 1878 after some particularly brutal massacres of Bulgarians a limited form of independence was granted to Bulgaria at the treaty of Berlin; the earlier treaty of San Stefano in the same year had given a much greater area to Bulgaria, but between 1878 and 1912 there was still a large area of Turkish territory disputed between the Exarchists and the Patriarchists.

This dispute was eventually settled by the Balkan Wars. In 1912 Greek, Serbian, and Bulgarian armies invaded Turkish territory. While the Serbs advanced as far as Bitola and the Greek army arrived at Thessalonica just before the Bulgarians, the main brunt of the fighting was borne by the Bulgarians in Thrace with little in the way of territorial gains. It looked as if the combatants were going to be rewarded with what their armies had gained. Enraged by this, the Bulgarians started the Second Balkan War in 1913. This they lost, and they lost more territory as a result. Western Thrace, largely inhabited by Muslims with some Greeks in the towns, became Bulgarian briefly, but the bulk of Macedonia was divided between Serbia and Greece, although generally inhabited by a people speaking a language very like Bulgarian. In World War I Bulgaria was again on the losing side and lost western Thrace to Greece in the subsequent peace treaty.

Not surprisingly, as the enemy in the guerrilla wars since 1880, and the enemy in the Second Balkan War and World War I, Bulgarians were not popular with Greeks. There was a nasty border incident near Petrič in 1925. Attempts under the aegis of France to achieve an alliance of Balkan states foundered when Bulgaria joined the Axis and was rewarded with most of Yugoslav Macedonia and western Thrace for its pains. Bulgarian rule over this territory was not successful, especially in Greece, where most of the Bulgarian population had left as a result of some well-managed population exchanges.

In 1944 Bulgaria deserted Germany and joined Russia. For Greece, which had first resisted the Axis and then fought a civil war against the communists, the Bulgarians remained enemies. The frontier was tightly guarded, and diplomatic relations remained frosty. The end of the Cold War and common coldness to the emergence of the Former Yugoslav Republic of Macedonia as an independent state meant a slight reduction of tension, although the economic instability of the new Bulgaria

Bulgars: illustration from the 11th-century chronicle of Skylitzes showing the Bulgar leader Peter Deljan in his tent during his siege of Thessalonica in 1040, Biblioteca Nacional, Madrid

and the presence of a large Muslim minority still aroused suspicion. In fact Bulgaria and Greece have much in common, sharing a Byzantine heritage, Eastern Orthodoxy, and a tradition of resistance against the Turks. But old enmities die hard.

T.J. WINNIFRITH

Summary

A non-Indo-European people from southern Russia, the Bulgars moved westwards at the same time as the Huns and Avars. In 681 they crossed the Danube and forced Byzantium to recognize a Bulgarian kingdom. At times this kingdom stretched from the Black Sea to the Adriatic. The Bulgars rapidly assimilated with the Slavs and by the 9th century ceased to be a separate ethnic group.

Further Reading

Browning, Robert, *Byzantium and Bulgaria: A Comparative Study across the Early Medieval Frontier*, London: Temple Smith, and Berkeley: University of California Press, 1975
Crampton, R.J., *A Concise History of Bulgaria*, Cambridge and New York: Cambridge University Press, 1997
Runciman, Steven, *A History of the First Bulgarian Empire*, London: Bell, 1930
Wolff, R., "The Second Bulgarian Empire", *Speculum*, 24 (1949): pp. 167–206

Bureaucracy

For most of antiquity, Greece remained a series of separate states, often in conflict. Hence, tracing patterns of bureaucracy is a difficult process at best. The Greek city states required administrative machinery to coordinate and produce documents, collect taxes, preside over laws, and maintain order. As a result, the development of a bureaucracy, or a core of professionals dedicated to the minutiae of state administration, became a requisite in nearly every state. City states developed similar patterns of administration. Increased efficiency, accompanied by advances in travel, produced government reforms on every level in almost every state. Greece was the first civilization effectively to develop a bureaucracy that incorporated those members of society who fulfilled the qualities of servitude and learning required to meet the needs of its citizens.

The duties of administration, responsibilities for the execution of those duties, and those permitted to function as part of the administration varied from state to state and period to period. Membership in many organizations was limited, by definition, to citizens. Affairs of the state and benefits that accompanied civil service were restricted to individuals belonging to a socially accepted group. Hereditary affiliation was the only means of inclusion within ancient Greek society. In some regions, however, slaves were employed for labour-intensive functions such as recording. Differences between the staffing of local governments were not important, however, since the benefits of government went to its citizens and to no one else.

The establishment of a bureaucracy indicated the creation of an institution that outlived its specific function. Although they varied by time and location, ancient Greek society became dependent upon the services provided by civil servants. The bureaucratic framework relied on flexibility to meet evolving demands in a changing society. In its most basic sense, the

bureaucracy facilitated distribution of obligations and benefits that accompanied citizenship. Through this distribution, Greek administrators promoted equity among the population and governmental advantage. The result of the Greek bureaucratic system was a society increasingly tied to local rule, and a general feeling of benevolence between government and citizen.

During the Archaic period public authority lacked direction and effectiveness. Evidence for this is found in Homer's *Odyssey*. City-state governments in this period failed to convene for decades. Citizenship indicated eligibility for public service, and, in return, society expected career terms of service from those elected. Other than the central composition of the government, usually a king, a council, and an assembly, little else is known about the daily functions of the government or its administration during the 8th century BC. With the limited number of persons involved in ruling a city state, there is likely to have been little interaction between ruler and subject, and little mutual concern.

Following the Archaic period, two events indicate the improbability of an established Greek bureaucracy. First, accounts of the Seven against Thebes suggest that the requisite conditions for a coalition – primarily an established bureaucracy – were missing. Second, Athenian intervention in the affairs of Miletus in 450 BC and Samos in 442 BC was limited to physical and not political domination. Athens lacked the required administrators to promote its policies and intentions. In both cases, Greece lacked the tools to capitalize on the success of its military campaigns.

Evolving through the ages of monarchy, aristocracy, and tyranny, three periods void of successful bureaucratic systems, democratic reforms in government produced similar changes in administration. Magistrates became crucial figures in most societies. Civil servants were elected annually and were not ordinarily eligible for reelection. Cities and states were administered by those professional civil servants who possessed no real power, but dedicated themselves to the execution of their duties. In any given city state, hundreds, even thousands of magistrates' positions existed, allowing a civil servant the opportunity to serve in several positions simultaneously without repeating a post assignment. Lower magistrates received a state-provided salary, while higher-ranking officials often came from wealthy families, demanding no compensation. It was during the 2nd century BC that magistrates achieved prominence within Greek society, and a permanent, professional core of civil servants was established.

By the 3rd century BC Greek bureaucratic reform produced more widespread and tangible results. In Thrace king Seuthes III organized the country on a Hellenistic model. He divided his kingdom into towns, provinces, and regions. At the lower levels local rule provided direction for daily government functions, while a smaller percentage of natives participated at the higher levels. Each level took direction from higher authorities, while preserving the appearance of self-rule.

In Egypt Hellenistic rulers inherited a bureaucracy many centuries old. Different from the civil servants that perpetuated the daily activities of the Greek city state, Egyptian bureaucrats often performed their scribal or accounting duties for their entire lives. Scribes were often illiterate, transferring the symbols from one sheet to the next, failing to understand their significance. Accountants, who could perform basic arithmetic, were likewise illiterate, and ignorant of their greater significance within society. Trained to serve the pharaohs, Egyptian civil servants introduced a new standard of detail to administrative duties. The success of the Egyptian bureaucratic model prior to the Greeks is questionable, since few civil servants recognized their job significance or benefited from their selfless service. During the period of Greek rule an abundance of trained civil servants, both native and imported, permitted the division of Egypt into cantons, districts, and villages that could be extraordinarily well controlled. Traditionally, Greek civil servants filled higher posts in the empire than their native counterparts. Accountability throughout Egypt achieved unparalleled proportions during the 3rd century BC.

The Ptolemaic kingdom was the most effective political organization to emerge from the Greek-speaking world. The constitution of the empire provided the basis for unequalled administrative success. The Ptolemies oversaw the Macedonian-Greek upper class and the Egyptian fellahin, a group dedicated to the patient and meticulous work of serving the pharaohs. Rather than replace the Egyptian bureaucratic system, the first two Ptolemies opted to augment the existing system with Greek reforms. The combination of a disciplined workforce and efficient administration produced the most effective government of the ancient world. Reforms in government administration and accountability in Ptolemaic Egypt provided the standard by which bureaucracies would be measured for decades. It was also during the 3rd century BC that bureaucratic service became not only an acceptable profession for the upper class, but an enviable one.

During the 2nd century BC Greek bureaucratic reforms were introduced throughout the eastern and western empires. Mithridates I emulated the Greek system, and employed Greek civil servants in large numbers. Iranian leadership instituted Greek reforms at the local level, and evidence of Greek bureaucratic influence appeared as far away as Kurdistan and India. The Greek model provided the basis for efficient administration of empires that continued to grow in size and complexity. By emphasizing self-rule, central governments freed themselves of the tedium associated with accounting and recording at the local level. The division of empires into subordinate organizations increased accountability and ensured the communication of supreme mandates.

Few changes occurred in Greek bureaucracy following antiquity. The Greek administrative model spread widely, appearing as the basis for the Roman system of administration, defining the Byzantine model of government, and finding great favour centuries later in the courts of Europe. Kingdoms in both east and west assimilated patterns of Greek government in their expanding and contracting empires.

Byzantium refined the Greek bureaucratic model. Gradually, a system of centrally controlled, self-governing institutions took shape. Although native-born inhabitants enjoyed the privileges of citizenship, the civil service provided an avenue towards acceptance and social mobility not previously available. Competition for bureaucratic positions improved the quality of candidates and their subsequent performance. Education eventually became the prerequisite for service, replacing citizenship in significance. Two distinct career paths guided bureaucrats, and provided nearly unlim-

ited potential for advancement. Civil servants specialized in finance or clerical careers. Both positions required literacy and advanced education. Similar to the ancient model, post holders were appointed or elected for a year, but the number of posts available in any given location allowed for civil servants to serve in many at one time. Bureaucratic positions occurred from the lowest to the highest levels of government, promising advancement for the most competent within a career field.

The chief institution within Byzantium was the commune. An established commune was a legal entity of one or several towns, providing self-direction, but enjoying the toleration of the administration. The *Kununname* was the first handbook to standardize and regulate the duties, responsibilities, and progressions of the bureaucrat. It facilitated efficient local rule, without extensive oversight from the central government. The *Kununname* further delineated two distinct career paths: accounting and clerical careers. Accountants levied and dispersed taxes at a local level, giving those who filled such a position great importance. Clerks not only performed as recorders, but also convened and presided over legal disputes. For the non-citizen, the authority and respect that accompanied civil service could not be found in any other career. As a result of Byzantine reforms, the world recognized the significant contributions of civil servants and welcomed their contributions, even in the most restricted societies.

During the period of Ottoman rule, Greek bureaucracy took a backward step. Plagued by a system of paternalism, government inefficiency reached a level not previously experienced. Local magistrates were exceptionally corrupt and appointed for long periods of time. Few local offices existed to address the needs of the population, while taxes increasingly supported programmes outside the community. Gradual erosion of the once effective Greek bureaucratic model resulted in a government incapable of the most basic administrative functions. Unable to recognize the limitations paternalism placed on the efficiency of the civil service, the Ottoman government failed in its ability to manage or administer its empire. It was during the period prior to the 19th century that Greek government at every level achieved new lows.

In terms of both national identity and social direction, Greece experienced great changes prior to the 19th century. As a consequence of Greek exposure to European nationalism, Ottoman practices seemed inadequate for a changing society. Shifting trends in the 19th century favoured western law codes, administrative processes, and a general return to effective government. The effort to redistribute both the wealth and the lands of those who had ruled Greece required an administrative system that promoted equity, similar to that of the Archaic period. For a brief period of time in the 19th century Greek paternalism or appointment through favour guided the assignment of civil servants. Paternalism resulted from exposure to European governments as well as the lingering effects of Ottoman rule. This policy proved ineffective in Greece as in most other European nations by the 20th century, giving rise to appointment by merit. This trend continues today. The modern Greek civil service requires strong skills in administration, diversity of character and talent, and dedication to advancing the goals of both the state and the citizens.

In antiquity Greece produced a significant and lasting model for bureaucratic efficiency. This Greek model effectively guided operations at every level of government, and succeeded in administering an empire that encompassed divergent cultures and concerns. Elements of Hellenistic bureaucracy survive in nearly every major government in the world today, a tribute to the vision of the early Greek thinkers.

SCOTT BLANCHETTE

Further Reading

Finley, M.I., *Politics in the Ancient World*, Cambridge and New York: Cambridge University Press, 1983

Fleischer, Cornell H., *Bureaucrat and Intellectual in the Ottoman Empire: The Historian Mustafa Ali, 1541–1600*, Princeton, New Jersey: Princeton University Press, 1986

Forrest, W.G., *The Emergence of Greek Democracy, 800–400 BC*, New York: McGraw Hill, and London: Weidenfeld and Nicolson, 1966

Glotz, Gustave, *The Greek City and Its Institutions*, New York: Barnes and Noble, and London: Routledge and Kegan Paul, 1965

Larsen, J.A.O., *Greek Federal States: Their Institution and History*, Oxford: Clarendon Press, 1968

Ure, P.N., *The Origin of Tyranny*, Cambridge: Cambridge University Press, 1922; New York: Russell, 1962

Burial Practices

The earliest burials in Greece date from the Mesolithic period (8th millennium BC). In the cave of Franchthi (Argolid) were found the undisturbed inhumation of a young man and several disturbed burials, together with two cremations thought to be the earliest in Europe. There are many more instances of Neolithic burials (5th–4th millennia BC). The standard practice was primary inhumation in pits, though secondary inhumation (after the body had been exposed or provisionally buried until the flesh had disintegrated) and cremation are also attested. Formal cemeteries are first found in the Late Neolithic (Kephala on Keos), but are not common, or indeed large, before the Early Bronze Age (3rd millennium BC), in the Cyclades and Attica; from then on, the practice of burying the dead within the house is mainly restricted to children. Monumental tombs for multiple burials (family, clan, or tribe) appear for the first time in the Early Bronze Age, but only in small numbers and certain areas (e.g. Leucas and Crete). Grave goods, which in the Neolithic were limited to simple pots, stone tools, or jewellery, become much more varied and reflect the socioeconomic differences in the community, the wealthy graves containing bronze weapons, clay and stone vases, gold and silver jewellery, and figurines of clay or marble. There is some evidence of ritual at the grave: vessels deposited on top of the grave, libations poured to the dead, and the ritual drink or "toasting" the dead, a custom better known from the Mycenaean period.

At the time of the first Minoan palaces (2000–1700 BC), the burial practices in Crete continue mostly unchanged, though jars (pithoi) or coffins (larnakes) were used more frequently. On the less prosperous mainland, burials were usually made within the settlements, in pits, stone cists, or in *pithoi*, and were scantily furnished with grave goods. Burying under tumuli, the only form of communal burial in this period, was an aristocratic practice, possibly restricted to particular tribes or clans, and largely confined to Messenia.

The Mycenaean period (1600–1100 BC) saw the change to the advice of multiple burial. Primary inhumation in family tombs became the norm. Single burials were uncommon and cremation an exception before the end of the period. The monumentality of the grave, the elaboration of the burial rites, and the quality and quantity of grave goods varied in relation to the status and wealth of the deceased in what was now a highly differentiated society. The earliest aristocratic cemeteries, Grave Circles A and B at Mycenae (1650–1550 BC), were circular stone enclosures, containing the graves of men, women, and children. The later, and richer, graves were deep shafts in which a number of dead were laid, and lavishly adorned with gold, including death masks for some of the men, headbands and shrouds decorated with gold discs for the women. Men were also provided with many weapons, and with drinking cups of precious metals, and women with gold jewellery. Later princely tombs were mostly of the tholos (beehive) type with corbelled vaults. The most monumental tholos tombs were built at Mycenae in the 14th and 13th centuries BC. Aristocratic funerals seem to have been lavish affairs, with funeral processions to the grave, the dead on horse-drawn chariots, the consumption of funeral meals, and the sacrifice of animals, sometimes even horses. Commoners were buried in larger cemeteries and simpler tombs dug in the rock, with a passage leading to a chamber (chamber tombs). Here multiple burials were often made over a period of several generations; earlier burials were pushed aside to make room for new burials after the flesh of the dead had disintegrated.

The so-called Dark Age (c.1200–700 BC) witnessed the reversion to single inhumation, in pit- or cist-graves. This is now believed to have been the result of the depopulation and fragmentation of society which followed the destruction of the Mycenaean centres, rather than of the arrival of newcomers. Only in some regions (Crete and to a lesser extent Messenia and Thessaly) was multiple burial in chamber or tholos tombs retained. During the Protogeometric and early Geometric periods (1050–800 BC) Attica and a few other regions (especially Crete) adopted cremation to the exclusion of inhumation, particularly for adults, children being mostly inhumed. But in the 8th century inhumation made a full comeback in Athens, and for the rest of antiquity the two rites then coexisted, though there were differences from region to region and period to period, cremation being more common than inhumation for adults in the Archaic period (7th–6th centuries BC), inhumation more popular in the Hellenistic period (4th–1st centuries BC). The two practices were a matter of choice and not of status or wealth. Inhumation graves were normally single burials, in simple shafts or pits, sometimes lined with stones or covered with tiles, or in containers such as sarcophagi, clay tubs, or pots (particularly for children). Cremation burials were normally placed in urns of clay or metal, which were often placed in lidded stone boxes. The graves were surmounted by mounds (tumuli) and often by grave markers. In the Archaic period the mounds were large and the grave markers could be tall sculptured gravestones or even over-lifesized statues (kouroi). In the Classical period, the age of democracy, laws were passed at intervals to curb the ostentatious display of wealth and to control the expense of funerals, and so the mounds, judging certainly from representations on vases, were much smaller, while in Athens at least sculptured stone grave markers seem to have gone out of fashion for most of the 5th century. Family plots and *peribolos* (precinct) tombs (tombs built of bricks or stones above the family plot) were used in Athens in the Classical period, but the grander type of built tomb was forbidden soon after its introduction in the late 5th century BC. Impressive examples of such tombs, with temple-like facades and sometimes vaulted and richly painted interiors, were built by the Macedonian kings and aristocracy from the 4th century BC onwards. They display a monumentality and wealth of grave goods (witness the unlooted tombs of Vergina) not found since the Mycenaean period.

The ancient Greek funeral as a three-staged process was already established by the time of Homer. The laying in state of the dead, or *prothesis*, most likely took place in the courtyard of the house after the ritual washing of the corpse by the women of the household. The dead was laid on a bier, wrapped in a shroud (or wedding dress in the case of unmarried or recently married women), the head supported by pillows and adorned with a crown. An important part of the *prothesis* was the mourning and singing of dirges, both formal (*threnoi*), sung by professional mourners, and improvised (*gooi*), sung by friends and members of the family. During the *ekphora* the dead was taken to the place of burial, on a horse- or mule-drawn cart (though Geometric representations, in keeping with heroic ideals, show chariots), and accompanied by a procession of mourners and sometimes a pipe-player. Less is known about the third stage, or deposition: a libation of wine was made to the dead, grave goods (personal belongings: strigils, mirrors, jewellery, toys, or vases) were placed in the grave or in special offering places or ditches nearby. Ceremonies were held during which burnt remnants of food, including the bones of small animals or birds, were also deposited. After the funeral, a funerary banquet (*perideipnon*) in honour of the deceased was held in the deceased's house. In the days and weeks which followed, libations and offerings were made at the grave by relatives of the deceased, particularly the women. Special rituals were the *trita* (third-day rituals), *enata* (ninth-day), and *triakostia* (thirtieth-day). Subsequently rituals were held to mark the annual anniversary or special occasions.

Funerary customs did not substantially change during the Hellenistic and Roman periods, though the graves are generally poorly furnished (the most common offering is the fusiform *unguentarium*, a container for ointment). The spread of Christianity naturally had repercussions on funerary practices. One important change was the disappearance of cremation. During the Byzantine period the dead continued to be buried in single graves, though these were now usually located in graveyards adjacent to, or inside, churches and chapels. The graves themselves were cists made of stone or brick, and marked with a grave slab with a cross on it, or with an actual cross. However the earlier custom of including vases and other objects, and even the coin which had previously been intended for paying the ferryman Charon, is found in Byzantine graves, and reflects the continuity of the pagan custom of providing for the passage from life to death.

In contemporary Greece the funerary customs are a mixture of Christian practices and long-standing traditions, which have many analogies with those of antiquity. In the cities, where the undertakers are responsible for the organization of the funeral and other rites, many of the traditions have been lost, but they are still observed in rural Greece. In many villages the dead is laid out on a bed at home, while relatives and friends mourn and sing laments before the dead is taken to church for the funeral. These laments (*moirologhia*), which are part of the Greek oral tradition and a survival of the ancient *gooi*, are also sung by women during the funerary procession and at the deposition. The priest presides at the formal funerary service in church, and recites prayers for the forgiveness of the sins of the deceased (the *trisagio*) at home and at the graveyard. A coffin of metal, wood, or concrete is normally used, and a cross or, if it can be afforded, a monument of marble is later erected above the grave. Food is brought to the graveyard at the funeral and on all later occasions when rites are performed. Indispensable are the *kollyva*, consisting of boiled wheat with spices and raisins decorated with icing sugar and silver sweets. Rites are held at the grave at prescribed days after the death of a person. The dates (the third, ninth, and most importantly the fortieth) are connected with the stages in Christ's progress between his death and the Ascension, but they closely correspond to ancient practices. The last important rite to be performed at the grave is the exhumation of the bones of the deceased, which usually takes place three to seven years after burial, by which time the flesh has disintegrated completely. This practice, which has connections with the prehistoric custom of secondary burial, marks the integration of the deceased into the world of the dead and the end of the obligations of the living to the dead. The exhumed bones are placed either in designated areas in the churchyard or in ossuaries, or else they are reburied beside the original grave. In the villages the rite is usually carried out by the women and provides the last occasion for mourning, the singing of *moirologhia*, and the sharing of *kollyva*.

CHRISTINA SOUYOUDZOGLOU-HAYWOOD

See also Death

Further Reading

Cavanagh, William G. and Christopher Mee, *A Private Place: Death in Prehistoric Greece*, Jonsered: Åström, 1998

Danford, Loring M., *The Death Rituals of Rural Greece*, Princeton, New Jersey: Princeton University Press, 1982

Garland, Robert, *The Greek Way of Death*, Ithaca, New York: Cornell University Press, and London: Duckworth, 1985

Jacobsen, T.W. and T. Cullen, "A Consideration of Mortuary Practices in Neolithic Greece: Burials from Franchthi Cave" in *Mortality and Immortality: The Anthropology and Archaeology of Death*, edited by S.C. Humphreys and Helen King, London and New York: Academic Press, 1981

Kurtz, Donna C. and John Boardman, *Greek Burial Customs*, Ithaca, New York: Cornell University Press, and London: Thames and Hudson, 1971

Vermeule, Emily, *Aspects of Death in Early Greek Art and Poetry*, Berkeley: University of California Press, 1979

Wilkie, N.C. and W.A. McDonald, "How the Mycenaeans Buried Their Dead", *Archaeology*, 37/6 (1984): pp. 40–47

Byron, George Gordon, Lord 1788–1824

Poet and philhellene

"While every man of any pretensions to learning" is tiring himself out studying "the harangues of the Athenian demagogues in favour of freedom, the real or supposed descendants of these sturdy republicans are left to the actual tyranny of their masters, although a very slight effort is required to strike off their chains." Byron's remark occurs in a note, written towards the end of his time in Greece and Turkey in 1809–11, to his *Childe Harold's Pilgrimage*, canto 2 (1812). This work (one of the most popular poems of the 19th century), and the series of eastern tales beginning with *The Giaour* (1813), had a profound influence on European and American philhellenism in the years just before the outbreak of the Greek War of Independence in 1821; subsequently the poet's own death while attempting to help strike off the chains in 1823–24 had even greater impact.

Childe Harold is neither actively hostile to ancient Greece – there are meditations at Marathon, Sunium, and the like – nor invariably favourable to modern Greece: Byron sometimes gives voice to the common contemporary belief that modern Greeks are degenerate, unworthy to inhabit the "land of lost gods and godlike men". But there is an unusual degree of interest in such "lands scarce noticed in historic tales" as the domains of Ali Pasha in Epirus and Albania, and it is clear that on balance he is sympathetic to a people whose ungodlike nature he regarded, more than most, as an unsurprising consequence of centuries of Turkish oppression. The poet engages closely enough with these moderns to go to the unusual lengths of learning "the Romaic or Modern Greek language", the appendix on which in *Childe Harold* includes the *Battle Hymn* (1797) of Rigas of Velestino, "who perished in the attempt to revolutionize Greece". Byron's close engagement with the Greeks prompts both sympathetic sentiment and a desire to inform; *Childe Harold* combines "exoticism with a sense of history and of place and a responsiveness to contemporary political realities" (Webb, 1993).

Byron's continuing philhellenic reputation was also enhanced by his disapproval, expressed in both the *Childe Harold* canto and *The Curse of Minerva* (1812), of Lord Elgin's removal of the Parthenon frieze, and his provision, in *Don Juan*, cantos 2 and 3 (1819), of both a sympathetic modern Greek heroine, Haidée (speaker of "good modern Greek / With an Ionian accent, low and sweet"), and a song that, taken out of its partly ironic context, became one of the anthems of philhellenism: "The isles of Greece, the isles of Greece! / Where burning Sappho loved and sung...".

Byron, who was sympathetic to liberal causes including that of the Italian *carbonari*, took some interest in the Greek War of Independence from its inception. He became more involved once the London Greek Committee approached him in April 1823. Edward Blaquiere, an Irish supporter of Greek independence, encouraged him on behalf of the committee to lend his aid in "resuscitating the land already so well illustrated by your sublime and energetic muse", and he was made a member in May. His departure for Greece was also a response to personal imperatives including a desire to do great deeds instead of writing poems, perhaps to improve his reputation at home, and to escape from his relationship with Teresa Guiccioli.

Having raised as much money as possible, Byron set off from Genoa in July. He went to Cephalonia, where the British resident, colonel Charles Napier, was both well disposed to the Greek cause and among those best able to brief his visitor on the complex internal divisions among the Greek leaders (a state of affairs little known to or idealistically ignored by the committee). Anxious about the implications of supporting or appearing to support a particular faction or grouping, Byron stayed in Cephalonia until late December. Finally in January 1824 he moved to Missolonghi, headquarters of prince Alexandros Mavrokordatos, although he attempted not to become too closely identified with him. Byron's time here was mostly difficult and unhappy – he was besieged in person or by letter by Greeks of every faction seeking money, attempted to pacify quarrelsome foreign volunteers, had difficulties in controlling the hundreds of unruly Suliotes and Albanians whom he for a time employed, and was irritated and confined by the persistent rain which made the already naturally damp Missolonghi "a mud-basket". Military supplies from the London Greek Committee were slow in coming and inadequate or unsuitable when they did arrive, and its promised loan, which Byron was to have administered, was not finalized until just before his death. Not surprisingly, he was less unambiguously committed to the cause than pious legend would have it; he stopped keeping a journal because he "could not help abusing the Greeks in it". But he was determined to honour his word, and expressed loyalty to newly awoken Greece and a heroic determination to seek "A Soldier's Grave" in one of his last poems, "On This Day I Complete My Thirty-Sixth Year". (The Byron myth has often stressed this aspect of the poem rather than its explicit origin as a reaction to unrequited love, particularly perhaps since the love was for a Greek boy, Loukas Chalandritsanos.) The loyalty was preserved inviolate by his death (from fever exacerbated by excessive medical bleeding) in April 1824. This was probably more useful to the Greek cause than anything Byron could have achieved while living.

He became immediately a martyr in the cause of liberty, saluted in a stirring funeral oration by Spiridion Trikoupis (itself an influence on subsequent tributes in verse), with solemn mourning and cannon shots in Missolonghi, and then with a national day of mourning. Through the 19th and early 20th century and beyond statues designed to stress his heroic qualities proliferated, and streets and children were named after him. (The best-known statue, of Byron and Greece in the Zappeion gardens in Athens, dates from 1896.) He was mourned in klephtic ballads, by Dionysios Solomos in his *Lyrical Poem on the Death of Lord Byron* (unpublished until after Solomos's death in 1857 but later influential), by Andreas Kalvos in "The Britannic Muse" (1826); later the academic poet Alexandros Soutsos, the popular poet Achilleus Paraschos, and many others continued to proclaim Byron's glorious sacrifice; there was a fresh rush of poetry to mark the centenary of his death in 1924, and he was the subject of plays by Alekos Lidorikis (1934) and Manolis Skouloudis (1964).

Interest in the hero's life led to some interest in his poems, most of which were available in translation from the 1850s. Solomos's *Hymn to Liberty* (1825), begun in 1823, echoes the

Lord Byron: statue at Missolonghi, erected in 1881, with the poet's heart buried beneath

"Isles of Greece" song – where the breasts of Byron's pre-rebellion Greek maidens must one day "suckle slaves", those of Solomos's maidens will suckle "courage and freedom" – and much 19th-century Greek poetry is more generally "Byronic". As late as 1912 Kostis Palamas (in "Pegasus") asserts that Pegasus has been riderless since Byron's death and only now does a Greek poet make bold to mount in his place. Nevertheless, in Greece as to some extent elsewhere, his life as mythically constructed since Missolonghi has remained much better known than his work or his actually more complex attitude to the Greeks.

MARTIN GARRETT

Biography

Born in London in 1788, Byron was educated at Harrow and Trinity College, Cambridge. He visited Greece and Turkey in 1809–11 after which (in 1812) he published the first two cantos of *Childe Harold's Pilgrimage*. Its lament on the bondage of Greece had a profound effect on European and American philhellenism. Byron himself sailed for Greece in 1823 and died of fever at Missolonghi in 1824.

Writings

Letters and Journals, edited by Leslie A. Marchand, 13 vols, London: John Murray, and Cambridge, Massachusetts: Harvard University Press, 1973–82

Complete Poetical Works, edited by Jerome J. McGann, 7 vols, Oxford: Clarendon Press, and New York: Oxford University Press, 1980–93

Further Reading

Buxton, John, "Byron and Greece" in *Byron and the Mediterranean*, edited by Peter Vassallo, University of Malta Press, 1986

Dover, K.J., "Byron on the Ancient Greeks" in his *The Greeks and Their Legacy*, Oxford: Blackwell, 1988

Fletcher, Robin, "Byron in Nineteenth-Century Greek Literature" in *The Struggle for Greek Independence: Essays to Mark the 150th Anniversary of the Greek War of Independence*, edited by Richard Clogg, London: Macmillan, and Hamden, Connecticut: Archon, 1973

Marchand, Leslie A., *Byron: A Portrait*, New York: Knopf, 1970; London: John Murray, 1971

Raizis, M. Byron, "The Greek Poets Praise 'The Britannic Muse'", *Balkan Studies*, 20 (1979) pp. 275–307

St Clair, William, *That Greece Might Still Be Free: The Philhellenes in the War of Independence*, London and New York: Oxford University Press, 1972

St Clair, William, "Byron and Greece" in *Greece Old and New*, edited by Tom Winnifrith and Penelope Murray, London: Macmillan, and New York: St Martin's Press, 1983

Solomou, K., "The Influence of Greek Poetry on Byron", *Byron Journal*, 10 (1982): pp. 4–19

Tsigakou, Fani-Maria (editor), *Lord Byron in Greece*, Athens: Greek Ministry of Culture and British Council, 1987

Webb, Timothy (editor), *English Romantic Hellenism 1700–1824*, Manchester: Manchester University Press, and New York: Barnes and Noble, 1982

Webb, Timothy, "Romantic Hellenism" in *The Cambridge Companion to British Romanticism*, edited by Stuart Curran, Cambridge and New York: Cambridge University Press, 1993

Byzantine Period, Early 330–843

In AD 324 Constantine the Great became sole ruler of a Roman empire that could still claim its territorial integrity. It was at this time that he took the momentous decision to build a new city on the shores of the Bosporus, on the site of ancient Byzantium. Constantine's city, Constantinople, was soon to be known as the "New Rome", and, although not designated at first to be the capital of the empire, it was to become so. Constantinople was positioned in close proximity to centres of Hellenistic culture; in time, and under Christian influence, it became the focal point and representative of the Christian Byzantine empire as Rome had been of the earlier pagan civilization of the Mediterranean.

The Christian author Sozomen relates how Constantine, after a long search for a suitable site for his city, was told in a dream to abandon his plan to build on the ruins of what was believed to be the legendary Troy, and consequently decided to raise his city on the ruins of Byzantium (Sozomen, *Historia Ecclesiastica*, 2. 3). Christian legend later told the story that when founding "New Rome" Constantine walked a great distance outlining the circumference of his city until those who accompanied him asked in wonderment: "How long, our Lord, will you keep going?" He reportedly replied: "I shall keep on until he who walks ahead of me will stop" (Philostorgius, *Historia Ecclesiastica*, 2. 9).

It was thus believed that Constantinople had been situated on the shores of the Bosporus on the site of Byzantium, the ancient colony of the Megarians, by divine intervention. The city commanded the entrances to the Black and the Mediterranean seas, and was placed on the border of two continents: Europe and Asia. The ancients had considered this location so advantageous that the Greek historian Herodotus told how the Persian general Megabazus, on arriving at Byzantium, called the inhabitants of the opposite shore at Chalcedon a blind people for having failed to build their colony on the better site, which was soon after occupied by the Megarians (Herodotus, 4. 1–44).

Constantine ordered materials to be brought from everywhere in the Roman empire, and pagan works of art were requisitioned by his agents and shipped to Constantinople from major imperial cities. The emperor's new city was dedicated on 11 May 330 with celebrations that lasted for 40 days. In order to protect his creation, Constantine surrounded the city with a wall that reached from the Golden Horn to the Sea of Marmora.

An insufficient number of monuments and buildings have survived the ravages of time to give us evidence of what the city must have looked like in the days of its founder. The church of St Irene, however, although rebuilt twice, during the reigns of Justinian the Great (527–65) and Leo III (716–41), dates back to the time of the first Christian emperor, and is preserved to this day. Of the pagan monuments brought to Constantinople, the famous serpent column from Delphi, given to the sanctuary of Apollo in commemoration of the Battle of Plataea, can still be seen in Istanbul today.

Not only architecture but Christian literature flourished under Constantine. The bishop Eusebius, the "father of ecclesiastical history", lived into the early 4th century and is the principal authority on Constantine the Great. His main work, the *Ecclesiastical History*, covers the time span from Christ to 324, when a victorious Constantine became sole ruler of the empire. The *History* is one of the most important sources for early Christianity, containing a wealth of documentary data. It is the first Church history to have been written, and thus sets the tone for later historians of Christianity. The spurious *Vita Constantina*, if written by Eusebius at all, is a panegyric rather than a history of the life of the emperor. The work of Eusebius was later continued by Socrates, Sozomen, Theodoret, and the Arian Philostorgius.

The intellectual life of the empire in this period was particularly rich and vigorous in Egypt, and especially so in Alexandria. Synesius of Cyrene, a scion of an old pagan family, began as a Neoplatonist but ended his life as the bishop of Ptolemaïs. Regardless of this, his sentiments remained coloured by his pagan past. Although not a historian, his work contains much that is of historical interest; but it is mostly as a stylist that Synesius set a standard that was much admired and copied by later writers. Athanasius, bishop of Alexandria, devoted his work to theological disputes during the long conflict with Arianism. In addition, he wrote a *Life of St Antony* in celebration of the founder of monasticism. He was followed by Palladius who, writing under the influence of Athanasius, presented in his work the ideal of the ascetic life. Cyril, another bishop of Alexandria, wrote letters and sermons that were no stylistic masterpieces since, by his own admission, he lacked a rhetorical education. Clearly, such training was still considered the cornerstone of the education of the elite.

An interesting woman whose impressive erudition stands out against the background of the savants of early Christianity is Hypatia, who lived in the early 5th century. The daughter of an Alexandrian mathematician, and a woman of great beauty, she became a philosopher in her own right. Alas the learned lady was finally killed by a fanatical crowd in Alexandria.

When Constantine died in 337, he left to his heirs an empire that once more had a well-established currency in the splendid *solidus* (*nomisma*), a gold coin that was to retain its value, and the respect it commanded throughout the Mediterranean world and beyond, for almost 700 years. The army that he had led so successfully in many battles was devoted to the house of Constantine, and, given the Achilles heel of an uncertain succession, it insisted that only the three living sons of the emperor could rule. This led to the massacre of all the other relatives of Constantine except for two very young boys, his nephews Gallus and Julian.

The three sons who followed him, Constantine, Constans, and Constantius, shared a combined reign from 337 to 340. With his brothers eliminated in 340 and 350 respectively after a period of conflict, Constantius became sole ruler of the empire for the rest of his reign. For lack of an heir, Constantius made his cousin, Julian, Caesar in 335. In 361 Julian's troops declared him emperor. Civil war was barely avoided when on his deathbed Constantius magnanimously designated Julian as his successor.

Julian (361–63), known as the "Apostate", had a brief reign during which he tried to bring back pagan worship. In his youth, when he was virtually an exile, he had cultivated the study of philosophy and, although baptized, loathed the Christian religion. Julian was a brilliant intellectual who was at home in various genres of literature: orations, letters, and

satire. His satirical work, the *Misopogon*, is an important biographical source for the emperor's life. He met an early death when he invaded Persia at the head of his armies. Subsequent rumours told that he had been struck down by a Christian among his own soldiers. Christianity had won the day, and the reign of Julian can be seen as a failed attempt to turn back the clock.

The empire faced troubled times as a result of both the renewed barbarian invasions and the calamitous Battle of Adrianople (378), in which the emperor Valens lost his life, and after which Gothic forces overran imperial territory. It was for reasons of such dangers that the emperor Gratian raised to the throne as co-emperor Theodosius, an able general who, on account of a conspiracy against his father that led to the latter's execution, had lived in exile in Spain. To satisfy dynastic sensibilities, Theodosius married Gratian's half-sister, Galla.

The emperor eventually established his two sons as successors: the older son, Arcadius, was to remain in Constantinople as senior Augustus while Honorius, his younger son, was to rule the West. Throughout his reign it had been the aim of Theodosius to maintain the unity of the empire but paradoxically, by designating his sons as rulers of an eastern and western territory respectively, the end of the 4th century foreshadows later developments leading to regional separation and a cultural parting of ways between East and West. In Church matters he was staunchly orthodox, and it was in his time that Christianity finally won its place as the religion of state. Theodosius' religious legislation granted a measure of tolerance to the Jews but was heavy-handed in dealing with pagans and heretics. A grateful Church would later call him "the Great".

The immediate successors in the Theodosian dynasty were singularly undistinguished. During their reigns the prominence at court of military men rather than men of culture is not surprising given the dangers surrounding the empire. In the year of Theodosius' death the Huns had overrun Syria and Mesopotamia while the Visigoths ravaged the Balkans. As a precautionary measure, Anthemius, praetorian prefect of the east under Theodosius II (408–50), surrounded Constantinople with additional defences, the Theodosian walls, which made the city virtually impregnable. The rule of Theodosius II is furthermore distinguished by the founding of a school of higher learning in Constantinople. This may have been due to the influence of the emperor's wife, the learned empress Eudocia. As a final achievement in 438, together with Valentinian III, he issued the Theodosian Code, which is the earliest imperial collection of laws.

The era was dominated by disputes over Christian dogma, and in 451 the emperor Marcian, who had succeeded Theodosius II, called the Fourth Ecumenical Council to meet at Chalcedon. It was to determine the thorny question of the nature of Christ, and ended condemning both the Monophysite and the Nestorian interpretations of the dogma. The council pronounced that Christ was both God and Man, and reaffirmed the status of the Virgin Mary as *Theotokos* ("one who gave birth to God"). The importance of the council lies furthermore in that it established Constantinople as ranking second only to Rome. Chalcedon remained a benchmark in the history of the Church, and further disagreements would inevitably be measured against the canons it had established.

Athens, ancient abode of Greek philosophy, although in decline, could still in the 5th century boast of being its centre. Proclus of Constantinople, the last important representative of Neoplatonic thought, taught there. The influence of philosophy may have been waning but there were many writers in this troubled century who recorded interesting aspects of the new enemies threatening the empire. One of them, Priscus of Thrace, had been a member of an embassy to the court of Attila, king of the Huns. He observed much about the customs of these people, and his work became a source for later authors such as Cassiodorus and Jordanes. The pagan writer Zosimus wrote a *New History*, which ends with the Visigothic siege and sack of Rome in 410. He contends that this calamity was brought about by the anger of the pagan gods for having been abandoned by the Romans, and he blames Constantine the Great for it. By contrast, he has the highest regard for the emperor Julian.

In this period three elements – Christianity, Hellenism, and the orient – provided the basis for the development of a distinctly Christian art; and imperial Constantinople became central to Christian culture in its eastern form. The "New Rome" was able to assimilate and transmute the various elements into a new artistic and cultural synthesis.

In the eastern Mediterranean the early churches of the Holy Land, such as those of Jerusalem, Bethlehem, and Nazareth, belong to the era of Constantine's dynasty. The monastery of St Simeon Stylites (Qalat Seman) between Antioch and Aleppo remains an impressive witness to this splendid early achievement, even as a ruin. Arcadius (395–408), the successor of Theodosius the Great, built a basilica in the Maryut desert near Alexandria over the grave of Menas, a revered Egyptian saint. There is thus evidence that imperial generosity and support for the Church reached well beyond the confines of the capital.

When the emperor Justin I died in 527, his nephew Petrus Sabbatius became emperor as Justinian I (527–65). His reign, although it has its critics, is generally regarded as a "golden age". It seems that Justinian's plans were oriented towards the West from the beginning. Latin was emphasized as the language of government, and religious orthodoxy, in the sense of the western Church, was enforced. The religious policy of Justinian aimed at orthodox conformity, in spite of his empress's Monophysite sympathies. His main effort, however, was to eradicate all traces of paganism. In this spirit, in 529 he closed the Academy in Athens, which had been founded 900 years earlier by Plato. By contrast, the school of higher learning that had been established earlier in Constantinople continued to flourish into the days of the emperor Maurice (582–602). The main aim of this institution was no doubt to provide the imperial government with educated bureaucrats.

The emperor himself was engaged in theological disputes, and wrote dogmatic tracts and hymnology. His many achievements, nevertheless, are celebrated by the historians of his reign. Foremost among the latter stands Procopius of Caesarea. Educated for a career in law, he became secretary to Justinian's general, Belisarius, the conqueror of Vandal Africa and Ostrogothic Italy. In this position he had access to letters, dispatches, and conversations that together with his personal observations inform his writings. In addition to Procopius'

official histories of Justinian's wars and building activities, in the *Anecdota* he launched a vicious attack on the emperor and his consort, Theodora. His works, for all their exaggerations, are nevertheless of great historical value, and are important for the information they contain on the early Slavic and Germanic peoples.

A contemporary of Procopius, Peter the Patrician, composed, among other things, a treatise on court ceremonies, part of which was later incorporated into the writings of Constantine VII Porphyrogennetos (913–59) in his own work on this subject. Procopius was followed by Agathias who wrote poems, epigrams, and a history of the reign of Justinian covering the period from 552 to 558. Agathias was in turn succeeded by Menander Protector who related events up to the accession of Maurice. Although extant only in fragments, Menander's history contains valuable information on geography and ethnography. It was continued by Theopylaktos Simokattes whose major work, a history of the reign of Maurice, and probably written early in the reign of Herakleios (608–41), is an important source.

A bureaucrat under Justinian, John the Lydian, wrote a treatise on the administration of the empire. John, it is said, was much valued by Justinian on account of his excellent education; so much so that he commissioned him to write an imperial panegyric. The era of Justinian furthermore produced works on a broad geographical scale, such as the *Christian Topography* of Cosmas Indicopleustes, and the statistical survey of the political geography of the empire, the *Synekdimos* of Hierocles. This latter work was to become an important source of geographical information for Constantine Porphyrogennetos. There were also writers of chronicles such as John Malalas. He was a Syrian from Antioch who could boast little education, but his chronicle, written in vulgar Greek, spans the time from the early Egyptians to the end of Justinian's reign. It became immensely popular, and exerted much influence beyond the borders of the empire when it was translated into Slavonic.

Church history in this era is represented by the Syrian Evagrius, who wrote about ecclesiastical events from the Council of Ephesus (431) to the year 593, and John of Ephesus (d. c.586), who wrote his work in Syriac. The latter's account is written from a Monophysite viewpoint. This bias is important since Monophysitism was then the prime theological dispute, and, by extension, a hot political issue as well. In addition to his *Ecclesiastical History*, which begins with the time of Julius Caesar and ends in 585, he also wrote a work on the lives of the eastern saints. Another contemporary of both Justin and Justinian was Leontius of Byzantium. His polemical writings, which expound an orthodox religious view, are typical of a Byzantine intellectual who moved gradually away from the once fashionable Neoplatonic thought and nearer to that of Aristotle.

There is finally a host of authors of hagiographical and devotional literature. Cyril of Scythopolis, a monk of the Palestinian lavra of Mar Saba, wrote saints' lives but his work remained incomplete. But, even so, his writings are a valuable source for cultural history. Another Palestinian monk, John Moschus, composed in Greek *The Spiritual Meadow* (*Leimon*) in which he gathers together the experiences gained in his travels to monasteries throughout the east. This work became favourite reading in the Byzantine empire and neighbouring countries. Given the interest of the reading public in matters of religion, the era may justly be called an "age of spirituality".

Romanos the Melodist, a writer of hymns, lived in the reign of Justinian. It is thought that he was the creator of the *Akathistos* hymn in praise of the *Theotokos*. It is worth noting that the Virgin Mary rose in the 6th century to her exalted place as the protectress of Constantinople, and that in the reign of the emperor Maurice her ascension into heaven became a feast day. Paul the Silentiary too was a contemporary of Justinian. He celebrated in Greek verse the beauty of the emperor's great church, Hagia Sophia, and particularly its splendid pulpit. Paul's poetry on this subject is still of much interest to art historians today.

The North African writer Corippus, who wrote his work in Latin, lived at first at Carthage but was later called to the imperial court at Constantinople. His works give testimony of the continued use of Latin into Justinian's reign. His *Johannis* was written in praise of John Troglita, the general who successfully put down a revolt against the imperial regime in North Africa. In addition, a panegyric of Justin II by Corippus contains interesting material on 6th-century court ceremonies. Finally, there was a body of entertainment literature such as romances and novels that was popular with the educated populations of the great cities of the empire. It is easy to conclude from the foregoing brief overview that the age of late antiquity preserved, and even expanded, its literary heritage.

As lawgiver, Justinian realized that the Code of Theodosius no longer served the needs of the law courts. It was largely incomplete, and earlier laws existed in scattered collections only. Thus he decided to replace it. A committee was established under the chairmanship of Tribonius, his quaestor, and in 529 the first edition of the new code was issued. But it had been too hastily compiled, and this made it necessary to produce a revised edition, in 534. Justinian's code consists of three parts: the *Institutes* (a legal textbook), the *Digest* (a commentary of jurists from the 2nd century onwards), and the *Corpus Iuris Civilis*, beginning with the praetor's edict under Hadrian and continuing to the time of Justinian. Later, Justinian's own legislation, the *Novellae*, was appended to the code. It remained a source of legal thought in Christendom, and when it was reintroduced in the West from the 11th century on, it became the foundation of civil law in continental Europe.

The other great achievement of the age of Justinian lay in his building activities, the most outstanding example of which is the monumental church of Hagia Sophia in Constantinople, built after an earlier church had been destroyed in the Nika rebellion of 532. Hagia Sophia is a domed basilica, with the enormous central dome rising over a longitudinal nave; and its interior is splendidly decorated with richly coloured mosaics and marbles. Throughout the ages, this church made such an impression on visitors to Constantinople that a whole body of legends and miraculous stories began to circulate, influencing even writers of Slavic and Islamic cultures. The other important church erected by Justinian, and designed by the same pair of architects who had planned Hagia Sophia, namely Isidore of Miletus and Anthemius of Tralles, was the church of the Holy Apostles which, originating in the time of Constantine the Great, was in such disrepair that the emperor decided to rebuild it. It remained as the burial place of the Byzantine emperors up to the 11th century but was destroyed in the Turkish conquest of Constantinople by Mehmet II to make room for his own mosque. Today the church of St Mark in Venice, which was modelled on the Holy Apostles, gives an indication of what its prototype in Constantinople must have looked like.

An outpost of Byzantine administration in the West in the 6th century, the exarchate of Ravenna had previously been first the capital of the western government under the emperor Honorius (395–423) and after that of Ostrogothic Italy. The period of the exarchate represents a brilliant phase in the architectural history of that city. When Ravenna fell to the conquering Byzantine army under the command of Belisarius, the church of San Vitale, the construction of which had already been started under the Ostrogoths, was then completed by order of Justinian. The other great church of this period is San Apollinare in Classe, the harbour of Ravenna. Grandiosely conceived in their architectural design, the most outstanding features of these churches are the mosaics. The apse of San Vitale contains the most discussed mosaics of Justinian's reign, showing on facing panels the emperor and empress, surrounded by their courts.

As recorded by Procopius in his *De Aedificiis*, Justinian built, in addition to these churches, fortifications, monasteries, baths, hospitals, and aqueducts. Little remains today of these buildings, and some are now known only through literary descriptions. Besides the great architectural and literary achievements of the age, the creations of the so-called "minor arts" should not be forgotten. These works in carved ivory, woven textiles, intricate metalwork, and colourful enamels still convey today the brilliance of the Byzantine achievement in late antiquity. As Gervase Mathew reminds us, "In Byzantine civilization these arts are never minor."

Tiberius' reign (578–82) ushered in a new era in Byzantine history. The emperor turned his attention to the affairs of the threatened East, abandoning much of Italy to the Lombards and leaving only the exarchate of Ravenna and parts of southern Italy under imperial control. A similar policy was pursued by Maurice who succeeded him in 582. He himself was an educated man who had risen in both the bureaucracy and the military, and presumably would have been sympathetic to the high culture of his day. This is supported in various sources that point to the achievements of his reign. But with the empire threatened once again by the might of Persia, and inroads of Avars and Slavs in the Balkans, there was little to spare for cultivating the arts. The so-called *Strategikon* (General's Handbook) of the emperor Maurice may have been written in his time, bearing testimony to the military concerns of the age. In the end, the emperor's political realism accompanied by stringent fiscal measures proved unpopular, and he fell victim to an army rebellion in 602.

The following reign, of Phokas (602–10) who had led the uprising against Maurice, is a dark page in the cultural life of the empire. The era is characterized by anarchy, foreign invasions, and internal conspiracies. With the coming of Herakleios, son of the exarch of Africa, the empire entered into a period of great military conflicts with Persia and the Avar power. Jerusalem was captured by the Persians who penetrated as far as Egypt. It was only in 628 that Herakleios was able to overcome the Persians and decisively crush Sassanian might. In the Balkans he established suzerainty over the Slavs following the waning of Avar control in the region.

In religion, too, Herakleios tried to find a solution to the vexing conflict with Monophysitism, issuing the *Ekthesis* or Exposition of Faith in 636, recognizing two natures but one will in Christ. The *Ekthesis* aimed at reconciling the Monophysites in the eastern provinces. It was, however, too late since at the same time the rapid conquest of these provinces by Arab forces under the banner of Islam had begun.

Ironically, the territorially shrunken Byzantine empire became more homogeneous as a result of having lost most of the provinces in which Monophysitism was strongest. This process was complete when Egypt too was conquered by Amr, the Muslim general, in 658. The empire became distinctly Greek in speech and culture in the time of Herakleios who, by taking the title of *basileus* (king), finally broke with the tradition of his predecessors who had styled themselves successors of the first Roman emperor, Augustus.

The early part of Herakleios's reign had been a struggle for the very existence of the empire, and the later period was overshadowed by the Arab menace. For this reason the intellectual life of the age was at an all-time low. Nevertheless, George of Pisidia, the deacon of Hagia Sophia, celebrated the reign of Herakleios in three historical works, and composed a panegyric in his honour on the occasion of his final victory in the conflict with Persia. George was later much appreciated by the 11th-century scholar Michael Psellos who considered him an equal of Euripides. The so-called *Chronicon Paschale* was composed in the reign of Herakleios and, although largely unoriginal, contains some interesting historical remarks about contemporary events.

The dynasty of Herakleios ended in 711 with the death of Justinian II. After a brief interlude of non-dynastic rulers, Leo III founded a dynasty that lasted until 802. The iconoclast emperors of Leo's house shook the very foundations of Byzantine religiosity when they legislated against religious art, and especially the veneration of icons, many of which were believed by the people of the empire to be heavenly manifestations "not made by human hands".

The period was also characterized by the great struggle between Byzantium and Islam. In an all-out offensive, the Muslims tried to take the capital, Constantinople, itself. The attempt failed thanks to the skilful use of Greek fire and the severity of a winter campaign that made the Muslim forces withdraw in 718. It was the last Arab attempt to take the "God-protected" city, and given the importance accorded to Leo's victory by later generations, it assumes historic significance. Constantinople had become the "sacred fortress" of Christendom in the minds of many.

Leo's reign is also remembered for the emperor's legislative activity. He realized that Justinian's code, which had been composed in Latin, no longer reflected the conditions of the Greek-speaking empire. His code, the *Ekloga*, was issued in the name of the "wise and pious emperors, Leo and Constantine".

Modern scholarship has tried to find connections between the Arab danger to the empire and Leo's iconoclast legislation. It is also thought that Leo, who was probably of Syrian origin, was influenced by Jewish and Muslim thought in the matter of images. Both religions considered the use of icons as a form of idolatry, and it has been noted in the historical analysis of iconoclasm that the caliph Yazid II forbade the Christians in his territory to venerate images three years before Leo's edict to the same effect.

Whatever provoked the emperor's stand on icons, his and his successors' legislation had far-reaching consequences, especially when after the Synod of Hieria (754) the destruction of sacred art was carried out with brutal efficiency. In this attempt to stamp out the worship of sacred images, icons, whether painted or in mosaic, sculpture, or illuminated manuscripts, were ruthlessly destroyed. This wholesale destruction was also accompanied by the annihilation of relics. Ironically, what remained of earlier religious art survived mostly in the provinces that had been lost to Islam and which were therefore beyond the reach of the imperial government.

It was in the reign of the empress Irene (797–802) that icon veneration was once more temporarily established. The second period of iconoclasm, however, ended only in the regency of Theodora, wife of the emperor Theophilos, who convened a council that reinstated the legality of icons throughout the empire in 843. The date of this event, 11 March, is to this day celebrated in the Greek Orthodox Church as the feast of Orthodoxy.

Much as the iconoclast emperors had achieved in their reigns, their policies hastened the rupture with the papacy, and made possible the crowning of Charlemagne as emperor of a renewed Roman empire in the west in 800.

FRANZISKA E. SHLOSSER

See also Chronicles, Hagia Sophia, Hagiography, Historiography, Hymnography, Iconoclasm, Law, Ravenna

Summary

From 330, the dedication of Constantinople by Constantine the Great, to 843, the triumph of Orthodoxy. Architecture and Christian literature develops under Constantine. Intellectual life flourishes in Egypt. Christianity becomes state religion under Theodosius I. Fourth Ecumenical Council at Chalcedon determines Christ's nature. Athens remains the centre of Greek philosophy. The Golden Age of Justinian in the 6th century as seen in Ravenna and elsewhere. Period of iconoclasm is followed by the triumph of Orthodoxy.

Further Reading

Ammianus Marcellinus, Works, translated by J.C. Rolfe, 3 vols, London: Heinemann, and Cambridge, Massachusetts: Harvard University Press, 1935–39 (Loeb edition)

Barker, John W., *Justinian and the Later Roman Empire*, Madison: University of Wisconsin Press, 1966

Barnes, Timothy D., *The New Empire of Diocletian and Constantine*, Cambridge, Massachusetts: Harvard University Press, 1982

Beckwith, John, *Early Christian and Byzantine Art*, 2nd edition, Harmondsworth and New York: Penguin, 1979; reprinted New Haven: Yale University Press, 1993

Brown, Peter, *The World of Late Antiquity*, London: Thames and Hudson, and New York: Harcourt Brace, 1971

Brown, T.S., *Gentlemen and Officers: Imperial Administration and Aristocratic Power in Byzantine Italy*, AD 554–800, London: British School at Rome, 1984

Browning, Robert, *Justinian and Theodora*, revised edition, London and New York: Thames and Hudson, 1987

Bryer, Anthony and Judith Herrin (editors), *Iconoclasm*, Birmingham: Centre for Byzantine Studies, University of Birmingham, 1977

Bury, J.B., *History of the Later Roman Empire from the Death of Theodosius I to the Death of Justinian*, 2 vols, London: Macmillan, 1923; reprinted New York: Dover, 1958

Byzantine Books and Bookmen, Washington, D.C.: Dumbarton Oaks, 1975

Cameron, Averil, *Continuity and Change in Sixth-Century Byzantium*, London: Variorum, 1981

Cameron, Averil, *Procopius and the Sixth Century*, London: Duckworth, and Berkeley: University of California Press, 1985

Downey, Glanville, *Constantinople in the Age of Justinian*, Norman: University of Oklahoma Press, 1960

Eusebius of Caesarea, *The History of the Church from Christ to Constantine*, translated by G.A. Williamson, Harmondsworth: Penguin, 1965

Gilles, Pierre, *The Antiquities of Constantinople*, 2nd edition, based on a translation of John Ball, New York: Italica Press, 1988

Haussig, H.W., *A History of Byzantine Civilization*, London: Thames and Hudson, and New York: Praeger, 1971

Hunger, Herbert, *Die hochsprachliche profane Literatur der Byzantiner*, 2 vols, Munich: Beck, 1978

Hussey, J.M., *The Byzantine World*, 4th edition, London: Hutchinson, 1970

Jones, A.H.M., *The Later Roman Empire, 284–602: A Social, Economic, and Administrative Survey*, 3 vols, Oxford: Blackwell, and Norman: University of Oklahoma Press, 1964

Kazhdan, A.P. (editor), *The Oxford Dictionary of Byzantium*, 3 vols, New York and Oxford: Oxford University Press, 1991

Kitzinger, Ernest, *Byzantine Art in the Making: Main Lines of Stylistic Development in Mediterranean Art, 3rd–7th Century*, Cambridge, Massachusetts: Harvard University Press, and London: Faber, 1977

Krüger, Paul (editor), *Corpus iuris civilis*, vol. 2: *Codex Justinianus*, Berlin: Weidmann, 1928

Lancaster, Osbert, *Sailing to Byzantium: An Architectural Companion*, London: John Murray, and Boston: Gambit, 1969

Mango, Cyril, *Byzantine Architecture*, New York: Abrams, 1976; London: Academy, 1979

Mango, Cyril, *Byzantium: The Empire of New Rome*, London: Weidenfeld and Nicolson, and New York: Scribner, 1980

Mathew, Gervase, *Byzantine Aesthetics*, London: John Murray, 1963; New York: Viking, 1964

Menander, *The History of Menander the Guardsman*, translated by R.C. Blockley, Liverpool: Cairns, 1985

Procopius of Caesarea, Works, translated by H.B. Dewing, 7 vols, London: Heinemann, and New York: Macmillan, 1914–40 (Loeb edition)

Sherrard, Philip, *Constantinople: Iconography of a Sacred City*, London and New York: Oxford University Press, 1965

Treadgold, Warren T., *A History of the Byzantine State and Society*, Stanford, California: Stanford University Press, 1997

Vasiliev, A.A., *History of the Byzantine Empire, 324–1453*, revised edition, 2 vols, Madison: University of Wisconsin Press, 1952

Weitzmann, Kurt (editor), *Age of Spirituality: Late Antique and Early Christian Art, Third to Seventh Century*, New York: Metropolitan Museum of Art, 1979 (exhibition catalogue)

Byzantine Period, Middle 843–1204

The middle Byzantine period began with the re-establishment of the veneration of icons in 843 and ended with the fall of Constantinople to the Crusaders in 1204. The period has been characterized as the "classic" phase of Byzantine civilization, when many of those features usually seen as most typically Byzantine from the modern point of view can be most clearly discerned.

Although the overall structure of imperial government and Church administration remained similar to that of earlier centuries, the social and economic role of local landowners and monasteries increased considerably compared with the early Byzantine period. Many new monasteries were founded, including the great monastic centres at Mount Athos and the Meteora in Greece, and these had a high degree of autonomy. The autonomy of the local aristocracies, within the thematic administrative structure already established, was also greater than in the early Byzantine period, and these rural "lords" came to play an important role in Byzantine society in general.

Accordingly, the middle Byzantine countryside was divided into large estates, owned by monastic houses or secular magnates. Rural society and economy became increasingly "feudal" in organization, especially at the end of the middle Byzantine period. There was a strict social hierarchy, although a degree of social mobility is apparent. However, the government in Constantinople retained control of the empire and was able to collect taxes, issue coinage, and enforce laws. Greek was the language of government, but religion – not language – became the defining feature of the Byzantine political and cultural identity, although a "Roman" identity was still also asserted.

Although an episcopal structure of Church administration remained, focused on the patriarch of Constantinople, the most distinctive characteristic of the middle Byzantine Church was the many monasteries, large and small. Middle Byzantine monasteries tended to share a similar layout, as exemplified both on Mount Athos and at the Meteora and on a smaller scale at many lesser monastic centres, as at Sagmata in Boeotia. Enclosed by a wall, with an elaborate main gate, they were centred on a church set in the middle of a courtyard. Around this were the monks' accommodation, refectory, and other buildings, often of more than one storey in height. As these examples show, in Greece and the Balkans especially, a large number of middle Byzantine monasteries still survive today as religious houses and many church buildings of this date also remain in use.

In cultural terms, probably the most important change affecting the middle Byzantine Church was the end of iconoclasm. This restored the veneration of icons to the liturgy and acted as a stimulus both to the arts (especially mosaic and painting) and to the monastic movement. Throughout the period the Church also actively supported a wide range of intellectual life, including literature and secular learning. In particular, Constantinople itself became a major centre for renewed academic and artistic activity. Thus, during the middle Byzantine period a distinctive new artistic style emerged that owed less to the Roman past than had early Byzantine art and which was often – although by no means universally – religious in its subjects.

Byzantine culture also began to encompass peoples outside the empire, as Orthodoxy gained new converts beyond the imperial frontiers. New Orthodox states were established following the conversion of the Bulgarian ruler (Boris I) in 864 and tsar Vladimir of Russia in 988. One result of this may have been the formation of a cultural, religious, and perhaps political zone centred on Constantinople, in which courts and the

Middle Byzantine Period: 9th- or 10th-century mosaic of Christ in Glory, church of Hagia Sophia, Thessalonica

Church in a number of independent states emulated Byzantine institutions: the "Byzantine Commonwealth".

It was in this period, too, that Byzantine church architecture began conventionally to employ the "cross-in-square" or "inscribed cross plan", which has remained a model for Orthodox churches ever since. During the middle Byzantine period this rapidly became the standard form of church building, and examples are known throughout the empire. Perhaps among the earliest churches of this form still standing are at Tirilye (in Bithynia), Side (in Turkey), and Skripou (in Boeotia). At Constantinople the first church employing this plan may well have been the Nea Ekklesia at the Great Palace (880). However, the oldest examples still in existence in the Byzantine capital are the Myrelaion and the Monastery of Constantine Lips churches, dating from the 10th century.

The origins of the cross-in-square church are obscure: some scholars have detected early Byzantine provincial (perhaps Armenian) predecessors to this distinctive plan; others think it originated from the architectural elaboration of cross-domed churches. Whatever its origins, the cross-in-square church is perhaps the archetypal middle Byzantine monument, although it is important to note that the rock-cut churches of Cappadocia include examples with many other plans. This may suggest that there was a wider diversity of middle Byzantine church forms than the evidence of free-standing buildings would imply, and the rock-cut churches themselves also remind us that regional constructional techniques and building types still existed.

Churches are associated with other architectural developments of the period. These include an increased emphasis on the exterior appearance of buildings; a tendency for smaller, more compact structures; and a formalization of the decorative programme of churches, so that different buildings tend to have similar schemes of art. These artistic programmes show biblical scenes, saints, and notables in a strict hierarchy throughout the church building, with Christ depicted in the (almost ubiquitous) dome.

Secular palaces known from middle Byzantine written sources also often seem to have adopted a plan similar to monasteries – that of a courtyard with central church – although rural aristocratic centres also included castle-like hilltop fortresses, appropriate to the military lifestyle of the secular rural elite.

In the borderlands where these "lords" were strongest, they

existed in a society that, while strongly Christian in its religion, was open to much Islamic cultural influence, as reflected in the fictional story of Digenis Akritis. The extent to which a fusion of cultures emerged in this border area is unclear. For example, there seems to have been some Islamic influence on the architecture of Byzantine palace buildings from the 9th century onward. This was not only in the eastern borderlands that were adjacent to Islamic polities, but even in Constantinople. The earliest instance of this is perhaps the palace built at Bryas (near Constantinople) by emperor Theophilos (829–42), which was explicitly modelled on buildings in Baghdad. Later, emperor John II Komnenos (1118–43) built a Seljuk-style pavilion (the Muchroutas) in the Great Palace at Constantinople.

Much more problematical is the extent to which Islamic architectural styles were employed in secular contexts in eastern Anatolia itself. In Cappadocia many middle Byzantine buildings – especially elaborately decorated churches – were cut into the soft tufa. Some have both Byzantine and Islamic architectural features, and it has been suggested that some may be the mansions of local secular landowners, although the more usual interpretation is that they all represent churches and monasteries.

Throughout the Byzantine empire both monastic communities and the rural aristocracy gained their economic support mainly from agriculture. The rural population lived in small villages, but little is known about such settlements archaeologically and they were seldom described in detail in texts. Most likely, they characteristically contained wooden or stonebuilt rectangular houses, with tiled or thatched roofs. Most villages probably also had a church, serving as the focus for the community.

However, although the economy was predominantly agricultural and the population mostly dwelt on the land, towns did exist, as at Thessalonica and Pergamum. Constantinople, the capital, was still by far the most important political, cultural, and trading centre and the largest city. In the 9th century both it and many of the provincial towns seem to have been smaller and very different in character from their early Byzantine predecessors. However, during the middle Byzantine period it seems that both Constantinople and other towns grew in size and acquired new commercial roles.

Characteristically, the middle-Byzantine period town contained closely packed stonebuilt houses (examples of which have been excavated at Athens and Pergamum) set along narrow streets, within a defensive wall. The civic buildings and other monuments of earlier periods were largely disused, and the principal public buildings in most of these towns (as in the villages) were churches. Monasteries were more common within middle Byzantine towns than had perhaps previously been the case, and crafts, including pottery production, were carried out within towns as well as in the monasteries and villages in the countryside.

Middle-Byzantine pottery is very distinctive. From the 7th century at the latest, Byzantine pottery was often glazed, and glazed and elaborately decorated pottery characterizes middle Byzantine assemblages. For example, "polychrome ware", glazed white vessels highly decorated with red, blue, and black paint, is characteristic of the middle-Byzantine period. A range of wall plaques, in the same style, adorned many buildings in Constantinople, as at St John Studios, the Myrelaion, and the Great Palace itself. Many other types of glazed pottery were also produced, as well as unglazed vessels and amphorae. These are commonly found at Byzantine town and monastery sites during excavation, but their study is hampered by a lack of well-dated archaeological contexts.

Other material changes in everyday life are also evidenced. For example, although wall mosaics were still made, floor mosaics – common in major buildings in the early Byzantine period – were no longer routinely laid. *Opus sectile* (a floor made of larger pieces of marble or other stone placed in designs) took their place. While this may be no more than a matter of fashion, some indications of technological change seem to be present. To give one example, aqueducts seem no longer to have supplied the needs of towns for drinking water. Instead, water was commonly stored in cisterns, one of the most widespread features of Byzantine sites of this date.

Thus, the middle-Byzantine period shows both continuities and discontinuities from the early-Byzantine period in culture, administration, society, economy, and in its material aspects. This has led to much debate over a range of related issues, including the connection between middle-Byzantine culture, society, economy, and technology and those of the Roman world, the degree of innovation present in the middle-Byzantine period, and the extent and character of both feudalism and urbanism. Nevertheless, few would doubt today that the middle-Byzantine period saw some of the greatest cultural and political achievements of Byzantine civilization.

KEN DARK

See also Commonwealth, Estates, Monasteries, Mosaic, Painting

Summary

Dated from 802 to 1204, the middle-Byzantine period is often regarded as the "classic" phase of Byzantine culture. Following the Triumph of Orthodoxy (the restoration of icons) in 843 many monasteries were founded. Religion, not language, became the criterion of cultural identity. The arts and learning flourished and the Church was their principal patron.

Further Reading

Angold, Michael, "The Byzantine State on the Eve of the Battle of Mantzikert", *Byzantinische Forschungen*, 16 (1990): pp. 9–34

Angold, Michael, *Church and Society in Byzantium under the Comneni, 1081–1261*, Cambridge and New York: Cambridge University Press, 1995

Angold, Michael, *The Byzantine Empire, 1025–1204*, 2nd edition, London and New York: Longman, 1997

Browning, Robert, *The Byzantine Empire*, London: Weidenfeld and Nicolson, and New York: Scribner, 1980

Brubaker, Leslie, *Byzantium in the Ninth Century: Dead or Alive?*, Aldershot, Hampshire: Ashgate, 1998

Fine, John V.A. Jr, *The Early Medieval Balkans: A Critical Survey from the Sixth to the Late Twelfth Century*, Ann Arbor: University of Michigan Press, 1983

Franklin, Simon and Jonathan Sheperd, *The Emergence of Rus, 750–1200*, London and New York: Longman, 1996

Harvey, Alan, *Economic Expansion in the Byzantine Empire, 900–1200*, Cambridge and New York: Cambridge University Press, 1989

Howard-Johnston, J.D. (editor), *Byzantium and the West, c.850–c.1200*, Amsterdam: Hakkert, 1988

Laiou, Angeliki E. and Dieter Simon (editors), *Law and Society in Byzantium, 9th–12th Centuries*, Washington, D.C.: Dumbarton Oaks, 1994

Magdalino, Paul, *The Empire of Manuel I Komnenos, 1143–1180*, Cambridge and New York: Cambridge University Press, 1993

Morris, Rosemary, *Monks and Laymen in Byzantium, 843–1118*, Cambridge and New York: Cambridge University Press, 1995

Mullett, Margaret and Dion Smythe (editors), *Alexios I Komnenos*, vol. 1, Belfast: Belfast Byzantine Enterprises, 1996

Obolensky, Dimitri, *The Byzantine Commonwealth: Eastern Europe, 500–1453*, London: Weidenfeld and Nicolson, and New York: Praeger, 1971

Rodley, Lyn, *Byzantine Art and Architecture: An Introduction*, Cambridge and New York: Cambridge University Press, 1994

Byzantine Period, Late 1261–1453

The final phase of Byzantine civilization presents a remarkable paradox of health within infirmity.

During the final two centuries of Byzantium's history, its political situation was one of consistent decline. The recovery of Constantinople in 1261 by the imperial regime in Nicaea seemed to vindicate Byzantium's humiliation of 1204. But when the first ruler of the new (and ultimate) dynasty of the Palaiologoi, Michael VIII (1259–82), boldly attempted to play a grand role in international politics, he was in fact stretching the capacities of his realm to near breaking-point. His successors were obliged to confront the realities of governing what had become a minor local state – "the empire of the Straits" it has been called – within a context of international affairs in which neighbours and rivals were far greater powers. External weakness was compounded by internal dynastic and social conflicts which made it the more vulnerable to the aggressions of its neighbours, especially the Serbians in the first half of the 14th century, and then the Ottoman Turks in the second half. Even before the beginning of the 15th century, a half-century before the final debacle of 1453, Byzantium was a ravaged spectre of a state: its lands reduced to Constantinople, a few islands, and other scraps of territory, its economy largely in the hands of others, and its government little more than a holding operation in the face of looming destruction.

Yet, for all the outward decay and degradation, Byzantine civilization remained remarkably vibrant and productive, even allowing for the reduction in patronage and economic resources. The sheer volume of its cultural legacy is extraordinary – and is still only beginning to be investigated and explicated in full.

The intellectual life of the Palaiologan era owed much to the cultural recovery launched under the Laskarid regime in Nicaea (1204–61). Nicaea (modern Iznik) was not the only refuge for institutional and cultural leadership among the fragments of the Byzantine world that had been smashed by the Fourth Crusade. But it soon became the most promising and consistent focus of claims to the traditions of Constantinople. From that great city's dispersed court came remnants of the intellectual elite who painfully strove to reconstruct in exile the earlier educational and scholarly life. The principal exemplar of the Nicaean revival was the learned Nikephoros Blemmydes (1197–c.1269), whose students included the philosopher-historian George Akropolites and even the future emperor Theodore II Laskaris. By the time Byzantine government was restored in Constantinople, a thriving cultural life was ready-made to be transferred back to the capital. Nor was Constantinople to be the only centre: Thessalonica could at times claim to rival the capital in artists and men of learning, while Mistra in the Morea also became a lively centre in the later Palaiologan epoch.

The scholarly circles identified with the first two Palaiologan emperors, Michael VIII and then Andronikos II (1282–1328), included such eminences as Akropolites's student, the polymath-historian George Pachymeres (1242–c.1310), the remarkable philologist Maximos Planudes (c.1255–c.1305), and Theodore Metochites (1270–1332), a facile scholar, artistic patron, and court politician of the highest rank. The next generation was best represented by his student, the highly versatile polymath-historian Nikephoros Gregoras (c.1292–c.1360). In the realm of historical writing, too, the ex-emperor John VI Kantakouzenos produced in his memoirs an outstanding example of its kind; though, in truth, the writing of history was to lapse until a constellation of 15th-century writers (Chalkokondyles, Doukas, Sphrantzes) gave it one final flourishing.

The most impressive scholar of the 14th century was surely Demetrios Kydones (c.1324–c.1398), who not only continued the Byzantine philosophical emphasis on Plato but who attempted a short-lived programme of studying and translating works of St Augustine, Anselm of Canterbury, and Thomas Aquinas. Just as with Planudes's earlier translations of Latin authors (Cato, Ovid, Cicero, Caesar among the ancients; St Augustine among Christians) for his circle of Constantinopolitan scholars, Kydones's later effort to alert Greek scholarship to what Latin literature and thought might offer proved fruitless in the face of Byzantine conservatism. Nevertheless, it symbolized the attraction of Latin culture to certain Byzantine individuals and, in the case of Kydones himself, was part of a mental reorientation leading him to accept Thomist thought and convert to Roman Catholicism. His students, such as the emperor Manuel II (1391–1425), continued his strictly Greek philosophical and literary tradition, without his ideology. But Kydones's protégé, Manuel Chrysoloras (c.1350–1415), extended further the older man's bridge to the West when he became (1387) the first Byzantine scholar of front rank to teach ancient Greek language and literature to the Italian humanists of the western Renaissance – becoming a Catholic himself in the process.

Chrysoloras wrote the first grammar book of Greek in Latin, and trained the first generation of Italian scholars in the language. His work represented a great breakthrough that for the first time opened the innermost circles of Byzantine learning to western scholars. It thereby initiated a flood of scholarly contacts, involving visits by Italian scholars to Byzantine centres and, above all, a steady flow of Byzantine scholars to the new lands of professional opportunity in Italy and beyond. The earlier of these included George Trapezountios (1395–c.1472), John Argyropoulos (c.1393?–1487), and Theodore Gaza (c.1400–c.1475), all of whom adopted Latin Christianity. Outstanding among these, however, was Bessarion of Trebizond (c.1400–72): his important role in achieving church union at the Council of Florence (1439) won him a cardinal's hat in the Roman Church, and thereafter he became a major intermediary for expatriate Byzantine scholars in Italy.

Byzantine learning has been criticized as archaizing pedantry, but its scholarly traditions created standards of philology and techniques of textual criticism that, together with knowledge of the ancient Greek language and access to the ancient texts, allowed Byzantine scholars to restore to western Europe a full knowledge of the literature of Classical Hellenism – a crucial contribution to the western Renaissance. A further intellectual influence was to direct Italian humanists to the study of Plato, which launched them in their decisive philosophical directions. This apparently resulted from discourses given during participation in the Council of Florence by Bessarion's teacher, the great scholar George Gemistos, who took the name of Plethon (c.1360–1452). Ironically, however, Plethon chose to remain a part of the Byzantine world rather than relocate in the West. In the final years of his long life, Plethon produced syntheses of his Platonic thought that were strikingly original and controversial. His intellectual opponent, the champion of Aristotle and upholder of Orthodox purity, George Scholarios, represents a kind of epilogue, in becoming the first patriarch of Constantinople under the Turks as Gennadios II.

The aforementioned are, of course, only among the most outstanding of a larger catalogue of scholars. Nor were philology and philosophy the only important areas of Palaiologan intellectual life. A final compilation of Byzantine law was achieved for immediate and practical use by Constantine Harmenopoulos in 1345. Though Byzantium has never been rated highly as a producer of great literary works, there was nevertheless, in its own terms, a considerable productivity in the Palaiologan era, not only in the rhetorical exercises of high culture that occupied the learned circles, but in popular writing as well. There was a particular flowering of the idiom of the Greek verse romance in the 14th century. Hagiography also enjoyed one final burst of activity, in a round of attention both to earlier saints and to contemporaneous holy men. This feature was hardly surprising in an epoch when the Church took on increasing prominence in a world in which the state was shrivelling so drastically: a world out of which the patriarch would survive the emperor as the force of leadership in the survival of Hellenic society and culture.

Accordingly, it is understandable that perhaps the most striking demonstration of Palaiologan cultural energy is shown in the sphere of theology. Beset by hostile ideological forces, Byzantine religious writers – both professionals and laymen – turned vigorously to the defence of their faith. There was a flourishing of debate with, and polemic against, Islamic religion, which had become such a potent threat with the progress of the Turkish conquest. The issue of church union with Rome – which was understood to threaten the compromising of Orthodox principles with Latin ones and the humiliating submission of Constantinople to Rome – was a recurrently provocative one for an era framed by two abortive union councils, those of Lyons (1274) and Florence (1439). Numerous treatises were composed to refute Latin doctrines, notably the so-called Double Procession of the Holy Spirit.

Even more stimulating to polemic, however, was the issue of hesychasm, the one significant theological controversy in Byzantium after the Christological debates and iconoclasm. Byzantine practices of mystical devotion, represented in private spiritual exercises in "silence" (hesychia), especially as a focus of monastic spirituality, were challenged in the 14th century and were given final definition by the last original Byzantine theologian, Gregory Palamas (c.1296–1359), whose ideas were adopted as official doctrine. The depth and virulence of the controversy over Palamism, however, partly reflected the increased importance and flourishing of monastic life itself in this late period. Nevertheless, the continuing transcendence of mystic theology over immediate polemic was exemplified in the writings of Nicholas Kabasilas, whose thought connects Palaiologan explication with the earlier traditions of Christian and Byzantine spirituality. The vitality of spiritual art is also reflected in lively activity in liturgical music, involving such important singer-composer-theoreticians as John Koukouzeles (d. c.1340) and Manuel Chrysaphes "the Lampadarios" who was active at the courts of the last two emperors.

In general, the particularly strong religious component of Palaiologan culture suggests an assumption, conscious or otherwise, by its participants that it was the spiritual dimension, rather than the political, which must provide the necessary guidance to those surviving the collapse of Byzantine government and society, and which must give the real meaning to what persisted of Hellenic identity.

In the realm of visual arts, of course, productivity is conditional upon the economic support system, whose decline or failure has its adverse effects. Building or rebuilding of monuments, especially churches, was extensive in the earlier part of the Palaiologan period, but gradually fell off. The survivals of late architecture are sporadic – few in Constantinople, more in provincial areas, especially in Thessalonica and, above all, in Mistra (numerous churches, the Palace of the Despots), whose prosperity in the late period contrasted ever more sharply with the capital's decline.

A last great burst of mosaic decoration attended the early Palaiologan decades. A great deal has been lost, but survives in the decoration of Holy Apostles' Church in Thessalonica, and in Constantinople in the magnificent Deesis panel in Hagia Sophia's south gallery. A climax was reached in the stunning ensemble of mosaics and frescoes in the reconstructed Chora Monastery (present-day Kariye Djami), as financed by Theodore Metochites and as restored to virtually complete glory today. The high cost of mosaic work reduced its role as a medium in the later Palaiologan period, but its place was filled more than robustly by the predominance of fresco painting. Artists in this medium explored more dramatic techniques of representation and extensions of iconography. Their achievements reached a peak in the 14th- and 15th-century churches of Mistra. But Byzantine monumental artists extended their work and influence not only through the provinces but into neighbouring areas, with rich results in such areas as Serbia, Russia, and Georgia. The continued vitality of Byzantine artistic style also provided inspiration for the flourishing in Italy of the so-called maniera greca in the 13th and 14th centuries, helping to shape such artists as Duccio. It is even argued that Byzantine innovations strongly influenced Giotto and other figures of what was to become early Renaissance art in Italy.

In addition to monumental art, the medium of manuscript illumination continued to prosper in Palaiologan Byzantium, even if with diminished court patronage. Finely illustrated books were produced not only in Constantinople but in other centres, such as Thessalonica, down to the early 15th century. Particularly important was Palaiologan icon painting, with surviving works of great power coming out of both the capital and Thessalonica – e.g. the Ohrid icon of the Annunciation from early 14th-century Constantinople. Some painters from this period are known by name, and by far the most interesting and perhaps important is Theophanes the Greek. He worked his way from Constantinople through Russian lands in the late 14th century, in the media of both fresco and icons, contributing greatly to the flowering of Russian painting thereafter, as extended in the work of Andrei Rublev (c.1365–1430) and his followers.

Likewise, the momentum of Palaiologan creativity would not be halted in the Greek world itself by the disaster of 1453, but would survive in traditions of fresco and especially icon painting under foreign rule. This was particularly true of the great icon painters of Crete and other islands under Venetian rule, whose lively productivity flowered on through the 17th century. It climaxed in one highly personal tangent followed in the West by Domenikos Theotokopoulos or "El Greco" (c.1548–c.1625), and it ended in the 18th-century Corfiote school, which was in turn made the basis for the present-day revival of icon painting that flourishes in the monasteries of Mount Athos and elsewhere in Greece. Once again, not even the attempted murder of Byzantine civilization could entirely end its life and influence.

In all, it has to be observed that the Palaiologan era constitutes not only a viable phase in the history of Byzantine art, but also one of its most important ones.

Over the centuries, Byzantium had repeatedly demonstrated the vitality of its society and the tenacity of its cultural traditions, surviving near-catastrophes and regenerating itself. The Palaiologan era displayed yet again those characteristics, amid the very cataclysm of its conclusion. Even when its political embodiment, the imperial state, had been wasted and destroyed, depriving it of outward independent structure, that civilization would still not truly die. It would live on to some degree under Turkish rule, eventually to feed into the modern regeneration of the Greek world. The stubborn vivacity of Palaiologan culture thus gives final testimony to the overall strength of Byzantine civilization as a whole, within the still larger context of the enduring and evolving Hellenic tradition.

JOHN W. BARKER

See also Hesychasm, Historiography, Icon, Mistra, Mosaic, Music, Painting, Renaissance (Palaiologan), Scholarship

Summary

From 1261, when Constantinople was recovered from the Latins, to 1453, when it fell to the Ottoman Turks. A remarkable cultural flowering known as the Palaiologan Renaissance, when there was great activity in the areas of scholarship, law, literature, theology, and the visual arts. Although politically the empire disintegrated in this period, Byzantine civilization was flourishing to the very end.

Further Reading

Angold, Michael, *A Byzantine Government in Exile: Government and Society under the Laskarids of Nicaea, 1204–1261*, Oxford: Oxford University Press, 1975

Beck, Hans-Georg, *Theodoros Metochites: Die Krise des byzantinischen Weltbildes im 14. Jahrhundert*, Munich: Beck, 1952

Belting, Hans, *Das illuminierte Buch in der spätbyzantinischen Gesellschaft*, Heidelberg: Winter, 1970

Clucas, Lowell, "The Triumph of Mysticism in Byzantium in the Fourteenth Century" in *Byzantine Studies in Honor of Milton V. Anastos*, edited by Speros Vryonis, Jr, Malibu, California: Undena, 1985

Constantinides, C.N., *Higher Education in Byzantium in the Thirteenth and Early Fourteenth Centuries, 1204–c.1310*, Nicosia: Cyprus Research Centre, 1982

Ćurčić, Slobodan and Mouriki Doula (editors), *The Twilight of Byzantium: Aspects of Cultural and Religious History in the Late Byzantine Empire*, Princeton, New Jersey: Princeton University Program in Hellenic Studies, 1991

Demus, Otto, *Byzantine Art and the West*, New York: New York University Press, 1970

Geanakoplos, Deno John, *Greek Scholars in Venice: Studies in the Dissemination of Greek Learning from Byzantium to Western Europe*, Cambridge, Massachusetts: Harvard University Press, 1962; as *Byzantium and the Renaissance*, Hamden, Connecticut: Archon, 1973

Geanakoplos, Deno John, *Interaction of the "Sibling" Byzantine and Western Cultures in the Middle Ages and Italian Renaissance, 330–1600*, New Haven, Connecticut: Yale University Press, 1976

Geanakoplos, Deno John, *Constantinople and the West: Essays on the Late Byzantine (Palaeologan) and Italian Renaissances and the Byzantine and Roman Churches*, Madison: University of Wisconsin Press, 1989

Hussey, J.M., *The Orthodox Church in the Byzantine Empire*, Oxford: Clarendon Press, 1986

Kazhdan, A.P. (editor), *The Oxford Dictionary of Byzantium*, 3 vols, New York and Oxford: Oxford University Press, 1991

Kianka, Frances, "Demetrius Cydones and Thomas Aquinas", *Byzantion*, 52 (1982): pp. 264–86

Kianka, Frances, "Byzantine-Papal Diplomacy: The Role of Demetrius Cydones", *International History Review*, 7 (1985): pp. 175–213

Meyendorff, John, *A Study of Gregory Palamas*, London: Faith Press, 1964

Meyendorff, John, *Byzantine Hesychasm: Historical, Theological, and Social Problems, Collected Studies*, London: Variorum, 1974

Meyendorff, John, *Byzantine Theology: Historical Trends and Doctrinal Themes*, New York: Fordham University Press, 1974

Mohler, Ludwig, *Kardinal Bessarion als Theologe, Humanist und Staatsmann*, 3 vols, Paderborn, 1923–42

Nicol, Donald M., *Byzantium: Its Ecclesiastical History and Relations with the Western World*, London: Variorum, 1972

Nicol, Donald M., *Church and Society in the Last Centuries of Byzantium*, Cambridge and New York: Cambridge University Press, 1979

Nicol, Donald M., *Studies in Late Byzantine History and Prosography*, London: Variorum, 1986

Nicol, Donald M., *The Last Centuries of Byzantium, 1261–1453*, 2nd edition, Cambridge and New York: Cambridge University Press, 1993

Ostrogorsky, George, *History of the Byzantine State*, revised edition, Oxford: Blackwell, 1968; New Brunswick, New Jersey: Rutgers University Press, 1969

Rice, David Talbot, *Byzantine Painting: The Last Phase*, London: Weidenfeld and Nicolson, and New York: Dial Press, 1968

Runciman, Steven, *The Last Byzantine Renaissance*, Cambridge: Cambridge University Press, 1970

Setton, Kenneth M., "The Byzantine Background to the Italian Renaissance" in his *Europe and the Levant in the Middle Ages and the Renaissance*, London: Variorum, 1974

Ševčenko, Ihor, *Society and Intellectual Life in Late Byzantium*, London: Variorum, 1981

Ševčenko, Ihor, "The Palaeologan Renaissance" in *Renaissances before the Renaissance: Cultural Revivals of Late Antiquity and the Middle Ages*, edited by Warren Treadgold, Stanford, California: Stanford University Press, 1984

Thomson, J., "Manuel Chrysoloras and the Early Italian Renaissance", *Greek, Roman, and Byzantine Studies*, 7 (1966): pp. 63–82

Trapp, Erich, *et al.* (editors), *Prosopographisches Lexikon der Palaiologenzeit*, Vienna: Akademie der Wissenschaften, 1976–

Vacalopoulos, Apostolos E., *Origins of the Greek Nation: The Byzantine Period, 1204–1461*, New Brunswick, New Jersey: Rutgers University Press, 1970

Vasiliev, A.A., *History of the Byzantine Empire, 324–1453*, revised edition, 2 vols, Madison: University of Wisconsin Press, 1952

Wilson, N.G., *From Byzantium to Italy: Greek Studies in the Italian Renaissance*, Baltimore: Johns Hopkins University Press, 1992

Wilson, N.G., *Scholars of Byzantium*, revised edition, London: Duckworth, and Cambridge, Massachusetts: Medieval Academy of America, 1996

Woodhouse, C.M., *George Gemistos Plethon: The Last of the Hellenes*, Oxford: Clarendon Press, 1986

Byzantines

The people to whom we conventionally apply this term would not have made much sense of it – a reminder that ex post facto historical labels and terms can often be very misleading.

The word "Byzantine" derives, of course, from the original name for the city on the Bosporus that was to become Constantinople. It was created in the mid-7th century BC by Greek colonists from Megara, and named Byzantion (or Byzantis) after Byzas, its supposed founder. When Constantine the Great expanded it as his new residence, to be called his city, *Konstantinoupolis*, it became the capital of the medieval "Greek" empire which is reckoned as lasting, from Constantine's refoundation in AD 324, for more than 11 centuries (with a brief interlude of Latin rule, 1204–61) until its storming by the Ottoman Turks in 1453.

It is true that Greek writers of the Middle Ages, at least those of intellectual circles enamoured of retaining ancient nomenclature at the cost of all reality, continued to use the name *Byzantion* in hyper-refined application to Constantinople itself, and such writers might also use the word *Byzantioi* for its citizens alone, as an archaizing artificiality. But even these writers would never describe their entire state and society as *Byzantion*, nor would they call themselves *Byzantioi* as a general population. It was rather the first generation of post-1453 western scholars, notably the German humanist Hieronymus Wolf (1516–80), who began the practice of calling the state "Byzantium" and its people "Byzantines". Other terminologies have also been brought into play, the imperial continuation of late antiquity being called such things as "Le Bas-Empire", or "later Roman" or "east Roman" empire, with "Byzantine" reserved for the phase of civilization running only from the 8th, or perhaps the 7th, century onward. Nevertheless, labels of "Byzantium" and

"Byzantine" have persisted and are generally applied uniformly in historical usages today to the full span of AD 324–1453.

As for the people of that time and civilization, for the most part, they would no more have called themselves "Byzantines" than they would have called themselves "Greeks" (*Hellenes*). In medieval usage, the word "Hellas" was a geographic and administrative term applied to part of what we think of as both ancient and modern Greece. But, by the late Roman era, "Hellene" became less an ethnic term than a cultural one, increasingly identified with paganism. The emperor Julian the Apostate (361–63) furthered that idea by identifying the cultural and religious paganism he hoped to revitalize as "Hellenism". Early Christian writers used "Hellene" consistently to mean "pagan" or "gentile", whereas secular scholars identified "Hellenes" as the writers of the ancient Greek tradition, to be admired for their wisdom and eloquence, but to be distinguished from savants since illuminated by Christian truth. Through the Greek Middle Ages, therefore, it was usually insulting to be called a "Greek". The Latin ambassador Liutprand of Cremona, for instance, learnt this to his peril in 968. His very life was endangered when documents connected with his embassy spoke of his German master as "emperor of the Romans" (*Imperator Romanorum*) while describing the sovereign of Constantinople as "emperor of the Greeks" (*Imperator Graecorum*).

What our "Byzantines" regularly and officially called themselves, in fact, was "Romans". While they understood "Rome" as the name for a specific city in Italy, they also regarded that city as bypassed and superseded by "the New Rome" of Constantinople, the older capital's very nomenclature now transferred eastward. What we have come to call "the Byzantine empire" was, to its citizens, "the empire of the Romans" (*basileia ton Rhomaion*), or simply *Romania*, and they were "Romans" (*Rhomaioi*). These usages continued all the way to the end of the empire, in the 15th century. Such terminology was known and acknowledged by neighbours beyond their frontiers: the Arabs (as would later the Turks) knew them as *Rumi*; the Greek word *Romania* was appropriated by Latins as the designation for the crusader world of Frankish feudalism on Greek soil; while the Ottomans were to designate their European territories as *Rumelia*.

For much of the Byzantine empire's history, this usage made perfect sense. The terms *Rhomaios* and *rhomaïkos* avoided the perspectives in which we are now so fixated, identified with ethnic consciousness and latter-day "national" concepts. Byzantium long continued the Roman empire's character as just that, a multiethnic and multilingual state containing numerous peoples, many of them conscious of distinctive identities, and even retaining their own local cultures. But the continuing refinement of *romanitas* developed a distinctly extra-ethnic meaning to the term "Roman" for those who used it.

Essentially, that term comprehended three important components. The first was the "Roman" heritage of law and divinely destined world sovereignty. The second was a "Hellenic" component of language and culture: among Byzantines, the verb *hellenizein* meant "to speak Greek [*to hellenikon*]" and one studied "the learning of the Hellenes", to become educated in the literature and thought of the old pagan

Greeks. The third component was the Orthodox Christian faith, increasingly as identified with the jurisdiction of the see of Constantinople.

As the empire's frontiers shifted and generally contracted over the generations, there were changes in ethnic composition and diversity, and one may wonder how much various population elements in the countryside understood of these three components. Latin was used in the earlier centuries essentially as an administrative tongue (dying out effectively by the 7th century). The educated were trained in a highly sophisticated, archaizing extension of Classical Attic Greek, while the urban classes in general spoke a simpler demotic street Greek. Local languages (Armenian, Syriac, Coptic; Slavic variants) might persist for a while, but even the uneducated must eventually have shared in some Greek as the working vernacular. What probably bound most together, however, would not have been secular culture but the beliefs and rituals of the Orthodox faith. Over the centuries, only the elite of the capital and other major cities would have understood fully the tripartite meaning of "Roman" identity.

Nevertheless, the "Roman" synthesis involved a dichotomy of pagan and Christian that could both persist and come apart. It is true that people we would call Greeks (mainly rural or small-town folk) continued to call themselves *Rhomaioi* well into the 20th century, preserving that combination of the two elements that emphasized the Christian, in contradistinction to the secular and citified stereotype of the *Hellenes* of modern Greece. By contrast, however, during the medieval era itself the Byzantines selectively rethought what "Hellene" might mean for them. By the 12th century, when the territories had been reduced to a more compactly Greek-speaking population which was painfully aware of the pressures of outside peoples, Byzantines began cautious use of the "Hellenic" label to apply to aspects of their life and identity without any negative (i.e. "pagan") associations. This process continued through the ensuing generations, with pride in the "Hellenic" cultural heritage becoming partially transferable as a sense of "national" identity.

The result was a blurring of distinctions between words and their meanings in late writings. Official use of the designation "Roman" continued for things Byzantine, but the word simultaneously began to be applied explicitly to "Western" peoples and things, in clear opposition to "Hellene" and "Hellenic" as words for Byzantines, who could now frankly be called "Greeks". For illustrations, we need look no further than two figures of the 15th century, otherwise bitterly hostile in their ideas. Thus, the controversial (even paganizing) philosopher George Gemistos Plethon proudly revelled in the identity of "Hellenes" as those linked to the glorious heritage of ancient (and pagan) Greece; while the churchman George Scholarios – as Gennadios II the first patriarch under the Turks – consistently used the word "Hellenes" to mean Greek Orthodox Christians. Each understood the word as carrying what we would recognize as ethnic implications, even if from distinctly different points of association.

We could, moreover, find an ironic parallel between the struggles of "Greeks" and "Turks" to establish their modern ethnic identities. We might suggest that there had to be made clear the same distinction between *Rhomaios* (imperial Byzantine Christian) and *Hellene* (modern Greek) as between

Osmanli (imperial Ottoman Muslim) and Turk (secular national), on the part of peoples whose anthropological backgrounds involved much intermixing of stocks and evolution within changing worlds.

The complexity of these usages suggests the dangers of relying blandly upon modern concepts of ethnicity, which do not apply equally to the earlier eras of late antiquity and early Christianity. There is no question that what we call "Byzantium" represents the medieval phase of the Hellenic tradition, in its broadest terms. To understand who "Byzantines" were, however, requires a sensitivity to what "Hellenism" variously meant in different ways at different times, as much as a linguistic or cultural label as an ethnic one.

JOHN W. BARKER

See also Identity, Language, Law, Orthodox Church, Rumeli

Summary

This term is applied conventionally today to the people who inhabited the Byzantine empire from AD 324 to 1453. They would not have called themselves Byzantines or even Greeks (Hellenes) but Romans. The three essential components of *romanitas* for them were: the "Roman" heritage of law and divinely ordained world sovereignty; Greek language and culture; and the Orthodox Christian faith.

Further Reading

Cavallo, Guglielmo (editor), *The Byzantines*, Chicago: University of Chicago Press, 1997

Garzya, A., "Visages de l'hellénisme dans le monde byzantin, IVe–XIIe siècles", *Byzantion*, 55 (1985): pp. 463–82

Gounaridis, P., "'Grecs', 'Hellenes', et 'Romains' dans l'état de Nicée" in *Aphieroma ston Niko Svorono* [Festschrift for Nikos Svoronos], edited by Vasiles Kremmydas *et al.*, Rethymno, 1986

Irmscher, J., "Der Hellenismus im Geschichtsverständnis der Byzantiner" in *Soziale Probleme im Hellenismus und im römischen Reich*, Prague, 1973

Irmscher, J., "'Griechischer Patriotismus' im 14. Jahrhundert" in *Actes du XIVe Congrès International des Études Byzantines*, Bucharest, 1975

Kazhdan, A.P. and Giles Constable, *People and Power in Byzantium: An Introduction to Modern Byzantine Studies*, Washington, D.C.: Dumbarton Oaks, 1982

Kazhdan, A.P. (editor), *The Oxford Dictionary of Byzantium*, 3 vols, New York and Oxford: Oxford University Press, 1991

Lechner, Kilian, "Hellenen und Barbaren im Weltbild der Byzantiner", dissertation, Munich, 1954

Mango, Cyril, "Byzantinism and Romantic Hellenism", *Journal of the Warburg and Courtauld Institutes*, 28 (1965): pp. 29–43

Mango, Cyril, *Byzantium: The Empire of New Rome*, London: Weidenfeld and Nicolson, and New York: Scribner, 1980

Rice, Tamara Talbot, *Everyday Life in Byzantium*, London: Batsford, and New York: Putnam, 1967

Runciman, Steven, *Byzantine Civilisation*, London: Arnold, and New York: Longman, 1933

Ševčenko, Ihor, "The Decline of Byzantium Seen through the Eyes of its Intellectuals" in his *Society and Intellectual Life in Late Byzantium*, London: Variorum, 1981

Vacalopoulos, Apostolos E., "Byzantinism and Hellenism", *Balkan Studies*, 9 (1968): pp. 101–26

Vacalopoulos, Apostolos E., *Origins of the Greek Nation: The Byzantine Period, 1204–1461*, New Brunswick, New Jersey: Rutgers University Press, 1970

Vryonis, Speros, Jr, "Byzantine Cultural Self-Consciousness in the Fifteenth Century" in *The Twilight of Byzantium: Aspects of*

Cultural and Religious History in the Late Byzantine Empire, edited by Slobodan Ćurčić and Doula Mouriki, Princeton, New Jersey: Princeton University Program in Hellenic Studies, 1991

Byzantium

City on the Bosporus, later known as Constantinople and Istanbul

Byzantium was founded at the southern end of the European shore of the Bosporus by Megarians, probably in association with other colonists from the Peloponnese and central Greece, in 668 or 659 BC according to respectively Herodotus (4. 144) and Eusebius (*Chronicle*). Its name is of Thracian origin, legend claiming the city's founders to be Byzas, son of the nymph Semestre or a Thracian king, and a certain Antes. Like any other settlement along the Bosporus and, to a lesser extent, the Hellespont (Dardanelles), Byzantium could potentially control maritime traffic from the Euxine (Black Sea) to the Aegean and the land route between Europe and Asia (Polybius (4. 38) details the city's mercantile advantages). Its defensible position, however, was such that the earlier Megarian colony of Chalcedon (now Istanbul's Asiatic suburb of Kadiköy) on the opposite shore of the Bosporus came to be known as "The City of the Blind". On a triangular peninsula bounded to the south by the Propontis (Sea of Marmara), to the east by the Bosporus, and to the north by the Golden Horn (a 7.2 km inlet which could serve as a protectable natural harbour), the city had only two drawbacks, exposure to the European hinterland to the west and a lack of drinking water. Both these were remedied in later centuries by the construction of increasingly massive walls and a system of aqueducts and vast open and underground cisterns.

The colonists settled on the eastern tip of the peninsula, which sparse archaeological finds suggest had been occupied as early as the 2nd millenium BC. Apart from traces of shrines to Aphrodite, Apollo, and Artemis between the churches of Hagia Sophia and Hagia Eirene, superimposition of later buildings has precluded the discovery of the Greek city. According to literary sources, however, a north–south wall of about 2 km with 27 towers and several gates enclosed to the east military headquarters, an agora, temples, sanctuaries (most notably to Zeus, Poseidon, Athene, and Dionysus), cisterns, a gymnasium, and a theatre.

Little is known of Byzantium's history until 512 BC, when the city came under Persian rule. Except for the period of the Ionian Revolt (499–494), this persisted until 478 when the Spartan Pausanias expelled the occupying garrison, only to be himself recalled by his government for alleged treason. Thereupon Byzantium joined the Delian League, although, when the Persian threat had receded and Athens was treating the member states as its empire, Byzantium twice attempted revolt (440–439 and 411–408). Its annual contribution to the league of 15 talents indicates a wealth at this time which was derived mainly from tuna fishing, tolls imposed on shipping in the Bosporus, and the resources of both European and Asiatic holdings. After the Battle of Aegospotami in 405 it came under Spartan control, but numismatic evidence proves that it joined the anti-Spartan sea league after the Battle of Cnidus in 394. Formally an ally of Athens from *c*.378, Byzantium revolted again in 357 in support of Rhodes, Cos, and Chios. Subsequently it came increasingly under Macedonian influence until, in alliance with Athens once more, it changed course and successfully held out against Philip II in 340–339 (to commemorate Hecate's succour at this famous siege the Byzantines put on their coinage her symbols of crescent moon and star, which were later adopted by the modern Turkish state). After the Battle of Chaeronea in 338 Byzantium came again under Macedonian sway, and in the 270s suffered severely from Galatian depredations.

In the following century its economic recovery was considerably aided by the privileged status granted to it as a reward for supporting the Romans during the Macedonian wars. This status was retained until Byzantium backed Pescennius Niger in his struggle for imperial power with Septimius Severus in AD 193–95. After a siege of two years, graphically and exaggeratedly described by Cassius Dio (75. 10–14), the Byzantines capitulated. Severus, however, rebuilt their devastated city, approximately doubling its area by constructing a new north–south wall about 800 m westward of its Greek predecessor from a point just east of the present Galata Bridge. Little of the layout of the Severan city is known, but a theatre and baths were built, the hippodrome commenced, and, probably, porticoes added around the agora from which a porticoed avenue led to the wall. (For the later history of the city, its topography, and monuments, see the entry on Constantinople.)

After an aborted attempt at building a new city in the Troad near the ancient Sigeum (at a location now known as Yenişehir) just south of the entrance to the Hellespont, Constantine I chose the site of Byzantium for his new and Christian capital. The city's perimeter was marked out on 8 November 324 and the dedication took place on 11 May 330. It is not certain what the emperor wished its name to be. Although it was most commonly referred to as Constantinople ("City of Constantine"), the Latin poet Publius Optatianus Porphyrius used (in *Carminae*, 4. 6) the expression "New Rome" as early as 324/25 (Cassiodorus' account of Constantine inscribing *Secunda Roma* on a marble column is, however, almost certainly legendary). Thereafter comparison with the ancient capital and rhetorical references to "New Rome" were increasingly favoured, but the earliest surviving attestation of this as an official name appears in Canon 3 of the First Council of Constantinople in 381. Used with considerable frequency by Byzantines over the centuries, "New Rome" was imitated later by the Seljuk Turks who, keen to uphold their imperial ambitions, named their capital at Iconium (modern Konya) "Rum". Later still, Moscow, as the new defender of the Orthodox faith, was described as "The New Constantinople" in 1492 and, from the early 16th century, as "The Third Rome". The Greek Ecumenical Patriarch was, and still is, officially "Bishop of New Rome", and for the Turks the patriarchate is *Rum Patrikhanesi*.

Constantinople was, however, increasingly referred to simply as "The City" (*I Poli*) and in the West as "The Great City" (Micklegard in the Icelandic sagas). The later Ottoman name of Stamboul or Istanbul is usually explained as a corruption of the Greek for "To the City", itself on occasion deliberately altered to Islambul or "Full of Islam". Owing to the archaizing of the Greek literati the name Byzantium (*Byzantion*) was preserved, and "Byzantines" therefore meant the inhabitants of the city alone. Since the empire was a continuation of the Roman empire, its inhabitants, when not referring to themselves as citizens of a specific city, called themselves "Romans", albeit usually and increasingly in Greek (*Rhomaioi*). At least until the coronation of Charlemagne on Christmas Day in 800, the western world also unquestionably accepted the empire as "Roman" (in the 10th century the Ottonian dynasty ambitiously established a rival "Roman" empire). Only after their empire had lost its polyethnic nature and was almost exclusively Greek-speaking did its inhabitants ever call themselves "Greeks" (*Hellenes*), a term by which they had earlier designated their pagan forbears. The use of the word Byzantine to cover the whole empire and its people is a modern anachronism of convenience: a few scholars beset by scruples have preferred to speak of an East Roman civilization.

The term "Byzantine" (or "byzantine") is used today in popular speech only pejoratively. In art it signifies either excessive ornamentation or two-dimensional rigidity, the latter largely a consequence of familiarity with post-Byzantine rather than genuinely Byzantine icons. In a ceremonial context it not inaccurately signifies lengthy and ritualistic formality with more show than substance. In argumentation it signifies either meaningless verbiage or hair-splitting logic: these derive from despairing Byzantine attempts to solve theological conundrums such as "the indivisibly divisible and divisibly indivisible" dual natures of Christ and the subtle formulations of Byzantine theologians which offended their more forthright western brethren. However, by far the most common misuse of the word suggests intrigue, secretiveness, deviousness, and deceit. This is quite unfair since Byzantium had no more palace cabals than many other states (and fewer than some, including its successors, the Ottoman Turks). The misapprehension is, however, of long standing and stems partly from the complexities of the Byzantine civil service, which bewildered many simple-minded western crusaders. More influential, however, has been the contempt of these crusaders, to whom war was largely a game of chivalric ostentation, for the Byzantine understanding of war as an evil to be undergone only when all the resources of diplomacy had been exhausted.

The word "Byzantine" is used more properly today in two technical contexts. The Byzantine era is a chronology that, though devised as early as the 7th century AD, did not come into general use in the Byzantine world until the late 10th. A modification of the Alexandrian era, it numbers solar years from the creation of the world in 5508 rather than 5492 BC. Its year began originally at the vernal equinox on 21 March, but in the late 9th or early 10th century this was changed to 1 September. The Byzantine Rite is a liturgical system of mainly Constantinopolitan and Palestinian rites. Commonly divided into Late Roman, Imperial, Stoudite, and Neo-Sabaïtic phases, it reflects successively the Antiochene origins of many early patriarchs of Constantinople, the imperial magnificence of Justinian in particular, the Palestinian monasticization of Theodore of Stoudios, and the Palestinian modifications of the Lavra of Mar Saba. It reached its definitive form under the Athonite hesychasts in the 14th century, by which time it was used throughout the Byzantine world with the exception of southern Italy and Russia.

A.R. LITTLEWOOD

See also Byzantines, Chronology, Constantinople

Summary

Founded in the 7th century BC by colonists from Megara, the city of Byzantium occupied a defensible position bounded to the south by the Propontis, to the east by the Bosporus, and to the north by the Golden Horn. Its disadvantages were exposure to its hinterland to the west and a lack of drinking water. It was refounded as Constantinople, the New Rome, by Constantine the Great in AD 324.

Further Reading

Dagron, Gilbert, *Constantinople imaginaire: Études sur le recueil des Patria*, Paris: Presses Universitaires de France, 1984

Dölger, Franz, *Byzanz und die europäische Staatenwelt*, Ettal: Buch-Kunstverlag, 1953, pp. 70–115

MacDonald, W.L., Byzantium entry in *The Princeton Encyclopedia of Classical Sites*, edited by Richard Stillwell *et al.*, Princeton, New Jersey: Princeton University Press, 1976, pp. 177–79

Newskaja, W.P., *Byzanz in der klassischen und hellenistischen Epoche*, Leipzig: Koehler & Amelang, 1955

Rice, David Talbot, *Constantinople – Byzantium – Istanbul*, photographs by Wim Swaan, London: Elek, 1965

C

Cacoyannis, Michalis 1922–

Film-maker, scriptwriter, theatre director, actor, and translator

Together with Thodoros Angelopoulos (1935–), Michalis Cacoyannis is the best-known film maker working in Greece today, with an established international reputation. In 1995 a retrospective of the director's work was staged at the Thessalonica Film Festival. Between 1954 and 1992 Cacoyannis directed 13 feature films, a documentary on the Turkish invasion of Cyprus, and the successful television drama *The Story of Jacob and Joseph* (1974). He has also worked as a theatre director and produced numerous plays both in Greece and abroad, as well as operas.

Cacoyannis was born in Limassol, Cyprus, on 11 June 1922. After studying law in Great Britain, Cacoyannis produced programmes for the BBC's Greek-language broadcasts during World War II, while attending the Central School of Dramatic Art (1944). He made his stage debut at London's Old Vic theatre in 1947 in Oscar Wilde's *Salome*, going on to perform in a number of different productions and taking the lead in Albert Camus's *Caligula* (1949). He visited the United States before returning to Greece in 1952, where he directed his first feature film, *Kyriatiko Xypanima* (Getting Up on Sunday, 1954; distributed in the UK as *Windfall in Athens*), which was screened at the Edinburgh Festival. Critical acclaim came with *Stella* (1955); this was followed by *To Koritsime ta Mavra* (*The Girl in Black*, 1956), a film about the tragic consequences of an Athenian writer's love for an island girl, which was made with the cinematographer Walter Lassally who has collaborated with Cacoyannis on many of his features.

Cacoyannis's early films share technical and thematic preoccupations with the European art cinema of the period, and in particular, with Italian neorealism which was introduced into Greece by Grigoris Grigoriou (1919–). The use of location filming and the frustrated hope of a postwar renewal that Cacoyannis's early films express, for example, owe much to postwar Italian cinema. All of them starred little-known actors who were later to build successful acting careers, including Elli Lambeti, Dimitris Horn, Yorgos Foundas, and Melina Mercouri, who made her screen debut with *Stella*. Together with those of Nikos Koundouros (1926–), Cacoyannis's films were the first independent Greek productions to attract international attention.

The script of *Stella*, which is characterized by its intense dialogue, was adapted from the play *Stella with the Red Gloves* by Ioakovos Kambanellis, with a score by Manos Chatzidakis. The action takes place for the most part in the bustling Monastiraki district of Athens and the narrative focuses on the tragic fate of the eponymous heroine (Mercouri), a singer in the bar Paradise, who is condemned for wanting to live in defiance of established moral codes. Cacoyannis's film charts Stella's doomed relationships, first with Alekos (Alekos Alexandrakis), who comes from an affluent bourgeois family in Patissia, and secondly with Miltos (Foundas), a brash football player from Piraeus. The heroine refuses to be pressured into marriage by her lovers and the denouement takes place in central Athens during the Ochi Day celebrations, as Stella goes to watch the parades while her fiancé Miltos waits with the guests in church. A parallel is intimated here between the nation's rejection of the Italian ultimatum and Stella's renunciation of the marriage to Miltos. At the end of the film, however, with Stella's murder by Miltos, the threat of a disrupted social order is quashed. Since the 1970s the character of Stella has been appropriated as a symbol of female emancipation and the film has often been construed as an index of authentic "Greekness", achieving an established position in the canon of Greek cinema.

Many of these social and political preoccupations are taken up again in the melodrama *To Televtaio Psema* (The Last Lie, 1958; distributed in the UK as *A Matter of Dignity*,) which was both written and directed by Cacoyannis and centres on a young Athenian woman's pledge to marry a rich man – in so doing relinquishing her chance of happiness – to save her family from bankruptcy. Like Stella, albeit in very different ways, the film explores social conventions and freedom in a rapidly changing society.

Cacoyannis's best works have been adaptations of plays or novels. In 1959 he produced a version of Kosmas Politis's masterful novel *Eroica* (1937), misleadingly translated into English as *Our Last Spring*. The film follows the adventures of a group of adolescents whose imaginary, heroic world is subdued by death and sexual desire. In 1964 Cacoyannis achieved international fame with the 20th Century Fox (a studio founded by the Greek entrepreneur Spyros Skouras) production of *Zorba the Greek*, starring Anthony Quinn and

Michalis Cacoyannis

Alan Bates and based on the novel by Nikos Kazantzakis (1946). Set to music by Mikis Theodorakis, this remains Cacoyannis's biggest international success, although the film has never been popular in Greece. As Cacoyannis himself has commented sardonically in a recent interview: "I was considered an artist when I made my early Greek films, but when *Zorba the Greek* was cast with Anthony Quinn, a Mexican-American actor, and the film made money, I was considered from then on as a commercial director!" The narrative of *Zorba* centres on an English writer of Greek parentage (Bates) who travels to Crete to claim his inheritance of a lignite mine. While waiting in Piraeus for the ship to take him there he is befriended by the ebullient Alexis Zorba (Quinn), described by the studio publicity as a "life force", who helps him to lose his inhibitions and waken his senses. Subsequently Quinn found it impossible to shake off the image of the extrovert Greek but agreed to act in Cacoyannis's Broadway musical based on the film which ran from 1983 to 1986.

Cacoyannis was to draw upon his theatrical background when he brought ancient drama to the screen for a wide modern audience in his successful adaptations of Euripides' tragedies inaugurated with *Electra* (1962), which starred Irene Papas and which won numerous international awards and an Oscar nomination. This was followed by *The Trojan Women* (1971), which starred Katharine Hepburn and Vanessa Redgrave, and *Iphigeneia* (1977). The films combine close-ups with dramatic long shots, and in so doing successfully balance convincing, poignant characterizations with an imposing mythic orientation.

Cacoyannis's more recent films have been less successful. *Sweet Country* (1986), a feature with an international cast, is

based on a novel by Caroline Richards and explores the fate of two women, Eva (Carole Laure) and Monica (Joanna Pettet), during the coup d'état led by General Pinochet in 1973 which overthrew the government of Salvador Allende in Chile; while Eva is caught and tortured, for no other reason than being the secretary of the President's wife, Monica joins the resistance. The comedy *Pano, Kato, kai Plagios* (*Up, Down, and Sideways*, 1993) maps out the frustrations of contemporary Athenian life over a period of 24 hours, focusing on the tensions between Maria, a widow (Papas), her adolescent son Stavros (Stratos Tzortzoglou), and Anestis (Panos Michalopoulos), the man who rekindles her passion. Other films include an Italian feature *Il Relito* (*The Wastrel*, 1961), and the British film *The Day the Fish Came Out* (1967), starring Tom Courtenay, Colin Blakely, and Sam Wanamaker, about the threat of radioactive contamination in the Mediterranean after a military aircraft crashes in the Aegean. The narrative, which is strangely reminiscent of Stanley Kubrick's comic call for disarmament in *Dr Strangelove* (1963), focuses on the efforts of a team of experts (who pose as agents of a hotel development company) to recover stray bombs. Finally, Cacoyannis's documentary *Attila 74* (1975) is a passionate account of dispossession that records the impact of the Turkish invasion of Cyprus in the summer of 1974.

Cacoyannis's last project of the 1990s was a screen adaptation of Anton Chekhov's *The Cherry Orchard*, entitled *Varya* (1999). It was filmed in Bulgaria with the support of the Onassis Foundation and starred Alan Bates and Charlotte Rampling.

ROBERT SHANNAN PECKHAM

See also Cinema

Biography

Born in Limassol, Cyprus, in 1922, Cacoyannis studied law in Britain and produced Greek-language programmes for the BBC during World War II. His first acclaimed film was *Stella* (1955); his best-known works are *Zorba the Greek* (1964), which won an Oscar for cinematography and art direction, and film adaptations of Euripidean tragedies. He has directed plays and produced three translations of Shakespeare into Greek as well as English versions of two plays of Euripides.

Writings

Diladi..., Athens, 1990 (in Greek)

Further Reading

Kolonias, Babis (editor), *Michalis Cacoyannis*, Athens, 1995 (in Greek)

Calabria

Region of southwest Italy

Calabria was colonized by the Greek city states from the 8th century BC. The south Italian colonies constituted "Greater Greece" or, as it is most commonly referred to, Magna Graecia. The establishment of Greek colonies in south Italy and Sicily was only the conclusion of a long period of contacts,

Calabria: the village of Bova, where a Greek dialect is still spoken

from the end of the 2nd millennium BC, between the Greeks of the mainland and the islands, who were seeking new markets, and the indigenous people in Italy. The colonization was extremely successful, especially when compared with the trading settlements of the Phoenician and Carthaginian settlers, which lacked the permanent character of the Greek colonies. The expeditions were led by aristocratic families. There was close cooperation with the mother city, which provided active support for the colony. Rapid economic and cultural development therefore soon followed.

One of the most famous Greek cities was Rhegium (modern Reggio di Calabria), an Ionian colony established by the Euboeans. Many philosophers were associated with the region of Magna Graecia and Calabria in particular, such as Pythagoras who emigrated from Samos to Croton, Timaeus in Locri, Parmenides and Zeno in Elea. The philosophical system of Pythagoras deeply influenced the cultural life of the colonies. Many of his ideas were enhanced by the Orphic cults that flourished in the area. Recent finds of gold coins with incised text found in tombs have increased our knowledge of the influence of the Orphic cult. Modern museums exhibit many traces of a glorious civilization and the archaeological sites are often breathtaking. Two of the most famous ancient statues, the Riace bronzes of approximately the 5th century BC,

were found in a shipwreck in 1972 and are now exhibited in the museum of Reggio. Rhegium was important culturally. The sculptor Pythagoras, the poet Ibycus, and the historians Hippys and Glaucus were associated with it.

Locri was a colony established by Dorians from Locris. The poet Xenocrates was associated with Locri; he devised the "Locrian harmony", a new type of musical composition that depended upon flutes rather than lyres. The Hellenistic female poet Nossis was also associated with Locri. She is known to us through some poems in the *Palatine Anthology*, and is believed to have written mainly epigrams in the sapphic metre. Ruins of an Ionic temple have been found near Locri, as well as a site associated with the cult of Persephone. Temples in the Ionic style are rare in Magna Graecia, where the Doric style prevails. A common feature of many cities in the area is the extramural sanctuary, such as the Heraion near Croton. Caulonia was a colony established by Locri that was destroyed in the wars between Pyrrhus and the Romans.

The region was conquered by the Romans by 212 BC and the cultural map changed significantly in the following centuries. Under Diocletian (AD 284–305) Calabria and Apulia formed one province, and until the 7th century the name Calabria designated all of southern Italy. There were major political and social upheavals in the area in AD 476 and towards the end of the western Roman empire. Until the first half of the 7th century the regions of south Italy (Bretia and Basilicata) constituted an eparchy directly dependent on the exarchate of Ravenna. The 7th century is important for Hellenic culture in the area, because this was when the first wave of immigrants came from Cappadocia, Syria, and Egypt. Also, due to the Islamic incursions on the eastern frontier of the empire, monks were taking refuge in Calabria and Sicily where they could practise true asceticism, especially in the mountains. In the 8th century Calabria became a *doukaton* (dukedom), dependent on the *strategos* (commander) of Sicily, which had been elevated to a Byzantine theme. Following the monastic immigration that came from the east, many monks came from the Greek mainland due to the religious turbulence associated with iconoclasm, especially after the edicts of Leo III. The foundation of monasteries also meant the establishment of Greek cultural centres.

The conquest of Sicily by the Arabs reshaped the south Italian world in the first half of the 10th century and persuaded the emperor Nikephoros Phokas to reorganize the administration of the empire. Religious matters also intervened, and became extremely important in view of the ongoing struggle between East and West. The Greek rite was imposed in all the churches of south Italy that belonged to the theme of Calabria, Lucania, and Longobardia (modern Puglia). Since Sicily was mainly in the hands of the Arabs, there was more immigration into Calabria, and that included the Sicilian monks. On the other hand, the Byzantine presence was not always well received by the local people due to the heavy taxation that was imposed on them, since it was an important region from a strategic point of view, and a large armed force had to be sustained in the area. The Normans occupied Calabria in 1040. Although there were still many Greek influences in customs, culture, and ecclesiastical matters, a gradual distancing started, and the Latin rite was gradually imposed in churches.

Trade continued with the Byzantines, and many monasteries were built in the following years. Calabria became an important refuge for scholars from the east, such as the monk Barlaam (*c.*1290–1350), and there was a significant circulation of Greek texts. Palaeographers identify a peculiar calligraphic style in many manuscripts as the Reggio script.

Today in the area of Aspromonte there are several villages where a distinctive Greek dialect is still spoken, mingled with many Italiot elements. There are various views as to the origin of this dialect, which is not quite the same as the one spoken in Puglia and the area of Salento, and often differs among villages of the same region. Many scholars argue that its origin is ancient Greek, others that it is Byzantine Greek, adducing many historical reasons related to the political turbulence in the area in the Middle Ages. The villages in which one finds Hellenophones today are Bova, Bova Marina, Condofuri, Amendolea, Roghudi, and Galliciano. There is a rich linguistic, literary, and musical Hellenic tradition that has shrunk significantly in modern times.

ANDROMACHE KARANIKA-DIMARGONA

See also Magna Graecia

Summary

The toe of Italy, Calabria was colonized by Greeks from the 8th century BC. Rhegium and Locri were major colonies and cultural centres. Under Diocletian Calabria and Apulia formed one province. Until the 7th century AD south Italy was an eparchy dependent on the exarchate of Ravenna. The 7th century brought refugees from Islam and the 8th from iconoclasm. Calabria was occupied by the Normans in 1040 but its culture remained largely Greek into the 14th century.

Further Reading

Caracausi, Girolamo, *Testi Neogreci di Calabria: indice lessicale*, Palermo: Istituto Siciliano di Studi Bizantini e Neoellenici, 1994

Casile, Antonella and Domenico Fiorenza, *Ellenofoni di Calabria: aspetti storici, linguistici e letterari*, Bova Marina, 1993

Karanastase, Anastasiou, *Historikon Lexikon ton Hellenikon Idiomaton tes Kato Italias* [Historical Lexicon of the Greek Dialects of Southern Italy], 2 vols, Athens, 1984–86

Lepore, Ettore, *Colonie greche dell'occidente antico*, Rome: La Nuova Italia Scientifica, 1989

Marchese, Nicola Gerardo, *La civiltà della Magna Grecia*, Rome: Consiglio Nazionale delle Ricerche, 1992

Pugliese Carratelli, Giovanni, *Le lamine d'oro orfiche*, Milan: Scheiwiller, 1993

Pugliese Carratelli, Giovanni, *The Western Greeks: Classical Civilization in the Western Mediterranean*, London: Thames and Hudson, 1996; as *The Greek World: Art and Civilization in Magna Graecia and Sicily*, New York: Rizzoli, 1996 (exhibition catalogue)

Rohlfs, Gerhard, *Historische Grammatik der unteritalienischen Gräzität*, Munich: Bayerischen Akademie der Wissenschaften, 1950

Calendar

Most ancient Greek states had their own individual calendars, often more than one for different purposes (e.g. civil and religious) as in many countries today (e.g. civil, religious, financial, scholastic). Like all calendars, the Greek suffered from the incommensurability of the units commonly used – solar day, synodic month, and tropical year. The solar day is the slightly variable period between successive apparent passages of the sun around the earth, and was usually taken to commence at sunset. The synodic month is the substantially variable period of a single cycle of the moon's phases as seen from the earth, and was deemed to commence with the appearance of the crescent of the "new moon". The tropical year is the period between successive passages of the sun across the celestial equator in March (the vernal equinox), although the dates of its commencement were extremely varied. The week of seven days, possibly inspired by Babylonian hebdomadism, entered the Graeco-Roman world from the Jews only in the 1st century BC, at the end of which the practice of naming its days for the planets, as found in most European languages today, was already being established (the Hebrew numbering of the days, however, persisted in Greek).

All ancient Greek calendars were originally, and most remained largely, lunar. Months were named after festivals or deities and one was intercalated periodically to achieve approximate correspondence with the solar year. Most surviving calendaric information relates to Athens, which used an astronomically controlled lunar calendar; a festival or archon's

lunar calendar (which through manipulation for political and religious reasons (mocked by Aristophanes in *Clouds*, 615–26) was often seriously at variance with the former); and a "prytany" calendar (used in dating governmental documents) which was based upon the annual presidential terms of the ten tribes in the *boule* (council). The years of the first two calendars were divided into 12 months of 29 or 30 days with a month being repeated when deemed necessary. The first day of each month was called the "new moon"; the next nine were numbered forwards as the "2nd to 10th of the waxing month", and the next nine simply as the "11th to 19th"; the 20th and 21st were called respectively the "20th" or the "earlier 10th" and the "10th of the waning month" or the "later 10th"; the 22nd to 28th were counted backwards as the "9th to 3rd of the waning month"; and the last day of the month was called "the old and the new", leaving the 29th in a 30-day month to be the "2nd of the waning month". Years were named after the eponymous archon (and in other states after other officials, priests, etc.). For the later numbering of years in a series, i.e. eras, see the article on Chronology.

Greek calendaric reform based upon cycles of years was made possible by the astronomical discoveries beginning in the 6th century BC with the sphericity of the earth, the obliquity of the ecliptic, etc. and, in the 4th century, by the theory of Eudoxus (which was refined by Callippus) of sun, moon, and planets moving in concentric spheres around the earth. Thus sometime before 432 the cycle of the *octaeteris* (cycle of eight years) was worked out by which the intercalation at intervals of three 30-day months during a period of eight lunar years made the period roughly synchronous with eight tropical years. The famous reform of Meton and Euctemon at Athens in 432 (of which not all the details are known) devised a more accurate cycle of 19 tropical years and 125 30-day ("full") and 110 29-day ("hollow") months. Around 100 years later Callippus proposed a cycle of 76 years which is one day shorter than four of Meton's cycles and thus accords more closely with astronomical phenomena. Later cycles of 2484 years (Aristarchus, who hypothesized heliocentricity) and 304 (Hipparchus) are also known, but, with the exception of the *octaeteris*, there has been much debate as to what extent any were used for civic as opposed to astronomical purposes.

In Greece itself states largely kept their own calendars into the early Roman period, some even persisting with the *octaeteris* until as late as c.AD 200. The conquests of Alexander, however, introduced over much of the eastern Hellenized world the Macedonian calendar of a year of 12 followed by a year of 13 lunar months, although this gave an excess of about seven days over a period of two solar years. The Greeks in Egypt, however, adopted the local calendar and the Seleucids adapted the Macedonian to the Babylonian.

Since by the mid-1st century BC the partly lunar Roman Republican calendar was substantially and increasingly out of phase with the seasons, Julius Caesar, in his capacity as Pontifex Maximus (chief priest), invited the Greek astronomer Sosigenes of Alexandria to advise on a new calendar, which was instituted in 46 BC and became known as the Julian calendar. Sosigenes first intercalated 67 days in addition to the regular biennial intercalation of 23 days (or 22 alternately in a quadrennial cycle) after 23 February, and then, to preclude a repetition of the Republican problem, proposed the adoption of a tropical (solar) year of 365.25 days. For practicality three years were to be of 365 days' duration with an extra day intercalated (between 23 and 24 February) every fourth year. However, because of confusion caused by Roman inclusive reckoning this was done every third year until the situation was gradually righted under Augustus between 9 BC and AD 4, by which time the months had been given their present number of days. The revision of this calendar, known as the Gregorian calendar, appeared in a papal bull of Pope Gregory XIII in 1582. By it the first three centennial years in every sequence of four are not bissextile (leap) years, since the true length of the tropical year (365.242199 mean solar days) puts the Julian Calendar approximately seven days behind the seasons every 1000 years.

The Byzantines largely used the Julian calendar, but with the days of the month numbered successively (rather than by Kalends, Nones, and Ides) and with the year beginning on 1 September, the traditional date for the beginning of an indiction (period of 15 years when annual tax was to remain unaltered). However, consular years (used until the 7th century for public and legal documents) still began on 1 January, while regnal years, patriarchal years (Constantinopolitan, Alexandrian, Antiochian, and Ierosolymite), papal years, and those of officials such as the praetorian prefect began upon accession or appointment. The problem of calculating the date of Easter begat a cycle of 532 years, the product of a 19-year lunar and a 28-year solar cycle, which gave precisely recurring Julian dates for the festival and its associated holy days. These cycles, with the rules for calculation, form the *computus*, tables from which survive in many manuscripts. The Church calendar was a combination of the Synaxarion, a list of calendarically fixed feasts and saints' days (often given separately with appropriate lections) and the Kanonarion, a list of the mobile Paschal feasts.

During the Tourkokratia Greeks were permitted to keep their civic and religious calendars. The modern state made the decision to change to the more astronomically correct Gregorian calendar in 1923, 16 February becoming 1 March, and the Greek Church swiftly followed, 10 March becoming 23 March. Nevertheless, outside the national Church there are still communities ("Old Calendarist") which abide by the Julian calendar, as do the monasteries of Mount Athos, where the day, itself divided into 12 hours of night and 12 of daylight, begins at sundown (except for Iviron which starts its day at sunrise).

A.R. LITTLEWOOD

See also Chronology, Old Calendarists

Further Reading

Bickerman, E.J., *Chronology of the Ancient World*, 2nd edition, London: Thames and Hudson, and Ithaca, New York: Cornell University Press, 1980

Grumel, V., *La Chronologie*, Paris: Presses Universitaires de France, 1958 (on Byzantine chronology)

Nilsson, Martin P., *Die Entstehung und Reliogiöse Bedeutung des Griechischen Kalenders*, 2nd edition, Lund: Gleerup, 1962

Samuel, Alan E., *Greek and Roman Chronology: Calendars and Years in Classical Antiquity*, Munich: Beck, 1972

Callas, Maria 1923–1977

Opera singer

Born on 2 December 1923 in New York and trained in Athens, Cecilia Sophia Anna Maria Callas went on to become one of the outstanding operatic sopranos of the 20th century. She was the second daughter of George Kalogeropoulos, a pharmacist from Meligala in the Peloponnese, and Evangelia Dimitroadou, the daughter of a military officer descended from prosperous Phanariots. The family surname was shortened to Callas when her parents emigrated to the United States several months before her birth, in what may have been an attempt to revitalize a marriage shaken by the recent death of their only son, Vasily. Unfortunately, the strains of immigrant life and financial difficulties, later compounded by the onset of the Great Depression, brought only further discord to the couple. Maria (or Mary, as she was then known) and her older sister Jackie (Iakinthy) were thus raised in an environment marked by constant bickering. Significantly, these marital disputes extended to music, reflecting in microcosm the cultural struggles that were being played out at that time in Greece. George preferred to listen to gramophone records of *rebetika* ("low-life" music) which his wife, whose musical tastes and cultural pretensions were those of the contemporary westernizing Greek bourgeoisie, would promptly disparage and replace with recordings of opera. Evangelia would also regularly listen to radio broadcasts from the Metropolitan Opera with her daughters, upon whom a substantial portion of the family's meagre financial resources were bestowed at her insistence for music lessons. Both girls studied piano, and Mary sang at school, in church, and, at her mother's behest, in radio competitions. In 1937 Evangelia separated from George and returned to Greece with the children, citing a desire to advance their musical careers.

In Athens Evangelia eventually managed to arrange an audition for her daughter Maria with Maria Trivella, a teacher of singing who secured a scholarship for her at the National Conservatory of the composer Manolis Kalomiris. Proving herself to be a determined and dedicated pupil, Maria Callas progressed rapidly and on 2 April 1939 she made her operatic debut as Santuzza in a student production of *Cavalleria Rusticana*. Emboldened by this achievement, Maria's mother presented her for an audition before Elvira de Hidalgo, a Spanish soprano of international stature who had come to Greece to teach at the more prestigious Athens Conservatory. Hidalgo was sufficiently impressed to arrange a full scholarship for her at the Athens Conservatory, where she sang in numerous concerts with the soprano Arda Mandikian and other students. Callas was hired by the Royal Theatre in 1940 and early in the next year (probably in February) she made her professional debut in the minor role of Beatrice in von Suppé's operetta *Boccaccio*. During the Axis occupation (1941–44) she graduated to leading roles with the Athens Opera while continuing to appear in concerts and recitals, albeit somewhat sporadically because of the adverse conditions. On 27 August 1942 she made her first appearance as Tosca, a role that she would sing to great acclaim towards the end of her career. She went on to sing in Athenian productions of *Cavalleria Rusticana*, *Fidelio*, d'Albert's *Tiefland*, and *O Protomastoras*

by Kalomiris, the only modern Greek opera she was ever to sing. After the liberation of Greece she continued to appear on the operatic and concert stages, but the refusal of the Athens Opera to renew her contract – a decision variously attributed to the jealousy of more established singers and accusations of collaboration with the occupiers – caused her to return to New York in September 1945 after her final appearances as Laura in Millöcker's operetta *Der Bettelstudent*.

Unable to advance her career sufficiently in America, Callas accepted an offer to sing the title role in Ponchielli's *La Gioconda* at the Arena in Verona, where she first performed on 2 August 1947 under the direction of Tullio Serafin. This successful appearance led to increasingly frequent engagements

Maria Callas: a still from Pier Paolo Pasolini's film *Medea* (1970), in which Callas took the title role

in Italy, Mexico, and South America to sing a wide variety of operas by Italian and German composers. Although initially prized for her dramatic interpretations of Aida, Isolde, Kundry, Brünnhilde, and Turandot, Callas soon abandoned heavy roles on Serafin's advice. She thereafter became known as a supreme interpreter of Italian operas from the later 18th to the mid-19th century, including works by Gluck, Haydn, Cherubini, Spontini, Bellini, Donizetti, and Verdi. Only after she had made her debut on the world's most prestigious operatic stages – for example, La Scala (12 April 1950), Covent Garden (8 November 1950), the Chicago Lyric Theatre (1 November 1954), and the Metropolitan (29 October 1956) – and had become an international celebrity was she engaged by the Athens Festival to sing in two concerts at the Herodes Atticus Theatre in August 1957. Despite political wranglings over the size of her fee and vocal troubles that caused her to cancel the first of these appearances, on 5 August Callas scored an artistic triumph over an initially hostile audience and thereafter began to renew her artistic and personal ties with Greece. At her suggestion, the new Dallas Civic Opera production of Cherubini's *Medea* was premièred on 6 November 1958 with direction by Alexis Miniotis of Greece's National Theatre and design by Ioannis Tsarouchis. In addition to helping to mount over the next four years further stagings of *Medea* at Covent Garden (1959), Epidaurus (1961), and La Scala (1961–62), Miniotis and Tsarouchis collaborated with Callas on the Greek National Opera's performances in August 1960 at Epidaurus of *Norma*, the first opera ever mounted in that ancient theatre. Callas, who donated the fees for all of her 1960 and 1961 Epidaurus engagements to a scholarship fund for poor singers, was given awards by the city of Athens and the government of Greece officially recognizing her contributions to art.

During the early 1960s Callas gradually withdrew from the operatic stage as her longstanding vocal troubles increased and her private life became centred on a relationship with the shipping magnate Aristotle Onassis. On 5 July 1965 she made her final operatic appearance as Tosca at Covent Garden, after which she made occasional recordings, gave infrequent concerts, starred in a non-operatic film of *Medea* directed by Pasolini, and led master classes. After completing a punishing two-year recital tour in 1974, she retired completely from public life and died in Paris on 16 September 1977.

Notwithstanding the relative brevity of her international career, the voice and personality of Callas have remained intensely fascinating to opera lovers and the general public, causing her to achieve near mythic status after her death. Her artistic work and glamorous life have been documented in exhaustive detail through numerous books and recordings. Most recently, she has begun to inspire authors both in Greece and abroad to create fictional accounts of episodes in her life, including Terrence McNally's play *Masterclass* and *Thymamai ten Maria* (I Remember Maria) by Menes Koumantareas, a short story describing how a young bellboy from Corfu heard Callas sing during her stay at the Grand Bretagne Hotel in 1957.

ALEXANDER LINGAS

See also Opera

Biography

Born in New York in 1923 to parents who had just emigrated to the USA, Callas returned to Greece with her mother in 1937. She won a scholarship to the Athens Conservatory in that year and made her professional operatic debut in 1940. She moved to New York in 1945, then back to Europe in 1947, and throughout the 1950s enjoyed international stardom. She gradually withdrew from performance in the 1960s and died in Paris in 1977.

Further Reading

Ardoin, John, "Maria Callas: The Early Years", *Opera Quarterly*, 3 (1983): pp. 6–13

Ardoin, John, *The Callas Legacy: The Complete Guide to Her Recordings on Compact Discs*, 4th edition, London: Duckworth, and Portland, Oregon: Amadeus Press, 1995

Callas, Evangelia, *My Daughter: Maria Callas*, in collaboration with Lawrence G. Blochman, 2nd edition, London: Leslie Frewin, 1967; New York: Arno Press, 1977

Callas, Jackie, *Sisters*, London: Macmillan, and New York: St Martin's Press, 1989

Galatopoulos, Stelios, *Maria Callas: Sacred Monster*, London: Fourth Estate, and New York: Simon and Schuster, 1998

Jellinek, George, *Callas: Portrait of a Prima Donna*, 2nd edition, New York: Dover, 1986

Koumantareas, Menes, *Thymamai ten Maria* [I Remember Maria], Athens, 1994

McNally, Terrence, *Master Class*, New York: Plume, 1996; London: Methuen, 1997

Scott, Michael, *Maria Meneghini Callas*, London: Simon and Schuster, 1991; Boston: Northeastern University Press, 1992

Stassinopoulos, Arianna, *Maria Callas: The Woman Behind the Legend*, London: Weidenfeld and Nicolson, 1980; New York: Simon and Schuster, 1981

Recording

La Divina Complete, 4 CD set, EMI, 1997

Callimachus *c.*320 BC–*c.*240 BC

Poet and scholar

Callimachus was one of the foremost literary scholars of the Hellenistic age and its most important poet. He produced an impressive array of works in prose and verse (the *Suda* ascribes more than 800 books to him, only a very small proportion of which has been preserved). Ingeniously taking up and reacting to earlier poetry, he became the very model of the *poeta doctus* for centuries to come.

Few details of Callimachus' life are known. He was born probably around 320 BC to a noble Cyrenean family. He may early on have had a position at the Ptolemaic court in Alexandria and could have attained his high standard of education at no better place than this. He spent long periods of his life in Alexandria and was intimately connected with its magnificent museum and royal library (both founded by Ptolemy I). Some other facts reported about him are probably fictitious: the *Suda*'s statement that he was at first a lowly schoolteacher is probably the product of slanderous invention, and the evidence for his supposed feud with his (somewhat younger) contemporary Apollonius Rhodius is late and shaky (e.g. the identification of Apollonius with the target of

Callimachus' curse-poem *Ibis*). Callimachus died probably around 240 BC.

Since dates for Callimachus' wide-ranging oeuvre are almost non-existent, it is best to present his work according to genre, following the order of the *Diegeseis* (summaries of his poems) preserved on papyrus (see below).

Callimachus' most famous poetic work is the *Aetia*, a collection of stories in four books relating the cause (*aition*, hence the title) and origin of certain peculiar customs and phenomena in the Greek world. Thanks to surviving papyri, this substantial work (possibly up to 6000 verses in elegiac couplets) can be reconstructed to a large extent. In the first two books (probably completed by 270 BC), the stories were framed by a conversation that Callimachus himself had (in a dream) with the Muses on Mount Helicon (a programmatic reminiscence of Hesiod). Books 3 and 4 were probably added considerably later (after 246 BC); they do not follow the narrative frame of the earlier books but consist of a collection of aetiological stories, the first and the last of which honoured Queen Berenice II, the wife of Ptolemy III Euergetes, thus providing a frame. At the beginning of book 3 the *Victoria Berenices* celebrates – in Pindaric fashion – the queen's chariot victory at the Nemean Games and gives the tale of the games' *aition*, Heracles' slaying of the Nemean Lion, told from a typically Callimachean angle. On his way to the fight, the hero spends the night in the lowly dwelling of the poor peasant Molorcus; this domestic setting was probably much more developed than Heracles' fight itself. Book 4 ends with the *Coma Berenices*, the tale of the lock of hair that the queen dedicated for the safe homecoming of Euergetes (who had gone to war in Syria); the lock vanished and was miraculously rediscovered in heaven as a new star (the charming story can still be read in Catullus' Latin translation). Another famous story (in book 3) is that of Acontius and Cydippe, admired and imitated in Latin (by Virgil, Propertius, and Ovid) as well as in later Greek literature (e.g. in the *Letters* of "Aristaenetus"). The most important – and most widely quoted – part of the *Aetia* was the prologue, which (contrary to what earlier scholars have surmised) was already the introduction to its original two books. In it Callimachus vividly and vehemently rejects the carpings of the Telchines, as he calls his critics (the name originally signified some malevolent spirits), who demand from him heroic epics on a massive scale; but he cites the well-crafted small-scale poems of Mimnermus and Philitas as his models and claims that from his very beginnings as a poet Apollo himself advised him to seek out yet untrodden poetic paths.

The epilogue at the end of the *Aetia* evokes the next category of Callimachus' poetry, the thematically and metrically very diverse *Iambi*, which adopt the tradition of the old Ionic iambus (and especially the work of Hipponax), as the *Aetia* took up Hesiodic catalogue poetry. In six of the *Iambi* (1–5 and 13) he adopted Hipponax' trademark metre, the "limping iambic"; in the rest he used a variety of other metres. In *Iambus* 1 Hipponax himself speaks; he is "on holiday" from Hades and now admonishes – of all people – the scholars of Alexandria (Callimachus' colleagues) to cease squabbling with each other; he then pointedly relates how magnanimously the Seven Sages behaved among themselves. *Iambus* 2 tells an Aesopian fable with satirical application at the end. *Iambus* 3 laments present bad times. *Iambus* 4, another fable about the

contest between the laurel tree and the olive tree that is interrupted by a neighbouring bush, is apparently connected to the framing story, in which a quarrel between Callimachus and a rival is similarly interrupted by a third person. In *Iambus* 5, in metaphorical language, the poet advises a pederastic schoolteacher not to pursue his vice any further. *Iambus* 6 offers a detailed (but badly preserved) description of the great statue of Olympian Zeus, apparently given by the poet to a friend who is about to visit Olympia; this is an intriguing mixture of a *propemptikon* (a farewell poem) and a traveller's guide. *Iambus* 7 gives an aetiological story about the wooden statue of Hermes Perphuraeus (told by the statue itself). Of *Iambi* 8–11 only a few verses remain, but we know their content from the *Diegeseis*: a victory ode in iambic trimeters containing another aetiological tale (8), a conversation between a statue of Hermes with erect phallus and a pederast (9), an *aition* for a curious pig sacrifice to Aphrodite (10), and an *aition* for a proverb (11). *Iambus* 12 returns to more poetical spheres. In this birthday poem for the newborn daughter of a friend the poet related how, when a similar feast was once celebrated on Olympus for the newborn Hebe, Apollo's hymn was judged the best among the presents then given; surely Callimachus himself wanted his own birthday poem to be judged similarly. In *Iambus* 13 Callimachus defended himself against critics carping at the diversity and multiformity of his poems. This could have been a fitting conclusion to the collection; recently, though, it has been argued that the book of *Iambi* did not only contain the 13 poems described above, but also the four following miscellaneous poems in various lyrical metres, as the *Diegeseis* do not really distinguish them from the preceding *Iambi* (Cameron, 1995, pp. 163–70).

The *Hecale* is Callimachus' response to Greek epic tradition; in this epyllion (little epic) he chooses – as in the Heracles story in the *Victoria Berenices* – a characteristically unexpected angle to retell a deed by the young Athenian hero Theseus. Having just escaped an assassination attempt by the sorceress Medea, Theseus is forbidden by his father Aegeus to seek a new danger and slay the mighty bull that ravages the Marathonian countryside; he ventures out nevertheless and, when surprised by a heavy downpour, finds hospitable refuge in the hut of a poor old woman, Hecale (and Callimachus describes this domestic scene with loving detail). Next day Theseus successfully captures the bull (this, it seems, was described only very briefly), but on his return finds the old woman dead; so he sacrifices the bull in her memory, and founds a new Attic deme, which he names Hecale, and a sanctuary to Zeus Hekaleios as well. The latter part of the poem is filled out mainly by the curious conversation between an old crow (which deeply delves into Athenian mythical history) and another bird (possibly an owl). The whole poem may have been 1000 to 1500 hexameters long.

The six *Hymns* to various deities, which take their cue from the so-called *Homeric Hymns*, are the only substantial part of Callimachus' poetry (except the *Epigrams*) to be preserved in medieval manuscript tradition. *Hymns* 1 (*To Zeus*), 3 (*To Artemis*), and 4 (*To Delos*; the island is divinized as the birthplace of Apollo) are written in a straightforward fashion. *Hymn* 3 especially contains scenes pervaded by typically Callimachean humour: little Artemis reaches in vain for her father's bearded chin and pulls hairs from the shaggy breast of the Cyclops Brontes, and when – after a hunting foray – she is welcomed on Olympus by Heracles, this well-known lover of great quantities of meat earnestly tells her not to hunt little hares but bigger animals like boar and oxen! *Hymn* 4 wittily includes an honorific mention of Ptolemy Philadelphus by way of a curious prophecy (162–95): when Leto approaches the island of Cos, Apollo, speaking from her womb, forbids her to bear him there, for this island is destined to become the birthplace of another god (Philadelphus). The other three *Hymns* are set within the frame of a ritual which is evoked by the poet's very words. *Hymn* 5 (*To the Bath of Pallas*), which unlike the other hymns is written in elegiac couplets and Doric dialect, unfolds within a ritual bathing scene for a statue of Athena; within this frame another (mythical) bath of Athena is described which cost Tiresias (who had inadvertently stumbled on the scene) his eyesight for seeing the bathing goddess. *Hymn* 6 (*To Demeter*, again in Doric dialect) within its ritual frame tells how Demeter punished Erysichthon for destroying her sacred trees by striking him with eternal hunger (which is then described in lurid and ludicrous detail). *Hymn* 2 (*To Apollo*) evokes the epiphany of the golden, youthful Apollo and ends with a peculiar section leading us back to Callimachus' convictions regarding poetry (105–12): Phthonos (personified Envy) approaches Apollo and whispers into his ear that he does not love poets who do not produce works on the scale of the sea, but Apollo kicks him away and declares his own preference for the clear and pure water of the modest fountain to the mighty, but muddy, Assyrian stream.

Of Callimachus' *Epigrams* about 60 have survived, almost all of them in the *Anthologia Palatina*. In an age famous for gifted epigrammatists, these little poems (rarely exceeding six lines) still hold their own for the strength of feeling that they express and the unexpected turn of thought that they often take.

Callimachus was as much a scholar as a poet, but of the astonishing amount of prose works he produced even more has been lost than of his poetry. According to the *Suda*, he wrote, among other things, *On the Names of the Months according to Peoples and Cities*, *The Settling of Islands and Cities and their Renaming*, *On Winds*, *On Birds*, *On the Rivers in the Inhabited World*, and *Collection of the Carvels of all the World according to Localities*. His greatest achievement as a scholar, however, was surely the *Pinakes*, or *Tables of Those who Distinguished Themselves in All Kinds of Learning and of their Writings*, a gigantic catalogue (in 120 books) which presented the contents of the great royal library in Alexandria ordered by genre, author, and single works.

Both as a scholar and as a poet Callimachus had far-reaching influence. The great Alexandrian scholars Eratosthenes and Aristophanes of Byzantium were his pupils, as were a number of lesser ones (Hermippus of Smyrna, Istrus, and Philostephanus). In the realms of poetry, the *Aetia* and *Hecale* acquired immediate and lasting fame. The *Aetia* secured Callimachus a place among the foremost elegiac Greek poets; echoes from the *Hecale* can be found in many Greek as well as Roman poets. In Hellenistic times Callimachus' presence could be felt in the works of Apollonius Rhodius, Lycophron, Rhianus, Eratosthenes, Euphorion, Nicander, and Parthenius; in imperial times in that of Dionysius Periegetes, the two Oppians, Quintus of Smyrna, Triphiodorus, the Christian

Gregory of Nazianzus, and Nonnus (both in the *Dionysiaca* and in the poetic paraphrase of St John's Gospel). In the little Egyptian village of Oxyrhynchus alone, papyrus fragments of nine separate copies of the *Hecale* have been found (ranging from the 2nd to the 6th or 7th centuries AD).

As Callimachus' poetry was never easy, even for native Greek-speakers, his works soon needed clarification. Perhaps as early as the final centuries BC the so-called *Diegeseis* (one might call them "Tales from Callimachus") were produced; largely preserved on papyrus, they provide valuable information on the content of Callimachus' work. Commentaries on Callimachus' poetry are known to have been written at least since the end of the 1st century BC: Theon, a scholar of Augustan times, and Epaphroditus (1st century AD) wrote commentaries on the *Aetia*; Archibius, the son of Apollonius, on the *Epigrams*; and Salustius (late antiquity) on the *Hecale* and perhaps other poems; this commentary was still used by Byzantine lexica (see below). Around AD 500 Marianus of Eleutheropolis produced a paraphrase of the *Hecale*, *Hymns*, *Aetia*, and *Epigrams* in 6810 iambic lines. The *Hecale* was cited by Archbishop Arethas (active in the late 9th/early 10th century), who also knew the *Aetia* and the *Hymns*; by the *Etymologicum Genuinum* (which, though itself lost, spawned various other *Etymologica* in the following centuries) in the 9th century and by the *Suda* (our most important source for the *Hecale* fragments apart from the papyri) in the 10th. The owner of the last known copy of *Hecale* (and probably *Aetia*) was Michael Choniates, metropolitan of Athens (1182–1204). This copy, however, in all likelihood perished when Athens was sacked by members of the Fourth Crusade in 1205. It was not until the 20th century that papyri would restore at least a part of what had been lost 700 years ago.

HEINZ-GÜNTHER NESSELRATH

Biography

Born *c.*320 BC in Cyrene, Callimachus was probably educated in Alexandria and lived there for much of his life. He was closely connected with the Museum and the royal library. He wrote extensively in poetry (*Aetia*, *Iambi*, *Hymns*, *Epigrams*) and prose (most notably the *Pinakes*, a catalogue in 120 books of the library's collections). His pupils included Eratosthenes and Aristophanes of Byzantium. He died *c.*240 BC.

Writings

Callimachus, edited by Rudolf Pfeiffer, 2 vols, Oxford: Clarendon Press, 1949–53

Hymns and Epigrams, translated by A.W. Mair, London: Heinemann, and Cambridge, Massachusetts: Harvard University Press, 1955 (Loeb edition)

Callimachus, translated by C.A. Trypanis and Thomas Gelzer, Cambridge, Massachusetts: Harvard University Press, and London: Heinemann, 1975 (Loeb edition)

Hymn to Zeus [First Hymn], introduction and commentary by G.R. McLennan, Rome: Ateneo & Bizarri, 1977

Hymn to Apollo [Second Hymn], commentary by Frederick Williams, Oxford: Clarendon Press, and New York: Oxford University Press, 1978

Iambi, edited by D.L. Clayman, Leiden: Brill, 1980

In *Supplementum Hellenisticum*, edited by Hugh Lloyd-Jones and Peter Parsons, Berlin: de Gruyter, 1983, pp. 89–144

Hymn to Delos, translated by W.H. Mineur, Leiden: Brill, 1984

Hymn to Demeter, edited by N. Hopkinson, Cambridge and New York: Cambridge University Press, 1984

The Fifth Hymn, edited by Anthony W. Bulloch, Cambridge and
New York: Cambridge University Press, 1985
Hecale, edited by A.S. Hollis, Oxford: Clarendon Press, and New
York: Oxford University Press, 1990 (includes commentary)
Aitia, Libri Primo e Secondo, edited and translated into Italian by
Giulio Massimilla, Pisa: Giardini, 1996 (includes commentary)

Further Reading

Cameron, Alan, *Callimachus and His Critics*, Princeton, New Jersey:
Princeton University Press, 1995
Harder, M.A., R.F. Regtuit, and G.C. Wakker (editors), *Callimachus*,
Groningen: Forsten, 1993
Hutchinson, G.O., *Hellenistic Poetry*, Oxford: Clarendon Press, and
New York: Oxford University Press, 1988, pp. 26–84

Canada

The first Greek to visit Canada may have been the
Cephalonian navigator Apostolos Valerianos, otherwise
known as Yannis Phokas, who in the employ of the Viceroy of
Mexico explored the Pacific coast of the Americas in 1592 and
for whom the Strait of Juan de Fuca, which separates
Vancouver Island from the state of Washington, was later
named. Although he was preceded by a few fellow-countrymen
along the shores of the Saint Lawrence in eastern Canada, the
first Greek immigrant of any importance was the soldier of
fortune George Kapiotis from Cyme in Euboea, who fought for
the British in the Crimean War, joined the gold rush to the
Caribou in the early 1850s, and settled in Victoria where he
married a local Songhee chief's daughter whom he taught
Greek (their grandson, the physician George Athans, was a
Canadian champion diver who competed at the Olympics of
1936). By 1900 there were still fewer than 300 Greeks in
Canada, almost exclusively males from the poorer areas of
Greece such as Arcadia, Laconia, and the islands, who had
arrived usually with the intention of making money and
returning to Greece rather than settling permanently. The rate
of immigration increased in the early decades of the 20th
century because of poverty and political persecution in Greece
and the Canadian need for cheap labour, but immigration policies biased against southeastern Europeans still kept the
numbers low, there being even by 1931 only 9450 persons of
Greek origin in the country. A postwar change of immigration
policy led to an influx of Greeks in the 1950s to mid-1970s
with a peak of over 10,000 in 1967, but growing unemployment in Canada ensured only a trickle in the 20 years up to
1998. According to the 1991 census there were 151,150 people
in Canada claiming single Greek descent and 40,330 claiming
part-Greek descent, with only a slight preponderance of males,
but these figures are probably too low. Approximately 30,000
were Greek Cypriots, whose immigration began in the 1960s
and reached its peak with the Turkish invasion of the island in
1974.

Although most immigrants were peasants and fishermen,
they largely chose to live in cities, especially Toronto,
Montréal, and Vancouver. In 1991 55 per cent resided in
Ontario and 29.5 per cent in the province of Québec. The men
worked at first mainly in labouring jobs and then increasingly
in their own businesses, of which in 1951 about 80 per cent

were restaurants (which frequently offered Canadian rather
than Greek food). The young women worked at first as domestic servants and later as partners in their husbands' businesses.
Since second-generation Greek Canadians had on average
more than twice as many years of schooling as their parents, so
many entered higher-paying occupations, and especially the
professions of teaching, law, engineering, and medicine, that in
the late 1990s retiring restaurateurs were finding it difficult to
keep their businesses in the family.

The first Greek Orthodox priest in Canada, Agathadoros
Papageorgopoulos, came to Montréal in 1906 from Greece,
although he was theoretically under the Ecumenical
Patriarchate, and from 1908 to 1922 the communities were
under the spiritual care, rather than effective jurisdiction, of
the Church of Greece. In 1922 Meletios, in his first official act
as the new ecumenical patriarch, created the archdiocese of
North and South America, which he had begun to organize on
a visit the preceding year. The Canadian parishes, originally
incorporated into the diocese of Boston, were formed into a
separate diocese with the installation of bishop Athenagoras
Kokkinakis in 1960. A further reorganization in 1996 saw the
enthronement on 26 September of Canada's first archbishop,
Sotirios Athanasoulas, under the direct jurisdiction of the
Ecumenical Patriarch. By May 1998 there were 65 parishes
(although no bishoprics had been created) and it was
planned to open a seminary in Toronto later that year. A very
few small Old Calendarist communities had been established
in Canada since the 1960s, and a small but growing number of
parishes of other Orthodox Churches such as the Antiochian
catered largely for second-generation Greeks and their often
non-Greek families who both needed the liturgy in English and
wished to escape Greek cultural domination. Since the late
1940s the traditionally wide-reaching and often authoritarian
role of the Church in community affairs was increasingly challenged, and often acrimonious struggles developed between the
clergy (born mainly in Greece) and secular leaders. Among the
factors involved were the influence of the generally more
secular Canadian society, the immigration of many communists persecuted in Greece at the end of the Civil War in 1949,
and the Church's support of the junta in Greece from 1967 to
1974.

The small numbers of Greeks in Canada always encouraged
the creation of tightly knit communities within the cities. In the
1970s and 1980s the federal government's deliberate fostering
of multiculturalism further aided a sense of ethnic distinctness.
Greek schools, for the teaching of the history and the modern
language, proliferated. Increasingly under lay direction, these
have operated in the evenings and on Saturdays, but have
rarely catered for children over the age of 14. Cultural, sporting, and philanthropic associations, some purely local, many
provincial or national or affiliated with US groups, have been
sponsored both by the Church and by the secular communities
(the first were in Montréal as early as 1906). In 1981 the
Hellenic Canadian Congress was founded as an umbrella organization largely to give these associations a more effective voice
in dealings with different layers of government. In 1998 there
were approximately 12 Greek newspapers in Canada, the earliest having appeared in Montréal in 1924. Greek television and
radio programmes have been based mainly in Toronto and
Montréal. Although these factors have all promoted ethnic

awareness, Canadian state schooling, the low level of Greek immigration in the 1980s and 1990s, and the growing tendency of young Greek-Canadians to practise exogamy had already begun to break down ethnic barriers and produce something more akin to the "melting-pot" of the USA.

Greek consciousness traditionally resulted in communities taking far more interest in Greek than in Canadian politics. Canadian Greeks returned to fight in the Balkan Wars of 1912–13, were divided between Venizelists and Royalists in and after World War I but joined forces in their opposition to the Germans in World War II, contributed generously to the Greek Relief Fund to aid the Nationalist Government against the communists in the Civil War, and later have been united in their opposition to the claims of Turkish Cyprus and the Former Yugoslavian Republic of Macedonia. In response to the junta in 1967–74 Andreas Papandreou, while a visiting professor at York University in Toronto, founded the Panhellenic Liberation Movement (PAK, later PASOK) before he returned to Greece as leader of the opposition and, in 1981, became its first socialist prime minister. In contrast the earliest serious interest in Canadian politics was not shown until the early 1960s when the Greek Association of the Liberal Party was founded in Montréal. By 1993 two senators, two members of the federal parliament, and one member of a provincial parliament (Saskatchewan) could claim a Greek origin.

Classical Greek (and Latin) language and literature and ancient history have traditionally been taught at Canadian universities in separate Classics departments, some of which in the 1990s became parts of larger departments of languages or Western civilization. Since the 1970s there has been a huge growth in courses on Greek (and Roman) culture, whose lack of a linguistic requirement has often resulted in enrolments of up to 300 students. A few universities have offered courses in Byzantine Studies and there is a Canadian committee affiliated to the Association Internationale des Études Byzantines. University courses in modern Greek have been rare and mainly in Montréal. Most Classics professors used to be both foreign born and trained (mainly in the UK and the USA), but, owing to a curb on immigration and a growth of graduate studies, most appointments made since the early 1980s have been of Canadians, though very few of these have been of Greek descent.

Publications by Canadian classicists were paltry until the 1950s, but since then there has been an upsurge of scholarly activity, much of very high quality. Since 1946 the Classical Association of Canada has published annually the internationally respected journal *Phoenix*, which has since been joined by *Classical News and Views / Echoes du monde classique* (1957, radically improved in 1982 as *Echos du monde classique / Classical Views* and issued with an annual fascicle of Canadian archaeological reports), *Teiresias: A Review and Continuing Bibliography of Boiotian Studies* (1971, now entirely electronic), *Cahiers des études anciennes* (1972), *Dionysius* (1977), and *The Ancient History Bulletin* (1987). In March 1989 the University of Western Ontario established the Centre for Olympic Studies (the first such centre in the world), which since 1992 has published annually its *International Journal of Olympic Studies* and biennially the *Proceedings* of its symposia. Byzantine studies have been remarkably fostered by the Hellenic Canadian Association of Constantinople which

since 1992 has regularly published as monographs the public lectures that it sponsors.

A.R. LITTLEWOOD

Further Reading

Chimbos, Peter D., *The Canadian Odyssey: The Greek Experience in Canada*, Toronto: McClelland and Stewart, 1980

Chimbos, Peter D., Greeks entry in *An Encyclopedia of Canada's Peoples*, edited by Paul Robert Magocsi, Toronto: University of Toronto Press, 1999, pp. 615–26

Efthimiou, M.B. and G.A. Christopoulos (editors), *History of the Greek Orthodox Church in America*, New York: Greek Orthodox Archdiocese of North and South America, 1984

Gavaki, Efrosini, *The Integration of Greeks in Canada*, San Francisco: R. & E. Associates, 1977

Gerber, D.E., "Canada: Greek and Latin Philology" in *La filologia Greca e Latina nel secolo XX*, vol. 2, Pisa: Giardini, 1989

Ioannou, T., *La Communauté grecque du Québec*, Montréal: Institute Québecois de Recherche sur la Culture, 1984

Vlassis, George D., *The Greeks in Canada*, 2nd edition, Ottawa, 1953

Canals

Until well into the 20th century difficulties of overland transport in Greece have led to a preference for water routes. A lack of navigable rivers has meant that long portages could not always be avoided, but Greece's deeply indented, irregular coastline has also provided opportunities to shorten both land and water passages through the construction of canals.

The most obvious site for a canal is at the isthmus of Corinth, which is a mere 6 km wide. A canal at this point was an objective of rulers from the 7th century BC to the modern era. The Cypselid dynasty, which ruled Corinth from the mid-7th to the early 6th century BC, was credited by ancient sources with a number of major projects linked to water transport. The dynasty's founder Cypselus was said to have dug a canal which separated Leucas (a Corinthian colony) from the mainland, making it an island. His son, Periander, constructed the artificial harbour at Lechaeum, on the north side of the isthmus. Late sources claim that he intended to dig a canal, but had to settle for a slipway, called *diolkos* in Greek. Traces of this construction, consisting of a paved roadway and two channels, are still visible, and archaeological as well as literary evidence supports the conclusion that it was originally constructed in the late 7th or early 6th century BC. The original purpose of this slipway is not entirely clear. The *diolkos* is near to neither of Corinth's ports, and was probably used by ships who were simply in transit. All the explicit mentions of its use involve the transport of warships. Still, this is unlikely to have been the *diolkos*' principal function as envisaged by its Corinthian builders who, after all, controlled harbours on both sides of the isthmus. It has been suggested (Cook, 1979) that the objectives of the original builders were commercial. Use of the *diolkos* allowed the Corinthians to levy tolls on those who were not actually trading with them but were passing through Corinthian territory. This slipway remained usable at least into the period of the early Roman empire, and there is some evidence that it was continuously in use up until the 9th century AD.

A canal at the isthmus of Corinth was supposedly contemplated by a variety of Hellenistic and Roman luminaries. The Roman historian Suetonius gives an account of Nero attempting to encourage the praetorian guard in this endeavour by breaking the ground and carrying the first basket of earth himself. This was not merely one of Nero's extravagant but empty gestures, since trenches 1.5 to 2 km long dating to his reign were visible before digging for the modern canal began. This canal was finally completed in 1893 during the administration of the prime minister Charilaos Trikoupis. It was one of many public works projects aimed at modernizing the country's infrastructure. For ships which can pass through the canal, the voyage from the Aegean to the Ionian Sea is shortened by some 325 km.

The second famous canal in Greece was the work of the country's enemies. The assistance that Athens and Eretria lent to the Ionian Revolt attracted the negative attention of Darius, king of Persia, who sent an expedition ostensibly to discipline those two cities. However, the expedition never progressed further than Macedonia because of excessive casualties on land and a disaster at sea. Attempting to sail round the Athos peninsula, the fleet was caught in a gale; Herodotus claimed that about 300 ships and over 20,000 men were lost as a result. A second attempt by Darius resulted in the great Athenian victory at Marathon. Herodotus presented Darius' successor Xerxes as eager to take revenge on the Greeks. He raised a force which dwarfed all the famous armies of the past and took extraordinary steps for the transport and provisioning of the expedition. In order to avoid a repeat of the Athos disaster he ordered that a canal be cut across the peninsula at its narrowest point, a distance of slightly more than 2 km. The project took three years to complete, and when finished the canal was the width of two triremes. Perhaps with the *diolkos* at Corinth in mind, Herodotus stated that Xerxes could easily have had the ships dragged across the narrow spit of land. He dismissed the canal as a work of ostentation, another manifestation of Xerxes' fatal hubris. Indeed, some ancient writers doubted that the canal had ever existed, or suggested that it had been only partially cut, with the ships being dragged the remainder of the distance. Nevertheless, European travellers of the 18th and 19th centuries noted traces of ditches and a chain of marshy lagoons along the line where the canal presumably ran. Recent geophysical investigations by the British School at Athens confirmed a V-shaped feature running along this line which agrees in its general dimensions with Herodotus' description (Isserlin *et al.*, 1994). The question of whether the cut completely severed the peninsula, turning it into an island, remains unsettled. The character of the soil along the southern portion of the presumed course of the canal would have made excavation much more difficult. Cores taken from the fill of the canal have no marine indicators, perhaps evidence that it had no direct outlet to the sea or that it was open only for a short time. Herodotus states that as part of the canal-building project breakwaters were constructed to keep the canal from silting up. No traces of these breakwaters have been found and, if they were in existence only for a short time, the canal itself may have had only a brief useful life (Isserlin *et al.*, 1996).

In post-Classical times Greek engineers had at their disposal more elaborate techniques for the building of artificial waterways. In the 3rd century BC Ptolemy II Philadelphus restored the Nile–Red Sea canal which had existed in the time of the pharaohs. Diodorus Siculus describes it as having a gate that could be opened and closed quickly, while Strabo mentions that boatmen could sail in and out easily. All of this suggests some kind of lock. Egyptian reliefs showing heavily laden ships voyaging between Egyptian Thebes and the land of Punt by way of the Red Sea attest to a much earlier canal which would also have been equipped with a lock (Moore, 1950, p. 99).

Roman military engineers assured the supply lines of the empire through a series of canals, dykes, and locks in the western European provinces. Pliny the Younger suggested to the emperor Trajan, while he was governor of Bithynia, that the construction of a canal between the city of Nicomedia and a lake in the interior might be a worthwhile project. The canal was never constructed, but in the 6th century AD Justinian proposed an even more ambitious scheme to connect the Black Sea with the Propontis. This was to involve reversing the current in the Sangarius river, which flows northeast into the Black Sea, so that it would instead flow southwest into the lake. From there, a canal would be used to convey ships to Nicomedia. However, the only evidence that construction was even begun is the existence of an absurdly large bridge over the Melas river. This insignificant stream was supposed to receive the flow of the diverted Sangarius, but the plan was never accomplished (Moore, 1950, p. 108–09).

BARBARA FIEDLER

See also Water Management

Further Reading

Cook, R.M., "Archaic Greek Trade: Three Conjectures", *Journal of Hellenic Studies*, 99 (1979): pp. 152–3

Curtis, Glenn E. (editor), *Greece: A Country Study*, 4th edition, Washington, D.C.: Government Printing Office, 1995

Herodotus, *The Histories*, translated by Aubrey de Selincourt, revised edition, with notes by John Marincola, London and New York: Penguin, 1996

Isserlin, B.S.J., "The Canal of Xerxes: Facts and Problems", *Annual of the British School at Athens*, 86 (1991): pp. 83–91

Isserlin, B.S.J., *et al.*, "The Canal of Xerxes on the Mt Athos Peninsula: Preliminary Investigation in 1991–1992", *Annual of the British School at Athens*, 89 (1994): pp. 277–84

Isserlin, B.S.J., *et al.*, "The Canal of Xerxes: Investigations in 1993–1994", *Annual of the British School at Athens*, 91 (1996): pp. 329–40

Moore, F.G., "Three Canal Projects, Roman and Byzantine", *American Journal of Archaeology*, 54 (1950): pp. 97–111

Salmon, J.B., *Wealthy Corinth: A History of the City to 338 BC*, Oxford: Clarendon Press, and New York: Oxford University Press, 1984

Candia, Fall of 1669

Determined to achieve supremacy throughout the eastern Mediterranean, and anxious to secure full control of the sea routes, the Turks eventually found a pretext for organizing a campaign to expel the Venetians for good from Crete and the

Levant. In 1644, off the island of Rhodes, a naval force of the Hospitaller Knights of St John captured a Turkish ship that was carrying functionaries of the Ottoman state on pilgrimage to Mecca. Among the captives was one of the wives of the sultan and their son. On their way back to Malta the knights anchored off Kaloi Limenes in Crete and released the Christians who had been slaves of the Turks, and took on supplies. Although the Venetian authorities on Crete had done their best to send the knights on their way as quickly as possible, the Turks nevertheless accused the Venetians of harbouring hostile forces, and declared war.

In 1645 the Turkish fleet commanded by Yusuf Pasha anchored in the port of Suda and a large military force disembarked close to the monastery of the Virgin at Gonia. Meeting no resistance, the Turks marched towards Chania, destroying villages and monasteries on the way. The Venetians tried to muster some counteroffensive, but to no avail. On 22 August 1645, after coming to terms, the town surrendered to the Turks. The conquest of Chania does not seem to have alarmed the European powers, who failed to appreciate the expansionist designs of the Ottomans. After repeated appeals for help from Venice, a small fleet of galleys sent by the pope, Spain, Malta, and the duke of Tuscany eventually arrived in Crete, some days after the surrender of Chania. Attempts to recapture the city were in vain; it was lost for good. In just a short space of time the Turks managed to establish control over most of western Crete, particularly the areas of Kissamos, Kydonia, and Apokoronas, reaching the gates of Rethymnon.

The siege of Rethymnon began in the autumn of 1646. At the start of the siege the Venetians had ordered the transfer of the population of the city to Candia in order to escape the continual bombardment from the Ottoman artillery and the food shortages. In the summer of the same year the city was afflicted by the plague, aggravated by the insanitary and squalid conditions of the besieged. At last, on 13 November of the same year, the *fortezza* of Rethymnon surrendered to the Turks.

The siege of Candia began in 1648, and it was to drag on for no less than 21 years, a duration that has few parallels in world history. Francesco Morosini, the last defender of Candia, was appointed head of the Christian forces in this critical contest between Christendom and Islam. Alongside him there were the reinforcements sent by the Knights of Malta, the pope, Spain, France, Tuscany, and the duke of Savoy. Yet despite the spirited resistance of the Venetians, the Cretans, and their allies, Candia could not hold out indefinitely against the Turkish onslaught. Before the superior might of the Turkish military machine under the leadership of the grand vizier Ahmet Köprülü, and under no illusion that defeat was avoidable, Morosini eventually opted for a diplomatic solution: on 16 September 1669 after long negotiations attended, on the Ottoman side, by the Greek interpreter Panayotis Nikousios, and on the Venetian side by the Scotsman Annant and the Cretan noble Stephanos Skordilis, an agreement was signed whereby the island of Crete, with the exception only of Grambousa, Suda, and Spinalonga, became Ottoman territory. Besides their arms and canons, the terms of the treaty allowed the Venetians to take with them their treasures and the government archive. It is for this reason that the valuable archive of the duke of Crete survived, brought back from Candia to Venice, where it is still preserved today. The transportation of the archive was supervised by the Greek Thomas Sakellaris.

The fall of Crete to the Ottomans was a severe blow to Venice, not only because it lost its most important dominion in the eastern Mediterranean, but chiefly because its prestige was irreparably dented. As they left the city, the Venetians dismantled the huge cross that they had erected in 1648 at the highest point of the city on the tower of Martinengo as a symbol of the city's strength. The immediate result of the Turkish conquest of Crete was a substantial reduction in the size of the population. Numerous Cretans, preferring flight to servitude, sought refuge in other Venetian dominions, and in particular in the Ionian islands or in Venice itself. This catastrophic war that shocked the Christian west, the plundering of the city's treasures, the destruction of the churches, and the expulsion of the population are described vividly for us in the long poem by the Rethymniot Marinos Tzanes Bounialis, *The Cretan War*.

CHRYSSA A. MALTEZOU

Further Reading

Chassiotis, I., "O Kritikos Polemos kai i epopoiia tis poliorkias tou Chandaka, 1645–69" [The Cretan War and the Epic Poem of the Siege of Chandaka, 1645–69] in *Istoria tou Ellinikou Ethnous* [History of the Greek Nation], vol. 10, Athens, 1974, pp. 334–51
Gryntakis, G., *I Kataktisi tis Dytikis Kritis apo tous Tourkous* [The Turkish Conquest of Western Crete], Athens, 1989
Vacalopoulos, A., *Istoria tou Neou Ellinismou* [History of Modern Hellenism], vol. 3, Thessalonica, 1968, pp. 472ff.
Valerio, Andrea, *Historia della guerra di Candia*, Venice, 1679

Canon Law

The Byzantine Church never produced an exhaustive and juridically consistent corpus of canon law, but it did recognize the permanent authority of a body of conciliar decrees and patristic opinions issued at various times and in various circumstances. Byzantine theology avoided rationally structured systematization, so the Byzantine Church never bound itself with an exhaustive code of ecclesiastical laws. The councils issued canons related to the structure and administration of the Church and to discipline, but all these texts reflected the requirements of particular situations. The canonical requirements were seen as absolute, inasmuch as they reflected the permanent norms of Christian doctrine and ethics, but in many cases the Byzantine Church also recognized the possibility that these same norms could be preserved not by applying the letter of the law, but by exercising mercy or condescension. Moreover the harmonious coexistence of the empire and the Church, as it was defined mainly by the emperor Justinian I (527–65), made it inevitable that imperial decrees came to be authoritative for the Church as, reciprocally, the empire recognized that ecclesiastical canons had the force of law. The text that comes closest to a theoretical definition of church–state relations in Byzantium is *Novella* 6 of Justinian I, which defines the priesthood and the imperial dignity as "the two greatest gifts of God" to mankind, and insists on their common divine origin. The ideal, as presented in the *Novella*, is a harmony between the two powers. In many cases of conflict between the two parallel systems the canon law prevailed. The result of this system was that many areas of Church discipline, such as the system for electing bishops and rule of marriage, were covered by imperial legislation, while in turn the emperors were formally bound by ecclesiastical canons (a famous case with many implications was the Church's opposition to the fourth marriage of emperor Leo VI).

Ecclesiastical canons and imperial laws regulated the election of patriarchs. Justinian (*Novella* 174, issued in 565) required that an electoral college of clergy and "important citizens" – similar to the college of cardinals in Rome – participate in the election, but the laity, with the exception of the emperor, were soon eliminated from the process. According to Constantine VII Porphyrogennetos (913–59), the metropolitans of the synod chose three candidates so that the emperors could pick one, while reserving for himself the option of making another choice as well. This openly admitted role of the emperor – which formally contradicted canonical proscriptions against the choice of clerics by civil rulers – was perhaps understandable in view of the political functions of the "ecumenical" patriarch in the state.

The sources of Byzantine canon law are the following:

Decrees of ecumenical councils. The decrees of Nicaea (325), Constantinople I (381), Ephesus (431), Chalcedon (451), the Quinisext Synod, also known as the Council in Trullo (692), which issued canons on behalf of Constantinople II (553) and Constantinople III (680–8), and Nicaea II (787).

Apostolic canons. These represent 85 disciplinary rules going back to the first half of the 4th century. Originating in Syria, they were given formal canonical authority by the Council in Trullo.

Canons of local councils. These were the canons of Ancyra (314), Neocaesarea (314–25), Antioch (341), Sardica (343), Gangra and Laodicea, and Constantinople (394). There were also the canons of Carthage (418), which included decrees of several councils of the north African episcopate held between the 3rd and the 5th centuries, as well as the later canons of Constantinople (859–80), sometimes referred to as the "Eighth Ecumenical Council".

Canons of the Fathers. These were a collection of patristic excerpts that were given formal canonical authority by the various councils. They included texts by Dionysius of Alexandria (died 265), Gregory of Neocaesarea (died 270), Peter of Alexandria (died 311), Athanasius of Alexandria (died 373), Basil of Caesarea (died 379), Gregory of Nazianzus (died 389/390), Amphilochius of Iconium (died 395), Timothy of Alexandria (died 355), Theophilus of Alexandria (died 412), Cyril of Alexandria (died 444), and Gennadius of Constantinople (died 471).

As for imperial legislation on ecclesiastical affairs, the most important compilation was the *Corpus Iuris Civilis* of Justinian I, followed by the *Novellae* (*Nearai* in Greek) issued by him and succeeding emperors. Other important sources of imperial legislation on ecclesiastical affairs are the *Ekloga* (731–41) and, particularly in the legislation of the Macedonians, the *Procheiros Nomos* (870–78), the *Basilics* (867–912), and the *Epanagoge*.

Nomokanon is a term used in Byzantine canon law to designate a collection presenting synoptically both ecclesiastical canons (*kanones*) and civil laws (*nomoi*) on ecclesiastical subjects. These were systematized collections of imperial laws and ecclesiastical rules arranged according to topic. The earliest was the *Nomokanon of 50 Titles*, assembled by an unknown compiler towards the end of the 6th century from two works by the lawyer-patriarch of Constantinople Ioannis III Scholastikos (565–77): the first one is the *Synagoge of 50 Titles*, a topical arrangement of conciliar canons to which Ioannis added the so-called apostolic canons, the African Code, and diverse excerpts from the letters of Basil the Great, and the second one a collection of civil laws in 87 chapters.

More influential was the *Nomokanon of 14 Titles*, assembled between 629 and 640 by the anonymous jurist usually known as Enantiophanes. Civil laws are drawn from a collection known as the *Tripartita*, while canons and the overall arrangement derive from the *Syntagma of 14 Titles*, which appeared in Constantinople in the later 6th century.

The *Nomokanon of 14 Titles* as well as the *Syntagma* went through several later compilations, these serving mainly to incorporate new canonical texts. Most famous is the compilation of the *Nomokanon* of 883, often ascribed to patriarch Photios, which not only enjoyed wide circulation in the Byzantine empire but also served as the basis for the major Slavic canonical collection known as *Kormchaya Kniga*, edited by St Sava of Serbia (13th century) and subsequently accepted in all the Slavic lands of the Balkans and Russia. Also noteworthy is the compilation of Theodore Bestes (in 1090), which gives an improved text for the imperial laws, and the extensive commentary of Theodore Balsamon (*c*.1170–78).

In late Byzantium the term *nomokanon* also came to be applied to manuals on penitential matters intended for the use of confessors. Such manuals circulated from the 9th century, often under the name of John the Faster (patriarch of Constantinople, 582–95). Their wide diffusion in the Slavic world, particularly in Russia, stems above all from the monastic communities of Mount Athos.

The authoritative commentaries on canonical legislation listed above appeared particularly in the 12th century. The commentary of Ioannis Zonaras attempted to classify canons according to their relative importance and authority. Alexis Aristenos emphasized their historical context. Theodore Balsamon, titular patriarch of Antioch during the reign of Manuel I Komnenos (1143–80), produced a major commentary on the entire *Nomokanon of 14 Titles* that attempted to coordinate the ecclesiastical legislation of the previous centuries and the civil legislation contained in the *Corpus Iuris Civilis* and the *Basilics*.

The permanent synod (*synodos endemousa*) at Constantinople regularly issued decrees on canonical and doctrinal issues. Since the archives of the patriarchate were almost totally destroyed by successive invaders (mainly after 1204), only a small part of the decrees have been preserved in their original text. In the last two centuries of the empire, as the power of the emperors diminished dramatically, the patriarchs assumed a wider role and greater competence in the affairs of society far beyond the shrinking borders of the empire. This new role was expressed in the concept of "universal leadership" (*kedemonia panton*) used in patriarchal decrees of that period (1261–1453), but their influence and their role were not comparable with those of the popes.

The entire legislative body of canonical texts was, according to Byzantine tradition, entrusted to the stewardship (*oikonomia*) of the bishops, with local provincial synods as well as the permanent synod at Constantinople acting as courts of appeal or as supreme tribunals. In the New Testament this term is used to designate God's plan for the salvation of mankind (Ephesians 1: 9–10, 3: 2–3) and also the stewardship entrusted to the bishops (1 Corinthians 4: 1; Colossians 1: 24–25; Titus 1: 7). This biblical origin of the term helps to explain the Byzantine canonical notion of *oikonomia*, which was not simply an exception to established rules but "an imitation of God's love for man" (Nicholas Mystikos), and implied repentance by the pardoned sinner. The principle of *oikonomia* implied a certain discretion given to the bishops in applying sanctions against repentant sinners. Politically minded patriarchs tended to expand the concept of *oikonomia*, more especially when imperial and political interests were involved, whereas the monks stood for a stricter interpretation of Church rules. On several occasions controversies, and even schisms, occurred over the issue of the use of *oikonomia*, for example the "moechian" schism in the early 9th century, on the occasion of the adulterous marriage of emperor Constantine VI, the "Tetragamy" of Leo VI in the 10th century, and the religious and political movement of hesychasm in the 14th century. However, everyone agreed on the principle that one could practice *oikonomia* only, in the words of Eulogius of Alexandria, "whenever orthodox doctrine remained unharmed", though there were many problems and misunderstandings.

A very important aspect of the Byzantine Church and of Byzantine canon law is the acceptance, at least as a principle, of a multiplicity of ecclesiastical centres. During the Palaiologan dynasty (1258–1453) the empire barely survived under the steady advance of Ottoman power in Asia Minor and, later, in the Balkans. During the same period the patriarchate of Constantinople, adapting to the new political situation, succeeded not only in maintaining its jurisdiction over vast territories but also in acquiring greater prestige and authority. When the Latins occupied Constantinople (1204–61), the patriarch went to exile in Nicaea, but continued to be recognized as the head of the mother Church of the Orthodox Slavs. From his exile he was more flexible and more generous towards them than his predecessors who had resided in the imperial city at the height of its power. In 1219 he appointed St Sava as the first archbishop of an independent Serbian Church. Sixteen years later he recognized the Bulgarian patriarchate of Tornovo. The Russian Church, destined to become the most powerful heir of Byzantine civilization, remained firmly under the patriarch's ecclesiastical control for the centuries to come. It was during the era of the grand prince Ivan III (1462–1505) that the Russians began to see in their powerful capital of Moscow a "new Constantinople" or a "third Rome". Nevertheless, it was still from Ottoman-held Constantinople that the Muscovite princes sought and obtained the recognition of their imperial title and, in 1589, the establishment of a patriarchate in Moscow.

That was the starting point for the development of autonomous ecclesiastical centres under the spiritual control of Constantinople. These ecclesiastical centres developed their own practices and their own canonic texts. The Church of Constantinople produced canon laws within its jurisdiction (more or less the territories of the Ottoman empire) and the patriarchate of Moscow for the territories of Russia. This trend created different sources of canon law for each autonomous Church in the Orthodox communion and currently the most accurate approach to the canon law of the Eastern Orthodox Church should be comparative. Of course the differences between the canon law systems of each "autocephalous" church are not essential, and in any case they carry the legacy of Christian Byzantium.

The Church of Greece, founded in 1833 and recognized by Constantinople in 1850, now has its own sources of canon law in addition to the ones that it has inherited. Most of these sources are the laws of the Greek state, which regulate every administrative and legal aspect of the Church. The general legal framework describing the relations between Church and state is provided by article 3 of the Greek Constitution:

> The prevailing religion in Greece is that of the Eastern Orthodox Church of Christ. The Orthodox Church of Greece, acknowledging our Lord Jesus Christ as its head, is inseparably united in doctrine with the Great Church of Christ in Constantinople and with every other Church of Christ of the same doctrine, observing unwaveringly, as they do, the holy apostolic and synodal canons and sacred traditions. It is autocephalous and is administrated by the Holy Synod of serving Bishops and the Permanent Holy Synod originating thereof and assembled as specified by the statutory Charter of the Church in compliance with the provisions of the Patriarchal Tome of 29 June 1850 and the Synodal Act of 4 September 1928. The ecclesiastical regime existing in certain districts of the state shall not be deemed contrary to the provisions of the preceding paragraph.

DIMITRIS A. KALOGERAS

See also Councils, Law, *Nomokanon*, Orthodox Church, Patriarchate of Constantinople

Further Reading
Beck, Hans-Georg, *Kirche und theologische Literatur im byzantinischen Reich*, Munich: Beck, 1959

Christofilopoulos, Anastasios, *Ellinikon Ekklisiastikon Dikaio* [Greek Ecclesiastical Law], Athens, 1965

Every, George, *The Byzantine Patriarchate, 451–1204*, 2nd edition, London: SPCK, 1962

Gofas, D., *Istoria kai Eisigiseis Romaikou Dikaiou* [History and Propositions of Romaic Law], Athens, 1985

Konidaris, I., *Zitimata Byzantinou kai Ekklisiastikou Dikaiou* [Problems in Byzantine and Ecclesiastical Law], Athens, 1990

Meyendorff, John, *Byzantine Theology: Historical Trends and Doctrinal Themes*, New York: Fordham University Press, 1974

Mortreuil, J.A.B., *Histoire du droit Byzantin ou du droit romain dans l'Empire d'Orient, depuis la mort de Justinien jusqu'à la prise de Constantinople en 1453*, vols 1–3, Paris: Guilbert, 1843–46; reprinted Osnabrück: Zeller, 1966

Obolensky, Dimitri, *The Byzantine Commonwealth: Eastern Europe, 500–1453*, London: Weidenfeld and Nicolson, and New York: Praeger, 1971

Scheltema H.J., in *The Byzantine Empire*, edited by J.M. Hussey,
    Cambridge: Cambridge University Press, 1967 (*The Cambridge
    Medieval History*, vol. 4, part 2)
Siciliano-Villaneuva, Luigi, *Diritto bizantino*, Milan: Società editrice
    libraria, 1906
Troianos, Spyros, *Piges Byzantinou Dikaiou* [Sources of Byzantine
    Law], Athens, 1986
Zužek, Ivan, *Kormčhaya kniga: Studies on the Chief Code of the
    Russian Canon Law*, Rome: Pontificum Institutum Orientalium
    Studiorum, 1964

Canonization

The concept of an abiding office and role of intercession for
certain leading disciples of Christ who have followed their
Lord into heavenly glory is one that is witnessed even in the
primitive Church. The apostles were promised thrones of glory
in the Kingdom (Matthew 19: 28), a promise that was always
understood to signify a continuing role of powerful influence,
even the exercise of judgement, within the context of the eschatological dominion of Christ. The early Church, from earliest
times, therefore, understood that certain elect disciples would
exercise an office of intercession with Christ that began in this
life but would endure into the next. While Paul called all the
members of the Christian assembly "the saints" it is clear
enough that the Christian populace soon regarded certain
"saints" as more significant than others. The central issue
seems to have been the extent of their intercessory power. The
first example of this attitude, observable in the New Testament
writings themselves, was the cult of the apostles. Among the
latter, Peter and Paul were given special pre-eminence.

In the persecutions of the 3rd and 4th centuries the extending cult of martyrs developed the idea of "saints" even further.
The Christians regarded those who had died for the sake of
their faith as surely guaranteed the reward of eternal life with
Christ. Already in the Book of Revelation the martyrs are
described as clothed in glorious white garments and praying
before God's throne (Revelation 6: 9f.), pointing yet again to
the centrality of the issue of intercession involved in the
Christian cult of the saints. Those who proved themselves
constant in time of persecution, but were spared the ultimate
penalty of death, came to enjoy great status in the Church. The
letters of Cyprian of Carthage in the 3rd century demonstrate
the conflict that could arise between these "confessors" and
the episcopate. The faithful clearly regarded the confessors as
sharing in the prerogatives of the martyrs, and able to exercise
on earth an intercessory power with Christ on behalf of
sinners. This belief paved the way for the fully developed cult
of saints which expanded from martyrs alone to embrace a
wider range of favoured disciples, such as ascetics and hierarchs; all of whom were "included in" the concept of martyrdom
(even if only symbolically) by themselves being called confessors, a title that became commonly used of later non-martyr
saints.

Archaeological evidence shows that the early Christians
often desired to be buried alongside their martyrs, hoping that
on the day of resurrection they would be in the presence of
elect souls who would intercede for them. Soon, especially
from the 4th century onwards, the bodies of martyrs were
transferred from common cemeteries and enshrined in special
churches. Their entombed bodies became focuses of pilgrimage. They were petitioned for intercession with God, especially
for healing miracles, and for the grace of forgiveness.

The beginning of the rationalization of the cultus of saints
can be traced to the late 2nd century, but it is really visible in
the 4th and 5th centuries. By this era the monastic ascetics
came to be regarded as a new paradigm of what would constitute an ideal disciple. Athanasius' *Life of Antony* enjoyed an
immense popularity and can almost be regarded as the progenitor of the genre of Christian hagiography. In this case the
great popular esteem with which Antony was regarded as a
Christian ascetic and holy man was reshaped by Athanasius,
an important Alexandrian hierarch, and brought to serve other
ecclesial ends – not least the furtherance of doctrinal orthodoxy. In the next generation the Cappadocian Fathers (especially Gregory of Nazianzus and Gregory of Nyssa) developed
the genre of hagiography in texts that were designed to highlight the sanctity of their own familial circle, and offer them as
ideal figures of Christian discipleship. The Cappadocians
developed Christian hagiography from the basis of Hellenistic
panegyric and, like Athanasius, their motive of shaping a form
of orthodox doctrine was never far from mind as they tried to
group a wider circle of the faithful around the ideal image of a
saint whom they idealized in their encomium (the *Life* of the
Saint) as a model of virtue and orthodoxy. Gregory of Nyssa's
Life of Macrina and Gregory of Nazianzus' *Funeral Sermons*
on members of his family are early examples of this hagiographical process. Panegyric texts such as these soon came to
have a special liturgical significance.

In the final stage of development, after the 5th century, all
the elements of the picture come together. Now, in addition to
a hagiographic text and the actual possession of a body (the
relics of the saint), the practical benefit of results is more insistently required. No longer is it enough to expect heavenly
intercession from the saint: some earthly manifestation of
benefit is also needed. The element of manifestation
(*epiphaneia*) is most commonly spoken about with regard to
miracles of healing. Frequently the older element of reconciliation, which the saint can effect with God, is presumed and
much of the healing genre (especially the healing of demoniacs)
can rightly be classed as a variant form of speaking about
reconciliation and release from guilt, a theme that was paramount in the earliest cult of martyrs.

The 5th century witnessed a number of *inventiones*: the
discovery by miraculous dream-intimations of lost relics of
great saints from earlier times. The empresses Pulcheria and
Eudoxia gained great status by their *inventio* of relics, and the
clearest example of how this cult of saints' intercession was
related to the exercise of power in Byzantium can be seen in the
legends of Constantine's mother Helena. The story of her
finding of the True Cross, the supreme relic in Byzantine estimation, is a classic of the type. So too is the story, preserved in
the writings of Cyril of Alexandria, of the discovery of the
relics of Cyrus and John, the Holy Unmercenaries (healer
saints), which Cyril translated to Menouthis in the early 5th
century to offset the continuing attraction of the Isis cult in
Egypt. The process of recognizing the places where the saints
lay hidden, or recognizing more generally that this person was
a powerful intercessor with God (*anagnorisis*) had by the 5th

century become a statement not only about the great power of the saint, but also about the spiritual acumen of those who oversaw the celebrations at the saint's shrine. All the elements for what we might therefore call a canonization (*anakeryxis*) were in place, but the acclamation that attended the proclamation of a saint was still largely a local and popular matter (however orchestrated it might sometimes be by hierarchs or princes) in Byzantium until well into the 13th century. The crucial elements can thus be established as: (*a*) a paradigmatic life (ideally a martyrdom; secondarily a radically ascetic lifestyle); (*b*) the possession in the local church of relics that were regarded as focal points for the saint's activity – especially on his or her feast day, or the day or anniversary of the "translation" of relics (when they had been moved into a position of honour within the church); (*c*) a hagiographic narrative that could be read out on the feast day recounting the merits of the saint and invoking his or her presence; and finally (*d*) an icon of the saint (the last element increasingly coming into place as the centuries developed).

From the 6th century onwards, and throughout all later Byzantine literature, the genre of the "Life of the Saint" came to rival even biblical and theological commentary. The Cypriot hermit saint Neophytos shows a classic example of this plastic process of "canonization" as it developed with all the necessary elements being carefully supplied in advance. Some later Byzantine hagiographies show the difficulty in trying to fit examples of married women (who did not fit the paradigm of ascetics) into the rigid categories of sainthood that had become established in the hagiographic genre. The attempt of Symeon the New Theologian in the 11th century to canonize his own spiritual father, Symeon Eulabes, earned him the censure of the Synod of Constantinople, and although other matters of conflict were at work in this case, it also serves as a clear sign that the process of canonization was being regularized from the time of Basil II onwards.

By the 13th century an official ecclesiastical process was beginning to be established to regularize the process of declaring saints. It is only from this period that we can properly speak of a Byzantine "canonization" process. It followed a similar movement in the West, visible from the late 10th century when the papal court attempted to restrict the right to declare new saints to itself. In Byzantium the first example of "official" canonization seems to have been that of patriarch Arsenios in the late 13th century, and more cases are witnessed in the 14th century, including those of patriarch Athanasios I and Gregory Palamas. A certain focus on leading hierarchs and teachers is noticeable. In the formalization of the process the same criteria – of exemplary life, actively powerful relics, and a hagiographic and iconic tradition – remain as standards, all of which, of course, could themselves be summed up as evidence of a lively popular cultus of the individual in question. Where the cultus was not popular or extensive (some pertinent examples are given in the collection of "Lives" of women saints recently translated by A.M. Talbot), the individual in question never seems to have entered the Byzantine Church's Synaxarion, the liturgical canon of saints invoked in the offices of prayer, and entered into the festal calendar.

In present Orthodox practice the right to declare saints falls to the Holy Synod, the supreme juridical legislature of the various autocephalous Churches, but it is still in a large

measure dependent on the ancient criteria – the prior existence of a lively cult of the saint (and thus the Christian acclamation (*anakeryxis*) that is at the heart of canonization resides, ultimately, in the spiritual sense of the Church at large), an expression of its faith in the closeness of Christ's leading disciples to their glorified master, and a sense that they enjoy special intercessory power with Christ, a power that they are still interested in exercising for the benefit of the "family" of Christians.

JOHN A. MCGUCKIN

See also Hagiography, Martyrdom

Further Reading

McGuckin, John, "The Influence of the Isis Cult on St Cyril of Alexandria's Christology", *Studia Patristica*, 24 (1992): pp. 191–99

McGuckin, John, "Martyr Devotion in the Alexandrian School (Origen to Athanasius)", *Studies in Church History*, 30 (1993): pp. 33–45

Macrides, R., "Saints and Sainthood in the Early Palaiologan Period" in *The Byzantine Saint*, edited by S. Hackel, London: Fellowship of St Alban and St Sergius, 1981

Talbot, Alice-Mary, Canonization entry in *The Oxford Dictionary of Byzantium*, edited by A.P. Kazhdan, 3 vols, New York and Oxford: Oxford University Press, 1991, vol. 1, p. 372

Talbot, Alice-Mary, *Holy Women of Byzantium: Ten Saints' Lives in English Translation*, Washington, D.C.: Dumbarton Oaks, 1996

Cappadocia

Region of central Anatolia

Cappadocia's southern border is the Taurus range of mountains. The Black Sea lies to the north, and its eastern boundary is set by Armenia and the Euphrates, with Lake Tata at its southern end. It consists of rugged plateau country, originally known for the breeding of horses, with limited agriculture, good grazing, and a fair degree of afforestation on the higher ground. The region is divided into a northern part, known as "Cappadocian Pontus", or more often simply "Pontus", and a southern part known as "Greater Cappadocia", or simply "Cappadocia".

Early in its history the region was invaded by Assyrians and Hittites (2nd millennium BC), followed by Phrygians and Cimmerians (*c*.1000 BC). The Persians, who came next (6th century BC), left their influence in art and religion. Although not directly conquered by Alexander the Great, Cappadocia came under Macedonian control from the 4th century, as the native monarchy assimilated Hellenized patterns. This process was well advanced in the 2nd century BC, when kingdoms such as Cappadocia were forced to take sides for or against the Romans. A spell of vacillation ended in support for Rome. As a client kingdom Cappadocia gained a measure of protection, benefiting particularly from Pompey's restoration of order in the east. Annexation followed in AD 17, when Cappadocia was for a time combined with Galatia. Between 107 and 113, it was joined with Pontus to form a new province, an arrangement which lasted until the reign of Diocletian (284–305). The strategic importance of this frontier province was recognized by the building of roads and the stationing of garrisons. The area became one of large estates, including imperial ones, clearly worth defending. It contrived to resist complete absorption into Roman life, maintaining an identity which included a form of the Cappadocian language which survived into the 3rd century AD.

Immigration was also an important factor in the history of Cappadocia, whether of Jews and Celts in the Hellenistic period or of Armenians in the 6th century AD. The diaspora Jews of Cappadocia were a significant element in the history of the Christian Church, mentioned in Acts 2: 9 as present at Pentecost and again referred to in 1 Peter 1: 1 as a notable part of the Jewish community, amenable to conversion. Christianity was established early in Cappadocia and the region came to play a notable part in its development. Mazaka became the capital in the 2nd century BC, but was renamed Caesarea (modern Kayseri) in 12–9 BC and became the provincial capital in AD 17, serving not only as an administrative centre but as a focus of literature and learning. This cultural primacy was encouraged by the emergence of a notable bishopric. St Firmilian (d. 268) was an impressive occupant of the see who was on intimate terms with Origen and was able to invite the Alexandrian teacher to Caesarea. Cappadocia did not escape persecution, whether under Emperor Maximinus "the Thracian" (235–38) or Decius, in the years 249–51. Throughout all this, Cappadocia maintained a reputation for Christian orthodoxy, in contrast to the sundry heterodox movements that developed in neighbouring Phrygia.

It was, however, in the 4th century, following Constantine I's acceptance of Christianity, that Cappadocia achieved its most noteworthy Christian status, through the birth there and lifelong work of the so-called Cappadocian Fathers, Basil of Caesarea, Gregory of Nazianzus, and Gregory of Nyssa. Associated with them were Macrina, the sister of Basil and Gregory of Nyssa, Amphilochius of Iconium, and Asterius of Nemesa. Cappodocia was also the birthplace of the emperor Julian, who came to be known as "the Apostate", for although brought up as a Christian he repudiated the faith and attempted to restore paganism, to the great anger of Basil and Gregory of Nazianzus who had been fellow-students in his Christian days. The preservation of the Nicene faith and its definitive expression at the Council of Constantinople in 381 owes much to the relentless exertions of the Cappadocian Fathers.

Alongside these searches for orthodox theological expression are the works of art of the Cappadocian Church. The region's rock-cut churches are decorated with complex wall-paintings that are variously primitive, bold, and direct in character and show a continuity of style, perhaps reflecting long traditions of monastic life and geographical remoteness. This isolation may well have been of importance during the iconoclastic controversy of the 8th and 9th centuries, allowing the secret preservation of works which might otherwise have been destroyed. The paintings were seen as valuable aids to meditation, with the potential to arouse strong emotions and to have an influence beyond their native region. Their distinctive character is thought to have affected painting styles in Thessalonica and possibly Italy. The 12th-century paintings of Elmale Kilisse, Qaranleq Kilisse, and Tchareqle Kilisse are particularly noteworthy.

Cappadocia maintained some measure of Greek identity until the Treaty of Lausanne in 1923, when the Greek population of Cappadocia, along with the communities of Pontus and Lycia, were repatriated under an exchange scheme agreed with the Turkish government.

D.A. SYKES

See also Basil the Great, Gregory of Nazianzus, Gregory of Nyssa

Summary

Region of central Anatolia, Hellenized from the 4th century BC in the wake of Alexander's conquests. There were significant Jewish, Celtic, and Armenian minorities, but Cappadocia was known for its Christian orthodoxy. Most notable were the so-called Cappadocian Fathers of the 4th century, Basil of Caesarea, Gregory of Nazianzus, and Gregory of Nyssa. Also distinctive are its rock-cut churches.

Further Reading

Baynes, Norman H. and H.St.L.B. Moss (editors) *Byzantium: An Introduction to East Roman Civilization*, Oxford: Clarendon Press, 1948

Beckwith, John, *Early Christian and Byzantine Art*, Harmondsworth and New York: Penguin, 1979

Broughton, Thomas and Antony Spawforth, Cappadocia entry in *The Oxford Classical Dictionary*, 3rd edition, edited by Simon Hornblower and Antony Spawforth, Oxford and New York: Oxford University Press, 1996, pp. 288–89

Hussey, J.M. (editor), *The Byzantine Empire*, Cambridge: Cambridge University Press, 1966–67 (*The Cambridge Medieval History*, vol. 4, parts 1–2, 2nd edition)

Jerphanion, Guillaume de, *Une Nouvelle Province de l'art byzantin: les églises rupestres de la Cappadoce*, 6 vols, Paris: Geuthner, 1925–42

Lassus, Jean, *The Early Christian and Byzantine World*, London: Hamlyn, and New York: McGraw Hill, 1967

Lietzmann, Hans, *From Constantine to Julian*, 2nd edition, London: Lutterworth Press, 1953 (*History of the Early Church*, vol.3)

Mango, Cyril, *Byzantium: The Empire of New Rome*, London: Weidenfeld and Nicolson, 1980

Mathew, Gervase, *Byzantine Aesthetics*, London: John Murray, 1963

Ramsay, W.M., *The Church in the Roman Empire before AD 170*, 2nd edition, London: Hodder and Stoughton, 1893

Rice, David Talbot, *The Beginnings of Christian Art*, London: Hodder and Stoughton, and Nashville: Abingdon Press, 1957

Runciman, Steven, *Byzantine Civilisation*, London: Arnold, and New York: Longman, 1933

Walbank, F.W. *et al.* (editors), *The Hellenistic World*, Cambridge: Cambridge University Press, 1984 (*The Cambridge Ancient History*, vol. 7, part 1, 2nd edition)

Carneades 214/13–129/28 BC

Philosopher

A pupil of Hegesinus the Academic, Carneades became the classic exponent of the sceptical interpretation of Plato. According to this, the essence of Plato's thought was to be found, not in the positive teachings of the later dialogues, but in the diffidence of Socrates, who maintained that he knew nothing, pronounced most of his arguments inconclusive, and was willing in the *Phaedrus* to deliver successive speeches on the same question in opposing characters. Carneades, however, also made himself familiar with a more dogmatic system under the Stoic teacher Diogenes of Babylon, and many of his discussions (which were not committed to writing but reported by his pupils) take the form of animadversions on Chrysippus, the most accomplished dialectician of that school. Indeed, he is reputed to have said that he would have been nothing without Chrysippus (Diogenes Laertius, *Lives of Philosophers*, 4. 62). Chrysippus averred that the wise man has no opinions, since he is able to distinguish between impressions that are dubitable or false and those that are truly cognitive. Carneades, on the other hand, believed that by exposing the flaws in the arguments of his great Stoic predecessor he had proved the fallibility of all reasoning, and had thus shown that the wise man is bound either to have opinions or to think of nothing at all.

The most famous of his polemics were directed against the Stoic belief in providence. Chrysippus had urged that since the gods are wise they are bound to love us, and, since they know the future, cannot fail to speak in times of need through oracles and omens. Carneades turned this reasoning on its head by saying that, if it is true that a deity who is wise is bound to love us, the presence in the world of many evils that belie this love compels the impartial thinker to doubt either the existence or the wisdom of the gods (Cicero, *Nature of the Gods*, 3. 32). He was a strong proponent of free will, and is said to have attempted a tripartite classification of the possible goals of life. Against the Stoics who followed Chrysippus in upholding divination, he retorted that the evidence of the senses, unreliable though it is, is still more worthy of trust than the private arts by which the seers profess to detect an occult significance in nature (Cicero, *On Divination*, 2. 9). From the frequency with which his name is cited in polemics against astrology, it is probable that he is the source of many specific arguments espoused by the later, Pyrrhonist branch of scepticism; nevertheless his views can be distinguished from those of the Pyrrhonists in two respects at least. First, he did not acknowledge that his doctrine of universal fallibility was itself a thesis open to refutation; secondly, he did not assert that all fallible opinions were of equal weight, but held that we may have reasons for considering one more probable than another. The Carneadean sceptic therefore lives according to his own conclusions and not, as the Pyrrhonist has to do, according to the custom of his neighbours. Nevertheless the criteria that determined probability for Carneades are far from clear, and even his disciples found it hard in many cases to ascertain his own belief.

The most notorious episode of his life was his visit to Rome in 155 BC, when he joined the Peripatetic Critolaus and the Stoic Diogenes in a petition for the waiving of a fine that the Senate had imposed on Athens. To demonstrate his prowess in philosophy he spoke on one day before the Senate in support of a certain thesis and on the next with equal cogency against it. So impressive was this exhibition that the Senate at once acceded to Cato's motion for the settlement of the fine and the expulsion of the philosophers from the capital (Plutrach, *Cato Maior*, 22). Nevertheless, there is something not entirely foreign to the Roman spirit in scepticism. Cato himself is said to have thought that augury was a sham, and Cicero borrowed liberally from Carneades in his works *On Divination* and *On Fate* which offer persuasive criticism of the Stoics. The third and ablest speaker in his dialogue *On the Nature of the Gods* declares that the Stoics have not convinced him, and that there-

fore he rests content with ancestral custom, the *mos maiorum*. This is the acquiescence of a Pyrrhonist, yet Cicero himself, in more Carneadean fashion, admits the force of the arguments on both sides, but opines without giving reasons that the Stoic enjoyed the best of the exchange. Carneades was for him the paradigmatic figure of the New Academy, of which he professed at times to be a member.

Under the Roman empire, systematic thought was once again in fashion among the Platonists, and Numenius of Apamea, a 2nd-century AD precursor of Plotinus, accused the New Academy of a progressive apostasy from the genuine teachings of the master. Around AD 200 the Christian writer Clement of Alexandria appealed to sceptical arguments to demonstrate the bankruptcy of philosophy, and deduced that no constructive thought was possible for those who were unwilling to put their faith in an infallible revelation (*Stromateis*, 5). The objections to astrology that were borrowed from Carneades by the Pyrrhonist Sextus Empiricus were borrowed in turn from Sextus by Hippolytus of Rome (died 235) and by Augustine. Nevertheless Augustine's work *Against the Academics* upholds dogmatic Platonism against the Carneadean method which assumes that it is possible to discover what is "like the truth" (*veri simile*) without the knowledge of anything that is certifiably true. The Christian tradition had good reason to treat the sceptic as its natural adversary, in the west as in the east: a Pyrrhonian suspension of belief could be the preface to orthodoxy, as in Descartes, but where the Carneadean spirit prevailed, as in Voltaire and Bayle, it allowed at most a lukewarm and conventional adherence to the Church.

MARK EDWARDS

See also Scepticism

Biography

Born in Cyrene in 214/13 BC, Carneades was a pupil of Hegesinus at the Academy and also of the Stoic Diogenes of Babylon. He became head of the Academy (or founder of the New Academy) before 155 BC. In that year he joined Diogenes and Critolaus on an embassy to Rome. He left no writings but his ideas were recorded by his pupil Clitomachus. He resigned in 137/36 and died in 129/28 BC.

Further Reading

Burnyeat, Myles (editor), *The Skeptical Tradition*, Berkeley: University of California Press, 1983

Long, A.A. and D.N. Sedley, *The Hellenistic Philosophers*, 2 vols, Cambridge and New York: Cambridge University Press, 1987, pp. 68–70

Schofield, Malcolm, Myles Burnyeat, and Jonathan Barnes (editors), *Doubt and Dogmatism: Studies in Hellenistic Epistemology*, Oxford: Clarendon Press, and New York: Oxford University Press, 1980

Carthage

Phoenician city in north Africa

The traditional date for the founding of Carthage is 814 BC. In the *Aeneid* Virgil immortalized the foundation myth of Queen Dido fleeing the Phoenician city of Tyre, and the murderous designs of her brother, to the shores of north Africa where she established her 'New City' (*Kart-Hadasht*).

Carthage became a prosperous city governed by an oligarchy with two chief magistrates (*suffetes*) elected annually, and supported by a Council of 300 and a popular assembly advising them. This constitution was admired by Aristotle in his *Politics* (2. 8). It evolved later into the Court of the 104 Judges, and the Boards of Five. The ruling class used this system to block any ambitious *suffet* from becoming too powerful with the help of the army.

Soon the Phoenician seafarers of Carthage began to colonize Andalusia, Malta, Sardinia, and parts of Sicily. Phoenician tombs in these regions, dated between 800 and 700 BC, attest to this activity. The following centuries saw the further expansion of Carthaginian territory along the north African coast. One group among the leaders of Carthage favoured branching out into the interior where they occupied land in the Bagradas valley, and successfully practised agriculture among the Berbers. The majority of the leading men in Carthage, however, concentrated their activity on seafaring and trade. Carthage became the foremost among the Phoenician settlements along the coast of Africa, drawing revenues from their ports, which made it the wealthiest city in the western Mediterranean.

Eventually, Carthage's colonizing zeal and mercantile activities brought it into conflict with the peoples of the northern shores of the Mediterranean: first the Etruscans and Greeks, and later the Romans. In 535 BC Carthage in alliance with the Etruscans fought a victorious battle against Phocaeans at Alalia in Corsica and in 509 BC, as an established power in the western Mediterranean, it signed a treaty with Rome.

A Carthaginian army under the leadership of Hamilcar, possibly encouraged by Persia which was involved in conflict with the Greeks in the east, attacked Sicily in 480 BC. The invasion failed due mainly to an alliance between Syracuse and Acragas. Gelon (*c.*540–478 BC), the tyrant first of Gela and later of Syracuse, was a military leader of talent who had established his authority over more than half of Sicilian territory. In league with Theron of Acragas (488–472 BC) and others, Gelon defeated the Carthaginians in 480 at Himera. Rich spoils in booty and prisoners were taken, and Gelon, mindful of Apollo, dedicated a golden tripod to the god at Delphi. Carthage was forced to buy peace, paying a large war indemnity.

The Greeks of Sicily were threatened again by Carthage when a Punic force captured Selinus and Himera in 409. In 405 Dionysius I (*c.*430–367 BC), the tyrant of Syracuse, acknowledged Carthaginian possessions in western Sicily where Himilco founded Lilybaeum, but was later able to drive them out of Sicily, leaving them by 392 in possession of the island's western extremity only. It was under his weaker son Dionysius II that Sicily was once again thrown into conflict.

In 348, 306, and again in 278 BC Carthage concluded further treaties with Rome. The last of these treaties had as its raison d'être in the danger posed to Carthage and Rome by the coming of Pyrrhus to Sicily. Regardless of this, the two states were later drawn into armed conflict, having both become entangled in Sicilian politics.

The First Punic War broke out in 264 and lasted until 241 BC. It was essentially a war triggered off by conflict of interest between Carthage and Rome; the former attempting to gain control over the Greek cities of Magna Graecia, and the latter seeing it as an interference in its sphere of influence. To recoup Carthage's losses resulting from the war, Hamilcar Barca abandoned all interest in Greek Sicily and established a Carthaginian empire in Spain. The capture of Saguntum by Hannibal in 219 BC provided the casus belli for the Second Punic War which saw Hannibal's spectacular crossing of the Alps into Italy and a string of impressive victories, but ended with Hannibal's defeat at the battle of Zama in Africa in 202 BC. In his statesmanship Hannibal belongs to the Hellenistic world of the Mediterranean, and in his generalship to the tradition of Alexander the Great and Pyrrhus, the Molossian king of Epirus (319–272 BC). After Zama Hannibal fled to the court of King Prusias I of Bithynia where he committed suicide in 183/82 BC. The Third Punic War was provoked by Rome's African ally Massinissa, and led to the destruction of Carthage by Scipio in 146 BC.

The territory of Carthage was pronounced cursed ground, and when Caius Gracchus tried to establish a Roman colony there, his enemies in the Roman Senate resisted, and he failed. It was later colonized by Caesar and Augustus, becoming the capital of proconsular Africa in the 2nd century AD. As such it was a flourishing Roman city, equally famous as a centre of education for orators and lawyers. Tertullian and Cyprian made it an important Christian city in the 3rd century AD; and in later years the bishop of Carthage was to play a significant role in Latin Christianity.

In AD 439 the Vandal king Gaiseric seized Carthage and made it the capital of his kingdom which lasted until AD 533/4, when Africa was conquered by Belisarius, the general of the emperor Justinian. Carthage remained the centre of the reconquered territory, and in time became the seat of the exarchate of Carthage. The exarchate was an administrative structure of the early Byzantine empire in which the exarch, appointed by the emperor in Constantinople as a kind of viceroy, wielded absolute power as chief administrator and military commander.

Justinian reconstituted Byzantine rule over Africa by appointing initially a *praefectus praetorio Africae*. He was not at first given military powers, and the emperor ordered Belisarius to take measures for the safety of the territory. The *praefectus praetorio* was directed to reside in Carthage, and was given a large, salaried staff to be divided between civilian and military departments. The administrative organization of the territory reflected the fact that Italy, to whose jurisdiction Africa had formerly belonged, was still in the hands of the Goths. When Belisarius left for Constantinople, one of his officers, Solomon, remained in Africa as the first *magister militum per Africam*. Soon afterwards, however, he was also appointed praetorian prefect in addition to his military command. The *Novels* of Justinian, issued in AD 535, regulating the question of land ownership and the re-establishment of the Church of Africa, are addressed to Solomon, *praefectus praetorio Africae*. Some historians see in this the possible beginnings of the exarchates which were to provide the model for the later thematic organization of the empire. Evidence points in this direction, since in the late 6th century the exarch of Africa is addressed as such in the correspondence of pope Gregory the Great.

The city maintained close ties with the Byzantine empire. It was from Carthage that Herakleios, the son of the exarch of the same name, came in AD 610 to overthrow the emperor Phokas whose tyrannical government had brought the eastern empire to near ruin. In the darkest days of his rule Herakleios is said to have contemplated moving the seat of government to Carthage, and as late as AD 663 Constans II (AD 641–68) attempted to govern the empire from Syracuse.

Carthage remained loyal to Byzantium into the final years of the 7th century, resisting the advances of Islamic armies on their westward drive, but was finally taken in AD 698 by an Arab force, bringing to an end Byzantine rule in north Africa.

FRANZISKA E. SHLOSSER

See also Africa (North), Phoenicians, Sicily

Summary

A Phoenician foundation near modern Tunis, Carthage became through trade the wealthiest city in the western Mediterranean. After early conflict with Greeks in Corsica and Sicily, Carthage fought a series of major wars against Rome, ending in the destruction of the city in 146 BC. Flourishing again by the 2nd century AD, Carthage fell to the Vandals in 439 but was reconquered by Byzantium in 533/34. Byzantine rule was ended by the Arabs in 698.

Further Reading

Aubet, Maria Eugenia, *The Phoenicians and the West: Politics, Colonies, and Trade*, Cambridge and New York: Cambridge University Press, 1993
Diehl, Charles, *L'Afrique byzantine: histoire de la domination byzantine en Afrique, 533–709*, 2 vols, Paris: Leroux, 1896
Gruen, Erich S., *The Hellenistic World and the Coming of Rome*, 2 vols, Berkeley: University of California Press, 1984
Harden, Donald B., *The Phoenicians*, revised edition, Harmondsworth: Penguin, 1980
Hurst, H.R., *Excavations at Carthage*, vol. 2, Sheffield: Department of Prehistory and Archaeology, University of Sheffield, 1984
Hussey, J.M. (editor), *The Byzantine Empire*, Cambridge: Cambridge University Press, 1966 (*The Cambridge Medieval History*, vol. 4, part 1, 2nd edition)
Lancel, Serge, *Carthage: A History*, Oxford, and Cambridge, Massachusetts: Blackwell, 1995
Ostrogorsky, George, *History of the Byzantine State*, 2nd edition, Oxford: Blackwell, 1968
Pedley, John Griffiths (editor), *New Light on Ancient Carthage*, Ann Arbor: University of Michigan Press, 1980
Pertusi, Agostino, "La Formation des thèmes byzantines" in *Berichte zum XI. Internationalen Byzantinisten Kongress*, Munich: Beck, 1958
Raven, Susan, *Rome in Africa*, 3rd edition, London and New York: Routledge, 1993
Warmington, B.H., *Carthage*, 2nd edition, London: Hale, and New York: Praeger, 1969

Cartography

In any consideration of cartography as practised by the Greeks, it quickly becomes apparent that there are two main divisions: the first is related to cosmology and theories about the origin and shape of the earth as a whole, while the second is rather more mundane and involves plans of a building, an area, a town, or a district, and may describe how to get from point A to point B, either by land or by sea. The ancients described these divisions as geography and chorography, respectively (cf. Ptolemy, *Geography*, 1. 1–5).

With regard to geography, early representations of the world survive from the Near East, the most famous perhaps being a clay tablet in the British Museum depicting Babylon and other districts and cities, along with the river Euphrates, all surrounded by a circular salt ocean with indications of mythical beasts and regions beyond the ocean. This object, dated *c.*600 BC, is surprisingly similar to the concept of the world promulgated by Thales of Miletus at about the same time, where the world is likened to an inverted bowl floating upon water: certainly the idea of the "River of Ocean" surrounding the land mass of the known world is remarkably persistent from Homer to late-Classical antiquity. As geographical knowledge improved, various writers recorded what they believed to be the spatial relationships of territories and peoples to each other, and it is from this information that many modern historical atlases present items such as "the world according to Hecataeus" or "Herodotus" or "Eratosthenes": actual ancient versions of these maps do not survive (indeed, modern versions seem to originate in the 1883 volumes of Bunbury), although there do exist Byzantine versions of Ptolemy's maps.

Circular maps were remarkably persistent, being found as late as the 1st century BC, even though Herodotus (4. 36) had mocked them in the 5th century. Of course, it is easy to confuse a circle with the representation of a sphere on a flat surface: the notion that the earth is spherical may have originated with Pythagoras and his followers in the late 6th century and certainly the idea was widely known by the 4th century, as can be seen from the production of "celestial spheres" (it is these, frequently with a zodiacal band, which appear in later statues of Atlas carrying a globe), all of which involved understanding of the equator, the tropics, and the polar zones, along with theories about inhabitable areas and the existence of "antipodes". Inevitably, people wanted to know exactly *where* they lived on this sphere and how *large* it was.

The gnomon (a vertical pointer, part of any sundial and possibly introduced from Babylon in the 6th century BC) made it possible to calculate latitude, if one knew the date and took one's readings at midday. Pytheas of Massalia (*fl. c.*320 BC) calculated the latitude of his home town to within about 13 km of the correct position; and from his famous voyage to the Tin Islands, around Britain, and possibly into the Baltic, he provided information about the length of solstitial days at various sites, which were later translated into degrees of latitude. (Longitude, of course, could not be calculated with any precision at all in antiquity, not that that prevented people from trying.) Eratosthenes of Cyrene (*c.*276–*c.*194 BC), chief librarian in Alexandria, was able, using a gnomon, to calculate that the distance from Alexandria to Syene (Aswan) was one fiftieth of the circumference of the earth, giving a result of 250,000 stades, which he later altered to 252,000 stades. There are several errors in Eratosthenes' calculations, notably that Syene lies on the Tropic of Cancer and that it is on the same meridian as Alexandria; however, these happen to cancel each other out and, depending on the length one accepts for a stade, his answer is either astonishingly close to the correct

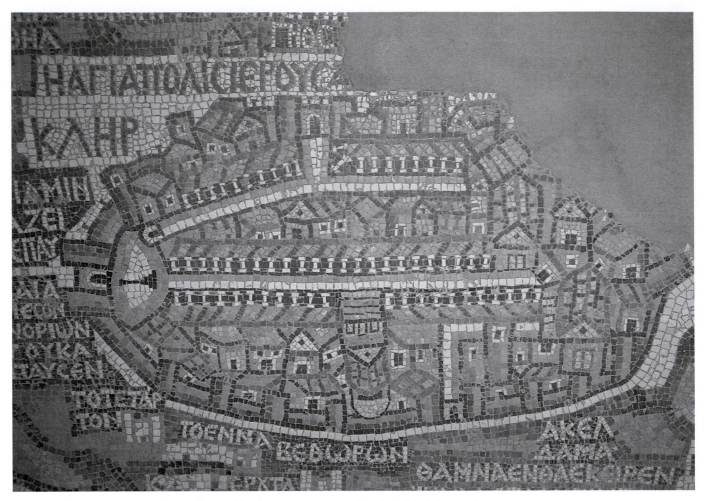

Cartography: mosaic map of Jerusalem, mid-6th century, from a church in Madaba, Jordan

figure, or it is merely the best approximation arrived at in antiquity.

In a major work on geography Eratosthenes then proceeded to calculate the size of the *oikoumene*, the inhabited portion of the world, as known in the 3rd century BC, and to produce a detailed map of it, using lines of latitude and a number of meridians to produce a grid, within which countries were placed, each having a generalized indication of its overall shape. Our knowledge of this map comes from later sources and, although it was somewhat crude and modern reconstructions of it may be rather misleading, nonetheless it formed the basis of all subsequent attempts in antiquity to produce maps of the inhabited world as they would be understood today.

By the middle of the 2nd century BC terrestrial globes were being produced, though large segments of them were inevitably hypothetical. Map makers tended, therefore, to focus on maps of the "known" world and they were, by this time, concerned with two problems: the representation of a section of a sphere on a flat surface and the type of scale to use. Crates of Mallus (who visited Rome *c*.168 BC) created a very large map which was 7 feet wide from east to west and intended to represent a scale of 1 foot to 10,000 stades; apparently the meridians did not converge. This map and others like it were clearly unsatisfactory; so the problem of establishing a suitable projection was tackled by Ptolemy (Claudius Ptolmaeus, *c*.AD 90–168),

who worked in Alexandria: he produced two projections, described in Book 1 of his *Geography*, and they constitute perhaps the greatest legacy from antiquity in scientific map making. In addition, the remaining seven books of the *Geography* catalogue by latitude and longitude about 8000 cities, mountains, islands, and the like, providing the raw material for the construction of a series of maps.

As for chorography, topographical representations have been identified in prehistoric carvings, and on rock and wall paintings and pottery, including an apparent "town plan" from Çatal Hüyük in Anatolia (*c*.6200 BC); and in Mesopotamia a seated statue of Gudea, ruler of Lagash in the mid-22nd century BC, shows on his lap a tablet bearing the plan of a large building with a scale along the top. In Egypt trigonometry and surveying instruments were developed in the early part of the Old Kingdom (*c*.2600 BC) to enable land allotments to be redefined after the annual inundation of the Nile; and many plans of estates, mines, and tombs survive from the period before 1000 BC. The Egyptian tradition of surveying and chorography became important for the rest of the Mediterranean world after the death of Alexander the Great, with the Ptolemaic dynasty and the scientific upsurge created by the Museum and Library in Alexandria. Alexander's expedition across the Middle East as far as India created huge logistical problems involving supplies and reinforcements, and Alexander, pupil as he was of Aristotle and curious about everything, had surveyors ("bematists") and geographers in his train. The result was an expansion of earlier Persian "route maps" and other representations of the world (cf. the story of Cleomenes I of Sparta and his discovery, from a map, that to travel the Royal Road from Sardis to Susa involved a march of three months: Herodotus, 5. 49–50), while Ptolemaic surveys in Egypt both of agricultural land and of distances undoubtedly influenced developments in Carthage and in Italy, where the Greek cities of the south and then the Romans evolved elaborate systems of land surveying and allocation (centuriation). The building of highways throughout the growing empire produced what today are known as "strip maps", culminating in the ancestor of the famous Tabula Peutingeriana and in various Itineraries, which reflect major routes for land travel in the Roman empire and later.

Although these developments involved Greek-speaking lands, traditionally the Greeks were seafarers and their interests are reflected in *periploi* ("sea routes around"), which correspond to modern "Pilots", with descriptions of sea distances, landfalls, coastlines, river estuaries, and harbours. The earliest *periplous* which can be hypothesized is "Homeric": any modern analysis of the wanderings of Odysseus is controversial, but it may not be entirely fanciful to see in the *Odyssey* some reference to knowledge of Italian, Sicilian, and north African waters acquired by the Greeks during the first phase of western colonization (c.750–650 BC): see, for example, Bradford's comparison of Odysseus' landfall among the Laistrygonians at *Odyssey*, 10. 87–97 with the (British Admiralty) *Mediterranean Pilot* account of Porte de Bonifacio in southern Corsica. Many such *periploi* appeared over the centuries, involving navigation all round the Mediterranean and also in the Atlantic, and in eastern waters too, after the voyage of Alexander's admiral Nearchus from the Indus to the Persian Gulf. Perhaps the most important of these is the *Periplus Erythraei Maris*, written by an Egyptian Greek about the middle of the 1st century AD: it describes routes around the coasts of east Africa and southern Arabia and the direct route, using the recently discovered monsoon, to the west coast of India.

Over time these two approaches to cartography, geography and chorography, drew on and enriched each other. For example, the huge map of the known world created by Marcus Agrippa at the behest of Augustus and displayed on a portico in Rome late in the 1st century BC was the result of the accumulation of chorographic as well as geographic information, while the huge engraved maps of the city of Rome created in the Flavian and Severan periods (of which stone fragments survive) represent the culmination of the tradition of detailed depiction of limited areas.

In the later Roman empire there seems to have been a decline in cartographic skill. For example, the mediaeval *mappae mundi* ("world maps"), which represent a mainly Christian development, are commonly circular or oval: they appear from as early as the 3rd to the mid-15th century and frequently have Jerusalem at their centre (especially from the beginning of the crusades), and their purpose seems to have been primarily didactic and moralizing. A similar development can be seen in the Greek east, where Cosmas Indicopleustes ("sailor to India"), an Alexandrian merchant and convert to Christianity (c.mid-6th century AD), wrote a *Christian Topography* in 12 books, in which the main tenets of spherical geography are rejected, the earth is seen as flat and rectangular, and the universe is a box-like structure, vaulted on top and resembling the biblical description of the Ark of the Covenant. However, this was probably not typical of the Greek east: besides the enormous mosaic map of Bible lands (c.24 × 6 m, of which 10.5 × 5 m survives, c.mid-6th century, from a church at Madaba in Jordan), depicting Jerusalem in considerable and accurate detail and showing some affinities to the Tabula Peutingeriana, *periploi* continued to be produced in the Byzantine era. These *periploi* are sometimes referred to as "Portolans", but the latter are a later, mainly western Mediterranean phenomenon, beginning c.1300 and involving use of the magnetic compass; there are a few Greek examples, but dating only from the 16th century.

The main Byzantine contribution to cartography came with the rediscovery of Ptolemy, of whom general knowledge seems to have died out in both the west and the east around 600, by the monk Maximos Planudes in 1295. The manuscript he found had no maps; so Planudes had a set made, and these so impressed the emperor Andronikos II Palaiologos that he had copies made for himself. There are two items to be noted here: first, there were in Constantinople c.1300 cartographers skilled enough to produce good maps from Ptolemy's text – cartography had not died out; second, all manuscripts (in the various recensions) of Ptolemy extant today are derived from Planudes's initiative. By 1406 there was a Latin translation of Ptolemy, dedicated to Pope Gregory XII, and the stage was set for the rebirth of European cartography.

CHARLES L. MURISON

Further Reading

Bradford, E.D.S., *Ulysses Found*, London: Hodder and Stoughton, 1963; New York: Harcourt Brace, 1964

Bunbury, E.H., *History of Ancient Geography among the Greeks and Romans*, 2 vols, London: John Murray, 1883; reprinted New York: Dover, 1959

Dilke, O.A.W., *Greek and Roman Maps*, London: Thames and Hudson, 1985

Engels, D., "The Length of Eratosthenes' Stade", *American Journal of Philology*, 106 (1985): pp. 298–311

Harley, J.B. and David Woodward (editors), *The History of Cartography*, vol. 1, Chicago: University of Chicago Press, 1987

Hunger, Herbert, *Die hochsprachliche profane Literatur der Byzantiner*, vol. 1, Munich: Beck, 1978

Cassius Dio c.AD 164 –after AD 229

Historian

Cassius Dio originally came from the prosperous city of Nicaea in Bithynia in northern Asia Minor, but was probably taken to Rome as a boy when his father Cassius Apronianus became a senator. Thus Dio, born in the Greek east and brought up in Rome, had a dual heritage. Following in his father's footsteps, he entered the Senate under Commodus (reigned AD 180–92), was awarded a praetorship by Pertinax (AD 193), and, probably around AD 204, was made consul by Septimius Severus (AD

193–211). His career continued to prosper under Severus Alexander (AD 222–35), who in quick succession appointed Dio proconsul of Africa (c.AD 223), legate of Dalmatia (c.AD 224–26), and legate of Upper Pannonia (c.AD 226–28). These appointments were certainly prestigious, but Dio, who was no longer a young man, was thereby prevented from spending much time in either Italy (where he had a pleasant villa at Capua) or Bithynia. In the end, Dio did not forget his eastern roots, although much of his adult life was spent serving Rome around the empire. After holding his second consulship in AD 229, he retired to Bithynia to nurse his bad feet (80. 4. 2–5. 3). The precise date of his death remains unknown.

Dio's most important achievement is his monumental historical work, the *Roman History*, which was written in Greek and originally contained 80 books narrating events from the origins of Rome until AD 229. The Bithynian senator claims that the impetus to write history came from Septimius Severus. This emperor had so much enjoyed Dio's earlier work on the dreams and portents that heralded his principate that he wrote a letter to say so (72. 23. 1): that same night Dio dreamed that a divine power ordered him to write a historical narrative of Severus' rise to power, and the success of this work eventually resulted in Dio composing the *Roman History*. Today we have *Roman History* 36–55. 9 (covering the years 69–6 BC) almost intact, but the remaining books are preserved only in fragments and epitomes. Proudly Dio claims that he spent 10 years conducting historical research and 12 years actually writing the narrative until the death of Severus in AD 211 (72. 23. 5). This assertion is designed to generate confidence in the *Roman History* as a well-crafted historical work and echoes the claims of previous historians writing in Greek: Diodorus Siculus claims to have spent 30 years on his history, and Dionysius of Halicarnassus 22 years. Above all, Dio was influenced by Thucydides, from whom phrases, ideas, and techniques were borrowed. So, Dio's Fabius Rullus argues against excessive retaliation for a Latin revolt (fr. 36. 1) in a way that recalls Thucydides' Diodotus during the Mytilenean debate. Dio's stylistic and intellectual debts to the 5th-century BC historian Thucydides can be seen as symptomatic of the Greek cultural revival known as the Second Sophistic.

At the same time, Dio owed much to the Roman historiographical tradition. For chronology the *Roman History* uses the official Roman year dated by consuls as the principal structural device, but, like Tacitus, Dio does not allow himself to be restricted by this potentially rigid annalistic format. So Dio organizes material along biographical lines, particularly when narrating the principate: individual emperors are often both introduced and allowed to leave the stage with separate character sketches. Likewise, Dio was prepared to narrate events that spanned several years in one continuous segment of narrative, particularly in the case of foreign campaigns (49. 19–33). Moreover, he clearly knew Latin: he appears to have read Seneca's *Apocolocyntosis* (60. 35. 3–4) and laments the fact that he cannot find a direct equivalent for the Latin word *auctoritas*, which he transliterates in Greek (53. 3. 4–5).

Ideologically, Dio valued the stability created by the principate and observed pithily that "Monarchy sounds unpleasant, but it is the most practical form of government under which to live" (44. 1. 2). This stance does not make him uncritical of incompetent emperors, and even Septimius Severus, who

inspired Dio to write history, is given a balanced treatment. We are repeatedly offered perspectives on the principate that reflect the senatorial point of view. So, when Commodus decapitates an ostrich and brandishes the head at the senators, Dio discreetly hints to his colleagues that they can avoid laughing by chewing on the laurel leaves of their crowns (72. 21. 1–2). In his narrative Dio's judgement on particular emperors often rests on how well they treated his fellow senators.

Nor does Dio's general approval of the imperial system lead him to ignore the difficulties of historical inquiry under the principate, when the size of the empire and the secrecy in which important decisions were taken made it difficult to reconstruct events (53. 19). Dio, who spent his professional life working under the emperors, was fascinated by the transition from republic to principate, as is clear from the fact that the *Roman History* devotes much more space to this period than to any other. Today historians especially value Dio's sophisticated and clear narrative of the triumviral era, and passages such as the unusually frank reassessment of Cicero (38. 12) show that Dio can offer us valuable alternative perspectives on leading historical figures of the period. Perhaps Dio's own experiences of confronting turbulent armies in Pannonia (80. 4) may have sharpened his interest in the triumviral age as a whole.

Dio was the last substantial writer of annalistic history from the ancient world whose work is at least partly extant. The Byzantine scholar Photios had read Dio and regarded him as a much clearer writer than Thucydides. Perhaps this enthusiastic response was partly because Dio's subject matter in the *Roman History* must by its very nature have appealed to educated readers in the Byzantine world, who saw their state as a continuation of the Roman empire. Many fragments of the *Roman History* have survived thanks to the efforts of the excerptors who worked for the emperor Constantine VII Porphyrogennetos (913–959). There is a useful epitome of books 36–80 made in the late 11th century by John Xiphilinos, who selected episodes from Dio that he regarded as particularly entertaining or enlightening. Moreover, early in the 12th century, John Zonaras wrote an *Epitome of Histories*, which was a universal history documenting events from the creation until AD 1118. A comparison between the *Epitome* and extant portions of the *Roman History* shows that Zonaras tended to paraphrase Dio fairly freely, but the Byzantine historian did preserve a version of *Roman History* 1–21 (now lost), which served as one of his chief sources for early Roman history. Subsequently, in Paris, the king's printer Robert Estienne produced in 1548 the first printed edition of Dio's *Roman History*, which ensured that the work was widely read. Finally, Dio's *Roman History* was competently edited by U.P. Boissevain (1895–1931), and his text still serves as the starting point for most modern editions.

RHIANNON ASH

See also Historiography

Biography

Born at Nicaea c.AD 164, Cassius Dio was educated in Rome and followed his father into the Senate. He held the consulship twice and after the second time (AD 229) he retired to Bithynia where he died (date unknown). Dio wrote in Greek a *Roman History* in 80 books, taking events from the origins of Rome to his own day, of which about 20 books survive intact (covering 69–6 BC) and fragments of the rest.

Writings

Roman History, translated by Earnest Cary, 9 vols, London: Heinemann, and New York: Macmillan, 1914–27 (Loeb edition; several reprints)

Further Reading

Aalders, G.J.D., "Cassius Dio and the Greek World", *Mnemosyne*, 39 (1986): pp. 282–304

Barnes, T.D., "The Composition of Cassius Dio's *Roman History*", *Phoenix*, 38 (1984): pp. 240–55

Brunt, P.A., "On Historical Fragments and Epitomes", *Classical Quarterly*, 30 (1980): pp. 477–94

Gowing, Alain M., *The Triumviral Narratives of Appian and Cassius Dio*, Ann Arbor: University of Michigan Press, 1992

Gowing, Alain M., "Cassius Dio on the Reign of Nero" in *Aufstieg und Niedergang der römischen Welt*, edited by Hildegard Temporini et al., 2. 34. 3, Berlin: de Gruyter 1997, 2558–90

Lintott, A., "Cassius Dio and the History of the Late Roman Republic" in *Aufstieg und Niedergang der römischen Welt*, edited by Hildegard Temporini et al., 2. 34. 3, Berlin: de Gruyter, 1997, 2497–2523

Marincola, John, *Authority and Tradition in Ancient Historiography*, Cambridge and New York: Cambridge University Press, 1997

Millar, Fergus, *A Study of Cassius Dio*, Oxford: Clarendon Press, 1964

Moscovich, M.J., "Historical Compression in Cassius Dio's Account of the Second Century BC", *Ancient World*, 8 (1983): pp. 137–43

Pelling, C.B.R., "Biographical History? Cassius Dio on the Early Principate" in *Portraits: Biographical Representation in the Greek and Latin Literature of the Roman Empire*, edited by M.J. Edwards and Simon Swain, Oxford: Clarendon Press, 1997

Rich, J.W., "Dio and Augustus" in *History as Text: The Writing of Ancient History*, edited by Averil Cameron, London: Duckworth, 1989

Swain, Simon, *Hellenism and Empire: Language, Classicism and Power in the Greek World AD 50–250*, Oxford: Clarendon Press, and New York: Oxford University Press, 1996

Swan, P.M., "Cassius Dio on Augustus: A Poverty of Annalistic sources?", *Phoenix*, 41 (1987): pp. 272–91

Swan, P.M., "How Cassius Dio Composed his Augustan Books: Four Studies" in *Aufstieg und Niedergang der römischen Welt*, edited by Hildegard Temporini et al., vol. 2. 34. 3, Berlin: de Gruyter 1997, 2524–57

Catalans

The origins of Catalonia and the Catalan language lie in the break-up of the Roman province of Tarraconensis by its Visigothic rulers before the invasion of Muslim armies from north Africa in the early 8th century AD. In 801 Charlemagne conquered Barcelona and in 865 the Spanish March based around Tarragona, Barcelona, and Girona was set up by Charles the Bald (843–77). It was he who appointed Guifre or Wifred the Hairy as count of the Spanish March. Latterday Catalans view Wifred's reign (870–97) as the beginning of a distinct Catalan political and cultural identity. In 1151 the crown of Aragon and the county of Barcelona were united by marriage. The two areas remained distinct but in a political confederation united by their count-kings. It was in the reign of James I (1213–76) that the commercial and territorial horizons of Aragon-Catalonia were dramatically enlarged and the maritime potential of Catalonia was extended from a local to a Mediterranean-wide role.

In the years 1229–31 the island of Majorca was conquered. By the mid-1280s the merchant marine of Barcelona and Majorca had established regular sailings to Meson, Palermo, Tunis, Alexandria, and Constantinople and outside the Straits of Gibraltar to Morocco, England, and Flanders. Catalan was set fair to be one of the commercial languages of the Mediterranean in the 14th century.

Politically and militarily the Aragonese-Catalan confederation took a major role in Mediterranean politics from the 1280s. As David Abulafia has pointed out, it is not clear whether trade followed the flag or whether the monarchs of Aragon-Catalonia had their political interests dictated by the commercial interests of their merchant communities. In 1282 Peter III of Aragon (1279–85) became king of Sicily through the right of his wife Constance, the granddaughter of the emperor Frederick II, and following the Sicilian Vespers, which had expelled Angevin garrisons from the island. The long and bitter war of the Sicilian Vespers (1282–1302) between the Angevins and their Aragonese rivals was to have repercussions for the Aegean area and for Catalan involvement in that region. In 1315 the Angevin–Aragonese struggle for Sicily spilled over to the Peloponnese when Ferrando of Majorca, cousin of the Aragonese ruler of Sicily, sought to wrest control of the principality of Achaea from the Angevin-backed ruler Louis of Burgundy. After a good beginning, Ferrando's over-confident behaviour led to his defeat and death at the Battle of Manolada near Elis on 5 July 1316.

The Treaty of Caltabellota (1302), which brought an end to the war of the Sicilian Vespers, also threw many Catalan mercenaries out of a job. Those in Aragonese employ in Sicily found a new war and a new employer in the Byzantine emperor Andronikos II Palaiologos who in 1303–05 used them to fight the Turks. Falling out with Andronikos, this Catalan Grand Company moved west to Thessaly, plundering its way there through the Byzantine provinces of Thrace and Macedonia, ostensibly in the pay of Charles of Valois who used their presence in the region to support the claims of his wife Catherine de Courtenay as titular Latin empress of Constantinople. In 1310 they were employed by Gautier de Brienne, the duke of Athens, to further his interests in Thessaly and they captured Domokos and Halmyros for him. In 1311 Gautier wished to dismiss most of his Catalan mercenaries now based at Halmyros. These defied him and he was forced to send an army to remove them. On Monday, 15 March 1311 the Frankish army of more than 700 knights was annihilated near Halmyros and control of the duchy of Athens and Thebes passed to the Catalan Company. In 1312 they recognized the overlordship of Frederick II of Sicily (1296–1337). Catalan rule over the duchy lasted until 1388.

PETER LOCK

Summary

From their capital Barcelona the Catalans became a major commercial and maritime power in the 13th and 14th centuries. Having fought in Sicily as allies of the Aragonese, many Catalans found employment as mercenaries to the Byzantine emperor Andronikos II who used them to fight the Turks in 1303–05. The duchy of Athens and Thebes was ruled by the Catalan Company from 1311 to 1388.

Further Reading

Abulafia, David, *The Western Mediterranean Kingdoms, 1200–1500: The Struggle for Dominion*, London and New York: Longman, 1997

Berg, B., "The Moreote Expedition of Ferrando of Majorca in the Aragonese *Chronicle of Morea*", *Byzantion*, 55 (1985): pp. 69–90

Hillgarth, J.N., *The Spanish Kingdoms, 1250–1516*, 2 vols, Oxford: Clarendon Press, 1976–78

Laiou, Angeliki E., *Constantinople and the Latins: The Foreign Policy of Andronicus II, 1282–1328*, Cambridge, Massachusetts: Harvard University Press, 1972

Lock, Peter, *The Franks in the Aegean, 1204–1500*, London and New York: Longman, 1995

Setton, Kenneth M., *Catalan Domination of Athens, 1311–1388*, Cambridge, Massachusetts: Mediaeval Academy of America, 1948; revised edition, London: Variorum, 1975

Catana

City in Sicily

The city of Catana lies on the coast in the centre of eastern Sicily, its harbour facing the Ionian sea – an excellent site for a port. It occupied the north side of a fertile volcanic plain in the shadow of Mount Etna; its sister city, Leontini, was situated to the south. No doubt the intention of the Ionians in founding the two cities was to control access to the rich agricultural plain. Catana was also located near a delta formed by three major river valleys reaching westwards into the interior, which was occupied by Sicels.

The Ionian colony at Catana was founded *c*.729 BC by Chalcidians from the mother colony of Sicilian Naxos, itself founded by a group of Chalcidians from Euboea. The *oikistes*, or founder, was Euarchus. In the early period a great variety of Greek pottery – Corinthian, Athenian, Chalcidian, Chian, East Greek, and Spartan – indicates that the native Sicels were well acquainted with the Greeks, primarily through trade. Once the Ionian colonists settled on the site, relations appear to have been relatively peaceful, with the archaeological evidence suggesting that the two groups lived amicably side by side. Thucydides (6. 2), however, says that the Sicels retreated inland and to the north with the arrival of the Ionians on the east coast of the island.

Catana was autonomous in the Archaic period, with a very active political and economic life. Greek goods gradually made their way into the interior along the river valleys; archaeological evidence indicates that the area was fairly well Hellenized by the end of the 6th century BC. The lawgiver Charondas (*c*.500) established one of the earliest codes of Greek law, pertaining primarily to the giving of evidence in court and rules governing contracts. These laws were successful in retaining aristocratic power without dissension among the colonists, and his law code became famous throughout Greece. Stesichorus, the choral lyric poet, was also resident in Catana at this time. Only fragments of his work survive, but they show that his treatment of myth was an important stage in the transition from epic to tragedy in Greek literature.

By the early 5th century BC the city had lost its autonomy and was under Syracusan control. In 475 Hieron I, tyrant at Syracuse, invaded Catana and expelled the inhabitants. He repopulated the site with Dorians and mercenaries and renamed the city Aetna, setting up his son Deinomenes as ruler, but the Catanians returned in 461 and the old name was restored. Later in the century, during the Sicilian expedition (415–413 BC), the city supported Athens, which used it as a base for attacks against Syracuse. When the Athenians were defeated, the city was occupied by Dionysus I, another tyrant ruling at Syracuse, who sold the entire population into slavery and settled his Campanian mercenaries there. From then on Catana formed part of the Syracusan empire. Diodorus Siculus (14. 59. 2) relates that the lands were given to the Sicels with the Ionians remaining in exile until 358, when the survivors moved to Tauromenium (Taormina). The Campanian mercenaries still inhabited Catana when it was conquered by Rome in 263 BC during the First Punic War.

In the 5th century the city was celebrated by the poet Aeschylus in his now lost play *The Women of Aetna* (*c*.470 BC), and it was the centrepiece for Pindar's *Pythian* 1, a choral lyric composed for the festival in honour of Apollo at Delphi, at which the major event was a musical competition for a hymn to the god.

Little is known about the physical appearance of the Greek city, as its remains were largely obliterated by the lava flow of 1669. Architectural fragments on the acropolis, a sanctuary of Demeter, long theatre walls, and the contents of Hellenistic graves outside the ancient city, do however attest to its presence.

In the 2nd and 1st centuries BC the city was given the status of a *civitas decumana*, flourishing under the Roman Republic, although it suffered damage in the First Slave War (135 BC). Catana became a Roman colony under Augustus (21 BC). Most of the extant physical remains in Catana date to the Roman imperial period, when the city was very prosperous. Having maintained and improved its port facilities, it served as a centre for the shipment of timber and basalt millstones.

The vast majority of Sicilian craftsmen were Greek-speaking, and the epigraphical evidence indicates that even into the Roman period roughly half the population on the island still spoke Greek, while the other half spoke Latin. The Greek calendar continued in use into the early imperial period, and the year was officially dated according to the eponymous priesthood of Zeus Olympios at Syracuse. It appears that Sicily was never fully Romanized and that Greek was widely spoken, especially in the rural areas, which were hardly affected by the Roman incursion. In fact, much of the island seems to have remained Greek until the end of the Roman empire. Catana retained its importance through the Byzantine period, and was one of the first and most important Christian communities in Sicily.

The Chalcidians were the earliest and most prolific colonizers on the eastern coast of the island, laying claim to the whole northeastern part of Sicily in two decades with the establishment of colonies there – one of the first settlements was located at Catana. Through peaceful coexistence with the native Sicels, Catana was a vital factor in the establishment of a Greek foothold on the eastern coast of the island, controlling as it did the agricultural products of the fertile volcanic plain and, by virtue of its excellent harbour, serving as a base for Greeks trading with settlements further to the west along the shores of the Mediterranean Sea. Catana played an important role in the Hellenization of the eastern central part of the island, a process so successful that the city was emblematic of a strong Greek presence in Sicily long after it became part of the Roman empire.

KATHLEEN DONAHUE SHERWOOD

See also Sicily

Summary

City in eastern Sicily founded by Ionian Greeks *c.*729 BC from Sicilian Naxos. Independent in the Archaic period, Catana came under Syracusan control in the 5th century BC and remained so until conquered by Rome in 263 BC. It became a Roman colony under Augustus but like the rest of Sicily remained largely Greek-speaking until the end of the empire.

Further Reading

Boardman, John, *The Greeks Overseas: Their Early Colonies and Trade*, 4th edition, London and New York: Thames and Hudson, 1999

Coarelli, Filippo and Mario Torelli, *Sicilia*, Laterza, 1984, pp. 326–38

Dunbabin, T.J., *The Western Greeks: The History of Sicily and South Italy from the Foundation of the Greek Colonies to 480 BC*, Oxford: Clarendon Press, 1968

Finley, M.I., *Ancient Sicily*, revised edition, London: Chatto and Windus, and Totowa, New Jersey: Rowman and Littlefield, 1979

Gabba, Emilio and Georges Vallet (editors), *La Sicilia antica*, Naples: Lombardi, 1992

Holloway, R. Ross, *The Archaeology of Ancient Sicily*, London and New York: Routledge, 1991

Holm, Adolf, *Catania antica*, Catania: Guaitolini, 1925

Libertini, Guido, *Scritti su Catania antica*, Catania: Rotary Club di Catania, 1981

Sjöqvist, Erik, *Sicily and the Greeks: Studies in the Interrelationship between the Indigenous Populations and the Greek Colonists*, Ann Arbor: University of Michigan Press, 1973

Stillwell, Richard (editor), *The Princeton Encyclopedia of Classical Sites*, Princeton, New Jersey: Princeton University Press, 1976, pp. 442–3

Vallet, Georges, *Le Monde grec colonial d'Italie du Sud et de Sicile*, Rome: École Française de Rome, 1996

Wilson, R.J.A., "Towns of Sicily during the Roman Empire" in *Aufstieg und Niedergang der römischen Welt*, edited by Hildegard Temporini *et al.*, 2. 11. 1, Berlin: de Gruyter, 1988, 123–36

Wilson, R.J.A., *Sicily under the Roman Empire: The Archaeology of a Roman Province, 36 BC–AD 535*, Warminster: Aris and Phillips, 1990

Caucasus

Region between the Black Sea and the Caspian Sea

The Caucasian mountains, which, with their many rivers, lakes, and passes, divide the northern Caucasus from Transcaucasia, were familiar to the Greeks, but they knew only the name and massiveness of this range. Herodotus was the first to give information about the mountains and the peoples who dwelt there, living a primitive and barbarian life. Alexander the Great was mistaken in thinking that the Hindu Kush was part of the Caucasian range. Although Strabo gives a good description of the mountains, ancient authors were wont to mislocate them to or conflate them with the Urals as well as the Hindu Kush.

This very distant and mysterious mountain region had its place in Greek mythology. The Caucasus was the land of Arimasps and of griffins, who guarded its gold treasure. Prometheus, having stolen the secret of fire and given it to man, was punished by being chained to Mount Elbrus, one of the highest peaks in the Caucasus, while an eagle sent by Zeus picked continuously at his liver until he was unbound by Heracles, who slew the eagle. There are several local versions of the myth and cult of Prometheus. In Georgian folklore Prometheus is called Amirani. In Greece itself there are many other versions: for example, in Athens he was worshipped by potters and in the Academy; in Thebes one of the Cabiri is named Prometheus and his son is Aetnaeus.

To the south of the Caucasian mountains lies Transcaucasia, known to the Greeks as home to the ancient civilizations of Colchis, Iberia, Armenia, and Albania, the first three being familiar to them but the latter beyond their interest and involvement.

Colchis was the best known thanks to the establishment of the Ionian colonies of Phasis, Gyenos, and Dioscurias on its Black Sea coast in the mid-6th century BC. In Greek imagination Colchis was the final destination of Jason and the Argonauts, who sailed there to retrieve the golden fleece. This, one of the most popular Greek myths, had a very strong impact on ancient art, and over several centuries artists depicted scenes from it. One of the most popular figures in Greek literature and art was Medea, the barbarian Colchian princess, granddaughter of Helios and daughter of Aeëtes, king of Colchis. Thanks to her sorcery and love Jason was able to depart from Colchis with the golden fleece; he also took Medea, and later married her. When he attempted to repudiate Medea she killed their children. The popularity of herbal medicines in ancient Greece was linked to Medea and her magical powers.

For Greeks Colchis was a land rich in gold, iron, timber, and honey. Ancient authors state that these natural resources and raw materials, together with slaves, were exported to Greece. In their writings it was alleged that particles of gold were washed up by the mountain streams of the Caucasus, and that Colchians used to place fleeces in the water to catch them. This is but one of many interpretations of the golden fleece in ancient Greek literature. It is thought that when Greeks initially arrived in the vicinity of Phasis they saw a very beautiful species of bird, previously unknown to them, which they started to export to Greece. They named it "bird from the Phasis river" (pheasant).

Colchian elite culture was strongly influenced by Greek. This is reflected in architecture, sculpture, goldwork, etc. Greek craftsmen were employed; the cults of Apollo, Dionysus, Helios, Heracles, and the Dioscuri were common; Greek was widespread as the official and religious language. Greek influence continued via Byzantium from the 4th century AD with the adoption of Christianity as the state religion of Egrisi (successor to Colchis; modern western Georgia) and Iberia (eastern Georgia). Early Christian church architecture showed strong Byzantine influence, and the Georgian Church itself was a

Byzantine offshoot. In the medieval period, Georgian icons were opulently decorated with enamel, initially influenced by Byzantine practice before a distinct Georgian school grew up (as was the case with religious mural painting and mosaics). A new wave of Greek settlers (known as Pontic Greeks) appeared from Anatolia in the wake of the Graeco-Turkish conflicts of the later l9th century. They settled in western Georgia in new villages which they established, and preserved their linguistic and cultural identity. Many "returned" to Greece following the collapse of the Soviet Union.

Iberia and Armenia were subject to weaker Greek influence. The predominant external influence was Achaemenid Persia. But the subsequent creation of Hellenistic kingdoms in the east brought the full weight of Hellenic culture to bear. This was reflected in the layout and architecture of cities, in crafts, and everyday life. Armenia was also Christianized and enjoyed close links with Byzantium.

GOCHA R. TSETSKHLADZE

Summary

A region to the east of the Black Sea, between it and the Caspian, the Caucasus was known to the ancient Greeks as a distant land of mysterious mountains. Many legends were located there. The Transcaucasian regions of Colchis (western Georgia), Iberia (eastern Georgia), and Armenia were Christianized early and subject to Greek influence. Many Pontic Greeks settled in western Georgia in the 19th century.

Further Reading

Boardman, John, *The Diffusion of Classical Art in Antiquity*, Princeton, New Jersey: Princeton University Press, and London: Thames and Hudson, 1994

Braund, David C., *Georgia in Antiquity*, Oxford: Clarendon Press, and New York: Oxford University Press, 1994

Chahin, M., *The Kingdom of Armenia*, London: Croom Helm, 1987

Tsetskhladze, Gocha R., *Die Griechen in der Kolchis*, Amsterdam: Hakkert, 1998

Cavafy, Constantine 1863–1933

Poet

Constantine Cavafy is widely regarded as the most important poet of modern Greece. Although he was contemporary with Kostis Palamas and began publishing in the same year (1886) as Palamas did, Cavafy's main creative period coincides with Palamas's decline. For Cavafy was, in his own words, "a poet of old age"; he did not reach poetic maturity until he was 40. Thus Palamas belongs more to the 19th century, while Cavafy is a poet of the 20th century, both chronologically and in spirit.

Cavafy has often been regarded by Greek critics as sui generis, since the Greek literary currents of his own day had little detectable influence on his mature poetry. This view, however, ignores the profound and lasting impact of Cavafy's English education, his exposure to Byzantium through Gibbon, his initial encounter with the Classics in English schoolbooks, and his extensive knowledge of English literature. Even Cavafy's metrical experiments can be traced to English prosodic forebears. Thus, rather than coming from nowhere in

literary terms, Cavafy can more plausibly be seen in the context of the English schooling he received between the ages of 9 and 16 in Liverpool and London.

Cavafy shows little interest in the preoccupations of late 19th- and early 20th-century Greek poetry: irredentism, the Greek landscape, and folk poetry. He does not advert constantly to Greece's glorious Classical past, preferring instead to explore the unfashionably decadent Byzantine and Hellenistic periods. The increasingly explicit homoeroticism of Cavafy's love poetry is another discordant feature, by contemporaneous standards.

Cavafy's enduring interest in Byzantium dates from a very early stage in his poetic career. The reason for this interest may well be connected with the fact that Cavafy had family roots in Constantinople. A second factor is that, for a Greek of the diaspora, late antiquity, when the centre of Hellenism was no longer Athens, held a particular fascination. Cavafy was able, by means of Byzantium, to lay claim to an elevated genealogy, both for himself (as a descendant of the Phanariots) and for his poetry, as central to (through being descended from) the poetic tradition of Byzantine Egypt, rather than peripheral to the modern Athenian school. Between 1882 and 1885 Cavafy lived in Constantinople. It was probably during this period that he began to acquire his prodigious knowledge of the Byzantine empire and its chroniclers.

Cavafy described himself as a "historian poet", and the vast majority of his poems are set in the recent or distant past. He divided his poetry into three categories: historical, philosophical, and erotic. Although there is some overlap between these categories, Cavafy's thematic collections (the most finalized arrangement of his poems) follow this distinction, grouping poems according to their predominant theme. In the historical sections of his thematic collections, poems are arranged in chronological order of the events to which they refer.

The philosophical poems, which have sometimes been called "didactic" by critics, are fewest in number and mostly fall into the earlier section of Cavafy's recognized (or canonical) poetry. Like many of Cavafy's poems, the philosophical poems can be read on two levels: as straightforward moralistic advice, or as satires on heroic attitudes.

The historical poems often take as their focus minor characters, such as Cleopatra's son Caesarion, or major characters in ignominious moments. Antony is depicted after his defeat at Actium, consoling himself with illusions of the Alexandria he will never reign over. Byzantine emperors are seen wearing jewels made of glass, or taking the schema in indecent haste just before dying, or again abandoning their finery like an actor's mask to sneak away. The historical moment is often one of transience: Christanity is replacing paganism; empires are crumbling; cultures, ideologies, and languages are under threat.

Cavafy's erotic poetry is distinguished by an apparent absence of higher sentiments, and a preoccupation with physical beauty and pleasure. Set in the past, these poems form a commentary, as do the historical poems, on historiography and the relationship between time, memory, and art. The erotic poems include epitaphs and poems of poetics. The epitaphs focus on beautiful, prematurely deceased, young men, who have usually lived lives of unbridled pleasure. The poems of poetics talk about art, mostly in the first person. One of the

Constantine Cavafy, Alexandrian poet

best-known erotic poems, "To Sensual Pleasure", describes this as sacred and the most important thing in life.

Cavafy was among the first Greek poets to break away from conventional metrical forms, though his experiments are by no means as extreme as those of Sikelianos in "Prologue to Life". Most of Cavafy's poetry is iambic, but line lengths vary, and syncopation and enjambment are widely used. His principal use of the 15-syllable line is for ironic effect. He is also very sparing in his use of rhyme, and never employs it for purely decorative effect. The prosodic understatement of Cavafy's poetry has led to its being perceived as prosaic, and Palamas famously dubbed it "historical journalism".

Cavafy's language is original, even idiosyncratic. It is quite unlike the intentionally poetic demotic of Palamas and his Athenian contemporaries, and makes frequent use of katharevousa morphology and syntax and also of Constantinopolitan idioms. Extreme demoticists and katharevousa supporters alike viewed this mixed language with hostility, and Palamas described Cavafy as "the Karaghiozis of demotic". Cavafy retaliated publicly by politely explaining that he could not understand Palamas's kind of lyricism, and privately by referring to his second-rate brandy as "the Palamas brandy".

Cavafy's reputation in Greece was largely founded posthumously. Admired during his lifetime by a small circle of Alexandrian literati and by a handful of foreigners, most notably E.M. Forster, with whom he became friendly in 1917, Cavafy was virtually ignored in Greece until the last decade of his life. Cavafy's idiosyncratic methods of disseminating his work, in privately printed pamphlets, broadsheets, booklets, and hand-pinned looseleaf collections, were a contributing factor in this lack of recognition. The first published volume of Cavafy's poetry appeared posthumously in 1935. As a perfectionist, constantly revising and even discarding his work, Cavafy seems to have been reluctant to make his poems publicly available in a permanent form.

Cavafy's work has proved puzzling, even to his admirers. Timos Malanos, who was the first to attempt a critical account of it, placed great emphasis on Cavafy's homosexuality, reading the poetry in Freudian terms as a mask for private obsessions. The Marxist critic Stratis Tsirkas attempted to read Cavafy's poems as veiled political allegory. A more influential approach has been George Seferis's attempt to demonstrate that Cavafy used the so-called "mythical method" of Eliot and Joyce, developing a constant parallel between past and present, although this approach may more fruitfully be applied to Seferis's own poetry. Perhaps more useful is the approach of Nasos Vayenas, who views Cavafy's poetic method as a continuous refining of the language of irony. As Cavafy himself, who remains the subtlest critic of his own work, pointed out, the pleasure derived from his poetry is intellectual, rather than emotional.

Cavafy's posthumous influence on Greek poetry, but also on world poetry, has been enormous. His description of himself, in a satirical French press release of around 1930, as "an ultra-modern poet" and "a poet for future generations" has proved uncannily accurate.

SARAH EKDAWI

See also Poetry (Lyric)

Biography

Born in Alexandria in 1863, Cavafy was the son of a wealthy merchant. Educated in England, he lived in Constantinople from 1882 to 1885 and thereafter in Alexandria where he worked for the Egyptian Ministry of Irrigation. His first (privately printed) collection of poems appeared in 1904 but he was little known outside his own circle of literati. He died in 1933 in Alexandria.

Writings

The Complete Poems, translated by Rae Dalven, with an introduction by W.H. Auden, London: Hogarth Press, and New York: Harcourt Brace, 1961; expanded edition, 1976

Further Reading

Bien, Peter, *Constantine Cavafy*, New York: Columbia University Press, 1964
Harvey, Denise (editor), *The Mind and Art of C.P. Cavafy*, Athens: Harvey, 1983
Keeley, Edmund, *Cavafy's Alexandria*, Princeton, New Jersey: Princeton University Press, 1976
Keeley, Edmund, *Modern Greek Poetry: Voice and Myth*, Princeton, New Jersey: Princeton University Press, 1983
Liddell, Robert, *Cavafy: A Critical Biography*, London: Duckworth, 1974; New York: Schocken, 1976
Robinson, Christopher, *C.P. Cavafy*, Bristol: Bristol Classical Press, and New Rochelle, New York: Caratzas, 1988
Sherrard, Philip, *The Marble Threshing Floor: Studies in Modern Greek Poetry*, London: Vallentine Mitchell, and Fair Lawn, New Jersey: Essential, 1956; reprinted Athens: Harvey, 1982

Celibacy

Celibacy refers mainly to a religious attitude towards sexuality that stresses physical chastity and the negation of carnal love. "Celibacy" must be distinguished from "virginity", which implies lifelong sexual abstinence. A virgin body is a celibate body, but the opposite is not necessarily true. Both terms designate not only a particular physical state but also a spiritual one, and sometimes are used interchangeably. The meaning of the Greek term *agamia* (celibacy) can best be understood by its opposition to *gamos* (marriage). In the cultural milieu of Greece, marriage for both sexes is axiomatic. Celibacy, therefore, is unacceptable, unless it is employed in the religious sphere. It is only within this context that celibacy offers to an individual an unconventional but socially acceptable alternative to traditional gender roles. Celibacy, therefore, in the Greek case, is used to indicate the unmarried state of bishops and monastics and in some cases of dedicated religious devotees.

By definition celibacy implies self-sufficiency and separation. It points to a hierarchy of relationships with the divine and establishes superiority. The celibate becomes the symbol of purity and the conveyor of special religious powers. In antiquity sexual abstinence was demanded of priests and priestesses of certain deities. However, in the case of priestesses the main idea of celibacy was that they lived in marital relation to the divine. Thus, old peasant women that could no longer have sexual intercourse were chosen for the position of Pythia at the temple of Apollo at Delphi, serving as "brides" of the god. A few days of sexual restraint were also required of participants in the cults and this was probably connected with the idea that sexual intercourse is polluting because it opens the possibility of demonic infection. As far as male celibacy in antiquity was concerned, one could distinguish two types: first, that of the priest whose celibacy was demanded for purely ritualistic reasons; and secondly the philosophically grounded celibacy of such groups as the Pythagoreans and the Stoic philosopher Epictetus, who saw the philosopher's task as necessitating a detachment from the mundane requirements of family care. Yet, it is worth noting here that in pre-Christian times celibacy was also considered, particularly by the Athenians, as "evil" because it prevented the reproduction of the human race and negated the "natural laws" of human existence. Plato and Plutarch even mention that special laws existed against celibacy.

Though in antiquity celibacy seemed primarily to serve a ritual function, in the early Christian Church it came to serve an ethical one as well. The celibate state was extolled by the Church Fathers and from then on was regarded as explicitly superior to being sexually active, even within the context of marriage. In the first centuries of Christianity, due to eschatological expectations, many Christians chose to live in celibacy, for, "when they rise from the dead, they neither marry nor are given in marriage, but are like angels in heaven" (Mark 12: 25). In the beginning, both celibate men and celibate women lived in the same communities and this cohabitation of the sexes was viewed as involving a more rigorous ascetical effort. Thus was created the institution of *syneisakton parthenon* or the *subintroductae* (celibate women cohabiting with clerics or monks), which, however, was condemned by the First Ecumenical Council in 325 (canon 3).

Celibacy as an anticipation of the "angelic life" led some monastics to the egotistic belief that this state of being was superior to the one followed by married Christians, and created a conflict with the ecclesiastical administration. Around 340 the Council of Gangra threatened with excommunication all those who believed that no person living in a state of marriage had any hope of approaching God. The Church Fathers defended the positive value of the nuptial union against any form of heresy which denied the body and the realities of marriage. They argued that marriage and celibacy, although they involved different practices, were based on the same theology and spirituality. Moreover, both celibacy and marriage were perceived by them as referring to a spiritual state of interiorized chastity – a chastity of the soul and mind. It is worth noting here that, when the Fathers spoke of virginity and celibacy, their positions were frequently antithetical and complementary. Thus, one cannot reduce them simply to a single insight. However, St John Chrysostom, who may be regarded as the best explicator of the essence of marriage, argued that its sum and substance is love and its main purpose the unification of humankind. Such love may be carnal at the outset, but gradually it should become spiritualized. Here, celibacy emerges as the natural development of marriage.

This positive view of marriage is also apparent in the context of sacerdotal celibacy, which was regarded in the East as a matter of personal choice. In the West the Council of Elvira (306) decreed the obligatory celibacy of all priests and bishops, but the eastern Churches were disinclined to take this position, hence allowing wedded bishops and priests as long as they had been married only once and their wives were neither widows nor divorcees (Apostolic Canon 17, 18). However, a later development of canon law reserved the highest ranks of the Church to unmarried clergy. This rule was established first in 528 by Justinian I and was confirmed by the decrees of the Quinisext Council in 629. Celibacy became mandatory for bishops by the 12th canon of the Council in Trullo (692), which remained in effect throughout the Byzantine era: readers and cantors could marry after ordination, while ordained priests, deacons, and subdeacons could retain already established marriages. Bishops, however, had to be separated from their wives, who had to enter a convent. Today Greek Orthodox priests are allowed either to marry or to take monastic vows prior to ordination. Thus, a hierarchy has been established in the Church in which the male celibates occupy the highest ranks. Wedded clergy are considered as spiritually advanced only when abstaining from sexual relations, a requirement for the celebration of the Eucharist. Such a view is derived from the association of purity with celibacy and of sexuality with pollution, particularly in the sacred sphere.

Celibacy is also a prerequisite for both male and female Orthodox monastics, who take vows to remain chaste. In this context, celibacy is considered necessary for spiritual advancement and is also viewed as betrothal to Christ in imitation of his union with the Church. It is worth mentioning, however, that women in the early Church were seen as having a greater need for celibacy than men, not only because they had an opportunity to serve God but also as a means of redemption. Although the institutional celibacy of nuns today is not connected with sacerdotalism, in the early Church it was associated with the order of deaconesses who, like deacons, were ordained to their office and assisted bishops and priests in the pastoral care of the faithful and especially of women. The Fourth Ecumenical Council in 451 prohibited marriage after ordination for deaconesses (canon 15) who were mainly selected out of female monastics, widows who had been married only once, or bishops' wives.

In Greece today non-institutional lay celibacy is found in the context of religious brotherhoods and sisterhoods, whose members choose to remain unmarried out of devotion, without, however, taking any monastic vows to that effect. This type of celibacy concerns particularly women since in the Greek cultural context there is no place for spinsterhood.

ELENI SOTIRIU

See also Bishops, Marriage, Priesthood

Further Reading

Clark, Gillian, *Women in Late Antiquity: Pagan and Christian Life-Styles*, Oxford: Clarendon Press, and New York: Oxford University Press, 1993

Cloke, Gillian, *This Female Man of God: Women and Spiritual Power in the Patristic Age, 350–450*, London and New York: Routledge, 1995

Ecumenical Patriarchate, "The Place of the Woman in the Orthodox Church and the Question of Ordination of Women", *Interorthodox Symposium*, edited by Gennadios Limouris, Katerini: Tertios, 1992

Evdokimov, Paul, *The Sacrament of Love: The Nuptial Mystery in the Light of the Orthodox Tradition*, Crestwood, New York: St Vladimir's Seminary Press, 1985

Evdokimov, Paul, *Woman and the Salvation of the World: A Christian Anthropology on the Charisms of Women*, Crestwood, New York: St Vladimir's Seminary Press, 1994

Galatariotou, Catia, "Eros and Thanatos: A Byzantine Hermit's Conception of Sexuality", *Byzantine and Modern Greek Studies*, 13 (1989): pp. 95–137

Gregory of Nyssa, *Traité de la virginité*, edited and translated by Michel Aubineau, Paris: Cerf, 1966 (Sources Chrétiennes 119)

Gregory of Nyssa, *Ascetical Works*, translated by Virginia Woods Callahan, Washington, D.C.: Catholic University of America, 1967 (The Fathers of the Church, vol. 58)

Gregory of Nyssa, *De Virginitate* in *Patrologia Graeca*, edited by J.-P. Migne, vol. 45, pp. 317–416

John Chrysostom, *De Virginitate* in *Patrologia Graeca*, edited by J.-P. Migne, vol. 48, pp. 533–96

John Chrysostom, *La Virginité*, edited by Herbert Musurillo and Bernard Grillet, Paris: Cerf, 1966 (Sources Chrétiennes 125)

John Chrysostom, *On Virginity: Against Remarriage*, translated by Sally Rieger Shore, Lewiston, New York: Mellen Press, 1983

Lefkowitz, Mary, R., *Women in Greek Myth*, London: Duckworth, and Baltimore: Johns Hopkins University Press, 1986

Meyendorff, John, *Marriage: An Orthodox Perspective*, Crestwood, New York: St Vladimir's Seminary Press, 1984

Špidlík, Tomaš, *The Spirituality of the Christian East: A Systematic Handbook*, Kalamazoo, Michigan: Cistercian Publications, 1986

Viscuso, Patrick, "The Theology of Marriage in the Rudder of Nikodemos the Hagiorite", *Ostkirchliche Studien*, 41 (1992): pp. 187–207

Ware, Timothy, *The Orthodox Church*, 2nd edition, Harmondsworth and New York: Penguin, 1993

Witherington, Ben III, *Women in the Earliest Churches*, Cambridge and New York: Cambridge University Press, 1988

Censorship

Censorship is a means of preventing the expression of ideas, speech, or behaviour. Social, religious, political, military, and other authorities practise censorship in the name of the common good of society, seeking to protect it from heresy, obscenity, treason, or ideological error. In one form or another censorship has existed universally throughout Greek history.

Most of the censorship among the ancient Greeks occurred over religious and political ideas. The common charge was impiety (*asebeia*). Since they believed that the gods could actively help or harm the city state, impious behaviour that might invoke divine wrath was punished. Sparta imposed a rigid system of censorship to protect its militarism: books, music, and even learned men were banned. Greek tyrants exercised censorship to silence and eliminate their opponents. Generally speaking, under the tyrants, and many other rulers, censorship was identical with harsh repression.

Artists were not usually censored, but one notable exception in the first half of the 4th century was the case of the Athenian courtesan Phryne, who was charged with impiety because she modelled for a nude statue of Aphrodite by Praxiteles. Hyperides, pleading her case, tore her clothes off at the height of his defence, and asked the all-male jury if there was anything about her body that was offensive to the gods or man. She was rather quickly acquitted.

Censorship of playwrights occurred on a number of occasions. Euripides, who played no active political role, was charged with *asebeia* by Cleon, as were other dramatists including Aristophanes. Humour was sometimes used to censure behaviour through the weight of public opinion, becoming thereby an unofficial form of censorship to those afraid of being satirized. Those mocked would occasionally seek to punish the jokers. Plato in the *Laws* advocates censorship of those forms of comedy that are cloaks for vicious personal attacks. Tragedies could also be banned. In 493 BC a tragedy written by Phrynichus and produced at the Dionysia on the theme of the failure of the Ionian revolt, and the fall of Miletus deeply moved the audience; fearing turmoil, the authorities fined Phrynichus and banned the play.

Athens, though democratic, censored many thinkers, artists, and intellectuals; they were exiled, imprisoned, or executed, or they took flight. Aeschylus was accused of violating the secrecy of the Eleusinian mysteries. Phidias was also accused of impiety and fled to Olympia. Protagoras, the famous sophist, was censored for his remark "Man is the measure of all things." Accused of atheism, he was banished from Athens and certain of his books were burned.

The beliefs of the Greek philosophers laid them open to various charges. Xenophanes criticized the morality of the Olympian gods as portrayed by Homer and other poets, arguing that their behaviour was shameful. This generated complaints of atheism (impiety) against him. Similarly, Anaxagoras of Clazomenae (c.500–428 BC) had argued that the sun was a hot rock. Convicted of impiety, he was banished from Athens and died in exile at Lampsacus. The real motive for the prosecution was probably to embarrass his patron Pericles.

The most famous case of censorship of a philosopher was the trial of Socrates on charges of corrupting youth (the moral charge) and impiety (the religious charge). The resulting judicial murder on these trumped-up charges was to have a profound influence on many including his most famous pupil, Plato. Oddly it is Plato who in the *Apology* stated the implications of a refusal to accept censorship, and later in the *Republic* himself instituted a system of censorship.

Plato's *Republic* has been widely read since it was first written and it has influenced many who would seek to impose censorship. Plato believed that whatever entered the soul would either develop it or corrupt it. In his utopian Republic a system of censorship is described that would mould the minds of all citizens, but especially the Guardian class, through a system of censored education. This included censorship of music, for Plato believed that music could have a profound impact on the soul and that it was important that the right music be heard at the right time. It should be noted that on several occasions intellectuals sought to censor those they disagreed with; Plato, for instance, wanted to burn the works of Democritus.

Aristotle also advocated a form of educational censorship in his *Politics*. Following the death of Alexander the Great, Aristotle himself became a victim of censorship. He was charged with impiety, but fled "lest Athens sin twice against philosophy".

During the Hellenistic period many states adopted a policy of punishing external political threats quickly, but they usually left native populations and cultures alone. One notable exception was the Seleucid policy of forced Hellenization, which censored any opposition to assimilation. This policy was violently resisted by conservative Jews, whose resistance and success in arms is described in the books of Maccabees and still celebrated at the festival of Hanukkah.

The establishment of great libraries at Alexandria and elsewhere led to two forms of literary censorship. When editors collated manuscripts, they often found variants in the copies and decisions had to be made about which was the "correct" version. Editors could also make important changes when issuing new editions of older works and thereby influence the interpretation of the text.

The other form of literary censorship was mob rule. On a number of occasions mobs or conquerors sacked and burned libraries. The library at Alexandria was damaged and burned during Julius Caesar's siege in 42 BC, by Christians in AD 391, and by Muslims in AD 642. In the Christian era political charges were brought against missionaries and other Christians. Because the worship of the emperor was equated with political loyalty, the Christian refusal to comply led to their persecution – in effect a violent form of censorship. St John was exiled to the island of Patmos and some scholars believe that the apocalyptic style of the book of Revelation was a religious cover that enabled the book to get past the censors.

With the conversion of the emperor Constantine and the legitimization of Christianity, a brief period of toleration occurred, which ended with the triumph of Christianity as the only licit religion. Under the emperor Theodosius I pagan religions were proscribed, sexual regulations were imposed, and the Olympic Games stopped. Theodosius, like Constantine before him and others after him, repressed unorthodox beliefs. The union of Church and state meant that heresies contrary to the Nicene Creed were viewed as political opposition and thus deserving of censure. The emperor Justinian I, seeking political unification through theological orthodoxy, also persecuted heresies, and he closed the philosophical schools in Athens (AD 529).

In the 8th century the iconoclasts vigorously censored the veneration of icons; the two periods of iconoclasm lasted for more than 80 years in total. The Latin conquest of Constantinople in 1204 and the occupation of its western lands led to the censorship of Orthodoxy and of other expressions of Greek culture, and it was only in 1261 that the restoration of Byzantine rule liberated most of the people. The Ottoman conquest involved the suppression of Greek faith and culture to a certain extent, but underground schools sought to preserve and extend Greek faith, language, and culture.

After Greek independence censorship took the forms typical of the modern nation state whose primary concern is state security from political enemies. Political challenges were usually suppressed. Political censorship was, however, limited by a general lack of opportunities in the undeveloped Greek state. One exception was the attempt of the Greek government to standardize Greek through the imposition of a pseudo-Classical language (katharevousa). Efforts were made to develop this artificial variant of Greek at the expense of the demotic form.

From World War I until late in the 20th century Greece experienced typical patterns of wartime censorship, or censorship of unpopular groups. In June 1925 the military rule of General Theodore Pangalos attempted sumptuary legislation to define the length of women's skirts. By the 1930s more serious efforts were made to censor the Greek Communist Party (KKE). In 1936 General George Metaxas became the virtual dictator of Greece and his nationalist ideology led to many forms of censorship. School textbooks either followed the nationalist line or were censored. Youth organizations were established to spread nationalist propaganda and rival organizations such as the Boy Scouts were banned.

During the German occupation in World War II ruthless Nazi censorship was imposed. Reprisal and intimidation occurred in a number of places. In the years after the war the right wing was able to suppress the leftist partisans and communists. In October 1947 the newspapers of the Greek Communist Party and of other leftist groups were banned and prisons were filled with their members.

The election of George Papandreou as Prime Minister in 1963 led to the adoption of policies of reconciliation that sought to end the civil strife of the previous decades and eliminated most censorship. The short-lived Papandreou government was followed by the coup d'état of the military junta in 1967. The lengths of women's skirts and of men's hair were subject to regulation and the media was rigorously censored. In 1974 the junta was replaced by the Karamanlis government and a new democratic era began. Most forms of censorship were then ended.

The current constitution of Greece shows a serious effort to balance individual rights with the responsibility of the government to protect society, but despite its high regard for "the rights of man", censorship is built into it. The Eastern Orthodox Church is described as the "prevailing religion" and translations of the Bible are forbidden unless given "prior sanction by the Autocephalous Church of Greece and the Great Church of Christ in Constantinople" (Article 3). According to Article 13 "Proselytism is prohibited", which means that the preaching of any faith other than Greek Orthodoxy is prohibited. Article 14 declares that the press is free and prohibits prior censorship, but seizure before or after circulation can be done if a publication "offends against the Christian or any other known religion; insults the President of the Republic; discloses state secrets (especially military secrets); or is obscene". Press offences must be punished according to law. The limited freedom of the press is not applied to other forms of mass communication. Article 15 permits censorship of electronic media and the film industry. The objective of communications control is to further the social and cultural mission of the country.

A.J.L. WASKEY, JR

See also Antisemitism, Atheism, Heresy, Iconoclasm, Junta, Media

Further Reading

Aristotle, *The Politics*, translated by Ernest Barker, New York: Oxford University Press, 1962

Barr, Stringfellow, *The Will of Zeus: A History of Greece from the Origins of Hellenic Culture to the Death of Alexander*, Philadelphia: Lippincott, 1961; London: Weidenfeld and Nicolson, 1962

Boatswain, Timothy and Colin Nicholson, *A Traveller's History of Greece*, Adlestrop, Gloucestershire: Windrush Press, 1989

Clogg, Richard, "The 'Black Hole' Revisited", *Index on Censorship*, 16/5 (May 1987)

Derenne, Eudore, *Les Procès d'impiété intentés aux philosophes à Athènes au Vme et au IVme siècles avant J.-C.*, Liege: Vaillant-Carmanne, 1930

Diogenes Laertius, *Lives of Eminent Philosophers*, translated by R.D. Hicks, 2 vols, London: Heinemann, and New York: Putnam, 1925 (Loeb edition)

Goodspeed, Edgar J. (translator), "The First and Second Books of Maccabees" in *The Apocrypha: An American Translation*, New York: Vintage, 1959

"Greece, Free Speech on Trial: Government Stifles Dissent in Macedonia", *Helsinki Watch*, 15/9 (July 1993)

Jaeger, Werner, *Paideia: The Ideals of Greek Culture*, 3 vols, Oxford: Blackwell, 1954–61; reprinted Oxford and New York: Oxford University Press, 1986

Kirk, G.S. and J.E. Raven, *The Presocratic Philosophers: A Critical History with a Selection of Texts*, Cambridge: Cambridge University Press, 1966

McDonald, Robert, "The Greek Press under the Colonels", *Index on Censorship*, 3/4 (Winter 1974)

McDonald, Robert, "A New Press Law", *Index on Censorship*, 6/6 (November–December 1977)

McDonald, Robert, "The Media since the Elections", *Index on Censorship*, 10/2 (March 1982)

Molho, Tony, "Letter from Thessaloniki", *Times Literary Supplement* (20 November 1998)

Nahm, Milton C., *Selections from Early Greek Philosophy*, 4th edition, New York: Appleton Century Crofts, 1964

Plato, *The Apology* [with other works], translated by Harold North Fowler, London: Heinemann, and New York, Macmillan, 1914 (Loeb edition; many reprints)

Plato, *The Laws*, translated by Trevor J. Saunders, Harmondsworth and Baltimore: Penguin, 1970

Plato, *The Republic*, translated by F.M. Cornford, Oxford: Clarendon Press, 1941; New York: Oxford University Press, 1945 (many reprints)

Plutarch, *Plutarch's Lives*, translated by Bernadotte Perrin, 11 vols, London: Heinemann, and New York: Macmillan, 1914–26 (Loeb edition; many reprints)

Popper, Karl, *The Open Society and Its Enemies*, 4th edition, 2 vols, London: Routledge, and New York: Harper, 1962

Sarafis, Marian, "The Black Hole", *Index on Censorship*, 15/2 (February 1986)

Stone, I.F., *The Trial of Socrates*, Boston: Little Brown, and London: Cape, 1988

Todd, S.C., *The Shape of Athenian Law*, Oxford: Clarendon Press, 1993

Vlastos, Gregory (editor), *The Philosophy of Socrates: A Collection of Critical Essays*, New York: Doubleday, 1971

Ceremony, Byzantine

The ceremony (*katastasis* or *taxis*, "arrangement") is a structure of rules and formulas intended to organize social coexistence. The actions, words, and gestures that accompany a ceremony often took on a symbolic character. Ritual actions mark important phases in the life of the Byzantines. Private processions, for example, could be performed for personal celebrations such as weddings, or for funerals; official processions were held by different social groups such as students, guilds, clergymen, and civil servants.

A particular, refined, and complicated form of ceremony was that of the Byzantine court, which controlled the emperor's meetings with his subjects. Furthermore, it reflected his relationship to governmental institutions and to the Church. It also illustrated the power and legitimacy of the imperial throne by means of public display. A strongly religious element is conspicuously associated with all ceremonial actions. Beginning in late antiquity, the Byzantine court ceremonial was continuously developed over the centuries.

The principal written source for Byzantine ceremonies – in addition to visual art (e.g. mosaics, miniatures) – is the so-called *Book of Ceremonies* (*De Ceremoniis*) of the 10th century, a compilation of earlier and contemporary sources inspired by the emperor Constantine VII Porphyrogennetos (913–59) and completed during his reign (he himself wrote the preface). It contains a great deal of information about the procedures at different festivities of sacred and profane character, such as processions on public holidays from the palace into the churches of Constantinople; the emperor's wedding and coronation; the departure and return of the emperor from and to the capital; triumphs after successful military actions; receptions of foreign rulers and diplomats; and banquets. The work therefore probably served as a manual both for the organizers and for the participants in these events. The rules of protocol concerning the motion and dress of the participants were very precise, as well as about which groups of people were allowed to appear when and how they were to pay homage to the emperor. Although the ceremonial was obliged to tradition, it was by no means inflexible, but adapted to changing conditions over time. This is demonstrated in an anonymous text of the 14th century called *De Officiis*. The author repeatedly calls his contemporaries' attention to the fact that certain elements of a ceremony are no longer in use or that some dignities and titles no longer exist. Non-Greek sources can also contribute to the elucidation of ceremonial procedures. The western bishop Liutprand of Cremona who in the 10th century stayed at the Byzantine court several times on official missions was able to observe some of the ceremonies very closely. Liutprand quite impressively describes the splendour and luxury of such spectacles. The throne room was equipped with artificial mobile animals and a mechanical throne that could be raised and lowered automatically. In addition, the *De Ceremoniis* gives an idea of the precious garments and gorgeous ornamentation of the rooms and the routes the processions took. Court ceremonies had their roots in the Roman empire, but their style was determined by Christianity. Furthermore, a certain oriental influence in behaviour and gestures is evident. The palace area, Hagia Sophia, the hippodrome, and some places and streets of Constantinople were the "stages" for these performances. There were high-ranking officials who were specifically charged to implement the protocol.

One special kind of ceremony was the audience, the meeting of the emperor with certain groups; this was also a relic from Roman times. There were daily morning receptions at which high-ranking officials and dignitaries appeared before the emperor in order to discuss current affairs, and receptions were also held on special occasions. Foreign ambassadors, for example, were led into audience halls reserved for that purpose. The emperor, dressed splendidly and carrying the insignia of his office, sat on a platform veiled with curtains.

The participants entered in groups (according to their rank or divisions) in company with the master of ceremonies. Porphyry disks in the floor served as markers for certain actions. Absolute silence was required, and only the master of ceremonies spoke, giving short instructions. People had to approach the emperor in a humble way, performing the so-called *proskynesis*, an attitude of subjection and supplication, which was expressed by different gestures such as bowing the head or the upper part of the body or prostrating. Exalting the emperor in such a way stemmed from his being seen as the representative of God on earth (the emperor himself performed *proskynesis* when praying to God). Thus, an initially pagan ceremony could persist and develop in Christian times.

Acclamations were another important element of ceremonies, i.e. rhythmic speaking choruses offered to the emperor by the people, members of the Senate, ministers, and especially by the leaders of the circus factions (the people's parties). They were the only outlet that the people were allowed to have; otherwise they had to remain silent. In the Roman period these were spontaneous demonstrations of praise, reproach, approval, refusal, demand, or congratulations. They became more and more formalized and professional in time, being mainly carried out by the representatives of the factions. The emperor was praised in a servile way according to stereotypical models. While in late antiquity Greek and Latin words were mixed in acclamations, in the following centuries Greek prevailed. Some frozen Latin expressions for certain occasions were however preserved until late Byzantine times.

There are some remnants of Byzantine ceremonies in the practice of the Orthodox Church. The Byzantine court ceremonial and the rites of the Greek liturgy show strong parallels, because they influenced each other over the centuries. Furthermore, the extraordinary and outstanding position of the emperor was preserved beyond the Byzantine period by the Russian tsars, since Russia saw itself as the successor of the Byzantine empire. This tradition even passed on to Soviet communism and to the socialist nations of Eastern Europe, demonstrated in the personality cults of the party leaders. Even ceremonial elements are to be found: Herbert Hunger has compared socialist slogans used at party congresses with Byzantine acclamations and has found some amazing parallels.

ASTRID STEINER-WEBER

Further Reading

Cameron, Averil, "The Construction of Court Ritual: The Byzantine Book of Ceremonies" in *Rituals of Royalty: Power and Ceremonial in Traditional Societies*, edited by David Cannadine and Simon Price, Cambridge and New York: Cambridge University Press, 1987

Hunger, Herbert: *Reich der Neuen Mitte: Der christliche Geist der byzantinischen Kultur*, Graz: Styria, 1965

McCormick, Michael, "Analyzing Imperial Ceremonies" in *Jahrbuch der Österreichischen Byzantinistik*, 35 (1985): pp. 1–20

Treitinger, Otto, *Die oströmische Kaiser- und Reichsidee nach ihrer Gestaltung im höfischen Zeremoniell: Vom oströmischen Staats- und Reichsgedanken*, 3rd edition, Darmstadt, 1969

Chaeronea, Battle of

Battle fought between Macedonians and the southern Greeks in 338 BC

It was in the territory of Chaeronea on 2 August (or possibly 1 September) 338 BC that the decisive battle was fought that enabled Philip II of Macedon to bring the Greek homeland under his control.

When Philip negotiated the peace treaty that ended the first war with Athens in 346 BC, his aim seems to have been to win the Athenians' friendship and cooperation, and he insisted that the treaty should be accompanied by an alliance. It failed, however, to effect a real reconciliation. The Athenians could not forget what they saw as his treachery over Amphipolis in 357 BC and they were not reassured by his treatment of their Phocian allies in the immediate aftermath of the treaty's conclusion. Thereafter, although in 344 BC he made an apparently genuine attempt to allay the Athenians' suspicions by offering to amend the peace terms, Philip persistently intervened in Greek affairs in ways that enabled Demosthenes and others at Athens persuasively to depict him as untrustworthy and hostile. In 340 BC he began to threaten the Athenians' corn-supply route from the Black Sea and attacked Perinthus on the Propontis (Sea of Marmora) and Byzantium. His failure to take either city and their own earlier success in expelling his friends from Euboea encouraged the Athenians, who at once declared war when Philip seized their corn fleet near the Bosporus in September.

To wage war positively, Philip needed to threaten Athens, but his old allies the Thebans had recently seized the pass of Thermopylae and seemed likely to bar his way (previously, in 346 BC, a treacherous Phocian general had enabled him to take it and subdue the Phocians). However, a dispute in the Delphian Amphictyony, of which he had been a member since 346 BC, led to a sacred war being proclaimed against Locrian Amphissa and, after the failure of the Amphictyons' first campaign, Philip was given the command.

In autumn 339 BC he advanced over the difficult pass into Doris, ostensibly to attack Amphissa, but unexpectedly turned eastwards down the Cephisus valley and took Elatea on the road from Thermopylae to Thebes, demanding that the Thebans assist him or at least facilitate his invasion of Attica. Demosthenes persuaded the Thebans to refuse and an Athenian force moved into Boeotia. Philip made no further move until the spring of 338 BC, when he took Amphissa. He then made a final attempt to achieve his aims without a battle, but his offers were rejected at both Thebes and Athens; he advanced into northwest Boeotia to find that his enemies were barring his way in a gap of about 2.5 km between the Cephisus and the low hills to the west.

In view of the battle's importance, the information provided by the sources is disappointingly meagre. It was a characteristically Greek head-on clash between two armies consisting of hoplites, heavily armed infantry in close formation, but there is no agreement on their relative strengths. Diodorus Siculus (16. 85) says that Philip with "more than 30,000 infantry and no less than 2,000 cavalry had the advantage in numbers", while Justin (9. 3) gives the Greeks numerical superiority, a conclusion suggested by the incomplete figures in Plutarch

(*Demosthenes*, 17). According to Demosthenes' speech *On the Crown*, contingents from Euboea, Achaea, Corinth, Megara, Leucas, and Corinth supported the Athenians and the Thebans.

As to the disposition of the forces, Diodorus (16. 86) says that Philip faced the Athenians on one wing and his son Alexander faced the Thebans on the other, but gives no further details; Plutarch, however, links Alexander with the river Cephisus on the Macedonian left (*Alexander*, 9).

Diodorus writes in general terms of the fierce fighting, both sides for a while having "hopes of victory", before Alexander's men gradually broke down their opponents and put them to flight (Diodorus' words give no support to the modern theory that his cavalry broke the Theban hoplites), while Philip did the same to the Athenians; although, according to Polyaenus, the collector of military stratagems writing in the 2nd century AD, this was only after a feigned retreat had lured them up a slope to disrupt their order – the only detail of the action provided by the sources.

Information about casualties is also sparse. The only figures in the sources are for the Athenians, more than 1,000 dead and at least 2,000 captured (Diodorus, 16. 86). Theban losses were probably heavier and Plutarch (*Pelopidas*, 18) reports that the Theban Sacred Band of 300 picked hoplites were totally destroyed, although excavations beneath the Lion monument erected in their honour revealed the remains of only 254 bodies.

Philip's victory was so emphatic that he did not need to press on to attack Thebes and Athens. The Athenians prepared to defend their walls, but, still preferring to win their cooperation rather than to crush them, the king paid the due honours to their dead and released their prisoners without ransom. Thereupon they readily accepted his peace terms, agreeing to renew their alliance with him and to dissolve what was left of their maritime confederacy in return for keeping inviolate their territory and institutions. The Thebans were less fortunate, having to ransom their prisoners and accept both a Macedonian garrison and an oligarchic regime dominated by Philip's friends. He then installed a garrison in Corinth and secured friendly regimes in other states, encountering resistance only at the borders with Sparta, where he used a little force to secure the frontiers of the Spartans' neighbours, but otherwise ignored their continuing defiance.

His military control established, Philip ensured his political supremacy by organizing a settlement along the lines of the earlier "common peace" treaties, designed to secure the peace and the loyalty of the Greeks. Confident of his domination, he persuaded them to appoint him leader of a Panhellenic invasion of the Persian empire. After his murder in 336 BC, the decisive quality of his victory was further shown in the meagre support mustered by the Thebans for their rising against Alexander the following year. Macedonian domination was re-emphasized by their swift suppression and the total destruction of the city at Alexander's hands, although it was never accepted and was seriously challenged in the confusion following his early death in 323 BC. Greek freedom was never fully restored, not even in the brief period (243–224 BC) when Macedonian garrisons failed to hold Corinth, and in 196 BC the Romans took indirect control of the peninsula, formally annexing it in 146 BC.

The significance of Philip's victory has continued to be recognized in the modern world. In his tenth sonnet (pub. 1645) John Milton referred to it as "that dishonest victory at Chaeronea, fatal to liberty" and George Grote, the first great British historian of ancient Greece, called Philip "the destroyer of freedom and independence in the Hellenistic world" (*A History of Greece*, 1846). The Lion monument was seen by Pausanias in the mid-2nd century AD, but was later demolished. Its fragments were accidentally discovered by the traveller George Lidwell Taylor in 1881, and it was restored and replaced on its ancient plinth beside the old main road north from Levadia by the Greek Archaeological Society in 1902–04.

T.T.B. RYDER

Summary

Battle in 338 BC at which Philip II of Macedon became master of all Greece. For practical purposes it marked the end of Greek self-determination until 1832.

Further Reading

Ellis, J.R., *Philip II and Macedonian Imperialism*, London: Thames and Hudson, 1976

Hammond, N.G.L. and G.T. Griffith, *A History of Macedonia*, vol. 2, Oxford: Clarendon Press, 1979

Hammond, N.G.L., *Philip of Macedon*, London: Duckworth, 1994

Lewis, D.M. *et al.* (editors), *The Fourth Century BC*, Cambridge: Cambridge University Press, 1994 (*The Cambridge Ancient History*, vol. 6, 2nd edition)

Chalcidice

Region of northern Greece

Lying as it does beyond the land routes that cross Macedonia and being separated from the rest of the country by natural barriers, Chalcidice has had a history that differs from that of mainland Macedonia. The western part of the country was closely associated with Thessalonica: whoever was in control of the city usually had control of western Chalcidice. Chalcidice as a whole is particularly rich in timber and minerals, which is why all powers with an interest in the north Aegean area made efforts to gain control of the region.

Chalcidice first entered Greek history in the 8th century BC with the founding of the first Greek colonies. The country was colonized by the Ionian cities of Euboea, notably, though not exclusively, Chalcis (which provides the etymology of the name Chalcidice). There was only one Dorian colony in Chalcidice, Potidaea on the isthmus of the Pallene peninsula, which was founded by Corinthians c.700 BC. Most significant of the other Greek colonies were Olynthus in southwest Chalcidice, Mende and Scione in the Pallene peninsula, Torone in the Sithonia peninsula, Acanthus and Stageira (birthplace of Aristotle) in eastern Chalcidice. The Greek colonization was mainly of an urban type and localized in the coastal areas of the country. An exceptional case was the colonization by Chalcis of rural southwestern Chalcidice which expanded over the area around Olynthus. There settlers from Chalcis lived side-by-side with the non-Greek Bottiaeans. The Greek colonies of Chalcidice became bridgeheads for the diffusion of Hellenic culture in the hinterland. The first to receive cultural influence from the Greek colonists were the earlier settlers of Chalcidice, the Thracians, Bottiaeans, and Pelasgians; they had become completely Hellenized by the Hellenistic era when Chalcidice became an integral part of the Macedonian state.

In the aftermath of the Persian Wars the cities of Chalcidice were included in the Athenian sphere of influence and all of them joined the Delian League. Events in Chalcidice were among the causes for the outbreak of the Peloponnesian War, as Potidaea was encouraged by its mother-city Corinth to break away from Athenian control in 432 BC. Athens sent an expeditionary force against Potidaea and managed to capture it after a two-year siege. The hostility to Athens, however, was not confined to Dorian Potidaea, but spread among the Ionian Chalcidians as well. Following the advice of the Macedonian king Perdiccas II, an enemy of Athens, the Chalcidians of the area around Olynthus were resettled inside the town in 432 BC, increasing its size and strength and making it a stronghold of anti-Athenian sentiment. More Chalcidian cities reversed their allegiances during the campaign of the Spartan general Brasidas between 424 and 422 BC. The cities that revolted against Athens, starting with Olynthus, made up the nucleus of the Chalcidian League which, after the end of the Peloponnesian War, expanded over the entire region. With a foreign policy dictated from Olynthus, the Chalcidian League built up particularly strong armed forces and, by switching alliances between Sparta, Athens, Thebes, Macedonia, and the Thracian kingdoms, played a leading role in north Aegean politics during the first half of the 4th century BC.

Chalcidian power was challenged when Macedonian imperialism took shape during the first years of Philip II's rule. His first involvement in the affairs of Chalcidice took place in 357 BC when he drove the Athenians out of Potidaea on behalf of the Chalcidian League. Soon, the cities of Chalcidice themselves became victims of Macedonian expansionism, as Philip occupied one after another. Faced with this threat, Olynthus turned for help to its old enemy, Athens, and this provided the occasion for Demosthenes to write his three renowned *Olynthiac* orations urging his fellow citizens to support by all means their former enemies in Chalcidice. Nevertheless, Olynthus fell in 348 BC, Chalcidice became an integral part of the Macedonian state, and, later on, was incorporated into the Roman province of Macedonia. The Hellenistic era is marked by the development of Cassandreia (founded by Cassander in 316 BC), which became one of the major cities in Macedonia and one of its few Roman colonies (Pella, Dion, and Philippi were the others).

Medieval Chalcidice developed in the shadow of Thessalonica and the Holy Mountain. The main towns of the region in that period were Cassandreia, Ierissos, Hermeleia, Rebenikeia, and Rentina, though none among them was particularly significant. Cassandreia, in particular, had lost much of the importance it had in Hellenistic and Roman times. From the 10th century onwards, when the monastic community was officially established on Mount Athos, the rest of Chalcidice became progressively the backyard of the Holy Mountain. The monastic domain expanded enormously by means of imperial and private donation, or through direct purchase of property by the monasteries, and incorporated a great deal of land and property in Chalcidice including entire villages. Collections of documents relating to these monastic possessions are still preserved in the archives of the monasteries and have become a prime source for the study of Byzantine rural society, economy, and demography, by taking the villages of Chalcidice as case studies.

The medieval monastic documents shed much light on the agricultural economy of Chalcidice. Mining, which was the second most important economic activity of the region, is better documented during the Ottoman period (Turkish occupation of Chalcidice began as early as 1387, followed by an interval of restored Byzantine rule and then Venetian rule in western Chalcidice between 1403 and 1430). Mining was undertaken in several villages of the region, mainly in the central and eastern areas, which later became known as "Mademochoria". The principal centre of mining was the town of Siderokausia in the northeast of the country. Particular attention was paid to the development of silver mining at Siderokausia during the reign of Süleyman I in the 16th century when the task of organizing and directing the extraction and processing of the ore was given to German masters, while more than 6000 workers and dealers, Greeks, Jews, Bulgarians, and others, were employed in the business.

The Ottoman government had granted a special administrative status as well as fiscal privileges to several villages in Chalcidice. In the 18th century some groups of villages with common status and the same privileges joined in confederations with communal authority. One of those confederations consisted of the villages that had been mining centres, known as Mademochoria, though the mining had declined sharply by then and stopped completely in the 19th century. Another confederation was formed by the so-called "Chasikochoria", in western Chalcidice, which constituted a domain (*hass*) of the sultan's mother. A third was composed of the villages of Cassandra (Pallene) peninsula, a *waqf* (pious donation) intended to provide subsidies for the poor of Mecca and Medina.

Chalcidice and the region of Mount Vermion, including Naousa, were the only parts of Macedonia where the Greeks rose in rebellion during the War of Independence. In the case of Chalcidice, this is explained by the revolutionary fervour and enthusiasm that was shown by many of the monks of Mount Athos who were members of the *Philike Hetaireia*, as well as by the possibility of support and supply by sea. In late March 1821 the Serrean patriot Emmanuel Pappas arrived in Mount Athos and began to stir up revolt. Fighting broke out in June at Polygyros, one of the "Mademochoria" in central Chalcidice and presentday capital of the region, and spread through the country. Nevertheless, the Greeks were not strong enough to repel the Turkish counteroffensive and, after losing the area of Polygyros, organized a last defence in Cassandra peninsula which was crushed in December 1821.

Ottoman rule in Chalcidice ended in 1912 as a result of the Balkan Wars. The history of the region in the 20th century is marked by the arrival of Greek refugees from Turkey after 1922. In order to provide for their rehabilitation the Greek government proceeded to confiscate the monastic estates, which still amounted to a large area of land in Chalcidice, undertaking to subsidize the monasteries in return. The economy of contemporary Chalcidice has grown remarkably due to tourism, while the recent discovery of gold deposits offers further opportunities for the development of the region, though it has given rise to controversies on environmental issues.

KONSTANTINOS P. MOUSTAKAS

Summary

Though officially part of Macedonia, Chalcidice has had a history of its own due to its geographical isolation. It was first colonized by Greeks in the 8th century BC, notably from Chalcis (whence its name). After the Persian Wars the cities of Chalcidice joined the Delian League, but later changed allegiance. They were absorbed by Macedon in 348 BC. From the 10th century the region was dominated by the monasteries of Mount Athos whose estates were confiscated in the 20th century to accommodate refugees from Asia Minor.

Further Reading

Dimitriadis, V., "Ottoman Chalkidiki: An Area in Transition" in *Continuity and Change in Late Byzantine and Early Ottoman Society*, edited by Anthony Bryer and Heath Lowry, Birmingham: University of Birmingham Centre for Byzantine Studies, and Washington, D.C.: Dumbarton Oaks, 1986

Laiou-Thomadakis, Angeliki E., *Peasant Society in the Late Byzantine Empire: A Social and Demographic Study*, Princeton, New Jersey: Princeton University Press, 1977

Lefort, Jacques, *Villages de Macédoine*, vol. 1: *La Chalcidique occidentale*, Paris: Boccard, 1982

Papazoglou, Fanoula, *Les Villes de Macédoine à l'époque romaine*, Athens: Ecole Française d'Athènes, 1988

Sakellariou, M.B. (editor), *Macedonia: 4000 years of Greek History and Civilization*, Athens: Ekdotike Athenon, Athens, 1983

Vacalopoulos, A.E., *History of Macedonia, 1354–1833*, Thessalonica: Institute for Balkan Studies, 1973

West, Allen Brown, *The History of the Chalcidic League*, Madison: University of Wisconsin, 1918; reprinted New York: Arno Press, 1973

Zahrnt, Michael, *Olynth und die Chalkidier*, Munich: Beck, 1971

Chalcis

City in Euboea

Chalcis is located on the narrowest point of the Euripus and is the capital of the district of Euboea. Today it is a bustling capital city of about 50,000 inhabitants and the town profits from trade in several important commodities (including livestock, butter, and agricultural tools). Modern Chalcis obscures the remains of the ancient city, which was famous for its manufacture of bronze (the city may have received its name from this trade, since *chalkos* means "bronze"). The Mycenaean city praised by Homer (*Iliad*, 2. 540) has yet to be discovered, but some ancient remains from the late Geometric period on have been found in the area of the modern town.

Chalcis played an important role in the developments of Geometric and Archaic Greece. The inhabitants were known for their commercial enterprise (including trade in pottery and metalwork) and colonizing ventures (founding colonies and trading posts on the coasts of Sicily, Italy, Chalcidice, Thrace, the islands of the Aegean, and possibly Syria). Perhaps most famous, while at the same time least understood, is the role that Chalcis played in the Lelantine War with Eretria. Apparently, during the late 8th century BC Chalcis and Eretria were in competition for land and power, which led to a war over the rich Lelantine plain. Strabo (*Geography*, 10. 1. 9) says that this plain was famous, among other things, for its curative hot-water fountains, which were even used by the Roman general Sulla. This early Hellenic conflict over the Lelantine plain involved, at least, Miletus, which supported Eretria, and Samos, which supported Chalcis. Thucydides implies that numerous other states were involved. While the 8th-century victor is unknown, Chalcis seems to have held the plain in the 7th century BC.

Chalcis was ruled by a monarchy until the 7th century BC, when its last king Amphidamus was killed in battle. (Aristotle, in *Politics*, 1304a, mentions a later, but otherwise unknown tyrant, Phoxus, who was overthrown by the elites of the city.) The aristocracy then took over, and eventually supported the Athenian tyrant Hippias who fled there after his expulsion from power. Tragically for their independence, the people of Chalcis allied with Boeotia against Athens, partly in an attempt to restore Hippias. The Athenians then attacked and defeated the Chalcidians, took their land for the settlement of 5000 cleruchs, dismantled their navy, and assumed control over their colonies in Italy and Sicily. The Athenians, proud of their success against Chalcis, set up a chariot on the Acropolis and inscribed it with news of their victory (Herodotus, 5. 77. 4; Diodorus, *Historical Library*, 10. 24. 3). In 480 BC the people of Chalcis supported the Athenians against Persia and sent at least 20 ships to the Greek fleet. Soldiers of Chalcis also fought in the Battle of Plataea.

Demosthenes in his orations on *Philip*, *On the False Assembly*, and *Against Midias* highlights the role that Chalcis played in early Macedonian attempts to influence and control Greece. Originally Callias, the general from Chalcis, supported Philip, but he then turned against Macedon in a successful attempt to rid the Euboean cities of Oreus and Eretria of tyrants. Nevertheless Philip took the city and garrisoned it in 338 BC. It remained important as a strategic control point and trade centre until 146 BC, when it was attacked and severely damaged by the Romans.

Once in the Roman sphere, the city, and Euboea, first became part of the province of Macedonia, and then in 27 BC the island became a part of the province of Achaea. Chalcis, due to its strategic location, remained economically viable throughout the Roman period. During the early Byzantine period, pagan temples were replaced with Christian monasteries and churches. By the 9th century AD silk was crucial to the economic life of the provincial Byzantine nobles in Chalcis. (In 1147 Roger II, king of Sicily, used his army to kidnap silk workers from Chalcis.) The Venetians captured and fortified the city in 1210, and made it the capital of Negroponte ("Black Bridge", referring to the whole of Euboea), the name deriving from a corruption of the Greek *ston Egripo* ("on the Euripus") and the Italian *ponte*, referring to the movable bridge built by Justinian. After a brutal battle in Chalcis against Sultan Mehmet II in 1470, the town fell to the Turks and then became the headquarters of *kaptan pasha* (admiral). The remains of the Turkish fortress, built in 1686 on top of the castle of Karababa (originally designed by the Venetians), apparently rest on even more ancient foundations – perhaps those of a Macedonian fort built c.334 BC. Chalcis remained in Turkish hands until 22 February 1833 when at last Chalcis and Euboea were freed from external rule, and Euboea was declared part of independent Greece.

The bridge spanning the Euripus channel at Chalcis also has an interesting history. The first fixed bridge was wooden, built in 411 BC, partly to interfere with Athenian maritime trade. In 334 BC towers, a wall, and gates were added to strengthen the defensive capabilities of the bridge. This structure remained more or less intact until Justianian replaced the fixed structure with a movable wooden bridge (intended to facilitate water-borne traffic). The Turks replaced Justinian's bridge with another fixed bridge, which remained in place until 1856, at which point a new swing bridge was constructed. The Belgians, in 1896, made major changes including enlarging the channel and erecting an iron swing bridge. The existing structure was created in 1962.

The city now houses a Folklore Museum, a storage house of medieval antiquities, and a small, well-kept Archaeological Museum. The Archaeological Museum displays Mycenaean pottery from local tombs and marble remains from Chalcis, Eretria, and Carystus. Sparse archaeological remains of buildings and graves have been found on the castle hill and fragments from other ancient structures may be seen built into the castle walls and other structures. The local synagogue, rebuilt in 1849 on its original foundations, includes in its walls tombstones from an ancient Jewish cemetery dating back at least 1,200 years. The modern city flourishes and is a popular route into Euboea for European and Athenian travellers.

CYNTHIA K. KOSSO

Summary

The largest city in Euboea located at the narrowest point of the Euripus, Chalcis played an important part in colonizing Sicily and Italy in the 8th century BC. It fought Eretria for possession of the Lelantine plain. In the Classical period it was dominated by Athens. In antiquity it was famous for its bronze working and in the Middle Ages for silk production.

Further Reading

Bakhuizen, S.C., *Chalcis-in-Euboea, Iron and Chalcidians Abroad*, Leiden: Brill, 1976

Bakhuizen, S.C., *Studies in the Topography of Chalcis on Euboea: A Discussion of the Sources*, Leiden: Brill, 1985

Evely, Doniert, Irene S. Lemos, and Susan Sherratt (editors), *Minotaur and Centaur: Studies in the Archaeology of Crete and Euboea Presented to Mervyn Popham*, Oxford: Tempus Reparatum, 1996

Popham, M.R., and L.H. Sackett (editors), *Lefkandi I: The Iron Age*, London: Thames and Hudson, 1979

Popham, M.R., P.G. Calligas, and L.H. Sackett, *Lefkandi II: The Protogeometric Building at Toumba*, 2 vols, Athens: British School of Archaeology at Athens, and London: Thames and Hudson, 1990–93

Sackett, L. *et al.*, "Prehistoric Euboea: Contributions Toward a Survey", *Annual of the British School at Athens*, 61 (1966)

Sakellaraki, E., *Chalkis*, Hellenic Ministry of Culture World Art Group, 1995

Sakellaraki, E., *Eretria*, Hellenic Ministry of Culture World Art Group, 1995

Sealey, Raphael, *A History of the Greek City States, c. 700–338 BC*, Berkeley: University of California Press, 1976

Chandris, Antony 1924–1984

Shipowner

Antony Chandris, president of the Union of Greek Shipowners from 1975 to 1981, succeeded in bridging the previously deep gulf between the Greek state and public opinion on the one hand and Greece's main industry on the other.

His father was a shipowner from Chios. He was educated at Athens College and as a marine engineer at the polytechnic in Lausanne. He and his brother Dimitri Chandris made Chandris Lines a leader in the 1950s and 1960s in passenger shipping, especially the movement of emigrants to Australia, but then switched the focus of their activities to tankers and cruise vessels.

Like most members of the shipping community, Antony and his wife Ourania Nikolaou lived in London. Greek politicians and public opinion felt that shipowners, who controlled by far the largest Greek industry, were contributing little to the country. On the other hand, there was resentment and suspicion following attempts by the government to impose retrospective taxation and to attach the insurance earnings gained from merchant ships sunk during World War II. In 1955, 80 per cent of Greek-owned tonnage flew foreign flags.

During this period the London-based Greek Shipping Cooperation Committee was influential. The chairmanship of his friend, John C. Carras (1963–65), brought ideas for a closing of the gap which found their way into the proposed five-year economic plan elaborated under the aegis of Andreas Papandreou in 1965. Some were, ironically, put into effect by the colonels after 1967, but the support of the dictatorship by many shipowners made Greek public opinion more hostile than ever.

Chandris was vice-chairman of the committee from 1967 to 1975. After the dictatorship fell in 1974, he stood for the presidency of the Union of Greek Shipowners. Narrowly failing in November 1974, he was triumphantly elected in January 1975, and unanimously re-elected in 1979. During his presidency the present institutional framework of Greek-owned shipping was put into place: with an eighth of total deadweight tonnage in 1980 the Greek merchant fleet was the largest in the world. The taxation system and other important provisions were entrenched under the Constitution of 1975. The year 1981 saw the highest proportion of Greek-owned tonnage ever under the Greek flag: 42 million tons to 12 million.

Chandris was a patient negotiator and determined bridge builder, and his humanity and warmth were proverbial. Under him the union succeeded for the first time in reaching out to a wide range of political opinion and integrating the interests of shipping with those of the country. He also organized its effective representation internationally, in the US, the European Union, and elsewhere.

A man of broad interests, Chandris invested substantially inside Greece. He was a co-founder of *Elliniki Etairia* (the Greek Society), Greece's main conservation organization, and supported important restoration work at the 11th-century church of Nea Moni on Chios. When he resigned in 1981 due to lung cancer, the shipping industry had become a respected partner both within and outside Greece.

COSTA CARRAS

See also Ships and Shipping

Biography

Born in 1924, Chandris was educated at Athens College and studied marine engineering at Lausanne Polytechnic. He and his brother Dimitri built up Chandris Lines, first as a leading passenger carrier, and later switched to tankers and cruise ships. Antony Chandris was President of the Union of Greek Shipowners from 1975 to 1981. He died in 1984.

Further Reading

Batis, Stathis, *Portraita se Ble Fondo* [Portraits with a Blue Background], Athens: Finatec Multimedia, 1999
Harlaftis, Gelina, *Greek Shipowners and Greece, 1945–75: From Separate Development to Mutual Interdependence*, London: Athlone Press, 1993
Harlaftis, Gelina, *A History of Greek-owned Shipping: The Making of an International Tramp Fleet, 1830 to the Present Day*, London and New York: Routledge, 1996

Chatzidakis, Georgios N. 1848–1941

Linguist

Chatzidakis is considered to be the pre-eminent linguist of Greece and one of the most influential individuals in shaping the study of the Greek language. Born in Mirtos in Crete, he studied Greek and Latin philology at the Philosophy Department of the University of Athens between 1873 and 1877, and received a scholarship to study linguistics in Germany, attending the universities of Leipzig and Berlin, as well as that of Vienna. He received a doctorate from the Philosophy Department at Athens University in 1883, with his thesis *Symvoli eis tin Istoria tis Ellinikis Glossis* (Contribution to the History of the Greek Language). He was designated interim professor of linguistics and of Indian philology at Athens University in 1885, appointed dean in 1905, and continued to teach at the university until 1923. He founded the University of Thessalonica, where he taught linguistics, and was dean from 1926 to 1928. He became a member of the Athenian Academy in 1926 and in 1927 was voted its president. He established the *Glossiki Hetaireia* (Language Society), as well as other scientific guilds. He died in Athens in 1941.

Despite its antiquity and remarkable importance for the illustration of linguistic principles and the evolution of words, the Greek language and its history, apart from the Archaic and Classical periods, had been mostly neglected by scholars. Chatzidakis's *Sintomos Istoria tis Ellinikis Glossis* (Short History of the Greek Language) was a succinct study, aimed primarily at a general readership.

A pupil of the philologist Kostantinos Kontos at the University of Athens, Chatzidakis used katharevousa (a form of Greek based on the spoken language but "purged" of modern elements) in his writings, but because he was a student of comparative linguistics and was thus able to view Greek bilingualism historically and objectively, he fought for its simplification, recommending, for example, that it be relieved of the infinitive and optative. Most significantly, he enabled the systematic study of demotic to be accepted at Athens university, where the "purist" language was used. He ultimately became one of the leading purists and used his influence between 1917 and 1920 to prevent the universal adoption of demoticism.

Chatzidakis was one of the first Greeks to study the medieval and modern Greek language, and in 1928 he founded the medieval archives of the Athenian Academy. The linguistic character of medieval texts was extensively and ardently debated by the two foremost Greek authorities on the subject, Chatzidakis himself and his adversary, Yannis Psycharis. Chatzidakis maintained that the beginnings of modern Greek could be traced as far back as the 6th century AD. He also argued that the language of medieval writers should not be taken as a manifestation of the popular speech of the day and, therefore, no emphasis should be placed upon it by historians of the language. Psycharis, on the other hand, contended that the formative period of modern Greek extended from the 10th to the 18th centuries, and believed that works written during this period were reliable witnesses to the dialects of their time, and thus could be relied upon for an understanding of the condition of the popular language in the last few centuries. Ultimately, Psycharis's theory met with little favour outside his own immediate circle, which was composed mainly of his former students. Nearly all modern Greek scholars concur with Chatzidakis, both in terms of the date of the beginning of modern Greek and with regard to the nature of the medieval written language. The linguistic struggle between Chatzidakis and Psycharis, on these and other issues, reached its height with the *Evangeliaka* (1901) and the *Orestiaka* (1903).

Chatzidakis also maintained that the Greek language, in spite of its peculiarities, remained the most Indo-European of all the languages in its group, exhibiting a comparatively true and accurate picture of the parent tongue, especially on such points as vocalism, verbal forms, and syntax. In one of his classic studies, *Peri tis Enotitos tis Ellinikis Glossis* (On the Unity of the Greek Language), Chatzidakis proved that Greek still uses or, at the very least, allows for the understanding of words used as far back as the composition of the New Testament. It was to this fact that he attributed the special bond that the Greek people feel for their language.

Without George Chatzidakis's work our understanding of the demotic language would have remained opaque. His scholarly study of this field dissipated much misguided teaching and increased our understanding of the Greek language. The fact that Chatzidakis did not use his influence and knowledge to promote the establishment of demotic as the official language is considered a failing, but it can only be assumed from his confidence in the language that demotic had not yet matured sufficiently to position itself as the official written language of Greece.

GEORGIA KEFALAS

See also Language

Biography

Born on Crete in 1848, Chatzidakis studied at the School of Philosophy of the University of Athens in 1873–77 and attended the universities of Leipzig, Berlin, and Vienna before taking his doctorate in Athens in 1883. He taught linguistics at Athens from 1885 to 1923 and was dean of the University of Thessalonica from 1926 to 1928. He championed the study of demotic and, in opposition to

Psycharis, traced its origins back to the 6th century AD. He died in Athens in 1941.

Further Reading

Babiniotis, G., *Lexiko tis Neas Ellinikis Glossas* [Dictionary of the Modern Greek Language], Athens: Kendro Lexikologias, 1998

Bien, Peter, *Kazantzakis and the Linguistic Revolution in Greek Literature*, Princeton, New Jersey: Princeton University Press, 1972

Chatzidakis, Georgios N., *Glossologikai Erevnai* [Philological Investigations], with an introduction by Dikeos Vayakakos, Athens, 1975

Costas, Procope S., *An Outline of the History of the Greek Language with Particular Emphasis on the Koine and the Subsequent Periods*, Chicago: Ukranian Academy of Sciences of America, 1936; reprinted Chicago: Ares, 1979

Chatzimichail, Theophilos 1873–1934

Folk painter

Theophilos (as he is usually known) began painting in his home at a very early age, but the tradition that he was taught by his maternal grandfather, the icon painter Kostantis Zografos, cannot be confirmed. His left-handedness made it difficult for him to follow his father's trade as a shoemaker; physically weak, and with a marked stutter, he was mocked by his peers and by early adolescence was socially isolated, devoted entirely to painting, traditional stories and songs, and an active fantasy life.

Before 1890 he left Mytilini on Lesbos for Smyrna, where he made his living as a painter, receiving lodging or a meal in payment for his work; his paintings from this period, on walls and furniture, have not survived. In Smyrna he adopted the fustanella as his everyday dress, sometimes with the full equipment familiar in the uniform of the National Guard, "dressing up" as a stereotypical Greek in a city of mixed culture, rather than wearing traditional costume, which on Lesbos meant *vrakia* (baggy knee-breeches). He also paraded about the city as Alexander with a gang of street children as his "Macedonians". It is now impossible to determine if his claim to have been a bodyguard at the Greek consulate in Smyrna had any basis in reality or was a reflection of these playacting fantasies.

After 1900 he moved to Thessaly, and continued to live by painting, receiving commissions both from residents of the villages on Mount Pelion and in the city of Volos. He returned to Mytilini in 1927. Soon afterwards, the Parisian art critic Tériade (Stratis Eleftheriadis, 1897–1983, a native of Skamnia on Lesbos) discovered his work, and in 1929 contracted to buy whatever Theophilos produced, providing him with supplies and encouraging him to move from wall painting to the more permanent and portable medium of canvas. In the following year an article by Kostas Ouranis in a national newspaper made Theophilos known more generally in Greece.

Both in the Pelion region and on Lesbos Theophilos was heir to a well-established tradition of wall painting in house decoration. What makes his work distinctive is that his painting was not restricted to the inner walls of bourgeois homes, but to a wide variety of surfaces, indoors and outdoors; his most famous work was the decoration of a taverna at Karini, on the way to a shrine of the Virgin at Ayiassos which attracts visitors from beyond Lesbos. Even more important was his choice of subjects; as well as traditional floral designs and landscapes, Theophilos decorated everything with paradigmatic figures of Greek traditional culture: ancient Greek gods and heroes, Alexander, Erotokritos, and the leaders of the War of Independence. The last, the subject of his most enduring fantasies and performances, are painted with a clarity and intensity that have few parallels. In the canvasses made for Tériade after 1929 he also portrayed a traditional way of life which was being rapidly replaced by a more homogenized modern (he would have said "Frankish") culture, symbolized by the aeroplanes he included in his latest paintings. In such paintings as his portrait of a musician from Lemnos and a representation of Mytilini in 1888 (before he left for Smyrna), there is the same vivid recall of a world now lost as in other works produced in Lesbos after the Asia Minor catastrophe, such as Elias Venezis's *Aeolia* and Stratis Myrivilis's *Vasilis Arvanitis*. Even though Myrivilis did not admire Theophilos artistically, he found him an appropriately archetypal figure to appear with his folk hero Vasilis Arvanitis in a nostalgic evocation of Greek traditional culture.

Along with his paints, Theophilos's workbox included a collection of postcards, photographs, and illustrations from school texts and popular literature. Some of his paintings are clearly derived from these pictures; but he produced works of startling originality, and even his most derivative works introduce new elements of light and colour, and are generally far more alive than their models.

For the poets Andreas Embeirikos, Odysseus Elytis, and George Seferis, the discovery of Theophilos in the 1930s was a critical point in their intellectual development. Like General Makriyannis's *Memoirs*, Theophilos represented a vital and authentically Greek popular tradition, as different from 19th-century academic European art as the general's Greek was from the artificial classicizing language of official culture. Theophilos's position as an iconic figure of Greek popular culture has since been enhanced by fictionalized treatments of his life, such as the *Myth of Theophilos* by Nestoras Matsas (1971) and the television film *Theophilos* by Lakis Papastathis (1987).

The largest collections of Theophilos's works are in the Museum of Theophilos in Varia outside Mytilini and the house of Yannis Kontos in Anakasia (Pelion); although the decoration of the taverna at Karini has largely disappeared, a decorated counter is still in use in a *kafeneion* in Ayia Paraskevi on Lesbos. Reproductions of several paintings are available on the World Wide Web, on sites maintained by the Greek Ministry of Culture (www.culture.gr).

HUGH J. MASON

See also Painting

Biography

Chatzimichail, usually known by his first name Theophilos, was born in Mytilini on Lesbos in 1873 and may have been taught to paint by his grandfather, the icon painter Kostantis Zografos. He moved to Smyrna and later to Mount Pelion, making a poor living as a journeyman painter of tavernas and coffee houses. Soon after his return to Mytilini in 1927 his talent was recognized by the Parisian critic Tériade. He died in Mytilini in 1934.

Further Reading

Crichton, Ronald, "Theophilos" in *Orpheus: A Symposium of the Arts*, edited by John Lehmann, vol. 2, London: Lehmann, 1949

Elytis, Odysseas, *O Zographos Theophilos* [The Painter Theophilos], Athens, 1973

Elytis, Odysseus, *Open Papers*, translated by Olga Broumas and T. Begley, Port Townsend, Washington: Copper Canyon Press, 1995, pp. 71, 165

Makris, Kitsos and Agapi Karakatsani, "Theophilos" in *Oi Ellines Zographoi* [Greek Painters], vol. 1, Athens, 1975

Myrivilis, Stratis, *Vasilis Arvanitis*, Armidale, New South Wales: University of New England Press, 1983, pp. 51–52, 105

Seferis, George, "Theophilos" in *On the Greek Style: Selected Essays in Poetry and Hellenism*, translated by Rex Warner and T.D. Frangopoulos, Boston: Little Brown, 1966; London: Bodley Head, 1967

Skopelitis, S.B., *Mansions in Lesbos: Wall Paintings*, Athens: I. Zacharopoulos, 1977

Theophilos Museum [Mouseio Theophilou], *Theophilos: Paintings*, Mytilini, 1990

Tsarouchis, Yannis (editor), *Theophilos*, Athens, 1966 (in Greek)

Chersonese, Thracian

The Thracian Chersonese, now known as the Gallipoli (Gelibolu) peninsula in modern Turkey, is a long, narrow peninsula forming the European side of the Hellespont (Dardanelles) and connecting the Sea of Marmara with the Aegean. It was always important as a wheat-exporting region, but even more because of its strategic location as a crossing point between Europe and Asia; before long, this attracted Greek colonization, mainly by Aeolians from Lesbos and Ionian Greeks from Miletus as early as the end of the 8th and the beginning of the 7th century BC. Attic black-figure vases started to reach the area from 600 BC, showing an Athenian interest in it that was to continue for centuries: probably already in the 6th century the Chersonese was a strategic point on the route along which grain imports vital for Athens moved (by the 4th century Athens imported about half of the grain it needed from the Black Sea region). The Athenian aristocrat Miltiades the Elder established a domain of his own and built a defensive wall across the Bulair isthmus to protect it against the native Thracians; the Chersonese remained his family's property until his nephew Miltiades the Younger abandoned it to Darius I of Persia (c.492 BC). According to the account given by Herodotus (6. 34–40, 6. 103f.), the Chersonese was originally held by the Thracian Dolonci, who consulted the Delphic oracle when they were attacked by another tribe, and then invited Miltiades to protect them. Miltiades died childless, and in about 516 BC the sons of the Athenian tyrant Pisistratus sent Miltiades the Younger to take control of the region. He established himself by maintaining an army of 500 mercenaries and married the daughter of the Thracian king Olorus, who became his ally. He fled back to Athens, however, before the Persian advance, and for the next 30 years the Chersonese was under Persian control.

After the Persian withdrawal from the Greek mainland in 479, Athens quickly moved to regain control of the Chersonese – conquering the strategically important Sestus – to ensure the safe passage of Black Sea grain; the Chersonese became a part of the Delian League. Moreover, the sending of colonists there was an outlet for surplus population (among the Athenian settlements known as cleruchies founded about the middle of the 5th century BC there is a dispatch of 1000 cleruchs to the Chersonese). After the Peloponnesian War (431–404) Sparta briefly controlled the area, but it reverted to the control of Athens, who once more sent settlers there in 353 and cruelly punished recalcitrant Sestus. In 338 Athens finally ceded the area to Philip II of Macedonia; later it became part of the Seleucid empire. In 188 BC the Romans gave the Chersonese to the Attalid Eumenes II of Pergamum; it became Roman in 133 BC. Under Augustus it was turned into an emperor's estate.

Since the beginning of Greek colonization, a number of Greek towns developed on the Chersonese. Of the lesser ones (Alopeconnesus, an Aeolian foundation; Crithote, founded by the elder Miltiades and in ruins in Roman times) not much is known; more importance – varying over time – was attained by Sestus, Cardia, Elaious, and (since Hellenistic times) Lysimacheia and Callipolis (which gave the peninsula its modern name).

Sestus was situated at the narrowest part of the Hellespont (just opposite Abydus) and therefore provided the best point of departure to and from Asia; originally a Thracian settlement and mentioned already in Homer's catalogue of the Trojan army (*Iliad*, 2. 836), it was colonized by the Lesbians in about 600 BC. In 480 BC Xerxes built his naval bridge there, and in 334 BC Alexander the Great crossed from there over to Asia. In 365 BC Sestus was held by the Persian satrap Ariobarzanes; in 360 BC the Thracians conquered the city. Under Attalid rule, Sestus seems to have retained a certain autonomy and minted its own coins; this stopped only in AD 250, when the city fell into decay. In the 6th century AD Justinian erected a fortress above the remains, and the place again had some importance in the fighting between the Latin emperors based in Constantinople and the Byzantine emperors at Nicaea in the early 13th century. As the Chersonese has not yet been much explored archaeologically (access to this military area of modern Turkey is restricted), the precise location of Sestus remains unknown.

Cardia, founded by the Milesians and occupied by the elder Miltiades and his colonists in 560 BC, had a strategic location on the west coast of the Chersonese where it opened up into mainland Thrace. In the Peloponnesian War Cardia was an Athenian naval base. Lysimachus destroyed it in 309 BC to incorporate its inhabitants into the newly founded Lysimacheia.

Elaious, situated at the southern tip of the Chersonese and dominating its entrance, was probably also an Athenian foundation and used by Miltiades as a harbour; it was famous because of its ancient sanctuary of Protesilaus (perhaps identical with the prehistoric tumulus of Eski Hisarlâk), which was pillaged by the Persian Artayctes, but apparently continued to exist until late antiquity; Alexander the Great sacrificed at Protesilaus' tomb before crossing over to Troy. Elaious served as an Athenian naval base in the Peloponnesian War and was a member of the Second Delian League from 375 BC; when the

Chersonese became the property of the Thracian king Cotys I, Elaious together with Crithote (see above) remained with Athens. Elaious still played a role in the battles between Constantine the Great and Licinius in AD 323 and was, like Sestus, refortified by Justinian.

Lysimacheia was founded at the northern end of Chersonese (near Cardia) in 309 BC by Lysimachus, who intended it to be his capital. After his death in 281 the city passed through several hands and was finally destroyed by the Thracian king Diegylis in 144 BC.

Callipolis, mentioned by sources only since the 3rd century BC (it was conquered in 209 BC by Philip V of Macedon), acquired greater importance in later antiquity when Byzantium became capital of the eastern empire. In 1354 or 1357 the city was the first place in Europe to be conquered by the Turks; it remained strategically important as a naval base for the defence of Istanbul. The modern town of Gallipoli was heavily damaged by an earthquake in 1912 and shortly afterwards suffered severe destruction during the fierce fighting of the Gallipoli campaign of World War I, in which determined Turkish resistance caused the invading Allies heavy losses. Today Gelibolu, a Turkish town of 14,500 inhabitants, is a commercial centre, fishing port, and marine base.

BALBINA BÄBLER

Summary
A long narrow peninsula, forming the European side of the Hellespont, the Thracian Chersonese was important in antiquity because of its fertility and its strategic location as a crossing point between Europe and Asia, and between the Black Sea and the Mediterranean.

Further Reading
Casson, Stanley, *Macedonia, Thrace and Illyria: Their Relations to Greece from the Earliest Times down to the Time of Philip, Son of Amyntas*, London: Oxford University Press, 1926

Isaac, Benjamin, *The Greek Settlements in Thrace until the Macedonian Conquest*, Leiden: Brill, 1986

Kahrstedt, Ulrich, *Beiträge zur Geschichte der thrakischen Chersones*, Baden-Baden: Grimm, 1954

Sealey, Raphael, *A History of the Greek City States, c. 700–338 BC*, Berkeley: University of California Press, 1976

Chersonesus

City in the Crimea

Chersonesus was a Greek colony in the southwest of the Crimea peninsula (near the modern city of Sevastopol). Throughout antiquity it had an important strategic position: whoever held the city had control over the northwest section of the Black Sea, i.e. the Danube delta and the entrance to the great northern gulf which receives the waters of the Dniestr, Bug, and Dniepr.

Until recently it was commonly agreed that Chersonesus was a Dorian colony, founded by Heraclea Pontica together with Delos in the later 5th century BC and that there had probably been an earlier, small Ionian emporium. New excavations, however, have brought to light Ionian and Attic black-figure vases and terracottas of the last quarter of the 6th century BC as well as a series of spectacular ostraca of the entire 5th century, showing that the colonists had the Milesian alphabet, but used chiefly Dorian names. This new evidence proves that already in the last quarter of the 6th century BC not only Heracleots but also Ionians from the south shore of the Pontus took part in the foundation of the polis. This earlier dating was confirmed when in 1986 an intact stratum of the Archaic period (containing the traces of a sanctuary of the end of the 6th century) was found in the northeast part of the city.

Chersonesus soon seems to have acquired a large territory. In the 4th century BC the city state covered most of the southwest Crimea and its fertile coast, including towns like Kerkinitis and Kalos Limen. Fortified farms with towers were built in this area, and at the same time the production of local amphorae began (for exporting wine). Coins were also minted from the 4th century BC.

In the 3rd century BC, however, the city state was badly affected by Scythian and Sarmatian invasions. Archaeological evidence shows that all surrounding settlements were destroyed and burned: several farmhouses contained human skeletons (apparently victims of a surprise attack) and in western Crimea coin hoards were found, hastily buried by the inhabitants. In Chersonesus itself the people, apparently expecting further attacks, built a new line of town walls from grave stelae of the city's necropolis. Chersonesus never fully recovered from this destruction; its agricultural settlements were in ruins, fields and vineyards destroyed, the export of goods and the production of amphorae almost brought to a standstill. At the end of the 2nd century Mithridates VI of Pontus protected the city against the Scythians, but Chersonesus lost its external territories; later it was integrated into the Bosporan kingdom by Asandros. When the Scythians besieged the city again in AD 60/61, Nero installed Roman soldiers and a naval detachment. Under Hadrian the Bosporanian king Cotys II also controlled Chersonesus; Antoninus Pius re-established the city's independence.

In the 2nd century AD Chersonesus was the starting point for the conversion of the Crimean population to Christianity. It was here that the banished bishop of Rome, St Clement, was martyred during the persecutions under the emperor Trajan. By the beginning of the 4th century Christianity was firmly established in Chersonesus.

During the Byzantine period, the city – now called Cherson (this name is attested at least since Hadrianic times) – gained great importance because of its strategic position in the empire's northern defence system and its control of the major sea routes. The Hellenistic town walls were repaired at the end of the 5th century and reinforced with towers and bastions in the reign of Justinian; further restorations took place in the 7th and 8th centuries. Moreover, between the 5th century and the end of the 10th some 30 churches were built in Cherson, among them four luxurious basilicas and a cruciform church. This last was discovered in 1897 and had an altar containing a silver reliquary bearing a monogram, bust, and control stamps of Justinian I. The city seems also to have been a place of exile for prominent persons, among them the pope St Martin (AD 655) and the emperor Justinian II (695). In the 8th century Cherson belonged to the Khazars, but Byzantine rule was re-established in the earlier part of the 9th century, and for the next three centuries Cherson was again the most important outpost of Byzantium in the northern Black Sea. It became a centre for Byzantine diplomatic, ecclesiastical, and military activity in relation to the peoples of the steppe. Knowledge of them proved to be of great value to the monks Cyril (originally Constantine the Philosopher) and Methodios, who spent the winter of 860/61 at Cherson before setting out on their missionary work. In the 10th century Cherson was a focal point for relations between Byzantium and the fledgeling Russian state. It was here that in 988 prince Vladimir of Kiev was baptized by the metropolitan of Cherson and married Anna Porphyrogenneta ("born in the purple"), the sister of Emperor Basil II (976–1025); the prelates of the metropolitanate of Cherson then accompanied the couple to Kiev, where they founded the Russian Orthodox Church. The same Vladimir had shortly before conquered and destroyed Cherson, because Basil had at first reneged on his promise to send Anna as Vladimir's wife-to-be in return for his help against a mutiny in Cappadocia.

The Byzantines rebuilt Cherson, but it did not fully recover and its strategic importance further dwindled following the Byzantine reconquest of the Danube delta. In 1081 the Seljuk Turks captured Sinope, Cherson's main supplier of wheat, for the first time, and again definitively in 1194. With the fall of Constantinople to the Franks and Venetians in 1204, Cherson lost its main centre of support. For a time this role was filled by the so-called empire of the Great Komnenoi of Trebizond (which had come into being as a spinoff of the disintegrating Byzantine empire), but the establishment of new commercial outposts by the Genoese and Venetians contributed to Cherson's decline. In 1299 the city barely survived a destructive invasion of Tatars and Mongols. Byzantine sources last mention it in 1396; it was finally abandoned some decades later.

BALBINA BÄBLER

See also Crimea

Summary

Greek colony in the southwest Crimea, near modern Sevastopol, founded by Heracleans and Ionians at the end of the 6th century BC. Flourished in the 5th and 4th centuries but lost its rich agricultural surroundings to the Scythians and Sarmatians in the 3rd century BC. Important role in Byzantine times and for the spread of Christianity in Russia. Destroyed by the Mongols in 1299, finally abandoned in the 15th century.

Further Reading

Koromila, Marianna, *The Greeks in the Black Sea from the Bronze Age to the Twentieth Century*, Athens, 1991, pp. 147–57 (in English)

Obolensky, Dimitri, "The Crimea and the North before 1204" in his *The Byzantine Inheritance of Eastern Europe*, London: Variorum, 1982

Saprykin, Sergei J., "Khersonesos Taurike: New Evidence on a Greek City-state in the Western Crimea" in *Proceedings of the First International Congress on the Hellenic Diaspora*, vol. 1, edited by John M. Fossey, Amsterdam: Gieben, 1991

Saprykin, Sergei J., *Heracleia Pontica and Tauric Chersonesus before Roman Domination, VI–I Centuries BC*, Amsterdam: Hakkert, 1997

Vinogradov, Jurij and M. Zolotarev, "Le Chersonèse de la fin de l'archaisme" in *Le Pont Euxin vu par les grecs*, edited by Otar Lordkipanidzé and Pierre Lévêque, Paris: Belles Lettres, 1990

Vinogradov, Jurij, "Die Entstehung des chersonesischen Territorialstaates" in his *Pontische Studien*, edited by Heinz Heinen, Mainz: Zabern, 1997

Children

For Hellenic culture the family is central and childlessness a catastrophe. Men need children to inherit their property and perpetuate the paternal line, while the primary function of wives has been to fulfil this patrilineal ambition. The childless have resorted to remedies of varying efficacy, from the ancient practice of incubation (documented in inscriptions from the shrine of Asclepius at Epidaurus, 4th century BC: *Inscriptiones Graecae*, 4. 2. 121–2) to today's more sophisticated medical interventions, but, since the traditional purpose of marriage is to produce heirs, often the consequence of infertility has been marital separation. Children have been important to Hellenic society in terms both military and political: in the 4th century BC Dinarchus claimed that a man without legitimate issue could become neither an orator nor a general (1. 71) and in Sparta bachelors were mocked publicly, while temporary relaxations in marriage laws in times of war and depopulation reflect anxieties about maintaining the birthrate.

While Greek culture has regarded unproductive marriage as anomalous, the partible inheritance system (in which an estate is divided among all its legitimate inheritors with no rule of primogeniture) which pertained at ancient Athens and in the Hellenistic and Byzantine worlds, together with the problem of poverty and the obligation to dower daughters, meant that children were not always a blessing. Large families were (and still are) a luxury; Polybius in the mid-2nd century BC claimed that family planning led to prosperity (36. 17. 5). High infant mortality rates due to primitive obstetrics and medical care limited family size, but contraception was largely ineffective (one 4th-century BC Hippocratic text suggests a posset of beans and water: *On the Nature of Women*, 98) and adoption for the ancient and medieval Greeks was not a means of finding a home for unwanted children but of ensuring an heir for the paternal estate, the usual adoptee being a male adult. Indeed at Athens foundling children could not be adopted since the consent of the child's father was needed. Furthermore, while the orphans of Athenian citizens killed in battle were supported at the expense of the state (Thucydides, 2. 45), state-run orphanages that cared for abandoned children did not appear until the Byzantine era, and they were few and far between.

Since contraception was unreliable and celibacy not an option (for pre-Christian Greeks at least), the standard methods of disposing of unwanted children were abortion and infant exposure. Abortion, legal in Greece today, is condemned by Orthodox teaching. However, pre-Christian concerns about abortion centred on the issue of paternal authority and the potential destruction of heirs rather than the sanctity of human life – only fathers (or, if the father was dead, the child's or embryo's agnatic kin) could decide to abort or expose offspring, and the mother who attempted to appropriate this power of decision was liable to prosecution (see Lysias, frr. 8a, 8b). Exposure must be distinguished from infanticide, which in Hellenic society has been almost invariably the object of religious proscription. Infants were left typically in places where people went, and they were intended to be found. The usual fate of foundlings was slavery and, for girls, the brothel. Ambrose suggested that, while the poor practised exposure, the wealthy favoured (or perhaps had access to effective methods of) abortion (*Lex.*, 5. 58). At Sparta the decision to raise a child belonged not to its father but to the elders of his tribe. "Defective" infants were cast into the Apothetae, a chasm under Mount Taygetus (Plutarch, *Lycurgus*, 16).

Demographic evidence suggests that the Greeks of antiquity practised selective female exposure; a letter of the 1st century BC from a soldier to his wife orders her to expose their unborn baby if it turns out to be a girl (*Oxyrhynchus Papyrus* 744). Indeed, Greek culture traditionally values sons more highly than their sisters, a partiality that illustrates the radical gender bias inherent in Greek society; at ancient Athens males alone could inherit and for Greeks ancient and modern the engendering of boys is a mark of masculinity. Even at the dawn of the 21st century sons may count for more than daughters; when asked how many children they have, Greek men may enumerate their sons only (see Vermeulen 1970).

The Greek Constitution now insists that both parents share equal rights and responsibilities in parenting (article 4, para 2, 1975) but earlier Hellenic society prioritized paternal authority. At Athens the father acknowledged paternity on the *dekate*, the tenth day after birth, while the formal rejection of an older child was possible (*apokeryxis*). In antiquity, as now, children were legal minors, subject to the authority of a guardian (*kyrios*), normally the child's father, although at Athens in the Classical period the archon was obliged to appoint a guardian – usually an agnatic male relative – for orphans. The children of divorced parents or widows belonged to their father's house and the modern assumption that children should live with their mothers in the event of marital breakdown or paternal death represents a radical reversal of ancient practice. Yet the trend has its roots in late antiquity; Byzantine law insisted that stepfathers adopt the children of a wife's previous marriage.

At Athens sons became their own *kyrioi* when they attained their majority (at about 18), although daughters, being perpetually legal minors, remained throughout their lives under the guardianship of either their male natal kin or their husbands. Although adult sons were legally independent, filial obligations remained strong; honour was due to one's parents as to the gods and sons could be disfranchised for mistreating their parents (Demosthenes, 10. 40–41; Lysias, 13. 91). In the Byzantine period the Roman law that legally subordinated adult children to their fathers (*hyperexousia*) was accepted by Justinian, and later the *Prochiron* (907) required that sons desiring legal independence should be formally emancipated from paternal power, although Leo VI (886–912) granted legal independence to sons who had established their own *oikoi* (households). Paternal authority persisting into adulthood led to tensions (John Chrysostom claimed that sons preferred their fathers not to live too long in *Colosseos*, 1. 3 – see *Patrologiae Cursus Completa, series Graeca*, 62. 303, edited by J.-P. Migne), yet the threat of disinheritance may have motivated

sons to keep on good terms with their fathers – while the legal minimum to be divided among all legitimate sons was one-quarter (later one-third) of the paternal estate, the amount could be divided unequally (Justinian, *Novellae*, 115. 3).

The children of "illegitimate" unions were dealt with variously. At Classical Athens a child was a bastard (*nothos*) if he did not result from a union legitimized by *engue* (betrothal) or *epidikasia* (legal process) in the case of an *epikliros* (heiress). *Nothoi* born to free Athenian parents were not members of the *oikos* but could inherit a residual portion of their fathers' estates in default of legitimate heirs; Justinian also allowed illegitimate children to inherit in the absence of legitimate sons (*Codex Iustinianus*, 5. 27. 8). The treatment of children of concubines and slaves underwent various changes; at Athens in the 5th century BC the children of citizens and free alien concubines could perhaps be legitimized, although this was no longer possible in the 4th century BC. Children of citizens and slaves, however, were slaves and belonged to their owners. In the Byzantine period Constantine insisted that children of freedmen and slave women remain slaves (*Codex Theodosianus*, 12. 1. 1, 4. 8. 7), although later Justinian rendered such children automatically free unless this was proscribed by the father's will. In 479 Zeno legitimized automatically children of free men and free concubines, a law extended by Justinian in 539 to embrace children of slave concubines. Children born of two slaves were throughout the period owned by their parents' masters. In post-Solonic Athens the law debarred parents from selling their children into slavery (Plutarch, *Solon*, 23. 2) and Byzantine children could be neither sold nor abandoned, although in 329 Constantine legalized the sale of children with the right of later repurchase.

Ancient literary representations of children begin with that of Astyanax in the *Iliad*. Erinna mentions little girls who play with dolls and are afraid of the "bogeywoman" Mormo (*Distaff, Greek Literary Papyri*, 3. 120, 4th century BC), while the death of children, from the horror of infanticide (Euripides' *Medea* and *Hercules Furens*) to the accidental death of 119 schoolchildren on Chios (Herodotus, 6. 27) evokes pathos and often signifies the end of the paternal line. *Choes* (pitchers) of the Classical period and Hellenistic art exhibit a particular interest in children, while Christian iconography frequently represents the infant Jesus.

In antiquity children were considered wild (Plato, *Timaeus*, 44a–b). Education was essential to "tame" children and to prepare them for adult roles and responsibilities – politics and war for boys, marriage for girls. A child's first learning experience was at home where the women of the household played an important part in the transmission of culture through storytelling and religious instruction (Plato, *Laws*, 887d–e). Many mothers took their children's education seriously – in the 2nd century AD Plutarch mentions a mother educating herself in order to educate her children (*Moralia*, 14b–c) and advises that wetnurses, who in the past, when weaning occurred at the ages of 2 or 3, exercised a significant influence on their charges, should be Greek-speaking and of good character (*Moralia*, 3e). Boys were removed from the sphere of female influence at 7 or 8. The Spartan *agoge* (education system) separated boys from their families at the age of 7, while elsewhere boys whose families could afford it were educated at schools where Homer and, later, Christian texts such as the Psalms formed the basis of a literary education, although many Christians such as Basil of Caesarea found pagan texts morally problematic as a didactic tool. Military training was crucial for boys and institutionalized homosexuality was an educational feature of many Greek states including Sparta (Xenophon, 2. 12) and Dorian Crete (Ephorus, fr. 70. 149). Physical education at the gymnasium and social education at the symposium were usually the province of boys, but music and dancing were common to both sexes; Alcman and Sappho in the 7th century BC attest to girls' choirs. However for girls education was essentially domestic: spinning and weaving were taught at home and up to recent times girls had limited access to formal education. Indeed, until the late 20th century Greek families financed the education of their sons but seldom that of their daughters.

The children of the poor and slaves worked at home, on the land, or at a trade; a papyrus from the Hellenistic period documents the case of a slave child apprenticed to a weaver (*Oxyrhynchus Papyrus* 1647). Childhood was short for many children in the past; girls were married young (although *Peira*, 49. 22 describes penalties for those who married girls under 12) and in the mid-7th century 10 was the minimum age for taking monastic vows. The 20th century has seen the extension of childhood into late adolescence as a much greater proportion of children, girls as well as boys, remain in education longer, while the minimum age for marriage in Greece is now 16 (18 without parental consent).

EUGÉNIE FERNANDES

See also Abortion, Adoption, Contraception, Divorce, Gender, Inheritance, Marriage

Further Reading

Antoniadis-Bibiacou, H., "Quelques Notes sur l'enfant de la moyenne époque byzantine (du VIe au XIIe siècle)", *Annales DH* (1973): pp. 77–84
Arjava, Antti, *Women and Law in Late Antiquity*, Oxford: Clarendon Press, and New York: Oxford University Press, 1996
Brulé, P., "Infanticide et abandon d'enfants: pratiques grecques et comparaisons anthropologiques", *Dialogues d'Histoire Ancienne*, 18 (1992): pp. 53–90
Calame, Claude, *Choruses of Young Women in Ancient Greece: Their Morphology, Religious Role, and Social Function*, translated by Derek Collins and Janice Orion, Lanham: Rowman and Littlefield, 1997
French, V., "Children in Antiquity" in *Children in Historical and Comparative Perspectives*, edited by Joseph M. Hawes and N. Ray Hiner, New York: Greenwood Press, 1991
Golden, Mark, "Did the Ancients Care when their Children Died?", *Greece and Rome*, 35 (1988): pp. 152–63
Golden, Mark, *Children and Childhood in Classical Athens*, Baltimore: Johns Hopkins University Press, 1990
Golden, Mark, "Continuity, Change and the Study of Ancient Childhood", *Echos du Monde Classique*, 36 (1992): pp. 7–18
Golden, Mark, "Change or Continuity? Children and Childhood in Hellenistic Historiography" in *Inventing Ancient Culture: Historicism, Periodization and the Ancient World*, edited by Mark Golden and Peter Toohey, London and New York: Routledge, 1997
Goody, Jack, *The Development of the Family and Marriage in Europe*, Cambridge and New York: Cambridge University Press, 1983
Harris, W.V., "The Theoretical Possibility of Extensive Infanticide in the Graeco-Roman World", *Classical Quarterly*, 32 (1982): pp. 114–16
Jaeger, Werner, *Paideia: The Ideals of Greek Culture*, 3 vols, Oxford: Blackwell, 1954–61; reprinted Oxford and New York: Oxford University Press, 1986
Lacey, Walter Kirkpatrick, *The Family in Classical Greece*, London: Thames and Hudson, and Ithaca, New York: Cornell University Press, 1968
Moffatt, A., "The Byzantine Child", *Social Research*, 53 (1986): pp. 705–23
Patterson, C.B., "'Not Worth the Rearing': The Causes of Infant Exposure in Ancient Greece", *Transactions of the American Philological Association*, 115 (1985): pp. 103–23
Patterson, C.B., "Those Athenian Bastards", *Classical Antiquity*, 9/1 (1990): pp. 39–73
Pelling, C., "Childhood and Personality in Greek Biography" in *Characterization and Individuality in Greek Literature*, edited by Christopher Pelling, Oxford: Clarendon Press, and New York: Oxford University Press, 1990
Pomeroy, Sarah B., "Infanticide in Hellenistic Greece" in *Images of Women in Antiquity*, edited by Averil Cameron and Amélie Kuhrt, revised edition, London: Routledge, and Detroit: Wayne State University Press, 1993
Shorter, Edward, *The Making of the Modern Family*, New York: Basic Books, 1975; London: Fontana, 1977
Strauss, Barry S., *Fathers and Sons in Athens: Ideology and Society in the Period of the Peloponnesian War*, London: Routledge, and Princeton, New Jersey: Princeton University Press, 1993
Vermeulen, C.J., *Families in Urban Greece*, Ithaca, New York: Cornell University Press, 1970

Chios

Island in the eastern Aegean

The island of Chios has been inhabited almost continuously from the Stone Age to the present day. This it owes at least in part to its fertile soil and to its geographical position, located in the eastern Aegean just off the coast of Asia Minor, from where over countless centuries it has been able to exploit the trade routes north to the Hellespont and the Black Sea and south, west, and east to the Mediterranean, the Levant, and Egypt.

The earliest evidence for human habitation comes from the cave site of Ayio Gala in the northwest of the island, and dates from the early Neolithic period in the 6th millennium BC. In the 5th millennium BC a settlement was also established at Emporio in the south, and continued in almost constant use through the Early, Middle, and Late Bronze Age. Then around 1100 BC Emporio, in keeping with other Mycenaean sites all over the Aegean, suffered catastrophic destruction by fire and abandonment by its population. Our understanding of the subsequent Dark Age period is confused, though probably around 1000 BC the island was colonized by Ionian Greek-speakers arriving from the west.

By the 8th century BC Chios shows evidence of increased activity, including the refoundation of a settlement at Emporio, the existence of a religious sanctuary at nearby Kato Phana, and clear indications of active overseas trade. The 7th century BC was a time of great expansion and development for the island, in terms both of its mercantile trade and also of its external cultural and political relations. Together with other Greek cities, it founded the trading station of Naucratis in Egypt and, joining with 11 other cities in the eastern Aegean,

Chios: monastery of Nea Moni, founded in the mid-11th century by the emperor Constantine IX Monomachos

established the Panionium or league of Ionian states. By the Archaic period the island was united under the control of Chios town, situated in the middle of the east coast. This was a time of great prosperity, when Chios emerged as one of the leading naval powers in the Aegean. Its products of gum mastic, turpentine, decorated pottery, fine cloth, figs, and wine were exported widely throughout the Aegean and beyond. So famous, indeed, was its wine that Chian coins were recognized by their emblem of the wine amphora. In addition to its commercial activities, Chios also became renowned for its school of sculptors: Chian artists such as Archermus, Bupalus, Micciades, and Glaucus exerted a strong influence on Archaic Greek sculptural style and were much sought after for their work. Also by the 6th century BC Chios had firmly established itself in the Greek poetic tradition: claiming to be the birthplace of Homer, a claim strongly contested by neighbouring Smyrna, the island became home to the Homeridae, a school of rhapsodes who asserted their descent from Homer himself. In the Classical period, too, Chios' influence on the arts and learning remained strong: the tragic poet Ion, the historian Theopompus, and the sophist Theocritus all numbering among its sons.

Although the early political history of Chios is scarcely understood, a fragment of an inscribed stele found on the island and dating to 575–550 BC represents one of the earliest extant documents in Greek constitutional history and shows that Chios was already attempting to move towards a democratic system of government. In its external relations the island prospered as long as the Lydians controlled western Asia Minor. In 545 BC, however, the Lydian kingdom was destroyed by the Persians, who imposed harsh tyrannical rule on the Ionian cities, including Chios. The Ionian response came in 499 BC in the form of a revolt in which Chios, as a naval power, played a major part. The subsequent defeat of the allies brought down a terrible reprisal on Chios in 493 BC, when the Persians marched across the island leaving death and destruction in their wake. The Persian domination persisted until their defeat at the hands of the Greeks in 479 BC. Independent once again, Chios now elected democratic leaders, and joined the Delian League under the leadership of Athens. Peace and prosperity returned to the island and the Chiots became famed for their wealth and luxurious lifestyle, which was supported by vast numbers of slaves. The Peloponnesian War (431–404 BC) proved a rude interruption to this idyll, especially when in 412 BC the Chiots revolted against their Athenian allies, an act that ended in Chiot defeat and fierce retribution by the Athenians. Following the close of the Peloponnesian War, Chios fell successively under Spartan and Athenian control. Subsequently it resisted the rise of Macedonian power, which led to its capture in 333 BC by one of the generals of Alexander the

Great and the imposition of a Macedonian garrison. In 332 BC Alexander sent a letter to the Chiots (inscription in Chios Museum) in which he ensured the restoration of the democracy, previously undermined by an oligarchic faction, and ordered a contribution of 20 Chiot triremes for his fleet. During the Hellenistic period the island regained its independence and passed in turn under the influence of Ptolemy I, the Seleucids, the Attalids, and the Macedonians. But its glorious days of wealth and power were now long over. Pro-Roman in its stance, Chios fared well in Roman hands, retaining its autonomy, but suffered severe damage in 86 BC during the Mithridatic wars. An earthquake of 17 BC brought further hardships, though these were in part offset by the aid extended to the island by Tiberius. In AD 70 the autonomy of Chios was abolished by Vespasian, and by the end of the 1st century AD economic decline had set in.

The early Christian history of Chios is obscure. St Isidorus, the island's patron saint, was at work there during the 3rd century, and the first official record of a Chiot bishop is of Tryphon in the 5th century. However, the archaeological evidence suggests that between the 4th and 7th centuries Chios enjoyed increased prosperity with basilica churches being built at Emporio, Chios town, and probably Kato Phana. The destructive Arab raids of the mid-7th century, however, ushered in a further period of decline and it is not until the 10th and 11th centuries that signs of recovery and development are again visible. The concern of the central Byzantine state for the security and welfare of the island now becomes clear in the construction of a fortress in Chios town, the presence of royal officers, and the founding of the monastery of Nea Moni. This highly important monument, endowed by the emperor Constantine IX Monomachos (1042–54), preserves some of the finest examples of Byzantine mosaic, painting, and architecture known to us.

By now once more attractive to foreign powers, attempts were made to seize Chios in the years 1125–71 by the Venetians, while between 1204 and 1225 the island fell subject to the Latin empire of Constantinople. In their turn, the Genoese set their sights on Chios, occupying it for the first time in the years 1307–29, and more permanently a second time between 1346 and 1566. Genoese interest in the island focused on the suitability of Chios as a mercantile depot for Black Sea commerce. Their administration of the island was controlled by Maona, a Genoese chartered company, most of whose members were drawn from the Giustiniani family while the "Podestà", or governor, was directly appointed by the Republic of Genoa. Although they ruled the native inhabitants with a heavy hand, the Genoese nevertheless ensured the security of Chios, building many defence towers and fortresses, and oversaw efficient agricultural production. Cultivation of citrus fruit and mastic and the manufacture of silk resulted in an increase in the wealth and population of the island, and the export of its products far and wide throughout the Mediterranean world. Mastic, a resin of the lentisk tree, grows only in the south of Chios and since antiquity the island had therefore possessed a monopoly on this valuable commodity, which was famed for its medicinal and other uses. Under Genoese encouragement, fortified mastic-producing villages, such as Pyrgi, Mesta, and Olympoi, now sprang up in southern Chios. They were located inland at a distance from the sea,

in order to escape the greedy eyes of pirates and Turks, were built around a central defence tower, and presented high, blank perimeter walls to the outside world. The Genoese, together with the old Byzantine noble families, meanwhile, built gracious mansions surrounded by citrus estates in the Kampos district to the south of Chios town.

In 1566 Chios was taken by the Turks. Thereafter, despite the attempts of the Florentine Knights of St Stephen (1599) and of the Venetians (1694–95) to wrest the island from them, Chios remained under Ottoman control until 1912. During this period, at least until 1821, the inhabitants enjoyed a considerable degree of political and religious autonomy and also economic prosperity, although they did have to remit heavy taxes to the foreign overlord. Trade continued to flourish, although Chios's position as the foremost mercantile port for ships plying between Constantinople and Europe, and between Constantinople and Syria-Egypt, had by the mid-17th century taken second place to nearby Smyrna. The island's prosperity and relative autonomy led, furthermore, to its fostering of cultural Hellenism. The School of Chios, founded in 1792 and financed by Chian merchants, possessed a library and printing press, the library owing much to the scholar Adamantios Korais. Another great scholar associated with the school was Neophytos Vamvas, a prolific writer on a number of subjects. Together with men such as Alexandros and Nikolaos Mavrokordatos, they safeguarded intellectual and spiritual Hellenism under the Ottoman occupation. When the War of Independence broke out in 1821, Korais was instrumental in encouraging the uprising. In 1822 the Chiots joined the rebellion, only to be punished by terrible massacres, enslavement, and destruction at the hands of the Turks. In revenge, Konstantinos Kanaris, commander of the powerful naval fleet of Psara, a small but important island lying off the west coast of Chios, destroyed the Turkish flagship. The Turkish massacres were vividly portrayed in Delacroix's famous painting (Paris, Louvre) of the outrage, a work of art that was to help shape western support for the Greek struggle for independence. The massacres of 1822 had deep and long-lasting effects on Chios. Many of those who survived fled the island and established settlements throughout Greece and overseas. The more fortunate of the refugees, such as the Rallis brothers, later became successful merchants in London, Paris, Marseilles, Palermo, Odessa, Alexandria, and elsewhere. In 1912, during the Balkan Wars, Chios was finally liberated and joined with the independent state of Hellas. Following the disaster of 1822 and also a catastrophic earthquake in 1881, which killed thousands and destroyed much property, shipping came to play an increasingly significant role in the revival of the Chian economy and, following the liberation, the merchant navy continued to expand. Many Greek shipping families, such as Chandris, Hadjipateras, Laimos, Livanos, Lyras, and Pateras, hailing from both Chios and the neighbouring islets of Oinoussai, generated great wealth during the 19th and 20th centuries. But despite its liberation, Chios' days of occupation were not yet over, for between May 1941 and September 1944 it suffered subjugation at the hands of the German forces during World War II.

Today the once teeming population of the island has declined as a result of urban drift and overseas emigration to countries such as America and Australia. Accordingly, agricultural production has shrunk, though mastic cultivation in the south of Chios continues to harvest a lucrative monopoly. Shipping also still plays an important role in the island's life and economy, and though some limited tourism has developed in recent years, this still prosperous island is by no means dependent on the tourist industry. Culturally, too, Chios fulfils a significant role as home to the Korais Library, rebuilt in 1886, and today one of the most important libraries in Greece.

LESLEY A. BEAUMONT

Summary

Chios has been inhabited since the early Neolithic period. In the Archaic period it helped found Naucratis and established the league of Ionian states. This was a period of great commercial and cultural prosperity. Sacked by the Persians, Chios joined the Delian League and enjoyed renewed prosperity in the 5th century BC. Gradual decline set in under the Romans and Arabs, but Chios flourished again in the 10th and 11th centuries. After rule by Venetians, Latins, and Genoese, Chios fell to the Ottomans in 1566. There were terrible massacres in 1822. The island was joined to Greece in 1912.

Further Reading

Argenti, Philip, *The Massacres of Chios*, London: John Lane, 1932

Argenti, Philip, *Bibliography of Chios, from Classical Times to 1936*, Oxford: Clarendon Press, 1940

Argenti, Philip and H.J. Rose, *The Folk-lore of Chios*, Cambridge: Cambridge University Press, 1949

Argenti, Philip, *The Occupation of Chios by the Genoese and their Administration of the Island, 1346–1566*, 3 vols, Cambridge: Cambridge University Press, 1958

Ballance, Michael *et al.*, *Excavations in Chios, 1952–55: Byzantine Emporio*, Athens: British School at Athens, and London: Thames and Hudson, 1989

Beaumont, L.A. and A. Archontidou-Argyri, "New Work at Kato Phana, Chios: The Kato Phana Archaeological Project", *Annual of the British School at Athens*, 94 (1999): pp. 267–87

Boardman, John, *Excavations in Chios, 1952–55: Greek Emporio*, London: British School at Athens, and London: Thames and Hudson, 1967

Boardman, John and C.E. Vaphopoulou-Richardson (editors), *Chios: A Conference at the Homereion in Chios, 1984*, Oxford: Clarendon Press, and New York: Oxford University Press, 1986

Bouras, Charalambos, *Chios*, Athens: National Bank of Greece, 1974

Bouras, Charalambos, *Nea Moni on Chios: History and Architecture*, Athens: Commercial Bank of Greece, 1982

Hood, Sinclair, *Excavations in Chios, 1938–55: Prehistoric Emporio and Agio Gala*, 2 vols, London: British School of Archaeology at Athens, and London: Thames and Hudson, 1981–82

Lamb, W., "Excavations at Kato Phana in Chios", *Annual of the British School at Athens*, 35 (1934–35): pp. 138–64

Miller, William, "The Genoese Colonies in Greece" in his *Essays on the Latin Orient*, Cambridge: Cambridge University Press, 1921; reprinted New York: AMS Press, 1983

Perikos, John, *Homer and Chios*, Chios: Perikos, 1994

Sarikakis, T., *I Chios stin Archaiotita* [Chios in Antiquity], Athens, 1998

Tsaravopoulos, A., "Syllogi Bibliographias (meta 1936) yia tin Archaia Chio kai ta Psara" [Collected Bibliography (post 1936) for Ancient Chios and Psara], *Horos*, 5 (1987): pp. 175–202

Zacharou-Loutrari, Athena, Vaso Penna, and Tasoula Mandala, *Chios: History and Art*, Chios: Chios Prefecture and the Society of Friends of Chios Archaeological Museum, 1989

Choricius of Gaza

Sophist and orator of the 6th century AD

Choricius lived and taught in his native city of Gaza in the age of the emperor Justinian (527–65). He was a pupil of the orator Procopius who had established a famous school of rhetoric there. Choricius succeeded his teacher as master of the school (c.538–50) and, as his speeches in front of the City authorities at festivals and other occasions suggest, he became the most acclaimed orator in the city of Gaza after Procopius. Choricius belongs to the rhetorical tradition which goes back to the Second Sophistic, a tradition of epideictic oratory favouring the composition of *declamationes* (*meletai*, rhetorical exercises on a given topic), rhetorical descriptions (*ekphraseis*), and speeches. Rhetoric was well established in the school curriculum, as was the teaching of grammar. The practice of declamation became particularly prominent in Greek schools of the period. Orators and sophists such as Aelius Aristides (2nd century AD) became models of this kind, while the handbooks of Hermogenes (2nd century AD) and Aphthonius (4th century) offered a systematization of this school rhetoric, the so-called *progymnasmata* (rhetorical exercises). This tradition reached a peak in Constantinople and Antioch with Libanius in the 4th century. Then in the 6th century Gaza became the new centre where rhetoric flourished. Rhetorical products of this kind required rigorous style and imaginative content and, despite their heavy rhetorical flavour, they often have considerable literary claims.

A number of Choricius' works have survived, which can be classified under three headings: speeches (8), declamations (12), and *dialexeis* (25), that is, a preliminary informal talk (basically an argument) preceding the delivery of a major speech. Several of his speeches and his declamations are prefaced with a *dialexis* and/or a *theoria*, an introductory piece containing information about the issue to be treated and the mode of its treatment. Unlike the *theoria*, the *dialexis* is not necessarily related to the main speech, but some of them discuss problems of declamation. Like Procopius and Aeneas of Gaza, Choricius himself was a Christian. Thus, in his encomiastic speeches to bishop Marcianus he employs traditional rhetorical means for the description of the architecture and the paintings of the churches of St Sergius and St Stephen in Gaza, built by Marcianus. But, these few works apart, in which we find allusions and references to the Bible, there are few traces of Christian influence in his work, which, faithful to rhetorical conventions, is permeated by pagan ideas and imagery. Choricius' speeches are both encomiastic and funereal. They address high-ranking local officials, and one funeral speech is devoted to his teacher Procopius. The themes of the declamations were determined by the rhetorical tradition – preeminently representations (*ethopoiiai*) of either stock characters (e.g. the avaricious older man) or mythical/historical pairs (e.g. Patroclus, Miltiades). They are often treated in pairs of opposites (Polydamas/Priamus, the young hero/the old miser). Choricius' versions of these stock themes are particularly elegant and his fictional discourse attains a high degree of sophistication.

Choricius' most interesting work for us today is his speech in defence of mimic theatrical performances entitled *Apology* for the Mimes (*Synegoria Mimon*). This is the last surviving text from antiquity concerning ancient theatrical performances. Although it is a mere rhetorical exercise, probably delivered in public in a theatre, it is invaluable for the information it contains about the popular genre of mime. The work presupposes mimic performances in Constantinople before 526, when Justinian issued an edict against theatre performances, but it may well have been written after this date. The Church targeted mimic performances on the ground that they had a bad effect on public morals, and John Chrysostom and Libanius were fierce critics of them. The topic thus lent itself to rhetorical advocacy. Choricius addresses the most important charges against mimic performances; the actors of the mime are defended against charges of immorality and the performances against charges of arousing bodily desire. The mime is presented as beneficial for the city, having a good effect on both the citizens and the authorities. Given the nature of his work, it is difficult to say what Choricius really thought about his subject, but this does not make his testimony less valuable.

Typical of the rhetorical products of this kind, Choricius' works are full of allusions and references to earlier Greek literature, on which he evidently was particularly knowledgeable. Homer, the Greek dramatic poets, Thucydides, Plato, and the Attic orators serve as examples of pure Attic style and colour every piece of Choricius' work. From among his contemporaries, he is most indebted to Libanius and to his teacher Procopius. Choricius writes Atticizing Greek and is particularly rigorous about his style. His works suffer from the weakness of the rhetorical works of this kind, namely excessive use of rhetorical schemes and poetic expressions, trivial ideas, rhetorical excess, and sophisticated style. However, they are valuable testimonies of his age. They contain important information about local personalities, history, and culture. His accounts of festivals (both pagan and Christian) and other cultural activities in Gaza are invaluable as they illustrate a gradual transition from paganism to Christianity. Choricius testifies to the survival of pagan customs and festivals in a largely Christianized society and sheds some light on the social life of Gaza, highlighting the role of the bishop and other local authorities. Choricius' works were used by subsequent generations of Byzantines; Photios, who read them, judges Choricius' style fairly and praises his Christian faith.

GEORGE E. KARAMANOLIS

Biography

Choricius (*fl.* 6th century AD) lived and taught in Gaza where he was a pupil of the orator Procopius. He succeeded Procopius as master of the school of rhetoric at Gaza and himself became a noted orator. Surviving works include speeches, declamations, and arguments which give valuable information about the society and architecture of Gaza and about contemporary attitudes to the theatre.

Writings

Opera, edited by Richard Foerster and Eberhard Richtsteig, Leipzig: Teubner, 1929
Synegoria Mimon, edited by I. Stephanes, Thessalonica, 1986

Further Reading

Hunger, Herbert, *Die hochsprachliche profane Literatur der Byzantiner*, vol. 1, Munich: Beck, 1978
Kennedy, George A., *Greek Rhetoric under Christian Emperors*, Princeton, New Jersey: Princeton University Press, 1983
Litsas, F.K., "Choricius of Gaza and his Descriptions of Festivals of Gaza", *Jahrbuch der Österreichischen Byzantinistik*, 32/3 (1982): pp. 427–36
Russell, D.A., *Greek Declamation*, Cambridge and New York: Cambridge University Press, 1983
Schmid, W., Chorikios entry in *Real-Encyclopädie der klassischen Altertumswissenschaft*, edited by August Pauly *et al.*, vol. 3, 1899, 2424–31

Chortatsis, Georgios

Cretan playwright of the late 16th century

Georgios Chortatsis is the most important figure in Cretan Renaissance drama, but, paradoxically, the one about whom least is known. Although there have been several attempts to identify the playwright with persons of the same name known from contemporary archival sources, none can be regarded as conclusive. All that can be said is that he was a native of Rethymnon, though he later lived in Kastro (Chandax), was active around the last decade of the 16th century, and was the author of at least three plays and two sets of dramatic interludes. Since his works are dated before any of the other surviving Cretan plays, he may have been the person responsible for the introduction of Renaissance drama in Greek (other Cretans are known who wrote plays in Italian a decade or two earlier). Among his circle of acquaintances were several influential persons of the time, including the Veneto-Cretan nobleman Markos Antonios Viaros and the lawyer Ioannis Mourmouris, to whom he dedicated *Panoria* and *Erofili* respectively. Internal evidence shows him to have been familiar with a wide range of Latin and Italian literature, particularly 16th-century works by Trissino, Speroni, Ariosto, Tasso, Guarini, and others.

The plays definitely known to have been written by Chortatsis include one of each of the three main dramatic genres of the time: the pastoral comedy (*tragicommedia pastorale*) *Panoria*, the tragedy *Erophili*, and the comedy *Katzourbos*. *Panoria* (which used to be known as *Gyparis*) is usually regarded as the earliest of the three works, dated around 1590. It is a work of Arcadian sophistication, but located in the Cretan countryside, specifically on Mount Ida; it is an Ida adapted to pastoral conventions, with goddesses and Nereids inhabiting its woods, shepherdesses hunting deer, and Cupid armed with bow and arrows. Chortatsis draws on Guarini's *Pastor Fido*, Tasso's *Aminta*, and perhaps also Grotto's *La Calisto* for some episodes, but borrowed material is artfully reworked to suit the plot requirements of the Cretan play. It centres on the loves of two pairs of shepherds, Gyparis and Panoria, and Alexis and Athousa. Two comic characters, Giannoulis, the father of Panoria, and the worldly-wise old woman Phrosyni, try to persuade the two shepherdesses to accept the advances of their swains. The successful outcome is brought about by the intervention of Aphrodite and her son Eros. The tragic posturings of the two love-sick shepherds are counterbalanced by the comic, and often bawdy, talk of the two older characters. Despite all the rustic humour, the liberated attitudes of the two shepherdesses have a very modern resonance. Chortatsis successfully adapts the conventions of pastoral drama to a Cretan context: his play is much more down-to-earth than the sophisticated artificiality of Italian pastoral.

Erophili was certainly completed after *Panoria* but can be dated only approximately to about 1595. It was the only one of Chortatsis' plays to be printed during the Cretan Renaissance period: an unsatisfactory edition was published in Venice in 1637, but a much better one appeared in 1676 and was several times reprinted. Three manuscripts have also survived. Chortatsis based his play on the plot of Giraldi's *Orbecche*; secondary sources include Tasso's *Il Re Torrismondo* and *Aminta* and Trissino's *Sofonisba*. Comparison with *Orbecche* reveals Chortatsis's superiority as a dramatist, in terms of both plot construction and characterization. The play is set in Egypt, where king Philogonos has usurped the throne after killing his brother. His daughter Erophili has secretly married Panaretos, a noble general. The drama reaches its height with the king's discovery of the marriage. In revenge for the affront to his honour he kills Panaretos and offers the dismembered remains to Erophili as a wedding present. Erophili commits suicide and, in the final scene, the king is killed by the chorus of the princess's handmaids. The chorus, which has commented on the action in choric odes at the end of each act, thus finally assumes an active and decisive role, avenging the heroine's death. The play's sophisticated construction is particularly noteworthy: alternating monologues and dialogues vary the pace, suspense and dramatic irony are artfully employed, and the speeches, particularly those of Erofili, are infused with a lyrical intensity. A set of four interludes associated with the play in the manuscripts and editions tell a contrasting and unrelated story: the episode of Rinaldo and Armida from Tasso's *Gerusalemme Liberata*. Words, music, and dance combine with elaborate effects to provide relief from the emotional intensity of the tragedy – if at least it can be assumed that the interludes were intended for performance between the acts.

Katzourbos was completed between 1595 and 1601, a dating based on allusions in the play to contemporary persons and events. It belongs to the tradition of *commedia erudita*, and makes use of stock characters such as the gluttonous servant, the pedantic schoolmaster, and the *miles gloriosus*. The plot is trivial enough: Nikolos is in love with Kassandra, the presumed daughter of the courtesan Poulisena, but is rivalled by old Armenis, who plans to buy a night of pleasure with Kassandra. An elaborate plan is laid to deceive Armenis by substituting Poulisena's maid Anneza for Kassandra. Armenis's amorous adventure is thwarted by his wife, and the intrigue is finally resolved by the discovery that Kassandra is really Armenis's long-lost daughter, who had been carried off from Naxos by Turkish pirates and sold in Crete. All ends happily with the marriage of Kassandra and Nikolos. Interwoven into the story line are various comic episodes involving the braggart captain, the schoolmaster, and the servants. Although there are some weaknesses in the plot (perhaps in part due to changes made by a later adapter), Chortatsis' comic inventiveness never flags. He exploits a wide variety of humorous effects, both verbal and visual, showing an awareness of contemporary Italian theories of laughter and rhetoric. Topical and local references to people, places, and

events would have enhanced the appeal to a Cretan audience. Chortatsis's comedy provided the model for another Cretan playwright, Markos Antonios Phoskolos, who composed his *Phortounatos* c.1655.

A further comedy, *Stathis*, has also been attributed to Chortatsis, but definite proof is lacking. The problem is complicated by the fact that *Stathis* survives only in an abridged three-act version made in the Ionian islands.

The three plays definitely known to be by Chortatsis are all in couplet-rhymed 15-syllable verse (with the exception of the choric odes of *Erophili*, which are in hendecasyllables with *terza rima*). They share the five-act structure prescribed for Neoclassical drama, and employ the Cretan dialect with many west Cretan elements. Chortatsis's poetic style is intricate and finely wrought, with long complex periods, much use of imagery, and a subtle feel for rhythm and rhyme. As K. Dimaras has written: "At no point, even in his least lyrical moments, can we forget that we are dealing with a genuine poet." Little is known about contemporary performances in Crete, but Chortatsis's work was transmitted to the Ionian islands (manuscripts of all three plays were copied there), and had a considerable influence on the development of a local dramatic tradition. Parts of *Erophili* also passed into oral tradition, either as ballads or as carnival entertainments, in various parts of Greece. All three plays have enjoyed successful revivals on the stage in recent years.

DAVID HOLTON

See also Renaissance (Veneto-Cretan)

Biography
Active in the last decade of the 16th century, though actual dates of birth and death are unknown. Born in Rethymnon, Chortatsis was the earliest and most important of the playwrights of the Cretan Renaissance. Three plays survive: *Panoria*, a pastoral comedy, *Erophili*, a tragedy, and the comedy *Katzourbos*.

Writings
Erophile in *Three Cretan Plays*, translated by Frederick Henry Marshall, London: Oxford University Press, 1929
Katzourbos: Komodia [Katzourbos: A Comedy], edited by Linos Politis, Herakleion, 1964
Panoria, edited by Emmanouil Kriaras, Thessalonica, 1975
Erophili, edited by S. Alexiou and M. Aposkiti, Athens, 1988
I Elevtheromeni Ierousalim: Ta Intermedia tis Erophilis [Jerusalem Liberated: The Erophili Interludes], edited by S. Alexiou and M. Aposkiti, Athens, 1992
Katsourbos, edited by S.E. Kaklamanis, Athens, 1993

Further Reading
Alexiou, Margaret, "Women, Marriage and Death in the Drama of Renaissance Crete" in *Images of Authority: Papers Presented to Joyce Reynolds on the Occasion of her Seventieth Birthday*, edited by Mary Margaret Mackenzie and Charlotte Roueché, Cambridge: Cambridge Philological Society, 1989
Bancroft-Marcus, Rosemary, "Georgios Chortatsis and his Works: A Critical Review", *Mantatophoros*, 16 (1980): pp. 13–46
Bancroft-Marcus, Rosemary, "The Editing of Panoria and the Prologue of Apollo", *Kritologia*, 10–11 (1980): pp. 135–63
Evangelatos, Spyros, "Georgios Ioanni Chortatsis (c.1545–1610)", *Thisavrismata*, 7 (1970): pp. 182–227
Holton, David (editor), *Literature and Society in Renaissance Crete*, Cambridge and New York: Cambridge University Press, 1991

Kaklamanis, S.E., *Erevnes gia to prosopo kai tin epochi tou Georgiou Chortatsi* [Researches into the Personality and Times of Georgios Chortatsis], Herakleion, 1993

Markomihelaki, Anastasia, "The Sixteenth-Century Cretan Playwright Georgios Chortatsis as a Parodist", *Kambos: Cambridge Papers in Modern Greek*, 3 (1995): pp. 71–93

Martini, Lidia (editor), *Stathis: Kritiki Komodia* [Stathis: A Cretan Comedy], Thessalonica, 1976

Pouchner, Valter, *Meletimata theatrou: to Kritiko Theatro* [Theatre Essays: The Cretan Theatre], Athens, 1991

Christianity

Few episodes in antiquity are so well documented as the beginnings of Christianity; perhaps for that reason, few are so obscure. That Jesus came from Nazareth, that he preached the Kingdom of God, that he was crucified by the Roman procurator Pontius Pilate are acknowledged facts in almost every study of the subject; every other detail of his life remains the stuff of unabated controversy. We know at least what emerged as Christianity: the recognition of Jesus as the Son of God, the Messiah or Christ of Israel, the Lord of life for his followers in the present world and the judge of all humanity in the next. In the New Testament all these claims are based on a belief in his Resurrection; if there was a community that revered him only as a human teacher, it must have perished quickly, and the history of the Roman world can show no other case in which a dead man, having first received the honours due to a human being, was subsequently worshipped as a god.

Faith in Christ was initially spread by Jewish missionaries, but (apart from a short-lived community in Jerusalem) the only Churches of which we have a reliable record were established among the Gentiles. The principal author of the Gentile mission was a Hellenized Jew from Tarsus in Cilicia, Saul or Paul, who had met the resurrected Christ but not the earthly Jesus. Paul maintains that only the Resurrection can deliver human nature from the sinfulness that clings to it as a consequence of Adam's first transgression. To practise a cult of manufactured idols, like the Gentiles, or of outward ordinances, like the Jews, is to live according to the flesh; only those who have died with Christ and have been incorporated into his body through the Church can walk according to the Spirit, knowing both release from punishment and liberty from sin. Faith in the Resurrection makes us righteous in the sight of God, and prepares us to be sanctified by the Spirit of obedience, who quickened Christ himself. True sanctity and everlasting life are possible only in the spiritual body, which will be given to the elect on Christ's return.

Paul thought this to be imminent, perhaps echoing a prophecy of Jesus (Mark 9: 1 etc.); but, as expectation waned, it was necessary to seek at least a partial realization of the Kingdom of God on earth. Some of the moral precepts in the Gospels may have been part of Jesus' ministry, but Matthew strikes a new note when he makes the Church the arbiter of judgement and forgiveness in the present. The communal meal or Eucharist came to signify, not so much the expectation of Christ's return, as the remembrance of his sufferings and a literal partaking of his body. Baptism, once the sign of faith in adults, was already being administered to children in some churches by the end of the 2nd century, being explained by Origen as the means whereby Christ purges the filth inherited or incurred at the time of birth. Above all, doctrine and discipline were maintained by appointed ministers who claimed direct descent from the apostles. The division of these into presbyters and deacons, perhaps with an *episkopos* or bishop as chief presbyter, was prevalent by the end of the 2nd century in the Greek-speaking communities of Syria, Asia, Italy, and Gaul.

The scriptures of the early Christians were in Greek, and at this period they comprised all or most of the present New Testament, together with the Septuagint, the Greek translation of the Hebrew Torah. The authority of the "apocryphal" books, which have no Hebrew original, was maintained by the eminent scholars Epiphanius and Origen, and even today the Orthodox revere them as canonical, arguing that the work of the Holy Spirit in the interpretation of scripture is continuous, and that while the Church is the heir of the apostles, the Bible is the creation of the Church. The argument is stronger if one holds, with the fourth evangelist St John and Origen, that prophecy is not the work of men, but of Christ himself, who as the Word of God has been active in creation, revelation, and redemption since the beginning of the world.

Scripture and the hierarchy sustained the Church in the face of the persecutions that it suffered from Jews, from pagan magistrates, from local mobs, and even from emperors. The readiness with which Christ's people followed him to martyrdom provoked the irony of pagan writers; their refusal to treat the emperor as a god was seen as treason; and their abstinence from public cults provoked the charge that they were not only atheists but practised atrocious rites. The catalogue of Greek martyrs includes Ignatius of Antioch, Polycarp of Smyrna, Origen of Caesarea, and Peter of Alexandria; it will be observed that the centres of persecution were the great cities, which were also the localities in which the Gospel spread most rapidly. It should also be noted, however, that, where it was not purposely invited, the violence of the magistrates was sparingly employed, and almost always fell on the leaders of the Church.

Laymen, bishops, and presbyters took a hand in the development of doctrine in the early Christian centuries. The chief concern of laymen, such as Justin, Athenagoras, and Aristides, was to express their faith in a form that would be acceptable to philosophers and innocuous to political authorities. The clergy saw their task as the protection of received tradition against the fallacious inferences, denials, and deviations of other teachers, whom they stigmatized as heretics. Thus Irenaeus defends the flesh of Christ, the Resurrection, and the Old Testament against an extravagant strain of Pauline teaching, which contended that the body and the Law could have no part in the economy of salvation. In the 3rd century primitive adherence to monotheism (an undisputed tenet of Christianity) was found to be in conflict with the Trinitarian formulas that had figured in prayer and liturgy since apostolic times. In its insistence on the "three hypostases", the school of Origen offered no equivalent description for the unity of the Godhead; but when the presbyter Arius declared that the Son was no God but a creature of the Father, the adjective *homoousios* ("consubstantial") was inserted in the credal declaration of the Nicene Council in AD 325.

Christianity: relief of an empty throne awaiting Christ's second coming, with lambs representing the apostles, 4th-century Byzantine, Frühchristlich-Byzantische Sammlung, Berlin

Western influence may be suspected here, since Constantine, the first Christian emperor, was also the convenor of the council. The patronage that the Christian Church enjoyed from Constantine and his successors had a number of important consequences: an official predilection for Christianity at the expense of Judaism, thus ratifying the separation of the two religions; the practice of settling differences in doctrine by ecumenical definitions, which elevated the status of the bishops who produced them, and superseded the more informal creeds of previous centuries; the exercise of royal power in the shaping and enforcement of ecclesiastical policy, especially in the East, where the dominant emperor tended to be resident; and a transference of political and cultural supremacy to Christians, which encouraged them to make explicit use of Greek philosophy and to imitate the ornate style of contemporary writings. It was the Christianity of Byzantium that preserved the masterpieces of pagan literature.

Not everyone embraced the world so readily, and it was in the late 3rd century that Antony left his village in Upper Egypt to overcome new temptations in the desert. His early imitators were also solitaries or eremites, and in Syria the ascetics (known as stylites) are reputed to have spent their lives on pillars. But from the mid-4th century the usual form of monasticism was the communal or cenobitic one, in which a spiritual director helped the novice to vanquish carnal passions. In the texts on prayer and contemplative piety that make up the *Philokalia*, a compilation of the 18th century, we often find the simultaneous presence of very different streams of thought such as the psychology of Plato and a belief in the glorification of the flesh. Nevertheless philosophy proved to be of little assistance in reconciling the full humanity of Christ with the full divinity accorded to him by supporters of the Nicene definition. This tenet, though rejected or diluted in conciliar pronouncements of the intervening period, was reaffirmed in 381 at the Council of Constantinople, together with the equal divinity of the Holy Spirit. The same assembly, however, had to condemn Apollinarius, who denied that Christ had possessed a human mind. His principal opponents, the Cappadocian Fathers, may be regarded as the founders of the Greek Orthodox tradition. This maintains the priority of the Father in the Trinity, with the rider that all three Persons share the incomprehensibile essence of God; at the same time, it adds that Christ could not have been the saviour of humanity had he not been perfect man.

It was not enough to affirm the full humanity of Christ without assenting to a true union of these natures. The patriarch Nestorius was condemned for his alleged denial of this at the Council of Ephesus in 431; in 451, however, the Council of Chalcedon condemned the opposing error of maintaining that the human nature had been absorbed by the divinity. The council upheld the doctrine of Rome, but at the cost of a double schism, which gave rise to anti-Chalcedonian churches in Egypt and the eastern parts of the empire. These churches, whether they favoured or opposed the "Nestorian" teaching, resisted the attempts of Byzantine emperors to suppress or reconcile them, frequently displaying their independence by using Syriac or Coptic rather than Greek. Meanwhile the chief refiners of the Chalcedonian formula were Leontius of Byzantium, who argued for a mutual penetration (*perichoresis*) of the two natures; Maximos the Confessor, who persuaded the Church that Christ had not one will but two in indissoluble union; and John of Damascus, whose digest of the faith was to exert great influence even in the West. Maximos held that things divine and heavenly were mirrored both in the Church and in human nature; the commentaries of Germanos and Kabasilas show what a central place the liturgy continued to hold in expositions of Orthodox theology. While it offers no philosophical theory to explain the efficacy of the Christian sacraments, the Orthodox Church believes that the body and blood of Christ are consumed in the Eucharist, and that baptism makes infants into members of his body. The principle that the Incarnation has permanently united God to matter underlies the cult of images, which was abolished temporarily by the iconoclastic rulers of the 8th century, but restored by the Seventh Ecumenical Council at Nicaea in 787.

The seventh is the last council to be regarded by the Greeks as ecumenical. All seven were attended by the legates of the Roman see, but never by the bishops. Among the further causes of estrangement were the new dignities that accrued to

Constantinople at the second and the fourth councils, the barbarian hegemony in Italy after 476, and the efforts of the iconoclast emperors to enforce the obedience of the Roman pontiff. When Rome transferred its allegiance from Byzantium to the Franks in 800, theological differences were intensified by political hostility. The breach was recognized, rather than created, by Rome's excommunication of the patriarchate of Constantinople in 1054, and despite the councils of Lyon (1275), Basle (1431), and Florence (1438) no reconciliation has been achieved. To the crusaders of 1204 the Greeks were already heretics. The main points that distinguish their theology from that of western Christendom are:

1. *The filioque*. Eastern theologians do not speak of a double procession of the Spirit from the Father and the Son within the Trinity, though they readily accept that the Spirit was "received from" the Son in his earthly mission as the Paraclete. Western thinkers have tended, on the other hand, to follow Augustine's teaching that the Spirit proceeds from the Father and the Son. Under the Frankish emperors the words "and the Son" (*filioque*) were inserted into the clause on the procession of the Spirit in the so-called Nicene Creed. Such additions had been proscribed by the Council of Ephesus in 431, and in 1054 the *filioque* supplied the principal ground of theological dispute between the Churches. The Greeks object that it postulates two sources in the Trinity, and thus accords to it only an abstract unity. For them the Father alone is the source of unity, whereas the Augustinian theory holds that the Spirit, as the joint offspring of the Son and Father, constitutes a bond of love between them. Early proponents of the *filioque* believed that it was a necessary defence against an Arian subordination of the Son to the Father, though nowadays the Greek position is better understood. So far is it from being true that the status of Christ is lessened by the Orthodox insistence on the priority of the Father that more prayers are addressed to Christ than in the western Churches, notably the Jesus prayer – "Lord Jesus Christ, Son of God, have mercy on me a sinner" – which remains a common devotional exercise. The invocation of Mary as *Theotokos* ("one who gave birth to God") is attested in the 4th century by Gregory of Nazianzus, and Nestorius' opposition to it was the cause of Cyril's first complaint against him. Admirers of the Greek tradition argue that, by stressing the coinherence of the Father, Son, and Spirit, it encourages us to think of the Godhead as a communion of persons; Zizioulas's study *Being as Communion* has commanded much attention in the West.

2. *Redemption*. Western theologians since Augustine have often held that the death of Christ discharged a debt that we were incapable of paying for ourselves; this is often accompanied by a doctrine of divine predestination, which asserts that even faith in the atoning work of Christ would be impossible without an act of grace. The Orthodox, however, reject the view that we are incapable of virtue in our natural state, as they also reject the Augustinian doctrine that we inherit the penalty of Adam's sin. Most Greek fathers (Cyril excepted) seem to have found no heresy in the Pelagian opponents of Augustine. Maximos the Confessor gave new currency to the notion, first proposed by Irenaeus, that humans were created in the image of God but not with the perfect likeness; this was manifested by the incarnation of Christ, and is attainable, with the help of the Holy Spirit, for anyone who elects to be incorporated into his earthly body. As we retain the image (which consists in our free will or rationality), we are free to make the initial act of faith, and are therefore fellow workers or *synergoi* with the redemptive love of God. The latter is not generally regarded as an offended Lord requiring satisfaction or as a judge inflicting punishment; rather, the divine Word who created us and took flesh in order to gather us into his body, thus enrolling us in his victory over Satan and reconciling our estranged hearts to himself.

3. *Life and death*. Faith is not so much an intellectual assent as a continuous participation in the body of Christ. The Incarnation has sanctified all matter, so that veneration of icons and partaking of the Eucharist can serve as regular instruments of salvation. The elaborate liturgy of Christmas and Easter teaches that Christ brings salvation through his Incarnation, Crucifixion, and Resurrection. Although the mysticism of Evagrius in the 4th century seemed to ignore the resurrection of the body, the usual aim of Orthodox spirituality has been rather to enhance the integrity of the human person: Symeon the New Theologian tasted the glorification of the body, while the Messalians of the 4th century and the Palamites of the 14th locate the centre of devotion in the "heart". Some hold that the cooperation of God with the believer continues after death, when the latter will undergo the fires of Purgatory – not so much to expiate his sins as to make him fit for heaven. A tradition going back to Origen holds that all humanity may eventually be saved, and that even the sinner's experience of hell arises only from his refusal to accept the warmth of love.

4. *Ecclesiology*. Women are not admitted to the priesthood, though as martyrs they may attain sainthood. The saints retain communion with the living, and may be addressed in prayer; Mary, the foremost of them, is supposed to have remained a virgin for the whole of her life, which many believe to have ended with her bodily assumption into heaven. By a decree of the Council in Trullo (692), bishops, when elected, should be unmarried; priests have always been allowed to marry provided their marriage took place before their ordination to the diaconate. Dogmatic resolutions can be taken only by councils, which must be ecumenical. The patriarch of Constantinople exercises primacy de facto, though a nominal pre-eminence is still allowed to Rome.

Since the fall of Byzantium the Greek world has contracted, and now that Greece is a state, its people do not need religion to sustain their nationhood. Nevertheless, attendance at the great services remains frequent, and even where there is little knowledge of dogma, the saints' days are remembered and observed. The monasteries of Mount Athos are probably flourishing more than those of the western denominations, and Justinian's church of the Holy Wisdom (Hagia Sophia) in Istanbul (Constantinople) is among the acknowledged glories of European architecture. The poems of the 6th-century "melodist" Romanos are regarded as the best works of Greek literature between the Classical period and the late 19th century. Here, as elsewhere, the modern intellectual is no friend to traditional religion; yet the novels of Kazantzakis (*Zorba the Greek*, *Christ Recrucified*, *The Last Temptation*, *God's Pauper*) testify to its hold upon the Greek imagination.

MARK EDWARDS

See also Baptism, Councils, Heresy, Liturgy, Martyrdom, Monasticism, New Testament, Orthodox Church, Schism, Septuagint, Theology

Texts

The Festal Menaion, translated by Mother Mary and Kallistos Ware, London: Faber, 1969

The Lenten Triodion, translated by Mother Mary and Kallistos Ware, London and Boston: Faber, 1978

The Philokalia: The Complete Text, translated by G.E.H. Palmer, Philip Sherrard, and Kallistos Ware, London and Boston: Faber, 1979–

Further Reading

Brown, Peter, *The Body and Society: Men, Women, and Sexual Renunciation in Early Christianity*, New York: Columbia University Press, 1988; London: Faber, 1990

Chadwick, Henry, *Early Christian Thought and the Classical Tradition: Studies in Justin, Clement and Origen*, Oxford: Clarendon Press, and New York: Oxford University Press, 1966

Frend, W.H.C., *The Rise of Christianity*, Philadelphia: Fortress Press, and London: Darton Longman and Todd, 1984

Gavin, Frank, *Some Aspects of Contemporary Greek Orthodox Thought*, Milwaukee: Morehouse, 1923, reprinted New York: AMS Press, 1970

Grillmeier, Aloys, *Christ in Christian Tradition*, London: Mowbrays, 1975–

Kelly, J.N.D., *Early Christian Creeds*, 3rd edition, London: Longman, and New York: McKay, 1972

Lossky, Vladimir, *The Mystical Theology of the Eastern Church*, London: James Clarke, 1957

Lossky, Vladimir, *In the Image and Likeness of God*, Crestwood, New York: St Vladimir's Seminary Press, 1985

Meyendorff, John, *Christ in Eastern Christian Thought*, Crestwood, New York: St Vladimir's Seminary Press, 1975

Meyendorff, John, *The Byzantine Legacy in the Orthodox Church*, Crestwood, New York: St Vladimir's Seminary Press, 1982

Pelikan, Jaroslav, *The Christian Tradition: A History of the Development of Doctrine*, vols 1–2, Chicago: University of Chicago Press, 1971–74

Torrance, Thomas Forsyth, *The Trinitarian Faith*, Edinburgh: Clark, 1988

Torrance, Thomas Forsyth, *Trinitarian Perspectives: Towards Doctrinal Agreement*, Edinburgh: Clark, 1994

Ware, Timothy, *The Orthodox Church,* 2nd edition, London and New York: Penguin, 1993

Zizioulas, John, *Being as Communion*, London: Darton, Longman and Todd, and Crestwood, New York: St Vladimir's Seminary Press, 1985

Chronicles

By convention, history writing can be classified as either annalistic (composed of brief annual entries) or narrative. The ancient Greek world provides the earliest European examples of both, on the basis of which the Greek-speaking medieval world of Byzantium developed Christianized varieties. Byzantine-style chronicles proved remarkably long lasting.

The earliest known Greek historical records are lists of public officials, such as the priestesses of Hera in Argos, the Athenian archons, or of victors in festivals, such as the Olympic Games. Such lists were kept in each community for local purposes and provided a basis for noting events of local significance. These were the first forms of chronicles. With the establishment of the multinational Hellenistic kingdoms in the wake of the conquests of Alexander it became of interest to establish synchronicities; hence the work of Timaeus (c.350–260 BC) and Eratosthenes (c.285–194 BC) on Olympic victor lists, which could function as a universal chronological framework within which significant events could be placed. The Parian Marble (of which two fragments survive, one in the Ashmolean Museum, Oxford, the other in the Paros Museum) lists a mixture of political, military, religious, and literary events from Cecrops, the first king of Athens, onwards, dated synchronously but corrrelated backwards from the archonship of Diognetus in Athens (264/63 BC, presumably the date of composition). Significant lists of rulers and dynasties, forerunners of the fully fledged chronicle, were compiled by such men as Apollodorus of Athens (c.180–120 BC), Castor of Rhodes (lst century BC), Manetho of Heliopolis (fl.280 BC), and Phlegon of Tralles (fl.AD 140).

These works of pagan late antiquity formed the background against which the (now lost) Christian *Chronicle* of Eusebius of Caesarea was written (two editions: before AD 303 and 325/26). Eusebius synchronized Old Testament and Graeco-Roman history into a continuous chronological sequence calibrated by years from Abraham and, from 776 BC onwards, by Olympiads. The Greek Eusebius has not survived. The work was in two parts, raw lists (surviving only in an Armenian version) and the chronicle proper (best preserved in Jerome's highly influential Latin translation). Its purpose was to demonstrate that God's plan for man's salvation encompassed the whole of history. Eusebius established a genre, the Christian world chronicle, which was to have a long history in the subsequent Byzantine centuries, though little has survived of his immediate successors (such as the Egyptian monks Annianus and Panodorus).

The first full-length chronicle in the Eusebian mould to be preserved is that of the 6th-century John Malalas, from Antioch, which recounts world history from Creation to the reign of Justinian (527–65), dealing with biblical and Near Eastern history as well as that of mythical Greece and imperial Rome. Malalas has an acute interest in Antiochene local lore and a fondness for a good story. The balance that he gave to ancient history – much emphasis on the Trojan War, little on the Greek city states or republican Rome – affected the presentation of the past by all later chroniclers, since his work was extensively excerpted. The old assumption that Byzantine chronicles of this sort were written for monastic audiences while secular history was written by and for secular officials of high rank has now been revised. The thought worlds, for example, of Malalas and his contemporary Procopius, a secular historian writing on the wars of Justinian, have much in common; it is chiefly the form and language that differ.

Other Christian world chronicles include the *Chronicon Paschale* (Easter Chronicle, so called because it attempts to provide chronological correlations between Easter and Creation; written c.630), the chronicle of George Synkellos (written before 810), and those of George the Monk (c.866), Constantine Manasses (c.1140), and Michael Glykas (mid-12th century). Chronicle writers in this tradition tend to copy out their predecessors, with changes reflecting the ideologies and realities of the time of writing, up to the period when the chronicler has personal access to oral sources. This last section becomes his personal contribution to the tradition.

The term chronicle is also applied to works in medieval Greek that cover longer periods of time and are largely independent of eyewitness accounts (the mark of the historian): into this category would come the chronicles of Theophanes (c.817) and Zonaras (c.1150); Zonaras is distinctive in naming some of his sources. There are two Byzantine chronicles in popular verse: the *Chronicle of the Morea* (14th century) describes the foundation and early history of the Frankish kingdoms in the Peloponnese, while the *Chronicle of the Tocco* (early 15th century) narrates the history of the Italian rulers of the Ionian islands and Epirus. Both used mixed language levels, which give interesting evidence of the spoken Greek of the time of composition.

From the late Byzantine period come a number of texts that provide succinct, secular, and at times enigmatic accounts of invasions: the *Chronicle of Monemvasia* (perhaps a 10th-century text, in 16th-century manuscripts), the *Chronicle of Galaxeidi* (written c.1703 but referring, among other topics, to Bulgarian invasions in the Peloponnese), the *Chronicle of Ioannina* (15th century, on the brutal rule of Thomas Preljubovic, d. 1384), and the *Chronicle of the Turkish Sultans* (16th century).

Lists of dated events in chronicle format also survive. The *Chronographikon* of patriarch Nikephoros I (806–13), which is a list of rulers from Creation to 829, was copied frequently: it may have become a schoolroom text. Notes in the margins of manuscripts of all kinds survive from the 10th century onwards (the so-called *Short Chronicles*), giving precise annotations of births and deaths, invasions, catastrophes, and natural phenomena, thus providing an annalistic counterpoint to the more discursive accounts of narrative historians.

The influence of the Byzantine world chronicle lingered long. Among several late 16th-century examples is the *Biblion Istorikon* known under the name of Dorotheos of Monemvasia, which takes as its basic structure a worldview that can be traced back to the 6th-century Malalas. Dorotheos's work was reprinted frequently in the 17th and 18th centuries, providing, it would seem, a textbook on world history for the Greek-speaking world of the Tourkokratia.

ELIZABETH M. JEFFREYS

See also Historiography

Further Reading

Adler, William, *Time Immemorial: Archaic History and its Sources in Christian Chronography from Julius Africanus to George Syncellus*, Washington, D.C.: Dumbarton Oaks, 1989

Croke, Brian, "The Origins of the Christian World Chronicle" in *History and Historians in Late Antiquity*, edited by Croke and Alanna M. Emmett, Sydney and New York: Pergamon Press, 1983

Croke, Brian, "City Chronicles of Late Antiquity" in *Reading the Past in Late Antiquity*, edited by Graeme Clarke et al., Canberra: Australian National University Press, 1990

Croke, Brian, "The Early Development of Byzantine Chronicles" in *Studies in John Malalas*, edited by Elizabeth Jeffreys, Sydney: Australian Association for Byzantine Studies, 1990

John Malalas, *The Chronicle*, translated by Elizabeth Jeffreys, Michael Jeffreys and Roger Scott, Melbourne: Australian Association for Byzantine Studies, 1986

Lurier, Harold E. (translator and editor), *Crusaders as Conquerors: The Chronicle of the Morea*, New York: Columbia University Press, 1964

Mosshammer, Alden A., *The Chronicle of Eusebius and the Greek Chronographic Tradition*, Lewisburg, Pennsylvania: Bucknell University Press, 1979

Scott, R., "The Byzantine Chronicle after Malalas" in *Studies in John Malalas*, edited by Elizabeth Jeffreys, Sydney: Australian Association for Byzantine Studies, 1990

Theophanes the Confessor, *The Chronicle of Theophanes the Confessor: Byzantine and Near Eastern History, AD 284–813*, translated by Cyril Mango and Roger Scott, Oxford: Clarendon Press, and New York: Oxford University Press, 1997

Whitby, Michael and Mary Whitby (translators), *Chronicon Paschale, 284–628 AD*, Liverpool: Liverpool University Press, 1989

Chronology

By "chronology" we mean the division of time, the ordering of events and the intervals between them on a fixed scale. The natural world has three ways of marking the passage of time: the daily cycle of night and day, the monthly cycle of the moon, and the annual seasonal cycle of the sun. The ancient and medieval Greek world had several ways of marking the succession of days in the month or year and the sequence of years, and of dating historical events whether within a short or a long time-span.

From at least the 5th century BC the full day was divided into night and day, each of 12 hours whose length varied according to season and latitude. Hours could be measured by a sundial or waterclock, but for most people internal divisions of the hour remained imprecise, though considerable precision could be achieved for astronomical calculations.

The week is an artificial temporal division not used in the ancient world. In the Greek-speaking world of the Christian east Roman empire a seven-day week, originally Hebrew but then Christianized, came into use. Each day had a mystical and liturgical symbolism sometimes apparent in the names (e.g. Paraskeve, Friday, "preparation").

By the 5th century BC Athenian astronomers had become aware that the lunar month was 29.5 days long and the solar year 365.25 days. There was no universal calendar and each Greek community used its own month names and individual date for the new year. The months were normally named after the festivals that fell within them, or after a deity. In the Byzantine world local month names remained predominant until late in the 5th century AD, but thereafter the Roman month names (Ianouaraios, Februarios, etc.) gradually prevailed.

In the Graeco-Roman world of antiquity prior to the reforms of Julius Caesar (44 BC) the calendar year was frequently at variance with the seasonal and solar year, despite the addition (intercalation) of days and months at irregular intervals, often for political rather than calendrical reasons. After the reform the year consisted of 365 days with one day inserted in the month of February every fourth (leap) year, a system that remained in force generally until the reforms introduced by Pope Gregory XIII in 1582 (the Gregorian calendar),

Chronology: ancient sundial at Cnidus in Caria

which removed leap-year status from century years, except for those divisible by 400 (e.g. 1600, 2000 etc.).

Between Meton (*fl.*432 BC) and Ptolemy (writing AD 146–170) an increasingly precise understanding of the lunisolar cycles was developed, giving rise to accurate predictions of eclipses, and also enabling public calendars to be set up that traced the movements of constellations throughout the year. In the Christian Byzantine empire lunisolar cycles were used to calculate the date of Easter (the results usually presented in paschal tables) and also to extrapolate to the date of Creation.

Dating of events in the short term in the ancient world (for legal documents, government decrees, some historical events) was normally by the year of the priest or magistrate into which they fell (e.g. Athenian archons, Roman consuls). Dynasties might be calculated roughly in terms of human generations. In the wake of the conquests of Alexander and the establishment of the Seleucid empire, a more precise reckoning by the Seleucid era (beginning from 312/11 BC) became widespread, together with an interest in establishing the synchronicity of rulers and events. Timaeus (mid-4th century–late 260s BC) constructed a synchronous list of Olympian victors, Spartan kings and ephors, Athenian archons, and priestesses of Hera; thereafter it became customary to date historical events in a longer perspective by years of the Olympic Games, i.e. by Olympiads. Eratosthenes in the 3rd century BC further refined

these lists and replaced a mythical prehistoric chronology with one based on what was believed to be the historical date of the fall of Troy (1183/82 BC). Other eras were also used, notably one calculating from the foundation of Rome (753 BC).

In the Byzantine world several systems of dating were in general use for short-term perspectives. Events could be dated by eponymous years (referring to an individual's holding of a particular office). These could begin and end at any point in the solar year: they included the regnal years of Byzantine emperors and foreign rulers, patriarchs of Constantinople, Alexandria, Antioch, or Jerualem, popes of Rome, etc. Until the 7th century AD dating was also by consulships, with each year named after one of two consuls appointed (with diminishing regularity) annually on 1 January. Numbered indiction years, within a 15-year cycle, were also used, though the indiction cycles themselves were not numbered. Events could also be dated by major natural phenomena, such as earthquakes, eclipses, and the appearance of comets. On a larger scale, dating by Olympiads continued, and also by local eras such as the Antiochene (starting from 49 BC). The *Chronicle* of Eusebius (2nd edition, AD 325) presented an influential synchronous table of world history from Creation with a Christian perspective. However, the most widely used dating reference came to be the so-called Byzantine era, from the date of Creation; the latter was arrived at by extrapolating backwards from the year of Christ's death and resurrection through the recurring synchronicity of the lunar cycle (19 years) and the solar cycle (28 years), making a combined cycle of 532 years. Until about the 9th century AD chroniclers and historians noted events by a multiplicity of overlapping systems; thereafter the regular dating method was by years from the Creation (normally deemed to have taken place 5,508 years before Christ's incarnation). Such dates are conventionally known as Year of the World (Anno Mundi; AM). Dating from the incarnation (Anno Domini; AD) was devised by the Scythian monk Dionysius Exiguus in the early 6th century, but did not come into use in the Greek world until late in the Byzantine period and was not widespread until long after the fall of Constantinople.

ELIZABETH M. JEFFREYS

See also Calendar

Further Reading

Adler, William, *Time Immemorial: Archaic History and its Sources in Christian Chronography from Julius Africanus to George Syncellus*, Washington, D.C.: Dumbarton Oaks, 1989

Bickerman, E.J., *Chronology of the Ancient World*, 2nd edition, London: Thames and Hudson, and Ithaca, New York: Cornell University Press, 1980

Croke, Brian, "The Origins of the Christian World Chronicle" in *History and Historians in Late Antiquity*, edited by Croke and Alanna M. Emmett, Sydney and New York: Pergamon Press, 1983

Grafton, Anthony, *Joseph Scaliger: A Study in the History of Classical Scholarship*, vol. 2, Oxford: Clarendon Press, and New York: Oxford University Press, 1993

Grumel, V., *La Chronologie*, Paris: Presses Universitaires de France, 1958

Mosshammer, Alden A., *The Chronicle of Eusebius and the Greek Chronographic Tradition*, Lewisburg, Pennsylvania: Bucknell University Press, 1979

Samuel, Alan E., *Greek and Roman Chronology: Calendars and Years in Classical Antiquity*, Munich: Beck, 1972

Chrysaphes, Manuel

Musician of the 15th century

Manuel Chrysaphes was undoubtedly the outstanding member of the Byzantine empire's last generation of church musicians. What little is known of his career as a cantor, composer, theorist, and scribe has been gleaned primarily from the brief notes attached to his compositions in musical manuscripts. These reveal that he was a *lampadarios* (a soloist and choir leader) among the "royal clergy" of the last Byzantine emperor, who also commissioned several of his works. Leaving Constantinople after its capture by the Turks in 1453, he continued to compose for the Orthodox Church in Serbia, Sparta, and Venetian-controlled Crete. Scholars have identified four codices written by Chrysaphes, three of which are in musical collections now on Mount Athos: the Kalophonic Sticherarion (MS Iviron 975, a collection of florid hymns for the Liturgy of the Hours which, according to Gregorios Stathis, predates 1453); the Akolouthia (MS Iviron 1120

("1458"), an important anthology containing the autograph of his theoretical treatise *On the Theory of the Art of Chanting and on Certain Erroneous Views that Some Hold about it*); and the Kalophonic Sticherarion (MS Xeropotamou 270, dated by Stathis to some time shortly after the fall of Constantinople). The fourth and presumably the latest of Chrysaphes's autographs is the MS. Istanbul Seraglio 15, a copy of the *Grammar* of Moschopoulos dated July 1463.

A highly versatile and prolific composer, Chrysaphes contributed both original melodies and arrangements of preexisting chants to nearly every genre of Byzantine liturgical music. For the three Eucharistic liturgies of the Orthodox Church he composed many settings of their more solemn chants, including music for the ordinary and festal Trisagia ("Holy God", "As many as have been baptized", and "We venerate Your Cross"); music in all eight modes for the Alleluia sung before the Gospel; multiple settings of the offertory chants "We who represent the Cherubim" and "Now the powers of Heaven"; and communion verses for ordinary weekdays, Sundays (in all eight modes), and the feasts of the liturgical year. Representing a variety of styles, these works range from elegant reworkings of traditional melodies – e.g. the *Dynamis* on fol. 491 of MS Iviron 1120, which is based on the standard Trisagion for hierarchical liturgies – to sprawling compositions in the highly embellished "kalophonic" idiom pioneered by St John Koukouzeles.

Chrysaphes's music for the Eucharistic liturgies is complemented by a much larger body of psalmodic and hymnodic chants for the morning and evening offices of the Byzantine monastic rite of St Sabas. For the festal psalms of these services, Chrysaphes followed the late Byzantine custom of composing elaborate settings, often extended through musical and textual troping, of selected verses with their refrains. These would have been performed alongside anonymous traditional melodies and settings by other composers during the chanting of such psalms as 1, 2, 3, and 103 at Vespers and 134, 135, and 136 at Matins. Falling outside the normal cycle of office psalms is Chrysaphes's moving lament for the fall of Constantinople, "O God, the nations have come into your inheritance", a setting of selected verses from Psalm 78 included by the composer in his autograph Iviron 1120. Other psalmodic chants from the same manuscript not belonging to the central repertory are found in his redaction of the "Service of the Furnace", a liturgical drama relating the story of the three children in the fiery furnace from the Septuagint book of Daniel that was performed on the Sunday before Christmas. Like his other settings of psalms and canticles, Chrysaphes's chants for this drama show the same stylistic diversity as his melodies for the Eucharistic liturgies. In contrast, although they continue to reflect a mix of old and new material, nearly all the hymns that Chrysaphes composed for the Byzantine offices are cast in the florid kalophonic style. Many are arrangements of traditional hymns appearing in the printed service books of the modern Orthodox Church, while others are set texts by such late Byzantine hymnographers as Nikephoros Xanthopoulos and St Mark Eugenikos of Ephesus. Like St John Koukouzeles and John Kladas, Chrysaphes also composed melodies for his own liturgical poetry, including approximately 20 poems in 15-syllable verse.

Innovations of a rather different sort were recently discovered among Chrysaphes's settings of kalophonic *stichera* (short hymns) by Stathis, who noted brief two-part passages in his autograph MS. Iviron 975. These would seem to suggest that some of the hymns were performed in a simple two-part style, presumably derived from the late medieval Italian practice of so-called "primitive polyphony". Such a style of composition was in fact occasionally employed by his predecessor Manuel Gazes and his contemporary John Plousiadenos, both of whom wrote two-part works. Polyphony, however, is never mentioned in Chrysaphes's treatise *On the Theory of the Art of Chanting*, which is focused on two issues of Byzantine performance practice, namely the proper realization of Byzantine notation and the execution of modulations. Regarding the first of these, Chrysaphes insists that rendering the intervallic neumes of a chant accurately is only a preliminary step towards a stylistically correct performance, the achievement of which depends on the singer's recognition and idiomatic realization of melodic patterns (*theseis*). The remainder of the treatise is devoted to an extended discussion of the Byzantine signs of modulation (*phthorai*) that remains frustratingly obscure because the exact tunings of the modes are never mentioned.

Throughout the period of Ottoman domination the musical works of Chrysaphes were frequently anthologized. Highly influential as models for post-Byzantine composers, these chants were subjected to melodic elaboration through a process of written and oral realization known as *exegesis*. At the beginning of the 19th century Chourmouzios the Archivist employed *exegesis* to transcribe in 17 volumes the complete works of Chrysaphes into the "New Method" of reformed Byzantine notation used by the modern Greek Orthodox Church. Select transcriptions were also made during the period of notational reform by Matthaios Vatopedinos and Gregorios the Protopsaltes, and the latter's florid realizations were published in the Constantinopolitan *Pandekte* of 1850–51. Most recently, Chrysaphes's theoretical writings about *theseis* and modulation have been cited frequently by Western and traditionalist Greek scholars attempting to interpret medieval Byzantine musical notation.

ALEXANDER LINGAS

Biography

Active in the mid-15th century, Chrysaphes was the leading church musician of his generation. He was a choir leader in the service of Constantine XI. Leaving Constantinople in 1453, he continued to compose for the Church in Serbia, the Morea, and Crete. A prolific composer, he wrote for almost every genre of liturgical music.

Writings

The Lampadarios: On the Theory of the Art of Chanting and on Certain Erroneous Views that Some Hold about It, translated by Dimitri E. Conomos, Vienna: Akademie der Wissenschaften, 1985

Further Reading

Conomos, Dimitri E., "The Treatise of Manuel Chrysaphes" in *Report of the Eleventh Congress of the International Musicological Society*, vol. 2, Copenhagen: Hansen, 1972
Conomos, Dimitri E., *Byzantine Trisagia and Cheroubika of the Fourteenth and Fifteenth Centuries: A Study in Late Byzantine Liturgical Chant*, Thessalonica: Patriarchal Institute for Patristic Studies, 1974
Conomos, Dimitri E., "Experimental Polyphony 'According to the...Latins' in Late Byzantine Psalmody", in *Early Music History*, 2 (1982): pp. 1–16
Patrinelis, Christos G., "Protopsaltae, Lampadarii and Domestikoi of the Great Church During the Post-Byzantine Period, 1453–1821" in *Studies in Eastern Chant*, vol. 3, edited by Miloš Velimirović, London and New York: Oxford University Press, 1972
Velimirović, Miloš, "Liturgical Drama in Byzantium and Russia", *Dumbarton Oaks Papers*, 16 (1962): pp. 351–85

Chrysoloras, Manuel c.1350–1415

Scholar and diplomat

Manuel Chrysoloras played a significant role in the development of Greek studies in Italy during the early Renaissance. A personal friend of the learned Byzantine emperor Manuel II Palaiologos (1391–1425), Chrysoloras was a member of the close circle of intellectuals that the emperor headed in Constantinople. Unusually for a Byzantine intellectual, he possessed a knowledge of Latin which made him invaluable as an ambassador to western Europe. Between about 1390 and 1415 he visited Italy, France, England, Spain, and the Holy Roman empire, in the hope of persuading their rulers to send military assistance to the beleaguered Byzantine empire against the Ottoman Turks. His ceaseless diplomatic activities may explain why, unlike other members of Manuel II's circle, his literary output was limited and unoriginal. His best-known work is *A Comparison of the Old and New Rome*, a discussion of the relative merits of the cities of Rome and Constantinople.

Yet it was as a result of a diplomatic mission that Chrysoloras came to have such an impact on Greek studies in Italy. In 1391, while in Venice, he gave some lessons in Greek to a certain Roberto Rossi, who then passed an enthusiastic account of his teacher to Coluccio Salutati, the chancellor of Florence. So impressed was Salutati that he decided to secure Chrysoloras's services, and in 1396 invited him to teach grammar and Greek literature at the University of Florence. Chrysoloras occupied this post only between 1397 and 1400, but in that period had a tremendous effect, prompting the Florentine historian Leonardo Bruni to claim, with only slight exaggeration, that Chrysoloras had singlehandedly revived in Italy the study of Greek letters that had been dead for 700 years. Among his pupils were numbered some of the foremost figures of the revival of Greek studies in Renaissance Italy, including Bruni himself, Guarino da Verona, and Palla Strozzi.

Chrysoloras's success in stimulating a revival in Greek studies and in imparting his knowledge so widely arose from his novel teaching methods. He carefully graded the authors that his pupils studied, beginning with prose authors before moving on to the poets, and among the poets beginning with Homer before passing to other epics, tragedies, and comedies. He was also able to simplify Greek grammar, his approach being later encapsulated in his textbook entitled *Erotemata* or "Questions", which cut through many of the complexities presented in traditional Byzantine grammar books. The *Erotemata* was translated into Latin by Guarino and was one of the first books to be printed in Italy, around 1471. Chrysoloras's methods and textbook placed the Greek

EMANVEL CHRYSOLORAS
GRAMMATICVS GRAECVS.

Patria, Roma Noua; est Vetus altera patria Roma:
In Latium per me Græcia ducta venit.

EMANVEL

Manuel Chrysoloras, a 16th-century engraving

language within the grasp of any keen and intelligent student, and some of his pupils were able to achieve a high degree of competence in only a year.

He also helped to make Greek literature better known in Italy in his activities as a translator. Along with Uberto Decembrio (d. 1427), he produced a Latin translation of Plato's *Republic*, a version that helped to stimulate the first awakening of interest in Plato's political thought in Italy. The success of Chrysoloras's translation was undoubtedly helped by his method, which was to abandon the word-for-word approach of previous translators in favour of a version that conveyed the spirit of the text and which had some literary merit in Latin, while at the same time avoiding an over-free rendering. His method was subsequently adopted by the Italian humanists as the standard approach to Greek translation, and inspired a generation of Italian scholars to produce new Latin versions of Aristotle to replace the old scholastic texts.

Chrysoloras left Florence in 1400, and after spending time in Pavia and Milan, where he may have continued his teaching, he returned to Constantinople in 1403. His later career was devoted to diplomacy rather than to teaching, although he may

have done something to stimulate Greek studies in France when in 1408 he presented a codex of the works of Dionysius the Areopagite (now in the Louvre, Paris), to the abbey of Saint-Denis on behalf of Manuel II. It was on a diplomatic mission that he died in 1415 while representing the Byzantine emperor at the Council of Constance.

Yet although Chrysoloras's teaching career in Florence had been brief, it was to have a significant impact in the long term, largely thanks to his pupil Guarino da Verona. Guarino followed Chrysoloras back to Constantinople in 1403 and remained there until 1408, acquiring a thorough grounding in the Greek language and Classical Greek literature. On his return to Italy, he became one of the foremost teachers of Greek, able to present Classical texts to Italians in a form in which they could be readily understood. In 1452, long after Chrysoloras's death, Guarino compiled the *Chrysolorina*, a collection of letters and texts that bore witness to the esteem in which his master had been held, and which constituted an act of homage to the man who was credited with having revived Greek studies in Italy.

JONATHAN HARRIS

Biography

Born *c.*1350, Chrosoloras was a friend of the emperor Manuel II Palaiologos who sent him on numerous missions to western Europe. He taught Greek at the University of Florence from 1397 to 1400 where his pupils included Guarino da Verona. Guarino did much to promote Greek studies in Italy and translated Chrysoloras's Greek grammar into Latin. Chrysoloras died at the Council of Constance in 1415.

Further Reading

Barker, John W., *Manuel II Palaeologus, 1391–1425: A Study in Later Byzantine Statesmanship*, New Brunswick, New Jersey: Rutgers University Press, 1969

Cammelli, Giuseppe, *I dotti bizantini e le origini dell'umanesimo*, vol. 1: *Manuele Crisolora*, Florence: Vallecchi, 1941

Geanakoplos, Deno John, *Constantinople and the West: Essays on the Late Byzantine (Palaeologan) and Italian Renaissances and the Byzantine and Roman Churches*, Madison: University of Wisconsin Press, 1989

Harris, Jonathan, *Greek Emigrés in the West, 1400–1520*, Camberley, Surrey: Porphyrogenitus, 1995

Setton, Kenneth M., "The Byzantine Background to the Italian Renaissance", *Proceedings of the American Philosophical Society*, 100 (1956): pp. 1–76

Thomson, I., "Manuel Chrysoloras and the Early Italian Renaissance", *Greek, Roman and Byzantine Studies*, 7 (1966): pp. 63–82

Wilson, Nigel G., *From Byzantium to Italy: Greek Studies in the Italian Renaissance*, London: Duckworth, and Baltimore: Johns Hopkins University Press, 1992

Church–State Relations

The relationship between Church and state in Greece is a matter of great importance with a long historical tradition. In order to understand, for example, the contemporary relations between Orthodoxy and politics – or more broadly the crucial role played by the Orthodox tradition in Greece – one has to take into consideration the specific sociopolitical developments since early Byzantine times. Before the Byzantine era, however, early Christian attitudes towards the Roman state and its power were far from consistent. Jesus Christ distinguished clearly between the "things of Caesar" and "the things of God" (Matthew 22: 21), while Paul (Romans 13: 1) admonished Christians to obey the governing authorities, because these derived their authority from God. On the other hand, Peter (Acts 5: 29) opined that in certain issues Christians must obey God rather than men. A radical and total negation of the state is also found in the book of Revelation. These cases reveal that Christianity was not altogether conservative in sociopolitical matters, but placed religious authority above all mundane powers. This is more apparent in the cases of numerous martyrs, who preferred to die rather than betray their Christian faith. Early Christians generally chose to remain loyal to the political authorities, but not when vital issues of their Christian identity (e.g. their radical monotheism) were at stake.

Byzantium, the New Rome, inaugurated a new chapter in Church–state relations when its founder, Constantine I (324–37), initially declared Christianity de jure as a *religio licita* and further as the official religion of the Roman state. Constantine's role, the political liberation he brought to the persecuted Church, and its public patronage were emphasized by Eusebius of Caesarea. Apart from occasional conflicts and matters of dispute, there always existed a very close collaboration between Church and state, between the *sacerdotium* (priesthood) and the *imperium* (imperial state), which was legally and religiously legitimized and stabilized, especially during the reign of Justinian I (527–65). On the basis of this mutual understanding, the Church commanded allegiance to the state, legitimized it, and tried to serve its goals – though usually not when matters of faith were at stake. On the other hand, the state protected the Church's interests and contributed to the solution of its problems (e.g. of dogmatic disputes through the summoning of Church councils). According to the principle of "symphony" (*consonantia*), both Church and state as a single organism affirmed that they had the same *Kyrios* (Lord), Jesus Christ. Neither of these two parties was the loser from this longstanding connection, which found its clear expression in Byzantine political ideology. The strength of the Byzantine empire and the culmination of its power were also attributed to this strong collaboration. The Byzantines generally felt superior to other people due to their Orthodox faith.

An area of dispute in modern scholarship concerning Byzantine Church–state relations has to do with the issue of Caesaropapism, i.e. the total subordination of the Church to the will of the emperor, who allegedly enjoyed unlimited rights over it. This was thought to be the outcome of the Church's submission to the imperial system and its bureaucracy. Yet the term "Caesaropapism" does not depict accurately the specific Byzantine situation. The political and religious authorities remained clearly distinguished, and the emperor never undertook the role of patriarch. Emperors could exert considerable influence upon the external affairs of the Church (e.g. on financial and material issues), but not on internal, theological issues, as the longstanding disputes over iconoclasm and the union of the Churches show. On the other hand, the Church, despite its strong connection with the state, tried through various means to preserve its autonomy, while in certain cases its ideological power was enormous and could even influence state legislation decisively. It is also important to note that the Byzantine model of Church–state relations has left its indelible mark upon Eastern Christendom, including Greece, and continues to function as an ideal pattern for the whole of society to imitate.

After the fall of Byzantium substantial changes occurred to existing Church–state relations. The Orthodox Church, due to the privileges bestowed upon it by the sultans, became the only Byzantine institution that survived the fall and continued to exist within the Ottoman empire. The patriarch of Constantinople became the leader of the entire Orthodox *millet* (community), to which not only Greeks belonged. Thus, during the long Ottoman domination (1453–1821) the Church acquired several other jurisdictions (e.g. in legal, educational, social, and political matters) far beyond the strictly religious domain. The gradual increase of its functions led to the transformation of the Church into a religio-political institution. Such a change implied a considerable strengthening of its social influence, which was naturally underscored by its own values and mode of thinking. Though the Church tried to preserve its traditional supranational role, it also provided a shelter for the preservation of various ethnic-cultural identities in the Balkans, including the Greek one, from the inroads of Islam and western propaganda. Orthodoxy was thus transformed into a crucial factor in the articulation of modern Greek identity. Nonetheless, the main challenge to the Church's supremacy came with the Greek Enlightenment of the late 18th century onwards, when demands were voiced for the limitation of the Church's broad influence and the concomitant differentiation of society.

This demand, however, was forcibly realized after the foundation of the Greek state during the reign of the young Bavarian king Otho (1833–62). This marked the beginning of a vigorous secularization process in an attempt to limit the jurisdiction of the Church solely to the religious domain and to foster the functional differentiation of the various societal sectors (e.g. law, administration, education). Thus, the autocephalous Church of Greece was unilaterally declared in 1833 through a split from the patriarchate of Constantinople, was totally subjected to the state, and was controlled by a government procurator. These and other developments (e.g. the closing of numerous monasteries and the confiscation of their property) caused a reaction among many Orthodox believers and led to a worsening of the Church's situation during the 19th century. Despite these difficulties, the ideological power of the Church was still left untouched, and it was able to adjust to the new situation by supporting wholeheartedly Greek nationalism in the frame of the "Great Idea". This meant also its transformation into an organ of the state and into a purely national Church, which signified the unavoidable end of Orthodoxy's previous supranational tradition in the east. Apart from this, from the 19th century onwards an entire mythology was created to support the diachronic correlation and ideal synthesis of Hellenism and Christianity throughout history. All these factors attest to the new opportunities offered to the Church to retain its pivotal role within Greek society.

The Church's overall situation was later impoved substantially during the reign of king George I (1863–1913). The constitution of 1864 gave greater freedom to the Church, while state legislation catered for the amelioration of the pecuniary condition of the clergy and the parishes. The Church, however, still remained dependent on the state at many levels and was thus affected by political corruption, factional rivalries, and multifaceted, intertwined interests. The political scandal of the *Simoniaka* (1874–78) and the gospel riots (*Evangeliaka*) of November 1901 demonstrate the interplay between religion and politics in this period. The same can be observed later when during World War I Greece was divided between the followers of the prime minister E. Venizelos and the followers of king Constantine I. The Church was divided too, and its royalist faction anathematized Venizelos in 1916 when the latter established a provisional government in Thessalonica. The dependence of the Church on political developments continued to exist even later, for example during World War II and the ensuing Civil War (1946–49), whereas the dictatorship of 1967–74 created a major internal split within the body of the hierarchs, whose repercussions in various domains have dogged the Church until now.

An important development in Church–state relations was the legal recognition by the Greek parliament (Law 590/1977) for the first time of the Constitutional Charter of the Church of Greece, published in the *Government Gazette* (Issue 146 of 31 May 1977). This marked the beginning of a new era in the relations between these two major institutions, which moved to the status of mutual alliance and collaboration in various domains. It was also stated that the administration of the Church would be free from state intervention, especially with regard to the election of the archbishop, in which there had been constant interference throughout modern Greek history. Yet various problems and contentious issues in Church–state relations have appeared in recent years too. Among the most hotly discussed matters were the following: the issue of "the automatic divorce", i.e. divorce on the grounds of long separation; the introduction of civil marriage as equivalent to the religious one; the nationalization of ecclesiastic and monastic property; the legalization of abortion; the depenalization of adultery; the compulsory record of religious affiliation on identity cards for all Greek citizens; the consequences of the Schengen Treaty; the revision of the constitution regarding religious freedom and the rights of religious minorities; and finally, the major "ecclesiastical problem" referring to the deposition of 12 metropolitans in 1974 by archbishop Serapheim, their later attempts at reinstatement through civil and other means, and the concomitant violent conflicts in some dioceses (1989–98).

In order to understand these problems between Church and state, it is vital to consider first that the Greek state is in principle a modern, secular institution, which belongs to the European Union, collaborates with all major international fora, and tries to conform to transnational regulations. At the same time, it is deeply influenced, both explicitly and implicitly, by the predominant Orthodox tradition, which it uses for various purposes (e.g. national) in the present globalized environment. But Orthodox doctrine, considered as the only true revelation of God, is in many cases out of line with the exigencies of a modern state and its policies of assimilation and adaptation to the world system. The lack of balance between these two situations creates occasional problems that spoil the apparently smooth surface of Greek Church–state relations.

It is quite characteristic of both that neither the state nor the Church wants to terminate their close connection and collaboration, though they have occasionally declared that such a development would perhaps be beneficial for both of them. The PASOK party in its founding manifesto of 1974 promised that it would implement a complete administrative separation of Church and state, a pledge that has not been fulfilled, although PASOK has sought looser ties with the Church. Especially after the collapse of communism in eastern Europe, where the Orthodox Church traditionally had firm footholds, the consequent revival of Orthodoxy there, and its active reappearance in political life, visions of a prospective separation between Church and state in Greece have almost completely vanished. After all, such a development would certainly be against the demands of the times. From this point of view, it can be said that in Greece Church–state relations have reached a normal level of compromise and coexistence. There is a single Ministry of Education and Religious Affairs, and the Church functions as a legal entity in public law. Needless to say, there exist several areas of overlapping interest between Church and state (e.g. in the civil code, and the finances of the Church). Finally, the Constitution of 1975/86, beginning with an invocation of the Holy Trinity, acknowledges the privileges of the Eastern Orthodox Church as the "dominant, prevailing religion" on Greek territory.

In this context, it is not surprising that Orthodoxy is very often used by the state and various politicians for a number of purposes (e.g. as an ideological tool for social control and cohesion, as a mechanism against acculturation and for social integration, as a decorative element in ostentatious ceremonies, and as a means for the worldwide promotion of Hellenism). This signifies that Orthodoxy is an indispensable element in the Greek sociopolitical system. Suffice it to say that the archbishop of Greece can become at turbulent historical moments the "ethnarch", i.e. both political/national and religious/spiritual leader of the Greek *ethnos* (nation). One example was when archbishop Damaskinos Papandreou became also viceroy (1944–46) and prime minister (1945). This is indicative of the strong interpenetration between the religious and the political spheres in Greece. In addition, the overwhelming majority of Greeks, though indifferent and sometimes very critical towards the Church, do not generally favour its separation from the state. Instead they support the improvement of their relations, because they think that the Orthodox Church has played a pivotal role for the Greek nation in the past. Thus, Orthodoxy prevails today in Greece largely because it is closely related to the ethnic and cultural identity of the people, a fact that influences decisively the positive attitude of most political parties towards the Church.

Generally, it seems that Church–state relations in Greece are paradoxical and even contradictory in certain ways, but this situation has a plausible explanation. If one may use a revelatory metaphor, Church–state relations in Greece resemble very closely the life of a married couple who have problems, but are not yet divorced. Both spouses continue to live together, follow their own life-styles, and collaborate on issues of common interest and profit. At the same time, they do not share a bedroom, occasionally have serious quarrels, and threaten to sue for divorce. But these threats remain solely verbal and both parties prefer to continue the status quo for practical reasons. It goes without saying that this situation is far from ideal and constitutes a tenacious source of problems for Church and state alike.

VASILIOS MAKRIDES

See also Orthodox Church, Orthodoxy and Hellenism, Orthodoxy and Nationalism

Further Reading

Ahrweiler, Hélène, *L'Idéologie politique de l'Empire byzantin*, Paris: Presses Universitaires de France, 1975

Aland, Kurt, "The Relation between Church and State in Early Times: A Reinterpretation", *Journal of Theological Studies*, new series 19 (1968): pp. 115–27

Alivizatos, Nicos C., "A New Role for the Greek Church", *Journal of Modern Greek Studies*, 17 (1999): pp. 23–40

Basdekis, Athanasios, "Between Partnership and Separation: Relations between Church and State in Greece under the Constitution of 9 June 1975", *Ecumenical Review*, 29 (1977): pp. 52–61

Boumis, Panayotis I., *Oi Epemvaseis tis Politeias stin Ekklisia kai Idiaitera sto Thema Eklogis Mitropoliton (Aoratos kai Oratos Polemos)* [State Intervention in Church Affairs, and Especially in the Election of Metropolitans (Seen and Unseen Warfare)], Athens, 1995

Frazee, Charles A., *The Orthodox Church and Independent Greece, 1821–1852*, London: Cambridge University Press, 1969

Frazee, Charles, "Church and State in Greece" in *Greece in Transition: Essays in the History of Modern Greece, 1821–1974*, edited by John T.A. Koumoulides, London: Zeno, 1977

Frazee, Charles, "The Orthodox Church of Greece: The Last Fifteen Years" in *Greece: Past and Present*, edited by John T.A. Koumoulides, Muncie, Indiana: Ball State University, 1979

Geanakoplos, Deno J., "Church and State in the Byzantine Empire: A Reconsideration of the Problem of Caesaropapism", *Church History*, 34 (1965): pp. 381–403

Georgiadou, Vasiliki, "Kosmiko Kratos kai Orthodoxi Ekklisia: Scheseis Thriskeias, Koinonias kai Politikis sti Metapolitevsi" [The Secular State and the Orthodox Church: The Relationship between Religion, Society, and Politics in the Changing Regime] in *Koinonia kai Politiki: Opseis tis III Ellinikis Dimokratias, 1974–1994* [Society and Politics: Aspects of the Third Greek Democracy, 1974–1994], edited by C. Lyrintzis et al., Athens, 1996

Hollerich, M.J., "Religion and Politics in the Writings of Eusebius: Reassessing the First 'Court Theologian'", *Church History*, 59 (1990): pp. 309–25

Hunger, Herbert, "Konstantinopel und Kaisertum als *Neue Mitte* des oströmischen Reiches" in his *Epidosis: Gesammelte Schriften zur Byzantinischen Geistes- und Kulturgeschichte*, Munich: Maris, 1989

Hussey, J.M., *The Orthodox Church in the Byzantine Empire*, Oxford: Clarendon Press, 1986, pp. 299–303

Karayannis, Yorgos, *Ekklisia kai kratos, 1833–1997: Istoriki episkopisi ton scheseon tous* [Church and State, 1833–1997: A Historical Review of their Relationships], Athens, 1997

Kokosalakis, Nikos, "Populare, offizielle und Zivilreligion: Zur Soziologie des orthodoxen Christentums in Griechenland" in *Volksfrömmigkeit in Europa: Beiträge zur Soziologie popularer Religiosität aus 14 Ländern*, edited by Michael N. Ebertz and Franz Schultheis, Munich: Kaiser, 1986

Kokosalakis, Nikos, "The Political Significance of Popular Religion in Greece", *Archives de Sciences Sociales des Religions*, 64 (1987): pp. 37–52

Kokosalakis, Nikos, "Church and State in the Orthodox Church with Special Reference to Greece" in *Identità europea e diversità religiosa nel mutamento contemporaneo*, edited by P. Antes et al., Florence: Pontecorboli, 1995

Kokosalakis, Nikos, "Orthodoxie grecque, modernité et politique" in *Identités religieuses en Europe*, edited by Grace Davie and Danièle Hervieu-Léger, Paris: Découverte, 1996

Kompos, Antonios G., "Thriskevtiki kai Kosmiki Exousia kata tin Kainin Diathikin" [Religion and Secular Power According to the New Testament], dissertation, University of Athens, 1969

Konidaris, Ioannis M., "Die Beziehungen zwischen Staat und Kirche im heutigen Griechenland", *Österreichisches Archiv für Kirchenrecht*, 40 (1991): pp. 131–44

Konidaris, Ioannis M., *O nomos 1700/1987 kai i prosphati krisi stis scheseis Ekklisias kai Politeias* [Law 1700/1987 and the Recent Crisis in the Church–State Relations], Athens, 1991

Konidaris, Ioannis M., *Ekklisia kai politeia* [Church and State], Athens, 1993

Konidaris, Ioannis M., *I Diapali Nomimotitas kai Kanonikotitas kai i Themeliosi tis Enarmoniseos tous* [The Conflict of Legality and Canonicity and the Basis for their Harmonization], Athens, 1994

Kratiki exousia kai Orthodoxi Ekklisia: Provlimata scheseon Ekklisias kai Politeias [The Power of the State and the Orthodox Church: Problems in Church–State Relations], Athens, 1995 (articles by S. Agouridis, P. Boumis, G. Metallinos et al.)

Makrides, Vasilios N., "Orthodoxy as a *conditio sine qua non*: Religion and State Politics in Modern Greece from a Socio-historical Perspective", *Ostkirchliche Studien*, 40 (1991): pp. 281–305

Makrides, Vasilios N., "The Orthodox Church and the Post-War Religious Situation in Greece" in *The Post-War Generation and Establishment Religion: Cross-Cultural Perspectives*, edited by W.C. Roof et al., Boulder, Colorado: Westview Press, 1995

Metallinos, Georgios, *Elladikou Avtokephalou Paraleipomena: Meleti istorikophilologiki* [What's Missing from Greek Independence: A Historico-Philological Study], 2nd edition, Athens: Domos, 1989

Meyendorff, John, "Justinian, the Empire and the Church", *Dumbarton Oaks Papers*, 22 (1968): pp. 45–60

Mouratidis, Konstantinos D., *Ekklisia – Politeia – Syntagma* [Church – State – Constitution], Athens, 1975

Nanakos, Sabbas, "Staat und Kirche in der griechischen Orthodoxie", *Ostkirchliche Studien*, 6 (1957): pp. 268–81

Petrou, Ioannis S., *Ekklisia kai Politiki* [Church and Politics], Thessalonica, 1992

Prodromou, Elisabeth, "Democratization and Religious Transformation in Greece: An Underappreciated Theoretical and Empirical Primer" in *The Orthodox Church in a Changing World*, edited by P. Kitromilides and T. Veremis, Athens, 1998

Ramiotis, Konstantinos, *I Ekklisia mesa stin Elliniki Politeia* [The Church in the Greek State], Athens, 1997

Rexine, John E., "The Church in Contemporary Greek Society", *Diakonia*, 7 (1972): pp. 200–21

Runciman, Steven, *The Orthodox Churches and the Secular State*, Auckland: Auckland University Press, 1971

Runciman, Steven, *The Byzantine Theocracy*, Cambridge and New York: Cambridge University Press, 1977

Savramis, Demosthenes, "Die religiösen Grundlagen der neugriechischen Gesellschaft" in *Die verhinderte Demokratie: Modell Griechenland*, edited by Marios Nikolinakos and Kostas Nikolaou, Frankfurt: Suhrkamp, 1969

Savramis, Demosthenes, "Altar und Thron: Zur Lage der griechischen Kirche", *Wort und Wahrheit*, 25 (1970): pp. 317–30

Savramis, Demosthenes, "Der Ethnarches als Typos religiöser Autorität", *Hellenika* (1970/71): pp. 5–10

Savramis, Demosthenes, "Ursachen und Wirkungen der Sakralisierung des politischen Raumes durch die orthodoxe Theologie und Kirche", *Hellenika* (1985): pp. 86–98

Spyropoulos, Philippos C., *Die Beziehungen zwischen Staat und Kirche in Griechenland unter besonderer Berücksichtigung der orthodoxen Kirche*, Athens, 1981

Stavrou, Theofanis G., "The Orthodox Church of Greece" in *Eastern Christianity and Politics in the Twentieth Century*, edited by Pedro Ramet, Durham, North Carolina: Duke University Press, 1988

Stewart, Charles, "Who Owns the Rotonda? Church vs State in Greece", *Anthropology Today*, 14/5 (1998): pp. 3–9

Troianos, Spyros, "Die Beziehungen zwischen Staat und Kirche in Griechenland", *Orthodoxes Forum*, 6 (1992): pp. 221–31

Ware, Kallistos, "The Church: A Time of Transition" in *Greece in the 1980s*, edited by Richard Clogg, London: Macmillan, 1983

Wenturis, Nikolaus, *Griechenland und die Europäische Gemeinschaft: Die soziopolitischen Rahmenbedingungen griechischer Europapolitiken*, Tübingen: Francke, 1990, pp. 21–26, 137–76

Wittig, Andreas Michael, *Die orthodoxe Kirche in Griechenland: Ihre Beziehung zum Staat gemäss der Theorie und der Entwicklung von 1821–1977*, Würzburg: Augustinus, 1987

Zacharopoulos, Nikos, *Istoria ton scheseon Ekklisias–Politeias stin Ellada* [History of Church–State Relations in Greece], vol. 1, Thessalonica, 1985

Cilicia

Region of southern Asia Minor

Cilicia commonly (but not invariably) names the area of southern Turkey bounded by the river Melas (Turkish Manavgat) to the west, the Taurus to the north, the Amanus as far south as Cape Rhosus (Hınzır Burnu) on the gulf of Issus to the east, and the Mediterranean to the south.

West of the river Lamus (Lamas) Cilicia is mountainous and the coastline mainly abrupt; it was named "rough" (Greek Tracheia); to the east as far as the Amanus it is a fertile plain (hence Greek Pedias). The mountainous mass of Rough Cilicia, jutting out into the sea, threatening not only Pedias but also the Pamphylian plain to its own west, difficult to penetrate or pacify, is a defining feature of Cilician history. Another is the location of Pedias on a main land route between east and west.

The Cilicians were an Anatolian people; Hittite and neo-Hittite sites have been uncovered (strikingly at Meydancık Kale near Gülnar and at Karatepe). Greek settlement began in the Archaic period at coastal sites in Tracheia (e.g. Kelenderis, Nagidus, Soli). Later legend attributed some native cities (Mallus, Mopsuestia, Olba, Tarsus) to Greek foundation in the heroic age. What history underlies this is obscure; a name resembling Mopsus (who figures in the legends) is borne by an ancestor in a royal inscription of the 8th century BC at Karatepe.

There were native kings at Tarsus under the Persians until the early 4th century BC. After Alexander's conquests control was disputed by the Seleucids and the Ptolemies. At first the whole was probably Seleucid; two of Seleucus Nicator's lasting monuments, Seleucia ad Calycadnum (Silifke) and the temple of Zeus at Olba, are in Tracheia. But by the middle of the 3rd century Tracheia had Ptolemaic garrisons which were ejected in 197 BC.

Seleucid weakness resulted in the pirate "kingdom" in western Tracheia around 140 BC. With the connivance or tolerance of other states the pirates grew in strength; only in 101 BC was a Provincia Ciliciae (which did not include Cilicia) created by Rome to deal with them. For the next 30 years efforts were

unsuccessful. Meanwhile in 83 BC Pedias was conquered by Tigranes of Armenia. A pirate raid on Ostia in 68 BC provoked a decisive response from Rome in the appointment and successful campaign of Pompey the following year. Tigranes also withdrew from Pedias. Pompey resettled pirates in the cities of Pedias and eastern Tracheia (including Soli, refounded as Pompeiopolis) and organized Pedias as a group of city states; rougher territory to the east was handed to a local dynast, Tarcondimotus. A policy of leaving such territory to clients endured until the Flavian period.

The Provincia Ciliciae of 64 BC extended beyond Cilicia proper. Between 58 and 47 BC it included Cyprus, and between 56 and 49 BC stretched to Phrygia. Around 44 BC Pedias became part of the province of Syria. Soon after, Tracheia (excluding the free city of Seleucia) was given to Egypt. It remained under client kings for about a century after Actium (Amyntas of Galatia to 28 BC, Archelaus of Cappadocia and his son, also Archelaus, to AD 38, and finally Antiochus IV of Commagene to AD 72). The kingdom of Olba in eastern Tracheia remained under the native dynasty until AD 41 when it was given to Polemo II of Pontus. A number of cities of Tracheia were founded in this period, perhaps with civilizing intent; Titiopolis and Domitiopolis probably by Cleopatra; Iotape, Irenopolis, Germanicopolis (still Turkish Ermenek), and Philadelphia by Antiochus IV; and Claudiopolis (Turkish Mut) by Polemo II. Two uprisings by the tribes (in AD 36 and 52) were serious enough to be recorded by Tacitus and needed Roman troops for their suppression.

In AD 72 Vespasian deposed Antiochus IV and united Pedias and Tracheia (except its western fringe) in a single province of Cilicia. Then they were divided again (perhaps in the mid-2nd century). Tracheia was thenceforth known as Isauria. In the second half of the 3rd century there were uprisings of the Isaurians and invasions by the Persians who in 260 advanced as far as Corycus and subsequently as far as Selinus. In the Diocletianic reform the province of Cilicia was subdivided, with Cilicia I having its capital at Tarsus and Cilicia II at Anazarbus. Both Cilicias and Isauria were part of Oriens and later were ecclesiastically subject to Antioch.

In 353 the Isaurians attacked Lycaonia and Pamphylia, in 354 Palaeae and Seleucia, in 368 Pamphylia again, in 400 Syria and Palestine. Sites were fortified (e.g. Anemurium in the 380s, Korasion around 370, and the shrine of St Thecla near Seleucia by 384); Isaurian fortresses were captured and regarrisoned without effect. There are vivid glimpses of these troubles in the 5th-century Miracles of St Thecla.

Zeno, an Isaurian who had become a favourite and son-in-law of Leo I, became emperor in 474. His rule was marked by civil wars, two of which in 474–76 and 483–88 took place in Cilicia. Zeno attributed his success in the first to St Thecla and rebuilt the sanctuary. What of the little that survives is Zeno's has been debated; the suggestion that some of the splendid churches still standing in eastern Tracheia (e.g. at Alahan, Canytela, Corycus, and Dag Pazarı) belong to Zeno's reign, on the grounds that the flow of patronage ceased afterwards, is plausible. The Isaurians were reputed as masons; they are later recorded at St Saba, St Symeon Stylites, and Hagia Sophia. Isaurian power ended with Zeno in 491. The Isaurians took on Anastasius and lost; reduction of their fortresses took seven years.

Cilicia: the land castle at Kizkalesi, built in the 12th century when the area was part of the Cilician kingdom of Armenia

Cilicia was lost to the Persians between 613 and 629. The Arabs first reached Tarsus (which its inhabitants abandoned) in 637, the first invasion of many throughout the century. Pedias remained nominally Roman till the beginning of the 8th century. Thereafter the frontier moved west to the Lamus and, despite raid and counter-raid, remained stable for more than two centuries. The devastation of these wars in Pedias is obvious; there are almost no standing remains from antiquity (Tarsus was described as in ruins in 778). By contrast in Tracheia urban life seems only gradually to have petered out; its subsequent depopulation has left a very rich collection of monuments.

The Byzantines recovered Pedias in 950 and retained it for little more than a century. After Manzikert they had to compete with other contenders (the Turks, the crusaders, and the Armenians). The Byzantine campaigns of 1137 and 1159 had shortlived effects and by the third quarter of the century their power had melted away. Cilicia now belonged to the Armenians but did not long remain at peace. Raids by the Mamluks began in 1266 and continued with devastating effect till their final conquest in 1375. Cilicia became wholly Ottoman in 1515.

The 19th century saw Greek immigration from Cappadocia, Cyprus, and the Aegean. Near its end Cuinet counted 46,200 Orthodox Greeks in a population of 403,439 (of whom 173,389 were Christians) in the vilayet of Adana (which covered Cilicia). Those remaining in the French zone (covering Pedias) were evacuated in November 1921 after the French agreement with Angora. The treatment of those under Turkish rule further west was less ordered; by 1923 they too had all gone.

GEORGE LEMOS

Summary

A region of southeastern Anatolia, the coast of Cilicia was settled by Greeks in the Archaic period. After Alexander's conquests it was disputed by the Seleucids and Ptolemies. A Roman province of Cilicia was created in 101 BC, part of which remained nominally Roman until the 12th century – the Byzantines reconquered it from the Arabs in 950 but lost control to the Turks by the later 12th century.

Further Reading

Boase, T.S.R. (editor), *The Cilician Kingdom of Armenia*, Edinburgh: Scottish Academic Press, and New York: St Martin's Press, 1978

Dagron, Gilbert and Marie Dupré la Tour (translators and editors), *Vie et miracles de Sainte Thècle*, Brussels: Société des Bollandistes, 1978 (Greek text of the *Acts of Paul* and *Thecla* with French translation and commentary)

Heberdey, Rudolf and Adolf Wilhelm, *Reisen in Kilikien ausgefuehrt 1891 und 1892 im Auftrage der kaiserlichen Akademie der Wissenschafter*, Vienna: Gerold, 1896

Hild, Friedrich and Hansgerd Hellenkemper, *Kilikien und Isaurien*, 2 vols, Vienna: Österreichische Akademie der Wissenschaften, 1990

Hill, Stephen, *The Early Byzantine Churches of Cilicia and Isauria*, Aldershot, Hampshire: Variorum, 1996

Jones, A.H.M., *The Cities of the Eastern Roman Provinces*, Oxford: Clarendon Press, 1937; revised by Michael Avi-Yonah *et al.*, 1971

Keil, Josef and Adolf Wilhelm, *Denkmäler aus dem Rauhen Kilikien*, Manchester: Manchester University Press, 1931

Mitford, T.B., Roman Rough Cilicia entry in *Aufstieg und Niedergang der römischen Welt*, edited by Hildegard Temporini *et al.*, 7. 2, Berlin: de Gruyter 1980, 1230–61

Cimon *c.*510–*c.*450 BC

Athenian aristocrat

Cimon has not been as well served by ancient tradition as some of his slightly older or younger contemporaries, because his era of dominance at Athens fell slightly after Herodotus' period of focus, but slightly before that of Thucydides. Plutarch's *Life of Cimon*, which contains most of what we know of him, is much shorter than his *Lives* of Themistocles or Aristides. Although Plutarch did not lack sources, it is evident that Cimon's personality did not generate as much interest in later generations as those of his more intriguing adversaries Pericles and Themistocles.

A relative of Thucydides, Cimon was from a very distinguished Athenian family, the Philaidae. He was the son of one of its most distinguished members, Miltiades, who, as ruler of the Chersonese, had promoted Athens' colonial ambitions keenly until his support for the Ionian Revolt so angered the Persians that he was forced to escape to Athens (493 BC). The climax of his career was his generalship at the Battle of Marathon (490 BC), but his subsequent campaign against Paros for its Persian sympathies was a failure. At the instigation of Pericles' father Xanthippus, he was fined 50 talents, but died from a battle wound before he could pay it. Cimon inherited not only his father's debt, but also his policies of hostility to Persia and Athenian imperial expansionism.

After an impressive performance at Salamis, Cimon was made an Athenian envoy to Sparta in 479 BC, and his name is associated with the most important campaigns of the early Delian League, from 478 BC to 463 BC, working with its organizer Aristides, who is said to have championed the young Cimon as his ally against Themistocles. In 478 the Spartan general Pausanias was still in charge of the Greek forces, but according to Athenian tradition his arrogance began to alienate them, and they were won over by the kindness of the Athenian generals. Once the Spartans recalled Pausanias on a charge of treason, control over the anti-Persian operations was definitively ceded to Athens, thereby laying the foundations for Athenian dominance over the Aegean during the 5th century BC. Acquitted, Pausanias took Byzantium, but he was driven out by Cimon himself, who then triumphed in his father's old stamping ground by removing Eion in Thrace from Persian hands (476/75 BC). Soon after this, he won Scyros for Athenian colonists and, in an effective personal coup, returned the alleged bones of Athens' national hero Theseus to the city for burial, to great acclaim. Sources do not explicitly say that he led the early campaigns of the league to crush allied rebellion,

at Carystus and Naxos (473–469 BC), but his usual enthusiasm for Athenian expansion makes his presence there very likely.

Soon after Naxos the Athenians undertook a major campaign in the southeast Aegean, perhaps to mollify allied discontent at their use of the league to police its own members. Cimon's greatest triumph followed at Eurymedon in Pamphylia (*c.*468 BC), when his troops wiped out the Persian fleet, and cities as far east as Phaselis joined the league. His generalship brought material wealth to Athens, and an immense sense of pride to a city that had been sacked by the Persians only some 12 years earlier, but was now carrying vengeance right into the Great King's territory. Cimon's comprehensive victory may be said to have paved the way for the Peace of Callias, *c.*450 BC, whereby Greek freedom from Persian interference was finally secured.

At this time, however, Cimon continued to pursue the Persians relentlessly, returning to the Chersonese and driving out those who remained, before besieging the Thasians who had now seceded from the league (465–463 BC). The Spartans, actively working against their former allies in the Persian Wars, had promised the Thasians that they would help them by invading Attica, but an earthquake and a helot revolt frustrated this plan. Meanwhile, Cimon crushed Thasos and returned to Athens, to be prosecuted (unsuccessfully) by the up-and-coming Pericles on a charge of bribery for having made no territorial gains in Macedonia. Unlike Pericles and others, Cimon clung to the old view that Sparta was Athens' partner, not its rival in Greek leadership (in spite of his service in the expansionist Delian League), and in 462 BC he persuaded Athens to help the desperate Spartans. It was perhaps while he was away that Ephialtes introduced the democratic reforms that took most jurisdiction away from the Areopagus and gave it to the people's courts instead: whether or not this was the cause, the Spartans decided that the Athenian army could not be trusted not to help the helots, and sent them away. This ignominious dismissal severely damaged Cimon's credibility in Athens, and, after a failed attempt to reverse Ephialtes' work, he was ostracized in 461 BC. Athens also broke irrevocably with Sparta by allying with its enemy, Argos.

Cimon's next known action was to patch up relations between Athens and Sparta with a five-year truce, *c.*451 BC. The two cities had been testing one another's strength throughout the decade, at the battles of Tanagra (won by Sparta) and Oenophyta (won by Athens), and after the loss of 200 Athenian ships in Egypt in 454 BC, both sides were ready for a brief respite. It seems clear that Cimon still hankered after the past when Sparta was an ally, not an enemy, and his last campaign was also a throwback to the 470s BC. He mounted another expedition to Persia to recapture Cyprus, but he died there, and aggressive Athenian expansion in the east ceased thereafter.

The sources, perhaps derived from Critias, say that Pericles instituted jury pay in order to counter Cimon's personal generosity. Cimon's family was wealthy anyway, and his huge campaign revenues brought him popularity as he opened up his estates to the poor, and gave them public dinners and financial handouts. Payment became necessary after the Ephialtic reforms, which brought a greater volume of business to the democratic courts, so that larger issues of practicality rather than small-scale politicking may have caused Pericles' move, but it is certainly true that Pericles opposed the traditional, almost feudal patronage practised by those from rich families, such as Cimon's, because this was damaging to democracy. A number of artefacts associated with Cimon indicate that he was keen to assert himself in a traditionally aristocratic manner: the Painted Stoa, commissioned by his brother-in-law, bore a picture of Marathon in which Miltiades was prominent, and a Delphic dedication associated a statue of Miltiades with those of Athena, Apollo, and the Athenian tribal heroes. By rehabilitating his father, Cimon augmented his own status as the inheritor of Marathonian glory over that of Themistocles, whose victory had been Salamis.

There is, therefore, some truth in the schematizations of later sources that pit Cimon the conservative against Pericles the democrat. His foreign policy was conservative in that it was based on traditional Greek affiliations at a time when new alignments were beginning which would lead to the Peloponnesian War. The names of two of his sons – Lacedaemonius and Eleius – are revealing. In other ways, however, he was as imperially minded as Pericles, leading the campaigns that created the Athenian empire, encouraging the Athenian naval activity that later writers associate with radical democracy, and vigorously opposing secession from the league. Both he and Aristides, though not as brilliant as Themistocles, played a huge part in the creation of 5th-century democracy.

SOPHIE MILLS

Biography

Born c.510 BC to a noble Athenian family, Cimon was the son of Miltiades, ruler of the Thracian Chersonese. As a general he actively pursued the war against Persia but was keen to retain Sparta as Athens' partner, not rival, in leadership of Greece. He was ostracized in 461 BC but recalled in 451 to mend fences with Sparta. He died soon after in Cyprus, attempting to recapture that island from Persia.

Further Reading
Gomme, A.W., *A Historical Commentary on Thucydides*, vol. 1, Oxford: Clarendon Press, 1945
Hornblower, Simon, *The Greek World, 479–323 BC*, revised edition, London and New York: Routledge, 1991
Plutarch, *Life of Kimon*, translated by A. Blamire, London: Institute of Classical Studies, University of London, 1989
Rhodes, P.J., *A Commentary on the Aristotelian Athenaion Politeia*, Oxford: Clarendon Press, and New York: Oxford University Press, 1981

Cinema

Cinema in Greece, as a form of mass popular entertainment, is largely a postwar phenomenon, although a tradition of Greek film making can be traced back to the early decades of the 20th century. The first Lumière films were shown in central Athens in 1897 to a mixed public response: members of the audience reportedly fainted, while others threw stones at the screen. Nevertheless, a cinema was established in the capital several years later.

The first full-length feature film to be made in Greece was a bucolic romance entitled *Golpho* (1914) by Kostas Bachatoris, which was adapted from the popular play by Spiridon Peresiadis and premiered at the Pantheon cinema on 22 January 1915. *Golfo* was followed in the same year by Michalis Glitsos's adaptation of Konstantinos Christomanos's Athenian novel *I Kerenia Koukla* (Waxen Doll, 1911), again starring Verginia Diamanti in the leading role.

Documentaries, however, such as those by the Hungarian royalist Josef Hepp, were also produced during this period, notably *The Entry of the Greek Army into Thessalonica* (1912), in which Hepp recorded the Greek military successes of the First Balkan War. The first film made in Greece was a newsreel of the 1906 interim Olympic Games.

In 1927 the DAG production company was formed and produced a number of features, including *Astero* (The Star), the first Greek feature to penetrate foreign markets, appealing, in particular, to Greeks of the diaspora. The director of this film, Dimitris Gaziadis (1899–1965), who went on to make a further five films, had studied in Berlin and later established a school of film making (1928). He was also the author of the first Greek book on cinema entitled *How Can I Act in Cinema?* (1926). In 1932 the first talkie was made by Dimitris Tsakiris, again a romance entitled *Agapitikos tis Voskopoulas* (The Lover of the Shepherdess), based on the play by Dimitrios Koromilas. The Greek film industry, however, lacked sufficient financial resources to rise to the challenge of the new technology and, consequently, few films were made in the 1930s.

World War II and the ensuing German occupation (1941–44), which was followed by the Civil War (1947–49), largely undermined attempts at rehabilitating the film industry in Greece. Despite the political and social turmoil, however, this period did see the founding of a major production company. The rise of the Greek cinema in the postwar years is closely connected to the establishment by the entrepreneur Philopoimin Phinos (1908–77) of the Phinos Films production company, which was launched with the film *Phoni tis Kardias* (Voice of the Heart) in 1943. Phinos Films was self-consciously styled on Hollywood production companies and oversaw production from the initial shooting, through the processes of editing, distribution, and marketing. Phinos produced mainly comedies and melodramas, as well as Hollywood genres such as the musical and the western. Among its greatest successes were the many features starring Aliki Vouyouklaki (1937–96), undoubtedly one of the leading stars of the Greek cinema, who made her debut in 1954 with Nikos Tsiforos's (1912–70) *To Pontiaki* (The Little Mouse), although she came to prominence a year later with Dimis Dadiras's (1927–82) version of *Agapitikos tis Voskopoulas*.

By the mid-1950s numerous films were being produced. These were mainly comedies which drew upon a broad range of Greek comic drama from popular entertainment, such as farce, variety, and the shadow puppet theatre (*karaghiozis*), to Aristophanes. A local star system began to develop during this period which saw the emergence of distinct comic actors such as Vassilis Logothetidis, Kostas Hadjihristos, Dinos Iliopoulos, and Thanassis Vengos (1927–), a self-taught comedian who has made over 110 films, including such hits as *Ti Ekanes ston Polemo, Thanasi?* (What Did You Do in the War, Thanassi?, 1971), and who was introduced to cinema by the director Nikos Koundouros (1926–) after they met in the concentration camp on the island of Makronissos.

Cinema: Alan Bates and Anthony Quinn in *Zorba the Greek* (1964), directed by Michalis Cacoyannis

Two outstanding directors of comedy active during the 1950s were Yorgos Tzavellas (1916–76) and Alekos Sakellarios (1913–92). Tzavellas directed such classics as *O Methistakas* (The Drunkard, 1950), which broke box-office records in Greece, and *Kalpiki Lira* (Counterfeit Coin, 1955), which starred Logothetidis with music by Manos Chatzidakis, and followed the fate of a coin as it passed through a myriad of hands. Among the best-known of Sakellarios's 50 or so films are *Oi Germanoi Xanarchontai* (The Germans are Coming Back, 1947), *Laterna, Phtochia, kai Philotimo* (Barrel Organ, Poverty and Dignity, 1955), and *I Thia apo to Chikago* (The Aunt from Chicago, 1957).

With a few exceptions, the major output of commercial Greek cinema consisted of low-budget comedies and melodramas. These did not evince any degree of experimentation, although the legacy of the war is reflected in the uncomfortable narrative shifts and sometimes hysterical acting. Nevertheless, the early 1950s did see some independent film productions. It was Grigoris Grigoriou (1919–), the director of *Pikro Psomi* (Bitter Bread, 1951), who introduced what is often called "Greek neo-realism" under the influence of the Italian postwar cinema of Roberto Rossellini, Luchino Visconti, and Vittoria De Sica. Neo-realism was a postwar movement that exploited location filming and employed non-professional actors, drawing for its subject matter upon the experiences and struggles of the popular classes.

At the same time, two other independent film makers launched their careers: Michael Cacoyannis (1922–), a Greek Cypriot, with his film *Stella* (1955), which established the career of Melina Mercouri (1923–94), and Koundouros with his film *O Drakos* (The Ogre, 1956, distributed in the UK as *The Ogre of Athens*). Despite such classics as *Stella*, *To Koritsi me ta Mavra* (The Girl in Black, 1956), starring Elli Lambetti, and his screen versions of the Euripidean tragedies *Electra* (1961), *The Trojan Women* (1971), and *Iphigenia* (1977), however, Cacoyannis remains best known today for *Zorba the Greek* (1964), an adaptation of the novel by Nikos Kazantzakis (1883–1957).

It was in the 1960s, however, that film directors such as Alexis Damianos (1921–), Theodoros Angelopoulos (1935–), and Pantelis Voulgaris (1940–), among others, attempted to break with the mainstream commercial film industry and created an *auteur* cinema outside the studio system, in much the same way as the French New Wave had done. The "New Greek Cinema" is a general term often applied to these independent film makers such as Kostas Ferris (1935–), Nikos Nikolaïdis (1940–), Nikos Panayotopoulos (1941–), Yorgos Panoussopoulos (1942–), and Vassilis Vapheas (1944–), who rose to prominence in the 1960s and 1970s, in the wake of innovative films such as *Sky* (1962) by Takis Kanellopoulos (1934–90). The term "New Greek Cinema" itself was coined by the critic Photis Alexiou in a review of a film by Voulgaris and refers to a broad category of films which are intensely concerned with contemporary Greek social issues and with the nation's recent historical experiences of political repression and conflict. Many of the films adopt a critical – even defiant – stance towards authority and in retrospect the "New Greek Cinema" can perhaps best be understood as a reaction to the oppressive 1967–74 dictatorship, as well as an attempt by directors to reflect upon the meanings of Greekness during a period when Greece was increasingly falling under the political and artistic influence of the United States. At the same time, while for the most part it eschewed the narrative techniques of the mainstream Greek commercial cinema, the "New Greek Cinema" found inspiration in the experimentation that characterized European art cinemas. Many of these preoccupations were debated in the pages of the film magazine *Synchronos Kinimatographos*, which was published between 1960 and 1985 and to which Angelopoulos and Voulgaris contributed.

Two films can perhaps be singled out as marking a watershed in Greek cinema of this period: Angelopoulos's first feature film *Anaparastasi* (Reconstruction, 1970) and Damianos's *Evdokia* (1971), the second part of a loose trilogy which began with *Mechri to Ploio* (Until the Ship Sails, 1966) and concluded in 1995 with *Iniochos* (The Charioteer). *Evdokia* is a love drama that centres on the tragic relationship between a sergeant and a prostitute who meet one night in a taverna and who marry after a brief but intense affair. The film charts the break-up of the couple's relationship against a barren, semiurban, Attic landscape. Sensuality and tenderness are consistently juxtaposed against the harsh discipline of the military compound and the film explores the consequences of social marginality, as well as the tensions between repressive middle-class aspirations and freedom.

Notwithstanding the interest which the New Greek Cinema provoked, by the mid-1970s the Greek film industry was in a crisis under the impact of television, together with the commercial successes of Hollywood films. It was partly to bolster independent Greek film makers that the Greek Film Centre was inaugurated in 1970, originally as a subsidiary of the Greek Industrial and Development Bank. It acquired its present name, however, after the overthrow of the Colonels' regime in 1974 and in 1982 the then minister of culture, Melina Mercouri, undertook the promotion of Greek films. A scriptwriting fund was also established. Today many Greek film makers benefit from its coproduction programme and it remains the primary producer of new films in Greece. At the same time the Thessalonica Film Festival, which was founded in 1960, acted as an important boost for the domestic film industry, bestowing valuable awards. It remains the main annual cinematic event in Greece. In 1981 the running of the festival was taken over by the Ministry of Culture and in 1992 it was transformed into an international event.

Although relatively few films are produced in Greece today and of the 9 million tickets sold in Greece in 1997, only 550,000 were for Greek films, there have been exciting developments in recent years. Following in the path of Tonia Marketaki (1942–94), women directors such as Maria Iliou, Photini Siskopoulou, Angeliki Antoniou, and Olga Malea – whose raunchy feature debut O Orgasmos tis Ayeladas (The Orgasm of the Cow, 1996) was a box-office hit – are making their mark. Sotiris Goritsas's Balkanizateur (1997), the story of two men's pursuit of fortune in the black-market economies of the Balkans, was another success; between them the films sold some 300,000 tickets. Among promising younger directors, Renos Charalambidis burst on to the scene in 1997 with the prize-winning No Budget Story, while Menelaos Karamangiolis's ambitious thriller Black Out (1998) won general acclaim.

There is growing interest, too, in the Greek cinema abroad. Greek film has begun to be taught at foreign universities, including Cambridge, where an international conference entitled "Theatres of War: Fifty Years of Greek Cinema" was hosted in 1998. There has been a major retrospective of Greek cinema at the Centre Georges Pompidou in Paris (1995) and retrospectives of Angelopoulos at the Museum of Modern Art in New York in 1990 and at the Riverside Studios in London in 1998. With the support of the Greek Film Centre, a Greek film series was screened at the National Film Theatre in London in 1998.

ROBERT SHANNAN PECKHAM

Further Reading

Demopoulos, Michel (editor), Le Cinéma grec, Paris: Centre Georges Pompidou, 1995

Journal of Modern Greek Studies, special issue on Greek film, guest-edited by Stratos Constantinidis (2000)

Koliodimos, Dimitrios, The Greek Filmography, 1914 through 1996, Jefferson, North Carolina: McFarland, 1999

Mitropoulou, Aglae, Découverte du Cinéma grec: histoire, chronologie, biographies, films..., Paris: Seghers, 1968

Mitropoulou, Aglae, Ellinikos Kinimatographos [Greek Cinema], Athens, 1980

Schuster, Mel, The Contemporary Greek Cinema, Metuchen, New Jersey: Scarecrow Press, 1979

Soldaos, Yannis, Istoria tou Ellinikou Kinimatographou [History of the Greek Cinema], Athens, 1982

Cities

What is a city? Is it a community of buildings or a community of people? According to Aristotle, it is not a community of buildings but of people. For one could, for example, "enclose Megara and Corinth in a wall, yet they would not be one city". "But a city", he continues, "is a society of people ... not ... founded for the purpose of men's merely living together, but for their living as men ought" (Politics, 3. 9). On the other hand, when Pausanias, the 2nd-century AD traveller, came upon a little place in Phocis, he hesitated to call it a "city" (polis) as it possessed "no government offices or gymnasium, no theatre or agora or water flowing down to a fountain" (10. 4. 1). Gradually, "city", which is at the root of the word "civilization" (politismos), came to encompass both the buildings and the people of a permanent settlement.

In Mesopotamia evidence of permanent village agriculture dates back to 8000 BC and temple cities and city states date from 3500 BC. In Greece the earliest settlements were the Minoan (2000–1400 BC) and Mycenaean (1600–1050 BC) palace centres. At about 800 BC Archaic Greek societies began developing permanent city structures. While the Greeks did not invent the city as a form, they established it as a political institution. The polis, as an independent city state and a community of self-governing citizens, emerged in the Greek world in the 8th century BC. Its democratic underpinnings, governed by equality of all under the law (isonomia), were contrasted with the monarchical and despotic institutions of contemporary cities in Mesopotamia, Egypt, and the Persian empire.

Greek cities originated either from small villages that grew gradually, from several villages that came together to form a community (synoecism), or from colonial settlements. Athens was allegedly formed through synoecism. Colonial settlements, on the Ionian coast (modern Turkey in Asia Minor) and on the south Italian peninsula, were founded for purposes of commerce and retained ties to the mother city in mainland Greece. Many of the new settlements were planned on an orthogonal grid, while cities that evolved over time usually exhibited an irregular, "organic" street plan. Athens, established in Mycenean times, had an "organic" street plan that was first set out in the Archaic period. Miletus, on the coast of modern Turkey, was planned on an orthogonal grid by Hippodamus in 479 BC, following its destruction by the Persians in 490 BC. Though the ancient Greek cities possessed some of the characteristics associated with urban environments today – high concentration of population, division of labour, trade with other cities – they were all heavily dependent on agriculture. The connection of the city to the countryside remained most vital until the 20th century.

Of the approximately 700 cities of the Greek commonwealth in the Classical period, Athens was the largest and most famous. Public life took place in the Agora – the ancient civic centre and marketplace – while the city's tutelary goddess Athena was honoured by the Periclean building programme on the Acropolis: the Parthenon (447–432 BC), the Erechtheum (421–405 BC), and the temple of Athena Nike (427–424 BC). In contrast to the magnificence of the public building programme, residential architecture remained humble and inward looking. In the Classical Greek city no individual, no matter how powerful, could attach his name to the new civic structures, as it was the state and the citizens themselves (the free, male residents) who commissioned and paid for all public buildings. That changed during the subsequent periods, when Hellenistic rulers and Roman emperors endowed several of the Greek cities with larger and more luxurious public buildings that bore their names: the stoa of Attalus, Hadrian's library, etc. These private donations eroded the democratic ideals of the Classical polis whereby all men enjoyed equal footing. This practice of privately funded civic structures, named after wealthy individuals or corporations, similarly marks the urban landscape today.

The insularity of the Classical Greek city states, which often resulted not only in competition but also in warfare among them, was transformed in the ensuing Hellenistic period. As a result of the successful military campaigns of Philip II of Macedon, most of central and southern Greece became subjugated to the Macedonian kingdom. Philip's son, Alexander III the Great, undertook a campaign of expansion to the east, creating a kingdom that stretched from Cyrene in North Africa to India. As Alexander considered his mission to be a civilizing one, albeit imperialist, he founded several new cities, thus spreading the Hellenic language and culture across much of the known world. These cities were normally laid out in a grid pattern, adjusted to the existing topography in each case. While their building programme was based on the Classical Greek city – with an agora, temples, theatres, and other civic structures – their political system differed drastically. Whereas the classical Greek city was, at least in principle, politically autonomous, the Hellenistic city was a dependent member of an extensive empire. Alexandria in Egypt, the first and greatest of Alexander's cities, was founded in 332 BC. It soon became one of the most important trading centres of the Mediterranean, and an eminent centre for culture and philosophical studies, its Neoplatonic schools eventually rivalling the philosophy schools of Athens. "Alexandria is situated, as it were, at the crossroads of the whole world, ... bringing together all men into one place, displaying them to one another, and, as far as possible, making them of the same race", wrote Dio of Prusa in his *Alexandrian Speech* (*c*.AD 69/79). Thessalonica, founded in 316 BC, also rose to prominence under Roman rule, becoming the capital of the Roman province of Macedonia and an important military and commercial centre. It maintained its commercial and administrative importance in the subsequent Byzantine and Ottoman periods.

Greece became a Roman province in AD 146, after a war in which the Romans destroyed Corinth. Under the Roman empire Athens, though now a provincial city, still enjoyed a special status as a result of its cultural eminence. While its political significance atrophied, its physical image was enhanced by the new buildings endowed by the various emperors and high-ranking Roman officials. A resurgence of its philosophy schools in the 4th and 5th centuries infused new blood into its economy, until the emperor Justinian ordered their closure in AD 529, condemning Athens to obscurity.

The next major city to rise to prominence in the Graeco-Roman world was Byzantium, a Greek merchant settlement founded at the end of the 8th century BC on the shore of the Bosporus. Chosen by emperor Constantine the Great (307–337) as a capital of the eastern Roman empire, it was aggrandized and inaugurated in 330 as Constantinople. Constantinople was endowed with a unique triple identity: Greek, Roman, and Christian. Hailed as "the New Rome", its political, legal, and building structure certainly justified that claim. Also part of that structure, however, were the earliest layers of its Classical Greek and Hellenistic foundation, and its newly acquired Christian identity. Constantinople became the centre of the Byzantine empire, diffusing its imperial, religious, and commercial power over a vast territory. It reached its zenith under the reign of Justinian I (527–65), maintaining a key role until the period of the Latin rule (1204–61). The weakening of the Byzantine empire finally led to the fall of Constantinople in 1453 to the armies of the Ottoman sultan Mehmet II.

The legacy of Byzantine civilization did not disappear overnight with the fall of Constantinople. Just as the Byzantine emperors ensured the continuity of several Roman institutions, so too the Ottomans incorporated several aspects of Byzantine culture into their own governing system. Given the widespread destruction by the crusaders, many Greek cities, including Athens, considered Ottoman rule preferable. On the whole, the Ottomans preserved the existing urban structures, converting some of the churches into mosques, and building new mosques, *tekkes* (dervish convents), baths, and other civic buildings that imprinted on each city a new image. In fact, when Mehmet II arrived in Athens in 1458, so impressed was he with the city's ancient heritage that he conferred upon it special administrative and religious privileges. Athens, as well as other Greek cities, experienced a period of economic and population growth in the 15th–17th centuries, reflecting the overall prosperity of the Ottoman empire. Conditions deteriorated, however, in the late 18th and early 19th centuries, leading to the War of Independence (1821–27) and the establishment of the modern Greek kingdom in 1833.

The events of the 19th century caused a major rupture in the demographic and administrative structure of the Greek cities. After the departure of most Muslims, the centuries-old ethnic diversity of the population was replaced by a mostly homogeneous Greek population from the Greek countryside and the European diaspora. The traditionally decentralized administration, which enjoyed a considerable degree of autonomy and self-government, was replaced by a highly centralized monarchy modelled on the Bavarian prototype. The new capital, Athens, rose to prominence as the main administrative and economic centre, even though several other cities – Nauplia, Patras, Corinth, and Syros among them – had a much more prominent commercial profile. The charge of the new state was to forge a national Greek identity, connect the modern with the ancient past, and highlight the ancient legacy. New planning and architecture projects helped the nation's cities project a modern, uniform, and western image. The vestiges of the Classical, Roman, Byzantine, and Ottoman pasts, however, remained close to the new urban surfaces.

More recently, the European Union, of which Greece is a member, has been gradually recasting the political significance of national borders and national identities, moving towards the creation of a rich multicultural European mosaic. The annual institution of the "European City of Culture", a post already held by Athens and Thessalonica, the establishment of festivals and contests in various cities, and the widespread use of the English language have begun to create a new, shared, European identity. As individual cities and towns have begun to celebrate their own cultural histories for the benefit of a broader European public, identification with a particular city may prove, once again, more powerful than national identification.

ELENI BASTÉA

See also Town Planning, Urbanization

Further Reading

Bierman, Irene A., Rifa'at A. Abou-el-Haj, and Donald Preziosi (editors), *The Ottoman City and Its Parts: Urban Structure and Social Order*, New Rochelle, New York: Caratzas, 1991

Frantz, Alison, *The Middle Ages in the Athenian Agora*, Princeton, New Jersey: American School of Classical Studies at Athens, 1961

Freeman, Charles, *Egypt, Greece, and Rome: Civilizations of the Ancient Mediterranean*, Oxford and New York: Oxford University Press, 1996

Hastaoglou-Martinidis, Vilma, "City Form and National Identity: Urban Designs in Nineteenth-Century Greece", *Journal of Modern Greek Studies*, 13/1 (May 1995): pp. 99–123

Hoff, Michael C. and Susan I. Rotroff (editors), *The Romanization of Athens*, Oxford: Oxbow, 1997

Kostof, Spiro, *A History of Architecture: Settings and Rituals*, 2nd edition, revised by Greg Castillo, Oxford and New York: Oxford University Press, 1995

Lapidus, Ira M., "Cities and Societies: A Comparative Study of the Emergence of Urban Civilizations in Mesopotamia and Greece", *Journal of Urban History*, 12/3 (May 1986): pp. 257–92

Morkot, Robert, *The Penguin Historical Atlas of Ancient Greece*, London and New York: Penguin, 1996

Scarre, Chris, *The Penguin Historical Atlas of Ancient Rome*, London and New York: Penguin, 1995

Todorov, Nikolai, *The Balkan City, 1400–1900*, Seattle: University of Washington Press, 1983

Wycherley, R.E., *How the Greeks Built Cities*, 2nd edition, London: Macmillan, 1962; New York: Norton, 1976

City State

The city state (polis) was the prevailing political, cultural, religious, and social system among the Greeks from c.800 to c.300 BC. The map of ancient Greece was a mosaic of city states; each was independent, but some were linked with others by ties of kinship and military alliances.

The term "polis" originally apparently meant something like "the villages around". The Greeks used the term *synoikismos* to describe the unifying of the houses in the countryside (*oikoi*) and villages (*komai*) into a constitutional system (*politeia*). Most city states had an acropolis (a high city), a fortified area on a high rocky promontory overlooking the surrounding countryside, which served as a place of refuge in times of danger.

Geography was a factor in the rise of the city states, because the numerous islands of Greece, the very mountainous terrain of the mainland, and the isolation of small plains favoured small local units of government. Another factor was the collapse of kingship late in the Dark Ages; by the historical period most city states were ruled by councils controlled by aristocrats.

The territory of each city state was small. Some were only a few kilometres square: Athens with 2600 sq km of territory and Sparta with 8400 sq km were among the largest. Physically the city state might look urban or be composed of villages without walls, as at Sparta. The population was generally small. Slaves and foreigners (metics) were excluded from citizenship, while women, children, and sometimes "the dwellers around" (*perioikoi*) were classified as second-class citizens.

The full citizens (*politai*) of the polis were all males over the age of 18. Their births would be registered with the traditional brotherhood (phratry). Regardless of its location, the male citizens were the essence of the city state. They composed a corporate body, ordered by the principle of citizenship, which could be housed anywhere. All were expected to serve in defence of the city state.

The city states were varied and numerous, eventually numbering perhaps as many as 1200 or more. Their constitutions and history largely remain unknown. The Aeolian-, Ionian-, and Dorian-speaking Greeks developed different styles of city states; Athens and Sparta are the best known of the Ionian and Dorian types, respectively. Most of ancient Greek history is known through the histories of these two, the most famous; but other important ones included Corinth, Syracuse, Miletus, Ephesus, Thebes, and Chalcis. Tribal and cultic differences marked the city states with a jealous particularism. Most were isolated in small farming valleys with their own local shrines, laws, and dialects.

By the mid-8th century BC population increases led to the foundation of numerous colonies all around the Mediterranean, but especially on the shores of the Black Sea, in southern Italy, and in Sicily. Each of these usually became an independent city state. Sometimes the new colony was founded by two or more mother cities.

The government of most city states changed over the centuries. By the Archaic period most were ruled by aristocrats in a council, but an assembly of citizens and magistrates also participated in governing. In Athens the earliest council was the Areopagus, made up of elder statesmen; the members, archons, served for life. By the end of the 7th century BC growing tensions between the aristocrats and citizens from the lower orders, in Athens and other city states, often developed into class conflicts. When Solon was elected archon of Athens in 594 BC he began a programme of political reform that was to lead eventually to the establishment of Athenian democracy at the end of the 6th century BC.

Sparta resisted all reform and maintained an oligarchy based upon the laws of Lycurgus, which had organized the people into Spartiates (citizens), *perioikoi* (non-citizens with some rights), and helots (state serfs). There were two kings, elected from two royal families, who exercised limited power; one stayed at home and the other led the army into battle. Sparta was governed by five officials called ephors, elected to one-year terms by citizens, with the aid of a council. There was also a citizen assembly (*apella*).

War, an incessant feature of life, robbed the Greeks of their strength. During the Classical period cooperative efforts were made to limit the jealous particularism through leagues. While most were military alliances, some leagues served trade needs, and even managed some of the games. They included the Aetolian League, Boeotian League, Chalcidic League, League of Corinth, Delian League, Second Athenian League, Achaean League, Ionian League, and the Delphic Amphictiony, which managed the Pythian Games.

The sovereignty of the city states ended with the conquest of the Greeks by Philip II of Macedon in 338 BC. After the conquests of Alexander the Great, Graeco-Macedonian kingdoms were established throughout the empire. The individual

Greek city states were never again strong enough to regain their original power.

A.J.L. WASKEY, JR

See also Urbanization

Further Reading

Andrewes, Antony, *The Greek Tyrants*, New York: Harper and Row, 1963; London: Hutchinson, 1966

Aristotle, *The Politics*, edited and translated by Ernest Barker, Oxford: Clarendon Press, 1948; New York: Oxford University Press, 1962

Barker, Ernest, *Greek Political Theory: Plato and His Predecessors*, 5th edition, New York: Barnes and Noble, and London: Methuen, 1960

Barr, Stringfellow, *The Will of Zeus: A History of Greece from the Origins of Hellenic Culture to the Death of Alexander*, Philadelphia: Lippincott, 1961; London: Weidenfeld and Nicolson, 1962

Freeman, Kathleen, *Greek City-States*, New York: Norton, 1950

Littman, Robert J., *The Greek Experiment: Imperialism and Social Conflict, 800–400 BC*, New York: Harcourt Brace, and London: Thames and Hudson, 1974

Plato, *The Republic*, translated by F.M. Cornford, Oxford: Clarendon Press, 1941; New York: Oxford University Press, 1945 (many reprints)

Plutarch, *The Rise and Fall of Athens*, translated by Ian Scott-Kilvert, Harmondsworth and Baltimore: Penguin, 1975

Sabine, George Holland and Thomas Landon Thorson, *A History of Political Theory*, 4th edition, Hinsdale, Illinois: Dryden Press, 1973

Sealey, Raphael, *A History of the Greek City-States, c.770–338 BC*, Berkeley: University of California Press, 1976

Stockton, David, *The Classical Athenian Democracy*, Oxford and New York: Oxford University Press, 1990

Zimmern, Alfred, *The Greek Commonwealth: Politics and Economics in Fifth-Century Athens*, 5th edition, Oxford: Clarendon Press, and New York: Oxford University Press, 1961

Civil War 1945–1949

The Greek Civil War, rooted in the struggle for power between leftist and right-wing pro-monarchist forces, erupted after the liberation of Greece from the fascist forces of the Axis. Immediately after the withdrawal of the Nazis from Greece in October 1944, the British, who had already put Greece within their sphere of influence, intervened to establish a conservative pro-monarchist post-liberation government in Athens, in order to protect their geopolitical interests in the region. On 18 October 1944 British forces and the Greek government in exile of George Papandreou landed in Athens. Upon their arrival in Greece the British (*a*) demobilized ELAS (National Popular Liberation Army), the military wing of the EAM (National Liberation Front), who for more than three years had fiercely fought the occupation armies of the Axis, (*b*) formed a national Greek army under British tutelage, consisting largely of zealous ultra-right-wing volunteers, and (*c*) ignored public demands for the punishment of Greeks who had collaborated with the enemy during the occupation. After the clash of British troops and units of ELAS forces in Athens from 3 December 1944 to 11 January 1945, Greek army units were increasingly made up of selected ultra-conservative conscripts who were called up as army reservists.

The Varkiza Agreement of 12 February 1945, between the right-wing pro-monarchists and EAM/ELAS forces, called for a general amnesty and the recruitment of ELAS into the post-liberation Greek army. After the agreement EAM/ELAS showed a willingness to coexist peacefully within a democratic parliamentary system of government and avoid violent conflicts. The peaceful intentions of EAM/ELAS, however, were ignored by the British and their right-wing Greek friends, who insisted on the return of king George II and the exclusion of ELAS and many liberals from the conscription of the Greek armed forces.

Heinz Richter has indicated that from the lower ranks to the top commands the post-liberation Greek army was filled with royalists, anti-communists, former Nazi collaborators of the Security Battalions (*Tagmata Asphalias*), and members of the ultra-right-wing "Organization X". The police, a federal law enforcement agency, also used the same political-background criteria to select their officers. Both the army and the police showed little respect for democratic procedures or civil rights and increasingly became independent from civilian control, especially when they were attacking leftist Greek citizens.

This new right-wing social order received support from the wealthy Greeks, many of whom had profited from economic collaboration with the Nazis, or from speculating in scarce commodities during the occupation (1941–44). These entrepreneurs constituted an important and powerful social group of postwar Greek society.

From October 1944 to March 1946 the British appointed and deposed four Greek prime ministers for being unable to deal with the economic problems and political instability of the country. Finally, the first elections since 1936 were held on 31 March 1946, under the supervision of British, French, and American observers. The communists, under the leadership of Nikos Zachariadis, as well as some liberals, boycotted the elections, which resulted in a clear victory for the right wing under the leadership of prime minister Constantine Tsaldaris. The new government, headed by Tsaldaris, brought forward a rigged and coerced plebiscite on 1 September 1946, and king George II returned to Athens on 27 September. The restoration of the monarchy was seen by the right-wingers, as well as many republicans, as essential to the maintenance of traditional conservative Greek institutions and values, which had been challenged by leftist forces. The National Liberation Front (EAM), for example, had advocated postwar radical institutional changes and mass participation in the political process by all regional and social groups, including the underprivileged and women.

With a new vengeful right-wing government and the return of the king, repression and persecution against the left were intensified, driving former ELAS fighters and leftist political refugees back to the mountains. Many thousands of Greek civil servants, including university professors, who had joined the resistance movement (1941–44) against the Axis, were fired from their jobs on the grounds of being "anti-nationalists". Many were terrorized by the police and right-wing paramilitary groups, imprisoned, tortured, sent into exile, or executed. During 1946, 116 Greek leftist citizens were sentenced by

Civil War: ELAS guerrillas, who had fought the Axis in World War II, returned to the mountains in 1946 as Greece descended into civil war

court marshal and executed, and another 688 in 1947. The death penalty was given for offences such as criticizing the authorities or helping leftist insurgents.

Indiscriminate persecution and terrorism by the Greek right forced more communists and liberal anti-monarchists to resort to arms for protection and survival. Attacks by left-wing bands on police posts and army patrols also became common activities. An attack on the police station of Litochoro, a village near Mount Olympus, by communist insurgents on 31 March 1946, is often cited as the start of the Civil War; on the other hand, right-wing armed bands had attacked left- wing communities in the Peloponnese; and by September 1946 several hundred left-wing armed bands were organized throughout Greece, especially in the rural areas.

In October 1946 the Communist Party of Greece (KKE) announced the formation of the Democratic Army of Greece (DAG) under the leadership of Markos Vafiadis, a former ELAS leader. Vafiadis assumed command of the new army from a headquarters in northern Thessaly. Most of the DAG combatants, including the regional commanders, were members of former resistance organizations, especially ELAS. As soon as Vafiadis assumed leadership of the leftist forces, Tito of Yugoslavia ordered that the communist Slav-Macedonian Popular Liberation Front (SNOF) should, for their operations in Greece, be under the command of the Democratic Army of Greece. Slav-Macedonians exploited the opportunity to cultivate the idea of Slav-Macedonian secessionism, an extremely unpopular policy among Greeks of all political leanings. Under enormous pressure from rank and file, the communist leadership terminated the shaky alliance between the DAG and the Slav-Macedonian units of SNOF. The separation was not amicable, and it came late. In certain instances, SNOF and DAG units fought against each other; and the right wing had already succeeded in labelling the leftists as traitors to their nation, an image which was to haunt the communists in Greece for decades.

By the end of 1946 the national Greek army had just over 98,000 demoralized and poorly trained soldiers and officers. The Democratic Army of Greece, on the other hand, had nearly 10,000 combatants and sent detachments to different parts of Greece to promote military operations against the right-wing pro-monarchist forces. The Yugoslavs and Bulgarians provided the leftist armed forces in northern Greece with guns and ammunition. Attacks by left-wing forces were more ferocious against the police and right-wing paramilitary units such as X-ites, who were considered responsible for most of the atrocities committed against leftists and even liberal Greek citizens. The police, who were not trained for combat, suffered casualties three times as heavy as those of the army. Furthermore, the police and X-ites were more likely than regular soldiers to be executed after being captured by communist insurgents. Leftist forces also took revenge on ultra-right-wing civilians who were held responsible for collaborating with police and security forces.

On 31 March 1947 the British presence in Greece was officially terminated, leaving the Americans responsible for carrying on economic and military aid to the Greek government. Fearing a communist takeover in Greece, the Americans granted massive aid as a part of a programme known as the Truman Doctrine. Within a relatively short time American aid to Greece transformed the national Greek army into a disciplined and effective fighting force under the leadership of General Alexandros Papagos. As an ardently anti-leftist force the army remained insulated by American intervention from politicians and enjoyed a close relationship with its American patrons.

On 24 December 1947 the Communist Party of Greece announced the formation of a provisional democratic government in the mountains of northern Greece under the leadership of Markos Vafiadis. The objectives of the new leftist government included recognition of the full equality of all minorities (but not the establishment of an independent Macedonian state), nationalization of banks and heavy industry, agrarian reform, democratic reorganization of the country, the creation of a democratic army, navy, and air force, and resistance to foreign aggression.

The committed hard-core communists, as well as their left-wing supporters, came from all classes of Greek society. However, the vigorous political and military leaders and organizers came from the educated and professional classes, some for democratic reasons and some for radical socialist objectives. They saw the monarchy as a reactionary, fascist institution, and the British and Americans as imperialists who looked after their own interests and supported the worst elements in Greek society in order to achieve their ends.

Communist regimes in the Balkans refused to recognize the provisional government and to deal with it in other than clandestine ways. On 27 December 1947 the Communist Party of Greece was outlawed by the nationalist government of Greece and all "communist"-related activities were subjected to harsh punishment, including the death penalty. Some leftists were spared after signing a "declaration of repentance".

Under intensive pressure by the national army, the leftist Democratic Army of Greece started to rely on forced conscription of men, as well as women, in the areas it controlled. Most of the conscripts were young, from villages and small towns, who had little or no experience of guerrilla warfare. About 25 per cent of them were females, many of whom had risen to positions of junior command. By the spring of 1948 the DAG had reached its peak of 30,000 regular combatants and 70,000 reservists in auxiliary organizations. It controlled over 65 per cent of the rural population and half of Greece's surface area. More than 700,000 Greeks became refugees within Greece. The overwhelming majority of them were forced by the national army to leave their villages in order to deprive the communist insurgents of supplies and moral support.

The forced conscription of women and men by the DAG created suspicion and distrust, even among liberals who sympathized with the persecuted members of the left. Furthermore, the *pedomazoma* (abduction) of 28,000 children from the war zone of northern Greece to Eastern European countries by the Greek communist forces became the most contentious and emotive issue of the Civil War against the insurgents. According to the communists, the children, many of whose parents were in the DAG, were evacuated for their own protection; according to the Greek government, to be indoctrinated as young communists.

With the increase of military and economic aid from the United States, the national army of 147,000 men became an effective force in military operations against the Democratic

Army. Many tens of thousands of auxiliary military organizations (e.g. National Guard, police, and armed civilians) played an important supportive role for the national army. The final battles of the Civil War were fought in the summer of 1949 on the Grammos and Vitsi mountain ranges in northern Greece, where 16,000 combatants of the Democratic Army held heavily fortified positions. Other battles were fought in the mountainous regions of the Peloponnese. Overwhelmed by the superior nationalist armed forces, and battered by massive air strikes, the Democratic Army was finally defeated. Over 3000 leftist troops escaped to neighbouring Albania, Bulgaria, and Yugoslavia. Although minor clashes between the national army and small leftist units continued for several months throughout Greece, the Greek Civil War was over.

In his analysis of the war, the historian Richard Clogg indicates that there were at least four factors which contributed to the military defeat of the communist forces in Greece. First, the forced conscription of men and women by the Democratic Army and the abduction of children from the war zone to Eastern bloc countries. Because of these two unpopular policies the communists lost the support of the Greek liberal population, who might otherwise have been attracted to some of their political and economic objectives. Second, the inclusion of Slav-Macedonians in the Democratic Army, a very unpopular policy even among Greek leftists. The majority of the leftists would not fight for a cause which, if successful, would truncate their country. Third, the feud between Stalin and Tito. When Yugoslavia was expelled from the Cominform in 1948, the Greek communists sided with Moscow. As a consequence Tito closed Yugoslavia's borders with Greece in 1949, depriving the Democratic Army of much-needed supplies as well as important reserves. More than 4000 combatants of the Democratic Army were cut off in Yugoslavia and not permitted to cross back into Greece to assist their comrades. The fourth factor was the massive influx of American economic and military aid to the national army to contain Soviet expansionism. Furthermore, since Greece was within the British and American sphere of influence, the Soviets were unwilling to risk a confrontation with the West in order to secure a leftist victory in Greece.

During the Civil War over 158,000 Greeks lost their lives. Estimated casualties, according to the Greek government, included 29,000 leftist combatants and 11,000 of the national army. More than 40,000 leftists were sent to concentration camps by the pro-monarchist government. About 20,000 men and women were tried for crimes against the state and, of those, at least 5000 were executed.

After the defeat of the Democratic Army in northern Greece in August 1949, more than 70,000 men and women fled to Eastern Europe and the Soviet Union as political refugees. The systematic persecution and ostracism of the communists continued until July 1974 when the Greek parliament voted for the legalization of the Greek Communist Party.

The destruction of the Greek economy by the Axis occupation and the Civil War, along with high rates of unemployment during the 1950s and 1960s, forced hundreds of thousands of Greeks to leave their country in search of better social and economic opportunities in other countries, including Australia, Canada, and the United States. Most of them were economically deprived peasants with little academic attainment and occupational skills. Some peasants, however, emigrated to large cities, especially in the Athens area, to find jobs and improve their socio-economic status.

Political persecution against the left-wing elements by the right wing during the post-Civil War years also forced a large number of Greeks to emigrate to Australia and Canada, where they could find political freedom and better economic opportunities. At that time the US Embassy in Athens was very reluctant to issue visas of immigration to Greek citizens with leftist ideologies, especially those affiliated to the Communist Party.

Between 1951 and 1971 over 10 per cent of the Greek population had emigrated to foreign countries, mainly for economic and political reasons. These patterns of emigration, along with the introduction of new agricultural technology, contributed to a steady decline of the rural population in Greece. The proportion of the rural population was changed from 53 per cent in 1951 to 35 per cent in 1971.

PETER D. CHIMBOS

Further Reading

Clogg, Richard, *A Concise History of Greece*, Cambridge and New York: Cambridge University Press, 1992

Close, David, *The Origins of the Greek Civil War*, London and New York: Longman, 1995

Couloumbis, Theodore A., *et al.*, *Foreign Interference in Greek Politics: A Historical Perspective*, New York: Pella, 1976

Iatrides, John O. (editor), *Greece in the 1940s: A Nation in Crisis*, Hanover, New Hampshire: University Press of New England, 1981

Iatrides, John O. and Linda Wrigley (editors), *Greece at the Crossroads: The Civil War and its Legacy*, University Park: Pennsylvania State University Press, 1995

Richter, Heinz, "The Varkiza Agreement and the Origins of Civil War" in *Greece in the 1940s: A Nation in Crisis*, edited by John O. Iatrides, Hanover, New Hampshire: University Press of New England, 1981

Woodhouse, C.M., *The Struggle for Greece, 1941–1949*, London: Hart Davis MacGibbon, 1976; New York: Beekman Esanu, 1979

Classical Period *c.*479–323 BC

The Classical period of Greek civilization is framed by wars: at the beginning was the great conflict with the Persian empire culminating in the defeat of Xerxes' invasion of 479 BC; at the end was the war between Philip II, king of Macedon, and the alliance of Athens and Thebes, followed by the conquest of the Near East by Philip's son Alexander the Great. Undoubtedly these circumstances influenced the character of the period, though they are only one factor in its complex form. The period also witnessed the greatest achievements of the Greek city state and its varied political systems: in essentials, this was marked by the triumph of the voluntary cooperation of the free citizens who constituted these small communities over the monolithic and massive resources of an absolutist, autocratic empire. At the same time, however, the city state contained the seeds of its own decline. The need to build a larger political organization strong enough to continue the combat against the Persians led to empire and hegemony within the Greek states themselves (particularly that of Athens, which dominated the

Classical Period: sculpture from the west pediment of the Parthenon showing Iris, messenger of the gods, c.438 BC, British Museum, London

first half of the period), and the subsequent rivalry and quarrels that weakened that unity following the great war between Athens and Sparta, and their resulting collective weakness in the face of the aggressive monarchy of Philip II.

Classical art and literature grew out of the developments of the preceding Archaic period, though political success engendered a new confidence. It is noticeable in the fine arts, in both sculpture and (in so far as the evidence for it has survived) painting. Already in the late Archaic period sculpture had been evolving away from its oriental- (and particularly Egyptian-) derived formalism towards greater naturalism. The stiff, formal poses of the Archaic marble statues give way to more complex ones made possible by the rapid development of hollow cast bronze. Indeed, the extremely elaborate poses of some early Classical statues, such as the *Discus Thrower* of Myron, seem specifically to illustrate their freedom from the

restraints previously imposed by the marble block. This phase passed, and Classical sculpture is marked essentially by a relaxed, yet idealized, naturalism. But what were by repute its greatest achievements, the lost statues of gold and ivory (fixed on a wooden frame) made by Phidias as the focus of worship in the temples of Athena on the Acropolis of Athens and of Zeus at Olympia, must have had an awesome majesty and formality that transcended any natural representation.

Much of this sculpture was produced to satisfy the demands of official patronage rather than the private individual. Statues were set up as thank-offerings for victory, or to express the religious needs of the community, rather than as monuments to the prestige and power of ruling families. The city, the community, commissioned them, and the art reflected, very often, the political agenda set by the community itself. Not all of this was the triumphant militarism typified by Phidias' colossal bronze of *Athena the Champion* that dominated the Acropolis of Athens, and which was prominent enough to serve as a landmark to guide ships approaching the harbour of Piraeus, more than 6 km away. More subtle, and echoing the changed circumstances of the 4th century BC, was the personification of *Peace* and her infant *Wealth* made by Cephisidotus (of which later copies survive), while a surviving original bronze of *Athena*, plausibly attributed to the same sculptor, though armoured, seems to present no threat of military aggression. The emphasis, more and more, is on humanity, as in the *Hermes Playing with the Infant Dionysus* by Praxiteles, Cephisidotus' more famous son, which was found at Olympia and often thought to be an original, not a copy. But in many ways the logical and most influential development of Classical sculpture is seen in Praxiteles' *Aphrodite*, sensational in its own day on account of its nudity, and a forerunner of an endless sculptural interest in the naked female form (and, in this case, supposedly modelled not on an imaginary goddess but on the sculptor's own mistress).

Despite this, sculpture was very much a public art, and even the *Aphrodite* was purchased by the people of Cnidus in Asia Minor, to be set up there in a sanctuary of the goddess, where the statue became a tourist attraction. Statues were placed in religious sanctuaries and in public places such as the agora, a term better translated as the civic centre rather then the marketplace of the Greek cities. Sculpture also adorned public buildings, particularly temples, which, continuing the conventions of the Archaic period, carried relief decoration on their friezes, and sculpture in the round in their pediments, the supreme examples of the Classical period being the temple of Athena, the Parthenon, on the Acropolis of Athens, and the slightly earlier temple of Zeus at Olympia. Certainly at Athens, and in all probability at Olympia, this work did not simply pay tribute to the gods, but at the same time celebrated victory over the barbarian, the Persian invader. It is typical of the Classical attitude, however, that it did this by allegory (for example, Greeks defeating legendary Amazons) rather than by direct representation, an indication that the Greek approach was now radically different from that of the Near Eastern predecessors.

Painting, we know, was used to decorate public buildings, such as temples, porticos, and feasting rooms, such as at the entrance (Propylaea) to the Athenian Acropolis. Executed on wooden panels or plastered walls, it was essentially a fragile medium and is now largely lost. Decorated vases, their pictures fired in the kiln, give us some idea of developments – the move towards greater realism, perhaps in advance of sculpture, and the illusion of three dimensions and depth. The panel-painting technique of colour wash on a chalky white ground was used briefly in the last part of the 5th century BC in a special category of vase, made to be deposited in graves; the best illustrate the freedom that artists had then mastered. In 1977, the unearthing of the tombs of Philip II and other members of the Macedonian royal family revealed wall-paintings of dazzling mastery that anticipate uncannily the achievements of Renaissance artists, in the sense of liberation from long traditions and conventions: such work clearly went on to inspire artists in the Hellenistic and Roman periods.

Architecture was firmly rooted in the forms of the Archaic period – superficially, there is no great difference between the Doric temple of Artemis at Corcyra, of the early 6th century BC, and the Parthenon, the greatest Doric building of the 5th century BC. Developments can be seen in the improvement in technique, particularly the use of marble, and the refinement of detail. Yet there is more than this. Though it is not easily noticed by the naked eye, the Parthenon represents the application to building design of a rigorously thought-out sequence of mathematical proportions, particularly in the ratio of 4:9, that is 2 squared to 3 squared. It is in mathematics that some of the greatest advances of the Classical period can be discerned. Despite having – or perhaps, by virtue of having – hopelessly cumbersome numerical systems, the 5th century BC was the time at which the Greek interest in mathematics became fully awakened, not surprisingly through geometry, ratio, and proportion rather than arithmetic. Sculptors such as Polyclitus saw the ideal of human beauty in the mathematical relationship between the different parts of the human body. The mathematicians of the Classical period constituted a discipline that has continued uninterruptedly, through the succeeding Hellenistic and Roman periods, inspiring the Arabic mathematicians of the Middle Ages, and on to the present day. Thus the work of the 4th-century mathematician Eudoxus of Cnidus was incorporated by the Hellenistic Euclid into his fundamental textbook, the *Elements*, which was still an essential schoolbook in the 20th century.

In addition to mathematics, and also building on the pioneering achievements of the Archaic period, the natural sciences flourished. Much, inevitably, was theoretical, but in what we would term physics for instance, Greek scientists evolved the atomic theory. It was still essentially the age of the universalist, but so much had been achieved that the greatest of them, Aristotle, gathered together in his writings (which read more like lecture notes, carefully preserved for posterity, than published works) his systematical concepts of the whole range of scientific thought – and beyond. The philosophers – a term coined in the Classical period – also turned to the study of human behaviour, politics and the nature of political relationships, the concepts of law and order and justice, of religious and related matters, of poetry and the arts. The nature of the ideal state was investigated; in size and scope, not surprisingly, it resembled the Classical Greek city state, but the unsatisfactory nature of contemporary political forms meant that no existing city furnished an ideal model, although Aristotle

studied the constitutions, presumably all different, of some 150 of them.

How much of practical value this study of political theory achieved is dubious, though Plato went to Syracuse to advise the autocratic ruler of that city, and Aristotle was chosen by Philip II to be tutor to his son Alexander the Great. The principal achievement of the philosophers based in Athens, including Aristotle, who was not a native Athenian, was the institution of their own philosophical schools (again, with Archaic-period antecedents). These were based on the exercise grounds, the gymnasia, of the Classical city, and they survived and even developed as centres of intellectual life through the succeeding Hellenistic and Roman periods. Although as centres of paganism they were suppressed by the Christian emperor Justinian, they provided a model for Alexandria, for the Arabic centres of the Middle Ages, and so again through post-medieval Renaissance Europe to the present day.

During the Classical period there was a great flourishing of literature. Earlier literature, since the time and works of Homer, comprised exclusively poetry. Now a significant prose literature began. The writings of Herodotus in many ways typify the Classical achievement. First and foremost, he brought to Greece a great personal knowledge of the wider world within which the Greeks existed and operated. Born at Halicarnassus in Asia Minor, he was by birth a subject of the Persian king; his neighbours were the non-Greek Carians. He certainly visited Egypt and other parts of the Persian empire before arriving in Athens, at the period of its great rise to power and prosperity following the defeat of Xerxes' invasion. He knew the leading political families, who told him their family histories, which were so important a part of the city's development. He was inspired to record the history of the Persian Wars, as the first united achievement of the Greek peoples since the siege of Troy (which to him, of course, was equally historical). In a world where education included above all else a knowledge of the Homeric poems, he set out to produce his own epic of the Persian Wars – but written in prose, not verse. He included everything that seemed to him to have even the least bearing on the history of the war, and thus preserved for us a vast spectrum of contemporary knowledge. Above all, in doing this, he instigated the study of contemporary or near-contemporary events: as the "father of history" he certainly inspired his more methodical successor Thucydides, who wrote about the lesser war between Athens and Sparta, with a deeper insight into historical analysis that this tragic event required, and thereafter an endless sequence of historians, down to the present day. From this, too, prose became the natural medium of expression for the philosophers.

At the same time, drama was developed as a new form of poetic literature. Here, too, the roots lie in the Archaic period, in the choral odes sung and danced at religious festivals throughout the Greek world. Tragedy required the participation of individual actors, separated from the choruses. They played the roles of recognizable characters drawn from the almost limitless repertoire of traditional legend and myth. Significantly, actions based on contemporary events are almost unheard of; the main known – and surviving – example is Aeschylus' play the *Persians*, which again was based on the events of Xerxes' invasion. Comedy was more involved with contemporary affairs, particularly politics, and often portrayed real politicians or other public figures. It was all part of the ferment of contemporary intellectual life. The surviving examples of both tragedy and comedy come, almost inevitably, from 5th-century Athens. Drama went into a marked decline in the succeeding century, the only real survivor being the "new" non-political comedy of manners of the late 4th century BC. Until recent discoveries of these plays on papyri from Egypt, they survived only in Latin versions of the 3rd and 2nd centuries BC. From the Greek examples, later Latin plays, written as literary exercises rather than for production on the stage, in their turn inspired subjects for plays by Shakespeare.

It would be wrong to create the impression that Classical Greece was unified in its achievement. Some places – most obviously, Athens – predominate because their own position in the Classical world, their wealth, and their power were particularly inspiring. In these places the culture of the Classical period is very much a *Zeitgeist*, the spirit of the age. They might well stimulate achievement elsewhere. All the same, much of the Greek world was outside this achievement. Some cities, such as Sparta, quite deliberately turned their backs on it in a desperate attempt to preserve what were for them the more congenial virtues of the preceding Archaic period. Many places, poor and small and insignificant, remained outside through lack of opportunity or sheer ignorance. All the same, awareness of what was being achieved was widespread, and the excitement, if not the opportunity, was not restricted by political or geographical divisions. Aristotle, surely the greatest intellect of the Classical period, came from Stagira in northern Greece, a place that recent excavation has shown to be nothing more than a rather squalid village; to gain intellectual fulfilment he had to move away, not just to the wealth of Philip II's growing kingdom but to Athens, in political decline but still the epitome of Classical civilization.

R.A. TOMLINSON

See also Architecture, Comedy, Democracy, Historiography, Mathematics, Painting, Philosophy, Physics, Religion, Tragedy

Summary

Roughly 479–323 BC – from the end of the Persian Wars to the death of Alexander the Great. The period is notable for a cultural flowering in Greece – and especially in Athens – in almost every field which brought to maturity the seeds sown in the preceding Archaic period. Among other highlights, the tragedies of Aeschylus, Sophocles, and Euripedes, the philosophy of Socrates, Plato and Aristotle, and the sculptures of Phidias and Praxiteles are considered benchmarks in the development of Western civilization.

Further Reading

The list is immense. The following books give a good general overview, with full bibliographies of relevant material.

Austin, M.M. and P. Vidal-Naquet, *Economic and Social History of Ancient Greece: An Introduction*, London: Batsford, and Berkeley: University of California Press, 1977
Boardman, John *et al.* (editors), *The Oxford History of Greece and the Hellenistic World*, Oxford and New York: Oxford University Press, 1991
Burkert, Walter, *Greek Religion: Archaic and Classical*, Oxford: Blackwell, and Cambridge, Massachusetts: Harvard University Press, 1985
Davies, J.K., *Democracy and Classical Greece*, Hassocks, Sussex: Harvester Press, and Atlantic Highlands, New Jersey: Humanities Press, 1978
Dodds, E.R., *The Greeks and the Irrational*, Berkeley: University of California Press, 1951
Guthrie, W.K.C., *A History of Greek Philosophy*, 6 vols, Cambridge: Cambridge University Press, 1962–81
Kennedy, George, *The Art of Persuasion in Greece*, London: Routledge and Kegan Paul, and Princeton, New Jersey: Princeton University Press, 1963
Kerferd, G.B., *The Sophistic Movement*, Cambridge and New York: Cambridge University Press, 1981
Lacey, W.K., *The Family in Classical Greece*, London: Thames and Hudson, and Ithaca, New York: Cornell University Press, 1968
Lawrence, A.W., *Greek Architecture*, 5th edition, revised by R.A. Tomlinson, New Haven and London: Yale University Press, 1996
Lewis, D.M. *et al.* (editors), *The Fifth Century BC*, Cambridge: Cambridge University Press, 1992 (*The Cambridge Ancient History*, vol. 5, 2nd edition)
Lewis, D.M. *et al.* (editors), *The Fourth Century BC*, Cambridge: Cambridge University Press, 1994 (*The Cambridge Ancient History*, vol. 6, 2nd edition)
Pollitt, J.J., *Art and Experience in Classical Greece*, Cambridge: Cambridge University Press, 1972
Robertson, Martin, *A History of Greek Art*, 2 vols, London: Cambridge University Press, 1975
Wiedemann, Thomas (editor), *Greek and Roman Slavery*, Baltimore: Johns Hopkins University Press, and London: Croom Helm, 1981

Cleisthenes *fl.*525–505 BC

Athenian political leader

The clan of the Alcmaeonidae, to which Cleisthenes belonged, had been prominent in the old "Eupatrid" pre-Solonian aristocracy of Athens. One of its members, Megacles, was chief archon around *c.*630 BC when another noble, Cylon, attempted to seize power and set himself up as "tyrant". Megacles rallied the people and blockaded him on the Acropolis. Cylon escaped, but his followers, who had taken refuge at the statue of Athena, were killed, despite a promise of safe conduct. As a result the whole clan was tried, put under a curse, and exiled.

Restored, it seems, at the time of Solon's reforms (594 BC), the Alcmaeonidae emerged in the mid-6th century as leaders of the coast faction, the "Men of the Shore" in Herodotus' account (1. 59) of the political struggles that led to Pisistratus' three attempts to establish a "tyranny"; Aristotle (*Athenian Constitution*, 13) identifies this faction as the supporters of "the middle form of constitution", such as Solon had tried to bring about, and views Pisistratus as "a man who seemed inclined to democracy". The Alcmaeonidae went into exile (Herodotus, 1. 64) after Pisistratus' successful third attempt with strong foreign backing.

Cleisthenes, who at this time was at least an adolescent, if not an adult, presumably went with them. But at some point, probably after Pisistratus' death in 528/27 BC, he returned to Athens, now ruled by Pisistratus' son Hippias, for he was almost certainly the Cleisthenes who appears in one fragment, discovered in the Athenian Agora, of a late 5th-century BC list of chief archons, as holding office in what its editors identify as 525/24 BC.

Later Cleisthenes was again in exile with many of his clan, who, after failing to spark a popular rising against Hippias by means of an armed incursion into Attica, withdrew to Delphi, where they obtained the contract for rebuilding the fire-damaged temple of Apollo. Their lavish performance of the task won them influence with the Delphic authorities, who were persuaded to advise the Spartans, whenever they came to consult the oracle, to liberate Athens from the tyrant. This advice was probably instrumental in winning support at Sparta for such men as king Cleomenes, who had other reasons for removing Hippias. In the event, after a failed seaborne invasion in 511 BC, the following year Cleomenes took a substantial army by land from the Peloponnese, won a battle, and forced Hippias into exile.

Cleisthenes' role in these events is unknown, but he is identified by Herodotus (5. 66) as one of the two most powerful men in Athens after Hippias' expulsion, his rival being Isagoras, described by Aristotle (*Athenian Constitution*, 20) as a friend of the tyrants. Isagoras gained the upper hand, being elected chief archon for 508/07 BC, whereupon, as Herodotus puts it, Cleisthenes "took the people into his party", words echoed by Aristotle, who adds: "by proposing to give political power to the masses". The clear inference to be drawn from their wording is that they believed that this action was born of political expediency, a belief that the previous history of the Alcmaeonidae, for all their support of the Solonian reforms, cannot be said to refute.

Cleisthenes' appeal to the people must have met with a response, for Isagoras at once sought help from Cleomenes, who had worked with him in 510 BC. The Spartan king's reply was to call on the Athenians to expel Cleisthenes and others of "the accursed" (Herodotus, 5. 70) – the descendants of the Alcmaeonidae who had been punished with a curse after the massacre of Cylon's supporters in the late 7th century BC – and then to travel to Athens with a small force. Before he arrived, Cleisthenes himself left Athens, a move that, whatever his motive, enabled the people to decide on their best policy without the pressure of the curse, but Cleomenes still set about expelling as many as 700 households of Cleisthenes' supporters. He also tried to replace the Solonian Council of 400 with a body of 300 partisans of Isagoras, and then seized the Acropolis. The people rose against him and after a two-day siege forced him to depart under truce, expelled Isagoras, and recalled Cleisthenes.

Cleisthenes now carried out his promise to give power to the people. His principal reform was to create a new tribal structure for the political and military organization of the Athenian people, replacing the four old Ionian tribes based on kinship with ten new tribes based on 139 small local units, the demes, grouped in such a way as to minimize the influence of the wealthy landed nobles by making each tribe consist of people drawn from all over Athens and Attica. He linked demes together, not necessarily with their immediate neighbours, to form thirty *trittyes*, ten in each of three regions, the city, the inland, and the coasts, and then took one *trittys* from each region to form each new tribe. He thus aimed to preserve the unity of the state against the sort of powerful regional factions whose rivalries had led to Pisistratus' tyranny and whose re-emergence Isagoras' success seemed to foreshadow.

Cleisthenes then used the new tribes to reshape Solon's Council of 400. Enlarged to 500, it was to consist of 50 men from each tribe selected by lot from nominees of the demes, the members to change annually and no one to serve more than twice in his lifetime. These arrangements ensured that it could not be controlled by minority pressure groups, while educating a good proportion of the citizens in public affairs, and so it enabled the sovereign Assembly open to all citizens, whose business it prepared and whose decisions it carried out, also to be truly democratic and effective. The two essential institutions of Athenian democracy were now in place and functioning properly. Cleisthenes' enactment of the only other measure credited to him, the introduction of ostracism (Aristotle, *The Athenian Constitution*, 22), has been needlessly doubted on the grounds that the procedure was not used until 488/87 BC.

His name is not linked with any event after his reforms of 508/07 BC and it is not known what part, if any, he had in the successful defence of the new democratic Athens against threats from Sparta, Thebes, and Chalcis (506–505 BC), or even when he died. However, both Herodotus (6. 131) and Aristotle (*Athenian Constitution*, 29) refer to him without qualification as the one who "established democracy"; Isocrates in his *Areopagiticus* (c.354 BC) sees the system he set up as greatly preferable to the radical democracy of his own day. Under it, certainly, the Athenians were very successful. In the modern democratic era, although due weight has been given to the influence of Solon as the "father of democracy", and although some scholars have detected signs of pro-Alcmaeonid gerrymandering in allocating *trittyes* to tribes, the essential role of Cleisthenes in the democracy's development to maturity has been freely recognized, not least in the celebrations that marked the 2,500th anniversary of his laws.

T.T.B. RYDER

See also Democracy

Biography
A member of the Alcmaeonid clan, Cleisthenes (date of birth unknown) was probably chief archon in 525/24 BC during the tyranny of Hippias. After the expulsion of Hippias by Cleomenes of Sparta in 510 BC, Cleisthenes emerged as a popular leader and in 508/07 BC carried out political reforms that set in motion the machinery that would bring about the establishment of Athenian democracy. Date of death unknown.

Further Reading
Andrews, A., "Kleisthenes' Reform Bill", *Classical Quarterly*, 27 (1977): pp. 241–48
Aristotle, *The Athenian Constitution*, translated by P.J. Rhodes, Harmondsworth and New York: Penguin, 1984
Boardman, John et al. (editors), *Persia, Greece and the Western Mediterranean, c.525 to 479 BC*, Cambridge: Cambridge University Press, 1988 (*The Cambridge Ancient History*, vol. 4, 2nd edition)
Forrest, W.G., *The Emergence of Greek Democracy: The Character of Greek Politics, 800–400 BC*, London: Weidenfeld and Nicolson, 1966
Herodotus, *Works*, vol. 3, translated by A.D. Godley, London: Heinemann, and New York: Putnam, 1922 (Loeb edition; many reprints)
Herodotus, *The Histories*, translated by Aubrey de Sélincourt, 2nd edition, Harmondsworth: Penguin, 1972

Clement of Alexandria, St

*c.*AD 150 – *c.*AD 215

Christian writer

It is to a large degree thanks to Clement that the cultural and philosophical traditions of Hellenism were deemed to be a legitimate component of Christian theology. In the religious and philosophical melting pot that was late-antique Alexandria, Clement fought a two-sided battle that was in many respects successful. Against the tendency to reject the Hellenic tradition outright evinced in Tatian, Tertullian, and Irenaeus, Clement defended the utility of Hellenic learning for the defence and deepening of the faith. On the other front, Clement attacked the complex and seductive speculations of the Gnostics, which had proved so attractive to many educated Christians.

The bulk of Clement's work forms a kind of trilogy. The *Protrepticus* or *Exhortation to the Greeks* is an attack on the absurdities of pagan religion and a call to accept the only true religion, that which has been sublimely revealed by Christ, the *Logos* of God. The *Paedagogue* or *Teacher* takes up the instruction of those who have accepted baptism. Its aim is to teach the perfect accomplishment of the virtues. The *Stromateis* or *Miscellanies* are, as the title suggests, a collection of diffuse materials; they deal, among other things, with the relation between the Christian faith and Hellenic philosophy, with marriage, and with the ideal of the true gnostic. In addition Clement composed a small work, *Quis Dives Salvitur?* or *Who is The Rich Man that is Saved?* This piece is a commentary on Mark 10: 17–31. Clement argues that the Christian is not required actually to sell all his goods, but rather to be free from attachment to them. Other works survive only as fragments.

Clement's teaching is centred on the *Logos*, the creator, instructor, and perfecter of humankind. The *Logos* has revealed God to the Jews in the Law of the Old Testament, to the Greeks in their philosophy, and finally and most perfectly in his own Incarnation. Philosophy is therefore a legitimate tool of Christian theology. The difference is one of degree, not of kind.

In opposition to the Gnostic tendency to divide Christians into more or less predetermined classes, Clement insists upon the sufficiency of faith and the equal grace conferred upon all at baptism. Also against the Gnostics, Clement affirms the integrity of the material order and the goodness of the body. Against the tendency found among Christians and Gnostics alike to denigrate marriage, Clement upheld its sanctity. He goes so far as to suggest that the married Christian is on a level above the celibate. The celibate has fewer distractions and encumbrances; his task is therefore easier.

Notwithstanding the equality of grace received at baptism, the Christian must strive for perfection. Through the exercise of his free will, he must struggle for the gift of *apatheia*, or freedom from passions. God is radically unknowable, but is made known to those who love him. Clement's apophaticism is more than mere agnosticism. The true gnostic is led by the *Logos* to the contemplation of God. By way of this anagogy, man is deified. Clement speaks of man's deification with almost unprecedented clarity.

Of Clement's immediate background we know frustratingly little. He is very vague about his own teachers, naming only one of them, the Alexandrian lecturer Pantaeus. His work is suffused with Platonic philosophy and Stoic ethics, and marked by Aristotelian logic and vocabulary. His frequent allusions to Classical literature, no doubt intended to keep up the interest of his cultured audience, are drawn from both florilegia and direct acquaintance. He is patently indebted to the Jewish Platonist Philo of Alexandria, particularly in respect of the allegorical method of biblical exegesis, the incomprehensibility of God, and the ideal of *apatheia*. Clement's integration of the Hellenic tradition and Christianity is a more searching and critical development of that proposed by St Justin Martyr. Clement's *Exhortation* owes some elements to Tatian's *Exhortation*.

The influence of Clement has been profound. The fusion of Hellenic philosophy and moral teaching with Christianity proved to be a heady mixture. Origen, though a man of greatly different temper, continued the work of Clement, establishing Christian Platonisim as the hallmark of the school of Alexandria. The Cappadocian Fathers represent the greatest flowering of the tradition of Clement and Origen. Clement's influence is clearly perceptible in the works of Evagrius of Pontus and pseudo-Macarius, the two great fountainheads of monastic spirituality. Clement's conception of the angelic hierarchies may be regarded as an ancestor of that made famous by Dionysius the Areopagite. Clement is quoted with deep approval by St Maximos the Confessor. He continued to be an important authority for the Byzantines. While removed from the Roman martyrology in the late 16th century, he remains accounted a saint by the Orthodox Church.

MARCUS PLESTED

Biography

Born *c.*AD 150, probably at Athens, educated at Alexandria in the catechetical school of Pantaenus, whom he succeeded. Principal surviving works are: *Protrepticus* (*Exhortation to the Greeks*), *Paedagogue* (*Teacher*), and *Stromateis* (*Miscellanies*). He argued for the legitimate retention of Hellenic cultural and philosophical traditions in Christian theology. He left Alexandria in 202 before the persecutions of Septimius Severus and died between 211 and 216.

Further Reading

Bigg, Charles, *The Christian Platonists of Alexandria*, Oxford: Clarendon Press, and New York: Macmillan, 1886

Chadwick, Henry, *Early Christian Thought and the Classical Tradition: Studies in Justin, Clement and Origen*, Oxford: Clarendon Press, and New York: Oxford University Press, 1966

Mondésert, Claude, *Clément d'Alexandrie*, Paris: Montaigne, 1944

Cleomenes III 260–219 BC

King of Sparta

The lives of Cleomenes III (Agiad, reigned *c.*235–222 BC) and his predecessor Agis IV (Eurypontid, reigned *c.*235–222 BC) are the subject of numerous studies and novels, ancient as well as modern. After Lycurgus the lawgiver, Leonidas, and Agesilaus II, they are the most famous exemplars of Spartan culture.

Their achievements and significance, on the other hand, are the stuff of history.

Cleomenes probably acceded to the Spartan throne in 235 BC. He could not have chosen a more pregnant moment. For it was then that Aratus achieved the decisive gain for the Achaean League that imperilled Sparta's future, in a way that Macedonian suzerainty of Greece had not. Megalopolis, led by its ex-tyrant Lydiadas, threw in its lot with Achaea, whose foreign policy thereby took on a decidedly anti-Spartan flavour. Like all his royal predecessors since Agesilaus II, only more so, Cleomenes had to keep watch on Megalopolis, no matter how preoccupied he might be otherwise with internal upheaval or other external threats from inside or outside the Peloponnese. Unlike all his predecessors, Cleomenes not only recovered from Megalopolis the disputed borderland of Belminatis but actually destroyed the urban centre of the Great City itself. For this, among many other things, he earned the enduring hatred of Polybius, even though the historian was born in a resurgent Megalopolis, 20 years after the king's ignominious death in exile.

The only hope for Sparta to regain its important standing in the Peloponnese was to mobilize all its inner strength and deal with the urgent social problems that beset it. Cleomenes seems to have understood this at a very early stage, and, instead of following the example of his father Leonidas and his father's cousin Areus, he decided to emulate Agis. It came as a surprise to his contemporaries to see the principles of Agis adopted by the son of his most bitter enemy.

Cleomenes was neither a romantic dreamer nor a dogmatic rationalist, but a practical politician. He was determined to solve the urgent social problems of Sparta in order to increase its political and military power, and at the same time to strengthen his own position. He knew very well that he could not carry out the necessary reforms by persuasion alone, and therefore tried to gain popularity and fame through military feats.

This does not mean, of course, that these events cannot or should not be viewed within their wider context, particularly the continuing balance of power between the three great dynasts of Macedon, Egypt, and the Near East. Indeed, it was this stalemate and, particularly, the enfeebled Macedonian suzerainty over Greece as represented successively by Antigonus II Gonatas (c.277–239 BC) and Demetrius II (c.239–229 BC) that allowed the Aetolian League, the Achaean League, and then Sparta under Cleomenes the space for internal consolidation or transformation and external expansion. In fact, it was the resurgence of Macedon under Antigonus III Doson in the 220s BC, ironically precipitated by Cleomenes, that fully exposed the limitations of the single Greek city state as a power unit and put paid to Sparta's illusory independence and ephemeral social renewal.

Cleomenes had planned his coup well in advance with the collaboration of a small group of sympathizers, including his stepfather Megistonous, a rich landowner. Returning to Sparta one evening (probably in the autumn of 227 BC) he fell upon the ephors at supper, killing four of them and ten of their chief supporters, and seized power. Eighty opponents were proscribed. Cleomenes then proceeded to carry out the same revolutionary programme that had led to the downfall of Agis. All landed property was put into a common pool, debts were cancelled, and the land was divided into 4,000 Spartan lots. He raised the citizen body to perhaps 5,000 from the metics and *perioikoi* (dwellers round about), but in the reassignment of the land, lots were reserved for proscribed exiles, whose eventual reconciliation and return was evidently envisaged – or at least that was the impression that Cleomenes sought to convey. Equally important for his aims, the traditional Spartan *agoge* (upbringing), with military training, age groups for boys, and common messes for adults, was reintroduced. But Cleomenes' measures were not simply backward-looking. Now at last, a century after Alexander and after several Spartan defeats, he introduced the Macedonian type of phalanx and spent the winter drilling his troops in the use of the long pike, the *sarissa*. Constitutionally, he weakened the Gerousia by attenuating or removing some of its powers, and by making election to it annual rather than for life (a major source of its enormous prestige), and abolished the ephorate, which he condemned as an excrescence on the "Lycurgan constitution", a move that led his opponents to brand him as a tyrant. According to Pausanias, he established a new board of magistrates, the *patronomoi* (the title means "Guardians of Ancestral Law and Order").

The Cleomenean revolution struck a chord in the cities of Sparta's Achaean opponents, where the poor sub-hoplite citizenry yearned for debt cancellation and land redistribution on the Spartan model, which they obviously regarded as exportable. This, however, was a grave misapprehension, because Sparta's unique sociopolitical conditions could not simply be reproduced elsewhere, and because Cleomenes had no intention of exporting social or economic revolution of any kind. Ideological preference may have had something to do with this refusal, but a more powerful factor was the pragmatic consideration that Spartan hegemony over an association of cities dominated by mass movements of a genuinely democratic character was likely to be radically unstable and bound to attract the unwelcome attention of Macedon, which had made its views on popular social movements unequivocally clear from the very outset of its hegemony of Greece.

The Cleomenic War, the war against Cleomenes as seen from the Achaean standpoint, lasted from 229/28 to 222 BC. At the beginning Cleomenes was very successful, and almost provoked the collapse of the Achean League. By the beginning of 224 BC his military-political drive had not only brought Argos and most of Arcadia within the Spartan camp but had carried his victorious arms into and beyond the original Achaean heartland to the very gates of the Peloponnese at Corinth. The victory in the field at Hecatombeum in western Achaea in 226 BC was matched in 225 BC by the diplomatic triumph of the adhesion of Argos. Even Aratus' own Sicyon trembled before the blast and had its loyalties severely strained. A few months into 224 BC, however, the wily and perplexing Aratus, former liberator of the Acrocorinth and unifier of much of the Peloponnese on an ostensibly anti-Macedonian alliance, deployed his recently acquired authority as general plenipotentiary (*strategos autokrator*) to lead the Achaean League into an alliance with none other than the old enemy Macedon.

A century before, the decisive battle between a still independent Greece and Macedon at Chaeronea had preceded the formation in 338 BC of Philip's Hellenic League, usually known as the League of Corinth. In the 220s BC the decisive encounter between Macedon and a still independent Sparta succeeded the formation of a new Hellenic League conceived on significantly different lines. Not only was Doson's league directed specifically against Sparta and the generalized social revolution it was supposed to stand for, but this was an alliance of federations, not single poleis.

The battle that was to settle the war was fought near Sellasia on the northern borders of Laconia. But Cleomenes' cause was already lost, and Ptolemy IV Philopator acknowledged that he had become a poor investment by cutting off his subsidy just days in advance of the fighting. But so far as can be ascertained, the decisive factor in Macedon's victory was superiority in numbers. Cleomenes' losses were heavy; but he himself escaped with a handful of men to Sparta, and thence to Gytheum, where they embarked for Egypt, to join his mother as a refugee in Ptolemy's Alexandria. Antigonus proceeded to take Sparta and achieved what Philip II had scorned to attempt and Pyrrhus among others had failed to execute, the first capture of the city.

Cleomenes' political reforms were now cancelled and the ephorate was restored; the kingship was in effect left vacant. The fate of his social and economic measures is less certain. The cancellation of debts clearly could not be reversed. It seems on the whole likely that in this field Cleomenes' measures were not wholly abrogated but that some sort of compromise was reached.

A vaguely Cleomenean political tendency at Sparta survived the battle of Sellasia. But it was a lost affair, especially after the pathetic deaths of Cleomenes and his handful of supporters at Alexandria in spring 219 BC in a futile rising against the new Ptolemy IV Philopator. The legend of Cleomenes, however, was in safe hands, and his ideas influenced generations to come.

DIMITRIS A. KALOGERAS

Biography

Born 260 BC. Spartan king (235–222 BC) and political reformer. Cleomenes tried to solve the social problems of Sparta in order to increase its political and military power and at the same time strengthen his own position. He reinstalled the Lycurgan political system, cancelled debts, and redistributed land in equal portions. His reforms alarmed neighbouring states, especially Macedon. He was defeated in 222 BC at Sellasia and his reforms cancelled. He went into exile and died in Alexandria in 219 BC.

Further Reading

Africa, Thomas W., *Phylarchus and the Spartan Revolution*, Berkeley: University of California Press, 1961

Bernini, U., "Studi su Sparta ellenistica: Da Leonida II a Cleomene III", *Quaderni Urbinati di Cultura Classica*, 27 (1978): pp. 29–59

Cartledge, Paul and Anthony Spawforth, *Hellenistic and Roman Sparta: A Tale of Two Cities*, London and New York: Routledge, 1989

Chrimes, K.M.T., *Ancient Sparta: A Re-examination of the Evidence*, 2nd edition, Manchester: Manchester University Press, 1952

Daubies, M., "Cléomène III, les hilotes et Selasie", *Historia*, 20 (1971): pp. 665–95

Ollier, François, *Le Mirage spartiate: étude sur l'idéalisation de Sparte dans l'antiquité grecque*, 2 vols, Paris: Boccard, 1933–43

Pavel, Oliva, *Sparta and her Social Problems*, Amsterdam: Hakkert, 1971

Tigerstedt, E.N., *The Legend of Sparta in Classical Antiquity*, vol. 2, Stockholm: Almqvist & Wiksell, 1974

Walbank, F.W., *et al.* (editors), *The Hellenistic World*, Cambridge: Cambridge University Press, 1984 (*The Cambridge Ancient History*, vol. 7, part 1, 2nd edition)

Cleopatra 69–30 BC

Queen of Egypt

Cleopatra was born in 69 BC to Ptolemy XII Auletes, king of Ptolemaic Egypt, and (almost certainly) his sister-wife Cleopatra V. The third of their six children, Cleopatra grew up against the backdrop of her father's turbulent reign, in the course of which he was deposed and fled Egypt for some years. During this period Cleopatra's two elder sisters ruled as pharaohs, although one soon died and the other was killed after Ptolemy XII was restored with Roman support. Nothing is known about Cleopatra's early life, but when her father died in 51 BC, Cleopatra was his eldest surviving child and acceded to the throne as Cleopatra VII Philopator, ruling jointly with her younger brother Ptolemy XIII, whom she married in accordance with Ptolemaic custom.

On account of the machinations of ambitious ministers and the agitation of the Alexandrian populace, the Egyptian throne was still far from secure. A war was engineered between brother and sister, leading to Cleopatra's expulsion from Alexandria. During the course of the contemporaneous Roman civil war between the triumvirs Pompey and Julius Caesar, Pompey fled to Egypt after his defeat at the battle of Pharsalus, and was pursued by Caesar. Pompey was treacherously murdered by the supporters of Ptolemy XIII. When Caesar arrived with his troops he decided to support the claims of Cleopatra and fought on her behalf the Alexandrian War against her brother. Caesar was by now married to his third Roman wife and was in his early 50s; Cleopatra was a young woman of about 20. Tradition maintains that she came to meet him in secret wrapped in a linen sack, and that Caesar, susceptible to feminine wiles, was immediately captivated by her.

Roman forces won the war, in the course of which Ptolemy XIII was killed. Caesar restored Cleopatra to the Egyptian throne and had her married to her other younger brother Ptolemy XIV, ostensibly to rule jointly with him. It is after this that Caesar and Cleopatra took their legendary Nile cruise to explore the country of Upper Egypt, an episode which has been much romanticized in recent times. No details about this trip survive, but when Caesar left Egypt sometime in 47 BC, Cleopatra was pregnant, allegedly by him. Later that year she gave birth to a son, known as Caesarion ("Little Caesar"). In 46 BC, for reasons which remain obscure, Cleopatra and her son followed Caesar to Rome, where they remained until his assassination on the Ides of March in 44 BC.

After the murder of Cleopatra's great champion and protector, the queen returned to Alexandria. She engineered the murder of her brother Ptolemy XIV and installed her young son on the throne with her as Ptolemy XV. The political consequences of Caesar's murder were great. One of his major supporters was Mark Antony, who allied himself with Octavian, Caesar's great-nephew and posthumously adopted

Cleopatra: relief from the temple at Dendera, Egypt, showing Julius Caesar and Cleopatra, with their son Caesarion between them

son, against Caesar's assassins. After their defeat of the assassins, Antony and Octavian divided the territory of Rome between them, but gradually fell out with each other to the extent that civil war again ensued. Antony, whose power base was in the east, summoned Cleopatra to meet him in Cilicia in 41 BC. Ancient sources describe Cleopatra arriving in her spectacular state barge at Tarsus adorned as Aphrodite, having cunningly calculated the effect of her appearance and such a dramatic arrival. Although Antony was by now a mature man in his 40s married to his third Roman wife, he was instantly smitten by the queen. She invited him to a sumptuous feast aboard her barge, and was lavishly entertained by him the following day.

Antony and Cleopatra spent the following winter together at Alexandria, enjoying a life of luxury, the extravagant Ptolemaic court life clearly appealing to the self-indulgent Roman. Cleopatra bore him twins (a boy and a girl) in 40 BC. Antony left Egypt to deal with events in Rome, taking as his fourth wife Octavian's half-sister Octavia in an attempt to improve relations with his rival. There is no evidence that he saw Cleopatra again until 37 BC, when he met her in Syria. It appears that their relationship was further consolidated, though it stopped short of marriage since Antony was still legally married to Octavia. He acknowledged his paternity of their twins, and Cleopatra bore him another son the following year.

Relations between Antony and Octavian worsened, no doubt hastened by this insult to Octavia. Antony campaigned in Parthia and Armenia, with varying results, but the final break with Octavian came after a ceremony in Alexandria in 34 BC, known as the Donations of Alexandria. At a grand spectacle Cleopatra was confirmed as queen of Egypt and the surrounding lands in conjunction with her son Caesarion, and the rest of the eastern territories were divided between the two sons of Antony and Cleopatra. By this act Antony and Cleopatra claimed dynastic succession for their children even as he granted Roman territories to the half-Egyptian princes. War with Octavian was now inevitable, and large forces were mustered.

The combined forces of Antony and Cleopatra were defeated by Octavian in the naval Battle of Actium (off the west coast of Greece) in 31 BC. The tactics of the battle have occasioned great debate, but Cleopatra's ships, lined up behind those of Antony, fled the scene through a gap in the battle lines and headed for Egypt. In despair, Antony followed her, his ships were captured, and his land forces gradually defected to Octavian. The campaign was lost. It only remained for Octavian to capture his two foes.

Antony and Cleopatra slowly returned to Egypt, and resumed their relationship. They spent the winter of 31 BC in Alexandria in a life of profligate luxury, reminiscent of the early days of their courtship. They made plans for further warfare even as Octavian approached Egypt. Various embassies were sent to Octavian. Some sources attest that Octavian secretly told Cleopatra that he would spare her if she betrayed Antony; others that Octavian pretended to be in love with Cleopatra so that she would not kill herself and burn the colossal treasure which she had collected in her unfinished tomb. In any event, it appears that Cleopatra was terrified of capture and being forced to march as a captive in Octavian's Roman triumph, which the victor clearly intended.

Egypt was attacked in 30 BC, and Antony was ultimately unable to stave off defeat when many of his land and naval forces deserted to Octavian. At the news of the final defeat, Cleopatra locked herself and her servants into her tomb and apparently sent out a message to Antony that she was dead. Antony killed himself with his sword, and some days later, despite Octavian's efforts to keep her alive, Cleopatra was found dead in her tomb, allegedly killed by the bite of an asp although rumours of poison were known.

Cleopatra's death ended the rule of the Greek Ptolemaic dynasty of kings in Egypt, and the country became a province of Rome. It was her fate, for good or ill, to come into contact with two of the most powerful Romans of their day, and her love affairs with them have ensured her undying fame. In hostile Roman sources Cleopatra was depicted as an eastern witch who had seduced two noble Romans, yet she was a Greek and only the first of her dynasty to speak Egyptian. Her political cunning and capacity for survival, whether as victim or manipulator, meant that Egypt remained Greek and independent from Roman rule for longer than the other Hellenistic empires.

E.E. RICE

See also Ptolemies

Biography
Born in 69 BC the daughter of Ptolemy XII Auletes, Cleopatra became queen on the death of her father in 51 BC, ruling jointly with her younger brother Ptolemy XIII. In a war between the brother and sister Julius Caesar supported Cleopatra and restored her to her throne. In 47 BC she bore his child and lived in Rome 46–44 BC. After Caesar's murder she returned to Egypt and in 41 BC met Mark Antony in Cilicia. Their forces were defeated at Actium in 31 BC by Octavian. Antony and Cleopatra committed suicide in Alexandria in 30 BC.

Further Reading
Bowman, Alan K., *Egypt after the Pharaohs, 332 BC–AD 642: From Alexander to the Arab Conquest*, Berkeley: University of California Press, and London: British Museum, 1986

Bowman, Alan K., Edward Champlin, and Andrew Lintott (editors), *The Augustan Empire, 43 BC–AD 89*, Cambridge: Cambridge University Press, 1996 (*The Cambridge Ancient History*, vol. 10, 2nd edition), chapter 1

Bradford, Ernle, *Cleopatra*, London: Hodder and Stoughton, 1971; New York: Harcourt Brace, 1972

Dio Cassius, *Dio's Roman History*, translated by Earnest Cary, 9 vols, London: Heinemann, and Cambridge, Massachusetts: Harvard University Press, 1914–27 (Loeb edition)

Empereur, Jean-Yves, *Alexandria Rediscovered*, London: British Museum Press, and New York: Braziller, 1998

Flamarion, Edith, *Cleopatra: From History to Legend*, London: Thames and Hudson, 1997

Foss, Michael, *The Search for Cleopatra*, London: O'Mara, 1997

Grant, Michael, *Cleopatra*, London: Weidenfeld and Nicolson, 1972; New York: Barnes and Noble, 1992

Hughes-Hallett, Lucy, *Cleopatra: Histories, Dreams, and Distortions*, London: Bloomsbury, and New York: Harper and Row, 1990

Pelling, C.B.R. (editor), *Plutarch: Life of Antony* (commentary), Cambridge and New York: Cambridge University Press, 1988

Plutarch, *Plutarch's Lives*, translated by Bernadotte Perrin, 11 vols, London: Heinemann, and Cambridge, Massachusetts: Harvard University Press, 1914–26 (Loeb edition; Caesar in vol. 7; Antony in vol. 9)

Rice, E.E., *Cleopatra*, Stroud, Gloucestershire: Sutton, 1999

Samson, Julia, *Nefertiti and Cleopatra: Queen-Monarchs of Ancient Egypt*, London: Rubicon Press, 1985, 2nd edition, 1990

Shakespeare, William, *Antony and Cleopatra*, various editions

Tarn, W.W. and M.P. Charlesworth, *Octavian, Antony, and Cleopatra*, Cambridge: Cambridge University Press, 1965

Volkmann, Hans, *Cleopatra: A Study in Politics and Propaganda*, London: Elek, 1958

Climate

Greece has a Mediterranean-type climate similar to that of Spain or California, with harsh dry summers (the dead season) and warm wet winters (the growing season in the lowlands).

The year begins in September, when clouds start to gather and the sun no longer burns so relentlessly. The first rains, coming one to ten weeks later, awaken plant growth for the winter. Frost and snow are rare but significant: olives cannot be grown in hollows where cold air gathers. Soil moisture typically reaches a maximum in spring; then the rains tail off, the heat of the sun rises, and evaporation increases. Many plants settle down to their summer dormancy, but some – notably the vine – are less well adapted to the climate and remain active through the dry season, their deep roots extracting water from the bedrock.

Greece is the land of lazy days in the crushing sun of a summer beach, and active days in the genial warmth of a southern winter; but also of people dropping dead from heat in the streets of Athens, or drowning in a flash flood in an arid Cretan gorge; of distant mountains glittering with snow; of the clammy mists from which the volcano island Santorini draws its moisture; of fire-storms jumping gorges, blasted by the October sirocco; of mules struggling through the snow in the high passes of Crete in July. Deluges are rare but very significant: once in a lifetime half a year's rain falls within a day or two and transforms a landscape.

Greece in general has a wet west side and a dry east side. The areas frequented by tourists are mostly dry, especially the islands. Athens, in the east, is one of the driest cities in Europe; Olympia, Patras, and Corfu, in the west, are relatively wet. High mountains distort the pattern; each one has a rain-excess on its northwest side, where the rain-bearing winds strike it, and a rain-shadow on the southeast. The southeast corner of Crete has less than 300 mm of annual rainfall; the high mountains probably get over 2000 mm, most of it as snow. One can have the illusion of going from Wales to Morocco in an afternoon's walk.

At high altitudes plant growth is limited by winter cold as well as summer drought. In the Pindus the growing season may be as short as two months: cereals and vines can be grown there but not olives. Modern Greeks cannot bear the cold, and flee from it if they possibly can. The highest all-year settlement is at 900 m, less than half as high as in the Alps, and a little higher than in Norway; anything higher calls for transhumance. Settlement has been much higher in prehistory.

Dust is a significant factor. It is picked up by storms in the Algerian Sahara and is transported in the upper atmosphere, to fall as a "red rain" of mud, especially in Crete. Over the centuries this has been an appreciable addition to the soils of the island, and may contribute to Crete's unexpected fertility.

Has the climate always been so? Records of unusual weather are fairly copious from islands in later phases of the Little Ice Age (1590s and 1690s AD). These were decades of extreme weather – cold, heat, drought, deluges – greater than anything that seems to occur now. Crete then had many more permanent rivers than today.

Climatology was already a discipline in ancient Greece. Theophrastus' best surviving work was in this field. Unfortunately the interest of ancient philosophers in theories rather than data means that they have little to tell us. The climate of ancient Greece was not grossly different from what it is now, but without instrumental measurements it is impossible to verify whether the climate – as opposed to unusual weather – was quite the same. If the ancient Greeks really went naked as on vase-paintings, they should have shivered in the chill damp of spring and been tortured by sunburn. (Modern Greeks are fully clad, and enjoy shade and the summer night.) It is an open question whether the clear atmosphere attributed by modern writers to ancient Greece, unlike the hazy, often murky atmosphere usual today, is merely a proverbial platitude, or whether there has really been a change.

It is often conjectured that some change or other in early human affairs, for example the decline of the Mycenaeans, was due to a change of climate, such as drought. These claims lack independent evidence. There is, however, some evidence that winter snow was then less rare than it is now, and vegetation zones possibly lower. Theophrastus makes the definite (though secondhand) statement that settlement and cultivation reached higher into the mountains of Crete in the past than in his time.

The present Mediterranean climate, however, is not very much older than Greek history. During the ice ages, up to 14,000 years ago, Greece was drier and colder than it is now. There was then a period of wetter, less strongly seasonal climate than today, when northern trees such as lime and alder were common down to the south of Greece and even in Crete. The change to something like the present climate began in the 5th millennium BC and was completed in the Bronze Age. Agriculture, coming after the change, is reasonably well adapted to a summer-dry climate (except in the case of the vine), whereas wild vegetation has not had time to adapt and copes as best it may. Not many Greek trees lose their leaves in summer as one might expect.

OLIVER RACKHAM

Further Reading

Grove, A.T., and Oliver Rackham, *The Nature of the European Mediterranean*, New Haven, Connecticut and London: Yale University Press, 2000

Guillou, A., *La Civilisation byzantine*, Paris: Arthaud, 1974, pp. 41–100

Rackham, Oliver, and Jennifer Moody, *The Making of the Cretan Landscape*, Manchester: Manchester University Press, 1996

Sallares, J.R., *The Ecology of the Ancient Greek World*, London: Duckworth, 1991

Coinage

Ancient Greek coinage developed in Asia Minor, probably influenced by the circulation of Lydian coinage in the 7th century BC. The production of Greek coinage grew as the polis flourished and spread throughout the Mediterranean during the height of the colonization phase between c.700 and c.500 BC. As a result, coinage in antiquity was an essentially Greek phenomenon and became a medium of exchange, the legacy of which remains with us today.

Money had existed long before the introduction of coinage. But it is less clear in the Greek world, at least, what exactly constituted money. We know that bars of precious metal were used as currency in the 8th century BC. Smaller payments, which required smaller denominations of coinage than were offered by early silver coinage, were probably served by other forms of money. Arrowheads, for instance, were used from the mid-6th century BC in the Black Sea area.

The earliest known Greek coins belong to the 6th century BC, but our knowledge of them is limited by the availability of good, datable archaeological contexts. The earliest archaeo-

logical evidence for the existence of coins dates from the middle of that century at the temple of Artemis in Ephesus. The coins of the Lydian king Alyattes, of a gold and silver alloy called electrum, were marked and punched with designs. Most Greek coinage was to be made of silver. Electrum was retained by a few cities (e.g. Cyzicus, Mytilene, and Phocaea) and then only until the 4th century BC.

It is clear that by c.500 BC silver coinage had been adopted by Greek cities throughout the Mediterranean – in Greece, Italy, Sicily, and the Hellenized parts of the Achaemenid empire, primarily western Asia Minor. It was not until the conquests of Alexander the Great in the third quarter of the 4th century BC that we see the further expansion of Greek coinage into Babylonia, Bactria, and eventually India (Cribb 1983). Rome also began to imitate Greek coinage at the end of the 4th century BC (Howgego 1995, p.10).

The introduction of coinage has yet to be explained conclusively. Some have suggested that coinage was required to pay mercenary soldiers employed in campaigns, others that coins were used to facilitate large payments by and to states (Cook 1958; Kraay and Jenkins 1976, pp.317–28). Such speculation was limited until recently by the absence of small-denomination coins, but new examination has revealed in some quantity evidence for fractional coinage at least for the late 6th and 5th centuries BC. Small denominations have appeared so far only for silver coins: these small issues discovered would still retain some value, for example the smallest electrum coin represented a day's wages (Kraay, 1964). It is only with the introduction of base metal coinage, such as bronze, apparent in Greece from around the mid-5th century BC, that one can start to think of a more diverse role for coinage.

The development and spread of Greek coinage are inextricably linked with the development of the polis and the increase in the political and economic forces of Greek-speaking communities in and around the Mediterranean. The payments made by these city states were clearly facilitated by the development of coinage. Civic coinage was validated by markings that confirmed the value and legitimacy of the state's coinage; the Greek word for coin – *nomisma* – was linked to the legitimizing authority through the laws – *nomoi* – that regulated production. However not all Greek coinage was produced by states; often individuals issued coins, acting as or representing "states". The number of individuals issuing coins exploded at the end of the 4th century BC. Ptolemy I established a precedent for the other Hellenistic kings by having his portrait put on the obverse of Egyptian coinage around 305–304 BC.

Designs on Greek coinage were synonymous with the issuing city or authority. Towards the end of the 6th century BC Athens produced coins with an owl depicted on the reverse. The bird was associated with their tutelary divinity Athena – she appeared on the obverse – and the coins soon became known as "owls". Other states had their civic designs struck on the obverse: Aegina had a tortoise, Corinth a colt. Later in the 4th century BC the monarchic leaders were to introduce their own image on to the obverse face of their coinage. Coinage from the end of the 4th century BC becomes much more closely associated with individuals, typically the Hellenistic dynasts. In the later Hellenistic period the names of eponymous officials stamped on coins allows greater precision in dating.

Coinage was one way for a city or a ruler to extend his identity through the coin types. The circulation of coinage provided a useful means of conveying ideas and meaning. Coins were therefore an important means of spreading propaganda and political messages. Around 405 BC the cities of Rhodes, Cnidus, Iasos, Samos, Ephesus, Cyzicus, and Byzantium issued coins with the same obverse type of Heracles strangling a serpent, while retaining their own civic design on the reverse. By sharing the same coin type, these cities were able to display their support for Sparta. Under the leadership of Lysimachus, of Heraclid descent, they had defeated Athens, represented by a snake symbolizing Cecrops, the founder of Athens (Howgego 1995, p.63; Karwiese 1980).

Greek coinage circulated over a wide geographic area. The most popular coins in the Classical period were the Athenian silver "owls". Most coins were made from precious metals and their value equated loosely to the content of metal in the coin. Not all Greek cities observed the same weight standards, however; thus an Athenian, Corinthian, and Aeginetan drachma were all of different weights. The Athenian silver coinage was made from metal of a higher silver content than any other contemporary Greek coin. This, and the political might of Athens that the city enjoyed thanks to its 5th-century BC empire, ensured that its coinage was established as one of the most important issues in the Mediterranean. The Athenian weight standard eventually became the norm for many of the Hellenistic kingdoms from the end of the 4th century BC. The use of the Athenian system for Alexander issues preserved this weight standard in some areas until the 1st century BC. Posthumous Alexander issues remained popular for much of the Hellenistic period.

Reducing the weight standard was one form of monetary manipulation. Debasing coinage is known; Athens introduced a "copper" currency around 406 BC (Howgego 1995, p.111). A more familiar ploy was to reduce the precious-metal content in the coin. Ptolemy I introduced major reforms to Egyptian coinage between c.310 and c.290 BC, abandoning the Athenian weight standard and eventually lowering the weight of his silver tetradrachm by nearly 20 per cent. Egypt operated a closed economy, and all coinage had to be exchanged for local issues, a development paralleled within the Attalid kingdom at the start of the 2nd century BC.

Many Greek coin producers lacked local silver resources. Rich local deposits of precious metals were available in some areas. The Athenians in the Laurium hills of southwest Attica, those on the island of Siphnos until the flooding of the mines in the 5th century BC, and the people of Thrace, Macedon, and Thasos all had access to supplies of precious metals. At Pangaeum, in Thrace, east of Amphipolis, Philip II of Macedon increased the extraction of the silver and gold from the mines after 356 BC. His son Alexander the Great used the metal to produce coins that were to circulate over vast distances and dominate the Hellenistic world. But good local metal supplies were not always necessary for the widespread circulation of coin: the distribution of Corinthian and Aeginetan issues in the Archaic and Classical era indicates that commercial activity was the main reason for the spread of their coinage.

Coin production took place in mints. Skilled craftsmen produced the designs for the coins on metal dies, which were used to punch the desired image on to the two sides of the coin or flan. It was normal for one of the two dies to be gripped in an anvil. The impression made on the coin by this static die is known as the obverse; the other side of the coin is known as the reverse and the image here was created by striking the die on the upper side of the flan. The dies used to strike coins would eventually deteriorate and sometimes break; the lower die would almost always have the longer life expectancy. A number of "new" coins were produced by striking new images on to existing coins. Such coins are known as "overstrikes".

Mints could also copy the designs of other coins. A number of cities in Sicily and south Italy were particularly famed for the quality of their coins and the types used were imitated throughout the Mediterranean. The head of Arethusa, which appeared originally on a Syracusan issue created by the famous engraver Cimon, was clearly imitated in the shape of the nymph who appeared independently on 4th-century BC coins at Larissa in Thessaly and at Tarsus in Cilicia. A number of coin producers imitated the designs and types of other cities: the Athenian silver tetradrachm was copied in Babylon, Phoenicia, and Egypt during the Classical period.

Coin distribution evolved with changing political and economic circumstances. So the rise of the Hellenistic kingdoms from the late 4th century BC marked a significant shift. Two levels of coin circulation can be observed. Coins issued by the monarchs enjoyed a far wider international acceptability than those of many of the smaller Greek cities. The exception in the Hellenistic period was probably Athens which revitalized its coinage in the 2nd century BC with the production of the so-called New Style Athenian coinage. Like Rhodes, Athens continued to issue a silver coin down to the 1st century BC.

From the 4th century BC more local bronze coins were issued in Greece, and these enjoyed considerable regional success, rarely being found outside their immediate centres of production. The bronze issues played a major role in the local economy and coins were minted for specific religious festivals, such as the Eleusinia in Attica. Bronze issues increased and were widely employed by Greek cities as Rome dominated Greek politics from the early 2nd century BC.

The federal Greek states became important producers of coinage in the Hellenistic period; in Asia Minor Greek cities continued to mint coins following the treaty of Apamea. By the end of the 1st century BC many Greek cities were no longer issuing their own distinct coinage. By this time, and throughout the 1st–3rd centuries AD, local Greek coins had taken on the appearance of Roman coins and were restricted to being struck in bronze. Under the Roman empire more Greek-speaking cities in Asia Minor were issuing coins than at any other time in antiquity. In the 3rd century AD the local production and circulation of provincial bronze coins issued by Greek cities reflects considerable economic developments within the Roman empire.

The coinage of the Byzantine period continued to be influenced by the coins of the later Roman empire. Copper, silver, and gold were minted but there were periods when one or other of these metals fell into disuse. Silver coins are less common in the 5th and 6th centuries AD. Initally Latin dominated the coinage of the Byzantine period, but eventually Greek took hold from the 7th century and had largely replaced Latin by the 11th century. Byzantine coinage drove the economies of the 4th to 7th and 11th to mid-13th centuries and made Constantinople the centre of a prosperous empire.

The legacy of ancient Greek coinage for the development of coinage in modern Greece is considerable. The use of images and terms from antiquity on modern Greek coins does reflect the enormous heritage of the past. In this, of course, Greece is similar to many other countries that illustrate their own history and culture on their coins and banknotes. But for Greece there is particular importance attached to the ideology of Hellenism. The very Greekness of modern Greece is established by connection with its ancient history. The role of Alexander the Great as a force unifying the Hellenic world is as strong today as it was in the 4th century BC.

GRAHAM OLIVER

Further Reading

Carradice, Ian, *Greek Coins*, London: British Museum Press, and Austin: University of Texas Press, 1995

Cook, R.M., "Speculation on the Origins of Coinage", *Historia*, 7 (1958): pp. 257–62

Cribb, J., "Investigating the Introduction of Coinage in India: A Review of Recent Research", *Journal of the Numismatic Society of India*, 45 (1983): pp. 80–101

Grierson, Philip, *Byzantine Coins*, London: Methuen, and Berkeley: University of California Press, 1982

Hendy, Michael F., *Studies in the Byzantine Monetary Economy, c. 300–1450*, Cambridge and New York: Cambridge University Press, 1985

Howgego, Christopher, *Ancient History from Coins*, London and New York: Routledge, 1995

Karwiese, S., "Lysander as Herakliskos Drakonopnigon (Heracles the Snake-Strangler)", *Numismatic Chronicle*, 140 (1980): pp. 1–27

Kraay, Colin M., "Hoards, Small Change, and the Origin of Coinage", *Journal of Hellenic Studies*, 84 (1964): pp. 76–91

Kraay, Colin M., *Archaic and Classical Greek Coins*, London: Methuen, and Berkeley: University of California Press, 1976

Seltman, C.T., *Greek Coins: A History of Metallic Currency and Coinage down to the Fall of the Hellenistic Kingdoms*, 2nd edition, London: Methuen, 1960

Stancomb, W., "Arrowheads, Dolphins and Cast Coins in the Black Sea Region", *Classical Numismatic Review*, 18 (1993): pp. 5ff.

Colonization

It should be remarked at the outset that the term "colonization" to describe Greek expansion throughout the Mediterranean and Pontic areas is a coinage of modern scholarship. It is employed by historians to indicate the process whereby, from the 8th century BC through to the Hellenistic era, Greek cities took collective and conscious decisions to plant sections of their population on foreign soil under the leadership of an *oikistes* (founder) who was responsible for the distribution of land plots to his fellow colonists and the transfer of metropolitan cults to the new civic foundation which was generally independent of its metropolis (though Corinth seems to have continued to exercise some authority over its colonies). There are, however, three difficulties with this conventional definition.

First, while in modern historiography the colonizing process is distinguished sharply in both chronological and definitional terms from the migratory traditions regarding earlier movements of peoples such as the Dorians, Ionians, or Aeolians, ancient authors made no such distinction. Thucydides (1. 12. 4), for example, uses the same terminology to describe both the Athenian colonization of Ionia (the "Ionian migration") and the 8th-century BC Peloponnesian colonization of Italy and Sicily.

Secondly, it is not at all certain that the early colonial ventures of the 8th century BC were as organized and public in nature as the prevailing orthodoxy upholds. A case in point is the late 8th-century colonization of south Italy which the sources attribute to cities in Peloponnesian Achaea despite the fact that there is neither literary nor archaeological evidence for Achaean cities much before the 5th century BC. The fact is that the "mechanics" of early colonization are often and all too uncritically retrojected from foundation decrees of later periods, particularly those concerning the foundation of Naupactus (first quarter of the 5th century BC), Brea (third quarter of the 5th century BC), Black Corcyra (4th century BC), and Cyrene, where it is impossible to gauge the extent to which a 4th-century decree replicates–as it claims–an original foundation decree of the later 7th century BC (though the weight of scholarly opinion inclines towards scepticism). Similarly, literary accounts for colonial foundations rarely predate the 5th century BC: thus, the developed tradition concerning the founding of Cyrene (which is frequently–though not unproblematically–regarded as a "model" for colonial foundations in general) is not attested before Pindar and Herodotus (see further below). A related point concerns the chronology of foundations. Thucydides (6.3–5) gives dates for the earliest colonies of Sicily while a more complete list is presented by Eusebius of Caesarea (late 3rd century AD). In neither case is the source of their information certain nor how they reckoned their dates. Archaeological investigation can certainly assist in answering this question, though the commencement of colonial activity–as opposed to less formal transactions of trade or exchange–is not always immediately apparent in the material record and in any case our ceramic chronologies are based in part (and more than is often admitted) on the Thucydidean and Eusebian dates. In general, the probability is that the origins of the earliest colonies were more haphazard, mixed, and gradual than is often stated.

Thirdly, while it would be unsound to regard Mycenaean material objects found in south Italy, Sicily, and the Aeolian islands as reflections of an early Mycenaean colonization of these areas (Mycenaean material is also found well inland in Anatolia), it does now appear that colonial activity may in some instances predate the 8th century. Thucydides (4. 123. 1) regards the city of Mende in Chalcidice as a colony (*apoikia*) of Eretria and it has often been assumed that Mende along with Torone (also in Chalcidice) were Euboean foundations of the Archaic period, but recent excavations at both sites have recovered Euboean and Euboeanizing material that dates back as far as the 10th or even 11th century BC. It is possible that this colonial activity represents a "rehearsal" for the more numerous and distant colonies planted in the west in the 8th century.

Indeed, the Euboeans of Eretria and Chalcis appear to have been prominent participants within the early colonization of the west. Both are said to have founded Pithecusae on the

11. Areas of Greek settlement from the 8th to the 3rd century BC

island of Ischia in the Gulf of Naples (Strabo, 5. 4. 9) with the Chalcidian element transferring to Cumae on the mainland opposite (Livy, 8. 22. 5–6): archaeological evidence suggests a date of about 775 BC for Pithecusae and 725–700 BC for Cumae. According to Thucydides (6. 3. 1) the first Sicilian colony, Naxos, was founded by Chalcidians under the leadership of Theocles in 734 BC, with Leontini and Catana following in 729 BC, while a Euboean presence is attested before the end of the 8th century at Zancle and Rhegium on either side of the Straits of Messina. Corinthians under the Bacchiad Archias are said to have founded Syracuse in 733 BC (Thucydides, 6. 3. 2)–a city which was to participate in the "secondary" colonization of Acrae and Casmenae in the mid-7th century and Camarina at the beginning of the 6th century BC. Megara Hyblaea was supposedly founded in 728 BC by Megarians who had failed to settle Leontini (Thucydides, 6. 4. 1) and established its own colony at Selinus a century later. Rhodes and Crete are said to have founded Gela in 688 BC (Thucydides, 6. 4. 3), followed in 580 BC by Gela's foundation of Acragas (Strabo, 6. 2. 5). Finally, Achaeans are credited with the foundation of several colonies in south Italy–including Sybaris and Croton towards the end of the 8th century, Metapontum and Caulonia in the second half of the 7th century, and Posidonia in the early 6th century–while Tarentum was founded by Spartan dissidents in the last decade of the 8th century and Epizephyrean Locri by Locrians in the early decades of the 7th century BC.

The second major area of early colonial activity was in the region of the Hellespont, Propontis, and Black Sea. Milesian foundation is attributed to Abydus on the Hellespont (670 BC?), Cyzicus in the Propontis (756 BC?), and Sinope (631 BC?) together with a host of other colonies in the Black Sea; Miletus

is also said to have participated with Paros and Erythrae in founding Parion in 709 BC. The Megarians planted the colonies of Astacus, Chalcedon, Selymbria, and Byzantium at the eastern end of the Propontis in the course of the 7th century and collaborated with the Boeotians in founding Heraclea Pontica c.560 BC. Towards the end of the 7th century, the Athenians founded Sigeum on the Hellespont and Samos established Perinthus on the northern shore of the Propontis, while the Tean colony of Phanagoria on the northern shores of the Black Sea probably dates to the mid-6th century BC.

In the far west, settlers and refugees from Phocaea are credited with the foundation c.600 BC of Massilia in southern France and Emporion in Spain. In the northern Aegean, the Chalcidice peninsula was settled by Eretrians, Chalcidians, Achaeans, Corinthians, and Andrians while Paros led a Panhellenic venture to colonize Thasos in the mid-7th century and Samians are said to have settled Samothrace in the second half of the 6th century BC. Finally, Libyan Cyrene is said to have been colonized by Thera c.630 BC and archaeological evidence suggests that other settlements were established in Libya at Tocra, Euhesperides, and Barca from the last third of the 7th century to the middle of the 6th century BC.

The motives for early colonization are the subject of scholarly controversy and it is probably unwise to insist upon unicausal factors. Some colonies may have been established for the purpose of exploiting trading opportunities, though most were situated on headlands and estuaries in possession of fertile plains, so it may be that the increased sedentary conditions of mainland Greece in the 8th century (together with consequent demographic increase) led to a shortage of agricultural land at home–certainly the Theran version of the foundation of Cyrene claims that a seven-year drought prompted the consultation of the Delphic oracle which instructed the Therans to colonize Libya (Herodotus, 4. 151). Alternatively, since the early colonial ventures appear to coincide with the crystallization of the polis or "city state", it may be that the inclusionary/exclusionary process through which the community of citizens emerged inevitably resulted in social disaffection on the part of those who found themselves excluded or dissatisfied: in the Cyrenean account concerning the origins of Cyrene, the founder Battus is said to be the illegitimate son of a Theran aristocrat and a Cretan princess (Herodotus, 4. 154–55), and similar imputations of illegitimate birth may be inferred from the name of the Spartan Partheniai ("maiden-born") who are said to have colonized Tarentum (Strabo, 6. 3. 2).

It is most unlikely that prospective colonists were entirely ignorant of their destinations. A small quantity of Protogeometric (10th-century) material has been recovered in the region of Tarentum while Greek cups dating to Middle Geometric II (early 8th century) are attested at Etruscan Veii; Cumae, Capua, and Pontecagnano in Campania; Scoglio del Tonno in Puglia; and Villasmundo in eastern Sicily. This would suggest either direct knowledge of the west on the part of Greek traders or at least indirect knowledge passed to Greek manufacturers by mercantile middlemen (probably Phoenicians). In some instances colonies were established on virgin soil (e.g. Pithecusae)–sometimes with the explicit blessing of neighbouring indigenous populations (Megara Hyblaea, Cyrene)–though on other occasions the colonizing effort required forcible occupation of the land (Thasos) and often subjugation of the former population (Syracuse, Heraclea Pontica). Though a matter of controversy, it is probable that intermarriage fostered greater integration between new colonists and indigenous populations: Herodotus (1. 164–65) states that wives accompanied the Phocaeans who attempted to colonize Corsican Alalia, though in his description of the foundation of Cyrene (4. 153)–as well as the Athenian "colonization" of Ionia (1. 146.2–3)–there is mention of men only so the likelihood is that the colonists, who were normally young men, took indigenous wives upon their arrival at colonial sites. Diodorus of Sicily (5. 6. 5) explains that the native population of Sicily eventually adopted the Greek language and educated their children according to a Greek model and it is this "Hellenization" of Sicily and south Italy that would later exercise such a profound influence on the culture of the Romans.

Colonization continued–albeit on a reduced scale–throughout the Classical period. In the early 5th century eastern Locrians established a colony at Naupactus; in the 440s BC Athenians settled Brea in Thrace and participated in the collective foundation of Thurii on the site of ancient Sybaris in southern Italy; and in 426 BC the Spartans issued a general invitation for Greeks (with the exception of the Ionians, Achaeans, and some others) to join them in the foundation of Heraclea Trachinia in central Greece (Thucydides, 3. 92). For the first time, contemporary literary and epigraphic testimony reveals the precise workings of colonial ventures in this period, from consultation of the Delphic oracle seeking approval for the expedition to the provisions for choosing an oikistes, recruiting colonists, and formalizing the relationship between the mother-city and its colony as well as providing for the right of return in the event of colonial failure. It is debatable whether the practices attested in this period had also operated in the case of the earliest colonies: the literary accounts for the earlier foundations which were first consigned to writing at this time (though they are frequently preserved only in later sources such as Diodorus of Sicily) are characterized by recurring tropes – many focusing on the "outsider" status of the oikistes who is directed to found a colony when consulting the Delphic oracle on a completely unrelated matter–and it is tempting to believe that individual traditions were selectively moulded to fit this new genre of foundation stories. Indeed careful reading of literary accounts reveals the existence of multiple traditions in which colonial origins are attributed to varying populations and oikistai (both mortal and heroic) and oracular sanction sought from other sanctuaries besides Delphi. Colonial traditions were never transmitted for their own sake but to justify and legitimate claims to power and recognition in the present.

From the end of the 6th century BC, Athens began to found a new type of colony named a cleruchy. Although ancient authors often fail to make any terminological distinction between a cleruchy and a colony, the chief difference would appear to reside in the fact that, while colonies were normally established as autonomous foundations, residents of a cleruchy remained Athenian citizens, though the situation is complicated by the fact that later residents of Athenian colonies also often retained citizenship at Athens. In general, the function of the cleruchy seems to have been to act as a garrison over populations that were deemed hostile to Athens. Cleruchies were established at Chalcis and Salamis in the late 6th century; Andros, Chersonesus, Lemnos, Imbros, and Histiaea in the mid-5th century; Aegina, Lesbos, and Melos in the last third of the 5th century; and Samos in the mid-4th century.

A renewed wave of colonization was initiated by Alexander the Great and his Hellenistic successors, especially in Babylonia (Seleucia on Tigris), northern Syria (Antioch, Apamea), Asia Minor (Laodicea), and central Asia (Ai Khanoum). These colonies normally served the function of garrisons and were populated by both Greeks and Macedonians, though the new city of Alexandria, founded west of the Canopic mouth of the Nile Delta in 331 BC, was granted full civic status. Its original citizens were Greeks of various origins, but the city also had a large indigenous Egyptian and Jewish population.

JONATHAN M. HALL

Further Reading

Bérard, Jean, *La Colonisation grecque de l'Italie méridionale et de la Sicile dans l'antiquité: l'histoire et la légende*, revised edition, Paris: Presses Universitaires de France, 1957

Billows, Richard A., *Kings and Colonists: Aspects of Macedonian Imperialism*, Leiden and New York: Brill, 1995

Boardman, John, *The Greeks Overseas: Their Early Colonies and Trade*, 4th edition, London and New York: Thames and Hudson, 1999

Descoeudres, Jean-Paul (editor), *Greek Colonists and Native Populations*, Oxford: Clarendon Press, and New York: Oxford University Press, 1990

Dougherty, Carol, *The Poetics of Colonization: From City to Text in Archaic Greece*, Oxford and New York: Oxford University Press, 1993

Dunbabin, T.J., *The Western Greeks: The History of Sicily and South Italy from the Foundation of the Greek Colonies to 480 BC*, Oxford: Clarendon Press, and New York: Oxford University Press, 1948

Graham, A.J., *Colony and Mother City in Ancient Greece*, Manchester: Manchester University Press, 1964

Graham, A.J., "The Colonial Expansion of Greece" in *The Expansion of the Greek World, Eighth to Sixth Centuries BC*, edited by John Boardman and N.G.L. Hammond, Cambridge: Cambridge University Press, 1982 (*The Cambridge Ancient History*, vol. 3, part 3, 2nd edition), pp. 83–162

Malkin, Irad, *Religion and Colonization in Ancient Greece*, Leiden and New York: Brill, 1987

Malkin, Irad, *Myth and Territory in the Spartan Mediterranean*, Cambridge and New York: Cambridge University Press, 1994

Ridgway, David, *The First Western Greeks*, Cambridge and New York: Cambridge University Press, 1992

Tsetskhladze, Gocha R. and Franco De Angelis (editors), *The Archaeology of Greek Colonisation: Essays Dedicated to Sir John Boardman*, Oxford: Oxford University Committee for Archaeology, 1994

Comedy

Greece has furnished us with the earliest literary examples of comedy. As a form of popular entertainment, Greek comedy is probably of greater antiquity than tragedy. The origin of the word has been connected with *komos*, meaning "a band of revellers". Their processions, with unrestrained singing and jesting, were held in honour of Dionysus, so that comedy or "the song of the *komos*", like the tragedy and the satyr play, may have had its origin in the festivals of Dionysus. Tradition attributed its invention to the Dorian inhabitants of Megara, from where it was supposed to have spread to other Dorian communities.

In chapters 4 and 5 of the *Poetics* Aristotle gives a rather cursory account of the origin and development of comedy. The gist of his account is: the Megarians, both of Sicily and of the isthmus, claim to have originated comedy; its name is (erroneously) derived from *kome* ("village"); its origin lay in the preludes to the phallic songs; the steps by which it developed are uncertain; the Sicilians introduced plots in place of mere lampoons; and comedy took longer than tragedy to receive recognition in Athens.

The transformation of the local Doric farce of Sicily into a literary form is attributed to Epicharmus of Cos (*c*.540–450 BC). Other representatives of early Dorian comedy appear to have included his contemporary Phormus or Phormis and Dinolochus, said to be a pupil of the latter. The introduction of comedy to Attica (*c*.580 BC) is credited to Susarion, who is said to have transplanted it to the Attic deme of Icaria, which is known to have been the principal centre of the worship of Dionysus in Attica, and the home of Thespis, the pioneer tragic poet, as well as of Chionides and Magnes (*c*.550 BC), who are said to have given Megarian comedy a more artistic form. Its adoption at Athens during the time of the Persian Wars ensured for comedy a place in literature. At Athens comedy became an official part of the celebration of Dionysus in 486 BC.

The evidence suggests that the ingredients of the old Attic comedy came from sources widely differing in place and time. The existence of "animal choruses" is attested by an Attic black-figure amphora of the mid-6th century BC, which depicts men disguised as horses, with riders on their backs, accompanied by a flute-player, and a 5th-century Attic vase showing men dressed as birds. Vases of the 6th century also depict grotesque satyrs as well as dancers whose dress is exaggerated behind and in front for humorous effect. The unrestrained personal abuse and gross sexual humour are anticipated in the poems of Archilochus (7th century BC) and Hipponax, and need not be traced solely to Dionysiac rituals. The dramatic element may have been derived from the secular Dorian comedy without chorus that is said to have originated in Megara and been developed by Epicharmus at Syracuse.

The earliest phase of ancient Greek comedy is known as "Old Comedy". In practice, this term refers to the comedies produced at Athens during the 5th century BC. These plays are characterized by unrestrained satire of public persons and affairs, extremely irreverent treatment of mythology and the gods, outspoken political criticism and comment on literary and philosophical matters, as well as sexually oriented humour. The actors wore grotesque masks, and their costumes, though based on the dress of everyday life, included artificial exaggeration for comic effect. The short tunic could expose the large phallus each carried. They also wore masks of certain easily recognized types. Female roles were played by men. Accordingly, nude or exposed women must have been costumed representations of the female body. Although Old Comedy transformed ritual into art, it still retained traces of its ritual origin: the prominence given to the phallus in the earlier plays; the final festive union of the sexes in a party or marriage; and the expressed or implied references to the reproductive organs.

The heyday of Old Comedy was during the time of Pericles and the Peloponnesian War when Athenian democracy had reached its highest point of development. Cratinus (*c*.520–*c*.423 BC) and his younger contemporaries Eupolis (*c*.446–*c*.411 BC) and Aristophanes are believed to have been the foremost writers of Old Comedy. Others include Crates, Pherecrates, Hermippus, Teleclides, Phrynichus, Ameipsias, Plato (not the philosopher), and Theopompus.

The plays were composed of a blend of song, dance, personal invective, and buffoonery, and consisted of loosely related episodes. The plot was set in contemporary Athens. In most plays of Aristophanes the protagonist conceives a fantastic plan that runs counter to the natural order of things. He is opposed by the chorus whom he eventually succeeds in winning over to his side. A series of short episodes then demonstrate the consequences of the realization of his fantasy for various professions and types, usually involving a series of acceptances and rejections, and the play usually ends in a festive spirit.

From a consideration of the 11 extant plays of Aristophanes (9 of which happen to be the only completely surviving examples of Old Comedy), we may infer that, gradually, a six-part structure evolved: (1) a *prologos* or introduction in which the basic issue of the play is explained and developed: the protagonist conceives an extravagantly imaginative but absurdly impractical solution to a problem; (2) the *parodos* or entry of

Comedy: a production of Aristophanes' comedy *The Birds*, directed by Karolos Kun, Epidaurus, 1975

the chorus; (3) the *agon* or contest between opposing princi-pals, in which the hero defends his bright idea from attacks and invariably defeats his opponents; (4) the *parabasis* in which the chorus, on behalf of the poet, speaks to the audience and attacks prominent citizens: it consisted of an anapaestic passage followed by the *pnigos* (a long sentence to be uttered in one breath), an *ode* or invocation to a god, an *epirrhema* or satiric speech on current affairs, an *antode*, and *antepirrhema*; (5) a series of *epeisodia* or farcical scenes, usually without any sequential connection with each other but building up to a climax, lightly separated by songs of the chorus, demonstrat-ing the consequences of the realization of the hero's fantasy both on the protagonist and on typical figures, but occasion-ally carrying on the main plot; (6) *exodos* or final scene of rejoicing generally leading up to a banquet or wedding.

Attic comedies, like Attic tragedies, were performed at the great festivals of Dionysus, namely, the Dionysia and the Lenaea. Their inclusion in the latter dates from shortly before 440 BC. Five comic poets competed on each occasion, each presenting one play (the number of competitors was evidently reduced to three during the Peloponnesian War, but this has been debated). In the 4th century comedies were also given at

the rural Dionysia, but it is not known how far back this prac-tice went.

Like a tragedy, a comedy consisted of the dramatic dialogue (for which the iambic trimeter was generally used) and the lyrical choruses. However, whereas the tragic chorus consisted of 12 (later 15) singers, the comic chorus included 24. They were often divided into two half-choruses. They wore masks and grotesque dresses to suit their parts (e.g. as birds, wasps, etc.), but removed their outer cloaks for the purpose of their dances. Their role was not generally one of reconciliation, as in tragedy, but of exciting the disputants and finally siding with the victor. On occasion, the entry of the chorus presents a moment of violence and excitement. It may be hostile to the protagonist who is faced with the task of winning them over to his side. Once this has been achieved, they applaud and rein-force what he says and does. The chorus played an important part in the Old Comedy, and, at least in the case of Aristophanes, several of the plays were named after their choruses.

The freedom of political criticism enjoyed by poets of the Old Comedy appears to have been occasionally curtailed, but it was not permanently lost until the downfall of Athenian democracy in 404 BC. The loss of imperial power and political energy was gradually reflected by a choice of material of a less typically Athenian and more cosmopolitan nature. Most notable is the reduced importance of the comic chorus. The *parabasis* disappeared altogether, and the choral odes were replaced by interpolated pieces (*embolima*) not germane to the play.

The term "Middle Comedy", which is of Hellenistic origin, has been used to designate Attic comedies written between *c.*404 and *c.*320 BC. The term is used to describe these plays because they represent a transition from Old Comedy to New Comedy, both of which have certain features in common with it. Although plays with political themes were still produced, mainly (but not exclusively) in the earlier part of the period, and politicians such as Demosthenes and Callimedon were frequently ridiculed, broadly speaking Middle Comedy avoided outspoken political criticism and open attacks on individuals, and dealt instead with typical human faults and foibles. The authors concentrated on social satire and resorted to burlesque or parody of tragedy, mythology, and the lives of the philosophers, notably Plato and the Pythagoreans.

The observation of contemporary types, manners, and pursuits was a common characteristic. Typical characters of New Comedy, such as bullies, parasites (evolved from the flatterers of Old Comedy), cooks, pimps, soldiers, stern old men, young men in love, and courtesans figured in Middle Comedy as well, although some of them, such as the swaggering soldier, can be traced back to Old Comedy at least. Their occurrence leads us to conclude that New Comedy-type plots were also anticipated in Middle Comedy. Significant also in this connection is the impact of Euripides' plays such as the *Iphigeneia in Tauris*, the *Ion*, and the *Helen*. Middle Comedy represents a period of experiment and transition. Different types of play appear to have predominated at various times, so that one may not be justified in labelling one type of play as Middle Comedy to the exclusion of all others.

The most celebrated authors of Middle Comedy were Antiphanes of Athens and Alexis of Thurii, followed by Eubulus, Timocles, and Anaxandrides of Rhodes. It is interesting to note that many of the authors were of non-Athenian origin. They appear to have been extremely prolific. More than 800 of their plays are said to have survived as late as the 2nd century AD. Athenaeus, who has preserved the majority of fragments, mentions some 57 playwrights. However, no complete example has come down to us, but the last play of Aristophanes, the *Plutus*, no doubt reflects some of the changed features.

The period of New Comedy extends from about 320 BC to the mid-3rd century BC. Its main features are the representation of contemporary life by means of imaginary persons drawn from it, the development of plot and character, the substitution of humour for wit, and the introduction of romantic love as a theme. These plays were written largely during a time of political and moral disillusionment, when Athens was no longer a free state but had come under the sway of Macedon. Political references are rare and are subordinate to the depiction of the domestic life of fictitious characters.

New Comedy offers a mildly satiric view of contemporary Athenian society, especially in its familiar and domestic aspects. There is no parody of public figures and events as in Old Comedy. Instead we meet with representations of the private affairs of average but fictitious men and women depicted without supernatural or heroic overtones.

The common subject is the infatuation of a high-born young man for a slave girl. One of the lovers is usually a foundling, the discovery of whose true birth and identity finally makes their union possible. But the romantic element is not the only ingredient and is not very significant: the girl whom the hero wishes to possess does not always appear on stage, or when she does, she often does not speak. Intrigue (especially on the part of crafty slaves on behalf of their young masters) plays an important part in the plots of New Comedy, which are articulated to a far greater extent than those of Old Comedy. The names of the slaves (Getas, Libys, etc.) reflect the economic expansion in the wake of Macedonian conquest. The resulting cosmopolitan atmosphere is matched by the mobility of the people, who constantly go abroad, be it on business, mercenary service, or as the result of misfortune. Although the characters have fixed names and masks, they differ vividly and come to life as individuals, at least in the better plays. Athenian laws of citizenship and marriage are integral to many of the plays. Yet the universality of the characters, situations, and relationships makes the plays enjoyable to those far removed from Athens in time and place. Menander, in particular, excelled at the sympathetic portrayal of various personal relationships and problems arising from ignorance, misunderstanding, and prejudice, in all of which one can recognize his debt to Euripides.

The dialogues of New Comedy are in the usual iambic trimeter, but there are trochaic tetrameters and lyrical passages too that may have been performed by the actors themselves. The chorus is so diminished in importance as to become a small band of musicians and dancers periodically providing light entertainment. The language is Attic, but closer to the koine of everyday speech. The play was apparently divided into five acts by the four choral interludes.

The most famous exponent of New Comedy was Menander (342–292 BC). His surviving work includes one complete play, the *Dyscolus*, and considerable portions of three others: *Perikeiromene*, *Epitrepontes*, and *Samia*. Some of his other plays, as well as those of his fellow New Comedy writers (Diphilus, Philemon, Philippides, Posidippus, Apollodorus of Carystus), are known to us only through their Latin translations and adaptations by the Roman comic poets Plautus (*c.*254–184 BC) and Terence (195/185–159 BC). The original Greek texts circulated widely until the 7th century AD, but were then completely lost. Until the discovery of the Menander papyri, New Comedy was known only through quotations, Roman adaptations, and echoes in later Greek authors such as Alciphron and Lucian.

Greek theatre did not survive in Byzantium, although dramas (including comedies) were copied and transmitted in manuscripts and during the Palaiologan period a number of scholars wrote commentaries on the various works. Naturally, we encounter here and there in Byzantine texts phrases and expressions from the comic poets – especially in satirical works. But these are philological remnants, so to speak. In *Epistle* 150 Photios shows knowledge of Aristophanes' *Plutus*, which he is likely to have encountered in the school curriculum. By contrast, Menander was still being read in the school at Gaza in the 6th century, but did not survive into the Middle Ages. Heliodorus wrote a commentary on the metres of Aristophanes, parts of which are found in the extant scholia. Among the sources most frequently used in the *Suda* are the text and scholia to Aristophanes, for which the *Suda* is in effect a fairly important witness. Of Eustathius' notes to Aristophanes no more is known than minute fragments preserved in late manuscripts. By the late 13th century it had become the custom to read three plays of each tragedian and Aristophanes, sometimes known as the "triad"; the habit may go back to the 12th century or earlier, for Tzetzes composed a full commentary on only the three Aristophanic comedies that later were standard reading, namely, *Plutus*, *Frogs*, and *Clouds*. The Ravenna Aristophanes is the only medieval manuscript to contain all 11 plays (Ravenna, Gr. 429). It has been suggested that Manuel Moschopoulos may have worked on a recension (possibly with annotations) of the Aristophanic triad since some scholia, especially on the *Plutus*, have been traced to him.

The pure Attic language of Aristophanes was studied and imitated by the ancient Atticists and their Byzantine successors. In his desire to create a modern Greek language, Adamantios Korais (1748–1833), the most important representative of the Greek Enlightenment, studied Aristophanic comedy with its rich linguistic heritage. However, these studies, as well as the earliest revivals of Aristophanic comedy, were affected by moral scruples: hence the relatively small number of translations, adaptations, and stage versions prior to 1900. For a long time Aristophanic performances were given by non-professional troupes both within and outside Greece, and this amateur spirit partly accounts for the high degree of audience appeal and participation associated with modern Aristophanic revivals in Greece. By the 1950s, however, the comedies had moved on to the official stage of the ancient drama festivals of Epidaurus (inaugurated 1954) and Athens (inaugurated 1955). The chief contributors to this promotion were Karolos Koun (1908–87) and his former student Alexis Solomos. These two directors, working independently and under widely differing conditions, set off a tradition of presenting the plays of Aristophanes to the large urban public, thereby ensuring their popularity in Greece.

Due to its contemporary relevance, revivals of Aristophanic comedy enjoyed vast success during the years of the military junta (1967–74), but declined in the two years following the fall of the dictatorship. There have been productions since 1977, but many of them have been characterized as events for tourists. However, during the same period, Aristophanic material has been put to alternative uses, such as Savvopoulos' musical version of the *Acharnians*, a shadow theatre adaptation of the *Birds* by P. Michopoulos in 1984, children's books and comics based on the plays, and productions staged in Greece by mostly English-speaking companies.

D.P.M. WEERAKKODY

See also Theatres, Tragedy

Further Reading

Arnott, W. Geoffrey, *Alexis, The Fragments: A Commentary*, Cambridge: Cambridge University Press, 1996

Bermel, Albert, *Farce: A History from Aristophanes to Woody Allen*, New York: Simon and Schuster, 1982; reprinted Carbondale: Southern Illinois University Press, 1990

Bowie, A.M., *Aristophanes: Myth, Ritual and Comedy*, Cambridge and New York: Cambridge University Press, 1993

Dobrov, Gregory W. (editor), *Beyond Aristophanes: Transition and Diversity in Greek Comedy*, Atlanta: Scholars Press, 1995

Dobrov, Gregory W. (editor), *The City as Comedy: Society and Representation in Athenian Drama*, Chapel Hill: University of North Carolina Press, 1997

Hubbard, Thomas K., *The Mask of Comedy: Aristophanes and the Intertextual Parabasis*, Ithaca, New York: Cornell University Press, 1991

Keaney, J.J., "Notes on Moschopoulos and Aristophanes-Scholia", *Mnemosyne*, 4/25 (1972): pp. 123–28

Konstan, David, *Greek Comedy and Ideology*, Oxford and New York: Oxford University Press, 1995

Lever, Katherine, *The Art of Greek Comedy*, London: Methuen, 1956

López Eire, Antonio (editor), *Sociedad, política y literatura: comedia griega antigua*, Salamanca: Logo, 1997

MacDowell, Douglas M., *Aristophanes and Athens: An Introduction to the Plays*, Oxford and New York: Oxford University Press, 1995

Menander, *Menander*, translated by W.G. Arnott, vol. 2, London: Heinemann, and Cambridge, Massachusetts: Harvard University Press, 1996 (Loeb edition)

Norwood, Gilbert, *Greek Comedy*, London: Methuen, 1931; New York: Hill and Wang, 1963

O'Regan, Daphne Elizabeth, *Rhetoric, Comedy, and the Violence of Language in Aristophanes' Clouds*, Oxford and New York: Oxford University Press, 1992

Parker, L.P.E., *The Songs of Aristophanes*, Oxford and New York: Oxford University Press, 1997

Pickard-Cambridge, A.W., *The Dramatic Festivals of Athens*, Oxford: Clarendon Press, 1953

Reynolds L.D. and N.G. Wilson, *Scribes and Scholars: A Guide to the Transmission of Greek and Latin Literature*, 3rd edition, Oxford: Clarendon Press, and New York: Oxford University Press, 1991

Russo, Carlo Ferdinando, *Aristophanes: An Author for the Stage*, revised edition, London and New York: Routledge, 1997

Scafuro, Adele C., *The Forensic Stage: Settling Disputes in Graeco-Roman New Comedy*, Cambridge and New York: Cambridge University Press, 1997

Slavitt, David R. and Palmer Bovie, *Menander*, Philadelphia: University of Pennsylvania Press, 1998

Taaffe, Lauren K., *Aristophanes and Women*, London and New York: Routledge, 1993

Van Steen, Gonda, "Aristophanes and the Modern Greek Stage", *Dialogus: Hellenic Studies Review*, 2 (1995): pp. 71–90

Van Steen, Gonda, *Venom in Verse: Aristophanes in Modern Greece*, Princeton, New Jersey: Princeton University Press, 2000

Vickers, Michael, *Pericles on Stage: Political Comedy in Aristophanes' Early Plays*, Austin: University of Texas Press, 1997

Webster, T.B.L., *Studies in Later Greek Comedy*, Manchester: Manchester University Press, 1953

Webster, T.B.L., *Monuments Illustrating New Comedy*, 3rd edition, 2 vols, London: University of London, Institute of Classical Studies, 1995

Whitman, Cedric H., *Aristophanes and the Comic Hero*, Cambridge, Massachusetts: Harvard University Press, 1964

Commonwealth, Byzantine

The Byzantine Commonwealth was first identified and described by the Oxford historian Dimitri Obolensky. The term is best known from his important publication of 1971, *The Byzantine Commonwealth: Eastern Europe 500–1453*. This book examined the way in which people living outside the borders of the Byzantine empire encountered aspects of Byzantine life, whether cultural, political, economic, or religious. Obolensky argued that many Byzantine influences successfully passed beyond the empire's borders, to the extent that they were subsequently incorporated into the everyday life of people who were not "Romaioi" and who may themselves have had no direct contact with Byzantium. Indeed, he found the levels of "Byzantinization" to be so high that he felt justified in claiming that an international community had existed that shared extensively in the life of Byzantium, although it was not incorporated into the empire itself. This alleged international community was termed the "Byzantine Commonwealth".

By focusing principally on the transnational character of the Byzantine tradition, Obolensky was pioneering a new approach within Byzantine studies. Hitherto, much of the scholarly work on the international relations of the Byzantine empire had been conducted by those seeking to shed light on Byzantine foreign policy, or on other aspects of the political history of the empire itself. This new work, however, examined the Byzantine Commonwealth in its own right. It discussed the process of "Byzantinization" with a view to ascertaining its impact on the subsequent development both of its member countries and of the region generally. In seeking to move away from a historiography that laid undue emphasis on formal political structures in defining its field of study, Obolensky could be said to have been incorporating aspects of the "history of civilizations" approach into Byzantine studies.

The subtitle of Obolensky's book suggests that the Byzantine Commonwealth was contained within the eastern European region. This may be true of the period *c*.800–1453, when it can be agreed to have extended from Kievan Rus and the lands to the north of the Black Sea, across to the eastern part of Hungary and the Transylvanian plain, and then south across the Danube to Romania and the Balkan peninsula. In the Balkans, the commonwealth included Serbia, Bulgaria (except between 1018 and 1187 when it was officially incorporated into the empire as a "theme" – a unit of provincial government), and various other territories over which the Byzantines did not exercise direct administrative control. Obolensky did not, however, include Byzantine overseas "dependants" – such as Sicily, Apulia, and Venice – in his definition of the commonwealth. These were, de jure, included in the formal structure of the empire for at least part of the period that the book covers.

Over the course of the millennium the borders of the Byzantine Commonwealth underwent some significant change. As the geographical frontiers of Byzantium itself shifted, so too did those of the commonwealth. Some areas left the commonwealth for political reasons, such as Bulgaria when it was (albeit temporarily) absorbed into the empire. Others, such as Croatia, moved away from the commonwealth in cultural terms: its geographical position on the far northeast of the

Adriatic littoral quickly exposed it to the influences of Latin Christendom. The result was that levels of "Byzantinization" in Croatia were never particularly high, and by the end of the 9th century Pannonian Croatia and some of Dalmatian Croatia were firmly orientated towards the West. Temporary acknowledgement of the Byzantine emperor's suzerainty by the Croats in the 11th century was not accompanied by the widespread adoption of other aspects of Byzantine culture. Conversely, some countries joined the commonwealth several centuries after its establishment. The lands that comprise modern Romania, for example, entered the commonwealth as late as the 14th century. Immediately before this their inhabitants were under the authority of the Hungarian princes, and prior to that the region had served as a temporary home to several different groups of peoples who were travelling west from the steppe. These latter groups did not form sedentary societies and so were more resistant to Byzantine influences, which were most attractive to societies at a higher level of political and social organization.

The constituent parts of the Byzantine Commonwealth were not, of course, homogeneous, even if they all comprised sedentary and centralized societies. They related both to the empire and to each other in sometimes very different ways, and where similar aspects of the Byzantine tradition *were* adopted, it was rarely at the same time. Profound differences in geography, history, economics, and political organization made sure of that. One should not be surprised, then, to discover that wars and violent conflicts were a common part of the political landscape of the Byzantine Commonwealth during the late antique and medieval periods. Indeed, one of the longest and most violent wars in eastern Europe took place between the empire and the country that had proved most receptive to Byzantine ideas and material goods: Bulgaria. For most of the 10th century these two polities were at war with each other, until 1018 when the Byzantine army finally defeated the Bulgarians and brought them under Byzantine subjugation. Clearly, a similar cultural tradition, even when that included similar ecclesiastical structures, education system, and political organization, did not prevent countries from waging war against one another.

Thus, the Byzantine Commonwealth was an organic entity; it was always in the midst of social and political changes, and the direction of the "Byzantinization" process was never fixed. A country could, for instance, be seeking political rapprochement with the empire's enemies, while at the same time increasing its demand for Byzantine products and developing a distinctly "Byzantine" artistic tradition. This was, for example, the case with early-13th-century Serbia as its ruler, grand zupan Stephan, sought to protect his political autonomy in the face of the Fourth Crusade. Although Stephan put himself under the religious authority of the pope in 1217, Serbia remained at the interface of East and West, and in economic and social terms started to move towards Byzantium. When, in the early 14th century, the territorial conquests of Stephan IV Dushan brought the country closer to Byzantine influences, Serbia became more entrenched in the Byzantine Commonwealth. In this way, the character of the commonwealth underwent significant change over the course of its 1,000-year history as its members responded to disparate events and circumstances. According to Obolensky's analysis, the greatest transition period for the commonwealth was the mid-12th century, as it moved from being a community whose strongest links with Byzantium – apart from Orthodoxy – were political, to one in which the most prominent Byzantine influences were cultural.

Nevertheless, there *was* extensive continuity in the character of the Byzantine Commonwealth, principally in the area of religion. Member societies all shared in the life and work of the Eastern Orthodox Church, acknowledging as they did so that this was an ecclesiastical organization whose spiritual and administrative base was the Church of Constantinople. A ruler who had recently converted to Christianity according to the Byzantine (that is, Eastern) rite was sent priests and bishops from the Patriarchal School in Constantinople. These men proceeded to establish dioceses of the Byzantine Church in the convert country. Thus, Bulgaria, whose ruler khan Boris had been baptized as a Christian in 865, had received significant numbers of Greek priests and a Greek archbishop by 870. Likewise, when grand prince Vladimir of Kiev accepted Christianity from the Byzantines in 988, he was sent Greek-speaking priests and bishops from Constantinople to facilitate the estab-

12. Byzantine Commonwealth in the 11th century

lishment of the new Russian Church. The setting up of the Orthodox Church in 13th-century Serbia conformed to the same pattern.

Yet, the conversion of eastern Europe to Orthodoxy, rather than Catholicism, was not inevitable, for missionaries from both denominations operated there until the 10th century. The attraction of Orthodoxy lay in the fact that, whereas the western missionaries believed that the scriptures should be read only in their original, "sacred" languages, Greek and Hebrew, and also Latin, the Byzantine missionaries agreed that new converts should be able to worship in the vernacular (citing 1 Corinthians 14 as justification). Moreover, since the Slavs (who had migrated into the region in the 7th century) did not have a written script for the Slavic language, the Byzantine Church invented one for it. Two monks, Cyril and Methodios, were sent to introduce the script to the Christian communities of eastern Europe, specifically Moravia, Bulgaria, and Kievan Rus. The script, known as Old Church Slavonic (from which the modern-day Cyrillic is derived), had unprecedented success. Although Moravia was later absorbed into the Catholic Church, the other countries that accepted and used the Slavonic script remained within the orbit of the Eastern Church through the Great Schism of 1054 and beyond. The exception is Croatia, which gradually orientated itself towards the West after the 8th century. Nevertheless, when the Synod of Spalatum was convened around 1069, there were still

Christians in the eastern part of Croatia who worshipped according to the Slavonic rite. The contribution of Cyril and Methodios, therefore, to the formation of the Byzantine Commonwealth is inestimable.

Political, as well as spiritual, consequences followed from accepting the liturgy of the Orthodox Church. These could not be separated from doctrinal beliefs, for Orthodoxy brought to bear upon its adherents a coherent system of thought, which encompassed the social and political realms, as well as the theological. Thus, the Byzantines conceived of the (Orthodox) eastern European countries as part of an indivisible Christian society, or *oikoumene*, over which God had appointed the emperor to be the guardian before Christ's return to earth. When a ruler (and hence his country) converted to Christianity, the imperial government held to an implicit belief that he had publicly acknowledged his subservience to the Byzantine emperor in Constantinople and had promised that in future he would help to defend the *oikoumene* against external attack. The empire's perceived hegemony was expressed diplomatically in the emperor's practice of standing as godfather to new Christian rulers, or, occasionally, by "adopting" a foreign ruler to be his "spiritual brother" or "spiritual son".

In theory, there was no room for dissent of any kind within the *oikoumene*. The Byzantines believed that dissent in one area would inevitably damage all of the Christian community. When, in the 1390s, for example, prince Basil I of Moscow made disparaging remarks about the relationship of the emperor to the Church, he received a stern letter from the patriarch of Constantinople: "It is not possible for Christians to have the Church and not to have the empire. For Church and empire have a great unity and community; nor is it possible for them to be separated from one another." Nevertheless, the political unity of the Byzantine Commonwealth should not be overemphasized. Whereas ecclesiastical unity was maintained, albeit with local variations of emphasis, throughout the Orthodox world, the notion that a political hierarchy existed among the rulers of the commonwealth, with the emperor at its head, was often a theoretical abstraction and seldom put to practical use. The list of foreign rulers, together with their ranking and mode of address, which appears in the mid-10th-century Byzantine source *The Book of Ceremonies* does not indicate the extent to which other countries were incorporated into the Byzantine orbit.

While direct political links between the commonwealth and the empire became less defined as the period progressed, the commonwealth's cultural identity became more evident. It was common for the rulers of eastern Europe to import Byzantine master craftsmen and architects so that their palaces and cathedrals could be built in the Byzantine style. The 11th-century rebuilding of Kiev is a case in point. Meanwhile, the popularity of the Slavonic script continued to grow, and with it the demand for literary works translated from the Greek. In monasteries across eastern Europe, and particularly on Mount Athos, the international monastic centre near Thessalonica, monks laboured in scriptoria, copying or translating into Slavonic the works of Byzantine and Classical scholars. The books – containing both theological and secular works – were then sent to libraries and churches in far-reaching parts of the commonwealth.

The intermediaries for the transmission of Byzantine cultural influences were not always people moving into the commonwealth from the direction of the empire. The assimilation, for example, of Kievan Rus into the commonwealth was greatly facilitated by Russian links with the Bulgarians. The Russian ruling elite obtained its first prolonged exposure to Byzantine culture in 967 when it attacked eastern Bulgaria on behalf of emperor Nikephoros Phokas. Impressed by the wealth of urban Bulgaria, grand prince Svyatoslav of Kiev refused to leave, writing in a letter to his mother Olga that life in Bulgaria was far preferable to that in Kievan Rus. When, eventually, in 971, the Russians were persuaded to return home, they took with them a new taste for Byzantine culture, as well as Byzantine literature, and at least one Byzantine woman – who was given in marriage to Svyatoslav's son. Nearly 50 years later, Kievan Rus was again the recipient of a Byzantine culture that had been filtered through a Bulgarian intermediary. After the Byzantine annexation of Bulgaria in 1018, many Bulgarians, including priests and other educated people, migrated north to Kiev. As well as their everyday possessions, they took with them Slavic translations of Byzantine literature, including law codes. The migrant Bulgarians were assimilated into Russian society and seem to have had a significant impact on Russian literary development, for philological research has shown that many of the medieval Slavonic scripts found in Russia are of Bulgarian origin.

The facets of Byzantine political, social, and religious life that were transmitted into eastern Europe during the period 500–1453 were not unaffected by the existing culture of the recipient peoples, or these peoples' own circumstances. Nor did the "Byzantinizing" process hinder the development of a unique social and political identity in the countries of the Byzantine Commonwealth. Indeed, having possession of Byzantine ideas about governance and social organization actually helped countries such as Bulgaria to break away from the empire's overlordship and to develop their own state structures in the later Middle Ages.

It is, therefore, difficult to offer a comprehensive description of the Byzantine Commonwealth, and the precise borders of this entity have eluded identification. Those scholars who have conceived of the commonwealth as an international community composed principally of formalized political linkages – such as dynastic marriages or the granting of court titles – have often been critical of the concept of a Byzantine Commonwealth. Yet, scholars more interested in the processes of cultural transmission have found that the concept provides a useful framework for examining the international relations of eastern Europe in the medieval period. This latter group of scholars has carried out more detailed historical research on aspects of Obolensky's argument, the result of which has been the further illumination of cultural linkages between the empire and its neighbours. New archaeological research has also illuminated such linkages, and has, interestingly, strengthened the view that the "Byzantinization" process was not confined to eastern Europe and the Christian *oikoumene*, but took place in parts of central and western Europe as well. The process can even be identified outside Obolensky's chronological remit of 500–1453. If the reign of Constantine the Great is taken to mark the inauguration of the Christian (Byzantine) empire, then those aspects of religious and cultural life that sprang – directly or indirectly – from the events of his reign can reliably be termed "Byzantine", rather than "late Roman". The transmission of these aspects of Byzantine culture across formal imperial boundaries (and even as far as the western-most parts of Europe) is reliably attested throughout the 4th and 5th centuries, albeit to differing degrees. It seems possible, therefore, that the formative years of the Byzantine Commonwealth are to be found rather earlier than was previously suggested by Obolensky, and that, moreover, the geographical area covered by it was broader than hitherto supposed. While the Byzantine Commonwealth continues to evade a precise characterization, therefore, it is likely to remain the subject of academic research.

ANTHEA HARRIS

Further Reading

Chrysos, E.K., "The Term *Basileos* in Early Byzantine International Relations", *Dumbarton Oaks Papers*, 32 (1992): pp. 29–75

Fine, John V.A., *The Early Medieval Balkans: A Critical Survey from the Sixth to the Late Twelfth Century*, Ann Arbor: University of Michigan Press, 1983

Fine, John V.A., *The Late Medieval Balkans: A Critical Survey from the Late Twelfth Century to the Ottoman Conquest*, Ann Arbor: University of Michigan Press, 1987

Franklin, Simon and Jonathan Shepard, *Byzantine Diplomacy*, Aldershot, Hampshire: Variorum, 1992

Gojda, Martin, *The Ancient Slavs: Settlement and Society*, Edinburgh: Edinburgh University Press, 1991

Mango, Cyril, *Byzantine Architecture*, New York: Abrams, 1974, reprinted New York: Rizzoli, 1985; London: Faber, 1986

Meyendorff, John, *Byzantium and the Rise of Russia: A Study of Byzantino-Russian Relations in the Fourteenth Century*, Crestwood, New York: St Vladimir's Seminary Press, 1989

Moyssidou, J., *Byzantium and its Northern Neighbours during the Tenth Century*, Athens, 1995 (includes summary in English)

Obolensky, Dimitri, *The Byzantine Commonwealth: Eastern Europe, 500–1453*, London: Weidenfeld and Nicolson, and New York: Praeger, 1971

Obolensky, Dimitri, *Six Byzantine Portraits*, Oxford: Clarendon Press, and New York: Oxford University Press, 1988

Papadakis, Aristeides and John Meyendorff, *The Christian East and the Rise of the Papacy: The Church, 1071–1453 AD*, Crestwood, New York: St Vladimir's Seminary Press, 1994

Rodley, Lyn, *Byzantine Art and Architecture: An Introduction*, Cambridge and New York: Cambridge University Press, 1994

Communist Party (KKE)

The Communist Party of Greece was founded on 10 November 1918 as the Socialist Labour Party of Greece (*Sosialistikon Ergatikon Komma Ellados*, SEKE); in April 1920 the party joined the Third International and was renamed SEKE(Kommounistiko); at its Third Extraordinary Congress in 1924 SEKE(K) changed its name to KKE (*Kommounistiko Komma Elladas – Elliniko Tmima tis Kommounistikis Diethnous*) (Communist Party of Greece – Greek Section of the Communist International).

Throughout the interwar years the KKE remained a party with marginal appeal; its share of the national vote was consistently small in the period until 1929, remaining below 4 per cent, and usually polling much less. This was partly the result of the policy of vigorous *ouvrierisme* the KKE pursued; a weakness that is hardly surprising, considering the numerical weakness of Greek industrial workers in the interwar years. The weakness was, however, attenuated by the continuous power struggles within the party: by 1931 the KKE had changed leader eight times, with the loss of leadership usually accompanied by the expulsion of the outgoing leader from the party. The party also had to overcome bouts of state measures intended to limit its effectiveness. In 1931 the Comintern sent Nikos Zahariadis to reorganize the KKE; he became its Secretary General in 1935, a post he retained until 1956. Under Zahariadis the KKE came out of its isolation, increased party membership tenfold, modified its highly unpopular position on the Macedonian Question, and even managed to elect 15 deputies in the elections of January 1936, enough to hold the balance in the hung parliament that ensued.

Under the Metaxas dictatorship, the KKE party organization was all but destroyed. Large numbers of real and suspected communists were arrested, imprisoned, or exiled, including virtually the whole of the party leadership. Maniadakis, the head of the Metaxas secret police, even created its own bogus KKE organization, complete with *Rizospastis*, the party newspaper, that sowed confusion in the ranks of the remaining communist supporters.

However, the KKE reached the peak of its popularity during the Axis occupation of Greece. It was the founding force and controlling influence in EAM and ELAS (*Ethniko Apelevtherotiko Metopo*, National Liberation Front, and *Ellinikos Laikos Apelevtherotikos Stratos*, Greek Popular Liberation Army), respectively the largest political and military resistance movements in occupied Greece. By the end of the occupation, party membership had multiplied and the KKE was claiming that its ideas and policies enjoyed the support of a very large segment of the population. The KKE (and EAM) had declared against the return of king George II to Greece after the end of the war, at least until a plebiscite had been organized; it was also initially against participation in the government of national unity formed under George Papandreou after the Lebanon Agreement in 1944. However, probably as a result of advice by a Soviet mission that was parachuted into the Greek mountains in July 1944, it suddenly reversed its position, cooperated with the British and the bourgeois parties, and accepted five relatively minor ministerial portfolios.

Following the liberation of Greece, the KKE's policy remained ambivalent. It seemed to fail to decide whether it wanted to seize power by force or not. The communist ministers resigned from the Papandreou government on 1 December 1944; what followed was the *Dekemvriana*, the events of December 1944 and January 1945, when ELAS forces fought pitched battles in Athens against British and Greek forces. The Varkiza Agreement of February 1945 ended the hostilities but not the conflict. For the next 18 months the KKE, once more under the leadership of Zahariadis (who had spent the war years in Dachau concentration camp), vacillated between participation in politics and armed struggle. The KKE controversially decided to abstain from the elections of March 1946, thus probably losing its last chance of peaceful integration in national politics. In the meantime the country was sliding towards civil war. The KKE adopted a policy of self-defence for its members, many of whom had been driven underground or to the mountains by extreme right-wing repression. By August 1946 armed bands were already formed; in October the KKE announced the formation of the Democratic Army; the KKE was declared illegal in December 1947; it was to remain illegal until 1974. In the summer of 1948, following the Tito–Cominform split, the KKE sided with Stalin, publicly condemning Tito, despite the fact that most of its supplies were coming from Yugoslavia. At about the same time, Zahariadis assumed the military leadership of the struggle and forced a change in tactics, which is usually credited (along with the massive US support for the Athens national government) with the defeat of the Communist Democratic Army in the Civil War.

Between 1949 and 1974 the KKE operated in exile, with headquarters in Bucharest and branches in other countries of the Eastern bloc. Zahariadis insisted on retaining the party on a war footing, even after it became clear that the armed struggle was no longer a realistic option. Following de-Stalinization in the Soviet Union and the satellites, Zahariadis was deposed and exiled to Siberia. Throughout the 1951–67 period, in politics in Greece itself, the KKE supported EDA (*Enomeni Dimotratiki Aristera*, United Democratic Left, founded in

1951), an umbrella of left-wing forces, which successfully contested all national elections between 1952 and 1967.

The KKE went through a major crisis in 1968, when it split into a Euro-communist faction named KKE(es) (KKE of the Interior) and the Moscow-oriented mainstream KKE. The party was legalized after the fall of the Colonels' regime in 1974; under the leadership of Harilaos Florakis, a resistance and Civil War veteran, the KKE established itself as the major party expressing the communist left in post-1974 Greece. The KKE contested all elections after 1974, either alone or in coalition with other left-wing parties; however, it never polled more than 12 per cent of the national vote: even in the elections of June 1989, when virtually all left-wing parties cooperated in an alliance, their collective share of the vote was 13.1 per cent. Between 1974 and the mid-1980s the party's influence was very considerable in the student movement, where KNE, the Communist Party youth, often dominated the scene.

While in the 1970s and early 1980s the party showing remained more or less stable, subsequently the KKE saw its fortunes gradually decline; this was in part the result of the rise and success of the more vigorous, left-of-centre Panhellenic Socialist Party (PASOK), which deprived the KKE of some support from moderate leftists.

During the period 1989–90 the KKE participated in government for the first time since 1944. Between July and November 1989 it was the junior partner in a coalition with the conservative New Democracy party; it subsequently participated in the "ecumenical" (grand coalition) government that governed between November 1989 and April 1990, as the elections of November 1989 had produced another hung parliament.

The KKE passed a serious crisis in 1989, when it supported the anti-Gorbachev coup in the Soviet Union. Though Florakis retired and there was some renewal in the leadership, more importantly the party failed to renew its policies in the 1990s, retaining an anti-Western, anti-capitalist rhetoric of diminishing relevance for the majority of the Greek electorate. This resulted in a further decrease of party support in the elections of 1993 and 1996, a decrease bringing electoral support for the KKE to roughly 1936 levels.

GEORGE KAZAMIAS

See also Civil War, EAM and ELAS

Further Reading

Exinta chronia Agonon kai Thysion: Chroniko tou KKE, 1918–78 [Sixty Years of Struggle and Sacrifice: The Chronicle of the KKE, 1918–78], 2 vols, Athens, 1978–79

KKE, Episisma Keimena [KKE: Official Documents], 6 vols, Athens, 1964–87

Kousoulas, George D., *Revolution and Defeat: The Story of the Greek Communist Party*, London and New York: Oxford University Press, 1965

Stavrakis, Peter J., *Moscow and Greek Communism, 1944–1949*, Ithaca, New York: Cornell University Press, 1989

Vlavianos, Haris, *Greece, 1941–49: From Resistance to Civil War: The Strategy of the Greek Communist Party*, London: Macmillan, and New York: St Martin's Press, 1992

Constantine I 1868–1922

King of the Hellenes

Constantine I ranks among the most controversial personalities of modern Greece. He was the eldest son of king George I and Queen Olga; in 1889 he married Princess Sophie Dorothea Hohenzollern, sister of kaiser Wilhelm of Germany. He trained as a soldier both in Athens and in Germany, but his reputation received a blow when he commanded the Greek army in Thessaly in the disastrous war of in 1897. However, though the defeat may have been to an extent due to his lack of experience, it was probably more directly linked to the lack of preparedness and inadequate training of the Greek army of the time. Despite demands for his resignation, Constantine retained his army position until the 1909 Goudi pronunciamento, when the Military League demanded that he and the other princes resign from army posts. He was reinstated by Venizelos in 1911, and was commander-in-chief of the Greek army in the highly successful campaigns of the Balkan Wars of 1912–13. In 1913, in an action that would be variously interpreted later, the kaiser presented him with the baton of a field marshal of the Prussian army.

He ascended the throne in 1913, at the age of 45, following the assassination of king George I in Thessalonica. He soon proved that, though he was a charismatic leader, he lacked his father's wisdom as well as experience. Constantine enjoyed considerable popularity, especially among the army: an army deputation had acted as godfather for his youngest child, princess Katherine, earning him the affectionate nickname *koumparos* (godbrother).

Initially Constantine cooperated well with prime minister Venizelos, but this ended with the outbreak of World War I. Venizelos was in favour of entering the war on the side of the Entente, and his arguments became even weightier after both Ottoman Turkey and Bulgaria, Greece's traditional enemies, joined the Central Powers (in November 1914 and September 1915 respectively). Constantine was in favour of remaining neutral, an attitude popularly described at the time as a view in favour of a "small and honourable Greece". This was linked to the view that consolidation of the territorial gains of the Balkan Wars should be the first priority, rather than further territorial expansion, as dictated by the Great Idea. To justify his involvement in active politics, Constantine claimed foreign affairs lay within his constitutional powers; Venizelos, disagreeing, resigned in March 1915, but won a clear majority in the elections of the following June. Venizelos regarded the result as a clear mandate in favour of Greek entry to the war alongside the Entente powers, but Constantine still refused to agree to this and once more demanded his resignation; Venizelos was subsequently dismissed and fresh elections were called. This disagreement was the beginning of the national schism.

Venizelos's party abstained from the elections of December 1915; other international and national events, among them the coup staged in Thessalonica by the National Defence movement, widened the rift between Constantine and Venizelos. By 1916 Greece was on the brink of civil war, with two governments: a royal government in Athens, formally neutral, controlling the southern half of Greece; and a Venizelist provisional government in Thessalonica, controlling the northern half and most of the islands, supporting and supported by the Entente. In June 1917 the Entente demanded that Constantine leave the country, using as pretext the violation of his oath to uphold the Greek Constitution. He left with the crown prince (later king George II), without formally abdicating, and was succeeded by his second son, Alexander. A government headed by Venizelos assumed power over the whole of Greece.

Constantine remained away from Greece (mostly in Switzerland) until Venizelos's defeat in the elections of November 1920. A rigged plebiscite, organized by the victorious Popular Party in December 1920, invited Constantine back to the throne. Once back, Constantine presided over the gradual unravelling of Greece's adventure in Asia Minor. Neither he nor the Populist government was strong or decisive enough to disentangle Greece from Asia Minor. Disaster came in August 1922, when the Turkish nationalist forces under Mustafa Kemal (later Atatürk) attacked and broke the front. The defeated Greek troops, evacuated to the nearby islands, revolted and demanded, among other things, the king's abdication. Constantine abdicated on 26 September 1922 and left Greece. He died in an obscure hotel in Palermo four months later.

As the popular support for him shows, Constantine was both charismatic and gifted; his shortcomings were mostly in that he saw the role of the monarch as much more active than the times (and the 1911 Constitution in force at the time) allowed. Indeed his involvement in politics dates from well before he became king: while still the crown prince he had been partly responsible for bringing down one of the Trikoupis administrations, when he openly participated in an anti-government demonstration. Once king, he elected to become an active political player, rather than the impassive umpire his father had been. He identified with the Populists and the more conservative elements in Greek society; his advocacy of neutrality during World War I, and the lengths to which he was prepared to go to advance it, gave him a reputation as a Germanophile, which he was never quite able to dispel. During the deepest rift of the national schism, he was even branded as a traitor, though very little evidence of direct links with the Central Powers has been uncovered.

Adoring supporters at the time called him Constantine XII, a numeral chosen to imply continuity between the modern Greek dynasty and the Byzantine emperors; and a proverb circulating at the time was claiming that as a Constantine was the last Greek emperor of Constantinople (in 1453), it would be a Constantine who would take it back from the Ottomans. Constantine got nearest to the realization of the dreams of the Great Idea, though this was more a result of Venizelos's foresight than his own policies. It is ironic that he would die in exile and remain, even after death, the object of hatred for half his people and of admiration for the other half.

GEORGE KAZAMIAS

See also Asia Minor Campaign, World War I

Biography

Born in 1868 the eldest son of king George I and queen Olga, Constantine trained as a soldier in Athens and Berlin. In 1889 he married princess Sophie, sister of Kaiser Wilhelm II. He commanded the Greek forces in the Graeco-Turkish war of 1897 and in the Balkan Wars of 1912–13. He came to the throne in 1913 and clashed with Venizelos about entry into World War I. He went into exile in 1917–20. Invited back, he abdicated after the Asia Minor disaster in 1922. He died in Palermo in 1922.

Further Reading

Dafnis, G., *I Ellas metaxy dyo polemon, 1923–1940* [Greece Between Two Wars, 1923–40], 2 vols, Athens, 1955

Dakin, Douglas, *The Unification of Greece, 1770–1923*, London: Benn, and New York: St Martin's Press, 1972

Gould-Lee, Arthur S., *The Royal House of Greece*, London: Ward Lock, 1948

Karolidis, P., *Istoria tou Ellinikou Ethnous* [History of the Greek Nation], vol. 20: *Apo ton A' Pagkosmio Polemo mechri to 1930* [From World War I to 1930], Athens, 1993

Ventiris, G., *I Ellas tou 1910–20* [Greece, 1910–20], 2 vols, Athens, 1932

Constantine I the Great 273/74–337

Emperor

Constantine the Great was born in Naissus (modern Niš, in Serbia) in 273/4, the son of the future emperor Constantius Chlorus and Helena his concubine (or perhaps wife). From 293, when his father became a member of the tetrarchy, as Caesar to the Augustus Maximian, Constantine served in the Roman army in the eastern part of the empire, first fighting in the Persian war and later serving with Galerius on the Danube; thereafter he seems to have been attached to Diocletian's court. The "Great Persecution" of the Christians began in 303, though in the west it was less severe than in the east, and in Gaul and Britain, where Constantius held sway, the persecution seems to have been limited to the demolition of churches. In 305 Diocletian, then seriously ill, and the other senior emperor, or Augustus, Maximian, resigned and were succeeded by their Caesars, Galerius and Constantius. Constantine (and Maximian's son, Maxentius) was passed over in the succession; two of Galerius' favourites, Severus (possibly his praetorian prefect) and Maximinus (his nephew), became Caesars.

After the reconstitution of the tetrarchy in Nicomedia, Constantius left for Britain, soon followed by his son. On 25 July 306, at York, Constantius died, and Constantine was immediately hailed by the army there as Augustus, his father's successor. He immediately announced his assumption of the imperial dignity to Galerius, the other Augustus, who compromised by appointing him Caesar, a position Constantine did not refuse, thus assuring beyond any doubt his legitimacy. The ensuing dissolution of the tetrarchy was a complicated business. Maxentius, initially with the support of his father, proclaimed himself Augustus in Italy. After Severus' failure to defeat Maxentius, Galerius appointed Licinius to the task, as Augustus. Galerius himself died in 311, having issued an edict of toleration, bringing to an end the persecution of Christians in the east. The following year Constantine advanced into Italy. On 28 October Maxentius left Rome and crossed the Tiber to

Constantine the Great: portrait of the emperor on a gold solidus minted at Nicodemia in 335, Barber Institute, Birmingham

confront the forces of Constantine. At the Battle of the Milvian Bridge he was defeated, and Constantine entered the city as the undisputed ruler of the western Roman empire. Rule of the eastern empire was now disputed between the two other Augusti: Maximinus, who had begun persecuting Christians again in Egypt and Palestine, and Licinius, whom Constantine supported. In 313 Constantine and Licinius met in Milan and extended to the whole empire the toleration Christians were already enjoying in the western part of the empire. Later that year Licinius defeated Maximinus. Harmony between the two Augusti, Constantine and Licinius, did not last long. There was an indecisive war in 316, and in 324 Licinius was finally defeated by Constantine, who thus became sole emperor, which he remained until his death.

Constantine's victory over Maxentius in 312 was presented in Constantine's propaganda as a victory for Christianity (though there is evidence that Maxentius supported the Christians too), and very soon there circulated stories that before the battle Constantine had had a dream (so Lactantius), or a vision in the sky (so Eusebius), in which he had seen the cross as an emblem of victory, which he was to use as his military standard: the *labarum*, bearing either the chi-rho or the *crux monogrammaticum* (so Lactantius, who says that it was inscribed on the shields of Constantine's soldiers). This dream or vision is presented as Constantine's conversion. There is in fact evidence that Constantine was far from unfamiliar with Christianity: the name of one of his half-sisters, Anastasia, may indicate longstanding Christian leanings in his family, and Constantine seems to have included Christian bishops in his entourage before the victory of 312. It is, however, clear that after 312 Constantine adopted Christianity as his favoured religion and made it the object of his considerable patronage. There is also evidence from coinage that like his father he maintained his devotion to *sol invictus*, the "unconquered sun", but it is not unlikely that, like later Roman Christians we hear of from pope Leo I (440–61), he had no problem in assim-

ilating Christ and the *sol invictus*. As to the motives for his conversion, there is continuing scholarly dispute over whether it was a response to the growing Christianization of the empire, or a precondition for its ensuing Christianization. The pagan rumour (preserved by Zosimus) that Constantine embraced Christianity as the only religion that could offer forgiveness to one who had murdered his wife and son in 326 is perhaps not entirely without foundation. At any rate, Constantine only became a baptized Christian on his deathbed in 337.

Constantine's support for Christianity is manifest in his providing funds for the building of churches, initially in the west, but soon in the east, and also in the introduction of changes in the law to meet Christian sensibilities (for instance recognizing bishops as legitimate legal arbiters). It is perhaps also manifest in his founding in 330 the city of Constantinople, named after him, or "New Rome". However, Eusebius' account of Constantine's planning a Christian city with many churches is not borne out by the surviving evidence: it seems that the only church begun by Constantine was the church of the Holy Apostles, intended as his mausoleum where his body would rest as that of the 13th apostle. The Christian Church, the object of Constantine's favours, very soon presented problems for him. In north Africa he found a Church divided by Donatism, and quickly discovered that Christian disunity was not easily dealt with. Even worse, when he had attained his ambition as sole emperor in 324, he found the Church in the east divided over the issue of Arianism. To solve this he convoked a synod, the first Council of Nicaea, which within a decade or so was to be regarded as the first ecumenical (or universal) council: Arius was condemned and the Christian faith defined in a creed (or symbol) drawn by the council. Constantine's involvement in the affairs of the Church has often been seen as the beginnings of Caesaropapism, though it has recently been forcefully argued (by Barnes) that Constantine and his immediate successors were scrupulous in respecting the government of the Church by bishops meeting in synod. Despite the clear decision of the Council of Nicaea against Arianism, Constantine seemed to compromise in his later years (at least in the eyes of the Orthodox) and received baptism from the hands of an Arian bishop, Eusebius of Nicomedia.

Constantine's reputation as the first Christian emperor was enormous: more of his successors bore the name of Constantine than any other, the last dying in defence of the city Constantine had founded in 1453. The vision of the cross that was the occasion of his conversion led to its becoming a symbol closely associated with Constantine (and the imperial office), which was enhanced in legend by his being closely associated with his mother Helena's discovery of the True Cross in 326. The shadow cast over his name by his having been baptized on his deathbed by an Arian was removed by the legend that he was baptized in Rome after his victory at the Milvian Bridge by pope Sylvester I. He is commemorated as a saint in the Orthodox Church, together with his mother Helena, on 21 May.

ANDREW LOUTH

See also Constantinople

Biography

Born at Naissus in Serbia in 273/74, the son of Constantius I and Helena, Constantine served in the Roman army from 293. When Constantius died at York in 306, Constantine was proclaimed as his successor by the troops there. After victory at the Milvian Bridge in 312 he entered Rome as ruler of the western part of the empire; and in 324 became sole ruler of the whole. Constantine was a supporter of Christianity and in 330 founded the city of Constantinople as a new, Christian, capital. He died near Nicomedia in 337.

Further Reading

Alföldi, Andrew, *The Conversion of Constantine and Pagan Rome*, 2nd edition, Oxford: Clarendon Press, 1969

Barnes, Timothy D., *Constantine and Eusebius*, Cambridge, Massachusetts: Harvard University Press, 1981

Baynes, Norman H., *Constantine the Great and the Christian Church*, 2nd edition, London: Oxford University Press, 1972

Lieu, Samuel N.C. and Dominic Montserrat (editors), *Constantine: History, Historiography, and Legend*, London and New York: Routledge, 1998

Schwartz, Eduard, *Kaiser Constantin und die christliche Kirche*, 2nd edition, Leipzig: Teubner, 1936

Constantine V 718–775

Emperor

Constantine V (741–75) earned unparalleled notoriety with Byzantine commentators due to his violent persecution of the supporters of icons during the first part of the iconoclastic controversy (726/30–784). The opprobrious nicknames given him included *Kopronymos* (the "dung-named", referring to a story that he had excreted in the font during baptism, an exceptionally bad omen) and *Kaballinos* (or "stable hand", a reference to his penchant for horses). In his day, however, he enjoyed a power base of military and to an extent political support that few other emperors before or after him could boast.

Constantine was the son and successor of the emperor Leo III the Isaurian (716–41) who initiated official iconoclast policies in either 726 or 730. The initial reaction to this policy appears to have been muted, thanks to popular approval of Leo's decisive actions in 717 when he helped to save Constantinople from a prolonged Arab siege. But it does not seem that he waged an all-out campaign of destruction against either icons or their supporters. All he asked for was an end to the actual veneration of icons, especially in public places and churches.

After Leo III's death in 741, Constantine appears to have enjoyed considerable support in the provincial, or *thematic*, armies, thanks to his father's victories against both Bulgars and Arabs, the like of which had rarely been seen since Herakleios's last campaigns against the Persians a century earlier. But the outset of Constantine's reign was marked by the revolt of his brother-in-law Artabasdos (*c.*741–43) who even managed to occupy Constantinople in 743, where he may have reversed iconoclast policies. Constantine finally crushed the revolt but the incident had impressed upon him the need to restructure the military and tie them more closely to his person.

The most important feature of Constantine's military reforms, beginning in the mid-740s, involved the creation of well-trained and well-maintained garrison units and field armies in and around Constantinople: these were collectively known as the *tagmata* (singular *tagma*, i.e. battalion) and were mostly recruited from the civic deme factions of the capital and destitute members of the mob. The crack troops of the *tagmata* eventually constituted Constantine's power base for his violent execution of iconoclast policies. The emperor's military prowess, his attention to the welfare of his troops, and his triumphs against the Bulgars (at Anchialos in 763 and Lithosoria in 773) and the Arabs (the capture of Germanikeia, Theodosioupolis, and Melitine in 752) associated his success with his iconoclasm in the military and popular mind. Consequently, anyone who opposed iconoclasm came to be identified as a personal enemy of the emperor and a traitor to the state.

The devastating plague of 746–47, during which Constantine may have briefly moved his court to Nicomedia, may have convinced him that God wanted him to take a tougher line against the icons and their venerators, the most vocal of whom were monks. After all, God had not failed him before. Furthermore, Constantine began to realize that, in order to refute the icons once and for all, theological arguments had to be presented at a Church council. This led to the Council of Hieria in 754 which, although proclaiming itself ecumenical, included no representatives from Rome or the eastern patriarchates, and even lacked a patriarch of Constantinople up to the very last session.

Constantine displayed prowess in his theological writings, of which the so-called *Peuseis*, or "Questions", is the only surviving example – if indeed there were originally others. Some historians have detected a Monophysite strain in his theology, claiming that his family's origins in north Syria predisposed him to such inclinations. This need not necessarily be the case. Nevertheless, Constantine may have influenced the synod's final pronouncements. Two of the most important points made in the *Peuseis* are that to portray Christ in an icon necessarily circumscribes the uncircumscribable divine nature in Him, and that the only true image (*typos*) of Christ was the Eucharist itself.

Imperial persecution of iconophiles (venerators of icons), mostly monks and nuns, increased around this time. Some, like St Stephanos the Neomartyr, were even publicly humiliated and executed. Later Byzantine sources claim that Constantine also waged an all-out war on holy objects (gospel books, chalices, vestments, etc.) in an attempt to eliminate monastic influence entirely. Some hostility towards the Virgin Mary is also noted, although this does not seem to have characterized the line taken by the official Church. These images of gross sacrilege deeply affected later historians and churchmen and more than anything contributed to the notoriety of both emperor and iconoclasm in their writings. These actions, however, were not part of any calculated iconoclast attack against the holy. Social and political factors (psychological dislocation in the wake of the plague, the hero cult around Constantine, short-term localized power interests, etc.) can help to explain them better.

Iconoclasm apart, Constantine showed a great interest in secular art, decorating his residences with scenes of his battles and his favourite charioteers. He also may have been responsible for the renovation of the church of Hagia Irene in

Constantinople, one of the most significant monuments of the period.

In his policy with the Caliphate he showed prowess, stemming Arab advances with a determination never previously seen. His iconoclast policies, however, isolated him in the iconophile West, and he may have been responsible for removing Calabria, Sicily, Illyricum, Macedonia, Crete, and Greece from the nominal jurisdiction of Rome and placing them under Constantinople. His hostile policies led to Rome drawing closer to the Franks in their struggle against the Lombards, and have long been regarded as contributing indirectly to the rise of Charlemagne.

Together with his father, Constantine may have been responsible for the publication in 741 of the *Ekloge*, the famous law code in which Christian attitudes to laws relating to the family, sexual offences, and criminal law begin to predominate over the more legalistic compilations of the Roman past. The *Ekloge* had a great influence on Byzantine law for centuries.

Constantine's war against the iconophiles subsided after his death in 775, indicating that its ferocity had much to do with his own personality. By 787, during the regency of his daughter-in-law Irene, the icons had been restored at the second Council of Nicaea and militant iconoclasm had abated.

Constantine's shadow loomed large over the events leading to the second period of iconoclasm, when soldiers and the mob invoked his name during a disastrous war with the Bulgars undertaken by iconophile emperors (809–16). The second period of iconoclasm, begun by Leo V in 815, owed much to his memory. The patriarch Nikephoros (806–15) attempted in his writings to refute the idea that Constantine's reign had been a "golden age". After 843 his name became synonymous with the powers of evil, and his bones were exhumed from the church of the Holy Apostles in Constantinople and discarded.

In modern Byzantine studies Constantine represents an anomaly that has fascinated historians, some of whom have regarded him as an enlightened despot trying to centralize the secular power of the state in the face of a "reactionary" iconophile Church. Protestant theologians see his iconoclasm as a precursor of the Reformation. Such evaluations, however, have more to do with modern concepts of progress and religion than with a realistic appraisal of events.

DAVID R. TURNER

See also Iconoclasm

Biography

Born at Constantinople in 718, Constantine succeeded his father Leo III in 741. Surviving a revolt by his brother-in-law Artabasdos in 741–43, he reorganized the military. In 754 he convened a church council at Hieria and thereafter pursued iconoclast policies which he supported with his own writings. He died at Strongylon in 775. After the triumph of Orthodoxy in 843 his bones were exhumed and scattered.

Writings

Peuseis, in *Textus Byzantinos ad iconomachiam pertinentes*, edited by Herman Hennephof, Leiden: Brill, 1969, pp. 141–87

Further Reading

Anastos, M., "Iconoclasm and Imperial Rule 717–843" in *The Byzantine Empire*, edited by J.M. Hussey, Cambridge: Cambridge University Press, 1966 (*The Cambridge Medieval History*, vol. 4, part 1, 2nd edition)

Gero, Stephen, *Byzantine Iconoclasm during the Reign of Constantine V*, Louvain: Corpus SCO, 1977

Haldon, John F., *Byzantine Praetorians: An Administrative, Institutional, and Social Survey of the Opsikion and the Tagmata, c. 580–900*, Bonn: Habelt, 1984

Herrin, Judith, *The Formation of Christendom*, Princeton, New Jersey: Princeton University Press, 1987

Lombard, Alfred, *Constantin V, empereur des Romains (740–775)*, Paris: Alcan, 1902

Mango, Cyril, "St. Anthusa of Mantineon and the Family of Constantine V", *Analecta Bollandiana*, 100 (1982): pp. 401–9

Rochow, I., *Byzanz im 8. Jahrhundert in der Sicht des Theophanes*, Berlin: Akademie, 1990 (extensive source references and bibliography)

Speck, Paul, *Artabasdos*, Bonn: Habelt, 1981

Turner, David, "The Politics of Despair: The Plague of 746/7 and Iconoclasm in the Byzantine Empire", *Annual of the British School at Athens*, 85 (1990): pp. 419–34

Constantine VII 905–959

Emperor

The name of Constantine VII, or Constantine Porphyrogennetos (913–59), is one inextricably linked with the so-called encyclopaedic trend of 9th- and 10th-century Byzantine literature, epitomized by such works as the *Book of Themes* (*De Thematibus*), the *Book of Ceremonies* (*De Ceremoniis*), and *On Governing the Empire* (*De Administrando Imperio*), all works commissioned, if not personally compiled, by Constantine VII. This literary role that characterizes Constantine is often ascribed to his exclusion from imperial power for so long.

Although born the son of the emperor Leo VI in 905 and crowned co-emperor in 908, Constantine VII had to wait from 912 (the date of the death of his father) until 945 to be an independent emperor. His uncle Alexander ruled from 912–913, then a regency was established for Constantine headed by the patriarch Nicholas. Constantine's mother Zoe Karbonopsina managed to oust Nicholas in 914 and establish herself as regent, but in 919 the admiral Romanos Lekapenos forced her to retire and gained control of Constantine. Constantine was married to Romanos's daughter Helena, then Romanos became emperor himself in 920, maintaining Constantine as a co-emperor but also establishing his own sons as co-emperors. Romanos I ruled until 944 when he was dethroned by his sons Stephen and Constantine. However they soon fell themselves in 945, and Constantine VII finally secured his birthright. Thus it was to fill his time during his exclusion from power that he turned to intellectual pursuits. Some sources also credit him with being a painter.

Perhaps the most famous of the encyclopaedic works linked with Constantine VII is the *Book of Ceremonies*. It was divided into two books, the second asserting that it was innovative because it drew on material that had previously been known only orally, though it too does contain pre-existing material, such as Philotheos's *Kletorologion* (a list of titles and offices), which was produced under Leo VI in 899. More significant perhaps are the ideas expressed in the prefaces – the importance of ceremony for *taxis* (order), the reproduction on earth of the harmony of the universe created by the Divinity. Here, as in other texts, Constantine's work is characterized by the qualities of compiling, cutting and pasting, preserving, and preface-adding.

The *On Governing the Empire* seems to be "a sort of encyclopedia of Byzantium's foreign policy" (Lemerle, p.320). It is prefaced by an address from Constantine VII to his son Romanos, asserting that the text is to be his guide to ruling over foreign nations well. The work consists of 53 chapters and is preoccupied especially with the Pechenegs (but seems hopelessly outdated on the Arabs and the West), and it also turns to internal diplomacy in its latter chapters. Here we find an emphasis (as in other texts connected with Constantine) on the language in which it is written – an everyday, understandable style.

The *Book of Themes* is a more problematic work. There is no address to Romanos, indeed no preface at all. It is divided into two books, one on the eastern themes, one on the western, and again its information seems less than up-to-date.

Of the other encyclopaedic works linked with Constantine, but not in his name, the most famous is probably the *Excerpta*. This was in 53 sections, each dealing with a particular topic, and each consisting of extracts drawn from pre-existing material, especially Hellenistic, Roman, and Byzantine histories, rather than the Greek classics of Herodotus, Thucydides, and Xenophon. In fact, the 26 authors known from the surviving list are notable for the reason that "almost half of them [are] grouped around the fifth to seventh centuries" (Lemerle, p.331). Each section was also topped by a preface, which appears to have been identical for each. Of this vast work only a tiny part has survived, notably Section 27 "On Embassies" and Section 50 "On Virtues and Vices". Lemerle remarks that "The scale of the tenth-century collection, as also the size of our loss, is astonishing" (p.325).

A well-known work in the encyclopaedic tradition dedicated to Constantine is the *Geoponica*, on rural life. It is divided into 20 sections, is headed by a preface, lists the authors consulted, and appears merely to use a pre-existing text (that of Kassianos Bassos Scholastikos).

Constantine seems also to have been the inspiration behind a corpus of strategic writings, including the *Taktika* of his father; and he appears to be the dedicatee of the famous *Synaxarion of Constantinople*. Thus the literary activity of his reign connected with him is broad and all-encompassing, pointing perhaps to a desire to possess all manner of human wisdom, casting the emperor in the role of the Old Testament king Solomon; indeed the preface to *On Governing the Empire* is marked by its use of the biblical Wisdom literature.

But it is not just encyclopaedism and the amassing and arranging of information that distinguish the work connected with Constantine VII. As a member of a dynasty that had come to power through bloody murder Constantine was not blind to the need to appropriate history. The works of Genesios and Theophanes Continuatus (so-called) were the result. A biographical impulse marks these texts, making them distinct from the chronographic concerns of Theophanes. Genesios's

Constantine VII: portrait of the emperor on a gold solidus minted in 945, Barber Institute, Birmingham

work covered the reigns of the four emperors Leo V, Michael II, Theophilos, and Michael III, the last also including material on Basil I the Macedonian. Theophanes Continuatus also wrote an account based on the reigns of emperors from Leo V onwards. Books 1–5 are divided into individual reigns, but then book 6 comprises the remaining reigns together, and probably postdates Constantine VII's life. Jenkins argues that here we have the beginnings of a less black-and-white, typically medieval characterization, inspired by the use of Classical authors such as Plutarch. This latter chronicle is also distinguished by its hostile account of the reign of Michael III, but especially by book 5, composed in a different style and genre. It is a life of Basil I the Macedonian based on the rhetorical principles of the *basilikos logos* (imperial encomium – and as such owes much to Leo VI's own *Epitaphios* on his parents), and, argues Jenkins (1954), inspired by the panegyrical *Life* of Augustus by Nicholas of Damascus. This section of the work has often been attributed to Constantine VII himself, though, as Ševčenko has pointed out, the title indicates that, although Constantine amassed the material, an unknown author was entrusted with the task of writing the *Life*.

Other works are also linked with Constantine. It is thought that he began the scholia on recent legislation, and that he encouraged the reappearance of medical treatises and veterinary science. Various works with religious themes have been linked with him, characterized by their commemoration of the translation of relics. Two exhortations to the army also exist in Constantine's name.

The sheer bulk and breadth of all this material can often blind one, but Ševčenko does not dodge the question of Constantine's own abilities. Pointing to a letter of Constantine to Theodore of Cyzicus as the only true example of the writing and literary ability of the emperor, Ševčenko doubts that Constantine wrote any of the texts associated with his name, and nominates ghostwriters. It is clear that texts could appear to be written by Constantine, with his name attached to them;

he became symbolic of the trend, if not the instigator behind it, which indeed had already begun in the 9th century. Further, it is important that the issues of Constantine's personal role or the quality of the product should not obscure the significance of the ideological impulse behind these texts. The desire to preserve and harness past knowledge for presentday use is very telling for the specific mood of Byzantium in the 9th and 10th centuries, and marks a stage in Byzantium's recovery of the past before its own flourishing in the 11th and 12th centuries.

SHAUN TOUGHER

Biography

Born in 905 and crowned co-emperor in 908, Constantine did not succeed as emperor until 945. A palace-based emperor like his father Leo VI, he contributed most to the systematization of knowledge and supported the compilation of (if he did not personally compile) such works as the *Book of Themes*, the *Book of Ceremonies*, and *On Governing the Empire*. He died at Constantinople in 959.

Writings

Le Livre des cérémonies, edited by Albert Vogt, 2 vols, Paris: Belles Lettres, 1935–67

De Thematibus, edited by Agostino Pertusi, Vatican City: Biblioteca Apostolica Vaticana, 1952

De Administrando Imperio, vol. 1: *Text and Translation*, edited by Gyula Moravcsik, translated by R.J.H. Jenkins, Washington, D.C.: Dumbarton Oaks, 1967

Three Treatises on Imperial Military Expeditions, edited and translated by J.F. Haldon, Vienna: Akademie der Wissenschaften, 1990

Further Reading

Ahrweiler, H., "Un Discours inédit de Constantin VII Porphyrogénète", *Travaux et Mémoires*, 2 (1967): pp. 393–404

Alexander, P.J., "Secular Biography at Byzantium", *Speculum*, 15 (1940): pp. 194–209

Beaud, B., "Le Savoir et le monarque: le *Traité sur les nations* de l'empereur Constantin VII Porphyrogénète", *Annales: Economies, Sociétés, Civilisations*, 45 (1990): pp. 551–64

Huxley, G.L., "The Scholarship of Constantine Porphyrogenitus", *Proceedings of the Royal Irish Academy*, 80 (1980): pp. 29–40

Jenkins, R.J.H., "Constantine VII's Portrait of Michael III", *Bulletin de l'Académie Royale de Belgique: Classe des Lettres et Sciences Morales et Politiques*, 5th series, 34 (1948): pp. 71–77

Jenkins, R.J.H., "The Classical Background of the Scriptores Post Theophanem", *Dumbarton Oaks Papers*, 8 (1954): pp. 13–30

Jenkins, R.J.H., *Constantine Porphyrogenitus: De Administrando Imperio*, vol. 2: *Commentary*, London: Athlone Press, 1962

Lemerle, Paul, *Byzantine Humanism: The First Phase*, Canberra: Australian Association for Byzantine Studies, 1986

Markopoulos, A. (editor), *Konstantinos Z'Porphyrogennetos kai he epoche tou* [Constantine Porphyrogennetos and his Times], Athens, 1989

Nickles, H.G., "The *Continuatio Theophanis*", *Transactions and Proceedings of the American Philological Association*, 68 (1937): pp. 221–27

Patlagean, E., "La Civilisation en la personne du souverain en Byzance, Xe siècle", *Le Temps et la Reflexion*, 4 (1983): pp. 181–94

Ševčenko, Ihor, "Re-reading Constantine Porphyrogenitus", in *Byzantine Diplomacy*, edited by Jonathan Shepard and Simon Franklin, Aldershot, Hampshire: Ashgate, 1992

Toynbee, Arnold, *Constantine Porphyrogenitus and his World*, London and New York: Oxford University Press, 1973

Constantine IX Monomachos *c.*1000–1055

Emperor

Born into a noble family around 1000, Constantine IX Monomachos (1042–55) was a prominent figure at court during the reign of Romanos III Argyros (1028–34), but he was exiled to Mytilene by Michael IV (1034–41) as being politically suspect. After public loyalty to the Macedonian dynasty had forced Michael V from the throne in 1042, and the subsequent joint rule of Constantine VIII's elderly and mutually antagonistic daughters Zoe and Theodora had rapidly proved a complete failure, Zoe in the same year recalled Constantine Monomachos to become her third imperial husband. Because she was well beyond childbearing age, and probably 22 years her husband's senior, she made no objection to the recall also of his mistress Maria Skleraina (the niece of his late second wife who had shared his exile) nor to the increasingly public role and elevated status as *Sebaste* (Augusta) that he gave her at court ceremonies. Skleraina died probably in 1044 (her position passing, after a series of paramours, to an Alan princess) and Zoe in 1050, while Constantine survived until 1055, when he was buried next to Skleraina in his church of St George of Mangana and was succeeded by his now very ancient sister-in-law Theodora.

During Constantine's reign both the strength of the army and the safety of the empire, which had been built up very successfully, especially by Basil II, were severely weakened. The army suffered from a series of revolts, most notably that of its leading general George Maniakes, when Constantine, at the very outset of his reign, had foolishly recalled him from southern Italy, siding with Maniakes's rival Romanos Skleros, a relation of his mistress. In 1047 he had to put down another, equally serious rebellion from his second cousin Leo Tornikios. His disbanding of certain *thematic* border armies was dictated not only by their often inadequate performance and his need for financial retrenchment, but also by a radical change of policy. Whereas Basil II had established well-defined frontiers defended by military strength, Constantine attempted, as had so often been done successfully in the past, to create more flexible frontiers by cultivating friendly relations with neighbouring states. To this end he initiated or strengthened alliances with the papacy, the German emperor Henry III, Serbia, and Hungary, while he made conciliatory gestures to the Seljuk Turks and even sent a large quantity of corn to help relieve a famine of their rivals, the Fatimids of Egypt.

Constantine's main military achievement was the destruction in 1043 by Greek fire of a major naval force of the Rus in the Bosporus, an interruption of the generally peaceful relations between Byzantium and the Rus that probably marks the latter's growing assertion of independence. This seems to have been acknowledged by Constantine in his willingness to pay reparations for damage and injuries suffered by the Rus during the war, in betrothing in 1046 a close relative (probably his daughter Maria to Vselevod, younger son of Yaroslav the Wise, and in permitting Yaroslav to appoint the first Russian-(rather than Byzantine-)born metropolitan in 1051. However, the effectiveness of the Kievan Rus as allies once more of Byzantium was reduced by the creation of a barrier between them when, by a series of miscalculations and military failures,

Constantine was forced to accept the settlement of Pechenegs south of the Danube. In the east the seemingly promising annexation of Ani in 1045, which had been willed to Byzantium by John-Smbat III but claimed by his nephew Gagik, removed a buffer between Byzantium and the Seljuk Turks who, after the latter's capture of Baghdad in 1055, confronted each other from the Caucasus to Syria. In the west Maniakes' gains in eastern Sicily were soon lost to the Arabs after his recall, and the Byzantine hold on southern Italy was increasingly threatened by the Normans.

The iron fist of Basil II had restrained the fissiparous elements in the state. Constantine, a member of the civil aristocracy, attempted to do the same by balancing their powers. In this he was aided by a group of youngish intellectuals who included Constantine Leichoudes, John Xiphilinos (both later patriarchs), John Mauropous, and Michael Psellos. Constantine lessened the strength of the urban aristocracy by creating new senators from a broad spectrum of society. He curbed the military aristocracy by creating a new judicial ministry (epi ton kriseon) to coordinate provincial administration by putting the thematic judges under its supervision, thus ensuring their complete independence from the military governors. At the same time he attempted to improve the paltry legal knowledge of the judges (Psellos had been appointed a thematic judge before he was 20 without any formal training) by establishing a law school in 1047 with Xiphilinos as its head (nomophylax, "guardian of the laws"); his duties included not only teaching but also supervising the examination of lawyers. Shortly afterwards Constantine established a parallel position for Psellos to teach rhetoric and philosophy and supervise the capital's schools. Partly out of piety and partly also to encourage another balancing force, Constantine lavishly patronized the Church. The most notable instance of this was his building of the monastery of St George Tropaiophoros, for which he prescribed the Typikon, in the region of Mangana on the eastern slope of the acropolis of the capital, but he also made a huge donation to Hagia Sophia, and helped lavishly in the restoration of the church of the Holy Sepulchre in Jerusalem, while there still survives today the monastery of Nea Moni on Chios with the magnificent mosaics of its katholikon (main church).

Despite his efforts Constantine lost support for his policies and his counsellors slipped away or were forced out. A year before his death the emperor effectively lost his ability to govern when he was worsted in a power struggle with his patriarch Michael I Keroularios. Constantine was negotiating for a papal alliance to curb Norman infiltration into southern Italy, but his patriarch was feuding with the papacy over its use of unleavened bread (azymes) in the Eucharist. In July 1054 (the very year in which the emperor began an annual donation to the Benedictine mother-house at Monte Cassino) the papal legate Humbert and the patriarch excommunicated each other, and Keroularios's affectation of purple imperial buskins now symbolized his victory over Constantine as well as an effective end to any surviving notion of a single Church. The emperor's loss of popular support was due both to a worsening military situation with the Pechenegs and to growing economic difficulties. Tactical indulgence of the expensive pious whims of the imperial sisters, his own tax exemptions and lavish donations to monasteries, his selling of salary-bearing titular offices at ludicrously low prices, or even the granting of them as gifts, his cash payments to demobilized soldiers, the subsequent necessity of paying mercenaries, and above all the expense of the wars against the Pechenegs were all serious drains on the imperial treasury. The inevitable result was the first major devaluation of the Byzantine nomisma (gold coin) from a nominal 24 carats to 18, since its introduction in 309, nearly 750 years before: the days of the nomisma as the respected international currency were over.

Constantine was Psellos's favourite emperor, but even he criticizes him for his indolence, extravagance, and sexual laxity. Later Byzantine historians (e.g. Zonaras, Epitomae Historiarum, 17. 16–21, edited by M. Pindar, vol. 3, Bonn, 1897) attribute most of the empire's woes to his frivolity, generosity, subservience to womenfolk, and above all his disbanding of frontier armies. Most modern historians follow suit. However, in the early period of his reign Constantine showed that he could be assertive, and his indolence was at least in part due to a muscular disease that left him in great and constant pain in his later years. Even then, Psellos relates how he would take his part in processions and, supported on his horse by attendants, conceal his agony by means of his facial expression and demeanour in order to carry out his public responsibilities. He was affable, kind, a patron of the arts, a builder (e.g. of the complex at Mangana, which included a hospital and a palace in addition to the church of St George), and an ardent if somewhat impatient landscape gardener. Above all, his military, diplomatic, and political actions were (as Angold points out) the direct result of carefully thought-out policies aimed at a genuine renovatio of the Roman empire: not all were obviously misguided without the benefit of hindsight. He thus contrasts favourably with his immediate predecessors and most of his successors who merely reacted to events.

Constantine's portrait may be seen in a mosaic in the south gallery of Hagia Sophia, Constantinople, showing Christ, Zoe, and Constantine (head only; the body was originally that of Zoe's first husband, Romanos III); in the frontispiece (together with Zoe and Theodora) of a copy of the homilies of St John Chrysostom (Sinai gr. 364, fol. 3r); on an enamel plaque now in Budapest from a crown believed to have been given to Andrew I of Hungary or his wife as an instrument of diplomacy; and probably in the features of the mural of king Solomon on the south wall of the katholikon of Nea Moni.

A.R. LITTLEWOOD

Biography

Born c.1000 to a noble family, Constantine was exiled to Mytilene by Michael IV. Recalled to marry Zoe as her third husband in 1042 and crowned the next day, Constantine curbed the power of the urban and military aristocracy and patronized the Church and the arts. Despite a notable victory over the Rus in the Bosporus in 1043, both the army and the empire were weakened during his reign. He died at Constantinople in 1055.

Further Reading

Angold, Michael, The Byzantine Empire, 1025–1204: A Political History, London and New York: Longman, 1984, especially pp. 36–48, 59–62

Cormack, Robin, Writing in Gold: Byzantine Society and its Icons, London: George Philip, 1985, especially pp. 182–94 and 211–14

Lemerle, Paul, *Cinq Etudes sur le XIe siècle byzantin*, Paris: Centre National de la Recherche Scientifique, 1977, especially pp. 195–248, 268–71, and 285–90

Mouriki, Doula, *The Mosaics of Nea Moni on Chios*, vol. 1, Athens: Commercial Bank of Greece, 1985, especially pp. 21–29

Ohnsorge, Werner, *Abendland und Byzanz*, Darmstadt: Gentner, 1958, especially pp. 317–32

Ohnsorge, Werner, *Ost-Rom und der Westen*, Darmstadt: Wissenschaftliche Buchgesellschaft, 1983, especially pp. 207–18

Psellos, Michael, *The Chronographia*, translated by E.R.A. Sewter, London: Routledge, and New Haven, Connecticut: Yale University Press, 1953; revised edition as *Fourteen Byzantine Rulers*, Harmondsworth and Baltimore: Penguin, 1966

Constantine XI Palaiologos 1405–1453

Emperor

Constantine was the fourth of the surviving six sons of the emperor Manuel II Palaiologos (1391–1425). His mother was the Serbian princess Helena Dragaš, and he alone among her sons took the name of Dragases as well as Palaiologos.

As a dynastic younger son he bore the title of despot (*despotes*). Although such younger sons were also normally given territorial appanages, during his father's lifetime Constantine never received any youthful assignment comparable to those of his elder brothers, Theodore (the Morea) and Andronikos (Thessalonica). Instead, he grew up in the capital, where he became particularly close to his eldest brother, the heir and successor to the throne, John VIII (1425–48). During their father's incapacity in his last two years, Constantine became his brother's trusted deputy. Thus, when John travelled to Venice and Hungary to plead for western aid, the 18-year-old Constantine served as his regent (1423–24), and it was he who signed a treaty (February 1424) that ended the recent outbreak of hostilities with the Turkish sultan Murad II.

The discontent of their brother Theodore prompted John to designate Constantine as his replacement, but Theodore, who was contemplating retiring to a monastery, suddenly changed his mind. Instead, after the death of their father (July 1425) and the formal accession of his brother, Constantine was given a small appanage of coastal territory around the capital extending from the Black Sea to the Sea of Marmora. But by 1427 he was transferred after all into the volatile sphere of the Morea, the one region in which Byzantium's arms were successful (against remnants of Latin rule in the Peloponnese) and its culture was flourishing. In concert with his brothers, Constantine participated in the seizures of Glarentza (1427) and Patras (1429–30) from their Latin lords. In the process, he acquired a Latin bride, Maddalena Tocco, as his first (if short-lived) wife. His youngest brother Thomas, by inheriting in 1432 the lands of his own Latin father-in-law, completed the Byzantine recovery of virtually the entire Peloponnese. Thereafter, Theodore, Constantine, and Thomas shared the rule of this region in an unstable division, which nearly dissolved into fighting in 1435 as a result of jealousies between the first two brothers.

In 1437 Constantine was summoned back to Constantinople as the emperor's most trusted deputy. While John VIII was in Italy (1437–40) attending the Council of Ferrara-Florence in order to negotiate Church union, Constantine served ably as his regent. After his brother's return, he contracted a second (and again short-lived) Latin marriage, to Caterina Gattilusio of the ruling family of Lesbos. He returned to the Morea in 1441, but was recalled to Constantinople the following year to help John resist an attempted coup by the most unstable and untrustworthy of their brothers, Demetrios. In the aftermath, newly shuffled assignments allowed Theodore – jealous of Constantine and anxious to be closer to the capital – to take up the Marmora appanage, while Constantine assumed control of the Byzantine Morea.

In 1443, therefore, Constantine took up his post in Mistra, sharing the Peloponnese with Thomas, who was ensconced in his Latin legacy in the northern regions. In the face of both internal and external difficulties, Constantine did his best to keep his territories secure from the Turks, though not always with success, while presiding over the one Byzantine region where cultural vitality and a new stirring of proud Hellenism were in full cry. Meanwhile, disillusioned by the stalemate of Church union and by the failure of hoped-for western aid, worn down in spirit and body, the emperor John died in October 1448. Ironically, his eldest brother, Theodore, who was awaiting the event nearby, himself died four months earlier, in June. Agitations in the capital on behalf of the irresponsible Demetrios were kept in control by their mother, the respected dowager empress Helena, thus clearing the path for the successor whom John himself had preferred. When the news of John's death reached Mistra, Constantine was secure in his rights. Nevertheless, he had himself crowned emperor at Mistra on 6 January 1449, before proceeding to the capital, deliberately avoiding the traditional rite of proper coronation in Hagia Sophia that would have involved his taking a stand on the divisive issue of union with Rome.

Accepted as the new – and, to be the last – Byzantine emperor, Constantine faced the suspicions of the increasingly outspoken opponents of union by pursuing mediation and postponing any commitment to it, allowing its formal proclamation only at the eleventh hour, in December 1452. His immediate task was to find allies and aid among Christian powers both eastern and western, which involved much busy but largely futile diplomacy. The urgency increased with the accession in 1451 of the new Turkish sultan, Mehmet II, whose determination to achieve the long-anticipated conquest of Constantinople soon became evident.

With ludicrously outnumbered forces and only token help from western Christian powers, Constantine prepared for the Turkish onslaught, which began on 6 April 1453. For more than seven weeks the attackers battered at the walls, which the defenders manned with stubborn courage. Constantine resisted all temptations to make terms or seek his own advantage and did his best to keep the disparate elements of Byzantines and Latins, of pro- and anti-unionists, reasonably united. When the final assault broke through on the morning of 29 May, Constantine flung himself into the last fighting and died as a common soldier.

For all our sources on the fall of Constantinople, there is no indisputable account of Constantine's death. Stories vary as to whether or not his body was ever found and, if so, what became of it. Almost immediately, however, tales began to circulate about his fate, embellished over the ensuing centuries: reports of a secret tomb, of his preserved possessions (especially a sword), and of his sleeping until a miraculous day of awakening to reclaim his realm. Both during and after the Tourkokratia, he became a symbol to be conjured with by Greek leaders who sought to revive Hellenic sovereignty and avenge the Turkish conquest.

Constantine's melodramatic death as the martyr of expiring Byzantium has inevitably coloured any objective assessment of his character. With no reliable image of him surviving, we do not even know what he looked like. His friend and retainer, the historian Sphrantzes, praised him liberally, and less biased observers seem to have found him an honourable man, a brave soldier, and a dutiful leader, perhaps not very sophisticated, but pragmatic and earnest. His personal feelings about Church union are unknown, but he seems to have viewed the matter in practical terms, with little concern for theological partisanship, if with presumed Orthodox loyalty. Although he was a genealogical mix of Greek, Serbian, and Italian strains, his ethnic sensibilities would probably be different from our own, and he would have regarded himself as a "Roman" (*rhomaios*). He has inevitably become, however, a symbol for latterly Greek national pride and mythology, a paragon of Hellenic heroism – as witness the fanciful statue of him, of which copies today stand in a square in the new town of Mistra and before the metropolitan cathedral of Athens.

JOHN W. BARKER

See also Constantinople (Fall of), Palaiologos Family

Biography

Born in Constantinople in 1405, the fourth son of the emperor Manuel II, Constantine grew up in the capital and deputized for his brother, the future emperor John VIII. In 1427 he moved to the Peloponnese which he ruled jointly at first with his two brothers Theodore and Thomas and after 1443 with Thomas alone. In 1448 John VIII died, predeceased by Theodore, leaving the throne to Constantine. He was the last Byzantine emperor and died fighting as the city fell to the Ottomans on 29 May 1453.

Further Reading

Carroll, Margaret, "Constantine XI: Some Problems of Image" in *Maistor: Classical, Byzantine, and Renaissance Studies for Robert Browning*, edited by Ann Moffatt, Canberra: Australian Association for Byzantine Studies, 1984

Chrysostomos, "Constantine XI", *Patristic and Byzantine Review*, 3 (1984): pp. 18–38

Kolias, George, "Constantin Paléologue: le dernier défenseur de Constantinople" in *Le Cinq-centième Anniversaire de la Prise de Constantinople, 1453–1953*, Athens: L'Hellénisme Contemporain, 1953

Mijatović, Čedomilj, *Constantine, the Last Emperor of the Greeks, 1448–1453: The Conquest of Constantinople by the Turks*, London: Low Marston, 1892, reprinted Chicago: Argonaut, 1968

Nicol, Donald M., *The Immortal Emperor: The Life and Legend of Constantine Palaiologos, Last Emperor of the Romans*, Cambridge and New York: Cambridge University Press, 1992

Nicol, Donald M., *The Last Centuries of Byzantium, 1261–1453*, 2nd edition, Cambridge and New York: Cambridge University Press, 1993

Pears, Edwin, *The Destruction of the Greek Empire and the Story of the Capture of Constantinople by the Turks*, London and New York: Longman, 1903; reprinted New York: Greenwood Press, 1968

Philippides, Marios, *Constantine XI Dragas-Palaeologus: A Biography of the Last Greek Emperor*, New Rochelle, New York: Caratzas, forthcoming

Sphrantzes, George *The Fall of the Byzantine Empire: A Chronicle*, edited and translated by Marios Philippides, Amherst: University of Massachusetts Press, 1980

Runciman, Steven, *The Fall of Constantinople 1453*, Cambridge: Cambridge University Press, 1965

Runciman, Steven, *Mistra: Byzantine Capital of the Peloponnese*, London: Thames and Hudson, 1980

Zakythinos, Denis A., *Le Despotat grec de Morée*, revised by Chryssa Maltézou, 2 vols, London: Variorum, 1975

Constantinople

The city of Byzantion or Byzantium, later called Constantinople and then Istanbul, was founded on a peninsula immediately south of the Golden Horn on the European side of Bosporus. Although this peninsula is bisected by the river Lycus, it is not well provided with water supplies. However, the narrow straits upon which the city was located were, and remain, an important trade route and enable control of sea traffic between the Aegean and the Black Sea.

Nearly a millennium after its founding in the 7th century BC (see the article on Byzantium), the city rose to new prominence in the early 4th century AD. In AD 326 – after considering several alternatives – the emperor Constantine I ("the Great") chose Byzantium as a new capital for the Roman empire. The city was then rapidly developed on a scale befitting a Roman capital, and once again new walls (the Constantinian walls) enclosed a much larger area. The city also now encompassed an area across the Golden Horn opposite the old Byzantium, Galata. This new city, formally established in AD 330, was the "New Rome" or "Constantinople" – the city of Constantine.

During the 4th and 5th centuries Constantinople continued to grow in size, and walls enclosing a much larger area were erected under Theodosius II in the 5th century (the Theodosian walls). These rendered the city virtually impregnable to land attack, and remained the principal defences throughout the Byzantine period.

Byzantine Constantinople reached a height of prosperity and sophistication between the reigns of Anastasius and Justinian I in the late 5th and 6th centuries. This phase of the city's development may serve to give an impression of its Byzantine topography, although of course the city was continually changing. Even within Justinian I's reign large areas of the city centre had to be rebuilt following the Nike riots in 532.

The principal imperial residence in late 5th- and early 6th-century Constantinople was the Great Palace. This was a sprawling complex of courtyards, halls, pavilions, and gardens, occupying much of the southeast of the city. Immediately to its north stood Hagia Sophia, the cathedral, with the palace of the patriarch (the head of the Byzantine Orthodox Church) adjacent. To the southwest of the Great Palace was the public chariot-racing arena known as the Hippodrome, and to the north of Hagia Sophia stood the city's original cathedral, Hagia Eirene. The Augusteum, a paved

Constantinople: the Golden Gate and Seven Towers Gate on the walls of Theodosius, the principal landward defences of the city

square, stood between the main entrance of the Hippodrome and Hagia Sophia, with the Senate House on its east, adjacent to the Great Palace. From a monumental milestone (the Milion) in this square, the city's main street (the Mese) ran westward through a series of four large paved fora, on the Roman model. The Mese was lined by porticos, and the fora were surrounded by porticos and adorned with monumental columns (notably the columns of Constantine and Arcadius), elaborate entrances, and statues.

As it approached the Constantinian walls, the Mese divided into a Y-shape, with branches heading for the northwest and southwest of the Theodosian walls. The northerly branch passed by the cruciform church of the Holy Apostles, the second most important church in the city and the burial place of the early Byzantine emperors, including both Constantine the Great and Justinian I. The branch to the southwest may have divided again in a Y-shape, to pass through the Second Military Gate in the Theodosian wall, and through the Golden Gate, the city's ceremonial entrance.

Outside the Theodosian walls, in addition to numerous suburbs, rural palaces, and monasteries, were the long aqueducts which fed the city's water supply. In the city, water was stored in both open and underground cisterns, of which the most famous is the underground Basilica Cistern (Yerebatan Saray) close to the Augusteum. Three large open cisterns – those of St Mocius, Aspar, and Aetius – were situated between the Theodosian and Constantinian walls. Another defensive wall (the Long Walls) enclosed the city's immediate hinterland.

Early Byzantine Constantinople contained numerous churches (some of which survive as buildings today, such as Sts Sergius and Bacchus) and monasteries, such as that of St John Stoudios, whose church is the oldest standing Christian religious building in the city. There were also the public buildings which one would expect of a major Roman city in the long-urbanized east Roman provinces, such as the baths of Zeuxippus near the Hippodrome, and Christian charitable institutions, such as the hospital of St Samson adjacent to Hagia Eirene. In addition to the Great Palace, there were other imperial palaces in the city, notably that at the Blachernae in the extreme northwest by the Theodosian walls.

There were also palatial houses belonging to aristocrats. Some were as grand as the most elaborate Roman villas of the 4th century AD, as is shown by the excavated buildings usually identified as the palace of Antiochus and Lausos close to the Hippodrome. Aristocrats also endowed churches and monasteries: the most lavish known example being the excavated church of St Polyeuktos (Saraçhane). Thus, while Constantinople was a major population centre – with perhaps half a million inhabitants in the early 6th century – and a trading port, its urban topography must have been dominated by public buildings, churches, monasteries, and palaces, at least within the Constantinian walls.

This magnificent phase of the city's history is thought to have come to an end in the 7th century. An intermittent, but devastating, plague beginning in the 530s – combined with increasing military, social, religious, and economic problems – led to dramatic urban decline. The exact extent to which these factors brought about the desertion and dereliction of the city and its public buildings is unclear, not least because of the difficulties in reconstructing urban change in 7th- and 8th-century

Constantinople in general. Nevertheless, throughout almost all of this period Constantinople remained the seat of imperial government, and was both the centre of the Orthodox Church administration and the principal Byzantine trading centre. Some building certainly continued, as is evident in the 8th-century reconstruction of Hagia Eirene.

Constantinople seems to have recovered after the late 8th century. Populations from the Balkans were relocated in the city and building projects initiated. Under emperor Theophilos in the 9th century, for example, new palace buildings and churches were constructed and the walls refurbished. The middle Byzantine city once again was a flourishing centre of intellectual and artistic life and commerce, and probably grew in size. It was adorned with a large number of churches, many of which still survive as buildings today. But the city remained somewhat smaller than it had once been and had lost some of its early Byzantine facilities. Nevertheless, new buildings of this period, such as the Myrelaion (Bodrum Camii) and the Nea Ekklesia, now lost, attest to the vigour of activity in the 9th-century city. This was maintained into the 11th century, with churches such as St Mary Peribleptos and Christ Pantepoptes being built on imperial commission.

In the 10th century Western (notably Venetian) trading communities were established inside the walls. This led to the city's trade coming under the control of non-Byzantines. The Genoese acquired concessions in Galata, which later developed a semiautonomous character with its governor sent from Italy. These developments were to play a central role in the later Byzantine history of Constantinople.

Constantinople remained in Byzantine hands continuously until 1204, when it was captured and sacked by the Fourth Crusade. Like all Byzantine lands captured by the crusaders, the city was divided among the westerners. The Venetians took three-eighths of the city, the remainder going to Count Baldwin of Flanders. The burned and ruinous shell of the city was recaptured in 1261, when it once again became the capital of the, now much reduced, Byzantine empire.

After the reconquest the Byzantine emperors and aristocracy attempted to restore and rebuild the city, as is well evidenced in the magnificent 14th-century decorations at St Saviour in Chora (Kariye Camii). But, while Hagia Sophia survived, many of the grandest buildings of the past – such as the Great Palace and Hippodrome – were abandoned and in ruins. The late Byzantine imperial palace was located on the walls, in the area of the earlier Blachernae, and new structures, such as that today known as Tekfur Saray, were added. Imperial burials were no longer made at the church of the Holy Apostles but in churches elsewhere in the city, notably at the church of the Pantocrator (Zeyrek Camii) and the monastery of Constantine Lips (Fenari Isa Camii). However, most of the city lay beneath fields and the rubble of collapsed structures, while occupation centred on much smaller areas. Thus, late Byzantine Constantinople was not merely a much smaller city, but one which bore little resemblance to the city of Constantine or Justinian – except in the survival of churches and the misunderstood monuments of earlier generations. Even so, late Byzantine Constantinople was the centre of Greek-speaking culture, as well as of Byzantine architecture and art.

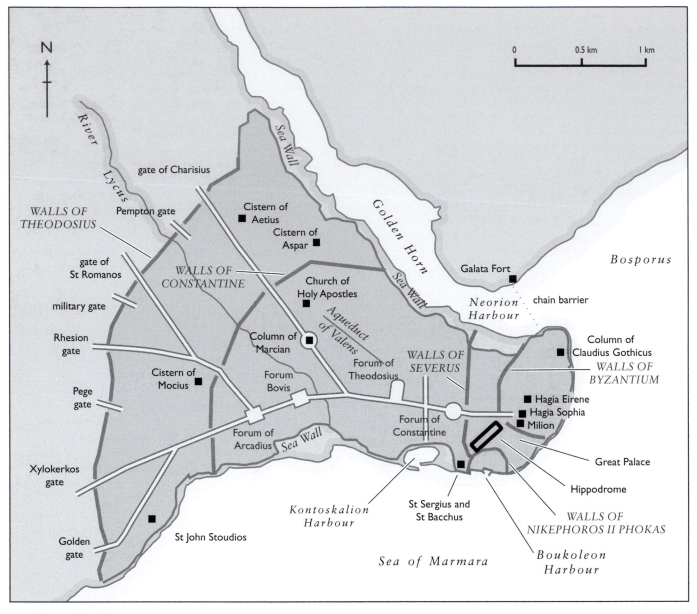

N

gate of Charisius

WALLS OF
THEODOSIUS   Pempton gate

Sea Wall

Cistern of
Aetius

Cistern of
Aspar

Golden Horn

Sea Wall

Galata Fort

Bosporus

gate of
St Romanos

WALLS OF
CONSTANTINE

Church of
Holy Apostles

Neorion
Harbour   chain barrier

military gate

Rhesion
gate

Column of
Marcian

Aqueduct
of Valens

Forum of
Theodosius   WALLS OF
SEVERUS

Column of
Claudius Gothicus
WALLS OF
BYZANTIUM

Pege
gate

Cistern of
Mocius

Forum
Bovis

Forum of
Constantine   Hagia Eirene
Hagia Sophia
Milion

Xylokerkos
gate

Forum of
Arcadius   Sea Wall

Great Palace

Hippodrome

Golden
gate

St John Stoudios

Kontoskalion
Harbour

St Sergius and
St Bacchus

Sea of Marmara

WALLS OF
NIKEPHOROS II PHOKAS

Boukoleon
Harbour

River Lycus

13. Constantinople

In 1453 the Turkish army led by Sultan Mehmet II (often called "the Conqueror") began an extended siege of Constantinople. Using batteries of large cannon – a weapon against which the Theodosian walls offered only limited protection – a sustained bombardment of the city was combined with continuous land and sea attack. The inhabitants of Constantinople, both Byzantine and Genoese, fought heroically against overwhelming odds. Despite appeals, no other western help arrived and the city came under attack from all sides. On 29 May Turkish troops entered the land walls and Giustiniani, the Genoese commander, was fatally wounded in the ensuing fighting. The Byzantine and Genoese resistance began to fail and many fled the city by sea as the Turkish army entered in ever greater numbers. Although the emperor Constantine XI Palaiologos was last seen fighting at the walls, no convincing account of his death was recorded and his body was never recovered, giving rise to much speculation about his

fate. Whatever the fate of the emperor, the siege was over within hours and by afternoon the city was in Turkish hands.

Sultan Mehmet rode to Hagia Sophia and gave orders that it was to be converted to a mosque. This was carried out in time for him to attend the first Muslim service in the Byzantine cathedral the following Friday. The capture of the city was followed by several days of extreme brutality, in which the city was stripped of its remaining treasures, its able-bodied inhabitants enslaved, and many atrocities committed against them.

The city was now even more ruinous and depopulated. This presented Mehmet with a problem, as the Turkish sultan wished to be seen as heir to the Caesars. He therefore set about repopulating Constantinople with groups from other parts of the Ottoman empire – including Greeks, Armenians, and Turks. He restored the Orthodox Patriarchate, both for symbolic reasons and as a means of governing the Orthodox citizens of the Ottoman empire. With Hagia Sophia in use as a mosque, the Patriarchate was located at the church of the Pammakaristos (Fethiye Camii) until 1586, before moving in 1601 to the rebuilt and much smaller church of St George in the Phanar district, where it still remains today.

In the following centuries of Ottoman rule, the urban topography was further Islamicized by the confiscation of many remaining churches and the construction of monumental imperial mosques, religious buildings, palaces, and tombs. The Greeks initially had only their churches as centres for communal life, although only one of these (the late Byzantine St Mary of the Mongols) remained continuously in Greek hands since before 1453. Nevertheless, during the Ottoman period specifically Greek-language schools and cultural institutions developed. Although under Ottoman rule the Greeks were only one of numerous population groups in the city, there were many of them. About 40 Greek churches existed in 18th-century Constantinople, and through the Patriarchate and the activities of scholars and clerics a sense of national identity and the continuity of Byzantine culture were maintained in the city. The wealth of merchants and officials, especially those of the Phanar district surrounding the Patriarchate, formed the core of the lay community. During the 19th century, in particular, the Greek-speaking community of the city was a vibrant cultural and intellectual centre within the broader Hellenic world.

This situation continued until the 20th century. The lot of the Constantinopolitan Greeks changed after World War I, first due to the Graeco-Turkish war of 1919–23, and later due to Greek emigration, and the Turkish immigration into the city, which has grown rapidly in size since 1900. The secularization of Turkey under Atatürk enabled the Byzantine heritage to be partially claimed by the state: for instance, Hagia Sophia was changed from a mosque into a museum. One other notable 20th-century development has been the change of the city's official name from Constantinople to Istanbul. Overall, while both the Orthodox Patriarchate and Greek-speaking community remain up to the present, the Greek community of the city is now reduced to just a few thousand people.

KEN DARK

See also Patriarchate of Constantinople

Summary

Originally founded as Byzantion by colonists from Megara in the 7th century BC, the city was of no particular significance until AD 326 when the emperor Constantine the Great chose it as the site of a new capital for the Roman empire. Perhaps at the height of its prosperity in the late 5th and 6th centuries when the population numbered about 500,000. Venetian trading communities were admitted in the 10th century. It was sacked by the Fourth Crusade in 1204 but reconquered in 1261. Fell to the Ottomans in 1453 but remained a cosmopolitan city and seat of the Orthodox Patriarchate, as it still is today.

Further Reading

Bardill, "The Palace of Lausus and Nearby Monuments in Constantinople: A Topographical Study", *American Journal of Archaeology*, 101 (1997): pp. 67–95

Batur, A. (editor), *Dünya Kenti: Istanbul* [Istanbul: World City], Istanbul, 1996

Çeçen, Kazim, *The Longest Roman Water Supply Line*, Istanbul: Türkiye Sinai Kalkinma Bankasi, 1996

Dagron, Gilbert, *Naissance d'une capitale: Constantinople et ses institutions de 330 à 451*, Paris: Presses Universitaires de France, 1974

Dark, K. and F. Özgümüù, "Rescue Archaeology in Istanbul", *Minerva*, 10/5 (1999): pp. 22–25

Dark, K., "The Byzantine Church and Monastery of St Mary Peribleptos in Istanbul", *Burlington Magazine*, 141/1160 (1999): pp. 656–64

Ebersolt, Jean, *Mission archéologique de Constantinople*, Paris: Leroux, 1921

Ebersolt, Jean, *Constantinople: recueil d'études d'archéologie et d'histoire*, Paris: Maisonneuve, 1951

Firatli, Nezih, *La Sculpture byzantine figurée au Musée Archéologique d'Istanbul*, Paris: Maisonneuve, 1990

Grabar, André, *Sculptures byzantines de Constantinople, IVe–Xe siècle*, Paris: Maisonneuve, 1963

Harrison, Martin, *A Temple for Byzantium: The Discovery and Excavation of Anicia Juliana's Palace-Church in Istanbul*, London: Miller, 1989

Janin, R., *Constantinople byzantine: développement urbain et répertoire topographique*, 2nd edition, Paris: Institut Français d'Etudes Byzantines, 1964

Janin, R., *La Géographie ecclésiastique de l'empire byzantin*, part 1: *Le Siège de Constantinople et le patriarcat oecuménique*, vol. 3: *Les Eglises et les monastères*, Paris: Institut Français d'Etudes Byzantines, 1969

Krautheimer, Richard (with Slobodan Ćurčić), *Early Christian and Byzantine Architecture*, 4th edition, New Haven and London: Yale University Press, 1986

Kuban, D., *Istanbul: An Urban History*, Istanbul, 1996

Magdalino, Paul, *Constantinople médiévale: études sur l'évolution des structures urbaines*, Paris: Boccard, 1996

Mango, Cyril, *The Brazen House: A Study of the Vestibule of the Imperial Palace of Constantinople*, Copenhagen: Munksgaard, 1959

Mango, Cyril, *Le Développement urbain de Constantinople, IVe–VIIe siècles*, Paris: Boccard, 1985

Mango, Cyril, *Byzantine Architecture*, New York: Rizzoli, 1985; London: Faber, 1986

Mango, Cyril, *Studies on Constantinople*, Aldershot, Hampshire: Variorum, 1993

Mango, Cyril and Gilbert Dagron (editors), *Constantinople and its Hinterland*, Aldershot, Hampshire: Variorum, 1995

Mathews, Thomas F., *The Early Churches of Constantinople: Architecture and Liturgy*, University Park: Pennsylvania State University Press, 1971

Mathews, Thomas F., *The Byzantine Churches of Istanbul: A Photographic Survey*, University Park: Pennsylvania State University Press, 1976

Müller-Wiener, Wolfgang, *Bildlexikon zur Topographie Istanbuls*, Tübingen: Wasmuth, 1977

Van Millingen, Alexander, *Byzantine Constantinople: The Walls of the City and Adjoining Historical Sites*, London: John Murray, 1899

Constantinople, Fall of 1453

Menaced and attacked time and time again, Constantinople had stood firm over the centuries – protected, its inhabitants believed, by no less a person than the Virgin Mary herself. Though its territories might be overrun, so long as the capital could hold out and the attackers be repulsed, the Byzantine empire could be safely reconstituted. The brutal storming and capture of the city in 1204 by the forces of the Fourth Crusade badly jolted Byzantine confidence. But, in a reversal of the past

Fall of Constantinople: 19th-century view of the siege of 1453 by Panayiotis Zographos, one of a series of scenes depicting the War of Independence commissioned by general Makriyannis in the 1830s

situation, the Byzantine world survived the loss of its capital. Out of its fragments came the successor state of Nicaea, which in 1261 was able to recover the battered city from the Latins and thereby vindicate Byzantine integrity.

Recovery of Constantinople in fact involved a burden of imperial pretension that could not be sustained by a regime of limited resources and weakened position in a rapidly changing world. Under the dynasty of the Palaiologoi the restored Byzantine state became a minor local power, ever more at the mercy of its neighbours. Losses first to the expansionistic Serbians and then to the aggressive Ottoman Turks reduced Byzantium during the 14th century to a rump state, holding a few islands and the Peloponnesian Morea but otherwise only small areas around Constantinople itself. The Turks even began a desultory siege of the city in 1394, which was broken only by the unexpected defeat and captivity of the Turkish sultan Bayezid I by Tamerlane at the Battle of Ancyra (1402).

Constantinople's ensuing breathing spell ended when sultan Murad II (1421–51) launched an attack on the city in the summer of 1422, during which cannon were first used to attack the walls. Byzantine diplomacy caused Murad's distraction and withdrawal, but stories of miraculous appearances by the Virgin strengthened anew popular convictions of the city's inviolability. Busying himself thereafter with rounding out the Turkish conquests in both Europe and Asia, Murad II made no further attempts on Constantinople. It fell to his son and successor, Mehmet II "the Conqueror" (1451–81), to claim the

city that was the necessary guarantee and capital of the empire that the Turks had been recreating out of the old Byzantine world.

Emperor John VIII (1421/25–48) had sought help from the Latin west, even at the terrible cost of submitting the Orthodox Church to papal domination and doctrinal compromise, but such efforts had proved futile, only leaving his population embittered and disillusioned. There was considerable sentiment among the clergy of Constantinople against resisting the Turks, not only out of hatred for the Latins but also out of a logical desire to reunite their ecclesiastical world now largely in Turkish hands – "better the turban of the Turk in the City than the Latin mitre" went a slogan of the day.

When Constantine XI arrived in Constantinople in March 1449 to become the last Byzantine emperor, the city was in wretched state, many of its areas desolate and its population reduced perhaps to fewer than 50,000 souls. Staving off any commitment to the divisive issue of Church union with Rome, Constantine conducted stumbling diplomatic efforts to win help. Meanwhile, carefully securing himself from any other distractions, sultan Mehmet took the provocative step of building a massive new fortress (Rumeli Hisar) up the Bosporus on the European side, as a staging point from which to menace the city.

Constantine found the Venetian community willing to cooperate, but the neighbouring Genoese colony of Pera on the Galata side of the Golden Horn remained officially neutral.

Despite promises from the pope and others, contributions of aid from the Latin west were pathetically minimal. A small troop of archers accompanied cardinal Isidore of Kiev, who arrived in December 1452 in order to proclaim Church union. A private force of some 700 under the Genoese adventurer Giovanni Giustiniani Longo arrived in late January 1453 and he was given command of the defences by Constantine.

Mehmet finally began his attack on 6 April 1453. His forces have been reckoned as numbering between 80,000 and 100,000 men, plus a fleet of 120 galleys, and augmented by a set of fearsome new cannon and bombards. The Byzantines had fewer than 7000 warriors both domestic and allied, and some 26 warships, plus a few small cannon on the walls – themselves unevenly maintained but still formidable.

Despite preliminary battering by the sultan's cannon, the walls held against the first Turkish assault, and all hands settled down for a prolonged and bitter siege. Concentrated on a vulnerable area of the land walls in the Lycus valley, the Turkish artillery inflicted terrible damage, which the defenders desperately repaired as best they could. The Turkish fleet failed to penetrate the harbour of the Golden Horn or to block the arrival of some Genoese grain ships, which brought hope to the defenders. But then, on 22 April, the Turks secured access to the Golden Horn upstream by the bold feat of hauling ships overland from the Bosporus. Turkish efforts at undermining the land walls were detected and neutralized by countermining. The fighting dragged on, ever more ferocious as successive Turkish assaults failed. The incessant artillery pounding sapped morale as well as the fortifications, while the hoped-for relief never came.

There was, in fact, a real possibility that the siege would fail, and some of Mehmet's advisers counselled withdrawal. That would only have postponed Constantinople's fate, not altered it, but it would have humiliated the sultan. He decided on one final effort, planned for 29 May. The night before, the Greek and Latin defenders shared a last communion in Hagia Sophia. The attack began in the earliest hours of the morning, with successive waves of assault driven back until, by dawn, Mehmet sent in his crack Janissaries. As they began to break through, first in the Blachernai area and then at the St Romanos Gate, Giustiniani Longo received a fatal wound and had himself carried away. This spread panic among the defenders as the Turks began to pour into the city. Constantine bravely led the final resistance and was killed in the fray. By midday the city was in Turkish hands, and there began three days of pillaging and violence allowed his troops by the sultan.

Now capital of the new empire on the Bosporus, that of the Ottoman Turks, Constantinople was once again to be a great ruling city, but no longer a Greek one. The event officially ended the moribund Byzantine state, of course, even though it was not until 1461 that Mehmet's final reduction of the Morea and his capture of the separate Greek regime of Trebizond completed the conquest of the Hellenic world. But the great (and extensively recorded) drama of 1453 readily assumed symbolic status.

In grand terms Constantinople's capture is sometimes taken to mark the terminal point of the Middle Ages. For the Hellenic tradition in particular, it initiates the long ordeal of the Tourkokratia and a new phase in the defining of Greek identity. Long a subject of enduring lamentation and pain in Greek expression, the fall of Constantinople became a verdict to be reversed some day. A strong neo-Byzantine dimension of the modern Greek mentality nurtured the so-called Great Idea (*Megali Idea*) which, well into the 20th century, imagined the Greek recovery of Constantinople as the ultimate goal and fulfilment of Hellenic destiny. This mentality still lurks below the surface of enduring Graeco-Turkish frictions down to the present.

JOHN W. BARKER

Further Reading

Babinger, Franz, *Mehmed the Conqueror and His Time*, Princeton, New Jersey: Princeton University Press, 1978

Le Cinq-centième Anniversaire de la prise de Constantinople, 1453–1953, Athens: L'Hellénisme Contemporain, 1953

Imber, Colin, *The Ottoman Empire, 1300–1481*, Istanbul: Isis, 1990

Inalcik, Halil, *The Ottoman Empire: The Classical Age, 1300–1600*, London: Weidenfeld and Nicolson, 1973

Melville Jones, J.R. (translator), *The Siege of Constantinople 1453: Seven Contemporary Accounts*, Amsterdam: Hakkert, 1972

Mijatović, Čedomilj, *Constantine, the Last Emperor of the Greeks, 1448–1453: The Conquest of Constantinople by the Turks*, London: Low Marston, 1892, reprinted Chicago: Argonaut, 1968

Nicol, Donald M., *The Immortal Emperor: The Life and Legend of Constantine Palaiologos, Last Emperor of the Romans*, Cambridge and New York: Cambridge University Press, 1992

Nicol, Donald M., *The Last Centuries of Byzantium, 1261–1453*, 2nd edition, Cambridge and New York: Cambridge University Press, 1993

Ostrogorsky, George, *History of the Byzantine State*, 2nd edition, Oxford: Blackwell, 1968; New Brunswick, New Jersey: Rutgers University Press, 1969

Pears, Edwin, *The Destruction of the Greek Empire and the Story of the Capture of Constantinople by the Turks*, London and New York: Longmans, 1903; reprinted New York: Greenwood Press, 1968

Philippides, Marios, *Constantine XI Dragas-Palaeologus: A Biography of the Last Greek Emperor*, New Rochelle, New York: Caratzas, forthcoming

Runciman, Steven, *The Fall of Constantinople, 1453*, Cambridge: Cambridge University Press, 1965

Setton, Kenneth M., *The Papacy and the Levant, 1204–1571*, vol. 2: *The Fifteenth Century*, Philadelphia: American Philosophical Society, 1978

Shaw, Stanford, *History of the Ottoman Empire and Modern Turkey*, vol. 1: *Empire of the Gazis: The Rise and Decline of the Ottoman Empire, 1280–1808*, Cambridge and New York: Cambridge University Press, 1976

Stacton, David, *The Crescent and the Cross: The Fall of Byzantium: May 1453* (as David Dereksen), New York: Putnam, 1964; as *The World on the Last Day: The Sack of Constantinople by the Turks, May 29, 1453: Its Causes and Consequences*, London: Faber, 1965

Vacalopoulos, Apostolos E., *Origins of the Greek Nation: The Byzantine Period, 1204–1461*, New Brunswick, New Jersey: Rutgers University Press, 1970

Constantinople, Sack of 1204

The sack of Constantinople by forces of the Fourth Crusade took place on the three days following the capture of the city on Monday, 12 April 1204.

The decision to divert the crusade to Constantinople had been taken at Zara on the Adriatic in early 1203 and had been confirmed in May when Alexios Angelos, the son of the deposed emperor Isaac II Angelos, had joined the army at Corfu. The decision had led to disputes within the crusading army, but the arguments for the diversion were sound, if some of the difficulties were skated over in the debates. Alexios had promised the sum of 200,000 marks, a Byzantine reinforcement of 10,000 men for one year, and thereafter, for the term of his life, a garrison of 500 men to defend the Holy Land. In addition, on ascending the throne, he would bring the Greek Church into canonical obedience to Rome. The crusading army had arrived at Constantinople in July 1203 and effected the restoration of Isaac Angelos and made Alexios joint emperor. Alexios was unable to fulfil his extravagant promises and Graeco-Latin relations had deteriorated. In August and November 1203 two fires started by Latins had caused much damage to residential property in the city, including the destruction of the mansion owned by Choniates. In March 1204 the Crusaders were in desperate straits, able neither to go on their way nor to stay without Greek support and provisioning. It was desperation that led to the plan to attack the city and on 12 April, much to their surprise, they managed to capture Constantinople, an enterprise that substantial Arab, Russian, and Varangian attacks in the past had failed to achieve.

As was traditional with a city captured by attack, the victorious forces were allowed three days of pillaging, but on this occasion it was to be looting limited by rules. Details of the horrendous events involved are given by the Greek civil servant and historian Niketas Choniates in his moving account of his own and his family's experiences in those three days. Western eyewitness accounts largely ignore the accumulated hatred and greed, the pillage and rape that accompanied their capture of the city. As the victors, surprised by their own success and seeing in it the hand of God judging the arrogant Greeks, the crusaders rapidly ran out of control and blatantly ignored the guidelines laid down by the crusading leadership prior to the assault on the city that women and churches should be left inviolate. The Latin commentators were clearly ashamed of the acts of their fellows. The crusading leadership took firm measures to re-establish control on 15 April by hanging looters, but it took some months before the details were reported to the pope in Rome. No Latin source even hints at rape and only one source mentions the looting of churches. The chronicle of Robert of Clari suggests that churches were indeed spared, yet he himself donated ecclesiastical spoils to the abbey of Corbie on his return to France. The sacking of the city was almost immediately condemned by Greek and Latin authorities in terms that were subsequently used to characterize the crusade itself and later Greek and Latin relationships in general. Niketas thought it better if Constantinople had been captured by the infidel rather than by these western Christians, drawing unflattering comparisons between the crusaders in 1204 and Saladin's restrained behaviour in Jerusalem in 1187. Innocent III, although his first letters referred to the capture of the city as an act of God, when he learned of details of the sack, condemned it: "those who should have used their swords against the infidel have covered them with Christian blood."

There has been much scholarly controversy as to what was taken and how much, a debate best summarized by Queller and Madden. Robert of Clari stated that neither Charlemagne nor Alexander had seen so much booty in one city and that there was more wealth in Constantinople than the world's 40 next richest cities combined. The plunder was to be gathered under guard into three churches in the city, but it was clear that much was held back by individual looters. The chronicler Geoffrey de Villehardouin records that a total of 300,000 silver marks was thus collected together, although he estimated that the total booty pillaged from Constantinople was in the region of 800,000 marks, a good 63 per cent kept by individuals. Most of these escaped detection and only a few were caught and hanged, like the unnamed knight recorded as belonging to the retinue of the Compte de Saint-Pol. For the poor among the crusading hosts expecting much from the wealthy city of Constantinople this was a source of great disappointment. In the final division each knight received 20 marks, each sergeant and cleric 10 marks, and each soldier 5 marks.

Constantinople was the richest repository of Christian relics, housing the Crown of Thorns, pieces of the True Cross, the hair of the Virgin, the head and arm of John the Baptist, as well as various parts of the apostles and other saints. These were unashamedly looted by western ecclesiastics such as Martin, abbot of Halberstadt, and others eager to endow a church or monastery back home.

Libraries did not escape the general destruction and some Classical texts read by Greek scholars before 1204 and otherwise unknown today were lost for ever at this time including works by Callimachus and Hipponax. Apart from precious gems and metals and relics, much damage was done to Classical statuary, which had been brought from all over the ancient world to adorn the city. Most of this was melted down to provide currency; other items, such as the four bronze horses from the Hippodrome, were taken west to adorn the entrance of San Marco in Venice.

PETER LOCK

See also Crusades

Further Reading

Cutler, A., "The *De Signis* of Nicetas Choniates: A Reappraisal", *American Journal of Archaeology*, 72 (1968): pp. 113–18

Ferrard, C., "The Amount of Constantinopolitan Booty in 1204", *Studi Veneziani*, 13 (1971): pp. 95–104

Queller, Donald E. and Thomas F. Madden, *The Fourth Crusade: The Conquest of Constantinople*, 2nd edition, Philadelphia: University of Pennsylvania Press, 1997

Constitution

Greece's political history is inextricably linked with its constitutions: ever since the War of Independence the constitutional texts have been a powerful symbol embodying the principles of the organization of Greece's political life as well as an image of the balance of power within society.

Among the first acts to be undertaken by the insurgent Greeks, once the military situation had somewhat stabilized, was the drafting of a constitution: as early as January 1822 representatives from different parts of revolutionary Greece voted for the first constitution in an assembly near the site of ancient Epidaurus. This first constitution was followed by another two, in 1823 and 1827 respectively. The constitutions of the revolutionary period were very liberal in their provisions. They drew from the French tradition, but were also influenced from pre-independence works, such as the writings of Rigas Velestinlis and the anonymous work *Elliniki Nomarchia* (The Greek Prefecture). The constitutions of the War of Independence provided (among other things) for an independent judiciary; power sharing between the legislative and executive branches of government; freedom of press, religion, and expression; they outlawed torture and slavery and declared that slaves arriving on Greek soil would be automatically considered free; and declared that no hereditary titles were recognized or conferred by Greece. They also declared that all Greeks living permanently in Greece as well as non-Greeks who had fought in the War of Independence would be entitled to Greek citizenship. Their most striking feature, however, was that they were republican, a practice contrary to what was the norm for European government at the time. The 1827 constitution was probably the least liberal, as it provided for a voluntary though temporary transfer of power from the legislative branch to Ioannis Kapodistria, the head of the executive, who had the title of Governor. Between the assassination of Kapodistria in 1831 and 1844 Greece did not have an operative constitution; the 1832 Convention of London declared Greece a monarchical and independent state; and a constitution was not a priority for either the regency or King Otho himself. However, in September 1843, an uprising in which the Athens garrison participated forced Otho to grant a constitution. The 1844 constitution, apart from the separation of the executive, legislative, and judiciary branches, also provided for a two-chamber assembly (the Boule and the Gerousia); it also provided for almost universal male suffrage (some property requirements were included).

After the fall of Otho and the election of George I, another constitution was drafted, the lengthy proceedings of the Constituent Assembly being speedily concluded at the insistence of the king. The new regime was one of *vasilevomeni dimokratia* (literally "a democracy under a king"); the king's role was to reign but not to rule; this was rather misleading, as the king had substantial powers, especially in the foreign-policy field. Nevertheless, to be valid the sovereign's actions had to be countersigned by the minister(s) responsible. The 1864 constitution was more liberal than its predecessor, providing for a single-chamber assembly (the Gerousia was abolished) elected by universal male suffrage; the members of the Assembly, it was declared, represented the nation (as opposed to their local constituencies). The new constitution further strengthened the popular rights and liberties; it also included provisions for local government. The 1864 constitution has been the longest-lasting to date, almost half a century elapsing before its revision in 1911.

The 1911 constitution was (as in 1844) the indirect result of another coup. Following the 1909 Athens garrison pronunciamento at Goudi, Eleftherios Venizelos was invited to assume government. At his insistence the 1864 constitution was revised, though not radically. The most radical change was the

addition of the principle of *dedilomeni* (literally "declared majority") stipulating that the sovereign has to ask the leader of the largest party of the Assembly to form a government. The principle had operated since 1875, but only in 1911 was it included in the constitution. Other changes included compulsory free education for all; the establishment of a Council of State (*Symvoulio Epikrateias*, high administrative court), tenure for civil servants, a prohibition against serving officers to be simultaneously in the armed forces and in Parliament, and a reduction of the quorum of the parliament (intended to reduce filibustering). Another change in the wording of the article regulating the conditions under which the state had the right of compulsory purchase of property in cases of public need (rather than for "public benefit" as in the text of the 1864 constitution) heralded the break-up of large estates and large-scale land redistribution, measures that would later be used extensively to solve the peasant and refugee problems in Greece.

The 1927 constitution was once more promulgated following an upheaval: the Asia Minor debacle and the antimonarchical movement that subsequently prevailed. It was the first republican constitution since the War of Independence, introducing the notion of *avasilefti dimokratia* (literally "democracy without a king"). The freedoms enshrined in the 1911 constitution were further safeguarded; the parliament became bicameral once more, with a second chamber (Gerousia) reintroduced; the state was provided with greater power to effect compulsory purchases of property in exceptional circumstances, something that made possible the redistribution of the remaining large estates to refugees and other landless peasants; and safeguards regarding the monastic state of Mount Athos incorporated to the Greek state after the Balkan Wars were also included; these latter were repeated almost verbatim in subsequent Greek constitutions.

The period from 1936 to 1952 was one of major turbulence for Greece: the 1927 constitution was suspended in 1936 when General Metaxas took power; war, the Axis occupation of Greece, and the Civil War effectively continued the suspension until 1949. Martial law was in force after 1947 and was only lifted in 1950. It was only in 1952 that a new constitution was drafted. It was more conservative than its predecessor; it formally restored the monarchy, returning to the *vasilevomeni dimokratia*; it abolished the upper house of parliament (Gerousia); and for the first time it gave the vote to women. Though it safeguarded individual rights, the safeguards were often theoretical, given the complexity of anticommunist "compulsory law" legislation in place since the Civil War period. The most serious shortcoming of the constitution was once more the relatively extensive powers of the king; and, in a more general sense, the cavalier way in which the palace dealt with the restrictions the constitution imposed on royal power. It was this rather than the shortcomings of the constitution that led to the instability of 1965 and eventually to the Colonels' coup.

During the 1967–74 period the military junta produced two constitutional texts, the first in 1968, the second in 1973. They were highly authoritarian constructions, institutionalizing the role of the armed forces in politics and according them a say in every important aspect of government. Beyond its undemocratic character, what is notable in the first of the two constitutional texts is a measure of republicanism in the form of the gradual erosion of the powers of the monarchy; however, this was the result of the king's abortive countercoup of December 1967 rather than of the republicanism of the drafters. The 1973 constitutional text actually abolished the monarchy, creating a presidential democracy, in which the president (with a seven-year term of office) held considerable powers and even appointed the three most important ministers and 10 per cent of the members of parliament. Neither of the two texts was ever fully put into effect; both were declared null and void after the fall of the Colonels' regime in 1974.

Upon his return in July 1974 Karamanlis reinstated the 1952 constitution, with the exception of the clauses related to the monarchy, until a plebiscite decided its future. Following the result of the plebiscite in December 1974, the monarchy was abolished and a new constitution was drafted.

The 1975 constitution had the strong imprint of Karamanlis. It declared Greece a *proedrevomeni dimokratia* ("republic headed by a president"). The model followed was to an extent that of the French constitution of 1958, almost creating a twin-headed executive. Though the regime was not presidential, the president (elected by the parliament with a special majority) had considerable powers, even though he could only exercise them in exceptional circumstances: under certain conditions he could call a referendum, grant amnesty for political crimes, even dismiss the prime minister. All these features gave the 1975 constitution in its initial form at least a degree of latent presidentialism. The system was never put to the test. The first president was the self-effacing academic Constantine Tsatsos, a close associate of Constantine Karamanlis, prime minister between 1974 and 1980. After 1981, when a conservative president (Karamanlis) "cohabited" with a socialist prime minister (Andreas Papandreou), the former carefully avoided using the powers given to him by the constitution.

The 1975 constitution was revised in 1986, at the initiative and under the influence of the PASOK government of Andreas Papandreou. The 1986 revision abolished almost all the powers of the president, making him simply a figurehead; it also proportionately strengthened the office of the prime minister, moving the constitution towards a more orthodox republican parliamentary system.

There have been a number of criticisms levelled at the 1975/1986 constitution. Its critics say that it failed to disestablish the Church; that it has not limited the number of members of parliament (currently 300), judged by some as excessive for a country with a population of 10 million; and more importantly that it has not enshrined the electoral law in the text of the constitution, allowing successive governments to change it according to what they expect to be the most beneficial model for them. All these, as well as the redefinition and strengthening of the role of the parliament, are being debated in view of another projected revision of the constitution.

GEORGE KAZAMIAS

See also Government

Further Reading

Alivizatos, N., *Eisagogi stin Elliniki Syntagmatiki Istoria* [Introduction to Greek Constitutional History], Athens: Sakkoula, 1981
Kaltchas, Nicholas Stavrou, *Introduction to the Constitutional History of Modern Greece*, New York: AMS Press, 1970
Kourvetaris, Yorgas A. and Betty A. Dobratz, *A Profile of Modern Greece: In Search of Identity*, Oxford: Clarendon Press, and New York: Oxford University Press, 1987
Manesis, A., *Elliniki Syntagmatiki Istoria* [Greek Constitutional History], Thessalonica: Sakkoula, 1980
Pantelis, A., *Keimena Syntagmatikis Istorias* [Constitutional History Text], Athens, 1993
Petridis, P., *Politikoi kai Syntagmatikoi Thesmoi sti Neoteri Ellada, 1821–1843* [Political and Constitutional Institutions in Modern Greece, 1821–1843], Thessalonica, 1990
Svolos, Alexandros, *Ta Hellenika Syntagmata, 1822–1952* [The Greek Constitutions, 1822–1952], Athens, 1972
Tsatsos, D., *Syntagmatiko Dikaio* [Constitutional Law], 4th edition, 3 vols, Athens, 1994
Venizelos, E. (editor), *To Syntagma tes Helladas, 1975–1986* [The Constitution of Greece, 1975–1986], Thessalonica, 1986

Contraception

Ancient and medieval Hellenic peoples employed contraceptive drugs administered topically and orally as one of a variety of means of birth control. Soranus (*fl.* AD 98–117) said that "a contraceptive (*atokion*) differs from an abortive (*phthorion*), for the first does not let conception take place, while the latter destroys what has been conceived." Even though the Greek language distinguished conceptually between contraception and abortion, writers often mixed the two actions, according to modern scientific nomenclature. Generally the pharmaceutical actions were hormonal, usually stimulating or decreasing either oestrogen or progesterone, resulting either in contraception or disruption of implantation. The latter we call an abortifacient, but to early Hellenic people the distinction was not so sharp. In ancient and Byzantine times it was thought that the sperm remained in the womb for a period of weeks before acceptance and foetal formation.

Plato and Aristotle regarded population control as a function of the state, whereas Polybius and other Hellenistic figures thought that a decline in Greek influence was attributable to decisions by families to have fewer children. Medical sources regarded contraception as preferable to abortion because of the relative safety of the former. A Homeric hymn, for example, thought that Zeus permitted the Trojan War because the earth had too many people. In the Greek myth, Persephone was told not to eat anything but she disobeyed by eating a pomegranate, a widely used contraceptive in Greek and earlier Near Eastern cultures.

The most famous contraceptive was silphium, the name given to a small tree of the *Ferula* genus, whose contraceptive qualities were discovered and marketed by Greek colonists in Cyrene. The Cyreneans enjoyed a virtual monopoly because attempts to transplant and cultivate it failed. By the 1st century AD the plant was very scarce and expensive. The last reference to it occurs in a letter by Synesius of Cyrene (4th century) who reported that his brother had some growing on his farm. The plant is known to have been an effective contraceptive because plants of related species that later Greeks substituted for the extinct silphium have been proven to be effective contraceptives in animal and human testing.

Coitus interruptus was seldom employed as a contraceptive measure to judge by the paucity of references to it. Those few references, however, indicate that the procedure was known. Barrier methods were not known. Some pessaries prepared as drug prescriptions with specific ingredients and administered on wool pads could possibly have resulted in mechanical blockage of sperm progression. The Hippocratic work *On Generation* (5. 1) said that the practice was for women who did not wish to have a child to expel "the sperm from both partners". Contrary to a number of philosophers, Aristotle regarded males as the sole providers of sperm, and hence the source of life, with women supplying only nourishment.

Magical devices in the form of amulets, talismans, and incantations were employed as contraceptive means. Soranus, the gynaecologist of the early 2nd century, ridiculed such means, although Galen and other Greek medical writers sometimes included these devices among the contraceptive prescriptions. The anomaly is that from the standpoint of modern pharmaceutical knowledge the drug prescriptions were to some degree effective. For example, Aetius of Amida (*fl.*AD 502–25) attested to the efficacy of wearing weasel liver, this among otherwise perfectly rational medical lore.

The existence of male contraceptives was known but seldom were details related. Dioscurides (*fl. c.*AD 50–70) related that a plant called *periklymenon* was a male contraceptive, but this plant has never been identified. In Talmudic sources there are references to unspecified root poisons that prevent conception when used by both males and females. Galen said that the chaste tree (*Vitex agnus-castus* L) was employed by athletes and certain priests to prevent erections. Recent tests using an extract of the plant show that in dogs its action is to disrupt sperm production. The paucity of references to male contraception, however, probably indicates a seldom-employed practice.

Christianity did not make a great distinction between contraception and abortion. It is not until the 19th century, with developments in embryology and instrumentation, that the distinction between a quickened (a formed, hence, ensouled) foetus and an unquickened (unformed, no soul) foetus was dropped in the West. The Eastern Churches, however, were more definitive about early abortions. Generally, the Churches were against any form of human interference with fertility. Contraceptives and fertility-enhancement drugs all were condemned. Even so the medical records in Greek during the Byzantine and early modern periods continued to have information about contraceptive and fertility-enhancing drugs.

JOHN M. RIDDLE

See also Abortion

Further Reading

Feen, Richard, "Abortion and Exposure in Ancient Greece: Assessing the Status of the Fetus and 'Newborn' from Classical Sources" in *Abortion and the Status of the Fetus*, edited by William B. Bondeson *et al.*, Dordrecht and Boston: Reidel, 1983

Harris, W.V., "Child-Exposure in the Roman Empire", *Journal of Roman Studies*, 84 (1994): pp. 1–22

McLaren, Angus, *A History of Contraception: From Antiquity to the Present Day*, Oxford and Cambridge, Massachusetts: Blackwell, 1990

Noonan, John T., Jr, *Contraception: A History of its Treatment by the Catholic Theologians and Canonists*, revised edition, Cambridge, Massachusetts: Harvard University Press, 1986

Poulakou-Rebelakou, E. *et al.*, "Abortions in Byzantine Times, 325–1453 AD", *Vesalius: Acta Internationalia Historia Medicinae*, 2/1 (1996): pp. 19–25

Riddle, John M., *Contraception and Abortion from the Ancient World to the Renaissance*, Cambridge, Massachusetts: Harvard University Press, 1992

Riddle, John M., *Eve's Herbs: A History of Contraception and Abortion in the West*, Cambridge, Massachusetts: Harvard University Press, 1997

Conversion to Islam

Conversion to Islam is deceptively simple: it is by attestation and circumcision. It is absolute and, under sharia law, the penalty for reversion is death. This entry is limited to examining the conversion of Orthodox Christians within the former Byzantine empire to Sunni Islam between 1071 (when the Seljuk Turks, themselves relatively recent converts to Islam, entered Anatolia) and 1839 (when apostasy from Islam ceased to carry the death sentence under Ottoman civil law). It omits cases, particularly during the 14th century, of conversion from Islam to Orthodoxy, of conversion to Judaism (which both St Gregory Palamas and a mullah agreed heartily to condemn in Nicaea in 1354, the Muslim position being that only conversion in the forward direction of the "sequence of revelation", from Judaism to Christianity to Islam, was acceptable), and of conversion through ecstasy or revelation (converts such as St Paul who was granted light on the road to Damascus are statistically insignificant, although their subsequent evangelism should not be overlooked). Most convert through external factors, yet without overt coercion, for social and economic reasons. Given that generalization, further factors may be considered as to how Christian Anatolia became Muslim Turkey. They are that Islam is a culture as well as a faith; that while conversion is a matter of a moment, subsequent acculturation may take generations; that in the early Ottoman state there was a demographic problem in that there were too few Muslims and of these too few were Turks; that converts try harder but are least appreciated by their new community; that in the folk religion derived from local and ancient cults there was a no man's land between the official orthodoxies of the Church and Islam over which a common Anatolian peasant culture could stray (few actually "converted" from either); that official Orthodoxies were associated with the secular rulers of Constantinople (which is why local Churches, such as the Armenian, might fare better under Islam than an imperial or *Melkite* Church); that while it cannot be demonstrated that Ottoman *defters* (tax registers) are any more reliable than most medieval registers, their classification of households by religion offers the first statistics of conversion that we have (though they were made for secular purposes, which in some respects makes them more trustworthy).

These questions may be illustrated within two major phases, of symbiosis and transition up to about 1520, and of consolidation thereafter. In the first phase Christians lost their daughters, their official faith, and their demotic language –

usually in that order. In intermarriage the Greek dowry and Turkish bride-price were directly opposed, and in such situations the bride-price usually won. But both were a luxury except among the extensive sequence of marriages between Orthodox princesses and Muslim rulers from 1297 to 1461, in almost all of which the bride kept her faith, at the price of none being regarded as a marriage under Orthodox canon law, or the bride became senior consort (*ulu hatun*), unless converted. The position of these women was part hostage and part protector of Christians in Muslim lands, and ended in 1476 with the death of Mara Brankovich, Sultan Mehmet II's revered Christian stepmother, when there were no further Orthodox rulers to take notice of. Of the more extensive seepage of women into Turkish hands there is less record. The Ottoman invasions of Europe from 1354 required manpower. The system of *devshirme* ("recruitment" in Turkish) or *paidomazoma* ("harvest of children" in Greek), in which children were brought (and converted) into Ottoman service, was in place by 1395. A dynamic of the self-perpetuating Ottoman Balkan expansion of the next century consisted of first-generation converts conquering the next, turning east only to take Byzantium before dealing with older Muslim powers in Anatolia – a repetition in miniature of the original expansion of Islam. The shockingly swift collapse of the Orthodox Church in Anatolia after 1071 followed the loss of imperial patronage, while its economic base passed to successive Muslim states, usually as *waqf* (charitable foundation). The collapse of the imperial Church with its state was halted only by its adoption as an instrument of government by the Ottomans after 1453. In Anatolia conversion was eased by Bektashi, dervish, or seductive Sufi teaching of many ways to truth, and of syncretistic texts, such as the so-called Gospel of Barnabas – a twilight world in which the Anatolian peasant could find his way around.

Although there were still exceptions, the basic social and economic distinction between Christians who paid head-tax and Muslims who entered military or administrative service was well established by 1453, which made it crucial for the state to identify who were Muslims and who Christians. Marriage and *devshirme* added to natural conversion to Islam, but they were not enough. Mehmet targeted cities and used resettlement (*surgun*), encouraging Muslim settlers and moving the former Christian elites elsewhere. By 1477 Constantinople was 58 per cent Muslim, but was restored to its position as the largest Orthodox city in the world; few of its citizens had known the capital before 1453 and local mosques, such as Rum Mehmed Pasha's of 1471 in Chrysopolis (Üsküdar), were built by converts.

Two other cities raise questions of population and conversion. When Mehmet II took Trebizond (Trabzon) in 1461, it had a notionally 100 per cent Christian population of about 4,000. By *surgun* he brought in Muslims, some evidently Albanian converts, with the result that by 1486 the Muslim to Christian ratio was 19:81 per cent. But it did not work. By 1523 the ratio was 14:86 per cent. The place was in danger of becoming wholly Christian again. There was a second *surgun*. In 1553 the Muslim to Christian ratio was 47:53 per cent and by 1583 had turned tables to 54:46 per cent, when the city had a population of more than 10,500 and still more Christians than there were to start with. The critical time is when the

Muslim/Christian ratio reaches about 45:55 per cent, when whole parishes, paying fixed levies, convert in landslides. Two points may be made. First, by 1583, 43 per cent of the Muslims of Trabzon are identifiable as first- or second-generation converts, which suggests that (unlike Constantinople) more than 70 per cent of its citizens were linked to its population of a century before. One may convert overnight, but it is more difficult to wake up speaking Turkish in the morning. Thus some Pontic people speak conservative Greek and are, or become thereby, conservative Muslims. The second point is that from the reign of sultan Suleyman the Lawgiver (1520–66) those who were going to convert did so. But nothing is typical.

One case is Thessalonica (Slav Solun, Turkish Selanik, Hebrew Slonki), which was conquered in 1430. From 1478 to 1519 it tripled in population to around 30,000 souls, but they were different tenants of the same Macedonian city. In 1478 the Christian element had an absolute majority of 59 per cent; by 1500 the Muslim population had grown to a simple majority of 42 per cent, when a third category appears, of Sephardic Jews, expelled from Spain after 1492 and astutely welcomed by the Ottomans to Thessalonica to make a demographic balance, where in 1519 Hebrews are registered with an absolute majority of 54 per cent, which they maintained in the largest Jewish city in the world until 1666. In that year a Thessalonian Jewish false Messiah, Sabbatai Zavi (1625–76), converted to Islam. He had been a nuisance to the Ottoman civil order, but that was not a solution, for he took large numbers of his flock with him, creating further problems of identity.

The followers of Sabbatai, called *dönme* in Turkish, are a common enough phenomenon in a world of secret, or dual, faiths and simple misregistration. When in 1571 the Ottomans took Cyprus and restored the economic and political status of its Orthodox Church, Roman Catholics had no recognized status. There was the theoretical choice of Orthodoxy or Islam. Some at least became *linobambakoi*, crypto-Christians, and preferred to remain so long after it was safer to conceal one's faith. Dual faiths had political and economic advantages, depending on whether it was a head-tax collector or a recruiting officer who asked the questions. Eighteenth-century Albanian transhumants traditionally changed their faith by season. Politically the great Druse emir Bashir II Shihab (1788–1840) of the Lebanon found that the best way to square the demography of that country was to become a Maronite Christian as well. But the largest group of crypto-Christians, perhaps seeking the best of both worlds, were from the Pontus, and "came out" in 1867. They were Christians indentured to the silver-mining economy of Gümüşhane, who were excused head-tax in return for a corvée. When the mines were exhausted after 1829, they declined either to pay Christian tax or to undergo Muslim military service. Significantly the Orthodox Church was slower to recognize them as Christian than the Ottoman state, which had always been reluctant to carry out the penalties of sharia law. Martyrs are troublesome and after 1839 apostasy was no crime. But this is not to question faith. The last recorded Neomartyr of the Orthodox Church was St George of Ioannina, also known as Hasan, who, accused of apostasy from Islam, died steadfast in his faith on 17 January 1838.

ANTHONY A.M. BRYER

Further Reading

Balivet, Michel, *Romanie byzantine et pays de Rûm turc: histoire d'un espace d'imbrication gréco-turque*, Istanbul: Isis, 1994

Bryer, Anthony, *Peoples and Settlement in Anatolia and the Caucasus, 800–1900*, London: Variorum, 1988

Bulliet, Richard W., *Conversion to Islam in the Medieval Period: An Essay in Quantitative History*, Cambridge, Massachusetts: Harvard University Press, 1979

Hasluck, F.W., *Christianity and Islam under the Sultans*, Oxford: Clarendon Press, 1929

Vryonis, Speros, Jr, *The Decline of Medieval Hellenism in Asia Minor and the Process of Islamization from the Eleventh through the Fifteenth Century*, Berkeley: University of California Press, 1971

Copais, Lake

Drained lake in Boeotia

Lake Copais is the fourth in a series of basins in a great valley running with the river Kiphisos from west–northwest to east–southeast for some 130 km. The corridor is separated from the Gulf of Corinth to the south by the ranges of Mount Parnassus and Mount Helicon, the latter directly south of Lake Copais. The lake was formed through crustal disturbance and enlarged through erosion and dissolution of the surrounding limestone. It was fed by the waters of the Kiphisos, which then progressed towards the sea through limestone ridges and the lakes Iliki and Paralimni. Sedimentation in the lake bed led to an increasing shallowness of the water; before 1886, seasonal changes in temperature caused an alteration between lake in winter and swamp in summer.

Archaeological survey and excavation have revealed Palaeolithic and Neolithic occupation around the lake, and shown that the region was relatively densely inhabited in the Bronze Age. Tradition recorded by Strabo (9. 415) and by Pausanias (1. 9. 3, 8. 33. 2, 9. 38. 7) held that the "Minyans" (after the mythical king Minyas) had drained the lake and cultivated the plain. The archaeological evidence for the drainage of the lake rests on two bases: observations of dykes, drainage, and canal works in and around the lake, and an apparent system of fortified enclosures or settlements encircling the lake.

The known ancient drainage works include two immense canal projects: one canal was created on the south and east side of the lake, the other on the north side; these were united at Agia Marina, in the northeast corner of the lake and about 1 km north of Gla. These canals are breathtaking examples of Mycenaean hydrological engineering works. With a combined length of over 50 km, they seem to have been designed to channel the waters of the Kiphisos and Melas rivers, and perhaps of smaller tributaries, away from the central bed and towards the north and east, where natural sink holes take the water to the sea. The canals are massive, in correspondence to the volume of water involved. At one point on the southern route the channel is 41 m wide and enclosed on one side by a dyke 19 m thick. Where the two routes meet, the channel is as much as 60 m wide. Archaeological investigations have been sporadic, but where observations have been possible the dykes have been revealed to be stone-built constructions.

Gla is the largest of a series of Mycenaean fortified sites around the lake. In the northeast section alone three other fortified sites overlook the plain, and elsewhere they include a fort at ancient Haliartos overlooking the southern channel and several sites on the north side. Although Gla is the only one of these sites to have been seriously investigated, the indications are that, with Gla, all of these sites were founded in the Mycenaean heyday and their period of use did not extend much beyond the end of the Mycenaean palace period. This suggests very strongly that the entire system of fortified sites and drainage projects formed a cohesive unity in draining, maintaining, and protecting the lake bed.

Gla is by far the largest of Mycenaean fortified sites, enclosing an area ten times that of Mycenaean Athens or of Tiryns, and seven times that of Mycenae itself. A massive Cyclopaean wall generally 3 m thick runs for 2.8 km around the perimeter of a rocky outcrop that would have been an island before the lake was drained. It is pierced by four gates, one of them double; from two of these gates, roads have been traced for some distance into the plain, further proof of the effectiveness of the drainage operations. The enclosed area, nowadays barren rock and scrub, appears to have been relatively open in Mycenaean times: only a central portion in front of the southern gate and running to the north wall was built upon. Part of this appears to have been taken up with stables and storerooms. Towards the north, where the rocky islet reaches its summit, an L-shaped block of rooms forms what is assumed to have been the administrative and perhaps religious centre of the site. These rooms, generally small, were plastered and painted and show some of the refinements of Mycenaean palatial architecture. The built area occupies less than one quarter of the enclosed area of Gla; it may be that temporary structures occupied the rest of the area, especially during the construction phase of Gla itself and the drainage projects in the lake.

Important Mycenaean sites are located at Thebes to the southeast and Orchomenus to the west. Recent fieldwork suggests that hydrological works extended as far as Orchomenus in the form of a small artificial lake created in the vicinity of the town. Orchomenus is thought to have been the site of a Mycenaean palace and certainly boasted the greatest of all tholos tombs, the Treasury of Minyas, which was modelled on the Treasury of Atreus at Mycenae. It seems logical to assume that the drainage of Lake Copais was orchestrated from there, and that, beginning with Gla, a number of fortified settlements were constructed to maintain and control the drainage system and the agricultural land that resulted from it. If Thebes were in any way a hostile centre, that would further explain the fortifications.

By the historical period the drainage system seems largely to have collapsed, probably in the wake of the collapse of Mycenaean political structures c.1200 BC. Sporadic attempts were made either to repair the system or to undertake new drainage projects, some of which may well have been smaller-scale but nevertheless successful. Crates of Chalcis, under the tutelage of Alexander the Great, is supposed to have attempted to drain the lake; perhaps the most striking remnant of this period is a tunnel at the northeast end of the lake, unfinished but destined to carry the waters off to the sea in much the same direction that the (presumably blocked) sink holes had done in previous years. Other repairs were undertaken in the Roman period, but it appears that the lake was never again drained in any systematic manner; instead small-scale, localized projects were undertaken.

In 1873 the Anglo-Hellenic Copais Company was formed to undertake a project of drainage at the invitation of the government, after an unfulfilled attempt in 1865 by a French company. The drainage was complete by 1886, at which time 25,000 hectares of land were reclaimed. The drainage was achieved by a system of canals converging on a tunnel which leads to Lake Iliki, whose consequently raised level enabled the waters to flow to Lake Paralimni and thence to the sea. The fertile basin, divided by canals and roads into a flat patchwork of cotton and wheat fields, contrasts with the otherwise variable Greek countryside. Settlements have remained strung around the lake, so that the basin is largely uninhabited.

MICHAEL J. BOYD

Summary

Lake Copais in Boeotia was, before being drained, the largest lake in Greece. Two canals with a combined length of 50 km were built in the Mycenaean period to channel the waters to the sea. Fortified sites around the lake include Gla. The system seems to have collapsed at the end of the Mycenaean period. The lake was drained again in the 19th century.

Further Reading

Hope Simpson, R., *Mycenaean Greece*, Park Ridge, New Jersey: Noyes Press, 1981, pp. 59–69

Iakovidhis, S.E., *Glas I: I Anaskaphi 1955–1961* [Glas I: The Excavations 1955–1961], Athens, 1989

Iakovidhis, S.E., *Glas II: I Anaskaphi 1981–1991* [Glas II: The Excavations 1981–1991], Athens, 1998

Knauss, J., B. Heinrich, and H. Kalcyk, *Die Wasserbauten der Minyer in der Kopais: die älteste Flussregulierung Europas*, Munich: Technische Universität, 1984

Knauss, J., *Die Melioration des Kopaisbeckens durch die Minyer im 2. Jh. v. Chr: Kopais 2 – Wasserbau und Siedlungsbedingungen in Altertum*, Munich: Technische Universität, 1987

Knauss, J., *Kopais 3: Wasserbau und Geschichte minische Epoche – Bayerische Zeit (vier Jahrhunderte – ein Jahrzehnt)*, Munich: Technische Universität, 1990

Copper and Tin

Copper was one of the earliest metals to be exploited, partly for its metallurgical qualities, but also because, like gold, it can occur in nature in its native form. However, the native metal was never a major ore in antiquity and it was an important step when it was realized that copper could be produced from other disparate-looking materials. The earliest copper production probably began in the Sinai peninsula, but the most important source of copper in the Bronze Age was the island of Cyprus. There were no major sources of copper in mainland Greece that were exploited in antiquity, although recently it has been mined on the Chalcidice peninsula. Other minor sources were in Anatolia and Palestine.

Initially, copper was used in its pure state to make tools and weapons. However, the usefulness of this material was limited by its relative softness. It was only when it was discovered that the hardness could be increased by alloying with arsenic, and later tin, that bronze became widely used, principally in armour, weapons, bowls, tripods, statuary, and tools. It was always an expensive material as all the ingredients had to be imported. It was eventually partly supplanted by iron and steel, possibly in response to a shortage of tin.

Copper production started on Cyprus in the Chalcolithic Age, 3800–2500 BC, but only reached its peak during the late Bronze Age, 1600–1100 BC. The predominance of Cyprus was due to the richness of the ores, and their early discovery. The earliest ores to be exploited were from colourful altered zones on the surface – iron and copper-rich rocks called gossan. However, the early Cypriots discovered that beneath many of the gossans lay rich deposits of primary sulphide ore, that were easier to work than the deposits on the surface. Every gossan on the island was explored for copper at this time. Production was at its maximum in the early 13th century BC, when the characteristic "oxhide" ingots were produced. The coming of the Iron Age reduced the importance of copper, but exploitation continued until the end of the Roman empire. The only ancient description of copper exploitation was given by Galen, the Roman physician, in AD 162.

The ancient mines and smelters were centred around Skouriotissa and Kalavasos. The volume of the slag heaps indicates that about 200,000 tonnes of copper was produced, mostly before Roman times. The mining was mostly underground, at depths of 185 m. Water pumps have not been found, hence the mines must have been constructed to drain naturally.

The copper deposits of Cyprus formed on the ocean floor, which was lifted up to form the Troodos mountains during the convergence of Africa and Europe. The upper part of the ocean floor was formed by volcanic eruptions of basalt. Ocean water circulated through these piles of hot lava and dissolved some of their minerals. Where these hot springs debouched, underwater cooling caused precipitation of the dissolved minerals to build chimneys and mounds – these are the well-known hydrothermal vents, or "black smokers", still to be found at mid-ocean ridges, particularly in the Pacific. These chimneys are rich in sulphide minerals, such as pyrite and chalcopyrite, the main copper mineral. The copper ore of Cyprus always contains a little gold, but not usually enough to be exploitable. However, some gold was concentrated during weathering of sulphide deposits on the sea floor to produce ochre. This was exploited for gold in antiquity, but was never a major source of the metal.

The copper ores were smelted in several steps. The sulphide ore was roasted in air to convert it to the oxide. This was mixed with a flux of quartz and iron-manganese oxides (umber), to increase the fluidity of the molten material, and charcoal to react with the oxygen and convert the oxide to the metal. The raw metal was refined by remelting and cast in "oxhide" ingots weighing about 20 kg.

Copper has many useful qualities, but it is not a hard metal. This is why the discovery that the hardness of copper could be improved by alloying with other metals was so important. The first alloys were with arsenic. This occurs with copper at a few deposits in Cyprus (Pevkos, Laxia tou Mavrou), and smelting would have made a natural alloy. Later it was found that the addition of tin made the best bronze. This discovery was long in coming, partly because tin and copper occur together so rarely.

Most deposits of tin are associated with granite. The main ore mineral is the oxide, cassiterite, which crystallizes in the granite itself or from watery fluids released during crystallization. This heavy, resistant mineral is released when the rock is weathered and can be concentrated in river sediments in the same way as gold. Such placer deposits were easily exploited once the value of the mineral was determined. There are no major sources of tin in the Aegean region. A minor source in eastern Turkey was exploited in the Bronze Age, but most tin must have come from much more distant sources. There are minor deposits of placer tin in the Eastern Desert of Egypt, but tin-bronze was not used there before 2000 BC, and there is no evidence that it was exported. One possibility is that tin came from Malaysia, a region still rich in tin today. Later on, the Iberian peninsula became an important source. Southwest Britain may have been another source – it was certainly exported from there by Roman times. Cassiterite was smelted by heating with charcoal.

Another important copper alloy is brass. This copper-zinc mixture seems to have been known in Greece from about 700 BC, possibly by the name *oreichalkos* (copper of the mountain). Early brass may have been made by smelting natural mixed copper-zinc ore, possibly in Cyprus or Asia Minor, but it is difficult to get much zinc into the copper by this process. Later on, high-zinc brass must have been made by deliberately alloying zinc and copper. This is difficult as zinc boils at a lower temperature than copper metals. It is possible by heating copper metal, zinc ore, and charcoal powders in a closed crucible at 920° to 1000°C.

MICHAEL D. HIGGINS

See also Geology, Metalwork

Further Reading

Craddock, Paul T., *Early Metal Mining and Production*, Edinburgh: Edinburgh University Press, 1995
Franklin, Alan D., Jacqueline S. Olin, and Theodore A. Wertime (editors), *The Search for Ancient Tin*, Washington, D.C.: Smithsonian Institution, 1978
Higgins, Michael Denis and Reynold Higgins, *A Geological Companion to Greece and the Aegean*, Ithaca, New York: Cornell University Press, and London: Duckworth, 1996
Muhly, J.D. (editor), *Early Metallurgy in Cyprus 4000–500 BC*, Nicosia: Pierides Foundation, 1982
Yenar, K.A. *et al.*, "Kestral: An Early Bronze Age Source of Tin Ore in the Taurus Mountains, Turkey", *Science*, 244 (1989): pp. 200–203

Copts

The term "Copts" was first used to identify the native Egyptians (as opposed to the Macedonian-descended Alexandrians) possibly as early as the Ptolemaic period, but from the 4th century AD it was applied predominantly to Egyptian Christians. It was in all likelihood associated with *Aigyptios* (Egyptian), but reduced to the root consonants *KPT* and pronounced "copt".

The Coptic language, however, seems to be older than the Ptolemaic era, appearing in demotic and on some later hieroglyphic monuments. Under the Ptolemies, the Egyptians began to adopt the Greek alphabet, to which they added seven new letters to express sounds that were entirely Egyptian. The earliest "proto-Coptic" manuscript is Papyrus Heidelberg 414 dating from the 3rd century BC.

In the Roman period Coptic probably existed alongside Greek as the normal language of the Egyptian peasantry, much as Berber was used alongside Latin among the north African native population. It was Christianity that brought Coptic into prominence as the language of native Christians. In 270 St Antony heard the gospel preached in Coptic and obeyed the injunction to "sell all" and devoted himself to Christ (*Vita Antonii*, 2). In the 4th century Coptic was the language of the Pachomian monasteries, and Alexandrians, i.e. Greek-speakers, were obliged to become familiar with it.

The language would have been Sahidic Coptic, but at this time there were other Coptic dialects in the Nile valley, and probably in use in the monasteries. Thus, many of the items in the Nag Hammadi library were written in Subakhminic or Lycopolitan, and some Manichaean works were also compiled in this dialect. Sahidic Coptic, however, dominated the scene between 450 and 700. During the first two generations of the Arab conquest (642–c.700) the free Coptic (Monophysite) Church was flourishing, sustained by the Coptic language. Thereafter, however, decline was slow but continuous. One of the early blows was the decision in 706 of the emir Abd el-Malik that Arabic would be the sole language of his emirate's administration. With this decree began a steady seepage of educated Copts to Islam and a corresponding weakening of the Coptic language. At the end of the 10th century the emir al-Hakim (996–1026) tried to forbid the use of Coptic even as the language of the Christian liturgy. This failed, but, combined with the decline of monastic institutions at this time and the general use of Arabic among the people, the Coptic patriarch Gabriel II was induced to permit the use of Arabic in the liturgy (12th century). However, the commendation (Letters Testimonial) sent with bishop Timotheos of Ibrim in Nubia after his consecration by Patriarch Gabriel IV (1372–80) was written in Coptic on the finest paper with an Arabic translation. It shows the continued use of Coptic as a church language to the end of the 14th century. The text was not only written in the patriarchate but was witnessed by four bishops from Upper Egypt who also wrote their commendations in Coptic. By this time Bohairic, originally the dialect of the people of the Nile delta, had replaced Sahidic as the language of such Copts as had survived. Even this became extinct as a written and spoken language, probably in the course of the 16th century.

Coptic culture was expressed in art, pottery, and sculpture as well as in devotion to the one-nature, "Monophysite" understanding of the person of Christ. From the 4th to the 8th century practically all art forms in Egypt may be characterized as Coptic; some of the best examples of Coptic art come from the monastery of Apa Apollo at Bawit, which included two churches in which were carvings and frescos, one of the latter being a full-length painting of St George. Tombs of the monks

Copts: Coptic church of the Virgin in Old Cairo

buried generation after generation often contained paintings of Christ enthroned in glory with the Apostles and the Virgin standing in intercession for the soul of the deceased.

French cultural initiatives and the archaeological policies furthered during the British occupation of Egypt (1882–1922) helped to bring about a revival of Coptic studies and the consequent consolidation of the Coptic Christian minority. Notable in the development were Amélineau's studies of the Coptic Church and its martyrs and W.E. Crum's *A Coptic Dictionary* (Oxford, 1939). The discovery of the library of Coptic-Gnostic documents at Nag Hammadi has given a further impulse to Coptic studies, particularly in American and German universities. The Coptic heritage will not be allowed to perish.

WILLIAM H.C. FREND

See also Monophysites

Summary

The Copts are the descendants of the original inhabitants of Egypt in pharaonic times. From the 4th century AD the term has applied mainly to the Egyptian Christians. The language predates the Ptolemaic period, but under the Ptolemies the Egyptians began to adopt the Greek alphabet. The Coptic Church follows the Monophysite understanding of the person of Christ.

Further Reading

Atiya, Aziz S. (editor), *The Coptic Encyclopedia*, 8 vols, New York: Macmillan, 1991 (especially the articles on Calendar, Ceramics, Art, and Language, all in vol. 2; and the articles on Bohairic and Sahidic in vol. 8)

Crum, W.E. (editor), *A Coptic Dictionary*, Oxford: Clarendon Press, 1939; reprinted 1979

Plumley, J.M., *The Scrolls of Bishop Timotheos: Two Documents from Medieval Nubia*, London: Egypt Exploration Society, 1975

Corfu

Ionian island

Corfu (Corcyra in Latin, Kerkyra in Greek) has never been as "far from the busy haunts of men" as the Scheria of the *Odyssey* with which, by Classical times, it was commonly identified. Its advantageous position on the main trade route between Greece and Italy attracted Corinthian colonists (probably in 734 BC, certainly by about 705), the Eretrians from Euboea whom the Corinthians apparently expelled, and their many successors.

The main Corinthian settlement was on the Palaeopolis peninsula and included, by about 600 BC, an Archaic temple to Hera. Corfu prospered rapidly and as a result became even more independent of the mother city than most Greek colonies; in about 664 BC it inflicted a naval defeat on the Corinthians. Nevertheless, the history of founder and colony continued to intertwine: they were co-founders of the colonies of Epidamnus (c.625 BC; Roman Dyrrachium; modern Durazzo and Durrës) and Apollonia (c.600 BC) in Illyria; for a time Corfu was controlled by the Corinthian tyrant Periander (d. 586 BC); and conflict between the two states was a prelude to and a cause of the Peloponnesian War.

In 435 tension between Corfu and Corinth, the result chiefly of the islanders' perceived lack of respect for the Corinthians and lack of interest in Greek affairs more generally, became an open quarrel over the affairs of Epidamnus. Broadly speaking, Corinth supported the *demos* (ordinary citizens) of Epidamnus and Corfu reacted by supporting the oligarchs. Again the Corinthians were defeated at sea. Epidamnus was taken and Corfu, for the time being at least, was established as the dominant power in the region. The islanders could not, however, afford to stand alone, given the place of Corinth in a pattern of powerful alliances, notably with Sparta. Therefore, in 433, they formed an alliance with Athens. To avoid breaking the existing Athenian entente with Corinth this was conceived as "defensive". But later, in 433, Athenian reinforcements played a crucial role in averting the defeat of the islanders by a Corinthian armada of 150 ships; the larger war – which broke out in 431 – became more likely.

In 427 BC Corfu was riven by complicated civil war. Oligarchs and their supporters fought elements of the *demos*, who were themselves subject to internal feuding, and Athens, Corinth, and Sparta were involved both as aggressors and as mediators. When the Peloponnesians, having ravaged the south of Corfu, had withdrawn, massacres of their supporters began; the Athenians, who had 60 ships offshore, did nothing to interfere. According to Thucydides, the victims "were accused of conspiring to overthrow the democracy, but in fact men were often killed on grounds of personal hatred or else by their debtors. ... There was death in every shape and form. ... Men were dragged from the temples or butchered on the very altars." For Thucydides these events provided a paradigm of the moral degeneration, cyclic violence, and collapse of law which would increasingly afflict all participants in the Peloponnesian War. In Corfu the fighting continued; there was a new Athenian expedition in 425 and further massacre.

The alliance with Athens was eventually ended in 410 BC but was re-established in response to Spartan activities in the Adriatic in 375. Interventions by other powers continued to be frequent; the Illyrians seized Corfu but were expelled by Rome, whose overlordship the island perforce accepted, in 229. The island served as an important bridgehead for subsequent Roman campaigns in Illyria, Macedonia, and Greece.

Under late Roman and Byzantine rule the island continued to attract the attention of outsiders. It was raided, between the 5th and 9th centuries, by Huns, Vandals, Ostrogoths, Bulgars, and Slavs. More sustained assaults came from the Normans of southern Italy and Sicily (1081 and 1147–49), seeking a stepping stone to their Greek fiefs (or intended fiefs). Later it passed to Venice (1204), the despots of Epirus (1214), Manfred of Sicily (1259), and the Angevin kings of Naples (1267). Under Angevin rule feudalism was introduced to the island; the maintaining of the rights and lands of the nobility was one of the Corfiotes' conditions for the acceptance of de facto rule by Venice in 1386 (formalized in 1402).

Through all these changes of overlord – and those that were to come – the Greek language and Orthodox religion maintained the Corfiotes' sense of Hellenic identity. (In the mid-17th century this was reinforced by the arrival of refugees from Crete, including the painters Emmanuel Tzanes (1610–90) and Theodoros Palakis (1622–92).) The Angevins had vigorously promoted the Catholic rite, but failed to make much headway against their subjects' Orthodoxy. Venice, by contrast, adopted, as in its other Greek outposts, a policy of prudent toleration. Both the Catholic and Orthodox Churches participated in public ceremonial and the Venetian republic encouraged the cult of St Spyridon, the patron saint of Corfu whose remains arrived there in 1456 and who has ever since remained central to Corfiote tradition and identity. (The basilica of St Spyridon dates from 1589.)

Venetian rule kept Corfu from Ottoman occupation. Its position on the eastern Adriatic made it valuable to the republic in both trade and war (increasingly so after the loss of mainland Greek outposts in the 15th century). Well-maintained fortifications together with a huge storm beat off the Ottoman siege of 1537; the New Citadel was completed (at enormous cost) in 1588 and further work on defences continued until 1645; in 1716 renewed fortifications, a daring sortie, and another violent storm raised a second Ottoman siege.

But if outside attacks were repelled, within Corfu the administration became increasingly corrupt; the affairs of the Council of 150 and inner oligarchy of 12 were dominated by bribery, violence, and feudal privilege. When the French took the island in 1797, soon after the fall of Venice itself, major reforms were promised and begun, but the liberators' irreligion and general failure to understand local traditions and sentiments soon lost them their initial popularity. Under the

Septinsular Republic, which replaced French rule in Corfu after a long siege by Russia and Turkey in 1798–99, various constitutions were tried out. Noble privileges were restored, again removed, and again restored. (The definition of nobility was, however, broadened.) Modernization was achieved in a number of areas – especially education – under the lead of one of the republic's most active ministers, the future president of Greece, Count Ioannis Kapodistria. But heavy taxes were levied and increasing Russian domination went far to undermine the autonomy of Corfu and the other islands of the Septinsular Republic.

Greater stability was at last achieved when the French regained control of Corfu between 1807 and 1814. This time religious sensibilities were treated respectfully. The nobility retained many of its privileges but public administration and justice became somewhat more efficient and considerable progress was made with agricultural reform. Newspapers in French and Italian were printed and in 1808 the first Ionian Academy was set up.

The British protectorate (1815–64) provided roads, fine architecture (including the palaces of St Michael and St George and of Mon Repos), and an enduring tradition of playing cricket. For many Corfiotes this was a period of frustration as the movement for Greek independence and then for enosis (union) grew. Successive Lord High Commissioners ruled essentially as autocrats, allowing on the whole only token involvement of the Senate and Assembly; favoured Corfiotes were offered membership of the grand but powerless Order of St Michael and St George established by the first Lord High Commissioner (1815–24), Sir Thomas Maitland. Nevertheless Greek culture did flourish under the protectorate. Inspired by the struggle across the water but safe from war (and civil war) and spared the birthpangs of the troubled new state, Dionysios Solomos and his followers produced the first modern demotic Greek poetry. (Solomos, attracted by the opportunities for social and literary life, moved to Corfu from Zakynthos in 1828 and died there in 1857; Andreas Kalvos – also a patriotic poet and in part a demotic one – lived in Corfu from 1826 to 1851.) Also important in the raising of Hellenic consciousness was the setting up in 1824, by Frederick North, Earl of Guilford, of a new Ionian Academy. Andreas Kalvos and the historian and diplomat Spyridon Trikoupis taught for a time at this, the first modern Greek university. (The Academy, by then ailing, fused with the University of Athens in the 1860s.)

Some concessions in the direction of greater local autonomy were made in 1849. Continued agitation for enosis, together with the coming in Greece of a constitutional monarchy acceptable to Britain, finally resulted in the union of the Ionian islands with Greece in 1864. Contacts with the west, however, remained frequent through trade and increasingly through tourism, especially in the second half of the 20th century. Until the end of communism in Albania Corfu, between East and West, retained its strategic and symbolic importance. Mussolini found a pretext (the assassination of his border commissioner on the mainland) temporarily to seize Corfu town in 1923; in 1941 the Italians returned and unsuccessfully attempted "re-Italianization". They were displaced by the

Corfu: view of a street in Corfu town where vestiges of Venetian influence are still apparent

Germans, who were removed only after a heavy Allied bombing campaign in 1944.

MARTIN GARRETT

See also Ionian Islands, Venetokratia

Summary

Most northerly of the Ionian islands, Corfu (Latin Corcyra, Greek Kerkyra) was first settled by colonists from Corinth in the 8th century BC. For much of the Classical period it was allied with Athens. It served as a valuable stepping stone for any power anxious to make a bridgehead across the Adriatic. It was therefore often under attack and changed hands frequently during the Middle Ages and later. Finally incorporated in the kingdom of Greece in 1864.

Further Reading

Bacchion, E., *Il dominio veneto su Corfù (1386–1797)*, Venice: Altino, 1956

Flamburiari, Spiro and Frank Giles (editor), *Corfu: The Garden Isle*, London: John Murray, and New York: Abbeville Press, 1994

Lewis, D.M., "The Archidamian War" in *The Fifth Century BC*, edited by D.M. Lewis *et al.*, Cambridge: Cambridge University Press, 1992 (*The Cambridge Ancient History*, vol. 5, 2nd edition)

Norwich, John Julius, *A History of Venice*, London: Allen Lane, and New York: Knopf, 1982

Pratt, Michael, *Britain's Greek Empire: Reflections on the History of the Ionian Islands from the Fall of Byzantium*, London: Collings, 1978

Thucydides, *History of the Peloponnesian War*, translated by Rex Warner, revised edition, Harmondsworth and Baltimore: Penguin, 1972

Corinth

City in central Greece

The importance and fortunes of Corinth derive in the first instance from its position at the isthmus which bears its name; as Thucydides commented, not only did this mean that Corinth controlled the only land passage from southern Greece (the Peloponnese), to central and northern Greece, but it also gave the city access to the seas, to the Aegean and the east, via the Saronic gulf, and to the west, to the Adriatic, Italy, and Sicily, via the gulf of Corinth, thus placing the city in a most favourable position for trade.

There are prehistoric settlements in the vicinity, but none seem to be of any particular significance, and certainly do not compare to the main Mycenaean sites in the Argolid. Following the collapse of the Late Bronze Age systems, Corinthia was another area into which Dorian settlers migrated, forming a small community below the conspicuous hill of the Acrocorinth, where the spring Peirene, with others, provided an abundant water supply. The place remained small until the 8th century BC, when it began to develop rapidly under the control of its principal Dorian clan, the Bacchiadae, a closeknit group who adhered more or less strictly to a custom of endogamy. Corinth then took over nearby communities, incorporating their land and sending part, at least, of their populations overseas to colonies, the most significant being Syracuse, founded probably in 733 BC. This Bacchiad supremacy lasted, according to later authors, for a period of 90 years (i.e. three generations) after which they were overthrown by a tyrant, Cypselus, the son of a female Bacchiad, Labda, and a member of another group called the Lapiths (who may have been non-Dorians): the breaking of the tradition of endogamy puzzled later Greeks, who explained it by guessing that Labda was physically unattractive. Whatever the reality, Cypselus and his son Periander consolidated the state in a reign lasting 70 years; the last of the dynasty, Psammetichus (significantly, an Egyptian name), was overthrown after ruling for only three and a half years. Thereafter Corinth had a restricted form of government, in which control was exercised by the landed well-to-do, almost certainly only a minority in the population, who therefore turned to Sparta, whose similarly restricted constitution made it the natural friend of states like Corinth. From this time Corinth was an important but essentially second-rate city. It continued its naval interests, forming in effect the fleet of Sparta. Later, in the early 4th century BC, the Corinthians turned against Sparta and in the process almost certainly broadened their constitution.

After the Battle of Chaeronea (338 BC), and following the defeat of Athens and Thebes, Corinth, or more particularly its extramural sanctuary of Poseidon at Isthmia, was chosen by Philip II of Macedon as the locale for the great conference he called to decide the future relationship between the Greek cities and himself; the result is popularly known as the League of Corinth. Probably in reality an instrument of Macedonian control, the organization lapsed in the wars of the Successors of Alexander, but was revived in 306 BC by Antigonus Monophthalmus who was the most powerful of them. For the whole of this time, and for much of the 3rd century, the Acrocorinth was held by a Macedonian garrison; part of the fortifications built by Antigonus' son, Demetrius the Besieger, are still visible, incorporated into the later medieval and Turkish walls. Corinth was one of the "fetters of Greece" and its liberation by Aratus of Sicyon, who incorporated the city into his Achaean League, was a serious blow for the Macedonians. The freedom of Corinth was finally secured by the Roman defeat of Philip V: the Roman commander, Titus Quinctius Flamininus, ironically – and knowledgeably – proclaimed the freedom of Greece at Isthmia, in the very sanctuary where Philip II had effectively ended it. The later disloyalty of Corinth, which took the Roman freedom too literally and participated in an Achaean counteraction against Roman domination in Greece, led in 146 BC to the destruction of the city by Mummius, and the ransacking of its works of art.

Yet the site was too important to be obliterated, and a century later the city was refounded by Julius Caesar, but as a Roman, Latin-speaking colony. Some of the buildings of the Greek city survived, such as the 6th-century BC temple to Apollo, built shortly after the downfall of the tyrants. Others, such as the ruined long portico or stoa, to the south of the temple, were refurbished to serve as public buildings in the new city. The area between temple and stoa, which had been a gymnasium complete with a running course, became the forum of the Roman colony, with Roman-type temples constructed at its western end. The Roman colonists were presumably allotted estates, but it is clear that a Greek population still survived – St Paul wrote his epistle to the Corinthians in Greek, and in the course of time Greek ousted Latin. The city flourished. Although Athens was the academic centre of Roman Greece,

Corinth: Temple of Apollo, dating from the mid-6th century BC

Corinth was its political capital. This continued into the Byzantine period; one of the largest basilical churches in Greece was constructed at Lechaeum, Corinth's harbour on the gulf of Corinth. This prosperity persisted well into the middle Byzantine period, after which it suffered a sharp decline. There was a revival in the 10th century AD, and subsequently. Corinth was occupied by the Franks, and recent excavations are beginning to reveal good-quality buildings of this period. The final decline came with the Turkish occupation (1460). Acrocorinth, still a strategic key to the control of Greece, was refurbished and occupied by a Turkish garrison until the Greek War of Independence, but the town dwindled to an insignificant village. The revived Corinth of modern times was shifted to a more convenient location by the sea, on the gulf of Corinth.

Corinth's contribution to Greek civilization was considerable. Its trade links in the late 8th and 7th centuries BC both with the Near East and with the west not only brought it prosperity, so that its wealth was proverbial – "not everyone is fortunate enough to sail to Corinth" – but were also responsible, to a large extent, for the development of oriental motifs and forms in Archaic Greek art. Its painted pottery of this period seems to have been prized over a wide area (perhaps for the contents of the perfume flasks as much as their decoration) and is found ubiquitously. Less well preserved, but certainly more highly valued in antiquity, was Corinthian bronze ware. Much of this was buried in graves at Corinth itself, and after Mummius' sack of the city created a taste for Corinthian metalware in Rome. Nekrokorinthia – funerary items plundered from the graves–were highly prized by the wealthy Romans who could afford to collect them. Perhaps the most lasting contribution of the Corinthians was the creation, in the early 7th century BC, of the Doric order of architecture, for which the earliest evidence is at Corinth and Isthmia (the Corinthian order is later and developed elsewhere). All this impetus came in the crucial Archaic period. Though Corinth was less important later, its contribution to later civilization has endured to the present day.

R.A. TOMLINSON

Summary

Situated at the isthmus between the Peloponnese and central Greece, Corinth flourished as a trading city. Prosperity came early under the Bacchiads (8th century BC) and continued under the tyranny of the Cypselids (c.657–585 BC). For much of the Classical period Corinth sided with Sparta. Freed from Macedonian control by Rome, the city was destroyed in 146 BC. Rebuilt, the city flourished again and became the political capital of Greece during the Byzantine period. Decline set in with the Turkish period.

Further Reading

Ancient Corinth: A Guide to the Excavations, 3rd edition revised and enlarged, Athens, 1936

Engels, Donald, *Roman Corinth: An Alternative Model for the Classical City*, Chicago: University of Chicago Press, 1990

Salmon, J.B., *Wealthy Corinth: A History of the City to 338 BC*, Oxford: Clarendon Press, and New York: Oxford University Press, 1984

Will, Édouard, *Korinthiaka: Recherches sur l'histoire et la civilisation de Corinthe des origines aux guerres médiques*, Paris: Boccard, 1955

Corinth, Sack of 146 BC

The sack of Corinth was the event that symbolized the end of Greece's autonomy in antiquity. Its destruction had its roots in the declaration of Greek independence made by the Roman general Titus Quinctus Flamininus at the Isthmian Games in 196 BC. After defeating Philip V, king of Macedon, in the Second Macedonian War, the Romans decided not to cripple the Macedonian kingdom because they had no imperialistic ambitions in Greece; rather, they wanted Macedonia to serve as a buffer against the powers in the east, the barbarians in the Balkans, and even Greece itself. The Romans thus granted Philip favourable terms, with the stipulation that he withdraw completely from Greece, and decreed that all Greek cities were to be free and governed by their own laws. The Greeks and Romans had conflicting views on what freedom (Latin: *libertas*; Greek: *eleutheria*) meant, however. The Greeks interpreted their newly bestowed freedom as complete autonomy and the absence of Roman interference in their affairs. The Romans, on the other hand, expected the Greek states to give them their loyalty and support. As Ernst Badian has shown, foreign policy was a microcosm of the patron–client relationship in republican Roman society, and the Greeks failed to perceive this. Whereas Rome expected cooperation and a sense of loyalty, the Greeks displayed a callous disregard for them and continued to carry out their centuries-old internecine wars and struggles.

Many Greeks resented Rome's settlement with Philip. Sparta, for example, was angry that it had lost the city of Argos, while the Aetolian League was embittered when it did not receive, as it had hoped, all of Thessaly but instead saw most of the territory divided into four separate confederate states. Relations between Rome and Greece quickly deteriorated, proving the folly of Rome's hands-off policy expressed by Flamininus at Isthmia. The Aetolians invited into Greece Antiochus III, king of Syria, who was quickly taken care of by the Romans in 191 BC: Antiochus' forces were overwhelmed at Thermopylae, forcing him to beat a hasty retreat to Asia Minor. The Third Macedonian War (171–168 BC), waged by the Romans against Philip's son Perseus, proved disastrous for Greece. Although few Greek cities actually sided with Perseus, Rome's anger did not fail to fall on Greece. One thousand Achaeans were deported to Rome because of suspicious loyalty; 500 Aetolians were executed after a farcical trial; 70 Epirot cities were destroyed, with 150,000 of the population sold into slavery; and the island of Rhodes was economically crippled by the establishment of Delos as a free port.

The end of Greek independence was the result of the actions of the Achaean league. In 150 BC the surviving 300 of the original 1,000 Achaean detainees returned and found the League in conflict, yet again, with Sparta, this time over a boundary dispute. The Spartans, although members of the league, appealed to Rome for arbitration. The league, which could not tolerate such insubordination by one of its members, decided to punish Sparta; because Rome had not previously interfered with how it conducted its business, the league felt at liberty to bring Sparta forcibly back into its political alliance. Embassies from Sparta and the Achaean League went to Rome on three occasions, yet Rome did not respond, its hands too occupied with a revolt in Macedonia (150–148 BC) led by Andriscus, a pretender to the throne. In 148 BC Sparta declared its secession from the Achaean League, which then went on the offensive, quickly reducing Sparta to the brink of surrender. At this point a Roman embassy, led by Lucius Aurelius Orestes, arrived at Corinth to ask the league to see reason; Orestes even threatened (although he was probably bluffing) to dissolve the league by removing from the alliance the cities of Sparta, Corinth, Argos, Arcadian Orchomenus, and Heracleia-ad-Oetam. The reaction was furious, and a second Roman embassy, led by Sextus Iulius Caesar, failed despite conciliatory overtures. In the spring of 146 BC Quintus Caecilius Metullus, the Roman general in Macedonia, sent yet another embassy to the league, which had assembled at Corinth. The envoys were rudely treated by the assembly, heavily composed of lower-class workers who, traditionally, were hostile to Rome because of its policy of supporting local aristocracies. The League then officially declared war on Sparta, although this was tantamount to war on Rome. The Roman Senate reacted by instructing Metullus to march south from Macedonia and the new consul, Lucius Mummius, to set sail for Greece with a fleet. As Erich Gruen has convincingly argued, the league was shocked and stunned by this development: in the past the Romans had not interfered in Greek internal struggles, and so the league had assumed that it was free to punish a city that had defected from its membership. But Rome's patience had worn out and foreign policy was no longer in the hands of men like the Scipios and Flamininus; more importantly, Rome could not tolerate a war in the Peloponnese at the very time that it was settling affairs in northern Greece.

The league struck first by marching against Heracleia-ad-Oetam. Metullus soon arrived and cut the Achaeans to pieces in three separate battles. The league then ordered 12,000 slaves freed to serve as reinforcements to a ragtag army raised to defend the isthmus. Meanwhile Mummius had assumed command of the Roman army and met the Achaean army at Leucopetra on the isthmus. The Achaeans were annihilated, and Corinth was captured without resistance. Rome decided to make an example of it. All survivors were sold into slavery. The city was sacked, burned, and levelled to the ground, and its land declared *ager publicus* ("public land") and handed over to the neighbouring town of Sicyon to till. Anything that could be carried off was taken to Rome. Stories circulated of Mummius taking out "insurance policies" on priceless art treasures in the event of their being lost on the voyage home, and of soldiers playing dice on masterpieces of Greek sculpture. Greece itself was subjected to a "final solution". All leagues were dissolved, democracies were abolished and replaced by aristocracies, and the whole of Greece was put under the responsibility of the governor of Macedonia. Later, in 27 BC, the province of Achaea was established to govern southern Greece, although this merely formalized Greece's existing total subservience. Individual cities achieved varying levels of prosperity during the empire, but mainland Greece as a political concept no longer existed. Greek independence had come to an end, but so had hundreds of years of internal strife and war.

STEVEN M. OBERHELMAN

Further Reading

Derow, P.S., "Rome, the Fall of Macedon, and the Sack of Corinth" in *Rome and the Mediterranean to 133 BC*, edited by A.E. Astin *et al.*, Cambridge: Cambridge University Press, 1989 (*The Cambridge Ancient History*, vol. 8, 2nd edition)

Fuks, Alexander, "The Bellum Achaicum and its Social Aspect", *Journal of Hellenic Studies*, 90 (1970): pp. 78–89

Gruen, Erich, "The Origins of the Achaean War", *Journal of Hellenic Studies*, 96 (1976): pp. 46–69

Gruen, Erich, *The Hellenistic World and the Coming of Rome*, Berkeley: University of California Press, 1984, vol. 2, pp. 481–528

Larsen, J.A.O., *Greek Federal States: Their Institutions and History*, Oxford: Clarendon Press, 1968

Coronation

The silence of literary sources about any ceremony of investiture of a new Greek ruler before the beginning of the Hellenistic period, when eastern influences began to be felt, attests to the simple assumption or seizure of power, perhaps celebrated by a banquet at which laudatory speeches could be delivered. The exception is Macedon, since at least theoretically the king was elected there by acclamation of the army. A vestige of this practice persisted in Ptolemaic Egypt where, certainly until its severe ethnic adulteration in the early 2nd century BC, the Macedonian royal bodyguard retained the right of approval of new sovereigns.

Crowns (at least in the form of garlands) did exist in Classical Greece, but they were worn by priests in the exercise of their rituals, orators, and especially symposiasts. Initially vegetal, they came to be made of gold, and some delicate funerary examples of this latter type have survived. The awarding of crowns for excellence at athletic and dramatic festivals encouraged their increasing use as symbols of merit in other spheres (the most famous example is Ctesiphon's proposal that Demosthenes be crowned at the Dionysia for his sage political advice). Such crowns could be awarded also to a whole state and were so frequently expected and received by rivals in the Wars of the Successors after the death of Alexander the Great that their value was often demanded in cash in lieu of the actual artefacts, a practice which by the Byzantine period had been formalized as a tax. As symbols of their position Hellenistic monarchs held a sceptre and wore purple garments and a diadem consisting of a white cloth knotted behind with free-flowing ends (this last was first assumed by Alexander, probably to advertise his conquest of Asia since Greeks had hitherto not worn diadems to indicate kingship, while Persians had).

Early Byzantine emperors naturally followed Roman tradition, since they were Latin-speaking and nobody recognized any break in the continuity of the empire despite its new orientation. Augustus' fiction of the re-establishment of the republic meant that in theory emperors were chosen simply as "first citizens" by the will of the people, which in practice ensured that after they had taken power peacefully or by violence they were begged to assume that same power by a compliant senate. Frequently they were first acclaimed *imperator* by their soldiers, a practice that evolved from this title being temporarily bestowed upon triumphing generals by their troops. Acclamations of welcome are first documented at Trajan's accession in AD 98 and thereafter were an increasingly ritualized part of these (and numerous other) imperial occasions. An important act at accession became the distribution of largesse to soldiery and populace. The diadem, famously refused by Julius Caesar in 44 BC, was not worn by the early emperors, but in radiate form it had become the chief imperial numismatic *insigne* by the 3rd century AD.

Roman and Byzantine usurpers were regularly acclaimed initially by the army, but from the time of Julian (361) to Phokas (602) two foreign customs were frequently observed. As a ceremony of accession the soldiers would raise the new emperor in Germanic manner on a shield, an act that may have been invested with solar symbolism. They also placed upon his head a torque, which was originally a (probably Scandinavian) protective collar but whose numerous types, some heavily bejewelled, came to be worn in the Byzantine period by slaves and various military officers and civil servants.

Christianization of the ceremony of investiture was slow except in one crucial detail: the appointment of an emperor (now the vicegerent of God rather than a deity in his own right) was deemed to be made by God, whether it came about through the approval of a reigning emperor's or widow's choice by one or more of the senate, army, and people or through an actual election by one or more of these bodies. Legal and other texts, moreover, claim that emperors were crowned by the hand of God, and middle Byzantine depictions – notably a few ivory plaques – show Christ as officiant. Nonetheless, in the 4th century the site was often the Hebdomon, an army camp in the suburbs of Constantinople, and when the ceremony was transferred in the 5th or 6th century it was to the Hippodrome, a move that still emphasized its popular if not completely secular importance. Although Constantine VI was crowned in the latter as late as 776, the coronation of Constans II in the ambo of Hagia Sophia in 641 marks the increasing role of the Church, which is emphasized by the scheduling of coronations to coincide with major feasts of the ecclesiastical year. Notwithstanding, co-emperors (in Hagia Sophia) and empresses (in the Augustaion or at the church of St Stephen of Daphne) were crowned by the senior emperor, rather than the patriarch (apart from one instance in 748); and on the less usual occasions when there was no senior emperor available, the patriarch probably acted more as the leading citizen than specifically as a churchman. Furthermore, emperors remained standing during the actual coronation, as they did during the preceding and following acclamations. Accessions continued to be celebrated with banquets, chariot-racing, and the distribution of largesse. The *Book of Ceremonies* compiled by or at the instigation of Constantine VII Porphyrogennetos (913–59) exhaustively details receptions by courtiers and the factions, the actual coronation, the acclamations, and the emperor's ascent of the throne to receive *proskynesis* (gestures of submission and reverence).

During the period of the Nicene emperors (1204–61) the coronation of co-emperors was abandoned and shield-raising reinstituted. The anonymous 14th-century *Treatise on the Dignities and Offices* (Pseudo-Kodinos) describes shield-raising outside Hagia Sophia by the patriarch and important officials in order of rank before the anointing. Pre-13th-century mention of the latter in connection with the accession of Byzantine emperors may have been just metaphorical, instigated by frequent reference in the Septuagint and reaffirmed by the Byzantine iconography of Davidic kingship, but from 1205 at the latest it was certainly actually practised immediately before the coronation itself. The inspiration may have been initially western, but Byzantines invested it with the Christomimetic symbolism of the Holy Spirit.

The Palaiologans (1259–1453), in addition to restoring the coronation of co-emperors, made a major addition in the emperor's profession of Orthodoxy that began the ceremony. This was now thoroughly integrated into the Eucharistic liturgy, but culminated in a *prokypsis* (manifestation) in which the removal of a curtain suddenly revealed on a platform the brilliantly lit emperor, who then received acclamations from an assembled throng of courtiers and clergy.

It is not clear whether all the imperial insignia were real objects (when not in use kept safe in the palace by court eunuchs) or merely iconographic (and especially numismatic) symbols. The most important was the crown, in origin the Hellenistic diadem which by the time of Constantine I had taken the form of a purple band fitted with pearls and jewels; it later developed *prependoulia* (hanging ornaments) and a superimposed cross. Late crowns (known as *kamelaukia*) contained a golden covering of the head. They were all personal, not hereditary, and were of different forms for different occasions. Remains of two 11th-century Byzantine crowns (both now in Budapest) survive. One, with enamel plaques of Constantine IX and his sisters, dancing women, and personifications of Humility and Truth, may have been made for the coronation, or wedding, of an empress. The other is the lower part of the Hungarian "Crown of St Stephen" which was given, in accord with common diplomatic practice, to Géza I, and displayed plaques to demonstrate his subordination to Michael VII and his son (or brother). The *sphaira* (orb) shown in one hand of an emperor was probably only an artistic symbol. It was of Roman origin and signified mundane dominion, but the substitution by Theodosius II (408–50) of a cross for its superimposed imperial eagle demonstrated that this power was only for and through God. The eagle- and, by the 8th century, cross-capped sceptre was a survival of the Roman consular symbol of authority which emperors assumed: it probably existed as a tangible object only at certain periods of Byzantine history and became important mainly in and after the 10th century. The *akakia*, held usually in the emperor's right hand, was a pouch of purple silk containing dust to signify the transience of temporal power. The throne was not only an imperial but also a divine symbol already in pagan antiquity, but in Byzantium, where it was regularly furnished with a foot-stool, it became even more potent through association with the biblical throne of Solomon.

The emperor wore a wide variety of vestments for different stages of different ceremonies, but they were all marked by a chromatic monopoly of imperial purple. At his coronation he usually wore a purple *divetesion* (a long, belted silk tunic, probably later replaced by the somewhat similar *sakkos*), over which was laid during the actual rite a purple *chlamys* (a cloak bordered with gems or pearls) with two attached golden *tablia* (richly embroidered rectangular or trapezoidal pieces). In 14th-century coronations the emperor donned a golden *mandyas* (cloak), probably instead of the *chlamys*. Ornamented red *tzangia* (high boots) became by the 10th century at the latest an imperial symbol and a sufficiently important part of the coronation ceremonial that their use by a subject signalled attempted usurpation of the throne. The *loros*, a stole with a long Byzantine history which was taken to symbolize either the cross or the winding-sheet of Christ, adorned Byzantine emperors on various festive occasions but not at their coronation. It was, however, worn by the Latin Baldwin of Flanders when he was crowned in Hagia Sophia in 1204.

Although a crown was made for the Bavarian Otho, when he accepted the throne of the newly independent Greek state in 1832, there was no actual coronation; and his successor George I did not even possess a crown since there was no constitutional use for one. Nevertheless, the Byzantine coronation ritual, regalia, and vestments survived with only minor changes up to the early 20th century in Russia. Western European coronations have also been indebted to Byzantium, most notably still at the end of the 20th century in Britain. There the crowns of Saxon kings had already been copied from early Byzantine exemplars and the English coronation order was modelled on the Byzantine by the 10th century, while most of the ceremonial and regalia at the coronation of Elizabeth II in 1953 derived from Byzantium, even to the extent of the the *loros* and the *chlamys* or *mandyas* surviving respectively in the Stole Royal and the Robe Royal of Cloth of Gold.

A.R. LITTLEWOOD

Further Reading

Anastos, Milton V., "*Vox populi voluntas Dei* and the Election of the Byzantine Emperor" in his *Studies in Byzantine Intellectual History*, London: Variorum, 1979

Christophilopoulou, A., *Ekloge, Anagorevsis kai Stepsis tou Byzantinou Autokratoros* [Selection, Election, and Coronation of the Byzantine Emperor], Athens, 1956

Constantine VII Porphyrogennetos, *Le Livre des cérémonies* [*De Caerimoniis*], edited and translated into French by Albert Vogt, vol. 2, Paris: Belles Lettres, 1967, pp. 1–23

Deér, Josef von, *Byzanz und das abendländische Herrschertum*, Sigmaringen: Thorbecke, 1977

Grabar, André, *L'Empereur dans l'art byzantin*, Paris: Belles Lettres, 1936; reprinted London: Variorum, 1971

Lilie, R.-J., Krönung entry in *Reallexikon zur byzantinischen Kunst*, vol. 5, Stuttgart: Hiersemann, 1991, columns 439–54

McCormick, Michael, *Eternal Victory: Triumphal Rulership in Late Antiquity, Byzantium, and the Early Medieval West*, Cambridge and New York: Cambridge University Press, 1986

Nelson, J.L., "Symbols in Context: Rulers' Inauguration Rituals in Byzantium and the West in the Early Middle Ages", *Studies in Church History*, 13 (1976): pp. 97–119

Nicol, Donald M., "*Kaisersalbung*: The Unction of Emperors in Late Byzantine Coronation Ritual", *Byzantine and Modern Greek Studies*, 2 (1976): pp. 37–52

Pseudo-Kodinos, *Traité des offices*, edited by Jean Verpeaux, Paris: Centre National de la Recherche Scientifique, 1966, pp. 252–73

Restle, M., Herrschaftszeichen entry in *Reallexikon für Antike und Christentum*, vol. 14, Stuttgart: Hiersemann, 1987–88, columns 943–66

Ritter, H.-W., *Diadem und Königsherrschaft: Untersuchungen zu Zeremonien und Rechtsgrundlagen des Herrschaftsantritts bei den Persern, bei Alexander dem Grossen und im Hellenismus*, Munich: Beck, 1965

Schramm, P.E., *Herrschaftszeichen und Staatssymbolik: Beiträge zu ihrer Geschichte vom dritten bis zum sechzehnten Jahrhundert*, 4 vols, Stuttgart: Hiersemann, 1954–78

Twining, Lord, *European Regalia*, London: Batsford, 1967

Walter, Christopher, "Raising on a Shield in Byzantine Iconography", *Revue des Etudes Byzantines*, 33 (1975): pp. 133–75

Walter, Christopher, "The Significance of Unction in Byzantine Iconography", *Byzantine and Modern Greek Studies*, 2 (1976): pp. 53–73

Wessel, K., E. Piltz, and C. Nicolescu, Insignien entry in *Reallexikon zur byzantinischen Kunst*, vol. 3, Stuttgart: Hiersemann, 1978, columns 369–498

Corruption

The 1997 European Union convention on corruption involving officials of the European Community or of member states (OJ No. C195, 25.6.1997, p. 2) defines corruption as the deliberate, direct, or indirect action of requesting, receiving, or accepting a promise on the one hand (passive corruption), or promising or giving on the other (active corruption) an advantage, to act or refrain from acting in breach of official duties.

This definition, which has been reiterated in the EU joint action on corruption in the private sector (OJ No. L358, 31.12.1998, p.2), reflects the perception of corruption as the occult exchange between the political and administrative and the economic and social market, violating public, legal, and ethical norms and sacrificing the common good to private interest (Della Porta and Meny, 1997). Such a broad definition is necessary in order to embrace the many different aspects of corruption, which are closely interrelated to parallel phenomena of clientelism and maladministration.

In his analysis of the causes of one of the main manifestations of the phenomenon, of political corruption, Paul Heywood (1997) provides a useful overview of the various approaches to the topic. The "structural" approach focuses on the nature of state development, examining variables such as administrative organization, efficiency, and the institutionalization of the political order. The "economic" approach associates political corruption with growing state intervention. And the "institutional" approach focuses on the function and financing of political parties and factors such as longevity in power.

The applicability of these approaches to instances of corruption in the Classical and Byzantine world is limited, due to the differences in the structure of state and polity. The preceding definition of corruption is inextricably associated with the development and specific characteristics of contemporary state organization and social structures. The conceptualization of corruption is considerably different in both Classical and Byzantine times, when characteristic types of political organization led to a broader perception of the term. The Classical period is thus characterized by a series of corruption claims, mostly linked with political disclosure. Corruption was thus a weapon to be used against political opponents, usually as part of a moral crusade aimed at the demonization of the opponent. Similar claims in the Byzantine period were triggered not by the purchase of offices and titles – largely held to be legitimate at the time – but rather by arbitrary administrative actions in the pursuit of profit.

All three approaches have, however, been employed in analyses of political corruption in the modern Greek state. The structural and economic approaches are interrelated in assessing corruption in the development of the Greek polity during the 19th century. Foreign interference and the emergence of a powerful and omnipresent state are viewed as significant factors, related to the immaturity of political institutions and parties, clientelism, and the "oscillation between authoritarian and democratic regimes" (Lyrintzis, 1984). Such articulation of powers in the "procapitalist" Greek society, between weak social and economic forces on the one hand and a very strong state machinery on the other, is critical in strengthening family and clientelistic networks and contributes towards a defensive perception of the role and function of politics, its aims being the protection of the individual from social conflict (Diamantouros, 1983). In this manner clientelistic networks compensate for the absence of strong social classes (Koutsoukis, 1998).

The situation changed with the military coup of 1909, which signalled the end of the 19th-century oligarchic parliamentary system of government (Mouzelis, 1987). The emergence of class interests and their articulation through better-organized political parties gave rise to more centralized forms of "party and state-oriented patronage". According to Mouzelis, the years up to World War II, notwithstanding the increasing significance of ideology, social division, and political conflict, did not witness the eclipse of the patron–client system, but rather the transition from oligarchic/traditional to state/ bureaucratic forms of patronage.

The end of the war and of the Greek Civil War brought about a further turn in the political situation of the country. Emergency legislation, increasing state control in the – in any case – limited exercise of social and political rights, and the proscription of the Communist Party and harassment of its followers made the development of participatory political structures impossible and paved the way for a political system dependent on recourse to patron–client relationships (Gravaris, 1998). Instead of being influenced by local notables, however, clientelism in this period witnessed the pivotal role of the central party leadership in distributing favours. The central role of the state apparatus in the development of clientelistic networks marks further the transition from "party-directed patronage" to a system of "bureaucratic clientelism". This term denotes the infiltration of state institutions by the supporters of the dominant political party, along with phenomena of favouritism, inextricably linked with the expansion of the public sector.

A genuine trend towards bureaucratic clientelism did not appear, however, until after the junta, coinciding with the emergence of well-organized political parties. The persistence of clientelistic phenomena in this period renders the "institutional" approach a useful analytical tool. Notwithstanding the important steps taken towards the consolidation of parliamentary democracy, New Democracy, the conservative party in power between 1974 and 1981, continued to rely on the personal influence and clientelistic networks of its leading members. The socialist government of PASOK on the other hand, in its first period in office from 1981 to 1989, in spite of the elaborate party organization, maintained clientelistic networks due to the overextension of the public sector and the emergence of the state as employer. The new "public ethic" endorsed by the socialist government led Koutsoukis to refer to the appearance of a form of "structural corruption" taking the form of scandals.

The 1990s witnessed an attempt to resolve such complex issues through recourse to the judiciary. The outcome of the corruption trials was of dubious significance for the elimination of the structural roots of corruption in the political system. The economic changes associated with the narrowing of the public sector, along with changes in party organization and perception, may add novel variables to the evolution of the phenomenon in Greece. At the same time, different forms of corruption are highlighted, such as police corruption, public corruption related to organized crime, and corruption in the private sector. In the Corruption Perceptions Index of 1998 issued by Transparency International, Greece holds the bottom position among EU countries after Italy (Transparency International and Göttingen University, 1998).

This and other findings led to an anti-corruption drive by the Greek Supreme Court, modelled on the recent "mani pulite" initiative in Italy (To Vima, 4 April 1999, article code B12539A501). At the same time, Greece has introduced a law ratifying the OECD convention on combating bribery of foreign public officials in international business transactions and, as a member of the European Union, implements the EU anti-corruption initiatives. The effectiveness of such legislative and judicial attempts to eliminate the structural roots of corruption remains to be seen.

VALSAMIS MITSILEGAS

Further Reading

Della Porta, Donatella and Yves Mény, "Introduction: Democracy and Corruption" in Democracy and Corruption in Europe, edited by Della Porta and Mény, London: Pinter, 1997

Diamantouros, N.-P., "I Enoathidrisi tou Koinovouleutismou stin Ellada kai I Leitourgia tou to 19o Aiona" [The Establishment of Parliamentarism in Greece and Its Function in the 19th Century] in Opseis tis Ellinikis koinonias tou 19ou Aiona [Aspects of Greek Society of the 19th Century], edited by D.G. Tsaoussis, Athens, 1983, reprinted 1998

Gravaris, D., "'To Ktisimo' tou Koinonikou Kratous: Apo ton Kommatiko Logo se Kratikes Politikes" [The 'Building' of the Social State: From Party Discourse to State Policies] in PASOK: Komma–Kratos–Koinonia [PASOK: Party–State–Society], edited by M. Spourdalakis, Athens, 1998

Heywood, P., "Political Corruption: Problems and Perspectives" in Political Corruption, edited by Paul Heywood, Oxford and Malden, Massachusetts: Blackwell, 1997

Koutsoukis, K., "I Diaphthora os Istoriko Phainomeno sto Syngchrono Elliniko Kratos" [Corruption as a Historical Phenomenon in the Modern Greek State] in Kratos kai Diaphrhora [State and Corruption], edited by A.P. Nicolopoulou, Athens, 1998

Lyrintzis, C., "Political Parties in Post-Junta Greece: A Case of Bureaucratic Clientelism?", West European Politics, 7/2 (April 1984): pp. 99–118

Mouzelis, N., Politics in the Semi-Periphery: Early Parliamentarism and Late Industrialisation in the Balkans and Latin America, London: Macmillan, and New York: St Martin's Press, 1986

Mouzelis, N., "Continuities and Discontinuities in Greek Politics: From Eleftherios Venizelos to Andreas Papandreou" in Political Change in Greece: Before and After the Colonels, edited by Kevin Featherstone and Dimitrios K. Katsoudas, London: Croom Helm, 1987

Website

Transparency International, press releases, including the annual Corruption Perceptions Index, can be downloaded from http://www.transparency.de/documents/press-releases

Corydalleus, Theophilos c.1574–1646

Philosopher

Theophilos Corydalleus was the most eminent philosopher of the Greek world after 1453 until the period of the Enlightenment and his influence persisted even down to the 18th century. He was born in Athens where he completed his first studies. Between 1604 and 1608 he was educated at the Greek Catholic College of St Athanasios in Rome. Afterwards he enrolled in the University of Padua to study philosophy and medicine and obtained his doctorate on 5 June 1613. There he met Cesare Cremonini and was influenced by Neoaristotelianism, a predominant philosophical current of the day. Its intention was not to interpret Aristotle as a means of corroborating Christian doctrine, as was the case earlier with medieval Scholasticism and Averroism. Rather it aimed at liberating Aristotle from ecclesiastical control and apologetic objectives and considering his works in their own terms. Such a perspective rendered Neoaristotelians suspicious to Church authorities, because they were thought of as professing non-Christian and even atheistic views.

Despite these shortcomings, Corydalleus's Neoaristotelianism was rather carefully articulated and avoided any serious confrontation with Orthodox doctrine. Aside from his teaching activity in Venice (1608–09), in Athens (1590, 1613–19, 1643–46), in Cephalonia (1619–21), and in Zakynthos (1621–22, 1628–36), Corydalleus was distinguished as director of the Patriarchal Academy in Constantinople (1622–23, 1625–28, 1636–40). He was initially appointed there through the intervention of patriarch Cyril Lukaris. Corydalleus restructured the entire curriculum along the Neoaristotelian model, which contributed to the relative emancipation of philosophy from theology. His teaching was characterized by a methodical, systematic, and clear exposition of his ideas. Corydalleus's impact was long-lasting, for he had many admirers among his students. Some of his works have been republished for didactic purposes. Numerous manuscripts of his writings also survive today in various libraries, a fact attesting to the wider dissemination of his ideas.

Corydalleus was a major scholiast of Aristotle's main works and contributed immensely to the reorientation of the Greek world towards Aristotelian philosophy. Aristotle's authority thus became established at that time so that he was referred to generally as "the Philosopher". Corydalleus's works, both published and unpublished, contain commentaries on Aristotle's philosophical and scientific texts as well as other writings (see Tsourkas). Corydalleus helped also the development of free thought in the Balkans by liberating Aristotle's interpretation from religious expediencies. To avoid potential conflicts with the Church, he supported the Neoaristotelian doctrine of the "double truth", namely that there existed two separate truths, one based upon the Bible and the Christian doctrine, and the other upon Aristotle. Corydalleus was neither anti-metaphysical nor anti-religious. He adhered to the Christian faith and considered it superior to philosophy. But he also intended to remain faithful to Aristotle, and the doctrine of the "double truth" provided a useful outlet. The latter theory, however, was severely criticized as unfounded and erroneous by other Christian Aristotelians, such as Nikolaos Koursoulas, who tried to prove the full coincidence of Christian and Aristotelian opinions.

Though Corydalleus was ordained as presbyter under the name Theodosios in 1622 and served as archbishop of Arta and Naupactus (1640–42), he was not a truly ecclesiastical man, for his scholarly and didactic activities held priority in his scale of interests. This was probably the reason why he abandoned his priesthood as early as 1625 and later his archbishopric in order to devote himself to his teaching goals. Corydalleus was even met with opposition and criticism from his contemporaries for theological reasons. In some cases, he was suspected and accused of atheism, materialism, and even Calvinism – the last being the accusation brought against patriarch Cyril I Lukaris too.

Corydalleus represented an important moment in the post-Byzantine philosophical tradition of southeastern Europe. His Neoaristotelianism found unexpected fertile ground in the educational tradition of the Orthodox east. This was probably due to the uninterrupted presence of the Aristotelian tradition in the Greek world. Among the consequences of Corydalleus's educational renewal was the relative marginalization of religious and grammatical lessons in school curricula. Corydalleus had numerous students who distinguished themselves at that time, among then patriarch Nektarios of Jerusalem, Ioannis Karyophyllis, Meletios Syrigos, Evgenios Yannoulis, Alexandros Mavrokordatos, and Georgios Sougdouris. Some of them disseminated his philosophical tradition in various parts of the Balkans, such as Germanos Lokros and later Sevastos Kyminitis at the Princely Academy in Bucharest. In this way, Corydalleus's Neoaristotelianism became the most important programme of philosophical education in southeastern Europe in the 17th and 18th centuries. It is no wonder therefore that the libraries of Bucharest and Jassy nowadays house numerous manuscripts containing his works.

In time, however, Corydalleus's influence and authority became so strong and suffocating that they did not allow other systems of thought to develop and flourish. This absolutization of Neoaristotelianism, sanctioned by the Church, became known later as "Corydalism", a term of opprobrium for those who were profoundly attached to and could not look beyond that philosophical system. Whenever Neoaristotelianism was challenged, reactions usually arose both from the teaching staff as well as from the Church. Indicative of such a case was the condemnation of Methodios Anthrakitis in 1723, who had abandoned Aristotelianism and was teaching modern western philosophy. In his reinstatement by the Church in 1725, Anthrakitis was given the order to teach solely Aristotelian philosophy according to Corydalleus's tradition, which was thought to pose no threat to the Orthodox faith. This is evidence of the official sanction of Corydalleus's system by the Orthodox Church, a fact manifested in other cases too (e.g. in the answer of the Eastern Orthodox Patriarchs to the Anglican Nonjurors in 1718). In the first half of the 18th century there were also various debates between Aristotelians (e.g. Dorotheos Lesvios) and non-Aristotelians (e.g. Nikolaos Zerzoulis). The latter tried systematically to undermine Aristotle's authority in ecclesiastical circles by showing the conspicuous and unbridgeable discrepancies between several Aristotelian and Christian views.

The most important challenge for Corydalleus's tradition came from the growing influence of the Enlightenment in the Greek world in the second half of the 18th century, which presented an attractive alternative model of philosophical and scientific tradition beyond Aristotle. As a result, Aristotelian physics as well as Ptolemaic cosmology came under denigrating attack from the proponents of the modern scientific developments in the West. However, Corydalleus still managed to exercise certain influences until the beginning of the 19th century, since his works continued to be taught in several schools. This happened at the Patriarchal Academy of Constantinople too, where Sergios Makraios taught Aristotelian philosophy and science and remained bound to this tradition until his death in 1819. Despite these much later developments, for which he was not responsible, Corydalleus's contributions were of great importance to the development of Greek learning and education in a period of transition from the post-Byzantine era to the age of the Greek Enlightenment.

VASILIOS MAKRIDES

Biography

Born c.1574, Corydalleus was educated in Athens, Rome, and Padua where he was influenced by the Neoaristotelianism of Cesare Cremonini. After teaching in Venice, Athens, Cephalonia, and Zakynthos, he was appointed director of the Patriarchal Academy in Constantinople by Patriarch Cyril Lukaris. He also served briefly as archbishop of Arta and Naupactus (1640–42) but resigned to devote himself to teaching. His programme dominated philosophical education in southeastern Europe in the 17th and 18th centuries. He died in 1646.

Writings

Introduction à la Logique / Prooimion eis Logikin, edited by Athanase Papadopoulos, translated into French by Constantin Noica, Bucharest: Association Internationale d'Etudes du Sud-Est Européen, 1970

Commentaires à la métaphysique / Metaphysiki Aristotelous, edited by T. Iliopoulos, translated into French by Constantin Noica, Bucharest: Association Internationale d'Etudes du Sud-Est Européen, 1972

Further Reading

Benakis, Linos, "O allote 'Kodix Phrontistiriou Trapezountos 16' (Theophilou Korydaleos, *Eisodos Physikis Akroaseos kat' Aristotelin*) kai o Ioannis Ierevs kai Oikonomos Trapezountos" [The Former 'Codex 16 of the Trapezous Phrontisterion'

(Theodore Corydalleus, *Introduction to Aristotle's Physics of Hearing*) and John, Priest and Oeconomos of Trapezous], *O Eranistis*, 5 (1967): pp. 86–97

Benakis, Linos, "Apo tin Istoria tou Metavyzantinou Aristotelismou ston Elliniko Choro" [From the History of Post-Byzantine Aristotelianism in Greece], *Philosophia*, 7 (1977): pp. 416–54

Benakis, Linos, "Anekdoto Keimeno tou Nikolaou Zerzouli (1706–1773). Mia Proimi Syngrousi me ton Dorotheo Lesvio se Themata Theologias, Philosophias kai Epistimis" [An Unpublished Text of Nicholas Zerzoulis: An Early Argument with Dorotheos of Lesbos on the Topics of Theology, Philosophy, and Science], *Devkalion*, 21 (1978): pp. 86–95

Benakis, Linos, "Neoteriki Kritiki tou Metavyzantinou Aristotelismou ston Elliniko Choro kata ton 18o Aiona" [New Criticism of 18th-Century Post-Byzantine Aristotelianism in Greece] in *Praktika tou Pangosmiou Synedriou "Aristotelis"*, vol. 2, Athens, 1981

Benakis, Linos, "I cheirographi paradosi ton Scholion sto *Peri Psychis* tou Aristoteli ton Nikolaou Koursoula kai Gerasimou Vlachou" [The Manuscript Tradition of Nicholas Koursoulas and Gerasimos Vlachos's scholia to Aristotle's 'On the Soul'], *Deltion tis Ioniou Akadimias*, 2 (1986): pp. 141–67

Gritsopoulos, Tasos, *Patriarchiki Megali tou Genous Scholi* [The Great National Patriarchal School], vol. 1, Athens, 1966, pp. 154–87

Henderson, George, *The Revival of Greek Thought, 1620–1830*, Albany: State University of New York Press, 1970, pp. 12–19

Jochem, Otto, "Scholastisches, Christliches und Medizinisches aus dem Kommentar des Theophilos Korydalleus zu Aristoteles' Schrift von der Seele", dissertation, University of Giessen, 1935

Noica, Constantin, "La Signification historique de l'oeuvre de Théophile Corydalée", *Revue des Études Sud-Est Européennes*, 11 (1973): pp. 285–306

Podskalsky, Gerhard, *Griechische Theologie in der Zeit der Türkenherrschaft, 1453–1821*, Munich: Beck, 1988, pp. 194–99

Tsourkas, Cléobule, *Les Débuts de l'enseignement philosophique et de la libre pensée dans les Balkans: la vie et l'oeuvre de Théophile Corydalée (1570–1646)*, 2nd edition, Thessalonica: Institute for Balkan Studies, 1967

Cos

Island in the Dodecanese

The island of Cos is the largest of the Dodecanese after Rhodes (although only about one-fifth of its area), and lies close to the coast of Asia Minor; its long, narrow shape, with an area of 282 sq km, extends, at its northeastern end, into the gulf separating the headlands of Halicarnassus (now Bodrum) and Cnidus. It has been known by several names, from the Cos Meropis of Strabo and the Caris of Stephanos of Byzantium to the medieval Lango (referring to its long shape) and the Turkish Istanköy.

The island has two prominent mountain formations, with the two highest points being Oros Dikaios towards the northeast (846 m) and Oros Latra in the southwest (428 m). Most of the rest of the island is quite fertile, with a light, sandy soil, and has always produced much fruit, vegetables, and wine, while its silk was famous in antiquity for its fine texture.

Although populated since earliest times, and later colonized by both Carians from Halicarnassus and by Dorians, the island did not play a part of great importance in Greek history until the mid-4th century BC, with the foundation of the city of Cos.

Thereafter it rapidly became one of the main maritime and trading centres of the Aegean, and was later to be the second city of the province of the Islands.

The artist who was perhaps the most famous painter of the ancient world, Apelles, was a native of Cos, and although his renown meant that he worked in many other parts of Greece, Pliny (*Naturalis Historia*, 35. 80) in his account of his life said that he was working at Cos on a painting of *Aphrodite Anadyomene* when "death grew envious of him" and he died with the work unfinished. Also on Cos was a marble statue of *Aphrodite* by the equally famous 4th-century BC sculptor Praxiteles; he had carved two versions, one clothed and one naked, and offered them both for sale at Cnidus; Pliny (*Naturalis Historia*, 36. 20) relates how the people of Cos chose the clothed one, "thinking that this was the sober and proper choice to make".

It was to be the association of the island with Hippocrates, the father of the medical tradition who was born there c.460 BC, that lay behind the foundation of the Asclepieum; this was to bring worldwide fame to Cos as a centre of healing. The "Hippocratic oath", named after him, still forms the basis of contemporary medical ethics throughout most of the world, and must be seen as one of the main gifts of the Hellenic world to international medical culture; in revised form it is still actively applied. The Asclepieum was founded after the death of Hippocrates in the mid-4th century BC, and its priests, the Asclepiadai, became known for performing medical cures that followed the teaching of Hippocrates. It developed and prospered over several centuries, eventually reaching the hugely impressive monumental complex that has now been excavated, before major destruction in the 6th century AD. Today it is the island's most visited site.

It may have been the fame of the island in late antiquity that accounts for its importance in early Church history. It was to be one of the three Aegean islands that were represented by bishops at the First Church Council at Nicaea of AD 325 (the other two were Rhodes and Lemnos), and the bishop of Cos, as a suffragan of Rhodes, was present at all major subsequent councils. Several important early Christian basilicas were built on Cos, and those excavated at Hagios Stephanos, Zipari, Mastichari, and in the town of Cos itself all have impressive floor mosaics. During the 11th century the island was attacked by the Arabs, and its position meant that it was sufficiently important to the Byzantines for it to be governed (and defended) directly from Constantinople by appointed officials; in the 12th century members of the imperial family controlled the island. A visitor early in that century, the Russian *higumen* (abbot) Daniil, described it as "large, populous, and rich in cattle".

After 1204 the Deed of Partition allocated Cos to the Latin emperor of Constantinople, but he was never able to exercise control and it was taken over by the Genoese. Around 1225 the navy of the Byzantine government in exile in Nicaea, under John Vatatzes, occupied Cos, incorporating it into the Nicene empire, and after 1261 into that of Byzantium. The hilltop village of Palaiopyli, now deserted, represents well the kind of rural existence that developed during these centuries, with a castle crowning its summit that would have provided shelter for local families.

Cos: view of the Asclepieum founded in the mid-4th century BC

From 1304 until 1947 control over the island was largely lost to the Greek people. It was occupied first by the Genoese, under the Zaccharia family, and then from c.1319 by the Turks. They in turn were ousted c.1337 by the Hospitallers, who gave the island a period of stability and relative importance that lasted almost two centuries, until they were driven from their home stronghold of Rhodes. The position and size of Cos meant that it was an ideal base from which they could defy, and be seen to defy, the Islamic power such a short distance away across the narrow straits. Besides the large castle of Antimachia that they built inland, the massive fortress that they built overlooking the harbour of Cos was the largest of their fortifications after that of Rhodes, and its latest phases, constructed in the early 16th century, represent the finest achievements of European military building of its day.

When the Hospitallers were forced to leave Rhodes in January 1523, the Turkish power finally completed their occupation of the whole island: they were to remain in control until 1912 when, with the rest of the Dodecanese, Cos was seized by the Italians to ensure that Turkey fulfilled the pledge made that year at the first Treaty of Lausanne. In the Treaty of Sèvres of 1920 the islands were formally made over to Italy, under whom they were to remain, in spite of undertakings to the contrary, until 1947. Only then did Cos formally re-enter Greek tutelage.

PAUL HETHERINGTON

Summary

One of the Dodecanese, the island of Cos lies off the coast of Asia Minor near Bodrum. The city of Cos, founded in the mid-4th century BC, became a major trading centre. It was the birthplace of Apelles and Hippocrates. The Asclepieum became an international medical centre. Cos was occupied by the Hospitaller Knights of St John c.1337–1523, by the Turks until 1912, and by the Italians until 1947.

Further Reading

Balducci, Hermes, *Basiliche protocristiane e bizantine a Cos*, Pavia, 1936

Luttrell, Anthony, *Latin Greece, the Hospitallers and the Crusades, 1291–1440*, London: Variorum, 1982

Luttrell, Anthony, *The Hospitallers of Rhodes and their Mediterranean World*, Aldershot, Hampshire: Variorum, 1992

Miller, William, *Essays on the Latin Orient*, Cambridge: Cambridge University Press, 1921; reprinted New York: AMS Press, 1983

Cosmology

One of the most significant contributions of Greek civilization to the world is the speculative study of the universe. In the 6th century BC the earliest Greek philosophers made the momentous step of viewing the world as a product, not of divine beings exercising supernatural powers, but of natural substances exhibiting natural powers. Why precisely the Greeks of the 6th century made this step is not clear, but modern science can be identified as the legacy of that tradition.

The mythographers of the 8th century BC, Homer and Hesiod, accepted from tradition a world in which a flat circular earth, bounded at its edge by the ocean, lay between a firmament of heaven (Ouranos) above and gloomy underworld (Tartaros) beneath. According to Hesiod, the world arose when Chaos (a yawning gap) was born, followed by the birth of Earth, Heaven, and other cosmic deities. Rejecting such supernatural explanations as this, the philosophers of Miletus gave naturalistic accounts of the world and how it arose. Little is known about the theories of the first philosopher, Thales, except that he is said to have derived all things from water and conceived of earth floating like a raft on a vast sea. His successor, Anaximander, theorized that the earth was a disk with its diameter three times its height, surrounded by circles of fire veiled in mist. The fire shone through holes like spoke-holes on a wheel, appearing as the sun, the moon, and the stars. The world came to be when something productive of hot and cold separated off from the "boundless" matter of the universe. Anaximander's successor, Anaximenes, pictured a flat earth that rode on a cushion of air. The heavens rotated around the earth like a felt cap, surrounded by a boundless expanse of air.

Challenged by criticisms of Parmenides and his followers that what-is cannot arise out of what-is-not, natural philosophers of the 5th century BC emphasized the construction of the world from pre-existent elements. Empedocles envisaged a universe in which a world like ours cyclically alternates with a perfectly homogeneous sphere in which all of the four elements (earth, water, air, fire) have become completely mixed. Anaxagoras posited a world which arose out of an original chaos when a vortex motion separated the elements into distinct layers. The atomists posited an infinite void in which indivisible particles of matter, the atoms, combined and separated to create multiple worlds and their contents. The early philosophers had learned to distinguish between a world-order or world (*kosmos*), of which there might be many, and the universe (*to pan*) which contained one or more ordered worlds and all unordered matter.

The break from mythological thinking was not complete or sudden. The philosophers of Miletus tended to endow the original stuff of the universe–water, "the boundless", or air–with divine qualities and to view it as an autonomous agent. Empedocles and Anaxagoras posited personified forces alongside their elements: Love and Strife (i.e. attraction and repulsion) for Empedocles, a cosmic Mind for Anaxagoras. The atomists finally did away with personified agents altogether, accounting for all changes merely on the basis of the motions of atoms. Early Greek philosophy had arrived at mechanistic explanations of the natural world.

In the 4th century BC the philosophical tradition turned strongly against such approaches to cosmology. Steeped in Socrates' ethical philosophy, Plato criticized natural philosophers for describing how natural phenomena took place while ignoring the fact that the world is organized for the best. To the scientist, mechanical explanations should be preliminary to teleological explanations. In the *Timaeus* Plato sets out to produce a new kind of cosmology based on his principles. Introducing a divine craftsman, the Demiurge, Plato shows how he must have arranged the world for the best, as a copy of an eternal paradigm. The Demiurge forms the earth as a spherical body enclosed in a heavenly sphere pervaded by soul. Outside the cosmos there is nothing. The traditional gods, who are born later, design the human body as the best vehicle for the human soul. Plato explains the motion of the heavenly bodies as circular orbits carried at uniform speeds; apparently irregular motions of the planets are the result of compound motions of several circles.

Although Plato's theory seems unscientific by modern standards, it was important in several ways. First, it allowed for a synthesis of scientific explanation and human values, which seemed to be undermined by materialistic theories of the early philosophers, and hence prepared the way for an acceptance of scientific explanation by popular opinion. Second, it made teleological explanations central to science, allowing for a flourishing of biological sciences. Third, his account allowed for the possibility of developing mathematical models of the heavens, which would lead to a flourishing of astronomy. Fourth, his theory that the earth is spherical was correct, and would henceforth become the standard view on the shape of the earth.

Plato's student Aristotle devoted much effort to working out the details of a cosmos inspired by Plato. Rejecting the hypothesis of a divine craftsman, Aristotle argued that the world was not created, nor would it be destroyed. Rather it exists forever, repeating its meteorological cycles. The four elements are arranged concentrically, with a spherical earth at the centre, surrounded by a shell of water (the seas), a shell of air (the atmosphere), and a shell of fiery matter. Earth and water naturally travel towards the centre of the universe (located at the centre of the earth), air and fire outwards to the periphery. From the region of the moon outwards the heavens consist of a fifth element that some identify with ether, which naturally moves in a circle, but which participates in no other kinds of change. Hence the heavenly bodies are all changeless except for their daily and yearly motions, while all things below the moon are subject to change along with the four elements of which they are composed, which elements are transformed into one another in daily and annual cycles. The heavens are further composed of concentric spheres and the heavenly bodies that move with them. These bodies move in imitation of a first unmoved mover, which we may identify with God, a being that lives the best kind of life by exercising pure mental activity. In Aristotle's world, as in Plato's, everything is arranged for the best; for Aristotle, however, the order is not imposed from without by a craftsman but achieved by natural processes.

Aristotle provided the standard picture of the cosmos for most thinkers in Europe and the Middle East down to the early modern era. The only serious contender was the conception of Epicurus, who revived atomism with a few modifications *c*.300 BC. But because Epicureans apparently clung to the view that the earth was flat at a time when scientific arguments for sphericity had already been given (by Aristotle) and the circumference of the earth had actually been calculated by scientists to a fair degree of accuracy (e.g. Eratosthenes in the 3rd century BC), Epicurus' theory was in effect obsolete from the time he propounded it. Meanwhile, Plato's conception of the heavenly bodies moving in circles with uniform speed inspired increasingly accurate mathematical models of planetary motions, culminating in the use of epicycles, small circles drawn from a point moving on the orbits of planets. The use of epicycles and other devices allowed astronomers to describe the motions of planets very closely. But the mathematical models produced another problem: no physical theory (Aristotle's was still the most influential) could account for the epicyclic motions of planets. The more accurate mathematical description became, the less satisfactory physical theory proved to be.

In almost all Greek theories of the cosmos, the earth was at the centre. But there were exceptions: Philolaus in the 5th century BC had posited a central fire around which the earth and all other heavenly bodies revolved. In the 3rd century BC, Aristarchus of Samos put forward the correct view that the planets revolve about the sun. His theory, however, never caught on. In the 2nd century AD Ptolemy combined traditional cosmology with the latest methods in mathematical astronomy and fresh observations to produce the most comprehensive astronomical account of the ancient world as well as the best geography of the earth. His treatises subsequently became the standard textbooks for astronomy and geography.

By the 3rd century AD Neoplatonism was becoming dominant among intellectuals. Mixing mysticism with Platonism, Plotinus saw the ultimate reality as an ineffable One from which emanated a cosmic Mind, in which the Platonic Forms found place, from which emanated soul, from which in turn emanated matter. Emanation was not to be understood as generation in time but as a timeless causation from the higher to the lower. The world, then, did not come to be in time, but always was, conforming to the perfect Forms of Mind. Neoplatonic theory did not so much revise the concept of the cosmos as locate it within a hierarchy of beings. About the same time as Neoplatonism became influential, Christianity began to emerge as a leading religion. Church Fathers sought to ground Christian theology in the dominant philosophy of the time, Neoplatonism, but were forced to modify philosophical theories to accommodate their religious doctrines. The world was not everlasting, but created by God, in accordance with the Forms, which were now understood the be in the Mind of God. The heavenly spheres of Aristotle were now understood to be peopled by angels and the Classical cosmos was Christianized. But essentially the cosmos of the Christian Middle Ages, both in the East and West, was Aristotle's cosmos located in a Neoplatonic hierarchy of beings and populated with demons and angels as well as humans, created and ruled by a transcendent God, who could be identified in different contexts with Plato's Demiurge, Aristotle's unmoved mover, and Plotinus' One.

DANIEL W. GRAHAM

Further Reading

Bailey, Cyril, *The Greek Atomists and Epicurus*, Oxford: Clarendon Press, 1928

Dicks, D.R., *Early Greek Astronomy to Aristotle*, Ithaca, New York: Cornell University Press, and London: Thames and Hudson, 1970
Furley, David J., *The Greek Cosmologists*, vol. 1, Cambridge and New York: Cambridge University Press, 1987
Furley, David, *Cosmic Problems: Essays on Greek and Roman Philosophy of Nature*, Cambridge and New York: Cambridge University Press, 1989
Heath, Thomas Little, *Aristarchus of Samos, The Ancient Copernicus: A History of Greek Astronomy to Aristarchus*, Oxford: Clarendon Press, 1913
Kahn, Charles H., *Anaximander and the Origins of Greek Cosmology*, New York: Columbia University Press, 1960
Kerschensteiner, Jula, *Kosmos: Quellenkritische Untersuchungen zu den Vorsokratikern*, Munich: Beck, 1962
Mohr, Richard D., *The Platonic Cosmology*, Leiden: Brill, 1985
O'Brien, Denis, *Empedocles' Cosmic Cycle: A Reconstruction*, London: Cambridge University Press, 1969
Plato, *Plato's Cosmology: The Timaeus*, translated by F.M. Cornford, London: Kegan Paul Trench Trubner, and New York: Harcourt Brace, 1937
Sambursky, Samuel, *The Physical World of the Greeks*, London: Routledge, 1956
Solmsen, Friedrich, *Aristotle's System of the Physical World: A Comparison with his Predecessors*, Ithaca, New York: Cornell University Press, 1960
Tannery, Paul, *Pour l'Histoire de la science hellène*, 2nd edition, Paris: Gauthier-Villars, 1930
Theiler, Willy, *Zur Geschichte der teleologischen Naturbetrachtung bis auf Aristoteles*, 2nd edition, Berlin: de Gruyter, 1965
Vlastos, Gregory, "Equality and Justice in Early Greek Cosmologies", *Classical Philology*, 42 (1947): pp. 156–78
Vlastos, Gregory, *Plato's Universe*, Seattle: University of Washington Press, and Oxford: Clarendon Press, 1975

Councils, Ecumenical

Ecumenical (or general) councils are those councils of the Christian Church whose decisions are recognized as binding by the entire Church. The precedent for settling controversies within the Church by means of a council is found in the New Testament (Acts 15). In post-Apostolic times councils continued to be held on a local basis. But the era of truly "ecumenical" councils began with the legal toleration of Christianity in the Roman empire during the 4th century AD. As Christianity became the official religion of the empire, seven ecumenical councils (covering the period from 325 to 787) were called for the purpose of preserving Christian unity within the Roman (and later the Byzantine) empire. These councils were convoked by the Roman emperor and held in cities of the predominantly Greek-speaking Roman east. The Roman empire and its satellites were considered coterminous with the civilized world, the *oikoumene*, whence the term "ecumenical" is derived. The councils produced creeds, or definitions of faith, in response to particular controversies that arose in the life of the Church. In the formulation of these doctrinal statements Greek philosophical terms were redefined to help explain the mysteries of the Christian faith. While only the first seven councils are recognized as ecumenical by the Orthodox and some Protestant Churches, the Roman Catholic Church recognizes 21, the last being Vatican II (1962–65). Two of these later councils dealt with the question of reuniting the

Christian Church after the schism between the Orthodox and Roman Catholic Churches in 1054.

Nicaea I, 325

The emperor Constantine I (324–37) called the first ecumenical council, at Nicaea in 325. The need for a council was precipitated by the teaching of an Alexandrian priest, Arius, who promoted a rigidly monotheistic concept of God. Arius taught that Jesus (the Word) was not God, but was created by him to serve as an intermediary between God and his subsequent creation; there was a time when the Word did not exist. At the incarnation the Word took the place of the rational soul in the person Jesus and became a man. Arius conceded that Jesus was called God, but argued that Jesus was God only by participation in divine grace, not by virtue of his own nature. The question of the nature, essence, or being of God and the relationship between God the Father and God the Son therefore became the point of debate at Nicaea. The council promulgated a statement of faith, the basis of what we now call the Nicene creed. In this statement the Greek term *homoousios* (of the same essence, or substance) was used to describe the relationship between the Father and the Son in the Trinity, thus safeguarding the full divinity of Jesus and his role in the salvation of mankind. The use of *homoousios* in the Nicene creed is evidence of the ongoing redefinition of Greek philosophical terms in a new Christian context. The council also dealt with various disciplinary matters and the administrative structure of the Church. The bishops of the greatest cities of the empire, Rome, Alexandria, and Antioch, were given supervisory powers over other bishops. The bishop of Jerusalem was to be held in honour next to these, because of the city's association with the earthly life of Christ.

Although the Nicene council had produced a creed endorsed by the majority of the bishops and supported by the emperor, the Arian controversy refused to die easily. The recognition of Nicaea as an ecumenical council took another 50 years and the confirmation of its status by the Council of Constantinople in 381. As the example of Nicaea shows, regardless of any declarations of ecumenicity at the outset, the ecumenical status of a council depended most of all on its subsequent recognition and confirmation.

Constantinople I, 381

In 381 the first Council of Constantinople was called by the emperor Theodosius I (379–95) to endorse the theology of Nicaea. Although it was convoked as an eastern regional council, Constantinople was recognized as the second ecumenical council by the Council of Chalcedon in 451. The fathers at Constantinople ratified the faith of Nicaea and further developed its creed. In response to a controversy over the deity of the Holy Spirit, this council confessed belief in the "Holy Spirit, the Lord and Life-giver, Who proceeds from the Father, Who is worshipped and glorified together with the Father and the Son, Who spoke through the prophets". Constantinople defended the Holy Spirit as God, just as Nicaea had defended Jesus as God. Also as at Nicaea, the Council of Constantinople dealt with the administration of the Church. The city of Constantinople had replaced Rome as the capital of the empire in 330. In recognition of its status as the "New Rome", the council decided to honour the bishop of Constantinople as second in rank only to the bishop of Rome. Although no western bishops were present, the Roman Church confirmed the decisions of Constantinople I at the Council of Chalcedon, with the exception of the canon regarding the rank of the bishop of Constantinople. This foreshadowed the growing rivalry between the two sees that eventually led to the schism between the Orthodox and Roman Catholic Churches.

Ephesus, 431

After dealing with the doctrine of the Trinity at Nicaea and Constantinople, theology in the 5th century turned to the question of Christology – in what way was Jesus Christ both God and man? Nestorius, bishop of Constantinople, and Cyril, bishop of Alexandria, were the primary figures in this controversy. Nestorius was trained in the Antiochene theological tradition, which tended to emphasize Jesus' humanity. He declined to call the Virgin Mary *Theotokos* (One who gave birth to God), a term in use since the 2nd century, preferring instead the term *Christotokos*. His reasoning was that while Mary did bear the person of Christ in her womb, she was mother only of his humanity, not his divinity, and so could not properly be called *Theotokos*. Although Nestorius attempted to do justice to both Jesus' humanity and his divinity, his position implied a separation between the two that threatened to make two persons out of Jesus rather than one. Cyril, representing the Alexandrian theological tradition, stressed the unity of Jesus' person (*prosopon/hypostasis*) in the incarnation as expressed in the Gospel of John: "The Word was made flesh" (John 1:14). This controversy was addressed at the Council of Ephesus in 431. Cyril led the attack on Nestorius in the church of the Virgin Mary. Nestorius himself refused to attend the council because Cyril had set himself up as both the prosecutor and the presiding judge. Not surprisingly, Cyril triumphed and Nestorius' position was condemned. A countercouncil was held by John, bishop of Antioch, in support of Nestorius; in the end, both sides appealed to imperial intervention. An agreement was reached whereby Nestorius resigned his see and was sent back to his monastery in Antioch, while Cyril and John worked out a compromise formula of union. The statement endorsed the term *Theotokos* and acknowledged Jesus Christ as "perfect God and perfect man ... For of two natures a union has been made. For this cause we confess one Christ, one Son, one Lord". The Council of Ephesus provoked the first lasting schism in the Christian Church – Nestorianism spread among the Christians of the Persian empire and survives today among the Assyrians of northern Iraq.

Chalcedon, 451

The declaration of the unity of Jesus' person at the Council of Ephesus provoked a strong reaction against any hint of Nestorianism. Eutyches, a monk in Constantinople, took Cyril's theology to an extreme. Eutyches taught that before the incarnation Jesus was of two natures, but afterwards only of one, in which the divine nature in effect swallowed up the human one. This "one-nature" theology is the origin of the term Monophysite (*physis* = nature) that is used to describe the theology of Eutyches and his sympathizers, which included Dioscurus, bishop of Alexandria. At issue were the use of the Greek terms *physis*, *hypostasis*, and *prosopon*, to explain the humanity and divinity of Jesus. For Eutyches and the Alexandrians, these terms were essentially synonymous – to be one person Jesus had to have one nature. Those who professed two natures seemed to fall into the error of the Nestorians, dividing the person of Jesus. Another council was held at Ephesus in 449, which supported the Alexandrian position. But the decisions of this council were overturned by the Council of Chalcedon in 451. Here an attempt was made to be true to Cyril's Christology while maintaining the reality of both Jesus' divinity and his humanity. This council accepted the explanation articulated by Leo, bishop of Rome, in his *Tome*: Jesus was "to be acknowledged in two natures ... in one person, and in one hypostasis". Unfortunately, this formula did not satisfy the Alexandrians, who while rejecting the heresy of Eutyches preferred to retain Cyrillian terminology. Thus began the schism between the Monophysites and the Orthodox Catholics. The Monophysite (also known as the non-Chalcedonian or Oriental Orthodox) Churches exist to this day, among the Coptic Egyptians, Ethiopians, Jacobite Syrians, Armenians, and Malankar Indians. Currently, ongoing theological discussions between Oriental Orthodox and Eastern Orthodox hierarchs have affirmed that the separation between the two Churches is one of terminology rather than theology, and they hope to achieve full communion in the near future.

The assembly at Chalcedon ratified the decisions of Nicaea I, Constantinople I, and Ephesus, thereby recognizing them as the first three ecumenical councils. The council also solidified the structure of Church government by granting the bishops of Rome, Constantinople, Alexandria, Antioch, and Jerusalem the title of "patriarch" and jurisdiction over all churches in their territories.

Constantinople II, 553

The Council of Constantinople II, held in 553, was an effort to reconcile with the Monophysites. Justinian I (527–65), like other Roman emperors before him, was interested in maintaining religious unity among his subjects. The council condemned the so-called Three Chapters – the writings of three theologians, Theodore of Mopsuestia, Theodoret of Cyrus, and Ibas of Edessa, whose work was considered by the Monophysites to be Nestorian. The council also tried to answer Monophysite objections to the definition of Chalcedon by explaining more concretely how two natures unite as one person in Jesus Christ: "For in saying that the only-begotten Word was united by hypostasis [personally] we do not mean that there was a mutual confusion of natures, but rather we understand that the Word was united to the flesh, each [nature] remaining what it was." The Council of Constantinople II also condemned the teachings of the 3rd-century theologian Origen, whose philosophical speculations were popular among certain eastern monks. Despite the efforts of the council and the emperor, the Monophysites were not reconciled and remained in schism.

Constantinople III, 680–81

The sixth ecumenical council, Constantinople III (680–81), condemned the Monothelite heresy. Monothelitism was a doctrine that proposed that while Jesus had two natures, he had only one will, the divine predominating. This formula, promoted by the emperor Herakleios (610–41), was yet another attempt to reconcile with the Monophysites. The Church as a whole rejected the doctrine of the "one will" as contrary to the faith as defined by the previous ecumenical councils – if Jesus had two natures, he must have two wills, both divine and human. With this affirmation, the council provoked another schism – the Maronites, a group of Syrian Christians, would not renounce Monothelitism. The Maronite Church later joined in communion with the Roman Catholics in 1182, and they exist today as an Eastern-rite Catholic community.

Nicaea II, 787

The seventh ecumenical council was called in response to the iconoclast controversy. Emperor Leo III (717–41) began an attack on the Christian practice of venerating icons, pictorial representations of Jesus and the saints. Apparently, he believed that God was angry with the Christians for their "idolatry" and was punishing them. This was at a time of natural disasters and the loss of imperial territory, especially to the Muslims, who abhorred the use of religious images. Iconoclasm was primarily an imperial heresy, in that it was imposed by the emperors on the Church. It was enforced in two stages, from about the years 726 to 780, and then again from 815 to 843. The first restoration of the icons occurred under the empress Irene (797–802, regent from 780), who convoked the second Council of Nicaea in 787. This council rejected the ecumenical claims of the iconoclastic Council of Hieria (753), and set forth the theological argument in favour of the veneration of icons. It made it clear that icons are useful in teaching the faithful and that the images are venerated or honoured, not worshipped, as worship properly belongs to God alone. The honour due to the icon is bestowed upon the person it represents, not the material out of which the icon is made. Most importantly, icons of Jesus expressed the truth of the incarnation. In the words of John of Damascus: "Of old God the incorporeal and uncircumscribed was not depicted at all. But now that God has appeared in the flesh and lived among men, I make an image of the God who can be seen." After a return to iconoclasm under a series of emperors in the 9th century, another empress, Theodora, presided over the final restoration of icons in 843. This event is commemorated in the Orthodox Church as the "Triumph of Orthodoxy", celebrated on the first Sunday in Lent. This liturgy affirms the faith of the seven ecumenical councils.

After Nicaea II the western Church, under the leadership of the pope of Rome, and the eastern Church, under the patriarch of Constantinople, grew increasingly apart, culminating in a schism that is conventionally dated to the year 1054. After this date one may speak of separate Roman Catholic and Eastern Orthodox Churches. The Roman Church continued to recognize its own councils after the schism as ecumenical; two of the most notable were the council of Lyons II (1274) and Ferrara-Florence (1438–39). These councils attempted to heal the schism between the two Churches, but because they enforced the Roman tradition over the Constantinopolitan, the East found it difficult to agree to any lasting reunion.

CONSTANTINA SCOURTIS

See also Heresy, Iconoclasm, Schism

Further Reading

Davis, Leo Donald, *The First Seven Ecumenical Councils, 325–787: Their History and Theology*, Wilmington, Delaware: Glazier, 1987

Geanakoplos, Deno, *Emperor Michael Palaeologus and the West, 1258–1282: A Study in Byzantine–Latin Relations*, Cambridge, Massachusetts: Harvard University Press, 1959

Gill, Joseph, *The Council of Florence*, Cambridge: Cambridge University Press, 1959

Leith, John H. (editor), *Creeds of the Churches: A Reader in Christian Doctrine, from the Bible to the Present*, 3rd edition, Atlanta: John Knox Press, 1982

Ware, Timothy, *The Orthodox Church*, 2nd edition, Harmondsworth and New York: Penguin, 1993

Crates of Mallus

Stoic philosopher and literary critic of the 2nd century BC

Mallus in Cilicia, in southeast Asia Minor, lay in an area that was an important centre of Stoic studies from the 3rd century BC until at least the 2nd century AD. Exactly when Crates, son of Timocrates, was born there is unclear; however, we learn from the *Suda* that he was a contemporary of Aristarchus of Samothrace (c.216–144 BC), from Strabo that he was also a contemporary of Demetrius of Scepsis (born c.214 BC), and from Suetonius that he was sent from Pergamum to Rome on a diplomatic mission at about the time of the death of Ennius (169 BC). All of this suggests that he moved to Pergamum at the time of Eumenes II (197–158 BC), the most culturally ambitious and the most tireless promoter of scholarship and the arts of all the Attalid dynasty. Crates had followers (we hear of "Cratetians"), but these may simply have been students in the Stoic tradition (the most distinguished was Panaetius) rather than members of a "school" deliberately established in Pergamum to oppose the scholarship produced in the Museum and Library at Alexandria.

Crates is much quoted in scholia, lexica, and collections of "opinions" generally (in Mette's two volumes (1936, 1952) there are 18 items of "testimonia" and 86 "fragments" – rather more voluminous than what is meant by this term in other collections – covering a total of 313 pages of printed text; see also Mette's indexes of sources). Of his works on literature only two titles appear reasonably certain: the first (?*Diorthotica*) seems to have been a commentary with textual criticism of the *Iliad* and *Odyssey* in nine books, while the second (*Homerica*) may have dealt with problems of geography and even cosmology. We have, however, no idea of the total range of Crates' writings on literary topics: there may have been many other works, since we have "fragments" citing his opinions on Hesiod, on Alcman, on Euripides, and on

Aratus, for example; but these may simply be obiter dicta to his works on Homer.

What seems fairly certain, however, is that Crates' approach to literary studies was primarily Stoic and this determined the type of scholarship that he produced. Cicero tells us that Chrysippus, another native of Cilicia, the third head of the Stoa and the person who, in his voluminous writings, gave the definitive statement of the principal Stoic doctrines, had "wanted to harmonize [*accommodare*] the myths in Orpheus, Musaeus, Hesiod, and Homer with his own views ... about the immortal gods, so that even the earliest poets, who had not the slightest idea about these views, would appear to have been Stoics" (*De Natura Deorum*, 1. 41). Given this manner of proceeding, it became possible for a literary critic of the Stoic persuasion to elucidate the "true" meaning that lay behind the words of an early poet, as Crates did for Homer most spectacularly (and bizarrely) when he interpreted the shield of Agamemnon (*Iliad*, 11. 32–40) as a representation of the cosmos and the shield's ten circles of bronze (line 33) as standing for the ten cosmic spheres and so on, with every detail "explained" by means of allegory (Eustathios on *Iliad*, 11. 32–40 = Mette, 1936, fr. 23a; Mette also argued for the same interpretation by Crates of the shield of Achilles, famously described at *Iliad*, 18. 463–608: cf. Mette, 1936, pp. 36–42). Likewise, a person with a good understanding of Stoic doctrines (the "truth") could see where the essential message had been corrupted, either because the poet had failed to apprehend it correctly or because errors had crept into the manuscript tradition: in either case the text could now be properly emended. This somewhat circular reasoning does not explain every emendation of Homer proposed by Crates, but it does go some way towards accounting for the remarkable freedom with which he, and other scholars, expounded the text.

Crates' great rival among literary critics was Aristarchus of Samothrace, who became chief librarian in Alexandria around 153 BC. Their differing approaches to a problem are well exemplified in a lengthy passage in the *Geography* of Strabo (1. 2. 24–28), where they are described as "the leading figures in this field of knowledge [sc. literary criticism]"; where Aristarchus is replying to an emendation of *Odyssey*, 1. 24 and a hypothesis of Crates about the Ethiopians; where Strabo dismisses the arguments of both as wrong (because, in his view, each has misunderstood what Homer is saying); and where Aristarchus, whose reading is the one found in standard texts today, is described as "also indulging in a petty and pointless discussion of the text"! Overall, one has the impression not so much of a clash of "schools" but of a personal rivalry between leading scholars, such as is still found today: they do, of course, agree on some things but disagree about much more.

Neither Crates nor Aristarchus was in any sense a narrow specialist and the passage just cited shows their interest in cosmology and geography. In Crates' case this led to what seems to have been a major innovation: according to Strabo (2. 5. 10), since the known, inhabited part of the world (that is, Eurasia and the northern portion of Africa) occupies but a small part of the total land mass of the globe, anyone who wishes to represent it accurately must make a large globe of the world (no less than 10 feet in diameter) "just like that of Crates".

There is another area, the study of the formal structure of language, where Crates and Aristarchus are contrasted in our sources. In Alexandria principles of regularity in the declension of nouns had been analysed and described, and to this principle the term *analogia* had been applied; by contrast, the Stoic Chrysippus had argued that words and the things they described frequently did not stand in any sort of harmonious relationship, and this situation he called *anomalia*, writing four books on the subject. By the time of Crates this area of study was being called *grammatike* (sc. *techne*), and Aulus Gellius tells us that "two distinguished Greek *grammatici*, Aristarchus and Crates, made a habit of defending with the utmost vigour, the former analogy, and the latter anomaly" (*Noctes Atticae*, 2. 25. 4). Obviously both ideas can be observed in declensions and conjugations; moreover, it was the Stoics in Crates' day who made the greatest contributions to the study of *grammatike*. It should, however, also be noted that Crates preferred to call himself *kritikos* (a critic), regarding criticism as "a master-science of language, comprising grammar, linguistics, and literary criticism" (Asmis 1992, p.139).

Finally, in his work *On Grammarians* Suetonius states that in his view, it was Crates of Mallus who introduced the study of grammar to Rome: during his embassy from Pergamum he had the misfortune to fall into a sewer opening and broke his leg, so that the public lectures and seminars that he had already been giving were continued into the period of his convalescence (*De Grammaticis*, 2). It is highly unlikely that Crates could have discussed grammar without at least some mention of basic Stoic ideas; accordingly, it may not be unreasonable to see in Crates one of those Greek philosophers who presented Stoicism, possibly in a somewhat simplified form, in Rome in a manner both accessible to, and welcome among, upper-class Romans – with enormous consequences for Roman conduct in the future.

In the 20th century our knowledge of Crates' activities and importance has been greatly enhanced by the work of H.J. Mette; some of his theories, however, especially the connection posited between the close scrutiny of anomaly and the ideas of the "empirical" school of medicine, remain controversial. More recently, E. Asmis, in an important and carefully argued paper analysing the discussion of Crates in book 5 of Philodemus' *On Poems*, has attempted to reconstruct Crates' theory of poetry; in addition, and more surprisingly, she concludes that he was not a Stoic philosopher, but as a "critic" simply adopted some Stoic principles and rejected others (p.161).

CHARLES L. MURISON

Biography

Born at Mallus in southeast Asia Minor *c.*215 BC, Crates seems to have moved to Pergamum from where he was sent on a mission to Rome in 169 BC. As a literary scholar he worked mostly on Homer and was the rival of Aristarchus of Samothrace. Suetonius says that he introduced the study of grammar to Rome. He took his linguistic principles from Stoic philosophy. His date and place of death are unknown.

Further Reading

Asmis, E., "Crates on Poetic Criticism", *Phoenix*, 46 (1992): pp. 138–69

Mette, Hans Joachim, *Sphairopoiia: Untersuchungen zur Kosmologie des Krates von Pergamon*, Munich: Beck, 1936
Mette, Hans Joachim, *Parateresis: Untersuchungen zur Sprachtheorie des Krates von Pergamon*, Halle: Niemeyer, 1952
Pfeiffer, Rudolf, *History of Classical Scholarship from the Beginnings to the End of the Hellenistic Age*, Oxford: Clarendon Press, 1968, pp. 234–45

Crete

Aegean island

"Out in the dark blue sea lies a land called Crete, rich and lovely land, washed by the waves on every side, densely peopled and boasting ninety cities. Each of the several races of the isle has its own language. First there are the Achaeans; then the genuine Cretans, proud of their native stock; next the Cydonians; the Dorians with their three clans; and finally the noble Pelasgians. One of the ninety towns is a great city called Knossos, and there, for nine years, King Minos ruled, and enjoyed the friendship of almighty Zeus" (*Odyssey*, 19. 172ff., translated by E.V. Rieu). Thus Odysseus described this Aegean island which has often played an important and intriguing role in the history of the Hellenic world, especially in pre- and protohistoric times – a pre-eminence which may be partly reflected in the fact that Crete is the home of many famous Greek myths and legends, from the story of Zeus' birth in one of the island's numerous caves to Theseus' slaying of the Minotaur, Minos' stepson, a creature half man and half bull, the offspring of the union between the king's unfaithful wife, Pasiphae, and a handsome bull.

Crete is the largest Aegean island. It is approximately 250 km long and its width ranges from 58 km at its widest point, across the Psiloriti massif, to 12.5 km at its narrowest, across the isthmus of Ierapetra; it lies across the southern Aegean basin, between the southeast tip of the Peloponnese and the island of Cythera (to the west) and the Dodecanesian islands of Kasos, Karpathos, Rhodes, and the southwest coast of Turkey (to the east); the Libyan Sea separates it from the north coast of Africa (about 300 km to the south) while the Aegean Sea and the Cyclades lie to the north.

Crete is now divided into four "nomes" or prefectures grouped around the main urban centres of Herakleion, Chania (ancient Kydonia), Rethymnon, and Sitia. About 20 per cent of the present population (a little over 500,000) reside in Herakleion.

The wild, rugged, and varied landscape is largely dominated by chains of limestone mountains forming the island's backbone. The main ranges are the White Mountains (2453 m) in the west, Psiloriti or Mount Ida (2456 m) in the centre, and Lassithi or Mount Dykte (2148 m) in the centre-east. The smaller Sitia mountains lie at the eastern end of the island, beyond the isthmus of Ierapetra, and the Asterousia Mountains are situated in the centre-south, between the Mesara plain and the Libyan Sea.

Crete's main mountains slope more gently towards the north coast, where there are several small coastal plains, but the largest piece of flat land is the Mesara, in the centre of the island, on the south coast. A characteristic feature are the small

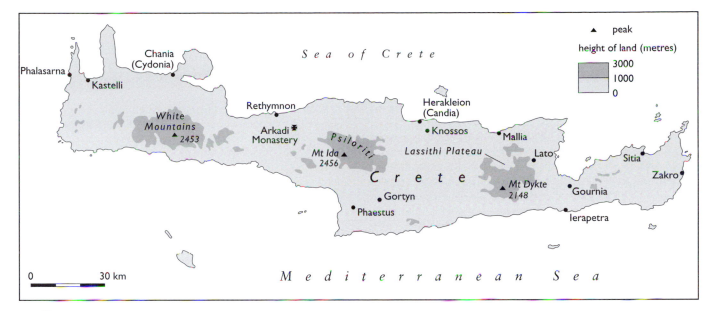

14. Crete

high upland plains, of which the best known are the Lassithi plateau, Nida (on Psiloriti), and Omalos (in the White Mountains), from which starts Samaria, the longest (17 km) and most spectacular of many gorges scarring the Cretan landscape.

There are few rivers, often reduced to little more than a trickle in the summer, such as the Kairatos near Herakleion, and the Ieropotamos in the Mesara, which is believed to have been partly navigable in antiquity. There is also one small freshwater lake, Kournas, a short distance inland from the north coast between the modern towns of Rethymnon and Chania.

Crete has been renowned since antiquity for its wild plants and flowers, of which over 100 are exclusive to the island. Among the fauna it is worth mentioning the wild goat (*agrimi* or *kri-kri*), often depicted in Minoan art and still surviving in the wild.

Crete is most famous for its long-lived Bronze Age civilization, called Minoan after the mythical king Minos, but the whole of the island's history is equally intriguing, as varied and rough as the landscape.

The earliest traces of human habitation go back to the Neolithic period (c. 7000–3500 BC). The first inhabitants were probably a small group of farmers from Anatolia, who crossed the Aegean Sea and settled at Knossos, sometime before the end of the 8th millennium BC. In the following millennia their first settlement expanded, more or less steadily, and from there groups of settlers spread to the rest of the island.

Knossos, the first as well as the largest Neolithic settlement on Crete, maintained its pre-eminence also during the following Bronze Age (c.3500–1100 BC), which saw the emergence and demise of the Minoan civilization. What language (or languages) the Minoans spoke is unknown, for their surviving documents were written in two scripts, known as Cretan Hieroglyphic (or Pictographic) and Linear A, which, so far, have not been convincingly deciphered: all one can say is that these scripts do not represent a form of Greek. (Indeed, a non-Greek language continued to be spoken in the east of Crete as late as the 3rd century BC, as shown by surviving inscriptions found at Praisos). The Minoans, however, had a significant and lasting influence on the population of the other Aegean islands and on the Greek-speaking population of mainland Greece, the Mycenaeans, before eventually succumbing to their power.

When exactly the Mycenaeans gained political supremacy in Crete is still a matter of debate, but most scholars believe that this may have happened towards the end of the Late Minoan IB period, that is around 1450 BC (low chronology) or 1550 BC (high chronology). That at some point during the second half of the 2nd millennium BC Mycenaean Greeks gained control in Crete is demonstrated by the Linear B tablets found by Sir Arthur Evans at Knossos at the beginning of the 20th century. Linear B, which is a development of Linear A, was deciphered as Greek by the British architect Michael Ventris in 1952.

Crete continued to flourish until the collapse of the Mycenaean palaces on mainland Greece (c.1200 BC), which heralded a period of insecurity and movements of people throughout the Aegean. In Crete this is indicated by the emergence, in the 12th century BC, of settlements on naturally defended high ground, such as Kastri, Vrokastro, and Karphi. The following period, the Early Iron Age (Geometric and Orientalizing periods, c.1100–700 BC) witnessed the gradual infiltration of a Dorian population as well as the emergence of the polis or Greek city state. The Dorians eventually came to dominate the island, building substantial cities, such as Lato and Dreros, often at war with each other. Throughout these changes, several Minoan cult places – such as the sanctuary at Syme, and the sacred Dyktean and Idean caves – continued to function as places of worship. Some of the finds from the Idean cave, namely the famous votive bronze shields with figurative relief, together with lively local pottery production, show that the island was one of the earliest centres in the Hellenic world to adopt the new orientalizing fashion. Crete is also the likely home of the Daidalic style of sculpture which had an important influence in the artistic development of the Archaic period throughout Greece.

In the Classical period Crete seems to have been relatively untouched by the momentous events occurring on the mainland and in the rest of the Aegean. Plato, however, admired Crete's ordered and conservative society, of which the famous inscription of the laws of Gortyn (dating from the first half of the 5th century BC) offers some picture; the Cretans also enjoyed a certain reputation in the Greek world at least as pirates and mercenary archers.

In the Hellenistic period Crete's advantageous position over sea routes brought new prosperity, despite the constant state of petty warfare among its city states, with Knossos, Lyttos, Gortyn, and Kydonia as the main contenders for supremacy.

Rome, after its conquest of mainland Greece in the mid-2nd century BC, became increasingly involved in Cretan affairs. In 68–66 BC Quintus Caecilius Metellus (who later gained the name of Creticus) led a successful expedition to conquer the island. Under Roman rule (67 BC–AD 330) the town of Gortyn became the capital of a province which also included Cyrenaica in north Africa. To judge from the abundance and type of settlements (e.g. isolated farmsteads reappeared for the first time since the Minoan age), this was one of the most prosperous periods for the island. Titus was sent by St Paul to spread Christianity, and he eventually became the island's patron saint.

The triumph of Christianity and the foundation of Constantinople in AD 330 mark the beginning of the early Byzantine era. In the division of the Roman empire in AD 395 Crete, naturally, was included in the eastern part and for centuries shared its fortunes. The island's wealth and stability during the early Byzantine period are reflected in the remains and sites of about 70 Christian basilicas, most dating from the mid-5th to mid-6th centuries AD. The most impressive example is that of Hagios Titos at Gortyn, while that of Vizari, in the Amari valley, is notable for it dates in the late 8th century, that is shortly before the Arab conquest of the island.

Crete had already been attacked by Arab raiders in 673 and 715, and in 824 fell into the hands of a group of Arab marauders based in Alexandria, but originally from Spain. Led by Abu-Hafs-Omar, they set up a fortified camp on the site of modern Herakleion, and surrounded it with a huge ditch – in Arabic el-Khandak, from which the name of Candia, frequently applied to both the town and the island until this century – was derived. Arab rule (824–961) lasted well over a century, but little has been recovered from this period.

Crete was recaptured by the Byzantine general Nikephoros Phokas in 961 and remained in Greek hands until 1204, when the Venetians gained control of the island, after negotiations following the Latin sack of Constantinople, and a brief war with rival Genoese forces. During the middle Byzantine period several basilicas were rebuilt and the Christian ruling class, the Archontopouli (Sons of Nobles), was drawn from 12 aristocratic families sent out from Constantinople.

Venetian administration (1204–1669) left many traces on the island, such as the impressive fortresses at Herakleion and Rethymnon as well as several other fine buildings. The Venetians, however, were unpopular masters, and their rule was punctuated by rebellions. The most serious was in 1363, when the Cretans declared the short-lived republic of St Titus. Throughout the period of Venetian rule, the Greek population maintained its links with Constantinople through language

and religion, for the Venetians left the Orthodox Church virtually untouched. The Cretan Archontopouli remained strong and continued to build their own small churches and chapels. A fine example of 13th- and 14th-century wall painting survives in the church of Panagia Kera near the village of Kritsa.

With the Turkish capture of Constantinople in 1453, Crete became an important asylum and staging post for Greeks fleeing to the west. This brought new vitality to the cultural life of the island, creating a sort of Cretan Byzantine renaissance: monasteries such as Arkadi, Gonia, and Angarathos became notable centres of manuscript copying and learning, with Hagia Aikaterini in Herakleion gaining particular distinction in the 16th century.

This renewed intellectual atmosphere also produced interesting paintings, exemplified in the works of Mikhail Damaskinos and Domenikos Theotokopoulos (El Greco) as well as some literary efforts, of which the most notable is Vintsentzos Kornaros's long poem, the *Erotokritos* (probably written in the mid-17th century, but published in Venice in 1715).

Crete eventually succumbed to the Turks in 1669, when Candia (Herakleion) capitulated after a siege of over 20 years. Like their Venetian predecessors, the Turks were detested masters, and their period of rule (1669–1898) was marked by several insurrections, such as those of 1866, which ended with the blowing up of the Arkadi monastery, and of 1878, which inspired the powerful novel *Freedom and Death* by Nikos Kazantzakis (1883–1957), one of Crete's best-known writers. Further violent uprisings eventually forced the great powers to intervene, and in 1898 Crete was granted autonomous status under nominal Ottoman suzerainty, with prince George, the heir to the Greek throne, appointed as High Commissioner. Union with Greece seemed very close, but the island became part of the Greek state only in 1913, a few years after an ambitious lawyer from Chania, Eleftherios Venizelos, became Greece's Prime Minister.

During World War II, in 1941, Crete was invaded and briefly occupied by Germany, before being liberated by the Allied forces – the island's wild mountains and the fiery independent character of its inhabitants once again playing an important part in the organization of the resistance.

Today Crete is one of the most prosperous regions of Greece, thanks to greatly improved – and largely EU-subsidized – agriculture and tourism. Since the 1980s, however, this prosperity has also brought a massive amount of hideous building, which has ruined large tracts of land, especially on the north coast.

NICOLETTA MOMIGLIANO

See also Arabs, Dorians, Linear B, Minoans, Mycenaeans, Renaissance (Veneto-Cretan), Venetokratia

Summary

The largest Aegean island, Crete is best known for its Minoan civilization which flourished during the Bronze Age until overtaken by Mycenaeans c.1500–1200 BC. A backwater in the Classical period, Crete prospered again in the Hellenistic and Roman periods and was an early centre of Christianity. Held by Arabs from 824 to 961, then Byzantine again until 1204, it was a Venetian possession until 1669 enjoying a cultural flowering after 1453. After 230 years of Turkish rule Crete gained autonomy in 1898 and was united with Greece in 1913.

Further Reading

Admiralty, Naval Intelligence Division, "Crete" in *Greece*, vol. 3: *Regional Geography*, London: Naval Intelligence Division, 1945

Allbaugh, Leland G., *Crete: A Case Study of an Underdeveloped Area*, Princeton, New Jersey: Princeton University Press, 1953

Beevor, Antony, *Crete: The Battle and the Resistance*, London: Penguin, 1991; Boulder, Colorado: Westview Press, 1994

Branigan, Keith, *The Tombs of Mesara: A Study of Funerary Architecture and Ritual in Southern Crete, 2800–1700 BC*, London: Duckworth, 1970

Branigan, Keith, *The Foundations of Palatial Crete: A Survey of Crete in the Early Bronze Age*, London: Routledge and Kegan Paul, and New York: Praeger, 1970; 2nd edition Amsterdam: Hakkert, 1988

Buondelmonti, Cristoforo, *Descriptio insule Crete; et Liber insularum*, Herakleion, 1981

Cadogan, Gerald, *Palaces of Minoan Crete*, revised edition, London and New York: Routledge, 1991

Cameron, P., *Crete*, 5th edition, London: A. & C. Black, and New York: Norton, 1988 (*Blue Guide* series)

Christides, Vassilios, *The Conquest of Crete by the Arabs, c.824: A Turning Point in the Struggle between Byzantium and Islam*, Athens: Akademia Athenon, 1984

Curuni, Spiridione Allesandro and Lucilla Donati, *Creta veneziana: L'Istituto Veneto e la missione cretese di Giuseppe Gerola, collezione fotografica, 1900–1902*, Venice: Istituto Veneto di Scienze, Lettere ed Arti, 1988

Davaras, Costis, *Guide to Cretan Antiquities*, Park Ridge, New Jersey: Noyes Press, 1976

Detorakis, Theochares E., *Istoria tes Kretes* [History of Crete], Herakleion, 1990

Evans, Arthur, *The Palace of Minos: A Comparative Account of the Successive Stages of the Early Cretan Civilization as Illustrated by the Discoveries at Knossos*, 4 vols, London: Macmillan, 1921–35; reprinted New York: Biblo and Tannen, 1964

Gallas, Klaus, Klaus Wessel, and Manolis Borboudakis, *Byzantinisches Kreta*, Munich: Hirmer, 1983

Gerola, Giuseppe, *Monumenti veneti nell'isola di Creta*, 4 vols, Venice: Istituto Veneto di Scienze, Lettere ed Arti, 1905–32

Graham, James Walter, *The Palaces of Crete*, revised edition, Princeton, New Jersey: Princeton University Press, 1986

Holton, David (editor), *Literature and Society in Renaissance Crete*, Cambridge and New York: Cambridge University Press, 1991

Hood, Sinclair, *The Minoans: Crete in the Bronze Age*, London: Thames and Hudson, 1971

Hopkins, Adam, *Crete: Its Past, Present and People*, London: Faber, 1977

Hutchinson, R.W., *Prehistoric Crete*, Harmondsworth: Penguin, 1962

Kalokyris, Konstantin, *The Byzantine Wall Paintings of Crete*, New York: Red Dust, 1973

Kazantakis, Nikos, *Zorba the Greek*, translated by Carl Wildman, New York: Simon and Schuster, and London: Lehmann, 1952

Kazantzakis, Nikos, *Freedom and Death: A Novel*, translated by Jonathan Griffin, New York: Simon and Schuster, and Oxford: Cassirer, 1956

Lear, Edward, *The Cretan Journal*, translated by Carl Wildman, edited by Rowena Fowler, Athens: Harvey, and Dedham, Essex: Sanctuary, 1984

Myers, J. Wilson, Eleanor Emlen Myres and Gerald Cadogan (editors), *The Aerial Atlas of Ancient Crete*, London: Thames and Hudson, and Berkeley: University of California Press, 1992

Pashely, Robert, *Travels in Crete*, London: John Murray, 1837; reprinted Amsterdam: Hakkert, 1970

Pendlebury, J.D.S., *The Archaeology of Crete: An Introduction*, London: Methuen, 1939; reprinted 1979

Powell, Dilys, *The Villa Ariadne*, London: Hodder and Stoughton, 1973

Psychoundakis, George, *The Cretan Runner: His Story of the German Occupation*, London: John Murray, 1955

Rackham, Oliver and Jennifer Moody, *The Making of the Cretan Landscape*, Manchester: Manchester University Press, 1996

Sanders, I.F., *Roman Crete: An Archaeological Survey and Gazetteer of Late Hellenistic, Roman and Early Byzantine Crete*, Warminster: Aris and Phillips, 1982

Sapouna Sakellaraki, E., *Minoan Crete: An Illustrated Guide with Reconstructions of the Ancient Monuments*, Rome: Vision, 1994

Spratt, T.A.B., *Travels and Researches in Crete*, London: van Voorst, 1865

Warren, Peter, *The Aegean Civilisations*, 2nd edition, Oxford: Phaidon, and New York: Bedrick, 1989

Willetts, R.F., *Aristocratic Society in Ancient Crete*, London: Routledge, 1955

Willetts, R.F., *Cretan Cults and Festivals*, London: Routledge, and New York: Barnes and Noble, 1962

Willetts, R.F., *Ancient Crete: A Social History*, 2nd edition, London: Routledge, 1974

Willetts, R.F., *The Civilization of Ancient Crete*, London: Batsford, and Berkeley: University of California Press, 1977

Zachariadou, Elizabeth A., *Trade and Crusade: Venetian Crete and the Emirates of Menteshe and Aydin, 1300–1415*, Venice: Istituto Ellenico di Studi Bizantini e Postbizantini, 1983

Crimea

The Crimea is a lozenge-shaped peninsula roughly 250×150 km in size on the northern Black Sea. Successively known as the Tauric Chersonese, Gothia, and Khazaria, it served as the historic interface between the western Greek and northern "barbarian" worlds, represented in turn by Scythians and Mongols. As a sort of ethnic sump, the Crimea long retained communities of invaders, traders, and refugees who passed through: for example, it was a "Little Armenia" in the late Middle Ages, while fundamentalist Karaite Jews outlasted the last metropolitan of Gothia, who died in 1786. Even today the Crim-Tatars, who arrived in the 13th century, are making a notable come-back, only to find their home is in the Ukraine but full of Russians. Of all the Crimea's peoples, the Greeks have been, until recently, the most persistent.

Despite such ethnic diversity, the Crimean interface is marked precisely by geography and economy. A sharp mountain range, topped by high summer pastures, runs along the southeastern coast from Cherson (ancient Chersonesus), near modern Sebastopol, to Pantikapaion, near modern Kerch, on the Cimmerian Bosporus at the entrance to the Maiotic Sea of Azov. The mountains hem the sea to a coastal strip which with its high rainfall, viticulture, and fish pans attracted colonists from the south and west to trading and listening posts. Behind the mountains most of the Crimea is steppe: grazing land when in the hands of Scythian, Pecheneg, or Tatar pastoralists, but at other times rich enough to become in turn a granary of ancient Athens (reflected in Euripides' play *Iphigeneia in Tauris*, which puts the near-sacrifice of her brother Orestes at Fiolente near a place of commercial importance); a granary of Genoa from the 1270s to the closing of the Black Sea by the Ottomans in 1475 (when the Genoese colonial capital was at Caffa [Theodosia, Feodosiya which in the 1340s also exported both slaves and the Black Death to the west); and finally in the 19th century when, just before the Crimean War, its grain won a gold medal in London at the Great Exhibition of 1851.

The Greek sequence begins with the meeting of Carian adventurers with Tauric Scythians long before the establishment of an Ionian colony at Cherson in the 6th century BC. As a self-consciously Greek entrepot and grain exporter, Cherson was especially prosperous in the Hellenistic, Roman, and early Byzantine periods and remained a pivotal and sometimes semiautonomous place thereafter, depending on the relative influence of Constantinople and Bosporan, Khazar, and other powers. Pope Martin I (d. 655) and Emperor Justinian II (d.711) were exiled there, and after it became a 9th-century Byzantine theme, it played an essential part in the evangelization of Kievan Russia: by tradition Prince Vladimir I was baptized in Cherson in 988/9.

After 1204 centres of importance moved east. The Grand Komnenoi of Trebizond claimed the Byzantine inheritance in the Crimea in theory and were closely related to the Greek princes of Sts Theodores (Mangup) in practice, reviving the political links that were first established between the Crimea and the Pontus when Mithridates VI, king of Pontus, died old and in despair at Pantikapaeum in 63 BC. Italian merchants and missionaries revived most of the ancient Greek commercial colonies of the coast and traded with the Golden Horde, the last of the sequence of steppe powers. This period came to an end in 1475 when the Ottomans concluded their conquests of Constantinople (1453) and Trebizond (1461) by taking Caffa and Mangup and making tributary the Giray khans of Crim-Tatary, who governed from north of the mountain divide at Bahchesaray, near the Karaite centre at Chufut Kale and not far from Mangup. The Armenians moved on up the Danube.

After the Russian conquest of the Crimea from 1783 under Catherine the Great, ancient Greek colonies, Italian trading posts, and Tatar fishing villages entered a new lease of life: for example, Symbolon (Italian Cembalo) is today better known as Balaclava, Kalamita as Inkerman, and Yalita (Tatar Dzalita) as Yalta, a resort twinned with Margate in England, which has today resumed more ancient commercial ties with Sinope (Turkish Sinop). After 1783 Pontic Greeks began a further migration north to the new towns of Odessa, Mariupol, and Rostov. But in the Crimea excavations of the vast Classical sites, of Cherson and Pantikapaeum especially, begun in the 19th century, continue to yield evidence of a continuity of settlement and economy. Genoese Caffa awaits further serious investigation.

ANTHONY A.M. BRYER

Summary

First colonized by Greeks in the Archaic period when it was known as the Tauric Chersonese, the Crimea was important chiefly as a source of grain. It was especially prosperous in the Hellenistic, Roman, and Byzantine periods. Italian merchants moved in from 1204 to 1475 when it fell to the Ottomans. Greek contact was revived after the Russian conquest in 1783.

Further Reading

Vasiliev, A.A., *The Goths in the Crimea*, Cambridge, Massachusetts: Mediaeval Academy of America, 1936 (remains an essential starting point amid a vast bibliography)

Croatia

Today an independent South Slav state in the northwestern Balkans, Croatia emerged from the disintegration of Titoist Yugoslavia, within which it had constituted a federal republic until 1991. Croatia is properly regarded as the region that follows the state borders with Slovenia, Hungary, and Bosnia, is blocked off from the Adriatic coast by the mountains of Velika and Mala Kapela (Gvozd), and fuses to the southeast with the adjacent Slavonia – the region between the Drava and Sava rivers – into one natural but not always historical entity. Historically, from the 13th century onwards, the lands of Croatia proper were called Slavonia, while the name Croatia (and Dalmatia) designated the littoral region between the Gvozd mountains and the Adriatic.

In Roman times the region corresponded roughly to the lowlands of the province of Pannonia below the Drava river, which was named after its ancient inhabitants, the Paeones, a heterogenous Illyrian-Celtic tribe who succumbed to the Romans at the time of Octavian, in 35 BC. There emerged in time one of the two medieval Croatian principalities, namely Pannonian (Great or White) Croatia, after Croat settlers massively infiltrated this pagan area around the Drava and Sava rivers (Pannonia Savia) in the 6th and 7th centuries during the South Slavic migrations. In fact, Croatian infiltration and eventual establishment in the northwestern Balkan borderlands of Byzantium are believed to have been encouraged by the emperor Herakleios (610–41) who sought to use the Croats to contain Avar incursions. Because of the Slavonic descent of the settlers the region was to be called Slovinje and later Slavonia. Another branch of Croats was directed to and populated the Adriatic littoral, the so-called Coastal or Dalmatian Croatia extending along the seaboard from the Raša to the Cetina rivers. Its core area was the triangle formed by the towns of Šibenik, Nin, and Knin, where there gradually evolved a matrix Croatian state which, in the 10th century, was to unify the two principalities into a strong and expanded Croatian kingdom.

Like Dalmatia, Croatia proper occupied a position that formed a channel for both communication and confrontation between peoples and cultures, a factor of major significance for Croatian history. Situated astride the route to and from central Europe, and at the same time a natural continuation of the wide Pannonian plain, Croatia formed a part of a broader geopolitical entity. This exposed the Croats to foreign influences, and in particular directed their orientation towards the Roman/western sphere of culture; but it also left them vulnerable to the multifarious rivalries that developed in the Pannonian basin, and this explains why the Croats experienced difficulty in attaining lasting national statehood.

Initially allotted to the western half of the Roman empire, the lands later inhabited by the Croats were transferred to Constantinople following the collapse of the West in 476 in the wake of the Germanic invasions. Nevertheless, both the inland regions and the coastal Roman towns remained culturally attached to Rome. This cultural tradition proved sufficiently resilient to survive latently the disruption of Illyrian-Roman civilization brought about by the South Slavic colonization. In the Dalmatian towns, in particular, there still lived a large number of Romanized Illyrians who were vehicles of Latin culture. Centuries later this heritage would prove an asset to Rome in preserving the universality of Latin Christianity in the Croatian lands in opposition to the Byzantine cultural influence promoted through the Slavic script and liturgy.

The first two centuries of the Croats' history after they settled in the Drava-Sava area are obscure – apparently a transitional period in which their social organization must have remained sketchy. At the end of the 8th century Charlemagne extended Frankish sway over Croatian Pannonia, but left it to be administered by local Croat dignitaries. At this time the Croats were won over to Christianity, and Charlemagne assigned their ecclesiastical jurisdiction to the Aquileia patriarchate. In this way the Franks became the harbingers of Latin Christian culture to pagan Croatian Pannonia.

Now for the first time all the Croat-inhabited lands (both Pannonian and Dalmatian Croatia) were brought together under Frankish suzerainty, a fact that produced nascent movements for a Croatian polity. In 819 prince Ljudevit, a Croat nobleman, gave expression to such aspirations in the revolt he led of Pannonian Croatians against the Franks; but his movement was defeated and Frankish control was restored. In the ensuing years Croatia experienced unrest generated by the Frankish–Bulgarian struggle in the Drava and Sava area. When the Frankish state was eventually divided by the Verden treaty of 843, inland Croatia was subordinated to the eastern state (Germany), which was soon plunged in internal feuds. Coastal Croatia, on the other hand, was annexed to the western state (Italy), achieving de facto independence in the second half of the 9th century.

Once more, a foreign presence induced the Croats to pursue a state organization of their own. This time it was the Magyars, whose massive arrival in the Pannonian plain placed the adjacent Croats under threat. The latter reached an accord with their kindred in Dalmatian Croatia under prince Tomislav (c.910–28) who, after he fought wars with the Magyars as well as the Bulgarians, effected the unification of inland and coastal Croats in the first Croatian state extending from the Drava to the Adriatic coast. A former ally of Byzantium in Dalmatia, Tomislav turned later to Rome, which in 925 acknowledged him as king – the first in Croatian history.

This was a crucial stage in the papacy's campaign to ensure the dominance of the Latin Church among the Croats. The Dalmatian towns always represented bastions of Latin culture, while the Pannonian Croats espoused Latin Christianity through Franco-German influence. But after 863, when Byzantium embarked on its mission to convert the Moravian Slavs to Christianity by means of the Slavonic language, the trend towards Slavonic liturgy (which meant that church services were conducted in the native language of the congregation and not in Latin) made inroads into the Croatian lands, especially among the common people. To suppress its appeal, the Latin bishops of the Dalmatian towns sought to extend inordinately the ecclesiastical jurisdiction of the papal archbishopric of Split over the unified Croatian lands. This policy was pursued at the cost of the bishopric of Nin on the Croatian Adriatic which, under its bishop Gregory, represented the Slavonic-Croatian ecclesiastical movement. The mutual interests of the Croatian ruling elite and Rome effected the subordination of the Croatian lands to the spiritual jurisdiction of the archbishop of Split and the establishment of the Latin

liturgy in Croatian churches. The Slavonic liturgy was banned (in fact it was marginalized in peripheral churches) and the bishopric of Nin was abolished. By these decisions, taken in two ecclesiastical synods in Split in 924 and 928, the Croats were placed firmly in the Roman-Latin cultural orbit.

Tomislav's successors struggled to sustain the Croatian state despite incipient Venetian antagonism on the eastern Adriatic. Croatia reached its height in the reign of king Petar Kresimir IV (1068–74) who annexed the Dalmatian towns as integral territory to his state, suppressing any residual Byzantine presence even as nominal overlord. In the ecclesiastical domain Kresimir, who had been brought up in Venice, encouraged an intensification of the role of the Latin in Croatia. As a result of new synods convened in Split (1060 and 1074) a purist campaign was launched by the Latin Church to discard any eastern elements in worship surviving from the earlier alternation of ecclesiastical authority between Constantinople and Rome over the Adriatic provinces. True, in the face of reactions among the people and the lower clergy, a more indulgent attitude was adopted following the synod of Split in 1079, and both the Church Slavonic language and the Glagolitic script (the first Slavonic alphabet devised by St Cyril) were permitted in central Dalmatia. In fact in some areas of Croatia the Glagolitic alphabet was adopted by Latin monks as a bulwark against surviving Greek Orthodox influences, to the point that it became known (falsely) as a Croatian script. Be that as it may, the final incorporation of the Croats into the Latin Church was a reality, and the Latin Christian faith became the vehicle of the Croats' accession to the culture of the western world.

In 1102, following a phase of instability, Croatia was united with Hungary in a "personal union", with the Hungarian king being separately crowned as king of Croatia too. Although this special coronation was omitted in the 13th century, the Croatian lands retained the status of annexed (partes adnexae) and not conquered lands (partes subiugatae). This settlement was to invite divergent interpretations as to the nature of the relationship between Hungary and Croatia, and the latitude of Croatian sovereignty it implied; the Croats, at any rate, never regarded this union as annulling the distinct status of their state.

Thenceforward Croatia was permanently removed from the Greek-Byzantine world, to which it had only briefly and half-heartedly subscribed. A brief restoration of Byzantine control in the mid-12th century over a large part of Croatia by the emperor Manuel I Komnenos was strictly a political episode with no cultural consequences. Following his death, Hungary acquired all the Byzantine possessions in Croatia and Dalmatia. There the Roman-Byzantine judicial tradition survived in the statutes of the coastal cities, which ensured their autonomy whether under Hungarian or Venetian rule. In modern times, from the early 18th to the mid-19th century, certain cities in Croatia (Zagreb, Karlovac, Osijek, and Slavonski Brod) accommodated some of the flourishing Greek colonies that were scattered in the ex-Yugoslav lands during Ottoman rule in Greece.

RENNOS EHALIOTIS

Further Reading

Božić, Ivan (editor), *Istorija Jugoslavije* [History of Yugoslavia], 2nd edition, Belgrade, 1973 (in Serbo-Croatian)

Carter, Francis W., "Urban Development in the Western Balkans, 1200–1800" in *An Historical Geography of the Balkans*, edited by Francis W. Carter, London and New York: Academic Press, 1977

Constantine Porphyrogenitus, *De Administrando Imperio*, Greek text edited by Gyula Moravcsik, English translation by R.J.H. Jenkins, Washington, D.C.: Dumbarton Oaks Center for Byzantine Studies, 1967; reprinted 1985

Črnja, Zvane, *Cultural History of Croatia*, Zagreb: Office of Information, 1962

Dvornik, Francis, *Les Slaves, Byzance et Rome au IXe siècle*, Paris: Champion, 1926

Dvornik, Francis, *The Slavs: Their Early History and Civilization*, Boston: American Academy of Arts and Sciences, 1956

Eterovich, Francis H., *Croatia: Land, People, Culture*, 2 vols, Toronto: University of Toronto Press, 1964–70

Ferluga, Jadran, *Byzantium in the Balkans: Studies on the Byzantine Administration and the Southern Slavs from the VIIth to the XIIth Centuries*, Amsterdam: Hakkert, 1976

Fine, John V.A., *The Early Medieval Balkans: A Critical Survey from the Sixth to the Late Twelfth Century*, Ann Arbor: University of Michigan Press, 1983

Guldescu, Stanko, *History of Medieval Croatia*, The Hague: Mouton, 1964

Hauptmann, L., "Les Rapports des byzantins avec les slaves et les avares pendant la seconde moitié du VIe siècle", *Byzantion*, 4 (1927/28): pp. 137–70

Ivančević, Radovan, *Art Treasures of Croatia*, Zagreb: ITP Motovun, 1993

Klaić, Nada, *Povijest Hrvata u razvijenom srednjem vijeku* [The History of the Croats in the Late Middle Ages], Zagreb, 1976 (in Serbo-Croatian)

Klaić, Vjekoslav, *Povijest Hrvata* [The History of the Croats], 5 vols, Zagreb, 1899–1911, reprinted Zagreb, 1985 (in Serbo-Croatian)

Novak, V., "The Slavonic–Latin Symbiosis during the Middle Ages", *Slavonic and East European Review*, 32 (1953–54): pp. 1–28

Obolensky, Dimitri, "Byzantium and its Northern Neighbours, 565–1018" in *The Byzantine Empire*, edited by J.M. Hussey, Cambridge: Cambridge University Press, 1967 (*The Cambridge Medieval History*, vol. 4, part 2)

Ostrogorsky, George, *History of the Byzantine State*, revised edition, Oxford: Blackwell, and New Brunswick, New Jersey: Rutgers University Press, 1969

Tanner, Marcus, *Croatia: A Nation Forged in War*, New Haven and London: Yale University Press, 1997

Crusades

The crusades were a military movement first launched by pope Urban II in 1095. They were directed against the enemies of the Church – initially the infidels who had occupied Jerusalem and were then threatening the Christians of the Byzantine empire. In conception the crusades were seen as a sort of armed pilgrimage undertaken at the behest of the pope and attracting certain privileges for participants, in the form of the protection of their family and property while they were away, and remission of their sins on the completion of their crusading vow. The response to Urban's appeal in the West was far beyond his expectations and reflects the heightened religious mood of the 11th century marked in part by increased pilgrim traffic following the millennium of Christ's birth. There was no

Crusades: Byzantine relief icon of the Archangel Michael, probably 11th century, looted by crusaders in 1204 and now in the Treasury of San Marco, Venice

one generally used term for crusading and for the crusader in the medieval period. By the early 13th century crusading had come to embrace expeditions directed not just to the recovery and defence of the Holy Land but also to the Iberian peninsula and northeastern Europe against heretics and schismatics and against other Christian lay powers dubbed the enemies of the popes. Quite when crusading came an to end is a matter for debate: the seizure of Malta from the Knights of St John by Napoleon in 1798 is a generally convenient terminal date, providing as it does seven centuries for the existence of the crusading movement.

With the coming of the crusades the period 1095–1204 witnessed the increasing presence of the Latins and their influence in the Greek east. As a result of the crusades in the 12th century knowledge and awareness of Byzantium were to be more widespread in the west and its wealth and commercial potential were to act as a lure to many. At the end of the 11th century the Byzantine empire was internally weak and surrounded by external enemies. The emperor Alexios I Komnenos (1081–1118) looked to the West for help and in that sense was responsible for bringing about the unhappy relations between Byzantium and the crusaders. There is no real evidence that he actually asked for a crusade. The letter written in Latin (not Greek) to Robert of Flanders stating that the empire was doomed if the faithful Latins did not help is almost certainly a forgery. The presence of Greek envoys at the

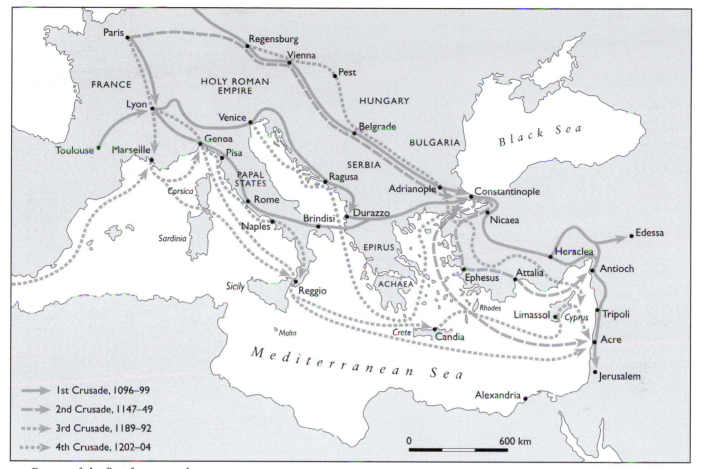

15. Routes of the first four crusades

Council of Piacenza on 1–7 March 1095 establishes that Alexios asked for help, but not what sort of help he wanted. On 27 November 1095 pope Urban II proclaimed the crusade at Clermont. What he actually said does not survive, but only garbled accounts written down from memory after the fall of Jerusalem which place the speech at the beginning of an inevitable process of triumph. It appears that Urban appealed for the relief of Christians in Palestine just as much as for the relief of eastern Christians within the former territories of Byzantium.

The West was already familiar with the idea of holy war or at least the idea of waging war with God's help, as is evident from the correspondence of pope Gregory VII (1073–85), the Norman invasion of England in 1066, and the case of El Cid in Spain. In many ways for the Greeks all wars were holy wars since they were fought in defence of the empire and for God's anointed, the emperor. It was the military aspect of the crusades that distinguished them from pilgrimages, and the idea of a penitential war-pilgrimage was something distinctly new in the late 11th century.

The crusaders had a mixed reception in Byzantine territory. In general, Byzantine organization stood up well to the demands for food made by these large contingents of crusaders passing through their territory. There were clashes brought about by hunger, the demands for markets, and cultural and linguistic differences. The Pecheneg cavalry, sent to escort some of the crusading contingents, often provoked a hostile reaction

and villagers thought to be holding back much-needed food supplies or to be overcharging incited violence and plunder on the part of the crusaders. There was the baggage of history too to cope with. Anna Komnene reacts with suspicion and dislike of Bohemond, who just 10 years before had been campaigning in Thessaly against her father. For his part too he carefully stayed clear of areas with concentrations of Byzantine troops and was at pains to pick a route to the south and east of Durazzo that had not suffered from his depredation in 1085. In the hinterland of Constantinople Peter the Hermit's contingent, which arrived on 1 August 1097, reacted to food shortages by pillaging and, despite the friendly reception and advice that Alexios gave to Peter, he was relieved when this first army crossed over to Asia Minor. Nevertheless he sent a flotilla to rescue survivors of Peter's army after the disaster at Xerigordo. In December 1097 the troops with Godfrey of Bouillon ravaged the area around Adrianople in response to false rumours that numerous western leaders had been imprisoned by Alexios. There was suspicion and fear on both sides, which come through both in the pages of Anna Komnene and in western accounts of the crusade written after the capture of Jerusalem and in the perceived lack of support given to the cause by Alexios. The Greeks are stigmatized as treacherous and crafty, the westerners as untrustworthy, impulsive, violent, and rapacious.

At no time did Alexios seek to place himself at the head of this western army. Instead he persuaded the crusading leadership to take an oath to return all cities and territories formerly in Byzantine hands, he offered advice on fighting the Turks, and he sent along his trusted general Tatikios (fl.1057–99) together with a small Byzantine force. Tatikios received the surrender of Nicaea in 1097. The events surrounding the siege revealed that western and Byzantine views of Islam differed markedly. The westerners had had little contact with Islam except in Spain and Sicily and their approach was based on ignorance and intolerance. Their crusading mission was to kill the enemies of God, while the Greeks kept their relations with Islam on a political level. All of this reinforced suspicion of the Byzantines in western eyes. Tatikios remained with the crusading army until February 1098 when during the siege of Antioch (December 1097–June 1098) he was forced to withdraw to Cyprus due to disagreements with Bohemond. In mid-June 1098 Alexios arrived at Philomelion in eastern Turkey with the intention, according to Anna, of marching to the assistance of the crusaders at Antioch. The distance between the two towns is more than 600 km and it is unlikely that this was the case. Western sources do not mention this intention and instead concentrate upon the treachery of Stephen of Blois and the other deserters from the camp at Antioch who are said to have spread false rumours of the crusader surrender to the Turks. The withdrawal of Tatikios and the non-appearance of Alexios at Antioch were conveniently taken by the crusading leadership to mean that their contract with Alexios made in Constantinople was at an end and that anything they conquered was their own. According to Anna, Alexios saw this failure of the crusaders to return Antioch as proof that the empire had gained nothing from the toil and expense of supporting the crusade. As a result the relations between Byzantium and the northernmost crusader states were uneasy. In 1108 (Treaty of Devol) Bohemond of Antioch swore allegiance to Alexios and acknowledged him as his suzerain. In 1158–59 the emperor Manuel I occupied Antioch and forced its ruler (Renaud de Chatillon) to acknowledge imperial overlordship and to accept an Orthodox patriarch. The relations between Byzantium and the other crusader states was far less clear cut.

The crusades of the 12th century were marked by western concerns to secure the route to Jerusalem by occupying the city of Constantinople. This concern surfaced early as Alexios was accused of sabotaging the crusade of 1101. In 1107–08 Bohemond launched an attack on Albania from Apulia; he captured Avlona and besieged Durazzo. Alexios blockaded Bohemond and forced him to agree to the Treaty of Devol (September 1108) by which Bohemond took an oath of vassalage for his principality of Antioch in western style and agreed to return to Italy. The Second crusade, called on 1 December 1145 as a response to the fall of Edessa the previous year, brought out into the open Byzantine fear of a crusader attack on Constantinople and the intention on the part of the crusading leadership to mount such an attack. The passage of the armies of both Conrad III and Louis VII had witnessed the usual tensions between Greeks and Latins. Manuel I had strengthened the defences of Constantinople. In September 1147 Conrad arrived at Constantinople ignoring Manuel's request that he bypass the city and cross over to Asia at Sestos. The two rulers never met, and it is said that Conrad eyed the defences of the city with interest with a view to returning the

following year to capture it. He and his army moved off to Asia Minor, leaving room for the arrival of Louis VII in October. Again there were those in the French army who urged an attack on Constantinople either on their own or in alliance with Roger II of Sicily. Nothing came of these aggressive proposals, but they had been voiced. Roger II had declined to take the cross and during 1147 had captured the islands of Corfu and Cephalonia and sent raiding expeditions to attack Thebes, Corinth, and Euboea. Manuel had tried to raise German and French troops from the crusading armies at Constantinople to attack Roger, but without success.

In the run up to the Third crusade in 1188 Isaac Angelos was rumoured in the west to have received payment from Saladin to delay the crusading armies. This rumour may have played some part in the preference of both Philip Augustus and Richard I to go by sea to Palestine. Only Frederick I Barbarossa used the land route through Constantinople and his relations with the Byzantines led to serious fighting in Thrace and preliminary negotiations with the Hungarians and the Bulgarians to join in an attack on Constantinople. The re-establishment of the Bulgar kingdom in 1186 had damaged the Byzantine empire close to its capital. The breach between Byzantium and the west caused by Frederick Barbarossa was not healed, and the occupation of the city by westerners so that the approach to Jerusalem would be in reliable hands was now definitely on the agenda. The crusades had raised awareness of Byzantium and its wealth in the west, while at the same time Byzantium had lost much face in western eyes by its perceived treachery and its vacillation in the face of western aggression. The diversion of the Fourth crusade to Constantinople in July 1203 was in many ways the logical outcome of the crusading movement; the tensions and animosity had been there right from the start. The capture and sack of Constantinople on 12 April 1204 are generally regarded as the great tragedy of the Middle Ages because so many books and works of art were destroyed.

Following the Fourth crusade a number of crusader states were set up around the Aegean, nominally acknowledging the suzerainty of the Latin empire of Constantinople. Surrounded on all sides by hostile neighbours – Bulgarians, Greeks in Nicaea, and Greeks in Epirus – this empire had a short and threatened existence (1204–61). The papacy was prepared to issue crusading indulgences in defence of the empire both as a means of maintaining a secure avenue of approach for the recovery of the Holy Land and as a means of fostering Church union between the Greek and Latin communions, and this happened on numerous occasions between 1223 and 1320. Constantinople and the Aegean lacked the appeal of Jerusalem as a crusade destination and the response was poor except for those rulers such as the Montferrats and the Angevins with crucial political interests in the Latin empire.

During the latter part of the 14th century the advance of the Turks into the Balkans and the Aegean focused western attention on the defence of Constantinople as a bastion of western Europe itself in the face of Turkish attack. Despite scepticism in some quarters as to the efficacy of crusading, it still had much support and no shortage of new ideas both as to strategy and as to tactics. Alongside conventional land crusading such as the expeditions to Nicopolis (1396) and Varna (1444), there developed a variety of naval crusades such as the attacks on

Smyrna (1344), Lampsacus (1359), Alexandria (1365), Vonitsa (1378), Lepanto (1571), the continued resistance to the Ottomans mounted by the Knights of St John from their naval bases on Rhodes (1309–1523) and Malta (1530–1798), and the campaigns mounted by the Venetian Republic in the Aegean and Peloponnese down to 1718. Crusading as a movement and as an idea lasted for more than seven centuries and in each of those centuries left its mark on Greek lands: first in cooperation, then in opposition, and finally in defence. Indeed it is debatable just what role crusading ideology played in the philhellenism that recruited support for the Greeks in their War of Independence: perhaps the battle of Navarino on 20 October 1827 was the last naval crusade.

PETER LOCK

See also Constantinople (Sack of), Normans

Further Reading

Housley, Norman, *The Later Crusades, 1274–1580: From Lyons to Alcazar*, Oxford and New York: Oxford University Press, 1992

Riley-Smith, Jonathan (editor), *The Oxford Illustrated History of the Crusades*, Oxford and New York: Oxford University Press, 1995

Setton, Kenneth M. (editor), *A History of the Crusades*, 2nd edition, 6 vols, Madison: University of Wisconsin Press, 1969–89

Cult

This article deals exclusively with pagan antiquity, because the change in the nature of belief and ritual with the coming of Christianity was so marked that it would be misleading to treat any aspect of Christian practice as having developed out of a pagan forerunner. Within the context of ancient Greek religion, "cult" refers to the rites and ceremonies of worship.

Most of the evidence for cult activity concerns official, public, service to the gods (*latreia, therapeia*). Participation in communal worship was one of the responsibilities of the citizen: at his trial, Socrates attempted to defend himself against the charge of not believing in the gods of the state by pointing out that he had been sacrificing regularly at the common festivals and on public altars (Xenophon, *Apology*, 10–11; cf. Plato, *Apology*, 26c).

But already in the Classical period, not even mere presence at ceremonies could be enforced, and at Athens at least, recourse was made to the "theoric fund", which provided the working poor with compensation for lost income so that they could attend public festivals. During the Hellenistic period it was not uncommon to declare public holidays during festivals, when businesses shut and people were adjured to take part. Schoolboys were often required to participate by marching in sacral processions.

The purpose of ritual was manifold: to avert the wrath of the deity, to obtain her or his goodwill, above all to establish a rapport between god and worshipper. The forms – more or less strictly adhered to – were based where possible on Homeric precedent. Thus the sacrifice performed by Nestor in *Odyssey*, 30. 418–63 served as a model for full-scale public sacrifices throughout antiquity, just as Odysseus' visit to the underworld (*Odyssey*, 11. 23–50) was the model for the worship of heroes

Cult: sacrifice at an altar before a statue of a god, Museum für Vor- und Frühgeschichte, Frankfurt

and other ground-dwelling deities. In this sense, of being mined for guidance to correct procedure, the Homeric poems were the nearest the Greeks came to having a "Bible".

Invocations of and prayer to the deity were less important in themselves than they were to worshippers in the Judeo-Christian traditions; rather, they were integrated into the central act of public worship, that is, the donation of gifts in the form of sacrifices or votive offerings.

Animal sacrifice is the most spectacular example of this transaction. It is a procedure that the ancient Greeks had in common with peoples of the Near East (well summarized by West). Depending on the nature of the deity, the animals sacrificed were entirely consumed by fire, or were shared as food by both gods and men. Sacrifices of the first kind (*sphagia, enagismata*) were made to heroes and gods who were believed to reside underground. Heroes were dead humans whose mortal remains were worshipped, usually at the place of their burial. The purpose of sacrifice in these cases was to rejuvenate and/or revive the heroes so that they might come to the aid of the worshippers. Heroes were usually bound to a restricted geographical area. The standard method of sacrifice was to lay a fire in a pit (*bothros*), slaughter the animal over it, catch the blood and pour it or other liquids into the ground at or near the "tomb", and burn the whole carcass up. The invocation of the spirit of Agamemnon in Aeschylus' *Choephori* (84–164) is a good example of the procedure, with, in this case, a liquid offering (*pelanos*) poured out at the tomb.

The status of hero was accorded to a wide variety of persons: distant ancestors, founders of colonies (oecists), figures from epic; but in many cases the names, if they ever had them, are unknown to us. Generally speaking, when a hero's parents were known, one was divine, the other mortal (usually the mother: Achilles is a noteworthy exception). Two such — Heracles and Asclepius – became famous well beyond their original spheres, and reached the status of hero-god.

Gods, particularly those whose conventional abode was on Mount Olympus, received *thysiai*, the sacrifice of parts of animals burned on a raised altar (*bomos*). Here the model is Hesiod, who tells the "just-so" story of how the Titan Prometheus – a friend to mankind – duped all-knowing Zeus into accepting as his share of the sacrifice the fat and bones of the beast, leaving the edible meat and hide to man (*Theogony*, 538–42). In this kind of sacrifice the animal is consumed jointly by god and worshipper alike, and usually within the sanctuary itself. The valuable hides normally formed one of the perquisites of the priest.

Sacrifices often, but by no means always, took place within the context of a formal festival. There were also bloodless offerings, often occasional, such as the first fruits, and objects (ranging from items of clothing or armour to full-sized statues) symbolizing the dedicator or their achievements, offered as gifts. Some were thank-offerings for favours received (good crops, successful delivery from life's crises, such as illness or war); others were supplicatory.

The rituals of the cult were performed by "doers of sacred acts", *hiereis*, a term usually translated as "priests", which is misleading to us, because these people were functionaries rather than members of a discrete caste, the only exceptions being those officiants who introduced initiates into various mysteries, and who usually belonged to a hereditary priesthood. But even they were not set apart from their fellow citizens, except in the actual performance of their duties: for example, Callias son of Hipponicus, torchbearer of the Eleusinian mysteries and one of the richest men in Athens in the 5th century BC, negotiated the peace settlement with Persia that bears his name. Even the transmitters of the god's will at oracular sanctuaries were not priestly in our sense. Occasionally a priesthood might be restricted to a man or woman of a certain age, whose term of office might be measured in lifetimes. Most often, however, priesthoods were annual magistracies like any other.

Cult activity normally took place in a sanctuary, an area cut off (*temenos*) from the secular world and consecrated to the deity involved (*hieron temenos*, conventionally abbreviated to *hieron*). The seclusion could be marked by a wall or a series of boundary stones. It was rare for a sanctuary to be deconsecrated (there are examples in Greek settlements in Italy). The only essential feature was a space where people could gather. Most sanctuaries had an altar for the sacrifice, and many, but not all, had a structure, the temple (*naos*, dwelling place) to house the cult image and objects dedicated to the god. The sanctuary might also include semisecular structures, such as dining rooms for the consumption of the sacrificial meals. The cult image itself represented the god as his or her proxy: the Greeks were well aware of the fact that their gods were not to be tied to any one place, and that they would favour now one, then another.

Most public cults were open to all comers. Some, however, limited their clientele depending on the nature of the ritual. The Thesmophoria, for example, were restricted to women, while some sanctuaries of Heracles barred women altogether. Mystery cults, after initial screening for ritual purity, accepted almost anybody, but the central rites themselves remained a close secret known only to initiates. It is a measure of the respect in which the ancient Hellenes held their gods that to this day we know almost nothing about these rites. This is a salutary lesson to anyone who may think that the ancient Hellenes were not serious and pious believers.

ALBERT SCHACHTER

See also Religion, Sacrifice, Sanctuaries

Further Reading

Bingen, Jean and Albert Schachter (editors), *Le Sanctuaire grec: huit exposés suivis de discussions*, Geneva: Fondation Hardt, 1992

Burkert, Walter, *Greek Religion*, Oxford: Blackwell, and Cambridge, Massachusetts: Harvard University Press, 1985

Kearns, Emily, *The Heroes of Attica*, London: University of London, Institute of Classical Studies, 1989

West, M.L., *The East Face of Helicon: West Asiatic Elements in Greek Poetry and Myth*, Oxford: Clarendon Press, and New York: Oxford University Press, 1997

Cyclades

The Cyclades were named from their clustering in a rough circle round the ancient sacred island of Delos. In antiquity 12 to 15 islands were counted as part of the group. In the modern *nomos* (prefecture) there are a total of about 30 islands and islets, with the capital on Syros. The name is used in Byzantine sources with a quite different significance (see below).

Throughout prehistory people were drawn through the Cyclades, to Melos, at the southwest of the group, in quest of obsidian – a dark volcanic glass that was highly valued for cutting edges for tools and weapons. In the Early Bronze Age (mid-4th to late 3rd millennium BC), the culture of the Cyclades was distinct from that of the rest of the Aegean. During the ascendancy of the Minoan and Mycenaean palaces (2nd millennium BC), the islands shared in their cultures and were probably subject to their authority. The Cyclades were presumably part of the "Thalassocracy of Minos" mentioned by Thucydides. Their main contribution to Aegean culture of the time may have been as middlemen and experienced seafarers.

During the period of movement and change which followed the decay of Mycenaean civilization (11th century BC) new settlers arrived, mainly from Ionia (the coast of Asia Minor), but also from mainland Greece. Several of the communities which they founded then and in the following centuries grew into important centres. In the Archaic and Classical periods Naxos and Paros played important parts in the development of monumental architecture and sculpture, and various islands (Mykonos, Melos, Thera) had their own distinctive styles of pottery decoration. Several islands (Naxos, Paros, Thera, etc.) were active in the colonial movement and thus in the spread of Greek culture, especially to Italy and Sicily.

In the Persian Wars they were at first overrun by the enemy. Subsequently they joined the Delian League and became subject to Athenian control. In the late-Classical and Hellenistic periods they were controlled by the Macedonians and the Ptolemies, then by Rhodes, and finally the Romans.

From the Archaic period, or possibly earlier, the important sanctuary of Apollo on Delos drew people and wealth into the Cyclades. In Hellenistic and Roman times the island also

Cyclades: a "star-gazer" figure of the Louros type, made by people of the Grotta-Pylos culture, *c.*2800-2700 BC, private collection

became an important commercial centre, further stimulating activity in the area.

The remains of early Christian basilicas show that Christianity had taken hold in the Cyclades between the 4th and 6th centuries AD. In the early years of the Byzantine empire the Cyclades suffered at the hands of raiders from both east (Arabs) and west (Slavs etc.). Later they were divided between different areas of the Byzantine military command. At one time they belonged to a Province of the Islands. In the late 11th century the theme of the Cyclades included such islands as Ikaria and Karpathos not normally thought of as part of the group. In the 12th century Naxos may have been the base of a province called the "Dodecanese". Church construction suggests renewed prosperity at this time.

Following the establishment of the Latin empire at Constantinople in AD 1204, the Cycladic islands were assigned to Venice and by it to individual families, resulting in the estab-lishment of local island or regional dynasties. Their castles and strongholds can still be seen on many islands. During the following centuries some of the local population became Catholic, and Catholic communities still flourish on some islands (e.g. Tinos, Syros) and survive on others (e.g. Naxos). Contacts have been maintained with western European Catholic countries. Naxos became an educational centre in the 17th century, when a French school and an Ursuline convent were founded. Earlier western connections were initially the result of the trading activities of the Italian maritime states in the Aegean; later, Greek traders were resident in Ancona (early 16th century). The islands were torn by the Veneto-Genoese wars in the 13th and 14th centuries and, ravaged by pirates, were depopulated in the 15th century.

After the fall of Constantinople in 1453 the islands were gradually (Tinos not until 1714) taken over by the Turks, who did not much interfere, though they levied taxes which were sometimes high.

In the 17th century the sanctuaries on Delos, Melos, and other places were looted of antiquities by English adventurers including the agents of Charles I and of Lord Arundel – a process which began the establishment of substantial collec-tions of Greek antiquities in foreign countries. After 1770 some of the islands were annexed by Russia in the course of its war with Turkey.

After the Greek wars of independence, in which the islanders played their part, Syros became an important commercial centre (1829). Its capital Ermoupolis was founded by refugees and endowed with extraordinarily fine public buildings and houses for an island town. One sign of the wide external contacts is the Syrian commemorative plates (Syriana) which were manufactured in Britain for the island market in the 19th century. Other evidence of the commercial importance of the islands comes from Melos whose pilots had a high repu-tation, going back at least to the 16th century, and where there were resident consuls in the 19th century. One, the Frenchman Louis Brest, was responsible for the removal of the Venus di Milo to the Louvre.

After the discovery of the famous icon on Tinos in 1822 the island, and thus to some extent that part of the Cyclades, became one of the most important focuses for pilgrimage in the Greek Orthodox world.

In the 19th century travelling potters from the island of Siphnos operated throughout Greece: some settled in Athens (Maroussi). Many other islanders emigrated to Athens, attracted by work available in the new capital. The quarter of Anaphiotika, high on the slopes of the Acropolis, takes its name from settlement by people from the island of Anaphi, and other Athenian street names bear witness to migration, both then and later.

Since the Cyclades were hardly more than an artificial grouping, their contribution to the Greek tradition lies rather in the special circumstances which prevailed on specific indi-vidual islands from time to time, and the extent to which they were subjected to similar political or economic pressures because of their geographical situation. Thus, in the Bronze Age many of them were on trade routes between the mainland and Crete (and further south and east) and Melos was visited for its obsidian products. In the Dark Ages they provided secure refuges for the establishment of refugee communities.

Their natural affinity with the sea and interest in commerce and foreign settlement to augment their meagre resources chimed in with the preoccupations of other Greek states in the Archaic period. In later antiquity they shared in the fortunes of the wider Aegean. The presence of the Italian dynasties has left its mark on the Cyclades, not only in defensive fortification, but also in helping to establish Catholicism as the religion of a significant number of the local population. Pilgrims have been attracted to the area in antiquity by the sanctuary of Apollo on Delos, in modern times by the icon of the Virgin on Tinos.

ROBIN L.N. BARBER

Summary

Group of originally 12 to 15 islands that encircled Delos, the modern province includes about 30 islands and has its capital on Syros. Obsidian on Melos attracted visitors throughout prehistory. Part of the Delian League after the Persian Wars. Commercially important in the Hellenistic and Roman periods. Assigned to Venice after 1204 when some islands became (and remain) largely Catholic. Tinos is a major centre of pilgrimage today.

Further Reading

Barber, R.L.N., *The Cyclades in the Bronze Age*, London: Duckworth, 1987

Bruneau, Philippe and Jean Ducat, *Guide de Délos*, 3rd edition, Paris: Boccard, 1983

Drosou, D., *Istoria tis Nisou Tinou* [History of the Island of Tinos], Athens, 1870

Ekschmitt, Werner, *Kunst und Kultur der Kykladen*, 2 vols, Mainz: Zabern, 1986

Exploration archéologique de Délos, Paris: Fontemoing, 1909

Hatsidakis, I., *Istoria tis Nisou Milou* [The History of the Island of Melos], Athens, 1927

Koukkou, Helene E., *Oi Koinotikoi Thesmoi stis Kyklades kata Tourkokratia* [Village Institutions in the Cyclades during the Turkish Domination], Athens, 1980

Lock, Peter, *The Franks in the Aegean, 1204–1500*, London and New York: Longman, 1995

Morris, Jan, *The Venetian Empire: A Sea Voyage*, London and New York: Faber, 1980

Slot, B., *Archipelagus turbatus: les Cyclades entre colonisation latine et occupation ottomane, c.1550–1718*, Istanbul: Nederlands Historisch Archaeologisch Instituut te Istanbul, 1982

Slot, B., "The Frankish Archipelago", *Byzantinische Forschungen*, 16 (1991): pp. 195–207

Travlos, John and Angeliki Kokkou, *Hermoupolis: The Creation of a New City on Syros at the Beginning of the 19th Century*, Athens: Commercial Bank of Greece, 1984

Cynics

The epithet "Cynic" ("doglike") was first applied to Diogenes of Sinope (?403–?321 BC), as a comment on the shamelessness with which he engaged in acts that were abhorred by other Greeks. Diogenes pursued a life of unqualified self-sufficiency, with only a barrel for warmth and a club for protection, styling himself a cosmopolitan or "citizen of the world". Arguing that actions which are based on natural impulses can never be unnatural, he defended even cannibalism and incest, and practised sexual intercourse in public. Freedom of action and freedom of speech were his watchwords, and he believed that

he had found a way to make these common to everyone, not merely to the holders of civic privilege. It is said that when Alexander the Great, admiring his fortitude, asked if he could do anything for Diogenes, the latter asked him simply to "stand out of my way, because you are blocking the sun". Plato too was a victim of his calculated insolence, and the lost *Republic* attributed to him was evidently a riposte to Plato's dialogue of that title. For all that, Diogenes was regarded by many ancient writers not as a pure innovator, but as a "Socrates gone mad". The bridge between the ascetic of the 5th century and the fanatic of the 4th was Socrates' pupil Antisthenes (*fl.*400 BC), who held up self-denial as the chief principle of the philosophic life. Though never called a Cynic in his lifetime, he was regarded by some later commentators as the true founder of the school.

Most notable of Diogenes' early followers was Crates of Thebes (*c.*368–288 BC), who differed from other Cynics in his willingness to curtail his freedom by marriage; he and his wife Hipparchia are reported nonetheless to have shared Diogenes' indifference to prevailing sexual customs. Crates was for a time the teacher of Zeno, who is usually regarded as the founder of the Stoics. While the Stoics could not condone the licentiousness of Diogenes and Crates, there were some, like the slave Epictetus (*fl.*AD 100), who represented the better kind of Cynic as an imitator of Heracles and a model of virtuous living. Epictetus is one of many moralists who adopted the homely and trenchant style of the Cynic diatribe. This form was devised to bring philosophy to the masses by Bion of Borysthenes, who taught around 315 BC in Athens, and does not seem to have adhered uniquely to any sect. In his ethics, which was the whole of his philosophy, he reduced all goods to pleasure and all knowledge to sense-perception in the manner of another Socratic school, the Cyrenaics; while he looked back to a golden age of virtuous frugality in which each man was his own governor, he did not dispute the present rights of kings. The diatribe was adapted to new purposes in the pseudo-Platonic *Clitophon*, the *Hermetica* (Treatise 7), and above all in the polished works of the orator Dio of Prusa (Dio Chryosostom, 1st century AD), who composed fictitious speeches for Diogenes and Socrates, but reserved his most obsequious and eloquent precepts for the emperor Trajan.

Another form which the Cynics bequeathed to literature is the medley of prose and poetry known as Menippean satire, named after its originator Menippus of Gadara (3rd century BC). Its most prolific exponent was probably Oenomaus, a Hellenized Jew of Gadara (*fl.* AD 120), whose works, like those of his fellow townsman, have not survived in any quantity. Menippus, however, figures frequently in the dialogues of the 2nd-century satirist Lucian. Famous for his ridicule of philosophers, society, and the gods, Lucian repudiates the more disgusting habits of the Cynics while expressing admiration for their ideals. Nevertheless, when others praised the sacrifice of Proteus Peregrinus, who threw himself on a pyre of his own construction at the Olympic Games of AD 169, Lucian denied that he could be called a second Heracles or even a genuine Cynic; he undertook to demonstrate instead that he was a renegade from the Church.

Though Lucian need not be believed, the hypothesis that Jesus was a Cynic has been entertained by a number of recent scholars, especially those who hold that the common source of

Luke and Matthew ("Q") is the most authentic record of his teaching. Evidence is found in the aphoristic sayings of Jesus (reminiscent of Diogenes and Lucian's teacher Demonax), and the poverty of his disciples, who carried only a staff and a wallet in their mission to the Galilaean cities. It must, however, be emphasized that Cynics worked no miracles, did not live in communities, did not commend humility, and (whatever they thought of kings) never promised anyone a kingdom. The manner of Jesus is evidently different from that of Paul, yet it has been maintained that the latter was indebted to the diatribe as a model for his letters. The arguments for this position, while copious and occasionally impressive, are always vitiated by the difficulty of determining what ought to count as a specimen of the form.

Popular opinion in antiquity, noting that Christians held aloof from sacrifice and occasionally from marriage, appears to have equated them with Cynics and to have suspected them of similar or worse atrocities. Perhaps it was the desire to maintain a distance that led Justin Martyr into his fatal feud with the Cynic Crescens; yet Tatian's pupil Justin has been suspected of adopting Cynic tenets when he founded a community of "encratites", who eschewed both meat and sexual intercourse. In fact, though some later Cynics may have practised vegetarianism, the dietetic axiom of Diogenes and Menippus was that nothing is forbidden; and when Cynics avoided marriage, it was only because they wished to maintain the right to promiscuity. When Christian writers speak of Peregrinus as a paradigm of fortitude, it is not because they regard him as a Christian; and even if the dirtiness and illiteracy of Christian monks reminded pagan observers of the Cynics, their cenobitic lifestyle and the worship of God were practices which that antisocial movement could not share. It was the emperor Julian "the Apostate" who proposed the loftiest interpretation of Cynicism, arguing that the vices of Diogenes concealed a profound critique of human laws (*Orations*, 6–7). The Church itself did little to foster the sect, which disappeared in the 6th century AD. As its legacy to Greek culture it left the adjective "cosmopolitan" (adopted by the Stoics and applied to Abraham by Philo, the Jewish precursor of Christian allegory), and the works of Dio and Lucian, the latter of whom can still be read for amusement, as well as for the elegance of his style.

MARK EDWARDS

Biography

Cynics were followers of Diogenes of Sinope (?403–?321 BC) who was called *kyon* ("dog") for his rejection of social conventions, though some regarded Antisthenes (*fl*.400 BC) as the true founder of the school. Diogenes' most notable successor was Crates of Thebes. The sect survived until the 6th century AD.

Further Reading

Bernays, Jacob, *Lucian und die Kyniker*, Berlin: Hertz, 1879

Downing, F. Gerald, *Cynics and Christian Origins*, Edinburgh: Clark, 1992

Dudley, Donald R., *A History of Cynicism from Diogenes to the 6th century AD*, London: Methuen, 1937; 2nd edition, London: Bristol Classical Press, 1998

Höistad, Ragnar, *Cynic Hero and Cynic King: Studies in the Cynic Conception of Man*, Uppsala: University of Uppsala, 1948

Cyprus

The island of Cyprus is the third largest in the Mediterranean and lies in its northeastern corner, just 70 km from the Turkish coast to the north and 103 km from Syria to the east. The nearest Greek island is Castellorizo, 270 km to the west, followed by Rhodes at 386 km to the west. Cyprus itself has a maximum length from east to west of 222 km, and a maximum width of 95 km. Geographically, it is dominated by the igneous Troodos mountain range in the centre of the island, rising to a height of 1951 m at the pineclad Mount Olympus, and by the long Kyrenia (or Pentadaktylos) range stretching along the north coast. Between them and extending to the east coast is the fertile Mesaoria plain. The west and northwest areas of the island are mountainous and often rugged; the south and east coasts depend on the rivers coming down from the Troodos mountains; the coastal plains in the north are fertile and well watered. The climate is semi-arid, and throughout its history human settlement has been heavily influenced by the need for water.

The first contacts with the Aegean world date from the Middle Bronze Age (*c*.2000–1600 BC), with a series of vases imported from Crete, mostly found in tombs along the north coast. The first large-scale contacts came during the Late Bronze Age (*c*.1600–1050 BC). During much of this period Cyprus had a complex urban civilization based on agriculture and copper production, with extensive trade links throughout the eastern Mediterranean. Important cities such as Enkomi on the east coast and Hala Sultan Tekke and Citium on the south coast near Larnaca clearly controlled large parts of the island both economically and politically, and one or more of them seems to have been the "Alashiya" mentioned in Near Eastern texts. The Cypro-Minoan script of this period, so-called because of its apparent similarities to Linear A on Crete, was probably used for bureaucratic purposes in large administrative buildings in the main cities. Although it has not been deciphered, it is clearly not Greek.

During the 14th century BC there was a great increase in the amount of Aegean pottery coming to Cyprus, mostly from Mycenae, and by the 13th century BC Mycenaean-style pottery was being manufactured on Cyprus. Pottery alone is insufficient evidence for the arrival of a Greek-speaking population on the island, but it is abundantly clear that by the Iron Age most Cypriots were speaking a dialect of Greek. The most plausible occasion for this demographic change is in the upheavals of the 13th and 12th centuries BC, when the "Sea Peoples", migrants and refugees from the west, were travelling, raiding, and settling across the eastern Mediterranean. The first known Greek inscription in Cyprus was found in an 11th-century BC tomb in Palaipaphos in the west, a bronze spit with the name "Opheltes". Although clearly a Greek name, and using a grammatical form characteristic of the Arcadian dialect of Greek, this is written in the Cypriot syllabary, a development of the Cypro-Minoan script adapted for the use of the Cypriot dialect of Greek.

The earlier part of the Iron Age (*c*.1050–475 BC) seems to have been characterized by a low population and simple social structure. In the 8th century BC the characteristic city kingdoms began to develop, with local elites maintaining their power using elaborate ceremonial and luxury goods imported from

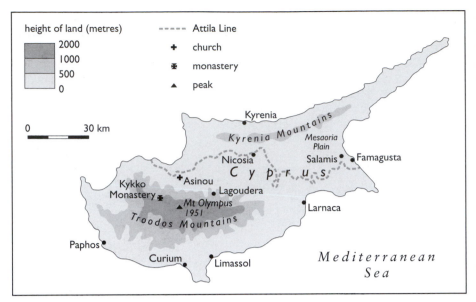

height of land (metres)
2000
1000
500
0

----- Attila Line
+ church
✳ monastery
▲ peak

0   30 km

Kyrenia

Kyrenia Mountains

Mesaoria Plain

Nicosia

Salamis

Famagusta

C y p r u s

Kykko Monastery ✳   + Asinou   Lagoudera

▲ Mt Olympus 1951

Troodos Mountains

Larnaca

Paphos

Curium   Limassol

Mediterranean Sea

16. Cyprus

the east. During this period there is an increasing number of inscriptions in Greek, written in the Cypriot syllabic script. This culminated in the 6th century BC, when a significant number of people were literate enough to write names on tombstones or dedications at sanctuaries. At the same time there was a considerable increase in imported pottery from Greece, particularly from east Greece and Athens, and Greek styles of sculpture had a strong influence on local Cypriot traditions, as seen in the many dedications in rural and urban sanctuaries.

From the beginning of the 5th century BC Cyprus appears regularly in the Greek written sources. We have an account in the pages of Herodotus about the participation of most Cypriot cities in the Ionian Revolt against the Persians in 499 BC, though they were retaken by the Persians in the following year. In political terms the 5th and 4th centuries BC were largely taken up with struggles against the Persians. The Athenian general Cimon led an expedition to Cyprus in 450 BC, but he died the next year, and his forces, after failing to take Salamis, returned home. A local player who acquired major influence in these power games was Evagoras I, king of Salamis from 411 to 374/73 BC, whose reign was vividly though uncritically described by his eulogist, the Athenian orator Isocrates. Resolutely pro-Athenian, he used his political and diplomatic skills to resist the Persians, increase his own power over the other city kingdoms of Cyprus, and disseminate Athenian art and culture. It was during his reign that the Greek alphabet began to displace the ancient Cypriot syllabary.

When Alexander the Great laid siege to Tyre in 332 BC, he was aided by 120 Cypriot ships, and although he never actually came to Cyprus, he made it clear that he was the island's master by issuing coins in his own name. At his death in 323 BC Cyprus, like most of his empire, was fought over by his successors, particularly Ptolemy and Antigonus. The city kingdoms aligned themselves on each side of the dispute; when Ptolemy sent an expedition there in 312 BC, the cities that had opposed him were punished and, in the case of Marion, destroyed. From this time until the Roman annexation in 58

BC, apart from one brief interlude, Cyprus was part of the Hellenistic empire of the Ptolemies of Egypt, sharing in the common Greek civilization and culture of the eastern Mediterranean.

Cyprus was annexed by the Romans in 58 BC, ostensibly because of the island's support of pirates. After being restored to Cleopatra of Egypt, it was taken by the future emperor Augustus in 31 BC, and transferred to the Senate in 22 BC. Apart from the Jewish insurrection in AD 116 and several earthquakes, this was a peaceful period in the island's history. The cities of the island boasted the usual trappings of the Roman provinces of the Hellenized east: bath houses, theatres, gymnasiums, temples, villas, honorific statues, inscriptions in Greek, and also local elites who benefited greatly from their role in the Roman administration of the province. In the countryside there was a considerable population, which supported itself through agriculture and produced wine, olive oil, flax, timber, and copper in sufficient quantities for export. Most famous of the works of art of the Roman period are the mosaics from villas in Paphos and Curium, which depict a wide variety of scenes from Greek mythology.

In AD 45 St Paul and the Cypriot St Barnabas visited the island, and according to the Acts of the Apostles they converted the Roman governor in Paphos. There was little sign of the spread of Christianity in the island until the 4th and 5th centuries, when considerable numbers of basilican churches were built in towns and cities across the island, and Cypriot bishops attended the great ecumenical councils and synods at Nicaea and elsewhere. The long campaign by the Cypriot Church to be independent from the patriarchate of Antioch was finally won in 488, when the remains of St Barnabas were discovered near Salamis and as a result the emperor Zeno gave the archbishop of Cyprus full autonomy. Treasures such as the 6th-century mosaics from the church of Panagia Kanakaria and the 6th- and early 7th-century gold and silver vessels from Lambousa bear witness to a rich artistic tradition during this period.

The large population and rich culture of the early Byzantine period were interrupted by the Arab invasions, which began in 649. For more than three centuries Cyprus existed uneasily under a condominium of the Byzantine emperor and the Arab caliph. Conditions improved in 965 when the island was reoccupied by the emperor Nikephoros Phokas, and during the 12th and 13th centuries there was an increase in population and a flowering of Byzantine ecclesiastical art and architecture. The frescos of mountain churches such as that of Panagia tou Arakou at Lagoudera (c.1192) are as fine as any in the Greek Orthodox world.

The political status of Cyprus changed abruptly in 1191. When part of the fleet of Richard I of England, on his way to the Third Crusade, was blown off course, it landed in Limassol and was opposed by the semi-independent ruler, Isaac Komnenos. When Richard himself arrived, he postponed his crusade for long enough to campaign against Isaac, who finally surrendered later in the year. Because of the expenses of the crusade, Richard attempted to sell Cyprus to the Knights Templar for 100,000 byzants, but in spite of their oppression of the local people the knights could not raise this sum. Richard repossessed the island in 1192 and gave it Guy of Lusignan, the recently ousted king of Jerusalem. So began a period of Frankish rule that lasted for almost 300 years.

Cyprus under Lusignan rule was organized in a classic feudal system. Land was owned either by the state or by Frankish feudal barons. The Greek subjects were divided into serfs, those who paid an extra annual tax to give themselves a modicum of independence, and those who held their land by free tenure. Serfs had to pay a tithe usually amounting to a third of their produce and a heavy poll tax, and owed two days of forced labour a week. For most Greek Cypriots under Lusignan rule life was a matter of hard and unrewarded agricultural labour. The Orthodox Church fared little better. In 1196 a Latin archbishopric and three bishoprics were established, fully endowed with land and tithes from the Greek subjects, and before 1220 no Orthodox prelates were permitted at all. According to the *Bulla Cypria* of 1260, the Orthodox archbishop and bishops were made formally subordinate to their Latin equivalents.

A slight improvement in general conditions for the Greek populace of Cyprus came in 1432 with the accession of John II, whose wife Eleni Palaiologina was the daughter of the despot of the Morea in the Peloponnese. For all her severity towards her husband (and his mistress) she was a strong supporter of the Orthodox Church and the Greek language in Cyprus, and it was during the 15th century that the use of Greek spread to the upper classes as well as the peasantry. John II's daughter and successor, Charlotte, was another Greek-speaker, but in the characteristic machinations of the period she was usurped by her father's bastard son James II. James was succeeded by his Venetian wife Caterina Cornaro, who in spite of her liking for the people of the island was unable to resist the power and greed of her compatriots, and in 1489 she was forced to abdicate in favour of the Venetians.

Conditions under Venetian rule were, if anything, worse than before, since Cyprus was now merely a distant province of the imperial city. Venice's main interest was to increase its own wealth, both that of the state and of its aristocratic families, by means of heavy taxation, the control of monopolies such as salt, and large estates producing crops such as sugar for export. An uprising in 1562 was led by two Greeks, a teacher and a cavalry officer, and supported by many local noblemen, but was betrayed and its leaders executed. The protests by the Greek populace following this demonstrated the widespread antipathy to Venetian rule. Only the Orthodox Church fared better during this period, and apart from its low revenues it had more equable relations with the Latin Church. Clear western influences can be seen in the Orthodox Church architecture and icon painting of the period.

The Venetians' lack of interest in developing and protecting the island meant that defences against the growing Ottoman threat were begun too late, and it was only in 1567 that work was started on the fortifications of Nicosia and Famagusta. In 1570 the Ottoman sultan Selim II demanded that the Venetians cede Cyprus to him; the Venetians naturally refused, but their relief expedition never reached the island. The Ottomans landed in July, and took Nicosia in September after a six-week siege. Famagusta held out for longer, but finally fell in August 1571, its defenders starving and vastly outnumbered. The Venetian officers were massacred, and their commander, Marcantonio Bragadino, was flayed alive.

In many ways Ottoman rule was a welcome relief to the Greek Cypriots. Taxation was reduced and rationalized, with tithes being set at one-fifth and forced labour reduced. With the expulsion of all Frankish Catholics, the Orthodox Church was reinstated as the principal Church of the island. Under the Ottoman *millet* (community) system, it was responsible to the authorities for the political control of the Orthodox Greeks, as well as for the extraction of taxes from them. This gave the archbishop and his prelates genuine power, particularly since they could appeal to Constantinople over the head of the Ottoman governor. By the 18th century the Greek *dragoman* or "interpreter" who managed the administration of the Greek *millet* was often a rich and powerful figure in his own right, as for example was Hadjigeorgakis Kornesios at the end of the century.

A system that should have worked well in theory was less successful in practice. Governors were keen to recoup what they had spent on bribes to gain their appointment, and with frequent corruption and extortion at many other levels, the peasant farmer was hard put to produce enough to pay the necessary taxes and bribes as well as supporting himself and his family. These difficulties were compounded by the frequent droughts, locust attacks, and plagues, and during the 17th century the population of Cyprus dropped dramatically, owing to deaths through plague or starvation and to emigration. Another reaction to excessive taxation was a series of "tax rebellions", for example that against the governor Chil Osman Agha in 1764, when Greeks and Turks together protested against his extortions. When the Greek War of Independence broke out in 1821, the governor Küçük Mehmet called for reinforcements from the sultan and began executing Christians. In July 1821, in spite of no further actions against the authorities, the archbishop was hanged and the three bishops beheaded. Further massacres continued, Church property was plundered, and a considerable number of Greek Cypriots fled the island.

As the 19th century wore on, desultory attempts at reform and greater economic contacts with Europe brought about a general improvement in conditions. A more radical change came in 1878, when according to a deal struck behind the scenes at the Congress of Berlin, the sultan agreed to allow the British to administer Cyprus in return for their support against Russia. In July the British fleet anchored off Larnaca, and the remaining Turkish authorities handed over power without argument. The Greek Cypriots initially welcomed this change in status, even though they had not been consulted about it. The British cession of the Ionian islands to Greece in 1864 was taken as an indication of a similar attitude towards Cyprus, and in 1882 the new Liberal government in Britain allowed the Greek community to teach in Greek and control its own educational system. In spite of this, the British gave no genuine political participation to the Cypriots, and spent little on the development of the island, particularly as every year they extracted a sum of £92,800 as "tribute" to the sultan (or rather to his creditors). During the 1920s and 1930s demands for *enosis* or union with Greece grew, and they culminated in a demonstration in October 1931 at which Government House was burnt to the ground. The British governor suspended the constitution, disbanded the Legislative Council, which was never to be reinstated, and outlawed the flying of the Greek flag.

Apart from a significant Greek Cypriot contribution to the Allied war effort in World War II, relations between the Greek Cypriot community and their British rulers remained poor. The governor's proposals in 1947 for an elected legislature were rejected, and in 1950 a plebiscite of Greek Cypriots showed 96 per cent in favour of *enosis*. In April 1955 the National Organization of Cypriot Fighters (EOKA) began its armed campaign to expel the British and win *enosis* with Greece. A series of bombs exploded, and leaflets proclaimed that with God's help and the support of all the forces of Hellenism, the struggle to throw off the British yoke had begun. This struggle took four years, during which many more bombs were thrown, archbishop Makarios was exiled to the Seychelles, civilians and policemen were killed, and nine Greek Cypriots hanged. After long-drawn-out negotiations a compromise among Greek Cypriots, Turkish Cypriots, and the British was agreed: instead of *enosis*, Cyprus would become an independent state within the Commonwealth, with a Greek Cypriot president and a Turkish Cypriot vice-president. This came into effect with the raising of the flag of the Republic of Cyprus on 16 August 1960.

The new constitution was complex and artificial, and turned out to be unworkable. At the end of 1963 president Makarios's proposals to alter it were rejected by Ankara, and intercommunal fighting quickly broke out. A mission from the United Nations arrived in 1964 to try to maintain peace between the two communities. After further intercommunal clashes in 1967, the new military junta in Athens withdrew its Greek forces, and the island was in political terms almost entirely divided. On 15 July 1974 the right-wing Greek junta orchestrated a coup against the more moderate president Makarios, during which the presidential palace was shelled and destroyed. On the pretext of protecting Turkish Cypriots from an extremist Greek regime, the Turkish army invaded Cyprus, with its first landings on the north coast taking place on 20 July. By the time the ceasefire line was drawn across the island on 18 August, 200,000 Greek Cypriots had been made refugees, 1619 were listed as missing, and the Turks had captured 37 per cent of the island's territory, including the fertile Mesaoria plain.

Since the invasion there have been sporadic intercommunal meetings and UN-sponsored negotiations, but little or no progress has been made. The island is divided by the "Dead Zone" and its minefields and observation posts, while through the centre of Nicosia runs a scar of barbed wire, sandbags, and weed-choked streets. In the occupied areas the names of streets and villages have been changed from Greek to Turkish, while churches have been closed, abandoned, or turned into museums. In the government-controlled areas new settlements house the refugees, while road signs still point hopefully northwards to Kyrenia and Famagusta. In spite of this catastrophe, however, an awareness of Cyprus's long and rich history, especially its distinguished Hellenic heritage, is very much alive in contemporary Greek Cypriot society, and plays a powerful role in the country's education system and in its cultural and political life.

MICHAEL GIVEN

See also Enosis, Venetokratia

Summary

The third largest island in the Mediterranean, Cyprus has had close contact with the Aegean since the Bronze Age. Mycenaean-style pottery was made on Cyprus by the 13th century BC. The earliest Greek inscription dates from the 11th century BC. City states began to develop in the 8th century and by the 6th century Greek artistic styles were prevalent. War with Persia dominated the 5th and 4th centuries. After Alexander Cyprus was ruled mostly by the Ptolemies until taken by Rome in 31 BC. From 649 to 965 the Byzantines shared rule with the Arabs. In 1191 Richard I of England took Cyprus and gave it to Guy of Lusignan. Taken by Venice in 1489 and by the Ottomans in 1570/71, Cyprus was a British possession from 1878 to 1960 when it became a republic. Since 1974 northern Cyprus has been under Turkish occupation.

Further Reading

Cobham, C.D. (editor), *Excerpta Cypria: Materials for a History of Cyprus*, Cambridge: Cambridge University Press, 1908; reprinted, New York: Kraus, 1969

Edbury, Peter W., *The Kingdom of Cyprus and the Crusades, 1191–1374*, Cambridge and New York: Cambridge University Press, 1991

Gunnis, Rupert, *Historic Cyprus: A Guide to its Towns and Villages, Monasteries and Castles*, London: Methuen, 1936; 2nd edition 1947

Hill, George, *A History of Cyprus*, 4 vols, Cambridge: Cambridge University Press, 1940–52

Hitchens, Christopher, *Hostage to History: Cyprus from the Ottomans to Kissinger*, 3rd edition, London: Verso, 1997

Hunt, David (editor), *Footprints in Cyprus: An Illustrated History*, 2nd edition, London: Trigraph, 1990

Karageorghis, Vassos, *Cyprus: From the Stone Age to the Romans*, London: Thames and Hudson, 1982

Kyrris, Costas P., *History of Cyprus*, 2nd edition, Nicosia: Lampousa, 1996

Peltenburg, Edgar (editor), *Early Society in Cyprus*, Edinburgh: Edinburgh University Press, 1989

Cyrenaica

Region of north Africa

Cyrenaica forms the eastern territory of modern Libya. There are two distinct areas of occupation — the uplands and the fertile coastal plain. The account of the Greek colonization of Cyrenaica is provided by Herodotus (4. 150–59). The Delphic oracle directed Grinnos, the king of the island of Thera (modern Santorini), to go and found a city in Libya. This advice was ignored, and after a seven-year drought on the island, the oracle reminded the islanders that they should send a colony to Libya. The Therans sent to Crete for advice about Libya, and as a result they came to the island of Platea (the site of which is disputed) and left a Cretan fisherman there while they returned to Thera. The Therans then sent out a group of colonists selected by lot under the leadership of Battos, and a settlement was established on the island. After further inter-

Cyrenaica: view of the 6th-century basilica at Apollonia, the port of Cyrene

vention from the oracle, a mainland settlement was established opposite the island of Aziris in eastern Cyrenaica. The site itself has been plausibly identified by the presence of Protocorinthian, East Greek, Cretan, and Greek pottery at the mouth of the Wadi el-Chalig. Eventually a settlement was established at Cyrene, and the numbers of Greek settlers in Cyrenaica were supplemented after a further oracle from Delphi.

Details about the establishment of Cyrene are recorded on a 4th-century BC inscription which gave the people of Thera honorary citizenship in recognition of the earlier links with the city. A section within the decree purports to be a record of the original decision of the Therans. There were apparently conditions about staying in Libya for five years before being allowed to return to Thera if the colony did not succeed.

After the foundation of the Greek colonies during the 7th century BC, Cyrenaica came into increasing contact with its eastern neighbour Egypt. The Egyptian pharaoh Apries marched against Cyrene in 570, but this attacked was foiled and led to the fall of Apries and his succession by Amasis as pharaoh. Amasis, who according to Herodotus established the Greek trading establishment of Naucratis in the Nile delta, fostered links with the Greek world, and in order to establish a link with Cyrene, married Ladice, a member of one of Cyrene's leading families. In 525 Egypt was annexed by Persia,

and Cyrenaica soon became part of its larger empire following a Persian invasion which reached as far as Euesperides. Cyrene regained some independence during the 5th century BC.

Cyrenaica supported Alexander the Great and subsequently became part of the Ptolemaic kingdom. This period is reflected in the way that some Cyrenaican cities were renamed in honour of the Ptolemies: Euesperides became Berenice, Taucheira became Arsinoë, and Barca became Ptolemais. Evidence from Apollonia shows that the walls of Apollonia were constructed in the late 2nd to early 1st century BC according to an Egyptian unit of measurement. Cyrenaica was finally bequeathed to Rome on the death of Ptolemy Apion in 96 BC.

As part of the Roman world, Cyrenaica was initially a joint province linked with Crete. The status of the Greek community is reflected in the edicts of Augustus, dating to 7/6 BC and 4 BC, which demonstrate the perceived tension between Greeks and Romans in the province. It is not clear how far the Greek constitutions of the Cyrenaican cities continued into the Roman period. One decree from Tocra, dating to the 1st century BC, seems to suggest that the citizen body had diminished, though a number of villages across Cyrenaica probably retained their Greek identity into the imperial period. Through the 1st century it is clear from a number of inscriptions that Jews were being allowed to take part in Cyrenaican civic life. The rivalry between the two parts of the population led to a revolt in Cyrenaica and Egypt under the Roman emperor Trajan when, as Eusebius (*Ecclesiastical History*, 4. 2) described it, the Jewish population "broke into factious strife against their fellow Greek citizens".

Cyrenaica's identification in the Greek world was re-emphasized by the inclusion of Cyrene in the Panhellenion established in Athens by the emperor Hadrian; indeed one citizen of Cyrene served as an official of the Panhellenion in 157. Hadrian's patronage of Cyrenaican cities in the aftermath of the destruction of the Jewish revolt placed an emphasis on Cyrene's origins in the Greek world and the colonists from Thera.

Cyrene had a number of major sanctuaries including temples of Apollo and of Zeus Ammon, the latter a cult linked to the famous Egyptian oracle in the Western Desert. Both seem to have been constructed in the 6th century BC. Outside the city was a major sanctuary of Demeter. Analysis of the bones from the sanctuary shows that pigs were a favoured sacrifice, as might be expected in a sanctuary of Demeter. Archaic sculpture from the city included *kouroi* and *korai* of a type found elsewhere in the Greek world. Cyrene itself issued silver coinage, probably from the late 6th century BC onwards.

Barce, on the west side of the Cyrenaican upland, was next to be established, apparently during the reign of Arcesilas II, perhaps in the 560s. This was followed by expansion in the coastal areas, with the creation of Apollonia (later renamed Ptolemais as the harbour for Cyrene, and the city of Euesperides (later replaced by the Hellenistic city of Berenice, and now the modern Benghazi) in the west. Excavations at Euesperides have revealed a carefully planned city; the earliest grid and settlement can probably be dated to at least the middle of the 6th century BC, though some deep excavations on the Sidi Abeid indicate an earlier settlement is likely. A further settlement was located on the coast at Taucheira where part of the sanctuary of Demeter and Kore has been excavated. Both Apollonia and Taucheira are recorded as being foundations of Cyrene, though Herodotus (4. 171) records that the latter was a polis of Barce.

Cyrenaica was well known for its agricultural produce. For example, probably during the 320s BC, Cyrene sent grain to some 41 Greek cities in response to a severe food shortage; Athens alone received the equivalent of 6000 tonnes, and the total gift was around 50,000 tonnes. Cyrene's prominence in the second half of the 4th century BC is perhaps also reflected in the construction of a Doric treasury at Delphi, probably in the 330s. Cyrenaica was also the source for silphium which was used for medicinal purposes among other things. The plant was used as an emblem on the coins issued by Cyrene. Members of the Cyrenaica elite enjoyed the benefits of horse rearing; a number of Pindar's odes (Pythian 4, 5, and 9) celebrate victories by Arcesilas IV and Telesicrates in the Pythian Games.

DAVID W.J. GILL

Further Reading

Barker, Graeme, John Lloyd, and Joyce Reynolds, *Cyrenaica in Antiquity*, Oxford: British Archaeological Reports, 1985

Boardman, John, *The Greeks Overseas: Their Early Colonies and Trade*, 4th edition, London and New York: Thames and Hudson, 1999

Buzaian, A. and J.A. Lloyd, "Early Urbanism in Cyrenaica: New Evidence from Euesperides (Benghazi)", *Libyan Studies*, 27 (1996): pp. 129–52

Chamoux, François, *Cyrène sous la monarchie des Battiades*, Paris: Boccard, 1953

Dore, J.N., "Excavations at El Merj (Ancient Barca): A First Report on the 1990 Season", *Libyan Studies*, 22 (1991): pp. 91–5

Dore, J.N., "Excavations at El Merj (Ancient Barca): A First Report on the 1991 Season", *Libyan Studies*, 23 (1992): pp. 101–05

Goodchild, R.G., J.G. Pedley, and D. White, *Apollonia, the Port of Cyrene: Excavations by the University of Michigan 1965–1967*, Tripoli: Department of Antiquities, 1976

Johnson, Douglas L., *Jabal al-Akhdar, Cyrenaica: An Historical Geography of Settlement and Livelihood*, Chicago: University of Chicago Department of Geography, 1973

Lloyd, J.A., "Urban Archaeology in Cyrenaica 1969–1989: The Hellenistic, Roman and Byzantine Periods", *Libyan Studies*, 20 (1989): pp. 77–90

Reynolds, Joyce, "A Civic Decree from Tocra in Cyrenaica", *Archaeologia Classica*, 25/26 (1974): pp. 622–30

Reynolds, Joyce, "Twenty Years of Inscriptions", *Libyan Studies*, 20 (1989): pp. 117–26

Reynolds, Joyce (editor), *Cyrenaican Archaeology: An International Colloquium*, London: Society for Libyan Studies, 1994

Reynolds, Joyce, "Cyrene", in *The Augustan Empire, 43 BC–AD 89*, edited by Alan K. Bowman, Edward Champlin, and Andrew Lintott, Cambridge: Cambridge University Press, 1996 (*The Cambridge Ancient History*, vol. 10, 2nd edition)

Spawforth, A.J.S. and S. Walker, "The World of the Panhellenion II: Three Doric Cities", *Journal of Roman Studies*, 76 (1986): pp. 88–105

Vickers, M., D. Gill, and M. Economou, "Euesperides: The Rescue of an Excavation", *Libyan Studies*, 25 (1994): pp. 125–36

White, Donald (editor), *The Extramural Sanctuary of Demeter and Persephone at Cyrene, Libya*, vol. 1: *Background and Introduction to the Excavations*, Philadelphia: University Museum, University of Pennsylvania, 1984

Cyrene

City in north Africa

Cyrene was the most important of the Greek colonies founded in north Africa during the 7th century BC and later. The region (to which Cyrene gave its name, Cyrenaica) was reasonably well watered and therefore fertile, but had the Sahara to the south, and was separated from Egypt by the Western Desert, with further difficult country to the west isolating it from Tripolitania (which in antiquity was a region of Phoenician and Carthaginian settlement). Cyrenaica was thus in effect a self-contained region, eventually divided among a number of Greek foundations. Contacts with the Aegean world preceded the period of colonization, and must already have existed in the Bronze Age. The Minoan harbour town of Kommos, on the south coast of Crete, with its great built shipsheds would have served for maritime links with the coastal regions of Africa immediately to the south. Even in the 1st millennium BC the coastal waters of Cyrenaica were visited by Greeks (the area produces excellent sponges) before Greek settlement took place.

Cyrene is important in the history of Greek colonization not only for the detailed account of the circumstances of its foundation in Herodotus (4. 145–50) but also for the inscription,

Cyrene: view of the ancient city which was colonized by Greeks from Thera, *c.*630 BC

found in Cyrene itself, which gives the text (perhaps a later edited version) of an oath supposedly sworn by the founders. The colony was sent out, around 630 BC, by the Aegean island of Thera (modern Santorini) after consultation of the oracle at Delphi. The reason was overpopulation, and the Therans had to order the colonists to stay for at least five years after the first attempt at settlement in Africa proved unsuccessful. They eventually settled on a small offshore island, then on the mainland, eventually moving inland to the site of Cyrene itself. Most Greek colonial foundations in overseas, non-Greek districts remained adjacent to the coast and safety. Cyrene was unusual in being situated well inland, 25 km away from the sea, on the edge of the inland plateau that stretches southwards to the Sahara. It is not clear how this was achieved in the presence of an indigenous population; either they were too few to resist, or, for some reason, they welcomed the Greek settlers. The latter is more likely, since the settlers themselves would not have been that numerous, and a non-Greek stratum persisted in Cyrene throughout its history.

The settlement was led by a man called Battos. He and his descendants ruled Cyrene as kings until their overthrow in the 5th century BC. The city prospered considerably. It produced corn on a large scale (at one critical moment in the late 4th century BC, when there was a failure of the harvest in mainland Greece and Egypt withheld supplies of corn in order to boost the price, Cyrene was able to provide an alternative source of

supply, an act recorded with gratitude in Greece itself). Equally important was the product of a plant called silphium, which seems to have been a form of drug much prized in Greece, and which was so important to Cyrene that it is represented on its coins. There is an important Greek vase, a cup made in Laconia, which depicts King Arcesilas II of Cyrene supervising the loading of bales (of silphium? or more prosaically wool, another export) into the hold of a ship. The choice of subject suggests that Sparta had close contacts and hence, a very real knowledge of Cyrene. Indeed, so much Laconian pottery has been found in Cyrenaica that it was originally thought to be of local origin.

Cyrene grew up round an abundant spring of the nymph Cyrana, who gave her name to the city. Below the spring was the central sanctuary of Apollo which, though later rebuilt, contained an important example of an early Doric temple. The main part of the town lay above and to the south of the temple. A road led up to the agora, which included the tomb of the founder Battos (though the actual structure of the tomb is 4th-century BC in date). Beyond this was the greatest of the city's temples, an early 5th-century dedication to Zeus. The city itself, like most colonial foundations, was laid out to a grid plan.

Cyrene remained largely aloof from the mainstream history of Greece: its retention of a monarchy until well into the 5th century is in some respects an indication of this. With the conquest of Egypt by the Persian king Cambyses, Cyrene became attached (loosely, again because of its geographical position) to the Persian empire. Similarly, after Alexander the Great had added Egypt to the area of his rule, the Cyrenaicans deemed it prudent to make their submission to him. With the break-up of Alexander's empire Cyrene was once more independent, but eventually became part of the kingdom of the Ptolemies based on Egypt and Alexandria. Ptolemy III married a Cyrenaican, Berenice, as his queen, and other prominent Cyrenaicans (such as the poet Callimachus) were attracted to the court at Alexandria. With the decline of the Ptolemies, Cyrene became a separate kingdom, ruled by a branch of the Ptolemaic royal family. The last of these, Ptolemy Apion, bequeathed his kingdom to the Romans on his death in 96 BC.

Under the Ptolemies a substantial Jewish population established itself at Cyrene, as at Alexandria. In the 2nd century AD the Jews of Cyrene joined in the widespread Jewish rebellion against the Romans, and Cyrene was badly damaged in the resulting turmoil. Subsequently the city revived, but the temple of Zeus, though reroofed, did not have its fallen colonnade re-erected. Cyrene continued to flourish in the late empire. There are (as in the other Cyrenaican cities) important early Christian churches there, but the main centre seems to have shifted to the harbour town of Apollonia. Cyrene itself gradually withered, and with the Arab conquest ceased to be a place of any significance.

Paradoxically, this withering away resulted in a remarkable degree of preservation of its ancient remains. With the Italian occupation of Cyrenaica much excavation was carried out and was continued after the war by the Libyans under their Director of Antiquities, Richard Goodchild. Much was restored. The great gymnasium, turned by the Romans into a Caesareum, which had fallen in an earthquake, was re-erected. But the most poignant survival (now less well preserved) was the surrounding environment with its ancient roads, lined with monumental cemeteries and running out into the hinterland through a field system which still retained its ancient boundaries.

R.A. TOMLINSON

Summary

Colony founded on the north African coast by Greeks from Santorini c.630 BC led by Battos. His descendants ruled Cyrene until the 5th century BC. Ptolemaic Cyrene produced Callimachus and Berenice, queen of Ptolemy III; it also housed a large Jewish population. Christianity was established at nearby Apollonia. Cyrene was taken by the Arabs in the 7th century and lost its significance in the Greek world.

Further Reading

Cassels, J., "The Cemeteries of Cyrene", *Papers of the British School at Rome*, 23 (1955): pp. 1–42

Chamoux, François, *Cyrène sous la monarchie des Battiades*, Paris: Boccard, 1953

Goodchild, Richard, *Cyrene and Apollonia: A Historical Guide*, Antiquities Department of Cyrenaica, 1959

Graham, A.J., *Colony and Mother City in Ancient Greece*, 2nd edition, Chicago: Ares, 1983

Smith, R. Murdoch and E.A. Porcher, *History of the Recent Discoveries at Cyrene*, London: Day, 1864

Stucchi, Sandro, *Architettura Cirenaica*, Rome: Bretschneider, 1975

White, Donald (editor), *The Extramural Sanctuary of Demeter and Persphone at Cyrene, Libya*, Philadelphia: University Museum, University of Pennsylvania, 1984–

Cyril I Lukaris 1570–1638

Patriarch of Constantinople

Cyril Lukaris, ecumenical patriarch of Constantinople (1620–35 and 1637–38), was a prelate of distinctive character, who strove to secure the enlightenment of the Greek people, and particularly the Orthodox clergy. His activities belong to a period when the Catholic Church was waging war on the Reformation, and he played a pioneer's role in the project to establish a Greek press in the East, with the aim of spreading the faith, which was threatened by the proselytizing policy pursued by Rome.

Konstantinos Lukaris was born in Herakleion, Crete, in 1570, and took the name Kyrillos (Cyril) when he became a monk. Descended from a well-known family, he studied in Crete under the theologian Meletios Vlastos, and went on to complete his studies in Italy with the aid of his uncle and mentor, Meletios Pigas, patriarch of Alexandria. He perfected his knowledge of Greek, Latin, Italian, and theology in Venice under the famous scholar Maximos Kargounios, and also availed himself of the opportunity to attend the lectures given by Cesare Cremonini in Padua. It was at this time, moreover, that he began to correspond with David Hoeschel and Friedrich Sylburgius, both of whom were men of letters, reformers, and publishers of important works of Greek literature.

In 1592 he broke off his studies and entered the service of the patriarch of Alexandria. He was swiftly appointed *protosynkellos* (chancellor) of the patriarchate by his uncle, who assigned to him the mission of travelling to Poland as exarch in order to avert the unification of the Orthodox Ukrainians and White Russians with the Catholic Church. Lukaris left Poland in January 1601 without achieving this aim; he began to realize, however, that the two Churches should come together again in the interests of Christendom. This same year Meletios Pigas died, and was succeeded by Lukaris on the patriarchal throne of Alexandria.

Little is known about Lukaris's activities as patriarch of Alexandria, except that he worked strenuously to restore the finances of the patriarchate. During a visit to Constantinople in 1611, he became acquainted with the ambassadors of England, Thomas Rowe, and of Holland, Cornelius Haga, who played leading roles in countering Jesuit propaganda in Turkey. In 1604, moreover, a close alliance had been created between England, Turkey, Holland, and Sweden, with the aim of checking the ambitions of the Catholic Church.

In 1612, Lukaris was appointed "Overseer" of the ecumenical throne, and in the same year Timotheos II became ecumenical patriarch (1612–20). From this time on, Lukaris' enemies began to defame him in every way possible, judging him from his ideas and actions to be a Lutheran. Lukaris did not change his views, however, and continued zealously to enter into relations with Protestant theologians, church dignitaries, rulers,

Cyril I Lukaris: 17th-century portrait

and kings, who were using all possible means to oppose the Roman Church and its proselytizing methods.

After the death of Timotheos II the Holy Synod elected Lukaris as patriarch of Constantinople on 4 November 1620. Immediately after his installation, he turned his attention once more to the Union of Brest, which for two and a half decades had caused disquiet in the Eastern Church, and particularly in the patriarchate in Constantinople, despite the fact that the Greeks of Constantinople had made clear their hostility to the Polish king, Sigismund III. In 1610 the Polish armies captured Moscow and Sigismund's son was elected Catholic tsar of Moscow.

In his anti-Catholic arguments Lukaris sought to implement views adopted by the Orthodox tradition, many of which were apparently of a reforming nature. Certainly, the ecumenical patriarch continued until his death to believe that the Calvinists and the Orthodox should unite forces against Rome, at the same time aiming at a gradual rapprochement with the teaching of Calvin. Lukaris believed that in this way he would purify Orthodoxy of distortions, perversions, and the influence of Rome, and eventually arrive at the point when the "true" Orthodoxy would be identical with the Reformation.

The main reason that impelled Lukaris to attempt to establish a printing press in the Phanar was his concern at the fact that it was impossible for Orthodox clergy to be educated in anything other than Catholic schools and universities, such as the theological school founded by the Jesuits in Constantinople. In 1616 he entered into a correspondence with George Abbot, the archbishop of Canterbury, asking that some gifted students of theology be admitted to higher education in English universities. One of those who benefited from Lukaris's policy was Nikodimos Metaxas, who studied in London from 1622 to 1626.

Lukaris's great desire to found a Greek press was one of the main reasons for sending Metaxas to London, where, in addition to his theological studies, he could become initiated in the printer's art. Lukaris had already attempted to found a Greek press some time previously. When he was in the town of Lvov in Poland, as emissary of Meletios Pigas, he had succeeded, in cooperation with Arsenios, archbishop of Elasson, in printing four books between 1591 and 1593, with Greek texts and parallel Slav translations.

After Metaxas had worked in London as an apprentice printer, he assembled the necessary printing materials and in June 1627 embarked on the ship *Royal Defence*, bound for Constantinople, accompanied by two assistant printers. On his arrival in Constantinople in 1627 he printed a book with the title *Of our most Blessed and most Wise Father*, written by the patriarch Cyril Lukaris. This initiative by Lukaris alarmed those opposed to his intentions, who were urged on mainly by the Jesuits and the French ambassador, and the Turks raided Metaxas's home on 22 June 1628, impounded all the printing materials, and expelled Metaxas. This brought an inglorious end to the first attempt to establish a Greek printing press in the East.

Lukaris's administrative activities, his struggle against Catholic propaganda, and the foundation of a printing press were not in conflict with the Orthodox tradition, and only a few who kept his company or corresponded with the patriarch were in a position to know of his reforming programme. Lukaris desired to come into contact and become acquainted with the official representatives of the Reformation Church, and his close colleague Mitrophanis Kritopoulos travelled to Germany, England, and Switzerland to examine the *Confessio Helvetica* and the *Confession* of Basel, in order to assess how far these views were consistent with Orthodox beliefs.

Beginning in 1628, the Propaganda Council in Rome had begun to publish a large number of books in the Greek language supporting unification, many of which were distributed free to the Orthodox population. The Dutch ambassador Haga sought to convince Lukaris that the time was right to publish his own *Confession*. The Patriarch intended publishing it on the press in the Phanar. After the violent closure of this press, however, the Latin text of the *Confession* was printed in 1629, possibly in Geneva, containing an explicit confirmation of its authenticity by the Dutch ambassador.

The work shook public opinion in both the West and the East as few others have done, and provoked a savage reaction, fuelling an impressive number of publications, for in his *Confession* the ecumenical patriarch declared openly that he embraced the teaching of Calvin. Most of the Orthodox prelates were naturally opposed to the views expressed by Lukaris in his *Confession*, but he also had his supporters, including Theophilos Corydalleus, who in 1639 wrote that the *Confession* was in conformity with the teaching of the Greek Church. Strong doubts were immediately expressed about the authenticity of the work, and within a short space of time

Lukaris's *Confession* saw several reprints and translations, and there were written criticisms calling into doubt the authorship of the text generally. Whatever the truth of the matter, the authenticity of the *Confession* has continued to be a vigorously disputed issue down to the present day.

From as early as 1618, Lukaris had planned to write a catechism in the demotic language; in the end, what he succeeded in doing was to make the Bible generally accessible through his translation of the New Testament into demotic Greek. With the fervent support of Antoine Leger, parish priest at the embassy of the Netherlands in Constantinople, the work was published in Geneva, at the press of Pierre Aubert, in 1638. The difficult task of editing the text was assumed by the monk Maximos Rhodios from Galipoli, who died in 1633 leaving the work unfinished; at this stage a large number of uncoordinated proofreaders took over who were not Greek, and when the book was eventually published it contained a great many serious linguistic errors.

The publication of Lukaris's *Confession* exercised a decisive influence on the development of the doctrines of the Orthodox Church and the position of the Patriarch within it, as well as on foreign relations. In March 1635 the Jesuits succeeded, after long efforts, in having Lukaris dethroned. He was replaced by Kyrillos Kontaris. About two years later, in March 1637, Lukaris was restored to his throne.

Lukaris's enemies were not disheartened, however, and, led by Kyrillos Kontaris, they wove a tissue of false accusations against him to the vizier Vayram Pasha during the absence of the sultan, Murad II, as a result of which the patriarch Cyril Lukaris was put to death by strangulation on 27 June 1638.

KONSTANTINOS STAIKOS

Biography

Born Konstantinos Lukaris in 1570 in Herakleion, Crete, he took the name Cyril on becoming a monk. He was educated in Crete and in Venice and Padua. In 1592 he joined the staff of the patriarch of Alexandria and was sent on a mission to Poland. In 1612 he became Overseer of the ecumenical throne and in 1620 was elected patriarch of Constantinople. Publication of his *Confession* in 1629 in which he accepted Calvinist doctrines made him many enemies, and in 1638 he was strangled.

Further Reading

Hering, Gunnar, *Ökumenisches Patriarchat und europäische Politik, 1620–1638*, Wiesbaden: Steiner, 1968

Mihalcesco, J., "Les Idées calvinistes du patriarche Cyrille Lucaris", *Revue d'Histoire et de Philosophie Religieuses*, 11 (1931): pp. 506–20

Ovannikov, E., *Kyrill Lukaris ego bórba s rimo-katoličeskoju propagandoju na Vostokě*, Novočerkassk, 1903

Papadopoulos, Chrysostomos, *Kyrillos Loukaris*, Athens, 1939 (in Greek)

Roberts, R.J., "The Greek Press at Constantinople in 1627 and its Antecedents", *The Library*, 5th series, 22 (1967): pp. 13–43

Runciman, Steven, *The Great Church in Captivity: A Study of the Patriarchate of Constantinople from the Eve of the Turkish Conquest to the Greek War of Independence*, London: Cambridge University Press, 1968, pp. 259–88

Schlier, Richard, "Der Patriarch Kyrill Lukaris von Konstantinopel: Sein Leben und sein Glaubensbekenntnis", dissertation, Marburg University, 1927

Cyril, St 826/27–869

Missionary to the Slavs

St Cyril (Constantine the Philosopher) was, together with his older brother St Methodios, the inventor of the Slavic Glagolitic alphabet and a prominent Byzantine diplomat. His baptismal name was Constantine; Cyril was the monastic name that he adopted shortly before his death in Rome on 14 February 869. The seemingly interminable dispute as to the ethnic origins of "the Apostles of the Slavs" has not been resolved. Born in Thessalonica in 826 or 827 to a Byzantine army officer of middle rank and a mother who some scholars have hypothesized was Slavic, Constantine went to Constantinople to pursue studies that would lead to a career in the imperial service. The main source on his career, the *Life* written (in Old Church Slavonic) at the instigation of his brother Methodios shortly after Cyril's death, mentions that St Cyril studied in Constantinople with the future patriarch Photios (858–67 and 877–86), one of the greatest Byzantine intellectuals and an imperial adviser. In addition to receiving a broad grounding in secular and religious subjects, Constantine the Philosopher showed an extraordinary talent for languages, which equipped him admirably for diplomatic missions. After a short service in the chancery of the patriarch and an intermittent academic career, he went on a diplomatic mission (851 or 855–56) to the Arab caliph Mutawakkil (847–61). Later he joined his brother in a monastery on Mount Olympus in Asia Minor. Photios soon called on him to participate in a mission to the Khazar court (860–61), where he again demonstrated his abilities in religious polemic, this time against Jewish and Muslim proselytizers.

The historically most significant mission of SS Cyril and Methodios was the one to Moravia (862–63), where the "Apostles of the Slavs" introduced for the first time an Old Church Slavonic liturgy written in the Glagolitic alphabet. It is unknown when they devised the Glagolitic alphabet, which was derived partly from the Greek minuscule script, partly from Syriac and Coptic, and partly an original invention of St Cyril. The statement in a 13th-century Bulgarian *Life* of St Cyril that he had introduced the Slavic liturgy into southern Macedonia before the Moravian mission appears to be groundless. In any case, when the Moravian prince Rastislav (846–70) requested Christian missionaries acquainted with the Slavonic language, the patriarch Photios chose the two brothers from Thessalonica. Political and religious motives seem to have converged both in Rastislav's request and Byzantium's response. Moravia, which historical scholarship has traditionally located in the Czech and Slovak lands, had already begun to be incorporated into the Frankish ecclesiastical structures, but Latin was an incomprehensible language to the Slavs of central Europe. In addition, both prince Rastislav and the emperor Michael III seem to have considered a Frankish–Bulgarian alliance threatening. The patriarch Photios had his own reasons for favouring the introduction of a vernacular Slavic liturgy, because he was competing with the papacy for the spiritual allegiance of the Slavs. The Cyrillo-Methodian mission proved a short-term success in Moravia, although its long-term consequences lay elsewhere. A Slavic Church was set up in Moravia, and Cyril translated the gospel and liturgical texts, such as the liturgy of St John Chrysostom, from Greek into Old Church Slavonic. He thus laid the groundwork for the development of Old Church Slavonic as a written literary language.

Cyril's and Methodios's mission in Moravia stumbled, however, over the strong opposition of the Frankish bishops supported by the eastern Frankish emperor Louis the German (817–76). The Byzantine missionaries fervently opposed the "three-language heresy" of the Franks, who claimed that the divine liturgy was permissible only in Hebrew, Greek, and Latin. In this way, Byzantium showed a more flexible attitude towards the formation of "national" churches under the spiritual aegis of Constantinople. A temporary support for the Slavic cause was found in the papacy. At the invitation in 867 of pope Nicholas I, who was interested in reducing the influence of the local Frankish bishops, Cyril and Methodios journeyed to Rome. There they received the blessing of the new pope, Hadrian II (867–72), who solemnly authorized the use of the Slavonic liturgy and ordained their disciples. After the death of St Cyril in 869, the furtherance of a Slavonic Church devolved on Methodios.

The momentous long-term consequences of the Moravian mission lay not in central Europe, but in the Balkans and in Russia. Moravia fell out of the Byzantine orbit in the 880s, while the Glagolitic alphabet was supplanted almost entirely by the Cyrillic (apart from Croatia, until the late 20th century). Nevertheless, the translations prepared by St Cyril were the first steps in the emergence of a Byzantine-Slavic Commonwealth bound by a common religious and cultural heritage. After their expulsion from Moravia the disciples of SS Cyril and Methodios successfully introduced the Slavic liturgy into Bulgaria which had been converted to Byzantine Christianity in 864. Bulgaria salvaged and expanded the Cyrillo-Methodian heritage, especially during the culturally productive reign of king Symeon (893–927). From here, Slavic writings and the alphabet spread to Serbia and Russia. New translations of Byzantine theological, literary, and legal texts were prepared by Bulgarian scholars working at Symeon's court. The Cyrillic alphabet was a result of an attempt by St Cyril's and St Methodios's disciples in Bulgaria to adapt the Greek uncial script to the phonetic peculiarities of the Slavonic tongue. The process of transliteration of Glagolitic texts into Cyrillic was almost entirely completed by the 11th century. To the present day the modern alphabet of the Orthodox Slavs – the Bulgarians, the Serbs, and the Russians – is a simplified version of the Cyrillic script introduced into medieval Bulgaria.

Another long-term effect of St Cyril's work of translation was the emergence of Old Church Slavonic as the lingua franca of the Orthodox Slavs. Because St Cyril managed to render masterfully in Slavonic the rich variety of Greek vocabulary and syntax, and because Slavic languages were relatively close to each other at that time, Old Church Slavonic established itself as the third literary language in Europe. A trained Byzantine diplomat sent on an imperial mission, but also a person sympathetic to the fate of the Slavs, St Cyril left a double-sided legacy: he drew the Orthodox Slavs irreversibly into the orbit of Byzantine civilization and contributed to the development of their own cultural identity.

DIMITER G. ANGELOV

Biography

Born in Thessalonica in 826 or 827 and baptized Constantine, St Cyril (the monastic name by which he was later known) was educated in Constantinople, where he was a pupil of the future patriarch Photios and perhaps of Leo the Mathematician. He taught philosophy at the Magnaura school (whence his soubriquet "the Philosopher"). But he is best known for his mission, undertaken in 863 with his brother St Methodios, to the Slavs for whom he devised both an alphabet (the Glagolitic) and a liturgical language (Old Church Slavonic). He died in Rome in 869.

Further Reading

Bowlus, Charles R., *Franks, Moravians, and Magyars: The Struggle for the Middle Danube, 788–907*, Philadelphia: University of Pennsylvania Press, 1995

Duichev, Ivan (editor), *Kiril and Methodius: Founders of Slavonic Writing: A Collection of Sources and Critical Studies*, Boulder, Colorado: East European Monographs, 1985

Dvornik, Francis, *The Making of Central and Eastern Europe*, London: Polish Research Centre, 1949

Dvornik, Francis, *Les Légendes de Constantin et de méthode vues de Byzance*, Prague, 1933; 2nd edition, Hattiesburg, Mississippi: Academic International, 1969

Dvornik, Francis, *Byzantine Missions among the Slavs: SS. Constantine-Cyril and Methodius*, New Brunswick, New Jersey: Rutgers University Press, 1970

Eggers, Martin, *Das "Grossmährische Reich": Realität oder Fiktion? Eine Neuinterpretation der Quellen zur Geschichte des mittleren Donauraumes im 9. Jahrhundert*, Stuttgart: Hiersemann, 1995

Obolensky, Dimitri, *The Byzantine Commonwealth: Eastern Europe, 500–1453*, London: Weidenfeld and Nicolson, and New York: Praeger, 1971

Obolensky, Dimitri, *Byzantium and the Slavs*, Crestwood, New York: St Vladimir's Seminary Press, 1994

Ševčenko, Ihor, "Three Paradoxes of the Cyrillo-Methodian Mission" in his *Ideology, Letters and Culture in the Byzantine World*, London: Variorum, 1982

Ševčenko, Ihor, "On the Social Background of Cyril and Methodius" in his *Byzantium and the Slavs in Letters and Culture*, Cambridge, Massachusetts: Harvard Ukrainian Research Institute, 1991

Soulis, G., "The Legacy of Cyril and Methodius to the Southern Slavs", *Dumbarton Oaks Papers*, 19 (1965): pp. 19–43

Vavrínek, V. and B. Zásterová, "Byzantium's Role in the Formation of Great Moravian Culture", *Byzantinoslavica*, 43 (1983): pp. 161–88

Vlasto, A.P., *The Entry of the Slavs into Christendom: An Introduction to the Medieval History of the Slavs*, Cambridge: Cambridge University Press, 1970

Cyril of Alexandria, St *c.378–444*

Patriarch of Alexandria

Cyril of Alexandria is one of the most important of the Christian Greek theologians, and was a major protagonist in the great Christological crisis of the 5th-century Church. The conciliar debate that he initiated at the Council of Ephesus (431) went on to determine the agenda of three following ecumenical councils up to the 7th century. To this extent he is rightly regarded as the chief architect of Byzantine Christology, even though his work was built upon important predecessors (especially theologians in the Alexandrian tradition) and was frequently modified in its later reception. The longterm political implications of these complex and often bitter Christological arguments, allied with the Arab invasions of the 7th century, had the effect of disconnecting important Christian Churches in Syria and Africa from Byzantine and Latin currents, and made severe divisions in the ecclesiastical polity of the East (the so-called Monophysite schism) that have remained active to this day.

Cyril was born some time around 378. His uncle Theophilus became Archbishop of Alexandria in 385, and brought Cyril to Alexandria to be educated. From his youth, then, he observed the ascendant power of the Christian Church in one of the most volatile cities of the empire. His education is apparent from his mature works, and shows that he received rhetorical training, as well as a substantial grounding in biblical exegesis and the theological tradition of the previous Fathers, especially the writers of the Alexandrian school. His Classical allusions (in his *Contra Julianum*) are derived from earlier Christian literature. He himself probably thought that his great biblical commentaries would have earned him lasting fame, but it was his Christological apologetic writing that achieved this result.

At the end of his studies, around 403 when he was 25 years old, Cyril was ordained lector of the Alexandrian Church, and was closely attached to his uncle's court. In the same year he attended Theophilus at the notorious Synod of the Oak, which deposed John Chrysostom. Cyril had learned his craft of leadership from a turbulent master, and when his uncle died on 15 October 412, the Byzantine administration of the city tried to pre-empt his election as a successor. The governor's office pushed forward the candidacy of the archdeacon Timothy, but it was Cyril's party that won the day. The clash between the ecclesiastical factions caused grave disturbances in the city. Cyril was consecrated as archbishop on 18 October 412; he was 34 years of age. The historian Socrates recounts the troubles of his early administration: his confiscation and seizure of the Novatianist churches (continuing in a milder manner the "aggressive" policy of his uncle Theophilus as permitted by a wider policy of the Theodosian dynasty); mob violence involving attacks on Jewish elements who had purportedly fired a Christian church; the infamous murder by Church factions of the philosopher Hypatia; and increasing friction with the Christian governor Orestes. In 416 an imperial investigation into Alexandrian affairs determined to restrict the guild of *parabalanoi* (the unofficial bodyguard of the archbishop), but within two years the number was again increased to more than 600 and officially placed under Cyril's personal direction, a mark of high imperial confidence. During this earlier period of Cyril's administration, he was also engaged in the active process of the evangelization of an Egypt still strongly devoted to the old religions, especially the cult of Isis. Fragments of sermons and discourses survive from 427 relating his establishment of a new healing shrine of the Unmercenaries Cyrus and John adjacent to the famous shrine of Isis at Menouthis. In this deliberate attempt to undermine the old religion Cyril portrayed himself as both "holy seer" and strong power. His policy of active, and sometimes aggressive, evangelization was advanced by marauding monastics, such as those communities under the control of Shenoudi of Atripe.

After 428 Cyril's life changed dramatically. In that year the patriarchal throne of Constantinople was taken by Nestorius,

a monk from Antioch. Nestorius assumed office in a city that had been wracked by disputes, and unsuccessful parties to the election gave him a hostile reception from the start. In his early days he was asked to adjudicate in a seemingly minor semantic problem about whether Mary could be rightly called the Mother of God (*Theotokos*). He tried an eirenic compromise by suggesting that she would be more correctly called "Mother of Christ". The local dispute flared from that point and it soon emerged that what was really at issue was a major collision between the Antiochene Christological tradition (that of Diodore of Tarsus and Theodore of Mopsuestia) and the Alexandrian school (Athanasius and Didymus) of the previous generation.

Cyril was well aware of all the ramifications of the argument from the outset, by means of his political staff in the imperial city, but he did not intervene directly until after Christmas 428, when Nestorius had been publicly denounced by enemies in his own cathedral. In the spring of 429 Cyril composed a paschal letter to his own extremely large archdiocese, insisting that Christ must always be regarded as a single divine person, and that the reality of his humanity must not distract the Christian mind from that fundamental position. It is, though embryonic in exposition, the base of all his detailed arguments that were to follow. By 430 Cyril had prepared the ground well, and sent for the information of the Roman Church a dossier of damaging information about his opponent. He was laying the basis of a formal charge against Nestorius. Rome reacted quickly, putting the matter on the agenda for a synod to be held later that same year. In Constantinople Nestorius pushed ahead, now teaching that only Antiochene theology should be regarded as the normative discourse of the imperial Church. The city was much disturbed by his agenda and, though the emperor seemed to be on his side, the Augusta Pulcheria, many monks, and several sections of the aristocracy were becoming increasingly hostile. In 430 Cyril composed his five-book *Against Nestorius*, which engaged battle directly. In August 430 the Roman synod announced that it condemned Nestorius' teaching, and supported that of Cyril. In response, Cyril summoned a synod of his own Church and sent off a demand that Nestorius should recant. Trying to disarm matters, the emperor Theodosius II called for the whole dispute to be settled by an international synod, which met at Ephesus in the summer of 431. Cyril manoeuvred the complex and confused proceedings and took the role of president himself. Nestorius refused to appear on such terms, and objected to matters beginning before the (late) delegation from the Antiochene Church arrived. By a significant majority, Nestorius' teaching was rejected, but a few days later, when the Syrian bishops finally arrived, they held a minority countersynod anathematizing the first. All the chief parties were then held under house arrest by the frustrated imperial officers, while the emperor called a series of meetings at Chalcedon to resolve the impasse. On 25 October 431 a new archbishop was elected in Nestorius' place. Nestorius himself was sent back in disgrace to his monastery in Syria; Cyril was freed to travel back in triumph to Egypt.

During the following years, between 432 and 444, there was a slow healing of the breaches between Alexandria and the Syrian Churches, patiently presided over by imperial negotiators. Eventually in 433 a compromise was reached in which the important points of the Antiochene position (Christ had two authentic natures – both human and divine) could be reconciled with Cyril's insistence that Christ was a single reality, one divine person. But the precise ramifications of that agreement still needed much clarifying debate, and without this it was inevitable that the intellectual argument would soon break out again with even greater force. It did so with greater bitterness in the following generation. In his later years Cyril continued a relentless attack on Antiochene theological traditions, but by then he had reached an acclaimed international status as a theologian, and ever afterwards his works became a kind of standard for the majority eastern Christian tradition, setting the agenda (though not unopposed) for the councils of Ephesus (449 – not regarded as ecumenical), Chalcedon (451), and Constantinople (553 and 680–81). He died on 27 June 444, a little short of his 70th year.

Cyril's role as one of the most powerful brokers of ecclesiastical power in the Theodosian dynasty has commanded much scholarly attention. His formative impact on Christian theology concerning the person of Christ and the effects of salvation (especially later Byzantine "deification theory") and his exegetical works remain of enduring importance.

JOHN A. McGUCKIN

See also Monophysites

Biography

Born *c*.378 at Mahalla in Egypt, Cyril was educated in rhetoric and biblical exegesis at Alexandria under the tutelage of his uncle, Archbishop Theophilus. Ordained *c*.403, he succeeded his uncle as patriarch in 412. His early administration was marked by conflicts of factions in a turbulent city, but he was an active evangelist and after 428 campaigned vigorously and successfully against Nestorius, Patriarch of Constantinople. He died in Alexandria in 444.

Writings

On the Unity of Christ, translated by John A. McGuckin, Crestwood, New York: St Vladimir's Seminary Press, 1995

Further Reading

Du Manoir de Juaye, Hubert, *Dogme et spiritualité chez Saint Cyrille d'Alexandrie*, Paris: Vrin, 1944

Gebremedhin, Ezra, *Life-Giving Blessing: An Inquiry into the Eucharistic Doctrine of Cyril of Alexandria*, Stockholm: Almqvist & Wiksell, 1977

McGuckin, John A., "The Influence of the Isis Cult on St. Cyril of Alexandria's Christology", *Studia Patristica*, 24 (1992): pp. 191–99

McGuckin, John A., *St. Cyril of Alexandria: The Christological Controversy, Its History, Theology, and Texts*, Leiden and New York: Brill, 1994

Norris, R.A., "Christological Models in Cyril of Alexandria", *Studia Patristica*, 13 (1975): pp. 255–68

Romanides, J.S., "St. Cyril's 'One Physis or Hypostasis of God the Logos Incarnate' and Chalcedon", *Greek Orthodox Theological Review*, 10 (1964–65): pp. 82–107

Wilken, Robert L., *Judaism and the Early Christian Mind: A Study of Cyril of Alexandria's Exegesis and Theology*, New Haven, Connecticut, and London: Yale University Press, 1971

Cythera

Island off the southern Peloponnese

Throughout its history Cythera, renowned in antiquity as the island sacred to Aphrodite (hence the title "Cytherean" Aphrodite), was involved either with the course of events in the Peloponnese or with Crete. During the Byzantine period it became closely linked with developments in the southern Peloponnese, while during the Venetian period Cythera became more closely associated with Cretan affairs. This double orientation of Cythera was naturally a result of its position, midway between the Peloponnese and Crete.

Cythera is mentioned in Ptolemy's *Geography* and in the *Geography* of the Anonymous of Ravenna, as well as in the *Tabula Peutingeriana* and the *Synekdemos* of Hierokles. A coin from Kastri identified as depicting the emperor Constantius II suggests that travellers were coming to the shores of Cythera in the mid-4th century AD. People may still have been coming to the island in order to worship Aphrodite; or fishermen may have come to gather the highly prized purple-yielding shellfish from which the island had acquired a second name, Porphyrousa. In the subsequent early Byzantine centuries no known written sources refer to the island. It is only thanks to archaeological excavations at Kastri that we know, from numismatic and ceramic evidence unearthed there, that the island was inhabited in the 7th and 8th centuries.

After the Arab conquest of Crete (*c*.824) the rocky indented coastline of Cythera served as a shelter for Saracen pirates. The 10th-century life of St Theodore describes the island as deserted and unapproachable because it was a "haven for the godless Agarenes" (Saracens). St Theodore, who subsequently became patron saint of Cythera, was born in Coroni in the southern Peloponnese. During the reign of the emperor Romanos I Lekapenos he came from Monemvasia to the island of Cythera in order to become a hermit. With the reconquest of Crete by the Byzantine emperor Nikephoros Phokas in 961, piracy in the region declined markedly. It is at this time that Cythera was settled anew. The governor (*gastaldo*) of the island in the following period was a certain George Pachys of Monemvasia. Towards the end of the 12th century the island was granted to the powerful family of Eudaimonoyannis of Monemvasia. Cythera now entered a period of relative tranquillity and prosperity, and it was probably at this time that the fortified settlement of Hagios Dimitrios was built. In 1238 Nicholas Eudaimonoyannis, realizing that the Venetians would eventually gain control of the Aegean, seems to have engaged in a policy of *realpolitik* in order to retain a measure of influence in Cythera: he married his daughter to the Venetian lord of Crete, Marco Venier, including the island of Cythera in the dowry. In effect this marriage marked the beginning of the period of Venetian rule in Cythera.

The participation of the Venier brothers in the unsuccessful uprising of the lords of Crete against Venetian rule in 1363 – the so-called St Titius rebellion – prompted Venice to deprive the Venier family of all authority and to impose direct control on Cythera from Crete. Apart from a very brief period of Turkish occupation (1715–18), Cythera – referred to in the Venetian sources as Cerigo or the Isola di Venere – remained under Venetian control until the final fall of the Venetian republic in 1797. Since then it has shared the fortunes of the Ionian islands.

Throughout the course of the Venetian period Cythera was divided into five administrative districts (*distretti* or *territori*): Fortezza-Borgo, Livadhi, Kastrissianika, Potamos, and Mylopotamos. Until the middle of the 16th century Cythera had three castles: Hagios Dimitrios, Kapsali, and Mylopotamos. The castle of Hagios Dimitrios, which guarded the Byzantine city of the Eudaimonoyannis family, was destroyed in 1537, after the invasion by Khayr al-Din Barbarossa. The district subsequently came to be known as Paliochora (Old Village), a toponym often used in the Greek language to indicate deserted villages or towns.

Two social strata developed on the island: the peasants (*popolani*) and the town dwellers (*cittadini*). The early centuries of Venetian domination in the island do not appear to have provoked substantial animosity or opposition, in contrast to nearby Crete. The long Venetian presence seems rather to have led to gradual convergence of habits and traditions.

After the Turkish conquest of Canea (modern Chania) and Candia (modern Herakleion) in Crete many families fled to Cythera, either settling there permanently and thus influencing many aspects of Cytheran life, or moving on from there to the Ionian islands of Zante or Corfu. Among those refugees from Crete were Frangiscos Salamon and his wife Anesina Podocataro, ancestors of modern Greece's national poet Dionysios Solomos.

CHRYSSA A. MALTEZOU

Summary

Lying off the south coast of the Peloponnese, Cythera was sacred to Aphrodite in antiquity. It was a source of *murex* (used to make purple dye), whence its alternative name Porphyrousa. After the fall of Crete (824) it was a haven for Arab pirates. Piracy declined after the Byzantine reconquest of Crete (961) and the island flourished. It was ruled by Venice from the mid-13th century until 1797. Since then it has shared the fortunes of the Ionian islands.

Further Reading

Maltezou, Chryssa A., *Venetike parousia sta Kythera: Archeiakes Martyries* [The Venetian Presence on Cythera: Documentary Evidence], Athens, 1991

Maltezou, Chryssa A., "Apo ta Vyzantina sta Venetika Cythera" [From Byzantine to Venetian Cythera] in *Euretirio Vyzantinon Toichographion Ellados* [Inventory of Byzantine Wall Paintings in Greece], edited by M. Chatzidakis and Ioanna Bitha, Athens, 1996

D

Dalmatia

Today a region of the Republic of Croatia, Dalmatia is the strip of land that hugs the indented eastern coast of the Adriatic from Zadar to the bay of Kotor, separated from the Balkan hinterland by the massif of the Dinaric Alps. A coveted region, which witnessed a succession of settlers, invaders, and conquerors in its history, Dalmatia was for several centuries a battleground for conflicting influences between East and West. Not surprisingly, its geographical position made it attractive to cultural forces emanating from across the Adriatic rather than the interior of the Balkans.

Named after the ancient town of Dalmion or Dalminion, the region was first populated by Illyrians. Scattered Greek settlements ensued. From the mid-2nd century BC the Romans extended their sway over a part of Dalmatia, but not until AD 23 did they definitively subdue its contumacious inhabitants and incorporate the region into the Roman province of Illyricum. Rome destroyed the ancient civilization of Illyria; still the latter gave Rome 13 rulers and defenders (*restitutores orbis*) of whom the emperor Diocletian (284–305) was the greatest. Latin was the language most commonly spoken, but Christianity had not much infiltrated the region by the time the capital was transferred to Constantinople. With the division of the Roman empire in 395, Dalmatia constituted the eastern-most region of the western Roman state until it collapsed in 476.

Briefly dominated by the Germanic ruler Odoacer, and in turn overrun by waves of Ostrogoths, Dalmatia was restored to Byzantium in 535 in the reign of the emperor Justinian, at the start of his 20-year struggle to restore the empire to its ecumenical extent. A proconsular province, it was composed of the Istria–Kotor coast and the offshore islands. Throughout the migrations of the 5th and the 6th centuries people from the disrupted northern provinces of the state fled as refugees to the Dalmatian coastal towns.

Among the peoples who ravaged the Roman world, during the 6th century the Slavs, whose social organization was similarly embryonic, flooded the Danubian basin causing depredations in the Balkan lands. In Dalmatia, specifically, the massive influx of Slavs shattered the foundations of Christian culture, at that time under the supervision of the papacy, and ruined urban life; Salona and Epidaurus, the major coastal centres, were destroyed in the early 7th century. Yet, unlike the other barbarian tribes pursuing principally marauding purposes, the South Slavs firmly bound their lot with these provinces and established themselves as permanent settlers. Dalmatia acquired its Slavic ethnic character, and new centres – Ragusa (Dubrovnik) and Zara (Zadar) – in time replaced the ruined Roman ones. In fact, if credence is to be given to the writings of the emperor Constantine VII Porphyrogennetos (*De Administrando Imperio*), the South Slavs (Serbs and Croats) who infiltrated Dalmatia and other Byzantine regions did so with the agreement of the emperor Herakleios (610–41). They were allowed in as settlers to populate and defend the Byzantine borderlands, having first acknowledged the emperor's suzerainty. To Herakleios also is attributed the first attempt to Christianize the South Slavs.

In contrast to the confused background, and to the overall trend of urban decay characterizing Byzantine provinces after the Avaro-Slavic invasions, in Dalmatia intercourse between east and west favoured conditions for social organization. The region with its nearby islands remained a Byzantine province with its capital at Zara, administered by an *archon* (prior), probably a Byzantine dignitary or a local nobleman. But its ecclesiastical authority alternated between Rome and Constantinople; and in 732–33 the emperor transferred the spiritual jurisdiction of Illyricum (together with the southern Italian provinces of Calabria and Sicily) to Constantinople. This happened at a time when the iconoclast controversy was at its height, and Lombard and Frankish raids on the Italian peninsula caused an irreparable rift with Byzantium's European provinces. The Byzantine east emerged progressively as a clear-cut political and cultural entity following the collapse of Byzantium's sway over the greater part of Italy by 751. Yet Dalmatia's engagement with Constantinople's sphere was mainly political and never able to strike roots. The region's position on the Adriatic fringe of the empire and a lingering memory of its Roman-Latin heritage in the towns kept it culturally attached to Rome.

Charlemagne sought to extend Frankish sway over the Adriatic dominions of Byzantium, and, after he conquered Venice in 810, he subjugated Dalmatia, which was administered briefly by a Frank *dux Jaderae* (duke of the Adriatic). Although by the treaty of Aix-la-Chapelle (Aachen/Akyisgranon) of 812 Byzantine authority over Dalmatia was restored, it remained nominal. In practice Dalmatia was independent in the first half of the 9th century, and the South Slavic tribes of the region established close bonds with their kindred in the Balkan hinterland who at the time were attempting to set up an inchoate political entity. But in the face of Arab raids on the Adriatic littoral, the Dalmatians called for Byzantine help. In response, the emperor Basil I, on ascending the throne in 867, sent the Byzantine fleet and recovered Dalmatia, which was organized as a Byzantine theme according to the new administrative system of the empire, already in existence in the European provinces since the 8th century. Ecclesiastically, it constituted a metropolis dependent on Constantinople.

Despite Dalmatia's integration into the Byzantine thematic system, especially under the centralist Macedonian dynasty, it remained one of the few exceptions enjoying a de facto autonomy, along with Venice and Cherson (in Crimea). At a time when most provinces saw their local immunities suppressed, Dalmatia retained its local privileges and municipal franchises, which ensured broad self-rule in the maritime urban centres. The theme of Dalmatia was placed under the administration of a Byzantine general, but the towns had their local notables and dignitaries. This status was further strengthened by a renewed flourishing of urban and commercial life in the empire, which had been suspended in the wake of the Avaro–Slavic disarray. Byzantine overlordship in the Dalmatian theme steadily diminished to a nominal authority. By 880 Croatian Dalmatia, extending southwards as far as the Cetina river, freed itself entirely under prince Branimir from Byzantine control. Along with a spirit of urban autonomy, most of Dalmatia became increasingly receptive to non-Byzantine influences, namely Croatian and Venetian.

Dalmatia was still recorded as a Byzantine theme in the 11th century, shortly after a revision of the Byzantine administrative system took place in the Balkan provinces; but the region itself was irretrievably lost to foreign administrations in later medieval times. The Byzantine presence was principally threatened by the ascendancy of Venice as a maritime power, and by the strong Croatian state, reaching as far down the Dalmatian coast as the Neretva river in the mid-11th century. Croatian control of Dalmatia from the time of king Tomislav (c.910–28), and a short-lived Venetian domination around 1000, already marked the decline of Byzantine influence. The latter, apart from being politically diminished, was culturally displaced by the Latin Church, whose bishops in the Dalmatian towns were encouraged by the Croatian rulers to ensure Dalmatia's incorporation into the sphere of Roman-Latin culture. Soon the role of Byzantium was eclipsed, despite an ephemeral restoration in the reign of the emperor Manuel I Komnenos (1143–80) who pompously assumed the title "ruler of Dalmatia". With Manuel's death Bela III of Hungary (1172–96) subjugated all the Byzantine possessions in the region.

In the 13th–14th centuries Dalmatia experienced complicated changes of overlord; characteristically, at one stage the southern half belonged to Serbia, the northern to Croatia-Hungary, the Adriatic islands and littoral sites to Venice, and Ragusa (Dubrovnik) constituted an independent city state. In cultural and economic terms this territorial fragmentation was tantamount to Dalmatia's irrevocable transfer to the Roman-Latin sphere. Even within the medieval Serbian state, whose Orthodox rulers may have grown politically combative but remained culturally receptive to Byzantium's civilizing impact,

Serbian Dalmatia represented a channel of Latin influence, which included Italian art. The long Venetian-Hungarian rivalry over Dalmatia, which spanned three centuries, culminated in the victory of Venice in the early 15th century.

In early modern times, when Ragusa emerged as a flourishing maritime republic, Greeks and Dalmatians came into close contact since Ragusan ships traded at Greek ports, and also as naval crews in the ships of Venice.

Historically, Dalmatian culture was heavily characterized by Italian influences, both Latin and Renaissance, but blended with a native Slavic element. Greek-Byzantine culture had a markedly secondary impact, though archaeological and architectural evidence bears witness to its presence. Diocletian's magnificent palace in Split (Spalato), a site already occupied by a Greek settlement (Aspalaton), was erected by builders invited from the East who echoed eastern palace architecture. More evident is the early Christian architecture, the basilicas of the 6th and 7th centuries. Later, Andrija Buvina, a great sculptor of the 13th century, drew partly on the Graeco-Roman heritage and the Byzantine tradition in creating his well-known reliefs on the doors of Diocletian's Mausoleum in Split. In Dalmatian literature, Classical Greek lyrics inspired some poets in Dubrovnik through Italian humanism, such as Dinko Ranjina (1536–1607) who in his lyrical poetry imitated Moschus and Theocritus. Lastly, Romano-Byzantine law had a remarkable effect on the statutes of the Dalmatian coastal towns and islands, which outlived Byzantine rule in Dalmatia.

RENNOS EHALIOTIS

See also Croatia, Illyrians, Serbia, Slavs

Summary

Dalmatia is the eastern shore of the Adriatic Sea from Zadar to the bay of Kotor. Isolated Greek settlements were made from the 6th century BC but the region was Latinized by the Roman conquest. Restored to Byzantium in 535, Dalmatia remained a Byzantine province until the 11th century. Venetian influence was strong thereafter.

Further Reading

L'Art Byzantin chez les Slaves, vol. 4: *Les Balkans*, 2 parts, Paris: Geuthner, 1930

L'Art Byzantin chez les Slaves, vol. 5: *L'Ancienne Russie, les Slaves Catholiques*, 2 parts, Paris: Geuthner, 1932 (especially "Sur Quelques bas-reliefs Byzantins en Dalmatie" by M. Abramić and "Notes sur l'Art Byzantin et les Slaves Catholiques de Dalmatie" by L. Karaman, both in part 2)

Babić, I., *Trogir's Cultural Treasures*, Zagreb, 1990

Bjelovučić, Harriet, *The Ragusan Republic: Victim of Napoleon and Its Own Conservatism*, Leiden: Brill, 1970

Božić, Ivan (editor), *Istorija Jugoslavije* [History of Yugoslavia], 2nd edition, Belgrade, 1973 (in Serbo-Croatian)

Carter, Francis W., *Dubrovnik (Ragusa): A Classic City-State*, London and New York: Seminar Press, 1972

Carter, Francis W., "Urban Development in the Western Balkans 1200–1800" in *An Historical Geography of the Balkans*, edited by Carter, London and New York: Academic Press, 1977

Constantine Porphyrogenitus, *De Administrando Imperio*, Greek text edited by Gyula Moravcsik, translated by R.J.H. Jenkins, Washington, D.C.: Dumbarton Oaks, 1967

Ćurčić, Slobodan, "The Byzantine Legacy in the Ecclesiastical Architecture of the Balkans after 1453" in *The Byzantine Legacy in Eastern Europe*, edited by Lowell Clucas, Boulder, Colorado: East European Monographs, 1988

Diehl, Charles, *Manuel d' Art Byzantin*, 2nd edition, 2 vols, Paris: Picard, 1925–26

Dusa, Joan, *The Medieval Dalmatian Episcopal Cities: Development and Transformation*, New York: Peter Lang, 1991

Dvornik, Francis, *Les Slaves, Byzance et Rome au IXe siècle*, Paris: Champion, 1926

Dvornik, Francis, *The Slavs: Their Early History and Civilization*, Boston: American Academy of Arts and Sciences, 1956

Dyggve, Ejnar, *History of Salonitan Christianity*, Oslo: Aschenhoug, and Cambridge, Massachusetts: Harvard University Press, 1951

Ferluga, Jadran, *Byzantium on the Balkans: Studies on the Byzantine Administration and the Southern Slavs from the VIIth to the XIIth Centuries*, Amsterdam: Hakkert, 1976

Hauptmann, L., "Les Rapports des Byzantins avec les Slaves et les Avares pendant la seconde moitié du VIe siècle", *Byzantion*, 4 (1927–28): pp. 137–70

Jackson, T.G., *Dalmatia, the Quarnero and Istria with Cettigne in Montenegro and the Island of Grado*, 3 vols, Oxford: Clarendon Press, 1887

Klaić, Nada, *Povijest Hrvata u razvijenom srednjem vijeku* [The History of the Croats in the Late Middle Ages], Zagreb, 1976 (in Serbo-Croatian)

Klaić, Vjekoslav, *Povijest Hrvata* [The History of the Croats], 5 vols, Zagreb, 1899–1911, reprinted Zagreb, 1985 (in Serbo-Croatian)

Novak, V., "The Slavonic-Latin Symbiosis during the Middle Ages", *Slavonic and East European Review*, 32 (1953–54): pp. 1–28

Obolensky, Dimitri, "Byzantium and its Northern Neighbours, 565–1018" in *The Byzantine Empire*, edited by J.M. Hussey, Cambridge: Cambridge University Press, 1967 (*The Cambridge Medieval History*, vol. 4, part 2)

Ostrogorsky, George, *History of the Byzantine State*, 2nd edition, Oxford: Blackwell, 1968; New Brunswick, New Jersey: Rutgers University Press, 1969

Skok, P., "L' Importance de Dubrovnik dans l' histoire des Slaves", *Le Monde Slave*, 8 (1931): pp. 161–71

Villari, Luigi, *The Republic of Ragusa: An Episode of the Turkish Conquest*, London: Dent, 1904

Vojnović, Lugo, *Histoire de Dalmatie*, 2 vols, Paris: Hachette, 1934

Damaskinos, Michael c.1530–c.1592

Painter

Michael Damaskinos was an important figure in the 16th-century renaissance of Cretan painting. He appears to have been born in Candia (Herakleion), the flourishing capital of Crete under Venetian rule, where previous generations of painters had established a solid artistic tradition. He certainly served his apprenticeship there, possibly with a painter of the circle around Theophanis Strelitzas-Bathas, and produced his first mature works between about 1555 and 1565.

A bearer of the Byzantine painting tradition, Damaskinos was also receptive to new trends in western European painting. Following the example of his fellow Cretan Domenikos Theotokopoulos (El Greco), he went to paint in Venice, at a time when some of the most brilliant Venetian painters (most notably Titian, P. Veronese, Tintoretto) were at their height. In Venice he signed a contract in 1569 to work for two years in Sicily. From 1574 to 1582/83 he was again in Venice. Working within the Greek Orthodox Confraternity of Venice (of which he was a member, with contributions registered in the years 1577–82), he painted icons for the church of San Giorgio dei Greci, many of which are still in situ today, in the sanctuary and on the iconostasis. On two occasions he sought election to the council of the confraternity, but without success. During these years he also worked for Catholic institutions and executed private commissions. In Venice he made the acquaintance of the sculptor Alessandro Vittoria, to whom, in 1581, he sold a collection he had amassed of drawings by Italian artists, particularly by the Mannerist Parmigianino. He also met the painter Palma Giovane and probably had some contact with the workshop of Tintoretto, whom he followed in some of his works.

When he returned to Candia (1583) he gave his only daughter Antonia in marriage to the painter Ioannis Mavrikas-Mandouphos and continued his professional career in a climate of general appreciation of his work but also, paradoxically, of financial difficulties. He undertook a variety of commissions and produced some of his finest works, now in Crete and Corfu. In 1588 he was invited most insistently by the Greek Orthodox Confraternity of Venice to return and paint the dome of San Giorgio dei Greci, but declined the invitation, citing family and financial reasons. The last references to his activities date from 1591, and he probably died in 1592, while still at a productive age.

The unconfirmed tradition that Damaskinos became a monk in the Vrondisiou monastery in the province of Kainourio in the southwest of the prefecture of Herakleion seems to derive from the fact that there was formerly a series of six icons by him in the monastery (now in the collection of St Catherine of the Sinaites, Herakleion). As a painter, he was much in demand during his own time, both in Crete and elsewhere. He also gained considerable posthumous fame: Panayiotis Doxaras, the painter and theorist of early modern Greek painting, in his *Art of Painting* (1720), considers Damaskinos to be one of the most important Greek painters.

Works by Damaskinos are to be found in many parts of Greece (Mount Athos, Athens, Corfu, Crete, Galaxidi, Patmos, and Zakynthos) and the rest of Europe (Italy, Switzerland, for example), on Mount Sinai, and in private collections in the United States. According to recent estimates, his known works amount to about 100. More than half are unsigned but are securely attributed to him on the basis of historical evidence or stylistic criteria; conversely, several works that falsely bear his signature have been removed from his oeuvre. Only two of his works bear a date: the *Beheading of John the Baptist* (1590; Municipal Cemetery of Corfu) and the *First Ecumenical Council* (1591; St Catherine of the Sinaites, Herakleion). A few more, executed in Venice, may be dated on the basis of archival evidence. In most cases, however, it is difficult to date Damaskinos' work, particularly since his style exhibits considerable differences, often during the same period.

The demands of his profession and the broad spectrum of his clients in Greece and Italy (Orthodox and Catholic churches and monasteries, private individuals of both creeds and from all social classes, Venetian noblemen, and Cretans from the lower and middle classes) undoubtedly influenced his work. His output was always of a high standard and exhibits great variety in terms of the genre, technique, style, and iconographic schema. He executed large-scale works for public places of worship and monasteries (despotic icons, iconostases for churches, and western-type altarpieces), and also small icons and triptychs designed for private piety. With unrivalled skill, he created individual devotional figures of saints in an imposing monumental style, and also complex narrative scenes of a miniature character. A large number of his works are in a traditional style, based on late Palaeologan models and Cretan painting of earlier generations. He never rejected this style, though towards the end of his career he added to it a distinct element of plasticity and a barely perceptible misty chiaroscuro. Many of his works also reveal the influence of western European art, sometimes confined to details, and sometimes more pervasive, using as models foreign Renaissance and Mannerist paintings and engravings. They retain a unity of style, however, thanks to the use of a single medium (normally traditional egg tempera, probably with an admixture of oil), and a uniform range of colours.

From a technical point of view, Damaskinos generally showed a preference for a brown underpaint, using pinkish flesh tones with a few greenish shadows, and lighting prominent points of exposed flesh with discreet white brushstrokes. Drapery sometimes retains the geometric character and rhythmical arrangement of early Cretan painting and sometimes acquires the soft folds and fluidity associated with western taste. The predominant colours in his work are red and green, with a rich tonal scale ranging from pale rose-red to deep purple, applied in successive thin layers.

In works whose iconography is of purely western origin Damaskinos adopted the appropriate style, strongly influenced by Titian and Tintoretto. It is to these painters that his preferences incline, along with others of the Venetian school, such as J. Bassano and P. Veronese, and other central and north Italian painters of the High Renaissance and Mannerist periods (Raphael, known mainly to Damaskinos through engravings by Marcantonio Raimondi, Parmigianino, and Andrea Schiavone), and more rarely from northern Europe. For a single work he gleaned elements from different sources, rarely copying figures or groups in their entirety.

Damaskinos's artistic aspirations find tangible expression in compositions which, while retaining their Byzantine core, distance themselves from the established schemes of that tradition. This results in multifigural works, with the main subject framed by other related episodes executed in miniature, revealing his assimilation of western influence. These works, which exhibit some originality with regard to the tradition in which they are set, and justify the painter's signing them with the word *Poiema...* (Creation of...) instead of the traditional *Cheir...* (Hand of...), are in accord with the mixed nature of Cretan society in the Venetian period. The most important of them are the six icons now in the collection of St Catherine, Herakleion, and a number in Corfu.

Among the artist's innovations, particular interest attaches to the use of linear perspective (an issue of serious concern to Renaissance art theorists and painters), the use of genre elements rendering details from everyday life, the incorporation of Renaissance features and semi-naked bodies of Mannerist taste, the correct perspective rendering of objects, architectural decoration, and the contorted *figura serpentinata*. Some of his works also reflect the concerns of the day, such as debates on doctrinal issues.

Damaskinos made a highly important contribution to the renewal of the traditional iconography of post-Byzantine painting. Many of the new iconographic compositions that he created were copied by known 16th- and 17th-century painters, such as Emmanuel Lambardos, Victor, Frangiskos Kavertzas, Philotheos Skouphos, Emmanuel Skordilis, Ioannis Moskos, and others – and also many anonymous painters. Though they fall short of the quality of their models, they indicate the esteem in which Damakinos' work was held by his fellow artists and the wide circulation of his drawings. With their excellent quality, their original treatment of their subjects, and the strong physical presence of the figures depicted, his works are also used as models by modern religious painters. Indeed, given the vast increase in the publication of books illustrating original icons in recent years, as well as a new interest in icon painting, they are now being copied more frequently than ever.

MARIA CONSTANTOUDAKI

Biography

Born *c*.1530 in Herakleion (Candia), Crete, Damaskinos served his apprenticeship in his native city, perhaps under a painter of the circle of Theophanis Strelitzas-Bathas (Theophanes of Crete). He moved to Venice in the 1560s and with a two-year break in Sicily stayed there until *c*.1582, working mainly for the Greek Orthodox Confraternity. In 1583 he returned to Herakleion and continued to paint. About 100 of his works are known. He died probably in 1592.

Further Reading

Further Reading

Acheimastou-Potamianou, Myrtali (editor), *From Byzantium to El Greco: Greek Frescoes and Icons*, London: Royal Academy of Arts, 1987 (exhibition catalogue)

Acheimastou-Potamianou, Myrtali, *Eikones tis Zakynthou* [Icons of Zante], Athens, 1997

Acheimastou-Potamianou, Myrtali, *Eikones tou Vazantiyou Mouseiou Athinou* [Icons of the Byzantine Museum in Athens], Athens, 1998

Alvarez Lopera, José (editor), *El Greco: Identity and Transformation – Crete, Italy, Spain*, New York: Abbeville, and London: Thames and Hudson, 1999

Bourboudakis, M. (editor), *Eikones tis Kritikis Technis* [Icons of Cretan Art], Herakleion and Athens, 1993 (exhibition catalogue)

Chatzidakis, Manolis, *Icônes de Saint-Georges des Grecs et de la collection de l'Institut*, 2nd edition, Venice: Institut Hellénique d'Etudes Byzantines et Post-Byzantines de Venise, 1975

Chatzidakis, Manolis, *Icons of Patmos: Questions of Byzantine and Post-Byzantine Painting*, Athens, 1985

Chatzidakis, Manolis, *Ellines Zographoi meta tin Alosi (1450–1830)* [Greek Painters after the Conquest (1450–1830)], vol. 1, Athens, 1987

Constantoudaki-Kitromilides, Maria, "Michail Damaskinos (1530/35–1592/93): Symuoli sti Meleti tis Zographikis tou" [Michael Damaskinos (1530/35–1592/93): A Contribution to the Study of his Paintings], 3 vols, dissertation, University of Athens, 1988

Constantoudaki-Kitromilides, Maria, "La pittura di icone a Creta veneziana (secoli XV e XVI): Questioni di mecenatismo, iconografia e preferenze estetiche" in *Venezia e Creta*, edited by Gherardo Ortalli, Venice: Istituto Veneto di Scienze, Lettere ed Arti, 1998

Constantoudaki-Kitromilides, Maria, "L'arte dei pittori greci a Venezia" in *La pittura nel Veneto*, vol. 3: *Il Cinquecento*, edited by Mauro Lucco, Milan: Electa, 1999

Hadjinicolaou, Nikou (editor), *Domenikos Theotokopoulos Kres / El Greco of Crete*, Herakleion, 1990 (exhibition catalogue in Greek and English)

Vocotopoulos, P., "Icones de Michel Damaskinos à Corfou", *Byzantion*, 53 (1983): pp. 35–51

Vocotopoulos, P., *Eikones tis Kerkyras* [Icons of Corfu], Athens, 1990

Dance

From the evidence of both literature and art, it is clear that in ancient Greece dancing – the art traditionally dedicated to Terpsichore, one of the Muses – was widespread and important, whether as part of private entertainment or public ceremonial. Attendance at dancing classes in the tribal divisions of society was an obligatory part of the education of young Athenians. Spontaneous or formalized dancing in groups, usually of the same sex (since many ritual occasions demanded segregation of the sexes), and solo dancing of an expressive or imitative nature, with attention to movements of the hands (*cheironomia*), are both well attested; but, surprisingly to us, dancing together in pairs of opposite sexes, as in western ballroom dancing, seems to have been quite unusual.

In the description of the scenes on the shield of Achilles in *Iliad* 18, however, youths and maidens dance in adjoining lines, accompanied by two tumbling acrobats, and the dance floor is compared to the one made by Daedalus for Ariadne at Knossos. Crete was in fact thought to have made the major contribution to the development of dance, going back to the very birth of Zeus, when the leaping, foot-stamping, and weapon-clashing of the Curetes, fertility demons, concealed the child from the cannibalistic intention of his father Cronus. A late fragmentary hymn describing the occasion, with the theme of leaping to promote fertility, was found in excavations at Palaikastro. The lively dance called *hyporchema* was also believed to have been a Cretan invention, and was occasionally introduced into the choreography of Classical Attic tragedy. Plutarch (*Theseus*, 21) also describes a dance called *geranos* ("crane"), said to have been danced by Theseus and other youths on their escape from the labyrinth of Minos, and the agility in battle of a minor warrior of the *Iliad*, the Cretan Meriones, was attributed to his dancing skill.

The association of dancing with warfare – called "fierce Ares' dance" in *Iliad*, 7. 241 – and the manipulation of weapons are highlighted in the so-called Pyrrhic dance, also said to have derived from a divine birth, this time not of Zeus, but from his head, when Pallas Athena leapt out vigorously, fully armed. The motif of the dramatic emergence of a warrior continued to be a feature of the Pyrrhic, which was performed particularly at the Panathenaic festival by youths, naked but armed with helmet, shield, and spear, like the goddess. Socrates (Athenaeus, 628f.) is said to have declared that "those best at dancing are also best at war", and Plato (*Laws*, 815) described how this dance imitated defensive and offensive postures of combat. The Pyrrhic was alternatively attributed to Achilles' son Neoptolemus (also called Pyrrhus), whose desperate self-defence against Delphians is likened to the dance in a memorable passage of Euripides' *Andromache* (1129ff.).

Aristophanes (*Clouds*, 988–89) complained that the effete younger generation in Athens could not adequately perform the shield-twisting movement in honour of Athena, and it seems that a sophisticated stereotype in the dance might replace the actual shield, with a folded cloak covering the left arm to mimic the true armed pose. The Pyrrhic is the dance most often represented in art, both in sculpture and in vase painting. A pose showing sideways or backward turning of the head is another motif, sometimes associated with another exploit of Athena, when she instructed Perseus how to avoid the fatal glare of the Gorgon in their famous combat, or even herself performed the slaying of the monster. Armed dancers were popular elsewhere in Greece, especially Sparta with its prominent tradition of military training, and an elaborate account by Xenophon (*Anabasis*, 6) gives a detailed description of these in entertainments provided by different Greek mercenaries during Cyrus' famous march through Asia Minor. Included are a Persian dance featuring crouching and jumping, and one named *karpaia*, in which a farmer takes arms to protect his property against rustlers. The Pyrrhic is here danced as a solo by a young girl.

In *Laws* 815 Plato declares that there are two desirable types of dance, the warlike (as described above) and the peaceful, among which the stately and graceful *emmeleia* is singled out. *Iliad* 16. 183 refers to maidens dancing in the choir of Artemis, and a feature of Attic ritual was the chorus of young girls dressed as bears dancing in her honour in the township of Brauron. Dances imitative of animals and birds were widespread throughout Greece. When Odysseus is entertained at the Phaeacian court (*Odyssey*, 8. 256) he watches a pair of local youths dance, where jumping and throwing balls to each other are featured. The maiden songs (*partheneia*) with choral dancing of Alcman were notable, often celebrated at a night festival (*pannychis*). *Paeans*, mostly associated with Apollo, were composed by poets like Pindar, along with processionals (*prosodia*), marriage songs (hymeneals, epithalamia), dirges (*threnoi*), and the victory odes (*epinicia*) for which he is most famous. Ecstatic dancing was a feature of the cult of Dionysus and his crazed maenads (most memorably featured in Euripides' *Bacchae*). Other deities of oriental origin, such as Cybele, Attis, Sabazius, and their acolytes the Corybants, were also worshipped with the sort of dancing to musical accompaniment performed by ecstatic votaries which aroused apprehension about the disruption of civic order in some communities.

The dance particularly honouring Dionysus was the dithyramb. Whether Aristotle was right to see Attic tragedy (certainly associated with that god, and performed in his theatre) as developing from the dithyramb remains controversial, and the latter continued to be danced independently in a circular group of 50 in inter-tribal competitions, while the tragic chorus was danced in more formal rectangular patterns of 12 or 15 performers. Having entered by the *parodos*, they performed in the dancing place (orchestra) and remained on stage during the acted portions which were punctuated by their stationary songs (*stasima*), before marching out, usually to an anapaestic rhythm, in the *exodos*. Sophocles was himself said to have been an elegant dancer, and to have written a handbook *On the Chorus*. The group of three tragedies (trilogy) was followed by a satyr play, where the chorus, sometimes in

Dance: female dancers depicted on a *krater* in the Museo Archeologico Nazionale, Ferrara

the guise of attendants of Pan or Silenus, indulged in grotesque parodies of the statelier tragic dances, and we hear too of frankly indecent dances like the *sikinnis* and *kordax*. The chorus in Aristophanes' comedies performed the energetic dances appropriate to revelry (*komos*). Dancing was a popular feature of symposia in Athens and elsewhere, and Xenophon's *Symposium* in particular describes a typical party. Courtesans (hetaerae) were frequently called upon for these entertainments, with the music of the double *aulos* and castanets.

When Greek culture began to penetrate southern Italy, the so-called *phlyakes* plays, of similar hilarious type, became popular, and the dances that accompanied them are represented on vases. It was in the Roman era that the craze for virtuoso dancing by Greek *pantomimi*, interpreting different mythical roles, not only spread in theatrical performance, but attracted the favour of the imperial courts. Nero's own patronage of dancing, and his taking the stage himself, were notorious. Moralists and satirists such as Cicero, Seneca, and Juvenal may have expressed their disgust at the lewdness of much professional dancing, and in the Christian era the suppression of such exhibitions was sought. Nevertheless in the 6th century the notorious dancer Theodora became Roman empress through her marriage to Justinian.

In the pantomime the same dancer acted out a series of roles, representing either sex, and changing masks accordingly, with the mimicry of a dumbshow in steps, postures, and gestures. Although in the Byzantine period stage performance declined, pagan festivals and carnivals such as the Kalends and Brumalia survived and continued to be celebrated, while more decorous dances were performed at weddings and court ceremonials. In spite of theatrical censorship, low-class dances were still to be seen in taverns, accompanied by wind instruments and percussion.

The popularity of mythological themes in French *tragédie lyrique* and opera-ballet in the 17th–18th centuries revived interest in Greek theatrical dancing. A notable example of a famous Attic tragedy restaged (in translation) in the following century was Mendelssohn's *Antigone* at the Prussian court in Potsdam in 1841. Though it was a great success, when it reached London four years later, *Punch* magazine reviewed it with facetious contempt for the costume, singing, and dancing of the chorus! A century later, staging Attic tragedy attracted the attention of Carl Orff. His *Antigonae* (which has been performed in the Athenian theatre of Dionysus) and *Oedipus der Tyrann* were set to German translations, but his later *Prometheus* was staged to Aeschylus' Greek text.

In modern Greek society, folk dancing is ubiquitous, with dances such as the *tsamikos*, *zeibebiko*, *hasapiko*, *kalama-*

tianos, and *syrtos* – a dance actually attested as early as the 1st century. In the 20th century attempts have been made to reconstruct for performance elements of what is known of ancient Greek dance from art and literature (especially Lucian's essay *On the Dance*); and mention could be made of the eurhythmic movement of Jaques-Dalcroze and the dancing of Isadora Duncan, who derived ideas from depictions of dancing in Greek art, and of Martha Graham. Now that the staging of Greek drama, either in the original Greek or in translation, has been revived, and performances are more frequent – those by the Greek Art Theatre of Karolos Koun, and the London Festival of Greek Drama have been successful, and even the stylized Japanese theatre has turned attention to Greek tragedy – producers have come to decisions as to how best to represent the choral interludes and dances of the ancient theatre.

E. KERR BORTHWICK

See also Music, Theatre

Further Reading

Borthwick, E.K., "Trojan Leap and Pyrrhic Dance", *Journal of Hellenic Studies*, 87 (1967): pp. 18–23

Borthwick, E.K., "The Dances of Philocleon and the Sons of Carcinus in Aristophanes' *Wasps*", *Classical Quarterly*, 18 (1968): pp. 44–51

Borthwick, E.K., "P.Oxy. 2738: Athena and the Pyrrhic Dance", *Hermes*, 98 (1970): pp. 318–31

Calame, Claude, *Les Choeurs de jeunes filles en Grèce archaïque*, Rome: Ateneo & Bizzarri, 1977

Emmanuel, Maurice, *The Antique Greek Dance, after Sculptured and Painted Figures*, New York and London: Lane, 1916

Fitton, J.W., "Greek Dance", *Classical Quarterly*, 23 (1973): pp. 254–74

Georgiades, Thrasybulos Georgos, *Greek Music, Verse, and Dance*, New York: Merlin Press, 1956

Latte, Kurt, *De Saltationibus Graecorum Capita Quinque*, Giessen: Töpelmann, 1913

Lawler, Lillian B., "The Dance in Ancient Crete" in *Studies Presented to David Moore Robinson*, vol. 1, St Louis: Washington University, 1951, pp. 23–51

Lawler, Lillian B., "Phora, Schema, Deixis in the Greek Dance", *Transactions and Proceedings of the American Philological Association*, 85 (1954): pp. 148–58

Lawler, Lillian B., *The Dance in Ancient Greece*, London: A. & C. Black, 1964; Middletown, Connecticut: Wesleyan University Press, 1965

Lonsdale, Steven H., *Dance and Ritual Play in Greek Religion*, Baltimore: Johns Hopkins University Press, 1993

Lucian, "On the Dance" in *Lucian*, translated by A.M. Harmon, vol. 5, London: Heinemann, and Cambridge, Massachusetts: Harvard University Press, 1955 (Loeb edition)

Pickard-Cambridge, Arthur Wallace, *The Dramatic Festivals of Athens*, 2nd edition, London: Oxford University Press, 1968 (see especially chapter 5, "The Chorus")

Poursat, J.-C., "Les Représentations de danse armée dans la céramique attique", *Bulletin de Correspondance Hellénique*, 92 (1968): pp. 550–615

Prudhommeau, Germaine, *La Danse grecque antique*, 2 vols, Paris: CNRS, 1965

Roos, Ervin, *Die tragische Orchestik im Zerrbild der altattischen Komödie*, Lund: Gleerup, 1951

Séchan, L., *La Danse grecque antique*, Paris: Boccard, 1930

Webster, T.B.L., *The Greek Chorus*, London: Methuen, 1970

Dark Age   1200–700 BC

The term "Dark Age" is a relatively recent coinage of modern scholarship, applied to the period that intervenes between the collapse of the Mycenaean palaces around 1200 BC and the emergence of a new state form (the polis) in the course of the 8th century BC. Ancient writers seem to have been unaware of any major disjuncture between the heroic age and the historical period. Hesiod, writing around 700 BC, paints a gloomy picture of a gradual decline, symbolized by the successive "five ages" of gold, silver, bronze, heroes, and iron (*Works and Days*, 109–76). Conversely, Thucydides' conception of early Greek history (1. 1–18) is predicated on the notion of a steady evolutionary growth of resources and power; although the period immediately following the Trojan War is characterized by instability and migration (1. 12), there is no real sense of a cultural or economic "trough" that stands in stark contrast to conditions before the Trojan expedition, nor again of a "renaissance" associated with the rise of the polis – in fact, most Greeks believed that poleis had existed from time immemorial.

Up to the 1870s, most scholars accepted – at least in principle – Thucydides' general schema of early Greek history, though many (George Grote in particular) believed that the lack of contemporary written evidence made it impossible to construct a properly historical narrative of Greece before 776 BC (the traditional date for the foundation of the Olympic Games). However, Heinrich Schliemann's excavations at Troy (1870–90), Mycenae (1876), and Tiryns (1884) made it clear for the first time that an earlier, civilized culture had flourished on the Greek mainland; it also soon became evident that the palaces associated with this "Mycenaean" civilization had experienced an abrupt end. Following Flinders Petrie's publication in 1890 of Mycenaean pottery in Egyptian contexts of the 18th and 19th Dynasties and his conclusion that the Mycenaean palaces had been destroyed around 1200 BC, it became evident that there was a gap of approximately five centuries between the collapse of the palaces and the first extant literature as represented by Hesiod and the lyric poets of the 7th century BC. The sheer paucity of evidence for this intervening period had already by the last decade of the 19th century led historians to term it a "Dark Age" or "the medieval epoch of Greece".

It is sometimes stated today that the Dark Age is simply a "subjective" perception in the mind of the modern historian, generated by the lack of any contemporary literary evidence, and that archaeological investigation is revealing the period to be anything but obscure in "objective" terms. In fact, if anything, the opposite is more correct. It is certainly true that direct and contemporary literary evidence is lacking for the period. The Linear B tablets, which offer precious testimony for economic, social, and military conditions in the Late Bronze Age, disappear with the destruction of the Mycenaean palaces as the bureaucratic necessity for scribal literacy evaporated; literacy – this time in alphabetic form – is not attested again in Greece proper until the middle of the 8th century BC (though a possible example of the Greek script of the early 8th century BC is claimed at Osteria dell'Osa to the east of Rome). Nor has Moses Finley's argument that the Homeric epics reflect the social conditions of the 10th and 9th centuries BC met with much scholarly consensus. Nevertheless, while recent decades of archaeological exploration have certainly served to illuminate our knowledge of the Dark Age and to trace certain low-level continuities throughout these centuries that should urge caution against too rigid a periodization, it is still the case that our increased understanding of this period ultimately confirms that settlement patterns, interactions between communities, religious behaviour, and artistic and technological traditions were indeed somewhat different from the situations that had existed earlier and were to exist subsequently.

The collapse of the Mycenaean palaces seems to have instigated certain population movements, revealed by the occupation of new areas such as eastern Attica, Lefkandi on Euboea, Emborio on Chios, Ialysus on Rhodes, Cyprus, and the north Aegean. Yet many of these sites were short-lived and by the first half of the 11th century BC the number of known settlements in Greece is less than half the 220 sites attested for the period 1200–1150 BC. This may indicate overall demographic decline but there is also the possibility that new sites were occupied on a more temporary or seasonal basis (thus potentially escaping archaeological retrieval) and it is often suggested that instability and insecurity were both the cause and effect of a shift from sedentary agricultural practices to a more pastoral lifestyle. From the 10th century BC the number of known sites begins to rise again but it is not until the 8th century BC that a sharp increase in site numbers and evident signs of urban nucleation signal a return to more settled conditions – a phenomenon that may have been triggered by, but would certainly help to foster, demographic growth.

The communities of this period were also far more isolated than had been the case earlier when the Mycenaean cultural koine had embraced much of the Mediterranean and the Near East littoral; one apparent indication of this new isolation is the increasing regionalization of pottery styles. Nevertheless, not all contacts were severed entirely: imported grave goods are still attested – albeit in smaller quantity – at sites in both central and southern Greece, while the diffusion of iron metallurgy should suggest some continued contact with the east – almost certainly with Cyprus as an intermediary. Crete in particular maintained links with Cyprus and possibly even Italy and Sicily. One of the most important "type-sites" for the period is Lefkandi on the island of Euboea where, from the 1960s onwards, excavations have brought to light part of the settlement (whose ancient name is unknown) and its cemeteries. The mid-11th-century BC tombs at Lefkandi contained artefacts from Cyprus and the Levant, though there followed a period of apparent isolation until the middle of the 10th century BC, when an imposing peripteral building, constructed from timber and mudbrick and erected over a "princely" burial, testifies to the emergence of a hierarchy within this newly prosperous (but still fairly small) community. Immediately afterwards the building was surrounded by a number of elite burials whose grave goods indicate renewed contacts with Athens, Thessaly, Macedonia, Cyprus, and the Near East. It is fair to say, however, that Lefkandi is very much the exception to the rule: at other Greek sites it is generally not until the 9th and 8th centuries BC that more distant links are resumed as a prelude to the colonization of the west.

While the appearance of many recognizably Greek divinities in the Linear B tablets points to some continuity in religious traditions, archaeological evidence that might suggest a continuity in ritual behaviour is more elusive. A few sites certainly attest a continuity of cultic enactment from the late Mycenaean period throughout the Dark Age (Kalapodi in Phocis, Kato Syme Viannou on Crete, and possibly the Polis Cave on Ithaca), and several sanctuaries were already functioning by the 10th century BC (Munychia, Brauron, and Mount Hymettus in Attica; Olympia and Kombothekra in Elis; Amyclae in Laconia; the Heraion on Samos; Tegea in Arcadia; and Isthmia in Corinthia), but there is little or no evidence for cultic activity much before the 8th century BC at some of the more famous sanctuaries of the historical period, such as Eleusis, Delos, and Delphi, and this is also the period that witnesses the earliest cultic buildings, even in sanctuaries that had been functioning for several centuries.

Finally, the period witnesses the disappearance of certain technological and artistic traditions such as ivory working, figured pictorial representations on pottery, and monumental stone architecture. It is the apparently seamless resumption of these techniques from the 9th and 8th centuries BC onwards that has suggested to some scholars that the Dark Age is nothing other than a scholarly mirage, produced as a result of synchronizing the Mycenaean ceramic sequence with faulty Egyptian dates; it has been argued that a recalibration of the Egyptian sequence yields a destruction date for the Mycenaean palaces of 950 BC rather than 1200 BC, thus halving the five-century "gap" that troubled earlier scholars. The thesis has little to recommend it, though it provides a salutary reminder as to the fragility of pottery chronology in the ancient Mediterranean and Near East.

JONATHAN M. HALL

See also Political History to 490 BC

Summary
The period from the destruction of the Mycenaean palaces c.1200 BC to the emergence of the polis as a state form c.700 BC. Archaeological evidence of settled communities and cultic activity is slight before the 8th century BC. Traditions of ivory working, figured decoration on pottery, and monumental stone architecture disappeared. Type-sites such as Lefkandi testify to the isolation of the society.

Further Reading
Coldstream, J.N., *Geometric Greece*, London: Benn, and New York: St Martin's Press, 1977

Desborough, V.R. d'A, *The Greek Dark Ages*, London: Benn, and New York: St Martin's Press, 1972

Hurwit, Jeffrey M., *The Art and Culture of Early Greece, 1100–480 BC*, Ithaca, New York: Cornell University Press, 1985

James, Peter *et al.*, *Centuries of Darkness: A Challenge to the Conventional Chronology of Old World Archaeology*, London: Jonathan Cape, 1991

Morris, Ian, "Periodization and the Heroes: Inventing a Dark Age" in *Inventing Ancient Culture: Historicism, Periodization, and the Ancient World*, edited by Mark Golden and Peter Toohey, London and New York: Routledge, 1997

Osborne, Robin, *Greece in the Making, 1200–479 BC*, London and New York: Routledge, 1996

Polignac, François de, *Cults, Territory and the Origins of the Greek City-State*, Chicago: University of Chicago Press, 1995

Snodgrass, Anthony M., *The Dark Age of Greece: An Archaeological Survey of the Eleventh to the Eighth Centuries BC*, Edinburgh: Edinburgh University Press, 1971

Snodgrass, Anthony M., *An Archaeology of Greece: The Present State and Future Scope of a Discipline*, Berkeley: University of California Press, 1987

Dead, Cult of the

Although Homer represents the dead in Hades as devoid of physical and mental power, and Hesiod credits the disembodied spirits of the golden race with being altruistically beneficent, the common Greek belief was that the behaviour of the dead was influenced by the conduct of the living. They behave beneficently when propitiated, but maleficently when neglected or spurned. Being capable of doing good or evil, they had to be gratified with pious attentions in order to induce them to do good. Accordingly, a ritually correct burial or cremation, costly grave gifts, and periodical offerings of food and drink were vital elements in the tendance of the dead.

The history of the Greek cult of the dead is to some extent related to the prevalence of the two chief modes of disposal, namely cremation and inhumation, although they do not reflect different eschatalogical beliefs. Whatever the method of disposal, it was essential to cover the body with earth, and three handfuls were sufficient to fulfil the requirements for a ceremonial burial. Thus in Sophocles' *Antigone* (255–56) the heroine scatters a thin coating of dust over Polynices. This covering cut the dead off from the sight of the heavenly gods, to prevent them from being offended and their altars polluted (cf. Sophocles, *Ajax*, 589, *Antigone*, 1716f.). It was also an act of kindness to the departed, because they could not enter the underworld unless their mortal remains were buried (Homer, *Iliad*, 23. 71ff.). To grant burial to a dead person, be he friend or enemy, was therefore universally recognized as a pious act. However, burial was denied to executed criminals, traitors, and occasionally to suicides.

When the body had been bathed, it was dressed in clothes such as the deceased might have worn in life, and laid on a couch (*prothesis*). Laments were made by the relatives and others present, and moderation in this respect (as well as in the elaborateness of funeral pyres and the amount of grave goods buried or burned with the body) was recommended, and sometimes required by law. Finally, the body was carried to the place of burial or cremation accompanied by a crowd of mourners (*ekphora*). Only the *prothesis* and *ekphora* are depicted on geometric vases, but the Athenian white-ground lekythoi frequently depict tomb cults. In the case of cremation, the ashes were placed in a vessel whose shape, size, and material varied according to place, time, and circumstances. Coffins were normally used for burials, while elaborately carved sarcophagi became fashionable among the well-to-do in later times. It was customary to hold a funeral even in the absence of a body, and dummies may have been used occasionally. Family rituals for the dead were held at the tomb not only after the burial, but also at intervals thereafter.

Although Minoan and Mycenaean tombs show variations in size, elaboration, and the number and value of their grave offerings, we know little or nothing of their funerals. Homer describes elaborate funeral ceremonies, such as those in honour of Patroclus in *Iliad* 23. The funeral was followed by elaborate games in which every contestant received a prize of some sort. Some of these were the property of the dead person, and it has been suggested that the prizes may represent a compromise between burning all the dead man's goods with him and allowing them to be inherited. During the Archaic period the funeral became an occasion to display aristocratic wealth, power, and prestige, and laws were passed to limit extravagance.

Greek literature frequently refers to the need for burial rites and the insult to human dignity if they are omitted. Though the dead themselves had no power, they had access to infernal powers, notably Hades and Persephone. Accordingly, *katadesmoi* or folded lead plaques inscribed with curses bearing the name of the person to be "bound down" were occasionally placed in graves. The dead person's journey to the next world was effected by elaborate ritual conducted by relatives, primarily women. Priests were not allowed at funerals for fear of incurring pollution, and there was no "burial service" as such. No tomb cult was practised in early times, but in Classical Athens women paid regular visits to the grave. Offerings included cakes and libations, mainly of pure water. Aeschylus has dramatized such visits in the *Choephori* and the *Persians*, but with differences of time and place. It was considered so important at this time for the dead to receive the attention of the living that it constituted a reason for adopting an heir (Isaeus, 2. 36. 7, 30).

From Classical times we have descriptions of magnificent public funerals (complete with orations honouring the dead), especially those given at Athens to citizens killed in war (Diodorus Siculus, 11. 33. 3; Thucydides, 2. 34). Their magnificence is matched by the sculptured gravestones of Classical Athens with their restrained expression of grief. The dead are often depicted performing some familiar act for the last time. The brief inscriptions usually record only the name and parentage, and sometimes the word "farewell" is added. Those who died unmarried at marriageable age received special sympathy, their pathos being underlined by a stone grave marker in the form of a *loutrophoros* or vase used in the nuptial bath. According to Plutarch (*Aristides*, 21), the heroic dead were so powerful that even in his own day (*c*.AD 46–*c*.120) they received blood sacrifice. Those who visited a funeral underwent some defilement, so water from another house was provided on leaving for cleansing: see Hesiod's advice not to make love on returning from funerals. Cypress branches were fixed to the door to indicate a death within.

Sacrificial offerings were made to the dead from the time of the burial and at the grave. Solon expressly forbade sacrifice of oxen at the grave. Burial was followed by a funeral feast. The soul of the dead man was thought to be present, even to be the host. On the third and ninth days after the funeral, meals were given to the dead man at his grave; the ninth day ended the period of mourning (in Sparta the eleventh). On the fifth day of the month of Boedromion a general *genesia* (birthday) was held by the entire Athenian public for their dead relatives; we also hear of a feast called *nemesia* probably to avert their anger.

At Athens the chief festival was held at the close of the Dionysiac feast of the Anthesteria, in spring, of which it formed the concluding day. On this day the dead swarmed back to the world. Each family made offerings to their own dead. Hermes, on behalf of the dead, was offered cooked vegetables and seeds in pots (hence the name Chytrai). After the feast the souls were asked to leave.

We learn from Plato (*Republic*, 2. 365a) that during the 4th century BC there were many Greek manuals attributed to Orpheus, Musaeus, and other sages, full of mythology and formulas for initiations. They also contained instructions for calling up the dead for consultation, Hermes being the intermediary. Such formulas are also found in the magical papyri.

In spite of philosophical discussions on reincarnation and the transmigration of the soul, it is strange that such views have left hardly any trace on Greek tomb inscriptions: there are no prayers for a better life at the next birth or for a safe return to old haunts. The doctrines of the religious and philosophical teachers in this regard apparently had little influence on the life and thought of the common people.

Quite different was the case of the Christian teaching of a purgation of the dead, as borne out by Paul's discovery that at Corinth some Christians were undergoing a second baptism on behalf of dead relatives (1 Corinthians 15:29). Similarly, Byzantine Christians, believing in the power of the living to influence, through prayers and intercessions, the destiny of the souls of the departed, made lavish donations to churches and monasteries in order to guarantee the proper commemoration of their dead relatives.

Death was viewed by both Christians and Neoplatonists as a liberation from captivity. Nevertheless, both laid greater emphasis on the positive aspect of death as the beginning of a new life. Loud and excessive mourning over the dead was therefore criticized by theologians such as Basil the Great and John Chrysostom, while some radical monastic circles even objected to a special burial service.

Christianity transformed in a special way the rites of the funeral liturgy and certain representations of the hereafter that derived from pre-Christian customs and beliefs. Among the beliefs thus taken over and transformed by the Church Fathers were the soul's journey after death escorted by the *psychopompoi*, a role now ascribed to the angels; Charon's ferry, whose role is now taken by the Church – the ship of souls; the *ephodion* or sustenance for the journey, now provided by the Eucharist or "Holy Viaticum". This last concept is sometimes given a wider meaning to include faith, baptism, or the monastic life. Meanwhile, the traditional funeral meal conducted by relatives at the tomb of the deceased gave rise to the custom of distributing *kollyva* (small round cakes). This practice was unanimously opposed by the Western Church as a pagan superstition, but it survived in the Byzantine Church. The 3rd, 7th (or 9th), and 30th (or 40th) days after death were specially commemorated by the distribution of *kollyva* and the offering of liturgical prayers, which were thought to accompany the dead person on his or her journey, these dates being regarded as marking important stations on the soul's journey either to the final vision of, or banishment from, God. The dead were also commemorated on the anniversary of their death and on the Saturday before Meatfare Sunday.

D.P.M. WEERAKKODY

See also Afterlife, Burial Practices, Death

Further Reading

Abrahamse, D., "Rituals of Death in the Middle Byzantine Period", *Greek Orthodox Theological Review*, 29 (1984): pp. 125–34

Alexiou, Margaret, *The Ritual Lament in Greek Tradition*, Cambridge: Cambridge University Press, 1974

Antonaccio, Carla M., *An Archaeology of Ancestors: Tomb Cult and Hero Cult in Early Greece*, Lanham, Maryland: Rowman and Littlefield, 1995

Fedak, Janos, *Monumental Tombs of the Hellenistic Age: A Study of Selected Tombs from the Pre-Classical to the Early Imperial Era*, Toronto: University of Toronto Press, 1990

Fedwick, P.J., "Death and Dying in Byzantine Liturgical Tradition", *Eastern Churches Review*, 8 (1976): pp. 152–61

Garland, Robert, *The Greek Way of Death*, London: Duckworth, and Ithaca, New York: Cornell University Press, 1985

Humphreys, S.C. and Helen King (editors), *Mortality and Immortality: The Anthropology and Archaeology of Death*, London and New York: Academic Press, 1981

Kurtz, Donna C. and John Boardman, *Greek Burial Customs*, London: Thames and Hudson, and Ithaca, New York: Cornell University Press, 1971

Morris, Ian, *Death-Ritual and Social Structure in Classical Antiquity*, Cambridge and New York: Cambridge University Press, 1992

Rohde, Erwin, *Psyche: The Cult of Souls and Belief in Immortality among the Greeks*, translated by W.B. Hillis, London: Kegan Paul Trench Trubner, and New York: Harcourt Brace, 1925 (German edition, 1894)

Sourvinou-Inwood, Christiane, *"Reading" Greek Death: To the End of the Classical Period*, Oxford: Clarendon Press, and New York: Oxford University Press, 1995

Vermeule, Emily, *Aspects of Death in Early Greek Art and Poetry*, Berkeley: University of California Press, 1979

Walter, C., "Death in Byzantine Iconography", *Eastern Churches Review*, 8 (1976): pp. 113–27

Death

In ancient Greece death was an everyday occurrence, being prevalent among people of all age groups whether as a result of disease, accident, childbirth, or warfare. Furthermore, it was a far more immediate aspect of the life of the community than is the case in many modern societies. Since there were no hospitals, most deaths occurred either at home or on the battlefield. If death occurred at home, it was the duty of the relatives of the deceased to prepare the body for burial, transport it to the burial ground, and lay it in the earth. Since funerals provided an opportunity for the display of wealth and prestige, many communities, including that of Athens, introduced legislation designed to limit their scale and magnificence.

The most striking evidence of burial practices in Bronze Age Greece is provided by the so-called shaft graves at Mycenae. These graves, dated to the 16th century BC, are cut into the living rock to a depth of several metres. They have yielded some of the richest finds ever discovered on the mainland. In the 15th century a different style of burial developed, in the form of beehive tombs, so named because of their domed appearance. Recent excavations at Lefkandi on Euboea dating to the 10th century BC have yielded evidence of the ritual slaughter of a young woman and four horses on behalf of a warrior, presumably so that they could accompany the warrior to the underworld.

In Homer death is characteristically described in terms of the departure of the psyche "lamenting its fate", from either the mouth or a gaping wound. However, it is worth noting that, of the 240 deaths in the *Iliad*, only four are described in this way. The psyche is, moreover, a biologically indistinct entity which is rarely referred to except at the moment of death. No other Greek writer gives any explanation as to why the human organism dies, except for Aristotle, who claimed that it was caused by loss of vital heat. Mythologically the idea of a painless death was epitomized by the gentle arrows of silver-bowed Apollo.

Because a corpse was believed to be highly polluting, relatives were required to take elaborate precautions to prevent the pollution from seeping out of the house and into the community. Solon legislated that only close family members and women over the age of 60 were permitted to enter the house of the dead and take part in the funeral. In order to contain the pollution, a bowl of water was placed outside the house so that visitors could purify themselves, and flasks containing olive oil were placed around the couch on which the dead was laid out. In addition, a cypress branch was hung on the door to warn passers-by of the presence of contagion within.

Death was handled almost exclusively by the relatives of the deceased, who were under a sacred obligation to ease transition "from here to there", as the Greeks phrased it. Though there are occasional references to undertakers in ancient sources, their duties were confined to transporting the corpse from the house to the grave and preparing the ground for burial. It is a reasonable assumption that the Greeks would have regarded the idea of handing over the corpse of a dead relative to strangers as both incomprehensible and inexcusable. This had much to do with the belief that in the period between death and burial the deceased was in a dangerous liminal condition and needed help from his or her relatives in order to secure entry to Hades.

Greek culture not only tolerated but expected extravagant manifestations of grief. Both men and women tore out their hair, rent their garments, beat and lacerated their breasts, and rolled on the ground in the dust. In part this behaviour was prompted by the belief that the deceased took pleasure in witnessing the exaggerated displays of grief that their death occasioned.

As soon as death occurred, the corpse would be prepared for the *prothesis*, or "laying out", which took place in the house where the deceased lived. First, the eyes and mouth were closed. Female relatives washed the corpse, anointed it with olive oil, clothed it, and then wrapped it in a winding sheet. Finally they laid it out on a couch with the head on a pillow and the feet facing the door. Visitors then came to view the body and dirges were sung in its presence. On the day of the funeral the bereaved accompanied the corpse to the burial site. If the family could afford it, it would be placed in a simple wooden coffin, though owing to the scarcity of wood it might only be covered with a few branches. The corpse was either borne by pall-bearers or transported in a cart.

Little is known about what took place at the burial service itself, other than the fact that ritualized laments were delivered. Though both inhumation and cremation were practised with varying degrees of popularity in antiquity, cremation was generally regarded as more prestigious, in part because this is how the bodies of Homeric heroes were disposed of. (The most detailed description of a cremation burial is that of Patroclus in Homer's *Iliad*, book 23.) After cremation the ashes were placed in an urn, which was then buried. Once the grave had been filled in, a grave marker was erected. The mourners then returned to the house of the deceased for a commemorative meal. Lastly, the house was ritually purified. Inscriptions from various parts of the Greek world indicate that it was customary to debar relatives from participating in the life of the community for several weeks.

The Greeks did not have cemeteries as such. Those who dwelt in rural areas buried their dead on their estates, whereas city dwellers buried them beside major roads. From around 500 BC the practice of burial within the city of Athens abruptly ceased, perhaps due to a law introduced by the politician Cleisthenes. The ban was no doubt connected primarily with the fear of pollution, but it may also have been due in part to the need to conserve as much residential space as possible. The busiest roads henceforth provided the most popular burial spots for wealthy families, as is indicated by the large number of tombs outside the Dipylon and Sacred Gates on the west side of the city in the neighbourhood known as the Ceramicus, or potters' quarter. In the final decades of the 5th century BC family plots became extremely popular among the wealthy. These were large rectangular spaces walled along the front and at the sides, access being gained from the rear. The popularity of this style of burial may be connected with the belief that members of the family could be reunited in the hereafter if they were buried together.

In Classical Athens concern for the well-being of the dead did not cease after burial. On the contrary, relatives continued to maintain a close attachment to the deceased long after death had occurred, since their welfare in Hades was believed to be dependent upon the attention they received from the living. The anniversary of the day of death was especially important. The dead were believed either to dwell close to the grave or at least to be capable of visiting it when summoned. For this reason a variety of gifts were deposited on the steps of the tomb, including jars of olive oil, myrtle branches, wreaths, cakes, and wine. In addition, the gravestone was anointed with olive oil and coloured sashes were wound around it. In Classical Athens the care of the dead was considered to be so important that it constituted a reason for adopting an heir.

Festivals in honour of the dead were major features of the sacred calendar. One such was the second day of the Anthesteria festival, which was equivalent to All Souls' Day, since the dead were thought to leave Hades and wander abroad. Most spectacular of all was the annual ceremony in honour of the war dead, which took place in early winter at the end of the campaigning season. An account of the ceremony conducted on behalf of those who died in the first year of the Peloponnesian War was provided by Thucydides (2. 34ff.), who also included the speech delivered by Pericles on that occasion. Only the most courageous war dead were accorded the privilege of being interred on the field of battle. They included the 192 Athenians who fell at the battle of Marathon, around whom a cult was established. The most revered dead were heroes such as Theseus, Oedipus, and Orestes, who were believed to be capable of exerting considerable power within the vicinity of their graves. Their services could be invoked by animal sacrifice. A clay pipe was sometimes inserted into the grave to enable the blood to reach the hero directly. Other important categories of the dead who received special rites include those who had been murdered, suicides, and those struck by lightning.

The Greeks felt particular sympathy for those who died at a marriageable age but who were unmarried. To underline their sad plight, a stone marker in the form of a *loutrophoros*, the vase used for the nuptial bath, was placed over the grave. Generally, however, Greek funerary art is remarkably reserved in its depiction of death and all sentimentality is eschewed. Sculpture depicts the deceased in a domestic setting in the company of family members. A particularly common image is that of two people, either standing or seated, shaking hands. In such cases it is usually impossible to discern which is the deceased and which the living, and we are left wondering whether the handshake is one of farewell between the living and the dead or one of greeting between the newly arrived in the underworld and those less recently arrived.

By definition death separates the world of mortals from that of the gods. Though the Olympian deities occasionally mourn the passing of a favourite, for the most part they are indifferent to human loss. Their removal from the physiology of death was due to the fact that proximity to the dying and the dead exposed them to risk of pollution caused by death. As Artemis observes in Euripides' *Hippolytus* (1437f.), it is not permitted by divine law for a deity "either to look at the dead or to sully their eyes with the expirations of the dying". For the same reason no priest or priestess was allowed to enter the house of the dead or attend a burial.

There are a number of parallels between modern and ancient Greece in regard to the treatment of death. Modern Greeks, like the ancients, tend to accept the physiological aspect of death as a natural fact of life. They are also much more likely to die in the comfort of their own beds than is the case in either Britain or the USA. When death is imminent the Orthodox priest performs the sacrament known as the Anointing of the Sick, or Unction. The belief still persists that the soul leaves the body through the mouth. Women continue to play the leading role in the care of the dead. A young woman who dies unmarried is sometimes buried wearing the bridal dress and crown that she was unable to wear in life. Fondling and kissing the corpse frequently occur, as they did at an ancient *prothesis*. Laments are sung by women both in the house of the deceased and at the graveside. Coins are placed in the coffin before it is lowered into the grave. On returning from the burial, those who have come into contact with the deceased are required to wash in order to purify themselves. *Kedeia*, the ancient Greek word for "funeral", which literally means "caring for", is still in regular use. The soul of the deceased is believed to linger on earth for 40 days before ascending to heaven.

The Greek Orthodox Church permits only inhumation, not cremation. The wealthy favour costly marble monuments to the dead. In addition, a glass case containing an oil lamp and a photograph of the deceased may be placed at the head. Periodic visits to the cemetery take place up to three years after burial. Close relatives of the dead remain in mourning throughout that period, observing dietary restrictions and wearing black, though a widow may wear black for the rest of her life, especially in rural areas. Partly for economic reasons, after three years have elapsed it is customary to exhume the dead and transfer the remains to the community ossuary, though the wealthy may elect to leave the dead in a family plot. By this time the flesh has usually disintegrated. Its failure to do so is sometimes interpreted as a sign that the deceased was evil. So ingrained is this belief that an extension is often granted in the case of those who underwent medical procedures, such as chemotherapy, that may delay the rate of decay.

ROBERT GARLAND

See also Afterlife, Burial Practices, Dead (Cult of the)

Further Reading
Alexiou, Margaret, *The Ritual Lament in Greek Tradition*, Cambridge: Cambridge University Press, 1974
Antonaccio, Carla M., *An Archaeology of Ancestors: Tomb Cult and Hero Cult in Early Greece*, Lanham, Maryland: Rowman and Littlefield, 1995
Danforth, Loring M., *The Death Rituals of Rural Greece*, Princeton, New Jersey: Princeton University Press, 1982
Garland, Robert, *The Greek Way of Death*, London: Duckworth, and Ithaca, New York: Cornell University Press, 1985
Morris, Ian, *Death-Ritual and Social Structure in Classical Antiquity*, Cambridge and New York: Cambridge University Press, 1992
Rohde, Erwin, *Psyche: The Cult of Souls and Belief in Immortality among the Greeks*, translated by W.B. Hillis, London: Kegan Paul Trench Trubner, and New York: Harcourt Brace, 1925 (German edition, 1894)
Sourvinou-Inwood, Christiane, *"Reading" Greek Death: To the End of the Classical Period*, Oxford: Clarendon Press, and New York: Oxford University Press, 1995
Vermeule, Emily, *Aspects of Death in Early Greek Art and Poetry*, Berkeley: University of California Press, 1979

Delian League

Major source of Athenian power in the 5th century BC

The Delian League, a modern name for what was originally called "the Athenians and their allies", was established in the winter of 478/77 BC and lasted until the defeat of Athens by Sparta in 404 BC. It arose from discontent with Spartan leadership of the Greek war effort against Persia in the aftermath of the great victories in 480–479 and, particularly, with the conduct of the regent Pausanias in 478. According to Thucydides, the non-Peloponnesian allies, and especially the Ionians and those recently freed from Persian rule, approached the Athenians to lead them and they decided to take advantage of the situation (1. 95. 1–2).

The Athenians quickly settled on the contributions to be paid by members of the new alliance, either ships fully equipped for a campaigning season or money in lieu of personal service (*phoros*, usually translated as "tribute"), and arranged for a council (*synodos*), at which each member had one vote, to meet at Delos, where the treasury was established. Alliances at this time usually had a specific duration, but here the allies threw lumps of iron into the sea to bind everyone, including the Athenians, for ever.

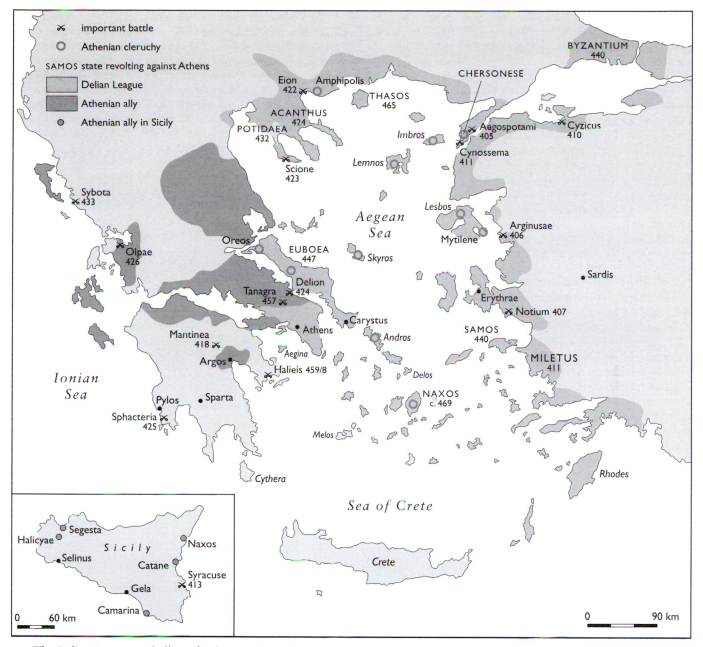

Legend:
- ✗ important battle
- ◯ Athenian cleruchy
- SAMOS state revolting against Athens
- ▨ Delian League
- ▨ Athenian ally
- ● Athenian ally in Sicily

17. The Delian League and allies of Athens, 460–446 BC

Several aspects of the alliance remain controversial, including its purpose, its extent, and the size of its revenues. Regarding its purpose, Thucydides says that the "pretext" (*proschema*) was to punish Persia for damage done (and to liberate any Greeks still enslaved: 1. 96. 1; cf. 3. 10. 3; 6. 76. 3); so this was not really a *symmachia*, an alliance whose members swore unconditionally to have the same friends and enemies (the word "pretext" may refer to later Athenian practice, when the league had become an Athenian empire and its resources were used for general Athenian purposes). As for its extent, there is no specific information about its membership at the beginning, though it seems likely that most non-Dorian islands of the Aegean plus coastal cities in northern Greece/Thrace, the Hellespontine area, Aeolia, and Ionia quickly joined; ultimately, there were over 200 members (cf.

the Athenian tribute lists for 447–446 BC). With regard to finance, Thucydides states that the "*original* tribute" was 460 talents (1. 96. 2), which implies subsequent adjustment; and indeed, in speaking of Athens' finances at the outbreak of the Peloponnesian War in 431 BC, he says that 600 talents of *phoros* came from the allies each year on average, exclusive of other revenue; there was also a reserve of 6000 talents, which had once been as large as 9700 talents. However, the detailed records of league monies entrusted to Athena for safekeeping after the transfer of the treasury from Delos to Athens (probably in late 454 BC) suggest that the revenues deposited in Athens rarely, if ever, exceeded 400 talents per annum in the period 454–426 BC. Various attempts to explain this seeming contradiction include failure to pay/late payment by the allies, reduction of the tribute after c.467, and error on Thucydides' part: none of these suggestions is satisfactory and probably the best that can be done with this problem is Unz's suggestion (1985) that the amounts deposited in Athens represent surpluses from fleet operations, costs of maintaining bases and garrisons, and possibly shipbuilding in allied yards, all of which items were paid for on the spot from local or district revenues.

It cannot be denied that the league fulfilled its initial purpose: Persian bases in the north Aegean area were captured, the Dorian cities of southwest Asia Minor were liberated, an apparent Persian invasion force was intercepted and smashed in battle near the mouth of the river Eurymedon in Pamphylia, expeditions were sent to Cyprus on at least two occasions, and there was a major attempt to detach Egypt from the Persian empire (459–454 BC), all of which resulted in either a formal peace ("the Peace of Callias") or an agreed informal cessation of hostilities in c.450–449 BC. At the same time, however, the Athenians saw and seized upon opportunities for their own benefit and power: certain states were forced to join the league, many were prevented from leaving, and those that fell foul of Athenian rigour in insisting on punctilious fulfilment of membership obligations found themselves reduced to the level of "subjects" through the imposition of separate, bilateral "agreements" between themselves and Athens. The results of this were often humiliating – surrender of warships, dismantling of fortifications, obligations to submit certain types of court case to Athens for final judgement, acceptance of garrisons and overseers, imposition of "democratic" constitutions, provision of troops over and above the payment of *phoros*, adherence to Athenian standards in weights and measures, enforced participation in Athenian religious festivals, and, finally, a requirement that all adult citizens swear various oaths proclaiming loyalty, goodwill, and even love towards Athens.

The conversion of an originally free and voluntary alliance into an Athenian *arche* (empire) was well under way by 450 BC, and after this empire had received formal acknowledgement in the Thirty Years' Peace (446/45 BC), the Athenians would refer to it as such, quite casually, and even argue that they had a perfect right to it. This attitude gave rise to increasingly severe punishments for rebellion, as in the case of Mytilene in 427 BC, outrages such as the destruction of Melos for refusing to accept Athenian control (416/15 BC), and the culminating *hubris* of the Sicilian expedition of 415–413 BC.

Throughout history, assessments of the significance of the Delian League have tended to be ambivalent. The radical democracy of the Periclean age owed much to the cash from the league, which made possible many of the benefits widely available to Athenians, while the stored-up surplus (see above) paid for the great building programme undertaken on the Acropolis after 450 BC. However, Pericles was criticized at the time for "decking out the city like some vain woman ... with thousand-talent temples" (Plutarch, *Pericles*, 12. 2; cf. the witty and sarcastic oligarchic pamphlet known as Pseudo-Xenophon, *Athenaion Politeia*), and although Athenian opinion in the 4th century regarded Periclean democracy as a class system whereby the "many" exploited and bullied the "few", there was, especially after the humiliating "King's Peace" of 387 BC, great pride in the power that Athens had wielded through the Delian League.

In modern times the period of the league has always been regarded as the "golden age" not only of Athens but of Classical Greece as a whole. However, even attitudes towards the league itself are still hotly debated: for example, in the 1950s and 1960s the question of whether or not the Athenian empire was "popular" among its subjects became an issue of Cold War rhetoric, with an English Marxist scholar arguing that it represented a liberation movement for oppressed masses in the various member states, while a US historian denied this with mutterings about "these days of 'People's Democracy'". Though this debate was conducted in somewhat simplistic terms, deeper consideration of the reality of the Delian League serves to remind us of two important truths: first, when Pericles describes the Athenian empire as a "tyranny" and when Cleon echoes this and describes its subjects as "disaffected conspirators", these are *politicians* attempting to persuade people to do something which they would not normally wish to do: politicians do not always tell the truth; second, given the polarization of Greece in the 5th century BC between Athens and Sparta, the average small state, although possessed of a typical Greek love of autonomy, was faced with a disagreeable choice: it is possible to *prefer* one of two options without particularly *liking* either of them (cf. the thoughts of Phrynichus described by Thucydides at 8. 48. 5–6).

CHARLES L. MURISON

See also Imperialism, Political History 490–318 BC

Summary

The Delian League is the modern name for the alliance that the Athenians established in 478/77 BC. Originally intended to punish Persia for damage done in the recent wars, it became the chief source of Athenian power in the 5th century BC. Its members numbered more than 200. The treasury was moved from Delos to Athens probably in 454 BC. By 450 the league had turned from a voluntary alliance into an Athenian empire. It lasted until the defeat of Athens by Sparta in 404 BC.

Further Reading

Bradeen, D.W., "The Popularity of the Athenian Empire", *Historia*, 9 (1960): pp. 257–69

Fornara, Charles W., *Archaic Times to the End of the Peloponnesian War*, 2nd edition, Cambridge and New York: Cambridge University Press, 1983 (*Translated Documents of Greece and Rome*, vol. 1)

Gomme, A.W., Antony Andrewes, and K.J. Dover, *A Historical Commentary on Thucydides*, 5 vols, Oxford: Clarendon Press, 1945–81

Hornblower, Simon, *A Commentary on Thucydides*, Oxford: Clarendon Press, 1991– (vol. 1: books 1–3; vol. 2: books 4–5.24)

Lewis, D.M. *et al.* (editors), *The Fifth Century BC*, Cambridge: Cambridge University Press, 1992 (*The Cambridge Ancient History*, vol. 5, 2nd edition): see especially the chapters by P.J. Rhodes, D.M. Lewis and A. Andrewes

Meiggs, Russell, *The Athenian Empire*, Oxford: Clarendon Press, 1972

Meritt, B.D., H.T. Wade-Gery, and M.F. McGregor, *The Athenian Tribute Lists*, vol. 3, Princeton, New Jersey: Princeton University Press, 1950

Raaflaub, K., "Beute, Vergeltung, Freiheit? Zur Zielsetzung des Delisch-Attischen Seebundes", *Chiron*, 9 (1979): pp. 1–22

de Ste Croix, G.E.M., "The Character of the Athenian Empire", *Historia*, 3 (1954–55): pp. 1–41

Thucydides, *The Peloponnesian War*, translated by Steven Lattimore, Indianapolis: Hackett, 1998

Unz, R.H., "The Surplus of the Athenian *Phoros*", *Greek, Roman and Byzantine Studies*, 26 (1985): pp. 21–42

Deliyannis, Theodoros 1826–1905

Statesman and prime minister of Greece

Theodorus Deliyannis was the son of Panagos Papayannopoulos, scion of a family of notables from Langadia in the Peloponnese who had made their fortune during the last five decades of Ottoman rule in Greek lands and who had become leaders in the War of Independence. It was during these years that the family name was changed to Deliyannis.

After studying law at Athens University Theodoros Deliyannis entered the civil service and in 1859 became general secretary of the ministry of the interior. During these years as a civil servant he acquired an expertise in the running of government, which distinguished him from other contemporary Greek statesmen.

Deliyannis first became involved in politics as representative of Gortynia, his constituency, in the Second National Constitutional Assembly in 1862 which followed the overthrow of King Otho. His first ministerial post was that of foreign minister in the Roufos cabinet (1863) and the Kanaris cabinet (1864). Between 1867 and 1868 he served as Greek ambassador in Paris and brought about Greek participation in the 1867 international exposition there.

On his return to Greece he resumed his ministerial career at the foreign ministry and the finance ministry in the shortlived cabinets of Thrasyvoulos Zaimis that were so characteristic of the first years of King George's reign. His cabinet positions, and his cultivation of the patronage networks that were already in place through his family's long-standing influence, permitted him to strengthen his political leverage with his constituents. Supported by a small group of deputies, Deliyannis was therefore able to maintain a relatively independent attitude towards all the other party leaders.

His political importance was acknowledged in 1877 during the crisis which developed into the Russo-Turkish War. Deliyannis was invited to join the all-party cabinet under admiral Constantine Kanaris as minister for education. Alexandros Koumoundouros then chose Deliyannis as his foreign minister in his cabinet of January 1878 and appointed him Greek delegate to the Congress of Berlin to present Greek national claims. After 1880 Deliyannis openly opposed Koumoundouros, accusing him of a conciliatory attitude towards the Great Powers on the issue of the future annexation of new lands.

After Koumoundouros' death in March 1883, Deliyannis became leader of the parliamentary opposition and by the end of the year had given unity to its diverse forces. By targeting his rhetoric on attacks against the policies of Charilaos Trikoupis, and by promising the electorate to undo Trikoupis' reforms, Deliyannis won the elections of April 1885 and became prime minister.

In his first term Deliyannis accomplished very little as his party was divided on financial issues and was soon faced with an international crisis. The annexation of eastern Rumelia by Bulgaria in 1885 was once again destabilizing the Balkans. Impatience for the fortune of Greek claims to Macedonia created tensions within Greece. The government mobilized the army but the Great Powers, fearing a Greek attack on the Ottoman empire, blockaded Greek ports to force the government to demobilize. Deliyannis was compelled to resign in May 1886.

He returned to office in November 1890, having won election on an anti-Trikoupis programme. His financial policies, however, created tension with the country's foreign creditors and with king George, who dismissed his cabinet in March 1892 amid antiroyalist popular protests; but Deliyannis returned three years later after defeating Trikoupis at the 1895 elections, which marked the end of Trikoupis's career. In December 1893, however, Greece had defaulted and its creditors were pressing for a settlement of its international debt that would permit them to control public revenue earmarked to service the loans. Both Trikoupis and Deliyannis resisted these pressures as restrictions upon national sovereignty. Finally Greece was forced to yield after its defeat in the Graeco-Turkish War of 1897, a war which had been forced upon Deliyannis's weak government by public nationalist excitement. In April 1897 Deliyannis was once more forced to resign. Deliyannis became prime minister on two further occasions, in December 1902 and December 1904. He was assassinated in June 1905 by the owner of a gambling club as a result of the legislation against gambling that he had put into effect.

Deliyannis's policies favoured financial retrenchment and distribution of patronage through government appointments. He also paid special attention to educational reform and to the economic hardships of the landless tenant farmers of Thessaly. Unlike his opponent Trikoupis, Deliyannis was conservative in his estimates of Greece's capability for rapid economic development. He was furthermore unwilling to encourage Greek and European bankers in search for capital to stimulate material development. He expressed his political views through *Proia*, his party newspaper. His party was kept together in opposition by patriotic, populist, and, at times, anti-western rhetoric but when in power proved incapable of implementing a consistent policy. His inability to withstand pressures from within his own party and from public opinion seriously impaired his international standing. These shortcomings contributed to the demise of the Greek two-party system, which had emerged in the 1880s and 1890s.

KATERINA GARDIKAS

See also Political History since 1832

Biography

Born in 1826 to a Peloponnesian family, Deliyannis studied law at the University of Athens. He first entered parliament as deputy for Gortynia in 1862–64. In 1867–68 he was ambassador to Paris and in 1878 he led the Greek delegation to the Congress of Berlin. He was prime minister of Greece in 1885–87, 1890–92, 1895–97, 1902–03, and 1904–05. He was assassinated in 1905.

Further Reading

Clogg, Richard, *A Concise History of Greece*, Cambridge and New York: Cambridge University Press, 1992

Levandis, John Alexander, *The Greek Foreign Debt and the Great Powers, 1821–98*, New York: Columbia University Press, 1944

Tatsios, Theodore George, *The Megali Idea and the Greek–Turkish War of 1897: The Impact of the Cretan Problem on Greek Irredentism, 1866–97*, New York: Columbia University Press, 1984

Woodhouse, C.M., *Modern Greece: A Short History*, 5th edition, London: Faber, 1991

Delos

Aegean island

Delos is a small island, surrounded by a circle of larger islands known collectively as the Cyclades. It is largely waterless and with little agricultural land. Its importance in antiquity therefore derived primarily from its religious significance, as one of the principal and international sanctuaries of Apollo. Greek mythology related that when Leto, pregnant by Zeus, was about to give birth, no place would receive her in case it incurred the wrath of Hera. Delos, which was then an unfixed, floating island, was the exception, and sheltered Leto, who gave birth there to Artemis and Apollo. In gratitude, Apollo fixed the island in its present location. Like most myths, this is a preposterous story, but there is no clear material reason why the island should have assumed its sacred character.

Evidence for activity on Delos dates at least as far back as the Late Bronze Age. Mycenaean remains, traces of walls and deposits of objects including figurines have been found in the area of the later Classical sanctuary. A revival or redevelopment of the island came with the general reawakening of the Greek world in the 8th century BC, and as a result of interest from the surrounding Cyclades. Particularly significant was the island of Naxos. By the end of the 7th century the Naxians had built a simple rectangular structure, its ridge supported eventually by a single row of thin marble columns, and later referred to as their Oikos, or house; it is very likely that this was in fact the first temple dedicated to Apollo. The marble for the columns was quarried on Naxos and shipped to Delos. Also of Naxian marble, and very spectacular, was a colossal statue of Apollo erected around 600 BC at the side of the Oikos. Only fragments survive, but they give an indication of the statue's original size. It stood on a single enormous block of marble, *c*.5 × 3 × 0.82 m, estimated to weigh about 32 tonnes; the statue itself was about four times life size, and therefore larger than the colossal statue in the sanctuary of Hera at Samos (much better preserved), which is about three times natural size. The Apollo statue copies the pose of the colossal statues of Egypt but, unlike them and like the Samian statue, was probably nude.

Towards the end of the 6th century Naxian influence waned, and eventually Delos came to be dominated by Athens, a domination that was to endure, with intervals of independence, for much of the island's history. During this first period a limestone temple was dedicated to Apollo; the building technique is similar to that of Athenian buildings. Delos was treated with respect by the Persians, with the intention of securing the sympathy of the Greek states, but after the defeat of Xerxes in 479 BC Delos became instead, under the protection of Apollo, the centre of the Delian League dominated by Athens with the purpose of keeping the Persians out of the Aegean and liberating the east Greek cities. Twenty years later, with the renewal of the Persian threat, the treasury and control of the league were transferred to Athens. The festival of Apollo continued and was of great significance still to the Athenians, who would dispatch each year one of the state triremes, the oared warships which had won the battle of Salamis. In 426 BC the Athenians went even further. Concerned that the plague which had decimated the population of Athens indicated that they had incurred the wrath of Apollo, the god of healing, the Athenians "purified" the island. Because of its sacred character laws prohibited birth and death on the island: pregnant women, and all those about to die, had to leave for the neighbouring island of Rheneia. Despite this there were many graves there (many perhaps dating to the prehistoric period). These were cleared and the contents shipped to Rheneia. The Athenians also built a new, marble temple to Apollo, in the Doric order: uniquely, it shows in its design the influence of the Parthenon.

By this time the island certainly had its own resident population, though as yet there is little archaeological evidence of the settlement they inhabited. With the defeat of Athens in the Peloponnesian War they attempted to reassert their independence, only to have the Athenians return in 394 BC. It was not until 80 years later, in the very changed world that followed the Macedonian conquest and the confusion that resulted from the break-up of Alexander's empire, that Delos became independent. All the same, it was used by the various successors of Alexander, particularly Ptolemy I and then Antigonus Gonatas, as the centre for their own island leagues by which they hoped to control the Aegean. This domination also meant patronage. The kings founded festivals (in their own honour, as much as Apollo's); they also had buildings constructed in and around the sanctuary, particularly porticoes (stoas). Most intriguing is a long narrow building east of the temples, the so-called Monument of the Bulls, because of the bulls' heads that rise above two internal half-columns. It was probably the Neorion, a ship shed in which one of the Hellenistic kings – almost certainly an Antigonid since these kings used the bulls' head motif elsewhere as in the Stoa of Antigonus – dedicated a ship in consequence of a naval victory; either Demetrius Poliorcetes, after the crucial battle of Cypriot Salamis in 306 BC, or his son Antigonus Gonatas, after the battle of Cos in the mid-3rd century BC.

In many ways the heyday of the island was in the 2nd century BC, particularly the years after the final Roman defeat and dismemberment of the Macedonian kingdom. The Romans restored the island to Athenian control, but this was a much weakened Athens, and the reality was Roman domination under a suitable disguise. Delos was declared a free port, and as such seriously interfered with Rhodian trade when that island, an erstwhile loyal supporter of Rome, displeased the Romans through half-hearted support in the war against Macedon. The island received an influx of Roman and Italian settlers, along with traders from other places, such as Berytus (modern Beirut). Under the settlers and the Greek inhabitants the area of the town increased considerably, with many luxurious houses, typically with splendid (though later robbed)

Delos: view of the sanctuary of Apollo, focus of political institutions as well as religious activity on the island

mosaic floors, marble columns round courtyards (beneath which were deep storage cisterns to alleviate the perennial water shortage), and walls built of local stone which were plastered and decorated with elaborate painted designs. Trade was vigorous; Delos, despite its religious significance, was an important place for the sale of slaves, many derived from the hinterland of Anatolia.

In the disintegrating political conditions of the 1st century BC, after the kingdom of Pergamum was bequeathed by its last king to the Romans, piratical raids from the harbours of southern Anatolia grew in intensity. Delos, a small island with no defensive system, was particularly vulnerable. In 88 BC it was seized by the troops of Mithridates king of Pontus in his war against the Romans, and pillaged. The destruction was completed by his allies, the pirates of Athenodorus, in 69 BC. Even the special centre sections of the mosaic floors were removed, and the town abandoned.

Thereafter, though the island continued to function religiously, activity was on a small scale. There are indications of a Christian population in the 3rd century AD, but the island was finally sacked in the 8th century AD, and then awaited its rediscovery by western scholars, beginning with Cyriac of Ancona who visited the island in 1445.

R.A. TOMLINSON

See also Delian League

Summary

An island in the Cyclades, Delos is traditionally the birthplace of Apollo and Artemis. After the Persian Wars Delos became the centre of the Delian League, which was dominated by Athens and designed to protect Greece from further Persian aggression. Independent from 314 BC, the island prospered especially in the 2nd century BC as a free port and centre of trade. Sacked in 88 BC by soldiers of Mithridates and in 69 BC by pirates, it never regained its prosperity.

Further Reading

Bruneau, Philippe and Jean Ducat, *Guide de Délos*, 3rd edition, Paris: Boccard, 1983
Ecole Français d'Athènes, *Exploration archéologique de Délos*, Paris: Fontemoing, 1909–
Laidlaw, William Allison, *A History of Delos*, Oxford: Blackwell, 1933 (out of date, but the only account in English)
Rauh, Nicholas K., *The Sacred Bonds of Commerce: Religion, Economy and Trade Society at Hellenistic Roman Delos, 166–87 BC*, Amsterdam: Gieben, 1993
Reger, Gary, *Regionalism and Change in the Economy of Independent Delos, 314–167 BC*, Berkeley: University of California Press, 1994

Delphi

Ancient sanctuary of Apollo in central Greece

Delphi was the principal sanctuary of Apollo on the Greek mainland, situated on a shelf of land on the southern slopes of Mount Parnassus, and looking out to the sea at Itea and the gulf of Corinth. It was therefore accessible from the Peloponnese by sea across the gulf. Land routes linked it with the isthmus of Corinth and Athens by way of Thebes in

Delphi: tholos of the sanctuary of Athena Pronaia, built *c*.390 BC

Boeotia, while another route passed directly to the north, to the back of the mountains above Thermopylae and down to the plain of Lamia. Geographically it belonged to the district of Phocis (whose most important city, Amphissa, was only a short distance away), but such was its religious importance that it was controlled rather by a special international body, the Amphictyonic Council, the council of "those who dwell around", i.e. the surrounding communities which had a special interest in the religious significance of the place. In addition to the sanctuary there was a small adjacent town, but this was little more than ancillary to the religious function.

The reason for its religious significance (outside the mythology attached to it) is nowhere stated, but it was probably a combination of its generally awesome character, with the towering cliffs of the mountain immediately above, and the abundant supplies of water from its springs, including what was probably the most renowned spring in Greece, Castalia. Delphi originated in prehistoric times, and there are traces of walls and the usual deposits of figurines from the Late Bronze Age. According to myth, Apollo took over the sanctuary from its previous owner, Gaia. This may represent a change of

presiding deity during the period that followed the political and cultural collapse of the Late Bronze Age communities, but everything seems to have been on a small scale, and there are no significant remains until the 6th century BC.

From the religious point of view, Delphi was most famous for its oracle. Pilgrims to the sanctuary could present their enquiries to the Pythia, the priestess, who mounted the sacred tripod in order to respond: the belief that she would go into a trance and rave is now discredited. Most famously, the enquiries were for predictions of the future, many of which are recorded by Herodotus, most notoriously the reply given to the non-Greek king of Lydia, Croesus (who was a great supporter of the sanctuary, showering it with expensive dedications, having been impressed by its efficacy). His last consultation was to enquire what would happen if he engaged in war with Cyrus, king of Persia. The oracle replied that a great empire would be destroyed, but omitted to say which. Croesus thought it meant the Persian empire, so went to war: in the event, it was his own empire that was destroyed. Most of these apparent oracular responses were probably inventions, and actually postdate the events they were meant to predict. They

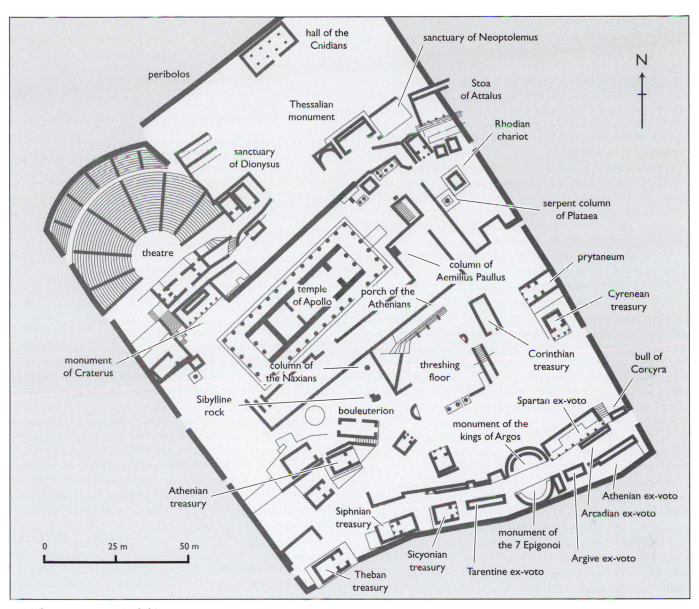

18. The sanctuary at Delphi

tended to obscure the true nature of the questions and responses, which was to seek guidance concerning the proper course of action to be followed in given circumstances. These could be for an interpretation of religious behaviour—what was right and proper – where the oracle was believed to have specialist knowledge and status far removed from mere fortune telling. The oracle, and its representatives, must have acquired a fair general knowledge of the world in which the Greeks lived, practical as well as religious. Advice was given on whether to send out a colony, or where, and what procedures would be desirable. The oracle was not above being influenced by others. In the last quarter of the 6th century BC a splendid new temple was built to Apollo, surrounded by a complete peristyle of Doric columns. It was to be built, as was most Delphian architecture, in the local limestone. The Athenian politician Cleisthenes undertook the contract (which meant he was financially liable if the work did not come up to the required standard), but for the east front and its pediment sculpture he provided at his own expense costly imported white marble from Paros. This was not altruistic; in return, the oracle responded to consultations by the Spartans by putting pressure on them to intervene and secure the return of Cleisthenes from exile to Athens. It worked.

The sanctuary consisted of a series of terraces, rising one above the other and linked by a "sacred way", a processional route which zigzags from the lowest terrace to the front of the temple at the middle level. Cleisthenes' temple was destroyed by a fall of rock in the 4th century BC, but was rebuilt to the same plan and design, the funds this time being collected by contributions solicited from the whole of Greece. Lining the sacred way were dedications to Apollo given by cities which had cause to be grateful to him. These included statues, or groups of statues set on bases of various forms and elaboration, up to complete buildings, the so-called treasuries (a misleading translation of the Greek term *thesauros*) some of which were elaborately decorated miniature temples. The most elaborate example was that given by the Cycladic island of Siphnos in gratitude for the discovery of a rich vein of silver on the island. Female figures (usually called Caryatids) replaced the more usual columns of the porch, which in this case would have been in the Ionic local to Siphnos, not the Doric of the mainland. Lavish sculpture also decorated the frieze and pediments. Nearby is the treasury of the Athenians, which perhaps celebrated Cleisthenes' return and the restoration of democracy at Athens, though many scholars believe it was a thankoffering for the victory at Marathon some 20 years later. Another famous offering was the tripod, a bronze cauldron supported on a column formed by intertwined snakes of bronze. This celebrated the Greek victory over the Persians at Plataea. The commander of the Greek allies, the Spartan regent Pausanias, boastfully put his own name on it. This caused offence, and the name was removed; instead the column was engraved with the names of the Greek states which had fought together against the Persians. It was eventually removed in the early 4th century AD by the Roman emperor Constantine, who took it to his New Rome, Constantinople, where part of it still survives.

There were many more memorials, and the sanctuary was enlarged in stages to accommodate them all. Round it was a substantial perimeter wall, the *peribolos*, also extended and improved over the ages, but which eventually, in the Hellenistic age, burst its seams with some buildings, such as the Stoa of Attalus, being constructed over it. In addition, several buildings were built below the main sanctuary including a second, smaller sanctuary, with a succession of temples of Athena, more treasuries and the circular Tholos, a Doric building of the 370s BC, the purpose of which, and, indeed, proper name, is uncertain. Nearby stood a gymnasium.

The sanctuary continued to flourish in the Hellenistic age. It was consulted by the Athenians early in the 1st century BC, when they wanted to restore religious practices which had ceased with the passage of time. It was supported by the Romans, and continued to be consulted and respected into the 2nd century AD. In the confusion of the 3rd century AD it fell into decline and evident disrepair. Attempts were made to tidy it up, but with the conversion of the empire to Christianity its purpose was lost. The emperor Julian tried to revive it as part of his restoration of paganism in the 360s, but the authorities had to make the sad reply "Tell the emperor that my hall has fallen to the ground. Phoebus no longer has his house, nor his mantic bay nor his prophetic spring: the water has dried up."

Parts of the sanctuary and some buildings were converted to Christian use, but Delphi never regained the same importance. By the 19th century, the site was covered by a squalid village, which was rebuilt on an adjacent site so that the French School at Athens could begin excavations.

R.A. TOMLINSON

See also Oracles, Sanctuaries

Summary

Delphi is the site of a major sanctuary of Apollo, best known for its oracle. As a shrine of supranational significance, its political independence was vital. It was therefore administered by a confederacy known as the Amphictyonic Council. There are no significant remains from before the 6th century BC. The oracle continued to be consulted into the 2nd century AD and was finally closed by Theodosius I in AD 390.

Further Reading

Amandry, P., *Delphi and Its History*, Athens, 1984

Bommelaer, Jean-François, *Guide de Delphes: le Site*, Paris: Boccard, 1991

Ecole Français d'Athènes, *Fouilles de Delphes*, Paris: Fontemoing, 1902–

Fontenrose, Joseph, *The Delphic Oracle: Its Responses and Operations, with a Catalogue of Responses*, Berkeley: University of California Press, 1978

Morgan, Catherine, *Athletes and Oracles: The Transformation of Olympia and Delphi in the Eighth Century BC*, Cambridge and New York: Cambridge University Press, 1990

Parke, H.W. and D.E.W. Wormell, *The Delphic Oracle*, Oxford: Blackwell, 1956

Demetrius, St d. *c*.300

Patron saint of Thessalonica

Demetrius is one of the Byzantine military saints, and as such is often depicted as a warrior, in full armour, sometimes on horseback, often in the company of St George, from whom he can sometimes be distinguished only by his hairstyle (less full, and seldom covering his ears). Like several other military saints (Procopius, for instance), his military career is a posthumous invention. So too, most likely, is his association with Thessalonica, of which city he had became the patron saint by the end of the 6th century. His earliest association was with Sirmium, and it is here that he was probably martyred and his cult first established. The cult of St Demetrius seems to have been transferred to Thessalonica along with the prefecture of Illyria in the mid-5th century.

In the accounts of his martyrdom Demetrius' fate is bound up with a young man called Nestor. The oldest account seems to be that preserved by Photios (*Bibliotheca*, cod. 255), in which Demetrius is martyred by the emperor Maximian as a result of the emperor's anger after the death in the arena of his favourite gladiator Lyaeus at the hands of Nestor. Other accounts make a closer link between Demetrius and Nestor: Demetrius becomes a teacher of Christianity, with Nestor as one of his pupils, who dies calling upon the "God of Demetrius". Still later accounts make Demetrius a noble senator and military commander, in this reflecting Demetrius' posthumous military career.

We know more about the cult of Demetrius than about his earthly life. Already by the end of the 6th century a series of miracles were attributed to him, in which he shows his care for the people of Thessalonica. This earliest collection of miracles was put together by John, archbishop of Thessalonica, shortly after 610. From this it is clear that there was no tradition in Thessalonica as to the whereabouts of his relics: the cult was focused on the icon of the saint (which does not survive) in a shrine, surmounted by a ciborium, in the church dedicated to him. It is only in the last 3 (out of 15) of these miracles, which concern the siege of Thessalonica by the Slavs in 586, that Demetrius appears in a military capacity, leading the resistance to the siege. A second, anonymous collection of miracles

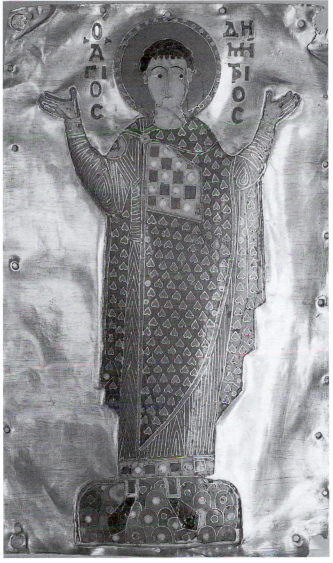

St Demetrius: icon in enamel, 12th century, Museum of Islamic Art, Berlin

concerns Demetrius' care for the city of Thessalonica during the episcopate of John (c.605–20), especially during the Slav attack on the city of 614, and in the defence of the city against siege by the khagan of the Avars at harvest-time in 618, during which John rallied his fellow citizens on the city walls, after a premonitory dream in which St Demetrius appeared, assuring him of the city's safety. Demetrius' care for the city continued and there are several later accounts of his miracles. Perhaps, in part, because of the role played by the saints of Thessalonica, Constantine/Cyril and Methodios, in the beginnings of Slav Christianity, the cult of St Demetrius became widespread among the Slavs.

Thessalonica itself became a centre for pilgrimage because of the cult of St Demetrius. The first basilica of St Demetrius, in the central part of the city, was built in the last quarter of the 5th century. This church was damaged by fire in the early 7th century and immediately restored; it was again virtually destroyed by fire in 1917 and rebuilt, so far as was possible, from the original materials. The focus of the cult was the icon,

from which issued, from time to time, healing oil, hence the saint's epithet, *myrovlytos*, "oil-gushing". The church itself was decorated with mosaics and frescos: some of the surviving mosaics date from the late 6th and late 7th centuries, and, since they depict the patrons who commissioned them, give valuable evidence for the changing balance between secular and ecclesiastical power in the 7th century. *Encolpia* (pendents), depicting the saint lying in his tomb, were made as souvenirs for pilgrims.

Demetrius has remained a popular saint, in both the Greek and the Slav worlds, as is evidenced by the popularity of the name (in its Slav form, Dmitri).

ANDREW LOUTH

See also Thessalonica

Biography

Little is known of the life of Demetrius except that he was a teacher in Sirmium who was executed by the emperor Maximian (286–305). His cult seems to have moved to Thessalonica in the 5th century where as a soldier saint he was credited with many miracles, notably in defence of the city. His icon (now lost) became a focus of pilgrimage.

Further Reading

Cormack, Robin, *Writing in Gold: Byzantine Society and Its Icons*, London: George Philip, and New York: Oxford University Press, 1985: pp. 50–94

Lemerle, Paul, *Les Plus Anciens Recueils des miracles de Saint Démétrius et la pénétration des Slaves dans les Balkans*, 2 vols, Paris: CNRS, 1979–81

Democracy

When the Athenians finally settled on "democracy" to describe their characteristic form of government, the term won out over several competitors: *iso-kratia* (equality of power), the Ionic word *is-egorie* (equality of expression), perhaps also *iso-moiria* (equality of sharing). Originally, "demos" meant the whole people, including aristocrats, but by the 5th century BC it came to imply, if not actually connote, the common people, the plebs. *Demo-kratia* means "power (*kratos*) exercised by the whole people (*demos*)", and it was used in explicit contrast to other more restricted forms of government such as *aristo-kratia* (power held by "the best") and *olig-archia* ("rule by a few").

Democracy had roots and antecedents. Already in Homer's day (perhaps 725 BC) rulers had lost, or were losing, whatever autocratic power they may have once possessed. The Greek high command at Troy felt it prudent, if not necessary, sometimes to summon assemblies to hear proposals and – ideally – ratify them without significant opposition. In *Iliad* 18 Achilles' shield is described as depicting some kind of popular gathering engaged in judging conflicting legal claims. At the end of the *Odyssey* the Ithacans assembled to debate alternative courses of action in response to Odysseus' slaying of the suitors. "Dark-Age kingship", a shadowy and poorly documented period, gave way in most Greek cities to oligarchic rule by a fairly wide circle of aristocratic families. Best attested is the government of the Bacchiadae at Corinth, and in many states, e.g. Thebes, this was the form that prevailed, with variations, through the historical period.

Sparta was an exception to this pattern. Here, in the mid-7th century, there occurred an experiment in a kind of proto-democracy. A document known as the "Great Rhetra" records a brief interval around 650 BC when the assembly of all Spartan citizens had the right to "speak in opposition" and make modifications to legislation introduced by their two kings and council of elders. The privilege lasted a generation at most, after which the legislative process reverted to the system familiar from other oligarchies in which the popular assembly served as little more than a rubber stamp of proposals put to it by the ruling council. Also of interest is an inscription from the island of Chios dated 575–550 BC that details a judicial procedure involving "(legislative) enactments of the *demos* [people]" and a "council of the *demos*" to hear judicial appeals.

First moves were made towards democracy at Athens when Draco produced a law code about 621 BC. Although it was remembered as having been extremely harsh, the very fact that it was written down was a step towards justice for the ordinary citizen, who now had some recourse against arbitrary decisions by the aristocrats. A reasonable claimant to the title "Father of Athenian Democracy" was Solon, a far-sighted and imaginative individual who revamped the Athenian law code in 594 BC. Athens was on the brink of class warfare brought about in part by an antiquated system of land tenure that allowed wealthy landowners to take over smallholdings and reduce their former owners to the status of indentured serfs. One of the slogans attributed to Solon was "equality breeds no war", but what he brought about was equality not of possessions – he resisted demands made by the poor to redistribute the land – but rather equality before the law. He is reported to have said, when asked what he considered the best city to live in, "the one in which those people who are not wronged, no less than those who are, come forward and punish the wrongdoer". From now on anyone who wished could seek legal redress on behalf of one perceived to have been a victim of injustice, and magistrates' decisions could be appealed to a jury court. According to Aristotle, "Solon appears to have set up the democracy by constituting the jury courts from all the citizens" (*Politics*, 1274a1ff.).

The period after Solon was marked by civil unrest and a spell of "tyranny" by Pisistratus and his sons. Luckily for the Athenians, their lawcode was left intact; the Pisistratids merely manipulated it in such a way that their own supporters were usually in positions of authority. After the tyrants were driven out in 510 BC there was a danger that matters would collapse into a melee of aristocratic infighting, but one of the contenders, Cleisthenes the Alcmeonid, swung the balance in his favour by promising the *demos* reforms. Cleisthenes effectively cut through and dismantled local fiefdoms based on the aristocrats' control of religious and political activity within their own regions. Cleisthenes regrouped the citizen body along national lines. Voting on important matters and serving in the army were henceforth to occur within a complex and artificial system of ten newly created tribes, whose distinctive feature was that they were composed of members from widely disparate districts of Attica. Moreover, Cleisthenes either created a legislative council for the first time or drastically refashioned an earlier and more primitive *Boule* (council) instituted by Solon. As will be seen, the Boule was the pivot around which the whole democratic legislative apparatus functioned.

A further important step towards democracy was made by the reform of the Areopagus, Athens' senior council, by Pericles and Ephialtes in 462 BC. Most of the judicial functions of this venerable body were distributed among the Council of 500, the Assembly of the people, and the lawcourts. Probably at this same time Pericles also introduced a bill that provided a daily allowance to members of the juries. This made it possible for poorer citizens to put their names forward to serve on the juries, and gave substance to the claim that an Athenian brought before a court of law was given a trial before a "jury of his peers". It was a characteristic of the full-blown democracy that payment was subsequently instituted for other kinds of public service: discharge of duties as a councillor, infantry duty, rowing in the fleet, and, finally, attendance at meetings of the Assembly and, for citizens who could demonstrate financial need, admittance to the major dramatic festivals.

What made Athenian "democracy" truly democratic in practice was the ubiquity of the lot as an instrument of selection. Certain officials were elected: the ten generals, one from each of the (Cleisthenic) tribes, and other officers whose functions were rather specialized, like treasurers. Otherwise, allotment to office was the rule, from the annual archons down. This system of allotment was all-pervasive. There are references to boards of "contractors", "market supervisors", "weight-and-measure superintendants", "inspectors of dockyards", and so on, so that the figure of 700 for such annually rotating officers, preserved in the *Constitution of Athens* but sometimes doubted, seems entirely believable.

If sovereign power rested with the *demos* collectively assembled, which had responsibility for war and peace, taxation, foreign affairs, and other important matters touching on the welfare of the body politic, what assured relatively smooth functioning of the whole apparatus was the Boule or Council of 500, ten tribal contingents of 50 chosen annually by lot and known as *prytaneis* (with the tenth part of the year in which they served known as a "prytany"), who took it in turn in a sequence decided by lot at the end of the preceding prytany to prepare the agenda for the Assembly. The 50 *prytaneis* met daily and actually lived together for their 35 or 36 days in a special building, the Tholos. Effectively, the day-to-day running of the Athenian state fell to them. They had the further duty of selecting, also by lot, one of their number to preside at their own meetings and at the meetings of the Assembly, which were held normally four times each prytany, that is, 40 times a year. On a famous occasion the lot fell to Socrates, whose tribe held the prytany at that crucial juncture, to act as president of the Assembly when the motion was brought to try as a group the generals who had been charged with dereliction of duty for failing to rescue survivors after a naval battle off Lesbos in 406 BC. Because he was unwilling to contravene a law requiring defendants to be tried individually and not as a group, Socrates refused to have any part in the proceedings. He was replaced by someone (whose name is not recorded) more willing to compromise his principles and connive at illegality.

No councillor could serve more than twice in his lifetime, and then not for two years in succession. Thus, there was no possibility of a cadre being formed, or the development of any continuity of interest, especially covert. Figures for the total population of Athens in the Classical period can only be guesses, and estimates of the percentage of male Athenian citizens who would have served on the Boule at least once in their lifetimes range between one-third to one-half (J. O'Neil) and 70 per cent (R. Osborne). The whole system was one of absolute equality. Men of varying interests, abilities, and backgrounds served together, on a temporary basis, and because of the transregional nature of the tribal membership noted above, it was the city as a whole whose needs were being served, not those of individual districts, nor of segments or interest groups within the population.

There is evidence of a cult of Demos, the Athenian populace conceived of as a collective abstraction, on the Hill of the Nymphs near the Pnyx at Athens from before 450 BC. Before the end of the 5th century the abstractions Demokratia and Oligarchia appear as personified opponents, and a cult of Demokratia is attested on inscriptions from the 330s. In this period also Boule, the personified Council, appears as a parallel abstraction. A surviving relief sculpture on a decree dated 337/6 from the Athenian Agora shows Demokratia crowning a dignified-looking, sceptred Demos who is seated on a throne. Athens was not alone in iconographically honouring Demokratia, for a statue of the goddess is depicted on a coin of Cnidus dated 300–190 BC.

Democracy defined the Athenian political ethos as at no other ancient Greek city, but there are traces of democratic periods elsewhere: Syracuse, Mantineia, Argos, Corfu, Rhodes, Thurii, Tarentum, Heracleia on the Pontus, Thasos, Epidamnus, and possibly Megara. When at the height of their imperial power, the Athenians tried to impose their democratic system on various dependent states, among them Boeotia and, in Ionia, Erythrae and possibly Miletus.

Aristophanes in *Knights* and Plato, the comic writer, in a play whose title is not preserved made fun of Demos as a cantankerous old man all too willing to be flattered, duped, and led astray by wily but unprincipled politicians. Other critics, such as the historian Thucydides and the philosopher Plato, were more scathing. What such critics feared was the tendency of an electorate to disintegrate into an unruly mob, like (in Plato's vivid image) a raging beast, unwilling to take direction from enlightened (i.e. aristocratic) leaders and yielding instead to the self-serving cajolery of (plebeian) demagogues. This continues to be the paradox of any modern democratic system, where large populations and an inflated governmental apparatus seem to require some kind of representation rather than the direct democracy of ancient city states: since election to office today depends upon heavy financial outlay by candidates, who, if elected, must then spend much of their time trying to divine the voters' sometimes only vaguely formulated and often inconsistent desires, the term "politician" has become more a label of disparagement than a job description.

Long after Athens had lost any claims to importance on the world stage or independence of political action, it maintained the forms of its democratic past: a decree survives from about AD 220 mandating a revival of the Eleusinian festival that opens with the characteristic formula, "It was decreed by the Demos". Such associations with popular government, however, gradually lost favour during the Roman period. By the 5th century AD the word "democracy" had acquired distinctly adverse connotations and for the Byzantines it came to mean a popular disturbance or riot.

ANTHONY J. PODLECKI

See also Government (Theories of)

Further Reading

Alexandri-Tzahou, Olga, Demokratia and Demos entries in *Lexicon Iconographicum Mythologiae Classicae*, vol. 3.1, Zürich: Artemis, 1986, pp. 372–74 and 375–82

Euben, J. Peter, John Wallach and Josiah Ober (editors), *Athenian Political Thought and the Reconstruction of American Democracy*, Ithaca, New York: Cornell University Press, 1994

Farrar, Cynthia, *The Origins of Democratic Thinking: The Invention of Politics in Classical Athens*, Cambridge and New York: Cambridge University Press, 1988

Glover, T.R., *Democracy in the Ancient World*, Cambridge: Cambridge University Press, 1927

Hansen, Mogens Herman, "Demos, Ecclesia and Dicasterion in Classical Athens", *Greek, Roman and Byzantine Studies*, 19 (1978): pp. 127–46

Hansen, Mogens Herman, "The Origin of the Term *demokratia*", *Liverpool Classical Monthly*, 11 (1986): pp. 35–36

Hansen, Mogens Herman, "On the Importance of Institutions in an Analysis of Athenian Democracy", *Classica et Mediaevalia*, 40 (1989): pp. 107–13

Hansen, Mogens Herman, "Solonian Democracy in Fourth-Century Athens", *Classica et Mediaevalia*, 40 (1989): pp. 71–99

Hansen, Mogens Herman, *The Athenian Democracy in the Age of Demosthenes: Structure, Principles and Ideology*, Oxford and Cambridge, Massachusetts: Blackwell, 1991

Headlam, J.W., *Election by Lot at Athens*, Cambridge: Cambridge University Press, 1891

Holden, Barry, *The Nature of Democracy*, London: Nelson, and New York: Barnes and Noble, 1974

Jones, A.H.M., *Athenian Democracy*, Oxford: Blackwell, 1957; New York: Praeger, 1958

Manville, Philip Brook, *The Origins of Citizenship in Ancient Athens*, Princeton, New Jersey: Princeton University Press, 1990

Meier, Christian, *The Greek Discovery of Politics*, Cambridge, Massachusetts: Harvard University Press, 1990

Ober, Josiah, *Mass and Elite in Democratic Athens: Rhetoric, Ideology, and the Power of the People*, Princeton, New Jersey: Princeton University Press, 1989

Ober, Josiah, *The Athenian Revolution: Essays on Ancient Greek Democracy and Political Theory*, Princeton, New Jersey: Princeton University Press, 1996

O'Neil, James L., *The Origins and Development of Ancient Greek Democracy*, Lanham, Maryland: Rowman and Littlefield, 1995

Osborne, Robin, "The Demos and Its Divisions" in *The Greek City from Homer to Alexander*, edited by Oswyn Murray and Simon Price, Oxford: Clarendon Press, and New York: Oxford University Press, 1990

Palagia, Olga, "A Colossal Statue of a Personification from the Agora of Athens", *Hesperia*, 51 (1982): pp. 99–113

Raubitschek, Antony E., "Demokratia", *Hesperia*, 31 (1962): pp. 238–43

Roberts, Jennifer Tolbert, *Athens on Trial: The Antidemocratic Tradition in Western Thought*, Princeton, New Jersey: Princeton University Press, 1994

Robinson, Eric W., *The First Democracies: Early Popular Government Outside Athens*, Stuttgart: Steiner, 1997

Saxonhouse, Arlene W., *Athenian Democracy: Modern Mythmakers and Ancient Theorists*, Notre Dame, Indiana: University of Notre Dame Press, 1996

Sinclair, R.K., *Democracy and Participation in Athens*, Cambridge and New York: Cambridge University Press, 1988

Snodgrass, Anthony, *Archaic Greece: The Age of Experiment*, London: Dent, and Berkeley: University of California Press, 1980

Stockton, David, *The Classical Athenian Democracy*, Oxford and New York: Oxford University Press, 1990

Demography

Demography as a scientific study of the size, distribution, and composition of human populations did not exist among the ancient Greeks. Moreover, in studying the population of ancient Greece and the relations between its component parts (such as old and young, male and female, slave and free, etc.), modern demographers are hampered by the lack of reliable figures and statistical information.

After the rediscovery and spread of the art of writing, and at least from the 6th century BC, the Greek states must have kept records concerned with the status and duties of citizens or with financial obligations and benefits, but such records would have applied to free men rather than slaves, and to adult men rather than women and children except in so far as these latter were involved in matters of citizenship. There are more inscriptions from the 4th century BC onwards, but these are generally religious, social, or honorific and it is uncertain to what extent local figures of population levies were consolidated and recorded in any permanent fashion.

Due to the emphasis that ancient historiography placed on warfare, most available data relate to the size of military forces or to the manpower available for military purposes. In other words, they refer only to adult male citizens. From such numbers attempts have been made to estimate the size of the entire population including women, children, and slaves. For example, Gustave Glotz's estimate (in *Ancient Greece at Work*) of the population of Attica during the Classical period is based on the number of Athenian hoplites at the beginning of the Peloponnesian War, as stated by Thucydides: according to this calculation there were then some 40,000 adult Athenian citizens of all classes, making with their families a total of 140,000, with about 70,000 metics and probably between 150,000 and 400,000 slaves.

Censuses of citizens were rare in the ancient Greek world. Only one census is recorded for Classical Athens, the one carried out by Demetrius of Phaleron in the late 4th century BC, whose results are preserved by Athenaeus (6. 272c). No results for Greece or any other region are preserved from the Roman censuses mentioned in the Gospel story of the birth of Christ (Luke 2: 1–2).

Information regarding changes in settlement patterns in ancient Greece, probably connected to population fluctuations, is supplied by intensive archaeological field surveys. Although there are local variations during all periods, the general pattern is of a sparsely populated landscape in the 11th and 10th centuries BC, followed by a substantial increase in most areas from the 9th century BC, culminating in the period from the 5th to the 3rd centuries BC and declining in the last two centuries BC and during the Roman empire. It is thus possible to accept the growth of population as at least a partial cause of Greek colonization from the 8th century BC onwards, as it undoubtedly was after the time of Alexander the Great. It is, however, difficult to say whether the colonizing activity of the Archaic period led to a long-term reduction of population in mainland Greece. This activity continued until the 6th century BC, after which there was opposition in the West from the Carthaginians, Etruscans, and Illyrians; and the suitable sites around the Aegean Sea were all occupied. Cities then began to grow, and to produce goods, with the help of captured slaves, partly in order to pay by exports for the corn they now had to import.

There were no birth or death certificates in ancient Greece and, consequently, ages given in literary sources are generally unreliable. However, a study of the relationship between the age and sex of a skeleton and particular grave goods can be useful in the investigation of prehistoric social organization (Halstead, 1977). Study of the skeletal remains of male individuals of the Early, Middle, and Late Helladic periods from the Greek mainland and the islands reveals a morphological homogeneity of the population throughout the Bronze Age (Xirotiris, 1980).

A high level of infant and child mortality in Classical Greece is suggested by excavations of cemeteries. There is even less evidence for fertility rates than mortality rates, but fertility levels must have been much higher than in advanced modern societies. For, although family limitation measures such as infanticide or abortion may have been practised in some social classes, religions, or periods, the high infant mortality must have encouraged large families to ensure that some children reached adulthood to inherit the property, provide additional farm labour, and support the parents in old age. A very important factor influencing fertility levels is the average age of marriage, particularly for women, and the few references in literary sources (e.g. Hesiod, *Works and Days*, 695–98) suggest a pattern of late marriage for men (around 30) and early marriage for women (mid- to late teens), the latter making high fertility rates possible. In their ideal states both Plato and Aristotle provided that parents should breed only when in their prime. Plato puts this for women at from 20 to 40 years of age, for men from the end of their prowess at racing until 50 (just like stud horses). Aristotle wished women to marry at 18, men at 37: they were then in the prime of life respectively, and the decline in the powers of both would coincide.

On the other hand, the emancipation of women in the Hellenistic age was accompanied by a revolt against wholesale motherhood, and the limitation of the family became the outstanding social phenomenon of the age. Abortion laws became more lenient, and exposure of children more common. In the old cities families raising more than one daughter would be one in a hundred: according to Poseidippus, "even a rich man always exposes a daughter". Sisters were a rarity, but one-child or childless families were common. Around 200 BC, out of a total of 79 Milesian families, 32 had one child, 31 had two; altogether they had 118 sons and 28 daughters (Gustave Glotz, *Ancient Greece at Work*, 1965, p.298; W.W. Tarn, *Hellenistic Civilisation*, 1927, p.86). At Eretria only one out of 12 families had two sons, and hardly any had two daughters. Infanticide received the approval of some philosophers (though not of Socrates/Plato in the *Republic*, who recommends only the separation of inferior children from the guardian class: cf. Mulhern, 1975) as a means of reducing the pressure of population; but the practice spread among the masses to such an extent that the death rate overtook the birth rate. The extent of family limitation may be gleaned from the fact that by forbidding it Philip V of Macedon raised the manpower of his country by 50 per cent in 30 years (Tarn, p.88). Around 150 BC Polybius (36. 17) lamented the desertion of the cities and the unproductiveness of the land resulting from a low birth rate and a general decrease in the population. He ascribed this to selfishness and indolence, and to a desire to give one's children too high a standard of living. But it may equally well have been due to demoralization and reluctance to bring children into a world of incessant war, revolution, banditry, and violence in general, with a high chance of poverty, enslavement, or early death. And if it is true that Aemilius Paullus, after defeating king Perseus of Macedon at Pydna in 167 BC, carried off 150,000 into slavery from the region of Epirus alone, there we have an example of one cause of depopulation, and of demoralization among the remnants (Wilkinson, 1979, ch.1).

It has been suggested that some 10 per cent of females may have been exposed at birth in order to avoid an excess of marriageable women (Golden, 1981). But this hypothesis cannot be demonstrated, and would require the unwarranted assumption that the Graeco-Roman era had a sustained surplus of births over deaths. It has been pointed out that a high rate of female infanticide was impossible for any ancient population since it would cause a decline in a nearly stable population (Engels, 1980, 1984).

Our extant evidence is mainly concerned with Athens and largely confined to the 4th century BC. It consists of fragmentary sources such as lists of *epheboi* (young men undergoing military training), *bouleutai* (councillors), and *diaitetai* (elderly men serving as arbitrators). It is not clear whether these groups were recruited from the entire body of adult male citizens or from only among the hoplites and the upper classes. According to Hansen (1989) ephebic rosters cannot be used to calculate accurately the total number of Athenian citizens during the 4th century BC. Every Athenian boy of 18 was registered in the deme of his father, and the total of these deme registers formed the list of those entitled to take part in the assembly. Similarly there were lists of 18-year-old boys eligible to become *zeugitai* liable to hoplite service and *thetes* liable to service in the Athenian navy. Both boys and girls were enrolled in their phratries, but there were no other records of citizen women. Demetrius' census enumerates 21,000 citizens, but it is uncertain whether this figure includes all citizens or merely those liable and fit for hoplite service. The number of metics, which is given as 10,000, is the only figure for this status group that has come down to us. Metics were required to pay a tax and were registered in their deme of residence.

The suggestion of Herodotus (5. 97. 2) that there were about 30,000 Athenian citizens in the early 5th century BC has sometimes led to the indiscriminate assumption of this figure for the rest of the Classical period as well. However, evidence of the size of Athenian military forces during the 5th-century BC empire suggests that by the middle of that century there were at least 50,000 or possibly even 60,000 citizens, thus indicating a substantial growth since the early 5th century BC. This level was maintained until the beginning of the Peloponnesian War, when it began to decline as a result of the plague and the heavy casualties in battle, especially during the expedition to

Syracuse in 415–413 BC. Moreover, after the introduction of Pericles' citizenship law of 451 BC, the Athenian citizen population was doomed to be stationary or to decline. Any significant increase in the number of citizens was ruled out by the strict rules for accepting new citizens combined with the continuous emigration from Attica (Hansen, 1982).

Most uncertain of all is the number of the slave population. The Athenian census of Demetrius records their number as 400,000, and similar incredibly high figures are given for Aegina and Corinth as well in sources of varying reliability. Thus, around 350 BC, Aristotle calculated that Aegina had a population of half a million, of whom 470,000 were slaves (Calhoun, pp.30–31). Nevertheless, there may have been considerably more slaves in the time of the 5th-century BC Athenian empire than there had been earlier.

Although Laconia had much of the richest land in Greece, it was thinly populated. According to Herodotus (7. 234. 2; 9. 10. 1), Sparta had 8000 potential soldiers in 480 BC, and in 479 BC 5000 actually took part in the Battle of Plataea. However, by Aristotle's time the citizen population seems to have come down to fewer than 1000 and the causes of this decline have been much debated: such diverse factors as the structure of Spartan society, casualties in war, inheritance patterns, and the earthquake of c.464 BC have been invoked to explain it. In the opinion of Aristotle (*Politics*, 1270a29–34) this serious problem of manpower shortage was the reason for Sparta's downfall. Yet we must remember that the citizens comprised only a small proportion of the total population. Although figures for the number of Spartiates between the ages of 21 and 50 and *perioikoi* ("dwellers round") in the army are given, their proportion to the total number of Spartiates or *perioikoi* can only be conjectured. The number of helots is still less well known, except that they were relatively more numerous in proportion to the free population than were serfs in any other state. At all events we know that at some time Sparta introduced severe penalties for celibacy as well as rewards for child-bearing. It was seriously concerned even about the loss of the 124 Spartiates trapped by the Athenians on the island of Sphacteria in 424 BC. By the time of its debacle at Leuctra in 371 BC it had only 1000 of these; whereas Aristotle calculated that its territory could have maintained 30,000 infantry and 1500 cavalry. An unwillingness to breed because of a decadent obsession with personal wealth seemed to be the chief cause of the population decline. Nor was there, as in Athens, a strong religious cult of ancestors to motivate perpetuation of the family.

The citizen population of Argos and Boeotia during the 4th century BC may not have been dissimilar to that of Athens, to judge from their military strength, but they probably had fewer resident aliens and slaves. Corinth, which in the 5th and 4th centuries BC had less than half the hoplites of Athens, may have had half as many inhabitants as Athens, if not fewer. The poor and mountainous country of Arcadia produced many emigrants; and yet it had 6000–7000 hoplites in the 4th and 3rd centuries BC. By comparison with Attica this would mean a citizen population of about 80,000–90,000. On the other hand, the prosperous Greek colonies of Sicily and Italy were densely populated and, despite the lack of evidence, we may assume that the size of their populations exceeded that of virtually every state in mainland Greece. To take just one example, according to Diodorus Siculus (3. 9) the wealthy and prosperous city of Sybaris had 300,000 inhabitants.

Sources for demography in the Byzantine age are also fragmentary. Apart from some judicial compilations that provide insights regarding the size and stability of litigant families, one has to depend on physical evidence or surviving government records. From the size and number of excavated houses A. Jakobson (in *Vizantijskij Vremennik*, 19 (1961): pp.154f.) estimated a population of 5000 for the average 10th- or 11th-century city. Evidence for births and mortality from funerary inscriptions is often insufficient or unsuitable for statistical analysis. The most important sources are the *praktika* (tax records), primarily of 14th-century southern Macedonia. Many offer detailed listings for members of peasant families dwelling on the estate; since a number of areas were assessed repeatedly, their *praktika* give some indications concerning household stability. However, being fiscal documents, they tend to omit what is considered not essential for taxation. Thus the ages of the population are not recorded, and it is not certain at what age a child was first enrolled. It is also possible that women, when not acting as heads of households, were persistently undercounted, and insufficient account appears to have been taken of newly arrived families or those who no longer worked on the estate but might remain in the same (or a neighbouring) village (D. Jacoby, review of *Peasant Society in the Late Byzantine Empire* in *Speculum*, 61 (1986): pp. 677f.). Isolated population figures for individual cities during particular periods are provided in literary sources.

The population of Byzantium grew steadily during the 4th and 5th centuries AD but declined precipitously during the 6th and 7th under the recurring impact of famines, plagues, and foreign invasions; this was followed in turn by a period of slow recovery. The empire lost a large portion of its population with the territorial losses of the late 11th century; and from 1200 onwards the population in the remaining areas appears to have dropped continuously. During the 14th century this downward trend was accelerated by civil wars, the Black Death, and the disruptions caused in Macedonia by marauding mercenaries of the Catalan Grand Company.

Modern Greece has a total area of 131,990 sq km, of which the mainland constitutes 81 per cent (106,821 sq km) while 19 per cent (25,169 sq km) is taken up by the islands. In 1861 there were 1,096,810 inhabitants, 567,334 male and 529,476 female, with a density of 23.08 per sq km. By 1991 there were a total of 10,264,156 inhabitants (77.78 per sq km), 5,029,710 of whom were male and 5,234,446 female. By 1996 the population had risen to 10,475,000 with a density of 79 persons per sq km. The urban population was 65 per cent in 1994 as opposed to 43 per cent in 1960.

The urban network of Greece is structured as a whole around two poles of different importance, Athens (population 3,096,775) in the south and Thessalonica (739,998) in the north. The periphery of these metropolitan centres is occupied by a series of satellite cities of varying size. The only other cities with a population of more than 100,000 are Patras (172,763), Volos (106,142), Larissa (113,426), and Herakleion in Crete (127,600). Like the rest of Europe, Greece has low birth rates and a rising trend in the average age of the population. Life expectancy is 77.8 years, and adult literacy 96.7 per cent.

In the recent past migration (both internal migration and emigration) was a significant feature of Greek demography. Internal migration was high before the 1980s and was reflected in the falling population figures for the mountainous areas and the islands. However, this trend has stopped since the 1980s so that these regions now show an increase of population. Emigration to America has been going on since the end of the 19th century while emigration to Australia, which began after 1945, has been supplemented since the 1960s by labour migration to Western Europe in general and to Germany in particular. However, the process of emigration has more or less come to an end, and remigration is stronger at present than out-migration, which remains steady at quite a low level. In fact, the faster growth in population when compared with the rest of Europe is due less to fertility than to high immigration and remigration.

Although Greece has on average a low population density, there are sharp regional variations. Attica is the most thickly populated area, while the mountainous regions and the islands have a low population density. Regarding fertility, there are no significant regional variations: the fertility rate in all regions is below the European average, and is now below replacement level. The mortality rate is also very low, and life expectancy is rather high, despite the low expenditure on health by the government. The infant mortality rate is somewhat higher than Europe on the average, but there is no fundamental difference in the age structure. Central Greece, Crete, and the Aegean islands have a smaller active age group and a higher proportion of elderly than the rest of the country, reflecting the consequences of internal migration processes, with the active persons migrating to the big urban centres while the young and the old stay behind. Compared to the rest of Europe, the female activity rate is lower (by more than 10 per cent), youth unemployment is much higher (except in the islands), and the annual growth-rate of the population is still somewhat higher (0.1 per cent) and on the increase although, as mentioned above, this last may be due to a much higher net migration.

D.P.M. WEERAKKODY

See also Emigration, Family, Slavery

Further Reading

Alden, Maureen Joan, *Bronze Age Population Fluctuations in the Argolid from the Evidence of Mycenaean Tombs*, Gothenburg: Åström, 1981

Bryer, Anthony and Heath Lowry (editors), *Continuity and Change in Late Byzantine and Early Ottoman Society*, Birmingham: University of Birmingham Centre for Byzantine Studies, and Washington, D.C.: Dumbarton Oaks, 1986

Calhoun, George Miller, *The Business Life of Ancient Athens*, Chicago: University of Chicago Press, 1926; reprinted Rome: Bretschneider, 1965, New York: Cooper Square, 1968

Carothers, S.J. and W.A. McDonald, "Size and Distribution of the Population in Late Bronze Age Messenia: Some Statistical Approaches", *Journal of Field Archaeology*, 6 (1979): pp. 433–54

Charanis, Peter and Speros Vryonis (editors), *Studies on the Demography of the Byzantine Empire*, London: Variorum, 1972

Cohen, G.M., "Colonization and Population Transfer in the Hellenistic World" in *Egypt and the Hellenistic World*, edited by E. Van't Dack *et al.*, Louvain: Studia Hellenistica, 1983

Dow, Sterling, *Prytaneis: A Study of the Inscriptions Honoring the Athenian Councillors*, Athens: American School of Classical Studies, 1937

Engels, D., "The Problem of Female Infanticide in the Graeco-Roman World", *Classical Philology*, 75 (1980): pp. 112–20

Engels, D., "The Use of Historical Demography in Ancient History", *Classical Quarterly*, 34/2 (1984): pp. 386–93

Figueira, T.J., "Population Patterns in Late Archaic and Classical Sparta", *Transactions of the American Philological Association*, 116 (1986): pp. 165–213

French, A., *The Growth of the Athenian Economy*, New York: Barnes and Noble, and London: Routledge, 1964

Golden, M., "Population Policy in Plato and Aristotle: Some Value Issues", *Arethusa*, 8 (1975): pp. 345–58

Golden, M., "Demography and the Exposure of Girls at Athens", *Phoenix*, 35 (1981): pp. 316–31

Gomme, A.W., *The Population of Athens in the Fifth and Fourth Centuries BC*, Oxford: Blackwell, 1933

Gomme, A.W., "The Slave Population of Athens", *Journal of Hellenic Studies*, 66 (1946): pp. 127–29.

Gomme, A.W., "The Population of Athens Again", *Journal of Hellenic Studies*, 79 (1959): pp. 61–68

Halstead, P., "Bronze Age Demography of Crete and Greece: A Note", *Annual of the British School at Athens*, 72 (1977): pp. 107–11

Hansen, Mogens Herman, "Demographic Reflections on the Number of Athenian Citizens, 451–309 BC", *American Journal of Ancient History*, 7 (1982): pp. 172–89

Hansen, Mogens Herman, "Political Activity and the Organization of Attica in the Fourth Century BC", *Greek, Roman and Byzantine Studies*, 24 (1983): pp. 227–38

Hansen, Mogens Herman, *Demography and Democracy: The Number of Athenian Citizens in the Fourth Century BC*, Herning, Denmark: Systime, 1985

Hansen, Mogens Herman, "Demography and Democracy Again" in *Zeitschrift für Papyrologie und Epigraphik*, 75 (1988): pp. 189–93

Hansen, Mogens Herman, "Demography and Democracy? A Reply to Eberhard Ruschenbusch", *Ancient History Bulletin*, 3 (1989): pp. 40–44

Jones, A.H.M., *Athenian Democracy*, Oxford: Blackwell, 1957; New York: Praeger, 1958

Mulhern, J.J., "Population and Plato's Republic", *Arethusa*, 8 (1975): pp. 265–81

Russell, Josiah Cox, *Late Ancient and Medieval Population*, Philadelphia: American Philosophical Society, 1958; as *The Control of Late Ancient and Medieval Population*, 1985

Sallares, Robert, *The Ecology of the Ancient Greek World*, London: Duckworth, and Ithaca, New York: Cornell University Press, 1991

Salmon, P., "La Population de la Grèce Antique", *Bulletin de l'Association Guillaume Budé, Supplement Lettres d'Humaniti*, 18 (1959): pp. 448–76

Sanders, G.D.R., "Reassessing Ancient Populations", *Annual of the British School at Athens*, 79 (1984): pp. 251–62

Todd, M, "Economic Conditions" in *The Fifth Century BC*, edited by D.M. Lewis *et al.*, Cambridge: Cambridge University Press, 1992 (*The Cambridge Ancient History*, vol. 5, 2nd edition)

Wilkinson, L.P., *Classical Attitudes to Modern Issues: Population and Family Planning, Women's Liberation, Nudism in Deed and Word, Homosexuality*, London: Kimber, 1979

Xirotiris, N.I., "The Indo-Europeans in Greece: An Anthropological Approach to the Population of Bronze Age Greece", *Journal of Indo-European Studies*, 8 (1980): pp. 201–10

Demons and Spirits

Our word "demon" comes from the ancient Greek *daimon*, from the verb *daiein*, "to distribute". In the Homeric and Classical periods *daimon* could be used as a synonym of *theos* to mean simply "god". More frequently, however, *daimon* referred to "divine power" in the abstract as opposed to the personified deity denoted by *theos*. In a wide range of Classical sources *daimon* could mean "the power controlling the destiny of individuals". It carried overtones of "a portion" (*moira*) in the sense of "fate". A *daimon* was both the distributor of destinies and the destiny itself.

In contrast to the Olympian gods, the *daimones* were not honoured by any cult or shrine within the polis. Nor were they represented in myth, drama, vase painting, or sculpture. They were a nameless, ill-defined plurality of supernatural beings, yet this semantic vagueness suited them for new applications in the course of time, especially in the area of psychology.

A productive set of meanings for *daimon* derived from Hesiod, according to whose *Works and Days* the souls of men from the golden age became good *daimones* who watched over and protected mortal men. In the *Timaeus* Plato allocated them to the *aither* (upper air), above the *aer* (lower air) where heroes and departed souls resided. Souls and *daimones* alike were physically composed of *aither*, a mysterious fifth element (*quinta essentia*). The *daimones*' position between heroes and gods was not, however, stable, and Plato elsewhere equated all fallen soldiers with *daimones*, while during the Hellenistic period any deceased person could be called a *daimon*. In this sense *daimon* came close to the ideas of soul (*psyche*) and spirit (*pneuma*).

Daimones also had associations with human emotions, beginning with the *Symposium*, where Diotima introduced Eros as a *daimon*. Plato furthermore (*Timaeus*, 90c) considered that humans should pursue learning and true thoughts in order to achieve "happiness" (*eudaimonia*) – a state in which the good internal *daimon* comes to the fore. It was Plato's pupil Xenocrates who conceptualized demons as dark, lustful forces, thereby initiating the shift of the *daimones* from elements of a scientific, philosophical cosmology to elements of a moral one. This would be a slow and uneven transition lasting centuries and not definitively finishing until the rise of Christianity. During the Hellenistic period *daimones* continued to be treated as intermediaries. For example, it was thought that they sent dreams. In Neoplatonic magic, as represented by the Chaldaean Oracles, the *daimones* could be addressed and their aid enlisted through elaborate rituals involving the spinning of a top, or *iunx*. Alternatively, messages enlisting demonic help against an enemy could be written on lead tablets and buried along with the dead. Or the *daimones* could be appealed to, or controlled by resort to more powerful gods, through elaborate spells recorded on magical papyri.

The Christianization of the Greek-speaking world did much to polarize the demons as exclusively evil spirits located on, or in, the earth. The already many-stranded traditional conception of *daimones* was reoriented by the Judaeo-Christian story of Satan who, in an act of hubristic jealousy, attempted to place his throne higher than God's. In recompense he was cast down from the heavens, along with his conspiring angels who became demons – a word that, through phonological changes in the language, was now pronounced *demones* (as indeed it still is in modern Greek). Demons in the Christian world were unequivocally evil, associated with matter, sin, corruption, and the body, as opposed to the values of Christian purity, restraint, and spirituality overseen by God and Christ.

"The gods of the gentiles are demons", the early Church Fathers exhorted. Thus, in the baptismal ceremony that converted pagans into Christians evil spirits were exorcized from the body of the initiate who was then instilled with the Holy Spirit. Finally, in the act of chrismation, his or her sensory organs and bodily orifices were symbolically "sealed" against future demonic incursions. Possession by demons was nonetheless still a danger and the priesthood retained the power to perform exorcisms just as Christ did in the New Testament. One of the primary techniques in Greek Christian exorcism was, and still is, to learn the name of the demon. If one can name a demon, one can control it, and this is accomplished either by verbally abusing the demon, or by reciting long lists of demonic names in the hope that one of these may be correct.

Christianity called for spiritual refinement as a means to ultimate union with God. This meant constant combat with dangerous passions and desires that threatened moral perfection. The monastic tradition, beginning with St Antony in the 4th century, offers many detailed accounts of how the Devil, or demons, tempted monks to stray from the path of goodness. The "deadly sins" – stabilized at seven in the Catholic west, but fluctuating between seven and eight in the Greek east – were conceptualized as demons that attacked one and had to be fought off by ascetic cultivation of the appropriate Christian virtues. Monastic texts such as those compiled in the *Philokalia* developed a chain-effect explanation of the emotions whereby submission to a particular demon "of the first rank" brought increased vulnerability to certain other demons in its wake. These demonologies were precursors of contemporary psychology.

The Orthodox Church oversaw a standard, or doctrinal, conception of demons according to which the Devil's helpers were fundamentally immaterial, powerless, and plural. This perhaps explains why the iconography of demons and the Devil did not begin much before the 7th century. That such an iconographic tradition did finally begin might be taken to indicate the pressure that alternative traditions exerted on the Church. Local popular beliefs attributed more independent power and specific characteristics to demons than Church doctrine would allow. Different views on this matter were at the root of high medieval dualist heresies such as Bogomilism, which asserted that the entire earthly world was demonic.

In modern Greece folklorists and anthropologists have uncovered a wide range of Greek beliefs in demonic supernatural beings such as the *neraides*, dangerous female spirits, or the *gelloudes*, child-snatching demons. Some of these, such as the above, bear names that connect them to ancient Greek supernatural beings. If they were not initially demons, then the Church has succeeded in demonizing them over the years. Demons in contemporary Greece – not uniformly believed in by a late 20th-century population exposed to modern science – form a large category comprising 30 or more differently named spirits known generically as *xotika* (things from outside), *aerika* (air spirits), or *demonika*. They account for illness or misfortune in terms that make them morally intelligible at the personal level, something universal science is unable to do. Throughout Greek tradition demons have always served as a labelling and categorizing principle enabling people to chart and comprehend the unknown, whether in outer space or in the recesses of the human psyche.

CHARLES STEWART

See also Folklore, Spells

Further Reading

Betz, Hans Dieter (editor), *The Greek Magical Papyri in Translation, Including the Demotic Spells*, Chicago: University of Chicago Press, 1986

Detienne, Marcel, *La Notion de daïmôn dans le Pythagorisme ancien*, Paris: Belles Lettres, 1963

Faraone, Christopher A. and Dirk Obbink (editors), *Magika Hiera: Ancient Greek Magic and Religion*, Oxford and New York: Oxford University Press, 1991

Greenfield, Richard P.H., *Traditions of Belief in Late Byzantine Demonology*, Amsterdam: Hakkert, 1988

Luck, Georg (translator), *Arcana Mundi: Magic and the Occult in the Greek and Roman Worlds: A Collection of Ancient Texts*, Baltimore: Johns Hopkins University Press, 1985

Onians, Richard Broxton, *The Origins of European Thought about the Body, the Mind, the Soul, the World, Time and Fate*, 2nd edition, Cambridge: Cambridge University Press, 1954

Provatakis, T.M., *O diavolos eis tin Vyzantinin Tekhnin* [The Devil in Byzantine Art], Thessalonica, 1980

Smith, Jonathan, "Towards Interpreting Demonic Powers in Hellenistic and Roman Antiquity" in *Aufstieg und Niedergang der römischen Welt*, edited by Hildegard Temporini et al., 2.16.1, Berlin: de Gruyter 1978, 425–39

Stewart, Charles, *Demons and the Devil: Moral Imagination in Modern Greek Culture*, Princeton, New Jersey: Princeton University Press, 1991

Demosthenes 384–322 BC

Orator

Demosthenes was the son of a wealthy Athenian manufacturer of swords and cutlery. His father died when he was 7 years of age, leaving him under the control of three guardians who embezzled most of the inheritance. After studying rhetoric with Isaeus, Demosthenes began a series of prosecutions against his former guardians and recovered some of the lost money (364 BC), but more significantly, gained a reputation as a speech writer. He also taught rhetoric, but he had grander ambitions and overcame a speech impediment by practising declamation with pebbles in his mouth and shouting above the noise of the waves at Phalerum.

Demosthenes' political career began in 355 BC, when he was commissioned to write *Against Androtion* for a political trial. In the early period he may have opposed the policy of Aristophon, who was advocating war with Persia, and he attacked Eubulus in *On the Syntaxis* (353/52 BC). By 351 BC he recognized the dangers posed by Philip II and delivered the unsuccessful *First Philippic*, followed by the three *Olynthiacs* (349 BC). In the third of these Demosthenes alludes critically to Eubulus' policies, which in 348 BC led to costly Athenian intervention in Euboea. In the same year he became involved in litigation against Meidias, a leading supporter of Eubulus, who slapped Demosthenes' face at the Dionysia. The *Against Meidias*, however, was never actually delivered, since the two reached an out-of-court settlement.

In 348 BC Demosthenes successfully defended Philocrates, when he was prosecuted for proposing negotiations with Philip, but soon afterwards Olynthus fell, and Demosthenes helped to secure the Peace of Philocrates (346 BC). Aeschines attacked Demosthenes for the poor part he played in the negotiations, and it was Aeschines who championed the treaty before the assembly, which knew that Philip was already threatening Phocis. It is unclear what Demosthenes tried to propose at this meeting before being shouted down, but he subsequently worked to undermine the peace, gathering supporters to strengthen his anti-Macedonian position, including Hyperides and Lycurgus. He was also plotting his revenge on Aeschines, claiming that he had been bribed by Philip, but his attack on him through the agency of Timarchus was a failure. This was, however, only a temporary setback. In 344 BC, with Philip interfering in Thessaly and rumours circulating about his proposed intervention in the Peloponnese, Demosthenes persuaded the assembly not to renew the peace by his *Second Philippic*. Hyperides successfully prosecuted Philocrates (343 BC), while Demosthenes prosecuted Aeschines with *On the False Embassy*. Demosthenes' case was weak, but despite the support of Eubulus and the prominent general Phocion Aeschines was only narrowly acquitted.

In 342/41 BC Philip turned his attention to the Chersonese, threatening Athens' corn supply from the Black Sea, and his supporters in Athens demanded the recall of Diopeithes from Thrace. Demosthenes supported Diopeithes in *On the Chersonese* and the *Third Philippic*, one of his finest speeches, in which he spelled out Philip's designs on Greece and urged the Athenians to defend the Chersonese and Byzantium. An alliance was formed with Byzantium (341/40 BC), and although Philip seized Athens' corn fleet, his advance on Byzantium was checked. Demosthenes was now supreme in Athens and had the allocation of surplus revenues to the Theoric Fund suspended, but could not prevent Aeschines fomenting a Sacred War in 339 BC. Philip marched into Phocis and took Elatea, and Demosthenes persuaded the Athenians to make an alliance with their old enemy, Thebes. The allies met Philip at Chaeronea, but were crushed (338 BC).

Demosthenes continued to work energetically on the city's behalf after the Macedonian conquest and delivered the public Funeral Oration of 338 BC. In 337/36 BC he was theoric commissioner, and Ctesiphon proposed that he be honoured with a gold crown at the Great Dionysia for his services to Athens. Aeschines immediately indicted Ctesiphon for making an illegal proposal, but let the case drop because the political climate in Athens changed with the death of Philip. After Alexander had reestablished Macedonian control and defeated Persia, Aeschines resumed his attack (330 BC), blaming Athens' troubles on Demosthenes, but Demosthenes' masterpiece, *On the Crown*, easily won the day. He remained a prominent figure in Athens until the Harpalus affair (324 BC). Alexander's treasurer Harpalus arrived in Athens with a vast sum of money, and Demosthenes proposed that he be imprisoned and the money stored on the Acropolis. Harpalus escaped, and it was discovered that some of the money was missing. The

Demosthenes, the great Athenian orator, Ny Carlsberg Glyptothek, Copenhagen

Areopagus cited Demosthenes, who was prosecuted by Dinarchus and Hyperides; fined 50 talents, he retired into exile. He returned to Athens after Alexander's death (323 BC) and advocated renewed resistance to Macedon in the Lamian War, but the Greeks were defeated at Crannon by Antipater (322 BC). Demosthenes, Hyperides, and their supporters fled; Demades proposed that they be sentenced to death, and Demosthenes committed suicide on the island of Calauria.

Judgements of Demosthenes' leadership have inevitably been affected by the brilliance of his speeches, and his championing of liberty tends to be seen in too simple a contrast to the servile acceptance of Macedonian rule by his opponents, whom he constantly accused of being bribed. In truth, other politicians were probably making proposals that stood a greater chance of success in maintaining Athens' freedom, particularly the uniting of the Greek states in a common peace. Athens alone lacked the resources to resist Philip in the way Demosthenes advocated, and his policy of fighting a war in the north was not popular with other Greek states, who realized that a successful outcome would result primarily in the greater glory of Athens. But this is not to deny Demosthenes' stature as one of Athens' greatest leaders.

From the literary point of view Demosthenes has been recognized by both ancient and modern critics as the best of the Attic orators. One of his outstanding qualities was the ability to vary his style to suit the occasion of the speech. There is some evidence that the speeches, always carefully prepared, were revised for publication, but Demosthenes creates an impression of spontaneity by mixing long periods with shorter, simpler sentences. He tended to avoid hiatus and also runs of more than two short syllables. There is disagreement over how far this was a conscious rather than instinctive practice, but its effect is one of solemnity and dignity. Demosthenes writes in pure Attic Greek, and in narrative passages he regularly employs a plain style of writing; but elsewhere his sentences can be quite complex. He uses repetition, bold metaphors, and colloquialisms, varies his tone, and indulges in the vulgar personal abuse that was popular in his day. It was the combination of simplicity and complexity into a "middle" style that the Augustan critic Dionysius of Halicarnassus regarded as producing the most effective oratory.

The Demosthenic corpus comprises 60 speeches, an *Erotic Essay*, a collection of 56 proems (prefaces, written as models for imitation by his pupils), and six letters; but a number of the private orations, the *Funeral Speech,* and the *Erotic Essay* are spurious. His earliest forensic speech, *Against Aphobus I,* already displays the hallmarks of Demosthenic oratory, with its forcefulness and variety, and a somewhat imperious ethos. Demosthenes continued writing speeches for wealthy clients throughout his life, though he did not appear in person in private cases after the late 350s BC but even private suits might have their political side. He composed *Against Stephanus I* (349 BC) for Apollodorus, when he was prosecuting Stephanus for perjury on behalf of Apollodorus' stepfather, the banker Phormio. He attacks Phormio bitterly, yet at the original trial in 350 BC he had written *For Phormio,* in which he bitterly attacked Apollodorus. Demosthenes probably changed sides because Apollodorus had begun, like Demosthenes, to advocate the use of the Theoric Fund to finance the struggle against Philip, but centuries later Plutarch criticized his morality.

Demosthenes' forensic speeches cover a wide range of subjects in both private and public cases, and demonstrate a talent for character portrayal and logical argument. One of his best private orations is *Against Conon*, an action for battery brought by Ariston. In a vivid narrative Ariston tells how he first met Conon's permanently drunk sons and describes the fight in which he was nearly beaten to death, though the decent youth cannot repeat the abusive language used by his brutal attackers. Demosthenes is an unashamed patriot, and national character is the underlying theme of many of his most famous speeches, both political and judicial. In *On the Crown* he gives an extended account of his public services and conceals the fact that his policy had failed at Chaeronea by emphasizing Athens' greatness – and his own role as the city's greatest champion.

Demosthenes' patriotic stance against Philip and his judicial defeat of Aeschines laid the foundations for his reputation in the later Classical world and beyond. A full-length biography was composed in the 2nd century AD by Plutarch, who paired Demosthenes with Cicero in his *Parallel Lives*; an extensive life is found in the pseudo-Plutarchan *Lives of the Ten Orators* of the same period; while briefer notices were written by Libanius and Zosimus (one of various scholars of that name living in the 5th–6th centuries AD). In the 9th century Photios wrote a biography based on pseudo-Plutarch, and further biographical details may be found in the *Suda*. This material is generally favourable, and St Nicholas of Myra regarded Demosthenes as the embodiment of virtue, in stark comparsion with Aeschines. But a hostile tradition is represented by Tzetzes, who perversely makes Demosthenes rather than Aeschines the venal politician. Theodore Metochites (1270–1332) similarly compared Demosthenes in part unfavourably to Aelius Aristides, though he regards Demosthenes as the greater rhetorician. Finally, a statue of Demosthenes was placed in the Baths of Zeuxippos in Constantinople and described by the 5th/6th-century poet Christodorus of Coptus.

Demosthenes' speeches were, in the eyes of most critics, the supreme models for imitation. Already in the 2nd century AD they were being drawn on extensively by rhetoricians such as Hermogenes, who calls Demosthenes "The Orator". Hermogenes' use of Demosthenes is highly significant, since later rhetoricians were in turn deeply influenced by him. Tiberius wrote *On the Figures of Demosthenes* in the late 3rd or early 4th century AD; Epiphanius the Syrian, a candidate for the chair of rhetoric in Athens after the death of Julian of Caesarea (c.AD 330), wrote a commentary on Demosthenes; and, most famously, in the 4th-century AD Libanius of Antioch wrote *Hypotheses* to the speeches in Constantinople. The *Suda* attributes another commentary to Zosimus. In the 6th century AD Choricius used Demosthenes as a model for his speeches; the curriculum in the schools of rhetoric in this period included the Attic orators, especially Demosthenes, as well as Isocrates and Aeschines, and extensive use of Demosthenes is attested by the numerous scholia – and by the abuse of Demosthenes, along with Homer, Plato, and Aratus, in the hymns of Romanos. The earliest manuscripts of Demosthenes are datable to the 9th and 10th centuries AD, when the revival of interest in the Classics led to further activity by scholiasts. Numerous papyri have also been recovered from Byzantine Egypt (they indicate the position of Demosthenes alongside Homer, Euripides, and Menander as one of the central

Classical authors), and Demosthenes' position as the greatest Classical Greek orator and the best source of suitable material for quotations was maintained throughout the Byzantine period to the 15th century. In the 11th century Michael Psellos compared Demosthenes with Gregory of Nazianzus, who synthesized Classical rhetoric and Christianity; while in the 12th century Gregory of Corinth recommended Demosthenes among his models for deliberative and judicial oratory. His rousing *Philippics* in particular have ever since been seized on by politicians; during the War of Independence the *Appeal to the French People* recalled the place of Demosthenes in Greece's glorious past, while in 1827 Lord Cochrane quoted the *First Philippic* to Kolokotronis in an exhortation to unity.

MICHAEL J. EDWARDS

See also Rhetoric

Biography

Born into a landowning Athenian family in 384 BC, Demosthenes studied rhetoric under Isaeus and became a professional speech writer. His political career began in 355 BC when he initially advocated peace, against the policy of Aristophon. By 351 BC he recognized the threat to Greece posed by Philip II of Macedon and devoted the rest of his career to warning aginst it. Despite the defeat at Chaeronea (338 BC) Demosthenes remained in office until 324 BC when he was charged with corruption. In 322 BC he fled and committed suicide on the island of Calauria.

Writings

Selected Private Orations, 3rd edition, edited by F.A. Paley and J.E. Sandys, 2 vols, Cambridge: Cambridge University Press, 1896–98, reprinted New York: Arno Press, 1979

Demosthenes, translated by C.A. Vince *et al.*, 7 vols, London: Heinemann, and Cambridge, Massachusetts: Harvard University Press, 1926–49 (Loeb edition; many reprints)

Six Private Speeches, commentary by Lionel Pearson, Norman: University of Oklahoma Press, 1972

De Corona, edited by W.W. Goodwin, Bristol: Bristol Classical Press, 1982

Selected Private Speeches, edited by C. Carey and R.A. Reid, Cambridge and New York: Cambridge University Press, 1985

Against Meidias (Oration 21), edited by Douglas M. MacDowell, Oxford: Clarendon Press, and New York: Oxford University Press, 1990

On the Crown: De Corona, translation and commentary by Stephen Usher, Warminster: Aris and Phillips, 1993

Further Reading

Cawkwell, George, *Philip of Macedon*, London and Boston: Faber, 1978

Goldstein, Jonathan A., *The Letters of Demosthenes*, New York: Columbia University Press, 1968

Pearson, Lionel, *The Art of Demosthenes*, Meisenheim: Hain, 1976

Sealey, Raphael, *Demosthenes and His Time: A Study in Defeat*, Oxford and New York: Oxford University Press, 1993

Dialectic

Dialectic is variously a practice, a method, and a science in Greek philosophy. The basic precept of dialect is based on conversation – and perhaps disputation – between at least two distinct parties. Dialectic lies at the very heart of all Greek philosophy and represents one of its most characteristic contributions to the sum of human thought.

The modern English word is a near-transliteration of the Greek word *dialektike*, meaning "the art or skill of discussing". Conversational encounters, as the ancient Greeks knew, may consist of unproductive pleasantries, or be hostile confrontations, or serve as mutually productive exchanges between two minds concentrating on the same issue from different initial perspectives. Serious dialectic concerns the latter; but Greek philosophers realized that without proper regulation the exercise could degenerate into one of the other forms of encounter. The more pressing danger came from the tendency to ill-disciplined disputation, which was given the pejorative title of "eristic", or contentious argument.

We learn about dialectic mainly from the practice of Plato's dialogues, where there occur specimen dialectical exchanges interspersed with some comments on sound and unsound method, and more thoroughly from Aristotle's *Topics* and *Sophistici Elenchi*, which describe the practice of dialectic and set out his thoughts on its philosophical purpose and value. Dialectic continued to be studied after Aristotle, particularly by such early Stoic logicians as Chrysippus. However, by this stage dialectic had come to be included in the study of logic, with specific reference to the more pragmatic aspects of the theory of argument; there is little evidence of the actual practice of dialectic from this period. On the other hand, philosophers after Aristotle continued to exhibit a dialectical style in their handling of problems; and to that extent dialectic is an enduring feature of all Greek philosophy, not merely a dominant aspect of its seminal period in the 5th and 4th centuries BC.

In a dialectical exchange there is a clear division of function between two participants – the questioner and the answerer. An issue is proposed: for example, *Is virtue teachable or not?* or *Should we return to people what is their due or not?* The answerer chooses one of the two possible responses, and thereafter answers questions which are designed to lead him to say something incompatible with his original answer. The questioner holds the initiative, but the answerer is at liberty to respond at any stage as he sees fit. Rational insight, and even logical dexterity, are needed if the questioner is to elicit an answer which fails to cohere with the answerer's original response.

Dialectic hinges on winning or losing a contest, and its purpose is to advance the pursuit of truth. These aims were articulated as the exercise progressed, and a sense of their significance always imposed discipline and regulation on its conduct. For example, questions must be clear cut; they must not leave open a plurality of responses beyond a straightforward yes or no. Measures must be taken to avoid or expose ambiguity, whether in a single word or in a larger unit of language; otherwise the value of any particular dialectical response will be uncertain. By these means, those who practised and theorized about dialectical exercises came to assist the creation and development of logic. But all such dialectical rules or sanctions were themselves subject to appraisal and acceptance or rejection within the context of the particular philosophical encounter. Everything was subject to consideration, save perhaps for the very freedom of enquiry which the exercise presupposed.

Plato had a strong insight into the potential of dialectic for the advancement of understanding. He understood that the open-ended, autonomous nature of the exercise made it an ideal method for securing knowledge which was based on deep and sustained conviction. The practised dialectician is able to defend his insights against every kind of attack; and how could there be a better basis than this for anyone to support a claim to have genuine knowledge?

Yet Plato was simultaneously developing stringent criteria defining what was to count as knowledge – for example, that it be not subject to revision, and that it be based on rational reflection. Thus he proposed that dialectic should be a science rather than merely a method. This revision was secured by placing dialectical method on a foundationalist basis; effective practice of the method was to be dependent on a grasp of the truth conveyed by an intuition of the nature of goodness. By using value as the fundamental concept of the science, Plato preserved a Socratic insight into the pervasive philosophical significance of matters of value, whatever particular topic might be under consideration. Nevertheless, the progression of dialectic from a method to a science transmutes an essentially open-ended sceptical stance into a commitment to the pursuit of certainty and truth.

Aristotle sought to restore dialectic to its earlier role as a training exercise and at the same time to establish its connection with the distinct spheres of science and philosophy. The philosophical value of dialectic resides both in its capacity for training and, above all, in its role in the examination of the scientific axioms. Dialectic can help those who wish to discover first principles; it provides an essential preliminary phase to the operation of axiomatic scientific demonstration. Scientists then take over the task of demonstrating the deductive consequences of these axioms.

Aristotle's practice when engaged in philosophy diverges somewhat from this official position. He begins almost every discussion – both of general topics and of detailed problems within them – with a review of previous views on the given question and an elaboration of the difficulties which are generated if we try to combine them. However, dialectical method dominates the entire discussion of these problems. It is not a preliminary, which will give place to a less tentative phase of enquiry in the subsequent examination. Instead, the teasing out of problems forms the very substance of Aristotelian philosophy, and in this sense philosophy is dialectical through and through.

In Aristotle the theory of dialectic is linked to the studies of logic and of fallacies. Many of the concepts of dialectic – such as argument, deduction, premise, and reduction – are also used in his theory of the syllogism. But logic is independent of the context of investigation, while dialectic is not. The study of fallacies, which Aristotle inaugurates in *Sophistici Elenchi*, is unintelligible without reference to dialectic. For example, the fallacies of many questions and begging the question arise essentially in a question-and-answer context, as their names make clear.

Many philosophers after the ancient Greeks have assigned philosophical significance to dialectic; perhaps the most notable in this company are Kant, Hegel, and Marx. Their very different interpretations and valuations of dialectic all owe much to the accounts of the matter in Plato and Aristotle. Moreover, the cut and thrust of dialectical method is still very apparent in the problem-oriented style of modern analytical philosophy. The original inspiration for this very fertile philosophical idea is firmly rooted in 5th- and 4th-century Greek thought, and it repays study in that context.

J.D.G. EVANS

See also Aristotle, Plato

Further Reading

Evans, J.D.G., *Aristotle's Concept of Dialectic*, Cambridge and New York: Cambridge University Press, 1977
Hamlyn, D.W., "Aristotle on Dialectic", *Philosophy*, 65/254 (1990): pp. 465–76
Irwin, Terence H., *Aristotle's First Principles*, Oxford: Clarendon Press, and New York: Oxford University Press, 1988
Robinson, Richard, *Plato's Earlier Dialectic*, 2nd edition, Oxford: Clarendon Press, and New York: Oxford University Press, 1953, reprinted 1984
Ryle, Gilbert, *Plato's Progress*, Cambridge: Cambridge University Press, 1966, chapter 4

Dialects

Those Indo-Europeans who arrived in the Balkan peninsula in the late 3rd or early 2nd millennium BC – whom we may call the Proto-Greeks – were themselves members of a dialectal subgroup of the Indo-European family of languages and peoples. Common linguistic innovations suggest that the ancestors of the Greeks, Indo-Iranians, and Armenians spoke related varieties of late Indo-European. We would expect that even among that body of Proto-Greeks penetrating into the Balkans there was dialectal heterogeneity (if only on the sociological level), since all speech communities are linguistically heterogeneous. Beyond this, however, documentary evidence clearly reveals that by the mid- to late 2nd millennium BC, and much more so in the 1st millennium BC, the Greek language was characterized by distinct dialectal forms.

Before Michael Ventris's decipherment of the Linear B script in the 1950s, scholars had long been classifying the already known dialects of ancient Greek into several groups. With the decipherment of the Mycenaean tablets, yet another dialect was revealed – one that showed close similarities to certain of the post-Mycenaean dialects, though not complete identity with any. As analysis of the Mycenaean texts progressed, an awareness developed of the existence of not one, but two dialects preserved in the Linear B corpus (see Risch 1966; Nagy 1968; Woodard 1986). Moreover, folding the Mycenaean evidence into the analysis of Greek dialectology of the 1st millennium BC gave rise to speculation that no fewer than four distinct dialects of Greek must have existed in the Mycenaean era (see Cowgill 1966).

Those two attested varieties of Mycenaean Greek have been commonly dubbed "Normal Mycenaean" (since it is the more frequently occurring dialect) and "Special Mycenaean". There are at least four linguistic differences (or isoglosses) which distinguish the two dialects. Normal Mycenaean is characterized by each of the following features: (1) the third declension dative singular ending -ei; (2) the development of Proto-Indo-European syllabic nasals into the vowel o, in the vicinity of a labial consonant; (3) the change of *e to i, also in the environment of a labial consonant; (4) the "assibilation" of inherited *ti to si. Special Mycenaean, on the other hand, shows a distinct set of developments: (1) the corresponding dative ending is -i; (2) syllabic nasals become a; (3) *e is preserved; (4) also preserved is the sequence *ti. Of the four dialect features characterizing Normal Mycenaean, only one is attested among the known Greek dialects of the 1st millennium BC (the change of *ti to si); otherwise it is the Special Mycenaean isoglosses alone that have survived.

The Greek dialects of the 1st millennium BC are divided into five major groups: Attic-Ionic, Arcado-Cypriot, Aeolic, Doric, and Northwest Greek. Of these, the most familiar to modern students of Greek is Attic-Ionic, consisting of the closely related dialects of Athens and surrounding Attica, and of the Ionians of Anatolia (East Ionic), of

19. The dialects of ancient Greece

the Cyclades (Central Ionic), and of the region of Euboea (West Ionic). Distinct linguistic features of the Attic-Ionic dialect include the change of *ā to ē (the vowel of eta), except after e, i, and r in Attic; and the process of "quantitative metathesis", whereby certain sequences of long vowel + short vowel become short vowel + long vowel (e.g. ēo gives eō).

Of the Greek dialects of the 1st millennium BC, the one most closely related to the language of the Mycenaean Greeks is Arcado-Cypriot. Though far-flung geographically – its speakers ranging from the central Peloponnese to the island of Cyprus in the eastern Mediterranean – the dialect is internally quite homogeneous. Its uniformity is plainly the consequence of common ancestry: Mycenaean peoples who, on the one hand, remained or settled in mountainous Arcadia and who, on the other, came as émigrés to Cyprus with the eclipse of the Mycenaean civilization of Greece. The Greek language of Pamphylia in southern Anatolia shows some similarity to this same dialect group. Arcado-Cypriot is characterized by a peculiar development of early Greek labiovelar consonants when they occur before the vowel i. Thus, Proto-Greek *kʷis "anyone" gives Cypriot sis (tis in other dialects); Arcadian writes the sound with a special symbol (a form of san) – И.

The Aeolic dialect group, like the Ionic, consists of members separated by the Aegean Sea. Lesbian is the dialect of the Aeolian islands and the Aeolian region of Anatolia. Boeotian and Thessalian were spoken in Boeotia and Thessaly respectively; the latter dialect itself is composed of two distinct varieties – Pelasgiotis and Thessaliotis. The Aeolic dialects are characterized by a bilabial development of the labiovelar consonants occurring before e-vowels; thus Proto-Greek

*penkʷe "five" gives Aeolic pempe (cf. Attic pente, with the common dental reflex t). Within Thessalian, Pelasgiotis and Thessaliotis exhibit two salient differences: (1) the genitive singular of the second declension is -oi for the former and -ō or -ou for the latter; (2) the present infinitive of the omega-conjugation is formed with -emen in Pelasgiotis, but with -en or -ein in Thessaliotis.

Doric is that group showing the greatest number of constituent dialects. Distinct varieties from the Peloponnese include Laconian, Messenian, Argolic, Sicyonian, and Corinthian. From the isthmus of Corinth comes Megarian. Greek islands attesting distinct Doric dialects include Crete, Thera, Cos, and Rhodes (with Doric also spoken on the associated Anatolian coast). The various Doric dialects show numerous unique linguistic features as well as features common to both Doric and Northwest Greek, discussed immediately below. Cretan, the best attested of the Doric dialects, shows several specific dialect characteristics, such as a particular propensity for consonant assimilation.

The remaining dialect group, Northwest Greek, is closely related to Doric. Dialects of this type are attested from Phocis, Locris, and Elis. Characteristic of both Northwest Greek and Doric is the preservation of the sequence *ti (as in Special Mycenaean), without the development to si found in other dialects. Elean is interesting in displaying the shift of long ē (eta) to ā – the very reverse of that vowel change distinctive to Attic-Ionic (see above). Also common to Northwest Greek and Doric (Cretan excepted) are the nominative plural articles toi (masculine) and tai (feminine), rather than the hoi and hai of other dialects.

Modern scholars have conventionally divided these various dialects into two major groups, East Greek and West Greek, implying some sort of bifurcation in evolutionary descent from Proto-Greek. East Greek subsumes Attic-Ionic, Arcado-Cypriot, Mycenaean, and Aeolic. West Greek is then made up of those two dialects we have already seen to be closely related, Doric and Northwest Greek. The adequacy of this interpretation was, however, called into question by Ernst Risch in 1955 in a careful and probing re-examination of the dialect features that distinguish and bind the regional dialects ("Die Gliederung der griechischen Dialekte in neuer Sicht", reprinted in Kirk, 1964). In summary, Risch argued that the relative antiquity of the various dialect features (isoglosses) must be taken into consideration when determining genetic relationships among the dialects. Those features that place Aeolic within East Greek are relatively late in origin and are characteristic of Lesbian, not Thessalian and Boeotian. Contending that Lesbian acquired these innovating characteristics in conjunction with their development in neighbouring East Ionic, Risch realigned Aeolic, placing it with Doric and Northwest Greek. The resulting dialect structure is then one of South Greek (Attic-Ionic, Arcado-Cypriot, Mycenaean) versus North Greek (Aeolic, Doric, Northwest Greek). The proper genetic grouping of the ancient Greek dialects awaits resolution.

The literary language of pre-Classical and Classical Greek, in its various forms, likewise displays linguistic features that are characteristic of the geographic dialects of the 1st millennium BC. However, the literary dialects are for the most part linguistically artificial. That is to say, they are contrived from elements of different regional dialects and are not themselves identical to any single dialect of spoken Greek – the products of local literary expression that have spread beyond their regional boundaries and have been fused by adapting literary artists. The language of Homer and Greek epic consists chiefly of East Ionic and Aeolic elements, along with bits of Arcado-Cypriot vocabulary. Lyric poetry is composed in several linguistic forms. The Lesbian poets Alcaeus and Sappho write in their Aeolic dialect, but preserve elements of epic language. Archilolochus, Solon, and others write in epic dialect, tempered with their own native Greek dialects. The language of choral lyric is fundamentally Doric, though generally unlike any single regional Doric dialect, mixed with Aeolic and epic. Tragedy's dialect is Attic, with elements of Doric, Aeolic, and epic woven in; choral passages are more heavily Doricized (achieved often by the use of long *ā* where Attic has *eta*). Herodotus and earlier prose authors wrote in Ionic. By the end of the 5th century BC, Attic had become the language of prose, though marked Atticisms (such as *-tt-* where Ionic has *-ss-*) tended to be avoided for a time. With the rise of Athenian political prominence, Attic was the widely used prestige dialect throughout the Greek-speaking world; it remains the dialect of the 4th-century prose authors.

Philip II, a Macedonian, chose to install Attic Greek as the official language of his realm. Greek culture and the Attic dialect trailed in the conquering footsteps of Philip's Greek-educated son, Alexander; Attic Greek thus became the lingua franca of Alexander's vast empire. The particular form which this lingua franca developed is that of a modified Attic, usually called Attic Koine or simply Koine Greek. This is the language of the Greek New Testament and of the Egyptian papyri.

Attic Koine displaced regional dialects within Greece, with the result that almost all modern Greek dialects appear to trace their roots to Attic. The notable exception is the dialect of Tsakonian. In response to Slavic incursions into the Peloponnese in the 6th and 7th centuries AD, the Greeks of Laconia are reported to have fled into the rugged mountains of Tsakonia. The modern dialect that developed in this remote area appears perhaps to be a descendant of Laconian, or at least of some form of Peloponnesian Doric which had resisted the influx of Attic Koine.

Modern Greek dialects have not been as carefully catalogued and analysed as either the ancient Greek dialects or the modern dialects of other European languages. A noticeable dialect difference is one that roughly divides the speech of contemporary Greece into a northern–eastern group and a southern–western group (see Browning, 1983 pp. 120–23 for a detailed description). The former, in contrast to the latter, is characterized by loss of the unaccented high vowels *i* and *u*, and an upward shift of unaccented *e* and *o* to become *i* and *u* respectively. The result is the occurrence of a great many consonant clusters in the northern–eastern group that are not found in the more conservative area.

The spoken vernacular of modern Greece is commonly called demotic. In contrast, there exists the artificial, cultured speech called katharevousa, a self-consciously archaizing official dialect that looks to antiquity for its inspiration and validation. Its use has declined precipitately since the mid 1970s.

ROGER D. WOODARD

See also Language

Further Reading

Browning, Robert, *Medieval and Modern Greek*, 2nd edition, Cambridge and New York: Cambridge University Press, 1983

Buck, Carl Darling, *The Greek Dialects*, Chicago: University of Chicago Press, 1955 (revised edition of *Introduction to the Study of Greek Dialects*, 1910)

Coleman, Robert, "The Dialect Geography of Ancient Greece", *Transactions of the Philological Society* (1963): pp. 58–126

Cowgill, Warren, "Ancient Greek Dialectology in the Light of Mycenaean" in *Ancient Indo-European Dialects*, edited by Henrik Birnbaum and Jaan Puhvel, Berkeley: University of California Press, 1966

Kirk, G.S. (editor), *The Language and Background of Homer*, Cambridge: Heffer, 1964; New York: Barnes and Noble, 1967

Nagy, Gregory, "On Dialectal Anomalies in Pylian Texts" in *Atti e memorie del 1° congresso internazionale di micenologia*, vol. 2, Rome: Ateneo, 1968

Palmer, Leonard R., *The Greek Language*, Atlantic Highlands, New Jersey: Humanities Press, 1980, reprinted Norman: University of Oklahoma Press, 1996

Risch, Ernst, "Les Différences dialectales dans le mycénien" in *Proceedings of the Cambridge Colloquium on Mycenaean Studies*, edited by Leonard R. Palmer and John Chadwick, Cambridge: Cambridge University Press, 1966

Thumb, Albert, *Handbuch der griechischen Dialekte*, 2nd edition, 2 vols, Heidelberg: Winter, 1932–59

Woodard, Roger, "Dialectal Differences at Knossos", *Kadmos*, 25 (1986): pp. 49–74

Diaspora

From the first period of Greek colonization in the early 8th century BC to the recent emigration movements to the "new worlds" the Greek consciousness has been profoundly marked by the experience of the diaspora. The reality of wandering in faraway places, whether for trade, expedition, settlement, or exile, is coterminous with the dawn of Greek literature and it has permeated both poetry and myth with symbolic representations of alienation, separation, and reunion, as well as with questions of identity, which are linked to the classical theme of the hero's quest. The *Odyssey*, the Argonautic legends, Io's wanderings in the Middle East, the founding of cities on sites identified with the transformation of Nymphs, point to a quasi-metaphysical understanding of the experience of diaspora engraved since time immemorial in the Greek consciousness.

Although the first colonization stories are enveloped in mystery, the wish of the settlers to maintain a more than symbolic link with the *metropolis*, their original mother-city, points to a willingness to see themselves as a people dispersed, as *apoikoi*, from their initial geopolitical centre. In the Hellenistic era their close contacts with the Judaic civilization contributed to a new understanding of the reality of diaspora. This notion of being scattered "abroad upon the face of all the earth" is first developed in the Genesis story of the tower of Babel, where it is linked to the theme of confusion, dispersion, and estrangement from God (Genesis 11: 9). The subsequent Judaic understanding of dispersion emphasizes the experience of exile from Jerusalem as a result of falling captive into the hands of Israel's enemies. However, the dispersed community may reconstitute itself in a *synagoge*, that is a congregation of its scattered members. The institution of the synagogue as a substitute for the Temple worship found its fullest expression among the dispersed Jews in the Hellenic world. It is noteworthy that the dispersed members of Israel formed their synagogues within the communities of the diasporas of the Greeks in the Hellenistic cities of the east.

The Stoics had already prepared the ground for a particular acceptance of a newly worked notion of diaspora by stressing the cosmopolitan nature of the Hellenistic civilization. Just as the Stoic *spermatikos logos* orders rationally the spiritual faculties of men, so the cosmopolis is an image of a rationally ordered natural world composed of a universal commonwealth of men and women dispersed throughout the Graeco-Roman world. The empire is held together spiritually by the operation of the *spermatikos logos*, whose seeds (*spermata*) are scattered throughout the universal dominion, the *oikoumene*. It is to this diaspora of the *Logos*, a metaphysical principle elaborated by Philo Judaeus in Alexandria, that the empire owes its internal cohesion. These doctrines, expressed in an embryonic form by Zeno and later developed by Posidonius, had been influenced to a great degree by the Semitic origins of the founders of the Stoa.

By the 1st century AD the communities of the diaspora, which had been established as *apoikiai*, that is as settlements "away from home", had become autonomous entities within the political administration of the Roman empire. However, the Semitic notion of the diaspora had struck a responsive chord among the Christians, who viewed their existence in this world of the secular kingdom as a temporary exile from their true home, the eternal kingdom of God. It is to these *parepidemois diasporas*, resident aliens in the diaspora of the world, that Peter addresses his First Epistle (1:1).

These assemblies, *ekklesiai*, which had been former synagogues, would now constitute themselves into *paroikiai*, parishes, retaining the diasporic notion of being away from home. Nevertheless, an important element transcended the temporal character of the local assemblies of the Church and constituted them into ecclesial communities: by being called together in one place to partake and be members of the body of Christ they experienced a remarkable sense of unity (1 Corinthians 10:16). Even though strangers and sojourners in the world, Christians formed a local *paroikia* thanks to their unity in Christ; they were already experiencing eschatologically the kingdom of God here on earth. In this spirit the author of the letter to Diognetus (6. 8) mentions the Christians dwelling here on earth "as aliens in the corruptible world, awaiting heavenly incorruptibility". The Eucharistic presence of Christ in the *paroikia* conferred on the community a total (*katholon*, catholic), integral, and internal universality, which had ultimately transcended the limitations of the exilic, diasporic existence. The centre was no longer Jerusalem but the universal, catholic, total experience of life found within Christ in the local assembly, the *ekklesia*, the living body of Christ formed by the individual members of the *paroikia*. If there would be one Jerusalem to return to, this would clearly not be the Jerusalem of this world, "for here have we no continuing city, but we seek one to come" (Hebrews 13: 14).

The Christian Roman empire had provided its citizens with the political frame of a coherent, ecumenical structure based on metaphysical convictions regarding the universal brotherhood of humanity; within that mutual consistency of its members, allowed to come into play by common Orthodox dogmas, the various diasporas had been absorbed by the all-embracing ecumenicity of the empire. This social mode of coexistence of the various ethnic diasporas had certainly been influenced by the message of the Church, which sought to unite all the scattered members of the body of Christ into one body. The Eucharistic experience, which made this union possible, occupied the central place in the ecclesial life of the Christian citizen.

Viewed in this light all former notions of diasporas had become obsolete; the only one still persisting in its old ways was associated with the messianic expectation of the eschatological *synagoge* of the elect people of God, the final assembly at Jerusalem, when the Messiah will abolish the divisive dispersion of his people.

The meaning of diaspora remained inoperative in the Greek world until the Ottoman conquest. As the seat of the Roman empire and the centre of medieval Hellenism fell into the hands of heterodox masters, an increasingly large number of Greeks took the road to exile. Since the seat of the patriarchate, the Great Church, was in unredeemed captivity, a profound hope for the restoration of the empire to its legitimate Romaic and Orthodox masters became widespread and was gradually enshrined in the consciousness of those who had fled to the centres of the Greek diasporas abroad. This profound hope was invested with a messianic vision of an eventual return to the lost imperial and metaphysical centre of modern

Η παρέλαση στη Νέα Υόρκη για την εθνική μας επέτειο

Παρών στην παρέλαση και ο Σύλλογος Μυστριωτών Αμερικής «Παντάνασσα» με το σύμβολο του Βυζαντίου που επιδεικνύουν υπερήφανα οι δύο χαριτωμένες κοπέλες της Μυστριώτικης παροικίας.

Diaspora: news report on a Greek parade in New York

Hellenism. The legend of the last emperor who turned to stone in Hagia Sophia, when the divine liturgy was interrupted as the Turks entered the city, and will be revived at the repossession of the city when the liturgy will be completed, points poignantly to the messianic hopes of the Greeks who had fled the city to seek protection in Christian lands.

The refugees who had settled in Venice, Florence, Padua, Budapest, Vienna, and in other European cities formed the modern communities of the diaspora and appropriated biblical notions of dispersion while nurturing eschatological ideas for an eventual *synaxis* (gathering) in the redeemed centre of their cultural, religious, and political identity. For the Hellenism of the diasporas the heavenly Jerusalem was replaced by Constantinople, which had now become the Polis, the city par excellence, with its Temple, Hagia Sophia, held by the infidels.

This intense longing to return to one's homeland was ever present in Greek literature, in folk songs, traditional tales, and in the popular imagination, constantly fed by the ancient, Odyssean craving for *nostos* (return). However, this primeval desire for *nostos* is now checked by the harsh reality of *xenitia*, life in foreign lands imbued with an unredeemed sense of political impotence. Although the theme of *xenitia*, wandering away from home, had been extensively used by the Church Fathers (the third chapter of St John Climacus' *Ladder* is titled "On Xenitia") to indicate an important spiritual trait in the life of the anchorite, the theological implications of *xenitia*, when elaborated by Church Fathers living under foreign occupation, begin to take on an increasingly secular meaning which is closer to worldly notions of diaspora.

The earliest transfer of meaning from the practice of *xenitia* as a longing for the heavenly home (*en Edem patris*) to a longing for the earthly homeland (*epigeios patris*) comes from a poem of the Cypriot saint Neophytos the Recluse, written in the latter part of the 12th or the early 13th century, when the island was ruled by Guy Lusignan. The wish to be released from the "enemy's bondage" and to regain the "ancient homeland" is expressed in such terms that it becomes ambivalent whether Neophytos is speaking of the dominion of Satan who prevents him from reaching his original home, the garden of Eden, or of the foreign master who has forced so many of his compatriots to experience *xenitia*, to flee from their island in order to live abroad; however, some verses lean towards the political situation that has forced so many Cypriots to live as strangers abroad. In this the poem is similar to other popular works written to lament the unenviable position of the Greeks living in the diasporas of Europe. As in Neophytos's poem, the various *Peri tis xenitias* (On Exile) or *Alfavitos xenitias* (The Alphabet of Exile) poems mainly deal, in a dirge-like manner, with the plight of strangers living in the diaspora: "The stranger is always sorrowful, unceasingly is he crying, the stranger always laments, having no consolation." This theme is increasingly reproduced in folk songs and traditional tales in the 15th and 16th centuries as the Turkish occupation of the Greek world spreads far and wide; nevertheless, it must be noted that it had begun to develop in Cyprus under Frankish, and later on in Crete, under Venetian occupation.

The notions of diaspora and *xenitia* began to loosen their firm hold on the Hellenic consciousness as the Greeks abroad showed signs of recovery from the initial shock of conquest and began to form communities within and through which they would exercise some rudimentary political rights. The Confraternita dei Greci founded in 1498 in Venice, the Greek Company of Sibiu in 1636, of Brasov in 1678, of Vienna, which secured its political rights at the treaty of Karlowitz in 1699, the political presence of the Phanariots in the Danubian principalities beginning in 1709, constitute some examples of a robust mercantile and political presence which, by the middle of the 18th century, had evolved into a full-fledged institution. It must be noted that the above dates mark the maturing point of the Hellenic communities of the diaspora and they should not be interpreted as a terminus a quo of their existence. The Hellenic community of Trieste obtained its official charter from the empress Maria Theresa and built its church and school in 1783, but it was settled by Greeks at least two centuries earlier, since there are accounts of Greeks leaving Pola (Pulj) for Trieste at the arrival in the former city, in 1562, of 180 families fleeing from the Turkish sack of Nauplia. The same remark applies to the Hellenic communities in Venice or in Pisa, which were in existence at least since the granting of trade privileges to those cities by the Byzantine emperors in the 12th century, and which were invigorated by the arrival of new waves of settlers in the 18th century.

An important line of distinction should be drawn here between the permanent settlements of Greeks outside the borders of the modern Greek nation and recent settlements receiving successive waves of settlers who had fled from their land as a result of foreign occupation. Whereas Paomia, and later Cargese in Corsica were settled in 1676 and 1775 respectively by Maniot Greeks, and may be qualified as centres of diaspora, the same cannot be said of Bulgarian Sozopolis, which was uninterruptedly inhabited by a Greek indigenous population. Neither the ancient cities of Asia Minor nor Constantinople itself could in any sense be portrayed as centres of the diaspora, since they had always been inhabited by Greeks and they were established as cultural and economic cradles of a larger Hellenism, which had survived there since antiquity.

By the beginning of the 19th century, when the Hellenic communities of the diaspora had achieved a satisfactory degree of self-government, the seeds of resistance against the oppressor matured into a full-scale uprising which, appropriately enough, was initially orchestrated from the Danubian principalities. When the descendants of the most prominent Phanariot families, Alexander Mavrokordatos and Dimitrios Ypsilantis, joined the war of liberation in Greece, their ambitions were motivated by the long-held aspiration of restoring the centre of Hellenism, Constantinople, to its rightful owners, the Greeks who had been dispersed in the diasporas of the world. When it became obvious that modern Hellenism was to be restricted within the small enclave of the Greek mainland, leaving the Hellenism of the periphery outside its borders, the Greeks of the centres of the diaspora began to pour into the liberated segment of Greece, thus precipitating the end of the age of the diaspora.

The wave of immigration to the Americas, Australia, and parts of Africa also had its great periods, especially as an aftermath of major national disasters such as the massive exodus of Greeks from Asia Minor in 1922, but it was totally deprived of the metaphysical or messianic motives that had conferred of old on the theme of the diaspora its mythopoeic qualities.

LAMBROS KAMPERIDIS

See also Colonization, Emigration

Further Reading

Geanakoplos, Deno John, *Byzantine East and Latin West: Two Worlds of Christendom in Middle Ages and Renaissance*, Oxford: Blackwell, and New York: Harper and Row, 1966

Iorga, Nicolae, *Byzance après Byzance*, Bucharest: Institut d'Etudes Byzantines, 1935, reprinted Bucharest: Association Internationale d'Etudes du Sud-Est Européen, 1971

Kamperidis, Lambros, *Early Signs of Greek Presence in the Modern Balkans*, Amsterdam, 1997, pp.95–106

Karathanassis, A.E., *L'Hellénisme en Transylvanie*, Thessalonica: Institute for Balkan Studies, 1989

Mavromatis, Y., *Ta peri tis xenitias poiemata* [Poems of Exile], Herakleion, 1995

Digenis Akritis

Hero of a Byzantine romance

Digenis Akritis is the hero of an epic-romance of Byzantine date and of ballads in 15-syllable verse collected in the 19th and 20th centuries. According to the romance, an Arab emir abducted, then married, the daughter of a Roman (i.e. Byzantine) general in the frontier area between Cappadocia and Syria. Their son Digenis ("of two races") proved a youthful prodigy in skirmishes with bandits (*apelatai*) and in hunting wild beasts. He too abducted a bride, another general's daughter, and defended her honour against bandits (including the female warrior Maximou) and supernatural beings. He imposed law and order in the region, acquiring the name Akritis ("frontiersman"). He then settled down with his wife on the banks of the Euphrates, to pass the rest of their lives in peaceful isolation in the magnificent castle he had constructed. This was not to be: Digenis succumbed to a fatal illness and, unable to bear the grief, his wife expired with him. Mourners came from far and wide to honour the youthful couple and to inter them in a conspicuous tomb.

This romantic story, which has epic overtones in its battle scenes, survives in six manuscripts dating from the early 13th century to 1672. All follow a similar plot but with considerable variation in wording. The two primary versions are those in manuscripts now kept in the Grottaferrata monastery near Rome (G, 13th century) and in the Escorial Library near Madrid (E, late 15th century). G's text, divided into 8 books, is written in an at times poorly controlled form of the Byzantine Koine. However, the narrative is reasonably well organized and coherent. E, an undivided yet episodic narrative, is less convincing as regards its plot, and its more popular language is seriously disturbed in the manuscript. There is much dispute over the relationship between these two versions: did G change into E or was a text like E rewritten to form a text like G? Recent work suggests that neither case is likely. Both versions probably draw loosely on a common original poem, the outline of whose plot can be perceived from close similarities between G and E but the details of which cannot now be reconstructed. The remaining four manuscripts represent versions of an early 16th-century compilation, made possibly in Venice for a printing which was never executed. The compilation was made on the basis of a text like G and the actual manuscript E.

The original poem that lies behind G and E had probably been composed in the mid-12th century, during the literary renaissance at that period when experiments were made with the literary use of vernacular Greek and there was a revival of interest in the novels of the ancient world. Reflections of the ancient novels and their Komnenian counterparts can be seen in *Digenis Akritis*, especially in G. There are also many historical allusions which hark back to the Byzantine–Arab wars of the 9th and 10th centuries, loosely reflecting the administrative structures of that period. It is very likely that the 12th-century poem was written in Constantinople, its narrative constructed from lays or ballads that had been circulating for many years in Anatolia, some concerned with the now legendary members of the Doukas family.

No doubt there were Byzantine folk songs on Digenis, but no direct signs of their existence are known before the mid-17th century. More surviving examples were collected in Pontus from around 1870 onwards, at about the time of the first rediscovery of a manuscript of the Byzantine romance in the Soumela monastery of Trebizond. The subjects include the abduction of Digenis' bride, the building of a castle, and his encounters with strange beasts. Variants on one of the most dramatic ballads, on Digenis' struggle with Charon, have been recorded throughout Anatolia and the Greek islands. It has been suggested that the ballads are the remains of the lays out of which *Digenis Akritis* was constructed, but it is more probable that the similarities are due to a common pool of traditional folk material. They continue to be sung to this day.

A number of ceramic plates, some, it seems, of 12th-century date, have been found in places such as Constantinople, Corinth, Athens, and Sparta, depicting scenes that arguably represent episodes from the epic or the ballads: these include a soldier in a pleated kilt (Digenis' traditional garment), a dragon pierced with darts, and a female warrior (Maximou?).

When the manuscripts of *Digenis Akritis* were brought to light at the end of the 19th century, this poem was hailed as Greece's medieval equivalent to Homer and to the European *Beowulf* and *Chanson de Roland*; its hero was claimed as a powerful national symbol, despite his explicitly mixed ancestry. Literary resonances from the epic can be found in the work of 20th-century writers, especially that of Kostis Palamas.

ELIZABETH M. JEFFREYS

See also Poetry (Epic, Antiquity)

Biography
Digenis Akritis is the mythical hero of an eponymous Byzantine epic-romance, compiled perhaps in the 12th century. Six manuscripts of the poem survive, of which two are early but display considerable variation. Episodes from the life of Digenis also feature in folk song and as illustrations on early ceramic plates. When the MSS first appeared (late 19th century) the poem was hailed as a medieval equivalent to the work of Homer.

Further Reading
Alexiou, S., *Vasileios Digenis Akritis kai to Asma tou Armouri* [King digenis Akritis and the Song of Armouri], Athens, 1985
Beaton, Roderick, *Folk Poetry of Modern Greece*, Cambridge and New York: Cambridge University Press, 1980
Grégoire, Henri, *Autour de l'Epopée byzantine*, London: Variorum, 1975
Jeffreys, Elizabeth (editor and translator), *Digenis Akritis: The Grottaferrata and Escorial Versions*, Cambridge and New York: Cambridge University Press, 1998
Kechaioglou, G., "Tyches tis Byzantinis Akritikis Poiisis sti Neoelliniki Logotechnia: Stathmoi kai Chriseis" [The Fortunes of the Byzantine Akritic Poem in Modern Greek Literature: Landmarks and Uses], *Ellenika*, 37 (1986): pp. 83–109
Notopoulos, J.A., "Akritan Ikonography on Byzantine Pottery", *Hesperia*, 33 (1964): pp. 108–33
Oikonomides, N., "L'Epopée de Digenes et la frontière orientale de Byzance aux Xe et XIe siècles", *Travaux et Mémoires*, 7 (1979): pp. 37–97
Saunier, G., "Le Combat avec Charos dans les chansons populaires grecques", *Ellenika*, 25 (1972): pp. 119–53, 335–70
Trapp, Erich, *Digenes Akrites: synoptische Ausgabe der ältesten Versionen*, Vienna: Böhlau, 1971

Dimaras, K.T. 1904–1992

Historian of ideas

Konstantinos Thiseos Dimaras was one of the most important Greek thinkers of the 20th century. He was one of the leading representatives of the "1930s generation" and befriended many of them, including George Theotokas and George Seferis. He was one of the founders of comparative literature in Greece, focusing his research mainly on the "history of ideas". Although his whole work emits a universal and transcendental feeling of Hellenism from antiquity to the present, he is considered to be the first, as well as the most important, scholar of the Modern Greek Enlightenment. Besides, it is he who established this term.

As he himself effectively put it, both his parents' families "were merchants, and for this reason they loved education". He had his father's and maternal grandfather's large libraries at his disposal. He grew up in a loving, scholarly environment: Nikolaos Dimaras, law professor, was his father's brother, while Constantine Raktivan, a great jurist, was his mother's brother. Prominent personages of the time frequented his house, including the Delta family, Dimitrios Balanos, and the linguist Manolis Triantaphyllidis, a distant relative who introduced the young Dimaras into the conflict over the predominance of demotic Greek. After that, Dimaras maintained a stable and, at the same time, critical relationship with the demotic Greek movement. He attended the Makris school where his contact with the strong personality of Ioannis Apostolakis was crucial, since it was to this scholar that he owed his introduction to "idealism". In 1926 Delmouzos and Apostolakis invited him to contribute to *Ellinika Grammata* (Greek Literature), which was edited by Kostis Bastias.

The philosophical quest of his youth was very strong, hence his registration at the Faculty of Philosophy of the University of Athens in 1921, where he was significantly influenced by Theophilos Voreas. He concluded that he had to study the sciences in order to "philosophize". As a result he studied physics and mathematics for four years and subsequently registered as a student at the medical school. This period left its mark on him, as it equipped him with many of the methodological tools that he would later use in his historical and philological research. He returned to the Faculty of Philosophy in 1925, where Constantine Amantos steered him towards the history of literature.

In retrospect, Dimaras later revealed his first serious readings: "I read incessantly ... I read many of the ancient authors ... the Presocratics, as well as Philostratus, Diogenes Laertius, and minor authors of ancient Greek literature." As for modern literary production, he was fascinated by Adamantios Korais and Kostis Palamas. Dimaras was a genuine representative of the "1930s Generation"; he retained close and fertile contact with European, particularly French, culture. He was attracted by the religious philosophy of Abbé Brémont; he read Maritain, and René Guénon, with whom he also corresponded. He studied the New Testament, Plato, Aristotle, Spinoza, Pascal. He included in his lectures authors who were ideologically conservative, like Charles Maurras, Léon Daudet, and the circle of Action Française. He described André Gide as "a great master of virtue" through his *Nourritures Terrestres*,

programmatic aims, as in the case of his opinions of June–August 1942, particularly the one entitled "Means and Ends". In this article Dimaras outlined "a programme for the study of Modern Greek literature, particularly during the period of the Turkish Occupation". Through the number and variety of these publications one can discern what the critic Alexandros Argyriou justly called "a free thinker". In his publications Dimaras expressed his philosophical and aesthetic tendencies, his "eusebism", which, during his mature period evolved into "adiaphorism", his curiosity, as well as his gradual passage through the various stages of the Greek literary tradition from antiquity to the Middle Ages and the modern period. His first two treatises, that were forgotten for many years, presented a particular interest: *Treatise on the Physical Theology of the 5th-century* BC *Sophists* (1926), which stemmed from a course of Theophilos Voreas. It dealt with the much-discussed subject of the Sophists' atheism. In his 1927 treatise entitled *Parmenidis: Introduction to the Philosophy of Parmenidis and Translation of his On Truth* Dimaras advocated the idea of the separation of philosophy from science.

In 1933 he published in *Nea Estia* a short comment entitled "Memorial for Korais", thus inaugurating a long period of study of the man and his work, which resulted, among other things, in the definitive edition of the voluminous correspondence of Adamantios Korais in six volumes (Athens, "Group for the Study of Greek Enlightenment", 1964–84).

Dimaras expressed his interest in poetry very early. In 1932 he published his study "Some Sources of the Art of Cavafy" in the journal *O Kyklos*, while in 1934 he published an anonymous review of the first collection of George Seferis entitled *Strophi* (Turn) in the journal *Vivlia* (Books). The following year he published the important theoretical treatise "Seven Chapters on Poetry" in the journal *Nea Grammata*. Among his later contributions, were his monograph *Kostis Palamas: Hi poreia tou pros tin techni* [Kostis Palamas: His Road to Art] (1947), and the translation of Constantine Cavafy's poems into French, in collaboration with Marguerite Yourcenar in 1958 (2nd edition 1978).

However, his detachment from aesthetic evaluations, as well the influence that his thinking received from the methods of comparative literary history, took place around 1940. The influence of Kostis Palamas, and the intellectual debate of the "1930s Generation" also contributed to this development. Dimaras believed that modern Greek studies "belonged to a large context which not only involved chronological antiquity, but also involved the geographical west". The great compositions of Daniel Mornet, Paul Van Tieghem, Paul Hazard, etc., expanding the field of research, relationships, and coincidence (*coincidences, simultanéités*), fitted his psyche, and he consequently adhered to the emerging "history of ideas". Dimaras followed the so-called French School, which was based on the literary history of Gustave Lanson. He did not adhere to the various innovative trends which flourished from the 1950s on. By totally emphasizing the "empirical" character of phenomena, the tracking of "multiple causes", and the practice of "successive approaches", and by declaring the absolute supremacy of historical continuity, he believed that literature or history (including historiography) can only be comparative. He based this theory on the fact that "one cannot isolate a

K. T. Dimaras, historian of ideas

and when Gide visited Greece, he met him in person. He also mentions Julien Benda. He was considerably influenced by Albert Thibaudet as well; it was from him that Dimaras adopted the use of the term "generation", which seriously preoccupied him, and which he consistently elaborated in his work.

A freelance period started in 1926. Dimaras contributed articles to several philological periodicals of the time, *Ellinika Grammata* (Greek Literature), *O Kyklos* (The Circle), *Eos* (Dawn), *Idea*, *Nea Estia* (New Hearth), etc., sometimes under an alias like "KONST(antinidis)", "Philonous", "P. Raphael". He later contributed articles to *Philologiki Protochronia*, *Aggloelliniki Epitheorisi*, *L' Hellénisme Contemporain*, *Epoches*, etc. He also contributed entries to the *Megali Elliniki Egkyklopaideia*. These articles were followed by his "Opinions" in the daily press, *Proia*, and *Politeia*. As of 1936, an important stage in his career began with his regular, weekly collaboration with the *Eleutheron Vima* (the later *Vima*), in which he wrote the column "The World of Culture". However, he did not confine himself to literary criticism and book reviews for long. His opinions "gradually turned from literary criticism towards the history of literature and ... methodology". There are more than 2000 of these articles which date from 1936 to 1987, when he stopped his collaboration with *Vima*, and cumulatively they function as a "national inventory", in sympathy with Dimaras's aims. At times, they carried

cultural phenomenon in one area, and cannot avoid continuously correlating different cultures". By using comparativism as a tool, a science of convergence, as well as "a science of differences", one is able to penetrate the specificity of Hellenism.

From the end of the 1930s it is possible to discern an evolutionary course and, most importantly, duration in Dimaras's work. Comparativism was present in its various aspects as the study of literary movements and genres; as the stamp of the "prerequisites" for their entrance into Greek cultural life; as a tracking of "sources" and "influences" (*Romantika Simeiomata* [Notes on Romanticism], 4 vols., 1944–46, *Phrontismata 1: Apo tin Anagenisi ston Diaphotismo* [Phrontismata, Part One: From Renaissance to Enlightenment], 1963 etc.); as an interpretative approach to "social" and "cultural" groups; and as the crystallization of new ideas and concepts. Dimaras's trajectory can be summarized as follows: from the "history of ideas" he moved to the "history of culture" (from the period of the German occupation on), and then to the "history of conscience".

During the period of the German occupation Dimaras gave a series of ten courses that formed the first kernel for his history of literature. He was encouraged by Konstantinos Amantos, the lectures of 1946 at "Athenaeum" followed, and, last but not least, he received a commission to write a history of literature from Ikaros Publishers. Dimaras's most important work, the *Historia tis neoellinikis logotechnias* [History of Modern Greek Literature], was published in 1948 and 1949 in two volumes. It was reprinted many times (eight to date), as well as translated into other languages (French, Romanian, Bulgarian, and English). It constitutes a fundamental tool which respects the totality of Hellenism and "attempts to define the term Modern Greek". By juxtaposing it to the term "post-Byzantine", which survived in various sectors, including art and law, Dimaras traced the formation of a "pre-Modern Greek" element in the Byzantine civilization, already present in the 13th century BC. This work is a synthesis that also identifies multiple causes while attempting to define the "character" of Hellenism within the greater geographic area of southeast Europe, where it developed. Its history is not based on extraordinary cases, on the aesthetic evaluation of a certain number of masterpieces. In the succession of phenomena, average works, minor thinkers, translations, the non-literary, scientific discourse occupy an important interpretative position, next to the "peaks".

In his later years Dimaras concentrated more on aspects of lexicography and ideology, as is obvious from the important Introduction to the reprint of the *Synagogi Neon Lexeon* [Collection of New Words] by Stephanos Koumanoudis (1980). He also dealt with aspects of the historiography of modern Hellenism, a subject which he treated in his studies, several of which were included in the volume *Ellinikos Romantismos* [Greek Romanticism] (1982). He was occupied by the individual factor in history, the relationship of the individual to collective bodies in great national or international affairs. He oriented himself to a renewed view of biography, as is evident in his important study entitled *Constantine Paparigopoulos: His Time, His Life, His Work* (1986), as well as his study of educational institutions and his treatise on the founding of the University of Athens entitled *Athens, 3 May 1837: A Historical and Philological Study*.

Dimaras has been recognized as the scholar of the Modern Greek Enlightenment par excellence. He already made use of the term in his 1945 article entitled "The French Revolution and Greek Enlightenment" in the journal *Dimokratika Chronika* (Democratic Chronicles). In a multitude of articles and studies, in which the work of Dimitrios Katartzis was discovered and made known, and which culminated in the publication of *Euriskomena* (Extant Opus; 1970), Dimaras dealt with all aspects of the phenomenon. In 1965 he published a small volume entitled *Symposiaka (Symptoseis–glossa–genees)* [Symposiaka (Coincidence–Language–Generations)], while in 1969 he published a small, though essential, compilation of studies in French which was entitled *La Grèce au temps de Lumières* (Geneva, Droz). In 1977 he published his compilation entitled *Neoellinikos Diaphotismos* (Modern Greek Enlightenment), which was reprinted many times. In his introduction he mentions several key concepts that are crucial in his work: the quest for "collective or national characterology"; the prosopographical and psychographical interest that preoccupied him after his youth; a need to "measure"; and the "statistical conscience" which is indispensable to the history of ideas, mentalities, and of conscience.

Dimaras was a scholar who was dedicated to his work, although he also happily contributed to public affairs, in his own way, by creating and establishing important and, in their time, pioneering institutions. In 1951 George Papandreou, then Minister of Education, asked him to organize and direct the Foundation for State Scholarships. Already in an opinion dated 1946 Dimaras had underlined the need for such an institution. In 1959, aided by Leonidas Zervas and Ioannis Pesmazoglou, he contributed to the founding of the Royal Foundation for Research, currently the National Hellenic Research Foundation (NHRF). He became the first Directing Adviser and Director of the Centre for Neohellenic Research (CNR) which was founded in December 1960. In the CNR, which was his spiritual child, he laid the foundations for his research strategy through the compilation of seminal works for the "national census" of later Hellenism. He held this position until 1970, when he was removed from it by the April dictatorship. In 1961 he founded, together with Dimitrios Ginis and a group of scholars, the "Group for the Study of Greek Enlightenment", which was one of the earliest of such societies in Europe. He also laid the foundations for the series "Nea Ellinika Keimena" (Modern Greek Texts), and for the journal of this group entitled *O Eranistis*. After his removal from the NHRF, he was invited to assume the direction of Neohellenic Institute of the Sorbonne, where he also occupied the chair of Modern Greek Literature. He retired from that position in 1978. After that he did not hold any office and dedicated himself to writing. Although Dimaras reluctantly accepted his professorial position, he acquired, directly and indirectly, many disciples. Through his methodology, as well as his long career in Greek letters, he exercised a considerable influence on his contemporaries, as well as on the following generations.

ANNA TABAKI

See also Enlightenment

Biography

Born in Athens in 1904 to a family of merchants, Dimaras studied physics, mathematics, and philosophy as well as the history of literature at the University of Athens. He became a leading representative of the "1930s generation", contributing to various periodicals and newspapers. His *History of Modern Greek Literature* appeared in two volumes in 1948–49. He was Director of the Centre for Neohellenic Research in Athens from 1960 to 1970 before becoming professor of Modern Greek Literature at the Sorbonne, 1970–78. He died in Paris in 1992.

Writings

"Epta kephalaia gia tin poiisi" [Seven Chapters on Poetry], *Ta Nea Grammata*, 1 (1935)

Romantika Simeiomata [Notes on Romanticism], 4 vols, Athens, 1944–46

Kostis Palamas: Hi poreia tou pros tin techni [Kostis Palamas: His Road to Art], Athens, 1947

Historia tis neoellinikis logotechnias, Athens, 1948–49; translated as *A History of Modern Greek Literature*, Albany: State University of New York Press, 1972

Présentation critique de Constantin Cavafy, 1863–1933, with Marguerite Yourcenar, Paris: Gallimard, 1958, 2nd edition, 1978

Phrontismata, 1: *Apo tin Anagenisi ston Diaphotismo* [Phrontismata, part 1: From Renaissance to Enlightenment], Athens, 1962

Symposiaka (Symptoseis–glossa–genees) [Symposiaka (Coincidence–Language–Generations)], Athens, 1965

La Grèce au temps du Lumières, Geneva: Droz, 1969

Neoellinikos Diaphotismos [Modern Greek Enlightenment], Athens, 1977

Ellinikos Romantismos [Greek Romanticism], Athens, 1982

Constantine Paparigopoulos, Athens, 1986

Further Reading

"Ergographia K. Th. Dimara" [The Works of Dimaras], offprint from the volume *Neoellinikos Diaphotismos: Aphieroma ston K. Th. Dimara* [Modern Greek Enlightenment: Dedicated to Dimaras], 1974, 1980

Peninta chronia neoellinikis paideias: Hi parousia tou K. Th. Dimara stin epistemi ton neoellinikon gramaton [Fifty Years of Greek Culture: Dimaras' Presence in the Science of Greek Letters], Athens, 1985

Politou-Marmarinou, Helen, "Ho K. Th. Dimaras, themeliotis tis Synkritikis Philologias stin Ellada [Dimaras, Founder of Comparative Literature in Greece], *Synkrisi / Comparaison*, 4 (June 1992): pp. 2–6

Tabaki, Anna, "La Méthode comparatiste dans l'oeuvre de Dimaras", *Synthésis*, 20 (1993): pp. 93–101

Dio Cocceianus *c.*AD 40–112

Orator and philosopher

The life and career of Dio Cocceianus not only form the background to his literary work, but also provide valuable insights into the situation of the Greeks under Roman rule during the so-called "high" empire (1st and 2nd centuries AD). Born into an influential family in Prusa in the province of Bithynia (northeastern Asia Minor), Dio first attained a prominent position as a well-educated Greek intellectual in Rome under the Flavian emperors. When, however, he (apparently) became implicated in the disgrace of a prominent Roman, Flavius Sabinus, under Domitian, he was banned from Rome and his home province; suddenly destitute, he took up the life of a wandering philosopher with Cynic affinities, roaming as far as the very outposts of Greek culture on the northern shore of the Black Sea. With the accession of the emperor Nerva (and his adoptive son Trajan) in AD 96, Dio was able to return to Prusa, where he regained his family's leading position and apparently played a major (though not uncontroversial) role in local and provincial politics until his death. Most of Dio's so-called *Bithynian Speeches* were written during this time and give valuable insights into the numerous rivalries not only within Greek provincial cities but also among them, and into their relations with Roman authorities.

Dio did not confine his public appearances to his home province, but also exhorted a number of other cities in Asia Minor (and even Alexandria in Egypt) to remain true to their former ideals and to keep the peace with each other and within themselves. He also addressed four speeches *On Kingship* to the emperor Trajan, with whom he developed a relationship marked by mutual respect and friendship. Apart from such speechmaking, Dio's oeuvre comprises an astonishing variety of themes and literary forms: essays on moral themes (*On Servitude, On Liberty, On Fate, On Philosophy*, etc.); lively dialogues that often feature the colourful figure of Diogenes the Cynic; treatises on literary subjects (e.g. a comparative study of the three Philoctetes plays written by the great Classical tragedians); a guide to suitable literary models for rhetorical imitation; and even writings on art (the *Olympic Discourse* is centred on Phidias' magnificent statue of *Zeus* at Olympia and the religious awe it conveyed). An especially entertaining part of this production consisted in so-called "sophistic" display rhetoric and treatments of paradoxical themes (the *Praise of the Parrot* is lost, and of the *Praise of Hair* some excerpts were incorporated by Synesius in his *Praise of Baldness*); an impressive tour de force is the *Trojan Discourse To Show that Troy Was Not Captured*, directed against the monumental work of Homer himself (but not really meant seriously, because Dio in many other essays quite happily accepts Homer as a model and teacher). Not all of this enormous production (the transmitted corpus contains 80 items, including two false attributions; but a number of works have been lost, some of which are still cited by their title in the late 10th-century *Suda* lexicon) can be securely dated. A number of works certainly go back to the time before Dio's exile, but the greater part was probably written afterwards (in exile he collected material for a now lost *Getica*, a historical description of this Scythian people).

The wide range of Dio's literary work prompted a lively debate about his exact position within the cultural currents of his times: was he to be reckoned more as a philosopher or as a rhetorician? This debate started soon after his death, and its long duration was one of the marks of his continuing influence: the philosopher Epictetus judged Dio to be only a rhetorician, more intent on form than on content, but Dio's pupil Favorinus regarded him – more positively – as a guiding moral authority even after his death, even seeing him in dreams. Lucian – in *De Morte Peregrini* – placed him beside the philosophers Musonius and Epictetus himself, both of whom suffered exile for their persuasions. In the 3rd century AD the "historian of sophists" Philostratus gave two pictures of Dio not wholly consistent with each other: in his *Life of Apollonius* he made Dio participate in a momentous (but fictional) "Constitutional Debate" with Euphrates of Tyre and Apollonius of Tyana, in the presence of the future emperor Vespasian; in the *Lives of the Sophists* he characterized him as a philosopher-sophist, whose philosophical disposition was clothed in the rhetorical abilities of a Sophist. In the latter part of the 4th century the philosopher-rhetor Themistius mentions Dio within a series of philosopher-advisers of Roman emperors; in the *Lives of the Philosophers and Sophists* of Eunapius, he is similarly ranked as a philosopher. A few years later, a more discriminating and in later times very influential picture of Dio was outlined by the Neoplatonist (and later bishop) Synesius of Cyrene: according to him, Dio set out as a clear-cut sophist, who even wrote strident tracts against philosophy, and only turned philosopher during and after his exile, so that his writings should be carefully divided into pre- and post-exile productions.

The other enduring aspect of Dio's influence was the style and content of his various works which provided stimulants and stylistic models until the end of Byzantium. Already in Lucian's writings many features of Dio's work reappear. In the 3rd century AD Menander of Laodicea (who was the first to record Dio's later canonical name "Chrysostomus") cites Dio as an example of an easy-running and graceful style, and as such he continues to be read. Our first witness for the importance of Dio in Byzantine times is – as so often – Photios, who in a detailed account in his *Bibliotheca* (Codex 209) not only discusses Dio's life and style of writing but also gives an item-by-item outline of the corpus of his works as it was extant in his day (this, incidentally, is identical with what is still preserved). Soon after, Arethas of Caesarea (though he strangely misplaced Dio by making him a contemporary of Nero and Vespasian and even more strangely explained his surname "Chrysostomus" as a euphemism for "stinking-mouth") not only ensured the ongoing transmission of Dio's works, but also added numerous and rich explanatory notes to the manuscript that was produced on his initiative. Arethas especially commented on those writings of Dio that were to be at the centre of the Byzantines' interests for centuries to come: the speeches *On Kingship*, the *Euboean Discourse* (a charming picture of the simple rural life on Euboea combined with moral advice for the urban poor), the *Borysthenitic Discourse* (a vivid description of Dio's visit to Olbia on the Black Sea and the cosmological myth he told there), and the *Trojan Discourse*. In the 11th century John Mavropous wrote a speech for the emperor Constantine IX that drew on Dio's *Borystheniticus* and kingship speeches; the latter also provided a model for the address to Constantine X written by Theophylact, archbishop of Ochrid. In the 12th century Dio's *Troicus* aroused the ire of John Tzetzes, who severely condemned every attempt *not* to take Homer's *Iliad* allegorically. Even Eustathios, the indefatigable commentator on the Homeric poems, seems to have taken Dio's anti-Homeric tour de force seriously. The last major witness to the Byzantines' unflagging interest in Dio is the essay on him by Theodore Metochites (1270–1332), wherein he subtly compares him to Synesius, Dio's most prominent admirer in late antiquity, and stresses the artfulness of his seemingly simple style. Because, however, even this simplicity moved within the confines of a long since obsolete literary language (the Attic of the 4th century BC), Dio's literary influence ended with the Byzantine empire.

HEINZ-GÜNTHER NESSELRATH

Biography

Born *c*.AD 40 at Prusa, Dio moved to Rome as a rhetorician, but was banished for political intrigue and spent many years wandering about the Greek-speaking world. In 96 he was able to return to Prusa where he played a part in local politics until his death *c*.112. His surviving works, a total of 78, include speeches, essays, and dialogues on philosophical as well as rhetorical topics.

Writings

Dio Chrysostom, translated by J.W. Cohoon and H.L. Crosby, 5 vols, London: Heinemann, and Cambridge, Massachusetts: Harvard University Press, 1932–51 (Loeb edition)

Orations 7, 12 and 36, edited by D.A. Russell, Cambridge and New York: Cambridge University Press, 1992

Discours bithyniens, translation and commentary by Marcel Cuvigny, Paris: Belles Lettres, 1994

Further Reading

Brancacci, Aldo, *Rhetorike philosophousa: Dione Crisostomo nella cultura greca e bizantina*, Rome: Bibliopolis, 1985

Desideri, Paolo, *Dione di Prusa: Un intellettuale greco nell'impero romano*, Messina and Florence: d'Anna, 1978

Harris, B.F., "Dio of Prusa: A Survey of Recent Work" in *Aufstieg und Niedergang der römischen Welt*, edited by Hildegard Temporini *et al.*, 2. 33. 5, Berlin: de Gruyter, 1991, 3853–81

Jones, C.P., *The Roman World of Dio Chrysostom*, Cambridge, Massachusetts: Harvard University Press, 1978

Moles, J., "The Career and Conversion of Dio Chrysostom", *Journal of Hellenic Studies*, 98 (1978): pp. 79–100

Moles, J., "The Kingship Orations of Dio Chrysostom" in *Roman Poetry, Drama, Greek Epic, Comedy, Rhetoric*, edited by Francis Cairns and Malcolm Heath, Leeds: Cairns, 1990

Moles, J., "Dio Chrysostom, Greece, and Rome" in *Ethics and Rhetoric: Classical Essays for Donald Russell on his Seventy-Fifth Birthday*, edited by Doreen Innes, Harry Hine and Christopher Pelling, Oxford: Clarendon Press, and New York: Oxford University Press, 1995

Swain, Simon, "Dio and Lucian" in *Greek Fiction: The Greek Novel in Context*, edited by J.R. Morgan and Richard Stoneman, London and New York: Routledge, 1994

Swain, Simon, *Hellenism and Empire: Language, Classicism, and Power in the Greek World, AD 50–250*, Oxford: Clarendon Press, and New York: Oxford University Press, 1996, pp. 187–241

Diocese

Unit of administration

The term diocese refers to various administrative units, all of which suggest divisions or subdivisions for the purposes of organized management. The use of the term for administrative units is Hellenistic in origin. It had a profound conceptual influence on forms of imperial and ecclesiastical administration, even as the term itself took on various meanings in different contexts. The early uses of the term refer to the responsibilities of treasury officials; later it was used to refer to different types of territorial divisions within Roman and Byzantine imperial and/or ecclesiastical structures. Through a process of linguistic generalization, the term also came to be used for an ordering by Christ, the angels, the Church, etc. The history of the term begins in the Hellenistic period with reference to the *dioiketes*, a Ptolemaic official responsible for the financial and interior matters of the king (see Bagnall, 1976). Early in the Roman empire the term was used synonymously with *conventus*, a provincial subdivision that defined a community for the purposes of administration. The sense of diocese as *conventus* would persist in some areas of the Roman empire into the 4th century AD and perhaps beyond, even after Diocletian divided the empire into 12 dioceses for centralized administration in the late 3rd century AD. Diocese also became a territorial unit of ecclesiastical administration, in which capacity it persisted, in concept, in the Byzantine Church into the 12th century. The more recent division of church diocese is related to these earlier divisions, but only in the sense of the organized territorial division of a larger entity, not literally in terms of the geographic areas of these older divisions.

The first territorial use of the term diocese, apart from the implications for financial administration suggested by the Ptolemaic *dioiketes*, occurs in Greek writings describing the Roman administration system of *conventus*. Strabo, for example, describes dioceses as units of territorial and legal division in the same areas that other authors describe as *conventus* (*Geography*, 3. 4. 19–20). The *conventus* as a subdivision of a province is attested most notably in Spain, Dalmatia, Asia, Cilicia, and Sicily. The *conventus* functioned as an administrative unit for taking assizes and later formed literal divisions of provinces in some areas for the purposes of legal administration and as a subdivision of the imperial cult. Some scholars have argued that the *conventus* system itself was borrowed from a Pergamene institution, although this explanation has been challenged convincingly (see Burton, 1975). In most areas, *conventus* divisions appear to have been obviated early in the empire as older provinces were subdivided into newer, smaller provinces; but in some areas, such as Spain, they persisted. Cicero describes as dioceses the divisions known by Pliny the Elder and others as *conventus*, thus further suggesting that the term diocese was the Greek term for the Latin *conventus* (see Albertini, 1923). It was the Greek term rather than the Latin that would be more prominent in the later administrative structures of the empire and, with it, the Church.

With Diocletian's restructuring of the empire in the late 3rd century AD the term diocese was used to refer to the larger supraprovincial divisions of the empire presided over by a *vicar*. The Verona List (*c.*AD 297) records 12 such dioceses: Africa, Asia, Britain, Gaul, Italy, Moesia, Oriens, Pannonia, Pontus, Seven Provinces, Spain, and Thrace. Some of these were subdivided later – Italy was divided in two with capitals at Rome and Milan; Moesia became Dacia and Macedonia; Oriens became Egypt and Oriens. According to some historians, the division of provinces sounded the death knell for the few remaining *conventus* dioceses remaining in the empire, since their usefulness was challenged by the smaller administrative units. Some *conventus* divisions continue to appear in the sources, however, such as the 5th-century *Chronicle* of Hydatius and the Council of Toledo (*c.*400). Nevertheless, Diocletian's division did incorporate the lines of some of the earlier *conventus* dioceses in the few areas they are still attested. Diocletian's diocesan system stopped working effectively during the 5th century (Jones, 1964, p.374). More than one emperor during this century and after deemphasized the role of the vicar and diocese in the administration of the empire. References to the diocesan system disappear during the 7th century.

Ecclesiastical dioceses followed the lines set out by Diocletian's redivision. Church councils and other writings of the 4th century (First Council of Constantinople, John Chrysostom, Socrates) refer specifically to most of the Diocletianic dioceses as basic units of church administration. The bishops of dioceses became known as exarchs and/or patriarchs. Ecclesiastical dioceses were subsequently divided into episcopal provinces, known as *eparchiai* and *paroikia*. The *eparchia* was associated with the metropolitan bishop, and the *paroikia* with those in surrounding areas. In its capacity as a unit of Church organization in the East modelled loosely on the provincial organization, the term diocese persisted into the 12th century, when it appears in the writings of canonists. Some canonists suggest that the term had undergone changes in exact administrative usage since the 4th century. Balsamon (*Patrum Graecorum*, 137. 420) specifically suggests that the privileges and powers of metropolitans vis-à-vis exarchs had changed somewhat in favour of the metropolitans, who appear to be no longer under the authority of exarchs. After the 12th century the term diocese in this sense no longer appears in reference to Church administration. The hierarchy of patriarch / metropolitan / bishop, however, became permanently written into the Byzantine Church, and has affected subsequent Church organizations.

As a Greek term and inspired by Hellenic and Hellenistic adminstrative structures and concepts, the diocese had an important influence. Administrative structures in the Roman and Byzantine empires as well as in the ecclesiastical administration of the Byzantine Church and its progenies were shaped, if only by homology, by the diocesan concept of administration and organization.

MARK W. GRAHAM

Further Reading

Albertini, Eugène, *Les Divisions administratives de L'Espagne romaine*, Paris: Boccard, 1923

Anderson, J.G.C., "The Genesis of Diocletian's Provincial Reorganization", *Journal of Roman Studies*, 22 (1932): pp. 23–32

Bagnall, Roger S., *The Administration of the Ptolemaic Possessions outside Egypt*, Leiden: Brill, 1976

Barnes, Timothy D., "Emperors, Panegyrics, Prefects, Provinces and Palaces, 284–317", *Journal of Roman Archaeology*, 9 (1996): pp. 532–52

Burton, G.P., "Proconsul, Assizes and the Administration of Justice under the Empire", *Journal of Roman Studies*, 65 (1975): pp. 92–106

Dolores Dopoico Cainzos, M., "Los conventus iuridici: origen, cronologia y naturaleza histórica", *Gerion*, 4 (1986): pp. 265–83

Engelmann, H. and D. Knibbe, "Das Zollgesetz der Provinz Asia: eine neue Inschriften aus Ephesos", *Epigraphica Anatolica*, 14 (1989): pp. 1–206

Fliche, Augustin and Victor Martin, *Histoire de l'Église*, Paris: Blond & Gay, 1936, pp. 437–87

Jones, A.H.M., *The Later Roman Empire, 284–602: A Social, Economic and Administrative Survey*, 3 vols, Oxford: Blackwell, and Norman: University of Oklahoma Press, 1964

Kallet-Marx, Robert Morstein, *Hegemony to Empire: The Development of the Roman Imperium in the East from 148 to 62 BC*, Berkeley: University of California Press, 1995

Noethlichs, K.L. "Zur Entstehung der Diözasen als Mettelinstanz des spätrömischen Verwaltungssystems", *Historia*, 31 (1982): pp. 70–81

Diodorus Siculus

Historian of the 1st century BC

One seldom encounters a figure so wrapped in the Greek tradition as Diodorus Siculus. Neglected by his contemporaries and often discounted by modern scholars, his work preserves priceless portions of Greek history and historiography. His *Library of History* claims to trace the history of the entire world from creation up to Diodorus' own days, formally ending with Caesar's consulate in 60 BC. Of Diodorus himself we know little, except for what we can glean from this work, which he claims was 30 years in the making. He was a native of Agyrium in Sicily, visited Egypt around 60–56 BC, and had some familiarity with Latin and Rome. The last event he mentions seems to be from 36 BC. Apart from ethnographic excursions in the early books, Diodorus' focus is almost entirely on Greece, Rome, and Sicily. Of the *Library*'s 40 books only 15 survive intact (1–5, 11–20), as well as substantial fragments from the remaining 25. These remains form the largest corpus of Greek history to survive from antiquity to our own day.

Diodorus' *Library* provides an intriguing glimpse into many varieties of Greek historical writings that would otherwise be largely unknown to us. The *Library* incorporates – relatively faithfully and relatively uncritically – a vast amount of otherwise lost literature in abridged form. After a brief account of the creation of the world, he gives an ethnography of Egypt, mostly from Hecataeus of Abdera; a legendary history of Mesopotamia, from Ctesias; and an account of India from Megasthenes. He then gives copious summaries of myths, canonical and deliberately outrageous, relying on Dionysius Scytobrachion and several others. In subsequent books he preserves tales about the Seven Sages, legendary lawgivers, and Themistocles, giving us a window into Greek traditions. His version of the Peloponnesian War and its origins, based on Ephorus and possibly Philistus, provides an interesting contrast to Thucydides. Diodorus provides our only continuous narrative of the history of 4th-century BC Greece, including book 16, which is devoted entirely to Philip II of Macedon. Book 17 is the earliest continuous surviving narrative of the campaigns of Philip's son Alexander, an account possibly adapted from Cleitarchus. Books 18–20, based on the work of Hieronymus of Cardia, are our best source for the wars of Alexander's successors. In addition to all of this material, Diodorus often shifts the scene and discusses contemporary developments in his native Sicily, using the histories of such fellow Sicilians as Timaeus and Philinus. It has been aptly said that a history of that island would be impossible without Diodorus. Later fragments, including a large narrative of the Sicilian Slave War of *c*.136–132 BC, may ultimately derive from the work of Posidonius. In addition to many historical works, mythographies, and ethnographies, Diodorus summarizes at least one novel, *The Islands of the Sun* by Iambulus.

Diodorus' intent was to produce an all-encompassing, chronologically accurate, handy compendium of world history. He was neither a deep historical thinker nor an adept prose stylist. He avoids elevated language and overtly strives for a monotonous consistency in style. These considerations – combined with the patently derivative nature of his work – kept him from gaining acclaim or respect among his Augustan contemporaries. He is first mentioned in a backhanded compliment from Pliny, who notes that the *Library* of Diodorus, unlike most second-hand anthologies, has an honest title. However, generations of Greeks found his compendium so useful that it was preserved, while almost all other Hellenistic prose literature – stylistically out of fashion – was consigned to oblivion. Aelian was apparently familiar with him and Athenaeus cites him. He receives copious praise and use from chronographers and writers from Eusebius in the 4th century AD to John Tzetzes in the 12th. These writers valued utilitarian history over good style or subtle theories of causation. Chronographers clearly also appreciated Diodorus' original integration of Roman and Greek chronology: even today he remains our earliest and most important source for the Roman *Fasti Consulares*. Diodorus was not always successful at synchronizing the Roman calendar with the Athenian one, and his work suffers from the embarrassing lapses one would expect from such a vast, self-published encyclopaedia. In the *Library* events are rigidly divided annalistically by archon and consular years, often interrupting the narrative and resulting in doublets and confusion.

In the Byzantine empire Diodorus' vision of a historical reference book seems to have found kindred spirits. Diodorus was summarized by Photios (Codex 70) whose praise is particularly effusive, complimenting his clear and unaffected style as well as his historical acumen. Another index of Diodorus' later popularity is the note in the *Suda* that Diodorus lived past the reign of Augustus, which possibly indicates a posthumous continuation of his work. Large fragments of lost books of Diodorus are preserved in the excerpts compiled under the direction of the emperor Constantine VII Porphyrogennetos (913–59), divided into convenient sections ostensibly for the purpose of ready reference by statesmen and scholars. The rediscovery of Diodorus in the west was also greeted with enthusiasm by a Renaissance reading public eager to learn more of the Greek past. This enthusiasm became muted in the following three centuries as Diodorus' intellectual poverty, his often compressed and muddled narrative, and frequently faulty chronology became more apparent.

Increasingly scholars are exploring the complex relationship between Diodorus' text and his sources. Even where it can be shown that Diodorus is rewriting earlier narratives, simply abridging and changing the style, he also adds his own interpretations and emphases. These interpretations, as well as the grand design of the work, provide an interesting picture of one Greek's view of history from a small town in Sicily during the Augustan era.

KENNETH MAYER

Biography

Born at Argyrium in Sicily, Diodorus "the Sicilian" wrote a world history from the creation down to his own time, ending in 60 BC. He visited Egypt c.60–56 BC after which he may have settled in Rome, completing his history c.30 BC. Of its 40 books only 15 survive intact, plus fragments of the rest. Despite many inaccuracies his work remains of value.

Writings

Bibliotheca historica, edited by Friedrich Vogel and C.T. Fischer, 5 vols, Leipzig: Teubner, 1888–1906

Diodorus of Sicily, translated by C.H. Oldfather *et al.*, 12 vols, London: Heinemann, and Cambridge, Massachusetts: Harvard University Press, 1933–67 (Loeb edition)

Bibliothèque historique, edited by François Chamoux *et al.*, Paris: Belles Lettres, 1972–

Further Reading

Ambaglio, Delfino, *La Biblioteca storica di Diodoro Siculo: problemi e metodo*, Como: New Press, 1995

Burton, Anne, *Diodorus Siculus*, Leiden: Brill, 1973 (commentary on book 1)

Galvagno, E. and C. Molè Ventura, *Mito, storia, tradizione: Diodoro Siculo e la storiografia classica*, Catania: Prisma 1991

Palm, Jonas, *Über Sprach und Stil des Diodoros von Sizilien*, Lund: Gleerup, 1955

Rawson, Elizabeth, *Intellectual Life in the Late Roman Republic*, Baltimore: Johns Hopkins University Press, 1985

Rubincam, C., "The Organization and Composition of Diodorus' *Bibliotheke*", *Echos du Monde Classique / Classical Views*, 31, new series 6 (1987): pp. 313–28

Sacks, Kenneth S., *Diodorus Siculus and the First Century*, Princeton, New Jersey: Princeton University Press, 1990

Diogenes Laertius

Biographer of the 2nd or 3rd century AD

Diogenes Laertius is the author of an extant compendium on the lives and doctrines of ancient philosophers that comprises ten books. In addition to this work, he wrote epigrams and he implies (1. 39) that he published a separate collection of them entitled *Pammetros* (Poems in Various Metres) in at least two books. Some of these epigrams on various philosophers are quoted in his historical work. Nothing is known about the author himself and the few references to himself in his work do not reveal much. There is no secure dating either of him or his work. The usual practice is to date him on the basis of the philosophers that he mentions (and does not mention). The latest figures that Diogenes refers to are Sextus Empiricus and Saturninus, both of them Pyrrhonian sceptics usually dated in the late 2nd century AD, while he does not mention any Neopythagorean or Neoplatonist philosopher. He probably lived in the late 2nd or early 3rd century AD. We know nothing of Diogenes' education, where and with whom he studied philosophy for instance, and his philosophical allegiance is a matter of speculation. Neither do we know anything about the composition of his work except that it was apparently dedicated to a lady who had an interest in Plato (3. 47).

Diogenes begins with a general introduction in which he deals with some elementary questions such as the rise of philosophy, the spread of philosophy among the Greeks, and the main philosophical divisions. He advocates the idea that philosophy was a Greek and not a barbarian invention, despite certain intimations of wisdom among barbarian nations. More importantly, in his prologue Diogenes introduces two notions that are crucial for the arrangement of his entire work, namely the notion of succession (*diadoche*) and that of a philosophical sect (*hairesis*). He arranges philosophers in two main successions, the Ionian and the Italian. The Ionian succession starts with Anaximander (going back to the Seven Sages) and goes down to the Stoics through Socrates, Plato, and the Peripatetics (it covers books 1–7), while the Italian succession starts with Pythagoras and continues with the Eleatics and the Atomists to end with Epicurus (books 8–10). Diogenes also distinguishes between dogmatic and sceptic (ephectic) philosophies. Then, following ancient doxographical literature, he gives us a list of the various philosophical sects and the names of their founders. Philosophers who do not belong to a sect and are only part of successions, like the Presocratics, are dispersed in various parts of the work.

The work seems finished as we have it (cf. 10. 138) but book 7 appears incomplete in the existing manuscripts, which leave off in the middle of a title in the list of Chrysippus' works. Each section in Diogenes' works has two main components, the biographical and the doxographical. Diogenes tends to follow a certain order in the arrangement of his material (origin, education, place in succession, sayings, anecdotes, works, doctrines, documents, other men with the same name). His usual practice is to give only the doctrines of the founder of the school, ignoring the additions and variations brought up by the successors. The sole exception is the Stoic school (book 7). The idea is that the founder's doctrines determine the philosophical point of the entire sect. Plato and Epicurus occupy one book each; Zeno the Stoic also enjoys an extensive presentation. The account of Plato presents clear similarities with Middle Platonist treatises of the 2nd century AD such as Albinus' *Isagoge* and Alcinous' *Didaskalikos*. The lists of works that Diogenes gives are invaluable since they tend to be quite comprehensive. Nevertheless Diogenes himself is unlikely to have consulted the original works of the philosophers he discusses, though in the case of Epicurus he cites three original Epicurean texts.

Diogenes' treatment of the various philosophers and philosophical schools is very uneven, and this obviously reflects the state of his sources. As far as the biographies are concerned, some of them consist of just anecdotes and apophthegms (Thales 1. 22–44, Polemo 4. 16–20), some contain only doxography (Anaximander 2. 1–2, Leucippus 9. 30–33), some are very long and well informed (Plato 3, the Stoics 7), others are very short (e.g. Aristotle 5. 28–40). As far as his doxography is concerned, the Stoic one is clearly the best of his whole work, whereas Aristotle's doxographical section is very poor in extent as well as in quality.

The problem of Diogenes' use of the sources is a complicated one. He does not seem to follow any one principal source in his work, and in most cases he uses more than one authority, which he usually names. His principal sources are Antigonus of Carystus, Sotion, Hippobotus, Hermippus, Favorinus, Apollodorus of Athens. Like his sources, Diogenes' technique is to combine and excerpt various authorities (cf. 4. 1, 10. 29). This, however, does not mean that his book is merely patchwork. There is a clear structure behind the whole work, and there are also certain features that characterize his authorship. Yet the use of sources often determines Diogenes' reliability, which varies considerably from book to book and from section to section.

Diogenes' work is definitely a bad history of philosophy by our standards. The author is uncritical about the doxographical material that he reproduces; he does not venture any personal comments; the quality of his information varies considerably; and he has little sense of history. Yet Diogenes did not mean his work to be a history of philosophy in the modern sense. His intention was to present philosophers rather than their philosophy or the historical development of philosophy. His work is chiefly indebted to the genres of successions (*Diadochai*) and of philosophical sects (*Peri haireseon*) that provide the main components of his work, namely the historical-biographical part and the systematic doxographical part respectively. Yet it is difficult to classify Diogenes' work under a specific genre since, for all we know, no earlier work is exactly like his.

Diogenes' work is invaluable today because it is so rich in material from sources that have been lost. This is the only work of its kind that has survived intact from antiquity. Many Hellenistic sources are principally or solely known from Diogenes. His account of Stoic logic, for instance, is important for the reconstruction of Stoic logic. His work is not mentioned by later ancient sources. It seems, however, that it was used by the Byzantines. Stephanos of Byzantium (6th century) quotes Diogenes. The Byzantine lexicon of the *Suda* (10th century) draws heavily on his work for its philosophical entries. Furthermore the compiler of the *Anthologia Palatina* also knows and makes use of Diogenes.

GEORGE E. KARAMANOLIS

See also Biography

Biography
Diogenes probably lived in the late 2nd or early 3rd century AD but nothing is known of his life or background. He wrote an extant work in 10 books entitled *The Lives and Opinions of Eminent Philosophers*. He also wrote a (lost) collection of epigrams, some of which are quoted in the *Lives*.

Writings
Lives of Eminent Philosophers, translated by R.D. Hicks, 2 vols, London: Heinemann, and New York: Putnam, 1925 (Loeb edition; many reprints)
Vitae Philosophorum, edited by H.S. Long, 2 vols, Oxford: Clarendon Press, 1964 (text and commentary)

Further Reading
Elenchos, 7 (1986); special issue: *Diogene Laerzio, storico del pensiero antico* (important collection of articles in various languages)
Mejer, Jørgen, *Diogenes Laertius and His Hellenistic Background*, Wiesbaden: Steiner, 1978
Mejer, Jørgen, Diogène Laërce entry in *Dictionnaire des Philosophes Antiques*, vol. 2, edited by Richard Goulet, Paris: CNRS, 1994, pp. 824–33
Schwartz, E., Diogenes Laertios entry in *Real-Encyclopädie der klassischen Altertumswissenschaft*, edited by August Pauly *et al.*, vol. 5.1, 1903, 738–63

Temporini, Hildegard *et al.* (editors), *Aufstieg und Niedergang der römischen Welt*, 2. 36. 5 and 2. 36. 6, Berlin: de Gruyter, 1992

Diogenes of Sinope
Philosopher of the 4th century BC

The oddest group of philosophers in ancient Athens were the Cynics, the dogs of philosophy, whose best-known representative was Diogenes of Sinope. It is not merely that people found (and still find) it easy to make fun of their way of life, for Athenians also poked fun at Socrates (most notably portrayed as a woolly-minded thinker and teacher of sophistries in Aristophanes' *Clouds*), Plato (also a target of comic poets), and Epicurus (whose moderate hedonism was exaggerated beyond recognition). Their oddity lies in the fact rather that they were considered philosophers at all, given that their odd way of life was based on a kind of return to nature that seems antithetical to the reasoned arguments of philosophy such as were found in Plato's Academy, Aristotle's Peripatos, Epicurus' Garden, and Cleanthes' Stoa. As Antisthenes, the first Cynic, said, "Virtue lies in action, not arguments or learning", requiring nothing more than "Socratic strength". Ideology, then, or movement, rather than philosophy, better describes ancient Cynicism.

Humankind is not only unique among creatures in being capable of advance through intellect and technology, but in also being capable of arguing that it has gone too far and should regress and, to quote a Cynic, "live in accord with nature". One finds the germ of this implicit in the general Greek belief that life need not be luxurious and that one can be happy without the fancy clothes, perfumes, and food of the Persians and Lydians. Socrates, Aristotle, and others specifically argued that wealth contributes nothing of essence to true happiness. It was the Cynics, however, who set out the results of their animal studies showing that mice and dogs seem happy without clothes, fancy food, and any but the most primitive housing, and, perhaps most significantly, with little in the way of social niceties. If dogs can snarl, why should humans gloss over the truth with social pieties?

The Cynics' status as philosophers was maintained, presumably on the basis of their arguments for their way of life, but none of their undoubted philosophical writings are extant (except for some spurious letters). What we have instead is primarily a series of telling, Zen-like, anecdotes designed to demonstrate in summary fashion the Cynics' attitude towards themselves and their fellow humans. Anecdotes of this sort are usually to be treated with great distrust, since all conform to the new Hellenistic fondness for literary biography; if used cautiously, however, they probably do paint a generally true picture of the Cynics' manners and teaching technique. Many of those anecdotes ascribed to Diogenes, moreover, depend upon a wicked (i.e. cynical) love of verbal play (almost always lost in translation) which grants them greater credence. In front of two badly painted Centaurs, for example, Diogenes asks "Which of them is Cheiron?", the famous Centaur whose name can also be read as *cheiron*, "worse".

The origin of the school was traced to Antisthenes, a follower of Socrates who was present at his death. It may well have been that the Cynosarges (White Dog) gymnasium where Antisthenes taught originally suggested the name Cynic for the school associated with him, but the association with dogs was one that the Cynics themselves would happily embrace. From Socrates, Antisthenes learned to emphasize the teaching of virtue for man's happiness; he also learned to emulate Socrates' endurance of physical hardship, raising this, as Socrates did not, to a tenet of his moral philosophy. Diogenes extended this to such an extent that he was said to be "Socrates gone mad".

Whether Antisthenes actually called himself a Cynic and whether others so regarded him is disputed. There is no doubt, however, that Diogenes, from the town of Sinope on the Black Sea, became and remains today even in popular belief the Cynic par excellence: living in a pithos (a large ceramic vessel) which he chilled in winter and heated in summer, eating without utensils, and snarling in mock canine fashion at all who approached him civilly, he outdid Timon of Athens in misanthropy. A particularly apt biographical anecdote has him forced to flee Sinope for having debased the coinage, erroneously having taken an oracle of Apollo too literally: it was rather the metaphorical coinage of civility that he was meant to debase. In Athens, the natural place for a philosophically inclined youth to visit, he fell in with both Antisthenes and Plato. With the former he developed his cynical ideas; to the metaphysical and political views of the latter he developed a marked antipathy which shows up in many of the stories. When, for example, Plato defined man as a featherless biped, Diogenes held up a plucked chicken as something that met the two criteria. Plato's theories of Ideas came in for even harsher criticism. It is usually assumed that Diogenes' *Republic* was written to counter and doubtless to mock Plato's *Republic*.

Whether Diogenes did in fact write this or any other work is a matter of dispute, however. Whereas some sources specifically say that he wrote nothing, others not only list the genres in which he was said to have written, they also quote passages from them. In addition to philosophical dialogues and epistles, Diogenes is credited with tragedies in which he seems to have defended strange positions. In the *Atreus*, for example, the eating of human flesh was shown in a favourable light, just as Diogenes seems to have argued in his prose.

It is understandable that anyone who called himself a Cynic would regard Diogenes as a model. Suitably tempered, however, Cynic ideas of endurance, self-sufficiency, living in accord with nature, and deriving pleasure from the bare necessities of life proved attractive to other schools of philosophy, especially the Megarians, Stoics, and Epicureans. Diogenes' skilful manipulation of words, moreover, provided a model for such Cynical writers as Menippus, Meleager, and Cercidas among Hellenistic Greek writers, and, among the Romans, Seneca, whose *Apocolocyntosis*, a biting satire in both prose and poetry on the emperor Claudius, was modelled on Menippus' satires.

DAVID SIDER

See also Cynics

Biography

Born towards the end of the 5th century BC in Sinope, Diogenes was the archetypal Cynic philosopher. Exiled some time after 362 BC, he

moved to Athens where he associated with Antisthenes and Plato. Living as close to nature as possible, he took shelter in a *pithos* and behaved like a dog. His writings have not survived. He died in the 320s BC.

Further Reading

Branham, R. Bracht and Marie-Odile Goulet-Cazé (editors), *The Cynics: The Cynic Movement in Antiquity and Its Legacy*, Berkeley: University of California Press, 1996

Diogenes Laertius, *Lives of Eminent Philosophers*, translated by R.D. Hicks, 2 vols, London: Heinemann, and New York: Putnam, 1925 (Loeb edition, many reprints; Diogenes Laertius' section on Diogenes of Sinope (book 2. 20–81) is the greatest source of ancient testimony)

Dudley, Donald R., *A History of Cynicism from Diogenes to the Sixth Century AD*, London: Methuen, 1937; reprinted New York: Gordon Press, 1974

Paquet, Léonce, *Les Cyniques grecs: fragments et témoignages*, Ottawa: Editions de L'Université d'Ottawa, 1975 (French translation with notes of the ancient testimony, pp. 59–108)

Sayre, Farrand, *Diogenes of Sinope: A Study of Greek Cynicism*, Baltimore: Furst, 1938

Dionysios of Phourna *c.*1670–after 1744

Painter and writer

The Hieromonk (priest-monk) Dionysios, who was also a painter and writer, was born *c.*1670, the son of the village priest of Phourna, a remote village in Eurytania, central Greece. He was orphaned as a child, and at the age of 12 travelled to Constantinople, probably to complete his education. At the age of 16 he went to Mount Athos, and from the early 18th century became established as a painter there; in 1711 he carried out the fresco painting of what may have been his first extant work, the *kellion* (small monastic settlement) that he had dedicated to St John the Baptist in Karyes. He continued working as a painter throughout his life, and his known oeuvre contains a number of other paintings, both frescos and portable icons; among the latter are six icons which are still kept in the church of his native village of Phourna. Wall paintings attributed to him include those on Mount Athos in a *parekklesion* (minor church) of Vatopedi and in the *katholikon* (main church) of Docheiariou; the painting of the interior of the village church at Phourna, dedicated to the Transfiguration, which was destroyed in 1821, was also by him.

Dionysios was also the author of two liturgical works, *akolouthies* (rites) of the holy martyr Seraphim, metropolitan of Phanarios, who was martyred in 1611, and of the Virgin of the *Zöodochos Pigi* (Lifegiving Spring). He died some time after 1744, but the date and place of his death are unrecorded.

Although he had a number of pupils, Dionysios' fame rests almost entirely on a text which he wrote probably during a second visit to Mount Athos in the years 1730–34; he called it the *Hermineia tis Zographikis Technis* (Explanation of the Painter's Art). While the work can be seen in the long tradition of medieval artists' manuals, which were largely technical in their approach, its scope is far wider than any previous compilation of this kind. Its importance for the Hellenic tradition lies in two separate aspects of the text and its treatment. The first aspect concerns the way that its content and approach are related to the historical conditions against which it was produced. By Dionysios' lifetime Greece had for over two centuries been occupied by a foreign, Muslim power, with no apparent prospect of liberation, and to a large extent Dionysios probably saw his task as one of codification of the long tradition of Byzantine and post-Byzantine artistic practice as it had developed down to his day. The second is due to the wide dissemination of the *Hermineia* in the Eastern Orthodox Church, which took place mostly after his death, but which had the effect of transmitting the practice of what he wrote to a much wider audience than he could have anticipated.

The *Hermineia* is divided broadly into three parts. After initial instructions regarding the artist's preparations for his work, the first part deals exclusively with instructions of a technical nature, including the making of brushes, the mixing of different colours, the preparation of varnishes, and the correct proportions of the human figure. In this respect the *Hermineia* follows the medieval or late medieval tradition of artists' manuals, the best known of which are those by the 12th-century monk Theophilos and the 14th-century Italian painter Cennino Cennini; passages from both these authors are traceable in Dionysios' work.

It is in the second part, which forms more than half the text, that Dionysios gathers together and presents the iconographic traditions of a wide range of Byzantine art as they had developed in the post-Byzantine period. This remains the most significant and widely used part of the *Hermineia*. Major episodes from the Old and New Testaments are covered here, including sections devoted to the life and parables of Christ, the life of the Virgin, and the whole of the Revelation of St John, with the *Akathistos Hymn,* the Ecumenical Councils, and miracle cycles of individual saints. Dionysios includes a martyrology for the whole of the ecclesiastical year and lists many groups of biblical and post-biblical figures: the ancestors of Christ, the holy women of the Old and New Testaments, the prophets with their relevant texts, the apostles, the bishops with their texts, the stylites, deacons, martyrs, hymnographers, and many other saints are all mentioned. He also describes at length how large-scale compositions only began to appear in post-Byzantine art such as the *Pasa Pnoi* ("Let everything that hath breath") and the *Anothea i Prophitai* ("Prophets from above").

Dionysios' method is to describe the essential elements of each scene, or the characteristics of each individual, in a way that provides an artist with sufficient basic information to depict the subject. A few sources that Dionysios must have used have been identified; the sequence of scenes of the Apocalypse is based on an early 16th-century series of woodcuts published in Basel, and the group of hymnographers that he calls The Poets derives from the title-page of a Greek service book published in Venice in 1600 by a Greek bishop, Michael Margounios. For the most part, however, this section of the *Hermineia*, in which the practice of post-Byzantine artists working in Greece at that period is gathered and codified, must have been substantially compiled by Dionysios himself. Indeed, he wrote that his work had been one of lengthy assemblage and compilation.

The third part of the *Hermineia* concerns the distribution of the canon of Byzantine subject-matter, as described in the second part, within the various buildings of an Orthodox monastery: the *katholikon*, refectory, and fountain (the scenes within a *katholikon* can of course be found in any post-Byzantine church).

Although Dionysios' text could never have had the force of ecclesiastical law, its importance lies in the way that it seems to have been adopted by artists of that and subsequent periods as representing an accepted tradition which should be followed when any subjects within the normal canon of post-Byzantine art were to be depicted. The fact that it appears to have fulfilled a need that was widely felt at the time is shown by the large number of versions of the text which were produced in the later 18th and 19th centuries. There are seven manuscript versions in the monastic libraries of Mount Athos, and further examples in public collections elsewhere in Greece. A translation into Romanian in the early 19th century, of which several versions are preserved in Bucharest, disseminated the text further in that area of the Orthodox world. A number of manuscript versions remain in private hands. All extant versions differ from each other in some degree.

The autograph of Dionysios' text has never been located, and the most complete manuscript is in St Petersburg; it is this version which was edited and published in 1909. This edition was inaccurate in a number of ways, and in 2000 a revised text was published giving the corrected form of the St Petersburg manuscript.

PAUL HETHERINGTON

See also Painting

Biography

Born at Phourna in Eurytania *c.*1670, Dionysios was orphaned young. He was educated in Constantinople and went to Mount Athos at the age of 16. From the early 18th century he worked there as a painter. His best-known written work is the *Hermineia tis Zographikis Technis* (Explanation of the Painter's Art) which represents the accepted tradition of Byzantine iconography. He died after 1744.

Writings

Ermineia tis Zographikis Techni [Dionysios of Phourna: Explanation of the Painter's Art], edited by A. Papadopoulos-Kerameus, St Petersburg, 1909

The "Painter's Manual" of Dionysius of Fourna: An English Translation, with Commentary of cod. Gr. 708 in the Saltykov-Shchedrin State Public Library, Leningrad, translated by Paul Hetherington, London: Sagittarius, 1974; 2nd edition in Greek, with revised Greek text, Athens, 2000

Further Reading

Didron, M., *Manuel d'iconographie chrétienne grecque et latine*, Paris: Imprimerie Royale, 1845; reprinted New York: Burt Franklin, 1967

Grecu, Vasile (editor), *Cărti de pictură bisericească bizantină*, Cernauti, 1936

Hetherington, Paul, "'The Poets' in the 'Hermeneia' of Dionysius of Fourna", *Dumbarton Oaks Papers*, 27 (1973)

Heydenreich, L.H., "Der Apokalypsen-zyklus im Athosgebiet und seine Beziehungen zur Deutschen Bibelillustration: der Reformation", *Zeitschrift für Kunstgeschichte*, 8 (1939): pp. 1–40

Dionysius I *c*.430–367 BC

Tyrant of Syracuse

The most significant Greek ruler before the great Macedonians, whom he prefigured in many respects, Dionysius belonged to the upper class of Syracuse in Sicily. The most powerful of western Greek cities, Syracuse resembled Athens in some ways, except for the political instability that characterized it in common with most other Siceliot cities – constitutional government tended to alternate with lengthy periods of tyranny. A number of factors were responsible for this, the most important being the ever-present danger of conquest by Carthage. The establishment of Dionysius' autocracy was the direct outcome of the large-scale Carthaginian invasions of Sicily of 409 and 406 BC. His rise to power was a classic instance of how tyranny could be achieved through demagogy, and it is cited as such by Aristotle in the *Politics*. Threatened by the complete collapse of Greek Sicily in the face of the advancing Carthaginian army, the people of Syracuse elected Dionysius first as a general and then as sole general with full powers to deal with the danger that threatened. Shortly afterwards he tricked the army into providing him with a bodyguard, and instead of a saviour Syracuse found itself saddled with a master. Some time passed, however, before Dionysius was firmly in control and during this time he withstood two revolts, the first by the aristocratic cavalry and the second by the people in general. The latter revolt was suppressed, it would appear, with the help of Sparta. This marked the start of close cooperation between Sparta and the tyrant that served the interests of both, but gained Sparta much opprobrium. Between the revolts Dionysius signed a treaty with Carthage whereby the Carthaginians were left in control, whether direct or indirect, of most of Sicily, including all the Greek cities they had captured, while the tyrant was confined to little more than Syracuse (405 BC).

During the next few years Dionysius first extended his rule in eastern Sicily and then embarked on a programme of massive rearmament aimed against Carthage. Clearly he had not intended the settlement of 405 BC to be of any permanence. We hear of new types of warships and war engines being invented at this time. Launched in 398 BC, his attack on Punic-controlled Sicily met with initial success, including the capture of Motya, the Punic stronghold in western Sicily. He was then, however, forced to retreat after a counter-attack and, when his fleet was defeated off Catane, he found himself besieged at Syracuse. At this critical juncture a plague killed many of the besieging forces. Attacking, Dionysius destroyed most of the Carthaginian fleet and then, as a result of a secret deal (or so we are told), allowed the Carthaginians themselves (as opposed to their allies and mercenaries) to sail away with what remained of their navy (396 BC). Though seriously weakened by his reverses, he recovered quickly and was able to check another Carthaginian campaign initiated in 393 BC. A stalemate having been reached, a new peace treaty was concluded (392 BC) which was much more favourable to the tyrant: all Greek Sicily was to be under Dionysius, and Carthage retained only the western corner of the island.

It was now the turn of Greek Italy. By a combination of military victories and clever diplomacy Dionysius soon succeeded in weakening the Italiot League and, having come to terms with it, in capturing Rhegium, a bitterly hostile city. He thus gained control of the strait of Messana, and annexed to his territories the whole of the toe of Italy. By 387 BC he was free to send to the Aegean a strong naval squadron to assist Sparta and Persia in imposing on Greece the infamous King's Peace. The 380s BC also witnessed the expansion of Dionysius' empire into the Adriatic, where he planted colonies and formed an alliance with the Illyrians. His main aim must have been the acquisition of vital resources in men, but above all of materials. A punitive raid in strength against the Etruscans (*c*.384 BC), traditional allies of the Carthaginians against the Greeks, must also have been motivated by a wish to improve his finances further, in preparation for another war with Cathage.

The Third Carthagianian War broke out in 383 BC and continued well into the 370s BC. It was fought by Dionysius on two fronts, in Sicily as well as in Italy, against both the Carthaginians and the Italiots who made common cause with Carthage. It is unfortunate that our main source for Dionysius (Diodorus Siculus) chose to give only a very brief and vague summary of what clearly was a major conflict. Victory went to Carthage. In the treaty that ended the war Dionysius was forced to recognize Himera as well as all Greek land west of the river Halycus as belonging to Carthage. He also had to pay a heavy indemnity. There was to be yet a Fourth Carthaginian War. Carthage, weakened by plague and a revolt of its subjects, invited attack by Dionysius in 368 BC. By then he had recovered sufficiently to be able to send mercenary forces to aid the Spartans (hard pressed after the disaster at Leuctra in 371 BC) at the same time as fighting Carthage. As in 398 BC, initial success was followed by reverses. Having concluded a truce in the winter, Dionysius died in the following year (367 BC). His son and successor Dionysius II subsequently made peace with Carthage on the same terms as his father in the 370s BC.

Though clearly a tyrant in the traditional Siceliot mould, characterized above all by disregard for convention and in holding life cheap, Dionysius nevertheless was a military despot on an altogether grander scale. In the level and range of his activities he bears comparison with the Hellenistic rulers, not least in the way he prepared for and waged war, on both land and sea. Here he was way ahead of his time. Brave, energetic, ambitious, cultivated (he was a poet of some ability), resourceful, with few scruples to inhibit his actions, Dionysius exercised absolute control over a much larger area and population than any other Greek before him. In an age when oligarchy and monarchy were viewed with ever-increasing favour by the Greek intelligentsia at the expense of democracy, Dionysius' one-man rule could not fail to attract attention. No less a thinker than Plato took the trouble to visit the tyrant, and the influence that Dionysius exerted on Greek political philosophy, for better or worse, is one of his main, if rather intangible, legacies. On the one hand Dionysius can be said to have stemmed, temporarily at least, the advance of Carthage in Sicily. His policies, on the other hand, all calculated to increase and maintain his power, especially his reliance on (mostly barbarian) mercenaries and the wholesale destruction of Greek cities and the transplantation of their populations, undoubtedly undermined the morale and sapped the stamina of western Hellenism.

P.J. STYLIANOU

Biography

Born *c.*430 BC, Dionysius came to power in Syracuse in 405 BC as a direct result of Carthaginian attacks on Sicily in 409 and 406 BC. Consolidating his position with the help of Sparta, he made himself master of all Greek Sicily, confining Carthage to the western corner. He then (387 BC) extended his influence into south Italy as far as the Adriatic and was active against the Etruscans. After further fighting with Carthage he died in 367 BC and was succeeded by his son Dionysius II.

Further Reading

Berve, Helmut, *Die Tyrannis bei den Griechen*, Munich: Beck, 1967, vol. 1, pp. 221 ff.

Caven, Brian, *Dionysius I: War-Lord of Sicily*, New Haven, Connecticut: Yale University Press, 1990

Lewis, D.M. *et al.* (editors), *The Fourth Century* BC, Cambridge: Cambridge University Press, 1994 (*The Cambridge Ancient History*, vol. 6, 2nd edition), chapter 5

Sanders, L.J., *Dionysius I of Syracuse and Greek Tyranny*, London: Croom Helm, and New York: Methuen, 1987

Stroheker, K.F., *Dionysios I: Gestalt und Geschichte des Tyrannen von Syrakus*, Wiesbaden: Steiner, 1958

Stylianou, P.J., *A Historical Commentary on Diodorus Siculus, Book 15*, Oxford: Clarendon Press, and New York: Oxford University Press, 1998

Dionysius of Halicarnassus

Historian of the 1st century BC

In the second half of the 1st century BC a literary trend developed which was to have the greatest impact on the future course of Greek literature down to the Byzantine age and even beyond. It was the time of the quite spectacular breakthrough of Atticism, according to which speeches and literature should be modelled after the great authors of Classical, i.e. pre-Hellenistic, times. Most prominent among the initiators of this movement were the rhetoricians and historians Caecilius of Caleacte and Dionysius of Halicarnassus.

When Dionysius arrived in Rome in 30/29 BC, the capital had already become a centre for Greek intellectual activity. Dionysius does not seem to have had any difficulties in finding Greek and Roman friends and patrons, among whom Caecilius was the most remarkable literary figure and Quintus Aelius Tubero, jurist, annalist, and father of two consuls, the most influential political personality. Dionysius wrote many rhetorical and critical treatises for these friends and was a private teacher to their sons. But he devoted most of his time to composing his monumental work on early Rome, the *Roman Antiquities*.

In the preface to his study *On Ancient Orators* – a singular manifesto-like text – Dionysius unfolded a tripartite conception of history: the heyday of the "old philosophical rhetoric", he declared, was followed by a period of decay after the death of Alexander the Great, but the time in which he lived saw a powerful revival of the time-honoured "Attic" rhetoric.

Dionysius attributed this change to the influence of Rome and its well-educated elite. In this conception, the orators and authors of the good, older time were regarded as classical models with normative power, whereas the whole literature of the Hellenistic period he rejected as "Asianic". In order to produce good speeches and literature, so Dionysius argued, one had to turn to the classics and imitate them. In his rhetorical and critical studies Dionysius attempted to show which authors were worthy of imitation (*mimesis*), how imitation should work, and which qualities in particular should be espoused, and which mistakes avoided. Dionysius thus proposed an eclectic procedure combining the good qualities of several Classical authors and at the same time avoiding all their flaws. By this means one could hope to rival the classics or even to surpass them. Dionysius took it for granted that the Classical authors had already proceeded in this way themselves: most successful of all the Attic orators, according to Dionysius, was Demosthenes, whose "mixed style" he therefore preferred.

The tremendous success of Atticism is clearly illustrated by the fact that, whereas Hellenistic literature was for the most part lost (except for some more technical works handed down because of their content), the works of the Classics (as well as those of the Classicists) have been preserved to a remarkable extent. This was possible only because Classicism was readily embraced and disseminated by the rhetorical schools. As far as we can see, it is in Dionysius' treatises that literary criticism is for the first time pursued not primarily as a means to explain a given text or author but almost exclusively in order to provide material for imitation. It is obviously for their practical value that these critical studies have often been read and thus have mostly been preserved. In the 1st century AD they were cited several times by the Roman rhetorician Quintilian, and the unknown author of *Peri Hypsous* (On the Sublime) clearly knows them, although there is no explicit reference. For instance, the latter used the critical device developed by Dionysius of rewriting a certain passage in order to show how important its rhythm is. The unknown author of the pseudo-Plutarchean treatise *On the Ten Orators* uses many passages from Dionysius without indicating his source, whereas an anonymous commentator on book 2 of Thucydides replies to some of the criticism made by Dionysius in his study *On Thucydides* (P.Oxy. 853; 2nd century).

In the 2nd and 3rd centuries AD Atticism became increasingly concerned or even obsessed with the purity of language. Purists of the time would accept only the vocabulary and the syntactical formations found in the Attic authors. For Dionysius and Caecilius, Atticism had been primarily a matter of style, but clearly the purism of the Second Sophistic would not have been possible without the success of stylistic Atticism. Indeed, in the 9th century the patriarch and scholar Photios was to criticize Dionysius' use of neologisms (cod. 83), which were, of course, profoundly antipathetic to purists. Nevertheless, Dionysius' treatises continued to be used – for example, by the rhetorician Hermogenes, still in the 2nd century – although direct references are rare, and even more extensively with many direct citations by his commentators, namely Syrianus (4th/5th century). As the Hermogenic corpus became the standard rhetorical textbook for the whole Byzantine period and was still much in use in the Renaissance,

Dionysius' authority remained unquestioned throughout the centuries. He was read by the rhetorician Libanius and the sophist Lachares (4th/5th century). An anonymous rhetorician, perhaps John Doxapatres (11th century), was a particularly fervent admirer, as he calls Dionysius "the master and good father of our art". Another anonymous rhetorician of the 10th/11th century, who wrote a commentary on Hermogenes, cited passages from many different treatises and seemed to know the whole of Dionysius' critical work. John Sikeliotes (12th century), a better-known commentator on Hermogenes at the time, refers directly to Dionysius. Epitomes have been made of the studies *On Imitation* and – probably in the 10th century or perhaps by Maximos Planudes (13th century) – *On Stylistic Composition*. The latter work was also widely used by Psellos (11th century), whose study *On the Composition of the Parts of Speech* consists to a large extent of extracts from it.

Of the 20 books of the *Roman Antiquities*, books 1–10 have been preserved entirely and book 11 partly. Books 12–20 survive only in excerpts, about one half of them from the collection made of Classical and later historians by order of the emperor Constantine VII Porphyrogennetos (10th century), and the other half from an epitome preserved in a 15th-century manuscript. According to Photios, who could still read the complete work (cod. 84), Dionysius had himself made an epitome in five volumes. The history extends "from the oldest myths ... to the beginning of the First Punic War" (1. 8. 1f), i.e. the year 264 BC, with which Polybius' history begins. Dionysius designed the *Antiquities* as a model for what can be produced by eclectic *mimesis*, but he also had a political message and an educational aim: he attempted to show that Rome was in fact a Greek foundation, Latin a Greek dialect, and the early Romans indeed Greeks – not only ethnically, but also in terms of their high moral standards. Dionysius thus justified Roman rule over the Greeks and at the same time presented Roman statesmen of the past as models for those of the present. Dionysius wished to be an educator like Isocrates, aiming to teach both good behaviour and good speaking.

The *Roman Antiquities* seems to have been quite popular, although direct references are few. Josephus' *Jewish Antiquities* in 20 volumes is obviously modelled on it, as are some aspects of his style. Plutarch used it for some of his *Lives*; in some cases (e.g. for the *Coriolanus*) it was his main source. Appian and Cassius Dio also seem to have referred to the *Antiquities*, though perhaps through an intermediary source. As a note by an anonymous writer in the earliest manuscript of Appian makes plain (cod. Vat. graec. 141; 11th/12th century), the account of Italian history and the earliest history of Rome were the most popular parts (hence perhaps the loss of the later books). In the Byzantine period the *Roman Antiquities* was used by Constantine Manasses, who drew on it for his *Chronike Synopsis* (12th century), as did John Kanabutzes (15th century) for his little geographical-historical miscellany *In Dionysium Halicarnassensem Commentarius*.

Over the last 200 years Dionysius has often been criticized and even despised for his hated Classicism and his positive approach to Rome. It should be borne in mind, however, that his Isocratean ideal of education (*paideia*), based on a sound knowledge of the Classical authors, proved to be one of the most important and persistent factors of Greek elite identity for many centuries.

THOMAS HIDBER

See also Rhetoric, Second Sophistic

Biography

A native of Halicarnassus, Dionysius moved to Rome in 30 BC where he taught rhetoric for many years. He also wrote many works of literary criticism, notably on Thucydides and the Attic orators. But his principal work was entitled *Roman Antiquities*, a history of Rome from its beginnings to the start of the First Punic War (where Polybius begins), in 20 books, of which books 1–10 survive intact, book 11 in part, and the rest only in excerpts. His thesis was that Rome was a Greek city, Latin a Greek dialect, and Romans really Greeks.

Writings

The Roman Antiquities, translated by Earnest Cary, 7 vols, London: Heinemann, and Cambridge, Massachusetts: Harvard University Press, 1937–50 (Loeb edition)
The Critical Essays, translated by Stephen Usher, 2 vols, London: Heinemann, and Cambridge, Massachusetts: Harvard University Press, 1974–85 (Loeb edition)
On Thucydides, translation and commentary by W. Kendrick Pritchett, Berkeley: University of California Press, 1975
Epistola a Pompeo Gemino, edited by Sotera Fornara, Stuttgart: Teubner, 1997 (text and commentary)
Sull'Imitazione, edited by Daniela G. Battisti, Pisa: Istituti Editoriali e Poligrafici internazionali, 1997 (text, Italian translation, and commentary)

Further Reading

Aujac, G., "Michel Psellos et Denys d'Halicarnasse: Le traité 'Sur la composition des éléments du langage'", *Revue des Etudes Byzantines*, 33 (1975) pp. 257–75
Bonner, S.F., *The Literary Treatises of Dionysius of Halicarnassus: A Study in the Development of Critical Method*, Cambridge: Cambridge University Press, 1939
"Denys d'Halicarnasse: Historien des origines de Rome", *Pallas*, 39 (1993)
Fox, Matthew, *Roman Historical Myths: The Regal Period in Augustan Literature*, Oxford: Clarendon Press, and New York: Oxford University Press, 1996, pp. 49–95
Gabba, Emilio, *Dionysius and the History of Archaic Rome*, Berkeley: University of California Press, 1991
Hidber, Thomas, *Das klassizistische Manifest des Dionys von Halikarnass: Die Praefatio zu 'De oratoribus veteribus'*, Stuttgart: Teubner, 1996
Kennedy, George A., *A New History of Classical Rhetoric*, Princeton, New Jersey: Princeton University Press, 1994, pp. 160ff.
Sacks, K.S., "Historiography in the Rhetorical Works of Dionysius of Halicarnassus", *Athenaeum*, 61 (1983): pp. 65–87
Schultze, C.E., "Dionysius of Halicarnassus and His Audience" in *Past Perspectives: Studies in Greek and Roman Historical Writing*, edited by I.S. Moxon *et al.*, Cambridge and New York: Cambridge University Press, 1986, pp. 121–41
Schultze, C.E., "Dionysius of Halicarnassus and Roman Chronology", *Proceedings of the Cambridge Philological Society*, 41 (1995): pp. 192–214
Swain, Simon, *Hellenism and Empire: Language, Classicism, and Power in the Greek World, AD 50–250*, Oxford: Clarendon Press, and New York: Oxford University Press, 1996
van Wyk Cronjé, Jacobus, *Dionysius of Halicarnassus: De Demosthene: A Critical Appraisal of the Status Quaestionis*, Hildesheim: Olms, 1986

Dionysius the Areopagite, pseudo-

Author of a corpus of Christian writings of *c*.AD 500

The Dionysian corpus includes ten letters and four treatises, which most manuscripts arrange in the following order: the *Celestial Hierarchy*, the *Ecclesiastical Hierarchy*, the *Divine Names*, and the *Mystical Theology*. The author purports to be the Dionysius who was converted by Paul's speech on the Areopagus (Acts 17: 34), and was subsequently identified both with the first Athenian bishop and with St Denis of France. The Renaissance scholars Lorenzo Valla and Erasmus, however, proved to the satisfaction of most Protestants that the ascription is pseudonymous, and since the work of Josef Stiglmayr and others in the early 20th century, even Roman Catholics have generally admitted that Dionysius wrote under the influence of the Neoplatonist Proclus, who died in AD 485. Since the first external attestation of his work occurs in 532, it is plausible to suggest that he wrote between these dates; the conjecture is confirmed by his assumption that the Nicene Creed is a regular part of the Eucharistic liturgy, which was not true anywhere before 476. Most scholars assign the author to a Syrian (though not Syriac-speaking) region, and since his doctrine of the Incarnation seems to dwell on Christ's divinity at the expense of his humanity, it is generally supposed that he was trying to lend an apostolic colour to the Monophysite position after the Council of Chalcedon of 451. At the same time, the philosophical elements in his work suggest that he hoped to make his own religion credible to pagans, or else to make philosophy more palatable to Christians in the years before Justinian's closure of the Athenian schools in 529.

The apogee of Dionysian thought is reached in the *Mystical Theology*, which asserts that every positive or kataphatic statement about the Deity is bound to be inadequate, and his nature is best apprehended through the negative or apophatic language that denies him every mundane attribute. Even the negations are alleged to partake of falsehood, since no phrase will suffice to comprehend the divine infinity; a simultaneous denial of every predicate, transcending all particular negations, would appear to be our closest approximation to the majesty of God. Nevertheless, Dionysius knows that scripture and tradition allow us to say that God is good, wise, just, and even beautiful; according to the *Divine Names*, it is possible to credit him with these properties (and goodness first of all) because he is the cause of them in us. In his own being God has them "superessentially"; in a single act they constantly proceed from and revert to his inner nature, so as to be at once imparted to us and recognized as his. In a passage ascribed to one "Hierotheus" this benevolence is said to express the love that is of God's essence; the biblical word *agape* is regarded as interchangeable with *eros*, which in the Neoplatonic vocabulary denotes the yearning of the soul to be like God (*Divine Names*, 4. 13–17). The Neoplatonic influence is most marked in the subsequent digression on the origin of evil (4. 18–35), which is said to stem not from God but from his creatures and to be nothing but a deficiency of good.

Affirmation descends from what is most like God, negation ascends from what is most unlike him. From symbols such as light or rock, we ascend to reflective knowledge, then from knowledge to an awareness of our unknowing. Knowledge of God is both conveyed and symbolized by the ninefold order of angels and the threefold order of clergy, which constitute the celestial and ecclesiastical hierarchies. The purpose of the clergy is to purify and illuminate the soul, which is thus made perfect for communion with God. There is a threefold order of laymen (including monks) to match the clergy, and in all the ranks of being it is a rule that the higher is present in the lower, but not vice versa. The consequence is that people can receive true knowledge of God through various symbols, according to their capacity for reception; such material sacraments as baptism and the Eucharist are always efficacious, though only when their meaning has been fully understood can they accomplish the perfection of the soul. The letters, addressed to fictitious correspondents, introduce the thought of the writer, and supply historical details to corroborate his pretensions. Reference is also made to a *Symbolic Theology*, which (if it ever existed) is now lost.

From the first discovery of his writings, Dionysius was suspected of being more Platonist than Christian; even in the latter guise, he appeared to show undue favour to the Monophysites and to be deficient in knowledge of the Trinity. The commentary of John of Scythopolis dissipated most of the objections, and the advocacy of Maximos the Confessor, who was certainly no Monophysite, secured Dionysius' place among the Fathers of the Eastern Church. Where the careless author had cited Clement of Alexandria (*Divine Names*, 5. 9, thus according to this late-2nd-century writer his true deserts as the founder of the apophatic tradition), Maximos pretended that he meant the 1st-century bishop Clement of Rome. It is all the more remarkable that when Maximos composed a mystical commentary on the Liturgy, he put the Incarnation at the centre, and made little use of the author whom he believed to have been a friend of the apostles. John Damascene treats him as a sure authority, and during the hesychast controversy both Palamites and their adversaries took refuge in his name. Even now, many monks would be unwilling to accept that "Dionysius" is a pseudepigraphic title.

Just as he transcended the division between Monophysites and Chalcedonians, so Dionysius was able to bridge the schism between the Eastern and Western Churches. The West first learned of him through John Scotus Eriugena (*c*.900), who translated the commentary by John of Scythopolis, together with some works by Maximos; from this time on, despite the heterodoxy of Eriugena, it was difficult to join a debate within the Roman Church without deferring to the Dionysian writings. Protestants have until recently portrayed him as the archpriest of the "*eros*-type" theology, which exaggerates our natural worth and puts our own self-seeking love of God in place of his sacrificial love for us. Yet the God of Dionysius is never so impersonal as the One of the Neoplatonists; the symbols of procession and reversion express his loving condescension to humanity, and *eros* in the Dionysian writings, as in Origen and Ignatius, is an appellation of Jesus on the cross. Modern scholars, stressing his use of scripture, his belief in the Incarnation, and his devotion to the sacraments, have generally agreed that Dionysius was a Christian before he was a philosopher, and that his churchmanship is more than a veneer.

MARK EDWARDS

Biography

Although in his writings he purports to be the Dionysius who was converted to Christianity by Paul's speech on the Areopagus, it is now generally agreed that the attribution is pseudonymous and that this anonymous writer wrote c.500. He stressed that the nature of God can only be defined by negatives, and was much influenced by Neoplatonism.

Writings

The Complete Works, translated by Colm Luibheid, London: SPCK, and New York: Paulist Press, 1987

Corpus Dionysiacum, edited by Beate Regina Suchla, 2 vols, Berlin: de Gruyter, 1990–91

Further Reading

Louth, Andrew, *Denys the Areopagite*, London: Chapman, and Wilton, Connecticut: Morehouse Barlow, 1989

Nygren, Anders, *Agape and Eros: A Study of the Christian Idea of Love*, 3 vols, London: SPCK, 1932–39

Rorem, Paul, *Biblical and Liturgical Symbols within the Pseudo-Dionysian Synthesis*, Toronto: Pontifical Institute of Mediaeval Studies, 1984

Rorem, Paul, *Pseudo-Dionysius: A Commentary on the Texts and an Introduction to Their Influence*, Oxford and New York: Oxford University Press, 1993

Dioscurides fl. c.AD 45–75

Physician

Pedanius Dioscurides of Anazarbus in Roman Cilicia (southeastern Asia Minor) wrote *On Materia Medica*, one of the more influential pharmacological works of the pre-modern period. The preface suggests that he studied under Arius in Tarsus and that he travelled extensively to collect information on the medicinal uses of plants, animal products, and minerals. His journeys probably took him to many of the places mentioned in his work, including much of Asia Minor, the Greek mainland, northern Egypt, Syria, Crete, Cyprus, and the Nabataean capital Petra. Following earlier traditions, he also described exotic substances from more remote areas (including Britain, Gaul, Iberia, Ethiopia, Armenia, and India), few of which he is likely to have visited. His explicit association of his pharmacological odyssey ("traversing much of the earth", Preface 4, an echo of *Odyssey*, 4. 268, 2. 364, etc.) with a "military" or "soldierlike life" prompted later writers to draw the controversial inference that he had been a physician in the Roman army.

Several other extant Greek texts are attributed to Dioscurides by later ancient writers and by Byzantine authors and scribes. These include *On Noxious Drugs*, *On Venomous Animals*, and *On Simple Drugs* (also transmitted as *Euporista*, "Readily Accessible Remedies"). A modern critical consensus has, however, rendered their authenticity doubtful.

In scope, thoroughness, and detail, Dioscurides' *On Materia Medica* probably exceeded its many ancient predecessors. He discussed the medicinal properties of more than a thousand natural substances (about 800 of these botanical, the rest mineral and animal), and recorded well over 4,000 uses for them, whereas the works attributed to Hippocrates, for example, had referred to fewer than half as many substances.

In his preface Dioscurides criticizes different predecessors by name for different flaws: omitting useful substances, imprecision, false information, second-hand knowledge, and poor structure, resulting in works that are impossible to memorize. His own work, he promises, will be superior in its completeness, accuracy, organization, systematicity, and detailed personal observation, with careful attention to topography, climate, seasons, and local botanical variations, as these pertain to the collection, cleaning, preparation, preservation, and storage of drugs.

Dioscurides' predecessors had listed pharmacological substances under individual disorders (e.g. Hippocratic Corpus) or alphabetically (Crateuas) or according to external, often morphological characteristics (Sextius Niger), whereas the sequence adopted by Dioscurides in his five books is as follows: (1) aromatics, oils, ointments, trees, shrubs; (2) animals, animal products (honey, milk, fat), cereals, vegetables, garden herbs; (3) roots, botanical juices, further herbs, seeds; (4) further roots and herbs; (5) wines, other potables, minerals. The organizational principles that prompted this arrangement are far from transparent, but a recurrent structural device might be grouping together substances according to affinities displayed by their *dynameis* (usually translated "properties"), i.e. by their "powers" to act upon something, for example, by having a heating, softening, astringent, diuretical, drying, cooling, "ripening", somniferous, relaxing, dispersing, aphrodisiac, or antaphrodisiac effect. In all, he identifies more than 300 kinds of qualitative medicinal effects. Yet Dioscurides never explicitly claims such similarities in the "power to effect" as the principle that informs his overall arrangement, and some later readers, not recognizing any consistent, clear structure, reorganized his text to give it a more accessible arrangement. An alphabetical version, probably produced between the 2nd and 4th centuries AD, is extant in a 6th-century manuscript (the "Vienna Dioscurides", see below) and in later manuscripts.

A subsidiary ordering sequence, discernible in the botanical sections, is testimony to Dioscurides' attempt at thoroughness. One chapter is devoted to each plant, and within each chapter the following pattern tends to be maintained: name of the plant; synonyms; typical location; botanical description, medicinal properties; preparation and application; occasional references to harmful side effects; dosage; collection, processing, and storage; forgeries and how to detect them; at times, veterinary, magical and non-medical uses; sometimes geographic distribution.

Each botanical chapter was probably also accompanied by an illustration of the plant, as in the earliest surviving Greek manuscript, the "Vienna Dioscurides". Now in Vienna (Österreichische Nationalbibliothek) this manuscript preserves an alphabetical version of Dioscurides' work. Copied in AD 512–13 in Constantinople for Princess Anicia Juliana, daughter of Placidia the Younger and of the western emperor Olybrius, the Vienna Dioscurides is the most lavishly produced of extant Byzantine scientific manuscripts, preserving almost 500 miniatures, mostly full-page paintings of plants. Different visual traditions are, however, discernible in the manuscript tradition, and it is unclear which, if any, of these derive from Dioscurides' original work. In the Vienna Dioscurides art historians have differentiated between a more abstract group of illustrations and a more naturalistic group, and a Neapolitan manuscript of the 7th century AD (now in the Biblioteca Nazionale, Naples), containing 403 plant illustrations of an inferior quality, also appears to represent more than one visual tradition. Illustrated pharmacological and other medical works none the less are well attested at least from the Hellenistic period and, modern expressions of doubt notwithstanding, it is likely that Dioscurides' original text, too, was illustrated.

The high regard in which Dioscurides' *On Materia Medica* was held in the Greek world until the early modern period is evident from the frequency with which later Greeks referred to him, quoted him, annotated his text, copied it, and plagiarized it. Dioscurides' contemporary Erotianus quoted him in his Hippocratic lexicon, and in the next generation two great Greek pharmacologists of the Flavian period, Asclepiades the Younger ("Pharmakion") and Andromachus the Younger, took ample account of Dioscurides' work. At the time of the emperor Trajan, Rufus of Ephesus explicitly acknowledged Dioscurides as an eminent authority, and under Hadrian another Ephesian, Soranus, drew on him in his Hippocratic glossary (fragments of which seem to survive in Hesychius' 5th-century lexicon of rare words). In the last six books of his work on simple drugs Galen by and large adapted Dioscurides' views to his own pharmacological system. In the 4th century AD Oribasius (*Collectiones Medicae* 11–13) recorded many lengthy verbatim excerpts from Dioscurides, arranged alphabetically. Writers of the 6th and 7th centuries who drew on (or knew of) Dioscurides' work include Aëtius of Amida (who offers excerpts), Alexander of Tralles, Stephanus of Byzantium, and Paul of Aegina. In the 9th century Photios seems to have had direct access to the *Materia Medica*, which he held in very high regard (*Bibliotheca*, cod. 178).

An impressive copy of the Vienna Dioscurides (New York, Pierpont Morgan Library) was produced in the 10th century. At about the same time Romanos II (emperor 959–63) sent another illustrated version from Constantinople to the caliph of Cordoba. Further evidence of Dioscurides' popularity throughout the Byzantine period is provided by the numerous comments entered in manuscripts of his text by physicians and others. Greek monks in the monastery of St John Prodromos in Petra, for example, made many annotations in the Vienna Dioscurides in the 14th and 15th centuries. A further measure of Dioscurides' influence was the active reception of his work both by the Latin west and by medieval Islam. Early Latin, Syriac, and Arabic translations ensured that for centuries Dioscurides served as a paradigm and source for three major cultural areas: the eastern Greek culture of Byzantium, Islamic civilization, and the western Christian Latin realms.

HEINRICH VON STADEN

See also Botany, Galen, Health, Hippocrates, Nicander

Biography

Born at Anazarbus in Cilicia, Pedanius Dioscurides (*fl. c.*AD 45–75) studied under Arius of Tarsus and travelled widely in the eastern Mediterranean to gather information about medicinal uses of plants, animal products, and minerals. His work *On Materia Medica* in five books is an extensive and influential study of the uses of drugs in medicine. Several of its surviving manuscripts are beautifully illustrated.

Writings

De materia medica libri quinque, edited by Max Wellmann, 3 vols, Berlin: Weidmann, 1906–14 (the standard modern edition)

The Greek Herbal of Dioscorides, Illustrated by a Byzantine AD *512, Englished by John Goodyer* AD *1655*, edited by Robert T. Gunther, Oxford: Oxford University Press, 1934; reprinted New York: Hafner, 1959

Codex Vindobonensis med. Gr. 1 der Österreichischen Nationalbibliothek, edited by Hans Gerstinger, 2 vols, Graz: Akademische Druck- und Verlagsanstalt, 1965–70 (facsimile of the Vienna Dioscurides with commentary)

Further Reading

Kádár, Zoltán, *Survivals of Greek Zoological Illuminations in Byzantine Manuscripts*, Budapest: Kiadó, 1978, pp. 52–76 and plates 59–101

Mazal, Otto, *Pflanzen, Wurzeln, Säfte, Samen: Antike Heilkunst in Miniaturen des Wiener Dioskurides*, Graz: Akademische Druck- und Verlagsanstalt, 1981 (on the Vienna Dioscurides)

Riddle, John M., in *Catalogus Translationum et Commentariorum: Mediaeval and Renaissance Latin Translations and Commentaries*, edited by F. Edward Cranz and Paul Oskar Kristeller, vol. 4, Washington, D.C.: Catholic University of America Press, 1980, pp. 1–143

Riddle, John M., *Dioscorides on Pharmacy and Medicine*, Austin: University of Texas Press, 1985

Sadek, M.M., *The Arabic Materia Medica of Dioscorides*, Quebec: Sphinx, 1983

Scarborough, John and Vivian Nutton, "The Preface of Dioscorides' Materia Medica: Introduction, Translation, Commentary", *Transactions and Studies of the College of Physicians of Philadelphia*, 4 (1982): pp. 187–227

van Buren, Anne, in *Illuminated Greek Manuscripts from American Collections: An Exhibition in Honor of Kurt Weitzmann*, edited by Gary Vikan, Princeton, New Jersey: Princeton University Art Museum, 1973, pp. 66–69

Weitzmann, Kurt, *Studies in Classical and Byzantine Manuscript Illumination*, edited by Herbert L. Kessler, Chicago: University of Chicago Press, 1971, pp. 25–36, 43, 135–39, 146–48, 154–60, 186, 198

Weitzmann, Kurt, *Late Antique and Early Christian Book Illumination*, New York: Braziller, 1977, pp. 60–71, and plates 15–20 (Vienna Dioscurides)

Diplomacy

Diplomacy is the peaceful conduct of relations between recognized political entities by means of negotiations. The word "diplomacy" is derived from the French *diplomatie*, which is in turn derived from the ancient Greek *diploun*, "to double". The Latin word *diploma*, so called because it consisted of two sheets of metal shut together like the leaves of a book, denoted important legal documents such as passports, licences to travel, or certificates conferring privileges. Renaissance humanists, perhaps a trifle pedantically, applied the term to all acts of sovereign authority; and eventually the term came to embrace all medieval documents. The word "diplomacy", according to Dr Murray's *New English Dictionary*, was first used in the Anglophone world as late as 1796, by Edmund Burke. Indeed, diplomacy as a uniform system guided by generally recognized rules and conventions is of comparatively recent date, with the rights and privileges of diplomatic agents being defined in a binding manner at the Congress of Vienna of 1815. The growth of the practice of diplomacy, however, goes back to ancient times. The contribution of the Hellenic world to the evolution of diplomacy is that of ancient Greece and the Byzantine empire.

Ancient Greece

Whether extant evidence of diplomatic activity in Mesopotamia and pharaonic Egypt points to the existence of a diplomatic system is still the subject of academic debate. Evidence of such a system in the case of ancient Greece, by contrast, is abundant and undisputed. Significantly, however, the practice of diplomatic exchanges was confined almost entirely to the Greek world. By virtue of its geographical position ancient mainland Greece was for long periods of its development free from external pressure (although this was of course not so in the case of settlements in the eastern and western peripheries of the Greek world). Under such conditions a cluster of small states emerged, often misleadingly referred to as "city states". The rise of the polis, the "self-governing state", was no doubt aided also by these states' relative isolation in the mountainous terrain of the mainland, which could not easily be traversed. Thus separated by topography, but connected by sea routes, the states needed to develop a means of regular communication. A further incentive for the growth of this protodiplomatic traffic was the fact that no single polis was powerful enough to establish some form of hegemony over the others. The relative equilibrium that resulted and the absence of external pressure meant that individual states dealt with each other on a basis of equality. Their common cultural background and a shared language obviously facilitated the transaction of diplomatic business. Yet, it is also true that Greek diplomacy possessed no conception of norms and rules of proper diplomatic conduct. So intense was the citizen's loyalty to his polis, and so deep was his suspicion of the *xenoi*, the foreigners from beyond the boundaries of his state, that inter-polis relations were highly quarrelsome. But while this characteristic tended to increase the frequency of diplomatic exchanges, it also prevented the emergence of a recognized uniform diplomatic system. What, however, did emerge was a pattern, both administrative and behavioural, that bore surprising similarities to modern international diplomacy.

The modern practice of maintaining permanent diplomatic missions in foreign capitals was, of course, unknown to the Hellenic world. Indeed, this did not become established practice until the heyday of Venetian diplomacy in the 15th century. The hallmark of ancient Greek diplomacy, by contrast, was the frequent dispatch and reception of temporary, or *ad hoc*, legations. The Greeks dealt with foreign-policy issues as and when they arose. The ancient equivalent to the modern ambassador or envoy was the *presbys*, or elder. Chosen for his known respectability and his knowledge of political affairs, he was appointed to a temporary mission to negotiate the settlement of a specific problem with a foreign state.

To the modern observer the most striking feature of Greek diplomacy is its relative openness and the suspicion with which the *presbeis* were often regarded by their own people. Greek ambassadors were generally chosen, by the assembly of their polis, not so much for their skills as negotiators but rather for their representative qualities. The policy to be pursued by the envoys was debated publicly by the assembly, and the negotiating strategy laid down in detailed, and usually restrictive, instructions. The modern practice of furnishing ambassadors with plenipotentiary powers seems to have been virtually unknown in ancient Greece. Such was the suspicion of their own diplomats that the Greeks tended to send missions on a large scale, usually composed of several *presbeis*, not infrequently as many as ten. This practice served a dual purpose. The large number of usually highly skilled orators as envoys was meant to increase the weight of the sending state's case. But, most importantly, it was a device to address domestic needs. Different envoys represented different factions at home. A large mission was therefore broadly representative of the different points of view entertained by the assembly at home. The accommodation of domestic animosities was, however, not conducive to diplomatic effectiveness. Instead of conveying an impression of unity of purpose, a large mission suggested to the receiving polis domestic strife in the sending state. An often quoted example of this was the Athenian mission to the court of Philip of Macedon in 346 BC, which was remarkable more for the strictures uttered by the celebrated rival orators Aeschines and Demosthenes against each other than for its negotiating success. Such personal animosities in large, mixed embassies were thus liable to be exploited by the receiving state. It is indeed remarkable, as Harold Nicolson noted, "that intelligent people should have permitted so bad a diplomatic method to survive".

The openness of Greek diplomacy extended not only to the appointment and dispatch of embassies but also to the transaction of their business abroad. Equipped with credentials issued by their own assemblies, the *presbeis* were led on their arrival to the assembly of the host state. Diplomatic negotiations were conducted orally and, it seems, publicly. The individual members of the mission each delivered a set speech along the lines fixed by their home assembly; open negotiations would then ensue. If an agreement resulted, its terms were engraved in a tablet, to be displayed in public. The ratification of any such agreement was by public exchange of oaths. The public nature of Greek diplomacy may also account for the frequent censuring of the returning mission by its own polis. Occasionally the returning ambassadors were even prosecuted, as for example was Aeschines, whose character had been tarnished by his accepting a bribe from the Macedonian prince, and who was consequently banished to Rhodes.

Another important feature of Greek diplomacy was the evolution of the office of *proxenos*, which was roughly that of the modern consul. In contrast to his modern successors the *proxenos* was a native of his polis, in which he resided while acting on behalf of another state and protecting the interests of the latter's citizens; it did not, however, include conducting diplomatic negotiations. Although the post of *proxenos* was one of honour, and many distinguished men strove to obtain it, the *proxenoi* were also often the leaders of the political faction which was favourably disposed towards the state they represented.

Its ad hoc nature and its public character, the lack of any administrative structure and of record keeping no doubt hampered Greek diplomacy. It was largely inconsistent, and the lack of domestic unity often rendered it ineffective. But the constancy and intensity of diplomatic exchanges, the recognition of diplomatic immunity, or the accepted principles of declaring war and concluding peace all indicate that the Greeks had developed a sophisticated and elaborate diplomatic apparatus. The Amphictionic Council, the leagues, and alliances demonstrate that the ancient Greeks understood the importance of the combinations of forces. The Delian League, for instance, organized and maintained under the hegemony of the Athenians for the better part of the 5th century BC, brought together 200 states in an anti-Persian combination. Without a sophisticated web of diplomatic exchanges such a feat would have been impossible.

Byzantium

Whereas the diplomacy of ancient Greece dealt largely with intra-Greek matters, the later Roman empire at Byzantium developed its diplomatic methods almost exclusively in response to external pressures. Surrounded on all sides by nomadic tribes, and faced with the prospect of frequent incursions by the barbarians, the effective protection of imperial possessions was of vital importance. In this, diplomacy was as important a weapon as traditional military means. Indeed, in view of the ephemeral nature of the "barbarian" political organizations and the protean nature of the threat they posed to the empire, military success often proved elusive. In maintaining peace on the frontiers, the Byzantine government relied not so much on strong defensive installations but above all on the skilful management of the frontier peoples. Especially under the emperor Justinian (527–65) Byzantine diplomacy was developed into "the science of managing the barbarians" (J.B. Bury, writing in the 11th edition of *Encyclopaedia Britannica*, 1911).

The primary objective of Byzantine diplomacy was thus to divide its enemies and to neutralize them by fomenting rivalries among them. It was an elaborate system of keeping one people in check by another, thereby preventing potential adversaries from invading the empire. Given the preoccupation of the Byzantine court with the barbarian world, it is not surprising that one of the bureaux of the central chancellery was the *Skrinion Barbaron*, or "barbarian bureau". The Byzantines were the first to organize a separate government department for external affairs, though very little evidence has survived as to the exact organization of the Byzantine diplomatic service. The foreign office was presided over by the *Logothetes ton Dromon* (the central tax collector), who also controlled the communications between other ministers and the emperor, whom he saw daily. In the 11th and 12th centuries he was principal secretary of state, under the name of Grand Logothete. The Logothete was responsible for the conduct of imperial diplomacy; and, as the latter was primarily concerned with the barbarians, the Logothete's chief responsibility was the collection and organization of information on imperial neighbours so as to facilitate the subtle manoeuvres involved in managing the barbarians. Occasionally the Logothetes also issued general statements on the principles of imperial foreign policy, such as that contained in *De Administrando Imperio* (c.950) by Constantine VII Porphyrogennetos.

Among the Logothete's other responsibilities was the reception and formal introduction of foreign envoys to the emperor.

Throughout their visit to Constantinople the foreign representatives remained under the strict supervision and constant surveillance of the Logothete; for this purpose they were confined during their stay in the imperial capital to the *Xenodochium Romanorum*, a special government residence for visiting dignitaries. The object of such attention was to ensure that the visitors returned home deeply impressed by the power and riches of Byzantium.

Arguably the most striking external feature of Byzantine diplomacy was its stiff formality, again designed to enhance imperial dignity and to impress foreign representatives. Emperor Constantine Porphyrogennetos' *De Ceremoniis*, a long treatise on the subject of protocol and ceremonial, seems to have served as a manual for his successors. The conjunction of secular and spiritual powers in the hands of the emperor facilitated that task for Byzantine diplomacy. While the foreign representative remained prostrate before the impassive emperor in the sumptuous surroundings of the palace, automata were set in motion to heighten the dazzling effect of glamour and mystery: golden lions began to roar, golden birds sang in trees, and the emperor's throne was lifted heavenwards.

Equally efficient in the manipulation of the frontier peoples was the liberal use of Constantinople's wealth. Ample subsidies were paid to the frontier tribes; and in return they undertook to defend that section of the imperial frontier adjacent to their own territory. The object of such "wise investment" (Steven Runciman) was that of all Byzantine diplomacy: it was to bring the barbarians under Roman influence, thereby eliminating them as a threat to imperial security. Often their chiefs were showered with Byzantine decorations and honours; barbarian princes were married to Roman brides. And the pretenders to the thrones of hostile frontier tribes were always welcome at Constantinople. Once under Byzantine influence, they were then foisted upon their own peoples.

Under the emperor Justinian a new facet was added to Byzantine diplomacy: the close intertwining of religion and politics. Christian propaganda complemented military conquest. The Christian missionary proved an excellent agent of imperial diplomacy, aiding the expansion of Byzantine influence through conversion to Christianity. Subsidies and the sword bought or forced the offering of barbarian support. But Justinian's religious diplomacy engendered their transformation through the penetration of Byzantine ideas. Although this new diplomatic strategy was successful, as for example in Nubia, Ethiopia, southern Arabia, the Caucasian region, and the coast of the Euxine, it was not without risks. Concessions on the part of the imperial power revealed the riches of the empire, and often led to renewed demands from its neighbours. Such a system could not be permanently successful unless it was supported by financial resources and backed up by military power. Byzantine diplomacy involved enormous expense. It flourished for as long as Constantinople's treasury was full. The city's decline as the commercial and financial centre of the Western world also meant the decline of Byzantine diplomacy.

In the 10th century imperial foreign policy was once more reformed and placed on a new basis of carefully formulated principles. Faced with a new powerful threat from two northern nomadic tribes, the Magyars and Bulgars, the science of managing the barbarians reverted to its old technique of creating an artificial equilibrium among its enemies. Each hostile people had its own potential enemies that could be used as a check and counterbalance. This strategy was set out in detail by Constantine VII Porphyrogennetos in his *De Administrando Imperio*. To be successful, however, Byzantine diplomacy as the art of keeping one enemy in check by another needed to be systematic and well organized. It required above all the constant collection and evaluation of information. Arguably this is the lasting legacy of Byzantine diplomacy. The system of regular reports by ambassadors sent to barbarian peoples or by imperial agents within the empire was adopted by the Venetians in their famous system of the *Relazioni*. "It was the Byzantines who taught diplomacy to Venice; it was the Venetians who set the pattern for the Italian cities, for France and Spain, and eventually for all Europe" (Harold Nicolson).

T.G. OTTE

See also Ceremony

Further Reading

Diehl, Charles, *Byzance: grandeur et decadence*, Paris: Flammarion, 1919
Mosley, D.J., "Diplomacy in Ancient Greece", *Ancient Society*, 3 (1972)
Nicolson, Harold, *The Evolution of Diplomatic Method*, London: Constable, and New York: Macmillan, 1954
Obolensky, Dimitri, "Principles and Methods of Byzantine Diplomacy" in his *Byzantium and the Slavs*, London: Variorum, 1971, reprinted Crestwood, New York: St Vladimir's Seminary Press, 1994
Runciman, Steven, *Byzantine Civilization*, London: Arnold, and New York: Longman, 1933
Westlake, H.D., "Diplomacy in Thucydides", *Bulletin of the John Rylands Library*, 53 (1970)

Disease

The earliest aetiological explanation of disease (*nosos, nousos*) in Greek literature is found in Hesiod's mythical description of the Golden Age of man in his *Works and Days* (90–105), a text dating from the 8th century BC. Hesiod envisages a purely masculine society free from the adversities that beset men nowadays – women, toil, and, significantly, disease: only when the first woman, Pandora, opens the jar are diseases released into the world as a punishment to men from Zeus. Henceforward, diseases roam the earth of their own accord, a constant bane to mortals.

This ancient notion of disease, that they are divine in origin and may be a symptom of divine displeasure at mortal misdeeds, was a persistent feature of Hellenic thinking from Homer onwards: at the very beginning of the *Iliad* Apollo sweeps a terrible plague through the ranks of the Achaeans because Agamemnon has insulted one of his Trojan priests (1. 10f.); the plague that devastates Sophocles' Thebes is a result of the religious pollution (*miasma*) brought upon the whole community by Oedipus; "the Sacred Disease", epilepsy, was attributed in antiquity to divine visitation; in the medieval period illnesses such as leprosy could be interpreted as divine retribution.

Yet just as diseases were thought to be inflicted by the gods, so their remedy was sought in prayer and sacrifice. In Greek antiquity many gods and heroes had the power to send and relieve sickness – for example, Artemis was invoked as a healer of women, but Apollo in particular was both the bringer and healer of disease, given the epithets of "doctor" (*iatros*) and "saviour" (*epikourios*). Both Homer's Achaeans and Sophocles' Thebans find a cure for their communal sickness by supplicating Apollo, while in 430 BC at the end of the great plague of Athens a shrine was dedicated to Apollo the Helper at Bassae.

Also important as a healer of disease was Apollo's son Asclepius, the father of Hygeia (Health) and the exemplary physician of the earliest Greek poetry (Homer, *Iliad*, 11. 833; *Hymnus Homericus ad Apollinem*, 210; Hesiod, fr.50), whose staff with a snake coiled around it is a symbol of the medical profession still. Asclepius had many cult sites throughout Greece, the largest of which was established at the end of the 6th century BC at Epidaurus; there were important sanctuaries too at Pergamum and Cos. The sick sought a cure for their disease through purification, sacrifice, and, above all, the practice of incubation – the patient slept in the sanctuary in the hope of being granted a direct cure or at least of receiving helpful instructions from the god in a dream.

Such appeals to the supernatural for relief from sickness reflect the paucity of defences available in antiquity against disease of often epidemic proportions. Thucydides' account of the Athenian plague in the late 5th century BC (2. 47ff.) is a powerful reminder of the despair and social devastation that such widespread and uncontrollable attacks of disease could produce, while Sophocles' *Oedipus Tyrannus*, produced during the same plague, dramatized the helplessness of a city ravaged by disease. Such epidemics raged through the Hellenic world on a regular basis: in AD 542 devastating bubonic plague gripped Byzantium and the whole Levant; in AD 744–47 plague resulted in the serious depopulation of Constantinople; and outbreaks of plague recurred throughout the medieval period. Whole populations were affected by other diseases too; there was an epidemic of leprosy at the beginning of the 3rd century BC in Alexandria and the disease was endemic throughout Europe in the 11th and 12th centuries, perhaps spread by the Crusaders, while malaria (which was said to have killed Alexander) was rife in the Classical period and again after the fall of Byzantium. Poor sanitation and urban overcrowding, especially in times of war and its aftermath, contributed to the spread of contagious diseases as did travel and trade within the Mediterranean and beyond to the East, to Africa, and to central Europe. Thucydides reports that the great plague of Athens started at the Piraeus.

Yet alongside supernatural ideas about illness which persisted into the Christian era, when saints took over the role of the ancient gods and heroes as healers of the sick, the Greek thinkers of antiquity sought natural explanations for the origins of disease. From the 5th century BC onward in Greece, Ionia, and Sicily there developed a body of knowledge about diseases, their classification, diagnosis, origins, treatment, and even prevention. Theories of disease were linked with contemporary scientific and philosophical doctrines and indeed writers outside the medical profession were interested in the nature of sickness and health; Plato gives a detailed account of the origin of disease in the *Timaeus* while Aristotle often discusses disease and may have written a work on the subject.

The most important extant collection of writing on disease from the ancient Hellenic world, however, is the Hippocratic corpus, which comprises about 60 treatises, most of which were written between 430 and 330 BC and which was assembled as a body of work probably by Alexandrian scholars in the 3rd century BC. This collection, the first systematic investigation and analysis of diseases and their treatment, takes its name from Hippocrates, the most famous member of a 5th-century BC guild of doctors from Cos who claimed Asclepius as an ancestor. However, no treatise of the corpus can be attributed directly to Hippocrates – the works are anonymous, written by an assortment of medics from Cos, Cnidus, and elsewhere who express a variety of opinions on diseases and their treatment. Some of the treatises are lectures on physiology and anatomy (*On the Nature of Man*, *On the Nature of the Child*, *The Heart*); some deal with the diseases of women in particular (*On the Diseases of Women 1 and 2*, *On the Diseases of Young Girls*); and some offer theories of the influence of environment on disease (*Airs, Waters, Places*) or advice on the treatment or prevention of disease (*Regimen in Acute Diseases*, *A Regimen for Health*). One significant and influential feature of the corpus is the emphasis given to the systematic observation of patients' symptoms – seven books of the collection consist of case notes (*Epidemics 1 and 3* are the earliest and most interesting) and, while retrospective diagnosis can be problematic, many specific diseases from diphtheria to tuberculosis can be identified from these detailed accounts.

Various theories regarding the origin of diseases are put forward by the Hippocratic writers and their ideas are sometimes at variance. There are, however, several unifying features, the most significant of which is an insistence that all diseases are natural rather than supernatural in origin, that "each disease has a natural cause and nothing happens without a natural cause" (*Airs, Waters and Places*, ch. 22; cf. *Science of Medicine*, ch. 6). Even epilepsy is given a natural aetiology by one medical writer who devoted a whole treatise (*The Sacred Disease*) to a discussion of the cause of the sickness and who attacks the "witch doctors and charlatans" who attribute epilepsy to a divine element.

The Hippocratic corpus contains several theories of the natural causes of disease. Environmental factors such as climate and water supply were thought to be responsible when many people in a locality exhibited common symptoms, and the concept of contagion was recognized by Thucyidides at least; but a variety of diseases in a population indicated that the cause lay in the individual, specifically in relation to his or her diet and habits. Perhaps the most influential aspect of Hippocratic nosology is the common theory that diseases resulted from an imbalance in the constituents of the body. This idea can be traced back to a follower of Pythagoras, Alcmaeon of Croton, who was influenced too by the theories of the Presocratic philosopher Empedocles who posited that everything consists of four primary elements – air, fire, earth, and water. Alcmaeon claimed that "health is the mixture of the qualities in the proper proportion" (fr. 4 Diels-Kranz, from *c*.500 BC) and that, if this equality of influence (*isonomia*) were disturbed, disease would result. Alcmaeon and many of the

Hippocratic writers suggested that imbalances between "primary opposites" such as hot and cold, wet and dry, were responsible for diseases, while other pathological theories were based on an imbalance of humours, in which deficiencies or excesses of the body's "juices" (*chymoi*), particularly bile and phlegm, gave rise to diseases (see for example *Diseases 1*, ch. 2; *Affections*, ch. 1; *Epidemics 1 and 2*). The writer of the treatise *On the Nature of Man* added two additional humours, black bile (choler) and blood, to this scheme, and this doctrine of four humours formed the basis of Western medical theory throughout the medieval period and beyond. Physical imbalances that caused disease could result from environmental factors such as geographical location or climatic conditions which rendered individuals "phlegmatic" or "bilious" and thus susceptible to particular pathological conditions (*Airs, Waters, Places* deals with this theme), while an overindulgence in food, drink, and sex was considered especially deleterious to the health – the Apollonian maxim "nothing to excess" exemplifies the Greek attitude to unrestrained behaviour and its consequences in matters of health as elsewhere.

The medical writers of antiquity recognized the importance of preventative medicine as a factor in the avoidance of disease; the treatise *A Regimen for Health* in particular offers advice on diet and exercise. Indeed the typical Greek diet of fruit and vegetables, whole grains, olive oil, and fish, combined with few animal fats and refined food, which remained largely unchanged until the very recent past, may have conferred some protection against many pathological conditions such as heart disease and various cancers.

In the ancient and medieval Hellenic world, prevention was most certainly better than a cure for disease, if indeed a cure could be found. Doctors (*iatroi*) regularly bled and purged their unfortunate patients and, while the efficacy of plants in the treatment of sickness was recognized at least as long ago as Homeric epic and drug therapy may have provided some relief from the symptoms of illness, prescriptions from the ancient pharmacopoeia supplied few if any effective cures for disease. Patients were treated at home. The first civilian hospital was founded in the middle of the 4th century AD by St Basil the Great, bishop of Caesarea, yet hospitals benefited only a few and attempts to prevent and treat disease were largely inadequate until the very recent past; as recently as the 1960s one study of health and disease in the population of rural Greece discovered a remarkable similarity to the nosology of the Hippocratic texts of the 5th century BC (see Blum and Blum, 1965). During the second half of the 20th century, however, there has been a revolution in the knowledge and treatment of diseases with regard to scientific advances and the development of effective drug therapies, vaccination, and surgical procedures, and, perhaps even more importantly, improved sanitation and access to health care – the provision of clean drinking water and the alleviation of poverty are the most effective weapons against disease.

One particular chronological and geographical continuity that links the Hellenic societies of the past to those of the present is that of hereditary disease. The medical writers of antiquity recognized that conditions such as epilepsy and strabismus could be passed down from parent to child, but there are two pathological conditions of particular interest, both of which can be traced back to ancient Greece and both of which still affect the Greek population and Greek communities overseas: favism and thalassaemia.

Favism, or lathyrism, describes an acute haemolytic anaemia (the decomposition of red blood cells) which results when an individual suffering from a hereditary deficiency of the enzyme glucose-6-phosphate dehydrogenase (G6PD) eats fava beans (*Vicia faba*, or broad beans). The Mediterranean or beta minus variant of G6PD deficiency (which itself has many minor variants classified by region – Athens, Attica, Corinth, and so on) is prevalent in Greece, in areas of ancient Greek colonization, and in individuals of Greek descent throughout the world. The disease was not recognized in antiquity, although one Hippocratic treatise links a diet high in pulses to symptoms characteristic of the pathological reactivity which the defect can induce (*Epidemics* 2, ch. 4), and the current geographical distribution of G6PD deficiency, present in all of the oldest Greek settlements (more than 12 per cent in Athens, the Peloponnese, Epirus, and Thessaly and even higher in Cyprus and Rhodes), suggests that the defect was present in the population of archaic Greece.

Thalassaemia, another anaemia, compromises the production of haemoglobin; the predominant form of the defect in individuals of Greek descent is beta-A2. The thalassaemic trait is widespread on mainland Greece where 5–10 per cent of the population are carriers of the defective gene, while on the Ionian islands and Rhodes the figure rises to 14–16 per cent and on Cyprus reaches 16–20 per cent. Like G6PD deficiency, this defect too was present in the ancient Greek world (see Grmek, 1989, ch. 10, for a discussion of the evidence). In its minor form (when one parent of the affected individual is a carrier of the defective gene) the defect produces only a mild anaemia and there is usually no clinical disability. In its major form, however (when both parents are carriers), the disease has severe and frequently fatal effects – crippling anaemia, often followed by heart failure; a foetus with the major form of the disease can now be identified by DNA analysis and termination of the pregnancy may be advised.

Both G6PD deficiency and thalassaemia are serious and sometimes fatal diseases, yet the genetic defects that produced them have persisted in the Greek population from the very ancient past to the present. The explanation as to why such potentially damaging defects have continued through time lies in recent research that suggests that the common link between the diseases is the protection they afford against malaria: the G6PD defect provides increased resistance to malaria and indeed there is selection for a more severe trait if it provides greater protection, while the thalassaemic trait is most common in places where malaria was a particular problem in ancient Greece. The interrelationship between disease and its effect upon a population through time is a complex one; in this case the distribution of a contagious disease in Greek antiquity, malaria, together with the geographical, meteorological, and social environments that produced it, has affected the pattern of disease and even the genetic make-up of the Greek population three millennia later.

EUGÉNIE FERNANDES

See also Health, Medicine

Further Reading
Allison, A.C., "Malaria and Glucose-6-Phosphate Dehydrogenase Deficiency", *Nature*, 197 (1963): pp. 609 ff.
Blum, Richard and Eva Blum, *Health and Healing in Rural Greece: A Study of Three Communities*, Stanford, California: Stanford University Press, 1965
Brothwell, Don and A.T. Sandison (editors), *Diseases in Antiquity: A Survey of the Diseases, Injuries, and Surgery of Early Populations*, Springfield, Illinois: Thomas, 1967
Cockburn, T.A., "Infectious Diseases in Ancient Populations", *Current Anthropology*, 12 (1971): pp. 45–62
Craik, E., "Diet, Diaita and Dietetics" in *The Greek World*, edited by Anton Powell, London and New York: Routledge, 1995
Edelstein, Ludwig, *Ancient Medicine*, edited by Owsei Temkin and C. Lilian Temkin, Baltimore: Johns Hopkins University Press, 1967, reprinted 1994
Grmek, Mirko D. (editor), *Hippocratica*, Paris: CNRS, 1980
Grmek, Mirko D., *Diseases in the Ancient Greek World*, Baltimore: Johns Hopkins University Press, 1989
Hanson, A.E., "Hippocrates: *Diseases of Women 1*", *Signs*, 1/2 (1975): pp. 567–84
Huheey, J.E. and D.L. Martin, "Malaria, Favism and Glucose-6-Phosphate Dehydrogenase Deficiency", *Experientia*, 31/10 (1975): pp. 1145–47
Jones, W.H.S., *Malaria and Greek History*, Manchester: Manchester University Press, 1909, reprinted New York: AMS Press, 1977
Kibre, P., "Hippocratic Writings in the Middle Ages", *Bulletin of the History of Medicine*, 17 (1945): pp. 371–412
Lloyd, G.E.R., *Magic, Reason and Experience: Studies in the Origin and Development of Greek Science*, Cambridge and New York: Cambridge University Press, 1979
Lloyd, G.E.R., *Science, Folklore and Ideology: Studies in the Life Sciences in Ancient Greece*, Cambridge and New York: Cambridge University Press, 1983
Matsaniotis, N. and C. Kattamis, "Thalassemias: A Social Problem in Greece", *Annales de la Sociétés Belges de Médecine Tropicale*, 49 (1969): pp. 223–30
Moller-Christensen, V., "Evidence of Tuberculosis, Leprosy and Syphilis in Antiquity and the Middle Ages", *Proceedings of the XIXth International Congress for the History of Medicine, Basel, 1964*, Basel: Karger, 1966
Parker, Robert, *Miasma: Pollution and Purification in Early Greek Religion*, Oxford: Clarendon Press, 1983
Scarborough, J., "Theophrastus on Herbals and Herbal Remedies", *Journal of the History of Biology*, 11 (1978): pp. 353–85
Spiller, Gene A. (editor), *The Mediterranean Diets in Health and Disease*, New York: Van Nostrand Reinhold, 1991
Stamatoyannopoulos, G. *et al.*, "The Distribution of Glucose-6-Phosphate Dehydrogenase Deficiency in Greece", *American Journal of Human Genetics*, 18 (1966): pp. 296–308
Vikan, G., "Art, Medicine and Magic in Early Byzantium", *Dumbarton Oaks Papers*, 38 (1984): pp. 65–86
Weatherall, D.J. and J.B. Clegg, *The Thalassaemia Syndromes*, 3rd edition, Oxford: Blackwell 1981

Dithyramb

The dithyramb was a choral song performed in honour of Dionysus. The original meaning of the word itself is obscure; the root -amb may be pre-Greek, but it nonetheless suggests a kinship with *iambos*, *thriambos*, and *ithumbos*, all terms for songs with early connections with Dionysus. Surviving evidence seems to indicate that the history of the genre can be divided into three phases: dithyramb as pre-literate cult song, the incorporation of choral dithyramb into formal competitions in the 6th century BC, and the drastic renovation of the genre at the hands of the poets of the "new music" in the latter part of the 5th century.

Earliest evidence of the dithyramb comes from Archilochus of Paros in the 7th century BC. Although the passage in question does not itself appear to be dithyrambic, Archilochus speaks of knowing how "to lead off the dithyramb of lord Dionysus" when his "wits are thunderstruck with wine" (fr. 120 West²). Archilochus' use of the verb *exarchein* ("to lead off") finds a parallel in a number of early texts describing the formal conduct of communal songs such as the lament and wedding song (*Iliad*, 24. 723; *Odyssey*, 4. 15–19), and Archilochus himself also used it of the paean (fr. 121 West²). These passages suggest a kind of song in which a leader engages in exchanges with a chorus, although the precise nature of such songs and the kind of Dionysiac occasion in which the dithyramb was performed remain uncertain. Aristotle seemed to be thinking in similar terms when he recorded that tragedy originated "from those leading off the dithyramb", just as comedy arose from the leaders of the phallic song (*Poetics*, 1449a10). Similarly Proclus finds the origin of the dithyramb in "rustic play and festivities at drinking parties" (*Chrest.* 51 [320b21]). Aristotle also adds that drama came into being from an "improvisatory beginning", and this may be taken to indicate that early dithyrambs were not formal poetic compositions that were preserved in writing. In this light it is hazardous to make inferences concerning this period from the later dithyramb, especially since the genre underwent significant change in the 5th century BC. It is particularly important to note that the frequent assertion that the early dithyramb was a vehicle for myth, detailing the nature of Dionysus and his history, is not directly supported by the evidence, but is an uncertain inference drawn from later practice.

Herodotus records that Arion of Methymna "was the first man that we know of to compose a dithyramb and so name it and produce it in Corinth" (1. 23). This statement has aroused considerable controversy, especially concerning the precise implications of *onomasanta* ("having named it"). In light of the earlier evidence of Archilochus, it is very unlikely that Arion can have invented the genre itself. Accordingly, it has been plausibly suggested that Herodotus is referring to the formal introduction in Corinth of a choral song performed by a trained choir, to which the name "dithyramb" was given. The alternative view, that *onomasanta* means "entitled", has been widely held, but it unconvincingly pushes back into the 7th century BC the practice of applying titles to dithyrambs, a practice that is only securely attested for the 5th century BC.

Arion's activities in Corinth should be understood within the broader context of the initiatives of the early tyrants in numerous Greek cities, where local pride was fostered and civic ideology promoted through the establishment of poetic contests. Such contests were regularly part of religious festivals, and attracted competitors from across Greece. Little is known of the details of Arion's activity at Corinth, but it seems to have been well known to later practitioners of the genre. When Pindar asks in a victory ode composed for a Corinthian victor, "Whence came the delights of Dionysus with the ox-driving dithyramb?", the ancient commentators tell us that he is referring to Arion, and we can make the further inference that the dithyramb is called "ox-driving" (*boelatas*) because oxen were the prizes in the dithyrambic competition and they were sacrificed as part of the festival. There were no doubt strong similarities between such dithyrambic contests and the better-attested tragic competitions in Athens.

As is regularly the case, more is known about Athenian practice. Lasus of Hermione (b. 548/4 BC) is said to have established the dithyrambic competitions at Athens. We have some idea of the way in which the contests were organized: each of the ten Athenian tribes competed with one chorus of men and one of boys, and the size of these choruses was fixed at 50 in each case. As in the case of the dramatic competitions, a producer, called a *choregos*, presided over the performance, not only seeing to the equipping of the chorus, but also providing fees for the poet, the choral trainer (*chorodidaskalos*), and the accompanist, the *auletes*, who played the *aulos*, a double-reed instrument. There is evidence for dithyrambic performances at a number of Athenian festivals: the City Dionysia, Thargelia, Panathenaea, Prometheia, and the Hephaestia. Hypodicus of Chalcis, who is now little more than a name, was the first victor at the Dionysia in 509/8 BC, and this may imply that the dithyrambic competition postdated the formal institution of the tragic competitions, an event traditionally assigned to *c*.535 BC. The poets are never mentioned in inscriptions commemorating victories, and this suggests that the contests were a competition among the tribes, who commissioned dithyrambs from distinguished poets from around the Greek world. The victorious *choregos* typically set up in the Street of Tripods a tripod with a dedicatory inscription.

In the first part of the 5th century BC the most successful poets of the dithyramb were Simonides, Pindar, and Bacchylides. An anonymous epigram, usually dated to the Hellenistic period, mentions that Simonides won 56 victories in dithyrambic contests, but there is only a single mention among the ancient sources of a Simonidean dithyramb: Strabo (15. 3. 2) refers to a dithyramb entitled *Memnon*, which was part of Simonides' *Deliaca* (possibly poems composed for the Delians). Thanks largely to papyrus finds, we have a better impression of the poems by Pindar and Bacchylides collected together as dithyrambs by Alexandrian editors. The remains of Pindar's dithyrambs (frr. 70–88 Maehler) are noteworthy for the prominence of Dionysiac elements, and this suggests a conscious acknowledgement of the Dionysiac roots of the genre. As in the case of Pindar's victory odes, there are also passages that treat the occasion of the poem and the polis that commissioned it, as well as mythic narrative (including myths that do not appear to be connected with Dionysus). In sharp contrast to Pindar's dithyrambs, those by Bacchylides (15–20, possibly frr. 21–22 Maehler) betray no interest in Dionysiac myth or religion, nor do they appear to give any clear indication of the occasion for which they were intended; they are simply lyric narratives of a variety of myths. It is possible that Bacchylides' poems indicate the degree to which the dithyramb had moved away from its Dionysiac roots, but it is not at all certain that these poems are in fact dithyrambs. There is little firm evidence for the criteria employed by Alexandrian scholars for classifying such poems, and there is some suggestion that the situation was anything but clear, even when scholars were working with complete texts. A scholium (P.Oxy. 2368) preserves traces of an ancient dispute between Aristarchus and

Callimachus over the classification of the *Cassandra* (fr. 23 Maehler), and that debate has been echoed by modern scholars, especially concerning *Dith.* 17.

Many of the uncertainties concerning the nature and character of earlier dithyramb arise from the fact that in the latter half of the 5th century BC the dithyramb became a favourite vehicle for the musical experiments of the poets of the "new music". The comic poet Pherecrates provides a list of offences committed against Music by the leaders of the movement (fr. 155 *PCG*), among whom he names Cinesias, Melanippides, Timotheus, and Philoxenus. In particular, the *Persae* by Timotheus provides an extended example of "dithyrambic" style, although that poem is technically a *nomos*. A number of other extant passages give us a glimpse into the nature of a genre in which the traditional rigour of triadic structure has been replaced by astrophic form, and words have been subordinated to music. Accordingly, the emphasis seems very much to have been on the music, and there are reports of outrageous instrumental effects. Elaborate vocabulary and complicated imagery rendered the texts obscure to many, and these poets were much criticized on such grounds by later writers. In fact, the obscurity of dithyrambic poets became proverbial: "You make even less sense than a dithyramb", runs a proverb quoted by a scholiast to Aristophanes (*Birds*, 1393). This "dithyrambic style" was regularly pilloried by comic poets in the 4th century BC.

Dithyrambs continued to be performed in the post-Classical world. There is evidence for such performances on Delos in the Hellenistic period, at both the Delia and the Apollonia, and in Athens at the City Dionysia, at least until the 2nd century AD. The fragments from this period offer no firm basis for speculation, and it is tempting to suppose that activity of the poets of the "new music" so undermined the character of the dithyramb that the genre never fully recovered.

CHRISTOPHER G. BROWN

See also Poetry (Lyric), Song

Further Reading

Froning, Heide, *Dithyrambos und Vasenmalerei in Athen*, Würzburg: Triltsch, 1971

Maehler, Herwig, *Die Lieder des Bakchylides*, vol. 2: *Die Dithyramben und Fragmente*, Leiden and New York: Brill, 1997

Pickard-Cambridge, Arthur Wallace, *Dithyramb, Tragedy, and Comedy*, 2nd edition revised by T. B. L. Webster, Oxford: Clarendon Press, 1962

Pindar, *The Dithyrambs: Introduction, Text, and Commentary*, edited by M. J. H. van der Weiden, Amsterdam: Gieben, 1991

Zimmermann, Bernhard, *Dithyrambos: Geschichte einer Gattung*, Göttingen: Vandenhoeck & Ruprecht, 1992

Divination

Divination, the supposed ability to acquire knowledge of the future or of other normally inaccessible matters by supernatural means, has always found a place in the Greek tradition from antiquity to the present day, but while some forms have enjoyed cultural approval, others have been condemned.

All the methods of divination in the Greek tradition, from the most sophisticated to the most crude, operate on the same basic principle: the belief that supernatural forces (whether gods, angels, demons, or spirits of the dead), endowed with greater understanding than humans, may reveal part of their superior knowledge through the phenomena being experienced or observed. Scholarship, following distinctions drawn in antiquity, has traditionally divided the methods of divination known in the Greek world between the "natural" or "intuitive" (those based simply upon direct inspiration in a natural or dream state) and the "artificial" or "inductive" (those involving deliberate observation, manipulation, and intervention on the part of the diviner). Such groupings, however, tend to be confusing since, even in the most apparently intuitive methods, some manipulation may be thought possible or necessary; they also impose a distinction not perceived by the great majority of actual participants, and have further been understood in different ways by different scholars. They are thus avoided here.

Oracular prophecy undoubtedly enjoyed the highest cultural esteem in the ancient Greek world. It was conducted at all manner of holy places, some of which transcended state boundaries and were highly institutionalized, although most were very local, catering to small communities and individuals. It also encompassed a broad spectrum of techniques, ranging from ecstatic utterance or frenzied behaviour to the interpretation of the rustling of leaves in a sacred tree or ripples in a sacred pool. The most famous site was probably Delphi, where Apollo was believed to speak through an inspired individual, the Pythia, but there were a number of other major oracles of similar standing, that of Zeus at Dodona for example. At these important centres a variety of complex rituals of consultation were conducted in correspondingly elaborate physical surroundings to produce the oracular response; questions were often posed by the representatives of cities and other such groups and concerned important matters of state policy and law, although individuals might also make enquiries. Another type of oracle, operating at a high cultural level and best exemplified by the tradition of Sibylline ecstatic prophecy, did not offer answers to specific questions but rather spoke generally about the future.

Closely related to oracular prophecy was the interpretation of dreams, which were taken to be inspired by supernatural powers. At some major sites, and at a great number of lesser ones, a god was believed to inspire the sick who slept there with dreams that either healed directly or told how a cure might be effected (incubation); most notable perhaps was the shrine of Asclepius at Epidaurus. People also commonly interpreted their own dreams as predictions of the future, or else they might employ professionals who had training and access to the many textbooks of dream interpretation (*oneirokritika*) that developed over the centuries and, in some cases, incorporated material from outside the Greek tradition. Dream interpretation illustrates quite clearly the problems of drawing sharp distinctions between "natural" and "artificial" forms of divination, for although it might appear to be a purely intuitive technique, in many cases there was an obvious perception that dreams might be *induced*, either in the self or another, and the powers producing them manipulated. Related to this notion, indeed, was a whole range of other divinatory techniques that involved the inducement of inspiration. Thus in practices such as hydromancy, lekanomancy, and katoptromancy (where the behaviour of objects or substances in a vessel of water was observed or where, in more complex forms, a medium saw visions on the surface of water or some other shining or reflective material) it was believed that supernatural powers could be induced or forced by a diviner or sorcerer to reveal hidden knowledge; often these powers were thought to be the spirits of the dead and hence such techniques were perceived to be forms of necromancy.

Other common and highly developed methods of divination in the pre-Christian period include augury, in which the behaviour of birds was noted, and hieroscopy, in which the behaviour of sacrificial victims and, even more importantly, the formation, development, and marking of their various organs, such as the liver or shoulder blades, were observed. Also subject to interpretation were the chance utterances of people and involuntary movements of the body (such as twitching, sneezing, itching, and the like), as well as the patterns found on various parts of the body, like the palms (chiromancy). Natural signs were thought to predict coming weather, while heavenly events, from thunder and lightning to the appearance of comets and shooting stars, were believed to be very significant. From Hellenistic times the sometimes immensely complex and "scientific" technique of astrology developed under eastern influence; using observation of the regular and irregular movements of heavenly bodies, this either predicted the future or determined the most appropriate course and timing of action. Other simple, and consequently very common, techniques involved reading the pattern in which cast objects, such as dice, grain, knuckle bones, or other lots, fell, or the order in which they were extracted from a container. The point at which spinning objects stopped was believed to be revealing, for example of the identity of a thief, and significance might be derived from passages determined by some random method of selection in written texts.

With the rise of Christianity to dominance in the Greek world, the old officially sanctioned forms of divination ceased to be culturally acceptable; most had been formally banned by the 4th century AD and gradually fell into disuse. Oracular prophecy thus almost completely disappeared as a result of the Church's need to preserve the authority of its canon, despite having enjoyed some prominence in the form of directly inspired utterance in primitive Christianity and in some heretical sects; the various types of divination related to animal sacrifice also vanished along with the sacrificial rituals themselves. But although the new Christian orthodoxy claimed that all forms of pagan divination were evil and nothing but vehicles of demonic deceit, practice at the popular level dictated that some at least would continue relatively unchanged. In the public sphere incubation, for example, carried on without interruption, churches taking the place (sometimes quite literally) of pagan shrines and Christian holy figures substituting as the source of inspiration. There is also abundant evidence throughout Byzantine times and down to the modern period that very many of the more private and individual forms of divination continued to be practised, not only at the local level but sometimes even in such places as the imperial court.

It is thus clear that people in the Byzantine and early modern Greek world still engaged in the whole diverse range of minor divinatory techniques: taking note of unusual bodily sensations or markings on the skin, watching the behaviour of birds and animals, studying the patterns in which scattered barley, beans, bones, or stones would fall, extracting lots from jars of water (*klidonas*), and so forth. The use of icons for divination, for example by noting apparent changes in their colour, found acceptance due to their role in culturally approved Christian religious practice; the same is true of bibliomancy where random consultation of the Bible and particularly the Psalms was valued. Astrology also flourished and, indeed, was developed in intellectual circles, despite periodic bouts of condemnation, and the old techniques of dream interpretation, along with their manuals, continued to be employed at all levels of society: the emperor Manuel II Palaiologos is known to have had an interest in the subject and is even credited with a book on it. Also popular among professional diviners were versions of the ancient methods using a shining, reflective surface. In their more sophisticated forms these involved elaborate rituals of invocation and manipulation of spirits (usually thought to be evil) and perhaps the souls of the dead. Information was channelled through a child (hence virgin and pure) medium, and the ritual, which might involve considerable knowledge of complex astrological and cosmological theory as well as the deliberate manipulation of sense perception, usually took place within the confines of a magic circle.

Although it evidently continued almost unchanged into the early years of the 20th century, the serious practice of divination has diminished considerably since then, but some traditional forms still continue and these have been supplemented by methods imported from other cultures. Thus incubation regularly takes place at churches with a particular reputation for healing, and other dreams are analysed for what they may predict of the future; in some cases, rituals are performed, for example on the first Saturday in Lent, to induce dreams of a future spouse. Common rituals for determining affliction by the evil eye are often closely related to older types of divination involving oil and water (*lekanomandia*), while as recently as the 1970s more complex forms of this art were still being attributed to professional sorcerers thought capable of providing information about such things as lost objects or appropriate courses of action. Divination by icons continues and some memory of simple forms of augury persists. Another of the old practices still appearing in places is the *klidonas* ceremony in which personal objects are drawn from a jar of water, usually to predict marriage partners, while divination by means of the observation of markings on the shoulder blades of sheep (scapulomancy) is known from many regions, as is that which looks at the patterns made by dropped beans or grain. Closely related, and perhaps the most common of all modern practices, is reading the patterns made by the grounds in the bottom of coffee cups. Astrology, in the form of horoscopes, is found as widely in Greece as in any modern western country, while other types of divination that do not belong to the Greek tradition, such as tarot or playing-card reading, are also known.

The credibility and efficacy of divination were certainly accepted by most people in the ancient world and, although Christianity condemned it as implying a separate source of inspiration from that controlled and approved by the Church, it did little to challenge the underlying notion that information could be obtained by such means, hence its persistence in the Greek tradition. This is not to say that there were no sceptics in antiquity or Byzantine times and some certainly preferred rational explanations to the supernatural ones usually offered for the operation of divination, or else dismissed most, if not all, such practices as the work of charlatans. The Church's constant criticism of divination during Byzantine and modern times has meant that ordinary people have often regarded it with some ambivalence, though this has often had more to do with the question of its sinfulness than its efficacy. Professional divination has tended to be viewed with particular suspicion, and even its practitioners have understood themselves to be working with evil powers, but minor types have been considered far less dangerous, especially by those unaffected by the niceties of theology. Thought to operate through the power of either neutral, natural forces, or else those of Christianity itself, such divination has been seen as a relatively legitimate activity. In recent times, however, as in most developed countries, all divination has increasingly come to be regarded with what has been described as a mixture of curiosity and mockery. Even among those who are still happy to engage in some of the rituals, the great majority are no longer prepared to accept the basis of belief in the supernatural required for their explanation. An example may be found in the practice of *klidonas*, deliberately revived by folklorists in some parts of Greece to preserve cultural heritage, or in the consultation of coffee cups or shoulder blades, prediction by which is not totally dismissed, but not taken particularly seriously by anyone either.

RICHARD P.H. GREENFIELD

See also Astrology, Dreams, Oracles

Further Reading

Bouché-Leclercq, Auguste, *Histoire de la divination dans l'antiquité*, 4 vols, Paris: Leroux, 1879–82; reprinted New York: Arno Press, 1975

Dodds, E.R, *The Greeks and the Irrational*, Berkeley: University of California Press, 1951

Dodds, E.R., *The Ancient Concept of Progress and Other Essays on Greek Literature and Belief*, Oxford: Clarendon Press, 1973

Eitrem, Samson, "Dreams and Divination in Magical Ritual" in *Magika Hiera: Ancient Greek Magic and Religion*, edited by Christopher A. Faraone and Dirk Obbink, Oxford and New York: Oxford University Press, 1991

Flacelière, Robert, *Greek Oracles*, translated by Douglas Garman, London: Elek, 1965

Fontenrose, Joseph, *The Delphic Oracle: Its Responses and Operations, with a Catalogue of Responses*, Berkeley: University of California Press, 1978

Fontenrose, Joseph, *Didyma: Apollo's Oracle, Cult, and Companions*, Berkeley: University of California Press, 1988

Greenfield, Richard P.H., "A Contribution to the Study of Palaeologan Magic" in *Byzantine Magic*, edited by Henry Maguire, Washington, D.C.: Dumbarton Oaks, 1995

Halliday, W.R, *Greek Divination: A Study of Its Methods and Principles*, London: Macmillan, 1913

Hart, Laurie Kain, *Time, Religion and Social Experience in Rural Greece*, Lanham, Maryland: Rowman and Littlefield, 1992

Herzfeld, Michael, *The Poetics of Manhood: Contest and Identity in a Cretan Mountain Village*, Princeton, New Jersey: Princeton University Press, 1985

Lewis, Naphtali, *The Interpretation of Dreams and Portents*, Toronto and Sarasota, Florida: Stevens, 1976

Lewy, Hans, *Chaldean Oracles and Theurgy: Mysticism, Magic and Platonism in the Late Roman Empire*, new edition, edited by Michel Tardieu, Paris: Etudes Augustiniennes, 1978

Luck, Georg, *Arcana Mundi: Magic and the Occult in the Greek and Roman Worlds: A Collection of Ancient Texts*, Baltimore: Johns Hopkins University Press, 1985

Parke, H.W., *Greek Oracles*, London: Hutchinson, 1967

Parke, H.W., *The Oracles of Zeus: Dodona, Olympia, Ammon*, Cambridge, Massachusetts: Harvard University Press, and Oxford: Blackwell, 1967

Parke, H.W., *The Oracles of Apollo in Asia Minor*, London: Croom Helm, 1985

Parke, H.W., *Sibyls and Sibylline Prophecy in Classical Antiquity*, edited by B.C. McGing, London and New York: Routledge, 1988

Stewart, Charles, *Demons and the Devil: Moral Imagination in Modern Greek Culture*, Princeton, New Jersey: Princeton University Press, 1991

Divorce

Greek attitudes to divorce and the practicalities of its execution have undergone radical revision since antiquity and these revisions are revealing, reflecting as they do upon the changing roles of state and religion within the institution of marriage and indeed of the perceived nature and function of marriage itself. Evidence from Classical Athens suggests that divorce was common and simple to accomplish, requiring state authorization in only a few particular cases, a situation that mirrors the concept of marriage as an essentially private matter between individual families in which the state played no formal role. We possess less evidence for areas outside Athens, but the Gortyn law codes of Crete and the apparent flexibility of the marriage bond at Sparta suggest that divorce was easily obtainable throughout Greece.

At Athens there were, broadly, three categories of divorce, the defining characteristic of each being the agent who effected the separation. First, the husband could send his wife away (*apopempsis*), an action that required no justification and so was a potential area of insecurity for women. However, it is likely that such divorces were discouraged by social and family pressures and by the convention that demanded the return of the dowry to the wife's natal family in all cases of divorce, whatever the reason. There was however one circumstance in which the sending away of a wife was compulsory on pain of the loss of civil rights (*atimia*) for her husband, that of the wife's adultery (for an example, see Lysias, 14. 28).

Second, the wife could leave the marital home (*apoleipsis*). Plutarch claims that Hipparate, the wife of Alcibiades, registered her intention to divorce her errant husband with the archon (Plutarch, *Alcibiades*, 8), suggesting that Athenian women lacked the requisite authority to effect a divorce personally and so, unlike their husbands, required the ratification of the state. The evidence for wives initiating divorce is problematic, however, since no other text describes such an event, although Euripides, in the context of the possibility of a woman leaving an unhappy marriage, suggests that divorce brought women a bad reputation (*Medea*, 236–37), while the children of a marriage belonged to their father and remained in his household, perhaps another disincentive for wives to seek divorce.

The third and perhaps most common category of divorce was that of *aphairesis*, the dissolution of marriage by the wife's natal guardian (*kyrios*). A woman's father and brothers had the right to insist upon her divorce and the return of her dowry, and the reasons that motivated them to do so highlight several functions of marriage in antiquity (and beyond). Childlessness is attested as a reason for divorce and the wife who did not provide her husband with heirs faced being sent back to her father's house. However, two lawcourt speeches voice a concern for the wives of infertile husbands; in one a husband unselfishly asks his wife's father to retrieve her and remarry her to another man so that she might have the chance to bear children (Isaeus, 2. 7–8), while in another a speaker criticizes the brother of a married but childless woman for not effecting her divorce and finding her another husband (Isaeus, 8. 36). The fate of the adulteress, compulsorily divorced, reflects too upon the notion that the primary purpose of marriage is the provision of legitimate children; the seduced woman can no longer be relied upon to fulfil this wifely function and so must be dismissed.

Marriage was important too as a site for social and interfamilial alliance, engendering and cementing kinship ties between and within families. Conversely, when conflict arose, divorce could result (Demosthenes, 4. 4), while social and financial ambition could also lead to the dissolution of an unprofitable marriage; in one text a daughter begs her father not to divorce her from the husband she loves to marry her to a richer man (Menander, Papyrus Didot 1). The case of the *epikliros* is particularly instructive here. The estate of a man who died without sons could be claimed by his nearest male kin, who was constrained also to marry any daughter of the deceased, the *epikliros*, who thus pertained to the estate. Such claims were legally adjudicated in a special court hearing (*epidikasia*). Significantly, a married woman who became an *epikliros* was divorced from her present husband in the interests of inheritance and the production of legitimate heirs for her natal family and thus, as the speaker in a 4th-century BC court case insists, "many men are deprived of their wives" (Isaeus, 3. 64).

Such pragmatic concerns about the legitimacy of children and socio-economic factors continued to inform marital alliance and separation in the Hellenic world, but the new perspective on marriage introduced by Christian teaching produced a pronounced change in attitudes to divorce. While the early Church's view on wedlock was divided, on the whole it promulgated the sanctity of marriage which thus was accorded an extra religious dimension and status. Furthermore, in marked contrast to the easily dissoluble marriage ties of antiquity, Christian marriage was regarded as a bond for life, and divorce was thus anathema. A further disincentive to divorce lay in the Christian notion that remarriage constituted adultery, even in the case of widowhood and especially with regard to divorce.

Today, while Orthodoxy regards marriage as a holy sacrament, the Church does permit divorce, although theoretically Orthodox canon law allows divorce and remarriage only in cases of the wife's unchastity, referring to the authority of Matthew 19: 9, an interesting parallel to the law of Classical Athens. In practice, however, the Church may make exceptions and will allow divorce for other reasons. Divorce ratified by the state may be easily obtainable in Greece and for the many Hellenic communities overseas, but for remarriage within the Church a divorce granted by the state is insufficient.

EUGÉNIE FERNANDES

See also Adultery, Dowry, Marriage

Further Reading

Antti, Arjava, *Women and Law in Late Antiquity*, Oxford: Clarendon Press, and New York: Oxford University Press, 1996

Beaucamp, Joëlle, *Le Statut de la femme à Byzance, 4e–7e siècle*, 2 vols, Paris: Boccard, 1990–92

Goody, Jack, *The Development of the Family and Marriage in Europe*, Cambridge and New York: Cambridge University Press, 1983

Hunter, Virginia J., *Policing Athens: Social Control in the Attic Lawsuits, 420–320 BC*, Princeton, New Jersey: Princeton University Press, 1994

Isaeus, *The Speeches, with Critical and Explanatory Notes*, edited by William Wyse, Cambridge: Cambridge University Press, 1904; reprinted New York: Arno Press, 1979

Just, Roger, *Women in Athenian Law and Life*, London and New York: Routledge, 1989

Lefkowitz, Mary R. and Maureen B. Fant, *Women's Life in Greece and Rome: A Source Book in Translation*, 2nd edition, London: Duckworth, and Baltimore: Johns Hopkins University Press, 1982

Meyendorff, John, *Marriage: An Orthodox Perspective*, 3rd edition, Crestwood, New York: St Vladimir's Seminary Press, 1984

Patterson, C., "Marriage and the Married Woman in Athenian Law" in *Women's History and Ancient History*, edited by Sarah B. Pomeroy, Chapel Hill: University of North Carolina Press, 1991

Pomeroy, Sarah B., *Women in Hellenistic Egypt: From Alexander to Cleopatra*, New York: Schocken, 1984; revised edition, Detroit: Wayne State University Press, 1990

Rosivach, V.J., "Aphairesis and Apoleipsis: A Study of the Sources", *Revue Internationale des Droits de l'Antiquité*, 31 (1984): pp. 193–230

Sealey, Raphael, *Women and Law in Classical Greece*, Chapel Hill: University of North Carolina Press, 1990

Todd, S.C., *The Shape of Athenian Law*, Oxford: Clarendon Press, 1993

Ware, Timothy, *The Orthodox Church*, 2nd edition, London and New York: Penguin, 1993

Willetts, R.F. (editor), *The Law Code of Gortyn*, Berlin: de Gruyter, 1967

Wolff, H.J., "Marriage Law and Family Organization in Ancient Athens", *Traditio*, 2 (1944): pp. 495 ff.

Dodecanese

Aegean islands

Today the "Dodecanese" (literally "group of 12 islands") includes Astypalia, Chalki, Cos, Kalymnos, Karpathos, Kasos, Kastellorizo, Leros, Leipsoi, Nisyros, Patmos, Rhodes, Symi, and Tilos, as well as a few other small islands, one or two of which are inhabited but do not have independent (deme) status. That is a total of 14 islands. The original 12, which included Ikaria but excluded Rhodes and Cos, got their group status following a collective protest in 1908 at the proposed removal of privileges which they had enjoyed from the

Dodecanese: view from Rhodes, the largest island of the group of 14

Ottoman authorities since the 16th century. These were taxation at a modest level and by community not by individual, and freedom from the permanent presence of Ottoman officials. The very importance of Rhodes and Cos was of course the reason why they were, from the start, excluded from privileged status. In fact the term "Dodecanese" was used as early as the 12th century AD but in a quite different sense. In this article it is used with the meaning it bears today.

Although the Dodecanese are geologically, and in details of climate and fauna and flora, more closely related to continental Asia Minor than to the Aegean archipelago, and in early prehistory were close in culture to Asia Minor, from the time of the Minoan palaces (c.2000 BC) they were part of Aegean spheres of influence (which included coastal Anatolia).

Both Minoan and Mycenaean remains have been found widely in these islands and it is clear that the Dodecanese belonged, in succession, to these cultural areas. Their history in the early Iron Age and down to c.600 BC is not known in much detail but they certainly received settlers from various parts of Greece and acquired their Dorian character. The islands (especially the three cities of Rhodes – Ialysus, Camirus and Lindus) were prosperous in the Archaic period (6th century BC) and the Rhodians participated in the establishment of the Greek trading emporium of Naucratis on the Nile delta and founded colonies abroad, contributing substantially to the spread of

Greek culture. In the Persian Wars of the early 5th century BC, the colonies were squeezed between the opposing sides, not least because of their geographical position. In the Classical period there were synoecisms, accompanied by the foundation of new urban centres, on both Rhodes and Cos. The smaller islands were subordinate to them and were sometimes formally incorporated into their administrative structure. Rhodes and Cos were especially prosperous and important artistic centres in the Hellenistic period, when they were subject to the Ptolemies of Egypt. Rhodian sculptors were responsible, inter alia, for the works in the Cave of Tiberius at Sperlonga in Italy, and played an important part in the transmission of Greek stylistic influences on Roman sculpture. After the advent of the Romans, Rhodes was punished for its support of the anti-Roman Macedonian king Perseus, and lost its economic and maritime influence when Delos was made a free port in AD 166.

When Constantinople became the capital of the Christianized Roman empire in AD 330, geography again determined the allegiance of the Dodecanese as is clear from the remains of numerous early Christian basilicas in the islands. In the 7th and 8th centuries AD they were plagued by Arab raiders, who may even have established a base on Karpathos (Sokastro). Under Byzantine administration the islands later belonged to the themes of Cibyra and the Aegean Sea. The monastery of St John on Patmos was founded in 1088 and other ecclesiastical architecture reflects the islands' prosperity in the Middle Byzantine period (843–1204).

In the 11th and 12th centuries, with the advent of the Crusaders, and of Genoese and Venetian traders, contacts were established with the west which were to be so important in the history of the Dodecanese. In 1309 Rhodes was captured by the Hospitaller Knights of St John who had been expelled from the Holy Land (and later from Cyprus). The knights, who remained until 1523, rapidly established control over most of the Dodecanese. During their ascendancy local culture was maintained, most effectively by the Church, but material culture was somewhat diluted by the introduction of western elements in art and architecture.

In the 14th and 15th centuries many of the islands were attacked by the Ottomans and in 1523 the knights were expelled from Rhodes after a long siege. This event inaugurated nearly 400 years of subjection to Ottoman Turkey. Although the smaller islands were largely untouched by the Ottomans, Rhodes and Cos were much more closely controlled – a fact which is substantiated by their architectural history. Only on those islands are there widespread signs of Ottoman presence, with purpose-built mosques, schools, bath houses, etc., as well as churches converted for Muslim worship. Nevertheless the two communities were not integrated: no Greeks, for instance, were permitted to reside within the walled old town of Rhodes; churches in Byzantine style continued to be built and decorated in traditional fashion and Greek customs were maintained. The problems of 1908 are however symptomatic of greater interference by the Ottoman authorities in the 19th century.

The islanders took part in the wars of independence, with notable contributions from the sailors of Kasos and the shipbuilders of Symi but, although they were originally assigned to the new Greek kingdom of 1833, they were subsequently exchanged for Euboea, which was initially to go to Turkey.

Italy took the Dodecanese in 1912 in the Italo-Turkish war. Under the first and second Treaties of Lausanne the islands were first destined for Turkey, then Italian possession was confirmed (1924). This situation lasted until 1947. In the years before World War II strenuous attempts were made to impose Italian language and culture, leading to riots and bloodshed, especially on Kalymnos. Under the Italians there was a governor in Rhodes and a regent on Cos. In both these towns, and on Leros where there was an important naval base, the grandiose public buildings of the period are strikingly un-Greek. There are occasional examples too on other islands (the police station on Patmos). The architecture of the Greek churches was not affected, however, that of private houses only occasionally and in minor details.

During the war the Germans took over some of the islands which later came under British military administration. The German surrender of the Dodecanese was signed on Symi on 8 May 1945.

Although there was considerable emigration from the Dodecanese in the 19th century, the islands mostly maintained substantial populations (Kasos – only 1100 today – had 11,000 until 1824, when it was ravaged by Egyptians) up to the Italian period when their main industry (sponge fishing) was hard hit by a ban on working off the coast of North Africa, which was exploited by other Italian colonies. One result of the subsequent emigration was the Dodecanesian colony of sponge fishers at Tarpon Springs in Florida.

Three points should be emphasized in considering the contribution of the Dodecanese to the Greek tradition. First, the three periods of substantial foreign interference introduced some significant non-Greek elements into local culture, but these were material rather than spiritual. Secondly, while these elements may superficially have enriched that culture, they have done nothing to affect its essential Greekness (and close affinity with the rest of the Aegean) which was energetically maintained. Thirdly, both in antiquity and in more recent times, Dodecanesian emigrants have played an important part in establishing Greek culture in other parts of the world. In recent times this has helped maintain the viability of small local communities by remittances.

R.L.N. BARBER

Summary

Group of "12" (now redefined to include 14) islands in the southeast Aegean. Rhodes and Cos became especially prosperous during the Hellenistic period. The 11th and 12th centuries brought contact with crusaders and traders from the west, and from 1309 to 1523 Rhodes was held by the Hospitaller Knights of St John. After four centuries of Ottoman rule, the islands became Italian from 1924 to 1947. Their Greek culture was however maintained throughout.

Further Reading

Barber, Robin, *Rhodes and the Dodecanese*, London: A. & C. Black, and New York: Norton, 1997 (*Blue Guide* series)

Doumanis, Nicholas, *Myth and Memory in the Mediterranean: Remembering Fascism's Empire*, London: Macmillan, and New York: St Martin's Press, 1997

Karouzos, C., *Rhodes*, Athens, 1973

Kollias, Elias, *The Knights of Rhodes: The Palace and the City*, Athens, 1991

Matton, Raymond, *Rhodes*, 4th edition, Athens, 1959

Mee, C., *Rhodes in the Bronze Age: An Archaeological Survey*, Warminster: Aris and Phillips, 1982

Papachristodoulou, X.I., *Istoria tis Rodou* [History of Rhodes], 2nd edition, Athens, 1994

Tarsouli, A., *Dodecanesa* [The Dodecanese], Athens, 1947–50

Dodona

City in Epirus

Dodona was the site of reputedly the oldest oracle in ancient Greece and dedicated to the worship of Zeus. Located at the head of the valley of Tsarkopvitsa at the foot of Mount Tomaros, the ancient site is 22 km south of Ioannina. In Classical times pilgrims reached the site from the south, up the valley of the river Louros to the town of Kopani. In Roman times Dodona lay directly on the inner main Epirote road heading north from Nicopolis; its centrality explains the revival in the 2nd century AD of the Zeus Naia festival and games and the establishment of a bisphoric two centuries later.

In the 3rd millennium BC Dodona saw continuous habitation in the form of primitive shepherd communities. No build-

Dodona: view of the theatre, built in the 3rd century BC to seat 18,000 spectators

ings survive from this period, although numerous stone tools, loom weights, pottery, and a clay hearth have been found. Seasonal habitation is suggested, that is, shepherds brought their herds to Dodona each summer to take advantage of the pastures, springs, forests, and cool temperatures. These non-Greek-speaking shepherds are identified in Greek tradition as Pelasgians. At the end of the Early Bronze Age or shortly thereafter, Greek-speaking peoples moved into the area, perhaps bringing with them the worship of Zeus. (Some scholars hypothesize that an original cult to the mother-earth goddess, Gaia, was supplanted by Zeus' cult; Gaia then became Zeus' consort, only to be replaced ultimately by Dione Naia, who is known from numismatic and inscriptional evidence to have shared the sanctuary with Zeus in the historical period.)

Dodona appears in both the *Iliad* and the *Odyssey*. In the *Iliad* (16. 233ff.) Achilles mentions priests called Selloi who had unwashed feet, slept on the ground, and acted as interpreters of Zeus; some scholars explain the unparalleled behaviour of unwashed feet and sleeping on the ground as indicative of an earlier Gaia cult, wherein priests strove to stay in communication with mother earth. Odysseus (*Odyssey*, 14. 327–28) travelled to Dodona to hear the will of Zeus uttered from a sacred oak tree. It is not clear from the text whether Zeus spoke from the oak, the oak itself spoke, or the priests interpreted the rustling of the oak's leaves or the moving of its branches. Hesiod (fr. 240, 319M-W) goes further, stating that Zeus spoke through doves within the oak; this may refer to the birds' cries or to their flight. Herodotus (2. 55) mentions the presence of three priestesses, whom he calls "doves"; his silence on the Selloi suggests that the male priests of Homer had been supplanted by priestesses sometime during the Archaic period. Scholars explain the move to priestesses as Dodona's attempt to emulate the oracular practices at the more famous sanctuary of Delphi. Whatever the reason for the change, the priestesses now assumed charge of the oracle, which had come to consist of consultation by lots. (Plato's assertion in the *Phaedrus* that the priestesses underwent ecstatic trances is a fantasy.) The use of lots would be logical if the sacred oak tree, which by now would have been 600 years old, had begun to die; moreover, the oracle at Delphi occasionally resorted to the use of lots, and so Dodona may have copied that practice.

The method of consultation was quite simple. The enquirer wrote his query onto a ribbon strip of lead and folded it over three or four times. The folded lead was marked on the outside for identification purposes and placed in a jar. A priestess then pulled from the jar an enquiry at the very time that she drew from another jar one of several responses, either a "yes" or "no" answer or the name of a deity to whom proper sacrifices needed to be made. These responses may have been written on oaken tablets (thereby perpetuating the tradition of the prophetic oak), although the use of other materials such as beans cannot be precluded. Over 150 enquiries have been discovered, the majority now housed in the Ioannina Museum. Only a few enquiries dealt with state affairs; the rest came from private individuals, most of them local, who wanted to receive foreknowledge about such matters as marriage, children, health, and employment. The lead tablets date from 500 to about 250 BC, when the oracle fell into disuse.

The city of Dodona flourished even after the oracle declined. Pyrrhus, king of Epirus, made it the religious centre of his kingdom and transferred there the mint of the Epirote alliance. With the subsequent establishment of the festival of Zeus Naia honouring the god, Dodona saw its first major building programme. Previously the site had consisted of only a small, early 4th-century temple to Zeus, a stone circuit wall that enclosed the temple and sacred oak, and a temple of Dione; in as much as the oracular cult required no elaborate structures (other than a few tables, jars, and consulting area), the sparse remains are wholly expected. During Pyrrhus' reign, the temple of Zeus was enlarged, two temples (to Heracles and to Aphrodite) were constructed, and a vast theatre was built on the hillside. The theatre's large seating capacity (up to 20,000) can be explained only by its connection with the Naia festival. The city was also fortified by an extensive circuit wall, with towers on three of its sides. The city proper, located on the acropolis north of the theatre, is mostly unexcavated. In 219 BC the Aetolians, under the generalship of Dorimachus, invaded Epirus and ravaged the site. The site was immediately restored by Philip V, king of Macedon. The temple of Zeus was further enlarged; also erected were a new temple of Dione and, in conjunction with the festival of the Naia, a council house, guesthouse, and a stadium to the southwest of the theatre. The oracle had by now fallen silent, as evidenced by the dearth of votive offerings and enquiry tablets. In 167 BC the Romans under Aemilius Paullus sacked Dodona to punish the Epirotes who had assisted the Macedonian king Perseus in his revolt. Dodona never recovered from this destruction. A ravaging in 88 BC by troops of Mithradates VI, king of Pontus, only exacerbated the situation. The Naia did continue on, however, until at least the mid-3rd century AD. The oracle remained silent, although Roman and Christian Greek writers penned fanciful descriptions of mantic activities like the banging of bronze cauldrons or gongs and the presence of oracular springs. The Naia ceased with the establishment of Christianity. A Byzantine basilica was built in the sanctuary in around 400, and the Council of Ephesus (431) records a bishop from Dodona in attendance.

STEVEN M. OBERHELMAN

See also Oracles

Summary

City in Epirus, site of the oldest oracle in Greece, dedicated to Zeus. Ritual is described by Homer, Hesiod, and Herodotus. Enquiries were later written on strips of lead, of which some 150 are preserved, dating from c.500 to 250 BC when the oracle fell into disuse. There are remains of various other buildings including a vast theatre used for the celebration of the Zeus Naia festival.

Further Reading

Carapanos, Constantin, *Dodone et ses ruines*, Paris: Hachette, 1878
Cook, Arthur Bernard, *Zeus: A Study in Ancient Religion*, 3 vols, Cambridge: Cambridge University Press, 1914–40
Dakaris, S.I., "Das Taubenorakel von Dodona und das Totenorakel bei Ephyra" in *Neue Ausgrabungen in Griechenland*, Olten: Urs Graf, 1963
Dakaris, S.I., *Archaeological Guide to Dodona*, Ioannina, 1967
Dakaris, S.I., "The Sanctuary of Dodona" in *Temples and Sanctuaries of Ancient Greece: A Companion Guide*, edited by Evi Melas, London: Thames and Hudson, 1973

Flacelière, Robert, *Greek Oracles*, translated by Douglas Garman, London: Elek, 1965

Hammond, N.G.L., *Epirus: The Geography, the Ancient Remains, the History and Topography of Epirus and Adjacent Areas*, Oxford: Clarendon Press, 1967

Kekulé von Stradonitz, Reinhard and Hermann Winnefeld, *Bronzen aus Dodona in den königlichen Museen zu Berlin*, Berlin: Reimer, 1909

Myers, F.W.H., "Greek Oracles" in his *Essays Classical*, London: Macmillan, 1911

Parke, H.W., *The Oracles of Zeus: Dodona, Olympia, Ammon*, Cambridge, Massachusetts: Harvard University Press, and Oxford: Blackwell, 1967

Pomtow, H.R., "Die Orakelinschriften von Dodona," *Jahrbuch für klassische Philologie*, 127 (1883): pp. 306–60

Dorians

Ancient ethnic group

The ancient Greeks believed that the Hellenic people was constituted by the totality of various ethnic subgroups, of whom the Dorians (along with the Ionians, Aeolians, and Achaeans) were considered to be the most important. By the Classical period, various cities in the Peloponnese (Sparta, Argos, Corinth, Sicyon, Megara), Crete and the southern Cyclades (Melos, Thera), the Dodecanese (Rhodes, Cos), southwest Asia Minor (Cnidus, Halicarnassus), North Africa (Cyrene), Sicily (Syracuse, Megara Hyblaea, Gela), and south Italy (Tarentum) claimed that they were Dorian foundations on the basis of perceived similarities in dialect, rituals, customs, and common origins.

According to ancient authors the Dorians had originally lived in central and northern Greece but had, towards the end of the heroic age, migrated south to the Peloponnese in the company of the Heraclidae (descendants of Heracles); a second migratory wave carried Dorians across the southern Aegean to Asia Minor, while the period of colonization from the 8th century BC onwards resulted in the Dorian foundations in Italy, Sicily, and Libya. The tradition for the so-called "Dorian invasion" of the Peloponnese is most fully attested in the universal history of Diodorus Siculus (1st century BC) and in the early imperial work known as the *Library* which was erroneously ascribed to Apollodorus of Athens. There are, however, earlier references: in the 5th century BC Herodotus (9. 26) mentions the first (unsuccessful) assault on the Peloponnese by the Heraclidae and Thucydides (1. 12) notes the second (successful) invasion by the Dorians and Heraclidae – an event which he places 80 years after the sack of Troy – while the 7th-century BC Spartan poet Tyrtaeus (fr. 2) proclaims that Sparta was granted by Zeus and Hera "to the Heraclidae, with whom we [Dorians] left windy Erineus and arrived in the broad island of Pelops". Despite the fact that his subject matter ostensibly deals with the premigratory phase of the heroic age, Homer (*Odyssey*, 19. 177) remarks on the presence of Dorians in Crete, alongside Achaeans, Eteocretans, Cydonians, and Pelasgians.

Although attempts were made in the 19th century to find archaeological confirmation for the Dorian invasion in the destructions of the Mycenaean palaces, it is now generally believed that the collapse of the palatial system was due to natural disaster, internal conflict, or economic failure rather than to external enemy action. Furthermore, apparent innovations in cultural forms and artifacts that were once attributed to the arrival of the Dorians (e.g. iron working, protogeometric pottery, cremation, burial in cist tombs, and new types of weapons and jewellery) have proved to be either earlier than the palatial destructions or first attested in areas such as Attica and Euboea which did not claim to be Dorian.

Similar scepticism concerning the tradition has recently been expressed by linguists who note that while the "Doric" dialects spoken in various cities share certain structural correspondences, no single linguistic innovation can be isolated that is not also found in at least one other non-Doric dialect and that therefore the Doric dialects need not derive from one proto-Doric idiom once spoken in central or northern Greece. In addition some Dorian cities seem not to have used the Doric dialect: by the 5th century BC, Halicarnassus was apparently employing the Ionic dialect for its official inscriptions.

Thucydides (6. 4. 3; 6. 5. 1) implies the existence of recognizably Dorian customs, though these are not explicitly identified. They may have concerned issues of constitution, law, political subdivision into the three "Doric" tribes of the Hylleis, Dymanes, and Pamphyloi, calendars, and religious festivals (for example, the festival of the Carnea), but it is far from clear that such customs were universal to all Dorian cities. Similarly, despite its origins in Corinthia, there is no reason to regard the "Doric" order of architecture as exclusively Dorian; the same is true of the "Doric" mode in music. Finally, various versions of the tradition appear to attribute to the Dorians different ancestors (Dorus, Aegimius) and different primordial homelands (Doris, Hestiaeotis, Thessaly, Macedonia) which might suggest that the legend of the Dorian invasion was in fact a compilation of earlier traditions that evolved towards the end of the Dark Age.

The earliest mobilization of Dorian identity for extrapolitical purposes would appear to be the Dorian Hexapolis—a league which, according to Herodotus (1. 144), was centred on the sanctuary of Apollo Triopios on the Cnidian promontory and which included the Rhodian cities of Lindus, Ialysus and Camirus together with Cos, Cnidus, and Halicarnassus (later expelled). If, as seems likely, the league was a Dorian response to the Ionian Dodecapolis (centred on the Panionion at Cape Mycale), then its origins should date back to at least the beginning of the 6th century BC. By contrast, Herodotus' account of Cleisthenes of Sicyon (5. 67–68) seems to imply that appeals to Dorian ancestry in the Peloponnese may have been restricted to the ruling elites.

In the 5th century BC appeals to a collective Dorian identity became more frequent in mainland Greece, particularly at Sparta whose evocation of Dorian kinship served to justify its intervention in the central Greek region of Doris in 457 BC (Thucydides 1. 107). The exploitation of Dorian solidarity reached its apogee, however, in the course of the Peloponnesian War as Sparta employed the motif of common kinship with its Peloponnesian and Sicilian allies in opposition to Athenian appeals to an Ionian heritage: on several occasions, Thucydides has his Spartan or Syracusan speakers contrast the freedom and courage of the Dorians with the enfeebled slavishness of Athens' Ionian allies (e.g. 5. 9; 6. 77).

From the 4th century BC onwards fewer appeals were made on the basis of Dorian identity, although renewed interest in Dorian origins accompanied the emperor Hadrian's foundation of the Panhellenion in AD 131/32 when adduced proof of being a Dorian foundation was frequently the prerequisite for admission into the league (both Cyrene and Synnada in Phrygia guaranteed their admission by these means). In the same period, Sparta attempted to revitalize its prestige by capitalizing upon its earlier status as an archetypal Dorian city and reviving its ancient customs in an archaizing form (including a "hyperdoricization" of its dialect). In general, however, the ethnic, cultural, and religious connotations of the term "Dorian" became gradually less significant compared with the linguistic definition as grammarians sought to identify a literary Doric dialect (alongside Attic, Ionic, and Aeolic) on the basis of the Doric idiom employed by earlier poets such as Tyrtaeus, Alcman, and Pindar. While the Dorians have figured prominently in the historiography and ideology of western Europe (particularly among German romantics of the 19th century and later the Nazi party), their role within the Hellenic tradition has been less significant, although it is often claimed that the modern dialect of Tsakonian (spoken in the northern Parnon range of the eastern Peloponnese) attests linguistic archaisms that find parallels with the ancient Doric dialect of Laconia.

JONATHAN M. HALL

See also Dialects, Hellenes

Summary

One of the main ancient ethnic groups of the southern Balkans, thought in antiquity to have moved south into the Peloponnese at the end of the heroic age (*c.*1200 BC) and then on into the south Aegean and Asia Minor. There is no archaeological or linguistic evidence to support this; but Dorians felt a shared racial identity in the Classical period which was often exploited for political purposes, especially by Sparta.

Further Reading

Alty, John, "Dorians and Ionians", *Journal of Hellenic Studies*, 102 (1982): pp. 1–14

Beloch, Karl Julius, "Die dorische Wanderung", *Rheinisches Museum für Philologie*, 45 (1890): pp. 555–98

Brillante, Carlo, "L'invasione dorica oggi", *Quaderni Urbinati di Cultura Classica*, 16 (1984): pp. 173–85

Chadwick, John, "Who Were the Dorians?", *La Parola del Passato*, 31 (1976): pp. 103–17

Craik, Elizabeth M., *The Dorian Aegean*, London and Boston: Routledge, 1980

Haley, J.B. and Carl Blegen, "The Coming of the Greeks", *American Journal of Archaeology*, 32 (1928): pp. 141–54

Hall, Jonathan M., *Ethnic Identity in Greek Antiquity*, Cambridge and New York: Cambridge University Press, 1997

Hammond, Nicholas, "The End of the Mycenaean Civilization and the Dark Ages: The Literary Tradition for the Migrations" in *History of the Middle East and the Aegean Region, c.1800–1380 BC*, edited by I.E.S. Edwards *et al.*, Cambridge: Cambridge University Press, 1973 (*The Cambridge Ancient History*, vol. 2, part 2, 3rd edition)

Hooker, James T., "New Reflexions on the Dorian Invasion", *Klio*, 61 (1979): pp. 353–60

López Eire, A., "El retorno de los Heraclidas", *Zephyrus*, 28–29 (1978): pp. 287–97

Müller, C.O., *The History and Antiquities of the Doric Race*, 2 vols, Oxford: Murray, 1830

Musti, Domenico (editor), *Le origini dei Greci: Dori e mondo egeo*, Rome: Laterza, 1985

Nixon, Ivor Gray, *The Rise of the Dorians*, Puckeridge, Hertfordshire: Chancery Press, and New York: Praeger, 1968

Parker, Victor, "Zur Datierung der dorischen Wanderung", *Museum Helveticum*, 52 (1995): pp. 130–54

Rawson, Elizabeth, *The Spartan Tradition in European Thought*, 2nd edition, Oxford: Clarendon Press, 1991

Will, Edouard, *Doriens et ioniens: essai sur la valeur du critère ethnique appliqué à l'étude de l'histoire et de la civilisation grecques*, Paris: Belles Lettres, 1956

Doukas family

Doukas, or Doux, probably a Hellenized form of the Latin military rank *dux*, occurs as a family name in Byzantium from the mid-9th century onwards. Bearers of the name eventually became widespread at all levels of Byzantine society from the emperor downwards, but not all seem to have belonged to the same family or clan (unlike the Komnenoi, for instance). Origins in Armenia have been suggested for some Doukai, but this is unprovable and rather unlikely. In his history (written before 1138) Nikephoros Bryennios claims for the first Doukas an anachronistic rank and relationship with Constantine the Great, saying that he had been appointed Dux of Constantinople by Constantine. The 11th-century imperial Doukai seem to have had connections with Paphlagonia, perhaps the seat of the family estates and the source of their wealth.

Three groups of Doukai can be distinguished in the period before 1204. Around 855 a "son of Doux" was involved in the persecution of the heretical Paulicians. Some 50 years later, and possibly related to this Doux, there appear Andronikos Doux (d. *c.*908), his son Constantine (d. 913), and Constantine's three sons, military commanders who were successful against the Arabs in Asia Minor. Andronikos was drawn into rebellion, defected to Islam, and died in obscurity. Constantine, apparently a charismatic personality, was reinstated in his military position and became involved unsuccessfully in schemes to make him co-emperor and guardian of the young Constantine VII Andronikos and Constantine became the subject of legend.

The second group, Andronikos Doux Lydos (d. *c.*979) and his two sons, probably unrelated to the earlier Doukai, were prominent under Basil II and were involved in the revolt of Bardas Skleros and the magnates of Asia Minor.

The third group, again probably unrelated to the above, are the Doukai who became emperors and high imperial officials in the late 11th century, emerging from among rival aristocratic clans in the confused years following the demise of the Macedonian dynasty. Constantine X Doukas (emperor 1059–67), a representative of the civil administration rather than the military, owed his promotion as emperor to a network of court contacts. He was marked more by piety, restraint, and financial prudence than incisive activity. His sole military venture, against the invading Uzes in 1064–65, was an abject failure. During his reign little attempt was made to respond to the increasing Turkic penetration into Asia Minor. On his death the military party put forward the general Romanos Diogenes, whose imperial status (as Romanos IV Diogenes, 1068–71) was legitimized by marriage to the widow of Constantine X, Eudokia Makrembolitissa. When Romanos fell into Turkish hands following the battle of Manzikert (1071), Constantine's son Michael was proclaimed emperor as Michael VII Doukas (emperor 1071–78; d. c.1090). A pupil of the statesman-philosopher Psellos, Michael was an unsatisfactory personality, perhaps simple-minded, with little taste for the military activity which circumstances demanded. Partly as a result of the Turkish devastation of Asia Minor, Byzantine coinage was seriously devalued during his reign; his nickname, Parapinakes, derives from the diminution of corn measures by the fraction known as a *pinakion*. He was eventually deposed in favour of the general Nikephoros Botaneiates and lived out his last days as a monk. Lively biographies of both Constantine and Michael are to be found in Psellos' *Chronographia*.

During and after the reign of Constantine, Michael's brother John (d. 1088), known as the Caesar John, played a prominent role both as a military commander and a schemer. Having engineered the disastrous retreat at Manzikert and the subsequent blinding of Romanos IV, he was instrumental in ensuring the eventual succession of Michael VII, his nephew. He became involved in the subsequent jockeying for power between the Doukas and Komnenos families, ultimately falling from his nephew's favour and becoming an adherent of the Komnenos faction. He set up a marriage between his granddaughter Irene and the rising young Alexios Komnenos, later emperor Alexios I. Like his brother and nephew, he seems to have exerted influence more as a result of his social position and wealth than through force of personality.

Of the numerous Doukas progeny, who formed a dense network of marriage alliances with other aristocratic families, the last with a serious chance of becoming emperor was Constantine (d. after 1094), the son of Michael VII. Though deprived of his right of succession on his father's fall from power, he was in 1083 betrothed to Anna Komnene, the eldest child of Alexios I and the future historian. Until the birth of John Komnenos in 1087, Constantine was acclaimed with Anna as future ruler.

Irene Doukaina, granddaughter of the Caesar John and wife of Alexios I Komnenos, united the two major aristocratic clans of the late 11th century and, by giving birth to seven children, themselves all with numerous offspring, did much to ensure the dynastic dominance of this family grouping. Accepted at first only with reluctance by Alexios, she came to be a valued and influential counsellor. She played an important cultural role as the patroness of such writers as her son-in-law Nikephoros Bryennios and the poet-scholar Theodore Prodromos. She endowed a monastery, of Our Lady Full of Grace, whose foundation document survives as an invaluable source of information on monastic practices as well as the prosopography of her family.

From the mid-12th century onwards the Doukas family became inextricably intermingled with other aristocratic groupings and the name Doukas appears increasingly only in combined form, such as Komneno-Doukas, attached to other families (such as Kamateros or Vatatzes), or in strings such as Michael Doukas Angelos Komnenos Palaiologos (Michael VIII, died 1282).

Later prominent bearers of the name include the historian Doukas (c.1400– after 1462), who recounted the last days of Byzantine rule in Constantinople. In the service of the Genoese Gattilusio family in Lesbos, he was an eyewitness to many of the events that he described. He supported the union of the Orthodox Church with Rome and viewed the Turkish conquest as God's punishment for Byzantine sins, though he was under no illusions about Turkish cruelty.

Such was the fame of the 10th-century Doukai that it would seem that reflections of their deeds have lingered on in stories and songs that have influenced the epic-romance *Digenis Akritis*. The personal roles of both Constantine and Andronikos are discernible in the epic, and especially in more recent Akritic songs, while the name of Doukas itself is part of the family background of both the hero Digenis and his bride.

ELIZABETH M. JEFFREYS

Further Reading

Bryennius, Nicephorus, *Histoire*, edited and translated by Paul Gautier, Brussels: Byzantion, 1975
Doukas, *Decline and Fall of Byzantium to the Ottoman Turks*, edited and translated by Harry J. Magoulias, Detroit: Wayne State University Press, 1975
Komnene, Anna, *The Alexiad*, translated by E.R.A. Sewter, Harmondsworth and Baltimore: Penguin, 1969
Ostrogorsky, George, *History of the Byzantine State*, 2nd edition, Oxford: Blackwell, 1968; New Brunswick, New Jersey: Rutgers University Press, 1969
Polemis, Demetrios I., *The Doukai: A Contribution to Byzantine Prosopography*, London: Athlone Press, 1968
Psellos, Michael, *The Chronographia*, translated by E.R.A. Sewter, London: Routledge, and New Haven, Connecticut: Yale University Press, 1953; revised edition as *Fourteen Byzantine Rulers*, Harmondsworth and Baltimore: Penguin, 1966, reprinted 1982
Trapp, Erich (editor), *Prosopographisches lexikon der Palaiologenzeit*, nos. 5676–99, Vienna: Akademie der Wissenschaften, 1976–91

Dowry

The institution of dowry (*proix*) has been a significant feature of marriage within the Hellenic world from antiquity until well into the 20th century as a material marker of both socio-economic status and interfamilial alliance; and, while the abolition of the dowry system was part of a relatively recent parcel of legal reforms relating to marriage and the family in Greece (Family Law Act 1983), there is evidence to suggest that the practice persists, in rural areas at least (see Kourvetaris and Dobratz, 1987).

In antiquity, dowry in the form of money, goods, livestock, or land represented the bride's family's contribution towards the establishment of the new household and, while not legally obligatory, was a normal and expected element of prenuptial negotiations, fixed at the time of betrothal. Indeed, since marriage was a private matter between individuals, the provision of a dowry was one indication that a sexual relationship was equivalent to marriage (Isaeus, 3. 78). Dowry was an important expression of social standing and wealth; at Athens in the Classical period dowries for women from rich families could amount to 5–10 per cent of the paternal estate, while for poorer families the proportion of the family property may have been greater still. Dowering the females of the family could represent an onerous financial burden, especially where there were many daughters, and the system may have contributed to the ancient practice of selective female infanticide (Golden, 1981, suggests a 10 per cent rate of female infanticide for Classical Athens). Nevertheless, particularly where women had little if any financial and legal power, dowry was an arrangement that worked to protect women's interests within marriage and to maintain links with their natal families; as such, it must be distinguished from the giving of "bridewealth" where the groom pays money to the bride's family.

Athenian women did not themselves take possession of their dowries; dowry was given by the bride's guardian (*kyrios*, usually her father or brother) to her husband and he administered it, dowry being essentially a transfer of property from *kyrios* to *kyrios*. Yet this transfer was, crucially, conditional; the husband's control of the dowry depended upon his continuing control and support of his wife and, if the marriage failed, the dowry was returned to the woman's original *kyrios*. The return of dowry on divorce was compulsory, including those cases when the wife's natal family instigated the separation and even when divorce was enforced legally upon a husband by his wife's adultery. Failure to return dowered property constrained the husband to pay interest on the original amount at a rate of 18 per cent per annum and failure to do this could result in a legal prosecution. In the case of large dowries, a mortgage (*apotimima*) equivalent to the value of the dowry was a common prerequisite to ensure repayment in the event of divorce. The destination of the dowry in the event of the death of either spouse depended upon the existence of children: if the wife died childless, her dowry was returned to her father; if the husband died childless, his widow was returned together with her dowry which could be used to redower her for a second marriage. If there were sons, however, they inherited their mother's portion (*metroia*) when they reached the age of majority, yet were obliged to maintain her for life.

A returnable dowry had several important implications. First, it reduced the likelihood of husbands divorcing their wives for trivial reasons and perhaps provided them with a financial incentive to treat their wives well; several texts attest to the power over her man that a large dowry could confer upon a wife through the threat of divorce (Menander, fr. 333 Koerte; Plato, *Laws*, 774c–e). Second, a widowed or divorced woman could return to her father's house with her dowry as a means of support, while the same property in the form of a second dowry could provide an opportunity for remarriage, a frequent occurrence in antiquity. Indeed, the role of the dowry system in the protection of women's interests in marriage is recognized by a legal speech from 4th-century BC Athens which suggests that the rich man who marries a poor girl ought to provide a fictitious dowry that he would be obliged to return in the case of divorce (Isaeus, 3. 35–36). Thus in a society such as Athens, where women did not inherit, dowry can be seen as a daughter's share in the household patrimony, the counterpart of (although not equivalent to) a son's inheritance and, as a form of security, a maintenance fund that attached to a woman throughout her life and which her sons would inherit.

In later Hellenic societies dowry retained its importance within the marriage contract, yet its uses underwent subtle changes. Where women exercised greater financial control, they are found disposing of and bequeathing their dowries in the form of a maternal inheritance, for example, in Hellenistic Egypt, where a daughter's dowry could equal a son's inheritance and could be provided by mothers as well as fathers, taking the form of money and personal property, although not of land. One Alexandrian marriage contract from 92 BC in which the dowry settlement is the crucial component insists that, if the wife voluntarily leaves the marriage, her husband must return her dowry within ten days and, failing this, must forfeit the amount plus one half (Tebtunis Papyrus 104). In the Byzantine period bridegrooms contributed an amount equal to that specified in the bride's dowry contract (*proikosymbolia*) and, while husbands administered the marital funds, the alienation of their wives' dowries was subject to considerable legal restrictions.

Christianity provided a new role for dowry as a means of financial support for women wishing to embrace monasticism – a woman was expected to bring money to the Church, just as she would on marriage. While often a father's approbation was required (and denied), an 11th-century ruling decreed that married women wishing to enter convents were allowed a six-month trial period, after which they were granted their dowries (Peira, 25. 4).

Well into the late 20th century Greek families have worked to finance sons' educations and daughters' dowries and the provision of dowry has been often a joint enterprise to which the whole family contributed, the strength of the obligation being such that Greek emigrants commonly sent home money to dower their daughters, sisters, and nieces. Yet this very Hellenic institution which has persisted from antiquity to the very recent past has now largely disappeared from Greece, a development informed by the radically changing role of women in the second half of the 20th century. Education and a career are now the concerns of girls as well as boys; married women contribute financially to their households and do not need a maintenance fund for their support. Furthermore, women no longer need to receive their share of patrimony in the form of dowry since they can inherit directly. Significantly, the abolition of the dowry system in 1983 was part of a reform package designed to encourage and recognize female equality and is a reflection of the enhanced social, legal, and economic status of women in modern Greek society.

EUGÉNIE FERNANDES

See also Children, Divorce, Inheritance, Marriage

Further Reading

Antti, Arjava, *Women and Law in Late Antiquity*, Oxford: Clarendon Press, and New York: Oxford University Press, 1996

Bremen, Riet van, "Women and Wealth" in *Images of Women in Antiquity*, revised edition, edited by Averil Cameron and Amélie Kuhrt, London: Routledge, and Detroit: Wayne State University Press, 1993

Campbell, J.K., "Traditional Values and Continuities in Greek Society" in *Greece in the 1980s*, edited by Richard Clogg, London: Macmillan, and New York: St Martin's Press, 1983

Clark, E.G., *Women in Late Antiquity: Pagan and Christian Lifestyles*, Oxford, Clarendon Press, and New York: Oxford University Press, 1993

Comaroff, J.L., *The Meaning of Marriage Payments*, London and New York: Academic Press, 1980

Foxhall, L., "Household, Gender and Property in Classical Athens", *Classical Quarterly*, 39 (1989): pp. 22–44

Golden, M., "Demography and the Exposure of Girls at Athens", *Phoenix*, 33 (1981): pp. 316–31

Goody, Jack and S.J. Tambiah, *Bridewealth and Dowry*, Cambridge: Cambridge University Press, 1973

Herlihy, David, *Medieval Households*, Cambridge, Massachusetts: Harvard University Press, 1985

Herrin, J., "In Search of Byzantine Women: Three Avenues of Approach" in *Images of Women in Antiquity*, revised edition, edited by Averil Cameron and Amélie Kuhrt, London: Routledge, and Detroit: Wayne State University Press, 1993

Kourvetaris, Yorgos A. and Betty A. Dobratz (editors), *A Profile of Modern Greece in Search of Identity*, Oxford and New York: Clarendon Press, 1987

Lefkowitz, Mary R. and Maureen B. Fant, *Women's Life in Greece and Rome: A Source Book in Translation*, 2nd edition, London: Duckworth, and Baltimore: Johns Hopkins University Press, 1982

Levy, H., "Inheritance and Dowry in Classical Athens" in *Mediterranean Countrymen: Essays in the Social Anthropology of the Mediterranean*, edited by Julian Pitt-Rivers, Paris: Mouton, 1963

Pomeroy, Sarah B., *Women in Hellenistic Egypt: From Alexander to Cleopatra*, New York: Schocken, 1984; revised edition, Detroit: Wayne State University Press, 1990

Pomeroy, Sarah B., "Infanticide in Hellenistic Greece" in *Images of Women in Antiquity*, revised edition, edited by Averil Cameron and Amélie Kuhrt, London: Routledge, and Detroit: Wayne State University Press, 1993

Rowlandson, J., "Women and Economic Opportunity in Early Ptolemaic Egypt" in *The Greek World*, edited by Anton Powell, London and New York: Routledge, 1995

Schaps, David M., *The Economic Rights of Women in Ancient Greece*, Edinburgh: Edinburgh University Press, 1979

Sommerstein, A.H., "Preverbs and Dowries", *Classical Quarterly*, 37/1 (1987): pp. 235–40

Todd, S.C., *The Shape of Athenian Law*, Oxford: Clarendon Press, 1993

Zepos, I. and P. Zepos (editors), "Peira of Eustathios Romaios" in *Ius Graeco-Romanum*, vol. 4, Athens, 1931; reprinted Aalen: Scientia, 1962

Doxiadis, Constantinos Apostolou

1913–1975

Architect and planner

Constantinos Doxiadis was an architect and planner who played a central role in the reconstruction and development of Greece after World War II. During the 1950s and 1960s his theory, teaching, and practice resonated beyond the architectural culture of Greece, and constituted a primary reference on development around the world.

Doxiadis was born in Stenimachos, in Bulgaria, and grew up in Athens. He received a degree in architecture and engineering from the National Metsovion Technical University of Athens (1935) and a Ph.D. in planning from the Berlin-Charlottenburg University (1936). His dissertation contended that the seemingly disordered layout of ancient Greek religious communities was derived from angles of vision, radial distances, and mathematical and philosophical principles of human cognition. Originally published in German in 1937 and soon translated into Greek, this first major study by Doxiadis was highly acclaimed for its originality, but some architects and archaeologists in Greece criticized its rationalist leanings.

Doxiadis began his professional career in 1937 as a chief town planner for Greater Athens. In 1939 he became chief of the Department of Regional and Town Planning in the Ministry of Public Works, where he was instrumental in promoting research for large-scale regional planning. When Greece entered World War II in 1940, Doxiadis was sent to the Albanian front, where he was decorated for bravery. During the Nazi occupation of Greece, he returned to his job at the Ministry of Public Works and coordinated a team effort to evaluate war damage in Greece looking towards future reconstruction; at the same time, he joined the resistance and led a team which gathered information on military objectives and passed it along to the Allies. This direct exposure to the devastation of the war intensified his position that the problems of shelter in Greek towns and villages called for an all-encompassing plan of action. As Doxiadis acknowledged, his experience during the war years was instrumental in the crystallization of his planning theory.

With the end of the war, Doxiadis came to the forefront of the efforts for the rehabilitation of the country, putting to test some of his ideas. As early as November 1944 Doxiadis organized a large exhibition which mapped the destruction of Greece and outlined a plan for its regeneration. The scope of the exhibition impressed Greek officials and foreign representatives as a pioneering effort. The exhibition later travelled to Paris, London, and San Francisco at the founding of the United Nations, where Doxiadis represented Greece seeking foreign aid. Soon afterwards he was assigned the Ministry of Reconstruction and then he became Associate Minister for Coordination. Between 1948 and 1951 he supervised the handling and distribution of American aid to Greece through the Marshall Plan and he represented his country at many international meetings on postwar reconstruction and development. Doxiadis became actively involved in all aspects of Greece's recovery programme – the restoration of transportation and communication networks, the rebuilding of the rural economy, the rehabilitation of fisheries and harbours, the provision of housing and education. His efficiency and resourcefulness in addressing the country's needs quickly and with limited means were often praised inside and outside Greece, while some criticized the boldness and assertiveness of his work. In 1951, while the implementation of the Marshall Plan was approaching completion, Doxiadis's cabinet post was abolished by the Greek parliament as a result of political rivalry. The abrupt and disappointing interruption of his work for the government lead Doxiadis to establish a private enterprise, Doxiadis Associates, which was the first private office in Greece that supported research in addition to design and building.

The practice of Doxiadis Associates was in large part based on the planning principles of "Ekistics", or the "Science of Human Settlements". The term Ekistics was coined by Doxiadis and was derived from the Greek word *oikos* meaning "house". It emerged as a rejection of customary architectural and planning practices – which, being the product of individual experts, Doxiadis argued, were inadequate to cope with the rapid increase of global population, the chaotic expansion of cities and regions, the immense demands of transportation and space, and the environmental problems that accompanied modern technology. Ekistics proposed the synthesis of all branches of knowledge, so that economic, social, political, administrative, technical, environmental, and aesthetic aspects of the built environment are all coordinated in a comprehensive manner to encompass all scales of human settlements from the individual neighbourhood to the global environment.

During the 1960s Doxiadis Associates grew to be one of the largest development consulting firms in the world. Doxiadis's Greek identity allowed him to take up many jobs in nations freed from colonial rule, because—unlike his western counterparts who carried an imperialist stigma—he gained the confidence of many local governments who struggled to cope with new urban needs. A charismatic speaker and a skilful coordinator, he worked as a consultant for the United Nations, the International Bank for Reconstruction and Development, the International Cooperation Association, the Ford Foundation, the Redevelopment Land Agency of Washington, DC, and for the governments of Ghana, India, Iraq, Jordan, Lebanon, Pakistan, Spain, the Sudan, and Syria. Within Greece his projects included, among others: a redevelopment project for the Saronic coast (1959); Aspra Spitia, Antikyra – a housing project for the personnel and workers of a large aluminium plant (1965); feasibility studies for highways (1963); feasibility studies for tourist development for the western Peloponnese and the Ionian islands (1964); and the Apollonion Vacation Development, Hagios Spyridon, Porto Rafti (1970–81). Doxiadis Associates also designed industrial plants and made surveys for the Greek Government regarding infrastructure development. In the late 1950s Doxiadis Associates made a master plan for Athens which was based on Doxiadis's generic scheme for the future city, "Dynapolis", which had a dynamic core that would expand along a controlled axis.

Along with his practice, Doxiadis also established the Athens Technological Institute which trained specialized assistants and technicians both from Greece and from abroad. In 1963 he became a lecturer in town planning at the Technical University of Athens. (He was also a visiting lecturer at many prestigious universities in the United States.) At the same time, he was a prolific writer and produced many books and articles on Ekistics. One of Doxiadis's most significant ventures was the Delos symposium in July 1963 to which he invited 30 thinkers, planners, architects, sociologists, anthropologists, geographers, lawyers, economists, geneticists, physicists, and administrators on a cruise around the Greek islands to discuss the problems of urban explosion in the world, an event which further increased the international profile of Ekistics.

Doxiadis continued his work until his death in 1975. With the theoretical shifts in the architecture and planning of subsequent decades, Doxiadis's large-scale interventions came under scrutiny for overlooking cultural particularity; but the contributions of his theory of Ekistics to the realms of architecture, planning, and policy making in the period after World War II have not yet been sufficiently explored.

PANAYIOTA PYLA

Biography

Born in Stenimachos, Bulgaria, in 1913, Doxiadis was educated in Athens and Berlin and began his career in 1937 as a town planner for Athens. His experience of the devastation caused by World War II led him to believe that a concerted plan of action was required for the problems of shelter in Greek towns and villages. He supervised the administration of US aid to Greece in 1948–51. He developed a science of human settlements based on "Ekistic" principles which involved a synthesis of all branches of knowledge. He died in 1975.

Writings

In *The Sacrifices of Greece in the Second World War*, Athens: Graphic Arts Aspioti-Elka, 1946
"Ecumenopolis: The Coming World City" in *Cities of Destiny*, edited by Arnold Toynbee, London: Thames and Hudson, and New York: McGraw Hill, 1967, pp. 16–38
Ekistics: An Introduction to the Science of Human Settlements, New York: Oxford University Press, and London: Hutchinson, 1968
Architectural Space in Ancient Greece, translated by Jaqueline Tyrwhitt, Cambridge, Massachusetts: MIT Press, 1972

Further Reading

Deane, Philip, *Constantinos Doxiadis: Master Builder for Free Men*, Dobbs Ferry, New York: Oceana, 1965
Doxiadis Associates, *Doxiadis Associates: Consultants on Development and Ekistics*, Athens, 1965
Rand, Christopher, "Constantinos Doxiadis: The Ekistic World", *New Yorker*, (11 May, 1963): pp. 49–85
Robinson, Donald B., "Constantinos Doxiadis", in his *The 100 Most Important People in the World Today*, New York: Putnam, 1970

Dreams

Dreams are a universal human phenomenon. Everyone dreams, although not everyone is able to remember their dreams. It is, therefore, unsurprising that people in Greece have always dreamt. What is interesting is the unusually detailed historical record of dreams from Homer to the present day. This textual span allows one to study the cultural history of dreams in Greece in a manner possible in only a few other places such as China and India.

Dreams had begun to be used for divining the future already in ancient Mesopotamia and Egypt. Indeed, the Greeks may well have borrowed from these two great civilizations. The earliest Greek dream on record is Agamemnon's in book 2 of the *Iliad*. It is a false dream sent by Zeus counselling Agamemnon that he will achieve victory if he launches an immediate all-out attack on the Trojans. Homer describes this as an *oulos oneiros*. Although scholars have always translated this as "destructive dream", the adjective *oulos* could also mean "woolly" or "kinky". In the *Odyssey* (book 19) Penelope explains that there are two kinds of dreams: those that come down to mortals through a gate of ivory are false; those that pass through a gate of horn are trustworthy. One speculative commentator ventured that this symbolism arose because ivory is always opaque while horn, if sliced thinly and polished, can be translucent.

The dream in Homer was generally conceived as a personified force that travelled from the realm of the gods to the beds of humans. This view was debated in the Classical period as can be seen in Herodotus' account of the dreams that came to

Xerxes, encouraging him to attack Greece. Convinced that these dreams were sent by the gods, Xerxes persuaded his adviser, Artabanus, to impersonate him and sleep in his bed to verify this momentous dream. Artabanus at first protested that dreams are purely products of the inner self: "nearly always these drifting phantoms are the shadows of what we have been thinking about during the day". Yet when he slept in the king's bed, the same dream not only appeared to him, but recognized him as the king's adviser and threatened to burn out his eyes with iron rods if he did not approve the plan to wage war. In later historical periods dreams came to be viewed more as internal states. Although grammatical gender does not necessarily reflect a real-world perception of animateness, it is interesting to note the sex change undergone by the word for dream. It began as a neuter form *to onar*, developed a personified masculine form *ho oneiros*, freely alternated for a long while between masculine and neuter forms, but then exclusively assumed the neuter noun form – *to oneiro* – that it possesses today.

The recognition that dreams were products of the human imagination did not exclude the possibility that they could also be prophetic. Aristotle addressed just this question in his tract *On Prophecy in Sleep* where, like Artabanus, he sceptically contended that dreams were just representations of personal wishes or stimuli felt during sleep; they could only be prophetic in minor ways such as predicting the onset of illness in the dreamer. Dreams were, indeed, embraced as a diagnostic tool by the Greek medical tradition as attested by the Hippocratic texts and by Galen.

Aristotle's sceptical views notwithstanding, the general population continued to hold that dreams could be interpreted to forecast the future. Artemidorus' 2nd-century AD text, *The Interpretation of Dreams*, attested to this public conviction. Artemidorus was a professional interpreter of dreams and the latter portion of his book was dedicated to his son who would succeed him. His instructions are extremely valuable for, unlike dream-interpreting keys (*oneirokrites*) that simply matched symbols to interpretations in dictionary fashion, Artemidorus explained how and why he reached his interpretations of dream symbols. Artemidorus thought it important to travel to understand the customs and cultures of the people whose dreams he was asked to interpret. He also thought that the meaning of symbols varied depending on the individual. One man reported the same dream of himself without a nose at three different moments of his life. The first time meant that he would lose his perfume business; the second time that he would be disgraced (lose face); and the third time, that he would die (since a skull has no nose).

In a gesture towards Aristotle, Artemidorus differentiated so-called "state dreams" (*enypnia*) – produced by current worries, feelings, or wishes – from prophetic dreams (*oneiroi*) that could literally or allegorically tell the future. It was only this latter category of *allegorikoi oneiroi* that required the services of a dream interpreter, although it must have been difficult for anyone to know in advance exactly which kind of dream had been had. Subsequent dream interpreters, including the 4th-century AD Neoplatonist Latin writers Macrobius and Chalcidius, proposed similar divisions of dreams into four or five classes, depending on whether they were true or false, divine or physical, interpretable or not. In denying the signifi-

cance of "state dreams", ancient dream interpretation dismissed the very sorts of dreams to which Freud would later attach the most significance.

The first response of Christianity to dream interpretation was to outlaw it – a step formally taken at the Council of Ankara (AD 314). In the Christian view the future belonged to God alone to decide and reveal. Prophecy was neither an appropriate nor a feasible endeavour for lay dream interpreters to engage in. One particular cult the early Church was eager to eradicate was that of Asclepius which boasted hundreds of shrines up and down Greece. Asclepius was a healing god and one of his modes of operation was through a practice that scholars have labelled "incubation". This involved pilgrims attending these Asclepian shrines, and sleeping in the inner sanctuary. There the god would appear to them in dreams, sometimes in the form of a snake, and he would either prescribe a remedy or else directly cure the ailment. The chronically ill 2nd-century AD rhetorician Aelius Aristides presented, in his book *The Sacred Tales*, a record of the dreams he saw and the cures Asclepius recommended he undertake.

The Church realized that it could not wipe out popular beliefs in healing dreams and so adopted a strategy of appropriation. The shrine of Asclepius at the foot of the Acropolis, for example, was converted into a church dedicated to St Andrew, patron of the sick, where people continued to practise incubation. New healing saints and Christian sites for incubation arose throughout the Middle Ages, an example being the church of St Artemios in 9th-century Constantinople where men went to be cured of hernias. Books of dream-interpreting symbols continued to circulate in Byantium, some with titles such as the *Oneirokritikon of Achmet* that related them to the East. This was not just because the East was a place where the prophetic arts were more advanced. Some of these were originally Greek dream books such as that of Artemidorus, that had been translated into Arabic, and then back into Greek.

The proliferation of such texts attests to the popular interest in dream-interpretation through the Byzantine and Ottoman periods up to today. *Oneirokrites* circulate in cheap editions in Greece today, and many households possess a copy of one and/or a family member skilled in the predictive interpretation of dreams. The Church still maintains that lay people lack the faculty of discernment necessary to separate demon-inspired false dreams from divine-sent true dreams. Clerical guidance should be sought.

CHARLES STEWART

See also Divination

Further Reading

Artemidorus, Daldianus, *The Interpretation of Dreams: Oneirocritica*, translated by Robert J. White, Park Ridge, New Jersey: Noyes Press, 1975

Devereux, George, *Dreams in Greek Tragedy: An Ethno-Psychoanalytical Study*, Oxford: Blackwell, and Berkeley: University of California Press, 1976

Dodds, E.R., "Dream Pattern and Culture Pattern" in his *The Greeks and the Irrational*, Berkeley: University of California Press, 1951

Edelstein, Emma J. and Ludwig Edelstein, *Asclepius: A Collection and Interpretation of the Testimonies*, 2 vols, Baltimore: Johns Hopkins University Press, 1945

Hamilton, Mary, *Incubation; or, The Cure of Disease in Pagan Temples and Christian Churches*, London: Simpkin Marshall, 1906

Kessels, A.H.M., *Studies on the Dream in Greek Literature*, Utrecht: HES, 1978

Le Goff, Jacques, "Christianity and Dreams, Second to Seventh Century" in his *The Medieval Imagination*, Chicago: University of Chicago Press, 1988

Lieshout, R.G.A. van, *The Greeks on Dreams*, Utrecht: HES, 1980

Miller, Patricia Cox, *Dreams in Late Antiquity: Studies in the Imagination of a Culture*, Princeton, New Jersey: Princeton University Press, 1994

Oberhelman, Steven M., *The Oneirocriticon of Achmet: A Medieval Greek and Arabic Treatise on the Interpretation of Dreams*, Lubbock: Texas Tech University Press, 1991

Price, Simon, "The Future of Dreams: From Freud to Artemidorus", *Past and Present*, 113 (1986): pp. 3–37

Stewart, Charles, "Fields in Dreams: Anxiety, Experience and the Limits of Social Constructionism in Modern Greek Dream Narratives", *American Ethnologist*, 24 (1997): pp. 877–94

Dress

Dress reveals much about society and culture. Generally, the further one goes back in time, the more difficult it is to establish an accurate history of dress. Greece's climate is detrimental to the preservation of textiles, so scholars must rely on visual and written evidence to determine the dress worn in Greece before modern times.

The earliest evidence for Greek dress dates from the Middle and Late Minoan periods (2100–1150 BC). Frescos, statuettes, vases, sarcophagi, and seals from Crete, Thera, Mycenae, Tiryns, and Tanagra help historians to reconstruct a general picture of Minoan dress. Substantial amounts of gold jewellery survive, including necklaces, earrings, rings, diadems, bracelets, and belts.

The snake goddesses from Knossos in Crete are famous in dress history for their bare breasts. These figurines, made of faience, wear fitted bodices that fasten just below the bustline. Some scholars believe that only goddesses and priestesses wore such revealing bodices since other artwork shows women wearing close-fitting tunics that cover the breasts. Women of all ranks wore bell-shaped tiered skirts, curved apron-like garments that covered both front and back, and belts that cinched their waists. They wore crowns, festoons of pearls, and diadems over dark, curled tresses. A fresco of a woman with reddened lips and accentuated eyes known as La Parisienne makes Minoan women out to be quite glamorous. Women who participated in bull riding wore the same attire as male participants – double aprons with narrow rolled belts and protective coverings around the ankles – suggesting an egalitarianism that women in Greece have not enjoyed since then.

Men appear less frequently in Minoan art than women. Frescos at Knossos and Thera depict men wearing either loincloths or patterned loin skirts decorated with tassels in front. Sometimes men wore tunics edged with decorative bands. Men's hair, like women's, was long and curly. Some images of men, such as the Prince of the Lilies at Knossos, have exceptionally narrow waists, possibly a result of rolled leather or metal belts placed on their bodies in childhood. From the

Dress: inhabitants of the Mani, dressed to kill, French engraving from 1881

frescos at Thera, it appears that boys wore little more than strings around the waist, or even nothing at all. Children's heads were partially shaved, possibly to prevent ringworm. When not barefoot, Minoans wore sandals or soft pointed shoes.

Minoans had a love of colour and pattern. Clothes were decorated at the edges with patterned bands. Barber (1991) argues that the patterns were woven, but such designs could also have been embroidered or painted on cloth. Remains of a linen tunic discovered in a bronze amphora dated 1000 BC from Lefkandi in Euboea reveal edges decorated with woven and embroidered bands. Ornaments on such bands and in jewellery include rosettes, lilies, birds, saffron flowers, butterflies, double axes, bull's horns, and bees. Minoan dress reveals knowledge of sophisticated cutting and fitting that is atypical of the time. Draping cloth around the body was the norm for contemporaries of the Minoans as well as a mark of civilization. Scholars believe that among early civilizations tailored clothes derived from the wearing of skin garments which were fitted and stitched to accommodate the size and shape of skins.

After the decline of Crete and the destruction of Thera around 1450 BC, Mycenae achieved dominance over Greece. Archaeological finds from Mycenae, Tiryns, and Tanagra show that dress on the mainland was indistinguishable from that worn on Crete and Thera during the Middle and Late Minoan periods. Mycenaean soldiers are shown wearing fringed tunics,

Dress: officials of the *epistasia* on the streets of Karyes on Mount Athos, wearing the official foustanella for a ceremonial event

helmets, and protective coverings for their shins. During Greece's Dark Ages the fitted bodices, tiered skirts, and loin cloths disappeared along with the elaborate patterned fabrics. By the time the Archaic period began, the Greeks had donned uncut rectangles of cloth draped on the body. The cloth came off wide, warp-weighted looms, and required no cutting or stitching for use as garments.

The basic piece of clothing for both men and women was the chiton, a tunic-like garment that fastened at the shoulders. It could be long or short depending on the wearer's gender and age. Women generally wore ankle-length chitons while active males and youths wore short ones. The chiton was draped in one of two basic ways – Doric or Ionic – so-called today because each resembled the capitals on architectural columns. The wool Doric chiton was folded over at the top and pinned once at the shoulders with large straight pins. The overfold, which often ended in a patterned band, extended to the waist. This style, termed *peplos*, originated during the Archaic period. The Ionic chiton, an innovation adopted from Ionia, had no overfold. The fabric, either linen or lightweight wool, was fastened several times at the shoulders and along the arms with stitches or small brooches called fibulae, creating a sleeve effect. Belts or loose stitching kept the garment, which was open down the side, in place. Belts with tassels apparently had a seductive quality about them. In the *Iliad* Homer tells of Hera's tasselled belt which Zeus found irresistible.

The chiton has an interesting social history. According to Herodotus, during the Persian Wars the Athenians outlawed the Doric chiton after Athenian women killed the lone survivor of a military campaign by stabbing him with the pins from their dresses. It was replaced with a foreign innovation, the softly pleated Ionic chiton. After the Persian Wars ended, the patriotic Greeks returned to the older indigenous form of dress, the Doric chiton. The Ionian style returned during the Classical and Hellenistic periods. During the Hellenistic period the chiton was belted high, creating an "Empire" waistline. The changing preferences in chitons are evident in sculpture. Artists took great pains to render the details carefully, as seen in the *Charioteer* at Delphi, who wears a long Ionic chiton, and the Caryatid maidens at the Acropolis, who sport Doric chitons.

Greeks wore a variety of wraps, most commonly the himation. In wide use by the late 6th century BC, it was almost always worn over the chiton. The most common method of draping the himation allowed the right arm to be free. Women used their himations as veils when outside the house, since respectable women would cover themselves. Other coverings included the smaller *diplax* and the square chlamys, a cloak preferred by travellers and soldiers since it doubled as a blanket.

Male athletes sometimes performed naked, at other times in a simple loincloth. Greeks prized athletic bodies, grooming and anointing themselves with fragrances and oils. Working-class men and slaves wore a short, rectangular garment called *exomis* which fastened at the left shoulder. Both men and women wore sandals. Jewellery included necklaces, earrings, rings, and pins.

Although we know that the ancient Greeks wore coloured clothes from the paint remaining in the crevices of sculpture and from written sources, our knowledge of colour from visual sources is limited because vase painting does not reveal colour, and the pigment has worn off statues. Pliny mentioned the "flowered colours" of women's clothes. Men and women sported a variety of hairstyles and headgear. Men were bearded with long hair during the Archaic period, but during the Classical period short haircuts and a clean-shaven look prevailed. A broad-brimmed hat called a petasus offered protection from sun or rain. The popular Phrygian bonnet, a brimless peaked cap, reappeared in the Middle Ages, and again during the French Revolution as a symbol of democracy. Women wore their hair long during the Archaic period but bound it in knots and chignons in the Classical and Hellenistic periods with bands, nets, cloth, and metal filets to keep the hair in place.

The dress of Classical Greece has had widespread influence throughout history. During antiquity Greek dress spread to other Mediterranean areas including the Etruscan and Roman worlds. Centuries later, whenever Greek politics, art, or philosophy was ascendant, fashionable dress took on the lines, colours, and details of ancient Greek dress.

Actual garments survive from as early as the 3rd century AD to inform us about the fabrics and construction of clothing during the Graeco-Roman period. Whole tunics come from the Copts, a Christian religious sect living in Egypt who buried their dead fully dressed in the desert. Initially woven of linen on wide vertical looms, the tunic (a Roman innovation) was seamed only at the sides. With the adoption of horizontal looms, the Copts (and presumably others in the Mediterranean) started piecing tunics from narrower widths of fabric and sewing on sleeves. Skilled weavers added colourful tapestry-woven stripes (*clavi*), squares, and roundels of wool. These tunics display motifs typical of the Hellenistic period including detailed portraiture. Gradually, the motifs took on Christian symbolism or changed to Christian imagery.

The inhabitants of the Byzantine empire wore similar tunics with mantles and cloaks. The difference lay in the fabrics. Extant mosaics and statuary show garments embellished at the hems and seams, sometimes with jewels. The Byzantines were avid consumers of complex patterned silks woven in Near Eastern textile centres and eventually established their own thriving silk industry. The colour purple was highly desirable in dress, although its use was limited to the most wealthy. Byzantine silks survive in church treasuries throughout Europe, particularly in the Vatican.

With the collapse of the Byzantine empire in 1453, much of Greece fell under the control of the Ottomans. Italian city states controlled some islands and parts of the mainland. Albanians and other ethnic groups in flight from the Turks settled in parts of Greece. This complex cultural landscape left a multilayered sartorial history that is evident in Greek traditional dress of the 19th and 20th centuries. Regional customs dictated dress practices and served to locate the wearer geographically. Clothing also signalled ethnicity during this period, especially on the mainland where each ethnic group had its own distinctive attire.

By the 19th century the inhabitants of mainland villages wore Byzantine-inspired dress. Men wore simple tunics over woven or knitted leggings. Women wore white chemises, woollen coats or jackets, headscarves, and belts. Female dress denoted age, marital status, and social rank. Some clothing had magico-religious connotations, particularly when associated with women of childbearing age. The colours red and black, embroidered hems and seams, and fringes had symbolic connotations that figured prominently in the most conservative forms of village dress.

In areas under Italian influence, such as the Ionian islands, some of the Aegean islands, and parts of Crete, local dress was inspired by the styles of Renaissance Europe. Chemises cut with full sleeves and skirts gathered at the waistline reflect western European influence. Conversely, in areas under Turkish rule, women donned caftan-like garments and under-trousers of Turkish fabrics. Their chemises were cut like those found in the dress of Turkish women. Turkish influence continued to be strong in areas that remained under Ottoman rule until the 20th century. Island men wore knee-length *vraka* (Turkish-style breeches) while the Vlachs and Sarakatsans on the mainland wore ankle-length trousers.

During the Greek War of Independence, resistance fighters adopted the dress of the Albanian soldiers that consisted of a white pleated skirt called a fustanella (one of the few examples of men in skirts in modern times), wide-sleeved shirt, waistcoat, fez, knitted stockings, and tasselled shoes. After the war, fancy versions of this costume became the official attire as established by Otho, Greece's first king. Lord Byron was painted in this costume. Village Greeks of Albanian heritage wore the fustanella or the *poukamiso* (an elongated shirt) on a daily basis well into the 20th century. Soldiers guarding the Tomb of the Unknown Soldier in Athens wear the fustanella today. Greek schoolboys dress up in a fustanella for holidays, for it has become the national costume. The corresponding costume for females is the Amalia costume, so named after Greece's first queen. It consists of a tight-fitting embroidered jacket, long silk skirt, and fez cap.

After Greece's liberation from Turkish rule, traditional dress was gradually abandoned. The first to give it up in favour of fashionable French styles were the inhabitants of the main towns and cities. Next came islanders with commercial ties to European cities. The inland villagers retained their customary dress longer. The Arvanites in Messoghia, for example, wore their traditional dress until after World War I, while the Karaghounes in Thessaly kept theirs until the mid-20th century.

The dress of Classical Greece influenced fashionable dress outside Greece at numerous times in the 18th, 19th, and 20th centuries. With the excavation of Pompeii in 1719 and Herculaneum in 1748, Europeans rediscovered the ancient Mediterranean world. Artists portrayed sitters in Classically draped fabrics. Aristocratic women in England and France, including the French queen Marie Antoinette, wore white cotton dresses for informal wear. After the French and American revolutions of the late 18th century came a renewed appreciation of Greek and Roman Classical drapery as visual representations of democracy and republican ideals. Women throughout Europe and America wore classically inspired white gowns, hair arranged *à la grecque*, and himation-like wraps. Such Neoclassical styles dominated fashion during the French Directoire and Empire periods.

Neoclassicism in dress eventually gave way to Romanticism which inspired the tight corsets and voluminous skirts of the mid-19th century. In the 1870s and 1880s exaggerated, fussy styles replete with bustles, drapes, and swags brought forth critics who recalled the elegance and simplicity of ancient Greek dress. Artists such as Frederick Leighton and Edward Burne-Jones who were associated with the Aesthetic Movement in Britain painted women in Greek chitons in soft ethereal colours. The Classical styles depicted by these artists influenced the dress designs of women in artistic circles. Dress reformers also idealized the uncluttered lines of ancient Greek dress, promoting it in their publications and exhibitions.

Not until the first decade of the 20th century did a Paris couturier incorporate Classicism in dress, eventually influencing mainstream fashion. The Frenchman Paul Poiret, who designed from 1903 to 1926, is credited with freeing women from the corset by garbing them in simple Empire-waisted tunics. A dress of 1910 called "Pénélope" consisted of an overblouse printed with Greek-inspired motifs and a finely pleated white skirt. The Spanish-born designer Mariano Fortuny, who worked in Venice, incorporated ideas from Minoan and Classical Greece into his designs. His Knossos veil used motifs inspired by Minoan frescos while his most famous creation, the Delphos dress, consisted of a tube of finely pleated silk either draped with an overfold like the Doric chiton or clasped at the shoulder with Venetian glass beads in imitation of the Ionic chiton. Fortuny stated that this dress, named after the *Charioteer* of Delphi, was "derived from the Classical robe".

Other 20th-century dress designers inspired by the Hellenic tradition include Alix Grès and Mary McFadden. Mme Grès, who opened her Paris couture house in 1934, specialized in beautifully draped gowns of neutral-coloured silk jersey. Beginning in 1976 in New York, McFadden used the thermoplastic nature of polyester to create permanently pleated evening gowns. Fashion critics consider the designs of Grès and McFadden to be classics, lending credence to the longevity and timeless appeal of the Hellenic tradition in dress.

LINDA WELTERS

See also Jewellery, Silk, Textiles

Further Reading

Barber, Elizabeth Wayland, *Prehistoric Textiles: The Development of Cloth in the Neolithic and Bronze Ages with Special Reference to the Aegean*, Princeton, New Jersey: Princeton University Press, 1991

Barber, Elizabeth Wayland, *Women's Work, the First 20,000 Years: Women, Cloth, and Society in Early Times*, New York: Norton, 1994

Hatzimichali, Angeliki, *The Greek Folk Costume*, 2 vols, Athens, 1979–84

Houston, Mary G., *Ancient Greek, Roman and Byzantine Costume and Decoration*, 2nd edition, London: A. & C. Black, 1947, reprinted New York: Barnes and Noble, 1965

Jenkins, Ian, *Greek and Roman Life*, Cambridge, Massachusetts: Harvard University Press, 1986

Osma, Guillermo de, *Fortuny: Mariano Fortuny, His Life and Work*, New York: Rizzoli, 1980, 2nd edition, 1994

Papantoniou, Ioanna, *Greek Costumes*, Navplion: Peloponnesian Folklore Foundation, 1987

Tortora, Phyllis G. and Keith Eubanks, *Survey of Historic Costume: A History of Western Dress*, 3rd edition, New York: Fairchild, 1998

Welters, Linda (editor), *Folk Dress in Europe and Anatolia: Beliefs about Protection and Fertility*, Oxford: Berg, 1999

Dyrrhachium

City in modern Albania

Dyrrhachium (now Durres in Albanian, Drasch in Turkish, Durazzo in Italian), situated on the Albanian coast, was founded in 627 BC by the Corcyreans and Corinthians (Thucydides, 1. 24) and remained an important port and commercial town in antiquity and medieval times; the coins of the town show a cow suckling its calf, symbolizing the dependence of the colony on the mother city. The Greeks named the town Epidamnos; but the Romans preferred the Illyrian name of Dyrrhachion/Dyrrachium (which at first was used only for the upper part of the town), probably because they regarded the second part of the Greek name (recalling the Latin word *damnum*, "damage") as a bad omen.

The Greek town Epidamnos had an oligarchic constitution; trade with its Illyrian neighbours soon made it so prosperous that it could afford to build a treasury at Olympia (Pausanias, 6. 19. 8). Inner conflicts in the 430s BC which then involved Corcyra (modern Corfu), Corinth, and Athens were one of the triggers of the Peloponnesian War. In 314 BC the Macedonian king Cassander took the city, but lost it soon afterwards to the Corcyreans who gave it to the Taulantian king Glaucias. In later Hellenistic times Epidamnos had the reputation of being a dissolute sea port.

As for the buildings of Greek times, several temples are mentioned in inscriptions, among them one of Athena/Minerva and another of Artemis/Diana. Only the sanctuary of Aphrodite has been excavated, bringing to light about 6 tons of mostly late Hellenistic votive figures in terracotta varying greatly in size. Many of them wear Illyrian costume, as also do many people depicted on the numerous grave stelai found in nearby cemeteries, which are often a source for Illyrian names. Although Albanian scholars used to stress the continuity of Illyrian traditions from ancient times until today, there can be no doubt that by the 4th century BC, at the latest, the Greek element dominated the country surrounding Dyrrhachium; many centuries later, Albania's national hero Skanderbeg not only received the inspiration for his name from Alexander the Great (Skanderbeg derives from Alexander bey), but also his helmet with two horns (a copy of which is preserved) was modelled on a similar helmet worn by Pyrrhus of Epirus in 287 BC.

At the end of the First Illyrian War (229 BC) Dyrrhachium came under Roman protection. A *civitas libera* already in republican times and a *colonia* under Augustus, Dyrrhachium was important because of its geographical situation: from the

1st century BC onwards the town was the starting point of the Via Egnatia leading to Thessalonica and then on to Byzantium; it was also the usual port for ships coming from Italy (Brundisium, modern Brindisi) and therefore played a significant role in the Roman civil wars; in 48 BC Pompey had his camp there and was besieged in vain by Caesar.

Dyrrhachium's apogee came after Augustus had stabilized the Roman empire; many remains of imperial times have been found, though modern Durres, with about 80,000 inhabitants and the second largest city after Tirana in Albania, covers most of the ancient city, thus making excavation nearly impossible. In the northern part of the city the Roman amphitheatre (already mentioned in 1510 in Marinus Barletius' biography of Skanderbeg) has been excavated to reveal a typical Roman building, a very rare occurrence in the Greek east but to be explained by the settlement of Roman army veterans. Constructed during the reign of the emperor Hadrian (117–38), the huge, oval ampitheatre measures of 127 × 103 m (arena 63 × 39 m) and could seat about 15,000 spectators; people moved in and out by way of subterranean stairs and galleries, which are well preserved in places, while the animals and gladiators entered the arena through big gates in the north and south of the building; an inscription records that 12 gladiatorial fights were given to celebrate the inauguration of a new library. In the western part of the amphitheatre a little chapel was later inserted (probably in the second half of the 6th century); on its southern wall one of the very few preserved wall mosaics of the early Byzantine era (the only one in Albania, in fact) shows the Virgin Mary as queen of the heavens in imperial garb, accompanied by Michael and Gabriel, and nearby St Stephen praying. During the reign of Hadrian a 15-km aqueduct was also built (restored by Severus Alexander 222–35) of which leaden water pipes with inscriptions mentioning the emperor and the officials in charge of the water supply have been preserved; great baths of the 2nd century AD with floor heating and sumptuous floor mosaics have been partially excavated. It is still unknown where the Greek and Roman fortifications were located.

Dyrrhachium was destroyed by earthquakes in AD 314 and 522, and in 481 it was besieged by Theodoric the Ostrogoth; nevertheless the town flourished as an episcopal see and capital of the province Epirus Nova, later a theme of the Byzantine empire. The emperor Anastasius I (491–518), who was born in Dyrrhachium, erected a new city wall (built of bricks and fortified by pentagonal towers) after the destructions caused by

earthquakes and the Gothic invasion; it is well preserved in the western part of the town. There are also foundations of a large 6th-century church, whose donor Martinia is commemorated in a floor mosaic. There must have been several other impressive buildings (mainly churches) in the 5th and 6th centuries of which few traces are left.

More sieges followed: by the Bulgarians in the 10th and 11th centuries, and by the Normans in the 11th and 12th centuries, as Dyrrhachium lay on their route for advancing into the Balkans; it was taken by Robert Guiscard in 1081 and by William II in 1185. Although the town still prospered in these times and sources mention numerous churches, almost nothing of its medieval architecture has survived; there are, though, some reliefs and the fragment of an ambo dating from the 11th and 12th centuries. During the Latin empire Dyrrhachium was the capital of the despot Michael of Epirus; his successor Theodore renewed the town walls (one of the mighty wall towers bears an inscription with his name and the date 1235).

In 1273 another earthquake started an irreversible decline that continued during the reign of the house of Anjou and the Venetian empire (1386–1501); under the Ottoman empire the town dwindled to 1200 inhabitants. It recovered, however, and in 1912 it was for a short time capital of the newly founded Albania.

BALBINA BÄBLER

See also Epirus

Summary

Now Durres, city in modern Albania on the Adriatic Sea, founded in 627 BC by Greek colonists, Dyrrhachium was later a Roman colony and flourished as a free city in the 2nd century AD. It remained strategically and commercially important as a port throughout ancient and medieval times. Decline set in from the 13th century. Today it is the second city of Albania.

Further Reading

Andrea, Zoe, *British Archaeological Reports for 1983–84*, Oxford: Tempus Repartum, 1984, pp. 102–19

Bakhuisen, S., "Between Illyrians and Greeks: The Cities of Epidamnos and Apollonia", *Iliria*, 16/1 (1986): pp. 165–77

Koch, Guntram, *Albanien: Kunst und Kultur im Land der Skipetaren*, Cologne: DuMont, 1989

O'Sullivan, Firmin, *The Egnatian Way*, Newton Abbot, Devon: David and Charles, and Harrisburg: Stackpole, 1972

Wilkes, John, *The Illyrians*, Oxford and Cambridge, Massachusetts: Blackwell, 1992

E

Eagle, Double-Headed

Emblem of the Byzantine empire

The mythological presentation of the eagle with two heads and its possibly apotropaic, and protective, character was a common figure among the prehistoric cultures of Mesopotamia, Syria, Asia Minor, and Egypt. Its appearance in the Hellenic tradition goes back to the period of the Mycenaean civilization, as suggested by finds from Mycenae and the south Peloponnese.

The reappearance of the double-headed eagle on Greek soil takes place in the Byzantine empire during the reign of the Palaiologan family in the 13th century. One of its first representations in Byzantine art can be found on the chapter of the iconostasis at the Porta Panagia church (1283) in Thessaly as well as on the founder's inscription at the Paragoritissa church (1294/6) in Arta. From the archaeological evidence it would seem that the symbol of the double-headed eagle was introduced into the Byzantine empire not by the Komnenian dynasty, as some scholars believed in the past, but by the Palaiologan emperors. During the Byzantine period and until the fall of Constantinople in 1453 the double-headed eagle was used as an emblem of the empire and definitely not as the coat of arms of the ruling Palaiologan family. That it was also used by the Kantakouzenos family among others, as well as by some merchant ships of the Italian peninsula to show their tax-exempt status, supports this thesis.

The double-headed eagle is depicted on a variety of icons, frescoes, illuminated documents, ceramics, jewels, and reliefs, while most Byzantine leather bindings of manuscripts that have survived from the 15th century are stamped with this motif. Its representation varies: it can be crowned (with one, two, or three crowns) or not and occasionally it is found carrying a sceptre and the imperial orb. Similar representations, mainly on wall paintings in neighbouring kingdoms (e.g. Serbia, Bulgaria), demonstrate the attempt to imitate Byzantine imperial ritual and symbolism.

After 1453 the double-headed eagle was adopted by various rulers of the Greek islands and Venetian colonies, who were interrelated with the Byzantines, either in order to legitimize their power or in order to declare their dominion as the legitimate successor to Byzantium; for the same purpose a double-headed eagle decorated the throne of Ivan III of Russia after his marriage to the last Byzantine princess Zoe.

The Ottoman empire passed on to the Orthodox patriarch of Constantinople many of the former emperor's functions and insignia including the double-headed eagle which was adopted by the patriarch as the symbol of the Orthodox Church. As the prosperity of the semiautonomous principalities of Walachia and Moldavia grew, their rulers, who became great benefactors of the Orthodox churches and monasteries, also imitated the Byzantine style and decorated their clothes and arms with the double-headed eagle. During the Tourkokratia, the double-headed eagle was used in church decoration and was often depicted on the carved iconostasis or in the middle of the floor as an *omphalion* (centrepiece) as well as in private homes on doors, embroideries, and on furniture.

The question of its meaning cannot be answered with absolute certainty. In the prehistoric period the double-headed eagle was probably a protective, magical, or apotropaic symbol; in other cases, it personified the "multiplied wisdom" of the god. Its representation on coins, seals, and manuscript illuminations in medieval Europe from the 12th century onwards relates to its heraldic meaning as a symbol of a city or as a coat of arms of a noble family. In imperial iconography it was also used in order to distinguish the emperor (double-headed eagle) from the king (one-headed eagle). As for Byzantine iconography, apart from some miscellaneous information about its significance as an imperial emblem, most of the references derive from Tourkokratia and from western sources. According to them, the two heads of the eagle symbolize the claims to both eastern and western halves of the Roman empire and refer either to the eschatological elements of the emperor cult based on the apocalyptic eagles of Ezekiel's prophecy or to the temporal and spiritual power of the emperor. However, during the Tourkokratia the double-headed eagle acquired the significance of the restoration of the Byzantine empire; and nowadays the black double-headed eagle on a yellow background is used as a symbol of the Orthodox Church all over the world.

CHARALAMPOS CHOTZAKOGLOU

Further Reading

Baum, Wilhelm, *Kaiser Sigismund: Hus, Konstanz und Türkenkriege*, Graz: Styria, 1993, 247ff.

Double-Headed Eagle: 13th-century relief in the Cathedral of St Demetrius, Mistra

Chotzakoglou, Charalampos, "Die Palaiologen und das erste Auftauchen des byzantinischen Doppeladlers in Byzanz", *Byzantinoslavica*, 57/1 (1996): pp. 60–68

Fourlas, Athanasios, "Adler und Doppeladler" in *Thiasos ton Mouson: Studien zu Antike und Christentum*, edited by Dieter Ahrens, Cologne: Böhlau, 1984

Kabbadia-Spondyle, Aristea, "Paratereseis se anaglyphe plaka tou Mystra" [Observations on a Relief at Mystra], *Archaiologikon Deltion*, 39 (1984): pp. 48–57

Oncarov, N., "La Représentation de l'aigle à deux tetes comme symbole de la dignité du souverain au XVe siècle", *Archeologia* (1994): pp. 19–24

Theodorescu, R., "Autour de la 'Despoteia' de Mircea l'ancien", *Actes du XIVe Congrès international des Etudes byzantines, Bucarest, 6–12 September 1971*, edited by M. Berza and E. Staeanescu, Bucharest: Academiei Republicii Socialiste Romania, 1974, vol. 2, pp. 625–35

Weyss, N., *Der Doppeladler in aller Welt*, Mödling: Historisches Museum der Stadt Mödling, 1994

EAM and ELAS

EAM (*Ethniko Apelevtherotiko Metopo*, National Liberation Front) and ELAS (*Ellinikos Laikos Apelevtherotikos Stratos*, Greek Popular Liberation Army) were respectively the largest political and military resistance organizations in occupied Greece during the period 1941–44.

EAM was founded on 27 September 1941, following the Seventh Plenum of the Communist Party (KKE) Central Committee earlier that month. It was formed and dominated by the KKE, although another three much smaller parties (SKE, Socialist Party of Greece; ELD, Union of Popular Democracy; and AKE, Agrarian Party of Greece) also participated in it, even signing the charter of EAM.

In April 1942 EAM formed ELAS as its military branch (later ELAN, the navy equivalent, and EtA, *Epimeliteia tou Antarti*, the commissariat, were added); it was also complemented by branches in other fields, such as the EEAM (*Ergatiko Ethniko Apelevtherotiko Metopo*, National Workers Liberation Front), EPON (*Eniaia Panelladiki Organosi Neon*, a youth movement), and the EA (*Ethniki Allillengyi*, National Mutual Aid). By 1943 EAM and its subsidiary branches had in effect formed an alternative government organization, controlling large parts of Greek territory that were not occupied by the Axis; this was complemented in March 1944 by the PEEA (*Politiki Epitropi Ethnikis Antistaseos*, Political Committee of National Liberation). Throughout the period of German occupation EAM remained the only truly nationwide resistance organization, and ELAS the most powerful military resistance group. EAM and ELAS were singularly successful in recruiting and mobilizing large sections of the population and by October 1944, when Greece was liberated, claimed (probably not without justification) a joint membership of 2 million, almost a third of the total population of Greece. As it was in effective control of large parts of Greece, EAM enacted a series of wide-ranging reforms, including granting women the vote and allowing justice to be dispensed by local committees.

Despite their appearance as umbrella organizations composed of several parties, both EAM and ELAS remained firmly under communist control; however, the vast majority of rank-and-file members of EAM were neither communists nor even necessarily leftists. Similarly in ELAS the majority of professional officers were of liberal (Venizelist) leanings; control was exercised by allocating key posts to Communist Party cadres and, in the case of ELAS, by attaching to the military heads of guerrilla units political "commissars", usually communists.

EAM/ELAS almost from the outset attempted to remain the only resistance organizations, going to considerable lengths to discourage or destroy any rival groups. After October 1943 EAM and ELAS attempted to eliminate all other resistance organizations by force of arms, in what was later to be named the first "round" of the civil war; they were successful in that by the end of the occupation only Zervas' EDES (*Ethnikos Dimokratikos Ellinikos Syndesmos*, National Democratic Hellenic Union) and some small nationalist groups in eastern Macedonia and Thrace had managed to keep armed bands in the field, all others (including Psaros' EKKA) having been destroyed and/or dissolved. Subsequently, in an attempt to prevent the complete domination of the resistance movement by EAM/ELAS, the British cut off material support from it. However, with the collapse of Italy in 1943, large stocks of arms and war material had fallen into the hands of EAM/ELAS, making it largely independent of this support.

Following the sudden volte-face of July 1944, EAM agreed to participate in the coalition government of G. Papandreou; EAM ministers continued to serve for a brief period after the liberation of Greece in October 1944; however, disagreements over the question of demobilization of ELAS and the other armed groups in Greece led to the withdrawal of EAM from the coalition government. The demonstration organized on 3 December 1944 led to the outbreak of fighting in Athens and its area, the Dekemvriana, in the course of which ELAS forces fought British and loyalist Greek forces. During the fighting

EAM sided openly with the Communist Party despite dissenting voices from the junior partners in the nominal coalition, including Svolos, the former president of the PEEA.

The end of hostilities in mid-January 1945 (when an armistice was signed) and the Varkiza Agreement of February 1945 also marked the end of ELAS, which was demobilized and handed in a substantial part of its arms (though some were hidden). As a political force, EAM survived for a while longer. Indeed it was reinvented in April 1945, as a complementary political movement to KKE, a movement that would retain the wider support that EAM had enjoyed during the occupation. Needless to say, EAM was under almost complete KKE domination. Probably its last momentous political act was the decision to urge its members to abstain from the elections of March 1946, following the policy adopted by the KKE; again dissenting voices from junior partners were not heeded. At least some EAM supporters along with the hard communist core of ELAS fighters subsequently formed the basis for the Democratic Army of Greece (*Dimokratikos Stratos Elladas*, DSE), the communist insurgent force that fought the Civil War. However, the refusal of the non-KKE participants to join the communists in forming the provisional government in 1947 virtually broke the new EAM. It faded into obscurity, especially after the leftist newspapers were banned in October 1947; EAM was later itself outlawed and largely ignored by the communists for the duration of the Civil War.

During the period from the end of the Civil War until 1974, participation in EAM or ELAS was enough to colour one as a communist sympathizer (or even a communist), with all the disadvantages this had. The EAM and ELAS wartime resistance remained formally unrecognized in Greece until the early 1980s, when the PASOK government passed a bill in parliament rewarding the resistance activity of both organizations' members.

GEORGE KAZAMIAS

See also Civil War, World War II

Further Reading

Fleisher, H., "EAM 1941–47: A Reassessment" in *Greece at the Crossroads: The Civil War and its Legacy*, edited by John O. Iatrides and Linda Wrigley, University Park: Pennsylvania State University Press, 1995
Glinos, D., *Ti einai kai ti thelei to EAM* [What EAM Is and What it Wants], Athens, 1944
Mazower, Mark, *Inside Hitler's Greece: The Experience of Occupation, 1941–44*, New Haven and London: Yale University Press, 1993
Papastratis, Procopis, *British Policy towards Greece during the Second World War, 1941–44*, Cambridge and New York: Cambridge University Press, 1984
Sarafis, Stefanos, *ELAS: The Greek Resistance Army*, London: Merlin, 1980

Earthquakes

The Aegean region has the highest incidence of earthquakes (seismicity) in Europe. This has had an important effect on both the civilizations and the landscape of the region. Most of

Earthquake: front page of *Akropolis* on 8 September 1999, the day after an earthquake measuring 5.9 on the Richter scale struck Athens

these earthquakes were produced by forces connected with large-scale movements of the earth's crust and mantle (plate tectonics).

Earthquakes are vibrations of the earth that are produced when rocks juxtaposed across a fault slide past each other. Some faults slide very easily, so stress on the fault is dissipated continually. However, many faults are "sticky" and the stress can build up to much higher levels before the energy is released in an earthquake. The magnitude of an earthquake (the well-known Richter scale) is not a measure of destructiveness but merely indicates how much energy is released. It varies according to the amount of movement of the rocks (from a few centimetres to several metres) and the surface area of the fault that moved (from a few square metres to tens of square kilometres). The amount of vibration felt at a particular place on the earth, and hence the local destructiveness of an earthquake, is called the intensity. It is measured on the Modified Mercalli scale and varies with location. Therefore, each earthquake has only one magnitude but many intensities. The intensity depends on the distance to the centre of the earthquake, its depth, and the local geology. Many sediments, especially those in recently drained lakes, can amplify considerably the earthquake vibrations and increase the intensity.

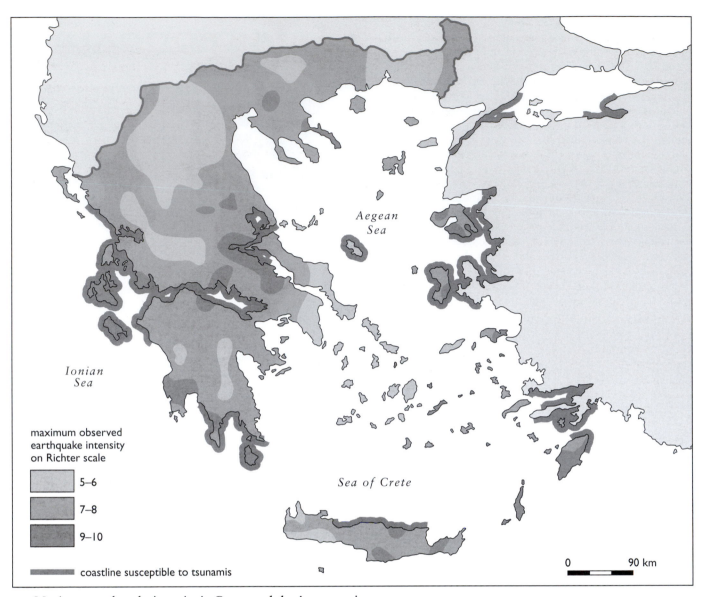

maximum observed
earthquake intensity
on Richter scale

5–6

7–8

9–10

coastline susceptible to tsunamis

Ionian Sea

Aegean Sea

Sea of Crete

0   90 km

20. Maximum earthquake intensity in Greece and the Aegean region

Underwater earthquakes or landslides can produce extraordinary waves on the sea called tsunamis (or less correctly, tidal waves). In the open sea tsunamis are typically less than 50 cm high, travel at speeds of up to 200 km per hour, and have a wavelength of the order of tens of km: hence they are not noticed generally by people in boats. Near to the coast their character changes dramatically – as the sea becomes shallower the wave height increases to up to 50 m. Such waves can be extremely destructive in coastal communities.

The movements associated with an earthquake will generally produce changes in the height of the land across the fault of up to several metres. Along the coast these changes in height will appear as local changes in sea level. Such changes have submerged coastal cities and quarries and left harbours dry. Such local effects should be distinguished from global long-term sea-level rises caused by melting of the ice caps since the peak of the last glacial period 20,000 years ago.

Just before an earthquake there are often changes in the environment, some of which have been used to try to predict the timing of the earthquake. Among these are changes in the water level in wells and in the discharge of springs. The general level of ground noise (very small earthquakes) may also change before an earthquake. Lastly, many people have noticed unusual animal behaviour before an earthquake. If true, this may be related to any of the effects listed above or to changing magnetic and electrical fields. As yet, there has been little success in the prediction of earthquakes.

Seismic risk can also be measured in several different ways, but the most important from a cultural point of view is the maximum intensity or destructiveness of the earthquake. The maximum intensity is much higher in some parts of the Aegean because they lie close to the edge of tectonic plates. The high maximum intensity of the Ionian islands and southwestern Peloponnese is due to the subduction of the ocean floor (albeit thicker than normal) beneath the Aegean Sea. The ocean floor has to bend in order to go down the subduction zone, and this movement causes the earthquakes. High maximum intensity on Crete and Rhodes is also related to the same plate motions, but here the direction of movement is almost parallel to the Hellenic arc (now the Ionian islands, the western Peloponnese, the islands of Crete, Karpathos, and Rhodes, and southeastern Turkey), and hence the two plates slide past each other along transform faults. A zone of earthquakes associated with a tectonic plate boundary extends from the northern Aegean through the Sea of Marmara and across northern Turkey. Most of the other zones of high maximum intensity are related to crustal extension north of the Hellenic arc: this has produced a series of approximately east–west grabens (tectonic valleys). There are still important movements on the Corinthian and Euboean gulf grabens, hence their high maximum intensity. The high maximum intensity of many of the islands in the eastern Aegean is probably related to grabens that stretch from the Aegean Sea itself deep into the Turkish mainland.

There were many earthquakes in antiquity, but few have been identified and studied in detail. The earliest has been only identified by the effects of the accompanying tsunami. This was an earthquake, or possibly a landslide, associated with the great Minoan volcanic eruption of Thera (modern Santorini) in 1650 or 1450 BC. The tsunami deposited sediments on the adjacent island of Anafi up to a height of 40 m and was still 7 m high when it reached Israel. It must also have devastated settlements on the northern shore of Crete. The earthquake of 464 BC that destroyed Sparta was an important historical event of the Classical period. It was a medium to large earthquake produced by vertical movement on the fault at the base of the Taygetus Mountains. The earthquake and tsunami of 373 BC in the gulf of Corinth were responsible for the destruction of the city of Helice, remains of which have not been located. It was probably 7 km west of Aigion, on the western gulf. Contemporary writers noted that wild animals and insects left the city during the five days preceding the earthquake, and this has often been cited when premonitory animal behaviour is discussed. The city was submerged by movements on the fault, and its destruction was completed by the tsunami and further earthquakes along this fault. The earthquakes that toppled the Colossus of Rhodes in 222 BC caused parts of the land to rise almost 4 m, which was one of the largest earth movements in the region during the last 10,000 years. The harbour at Phalasarna in western Crete has been lifted up by over 7 m since antiquity. This must have occurred during several earthquakes, including the devastating earthquake of AD 365 centred south of Crete. The ensuing tsunami caused the loss of thousands of lives and extensive damage throughout the eastern Mediterranean. Another earthquake in AD 551 is known to have caused drastic damage further east, and may have also contributed to the uplift. A recent tsunami associated with a volcanic eruption was that of the Colombo Bank volcano in AD 1650 that produced waves 20 m high on the coast of Thera. Devastating earthquakes occurred even more recently in the Cyclades in 1956, Corinth in 1961, and Kalamata in 1986.

MICHAEL D. HIGGINS

Further Reading

Burton, P.W. *et al.*, "Seismic Risk in Turkey, the Aegean and the Eastern Mediterranean: The Occurrence of Large Magnitude Earthquakes", *Geophysical Journal of the Royal Astronomical Society*, 78 (1984): pp. 475–506

Institute of Geology and Mineral Exploration (IGME), Seismotectonic Map of Greece, scale 1:500,000 in two sheets, 1989

Makropoulos, K.C. and P.W. Burton, "A Catalogue of Seismicity in Greece and Adjacent Areas", *Geophysical Journal of the Royal Astronomical Society*, 65 (1981): pp. 741–62

Papadopoulos, G.A. and B.J. Chalkis, "Tsunamis Observed in Greece and the Surrounding Area from Antiquity up to the Present Times", *Marine Geology*, 56 (1984): pp. 509–17

Stiros, S. and R.E. Jones (editors), *Archaeoseismology* (Fitch Laboratory Occasional Paper 7), Athens: British School at Athens, 1996

Ecology

Greek ecosystems go back to the Tertiary period, several million years ago, when the climate was much wetter than today and the predominant vegetation was probably evergreen forest. These subtropical "laurisylvan" forests perished in the cold, drought, and fire of the Quaternary period, but their rustle and scent still faintly echo and breathe in the laurel and arbutus jungles on the north sides of west Cretan mountains.

Mediterranean ecology is determined partly by its history. For most of the last two million years Greece was colder and drier than it is now, the local effect of the glaciations of higher latitudes. Mediterranean-type plants retreated to favourable localities. The predominant vegetation was steppe-like grassland, sometimes with scattered trees. Forests were very local. Endemic plants – those confined to Greece – had nowhere to retreat to, and presumably sat out the glaciations on or near the mountains and gorges where many of them now grow. Significantly, very few endemics are forest plants.

Hundreds of thousands of years of cold and drought were interrupted by periods of thousands of years of climate more like the present. The present such interglacial began some 14,000 years ago. In the first half, Greece was populated mainly by deciduous trees like those of central Europe today: deciduous oaks, lime, alder, hazel, and even such a northern tree as birch. These indicate a wetter, probably less seasonal climate. From the 5th millennium BC onwards, the climate changed to approximately the semi-arid present. Middle European trees died out or retreated to unusually cold places and what are now thought of as Mediterranean plants became dominant.

The soils of Greece are varied, but mostly rich in lime. Soils come from three sources: weathering of the underlying rock; material eroded and washed in from elsewhere; and wind-blown dust from the Sahara. Weathering and erosion have been more active at times in the past than they are now. Erosion has washed material off hillsides and out of gullies and the resulting deposits have built up most of the basins and river deltas which are the best agricultural land. Lack of soil precludes most agriculture but not wild vegetation: many forests in Greece, and some olive groves, grow out of pockets and fissures in bare limestone.

Greece has always had browsing animals. Elephants and other great tree-breaking beasts were probably exterminated by Palaeolithic men, and do not appear in this interglacial. Deer, wild oxen, wild swine, and smaller herbivores such as hares survived into historical times. From the Neolithic onwards, people have replaced wild herbivores by domestic livestock. Each species of animal has its likes and dislikes: goats, for example, are fond of prickly-oak (despite the prickles) but will not eat pine unless they have to. How the impact of wild beasts differed from that of domestic animals is not known: we do not know how many deer there were in aboriginal times, still less what they ate.

Crete, and probably the other islands, tells a different story. It had tiny elephants, mini-hippopotamuses, and slow deer, but no carnivore fiercer than a badger. Lacking predators, these animals would have produced a state that a modern ecologist would regard as excessive browsing. The transition after human settlement to an island dominated by sheep and goats may have had less effect than on the mainland.

Fire is a major ecological factor. Every summer there are countless wildfires in Greece, which are regarded as an abnormality and a tragedy. In reality trees and plants are combustible not by misfortune but by adaptation. They burn because they make flammable oils and resins; it is their business in life to catch fire (by lightning or otherwise) and burn up their less fire-adapted competitors. Some survive a fire by their thick bark or well-insulated growing points; others perish but come again from seed.

During the Neolithic and Bronze Ages the landscape was affected both by increasing human activity and by a change to a drier climate. People grubbed out (uprooted) forests on good soils to create farmland; on the remaining roughland they replaced the native mammals by goats, sheep, and cattle. Forests retreated to places with moisture or good root penetration, being replaced by maquis or savanna. Undershrubs benefited from the changes to establish areas of phrygana. The date, nature, and consequences of deforestation are controversial, but there is no good evidence that Classical Greece was more wooded than Greece is today.

These changes had more effect on some groups of plants than others. Cliff plants were little affected. Plants requiring deep soils were almost annihilated by agriculture, which changed the balance of the vegetation. Part of the reason why Greece is now thought of as a land of evergreen trees is that deciduous trees, especially oaks, grew on soils suitable for cultivation and were thus subtracted from the landscape: in recent decades, as cultivation has retreated, they have recovered some of the lost ground.

By Classical times the ecological changes were largely completed. Mostly the landscape looked not very different from Greece today, leaving aside urbanization, road making, and bulldozing. One important difference is the disappearance of fens, mostly destroyed in the 19th century. Another factor that the modern visitor may not appreciate is the great historic importance of woodcutting. Most Greek trees (even some conifers) sprout when felled and form coppice stools. In many areas wood was scarce, and even on cliffs trees were repeatedly cut down, and repeatedly sprouted, down to the mid-20th century.

In the last few decades, as land uses have been concentrated and intensified, much land that was once farmland or pasture has been abandoned. Woodcutting has almost disappeared: such firewood and charcoal as are still used come mainly as a by-product from an increasing area of olives and walnuts. Greek vegetation is very resilient, and the result is a great increase in the quantity of natural vegetation. Terraces become roughland, maquis grows up into forest, rivers are lined with jungle, and savanna becomes infilled into forest. One consequence is an increase in fires, since much of the new vegetation consists of pines and other fire-promoting plants.

OLIVER RACKHAM

See also Climate, Forestry, Plants

Further Reading

Rackham, Oliver "Ecology and Pseudo-Ecology: The Example of Ancient Greece" in *Human Landscapes in Classical Antiquity: Environment and Culture*, edited by Graham Shipley and John Salmon, London and New York: Routledge, 1996
Rackham, Oliver and Jennifer Moody, *The Making of the Cretan Landscape*, Manchester: Manchester University Press, 1996
Rackham, Oliver and A.T. Grove, *The Nature of the European Mediterranean*, Yale University Press, 2000

Economy

The modern concept of a national economy is far removed from the origins of the term itself. Modern economists have developed abstract and analytic concepts and built up mathematical models to measure and quantify economic activities. Gross national product, inflation, and levels of employment are all criteria which are used today to analyse a country's economy. Such criteria cannot easily be applied to ancient Greece, so that economic quantification often proves controversial or elusive.

The discipline of ancient and modern economists differs in many ways. Modern study of the ancient Greek economy was transformed by the publication of M.I. Finley's *Ancient Economy* in 1973. To understand the economy of ancient Greece, and to consider the economy in the Hellenic tradition, we must embrace the changing attitudes towards our understanding of the Greek economy.

The word "economy" derives from the ancient Greek term *oikonomia*. In antiquity *oikonomia* had a meaning different from that of "economy" as we understand it today. *Oikonomia* was far more closely associated with the organization and management of the household (*oikos*). The use of the word later extended beyond its strict application to the household but there is only limited evidence to suggest that the "national" economy was considered. The ancient Greeks had no developed literature on or theory of economics. Xenophon's *Oeconomicus* is concerned with running the household and estate of a wealthy citizen; his *Poroi* (Resources) discusses ways of increasing revenue for the city, but is limited in explaining the means by which such improvements might be made. The *Oeconomicus* attributed to Aristotle is a collection of anecdotal stories about fundraising and the use of money, with minimal analysis of economic systems. Finley sought in vain for discussions and conscious theorizing about economics in ancient literary sources.

In ancient Greece the principal economy was that of the household. This was predominantly a rural economy. Agriculture was supplemented by the raising of livestock and in some areas by fishing. Other spheres of economic activity are also discernible. The Greek ideal of self-sufficiency (*autarkeia*) was aspired to but rarely achieved. Not all communities were able to provide all their own produce from their local rural environment. As a result, produce, among other things, was traded over varying distances in order to provide communities with the goods that they required. This trade existed on different geographic scales – local, regional, and international. Not all communities needed to rely on long-distance trade or had populations large enough to make demands beyond their immediate region. In this respect, Athens was exceptional among Greek communities not only for the large size of its population but also for its need to supplement its large domestic produce with the import of agricultural produce from abroad.

The primacy of the rural economy in ancient Greece appears as only one dynamic element in what is emerging as a complex picture of the economies of ancient Greece. The function of slaves and of non-slave labour, the role of money and coinage, the social behaviour and value systems of the urban elites in ancient Greek communities, the role of religion and temple economies, the importance of natural resources (mineral, geological, and timber), the dependence on maritime transport, and the significance of war, are all essential factors to be taken into account in understanding ancient Greek economies.

The ways in which the economies of ancient Greece have been approached in recent years have changed, and the different methods of analysing them have shed light on their nature. The established views of the past are being rejected in favour of more contextualized views of economic activities in ancient Greece.

Distinctive spheres of activity in ancient Greece can be labelled "economic" in so far as they related to the use of money, affected the finances and distribution of resources in the community, or dictated or involved the role of wealth. But understanding these spheres of activity is now seen as impossible unless their social, political, and cultural context is also taken into account.

Traditionally, students of the ancient Greek economy have been divided into "primitivists" and "modernizers". The primitivists have concentrated on the wider activities of society, paying less attention to the small minority, the elite, who have tended to dominate the surviving source evidence. The modernizers, by contrast, have tended to overestimate the importance of the elite and neglected the interaction of the numerically greater sectors of society. This polarization of approaches makes it impossible to see how all levels of Greek society interacted.

Another feature of the debate on the ancient Greek economy has been a distinction between the approaches of the substantivists and the formalists. The substantivists believe that the ancient Greek economy, while not as sophisticated and developed as the modern economy, betrays features and rationales which can be isolated and analysed independently of their socio-politico context. By contrast, the formalists believe that the ancient Greek economy was not only less developed than the modern economy, but was embedded within society. The ancient economy can be understood only in terms of social and political relationships. Movement of goods, for instance, may not have been motivated by economic gain, but by considerations of reciprocal gift-giving.

There has been a move away from these two sets of polarized approaches towards a more comprehensive and pluralistic understanding of the ancient Greek economy. It is more accurate to speak of ancient Greek economies, since there was no monolithic Greek economy. Greece never existed as a single cellular entity but consisted of many different communities which interacted individually with the communities and peoples of the Mediterranean and beyond. The economy of ancient Greece should therefore be seen as numerous interrelated dynamic economic activities. These activities sometimes involved only some segments of or groups within a community, and at other times affected the whole community.

The central importance of agriculture to Greek communities led to the movement, often over large distances, of both essential and luxury items. Trade in grain in antiquity is a feature of political and economic history. Athens in the 5th and 4th centuries BC had developed such a large population that there was no guarantee that the large supplies of grain from Athenian territory, including the important islands of Lemnos, Imbros, and Skyros, could provide for the city. In some years a shortfall in domestic production would have signalled shortages in Athens. The demand for grain stimulated an increase in the movement of merchants to Athens. Virtually all the grain supplied to Athens arrived by sea. This ensured that the Piraeus, Athens' harbour, prospered and attracted numerous foreigners and traders. While it would be unfair to say that the economic prosperity of the Piraeus grew out of the trade in grain, the movement of staple crops obviously provided an essential commodity to a highly demanding market. In the 5th century BC the growth of the Athenian empire had the important effect of providing considerable security for maritime transport in and around the Aegean. The loss of its empire by the end of the 5th century BC forced Athens to rely much more heavily on foreign alliances and institutional or legal reforms to regulate and control the movement of grain to the city.

For Athens, the most developed of the Greek polis economies, much more evidence exists for the use of credit and the role of banks and moneylenders than exists for any other ancient Greek community. Banking played an important role not only in financing maritime commercial enterprises but in all kinds of economic activity. Financial confidence was often entrusted to ad hoc groups of individuals who would act as guarantors of capital. Many surviving documents, the majority in the form of inscriptions on stone, provide information us about the use of security and capital.

Unlike many communities, Athens had the advantage of enormous wealth in its silver mines. The extraction of silver from the hills of Laurium provided the city with the raw material with which it manufactured its famous silver coinage, characterized by the owl stamped on the coin. The Athenian owl became a symbol of a guaranteed high-quality silver coinage. Its circulation during the 5th and 4th BC centuries was greater than that of any other Greek coin. The silver mines of Attica therefore played a huge role in promoting the economic welfare of the city.

The extraction of silver from Laurium depended on slave labour. Many Greek communities relied on unfree labour for their workforce. The very different and almost exclusively agrarian-based economy of Sparta was founded upon the peasant workers, the helots, who were subordinate to the Spartans. In Athens too the slave labour force which worked in the Laurium district was an essential part of the mining economy. Slaves played an important role in other areas of life. In Athens, however, it is less than certain that all farms would have used slave labour. Unlike Sparta, with its subjugated helot workforce, the typical Athenian farm was probably a small-holding providing at least sufficient produce for the household. Slaves worked in many other areas – in industries such as shieldmaking,or in crafts such as painting pots, for example, and in construction, such as on the building projects of the Acropolis in the 5th century BC.

But the economies of Greek communities also exploited a more fluid population of non-citizens: foreigners. In Athens, resident foreigners were designated as "metics" and would pay a special tax. In other commercial centres also foreigners played an important role, such as on Delos, Rhodes, and in Corinth. It was normal that only citizens could own land in a Greek city; foreigners were sometimes granted the right to do so, but only as a reward for services to the city. The non-citizen population of the Greek city was highly fluid and transitional. Warfare and economic depression would probably see falls in this mobile population. Some cities, including Athens, had sufficiently large foreign populations to establish foreign cults and maintain a more permanent community.

Religion and warfare were of central importance to the economies of the Greek world. Religion, centred on the worship of gods in temples, encouraged the rise of temple economies. The built temple often served as a storehouse for the wealth and dedications offered to a god. The temples of Apollo at Delphi and Athena at Athens contained vast amounts of wealth at the heights of their success. Revenue from the cities of the Athenian empire was hived off as offerings to Athena in her temple on the Acropolis, and the monies dedicated to her from Athens' allies were recorded on stones and displayed outside the temple (the so-called Athenian tribute lists). The role of the temple in the movement of wealth and as a repository for wealth which could be used by a Greek city is best illustrated by Pericles' statement of the Athenian financial reserves at the opening of the Peloponnesian War (Thucydides, 2. 13. 2–6).

One of the greatest drains on the economic resource of a Greek community, and particularly a city, was warfare. The citizens of the polis in the Archaic and Classical periods typically provided the main infantry fighting force for the army. This minimized the expenditure a community had to meet for sending out a military force. The expense of warfare put an immense strain on many communities. In the 5th century BC Athens spent more on warfare than any other city. The cost of running a navy of 100 or more ships was huge. The services that the wealthiest Athenians were required to perform on behalf of the city included trierarchy – providing for the equipping and manning of warships – which helped to reduce the cost to the city of maintaining a fleet. For many Greek cities such expenditure was impossible. The other great expense of warfare was the cost involved in building and maintaining the defences of a community, in particular the cost of building city walls. Emergency taxes were sometimes required to meet the cost of military operations; special taxes were on occasion imposed if defences were required hastily. Expenditure on civic defence was large, as was the cost of providing patrols and mobile defence forces such as cavalry. Cavalry power was often provided by the wealthiest citizens of any community; the cost of maintaining a horse throughout the year was high. Despite the dependence on the wealthy elite to defray some of the expenses of warfare, it was inevitable that many cities relied on their own finances to pay for military activities. The use of the financial reserves of temples was central to providing money to the city.

The economy of the Greeks in later periods, such as the Byzantine era, continued to be based on agriculture. Even in times of wider economic depression, the supply of agricultural produce was often sufficient to support a local economy. The Byzantine state played a major role in the economy of this period, raising money through taxation and paying out vast sums for its army and bureaucracy. On a local level signs of continuity are visible, but overseas trade was vulnerable to the fluctuations of the political world.

It becomes clear that the economic organization of ancient Greek communities differed in many respects from those of a modern state. Individuals and households were essential to the shaping of ancient Greek economies. In the same way, the community depended to large extent on the household and the individual for financial support of the city. Over time the smaller-sized community of the polis was overtaken by the much more richly endowed political systems of the kingdoms which dominate the Hellenistic period. The Roman domination of the Mediterranean illustrates the rise of an even greater power than the Hellenistic kingdoms. Despite the changing shape of the political world, the economies of the Greek communities which made up the ancient world remained remarkably consistent and dependent on the household economy and the wealth of the richer individuals or elites within the community.

GRAHAM OLIVER

See also Agriculture, Banking, Coinage, Finance, Slavery, Taxation, Trade

Further Reading

Austin, M.M. and J.-P. Vidal-Naquet, *Economic and Social History of Ancient Greece: An Introduction*, London: Batsford, and Berkeley: University of California Press, 1977

Austin, M.M., "Hellenistic Kings, War and the Economy", *Classical Quarterly*, 36/2 (1986): pp. 450–66

Cartledge, Paul, "The Economy (Economies) of Ancient Greece", *Dialogos*, 5 (1998): pp. 4–24

Cohen, Edward E., *Athenian Economy and Society: A Banking Perspective*, Princeton, New Jersey: Princeton University Press, 1992

Davies, J.K., "Ancient Economies: Models and Muddles" in *Trade, Traders and the Ancient City*, edited by Helen Parkins and Christopher Smith, London and New York: Routledge, 1998

Finley, M.I., *Economy and Society in Ancient Greece*, edited by Brent D. Shaw and Richard P. Saller, London: Chatto and Windus, 1981; New York: Viking, 1982

Finley, M.I., *The Ancient Economy*, 2nd edition, London: Hogarth Press, and Berkeley: University of California Press, 1985

Gallant, Thomas W., *Risk and Survival in Ancient Greece: Reconstructing the Rural Domestic Economy*, Stanford: Stanford University Press, and Cambridge: Polity Press, 1991

Garlan, Yvon, *Slavery in Ancient Greece*, Ithaca, New York: Cornell University Press, 1988

Garland, Robert, *The Piraeus from the Fifth to the First Century BC*, London: Duckworth, and Ithaca, New York: Cornell University Press, 1987

Garnsey, Peter and C.R. Whittaker (editors), *Trade and Famine in Classical Antiquity*, Cambridge: Cambridge Philological Society, 1983

Garnsey, Peter, Keith Hopkins, and C.R. Whittaker (editors), *Trade in the Ancient Economy*, London: Chatto and Windus, and Berkeley: University of California Press, 1983

Garnsey, Peter, *Famine and Food Supply in the Graeco-Roman World: Responses to Risk and Crisis*, Cambridge and New York: Cambridge University Press, 1988

Glotz, Gustave, *Ancient Greece at Work: An Economic History of Greece from the Homeric Period to the Roman Conquest*, London: Kegan Paul Trench Trubner, and New York: Knopf, 1926

Hendy, Michael F., *Studies in the Byzantine Monetary Economy, c. 300–1450*, Cambridge and New York: Cambridge University Press, 1985

Hendy, Michael F., *The Economy, Fiscal Administration and Coinage of Byzantium*, Northampton: Variorum, 1989

Kourvetaris, Yorgos A. and Betty A. Dobratz, *A Profile of Modern Greece in Search of Identity*, Oxford: Clarendon Press, and New York: Oxford University Press, 1987, chapter 5

Millett, Paul, *Lending and Borrowing in Ancient Athens*, Cambridge and New York: Cambridge University Press, 1991

Osborne, Robin G., *Classical Landscape with Figures: The Ancient Greek City and its Countryside*, London: George Philip, and Dobbs Ferry, New York: Sheridan House, 1987

Pirounakis, Nicholas G., *The Greek Economy: Past, Present and Future*, Basingstoke: Macmillan, and New York: St Martin's Press, 1997

Pomeroy, Sarah B., *Families in Classical and Hellenistic Greece: Representations and Realities*, Oxford: Clarendon Press, and New York: Oxford University Press, 1997

Price, B.B. (editor), *Ancient Economic Thought*, London and New York: Routledge, 1997

Reden, Sitta von, *Exchange in Ancient Greece*, London: Duckworth, 1995

Sallares, Robert, *Ecology of the Ancient Greek World*, London: Duckworth, and Ithaca, New York: Cornell University Press, 1991

Sbarounes, A.I., *Economic Development of Greece*, Athens, 1959

Starr, Chester G., *The Economic and Social Growth of Early Greece, 800–500 BC*, New York: Oxford University Press, 1977

Ecumenism

Although a definitive lexical study of the words *oikoumene* and *oikoumenikos* has not yet been written, it is possible to distinguish, from antiquity to the present, at least seven meanings in them: (1) pertaining to, or representing, the whole (inhabited) earth; (2) pertaining to, or representing, the whole of the (Roman) empire; (3) pertaining to, or representing, the whole of the Church; (4) that which has universal or ecclesiastical validity; (5) pertaining to the worldwide missionary outreach of the Church; (6) pertaining to the relations between and unity of two or more Churches (or of Christians of various confessions); (7) that quality or attitude which expresses the consciousness of and desire for Christian unity.

The term, derived from *oikein* (to inhabit), has been used since Herodotus; and in the Hellenistic period it found application in secular contexts, where it referred politically to the realm of the Graeco-Roman empire or to the civilized world in cultural contradistinction to the lands of the barbarians.

Biblical writings generally follow the secular usage, taking *oikoumene* as a synonym for "earth" (Ps. 23: 1, LXX), yet without giving particular prominence to the term. In the New Testament its political connotation is observable in Luke 4: 5–7 (cf. also Luke 2: 1; Acts 17: 16) and in the Apocalypse (esp. 16: 14). For the writer of Hebrews, the expected reign of God can be called the "*oikoumene* to come" (2: 5).

The subsequent, much more widespread, ecclesiastical use of the term is linked with the extension of the Greek-speaking Christian community across the entire Roman empire. By the 4th century the *oikoumene* had become the "Christian world", with the double (political and religious) meaning of the "Christian empire" and the "whole Church". The adjective *oikoumenikos* refers to everything that has universal validity. Thus, "ecumenical" is a quality claimed for particular councils and their dogmatic decisions. It is also used as a title of honour for specific patriarchal sees or for respected teachers of the whole Church. In the Orthodox tradition, which preserved the memory of the early link between Church and empire, the term remained in use, though its meaning became more and more specific. Today it serves to describe the new reality of the organized ecumenical movement, as represented in particular by the World Council of Churches (established in 1948), and the different ways of reacting to this reality.

The Orthodox Churches have participated actively in the ecumenical movement from the beginning. Indeed, an encyclical from the ecumenical patriarchate to the sister autocephalous Churches in 1902 inaugurated the journey of Orthodoxy towards dynamic dialogue, conciliation, and cooperation in order to respond more fruitfully to the urgent need of reuniting fragmented Christianity. This encyclical was the first document to raise at an official level the issue of relationships, first, between Constantinople and the Oriental Orthodox Churches and, secondly, between Orthodoxy and Western Christendom, in an ecumenical perspective.

A second, landmark encyclical, issued in January 1920 from the Phanar and addressed to "all the Churches in the *oikoumene*", introduced a fundamental programme of contemporary ecumenism and called for the formation of a "league of Churches", to be modelled on the newly established League of Nations. The document laid down two essential conditions on which rapprochement and fellowship could be achieved: (1) the elimination of "mutual distrust and bitterness between the different Churches", and (2) the rekindling and strengthening of love among them. This letter signified a departure from the usual cautious attitude of the Orthodox towards the West, and showed the desire of some at least among their hierarchs to take the lead in the movement towards closer fellowship.

As an outcome of this remarkable change of mind, a large delegation came to Geneva (12–20 August 1920) to the preparatory Conference of the Faith and Order movement. Three of these delegates were also present at the preparatory meeting of the Life and Work movement, which took place in Geneva at the same time. For many of the Orthodox delegates, this was the first occasion of meeting with representatives of non-Orthodox Churches, and the initial contacts were not always easy. Some of the Orthodox were particularly troubled by the proselytizing missions supported by certain American and British groups, and made the cessation of all such activities the condition for their further cooperation. In spite of these tensions, the impression produced upon the Orthodox by the leaders in Faith and Order was highly favourable, and convinced a number of them of the sincerity and genuine desire for unity animating many representatives of these new endeavours towards reconciliation.

Two major attempts at achieving reunion between the Greek East and the Latin West took place at the Second Council of Lyons in 1274 and the Council of Florence in 1438–39. But in both cases, although a formal union was promulgated, it was ultimately rejected by the general Orthodox population. Centuries of mutual isolation and hostility ensued, with each Church de facto denying the ecclesial reality of the other.

The situation began to improve only in the 1960s, when important changes in attitude took place within both the Catholic and the Orthodox Churches. From the Catholic perspective, the convocation of the Second Vatican Council with its Orthodox observers marked a greater openness to the East. From the Orthodox perspective, the third Pan-Orthodox Conference (Rhodes, 1964) encouraged the local Orthodox Churches to engage in studies preparing for an eventual dialogue with the Roman Catholic Church.

Two other notable events took place in the same decade. In January 1964 pope Paul VI and the ecumenical patriarch Athenagoras met for the first time, in Jerusalem. In a common declaration issued by them on 7 December 1965 the mutual excommunications of 1054 were "erased from the memory of the Church". In 1967 the pope and the patriarch exchanged visits in Rome and Constantinople. Between 1980 and 1990 six official meetings of the Joint International Commission for theological dialogue between the Orthodox Church and the Roman Catholic Church were held. This dialogue is still in its early stages, but progress is being made in the effort to establish a common foundation, on the basis of which the more difficult issues, especially the role of the Church of Rome and its bishop among the local Churches, can be most fruitfully discussed.

The first official international dialogue between the Orthodox Churches and the World Alliance of Reformed Churches took place in 1988 in Leuenberg, Switzerland, under the leadership of the metropolitan Panteleimon Rodopoulos (ecumenical patriarcharte) and Dr Lukas Vischer (World Alliance). The second was held in Moscow in 1990.

Behind these meetings lies a long history of Orthodox and Protestant contacts. The earliest exchange of letters took place between the Lutheran theological faculty of the University of Tübingen and the ecumenical patriarch Jeremias II from 1573 to 1581. For the Calvinists, the first Orthodox–Reformed discussions centred on the stormy debate over the "unorthodox" confession of faith of the ecumenical patriarch Cyril Lukaris (ruled 1620–38). In the light of this history both groups consider it essential to establish firm grounds on which both traditions can confess the essentials of their Christian faith in common. Hence the decision for the official international dialogues to focus on the doctrine of the Trinity, based on the Nicene Creed.

DIMITRI CONOMOS

Further Reading

Beek, Huibert van, and Georges Lemopoulos (editors), *Proclaiming Christ Today: Orthodox Evangelical Consultation*, Geneva: World Council of Churches, and Bialystok: Syndesmos, 1996

Belopopsky, A. and A. Talvivaara (editors), *Orthodox Youth and Ecumenism Resource Book*, Geneva: World Council of Churches, and Bialystok: Syndesmos, 1998

Chaillot, Christine and Alexander Belopopsky (editors), *Towards Unity: The Theological Dialogue between the Orthodox Church and the Oriental Orthodox Churches*, Geneva, 1998

Florovsky, Georges, "The Orthodox Churches and the Ecumenical Movement Prior to 1910" in *A History of the Ecumenical Movement 1517–1948*, edited by Ruth Rouse and Stephen Charles Neill, 2nd edition, London: SPCK, and Philadelphia: Westminster Press, 1967

Lemopoulos, George (editor), *The Ecumenical Movement, the Churches, and the World Council of Churches*, Geneva: World Council of Churches, and Bialystok: Syndesmos, 1996

Lossky, Nicholas *et al.* (editors), *Dictionary of the Ecumenical Movement*, Geneva: World Council of Churches, and Grand Rapids, Michigan: Eerdmans, 1991

Sabev, Todor, *The Orthodox Churches in the World Council of Churches: Towards the Future*, Geneva: World Council of Churches, and Bialystok: Syndesmos, 1996

Zernov, Nicholas, "The Eastern Churches and the Ecumenical Movement in the Twentieth Century" in *A History of the Ecumenical Movement, 1517–1948*, edited by Ruth Rouse and Stephen Charles Neill, 2nd edition, London: SPCK, and Philadelphia: Westminster Press, 1967

Education

The poems of Homer depict aristocratic youths attending their seniors much in the manner of esquires attending the knights of the western Middle Ages. There was doubtless a similar educational purpose, both in teaching skills of warfare and in inculcating heroic *arete* (valour). Apart from the long list of the centaur Cheiron's students (which gave rise to the lost Hesiodic *Praecepta Chironis*), the tale of Phoenix's instruction of Achilles (*Iliad*, 9. 432–619) involves the employment by a father of a private tutor. His noble birth possibly foreshadows (unless it is a later ad hoc invention) a formal institution known among the aristocracy of some states in the Archaic and Classical periods, when it involved a strong pederastic element. In this institution an older man courted (in Crete abducted) a youth whom he initiated into all aspects of civic life.

Other poets too were a major early source of education for the Greeks but although they did give practical information they, like Homer himself, were regarded chiefly as teachers of ethical ideals. Although their position was assailed by philosophers (first as early as the 6th century but most notably by Plato), it survived to the end of the Classical period. Thereafter the poets were read more for their artistry. Homer's paramountcy (and longevity) is marked by the commentary of

Eustathios, a 12th-century bishop of Thessalonica, which is the lengthiest commentary ever written on any ancient author.

The earliest formalized education in the Greek world was probably the Spartan *agoge* (training). Though attributed to a single early enactment, this was probably a gradual development resulting from the need for internal self-defence by the vastly outnumbered Spartiates. By the Classical period it certainly involved the compulsory, state-run education of males from the ages of 7 to 29. Since the aim was military preparedness, it gave minimal attention to literacy and maximum attention to training for war through sport and dancing as well as mock fighting and hunting. Toughness was attained through starvation, inadequate bedding in winter, and sleeping rough (excesses of severity, such as the whipping competitions that could lead to death, belong to the Roman period). Girls were given a similar but less rigorous training. A gentler and briefer Athenian analogue was the 4th-century *ephebeia*, which gave primarily military instruction to youths who entered barracks (as at Sparta) in their eighteenth year. No longer compulsory by 305 BC, the two years of service were reduced to one in 282 BC, and thereafter the *ephebeia* became increasingly pacific. Except in Macedon, where ephebes continued with strictly military training until 168 BC, parallel institutions in other cities degenerated into young gentlemen's associations, but in places lasted until the 4th century AD.

It is not known when private group schooling came into existence. The earliest schools reliably mentioned were at Chios (Herodotus, 6. 27) and Astypalaea (Pausanias, 6. 9. 6) in the 490s BC and at Troezen (Plutarch, *Themistocles*, 10) in 480 BC. The number of schools grew throughout the Classical period even in small cities (Boeotian Mycalessus must have possessed at least three schools in 413 BC, because Thucydides [7. 29. 5] reports the slaughter by Thracian mercenaries of all the boys in "the largest one"). The early, aristocratic emphasis was on gymnastics and music, the latter constituting poetry, dancing, singing, and the playing of an instrument (by the early 4th century BC the lyre had ousted the *aulos*). It is not known if there were any schools for literacy in the early part of the 5th century, but by its end these predominated.

Most of the information known about Classical education is 4th-century BC Athenian. Boys (and girls according to the evidence of vase painting) attended – but not necessarily all of – the usually separate schools of the *paidotribes* for gymnastics, the *kitharistes* for music and lyric poetry, and the *grammatistes* for reading, writing, other literature, and arithmetic. At the end of the Classical period Sicyon introduced drawing into the artistic curriculum. Teachers were freemen, sometimes with slaves as assistants, poorly paid and held in low regard. Boys were accompanied to school by a *paidagogos*, a trusted slave responsible for behaviour and moral upbringing. Lessons were learned largely by rote and encouraged by the cane and regular public competition (Plato (*Laws*, 819b–c), approvingly mentions arithmetical games). Holidays coincided with festivals.

Higher education was provided in the last third of the 5th century BC by sophists, itinerant teachers who lectured for a fee on a wide range of subjects. Hippias' professed expertise in arithmetic, geometry, astronomy, and music is the origin of the western medieval quadrivium, while Gorgias' instruction in Sicilian techniques of rhetoric transformed prose writing and ultimately the future direction of education. In the 4th century BC Isocrates and Plato opened schools, the former to all who could pay the fee, the latter only to chosen students. Both men were influential educational innovators (Plato in part through the utopian theories of his *Republic* and *Laws*). Isocrates' aim was to produce future political leaders, primarily through rhetoric, a subject that Plato was late in allowing at his Academy, where philosophical and mathematical studies were supreme. Plato's insistence on propaedeutic courses in geometry and his use of specialist teachers may be seen as the origin of secondary education, while his scientific interests inspired Aristotle, his pupil of 20 years, to open a school of his own (the Lyceum) in 335 BC where the natural sciences were vigorously pursued.

During the Hellenistic period there was both a huge expansion and a definitive formalizing of education that extended to the introduction of examinations. Whereas Diodorus Siculus' claim (12. 12. 4, 12. 13. 3–4) that Charondas deemed literacy so important that he legislated for universal education at public expense is a muddled retrojection (to the 6th century BC, and a transplantation from Catana to Thurii that was founded in 444/43 BC), Teos, Miletus, and Rhodes now certainly received huge benefactions that made universal education (for boys) a possibility, while elsewhere schools were regularly subsidized by the municipality that itself contracted the teachers. Education for girls definitely expanded, and evidence suggests that even slaves were occasionally allowed schooling (there is firm later documentation from Graeco-Roman Egypt). All children's educational activities, including gymnastics and music, were now concentrated into a single building. The age of entry to primary school varied: the Stoic Chrysippus, who emphasized the pedagogic importance of well-spoken nursemaids, suggested three, Aristotle five, and Plato six, but seven was more normal. Writing materials were more readily available and tablets with copied exercises survive. Literacy was taught through letters, syllables, words, and finally short continuous passages that were always difficult to read for lack of word division. Memorization was still dominant. Arithmetic involved little more than counting. Secondary education was largely for the study of Classical literature under the *grammatikos*, but a general education (*enkyklios paideia*) of mathematical subjects, astronomy, and music played a minor role. Higher education in literature, rhetoric, and philosophy was available in many larger centres, but most of the best teachers worked in Alexandria, Athens, and Pergamum. Medicine was taught chiefly at Alexandria, Cos, Ephesus, and Pergamum.

Roman education was closely patterned on Greek: any Roman with cultural pretensions was bilingual; Roman aristocrats employed Greek-speaking tutors for their children; some if not all of the earliest Roman schools taught Greek; and the curriculum of the Latin schools was based on the Greek. The main changes in the Greeks' own education was the introduction of the study of grammar in its own right in the 1st century BC through the influence of Dionysius Thrax, the deliberate choice of an archaizing form of the language increasingly distinct from that which was spoken, and an increasing emphasis upon rhetoric. This latter involved training in often extemporary forensic and epideictic oratory, the analysis of numerous kinds of speeches, and the formulation of strict rules for them. During the Second Sophistic (c.AD 60–410) declamatory

Education: Vlach priest giving religious instruction to some Vlach children at Voskopoje in eastern Albania

displays became a major form of entertainment (and tool for the recruitment of students).

Christian emphasis on God's written revelations and the need for their interpretation fostered literacy in the Byzantine world (Maximos Planudes' complaint that it was not lucrative is satirical). Despite periodic monastic attacks, pagan literature continued to form the base of secular education: its defenders claimed that it was allegorical, foreshadowed Christianity, or that its resplendent form should be imitated even if its content was rejected (see St Basil's *Address to Young Men*). Persecution for paganism (most notably of John Italos in the 11th century) was remarkably infrequent and mild. Scientific subjects, however, were not usually encouraged.

In the early centuries of the Byzantine empire there was little change in education, schools being largely a municipal responsibility. Privatization after the 6th century AD resulted, however, in a drastic reduction in their number. Although the occasional small elementary school still existed, most children were taught reading, writing, arithmetic, and some knowledge of the Bible by their parents, or by priests, notaries, or other literate persons (Michael Psellos praises his mother for the rudiments of his own education). Monastic schools satisfied the needs of illiterate novices and sometimes accommodated lay children. Formal secondary education was also rare and usually a matter of private arrangement. At this level the emphasis was upon Classical literature and grammar (though not of the spoken language) with occasional forays into subjects of the quadrivium. With the revival of learning in the mid-9th century a school was opened at the Magnaura Palace and later emperors sometimes subsidized private schools. An illuminating collection of letters by an anonymous Constantinopolitan teacher of the 10th century deals with the school programme, teaching methods (including the use of older boys to instruct younger ones), truancy, behavioural problems, and struggles to extract from parents the fees that he was forced to supplement by the copying of manuscripts. Thomas Magistros in the early 14th century emphasizes the importance of choosing teachers both knowledgeable and of good character.

Institutional higher education was sporadic and information on it is both vague and occasional. The Neoplatonic Academy of Athens was the centre of pagan studies (apart from a brief period of Alexandrian superiority around AD 500) and survived, albeit probably for only a few decades, the ban imposed by Justinian I in AD 529 on the teaching there of philosophy and law. Theodosius II established (or reorganized) at Constantinople in AD 425 a "university" with 31 chairs, mainly in Greek and Latin but including philosophy and law. Its demise, probably in the late 6th century, is obscure. Constantine VII's school in the palace in the mid-10th century may have involved higher as well as secondary education. In 1047 Constantine IX established a law school and shortly thereafter one for the teaching of rhetoric and philosophy that was headed by Michael Psellos, from whom survive various short works addressed to his students. In 1107 the Patriarchal School was organized (its possible earlier existence is a contentious issue) in Hagia Sophia for the teaching of theology, but by the middle of the century rhetoric had been added. In the 1440s the scholars Michael Apostoles and John Argyropoulos, both of whom were interested in rhetoric and

philosophy, are known to have taught at a school attached to the Xenon of the Kral of the Petra monastery in the capital. Medical schools were sometimes attached to hospitals. In addition up to c.1300 many Byzantines and foreigners sought higher education from private teachers mainly, but not exclusively, in Constantinople.

Outside the Greek-speaking areas Byzantine culture and education were exported, largely through churchmen and with profound effects still very evident at the end of the 20th century, to the countries of the Caucasus, throughout the Balkans, to the Kievan Rus, and later to Moscow. Many foreigners, most notably Symeon the future tsar of Bulgaria, were educated in Constantinople itself. Arab courts openly solicited Byzantine scholars and were far more receptive to their knowledge than Byzantines were to the Arabs'. Many aspects of both Seljuk and Ottoman cultural life were modelled on that of the Byzantines. Scholarly émigrés mainly from Constantinople, beginning with Manuel Chrysoloras in the last decade of the 14th century, had more to do with the Renaissance than westerners usually admit.

In the first few decades after the fall of Constantinople in 1453, poverty was primarily responsible for the small number of schools for the Greek inhabitants of the Ottoman empire; but the situation was never as dire as some intellectuals thought, who went so far as to question the very survival of the language (some Greeks in Asia Minor, the so-called Karamanli Christians, did, however, adopt Turkish, though writing it in the Greek alphabet). Even higher education did not entirely disappear, because the Patriarchal Academy was restored by Gennadios II Scholarios, and taught rhetoric and philosophy in addition to theology, while there are hints of private individuals teaching at Thessalonica, Adrianople, and elsewhere. Most children in rural areas, and even in many towns, gained what knowledge they did orally at home and at church. Schooling was rudimentary and available in many areas only at the local monastery where many of the monks were themselves illiterate (Athos, nevertheless, enjoyed several genuine intellectual revivals). In time, however, a few communities benefited from schools and libraries financed by natives who had improved their lot elsewhere. All Greek education was the responsibility of the Greeks themselves and not of their Turkish overlords. Indeed there was sporadic Turkish oppression of Greek education, dependent increasingly upon the whims of local pashas and beys; and until the late 17th century many of the more intelligent (and good-looking) Christian boys were taken away at an early age through a levy (*devshirme* or *paidomazoma*) to be trained as soldiers or civil servants. Outside the areas of Ottoman rule the situation was better, especially in the Venetian-ruled Ionian islands and Crete, from which the sons of the wealthy flocked to Italy, and in particular to the medical school at Padua, where they were joined in the 16th century by Phanariots whose commercial activities had by then brought considerable economic success.

When Jeremias II reorganized the Patriarchal Academy in 1593 the various departments, which included some sciences, were all headed by Padua-educated Phanariots, whose acquired contempt for Byzantine traditions and collaboration with the Ottoman government created permanent distrust and antipathy between them and Greeks elsewhere under Turkish rule. To the north further centres of Greek culture, though influenced by current western European trends, were established through the School of the Three Hierarchs at Jassy and the Bucharest Academy (founded in 1644 and 1679 respectively), which were made possible by the Phanariots' monopolization of the position of *hospodar* (prince) in Moldavia and Wallachia. After about 1750 the increasingly apparent decline of the Ottoman empire encouraged a revitalization of education among the Greeks, most dramatically shown by the astonishingly large number of books published (albeit mainly abroad). Intellectuals, most notably Adamantinos Korais, proclaimed that national consciousness entailed linguistic identity, a belief that engendered even an artificial language (katharevousa, literally "purifying") that rejected Turkish loan words and reverted to many Classical grammatical forms. Diglossia, which for the Byzantines had been purely cultural, was now, therefore, politicized (the Epirot Alexandros Pallis's demotic translation of the New Testament caused riots in the streets of Athens when it was published in 1901) and bedevilled education until the late 20th century. The peasantry, meanwhile, formed so many so-called "secret schools" for the preservation of both the culture and the language that at the outbreak of war in 1821 rudimentary literacy was fairly widespread.

For nearly a century and a half after independence was achieved few children advanced beyond elementary education, since the *gymnasia* (secondary schools), accessible only through examination, maintained rigorous academic standards with an emphasis upon arts subjects – and especially ancient Greek – and were primarily intended as preparatory to university. Eleftherios Venizelos (who in 1911 had made primary education free and compulsory) even reduced the number of *gymnasia* with a corresponding decrease of enrolment from 96,000 in 1928 to 57,000 in 1932. Moreover, instruction, until 1917 even in the elementary schools, was in the rarely spoken katharevousa rather than the *dimotiki* (demotic) of the majority of the population. All education was underfunded, highly centralized, and, partly through the influence of the Church, conservative.

The most important reforms of the late 1950s concerned the creation of both parallel technical-vocational schools and a separate and far less popular scientific stream for the fourth to sixth years of the *gymnasia*. Major reforms were made in 1964, largely at the initiative of the Minister of Education E.P. Papanoutsos, who had studied education (and philosophy) in Germany and France. Although these were swept away three years later by the military junta (which also purged atheist teachers and abolished corporal punishment in schools as "contrary to modern educational principles"), they were largely reintroduced at its demise in 1974. *Dimotiki* now became the medium of instruction at all levels, and three years' attendance at *gymnasia* (for a total of nine years of schooling) became compulsory, with ancient literature being taught only in modern translation. The final, optional, three years of secondary schooling involved two parallel streams at the General or Technical-Vocational *Lykeia*, of which only the former could lead to university, where education was now free. In 1981 the school week at both elementary and secondary levels was changed from six to five days, but with minimal diminution of hours. Subsequent reforms by socialist governments introduced greater democratization rather than structural changes. The OECD report of 1995 emphasized the need to dilute the rigid centralization of all educational policy-making.

In 1991 only 37.4 per cent of the population aged 25 and over had progressed past the elementary school level. Although total expenditure on public education was low at 3.7 per cent of GNP (1995), the student–teacher ratio at elementary schools dropped most encouragingly from 50:1 in 1955–56 to 24:1 in 1980–81 to 17:1 in 1993–94 with a large associated diminution in the number of single-teacher rural schools. In 1993–94 there were also 5588 non-compulsory pre-primary schools serving about 45 per cent of children aged between three and a half and five and a half.

The first modern tertiary-level educational institution on Greek soil was the Ionian Academy, opened under the British Protectorate at Corfu in 1824 (after an aborted attempt in Ithaca) largely through the instigation of Frederick North, 5th Earl of Guilford, who became its first chancellor (the earlier French Ionian Academy was a society of savants). It finally closed after a chequered history in 1864, having served mainland as well as Septinsular students. The oldest university established in independent Greece is the National and Capodistrian University in Athens, which from 1837 was the sole university in the country until the Aristotelian University of Thessalonica was opened in 1925. Since 1964, with one at Patras, small universities have been created elsewhere in Greece in addition to various other institutions of which some have university standing (in 1995 there were 18 universities, 12 technological educational institutions, and 61 higher professional schools).

Keen competition for places gave rise to numerous *phrontisteria* (expensive private tutorial schools), and still in the 1990s only one out of four applicants attained a place at university. Total enrolment at all institutions of tertiary education, however, increased from just over 120,000 in 1980–81 to nearly 300,000 in 1993–94, with almost half of 18-to-21-year-olds in some form of education, despite the labour market's inability to provide employment appropriate to qualifications. Efforts were made to combat the Greek predilection for arts subjects, which had surprised foreigners as early as the mid-19th century, by changing emphases at both secondary and tertiary levels. Nevertheless in 1993 there were still only 774 scientists and engineers and 314 technicians per million of the population, while Research and Experimental Development accounted for a mere 0.6 per cent of GNP.

A.R. LITTLEWOOD

See also Literacy, Rhetoric, Schools, Sophists

Further Reading

Barclay, William, *Educational Ideals in the Ancient World*, London: Collins, 1959
Beck, Frederick A.G., *Greek Education, 450–350 BC*, London: Methuen, and New York: Barnes and Noble, 1964
Beck, Frederick A.G., *Album of Greek Education: The Greeks at School and Play*, Sydney: Cheiron Press, 1975
Browning, Robert, *Studies on Byzantine History, Literature and Education*, London: Variorum, 1977
Buckler, G., "Byzantine Education" in *Byzantium: An Introduction to East Roman Civilization*, edited by Norman H. Baynes and H. St L.B. Moss, Oxford: Clarendon Press, 1948, pp. 200–20

Constantinides, C.N., *Higher Education in Byzantium in the Thirteenth and Early Fourteenth Centuries, 1204–c.1310*, Nicosia: Cyprus Research Centre, 1982

Euangelides, T.E., *I Paideia epi Tourkokratias: Ellinika Scholeia apo tis Aloseos mechri Kapodistriou* [Education in the Turkish Period: Greek Schools from the Conquest up to Kapodistria], 2 vols, Athens, 1936

Geanakoplos, Deno John, *Greek Scholars in Venice: Studies in the Dissemination of Greek Learning from Byzantium to Western Europe*, Cambridge, Massachusetts: Harvard University Press, 1962

Henderson, G.P., *The Ionian Academy*, Edinburgh: Scottish Academic Press, 1988

Hussey, J.M., *Church and Learning in the Byzantine Empire, 867–1185*, London: Oxford University Press, 1937

Jaeger, Werner, *Paideia : The Ideals of Greek Culture*, 3 vols, Oxford: Blackwell, 1954–61; reprinted Oxford and New York: Oxford University Press, 1986

Lemerle, Paul, *Byzantine Humanism: The First Phase*, translated by H. Lindsay and A. Moffatt, Canberra: Australian Association for Byzantine Studies, 1986, pp. 281–308

Marrou, Henri Irénée, *A History of Education in Antiquity*, translated by G. Lamb, London and New York: Sheed and Ward, 1956 (7th French edition, 1977)

Nilsson, Martin P., *Die hellenistische Schule*, Munich: Beck, 1955

Organization for Economic Co-operation and Development, *Reviews of National Policies for Education: Greece*, Paris: OECD, 1997

Runciman, Steven, *The Great Church in Captivity: A Study of the Patriarchate of Constantinople from the Eve of the Turkish Conquest to the Greek War of Independence*, London: Cambridge University Press, 1968, pp. 208–25

Unesco Statistical Yearbook, Paris: United Nations Educational, Scientific, and Cultural Organisation (annual publication)

Wilson, Nigel G., *From Byzantium to Italy: Greek Studies in the Italian Renaissance*, London: Duckworth, and Baltimore, Maryland: Johns Hopkins University Press, 1992

Egypt

It was from the time of the New Kingdom (1550–1069 BC) that contact between Greece and Egypt became established. By that time Egypt was already a land of great antiquity with a flourishing native civilization. Over the years the Greeks established trade and political links with Egypt. Parts of the country gradually became famous centres of Greek civilization, coexisting alongside the ongoing native culture.

After a period of internal political instability in the 7th century BC, Egypt was reunited and stabilized during the reign of the pharaoh Psammetichus I (664–610 BC). Needing economic resources to make of Egypt the great nation that once it was, he developed a large-scale policy of trade relations with the Greeks and with the Phoenicians in the Levant. One very important result was the foundation of the Greek colony of Naucratis in the Nile delta, some 80 km southeast of the later Greek city of Alexandria, on the Canopic (or Rosetta) branch of the Nile. Naucratis was an important town in antiquity, though very little of it remains today. Excavations there have produced important finds of closely datable Greek pottery. In the 6th century BC the pharaoh Amasis permitted the Naucratites to levy taxes on imports and exports from river traffic, thereby ensuring their prosperity, and the Greek historian Herodotus, who wrote about Egypt in his *Histories*, mentioned various Greek temples in the city. During the reign of Amasis, the Hellenion, a Greek shrine, was established at Naucratis jointly by Ionian, Dorian, and Aeolian Greeks from the Greek islands and Asia Minor. The most famous native of Naucratis was the Greek writer Athenaeus (*fl. c.* AD 200), the author of the *Deipnosophistai* (*The Learned Banquet*), a highly important work relating supposed conversations at a fictional banquet lasting several days. It contains a wealth of antiquarian information and excerpts from a vast number of earlier, largely disappeared Greek texts. Greeks from all over the Greek world also came to live elsewhere in Egypt at this early period, many enrolling as mercenaries in the pharaonic armies.

Egypt was conquered by the Persian great king Cambyses in 526/25 BC and, though there were periods of revolt and independence, it remained an uneasy, far-flung province of the Persian empire (as such becoming a theatre of minor operations in the Peloponnesian War when Persia became involved in this Greek conflict) until the arrival of Alexander the Great in 332 BC. Alexander invaded and conquered Egypt in the course of his campaign to subdue the Persian empire. He was welcomed as an alternative to the hated Persian rule. Either before or after his legendary trip to the Siwa oasis in the Western Desert, where he visited the oracle of Ammon and allegedly sought recognition as the god's son, Alexander founded his first city named "Alexandreia", on the Mediterranean coast on the western branch of the Nile delta. It is at this point that we can meaningfully begin to speak of a Greek Egypt, although Alexander did not live to return there.

After Alexander's death in Babylon in 323 BC and the subsequent division of his empire, the satrapy (province) of Egypt came under the control of his Macedonian boyhood friend and later general, Ptolemy, son of Lagus. Ptolemy diverted the funeral cortege of Alexander (en route to Macedonia) to Egypt, burying the coffin first at the old dynastic capital Memphis (south of Cairo) and then in a magnificent tomb in Alexandria which later became the burial place of the Ptolemaic kings and the focus of their ruler cult. The site of the tomb has not been discovered.

Alexandria had functioned as a Greek city from soon after its foundation and, after Ptolemy declared himself king of Egypt in 305/04 BC, became the glittering capital of the Hellenistic empire, called Ptolemaic after his name. Over time Alexandria replaced Athens as the greatest city of Greek culture. The city was endowed with splendid buildings aligned on a grid system with wide thoroughfares, and it was proverbially wealthy in the works of contemporary authors. The Ptolemies actively encouraged Greek immigrants to Egypt. Many were merchants lured by the economic prospects of Alexandria (which soon became a great trading centre); others were professional soldiers given ownership of allotments of land (known as cleruchic land) throughout Egypt in return for their military service. The early Ptolemies actively fostered the development of the famous library of Alexandria, to which we can credit the preservation, copying, and transmission of much ancient Greek literature, and the Mouseion (literally "the shrine of the Muses"), a residential study centre for scholars which acted as a magnet for the greatest Greek writers and thinkers of the day.

Egypt: bronze head of queen Arsinoe III, sister and wife of Ptolemy IV, late 3rd century BC, Antiquarium Gallery, New York

Greek cities, many with Ptolemaic dynastic names such as Ptolemais, or Greek theophoric names such as Apollinopolis, grew up throughout Egypt. Important collections of Greek documents written on papyri (a writing material made from joined strips of the papyrus plant, native to Egypt and used for native Egyptian hieroglyphic writing for millennia) attest to a vibrant Greek lifestyle in many provincial areas of Egypt. The desert environment of much of Egypt is ideal for the preservation of papyrus, although little remains from the city of Alexandria or the rest of the Nile delta because of its comparatively moister climate. The Zenon, Tebtunis, and Oxyrhynchus collections of papyri, to name but a very few, have greatly increased our knowledge about the Greek way of life in Ptolemaic Egypt, and the interaction between Greeks and Egyptians, a very important subject for the question of the Hellenization of Egypt. Occasionally the papyri contain political insights, and fragments of hitherto lost Greek literature, most notably large sections of the plays of the 4th-century BC Greek comic poet Menander of Athens (which attests to his considerable popularity in Egypt). There are also private letters, wills, contracts, marriage agreements, and financial accounts, written both in Greek and in the native language known as demotic, with the result that we know much more about the private lives of the Greeks living in Ptolemaic Egypt than we do about Greeks elsewhere in the Hellenistic empires. It appears that the Greeks remained largely Greek, although many native Egyptians tried to assimilate themselves by learning the Greek language, and adopting the veneer of a Greek

way of life in order to ascend the social and professional ladder. Archaeology shows that Egyptian decorative motifs were adopted by Greeks living in Egypt from early on, but these tended to be grafted on to identifiable Greek structures. The current excavations in the harbour of Alexandria may well extend our knowledge in this area.

Ptolemaic Egypt grew into arguably the most powerful of the Hellenistic empires in the 3rd century BC. At that period it was characterized by good kings and relatively stable government, and the development of the most powerful ancient navy of all time under Ptolemy II Philadelphus (ruled 285–246 BC) meant that Ptolemaic Egypt became a major player on the Mediterranean stage. Its navy took on the protection of the Greek islands against the scourge of pirates in the Aegean (attested through honorary inscriptions at Delos and elsewhere). Egypt also established hegemony over Cyrenaica (which had been colonized by the Greeks since the 7th century BC) and Cyprus, and developed a flourishing commercial relationship with the independent Greek island of Rhodes. Military outposts were established in several places, and Egypt was always an active observer of, if not always an active participator in, political events in Greece and Asia Minor. There is evidence of some involvement against the Macedonian Antigonid kingdom in mainland Greece, and several wars were fought in the 3rd and 2nd centuries BC against the Seleucid empire of Syria over the area known as Koile ("Hollow") Syria, roughly the area we consider as the Levant, or Middle East.

Greek relations with Upper Egypt (the area known as Nubia) were not always happy, and native revolts and even temporary secession are attested at the end of the 3rd century BC. Perhaps as a means towards internal cohesion, the Greek kings allowed, or possibly ordered, themselves to be depicted in Egyptian garb in statues and temple reliefs for native consumption, many examples of which exist today. Several took pains to foster the ancient native religion of Egypt and generously endowed various non-Greek cults and temples, such as those of the Apis bulls at Saqqara, near the old dynastic capital Memphis. During the Ptolemaic period, huge temples very much in native style were built at Kom Ombo (Ombos in Greek), Edfu (Apollinopolis Magna), and Dendera (Tentyra), and Ptolemy V had a coronation ceremony in which he was crowned pharaoh, a fact to which the famous Rosetta Stone refers. Ptolemy I is usually credited with the creation of the hybrid cult of the Graeco-Egyptian god Sarapis, perhaps intended to appeal to both nationalities, who was worshipped at important shrines at Memphis and Alexandria. Still, it appears that the Greek kings remained very much Greek in their upbringing, outlook, and personal behaviour, and the ancient evidence attests that the last Ptolemaic ruler, Cleopatra VII, was the first monarch to speak native Egyptian. From the time of Ptolemy II, the kings with a few exceptions (i.e. marriages to politically useful Greek princesses from other Hellenistic empires) practised brother–sister marriage, and this remained the norm until the end of the dynasty. As a result, the family line remained Greek, despite occasional evidence of adulterous liaisons.

In common with the other Greek empires of the east, the Ptolemaic dynasty could not ignore the growing might of Rome, which from the 2nd century BC onwards gradually incorporated the Hellenistic kingdoms into its own territory. Roman power was invoked on one or other side of disputing Ptolemies, and by the beginning of the 1st century BC the Greek throne of Egypt was secure only through the intervention of Rome. After her famous liaisons with Julius Caesar and Mark Antony, and the defeat of her forces and Antony's by Octavian (later to be Augustus, the first emperor of Rome), Cleopatra committed suicide in 30 BC and the Ptolemaic dynasty ended. Her sons by both Romans were soon killed. Egypt passed into the possession of Rome and soon became the personal property of the Roman emperor of the day, governed for him by an equestrian prefect.

The Greek population of Egypt, however, remained and carried on with their lives much as they had always done, with the exception that there was now a foreign overlord. But Greek language and administrative procedures were retained for another 300 years. The flourishing economy created by the Ptolemies over centuries meant that Egypt's prosperity was a jewel in Rome's crown, and the huge grain ships which sailed from Egypt every year were a vital source of food for the Roman people. Alexandria grew into one of the largest cities of the Roman empire, and continued the tradition of Greek scholarship (both pagan and Christian) championed by it since the 3rd century BC. At the end of the 3rd century AD Egypt passed into the control of the Greek Byzantine empire based in Constantinople, but it was too far away from the political centre for much effective involvement on the part of the imperial government. In AD 642 Egypt was conquered by the Arabs who were gradually eroding the fringes of the Byzantine empire, but still Greeks continued to live there under yet another foreign ruler. There were large communities of Greeks in Cairo and Alexandria well into the 20th century, who contributed greatly to the commercial success of Egypt, and who, in common with other resident foreign enclaves, created the cosmopolitan and exotic mixture of peoples and atmosphere which characterized these cities. During World War II and against the backdrop of severe political turmoil in Greece, king George II of the Hellenes and the Greek royal family were forced to flee Greece, and established their court in Cairo for five years (1941–46).

E.E. RICE

See also Africa, Ptolemies

Further Reading

Astin, A.E. et al. (editors), Rome and the Mediterranean to 133 BC, Cambridge: Cambridge University Press, 1989 (The Cambridge Ancient History, vol. 8, 2nd edition)
Bell, H. Idris, Egypt from Alexander the Great to the Arab Conquest: A Study in the Diffusion and Decay of Hellenism, Oxford: Clarendon Press, 1948
Bevan, Edwyn R., A History of Egypt under the Ptolemaic Dynasty, London: Methuen, 1927; as The House of Ptolemy: A History of Egypt under the Ptolemaic Dynasty, Chicago: Argonaut, 1968
Bilde, Per et al., Ethnicity in Hellenistic Egypt, Aarhus: Aarhus University Press, 1992
Bowman, Alan K., Egypt after the Pharaohs 332 BC–AD 642: From Alexander to the Arab Conquest, Berkeley: University of California Press, and London: British Museum, 1986
Bowman, Alan K., Edward Champlin and Andrew Lintott (editors), The Augustan Empire, 43 BC–AD 89, Cambridge: Cambridge

University Press, 1996 (The Cambridge Ancient History, vol. 10, 2nd edition)
Butler, Alfred J., The Arab Conquest of Egypt and the Last Thirty Years of Roman Dominion, 2nd edition, edited by P.M. Fraser, Oxford: Clarendon Press, 1978
Cary, M., A History of the Greek World from 323–146 BC, 2nd edition, London: Methuen, 1972
Fraser, P.M., Ptolemaic Alexandria, 3 vols, Oxford: Clarendon Press, 1972
Goudriaan, Koen, Ethnicity in Ptolemaic Egypt, Amsterdam: Gieben, 1988
Gruen, Erich S., The Hellenistic World and the Coming of Rome, Berkeley: University of California Press, 1984
Lewis, Naphtali, The Greeks in Ptolemaic Egypt: Case Studies in the Social History of the Hellenistic World, Oxford: Clarendon Press, and New York: Oxford University Press, 1986
Pollitt, J.J., Art in the Hellenistic Age, Cambridge and New York: Cambridge University Press, 1986
Pomeroy, Sarah B., Women in Hellenistic Egypt: From Alexander to Cleopatra, New York: Schocken, 1984; revised edition, Detroit: Wayne State University Press, 1990
Rodenbeck, Max, Cairo: The City Victorious, London: Picador, 1998
Rostovtzeff, M.I., A Large Estate in Egypt in the Third Century BC: A Study in Economic History, Madison, University of Wisconsin Press, 1922
Rostovtzeff, M.I., The Social and Economic History of the Hellenistic World, 3 vols., Oxford: Clarendon Press, 1941
Samuel, Alan E., The Shifting Sands of History: Interpretations of Ptolemaic Egypt, Lanham, Maryland: University Press of America, 1989
Seton-Williams, Veronica and Peter Stocks, Egypt, 2nd edition, London: A. & C. Black, 1988 (Blue Guide series)
Smith, R.R.R., Hellenistic Sculpture: A Handbook, London and New York: Thames and Hudson, 1991
Tarn, W.W. and G.T. Griffith, Hellenistic Civilization, 3rd edition, London: Arnold, 1952
Thompson, Dorothy J., Memphis under the Ptolemies, Princeton, New Jersey: Princeton University Press, 1988
Walbank, F.W. et al. (editors), The Hellenistic World, Cambridge: Cambridge University Press, 1984 (The Cambridge Ancient History, vol. 7, part 1, 2nd edition)
Walbank, F.W., The Hellenistic World, revised edition, London: Fontana, and Cambridge, Massachusetts: Harvard University Press, 1992
Winter, John Garrett, Life and Letters in the Papyri, Ann Arbor: University of Michigan Press, 1933

Eleusis

City in Attica

The most important town in ancient Attica after Athens and the Piraeus, Eleusis is located 24 km northwest of Athens on a landlocked bay and at the head of the fertile Thriasian plain, in antiquity the region's main wheat and barley grain producer. In Greek mythology the Thriasian plain was the first to be sown with seed and to yield crops. Eleusis was strategically placed, as it lay opposite the island of Salamis and at the junction of the trade routes from Attica, central Greece, and the Peloponnese. Eleusis, Panacton, and Phyle served as border forts for the western defence of Attica.

The site dates back to at least the Early Bronze Age. Current excavations have revealed on the west slope of the acropolis a small deposit of Early Bronze Age remains, Middle Bronze Age

Eleusis: looking south over the Telesterion or Hall of Mysteries, the large square building in the foreground, with the island of Salamis in the distance

house walls, and Late Bronze Age walls; in the 15th century BC a porched hall (megaron) was built on the site of the Hall of Mysteries, the main cult site of the ancient city. The relationship between Athens and Eleusis during the prehistoric period is not clear, although Athenian legends speak of wars between Athens and Eleusis during the Late Bronze Age, until Theseus unified Eleusis and 11 other Attic towns under the hegemony of Athens. All that can be said with certainty is that, on the basis of archaeological and historical evidence, Eleusis was subject to Athens at least as early as the 8th century BC. In subsequent centuries Eleusis grew ever greater in size and importance, thanks to its Panhellenic Mysteries of Demeter and Persephone. Eleusis was devastated in 480/79 BC by the Persians (whose breach of the walls is still evident), but was almost immediately rebuilt by the Athenians. The city enjoyed prosperity throughout the Classical and Hellenistic periods. Later on, Roman aristocrats and emperors like Hadrian built up the sanctuary. After the Sarmatian Costobocs invaded and sacked the city in AD 170, the emperor Marcus Aurelius restored the site upon his initiation (in 176 he had become the only lay person to enter the "Holy of Holies" in the sacred Hall of Mysteries). Eleusis suffered irreparable damage at the end of the 4th century: in 391 Theodosius I proscribed all pagan cults, including the Eleusinian Mysteries, and then four years later the Visigothic army of Alaric destroyed the site. Eleusis was the victim of further attacks, but this time at the

hands of Christians, and was deserted in the Byzantine era, remaining so until the 18th century. Modern Eleusis is an industrial city of cement, chemical, and steel factories. The bay is home to shipbuilding, oil tankers, ship repair docks, and a naval training academy. Pollution is heavy, the traffic unbearable, and many refineries and factories are in need of modernization.

Eleusis's fame rested on the Mysteries of Demeter and Persephone, the most renowned and important of Greek mystery cults. According to the ancients, the rites were established in the 15th century BC; however, there is no firm archaeological evidence for Late Bronze Age cult activity. It is clear, though, that the rites were known throughout Greece by the time of the *Homeric Hymn to Demeter* (650–550 BC), according to which the mysteries were established to celebrate the return of Persephone to her mother Demeter, the goddess of grain. According to the legend, Persephone was raped by Hades and carried off to his underworld realm. In her grief Demeter wandered the earth, searching for her daughter. She came to rest at Eleusis, where she befriended the king and promised to teach the Eleusinians her rites and mysteries. Demeter refused to allow crops to grow until Persephone was released, and so humankind was brought to the brink of starvation and sacrifices to the gods were in danger of ceasing. Hades yielded to the entreaties of Zeus and released Persephone who, however, since she had eaten food (a pomegranate seed) in the underworld, could not be fully restored to the upper world. Thus, although Persephone could spend eight months a year with her mother, she was compelled to spend the rest of the year in the underworld. This arrangement explains the growing cycle: during the reunion of mother and daughter, crops grow and lush vegetation spreads throughout the world, but on Persephone's return to Hades, the growing season comes to an end.

The *Homeric Hymn to Demeter* states that, after Persephone was first returned to her mother, Demeter revealed her mysteries to the leading citizens of Eleusis. Many of the sacred rites that form the essence of the Eleusinian Mysteries are not known, as disclosure of the rites was punishable by death; for a millennium and more that secrecy was preserved. (The great tragic poet Aeschylus, a native of Eleusis, was nearly lynched by an angry mob because the audience at one of his plays thought he had revealed some of the rites, while the famous Athenian general Alcibiades was condemned to death, in absentia, for conducting a parody of the mysteries.) What transpired in the mysteries may be reconstructed as follows. The cult was run by the city of Athens, although two families from Eleusis, the Eumolpidae and Ceryces, controlled the priesthood. Candidates for initiation (*mystai*) came to Athens in the early spring for the ritual called the Lesser Mysteries, the purpose of which was to prepare the candidates for initiation into the Greater Mysteries. Anyone who could speak Greek and was free of blood-guilt was eligible; the inclusion, in a Greek cult, of women, slaves, and Greek-speaking foreigners was remarkable. The *mystai* returned to Athens for the Greater Mysteries, a nine-day festival in the month of Boedromion (September/October). After six days of purification, washing, fasting, and sacrifices, a procession of priests and *mystai* left Athens for Eleusis via the Sacred Way. Stopping frequently for sacrifices, dancing, and singing, the procession arrived at night at the sanctuary. (A 35-m stretch of the Sacred Way has been unearthed near the 2nd-century AD bridge over the Cephisus river outside the city.) That night in the Hall of Mysteries the *mystai*, about 2000–3000 strong, were initiated into the mysteries and became *epoptai* ("those who have seen"). The ritual probably included a sacred meal, the revealing of the sacred objects of the cult, a re-enactment of the story of Demeter and Persephone, and dancing and sacrifices. Ancient sources relate that the *epoptai* were guaranteed a better life on earth and the promise of an afterlife. *Epoptai* could participate in the ritual as many times as they wished, and many did because of the intensely emotional spiritual experience. The personal communion with a deity, the promise of immortality, and the intensity of a shared bond with other worshippers made the mysteries a sharp contrast to state cults. The mysteries fulfilled spiritual yearnings in ways that mythology, legends, and official cults could not.

The archaeological remains at Eleusis are connected for the most part with the mysteries. The entire site is enclosed by magnificent fortifications from the Archaic to late Classical periods; the west wall, with its round and square towers, is perhaps the finest example of 4th-century BC fortification. The sacred precinct, lying on the south slope of the acropolis, was entered through two propylaeas: the Greater Propylaea, built by Marcus Aurelius in imitation of the Propylaea on the Athenian Acropolis, and the Lesser Propylaea, erected in the mid-1st century BC by the Roman aristocrat Appius Claudius Pulcher and his two nephews. Just inside the sanctuary, to the immediate right, is a cave with a small 4th-century BC temple dedicated to Hades; the cave was believed to be the entrance to the underworld. Just to the west is the Temple of Demeter or the Hall of Mysteries (Telesterion). A megaron from the Mycenaean age was built here, but it may not have had any cultic significance. The Telesterion had ten different building phases. In its final phase the hall was 56 m ¥ 66 m, with eight tiers of seats on each side. Forty-two columns supported the wooden roof. In the centre was the *anaktoron* ("Holy of Holies"), which contained the cult's sacred objects, and the high priest's chair. Except for the doors on three sides, the walls were solid, creating a dark, mysterious atmosphere. To the west of the Telesterion are remains of the council house, a 7th-century BC hero shrine, a Roman cult building dedicated to the sun god Mithras, and a gymnasium. On the acropolis are remains from the Bronze Age and the Hellenistic period. Immense Roman bath complexes have been found around the sacred precinct and in the modern town. To the south of the ancient site are a stadium and theatre; these should be understood in connection with the Eleusinia, which were games held every fourth year (that is the third year of the four-year cycle of the Olympiad) and to a lesser extent two years later. For Athenians, the Eleusinia ranked behind only the Panathenaic games in prestige.

Eleusis may have lost its importance after its destruction in the 5th century AD, but the mysteries and the *Homeric Hymn to Demeter* continued to exert influence. The rape of Persephone proved popular in literature, and the legend and the Mysteries have attracted scholars in such fields as psychoanalysis, religion, feminism, gender studies, folklore, comparative mythology, and sociology. Moreover, the mysteries, with their promise of an afterlife and intense intense emotional transformative experience, tapped into the spiritual cravings of the ancient Greeks and Romans, and so paved the way for religions like Christianity and Mithraism.

STEVEN M. OBERHELMAN

See also Afterlife

Summary

City in Attica, 24 km northwest of Athens, Eleusis was strategically sited at the junction of trade routes from the Peloponnese, central Greece, and Attica. There are remains from the Early Bronze Age but no evidence of cult activity from that time. Eleusis is famous for the mystery cult of Demeter and Persephone which was well known by the Archaic period and attracted initiates from all over Greece. The cult was proscribed by Theodosius I in AD 391.

Further Reading

Burkert, Walter, *Ancient Mystery Cults*, Cambridge, Massachusetts: Harvard University Press, 1987

Cosmopoulos, Michael B., "The University of Manitoba Excavation at Eleusis: An Interim Report", *Classical Views*, 35 (1995): pp. 75–94

Foley, Helene P. (editor), *The Homeric Hymn to Demeter: Translation, Commentary, and Interpretive Essays*, Princeton, New Jersey: Princeton University Press, 1994

Kourouniotes, Konstantinos, *Eleusis: A Guide to the Excavations and the Museum*, Athens: Hestia, 1936

Mylonas, George E., *The Hymn to Demeter and Her Sanctuary at Eleusis*, St Louis: Washington University Studies in Language and Literature, 1942

Mylonas, George E., *Eleusis and the Eleusinian Mysteries*, Princeton, New Jersey: Princeton University Press, 1961

Osborne, R., "A Crisis in Archaeological History? The Seventh Century in Attica", *Annual of the British School at Athens*, 84 (1989): pp. 297–322

Parker, R., "The *Hymn to Demeter* and the Homeric Poems", *Greece and Rome*, 38 (1991): pp. 1–17

Richardson, N.J. (editor), *The Homeric Hymn to Demeter*, Oxford: Clarendon Press, 1974

Travlos, John, "The Topography of Eleusis", *Hesperia*, 18 (1949): pp. 138–47

Travlos, John, "Eleusis: The Origin of the Sanctuary" in *Temples and Sanctuaries of Ancient Greece: A Companion Guide*, edited by Evi Melas, London: Thames and Hudson, 1973, pp. 75–87

Elytis, Odysseus 1911–1996

Poet

Odysseus Elytis was born in Crete of parents from Lesbos. He published his first poems in 1935 and established himself as one of the leading figures in the "1930s Generation", which also included Greece's other Nobel laureate, George Seferis. He travelled widely and, after World War II, lived in France for long periods, associating with leading poets and artists of his generation. He published 17 collections of poetry, a number of translations from ancient Greek and modern European poets, and two large volumes of prose writings. He was also an accomplished artist. In 1979 he was awarded the Nobel Prize for Literature.

Elytis began his poetic career clearly influenced by French Surrealism, and by Éluard in particular. Less emphasized by critics is the influence in his later works of the German Romantics, notably Hölderlin. However, he was always keen to emphasize his link with what he considered to be the genuine Greek tradition, in which he included poets such as Homer, Pindar, Sappho, the ancient lyric poets, Romanus the Melodist, Dionysios Solomos, and Andreas Kalvos.

It is indicative that he translated Sappho and Crinagoras (both poets from his native isle of Lesbos), and referred to Sappho as "a distant cousin", in the sense that they both worked with the same concepts and words. Similarly, he wrote extensive studies of Romanos and Kalvos, and often expressed his adulation for Solomos, whom he referred to as "one of the greatest lyric poets throughout the world and throughout the ages". And elsewhere, he spoke of his debt to Solomos, the poet who, together with Hölderlin, followed Elytis "with a watchful eye". Less obvious, though equally genuine debts are due to the ancient philosophers Heraclitus, Plato, and Plotinus. Elytis referred to them regularly in both his poetic and his prose works. Many of Elytis's poetic utterances, particularly in his later works, could be almost "presocratic" in their obscurity and polysemy, and the assertion by Georgousopoulos that "Elytis descends directly from the presocratic logos" is certainly justifiable.

In his address to the Swedish Academy on receiving the Nobel Prize in 1979, Elytis set out his views on the Greek poetic tradition. He stressed that he wrote in a language that is spoken by only a few million people, yet one that has been spoken for two and a half thousand years without interruption and with a minimum of changes. He went on to point out the difficulties that a poet faces when he uses for the things most dear to him the same words used, for example, by Sappho or Pindar – without, however, his having the same impact that they had throughout the then civilized world. It must not be forgotten, he said, that over a span of 25 centuries there was not one century when poetry was not written in Greek and that every Greek poet has to face the great weight of tradition borne by the Greek language.

Elytis maintained that the sphere formed by modern Greek poetry has, like every sphere, two poles. At one end he placed Solomos, who, he believed, from the point of view of expressiveness, succeeded – before the appearance of Mallarmé in European letters – in formulating with complete consistency and rigour the idea of a *poésie pure* with all its consequences: subjugating sentiment to intellect, refining expression, and making full use of the instrument of language in moving towards the miracle. At the other pole he placed Constantine Cavafy, who, like T.S. Eliot, had arrived at extreme economy of expression, at the greatest possible precision, eliminating all form of turgidity in the expression of his personal experiences. Between these two poles, some nearer to one, some nearer to the other, he placed other major Greek poets: Andreas Kalvos, Kostis Palamas, Angelos Sikelianos, Nikos Kazantzakis, and George Seferis. This schematic representation of Greek poetry is important as it provides an insight into how Elytis saw the Greek poetic tradition and his place in it.

He elaborated on this even further in his essay entitled *Romanos O Melodos* (Romanus the Melodist), in which he distinguished and contrasted two types of poetry which he termed "prismatic" and "plane". The terms are novel, as is the classification of Greek poetry that is put forward. What is of concern is not the question of the objective validity of this distinction, but its importance for understanding Elytis's poetics. The features of these two types of poetry may be summarized as follows. In prismatic poetry, words are never on the same plane but *undulate*. The poetic text is organized around certain "nuclei" which stand out like peaks within the poem and which, in retrospect, can be seen to hold the poem together. These "nuclei" are not necessarily images, but are rather phrasal units with a self-generating radiance, in which the combination of the word's image and sound coincides with the cognitive meaning to such a degree that it is impossible to decide whether the poetic effect comes from *what* the poet says or the *way* he says it. The repetition of this feature gives a prismatic form to the poetic expression. Poems containing this feature affect the reader not only as a whole, but also in their parts, precisely because of these peaks, these concentrated and laconic crystallizations of the poetic spirit. They are utterances, Elytis maintained, in which the cast of the language and the images produced are fused and in which the formulation of a truth gives rise to another perception of the world as apprehended through the imagination. The test of this type of poetry is to imagine that 90 per cent of the poetic text has been lost and to examine whether the fragments that remain still function as poetry. Here, he cited the case of Sappho. Prismatic poetry, according to Elytis, is that feature which characterizes

Odysseus Elytis, poet and Nobel laureate

the true Greek poetic tradition, and is a feature of Homer, Pindar, Sappho, and the ancient lyric poets, Romanos, Kalvos, and, by inference, Elytis himself.

Plane poetry, on the other hand, is characterized by a flat, linear form of expression. It is narrative in style and has a poetic value not in its parts but only when taken as a whole. If such poetry is fragmented, all that remains is "plain statements". As exponents of this kind of poetry, he mentions Seferis and Cavafy. He attributed the appearance of this kind of poetry in the Greek (prismatic) tradition to the excesses of the other kind and to the influence of foreign, particularly Anglo-Saxon, poetry. Elytis did not reject this poetry but considered it as being outside the true Greek tradition. Without explicitly saying so, Elytis makes it clear that he favoured the tradition of prismatic poetry, his description of which corresponds entirely to the features of his own poetry. As one critic rightly remarked: "In this contrast [between prismatic and plane poetry], we find the clearest expression of his own poetics."

His views concerning a particular poetic mode of expression are, of course, linked with his views as to the deeper function of poetry. Poetry, for Elytis, was not a pastime but a mission. It "rises up at the point where rationalism lays down its arms for poetry to take them up and advance into the forbidden zone". And it is perhaps not without significance that here too he took issue with the Western conception of poetry, just as he did with Anglo-Saxon poetry in terms of poetic expression. He understood poetry as having come about "to correct God's mistakes; or, if not, then to show how mistakenly we perceive His gift" and he asserted that the pile of materials that consti-

tute this world could, with a different method of assembly, dictated by our sentiments, produce a more inhabitable dwelling. Yet, in trying through poetry to reassemble the elements of the world, to make a Heaven out of a Hell, "we came up", he says, "against an unbreachable wall: the Western perception of art, that because of its inability to move on a mythical level, has come to confine itself to observation and analysis, transferring the area of a poem from a nucleus of mysterious radiances to a simple melancholic confessional".

It can be seen from the above that Elytis set himself firmly within the Greek poetic tradition (as he defined it) and outside the 20th-century Anglo-Saxon tradition, which may partly explain the relative lack of acceptance of his work in the English-speaking world, at least in comparison with Cavafy and Seferis.

DAVID CONNOLLY

Biography

Born in 1911 in Crete of parents from Lesbos, Elytis published his first poems in 1935 and established himself as one of the leading figures in the "Generation of the 1930s", which also included Greece's other Nobel laureate, George Seferis. He travelled widely and, during the postwar years, lived in France for long periods. He published 17 collections of poetry, a number of translations from ancient Greek and modern European poets, and two large volumes of prose writings. In 1979 he was awarded the Nobel Prize for Literature. He died in 1996.

Writings

The Sovereign Sun: Selected Poems, translated by Kimon Friar, Philadelphia: Temple University Press, 1974; Newcastle-upon-Tyne: Bloodaxe, 1990

Selected Poems, translated by Edmund Keeley, Philip Sherrard, George Savidis, John Stathatos and Nanos Valaoritis, New York: Viking, and London: Anvil Press, 1981

Open Papers, translated by Olga Broumas and T. Begley, Port Townsend, Washington: Copper Canyon Press, 1995

The Oxopetra Elegies (bilingual edition), translated by David Connolly, Amsterdam: Harwood, 1996

The Collected Poems, translated by Jeffrey Carson and Nikos Sarris, Baltimore: Johns Hopkins University Press, 1997

Carte Blanche: Selected Writings, translated by David Connolly, Amsterdam: Harwood, 1999

Further Reading

Connolly, David, "Odysseus Elytis: Obscure Verbs and Metalingual Poetry" in *Greek Modernism and Beyond: Essays in Honour of Peter Bien*, edited by Dimitris Tziovas, Lanham, Maryland: Rowman and Littlefield, 1997

Elytis, Odysseus, "Odysseus Elytis on His Poetry: From an Interview with Ivar Ivask" in *Books Abroad*, 49/4 (1975): pp. 631–43

Emigration

Emigration is the act of moving from one country or region to another as a place of abode. The very making of Greece was the result of emigration of Greek-speaking tribes from the north into the Greek peninsula during the Bronze Age. In the centuries between the penetration and diffusion of the Greek-speaking tribes into the Greek peninsula and its conquest by the Romans, emigration was practised as an answer to various kinds of problems: war, famine, demographic pressure, poor standard of living. Emigration, constantly present in ancient Greek society, is a complex phenomenon addressing in different sociohistorical circumstances different needs. This article covers the great migratory movements of ancient Greek history through to the emigrations of Greeks in medieval and modern times.

The first extensive emigration took place between 1125 and 800 BC. There occurred three types of emigration during this period: (a) of Greeks who had previously settled in mountainous parts of the mainland and whose development lagged considerably in comparison to the tribes who participated in the Mycenaean civilization; once the decline of the Mycenaeans set in, these mountainous Greek tribes moved to the sites of the Mycenaean acme; (b) of refugees created by the first type of migratory movement; and (c) of early colonization of the east Aegean.

During the Archaic and Classical periods emigration was almost exclusively conducted by poor citizens of the city states. The majority of peasants owned small plots of land which were often insufficient for their sustenance. The situation was aggravated by inheritence rules, which prescribed the equal distribution of land among all male heirs, and which led to considerable land fragmentation. In addition, within the city states mechanisms of wealth transfer from the peasants to the city were also at play. In such a situation poor citizens often emigrated in search of a better life.

The character of emigration was profoundly changed in the time of Macedonian splendour. The annexation of territory in Egypt and Asia Minor by Alexander the Great gave rise to extensive emigration to these new lands. All through the 4th century BC large numbers of emigrants were drawn to the east in the hope of a career in the administration or the army, or even in the hope of acquiring land. As it was required of administrators and various officials to master the Greek language, the annexed territories offered great opportunities for career advancement to those Greeks who emigrated there.

In Byzantine times wars and the search for resources were the major causes of emigration. Invasions by enemy troops created a climate of instability in the countryside leading whole families to emigrate to areas or cities considered safe. Towards the end of the 6th century AD, when the northern borders of the empire collapsed, there was an emigration wave westwards to the Ionian islands and Italy. Although emigration was usually practised by the most needy members of the population, the economic pressures exercised on peasant households forced even wealthy peasants to emigrate. A different kind of emigration emerged just before the fall of the Byzantine empire. After the defeat of the crusaders at Nicopolis in 1396 many intellectuals fled west to Italy and north to the states of the Dunav. Here Greek emigrants formed sizeable communities which later played an important role in the formation and development of the Greek nation.

Emigration was not halted by the Ottoman conquest of the Byzantine empire. On the contrary, the hardship of Ottoman rule often forced Christians to emigrate. Thus, by the 17th and 18th centuries Greeks had formed dispersed communities in the Mediterranean countries – especially Romania, Russia, and Egypt. The Greeks who emigrated during this period were predominantly peasants who moved from small villages to urban centres of central Europe and Egypt, and from agriculture to trade and services. The transition from peasant status to city-based occupations was viewed as a step up the social ladder. This upward social mobility was desirable not only to the emigrant as an individual, but also to his family in Greece, as the family of origin gained both materially and in prestige by the emigrant's new elevated status. In this sense, emigration during the 17th and 18th centuries was largely part of a family policy which aimed at individual and family upward social mobility.

The wave of Greek emigration to the cities of central Europe was halted by the weakening of the Ottoman empire and the Greek War of Independence in the 19th century. Equally important was the rise of nationalism in the young Balkan states and the formation of a local middle and enterpreneurial class; as a result, outsiders, such as Greek emigrants, were excluded from these positions in the social and economic hierarchy.

Shortly after the establishment of the Greek nation state in 1830 there was a new emigration wave. The economy of Greece was largely based on agriculture, the structural problems of which were clearly felt very soon after the establishment of the state. The typical small-scale independent agricultural holding which resulted from the distribution of lands formerly belonging to Turks proved devoid of potential for further development and unable to sustain the growing village population. The beginning of the 20th century saw a demographic boom in the Greek countryside. At the same time, inheritance rules precluded the accumulation of land; on the contrary, they led to its further fragmentation, thus posing serious obstacles to the development of the rural economy. This provided the basis for the ensuing manpower surplus in Greek villages and the underemployment of Greek peasants. Under these conditions emigration emerged as a means not for social mobility, but for securing employment.

The rapid development of capitalism in the USA in the early 20th century, and the need created there for working hands to support the industrialization of the country, attracted the first big emigration wave from the young Greek nation state: from 1900 to 1920 over 400,000 Greeks emigrated, most to the USA and Australia. The numbers of Greek emigrants directed to other countries of reception, such as Brazil or Canada, were insignificant. Most of these emigrants were men of working age, between 19 and 45 years of age.

Once the link with the USA was established, Greek emigrants formed networks of reception for newcomers from Greece. This allowed new emigrants to organize better their transition to the country of reception. Furthermore, the existence of these networks of relations and the accumulated knowledge of the society and its market enabled Greeks in the USA to move from manual work to the sector of services and trade.

The emigration wave towards the USA was seriously halted after 1922 for a number of reasons. In the USA the Act on "quotas", which was passed in 1922, posed limitations on the number of emigrants accepted from each country of origin. It was, therefore, only possible for a certain number of Greeks to emigrate to the USA. At the same time, the situation created in Greece by the annexation of new territories, the process of urbanization, and the attraction exercised by the new urban centres within the country created hopes in Greeks that they could attain a better standard of living within their own country.

The promise of development, however, was not carried out and, in the aftermath of the two successive wars – World War II and the subsequent Greek Civil War – Greece was faced with extensive poverty. The problems of Greece as a dependent country on the periphery of Europe became more pronounced after the wars as investment in the productive sectors of the economy was minimal. In the cities unemployment grew, while the rural sector remained stagnant. Agricultural holdings were to a great extent maintained through money transfers from abroad. The problems associated with land fragmentation and the low mechanization of agriculture continued and were aggravated by state policies which often proved a hindrance to agricultural development. Low productivity and the underemployment of peasants resulted in stagnation in rural Greece and, in turn, drove large numbers of peasants to migration, internal and abroad. Added to the above was the climate of insecurity in postwar Greece, characterized by political instability and the persecution of left-wing citizens, which, again, drove people out of the villages and to the cities of Greece and Europe. The late 1950s and 1960s were decades of modernization, rural exodus, and rapid urbanization for Greece. City life became an ideal, while villages presented an image of abandonment; emigration under these conditions provided the opportunity for a desirable life-style and the acquisition of goods not available in the villages.

Under these conditions there was a resurgence of emigration in the postwar period. This new emigration wave was most pronounced between 1955 and 1975. What differentiated this new emigration wave from that at the beginning of the 20th century was that, along with the USA, Australia, and other overseas destinations, the countries of northern Europe emerged as major recipients of Greek emigrants. After World War II the countries of northern Europe entered a phase of rapid industrial development and were therefore in need of working hands. The surplus manpower in Greece and other countries of southern Europe supplied the labour which made possible the development of northern Europe.

The first European recipient of Greek emigrants in the 1950s was Belgium, where emigrant workers were employed in the coal mines. It was West Germany, however, which later developed into the major recipient of Greek emigrants. The years subsequent to World War II saw the rapid development of West Germany, often referred to as a miracle. In order for this "miracle" to take place, emigrant workers, known as *Gastarbeiter*, were employed in German industries as unskilled labourers in positions largely considered inferior by the German citizen.

Emigration towards West Germany shared most of the characteristics of the earlier emigration wave to the USA. Emigrants were again recruited from the productive age groups – between 19 and 45 years of age – as well as from the healthier and more energetic among the population. Indicative of the situation of emigrants is that only 4.3 per cent of the Greek emigrants in West Germany in 1971 lacked formal education while the relevant percentage of those remaining in Greece was 12 per cent. Once the first emigrants settled in Germany they acted as attraction poles for their friends and relatives in

Greece. In this way whole communities of emigrants from the same town or village of origin were formed in Germany. The geographical proximity of West Germany to Greece allowed for more frequent visits of emigrants to their home country, helping the maintainance of close ties with the country of origin.

The influx of Greek emigrants in West Germany followed the fluctuations of its economy, emigrant numbers falling in times of economic depression and rising again in times of prosperity. In 1973, however, the German emigration recruitment office in Greece was closed, causing a serious cutback on Greek emigration. The waning of emigration to Germany signalled the end of mass emigration movements from Greece and attention shifted to the problems associated with repatriation.

GABRIELLA-EVANGELIA ASPRAKI

See also Diaspora, Urbanization

Further Reading

Bottomley, Gillian, *From Another Place: Migration and the Politics of Culture*, Cambridge and New York: Cambridge University Press, 1992

Costa, Janeen Arnold, "Migration and Economic History in Rural Greece: A Case Study", dissertation, Stanford University, 1983

Costa, Janeen Arnold, "The History of Migration and Political Economy in Rural Greece: A Case Study", *Journal of Modern Greek Studies*, 6 (1988): pp. 159–85

Dimen, Muriel and Ernestine Friedl (editors), *Regional Variation in Modern Greece and Cyprus: Toward a Perspective on the Ethnography of Greece*, New York: New York Academy of Sciences, 1976

Essays on Greek Migration, Athens: Social Research Centre, 1967

Kayser, Bernard, *Géographie humaine de la Grèce: éléments pour l'étude de l'urbanisation*, Paris: Presses Universitaires de France, 1964

Kolodny, Emile, "Neokaisaria (Pierie): exemple d'émigration massive récente à partir d'un village de Macedoine occidentale vers l'Allemagne Fédérale" in *Aspects du changement social dans la campagne grecque*, edited by Stathis Damianakos, Athens: Centre National de Recherche Sociales, 1981

Kouvertaris, George, *First and Second Generation Greeks in Chicago: An Inquiry into their Stratification and Mobility Patterns*, Athens: National Centre of Social Research, 1971

Laiou-Thomadakis, Angeliki E., *Peasant Society in the Late Byzantine Empire: A Social and Demographic Study*, Princeton, New Jersey: Princeton University Press, 1977

Patiniotis, Nikitas, *Exartisi ke Metanastefsi: I Periptosi tis Elladas* [Dependence and Emigration: The Case of Greece], Athens: National Centre of Social Research, 1990

Saloutos, Theodore, *The Greeks in the United States*, Cambridge, Massachusetts: Harvard University Press, 1964

Tsoukalas, Constandinos, "Dépendance et reproduction: le rôle des appareils scolaires en Grèce", dissertation, Paris: Sorbonne, 1976

Vacalopoulos, Apostolos, *Origins of the Greek Nation: The Byzantine Period, 1204–1461*, New Brunswick, New Jersey: Rutgers University Press, 1970

Empedocles *c.*492–432 BC

Philosopher

A native of Acragas (modern Agrigento) in Sicily, Empedocles was a leading philosopher of his time. He is difficult to classify because of the complexity of influences he manifests. He is at once a philosopher and a medicine man: while he constructs a rational cosmology, he also claims to have magical powers to raise the dead and change the weather. In his thought he both preserves Pythagorean religious teachings from the western Greeks and continues the scientific research of the eastern Greeks in Ionia. He accepts Parmenides' denial of coming to be, yet propounds a philosophy of natural change. Though a philosopher, he writes epic verse in a florid style; appealing to the authority of reason and argument, he also presents his theory as a revelation from the deities of Greek religion.

The most immediate philosophical influence on Empedocles is Parmenides. Empedocles adopts from him both the device of using epic conventions and diction to express his views, and some of his views as well, echoing Parmenides' own language. Most importantly, he accepts the principle that nothing can come to be from what is not. Furthermore, he agrees with Parmenides that the senses are suspect, though he ultimately accepts the testimony of the senses if they are used properly. But Parmenides seems to go on to use his principle that nothing comes from what is not to argue that there is no change at all, and that what our sense experience presents us with is no more than illusion. Empedocles, to the contrary, offers a positive account of how change is possible.

While there is no coming to be or perishing, strictly speaking, there are elements that can combine and separate to present the appearance of things coming into being and changing. The many substances of the world are on this theory mixtures of elements. Empedocles uses the simile of artists painting with a set of colours. By combining a few colours and drawing appropriate shapes with them, the painter may represent the infinite variety of things in the world. So nature produces the world with a few elements. Empedocles presents four elements, which he call "roots" (*rizomata*): earth, water, air, and fire, as combining in whole-number ratios to form compounds. For instance, bone consists of two parts earth, two parts water, four parts fire. The elements are acted upon by two forces, which he personifies as Love and Strife, or, roughly, attraction and repulsion.

The elements and forces take part in an elaborate cosmogony. At one time, in the present cosmos, the elements were separated out into concentric layers of earth, water, air, and fire, while Strife played an important role. But gradually Love comes to dominate in the world, combining the elements more and more until at last all the materials of the world are completely harmonized into a homogeneous sphere (*sphairos*) pervaded by Love. In the sphere there are no differences manifest, and hence no living things, no world as we know it. But at some point Strife attacks the sphere from the periphery and causes the elements to separate from one another, whereupon the cosmos begins to form. This alternation between the sphere and the cosmos forms a never-ending cycle of cosmic change.

Empedocles' theory of soul is deeply influenced by Pythagorean thought. The soul falls into a body as a result of the influence of Strife. It undergoes a cycle of reincarnations in plants, animals, and humans until it is purged and purified. The evils of mortality are compounded by the shedding of blood; Empedocles compares the eating of meat to cannibalistic consumption of one's relatives. Souls may progress to higher forms of plant and animal life and eventually to human life and its highest manifestations, from which they return to the status of gods. Empedocles announces that he "goes about as a mortal god, no longer mortal, honoured by all" (fr. 112. 4–5). He seems to be claiming to have achieved a state of purity that precludes further reincarnations, one that confers on him the magical powers to which he pretends. His philosophy thus forms part of a larger religious vision. Empedocles recognizes traditional gods, but calls them "long-lived" rather than "immortal", suggesting that they are beings subordinate to the cosmic cycle who will eventually be absorbed into the sphere. In his anthropology he looks back with longing to a primitive golden age in which humans and animals lived in harmony under the rule of Love, and worship was carried on without animal sacrifices.

Empedocles' views on nature, including specific discussions of biology, influenced Greek medical writers from the 5th century BC onwards, some of whom criticized him, but in doing so recognized his influence on medical studies. His great contribution to the scientific tradition was the theory of a finite set of elements forming an unlimited number of compounds by their combinations in whole-number ratios – a theory that has become the basis of modern chemistry. His specific set of four elements became standard by the following century and remained the basic substances of physical theory in both the Greek world and the west until the beginning of the modern era. Empedocles' religious ideas became part of the Neopythagorean and Neoplatonic traditions of later centuries.

DANIEL W. GRAHAM

Biography

Born *c.*492 BC at Acragas in Sicily, Empedocles came from an aristocratic family which had taken part in the Olympic Games. He himself seems to have been a doctor and to have been active in politics as well as in religious and philosophical circles. He was clearly influenced by Pythagoreanism as well as by the thought of Parmenides. He wrote two poems, one physical (*On Nature*), the other religious (*Purifications*), of which only fragments survive. He died in 432 BC.

Writings

The Proem of Empedocles' Peri Physeos, edited by N. van der Ben, Amsterdam: Grüner, 1975
The Extant Fragments, edited by M.R. Wright, New Haven, Connecticut: Yale University Press, 1981
The Poems, edited and translated by Brad Inwood, Toronto: University of Toronto Press, 1992

Further Reading

Bollack, Jean, *Empédocle*, 3 vols, Paris: Minuit, 1965–69
Graham, Daniel W., "Symmetry in the Empedoclean Cycle", *Classical Quarterly*, 38 (1988): pp. 297–312
Kingsley, Peter, *Ancient Philosophy, Mystery, and Magic: Empedocles and Pythagorean Tradition*, Oxford: Clarendon Press, and New York: Oxford University Press, 1995
Long, A.A., "Empedocles' Cosmic Cycle in the 'Sixties'" in *The Pre-Socratics: A Collection of Critical Essays*, edited by Alexander P.D. Mourelatos, revised edition, Princeton, New Jersey: Princeton University Press, 1993
Mourelatos, Alexander P.D., "Quality, Structure, and Emergence in Later Pre-Socratic Philosophy", *Proceedings of the Boston Area Symposium in Ancient Philosophy*, 2 (1987): pp. 127–94
O'Brien, Denis, "The Relation of Anaxagoras and Empedocles", *Journal of Hellenic Studies*, 88 (1968): pp. 93–114

O'Brien, Denis, *Empedocles' Cosmic Cycle: A Reconstruction from the Fragments and Secondary Sources*, London: Cambridge University Press, 1969

O'Brien, Denis, "Empedocles Revisited", *Ancient Philosophy*, 15 (1995): pp. 403–70

Osborne, Catherine, "Empedocles Recycled", *Classical Quarterly*, 37 (1987): pp. 24–50

Solmsen, Friedrich, "Love and Strife in Empedocles' Cosmogony", *Phronesis*, 10 (1965): pp. 109–48

Enamel

Enamel is essentially coloured glass. When heated to its melting point, glass fuses with the metal with which it is in contact, and craftsmen have long exploited this property by decorating metal with boldly coloured opaque or jewel-like translucent enamel. It may well have been a Mycenaean invention: the earliest occurrence is thought to be on gold-relief beads from chamber tombs at Mycenae of *c*.1400 BC (Athens, National Archaeological Museum, Mycenae graves 88, 103). Blue enamel was fused into depressions in the repoussé-work, sometimes ringed by tiny spheres of gold.

The earliest cloisonné enamel to have survived is probably that on finger rings found in a tomb of the 12th century BC in Cyprus (Nicosia, Cyprus Museum, Kouklia Evreti grave 8/33). The design was created, and the different colours of glass separated, with strips of gold set on edge in glass disks, which were then mounted on the bezels of the rings. The fully developed cloisonné technique, in which the metal strips are attached to a metal backplate, is found on the bezel of a ring from a Minoan tomb of *c*.1425–1400 BC near Knossos (Herakleion, Archaeological Museum, Sellopoulo grave 3, J 6) and on the famous Kourion sceptre (Nicosia, Cyprus Museum, J 99); however, the vitreous material on the ring may not be enamel, and the sceptre may belong to a later culture.

There is little further evidence for the use of enamel in the Greek world before the 6th century BC, when filigree enamel – glass fused to the surface of an object inside loops of decorative wire – seems to have come into fashion, with blue and green the most common colours; it remained popular during the Classical and Hellenistic periods. Between the 3rd and the 1st centuries BC small pendants to be attached to jewellery were enamelled in the round, probably by being heated and dipped in molten glass, which was almost always white.

Late-antique and early-Byzantine goldsmiths may well have carried on the tradition of filigree enamel, but evidence is lacking: a medallion (Paris, Bibliothèque Nationale, Cabinet des Médailles, M 1688) with a bust of Licinia Eudoxia, daughter of the eastern Roman emperor Theodosius II (408–50) and wife of the western emperor Valentinian III (425–55), was almost certainly made by the goldsmith responsible for another filigree enamel medallion, depicting a cross and two orbs (Baltimore, Walters Art Gallery, 44. 304), which has been shown to be of recent manufacture (post-17th, and probably late-19th century).

The only incontrovertibly late-antique or early-Byzantine enamel is on jewellery characterized by isolated motifs, typically birds, standing proud of the surfaces of the objects. A pendent cross (Washington, D.C., Dumbarton Oaks Collection, 58. 40) comes from a hoard of the late-6th century AD said to have been found in Syria; another example is part of a Byzantine necklace (Mainz, Römisch-Germanisches Zentralmuseum, O 37809) with components stylistically datable to around 600. The whole group is therefore likely to date from the late 6th or early 7th century. The enamel on this jewellery is contained within a gold strip hard-soldered edge-on to the surface of the object. There is no enamel outside the main outline, where details are executed in round-section wire; both these features belong to the tradition of filigree rather than cloisonné enamel.

The technique of cloisonné enamel was reintroduced from western Europe at the end of the iconoclast period in 843 (the Poitiers triptych, once believed to have been commissioned by the Byzantine emperor Justin II (565–78), is now dated to the 11th or 12th century). In the 9th and the first half of the 10th centuries Byzantine goldsmiths produced western-style cloisonné enamel, with the figures and busts of saints, as well as other motifs, in backgrounds of translucent enamel, which was almost always green; reasonably securely dated examples are on the votive crown of an emperor Leo (Venice, San Marco, Tesoro, 116), who can almost certainly be identified with Leo VI "the Wise" (886–912). Later, from around the middle of the 10th century, the cloisonné enamel subject, instead of having a background of translucent enamel, was set into and surrounded by the metal of the plaque; this development produced what is popularly regarded as the "typical" Byzantine enamel – representations of saints silhouetted against gold, a technique that has become known as *Senkschmelz* (German: "sunk enamel"), in contradistinction to the earlier *Vollschmelz* (German: "full enamel"), where the subject or motif had a background of enamel. The earliest strictly datable *Senkschmelz* appears on a staurotheca (a reliquary for a fragment of the True Cross) commissioned by Basil the Nothos (*Proedros* from 963 to 985) and now in the Limburg an der Lahn, Domschatz. However, comparisons between the staurotheca and two chalices with inscriptions mentioning an emperor Romanos (Venice, San Marco, Tesoro, 65, 70) make it virtually certain that this emperor is Romanos II (959–63). If this is the case, the earliest evidence for *Senkschmelz* is around 960. Allowing time for development, a mid-10th-century date for the introduction of the technique seems reasonable.

Late in the 12th century there was a return to *Vollschmelz*, but, instead of translucent enamelled backgrounds, as in the 9th and the first half of the 10th centuries, the backgrounds are now opaque. Dated examples of this type of enamel are found on an enkolpion (Budapest, Magyar Nemzeti Múzeum) that belonged to Béla III (1172–96) and a cross (Copenhagen, Nationalmuseet, 9088) found in the tomb of the Danish queen Dagmar (died 1212) or that of her sister-in-law. *Senkschmelz* was not replaced by this later *Vollschmelz* but coexisted with it.

The three-dimensional face of St Michael on a famous icon of the saint depicted full length (Venice, San Marco, Tesoro, 6) is executed in relief enamel, the precursor of the *émail en ronde bosse* of the Gothic period in western Europe. The technique is also used on an equestrian icon of St Demetrius in the Guelph Treasure (Berlin, Kunstgewerbemuseum, W 3), which is probably to be dated to the middle of the 13th century.

Enamel: 10th-century Byzantine enamelled pendant cross, showing the Virgin flanked by St Basil the Great and St Gregory Thaumaturge, British Museum, London

A different sort of relief enamel, sunk instead of raised, decorates a copper funerary censer (Athens, Benaki Museum, 11469) of a type used in the 13th and 14th centuries. The technique imitates western champlevé enamel, but the metal is actually embossed copper sheet. Genuine champlevé enamel in a late-Byzantine context is found on a pair of copper candlesticks (Riggisberg, Abegg-Stiftung Bern, 8.185.72, 8.186.72). With the revival of *Vollschmelz* in the late 12th century, when an opaque enamel background obscured the metal of the substrate, the use of gold may have been considered something of a luxury; certainly there was an upsurge in the use of copper cloisonné enamel in place of gold, most examples belonging to the 13th and 14th centuries. The use of the cheaper metal, which could of course be gilded, removed one of the constraints on size, and some of the enamels on copper are considerably larger than their earlier gold counterparts.

Revived or reinvented by the Venetians in the 14th century, the technique of filigree enamel was practised in the Balkans by the 15th or 16th century, becoming the characteristic enamel of the post-Byzantine Greek world. While painted and champlevé enamel were used (for instance in the pendant and pastoral staff of bishop Parthenios of Caesarea, 1738, now in the Benaki Museum), it is filigree enamel that customarily decorates book-covers and liturgical objects. On the Greek islands earrings and pendants often took the shape of sailing ships decorated with filigree enamel. The types of ship can be used to date such jewellery to the 16th, 17th, and 18th centuries, inscriptions on some of the later examples suggesting manufacture by Greek goldsmiths working in Venice (Athens, Benaki Museum, no. 7669).

DAVID BUCKTON

See also Glass, Jewellery

Further Reading

Bouras, Laskarina, "Palaiochristianika kai vizantina thumiatiria tou Mouseiou Benaki" [Early Christian and Byzantine Censers in the Benaki Museum], *Archailogia*, 1 (1981): pp. 64–70

Brown, Katharine R., *The Gold Breast Chain from the Early Byzantine Period in the Römisch-Germanisches Zentralmuseum*, Mainz: Römisch-Germanisches Zentralmuseum, 1984

Buckton, David, "Enamelling on Gold, a Historical Perspective", *Gold Bulletin*, 15 (1982): pp. 101–09

Buckton, David (editor), *The Treasury of San Marco, Venice*, Milan: Olivetti, 1984 (especially nos 8, 10, 11, 19)

Buckton, David, "Byzantine Enamel and the West" in *Byzantium and the West, c.850–c.1200*, edited by J.D. Howard-Johnston, Amsterdam: Hakkert, 1988

Buckton, David (editor), *Byzantium: Treasures of Byzantine Art and Culture from British Collections*, London: British Museum Press, 1994 (especially p. 18, nos 98, 141, 142, 165, 200, 201)

Buckton, David, "'All That Glisters': Byzantine Enamel on Copper" in *Thumiama, sti mnimi tis Laskarinas Boura* [An Offering to the Memory of Lascarina Voura], edited by Maria Vassilaki *et al.*, 2 vols, Athens: Benaki Museum, 1994 (vol. 1: pp. 47–49; vol. 2: colour plate V, plates 20–21)

Buckton, David, "'Chinese Whispers': The Premature Birth of the Typical Byzantine Enamel" in *Byzantine East, Latin West: Art-Historical Studies in Honor of Kurt Weitzmann*, edited by Christopher Moss and Katherine Kiefer, Princeton, New Jersey: Department of Art and Archaeology, Princeton University, 1995

Buckton, David, "The Gold Icon of St Demetrios" in *Der Welfenschatz und sein Umkreis*, edited by Joachim Ehlers and Dietrich Kötzsche, Mainz: Zabern, 1998

Chatzidakis, Manolis, *Benaki Museum*, Athens: Ekdotike Athenon, 1989

Drayman-Weisser, Terry and Catherine Herbert, "An Early Byzantine-style Gold Medallion Reconsidered", *Journal of the Walters Art Gallery*, 49/50 (1991–2): pp. 13–25

Durand, Jannic (editor), *Byzance: l'art byzantin dans les collections publiques françaises*, Paris: Réunion des Musées Nationaux, 1992 (especially no. 241)

Durand, Jannic, "Le Reliquaire de la Vraie Croix de Poitiers: nouvelles observations", *Bulletin de la Société Nationale des Antiquaires de France* (1992): pp. 152–67

Evans, Helen C. and William D. Wixom (editors), *The Glory of Byzantium: Art and Culture of the Middle Byzantine Era, AD 843–1261*, New York: Metropolitan Museum of Art, 1997 (especially nos 333, 335)

Fleischer, Jens, Øystein Hjort and Mikael Bøgh Rasmussen (editors), *Byzantium: Late Antique and Byzantine Art in Scandinavian Collections*, Copenhagen: Ny Carlsberg Glyptotek, 1996 (especially no. 96)

Goring, Elizabeth, "A Flash in the Pan? The First Appearance of Enamelling in the Ancient Near East", *Jewellery Studies*, 3 (1989): p. 83

Goring, Elizabeth, "The Kourion Sceptre: Some Facts and Factoids" in *Klados: Essays in Honour of J.N. Coldstream*, edited by Christine Morris, London: University of London Institute of Classical Studies, 1995: pp. 103–10

Henderson, Julian, "A Scientific Analysis of the Enamel Decorating a Gold Medallion in the Walters Art Gallery", *Journal of the Walters Art Gallery*, 49/50 (1991–92): pp. 27–31

Higgins, Reynold, *Greek and Roman Jewellery*, 2nd edition, London: Methuen, and Berkeley: University of California Press, 1980

Higgins, Reynold, *Minoan and Mycenaean Art*, revised edition, London: Thames and Hudson, 1997

Ogden, Jack, *Jewellery of the Ancient World*, London: Trefoil, and New York: Rizzoli, 1982

Otavsky, Karel, "Two Greek Candlesticks in the Abegg Foundation" in *Thumiama, sti mnimi tis Laskarinas Boura* [An Offering to the Memory of Lascarina Voura], edited by Maria Vassilaki, *et al.*, 2 vols, Athens: Benaki Museum, 1994 (vol. 1: pp. 239–40, vol. 2: plates 125–30)

Popham, M.R., "Sellopoulo Tombs 3 and 4: Two Late Minoan Graves near Knossos", *Annual of the British School at Athens*, 69 (1974): p. 219, figure 14h, plates 37e and g

Ševčenko, Nancy P., "The Limburg Staurothek and its Relics" in *Thumiama, sti mnimi tis Laskarinas Boura* [An Offering to the Memory of Lascarina Voura], edited by Maria Vassilaki, *et al.*, 2 vols, Athens: Benaki Museum, 1994 (vol. 1: pp. 289–94, vol. 2: plates 166–67)

Skubiszewski, Piotr, "La staurothèque de Poitiers", *Cahiers de civilisation médiévale*, 35/1 (1992): pp. 65–68, 71–75, plates VI–VII

Tatton-Brown, Veronica (editor), *Cyprus BC: 7000 Years of History*, London: British Museum Publications, 1979

Wessel, Klaus, *Die byzantinische Emailkunst vom 5. bis 13. Jahrhundert*, Recklinghausen: Bongers, 1967

Williams, Dyfri and Jack Ogden, *Greek Gold: Jewellery of the Classical World*, London: British Museum Press, and New York: Abrams, 1994

Enlightenment

The Neohellenic Enlightenment cannot be restricted to the confines of a national – let alone geographical – definition. It is the reflection of a complex interweaving of currents of renewal in the Balkans under Ottoman rule, where the Greek language took on the role of a *langue véhiculaire*, a lingua franca, but was also the language of learning, particularly in some specific cases such as, for example, in the Danubian principalities. It had an influence in the broader geopolitical area of southeastern Europe, and indeed the eastern Mediterranean basin, not to mention the strong cores of learning which appeared (as a result of the convergence of favourable trading conditions) in the Greek communities of central Europe, southern Russia (Odessa), and western Europe (Venice, Vienna, Paris, etc).

From the 18th century onwards, the crisis in the social structures and political institutions of the Ottoman empire provoked the diverse national groups which made up the social and cultural mosaic of the Balkan peninsula to seek a new social model, based on a system of values oriented towards the west. Through a series of social changes and a process of cultural osmosis, the Enlightenment was introduced into southeastern Europe by the rising urban merchant classes. Over time this led to the formulation of national demands, and culminated in the creation of nation states. Changes to the way of life were adopted gradually, and were assimilated in the face of considerable resistance. It is possible to detect them in many areas of society, both economic and intellectual, and in the transition undergone by the natural environment as the system of urban planning was being developed. The result was the emergence of new symbols and images which attempted to transcribe and to explain the innovations taking place in society.

With regard to the major western movements, modern Hellenism became receptive to the influence of the Italian Renaissance relatively late, during the 17th century. This cultural phenomenon took root not in mainland Greece but in Venetian-ruled Crete, from where it radiated out to other strongholds of Italian culture, particularly the Ionian islands. Consequently, the major part of Greece experienced the Enlightenment without having come under the influence of the Renaissance. Neohellenic culture before the Enlightenment was thus dominated by the Orthodox Christian ethic: education was based on Aristotelianism, as well as on a fixed, stereotyped choice of texts from Classical and Byzantine literature. However, from an early stage it is possible to detect the coexistence of two decisive elements: tradition and renewal. It has been said that in Greek intellectual life the development of ideas from the 16th to the 19th century is distinguished by a continuous "assimilative capacity", by a living tradition capable of receiving new elements and embracing modernity.

The first attempts to trace the development of the Neohellenic Enlightenment date from as long ago as the early 19th century, by scholars who were themselves vehicles of the movement (Adamantios Korais, Iakovos Rizos Neroulos, etc.). The Greek term for the Enlightenment, *Diaphotismos*, was coined much later, however, its appearance dating to around 1862, and probably derived from the German term *Aufklärung*. Its use is first recorded in the writings of Dimitrios Vernardakis.

The Greek *Diaphotismos* is considered to be an offshoot of the main European Enlightenment. If this neologism was created in connection with the corresponding European terms (*Lumières*, *Aufklärung*, and *Illuminismo*), the expressions of *phota* (lights), lights of Europe (*lumières de l'Europe*), enlightened nations (*nations éclairées*), which lead us to the connotations of the French term *lumières*, do not belong to the field of neologisms. The symbolic meaning of light belonged to a centuries-old linguistic arsenal, from Classical rhetorical models and humanistic learning, to the vocabulary of "religious humanism" of the 17th century (where the exhortation for the Enlightenment of the *genos* (racc) led to a symbiosis of Classical learning with Byzantine tradition). In the 18th century the term was incorporated into a new frame of reference and was enriched with new, dynamic semantic connotations. The alignment with the achievements of western thought is clear; but this process presupposes a rehabilitation of values, from antiquity through the western Renaissance to an enlightened Europe, and from there to modern Hellenism, a course which leads, in a term later coined by Korais, to the *metakenosi* (expulsion) of western knowledge and to the recovery of a traditional heritage of Classical learning.

The Byzantine "ecumenical" idea survived through the ecclesiastical edifice and in many ways through the Phanariot ideology, while the national awakening gradually taking place was based to a large degree on the recovery of the ancient heritage. The idea of orthodoxy continued to be identified with that of the *genos*. In the collective memory of the peoples of southeastern Europe, in popular tradition, and in legends, the lost Christian empire was present. Moreover, the expectations for Russian intervention in the east were founded on the common religion. On the other hand there is the reconnection with antiquity. The "Classical vision" and its revival, a commonplace of European Classicism since the Renaissance, acquired greater force with the outbreak of the French Revolution – "heroic Neoclassicism" became a social experience. To a great extent, the Greek Enlightenment embraced these models.

The Neohellenic Enlightenment gave rise to a number of secondary phenomena which demonstrate not only its internal dynamics and development but also its individuality. According to the original division of Dimaras, we can speak of a period of 50 years, from 1770 to 1820, with a backward margin of 20 years, to include the events of the 1750s, and reaching to the 1830s, when the Enlightenment met the spirit of Romanticism. The disintegration of the Enlightenment began to be seen during the 1830s, although some cores of resistance remained until the 1850s, and even later.

However, in southeastern Europe the period from 1700 to 1750 can be equated with the "early Enlightenment" (*Frühaufklärung*). The Mavrokordatos family is a good example. Polyglots, and extremely cultivated, the family aligned themselves with the moderate ideals of enlightened authoritarianism (*despotisme éclairé*). They were exceptionally well informed about literature, maintained a much-envied library (their collections prompted the interest of Louis XIV and Colbert), and had contact with western men of letters such as Jean Le Clerc. They were without doubt equal citizens of the ideal Republic of European Letters. The family included Alexander "*o ex Aporriton*" ("Minister of the Secrets"), the head of the dynasty, and Nicholas, the first Phanariot prince of Moldavia (1709), who acted as vehicles for new ideas in ethics and political thinking (such as the theory of natural law) and knew the French *moralistes* (La Rochefoucauld). In Nicholas's novelistic work *Philotheou Parerga* (1713), we can see the influence of the great philosophical discussions of the age: "the *Querelle* of the Ancients and the Moderns", the morality of the spectacle, historical criticism, etc. Nicholas, breaking away from the established neo-Aristolenianism, turned towards Plato and makes reference to the philosophy of his contemporaries (Locke, Hobbes, Bacon). It is through the hegemonic Mavrokordatos family that the first signs of interest in modern western narrative forms, literature, the novel, and the theatre can be seen (Fénelon, Cervantes, Molière, Gracian y Morales, etc).

Theophilos Corydalleus, the 17th-century neo-Aristotelian philosopher, dominated the educational system of southeastern Europe for a long period, since his writings in the fields of logic and philosophy and his rhetoric were widely disseminated as teaching handbooks, and were in use until around 1827, when the Greek state was founded.

At the beginning of the 18th century can be seen the first faltering steps marking a rift, a gradual distancing from the absolute spiritual leadership of the Church, doubts over Aristotelianism, a turning towards the outside world and observation, the desire for historical knowledge, familiarity with the natural world, the environment, ultimately a faith in experimentation and empiricism. These changes are anticipated in *Introduction to Geographics and Spherics* (1716) by

Chrysanthos Notaras, the patriarch of Jerusalem, although he disputes the position of Copernicus. The first examples of rationalist thought are encountered in the works of Vincentios Damodos, Methodios Anthracites, and Theodoros Cavalliotes. Damodos, without deviating from Orthodoxy, accepts the Cartesian theory concerning the genesis of the passions. The works of Methodios Anthracites were influenced by Malebranche. He expresses the movement towards mathematics and the natural sciences as well as an early eclecticism which would later prove to be one of the most fundamental features of the Greek movement. His teaching was condemned as heterodoxy in 1721. Finally, Theodoros Cavalliotes, from Moschopoli, was a student of Evgenios Voulgaris (1716–1806) in Ioannina. In his writings he refers to Descartes and Leibniz. The influences of the German *Frühaufklärung* on Greek culture later become more noticeable, particularly through the popularization of the writings of Leibniz and Wolff, Baumeister and Heinecke. After 1760 modern Hellenism began to become familiar with Italian thought: Muratori, Genovesi, Soave, Beccaria, and Vico.

As far as education is concerned, the 18th century was for the most part dominated by the coexistence of Classical and Byzantine learning: lyric and dramatic poetry, Classical and ecclesiastical rhetoric, admonitory texts, etc. This was characteristic both of the humanistic and of the exact sciences. The teaching of astronomy, of mathematics, and of geometry was dominated by the influence of 17th-century religious humanism. Theophilos Corydalleus, Chrysanthos Notaras, and Methodios Anthracites continued this Greek-Byzantine tradition, enriching it with new elements. They gave way to new, more radical generations, firmly oriented towards western thought. The desertion of tradition, the acceptance of a spirit of renewal and of modern scientific theories introduced from the west filtered through during the final third of the 18th and the first decades of the 19th century. However, it is rare to find serious examples of Christian dogma being disputed, and even rarer for cases of atheism to appear. The clash with the official Church would take place later, after the outbreak of the French Revolution.

Between 1750 and 1770 the characteristic features of the Greek movement were taking shape. There was a strong increase in publishing activity, the decline of ecclesiastical and service books, the cultivation of a systematic interest in history (ancient and modern), and the development of translation from foreign, western languages. It is then that we can observe the introduction of the exact sciences by Nikephoros Theotokis and of modern philosophy by Evgenios Voulgaris, who introduced the thinking of John Locke with his *Logic* (1766) and was the first to translate Voltaire with *Memnon* (1766) and *Essay on the Discord in the Church of Poland* (*Essai sur les dissensions des églises en Pologne*, 1767) to which he added his *Treatise on Religious Tolerance*, inspired by the French philosopher's famous *Traité sur la tolérance* as well as by the thinking of John Locke. He left us with the neologism *anexithreskeia* (religious tolerance). Vulgaris was attached to the model of enlightened authoritarianism, particularly during the time he spent as librarian in the court of Catherine the Great (1772–74). It was then that he translated a number of Voltaire's political pamphlets, with the aim of increasing Russian influence in the eastern Mediterranean basin.

The appearance of Voltaire breathed new life into Greek intellectual life. Josephos Moisiodax also appears at this stage. He exemplifies the Hellenized Balkan scholar whose interests, including moral philosophy, geography, physics, mathematics, and pedagogics, reflected a vital curiosity. Among his writings, the *Apologia* (1780) is particularly important. He refers in his works to Newton and Locke, and in 1765, during a public lesson at which the prince of Moldavia was also present, he referred to Voltaire.

The second period of the Neohellenic Enlightenment thus extended from 1750 or 1760 to 1800. The first decades of the second half of the 18th century were distinguished by an increased occurrence of interrelated events. Contact with western thought became regular and more continuous, and changes in the way of life and in the way of thinking began to be noticeable and were manifested more strongly in urban centres. Renewal, as represented by the ascending urban merchant class, began to crystallize. Publishing strategies aimed mainly at education and the scholars (Moisiodax, Katartzis) who were the vehicles of the Enlightenment gave absolute priority to educational matters.

A number of innovations were applied in educational institutions, which began to multiply in widely disseminated centres of Hellenism, and reached their greatest number in the early 19th century, even if conservatism often coexisted with renewal: the Hegemonic Academies in Bucharest and Iasi, the Athonias, the Patriarchal School, schools in Epirus and western Macedonia (Ioannina, Arta, Metsovo, Kastoria, Kozani, Moschopoli, Siatista); Patmos; Ambelakia and Tyrnavos in Thessaly; Milies and Zagora in Pelion; Dimitsana, Chios, the School of Kydonies, the Evangelical School and the Philological Gymnasium of Smyrna, the Ionian Academy, etc.

The spirit of French encyclopedism gained ground. The second period, according to Dimaras, was characterized by the influence exerted by the French *Encyclopédie* in southeastern Europe. One of its most typical representatives was the Phanariot Dimitrios Katartzis (c.1730–1807) together with some of his students such as Rigas Pheraios, otherwise known as Velestinlis (1757–98). Information and theories were drawn from the French encyclopedia regarding the natural language, the general grammar, and the practice of translation (Katartzis); on the definition of the philosopher and the content of philosophy (Christodoulos Pamblekis, *On Philosophy*); and even on natural sciences (Rigas, *Physikis Apanthisma* [Physics Anthology]). The renewal of geography as a science was confirmed in a major work of the Neohellenic Enlightenment, *Modern Geography* (1791) by the Peliots Daniel Philippides (c.1755–1832) and Grigorios Konstantas (1758–1844), who took Marmontel's *Encyclopédie méthodique* as a model. This period of maturity gave clear priority to the exact sciences, to experimentation, which was considered a driving force, and the liberation of the individual from the shackles of ignorance and superstition. Finally, in the field of historiography, a long tradition of chronography was left behind, giving way increasingly to a developing interest in antiquity as well as the interpretation of the modern period (Rollin, Domenico Caminer, etc.). The modernization of structures, both social and intellectual, also began to spread at this time, and remained the dominant demand of the Enlightenment.

The French Revolution had its repercussions in the Balkans. Its outbreak and development allowed a radical spirit to be articulated, in which three focal points of expression can be discerned: the liberation movement of Rigas, the centres (Greek communities) of the diaspora, and Ionian radicalism (presence of French republicans in the Ionian islands, overthrow of the old feudal system, burning of the *libri d'oro*, manifestos, trees of freedom, Jacobin clubs, etc.). In 1791, in the *Ephimeris* of the Markidon Pouliou brothers, the *Manifesto of the Rights of the Individual and of the Citizen* was published. On the other hand, the revolutionary events and the excesses in France (the Terror, the regicides, etc.) would cause somewhat delayed negative protestations on the part of the official Church, or rather of the patriarchate, which reacted in 1797 or 1798 with a fulmination condemning the blasphemous philosophy of the French atheists Voltaire and Rousseau (*Patriki Didaskalia, Christianiki Apologia* [The Teaching of the Fathers: A Christian Defence]).

The practice of criticism, one of the fundamental demands of European thinking of the time, was articulated in Greece in three fields: cultural criticism, which already existed in texts such as *Modern Geography*; criticism of social structures, which was channelled into satirical texts at the beginning of the 19th century (*Rossanglogallos* [Russanglofrench], 1805) or into texts full of ideas of the Enlightenment or of national revolution (*Helliniki Nomarchia* [Greek Prefecture], 1806); and finally, criticism of the Church and of traditional religion. Of course, the Greek Enlightenment – as elsewhere in Europe – was not anti-Christian. The question of religion was for the Christian population of the multiethnic Ottoman empire, whether Orthodox or not, an extremely sensitive point, since religious diversity was a legal right, recognized by the Turks, which distinguished them and made them an entity in the face of authority. It was also a cohesive link with a single cultural tradition. There are very few examples of real religious dispute (*Anonymous*, 1789, *Peri Theokratias* [On Theocracy] by Christodoulos Pamblekis). Criticism was for the most part confined to anticlericalism, and demanded the purge and rationalization of religion, and a return to evangelical love and faith (e.g. Adamantios Korais).

In the field of ideas, the final decade of the 18th century focused on the search for a new ethic. If, during the period of the early Enlightenment, ethical questions had offered rich and fertile ground to the Mavrokordatos family, who followed the lead of the widespread form of the *Mirror of Princes* (the link of the ancient Graeco-Roman with the Christian sophiological tradition), from 1760 the search for a new moral philosophy was a serious concern of the modernizing men of letters. In 1760 Josephos Moisiodax translated Muratori's *Moral Philosophy*. Yet only in about 1790 did this process break away from the remaining theocratic morality and make its aim an earthly, anthropocentric happiness. Its natural, deterministic search and the harmonious symbiosis of the individual and his environment in a civil society are at the very centre of the issue raised by a host of books on ethics and behaviour (*True Path to Happiness, Handbook to Benevolence, Flower of Virtue and Knowledge*, etc.). Writers who used their works to popularize the new social ideal were published in adaptations and translated extracts: Restif de la Bretonne, *Les Contemporaines*, which inspired the novellas of *School for Delicate Lovers* by Rigas (1790); the Utopian Louis-Sébastien Mercier, *L'An 2440 ou rêve s'il en fut jamais*, from which Stephanos Dimitriadis drew selections for his book, *Apanthismata* (Florilegium, 1797); or even the revolutionary *Catechism* of La Chabeaussière. In the final years of the century translations increased the number of works dedicated to the exact and natural sciences, and writers such as Montesquieu and Jean-Jacques Rousseau also appeared for the first time. But the recovery of antiquity, a process which assumed an ideological load and led to national awareness, was realized in many ways through the dissemination of the famous work of the Abbé Barthélemy, *Voyage du jeune Anacharsis*. The first volume was published in a translation by Georgios Sakellarios, while the fourth was translated by Rigas and Georgios Ventotis.

Between 1800 and 1830 the movement of the Enlightenment completed its course. This stage was the most dynamic, as it became involved with the ideological preparation for the national revolution of 1821. There was one aim: the enlightening of the *genos*, which would lead to national awakening and liberation. The exhortation of Korais for "the lights of Europe to be decanted" (*metakenosi*) was applied in a consistent and methodical manner. The colossal oeuvre of the grand old man of letters Adamantios Korais (1748–1833), particularly through the editions of ancient classics (the famous *Helliniki Bibliothiki* [Greek Library]) and the extensive annotations, is the most irrefutable evidence of the dialectical relationship which united the conquest of learning with the regaining of freedom. A moderate visionary of the national renaissance, associated with the French Ideologues and an adherent of their analytical theory, he represents a cohesive image of the final phase of the Greek movement through his writings and his famous linguistic and political proposal of the "middle road". The reading of ancient writers in the light of the social thinking of the Enlightenment constituted what has been termed the intellectual matrix of his political theory.

The admonitory and pedagogical character of the Neohellenic Enlightenment was at its peak. Korais and a host of scholars, including those who travelled in the same direction without their paths meeting, his supporters but also opponents of his theories, played a leading part (Athanasios Psalidas, Neophytos Doukas, Anthimos Gazis, Theoclitos Pharmakidis, Constantinos Kokkinakis, Neophytos Vamvas, Constantinos Oikonomos, Constantinos Koumas, Veniamin Lesvios, Stephanos Doungas, Theophilos Kairis, Panagiotis Kodrikas, etc.). Publications written with the purpose of moral teaching multiplied, as did schools and libraries, while literary journals made their first appearance: *Hermes o Logios*, *The Hellenic and Philological Telegraph*, *Athina*, *Calliope*, and *Melissa*. There was a close relationship between most of the prerevolutionary publications and the journals of the Ideologues. The first public theatrical productions clearly prompted by national revolution took place. The heroic, revolutionary Neoclassicism of the French and the scientific theories of the Ideologues influenced the Greeks to a significant degree: Cabanis, Thurot, Condillac, Lalande, Brisson, Volney, Destutt de Tracy (*Eléments d'idéologie*), and even Daunou's views on history, the Hellenists, Etienne Clavier, D'Ansse de Villoison, the orien-

talist Silvestre de Sacy, the linguistic theories of De Gérando, the political economy of Jean-Baptiste Say.

Paris on the one hand, Vienna on the other, shaped the "new philology of the Greeks". Nor were German influences by any means insignificant. Increasing numbers of young men from the Balkans studied in German universities at the end of the 18th and beginning of the 19th century. The philosophical spirit of Kant and Schelling, the example of Goethe, and a host of other names entered Greek intellectual life through their writings, which were translated or used for educational purposes: the philosophical ideas of Wilhelm Traugott Krug; the historical views of Johann Christoph Gatterer, Julius August Remer, Mathias Schröck, and Johann Gottfried Gruber; the pedagogics of Joachim Campe; the literary works of Salomon Gessner, Christoph Martin Wieland, and August Kotzebue; the aesthetic ideas of A.G. Suilzer, etc.

The Neohellenic Enlightenment was receptive to and eclectically assimilated different tendencies characteristic of the corresponding western movements. Its end was in fact a beginning in the political history of the Balkans: if the age of Rigas had seen the Utopian idea of a multiethnic Balkan state called the "Hellenic Republic", the Enlightenment concluded in the formation of the modern states. The Balkan century of the Enlightenment exploited the multiethnic Ottoman empire. On this basis, and after a long period of awakening, it acted as a catalyst in the emergence of national traditions.

ANNA TABAKI

See also Humanism, Neoclassicism, Phanariots, Romanticism

Further Reading

Argyropoulos, Roxane D., "La Pensée des Idéologues en Grèce", *Dix-huitième siècle*, 26 (1994): pp. 423–34

Camariano-Cioran, Ariadna, *Les Académies princières de Bucarest et de Jassy et leurs professeurs*, Thessalonica: Institute for Balkan Studies, 1974

Dimaras, K.T., *La Grèce au temps des Lumières*, Geneva: Droz, 1969

Dimaras, K.T., *Neohellinikos Diaphotismos* [Neohellenic Enlightenment], 1977

Dimaras, K.T., *Hellinikos Romantismos* [Greek Romanticism], 1982

Iorga, Nicolae, *Byzance après Byzance: continuation de l'histoire de la vie byzantine*, Bucharest: AIESEE, 1971

Kitromilides, Paschalis, *I Galliki Epanastasi kai Notioanatoliki Evropi* [French Revolution and South-East Europe], 1990

Kitromilides, Paschalis, *The Enlightenment as Social Criticism: Iosipos Moisiodax and Greek Culture in the Eighteenth Century*, Princeton, New Jersey: Princeton University Press, 1992

Kitromilides, Paschalis, *Enlightenment, Nationalism, Orthodoxy: Studies in the Culture and Political Thought of South-Eastern Europe*, Aldershot, Hampshire: Variorum, 1994

Kitromilides, Paschalis, "John Locke and the Greek Intellectual Tradition: An Episode in Locke's Reception in South-East Europe" in *Locke's Philosophy: Content and Context*, edited by G.A.J. Rogers, Oxford: Clarendon Press, and New York: Oxford University Press, 1994

Kitromilides, Paschalis, "Le Retentissement des idées de Jean-Jacques Rousseau au sein du radicalisme balkanique à l'époque de la révolution française", *Studies on Voltaire and the 18th Century*, 324 (1994): pp. 121–39

Kitromilides, Paschalis, *Tradition, Enlightenment, and Revolution: Ideological Change in 18th and 19th Century Greece*, Cambridge, Massachusetts: Harvard University, 1978; revised edition as *Neohellinikos Diaphotismos* [Neohellenic Enlightenment], Athens, 1996

Makrides, Vasilios, "Science and the Orthodox Church in 18th and Early 19th Century Greece: Sociological Considerations", *Balkan Studies*, 29/2 (1988): pp. 265–82

Makrides, Vasilios, *Die Religiöse Kritik am kopernikanischen Weltbild in Griechenland zwischen 1794 und 1821: Aspekte griechisch-orthodoxer Apologetik angesichts natur-wissenschaftlicher Fortschritte*, Frankfurt: Peter Lang, 1995

La Révolution française et l'Hellénisme moderne, Athens: Centre for Neohellenic Research, 1989

Symposium "L'époque phanariote", 21–25 octobre 1970, Thessalonica: Institute for Balkan Studies, 1974

Stassinopoulou, Maria A., *Weltgeschichte im Denken eines griechischen Aufklärers: Konstantinos Michail Koumas als Historiograph*, Bern: Peter Lang, 1992

Tabaki, Anna, "Un Aspect des Lumières néohelléniques: l'approche scientifique de l'orient: le cas de Dimitrios Alexandridis", *Hellinika*, 35 (1984): pp. 316–37

Tabaki, Anna, "Les Dominantes idéologiques et esthétiques du discours théâtral au temps des Lumières en Grèce", *Studies on Voltaire and the 18th Century*, (1989): pp. 1317–21

Tabaki, Anna, *I neohelliniki Dramatourgia kai hi Dytikes tis Epidraseis, 18os-19os ai: Mia Syngkritiki Prosegisi* [The Modern Greek Drama and its Western European Influences, 18th-19th Century: A Comparative Approach], Athens, 1993

Tabaki, Anna, "La Réception du théâtre de Voltaire dans le sud-est de l'Europe, première moitié du XIXe siècle" in *Voltaire et Ses Combats*, Oxford: Voltaire Foundation, 1997, pp. 1539–49

Tabaki, Anna, "Identité et diversité culturelle: le mouvement des traductions dans le sud-est de l'Europe, XVIIIe siècle–début du XIXe", *Synkrisi/Comparaison*, 9 (1998): pp. 71–91

Enosis

The newly formed Greek state, first ruled by Count Ioannis Kapodistria (1828–31) as its *Kyvernitis* (President) and then by king Otho (1833–62), contained only a minority of the Greek people. The majority were still living under Ottoman rule, while the Ionian islanders had been under British protection since 1815. Although the desire for *enosis*, unification (with Greece), led to agitation in the Ionian Islands, unrest in Crete, and repeated infiltration by nationalist armed bands in Ottoman-occupied Thessaly and areas beyond, there was no extension of the country's borders before the reign of king George I (1863–1913). As a gesture of good will towards the new king, Britain ceded the Ionian islands to Greece (1864). Insurgency continued in Crete, most notably in 1866–69, and another revolt broke out during the Russian-Turkish War of 1877–78. Concurrently, Greek irregulars carried out raids in Thessaly and Macedonia, while the Greek army was mobilized. Following the Congress of Berlin (1878), the Great Powers invited the Porte to make some frontier concessions; it was only after Greek mobilization and pressure by the Powers, however, that the Turks agreed to yield Thessaly and the Arta region to Greece (1881). In the wake of another Cretan revolt, in 1895, Greece went to war with Turkey but suffered a humiliating defeat (1897). The one positive outcome of the peace settlement was that Crete was given autonomous status under Ottoman suzerainty and prince George (king George's second son) was appointed High Commissioner on the island. After two more unilateral proclamations of *enosis* (1905, 1908), Crete was formally united with the mainland at the end of the Balkan Wars. Meanwhile, multi-ethnic Macedonia was the scene of guerrilla warfare; largely ignited by Bulgarian expansionist initiatives, it was not so much directed against the Turks, but rather waged between Greek and Slav nationalist bands, reaching its culmination during the years 1904–08.

For many of those Greeks living under Ottoman rule the wish for *enosis* was fulfilled with the Balkan Wars (1912–13) when, under the premiership of Eleftherios Venizelos and in alliance with Serbia, Bulgaria, and Montenegro, Greece declared war on the Ottoman empire. The allies achieved swift and spectacular victories but disputes over the spoils led to a second war, with Bulgaria attacking Greece and Serbia and being defeated by them. Greece emerged from these conflicts having secured most of the territories contained within its present boundaries. After the end of World War I and the Treaty of Sèvres (1920) the dream of a greater Greece extending into Asia Minor, cherished for generations and known as the "Great Idea", seemed briefly realizable. Such hopes were abruptly ended by the Asia Minor Catastrophe (1922). Over a million Greeks were forced to leave their native land and flee to Greece. Following the end of World War II, with the Treaty of Paris (1947), Italy was obliged to give up the Dodecanese, which it had seized from the Ottoman empire in 1911. A year later, in 1948, these islands were formally united with Greece.

After the Asia Minor Catastrophe, the subsequent exchange of populations (1923), and the Dodecanese settlement, the largest remaining area predominantly peopled by Greeks outside the confines of the Greek State was Cyprus. Here, too, the call for *enosis* had a long history. In August 1828 the archbishop, the bishops, and other notables of Cyprus sent a letter and a deputation to Kapodistria asking for his help. This led him to recommend to the British, French, and Russian ambassadors to the Porte, soon to meet on Poros to consider proposals for the frontiers of Greece, that Cyprus and Rhodes be included within the national boundaries. In 1830 an agent was again sent to Kapodistria, this time to persuade him to annex Cyprus to Greece. As he was obviously unable to do anything about it, the enterprising Cypriots took it upon themselves to turn the island into "a Greek colony". The relevant section from a report (1831) the British consular agent in Cyprus sent to the consul-general in Constantinople reads:

> In several of my reports I have called your attention to the emigration of these islanders; the bulk of them go to Greece and return to their native country with Greek passports, which are accorded easily and without delay. Thus they enter again into possession of their goods and their houses, exempt from all tribute and with the privileges of the Franks. To such an extent has this process been adopted by peasants and persons of all conditions, that, were it to continue the island would shortly become a Greek colony, and the Sultan be left with the empty title of suzerain (*padrone*). An order has therefore been issued that these persons must revert to the category of *rayah* [subjects]; several have already been arrested, and it appears that rigorous measures will be taken to check this practice.

> (Luke, 1921, p. 169)

By the Cyprus Convention of 1878 the Ottoman government agreed to British occupation and administration of the island; the sultan was to retain his sovereignty over it and the

Enosis: demonstration in Pirgos in the Peloponnese in support of Cypriot demands for unification with Greece, 1955

British undertook to pay to the Porte the surplus of revenue over expenditure. This change of administration, ending three centuries of Ottoman rule, was particularly welcome to the Greek Cypriots both in its own right and because they saw it as the first step towards unification with Greece – the ceding of the Ionian islands was still very fresh in everybody's mind. Writing in the late 1940s, the island's historian George Hill devoted a whole chapter to "The Movement for Enosis". He offered an apology for tracing its history at such length and sought to forestall any criticism by the reader: "The constant repetition of the same cry may be tedious, but it proves the persistence of the movement, and gives some impression of what the administration had to face. ...Hardly a year has passed since the [British] Occupation without the 'Hellenic idea' finding expression in some form or other" (Hill, 1952, 4. 495–96).

In 1914, with the Ottoman empire entering World War I on the side of the Central Powers, Cyprus was formally annexed to the British Crown. A year later Britain offered to cede the island to Greece if the latter were to enter the war on the side of the Entente powers. Divided as it was at the time on the issue of war, the Greek government refused the offer. In 1923, by the Treaty of Lausanne, Turkey recognized British sovereignty over Cyprus, which was proclaimed a Crown colony two years later.

In October 1931 pro-*enosis* agitation, coupled with resentment over newly imposed duties and taxes, led to violent demonstrations which, in Nicosia, resulted in the burning down of Government House. The administration, already hardening its position since the late 1920s, adopted a series of repressive measures which were only partly relaxed at the beginning of World War II. As in World War I, thousands of Greek Cypriots once again enlisted voluntarily in the British forces. The conviction grew that, if the Allies were successful, their participation in the Middle East campaigns and Greece's role in the war effort would bring the reward of *enosis*. Yet, the attempts made by the Greek government to raise this issue, during and just after the war, fell on deaf ears. The Cypriots were told that there would be no change in the status of the island, which was to remain under British sovereignty, and were offered instead constitutional reforms, the re-establishment of the Legislative Council (dissolved since 1931), and a ten-year programme of social and economic development. These proposals were welcomed by the Turkish minority (representing 18 per cent of the population) and rejected by the Greek majority (representing 80 per cent of the population), who insisted on their demand for union with Greece. In January 1950 a plebiscite organized by the Orthodox Church among Greek Cypriots produced a 95.7 per cent vote in favour of *enosis*.

Towards the end of 1952 Archbishop Makarios (1950–77) asked the newly elected Greek prime minister, field-marshal Alexandros Papagos, to take the Cyprus question to the United Nations. Favouring a direct approach to the United Kingdom first, Papagos raised the matter with the British foreign minister, Anthony Eden, but was rebuffed. His attempt, moreover, to bring the question of Cypriot self-determination before the General Assembly of the United Nations in 1954 was unsuccessful. A serious consequence of this failure was that on 1 April 1955 the armed struggle began in Cyprus under the banner of EOKA (*Ethniki Organosis Kyprion Agoniston*, the National Organization of Cypriot Fighters) headed by George Grivas, a retired colonel of the Greek army, who adopted the codename "Digenis". The British government responded by sending troops and field-marshal Sir John Harding as governor and commander-in-chief. Emergency laws were imposed, imprisonments, torture, and executions took place. It would be idle to deny the effectiveness, courage, and heroism of the EOKA fighters. It would also be idle to deny that during the period they were active (1955–58) innocent people were killed. Moreover, intercommunal strife became inevitable with the formation of TMT (*Türk Müdafaa Teskilati*, the Turkish Defence Organization), an anti-EOKA Turkish Cypriot underground organization.

The year 1955 also saw Turkey being brought into the picture. According to the historian Richard Clogg (p. 172), "The British authorities sought to use the Turkish community on the island as a counterweight to the demands of the Greek Cypriots and the Turkish government, which had hitherto been rather indifferent to the fate of the Turks on the island, was encouraged to consider itself as having an interest in the island comparable to that of Greece." In June the British government invited Greece and Turkey to a tripartite conference to discuss a qualified degree of home rule in Cyprus. On 6 September, a day before the discussions ended in failure, an organized outburst of violent "popular anger" broke out in Istanbul; it was aimed at the then 100,000-strong Greek minority. Negotiations between Harding and Makarios likewise broke down in the following year; the latter was deported to the Seychelles, not to be released until April 1955, and even then he was forbidden to return to Cyprus. During 1955 the question of Cyprus was discussed at the United Nations and a resolution was passed expressing the wish that a settlement be reached in accordance with the principles of the UN. Yet, with the Greeks insisting on *enosis*, the Turks on partition, and the British pressing for a seven-year-long period of transition during which the three countries would "partner" each other in the administration of the island, the situation was at an impasse. In September 1958 Makarios indicated that he was prepared to accept independence instead of *enosis*. After that events moved swiftly: talks in Paris between the foreign ministers of Greece and Turkey were followed by talks in Zürich between Constantine Karamanlis, the successor of Papagos (who had died in 1955), and his Turkish counterpart Adnan Menderes. A draft agreement resulted. This was finalized in London, ratified by the prime ministers of the United Kingdom, Greece, and Turkey, and presented for signing to the leaders of the two Cypriot communities, Makarios and Dr Fazil Kutchuk (February 1959). Accordingly, Cyprus was established as an independent republic on 16 August 1960 and admitted to the Commonwealth in March 1961.

It soon became clear that the constitution of the new republic was unworkable, and in November 1963 president Makarios presented 13 proposals for amending it to vice-president Kutchuk; he rejected them, but only after the Turkish government had done so. Amid mounting frustration and mutual distrust, intercommunal fighting broke out on 21 December. The months that followed saw further conflict between the two communities, the return of General Grivas to the island, Turkish air raids, an increase by Greece and Turkey of the number of troops officially permitted to them in Cyprus, and Turkish Cypriots concentrating in enclaves. British troops from the bases at Dekelia and Akrotiri (over which the United Kingdom retained sovereignty) were sent to Nicosia as peace-keepers, to be replaced in March 1964 by a UN peace-keeping force, and the American president, Lyndon Johnson, twice intervened to warn the Turkish government against invading the island. Moreover, Johnson entrusted the former secretary of state, Dean Acheson, with the task of reporting on Cyprus and its future. The solution Acheson proposed was a kind of double *enosis*: the republic would be dissolved and most of the island would be united with Greece, but its northern part would become a Turkish military base as well as a political canton. A number of other Turkish cantons would exist autonomously within the Greek part of Cyprus and, in addition, Greece would cede to Turkey the small island of Kastellorizo. The Turkish government accepted the plan only as a basis for negotiations; Makarios rejected it outright and, after some initial hesitation, so did the Greek government led by George Papandreou. Nevertheless, in its essential features, the Acheson plan continued to exert its influence on subsequent developments.

In the polarized atmosphere of the cold war, Makarios's increasingly neutralist foreign policy and independent line were not to the liking of the West. He had rejected the Anglo-American proposal for a NATO peace-keeping force insisting on a UN one, he was prepared to appeal to the Soviet Union, and he sought the support of non-allied countries; by rejecting the Acheson plan, moreover, he effectively kept Cyprus out of the reach of NATO, of which both Greece and Turkey were members. The Americans were suspicious of him and the Greek government itself, though siding with him over the Acheson plan, had allowed Grivas to return to Cyprus and help organize the Cypriot National Guard. Ready to fight for *enosis* in any form, Grivas was thought of as a counterweight to Makarios.

With the Greek coup d'état of 1967 the situation deteriorated. At a conference between the Greek and Turkish governments in September of the same year the Greek side proposed *enosis* based on a modified version of the Acheson plan; but this was rejected by the Turkish delegation. An attack by Grivas on two Turkish Cypriot villages shortly after brought about an ultimatum from Turkey. The Colonels capitulated over the Turkish demands and recalled Grivas and all Greek troops exceeding the 950 laid down by the Zürich and London agreements.

Although relations between the Greek junta and the Republic of Cyprus remained formally (if frigidly) correct, the Colonels became convinced that *enosis* could only be achieved if Makarios was removed from the scene. Allegedly behind an attempt on his life in 1970, in the following year they also helped general Grivas to return to Cyprus clandestinely and organize EOKA-B, an extremist right-wing, pro-*enosis*, underground organization. There followed, on 15 July 1974, a coup against Makarios inspired by the junta and staged by the Cypriot National Guard. Nikos Sampson was installed as president, but contrary to the conspirators' plans, Makarios had managed to escape and was flown, via Malta, to London. The Turkish government urged the British to take joint action in order to restore the status quo, but as they declined, Turkey acted unilaterally under the 1960 Treaty of Guarantee and invaded Cyprus from the north on 20 July. The UN Security Council passed a resolution calling for a ceasefire which became effective on 22 July and was broken a few days later.

Meanwhile, following mobilization which also proved a fiasco, the Greek junta collapsed and with it the Sampson regime. In Makarios's absence, Glaphkos Clerides, president of the House of Representatives, took over as acting president of Cyprus. Karamanlis was invited from his self-exile in Paris to restore democracy to Greece. He arrived in Athens in the early hours of 24 July, was sworn in as prime minister, and formed a government of national unity. The foreign ministers of the three guarantor powers (the United Kingdom, Turkey, and Greece) met in Geneva and, on 30 July, signed a ceasefire. Talks at the second Geneva Conference, convened to seek a political solution, collapsed on 14 August. Within hours the Turkish forces went on the offensive, advancing until they reached their objective, the so-called Attila Line. After repeated UN Security Council resolutions calling for the termination of the military operations, the withdrawal of all foreign troops in the island, and the resumption of talks, a new ceasefire was signed on 16 August; it proved more lasting, but by then the Turkish army was in control of almost 40 per cent of the island and some 180,000 Greek Cypriots had fled that area.

President Makarios returned to Cyprus in December, and in January 1975 talks began between Glaphkos Clerides and Rauf Denktash, representing the two communities which were becoming increasingly concentrated in the south and the north, respectively. The following month Denktash proclaimed the Turkish-occupied north the "Turkish Federated State of Cyprus" and, in November 1983, the "Turkish Republic of Northern Cyprus". In either case, Denktash's state has not been recognized by the international community (with the exception of Turkey and Pakistan). In November 1975 a resolution had been passed by an overwhelming majority of the UN Assembly calling for the withdrawal of all foreign troops in Cyprus, the return of the refugees to their homes, and the resumption of peace talks under the aegis of the Secretary General. The years that followed have been marked by talks and UN resolutions, by fresh initiatives and further negotiations; yet little progress towards a solution has been made to date.

Enosis was specifically excluded by the 1960 settlement, but hope for an eventual *enosis* was too deeply rooted to be abandoned so easily. It persisted for another 14 years affecting individual actions and national policies. It is true to say, however, that although Greece remains the natural ally and traditional advocate of the Greek Cypriots, since the tragic events of 1974 the *enosis* dream has been laid to rest.

KATERINA KRIKOS-DAVIS

Further Reading

Averoff-Tositsas, Evangelos, *Istoria Chamenon Evkairion: Kypriako, 1950–1963* [A History of Lost Opportunities: Cyprus, 1950–1963], 2 vols, Athens, 1981–82

Clogg, Richard, *A Short History of Modern Greece*, 2nd edition, Cambridge: Cambridge University Press, 1986
Davis, Thomas W., "The Rôle of the United States in the Cypriot Dispute - Past and Present" in *Greece in Transition: Essays in the History of Modern Greece, 1821–1974*, edited by John T.A. Koumoulides, London: Zeno, 1977
Hill, George Francis, *A History of Cyprus*, vol. 4, Cambridge: Cambridge University Press, 1952
Hitchens, Christopher, *Hostage to History: Cyprus from the Ottomans to Kissinger*, 3rd edition, London: Verso, 1997
Koumoulides, John T.A., *Cyprus and the War of Greek Independence, 1821–1829*, revised edition, London: Zeno, 1974
Kranidiotis, Nikos, *Dyskola Chronia: Kypros, 1950–1960* [Difficult Times: Cyprus, 1950–1960], Athens, 1981
Luke, Sir Harry, *Cyprus under the Turks, 1571–1878: A Record Based on the Archives of the English Consulate in Cyprus under the Levant Company and After*, London and New York: Oxford University Press, 1921; reprinted with new introduction, London: Hurst, 1969
Martin, Ian, "The 'Cyprus Troubles', 1955–1960", *Kambos: Cambridge Papers in Modern Greek*, vol. 1 (1993): pp. 65–83
Orr, C.W.J., *Cyprus under British Rule*, London: Scott, 1918; reissued, London: Zeno, 1972
Panteli, Stavros, *A New History of Cyprus: From the Earliest Times to the Present Day*, London: East–West Publications, 1984
Panteli, Stavros, *The Making of Modern Cyprus: From Obscurity to Statehood*, New Barnet, Hertfordshire: Interworld, 1990
Papandreou, Andreas, *Democracy at Gunpoint: The Greek Front*, New York: Doubleday, 1970; London: Deutsch, 1971
Richter, Heinz, "The Greek-Turkish Conflict" in *Background to Contemporary Greece*, edited by Marion Sarafis and Martin Eve, vol. 2, London: Merlin Press, 1990
Tenekidis, G. and Y. Kranidiotis (editors), *Kypros: Istoria, Provlimata kai Agones tou Laou tis* [Cyprus: The History, Problems, and Struggles of its People], Athens, 1981
Vlachos, Angelos, *Deka Chronia Kypriakou*, Athens, 1980
Woodhouse, C.M., "Cyprus and the Middle Eastern Crisis", *International Journal*, 11/1 (Winter, 1955–56): pp. 1–15
Woodhouse, C.M., *Capodistria: The Founder of Greek Independence*, London and New York: Oxford University Press, 1973
Woodhouse, C.M., *The Rise and Fall of the Greek Colonels*, London: Granada, and New York: Watts, 1985

Epaminondas

Theban statesman of the 4th century BC

Epaminondas, son of Polymnis, sprang from a venerable family, distinguished by birth but not by political accomplishments. His date of birth is unknown, but he received an excellent education in music and dance, rhetoric, and especially philosophy. During his early adult life he participated in the liberation of Thebes from Spartan occupation, but played no conspicuous role in the years of subsequent fighting. Epaminondas came to the fore in 371 BC when at a Panhellenic peace conference he defied the authority of Sparta and its king Agesilaus. When the Spartans invaded Boeotia later that year, he commanded the Theban army. At the Battle of Leuctra he crushed the enemy by a combination of brilliant tactics and superbly trained troops, destroying Sparta's ascendancy in Greece. In its place he established the Theban hegemony, which lasted until 362 BC, and made possible Theban predominance well into the Sacred War of 355–346 BC.

Anger over Spartan policies had long alienated many of the Peloponnesian states, and the victory at Leuctra released this pent-up animosity. Elis, Arcadia, and Argos allied with Thebes in 370 BC to oppose Sparta, and Agesilaus' ineffectual efforts to disrupt Arcadia provoked a military campaign by the new allies. Epaminondas and Pelopidas led the combined army on a massive invasion of Laconia. They assaulted Sparta unavailingly, but immediately turned their attention to ravaging unspoiled Laconia. Epaminondas next led them to Messenia, which they liberated from Sparta. The emancipated Messenian helots joined the allies, and together they encircled Sparta. Epaminondas directed the building of Messene, the capital of the new polis, in 369 BC. Next year he helped the Arcadians to build their new capital at Megalopolis.

On their return to Thebes, both Epaminondas and Pelopidas were tried by envious political opponents, but won easy acquittal. Reassembling the army, Epaminondas again in 369 BC penetrated the Peloponnese, but this time his target was Corinth and its surrounding allies. Although he devastated Corinthian territory and attacked the capital, his army were unable to do the well-fortified city any real harm. He was more successful in assailing neighbouring Sicyon, Epidaurus, Troezen, and Pellene. Though hardly spectacular, Epaminondas' gains deprived Sparta and Corinth of additional allies and denied them a portion of the northeastern Peloponnese.

Epaminondas' Peloponnesian policy had achieved remarkable results in a short time, but events in 368 BC proved that his work was inadequate. Athens had concluded an alliance with Sparta the previous year, but as yet was more of a nuisance than a threat. Of greater urgency was a serious dispute between Elis and Arcadia over the border territory of Triphylia. The two states were the warders of Sparta, and enmity between them threatened to undo all of Epaminondas' work. The quarrel also underlined a fundamental flaw in his system of alliances, from which he cannot be absolved. At the creation of the alliance, all members tacitly but actually acknowledged Theban hegemony. Yet this understanding was never formally endorsed. Nor was there any joint body or *synedrion* to resolve differences among the allies. In this diplomatic arena the Theban army was of little use, for armed intervention against any of the city states would disrupt the entire alliance. An additional fault was Epaminondas' failure to apply diplomatic pressure in order to obtain a peaceful solution to the problem. As a result, the quarrel split the alliance. Mutual and antagonistic ambitions did more damage to the united front than Sparta could ever have done. Thereafter, Epaminondas faced the relatively easy problem of Sparta and the far thornier matter of his allies.

Further diplomatic failure confronted Thebes in 366 BC, when Pelopidas won the approval of the Persian king for a new general peace, only to see its wholesale rejection in Greece. The affair ended in deep embarrassment. Epaminondas tried to recover Theban fortunes by another military expedition, this one aimed at Achaea, but the effort was pointless, because Achaea had hitherto neither supported Sparta nor opposed Thebes. Achaea fell easily, but unpopular Theban measures soon goaded a strong group of Achaeans to throw off its authority. Moreover, Achaea immediately joined Sparta, which additionally weakened the Theban position within the Peloponnese.

One of the oddest episodes of the Theban hegemony is Epaminondas' naval programme, which grew out of the Theban–Persian accord of 366 BC, and was aimed at Athens, despite the fact that Thebes had suffered virtually nothing at Athenian hands, and the project was of little strategic value to its ambitions. The Persian king subsidized the construction of 100 triremes and in 364 BC Epaminondas put to sea. At the end of the summer he returned to Boeotia without results – and nothing more is heard of his fleet.

The final crisis for both Epaminondas and Thebes stemmed from the breakdown of their system of Peloponnesian alliances. By 362 BC the Peloponnesians were at open war with one another, Theban leadership disregarded, and Spartan resurgence a distinct possibility. Realizing that Thebes had virtually lost control of the situation, Epaminondas intervened to re-establish its authority. He led an army of 25,000–30,000 men against a coalition of Sparta, Athens, Elis, and some Arcadians, numbering some 22,000 soldiers. Epaminondas encamped at Tegea, his enemies at Mantinea in the Arcadian plain. The Spartans were late to arrive, so he seized the opportunity to attack the unprotected city of Sparta, but was repulsed. He retraced his steps without hesitation, and with his cavalry made a surprise stab at Mantinea, which also failed. Pitched battle was now the only option. He confronted the enemy south of Mantinea; and, as at Leuctra, drew up his striking force on the left with his allies on the right. Opposite him were the Spartans under Agesilaus. Epaminondas' men charged and cut through the Spartan line easily, but at the height of the action Epaminondas fell, mortally wounded. This effectively ended the battle: Epaminondas died on the field, and with him died the Theban hegemony.

Epaminondas had raised Thebes to the height of its power, but he alone could not sustain its position. The Theban hegemony proves rather that no one state could bring political unity to Greece. None the less, Cicero considered Epaminondas first among the Greeks, and most Greeks considered him the architect of the hegemony. The western intellectual tradition has uniformly held him as the model of the noble, far-sighted, and virtuous philosopher-statesman. He was also the paradigm of the cultured gentleman and man of action. A modern statue of him still stands in Thebes.

JOHN BUCKLER

Biography

Epaminondas, whose date of birth is unknown, came from a noble Theban family and received a good education. In 371 BC he represented Thebes at a Panhellenic peace conference at Sparta and made his mark by defying Sparta's king Agesilaus. Re-elected a Boeotarch, he led the Thebans at the Battle of Leuctra which destroyed Spartan supremacy and established Theban hegemony. He was killed in the Battle of Mantinea in 362 BC and Theban hegemony of Greece died with him.

Further Reading

Buckler, John, *The Theban Hegemony, 371–362 BC*, Cambridge, Massachusetts: Harvard University Press, 1980
Buckler, John, "Plutarch on Leuktra", *Symbolae Osloenses*, 55 (1980): pp. 75–93

Buckler, John "Epaminondas and the New Inscription from Knidos", *Mnemosyne*, 51 (1998): pp. 192–205

Cawkwell, G.L., "Epaminondas and Thebes", *Classical Quarterly*, 66 (1972): pp. 251–78

Fortina, Marcello, *Epaminonda*, Turin: Società Editrice Internazionale, 1958

Ephesus

City in western Asia Minor

Ephesus, which became the greatest city of Asia Minor, was a centre of Hellenism for over 2,000 years. According to tradition it was founded by Androclus, son of the king of Athens, in the 10th century BC. He chose a defensible site on a gulf near the mouth of the Cayster river. Ephesus thrived as an independent city through the Archaic period, becoming a centre of the Ionian renaissance. It adopted the worship of a local goddess identified with Artemis, whose images and priests, however, retained distinct local characteristics. Her first temple was destroyed by the Cimmerians in the 7th century BC.

Croesus of Lydia conquered the city in 560 BC, and moved its inhabitants to a new site near the new temple of Artemis, which he adorned with elaborate columns. Despite its incorporation into the Persian empire in 547 BC, the city retained considerable autonomy and flourished as a centre of Greek culture. Its most famous sons were the philosopher Heraclitus and the satiric poet Hipponax.

Ephesus supported the Ionian revolt of 499 BC, and in 478, now independent, joined the Delian League, where its high tribute marked it as one of the richest members. The Persians took it again in 387 BC, and held it until its capture by Alexander the Great in 334. Alexander made generous gifts to the temple of Artemis which had been burned in 356 BC, on the night when he was born. The new temple, built on an even grander scale, was soon recognized as one of the seven wonders of the ancient world. It functioned as a financial centre, and had the right of asylum.

Because of silting of the harbour, Lysimachus, who controlled the region from 287 to 281 BC, moved the city to a new site, where it flourished until the Middle Ages. The new Ephesus had a rectangular street pattern, with a great theatre and agora in the centre. The major remains of his work are the

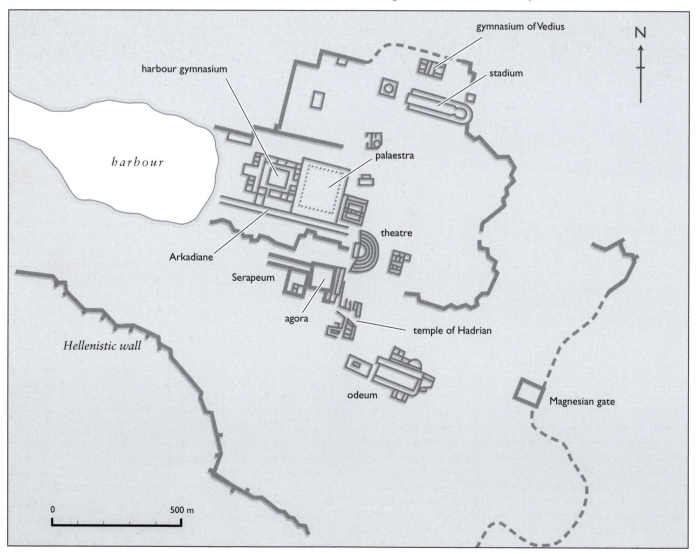

21. Ephesus

Ephesus: remains of the city centre which was the greatest Roman city of Asia Minor

massive fortifications, 10 km long. Ephesus was subsequently ruled by the Seleucids and Pergamum until it became Roman in 133 BC. Despite joining Mithridates in 88 BC, the city remained a major centre, receiving the visits of Cicero and Mark Antony, who made a dramatic entrance in the guise of Dionysus.

Ephesus reached its height under the Roman empire, when it was the residence of the proconsul of Asia (the most famous was the future emperor Antoninus Pius), and seat of the imperial cult. Surviving remains illustrate the growth that made it one of the three largest cities of the eastern half of the empire. They include four huge gymnasia, the theatre, stadium, agora, library, civic centre, temples, lavish houses, and streets paved with marble and lined with colonnades. The greatest monument was still the temple of Artemis, on the ancient site. Building activity was most intense in the 2nd century AD.

By that time, Ephesus had become a centre of Christianity and home of some of its most sacred sites. St Paul visited in a famous and well-documented scene (Acts 19). An ancient tradition had St John and St Timothy buried here and a legend associated the last years of the Virgin Mary with the city.

Although a Gothic attack in AD 262 destroyed much of the centre, late antiquity brought revival and continuing prosperity. The Roman city was maintained but transformed. Temples were destroyed and used as quarries, churches were added to the urban fabric, and bazaars grew up along the colonnaded streets. Mosaics and wall paintings produced a colourful impression. Ephesus took on a distinctly Christian appearance, most notably in two great churches. St Mary's, built into the ruins of the precinct of Hadrian's temple, was the seat of two church councils, the Third Ecumenical Council of 430 which established the adoration of the Virgin, and the so-called Robber Council of 449, not recognized by the Orthodox Church. These meetings brought an influx of visitors and widespread public disturbance as the various doctrines were debated and fought over. The church of St John, built over the apostle's tomb on the hill above the temple of Artemis, was rebuilt in the 6th century on a grandiose scale by Justinian I. It soon became the seat of the metropolitan bishop, and the goal of pilgrims from every part of the empire. The 5th century had added another holy site, the tomb of the Seven Sleepers, youths who had survived persecution by miraculously sleeping for 200 years. This, too, became a goal of pilgrimage.

Large parts of the city were destroyed in the early 7th century, probably by the Persians. They were followed by the Arabs, who occupied it in 654. Ephesus never recovered. The medieval city was confined to a small part of the ancient centre, surrounded by new walls built from the remains of earlier buildings. Although this site had remained an important port and seat of a large regional fair, silting of the harbour caused the centre to shift to the heavily fortified community around the church of St John by the 11th century. Consequently, medieval Ephesus is usually called Theologos, a title of the saint. Pilgrims continued to visit the apostle's tomb through the Byzantine period, especially to collect the sacred dust, or manna, that issued from the tomb and supposedly had miraculous powers.

Byzantine (and Hellenic) Ephesus flourished for the last time under the Laskarids (1204–61) when it was an important centre of education and home of the greatest scholars of the time. The Turkish conquest of 1304 introduced a period of renewed prosperity, the greatest since the 6th century, but Ephesus was now a Turkish city. The Greek population rapidly disappeared or was converted, and the church of St John became a mosque. It was finally destroyed in civil wars in the early 15th century. In the Ottoman period, only a few Greek Christians remained in a declining town that suffered from malaria and nomadism. The arrival of the English archaeologist John Wood in 1863 introduced a period of revival. His discovery of the temple of Artemis was the prelude to the extensive excavations that the Austrians have been carrying out successfully since 1895, revealing the ancient city.

CLIVE FOSS

Summary

A city on the west coast of Asia Minor, Ephesus was a great centre of Hellenism for over two millennia, from the 10th century BC to the 13th century AD. It was best known for the temple of Artemis which was one of the Seven Wonders of the Ancient World. It flourished in the Classical and Hellenistic periods and reached its height under the Romans, prospering until the 6th century AD. As a centre of Christianity it was the site of the Third Ecumenical Council and the tomb of St John. Though devastated in the 7th century, it remained Greek until the early 14th century.

Further Reading

Bean, George E., *Aegean Turkey: An Archaeological Guide*, London: Benn, and New York: Praeger, 1966

Foss, Clive, *Ephesus after Antiquity: A Late Antique, Byzantine, and Turkish City*, Cambridge and New York: Cambridge University Press, 1979

Koester, Helmut (editor), *Ephesos, Metropolis of Asia: An Interdisciplinary Approach to Its Archaeology, Religion, and Culture*, Valley Forge, Pennsylvania: Trinity Press, 1995

Scherrer, Peter (editor), *Ephesos der neue Führer: 100 Jahre österreichische Ausgrabungen, 1895–1995*, Vienna: Österreichisches Archaeologisches Institut, 1995

Ephorus

Historian of the 4th century BC

Ephorus was a major historian of the 4th century BC who came from Cyme in Aeolis (Asia Minor). The tradition is unanimous that he studied at Athens under Isocrates, and in fact the surviving fragments and that part of the text of Diodorus Siculus that is based on Ephorus (Ephorus' own works are all lost) preserve an unmistakable Isocratean flavour. Equally in evidence is a strong admiration for Athens. Apart from his main work, the *Histories*, we hear, *inter alia*, of a local history of Cyme, a book on literary style, and one on discoveries.

The *Histories* were a general, or universal, history from the Dorian invasion up to Ephorus' own day that, while concentrating on the Greeks, tried also to include the actions and achievements of non-Greek people, to the extent at least that these impinged on Greece. In this respect he was following in the footsteps of Herodotus rather than Thucydides; and not only in this, but also in his broader interpretation of history and its scope. For instance, two whole books were devoted to geography, and in the early books necessarily, but in the later

historical books as well, whenever appropriate, he related much that was known in the 4th century BC about Greek colonization and the foundation of cities (reputedly an Ephoran speciality), ethnology, religion, culture in general, and science. According to Polybius, Ephorus was the only historian (apart from himself of course) to have attempted a universal history. Herodotus had been inspired to write what he did by the titanic clash between east and west, Europe and Asia, Greeks and barbarians (led by Persia), which culminated in the crossing of Xerxes from Asia to Europe in 480 BC where he met with defeat and disgrace. The unification of Greece under Philip of Macedon and the reverse crossing of Alexander the Great from Europe to Asia in 334 BC, which resulted in the conquest of the Persian empire, a stupendous event, would appear to have provided Ephorus with his main theme: he had intended to cover the period of Greek (and related barbarian) history from the return of the Heraclidae (the Macedonian royal house claimed descent from Heracles) in the 11th century BC to 334 BC, but he was forced (by old age or illness) to stop with the year 341/40 BC, having written 29 books. A 30th book was added by his son Demophilus, which still did not complete Ephorus' original purpose.

Ephorus was above all a didactic historian. In line with most contemporary historiography he wrote primarily for the purpose of instructing. The moral appraisements of public men (praising the good and censuring the bad) that we find in books 11 and 15 of Diodorus Siculus had their origin in Ephorus, who in turn applied to historical writing Isocratean theory on the subject. Rhetoric and a fine style, whether in writing or in speaking, were not ends in themselves for Isocrates, but merely tools to be employed, along with anything else that could be so utilized, for the attainment of correct, virtuous conduct, above all by political leaders. Writing at a time when Greece had succumbed to Macedon, Ephorus, naturally enough, sought to explain the collapse of the leading states of Greece and the rise of Macedon: ethical and pious conduct, whether by individuals or by states, in private no less than in public life, was Ephorus' (and Isocrates') recipe for success, one entirely in keeping with conventional Greek morality. For Ephorus, therefore, the failure of Greece was essentially a moral matter, as was also Philip's corresponding success.

Conventional in his outlook, as a historiographer Ephorus was nevertheless highly innovative and influential. He appears to have been the first writer to divide his work into books, providing each with its own preface. Within books events were narrated, in so far as it was possible, from beginning to end without interruption, and they were grouped together so as to form a thematic unity. There can be little doubt that this was a conscious attempt to improve on the annalistic presentation of Thucydides and the Oxyrhynchus historian, both of whom Ephorus employed as sources. The belief, almost universally held by scholars, that, always and as a matter of principle, each book was devoted exclusively to the history of one of the four major regions with which the *Histories* were concerned, that is, mainland Greece, the west, the east (Persia), and (after 360 BC) the north (Macedonia), can be shown from the fragments and the text of Diodorus Siculus to be wrong. Ephorus' method was not inflexible. Events from different regions were often related in close sequence in the same books, with any connections between them highlighted.

Often uncritical in the use of his sources, prone to exaggeration (for example, he habitually inflated figures for barbarian forces, even when he knew better), and to smoothing over difficulties, Ephorus falls short of the high standards of the greatest of the Greek historians. Even so, his achievement in composing for the first time a general and systematic history of the Mediterranean world was considerable, and the *Histories* remained canonical reading for as long as the ancient world was able to handle works on such a scale. Its popularity is indicated by the extent to which it was used and imitated by other writers. Diyllus, the Athenian historian, made the year 340 BC (where Ephorus broke off) the starting-point of his own general, Greek and barbarian, history. Strabo, the eminent geographer, made extensive use of Ephorus, quoting him on numerous occasions; and of course much of the surviving work of Diodorus Siculus is in essence Ephorus, abridged and paraphrased. We would have a much poorer understanding of the 4th century but for Ephorus, as he has come down to us in Diodorus.

P.J. STYLIANOU

Ephorus

Born c.400 BC at Cyme in Aeolis in Asia Minor, Ephorus seems to have been a pupil of Isocrates at Athens. His principal work was the Histories in 30 books, a universal history from the Dorian invasion to his own day (the last book was written by his son). He also wrote a local history of Cyme, a book on style, and a book on discoveries. All his works are lost, but the Histories was an important source for other historians, notably Diodorus Siculus. He died in the 320s BC.

Writings

In *Die Fragmente der griechischen Historiker*, edited by Felix Jacoby, Leiden: Brill, 1923–, no.70

Further Reading

Barber, Godfrey Louis, *The Historian Ephorus*, Cambridge: Cambridge University Press, 1935
Schepens, G., "Historiographical Problems in Ephorus" in *Historiographia Antiqua: Commentationes Lovanienses in honorem W. Peremans septuagenarii editae*, edited by Tony Reekmans, Leuven: Leuven University Press, 1977, pp. 95–118
Stylianou, P.J., *A Historical Commentary on Diodorus Siculus, Book 15*, Oxford: Clarendon Press, and New York: Oxford University Press, 1998

Ephraim the Syrian, St c.306–373

Poet and theologian

The Syriac poet and theologian Ephraim lived most of his life in Nisibis, a border town on the eastern frontier of the Roman empire (modern Nusaybin, in Turkey), serving as a deacon under St James, bishop of Nisibis (died 338) and his successors, until 363, when the town was ceded to the Persians following the death of the emperor Julian. Ephraim moved to Edessa (modern Urfa, also in Turkey), where he spent the last ten years of his life (he died on 9 June 373). Although he was often described and portrayed in later tradition as a monk, he was not a monk in the later sense, but a member of the *bnay qyama*, which can variously be translated as "members of the covenant", or "sharers in the pact, or promise", who undertook certain ascetic promises (probably at adult baptism) but continued to live and work within the urban (or village) Christian community. His extensive Syriac writings consist of: (1) lyric poems (*madrashe*), some 500 of which survive; (2) narrative poems (*memre*; the authenticity of many of these is uncertain); (3) artistic prose (a homily "On Our Lord" and a letter to Publius); and (4) ordinary prose (works against Marcion, Bardaisan, and Mani; commentaries on Genesis, part of Exodus, the Diatessaron, Acts, and the Epistles, the last two of which survive only in Armenian translation). Although many of these works already feature in the great 18th-century edition of Ephraim's works in both Syriac and Greek, it is only in the last half-century that reliable editions of the Syriac texts have appeared.

Ephraim lived in a milieu that was probably largely bilingual, though he himself belongs primarily to the Syriac cultural world and it is uncertain whether he read Greek; nevertheless he has some awareness of the Greek cultural world: in his prose works Plato, the Stoics, Hermes (Trismegistus), and Albinus all receive mention, while in his poetry he alludes to Greek mythology on at least two occasions.

Ephraim's fame was already known to Jerome, who devotes a chapter on him in his *On Famous Men* (written in 392), and notices on him subsequently feature in a number of Greek 5th-century works, notably in Palladius' *Lausiac History* (chapter 40) and in the *Ecclesiastical Histories* by Sozomen (3. 16) and Theodoret (4. 29); Sozomen accords him the highest praise, describing him as "the greatest ornament of the Catholic Church", and as someone who "comprehended with ease the most abstruse theorems of philosophy", and whose "style of writing was so filled with splendid oratory ... that he surpassed the most approved writers of Greece". The Syriac *Life* of Ephraim, of which a Greek adaptation also survives, can hardly date before the mid-6th century, and it simply expands upon material to be found in the earlier Greek sources. The *Life* further contains the famous episode of the saint's visit to St Basil in Caesarea, which features in the Greek encomium on St Basil falsely attributed to St Ephraim himself, pseudo-Amphilochius' *Life* of St Basil, and pseudo-Gregory of Nyssa's *Encomium on St Ephraim*. The seeds of this legend go back to the mistaken identification of "a Syrian", mentioned by St Basil, as Ephraim (this "Syrian" is now known to have been Eusebius of Emesa).

Less than 20 years after Ephraim's death Jerome reports that he had read a work on the Holy Spirit by Ephraim in Greek translation. Although this particular work cannot be identified for certain, more than 250 texts in Greek attributed to Ephraim do survive. Much work on sorting out the many problems connected with this large corpus, however, still remains to be done: thus attributions in the manuscripts and versions are often at variance (Macarius and John Chrysostom are quite frequent alternatives), and many works come down in multiple forms. Critical editions are absent except in a few cases, and so for the most part the 18th-century edition by J.S. Assemani remains the standard (it serves as the basis for the recent new edition by K.G. Phrantzolas). In general terms, the Greek corpus can be divided into four main categories: (1)

texts for which a Syriac original, probably by Ephraim himself, can be identified; this applies to the long verse homily on *Jonah and the Repentance of Nineveh*, where the Greek translator adopts the seven-syllable metre of the original; (2) texts for which a Syriac original exists, but is not by Ephraim: examples of this are the influential *Sermo Asceticus*, which is built up from several different Syriac sources, the *Testament of Ephraim*, and the *Life of Abraham and his niece Mary*; (3) texts in syllabic metre (suggesting a Syriac origin), for which no Syriac survives; some of these may go back to lost Syriac originals, but more often they seem to be Greek compositions; thus the homily on Abraham and Isaac uses the Septuagint text of Genesis, and the Greek homily on Elijah is quite different from the Syriac one, which is also attributed to Ephraim; (4) prose texts that were certainly written in Greek. A few of these may well belong to the 6th-century Ephraim, patriarch of Antioch, while others will belong to that large throng of unknown authors of (especially) the 5th and 6th centuries whose works came to be attributed to more famous names. The famous Lenten prayer of St Ephraim, beginning "O Lord and Master of my life", seems to belong to this category, for no trace of a Syriac original is to be found.

Of Ephraim's poetry it was only the narrative poems, in seven-syllable couplets, that were translated, and the Greek translations of these, which reproduce the syllabic metrical pattern of the originals, may well have helped to introduce into Greek this new metrical form, so different from Classical Greek metre. Although none of the lyric poems appears to have been translated, it is very possible that their poetic form may have provided some of the inspiration for the creation of the kontakion, the oldest examples of which go back to the late 5th century; the kontakion, however, introduces a new element, in the form of homotony. It is also quite possible that Romanos, a 6th-century native of bilingual Syria and the greatest exponent of the kontakion form, would have been able to read Ephraim's *madrashe* and so borrow some of his motifs.

Ephraim's discourses were often prescribed for Lenten reading in monasteries, and excerpts from them feature prominently in a number of monastic florilegia, such as the *Synagoge*, or *Evergetinos*, of Paul (d. 1054) of the monastery of the Theotokos Evergetis. Many of the Greek texts attributed to Ephraim were subsequently translated into a wide variety of other languages – Latin, Coptic, Georgian, Armenian, Arabic, Ethiopic, Christian Palestinian Aramaic, and Slavonic.

Descriptions of the Second Coming in a number of the Greek works have influenced the iconographical tradition. The earliest portrayal of St Ephraim himself is on a mid-10th century icon in St Catherine's Monastery, Sinai: the upper two panels of the icon portray the apostle Thaddaeus and king Abgar of Edessa with the Mandylion, while the lower two have St Paul and St Antony on the left, and St Basil and St Ephraim on the right. A popular theme in the post-Byzantine period is the death of St Ephraim: 16th-century examples can be found in icons in Jerusalem, Patmos, and the monastery of Iviron (Athos), and in paintings in the *katholikon* of the monastery of Docheiariou (Athos) and elsewhere. St Ephraim's liturgical commemoration is on 28 January.

SEBASTIAN BROCK

Biography

Born *c*.306 at Nisibis (modern Nusaybin) where he spent most of his life, Ephraim was ordained a deacon. After the Persians occupied Nisibis in 363, he moved to Edessa (modern Urfa) where he died in 373. His copious writings, composed in Syriac, include lyric and narrative poetry as well as exegetical, dogmatic, and ascetic prose works. Several were translated into Greek (where many more were attributed to him) and had a significant impact on the subsequent tradition.

Writings

English translations of Syriac works

The Harp of the Spirit: Eighteen Poems, translated by Sebastian Brock, 2nd edition, London: Fellowship of St Alban and St Sergius, 1983

Hymns, translated by Kathleen E. McVey, New York: Paulist Press, 1989

Hymns on Paradise, translated by Sebastian Brock, Crestwood, New York: St Vladimir's Seminary Press, 1990

Commentary on Tatian's Diatessaron: An English Translation of Chester Beatty Syriac MS 709, edited by Carmel McCarthy, Oxford: Oxford University Press, 1993

Selected Prose Works, translated by Joseph P. Amar and Edward G. Mathews, Washington, D.C.: Catholic University of America Press, 1994

Greek texts under Ephraim's name

S. Ephraem Syri opera, 1: *Sermones in Abraham et Isaac, in Basilium Magnum, in Eliam*, edited by S.J. Mercati, Rome, 1915

"Sermon sur Jonas", edited by D. Hemmerdinger-Iliadou, *Le Museon*, 80 (1967): pp. 47–74 (includes Syriac text)

Schriften des Makarios/Symeon unter dem Namen des Ephraem, edited by Werner Strothmann, Wiesbaden: Harrassowitz, 1981

Osiou Ephraim tou Syrou [Collected Works], translated into modern Greek by K.G. Phrantzolas, Thessalonica, 1988–

"Une Homélie grecque inédité attribuée à Ephrem: CPG 4107", edited by M. Aubineau and F.J. Leroy, *Orpheus*, 14 (1993): pp. 40–75

Further Reading

Brock, Sebastian, *The Luminous Eye: The Spiritual World Vision of Saint Ephrem*, Rome: Center for Indian and Inter-Religious Studies, 1985; Kalamazoo, Michigan: Cistercian Publications, 1992

Brock, Sebastian, "From Ephrem to Romanos", *Studia Patristica*, 20 (1989): pp. 139–51

Geerard, Maurice, *Clavis Patrum Graecorum*, vol. 2, Turnhout: Brepols, 1974, nos 3905–4175, and *Supplementum*, 1998, pp. 227–50 (essential guide to the Greek texts attributed to Ephrem)

Hemmerdinger-Iliadou, D. "Ephrem grec et latin" in *Dictionnaire de spiritualité*, vol. 4, edited by André Rayez, Paris: Beauchesne, 1960, pp. 800–19

Martin, J.R., "The Death of Ephrem in Byzantine and Early Italian Painting", *Art Bulletin*, 33 (1951): pp. 217–25

Epicurus 341–270 BC

Philosopher

Though an Athenian by citizenship, Epicurus was born and brought up in Samos, after his father Neocles emigrated to the Athenian cleruchy there. He was educated in Athens by the Platonist Pamphilus and the Democritean Nausiphanes. After a period teaching philosophy in Mytilene and Lampsacus he returned to Athens (307/06 BC) and bought a house with a garden (on a site between the Dipylon Gate and Plato's Academy) where he set up his own philosophical school (sometimes referred to simply as "the garden"). He created scandal by including both slaves and women in the community of followers who gathered around him.

Philosophically, Epicurus was a hedonist, in that he believed that pleasure was the goal of all activity, but his conception of pleasure was a very austere one. The supreme pleasure, he claimed, could be enjoyed only in the absence of all pain (and indeed in some sense pleasure consisted of the removal of pain, as in drinking when we are thirsty, or eating when we are hungry). Since an unfulfilled desire is a pain, then the happy life can be achieved only if we restrict our desires to those that are related to natural, satiable, appetites (e.g. for food or drink), and remove those that spring from unnatural appetites (for gourmet meals, for example, or wealth, fame, and power); such desires, being unnatural, have no natural limit, and so can never be satisfied. He recommended, then, a simple life of unambitious obscurity. To the objection that uncontrolled pain in this life, and punishment by the gods in the life to come, might overbalance any pleasure we may achieve, he responded that death was our guarantee that no pain could become so great as to overcome pleasure entirely; death limits the amount of pain we can suffer, because it is the end of all sensation: "Death is nothing to us, for when we are death is not, and when death is we are not." So far as the gods are concerned, they would not be able to live lives of perfect pleasure if they bothered themselves with the running of the world, and so, he argues, like perfect Epicureans they enjoy an existence of eternally undisturbed blessedness, taking no interest in us or our activities. He supported these positions by adopting a modified form of the atomism of Democritus, which enabled him to explain the creation and existence of the world in purely mechanical terms, as the result of random collisions of atoms, without having to bring in a divine creator. Since the human soul also consisted of atoms, which dispersed at death, there could be no afterlife, and death need no longer be feared. His principal modification of Democritus' system was the introduction of an uncaused swerve that some atoms made at random times; this seems to have been Epicurus' attempt to escape the risk that Democritus' purely mechanistic universe would rule out human free will, but the fragmentary nature of the evidence makes it difficult to be certain how he thought of this as working. He went on to develop a sophisticated theory of perception (sight, for example, being caused by thin films of atoms that are constantly being cast off by physical objects, and which are brought into contact with our soul-atoms through our eyes), and on the basis of this a theory of knowledge that rested on the absolute reliability of all sense perception (but not of our interpretation of it).

Though Epicurus was reputedly a prolific writer, very few of his works survive. Diogenes Laertius' *Lives of the Philosophers* preserves three "letters" (really short essays) on ethics, astronomy, and physics, together with a collection of 40 sayings, the *Principal Doctrines*. Another similar collection is preserved in a manuscript found in the Vatican in the 19th century. In addition, in the 18th century, scrolls of his major work, *On Nature*, were discovered preserved by volcanic ash in the Villa of the Papyri at Herculaneum; attempts to unroll and read them have been successful only recently. Otherwise we are dependent on an account in verse of his physics written by the Roman poet Lucretius, and summaries of his doctrines by writers such as Cicero and Plutarch, given from the point of view of his philosophical opponents.

Unlike many ancient philosophical schools, the Epicureans were enthusiastic proselytizers, and made an effort, with popularizing accounts of their doctrines, to make a wide appeal, and their success attracted the hostility and contempt of the followers of more conservative schools. A striking example of the degree of enthusiasm that the school could arouse in its followers is shown by a massive inscription (covering a wall about 80 m long) put up in the Lycian city of Oenoanda in the 2nd century AD by the Epicurean Diogenes for the edification of his fellow citizens, and containing among other things treatises on ethics and physics, and a collection of maxims. There is no evidence that the school survived into the 3rd century AD.

Though Epicureanism, with its emphasis on community and moderation, its enthusiasm for proselytizing, and its hostility to conventional religion and superstition, might be thought to have many points of resemblance to Christianity, Christian writers treat it on the whole unsympathetically. Although some Epicurean teachings (that the soul is a physical thing, for example, and that the world had a beginning and an end) gave welcome support to the Christian position in controversies with other philosophical schools, so that in these contexts Epicurean views could be cited with approval, Christians in general were unsympathetic to Epicureans. Their denial of a life after death, their belief that the gods did not concern themselves with what happens in the world, and their elevation of pleasure as the ultimate goal of all activity made them the representatives of all that was wrong with non-Christian thought. A very few Christian writers saw their virtues (Gregory of Nazianzus, for example, praises Epicurus for his moderation), but in general they do no more than repeat anti-Epicurean polemic picked up from the writings of rival philosophers, and played a great part in perpetuating the caricature of Epicureans as vulgar hedonists.

RICHARD WALLACE

Biography

Born in Samos in 341 BC, Epicurus was educated in Athens where he was a pupil of the Platonist Pamphilus and the atomist Nausiphanes. In 309 he began teaching and opened schools in Mytilene and Lampsacus. In 307/06 he returned to Athens and opened a school called "the garden" which continued to teach Epicureanism until the 2nd century AD. Apart from some surviving fragments his writings are best known through the *De Rerum Natura* of Lucretius. He died at Athens in 270 BC.

Further Reading

Bailey, Cyril, *The Greek Atomists and Epicurus*, Oxford: Clarendon Press, 1928

Farrington, Benjamin, *The Faith of Epicurus*, London: Weidenfeld and Nicolson, and New York: Basic Books, 1967

Inwood, Brad and L.P. Gerson, *The Epicurus Reader: Selected Writings and Testimonia*, Indianapolis: Hackett, 1994

Jones, Howard, *The Epicurean Tradition*, London and New York: Routledge, 1989

Long, A.A. and D.N. Sedley, *The Hellenistic Philosophers*, Cambridge and New York: Cambridge University Press, 1987

Nussbaum, Martha C., *The Therapy of Desire: Theory and Practice in Hellenistic Ethics*, Princeton, New Jersey: Princeton University Press, 1994

Rist, J.M., *Epicurus: An Introduction*, Cambridge: Cambridge University Press, 1972

Epidaurus

City in the eastern Peloponnese

Epidaurus is a typical small Greek city, hardly bigger than an English village, situated on the coast at the south side of the Saronic gulf. It is important for one reason only, the existence in its southern hinterland of the remains of the ancient sanctuary of Asclepius the healing god, the most significant of his sanctuaries in mainland Greece.

Asclepius was something of a parvenu among the Greek gods. According to his mythology, he was the son of Apollo and a mortal woman Coronis; originally a mortal, he was only subsequently deified. There is no real trace of his cult in the early Greek tradition, and his sanctuary at Epidaurus was grafted on to an existing sanctuary of Apollo. At first it was completely nondescript, an altar and a small adjacent building. Apollo himself had little more, and the whole is typical of the modest sanctuaries that were sufficient for and all that could be afforded by the less wealthy Greek communities. It is thus possible to trace its deliberate conversion, the reason and means whereby this was achieved, into one of the major sanctuaries of Greece.

The cause seems to have been the great plague which struck Athens during the early years of the Peloponnesian War, when the rural population was evacuated into the area defended by the walls that linked Athens to Piraeus, in squalid conditions with no sanitation. At this time, the last third of the 5th century BC, Greek medicine was developing along scientific – certainly pragmatic – lines. It is the time of Hippocrates the "father" of Greek medicine. But parallel to this was a firm belief, certainly among the mass of the population, in miracle cures brought about by the intervention of a deity. Asclepius, through his father, was the appropriate focus for such beliefs, and duly acquired divine status. Since conventional doctors had no cure for the plague, anyone who recovered, or any community which escaped, could only credit this to the intervention of the god, and the reputation of Asclepius was thereby greatly increased. A small sanctuary (again, grafted on to one of Apollo) was established in 416 BC on the south slopes of the Acropolis at Athens; but it was Epidaurus (which seems to have escaped the spread of the plague) that benefited the most.

The sanctuary was supposedly at the place, or, rather, one of the places, where it was believed that Asclepius was born. During the 4th century BC the amount of patronage attracted

Epidaurus: view of the theatre, built in the 4th century BC to seat 14,000 and still in use today

to the sanctuary, and, by implication, the amount of revenue it raised for the cult, enabled a substantial building programme to be carried out. The contracts for the various necessary building projects were recorded by inscriptions on stone. Many of these have survived, and record the progress of the sanctuary's development, and the means by which this was achieved. The work was under the control of an official board of commissioners, who were entrusted with, or more likely actively collected, the necessary funds. They appointed roving ambassadors who visited cities up and down the Greek world asking for financial support. They let the contracts, to quarrymen, to transporters, and to craftsmen. They appointed the architect. They also appointed guarantors, wealthy citizens of Epidaurus, who would be liable to financial penalties if the work was not carried out to the satisfaction of the commissioners. These inscriptions record the cost of materials and their transport, the wages of the craftsmen, and the salary paid to the architect (he got double the rate of an ordinary workman, which suggests that his pay was regarded basically as expenses only). It is possible to calculate, when the inscriptions are well enough preserved, the actual cost of the buildings, and these make clear that figures given in later literary sources for other building projects, particularly those on the Acropolis of Athens, are grossly exaggerated.

The first essential in the building programme was the Doric temple of Asclepius, in limestone, brought mostly from Corinth, and with Pentelic marble for the sculptural decoration. In front of this was the altar, and to the north a long enclosed building, the Abaton, which was the place of healing: in this the patients slept, and during the night were supposedly visited and healed by the god. Next came the most ornate structure, a circular Doric building called the Thymele. It once had important painted wall decoration, described by Pausanias but now irretrievably lost. The circular cella had a decorative interior colonnade of Corinthian columns. (There were probably Corinthian columns also in the temple but these have totally vanished.) It all rested on a maze of circular foundations, each ring accessible to the next through doorways. Its purpose is enigmatic, but it is probably best interpreted as a cenotaph, representing the burial place of the human Asclepius before he was deified. The inscriptions for this building cover a period of over 30 years, in the second half of the 4th century BC, a time when, it is clear, funds were coming in erratically. Another important building of this period is the great theatre, the best preserved in mainland Greece, attributed by Pausanias, together with the Thymele, to Polyclitus, who he seems to have thought was the famous Argive sculptor. But the dates are wrong, and unless this is a total mistake, the architect was probably a descendant of the sculptor.

Construction work continued well into the 3rd century BC, buildings often being paid for by single donors. They include a large courtyard building, with an elaborate ramped entrance for processions, and surrounded by rooms equipped for ritual feasting in the Greek manner, the participants in the sacred meals reclining on simple couches. There is a propylon, or gateway building, not an effective barrier, since it can be bypassed to either side. Its function is to mark the entry into the sanctuary; there was a rule that all the sacrificial meat had to be consumed within the boundary. There was quite elaborate provision for water supplies; the abundance of water, still

a feature of the site, is undoubtedly the reason the sanctuary developed at this particular spot. There is a stadium for athletic contests. There are also temples and altars to other deities, to Apollo's sister Artemis, and to other gods whose identity is not recorded.

The sanctuary flourished throughout the Hellenistic period, when many of the cures effected were recorded on inscriptions ("publication promised"). It was ransacked in the disturbed times of the 1st century BC, but revived and flourished again under the Romans, when buildings were repaired and a bath building added. The last recorded cures date to the 4th century AD, but the whole cult, its beliefs and practices, had such close parallels to Christianity (which was certainly influenced by this and similar cults) that it was regarded as a blasphemy, and ceased to function. The buildings fell into ruin, except for the theatre the seats of which were covered by earth slips. In the late 19th century the theatre was excavated and now plays an important role in the continuity of the Hellenic tradition, as a venue for the modern production of classical Athenian drama.

R.A. TOMLINSON

Summary

City in the eastern Peloponnese, Epidaurus is best known at the principal sanctuary of Asclepius in mainland Greece. The cult, associated with the birthplace of the god, seems to have originated at the time of the plague in Athens (430 BC). Most of the surviving buildings, including a well-preserved theatre, date from the 4th century BC.

Further Reading

Burford, Alison, "Notes on the Epidaurian Building Inscriptions", *Annual of the British School at Athens*, 61 (1966)

Burford, Alison, *The Greek Temple Builders at Epidauros: A Social and Economic Study of Building in the Asklepian Sanctuary, during the Fourth and Early Third Centuries BC*, Liverpool: Liverpool University Press, 1969

Gerkan, Armin von and Wolfgang Müller-Wiener, *Das Theater von Epidauros*, Stuttgart: Kohlhammer, 1961

Tomlinson, R.A., *Epidauros*, London and New York: Granada, 1983

Epigram

Originally an epigram (from the verb *epigrapho* – "I write upon") was an inscription on an object or a monument. Its original application determined the characteristic features of what was to become a literary genre; it was brief and in verse, while its content was usually dedicatory or funereal. The literary genre of the epigram in its non-inscriptional form was developed and cultivated intensively in the Hellenistic and imperial periods. The epigram is perhaps the sole ancient literary genre that has been practised unremittingly down to modern times. Although the genre underwent considerable changes in the Byzantine period, the basic characteristics remained the same, while its original association with inscriptions was not entirely lost.

Archaic epigrams are inscriptions. The earliest known (8th century BC) are in hexameters but very soon the predominant metre became the elegiac couplet which was to become the classic metre of the epigram. The epigrams of the Archaic period are mostly epitaphs or inscriptions on an object, and they consist largely of formulas.

Many inscriptional epigrams from the Classical period are anonymous. The first known epigrammatist was Simonides of Ceos (557/56–468 BC) who wrote funeral epigrams on the fallen in the Persian Wars. Yet only a few of the epigrams attributed to him are certainly his. Some renowned figures such as Aeschylus, Euripides, Plato, and Aristotle also composed epigrams which now became increasingly elaborate in form and content. Their aim is often to edify, but human feelings are also given expression.

The beginning of the Hellenistic age marks a turning point in the history of the epigram. Two important changes raised it into a literary genre: it became less factual as it gradually lost its association with actual events and objects, and thus served no practical function; and it was published mainly in book form. The epigram now became a vehicle for the expression of personal feelings, assuming the role traditionally played by lyric and sympotic poetry. Allusiveness, conciseness, density of expression, wit, and a constant search for variation now became characteristics of the genre. Two schools of early epigrammatists may be distinguished: the Dorian-Peloponnesian and the Ionian-Alexandrian. In the first the leading figure was Leonidas of Tarentum, as well as the female poets Anyte, Nossis, and Moiro. They show a preference for the traditional inscriptional epigram, i.e. dedicatory and funereal. The ordinary and idyllic replace the heroic aspect, but the style is often ornate or even pompous. Callimachus, Poseidippus, and Asclepiades are eminent figures of the Ionian-Alexandrian school. Witty language and the art of allusion are skilfully used to describe the pleasures of life, wine, love, song, women, boys. In the 1st century BC the epigram blossomed with Antipater of Sidon and Meleager of Gadara (Phoenician school). The latter compiled the first anthology of epigrams known as "Garland" (Stephanos). It became a characteristic of the literary epigram to appear in anthologies. The most important were the Garland of Philip (c.AD 40), the Cycle of Agathias (6th century AD), and later the Palatine Anthology (c.980) and the Planudean Anthology (1301).

The epigram flourished in the imperial age and was taken over by Roman poets. There is a noticeable change not only in the themes of epigrams but also in their tone. Ecphrastic and epideictic epigrams for various occasions – epigrams on events of everyday life, to accompany gifts, to console or to congratulate, to thank or invite now predominate – and satirical epigrams also became very fashionable. Many Greek epigrammatists, such as Philodemus, Crinagoras, and Antipater of Thessalonica, frequented Roman high society. In the 2nd century AD the epigram went through a classicizing phase; and the erotic epigram was revived with Rufinus and Strato, who wrote pederastic ones.

The epigram was cultivated widely during the Byzantine millennium. In the first two centuries of the empire epigrams were still written in Classical metres, in an archaizing language and on Classical themes. This manner of epigrammatic poetry was to be fashionable again in the last two centuries of the empire, when nostalgia for the Classical past revived classizing tendencies. Yet relatively few Byzantine epigrams are written in the ancient metres: the Greek language had long since lost its ancient prosodic features and was now based on stress. The

most fashionable metre was the iambic in 12 syllables (with the penultimate stressed) and later in 15 syllables ("political verse"). The Byzantines also developed the sacred epigram, i.e. the epigram on Christian themes (icons, saints, Church festivals), although dedicatory or satirical epigrams were also popular.

In the 4th century the literary epigram enjoyed a revival in the hands of a pagan and a Christian poet, Palladas and Gregory of Nazianzus. Palladas wrote a number of satirical epigrams as well as laments for the decline of paganism. The profane epigram was cultivated with remarkable success up to the 6th century by such skilled poets as Agathias and Paul Silentiarius who, though Christians, followed the model of the Hellenistic epigram. George of Pisidia (7th century) did much to establish the sacred epigram and became a model for future generations. The most important period for the Byzantine sacred epigram came with the end of iconoclasm (843). At this time the Byzantine epigram began to detach itself from classicizing models and to form its own distinct characteristics. Theodore of Stoudios (d. 826) channelled his theological views into epigrams, aiming both to instruct and to edify. In the 10th century the popularity of the epigram combined with the revival of interest in Classical antiquity led to the compilation of anthologies. Constantinos Kephalas compiled a substantial anthology (now lost) that served as the basis for the Palatine Anthology; the latter contains 3,700 epigrams from the 6th century BC to the 10th century AD arranged in 15 books. (A shorter anthology was compiled in 1301 by Maximos Planudes). The genre continued to be practised on a wide range of topics in the following centuries and reached its golden age with poets such as John Geometres (10th century), John Mavropous, Christophoros Mytilenaios (11th century), and Theodore Prodromos (12th century). In the last two centuries the number of epigrams in Classical metres increased, while the epigram in Byzantine metres declined in the hands of Manuel Philis (14th century).

The revival of Classical learning during the Italian Renaissance is clearly reflected in the flourishing of classicizing epigrams in ancient metres and archaizing language. The genre was first practised by Greek émigré scholars such as Janus Laskaris, the first editor of the Planudean Anthology (1494), but soon it became very fashionable among western humanists who gave an enthusiastic reception to the Planudean Anthology (the Palatine Anthology – Vatican Library cod. Palatinus Gr. 23 – remained unknown until 1607). Yet this was more a scholarly than a poetic enterprise. Epigrams of this kind were pièces d'occasion, mostly dedicatory or complimentary, usually placed in the prefaces of books rather than separately published. Poliziano (1454–94) was one of the first western humanists to write such epigrams. In the 17th century polymaths such as J. Auratus, J.J. Scaliger, I. Causabon, and M. Crusius were prolific practitioners of the genre, also cultivating the bilingual epigram (i.e. in Greek and Latin). Notable Greek scholars who wrote classicizing epigrams were M. Mousouros, F. Portos, M. Margounios, and J. Kottounios.

Epigram is a rather ambiguous term in modern European literature since it lacks distinct formal characteristics; short, witty poems often qualify as such. Yet it is difficult to talk about a clearly distinct genre of epigram in modern Greek literature. Short poems with or without rhyme striving for point were composed by many poets. The poems of Christopoulos (1772–1847) and Valaoritis (1824–79) could be regarded as epigrams, and also the work of poets of the generation of 1880 (Drosinis, Vizyinos, Polemis, and Pallis).

GEORGE E. KARAMANOLIS

See also Anthology

Texts, Translations, Commentaries

Friedländer, Paul and Herbert B. Hoffleit, *Epigrammata: Greek Inscriptions in Verse from the Beginnings to the Persian Wars*, Berkeley: University of California Press, 1948; reprinted Chicago: Ares, 1987

Gow, A.S.F. and D.L. Page (editors), *The Greek Anthology: Hellenistic Epigrams*, 2 vols, Cambridge: Cambridge University Press, 1965

Gow, A.S.F. and D.L. Page (editors), *The Greek Anthology: The Garland of Philip and Some Contemporary Epigrams*, 2 vols, London: Cambridge University Press, 1968

Page, D.L. (editor), *Further Greek Epigrams: Epigrams before AD 50 from the Greek Anthology and Other Sources, Not Included in Hellenistic Epigrams or The Garland of Philip*, Cambridge and New York: Cambridge University Press, 1981

Paton, W.R. (editor and translator), *The Greek Anthology*, 2nd edition, 5 vols, London: Heinemann, and Cambridge, Massachusetts: Harvard University Press, 1948–53 (Loeb edition)

Peek, Werner (editor), *Griechische Grabgedichte, griechisch und deutsch*, Berlin: Akademie, 1960

Further Reading

Beckby, Herman, *Anthologia Graeca*, vol. 1, Munich: Heimeran, 1957, pp. 9–95

Cameron, Alan, *The Greek Anthology: From Meleager to Planudes*, Oxford: Clarendon Press, and New York: Oxford University Press, 1993

Hunger, Herbert, *Die hochsprachliche profane Literatur der Byzantiner*, vol. 2, Munich: Beck, 1978, pp. 165–73

Hutton, James, *The Greek Anthology in Italy to the Year 1800*, Ithaca, New York: Cornell University Press, and London: Oxford University Press, 1935

Hutton, James, *The Greek Anthology in France and in the Latin Writers of the Netherlands to the Year 1800*, Ithaca, New York: Cornell University Press, 1946

Keydell, R., Epigramm entry in *Reallexikon für Antike und Christentum*, edited by Theodor Klauser, vol. 5, Stuttgart: Hiersemann, 1962, pp. 539–77

Kominis, A.D., *To Vyzantinon ieron epigramma kai oi epigrammatopoioi* [The Byzantine Sacred Epigram and the Epigrammatists], Athens, 1966

Pfohl, Gerhard (editor), *Das Epigramm*, Darmstadt: Wissenschaftliche Buchgesellschaft, 1969

Politis, Linos, *A History of Modern Greek Literature*, Oxford: Clarendon Press, 1973

Reitzenstein, Richard, *Epigramm und Skolion*, Giessen: Ricker, 1893

Reitzenstein, Richard, Epigramm entry in *Real-Encyclopädie der klassischen Altertumswissenschaft*, edited by August Pauly et al., vol. 6, 1907, 71–111

Tarán, Sonya Lida, *The Art of Variation in the Hellenistic Epigram*, Leiden: Brill, 1979

Trypanis, C.A., *Greek Poetry: From Homer to Seferis*, Chicago: University of Chicago Press, and London: Faber, 1981

Voutierides, E.P., *Syntomi Historia tis Neoellinikis Logotechnias* [A Short History of Modern Greek Literature], Athens, 1924; 2nd edition 1966

Epiphanius of Salamis, St

Theologian of the 4th century

Epiphanius occupies a prominent place among the Church Fathers of the 4th century because of his theological writings. He is also considered an important saint of the Church in Cyprus, where he lived for nearly four decades as a miracle-working bishop.

His biography, which has to be patched together from different sources, can be traced as follows. He was born sometime between 310 and 320 near Eleutheropolis in Palestine. That his family were Jews is affirmed by the *Life of Epiphanius*, composed in the 5th century, and later repeated by Byzantine theologians such as the patriarch Nikephoros (808–15). Orphaned at a very young age, he was taken into the household of a rabbi who provided him with a traditional religious education. Soon after the rabbi's death, Epiphanius converted to Christianity under the impression of a divine vision. He travelled to Egypt where he became acquainted with the monastic life of the Desert Fathers and on his return to Palestine founded a monastery in the vicinity of his birthplace.

In 367, while visiting the island of Cyprus, he was ordained bishop of the see of Constantia (ancient Salamis, modern Famagusta), which had recently fallen vacant. Under Epiphanius' energetic guidance, Christianity established a firm hold among the largely pagan population of this wealthy and thriving port. In order to accommodate the growing number of Christians, he initiated the construction of a large five-aisled basilica – today in ruins – which eventually became the resting place of his relics.

Epiphanius played an active role as a defender of orthodoxy in the theological controversies of his time. In the Meletian schism that afflicted the Church of Antioch, Epiphanius lent his support to bishop Paulinus, on whose behalf he went to Antioch, lobbied at the Second Ecumenical Council in 381 in Constantinople, and even travelled to Rome in 382. His disapproval of the teachings of Origen prompted him to take a stand against John, patriarch of Jerusalem, who was known as an Origenist sympathizer. As the crowds were gathered for the feast of Encaenia in Jerusalem in 383, Epiphanius and John each delivered a sermon attacking the other. In the following year the rift between them deepened when Epiphanius ordained to the priesthood Paulinian, the younger brother of Jerome, within the jurisdiction, but without the explicit permission, of the patriarch.

Epiphanius had also offended the patriarch John on an earlier visit to Palestine, as they were both passing through the village of Anablatha. When he noticed in the church a curtain with the representation of a human image, either of Christ or of a saint, he immediately tore it down, declaring that it would be fit only for a burial cloth. John was offended at this rash gesture at first, but later mollified by Epiphanius' promise to replace the curtain at his own expense. This episode, first attested in Letter 51 of Jerome, was exploited more than four centuries later, for the first time in 815, in the iconoclast controversy when the iconoclasts adduced it in support of their anti-iconic stance. Although the iconophiles, such as John of Damascus, the patriarch Nikephoros, and Theodore the Stoudite, attempted to question the authenticity of this story, they were nonetheless eager to admit that "we recognize the holy father as a teacher of the universal Church".

The third and last involvement of Epiphanius in large-scale ecclesiastical politics was again prompted by his fervour for orthodoxy. John Chrysostom, the patriarch of Constantinople, had fallen under suspicion of harbouring Origenist sympathies. Spearheading the international coalition that was forming against him and that would eventually bring about his deposition and exile was Theophilus, the patriarch of Alexandria, who urged Epiphanius to become involved. Epiphanius first obtained the condemnation of Origen's teachings from a synod in Cyprus, and then, despite his advanced age, travelled to Constantinople where he made contact with the enemies of John, while refusing the patriarch's hospitality. He was on his way to deliver a public sermon against John when the latter alerted him to the imminent danger of riots in the capital. Thereupon, Epiphanius departed in great haste. He died aboard the ship that was carrying him to Cyprus, in the spring of 403, and was buried with great honours in the basilica of Constantia/Salamis. His feast day is 12 May.

Within two generations of his death, a saint's *Life* was composed in his honour, based in part on the eyewitness account of his disciples John and Polybius. It was translated into Coptic, Syriac, Georgian, and Latin, thus attesting to his fame throughout Christendom. The first translation of the *Life of Epiphanius* into modern Greek was the work of Kaisarios Dapontes, a monk on Mount Athos, in 1780.

Many miracles were attested at Epiphanius' tomb before the mid-7th century when Cyprus was invaded by the Arabs. The emperor Leo VI (886–912) eventually arranged for the transportation of his relics to Constantinople, but their subsequent history is unknown. Next to the apostle Barnabas, who was martyred by the Jews of Salamis, Epiphanius is the most prominent saint of Cyprus and is frequently depicted, dressed as a bishop, in local church decoration. His able and energetic administration of the episcopate not only helped to establish the city of Constantia as the location of the metropolitan see of the island, it also provided a forceful precedent when the autocephaly of the Church of Cyprus from the patriarchate of Antioch was debated and affirmed at the Council of Ephesus in 431.

Epiphanius' reputation as a Church Father rests upon his prolific literary production. He wrote several smaller treatises (*On Gems*, *On Weights and Measures*, *Catalogue of the Apostles*) that enjoyed enormous popularity even beyond the Byzantine empire. His most original works are the *Ancoratus* and the *Panarion*. The *Ancoratus* was completed in 374, seven years after his accession to the episcopate. Epiphanius had composed it at the request of the Church of Syedra in Pamphylia as an "anchor" (hence the title) of faith in the adverse winds of heresy. It gives a systematic treatment of Christian dogma. In some manuscripts it contains the earliest version of the Nicaeno-Constantinopolitan Creed. A few years later he published the *Panarion*. This work was intended as a "medicine chest" (the literal meaning of the title) against various heresies. Epiphanius deals with 80 heresies, comparing them to poisonous animals, expounding their teaching in some detail, then providing the antidote by refuting their doctrines and denouncing their religous practices. In gathering his material, he spared no effort to obtain relevant and reliable infor-

mation. This, combined with the fact that he is the only author to discuss many of them in detail, makes the *Panarion* a very significant source of information about dissenting groups within the early Church.

It was Epiphanius' ardent defence of orthodoxy, in his writing as well as in his life, that attracted the attention of Catholic scholars of the Counter-Reformation. The first edition of his works was published, in Latin, in Basel in 1571. At around the same time cardinal Sirlet, the cardinal librarian of the Vatican Library who had also attended the Council of Trent, showed his interest in Epiphanius when he noted down, in his own hand, excerpts from his saint's *Life*. Finally, it was a Jesuit scholar in Paris, Denis Petau, who produced the first edition in Greek of the *Ancoratus* and the *Panarion* in 1622, highlighting in his preface the importance of Epiphanius' work for the present struggle against the Protestants.

CLAUDIA RAPP

Biography

Born at Eleutheropolis in Palestine in the second decade of the 4th century to a Jewish family, Epiphanius was educated by a rabbi, but converted to Christianity soon after the rabbi's death. He spent some time in Egypt with the desert fathers and returned to Palestine where he founded a monastery c.335. In 367 he became bishop of Salamis on Cyprus, defending orthodoxy in his teaching and his writing until his death in 403.

Writings

The Panarion: Selected Passages, edited by Philip R. Amidon, New York: Oxford University Press, 1990

Further Reading

Clark, Elizabeth A., *The Origenist Controversy: The Cultural Construction of an Early Christian Debate*, Princeton, New Jersey: Princeton University Press, 1992

Dechow, Jon F., *Dogma and Mysticism in Early Christianity: Epiphanius of Cyprus and the Legacy of Origen*, Macon, Georgia: Mercer University Press, 1988

Norris, F.W., Epiphanius of Salamis entry in *Encyclopedia of Early Christianity*, 2nd edition, edited by Everett Ferguson, 2 vols, New York: Garland, 1997, pp. 380–81

Rapp, Claudia, "Epiphanius of Salamis: The Church Father as Saint" in *The Sweet Land of Cyprus: Papers Given at the Twenty-Fifth Jubilee Spring Symposium of Byzantine Studies*, edited by A.A.M. Bryer and G.S. Georghallides, Nicosia: Cyprus Research Centre, 1993, pp. 169–87

Epirus

Region in northwest Greece

Epeiros means "mainland" in ancient Greek. At first sight this seems rather a vague term, but the western coast of Epirus is the mainland opposite the northern Ionian islands of Corfu and its outliers. The eastern border is formed by the central Pindus massif running like a spine through northern Greece. To the north, the central Albanian plain beginning near Vlorë marks the end of Epirus, basically a mountainous region, while to the south the Gulf of Arta and the comparatively low-lying areas of Aetolia and Acarnania form a similar barrier. Three

Epirus: "Dark Suli's rocks ... robed half in mist" – the mountains between Ioannina and the sea

parallel high limestone ridges running from north to south dominate the landscape and make the area curiously enclosed, since invaders coming from the north can climb up the valleys of the Aoos (Vijosë) river and its tributaries, but eventually these lead nowhere. The alluvial valleys are quite fertile, but flooding is always a danger. There are few natural harbours, and these are liable to silting. Rainfall by Greek standards is plentiful, although winters are harsh, and melting snows cause deforestation.

Unlike Macedonia, Epirus is a compact, well-defined, and reasonably homogeneous entity, but both areas have caused controversy by their position half inside and half outside the Greek world. Thus in Classical times Epirots and Macedonians were seen as semibarbarians, and, whereas the territory of Classical Greece was independent in 1830, it was not until the Balkan Wars of 1912 and 1913 that Epirus, like Macedonia, was freed from the Ottoman yoke. In the early Middle Ages most of Epirus passed from Byzantine control, and for much of the later Middle Ages it was ruled by a Greek-speaking dynasty, but one different from that reigning in Constantinople. At all times the ethnicity of Epirus has been in dispute, with Greeks and Illyrians in ancient times, Greeks, Albanians, and a few other races in modern times, sharing the territory between them. At present Greeks still call southern Albania "northern Epirus", and it is possible to find Greek-speakers as far north as Vlorë. Up until World War II it was

still possible to find Albanian-speakers as far south as Preveza. The history of Epirus in ancient and medieval times is distorted by the wish to prove the antiquity of Greek or Albanian claims, although most of the evidence points to considerable movements of population, the infiltration of other ethnic groups, notably Slavs, Turks, and Latins, and a generally mixed population.

The *Odyssey* refers to Epirus as the mainland and to the possibility that Odysseus may have sheltered in Thesprotia, the area opposite Corfu which is still known by this name. Homer in the same poem talks of the oracle of Dodona, second only to Delphi in fame and to none in antiquity, situated in the mountains of eastern Epirus. Herodotus mentions Epirus as the home of the ancient Dorians and refers to the oracle at the mouth of the river Acheron in southern Epirus. The Persian and Peloponnesian Wars do not seem to have impinged much on Epirus, although the Persian invasion to the east, the conflict between Corcyra (modern Corfu) and Epidamnus to the west, and the campaigns of Demosthenes in Aetolia to the south must have made some mark.

In the 4th century BC the Greek world widened. Philip of Macedon was married to the sister of Alexander, a powerful king of the Molossians, who seems to have established hegemony over the rest of Epirus. He and his more famous cousin Pyrrhus tried to expand westwards in the same way that Alexander the Great had expanded the power of Macedon to the east, but both perished in the attempt. Nevertheless, the 3rd and 2nd centuries were prosperous times for Epirus in which powerful cities like Antigoneia and Amantia were built. Modern Albanian historians tend to see these as Illyrian foundations, but 4th-century inscriptions show the tribes of Epirus, including the Molossians, writing in Greek. The Molossian monarchy fell in 232 BC and was replaced by a federal republic with an assembly at Phoenice (modern Finiq) in the Greek-speaking part of southern Albania. In Rome's war against Macedon, Epirus changed sides and was punished for its faithlessness by the Roman sack of many Epirote towns and the enslavement of 150,000 captives in 168 BC.

Not surprisingly, Epirus fell into decline under Roman rule. Cicero's friend Atticus had rich estates at Buthrotum (modern Butrint) and Latin settlers and traders may have brought some prosperity to the coast near Italy, although both branches of the Via Egnatia passed further north. Augustus founded Nicopolis near Preveza and Hadrian Hadrianopolis near Gjirokastër. Roman foundations in Greek lands soon lost their Latin speech, but the influence of Latin should not be discounted as a factor in west Balkan ethnology, as it would help explain both the presence of large numbers of Vlachs in Albanian and Greek Epirus and the survival of Albanian, not giving way to Greek or Latin because neither was the dominant lingua franca.

Writing in the 1st century AD, Strabo gives a picture not only of Epirus in his own day, but also, apparently drawing on the 6th-century BC geographer Hecataeus, of conditions in the past. Tribes like the Chaones and the Molossians had long vanished by Strabo's time, but interestingly he describes them as neither Illyrian nor Greek, but Epirot. The ambiguous state of Epirus did not become any clearer when Roman authority collapsed. Alaric and his Visigoths occupied Epirus for quite a long period at the beginning of the 5th century before proceeding westwards. The revival of the east Roman empire in the 6th century under Justinian I, himself of Illyrian stock, temporarily revived the fortunes of Epirus, now divided into Vetus Epirus in the south and Nova Epirus in the north. According to the 6th-century historian Procopius, Justinian built or rebuilt extensive fortifications in both districts. Some of them may have been the work of Anastasius. But the fortifications proved useless in checking the Slav invasions which had already begun at the end of Justinian's reign. At the beginning of the 7th century Byzantine authority over the whole of the western Balkans would seem to have been lost. The extent and nature of the Slav invasions are a matter of dispute, particularly among Greek and Albanian historians who in minimizing the Slav presence point to the undoubted survival of the Greek and Albanian languages. On the other hand, the melancholy testimony of the few written records, the abundance of Slav place-names in Epirus, and the archaeological evidence with almost no churches being built between the 6th and 9th centuries, do suggest a hiatus in the Greek presence.

By the 9th century Byzantium was recovering. It still occupied southern Italy, and had a strong navy. Themes of Nicopolis and Dyrrhachium were established in southern and northern Epirus, although it is uncertain how far these themes extended inland. When in 1016 Basil II defeated the Bulgarians he recaptured the whole of the Balkans, and Epirus remained in the Byzantine empire for most of the next two centuries. The last Italian possession of the empire fell to the Normans in 1071, and towards the end of the 11th century Epirus was frequently invaded from the west by leaders like Robert Guiscard and his son Bohemond.

Manuel Komnenos was the last Byzantine emperor to harbour Italian ambitions and to control the western Balkans. Shortly after his death, the Serbs under Stefan Nemanja became independent, the Bulgars revolted, and the Albanian tribes of the interior, never exactly subservient, followed suit. The Fourth Crusade of 1204 divided what was left of the empire with Epirus falling into the hands of the famous Doukas family, also known as Angelos, related to the Komnenoi. For the next century the fortunes of this family and of Epirus waxed and waned. Sometimes, as when they occupied Thessaly and even Thessalonica, it looked as if they might succeed in recapturing Constantinople. After the Battle of Pelagonia in 1259 it was clear that the empire of Nicaea was the stronger and the last years of the despotate of Epirus were sad ones with the dynasty being propped up by the Angevins and the succession passing through the female line to the Italian family of Orsini.

The capital of the despotate was at Arta. In spite, or perhaps because, of its precarious political position Epirus saw much church building in the 13th and 14th centuries. In southern Albania, the great fortress church of Mesopotam is a 12th-century foundation. The last despot of Epirus was defeated in 1340, and momentarily Epirus passed into the hands of the incompetent Byzantine emperor Andronikos III. He built, or restored, churches in Epirus, but within a few years the province had been lost to the Serbs under Stephan Dushan. On Dushan's death in 1355 his empire fell apart, and Epirus was ruled in part or as a whole by a succession of different nationalities, Florentine, Albanian, and Serb. It was clear that with the collapse of any central authority Epirus was an easy prey to invasions from the north of Albanians and Vlachs, both of whom have left their mark in the modern era. The anonymous *Chronicle of Ioannina* gives a good account of the complicated history of these times.

Eventually the Ottomans, with surprising speed, conquered virtually the whole of Epirus. Although Venice held isolated outposts on the coast, and Scanderbeg kept up resistance in Albania during the 15th century, most of the land was Turkish for over 500 years. It was, however, not a time of complete stagnation. The presence of Venice and the proximity to Italy meant some degree of trade and cultural interchange with the west. As a backward province remote from the capital, Epirus was not liable to much Turkish immigration, although Ioannina began to look like a Turkish town. When the central authority grew weak, warlords like Ali Pasha could carve out virtually independent realms of their own. But, although Ali Pasha and his savage bands of Albanians destroyed some villages, his rule over a mixed Greek and Albanian domain stretching from Tepelenë to Preveza was not entirely harsh. The poverty of mountain districts drove many Epirots overseas, where engaged in trade they became rich, sending part of their wealth back to their native villages. The district was wild and uncivilized, and western travellers were baffled by the medley of different races and the presence of brigands or klephts, who sometimes combined their role with that of *armatoloi* or keepers of law and order.

With the death of Ali Pasha in 1821 and the establishment of Greek independence in 1830, Epirus became even more lawless. As in Macedonia, there was a series of gallant but not always scrupulous Greek heroes fighting for liberty with the advantage that there were no rival Slav bands. Albanians and Vlachs, though present in large numbers, were less nationalistically inclined, with most Vlachs being on the Greek side. Before meeting a martyr's death in 1779, the heroic St Kosmas had travelled the length and breadth of Epirus preaching Greek nationalism and founding new churches.

Turks and Albanians in Epirus put up a stiff resistance in the First Balkan War, and Ioannina was one of the last places to fall to Greek troops. The Great Powers found it hard to draw the Greek– Albanian frontier which eventually left many Greek speakers in Albania and Albanian speakers in Greece. Before, during, and after World War I Greece briefly occupied southern Albania or northern Epirus, as the Greeks liked to call it. After the peace treaties there was a bad feeling between the two countries with violent incidents and a great deal of lawlessness on both sides of the frontier. The educational rights of Greeks in Albania were curtailed; there were no Albanian schools in Greece. Italy first fomented trouble, and then in World War II invaded Greece in 1940, only to have its forces thrown back as far as Tepelenë. The German invasion of 1941 left the Greek army stranded on this advanced line.

During World War II both Greek and Albanian Epirus saw a different pattern of resistance from that followed by the rest of Greece and Albania. In Greece the forces of EDES (*Ethnikos Dimokratikos Ellinikos Syndesmos*, the National Democratic Hellenic Union) under Napoleon Zervas were able with difficulty to keep themselves free from the control of the communist ELAS (*Ellinikos Laikos Apeleftherotikos Stratos*, the Greek Popular Liberation Army). The Greeks in Albania tried to organize resistance in broad agreement with Zervas, but found it difficult to resist the nationalist, Muslim, and vaguely pro-Axis Balli Kombëtar or the equally nationalist, atheist, but fervently anti-Axis partisans under Enver Hoxha. Hoxha, an inhabitant of the northern Epirot town of Gjirokastër, prevailed. Under his authoritarian regime the Greek minority was allowed limited educational rights, but no contact with their fellow Greek-speakers in southern Epirus. In Greece Albanian-speaking Muslims, the so-called Tsams, were accused of favouring the Axis and expelled to Albania where Hoxha planted them in such a way that the Greek element in the population was diluted.

After the war Greek Epirus, though a mountainous area difficult of access without anything much apart from Dodona in the way of Classical sites, shared the benefits brought by tourism: Igoumenitsa became an international port and resorts like Parga were made more accessible. The collapse of communism in Albania in 1992 could have led to the equally beautiful coastline of Greek-speaking Albania being developed, perhaps in a more sensitive way, but in fact there was massive emigration from Albania to Greece. Consequently, the Greek villages of northern Epirus are now sadly neglected and suffering from the general lawlessness that followed the collapse of president Berisha's government in 1997. Greece has now formally renounced its claim to northern Epirus, and showed remarkable restraint when some Albanian Greeks were found guilty of plotting against the state, but is naturally interested in the future of what, with some reason, it regards as part of its people.

T.J. WINNIFRITH

Summary

A mountainous region of northwest Greece, Epirus—like Macedonia—has always been ambivalent about its membership of the Greek world. There were ancient oracles at Dodona and Ephyra. The reign of king Pyrrhus (319–272 BC) initiated a period of prosperity for Epirus which ended with the arrival of the Romans in 168 BC. Huns and Slavs interrupted periods of Roman/Byzantine rule. After 1204 Epirus became an independent despotate but from 1340 ownership was disputed between Florentines, Albanians, and Serbs until the Ottoman conquest in the 15th century. Epirus became Greek again in 1913 but the border with Albania has remained a running sore.

Further Reading

Cabanes, Pierre, *L'Epire de la mort de Pyrrhos à la conquête Romaine*, Paris: Belles Lettres, 1976

Cross, Geoffrey Neale, *Epirus: A Study in Greek Constitutional Development*, Cambridge: Cambridge University Press, 1932

Foss, Arthur, *Epirus*, London and Boston: Faber, 1978

Hammond, N.G.L., *Epirus: The Geography, the Ancient Remains, the History and Topography of Epirus and Adjacent Areas*, Oxford: Clarendon Press, 1967

Koliopoulos, John S., *Brigands with a Cause: Brigandage and Irredentism in Modern Greece, 1821–1912*, Oxford: Clarendon Press, 1987

Leake, William Martin, *Travels in Northern Greece*, London: Rodwell, 1835; reprinted Amsterdam: Hakkert, 1967

Lear, Edward, *Journals of a Landscape Painter in Albania, etc.*, London: Bentley, 1851; with introduction by Steven Runciman, London: Century, 1988

Nicol, Donald M., *The Despotate of Epiros, 1267–1479: A Contribution to the History of Greece in the Middle Ages*, Cambridge and New York: Cambridge University Press, 1984

Ruches, Pyrrhus J., *Albania's Captives*, Chicago: Argonaut, 1965

Winnifrith, Tom (editor), *Perspectives on Albania*, London: Macmillan, and New York: St Martin's Press, 1992

Woodhouse, C.M., *The Struggle for Greece, 1941–1949*, London: Hart Davis MacGibbon, 1976; New York: Beckman Esanu, 1979

Epistolography

Epistolography (from Greek *epistole* "letter" and *graphia* "writing") is letter writing. The term is used for a literary genre in which works are written in the form of letters. Such letters are known as literary letters – as distinguished from private and official letters – if they were either primarily destined for publication by their author or if they were published posthumously for the sake of their contents and what they reveal about the personality of the author (or of the addressee). A sharp line, however, cannot be drawn between literary and private letters. Private letters published afterwards should be assigned to epistolography if they are autobiographical and contemporary documents. In this case they are called literary private letters.

In Classical times folding wooden boards were used for correspondence. They were covered inside with wax to be written on and were used for answering letters after the initial message had been erased. Papyrus was also used – demonstrated by the large number of private letters written on papyrus – and, later on, parchment and paper. Since there was no public mail service, letters were sent by messengers who had to be privately hired in each case; another possibility was to send letters with travellers.

Letter writing is not a Greek invention: in the 2nd millennium BC the Egyptians were already collecting correspondence. A theory of letter writing was gradually developed by the Greeks during the Classical period around the 5th century BC, at a time when the contents and functions of literary forms were the subject of analysis. Moreover, the art of rhetoric became increasingly important. Since epistolography was regarded as an aspect of rhetoric, basic rules and principles for writing letters were developed. Some of the thoughts and general considerations about style of one of the oldest theoreticians, Artemon of Cassandreia (1st century AD), were indirectly passed on to us through statements of a late Hellenistic author, pseudo-Demetrius (c.1st century AD). In the 2nd century AD a certain Philostratus established a system of rules that classified the most important items for a cultivated and refined style. Here readers learn that a letter should be an image of the writer's soul. Letters are considered to be identical in character to conversation, hence great value is attached to forms of salutation and direct address in the text. The style should be distinguished by brevity and clarity; the language should be elevated but understandable. All this can be achieved by a moderate use of Atticisms and by avoiding rarely used words. Rhetorical ornamentation is allowed in principle but should be used with moderation. Metaphors, for instance, should be avoided, but the insertion of narratives and myths, literary allusions, quotations, and proverbs is encouraged.

In later centuries these theoretical principles were taken up and described repeatedly, but observed less and less in practice. Practical examples accompanied theoretical considerations. Pseudo-Demetrius, for instance, gives a survey of different letter forms (he mentions 21), quoting a sample letter for each type. In the Renaissance this author was still in demand in the Latin west, as revealed by occasional references to him by the famous humanist Erasmus of Rotterdam in his guide to letter writing.

Literary letters appear in various forms, and theoreticians who have tried to classify them strongly disagree over their number. Both the didactic epistle, which is often used in philosophical discussions, and the dedicatory epistle, used as a preface to literary works addressed to a specific person, are found, for example. Faked letters, which first became popular during the Hellenistic period and which were sometimes compiled as epistolary novels, were used for rhetorical exercises. In addition, there are private letters concerning friendship, comfort, requests, thanks, recommendation, praise, and reproach.

When writing a letter, certain conventions had to be observed. Letters usually consisted of three parts: the introduction or *praescriptum*, the actual text, and the final clause. The *praescriptum* originally contained only the salutation of the addressee, according to the scheme "A greets B", but this could be extended to a greater demonstration of friendship in the introductory and final parts, especially if the addressee's health became the main topic.

More or less private collections of correspondence are known for almost all famous people (though many only through references in other works), beginning with the Classical authors. In the Hellenistic period the writing of letters increased and gradually gained in importance over the following centuries. The extensive correspondence of the rhetorician Libanius (4th century AD) contains more than 1500 letters written to or by Libanius, some of them addressed to famous contemporaries. It is important to note that collections of private letters not only contain letters received by the respective addressee, but also letters written by him. When a letter was composed it was usual – especially with regard to later publication of the correspondence – to make a duplicate and retain it in a private archive. Before publication letters were sometimes subjected to a second rhetorical and stylistic revision. A letter was not only an instrument of communication, but a real literary product. A letter that was carefully drafted according to the rules of rhetoric was, naturally enough, enthusiastically received by the addressee. Many inspired passages were almost literally reproduced in subsequent letters of the recipient's own; this was not regarded as reprehensible but, on the contrary, as desirable. It was called *mimesis*, imitation. Moreover, it was customary to read elaborate letters aloud to interested circles in order to enjoy collectively a writer's language and expression.

Epistolography was also influenced by Christianization. The epistles of the apostle Paul to early Christian communities, for instance, had a partially didactic, partially encouraging purpose; they stand at the beginning of the tradition of the pastoral epistles and encyclica of the Christian Church. The letter was also an important instrument for the Fathers of the Church in the discussion of dogmatic, exegetical, and philosophical problems. Christian influence is evidenced by stereotyped phrases, modesty demanding that the sender – independent of his social position – assume an attitude of humility and place himself on a lower level in relation to the addressee. The form of salutation here is: "it is B that A greets" or "B is greeted by A".

In the Byzantine period epistolography remained within the tradition of the Classical and late-Classical as well as early-Christian periods. The Byzantines took particular delight in this literary genre. Almost every well-known personality in public life – writers (e.g. Michael Psellos, Maximos Planudes), emperors (e.g. Theodoros II Laskaris, Manuel II Palaiologos), clerical dignitaries (e.g. the patriarchs Photios and Nikolaos Mystikos) – left a collection of letters. There is no real Byzantine theoretical treatise before the 14th century, when Joseph Rhakendytes devoted one chapter of his rhetorical manual to letters, taking up the instructions on style known from antiquity. However, there was a large gap between theory and practice in Byzantine times. The inherited theoretical requirements were familiar but rarely taken into account. The epistle as a literary work was composed according to the principles of rhetoric and *mimesis*, because a written work would be accepted (which means that it would be copied and passed on to other readers) only if it contained an abundance of ornamentation with rhetorical figures and hidden allusions to Classical authors. On the other hand, the elaborate style and linguistic profuseness that often appear mannered led to a strong deconcretization (that is, lack of a concrete topic). As a result, the external form became more important than the content. Modern readers undeniably find this exaggerated or even repulsive. But for Byzantine intellectuals – and these were precisely the people to whom literary letters were directed – it became a social game: they enjoyed decoding a letter, that is, identifying Classical quotations and allusions and discovering rhetorical figures. Reading out a letter in front of an interested and competent audience could become a real performance (Greek *theatron*). If the listeners applauded the work, the writer's reputation and fame were enhanced. Byzantine epistolographers – like their Classical predecessors – collected duplicates of their letters so that they could rework them for possible publication. Such revised correspondence in turn was well received by other writers, who used it as a model or copied whole parts of it. The preface (*prooimion*) of a letter, being the rhetorically relevant part, was the most popular. The subjects of the letters were also modelled on Classical examples, and it has to be said that epistolographers insisted more on matters of style than on thematic variation. Because letters also had a social function, such topics as friendship and, in relation to this, the separation of penfriends, were prominent. A letter was then meant to provide comfort and encouragement, which although not replacing a personal meeting, was at least regarded as a certain makeshift. If requests were related to the writer himself, they sometimes articulated specific material wishes. This often led to begging letters of which there are numerous unpleasant examples from the Byzantine period. However, if a request was associated with a third party, it could be a letter of recommendation; the protégé then often acted as a messenger. Frequently, presents (e.g. books, works of art, food, or objects of daily life) were sent along with the letter. There was not necessarily a specific purposes to the many of the hymns of praise contained in such letters, which simply seem to be flattering: the writer often degraded himself, while the addressee was exalted. The exchange of compliments was also of great importance. The attempt to gain a correspondent's benevolence (*captatio benevolentiae* – a term that comes from forensic rhetoric) through adulation was a means of achieving some purpose. If a correspondent did not reply for a long time, he might be accused with reproachful formulations, often expressed in terms derived from legal language. In spite of their stereotyped manner and of the difficulties involved in puzzling out their precise contents, Byzantine letters offer rich material for research into the various fields of history and culture of the period, provided that the modern reader is not discouraged by the flowery diction or by the many allusions, which may appear rather mystical.

After the fall of the Byzantine empire many Greek scholars emigrated to western Europe, mainly to the centres of humanism in Italy. Acting as teachers, writers, and editors of Classical texts, they brought the knowledge of Greek language and literature into the Latin west; consequently, the antique and Byzantine traditions were never interrupted. Most of these intellectuals left series of letters among their works (e.g. Constantine Laskaris and Markos Mousouros in the 15th and 16th centuries) that provide important historical and cultural evidence of their time. Between the 15th and the 19th centuries precepts for a good letter-writing style (according to the theory of letters current in the late Classical period) were widespread.

Most letters were written in the vernacular language – due to the gradually changing state of the Greek language – and directed to the general public. Furthermore, compilations of specific aphorisms and expressions were produced for use in letters, to meet the increasing demand for popular and generally understandable letter-writing manuals.

A change in epistolographic style, i.e. the abandonment of rhetoric and the adoption of a more individual style, reflects the general development of European literature in the period between the 16th and the 19th centuries. Modern Greek epistolography, however, still continued to adhere to the models adopted from the Byzantines, although more specific and personal themes were dealt with in letters. It was only in the 20th century that the old patterns were gradually abandoned. In most cases correspondence is now an essential component of a writer's complete works. In addition to autobiographical information, it often contains statements that are essential for the interpretation of an artist's works.

ASTRID STEINER-WEBER

Further Reading

Hunger, Herbert, *Die hochsprachliche profane Literatur der Byzantiner*, vol. 1, Munich: Beck, 1978, pp. 199–239

Mullett, Margaret: "The Classical Tradition in the Byzantine Letter" in *Byzantium and the Classical Tradition*, edited by Margaret Mullett and Roger Scott, Birmingham: Centre for Byzantine Studies, University of Birmingham, 1981

Sykutris, Johannes, Epistolographie entry in *Real-Encyclopädie der klassischen Altertumswissenschaft*, edited by August Pauly *et al.*, supplement 5, 185–220

Erasistratus *c*.315–*c*.240 BC

Physician

Erasistratus is known as the father of physiology. Born into a medical family in Iulis on the island of Ceos, educated in Athens in the peripatetic philosophy of Aristotle and Theophrastus, he later learned medicine on the island of Cos. Aristotle's son-in-law Metrodorus taught him medicine. Around 293 BC he was a court physician to Seleucus I Nicator and worked mostly in Antioch in medical practice. By tradition, he became a member of the Museum in Alexandria. Later writers, such as Celsus, associated Erasistratus and Herophilus as colleagues in research in the Museum, but some modern scholars are sceptical that Erasistratus was actually in residence in Alexandria. More likely he conducted his anatomical research there, since it is doubtful that dissections could have been conducted elsewhere.

The leisurely research environment of the Museum and his previous philosophical and medical practice enabled Erasistratus to examine the physiology of the body in a comprehensive system. He provided original and important observations on the functions of blood, air, digestion, and nerves that were probably explained in his work *Oi Katholou Logoi* (*General Principles*). None of Erasistratus' works is extant, but, because later authors, especially Galen, referred to him extensively, his ideas are preserved. Although Erasistratus influenced physiology, medicine, and, to some degree, philosophy, his major influence was confined to specific contributions.

Erasistratus' system combined a mechanistic system of bodily functions influenced by his Stoic teacher, Chrysippus, and by his anatomist colleague at Alexandria, Herophilus. Also influential on his thinking were the peripatetic teleology of causation and an abiding commitment to empirical verification, perhaps derived from Strato. Dissection of human cadavers was conducted at the Museum. The Roman medical writer Celsus (early 1st century AD), attributed vivisection of condemned criminals to both Herophilus and Erasistratus. Later Christian writers (Tertullian and Augustine among them) repeated the accusation. Many modern scholars are sceptical because Galen, who employed Erasistratus' works extensively, made no mention of the practice, but he described Erasistratus' vivisection experiments with animals. However, Erasistratus himself did say that the examination of dead bodies can be deceptive in terms of what we may learn about the functions of live bodies.

Erasistratus wrote on abdominal pathology. Gargilius Martialis (fl. 3rd century AD) referred to Alexandrian deep autopsies for the cause of death. In particular he spoke of an examination of death by lice-induced typhus where death was detected by changes in cardiac tissue. Whereas Gargilius did not specifically name Erasistratus, he is the only one at Alexandria whose name is associated with autopsy.

Erasistratus' assertion that the heart was central to both the venal and the arterial systems has led some modern scholars to claim that he foresaw the circulatory system, but this is not the case. Erasistratus thought that the heart pumped blood through the venal system to all the parts of the body to convey nourishment. The liver transforms nutriments from the digestive tract. Galen would later assign a greater role to the liver because he did not accept Erasistratus' assertion that the heart completes the process started by the liver. To Galen the liver was the beginning of the venal system, not the heart. According to Erasistratus nourishment in the form of blood reaches its destination in tiny particles through very fine pores. The arterial system delivered vital spirits in air (*pneuma*), and some of the vital spirits in blood pumped by the left heart ventricle are transformed by the brain into psychic spirits (another *pneuma*) and subsequently conveyed through the nerves to all body parts. Each form of *pneuma* from veins, arteries, and nerves ultimately was delivered through such fine networks as to be invisible. Thus the organism was a combination of three mechanisms: appetites (*orexeis*), energies or forces (*dynameis*), and substances (*hylai*).

According to Erasistratus, the process which supplies nutriments in the form of blood from its production centre in the liver pumped by the heart to all parts, is analogous to the function of water in the garden. Just as in the garden, the water is consumed and so is the blood. The observation that a severed artery spurts blood is because of a vacuum created by the outflowing air. The vacuum's action (*horror vacui*) also causes the flow from the veins and nerves throughout the body. Perhaps Erasistratus' mechanical action was derived from or inspired by Strato.

Erasistratus demonstrated the metabolic process in a famous experiment with birds, the details of which are preserved in the tract *Anonymous Londinensis* of the 6th century AD. A bird or similar animal would be deprived of food for some time, then it would be weighed, as well as its excrement, over a period of time. The postulate is the loss of weight of the combination of excretions and the animal is accounted for by the equivalent consumption of nourishment.

He wrote in a lost work, *On Fevers*, that fevers resulted from inflammations, a theory rejected by Celsus and Galen. He regarded as a main cause of disease an excessive flooding of the blood, because excessive nourishment ultimately compresses *pneuma* in the extremities of the arteries, thereby causing inflammations. Like Herophilus, he thought that men and women had the same diseases, none being peculiar to a single sex. Both Erasistratus and Herophilus saw the differences between sensory and motor nerves. Erasistratus rejected most therapeutic uses for bloodletting, again supplying the rejection by later medical writers who knew his works.

Although many late Greek and Roman writers cited Erasistratus' works, especially Galen, none adopted his medical system, and yet all were influenced by Erasistratus' specific contributions about the body's functions.

JOHN M. RIDDLE

See also Anatomy

Biography

Born *c*.315 BC at Iulis on Ceos, Erasistratus was educated in Athens at the peripatetic school of Aristotle and Theophrastus and later in medicine on Cos. Then he moved to Alexandria and joined the Museum where he worked with Herophilus. None of his writing is extant but he had a great influence on subsequent work in physiology and medicine. He died *c*.240 BC.

Writings

Fragmenta, edited by Ivan Garofalo, Pisa: Giardini, 1988

Further Reading

Brain, Peter, *Galen on Bloodletting: A Study of the Origins, Development, and Validity of his Opinions, with a Translation of the Three Works*, Cambridge and New York: Cambridge University Press, 1986
Fraser, P.M., *Ptolemaic Alexandria*, 3 vols, Oxford: Oxford University Press, 1972
Longrigg, James, Erasistratus entry in *Dictionary of Scientific Biography*, edited by Charles Coulston Gillespie, vol. 4, New York: Scribner, 1971, pp. 382–86
Lonie, I. M., "Erasistratus, the Erasistrateans and Aristotle", *Bulletin of the History of Medicine*, 38 (1964): pp. 426–43
Staden, Heinrich von, *Herophilus: The Art of Medicine in Early Alexandria: Edition, Translation, and Essays*, Cambridge and New York: Cambridge University Press, 1989
Wilson, Nigel G., "Erasistratus, Galen, and the Pneuma", *Bulletin of the History of Medicine*, 33 (1959): pp. 293–314

Eratosthenes

Scholar of the 3rd century BC

Eratosthenes, son of Aglaos, was a renowned scholar, poet, and scientist. His family was Cyrenean and was probably not of substantial means, although it could afford to send him to Athens for his education. His birthdate cannot be established with certainty. The *Suda* places his birth during the 126th Olympiad (276/275–273/272 BC), but this is too late and scholars now put his birth in the mid-280s BC. Eratosthenes did not receive his education at nearby Alexandria, but rather went to Athens to pursue philosophy. He studied with Zeno, founder of the Stoic school, Arcesilaus, head of the Platonic Academy, and Ariston of Chios, who had established a new branch of the Stoa. His varied philosophical studies reflect the eclecticism that consistently informed his life's work.

In 245 BC, at the age of about 40 and on the strength of his growing reputation in the fields of poetry, mathematics, and geography, Eratosthenes was invited by Ptolemy III Eurgetes, king of Egypt, to come to Alexandria. After the retirement of Apollonius of Rhodes, he assumed the directorship of the Library of Alexandria, one of the most prestigious positions in the ancient world. He remained there until he was succeeded by Aristophanes of Byzantium. His death, which occurred during the reign of Ptolemy V Epiphanes, may be dated to between 205 and 195 BC.

Eratosthenes was an expert in philosophy, grammar, poetry, chronology, mathematics, astronomy, and geography, and the breadth and the versatility of his intellect were both praised and censured in antiquity. Admirers called him a "second Plato". Others preferred to call him *pentathlos* ("jack of all trades"), since he was versed in so many branches of learning, or *beta* ("second best"), since he never specialized in any one area but showed enough brilliance to be considered the second leading authority in many disciplines. Each term was used in both derogatory and complimentary contexts. Eratosthenes himself coined the term *philologos* ("scholar" or "lover of learning") to describe his scholarly activities.

His works are known only by title or through fragments. No comprehensive edition of the fragments exists, although fairly good editions of individual areas have been published. His three-volume work *Geography* and his *On the Measurement of the Earth* epitomize his scientific spirit. Eratosthenes broke from his predecessors in rejecting Homer and mythology as trustworthy sources of geographical information and relied instead on his training in mathematics and astronomy and on the immense resources available in the Library at Alexandria. The *Geography* was intended to describe the entire inhabited world. In book 1 he attacked the use of Homer in geographical studies and pointed out the flaws of previous geographical works, which had now been rendered obsolete by the extensive information garnered from the military expeditions of Alexander the Great. In book 2 he fixed the world's breadth and length, and in book 3, he used his measurements to construct a map of the world. Eratosthenes' anthropology, set forth in book 2, is remarkable, in so far as he rejected the traditional categories of "Greek" and "barbarian", preferring to regard people on the basis of good and bad qualities. In *On the Measurement of the Earth* he used his mathematical skills to calculate the earth's circumference, which he fixed at 252,000 stades or 24,662 miles (accurate to about 1 per cent).

Eratosthenes is accredited with establishing the field of scientific chronology. He revised the existing Olympic victor lists (widely used for determining dates) and published his revision in two books. Using those Olympic lists and, for prehistoric events, the lists of Spartan kings, he wrote his own

Chronology, which established a timetable from the Trojan War (which he dated to 1184/83 BC) down to the death of Alexander (323 BC). Eratosthenes divided this 860-year period into 10 epochs, with events listed in the form of chronological tables.

Eratosthenes was eclectic in his approach to philosophy. He received his training from the Platonist Arcesilaus and the Stoic Ariston; he also heard the teachings of the Cynic Bion of Borysthenes. Eratosthenes' philosophical writings, which survive only in a few fragments, probably predate his arrival at Alexandria. The *Platonicus*, penned in the traditional dialogue format, dealt with Platonic astronomy and mathematics. Other works, such as *On Freedom from Pain*, *Ariston*, and *On Good and Evil Qualities*, have been lost. Many later writers heaped scorn on Eratosthenes' philosophical treatises, but their attacks are heavily flavoured by sectarian biases.

Eratosthenes was considered one of the great mathematicians of his day; Archimedes dedicated a book to him and corresponded with him on mathematical problems. Little remains of his works, however. He developed a method for determining prime numbers, the so-called Sieve of Eratosthenes, which in modified form (needed, since the system does not work with high numbers) is still critical for number theory research; he wrote on progressions and proportions; he solved the problem of how to double a cube, for which he designed a mechanical instrument; and he discussed musical scales. He applied his learning in geometry to the fields of astronomy and mathematical geography. For example, he measured the distance to the sun as 804 million stades (= 78 million miles, versus the actual 92.9 million) and to the moon as 780,000 stadia (= 76,500 miles, versus the actual 239,000). The tilt of the earth's axis was calculated, with great accuracy, as 23 degrees, 51 minutes, 15 seconds. A lost treatise, *On Means*, has not survived, but it did form part of the Hellenistic edited collection *Treasury of Analysis*, which contained works by such famous mathematicians as Euclid.

In the field of literary criticism, Eratosthenes' most important work was *On Ancient Comedy*, in 12 books. This work was very highly regarded in antiquity. Evidently he wrote essays on a wide variety of topics, such as textual criticism, authorship of plays, dialectology, dates of performances, historical issues, and the interpretation of individual passages. Although he published no editions of the plays, Eratosthenes did collate available manuscripts to fix textual readings.

Very little of Eratosthenes' poetry survives. Traces of Callimachean Alexandrinism are evident. For example, Eratosthenes' short epic *Erigone*, dealing with Icarius and his daughter Erigone and her dog, evokes with its style and form Callimachus' *Hecale*. His didactic poem *Hermes*, which describes the god's ascent to the heavens, recalls the didactic poems of the 3rd century BC, especially when Eratosthenes describes the eight spheres of the universe. Otherwise, Eratosthenes displayed in his poetry his usual independence of thought. For example, he rejected Homer and mythology as useful sources of poetic material – a view that was severely criticized, since the Greeks generally believed in the centrality of Homer in culture, history, and literature; he also insisted that the purpose of poetry was to entertain, not to instruct (a principle he called *psychagogia*).

Eratosthenes was vastly unappreciated in antiquity. He had few disciples, and his writings were often subjected by later writers to scathing attacks. The nickname *beta* was an ingenious but unwarranted term for someone who was truly brilliant in so many areas. He was one of those rare people for whom the sciences and the humanities are complementary. Applying his powerful intellect to fields as diverse as mathematics, chronology, literary criticism, geography, and philosophy, Eratosthenes had few equals in his or any other era.

STEVEN M. OBERHELMAN

Biography

Born perhaps in the mid-280s BC in Cyrene, Eratosthenes was educated in Athens where he was a pupil of Zeno, Arcesilaus, and Ariston. At the invitation of Ptolemy III Eurgetes he moved to Alexandria in 245 BC where he succeeded Apollonius Rhodius as director of the Library. He made distinguished contributions to philosophy, grammar, poetry, chronology, mathematics, astronomy, and geography but was too versatile to be appreciated by his contemporaries. He died *c.*200 BC.

Writings

Carminum reliquiae, edited by Eduard Hiller, Leipzig: Teubner, 1872 (poetry)

De Lycophrone, Euphronio, Eratosethene comicorum interpretibus, edited by Karl Strecker, dissertation, Greifswald, 1884

In *Die Fragmente der griechischen Historiker*, edited by Felix Jacoby, Leiden: Brill, 1923– , nos. 241, frr. 5–8 and 241, frr. F1–3 (chronology)

In *Collectanea Alexandrina*, edited by John Undershell Powell, Oxford: Clarendon Press, 1925, fragments 1–16, 22–27, 58–68 (poetry)

Eratosthenes von Kyrene als Mathematiker und Philosoph, edited by E.P. Wolfer, Groningen: Noordhoff, 1954

Die geographischen Fragmente, edited by Hugo Berger, Amsterdam: Meridian, 1964

Eratosthenica, edited by Gottfried Bernhardy, Osnabrück: Biblio, 1968, pp. 186–202 (philosophy)

Further Reading

Blomqvist, Berker, "Alexandrian Science: The Case of Eratosthenes" in *Ethnicity in Hellenistic Egypt*, edited by Per Bilde *et al.*, Aarhus: Aarhus University Press, 1992

Fraser, P.M., "Eratosthenes of Cyrene", *Proceedings of the British Academy*, 56 (1970): pp. 175–207

Fraser, P.M., *Ptolemaic Alexandria*, 3 vols, Oxford: Clarendon Press, 1972 (the single most important source for Eratosthenes and his work)

Goldstein, B.R., "Eratosthenes on the Measurement of the Earth", *Historia Mathematica*, 11 (1984): pp. 411–16

Knaack, G., Eratosthenes entry in *Real-Encyclopädie der klassischen Altertumswissenschaft*, edited by August Pauly *et al.*, vol. 6, 1907, 358–88

Pfeiffer, Rudolf, *History of Classical Scholarship from the Beginnings to the End of the Hellenistic Age*, Oxford: Clarendon Press, 1968

Solmsen, Frank, "Eratosthenes as Platonist and Poet", *Transactions of the American Philological Association*, 73 (1942): pp. 192–213

Solmsen, Frank, "Eratosthenes' Erigone", *Transactions of the American Philological Association*, 78 (1947): pp. 252–75

Thomas, Ivor (translator), *Selections Illustrating the History of Greek Mathematics*, 2 vols, London: Heinemann, and Cambridge, Massachusetts: Harvard University Press, 1939–41 (Loeb edition)

Thomson, James Oliver, *History of Ancient Geography*, Cambridge: Cambridge University Press, 1948

Eretria

City in Euboea

Eretria is the second principal ancient city on the island of Euboea, the first being its immediate neighbour to the north, Chalcis. In 498 BC the Eretrians joined the Athenians in sending help to the east Greek Ionian cities in their rebellion against their Persian overlords; the Eretrians contributed 5 triremes and the Athenians 20, which Herodotus says were the cause of evil for both Greeks and Persians alike. Though this achieved little enough on behalf of the Ionians beyond sacking sanctuaries at Sardis, when the Persians in their turn attacked mainland Greece in 490 BC Eretria was one of their first targets. After forcing the surrender of the southernmost Euboean city, Carystus, the Persians disembarked at Eretria without opposition and put the walled city under siege. The city was betrayed to them after six days' resistance; they burnt and plundered the sanctuaries, in revenge for the burning of the sanctuaries at Sardis, and deported at least part of the population (they were settled by Darius near Susa, and they or their descendants were still there in Herodotus' time continuing to speak Greek, as he notes with some surprise). Doubtless more were left at Eretria following the surprise defeat of the Persians at Marathon, since there was no interuption in the continuity of the city.

The geographer Strabo, writing in the 1st century BC, mentions, in addition to the existing city of Eretria, the ruins of "Old Eretria", which he believed was the city destroyed by the Persians; the remains of houses were still visible there. Excavations at Eretria itself have demonstrated that this was not correct, that the walled city captured and plundered by the Persians was the same one that existed in Strabo's time, and which, indeed, had been the location of the city since much earlier, at least as early as the 8th century BC. What Strabo saw as "Old Eretria" was elsewhere. The most likely candidate is situated to the north of the Classical city, closer to Chalcis, on a promontory site known by its modern Greek name of Lefkandi. Here an earlier settlement and, adjacent, an extensive cemetery have been excavated going back to the turn of the 2nd and 1st millennia BC, including one extremely rich grave in a large apsidal structure surrounded by wooden posts. This site seems to have been abandoned gradually, at the same time that the site of Classical Eretria developed. Whether or not there is a direct connection, the movement of inhabitants from the one to the other, Lefkandi must be significant to the early history of the Eretrians.

In general, this area, including Chalcis, had benefited from its geographical position, facing on to the sheltered waters between Euboea and the mainland and the sea route to the southeast, past the islands of Andros and Tenos (which are a continuation of the Euboean land-mass) into the central Aegean and beyond, encouraging direct trade links through to the eastern Mediterranean (while Chalcis, situated at the narrows of the Euripus, also controlled the sea routes to the north). The link with the central Aegean had been important even in the Early Bronze Age, while the evidence from Lefkandi proves the existence of overseas contacts even at the beginning of the Iron Age when mainland Greece apparently survived in isolation. After this, Eretrian involvement in the Greek trading post at al-Mina in Syria and the distribution, to both east and west, of the Euboean pottery drinking cups decorated with suspended groups of semicircles (the "pendant-semicircle *skyphoi*") demonstrate the importance of overseas links. Both Chalcis and Eretria, possibly in conjunction, played a major role in the early colonization movement, such as the colony on the island of Ischia in the bay of Naples. Eretria is also credited with the earliest colonization of Corfu, though this was soon supplanted by a Corinthian foundation.

What the later Greeks remembered of this period was a war between Eretria and Chalcis, over possession of the Lelantine plain which was situated between them. Herodotus points out that the reason the Eretrians helped the Ionians in 498 BC was not support for the Athenians but because Miletus had earlier helped them in their war against Chalcis. Thucydides also mentions grand alliances, with the "rest of Greece" divided into supporters of one or other of the Euboean cities. Whether these alliances are a historical reality, or a projection back into the unrecorded early period of later political links, cannot be resolved. It may well be that defeat at the hands of Chalcis forced the Eretrians to abandon the site at Lefkandi and move to the Classical site of their city.

The early significance of Eretria is demonstrated by the archaeological discoveries there. The principal sanctuary in the city, that of Apollo Daphnephoros, boasted a major limestone Doric temple of the late 6th century BC with high-quality sculptural decoration in marble, fragments of which survive. It was sacked by the Persians. Its earliest antecedent was a small apsidal structure of the 8th century BC, one of the oldest temple buildings to be found in Greece. Other shrines included a heroon of the 7th century BC, and a Thesmophorion, also sacked by the Persians, where the finds include a deposit of drinking vessels, presumably used in the cult rather than left as offerings. Links with Athens were close: the arrangement of the late Archaic temple of Apollo Daphnephoros seems to anticipate the hexastyle Athenian temples such as that of Hephaestus (the "Theseum") and of Poseidon at Sunium, where the original construction is dated before the Persian Wars. At the time Eretria joined Athens to help the Ionians, the Athenians had just fought a successful war against Chalcis, seized a substantial part of Chalcidian territory, and placed Athenian settlers on it, a move that must have benefited Eretria – Herodotus, perhaps, is being a shade too knowledgeable when in effect he denies this as a reason for Eretria's support of Miletus in the Ionian revolt.

The city recovered from the Persian attack, and became part of the Athenian alliance, along with Chalcis and the other Euboean cities. Their importance was such that their rebellion in 446 BC forced the Athenians to make a quick deal with the Spartans so that they could suppress it. We have an inscription that details the harsh terms then inflicted on Chalcis, with enough evidence to show that similar conditions were meted out to Eretria. Part of Eretrian territory may have been occupied by Athenians; certainly, there was an Athenian stronghold there (but outside the city) in 411 BC, and the discovery at Eretria of large numbers of Athenian "white-ground" vases (*lekythoi*), of the sort favoured as burial offerings in Athens in the latter part of the 5th century BC, suggests the presence of an Athenian population. Eretria finally broke away from Athens

in 411 BC, after the Syracusan disaster, but in the succeeding century joined the second Athenian alliance. Philip of Macedon took the city into his sphere of interest – a Macedonian presence is subsequently attested by two vaulted Macedonian chamber tombs, one at Eretria itself and another by the road to Amarynthus to the south. During the Hellenistic period the strategic importance of this area was emphasized by the continued presence of a Macedonian garrison at Chalcis, one of the three vital strongholds, the so-called fetters of Greece. Eretria, under the shadow of this presence, seems to have had its own Macedonian garrison, at least at the time of the final war between the Romans and the Macedonian king, Philip V. During this, in 198 BC, the city was attacked and sacked by the Romans. After this, despite a short involvement in the subsequent war with Antiochus III, Eretria regained its freedom, and enjoyed a subsequent uneventful history as a small town of the Roman empire.

There are interesting architectural remains. The city walls, originally constructed in the 7th century BC (the date of the first west gate), have been partly uncovered. Sections of the early (pre-Persian) walls survive on the acropolis, while the existing traces of the walls of the lower town are probably late 4th century BC, with later repairs and additions. There are early Hellenistic houses, some of which have good-quality pebble mosaics. Most interesting of all is the theatre. Unlike most Greek theatres it was constructed on level ground, by hollowing out the orchestra and banking earth up against a surrounding support wall for the cavea. There is also an underground passage, of uncertain purpose, running from the stage area to the centre of the orchestra.

R.A. TOMLINSON

Summary

A city in Euboea, Eretria, like its neighbour Chalcis, played a part in colonizing Italy, Sicily, and the north Aegean. The two cities fought over possession of the Lelantine plain in the late 8th century BC. Eretria was a member of the Delian League and the second Athenian confederacy. It was sacked by the Romans in 198 BC.

Further Reading

Auberson, Paul, *Führer durch Eretria*, Bern: Francke, 1972

Boardman, John, in *The Prehistory of the Balkans; and The Middle East and the Aegean World, Tenth to Eighth Centuries BC*, edited by Boardman *et al.*, Cambridge: Cambridge University Press, 1982 (*The Cambridge Ancient History*, vol. 3, part 1, 2nd edition), pp. 754ff.

Eretria: Fouilles et recherches, several vols, Bern: Francke, 1968– (final report series of recent and current Swiss excavations)

Forrest, W.G.G., in *The Expansion of the Greek World, Eighth to Sixth Centuries BC*, edited by John Boardman and N.G.L. Hammond, Cambridge: Cambridge University Press, 1982 (*The Cambridge Ancient History*, vol. 3, part 3, 2nd edition), pp. 249ff.

Lewis, D.M., in *The Fifth Century BC*, edited by Lewis *et al.*, Cambridge: Cambridge University Press, 1992 (*The Cambridge Ancient History*, vol. 5, 2nd edition), pp. 135ff.

Popham, M.R. *et al.*, *Lefkandi*, London: Thames and Hudson, 1990– (joint British / Greek excavations at Lefkandi)

Estates

Much of the history of the Greek countryside has been characterized by the struggle between state, wealthy landowner, and peasant for control of the productive agricultural land. Given the very varied nature of the Greek landscape, it was often advantageous to produce a particular cash crop on a large scale and export it to less suitable areas. This mode of production tended to favour the wealthy landowner who controlled large estates.

The first evidence for estate agriculture, as opposed to communal or individual subsistence production, comes from the Bronze Age. During the 17th and 16th centuries BC a series of large rural structures in eastern Crete, generally termed "villas", shows evidence for mass storage, high-status residence, and administration. These were presumably involved in the production of the wine, olive oil, and wheat mentioned in the Linear A texts. In the Linear B tablets from the Mycenaean palace of Pylos, dating to about 1200 BC, many individuals are listed as owning estates. The king's estate, which may have been one of several royal estates, was 1800 times as large as the smallest one on the list, and three times as large as those of his most senior subordinates.

The Archaic and Classical periods were characterized by widespread small landholding, often by tenant farmers who were very vulnerable to their landlords and creditors. Archaeological survey shows a wide distribution of small structures and intensive cultivation during this time. In the course of the Hellenistic period this gradually changed, with small farmsteads being abandoned and larger landowners, often based in the cities, gradually controlling more of the land. By the early Roman period much of the Greek countryside was dominated by large estates. Few of these were actually owned by Romans; in general there is little evidence for imperial estates, colonies of veterans, or estates owned by Roman aristocrats. The pattern was more one of large estates owned by rich local families who favoured and were favoured by Roman rule. Often they were based on villas sumptuously decorated with mosaics and equipped with bath houses. This was just one aspect of the increasing social stratification and economic polarization that characterized the period.

Estates were also an important part of the Byzantine landscape, though in many cases landowners owned a series of small dispersed plots, or several estates in different areas. The tenant farmer or *colonus* was very much tied to the land and heavily taxed, as well as paying rent to his landlord. A typical large estate would include some sort of mansion, demesne land as well as land let out to tenants, and a whole series of productive assets termed *autourgia*, such as olive groves, watermills, salt pans, and pottery workshops. The estate often encompassed all or part of a village where hired workers or tenants would live. Many monasteries increasingly had their own estates, with *metochia* or branches of the monastery to house the monks who supervised them.

The advent of the Ottoman empire caused major changes in landholding and the rural economy. Each Ottoman *spahi* or cavalryman was allotted a fief of varying size according to his rank. Usually this would consist of an entire village, but rather than managing it as an estate he would merely extract a proportion of the villagers' produce, and this would constitute his income. Other villages were estates owned by a *waqf* or Islamic endowment, or else by members of the imperial family.

In Asia Minor, from the end of the 16th century, there was a general process of appropriating the land of peasant farmers, either by force or because of debt. This land was amalgamated into *çiftliks* or estates, originally referring to the amount of land that could be worked by a *çift* or pair of oxen. By the end of the 18th century the *çiftlik* system had arrived in northern Greece. Typically estates would consist of a manor, often fortified with a tower, huts for hired workers, stables, large storerooms, a bakery, a smithy, and a watermill. Usually they were associated with a village of tenant farmers.

During the 17th and 18th centuries the Church and individual monasteries acquired considerable amounts of land, usually by bequests from Greek peasants who wanted to avoid their property being taken by the Ottoman authorities. In Cyprus by 1844, for example, the Church owned some 16.4 per cent of all agricultural land. As with the secular estates, they were mainly concerned with the production of cash crops on a large scale, as well as a range of subsistence crops for local consumption. The export trade in commodities such as cotton and wheat greatly favoured an estate that had a large labour force, controlled the necessary water rights, and could produce on a large scale.

The end of the estate system came after World War I, following the land law passed in 1917 by Venizelos's government. Large estates were broken up and redistributed to each family that had been tilling the land as hired hands. This expropriation extended to many of the monastic estates, including those of the Mount Athos monasteries. After the Asia Minor defeat in 1922 many of these confiscated lands were given to incoming rural Greeks from Anatolia as part of the refugee settlement process. To some extent this meant that agriculture and landholding remained fragmented and often less efficient. It did, however, allow for a strong landowning rural class, as opposed to a dissatisfied and oppressed rural population of serfs and hired labourers, which throughout Greek history has so often been the end result of the estate system.

MICHAEL GIVEN

Further Reading

Alcock, Susan E., *Graecia Capta: The Landscapes of Roman Greece*, Cambridge and New York: Cambridge University Press, 1993

Chadwick, John, *The Mycenaean World*, Cambridge and New York: Cambridge University Press, 1976

Inalçik, Halil, "The Emergence of Big Farms, Çiftliks: State, Landlords, and Tenants" in *Landholding and Commercial Agriculture in the Middle East*, edited by Çaglar Keyder and Faruk Tabak, Albany: State University of New York Press, 1991

Kazhdan, A.P. (editor), *The Oxford Dictionary of Byzantium*, 3 vols, New York and Oxford: Oxford University Press, 1991

McGowan, Bruce, *Economic Life in Ottoman Europe: Taxation, Trade, and the Struggle for Land, 1600–1800*, Cambridge and New York: Cambridge University Press, 1981

Sant Cassia, Paul, "Religion, Politics and Ethnicity in Cyprus during the Turkocratia, 1571–1878", *Archives Européennes de Sociologie*, 27/1 (1986): pp. 3–28

Ethics

Although ethical precepts of a rudimentary nature are found scattered throughout early Greek poetry and the surviving fragments of the Presocratic philosophers, there was no real attempt to formulate a coherent ethical system before the time of Socrates, Plato, and Aristotle. The Delphic maxims and the sayings attributed to the Seven Sages, epigrammatic lines from Hesiod and the gnomic poets, and early philosophical fragments, such as those of Xenophon and Heraclitus, provide early examples of attempts to collect and codify ethical wisdom gathered through the experience of many generations. Even the Homeric epics, with their professedly recreational objectives, came to be treated as storehouses of advice on human conduct.

Pythagoras (*c*.580–*c*.500 BC) founded a brotherhood which (probably under Orphic influence) appears to have advocated vegetarianism associated with the belief in transmigration of the soul. The brotherhood's rules emphasized simplicity in speech, dress, and food; for Pythagoras believed that the intellectual nature is higher than the sensual, and that the best life is one devoted to mental discipline.

A note of scepticism was sounded in the 5th century BC when the Sophists questioned moral absolutes. Their common theme was that the traditional opposition of good and bad, or just and unjust does not reflect any objective fact of nature but is rather a matter of social convention. Protagoras of Abdera taught that "man is the measure of all things: of the things that are that they are, of the things that are not that they are not", meaning that human judgement is subjective, and that one's perception is valid only for one's self. The particular content of moral rules may differ, but rules of some kind are necessary, he argued, if life is to be tolerable.

But even this attempt to set up a new standard for interpreting moral actions fell before the onslaught of that very scepticism which Protagoras himself initiated. The laws and codes of society were shown to be themselves a perversion of the natural state of man. Society was depicted, as by Glaucon and Adeimantus in Plato's *Republic*, as the product of a social contract in which *physis* (i.e. natural law that "might is right") was prevented by *nomos* (i.e. established laws of society and the state) – an artificial code made by the weaker many to suppress the stronger few. Tyrants and suchlike were those who broke through these codes and asserted the primeval right of might. True justice was the interest of the stronger. It was better to do evil than suffer evil, and having done evil, it was better not to pay the penalty than to pay the penalty. The possible consequences of such a doctrine, if translated into action, can well be imagined if one reads its representation by Thrasymachus and Callicles in the *Republic* and *Gorgias* of Plato.

Despite his ruthless criticism of the Sophists, Plato was well aware that it was by countenancing their destructive criticisms that Socrates (470–399 BC) was able to establish ethical values on the sound basis of knowledge. Socrates' contribution to ethics is best described as a way of inquiry rather than a way of life. He would ask for a definition of a virtue such as justice, courage, piety, or temperance and then, through questioning, he would demonstrate the inadequacy of the definition as a complete account of the virtue in question, and suggest the need to reformulate the definition. This method of inquiry was bound to undermine the security of conventional beliefs, and Socrates was therefore tried on a charge of corrupting the youth of Athens and was put to death. He did not subscribe to the moral relativism of the Sophists, but maintained that virtue could be known and that the good person knew what constituted virtue or justice. However, he himself did not claim to have such knowledge. Nor did he distinguish sharply between the good and the advantageous, but maintained that those who knew what good was would in fact be good. If anyone did what was not good, it was because he was ignorant of the nature of goodness. Thus, a person can become good through education.

Socrates' life and teaching gave rise to many later schools of moral philosophy. Four such schools originated among his immediate disciples: the Cynics, the Cyrenaics, the Megarians, and the Platonists. The Cynics held that self-control was the essence of virtue and that it could be taught. This was, in particular, the view of Antisthenes. The Cyrenaics were hedonists: for them pleasure was the highest good, provided it did not dominate one's life. Pleasures could not be ranked by superiority; they could only be measured by intensity and duration. The best-known member of the school was Aristippus of Cyrene. The Megarians (founded by Euclid of Megara) maintained the unity of goodness despite its equation with wisdom, god, or reason. It is the final secret of the universe, and can be revealed only through logical inquiry.

For Plato (428/27–348/47 BC), goodness is an essential element of reality. It is the common element by which all good things are good, in other words, the pure form of goodness. Not only good things, but all other forms too (being themselves good) depend on the form of the good for their sustenance and manifestation, just as all things in our world depend on the sun. Evil has no independent existence; it is an imperfect reflection of the good reality. The virtue of anything depended on its function, and human virtue lies in the fitness of a person to perform that person's proper function in the world.

Plato believed in a tripartite soul (and its "bigger" version, the state) consisting of the rational, the emotional, and the appetitive, each with its corresponding virtue: wisdom, courage, and temperance. Justice, the fourth virtue, consisted in the harmony between these three elements, when each part of the soul kept to its appropriate place and function: intelligence must rule, emotion must obey, and the two together must control the appetite. While the unjust man lives in a state of internal strife, the just man, whose soul is thus harmoniously ordered, finds true satisfaction in the pursuit of knowledge. Plato doubtless saw in the life and death of Socrates the concrete embodiment of his ideal of the just man.

With Plato, just as with Socrates, the basic problem of ethics becomes a problem of knowledge. He who knows that moral virtue leads to happiness will naturally practise virtue. This is different from the view of many Christian thinkers who feel that the fundamental problem of ethics is one of will, since a person may know what is morally right, but may not have the willpower to carry it out.

Plato maintained that it is worse to do evil than to suffer it, because immoral conduct is symptomatic of a sick soul. Once a person has committed an unjust deed, Plato believed that it is better for him to be punished than to go unpunished, because punishment serves to cure the soul of its most serious ills.

For Aristotle (384–322 BC), the aim of life was happiness, which he defined as activity that accords with the specific nature of humanity. Although such activity is accompanied by pleasure, such pleasure is not its principal aim. Happiness results from the activity of reason (an attribute unique to mankind) functioning in harmony with human faculties.

While accepting the four-fold virtues of the Platonic system, Aristotle maintained the importance of other traits such as friendship, liberality, gentleness, truthfulness, and wit. But the most important was prudence (*phronesis*), i.e. the ability to discern the right course of action that leads to a good life. For him, virtues are essentially good habits acquired by constant practice, and he makes a distinction between moral and intellectual virtues. In connection with moral virtues, he introduces the famous doctrine of the mean. A moral virtue is a mean between two extreme vices, one of excess and one of deficiency. Thus liberality is a mean between avarice and profligacy, and courage is a mean between cowardliness and foolhardiness. Intellectual virtues such as knowledge lead to contemplation, which is the highest human activity. Both these kinds of virtue are only a means towards the attainment of happiness, which results from the full realization of human potential.

Aristotle makes a distinction between instrumental goods (which are good only because they lead to some other thing that is good) and intrinsic goods (which are good in themselves). He also distinguishes between distributive justice and remedial justice, as well as between theoretical wisdom and practical wisdom. Practical wisdom, the knowledge which leads people to right action and a happy life, is the subject of both politics and ethics.

Like Aristotle's other works, his *Nicomachean Ethics* prompted commentaries, glosses, and paraphrases from scholars of late antiquity and the Byzantine age. Two sets of scholia are known, the first and more ancient being anonymous, and the second by Aspasios. Partial commentaries by Michael of Ephesus, Eustratios of Nicaea, and an anonymous Byzantine scholar are preserved in a Latin translation by Robert Grosseteste, Bishop of Lincoln (1253). A paraphrase was copied for the emperor John VI Kantakouzenos. This exegetical material gave rise to summaries of ethics such as those by John of Damascus, Michael Psellos, and Joseph Rhakendytes.

The chief Stoic philosophers in Greece were Zeno of Citium, Cleanthes, and Chrysippus of Soli, while the development of Stoicism under the Roman empire is represented by Epictetus and the emperor Marcus Aurelius. There were also a number of popular moralizing anthologies, and a treatise *De Virtutibus et Vitiis* is attributed to Andronicus of Rhodes. Stoic impact on Byzantine writers is evident in works such as Plethon's treatise *On Virtues*. According to Zeno, the true end of man is an active life in conformity with nature, in other words, a life according to virtue, which is the will of God and hence the law of the universe. Happiness is produced by right conduct. Originating from the views of Socrates and Plato, Stoicism taught that nature was rational and orderly, and that the only good life was one led in harmony with nature. Since life is influenced by material circumstances, one should free oneself from them as much as possible. This freedom could be achieved by cultivating certain cardinal virtues such as practical wisdom, fortitude, discretion, and justice.

Whereas Plato believed that human passions and physical desires must be regularized by reason, the Stoics rejected passion altogether as a basis for deciding what is good or evil. Although one cannot completely eliminate physical desires, a wise person can appreciate the difference between wanting something (which is caused by our desires) and judging it to be good (which is caused by our reason). The wise man identifies himself with reason, not with desires, and will neither expect the fulfilment of physical desires nor be anxious about failing to attain them. Living in a state of wisdom and virtue is the only real good, and the efforts to attain it are not hampered by external circumstances as is the search for material wealth and bodily pleasure, since wisdom and virtue are intellectual matters and therefore are within our control.

The Stoics believed that all human beings have the capacity for reason, and therefore held a notion of equality much broader than the Greek sense of equal citizenship: common reason makes all individuals fellow citizens, observed Marcus Aurelius. From this followed the Stoic concept of a universal moral law appealing to all people. This universality of reason provided a basis for rejecting ethical relativism as taught by the Sophists. The pursuit of wisdom and virtue is open to all human beings irrespective of the external circumstances of their lives, and it is not surprising to find that the two principal exponents of Stoicism in the 2nd century AD were a slave and an emperor. Stoicism also exerted considerable influence on Byzantine monastic circles.

Plotinus (born *c.* AD 215), the founder of Neoplatonism, enjoined purification by self-discipline, with the object of ascending to the spiritual world and pursuing the divine out of love and enthusiasm. Some idea of the ethical theory of the Neoplatonists may be gained from its formulation in the *Sentences* of Porphyry. According to Proclus and Ammonius, evil is not a substance, but a privation of good; in particular, it was a moral turning away from God. This theory of evil and its reconciliation with free will and divine providence were adopted by Psellos and Isaac Komnenos. The Neoplatonists identified happiness as union with God. This was to be achieved in contemplation through purifying the soul of its corporeal existence by virtue. Through the Cappadocian fathers, this identification provided a fundamental structure to Byzantine moral theology. Psellos believed that Aristotelian ethics could be integrated into this structure in that "political virtue", which is the lowest type, concerns the rationally ordered and harmonious life of man as a union of soul and body, a life formulated by Aristotle and including practical wisdom and political action. To this, Porphyry had added purificatory and contemplative virtue, and Psellos saw in them the path that leads man as immortal soul to transcend the world and reach greater union with God. A similar integration of Stoic ethics (which prescribes the ideal life of man as he is) with the Platonic (concerned with life beyond this world) was proposed by Barlaam of Calabria in his *Ethics According to the Stoics*.

Epicurus (341–270 BC) taught that the only ultimate good was pleasure (being the only good known to the senses) and that the only ultimate evil was pain. The best pleasure, that which is accompanied by no painful want, is a perfect harmony of body and mind to be sought in plain living and in virtue. Intellectual pleasures were the more refined, and were higher than the coarser physical ones purely in terms of their quantity and durability. Tranquillity (*ataraxia*) is the highest pleasure obtainable, and comes from the removal of all emotional disturbances resulting from unsatisfied wants, through the elimination of all but the simplest needs which are then easily satisfied even by those who are not wealthy. What the Epicureans advocated, therefore, was a temperate, even ascetic, existence devoted to contemplative pursuits. If something increased pleasure and reduced pain, it was good as a means; otherwise it was not good at all. Justice was good only as a way of preventing mutual harm; but injustice brought pain and anxiety only through the perpetual fear of being discovered. The Epicureans placed high value on friendship and were famous for the warmth of their personal relationships; but friendship was good only because it tended to increase pleasure. It was believed that immediate pleasures should be postponed in order to attain more secure and durable satisfaction in the future. Therefore, the good life must be regulated by self-discipline. Religious beliefs and practices were considered harmful because they preoccupied men with disturbing thoughts of death and the uncertainty of life after death.

D.P.M. WEERAKKODY

Further Reading

Bonhöffer, A.F., *The Ethics of the Stoic Epictetus*, Bern and New York: Peter Lang, 1996

Irwin, Terence, *Plato's Ethics*, Oxford and New York: Oxford University Press, 1995

Nussbaum, Martha C., *The Therapy of Desire: Theory and Practice in Hellenistic Ethics*, Princeton, New Jersey: Princeton University Press, 1994

Reeve, C.D.C., *Practices of Reason: Aristotle's Nicomachean Ethics*, Oxford: Clarendon Press, and New York: Oxford University Press, 1992

Zanker, Graham, *The Heart of Achilles: Characterization and Personal Ethics in the Iliad*, Ann Arbor: University of Michigan Press, 1994

Etruscans

The Etruscans, a culturally unified people who settled in central Italy (between the Arno and the Tiber rivers) from around the beginning of the 1st millennium until the 1st century BC, were referred to by the ancient Greeks as the *Tyrrhenoi* (Tyrrhenians), a name that they also gave to the sea off Tuscany, still known today as the Tyrrhenian Sea. Undoubtedly, this name was given to the Etruscans because many Greeks believed that they had emigrated to Italy from the east, specifically from Lydia in Asia Minor, and were led away from a devastating famine by the son of the Lydian king, who was called Tyrrhenus (Tyrsenos). This story is preserved by the Greek historian Herodotus (1. 94. 2), writing in the 5th century BC, and is typical of traditional Greek explanations of the origins of people or city states, i.e. they began as the result of a migration under the leadership of a mythical founding

hero. Other Greek historians (e.g. Hellanicus and Anticleides) had similar beliefs about the eastern origins of the Etruscans and connected them with the Pelasgians, an ancient wandering people who eventually settled on the coast of Italy. The one ancient exception to this view is the Greek historian and rhetorician Dionysius of Halicarnassus (1. 25-30), writing towards the end of the 1st century BC, who argued that the Etruscans were autochthonous. This, according to Dionysius, was the Etruscan view of the matter. Indeed the Etruscans did not call themselves the Tyrrhenians at all, but referred to themselves as Rasenna or Rasna. This is also the view of most modern scholars who, as the result of decades of archaeological study, now believe that the Bronze Age inhabitants of central Italy (from c.3000 to 1000 BC) should be considered the ancestors of the Iron Age inhabitants, i.e. the Etruscans.

Unfortunately, because Etruscan civilization was relatively short-lived and because their once extensive literature was either obliterated by the Roman conquest or else simply failed to survive the process of transmission during the Middle Ages, very little is known about the internal events of Etruscan history. The archaeological record and the incidental references to the Etruscans by contemporary Greek and Roman writers are not complete or always reliable sources of information about Etruscan culture. However, these sources do yield considerable information about the trade relations between Greeks and Etruscans. For example, the early Euboean colonies at Pithecusae and Cumae were deliberately well situated for trade with Etruria and, by the end of the 8th century BC, Etruscan culture was largely transformed and Hellenized by Greek and other eastern objects and techniques that were introduced by the colonists. In the 7th century BC many Corinthian and east Greek vases made their way to Etruria, and by the 6th century BC the market was dominated by fine Athenian wares. There is also evidence that in the 6th century BC many Greek potters worked with Etruscan taste in mind. For example, the class of pottery known as "Tyrrhenian amphorae" features especially colourful narratives with nonsensical inscriptions that were unlikely to be recognized as such by the Etruscan buyers. Other ingenious potters, such as Nicosthenes, began supplying the brisk Etruscan market with types of vases familiar to the Etruscans from their own native *bucchero* pottery (e.g. the so-called Nicosthenic amphorae and *kyathoi* or wine ladles), but decorated in the popular Greek black-figured style.

In exchange for Greek pottery and other imported objects (Near Eastern seals, bronzes, etc.) it seems that the Etruscans mainly traded raw materials (metals). During the 8th and early 7th centuries BC, however, some Etruscan objects do begin to appear in the votive deposits at several international Greek sanctuaries (e.g. Delphi, Olympia, Dodona, and Samos). These objects are not trade goods but typical Italic votive offerings such as bronze helmets, shields, horse bits, and other ornaments. In fact, according to Pausanias (5. 12. 5), it was the Etruscan king Arimnestos who made the very first dedication (a throne) at Olympia. During the 6th century BC Etruscan merchants seem to have circulated more widely, since their native *bucchero* pottery has been found at nearly every major site in Greece except for the international sanctuaries of Delphi, Olympia, Isthmia, and Nemea, which instead attracted finer Etruscan donations, such as bronzes, art objects, and war trophies. Most of the *bucchero* vases found in Greece are tall stemmed cups with two vertical handles – a shape that inspired the development of the *kantharos* (large-handled cup) in Boeotia and Athens. The Athenian Agora has produced a few examples of Etruscan *bucchero*, although the bulk of Attic trade with the Etruscans occurred later than the production of this type of pottery. So, in the later 6th and 5th centuries BC, the Etruscans probably traded other goods such as bronze utensils, candelabra, tripods, and spouted pitchers (known today as *Schnabelkannen*) which were widely admired by the Greeks.

The influence of Greek imports on Etruscan art is easily recognized as well. Native artists copied the Euboean Geometric and early Orientalizing styles as well as all the Corinthian styles down to the middle of the 6th century BC. Greek shapes were introduced into *bucchero* pottery. Athenian black- and red-figured pottery was also imitated by local artists, and Greek subjects and styles were introduced into Etruscan tomb painting. Greek influence is additionally apparent in Etruscan metalworking (particularly in the production of certain fibulae) and in the Etruscan art of architectural terracottas which was developed as the result of trade relations with the Peloponnese.

There is also evidence of Greeks who actually lived and worked in Etruria. For example, according to Pliny (*Naturalis Historia*, 35. 152), Livy (1. 34), and Dionysius of Halicarnassus (3. 46), one Demaratus of Corinth emigrated to Tarquinia (with three Greek artisans) in the middle of the 7th century BC, carried on a prosperous business, married a local noblewoman, and sired the fifth king of Rome (Tarquinius Priscus). Tarquinia was also home to a significant school of Etrusco-Corinthian vase painting that has been linked to Corinthian immigration. In addition, the port city of Tarquinia, Gravisca, had a wealthy Greek quarter that included a sanctuary with Greek-style temples where a syncretism of Greek and Etruscan cults took place. The Etruscan city of Caere also seems to have been partly settled by Greeks, who called it Agylla and dedicated a treasury at Delphi. At Caere an itinerant Greek artist named Aristonothos produced an interesting and unusual hybrid *krater* (mixing bowl) depicting a naval battle and the blinding of the Cyclops Polyphemus by Odysseus and his men (Paris, Louvre).

Etruscan culture was influenced by the Greek imports and immigrants in other ways as well. For example, the Greeks brought to Etruria the alphabet and the art of olive cultivation. Greek-style hunts and athletics are depicted in many Etruscan tombs, although it seems unlikely that the Etruscans accepted the social ideals that went along with these sports in Greek culture. Etruscan weapons and warfare, including the use of warships as well as the organization of the cavalry and infantry (phalanx formation), also seem to have been influenced by Greek practice. In addition, Etruscan dress was closely related to Greek models, although the Greeks were known to have admired the native Etruscan sandals with their hinged wooden soles. The Etruscan elite also adopted the practice of banqueting on couches with drinking equipment of the type used at the Greek symposium. But unlike the Greeks, the Etruscans reclined together with their wives – a practice that the Greeks thought was barbarous.

Despite this apparent cultural dependence, Greek–Etruscan relations seem to have worsened after the large Etruscan fleet was defeated at Cumae in 524 BC by the Greeks and the Latin alliance. At this time, the Greeks controlled the overland routes into Campania and soon after they gained control of the seas as well. By the end of the 4th century BC, trade with Greece had declined considerably and very few dedications were made by Greeks in the sanctuary at Gravisca. Some Greek trade with Etruria continued in the 3rd century BC with areas as remote as southern Russia receiving a few Etruscan objects. In this small way, before they were conquered by the Romans, the Etruscans contributed to the *koine* (shared culture) of Hellenistic civilization.

ANN M. NICGORSKI

Summary

A people settled in central Italy for most of the 1st millennium BC, the Etruscans were believed in antiquity to have originated in Asia Minor, though this now seems unlikely. Trade with Greece began early and Etruscan culture was largely Hellenized by the 8th century BC. Relations with Greece cooled in the late 6th century and trade declined after the 4th century BC.

Further Reading

Boardman, John, *The Greeks Overseas: Their Early Colonies and Trade*, 4th edition, London and New York: Thames and Hudson, 1999

Bonfante, Larissa, *Etruscan Dress*, Baltimore: Johns Hopkins University Press, 1975

Bonfante, Larissa, *Out of Etruria: Etruscan Influence North and South*, Oxford: British Archaeological Reports, 1981

Bonfante, Larissa (editor), *Etruscan Life and Afterlife: A Handbook of Etruscan Studies*, Detroit: Wayne State University Press, and Warminster: Aris and Phillips, 1986

Brendel, Otto J., *Etruscan Art*, 2nd edition, New Haven: Yale University Press, 1995

Pallottino, Massimo (editor), *Les Etrusques et l'Europe*, Paris: Réunion de Musées Nationaux, 1992

Rasmussen, T.B., "Etruscan Shapes in Attic Pottery", *Antike Künst*, 28 (1985): pp. 33–39

Ridgeway, D., "The First Western Greeks: Campanian Coasts and Southern Etruria" in *Greeks, Celts, and Romans: Studies in Venture and Resistance*, edited by Christopher Hawkes and Sonia Hawkes, London: Dent, and Totowa, New Jersey: Rowman and Littlefield, 1973

Scullard, H.H., "Two Halicarnassians and a Lydian: A Note on Etruscan Origins" in *Ancient Society and Institutions: Studies Presented to Victor Ehrenberg on his 75th Birthday*, Oxford: Blackwell, 1966; New York: Barnes and Noble, 1967

Spivey, Nigel, *Etruscan Art*, London and New York: Thames and Hudson, 1997

Torelli, M., "Greek Artisans and Etruria: A Problem Concerning the Relationship of Two Cultures", *Archaeological News*, 5 (1976): pp. 134–38

Euboea

Island in the Aegean

Euboea is the second largest Greek island after Crete and runs for about 180 km along the eastern coast of mainland Greece. It is separated from the mainland by a strait, known as the

Euripus, that narrows at the mid-point along the west coast. Euboea is separated into three geographical areas, each region defined by a major peak. The well-watered and forested north is dominated by Mount Pyxaria (1341 m). The central, most fertile, region is south of Mount Dirfis (1745 m), the highest point on the island, and boasts forests of chestnuts and pines on the north side. Surrounding plains produce grains, vines, figs, and olives. The southern region of the island sits below Mount Ochi (1394 m). The island has substantial mineral wealth as well, including quantities of lignite and magnesite (now being exported), marble and asbestos. The marble (cipollino) of Carystus was widely popular in antiquity, particularly in Rome during the imperial era.

From the 5th century BC bridges across the Euripus have joined Euboea to Boeotia allowing access to the western portion of the island from the mainland. With the exception of the reasonably good port located at Kymi along the rocky east coast, Euboea was most accessible by sea at Chalcis and Eretria, also on the west coast and on the southern tip at Carystus. Important modern ports are still located at Chalcis and Carystus.

Throughout the history of Euboea, environmental and geographic divisions of the island were paralleled by sociopolitical divisions. According to tradition, Euboea was originally settled by people from Thessaly – the Ellopians in the north, the Abantes in the centre and west, and the Dryopes in the south. Each region included, and still includes, a major town. Histiaea-Oreos, the modern village of Orei in the north, is located on the coast. The town was important from the Bronze Age until Classical times when it became known as either Histiaea or Oreos (perhaps an old deme name). Histiaea-Oreos controlled a fairly large and fertile plain and was described by Homer as "rich in vines" (Iliad, 2. 537).

Chalcis, in the centre, is located at the narrowest part of the island, facing Boeotia. The town was a trade centre for pottery and metalwork and was important during the Dark Ages. Chalcis flourished despite losing its independence, first to the Athenians, then to the Macedonians, and then to the Romans. Carystus, in the south, is located on the coast below Mount Ochi. On top of Mount Ochi is an example of the famous "dragon houses" of Euboea – ancient structures whose use is unknown. Carystus' importance stems from its control of the southern entrance to the Euripus and of maritime traffic through the Andros straits as well as from its cipollino marble and asbestos. (Still visible in the ancient quarries are abandoned, but worked, columns from the Roman period.) Carystus suffered destruction at the hands of the Persians when its inhabitants were the first to try to oppose the invaders in 490 BC; it later came under Athenian control and may have had an Athenian cleruchy settled there. Near Carystus is Geristos, the site of a sanctuary of Apollo (first mentioned by Homer) and the one safe harbour on the southeast coast of Euboea. It was the first good stopping point for merchant ships travelling from the east and it is possible that this was the main port for Carystus in Classical times.

According to tradition, the original Euboeans were later joined by Ionians from Attica, Aeolians from Phthiotis, and Dorians from the Peloponnese. Because the textual record for the settlement and activities of early Euboea is limited, the site of Lefkandi and its rich material remains play an important role in recreating a picture of Late Bronze-Age and Dark-Age Euboea. At Lefkandi, located between Chalcis and Eretria (explored in 1965–66, 1969–70, and again in the 1980s by the British School at Athens), was found extensive early evidence for occupation from the Early to the Late Helladic and the Geometric periods, and in particular the site sheds light on the transition from the Mycenaean period to the early Dark Age. Of particular historical importance for an understanding of post-Mycenaean economic, social, and architectural developments in Greece is a cemetery found on Toumba hill (about 200 m north of Lefkandi village). At this site is the largest building known from Dark-Age Greece (c.1000 BC). It was an apsidal building, about 10 m wide and 45 m long, built of mud brick on top of a stone foundation. There was a double grave in the main room, one grave containing the richly adorned remains of a cremated male warrior and an inhumed woman. The other grave held four inhumed horses. The material remains show clear contact with other areas in the Mediterranean (such as Crete and Attica) and, more surprisingly, the existence of this structure testifies to a much more active economic role for Euboea than had been previously suspected for this early period.

During the 8th century the inhabitants of Chalcis and Eretria were among the first Greeks to found colonies and trading posts on the coasts of Sicily, Italy, Thrace, the islands of the Aegean, and possibly Syria. In fact, at Eretria, mentioned in the Homeric catalogue of ships and located about 18 km south of Chalcis, the earliest physical evidence dates to the Geometric period, when Eretrians established colonies abroad. Currently it is believed that in the late 8th century competition for land and power between these two cities led to the Lelantine War, named after the rich Lelantine plain. The victor in this war is unknown, but the war is reputed to have involved numerous Greek states. Herodotus says that Miletus supported Eretria and Samos supported Chalcis and Thucydides implies that other states were involved, but further details remain stubbornly elusive.

Euboea played an important role in many of the major historical events of the Archaic and Classical periods. For example, Hippias, the former tyrant of Athens, fled there after his expulsion from power. Indeed, after his arrival in Euboea, the Chalcidians allied with Boeotia against Athens, partly in an attempt to restore him. As a result, in 506 BC, the Athenians attacked and defeated the Chalcidians, then took their land for the settlement of 5000 cleruchs. Similarly, the inhabitants of Eretria angered the Persians because of their support of the Ionian revolt, so that in 490 BC the Persians attacked and burned Eretria, and then enslaved the citizens. Off the cape of Artemisium, a promontory on the northwest coast of Euboea, the Greeks and Persians fought one of their first important sea battles in 480 BC. (The statue of Zeus or Poseidon hurling a thunderbolt was also found there and is now located in the National Museum at Athens.)

Euboea joined the Greek forces to defeat the Persians and became a member of the Delian League until 411 BC. However, the Euboeans came to resent Athenian rule and revolted from the league in 446 and in 411 BC. The first revolt was put down by Pericles, who expelled the inhabitants of Histiaea-Oreos and settled at least 1000 cleruchs there (though after the Peloponnesian War the Spartans drove the cleruchs out and recalled the refugees). The second revolt, probably led by Eretria, was more successful, since the Athenians had been weakened by internal troubles and war with Sparta. Also in 411 the Chalcidians and Boeotians built a bridge over the Euripus, partly to interfere with Athenian maritime trade. Yet, between 378 and 376, due to dramatic changes in the balance of power in Greece, the Athenians induced most Euboean cities voluntarily to join a new maritime league. Thereafter, the populace of Euboea vacillated in their support between the Athenians and the Macedonians.

The Euboean alliance with Athens was not long lived. After the Battle of Leuctra in 371 BC, control of Euboea passed to the Thebans. In 358 the Euboeans were liberated by Chares, who restored the alliance with Athens. In 341 a Euboean confederacy was established, though after the Battle of Chaeronea (338) the island was incorporated under Macedonian control (Philip of Macedon recognized the strategic importance of Euboea and, indeed, claimed that the "master of Euboea is the master of Greece"). Chalcis sheltered at least one important refugee in this period – Aristotle died in Chalcis in 321, at the age of 62, after fleeing there because of persecution by an anti-Macedonian faction in Athens.

Roman interference in Euboean affairs began in earnest during the 2nd century BC. The Romans captured Histiaea in 199 and then in 198 captured and ransacked the city of Eretria, and in 87 BC Eretria was utterly destroyed and deserted. In 194 Euboea, as a whole, was taken from Macedon by the Roman general Flamininus, who briefly restored the Euboean confederacy. In 146 BC Chalcis was nearly destroyed for fighting with Macedon against Rome. The island was next attached to the province of Macedonia, until 27 BC when Greece became the province of Achaea. Though Euboea's political fortunes declined after incorporation into the province of Achaea, the island was still economically viable. Greek lands, including land in Euboea, became an important source of economic power and prestige for Roman elites and archaeological investigations reveal villas and other signs of wealth. Thus, for most of the period under Roman rule, Euboea did not show signs of serious economic decline, at least until early Byzantine times, in part because of its marble and in part because of its favourable position in the trading networks used by the Romans.

The early Byzantine period was one of profound social, religious, political, and economic transitions in the Graeco-Roman world. The now-Christian empire was more clearly divided into eastern and western sections (Euboea was in the east). A series of migrations and invasions from the north, to which Euboea was subject, changed the nature of land use and settlement on the island (people were more likely to cluster in defensible towns than remain on their unprotected rural homesteads). Pagan cult places were replaced with Christian monasteries and churches. During the 7th century AD the territories of the empire began to be reorganized into themes in an attempt to create a better system of defence. The development of the theme system probably had an immediate economic impact, even on Euboea, because local soldier-farmers were allotted lands in return for their military service.

By the end of the 9th century silk was nearly as important to the economy of the provincial Byzantine nobles in Euboea as the quarrying of marble had been in Roman times. During the Second Crusade in 1147, Roger II, king of Sicily, used his army to abduct silk workers from Thebes and Chalcis, because silk was considered so desirable in the west. Mulberry trees, food for silk worms, can still be found in abundance in some areas of the island (especially Carystus).

In 1209 Euboea was divided into the triarchies of Chalcis, Carystus, and Oreos, which were governed by Franks, who ruled from dramatic newly built castles, and who later recognized Venetian overlordship. The Venetians controlled Euboea for more than 200 years. (Above the modern town of Carystus sits Castel Rosso, a well-preserved Venetian fort – named after the reddish colour of its stone.) It was the Venetians who gave the island the name of Negroponte, "Black Bridge", which is a corruption of the Greek *ston Evripo*, "on the Euripus", already changed to *Egripo*, and additionally refers to the bridge (*ponte*) over the Euripus. Since Negroponte ranked as a "kingdom", its flag was one of three raised in St Mark's Square.

When in 1453 the Turks conquered Constantinople, it was only a matter of time before Euboea became part of the new Ottoman empire. So it was in July 1470 that the island fell to the Turks, after a brutal battle at Chalcis led by Sultan Mehmet II. Despite continued fierce resistance in the cities, rural Euboeans may have benefited under the new rule since villagers were no longer serfs (as when they were under the control of Byzantines and Venetians) and could even own property. Agricultural production began to improve as early as the 16th century, although the area around Eretria declined in productive capacity and became swampland until 1824, when a refugee settlement (Nea Psara) was located there. There is now an important regional museum located at Eretria which displays many antiquities including the well-known terracotta centaur of the 10th century BC from Lefkandi.

In the 19th century Euboea was finally released from external rule. Following the Greek War of Independence (1821–30) Greece became the first Balkan state to achieve independence from the Ottomans. Fighting in Euboea appears to have been limited and sporadic, and for three years after most of Greece became independent Euboea remained in Turkish hands. But on 22 February 1833 Euboea was finally declared part of the new Greek state.

The modern island flourishes and is a popular destination for European and Athenian travellers, partly due to its lovely beaches. Modern Carystus, for instance, a town of about 5000 inhabitants, founded after the War of Independence, receives numerous Athenian visitors throughout the summer, ferry services permitting. Many local ancient customs have been preserved, which can be seen in the numerous celebrations held in mountain and coastal villages and at monasteries throughout the year.

CYNTHIA K. KOSSO

Summary

Second largest island in Greece, Euboea was settled by the Neolithic and played a central role in the era of Greek colonization of the 8th and 7th centuries BC. Throughout Classical times it was often controlled by Athens. It remained central to Greek politics well beyond the Classical period because of its location and relative wealth.

Further Reading

Aalen, F., "The Cycladic House in South Evvoia, Greece", *Vernacular Architecture*, 13 (1982): pp. 5–19

Carpenter, J. and D. Boyd, "The Dragon-Houses of Southern Euboea", *Archaeology*, 29 (1976): pp. 250–57

Carpenter, J. and D. Boyd, "Dragon Houses: Euboea, Attica, Karia", *American Journal of Archaeology*, 81 (1977): pp. 179–215

Eretria: Fouilles et recherches, several vols, Bern: Francke, 1968– (final report series of recent and current Swiss excavations)

Evely, Doniert, Irene S. Lemos, and Susan Sherratt (editors), *Minotaur and Centaur: Studies in the Archaeology of Crete and Euboea Presented to Mervyn Popham*, Oxford: Tempus Reparatum, 1996

Popham, M.R., P.G. Calligas, and L.H. Sackett (editors), *Lefkandi II: The Protogeometric Building at Toumba*, London: Thames and Hudson, 1990

Sackett, L.H. *et al.*, "Prehistoric Euboea: Contributions toward a Survey", *Annual of the British School at Athens*, 61 (1966)

Sackett, L.H. and P.G. Themelis (editors), *Lefkandi I: The Iron Age*, London: Thames and Hudson, 1979

Schefold, K., "The Architecture of Eretria", *Archaeology*, 21 (1968): pp. 272–81

Schumacher, R., "Three Related Sanctuaries of Poseidon: Geraistos, Kalaureia and Tainaron" in *Greek Sanctuaries: New Approaches*, edited by Nanno Marinatos and Robin Hägg, London and New York: Routledge, 1993

Sealey, Raphael, *A History of the Greek City States, c. 700–338 BC*, Berkeley: University of California Press, 1976

Euclid

Mathematician of the 4th–3rd centuries BC

Hardly anything is known about Euclid's life (even in antiquity he was sometimes confused with the Socratic Euclides of Megara); even his dates are uncertain. Proclus (5th century AD) knew only that he was later than the pupils of Plato and earlier than Archimedes (which could be inferred from the surviving works of Euclid and Archimedes, and so probably does not rest on independent evidence). Proclus' guess that he lived in the reign of Ptolemy I Soter (305–282 BC) is a reasonable one, but is based only on anecdotes; his claim that Euclid's goal in pursuing mathematics was to give support to Platonism is certainly no more than an attempt to include the best-known mathematician of the ancient world within Proclus' own school.

A number of mathematical works by Euclid have survived. The *Data* defines and discusses what must be "given" in a geometrical proof; *On Divisions* (surviving only in Arabic) deals with problems about dividing figures into parts that have a given ratio to one another; the *Phaenomena* concerns the astronomical applications of spherical geometry; the *Optics* is on the geometrical aspects of optics. Another work attributed to him, the *Catoptrica,* which deals with the geometry of reflection, seems not to be by Euclid in its present form, but may contain much Euclidean material.

These works establish that Euclid was a substantial creative mathematician in his own right, but there is no doubt that he is most renowned not for this, but for a work that is a compilation and systematization of the work of his predecessors, the *Elements*. Euclid was not the first to compose such a work. The first attempt to compile and systematize geometry appears to have been made by Hippocrates of Chios in the late 5th century BC, and this may have been the basis of much of the earlier books of Euclid's work. It is unclear which (if any) parts of the *Elements* are Euclid's own. He certainly made use of Theaetetus' work on irrationals, and Eudoxus' on the theory of proportion (and he uses extensively the mathematical method devised by Eudoxus and usually called "the method of exhaustion"), and there is clear evidence that other sections of the material incorporated in the *Elements* predate him (for example, Common Notion 3, "if equals are taken from equals, the remainders are equal", is cited by Aristotle in a form very close to that of Euclid's own).

The *Elements* is in 13 books (the alleged 14th, on dodecahedrons and icosahedrons inscribed in a sphere, was written by Hypsicles in the 2nd century BC, and the 15th, on the regular solids, is a compilation of the 6th century AD or later). Book 1 begins with a statement of definitions and of the axioms of mathematics, the unprovable and allegedly self-evident assumptions that are the starting point of mathematical proofs (though even in antiquity some of them, e.g. Postulate 5, were controversial). It then goes on to deal with elementary theorems on triangles, intersecting straight lines, and parallelograms. Book 2 deals specifically with rectangles (the view once held that the theorems in this book constitute a kind of "geometrical algebra", that is a geometrical method of solving quadratic and other equations, is now no longer thought to be probable). The subject of books 4 and 5 is the geometry of the circle and inscribed and circumscribed rectilinear figures. Book 5 is devoted to the theory of proportion; it is probably dependent on the work of Eudoxus, and constitutes one of the most sophisticated and elegant surviving pieces of Greek mathematics. In book 6 the conclusions of book 5 are applied to plane geometry. Books 7, 8, and 9 are on number theory, and book 10 deals with irrationals. Finally, books 11, 12, and 13 deal with solid geometry, with a series of propositions parallel to those on plane geometry in the early books. Though the individual sections are impressive in isolation, Euclid's real achievement is to bring together a mass of mathematical material and to articulate it into a coherent and ordered system, based on the minimum of axioms.

Euclid's *Elements* subsequently became the basis of all mathematical education, not only in the Roman and Byzantine periods, but right down to the mid-20th century, and it could be argued that it is the most successful textbook ever written. His clear and logical exposition of mathematics facilitated the process by which geometry became an essential part of the educational syllabus, and a familiarity with its principles an indispensable accomplishment for every educated man. Certainly it helped to establish mathematics as one of the foundations of Hellenic culture, and the discovery of formal proof as one of Greece's most valuable and enduring legacies. A series of commentaries on the *Elements* demonstrates its continuing importance. The most important of them (on book 1) was written by Proclus in the 5th century AD. Proclus was primarily a philosopher rather than a mathematician, and his commentary stresses the significance of Euclid's geometry for Neoplatonism. Though the work was undoubtedly designed for students of philosophy who were beginners in mathematics (and may have been based on a series of lectures given by Proclus), there are signs that a general readership was also envisaged, which, if true, would be evidence of a continuing interest in Euclid's work among a wider educated public.

Like most school textbooks, the *Elements* was adapted by teachers to fit their own needs, and before the 19th century the text universally used was not Euclid's own, but an adaptation of it devised by Theon of Alexandria in the late 4th century AD. Theon corrected what he believed (often wrongly) to be errors in Euclid's mathematics, tidied up his diction, and introduced material (including whole propositions) with the intention of making the argument clearer. There are signs that some of the additions were not Theon's own, but were taken over from earlier adapted texts. It was only with the edition of F. Peyrard, completed in 1818 (and made possible by Napoleon's looting of manuscripts from Italian libraries), that a good text close to Euclid's own was made available. The *Elements* was first translated into modern Greek in 1820.

RICHARD WALLACE

See also Mathematics

Biography

The most famous Greek mathematician, even though almost nothing is known about his life. He may have lived in the reign of Ptolemy I (305–282 BC) in Alexandria. Surviving mathematical works include the *Data*, *On Divisions*, *Phaenomena*, *Optics*, and *Catoptrica*. His best-known work is undoubtedly the *Elements* in 13 books. It remained the standard textbook of geometry for 2000 years.

Writings

The Thirteen Books of Euclid's Elements, edited by Thomas L. Heath, 2nd edition Cambridge: Cambridge University Press, 1926

Further Reading

Heath, Sir Thomas Little, *Greek Mathematics and Science*, Cambridge: Cambridge University Press, 1921

Knorr, Wilbur Richard, *The Evolution of the Euclidean Elements: A Study of the Theory of Incommensurable Magnitudes and its Significance for Early Greek Geometry*, Dordrecht and Boston: Reidel, 1975

Neugebauer, Otto, *A History of Ancient Mathematical Astronomy*, Berlin and New York: Springer, 1975

Eudoxus *c.*390–*c.*340 BC

Mathematician and astronomer

Though he is reported to have taught at Cyzicus and studied in Egypt, most of Eudoxus' activity is associated with Plato's Academy in Athens, where he was working in the middle of the 4th century BC. None of his writings survives, and so we must reconstruct his work through reports in later writers. He was clearly a man of very broad interests. Aristotle (*Nicomachaean Ethics*, 10. 1172b) reports that in ethics he held that the supreme good is pleasure, on the grounds that pleasure is what all creatures desire; Aristotle remarks that his view attracted support, not from the cogency of the argument, but because of Eudoxus' own reputation for moral rectitude. He is also said to have done work in geography, and to have written a code of laws for his home city Cnidus.

Eudoxus is, however, best known for his work in astronomy. He did a good deal of detailed observational work. He appears to have been influential in marking the sun's annual movement in terms of the 12 signs of the zodiac, and to have introduced the practice of identifying individual stars in constellations by letters of the alphabet. He is the first Greek astronomer of whom we can say with reasonable certainty that he had access to the ancient astronomical knowledge of the Babylonians (though his supposed study in Egypt left no discernible trace); for example, in the placing of the solstitial and equinoctial points in the middle of the appropriate signs of the zodiac (rather than at the beginning), and in equalizing the lengths of the seasons, he is following Babylonian rather than standard Greek practice. His main contribution, however, was to apply contemporary mathematics, and particularly the geometry of the circle and the sphere, to astronomical problems. Both the fixed stars and the sun seem to move round the earth in circular orbits on the surface of a sphere. The moon and the planets, however, appear to move in much more complex ways (indeed the planets sometimes appear to move backwards). Eudoxus' system is an attempt to explain these movements mathematically in terms of combinations of circular orbits, the axes of which were not fixed but rotated around different axes – or, in other words, complex arrangements of concentric spheres. He believed that the movements of the moon and the sun could be explained by using three such spheres for each body, while the five visible planets needed four each, making, with the sphere of the fixed stars, 27 in all. The apparent retrograde movement of the planets is accounted for by having their third and fourth spheres rotate in opposite directions to one another, and around axes at an angle to one another, which produces movement in something like a figure-of-eight; Simplicius tell us that Eudoxus called this figure a *hippopede* (horse-fetter). Despite the mathematical sophistication of this system, it failed to account even for those movements that were well known to astronomers of his time (perhaps the most striking example being the inequality of the seasons). It soon had to be modified (and complicated) by Callipus of Cyzicus, a version of whose system was the one used by Aristotle, and it was later superseded by the more accurate systems of Eratosthenes, Hipparchus, and Ptolemy. Nevertheless, Eudoxus was the first to make a serious attempt to create a mathematical model of the movement of the heavenly bodies, and so can claim to be one of the founders of scientific astronomy. His system was an entirely mathematical one, and he made no suggestion that we know of as to the mechanism whereby the mathematics could be converted into actual moving bodies.

Important though his astronomical work is, however, there is no doubt that it was his contribution to mathematics that had the most permanent and creative influence. He is said to have been largely responsible for the material on proportion contained in book 5 of Euclid's *Elements*. He is credited with the discovery of a method of handling both commensurable and incommensurable magnitudes, which meant that it became possible to simplify and clarify proofs in a number of important areas, and opened up the way for significant new developments in geometry. Eudoxus seems also to been responsible for one of the most powerful and characteristic strategies for proof in Greek mathematics, the so-called "method of exhaustion". The name by which it is now generally known is seriously misleading. It is used to relate the areas or volumes of figures bounded by curves to those of figures bounded by straight lines, and its purpose is to avoid the difficulties posed by infinite division; for example, although a polygon can be inscribed in a circle as closely as you like to the circumference of the circle, it can never be inscribed so closely that another polygon cannot be inscribed between the first polygon and the circumference of the circle, and the space separating the two can never be entirely exhausted. Eudoxus' method avoids this problem by proving that, for example, a given polygon encloses an area that can be neither bigger nor smaller than that enclosed by a given circle, and so must be equal to it. This ingenious strategy enabled the solution of many problems (including those arising from attempts to square the circle) and is the basis of much of the geometry of Euclid and Archimedes.

RICHARD WALLACE

Biography

Born *c.*390 BC at Cnidus, Eudoxus was taught geometry by Archytas and medicine by Philistion. He is said also to have visited Egypt, Cyzicus, and Halicarnassus before settling in Athens to teach, where he was acquainted with Plato. None of his writings survive, but he made important contributions to mathematics and astronomy. He died *c.*340 BC.

Writings

Die Fragmente, edited by François Lasserre, Berlin: de Gruyter, 1966

Further Reading

Dicks, D.R., *Early Greek Astronomy to Aristotle*, London: Thames and Hudson, and Ithaca, New York: Cornell University Press, 1970
Heath, Thomas L., *Greek Mathematics and Science*, Cambridge: Cambridge University Press, 1921
Maula, Erkka, *Studies in Eudoxus' Homocentric Spheres*, Helsinki: Societas Scientiarum Fennica, 1974
Neugebauer, Otto, *A History of Ancient Mathematical Astronomy*, Berlin and New York: Springer, 1975

Eunuchs

"Eunuchs" may seem at first sight a jarring entry in an encyclopaedia of Greece and the Hellenic tradition, for eunuchs are primarily associated with the Orient. Indeed the Greeks of the Classical world linked them especially with Persia, where court eunuchs were prevalent, as on the Assyrian model. Herodotus alludes casually to the eunuchs to be found at the Persian court, but also to those in Median and Egyptian circles; in the *Acharnians* (91–122) Aristophanes has the Great King's Eye report to the Athenian assembly, flanked by two eunuchs; famously, Xenophon in his *Cyropaedia* presents an elaborate justification of the use of eunuchs by king Cyrus; while Ctesias' *Persica* is full of tales concerning eunuchs at the Persian court.

Yet eunuchs and castration did have a closer proximity to the Greeks. Castration was as much a part of Greek mythology as that of other Near Eastern religions. Hesiod in his *Theogony* (178–200) describes the castration of Uranus' genitals with a sickle by Cronus, the blood from which was received by Earth

who bore the Erinyes, the Giants, and the Meliae nymphs. The genitals themselves were thrown into the sea, from which grew Aphrodite. The effect of the castration of Uranus was disempowerment, and he was replaced by his son Cronus as the supreme deity. Castration also found a place in Greek epics (e.g. the mutilation of Melanthius in the *Odyssey*, 22. 474–77). In the real world, eunuch priests had their part to play in the Anatolian cults of goddesses, notably that of Cybele.

It is clear that eunuchs also impinged more directly on the Greek world. Herodotus records that Periander the tyrant of Corinth sent 330 boys of the leading families in Corcyra (modern Corfu) to the Lydian king Alyattes at Sardis to be castrated, though the people of Samos saved them. Perhaps more reliably, Herodotus states that during the Ionian revolt the Persians threatened to eunuchize Ionian boys, a threat which the historian says came to pass. Herodotus also relates the history of Hermotimus (the most favoured of Xerxes's eunuchs) who came originally from Pedasus east of Halicarnassus. He was bought as a prisoner of war by a Chian, Panionius, who castrated him as part of his regular trade in eunuchs, whom he would sell at Sardis and Ephesus. Plato even asserts that Callias, a wealthy Athenian in late 5th-century BC Athens, had a eunuch doorkeeper, though it is vital to remember that Plato was writing a century later. Other evidence for eunuch slaves in Athens is found in Terence's *Eunuch*, which was based on a work of the Athenian playwright Menander; in the extant Roman version the plot revolves around the fact that an Athenian woman has a eunuch slave whose place is taken by an uncastrated male so that he can gain access to the house and seduce a girl. In the 4th century BC Aristotle certainly seems very familiar with eunuch physiognomy, discussing for instance their impotency, gender status, and voice, though his knowledge may be based on the Hippocratic corpus (itself problematic) rather than on personal observation.

With the advent of Alexander the Great, the Greek world came into even closer contact with the tradition of political eunuchism. For when Alexander conquered the Persian empire he did not simply replace it with an extension of the Macedonian kingdom, but sought to present himself as the legitimate ruler of Persia. This entailed his adoption of the Persian royal style and its trappings, including the use of court eunuchs. In all the subsequent Hellenistic kingdoms (with the exception of Macedonia, which maintained its character undiluted) eunuchs are to be found. It is well known that the decision to murder Pompey after his flight to Ptolemaic Egypt following his defeat in the civil war with Julius Caesar was primarily encouraged by the eunuch Potheinus, a key figure in the regency of Ptolemy XIII. Eunuchs feature prominently in the stories of Mithridates VI, king of Pontus. A more unusual case marks the principality of Pergamum; the establishing figure of this was Philetaerus, said to have been eunuchized as a child when crushed in a crowd at a funeral.

With the shift of power in the Mediterranean to Rome, Greek political power took a back seat, but the Hellenistic court style, based on the Persian model, eventually triumphed at the Roman court of late antiquity; as a result of this eunuchs are a striking feature of the history of the later Roman empire. This development is associated primarily with Diocletian (284–305), who seems to have enhanced imperial status and ceremony to promote the authority and security of the emperor.

The phenomenon of the court eunuch, introduced to the Roman empire in late antiquity, reached an apogee in the Byzantine empire. One of the curiosities of the Byzantine system was, however, the internal production of eunuchs. Rome had expressed vehemently again and again that no Romans themselves were to be made eunuchs, or indeed that castration was not to occur within the empire, preferring to rely on the importing of foreign eunuchs, but in Byzantium there is clear evidence for the internal production of eunuchs. The 10th-century Arab historian Masudi states baldly that the Byzantines, like the Chinese, practised the castrating of their own children, while a hagiographical anecdote points to Paphlagonia as a region particularly given to the production of eunuchs. This latter story seems to find confirmation in the appearance in middle Byzantine history of a large number of Paphlagonian eunuchs, such as Constantine, Bringas, and John the Orphanotrophos. Undoubtedly this fact was due to the high demand for eunuchs at the imperial court, but also the high rewards that could be achieved. Another striking feature of Byzantine eunuchs, however, is the existence of a substantial group as free individuals, beyond imperial service. Eunuchs are met as actors, teachers, prostitutes, singers, monks, and clergy; some even became patriarch of Constantinople. In the case of Ignatios (patriarch from 847 to 858 and again from 867 to 878), he owed his eunuch state to the fact of his castration as a youth which was carried out to block him from imperial power, for he was a son of the deposed emperor Michael I (811–13).

Castration seems to have been a more general form of punishment also – rapists and homosexuals could expect to be castrated. There is no doubt then that in Byzantine times castration and eunuchs were a full part of the Hellenic tradition, but one that did not remain uncontroversial. Indeed, in the 12th century Theophylact of Ohrid wrote a defence of eunuchs, at the instigation of his eunuch brother.

A decline in the phenomenon of powerful court eunuchs occurs from the 11th century onwards, and is variously linked with the establishment of the aristocratic regime of the Komnenoi, the disaster of 1204, and the westernization of Byzantine society. Yet it seems that the general presence of eunuchs continued, and the system certainly provided a stimulus, if not a model, for the succeeding Ottoman empire. Here, this striking aspect of the Hellenic tradition continued to flourish.

SHAUN TOUGHER

Further Reading

Dunlap, J.E., *The Office of the Grand Chamberlain in the Later Roman and Byzantine Empires*, New York and London: Macmillan, 1924

Guilland, R., "Les Eunuques dans l'empire byzantin", *Revue des Etudes Byzantines*, 1 (1943): pp. 197–238

Guyot, Peter, *Eunuchen als Sklaven und Freigelassene in der griechischen-römischen Antike*, Stuttgart: Klett Cotta, 1980

Hopkins, Keith, *Conquerors and Slaves*, Cambridge and New York: Cambridge University Press, 1978, pp. 172–96

Kuefler, M.S., "Castration and Eunuchism in the Middle Ages" in *Handbook of Medieval Sexuality*, edited by Vern L. Bullough and James A. Brundage, New York: Garland, 1996

Nock, A.D., "Eunuchs in Ancient Religion" in his *Essays on Religion and the Ancient World*, vol. 1, Oxford: Clarendon Press, 1972

Patterson, Orlando, *Slavery and Social Death: A Comparative Study*, Cambridge, Massachusetts: Harvard University Press, 1982, pp. 299–333

Ringrose, K., "Living in the Shadows: Eunuchs and Gender in Byzantium" in *Third Sex, Third Gender: Beyond Sexual Dimorphism in Culture and History*, edited by Gilbert Herdt, New York: Zone, 1994, pp. 85–109, 507–18

Ringrose, K., "Eunuchs as Cultural Mediators", *Byzantinische Forschungen*, 23 (1996): pp. 75–93

Schlinkert, D., "Der Hofeunuch in der Spätantike: ein gefährlicher Aussenseiter?", *Hermes*, 122 (1994): pp. 342–59

Scholten, Helga, *Der Eunuch in Kaisernähe*, Frankfurt: Peter Lang, 1995

Stevenson, W., "The Rise of Eunuchs in Greco-Roman Antiquity", *Journal of the History of Sexuality*, 5 (1995): pp. 495–511

Tougher, S.F., "Byzantine Eunuchs: An Overview with Special Reference to Castration and Origin" in *Women, Men and Eunuchs: Gender in Byzantium*, edited by Liz James, London and New York: Routledge, 1997

Tougher, S.F., "Images of Effeminate Men: The Case of Byzantine Eunuchs" in *Masculinity in Medieval Europe*, edited by D.M. Hadley, London and New York: Longman, 1999

Euripides c.480–c.407/06 BC

Tragedian

Euripides spent the last two years of his life as a guest of Archelaus in Macedonia. He won his first victory in 441 BC and three others in his lifetime (including one with the trilogy that contained *Hippolytus* in 428 BC, and an additional one for the posthumous performances of *Iphigenia in Aulis* and *Bacchae* in 405 BC). Although he later became the most popular Greek tragedian, in his own lifetime Euripedes was less successful than Aeschylus and Sophocles.

Nineteen of his plays, out of some 90, survive (one of which, *Rhesus*, is probably by a later poet), including our only complete satyr play, *Cyclops*. In addition to the ten plays that survive because they were the most commonly read in the Hellenistic and Roman periods, a further nine survive through a lucky accident: they were preserved in a manuscript that presents them in a quasi-alphabetical order (they evidently formed one part of a collection representing *The Complete Euripides*). In addition, there are extended fragments of the *Antiope*, *Alexander*, *Archelaus*, *Bellerophon*, *Cresphontes*, *Cretans*, *Erechtheus*, *Hypsipyle*, *Captive Melanippe*, *Wise Melanippe*, *Phaethon*, and *Stheneboea*.

The dates of performance for nine of Euripides' surviving plays are known, and others are tentatively proposed on the basis of evidence provided by the scholia or other writers or of his own developing metrical practice: *Alcestis* (c.438 BC), *Medea* (c.431), *Heraclidae* (c.430), *Hippolytus* (c.428), *Andromache* (c.425), *Hecuba* (c.424), *Suppliant Women* (c.424–420), *Electra* (c.422–416), *Troades* (c.415), *Heracles* (c.415), *Iphigeneia among the Taurians* (c.414), *Ion* (c.413), *Helen* (c.412), *Phoenissae* (c.409), *Orestes* (c.408), *Cyclops* (uncertain), *Iphigeneia at Aulis* (c.405, posthumous), *Bacchae* (c.405, posthumous), and *Rhesus* (possibly post-Euripidean).

Euripides has been called the first psychological playwright. Longinus praised his depiction of madness and love (*On the Sublime*, 15. 3). Aristotle says that Sophocles claimed that he depicted men as they ought to be and Euripides as they were (*Poetics*, 1460b33ff.). Whereas in Aeschylus god confronts god, and in Sophocles man confronts god, in Euripides man confronts man, or woman, and often himself or herself. Only Medea can stop Medea: her main debate is with herself. In the works of other playwrights the traditional heroes are endorsed; Euripides focuses instead on women, children, and slaves. He shows us women doing noble acts (e.g. Iphigeneia, Macaria), children acting nobly (both characters just mentioned, and Menoeceus in *Phoenissae*), and the figure of the noble slave (e.g. in *Helen*).

Euripides questions traditional beliefs and attitudes, and his plays feature debates that were also popular among the Sophists of his time. In these debates both strong emotions and strong intellectual positions are expressed; examples are Hippolytus' confrontation with Theseus (*Hippolytus*) and Hecuba's with Helen (*Trojan Women*). This bothered many critics in the 19th century who would have preferred inspired emotionalism without philosophical debate (see Nietzsche's condemnation of Euripides for just this rationality, which he considered a debasement of the noble goals of tragedy).

Aristophanes' *Frogs*, which highlights a contest between Aeschylus and Euripides, shows the latter as an innovator and an iconoclast. It is from Aristophanes that we get the dubious impression that Euripides was a misogynist. He was instead a scientist of the emotions and focused on unconventional, passionate women. It may have been his idea to have Medea kill her children, the ultimate revenge against the husband she hated. His psychological characterization is outstanding; he gave the first instance of a guilty conscience (*Orestes*, 395–96), described as an internal disease rather than an externally imposed punishment as we find in Aeschylus and Sophocles.

Euripides' language is accessible, and at times colloquial. His structure varied from the most organized and conventional (*Bacchae*, *Iphigeneia among the Taurians*) to loose and episodic (*Trojan Women*, *Iphigeneia at Aulis*). He specialized in arias to enhance emotional states; he also excelled in debate (*agon*) as a revelation of character. His choruses can range from being integrated with the plot, to the less relevant. This may reflect a trend of the time.

There were regular revivals of Euripides' work after 386 BC. Around 330 BC the Athenian politician Lycurgus prescribed that copies of the texts of the plays should be deposited in the official archives, and that future performances should conform to these texts. The purpose was to safeguard the plays from adaptation and interpolation by actors and producers, of a kind to which they had already become vulnerable. These copies were lent to the Egyptian king Ptolemy I Euergetes, and will have passed into the Library at Alexandria, to form the basis of the critical edition made by the librarian Aristophanes of Byzantium (*c*.257–180 BC). Aristophanes divided the lyrics (previously written as continuous prose) into metrical cola. He also added brief introductory comments, probably making use of Aristotle's lost *Didaskaliai* (production records). Part of these comments survive in the *hypotheses* (plot summaries) that were prefixed to the plays by later scholars in the Roman

period. The composition of commentaries (scholia) on the plays was begun in the Hellenistic period (by scholars such as Aristarchus of Samothrace, ?217–145 BC, and Didymus, ?80–10 BC). Further scholia were added in the Byzantine period.

The Romans prized Euripides, and Ennius (239–169 BC) wrote adaptations: *Andromacha*, *Hecuba*, *Iphigenia*, and *Medea*; Pacuvius (*c*. 220–130 BC), *Antiopa*; and Accius (170–?86 BC) *Alcestis*, *Bacchae*, *Hecuba*, *Medea*, and *Troaïdes*. Half of the plays by Seneca (?AD 1–65) are from Euripides: *Hercules* [*Furens*], *Troades*, *Phoenissae*, *Medea*, and *Phaedra*.

The selection of the ten "school edition" plays that we possess was probably done in the 2nd or 3rd century AD, and scholia were included. After parchment gradually replaced papyrus (around the 4th century AD) the unselected plays gradually passed out of use. Stobaeus' anthology (5th century) of gnomic sayings often quotes lines from Euripides, including many from the lost plays. After the Athenian Academy was closed in AD 529, the Classical texts disappeared from sight for several centuries and did not re-emerge until the revival of learning in the middle Byzantine period, when they were copied from the uncial into the new cursive script. Among the scholars who wrote commentaries and handled the texts of the plays the most important are Thomas Magister (late 13th century), Manuel Moschopoulos (*fl*.1300), and Demetrios Triklinios (early 14th century). Triklinios brought a new metrical awareness to the amendment of the text, in particular the lyrics.

The nine alphabetical plays mentioned above are preserved only in two 14th-century manuscripts, L and its copy P. The earliest manuscript is the Jerusalem palimpsest from the 10th or 11th century and it includes the school selection. The Euripidean plays most commonly read in Byzantine times were *Hecuba*, *Phoenissae*, and *Orestes*. *Christus Patiens* was a play written in the 11th or 12th century on the passion of Christ using lines from Euripides, Aeschylus, and Lycophron, and some of the ending of the *Bacchae* has been reconstructed from it.

Medea, *Hippolytus*, *Alcestis*, and *Andromache* were first printed in Florence about 1494; an edition of 18 plays followed in 1503; *Electra* was not published until 1546. For the next 400 years there were revivals and reworkings of Euripides' plays in Europe, most notably by Racine, Goethe, Schlegel, and many others. In the 20th century Euripides is the playwright of social protest par excellence.

There have been many performances of Euripides' plays in modern times in Greece. A few of the most notable are: *Alcestis* in 1901 (music by Gluck, direction and translation by Constantinos Christomanos) and 1934 (Karolos Koun, director, and set by Giannis Tsarouchis); since 1868 *Medea*: 1942 (Takis Mouzenidis, director, music by Manos Hazidakis), 1956 (Alexis Minotis, director, music by Hadzidakis, starring Katina Paxinou), and 1989 (Aspasia Papathanasiou, director and star); *Hippolytus* since 1897: in 1937 (Dimitris Rondiris, director, Dimitris Mitropoulos, Alexis Minotis as Hippolytus, and Katina Paxinou as Phaedra) and 1965 (Dimitris Rondiris, director, music by Dimitris Mitropoulos; Aspasia Papathanasiou as Phaedra); *Bacchae* was notably done in 1962 (Alexis Minotis, director, music by Hadzidakis, Alexis Minotis as Kadmos, Basilis Kanakis as Pentheus, Katina Paxinou as

Agave), 1977 (Karolos Koun, director), and 1986–88 (Theodoros Terzopoulos, director, with his Attis theatre). Mikis Theodorakis's opera *Medea* (1991) is a parable of the history of Greece.

There are many films based on Euripides; Cacoyannis's *Trojan Trilogy* is based entirely on his work, with *Electra* (1961), *Trojan Women* (1971), and *Iphigeneia* (1976), all protesting in their own way against unjust oppression; Mikis Theodorakis composed the music for these films. Jules Dassin filmed *Phaedra* (1962) with a social message, contrasting the mass tragedy of loyal workers with the personal tragedy of dissolute jet-setters; he also based his *Dream of Passion* (1978) on *Medea*. Pasolini's *Medea* (1967) dealt with the myth behind the play in psychological and anthropological terms.

MARIANNE McDONALD

See also Tragedy

Biography
Born c.480 BC in Phyla, Euripides moved to Athens in childhood and first competed in the city Dionysia in 455 BC, winning his first victory in 441. He won four other victories (including one posthumously in 405). Of about 90 plays written, 19 survive (one of them spurious), including our only complete satyr play. He was less successful than Aeschylus and Sophocles in his lifetime but more popular than them later. He died in Macedon c.407/06 BC.

Writings (in translation)
The Plays (texts, translations, and commentaries), Warminster: Aris and Phillips, 1986–

The Complete Greek Tragedies (Centennial Edition), edited by David Grene and Richmond Lattimore, vols 3–4: *Euripides*, Chicago: University of Chicago Press, 1992

Euripides, translated by David Kovacs, Cambridge, Massachusetts: Harvard University Press, 1994– (Loeb edition)

Texts and Commentaries
Austin, Colin (editor), *Nova Fragmenta Euripidea in Papyris Reperta*, Berlin: de Gruyter, 1968

Collard, Christopher (editor), *Supplices*, 2 vols, Groningen: Bouma, 1975

Diggle, James (editor), *Phaeton*, Cambridge: Cambridge University Press, 1970

Diggle, James (editor), *Fabulae*, 3 vols, Oxford: Clarendon Press, 1981–94

Diggle, James (editor), *Tragicorum Graecorum Fragmenta Selecta*, Oxford: Clarendon Press, 1998

Harder, Annette (editor), *Kresphontes and Archelaos*, Leiden: Brill, 1985

Kannicht, Richard (editor), *Helen*, 2 vols, Heidelberg: Winter, 1969

Kannicht, Richard (editor), *Tragicorum Graecorum Fragmenta*, vols 5–6: *Euripides*, Göttingen: Vandenhoeck & Ruprecht, forthcoming

Lee, K.H., *Troades* (editor), London: Macmillan, and New York: St Martin's Press, 1976

Mastronarde, Donald J. (editor), *Phoenissae*, Cambridge and New York: Cambridge University Press, 1994

Schwartz, Edward (editor), *Scholia*, 2 vols, Berlin: Reimer, 1887–91

Works (texts and commentaries), Oxford: Clarendon Press, 1938–

Further Reading
Albini, Umberto, *Viaggio nel teatro classico*, Firenze: Le Monnier, 1987

Albini, Umberto, *Nel nome di Dioniso: vita teatrale nell'Atene classica*, Milan: Garzanti, 1991

Allen, James T. and Gabriel Italie, *A Concordance to Euripides*, Groningen: Bouma, 1970

Burian, Peter (editor), *Directions in Euripidean Criticism: A Collection of Essays*, Durham, North Carolina: Duke University Press, 1985

Conacher, D.J., *Euripidean Drama, Myth, Theme and Structure*, London: Oxford University Press, and Toronto: University of Toronto Press, 1967

Croally, N.T., *Euripidean Polemic: The Trojan Women and the Function of Tragedy*, Cambridge and New York: Cambridge University Press, 1994

Diggle, James, *Studies on the Text of Euripides*, Oxford: Clarendon Press, and New York: Oxford University Press, 1981

Diggle, James, *The Textual Tradition of Euripides' Orestes*, Oxford: Clarendon Press, and New York: Oxford University Press, 1991

Diggle, James, *Euripidea: Collected Essays*, Oxford: Clarendon Press, and New York: Oxford University Press, 1994

Easterling, P.E. (editor), *The Cambridge Companion to Greek Tragedy*, Cambridge: Cambridge University Press, 1997

Flashar, Hellmut (editor), *Inszenierung der Antike: das griechische Drama auf der Bühne der Neuzeit*, Munich: Beck, 1991

Flashar, Hellmut (editor), *Tragödie: Idee und Transformation*, Stuttgart: Teubner, 1997

Foley, Helene P., *Ritual Irony: Poetry and Sacrifice in Euripides*, Ithaca, New York: Cornell University Press, 1985

Gregory, Justina, *Euripides and the Instruction of the Athenians*, Ann Arbor: University of Michigan Press, 1991

Grube, G.M.A., *The Drama of Euripides*, London: Methuen, 1941

Jong, Irene J.F. de, *Narrative in Drama: The Art of the Euripidean Messenger-Speech*, Leiden and New York: Brill, 1991

Knox, Bernard, *Word and Action: Essays on the Ancient Theatre*, Baltimore: Johns Hopkins University Press, 1979

Lloyd, Michael, *The Agon in Euripides*, Oxford: Clarendon Press, and New York: Oxford University Press, 1992

McDonald, Marianne, *Terms for Happiness in Euripides*, Göttingen: Vandenhoeck & Ruprecht, 1978

McDonald, Marianne, *Euripides in Cinema: The Heart Made Visible*, Philadelphia: Centrum, 1983

McDonald, Marianne, *Ancient Sun, Modern Light: Greek Drama on the Modern Stage*, New York: Columbia University Press, 1992

MacKinnon, Kenneth, *Greek Tragedy into Film*, London: Croom Helm, and Rutherford, New Jersey: Fairleigh Dickinson University Press, 1986

Mastronade, Donald J. and Jan Maarten Bremer, *The Textual Tradition of Euripides' Phoinissai*, Berkeley: University of California Press, 1982

Mossman, Judith, *Wild Justice: A Study of Euripides' Hecuba*, Oxford: Clarendon Press, and New York: Oxford University Press, 1995

Pfeiffer, Rudolf, *History of Classical Scholarship*, 2 vols, Oxford: Clarendon Press, 1968–76

Pucci, Pietro, *The Violence of Pity in Euripides' Medea*, Ithaca, New York: Cornell University Press, 1980

Reynolds, L.D. and N.G. Wilson, *Scribes and Scholars: A Guide to the Transmission of Greek and Latin Literature*, 3rd edition, Oxford: Clarendon Press, and New York: Oxford University Press, 1991

Ritchie, William, *The Authenticity of the Rhesus of Euripides*, Cambridge: Cambridge University Press, 1964

Rosenmeyer, Thomas G., *The Masks of Tragedy: Essays on Six Greek Dramas*, Austin: University of Texas Press, 1963; reprinted New York: Gordian Press, 1971

Segal, Charles, *Dionysiac Poetics and Euripides' Bacchae*, Princeton, New Jersey: Princeton University Press, 1982; revised edition 1997

Segal, Charles, *Euripides and the Poetics of Sorrow: Art, Gender, and Commemoration in Alcestis, Hippolytus, and Hecuba*, Durham, North Carolina: Duke University Press, 1993

Webster, T.B.L., *The Tragedies of Euripides*, London: Methuen, 1967

Winnington-Ingram, R.P., *Euripides and Dionysus: An Interpretation of the Bacchae*, Cambridge: Cambridge University Press, 1948; 2nd edition, with foreword by P.E. Easterling, Bristol: Bristol Classical Press, 1997

Zeitlin, Froma I., *Playing the Other: Gender and Society in Classical Greek Literature*, Chicago: University of Chicago Press, 1996

Zuntz, Günther, *The Political Plays of Euripides*, Manchester: Manchester University Press, 1955

Zuntz, Günther, *An Inquiry into the Transmission of the Plays of Euripides*, Cambridge: Cambridge University Press, 1965

European Community and European Union

On 1 January 1981 Greece became a full member of the European Community (EC), which metamorphosed into the European Union (EU) when the Maastricht Treaty came into force on 1 November 1993. Greece was thus a "second generation" EC member. However, as the first state to apply for an Association with the European Economic Community, Greece had participated in the economic integration process from the early years.

The EEC, founded in 1957 by West Germany, France, Italy, the Netherlands, Belgium, and Luxembourg, initially entailed the creation of a common market based on the "Four Freedoms" – freedom of movement of goods, capital, labour, and services – plus a Common Agricultural Policy (CAP). From an economic viewpoint, the Greek application to the EEC on 8 June 1959 can be seen as the logical extension of the switch to an export-led development strategy adopted in 1953. By the end of the 1950s the EEC-6 already constituted the main outlet for Greek exports (over 30 per cent), and association facilitated access to Community markets. However, the motivation of Constantine Karamanlis's National Radical Union (ERE) government also appears to have been political, with the aim of consolidating Greece's links with its west European allies during a period of Cold War. Like European integration itself – which can be summed up as the quest by west European states to achieve "ever closer union" politically via an economic route – the Greek association pursued political ends through economic means.

Official negotiations began in March 1960, culminating with the signature of the Athens Agreement on 9 July 1961 and its coming into effect on 1 November 1962. The basis of the association was a customs union between Greece and the EEC-6, to be completed over a 22-year period ending in 1984. Reflecting the disparity in economic development levels, the dismantling of tariff barriers was to take place more rapidly on the EEC side, so that Greek products would gain access to European markets before the domestic economy opened up fully to foreign competition. Clauses not subsequently implemented provided for free movement of labour and the progressive harmonization of Greek agricultural policy with the CAP. A financial protocol attached to the association offered $125 million in subsidized development loans from the European Investment Bank – a significant recognition of the EEC's responsibility to support the economic development of its weaker partner. The association also declared that, when Greece could assume all the obligations of full membership, the contracting parties should "consider the possibility" of accession. While hardly a binding legal commitment, this can be regarded as a clear indication of intent by both parties. Thus, the association acknowledged this developing country, with a per capita GDP around 40 per cent of the EC average, as a potential full participant in the influential Community club.

This prospect seemed to be threatened when the military coup of 21 April 1967 resulted in the EC limiting the association to its "routine administration". While tariff dismantling continued on schedule, agricultural harmonization talks were suspended, free movement of labour was not implemented, financial aid was frozen, and political contacts significantly reduced. The unbalanced functioning of the association continued following the junta's fall in July 1974. Although the association was formally reactivated five months later, the EC declined to discuss free movement or agricultural harmonization, while agreement on the Second Financial Protocol required tough negotiation.

Greece's relative marginalization coincided with a rapid advance in European integration. In 1968 the EEC merged its institutions with those of the European Coal and Steel Community (founded in 1952) and the European Atomic Energy Commission (1957) to form the European Communities or, more simply, Community. In the early 1970s the EC expanded from six to nine members with the accession of the United Kingdom, Ireland, and Denmark; made an explicit move from the economic to the political sphere with the first timid steps towards foreign policy coordination (European Political Cooperation – EPC); and embarked on an ill-fated first attempt at Economic and Monetary Union (EMU).

The EC's rapid development, combined with the unbalanced functioning of the association, made full membership desirable sooner rather than later. The official application was submitted on 12 June 1975. Karamanlis's New Democracy government hoped accession would consolidate domestic democracy and enhance national security vis-à-vis Turkey, while regarding the challenge of the EC market combined with CAP support as an optimum framework for economic development. In the aftermath of the Turkish invasion of Cyprus and temporary Greek withdrawal from NATO's military wing, EC membership was also expected to restabilize Greece's links with its western allies, while simultaneously permitting the adjustment of the postwar patron–client relationship with the United States. On a symbolic level, Karamanlis's description of accession as Greece's "new *Megali Idea*" defined EC entry as the route to national regeneration – to be achieved, not through the pre-1922 dream of territorial expansion, but by Greece's transformation into a modern state in the contemporary European mould.

Accession was a controversial policy choice. Advocated by the right-wing New Democracy, the Centre, and (rather more critically) by the small Eurocommunist party (KKE-Esoterikou), it was adamantly opposed by the Panhellenic Socialist Movement (PASOK) and the orthodox Communist Party (KKE). While the two anti-EC parties promoted different alternatives – closer economic links with the Third World in the case of PASOK compared to the KKE's support for increased trade with the eastern bloc – their analyses of the EC were remarkably similar. Both parties regarded the Community as an imperialist creation and warned that accession would result in economic subordination to multinational monopolies, the distortion of democracy, and the betrayal of national foreign policy interests. While the dispute was clearly shaped by Cold War dynamics, on another level it represented a new phase in the long-running debate about Greece's cultural identity and relationship to Europe. The EC's supporters saw "Europeanization" and "modernization" as both synonymous and desirable, and regarded accession as a homecoming to the area where Greece rightfully belonged. In contrast, its opponents, continuing a tradition which viewed western Europe as an alien region inimical to Hellenism, warned that Greek culture was endangered by accession. On occasion, there appeared to be a curious convergence of views between the two anti-EC left-wing parties and Church circles which feared entry to the "Catholic" EC threatened the spiritual values of Orthodoxy.

The path to accession was not especially smooth. The European Commission's initial proposal for an extended pre-entry period was rejected by the Council of Ministers. But the negotiations, which formally opened in July 1976, were then threatened by the 1977 Spanish and Portuguese membership applications. The subsequent threat of "globalized" entry talks, delaying Greek admission, was apparently averted by the dynamic personal diplomacy of prime minister Karamanlis. He was clearly assisted by west European concerns to reestablish unity on NATO's southeastern flank and to ensure Greek accession before the election of an anti-Western government. The membership treaty, signed on 28 May 1979, included a five-year transitional period before the full application of the CAP (extended to seven years for certain products, including peaches and tomato paste, and seven years for free movement of labour). Opposition claims that Greek entry occurred on particularly onerous terms later seemed to be disproved when Spain and Portugal finally entered the EC five years later than Greece and with longer transition periods.

Despite 18 years of association, neither the economy nor the administration was well prepared for accession. The government's strategy appeared to be summed up by Karamanlis's famous remark to the Greek industrialists, that he was throwing them into the sea, confident that they would learn how to swim. Nor did PASOK's electoral victory ten months after Greek accession facilitate adjustment to membership. In particular, the party's first term in office (1981–85) saw intense ideological conflicts in the field of foreign-policy cooperation, frequent attempts to delay economic integration by seeking postponements and exceptions from EC rules, and adamant opposition to proposals for deeper political integration. A formal request for a special status, made in the Greek Government Memorandum of 1982, was rejected by the EC. However, the Community's offer of substantial funding through the Integrated Mediterranean Programmes provided the justification for a subsequent change of heart. In 1985, after a period of prevarication, prime minister Andreas Papandreou, claiming that PASOK had improved the terms of

participation, announced that Greece was in the Community to stay.

Subsequently, PASOK moved towards an increasingly pro-European stance. Public opinion was already convinced: from the mid-1980s polls showed clear pro-EC majorities. By the 1990s opposition to integration was no longer a mainstream political position. But by this time Greece had acquired an unflattering image among its partners, owing to its weak economic performance, foreign policy incompatibilities, and generally non-*Communautaire* stance. This picture only began to change during the premiership of Kostas Simitis after 1996.

Meanwhile, after the mid-1980s, the EC had acquired a new momentum: expanding from 10 to 12 and then 15 members; moving from the customs union to the single market and subsequently to EMU; enhancing supranational decision-making; and acquiring an explicitly political content with the adoption of the Common Foreign and Security Policy (CFSP) and Justice and Home Affairs Cooperation as the two new "pillars" of European Union alongside the existing economic Community. Membership of the current EU clearly has more far-reaching implications than the more limited Community which Greece initially joined. Over a historically brief period, accession has already had a deep and wide-ranging impact on Greece's economy, international standing, and domestic political system, which can only be schematically indicated here.

For instance, participation in the customs union has encouraged trade reorientation towards the EU, which by the 1990s accounted for over 60 per cent of both imports and exports. A growing trade deficit has been accompanied by the decline of industry's share in GDP. Increasing import penetration has stimulated significant lifestyle changes, including a startling growth in consumerism. For example, the rapid rise in meat imports, of which the EC accounted for almost 90 per cent by 1985, has been a notable factor in altered eating habits. On the other hand, it could be argued that such change was inevitable anyway, while EU membership provides some defence against the ubiquitous effects of globalization.

Membership has also promoted economic liberalization, encouraged by the single market programme and reinforced by the drive to meet the strict entry criteria for EMU. The consequences include the ending of state monopolies in many sectors, ranging from air transport and telecommunications to match production, and the stimulation of economic restructuring, e.g. in the banking sector. The overall effect has been a significant erosion of the Greek state's previously dominant economic role, upgrading the importance of market forces.

Net transfers from the EC/EU budget grew from 0.5 per cent of GDP in 1981 to over 6 per cent by the late 1990s. The lion's share (around 60 per cent) came from the CAP, accounting for over 35 per cent of national agricultural product by the late 1990s. This brought a visible new prosperity to the Greek countryside, narrowing the urban–rural divide in living standards; the CAP and tourism together stemmed the tide of the postwar rural population exodus. Meanwhile, by the mid-1990s, the Structural Funds (Regional, Social, and Agricultural Guidance) provided about one-third of total public investment. The Greek state's regional development policy, almost in its entirety, is now conducted in partnership with the EU. Sadly, the inflow of funding has failed to achieve real economic convergence: Greek GDP per capita as a proportion of the EC/EU average has actually declined since 1981.

Participation in EPC/CFSP has brought closer foreign-policy alignment with the EU partners. A prime example was diplomatic recognition of Israel, overturning Greece's previously pro-Arab stance. Traditionally an object rather than a subject of international power politics, Greece has acquired a greater voice in global affairs through its ability to influence EC/EU policy. Membership has also provided a powerful weapon in bilateral relations with the Balkan neighbours; this proved controversial when used to block international recognition of the Former Yugoslav Republic of Macedonia or EU financial aid to Turkey.

The implications of European integration for national sovereignty and democracy remain a topic of heated debate; but they are clearly not the same for Greece as for the former imperial powers. Since independence in 1830 Greece, as a small, weak state occupying a strategic position, was frequently an object of Great Power intervention, often with unsettling effects on domestic democracy. Membership of western Europe's most powerful club helped to break the pattern of dependence on foreign patrons, providing a stable framework for consolidation of the post-1974 democracy. While the transfer of legislative responsibilities to "Brussels" has undermined the role of the Greek parliament, the latter was traditionally weak anyway. Although not one of the more powerful players, within EU institutions Greece is now a policy-making participant with some decision-making influence.

Meanwhile, it has been argued that integration may be producing a more diffuse power distribution among different levels of government: for example, by effecting shifts in centre–periphery relations. Thus, EC/EU structural policy has broadened the horizons of Greek local government, and necessitated the creation of administrative regions as the basic units for EC/EU-funded programmes.

Despite entrenched resistance, "Europeanization", in the sense of the internalization of values, norms, and practices prevalent within the EU, is increasingly apparent throughout the political system. Examples range from the ideological and programmatic convergence of Greek political parties with their west European counterparts, to the introduction of new principles of planning and monitoring public works projects in response to the rules of EU-funded programmes. Meanwhile, public policymaking is increasingly driven by the constraints and opportunities of EU membership. For example, Greek environmental policy – still in a rudimentary phase at the time of accession – has essentially taken shape under the twin stimuli of the EU's legislative framework and financial inputs.

Thus, after two decades of Association and two of full membership, the European Union has essentially become the focal reference point for Greek economics, politics, and international identity. The extent and range of future EU influence will depend not only on how the Union itself evolves, but also on how well Greece responds to the continuing challenge of European integration.

SUSANNAH VERNEY

Further Reading

Coufoudakis, Van, "The European Economic Community and the 'Freezing' of the Greek Association, 1967–1974", *Journal of Common Market Studies*, 16/2 (1977): pp. 114–31

Featherstone, Kevin, chapter on Greece, in *Socialist Parties and European Integration: A Comparative History*, Manchester: Manchester University Press, 1988, pp. 170–90

Featherstone, Kevin and Kostas Ifantis (editors), *Greece in a Changing Europe: Between European Integration and Balkan Disintegration*, Manchester: Manchester University Press, 1996

Greek Government, *Greece, the European Economic Community and a European Free Trade Area*, Athens: Ministries of Coordination and Foreign Affairs, 1959

Ioakimidis, P.C., *Greece in the European Union: Problems and Prospects*, Reading: University of Reading, Graduate School of European and International Studies, 1994

Ioakimidis, P.C., "Measuring 'Ensomatosis': The Case of Greece in the European Union", in *The Southeast European Yearbook 1994–5*, Athens: Hellenic Foundation for European and Foreign Policy, 1995

Ioakimidis, P.C., *Evropaiki Enosi kai Elliniko Kratos: Oi Epiptoseis apo ti symmetochi stin Enopoiitiki Diadikasia* [European Union and the Greek State: The Effects of Participation in the Unification Process], Athens: Themelio, 1998

Kazakos, Panos and P.C. Ioakimidis (editors), *Greece and EC Membership Evaluated*, London: Pinter, and New York: St Martin's Press, 1994

Moschonas, Andreas, "European Integration and Prospects of Modernization in Greece", *Journal of Modern Greek Studies*, 15/2 (October 1997): pp. 325–48

Psomiades, Harry J. and Stavros B. Thomadakis (editors), *Greece, the New Europe, and the Changing International Order*, New York: Pella, 1993

Stephanidis, Ioannis D., "The Greek Pro-European Movement (1947–1967)", in *Hellenic Review of International Relations*, 5/6 (1985–86): pp. 244–70

Tsakaloyannis, Panos, "Greece: The Limits to Convergence" in *The Actors in Europe's Foreign Policy*, edited by Christopher Hill, London and New York: Routledge, 1996, pp. 186–207

Tsalicoglou, Iacovos S., *Negotiating for Entry: The Accession of Greece to the European Community*, Aldershot: Dartmouth, 1995

Tsatsos, Constantine, *Greece and Europe*, Athens: General Secretariat for Press and Information, 1977

Tsinisizelis, Michael, "Greece and the European Community: A Bibliographical Essay", *Modern Greek Society*, 18 (1990): pp. 1–120

Tsinisizclis, Michael, "Greece" in *The European Union and Member States: Towards Institutional Fusion?*, edited by Dietrich Rometsch and Wolfgang Wessels, Manchester: Manchester University Press, 1996

Tsoukalis, Loukas (editor), *Greece and the European Community*, Farnborough: Saxon House, 1979

Tsoukalis, Loukas (editor), *The European Community and its Mediterranean Enlargement*, London and Boston: Allen and Unwin, 1981

Veremis, Thanos and Dimitri Constas, "The Beginning of the Discussion on European Union in Greece" in *Documents on the History of European Integration*, vol. 3: *The Struggle for European Union by Political Parties and Pressure Groups in Western European Countries, 1945–1950*, edited by Walter Lipgens and Wilfried Loth, Berlin and New York: de Gruyter, 1985–91

Yannopoulos, George N., *Greece and the European Economic Communities: The First Decade of a Troubled Association*, Beverly Hills and London: Sage, 1975

Eusebius *c.*AD 260–339

Ecclesiastical historian

In his native Caesarea Eusebius was a pupil of the great Origenist Pamphilus, whose martyrdom he celebrates in his *Ecclesiastical History*, and whose name he honoured by adding it to his own. Like Pamphilus he admired both the theology and the scholarship of Origen, whose library must have furnished him with materials for his apologetic work, the *Preparation of the Gospel*. Written after AD 313, this was in response to the Neoplatonist Porphyry, who had written a damaging work against Christianity. The *Preparation*, far excelling both Origen and Pamphilus in its knowledge of and sympathy with Greek literature, remains our most abundant source of passages from the authors whom we now call Middle Platonist. With his monograph *Against Hierocles* (*c.*300) Eusebius refuted another disputant, who had argued that the miracles attributed to the pagan saint Apollonius of Tyana were both holier and greater than those of Christ. He completed his apologetic task with the *Demonstration of the Gospel*, which set out what he understood as the elements of theology, supporting them from scripture and drawing the first of many illegitimate comparisons between the Christian Trinity and the "three hypostases" (One, Mind, Soul) of Neoplatonism.

The most original of Eusebius' many talents were devoted to historical inquiry, which invariably led to the discernment of God's providential will in the affairs of his chosen people(s). More serviceable to later generations than his commentaries on Luke and Matthew were his *Onomasticon*, a glossary of the Hebrew names in scripture, and his (lost) *Chronicle*, which in Jerome's Latin adaptation supplies the modern historian with many of his dates. Eusebius' reckoning is by Olympiads, since his object was to match the biblical record with the events of secular history; in this, as in his concordance of the gospels, his success was not so great as he supposed. His most important labour was the *Ecclesiastical History*, the first seven books of which may have been complete before the persecution of Diocletian in 303. Taking the fall of Jerusalem in AD 70 as a proof that Christianity had supplanted Israel in the plan of God, he reckoned up the bishops of all the major sees, alluded to works by previous apologists, commemorated the lives of outstanding churchmen, and showed how the integrity of both scripture and the episcopate had been maintained against the assaults of heresy. His practice of quoting written sources, typical of Greek oratory but not of historiography, is a further indication of his apologetic motive. But if his purpose was (as one suspects) to be the Josephus of the Church and win the Romans to his party, he was undeceived by the years of persecution (303–13) which he recounts in his last three books and in the associated history of the Palestinian martyrs. The final version of these, however, was published after the Christian warlord Constantine assumed the throne of a united empire in 324, and Eusebius saw his reign as the consummation of God's purpose in the world.

He now had the opportunity to set out his optimistic view of history more fully in the second of his two *Theophanies*, which treats the supersession of the Jews as an accomplished fact and predicts an imminent judgement of the world. In his *Tricennalian Oration* of 336 he endows his sovereign with a benevolence, perspicacity, and promptitude of action scarcely inferior to those of the Almighty. The *Life of Constantine*, more a panegyric than a biography, was finished after its hero's death in 337, and credits him with a thoroughgoing policy for the conversion of the empire, which he never executed and may never have entertained. This work also preserves an embellished narrative of Constantine's conversion and the fifth book is an appendix that contains the emperor's one surviving sermon, the *Oration to the Assembly of the Saints*.

That this work is not a forgery by Eusebius is clear from several passages that contradict the teaching of the theological treatises that he was forced to write in the aftermath of the Council of Nicaea in 325. As bishop of Caesarea, he reluctantly put his name to the Creed that imposed the word *homoousios* ("being of one essence") on the clergy; but, as he showed in a letter to his own flock, he did not construe this term to mean that God and Christ were equal or identical. He set out the scriptural basis of his position in his writings against Marcellus of Ancyra, who, according to him, denied that the incarnate Christ possessed his own identity (*hypostasis*) and made him only a temporal emanation of the Father. Eusebius was prepared to speak of Christ as the second member of a triad, who existed with the Father before the ages and brought the cosmos into being, but he never calls him eternal or consubstantial with the Father. Following Origen, he held that the Father was God by nature (*ho theos*, *autotheos*), whereas Christ was only God by derivation (*theos*; cf. John 1: 1); in so far as he was equated with the Wisdom of Proverbs 8: 22, he could even be called a creature. At first it seemed that his position, upheld as it was by the Council of Antioch in 341, was likely to triumph over that of Athanasius, who maintained that all three persons of the Trinity were equally divine. The orthodox position after 381, however, was that Christ could not be called a creature (whatever we make of Proverbs 8: 22) and that the Father's priority in the order of generation does not entail the subordination of the Son.

Eusebius' theology thus became obsolete, but his scholarship did not. No historian undertook to do his work again, though some of his continuators offered a different view of Constantine. His narrative was taken up in Greek by Socrates, Theodoret, Sozomen, Gelsasius, and Philostorgius, and in the West by Rufinus, another Origenist. His enduring reputation is attested in the West both by Rufinus' Latin version of the *Ecclesiastical History*, and by the name of Rufinus' great contemporary Hieronymus Eusebius, better known to us as Jerome. His celebration of Constantine as God's vicegerent, with power to summon councils, to dictate a creed, and even to unseat religious dignitaries, strengthened the hands of later Eastern sovereigns in their dealing with the Church. Most of his works survived in Greek, for all Athanasius' efforts to portray him as an Arianizing heretic. This he was not, but rather a conservative and peaceful ecclesiastic; no doubt he spoke from the heart in his *Life of Constantine* when he alluded to Athanasius, without naming him, as one who had gratuitously sown discord in the Church. The consequence was that he, like his sympathetic master Constantine, failed to achieve the rigorous orthodoxy that enabled many worse men of his epoch to be recognized as saints.

MARK EDWARDS

Biography

Born c.AD 260 in Caesarea, Eusebius was a pupil of Pamphilus who gave him access to the library of Origen. Elected bishop of Caesarea c.313, he attended the Council of Nicaea in 325 and the Council of Tyre in 335. Of his many works the most important are his *Ecclesiastical History*, the model for all subsequent histories of its type, and a *Life of Constantine*. He died in 339.

Writings

Praeparatio Evangelica, edited by E.H. Gifford, 5 vols, Oxford: Clarendon Press, 1903

Against Hierocles in *Life of Apollonius of Tyana* [by Philostratus], *The Epistles of Apollonius, and the Treatise of Eusebius*, vol. 2, translated by J.C. Conybeare, London: Heinemann, and New York: Macmillan, 1912 (Loeb edition)

The Ecclesiastical History, translated by Kirsopp Lake, 2 vols, London: Heinemann, and New York: Putnam, 1926–32

Werke, edited by E. Klostermann *et al.*, Berlin: Akademie, 1954–

In Praise of Constantine: A Historical Study and New Translation of Eusebius' Tricennial Orations, by H.A. Drake, Berkeley: University of California Press, 1976

The History of the Church from Christ to Constantine, translated by G.A. Williamson, revised edition, London and New York: Penguin, 1989

Church History, Life of Constantine, Oration to the Saints, translated by A.C. McGiffert in *Nicene and Post-Nicene Fathers*, 2nd series, vol. 1, reprinted Peabody, Massachusetts: Hendrickson, 1994

Life of Constantine, translated by Averil Cameron and Stuart Hall, Oxford: Clarendon Press, 1999

Further Reading

Barnes, Timothy D., *Constantine and Eusebius*, Cambridge, Massachusetts: Harvard University Press, 1981

Grant, Robert M., *Eusebius as Church Historian*, Oxford: Clarendon Press, 1980

Lyman, J. Rebecca, *Christology and Cosmology: Models of Divine Activity in Origen, Eusebius, and Athanasius*, Oxford: Clarendon Press, and New York: Oxford University Press, 1993

Wallace-Hadrill, D.S., *Eusebius of Caesarea*, London: Mowbray, and Westminster, Maryland: Canterbury Press, 1960

Eustathios *c.1115–c.1195*

Archbishop of Thessalonica and scholar

Eustathios was a commentator on ancient literature and a composer of brilliant speeches. He belonged to a circle of learned men at the end of the 12th century that included famous scholars such as Michael and Niketas Choniates, Euthymios Malakes, and Gregory Antiochos.

He was born around 1115 in Constantinople, where he was a pupil of Nikolaos Kataphloron, who was a well-known rhetorician and perhaps also his uncle. He spent some time with other colleagues such as Euthymios Malakes, later the metropolitan of Neopatras, at the Euphemia monastery in Constantinople. Eustathios mentions his education only twice: he speaks about his severe teacher and an expedition with him

into the outskirts of Constantinople to visit the broken column at Pinakidion.

Eustathios started his career as a scribe at the patriarchate and soon became deacon with responsibility for the sacred treasures during the reign of patriarch Luke Chrysoberges (1157–69/70). Thus he was attached to the group from which the higher ranks of the clergy were chosen. After 1166 he is mentioned as master of the rhetoricians (*magistros ton rhetoron*), the highest teaching position at the patriarchal school, which he held until he left Constantinople. Following in the footsteps of his teacher Kataphloron, Eustathios became a very successful teacher and continued teaching after his move to Thessalonica. Sons of distinguished Constantinopolitan families were even sent to him there for lessons.

Eustathios rose up the ecclesiastical hierarchy and held several posts of a juridical and fiscal nature. During the patriarchate of Michael III Anchialos (1170–78) his career stopped for some time: he lost his post as a deacon at Hagia Sophia, because the deacon who had been dismissed by Luke Chrysoberges was reinstated. He complained about this in a short document (a so-called *hypomnestikon*) and sent a petition asking for support to Michael Hagiotheodorites, the powerful minister of transport and internal affairs (*logothetes tou dromou*). He was successful and was nominated for the see of Myra, but within a short time he was assigned on the orders of the emperor to Thessalonica, where he arrived around 1179. In 1185 the Normans conquered Thessalonica. Defending his diocese, Eustathios was captured but well treated. The occupation did not last long, and the Normans were soon routed by general Alexios Branas.

Eustathios had some problems with the local clergy and he published some critical remarks about the monks' lifestyle (e.g. his pamphlet *On the Improvement of Monastic Life*), which provoked his temporary expulsion from Thessalonica. In February 1191 he delivered a speech in front of Isaac II Angelos (1185–95) in Philippopolis and by the end of April he was back in Thessalonica. After his reinstallation by the emperor Isaac II a new conflict arose, but this time the patriarch Georgios II Xiphilinos personally acted for him and it seems that he lived the rest of his life without troubles until his death in 1195/96.

Eustathios, one of the best-known scholars, commented on a wide range of ancient literature. Two fragments of his commentary on Pindar are preserved. He wrote voluminous commentaries on the *Iliad* and *Odyssey* of Homer citing many ancient authors (some fragments are preserved only in Eustathios). And he did further philological work on Aeschylus, Dionysius Periegetes, and Strabo.

In his official capacity he composed a few speeches for the emperor Manuel I Komnenos (1143–80), whom he supported politically and sometimes dared to criticize. He delivered speeches on various subjects, including a shortage of water in the capital, on the marriage of Alexios II, son of Manuel, to Agnes of France (1179), and on the wedding banquet in the city. In 1180 he delivered the funeral sermon (*epitaphios logos*) for the emperor Manuel. Later he glorified Isaac II Angelos in several speeches.

The capture of Thessalonica (1185) by the Normans was a traumatic event for all its inhabitants. Eustathios's account (the *Capture of Thessalonica*) is in two parts: the first deals with the reign of Andronikos I Komnenos (1183–85); in the second part the author describes the capitulation of the city and his own capture. A collection of 47 of his letters also survives. Eustathios provides the modern scholar with valuable insights into ancient literature and also a window into the learned culture of the late 12th century.

MICHAEL GRÜNBART

See also Education, Homer, Manuel I, Pindar

Biography

Born *c.*1115 in Constantinople, Eustathios was a pupil of Nikolaos Kataphloron, who may also have been his uncle. He served as a scribe at the Patriarchate, was ordained a deacon, and subsequently became master of the rhetoricians (after 1166). Nominated first as bishop of Myra, he was sent instead in 1179 to Thessalonica as archbishop. Taken prisoner by the Normans in 1185, he was later released. He wrote extensive commentaries on ancient literature and a number of sermons and panegyrics. He died *c.*1195/96.

Writings

Commentarii ad Homeri Odysseam, edited by J.G. Stallbaum, 6 vols, Leipzig: Weigel, 1825–26
Opuscula, edited by G.L.F. Tafel, Frankfurt, 1832; reprinted Amsterdam: Hakkert, 1964
La espugnazione di Tessalonica, edited by Stilpon Kyriakides, Palermo: Testi e Monumenti, 1961
Commentarii ad Homeri Iliadem pertinentes, edited by Marchinus van der Valk, Leiden: Brill, 1971–87
Opera minora, edited by Peter Wirth, Berlin, 2000

Further Reading

Kazhdan, Alexander P. and Simon Franklin, *Studies on Byzantine Literature of the Eleventh and Twelfth Centuries*, Cambridge and New York: Cambridge University Press, 1984, pp. 115–95
Wirth, Peter, *Eustathiana: Gesammelte Aufsätze zu Leben und Werk des Metropoliten Eustathios von Thessalonike*, Amsterdam: Hakkert, 1980

Evagoras *c.*445–374/73 BC

Ruler of Cypriot Salamis

For much of the 5th century BC Cyprus was a bone of contention between the Greeks and Persia. When in 449 BC Athens, the leading Greek maritime power, and its alliance (the Delian League) were forced to come to terms with the Great King (the so-called Peace of Callias), whereby Cyprus was conceded as belonging within the Persian sphere of influence, the Greeks of Cyprus were effectively left to fend for themselves. The Persian-backed Phoenician minority quickly gained the ascendancy and Phoenician kings were imposed on a number of Greek Cypriot cities, including the most important, Salamis, which had been ruled by the Teucrid dynasty since the city's foundation at the close of the Bronze Age. A member of this dynasty, the youthful Evagoras, was forced to flee, but he returned a few years later (possibly in 415/14 BC), perhaps with Athenian help, expelled the Phoenicians, and restored Greek royal rule. It is commonly believed that Evagoras immediately submitted to Persia and paid tribute, but this is unlikely. At any rate his actions in helping Athens, an enemy of the Great King, do not point to such a conclusion.

The evidence for the career of Evagoras is none too plentiful and much of it is equivocal, but on balance it seems to point to his having been from the very start fixed on the policies we see him pursuing in later years. The development and strengthening of Salamis was the first and indispensable step to unifying the island under his rule and wresting it from Persian control. Close ties with Athens, the heart of Hellas, and the full Hellenization of the island went hand-in-hand with this aim. It should be stressed that Hellenization in the Cypriot context meant (for the Cypriot Greeks at least) a process of catching up with their fellow Greeks. Having lived in relative isolation for many centuries, the Cypriots still adhered to older ways of living and thinking.

By 412 BC Evagoras had rendered Athens, locked as it was in a life-and-death struggle with Sparta (the Peloponnesian War), services sufficiently important for both him and his sons to be rewarded with the city's citizenship. In 405 BC, when the Athenian fleet was destroyed by Sparta, the Athenian general Conon, with a number of warships and many hundreds of Athenians, took refuge with Evagoras in Cyprus. Together Conon and Evagoras planned the defeat of Sparta and the restoration of Athenian power. Because Persian money and resources were necessary for this, Evagoras made his peace with the Great King and agreed to be his tribute-paying vassal. In 394 BC at Cnidus the Spartan fleet was decisively defeated by a Persian-financed force led by Conon. The Spartan naval hegemony was over. A grateful Athens heaped honours on the two men, including the setting up of their statues in the Agora next to the image of Zeus Soter, an unprecedented and extraordinary gesture, extended only to two other men, Timotheus, the son of Conon, and, centuries later, Hadrian, the great Roman emperor and philhellene.

Evagoras now turned his attention to the unification of Cyprus, which meant the subjection of the other city kingdoms of the island, all of them tribute-paying clients of Persia. He seems to have been well on the way to achieving this when the Great King, fearful and suspicious, resolved to strike first and restore the status quo. War broke out around 390 BC and lasted for some ten years. Allied with Athens, who repeatedly sent ships and troops to the island, and Egypt, Evagoras initially went from success to success. He captured Tyre and caused much of Phoenicia and Cilicia to revolt against Persia. Citium in Cyprus, the main Phoenician stronghold on the island and always strongly pro-Persian, nevertheless held out, and the tide definitely turned against Evagoras when Sparta and Persia enforced the King's Peace in Greece in 386 BC. A central clause of the peace recognized Greek Asia and Cyprus as belonging to the Great King. Athenian forces evacuated the island and Evagoras stood alone, bereft of his vitally important Greek support. A mighty Persian armada invaded the island, probably in 385 BC, and though Evagoras fought well and bravely, and with considerable initial success, in the end he found himself besieged in Salamis and was forced to come to terms. He was still strong enough, however, to resist complete subjection to Persia and to insist instead on being granted his previous status of an autonomous, but tribute-paying, client king. He died a few years later, assassinated with his eldest son, in rather mysterious circumstances in 374/73 BC.

One of the most eminent of British historians summed up the career of Evagoras thus: "There are few more striking demonstrations in Greek history than the attempt ... of Evagoras of Salamis, with the limited resources of a small island, to challenge the great Persian empire and to make Cyprus more Greek than Greece" (J.B. Bury in *A History of Greece*, edited by Bury and R. Meiggs, 3rd edition 1951, p.73). That contemporary Greece, and in particular Athens, whose honorary citizen he was, would have concurred fully with this judgement is proved not merely by the high praise of the prominent Athenian orator Isocrates (above all in his pioneering oration, the *Evagoras*), but also by two new fragments (identified in 1979) of the stele bearing the decree voted in honour of Evagoras by the Athenian assembly in 393 BC (D.M. Lewis and R.S. Stroud, *Hesperia*, 48 (1979): pp. 180ff.). It would appear that the public herald was to proclaim on the occasion of a dramatic festival, *inter alia*, that Evagoras had done his duty by Greece and Greek freedom as a Greek ought.

While Evagoras' policy of the further Hellenization of Cyprus met with much success (the wholesale importation of Athenians and their culture left an indelible mark on the island), his political aims failed. After so many years of war, which exhausted the resources of Salamis, he was at the end no nearer his purpose than when he began. Nevertheless, his goal of a united island that would moreover form part of the wider Greek world, and the tenacity with which he pursued it, lived on to inspire the modern Greek Cypriots in their own equally long struggle for national rehabilitation.

P. J. STYLIANOU

Biography

Born *c.*445 BC as a member of the ancient Teucrid dynasty of Cyprus, Evagoras was at first forced to leave the island but returned *c.*415/14 to expel the Persian-backed Phoenicians and restore Greek rule. Allied with Athens, he united most of Cyprus. After the King's Peace (387/86) he defied the Persians and secured honourable terms. He was assassinated in 374/73 BC.

Further Reading

Gjerstad, Einar *et al.*, *The Swedish Cyprus Expedition: Finds and Results of the Excavations in Cyprus, 1927–1931*, vol. 4.2, Stockholm: Swedish Cyprus Expedition, 1948 (especially pp. 489 ff.)

Hill, George Francis, *A History of Cyprus*, vol. 1, Cambridge: Cambridge University Press, 1940, pp. 125 ff.

Spyridakis, Konstantin, *Euagoras I. von Salamis*, Stuttgart: Kohlhammer, 1935

Stylianou, P.J., "Cyprus: The Age of the Kingdoms" in *Meletai kai Hypomnemata* [Studies and Notes], 2 (1989): pp. 458 ff.

Stylianou, P.J., *A Historical Commentary on Diodorus Siculus, Book 15*, Oxford: Clarendon Press, and New York: Oxford University Press, 1998, pp. 143 ff.

Evagrius of Pontus *c.*345–399

Monk and theologian

Judging from the sophistication of his works, it is clear that Evagrius received a fine Classical education. His theological formation was with the Cappadocian Fathers – he was ordained a reader by St Basil and a deacon by St Gregory of Nazianzus; Evagrius described Gregory as the one who had "planted" him. After accompanying Gregory to the Ecumenical Council of Constantinople in 381, Evagrius fled for fear of causing scandal, first to Jerusalem and then to the Egyptian desert. There he came into contact with the great elders of the day, and particularly with St Macarius of Egypt and St Macarius of Alexandria. From the living experience of the Egyptian desert, Evagrius drew the substance of his teaching on the ascetic life.

Evagrius' genius lay in his ability to systematize what he had learned in the desert, and to present it in a form that was intelligible to the educated reader. His systematization of the spiritual life is presented in three major works: the *Praktikos*, 100 chapters on the ascetic struggle; the *Gnostikos*, 50 chapters on the proper conduct of the true gnostic; and the *Kephalaia Gnostika*, 6 centuries, each of 90 chapters, dealing largely with the more speculative aspects of his thought. In this last work Evagrius reproduces and reifies the cosmological speculations of Origen. He posits the pre-existence of a Henad of pure intellect, engaged in the contemplation of God. A rupture is produced by the fall of these rational beings from contemplation, due to satiety or negligence and occasioning the second, physical, creation, in which each intellect is given a soul and body so that it might return, by way of contemplation, to the original unity.

Evagrius' work is chiefly concerned with the stage of return. The path back to God shown by Christ requires a conscious turning from materiality, both in body (the struggle against the passions) and in intellect (the divestment of forms). One begins with the practical struggle that produces love. The intellect must then turn to the contemplation of nature, perceiving the inner realities of creation and then passing on to essential knowledge, true theology, the contemplation of the Holy Trinity. Each of these stages requires a proportionate divestment of the intellect from all forms, material and immaterial, until it is perfectly "naked" and reunited to unoriginate intellect. Thus the original state of all things is restored and the *apokatastasis* (restoration) is accomplished.

Evagrius died just before the outbreak of the Origenist controversy in Egypt. It is, however, clear that it is largely his brand of Origenism that was condemned at the Fifth Ecumenical Council of 553. This black mark against his name did not, however, put a stop to his influence. The Church tradition took the eminently sensible course of discarding his metaphysical speculations and keeping much of his spiritual teaching under a pseudonym, usually that of Nilus. Evagrius' work was simply too valuable to be lost for the sake of his overenthusiasm for metaphysical speculation. He had crystallized much of what was best in the Egyptian desert, not only in his *Praktikos* but also in other works, such as his *One Hundred and Fifty-Three Chapters on Prayer*, *Ad Monachos*, and *Texts on Discrimination*. The *Kephalaia Gnostika* disappeared from the Greek tradition, being preserved only in the Syriac.

Evagrius has often been criticized for giving a disproportionate role to the intellect. There is a great deal of truth in this observation, but it has to be nuanced. He had no antipathy to the material order – the body and soul are there to help the intellect, not to hinder it. Moreover, intellect, soul, and body form a whole, the soul forming the bond of unity. On the Last

Day, soul and body are to be raised to the level of intellect. Evagrius allows a certain role to the heart in the spiritual life, linking it to knowledge and wisdom and treating it as the locus of the spiritual struggle. He was certainly not a dualist, although it is true that his anthropology lacks balance.

Evagrius was a crucial figure in the shaping of the monastic spiritual tradition. St John Cassian and Palladius were early disciples, and did much to propagate his teaching. His work rapidly entered into the mainstream. His influence is palpable in the works of St Diadochus of Photice and St John Klimakos. St Maximos the Confessor made extensive use of Evagrian structures and terminology, noticeable throughout his work but especially in the *Chapters on Love*. His influence is also discernible in the *Centuries* of Thalassios and Hesychios of Batos. There is a significant section of Evagrian material in the *Philokalia*, ascribed to St Nilus in the original editions, but restored to Evagrius in the recent English translation. While his attempt to integrate the Christian philosophical tradition with the wisdom of the Desert Fathers was not entirely successful, it has been remarkably fruitful.

MARCUS PLESTED

Biography

Born *c*.345 at Ibora in Pontus, Evagrius was ordained a reader by St Basil the Great and a deacon by St Gregory of Nazianzus. With Gregory he attended the Council of Constantinople in 381 and then fled into the desert of Egypt to become a monk. He wrote a number of works on the ascetic life of which the most important are the *Praktikos*, the *Gnostikos*, and the *Kephalaia Gnostika*. He died in Egypt in 399.

Writings

The Philokalia: The Complete Text, translated by G.E.H. Palmer, Philip Sherrard, and Kallistos Ware, vol. 1, London and Boston: Faber, 1979 (includes several texts by Evagrius)
The Mind's Long Journey to the Holy Trinity: The "Ad Monachos" of Evagrius Ponticus, translated by Jeremy Driscoll, Collegeville, Minnesota: Liturgical Press, 1993

Further Reading

Driscoll, Jeremy, *The "Ad Monachos" of Evagrius Ponticus: Its Structure and a Select Commentary*, Rome: Benedictina Edizioni Abbazia S. Paolo, 1991
Guillaumont, Antoine, *Les "Képhalaia Gnostica" d'Evagre le Pontique et l'histoire de l'Origénisme chez les grecs et chez les syriens*, Paris: Seuil, 1962
Louth, Andrew, *The Origins of the Christian Mystical Tradition from Plato to Denys*, Oxford: Clarendon Press, and New York: Oxford University Press, 1981, chapter 6

Evil Eye

Many elements of belief associated with commonly held ideas of the evil eye are evident throughout the Greek tradition from antiquity to the present day. While the basic notion of the evil eye, that harm or damage may be caused by a glance, is found unequivocally at many points in this tradition, it is probably more helpful to see it in the context of a larger group of beliefs evident in Greek thought, which involves the idea that change in physical or emotional condition may be effected in humans, animals, and inanimate objects by means of the power of sight alone and without obvious physical contact. The ability to cause such change is not confined to human beings, for it is also attributed to various supernatural powers and forces; nor is the change thought to be necessarily evil, although it is without question most commonly associated with bad effects and the fear that an envious, jealous, or perhaps hateful glance may cause serious harm is particularly prominent. Care is to be exercised in relating the Greek tradition concerning the evil eye to superficially similar but often significantly divergent ideas found in a broad range of cultures around the Mediterranean and beyond.

Firm literary evidence for the existence of many elements within this complex of ideas goes back at least to the early Classical period, while cross-cultural comparison and archaeological evidence may well suggest that such beliefs were present in some form from the very beginnings of a recognizable Greek culture. Phrases directly equivalent to the term "evil eye", such as *vaskanos ophthalmos* or *ophthalmos poneros*, are attested only from later antiquity, but writers throughout the pagan tradition such as Aeschylus, Plato, Theocritus, Callimachus, Apollonius Rhodius, Libanius, and Heliodorus allude in a wide variety of contexts to the closely related idea of the malignant and communicable power of envy (*phthonos*) or jealousy (*vaskania*); indeed, it is probable that the verb *vaskainein* in ancient Greek is to be taken primarily as meaning "to bewitch", very much in the sense of casting the evil eye through jealousy. Kindred notions are also found in the powers attributed to the gorgon and basilisk of Greek myth. Plutarch (*Quaestiones Convivales*, 5. 7. 680–83) provides the fullest discussion of the topic in antiquity and proposes that the eyes of a jealous person emit a stream of particles that strike the victim and so transmit harm, a theory of explanation close to one suggested by Democritus (to which he alludes) and followed by several later writers. As Plutarch also reveals, the notion of malignant envy or the evil eye was sometimes treated with suspicion and scorn in antiquity, but nevertheless its persistence in the Greek tradition as a whole attests to its general acceptance.

A number of passages in the New Testament (e.g. Matthew 20: 15, Mark 7: 22, and Galatians 3: 1) are connected with this tradition and Church Fathers, such as Basil, John Chrysostom, and Eusebius, discuss the belief and its implications for Christianity. All conclude that the apparent power of the evil eye is to be attributed to the activity of the Devil, but all fail to deny completely the validity of the idea. Given the inability of such intellectual early Christian authorities to do so, it is not surprising that the literary and material record from the Byzantine period down to the present day indicates a widespread popular belief in the power of the evil eye and in apotropaic practices associated with it, many of which are scarcely Christianized.

Belief in the evil eye is thus very widely attested, though not universally accepted, in the popular culture of modern Greece. The term generally used is *kako mati* (evil eye) or simply *to mati* (the eye), although there are many other local and regional expressions, most derived in some way from the *ophthalmos* (eye) of ancient Greek (e.g. *thiarmos* in western Crete). Symptoms associated with "the eye" tend to be ill defined, since specific indications will normally suggest a more conventional diagnosis, but in general everything thought to have been affected by it will show signs of sickliness and loss of function. Symptoms in adults commonly include a feeling of malaise or depression, yawning, chronic feverishness, nausea, or headache; young children may sleep badly, lose their appetites, or cry constantly; animals will display signs of weakness, lethargy, and infertility; crops will fail to grow or will wither; and machinery will cease to function properly. Despite its vague symptoms the evil eye is thought to be very serious and, if left untreated, potentially fatal.

Explanations of the cause of the evil eye focus most usually on perceived jealousy or envy. It is commonly associated either with over-zealous admiration to the point at which the thing admired is actually coveted or else with the expression of insincere admiration. Some individuals are thought particularly likely to cause it, perhaps because of their social situation (e.g. elderly spinsters) or their unpleasant demeanour, while physical characteristics, such as blue or green eyes (usually an indication of foreignness), may also be thought to be signs of danger. Occasionally it may be thought to have been deliberately induced by magic. The view that the evil eye may be cast unknowingly and without any deliberate intent is, however, also widespread, making both detection of origin and prevention very difficult.

Practices to avert the evil eye are numerous and varied. Among the most common objects employed are cloves of garlic, blue beads or thread, the image of a staring eye (usually blue), and Christian symbols and objects such as the cross or an amulet containing holy material; these are either worn or placed in contact with whatever is being protected. Other techniques involve such things as spitting after making a compliment, or the invocation, either aloud or silently, of a spell or prayer.

Diagnosis and cure of the evil eye are also performed in a wide variety of ways, many of which show strong regional and local characteristics. Healers, often women, are to be found and openly acknowledged in most villages and towns. Among the commonest methods of diagnosis and cure, which usually form a single ritual, are those that involve dropping a substance or object (often oil but perhaps salt, incense, charcoal, or a cross) into a vessel of water. Affliction is determined through the behaviour of the material in the water, and, in the curative phase of the ritual, victims will drink some of the water or have it sprinkled on them; sometimes the healer will exhibit the victim's previous symptoms. The rituals, whatever their precise nature, are accompanied throughout by spells or prayers that almost always involve at least some overtly Christian elements, although these are often used in ways that are far from orthodox. Indeed, the Church, doctrinally speaking, disapproves of the popular notions of the evil eye since these tend to challenge the central Christian principle of the omnipotence and goodness of God. Nevertheless an acceptable explanation is found by seeing the supposed power of evil eye as a manifestation of the familiar activity of the Devil or his demons operating through humans, and the Orthodox Church has available, at least at a local level, a fully Christian ritual for removing it.

RICHARD P.H. GREENFIELD

See also Magic, Spells, Superstition

Further Reading

Blum, Richard and Eva Blum, *Health and Healing in Rural Greece: A Study of Three Communities*, Stanford, California: Stanford University Press, 1965

Blum, Richard and Eva Blum, *The Dangerous Hour: The Lore of Crisis and Mystery in Rural Greece*, London: Chatto and Windus, and New York: Scribner, 1970

Dickie, Matthew W., "The Fathers of the Church and the Evil Eye" in *Byzantine Magic*, edited by Henry Maguire, Washington, D.C.: Dumbarton Oaks, 1995

Dunbabin, K.M.D. and M.W. Dickie, "Invidia rumpantur pectora: The Iconography of Phthonos-Invidia in Graeco-Roman Art", *Jahrbuch für Antike und Christentum*, 26 (1983): pp. 7–37

Dundes, Alan (editor), *The Evil Eye: A Casebook*, Madison: University of Wisconsin Press, 1992

Elworthy, Frederick Thomas, *The Evil Eye: An Account of this Ancient and Widespread Superstition*, London: John Murray, 1895; reprinted New York: Julian, 1986

Herzfeld, Michael, "Meaning and Morality: A Semiotic Approach to Evil Eye Accusations in a Greek Village", *American Ethnologist*, 8 (1981): pp. 560–74

Herzfeld, Michael, "The Horns of the Mediterraneanist Dilemma", *American Ethnologist*, 11 (1984): pp. 439–54

Herzfeld, Michael, "Closure as Cure: Tropes in the Exploration of Bodily and Social Disorder", *Current Anthropology*, 27 (1986): pp. 107–20

Maloney, Clarence (editor), *The Evil Eye*, New York: Columbia University Press, 1976

Russell, James, "The Evil Eye in Early Byzantine Society", *Jahrbuch der Österreichischen Byzantinistik*, 32/3 (1982): pp. 539–48

Stewart, Charles, *Demons and the Devil: Moral Imagination in Modern Greek Culture*, Princeton, New Jersey: Princeton University Press, 1991

Walcot, Peter, *Envy and the Greeks: A Study of Human Behaviour*, Warminster: Aris and Phillips, 1978

Execias

Potter and painter of the 6th century BC

Execias worked as a vase painter from about 545 to 530 BC, but his career as a potter started earlier: his signature is recognized on an amphora representing Heracles and Geryon (now in Paris, Louvre F 53, from Vulci), which is assigned to the so-called Group E, as well as on a number of cups (e.g. Munich, Antikensammlungen 2044, from Vulci). He signed a neck amphora (Berlin, Staatliche Museen 1720, from Vulci) and a type A belly amphora (Vatican Museums 344, from Vulci) as both potter and painter: "Execias painted and made me". Execias' great contribution to the Athenian black-figure tradition lies in his potting as well as his painting. Although the number of vases attributed to him is not large, the range of shapes is very wide, including amphorae (type A and type B), neck amphorae, a Panathenaic amphora, a *dinos* (goblet), a *pyxis* (box), cups, a calyx crater, and funerary plaques. He was responsible for the development of the type A cup and the type A belly amphora – both vases are of large size, around 60 cm high – and probably invented the calyx crater since the earliest surviving example was decorated by him (Athens, Agora Museum, from the Acropolis north slope). He demonstrated a preference for amphorae, especially of the neck type and of type A, identified by its decorated flanged handles and a stepped foot.

The influence of the earlier Group E has been observed in his work, especially in his painting style as well as in his choice of ornaments and shapes. His scenes are simple, including only the essential elements of a composition. He demonstrated, however, an interest in the detailed representation of armour, manes, hair, and drapery, and experimented with the rendering of three dimensions. His workmanship is characterized by precision and his scenes of action by originality, since he seldom used standard motifs or compositions. He preferred to interpret well-known scenes anew, such as Ajax carrying Achilles, or invent others, such as Dionysus in his ship.

Execias has been considered a master of narration; by eliminating extraneous figures from his scenes, he focused on just those essential for his story. Despite the limitations of the black-figure technique, he often attempted to render some degree of emotion on the faces of his figures without distorting them, as on the mourners' faces on his funerary plaques. He preferred scenes that displayed strong tension in a subtle way, while occasionally depicting the moment before the action, as in the scene of Ajax's suicide (on a belly amphora, Boulogne Museum 553, France). In these respects Execias could be considered the forerunner of the Classical style.

Just as Execias had a liking for certain vase shapes, he also favoured specific patterns framing his pictorial scenes. Chains of lotuses and palmettes with separated and finely drawn leaves ornamented the neck or framed the panels of amphorae. The handles of his type-A amphorae are decorated with a tendril of ivy leaves.

His originality is also expressed in other forms. He broke the Attic convention of a tondo in the interior of cups and painted Dionysus sailing across the interior of a *kylix* (wine cup, Munich, Antikensammlungen 2044, from Vulci). Both the "coral-red" background of the scene and the pair of eyes decorating the exterior of the cup seem to be his inventions. Moreover, he was the first painter to depict ships sailing around the rim of a *dinos* (Rome, Villa Giulia Museum 50599). Execias often named not only his heroes but also their horses, the representations of which are classified among his favourite subjects.

Execias' iconographic repertoire is based on mythological scenes, especially those related to the Trojan War, but few of them followed established patterns. Unlike his contemporaries, he showed a lack of interest in the secular *komos* (revel) and the symposium, while the sole scenes from everyday life that he depicted are the *prothesis* (laying out) and the *ekphora* (carrying to burial) of the dead on funerary plaques. His Trojan scenes are devoted to episodes from the lives of Ajax and Achilles or to the events leading to their deaths and do not follow the versions of the myth found either in the *Iliad* or in any other of the known literary texts. Thus, Execias depicted Ajax and Achilles playing a board game – the scene appears here for the first time in Greek art and was repeated numerous times in vase painting thereafter – Ajax's suicide, Achilles killing Penthesilea, Ajax lifting the dead Achilles from the ground, the dead Patroclus fought over by Hector and Diomedes, as well as scenes with Memnon. Although Execias does depict the heroes Heracles, Theseus, and the Dioscuri, it was the two Trojan heroes that prevailed in his scenes. It has

therefore been suggested that Execias countered the heroic virtue that other artists portrayed through Heracles by his use of Ajax and Achilles.

Although Execias' interest in Heracles was not remarkable, the scene with Heracles wrestling with the lion introduced to Athenian vase painting the composition of the lion fight in a prone position. His treatment of the Dioscuri is also innovative: he represented the homecoming of Castor before Polydeuces and their parents, Leda and Tyndareus. Previously the two heroes had appeared either at the Calydonian boar hunt or at the wedding of Menelaus and Helen. Execias was less interested in the depiction of a specific mythological event than in the heroes themselves.

ELENI ZIMI

Biography

Execias of Athens was active as a painter and potter from about 545 to 530 BC. He signed two amphorae as both potter and painter and his contribution to Athenian black-figure vase decoration is recognized as combining both activities. He departs from convention to depict both the character of his subjects and the tension of the moment.

Further Reading

Beazley, J.D., *The Development of Attic Black-figure*, revised edition, Berkeley: University of California Press, 1986, pp. 58–68

Boardman, John, "Painted Funerary Plaques and Some Remarks on Prothesis", *Annual of the British School at Athens*, 50 (1955): pp. 51–66

Boardman, John, *Athenian Black-figure Vases*, London and New York: Thames and Hudson, 1974, pp. 56–58

Boardman, John, "Execias", *American Journal of Archaeology*, 82 (1978): pp. 11–25

Mommsen, H., *Exekias*, vol. 1: *Die Grabtafeln*, Mainz: Zabern, 1997

Moor, Mary B., "Horses by Execias", *American Journal of Archaeology*, 72 (1968): pp. 357–68

Neutsch, Bernhard, *Exekias: ein Meister der griechische Vasenmalerei*, Marburg: Kunstgeschichtlichen Seminars der Universität Marburg, 1949

Steiner, A., "Illustrious Repetitions: Visual Redundancy in Exekias and his Followers" in *Athenian Potters and Painters*, edited by J.H. Oakley, William D.E. Coulson, and Olga Palagia, Oxford: Oxbow, 1997

Exile and Detention

Myth repeatedly describes individual banishment, usually for murder, but also for incest and other forms of sacrilege, as religious purification of a whole community. The outcast, interdicted from fire and water, deprived of ancestral worship, and cursed with all his issue, was deemed legitimate prey for any man. His only possible safety came from supplication at alien shrines or courts, and mere sufferance was often his most ambitious hope. Survival of this religious element of banishment into the time of the city state can be illustrated by *inter alia* a historical event and a festival at Athens. Some years after Megacles, the head of the Alcmaeonidae, had in 632(?) BC sacrilegiously allowed the suppliant supporters of the defeated Cylon to be slain, not only was the whole clan exiled but the bones of its dead were exhumed and cast beyond the borders of Attica. At the purificatory festival of Thargelia in honour of Apollo, Athens still included in the Classical period the practice of beating and driving beyond its borders two *pharmakoi* (scapegoats) who at least theoretically took the evils of the city with them.

Banishment in the Archaic, Classical, and Hellenistic periods could be suffered by whole communities, groups, and individuals. Inhabitants of conquered cities were at the mercy of their victors, who sometimes chose to drive them out. That they could often then keep a sense of communal identity was due to allies who gave them shelter within their walls or found them land to settle, and they often later managed to regain their homes (all three of these fates befell the Plataeans driven out by the Thebans at the beginning of the Second Peloponnesian War). The survivors of the citizens sold as booty when Philip II sacked Olynthus in 348 were settled 32 years later by Cassander in his new foundation of Cassandreia.

Greek historians frequently do not make clear whether groups (or individuals) were exiled or fled voluntarily. In most cases their removal was due to governmental change in the struggles between tyrants, oligarchs, and democrats. Nearly all these exiles were from the upper classes, and could stay with sympathizers or had connections in other states, and frequently returned home at a change of government (that they themselves sometimes engineered) or upon an amnesty.

Individual exile was largely a political weapon. Most victims were politicians or generals, who suffered for real or alleged treason, military failure (as in the case of the historian Thucydides), or just unpopularity. The punishment, that was for either life or a set number of years, could be severe because it usually entailed deprivation of civic rights and confiscation of property. An exile returning illicitly ran the risk of summary execution; anyone harbouring an exile became himself liable to expulsion. Individual recalls and general amnesties were not, however, uncommon: Diodorus Siculus states (18. 8. 5) that according to Alexander the Great's decree in 324 BC, 20,000 Greek exiles were permitted to return to their homes. Voluntary exile could be chosen to avoid trial and even after the sentence of death had been passed (Socrates famously refused his friends' request to go into exile). In the 5th century BC the Athenian *ekklesia* was enabled to vote in favour of holding an ostracism, whereby if at least 6000 citizens took part the man whose name was recorded on the highest number of *ostraka* (potsherds) was exiled, without loss of citizenship or property, for ten years. Aristotle claims (*Athenaion Politeia*, 22) that the law was introduced by Cleisthenes in 508/07 BC, but the first ostracism was not held until 487. The last man ostracized was the demagogue Hyperbolus between 417 and 415, after which the *graphe paranomon* (indictment for offence of proposing an illegal law or decree) became the preferred means of attacking politicians. Forms of ostracism were employed also at Argos and at Syracuse – at the latter it was called *petalismos* ("leafing") since the names were written on olive leaves.

Information on detention is scant and largely Athenian. Non-productive long-term incarceration was extremely rare, its function served by deprivation of civil rights. Short-term incarceration, however, was occasionally used, sometimes in addition to a fine: otherwise the prison in Athens, under the supervision of the Eleven, held men on remand for certain crimes (e.g. maltreating parents or failing in military duties), men delinquent in the payment of some categories of fines, and men awaiting execution. Soldiers captured in battle were usually executed, taken or sold into slavery, exchanged, or ransomed. Occasionally they were held in detention as hostages, sometimes later to be exchanged (e.g. the Spartiates held by the Athenians in the city and elsewhere in their empire for nearly four years after their capture on Sphacteria in 425 BC). In contrast, the survivors of the Athenian expedition against Syracuse in 415–413 were imprisoned for life in nearby stone quarries, where some years later the dithyrambist Philoxenus, temporarily imprisoned for adversely criticizing the poetry of the tyrant Dionysius I, wrote one of his more famous pieces.

The most innovative penal theorist was Plato, who in his *Laws* prescribed varying terms of imprisonment and exile for different classes of criminals (citizens, metics, visiting foreigners, and slaves) and different crimes. More revolutionary, in addition to a large general and a purely punitive prison, he envisaged a reformatory (*sophronisterion*), where suitable offenders convicted of impiety were to be subjected to at least five years of counselling before being reintegrated into society (recidivists were, however, to be executed). Plato's ideas were largely ignored in antiquity.

Greeks under Roman rule were subject to Roman law, which, with modifications, survived in the Greek world until the Ottoman sack of Constantinople in 1453. Exile in the Byzantine empire was occasionally imposed upon economic offenders, but mostly upon the emperors' political opponents (often ecclesiastics). *Exoria* involved permanent or temporary exile without confiscation of property, *periorismos* restriction to a prescribed area with loss of property. Places of exile varied from remote borderlands and islands to monasteries and even personal estates. Conditions similarly differed, as can be seen from a wide range of letters written from confinement with complaints ranging from torture, starvation, and squalor to lack of books and nostalgia for life in the capital. Some politicians (e.g. Michael Psellos) voluntarily became monastic exiles until they deemed it safe to return to an active life.

In law prisons were regarded as remand centres, but in practice stay there was not always brief and, unlike in ancient Greece, they were common (there were five or six prisons within the complex of the Great Palace in Constantinople alone). They housed traitors, murderers, thieves, forgers, adulterers, magicians, and, if they could not be looked after at home, the insane, but only males since women were confined in convents to avoid risk of abuse from gaolers. Prisons fell into two types: those containing unchained and those containing chained inmates. In the former there were even some relatively comfortable single rooms, but conditions were particularly bad in the latter which were notoriously dark and cold and where food was scant and poor. According to legend one widow was so appalled that she offered her house for use as a prison, an offer accepted by the emperor Phokas (602–10), who nevertheless paid her the full price. Although the official in charge of prisons was subject to punishment if he illegally alleviated the lot of prisoners, some legislation attempted to ameliorate conditions, as did emperors, the nobility, churchmen, monks, and the pious with visits and donations of money and food. References are numerous also to emperors, the Church, and rich individuals paying the ransom of prisoners of war (and those held by bandits), who stood a far better chance of rescue than in antiquity. Constantinople had a prison specifically for Muslims: a letter from the early 10th-century patriarch Nikolaos Mystikos to the caliph Al-Muqtadir claims that there Arab prisoners suffered only the deprivation of their friends and family since, among other comforts, they enjoyed spacious quarters, clean air, and even an oratory set apart for their devotions. Although private prisons were banned by law, monasteries were frequently so used.

After the War of Independence (1821–29) the new state of Greece established its own prisons for both short- and long-term stay for a wide variety of crimes. Conditions varied, but stimulus towards reform was hampered by the frequent changes of governors consequent upon changes of government.

Modern prisons are divided into several categories: in 1998 there were 28 in all, of which 12 were for those serving light sentences or awaiting trial, 7 were closed prisons for those sentenced to over 5 years of incarceration, 4 were rural prisons where inmates did agricultural work during the day, 2 were medical/psychiatric prisons, 2 were closed prisons for minors (the minimum age was 12) and the last was an open prison where bread was baked for hospitals and other prisons in Athens. Although the last execution took place in July 1972, capital punishment was not abolished until 1993. The average custodial sentence in 1998 was from 2 to 5 years, with a "life"-sentence of at least 16 years.

The percentage of the population incarcerated fluctuated greatly, some regimes even resorting to internal exile. In 1970 Greece had one of the lowest rates among the member states of the Council of Europe at 0.0409 per cent of the population, but this rose rapidly to 0.0607 per cent by the end of 1997 despite minimal numbers of females and minors. Over-crowding (approximately 50 per cent above capacity) was a growing problem, but legislation aimed at alleviation was being thwarted mainly by a reluctance of judges to grant bail (in 1997 over 30 per cent of those incarcerated were awaiting trial) and a rapidly growing number of foreign convicts (in mid-June 1998 over 40 per cent of a total prison population of 7021), largely for drugs-related offences. Moreover, poor conditions in prisons, shortage of qualified educational and therapeutic staff (approximately a third of prisoners were on drugs-related charges) and low morale of both warders and prisoners were fostering increasing recidivism.

A.R. LITTLEWOOD

See also Ostracism

Further Reading

Amit, M., "Hostages in Ancient Greece", *Rivista di filologia e di istruzione classica*, 98 (1970): pp. 129–47

Balogh, Elemér, *Political Refugees in Ancient Greece from the Period of the Tyrants to Alexander the Great*, Johannesburg: Witwatersrand University Press, 1943; reprinted Rome: Bretschneider, 1972

Ducrey, Pierre, *Le Traitement des prisonniers de guerre dans la Grèce antique*, Paris: Boccard, 1968

Evert-Kappesowa, H., "Formy zesłania w państwie bizantyńskim" in *Okeanos: Essays Presented to Ihor Ševčenko on His Sixtieth Birthday*, edited by Cyril Mango and Omeljan Pritsak, Cambridge, Massachusetts: Ukrainian Research Institute, Harvard University, 1984

Guillou, A., "Le Monde carceral en Italie du sud et en Sicile au VIe-VIIe siècle", *Jahrbuch der österreichischen Byzantinistik*, 33 (1983): pp. 79–86

Janin, R., *Constantinople byzantine: développment urbain et répertoire topographique*, 2nd edition, Paris: Institut Français d'Etudes Byzantines, 1964, pp. 165–73

Koukoules, P. and R. Guilland, "Voleurs et prisons à Byzance", *Revue des Etudes Grecques*, 61 (1948): pp.118–36

MacDowell, Douglas M., *The Law in Classical Athens*, Ithaca, New York: Cornell University Press, 1978

McKechnie, Paul, *Outsiders in the Greek Cities in the Fourth Century BC*, London and New York: Routledge, 1989

Mullett, M., "Originality in the Byzantine Letter: The Case of Exile" in *Originality in Byzantine Literature, Art, and Music: A Collection of Essays*, edited by A.R. Littlewood, Oxford: Oxbow, 1995

Saunders, Trevor J., *Plato's Penal Code: Tradition, Controversy, and Reform in Greek Penology*, Oxford: Clarendon Press, and New York: Oxford University Press, 1991

F

Fable

A fable (*ainos*, *logos*, *mythos*) can best be defined as a fictitious, metaphorical narrative. It has been asserted that fables typically are about animals and have a moral purpose, but these restrictions do not take into account the genre's historical multiformity: fable collections traditionally include stories with rational as well as irrational characters, and the genre's functions may vary widely, notably from persuasive to satirical, from moral to explanatory, from didactic to illustrative. It is to this flexibility that the genre owes its remarkable, millennia-long vitality.

Throughout ancient literature fables are used in a variety of other literary genres. The oldest extant Greek fables occur in Archaic Greek epic (Hesiod) and lyric poetry (Archilochus, Semonides, Stesichorus, Ibycus, Simonides). In the Classical period fables are adduced in both prose and poetry; they are applied not only by tragedians (Aeschylus, Sophocles), satyric playwrights (Achaeus), and comedians (Aristophanes), but also by historiographers (Herodotus), rhetoricians (Aristotle), orators (Demosthenes (allegedly)), and philosophers (Socrates (allegedly), Plato, Xenophon). From the Classical period onwards fables are typically connected with the name of Aesop, the legendary fabulist. By then, already, fables were apparently so popular that authors could confine themselves to mere allusions, obviously presupposing the audience's knowledge of the rest of the story.

At the beginning of the Hellenistic period Demetrius of Phalerum compiled the first fable collection, probably an anthology of fables excerpted from the works of Archaic and Classical authors, made up as a repertory for orators looking for a fable that could appropriately be used in some speech or situation in accordance with the advice given by Demetrius' teacher Aristotle in what is the oldest extant treatise on fable as a genre (*Rhetoric*, 2. 20). Regrettably enough, Demetrius' collection has been lost but for its title (*Collections of Aesopic Fables*), preserved by Diogenes Laertius.

The extant fable collections all date from the imperial period of Greek literature. Most are in prose. Of the oldest one only fragments of 14 fables remain (*Rylands Papyrus* 493; early 1st century AD). The verse collection by Babrius (late 1st or 2nd century AD) has also been incompletely preserved, but 144 fables have come down to us in their original form, whereas knowledge of what has been lost may be gained from prose paraphrases. The largest collection is the so-called *recensio Augustana* (see below), consisting of 231 allegedly Aesopic, but really anonymous, prose fables concluded by *epimythia* (less felicitously called "morals"). In addition, we have three small prose fable collections, probably used in rhetorical education. One, by Aphthonius (4th century AD), includes 40 fables, all equipped with both a *promythion* (an introductory moral, serving as title) and an epimythion; another, by his contemporary Libanius, has only three fables; a third, anonymous collection (*Codex Brancatianus*) contains 14 fables with iambic *epimythia*.

At the same time, fables continued to be used in other literary genres. In the Hellenistic period fables are adduced not only by poets such as Callimachus and Nicander and by epigrammatists (Leonidas), but also by historiographers (Theopompus, Diodorus Siculus) and philosophers (Philodemus). In the imperial period fables occur not only in traditional genres – notably historiography (Dionysius of Halicarnassus, Flavius Josephus), oratory (Aelius Aristides, Dio of Prusa, Themistius), and philosophy (Philo) – but also in new genres such as epistolography (Julian, Libanius), romance (Aesop romance, Alexander romance, Achilles Tatius, Heliodorus), and biography (Plutarch).

Simultaneously, the theory of the fable was also studied. Of great importance is the treatise on fable by the rhetorician Theon (late 1st century AD), who formulated the oldest extant – and, according to some, the best possible – definition of the genre: "a fable is a fictitious story that gives the semblance of reality."

The polytheistic background of the ancient fables, traditionally featuring "pagan" gods, did not prevent the early Christian writers from using them in their own works, witness references in poems by St Gregory of Nazianzus, in epistles by St Basil the Great and St Gregory of Nyssa, in homilies by St John Chrysostom, and in apologetical works by Epiphanius of Salamis and Theodoret.

Byzantium preserved the heritage of the ancient fable tradition. On the one hand, the fables from antiquity were copied and paraphrased; on the other, they inspired Byzantine fabulists to write new versions or original fables of their own. The anonymous prose fables must have been very popular, demonstrated by the great number of manuscripts that regularly combine the "Aesopic" fables with the *Life of Aesop*. The fable collections can be subdivided into three classes, named after the library where its principal manuscript was found, or after its editor: the ancient *Augustana* (Augsburg); the Byzantine *Vindobonense* (Vienna; 127 fables); and the *Accursiana* (Bonus Accursius; 130 fables). They are also called, respectively, *recensio* I, II, and III: II is mainly based on I and Babrius, III on I and II. The exact date and purpose of these collections are still under debate.

Two other Byzantine collections also predominantly derive from ancient Greek models. The 89 *Tetrastichs* attributed to Ignatius (9th century) are mainly inspired by Babrius. The collection of 62 prose fables ascribed to Syntipas (the legendary Sindbad the Sailor) and translated from the Syriac possibly by Michael Andreopoulos (*c.*1100) largely goes back to Babrius on the one hand and to the *Augustana* on the other; all of these fables have *epimythia*. Both the pseudo-Ignatius and the pseudo-Syntipas collections contain some fables that have not been preserved elsewhere.

Throughout the Byzantine period fables were, as in antiquity, frequently used in other literary genres, both in poetry (John Tzetzes) and in prose, particularly by epistolographers (Theophylaktos Simokattes), lexicographers (Photios, the *Suda*), philologists (Eustathios), historiographers (Nikephoros Gregoras, John Kantakouzenos, John Zonaras), paroemiographers (Apostolios), orators and rhetoricians (Michael Psellos, Theodore Prodromos).

Typical of fables are easy transitions from and to other genres and forms of imagery. Thus, fables are often reduced to, or based upon, proverbs and comparisons. Conversely, fables can also be elaborated into beast epic, whose function is typically satirical. Famous examples are the ancient *Batrachomyomachia* (Frog-Mouse-War; 1st century BC/AD) and the late Byzantine *Legend of the Ass* (early 16th century).

In Byzantine times the Classical fable tradition was further enriched with fables of Indian provenance. Greek versions of two frame stories served as vehicles for this influx of oriental fables. First, the Christian romance of *Barlaam and Joasaph*, adapted from a Buddhist prototype by St John of Damascus (8th century), contains a number of fables. Second, the book of *Stephanites and Ichnelates*, translated from the Arab *Kalila wa Dimnah* (which in its turn goes back to the Sanskrit *Panchatantra*) by Symeon Seth (late 11th century, at the instigation of Emperor Alexios I Komnenos), is interspersed with fables. Both books were widely read, as is clear from the numerous medieval manuscripts.

The *Stephanites and Ichnelates* remained so popular that it was twice paraphrased into modern Greek by superior order: first by Theodoros Zygomalas, protonotary of the patriarch of Constantinople, in the 16th century; later by Demetrios Prokopios (1721), commissioned by John Nikolaos Mavrokordatos. Both modern Greek versions were, in their turn, copied several times.

The first translation of ancient fables into modern Greek prose was by the Corfiot Nikandros Noukios (Venice, 1543; 150 fables). It was to be followed by many others (e.g. by Ioannis Patousos, Venice, 1752). More original, but clearly also modelled on the Classical fable tradition, are two modern Greek verse fable collections (*Mythoi*), one by Georgios Aitolos from Corinth (1525–74; 144 fables), the other by Jannis Vilaras from Ioannina (1771–1823; 20 fables). The former's rhyming political verses may be considered to be a predecessor of the elegant versions by the famous 17th-century French fabulist Jean de la Fontaine, who is one of the latter's sources of inspiration.

In modern times the text of the ancient fables was published. A milestone along the road was the edition by the erudite scholar Adamantios Korais (Paris, 1810); typically enough for a man who contributed so much to the consciousness-raising of the Greeks, the title of Korais's *Collection of Aesopic Fables* referred back to the prototypical collection by Demetrius of Phalerum mentioned above. The first edition of the *recensio Augustana*, by Schneider, was to follow suit (Bratislava, 1812).

That the fable tradition from the golden age of Hellas continues to be popular without abatement in today's Greece is evident not only from the inclusion of a fable in the famous *Life and Works of Alexis Zorba* by Nikos Kazantzakis, but also from two really modern media: the edition of a series of stamps and comic strips with *Fables of Aesop*. The latter may therefore without exaggerating be said to embody the Hellenic tradition.

GERT-JAN VAN DIJK

Texts

Aesop, *Fables*, edited by Emile Chambry, 2 vols, Paris: Belles Lettres, 1925–26 (Budé edition)

Aesop, *Corpus Fabularum Aesopicarum*, edited by August Hausrath, H. Haas and Herbert Hunger, vol. 1: *Fabulae Aesopicae Soluta Oratione Conscriptae*, 2 parts, Leipzig: Teubner, 1959–70

Aesop, *Aesop without Morals: The Famous Fables, and a Life of Aesop*, translated by Lloyd W. Daly, New York: Yoseloff, 1961

Aesop, *Fables*, translated by S.A. Handford, London and Baltimore: Penguin, 1964

Aesop, *The Complete Fables*, translated by Olivia and Robert Temple, Hardmondsworth and New York: Penguin, 1998

Perry, Ben Edwin (editor), *Aesopica: A Series of Texts Relating to Aesop or Ascribed to Him or Closely Connected with the Literary Tradition that Bears His Name*, vol. 1, Urbana: University of Illinois Press, 1952; reprinted New York: Arno Press, 1980

St. John Damascene, *Barlaam and Ioasaph*, translated by G.R. Woodward and H. Mattingly, London: Heinemann, and Cambridge, Massachusetts: Harvard University Press, 1967 (Loeb edition)

Sjöberg, Lars Olof, *Stephanites und Ichnelates: Überlieferungsgeschichte und Text*, Stockholm: Almqvist & Wiksell 1962

Further Reading

Adrados, Francisco Rodríguez, *Estudios sobre el léxico de las fábulas esópicas*, Salamanca: Colegio Trilingüe de la Universidad, 1948

Adrados, Francisco Rodríguez (editor), *La Fable*, Geneva: Fondation Hardt, 1984

Adrados, Francisco Rodríguez, *History of the Graeco–Latin Fable*, translated by Leslie Ray, revised and updated by the author and Gert-Jan van Dijk, 3 vols, Leiden and Boston: Brill, 1999–2001

Bieber, Dora, *Studien zur Geschichte der Fabel in den ersten Jahrhunderten der Kaiserzeit*, Berlin: Simion, 1906

Carnes, Pack, *Fable Scholarship: An Annotated Bibliography*, New York: Garland, 1985

Dijk, Gert-Jan van, *Ainoi, Logoi, Mythoi: Fables in Archaic, Classical, and Hellenistic Greek Literature, with a Study of the Theory and Terminology of the Genre*, Leiden: Brill, 1997

Dijk, Gert-Jan van, *Ignatius Diaconus' Fabelkwatrijnen: Byzantijnse Tetrasticha*, Groningen: Styx, 2000

Falkowitz, Robert S. *et al.*, *La Fable: huit exposés suivis de discussions: Vandoeuvres, Genève, 22–27 aôut 1983*, Geneva: Fondation Hardt, 1984

Hale, C.B., "The Text Tradition of the Aesopic Fables Belonging to the So-Called Augustana Recension", dissertation, Urbana, Illinois, 1941

Holzberg, Niklas, *Die antike Fabel: Eine Einführung*, Darmstadt: Wissenschaftliche Buchgesellschaft, 1993

Hower, C.C., "Studies on the So-Called Accursiana Recension of the Life and Fables of Aesop", dissertation, Urbana, Illinois, 1936

Jedrkiewicz, Stefano, *Sapere e paradosso nell'antichità: Esopo e la favola*, Rome: Ateneo, 1989

Karadagli, Triantaphyllia, *Fabel und Ainos: Studien zur griechischen Fabel*, Königstein: Hain, 1981

Kovacs, R.S., "The Aesopic Fable in Ancient Rhetorical Theory and Practice", dissertation, Urbana, Illinois, 1950

Martín García, Francisco and Alfredo Róspide López, *Index Aesopi Fabularum*, Hildesheim: Olms-Weidmann, 1991

Nøjgaard, Morten, *La Fable antique*, 2 vols, Copenhagen: Nordisk Busck, 1964–67

Perry, B.E., *Studies in the Text History of the Life and Fables of Aesop*, Haverford, Pennsylvania: American Philological Association, 1936

Pugliarello, Mariarosaria, *Le origini della favolistica classica*, Brescia: Paideia, 1973

Wienert, Walter, *Die Typen der griechisch-römischen Fabel*, Helsinki: Suomalainen Tiedeakatemia, 1925

Fairs and Markets

Periodic markets take place monthly or more frequently, typically once a week. Fairs are less frequent, typically annual, and often serve multiple purposes: religious, political, social, as well as economic. Both are worldwide phenomena.

"Landings, sailings, numbers of people and goods and ships: these prove the merit of a fair, a harbour, or a market", said Dio of Prusa in the 1st century AD. Evidence of Greek fairs and markets is scattered and piecemeal. Demosthenes and Aristophanes are among sources for the Classical period; Hellenistic inscriptions supply details of trade regulations at fairs; in Roman times, special coin issues, commemorating local festivals, imply busy economic activity there.

The agora was the central public space of an ancient Greek city. The word also denoted the activity of a market, whether it took place in that public space, at a fair, or at a harbour.

In Classical Greece fairs (*panegyreis*) were chiefly religious festivals, but trade was a part of almost every *panegyris*. Thus, at a festival at Andania, "the priests shall indicate a place for all sales. The city *agoranomos* [market supervisor] shall ensure that sellers sell fairly and cleanly and use the city's weights and measures. He shall not restrict the sellers as to volume of sales, or as to time, or charge them for the site" (no. 65, lines 99–107 in *Lois sacrées des cités grecques*, edited by Franciszek Sokołowski, Paris: Boccard, 1969). An Amphictyonic decree of the 2nd century BC prescribes currency equivalents to be operated by "the money changers who sit in the cities or at the *panegyreis*". Fairs, often lasting several weeks, could be interrupted by a city's periodic market. At Oenoanda, in western Asia Minor, the quadrennial festival was suspended on the sixth of the month, the regular market day.

Some fairs attracted dealers and customers for a range of merchandise: in Roman times the twice-yearly fair near Tithorea in Phocis sold "slaves, cattle of all kinds, clothes, silver, and gold" (Pausanias). Other fairs too, including the Pylaea at Delphi, were noted for slaves. Domestic animals are mentioned in several sources as a typical purchase at an annual fair.

Fairs often attracted tax-free status, *ateleia*. Some fairs were held in cities or just outside them; others traditionally took place far from any centres of population, like the mountain-top fairs still known in the Balkans and first mentioned in a work attributed to Aristotle (*On Marvellous Things Heard*, 104).

The great religious festivals were major commercial events. According to the Roman historian Livy: "The Isthmian Games had always been well attended ... because of their excellent location, which enabled the Isthmus to deal in all kinds of commodities imported over two different seas. The market there was a fair for Asia and for Greece" (*Ab urbe condita*, 33. 32. 1–3, abridged).

In the Hellenistic period the regular political gatherings of the Aetolian and the Achaean Leagues were accompanied by some kind of commercial fair or market. Under Roman rule a provincial governor's judicial progresses attracted trade: "the courts are in session every year, bringing together a numberless throng – litigants, jurymen, orators, nobles, attendants, slaves, pimps, muleteers, hucksters, whores, and craftsmen. Those who have any goods to sell can get the highest prices; nothing in the city is out of work, neither the draught animals nor the households nor the women. This contributes noticeably to prosperity", Dio observed. But the most important fairs continued to be the religious ones. We hear of the struggles of conscience that Christians faced in attending them. "A believer must not go near a fair, except in order to buy a slave (and thus save his soul) or to buy one of the necessities of life", according to the *Apostolic Constitutions* of the 4th century AD. Yet they attended; and Christian festivals slowly replaced pagan ones as the occasion for fairs. In Byzantine Greece the fair that began six days before St Demetrius's Day at Thessalonica attracted traders from Catalonia, France, and Italy. The Ottoman traveller Evliya Çelebi described the annual fair of the salt beef merchants, "infidels of Moldavia and Wallachia", held outside the walls of Constantinople for 40 days beginning from St Demetrius.

Thus fairs have a long history in Greece. Periodic markets, weekly to monthly, are less talked of. In Roman times there may have been such markets in northern Greece. Certainly they existed near the Aegean coast of Asia Minor, where inscriptions record ten-day markets around Magnesia and monthly markets elsewhere.

Cities of some size certainly supported daily markets in Classical times, as they do now. Written sources refer to various specialized markets: a cattle market at Sparta; a covered market (stoa) specializing in spices at Megalopolis.

Classical sources are most informative about the market at Athens. This occupied a considerable area, centring on the Agora. It included sections such as *eis tous ichthyas*, the fish market, and *eis toupsa*, delicatessen. There was a distinct women's market: maids could be hired there. Characters in Athenian Middle and New Comedy spent a good deal of time boasting of their success at market or complaining of the price of fish. Athens also held a monthly fair or market on the day of the new moon (*noumenia*) at which slaves and animals were sold: a slave acquired on that day might be named *Noumenios*.

Fairs and Markets: The Central Market in Athens, successor to the ancient Agora

In coastal cities, and in the Greek islands, periodic markets are not recorded in ancient times and are not common nowadays. Trade here has been seaborne, dependent on sea conditions, and thus unsuited to a market timetable. Instead, the practice is for a market to be set up at the harbour when ships arrive. This is seen in many places today when a ferry puts in, often signalling its arrival with a blast on the foghorn. The evidence in Classical texts is of the arrival of fishing boats being announced by a harbour bell. Early sources, beginning with Homer and Herodotus, tell stories that depend on this practice of impromptu harbour markets.

ANDREW DALBY

Further Reading

Ligt, L. de, *Fairs and Markets in the Roman Empire: Economic and Social Aspects of Periodic Trade in a Pre-industrial Society*, Amsterdam: Gieben, 1993

Mitchell, Stephen, "Festivals, Games, and Civic Life in Roman Asia Minor", *Journal of Roman Studies*, 80 (1990): pp. 183–93

Schaps, D.M., "Small Change in Boeotia", *Zeitschrift für Papyrologie und Epigraphik*, 69 (1987): pp. 293–96

Stanley, P.V., "Agoranomoi and metronomoi", *Ancient World*, 2 (1979): pp. 13–19

Vryonis, Speros, "The Panegyris of the Byzantine Saint: A Study in the Nature of a Medieval Institution" in *The Byzantine Saint*, edited by Sergei Hackel, London: Fellowship of St Alban and St Sergius, 1981

Wycherley, R.E., *The Athenian Agora*, vol. 3: *Literary and Epigraphical Testimonia*, Princeton, New Jersey: Princeton University Press, 1957

Family

Throughout recorded Greek history, the family has functioned as the central social unit. In ancient Greek there is, however, no word for "family" in today's sense, and the nearest equivalent, *oikos* or "household", refers not only to the human members of the family group but also to its property, be that house, land, tombs, slaves, or animals. This is evident as early as Homer's *Odyssey*. Crucial, therefore, to the continuation of the *oikos* was the production of legitimate heirs to whom the family property could be passed. Ancient Greek society was patriarchal, as indeed it has been until almost the present day. However, whereas in Homer the male hero stood alone at the head of his *oikos*, the *oikos* of the Archaic and Classical Greek polis, or city state, was tied closely to the social, military, civic, and religious structure of the city. While the polis provided protection from enemies to the *oikos* and its property, the *oikos* provided the polis with its citizen soldiers. The *oikos* of the Archaic and Classical periods therefore functioned on both a public and a private level. Although patriarchal, the *oikos* nevertheless laid great value on the woman's role as wife and mother. Proper and chaste behaviour was highly prized, indeed expected, by Greek society as a means of ensuring legitimate family succession and inheritance. The woman also played a central role in household management, and in the conduct of proper death ritual (preparation of the corpse and mourning) for deceased family members.

Marriage in ancient Greece, and throughout subsequent Greek history, was based on the principle of monogamy and, as again until recent times, was an arranged affair involving agreement between the bride and groom's families; this included agreement on the dowry, usually a sum of money, that the woman would bring to the marriage. At Athens during the Classical period the bridegroom was generally aged around 30 while, in order to ensure her virginal status, the bride was usually half his age. Following the wedding, the bride moved from her father's house to that of her husband. There, although sharing the family house and concerns, man and wife led distinctly different lives, for while the adult male participated daily in the public citizen life of Athens, the female remained at home, leading a private existence concerned only with domestic matters. In the case of an unsatisfactory marriage divorce was possible and could be instigated, in theory at least, by either husband or wife. Athenian law required that on divorce a woman's dowry be returned to her; this protected her from becoming destitute and made her an attractive candidate for remarriage. Procreation of children within marriage was highly important, not only to safeguard the inheritance of family property, but also to provide care for the parents in old age: indeed the nuclear family was often extended to include elderly relatives within the household. The production of children, furthermore, ensured that the older generation would receive the appropriate death ritual and proper burial when the time came, and that the family tomb cult would be maintained. Since inheritance of family property operated through the male line, sons were especially desired; daughters, by contrast, had to be provided with a dowry. It has therefore been suggested that infant exposure, which is known to have occurred, involved more female than male children, though hard evidence for this is not forthcoming. It is also worth noting that, since all sons had an equal right to share in their father's property, the production of a number of male children could also be considered problematic. Inheritance matters were protected by complex legislation, necessary since the polis was founded on an agrarian basis; where, for example, a family lacked a male heir, a son could be adopted or, alternatively, property could pass through a daughter to her sons.

As a result of a bias in our evidence, most of what we know about the family in Classical Greece relates to the Athenian upper class. It is, therefore, interesting to compare the case of Sparta, where the state claimed a much greater degree of involvement in the family and household matters of the Spartan upper class. The underlying reason for this was the maintenance at Sparta of a professional standing army. Following marriage, which was compulsory, the groom returned to a communal military life until he was 30. Consequently, husband and wife did not live together for a number of years, resulting in Spartan women leading more public and active lives than their Athenian counterparts, and being able to exercise a degree of control over family property matters. They were, furthermore, able to own property and wealth independently. Unlike Athenians, Spartan women were not married until they were fully grown, and then generally to a man of similar age. According to Xenophon, a Spartan man could have children with the wife of another consenting Spartan male, and a young wife married to an elderly husband might also produce children with another man: these arrangements probably operated to combat cases of infertility, adoption of children also being practised. The decision to expose a child rested not with the parents, but rather with the tribal elders who had always in mind the military requirements of the Spartan community. Furthermore, the education of male children was not determined by their parents but by the state, which removed boys in their seventh year to communal barracks where they received a military, as well as traditional, education.

The Hellenistic period in Greek lands witnessed, as seen in the plays of Menander and others, a shift of focus towards the family's and individual's private affairs. This occurred as the polis structure weakened and the relationship between polis and *oikos* changed. For example, whereas in the Classical period at Athens one's membership of the polis depended on membership of an Athenian citizen family, in the Hellenistic period some states were happy to bestow citizenship on individuals descended from non-citizen parents. Furthermore, women in many states gained the ability to own and manage wealth and property in their own right, resulting in a new emphasis on their individual, as well as family, identity and worth.

During the Roman period the family underwent further evolution due, in part, to the introduction of Christianity. The most profound change revolved around the alternative roles now open to women. In the 4th century AD the emperor Constantine decreed that a woman did not have to marry, but could rather devote herself to the Church as a bride of Christ. This in turn impacted on inheritance law, for such women could now also bequeath property to the Church instead of to relatives. For the first time, priestesses aside, women could reject marriage and childbearing: either they could continue to live in their paternal home, or choose solitude, or reside within a community of women. This increase in celibacy and non-family life in the early Christian period applied equally to men as to women. Most men and women did, however, continue to marry and produce children. Marriages, as before, were arranged and contracts, recording financial agreements, were drawn up. As earlier, most girls were married by the time they reached 16, and a legal minimum of 12 years was set for brides. Now for the first time, Christian teaching established the requirement of fidelity within marriage for men as well as for women; further, in AD 326 Constantine went so far as to outlaw the ancient practice of concubinage, that is a stable sexual liaison between a married man and a woman not his wife. Many subsequent emperors, however, regarded this practice with greater tolerance. Divorce law, particularly relating to the grounds on which divorce was permitted, changed many times during the early Christian period, due perhaps in part to the influence of Christian teaching. Nevertheless, even though Christian belief stressed the indissolubility of human marriage as a reflection of the union between Christ and the Church, divorce continued to be a legal option. In the event of divorce, a woman's dowry had to be returned to her as before, while the children officially remained under their father's authority although they did not necessarily live with him. Abortion and infant exposure were now regarded with strong moral disapproval, though again the legal response was more liberal. Encouraged by the Church, some provision of care for orphans developed through private and local charity.

Throughout the Byzantine period the *oikos* comprised an essentially nuclear family. As earlier, however, no precise word for "family" exists in Byzantine Greek and the nearest equivalent, *syngeneia*, refers to both the nuclear family and the wider kinship group. Beginning in the late 8th and 9th centuries, these kinship groups began identifying themselves by adopting family names which were then passed to the next generation. Indeed, by the end of the 11th century these lineages were becoming, at the aristocratic level, the basis of political organization, giving rise to a "feudal" family network possessing great economic and political power. Marriage, therefore, represented an important family strategy for social and political advancement. By the 8th century the Christian marriage ritual was developing a definite form, with the exchange of rings, prayers, and blessings and the crowning of the couple with a floral wreath or later a metal diadem. Nevertheless until at least the end of the 9th century the marriage contract was a civil agreement, without any involvement of the Church in the legal aspect of the union. Gradually thereafter, however, the Church's marriage rite became the only acceptable way of joining man and woman in wedlock. Whereas in ancient Greece intermarriage between blood relatives had been commonplace, now incestuous marriage was severely prohibited, laws being passed as early as the late 3rd century AD: by the 11th century marriage was forbidden to any couple related up to the seventh degree. Furthermore, from the 6th century onwards, such prohibitions on marriage applied not only to blood relatives but also to those linked by the spiritual kinship of godparenthood. Although divorce continued to be a legal option, the grounds on which it was granted were strictly limited and remarriage was discouraged for both divorced and widowed spouses. Celibacy, on the other hand, claimed a higher moral status than marriage for both sexes, and individuals entering a monastery or convent were required to renounce their blood family in favour of spiritual kin. Except for the celibate, however, marriage, childbearing, and household management remained the prime female roles and, with the exception of a few women from imperial and aristocratic circles, the place of women generally remained confined to the secluded sphere of family life. In this context, the female as wife and mother commanded considerable prestige, enhanced by the all-important spiritual model of the *Theotokos*, Mary, as Mother of Christ. In the event of divorce, moreover, the children now no longer remained under the father's sole legal authority, the parental rights of mother and father having been balanced by the 8th century AD. Under Leo VI (886–912) a law was also passed to allow women to adopt children: consequently women who were virgins, or those who were barren, did not have to remain childless. Unadopted children were cared for in monasteries or orphanages, some having been abandoned in infancy even though infant exposure, like abortion, was legally forbidden. Regarding inheritance, the equal division of wealth and property among the family's children continued as earlier.

The centuries of Ottoman rule in Greece have thus far received relatively little study and have left scanty historical documentation relating to family life. Nevertheless, we can at least observe that, as long as the Greeks remitted the required Ottoman taxes and maintained a peaceful profile, matters of everyday domestic life were allowed to remain essentially under the authority of the Orthodox Church. This ensured a large degree of continuity in Greek family custom and inheritance law. A rare example of the involvement of the Ottoman state in the Greek family concerned the selection every four years by Ottoman officials of promising Christian children who were then removed from their families: these children were converted to Islam and brought up in the service of the state to become skilled administrators or members of the military elite. This practice continued until the mid-17th century.

Following the liberation of Greece from Ottoman rule and the establishment of the Greek nation state in the early 19th century, the factor which had perhaps the most profound effect on the Greek family was urbanization. Gradually the power of the old endogamous land-based "archon" families, which had grown and flourished under the Ottomans, was replaced by a developing merchant middle class. Marriage dowries for both men and women in the form of property, land, livestock, and cash, and a trousseau of fine clothes, jewellery, and household goods for women, all underwritten by a matrimonial contract, now provided a channel for the transmission of wealth and therefore the means of achieving social mobility. The institution of godparenthood was also strategically employed in the formation of desirable family alliances. As in antiquity a strong desire for the production of sons persisted, as also did the separation of male and female roles into public and domestic spheres respectively.

Since the end of World War II and the Greek Civil War, numerous changes have taken place in Greek family life, at least in the ever-growing urban centres. The amassing of increasingly large cash and property dowries, particularly for women, was brought to an end in 1983 by a new family law which abolished the age-old practice of dowry exchange. This, however, does not mean that unofficial dowry agreements are no longer made: the most common practice is for the bride to bring to the marriage a house or apartment. This has contributed to a trend for the newly wed couple to establish their own independent nuclear family unit, in contrast to the previous traditional arrangement under which the bride was transferred to the groom's family. Nevertheless, the modern Greek word for "family", oikogeneia, can refer either to the nuclear or the extended family, and much moral value is set by Greek society on the family caring for elderly or sick parents. Increasingly in the cities young people now choose their own marriage partners, representing a major departure from the time-honoured custom of arranged marital unions. Developing alongside this can be seen the growing social and economic power of women, many of whom now contribute to the family not only in domestic terms, but also as paid employees working outside the home. Further, though Greek society has traditionally strongly disapproved of divorce, current rising urban divorce rates suggest changes in the perception and expectations of married life. In recognition of this, the law of 1983 endowed both parents with equal rights in respect to their children. Greece's current low birth rate is a cause of considerable concern for the country's leaders. This results from a number of factors, not least the improved education of women. Effective birth control, in particular the use of abortion, though still contrary to the doctrines of the Greek Orthodox Church, is widely practised. Also significant for the relationship of Church and family is the law of 1983 which made a civil wedding ceremony a legal, though still not widely popular, alternative to the Orthodox marriage ritual. Nevertheless, both family and Church still represent powerful forces in Greek life, with marriage and the production of children being greatly desired, expected, and morally respected.

LESLEY A. BEAUMONT

See also Children, Divorce, Dowry, Inheritance, Marriage

Further Reading
Arjava, Antti, *Women and Law in Late Antiquity*, Oxford: Clarendon Press, and New York: Oxford University Press, 1996

Billigmeier, J.C., "Studies on the Family in the Aegean Bronze Age and in Homer", *Trends in History*, 3 (1984): pp. 3–18

"The Byzantine Family and Household" (symposium), *Dumbarton Oaks Papers*, 44 (1990): pp. 97–226

Campbell, John Kennedy, *Honour, Family and Patronage: A Study of Institutions and Moral Values in a Greek Mountain Community*, Oxford: Clarendon Press, 1964

Clark, Gillian, *Women in Late Antiquity: Pagan and Christian Lifestyles*, Oxford: Clarendon Press, and New York: Oxford University Press, 1993

Cox, Cheryl Anne, *Household Interests: Property, Marriage Strategies, and Family Dynamics in Ancient Athens*, Princeton, New Jersey: Princeton University Press, 1998

Foxhall, L., "Household, Gender and Property in Classical Athens", *Classical Quarterly*, 39 (1989): pp. 22–44

Humphreys, Sarah C., *The Family, Women and Death*, 2nd edition, Ann Arbor: University of Michigan Press, 1993

Just, Roger, *Women in Athenian Law and Life*, London and New York: Routledge, 1989

Lacey, Walter Kirkpatrick, *The Family in Classical Greece*, London: Thames and Hudson, and Ithaca, New York: Cornell University Press, 1968

Loizos, Peter and Evthymios Papataxiarchis, *Contested Identities: Gender and Kinship in Modern Greece*, Princeton, New Jersey: Princeton University Press, 1991

Patterson, Cynthia B., *The Family in Greek History*, Cambridge, Massachusetts: Harvard University Press, 1998

Pomeroy, Sarah B., *Families in Classical and Hellenistic Greece: Representations and Realities*, Oxford: Clarendon Press, and New York: Oxford University Press, 1996

Sant Cassia, Paul and Constantina Bada, *The Making of the Modern Greek Family: Marriage and Exchange in Nineteenth-Century Athens*, Cambridge and New York: Cambridge University Press, 1992

Shaw, B., "The Family in Late Antiquity: The Experience of Augustine", *Past and Present*, 115 (1987): pp. 3–51

Veyne, Paul (editor), *A History of Private Life*, vol. 1: *From Pagan Rome to Byzantium*, Cambridge, Massachusetts: Harvard University Press, 1987

Fascism

The word fascism derives from the *fasces*, bundles of elm or birch rods tied round a battleaxe and carried ahead of consuls as a symbol of state authority in ancient Rome. However, the term acquired its current usage in the 20th century. The ideology of fascism is the product of the economic and social crisis in Europe after World War I. Nevertheless, elements of fascism can be detected in the 19th century and beyond, as its roots reach back to the reaction of the ruling classes to the French Revolution.

Specifically, fascism refers to the 1919 movement formed by Benito Mussolini in Italy. The same movement brought him to power in 1922. Generically, fascism is an authoritarian movement, founded as Nazism in Germany, the Falanges in Spain, the Iron Guard in Romania, or the British Union of Fascists of Sir Oswald Mosley. Fascism was never a coherent ideological and social system comparable to Marxism, for example. In addition, fascist movements in various countries reflected their different national backgrounds.

In the case of Greece, the presence of fascism may be considered only in a broader sense. There has not been a fascist movement similar to those mentioned previously. On the contrary, the movements and politicians labelled fascist in Greece generally rejected the characterization as infamous. In fact, the term fascism was used against opponents of right-wing parties, against nationalists, and even sometimes against centrist-liberals. There is no doubt that during the era of dictatorships, such as that of Metaxas in 1936 or the colonels in 1967, fascist methods of violence and oppression were used. That happened also during the Greek Civil War (1944–49) and the era that followed it. However, these are methods used by a dictatorship or authoritarian regime whether civil or military.

The historical context of the development of what has been labelled Greek fascism remains linked to World War I and the catastrophe of Asia Minor in 1922. The brutal end to the long history of Hellenism in Asia Minor changed the whole social and political spectrum of Greece as two million refugees were suddenly added to the population. The destruction of national ideals had inaugurated a new era, a time of political and social crisis. In March 1924 the monarchy was abolished and the republic established. There soon followed political instability, coup d'état, social and economic crises, re-establishment of the monarchy, and finally the Metaxas dictatorsip in 1936 which marked this troubled period of modern Greek history.

The socialist and communist movements appeared simultaneously and the reaction against them soon followed in the form of nationalistic and authoritarian discourse. In May 1936 political disillusionment and depressed living conditions among workers and peasants led to strikes and social unrest, especially in Thessalonica. The refugees of Asia Minor reinforced the liberal and left labour movement. Within this context of domestic crisis, reinforced by an international economic and social crisis, fascist ideas appeared in Greece.

The Metaxas dictatorship was formally established on 4 August 1936, hence it has always been known as the regime of 4 August. It was an authoritarian regime using fascist methods against its opponents, especially left-wing liberals and communists. However, one should also remember that the Germanophile Metaxas, whose regime was sometimes considered fascist, was partly the creation of the Anglophile Greek monarch, king George II.

In one way or another, the regime of 4 August 1936 opened a long era of authoritarian government including the German occupation and the terrible Civil War, a struggle which in practice ended only with the fall of the colonels' dictatorship in July 1974. Yet authoritarian regimes are not synonymous with fascist regimes. For example, the colonels' regime, also labelled fascist, was a military dictatorship which had the acceptance and support of the USA, if not its blessing.

The real fascist movements in Greece after World War I remained as marginal as they were during the Civil War and the era following it. Nevertheless these marginal movements not only supported the dictatorships but also provided people who could be used by the regime and even by right-wing parties to carry out the oppression of the Greek public. This fact and, in a sense, the liberty of action allowed to small fascist groups gave the impression of a great fascist movement in Greece. In addition, both the communists and the left in general misused the term fascism as a weapon against their opponents. This linguistic abuse lent credence to the idea that dictatorships and right-wing authoritarian governments were in essence fascist.

However, from a sociological point of view, fascism never was a real political or ideological force in Greece. At this point it is useful to review the main traits of fascism: relatively coherent militaristic ideology, presence of a unique political party of the masses and a charismatic leader, significant popular support for the regime (e.g. the fascism in Italy or the nazism in Germany). Other traits of fascism are nationalism, populism, anti-communism, anti-liberalism, anti-democracy, monopoly of power, and the heavy use of propaganda and terror.

Greece has never had either a coherent fascist ideology or a unique fascist party of the masses and, of course, no significant popular support for dictatorships. Other traits of fascism observable in Greece, such as anti-communism, nationalism, anti-democracy, or the use of propaganda, are common characteristics of authoritarian regimes and even some liberal regimes (e.g. anti-communism or nationalism).

On the other hand, Greece, unlike France and a few other European countries, had no intellectuals developing fascist theories and ideas. Certainly there were nationalist intellectuals and some of their themes gave the impression of a fascist approach to Greek social problems. Indeed, some intellectuals were compromised by their links to dictatorships. However, they produced nothing in terms of fascist ideology and even proclaimed their faith in democracy and justified their support of dictatorships as necessary under the "special" circumstances in which the country found itself at that time.

In conclusion, it appears that dictatorships, reactionary, authoritarian, and right-wing parties or movements were generally lumped together and called fascist in Greece by their opponents. Nevertheless, one should recognize that at times this conservative front did use methods of fascist inspiration and did oppose liberal reforms and liberal visions of Greek society, thus amalgamating communism with liberal and progressive ideas and using the army as a barrier against these visions and ideas.

STEPHANOS CONSTANTINIDES

Further Reading

Campbell, John and Philip Sherrard, *Modern Greece*, London: Benn, and New York: Praeger, 1968

Dimaras, K.T., *Historia tis neoellinikis logotechnias*, Athens, 1948–49; translated as *A History of Modern Greek Literature*, Albany: State University of New York Press, 1972

Hellenic Studies / Études helléniques, 1983–

Kousoulas, D. George, *Revolution and Defeat: The Story of the Greek Communist Party*, London: Oxford University Press, 1965

Metaxas, Ioannis, *Prosopikon Imerologion* [Personal Journal], Athens, 1960

Meynaud, Jean, *Les Forces politiques en Grèce*, Lausanne: Etudes de Science Politique, 1965

O'Ballance, Edgar, *The Greek Civil War, 1944–1949*, New York: Praeger, 1966

Pentzopoulos, Dimitri, *The Balkan Exchange of Minorities and Its Impact Upon Greece*, Paris: Mouton, 1962

Sherrard, Philip, *The Greek East and the Latin West: A Study in the Christian Tradition*, London and New York: Oxford University Press, 1959

Svoronos, Nicolas G., *Histoire de la Grèce moderne*, 2nd edition, Paris: Presses Universitaires de France, 1964

Tsoucalas, Constantine, *The Greek Tragedy*, Harmondsworth: Penguin, 1969

Woodhouse, C.M., *Apple of Discord: A Survey of Recent Greek Politics in their International Setting*, London and New York: Hutchinson, 1948

Woodhouse, C.M., *Modern Greece: A Short History*, 5th edition, London and Boston: Faber, 1991

Fasts

The Greek word *nisteia* (fast) has the general meaning of "not having eaten" or "being without nourishment". Most often, however, it is used in a religious context to denote the total or partial abstention from particular foods at certain periods of the year or on certain days of the week.

The act of fasting in antiquity was prevalent among the Greeks and was primarily associated with rites of mourning. Its main purpose seemed to be an apotropaic one; the mourning fast was seen as a powerful medium of warding off demonic spirits that could enter the body through eating and drinking. Fasting was also considered by the ancient Greeks to be a means of expiation and purification that rendered the faster fit for union with the deities. In the festival of Thesmophoria, an Athenian cult in honour of Demeter, a one-day fast was demanded of women. In the Eleusinian mysteries fasting was imposed on the initiate in order to render them worthy of receiving the sacramental drink. Another context in which abstinence from food was required in antiquity was that of manticism. It was believed that the one who fasted was more receptive to divine revelation. Thus, preparation by austere fasting was a necessary precondition for the dream oracles through which the gods unveiled the future to their devotees and made promises to them. Yet, fasting in antiquity, apart from its ritual functions, had also therapeutic ones. The Greek philosophers often praised self-restraint for hygienic purposes and recommended fasting for the sake of philosophy. Notwithstanding such philosophical ideas, fasting in antiquity did not seem to have an ethical pertinence.

In early Christianity the position adopted towards fasting was different and exceptional. Jesus had criticized the ritual formalism of the Pharisees because it assumed precedence over ethical action. Jesus, however, did not eliminate fasting for he spent 40 days in the desert praying and fasting and he suggested that both could be used as effective means against the devil, a view which is reminiscent of ancient practices. Yet, because of the association of fasting with mourning, Jesus regarded fasting in his Messianic presence as meaningless (Mark 2: 18). Early Christianity, therefore, broke away from Jewish customs regarding fasting. Dietary restrictions were considered redundant by Christians since they were signs of the old Covenant. Hence, in the 1st century, Christians did not observe any voluntary fasts. Fasting at that period was connected only with the preparation for the revelation of the Holy Spirit to the Apostles for guidance in their decision making.

In the post-apostolic period, however, Christianity imposed its own rules with regard to fasting, which seem to have developed from Jewish ones. In the 2nd century the Easter fast was established. The duration of this fast was analogous to the period of time that Christ spent in the tomb. However, it was not associated with mourning, but rather was viewed as a preparatory period for the celebration that lasted from Easter to Pentecost and as an outward sign of the anticipation of spiritual fulfilment. During the course of the 4th century this fasting period was extended to 40 days in commemoration of Jesus' 40-day fast in the wilderness; from then onwards it was known as the Great Fast (Lent). Also, by the 3rd century, Wednesdays and Fridays were designated as fasting days for Christians (in contrast to Mondays and Thursdays, which were fasting days for Jews). These days were chosen because they were days of mourning: Wednesday in remembrance of the betrayal of Jesus and Friday in remembrance of his death. To fast on Sunday, the day of Christ's resurrection, was prohibited since fasting and joy were regarded as antithetical. Three other main fasts were subsequently introduced, observed first in monastic communities and much later being commonly kept by clergy and laity also. These were the Apostles' Fast (ranging for one to six weeks before 29 June – the feast of SS Peter and Paul – depending on the year), the Assumption Fast (1–15 August), and the Christmas Fast (15 November–24 December). Apart from these four main periods of fasting, some one-day fasts were also established in the Orthodox Church: that of the Exaltation of the Cross, the Beheading of St John the Baptist, and on the eve of the Epiphany. It is worth noting here that in the first centuries of Christianity fasting became a necessary practice for neophytes before baptism. Finally, a complete abstention from food and drink is required by Orthodox Christians before receiving Holy Communion.

The Orthodox fasts are of two types (cf. Schmemann 1969): ascetic fast and total fast. The first refers to the abstinence from particular food and to a drastic reduction in food intake. It is a means of eschewing physicality in an attempt to achieve spirituality. Its purpose is to subject the body to privation so as to free the spirit from bodily desires, which are seen as the tragic consequences of the Fall: sin entered into the world through the act of eating and it is abstinence from food that would allow us to be redeemed. Thus, physical hunger and thirst should be redirected to a continuing hunger and an unquenchable thirst for God. Of all the ascetic fasts the most severe and the most rigorously observed by the laity is the Lenten fast. During this period one should abstain from meat, fish, all dairy products, oil, and wine. Unlike ascetic fast, which is long in duration, "total fast" lasts only for a day or even half a day and involves total abstinence from food and drink and from sexual relations. Total fast is the last and ultimate preparation before one is fed on Christ. It is a state of spiritual concentration and waiting that precedes the coming of the Kingdom of God. Fasting may also be viewed as a sacrifice. By dying to bodily needs one symbolically offers one's body as a gift to God with the hope of salvation.

Fasting was also regarded by the Church Fathers as a necessary preparation for real prayer. Because of this connection with prayer, its rejection of bodily sensations, and its eschatological meaning, fasting seems essentially linked with monasticism. The dietary restrictions observed by monastics are more rigid than those imposed on the laity. There is a permanent abstention from meat. Apart from Wednesdays and Fridays, Mondays are also fast days for monks and nuns, on which only one meal, free from all animal products, oil, and wine (*xerophagia*, eating "dry food") is permitted. Athonite monks practise a total fast for the first three days of Lent, and take only a single meal (*monophagia*) on other fast days. As far as the laity is concerned, women normally fast more often and for longer periods than men, especially as they progress in age. In doing so they believe that they strengthen their own and their family's relationship with God.

Fasting in Orthodoxy is an act of unification and time-reckoning. It unites the soul with the body, the one who fasts with the divine, and also all Orthodox believers in the world in a shared action of alternate fasting and feasting.

ELENI SOTIRIU

Further Reading

Cross, Lawrence, *Eastern Christianity: The Byzantine Tradition*, Sydney and Philadelphia: Dwyer, 1988

Enisleidis, C.M., *O Thesmos tis Nistias* [The Institution of Fasting], Athens, 1959

Feeley-Harnik, Gillian, *The Lord's Table: The Meaning of Food in Early Judaism and Christianity*, Washington, DC: Smithsonian Institution Press, 1994

Kittel, Gerhard (editor), *Theological Dictionary of the New Testament*, vol. 4, Grand Rapids, Michigan: Eerdmans, 1964 (see especially entries for nistis, nisteuo, nistia)

Koutsas, Symeon, *I Nistia tis Ekklesias* [The Church's Fast], 6th edition, Athens, 1996

Miles, Margaret R., *Fullness of Life: Historical Foundations for a New Asceticism*, Philadelphia: Westminster, 1981

Porphyry, *Treastise on Abstinence*, 37–38 in *L'Ascèse monastique de saint Basile*, translated by Emmanuel Amand de Mendieta, Maredsous: Editions de Maredsous, 1948

Schmemann, Alexander, *Great Lent: Journey to Pascha*, Crestwood, New York: St. Vladimir's Seminary Press, 1969

Špidlík, Tomaš, *The Spirituality of the Christian East: A Systematic Handbook*, Kalamazoo, Michigan: Cistercian Publications, 1986

Ware, Timothy, *The Orthodox Church*, 2nd edition, London and New York: Penguin, 1993

Fate

The Greek words for fate – *moira*, *moros*, and *heimarmene aisa* – mean "portion". Apportionment is often said to be the work of gods, but the relation between fate and the other divine powers presented an acute problem to Greek thought. Usually a daimon is held responsible for an individual's allotted fate but often *moira* is the work of Zeus, the highest divinity of the Greek pantheon. Equally often *moira* appears to be determined independently of Zeus, and any interference with it amounts to upsetting the natural order of things (*Iliad*, 8. 70ff.,

16. 435f., 22. 174f.). In this sense fate is regarded as being arbitrary and irrational, and therefore inexplicable and more powerful than the gods. A power closely similar to fate was fortune (*tyche*), and often, especially in later literature, the distinction between fate and fortune is vague. Although fortune can crucially affect somebody, originally its realm is that of chance, whereas the realm of fate is that of (godly) determination and strict necessity (cf. Aristotle *Nichomachean Ethics*, 1099b10–12). Throughout the history of Greek culture fate is seen as determining both sad and happy events with a power of universal law. Fate determines first and foremost death, and sometimes (e.g. in inscriptions) it is identical with death. The belief in the inevitability of man's allotted fate is of fundamental importance in Greek tradition and permeates Greek literature and thought from the Homeric age through the Classical and Hellenistic era up to modern times. It is striking to see that formulaic phrases and such terms as *moira* and *tyche* pervade all periods of Greek cultural history.

In the Homeric poems fate, *moira* or *aisa*, is neither a person nor a god or goddess but a fact. *Moira* appears in two forms: as a synonym for death, but also as signifying what is seemly or fit for someone, e.g. a share of honour. In its first form, *moira* is often found in formulaic phrases as the cause of death and destruction (*Iliad*, 4. 517, 19. 409–10, 23. 119). The hero frequently begs the gods for a reversal of fate (*Iliad*, 19. 287–302, 315–39) and often able to reverse it or to worsen it by his own deeds (*Odyssey*, 9. 32f.), a situation described as *hyper moron* (beyond fate). In its second form *moira* reveals an ethical significance. One has to act and speak in accordance with one's own *moira*, taking into account social hierarchy, social and religious values, understanding of one's place and role in the social context.

Already in Hesiod fate becomes personalized in the figures of three old women spinning, the Moirai, the children of Night (*Theogony*, 219f.) or of Zeus and Themis (Righteousness) (*Theogony*, 904ff.); they were considered goddesses, able to "assign mortal men at their birth both good and ill" (*Theogony*, 217). Their functions are indicated by their names: Clotho spins the thread of life, Lachesis apportions destiny, Atropos makes final decisions. The Moirai appear in Greek iconography as early as the 6th century BC, and we know of the existence of their statues in various Greek cities, witnessing the cult of the Moirai. The power of Moira is stressed in the victory songs of Pindar and especially in tragedy. Aeschylus reserves a highly prestigious position for the Fates in the pantheon (*Eumenides*, 956f.), making even Zeus their dependant (*Prometheus Vinctus*, 511). The tragic heroes Ajax, Oedipus, Antigone, Philoctetes, and Alcestis lament their own fate and sing their own dirges. In Aeschylus' *Agamemnon*, Cassandra, endowed with the ability to prophesy, knows and laments her own fate and Agamemnon's.

The notion of *moira* plays a major role in funerary inscriptions and in the tradition of the literary epigram as well as in the magical papyri. A number of different formulae, many of them Homeric, are employed in funerary inscriptions to describe the work of Moira. Sometimes the deceased or the mourner directly addresses and reproaches Moira as the agent of their death. In funerary epigrams sentiments of grief are expressed for the inevitable action of Moira, especially when concerning premature death. From the 4th century Fortune appears to supersede Moira, especially in some genres, such as comedy. The role of Moira and Fortune is highlighted in the stories of love and adventure of the Hellenistic and late antique novels. Fortune plays an active role in these novels as a personified agent, and dramatic tension is created by the innumerable reversals of fortune against which the heroes and heroines often protest.

The problem of fate appears from very early on in Greek philosophy. Parmenides maintained that fate determines that nothing exists but the being (fr. 8. 36–38). The problem of fate is first seriouly addressed by the Stoics. For them the way the world evolves is determined by a divine plan which includes our choices and decisions. Yet the divine plan is contingent on our own choices. Something can be dependent on us and still fated (but not necessitated) since a person's soul, together with external circumstances, is part of the network of fate. The human agent has power only over his or her own impressions. One may choose freely among them but whether one succeeds in realizing them is a matter of divine providence. Thus one is free if one does not desire anything beyond one's power (Epictetus, *Dissertationes*, 4. 7. 9). For the Stoics one exercises one's free will only when one gives assent to the right impression, but to act rightly or virtuously is not in one's power. The Stoic notion of fate was highly influential but was also polemicized by the Epicureans who denied the existence of a godly imposed fate (*D.L.X.*, 133–134). They argued that to the extent that men are rational their actions are voluntary, in the sense that they are under rational control. Later Alexander of Aphrodisias in his *On Fate* (c. AD 200), which argues that the Stoic view seriously restricts freedom.

In late antiquity the problem of fate and predestination was much debated among pagans and Christians alike. Gnostic sects, for instance, maintained a strict determinism, holding that salvation is reserved only for the chosen ones. The Christian Fathers were opposed to the pagan notion of fate, and the pagan view of astral determination. They maintained that everything is directed and guided by God's will and there is no room for an impersonal force like fate or fortune to be the agent of anything. The difficulty of this position is twofold, namely that God is the cause of evils and also that God is responsible for discriminating among humans, endowing some of them more and some of them less. From very early on, Christian Fathers stressed the human free will and Origen argued that man is created free by a just God who made all humans equal. The Christian notion of free will, like the Stoic one from which it springs, is shaped by a particular notion of freedom. Our freedom consists of acting in the way that God wishes us to act. Acting against God's will, we do not display our free will but our subordination to passions.

In the Byzantine period the image of fate has an important presence in both literature and philosophy. Fate remained a philosophical problem to which the Byzantines devoted special attention. The question of the extent to which human life is predestined, what is the realm of free will, and how this is compatible with God's foreknowledge of everything was vividly discussed by Maximos the Confessor and John of Damascus. Photios (9th century), Nicholas of Methone (12th century), and Nikephoros Gregoras (14th century) also dealt with the problem. In the Byzantine novels of the 12th and 13th centuries the picture is very much the same as in the ancient novels. At the same time a folk image of fate makes its appearance. In *Kallimachos and Chrysorrhoe* (1329–46) Tyche appears in the guise of a beggar woman dressed in black, a picture occurring also in folk tales. We also encounter the idea of the thread woven by Fate the Spinner or the decree of Fate, written down at the birth of a child, the *moirographema*, as it is called in *Kallimachos and Chrysorrhoe*, *Belthandros and Chrysantza*, and *Libistros and Rhodamne*, and other novels. Folk tales mention the records of *moira*, and even today Greeks use the expression "it was written" to indicate the inevitability of an event. In the 15th century the philosophical discussion of the problem of fate was revived. Plethon in his treatise *On Fate* maintains a strong determinism, arguing that God's will was a fixed law. In reply Theodore Gaza attacked Plethon, arguing that both Plato, whom Plethon invoked, and Aristotle allowed for human free will.

In modern Greece the belief in fate survives despite its obvious contradiction of Orthodox Christian doctrines. The role of fate is crucial in folk poetry. In folk tradition the Fates are depicted as three old women, of whom one at least is engaged in spinning, another holds a book with records of the decrees of people, and the third carries a pair of scissors to cut the thread of life. In many fables the Fates are said to present themselves after the birth of a child to determine its destiny, a motif which can be traced back to antiquity (e.g. Pindar, *Olynthian Odes*, 6. 42, Plato, *Symposium*, 206d). We also find the belief that the Moirai can change their minds if they are offered various gifts and prayers. A widespread popular tradition has been that of *Moirologia*. These are songs lamenting the dead, sung by women over the dead body or the tomb, recounting and blaming the work of the merciless Moira.

GEORGE E. KARAMANOLIS

See also Death

Further Reading

Adkins, A.W.H., *Merit and Responsibility*, Oxford: Clarendon Press, 1960; reprinted Chicago: University of Chicago Press, 1975

Alexiou, Margaret, *The Ritual Lament in Greek Tradition*, Cambridge: Cambridge University Press, 1974

Amand de Mendieta, Emmanuel, *Fatalisme et liberté dans l'antiquité grecque*, Louvain, 1945; reprinted Amsterdam: Hakkert, 1973

Bianchi, Ugo, *Dios Aisa: destino, uomini e divinità nell'epos, nelle teogonie e nel culto dei Greci*, Rome: Signorelli, 1953

Burkert, Walter, *Greek Religion: Archaic and Classical*, Cambridge, Massachusetts: Harvard University Press, and Oxford: Blackwell, 1985

Dietrich, B.C., *Death, Fate and the Gods: The Development of a Religious Idea in Greek Popular Belief and in Homer*, London: Athlone Press, 1965

Dover, K.J., *Greek Popular Morality in the Time of Plato and Aristotle*, Oxford: Blackwell, and Berkeley: University of California Press, 1974; 2nd edition Indianapolis: Hackett, 1994

Eitrem, S., Moira entry in *Real-Encyclopädie der klassischen Altertumswissenschaft*, edited by August Pauly *et al.*, vol. 15, 1932, 2449–97

Greene, William Chase, *Moira: Fate, Good and Evil in Greek Thought*, Cambridge, Massachusetts: Harvard University Press, 1944

Lawson, John Cuthbert, *Modern Greek Folklore and Ancient Greek Religion: A Study in Survivals*, Cambridge: Cambridge University Press, 1910; New York: University Books, 1964

Mayer, August, *Moira in griechischen Inschriften*, Giessen, 1927

Federal States

The federal state was a major form of organization of the ancient Greek state. Its main characteristic was the union of various city states or tribal communities to form a single entity, which exercised certain political powers on behalf of its member states. By definition, the constituent parts of federal states enjoyed a specific degree of autonomy, including local government and the use of local citizenship, while the federal authorities were genuinely concerned with foreign policy. Political participation of the member states was achieved by the means of equal or proportional representation. Federal states were always founded on the basis of earlier Greek tribes – for instance the Boeotians, Arcadians, Achaeans (see below) – as a consequence of which tribal cults and ceremonies continued to play a prominent role in federal affairs. There is no single term to denote a federal state in ancient Greek. In the 5th and 4th centuries BC the term *koinon* is predominant, while in the Hellenistic period *ethnos* and *sympoliteia* are found.

One of the earliest – and one of the most important – federal states was the Boeotian League. Its chief officials, the Boeotarchs, appear to have been established by 519 BC, when Boeotian troops tried to incorporate Plataea into the Theban-led confederacy. Due to Theban Medism (support for Persia) in 480, the federal state was weakened after the Persian Wars. There was no official dissolution, but its political influence seems to have perished, and Boeotia came under Athenian domination in 457. A new confederacy was founded after the liberation from Athens a decade later, its polity being the best-attested form of representative government in antiquity. All Boeotia was divided into nine (in 427 extended to 11) electorate units, each of which provided one Boeotarch, 60 councillors, 1000 hoplites, 100 horsemen, and a certain number of jurors to the federal government. Active citizenship was confined to those who served in the federal troops (eligibility established by a so-called hoplite census). The constituencies were shared among the poleis according to their population. Both Orchomenus and Thebes were permitted two districts in 447, while smaller cities administered one or sometimes only a third of a district. In 386 the Spartans dissolved the federation on the grounds of the King's Peace. The League was soon re-established in the aftermath of the Theban revolution in 379. Its main political institution was the board of Boeotarchs, now reduced to seven. The representative councils were not revived. Instead, decision making rested with the primary democratic assembly in Thebes, which was open to all Boeotian citizens. Theban leadership soon became overwhelming. After the destruction of several poleis (most notably Orchomenus in 364), Boeotia was dominated by the Thebans alone. The sources tend to speak of the league in terms of a Theban *synteleia* (subordinate group), which indicates an amalgamation of polis structures and federal institutions. The confederacy was maintained in the Hellenistic age (despite the destruction of Thebes by Alexander in 335 BC), though its constitutional outline profoundly changed. At the head of government stood a board of seven (sometimes eight) Boeotarchs, who now were confined to one representative from any specific city. Next to them, the office of a military *strategos* (general) and a federal *synedrion* (council) were introduced. Another important improvement was the practice of taking the vote in the federal *synedrion* by cities. Effectively, no single polis seems to have dominated the federation until it was dissolved by Rome in 146 BC. In later periods the Boeotian *koinon* obtained cultural functions, such as hosting religious festivals.

In the north the Thessalian League was the leading federal state. It seems to have been established by the beginning of 5th century BC, emerging from the feudal kingdom of Thessaly. Its proper territory was divided into four tetrads (Thessaliotis, Phthiotis, Pelasgiotis, Hestiaeotis), each headed by a tetrarch. Initially, the office was monopolized by local aristocratic families (for instance the Aleuads of Larissa), who owned the vast majority of the Thessalian *kleroi* (land lots). Of these, each *kleros* was required to furnish 40 horsemen and 80 hoplites to the federal troops. With the growing importance of the *koinon*, the tetrarchs were replaced by four annual polemarchs. They were elected by the federal primary assembly of all free Thessalians. Like the polemarchs, the *tagos* (the head of state), was elective. His office embodied the supreme sovereignty of the league. However, the sources attest certain *atageiai*, which implies that there were substantial periods without a *tagos*. In the 4th century several tyrants of Pherae, most prominently Jason, sought to establish a lasting *tageia* over Thessaly. In resistance to their attempts, the league appealed to Philip II of Macedon, who was elected as federal archon and defeated the Pheraeans in a pitched battle in 352. Under his archonship the Thessalian League soon became a Macedonian protectorate. The tetrarchy was reintroduced, its officials being appointed by Philip. Further, he initiated a system of "decarchies" (boards of ten) in each of the cities, to anchor Macedonian interests. The next major reform was enforced by Flamininus in 194. The league, now detached from Macedon, obtained representative government, including a federal *synedrion* of city delegates. Apart from judicial and deliberative activities, its main objective was the annual election of the head of government, the *strategos*. Unlike most confederacies, this polity was officially maintained throughout the Roman empire, affiliated to the province of Achaea.

The Arcadian League presents a much shorter history. Founded after the Battle of Leuctra in 371, it was brought about by Mantinaean and Tegean democrats, who sought to unite their poleis against Sparta. To prevent rivalries between these prominent member cities, Megalopolis was founded as a new federal capital. The central political body was the primary assembly, the *myrioi* ("ten thousand" – that is, "all") in Megalopolis. This assembly was attended to a large extent by members of the federal army, the *eparitoi*, a mercenary force paid by the confederacy. At the head of the troops stood the *strategos*, the federal commander-in-chief. The most interesting institution was the federal *boule* (council) of 50 *damiourgoi* (councillors), who represented the cities approximately in proportion to their population. Despite this sophisticated combination of direct and representative bodies, the Arcadian League was soon crushed by internal civil strife and disintegrated in 364/63.

More successful was the Aetolian League, which – as well as its great opponent, the Achaean League – played a major role in the politics of Hellenistic Greece. Its origins can be traced back to the late 5th century BC, when Aetolia initially established some sort of federal government. The *koinon* had both tribal and city members. Foreign policy was in the hands of the federal state. The confederacy held two annual meetings (*Thermika* and *Panaitolika*), to determine the league's policy and to elect military commanders. As early as 327, a federal *boule* is attested, and it is clear that this council served as the administrative body. This constitutional framework was the basis for further development of the federal state in the 3rd century, when its territory expanded considerably. While maintaining a remarkable degree of local autonomy, new members (such as the Lokrian district) were conceded an equivalent status to the genuine Aetolian tribes and cities. More distant members were granted the status of *isopoliteia* (state with reciprocal civil rights). Consequently, the federal council soon grew from its original extent to a size of possibly up to 1000 representatives. For practical reasons, a certain number of these served as executive councillors (*apokletoi*). The chief magistrates were the *strategos* and the *hipparchos* (cavalry commander), both elected by the federal primary assembly in Thermon. In the 2nd century BC the Aetolian League increasingly came under Roman power. After the reduction of its territory to Aetolia proper in 167, the federal state lost its sovereignty and was finally incorporated into the province of Achaea under the principate.

The federal constitution of Achaea goes back to the 5th century BC. The early confederacy appears to have been divided into 12 *merea* (units), each of which sent a contingent of delegates to the federal board of *damiourgoi* and to the oligarchic assembly at Aigion. By 389 the league had adopted a system of double citizenship: in that year the *koinon* incorporated Naupactus on the north coast of the Corinthian gulf by granting federal citizenship to its inhabitants. After 324 the league seems to have been broken up by Demetrius, but it was revived in 281/80 on the initiative of four Achaean cities (Pharae, Dyme, Tritaea, Patrae). The newly established federal state soon rose to great prominence. From 251, when Sicyon joined, the league gradually expanded and finally embraced the whole of the Peloponnese. Its main political body was the representative council, the *synodos*, assembling at Aigion. Additionally, there existed a federal primary assembly, the *synkletos*, which was concerned with extraordinary business. In both the *synodoi* and the *synkletoi*, votes were taken by individual cities. The league's executive rested with the annual board of ten *damiourgoi* and two *strategoi* (after 255 BC reduced to one). Election took place in the *archairesiai* (election meetings) of the Achaean citizens. With Roman support, the federal state became the most important single power in mainland Greece in the 2nd century BC. However, economic crisis and class struggle soon led to strained relations and to open resistance against Rome. In 146 the Achaean federal state was dissolved by Lucius Mummius. Like the late Boeotian *koinon*, it continued to serve as a community for cultural and religious ceremonies, until the province of Achaea was established in 27 BC.

HANS BECK

See also Boeotia, Orchomenus, Thebes

Further Reading

Aigner Foresti, Luciano (editor), *Federazioni e federalismo nell'Europa antica*, vol. 1: *Alle radici della casa comune europea*, Milan: Vita e Pensiero, 1994

Alcock, Susan E., *Graecia Capta: The Landscapes of Roman Greece*, Cambridge and New York: Cambridge University Press, 1993

Beck, Hans, *Polis und Koinon: Untersuchungen zur Geschichte und Struktur der griechischen Bundesstaaten im 4. Jahrhundert. v. Chr.*, Stuttgart: Steiner, 1997

Buck, Robert J., *A History of Boeotia*, Edmonton: University of Alberta Press, 1979

Buckler, John, *The Theban Hegemony, 371–362 BC*, Cambridge, Massachusetts: Harvard University Press, 1980

Buckler, John, "Federalism: Greek and American", *Journal of Liberal Arts*, 2 (1995): pp. 5–16

Busolt, Georg, *Griechische Staatskunde*, 2 vols, Munich: Beck, 1920–26

Ehrenberg, Victor, *The Greek State*, 2nd edition, London: Methuen, 1969

Giovannini, Adalberto, *Untersuchungen über die Natur und die Anfänge der bundesstaatlichen Sympolitie in Griechenland*, Göttingen: Vandenhoeck & Ruprecht, 1971

Grainger, John D., *The League of the Aitolians*, Leiden: Brill, 1999

Hansen, Mogens Herman and Kurt Raaflaub (editors), *More Studies in the Ancient Greek Polis*, Stuttgart: Steiner, 1996

Hansen, Mogens Herman (editor), *The Polis as an Urban Centre and as a Political Community*, Copenhagen: Munksgaard, 1997

Helly, Bruno, *L'Etat thessalien: Aleuas le Roux, les tétrades et les "Tagoi"*, Lyon: Maison de l'Orient Méditerranée, 1995

Larsen, Jakob A.O., "The Early Achaean League" in *Studies Presented to David Moore Robinson on his Seventieth Birthday*, vol. 2, edited by George E. Mylonas, St Louis, Missouri: Washington University, 1953

Larsen, Jakob A.O., *Representative Government in Greek and Roman History*, Berkeley: University of California Press, 1955

Larsen, Jakob A.O., *Greek Federal States: Their Institutions and History*, Oxford: Clarendon Press, 1968

Lehmann, Gustav Adolf, "Erwägungen zur Struktur des Achaiischen Bundesstaates", *Zeitschrift für Papyrologie und Epigraphik*, 51 (1983): pp. 237–61

Sprawski, Slawomir, *Jason of Pherae*, Krakow: Krakow University Press, 1999

Walbank, F.W., *A Historical Commentary on Polybius*, 3 vols, Oxford: Clarendon Press, 1957–79

Walbank, F.W., "Were There Greek Federal States?", *Scripta Classica Israelica*, 3 (1976–7): pp. 27–51

Westlake, H.D., *Thessaly in the Fourth Century BC*, London: Methuen, 1935

Festivals

Antiquity

In a society that did not have the modern system of weeks – and accordingly, weekends – regularly recurring festivals offered opportunities not only for repose and entertainment, but also for maintaining contact with one's fellow citizens, and, on a more practical level, for eating meat. It is estimated that more than 60 days out of the Athenian year of 360 days were given over to festivals, when normal business – at least of an official nature – was suspended (the equivalent of our bank holidays). This compares well enough to modern western practice.

The Greek word for festival was *heorte*, which was used for most communal celebrations with a religious component. This would involve a sacrifice, conducted usually in the deity's sanctuary. This meant that the sacrificial beast had to be brought to the place of sacrifice, a requirement that easily developed into a procession (*pompe*), sometimes very elaborate, in which the beast was accompanied by the priest, the butcher, other cult and public officials, and the public. The Heraia of Argos, for example, began with a procession that led from the city across the Argive plain to the Heraion, which served to demonstrate to the people of the Argolid, and remind them of the fact, that the Argolid belonged to Argos.

The essential feature of any festival was the actual gathering of people to participate, and, depending on the nature of the celebration, to watch. The supposed birthdays of gods and heroes were marked by celebrations, monthly and/or annual. Many festivals marked stages in the agricultural cycle. Such was the basis of the various Dionysiac rites celebrated during the late winter and early spring, to signal – and in some cases to stimulate – the reawakening of plant and animal life after the rigours of winter: Lenaia, Dionysia, Thyia, Agrionia. Similarly, the successful growing of grain was the goal of a whole series of rituals focused on Demeter and Kore Persephone, the most notorious of which were the Thesmophoria, a rite restricted to women.

There were other rites in which participation was restricted. These included festivals devoted either wholly or in part to the initiation of new members into a relatively closed community. Mystery rites – *teletai* – are one example of this kind of festival. The best known were those at Eleusis and Samothrace, which admitted initiates regardless of citizenship. Then there were the various rites of passage from one age group to another in the course of progression from childhood to full citizenship, which were part of larger local festivals. Thus at Athens one day of the Apatouria was given over to the admission of ephebes to the status of manhood, while something similar lies behind the confused rituals of the Spartan *agoge* (education system).

Festivals might range from relatively simple commemorations to full-scale celebrations, with formal procession, sacrifice, competitions (*agones*), and an attendant market and fair (*agora*). The inscription that sets out the arrangements for the festival connected with the celebration of the mysteries at Andania in Messenia is a mine of information. It dates from 92 BC, when one Mnasistratos, to whose family the operation of the mysteries had been entrusted in the past, turned over the operation of the cult to the state. We learn that, in addition to the initiatory ceremonies proper, there were extensive public celebrations. The sanctuary was out in the countryside, and arrangements had to be made to house, feed, water, bathe, and police the multitude who came. All we are really told about the mysteries is that new initiates were sworn in by former initiates – male and female – and that all of them had to dress in specific kinds of clothing. The "open" festival included a procession in which all the officiants as well as the priests and priestesses of other sanctuaries in the region took part, and in which sacrificial beasts were escorted. There was a sacred feast from the meat of the sacrificed animals, and performances of music and dancing. Close attention is paid to the regulations for the market, which was clearly an important feature of the festival. The whole – festival, mysteries, market – was open to men, women, children, free or servile (indeed, an area was set aside for slaves to seek refuge).

The term *panegyris* (an Aeolic form meaning literally "gathering of all") is reserved for festivals with a wider than purely local appeal. It appears in a fragment attributed (possibly falsely) to Archilochus, which refers to a *panegyris* of Demeter and Kore (fr. 322 West). An early description of such a festival – although it does not employ the actual word – is the gathering of Ionians with their children and wives on Delos, where, according to the author of the *Homeric Hymn to Apollo*, they regularly delighted the heart of the god with competitions in boxing, dancing, and song. The festivities also included hymns sung by the girls of Delos in honour of Apollo and Artemis and their mother Leto.

From the other end of antiquity we have a long inscription from Oenoanda in Lycia, dating from the reign of Hadrian, which records the foundation of a *panegyris* by a local tycoon (Caius Julius Demosthenes). The document gives a detailed account of the programme of events of a musical and theatrical (thymelic) agon. The festival was spread over 22 days beginning on the first day of the month (in high summer) with a competition for trumpeters and heralds (essential features of any festival: the victorious trumpeter would summon the multitude, the herald would announce the programme and dispense other information). The second to fourth days were reserved for public business: meetings of the council and assembly of the polis. The first competitions proper (the sequence and range of competitions are more or less identical in surviving victors' lists from all over the Greek-speaking world) were held on the fifth, when composers of prose encomia (probably in honour of members of the imperial family and important local people) competed. The sixth day was given over to the market. On the seventh day epic poets competed, on the eighth and ninth aulos players with chorus, and on the tenth and eleventh comic poets. On the twelfth day of the month there was a sacrifice to Apollo Patroos (patron god of the polis), followed on the thirteenth and fourteenth by the competitions of tragic poets, and on the fifteenth by a second sacrifice to Apollo Patroos. Singers with cithara accompaniment competed on the sixteenth and seventeenth days, and the agon proper ended on the eighteenth with a final open competition for all (perhaps all the victors in preceding competitions). For all these, prizes were awarded, in most cases to those who finished second as well as first. From the nineteenth to the twenty-first, hired mimes, singers, and other entertainers performed, but not in competition, and finally on the twenty-second day there were gymnastic events open to citizens (the inclusion of a few athletic competitions in musical festivals – and vice versa – is not unusual under the empire). During this *panegyris*, which took place in the theatre, the agonothete (president of the competition), priests, functionaries, civic dignitaries, and representatives from surrounding towns and villages processed through the theatre, and each individual group sacrificed according to a fixed schedule. There were penalties for non-participation.

The earliest competitive festivals (*agones*) we read of are the funeral games in honour of Amphidamas of Chalcis, presumably a real person (Hesiod, *Works and Days*, 650–59), and the fictional games for Amaryntheus of Epeia (*Iliad*, 23. 629–45) and Patroclus, the last vividly described in *Iliad*, 23. 297–897. Such games would naturally have been casual occasions, but they provided the model for games celebrated annually in honour of heroes. The Herakleia were celebrated at about the time of the winter solstice, when the people of Boeotia performed public rites in honour of those who had died in the service of the state.

The best-known ancient Greek festivals were the four great Panhellenic gatherings at Olympia, Delphi, the sanctuary of Poseidon at the Isthmus of Corinth, and the sanctuary of Zeus at Nemea. Each of these sanctuaries was well placed to be a centre for an interstate festival: Olympia was at the confluence of the rivers Cladeus and Alpheus, and, as its name reveals, it was at the southern end of a land route used by transhumant herdsmen, linking the Peloponnese with the north and north-east of the Greek mainland, where Mount Olympus looms. Similarly, Delphi is at the southern end of an overland corridor joining the north to the Gulf of Corinth. Both Olympia and Delphi were also easily accessible by sea to the Greek settlements in the west, a fact that greatly accelerated the pace and extent of their growth from local to interstate/Panhellenic meeting place. Isthmia is at the southern end of the portage across the Isthmus, which linked the gulf of Corinth and the Saronic gulf. Nemea, although at first glance of lesser importance, in fact lies astride a major north–south land route in the Peloponnese.

All of these festivals – Olympia, Pythia, Isthmia, Nemea – began as purely local operations. The first to attract a wider clientele was Olympia, where the list of victors in the stadium race begins at 776 BC, a date that more or less matches the archaeological record. The Olympian games probably began relatively simply, with the foot race, other competitions being added as time passed. During its early years the Argives and Spartans were major patrons; in the early Classical period much interest was shown by rich and powerful Hellenes from Sicily and southern Italy. The Pythian games traditionally began with a single competition, the performance of a hymn in honour of Apollo. By early in the 6th century BC (traditionally after the so-called First Sacred War), the Pythia, which had originally been celebrated at intervals of eight years, had become, like the Olympic games, pentaeteric, that is, they were celebrated every four years (every five by the inclusive reckoning used in antiquity). Furthermore, athletic contests were added to the musical ones (the Olympic games, on the other hand, remained strictly athletic). Delphi too attracted the patronage of Sicilians and Italians. At about the same time – c.582 BC – the Isthmian games became Panhellenic, to be followed a few years later (c.573 BC) by the Nemean games. Both the Isthmian and the Nemean games were trieteric, celebrated every second year. The Isthmia were originally athletic only, with musical competitions being attested from the 3rd century BC. The Nemean games included both musical and athletic contests. The games of the cycle – the *periodos* – were preceded and followed by a Sacred Truce, so that competitors and visitors might have safe passage to and fro (not so much a "truce" as we know it, rather an agreement not to seize the persons or property of people travelling to and from the site of the festival: in later antiquity these arrangements were not limited to the Periodic games). Olympic and Pythian games were held at the same time of year (late August/early September) with a two-year interval between them; the Isthmian games were held in April/May of every Olympian/Pythian year, and the Nemean games in July of every off-year, giving, for example, the following sequence for an Olympiad:

488 BC Olympia and Isthmia; 487 BC Nemea; 486 BC Pythia and Isthmia; 485 BC Nemea; 484 BC Olympia and Isthmia.

These contests were what was later called *stephanitai*, that is, the prize for victory was not monetary, but in the form of a wreath (*stephanos*), of wild olive for the Olympia, bay leaves for the Pythia, pine, later dry celery for the Isthmia, and fresh celery for the Nemea. Victors in these games could count on receiving more material rewards at home, in recompense for the glory they brought their communities: at Athens, for example, victors at the Olympic games (at least those well enough off to have entered a horse or chariot) were fed at public expense in the Prytaneum. The glory of such victories is also reflected in the epinician odes commissioned from such poets as Simonides, Bacchylides, and Pindar.

The polis of Elis was responsible for the Olympic games. The Pythian games, like the Delphic oracle, were governed by a genuine interstate body, the Delphic amphictyony. The Nemean games seem to have begun as a festival shared between the towns of Cleonae and Phlious, but eventually came under the control of Argos. The Isthmian games were Corinthian, except during the period 156–44 BC when Corinth lay in ruins and the direction of the games was assumed by Argos. (Argos became one of the two headquarters – the other being Thebes – of the guild of actors and musicians called the "Isthmian and Nemean Artists of Dionysus": these Hellenistic guilds – the other major associations were the Athenian guild and the guild of artists of Ionia and the Hellespont – ensured the participation of professional competitors at agons great and small.) Despite the fact that three out of four of these festivals were run by a single state, all four reached and held the status of interstate, Panhellenic festival, probably because they were clearly tied to the rural sanctuary in which they were held, rather than to the state itself. By contrast, the Panathenaia of Athens, founded or expanded in the 6th century BC, which included both musical and athletic contests, and for which huge amphorae were given as prizes, never reached true Panhellenic status. This was probably because they were too closely linked with Athens: the name itself was a form of propaganda.

A significant change in the world of Greek competitive festivals came with the institution of the Soteria at Delphi, first founded to celebrate the defeat of the Gallic invasion of 279/78 BC, and in the mid-3rd century BC refounded as a pentaeteric festival of Panhellenic pretensions by the dominant Aetolian League. This started a veritable flood of new festivals, many of them pentaeteric, throughout the Hellenistic world, whose organizers sought acceptance of their new or enhanced status from the Aeolian-controlled Delphic amphictyony, as well as from any other political power that would grant it. The main attraction of these games for competitors was the prizes, usually in the form of wreaths of gold or silver. The holding of such a festival and its acceptance became an important feature of international relations during the Hellenistic period, and it is probably true to say that these festivals were one of the most powerful instruments in fostering and maintaining Hellenic identity in late antiquity.

Modern Times

The festivals of the modern Greek year reflect the needs of the changing seasons, as did many in antiquity, but now within the framework of the Orthodox Church. Again, as in antiquity, there are many local variations, as well as celebrations that might truly be called Panhellenic. A good example is the series of rites over the 12 days of Christmas, which include mummers' shows and rituals aimed at averting evil spirits. Many of the festivals are concerned with ensuring the fertility of crops, kine, and mankind, and there are numerous occasions on which the graves of the dead are visited and adorned. These rites and others recall ancient practice, and it is possible, in specific cases, to identify a modern festival with an ancient predecessor; here and there even animal sacrifice survives. But all this is at a local level, and it would be wrong to posit any system of direct survival. What has survived are not the individual festivals, but the underlying Hellenic preoccupations with physical well-being in a difficult environment, spiritual comfort in an uncertain world, and survival of the *ethnos* (nation). The Church has been the great unifying factor, both at the Panhellenic level and locally, where a multitude of saints (many of them multi-faceted) has assumed the age-old function of local heroes.

The modern festival year follows the agricultural seasons, beginning with St Demetrius' Day (26 October), which coincides with the opening and tasting of the new wine. This precedes the sowing of the main cereal crops, the midpoint of which is marked on 21 November by the festival of the *Eisodia tis Theotokou* (Entry of the Virgin). The festivals of the *Dodekameron* (the Twelve Days), from 12 December to 6 January , include feasting on Christmas Eve, special tending of the graves of the dead, rites to avert the evil spirits (*Kallikantzaroi*), and others to welcome the new year under the auspices of St Basil. It ends with Epiphany, the day of Christ's baptism, which signals a new beginning and is in many places accompanied by the opening of new wine.

The three-week period preceding Lent is the season of Carnival (*Apokreos*). There is much feasting, and the performance of masquerades by wandering groups of players, which recalls the rustic *komoi* of ancient Attica. The 40 days of Lent are punctuated by rites to honour the dead and commemorate the triumph of the faith. At the same time, the beginning of March is regarded in many places as the real beginning of summer and so celebrated, and of course 25 March, Independence Day and Feast of the Annunciation, is a special national festival throughout the Greek world.

Easter rites abound from the day before Palm Sunday over Easter itself and throughout the entire following week. Another Panhellenic day of celebration is 23 April, St George's Day, marked not only by the usual festivities but also by athletic games. May Day is celebrated as a festival of spring, symbolized in many places by a maypole procession. But the most important festival in May is the *Anastenaria* (21 May), the feast of SS Constantine and Helena: among the highlights are processions, dancing, and the sacrifice of bulls and rams.

The month of June is given over to the harvest, and consequently there is little time for elaborate festivals, although rituals aimed specifically at the harvest are conducted: 24 June, the birthday of St John the Baptist, is celebrated by the lighting of bonfires. July is the month of threshing, and this too has its special rites, but the major festival is that of the Prophet Elijah on 20 July. Many of his rites take place on mountain tops, and it is clear that the prophet has inherited characteristics of Zeus (the farmer's god) and Helios (the sun god). The main festival of August is the Dormition of the Virgin Mary (15 August), a time of pilgrimage, while September brings both the vintage and the Exaltation of the Cross (14 September), which is the turning point from one agricultural year to the next.

ALBERT SCHACHTER

See also Fairs and Markets, Fasts, Games and Sports, Sacrifice

Further Reading

Megas, George A., *Greek Calendar Customs*, 2nd edition, Athens, 1963

Mikalson, Jon, *The Sacred and Civil Calendar of the Athenian Year*, Princeton, New Jersey: Princeton University Press, 1975

Nilsson, Martin P., *Griechische Feste von religiöser Bedeutung*, Leipzig: Teubner, 1906

Parke, H.W., *Festivals of the Athenians*, London: Thames and Hudson, and Ithaca, New York: Cornell University Press, 1977

Polignac, François de, *Cults, Territory, and the Origins of the Greek City-State*, translated by Janet Lloyd, Chicago: University of Chicago Press, 1995

Raschke, Wendy J. (editor), *The Archaeology of the Olympics: The Olympics and Other Festivals in Antiquity*, Madison: University of Wisconsin Press, 1988

Sokolowski, Franciszek (editor), *Lois sacrées des cités grecques*, Paris: Boccard, 1969

Wörrle, Michael, *Stadt und Fest im kaiserzeitlichen Kleinasien*, Munich: Beck, 1988; also the review article by S. Mitchell, *Journal of Roman Studies*, 80 (1990): pp. 183–93

Finance

Finance is the process by which individuals or groups collect and expend funds. This article focuses on governmental revenue and expenditure.

The earliest preserved financial documents from Greece are records of inventories and payments dating to the Mycenaean period (*c.*1600–1100 BC). Mycenaean Greece was organized into kingdoms staffed by officials who collected mandatory contributions from the king's subjects. Payments were made "in kind", i.e. in the form of produce such as grain or objects such as axes. Some of this revenue was used to support the royal household and the military. The remainder was redistributed to the kingdom's subjects in proportion to each individual's position in the political hierarchy.

After the collapse of Mycenaean civilization, both government and finance were greatly simplified. A king with strictly limited powers drew revenue from a piece of public land called a *temenos*, the produce of which was given over to him as long as he held power. Significant gains were also won through war and piracy. The king's financial responsibilities included funding military and religious activities and the entertainment of local nobles and foreign visitors.

Around 800 BC more complex state forms emerged. A sense of the different kinds of financial arrangements which were found in Greece thereafter can be had by looking at three examples: Sparta, Athens under Pisistratus, and Athens under democratic rule.

The Spartan state was controlled by a military elite, the members of which neither worked nor paid taxes. They were supported by serfs called helots who tilled the estates of the elite and who were required to provide specified amounts of various foods to their master's household. No other regular taxes existed except for small gifts made to the kings. This remarkable absence of taxation was possible because governmental apparatus was minimal. The lack of revenue sources was, however, a problem in wartime when military expenses had to be met, sometimes only with difficulty, from the contributions of Sparta's allies, from the sale of booty, and from voluntary offerings by Spartan citizens.

Athens under Pisistratus presents a very different picture. Pisistratus became sole ruler (tyrant) of Athens in 546 BC. The primary source of revenue for his government was a tax on agricultural produce. State expenditures included the maintenance of police and military forces, the completion of a substantial building programme, and the celebration of religious ceremonies. A key feature of this financial system was the imposition of a direct tax on all inhabitants of Athens. (Direct taxes are levied on an individual's income or personal wealth. Indirect taxes are levied on services or transactions. Income taxes are an example of the former, sales taxes of the latter.) The obligation to pay direct taxes was seen as a form of subservience and thus as a sign of despotic rule.

The democratic government which came to power in Athens in 514 BC kept elaborate records, many of which are preserved. These, along with contemporary literary sources, provide unusually detailed evidence about financial practices.

The revenue of the Athenian state in the mid-5th century BC came from five sources: rents on state property, indirect taxes, direct taxes, tribute, and liturgies (see table). While indirect taxes were paid by all Athenians, direct taxes were normally paid only by resident aliens, each of whom was required to pay a yearly fee (a "head tax"). The Athenian state also derived revenue from the tribute it extracted from its allies. (Liturgies are discussed below.)

Revenue Source	percentage of Revenue Supplied
Rents on State Property	15
Indirect Taxes	15
Direct Taxes	5
Tribute	50
Liturgies	15

The revenues of the Athenian state were expended as follows. About 35 per cent of the total was used to support the military. Public works, particularly the massive building project which produced the Parthenon, consumed another 20 per cent. The internal administration of Athens involved the paid participation of thousands of citizens and thus resulted in heavy expenses for jurors (12 per cent) and for various other officials (7 per cent). Expenditures for religious ceremonies (10 per cent), for the support of orphans and invalids, and for the police force (about 6 per cent each) made up most of the rest.

In wartime, expenses increased significantly; this frequently put Athens in a difficult financial position, and upon occasion an emergency property tax (*eisphora*) was levied on all residents including citizens.

The administrative machinery which organized Athenian finance was quite simple. Governmental budgeting – projecting and adjusting total future revenue and expenses – did not make its appearance in Greece until the 19th century AD. All earlier governments administered their finances through "earmarking"; the proceeds of individual sources of revenue were kept in separate funds each of which was used to pay for one or more predetermined types of expenditure. This union of taxing and spending is reflected in the institution of liturgies. Many tasks of the Athenian state, including such items as the maintenance of warships, were carried out by assigning the task to a wealthy citizen. The liturgist was legally bound to supply all necessary expenses to complete the assigned project.

Of the three financial systems discussed above, the one used by Pisistratid Athens proved to be the most durable. The financial organization of the kingdoms which ruled most of Greece after the 4th century BC closely resembled that of Pisistratid Athens, despite obvious differences in scale. Revenues came from a direct agricultural tax on the entire population and were spent largely on maintaining the military and the leader's entourage.

This pattern of taxation and expenditure was remarkably persistent, existing well into the 19th century AD in spite of numerous changes in Greece's political situation. The revenues of the Byzantine empire were drawn primarily from direct imposts in the form of a land tax and a head tax. Of this revenue 80 per cent was expended on the military with most of the rest going to pay for public buildings, ceremonies and games, and the upkeep of the royal court. The Ottoman Turks made only minor changes in the system which they found in operation when they seized control of Greece in the 15th century. The same can be said of the various parties who ruled Greece in the first years of independence.

It was only in the 19th century that substantive changes in patterns of revenue and expenditure were implemented. The establishment of a national government organized along western European lines led to more thoroughgoing oversight by the state, beginning with a board of financial control (created October 1833).

In spite of the fundamental changes in the financial system of Greece which took place after the end of Turkish rule, a strong element of continuity with ancient practice is observable today. With the achievement of independence, a distaste for direct taxation resurfaced. The close parallel to the cessation of direct taxation on citizens in Athens after the establishment of the democratic government is significant. Direct taxation was associated with Turkish rule and was largely suppressed in favour of indirect alternatives. This predilection for indirect taxation continues to influence the financial practices of the Greek state. About 65 per cent of the national budget (excluding social insurance) is provided by indirect imposts whereas most European states derive the majority of their revenue from direct taxes.

PAUL CHRISTESEN

See also Taxation

Further Reading

Andreades, A.M., *A History of Greek Public Finance*, 2nd edition, Cambridge, Massachusetts: Harvard University Press, 1933

Baynes, Norman H. and H. St. L.B. Moss (editors), *Byzantium: An Introduction to East Roman Civilization*, Oxford: Clarendon Press, 1948

Eulambio, M.S. *The National Bank of Greece: A History of the Financial and Economic Evolution of Greece*, Athens: Vlastos, 1924

Finlay, George, *A History of Greece from its Conquest by the Romans to the Present Time, BC 146 to AD 1864*, revised by H.F. Tozer, Oxford: Clarendon Press, 1877; reprinted New York: AMS Press, 1970, vol. 7

Goldsmith, Raymond W., *Premodern Financial Systems: A Historical Comparative Study*, Cambridge and New York: Cambridge University Press, 1987

Legg, Keith R. and John M. Roberts, *Modern Greece: A Civilization on the Periphery*, Boulder, Colorado: Westview Press, 1997

National Bank of Greece, *Economic and Statistical Bulletin*, 1975– (annual statistical survey)

Petropulos, John Anthony, *Politics and Statecraft in the Kingdom of Greece, 1833–1843*, Princeton, New Jersey: Princeton University Press, 1968

Treadgold, Warren T., *The Byzantine State Finances in the Eighth and Ninth Centuries*, Boulder, Colorado: East European Monographs, 1982

Webber, Carolyn and Aaron Wildavsky, *A History of Taxation and Expenditure in the Western World*, New York: Simon and Schuster, 1986

Fire, Greek

Although "Greek fire" was never called by that name by its Byzantine originators, who referred to themselves as Roman, this appellation was adopted centuries ago (though exactly when is uncertain) to describe the Byzantine naval super-weapon, used from the late 7th century until the empire fell in the 15th century, that consisted of a flame that was "thrown" from a pipe at the front of a ship. Although its exact composition is unknown, sources agree that – like modern-day napalm – Greek fire was capable of burning on water and would cling to any available surface, and that it was virtually inextinguishable except by means of sand, vinegar, or urine (which contains phosphates).

J.R. Partington, the foremost 20th-century authority on Greek fire, has suggested that the liquid used to produce this effect was probably rectified petroleum or volatile petrol, with resins or solid combustibles dissolved in it to thicken it to a jelly. Thickening increased the range of projection and the stability of the flame when it was shot through a leather or bronze hose. Sources disagree about its exact nature, but either the liquid ignited spontaneously upon contact with water or a small flame at the hose's mouth would light the material as it streamed past. A double-action pump on board the ship would keep the stream moving steadily.

Incendiary weapons were well known to the ancient world, and were often used in land warfare. Naphtha (naturally occurring petroleum) was contained in breakable containers, set alight, and tossed at the enemy, though this procedure does not seem to have enjoyed common usage until after the time of Alexander the Great. The first hint of something similar to Greek fire was described by Aeneas Tacticus around 360 BC. He described a mixture of pitch, sulphur, pine shavings, and incense or resin, and mentions that pots of the material were often thrown on to the decks of wooden ships. Pliny the Elder was struck by the fact that a mixture of quicklime with an inflammable substance such as naphtha will inflame spontaneously when wetted. In fact, anhydrous quicklime is a compound that can bind chemically with water to make another compound, forming molecular bonds to make up a crystalline structure called a hydrate. In the process of hydration it gives off heat. When the hydrate form is heated, energy is absorbed in breaking down the chemical bonds, and when the dehydrated form is again wetted, heat is given off when the crystalline structure reforms. The heat could then ignite the petroleum. This reaction may be the base of the story of Medea's assassination of the Corinthian princess Glauke by offering her a garment that burned her to death when she put it on: Medea's homeland, Colchis, has abundant naphtha resources.

Theophanes claims that the inventor of Greek fire as a naval weapon was Kallinikos, a Syrian from Damascus who sold the secret to the Byzantine emperor Constantine IV sometime around 672. Sources disagree about exactly what it was that Kallinikos sold; it might have been the formula for the mixture, or the method of shooting the mixture out of a siphon mounted on a ship's prow. When Muslim forces besieged Constantinople in 673, they were met with this devastating new weapon. In the year 680, at the Battle of Cyzicus, the Byzantine navy burned the entire flotilla of Syrian and Egyptian ships, and the seven-year siege was broken: the Muslims signed a 30-year truce. As the historian Aziz S. Atiya puts it, "The spell of the invincibility of the Arab broke down at the gates of Constantinople."

Both Arab and Greek sources agree that this weapon surpassed previous incendiaries in its destructive and demoralizing capacities, and the powerful effect of its introduction has been compared to the introduction of nuclear weapons in 1945. Since there are records of the Muslim forces using some form of Greek fire with catapults in combat as early as the year 683 (by the general Ibn 'Uqbah, at Mecca) and throughout the crusades, the military secret clearly applied to its use in naval combat only.

It might seem surprising that a Syrian would be willing to sell out his own country to the Byzantine empire until one remembers that Damascus had been a part of the empire until the city was taken by the Arabs in the year 635, and Syria itself was not conquered until the following year. Public accounts were still kept in Greek until the dawn of the 8th century, and Syrian society, after 1000 years of Graeco-Roman domination, remained very Byzantine in flavour. Muslim incursions into Byzantine territory began in 633, in the wake of several years of war between Byzantium and Persia. Persia had taken Antioch and Damascus in 613, Jerusalem in 614, and Egypt in 619; the Byzantine emperor Herakleios defeated the Persians in 630 and took back the territory, but both empires had been severely weakened by the struggle. The Byzantine army in Syria, led by Herakleios's brother Theodore, was exterminated by Muslim forces six years later. Jerusalem became Muslim in 637–38, and Egypt followed in 641. In 655 the Muslim forces enjoyed naval supremacy, having trounced the Byzantines off the coast of Asia Minor and captured the young Byzantine emperor Constans II. Constantine IV was Constans II's son, and thus was acutely aware of the need to strengthen Byzantium's naval forces when he purchased Kallinikos's invention.

Throughout the existence of the Byzantine empire the secret of Greek fire was guarded obsessively. The emperor Constantine VII (913–59) wrote to his son:

If you are ever asked to divulge information about the making of liquid fire discharged through tubes, you must reply, "This was revealed by God through an angel to the great and holy Constantine, the first Christian emperor. And we are assured by the faithful witness of our fathers and grandfathers that it should be manufactured among the Christians and in their capital city and nowhere else."

In 941 Constantinople was again defended, this time against the Russians. According to Liutprand of Cremona, whose nephew was then an ambassador to Constantinople, the Russian flotilla of several thousand ships was defeated by 15 "semifracta chelandria" which threw liquid fire from prow, stern, and sides. The Russians hurled themselves from the burning ships; those weighed down by their armour were drowned, and those who could swim were burned.

To add to the awesome effect, Byzantine shipmakers designed the prows of the ships to look like the heads of ferocious animals, from which the Greek fire would issue. It has been suggested that its use against Viking invaders in the 10th century in this manner led to northern tales of fire-breathing dragons.

Because of its originators' obsession with secrecy, Greek fire was long thought to be a lost art. It seems, however, to have adapted into other forms and to have found its way into artillery and gunpowder. In the earlier stages of development Greek fire and cannon were sometimes used together. By projecting flammable substances instead of cannon balls, fires were started within the walls of siege targets. It was used in some form in almost all wars, up to and including World War I in 1917.

SUSAN SPENCER

See also Warfare

Further Reading

Atiya, Aziz S., *Crusade, Commerce, and Culture*, Bloomington: Indiana University Press, 1962

Bilkadi, Zayn, "The Oil Weapons", *Aramco World*, January/February 1995

Glubb, John, *A Short History of the Arab Peoples*, New York: Stein and Day, and London: Hodder and Stoughton, 1969

Lewis, Archibald R. and Timothy J. Runyan, *European Naval and Maritime History, 300–1500*, Bloomington: Indiana University Press, 1985

Newark, Tim, *The Barbarians: Warriors and Wars of the Dark Ages*, Poole, Dorset: Blandford Press, 1985

Partington, J.R., *A History of Greek Fire and Gunpowder*, Cambridge: Heffer, 1960; reprinted Baltimore: Johns Hopkins University Press, 1999

Shaw, M.R.B. (translator), *Joinville and Villehardouin: Chronicles of the Crusades*, Harmondsworth: Penguin, 1963

Theophanes the Confessor, *The Chronicle of Theophanes: An English Translation of anni mundi 6095–6305 (AD 602–813)*, edited by Harry Turtledove, Philadelphia: University of Pennsylvania Press, 1982

Website

Meyer, Robert, *Greek Fire*, at http://pantheon.yale.edu/~robmeyer/greek_fire.html

Fishing

The Mediterranean is an enclosed sea, consisting of deep basins with poor water circulation and therefore limited distribution of nutrients. Annual evaporation rates exceed replacement from rivers and as a consequence the sea is saltier than waters of the north Atlantic. Sea temperatures are lower and the important commercial fish stocks of the Atlantic, such as cod and herring, are absent. In general, the Mediterranean is lacking in fertility and, although evidence is not conclusive, this appears always to have been the case despite changes to sea level in the Pleistocene–Holocene transition.

Although the seas of the Aegean and eastern Mediterranean are less fertile than the waters of the north Atlantic, they support a wide range of species. Over 1500 species of marine invertebrate are reported for the Mediterranean as a whole, and around 100 of these are edible. In Greek waters 447 species of marine fish have been recorded, comprising important pelagic species such as tuna, mackerel, and anchovies as well as a great variety of demersal species including the important families of Serranidae (grouper), Sparidae (sea bream), Labridae (wrasses), Mugilidae (mullet), and Scorpaenidae (scorpion fish). Numerous species of edible shark and ray exist, and turtles and marine mammals are also present. The variety of species means that fishermen are able to engage in diversified fishing and are not dependent on single species, whose stock levels may fluctuate annually and interannually.

A variety of fishing methods are recorded for antiquity, and archaeological evidence suggests that many of these methods go back into prehistory. Many of these fishing methods are still in use today. In the 2nd century AD the writer Oppian described four methods, namely the use of hooks, nets, weels (wicker basket traps), and tridents. Line fishing using hooks can employ a stationary line (as with the set line, the *paragathi*), a trolling line pulled behind a moving boat, or involve the use of a rod. Nets include simple nets (gill nets, cast nets, drag nets, and seine nets) or complex nets such as the three-walled *manomena*, a trammel net. The madrague (or *tratai*) is a specialized fishing method employed for catching tuna. A lookout alerts fishing boats to the arrival of a shoal of tuna and the fish are chased through a series of nets placed parallel to the coast until they reach a death chamber where they are gaffed. In the ensuing melee, many fish are killed by others in a frenzy. Aeschylus compared the slaughter of the Persians at Salamis to this fishing method. Weels, baskets, and pots are used to catch a range of fish and shellfish. Tridents were often employed at night with lights.

The earliest evidence for marine exploitation occurs at the littoral zone. Eels are generally caught by trapping and these

Fishing: fisherman mending his nets, one of 13,000 Greeks still fishing by non-mechanized methods

and demersal and littoral species dominate the earliest evidence during the Final Palaeolithic and Early Mesolithic. Evidence for the use of boats corresponds with the appearance of tuna remains, together with obsidian from the island of Melos, in Upper Mesolithic levels at Franchthi Cave in the southern Argolid. The two key sites for the prehistoric period are Franchthi Cave and the Cave of Cyclops on the island of Youra in the north Aegean. Youra has produced the largest known collection of bone fish hooks and fish gorges for any period in Greece. At both sites the proportion of fish remains in the total food refuse declines dramatically at the beginning of the Neolithic.

Iconography during the Bronze Age is an important source of information about fishing and marine exploitation. The Minoans and the residents of Akrotiri (Thera, modern Santorini) were fond of marine imagery and the fresco of the fisherboys at Akrotiri shows a mixed catch of dolphin fish (*Coryphaena hippurus*) and mackerel (*Scomber sp.*). The extraction of purple dye from the shellfish *Murex brandaris* occurs from Middle Minoan times. The set line or *paragathi* is also attested from Middle Minoan times, and lead weights that could well have been used for trammel nets date from the Late Bronze Age.

Homer's heroes did not eat fish, but whether this reflects a common practice or is simply an indication of the social status attached to various foods is unclear. The poems do, however, make mention of spears, nets, rods, and handlines which suggests that fishing was widely practised. The low status of fishermen is apparent in later periods, as they are commonly the object of jokes in comic theatre.

Classical Greece, or more particularly Athens in the 5th century BC, imported a broad range of foodstuffs, and expensive fish were part of the conspicuous consumption of the urban wealthy elite. Greek food consisted of staples like bread (*sitos*), drink notably wine (*poton*), and *opson*, the relish that accompanied these staples. The term *opson* survives in modern Greek as the word for fish, *to psari*.

Some of the most important "relishes" that accompanied food were fermented fish products such as *tarikos*, known to the Romans as *garum* or *salsamentum*. The earliest mention of salted fish is in the Hippocratic Corpus and the first mention of fish sauce is in Dioscurides, but Greeks no doubt ate salted and preserved fish well before these literary references. A 5th-century BC house at Corinth produced Punic amphorae, the sherds of which have preserved fish attached. Various species of fish and shellfish could be used in the process and the result is comparable with the modern Vietnamese fish sauce, *nuoc-mam*. No fish-processing centres have yet been excavated in Greece, although salting factories are known for the Roman period. Roman fish tanks are found in eastern Crete at Siteia,

Chersonisos, and Mochlos. Such facilities could have been used to breed or store fish, but at none of these sites is there evidence for associated salting facilities.

Greece continues to have the most artisanal of all the fisheries of the European Economic Union. In 1990 full-time professional fishermen numbered around 20,000. Of these, 13,000 were involved in small-scale and local fishing, employing mainly artisanal, non-mechanized fishing methods. Besides these statistics on professional fishermen it is important to note that since 1970 catch and employment statistics have not included vessels with a motor of 19 horsepower or less, yet such boats are estimated to number approximately 12,000 and have an average monthly production of 150–200 kg per vessel. Accurate catch data are therefore difficult to obtain, but for the official statistical group of fishermen the total catch for 1990 was 112,202 metric tons. Key species in this catch included anchovies (14,668.6 metric tons) and pilchards (11,053 metric tons). Although 55 species were identified, 11,451.7 metric tons of the annual catch is simply recorded as "other species".

In terms of fish landed, the most important fishing grounds in Greece today are the Thermaic gulf, the gulf of Chalcidice, the Strymonian gulf, the gulf of Kavala, the gulf of Lamia, and the gulf of north and south Euboea. The Argolid and Saronic gulfs, the seas around the Cyclades and the islands of Lesbos, Chios, Samos, and Icaria, and the seas of Crete also produce significant catches.

JUDITH POWELL

See also Food and Drink

Further Reading

Curtis, Robert I., *Garun and Salsamenta: Production and Commerce in Materia Medica*, Leiden and New York: Brill, 1991
Dalby, Andrew, *Siren Feasts: A History of Food and Gastronomy in Greece*, New York and London: Routledge, 1997
Davidson, Alan, *Mediterranean Seafood: A Handbook Giving the Names in Seven Languages of 150 Species of Fish, with 50 Crustaceans, Molluscs and Other Marine Creatures, and an Essay on Fish Cookery Followed by 200 Mediterranean Recipes*, Harmondsworth: Penguin, 1972
Gallant, T.W., *A Fisherman's Tale*, Ghent: Belgian Archaeological Mission in Greece, 1985
Powell, Judith, *Fishing in the Prehistoric Aegean*, Jonsered: Åström, 1996
Thompson, D'Arcy Wentworth, *A Glossary of Greek Fishes*, London: Oxford University Press, 1947
Whitehead, P.J.P. et al., *Fishes of the North-eastern Atlantic and the Mediterranean*, Paris: UNESCO, 1984–89
Wilkins, John, David Harvey and Mike Dobson, *Food in Antiquity*, Exeter: University of Exeter Press, 1995

Florina

City in western Macedonia

According to the 14th-century memoirs of John Kantakouzenos, while Byzantium was facing a Serbian invasion in Macedonia in 1334, a notable from Constantinople, Sphrantzes Palaiologos, was appointed to the command of a province consisting of four small towns in western Macedonia,

Chlerenon, Soskos, Staridola, and Debre. The first-mentioned among them, Chlerenon, can be safely identified with Florina, being the original Slavic name of the town, which is still known as Lerin in Slavonic languages. Florina is the later, Ottoman, name of the town which was also adopted by the Greeks.

The mention of Florina in the text of Kantakouzenos is the earliest record of the town which had remained in obscurity until then. The town's insignificance is also reflected by the absence of any high ecclesiastical authority there. Florina remained under the jurisdiction of the bishop of Prespa until the late 19th century when it was transferred to the diocese of Moglena. However, efforts were made by the Bulgarian exarchate to establish a metropolitan see of its own in Florina in the late 19th century.

The town is described for the first time in an Ottoman fiscal register of 1481. According to the data it provides, Florina had a population of approximately 1201 people (981 Christian, 220 Muslim). The Christian element of Florina's population was of a mainly Slavic ethnic character, as suggested by the personal names recorded. The same register points to an economy based on agriculture, as most of the town's fiscal revenue was of an agrarian provenance. In later centuries the town retained the agrarian basis of its economy, with commerce and handicrafts catering for local demands. Yet, the proximity of Florina to the principal land route which followed the course of the Roman Via Egnatia facilitated its contact with adjacent and more distant regions. Florina had grown bigger by the second half of the 17th century when it is described by Evliya Çelebi as having 1500 houses (which corresponds to a population of about 7500 people), 14 mosques, three religious colleges (madrasas), and one dervish convent (*teke*).

The Christian population of Florina and the surrounding area was primarily Slavic, though the Vlachs had a considerable presence, and other ethnic groups, such as Greeks and Armenians, were no doubt represented during the Middle Ages and the centuries of Ottoman rule. The people of Florina were receptive to Greek cultural influences, first from the Greek-dominated Orthodox Church, then through the establishment of Greek schools during the 19th century. The intensification of Greek cultural influence coincided with the age of nation-building ideas. As a result, the adoption of Greek cultural features, including the language, first bilingually then exclusively, was accompanied by the building of a Greek national identity among people of different ethnic backgrounds, including a percentage of the Slavs, in the district of Florina. Bulgarian reaction in the late 19th century led to strong rivalry in the areas of religion and education as the Bulgarians established their own institutions in order to counteract Greek progress in shaping local national sentiment. This Graeco-Bulgarian confrontation culminated in fighting which was particularly intense in the district of Florina between 1904 and 1908.

After Florina was incorporated into Greece in 1912, the Hellenization of the local Slavs progressed rapidly as there was no alternative for educational and ecclesiastical purposes, while the arrival of Greek settlers including refugees from Turkey enforced the already existing Greek or Hellenized element. Nevertheless, a considerable proportion of the Slavic population strongly resisted the processes of assimilation and made the district of Florina one of the very few regions in Greek Macedonia where the presence of a minority created serious problems (31 per cent of the population in the district of Florina are recorded as Slavic speakers in the census of 1928). The Slavic communities of the district of Florina finally disappeared after the Greek Civil War (1946–49), as most of them sided with the leftist Democratic Army of Greece and had to flee the country facing defeat. The rest were completely assimilated to the virtual extinction of Slavic ethnicity in this region of Macedonia where it had been particularly strong. The recent history of Florina demonstrates the effectiveness and success of Greek policies and processes of assimilation.

KONSTANTINOS P. MOUSTAKAS

Summary

The city of Florina in western Macedonia is first recorded in 1334, and by 1481 it had a population of about 1200. Proximity to the Via Egnatia encouraged commercial expansion in subsequent centuries. Its Christian population was largely Slav and by the late 19th century there was serious rivalry between Greeks and Bulgarians for cultural influence. Slavs remained a significant minority until after the Civil War of 1946–49.

Further Reading

Kravari, Vassiliki, *Villes et villages de Macédoine occidentale*, Paris: Lethielleux, 1989

Regos A., *I B' Elliniki Dimokratia (1924–35): Koinonikes Diastaseis tis Politikis Skinis* [The Second Greek Republic, 1924–35: Social Dimensions of the Political Scene], Athens, 1988

Sokoloski, Metodija, *Turski Dokumenti za Istorijata na Makedonskiot Narod/ Documents turcs sur l'histoire du peuple Macedonien*, vol. 2, Skopje: Arhiv na Makedonija, 1973

Vacalopoulos, A.E., *History of Macedonia, 1354–1833*, Thessalonica: Institute for Balkan Studies, 1973

Folklore

Laographia is the term coined in 1884 by Nikolaos Politis, the noted Greek folklorist, to denote the systematic and scientific study of folk traditions, beliefs, customs, and oral literature, as he noted in his definition of the term published in the journal *Laographia*. Politis arrived at the term after thorough and careful consideration of the terms already available in the European academic vocabulary. He was interested in creating a term that would encapsulate the breadth of the English word *folklore* along with the thoroughness of the German term *Volkskunde*. To this end he engaged in extensive correspondence with leading European folklorists, primarily Bernard Schmidt. Politis had followed the European debates surrounding the establishment of folklore as a discipline, the appropriate terminology, and its contents. The English term "folklore" appeared in 1846 in the journal *Atheneum*, coined by the folklorist William Thoms who, writing under the pseudonym Ambrose Merton, proposed that a "good Saxon compound, Folklore" be used to replace the terms "popular antiquities" and "popular literature". Thoms proposed that the new term encompassed both the *study* (the discipline) and the *content* (the lore of the folk) of folklore, which he conceived of and

defined enumeratively and specifically as a people's manners, customs, observances, superstitions, ballads, proverbs, and so on. Thoms's work, like Politis's, lay resolutely within the romantic and nationalist intellectual context that interfaced with the archaeological and philological projects of 19th-century epistemologies, which were supported by and themselves supported the struggle for national and ethnic definitions and legitimations that appeared with the dissolution of the Ottoman empire and the attempts at unification by European states (especially Germany and Italy). These nationalist movements, which sought to establish the legitimacy of new sovereign states based on claims of historical continuity with the past, also concerned themselves with proving the continuity of the people's *spirit*. To this end exhaustive research was carried out in Germany, initially, in 1812, by the Grimm brothers (the famous fairy-tale tellers), in Italy by Giuseppe Pitré, and in France, Spain, and Greece by Claude Fauriel, among others. In every case, the study of folklore was meant to show, on a basis of scientific truth (as the term was understood at the time), the validity of the claims made by various ethnic groups as to their historical and unbroken presence at a specific place, which thus acquired ancestral status. This ancestral status became the cornerstone on which the emergence of new national states came to be established, often (as was the case in both Greece and Italy) through war and revolution. The continued intimate relationship between folklore (as a discipline) and national discourses can be found in a "cursory definition" of folklore given by the Greek folklorist Dimitrios Loukatos in 1978, as "the discipline that observes and interprets the spiritual, psychic, and artistic expressions of the life of the people, the ones that constitute the civilisation of the people and the nation" (p. 21). As to any possible claims of folklore to "objective research", Alki Kyriakidou-Nestoros (the late professor of Folklore at the University of Thessalonica) noted that

> if we cannot innocently claim, any longer, for any of the social or even the positivist sciences, "objectivity" of knowledge and scientific lack of bias, I am afraid that we have to admit that folklore, even more so, is a discipline inherently biased ... because the notion of the "people" is particularly fluid and one that is easily susceptible to ideological manipulations and misuse. (p. 10)

Loukatos classified the aims of folklore as follows: scientific, national, humanitarian, and internationalist. As *scientific* aims he identified the historical and cultural information provided about the past and current life of that segment of the population that generates "folk" culture. "We have the duty to know about our past just as a family has the duty to know about its ancestors", he notes. The second scientific aim is the correct contextualization of Greek cultural development alongside the development of neighbouring peoples. The last scientific aim is the contribution of folklore to neighbouring disciplines. As *national* aims Loukatos classifies national self-knowledge which will lead to national self-discipline and self-inspiration. Self-discipline, he suggests, would combat many of the national shortcomings, while self-inspiration would contribute to the continued production of a Greek tradition. Under *humanitarian* aims he mentions the possibility of in-depth knowledge of the human psyche, which in turn would

Folklore: a garland of wild flowers gathered on 1 May and nailed to a front door in Nauplia to welcome the arrival of spring. The discipline of folklore in Greece was initiated by Nikolaos Politis to describe and account for such customs as this.

lead to the deeper love and appreciation of the psyche of the "simple people", something which, in its own turn, could aid the state in its designing and implementing a social welfare system that would be based on folk models of understanding and actions. Finally, through comparative folklore one could prove the internationalist nature of humanity and of the commonality of the human folk experience and goals.

Despite the fact that a well-articulated theory of the discipline of folklore has been in existence since the mid-19th century, its study has been practised by both trained and amateur folklorists in close collaboration with each other. This is especially the case in Greece, where a long tradition of local historians has greatly facilitated the development of a parallel study of local folklore. As Dimitris Loukatos noted in 1978, the contribution of these local, amateur folklorists, who assume the cost of research and publication and make their findings available to trained folklorists for a more complete and methodical classification and taxonomy of the material, has been invaluable. With the firm establishment of folklore as part of the university curriculum and the parallel establishment of university chairs for the study of folklore, research has expanded from the confines of rural, non-literate traditions to include the study of urban and professional material (such as the practices of taxi drivers, urban housewives, hairdressers, truck drivers, schoolchildren, football, card-playing clubs, etc.).

NENI PANOURGIÁ

See also Politis

Further Reading

Dundes, Alan, *The Study of Folklore,* Englewood Cliffs, New Jersey: Prentice-Hall, 1965

Herzfeld, Michael, *Ours Once More: Folklore, Ideology, and the Making of Modern Greece,* Austin: University of Texas Press, 1982

Kyriakidou-Nestoros, Alki, *I Theoria tis Ellenikes Laographias: Kritiki Analysi* [The Theory of Greek Folklore: A Critical Analysis], Athens, 1978

Loukatos, Dimitrios, *Eisagogi stin Ellenike Laographia* [Introduction to Greek Folklore], 2nd edition, Athens, 1978

Thoms, William [Ambrose Merton], Letter to *The Atheneum,* 982 (22 August 1846): pp. 862–63

Food and Drink

The food and drink of Greece show a surprising degree of continuity from classical times, and even before, down to the present day.

Prehistoric evidence comes from archaeology and also from the Greek language. The Greek names for many plant foods, and for nearly all fish, cannot be paralleled in other Indo-European languages, suggesting that many of the foodstuffs of Greece were unfamiliar to the speakers of prehistoric Greek before their arrival in the Aegean region. But for cereals (emmer, barley, perhaps millet) and for some important food animals (oxen, swine, sheep, goats, ducks, and geese) the names used in Greek are of Indo-European origin, which indicates that the earliest Greek speakers of the region had brought a knowledge of these species with them.

Archaeologists find evidence of the use of deer and wild goats, of tunny, of shellfish and snails, and of a range of fruits and other plants at sites in Greece from about 10,000 BC and even before. Emmer and einkorn (primitive forms of wheat), barley, oxen, swine, sheep, and goats were farmed in Greece and Crete by 6000 BC. In subsequent millennia grapes, accumulates for a range of seafood. By 2000 BC wine and cheese were certainly familiar. Probably olive oil was already well known: the extent of olive cultivation in prehistoric times has aroused controversy, but quantities of oil are recorded on Linear B tablets. Coriander, dill, cumin, fennel, mustard, and parsley are among the early aromatics of Greece. The world's oldest-known man-made beehive comes from Akrotiri (Thera, modern Santorini), demonstrating that domesticated bees were kept there before the volcanic eruption that destroyed the town, and thus that honey was valued as a food.

For Classical and later Greece, literature becomes the main source. Although in the *Iliad* and *Odyssey* there is no evidence of any elaborate methods of cookery, by the 5th century BC a highly developed cuisine was practised in many Greek cities – partly under overseas influence. Some recipes were said to be Lydian (from the rich and civilized kingdom in western Asia Minor) or Ionian (from the Greek settlements in and near Lydia). Others derived from the prosperous Greek colonies in

Sicily; Sicilian cooks were famous. Growers of fruit and vegetables developed varieties that varied in quality, time of ripening, and soil and water requirements. Athens, rapidly expanding, depended on imports even for staple foods such as wheat.

The staple foods of Classical Greeks, when leading a settled life, were wheat and barley. At home these were baked into loaves in clay ovens or under ashes; travellers and soldiers probably more often boiled them as gruel or porridge. Poor people supplemented this diet with little more than fruit, mushrooms, and vegetables gathered from the wild. Many could afford to add olive oil and flavourings such as cheese, onion, garlic, and salt fish (e.g. anchovy, goby). On the tables of the wealthy the variety of fish and meat dishes and the many savoury and sweet confections were still typically preceded by wheat and barley loaves.

Much cooking was probably done out of doors, and took the form of grilling, roasting, frying or boiling over a fire, or baking in hot ashes; *klibanoi*, baking cloches or clay ovens, were used for bread. Cooks depicted in Athenian comedy of the 4th century BC happily list the methods they preferred. At least one cookery book, by Mithaecus, had been written; others would follow. The humorous gastronomic poem of Archestratus, now known only in fragments, shows that travel and trade were encouraging the appreciation of local produce and regional cuisine.

Comedy cooks sometimes list the range of ingredients they would expect to have at hand. These lists include thyme, oregano, fennel, dill, sage, rue, parsley, fig leaf, coriander leaf, and other herbs; raisins, olives, capers, and sumach; onions, garlic, and leek; cumin and sesame seed; almonds; olive oil, vinegar, grape juice; eggs, pickled fish, salt. Favourite kinds of wine, oil, and luxury foodstuffs criss-crossed the Aegean, but the only commonly used ingredients that had to come from far away were *silphion*, the now extinct aromatic from Cyrene; dates from the Levant; *horaion* and other forms of salted tunny, and *garos* (fermented fish sauce), both of which came from the Black Sea ports, as did much of the wheat that Greece imported.

Greeks commonly ate two meals a day, a lighter *ariston* at the end of the morning and a heavier *deipnon* in the early evening. Among the leisured classes, dinner might lead into a *potos* or *symposion* (drinking party). In Sparta and on Crete the typical meal in Classical times was a communal one, served in a public hall. In Athens and other cities private dinners were often held, at which guests reclined to eat, an eastern fashion. At the beginning of the meal a small table, freshly scrubbed, was placed in front of each diner or of each couch. Food from the serving dishes might be taken directly on to the table, or on to bread, and eaten with the fingers.

An elaborate dinner of the 4th century BC began with the serving of loaves in baskets. A relatively light first course consisted of appetizing relishes, *paropsides*, to eat with the bread. A selection of more generous fish, poultry, and meat dishes formed the main course. Fresh meat was spit-roasted or grilled, and required to be slaughtered and prepared by a professional *mageiros* (butcher-cook) with appropriate religious ritual. Dessert was called *deuterai trapezai* (second tables) because clean tables were brought in at this point. It consisted of cakes and sweetmeats, cheese, nuts, fresh and dried fruit. Between main course and dessert, wine was first served: it was normally mixed with water. Wines of Chios, Lesbos, Thasos, and the coast of Macedonia had lasting popularity. "Water is best", said Pindar, but the drinking of water "unmixed", without the addition of wine, was discouraged by many doctors.

Food was a medium of patronage and dependence. The dependants (*parasitoi*) of powerful Athenians and the courtiers (*kolakes*, "flatterers") of Hellenistic monarchs were fed by their masters, and paid for their food with more or less tangible services. Cities honoured their guests with dinner in the *prytaneion*, a public building containing dining rooms.

The Hellenistic cuisine of the eastern Mediterranean, after Alexander the Great's conquests, took on a new style influenced by Macedonian, Persian, and other cuisines and customs. Trade within the Mediterranean area continued to grow; crop varieties were exchanged and tested in new environments. New fruits (peaches, cherries, lemons) were introduced from the east; spices began to be imported from Persia, India, and beyond. Thus the Hellenistic menu differed from the Classical Athenian menu in many ways. New kinds of bread became popular, some apparently native to Cappadocia and Syria. Oven-roasting of meat was introduced from the East, allowing the development of large and elaborate stuffed meat dishes, which afterwards became typical of Roman cuisine. Macedonians liked to drink wine earlier in the meal and with less admixture of water (this, some said, killed Alexander).

No sudden change occurred when most of the region became part of the Roman empire. In the arts of luxury Rome deferred to Greece. The cookery of Rome came under strong Hellenistic influence – Greek cooks were in heavy demand – and Latin is full of Greek loanwords for food terms. From Roman times (about AD 200) comes the single most important source text for ancient Greek food and dining, the *Deipnosophists* ("professors of dining" or perhaps "professors at dinner") of Athenaeus of Naucratis. A second important text (not yet translated into English) is Galen's dietary survey, *On the Properties of Foods*.

Byzantine cuisine grew out of Greek and Roman influences, but Byzantium did not cease to innovate. Dried meat, a forerunner of the *pastirma* (preserved salted meat) of modern Turkey, became a delicacy. Among favoured game were gazelles and wild asses. The Byzantines appreciated salt roe, *oiotarichon* (literally "egg pickle": hence the modern term *botargo*); they were to taste caviar, *kabiari*, and kippered herrings, *rengai*. Fruits unknown to the Classical menu included the aubergine, *melitzana*, and the orange, *nerantzion*.

New flavours multiplied. It was probably the Byzantines who first tried rosemary as a flavouring for roast lamb, and who first used saffron in cookery: both these aromatics, well known in the ancient world, had not previously been thought of as food ingredients. Nutmeg was sprinkled on the pease pudding that was a fast-day staple. It is among spoon sweets and sweet drinks that the distinctive flavour of Byzantine cookery is best sensed. The increasing availability of sugar, *zachar*, assisted the confectioner's inventiveness: rose sugar, a popular medieval confection, may well have originated here. The flavoured soft drinks (required on fast days) and flavoured wines of Byzantium, distant ancestors of the *mastikha*, vermouth, absinthe, and pastis of the modern Mediterranean, were fine-tuned to give a healthy diet month by month: they

Food and Drink: woman kneading dough (5th century BC), an activity still performed by many women in rural Greece, Ashmolean Museum, Oxford

called for such ingredients as spikenard, gentian, yellow flag, stone parsley, gum benzoin, ginger grass, chamomile, and violet.

Medieval travellers to Byzantium did not always like the strange flavours they encountered. Fish sauce was still much used and was an acquired taste; so was squill vinegar. Most foreigners and even some Byzantines disapproved of retsina: "undrinkable", said the supercilious Liutprand of Cremona in the 10th century. But even strangers were seduced by the confectionery, the candied fruits, and the sweet wines.

The food of the poor of Constantinople was no doubt limited, though cheese, olives, and onions made up for a scarcity of meat. *Timarion*, a satirical poem of the 12th century, offers a salt pork and cabbage stew as a typical poor man's meal, eaten from the bowl with the fingers just as in contemporary western Europe. Inns and wine-shops generally provided only basic fare: though it is a 6th-century Byzantine source, the *Life* of St Theodore of Sykeon, that contains the earliest reference known anywhere in the world to an inn that attracted customers by the quality of its food.

Descriptions of the food of early Ottoman Greece display continuity with that of Byzantium, but by the 18th and early 19th centuries travellers were noting the relative poverty of Greece. Constantinople, still a Greek city but also the capital of a great Muslim empire, continued to attract the long-distance trade that it had always done. Its spice market was one of the wonders of the world, and the Seraglio consumed luxury foods from all over the eastern Mediterranean.

Modern Greek food and wine are the products of a long tradition. The importance placed on fine seafood recalls the preoccupations of Classical Athens. Cheese is still often stored in brine, as it was in ancient and medieval times. The aroma of Chian mastic, the world's first chewing gum, still used by many to freshen the breath, is as distinctive as that of the honey-soaked patisserie the ancestry of which can be traced in recipes preserved by Athenaeus. The EU hierarchies of *appellation contrôlée*, favouring local distinctiveness, are appropriate to the wines of modern Greece, grown in terrains that have not been ravaged by phylloxera, where local grape varieties tend to do better than the fashionable ones.

ANDREW DALBY

Further Reading

Archestratus, *The Life of Luxury: Europe's Oldest Cookery Book*, translated by John Wilkins and Shaun Hill, Totnes: Prospect, 1994

Athenaeus, *The Deipnosophists*, edited and translated by Charles Burton Gulick, 7 vols, London: Heinemann, and Cambridge, Massachusetts: Harvard University Press, 1927–41 (Loeb edition)

Dalby, Andrew, *Siren Feasts: A History of Food and Gastronomy in Greece*, London and New York: Routledge, 1997

Davidson, James N., *Courtesans and Fishcakes: The Consuming Passions of Classical Athens*, London: HarperCollins, 1997; New York: St Martin's Press, 1998

Lambert-Gócs, Miles, *The Wines of Greece*, London and Boston: Faber, 1990

Salaman, Rena, *Greek Food: An Affectionate Celebration of Traditional Recipes*, 2nd edition, London: HarperCollins, 1993

Slater, William J. (editor), *Dining in a Classical Context*, Ann Arbor: University of Michigan Press, 1991

Wilkins, John, David Harvey and Mike Dobson (editors), *Food in Antiquity*, Exeter: University of Exeter Press, 1995

Foreigners

Homer's Trojans are not markedly different in character from his Greeks. As knowledge of foreign peoples penetrated the Greek world, however, increasingly the Greeks came to define their own character in opposition to that of foreign peoples. Pindar spoke of how the man without a wagon was a nomad among the (nomadic) Scythians: the Greeks, by comparison with the archetypally rootless Scythians, saw themselves by definition as city dwellers. The lyric poets of the Archaic age already identified luxurious living and tyrannical government as characteristic of Asia. The contrast between Greeks and "barbarians" and the accompanying sense of a common Greek identity were given a new emphasis in the aftermath of the Persian Wars between the cities of the Greek mainland and the Persian kings Darius and Xerxes (490–479 BC). Herodotus famously encapsulated this common identity by making the Athenians deny a charge of betrayal by pointing to their "sharing the same blood and the same language, with common shrines to the gods and sacrifices, and the same way of life".

The common blood of the Greeks is, among these criteria of Greek identity, perhaps the one given least emphasis in our sources. However, the differences in way of life between Greeks and foreigners are often seen as dictated by innate characteristics. The Greek version of the origins of the monarchy of the Medes, for example, describes how, living in villages with no form of common organization, the Medes gradually turned for the settlement of disputes to the authority of a single man, their future king Deioces, who then imposed his own terms and conditions. The Medes, the story implies, naturally gravitate to a strong leader; the peoples of Asia – by contrast to the freedom-loving Greeks – are natural slaves.

Greek polytheistic religion was, at least overtly, a universal religion. The Greeks equated their own gods with those of foreign peoples, saying, for example, that Dionysus was the Greek name for Osiris or that the Ethiopians worshipped Zeus and Dionysus "alone of the gods". There was no duty of evangelizing in ancient Greek religion. The Greeks could even espouse an ideal that to mock the religion of another people was "madness". However, there were other more subtle ways of distancing the religion of foreigners. Toleration of foreign gods rarely – and only with great caution – led to the institution of those gods' cults. (Though there were "Panhellenic" sanctuary sites such as Delphi and Olympia, different Greek cities likewise had their own distinct cults of common Greek gods.) Some foreign gods proved untranslatable: the grounds are difficult to discover, but probably include the barbaric nature of their rites. Ironically also the intolerance of other peoples was itself the subject of disapproval. The Persians were (in some instances unfairly) charged with gross acts of sacrilege; a number of stories from the Persian Wars relate, with apparent relish, the come-uppances of the perpetrators of such crimes. The Greek destruction of foreign temples was, by contrast, accidental. The practice of *proskynesis* – probably the blowing of a kiss while leaning forward – offered by the Persians to their kings was inaccurately but persistently believed by the Greeks to represent a form of worship. While the Greeks often saw foreign lands, especially Egypt, as the privileged source of religious wisdom and the land from which (in the distant past) their own knowledge of the gods largely derived, it is noticeable that by their own time they had overtaken the Egyptians in the number of gods in their pantheon.

It was the incomprehensible babble of foreign languages that led to the Greeks terming foreigners *barbaroi* or barbarians. Greeks travelled widely for trade; Greeks served as mercenaries in Egypt in the Archaic period and as administrators and builders in the heart of the Persian empire at Persepolis. But though there must have been Greeks who were fluent in foreign languages, stereotyped caricatures of foreign languages continued; there is also little sign that the ability to speak a foreign language was given any status in the Classical period. The Athenian commander in the Persian Wars, Themistocles, was said to have learnt the Persian language within a year of exile in the Persian court, but there is little suggestion that this was a cause of admiration; rather it seems to have been adduced as another example of his extraordinary cunning. The story, recorded by Plutarch, that a Persian interpreter was killed for daring to express barbarian commands in Greek, is one of a number of anecdotes suggestive of a Greek chauvinism concerning their language. Similar chauvinism attached itself, however, to individual Greek "dialects" – the distinction of language and dialect is essentially a modern one – as to Greek as a whole.

In general also, a sense of national identity by contradistinction to foreign peoples was far less dominant in the ancient world than in the age of the modern nation state. Self-definition could take place as much by opposition to other Greeks, in terms of belonging to a city state (or polis) or to family and kinship groups, as in opposition to "barbarians". Nineteenth-century historians envisaged Greek history as a failed process of national unification. But though Panhellenism proved a convenient slogan for those resisting Persian conquest or for Alexander the Great in his expedition into Asia, any such sense of common purpose was fragile.

The modern Greek identity which emerged from under Ottoman rule was to a large extent dependent upon an imagined continuity between ancient and modern Greece. As Grigorios Paliouritis put it, the Greeks were awaking from a deep lethargy of ignorance of their own past. The resurgence of Greek nationalism in the early 19th century saw the revival of ancient names in preference to Orthodox Christian names. Many of the most prominent public buildings of the newly independent state were built in an ostentatiously Neoclassical style (associated particularly with the Danish architect Theophilus Hansen). Arguably the greatest contribution to this revival of a sense of Greek identity was made by the Austrian scholar J.P. Fallmerayer, who in the 1830s challenged the assumption that the Greeks were the lineal descendants of the ancients. This provoked an enormous reaction. Folklorists such as Nikolaos Politis or Dora Stratou were determined to prove the affinity between modern songs, folk-tales, or dance and ancient practices and rituals. The rawness of feelings on such questions, and the way in which ancient evidence is adduced, are well illustrated by the recent dispute aroused by the Former Yugoslav Republic of Macedonia, and in the common Greek claim that Macedonia has been Greek for 2500 years.

The main battlegrounds in the definition of modern Greek identity are certainly familiar. Already in the first decade of the 19th century there was dispute over the proper form of the Greek language: the spoken or "demotic" Greek, or katharevousa (literally "purifying"), a form of the language designed to enhance the similarities with ancient Greek. A middle course proposed by the intellectual Adamantios Korais was to purify demotic of foreign traces. Korais regularly compared Turks to wild beasts. The religious definition of the independent Greek state was also problematic. The term Hellenes initially denoted non-Christians. Many of the Orthodox citizens of the new state, even the inhabitants of Attica, Hydra, and Poros, spoke *arvanitika* (Albanian) rather than Greek; others in the Macedonian north spoke Bulgarian, although the later schism between the Orthodox and Bulgarian churches ensured that religious and ethnic distinctions ran in parallel. At the same time, the new identity of the Greek state tended to highlight the ancient past at the expense of the intervening Christian period. Before independence, Korais expressed his contempt for the religious obscurantism of the Byzantine past. It was only gradually, with the publication for example of a new study of Greek history by Paparrigopoulos, that this period of national history was reintegrated.

There were other difficulties in defining who was Greek and who foreign. There was considerable tension between the inhabitants of the Greek state (or autochthons) and the heterochthons, those who lived abroad, generally better educated and so given a greater share in the offices of the new state. The arrival of approximately one million new Greek citizens, many of whom could not speak Greek, at the time of the transfer of populations between Greece and Turkey in 1923 resulted in similar problems. The idea that a Greek can live (in the words of John Kolettis in 1844) "in any land associated with Greek history or the Greek race" is still sustained by the common practice of living in foreign lands, or *xeniteia*.

THOMAS HARRISON

See also Identity, Metics, Nationalism

Further Reading

Bacon, Helen H., *Barbarians in Greek Tragedy*, New Haven: Yale University Press, 1961

Baslez, M.-F., "Présence et traditions iraniennes dans les citées de l'Égée", *Revue des Etudes Anciennes*, 87 (1985): pp. 137–55

Bosworth, A.B., *Conquest and Empire: The Reign of Alexander the Great*, Cambridge and New York: Cambridge University Press, 1988

Bovon, A., "La Representation des guerriers perses et la notion de barbare dans la 1re moitié de Ve siècle", *Bulletin des Correspondances Helléniques*, 87 (1963): pp. 579–602

Drews, Robert, *The Greek Accounts of Eastern History*, Washington, D.C.: Center for Hellenic Studies, 1973

Goldhill, S.D., "Battle Narratives and Politics in Aeschylus' Persae", *Journal of Hellenic Studies*, 108 (1988): pp. 189–93

Hall, Edith, *Inventing the Barbarian: Greek Self-Definition through Tragedy*, Oxford: Clarendon Press, and New York: Oxford University Press, 1989

Hall, Edith, "Asia Unmanned: Images of Victory in Classical Athens" in *War and Society in the Greek World*, edited by John Rich and Graham Shipley, London and New York: Routledge, 1993

Harrison, T., "Herodotus' Conception of Foreign Languages", *Histos*, 2 (1998): http://www.dur.ac.uk/Classics/histos/1998/harrison.html

Hartog, François, *The Mirror of Herodotus: The Representation of the Other in the Writing of History*, Berkeley: University of

California Press, 1988:
http://www.dur.ac.uk/Classics/histos/1998/harrison.html

Long, Timothy, *Barbarians in Greek Comedy*, Carbondale: Southern Illinois University Press, 1986

Miller, Margaret Christina, *Athens and Persia in the Fifth Century BC: A Study in Cultural Receptivity*, Cambridge and New York: Cambridge University Press, 1997

Mitchell, Lynette G., *Greeks Bearing Gifts: The Public Use of Private Relationships in the Greek World, 435–323 BC*, Cambridge and New York: Cambridge University Press, 1997

Momigliano, Arnaldo, *Alien Wisdom: The Limits of Hellenization*, Cambridge and New York: Cambridge University Press, 1975

Momigliano, A., "Persian Empire and Greek Freedom" in *The Idea of Freedom: Essays in Honour of Isaiah Berlin*, edited by Alan Ryan, Oxford and New York: Oxford University Press, 1979

Walbank, F.W., "The Problem of Greek Nationality", *Phoenix*, 5 (1951): pp. 41–60

Wieshofer, Josef, *Ancient Persia from 550 BC to 650 AD*, London and New York: Tauris, 1996

Forestry

"Forestry" is a term not really applicable to pre-modern Greece. Modern forestry is a specialized art, concerned with growing trees merely as a timber crop. Usually it is done on the basis that trees begin by someone planting them and die when they are cut down. In earlier traditions of woodmanship, in contrast, trees are wild creatures, arising spontaneously, and many species survive being felled, and sprout from the stump. Modern forestry has been practised in Greece for over a hundred years, but has not come to dominate the landscape nor to supplant earlier, more complex relations between people and trees.

Trees grow in most parts of Greece, but in the drier eastern half of the country they are getting near the limit of their range and grow slowly, especially when close together. By modern standards they often make poor-quality timber: typical Mediterranean oaks are short, hard, crooked, and difficult to work.

In Classical Greece woodland was of rather limited extent and was to be found mainly in the mountains. Then, as now, the abundant trees were evergreen and deciduous oaks, juniper, various species of pine, fir at high altitudes, and (in Crete) cypress and plane. Trees had many uses: besides timber, they provided fuel, stakes for vineyards, leaves to feed animals, acorns, resin, stocks of pear and olive on to which to graft fruit-bearing varieties, oak bark for tanning leather, osiers for basket-making, fruit, drugs, etc. Fodder could be supplied by trees that, because of constant browsing, never grew larger than shrubs, as happens with the common Greek prickly-oak and many others. Firewood and some timber came also from olives and other cultivated trees.

Most trees in Greece other than pines and firs can be coppiced: when cut down (or burnt), they sprout from the base and yield further crops of produce. Regrowth is delayed and hindered by browsing animals. In modern Greece many trees are pollarded (cut at 3 to 4 m above ground) to protect the young shoots from browsing animals.

Ancient Greeks apparently managed their woods, though not by modern forestry methods. On Chios leases written on tables of stone mention coppice-woods attached to farms, which were expected to produce so much weight of wood each year for ever, either for consumption on the farm or by way of rent. The quantities, a ton or two per year, were quite small. One clause has been interpreted as meaning that the farmer was forbidden to let livestock browse on growing trees, but the text is damaged and the sense unclear at this point. Some big woods had names. The wood Skotitas in the Peloponnese, described by Pausanias, which also had its own god, is still extant. Wood in various forms was regularly imported to islands like Delos that were without woodland.

Athens, giant of Greek cities, was relatively well supplied with woodland, with pine and evergreen oak on Mounts Parnes and Cithaeron and in the Isthmus. Some of it was private property: a list of the lands of condemned criminals, graven in stone in 414 BC, includes an oakery and probably a pinery. Athens was apparently self-sufficient in wood and charcoal, supplied by professional woodcutters. Demosthenes, for example, mentions a farm where six donkeys were working all the time carrying wood to market. Woodland was probably less extensive and certainly less well grown than it is today.

Attic vegetation fuelled production from the silver mines at Laurium, whose output paid for imports of corn and timber. At a rough estimate, Laurium could have kept going indefinitely on the growth and regrowth of maquis on at most 30,000 ha of land. The Athenians were using perhaps one seventh of their land area as a fuel supply for what was by far their biggest industry.

Timber for shipbuilding or big construction came from far away. According to Theophrastus, the sources were Macedonia (the best quality), the Black Sea, Thessaly, Arcadia, Euboea, and Mount Parnassus (from which came the worst). Other documents and inscriptions record minor supplies from all over the Aegean and even Sicily. Athenian foreign policy had to maintain access to the timber of Macedonia: if the Athenians failed in this they had to do without a fleet. The quantities were not great, for a trireme was a huge, lightly-built racing rowing-boat; but specially long timbers were needed for keels and masts.

OLIVER RACKHAM

Further Reading

Dunn, A., "The Exploitation and Control of Woodland and Scrubland in the Byzantine World", *Byzantine and Modern Greek Studies*, 16 (1992): pp. 235–98

Meiggs, Russell, *Trees and Timber in the Ancient Mediterranean World*, Oxford: Clarendon Press, 1982

Rackham, Oliver and Jennifer Moody, *The Making of the Cretan Landscape*, Manchester: Manchester University Press, 1996

Rackham, Oliver and A.T. Grove, *The Nature of the European Mediterranean*, New Haven, Connecticut and London: Yale University Press, 2000

France

Greeks have lived in France since at least 600 BC. Finds of pottery from Marseilles and Hyères indicate that there were trading links as early as 700 BC, but the first colony, at Massilia

(Marseilles) was not founded until around 600 BC. The attraction of the area was the Rhône river which provided a trade route across France to the English Channel whence tin from Britain could be imported. This incidentally contributed to the development of the Celtic cultures of Hallstatt and La Tène, many of whose hillforts demonstrate Greek influence in their art, architecture, and fortifications. The Greeks were also responsible for introducing cultivation of the vine and olive to France. The Phocaean colony at Massilia prospered during the 6th century BC and established a string of settlements along the coast from Nicaea (Nice) to Emporion (Ampurias) in northern Spain. It also maintained close links with Greece and set up a treasury at Delphi. During the 5th century BC there was a shift in the balance of power in central Europe and the Greek trade route across France was broken. But the colony at Massilia survived and retained its reputation as a centre of Greek culture and learning well into the Roman period.

After the fall of the western Roman empire links between Byzantium and France were broken, but the Byzantines came to see the Franks as potential allies against the Arian Goths and later the Lombards in Italy. The coronation of Charlemagne, however, as "emperor of the Romans" in AD 800 was a severe blow to Byzantine prestige and brought the two empires into political and ideological competition with each other. Nevertheless, cultural and religious links with Byzantium persisted, particularly in Provence, and the emperor Manuel I Komnenos (1143–80) married his son Alexios II to Agnès of France in an attempt to forge an alliance against the Holy Roman emperor Frederick I Barbarossa. The French played a large part in the crusades and it was a Frenchman, Baldwin of Flanders, who became the first Latin emperor in 1204. After the Byzantine restoration in 1261 the emperors frequently appealed to France for support against the Ottoman threat but little help was forthcoming.

In later Renaissance and afterward, Greek communities were also established in France, more distant and with fewer political and commercial connections with Constantinople. In the 16th century, the nucleus of a Greek colony seems to have existed in Lyons, at which time silk-workers were settled, apparently to establish a silk industry in competition with the Italians. Greeks also appeared relatively early in the French capital, Paris. With the beginnings of interest in Greek studies in France in the later 15th and 16th centuries, a number of Greek savants, especially Cretans were to be found there. They included Janus Lascaris, who had firmly established Greek studies in Paris and became the French ambassador to Venice; George Hermonymus, who was a capable copyist of texts despite Erasmus's and Budé's denigration of his abilities; further the expert calligrapher Angelos Vergikios, who was official scribe to the French King and was awarded the post of royal librarian. Furthermore, some modern scholars believe that the original letters cut for the royal Greek press in France by Claude Garamond and by Henry Stephanus were modelled on Vergikios's handwriting. His son Nicholas wrote competent French poetry and mingled with the famous literary group called the Pléiade. Another Greek who appeared in Paris was Antonios Eparchos from Corfu, who presented a number of Greek manuscripts to Francis I, which were to constitute the nucleus for the royal library at Fontainebleau and later the famous Greek collections in the Bibliothèque Nationale, which

were also enriched during the reign of Louis XIV by the efforts of the writer and librarian Athanasius the Orator (1571–1663).

During the Middle Ages and the Renaissance, the study of Hellenism in France was the pursued by scholars who were interested in all aspects of Greek civilisation and had contributed generally both to the advancement of scholarship and the spread of Classical ideas. This aim was achieved in three important periods of France's subsequent intellectual history: humanism in the 16th century, classicism in the 17th and 18th centuries, when intellectuals discussed whether ancient or modern writers were more important, the "Querelle des Anciens et des Modernes", in which the ancient world provided an alternative to the present. Meanwhile the search for Greek manuscripts persisted at the French court of Louis XIV and his ministers Colbert and Mazarin organized missions to the Aegean to collect rare Greek manuscripts from monastic libraries.

Up to the 18th-century education in France meant a Classical education, but with the emphasis on Latin rather than Greek. Classical authors were studied and taught with didactic and ethical preoccupations in mind. For moral exemplars and heroic prototypes, the mind of an educated 18th-century Frenchman turned naturally to Greece and Rome; their history and literature were regarded as a vast treasurehouse of moral precepts and exemplary attitudes.

Hellenism as a concept was first introduced in French by Montaigne in 1580 in his *Essays*. Hellenists were, at that time, absorbed by the scolastic study of texts and their philological problems. Books such as the *Antiquité Expliquée* by Montfaucon (1719) the *Recueil d'Antiquités* (1750–67) by the Comte de Caylus, along with works of Winckelmann opened up a broader vision of Hellenism as a human reality. At the same time, Byzantium was also studied by French scholars: in 1648 P. Labbe's book *De Byzantinae Historiae Scriptoribus ad Omne per Orbem Eruditos Protreptikon* appeared, and a century later Charles Le Beau published an unfinished work in 21 volumes, the *Histoire du Bas-Empire* (Paris, 1757–1786). Difficulties of interpretation were resolved and there was increased specialization in Classical learning among professional scholars; minds shaped by the reading of Greek literature, were ready to welcome the new ideas.

The Enlightenment, which was a turning point in the apprehension of antiquity did not consciously cling to the past and could not ignore the differences produced by time. Among the Greek states it was not Athens with its pure form of democracy that was venerated by the French, but rather Sparta. Both Montesquieu and Rousseau judged Sparta to be a model of freedom and order, its people distinguished by public virtue, simple lifestyle, patriotism, vigour. Jean Schweighaeuser, D'Ansse de Villoison, and A.J. Letronne gave an impulse to the editing of Greek texts and tried to present some interpretations on the problems of the Greek world. Pierre-Charles Lévesque dedicated his whole life to Thucydides. New disciplines such as archeology, ethnology and cultural anthropology began to examine the cultural evolution of Greek antiquity. An idea that prevailed in France and which was expressed by Condorcet in his *Esquisse d'un tableau historique des progrès de l'esprit humain* (Paris, 1795) was that the history of ancient Greece is a microcosm of the history of human race. Jean-Pierre de

Bougainville wrote in 1764: "Il est certain que l'histoire de la Grèce, se peuplant et se poliçant par dégrés, est moins le spectacle des destinées d'une nation qu'une perspective où le genre humain se peint en raccourci dans différents états." ["It is certain that the history of Greece, which was progressively inhabited and civilized, is less the spectacle of a single nation's destiny than a perspective in which the human race is seen in a succession of different states."] Nevertheless, the works of such Hellenists as Chardon de La Rochette, Millin and Choiseul-Gouffier was not only important for understanding ancient Greece but more for modern Greece. Nor were Greece and its literature absent from the work of Madame de Staël, Ginguené, Sismondi and Fauriel.

Up to the end of the ancien régime modern Greece as a province of the vast Ottoman Empire, was considered in France as a phenomenon of degeneracy. For the French people, Ottoman rule was a paradigm of lawless tyranny, of a hierarchy of oppression in which each man lorded it over those beneath him. C.-F. Volney, for instance, who was a ideological believer in the primacy of reason, and equally opposed to the cult of feeling and absolutism, in his *Considérations sur la guerre actuelle des Turcs* (London, 1781), considered the question of Greece's survival to be identified rather with the restoration of antiquity; a similar aspiration underlay another work of the French Enlightenment, the *Voyage du jeune Anacharsis en Grèce*, (Paris, 1788) written by the abbé Barthélemy, who was followed by many French liberal writers who supported the emancipation of Greece such as the great philhellene René de Chateaubriand. However, the fervour of the Revolutionary France was also characterized by an awareness of a return to the civic virtues of Classical antiquity – in oratory, in painting and sculpture, in the decorative and applied arts, in design. Some years later the philhellenic movement took place, which had been nourished and strengthened by Romanticism and in which humanism and the ideas of the Enlightenment played still a major role. What is remarkable is that the French philhellenes who went to liberate Greece and took part in the war for Independence, such as Persat, Fabvier and Jourdain, were chiefly Bonapartists who wished by their success in Greece to show that their party was no mere relic of the past but a living force.

On the other hand, Napoleon's designs on the eastern Mediterranean were well received in Greece and it was a sign that French revolutionary fever had reached Greece when, in June 1797 a French expeditionary force took over the Ionian Islands. The principles of French Revolution were preached. It was an important moment for Greek political thought which, in the wake of Rigas Velestinlis, was progressing towards a broader conception of liberty and human rights. On the other hand, in Constantinople a strong opposition movement was represented by the traditionalists who fought French republican ideas and saw in the French Revolution the coming of the Antichrist. A typical example of this attitude is to be found in a well-known passage of a satire against Francophilia the *Moral Versification* of Alexandros Kalphoglou of Constantinople; the author characterizes the enlightened Frenchman as "an impious libertine"and says of the Greek intellectuals of that time that "they boast of being the pupils of Mirabeau, Rousseau, and Voltaire, even if they do not understand them, and have never read them".

By the second half of the 18th century the Greeks had made considerable economic and intellectual progress. A Greek colony was founded in the cosmopolitan port of Marseilles by merchants who came mainly from Smyrna and from the islands of Chios and Hydra. This Greek merchant colony of Marseilles provided an important channel for the transmission of republican political ideas to the Greeks. In this connection, wealthy families of merchants as the Zizinia, the Rodocanachi, the Prassacachi, the Agelasto, the Vlasto, the Ralli, the Schilizzi, and many others showed great interest in the achievements of the Greek War of Independence and together with the French formed philhellenic committees. The most important of these, was the *Association Philanthropique* which was first formed in Paris by personalities from political and intellectual life.

A few years before the outbreak of the War of Independence, the Greek community in Paris became of great importance for Greek diaspora and Greek intellectual life: Adamantios Korais, Constantine Nikolopoulos, Panayotis Kodrikas were residents there and contributed to the intellectual emancipation of modern Hellenism. Greek students were attending French universities as well as the newly founded Ecole Polytechnique; they studied medicine, mathematics, physics, and chemistry, liberal arts (Dorothéos Proïos, Benjamin of Lesbos, Néophytos Vamvas, Theophilos Caïris), and they carried back French scientific thought and literature to Greek schools. Greek books were printed by Firmin Didot and Greek magazines were published such as *Athena*, *Melissa*, *Mousseion*, and *Le Polyglotte*; in 1828 the *Société Hellénique* was founded.

After the emergence of the Greek state, French education and language played an important role as vehicles of cultural change. The translation of literary works and the adoption of cultural styles constitute a good index of this process of reception. Leading Greek figures attended French universities during the 19th and the 20th centuries. The Greek presence also made its mark in the cultural and artistic life of Paris; in the later 19th century Jean Moréas became a leading figure in French poetry, and Yannis Psycharis also played a part in French and Greek literary life; these cases can easily be multiplied for the twentieth century, for example with the painters Dimitris Galanis, Giorgos Gounaropoulos, Marios Prassinos, Thanassis Tsingos who lived and worked in Paris.

Following the expulsion of the Greek population from Asia Minor in 1922 many Greeks settled in France and strengthened the Greek communities. During the period of the military junta (1967–974) 20,000 Greeks lived in France, many of them active political exiles, sharing the ideas of the Greek progressives forces. Today Greek communities number 5000, and cultural relations between Greece and France include not only state-sponsored exchanges and festivals of the arts, but unrestricted communication and dialogue.

ROXANE ARGYROPOULOS

See also Enlightenment

Further Reading

Badolle, Maurice, *L'Abbé Jean-Jacques Barthélemy (1716–1795) et l'hellénisme en France dans la seconde moitié du XVIIIe siècle*, Paris: Presses Universitaires de France, 1926

Bertrand, Louis, *La Fin du classicisme et le retour à l'antique dans la seconde moitié du XVIIIe siècle et les premières années du XIXe en France*, Paris: Fayard, 1897, reprinted Geneva: Slatkine, 1968

Bruneau, André, *Traditions et politique de la France au Levant*, Paris: Alcan, 1932

Canat, René, *L'Hellénisme des romantiques*, vol. 1: *La Grèce retrouvée*, Paris: Didier, 1951

Echinard, Pierre, *Grecs et Philhellènes à Marseille: de la Révolution française à l'Indépendance de la Grèce*, Marseilles: Institut Historique de Provence, 1973

Egger, Émile, *L'Hellénisme en France: leçons sur l'influence des études grecques dans le développement de la langue et de la littérature françaises*, 2 vols, Paris: Didier, 1869, reprinted New York: Franklin, 1967

Gay, Peter, *The Enlightenment: An Interpretation*, vol. 1: *The Rise of Modern Paganism*, New York: Knopf, 1966; London: Weidenfeld and Nicolson, 1967

Grell, Chantal, *Le XVIIIe Siècle et l'antiquité en France (1680–1789)*, 2 vols, Oxford: Voltaire Foundation, 1995

Joret, Charles, *D'Ansse de Villoison et l'hellénisme en France pendant le dernier tiers du XVIIIe siècle*, Paris: Champion, 1910

Leduc-Fayette, Denise, *Jean-Jacques Rousseau et le mythe de l'antiquité*, Paris : Vrin, 1974

Loraux, Nicole and Pierre Vidal-Naquet, "La Formation de l'Athènes bourgeoise: essai d'historiographie 1750–1850", in *Classical Influences on Western Thought, AD 1650–1870*, edited by Robert Ralph Bolgar, Cambridge and New York: Cambridge University Press, 1979

Omont, Henri, *Missions archéologiques françaises en Orient aux XVIIe et XVIIIe siècles*, 2 vols, Paris: Imprimerie Nationale, 1902

Pingaud, Léonce, *Choiseul-Gouffier: la France en Orient sous Louis XVI*, Paris: Picard, 1887

Polites, Alexes, *I Anakalypse ton Ellenikon Demotikon Tragoudion: Proypotheseis, Prospatheies kai I Demiourgia tis protis syllogis* [The Discovery of Greek Popular Songs: Presuppositions, Attempts, and the Creation of the First Collections], Athens, 1984

Pomian, Krzysztof, *Collectionneurs amateurs et curieux: Paris, Venise XVIe–XVIIIe siècle*, Paris: Gallimard, 1987

Rawson, Elizabeth, *The Spartan Tradition in European Thought*, Oxford: Clarendon Press, 1966

Tabaki, Anna, "Les Intellectuels grecs à Paris (fin du XVIIIe siècle–début du XIXe siècle)", in *Corneliae Papacostea-Danielopolu: in Memoriam*, Bucharest, 1999

Tolias, Georges, *La Médaille et la rouille: l'image de la Grèce moderne dans la presse littéraire parisienne (1794–1815)*, Athens: Hatier, 1997

Freedom

W.G. De Burgh reiterates a cliché of Classical scholarship when he calls the ancient Greeks "the people who created science, who first grasped the meaning and worth of freedom in thought and action". Denys Haynes echoes the claim that "the relationship between freedom and necessity is the fundamental theme of Greek art", and adds that the idea of human freedom is "the highest achievement of Greek thought, distinguishing it from that of all the other peoples of the ancient world and laying the foundation of our modern Western civilization". Gilbert Murray goes further still, asserting that "of all peoples known to us in history, the Greeks were far and away the freest thinkers", and that (despite China and India) "there is no philosophy except in Greece or derived from Greece." In science, art, philosophy, and of course politics ancient Greece (especially Athens) has long been celebrated as the birthplace of freedom.

Recent critics have cited factors that complicate or contradict this traditional picture. The cultural authority of the West, of which Greece is supposed to be the foundation, has itself been called into question. Greek anti-barbarian sentiment is reconceptualized as the prejudice of "orientalism". Athenian democracy is scrutinized for its exclusions and oppressions (for example, women and slaves). Greek claims to priority in science, and even science's claims to intellectual pre-eminence, are challenged, in the name of multicultural fairness. In response, defenders of the traditional view insist that the challenges themselves rely on unacknowledged appeal to aspects of the Greek intellectual legacy. Such disputes are made more difficult by the fact that freedom is a complex and contestable concept to begin with. In a brief discussion it must suffice to sort freedom into three rough categories: practical, political, and philosophical. Greek thought and practice have made significant contributions to understanding all three.

Freedom in the practical sense is the power to live as one chooses. This notion of freedom is tied to the idea of self-rule (autonomy). Individuals are *un*free in so far as their lives are determined not by themselves (that is, by their values, desires, and beliefs) but by what is other than themselves. Since human beings do not appear to be immortal, let alone omnipotent, and since one person's power must often limit the power of another, this sort of freedom can only be possessed to a degree. One may hope to see such power expanded to more people, to more kinds of people, to more aspects of human life. The intellectual project of expanding human freedom through expanding human power runs from the ancient Greeks down to 14th-century "humanism" and the 18th-century "Enlightenment", and so on to the present. On the traditional account, Greek rationality was the enabling precondition for the subsequent development of western scientific inquiry; some recent critics, however, view this as naive and ethnocentric. In any event, one human's power is another's vulnerability, so the quest for freedom is not merely an intellectual or technological undertaking, but requires adjustment in social forms. Except in ideal circumstances, practical freedom requires social and political support (though the demands of political freedom can be viewed as themselves impinging on one's practical freedom).

Freedom in the political sense is the power to participate in a suitable way in the processes that determine the political structure in which one lives. Freedom in society requires limits, and therefore the transformation of external constraints into self-rule (*sophrosyne*). By incorporating aspects of social reality into the self, one can see regulations as expressions of the "civilized" self, which is a creation of the polis. In classical practice, this political conception of freedom can be praised for its natural affinity with notions of democracy, equality, privacy, and individual self-expression, or criticized in view of the restrictions on membership in the polis. To modern readers, Plato's attack on democracy and Aristotle's defence of slavery strike sour notes. Whether the cultural achievements of Athens' golden age "required" the material foundation of slavery on which it in fact relied, and whether such a requirement could serve in any measure to "justify" that society's abridgement of freedoms, are uncomfortable questions still often debated. Several scholars (for example, M.I. Finley and

Orlando Patterson) have suggested that the existence of slavery contributed conceptually to the development of the idea of freedom, which grew out of the very exclusions of Athenian democracy.

If the opposite of political freedom is slavery (and other forms of oppressive dependence), the opposite of philosophical freedom is determinism. The notion of fate or destiny (*moira*) colours early Greek religious thought, and connects to familiar philosophical questions about freedom of the will. Later, Stoic sages advise restricting desire to the sphere in which one is able to exert some control. While one may not have the power to live as one chooses, one can still choose to live one's life in conformity with the power that one does have. Freedom in this philosophical sense consists of adjusting expectations to the realities of one's situation; freedom requires acquiescing in necessity. This viewpoint is expounded in Greek by both slave (Epictetus) and emperor (Marcus Aurelius), with enduring influence on western thought. In the koine Greek of the New Testament, St Paul (whom Gilbert Murray called "one of the greatest Greek writers") adapts the paradox that true freedom consists of acquiescence in being bound by (religious) truth. Paul's frequent references to himself as the "servant" (*doulos*) of God and of Jesus, along with his exhortation to servants "to be obedient unto their own masters" (Titus 2: 9) – though these are part of the transvaluation of values that Nietzsche would later complain about – help to define a religious notion of freedom for Christianity, which plays a dominant role during the Byzantine period of Greek history and after. This religious version of the philosophical notion of freedom also has metaphysical concerns about the place of human action in a non-human world (ruled by God), and it raises political questions, particularly in connection with the idea of a Christian polity, whether that of an empire, like Byzantium, or that of a quasi-secular, henotheistic nation, such as modern Greece. (Additional religious and political complexities characterize the long interval of Turkish domination and the struggle for independence and national self-determination.)

The often expressed (but misleading) idea that Greek civilization was "centred on the individual" may serve to unite the three sorts of freedom, for the individual is a participant in the struggle to survive in nature and in society, as well as the subject of that play of power and desire whose rational articulation comprises the substance of philosophical freedom. Some will find the important expression of human freedom in the expansive, pleasure-seeking, Epicurean (even "Dionysian") approach, while others will hold that a realistic sense of human freedom is best discerned by the restrictive, desire-limiting Stoic (and, in terms of Nietzsche's influential dichotomy, "Apollinian") approach. In this sense, the debate about freedom is not likely to reach either an answer or an end, and it may well be that, in the words that E.R. Dodds quotes from T.H. Huxley, "A man's worst difficulties begin when he is able to do as he likes."

EDWARD JOHNSON

See also Democracy, Fate, Slavery

Further Reading

Berlin, Isaiah, *Four Essays on Liberty*, Oxford and New York: Oxford University Press, 1969
Cromer, Alan, *Uncommon Sense: The Heretical Nature of Science*, Oxford and New York: Oxford University Press, 1993
De Burgh, W.G., *The Legacy of the Ancient World*, London: Macdonald and Evans, and New York: Macmillan, 1924; revised edition 1947
Dodds, E.R., *The Greeks and the Irrational*, Berkeley: University of California Press, 1951
Farrar, Cynthia, *The Origins of Democratic Thinking: The Invention of Politics in Classical Athens*, Cambridge and New York: Cambridge University Press, 1988
Finley, M.I., *Ancient Slavery and Modern Ideology*, London: Chatto and Windus, and New York: Viking, 1980
Finley, M.I., *Economy and Society in Ancient Greece*, London: Chatto and Windus, 1981; New York: Viking, 1982
Hanson, Victor Davis, and John Heath, *Who Killed Homer? The Demise of Classical Education and the Recovery of Greek Wisdom*, New York: Free Press, 1998
Haynes, Denys, *Greek Art and the Idea of Freedom*, London: Thames and Hudson, 1981
Kagan, Donald, *Pericles of Athens and the Birth of Democracy*, London: Secker and Warburg, 1990; New York: Free Press, 1991
Meier, Christian, *The Greek Discovery of Politics*, Cambridge, Massachusetts: Harvard University Press, 1990
Moore, Barrington, Jr, *Privacy: Studies in Social and Cultural History*, Armonk, New York: Sharpe, 1984
Muller, Herbert J., *Freedom in the Ancient World*, New York: Harper and Row, 1961; London: Secker and Warburg, 1962
Murray, Gilbert, *Greek Studies*, Oxford: Clarendon Press, 1946
Oliver, James H., *Demokratia, the Gods, and the Free World*, Baltimore: Johns Hopkins University Press, 1960
Patterson, Orlando, *Freedom*, vol. 1: *Freedom in the Making of Western Culture*, New York: Basic Books, 1991
Pohlenz, Max, *Freedom in Greek Life and Thought: The History of an Ideal*, New York: Humanities Press, 1966
Roberts, Jennifer Tolbert, *Athens on Trial: The Antidemocratic Tradition in Western Thought*, Princeton, New Jersey: Princeton University Press, 1994
Ste Croix, G.E.M. de, *The Class Struggle in the Ancient Greek World: From the Archaic Age to the Arab Conquests*, London: Duckworth, and Ithaca, New York: Cornell University Press, 1981

Fundamentalism, Orthodox

The term "fundamentalism", coined in the US in the 1920s and referring to conservative Protestants reacting against liberal trends, was later used more broadly to describe a variety of different sociocultural phenomena. Though widely used, the term still retains a clear connection to the religious sphere, to which it was originally applied. Another related term is "integrism", referring to analogous phenomena within the Roman Catholic Church. Generally, the main fundamentalist intentions are the purity and authenticity of the doctrine; the emphasis on the "fundamentals" of a religious system; the improvement of practice and its consequential relationship with theory; and the return to a past, glorious epoch, in which the principles of the ideal society had been realized.

There exist numerous reasons and causes, both endogenous and exogenous, which may give rise to fundamentalist currents as protest movements in various socio-cultural contexts worldwide. Usually, fundamentalists react against modernist trends within their religious bodies and to radical changes in their social environments. The fundamentalist mentality must be distinguished generally from a full-fledged fundamentalist movement. While we may find aspects of a fundamentalist attitude in earlier periods too, fundamentalism is basically a modern phenomenon. Moreover, fundamentalism should not be equated simply with fanaticism, radicalism, extremism, reactionism, zealotism, traditionalism, conservatism, and other similar phenomena. Though in many cases closely related to them, fundamentalism points to a more inclusive attempt to reinterpret and incorporate such features into a wider protest movement.

Fundamentalist movements can also be observed within the Orthodox world in modern times (e.g. in Russia). This holds for Greece too, though the term "fundamentalism" has not been successfully rendered into Greek so far. In the Greek case, due to the apparent religious homogeneity of the country, the most marked feature of the fundamentalist movements is their distancing from the official Church, either through a schism (e.g. the Old Calendarists) or through the founding of an independent organization (e.g. the religious brotherhoods). In both cases, serious or milder criticism is exerted on the "pseudo-Orthodox" policies of the official Church, which is accused of playing a solely decorative role in Greek society and of allowing serious compromises with regard to its time-honoured traditions. Orthodox fundamentalists want to purify the Church by imposing certain therapeutic measures and by bringing it closer to a past and idealized golden age (e.g. the Patristic period).

Greek Orthodox fundamentalism is a multiform and multidimensional phenomenon. It cannot be reduced to one single group. Nowadays it is mainly represented by various groups of Old Calendarists, who call themselves the "true Orthodox Christians", and affiliated organizations (e.g. the Greek Orthodox Salvation Movement); by the religious brotherhoods (e.g. *Zoe*, *Sotir*); by various other independent organizations, such as the Panhellenic Orthodox Union with its journal *Orthodoxos Typos*; by numerous monks on Mount Athos and in other monastic communities, who are usually subsumed under the loose category of Zealots; and finally by some small political parties and movements, such as Christian Democracy, founded by N. Psaroudakis. Although there is often tension between them, these groups, which are not hermetically separated one from the other, occasionally collaborate on issues of common interest against the policies of the official Church and the state. It is worth mentioning, however, that several priests and sometimes even bishops of the official Church (e.g. metropolitan Avgustinos Kantiotis, who in 1952 founded in Athens the Orthodox Militant Association "Athanasios the Great") are in close relationship with such movements and share some of their principles and ideals.

The sociohistorical background of Greek Orthodox fundamentalism should be principally sought in late 18th-century Greece. On the eve of its independence Greek society under Ottoman rule underwent far-reaching changes under the impact of western ideas (e.g. of the Enlightenment and the French Revolution), which seriously affected its traditional Byzantine Orthodox culture. This process continued after the foundation of the Greek state, when the Church was subjected to state control and its overall condition deteriorated in many respects. Thus the protest movement of the Kollyvades in the 18th century as well as the cases of Kosmas Flamiatos and

Apostolos Makrakis in the 19th century, who were in serious tension with the official Church, can be considered as antecedents of contemporary fundamentalist trends.

The main and common characteristics of Greek Orthodox fundamentalists include a sense of exclusivity in possessing the sole true faith; a strong feeling of elitism (as being the elect or a faithful remnant); a spirit of self-righteousness and self-sufficiency that leads them to isolation, separatism, and tension with the official Church and the surrounding secular culture; anti-pluralist trends and a totalitarian mentality; a persistent enemy syndrome and conspiracy mentality, imbued with an apocalyptic spirit, that drive them to suspect dangers for Orthodoxy everywhere, initiated by the "Powers of Darkness" (e.g. Roman Catholicism, Protestantism, Freemasonry, Zionism, the ecumenical movement, the European Union) in the contemporary world system; fanaticism, militancy, and even violence (e.g. against beauty contests and carnivals, against the film *The Last Temptation of Christ* and Nikos Kazantzakis's works, the Rotonda incidents in Thessalonica in 1994–95) in implementing their ideals; a special emphasis on moral issues and promotion of their own puritanical, patriarchal ethics and lifestyles; a social activism in order to transform the Church and the world; hyper-Orthodox trends that finally force them to suspect each other of deviations from Orthodoxy; a total rejection of certain scientific (e.g. the theory of evolution) and technical developments; an opposition to intellectualism, freedom of thought, and academic theology; and a strong correlation between Orthodoxy and nationalism concerning the God-determined future glorification of Greece.

Although Greek Orthodox fundamentalists have not yet been very active in politics, they are still greatly interested in playing a more significant role in this domain. To this end, they are also approached by some politicians who occasionally support quite extreme fundamentalist demands and try to profit from the social influence that fundamentalists are able to exercise on certain social strata. The violent conflicts between fundamentalists of varied provenance and the official Church, supported by the state, in the diocese of Larissa (1989–98) over the election of a new bishop have demonstrated the effective structure, the considerable vigour, and the mobilization power of the fundamentalists. This has provoked a determined reaction from the official Church, which fears the long-term impact of such activities upon the wider Church body and the increased appearance of similar phenomena in the future. To this purpose, the Church has issued official encyclicals condemning fundamentalist views and actions as non-Orthodox and anti-ecclesiastical. It also threatened to consider them as schismatics and heretics (see the encyclical no. 2564 of 25 October 1993 against the Panhellenic Orthodox Union and its journal *Orthodoxos Typos*).

Generally speaking, Orthodox fundamentalism is not the most salient characteristic of Greek society as a whole. Yet it does constitute a specific feature of Greek religious life, is able to exert some pressure on official Church and state policies, and, as recent events have shown, may demand more access to positions of power and influence in the future.

VASILIOS MAKRIDES

See also Old Calendarists, Religious Brotherhoods, Zealots

Further Reading

Alexander, Daniel, "Is Fundamentalism an Integrism?", *Social Compass*, 32 (1985): pp. 373–92

Episkepsis, 522 (30 September 1995): pp. 13–37

Lossky, Nicolas, "Fidelité à la foi et intégrismes", *Service Orthodoxe de Presse*, 167 (1992): pp. 28–32

Makrides, Vasilios N., "Aspects of Greek Orthodox Fundamentalism", *Orthodoxes Forum*, 5 (1991): pp. 49–72

Makrides, Vasilios N., "Fundamentalismus: Provlimata ellinikis apodosis tou orou" [Fundamentalism: Problems with the Greek Rendering of the Term], *To Vima ton Koinonikon Epistimon* [Social Science Forum], 4/14 (June 1994): pp. 83–103

Makrides, Vasilios N., "Fundamentalismus aus religionswissenschaftlicher Sicht", *Dialog der Religionen*, 4 (1994): pp. 2–25

Mantzaridis, Georgios, *Prosopo kai thesmoi* [The Individual and Institutions], Thessalonica, 1997, pp. 79–98

Papandreou, Damaskinos, Metropolitan of Switzerland, *Logos Dialogou (I Orthodoxia enopion tis Tritis Chilietias)* [Grounds for Dialogue (Orthodoxy at the Start of the Third Millennium)], Athens, 1997, pp. 293–302

Stewart, Charles, "Who Owns the Rotonda? Church vs State in Greece", *Anthropology Today*, 14/15 (1998): pp. 3–9

Yannaras, Christos, "Die Herausforderung des orthodoxen Traditionalismus", *Concilium*, 28 (1992): pp. 249–54

Zacharopoulos, Nikos, "Kindynologia gia ta Ekklisiastikopolitika Pragmata tis Ellados ton Meson tou 19ou aiona: Dyo Anekdotes Epistoles tou Kosma Flamiatou" [Risk-Assessment in Greek Church Politics of the mid-19th Century: Two Unpublished Letters of Kosmas Flamiatos] in *Diakonia: Aphieroma sti Mnimi tou Vasileiou Stoyannou* [Ministration: An Offering to the Memory of Vasilios Stoyannos], Thessalonica, 1988

Furniture

The human activities of sitting, eating, lying down, and storing objects required furniture in the homes of ancient Greece. The development of hierarchic sociopolitical structures in the Bronze Age gave added impetus to furniture development, in the multiplicity of forms and decorative embellishments, as seen in the decorative ivory and gold inlays from the Mycenaean period.

Stationary furniture, such as dining couches, and outdoor furniture, such as benches in a theatre, was often sculpted out of bronze and stone. But furniture construction was generally within the province of carpenters, because wood was the typical material, being relatively lightweight, durable, and easy to fashion. Wood varieties mentioned by ancient Greek authors include maple, beech, oak, willow, cedar, cypress, yew, juniper, poplar, fir, lime, olive, elm, and pine. By the 6th century BC Greek carpenters had most of the possible hand tools for working wood – the adze, axe, saw, plane, hammer, chisel, borer, screwdriver, file, rule, level, plummet, and lathe. Joinery techniques depended on wood constructions of dowel and tenons, socket and tongues, butterfly cramps, and complex mitre joins rather than metal hardware. Steamed bent wood is seen in the chair backs of the 6th and 5th centuries BC. Finishing techniques included veneer, painting with geometric decorations, and oil polish.

The earliest references to Greek furniture are from the Mycenaean culture. The original 13 Linear B furniture tablets found in the palace at Pylos in 1939 (now in the National Archaeological Museum, Athens) record elaborate chairs, footstools, and tables made out of stone, crystal, yew, boxwood, or ebony inlaid with ivory decorations depicting cattle, lions, stags, trees, men, shells, and rosettes. Ivory ornaments have been found at several Mycenaean sites that are probably the inlaid remains of such furniture, from which the wood has disintegrated. Additional evidence comes from the miniature, crudely painted terracottas found in graves that portray low, simple beds and three-legged, sling-back chairs. Clay benches were common and found at Pylos, as was a big clay bathtub. A fresco from Pylos shows tall three-legged wooden tables carried by votaries.

Evidence for furniture from the Greek historical period consists largely of literary sources and images on pottery and sculpture, and consequently, our knowledge is limited primarily to Classical Athens. The types of ancient furniture included chairs and stools, benches, beds and dining couches, tables, and chests. Round metal or pottery oil lamps, which held a wick in the spout, provided light and could be placed on the floor, a shelf, or on tall bronze, single-legged stands. Personal possessions remained few, and clothing simple. Most household objects were stored by hanging them on the wall or placing them in chests (*kibotoi* or *larnakes*) or small boxes. Clothing in particular could be folded flat, since it was made of rectangular pieces of cloth, and stacked in large chests with a top lid. Thrones (*thronoi*) and footstools (*thrinyes*) were manufactured with animal legs, which had been popular in Egypt and Mesopotamia; lathe-turned legs, which become common in Greece only after the 7th century BC; rectangular legs; or solid sides extending to the floor. Thrones had a hierarchic meaning in that they elevated and enlarged the stature of the nobility and, of course, deities. The popular, lightweight chair (*klismos*) with curved back and legs was an extraordinarily graceful Greek invention that was used for domestic purposes; it was easy to lounge in while draping one arm over the back. Four-legged (*diphros*) or folding stools (*diphros okladias*) were also used for seating. Tables, usually three-legged (*trapezai*), were lightweight due to dining customs. Food was carried on these low portable tables from kitchen to dining-room and removed afterwards or pushed under the dining couches so that the space could be used for entertainment. The dining couches (*klinai*), on the other hand, were stationary, often the only permanent furniture in the house, and so could be solidly made and heavy, sometimes constructed of bronze. Eating while lying down was practised in the ancient Near East on waist-high couches, mounted by means of a footstool, but the long bow-curved end of the Assyrian couch was not adopted in Greece. Instead, the Greek couch extended two of its legs higher than the seat to support the arm-rest pillows. Dining couches carried specific social connotations, in that well-born men used them for sleeping or dining. They usually shared a couch with another man or a courtesan. Wives, however, dined in separate quarters, upright on chairs.

There is less evidence for furniture from the Byzantine era. Thrones are the predominant furniture shown in mosaics, ivories, and manuscripts, due to the prominence of saints and kings being portrayed. They were elaborately carved as seen on the ivory Harbaville Triptych in the Louvre of *c.*AD 950 or studded with jewels, as on the throne on the mosaic of the Virgin and Child enthroned in Hagia Sophia, of *c.*850.

Simple one-room houses with a ground floor and upper level were typical throughout the medieval era in Greece. The furnishings were sparse with wooden screens carved with vegetal motifs to hide the sleeping areas, built-in wooden cupboards with carved doors, low round tables, chairs, chests, and stools. Wooden furniture from Skyros and Crete was particularly well known for its high quality. The quality of wood carving remained high as carpenters were continually occupied by carving wooden iconostases and other church furnishings, particularly in western Macedonia and the islands.

By the 18th century a wealthy merchant class arose in Greece who built large homes in western Macedonia, Epirus, the Peloponnese, and the islands. Influenced by western European fashions, elaborate reception rooms were covered with wood panelling of open fretwork, carved flower panels, and complex mouldings, as can be seen in the room of such a house, built in Kozani in the late 17th century, and now on exhibition in the Benaki Museum in Athens. Furnishings in these merchant houses remained simple, with cupboards, armchairs, stools, and low tables.

Greek furniture has continued to follow European furniture styles from Neoclassicism to Modern and finally Postmodern design. Most furniture today comes from Athens and Thessalonica.

CATHERYN CHEAL

See also Woodworking

Further Reading

Baker, Hollis, *Furniture in the Ancient World: Origins and Evolution, 3100 BC–475 BC*, New York: Macmillan, and London: The Connoisseur, 1966

Higgins, R., "The Archaeological Background to the Furniture Tablets from Pylos", *Bulletin of the Institute of Classical Studies*, 3 (1956)

Hill, D.K., "A Bronze Couch", *Journal of the Walters Art Gallery*, 15–16 (1952–53): pp. 49ff.

Hill, D.K., "Ivory Ornaments of Hellenistic Couches", *Hesperia*, 32 (1963): pp. 293ff.

Picon, Carlos, "Table Support Decorated with Griffins", *Metropolitan Museum of Art Bulletin*, 53 (Fall 1995): pp. 8–9

Richter, Gisela M.A., "The Furnishings of Ancient Greek Houses", *Archaeology*, 18 (1965): pp. 26ff.

Richter, Gisela M.A., *The Furniture of the Greeks, Etruscans, and Romans*, London: Phaidon, 1966

Robsjohn-Gibbings, T.H. and C.W. Pullin, *Furniture of Classical Greece*, New York: Knopf, 1963

Seltman, C., "Two Athenian Marble Thrones", *Journal of Hellenic Studies*, 47 (1947): pp. 22ff.

Ventris, Michael, "Mycenaean Furniture on the Pylos Tablets", *Eranos*, 53 (1955): pp. 109ff.

G

Galen AD 129–?208/16
Physician and philosopher

Galen, a prolific Greek physician and philosopher born in Asia Minor (Pergamum), became the dominant influence on European medicine from the Roman empire until the Renaissance. The son of a prosperous architect, he was educated in rhetoric and studied philosophy under Platonists, Aristotelians, and Stoics in Pergamum before taking up the study of medicine. The effects of this early training on his thought and style remain amply visible in the more than 170 fully and partly extant treatises attributed to him (a substantial majority of which are of undisputed authenticity). After continuing his studies under distinguished physicians in Smyrna and Alexandria, Galen returned to Pergamum in AD 157, where he apparently became a spectacularly successful physician to wounded gladiators. In AD 162 he went to Rome, returning to Asia Minor in 166, only to be called back by Marcus Aurelius in 169 to serve the Roman imperial court, in whose service he remained thereafter.

Galen attempted to give a comprehensive, detailed account of all aspects of medicine: anatomy, physiology, nosology, aetiology, diagnosis, prognosis, pathology, therapeutics, dietetics, pharmacology, surgery, deontology, ethics, psychology, medical education, medical history, theory of scientific method, and so on. He constantly wove conceptual, doctrinal, epistemological, and methodological links between the different branches of his comprehensive enquiry, thus lending his project the appearance of a systematic, monumental, and scientific whole. Furthermore, he had many impressive prognostic, surgical, and other therapeutic successes (for example, removing a suppurating breastbone and often succeeding where all other practitioners had failed), proving that he was not merely a brilliant theorist but also an accomplished clinician.

Galen's public anatomical demonstrations, at which he dissected and vivisected various animals, appealed to the theatrical sense of a 2nd-century audience attuned to the "display" culture of the Sophists' public declamations. Unlike Herophilus and Erasistratus, he never performed systematic dissections of human cadavers, and his use of comparative anatomy at times led him to attribute non-human features to the human body. His meticulous dissections of monkeys, apes, pigs, goats, etc. (recorded in *On Anatomical Procedures*) nevertheless allowed him to correct numerous observations and theories of his predecessors.

A voracious reader, Galen eagerly displayed his encyclopedic knowledge of the works of his precursors and contemporaries, and, for the most part, he was unsparing in his criticism of them. Even to Plato and Hippocrates, whom he revered more than all others – and whose views, he argued at length, are essentially in agreement (*On the Doctrines of Hippocrates and Plato*) – Galen at times responded with independence and originality. By constantly incorporating the history of medicine and of philosophy in impressive, if often self-serving, critical detail, he positioned his treatises as superseding all others. An invaluable, if unintended, benefit of this Galenic strategy is that he is an invaluable source for the history of medicine between the Hippocratic Corpus and the 2nd century AD, providing numerous quotations from the lost works of Diocles, Herophilus, Erasistratus, Asclepiades, and others. He likewise preserves significant evidence concerning lost philosophical works (e.g. of Posidonius) and many fragments of Greek poetry.

Galen used his keen philosophical ability to lend his work the authority of a sophisticated logic of scientific demonstration. He viewed medicine as a completable axiomatic science. Any gaps, errors, and inaccuracies in scientific medicine arise, he believed, not from the nature of the medical *techne* itself but from human cognitive or linguistic failures or from quantitative imprecision. His mastery of logic – to which he made original contributions – as well as his teleology and his treatment of many psychophysical questions rendered Galenic medicine appealing to numerous philosophers, too, in subsequent centuries.

Anatomical investigations and physiological experiments provide scientific proof of the providentiality of nature, Galen insisted. "Nature does nothing in vain": on this point he agreed with Aristotle, but he defended a stronger version of teleology than perhaps any of his predecessors. In his principal work on physiology (*On the Usefulness of the Parts*), Galen attributes the pervasive purposiveness visible in the body to a divine, craftsman-like "Nature", evoking many echoes of Plato's *Timaeus* (on which he wrote a commentary). Though reserved on issues such as the immortality of the soul, Galen adapted the Platonic version of a tripartite soul to his anatomical discoveries, locating its three parts in the brain, the heart, and the liver, respectively. From the brain, he argued, psychic *pneuma*, derived from the vital *pneuma* in the arteries, is distributed through the nerves (making sensory and motor activity possible). All the principal physiological activities – respiration, heart-beat and pulse, ingestion and digestion, sensation, and voluntary motor activity – are interdependent and interactive, brought together in a single, coherent, teleological model. In pathology Galen appropriated the four-humour theory of the Hippocratic treatise *On the Nature of Humans*: the relative proportions of four juices or liquids in the body – phlegm, yellow bile, black bile, and blood – determine health and disease.

The medical authority of Galen's vast corpus was rarely challenged in the millennium after his death. Already in the 3rd century AD he was recognized as surpassing all other physicians. In the 4th century Nemesius, bishop of Emesa, made extensive use of Galen in his *On the Nature of Humans*. Galen's fervent advocacy of teleology made him acceptable to many Christians, and he was admired by a heretical sect, the Adaptionists, who tried to provide a rational, philosophical basis for Christian doctrine, perhaps prompted in part by Galen's criticisms of Christians and Jews. In the mid-4th century Oribasius initiated a long tradition of excerpting and summarizing Galenic texts. Aëtius of Amida and Alexander of Tralles (who was not uncritical of Galen) continued this tradition in the 6th century, as did Paul of Aegina in the 7th. In Alexandria physicians and Neoplatonists alike lectured on Galen throughout later antiquity; the Christian Neoplatonist John Philoponus (AD 490–570s) had high praise for Galen's original contributions to logic and science, as did his contemporary Simplicius.

The Alexandrian iatrosophists of late antiquity selected a canon of perhaps 16 Galenic writings to be read in schools, to be summarized, and to be commented upon. The first four treatises in the canon were *On Sects for Beginners*, *The Medical Art*, *On the Pulse for Beginners*, and *To Glaucon on the Method of Healing*. For the most part, the Alexandrians' selection and sequence do not correspond to Galen's own propaedeutic recommendations, but they became a decisive step in the Alexandrians' scholastic transformation of the Galenic oeuvre into a medical system that was to dominate European and much of Arabic medicine for centuries.

Among numerous other Byzantine writers who drew extensively on Galen, whether directly or indirectly, are Stephanos of Athens (who wrote a commentary on Galen's *To Glaucon on the Method of Healing*), Meletios the Monk, Theophilos Protospatharios, and John (Zacharias) Aktouarios.

A rare Byzantine attempt at refuting Galen occurs in a treatise by the 11th-century scientist Symeon Seth, who was equally familiar with Greek and Arabic traditions. Tensions between Aristotelians and Galenists grew as Aristotle and Galen came to be recognized as the two greatest representatives of a science rooted in logic and in systematic philosophy. Numerous translations, summaries, commentaries on Galen's treatises, and adaptations of his work in a variety of languages (e.g. Latin, Syriac, Arabic, and Hebrew) attest to his stature both in the East and in the West. Even when his authority began to be challenged, especially after the resumption of systematic human dissection in the early modern period,

Galenism remained a powerful force in European medical thought for several centuries.

HEINRICH VON STADEN

See also Anatomy and Physiology, Dioscurides, Health, Herophilus, Hippocrates, Nicander

Biography

Born in Pergamum in AD 129, Galen was the son of an architect. He studied rhetoric and philosophy in Pergamum before turning to medicine. After further study in Smyrna and Alexandria he returned to Pergamum in 157 and went to Rome in 162. Returning to Asia Minor in 166, he was recalled by Marcus Aurelius in 169 and remained in imperial service until his death in 208 or 216. He was a prolific writer on all aspects of medicine; more than 170 surviving works are attributed to him.

Writings

Opera Omnia, edited by Karl Gottlob Kühn, 20 vols, Leipzig, 1821–33; reprinted Hildesheim: Olms, 1964–65 (the most recent reasonably complete modern edition)
On the Natural Faculties, translated by Arthur John Brock, London: Heinemann, 1916
On Anatomical Procedures, translated by Charles Singer, London and New York: Oxford University Press, 1956
On the Usefulness of the Parts of the Body, translated by Margaret Tallmadge May, 2 vols, Ithaca, New York: Cornell University Press, 1968 (includes commentary)
Three Treatises on the Nature of Science, translated by Michael Frede and Richard Walzer, Indianapolis: Hackett, 1985
On the Therapeutic Method, books 1–2, translated by R.J. Hankinson, Oxford: Clarendon Press, and New York: Oxford University Press, 1991 (includes commentary)
Selected Works, translated by P.N. Singer, Oxford and New York: Oxford University Press, 1997 (with a useful bibliography)

Further Reading

Bowersock, G.W., *Greek Sophists in the Roman Empire*, Oxford: Clarendon Press, 1969 (chapter 5)
Debru, Armelle (editor), *Galen on Pharmacology: Philosophy, History, and Medicine*, Leiden: Brill, 1997
Haase, Wolfgang (editor), *Aufstieg und Niedergang der römischen Welt*, 2.37.2, Berlin: de Gruyter, 1994 (17 contributions on Galen [some in English], including a comprehensive bibliography by J. Kollesch and D. Nickel)
Kollesch, Jutta and Diethard Nickel (editors), *Galen und das hellenistische Erbe*, Stuttgart: Steiner, 1993 (some important contributions in English)
Kudlien, Fridolf and Richard J. Durling (editors), *Galen's Method of Healing: Proceedings of the 1982 Galen Symposium*, Leiden: Brill, 1991
Lloyd, G.E.R., *Methods and Problems in Greek Science*, Cambridge and New York: Cambridge University Press, 1991, chapter 17
López, Férez, J.A. (editor), *Galeno: obra, pensamiento e influencía*, Madrid: UNED, 1991 (includes articles in English)
Manuli, Paola and Mario Vegetti (editors), *Le opere psicologiche di Galeno*, Naples: Bibliopolis, 1988 (several important contributions in English)
Nutton, Vivian (editor), *Galen: Problems and Prospects*, London: Wellcome Institute, 1981
Nutton, Vivian, *From Democedes to Harvey: Studies in the History of Medicine*, London: Variorum, 1988 (especially chapters 1–3)
Ottosson, Per-Gunnar, *Scholastic Medicine and Philosophy: A Study of Commentaries on Galen's Tegni, ca. 1300-1450*, Naples: Bibliopolis, 1984
Rescher, Nicholas, *Galen and the Syllogism*, Pittsburgh: Pittsburgh University Press, 1966

Smith, Wesley D., *The Hippocratic Tradition*, Ithaca, New York: Cornell University Press, 1979 (especially "Galen's Hippocratism", pp. 61–176)

Temkin, Owsei, *Galenism: Rise and Decline of a Medical Philosophy*, Ithaca, New York: Cornell University Press, 1973

Walzer, Richard, *Galen on Jews and Christians*, London: Oxford University Press, 1949

Games and Sports

Influenced by the Minoans, and possibly also by the Egyptians, the Mycenaeans almost certainly engaged in athletic activities. Myth suggests the purposes as honouring a god (e.g. Zeus at the Olympic Games) or a dead hero (e.g. Patroclus' funeral games in book 23 of the *Iliad*) or just as entertainment (e.g. the Phaeacian games in book 8 of the *Odyssey*). By the classical period they were both an essential part of the school curriculum for boys and a pursuit for youths and men of all classes at the public gymnasia and the private palaestrae. The Greek attitude to them is most succinctly encapsulated in the famous phrase of Juvenal (10. 356), *mens sana in corpore sano* (a healthy mind in a healthy body), which does not, however, come from an athletic context. Alexander the Great's subjugation of the Near East in the 4th century BC spread this attitude to non-Greeks, most surprisingly, perhaps, to young Jewish priests who in the 2nd century BC forsook their duties in the temple for the delights of the discus (2 Maccabees, 4. 7–17). Even 300 years after Alexander's more evanescent conquests deeper into Asia, an Indian prince was throwing the discus and the javelin in an especially laid-out area of his palace. Athletic sports did not, however, have much appeal to the Romans, whose gladiatorial atrocities were in turn generally despised by the Greeks.

Although girls, especially in Sparta, participated in some athletic events including on occasion even wrestling, adult women were denied the opportunity. From the 6th century BC all males (except in equestrian events) competed naked, their bodies, to prevent dirt entering the pores, covered in olive oil which was later scraped off with a strigil. Homer describes chariot racing, boxing, wrestling, running, an armed joust, the throwing of a stone and of a piece of metal, and archery. In the classical period the events that comprised the competitions at the public games fell into four groups: running, the pentathlon, fighting, and equestrian events.

Apart from relay races with a torch for a baton, which were rather part of religious cult than athletically competitive, there were four running-races: the *stade* and the race in armour were one length of the stadium and the *diaulos* two, while the *dolichos* was a long-distance race. As the lengths of stadia differed, so did those of these races, but they approximated to a furlong (200 m), a quarter of a mile (400 m), and three miles (4.8 km) (the marathon is a modern commemoration of Phidippides' run from Marathon to Athens to announce the victory over the Persians in 490 BC). The *stade*, the original event in the Olympics, traditionally founded in 776 BC, carried the most prestige. In all races runners first started, at the sound of a trumpet, from a *gramme* (scratch-mark) in the sand, but in the 6th century BC this was replaced by a *balbis* (stone sill)

with grooves for the toes, to which was added in the 5th century a *husplex* (starting gate). This last was operated by a man behind the runners releasing simultaneously cords which were attached to horizontal bars on vertical posts in front of each runner (the remains at Isthmia provide the best archaeological evidence). Turning-posts were used in the *diaulos* and *dolichos*, but it is not known if each runner had his own post or if, more likely, they all turned round the same post. There was no finishing-tape, and if the judges could not distinguish a winner a rerun was held. Heats were used when more than the 16–20 runners that the varying widths of stadia could accommodate competed.

The pentathlon, first devised probably for the Olympic Games of 708 BC, comprised five activities: a jump, a discus throw, a javelin throw, a *stade* race, and wrestling, for the first three of which there were no separate competitions. The winner was the first athlete to win three events: running and wrestling presumably took place only if no clear winner had already been determined. Despite the pentathlon's popularity on vase-paintings, Plato's comment (*Amatores* 135e) that it was the opportunity for the second-rate athlete, and the small prizes for winners known from the Hellenistic period, suggest that it ranked low in prestige.

The jump was performed to the sound of pipes as a rhythmic aid by athletes who held *halteres* (jumping-weights) of 1.8 to 3.6 kg in their hands. Since the only three recorded distances are between 15 and 17 m, the jump is most likely to have been a multiple jump, perhaps the modern hop-step-and-jump or triple jump which was introduced as an interpretation of the ancient event. Aristotle claims (*De Incessu Animalius* 705a17) that the athletes jumped further with *halteres*, and modern athletes have found that weights can improve distance in the long jump (and, if they are released, even in the high jump), but it is difficult to see how this could be possible in a multiple jump unless they were released in the first segment. The evidence of both literature and vase-painting, however, points unanimously to their retention.

The discus was usually made of bronze in the Classical period. Surviving examples vary in diameter from 16 to 34 cm and in weight from 1.3 to 6.8 kg. Although the athlete threw forwards from an area demarcated in front and at the sides, and could consequently make a preliminary run, he is unlikely to have done this. Vase-paintings and sculptures show reversed feet, probably indicating at least a partial turn of the body, and a rope-like pull with the right arm. The only recorded throw is of 29 m.

The javelin was generally made of cornel wood tipped with bronze. It was thrown, after a run, by an athlete holding it roughly horizontal above his head, with a thong wrapped round the shaft and looped over the first or first two fingers of the throwing hand. This perhaps gave added leverage, but certainly enabled the javelin to spin on its own axis, thus being steadier in flight and, in its military equivalent, boring into its target like a bullet. It had at least to nick the ground on landing.

The three fighting events were wrestling, boxing, and the *pankration* with no weight divisions, rings, or rounds. Judges attended the fights and beat with canes those who infringed the rules. The longevity of some fighters was remarkable: Milon, a boxer from Croton in the 6th century, must have been a cham-

Games: terracotta figures playing knucklebone, *c.*340-330 BC, from southern Italy, British Museum, London

pion for at least 21 years since he won six Pythian crowns (and five Olympic). Weightlifting must largely be considered as a form of training for these fighting events rather than as a sport in its own right.

Wrestlers, who had to make their opponents' shoulders touch the ground three times in order to win, were not allowed any leg-holds, although their legs could be used to sweep opponents off the ground. Vase-paintings and sculptures show numerous holds, upon which the modern Graeco-Roman style is based.

The aim of the boxer was to incapacitate his opponent (there are only two recorded deaths, both the result of fouls), or to force him to submit by raising an index finger. As was probably the case in Minoan boxing, the head was the sole target, and vase-paintings frequently show boxers (always right-handed) with head held back and chest thrust forward. In the 1st century AD a remarkable athlete from Caria named Melancomas displayed a completely different technique by skipping out of the way of his more ponderous opponents until they gave up in exhaustion. He is reputed never to have been hit and to have engaged in one bout that lasted two days. In training, shadow boxing was practised and fighters wore ear-guards and, to avoid hurting each other excessively, padded gloves, but in competition they bound *himantes* (thongs) round the knuckles for self-protection: the nickname *murmekes* (ants), applied to these *himantes*, indicates how they stung .

The *pankration*, which had the same aim as boxing, was a fight in which everything was allowed except gouging and biting. To judge from the number of poems commissioned from Pindar by pankratiasts and the magnitude of Hellenistic prizes, this was an event which both carried considerable prestige and appealed to the upper class.

Chariot-racing was for aristocrats, owners rather than competitors receiving the prizes. Despite the pride of place given to it by Homer, it did not feature in the Olympic Games until the 25th celebration in 680 BC. Light chariots were pulled by teams of two or four horses, or two mules or two foals, completing up to 12 laps between two markers. Hippodromes varied enormously in size from about 275 m to one in Athens that allowed a race of about 1.6 km without a turn. At Olympia the track was about 550 m long, and at the sound of a trumpet a rope barrier across stalls set in a convex line was removed in such a way as to give all teams a fair start, each driver having a flying start on his inside rival. Over 40 teams are known to have taken part in a single race. Bareback riding was far less popular, but appeared at Olympia as early as 648 BC.

Although not recommended by medical practitioners, most Greeks could swim according to Herodotus (8. 89), who attributes the large number of survivors from the Battle of Salamis in 480 BC to this fact. The 6th-century Sicilian Olympic boxer Tisander used long-distance swimming for training. References are found to both breaststroke and front crawl, while beginners had the help of cork lifebelts and a fresco of the 5th century BC from Paestum shows a youth diving from what appears to be a diving-tower. There is literary evidence for occasional swimming races, while regattas for rowing were certainly held in the Imperial period.

Ball games were apparently aimed at healthy exercise (in the 2nd century AD Galen, in his *De Parvae Pilae Exercitu*, is particularly enthusiastic) and pleasure rather than serious competition, but they were important enough to form the subject of a lost treatise by the Laconian Timocrates (Athenaeus, 1. 15c). Homer describes Nausicaa and her attendants throwing a ball to each other, a late archaic bas-relief from Athens depicts what looks like a bully-off in hockey between two players while others with curved sticks look on, another bas-relief shows a throw-in in a team game, a black-figure vase shows a game in which an old man leaning on a stick is throwing a ball to three pairs of youths piggyback in front of him, a 5th-century relief has a youth bouncing (or balancing) a ball on his thigh (Spartan youths in the Roman period played a ball game with teams of 14 a side), and in the 2nd century AD Pollux describes (9.4) the game of *episkuros* that sounds a little like rugby football without any kicking.

Other games included hoop bowling (for youths as well as children), marbles, and, for the more sedentary, dice, knucklebones, and draughts, which last was played on a board of 36 squares with a "sacred line" down the centre to separate home from enemy territory. The most frequently mentioned game is *kottabos*, in which inebriated symposiasts, while reclining on their left elbows, threw with their right hands the last drops from their wine cups at varied targets such as saucers floating in water and objects that could fall when struck.

In Byzantium sport suffered from its pagan associations and Christianity's contempt for mundane activities. The most popular spectator sport was chariot-racing, but its style and organization of factions were Roman rather than Greek. With the waning of Roman influence it survived after the 7th century only in Constantinople and even there only as a part of imperial ceremonial. A total of 66 days' racing a year with about 24 races a day in the 5th century dropped to fewer than 12 days of only eight races by the 10th century and after 1204 the sport disappeared completely. It was to some degree supplanted by *tzykanion*, a Persian version of polo that resembled mounted lacrosse. It was introduced as early as the 5th century AD by Theodosius II, but was popularized in the 10th century by the Armenian-born John I Tzimiskes, and was the cause of a fatal injury to John I Komnenos Axouch at Trebizond in 1238. As military training John Tzimiskes introduced one cavalry game in which a horseman had to avoid or catch the blunted javelins of four opponents, and another in which galloping horsemen shot arrows at hats that they had hurled into the air (these games survive in Georgia as *isindi* and *kabakhi* respectively). Western influence brought to Constantinople the *tournemen* and the *dzoustra*, the massed tourney and the individual joust. Horsemanship was displayed also by aristocrats in the hunting of boar, bears, and deer both in the wild and, especially from the 10th century, in imperial game parks. The principal weapon was the spear, while dogs and even cheetahs were trained for the hunt. Most popular among smaller game were hares and quails. Fowling was always a method of supplying the table, but falconry became an aristocratic enthusiasm chiefly under the Komnenoi.

Although under Christian influence gladiatorial combat ceased in the 4th century, canon law did allow wrestling, boxing, running, jumping, and discus throwing. Archery was primarily for military training, while juggling and gymnastics were spectator sports in the hippodrome. Board games were frowned upon by the Church both for the associated gambling and the role of *Tyche* (chance). Dice, knucklebones, and chequers were, however, all known and Alexios I (1081–1157) played chess with members of his family.

As in most of the rest of the modern world, the favourite team sport of Greeks today is association football (soccer), in which their national and leading club sides enjoy fanatical support and have occasionally beaten more powerful sides without having ever won any European or world competitions (Greece did reach the finals of the World Cup in 1994, although it was well beaten in all its three matches in the first round). Basketball and volleyball come next in popular support. Most international success has been won in the individual sports of wrestling and weightlifting, which only in part explains the preponderance of successful male rather than female Greek athletes. In one sport Greece has enjoyed a fame quite out of proportion to its importance in the country. After Corfu was declared a British protectorate at the Congress of Vienna in 1815, soldiers of the British garrison played cricket on the Esplanade (until recently merely gravel), and in 1855 the first two local clubs of Greeks rather than expatriates began to play the game with a unique medley of Greek, English, and Italian terminology: official recognition came 140 years later when the International Cricket Council granted Greece affiliate membership. The most distinctive Greek game today, however, must be *tavli* (a form of backgammon): the clatter of its counters is the instantly recognizable sound of every *kafeneion*.

Greece's sporting legacy to the modern world is incalculable. Its emphasis upon athletic activity for young and old was a major impetus during the 19th century, first in England and thence elsewhere, in the introduction of sport into the educational curriculum and its acceptance as a respectable activity for adults of all classes. The modern Olympic Games are the abiding memorial of the Greek devotion to athletics.

A.R. LITTLEWOOD

See also Hippodrome, Olympic Games

Further Reading

Beck, F.A.G., *Album of Greek Education: the Greeks at School and Play*, Sydney: Cheiron Press, 1975 (especially plates 54–68)

Bryer, A.A.M., "Byzantine Games", *History Today* (July 1967): pp. 453–59

Cameron, Alan, *Porphyrius the Charioteer*, Oxford: Clarendon Press, 1973

Cameron, Alan, *Circus Factions: Blues and Greens at Rome and Byzantium*, Oxford: Clarendon Press, 1976

Decker, W., *Sport in der griechischen Antike: vom minoischen Wettkampf bis zu den Olympischen Spielen*, Munich: Beck, 1995

Finley, M.I. and H.W. Pleket, *The Olympic Games: The First Thousand Years*, London: Chatto and Windus, and New York: Viking, 1976

Forte, John, *Play's the Thing: A Medley of Corfu and Cricket*, London: Darf, 1988

Gardiner, Edward Norman, *Athletics of the Ancient World*, Oxford: Clarendon Press, 1930

Harris, H.A., *Greek Athletes and Athletics*, London: Hutchinson, 1964

Harris, H.A., *Sport in Greece and Rome*, London: Thames and Hudson, and Ithaca, New York: Cornell University Press, 1972

Koukoules, Phaidon, *Byzantinon Bios kai Politismos* [Byzantine Life and Culture], vol. 3, Athens, 1948, pp. 7–147

Kretzenbacher, "Ritterspiel und Ringreiten im europäischen Südosten", *Südost-Forschungen*, 22 (1963): pp. 437–55

Miller, Stephen G. (editor), *Arete: Greek Sports from Ancient Sources*, 2nd edition, Berkeley: University of California Press, 1991 (English translation of sources)

Yalouris, Nicolaos *et al.* (editors), *The Eternal Olympics: The Art and History of Sport*, New Rochelle, New York: Caratzas, 1979 (excellent source of illustrations)

Gardens

Finds of plant pots of clay or faience with holes at the base attest to the cultivation of flowers or herbs in the Aegean area in the 2nd millennium BC. The art of the Mycenaeans shows a persistence of floral motifs which is probably due to the non-Greek but associated and culturally influential Minoans, in whose frescos, glyptic art, metalwork, and painted pottery floral landscapes figure prominently. Although there is as yet no evidence that the Mycenaeans actually cultivated pleasure gardens, it is probable that the Minoans, under Egyptian inspiration, may have done so. A restored fresco of the Middle to Late Minoan period from a villa at Amnisos northeast of Knossos appears to show lilies arranged in a formal setting reminiscent of a garden. Excavation suggests the possibility of terraced gardens leading off porticoes in some Minoan palaces. At Phaestus in central Crete a rocky outcrop in the southeast area of the palace was not only cut back but also furnished with round holes, most likely once filled with soil and planted with flowers to create a tiny garden for the associated court and portico. The flowers in vases depicted in several frescos are, however, probably not growing but cut and wild.

The epics attributed to Homer, which frequently reflect the culture of the dark age rather than the preceding Mycenaean period, contain descriptions of gardens. Although these are mainly kitchen gardens and orchards providing grapes, olives, figs, apples, pears, pomegranates, and vegetables, there is also mention of groves associated with the shrines of gods and the graves of heroes. The almost lyrical delight in the beauties of nature shown in these poems is in sharp contrast to the harsh realities of practical agriculture in the roughly contemporary *Works and Days* of Hesiod.

Private gardens in the Classical period were again almost entirely utilitarian, even flower gardens having profit as their primary purpose in the sale of their produce for garlands. Unlike the situation in the Persian and the later Roman empires, horticulture and even agriculture were not considered gentlemanly pursuits in Greece. Urban houses were simple and small with no surrounding land but a central courtyard that rarely measured more than about 50 square metres, was usually paved, often contained a well and an altar, and served for many everyday domestic activities: it could have accommodated at best only a few potted herbs. The sole common private non-utilitarian gardens were the so-called Gardens of Adonis, but these were merely pots of fast-growing plants that died quickly and thus symbolized the life and death of the divine Adonis.

Public gardens in the Classical period were largely groves of trees (especially cypress, plane, and laurel) around shrines and were chosen for cultic reasons and to give shade. These sanctuaries sometimes also included stands of trees and fields of crops for commercial purposes. Two of the best-known groves were at the shrines of Aphrodite outside Athens and of Zeus and Aphrodite at Cyrene. The only one hitherto excavated surrounded the temple of Hephaestus in the Athenian Agora, but its date is as late as *c.*300 BC. Excavation of square pits dug into the bedrock indicates two straight rows of shrubs or small trees on three sides of the temple and small flowerbeds against the precinct wall. The pits contained deliberately broken pots used for the method of propagation known as layering by circumposition. Groves were planted also at gymnasia, which were themselves often associated with sanctuaries. Such is the origin of the schools of Plato and Aristotle, the Academy and Lyceum respectively, which set the pattern for later philosophical gardens, most notably that of Epicurus, which he left at his death to Athens as a public park.

The changes in the Hellenistic period are primarily due to two factors: the creation of new cities, most notably Alexandria in Egypt, enabled a more generous disposition of buildings with extensive open areas available for sanctuaries and public parks; and the substitution of autocracy for democracy or oligarchy encouraged rulers to spend public revenues on grandiose works that enhanced their prestige, these works including gardens in imitation of oriental monarchs. The most outrageous of these works was a ship designed by Archimedes in the 3rd century BC for Hieron II of Sicily that included a gymnasium with bowers of vines and numerous irrigated flowerbeds, while in the 2nd century Attalus III of Pergamum grew drugs on the deck of his flagship. Terrestrial parks often had artificial grottoes, fountains, sculptures, and an increasing range of plants, an interest attested by botanical treatises such as those of Theophrastus. Private homes, although often larger and more luxurious than earlier because of an increase in wealth, still tended not to include gardens, the central courtyard being often floored in mosaic.

Gardens in the Greek world under Roman rule were Roman in inspiration. The paved Greek courtyard became a peristyle garden with artistic fountains and formally arranged shrubs and flowerbeds. When space was cramped, roof gardens were created and walls were painted in the verisimilitude of gardens complete with birds. Grandees owned numerous villas that were single entities incorporating buildings, porticoes, terraces, arbours, shrubberies, and flowerbeds and occasionally included even a game park. Landscaping, topiary work, sculptures, elaborate fountains, grottoes, and fish ponds all became regular features and garden dining rooms were not uncommon. All cities boasted public parks and temple gardens. Excavation, especially around the Bay of Naples, has revealed a vast amount of information.

The Byzantine Greek world shows a continuation of the Roman tradition, but precise information is hard to glean. Archaeology has hitherto unearthed virtually nothing. Frescos and mosaics in churches and manuscript illustrations, though frequently showing vegetation, do not provide a single picture devoted even primarily to a garden. The literary sources are very imprecise, while the most detailed descriptions, inserted for their sexual connotations in 12th-, 14th-, and 15th-century romances, are of imaginary (though not unrealistic) gardens. The single surviving treatise that deals with horticulture, the 10th-century *Geoponica*, is largely antiquarian, but does include some specifically Constantinopolitan information. Byzantine delight in gardens is nonetheless evident everywhere, churches being liberally adorned with vegetal decoration, manuscript illuminations frequently including flowers and trees (even when quite inappropriate, as in desert scenes), and literature being permeated with horticultural imagery. This delight was both inherited from the Romans and encouraged by a religion which emphasized the natural world as the work of God and saw the garden as a pale reflection of the heavenly paradise – it is no surprise that the monks of Mount Athos claim their peninsula to be "the garden of the Mother of God". Health was also a consideration: a house would be rendered salubrious by "the circumambient air since it is infected by the exhalations of the plants", while the emperor Theophilos (829–42) hoped that fresh air and lovely views would wash away "the baneful lusts" of former prostitutes. For emperors gardens were often a matter of prestige and associated with the symbolism of imperial renewal.

In the Late Antique period increasing barbarian incursions, especially in the western part of the empire, necessitated more defensible country villas and a corresponding decline in the number, size, and elaboration of their attached gardens. There is only meagre evidence for extensive examples after the 6th century AD except in the immediate vicinity of Constantinople. The gardens of villagers and monks were almost exclusively utilitarian. Market gardens supplied the cities with a wide range of vegetables and fruits which generally enabled the Byzantines to enjoy a healthier diet than did their western European counterparts (the produce was often transported over considerable distances). Urban houses of the middle class contained small gardens that could contain fruit and decorative trees: two descriptions of such a garden (his own) by the 10th-century writer John Geometres survive. Manuscript illuminations suggest also a fondness for roof gardens. Urban churches were frequently surrounded by gardens of shady trees, flowerbeds, and paths for the enjoyment of the general public. The most extensive and elaborate pleasure gardens were those associated with the palaces of the emperors and, to a lesser extent, of high court officials. Some of these were suburban, often by the sea, designed to combat the heat of the summer and sometimes connected with a game park, but the most important was undoubtedly the Great Palace in Constantinople. This was not a single building but an agglomeration, dating from the 4th to the 12th centuries, of residential quarters, public reception- and dining-rooms, churches, chapels, baths, pavilions, pleasure and vegetable gardens, an orchard, a fish pond, and sports grounds all set on terraces descending from the Hippodrome to the Sea of Marmara. The literary sources dwell on the lush vegetation of the gardens and especially on the highly elaborate fountains and a golden tree with mechanically warbling birds. The gardens described in the romances, based on palatial exemplars, emphasize also artwork in the form of statues or paintings and mosaics in pavilions and bath houses, water-driven automata in the form of birds and mammals on the fountains, and, above all, the sound of the wind whispering through the leaves of intertwining branches.

Among the trees and shrubs, both useful and ornamental, found in literary and visual sources are pine, fir, cypress, black and white poplar, alder, cedar, willow, tamarisk, oak, ash, elm, beech, plane, maple, bay, myrtle, mastich, terebinth, arbutus, box, juniper, olive, apple, pear, sorb, peach, apricot, citron, quince, damson, sloe, cherry, pomegranate, fig, date-palm, jujube, medlar, carob, mulberry, hazelnut, walnut, pistachio, sweet chestnut, and the ubiquitous vine which frequently festooned trellises. Orange and lemon appeared late. The range of flowers, because of the problems of irrigation, was far more restricted. Pride of place was taken by the rose, grown in rows, spiralling up trees, and in pots. Violet, narcissus, lily, crocus, pimpernel, and, for ground cover, periwinkle are also found, while ivy too was used for decorative effect. Herbs include basil, marjoram, savory, coriander, saffron, dill, rue, fenugreek, cress, mallow, mint, borage, costmary, squill, tarragon, parsley, cumin, smilax, salsify, mustard, and monk's rhubarb. Illustrated copies of Dioscurides' extensive medicinal herbal of the 1st century AD continued to be produced and used and were even sent as gifts to Muslim rulers.

Trees were planted individually, in clumps, in straight rows and crescents, and to create arbours; flowers in separate and mixed beds and often between trees to take advantage of their shade and water channels. Topiary work seems not to have followed the extravagances of its Roman inventors but to have been restricted to a few favourite configurations. Landscaping was vigorously pursued, since gardens were designed to be enjoyed not only from buildings but also by strollers who appreciated ever-changing vistas. Particularly enthusiastic as a landscape designer was Constantine IX Monomachos (1042–55), whom Michael Psellos gently mocks for impatience and changes of mind in mid-course. Horticultural experiments in grafting, improving colour and fragrance, and enabling flowers to bloom out of season were laudable occupations of the upper class.

During the Tourkokratia Greek gardens, both private and monastic, were largely utilitarian, although arbours of vines and pots of fragrant herbs such as basil had an added aesthetic function. Since independence no distinctive Greek style has emerged. Towns and cities usually contain small and formal squares with shady avenues and sometimes geometric parterres. The Esplanade in Corfu is exceptional, but its large size (c.550 × 230 m at its widest point) is due to its origin as a Venetian parade-ground: it is unique too in Greece in that its northern part constitutes the famous and, until recently, gravelled cricket "field". Among palatial gardens that at Tatoï, outside the capital, is noteworthy in that the afforestation in unpromising soil is a scientific triumph. Although from 1836 queen Amalia designed the Royal Gardens (now known as the National Garden) in Athens, the few interesting gardens in Greece have been designed by foreigners, mostly British. Thomas Mawson was responsible for the initial landscaping in Athens on the Acropolis, Lykabettus, and the Philopappos Hill (his other plans for urban parks and royal gardens were unfortunately never carried out); Robert and Marina Adams between 1965 and 1982 encouraged the integration of gardens into the Greek landscape by the use of native materials. In more recent years Greek landscape-architects have done some good work, although they have been hampered by the lack of any modern gardening tradition beyond that of basic skills.

A.R. LITTLEWOOD

See also Dioscurides, Geometres, Plants

Further Reading

Barber, C., "Reading the Garden in Byzantium: Nature and Sexuality", *Byzantine and Modern Greek Studies*, 16 (1992): pp. 1–19
Carroll-Spillecke, Maureen, *Kepos: der Antike griechische Garten*, Munich: Deutscher Kunstverlag, 1989
Carroll-Spillecke, Maureen (editor), *Der Garten von der Antike bis zum Mittelalter*, Mainz: von Zabern, 1992, pp. 101–75, 213–48
Carroll-Spillecke, Maureen, "The Gardens of Greece from Homeric to Roman Times", *Journal of Garden History*, 12/2 (1992): pp. 84–101
Littlewood, A.R., "Romantic Paradises: The Rôle of the Garden in the Byzantine Romance", *Byzantine and Modern Greek Studies*, 5 (1979): pp. 95–114
Littlewood, A.R., "Gardens of Byzantium", *Journal of Garden History*, 12/2 (1992): pp. 126–53
Littlewood, A.R., "Gardens of the Palaces" in *Byzantine Court Culture from 829 to 1204*, edited by Henry Maguire, Washington, D.C.: Dumbarton Oaks, 1997, pp. 13–38
Maguire, H., "Imperial Gardens and the Rhetoric of Renewal" in *New Constantines: The Rhythm of Imperial Renewal in Byzantium, 4th–13th Centuries*, edited by Paul Magdalino, Aldershot, Hampshire: Variorum, 1994, pp. 181–97
Osborne, R., "Classical Greek Gardens: Between Farm and Paradise" in *Garden History: Issues, Approaches, Methods*, edited by John Dixon Hunt, Washington, DC: Dumbarton Oaks, 1992, pp. 373–91
Schissel von Fleschenberg, Otmar, *Der byzantinische Garten: seine Darstellung im gleichzeitigen Romane*, Vienna, 1942 (on the gardens in the romances)
Shaw, M.C., "The Aegean Garden", *American Journal of Archaeology*, 97 (1993): pp. 661–85

Gatsos, Nikos 1916–1995

Poet and translator

Regarded as a great innovator and an inventive revolutionary wit, Nikos Gatsos was undeniably a legend before the facts of his life were established or his texts had been thoroughly edited. Gatsos was said to be an obscure, private, and bizarre poet, the hyper-realist before hyper-realism who demonstrated an extraordinary ability to move freely between a hyper-realism that shrank from no sort of sordidness and a surrealism that was not to become a programme until half a century later. Gatsos was the erudite mind who, more than anyone else, clung to the inexhaustible stock of the Hellenic literary tradition and attempted to reinvigorate it by blowing on it the daring winds of European surrealism. In this way, he shed light on the hyper-realist elements of the Hellenic tradition that, although always present in it, had remained unknown, silent, and undiscovered. Thus Gatsos not only regenerated the Hellenic tradition and imparted a substantial knowledge to his own generation as well as the previous poetic generation but, most importantly, he was responsible for changing the momentum and transforming the course of modern Greek poetry.

Gatsos's poetic work includes only one collection published under the title *Amorgos* which circulated in two editions (1943 and 1964). Nevertheless, Gatsos composed a limited number of individual poems intended to be set to music as songs by famous Greek composers. He also translated dramatic texts and plays that were performed by numerous Greek theatrical companies. Among his most renowned translations were Federico García Lorca's *Blood Wedding*, and Tennessee Williams's *A Streetcar Named Desire* and *Something Cloudy, Something Clear,* through which he instilled his creative, original, and revolutionary ideas and transferred his poetic qualities to the modern Greek theatre. Thus he had an immense influence on the way of thinking of modern Greek dramatists, playwrights, and directors.

Gatsos was born in a village in Arcadia (Peloponnese) and attended the University of Athens where he completed his studies in Greek literature. Gatsos's dedication to poetry was never that of a potential professional writer or a man of letters. He was the poet who never encouraged a critic to delve into his poetry and analyse it or to approach him personally. This is evident from the limited amount of Greek critical bibliography relating to his work. After publishing just one collection, Gatsos never returned to poetry but instead he embarked on an enduring, extremely personal, intellectual, and philosophical adventure. It is no exaggeration to say that Gatsos's silence is comparable to that of Dionysios Solomos. This is because Gatsos never tried to be a prolific poet, but the real artist, able to communicate his presence and influence to a whole generation, to spell out his visions and truths, to enlighten the next generation through a single collection. Gatsos was able to maintain the delicate balance between the critical and the imaginative, idealistic elements in his poetry. When he sensed the balance tilting towards the critical element and his contemplative mind overtaking his visionary mood, he immediately denounced his art and suspended his writing.

Gatsos was destined to be compared in many respects with Andreas Kalvos. Although they made their appearance at different moments in time, both provided the Hellenic literary tradition with a large vision, a big idea. Although both were considered to be among the less productive of modern Greek poets they were able to renew the Hellenic tradition not by simply adopting external models but rather by incorporating the antithetical elements and uncovering new ones.

In evaluating the contextual framework of Gatsos's poetry and its overall effect, one could say that he derived his inspiration from the broader pantheon of Greek and European tradition and an amazing plethora of stimuli. By following in the steps of Alexandros Papadiamantis, Takis Papatsonis, Georgios Sarandaris, Odysseos Elytis, and George Seferis, he sought a connection with European philosophical thought and literature.

The unique phenomenon of Gatsos was not a purely surrealistic one like that of Egonopoulos or Andreas Embirikos. Gatsos employed several hyper-realistic elements but always remained conscious of his cultural and ideological context. He was not only an expert of the Hellenic tradition but he also succeeded in sheltering it in his work and renovating it from within. He made the first consistent attempt to prove that the Greek tradition contained important hyper-realistic elements. He relied on the tradition without exploiting it, while at the same time he incorporated the whole of Western thought produced between the two World Wars. As a result Gatsos has proved to be a two-dimensional poet: both deeply Greek and deeply European.

Also remarkable is the number of ways in which the Hellenic tradition functioned in his verse. Gatsos could converse with the characters of folk songs, flirt with the rhythms of ancient Greek poetry, and, at the same time, call upon an epigrammatic adage from Heraclitus. Following the example of Max Jacob, he constructed a vision strong enough to be expressed through the most unpoetic, flat, and solid expressions.

Having devoured the works of T.S. Eliot, García Lorca, Kafka, Sartre, and Valéry, as well as Cavafy and Solomos, Gatsos responded to the history of world literature according to his own perception of it. He discovered the tradition in the chorus of ancient tragedy, the hymns of Byzantium, and the popular songs of his ancestors. In this way, he taught the robustness of the organic function of rhyme, the aesthetic and moral quality of the Greek language. Gatsos was an "alchemist of the word" and an inventor of "the colours of the vowels". Sometimes in his poetry an expert reader can detect the pure magic of freely floating images and sounds operating more powerfully than Gatsos's acute intelligence and unabashed eye. His imagery is always as daring and surrealistic as it is in popular songs or in the texts of Cretan theatre. It evokes the past without any hint of nostalgia and it fluctuates incessantly. His obsession was to use the right words in the right order in his verse. Like Solomos he was a perfectionist. He attempted to convey his thoughts through a synthesis of traditional sounds, odours, colours, and images.

Gatsos's concentration on the hyper-realistic element in the Hellenic tradition made possible his transition from poetry to song writing. His songs are complete, self-sufficient, and independent. They are like one-act plays and they enabled him to popularize traditional surrealism among the Greek public. He also showed an extraordinary talent for translation. All his translations are direct, pure, and lyrical. Moreover, either through his translation of theatrical plays or by his attempt to adapt the theatrical text to the needs of the staging, Gatsos exercised a profound influence over the dramatists and directors with whom he collaborated.

It is no accident that Gatsos's poetry – which first appeared in the year of the German occupation of Greece (1943) – became the landmark for a whole generation of poets and the standard against which the next generation rebelled. He influenced every single aspect of Greek intellectual and cultural life.

He questioned all the conventional associations of poetry without neglecting the traditional element. Gatsos wanted to substitute a new meaning to all the things he saw – the Hellenic literary tradition as a whole – not as seen by human conventions but as they really are. His contribution is enormous since without him modern Greek poetry might have followed completely different directions.

MARIA ROUMBALOU

See also Elytis, Kalvos, Seferis, Solomos

Biography

Born in Arcadia in 1916, Gatsos studied Greek literature at the University of Athens. He published only one collection of poetry, *Amorgos*, in two editions (1943 and 1964), though it became a landmark for a whole generation of poets. In addition he wrote songs and translated the plays of Lorca and Tennessee Williams. He died in Athens in 1995.

Writings

Amorgos, translated by Sally Purcell, Hay-on-Wye, Herefordshire: Other Poetry, 1908; reprinted London: Anvil Press, 1998

A Greek Quintet: Poems by Cavafy, Sikelianos, Seferis, Elytis, Gatsos, , translated by Edmund Keeley and Philip Sherrard, 2nd edition. Limni, Evia: Harvey, 1992

Further Reading

Argiriou, A., *Dhiathoki kes Anagnosis Ellinon Iperrealiston* [Successive Research and Recurrent Analysis in the Works of the Greek Hyper-realists], Athens, 1986

Eleftheriou, M., "O Zontanos mithos ke to Allothi tis Amorghiou" [The Myth and the Alibi of Amorgos], *Lexi*, 52 (1986)

Karidis, N., "Enas Iperrealistis prin apo ton Iperrealismo" [A Hyper-realist Before the Hyper-realism], *Lexi*, 52 (1986)

Lignadis, T., *Dhipli Episkepsi se mia Ilikia ke se enan Pieeti* [Double Visit to an Age and a Poet], Athens, 1986

Gaza

City in Palestine

Gaza, on the route from Egypt to Palestine and situated a few kilometres from the sea, and its port, Maiuma, have a long history. Gaza appears in the Bible as a centre of the Philistines. Hellenization began after the city was captured by Alexander the Great in 332 BC. It was ruled by the Ptolemies, and destroyed by the Jewish ruler Alexander Jannaeus in 96 BC, only to be rebuilt by the Roman governor Gabinius on a new site. It received Roman settlers when it became a Roman colony in the reign of Hadrian, perhaps in AD 129. The city worshipped Greek gods, but these were probably Semitic deities whose names and cult had been Hellenized. This is clear in the case of Zeus Marnas, the principal god of the city. As late as 395 the majority of Gaza's inhabitants still adhered to paganism.

Mark the Deacon's account of how Bishop Porphyry with the support the empress Eudoxia and local imperial forces destroyed the Marneion and the other pagan temples in 402 and so inaugurated the conversion of the population to Christianity is remarkably vivid and informative. In the 5th and 6th centuries, Gaza was an important centre of education with a succession of distinguished teachers representing a Christian humanism, combining traditional rhetoric with Alexandrian philosophy and study of the Bible. Procopius (c.465–528) wrote a panegyric of the emperor Anastasius, rhetorical descriptions of works of art, and commentaries on a number of books of the Bible. He was one of the creators of the genre of catenas. His pupil Choricius was a Sophist in the tradition of Libanius. Choricius' orations give a vivid impression of Gaza in the first half of the 6th century. The *Theophrastus* of Aeneas of Gaza describes how Theophrastus, a pupil of Aristotle, is forced to accept Christian arguments concerning immortality and the Resurrection. Dorotheus of Gaza (500–60) was the author of the influential *Didaskaliai* (Teachings) of monastic life which were to be translated into Syriac, Arabic, Georgian, and Church Slavonic. The city was captured by the Arabs in 635.

J.H.W.G. LIEBESCHUETZ

Summary

An ancient city on the coast of Palestine, Gaza was first Hellenized after its capture by Alexander the Great in 332 BC. Paganism prevailed until the end of the 4th century but conversion to Christianity was initiated in 402. In the 5th and 6th centuries it was an important centre of scholarship whose teachers included Procopius, Choricius, Aeneas, and Dorotheus. It fell to the Arabs in 635.

Further Reading

Avi-Yonah, Michael and Ephraim Stern (editors), *Encyclopedia of Archaeological Excavations in the Holy Land*, 4 vols, London: Oxford University Press, and Englewood Cliffs, New Jersey: Prentice Hall, 1975–78, vol. 2, pp. 408–17

Downey, Glanville, *Gaza in the Early 6th Century*, Norman: University of Oklahoma Press, 1963

Downey, Glanville, Gaza entry in *Reallexikon für Antike und Christentum*, vol. 8, Stuttgart: Hiersemann, 1972, pp. 1123–34

Friedländer, Paul (editor), *Johannes von Gaza und Paulus Silentiarius: Kunstbeschreibungen justinianischer Zeit*, Leipzig and Berlin: Teubner, 1912

Friedländer, Paul, *Spätantiker Gemäldezyklus des Procopius von Gaza*, Vatican City: Biblioteca Apostolica, 1939

Glucker, Carol A.M., *The City of Gaza in the Roman and Byzantine Periods*, Oxford: BAR, 1987

Kaster, Robert A., *Guardians of Language: The Grammarian and Society in Late Antiquity*, Berkeley: University of California Press, 1988, pp. 83, 299–301, and 368–70

Kazhdan, A.P. (editor), *The Oxford Dictionary of Byzantium*, New York and Oxford: Oxford University Press, 1991, vol. 1, pp. 654 (Dorotheos) and 1065 (John); vol. 3, pp. 1732 (Procopius) and 1991 (Timotheus)

Marc le, Diacré, *Vie de Porphyre: évêque de Gaza*, edited and translated by Henri Grégoire and M.-A. Kugener, Paris: Belles Lettres, 1930

Martindale, J.R., *The Prosopography of the Later Roman Empire*, vol. 2, Cambridge and New York: Cambridge University Press, 1980

Seitz, Kilian, *Die Schule von Gaza: Eine Literargeschichtliche Untersuchung*, Heidelberg: Winter, 1892

Trombley, Frank R., *Hellenic Religion and Christianization: c.370–529*, vol. 1, Leiden: Brill, 1993, pp. 187–282

Wolf, A., Procopius von Gaza entry in *Real-Encyclopädie der klassischen Altertumswissenschaft*, edited by August Pauly *et al.*, vol. 23.1, 1957, 259–73

Gaza, Theodore c.1400–1475/76

Scholar

Theodore Gaza was one of the most prominent of the Byzantine émigré scholars who found refuge in Italy during the mid-15th century. In his activities as a teacher, translator, philosophical writer, and copyist of manuscripts, he helped not only to transmit classical Greek literature, especially the works of Aristotle and the ancient rhetoricians, to the Italian humanists but also to influence both their interpretation and their place in humanist education.

Throughout his career in Italy, Gaza was a popular teacher. He gave lessons in Greek to some of the foremost Italian scholars and humanists, including Ludovico Carbone, Ermalao Barbaro, the German astronomer Johannes Regiomontanus, and the Sicilian poet Antonio Beccadelli Panormita. Some insight into his teaching methods is given by his *Introduction to Greek Grammar*, which he wrote in the 1440s and which became the standard textbook for learning Greek. Erasmus regarded it as the best of the Greek grammars, and used it as the basis of his teaching at the University of Cambridge. In 1495 it was printed in Venice by the publisher Aldus Manutius and it remained in use well into the 16th century.

In his teaching Gaza laid stress on the Byzantine tradition of rhetoric drawn from the Greek orators of antiquity. In 1446, when he was appointed to the chair of Greek and Eloquence at the University of Ferrara, his first lecture series seems to have been on Demosthenes' oration *On the Crown*. His teaching of Greek rhetoric was undoubtedly helped by his mastery of Latin, a rare accomplishment among Byzantine scholars, which he had attained by studying under Vittorino da Feltre in Mantua between 1440 and 1446. Such was his proficiency that he was able to translate the orators Cicero and Claudian into Greek. Yet Gaza also appears to have believed, like his contemporary John Argyropoulos, that the whole of Greek Classical literature, and not only the rhetoricians, was worthy of study in humanist education. He used the occasion of his inaugural oration, entitled *On the Importance of Greek Studies*, to argue this point, stressing the role of Greek learning as a preparation for effective participation in political life.

It was, however, as a translator and paraphraser of Greek texts into Latin that Gaza was to make his name, especially in the work he produced in the years 1449–55 and 1464–73 when he resided in Rome, at the invitation of the humanist popes Nicholas V and Sixtus IV, and was one of the leading members of the Academy that met in the house of cardinal Bessarion. He produced Latin versions of Theophrastus' *On Plants*, Aristotle's *History of Animals* and *Problems*, and the pseudo-Aristotelian *Problems*, attributed to the Hellenistic commentator Alexander of Aphrodisias. He appears to have followed the method of translation adopted by Manuel Chrysoloras, abandoning a word-for-word rendering in favour of one that conveyed the spirit of the text. His translations were generally highly praised, but did not meet with universal approval; both Angelo Poliziano and George of Trebizond believed that his versions were too free.

In the process of translation, Gaza also made a significant contribution to the establishment of correct Greek texts: while translating the *History of Animals*, he noticed that in the

THEODORVS GAZA RHE,
TOR & GRAMMATICVS.

Altrix Roma, parens cui Græcia, Græcia Magna
Fit tumulus: linguæ Gaza vtriusq; vocor.
THEO-

Theodore Gaza, a 16th-century engraving

manuscript tradition books 7 and 9 had been transposed and he realized that book 10 was spurious. Both these judgements are accepted today. He was also active in the copying of manuscripts, which in the mid-15th century was still the only means of reproducing a text. A number of manuscripts survive in his elegant hand, including a copy of Homer's *Iliad*, made for the Milanese humanist Francesco Filelfo, now in the Bibliotheca Medicea Laurenziana in Florence (MS 32.1).

Gaza's contribution to the interpretation of Aristotle had less immediate impact but was to be influential well beyond his own lifetime. In 1459 he wrote his *On Fate*, a treatise in defence of Aristotle against George Gemistos Plethon and other admirers of Plato. The work was notable for its conciliatory tone, in sharp contrast to that adopted by George of Trebizond, and for its attempt to reconcile the philosophies of Plato and Aristotle rather than to emphasize the differences in their teachings. However, *On Fate* was written not only against the rising tide of admiration for Plato but also against the late scholastic interpretations of his work, based on the 12th-century Arab commentator Ibn Rushd Averroes, which still held sway in many Italian universities. Instead Gaza referred to the interpretations to be found in the early Byzantine commentators Simplicius, John Philoponus, Themistius, and Alexander

of Aphrodisias. His pupil, the Venetian Ermalao Barbaro, and others were converted to Gaza's belief that the truest interpretation of Aristotle was to be found in these writers rather than in Averroes, and, as a result, the Greek interpretation gained ground, especially in Venice. In 1497, some 20 years after Gaza's death, the Venetian senate appointed Nicholas Leonicus Tomaeus to lecture on the Greek text of Aristotle at Padua, an appointment sometimes seen as marking the eclipse of Averroism.

JONATHAN HARRIS

Biography

Born in Thessalonica c.1400, Gaza moved to Italy by 1440 where he taught Greek in Ferrara, Naples, and Rome. His pupils included some of the foremost scholars of the day – Ludovico Carbone, Ermalao Barbaro, and Johannes Regiomontanus. His *Introduction to Greek Grammar* became a standard textbook and his Latin translations of Aristotle and Theophrastus were highly praised. He died in Policastro (Calabria) in 1475/76.

Further Reading

Geanakoplos, Deno John, *Greek Scholars in Venice: Studies in the Dissemination of Greek Learning from Byzantium to Western Europe*, Cambridge, Massachusetts: Harvard University Press, 1962

Geanakoplos, Deno John, "Theodore Gaza: A Byzantine Scholar of the Palaeologan 'Renaissance' in the Italian Renaissance", *Medievalia et Humanistica*, 12 (1984): pp. 61–81

Harris, Jonathan, *Greek Emigrés in the West, 1400–1520*, Camberley, Surrey: Porphyrogenitus, 1995

Kraye, Jill, "Philosophers and Philologists" in *The Cambridge Companion to Renaissance Humanism*, edited by Jill Kraye, Cambridge and New York: Cambridge University Press, 1996, pp. 142–60

Lee, Egmont, *Sixtus IV and Men of Letters*, Rome: Storia e Letteratura, 1978

Monfasani, John, "The Byzantine Rhetorical Tradition and the Renaissance" in his *Byzantine Scholars in Renaissance Italy: Cardinal Bessarion and Other Emigrés*, Aldershot, Hampshire: Variorum, 1995

Taylor, John Wilson, *Theodore Gaza's "De Fato"*, Toronto: University of Toronto Library, 1925

Wilson, N.G., *From Byzantium to Italy: Greek Studies in the Italian Renaissance*, London: Duckworth, and Baltimore: Johns Hopkins University Press, 1992

Gems and Seals

The use of seals fashioned from engraved semiprecious stones (normally cornelian and other quartzes) has a long history in Greek lands. Their primary purpose was to secure valuable commodities with a mark of ownership or to guarantee the authority of a letter or contract. They comprise much of the best miniature art produced during the Aegean Bronze Age and over a period stretching from Archaic Greece to Roman times, and were certainly valued for their artistry. Apart from the gems themselves, clay sealings survive from destroyed archives such as those of Hellenistic or early Roman date at Delos, Edfu, and Cyrene. Only from the 4th century AD did it become the custom in the Byzantine empire to affix to documents and

Gems and Seals: gem with a representation of a Greek warship, British Museum, London

packages double-sided sealings, normally of lead and made with a pincer-like *bulloterion*.

Seal motifs used in Cretan palaces of the 2nd millennium BC, such as Knossos, were generally engraved on one side of a pierced bead which could be worn on a string around the wrist or neck. Subjects comprise much of the standard repertoire of Minoan art, including marine creatures, bulls, and ritual scenes, such as the bull-leaping attractively rendered on an agate flattened cylinder (Ashmolean Museum, Oxford). Seals are quite common as finds and there are also many examples of sealings fired in various conflagrations, which attest to the highly organized and bureaucratic nature of Bronze Age society. The use of seals spread to mainland Greece, and fine examples are recorded from all the major sites, including Mycenae, Tiryns, and Pylos. The collapse of high culture, and with it the decline of literacy, at the end of the 2nd millennium BC brought the use of seals to an end.

From the 9th century BC there was a tentative revival of seal-cutting on the Greek mainland, though the stamp seals that were produced are rather schematically carved, on ivory or soft stone. In the 7th century BC seals of much higher aesthetic quality, often imitating Minoan prototypes, were engraved in the Cyclades. The major revival in gem-cutting came only in the second quarter of the 6th century BC when the Greeks adopted the Egyptian custom of carving seals in the form of scarab beetles. These were worn on a swivel-ring, and the devices engraved on the undersides of these archaic scarabs were thoroughly Greek in character from the start, sometimes orientalizing in style. Popular subjects include satyrs, warriors, lions, and winged figures such as the "mistress of the animals". From about 500 BC the use of the scarab back was largely abandoned and the devices on seals of scaraboid form became more naturalistic, as can be seen in the case of a gem signed by the engraver Epimenes showing an ephebe restraining a horse (Museum of Fine Arts, Boston).

Scaraboids of the 5th century BC are generally larger, and often made of a beautiful grey-blue chalcedony. Classical artists tried to imitate nature meticulously, whether the subject was a nut, a sandal, or an erotic scene. There are many delightful vignettes of animal life, including two studies of herons carved by Dexamenus of Chios (both in the Hermitage, St Petersburg). The same engraver carved a bearded male head (Museum of Fine Arts, Boston) and a delightful scene of a lady with her maid (Fitzwilliam Museum, Cambridge). During the Classical period the use of Greek-style seals spread in the western satrapies of the Persian empire and far beyond, many Graeco-Persian gems depicting figures in Persian costume and mounted hunts carved in an unmistakably Greek style.

Rings with fixed bezels became usual in the following century and were normal in Hellenistic and Roman times. From the time of Alexander the Great the Greek tradition of gem use was spread throughout the eastern Mediterranean area and, indeed, as far as India. A Hellenistic portrait of Alexander in the Ashmolean Museum, Oxford, bears an inscription in an Indian language. Moreover it is carved from tourmaline, demonstrating that rarer stones from the east were now available. The typical Hellenistic medium was perhaps garnet obtained from the western Himalayas. The changed nature of society is reflected in Hellenistic glyptics, many seals now showing the portraits of Ptolemies, Seleucids, and other rulers, although deities and genre scenes were always more common.

The incorporation of the Greek world into the Roman empire did not mark any real break with the Hellenistic tradition. The Greek style of gem usage had entered northern Italy as early as the Archaic period, and although the Etruscans and other peoples clung to the scarab back for longer, Greek influence from Magna Graecia and beyond continued to be felt, not least in Latium. By the beginning of the 2nd century BC important Romans were commissioning the best Greek engravers. The emperor Augustus (27 BC–AD 14) employed the great Dioscurides for his signet, as we hear from Suetonius, Pliny the Elder, and Dio Cassius. A number of gems from his hand are extant, including a Hermes (Fitzwilliam Museum, Cambridge) and Diomedes stealing the Palladium from Troy (Devonshire collection, Chatsworth).

Among the many gems from Greek-speaking lands in the empire, a special class of gems cut with figured devices and/or magical texts on both sides was widely distributed, especially in the Levant. These could be used in gems as seals but served mainly as amulets. Otherwise, while the occurrence of the Greek language or a Greek name on an inscribed seal indicates a Greek-speaking owner, the style and subject of "Roman" gems from Scotland to Syria are very similar, demonstrating the dominance of the Greek tradition in this medium.

During Hellenistic and Roman times gems were used in all manner of jewellery, especially by women. Even engraved gems were sometimes simply used decoratively in brooches and rings, especially in the case of cameos, gems carved in relief. The best were works of art, cut in the workshops of Dioscurides and his contemporaries, though others were mass-produced, often love-tokens given by men to their girlfriends. Of especial interest here are those of the 2nd- or 3rd-century AD carved with Greek mottoes, found not only in Greek lands but as far away as Roman Britain.

Byzantine practice marked a break from earlier tradition. The double-sided lead sealing made with the *bulloterion* was more formal in appearance, generally incorporating a religious text as invocation, a portrait of Christ if the seal was imperial, or of the Virgin for the patriarch, while other important people might use a saint or a monogram. Gems were of course still very much admired but would now normally be worn as jewellery.

Although the Byzantine *bulloterion* was sometimes used in western Europe, notably for papal seals, it was normal in the Middle Ages to use a metal stamp or a finger ring engraved in intaglio, sometimes incorporating an ancient gem or a contemporary copy of it. The ancient Greek practice thus had a tenuous continuity into modern times. From the Renaissance, princely patrons such as Isabella d'Este (1474–1539) and later others such as Thomas Howard, Earl of Arundel (1585–1646), collected classical gems as objets d'art. This stimulated artists to emulate their Greek and Roman predecessors. Often completely new subjects were engraved, based on ancient or contemporary statues or paintings, as in the case of the 18th-century English engravers Nathaniel Marchant (1739–1816) and Edward Burch (1730–1814). It was thus by no means unusual for any European of the period of the Enlightenment to seal a letter with the image of Homer or Socrates.

MARTIN HENIG

See also Jewellery

Further Reading

Boardman, John, *Archaic Greek Gems: Schools and Artists in the Sixth and Early Fifth Centuries BC*, London: Thames and Hudson, and Evanston, Illinois: Northwestern University Press, 1968

Boardman, John, *Greek Gems and Finger Rings: Early Bronze Age to Late Classical*, London: Thames and Hudson, 1970; New York: Abrams, 1972

Boardman, John and Marie-Louise Vollenweider, *Catalogue of the Engraved Gems and Finger Rings, Ashmolean Museum*, Oxford: Clarendon Press, and New York: Oxford University Press, 1978

Brown, Clifford Malcolm (editor), *Engraved Gems: Survivals and Revivals*, Washington, D.C.: National Gallery of Art, 1997

Collon, Dominique (editor), *7000 Years of Seals*, London: British Museum Press, 1997

Henig, Martin, *The Content Family Collection of Ancient Cameos*, Oxford: Ashmolean Museum, 1990

Henig, Martin, *Classical Gems: Ancient and Modern Intaglios and Cameos in the Fitzwilliam Museum, Cambridge*, Cambridge and New York: Cambridge University Press, 1994

Plantzos, Dimitris, *Hellenistic Engraved Gems*, Oxford: Clarendon Press, and New York: Oxford University Press, 1999

Richter, Gisela M.A., *The Engraved Gems of the Greeks, Etruscans and Romans*, 2 vols, London: Phaidon, 1968–71

Spier, Jeffrey, *Ancient Gems and Finger Rings: Catalogue of the Collection*, Malibu, California: Getty Museum, 1992

Zazoff, Peter, *Die Antiken Gemmen*, Munich: Beck, 1983

Gender

In this essay, the term "gender" is to be understood as the social and cultural, as opposed to biological, identification of a person's sex, and the distinctions between the sexes.

Though a social construction, gender nevertheless has its ideological roots in biological differences, real or imagined, between the sexes. This is presented most clearly by the 5th-century-BC doctor Hippocrates, who wrote in his *Diseases of Women* (trans. A.E. Hanson, quoted in Halperin):

I say that a woman's flesh is more sponge-like and softer than a man's: since this is so, the woman's body draws moisture both with more speed and in greater quantity from the belly than does the flesh of a man ... And when the body of a woman – whose flesh is soft – happens to be full of blood and that blood does not go off from her body, a pain occurs, whenever her flesh is full and becomes heated. A woman has warmer blood and therefore she is warmer than a man. Because a man has more solid flesh than a woman, he is never so totally overfilled with blood that pain results if some of his blood does not exit each month. He draws whatever quantity of blood is necessary for his body's nourishment ...

Women are therefore bound to bleed, notably at liminal points of life: menstruation, defloration, and parturition; it is an essential aspect of the prime female role as giver of life. By contrast, it is the man's duty to bleed in warfare, which was understood by the ancient Greeks as the male counterpart to female parturition. Thus Euripides' Medea proclaims that she would prefer to face battle three times rather than give birth once (*Medea*, 250ff.), and the laws of Lycurgus allow marked burials only for men who died in battle and women who died in childbirth (Plutarch, *Life of Lycurgus*).

This dichotomy of the "soft, weak" female and the "strong" male pervades all aspects of the Greek understanding of gender distinctions. Since the female is weak in will and body, excess and temptation have received feminine attributes. In ancient Greece feminine deities personified strife (Eris) and madness (Lyssa), while in the Byzantine era sins acquired feminine personifications (Neophytos Enkleistos). Nevertheless, this weakness also counteracts the high potential for destruction and disruption, and the feminine is seen to be essentially *passive*, unable to exert active control over the self and often considered to be childlike.

By contrast, the male is understood to be strong in body and mind and is essentially *active* in character. As the strong body makes men fit for warfare, strength of mind gives them the potential for self-restraint, in Greek *sophrosyne*, or temperance. Thus the male is expected to control his appetites for food, drink, and sex along with overweening pride and anything else considered to be excessive (Aeschines, *Against Timarchus*). The male is in active control, stable and competent, while the female is passive but dangerous. This conception of male and female genders has changed little if at all since ancient times.

While the ideology of the strong, active male and the weak, passive female remains constant in Greek culture, there are various inversions of these roles, when men become "as women" and vice versa. In early Greece gender ambiguity is represented by Dionysus, god of wine, madness, and liminality. In the *Bacchae* he is described as fair-skinned, long-haired, and luxurious, and since he is feminine he also causes the youth Pentheus to adopt transvestitism. From the 4th century BC vase painters show Dionysus as beardless. Even greater gender ambiguity occurs with Heracles. While ultimately masculine in his superior strength, Heracles is forced into the feminine role throughout his career. On one occasion he must serve the Lydian queen Omphale, wearing her clothes and spinning thread at her feet, while she bears his cloak and club. In *Trachiniae* (1070ff.) suffering in his death, Heracles proclaims himself turned into a woman. As there are feminine men, so too are there masculine women in the Greek tradition, notably the maenads and Amazons, both of whom represent inversions of the "natural" order of society and civilization in the ancient Greek arts.

Beginning in the Byzantine era eunuchs also upset the engendered order. Contemporary views varied on the extent to which eunuchs represented a "third sex". The secular opinion was that eunuchs were neither male nor female, but other, while Theophylaktos of Ohrid (12th century), providing Church commentary, argued that they were "neither a third sex nor a third gender; they are simply men" (S. F. Tougher, in James, 1997, p.169). Nevertheless, physical and sexual differences were recognized in eunuchs; Theophylaktos himself noted that sexual purity was their inherent benefit (ibid., p.175); they had feminine voices, glossy skin, and corpulent physiques (Hopkins, 1978, pp.193–94); and the 10th-century Arab historian al-Masudi mentioned that their armpits did not smell (Masudi, 1989, pp.345–46).

Male homosexuality in ancient and modern Greece presents its own subversion of masculine gender. In ancient Greece the man was expected to be the *erastes*, the active lover. Only the female should be able to enjoy sex passively (*eromenos*), and the male who did so was given the derogatory epithet *kinaidos*. In modern Greece male homosexuality is regarded as the union of an active, extra-masculine male and a passive, feminine one known as the *poushtis* (Loizos and Paptaxiarchis, 1991, p.227). The latter is often regarded as subhuman, being of weak moral character and without dignity (ibid., pp.227–28). A lesser, although more commonly heard, insult of the male through likening to the female is the term *malaka*, meaning "soft". It carries inherently feminine overtones, and ranges in insult from casting aspersions on the masculinity of the term's recipient to verbally placing the recipient in the role of the *poushtis*. As in most modern, Western cultures, there is no corresponding insult likening the female to the male.

In all periods of Greek history the house interior is feminine space, while the outdoors, the city or farm, is the realm of the man. The white paint used to render females in Bronze Age and classical art in contrast to the red or black pigments used to colour men has mostly been attributed to this dichotomy. In modern Greece the house is still the proper domain of the woman (A. M. Iossifides, in Loizos and Papataxiarchis, 1991, p.141), and the respectability of (unmarried) females is often dependent on claims of "never leaving the house". By contrast men are expected to remain outdoors (J. K. Cowan, in Loizos and Papataxiarchis, 1991, pp.187ff.), either working in the fields or the city, or relaxing in male company at the *kafeneion* (one humorous aspect of modern Greek village life is the social impropriety of men going home during the day; on slow days they have little choice but to remain at the *kafeneion*).

While interior space is feminine and the civilized outdoors masculine, wild, uncultivated territories are seen as feminine. In the pagan tradition this area is sacred to Artemis, and it is to these regions that the maenads flee when possessed (Euripides, *Bacchae*). Unfortunately, little such territory remains in modern Greece.

STEPHANIE LYNN BUDIN

Further Reading

Fantham, Elaine *et al.*, *Women in the Classical World: Image and Text*, Oxford and New York: Oxford University Press, 1994
Halperin, David M., John J. Winkler and Froma I. Zeitlin (editors), *Before Sexuality: The Construction of Erotic Experience in the Ancient Greek World*, Princeton, New Jersey: Princeton University Press, 1990
Hopkins, K., *Conquerors and Slaves*, Cambridge and New York: Cambridge University Press, 1978
James, Liz (editor), *Women, Men and Eunuchs: Gender in Byzantium*, London and New York: Routledge, 1997
Kazhdan, A.P. (editor), *The Oxford Dictionary of Byzantium*, 3 vols, New York and Oxford: Oxford University Press, 1991
Laiou, Angeliki E., *Gender, Society and Economic Life in Byzantium*, Aldershot, Hampshire: Variorum, 1992
Loizos, Peter and Euthymios Papataxiarchis (editors), *Contested Identities: Gender and Kinship in Modern Greece*, Princeton, New Jersey: Princeton University Press, 1991
Masudi, *The Meadows of Gold: The Abbasids*, translated and edited by Paul Lunde and Caroline Stone, London and New York: Kegan Paul, 1989

Gennadios II Scholarios c.1405–c.1472

Scholar and Patriarch of Constantinople

Baptized as George, with the (maternal?) family name of Kourtesis, he was born in Constantinople c.1405. His parents, of Thessalian origins, had relocated in the capital. Little is known of his early life, but he clearly received the best education that the intellectual life of Constantinople could allow. His teachers included the philosopher-humanist John Chortasmenos, and the theologians Joseph Bryennios and Mark Eugenikos.

He developed early a love for philosophy and theology, and for their interrelationships. Impatient with the Platonism dominating Byzantine intellectual life – and represented by the maverick scholar George Gemistos Plethon – he became an ardent Aristotelian. Likewise disillusioned with what he considered the shallow level of Byzantine philosophical and theological scholarship, he learned Latin and studied the commentaries of Averroes and Avicenna (in Latin) as well as the works of Latin theologians, especially Thomas Aquinas. Particularly sympathetic to the Scholastic harmonization of Aristotle's thought with Christian theology, he translated some of Aquinas's writings, respecting Thomistic thought even into his own later years of hostility to Church union with the Latins.

George opened his own school of grammar, philosophy, and logic. Accused of being a "Latinizer" – an irony in view of his later ecclesiastical stance – he defended himself with the arguments that Latin philosophy had simply outstripped what the Byzantines knew, and that admiring the learning of the Latins did not necessarily mean accepting their religious doctrines or compromising his firmly held Orthodox beliefs.

George's intellectual activities won him the admiration and friendship of the emperor John VIII Palaiologos, who appointed him to significant court and judicial offices. From a post as the emperor's secretary he took the title of "Scholarios" which became firmly affixed to his name thereafter. His advice was understandably sought by the emperor as plans were made for a council in the West to consider the union of the Greek and Latin Churches, which at this point he favoured.

He served as an unofficial member of the Byzantine delegation to the union council which, opening in Ferrara in the spring of 1438, was transferred to Florence the following year. He was initially more in tune with the pro-unionist and fellow-student of Chortasmenos, Bessarion of Trebizond, than with his former teacher Mark Eugenikos, the principal opponent of union. In April 1439 he joined Bessarion in pleading with the Greek delegation to reach agreement with the Latins and thus secure aid against the Turks, arguing, in the process, that Latin learning and theological dialectic were now superior to Byzantine skills in these realms and had shown how seeming contradictions in Patristic texts could be reconciled. He attempted unsuccessfully to contribute a compromise position statement of his own, and he expressed a clear acceptance of the principles of the union.

Circumstances prompted his departure from the council before its proclamation of the union, to which he was thus not a formal signatory. Recognition of the hostility towards the union of Byzantine public opinion may already have begun to undermine his affirmative position, while he soon recognized that the hoped-for military aid from the West for which the union had been bargained would be of no consequence. When he returned to Constantinople, Scholarios remained officially a pro-unionist, or at least a favourably disposed neutral, if only out of respect for his master the emperor, on whom his career so much depended. But he became the target of Mark Eugenikos, the outspoken champion of anti-unionism. Apparently by the time of the latter's death (June 1445), Scholarios was won over to the opposition. Still observing caution, but at growing cost to his official status, he began to emerge as the chief exponent of rejecting compromise with Latin doctrines.

John VIII's death (October 1448) removed any remaining restraints. Scholarios joined those who attempted to withhold recognition from the new emperor, Constantine IX, unless he renounced the union. With his old life and livelihood gone, and either expelled or resigning from his remaining court positions, Scholarios became a monk, taking the name of Gennadios, by which he would henceforth be known. He began an active campaign of writing and preaching the cause of Orthodoxy and its preservation from Latin doctrinal perversions, supported by many of the clergy. When the threat of Turkish attack on Constantinople rose and his former schoolmate Isidore of Kiev arrived as a Roman cardinal and papal legate, Gennadios circulated his final denunciations of the union. After its belated proclamation in Hagia Sophia (December 1452), Gennadios isolated himself in his cell at the Pantokrator Monastery, taking no part in the ordeal of the city's beleaguerment until the following spring.

When Constantinople fell on 29 May 1453, Gennadios was captured and carried off to Adrianople among the enslaved prisoners. In already established Ottoman tradition, Mehmet the Conqueror appreciated the value of the Orthodox Church as a focus of Christian identity and, consequently, as an agency through which he might rule its faithful. Recognized by the sultan as a logical figure to reunite the Christian population, Gennadios was brought back to Constantinople and allowed to reconstitute his monastery. Meanwhile, Gennadios made a great impression upon the sultan, and a relationship of mutual respect and even friendship developed between them. Mehmet realized that, with his anti-union leadership and hostility to Rome, Gennadios would be a reliable leader of the Christian *millet* (communities) firmly under Turkish rule. They seem, by June 1453, to have worked out an understanding as to the revival and operation of the Greek Patriarchate of Constantinople. The last Byzantine patriarch had fled the city before its fall, so that new election procedures could be observed and, the following January, Gennadios could be properly and canonically enthroned in that office. He was at first headquartered in the church of the Holy Apostles, from which, however, he soon transferred his seat to the smaller (and safer) church of the Pammakaristos.

The Byzantine Patriarchate had been an agency of a Christian imperial state; it now was easily transformed into a component of an Islamic imperial state. Gennadios was assured, however, that his position, and that of the Church, were to be fully respected. Indeed, the tolerant and intellectually broad-minded sultan enjoyed at least three discussions of religious ideas with him. Gennadios may even have had hopes of converting the sultan when the latter commissioned him to write a concise exposition of Christian belief for translation into Turkish. On the other hand, the new patriarch was sensitive to internal challenges: believing the neo-pagan ideas of old Plethon to be dangerous, Gennadios went so far as to destroy most of the sole manuscript of Plethon's treatise, *On the Laws*. Nevertheless, Gennadios confronted the social strains suffered by his flock with a pragmatic flexibility (*oikonomia*) in interpreting canonical regulations that provoked much criticism from some of his clergy.

Wearied by his uncongenial burdens, after about two years Gennadios was allowed to retire from his office to monastic refuge. But shameful squabbles under his immediate successors prompted the sultan to recall him to the Patriarchate in 1463. He is said to have fled from his tasks after a few months, but he was recalled again for a final term of service (1464–65) before his definitive release. He spent his remaining years in the Monastery of the Prodromos near Serres (in Macedonia), resuming his devotion to theological writing and Thomistic scholarship. The date of his death is uncertain but may have been as late as 1472.

JOHN W. BARKER

Biography

Born in Constantinople *c.*1405, George (as he was baptized) was a pupil of such distinguished scholars as John Chortasmenos, Joseph Bryennios, and Mark Eugenikos. He taught logic and physics at his own school and studied the works of Averroes, Avicenna, and Aquinas. He accompanied the emperor to the council of Ferrara/Florence in 1438–39 but later abandoned his pro-unionist stance. After the fall of Constantinople sultan Mehmet II appointed him the first patriarch under Ottoman rule. He died *c.*1472.

Writings

Oeuvres completes, edited by Louis Petit, X.A. Sidérides and Martin Jugie, 8 vols, Paris: Maison de la Bonne Presse, 1928–36 (critical edition in Greek)

Further Reading

Gill, Joseph, *The Council of Florence*, Cambridge: Cambridge University Press, 1959

Gill, Joseph, "George Scholarius" in *Personalities of the Council of Florence and Other Essays*, Oxford: Blackwell, 1964, pp. 79–94; New York: Barnes and Noble, 1965

Inalcik, Halil, "The Policy of Mehmed II toward the Greek Population of Istanbul and the Byzantine Buildings of the City", *Dumbarton Oaks Papers*, 23–24 (1969–70): pp. 231–49

Karpat, Kemal H., "Ottoman Views and Policies towards the Orthodox Christian Church", *Greek Orthodox Theological Review*, 31 (1986): pp. 131–55

Nicol, Donald M., *The Immortal Emperor: The Life and Legend of Constantine Palaiologos, Last Emperor of the Romans*, Cambridge and New York: Cambridge University Press, 1992

Runciman, Steven, *The Fall of Constantinople, 1453*, Cambridge: Cambridge University Press, 1965, reprinted 1990

Runciman, Steven, *The Great Church in Captivity: A Study of the Patriarchate of Constantinople from the Eve of the Turkish Conquest to the Greek War of Independence*, London: Cambridge University Press, 1968

Runciman, Steven, *The Last Byzantine Renaissance*, Cambridge: Cambridge University Press, 1970

Turner, C.J., "The Career of George-Gennadius Scholarius", *Byzantion*, 39 (1969): pp. 420–55

Genoese

Genoa is a port on the gulf of Genoa in Liguria, some 120 km south of Milan in northwest Italy. It was first mentioned as a *municipium* in the 3rd century BC and had a bishop of its own by the mid-5th century AD. From 958 it was a free city ruled by its bishop. During the 9th and 10th centuries Genoa and the Ligurian coast were subject to Muslim raids from Sicily and Spain. In 1016–17, in alliance with Pisa, Genoa prevented the Muslim conquest of Sardinia and in 1087 raided Mahdia, to the south of Tunis. As part of the peace negotiations with the Muslims the Genoese secured the right to trade along the Tunisian coast. After 1090 and the conquest of Sicily by the Normans, Genoese trade was extended to southern Italy. The Genoese also traded with the Levant. In 1063 Ingulf, abbot of Croyland in Lincolnshire, returned from pilgrimage in a Genoese ship he boarded in Jaffa, and in 1094 or 1095 on pilgrimage to the Holy Land Godfrey of Bouillon sailed out and back in a Genoese ship called *La Pomella*. In 1097 a squadron of 12 Genoese ships took part in the First Crusade and helped capture the city of Antioch. As a reward Genoese merchants were granted a *fondaco* based around the church of St John and 30 neighbouring houses by Bohemond, the new ruler of the city.

Behind the Amalfitans (950?), Pisans (1111), and Venetians (1092), the Genoese did not conclude their first commercial treaty with the Byzantines until 1155. In the following year, partly to wean the Genoese from too close a commercial alliance with Byzantium, William I of Sicily granted them favourable trade concessions in the wheat and cotton trade of Norman Sicily. Nevertheless, the Venetians saw the Genoese as their main rival in Constantinopolitan trade, and in 1162 and again in 1171 attacked the new Genoese quarter. The Genoese inhabitants of Constantinople helped defend the city against the army of the Fourth Crusade, but its success placed trade with Constantinople firmly in Venetian hands, to the detriment of Genoese merchants who sought trade links with the Greeks of Nicaea. In 1261 by the Treaty of Nymphaeum the Genoese gave their support to Michael VIII Palaiologos's successful attempt to recapture Constantinople; in return in 1267 Genoese merchants received very favourable concessions together with a commercial base in Pera (Galata), from where an extensive Black Sea trade was built up.

The 14th century marked the apogee of Genoa's preeminence in Aegean and Black Sea trade. In 1275 Manuale Zaccaria had been granted a monopoly of the alum mines around Phocaea (modern Foggia) in northwest Turkey. Alum was the principal fixing agent used in the west for the dyeing of cloth, and the mineral from Phocaea was the best available outside the Black Sea area. In 1304 the monopoly was extended to Genoese merchants in general, though not before the Zaccaria family had amassed a fortune which elevated it to the ranks of the super-rich. In the same year the Genoese seized the island of Chios, both to protect their investments in Phocaea and to preserve the mastic gardens on the island from Turkish attacks. Mastic was the favoured toothpaste of the wealthy in the Middle Ages and Chios its only known source. The island reverted to Byzantine rule in 1329 but in 1346 was seized by a Genoese adventurer, Simone Vignoso. The Genoese government, unable to repay the cost of this expedition, passed the administration of the island and the exploitation of its resources to a company (*mahonna*) made up of those who had financed the expedition. The island remained in Genoese hands until 1566 and the *mahonna* became the earliest example of a chartered company administering a colonial possession. In November 1354, in return for helping John V Palaiologos to enter Constantinople, the Genoese family of Gattalusi were rewarded with the island of Lesbos and an imperial marriage with the emperor's sister Irene. The family established a ruling dynasty based on Lesbos which lasted till 1462. In the same period the Genoese retained their share of Levantine trade in the face of aggressive Venetian action to regain its own share of the market. Four major naval wars (1258–70, 1294–99, 1350–51, and 1375–81) resulted. With the capture of Constantinople by sultan Mehmet II in 1453 the Genoese rulers and merchants in Chios, Kaffa, Lesbos, and Pera sent embassies to offer their congratulations and to negotiate tribute payments to their new overlord. Thereafter the Genoese lost out to the expanding Ottoman power, which took Pera in 1453, Lesbos in 1462, Kaffa in 1475, and the island of Chios, the last Genoese possession in the Levant, in 1566.

Byzantine/Greek artistic influences were not as evident in Genoa as they were in Venice. They are, however, evident in two major schemes: the frescos in the cathedral of St Lawrence in Genoa painted around 1310 may have been the work of a Byzantine, but this together with a textile depicting the life of St Lawrence sent to Genoa by Michael VIII Palaiologos.

PETER LOCK

Summary

A relative latecomer to the Byzantine world, the Italian city-state of Genoa concluded its first treaty with Constantinople in 1155. The Genoese quickly became the Venetians' main trading rivals. The Genoese had a monopoly of the alum mines around Phocaea: they also ruled Chios from 1304 to 1566 (with a break in 1329–46) and Lesbos from 1354 to 1462.

Further Reading

Argenti, Philip, *The Occupation of Chios by the Genoese and Their Administration of the Island*, 3 vols, Cambridge: Cambridge University Press, 1958, reprinted 1966

Balard, Michel, *La Romanie génoise: XIIe–début du XVe siècle*, 2 vols, Rome: Ecole Française, 1978

Day, Gerald, *Genoa's Response to Byzantium 1155–1204: Commercial Expansion and Factionalism in a Medieval City*, Urbana: University of Illinois Press, 1988

Lock, Peter, *The Franks in the Aegean 1204–1500*, London and New York: Longman, 1995

Nelson R., *Art Bulletin*, 67 (1985): pp. 548-66

Geography

Although the Greeks were the creators of the science of geography and made considerable advances in mathematical and descriptive geography, they were hampered by the lack of good technical appliances and therefore could not obtain technical accuracy. Only a fraction of the world was actually known to them, and what was unknown was the subject of a priori deduction and fanciful speculation. With the exception of mathematics and astronomy, Greek geography did not as a rule rely on other sciences as does geography today.

A considerable appreciation of topography, world order, and theory is displayed in the various Homeric descriptions, some of which are quite elaborate. The catalogue of ships in book 2 of the *Iliad* is a systematic evocation of the homeland of the Greeks. Both Homer and Hesiod conceived the earth as a round land mass surrounded by Ocean and symmetrically vaulted by heaven above and Tartarus below.

It was among the Ionians of Asia Minor that Greek geographical enquiry and writing originated, and their geographical horizons were enlarged by the expansion of their commerce and the colonization movement. In choosing names for their new settlements they repeated place names from their homeland, a habit of thinking which reflects a geographical sophistication. Not only is this practice paralleled from other parts of the world and other ages, but the practice persisted among the Greeks themselves down to Hellenistic, Roman, and even modern times.

The first recorded attempt at drawing a map of the world is that of Anaximander of Miletus (6th century BC). This map probably represented the world as a circular land mass divided into two portions, Asia and "Europe", surrounded by Ocean as Homer described it. The map was corrected and enlarged by Hecataeus (530–490 BC) who also wrote a commentary on it (including descriptions of towns and peoples as well as geographical features), of which some fragments are preserved by Herodotus. Herodotus (traditionally 484–425 BC), the "father of history", carefully recorded his personal observations made during many years of extensive travel, thus combining the geographical and ethnographical perspectives. Following his example, almost all ancient historians regularly included geographical descriptions in their works, and many of them appreciated, though perhaps not adequately by modern standards, the impact of geography on historical events. Ephorus (c.405–330 BC) attempted ethnography and historical geography and devoted entire books to descriptive geography, while Timaeus (c.350–260 BC) dealt largely with the general geography of western Europe.

Meanwhile, the shape and nature of the earth itself was engaging the attention of the early Greek philosophers. Of the Milesians, Thales (c.625–547 BC) declared it to be like a log floating on water, Anaximander that it was cylindrical and that it remained steady due to its central position in respect to other heavenly bodies, Anaximenes (c.380–320 BC) that it was like a leaf floating in the air. By insisting that the earth had no limit below and that the air had none above, Xenophanes (c.570–478 BC) got rid of both Uranus and Tartarus. The sphericity of the earth was asserted by the Pythagoreans, referred to for the first time in extant literature by Plato (in the *Phaedo*), and proved by Aristotle and Eudoxus of Cnidus (c.400–347 BC). The last mentioned is also responsible for the division of the globe into five zones: one of torrid and two each of frigid and temperate climate. Heraclides of Pontus (388–315 BC) declared that the earth revolved round its axis, and Aristarchus of Samos (330–260 BC) believed that it might also be revolving round the sun (prior to this, the Pythagorean Philolaus had taught that the earth, together with the planets, revolved round a central fire).

The earliest surviving work of a purely geographical nature is a description of the Mediterranean coast, the so-called *Periplus of Scylax* (named, doubtless, after Scylax whom Darius sent to explore the Indus), in reality a work of the early 4th century BC. About 330 BC Pytheas of Massilia made his voyage of exploration towards the northwest as far as the northern end of the British Isles and the coasts of Germany.

At about the same time, the eastern campaigns of Alexander the Great opened to Greek research the whole of Asia as far as India, with prospects of further expansion. The work of his companions and followers served, more than anything, to establish a link between formal geography and political dominion. Moreover, through the development in their hands of the ethnographical tradition, these writers gave to geography an analytical content which, while relying on the techniques of description and cataloguing, outlasted them. Thus Nearchus' report on his voyage from the Indus received visual form in a new map by Aristotle's pupil Dicaearchus of Messana (c. 320 BC). He was the first writer to treat physical geography in a scientific manner. Though his estimate of the earth's circumference (40,000 miles) was exaggerated, he rightly assumed the existence of a southern hemisphere. His map remained the standard of its kind for a long time.

The southern and eastern parts of India were opened up even further under Alexander's successors, as a result of Seleucid military expeditions and the trips of ambassadors such as Megasthenes. Unlike Ctesias of Cnidus (c.400 BC) whose *Indica* has been criticized as being overloaded with fable, Megasthenes has been commended (though not without debate) for giving a good description of the Ganges valley, of which he had personal knowledge. The Arabian and East African coasts became better known as a result of the commercial expeditions of the Ptolemies, and this improved knowledge is reflected in Agatharchides' partially extant description of the Red Sea coast (c.120 BC) and in the geographical chapters of Diodorus Siculus (c.100–20 BC).

It was Eratosthenes of Cyrene (c.285–200 BC) who arranged into a truly scientific system the mass of geographical material collected up to his time. He rejected the Homeric tradition and insisted on a clear distinction between fictitious wonder-descriptions and the recording of scientific fact. He created a new genre by blending mathematical and descriptive geography. His achievements in mathematics and the physical sciences on the one hand and history and philology on the other equipped him ideally for his task. He was the first to attempt to estimate the earth's circumference by a measurement of degrees carried out over a space of 15 degrees of latitude, but the imperfections of his method caused him to arrive at an exaggerated estimate (by 15 per cent or less) of 25,000 geographical miles. But the estimate which came to be accepted for many centuries to come was that of Posidonius of Apamea (c.90 BC) who based his calculation on the measurement of the shortest distance from Alexandria to Rhodes, and arrived at a figure of 18,000 geographical miles.

The true founder of mathematical geography was Hipparchus of Nicaea (c.140 BC), for he applied geometrical length and breadth to determine the position of places on the earth's surface. He also replaced the then current (Eratosthenean) rectangular and equidistant projection of parallels and meridians with a projection approximating to modern usage. He represented the parallels by segments of a circle, and the meridians by straight lines or curves in keeping with the portion of surface to be represented, drawn at distances corresponding to the actual distances on the surface of the globe.

The most important surviving Greek work on descriptive geography and ethnology is the 17-book treatise of Strabo published around AD 20. It covers topography as well as physical, political, historical, and (with less enthusiasm) mathematical geography. His object was the edification of political and military leaders. Roman conquests enabled him (as they enabled Polybius and Posidonius) to give a more accurate description of the West than his predecessors. The first two books present a wide-ranging discussion of the aims and methods of geography and review earlier writings on the subject. The remainder is devoted to regional geography. The vanished writings of many of his predecessors are known to us mainly through his criticisms.

The geographical contribution of Claudius Ptolemy (mid-2nd century AD) was the concept of the tabulation of latitude and longitude of places, which could give precision to locations. Its defects are due chiefly to the inaccuracies in his data and his preference for a priori principles over data available from recent reports (which must have included works such as the anonymous *Periplus of the Erythraean Sea*, a work probably dating from the second half of the 1st century AD and preserved, with other minor geographical works such as the epitome of Strabo, in a 9th-century Heidelberg manuscript). Though most of Ptolemy's geographical data were not actually determined by astronomical observation, he expressed them systematically in reference to curved lines of latitude measured northwards from the equator and curved meridians measured eastwards from the Canary Islands. The special topographical features of Greece were served by Pausanias' *Guide to Greece*, while the didactic geographical hexameter poem of Dionysius Periegetes (2nd century AD) acquired so much popularity down the ages that it was translated into Latin by both Avienus and Priscian, paraphrased by Nicephorus and an anonymous

writer, and was commented on by Eustathios, the 12th-century bishop of Thessalonica.

Greek geographical writings after Ptolemy largely consist of compilations and extracts, such as the *Periplus of the Outer Sea* by Marcian of Heraclea (c.AD 400) and the *Anonymi Geographi Expositio Compendiaria* attributed to Agathemerus. Both these works were printed by C. Müller in the first volume of his *Geographi Graeci Minores* (1855). Towards the end of the 6th century Stephanos of Byzantium compiled a dictionary known as the *Ethnica* which has preserved a great quantity of geographical information from earlier writers now lost, and which was in its turn utilized by the emperor Constantine VII Porphyrogenitos in his *De Administrando Imperio* and *De Thematibus* which include historical and ethnographic data. Stephanos's main sources were Strabo and Pausanias. Cosmas Indicopleustes, an Egyptian merchant turned monk, wrote the 12-book *Topographia Christiana* in which he made a vehement attempt to disprove the pagan theory of the earth's sphericity, maintaining that the shape of the world was the same as that of the tabernacle which Moses built to house the Covenant.

Interest in descriptive geography, which had been fashionable in the late Roman period, dwindled after the 6th century, but was revived in the 9th century beginning with Epiphanios Hagiopolites, and with the resurgence of travel literature from the 11th century onwards. The history of Gregoras, covering the period 1204–1359, included a long account of his friend Agathangelos whose letters described his alleged journeys around the Mediterranean during 20 years. He was followed in the subsequent centuries by John Phokas, Andrew Libadenos, and Laskaris Kananos. Within this category of descriptive geography can also be included narrative accounts of ambassadors to foreign lands, such as Priskos of Panium and Nonnosus in the late Roman period, and Constantine Manasses, Nicholas Mesarites, and Theodore Metochites in the 12th–14th centuries.

Although Byzantine scholars, like their Greek predecessors, held various views regarding the shape of the earth (ranging from the domed cube of Cosmas Indicopleustes to the globe of Photios), the centre of their *oikoumene* (world) was the Mediterranean. This was surrounded by the three continents – Asia, Europe, and Libya – while the Ocean surrounded all of them. Britain, China, and Black Africa lay at the extremes of the earth and were generally presented in legendary form. India was either identified with Ethiopia or with the country round the Phison of scripture (identified with either the Ganges or the Indus). The Phison was one of four major rivers which originated in the terrestrial Paradise, the easternmost country of the world.

Byzantine geographical perceptions, like those of the ancient Greeks, were limited by various factors: (1) the need to reconcile observations and empirical findings with preconceived notions based on scripture; (2) the uncritical acceptance of bookish information as true, without reference to current conditions; and (3) the strong impact of folklore on geography, which led to reliable information being often blended with fantastic notions concerning foreign lands and peoples.

D.P.M. WEERAKKODY

See also Anaximander, Astronomy, Cartography, Constantine VII, Ephorus, Eratosthenes, Eudoxus, Hecataeus, Herodotus, Hipparchus, Metochites, Pausanias, Posidonius, Ptolemy, Strabo, Timaeus

Further Reading

Bunbury, Edward Herbert, *History of Ancient Geography among the Greeks and Romans*, 2 vols, 2nd edition, New York: Dover, 1959

Burton, Harvey E., *The Discovery of the Ancient World*, Cambridge, Massachusetts: Harvard University Press, 1932

Cary, Max and Eric Herbert Warmington, *The Ancient Explorers*, London: Methuen, and New York: Dodd Mead, 1929; revised edition Harmondsworth and Baltimore: Penguin, 1963

Jacob, Christian, *Géographie et ethnographie en Grèce ancienne*, Paris: Colin, 1991

Karttunen, Klaus, "Distant Lands in Classical Ethnography", *Grazer Beitrage*, 18 (1992): pp. 195–204

Neugebauer, Otto, *The Exact Sciences in Antiquity*, 2nd edition, New York: Dover, 1969

Passen, Christiaan van, *The Classical Tradition of Geography*, Groningen: Wolters, 1957

Sykes, Percy, *A History of Exploration from the Earliest Times to the Present Day*, 3rd edition, London: Routledge and Kegan Paul, 1950

Thompson, James Oliver, *History of Ancient Geography*, Cambridge: Cambridge University Press, 1948

Tozer, Henry Fanshawe, *History of Ancient Geography*, 2nd edition, Cambridge: Cambridge University Press, 1935

Warmington, Eric Herbert, *Greek Geography*, New York: Dutton, and London: Dent, 1934, reprinted New York: AMS Press, 1973

Geology

Our knowledge of the geological history of the Aegean region starts in earnest 200 million years ago. At that time the North Atlantic Ocean did not exist and both Africa (more correctly Gondwanaland, or Africa plus other continents) and Eurasia (Europe and Asia) were united with the North American continent to form a supercontinent named Pangea. Between the future continents of Africa and Eurasia there was a wedge-shaped ocean, named Tethys (after the daughter of the earth goddess Gaia), which opened out to the east, where it joined the other oceans. The southern part of Tethys was a wide, shallow tropical sea where limestone was being deposited, rather similar to the Bahama banks today. Much of the grey limestone seen today in Greece formed at this time. Low islands on this platform were later to form parts of the mountains of Macedonia, Thrace, and southwestern Turkey. The northern part of Tethys was a deep ocean basin that abutted mountains in southern Eurasia. This state of affairs changed when the North Atlantic Ocean began to form about 190 million years ago.

The Atlantic Ocean started to open from the south and a great tear extended northwards. Africa had to rotate anticlockwise to accommodate the new ocean and the Tethys Ocean started to close up. At the same time, between the wide platform where the limestone was forming and the core of the African continent, a new ocean was opening up, later to become the Mediterranean Sea. These two processes combined to force the limestone platform, with its islands and troughs, northwards towards Eurasia. The deep ocean floor could bend and descend into the deeper parts of the interior of the earth, but the islands and the platforms were too light to go down. Instead they were piled against Eurasia to form chains of mountains. The overall convergence between Africa and Eurasia slowed down after the Arabian peninsula hit Eurasia, but continued expansion of parts of the Mediterranean sea floor continued to force parts of the crust northwards, raising up further mountain ranges. This overall convergence continues today, which is why the Aegean region is so mountainous.

Within the overall Mediterranean context of convergence and compression there are regions where crustal stretching was and is important, such as parts of the Aegean. During crustal stretching the surface of the earth cracks along faults. Parts of the crust descend to form tectonic valleys called grabens (as opposed to erosional valleys formed by rivers) which can also extend under the sea, the intervening blocks remaining as mountains, peninsulas, and islands (horsts). Expansion was directly north–south in Asia Minor, giving major east–west grabens now occupied by rivers such as the Gediz and Büyük Menderes in Turkey. In the Peloponnese and southern Greece expansion produced northwest–southeast grabens, such as the Gulf of Corinth and the Euboean straits. In between these areas stretching was more complex, producing a series of isolated blocks, the Cyclades.

Mention should be made of an unusual event that occurred about six million years ago: the Mediterranean sea almost completely dried up. This happened when tectonic forces closed up the Straits of Gibraltar. Rivers flowing into the basin, principally from the Black Sea, were insufficient to maintain sea-level and the sea dried out, except for a few saline lakes resembling the modern Dead Sea. There may even have been a salty waterfall at Gibraltar, also feeding the lakes. Evaporation of water from the lakes produced deposits of gypsum (alabaster) and other minerals, seen today in Crete and elsewhere.

The climate of the last 1.6 million years has been marked by dramatic fluctuations. Within this period, loosely called the Ice Age, the climate has been generally cool, with warmer conditions typically lasting for about 10,000 years every 100,000 years. During the last glacial period, about 130,000 to 10,000 years ago, the climate of the Aegean was moist and cool. There were glaciers on the highest mountains of the Greek and Turkish mainlands and the island of Crete. Sea level was considerably lower that it is today, by about 120 m, and hence the river-beds were steeper resulting in more rapid erosion. Mountains were deeply incised, and broad, flat valleys were developed. The climate was coldest about 20,000 years ago. Warming began rapidly about 10,000 years ago, but by 8000 years ago the climate was more stable. Since then variation has been less extreme, especially during the last 4000 years.

Global climatic warming melted the glaciers and sea-level rose, stabilizing close to its present level about 6000 years ago. The sea invaded estuaries, drowning many Palaeolithic sites on the old, fertile river plains. The deep, protected bays that formed were useful harbours in antiquity, but many had a short life (e.g. Miletus and Ephesus). Sediments washed down by the rivers were deposited in the bays, commonly filling them almost completely (e.g. Thermopylae and the gulf of Malia). Agriculture increased erosion and hence aided this process. It should be noted that earthquakes can also produce local

Geology: the lofty pillars of the Meteora in central Greece, most of which are topped by monasteries. Made of conglomerates, the cliffs acquired their remarkable shapes by weathering and erosion

changes in sea-level that are superimposed on the global sea-level rise (e.g. Phalasarna and Western Crete).

Geological history is recorded by rocks – sedimentary, metamorphic, and igneous. Sedimentary rocks form on the surface by the accumulation of rock fragments (e.g. sand, mud), biological material (e.g. shells, bones, plant material), or by crystallization of minerals from water (e.g. gypsum, salt). Most sedimentary rocks form under the sea or in lakes. Loose sediments are transformed into hard rocks when minerals crystallize from the water between the grains and cement them together. This process can continue after a rock is quarried, making the rock harder as it dries out. Cementation of sediments commonly occurs on beaches, making "beachrock", which is common throughout the Aegean. Accumulation of the finest rock particles makes clay. There are many types of clay and not all are suitable for making pottery. However, good pottery clay is commonly formed in basins that also contain lignite, a low-grade coal (e.g. Corinth).

When rocks are piled on top of each other, for example during convergence, or in a sedimentary basin, those at the base are heated up and subjected to increased pressure. This is because the temperature increases with depth in the earth by an average of 30°C per kilometre. Many of the minerals that make up the rocks are not stable under these new conditions and will either recrystallize to form larger crystals or transform into new minerals, a process called metamorphism. The most common metamorphic rocks in Greece are marble, schists, and serpentinite, formed respectively from limestone, mud-rocks, and peridotite. Some areas of metamorphic rocks, such as the Cyclades, are considered to be the deeper equivalents of sedimentary rocks elsewhere. Others, like the Menderes massif south and east of Izmir, have a much more complicated history, with much older rocks and several cycles of metamorphism. Sometimes the rocks can become so hot that they melt to form plutonic rocks such as granites.

The geological structure of the oceanic crust is quite different from that of the continents – it is almost completely made of igneous rocks, that is those that were originally molten. Its base is dominated by plutonic rocks such as peridotite and gabbro that solidified deep in the earth, whereas the top is made of basaltic lavas that were erupted underwater. The lavas are in turn commonly covered by chert and limestone. Although there is no true oceanic crust in the Aegean region today, convergence of Africa and Europe has forced former parts of the oceanic crust up on to the land. The peridotites have been converted into the green or black rock serpentinite.

There are many volcanic rocks in Greece and western Turkey, mostly formed during the last 20 million years, and the activity continues today. These rocks formed when the sea-floor was thrust down deep into the earth. As the temperature rose, part of the rocks melted and the liquid made its way to the surface in volcanoes. Volcanic activity is now restricted to

Santorini (ancient Thera) and Nisyros, but in antiquity Methana and Melos were active for short intervals. There have been many different types of eruption. The largest was the "Minoan" eruption of Thera in 1650 or 1450 BC – almost 30 cubic km of volcanic ash was erupted. Since then activity has mostly been non–explosive, with the eruption of lava flows. On Nisyros volcanic activity has been marked by steam explosions with no lava or true volcanic ash.

Most metallic ore deposits, such as those of gold, silver, lead, iron, copper, and tin, are precipitated from hot watery fluids that circulate in the crust. These fluids start as surface water that descends into the crust. There it is heated, and metals, and other elements, dissolve in the water. They are precipitated as minerals when the water rises and cools. The heat necessary to drive circulation is sometimes associated with metamorphism, the emplacement of plutonic rocks such as granite or volcanism. Circulation of sea water into the oceanic crust also produces deposits of copper and other elements where these fluids vent on to the sea floor (e.g. the Troodos mountains of Cyprus).

The most common rocks in the Aegean region today are limestone and its metamorphic equivalent marble. These rocks are more resistant to erosion than other types of rocks and tend to form the hills, in the absence of tectonic movements. Paradoxically, both limestone and marble are soluble in rain water and prolonged erosion gives rise to a characteristic landscape called *karst*, after a region in Croatia. In these regions most drainage is not on the surface in valleys, but instead rain and snow-melt drain directly into swallow-holes (sink-holes). The drainage basins start as small conical depressions and can become quite large, with flat bottoms (there are many in Arcadia). Every swallow–hole is connected to a system of caves or fissures, that tend to be enlarged by continual solution of the rock. The springs can debouch many kilometres away, in some cases under lakes or the sea (e.g. the gulf of Argos). In many areas the fissure and caves system can store sufficient water for the springs to be perennial. Although *karst* caves are formed by solution of rock, precipitation of limestone from waters percolating into caves forms stalagmites and stalactites. This can only occur when there is little flow of water through the cave. A similar process deposits travertine around many *karst* springs. However, much travertine was quarried in antiquity.

Soils form by weathering of the underlying rock. Much of this weathering may have happened during the last glacial period when the climate was wetter, but glaciers were only on the peaks of the mountains. Limestone or marble gives a characteristic red soil called *terra rosa*. Although fertile, this soil is usually too thin on the hillsides for successful agriculture. In antiquity this soil was processed to give a red clay. The soft sediments that fill the grabens weather easily and tend to yield fertile soils. The best soils form on marls – sandy, clay-rich limestones. Soils washed from the hills accumulate in the valleys to form alluvial soils. The abundance of water and the renewal of these soils by material washed from the hills during storms has made these areas very productive. Drainage in antiquity and recently has greatly increased the availability of these soils (e.g. Lake Copais).

MICHAEL D. HIGGINS

See also Climate, Earthquakes, Volcanoes

Further Reading

Ager, Derek V., *The Geology of Europe*, London and New York: McGraw Hill, 1980

Bassiakos, Y.E., "Ancient Greek Mining and Metallurgical Activities and Relationships to the Geosciences", *Bulletin of the Geological Society of Greece*, 28/2 (1993): pp. 475–91 (in Greek)

Brinkmann, Roland, *Geology of Turkey*, Amsterdam and New York: Elsevier, 1976

Cornwall, Ian Wolfram, *Soils for the Archaeologist*, London: Phoenix House, 1958

Ford, Derek C. and P.W. Williams, *Karst Geomorphology and Hydrology*, London and Boston: Unwin Hyman, 1989

Higgins, Michael Denis and Reynold Higgins, *A Geological Companion to Greece and the Aegean*, London: Duckworth, and Ithaca, New York: Cornell University Press, 1996

Hsu, Kenneth J., *The Mediterranean Was a Desert: The Voyage of the Glomar Challenger*, Princeton, New Jersey: Princeton University Press, 1983

Jacobshagen, Volker, *Geologie von Griechenland*, Berlin: Borntraeger, 1986

Marinos, Paul G. and George C. Koukis (editors), *Engineering Geology of Ancient Works, Monuments and Historical Sites: Preservation and Protection*, 4 vols, Rotterdam: Balkema, 1988–90

Strothers, R. B. and M.R. Rampino, "Volcanic Eruptions in the Mediterranean before AD 630 from Written and Archaeological Sources", *Journal of Geophysical Research*, 88 (1983): pp. 6357–71

Tooley, Michael J. and Ian Shennan (editors), *Sea-Level Changes*, Oxford and New York: Blackwell, 1987

Geometres, John

Poet and prose writer of the 10th century

All that is known for certain about the life of John Geometres (or Kyriotes) is that he flourished in the second half of the 10th century. "Geometres" could refer to a profession as surveyor, to a post in the imperial fisc dealing with land measurement, or to his being a geometrician, but it may also be taken in the sense of "globe-trotter", i.e. a vagabond. "Kyriotes" probably refers to a district in southwestern Constantinople where he may have been born or possibly became a monk. There are a few slight indications that he may have been a member of the civil aristocracy: he refers to his father as an energetic servant of the empire who died in Asia; he himself owned a house on the principal street of the capital; one manuscript styles him *protospatharios*, a dignity that usually conferred membership of the Senate and in the 10th century was still mainly given to commanders of the empire's military and territorial divisions which were known as themes. The belief that he was at one time bishop of Melitene in Cappadocia is without substance. He was well read in the pagan and Christian classics and made important contributions to both prose and poetic genres.

Geometres revived and rescued from its scholastic sterility the genre of the *progymnasma*. This had lain dormant for a few centuries but, probably initially through his influence, became popular again in the 11th to 15th centuries. Designed originally as a preliminary exercise for students of rhetoric, it had speedily become a form of polished essay in its own right with numerous subgenres and rules. Three lively encomia of the apple and one of the oak and two *ekphraseis* of his own garden (the sole surviving prose descriptions of a private Byzantine garden) survive by him. His originality is shown in his introduction of humour, parody of 4th-century *progymnasmata*, and Christian elements (which on occasion even approach blasphemy, as when the medicinal virtues for physical ailments of a rotten apple are compared with the salvific virtues for spiritual ailments of Christ when he had taken on corruptible flesh). He also mixed subgenres in an unprecedented way, including an imaginary speech and an erotic myth of possibly his own invention in encomia of the apple, while his *ekphraseis* of his garden are addressed as letters to a friend and his encomia of the apple are covering letters for gifts of the fruit. His artistry in the *progymnasmata* is best shown in his encomium of the oak which follows all the hallowed rules of what topics should be included in the encomium of a plant, yet with almost imperceptible subtlety describes the life cycle of the tree in human terms from birth by immaculate conception to the role of grandparent.

Two homilies, on the Annunciation and the Dormition of the Virgin, alone survive (from at least four that he wrote). Though on traditional themes, they exhibit important differences from their simpler predecessors. Less concerned with the narrative of events and the personalities of the characters, they rather comment on stories with whose details their auditors are assumed to be familiar. They are thus more abstract and resemble theological tracts with scholarly and other digressions.

Geometres' rhetorical expertise, evident in both homilies and *progymnasmata*, extended to the theoretical. His commentaries on rhetoricians of the Second Sophistic survive only as lengthy quotations in the works of successors such as John Doxopatres, but in that form they became very influential in Byzantium. He was often more systematic than his predecessors and was one of the first rhetoricians to study the style of early Christian writers (most notably in an encomium on Gregory of Nazianzus and in commentaries on some of his works). He was also sufficiently a realist to reject the theoreticians' condemnation of obscurity, claiming that it is not in "every instance a vice; on the contrary it is often even a virtue".

In verse Geometres virtually invented a new genre, that of political poetry (this must not be confused with the metrical term "political verse"), through a series of compositions ranging from just 2 to more than 100 lines. These were written mainly in the reigns of Nikephoros II Phokas (963–69) and John I Tzimiskes (969–76), but a few probably date from just before 963 and one from probably as late as 989. They describe the achievements of the emperors and other events such as rebellions, a foreign (Georgian?) invasion, and an alliance of the Rus and Bulgarians against Byzantium. His favourite emperor is Nikephoros, whose assassin John he both praises and portrays in Macbethian manner as a lion reduced by his crime to a trembling hare frightened by false dreams. Other poems extol the beauties of nature or one of the defensive towers of the capital, praise saints or, more enthusiastically, ancient philosophers, mock a literary opponent or a man who could not distinguish in pronunciation between *l* and *r*, and mourn the barbarization of language and customs of Greece. In perhaps his most remarkable and innovative poem

he describes the natural and human devastation around Selymbria, saddened by which he set out for Constantinople only to hear of the even more lamentable destruction caused there by fire and earthquake. This poem combines *ethopoiia* (character-drawing) with *ekphrasis*, formulaic expressions with personal pathos, high poetry with autobiography.

Geometres' religious poetry includes a panegyric on St Panteleimon written in iambics. Such a thing, though not unique, was very rare and differed from both the usual prose Life and the much shorter poetic encomiastic sermon in the form of a canon (a type of hymn). Four hymns praise the Theotokos (the Virgin Mary) and shorter poems on traditional subjects concern the Annunciation, the Nativity, the Assumption, the individual instruments of the Passion, Lazarus, the Samaritan Woman, the discovery of the head of St John the Baptist, etc. A further collection of 94 quatrains on the monastic life is attributed in numerous manuscripts either, impossibly, to St Nilus or to Geometres. If the latter attribution is correct, they would add to his reputation through their frequently striking imagery, their occasionally original thought, and their sophisticated versification.

Geometres was one of the most attractive and innovative of Byzantine writers. An accurate assessment of his importance must, however, await the literary history of Byzantium that still remains to be written.

A.R. LITTLEWOOD

Biography
John lived in Constantinople in the second half of the 10th century. Little is known of his life except that he served in the army and later became a monk. He wrote essays (reviving the genre of *progymnasmata*) and homilies (on traditional themes) as well as religious verse (panegyrics), epigrams, and political poetry on contemporary events.

Writings
In *Patrologia Graeca*, edited by J.-P. Migne, vol. 106, cols 806-1002
Homily on the Assumption, with French translation, in *L'Assomption de la T.S. Vierge dans la tradition byzantine du VIe au Xe siècle: études et documents*, edited by Antoine Wenger, Paris: Institut Français d'Etudes Byzantines, 1955, pp. 185–205, 363–415
The Progymnasmata, edited by A.R. Littlewood, Amsterdam: Hakkert, 1972

Further Reading
Kustas, George L., *Studies in Byzantine Rhetoric*, Thessalonica: Patriarchal Institute for Patristic Studies, 1973, pp. 24–25, 90–93
Littlewood, A.R., "A Byzantine Oak and Its Classical Acorn: The Literary Artistry of Geometres, Progymnasmata 1", *Jahrbuch der österreichischen Byzantinistik*, 29 (1980): pp. 133–44
Scheidweiler, F., "Studien zu Johannes Geometres", *Byzantinische Zeitschrift*, 45 (1952): pp. 277–319
Trypanis, C.A., *Greek Poetry: From Homer to Seferis*, Chicago: University of Chicago Press, and London: Faber, 1981, pp. 457–58, 473–74

Geometric Period *c.900–c.700* BC

The Geometric period of ancient Greece is normally understood to last from *c.*900 to *c.*700 BC, taking its name from the "geometric" style of pottery decoration found throughout the

Greek world at that time. This style is characterized primarily by the use of rectilinear motifs in various combinations; while it may also include the pictorial representation of both animals and humans, especially in the 8th century, these also follow the prevailing artistic conventions and appear obviously "geometric" in form.

The Geometric period can be said to have begun in Athens, where the characteristic style first emerged *c.*900 BC, evolving from its predecessor, the Protogeometric, which itself developed there around the middle of the 11th century BC. The pottery decoration follows a definite stylistic evolution, so that the period can be divided into three phases, the Early, Middle, and Late Geometric (EG, MG, and LG respectively), each of which may be further subdivided into two phases. The traditional dates for these phases are: EGI 900–875 BC; EGII 875–850 BC; MGI 850–800 BC; MGII 800–760 BC; LGI 760–735 BC; and LGII 735–700 BC. A word of caution is needed, however, when referring to these dates since, strictly speaking, they apply only to Athens. In fact, the whole chronological framework of the period has recently come under attack due to the rather tenuous nature of the evidence supporting it; a heavy reliance has been placed on the stylistic development of the pottery, taken in conjunction with historical accounts, since other methods that might be expected to yield more precise information, such as radiocarbon dating and dendrochronology, have not proved particularly useful. Some confirmation for the dating scheme accorded to the pottery has been possible, for it has occasionally been found in association with Egyptian objects, particularly scarabs, which are datable to the reigns of individual pharaohs. Other information has been provided by relating the ceramic evidence to the traditional foundation dates of the Greek colonies in Italy as given by later writers such as Thucydides, but this is of limited value since it applies only to the last 50 years of the Geometric period; other historical events noted by ancient authors, such as the first Olympiad in 776 BC, have also been used, but in general there are very few fixed chronological points. Given this lack of corroborating evidence, some recent scholarship has suggested that all dates for the early Iron Age, including those for the Geometric period, should be lowered, but this view has itself met with much criticism and has failed to win general approval.

Dating for the various phases of the Geometric period also differs from place to place. The phases in Geometric decoration found in the Argolid and Corinthia match those at Athens very closely in development and date, but further afield the pace of the acceptance of change appears to have been somewhat slower and there is thus often a time lag in comparison to Athens. In Laconia and west Greece, for instance, the Protogeometric appears to have continued to the middle of the 8th century BC, while in east Greece the Early Geometric phase is very difficult to assess, and in Thessaly it is impossible to distinguish the end of the Late Geometric phase. Similar problems and uncertainties are also apparent in other areas, making it clear that the history of the Geometric style must take into account significant regional variation.

When the Bronze Age palace civilization came to an end at some point in the 12th century BC, all the components that had made that civilization what it was collapsed; the Greek world entered a new phase of its history, the Iron Age. The early part of the Iron Age (*c.*1200–900 BC, a period often also called the Dark Age) has traditionally been viewed as a time of poverty, isolation, and depopulation, and even though this picture may be more representative of our own relative lack of knowledge about the period, there is also some truth in the traditional view that the Greeks had, in a sense, to rebuild their civilization. By about 900 BC, however, when the Geometric period begins, some degree of stability appears to have returned. The Geometric period was thus a time of great change, a time when the Greeks finally overcame many of the difficulties associated with the so-called Dark Age, and a time of rebirth characterized by the appropriately named Greek renaissance of the later part of the 8th century BC (LG).

A great deal of information about the period comes from the graves that have been found all over Greece. From the Kerameikos and Areopagus areas in Athens, for example, comes a wealth of information about burial customs and about the pottery used in those burials. Generally cremation was employed, the bodies being burned on a pyre and then placed in a pot which was itself buried in a pit along with various possessions and gifts. The ash urns were different for men and women, and the goods contained in each also seem to have been gender-specific, weapons for instance in male burials, jewellery in female burials. Customs, however, varied at different times, and children were normally inhumed, often with their toys, while for a short time in the Late Geometric period, inhumation was also adopted for most adults. It is at this time that the very large Dipylon amphorae and kraters were used in Athens as grave markers. These pots, named after the area of the cemetery in which they were found, were all made in the same workshop and bear figured scenes representing the *prothesis* (lying in state) and *ekphora* (funerary procession). For many, these pots are the epitome of Greek Geometric art. Burial customs also differed in other areas of Greece, with some regions preferring inhumation, others cremation, while specific practices varied within these two categories. Interpretation of the burials and their contents has thus provided some understanding of social and economic organization among different individuals and groups at this time.

It was during the Late Geometric period, however, that the most significant changes occurred. This is the era of the Greek renaissance, so called because the substantial developments that took place at that time suggest a rebirth after the Dark Age. Some scholars take the very sharp rise in population that occurred in the 8th century BC as the catalyst provoking all the changes; consequent overpopulation, they argue, led to increased pressures on land and resources that in turn led to a growth in political centralization characterized by the emergence of the polis (or city state) ruled by aristocracies. Warfare among these newly established Greek states was also a very common occurrence in this period.

Essential to this renaissance are the contacts with the outside world which, although never entirely lost in the previous centuries, are now seen on a much grander scale. These contacts themselves can partly be viewed as the result of some of the pressures facing the Greeks in the 8th century BC, pressures caused by such factors as overpopulation, a shortage of good land, a need for access to more natural resources, and political dissatisfaction. Partly to alleviate some of these troubles and to find solutions to them, a great colonizing movement began *c.*750 BC. The Greeks from some of the most developed (and hence often most troubled) states, such as Corinth, Megara, and Euboea, sent colonies to south Italy and Sicily. In the east, trading centres were established at places such as Al Mina on the Levantine coast, and trade was extended to other areas that included the Near East, Asia Minor, and Egypt. These eastern contacts in particular would profoundly affect Greece.

In the religious sphere, change is also very noticeable, especially in the sanctuaries. Although some of these existed earlier in the Geometric period, archaeological evidence indicates that there was a strong increase in the level of activity taking place at them by the 8th century BC; masses of votive offerings have been found, particularly pottery and, by the later part of that century, metal goods also appear. By that time temples to the gods were also being constructed, most of rather modest construction, but a few of massive size.

Contact with the east also brought about the adoption of the alphabet, knowledge of which was obtained through the Phoenicians and adapted somewhat by the Greeks to suit their own language. Literacy had finally returned after an absence of more than 400 years. This was a monumental achievement and among its earliest manifestations are the great Homeric epic poems, the *Iliad* and the *Odyssey,* soon followed by the works of the didactic poet Hesiod.

The adoption of the polis meant that, in this period, the Greeks never developed a real sense of nationality as we would think of it, yet they certainly possessed a great sense of national consciousness and pride, a Hellenism that partly manifested itself in the growth of the great Panhellenic sanctuaries, such as Olympia and Delphi. Indeed, their renewed contacts with the outside world helped to foster their identity – they were Greeks, the others were barbarians. The transformations of the 8th century BC led directly to the significant achievements of the archaic period that followed the Geometric.

A. FOLEY

See also Alphabet, Burial Practices, Colonization, Pottery

Summary

The Geometric period, *c.*900–700 BC, is named after the geometric style of pottery decoration that prevailed at the time throughout Greece. Archaeology provides information of burial customs and of religious practices. Population growth inspired the colonization of areas in the central and eastern Mediterranean. From the east came knowledge of the alphabet which enabled the composition of the poetic works of Homer and Hesiod. Adoption of the polis (organization into city states) brought with it a sense of Panhellenic cultural pride.

Further Reading

Ahlberg-Cornell, Gudrun, *Prothesis and Ekphora in Greek Geometric Art*, Göteborg: Åströms, 1971
Boardman, John, *The Greeks Overseas: Their Early Colonies and Trade*, 4th edition, London and New York: Thames and Hudson, 1999
Coldstream, J.N., *Greek Geometric Pottery: A Survey of Ten Local Styles and Their Chronology*, London: Methuen, 1968
Coldstream, J.N., *Geometric Greece*, London: Benn, and New York: St Martin's Press, 1977
Davison, Jean M., *Attic Geometric Workshops*, New Haven, Connecticut: Yale University Press, 1961
Dunbabin, Thomas James, *Greeks and Their Eastern Neighbours: Studies in the Relations between Greece and the Countries of the Near East in the Eighth and Seventh Centuries BC*, London: Society for the Promotion of Hellenic Studies, 1957, reprinted Chicago: Ares, 1979
Hägg, Robin (editor), *The Greek Renaissance of the Eighth Century BC: Tradition and Innovation*, Stockholm: Svenska Institutet i Athen, 1983
Hägg, Robin, Nanno Marinatos and Gullög C. Nordquist (editors), *Early Greek Cult Practice*, Stockholm: Svenska Institutet i Athen, 1988
Mazarakis Ainian, Alexander, *From Rulers' Dwellings to Temples: Architecture, Religion, and Society in Early Iron Age Greece, 1100–700 BC*, Jonsered: Åströms, 1997
Morgan, Catherine, *Athletes and Oracles: The Transformation of Olympia and Delphi in the Eighth Century BC*, Cambridge and New York: Cambridge University Press, 1990
Morris, Ian, *Burial and Ancient Society: The Rise of the Greek City-State*, Cambridge and New York: Cambridge University Press, 1987
Polignac, François de, *Cults, Territory, and the Origins of the Greek City-State*, Chicago: University of Chicago Press, 1995
Schweitzer, Bernhard, *Greek Geometric Art*, London: Phaidon, 1971
Snodgrass, Anthony M., *The Dark Age of Greece: An Archaeological Survey of the Eleventh to the Eighth Centuries BC*, Edinburgh: Edinburgh University Press, 1971
Snodgrass, Anthony M., *Archaeology and the Rise of the Greek State*, Cambridge and New York: Cambridge University Press, 1977
Starr, Chester G., *The Origins of Greek Civilization, 1100–650 BC*, New York: Knopf, 1961, reprinted New York: Norton, 1991
Starr, Chester G., *The Economic and Social Growth of Early Greece, 800–500 BC*, New York: Oxford University Press, 1977
Whitley, James, *Style and Society in Dark Age Greece: The Changing Face of a Pre-Literate Society, 1100–700 BC*, Cambridge and New York: Cambridge University Press, 1991

George I 1845–1913

King of the Hellenes

King George I was the second son of Christian, Crown Prince of Denmark. Born in 1845 in Copenhagen, he was assassinated in Thessalonica in 1913. Despite his violent death, he was the longest-reigning sovereign of Greece. Throughout his reign he struck a balance between the international and domestic stability of his country.

Prince William George studied at the Danish Naval Academy and was appointed constitutional King of Greece by the three guarantor powers of Greece, namely Britain, France, and Russia, as successor of King Otho, by a treaty signed in London on 1 July (Old Style – OS)/13 July (New Style – NS) 1863. Otho had been deposed by revolution on 10 October 1862 (OS). The appointment of King George was considered to have been influenced by British interests in the eastern Mediterranean, partly because he had been chosen by Lord Palmerston, the British prime minister, and partly on account of the dynastic relationship between the Danish and the British royal families. Indeed, Britain demonstrated its favour towards the young king in 1864 by handing over to Greek sovereignty the Ionian Islands, a British protectorate since 1815. His title "King of the Hellenes" denoted the nation's perception of his role as king also of the unredeemed Greeks.

Upon his arrival in Greece in October 1863, King George faced a suspicious constituent national assembly, whose proceedings he was unable to influence effectively. Regardless of the king's opposition, the 1864 constitution provided for a unicameral political system, in which the country's leading politicians, who had overthrown the Bavarian dynasty, held virtually unlimited power in the name of the nation.

The king's most serious confrontation with parliament occurred during the Cretan insurrection of 1866, when the parliamentary majority endorsed prime minister Alexandros Koumoundouros and his policy of support for the Cretans against the Ottoman empire, a policy also encouraged by Russia. The king first alienated the Greek government by marrying the Russian grand duchess Olga in 1867, without the knowledge of the Greek prime minister, and then dismissed the Koumoundouros cabinet in January 1868, to avert a war with the Ottoman empire over Crete. Such a war threatened to destabilize the whole region. This royal initiative resulted in a long series of minority cabinets, serious tension between the king and the country's political forces, and, ultimately in 1874, a constitutional crisis. The crisis was resolved in April 1875, when king George turned to his radical opponent, Charilaos Trikoupis, and summoned him to form a government and to hold fair elections.

In his inaugural speech to parliament the following October the king pledged his commitment to majority governments; the speech was the work of prime minister Charilaos Trikoupis. The king's overall relationship with the Greek politicians improved thereafter. Once in office, Trikoupis moderated his earlier radical views and for the next 15 years became the king's trusted political leader. The king, on the other hand, saw in Trikoupis a source of political stability, a realistic prospect of modernization, and, not least important, pro-British foreign-policy priorities. Thus between 1875 and 1892 a two-party system functioned with hardly any royal interference. The king's main preoccupation was with Greece's national interests in his annual unofficial tour of the European capitals. Indeed, in moments of international tension, like that of the Eastern Crisis of 1878, he could argue convincingly and for the benefit of Greece's irredentist programme that, if he became unpopular with his subjects, the stability of his throne could be endangered. The crisis ended with the annexation of Thessaly and Arta to Greece in 1881.

In 1887 king George received kaiser Wilhelm of Germany for the wedding of his son, crown prince Constantine, to princess Sophia, Wilhelm's daughter, in Athens. In 1888 the Greek king celebrated the 25th anniversary of his reign. Both occasions were exploited by prime minister Trikoupis to enhance the king's popularity. This popularity however suffered when in February 1892 king George removed from office prime minister Theodore Deliyannis on account of his financial policies, despite his parliamentary majority, in transgression of the 1875 royal commitment to parliament. Greece, through the financial policies of Trikoupis, had borrowed heavily on foreign markets and its creditors were becoming anxious over its ability to meet its obligations. In his efforts to secure a ministry more amenable to the pressures of Greece's foreign creditors, king George unsuccessfully tried to create a third royalist political party by summoning K. Konstantopoulos and S. Sotiropoulos to form cabinets. As a result, the king incurred the hostility of the two dominant Greek political parties. His popularity further suffered after Greece's military defeat in the war with Turkey in 1897, for which the royal family and entourage were held responsible.

After an abortive attempt on his life in February 1898, the last years of his reign were marked by the revolt of the "Military League" in August 1909, whose anti–dynastic dispositions were tempered and channelled by the Cretan statesman, Eleutherios Venizelos, into a revision of the 1864 constitution in 1911. Thereafter, Venizelos and King George cooperated for the military and diplomatic preparation of Greece in view of its confrontation with the Ottoman empire for the acquisition of Macedonia, Epirus, Crete, and the Aegean islands. After the victory of Greece in the First Balkan War in 1912 and the liberation of Thessalonica, King George resided in that city to highlight Greece's legitimate rights to the region in the face of Bulgarian counter-claims. He was assassinated in Thessalonica on 5 March 1913 (OS). The motives of his assassins have remained obscure.

Through his capacity for compromise and his political sagacity, which are in striking contrast to the inflexibility of his successor, King Constantine I, King George secured for Greece a stable parliamentary regime and significant territorial gains.

KATERINA GARDIKAS

See also Constantine I, Deliyannis, Graeco-Turkish War, Trikoupis, Venizelos

Biography
Born in Copenhagen in 1845, George was the second son of king Christian IX of Denmark. After the deposition of king Otho in October 1862, he was chosen by the protecting powers (Britain, France, and Russia) to succeed as "King of the Hellenes". He married Olga, niece of tsar Alexander II, by whom he had seven children. He was assassinated in the newly liberated Thessalonica in 1913.

Further Reading
Dontas, Domna, *Greece and the Great Powers, 1863–1875*, Thessalonica: Institute for Balkan Studies, 1966
Kofos, Evangelos, *Greece and the Eastern Crisis, 1875–1878*, Thessalonica: Institute for Balkan Studies, 1975
Prebelakes, Eleutherios G., *British Policy Towards the Change of Dynasty in Greece, 1862–1863*, Athens: Christou, 1953

George II 1890–1947
King of the Hellenes

George II, son of Constantine I, was born in Athens in 1890. He became king of Greece in 1922 but in 1924 was overthrown after the proclamation of the republic of Greece. He then found asylum in Great Britain. The British strongly endorsed his restoration and he associated himself with British foreign policy. After an unsuccessful *coup d'état* by the Republicans on 1 March 1935, the monarchy was restored and George II returned to Greece. A manipulated plebiscite on 3 November 1935 produced a vote of 97 per cent in favour of the restoration of the king.

As soon as George II returned to Athens he became associated with his old friend General Ioannis Metaxas. After the death of the prime minister, Constantine Demertzis, in April 1936, George II promoted Metaxas from deputy prime minister to the post of premier, despite the fact that his party had only six deputies in parliament.

On 4 August 1936 George II approved Metaxas's right-wing dictatorship and rejected an offer from the leaders of the two major parties in parliament (the Liberals of Themistoklis Sophoulis and the Populists of Ioannis Theotokis) to form a coalition government. He supported all the oppressive measures of Metaxas's regime, including the imprisonment and exile of politicians and trade union leaders and the suppression of freedom of speech. Metaxas even censored Pericles' funeral oration in Thucydides' history.

After Metaxas's death in January 1941, which left Greece in a state of war against Italian fascist forces, George II made no attempt to restore constitutional order. When the German army invaded Greece in April 1941, the king and his government under Emanuel Tsouderos, together with units of the Greek army and navy, escaped to Cairo, where they established a Greek government in exile.

During the occupation of Greece by Axis forces (1941–44) George II lived in exile, moving between Cairo and London. The occupation of Greece and the resistance of the anti-monarchist National Liberation Front (EAM) and its military wing the Greek Popular Liberation Army (ELAS) led to a new constitutional crisis for the self-exiled king.

With the withdrawal of the Axis forces from Greece in the autumn of 1944 and the demobilization of the Greek Popular Liberation Army, the British, who had already brought Greece under their sphere of influence, made every effort to restore the monarchy along with a right-wing government in Athens. On 1 September 1946 a coerced plebiscite permitted George II to return as king. Although the validity of the plebiscite was disputed by the liberal parliamentary opposition and the Left in particular, the king received the support of the British and American Allies who looked upon the Greek monarchy as the sole bulwark against Soviet expansion in the area.

George II died in March 1947 under peculiar circumstances. He was succeeded by his brother, who came to the throne as Paul I. George II was an authoritarian personality who chose not to play the role of a constitutional king. He lost popular support by associating himself with unconstitutional practices and even more by endorsing the various dictatorial and authoritarian measures imposed by Metaxas and other right-wing governments. His successors Paul I and Constantine II (his nephew) continued in the same vein and brought the monarchy of Greece to its inevitable demise.

STEPHANOS CONSTANTINIDES

Biography

Born in Athens in 1890 the eldest son of king Constantine and queen Sophia, George studied at the Military Academy in Athens and in Berlin. He came to the throne in 1922 but left Greece in 1923, the year before a republic was declared. Recalled in 1935, he supported Metaxas's dictatorship. During the German occupation (1941–44) he lived in exile. He returned to the throne in 1946 but died in 1947.

Further Reading

Campbell, John and Philip Sherrard, *Modern Greece*, London: Benn, and New York: Praeger, 1968

Legg, Keith R., *Politics in Modern Greece*, Stanford, California: Stanford University Press, 1969

Svoronos, N., *Histoire de la Grèce moderne*, 3rd edition, Paris: Presses Universitaires de France, 1972

Woodhouse, C.M., *Apple of Discord: A Survey of Recent Greek Politics in Their International Setting*, London and New York: Hutchinson, 1948

Woodhouse, C.M., *The Story of Modern Greece*, London: Faber, 1968

George of Pisidia

Poet of the early 7th century AD

George is best known for his panegyrical poems in iambic trimeters that celebrate the Persian campaigns of the emperor Herakleios I during the 620s. Probably originally from Antioch in Pisidia, his working life was spent in Constantinople, where he was among the many deacons of Hagia Sophia and pursued a successful administrative career in the service of the patriarch Sergios, reputedly rising to the position of archivist and head of the patriarch's secretariat (*chartophylax*). Hence, as with Agathias's circle half a century earlier, poetry was George's second career; his ecclesiastical environment is an important key to understanding his writings.

George's literary activities formed part of a wider cultural revival promoted by Herakleios to help underpin his unconstitutional and insecure regime. Sergios too played a major role in this revival, and he is as prominent as the emperor in the dedications of George's poetry. The *History* of Theophylaktos Simokattes and the *Chronicon Paschale* (or *Easter Chronicle*, because of its interest in chronology and the dating of Easter) are products of the same era. The transferral of the Neoplatonic philosopher and polymath Stephen from Alexandria to Constantinople and the establishment of a library by Sergios should also be linked with it.

George's works have traditionally been divided into the two categories of panegyrical epics and religious poems, but all have a strong religious flavour: Herakleios's campaigns are justified as an attempt to establish the universal authority of God in the face of the Persian worship of moon, stars, and fire, elements that are God's creations. His one surviving prose work also has a religious theme: it elaborates the *Acts* of the contemporary martyr Anastasios the Persian. Like *On the Resurrection* (?624), George's principal work, a *Hexaemeron* (1900 lines), encompasses the two categories: it encloses an account of the wonders of God's Creation within a framework inspired by the immediate political context of Herakleios's victory over Persia in 628, culminating in a prayer for the emperor and his dynasty put into the mouth of the patriarch Sergios. A more useful distinction can be made between brief poems of 100 or so lines and longer works with a significant narrative element. The former group, transmitted as "impromptu" pieces, evoke the emotional atmosphere in Constantinople at particular moments (for example, *To Bonus*, calling for the emperor's return from campaign in the east to rescue the capital from the Avars in 626, and *On The*

Restoration of the Cross, celebrating the climax of Herakleios's achievement in restoring to Jerusalem in 630 the remnants of the True Cross which had been pillaged by the Persians in 614). The second group are elaborate, doubtless commissioned, pieces such as *On the Persian Expedition* (maximizing the achievement of Herakleios's first campaign in 622), *On the Avar War* (describing the near-successful Avar siege of 626), and *Herakleios* (a survey of the reign composed at the moment of victory). The Constantinopolitan perspective and the prominent religious undercurrent are fundamental to George's *oeuvre*.

By the 7th century Hellenic traditions of education and culture were struggling to survive. Hitherto the hexameter had been the traditional medium of imperial verse panegyric, and George's preference for iambics, while developing a Late-Antique custom of prefacing hexameter panegyric with an iambic prologue, doubtless also represents an attempt to maximize his accessibility. So too does his taste for the inclusion of brief maxims, many of them lifted from tragedy, probably via the compilations that proliferated in this period. But George sustains a high prosodic standard, combining quantitative accuracy with sensitivity to regulation of accent. The maxims have a structural function in articulating thematic transitions and are often combined with first-person interjections, a technique that has its roots in Pindar. Close philological study uncovers subtle and creative allusions to classical texts in both poetry and prose, while the vocabulary incorporates many prose formations (especially medical) and neologisms. Stylistically George is strongly influenced by contemporary taste for elaborate rhetoric and word-play, but deploys the familiar topics of panegyric with originality, often integrating metaphor and narrative with striking novelty. The slide from narrative to image is sometimes barely perceptible, while sustained images can have a daring that anticipates the Metaphysical poets (e.g. a comparison between Sergios and the Virgin, *Avar War*, 130–44). For George the integration of Classical and biblical is unproblematic, even exuberant, an advance upon the apologetic stance of 6th-century literary writers.

George's works were influential in Byzantium in several distinct areas. First for their content: the poems for Herakleios are a crucial source for the Persian wars of the 620s, quoted extensively (including lost works) in the prose chronicle of Theophanes (c.810), who may have used a prose/verse compilation produced by George himself. Second, George was greatly admired for his language and style: the 10th-century *Suda* lexicon includes 76 citations, roughly half from poems no longer extant. Most memorably, the 11th-century politician, historian, and academic Michael Psellos composed a brief essay, probably to impress his students, in response to the question "Who was the better poet, Euripides or Pisides?". Psellos's judgement is lost in a lacuna, but his discussion offers invaluable insight into tastes and attitudes to earlier literature among middle-Byzantine literati. Versification and diction and their adaptation to characterization and subject matter, rather than content or context, are paramount: Psellos is as interested in Euripides' lyrics as in his iambics, while it is George's ability to pull out rhetorical stops in vivid description that probably proved his superiority.

The main vehicle for the transmission of George's poems is an 11th-century anthology (cod. suppl. gr. 690, in the Bibliothèque Nationale, Paris), perhaps compiled in the reign of Basil II (976–1025). The *Hexaemeron*, however, enjoyed a flourishing manuscript tradition (approximately 50 manuscripts, as well as 14th-century Slavonic and Armenian translations), due to a false attribution to Cyril of Alexandria and the wide appeal of a topic that fell within an established tradition. But George's poem is innovative: it focuses on the individual's endeavour to comprehend God through progress in contemplating his created universe and incorporates contemporary Christian Neoplatonic thinking alongside biblical paradigms.

Today the juxtaposition of George with Euripides shocks, but Psellos's essay, together with the extensive interest of the *Suda*, signals George's Janus-position between Classical and medieval literature, as well as providing a salutary reminder of the limitations of modern perspectives.

MARY WHITBY

Biography

Nothing is known of George's time of birth, but he came from the region of Pisidia and was probably born in the town of Antioch there (not to be confused with the more famous Antioch on the Orontes). He lived most of his life in Constantinople where he was a deacon at Hagia Sophia and worked as archivist to the Patriarchate. He was active during the reign of the emperor Herakleios (ruled 610–41), and wrote panegyrical epics in praise of the emperor's campaigns. He also wrote religious poetry, notably the *Hexaemeron* on the wonders of the Creation and *Against Severus*. The date and place of his death are unknown.

Writings

Poemi, edited by Agostino Pertusi, vol. 1: *Panegirici epici*, Ettal: Buch-Kunstverlag, 1959
Carmi, edited by Luigi Tartaglia, Turin: Unione Tipografico Editrice Torinese, 1998
Propaganda at the Court of Heraclius: Select Poems of George of Pisidia, edited by Mary Whitby, Liverpool: Liverpool University Press, forthcoming

Further Reading

Flusin, Bernard, *Sainte Anastase le Perse et l'histoire de la Palestine au début du VIIe siècle*, 2 vols, Paris: Centre National de la Recherche Scientifique, 1992
Frendo, J.D.C., "The Significance of Technical Terms in the Poems of George of Pisidia", *Orpheus*, 21 (1974): pp. 45–55
Frendo, J.D.C., "Special Aspects of the Use of Medical Vocabulary in the Poems of George of Pisidia", *Orpheus*, 22 (1975): pp. 49–56
Frendo, J.D.C., "The Poetic Achievement of George of Pisidia" in *Maistor: Classical, Byzantine, and Renaissance Studies for Robert Browning*, edited by Ann Moffat, Canberra: Australian Association for Byzantine Studies, 1984, pp. 159–87
Frendo, J.D.C., "Classical and Christian Influences in the *Heracliad* of George of Pisidia", *Classical Bulletin*, 62 (1986): pp. 53–62
Howard-Johnston, J., "The Official History of Heraclius' Persian Campaigns" in *The Roman and Byzantine Army in the East*, edited by E. Dabrowa, Krakow: Jagiellonian University, 1994, pp. 57–87
Ludwig, C., "Kaiser Herakleios, Georgios Pisides und die Perserkriege" in *Poikila Byzantina*, vol. 11, edited by P. Speck, Bonn: Habelt, 1991, pp. 73–128
MacCoull, L.S.B., "George of Pisidia, *Against Severus*: In Praise of Heraclius", in *The Future of the Middle Ages and the*

Renaissance: Problems, Trends and Opportunities for Research, edited by Roger Dahood, Turnhout: Brepols, 1998, vol. 2, pp. 69–79

Nodes, Daniel J., "Rhetorical and Cultural Synthesis in the *Hexaemeron* of George of Pisidia", *Vigiliae Christianae*, 50 (1996): pp. 274–87

Olster, David M., "The Date of George of Pisidia's *Hexaemeron*", *Dumbarton Oaks Papers*, 45 (1991): pp. 159–72

Olster, David M., *Roman Defeat, Christian Response, and the Literary Construction of the Jew*, Philadelphia: University of Pennsylvania Press, 1994

Psellos, Michael, *The Essays on Euripides and George of Pisidia and on Heliodorus and Achilles Tatius*, edited by Andrew R. Dyck, Vienna: Akademie der Wissenschaften, 1986

Speck, Paul, "Ohne Anfang und Ende: Das *Hexaemeron* des Georgios Pisides" in *Aetos: Studies in Honour of Cyril Mango*, edited by Ihor Ševčenko and Irmgard Hutter, Stuttgart: Teubner, 1998

Sternbach, L., "Georgii Pisidae carmina inedita", *Wiener Studien*, 13 (1891): pp. 1–62; 14 (1892): pp. 51–68

Sternbach, L., *De Georgii Pisidae apud Theophanem aliosque historicos reliquiis*, Krakow, 1900

Trilling, James, "Myth and Metaphor at the Byzantine Court", *Byzantion*, 48 (1978): pp. 249–63

Whitby, Mary, "A New Image for a New Age: George of Pisidia on the Emperor Heraclius" in *The Roman and Byzantine Army in the East*, edited by E. Dabrowa, Krakow: Jagiellonian University, 1994, pp. 197–225

Whitby, Mary, "The Devil in Disguise: The End of George of Pisidia's *Hexaemeron* Reconsidered", *Journal of Hellenic Studies*, 105 (1995): pp. 115–29

Whitby, Mary, "Michael Psellus on Euripides and George of Pisidia" in *The Reception of Classical Texts and Images*, edited by Lorna Hardwick and Stanley Ireland, Milton Keynes: Open University Press, 1996, pp. 109–31

Whitby, Mary, "Defender of the Cross: George of Pisidia on the Emperor Heraclius and his Deputies" in *The Propaganda of Power: The Role of Panegyric in Late Antiquity*, edited by Mary Whitby, Leiden: Brill, 1998, pp. 247–73

George of Trebizond 1395–1472/73 or c.1484

Scholar

George of Trebizond, humanist teacher, rhetorician, and translator, was one of the expatriate Greek scholars whose activities in Italy during the 15th century helped to stimulate the development of Greek studies there. Originally from Crete, where his family had moved from Trebizond, he emigrated to Italy around 1416, and earned his living initially by teaching Greek in Vicenza and Venice, while studying Latin under Vittorino da Feltre and Guarino da Verona. From about 1440 he was living in Rome where he entered the papal curia as a secretary. He soon acquired a reputation for ill-temper: he denounced the scholar Lorenzo Valla as an ignoramus, came to blows with the humanist Poggio Bracciolini, and on more than one occasion was briefly imprisoned in the Castel Sant'Angelo.

In spite of his cantankerousness, his gifts as a scholar were soon recognized. He became the leading lecturer in humanist studies in Rome and, along with his rival Theodore Gaza, one of the greatest Greek teachers in Italy in the generation after Manuel Chrysoloras. He was also a prominent member of the Academy that met at the house of cardinal Bessarion. He was

Georgius Trapezuntius.

George of Trebizond, a 16th-century engraving

encouraged by the scholarly pope Nicholas V to make translations of Greek classical texts into Latin, and proved to be a prolific worker, making Latin versions of the works of Plato, Aristotle, Demosthenes, Ptolemy, Eusebius, and the Cappadocian Fathers. Unfortunately, his work was often criticized for inaccuracy by contemporaries, especially by Theodore Gaza and Bessarion. Although George's translations undoubtedly contained mistakes, the criticism seems to have stemmed in part from a difference in method: George himself favoured a literal, word-for-word approach, and if a passage was obscure it was his practice to elucidate the meaning with a marginal note. Gaza, on the other hand, preferred a freer rendering that conveyed the spirit of the text. In the next generation the merits of George's translations were perceived by the humanists Angelo Poliziano and Erasmus. His version of Ptolemy's *Almagest* became standard and was printed in 1538.

Another unfortunate episode in George of Trebizond's career was his estrangement from Bessarion and the other members of the Academy from about 1450, partly as a result of Bessarion's criticisms of his translations, and partly because George became alarmed at the increasing admiration for the philosophy of Plato and for the works of Bessarion's teacher, George Gemistos Plethon. In 1458 George wrote a strongly worded denunciation of Plato, entitled *Comparisons of Aristotle and Plato*, in which he claimed that Plato's ideas led inevitably to immorality and heresy, and denounced any attempt to reconcile Platonism with Christianity. For George, Plethon was a case in point, and he claimed that he had overheard Bessarion's teacher prophesying that Christianity and Islam would soon pass away and be replaced by a new paganism. However, in his strong antipathy to Platonism and its advocate, George found a formidable adversary. His assault prompted Bessarion to publish his *Against the Calumniator of Plato* in 1469, the "calumniator" being George himself. The controversy raged for more than a decade, with George being joined by his son, Andreas (died 1496) in his attack on the Platonists. Ultimately, however, it was Bessarion's reconciliation of Plato with Christianity that gained ground among the humanists, leaving George of Trebizond increasingly isolated.

Less contentious than his attack on Plato, and more successful than his translations, was his *Five Books on Rhetoric*, which he completed in Venice in 1434 and in which he attempted to provide a synthesis of the Latin and Greek rhetorical traditions. The work was to have a major impact on humanist education, revealing to the Italians for the first time the works of the great Byzantine rhetoricians. By taking examples both from Byzantine authorities such as Dionysius of Halicarnassus, Maximus the Philosopher, and Hermogenes, and from Latin writers, especially Cicero, Livy, and Virgil, George succeeded in producing an authoritative work on the subject that circulated throughout Europe and which remained in widespread use until the late 16th century. So highly regarded was it that the German Protestant theologian and humanist Philip Melanchthon justified his own short book on rhetoric solely because it would save students the expense of buying George's larger one. It was superseded only when translations and epitomes of Hermogenes became generally available.

George of Trebizond was also the author of a prodigious number of other works in Latin on logic, philosophy, astrology, and astronomy, as well as several theological works. His *Introduction to Dialectic*, written in about 1440, summarized Aristotle's teaching on dialectic in an accessible way, shorn of scholastic accretions, and in an elegant Latin acceptable to the humanists. He wrote a massive commentary on Ptolemy's *Almagest*, explaining Ptolemy's astronomic theories on the basis of the ancient Greek commentary of Theon of Alexandria. His *On the Truth of the Christian Faith* (1453), addressed to the Turkish sultan Mehmet II, called upon him to adopt Christianity and to become a universal ruler in imitation of Constantine the Great. Although a convert to Catholicism, George even ventured into traditional Byzantine hagiography in his account of the recent martyrdom of St Andreas of Chios. Yet even in this work he could not resist a jibe at his opponents, ending with a prayer to St Andreas, bidding him to "suppress by your intercession these Platonists rising here in Italy".

JONATHAN HARRIS

Biography

Born in Crete in 1395, where his family had moved from Trebizond, George emigrated to Italy c.1416 and taught Greek in Vicenza, Venice, and Rome. Having converted to Catholicism, he worked as a secretary in the papal curia. He translated many ancient Greek texts into Latin (though his versions were much criticized) and produced many works of his own including the influential *Five Books on Rhetoric*. The date of his death is unknown.

Further Reading

Classen, C.J., "The Rhetorical Works of George of Trebizond and Their Debt to Cicero", *Journal of the Warburg and Courtauld Institutes*, 56 (1993): pp. 75–84

Geanakoplos, Deno John, *Greek Scholars in Venice: Studies in the Dissemination of Greek Learning from Byzantium to Western Europe*, Cambridge, Massachusetts: Harvard University Press, 1962

Harris, Jonathan, *Greek Emigrés in the West, 1400–1520*, Camberley, Surrey: Porphyrogenitus, 1995

Monfasani, John, *George of Trebizond: A Biography and Study of His Rhetoric and Logic*, Leiden: Brill, 1976

Monfasani, John (editor), *Collectio Trapezuntiana: Texts, Documents, and Bibliographies of George of Trebizond*, Binghamton, New York: Renaissance Society of America, 1984

Monfasani, John, "The Byzantine Rhetorical Tradition and the Renaissance" in *Byzantine Scholars in Renaissance Italy: Cardinal Bessarion and Other Emigrés: Selected Essays*, edited by Monfasani, Aldershot, Hampshire: Variorum, 1995

Setton, Kenneth M., "The Byzantine Background to the Italian Renaissance", *Transactions and Proceedings of the American Philosophical Society*, 100 (1956): pp. 1–76

Wilson, N.G., *From Byzantium to Italy: Greek Studies in the Italian Renaissance*, London: Duckworth, and Baltimore: Johns Hopkins University Press, 1992

Georgia

The land of Georgia occupies the southern slopes of the central section of the main Caucasus range. To the west it is bounded by the eastern coast of the Black Sea. To the east it stretches to Azerbaijan in the direction of the Caspian Sea. To the south it is bordered by Turkey and Armenia, with a historical claim to a substantial portion of northeast Turkey (the Tao-Klarjeti of the Georgian tradition).

The name Georgia has encouraged the idea that this land was so named by the Greeks on account of its agricultural resources (*georgia* means "farming" in Greek). (Georgians use an entirely different term, *sakartvelo*, and term themselves *kartvelebi*.) However, the apparently Greek name is now taken to be a derivation from an Iranian root, *Gurj*. Greeks in antiquity did not use the term Georgia, but referred instead to western Georgia as Colchis (Byzantine Lazike) and to eastern Georgia as Iberia. The existence of these two Greek names reflects the principal geographical division within Georgia, caused by the so-called Surami ridge. As a result of this ridge, western Georgia looks across the Black Sea towards Europe and the Aegean, while eastern Georgia looks to Iran and Central Asia.

Greek knowledge of western Georgia is firmly attested by 700 BC in the poetry of Eumelus and Hesiod. The myth of the Argonauts, which was known to Homer, gave Colchis a particular significance in Greek culture from earliest times. However, according to archaeological evidence and later literary sources Colchis was not settled by Greeks until about 550 BC. From the 4th century BC Greek texts mention the towns of Dioscurias (modern Sukhumi), Guenos (near modern Ochamchira), and Phasis (near modern Poti) as Hellenic communities. In particular, Dioscurias and Phasis are said to have been founded by Greeks from Miletus, in the latter case led by one Themistagoras. The archaeological evidence also points to a significant Greek presence elsewhere on the coast of Colchis, at Eshera (north of Sukhumi), at Pitchvnari (near Kobuleti), at Tsikhisdziri, and perhaps in the environs of Batumi, which the Greeks of antiquity named Bathus Limen ("deep harbour"), whence its modern name.

Georgia: Byzantine church at Dörfkalise (now in Turkey). Blind arcading with ornate spandrels was a feature of 11th-century Georgian churches.

Greek influence spread up the numerous rivers of Colchis into the hinterland, but not across the Surami ridge into Iberia. When Hellenic culture reached eastern Georgia it came with the Seleucids, who claimed Iberia as part of their imperial sphere. In Iberia Greek culture met not only local culture but also strong influences from further east. In later centuries Iberia was to be the diplomatic and military battlefield upon which the Byzantine Greeks fought the Persian empire, especially in the 4th to 7th centuries AD. Iberia's conversion to Christianity in about AD 337 helped the Greek cause, but Arab conquest in the mid-7th century was conclusive. Ironically, the loss of Iberia followed hard upon the famous Byzantine victory at the siege of Tiflis (modern Tbilisi), captured by the forces of the emperor Herakleios in 627. However, Iberians continued to exert influence at Byzantium: in the 10th century the Iviron monastery was established on Mount Athos by St Evthymios and his father.

By contrast, western Georgia had become an integral part of the Greek world, albeit at its periphery (e.g. Plato, *Phaedo* 109b). Colchis was known in classical Athens as a mercantile destination (Aristophanes, *Holkades*), providing a famous type of linen which rivalled that of Egypt, according to Herodotus (2. 104–05). When Xenophon's 10,000 reached the Black Sea at Trapezus (modern Trebizond) in 400 BC, he saw the potential of Colchis and apparently contemplated settlement in the region of Phasis (*Anabasis* 5. 6. 36). In the Pontic empire of Mithridates VI Eupator, from about 100 BC, Colchis was a principal reservoir of resources, providing quality timber and all else needed for shipbuilding. The Greek geographer Strabo mentions that a member of his family had been Mithridates' viceroy there (11. 2. 18).

Byzantine Colchis was regularly known as Lazike, for the Lazoi had managed to establish an empire for themselves over the other tribes of western Georgia by the 4th century AD. They had done so with the support of the Byzantines, for whom the region was of particular significance because it could offer the Persians access to the Black Sea. The Byzantine historians Procopius of Caesarea and Agathias relate in detail the struggle between the two empires in Lazike in the 6th century AD, when Justinian I founded the new city of Petra at Tsikhisdziri.

A new process of Greek settlement in Georgia began around 1800, encouraged by imperial Russia, newly dominant there. Greek miners, craftsmen, and farmers, largely from the Ottoman empire, were encouraged to settle, not least in eastern Georgia. They were welcome both for their skills and for their manpower, a contribution to Christian resistance to the Turkish threat. On the eve of the World War I the number of Greeks in the Caucasus, most of them in Georgia, was 180,123. In 1920–21 it was therefore natural that many of the Greeks of the Kars region made their way to Greece through Georgia, particularly the old Greek colonies of the Black Sea coast. This can only have encouraged the Greeks of Georgia to join the many Greeks of the Soviet Union who now sought to obtain a new life in Greece proper.

That tendency was further encouraged by the Soviet persecution of Greeks, which began in 1929–35 as a by-product of the collectivization of agriculture, since many Greeks were farmers. However, Greek culture was tolerated and even encouraged until 1936–38, when Greek schools were closed, Greek printing presses stopped, and Greek cultural events

obstructed. Subsequently, the Greeks of Georgia suffered again, caught up with others of the region in Stalin's policy of deporting small ethnic groups away from the German front for fear of their treason. During the Gorbachev years (1985–91) and the emergence of the independent Republic of Georgia, the place of Greeks and Greek culture in Georgia was normalized, though the social and economic attraction of migration to Greece continues to exert a powerful influence.

DAVID BRAUND

See also Black Sea

Further Reading

Agtzideas, V., *Pareuxeinios diaspora: oi elleanikes egkatastaseis stis voreioanatolikes periokhes tou Euxeinou Pontou* [The Black Sea Diaspora: The Greek Settlements in the Northeast Part of Pontus Euxinus], Thessalonica, 1997

Allen, W.E.D., *A History of the Georgian People from the Beginning down to the Russian Conquest in the Nineteenth Century*, London: Paul Trench Trubner, 1932, reprinted London: Routledge and Kegan Paul, and New York: Barnes and Noble, 1971

Braund, David, *Georgia in Antiquity: A History of Colchis and Transcaucasian Iberia, 550 BC[-]AD 562*, Oxford: Clarendon Press, and New York: Oxford University Press, 1994

Conquest, Robert, *The Nation-Killers: The Soviet Deportation of Nationalities*, London and New York: Macmillan, 1970

Khasiotes, I.K. (editor), *Oi Elleanes teas Roasias kai teas Sovietikeas Enoaseas: metoikesies kai ektopismoi, organoase kai ideologia* [The Greeks of Russia and Soviet Asia: Migrations and Deportations, Organizations and Ideology], Thessalonica, 1997

Koromila, Marianna (editor), *The Greeks in the Black Sea: From the Bronze Age to the Early Twentieth Century*, Athens: Panorama, 1991

Lang, David Marshall, *A Modern History of Georgia*, London: Weidenfeld and Nicolson, 1962

Lang, David Marshall, *The Georgians*, London: Thames and Hudson, and New York: Praeger, 1966

Germanos I

Patriarch of Constantinople, 7th–8th century

Germanos, who is said to have been more than 90 years old when he died sometime between 730 and 750, was born into a noble Byzantine family that owned property at Platanion, near Constantinople. His father, Justinian, was reputed to have been a kinsman of the emperor Herakleios I (608–41), under whom he held high office. Germanos received a thorough classical education at Constantinople. In 688 his father was implicated in the murder of Constans II and executed, Germanos himself being castrated at the same time. He made his career in the clergy of the Great Church of Hagia Sophia in Constantinople, and eventually became their head. He is said to have been involved in both the Sixth Ecumenical Council held in Constantinople in 680–81, which condemned the Christological heresy of Monothelitism, and in the so-called Quinisext Council of 691–92, which put in hand a major reform and consolidation of the canon law of the Byzantine Church. There would be nothing surprising about his involvement, but there is no clear evidence. In the early years of the 8th century he was appointed metropolitan of Cyzicus. During the brief reign of the usurping emperor Philippikos-Bardanes, who convoked a synod to restore Monothelitism, Germanos seems to have been compliant. But when he was appointed to the patriarchal chair in 715, after Philippikos's fall, he promptly called a synod that condemned Monothelitism. He was patriarch during the last Arab siege of Constantinople in 717–18, the successful issue of which was attributed to the protection of the Mother of God. When the emperor Leo III (716–41) introduced iconoclasm by edict in 730, Germanos refused to accept the imperial will, resigned his patriarchate, and retired to his estate at Platanion. At the synod of Hiereia in 754, which proclaimed iconoclasm, he was anathematized, along with George of Cyprus and St John of Damascus; their memory was reinstated at the Seventh Ecumenical Council, the Second Council of Nicaea, in 787.

Germanos's literary oeuvre is in a confused state. Some sermons in honour of the Mother of God are his, as well as a certain amount of liturgical poetry, including examples of the newly fashionable "canons" (though it is difficult to know how much of this is genuinely his). From this it is clear that he had a genuine literary talent. There are also some letters, in which he defends the veneration of icons, which belong to his final years as patriarch. In his retirement he wrote a work *On Heresies and Synods*, which is an account of the (then) six ecumenical councils. Most other works attributed to him have been, or ought to be, ascribed to others, but there are two small but important works that are probably his: the oddly entitled *Church History and Mystical Contemplation* (which should perhaps be translated: "what happens in church and its hidden meaning"), and *On Predestined Terms of Life*, a significant example of a popular theological and philosophical genre concerned with the workings of divine providence.

Germanos's significance is threefold: as a stout defender of the veneration of icons against Leo III's iconoclasm; as a notable figure in the development of Byzantine devotion to the Mother of God; as an influential interpreter of the Byzantine liturgy. With St John of Damascus, Germanos represents the initial reaction of Byzantine churchmen to imperial iconoclasm. Although he does not have anything like the theological breadth and depth of the Damascene, he is clear in his repudiation of the iconoclast appeal to the second Mosaic commandment against the making of idols, drawing attention to the use of images in the ceremonial of the Jewish Temple, in his appeal to the Incarnation as inaugurating a new dispensation in which God has manifested himself in visible form, and in his repudiation of the emperor's claim to priestly authority in the defining of Christian doctrine.

In his sermons, and in some of his liturgical poetry, Germanos expresses a developed Mariology. The eight sermons that survive all have Marian themes: three are on the Dormition of the Mother of God, and another, on the *Akathist* hymn and the Dormition, celebrates the lifting of the siege of Constantinople on 15 August 718, the feast of the Dormition. Latin texts of the *Akathist* even ascribe one of the *prooimia* of the *Akathist*, *Tei hypermachoi strategoi* ("To you, Champion and Commander"), to Germanos, but it is probably at least a century older. In his praise of the Mother of God, he lays stress on her complete purity and the universal power of her intercession.

The *Church History and Mystical Contemplation* was to become an immensely influential commentary on the Eucharistic liturgy of the Byzantine Church. With some supplementation (mainly from St Maximos the Confessor's *Mystagogia*), it became a virtually official commentary on the liturgy, and was included in the first printed text of the liturgies of St John Chrysostom and St Basil, as well as in medieval manuscripts of the Slavonic service books. Every part of the church building, the sacred vessels, the vestments, the incense, the processions, and each event of the liturgy from the preparation through to the communion of the people: all are given a symbolic significance, the church building itself being both the temple of God and a miniature representation of the cosmos. The comprehensive decoration of the church with icons, which reached a settled form after the defeat of iconoclasm, finds its rationale in Germanos's understanding of the liturgical action.

ANDREW LOUTH

Biography

Born in the mid-7th century to a noble Byzantine family, Germanos was castrated when his father was executed for involvement in the murder of the emperor Constans II. Joining the clergy of Hagia Sophia, he became bishop of Cyzicus before being appointed patriarch of Constantinople in 715. He resigned in 730 when the emperor Leo III introduced iconoclasm. He wrote sermons and liturgical poetry, an account of the ecumenical councils to date, and an influential commentary on the Divine Liturgy.

Writings

In *Patrologia Graeca*, edited by J.-P. Migne, vol. 98
On Predestined Terms of Life, edited and translated by Charles Garton and Lendeert G. Westerink, Buffalo: Department of Classics, State University of New York, 1979
On the Divine Liturgy, edited and translated by Paul Meyendorff, Crestwood, New York: St Vladimir's Seminary Press, 1984

Further Reading

Lamza, Lucian, *Patriarch Germanos I. von Konstantinopel (715-730)*, Würzburg: Augustinus, 1975
List, Johann, *Studien zur Homiletik Germanos I. von Konstantinopel und seiner Zeit*, Athens: Verlage der Byzantinisch-neugriechischen Jahrbücher, 1939

Ghika 1906–1994

Artist

Nikos Hadjikyriakos was the son of a naval officer, whose family from the island of Psara had participated in the War of Independence, and of Eleni Ghika, who was descended from the branch of the well-known Albanian family that had settled on the island of Hydra in 1628 and had contributed substantially to its uprising in 1821. He used his maternal family name when signing his paintings in Paris in the 1920s, and it was by this name, "Ghika", that he became known as an artist both in Greece and internationally.

Ghika's family tradition and his father's continued participation in military and political events weighed heavily on his cultural and artistic formation. The exceptionally talented, socially and financially privileged youngster had a few elemen-

Ghika: *Hydra,* 1948 – a Cubist composition depicting the artist's own island

tary private painting lessons with Constantine Parthenis before going to Paris to study Greek literature. He soon abandoned the Sorbonne for the Académie Ranson, however, where he studied painting for two years under Roger Bissière and engraving under Dimitris Galanis. Ghika effectively came to belong to what is loosely known as the École de Paris and his early work in France shows no trace of Greek influence or so-called traditionalism. His art derived its main precepts from Cubism and a post-Cubist vision of space and objects.

Ghika acquired a more distinct artistic identity and became deeply preoccupied with questions of "Greekness" in the arts following his return to Greece in 1934 and the repair of his maternal family house in Hydra. Some of his most important paintings date from the late 1930s and are landscape composi-tions based on the barrenness of the rocky island and angular motifs of Aegean architecture. "A cool Hydra breeze often blows in Ghika's atelier", wrote Elytis. "It comes down the deserted streets with the walls and the prickly pears, it hits the heavy relief doors of the island and ends up violet in the distance on the slopes of Dhokos and Hermione." Hydra remained the principal source of Ghika's work until his house was accidentally destroyed by fire in 1960. Some of his most important pictorial inspirations during the next decade came from the similarly barren landscape and linear architecture of the island of Santorini.

Indeed, Hydra and Santorini offered Ghika the ideal visual stimulus and inspiration for the application of the Cubist pictorial rules that characterized his artistic idiom. It is difficult to say whether the principal influence in this happy marriage was that of the Greek traditional and visual impact over the geometrical rules of Cubism, or the other way round. Perhaps Ghika's analytical and systematic thinking, as expressed in his various writings and interviews, makes one inclined to opt for the latter. In any event, it could safely be said that the post-Cubist characteristics of his art were fused into and absorbed by the Greek landscape, by traditional island architecture, and the all-pervading Greek light. Ghika's perception of harmony and rhythm was logical, i.e. humanistic in the ancient Greek sense. That was why he had adopted the language of Cubism, as he himself said:

My compositions spring from the very rhythm and the very logical synthesis of the Greek landscape. The rock of Hydra and the island stone-walls were for me logical, rhythmical shapes. I stood reflecting and correlating Cubism with the Greek geometrical landscape. The roots of ancient Greek art, as in vase painting, were also geometric, and so was Greek architecture. Logic stood as my guide for the analysis and the reconstruction of Greek space through art.

Ghika applied Cubist pictorial rules to the Greek subjects of his paintings – mainly landscapes pervaded by the extraordinary limpidity of Greek light: "Light here is *par excellence sui generis*," he said; "it shapes and searches the objects, it traces on the ground the exact confines between the illuminated and the dark." In this way he not only acquired a unique artistic idiom but he also effectively renewed the visual conception of "Greekness". By combining western modernity with Greek traditionalism he revolutionized Greek painting and art in general. Indeed, he gave it a completely new orientation, rejecting the predominant influence of the academic teachings of the Munich School. Despite the fact that he did not create a school of followers (he had only a few untalented imitators), Ghika's bold and progressive pictorial idiom opened the way for younger Greek artists to feel free to work in a modern idiom and, in the process, to harmonize Greek art with modern and contemporary artistic movements.

Ghika combined his admiration of ancient Greek civilization and art with a deep knowledge of mythology, history, and literature as well as the means and media of artistic expression. From the Cycladic to the Byzantine era, through the Minoan, the Archaic, and the Hellenistic, he studied the immense variety of art forms and tried his own hand at various techniques (e.g. encaustic) and materials. He once said: « I do not know of any other art of any nation that shows such development and visual multiplicity. For over four thousand years Egyptian art has remained substantially unaltered; and the same applies, to a great extent, to the art of India. » Yet Ghika did not blindly join forces with those who idolized antiquity with an uncritical eye; nor did he ever become totally identified with the so-called 1930s generation of artists who expressed the need for a return to Greek tradition. It was then that the merits of the naive painter Theophilos and of the Karaghiozis shadow puppets were rediscovered and that folk art and traditional architecture began to be appreciated, as the artists of the 1930s generation sought to redefine the character of contemporary "Greekness" by re-evaluating Greek tradition.

Ghika, however, searched deeper and refused to reduce the notion of "Greekness" to the elementary attributes of various forms of popular art. He refused to accept "simplicity" and "functionality" as the foundation of modern theories of art and architecture. As a close friend of Le Corbusier, he knew well about such conceptions, which he considered as having failed. He believed that perfection can be found in simplicity, as in the case of a sea pebble or a clay vase; but this is a totally different kind of perfection from that, say, of the flutes of a Doric column: that sort of perfection presupposes both sensitivity and knowledge. Furthermore, apart from his western cultural and artistic upbringing, Ghika was also interested in oriental art and philosophy (he practised yoga and painted while in India and Japan in the late 1950s) and he did not hesitate to introduce oriental elements in his own painting and sculpture. "My art is essentially Greek", he said, "but with the difference that I tried to create a link between Greek, European and Oriental elements; between elements which, irrespective of their provenance, contain something Greek." In other words, Ghika's "Greekness" was not nationalistic or provincial; it was a free-spirited continuous process of artistic enrichment, an attempt to combine apparently disparate artistic elements, always within the context of a wisely constructed classical synthesis.

Between 1935 and 1937 Ghika financed and published (mainly with his friends Pikionis, Papatsonis, Papaloukas, and Karandinos) the pioneering magazine *To Trito Mati* (The Third Eye). The avowed double aim was to arouse interest in popular Greek art and in the preservation of the Classical architectural heritage. "We failed in both", Ghika admitted later, but *To Trito Mati* gave the culturally somnolent Athenians an invigorating shock, with challenging articles on literature, poetry, philosophy, painting, sculpture, architecture, and mathematics. Almost 60 years later, Ghika still had "many loves", as he said: "painting, architecture, sculpture, literature, love, Greece, history. They are all equivalent for me and they influence each other." At the time of his death in 1994, however, he was disillusioned with the status and the future of the arts in Greece. "Greek society is incapable of appreciating the value of art and the average Greek is more attracted to football", he had said two years earlier. Nevertheless, that was the way it had always been (Egyptian priests had spoken in this vein about the Greeks to Plato, he recalled) and he knew well that football (or its various equivalents) is still far more popular than art, even in the most developed countries of the world.

Until the last years of his life, when his sight progressively deteriorated almost to the point of blindness, Ghika maintained a clean line in his drawing and neat colours in his painting, avoiding the excessive use of shading and chiaroscuro. His work can be divided into three periods: 1921–37, the period of youthful experimentation; 1938–65, the period of accomplishment; and post 1966, the period of maturity followed by progressive decline. Among his main preoccupations were the effect of light on landscape and on the surface of objects, the organization of his compositions, and the combination of straight lines and angles with curves and spherical shapes. Ghika was widely respected and loved, both in Greece and abroad. After 1960 he came to spend long periods of time in London with his second wife Barbara (née St John Hutchinson). He was a close friend of many important personalities in the history of 20th-century art, among them Zervos, Raynal, Laurens, Braque, Le Corbusier, Arp, Cartier-Bresson, Lawrence Durrell, Henry Moore, Walter Gropius, Henry Miller, and many others.

NICHOLAS PETSALIS-DIOMIDIS

See also Painting

Biography

Born on Hydra in 1906, Nikos Hadjikyriakos adopted his mother's maiden name in the 1920s and was known as Ghika ever afterwards. Educated in Paris, he left the Sorbonne for the Académie Ranson in 1924. He exhibited in Paris from 1927 to 1934, when he returned to Athens. He was Professor of Drawing at the School of Architecture, Athens Polytechnic, in 1941–58. He is known primarily as a painter, but also as a sculptor, engraver, designer of theatrical sets and costumes, teacher, and writer on art. He died in 1994.

Writings

Ellinikoi Provlimatismoi [The Greek Way of Thinking], 1983; *I Anichnevsi tis Ellinikotitos* [In Quest of Greekness], 1985; and *I Gennisi tis Neas Technis* [The Birth of the New Art], 1987, all in *Evthini*, Athens

Letters to Tiggie, 1945-1955, edited by Ioanna Kritseli-Providou, Athens, 1991 (letters to his first wife; in Greek)

Further Reading

Iliopoulou-Rogan, Dora, *Ta Parallila* [The Parallel Works], Athens, 1980

Petsalis-Diomidis, Nicholas, *Ghika: Pleres Katalogos tou zographikou ergou, 1920-1940* [Ghika: Catalogue Raisonné of the Paintings, 1920-1940], Athens, 1979

Tsakona, Pitsa, *Ergographia–Bibliographia* [Ghika: Catalogue of Written Works–Bibliography, 1923–1996], Athens, 1997

Zervos, Christian, Stephen Spender and Patrick Leigh-Fermor, *Ghika: Paintings, Drawings, Sculpture*, London: Lund Humphries, 1964; Boston: Boston Book and Art Shop, 1965

Glass

Glass is a man-made material of great versatility. It is made by melting together three main ingredients: soda, lime, and silica. In antiquity silica came from sand that also contained the lime needed to make the glass water-resistant, and soda came either from natron, which occurs naturally in Egypt, or, in the east, from saline plants found in the deserts and marshy areas. If nothing was added to the basic mixture, glass was naturally bluish-green; coloured glass was made by adding specific metal oxides and varying the furnace conditions. Colourless glass, akin to modern crystal glass, used manganese or antimony as decolourizing agents. It seems likely that in antiquity glass itself was made from the raw materials in only a few places, and shipped around as ingots to different glassmaking centres.

The first glass objects known are from Mesopotamia and date from around 2500 BC. A technological breakthrough some 1000 years later led to the production of the first glass vessels. This was the invention of core-forming, whereby glass was formed around a rod covered by a core of dung and clay mixed with a little water. Decoration was added by trailing soft glass of different colours around the body and combing it into patterns with a pointed tool. After subsequent reheating the shoulders, neck, and rim were formed and any handles added. The core-covered rod was finally removed after the vessels had been annealed (placed in a warm place apart from the actual furnace to cool slowly). The first vessels made by this method seem to have been produced in northern Mesopotamia around 1500 BC. The glass industry was born in Egypt not much later, but core-formed vessels were not produced in any great numbers before the time of Amenhotep III (1390–1352 BC). By 1450 BC Mesopotamian glassmakers were also forming vessels of mosaic glass, made by fusing together slices of monochrome glass or multicoloured canes that were then shaped around a core or, for open vessels, slumped over a form (positive mould). Early Mesopotamian and Egyptian glassmakers were also responsible for a great variety of objects, including pendants and beads of many different varieties. Diplomatic correspondence from the royal archives of el-Amarna, the new capital of Egypt established by Akhenaten (1352–1336 BC), mentions consignments of raw glass being sent from Tyre (modern Lebanon) and neighbouring cities. This speaks already for the importance of this region, credited by the Elder Pliny (1st century AD) with the invention of glass. The same area (the Levant) was responsible for a series of core-formed vessels.

Glass became known to the Greeks in the Late Bronze Age when documents in Mycenaean Greek call it *kyanos*. Imported Egyptian core-formed vessels have been recorded, principally from Cretan sites of the 14th and 13th centuries BC, while from mainland Greece, notably Mycenae and Kakovatos, come some Mesopotamian beads and pendants. The first items evidently made in Greece were a bowl with indented sides similar to metal and stone vessels, a tiny bull figurine, and a hilt for a distinctly Mycenaean type of sword, all of translucent blue glass perhaps of Mesopotamian origin (all three pieces are now in the National Archaeological Museum, Athens). Gaming pieces may also have been made locally. A series of ornaments is exclusive to Mycenaean Greece and evidently made there. Normally of translucent blue glass with flat backs and suspension holes, they occur in many different shapes, the most common being rosettes and spirals, the latter perhaps representing locks of hair. Most date from 1400 to 1200 BC. Moulds of stone, usually steatite, have been found on several sites, suggesting that there were a number of manufacturing centres. Ornaments of gold foil, quite often found with the glass examples, could also have been made in these moulds, the gold and glass sometimes fitting together. Some of the blue glass used by the Mycenaeans evidently came from Egypt, as illustrated by cobalt-blue glass ingots of evidently Egyptian origin that were discovered in the wreck of a merchant ship on its way to Greece that sank off the coast of southwest Turkey at Ulu Burun towards 1300 BC. Very similar ingots have been found at Tell Brak in northeast Syria (Mesopotamia).

In the earlier Iron Age the Greek contribution to the glass industry was a remarkable series of core-formed vessels, initially made principally on the island of Rhodes between about 550 and 400 BC. This Rhodian production was evidently inspired by Mesopotamian core-formed vessels found in 7th-century-BC contexts on the island. These may have been imported or possibly made by migrant Mesopotamian glass-workers. The Rhodian vessels were designed as containers for perfume or scented oils, which were Rhodian products of the time, and take their shapes from the contemporary Greek repertory of vases in pottery and metal. The most common body colour is translucent dark blue, but some are opaque white, brown, red, or olive green. Decoration usually consists of opaque orange, yellow, white, or turquoise trails combed into zigzag, festoon, or feather patterns. Traded far and wide, initially perhaps in the hands of Phoenician seafarers (residents of modern Lebanon), they reached every major site in the Mediterranean and also travelled as far as the Black Sea. Everywhere they are concentrated in areas of Greek commercial activity.

The Rhodian factories ceased production at the end of the 5th century BC and more than two generations passed before core-forming was revived in Mediterranean workshops. This occurred some time after 350 BC, coinciding with the conquest of the Persian empire by Alexander the Great. It marked the beginning of an era of Macedonian supremacy, and it seems likely that some factories were located in Macedonia and supplied northern Greece and Russia. Fewer vessels were now produced and many of the forms were more massive than before. New shapes included jars (*stamnoi*), three-handled flasks (*hydriskai*), and bottles (*unguentaria*).

By the 5th century BC the Greeks had two names for glass, one, *lithos chyti*, meaning "poured (or melted) stone", an apt description of the core-formed vessels. The second, *hyalos*,

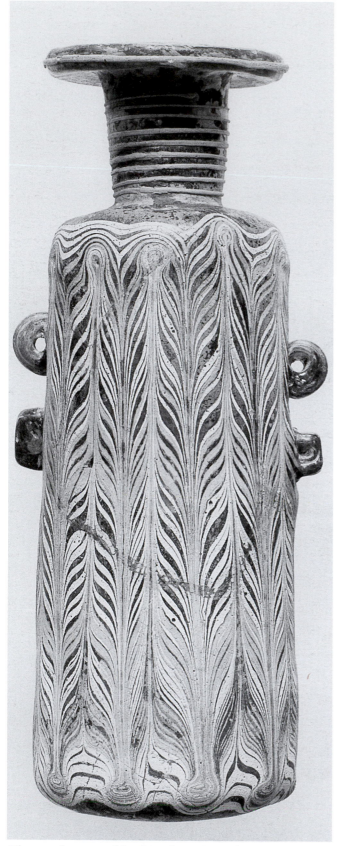

Glass: perfume vessel in glass, the variegated colours enhancing the elegance of these dainty vases, Ashmolean Museum, Oxford

signifies "transparency" or "clarity". This could refer to 5th-century BC ornaments of clear yellowish and greenish glass in the shape of three-pointed stars and parts of palmettes and flowers, cast in clay moulds, and found in the workshop of Phidias at Olympia (now in the Olympia Museum). They were evidently drapery decorations, and different-coloured glass insets were used to enhance contemporary Greek architecture.

The second group of core-formed vessels has already brought the story into the Hellenistic period. During this time the glass industry generally flourished as never before, and the Greek world seems to have played a part in production. Excavations on the island of Rhodes revealed the presence of a glass factory operating in the late 3rd or early 2nd century BC making beads, and also vessels formed of two clear glass bowls fitted one inside the other with patterns in gold leaf attached to the outside of the inner bowl, thus appearing "sandwiched". The Rhodian finds are fragments, but more complete sandwich gold-glass bowls with known findspots come from Italy (four examples), Gordium (Asia Minor), and Olbia on the Black Sea. Rhodes may have been a centre of production of these magnificent vessels, but this is still debated. The Hellenistic period in glassmaking was marked by the production of fine vessels of mosaic glass, and finds from the Greek world show the familiarity of the people with such glasses, although it is still not certain where they were made. From graves at Palaikastro, near the town of Karditsa in Thessaly, come two very fine "bottles" of a particularly beautiful type of mosaic glass that imitates agate, a semi-precious stone, showing spiral patterns of white and purple in a brown ground. From another grave came a similar bottle of clear glass. These probably all date from the 2nd to the 1st century BC, and can be seen in the National Archaeological Musuem, Athens. This was the time that a new type of tableware made by the slumping process was being produced in profusion at sites on the coast of Syria and Palestine. Bowls of various shapes were made, usually hemispherical or conical with pointed bottoms and decorated on the inside with grooved lines. Initially they were of clear greenish or brownish or colourless glass, and later sometimes of green, amber, blue, or wine-coloured glass as well. Known as "grooved bowls", they were made with little variation for nearly 100 years between about 150 and 50 BC.

Around 80 BC a ship was wrecked near Anticythera off the southwest coast of Greece. Its cargo included colourless and mosaic glass vessels (National Archaeological Museum, Athens). Among the colourless vessels were two glass *skyphoi* (wing-handled cups), a bowl with bossed decoration, another of the fluted series, and one of similar shape with a finely executed engraved design. Bowls of mosaic glass, on applied ring bases, were hemispherical or had outward-curving sides, new shapes in the repertory. The mosaic pattern included spirals and a network pattern that had been introduced earlier, but new at this time was a true striped effect achieved by fusing together canes of different colours laid side by side (coloured band glass). Similar glasses to these have been found on the island of Delos (and now in the Delos Museum) in a context dating from 125 to 69 BC, together with deep "grooved bowls" of bright opaque colours, known in later contexts of the early to mid 1st century AD at Knossos in Crete (Herakleion Museum). Three small workshops making glass beads were also discovered on Delos.

Whether any of the glasses just described were actually made in Greece is perhaps unlikely, but probably of Greek or specifically Cretan manufacture were cosmetic boxes. These are made of thick glass, green, yellowish-brown, or colourless with a greyish tinge, and most with known findspots come from Crete. In form they compare rather loosely with marble and pottery examples, and the glass is similar to that used for finger-rings, some of which come from 3rd-century BC contexts. The glass cosmetic boxes are perhaps of the same date. The lid was made by the slumping process, while the box was evidently mould-pressed, using two shaped "forms" between which the molten glass was compressed, before being cooled and then cut, ground, and polished. Much of the table-ware produced in Italy from the time of Augustus (see below) was made this way.

The discovery that glass could be blown revolutionized the industry. The first evidence for glass blowing comes from a collection of waste dumped in the Jewish quarter of the old city of Jerusalem around 50 BC (Israel Museum, Jerusalem), but blown-glass vessels did not become the norm for another 75 years. Thus in the late 1st century BC and earlier 1st century AD blown vessels are found alongside non-blown examples at Corinth (Corinth Museum) and in a grave group from Macedonia (National Archaeological Museum, Athens). The grave group includes five blown unguent flasks and a slumped shallow thin-walled bowl of a type made from about 25 BC to AD 25 in both brightly coloured and natural-coloured glass and recorded from all over the Mediterranean world. Many fragments of such bowls have been recorded from Knossos in Crete, but they were perhaps imported from Italy, where factories producing a fine series of tableware of monochrome brightly coloured glass and other vessels of intricate mosaic glass were certainly established in the time of Augustus (27 BC–AD 14). They seem to have supplied the Greek market, and to some extent to have reached Greek cities on the coast of Asia Minor as well. The same Italian factories were in part responsible for a series of bowls, often of mosaic glass, with evenly spaced ribs on the outside, known as "pillar-moulded bowls". The type seems to have originated in Syro-Palestinian glasshouses around 25 BC alongside, and in part preceded by, a series with less evenly spaced ribs. Both series are known from the island of Crete, but are rare on the Greek mainland.

Early blown glass, principally small bottles for perfume or oil, is known from the Greek city of Priene on the west coast of Asia Minor and the Greek island of Siphnos, as well as the sites noted above, suggesting that in the age of Augustus the blowing technique was rapidly being adopted in many parts of the Roman empire. Vessels from both eastern and western glasshouses also reached the Greek world in the 1st century AD and, since certain types are common to both areas, it is not always easy to decide their origin. Mould-blown glasses, first made around AD 25, mostly came from Phoenician and Palestinian glasshouses. Typical Italian types such as a large jug with embedded blobbed decoration from one of the Greek islands (British Museum, London), and small ribbed cups with coloured trails found in Crete, were also imported. Hemispherical cups, some with cut and abraded decoration, known from various sites in the Greek world, may also have come from Italy. An enamelled bowl from Greece (British Museum, London), which differs from the typical north Italian group in having a star rather than a rosette on the bottom, is perhaps from an eastern glasshouse that produced enamelled flasks known from sites on the Black Sea and on Cyprus.

By the end of the 1st century AD, when most glass vessels were blown and factories already established in the Syro-Palestinian area and in Italy increased their production, new glasshouses producing utilitarian glass vessels were established all over the Roman empire, no doubt including Greece, though actual evidence for Roman glassworking sites has yet to be revealed. Fine glassware was still imported. From Italy may have come tall beakers with facet-cut decoration recorded from Crete in late 1st- and early 2nd-century-AD contexts, and Italy may also have been the source of mould-blown square (and cylindrical) bottles that were produced from around AD 70 until the late 2nd or 3rd century, as well as jars, which were later used as cinerary urns, between AD 50 and 200. Bottles of the late 2nd century AD from Thermopylae and Corinth have short necks, restricted at the junction with the body, and cracked off rims, and are decorated with fine polychrome trailing. They may have come from a Syro-Palestinian workshop responsible for a series with trailed decoration of flowers and birds. A polychrome bottle of similar shape, but with a taller neck, from Karditsa in Thessaly is decorated with embedded yellow and white trails, and perhaps came from Italy where bottles of this type, but with cut decoration showing Italian landscapes, date from the later 3rd and 4th century. To the same years belong "pipette-shaped" bottles of a type current in both East and West and found on the island of Crete.

Our knowledge of glass of the early Byzantine period in Greece is limited. Roman traditions of glassmaking survived in the eastern Roman empire into the 7th century AD with most vessels being made of thinly blown glass in different shades of green as well as other natural colours. Excavations in Crete have revealed typical early Byzantine stemmed goblets and lamps, and a long-necked flask of the 6th century AD was found in a tomb near Athens. Two tombstones from Athens name glassworkers of the 6th century AD, and it is possible that at least one mould-blown jug was brought back to Athens by a pilgrim to Jerusalem about the same time (National Archaeological Museum, Athens).

By the end of the reign of the emperor Herakleios (610–41) Byzantine civilization was fully developed, but the role of Byzantium in the history of medieval glassmaking is still little understood. However, the products of the glassmakers of Greece, as well as other parts of the Byzantine world, must have played an important role in religious and secular art as well as in everyday life. The cargo of a ship that was wrecked off the coast of southwest Turkey around 1025 included three tons of broken glass vessels and glass cullet (glass fragments for a glassmaker to reuse), suggesting a flourishing trade in recycled glass. Excavations at a site in Constantinople revealed glassware of the 11th to 13th centuries. Predominant were wine glasses and lamps, similar in form to those of the earlier period, but made of fine-quality light blue-green to light bottle-green glass. There were also a few fragments of enamelled glass. The monk Theophilos, writing in Germany in the early 12th century, describes the making of glass goblets that the "Greeks" embellish with gold and silver, but by "Greeks" he simply means those living within the Byzantine empire, and so probably in the capital Constantinople, the most likely source of fine enamelled glassware. "Greeks" are also described as being responsible for glass wall tiles with gold cruciform decoration made in much the same way as late Roman gold-glass roundels, evidently produced in Rome in the 4th century AD. This was one of the traditions inherited by the Venetians who were to dominate glassmaking from soon after the sack of Constantinople in 1204, though not until the middle of the 15th century did they produce works that could rival the Byzantine in quality.

Little glass of the later Byzantine period has in fact been found in Greece itself. In 1937 two glassmakers' workshops were discovered at Corinth on the site of the ancient agora. One was represented by fragments of furnace pots and debris, but no structures. The other was more complete and included knobbed (or prunted) beakers, of a type that was to dominate German glass production from the 16th century, cups blown in patterned moulds, beakers with vertical mould-blown ribs, and bottles with tall necks and globular or ovoid bodies (Corinth Museum). These products are similar to glass made in Italy in the 13th and 14th centuries, and it now seems likely that this glasshouse at Corinth operated at that time during the Frankish occupation of Greece. The glassmakers, therefore, may well have been Italian. Thus the influence of Byzantine glassmaking in Greece on the glasshouses of medieval Italy and central Europe was nil.

Through the centuries the Greek world had contributed in various ways to the glass industry. However, while local factories must have produced utilitarian glasses for everyday use in more recent years, no specifically Greek traits can be identified in modern glass, whether the mass-produced glass tableware or the hand-made artistic pieces that to this day are blown, just as they were 2000 years ago.

VERONICA TATTON-BROWN

Further Reading

Hayes, J.W., "Late Roman, Byzantine and Ottoman Period Glass Finds" in *Excavations at Saraçhane in Istanbul*, vol. 2: *The Pottery*, edited by R.M. Harrison, Princeton, New Jersey: Princeton University Press, 1992, pp. 399–421

Liefkes, Reino (editor), *Glass*, London: Victoria and Albert Museum, 1997

Nenna, M.-D., "La Verrerie d'époque hellenistique à Delos", *Journal of Glass Studies*, 35 (1993): pp. 11–21

Nenna, M.-D., *Les Verres: Exploration archeologique de Délos*, vol. 37, Paris: Boccard, 1999

Parker, A.J., *Ancient Shipwrecks of the Mediterranean and the Roman Provinces*, Oxford: Tempus Reparatum, 1992

Price, J., L.H. Sackett, K. Branigan *et al*, "Hellenistic and Roman Glass" in *Knossos, from Greek City to Roman Colony: Excavations at the Unexplored Mansion*, vol. 2, Athens: British School of Archaeology, 1992, pp. 415–90

Stern, E. Marianne, *Roman Mould-Blown Glass*, Toledo: Toledo Museum of Art, 1995

Tait, Hugh (editor), *Five Thousand Years of Glass*, London: British Museum Press, and New York: Abrams, 1991

Weinberg, Gladys Davidson, *Glass Vessels in Ancient Greece*, Athens: Archaeological Receipts Fund, 1992

Whitehouse, D., "Glassmaking at Corinth: A Reassessment" in *Ateliers de verriers de l'antiquité à la période préindustrielle*, edited by D. Foy and G. Sennequier, Rouen: Association Française pour l'Archéologie du Verre, 1991, pp. 73–82

Gnostics

The term Gnostic is applied by early writers to a number of sects, all purporting to be Christian and to possess either a special revelation or a special understanding of the things revealed to others. These heresies were alleged to originate either with Simon Magus or with the Naassenes of Phrygia. Accounts of the former are largely fictitious, but the so-called Naassene Sermon, which assimilates Jewish and Christian beliefs to pagan mysteries in the course of a commentary on a hymn to Attis, is evidently genuine in substance, and of some antiquity (Hippolytus, *Refutation*, 5. 6–11). It finds the common theme of all religions in the oscillation of the human soul between the realms of spirit and matter, which are merely the upper and lower arms of a bifurcated stream. The Gnostics known to Irenaeus maintained, more pessimistically, that matter was wholly alien to spirit, and that the present world owed its origin to a schism in the Godhead, which imprisoned the divine Wisdom (or at least an offspring or reflection of it) in the underlying darkness. This myth was refined in the school of the Alexandrian Valentinus, which was probably not called Gnostic, either by itself or others, until the 4th century AD. The Valentinians held that even matter was an emanation of the fallen Wisdom, and that the task of the elect in the present world was therefore to liberate the soul from its gross environment, though not perhaps entirely from the body. In this they were helped by Christ and the Holy Spirit, who were brought forth from the fullness or *pleroma* of the Godhead in order to restore Wisdom to her previous state of knowledge. The elect in the present world are seeds of this repentant Wisdom, and the coming of Christ in human form delivered them from the bondage of the Law that the Creator had imposed upon the Jews. The somewhat earlier school of Basilides, another Alexandrian, appears to have taught that the present world is governed by the "third archon", who, in company with the elect, aspires to the spiritual condition of his superiors. The Neoplatonist Porphyry, whose master Plotinus attacked a group of Gnostics around AD 265, describes them as Christian heretics distinguished by the tenet that "the author of the cosmos is malign" (*Enneads*, 2. 9; cf. *Life of Plotinus*, 16). Yet this is not the teaching of either Basilides or Valentinus, both of whom ascribe to the creator a limited knowledge of, and share in, the goodness of the highest principle.

"Gnostic" is thus the name of a tendency rather than of a religion, and modern attempts to construct a unified faith called Gnosticism often rest on careless handling of the evidence. Nor is it true, on the other hand, that the Fathers themselves imposed the word promiscuously on every deviant movement; on the contrary, it was generally denied to those who claimed it, while philosophic Christians such as Clement of Alexandria were happy to apply it to themselves. It is even more tendentious to suggest, in the German manner, that the main Church was consistently opposed to a widespread principle of *gnosis* that was embraced by both the heretics and the pagan schools of the early Christian period; *gnosis* is nothing more than the Greek for "knowledge", which every creed and doctrine, including Christianity, declared to be its own prerogative. Many traits that modern theologians pejoratively characterize as Gnostic are of the essence of New Testament Christianity: the division between the substance of the Creator and of his creatures is stronger in orthodox teaching than in Valentinian theory, and the propensity to allegorize the Old Testament was most common among those Christians who believed the whole canon to be infallible.

The testimony of sources from the early Christian era has been partly vindicated by a number of texts discovered at Nag Hammadi in Egypt in 1945. The Apocrypha of John and *Zostrianus* contain the tenets denounced by Porphyry and Irenaeus, but the Valentinian writings of the "Jung Codex" show that the sect was less unorthodox than the Fathers made it seem. The central myth is greatly attenuated from the so-called Gospel of Truth, the *Epistle to Rheginus* seems to affirm the resurrection of the flesh, and the Tripartate Tractate substitutes the Logos for Wisdom and traces the creation to divine benevolence rather than to error. There is much to be said for the view that all the Gnostic myths were conceived as allegorical or encoded presentations of beliefs that differed little from those of orthodox Christianity. Of all the great heresiarchs who are said to have maintained that the present world is the creation of a lesser God, Marcion was the one who dispensed with parables, and neither our ancient sources nor the majority of modern scholars regard him as a Gnostic. Critical reflection on the evidence has now dispelled a number of ancient calumnies: for instance, that the Gnostics were determinists, that they practised immorality as a ritual, and that they taught their pupils to lie as a means of evading persecution. When they write as though all human choices were determined by our natures, they are borrowing the idiom of the Pauline and Johannine writings; far from eschewing material sacraments, they seem to have accorded to them a magical efficacy, as we learn not only from the Gospel of Philip in the Nag Hammadi collection, but from Irenaeus' satire on the impostures of Mark the Mage. Many of the Nag Hammadi codices err not in the antinomian direction, but in that of the extreme asceticism that was known as the encratite heresy; for that reason it makes little sense to ask whether such a document as the infamous Gospel of Thomas should be classed as Gnostic, encratite, or a conflation of the two.

The Nag Hammadi codices give little support to the thesis of Rudolf Bultmann and Richard Reitzenstein that the Gnostic myths developed independently of the biblical tradition; in any case, these views were always known to rest on inferences from later Mandaean and Manichaean writings (some no earlier than the 9th century), together with a precarious distinction between indigenous and Hellenized Judaism. It would, however, be equally rash to deduce from the predominance of Old Testament citations that the authors of the new documents were Jewish rather than Christian; Christians might confine themselves to the Jewish scriptures either for apologetic purposes or because they did not yet possess a canonical New Testament. Similarly, the fact that some of the Nag Hammadi texts evince no trace of Christianity may imply that they were meant for a pagan audience, but says nothing of their provenance or date. Pétrement argues plausibly that the Valentinian teaching is a cryptic version of Pauline Christianity, and proponents of a non-Christian or pre-Christian Gnosticism are still looking for an adhesive that would unite their speculations with the facts.

MARK EDWARDS

Summary

Gnostics (derived from *gnosis*, "knowledge") were regarded as heretics by early Christian writers, for being members of sects purporting to be Christian but who believed that they possessed either a special revelation or a special understanding of the revealed religion. The recent discovery of Gnostic texts has partly vindicated this view but also shown that the sects were less unorthodox than the Church Fathers claimed.

Further Reading

Bianchi, Ugo (editor), *Le origini dello Gnosticismo*, Leiden: Brill, 1967

Bultmann, Rudolf, *Primitive Christianity in Its Contemporary Setting*, London: Thames and Hudson, and New York: Meridian, 1956

Grant, R.M., *Gnosticism and Early Christianity*, 2nd edition, New York: Harper and Row, 1966

Jonas, Hans, *The Gnostic Religion: The Message of the Alien God and the Beginnings of Religion*, 2nd edition, Boston: Beacon Press, 1991; London: Routledge, 1992

Layton, Bentley (editor), *The Rediscovery of Gnosticism*, 2 vols, Leiden: Brill, 1980–81

Layton, Bentley, *The Gnostic Scriptures: A New Translation with Annotations and Introductions*, New York: Doubleday, 1987

Logan, Alastair H.B., *Gnostic Truth and Christian Heresy: A Study in the History of Gnosticism*, Edinburgh: T. & T. Clark, and Peabody, Massachusetts: Hendrickson, 1996

Perkins, Pheme, *Gnosticism and the New Testament*, Minneapolis: Fortress Press, 1993

Pétrement, Simone, *A Separate God: The Christian Origins of Gnosticism*, San Francisco: Harper and Row, 1990; London: Darton Longman and Todd, 1991

Quispel, Gilles, *Gnostic Studies*, 2 vols, Istanbul: Nederlands Historisch-Archaeologisch Instituut, 1974

Reitzenstein, R., *Poimandres: Studien zur griechischägyptischen und frühchristlichen*, Leipzig: Teubner, 1904

Robinson, James M. (editor), *The Nag Hammadi Library in English*, Leiden: Brill, and San Francisco: Harper and Row, 1988

Rudolph, Kurt, *Gnosis: The Nature and History of an Ancient Religion*, translated and edited by Robert McLachlan Wilson, Edinburgh: T. & T. Clark, 1983

Wilson, Robert McLachlan, *The Gnostic Problem: A Study of the Relations between Hellenistic Judaism and the Gnostic Heresy*, London: Mowbray, 1958

Wilson, Robert McLachlan, *Gnosis and the New Testament*, Oxford: Blackwell, and Philadelphia: Fortress Press, 1968

Gods and Goddesses

Ancient Greek religion was not only polytheistic, but also multifaceted, in the sense that there was an evolution in the notion of divinity. Even within the frame of specific divinities certain features changed with time. The crystallization of our notion of the gods and goddesses derives mainly from archaic poetry, and particularly from the Homeric and Hesiodic epics. The ambiguities and contradictions that are observed in the mythic narratives explain the multifaceted character of the ancient gods and goddesses. The ruling divinities were the Olympians, so called from Mount Olympus, which was believed to be their residence. Before them were some primordial beings. In Hesiod's *Theogony* the first beings were Gaia ("earth"), Chaos, Tartarus, and Eros. In the Hesiodic account the world was created essentially by Gaia, who gave birth to

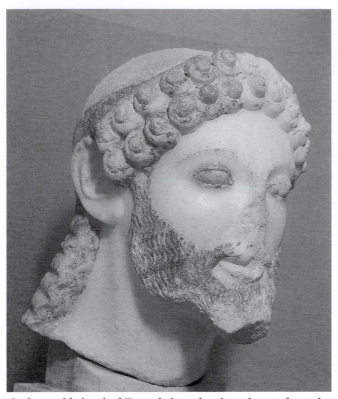

Gods: marble head of Zeus, father of gods and men, from the Archaic period, 6th century BC

Uranus ("sky"), and then, mating with him, produced the 12 Titans, the Giants, and the Cyclops. Some myths are about the fear of losing power and the eventual succession among different generations of divine creatures. Uranus kept his children inside Gaia because he was afraid that they might take his power. Gaia, in order to be liberated from such a burden inside her, made a sickle, which their son Cronus bravely used to castrate his father. In the Hesiodic version the goddess Aphrodite was born out of Uranus' castrated genitals, which fell on the sea's foam. In Apollodorus' version Cronus was persuaded by his mother to kill his father because Uranos had overthrown the Cyclops, the first children he had with Gaia. Cronus, in his turn, swallowed his children out of the same fear that his own father had. He was defeated by his son Zeus, who after the Titanomachy and the Gigantomachy acquired supremacy. Cronus and Rhea had six children, three sons and three daughters: Poseidon, Hades, Zeus, Hera, Hestia, and Demeter.

The notion of 12 gods and goddesses was established early in the consciousness of the Greeks, but the catalogue of them varies. The most common list of the 12 consists of the following: Zeus, Hera, Poseidon, Demeter, Apollo, Artemis, Athena, Hermes, Ares, Aphrodite, Hephaestus, and Hestia. There were local variations according to which Hades or Pluto takes the place of Hermes, or Dionysus takes the place of Hestia. Besides the principal gods, there is also a group of minor deities such as the Graces, the Muses, Eros (not the Hesiodic primordial creature, but rather the son of Aphrodite), Hebe, Eileithyia, Hecate, Pan, the Nymphs, the Horae, Themis, the Moirae, Nemesis, the Erinyes, and others with different degrees of importance. It is uncertain how many were regarded as deities

and with what specific role, and how they were worshipped. A general feature that is often pointed out regarding ancient Greek religion is anthropomorphism. Although they were believed to have power over nature and humans, the deities were subject to mortal needs such as food, drink, and sex. Political behaviour was not unknown among them and the Homeric epics present the gods as taking sides and making enemies even among their fellow gods. There is no representative of absolute perfection or absolute evil, but they were immortal, even though subject to mortal feelings as well.

Zeus was thought to be the father of gods and men. The expression "Zeus father" (Zeus *pater*) is equivalent to the Latin Jupiter. Besides the myths of succession that are associated with him, there are other myths related to his birth, the most common being the Cretan one. According to this myth the child was hidden in a cave on mount Ida so as not to be swallowed by his father, Cronus, and was nourished by the goat Amaltheia, while the Couretes danced around him and with their noise drowned his cries. Zeus was the god of weather and the one who makes thunder and lightning. Many of Zeus' Homeric epithets are related to his control of natural phenomena. He was notorious for his erotic liaisons that made him the father of many gods and heroes. By Hera he had Ares, Hebe, and in some versions Hephaestus and Eileithyia. By Leto, a Titaness, he had Apollo and Artemis. By Maia he had Hermes and by Semele, a mortal, Dionysus. In Homer he is also the father of Aphrodite by Dione. He gave birth to Athena, on his own, by swallowing her mother Metis. He was the father of Persephone by Demeter, of the Moirae, the Horae, the Graces, and the Muses. The most famous heroes claimed their descent from him: Heracles was his son by Alcmene, Perseus by Danae, the beautiful Helen by his daughter Leda. His many epithets are revealing of different emphases on various aspects of his divine identity in the mind of his worshippers. He is Zeus Herkeios, family protector, and also the protector of the domestic hearth (Ephesteios). As the god who soothes, especially at the end of the winter, he is worshipped as Meilichios. Freedmen used to worship Zeus Eleutherios in a sanctuary in Athens. As the ultimate lawgiver and bearer of justice he is Zeus Themistios.

Hera, daughter of Cronus and Rhea, was the sister and wife of Zeus. She is the feminine representation of natural forces, and the goddess of marriage and protector of women. In literature she is often depicted as the jealous wife who is constantly after her husband's lovers and offspring by them. In the Homeric *Hymn to Apollo* she delays the birth of Apollo and Artemis. Her persecution of Heracles is a beloved theme in literature and art. She is often referred to as Argeia, since Argos is one of the most ancient places of her worship, or as Zygia due to her patronage of marriage.

Demeter is another goddess closely connected with femininity, and particularly maternal powers. The evident etymology of her name ("earth-mother") has led to research into her relationship with the period of matriarchy in Greece. The main myth in which she features as a central figure is that of the quest for her daughter Persephone, who had been abducted by Hades. She finally finds her and makes the arrangement that Persephone will stay for some months with her husband in the Underworld, the mourning period for Demeter and winter for mankind, and for some time with her mother on earth.

Demeter was worshipped extensively at Eleusis, in the Eleusinian Mysteries in autumn time. The Thesmophoria was a widely celebrated female festival.

Poseidon is most commonly known as the god of the sea. Some of his Homeric epithets refer to him as the "earth-shaker". He was married to Amphitrite, but like his brother Zeus fathered many heroes. Some of his sons have monstrous features, like the Cyclops Polyphemus. He competed with the goddess Athena for the patronage of the city of Athens and lost. Athena, mostly known as the goddess of wisdom and prudence, is a multifaceted figure. She is the personification of feminine virginity combined with a warrior's virility. She was born from Zeus' head after he had swallowed her mother Metis; she therefore incarnates the *metis* (cunning intelligence) of her mother. Athena is an active participant in many myths due to her role as the protector-goddess of many heroes, such as Odysseus, Heracles, Perseus, and others. In Homer she fervently protects the Achaean side in the Trojan War, and accompanies her favourite Odysseus in the *Odyssey*. One of the most glorious ancient festivals, the Panathenaia in Athens, was dedicated to her. In Hesiod she is the one who teaches the art of weaving to Pandora, the first woman. One of her standard epithets is that of *ergane* ("worker"), revealing her relation with many women's works. An intriguing deity, she represents the ferocity of war and is easily recognizable in art by her attributes, a shield, spear, and helmet. She is also the guardian of peaceful community life.

Apollo and Artemis were twins, the children of Zeus and Leto. The first part of the Homeric *Hymn to Apollo* tells the adventure of their birth. Their mother was being pursued by Hera, and Delos was the only place that agreed to receive her; it therefore holds a central position for their cult. The second part of the Homeric *Hymn to Apollo* tells how Apollo came to be associated with Delphi, after killing a huge female serpent, Python. He was the god of divination and Delphi became the most famous oracle in antiquity. His epithet Loxias designates the oblique answers that he gave. He was also the god of medicine, healing, and music. In *Iliad* 1 he is the one who brings the plague. Apollo was also associated with the sun, hence the epithet Helios. He was the leader of the Muses, *Mousagetes*, and the patron of lyric poetry, particularly choric. Since he was the god so directly associated with mankind (through his link with medicine, music, and divination) he held a significant position in cult and was worshipped in many places, particularly Delos, his birthplace, where the Delia festival was celebrated every five years, and in Delphi, where there were many festivals, such as the Pythia and the Theoxenia. Artemis, Apollo's twin sister, was the goddess of hunting and represents untamed virginity. Unlike Athena, the other virgin goddess, she was not a city person, but rather dwelt in wild country, and was known as the lady of the wild beasts (*Potnia theron*). She was worshipped in many places, particularly in Sparta as Artemis Orthia. She was associated with many women's festivals, because she was worshipped with Eileithyia, the goddess who brought relief to pregnant women by granting them fast delivery.

There are two versions of Aphrodite's birth, the goddess of beauty and love. According to Hesiod (*Theogony*, 190–200) she belongs to the most ancient divine generation, before the Olympians ever existed, born from Uranus' castrated genitals that were combined with the sea's foam. In Homer her mother is Dione who mated with Zeus. Her epithets Kypria or Kythereia show her connection with the islands of Cyprus and Cythera, both claiming to be her birthplace. The same conflict arises regarding Eros, who in some versions is one of the primordial divinities, like Gaia, yet in most literary accounts and artistic depictions he is the son of Aphrodite and Ares, incarnating a warlike feature of passionate erotic desire. In Plato's *Symposium* Pausanias makes a distinction between Aphrodite Ourania ("heavenly"), and Aphrodite Pandemos ("of the people", "possessing a vulgar nature"). This difference has shaped the cult of Aphrodite and the reception of the goddess in religious terms.

Ares was the warlike god. Unlike Athena, he represents the passionate and irrational desire and insatiable thirst for war. The spear and the burning torch are his symbols. In Homer he is the lover of Aphrodite. He was worshipped everywhere, particularly in Sparta, Arcadia, and Elis. Hephaestus, associated with fire and artwork, is in Hesiod's version the son of Hera alone, and therefore, as a product of the female only, he is lame. He was the renowned maker of many wonderful objects of which extensive description (*ekphrasis*) is given in literature, such as the shield of Achilles in *Iliad* 18. In some accounts he is married to Aphrodite. He is associated with volcanoes, and was therefore worshipped in Sicily, especially near Mount Aetna, and the Lipari islands where he worked with the Cyclops. There was an annual festival in his honour in Lemnos, and in Athens the festival of Chalkeia in October. There was also a feast with the name Hephaestia.

Hermes and Dionysus were both offspring of Zeus, both involved in stories about coming to power. Dionysus' place of birth was Thebes. He was the son of Zeus and Semele, a mortal princess, the daughter of Cadmus. Semele, having fallen into Hera's trap, asked to see Zeus in all his glory, and was destroyed by lightning. Zeus took the baby Dionysus, who was born some months later from his father's thigh. The general consensus ascribes to Dionysus a Thracian or Phrygian origin. His cult was widespread in northern Greece and had an orgiastic character, adhered to particularly by women in a form that demanded religious ecstacy (*ekstasis*). Women were swept away by his divine nature and abandoned their life to join frenzied dances in the mountains, swinging thyrsi and torches. There are various artistic representations of maenads, as well as literary ones, the most famous being Euripides' *Bacchae*. Dionysus was popular as the god of wine and merriment, although wine does not seem to have had any significant role in the ancient orgiastic cults. The use of a mask was characteristic of his cult. The birth of drama is associated with the cult of Dionysus. The greatest theatrical festivals, the greater and the lesser Dionysia, were in honour of him. He was also associated with powers of fertility in nature, thus his most ancient representations consist of wooden images with the phallus as a symbol of fertility. The name Dionysus appears in Linear B tablets, which suggests that he was not unknown to the Mycenaean civilization. Hermes is another "young" god in myth, although probably quite old in origin. He was born on the Arcadian mountain of Cyllene and proved his characteristics of inventiveness, trickery, and versatility already from babyhood. The stories of the deception of Apollo by the baby Hermes who stole his cattle and of Hermes' invention of the lyre are found in the Homeric *Hymn to Hermes*. He is associated with the notion of transgressing limits. He is the one who accompanies mortals to Hades, known for that as *psychopompos* ("escorter of souls"). He is also the messenger. Together with Athena he protects heroes in perilous enterprises and is often depicted in art escorting heroes. His characteristic attributes in art are the winged cap and the herald's wand. Much associated with Hermes is Hestia, the representative of home and family life; her name means "hearth". She was closely connected with Zeus, her brother. She took an oath of eternal virginity. She is the least anthropomorphic god of all and is never mentioned by Homer.

It is a commonplace to talk about the fusion between ancient and Christian religion. In some places, such as the southern Mani and remote islands such as Lesbos, popular attachment to ancient religion was so strong that total Christianization did not come before the 9th century AD. The struggle between paganism and Christianity was a common topic for writers on both sides. There is intense scholarly debate as to the relation between Hellenism and Christianity and the mutual influence of the one on the other. Despite many attempts by the Church to eradicate the practice of ancient religion it is still alive today in some folk customs and ideologies. The ancient gods and their spheres of influence have been fused with the cult of the saints: St Nicholas is the protector of seamen; a certain St Demeter was worshipped until recently in the region of Eleusis. Some saints have a specific role as healers or guardians against evil. As Martin Nilsson remarks: "Christianity easily swept away the great gods, but the minor daemons of popular belief offered a stubborn resistance." The belief in Hades, although no longer as the brother of Zeus and Poseidon, has many of the archaic elements that may be seen in Homer. Historians of religion and other scholars interested in great battles, particularly in the period of late antiquity and Byzantium, often take sides according to their personal beliefs and fail to see the periods in question with a sympathetic eye. As is often the case with languages, the mythology of ancient gods has not totally disappeared, but has left its remains in modern beliefs.

ANDROMACHE KARANIKA-DIMAROGONA

Further Reading

Bremmer, Jan N., *Greek Religion*, Oxford and New York: Oxford University Press, 1994

Burkert, Walter, *Greek Religion: Archaic and Classical*, Oxford: Blackwell, and Cambridge, Massachusetts: Harvard University Press, 1985

Burkert, Walter, *Ancient Mystery Cults*, Cambridge, Massachusetts: Harvard University Press, 1987

Guthrie, W.K.C., *The Greeks and their Gods*, London: Methuen, 1950, reprinted London: Methuen, and Boston: Beacon Press, 1968

Megas, Georgios A., *Greek Calendar Customs*, Athens: Department of State, Public and Private Institutions and Societies, 1958

Nilsson, Martin, *A History of Greek Religion*, Oxford: Clarendon Press, 1925; 2nd edition Oxford: Clarendon Press, 1963, Westport, Connecticut: Greenwood Press, 1980

Nilsson, Martin, *Greek Folk Religion*, New York: Harper and Row, 1961, reprinted Philadelphia: University of Pennsylvania Press, 1998

Vernant, Jean Pierre, *Mythe et société en Grèce ancienne*, Paris: Maspero, 1974

Gold

Although one of the major metals of antiquity, gold was not the first metal to be exploited, even for decorative purposes. This is probably because its extreme malleability made it unsuitable for making tools. The earliest regular use of gold dates from the 5th millennium BC (Neolithic) in Bulgaria, where containers of sheet and cast gold were found, with gold-dust decorated pottery vessels. Two different types of gold deposit were worked in antiquity – those in solid rock (primary deposits) and those in the sediments of rivers (placers). However, in both gold occurs as the native metal and smelting thus largely consisted of melting the separated metal.

Primary gold deposits are of many different types but one of the commonest is the vein deposit. Here the gold occurs as minute metallic grains in veins of white quartz typically up to a few metres wide, commonly with pyrite (iron sulphide or "fool's gold") and other sulphides. Such deposits form from hot circulating watery fluids. The fluids are very dilute and are usually associated with granitic intrusions or metamorphism. Gold deposits of this type were exploited in antiquity, but required much labour because the hard rock had to be crushed before the gold could be extracted.

Placer gold occurs as dust, grains, and nuggets in sands and gravels deposited by rivers. Such deposits form by the weathering and breakdown of the hard rock in which the gold originally crystallized. Lighter minerals originally present in the rock are slowly swept away by the flow of the water in the river, and the heavier minerals, including the grains of gold, are left behind. A placer miner will search for gold in parts of the river protected from the full force of the river current, such as downstream of large boulders or on the inside of bends in the river bed. The gold can be separated from the sand and gravel of the river bed by a number of different methods, such as pans and sluices, all of which mimic the sorting action of the river. Herodotus described gold extraction in the Phasis river (modern Rioni) of Georgia thus: "The mountain torrents are said to bring down gold and these barbarians catch it in troughs perforated with holes and on fleecy skins." This technique no doubt gave rise to the legend of the Golden Fleece. When a river changes course, its placer deposit will become "fossilized", but can still be exploited in the same way.

Although placer gold deposits are mostly produced by mechanical processes of alteration and sorting, there is also a chemical part to the process. Early writers on mineralogy were aware of this and spoke of gold nuggets "growing" in rivers. When a rock is weathered, most of the gold remains in the solid, metallic form, but some goes into solution in the water. In the river bed the chemical conditions are different and the gold in the water is plated out on to gold grains already present. This is why gold grains in placer deposits can be much larger than grains in rocks.

Gold has been mined in Macedonia and Thrace since the Bronze Age, but serious exploitation did not begin until Philip II gained control of the mines in 358 BC. Almost all the rivers in this area had some placer deposits, but most were exhausted in antiquity. About 300 tonnes of gold were extracted in Macedonia and Thrace between 1200 BC and AD 50. In recent times the Axios and Gallikos rivers north of Thessalonica have yielded the most gold. This placer gold originated in the

Gold: stalk of wheat in gold, from Ptolemaic Egypt, the source of most Greek gold, Sotheby's, New York

metamorphic rocks of the region. Some of these primary deposits were also directly exploited by the Thracians on Mount Pangaeum, where the gold occurs in quartz veins with pyrite.

There were several gold mines on the island of Thasos, and those near Kinyra, visited by Herodotus in the 5th century BC, were considered to be the most important. Much of the gold here, and on Siphnos, occurs in primary deposits of quartz veins with pyrite and copper sulphides. However, recently it has been found that the highest concentrations of gold on Thasos occur in sediments filling cavities in the marble host-rock. These cavities form by solution of the carbonate minerals in percolating rainwater, exactly as caves form in limestones. Streams that ran through these passages washed in the gold-bearing sediments to make these underground placer gold deposits.

The most famous ancient gold deposits of the Aegean region were those of Lydia. Exploitation of these very rich placer deposits of the Pactolus river started around 700 BC, but were exhausted by Strabo's time. The gold originated in quartz-gold veins in the metamorphic rocks to the south. Weathering liberated the gold, which was then transported by rivers and laid down in sandstones and conglomerates in the Gediz valley, some of which underlie the acropolis of Sardis. At a later time these rocks were again weathered and the gold redeposited in the beds of the present rivers. It is this two-stage process that gave the unusually high concentrations of gold here.

Much ancient gold used in the Aegean region was probably imported from Egypt. There it was first extracted from placer deposits of the Nile valley. Later, quartz-gold veins in the Eastern Desert were exploited, first from opencast and then from underground mines. Gold was also obtained from Nubia to the south (*Nub* means "gold" in Ancient Egyptian).

Although gold commonly occurs as the native metal, it is not usually pure, but alloyed with silver and copper. The silver alloy was called electrum on account of its colour, which was said to resemble that of amber. On occasion silver was deliberately added to extend the more valuable gold. This process was called *diplosis* ("doubling") by the early Egyptian goldsmiths. The gold content of such alloys was determined by the use of touchstones. These are small smoothed pieces of fine-grained, dark rock, hard enough to abrade gold. The gold was rubbed on the rock and the colour of the streak was used to determine the purity. The best touchstones were said to come from near Sardis, hence the synonym "Lydian stone". Many different types of rock were used, such as chert, siltstone, hornfels, and tuff.

Another impurity in much ancient gold is represented by minute grains of white metal of the platinum group of elements. These metal grains occur in serpentinites and are concentrated in placer deposits. The common presence of these grains attests to the importance of placer, as opposed to primary gold. Such grains could be a nuisance to goldworkers but were rarely removed.

The earliest attempts at refining were probably concerned with the removal of copper from gold. This can be done by heating the molten metal in a stream of air. During this process of cupellation the copper would be oxidized to form a slag. Separation of silver from gold was more complex. It was first developed at Sardis during the late 7th century BC. Electrum was mixed with salt and brick dust in a pot. The pot was heated for a long time without melting the metal, so that all the silver would be converted into chlorides and absorbed into the brick dust.

The Byzantines held gold in high esteem and used it as widely as possible, not only in its pure form but also in alloys with silver and copper. Gold was used for coins, medals, jewellery, and liturgical vessels. Further applications included the use of gold foil in mosaic, icon painting, and book illumination. Emperors dined off gold plates; and the ultimate seal of authority in Byzantium was the imperial *chrysobull* or golden seal.

MICHAEL D. HIGGINS

Further Reading

Craddock, Paul T., *Early Metal Mining and Production*, Edinburgh: Edinburgh University Press, and Washington, DC: Smithsonian Institution Press, 1995

Healey, John F., *Mining and Metallurgy in the Greek and Roman World*, London: Thames and Hudson, 1978

Higgins, Michael Denis and Reynold Higgins, *A Geological Companion to Greece and the Aegean*, London: Duckworth, and Ithaca, New York: Cornell University Press, 1996

Rapson, W.S., "Mining, Extraction and Refining of Gold", *Interdisciplinary Science Reviews*, 17/3 (1992): pp. 203–12

Wagner, Günther A. and Gerd Weisgerber, *Antike Edel- und Bunt-Metallgewinnung auf Thasos*, Bochum: Deutsches Bergbau-Museum, 1988

Gortyn

City in Crete

The site of Gortyn lies 16 km inland from the south coast of Crete. Originally a Minoan settlement, it was refounded by Greek immigrants from Achaea, Thessaly, and Arcadia (central Peloponnese), followed by Dorians. From the 4th century BC Gortyn seems to have been involved in perpetual feuding with Knossos, each city striving for superiority over the other. When the Cretan cities became involved in war with Rome, Gortyn sided with the Romans in 66–65 BC and was rewarded by the victorious Quintus Caecilius Metellus with the title of *maxima civitas* and the position of provincial capital of the Roman province comprising Crete and Cyrene.

The early history of Gortyn is associated with the Gortyn law code of *c.*450 BC, found built into a wall of the odeum which was restored *c.*AD 100, though the inscription bearing the code may always have been visible. The code deals with a range of private legal matters, including family property, adoption procedures, slaves, mortgages, sureties, and donations. It reveals that slaves had certain rights, including that of permission to marry free women. Rape was a civil offence punishable by a fine, the amount depending on the status of the victim. A magistrate could use his discretion to decide whether a rape had been committed. This most important source of social and legal conditions in the Archaic–Classical period indicates the existence of a highly stratified society in which disputes over property rights and successions played a major part.

In the Roman period Gortyn continued to be the most important city in Crete. Christianity was preached early in the island. In the Pastoral Epistles Paul is represented as sending Titus to Crete "to set in order things that are wanting" and to ordain elders in every city (Titus 1: 5). Gortyn may have been one of these, for by *c.*170 AD we learn from Eusebius of Caesarea (*Eccles. Hist.* 4. 21 and 23) that Philip was bishop of Gortyn. He received a letter from Bishop Dionysius of Corinth praising him for his "many noble acts" and putting him on his guard against heresies. Gortyn had already won a good reputation which Philip was upholding against heresies, suggesting a relatively long-established Christian community there. Gortyn was the metropolitan see of Crete and the remains of seven churches have been found, including one dedicated to Hagios Titos, the presumed founder of the bishopric.

Exploration of the ruins of Gortyn up to World War I revealed the remains of a praetorium, baths, an amphitheatre, and circus as well as the Christian churches. The city, which covered an area of 150 hectares, was abandoned during the 7th century under increasing pressure from Arab raiders.

WILLIAM H.C. FREND

Summary

A city in central Crete, Gortyn was originally a Minoan settlement. It is famous for its law code (*c.*450 BC) which survives as an inscription on a wall of the odeum. In the Roman period it was the capital of the province of Crete and Cyrene. Christianity arrived early and remains of seven churches survive. Gortyn was abandoned in the 7th century AD.

Further Reading

Burchner, Gortyn entry in *Real-Encyclopädie der klassischen Altertumswissenschaft*, edited by August Pauly *et al.*, vol. 7, 1912, 1165–71 (includes map of the ruins discovered by that date)

Ehrenberg, Victor *et al.*, Gortyn entry in *The Oxford Classical Dictionary*, 3rd edition, edited by Simon Hornblower and Antony Spawforth, Oxford and New York: Oxford University Press, 1996, p. 643

Willetts, R.F., *The Law Code of Gortyn*, Berlin: de Gruyter, 1967

Goths

Germanic people

Jordanes, a writer of the 5th century AD, gives a southern-Scandinavian origin to the Goths who migrated early in the Christian period to settle around the lower Vistula. Archaeological evidence, however, only supports a migration from the lower Vistula region to an area north of the Black Sea in the second half of the 2nd century AD. In 238 they began raiding the Roman empire, especially the Balkans, Asia Minor, and Greece. Victories by the emperors Gallienus (253/260–68), Claudius (268–70), who won the title Gothicus for his exploits against them, and Aurelian (270–75) largely ended the land and seaborne attacks, but only after one group (later known as the Visigoths) occupied Dacia on the left bank of the Danube, forcing Aurelian to withdraw Roman troops and administrators from the area. Out of an unknown number of groups operating under separate chieftainships, a second major group emerged and established a strong presence in the Ukraine. A large number of these Goths (later they formed the Ostrogoths) were absorbed by the Huns in the early 370s and only rose to prominence after the collapse of the Hunnic empire in the middle of the 5th century.

The westward advance of the Huns, and perhaps tribal conflicts, drove two groups of Goths across to the right side of the Danube into Roman territory, creating a chaotic situation that resulted in the battle of Adrianople (378). The resounding Gothic victory over the Roman army and subsequent devastation of the Thracian countryside temporarily shook Roman confidence but the Goths were unable to exploit their military superiority in any significant manner. The emperors Gratian and, later, Theodosius, realizing that a stable and peaceful Gothic people benefited everyone, arranged treaties by which the Visigoths were allowed to settle as federates with special status within Roman territory: in Pannonia (380) and in Lower Moesia (382).

The terms of the treaties were far from perfect but the Goths maintained peace with the empire until after the battle of the Frigidus river (394) where Theodosius' eastern forces engaged those of the usurper, Eugenius. Here the Goths fought for Theodosius under the command of their own chieftain, Alaric I (395–410), but were subject to other commanders who cared little for them so long as the battle was won. The eastern forces prevailed at a terrible cost to the Goths who had been thrown almost as fodder against the enemy. More than half of their 20,000-strong force was lost. Their enforced idleness the next year at Milan, Theodosius' temporary base, must have produced a tension-filled situation. At least this would help to explain why Stilicho, the commander at Milan after Theodosius' death (395), released the Goths, who then returned east only to discover that their Moesian homes had been raided by the Huns.

Alaric immediately marched his force to Constantinople where he obtained better terms for his people, including high military office for himself. The treaty was satisfactory enough to convince the Goths to depart but did not resolve their needs. Over the next 15 years, led by their king Alaric, the Goths devastated large parts of Greece and the Balkans in an attempt to stabilize their situation. Fighting for their own sake, they sometimes aided the eastern empire, sometimes the western empire. All was done to secure their most urgent objective: a safe and permanent territory for their people.

Before a year had lapsed since the signing of the treaty of 395, changes at Constantinople had made Alaric and his Goths outsiders once again. Moving southward through Greece, they ravaged much of Boeotia and captured the Piraeus. Athens only escaped their depredations by bribing the Goths to bypass the city as they moved southward into the Peloponnese where they remained for over a year (396–97). After a confrontation with Stilicho's forces near Olympia that came to nothing, Alaric moved his Goths first to Epirus and then into Macedonia where, according to a new treaty, territory west of Thessalonica, between the Haliakmon and Axios rivers, had been set aside for the Goths to settle as federates.

More than once during this time the Goths had been at a military disadvantage, but Alaric managed to extricate his forces by employing what must have been considerable diplomatic skills. No doubt, his group's potential as a powerful ally helped in negotiations with both the eastern and western empires, yet Alaric had forged a unified Gothic entity that could, and did, become a serious threat to those who would use them. The lack of secure territory for settlement and the desire to have their own high-ranking commanders within the Roman military structure compelled the Goths continually to break with their imperial allies. Eventually the quest to fulfil these needs led to the Gothic invasion of Italy in 401, which culminated with the sack of Rome on 24 August 410. After temporarily installing their own emperor in Rome, the Visigoths moved into Gaul and Spain where they finally established their own kingdom centred first at Toulouse (418–507) and then in Spain (507–711/725).

The Goths who had remained under Hunnic control until the death of Attila (453) and the battle of the Nedao river (454/5) established themselves in two rival groups on the right bank of the Danube. One group, subdivided under the rule of three brothers, settled as federates of the eastern empire in Pannonia. The other band settled in Thrace, nearer to events in Constantinople.

The most important of these Goths was the son of the chieftain Thiudimir, Theodoric, who was raised in Pannonia until the age of eight. His next ten years were spent in Constantinople as a hostage where he became acquainted with activity at the court and observed barbarian commanders of high rank. At the age of 18 he returned to his people, becoming the leader of the united Goths of his region in 474. The year before, these Goths had moved into Macedonia to establish a kingdom but this was a short-lived venture. No later than 476 they had returned to the Danube in Lower Moesia where they secured a kingdom centred around Novae-Svistov (Bulgaria).

About this time, in 475, the emperor Zeno was driven out of Constantinople, partly through the influence of the Thracian Goths under the command of Theodoric Strabo (son of Triarius), who now became the supreme commander of the imperial army. Theodoric, son of Thiudimir, quickly allied himself with Zeno against their rivals on the promise of increased status for himself and recognition of his Goths.

Now these two eastern Gothic groups came into direct conflict as they competed for the favour of the emperor who attempted to play them off against each other. The following years were filled with chaotic conflicts as the Goths of Theodoric moved across the Balkan peninsula and into Epirus (c.479/80) where they established a fourth kingdom. The accidental death of Theodoric Strabo in 481 ended the strife between the Gothic groups, who soon were amalgamated into the Ostrogoths under Theodoric's command.

With this large unified force, Theodoric represented a serious threat to the eastern empire. Greece suffered great devastation in 482 and was only spared further disaster when Zeno made a treaty (483) granting the Goths land and making Theodoric supreme commander and consul-elect for 484. By 487, however, the relationship between the emperor and Theodoric had deteriorated to such a point that the Gothic king led his forces to the walls of Constantinople, forcing Zeno to negotiate once more.

The strategic solution was to send Theodoric and his Ostrogoths against Odovacar to recover Italy. Theodoric set out in 489 and by March of 493 had undisputed control of Italy following his brutal murder of Odovacar and his family. His own kingdom briefly united the Visigoths and Ostrogoths (511–26) before it fell to Justinian's onslaught in the middle of the 6th century.

Andrew N. Sherwood

Summary

The Goths were a Germanic people who originated in southern Scandinavia and settled in an area north of the Black Sea in the 2nd century AD. Driven west by the Huns, they defeated the Romans at the battle of Adrianople in 378. First accommodated and then slighted, the Goths under Alaric continued to harass Greece until 401 when they invaded Italy. These Visigoths (who later moved to Gaul and Spain) and the Ostrogoths (who remained in the east) remained a threat to the empire until the reconquests of Justinian.

Further Reading

Cameron, Alan and Jacqueline Long, *Barbarians and Politics at the Court of Arcadius*, Berkeley: University of California Press, 1993

Chrysos, Evangelos K., *To Byzantion kai hoi Gotthoi* [Byzantium and the Goths], Thessalonica, 1972

Goffart, Walter A., *Barbarians and Romans* AD *418–584: The Techniques of Accommodation*, Princeton, New Jersey: Princeton University Press, 1980

Gordon, Colin D., *The Age of Attila: Fifth-Century Byzantium and the Barbarians*, Ann Arbor: University of Michigan Press, 1960, reprinted 1966

Hachmann, Rolf, *The Germanic Peoples*, London: Barrie and Jenkins, 1971

Heather, Peter J., "The Crossing of the Danube and the Gothic Conversion", *Greek, Roman and Byzantine Studies*, 27 (1986): pp. 289–318

Heather, Peter J., "Cassiodorus and the Rise of the Amals: Genealogy and the Goths under Hun Domination", *Journal of Roman Studies*, 79 (1989): pp. 103–28

Heather, Peter J., *Goths and Romans, 332–489*, Oxford: Clarendon Press, and New York: Oxford University Press, 1991

Heather, Peter J. and John F. Matthews, *The Goths in the Fourth Century*, Liverpool: Liverpool University Press, 1991

Heather, Peter J., "Theodoric, King of the Goths", *Early Medieval Europe*, 4/2 (1995): pp. 145–73

Heather, Peter J., *The Goths*, Oxford and Cambridge, Massachusetts: Blackwell, 1996

Jones, A.H.M., *The Later Roman Empire, 284–602: A Social, Economic and Administrative Survey*, 3 vols, Oxford: Blackwell, and Norman: University of Oklahoma Press, 1964

Kazanski, Michel, *Les Goths: Ier.–VIIe. siècles après J.-C.*, Paris: Errance, 1991

Liebeschuetz, J.H.W.G., *Barbarians and Bishops: Army, Church, and State in the Age of Arcadius*, Oxford: Clarendon Press, and New York: Oxford University Press, 1990

Thompson, E.A., "The Visigoths from Fritigern to Euric", *Historia*, 12 (1963): pp. 105–26

Thompson, E.A., *The Early Germans*, Oxford: Clarendon Press, 1965

Thompson, E.A., *The Visigoths in the Time of Ulfila*, Oxford: Clarendon Press, 1966

Todd, Malcolm, *The Early Germans*, Oxford and Cambridge, Massachusetts: Blackwell, 1992

Wolfram, Herwig, *History of the Goths*, revised edition, Berkeley: University of California Press, 1988

Wolfram, Herwig, *The Roman Empire and Its Germanic Peoples*, Berkeley: University of California Press, 1997

Government, Theories of

The Classical approach to politics and government was concerned both with the institutional features of political regimes and with the question of the relationship between philosophy and government. The polis, the city state which presented the context for the development of that approach, was in many respects unique. From the perspective of the theory of government, the institutions of the polis can be illustrated by taking Athens as a model, since it was mainly Athens that provided the environment and the inspiration for political philosophy. The model, which was characteristic of Athens during the period of the city's greatest power, was based on the constitutional reforms of Cleisthenes (507 BC). Male citizens formed the Assembly (*Ekklesia*), the forum of direct democracy, which met regularly. The elected bodies were the Council of Five Hundred and the courts. But election to these bodies reflected a notion of representation very different from that which developed after the Middle Ages in Europe. The system of filling offices was a combination of election and lot: the townships (*demoi*) of Athens elected candidates and the holders of office were then chosen by lot from those elected. For the Athenians this system was democratic because it equalized the citizens' chances to hold office. The idea of citizenship was deeply participatory and left an unmistakable mark on Greek theories of government.

Political philosophy and the theory of government developed after the end of the Peloponnesian War and the defeat of Athens. The idealized account of the Athenian regime presented by Thucydides (in the Periclean Funeral Oration) emphasized both the civic commitment by the citizen and the confident and relaxed quality of life in Athens. The focus throughout was on the balance accomplished by Athenian political life between participation and freedom, public-mindedness and self-development. The civic greatness of the Periclean age was exemplified in a civilized way of life, in culture, and, characteristically, in the art of the 5th century BC. By contrast, the academic specialization of Athens came with the years of decline. Plato's Academy (385 BC) and, some 50 years later, Aristotle's Lyceum were founded in the aftermath of the humiliation of the model city state.

In the *Republic* Plato sought to define justice and asked whether justice can be found or created in the world of the polis. Plato's sublime exposition of his philosophical ideal in the *Republic* should be considered in conjunction with his account of "a half-way house between the actual and the ideal" (Barker, 1918, p. 183) in the *Laws*, written almost 30 years after the *Republic*. In the *Laws* an Athenian discusses with a Spartan and a Cretan the possible constitutional arrangements of government in a projected colony. Although there are also Spartan influences in Plato's thought, the Athenian model remains central in both positive and negative ways.

But the most important classical influence upon later theory comes from Aristotle, who was a member of Plato's Academy until Plato's death in 347 BC. Aristotle took over Plato's interest in political philosophy but approached its themes from a markedly different perspective. Aristotle's theory of political regimes in *Politics* proposes a classificatory model with three main types of organization of government: monarchy, aristocracy, and constitutional government. There are also three deviations: tyranny, oligarchy, democracy. Actual regimes vary, depending on the distribution of power according to rank and wealth. In addition to the analytical discussion in *Politics*, Aristotle undertook the empirical investigation of the operation of government in contemporary city states. These empirical studies, unarguably the first texts in the history of comparative political science, are lost, with the exception of the *Athenian Constitution*. Of equal significance has been the moral and political philosophy outlined in *Nicomachean Ethics*, a work of immense theoretical and methodological influence. For Plato the quest for truth was an ascent from mere opinions to the light of reality. There was an unbridgeable gap between the two. By contrast, Aristotle (and political science in the Western tradition since then) takes as a starting point common opinions in the polis, aiming to explicate and eliminate the inner difficulties which arise from an analytical consideration of these opinions. Regarding political methodology, Aristotle made two main contributions. First, he established political science as a comprehensive social science on the assumption that its comprehensive character corresponds to the comprehensive character of the political community. Other communities (social, religious, and so on) are parts of the political community which regulates them for the common good. Second, starting from the assumption that the choice of method (and degree of exactness) will depend on the subject matter, Aristotle put forward a distinct method of political inquiry, arguing that the objects of political science rest on human convention not nature.

The centrality of Plato and Aristotle for the future development of the theory of government cannot be readily gauged from an examination of the schools of political thought that immediately followed the two great thinkers. The schools of the Epicureans and the Cynics, which began some 30 years after Aristotle, followed new lines of thought which centred respectively on the pursuit of happiness through avoidance of pain and anxiety and on protest against social convention. These lines (which, despite their differences, converged in their withdrawal from the sphere of political activity) were to become influential at a later stage, more so in western Europe than in Greece. In the latter the theory of government evolved in interaction with the kingdoms of the Hellenistic world beyond the Greek peninsula. The most important school of thought in the century that followed Aristotle's death, the Stoics, tolerated and occasionally defended the new monarchies, which were aiming at the integration of Greeks and people living in Asia. The theory of the deified king as a symbol of unity became influential throughout the Hellenistic world and was later partly adopted by the Romans. By the end of the 2nd century BC, however, Stoicism was revised by Panaetius of Rhodes. The revision was meant to recultivate Stoicism's moral philosophical content and in the process began to look back to ideas drawn from Plato and Aristotle. Panaetius worked on a humanitarian and universalist version of Stoicism, according to which justice is the bond that keeps polities together. In so far as a polity becomes unjust, it loses that basis of harmony which makes it a polity. This approach had great influence on Cicero and Roman legal theory, but it also signified a degree of adaptation of Platonic and Aristotelian concerns in the new context of a Mediterranean world which was becoming increasingly integrated economically and culturally (Sabine and Thorson, 1973, pp. 151–52).

Although the role of Roman legal institutions and norms remained significant throughout the years between the inauguration of the eastern capital in Constantinople in AD 330 and its fall in AD 1453, the prevalent model of government in the Byzantine empire combined elements of the deified king of the Hellenistic period and of eastern theocratic traditions. The result was a model that stressed the sacred character of the person of the emperor. Under Ottoman rule the Patriarch of Constantinople was granted the authority of the spiritual and political leader (*Millet Basi*) of the Christians. The role of the Orthodox Church was religious and supranational (ecumenical), that is, the Church guaranteed the institutionalized distinction between Christians and Muslims and was responsible for both the religious and the administrative guidance of the former within the framework of Ottoman rule. But the actual organization of government was complex, varied from region to region, and manifested a variable mix of influences by local notables, the Orthodox Church, and the Ottoman rulers. It must be stressed that Roman (Justinianic) law remained significant in many regions throughout the years of Ottoman rule, thereby providing an important normative thread alongside the other elements of continuity, notably linguistic and religious.

After the establishment of an independent Greek state in 1830 the building of political institutions became the focus of political debate and controversy. During the War of Independence there were declarations by the national assemblies in republican directions, but geostrategic realities, foreign influences, and domestic complications eventually led to the imposition of monarchy. After the 1830s it became evident that different sociopolitical factions championed different models of government. Those who wanted to initiate a process of state-building in the Western tradition pushed for a centralized state with strong executive and rationalized administrative structures. On the other hand, those who wished to retain the power of local notables had a preference for more decentralized governmental structures. At the level of political ideas, the Enlightenment exerted considerable influence on important intellectuals, but the power structure of the new state was based on a conservative coalition that proved inimical to the widespread acceptance of liberalism and human rights theories (Kitromilides, 1994). The establishment of the University of Athens, in 1837, contributed to the cultivation of a Western cultural environment, but its main objective was the training of personnel for the state institutions. In 1833 the Greek Orthodox Church broke away from the Patriarchate of Constantinople, and less than two decades later its status as a state Church had become clear. The weakness of liberal ideas in combination with the establishment of Orthodoxy as a state Church resulted in a persistent democratic deficit in the treatment of other religions (Pollis, 1988).

Despite the power of the conservative local oligarchies, the Western governmental model prevailed. But the state apparatus soon became dominated from within by the so-called *tzakia*, influential families whose origins can be traced to those local notables (*proestoi*) who had played a critical role during the War of Independence. By and large, the *tzakia* increasingly favoured a loose parliamentary model, since the latter, adapted to 19th-century Greek conditions, would simultaneously constrain the capacities and the reach of central authority and assist these patrician families to strengthen their role in the state, based on their local power resources and their extensive presence in parliament. In 1875 the king accepted the parliamentary principle in government formation, although parliamentarism had already been declared in 1844. The balance thus achieved survived until 1909, when the coup set in motion developments that favoured the ascendancy of liberal statesmen and the prevalence of liberal institutions. The formation of a differentiated and operational political system, a rationalized bureaucracy, and a professional army was a slow and difficult process, and it was not before the 1920s that the Greek state can be said to have acquired a modern structure of governmental authority.

The study of government in modern Greek political science and political theory grew out of the study of constitutional law. In this respect the institutions of the Second (1924–35) and the

Third Republic (1974–) have been important as points of reference for the evolution of constitutional theory. The latter remains in continuous interaction with the theory of government, even as the scope of inquiry widens and a number of factors, both domestic and "external", are brought in.

Four different approaches in the study of goverment can be distinguished, which incorporate partly different concepts of government. First, there is the approach which concentrates on the structure of governmental authority and the formal arrangements of the offices of government. This is typical of much work in the field before the 1970s and reveals the legal background of Greek political science. The focus on the formal institutions of government resulted in certain important contributions, along with some descriptive work. It is noteworthy that this approach often combined a legal lineage and an interest in analytical Greek political theory. For example, in this approach classifications of government still rely to a considerable extent on the Aristotelian typology of regimes. Second, there is the approach which examines the executive authority in the state. This signifies a constraining and sometimes confusing identification of government with the executive authority. Again, work that can be grouped in this category reveals a legal background.

The third and fourth approaches distance themselves from the constitutional-legal terrain. It is important at this point to stress that certain influential constitutional theorists in the early decades of the 20th century proved sensitive to the political and social dimensions of government (notably N.N. Saripolos and Alexandros Svolos). But the theory of government in these approaches remained for the most part constrained by its subject matter, the structure and operation of the constitutional edifice. The third approach, then, is concerned with the process of governing, including the various formal and informal aspects of policy making and the ways in which sociopolitical interaction influences and becomes itself influenced by political power. Finally, the fourth approach possesses a philosophical lineage and is concerned with the art of government, the criteria for assessing good government, and the relationship between government and moral values.

The conservative modernization drive of the late 1950s and early 1960s under Constantine Karamanlis was combined with the quest for a strong executive. One particular aspect of the Platonic theory of government, the view of guardianship, resurfaced in the conservative constitutional theory of the 1950s and 1960s (in the work of Constantine Tsatsos), reflecting the efforts to anchor the semiauthoritarian modernization drive in Greek political philosophy. In 1967 a coup installed an authoritarian regime, apparently aimed at blocking the possibility of a centre-left government emerging from the planned elections of that year. The regime tried unsuccessfully to institutionalize itself and collapsed amid foreign policy crisis and domestic upheaval in 1974, changing dramatically the contours of the theory and practice of government. The authoritarian potential in conservative rule having exhausted itself, the new equilibrium which was reflected in the 1975 republican constitution allowed the operation of liberal institutions, lifted the ban on the communist left, and sought to reorient the role of the army in the political system. However, elements of continuity with the situation before the coup were equally significant. The emphasis on a strong executive essentially represented a continuity from political strategies before 1967, only this time the organization of relationships between the head of state, the government, and the parliament revealed the influence of French semi-presidentialism. Also the regime change in 1974 did little to challenge the inherited corporatist structures which govern the participation of organized interests in the making and implementation of policy. The transformation of interest politics was gradual and took place in the 1980s and 1990s through the shifts, abandonment, or step-by-step revision of the structures of policy making and collective action.

Despite its opportunist aspects, the limited constitutional revision of 1986 reflected a shift in the balance of both practical politics and theoretical views. The revision's aim was to enhance further the role of the prime minister and to constrain the president of the republic, whose role became largely ceremonial. To some extent, the revision was consistent with the socialist (PASOK) analysis of the 1975 constitution as arming the president with extensive powers and distorting parliamentarism. But in the precise form it aquired, the revision expressed the immediate political concerns of the then prime minister Andreas Papandreou and the experience of cohabitation between Papandreou and Karamanlis. In this sense, it was an unnecessarily drastic reduction of the powers of the head of state; a more reasoned revision might have resulted in more efficient organization of constitutional relationships. In fact, the revision reflected the populist majoritarian thrust of the PASOK governments' policy in the 1980s. One aspect of that approach was the combination of the strengthening of the executive authority in the state and the promotion of further politicization of the administrative structures (Makridimitris, 1992). Another aspect was a certain impatience with elaborate institutional checks and balances. In this particular respect, A. Papandreou's approach to governing was not very different from the early disregard of Karamanlis for the static quality of intricate politics.

Government changed in both form (governmental and administrative structures) and content (policies) as a result of increased participation in the process of European integration since 1981. The theory of government traces the impact of convergence and Europeanization on policies, institutions, and rules of the game (Lavdas, 1997; Ioakimidis, 1998). Changes in the spatial organization of government have been studied more extensively, concerning not only the growth of local governments but, more importantly, the attempted regionalization of a country which (like Portugal or Ireland) had no inherited regional tiers of government. The emergence of new models of government is closely linked to the emerging pluralism of the centres of policy-making and the multiplication of policy actors at various levels: local, regional, national, transnational, European, global. The overall picture in the 1990s is one of a transitional, mixed, and segmented pluralism, where pockets of corporatist-interest intermediation coexist with pluralist arenas. The possibility of later (after 2001) Greek participation in the euro opens up a rich field of debate on how to approach government and democratic accountability in a multilevel decision-making framework in which European institutional building falls behind developments in monetary and economic unification. In a framework, that is, in which government currently appears to follow economics.

KOSTAS A. LAVDAS

See also Aristocracy, Constitution, Democracy, Junta, Monarchy, Oligarchy, Republic, Tyranny

Further Reading

Alivizatos, Nicos C., *Les Institutions politiques de la Grèce à travers les crises, 1922-1974*, Paris: Librairie Générale de Droit et de Jurisprudence, 1979

Barker, Ernest, *Greek Political Theory: Plato and His Predecessors*, London: Methuen, 1918, reprinted New York: Barnes and Noble, 1960

Clogg, Richard (editor), *Greece 1981[-]89: The Populist Decade*, Basingstoke: Macmillan, and New York: St Martin's Press, 1993

Connor, W. Robert, *Thucydides*, Princeton, New Jersey: Princeton University Press, 1984

Contogeorgis, Georgios, "I Politiki Epistimi stin Ellada" [Political Science in Greece], *To Vima ton Koinonikon Epistimon*, 23 (1998)

Diamandouros, Nikiforos and Michalis Spourdalakis, "I Politiki Epistimi stin Ellada" [Political Science in Greece] in *Information Bulletin*, edited by Maria Mendrinou, Athens: Hellenic Political Science Association, 1997

Ioakimidis, Panayotis, *I Evropaiki Enosi kai to Elliniko Kratos* [The European Union and the Greek State: Effects from Participation in the Integrative Process], Athens: Themelio, 1998

Kitromilides, Paschalis M., *Enlightenment, Nationalism, Orthodoxy: Studies in the Culture and Political Thought of South-eastern Europe*, Aldershot, Hampshire: Variorum, 1994

Lavdas, Kostas A., *The Europeanization of Greece: Interest Politics and the Crises of Integration*, Basingstoke: Macmillan, and New York: St Martin's Press, 1997

Makridimitris, Antonis, *I Organosi tis Kivernisis* [The Organization of Government], Athens: Sakkoulas, 1992

Mavrogordatos, George T., *Stillborn Republic: Social Coalitions and Party Strategies in Greece, 1922-1936*, Berkeley: University of California Press, 1983

Mouzelis, Nicos P., *Modern Greece: Facets of Underdevelopment*, London: Macmillan, and New York: Holmes and Meier, 1978

Patrinelis, Christos, "Ekklesia kai Orthodoxia" [The Church and Orthodoxy], in *History of the Greek Nation*, vol. 10, Athens: Ekdotiki Athinon, 1974

Pollis, Adamantia, *Kratos, Dikaio kai Anthropina Dikaiomata stin Ellada* [The State, Law and Human Rights in Greece], Athens: Foundation for Mediterranean Studies, 1988

Sabine, George Holland and Thomas Landon Thorson, *A History of Political Theory*, 4th edition, Hinsdale, Illinois: Dryden Press, 1973

Tessitore, Aristide, *Reading Aristotle's Ethics: Virtue, Rhetoric, and Political Philosophy*, Albany: State University of New York Press, 1996

Zweigert, Konrad and Hein Koetz, *Introduction to Comparative Law*, 3rd edition, Oxford: Clarendon Press, and New York: Oxford University Press, 1988

Graeco-Turkish War 1897

The adverse impact of the 1897 war on the morale of the Greek nation and its delayed after-effects on Greek politics were certainly more significant than the event itself which commenced on 27 March (Old Style; 8 April New Style) 1897 and was terminated with the 7 (19) May armistice of that year.

This accidental conflagration was the undesirable byproduct of an irredentist ideology that had become the hallmark of Greek foreign policy throughout the 19th century. Between 1844 and 1897 Greece pursued its irredentist guerrilla warfare against the Ottoman empire with native irregulars or soldiers of fortune from Crete and Macedonia. Brigand groups were on many occasions granted pardon if they volunteered their services to the patriotic cause.

The culprits responsible for inflaming public opinion on the side of confrontation included the press, the political parties, the government of Theodoros Deliyannis, and the royal family. The most pernicious influence came from a clandestine organization bearing the name the "National Society", founded by young army officers in November 1894. A year later prominent civilians were admitted, but until early 1896 only eight out of 130 members were not officers. It was after the spring of that year that a stream of well-known Athenians began to enter the society.

In spite of the patriotic sound and fury, however, the morale of the Greek officer corps on the eve of the war was sagging. The 1893 default of Greece on its external debt had diminished the military budget from close to 59 million drachmas in 1895 to less than 20 million eight years later. The irredentist fever that seized the country in 1897 was certainly not compatible with the prevailing austerity in public finances. Nevertheless, in January 1897 the Cretans defied Ottoman rule and proclaimed their unification with Greece, while the latter responded by sending a small expeditionary force under Colonel Timoleon Vassos to their rescue. Although the naval forces of the great powers (with the exception of Britain) blockaded the island, Greek public opinion demanded of the government to stand by its decision to annex Crete.

The National Society played a pivotal role in pushing prime minister Theodoros Deliyannis over the brink. The episode that unleashed the dogs of war was the incursion of 3000 Greek irregulars into Ottoman-held Macedonia at the end of March. On 5 April the Sublime Porte severed diplomatic relations with Athens and declared war. From the outset hostilities erupted on two fronts, in Epirus and in Thessaly. The performance of the commander-in-chief, Crown Prince Constantine, left much to be desired. One week after the skirmishes commenced, the Greek forces retreated in disarray.

On 12 April the Turks captured the Thessalian city of Tirnavo, and on 13 April they entered Larissa. Between 14 and 24 April the decisive battle of Velestino was fought and lost by the Greek army. On 26 April the vital port of Volos was taken by the Ottomans and on 5 May the last battle was waged in Domokos.

The Ottoman army, superior in numbers and organized by German officers, found no match in the diminutive Greek forces. Faced with the imminent threat of collapse, Greece hurried to an armistice on 7 May. The peace terms, however, were lenient and, thanks to British intervention, no territorial losses were incurred by Greece. However, since the war indemnity of four million Turkish pounds to the Ottomans could not be paid by an insolvent state, Germany proposed that Greek finances be controlled by an international finance commission, which would also supervise the servicing of Greece's external debts.

Surprisingly, the apple of the particular discord, Crete, was granted complete autonomy and in 1898 Prince George, the second son of King George I of the Hellenes, became High Commissioner of the island.

One year after the first modern Olympic games, which were held in Athens, the self-esteem of the nation, elevated to heights of romantic delusion, plummeted to the depths of pessimism. The 1897 debacle obliged Deliyannis to step down from the premiership, an attempt was made against the life of King George, and members of the royal family were castigated by the press. Literature and poetry, in hot pursuit of 1897, produced works of despair, anger, and satire. The sarcastic verse of George Souris left neither the royal palace nor the exponents of the war unscathed, while scores of melancholy novels were based on the traumatic event. It was only in 1902 that the poet laureate, Kostis Palamas, with his *Flute of the King*, dared to revive the hope of national resurrection after the humiliation of 1897.

THANOS M. VEREMIS

See also Constantine I, Deliyannis, George I, Palamas

Further Reading

Campbell, John and Philip Sherrard, *Modern Greece*, London: Benn, and New York: Praeger, 1968, pp. 106–07

Koliopoulos, John S., *Brigands with a Cause: Brigandage and Irredentism in Modern Greece, 1821–1912*, Oxford: Clarendon Press, 1987, pp. 215–23

Lefkoparidis X. (editor), *Stratigou P. G. Dangli: Anamniseis, engrapha, allilographia* [The Archives of General P.G. Dangli: Reminiscences, Documents, Correspondence], vol. 1, Athens: Vayonaki, 1965, pp. 136–80

Pikros, I.P., "Pros ton polemo tou 1897" [Towards the War of 1897], *Istoria tou Ellinikou Ethnous* [History of the Greek Nation], vol. 14, Athens, 1977, pp. 88–125, 127–60

Veremis, Thanos, *The Military in Greek Politics: From Independence to Democracy*, London: Hurst, 1997, pp. 39–49

Grammar

The term "grammar" comes from the Classical Greek *grammatike techne* (later abbreviated to *grammatike*), which simply means "skill of writing" (Greek *gramma*, "alphabetic character", "writing"). Accordingly, the *grammatikos* was someone who knew the alphabetic characters, who was able to read. In Hellenistic times *grammatike* progressively took on the meaning of "linguistic and literary studies", i.e. the present sense of "philology". This was a result of the influence and development of various intellectual movements. Consequently the term *grammatikos* stood for a professional philologist, someone who was concerned with textual criticism and the interpretation of Classical works. In Late Antiquity a semantic narrowing occurred: grammar was now simply understood as phonology and morphology, which still form the central field of grammar. The Romans adopted the terminology together with the contents. The loan translation *litteratura*, however,

was not applied in this field, whereas the Greek loan word (*ars*) *grammatica* passed as a technical term into most European languages.

In antiquity the systematic scholarly exploration of language and the development of proper grammatical terms were the work of philosophers. Although they were simply considering their own language and not doing any comparative linguistics in a modern sense, the Greeks nevertheless managed to create a terminology that is still in use by observing and compiling linguistic facts and arranging them into different fields. The first philosophical discussions about language date from the time of the Sophists (5th century BC) with a focus on the relation between word and object. Rather casually, philosophers also touched on grammatical topics: they distinguished for instance three genders of the noun. Plato's *Cratylus*, in which he deals thoroughly with linguistic problems, offers the basics of phonology. Alphabetic characters are distinguished according to vowels and consonants, and words are analysed in syllables. Syntax is also addressed in addition to morphology; for the first time the denotations *onoma* ("noun"), and *rhema* ("verb"), are explicitly introduced as parts of speech. The terminology was taken up and partly refined by Aristotle. He explained that conjunctions and particles are also parts of speech, as are articles and demonstrative pronouns. In his writings we find the technical term *ptosis*, ("case", "inflection"), for the first time as a designation for all morphological variations of word forms, i.e. not only nouns but also verbs. His terminology was extended and concretized by the philosophical school of the Stoa (from about 300 BC), who established grammar as a scholarly field of its own. As to phonology, the Stoics defined a set of 24 alphabetic characters as "elements of words" and they distinguished seven vowels and six consonants. As to morphology, they examined the inflection of nouns and verbs. Moreover, the tenses and gender of verbs were systematically described. In the field of syntax they explained constructions of active and passive voice, and also the role of the nominative and oblique cases. Etymology was particularly studied, as it had been by Plato. Although they pursued it with true passion, the results were obviously rather naive from the perspective of modern linguistic knowledge. The numerous irregularities in word formation and use were interpreted by Stoic philosophers as following from a principle of anomaly prevailing in language. Their method was purely descriptive: they merely stated facts but refrained from finding reasons for inconsistencies.

Grammarians of the Hellenistic period, by contrast, above all the Alexandrians (*c.*2nd century BC) who were leaders in philology at that time, tried to put regularities of language in the foreground, considering irregularities as deviations from normality. Their basic principle of explanation, which they called analogy, has predominated ever since. This method had another starting point: whereas the Stoics proceeded from logical assumptions, Alexandrian philologists dealt with grammar for practical, i.e. didactic, reasons. As Greek civilization spread in the Hellenistic period, they tried to provide tools for non-Greeks to learn Greek language and literature. Morphology especially was understood as a system of analogies. Groups of identically inflecting words could be distinctly classified by corresponding rules so that patterns of declension and conjugation were set up and, at the same time, irregularities were registered. This method was also purely descriptive. The first systematic description of phonology and morphology was compiled by Dionysius Thrax (c.100 BC) under the title *techne grammatike* ("science of grammar": syntax, defined as the composition of words in a sentence, is mentioned but not treated in detail). This work was the first grammatical manual for didactic purposes and consequently achieved wide circulation. From about the 4th century AD it was regarded as a standard grammar for Greek, forming a basis for further research throughout the Byzantine period and up to the Renaissance. Dionysius defines grammar as the "knowledge of what is normally said by poets and prose writers". His work is divided into six parts: reading aloud, explaining literary expressions, commenting on words and knowledge, etymologies, finding regularities, and finally literary criticism. From his explanations it becomes obvious that the eight parts of speech (noun, verb, participle, article, pronoun, preposition, adverb, conjunction) are determined by the sentence as a whole and, consequently, considered as (relative) parts of the sentence. The order of enumeration is intentional: the most important parts of speech, noun and verb, are named first. This is in accordance with linguistic and philosophical reflections from the past, where these two elements were already regarded as determining a sentence. Moreover, the first five word classes are inflectional, the last three are not. Dionysius' classifications and terminology were adopted by Roman grammarians. They adapted the system to the Latin language, also translating technical terms into Latin. These still survive (for instance *ptosis* = *casus* = "case"). Apollonius Dyscolus (2nd century AD), basing himself on the Stoics and on Dionysius Thrax, dealt extensively with syntax in a way that was quite subtle for his time. He defined syntax as a combination of words considering the coherence of the whole sentence. He illustrates the central position of noun and verb in a sentence by remarking that a sentence will become senseless or at least indefinite if these two elements are omitted. He also wrote special studies on pronouns, adverbs, and conjunctions. Furthermore, he introduced the terms transitivity and intransitivity (in relation to verbs). With this grammarian, the separation between grammar and philology was fulfilled, so that the development of an independent discipline could begin.

In the Byzantine period, as the spoken everyday language and the Classicist literary language progressively separated, gradual linguistic changes also modified the demands that were made on grammar. Having been merely descriptive in the Classical period, it now became prescriptive with rules for correct pronunciation, orthography, inflection, etc. Although colloquial language developed in a very dynamic way over the centuries, only the Atticizing language was described in grammars. In the highly developed educational system material was needed both for elementary and for higher instruction in order to explain the language of literature and to assist the reading of classical authors. Thus, numerous commentaries on and compilations of earlier grammatical works exist. The so-called *epimerismoi* became very popular for instruction. These are comments on Classical writers (above all Homer) and on religious texts (e.g. the Psalms), partially written in the form of question and answer in order to underline the didactic purpose. In these Byzantine grammatical writings word-for-word explanations concerning phonology, orthography,

prosody, and morphology are in the foreground, while analysis of syntax is only treated marginally. From the 11th century a new technique called *schedographia*, related to that of the *epimerismoi*, comes into fashion. These are small exercises in prose (sometimes mixed with introductory verses) in combination with moral instructions. They were used to practise and apply grammatical rules. This method, however, was controversial among Byzantine intellectuals, since it was overemployed and commercialized by some grammarians so that it was no longer serious.

Michael Synkellos (9th century) was famous for his work on syntax. He is the first grammatical author since Antiquity to devote himself exclusively to this topic. His starting point is the isolated word and not so much the mutual relationships of words in sentences. He treats different verbs and prepositions and corresponding case constructions at length, interlarded with numerous examples. His work is a short and clear manual with instructions for the correct use of language rather than theoretical reflections. On the whole, Byzantine authors concerned with linguistic and/or grammatical problems were not conspicuous for their innovative tendencies or originality. Ideas that came from Antiquity and Late Antiquity were taken up again and again, annotated, and, at best, slightly added to. An exception is the versatile scholar Maximos Planudes (13th/14th centuries) who, within the framework of his works about syntax, developed a theory that may be traced back to Antiquity and the Hellenistic period: the so-called localist theory of case (this, however, being the modern term). Planudes explains that there are three interrogatives asking for the most important parts of speech, i.e. the three oblique cases: "whence" (genitive as the case of origin), "where" (dative for location), "whither" (accusative denoting destination). Greek prepositions governing all three cases demonstrate this theory in a very clear way. The localist point of view in the interpretation of case systems was and still is in use by linguists of the 19th and 20th centuries.

In the 14th and 15th centuries several scholars taught classical Greek in the Latin west, especially in Italy. By so doing they initiated a revival of Greek studies in western Europe. Manuel Chrysoloras, for example, gave lessons in Florence and wrote a grammatical treatise in the form of questions and answers, a method that had been popular since the 12th century. His grammar presented the Classical language of literature (phonology, morphology, syntax) in a vivid manner, with little theory, and it was meant as a practical guide for those who wanted to learn Greek as a foreign language.

The *Introduction to Greek Grammar* by Theodore Gaza (15th century) is probably the most comprehensive grammatical treatise of its time. In addition to orthography, phonology, and morphology, Theodore also devoted a whole book to syntax. The influence of this work was also very great in the Latin west (Erasmus of Rotterdam translated parts of it into Latin). The book was reprinted frequently up to the 19th century.

After the conquest of the Byzantine empire by the Turks many Greek intellectuals fled to the West. One of them was Constantine Laskaris who in the second half of the 15th century worked as a teacher of Greek in different Italian cities. He wrote a Greek grammar, a *Collection of the Eight Parts of Speech*, which in 1476 was one of the first books to be printed entirely in Greek types.

During the Tourkokratia new literary centres were formed outside the Ottoman sphere of influence (Cyprus, Rhodes, Crete, Ionian Islands) in which a daily spoken, popular language, with specific dialectal features, could flourish. At this time descriptions of the current language were gradually developed. The oldest grammar of vernacular Greek is by Nikolaos Sophianos of Corfu (16th century). Girolamo Germano, an Italian who lived in Chios for some time in the 17th century, presented a few grammatical observations as a preface to his Italian–Greek glossary. Simon Portius (17th century) adopted some of Nikolaos's thoughts in his grammar of vernacular Greek written in Latin.

A growing feeling of nationalism among the Greek people, together with the political independence that followed in the 19th century, resulted in the ambition to achieve a homogeneous (modern) Greek language for daily use above regional variations. Out of these attempts, however, different movements developed. Two directions emerged in the course of time that determined the further development of the Greek language down to the 20th century: *dimotiki*, popular language, and *katharevousa*, purified learned language. Accordingly, language manuals and grammars were also coloured differently. With the rise of historical and comparative linguistics towards the end of the 19th century, grammars were increasingly written from the perspective of diachronic linguistic study, i.e. as scholarly treatises rather than school grammars. Examples include the works of Yannis Psycharis (with emphasis on *dimotiki*) and Georgios Chatzidakis (with emphasis on *katharevousa*). In the 1950s André Mirambel wrote a comprehensive analysis of the modern Greek language (phonology, morphology, syntax, vocabulary, stylistics) taking into account both directions of the Greek language.

ASTRID STEINER-WEBER

See also Language

Further Reading

Browning, Robert, *Medieval and Modern Greek*, 2nd edition, Cambridge and New York: Cambridge University Press, 1983
Robins, R.H., *The Byzantine Grammarians: Their Place in History*, Berlin and New York: de Gruyter, 1993
Steinthal, Hajim, *Geschichte der Sprachwissenschaft bei den Griechen und Römern, mit besonderer Rücksicht auf die Logik*, Berlin: Deummler, 1863, reprinted Hildesheim: Olms, 1971

Great Idea

The *Megale Idea*, or Great Idea, was the central programme of Greek nationalism in the 19th century. The programme was often vaguely defined and shifting in its emphasis, but its general thrust was irredentist. The Great Idea envisioned the unification of all the Greeks of the Ottoman empire within the borders of a Greek state.

This programme grew out of the disappointing outcome of the Greek revolution of 1821. The revolutionary leaders had aspired to the liberation of all Greeks from Ottoman rule and the replacement of the sultan's rule with some sort of Hellenic authority. The expected borders of this new state were never clearly defined, but they were certainly much larger than those of the Greek state that actually came into being. By the time the treaty of 1832 was signed, regularizing Greece's position in the international community of nations, the new state occupied only the southern tip of the rocky Balkan peninsula, as well as a few Aegean islands. This out-of-the-way area had always been a marginal one within the context of the Ottoman empire as a whole, and it was not an important centre of Hellenism when compared to Constantinople, the west coast of Asia Minor, or the Danubian principalities. The population of the new state was roughly 800,000, no more than a quarter of the total Greek population in the Near East.

The political leader John Kolettis is often credited with the formal articulation of the Great Idea during his speech to the Constituent Assembly in January 1844. But irredentist aspirations were part of Greek political discourse from the very beginning of the kingdom's existence in 1833. At the first celebration of Independence Day (25 March) in 1838, the slogan "To the City!" (Constantinople) spread like wildfire. When sultan Mahmud died a year later, the expectation was high that king Otho was about to depart for the Ottoman capital where he would be crowned emperor. According to a Greek historian writing in the 1860s, he was only prevented from doing so by the fact that the kingdom's one steamship was under repair. Even earlier, in 1834, Kolettis had argued that Greece should not declare a formal capital city, since the real and only capital of the Greeks was Constantinople.

Kolettis's argument brings up the principal interest of the Great Idea for the history of modern Greece. The Great Idea was never seriously pursued in Greek foreign policy, except during the exceptional circumstances of the immediate post-World-War-I years. Greece was far too weak, and Europe far too hostile, for the Greeks to be able actively to pursue the extension of their borders at the expense of the Ottoman empire. Shifts in the international situation did, however, affect which aspects of the Great Idea were emphasized and which downplayed.

The Great Idea was much more important in domestic politics, helped along by the fact that there was virtually no dispute over its validity, just a debate over how best to translate it into actual policy. The policy question was essentially this: given that the national project had been arrested almost at the start, what was the place of the Greek kingdom in the larger framework of the national question, and how should it conduct itself? As John Petropoulos put it, the Greeks simultaneously held two totally different conceptions of statehood. On the one hand, it was felt that Greece, as a new member of the European family of nations, should regularize relations with its neighbours, concentrate on internal development, and, in general, settle down to peaceful pursuits. This was the idea behind the rhetoric of "the model kingdom". The pursuit of a "model kingdom" had the added virtue, according to its advocates, that a prosperous and peaceful Greece would be sure to retain the loyalty of all the unredeemed Greeks living in the Ottoman empire, and would attract the support of Europe as well. Radically opposed to this vision of the state was the conviction that the Greek kingdom was no more than a kind of "temporary and makeshift military base from which the already redeemed Greeks must carry on the national crusade on behalf of their unredeemed brethren", in Petropulos's memorable words.

Given the universal popularity of the Great Idea, it is not surprising that it was frequently enlisted as a tool in the ideological battles between liberals and conservatives that racked Greece from the very beginning of its national existence. In general, the liberals pulled more strongly in the direction of the "model kingdom" view of the Greek state. They were fervently committed to the development of a Western-style state in Greece, and had little love for the backward, as they saw it, institutions, such as the patriarchate, that were still so important in the Greek communities of the Ottoman empire. Their version of the Great Idea, then, saw the extension of the borders of the Greek kingdom to include all of the Greeks of the Ottoman empire. That way the Greeks would be not only united, but united under the aegis of a state that was properly Western in its orientation. Conservatives, on the other hand, could often barely disguise their scorn for the Western-style reforms that had been imposed on Greece, in their view, by a culturally alien West. The whole point of the Greek kingdom was to help the Greeks regain their ancient capital, Constantinople, where they would resurrect something like the Byzantine empire. These battles, of course, harked back to the revolution of 1821 and even the 18th century.

The Great Idea had a way of erupting into every policy debate in 19th-century Greece. Differences over the nature of the Great Idea were exposed in the 1830s debate on the place of the Church in the new kingdom of Greece. For liberals, it was self-evident that the Church in Greece should be autocephalous, that is, independent of Constantinople (which it did become), because the revolution had been almost as much against the patriarch as it had been against the sultan. It was simply unacceptable to envision an Orthodox Church in Greece that owed ultimate loyalty to the patriarch. The liberals' intent was to extend the authority of the king to Constantinople, not to come under the authority of the patriarch. Conservatives, who very much wanted to preserve the authority of the ecumenical patriarch and, more generally, the primacy of religion in the organization of society, argued that the establishment of an independent Church would fracture the formerly unified greater Greek nation. Thus, it would be an impediment to the realization of the Great Idea. Debates about economic policy often referred back to the Great Idea as well. Backers of the "model kingdom" argued that Greece should do its utmost to develop its existing resources, and in this way it would stand as an example of progress to the unredeemed Greeks. Others argued that the Greek kingdom was too small and too poor ever to become economically viable; the only hope for Greece was territorial expansion. The annexation of Thessaly in 1881 was viewed as a critical acquisition precisely because of its rich agricultural lands.

During the 19th century Greece gained the Ionian islands (1863) and Thessaly (1881) through diplomacy. But on balance its progress was felt to be unsatisfactory and the last quarter of the century was particularly discouraging. To the north an entirely new contender, Bulgaria, began to lay claim to lands just beyond Greece's northern border that the Greeks considered to be rightfully theirs. Mindful of the new Slavic threat, the shape of the Great Idea shifted yet again, this time towards some sort of Greek–Ottoman power sharing within the empire that still remained. Such an arrangement, it was felt, was the best way to protect Greek interests, both within the kingdom and in the Ottoman empire. Such a proposal, however, never got very far, in part because the Ottomans were not interested in sharing power with their former subjects.

It was only in the wake of World War I, with the Ottomans on the losing side and the Greeks just barely on the side of the victors (Greece abandoned its neutrality and entered the war on the side of the Allies five months before the war was over), that Greece finally had the opportunity to make the Great Idea a reality. During the course of the war the two principal Allied powers – Britain and France – had sought to win over to their side various countries by making promises of territorial enlargement once the war was over. Thus Italy, for example, was promised much of Dalmatia and the port of Vlorë in Albania, while Romania stood to gain Transylvania. Greece, for its part, was rewarded with the promise that it could occupy Smyrna and its hinterland on the west coast of Asia Minor, taking these lands, essentially, from the defeated Ottoman empire. The Greek communities in western Asia Minor, and in Smyrna in particular, were the wealthiest and the most illustrious in all the Greek world. Throughout the 19th century the Greeks had debated whether it would be best to try and extend their borders within the context of a general European war, or whether they should strike out on their own and hope that Europe would be forced to intervene. Now, with the prize of Smyrna being dangled in front of their eyes, it seemed that Greece had waited patiently until the day when European diplomacy would award it the territory it coveted. In May 1919 the Greek government began to land troops in Smyrna.

Given the long-standing disagreements over the policy implications of the Great Idea, it is perhaps not surprising that the actual pursuit of greater Greece provoked a profound political crisis. The country was already highly polarized as a result of the difficulties of incorporating the new territories gained during the course of the Balkan Wars (1912–13) and then of disagreement over Greek participation in World War I. When it looked as if the occupation of Asia Minor might actually require military campaigns, a significant portion of the war-weary Greek population began to sour on the entire operation. To the irredentist dream of the "Greece of Two Continents and Five Seas" the opponents of the war held up the concept of a "small but honourable Greece". In the fateful elections of November 1920 the Greek prime minister, Eleutherios Venizelos, the man who had succeeded in extracting the promise of Smyrna from the Allies, suffered a massive defeat. The royalists came to power. Although during the campaign they had relentlessly criticized the operations in Asia Minor, once in power they found that they could not bring themselves simply to withdraw from the lands that had been promised for Greece. Things rapidly went from bad to worse. Most unexpectedly, a new Turkish army, under the leadership of Mustafa Kemal (later Atatürk), was forming in the interior of Anatolia. In August 1921 he managed to stop the Greek advance and thus began the long process of Greek withdrawal that would end in Smyrna in September 1922. The Allies, watching the spirited Turkish resistance to the terms of the treaty of Sèvres, slowly retreated from their promises to Greece.

The dream of the Great Idea died in the flames that consumed Smyrna in September 1922. The long history of

Hellenism in Asia Minor came to an end. The remains of the Greek army, along with a stream of refugees, straggled back to Greece. The defeat engendered another round of political violence in Greece, as those who had supported Venizelos blamed the royalists for the disaster in Asia Minor. King Constantine was forced to abdicate and a newly formed Revolutionary Committee quickly returned indictments against eight ministers and military advisers. On 28 November 1922 six of the eight were executed by firing squad.

MOLLY GREENE

Further Reading

Alexandris, Alexis, *The Greek Minority of Istanbul and Greek–Turkish Relations, 1918–1974*, Athens: Centre for Asia Minor Studies, 1983

Herzfeld, Michael, *Ours Once More: Folklore, Ideology and the Making of Modern Greece*, New York: Pella, 1986

Mavrogordatos, George T., *Stillborn Republic: Social Coalitions and Party Strategies in Greece 1922-1936*, Berkeley: University of California Press, 1983

Petropulos, John Anthony, *Politics and Statecraft in the Kingdom of Greece, 1833-1843*, Princeton, New Jersey: Princeton University Press, 1968

Skopetea, Elli, *To "Protypo Vasileio" kai e Magale Idea: Opseis tou Ethnikou Provlematos sten Hellada, 1830-1880* [The Model Kingdom and the Great Idea: Aspects of the National Question in Greece 1830–1880], Athens, 1988

Great Palace

The emperors' palace in Constantinople

The Great Palace of the Byzantine emperors was established in the early 4th century AD by the emperor Constantine I in the southeast part of the city of Constantinople. The palace was the centre of Byzantine court life and government, and remained in use until the sack of the city in 1204.

The Great Palace was a complex of structures rather than a single building, and its partly sloping location required the southern and eastern areas of the palace to take the form of a series of artificial terraces above the sea walls. These structures included residential and administrative buildings, reception halls and throne rooms, and numerous churches and chapels. They were very elaborately decorated and furnished and set amid landscaped gardens, containing sculpture and fountains.

The palace was continually modified between the 4th and 12th centuries, although important elements of Constantine's original plan remained. By the time the Turks entered the city in 1453, however, it was already a ruinous shell, although a few of its churches survived. Today very little remains above ground and this naturally makes reconstruction extremely difficult, especially as very few archaeological excavations have been undertaken on the site. By far the most important of these, carried out by British archaeologists in the mid-20th century, revealed the remains of a Roman-style courtyard, with an attached apsidal reception hall decorated with elaborate floor mosaics. There has been little recent excavation at the site and without more direct material evidence one still gains the most clear-cut impression of the character of the complex from written sources.

Constantine I's palace seems to have been relatively modest compared to the structures that were eventually to comprise the Great Palace complex. It was bordered on the north side by the Augusteum, the imperial square, and on the west by the Hippodrome. Each of these was provided with a monumental entrance to the imperial area, a part of the complex that was later known as the Daphne. The entrance to the palace on the Augusteum (the Chalke) was a bronze-doored rectangular structure, decorated with mosaics.

Although modifications were made in the 5th century – such as the addition of the church of St Stephen, close to the Kathisma (the imperial box at the Hippodrome) – the next major phase of remodelling was undertaken by Justinian I in the 6th century. The Chalke was rebuilt, following the Nike riots that had damaged both this entrance and the area reserved for the palace guards immediately inside it. Justinian also ensured that the palace was made more defensible – bakeries, a cistern, and granaries were built to make the court more self-sufficient in the event of another insurrection. By this time the complex had four main areas. The Boukoleon (or Hormisdas palace) was a waterfront complex above a private imperial harbour, decorated with sculptures of animals and close to a lighthouse on the line of the walls. Part of its façade – the most complete remaining fragment of the palace – still survives, at the point where it fronted the sea walls. Along with this and the Daphne, already mentioned, the third complex was the Magnaura. Its exact extent and character are uncertain, but it was to the northeast of this complex near the Augusteum. Justinian linked these buildings with long porticoes, combining what had perhaps been separate imperial focuses into a single larger complex.

After Justinian I further modifications occurred. Tiberios I redesigned the north side of the complex, demolishing buildings and erecting new structures including baths and a stable. Justin II built what was to be the most important imperial throne room, the apsed rectangular building known as the Chrysotriklinos (Golden Hall). Later still, Justinian II built the Justinianos – another major structure – and strengthened the circuit wall of the palace. Thus, the complex continued to be rebuilt and changed during the later 6th and 7th centuries, with important construction projects taking place.

It was under the direction of the emperors Theophilos (829–42) and Basil I (867–86) in the 9th century, however, that perhaps the most ambitious programmes of remodelling were undertaken. This partly involved new work on old buildings but also included the dramatic expansion and elaboration of the whole palace. Written descriptions survive of both projects. Theophilos commissioned a series of colonnaded marble halls on terraces. These included a triconch reception room (aptly called the Triconchos), with a C-shaped courtyard (the Siama) decorated with fountains, other freestanding elaborate buildings such as the Mousikos, and the Margarites, his private quarters. The last comprised a colonnaded marble living room, with a domed summer bedroom roofed with a gold-speckled ceiling supported by dark marble columns. Theophilos also built a winter bedroom nearby, on a terrace on the eastern side of the palace, overlooking the court polo pitch (the Tzykanisterion). It was on the site of this polo pitch that the most important of the structures built under Basil was located. This was the Nea Ekklesia, a five-domed church, set amid porticoed courtyards and gardens. The southeastern part of the palace already had other important buildings, notably the church of St Mary of the Lighthouse, close to the sea walls, and the Porphyra, a porphyry-clad square structure overlooking the Boukoleon harbour.

Yet more changes took place in the 10th century, especially during the reign of Constantine VII Porphyrogennetos (913–59). Nikephoros II Phokas built a defensive wall around the Boukoleon area. Even in the 12th century the emperor Manuel I commissioned colonnaded halls for the Great Palace, decorated with mosaics. So, the complex was continually being modified and redesigned, and there is also evidence that the function of existing structures often changed. The dynamic character of the Great Palace must, therefore, be borne in mind. Nor was it the only imperial palace in the city. However, for centuries the Great Palace played a central role in both urban and imperial life.

KEN DARK

See also Architecture: palaces

Summary
Founded by Constantine I in the early 4th century AD, the Great Palace of the emperors was the centre of Byzantine court life and government. Located in the southeast part of the city, it remained in use until 1204. Originally built on a modest scale, it was much modified over the centuries and became an elaborate complex of residential and administrative buildings, reception roms, throne rooms, and churches.

Further Reading
Brett, Gerard (editor), *The Great Palace of the Byzantine Emperors*, 1st report, London: Oxford University Press, 1947

Brett, Gerard, "Automata in the Byzantine 'Throne of Solomon'", *Speculum*, 29 (1954): pp. 477–87

Cameron, Averil, "The Construction of Court Ritual: The Byzantine Book of Ceremonies" in *Rituals of Royalty*, edited by David Cannadine and Simon Price, Cambridge and New York: Cambridge University Press, 1987, pp. 106–36

Ebersolt, Jean, *Le Grand Palais de Constantinople et le livre de cérémonies*, Paris: Leroux, 1910

Jobst, W., B Erdal, and C. Gurtner, *Istanbul: Büyük Saray MozayiZi Istanbul / Istanbul: Das Grosse Byzantinische Palastmosaik Istanbul / The Great Palace Mosaic*, Istanbul: Arkeoloji ve Sanat, 1997

Krautheimer, Richard and Slobodan Ćurčić, *Early Christian and Byzantine Architecture*, 4th edition, New Haven, Connecticut and London: Yale University Press, 1986

Magdalino, P., "Manuel Komnenos and the Great Palace", *Byzantine and Modern Greek Studies*, 4 (1978): pp. 101–14

Maguire, Henry (editor), *Byzantine Court Culture from 829 to 1204*, Washington, DC: Dumbarton Oaks, 1997

Mango, Cyril A., *The Brazen House: A Study of the Vestibule of the Imperial Palace of Constantinople*, Copenhagen: Munksgaard, 1959

Mango, Cyril A., *The Art of the Byzantine Empire, 312-1453: Sources and Documents*, Englewood Cliffs, New Jersey: Prentice Hall, 1972

Mango, Cyril A., *Byzantine Architecture*, New York: Abrams, 1976; London: Faber, 1978

Mango, Cyril A., *Le Développement urbain de Constantinople, Ive–VIIe siècles*, 2nd edition, Paris: Boccard, 1990

Mango, Cyril A., "The Palace of the Bukoleon", *Cahiers Archéologiques*, 45 (1997): pp. 41–50

Müller-Wiener, Wolfgang, *Bildlexikon zur Topographie Istanbuls*, Tübingen: Wasmuth, 1977

Talbot-Rice, David (editor), *The Great Palace of the Byzantine Emperors*, 2nd report, Edinburgh: Edinburgh University Press, 1958

Gregoras, Nikephoros
Historian and scholar of the 14th century

A Byzantine historian, encyclopedic scholar, theologian, and imperial adviser, Nikephoros Gregoras was one of the great intellectuals of late Byzantium. He was born and brought up in Heracleia Pontike in Asia Minor. His uncle and first tutor, bishop John of Heracleia Pontike, sent the young Gregoras to Constantinople to study theology, philosophy, and grammar with the patriarch, John XIII Glykys (1315–19). Subsequently, Gregoras befriended the great scholar and statesman Theodore Metochites, from whom he learned astronomy. Metochites introduced him to the imperial court and Gregoras became an influential adviser to Andronikos II (1282–1328). The emperor entrusted Gregoras with an important mission to Serbia in 1326 during the civil war between the two Andronikoi (1321–28) and was persuaded by him of the need for a calendar reform that Gregoras had defended in a public plea. In spite of Gregoras's superb knowledge of astronomy, the conservative Church opinion of the day prevented the change to the Julian calendar, a century and half before pope Gregory XIII's reforms in 1574.

Although Gregoras was in the camp of the supporters of the elder Andronikos during the civil war, he continued to serve Andronikos III (1328–41) afterwards. In 1331 he defeated in a public dispute the Calabrian monk Barlaam, whose Aristotelian and rationalistic views seem not to have found favour with the Byzantines. After Theodore Metochites' death, Nikephoros Gregoras inherited his enormous library and began to teach in the Chora monastery, which Metochites had splendidly renovated. Andronikos III selected Gregoras to participate in a public debate with two papal legates in 1333, but he declined, convinced that theological debates could not lead to the union of the Latin and the Greek Churches, which he favoured for reasons of political expediency.

Gregoras's involvement in the hesychast controversy in the 1340s and 1350s occupied the later years of his life and proved to be his nemesis. After the synod of 1341 confirmed the orthodoxy of hesychasm, he began to oppose vehemently the teachings of Gregory Palamas and his followers. He tried to persuade John VI Kantakouzenos, his erstwhile friend and victor in the second civil war (1341–47), of the heretical nature of Palamism, but Kantakouzenos remained until his death a steadfast supporter of hesychasm. The Church synod of 1351 reconfirmed the orthodoxy of hesychasm and condemned Gregoras. Furthermore, he was sentenced to house arrest in the Chora monastery for three years (1351–54), where he devoted his time to composing theological treatises and anti-hesychast pamphlets. A substantial part of his history consists of a polemic against hesychasm as well. Gregoras was, however, doomed to be on the losing side of the dispute. In the 15th century the Church of Thessalonica included the name of

Nikephoros Gregoras in the anathemas annually pronounced on the day of the Feast of Orthodoxy.

In spite of his bad posthumous reputation in the Orthodox Church, Nikephoros Gregoras stands out, together with Theodore Metochites and Nikephoros Choumnos, as one of the leading intellectual figures in the culturally productive period of the 14th century, sometimes called the Palaiologan renaissance. Gregoras, like Metochites, was an admirer of Plato rather than Aristotle. His dialogue *Phlorentios, or On Wisdom* is a successful imitation of a Platonic dialogue and presents the dispute between him and Barlaam. The dialogue is an important source for the arguments held by Byzantine proponents of Plato against those of Aristotle. Gregoras also wrote treatises on the construction of the astrolabe and on solar eclipses, on mathematics, on grammar, and on musicology. He was the author of imperial panegyrics and funeral orations dedicated to Andronikos II and Andronikos III. A great deal of his correspondence has survived. His theological works include saints' lives, and he wrote the *vita* of his uncle, John of Heracleia. His polemical treatises (*Antirrhetika*) against hesychasm provide important information on the ecclesiastical disputes of the time.

Gregoras's *Roman History*, covering the period from 1204 until 1358, is a valuable source for Byzantine society in the first half of the 14th century though the historical account is quite unbalanced. Although the narrative begins with the fall of Constantinople to the Latins, the emphasis is mainly on events of Gregoras's own time, with particular attention paid to theological controversy. The last third of the *History* is a polemic against Palamism. Written in a heavily archaizing style in accordance with the cultural currents of the period, the work abounds in quotations from Herodotus and Thucydides and allusions to Classical mythology. Still, the *History* shows that Gregoras was aware of the main political problems of his own day. He recognized that the loss of Asia Minor to the Turks had put the empire in an extremely critical situation. He placed the blame for the empire's straits on the civil wars and on internal divisions, while recognizing the necessity of an alliance between Byzantium and its Balkan neighbours and the need for a union of the Greek and Latin Churches. For the early period Gregoras used primarily, but not exclusively, the histories of George Akropolites and George Pachymeres. The main historical value of the work lies in the account of the two civil wars, which complements the biased autobiographical history of the emperor John VI Kantakouzenos.

Dimiter G. Angelov

Biography

Born at Heracleia Pontike between 1290 and 1294, Gregoras was orphaned as a child and raised by his uncle, Bishop John of Heracleia Pontike. He later moved to Constantinople to study theology, philosophy, and grammar with the Patriarch John XIII Glykys and astronomy with Theodore Metochites. A prolific writer, his works include theological treatises against Gregory Palamas and the *Roman History* in 37 books covering the period 1204–1358. He died in disgrace in Constantinople between 1358 and 1361.

Writings

Rhomaische Geschichte, translated by J.L. Van Dieten, 5 vols, Stuttgart: Hiersemann, 1973–94 (includes commentary)

Further Reading

Guilland, Rodolphe, *Essai sur Nicéphore Gregoras: L'homme et l'oeuvre*, Paris: Geuthner, 1926

Hart, T., "Nicephorus Gregoras: Historian of the Hesychast Controversy", *Journal of Ecclesiastical History*, 2 (1951): pp. 169–79

Hunger, Herbert, *Die hochsprachliche profane Literatur der Byzantiner*, vol. 1, Munich: Beck, 1978, pp. 453–65

Gregory V 1745–1821

Patriarch of Constantinople

Gregory V is one of the best-known patriarchs of Constantinople from the Ottoman period (Tourkokratia). This is largely due to his execution by the Ottomans following the outbreak of the Greek War of Independence. Gregory was born in 1745 in Dimitsana (Peloponnese) and studied there, in Athens, in Smyrna, and in Patmos. Invited to Smyrna by Bishop Prokopios, Gregory worked there until 1785 when he succeeded Prokopios as Bishop of Smyrna. Through his manifold activities Gregory made a name for himself and was elected to the patriarchate of Constantinople, where he served three terms in total.

His first term (19 April 1797–18 December 1798) was marked by radical developments in the intellectual and political domain. Enlightenment ideas were infiltrating society on a large scale. In the wake of the French Revolution plans for a Greek revolution were at their peak. French activities in the Ionian islands and Napoleon's presence in Egypt triggered hopes among the subjugated Orthodox of eventual liberation. Gregory took several steps to inhibit the spread of these secular ideas. He established a patriarchal printing press with censors, imprimatur, and systematic control intended to protect the Orthodox flock from Western ideas. In 1798 he issued encyclicals condemning Rigas's revolutionary pamphlets and the godless and seditious influence of the French. In the same year a booklet entitled *Paternal Teaching* under the name of patriarch Anthimos of Jerusalem was published in an attempt to provide religious legitimacy for the God-ordained Ottoman empire. Gregory, among others, was suspected of having composed it. Several other anti-Enlightenment texts were published at that time including the *Christian Reply* in 1798. Despite these counter-revolutionary actions, Gregory was dethroned and spent seven years on Mount Athos.

He was re-elected patriarch for a second term (23 September 1806–10 September 1808) and once more faced serious developments, such as the Ottoman war against Russia and England. Gregory showed his loyalty by supporting with 1000 Greek workers the construction of fortifications in Constantinople against the approaching English fleet. In addition, Gregory followed his earlier defensive policy against the Enlightenment and Western liberalism. He took measures (encyclical of March 1807) to control the circulation of books. However, the Janissary revolt against Sultan Selim III and the subsequent counter-revolution again brought about Gregory's dethronment. He moved back to Mount Athos, where he stayed for nine years.

His third term as Patriarch (14 December 1818–10 April 1821) coincided with the eve of the Greek War of Independence. It was a critical period when revolutionary plans and anticlericalist currents were at their height. Gregory was aware of the *Philiki Hetaireia* (Friendly Society), but followed a very careful policy vis-à-vis the Ottoman rulers and the Greek seditionists. He organized Orthodox countermeasures against Western ideas, again including the printing press under Ilarion Sinaitis, a churchman who drew harsh criticism for his inquisitorial acts, such as compiling an index of prohibited books, and burning of books. In March 1819 Gregory issued a much-discussed encyclical concerning Orthodox education, which was critical of the teaching of science and mathematics, of new theories about the Greek language, and of the naming of Orthodox children after ancient Greeks. Probably having in mind the "Philological Gymnasium" of Smyrna, Gregory feared that such worldly interests would lead to indifference to or rejection of Orthodoxy and emphasized the value of traditional religious and grammatical lessons. In 1820, through the intervention of Ilarion Sinaitis, a radical text of the Greek Enlightenment, *Kriton's Reflections*, was publicly burnt in the grounds of the Patriarchate. This period was also marked by serious social conflicts within the Greek community in Smyrna due to the rise of a merchant class which intended to undertake a leading role in social matters, such as education, and to marginalize the Church. But in the summer of 1819 the progressive Philological Gymnasium of Smyrna was closed following organized attacks by the guilds and Bishop Anthimos, supported by patriarch Gregory. Similar problems occurred in 1820 in the schools of Kydonies and Chios. Finally, a patriarchal synod, directed against the followers of Adamantios Korais, condemned "philosophical and scientific studies" on 27 March 1821.

The most radical event of the day was undoubtedly the outbreak of the Greek War of Independence. In March 1821 the patriarchal synod issued an official excommunication of Alexandros Ypsilantis's uprising in the Danubian principalities. During that turbulent period, retaliatory measures against the Greeks in Constantinople were quite usual. When news came of the subsequent Greek uprising in the Peloponnese, Gregory was arrested and imprisoned. He was finally hanged on 10 April 1821 from the lintel of the Patriarchate's main gate at Phanar. His dead body was left for three days to public ridicule, dragged through the streets by the mob, and thrown into the sea in the Golden Horn. From there it was recovered by M. Sklavos, who brought it to Odessa. It was then buried with honours by the Greek community there. In April 1871 Gregory's relics were brought to Greece and were placed in a sarcophagus in the cathedral of Athens, while his statue was erected in front of the University of Athens. He was canonized in 1921 and is officially honoured as a national martyr. His symbolic significance for the Greek people remains great. The Patriarchate's main gate has remained closed ever since in memory of his execution.

Gregory has been a controversial figure in modern Greek historiography, for the assessments of his activities vary immensely. Some hail him as an important ecclesiastical personality and as a martyr for the Greek cause. His negative attitude towards the Greek insurrection is considered a clever subterfuge to mislead the Ottoman authorities, who were generally behind Gregory's actions and encyclicals. Others consider him a conservative Orthodox prelate, who wished to preserve the traditional establishment. They also characterize him as a Turkophile and as a staunch opponent of the Greek cause. Gregory was criticized not only by later generations but even by his contemporaries, including Korais.

Gregory undoubtedly opposed all radical changes within Greek society. His oscillation between loyalty to the Sublime Porte and to his Orthodox flock was extremely difficult and risky, and it cost him his life. It is true that he had received orders from the Ottoman authorities to resist the spread of revolutionary ideas in the East. But Gregory had other reasons to oppose the new ideas: for their danger to Orthodoxy and to the Byzantine supranational heritage of the Patriarchate. For Gregory, the time-honoured patristic and ascetic Orthodox tradition took priority in his scale of interests over the pernicious new ideas that could destroy the established order. His behaviour reflects the fact that he was a truly ecclesiastical man devoted to his religious duties. Hence, it is no wonder that his three terms in the patriarchate are noted for numerous anti-Enlightenment policies, which were unsuccessful in the long run. In fact, Gregory captured the underlying spirit of that critical period and foresaw with prophetic intuition the future impact of the Enlightenment upon Church and society. Needless to say, his predictions and fears were realized in many respects in the independent Greek state.

VASILIOS MAKRIDES

See also Korais

Biography

Born in 1745 at Dimitsana in the Peloponnese, Gregory studied in Athens, Smyrna, and Patmos. In 1785 he became bishop of Smyrna. He served three terms as patriarch of Constantinople – 1797–98, 1806–08, and 1818–21. He tried to counter the spread of revolutionary and Enlightenment ideas among the Orthodox subjects of the Ottoman empire, but his efforts were considered insufficient by the Ottomans, who hanged him on 10 April 1821. He was canonized in 1921 and is regarded as a national martyr.

Further Reading

Apostolopoulos, Dimitris G., *La Révolution française et ses répercussions dans la société grecque sous domination ottomane: Réactions en 1798*, Athens, 1997

Borovilos, Georgios E., "Peri tis katastaseos tou klirou sti Smyrni kata to devtero imisy tou 18ou aiona" [The Situation of the Clergy in Smyrna during the Second Half of the 18th Century], *Deltio Kentrou Mikrasiastikon Spoudon*, 8 (1990/91): pp. 65–86

Clogg, Richard, "Some Protestant Tracts Printed at the Press of the Ecumenical Patriarchate in Constantinople, 1818-1820", *Eastern Churches Review*, 2 (1968): pp. 152–64

Clogg, Richard, "The 'Dhidhaskalia Patriki' (1798): An Orthodox Reaction to French Revolutionary Propaganda", *Middle Eastern Studies*, 5 (1969): pp. 87–115

Clogg, Richard, "Anti-clericalism in pre-Independence Greece c.1750-1821" in *The Orthodox Churches and the West*, edited by Derek Baker, Oxford: Blackwell, 1976, pp. 257–76

Clogg, Richard (editor and translator), *The Movement for Greek Independence, 1770-1821: A Collection of Documents*, London: Macmillan, 1976, pp. 56–65, 86–89, 203–06

Eranos eis Adamantion Korain [Symposium on Ademantios Korais], Athens, 1965 (especially the articles by E. Hatzidaki and D. Gkinis)

Frazee, Charles A., *The Orthodox Church and Independent Greece, 1821-1852*, London: Cambridge University Press, 1969, pp. 15–48

Georgantzis, Petros A., *O "Aphorismos" tou Alexandrou Ypsilanti: Istoriki kai Theologiki Dierevnisi tou thematos* [The *Aphorism* of Alexander Ypsilantis: A Historical and Theological Investigation], Kavala, 1988

Gritsopoulos, Tasos, "Grigorios V, o Patriarchis tou Ethnous" [Gregory V: Patriarch of the Nation], *Deltion tis Istorikis kai Ethnologikis Etaireias tis Ellados*, 14 (1959): pp. 164–229

Gritsopoulos, Tasos, *Moni Philosophou* [Monastery of a Philosopher], Athens, 1960, pp. 305–72

Iliou, Philippos, *Koinonikoi agones kai Diaphotismos: I periptosi tis Smyrnis (1819)*[Social Struggle and the Enlightenment: The Case of Smyrna], 2nd edition, Athens, 1986

Iliou, Philippos, *Typhloson Kyrie ton Laon Sou: Oi proepanastatikes kriseis kai o Nikolaos Piccolos* [Lord, Make Thy People Blind: The Prerevolutionary Crises and Nikolaos Piccolos], Athens, 1988

Kekridis, Stathis N., *Ekklisia kai logokrisia stin Othomaniki Avtokratoria, 1700-1850* [Church and Censorship in the Ottoman Empire, 1700–1850], Kavala, 1995

Kitromilides, Paschalis M., *I Galliki Epanastasi kai i Notioanatoliki Evropi* [The French Revolution and Southeastern Europe], Athens, 1990

Lappas, Kostas, "Patriarchiki Synodos 'peri kathaireseos ton philosophikon mathimaton' ton Martio tou 1821. Mia martyria tou Kon. Oikonomou" [Patriarchal Synod "On the Purification of Philosophical Studies" of March 1821: A Testimony of Constantine Oikonomos], *Mnimon*, 11 (1987): pp. 123–53

La Révolution française et l'Hellénisme moderne, Athens: Centre de Recherches Néohelléniques, 1989

Skiadas, Nikos E., "To typographeio tou Patriarchi Grigoriou tou V kai oi ekdoseis tou" [The Press of Patriarch Gregory and Its Publications], *Nea Estia*, 100 (1976): pp. 880–90

Vranoussis, Leandros, "Agnosta patriotika phylladia kai anekdota keimena tis epochis tou Riga kai tou Korai: I philogalliki kai i antigalliki propaganda" [Unknown Patriotic Pamphlets and Unpublished Texts of the Time of Rigas and Korai: Pro- and Anti-French Propaganda], *Epetiris tou Mesaionikou Archeiou*, 15-16 (1965/66): pp. 125–329

Zacharopoulos, Nikolaos, *Grigorios V: Saphis ekphrasis tis ekklisiastikis politikis epi Tourkokratias* [Gregory V: A Clear Expression of Church Politics under the Turkokratia], Thessalonica, 1974

Zisis, Theodoros, *O Patriarchis Grigorios 5os sti syneidisi tou Genous* [Patriarch Gregory V in National Consciousness], Thessalonica, 1986

Gregory of Nazianzus, St *c.329–c.390*

Theologian

Gregory was born in Cappadocia, one of the Cappadocian Fathers alongside Basil of Caesarea and Gregory of Nyssa. His posthumously awarded title "the Theologian" was a tribute to his writings on the nature of the Godhead (*theologia*). His father, Gregory the Elder, was bishop of Nazianzus, in southwest Cappadocia. A good deal is known about his life, because Gregory was very, perhaps only too, willing to give accounts of it. These are contained in his autobiographical poem *De Vita Sua,* of 1949 lines; in other poems and orations dealing with phases in his career, often in self-defence or self-praise; and in letters that give a lively picture of his varied preoccupations and the range of his social contacts, some of which reflect a background that, like that of his friends Basil and Gregory, is at once privileged and pious. Like Basil, he was educated to a high standard over a period of 10 years, studying in Cappadocian Caesarea, followed by a period of rhetorical training at Caesarea in Palestine and a time in Alexandria, where he encountered Platonism. Later he went on to Athens, aged about 20, to share in the student life of his friends Basil and Julian; the latter, as the emperor who defected from Christianity ("the Apostate"), was to alienate Gregory on a spectacular scale. The account he gives of this time in his life shows openness to a wide range of academic interests, his teachers including Prohaeresius who was a Christian and Himerius who was not, though tempered by a sobering piety. Gregory's first reaction to completing his formal education was to debate the future course of his life. Should he join Basil in the solitary contemplation and asceticism of a monastic life or follow one of his talents by taking up a career in rhetoric (a choice that Basil had also faced and rejected)? Initially he did neither, acceding to his father's belief that he needed his son to be ordained priest, as he was reluctantly, to help in the day-to-day life of his see of Nazianzus. Basil, having himself left, for the time being at least, the monastic life to become bishop of the important see of Caesarea, had other ideas. He, too, felt in need of assistance and persuaded his friend to be consecrated bishop of Sasima, as support in an ecclesiastical dispute. This turned out to be a severe test of friendship, since Gregory saw himself, not without justice, as being manipulated into accepting a token bishopric that amounted to nothing more than a remote collection of hovels. His disillusionment found expression in a refusal even to visit the place. Instead, he found comfort in a solitary life, before yielding to persuasion and returning to work with his father. The elder Gregory's death in 374 brought renewed pressure, this time to succeed to the bishopric. This he resisted, preferring to live again a life of seclusion, in Seleucia.

That might have remained the pattern for the rest of his life, had he not felt himself summoned to take an active part in the pro-Nicene, anti-Arian, cause of the Church. With the death of the emperor Valens in 378 the Arian party lost a powerful supporter. Gregory, seeing a chance of loosening the Arian hold on Constantinople, took on a preaching campaign in the tiny Anastasia church. His sermons were soon attracting wide attention. The five *Theological Orations* of 380 did much to hearten the Nicene community, reviving under the encouragement of the emperor Theodosius. When the Arians were expelled from the capital by the emperor and he summoned a council to settle the doctrinal issues of the Church, Gregory was perceived to have played a major role in the reversal. This was recognized by his being declared the true bishop of Constantinople, in place of Maximus whose actions over several years in pursuit of power were seen, at best, as equivocal. Not only that, but on the death of Meletius, bishop of Antioch, in 381, Gregory was appointed president of the Council of Constantinople, which was to save for the Church the Creed of Nicaea of 325 and to give to all subsequent generations the form that became known as the "Nicene Creed", a centre point of the Eucharist. The acrimonious nature of the debate that preceded the settlement did not agree with Gregory's temperament and he resigned. Returning to Nazianzus, he stood in as an interim bishop until a successor could be appointed. Perhaps suffering from the bad health to which he often claimed to be subject, and possibly doubting the suitability of his successor, his cousin Eulalius, he gave the impression of retiring none too soon. From 383 he lived in contemplative and active literary retirement, on his family estates, until his death in 389 or 390.

In character Gregory may be accounted a rather strange mixture. The speaker who could deliver carefully crafted orations based on accepted rhetorical models was clearly aware of himself as a public figure. He shied away, however, from many of the administrative duties that might have gone with that role. Yet in his periods of solitary withdrawal he could never entirely rid himself of anxiety about his reputation in the active life that he claimed to have quit so gladly.

As a man of letters Gregory shows at least competence, and often distinction, in several spheres. The best of the orations have been taken as something of a high point in the harmonious synthesis of Classical and Christian cultural traditions, polished and often telling as they range over topics of central theological importance, events in the Christian calendar, personal statements, and eulogies of heroes such as Athanasius and Basil, or, less commendably, denunciations of the dead Julian. His 250 or so surviving letters, some very personal and others written with an eye to publication (a novelty), are generally models of style, well exemplifying his professed ideals of conciseness, clarity, and grace or beauty (*syntomia, sapheneia, charis*). Gregory's verse has been variously judged. There are tracts of tedious formal versification, while other poems merit careful reading. The autobiographical *De Vita Sua* contains fine passages, as do other poems written about his experience and variable emotions, while some of his "dogmatic" poems, particularly the *Arcana*, have some claim to stand in the literary tradition of didactic verse.

Showing throughout a good deal of his writing are philosophical influences, most of all Platonic. His theology draws on, among others, Irenaeus, Clement, and Origen. (He collaborated with Basil on the Origen selection in the *Philokalia*.) Of his contemporaries he shows especial veneration for Athanasius and Basil. Yet he emerges with an individual voice, as he vigorously defends the Nicene position, notably against the form of later Arianism that was championed by Eunomius. He was regarded as a foremost opponent of the views of Apollinarius, his opinions being cited at the Councils of Ephesus (431) and Chalcedon (451). Gregory held that, by denying the presence in Christ of a human mind, Apollinarius had deprived him of real humanity and thereby human beings of salvation. In his Trinitarian theology, while following the revered Basil, he achieves insights and modes of expression and emphases that are his own. He stresses the divinity of the Holy Spirit as a natural perception in a developing understanding of the Christian faith, speaking of "procession" from the Father. In Gregory are to be found clear enunciations of belief in the unity, equality, and distinct relationships of the three persons, each preserving individual characteristics.

In what was often the troubled seclusion of his last years, Gregory may well have wondered what his life had achieved. Successors were to prove more positive. Councils accepted his theology and posterity awarded him his title. For John of Damascus in the 7th/8th centuries Gregory is the most favoured of the earlier Fathers for the soundness of his thinking and the clarity of its expression. Translations into Latin by Rufinus brought orations of Gregory's to the West. As an orator, he was widely studied throughout the Byzantine period as a model for the successful union of Christian thought with the high, Attic style of eloquence, doing much to establish the official language of the Greek Church. It is fitting that his pictorial representations should enliven a number of manuscripts.

D.A. SYKES

See also Basil the Great, Cappadocia, Gregory of Nyssa

Biography

Born in Cappadocia c.329, Gregory was a close friend of Basil of Caesarea. They studied together in Caesarea in Palestine, and in Athens. Later they both became monks and (less willingly) bishops, Gregory of his native Nazianzus and later of Constantinople. He preached in strong support of Nicene orthodoxy and wrote widely in prose and poetry on (mostly) theological topics. He died in Cappadocia c.390 and was awarded the title "the Theologian" by the Council of Chalcedon in 451.

Writings

The Five Theological Orations, edited by Arthur James Mason, Cambridge: Cambridge University Press, 1899

De Vita Sua, edited and translated into German by Christoph Jungck, Heidelberg: Winter, 1974 (includes commentary)

Selected Poems, translated by John McGuckin, Oxford: JLG Press, 1986

Three Poems, translated by Denis Molaise Meehan, Washington, DC: Catholic University of America Press, 1987

Faith gives Fullness to Reasoning: The Five Theological Orations, edited by Frederick W. Norris, translated by Lionel Wickham and Frederick Williams, Leiden and New York: Brill, 1991 (supplement to *Vigiliae Christianae*, vol. 13)

Cyril of Jerusalem, Gregory of Naziansen, translated by C.G. Browne and J.E. Swallow, vol. 7 of *Nicene and Post-Nicene Fathers*, 2nd series, edited by Philip Schaff and Henry Wace, reprinted Peabody, Massachusetts: Hendrickson, 1994

Poemata Arcana, translated by D.A Sykes, Oxford: Clarendon Press, and New York: Oxford University Press, 1997

Texts and French translations of several works can be found in the series *Sources Chrétiennes*, Paris: Cerf, several dates

Further Reading

Armstrong, A.H. (editor), *The Cambridge History of Later Greek and Early Medieval Philosophy*, London: Cambridge University Press, 1967, reprinted 1970

Campenhausen, Hans von, *The Fathers of the Greek Church*, New York: Pantheon, 1959; London: A. & C. Black, 1963

Cross, F.L. (editor), *The Oxford Dictionary of the Christian Church*, 3rd edition, Oxford and New York: Oxford University Press, 1997

Demoen, Kristoffel, *Pagan and Biblical Exempla in Gregory Nazianzen: A Study in Rhetoric and Hermeneutics*, Turnhout: Brepols, 1996

Gregg, Robert C., *Consolation Philosophy: Greek and Christian Paideia in Basil and the Two Gregories*, Cambridge, Massachusetts: Philadelphia Patristic Foundation, 1975

Grillmeier, Aloys, *Christ in Christian Tradition*, vol. 1, 2nd edition, London: Mowbrays, and Atlanta: John Knox Press, 1975

Hanson, R.P.C., *The Search for the Christian Doctrine of God: The Arian Controversy, 318–381*, Edinburgh: T. & T. Clark, 1988

Hardy, Edward Rochie (editor), *The Christology of the Later Fathers*, London: SCM Press, and Philadelphia: Westminster Press, 1954

Kennedy, George A., *Greek Rhetoric under Christian Emperors*, Princeton, New Jersey: Princeton University Press, 1983

Meredith, Anthony, *The Cappadocians*, London: Geoffrey Chapman, and Crestwood, New York: St Vladimir's Seminary Press, 1995

Pelikan, Jaroslav, *Christianity and Classical Culture*, New Haven and London: Yale University Press, 1993

Quasten, Johannes, *Patrology*, vol. 3: *The Golden Age of Greek Patristic Literature from the Council of Nicaea to the Council of Chalcedon*, Utrecht and Antwerp: Spectrum, and Westminster, Maryland: Newman Press, 1960

Ruether, Rosemary Radford, *Gregory of Nazianzus, Rhetor and Philosopher*, Oxford: Clarendon Press, 1969

Stead, Christopher, *Philosophy in Christian Antiquity*, Cambridge and New York: Cambridge University Press, 1994

Winslow, Donald F., *The Dynamics of Salvation: A Study in Gregory of Nazianzus*, Cambridge, Massachusetts: Philadelphia Patristic Foundation, 1979

Gregory of Nyssa, St *c.330–c.395*

Theologian

Gregory was a younger brother of Basil of Caesarea and one of the Cappadocian Fathers. We know much less about his life than about that of Basil or their friend Gregory of Nazianzus: probably there is less to know. His writings show the depth of his education, yet there is no account of it to match the detailed curricula of their studies. He himself attributes his education to Basil's tuition, but it is likely that he supplemented this with a great deal of private study. The relatively quiet life that he led would have conduced to his emergence as one of the most scholarly men of his generation. Of the rest of Gregory's personal life only hints survive. A reference to his marriage is cryptic. Conjecture has suggested that his wife may have died or become a nun by the time he took up the monastic life. This meant that he, like Basil and Nazianzus, abandoned the possibility of a career in rhetoric. Unlike his brother, however, he found that elevation to the episcopate brought neither prestige nor personal fulfilment. The see of Nyssa was remote, deriving its little importance from being a subsidiary station in Basil's ecclesiastical territory. When Gregory went there in 372 he would have found little intellectual stimulus, though its minimal demands might have suited a man with small desire to be a bishop, and his removal three years later, on the grounds of staunch anti-Arian views in a period of Arian influence, would have caused as little heartache as his return, following the death in 378 of the Arian-minded Valens, would have produced jubilation. He had a gift for thinking and writing and was glad of any opportunity to exercise it. When, however, events demanded, he did not stand aside from activity. Though his appointment as bishop of Sebaste was no more successful than that of Nyssa, and of very short duration (he was glad to hand over to his brother, Peter), the intensity of his ardour for the Nicene position drove him, no less than Basil and Nazianzus, to powerful writing in its defence. He took part in the Council of Constantinople in 381, having previously written pointedly against the extreme Arianism of Eunomius. Indeed, he appears to have found after the council a new standing within the Church, recognized by the now Orthodox

imperial family. He was appointed by the emperor Theodosius to a position of doctrinal supervision and in 385 was invited to deliver funeral orations on the empress and her young daughter. The final decade of his life saw much activity as a preacher and as a creative theological writer.

For Gregory, seclusion, whether of the study or in remote territory, was the condition of his most vigorous and effective activity. Of the three Cappadocians, he was the prime intellectual, wide-ranging in his search for understanding and deeply probing with the instruments of honest inquiry. At home in the traditions of Classical literature, though sometimes in its more contrived forms in his writing, in his fundamental thinking he is able to draw on Platonic lines, particularly in the version mediated by Origen. In his expositions of scripture, he employs aspects of Origen's methods of eliciting mystical senses. Works in which this is most evident include the *Life of Moses*, homilies on Ecclesiastes, the Song of Songs, the Lord's Prayer, and the Beatitudes. Writings of this kind have an affinity with treatises directed towards the ascetic life. *On Virginity* also provides a link with some of the practical issues with which Basil was concerned. While his brother evolved rules for the monastic life, Gregory probed in a different way the principles of the vocation, looking for the theory behind the practice, finding in virginity an essential way into the life of holiness, evoking Platonic notions and Origen's concept of the human soul as the Bride of Christ. Gregory's ability to bring together Classical and Christian backgrounds is seen in the dialogue *On the Soul and Resurrection*, set at the deathbed of his sister Macrina and showing the influence of Plato's *Phaedo*. She is also the subject of a fine Life written by Gregory, very much aware of his family in his admiration for his sister, who is represented as a considerable intellectual force in her own right, no less than in deference towards the dominating Basil. This is widely shown in his work, as in *De Hominis Opificio* (On the Making of Man), seen as a respectful supplement to his brother's writing. Clear theological positions are to be discerned in his dogmatic writings. He is unyielding in his defence of the Nicene position, over against Eunomius, taking his place alongside the other Cappadocians in maintaining the divinity of the Holy Spirit and in developing a doctrine of the Trinity, in works that include *That There are Not Three Gods*. He joins Nazianzus in opposition to what he saw as Apollinarius' failure to give a due place to the human nature in Christ. Gregory's celebrated *Catechetical Oration*, written around 385, is a masterly attempt to set out in summary form, with room for discussion, major tenets of Christianity, and has been seen as a small-scale successor to Origen's *On First Principles*. The approach is to people at an impressive level of philosophical awareness who are willing to explore the relationship of biblical revelation to Platonic thought. It is in this context that Gregory deals with the Incarnation, salvation, and ultimate destiny, following Origen in his envisaging a final restoration of all to life in God. The work also fulfils the function of instructing catechumens in the understanding of the sacraments of baptism and the Eucharist.

Like his fellow Cappadocians, Gregory was notable as a correspondent, though his letters survive in smaller numbers. These testify to his social contacts as well as to his doctrinal interests and questions of Church practice.

Not awarded honorific titles such as "the Great" or "the Theologian", as were Basil and Nazianzus, Gregory has some claim to be thought the most original and most profound of the Cappadocians. Later generations have found in his reflective mind insights that have outlived the controversies of his time.

D.A. SYKES

See also Basil the Great, Cappadocia, Gregory of Nazianzus

Biography

Born *c.*330 in Cappadocia, Gregory was the younger brother of St Basil and the youngest of the "Cappadocian Fathers". Little is known of his life, but he seems to have married early before becoming a monk. Ordained bishop of Nyssa *c.*371 by his brother Basil, and later bishop of Sebaste, he took part in the Council of Constantinople in 381. After the death of Basil in 379 he wrote widely on theological topics and is regarded as the most intellectual of the Cappadocians. He died *c.*395.

Writings

The Catechetical Oration, edited by James Herbert Srawley, Cambridge: Cambridge University Press, 1903

From Glory to Glory: Texts from Gregory of Nyssa's Mystical Writings, edited by Jean Daniélou, translated by Herbert Musurillo, New York: Scribner, 1961

Dogmatic Treatises, translated by W. Moore and H.A. Wilson, vol. 5 of *Nicene and Post-Nicene Fathers*, 2nd series, edited by Philip Schaff and Henry Wace, reprinted Peabody, Massachusetts: Hendrickson, 1994

Further Reading

Armstrong, A.H. (editor), *The Cambridge History of Later Greek and Early Medieval Philosophy*, London: Cambridge University Press, 1967, reprinted 1970

Campenhausen, Hans von, *The Fathers of the Greek Church*, London: A. & C. Black, 1963

Cross, F.L. (editor), *Oxford Dictionary of the Christian Church*, 3rd edition, Oxford and New York: Oxford University Press, 1997

Grillmeier, Aloys, *Christ in Christian Tradition*, vol. 1, 2nd edition, London: Mowbrays, and Atlanta: John Knox Press, 1975

Meredith, Anthony, *The Cappadocians*, London: Geoffrey Chapman, and Crestwood, New York: St Vladimir's Seminary Press, 1995

Meredith, Anthony, *Gregory of Nyssa*, London and New York: Routledge, 1999

Pelikan, Jaroslav, *Christianity and Classical Culture*, New Haven and London: Yale University Press, 1993

Quasten, Johannes, *Patrology*, vol. 3: *The Golden Age of Greek Patristic Literature from the Council of Nicaea to the Council of Chalcedon*, Utrecht and Antwerp: Spectrum, and Westminster, Maryland: Newman Press, 1960

Richardson, Cyril C., in *Christology of the Later Fathers*, edited by Edward Rochie Hardy, London: SCM Press, and Philadelphia: Westminster Press, 1954

Stead, Christopher, *Philosophy in Christian Antiquity*, Cambridge and New York: Cambridge University Press, 1994

Texts and French translations of several works can be found in the series *Sources Chrétiennes*, Paris: Cerf, several dates

Williams, Rowan, *The Wound of Knowledge: Christian Spirituality from the New Testament to St. John of the Cross*, London: Darton Longman and Todd, 1979, Atlanta: John Knox Press, 1980, revised edition London: Darton Longman and Todd, 1990

Gregory Palamas, St 1296–1359

Theologian

St Gregory Palamas exercised an enormous influence not only on the development of Byzantine theology but also on the relation between that theology and the Hellenic tradition. Byzantium in the 14th century remained gripped by the debate between sacred and profane learning, between the patristic tradition and incipient humanism. Palamas played a pivotal role in determining the Church's attitude to the wisdom of the Greeks.

Against a series of detractors – the Calabrian monk Barlaam, Gregory Akindynos and Nikephoros Gregoras – Palamas developed a theology that was both creative and traditional. His initial debates with Barlaam were concerned with theological method. Palamas perceived Barlaam's anti-Latin arguments to be potentially dangerous in their apparent relativism. Barlaam claimed that the syllogisms of the Latins were not apodictic, or demonstrative, according to the definition of Aristotle. Citing Dionysius the Areopagite, he argued that no apodictic reasoning was possible vis-à-vis the divine. Palamas felt that this kind of argument equally undermined the Greek as the Latin position on the procession of the Holy Spirit. Furthermore, was God not revealed? Did he not unite himself with the saints? Palamas's *Apodictic Treatises* represent his first counter to Barlaam's theological agnosticism.

With the emergence of Barlaam's criticisms of the psychophysical methods of prayer used by the hesychast monks, the controversy began to heat up. Palamas began with a powerful demonstration of the integrity and wholeness of the human person, and the consequent appropriateness of the body's participation in the spiritual life. Palamas had a weighty patristic and biblical tradition behind him on this point, and was soon able to dispense with this aspect of Barlaam's critique. Barlaam had also defined the light of the Transfiguration, which the hesychast monks claimed to experience in the highest states of prayer, as a created light. Palamas argued, citing several patristic witnesses, that this light was in fact uncreated and divine. It was, in some sense, God. This raised the problem of how man can be said to participate directly in God, while maintaining divine transcendence.

Palamas's solution was essentially to posit a real distinction between the imparticipable and transcendent divine essence and the participable and immanent divine operations or energies. God is one according to essence, three according to hypostasis, and manifold according to energy. It is according to energy that man is united to God. This doctrine was strenuously opposed by Akindynos, and by many since his time. It was, however, received by the Church at the councils of 1347 and 1351, a vindication confirmed by the canonization of Gregory Palamas in 1368, only nine years after his death. His feast falls on the second Sunday of Lent, an exceptional honour that makes of it a second "Triumph of Orthodoxy".

Palamas's oeuvre is extensive. Most of it has now been published. Among his purely spiritual works, his *Life of St Peter the Athonite* should be mentioned. He also produced works on prayer and the monastic life. The bulk of his work is concerned, directly or indirectly, with the hesychast controversy. His most important works are the *Triads in Defence of*

St Gregory Palamas: fresco of the saint in the Chapel of the Hagioi Anargyroi at the monastery of Vatopedi, Mount Athos, c.1371

the Holy Hesychasts. Particularly worth looking at are the *Natural, Theological, Moral and Practical Chapters,* found in the *Philokalia.* There is also a substantial collection of homilies, delivered as archbishop of Thessalonica.

Palamas's sources are predominantly biblical and patristic. He cites the Cappadocian Fathers, St Athanasius the Great, St Cyril of Alexandria, and, especially, St Maximos the Confessor to support his case. He makes great use of Dionysius the Areopagite, albeit reading Dionysius very much in the tradition of Maximos. Among spiritual writers, he draws on the traditions of both Evagrius of Pontus and (pseudo-) Macarius, very much as Maximos had done.

More immediately, Palamas was an heir to the very constructive theology of Gregory of Cyprus, patriarch from 1283 to 1289. He was also much indebted to the teachings of Theoliptos of Philadelphia and Nikephoros the Hesychast and exhibited great admiration for patriarch Athanasios I of Constantinople (1289–93 and 1303–09).

One of the most interesting aspects of his thought is his attitude to the Hellenic tradition. Palamas received an excellent education, thanks to his family's connections with the ruling house. He studied under, and apparently greatly impressed, Theodore Metochites, the Great Logothete. He appears to have followed the trivium and quadrivium, which included the study of Aristotle but not of Plato. He gave up his studies and embraced the monastic life at the age of about 20. Palamas never entirely repudiated profane learning, so long as it was restricted to its proper sphere. Barlaam's Aristotelianism appeared to Palamas to be using philosophy to undermine theology, and to deny the very possibility of human knowledge of the divine. Palamas replied by allowing that man has a natural capacity to investigate the things of the world, and even that this capacity is a gift of God, but that such natural knowledge is inferior to the supernatural knowledge granted by God to man through grace. Philosophy never has absolute value in Palamite theology.

Palamas has often been accused of obscurantism, notably by the Byzantine humanist Nikephoros Gregoras. This is unfair, because Palamas did not seek to reject the Hellenic tradition outright, only to stress its inferiority in relation to divine revelation. Adherence to Palamite theology did not inhibit the flourishing of a Christian humanism in Nicholas Kabasilas. Furthermore, Palamism did not determine attitudes to union with the West. Mark of Ephesus, the leader of the anti-unionists at the Council of Florence in 1438–39, was a committed Palamite, whereas his successor as leader of the anti-unionist party, George (later Gennadios) Scholarios, was essentially a Thomist. The victory of Palamite theology is not, therefore, to be regarded as a rejection of the Hellenic tradition, but as the subordination of that tradition to the truths of revealed theology.

MARCUS PLESTED

See also Akindynos, Gregoras, Hesychasm

Biography

Born in Constantinople in 1296, Gregory received a good education as a pupil of Theodore Metochites but gave up his studies in 1316 to become a monk on Mount Athos. Most of his literary output was concerned with the hesychast controversy in which he was famously embroiled against Barlaam of Calabria. But he made a positive contribution to creative theology and was canonized in 1368. He died in Thessalonica in 1359.

Writings

The Triads, translated by Nicholas Gendle, New York: Paulist Press, 1983

Further Reading

Krivocheine, B., "The Ascetical and Theological Teaching of St Gregory Palamas", *Eastern Churches Quarterly* (1954)

Mantzaridis, Georgios I., *The Deification of Man: St Gregory Palamas and the Orthodox Tradition,* Crestwood, New York: St Vladimir's Seminary Press, 1984

Meyendorff, John, *A Study of Gregory Palamas,* London: Faith Press, 1964, 2nd edition, 1974

Ware, K.T., "God Hidden and Revealed: The Apophatic Way and the Essence-Energies Distinction", *Eastern Churches Review,* 7 (1975): pp. 125–36

Guilds

Compulsory or free associations of craftsmen or merchants are attested in large cities throughout the late Roman and Byzantine period (4th–15th centuries). Over these centuries, their organization, the extent of government control over their activity, as well as the conditions of admission and functioning, underwent considerable change. Special legislation was drafted for the guilds of Constantinople in the 10th century – *The Book of the Eparch* – which aimed at protecting the guild members from competition by craftsmen outside the guild and at securing better protection from the state.

After the fall of Constantinople to the Ottomans in 1453, there is no evidence of state involvement in the compulsory organization of Christian craftsmen into guilds. Nevertheless, the conditions of foreign conquest created the need for increased solidarity among the conquered peoples, which materialized into various forms of associations under Ottoman rule. The prevailing insecurity in the various manifestations of social life, as well as economic protectionism in the financial policy of the Ottoman empire, led to the creation or reorganization of two predominant forms of association: the community (of a political character) and the guilds (of an economic one). The associations of craftsmen were called *esnaphia* or *rouphetia*; those of the merchants were called "companies", *syntrophies*, or later, *systemata*, while those of the sheep and goat herd-owners *tselingata*, and of the shipowners *syntrophonaphtes*.

Besides the associations of individuals in guilds, there also existed associations of local communities of a given geographical area that jointly produced, processed, and, eventually, traded various products. These associations assumed the form of guilds or, in some cases, that of cooperatives. Examples were the Mademochoria in Chalcidice in Macedonia for cast iron, the Mastichochoria in Chios for the production, collection, and processing of mastic, Ambelakia in Thessaly for spinners and dyers of red yarn, and the village communities around the silver mines in the southern coast of the Black Sea (Pontus). Those associations that were important to the Ottoman economy were granted privileges by the sultans and, in some cases, the monopoly of production, processing, or trade of the product. The development and prosperity of the guilds were encouraged by the Ottoman system of taxation. The guild was a fiscal unit that paid as tax a lump sum, which was proportionately divided among its members; the tax could also be assessed in kind, in which case its members provided the share attributed to each one of them by the guild board. As guilds developed and prospered, they reached a higher level of organization and acquired administrative, police, even judicial jurisdiction.

Probably from the end of the 16th century – and certainly from the early 17th – guilds played a significant part in the organization and life of the Christian community. Representatives of the guilds participated, as a rule, in the administrative council of the Christian communities and their charities (hospitals, schools, etc.). The generous support given by the guilds to the Church and monasteries is also widely witnessed in documents. The importance of guilds in the system of self-government of the Christian communities lasted until the period of the Tanzimat, when the community administration had to comply with the General (or National) Regulations of 1860–62.

The administration of the guilds was based on the internal hierarchy of its members: apprentice, head apprentice, craftsman, head craftsman, master craftsman (*mathitoudi, tsiraki, paragios, kalphas, protokalphas, mastoras, protomastoras*). Promotion from lower to higher rank was open, but depended on craftsmanship which was examined and decided upon by the guild's elected board. Guilds functioned and were governed on the basis of unwritten by-laws well into the late 17th century. From the 18th century onwards, written statutes were often drafted and voted by the members' assemblies; they had to be confirmed by the local Orthodox bishop, usually with no further involvement of the Ottoman authorities. In some towns the guilds had common statutes. The large merchant guilds – "companies" – were a type of association observed among the Greeks outside the Ottoman empire, mostly in the Austrian empire where they traded in oriental goods and formed prosperous communities. Some of these are known to have been granted privileges by the Austrian emperors (in Hungary and Transylvania).

DESPINA TSOURKA-PAPASTATHI

Further Reading

Chatzimichali, Angeliki, "Selected Forms of Association of the Greeks in the Ottoman Empire: Guilds – Esnafia", *L' Hellénisme Contemporain*, issue dedicated to the 500th anniversary of the Fall of Constantinople (1953): pp. 279–303 (in Greek)

Kalinderis, M.A., *The Guilds and the Church under Ottoman Rule*, Athens, 1973 (in Greek)

Pantazopoulos, N.I., *Roman Law in Dialectic Interrelation to Greek Law*, vol. 3, Thessaloniki, 1979 (in Greek)

Pantazopoulos, N.I., *Corporations of Greeks in the Period of Ottoman Rule*, 2nd edition, Thessalonica: Yearbook of the Faculty of Law and Economics of the Aristotle University, vol. 19, fasc. 3, pp. 91–119, 1986 (in Greek)

Tsourka-Papastathi, Despina, *The Greek Merchant Company of Sibiu in Transylvania, 1636–1848: Organization and Law*, Thessalonica, 1994 (in Greek)

Gypsies

The first documents recording the presence of the Gypsies in Europe and the Mediterranean region date from the Byzantine period and also provide proof of their presence in Thrace. The Gypsies stayed in Thrace for longer than in many other regions and this had a significant influence on their language. The Life of St George the Athonite, written in Georgian by one of the saint's followers and dating from 1068, is regarded as the oldest known source. In another source dating from 1204, Theodor Balsamon reported on "satanic" people with the ability to predict the future. The Byzantine cleric called them *athinganoi* (*athinganos* in the singular) or *atsiganoi* (singular *atsiganos*), identifying them with followers of the heresy of this name, who were active in Asia Minor during the era of Emperor Michael II (820–29). The word *athinganoi* comes from the Greek verb *thingano*, to touch, and means "the untouchables". Linguists have not yet been able to ascertain whether the word *atsiganoi* is a derivative of *athinganoi*.

Whatever the case, the name *atsiganoi* (and its abbreviated form *tsiganoi*) was the source of names used for this group in several languages, as in the German *Zigeuner*, the Spanish *gitanos*, the Turkish *çingene*, and so on.

Following attacks by Turkish tribes on Thrace and Byzantium in the 14th century, the Gypsies moved from Thrace to Bohemia and then spread throughout Europe. Before this a few groups had emigrated southward to the Peloponnese, to Crete, Corfu, and the Ionian islands. References to their presence in Crete can be found in the stories of Franciscan monks Simon Simeonis and Hugo the Enlightened from 1322.

During the Ottoman empire it seems that a significant number of Gypsies continued to live in Thrace and Rumeli, as attested by official documents of the period (censuses, administrative documents, etc.). After the Graeco-Turkish War and due to the compulsory exchange of population between Greece and Turkey (ordered by the Treaty of Lausanne in 1923), Christian Gypsies joined the refugees from eastern Thrace, Istanbul, and Asia Minor and took up residence in Greece.

The Gypsies did not escape the devastation of World War II. During the German occupation of Greece many thousands of Gypsies were deported to concentration camps: the archives of Ravensbrück concentration camp provide evidence of this.

Today the Greek Gypsies generally call themselves *Tsiganoi*. The name *Gyphtoi* (*Gyphtos* in the singular) is also common, although it tends to be used by non-Gypsies and in a pejorative way. The word *Gyphtos* is an abbreviation of *aegyptios* ("Egyptian") and refers to the belief – current until the 18th century – that Gypsies came originally from Egypt. They are also called *Katsiveloi* (singular *Katsivelos* and feminine form *Katsivela*), a name that is found as early as the 14th century in Byzantine sources. According to linguistic studies the word comes from the Italian *cattivelo* (*cattivo* + *ello*), meaning "captive" and in the figurative sense "impoverished" or "destitute". Alongside these general names, other names are also used, such as *Kalo* (i.e. "the Dark One"), *Malele*, *Manouch*, and so on. Gypsies are also called by names which refer to their occupations or their geographic origin. Thus they can be called *romiogyphtoi* ("Greek Gypsies"), *turkogyphtoi* ("Turkish Gypsies"), *arnavout* ("from Albania"), or *chalkiades* ("smiths"), *demertzides* ("tanners"), *meskarides* ("bear trainers"), *tsabasides* ("cattle dealers"), *laoutarides* ("lute players"), and so on.

Artists have often been inspired by the lifestyle and philosophy of the Gypsies: for example the author Alexandros Papadiamantis with his novel *I Gyphtopoula* (The Gypsy Girl) or the poet Kostis Palamas with his important poetic work *O Dodekalogos tou Gyphtou* (The Twelve Words of the Gypsy). Very little attention has been paid to the Gypsies' contribution to Greek popular culture, although this seems to have been considerable: one needs only to think of their musical contribution to Greek popular festivals (*panigyria*). Unlike their culture, their language and their various dialects have been the subject of a number of studies by Greek and international linguists.

The Gypsies are probably the largest minority in Greece in numerical terms, although they have never been officially recognized. Their present population cannot be given exactly, as no data for minorities is available after the census of 1951.

The figure is estimated at around 120,000 to 150,000, taking into account the increasing emigration towards western Europe in recent years. The problem of estimating their population is further complicated by the fact that even today many Gypsies are not registered with the appropriate authorities.

In terms of their political status, the Greek Gypsies (with the exception of the Muslim groups living in western Thrace) were still stateless until a few years ago, as they were denied the right to Greek citizenship. It was not until 1978 that special regulations were introduced by the state, and in 1979 they were finally granted the right to full citizenship.

The Gypsies in Greece should not be regarded as a homogeneous group: they vary widely in terms of religion (Christian and Muslim, although the majority are Christian), in terms of language (mostly Romany but also Turkish and Greek), in terms of their degree of integration in Greek society, and their social status. Gypsies can be found throughout the country, although they live mostly on the outskirts of cities and provincial towns or in villages; generally they live in communities clearly separate from the rest of the population, often in ghettos which are rarely visited by outsiders. Although most of them have fixed places of residence, a significant proportion lead an itinerant lifestyle for financial reasons – because they are employed seasonally (in agriculture, for example) or live by trading. A good example of their heterogeneity can be found in three areas of western Athens: Agia Varvara, Ano Liosia, and Kolonos. Christian and Muslim Gypsies live in Kolonos, although there is scarcely any contact between them. While the Gypsies in Agia Varvara are regarded as the most fully integrated, the groups that live in Ano Liosia suffer from wretched living conditions and marginalization by non-Gypsies.

In general the Gypsies are marginal communities within Greek society: they are among the social groups who are most at risk, frequently living in conditions of great poverty. Illiteracy levels are high, as many studies of their social situation have demonstrated. Child labour is widely prevalent: their children are a common sight on the streets of cities and towns selling trinkets, washing car windscreens, or begging to earn a living.

On the initiative of several municipal councils the Intercommunal Roma-Network was founded in September 1995 in order to implement a nationwide plan to solve the most urgent problems facing the Gypsies. Objectives include the elimination of discrimination and marginalization by state and social bodies, and the support of nomadic or semi-nomadic groups.

SEVASTI TRUBETA

Summary

Gypsies, known in Greek as *athinganoi*, *atsiganoi*, *Gyphtoi*, or *Katsiveloi*, originated in India. In Europe they were first recorded living in Thrace before moving to Bohemia and elsewhere in the continent. They form heterogeneous groups in terms of religion, language, degree of social integration, and social condition. They are the largest minority in Greece and yet have never been officially recognized, though since 1979 they have been able to take Greek citizenship. As social groups they are marginalized and at risk.

Further Reading

Frazer, Angus, *The Gypsies*, 2nd edition, Oxford and Cambridge, Massachusetts: Blackwell, 1995

Giannakopoulos, Takis, *Oi Gyphtoi Kai to Dimotiko mas Tragoudi* [The Gypsies and our Folk Songs], Athens, 1979, reprinted 1981

Messing, Gordon M., "Influence of Greek on the Speech of a Greek Gypsy Community", *Byzantine and Modern Greek Studies*, 3 (1977): pp. 81–93

Messing, Gordon M., "Tsinganos and Yiftos: Some Speculations on the Greek Gypsies", *Byzantine and Modern Greek Studies*, 7 (1981): pp. 155–67

Messing, Gordon M., *A Glossary of Greek Romany, as Spoken in Agia Varvara (Athens)*, Columbus, Ohio: Slavica, 1988

Palamas, Kostis, *O Dodekalogos tou Gyphtou*, Athens; 1907; as *The Twelve Words of the Gypsy*, translated by Frederic Will, Lincoln: University of Nebraska Press, 1964; as *The Twelve Lays of the Gypsy*, translated by George Thomson, London: Lawrence and Wishart, 1969; as *The Twelve Words of the Gipsy*, translated by Theodore Stephanides and George Katsimbalis, London, 1974, Memphis: Memphis State University Press, 1975

Paspati, Alexander G., *Etudes sur les Tchinghianés ou Bohémiens de l'empire Ottoman*, Constantinople: Koromela, 1870

Soulis, George, "The Gypsies in the Byzantine Empire and the Balkans in the Late Middle Ages", *Dumbarton Oaks Papers*, 15 (1961)

Gyzis, Nikolaos 1842–1901

Painter

Like his lifelong friend and fellow Tinian the painter Nikephoros Lytras, Nikolaos Gyzis belongs to the so-called "Munich school" of Greek painters. But unlike Lytras, who returned to Greece to teach and work, Gyzis is an example of a Greek expatriate whose life and career unravelled entirely abroad without forsaking its distinctive Hellenic character. This character flourished in the context of the dual artistic trends – ethnographic genre and classicizing symbolism – prevalent in German art, especially in Munich, in the second half of the 19th century.

Hellenism was indeed a driving force in 19th-century Bavarian culture. In the first decades of the century, under the enlightened patronage of the philhellenic king Ludwig I, father of Greece's first king, Otho, Munich, the capital of Bavaria, became a lively cosmopolitan city adorned with handsome neoclassical buildings and museums, including Leo von Klenze's Propylaion, a modern echo of the celebrated gateway to the Athenian Acropolis, and his Glyptothek with its important collection of ancient Greek sculptures. By the second half of the century, Munich rivalled Paris as a centre for artistic instruction and lively artistic and intellectual exchange.

It was in Munich's celebrated Academy of Fine Arts that in 1865 the young Gyzis first came to study painting under the academic history painter Karl Theodor von Piloty (1826–86). He settled there permanently thereafter, with only rare trips abroad, to Greece and Asia Minor in 1872–74, and 1877; to Paris, along with Lytras, in 1876; and to Greece again in 1895. He achieved prominence as an artist in both his homeland and in Germany. In 1880 he was elected to honorary membership of the Munich Academy, and two years later was appointed full professor there. In Greece he was decorated by King George I in 1880.

His early works, up to the late 1880s, exemplify the contemporary fashion for sentimental, realistic, and anecdotal everyday-life scenes with a strong ethnographic flavour. In that sense, he followed the direction of contemporary Munich artists of his generation, including Ludwig Lofftz, Wilhelm Leibl, and the early Max Liebermann. Gyzis drew inspiration from a dual source: life during the times of the Greek struggle for independence from Turkish rule; and modern Greek customs and festivals. Among the former, *The Betrothal* (1875, National Picture Gallery, Athens) depicts the custom, prevalent in the rural countryside, of early engagements between children of well-to-do landed families intent to secure and expand their estates through profitable family connections during the uncertain times of Turkish rule. The painting known as *Children Gathering* (National Picture Gallery, Athens) refers to the brutal Turkish practice of abducting the first male offspring of Greek families to be raised as and become part of the fierce Turkish militia, known as the Janissaries. In turn, *The Secret School* (c.1885, private collection, Athens) is a scene of Greek resistance to Turkish efforts at cultural and linguistic levelling in occupied Greece. It represents a makeshift class of Greek children surrounding a Greek monk who teaches them how to read their native language in the secluded safety of a church interior, at night. A fully armed chieftain guarding the entrance is seated on a broken Ionic capital, a symbolic reference to the continuity of Greek culture from ancient to modern times.

The persistence of picturesque customs and festivals into contemporary times is the theme of paintings such as *The Grandmother's Tale* (1883, National Picture Gallery, Athens) with its attentively listening children clustering around the tale-telling grandmother. *Carnival in Athens* (c.1885, National Picture Gallery, Athens) is a scene of boisterous revelling and good-natured funmaking whose lavish ethnographic decor situates it in the coutryside rather than in urban Athens. These paintings depicted a colourful and highly idealized rural society that would appeal to middle-class Greek urban patrons as well as to an international clientele in a time of revived ethnographic interest throughout Europe.

Sometime in the early 1890s Gyzis gradually abandoned realistic genre for classicizing allegory with symbolist overtones. This redirection of his manner owes a great deal to the turn towards a more idealistic form of art inspired from ancient Greek myths and ancient Greek sculpture among the Munich avant-garde, and in Germany more generally. In Munich, the movement culminated in the creation of the first Munich Secession founded by artists such as Franz von Stuck and Georg Hirth, and the elaboration of the new style known as *Jugendstil*. Other painters included the Swiss Arnold Bocklin, who worked in Germany, and Hans von Marees who spent some time in Munich between 1857 and 1864.

Gyzis's work in that vein is anticipated by his painting *Spring Symphony* (1886, National Picture Gallery, Athens), a fantastic allegory of natural and spiritual renewal brought about by the sister arts of music and painting. His monumental work, *The Triumph of Bavaria* (c.1895; destroyed), a ceiling painting for the museum of applied arts in Nuremberg known through preliminary studies only, showed Bavaria in the guise of the goddess Cybele riding a lion-drawn chariot. Characteristic of his shift to symbolic allegory in a severe, classicizing style is also his painting commemorating the destruction of the island of Psara by the Turks as narrated in a poem of 1825 by Dionysios Solomos. Gyzis envisioned a gigantic, allegorical figure of victory or Nike mournfully surveying the burnt and ravaged island (1898–99; National Picture Gallery, Athens). From this phase, too, date numerous graphic works, posters, advertisements, and illustrated diplomas, including his design for the diploma of the 1896 Olympic Games.

Gyzis's artistic impact may be seen not so much on his immediate circle of Greek pupils trained in the Munich academy, such as the painters George Roilos (1867–1928) and Symeon Savvides (1869–1927), among others. Rather, his classicizing idealism provided the impetus for contemporary 20th-century painters, including Konstantinos Parthenis, George Moralis, and Panayotis Gounaropoulos.

NINA ATHANASSOGLOU-KALLMYER

See also Lytras

Biography

Born in Tinos in 1842, Gyzis studied in Munich under the painter Karl Theodor von Piloty and settled there permanently. Recognized as an artist in both Greece and Germany, he was made an honorary member of the Munich Academy in 1880 and a full professor there in 1882. In Greece he was decorated by King George I in 1880. His classicizing idealism influenced many 20th-century painters. He died in 1901.

Further Reading

Christou Chrysanthos, *Greek Painting, 1832–1922*, Athens: National Bank of Greece, 1981

Giofyllis F., *Istoria tis neoellinikis technis* [A History of Modern Greek Art], 2 vols, Athens, 1962

Oi Hellenes zographai [Greek Painters], 4 vols, Athens:, 1974–76, vol. 3, pp. 166–215

Kalliga, Marinou, *Nikolas Gyzis, he zoe kai to ergo tou* [Nikolaos Gyzis: Life and Work], Athens, 1981

Missirli, N., *Gyzis*, Athens, 1995

Montadon, Marcel, *Gyzis*, edited by H. Knackfuss, Bielefeld, 1902

Papanikolaou, Miltiades, "I helliniki ethographiki zographiki tou dekatou enatou aionos" [19th-Century Greek Ethnic Painting] (dissertation), Thessalonica, 1978

H

Hades

Hades, which in antiquity could denote both the subterranean kingdom of the dead and the god who ruled over it, means "that which is unseen", according to an ancient etymology. In the Classical period, however, "Hades" invariably referred to the god, never to his realm, which is described as "the house of Hades". He was the brother of Zeus, who ruled the upper air, and of Poseidon, who ruled the sea, though he never visited Mount Olympus. Rarely is mention made of any cult in his honour, due no doubt to the fact that he is characteristically described as "implacable" (*adamastos*) and "relentless" (*ameilichos*), and "most hated of all the gods". The most celebrated myth associated with his name involves his abduction of Demeter's daughter Persephone, whom he deceived into becoming his bride. In Greek mythology this is the explanation for the changing seasons, since Demeter, who succeeded in gaining her daughter's release from the clutches of Hades for eight months of every year (spring and summer), grieves and neglects the earth for the remaining four (autumn and winter).

Little is known about the appearance of the mythological kingdom of the dead. Its essential characteristic, however, was its impenetrable darkness. The earliest literary description is to be found in book 2 of Homer's *Odyssey*, where Odysseus visits the bounds of Oceanus in order to consult the denizens of the underworld. In book 24 the messenger god Hermes conducts the gibbering dead past Oceanus, the white rock, the gates of the sun god Helios, and the realm of dreams until they eventually reach the asphodel meadow.

The next literary description of Hades is provided by Aristophanes in his comic masterpiece *Frogs*. Having asked Heracles to describe to him the route by which he descended to the underworld to fetch Cerberus, the god Dionysus is informed that he will first come to a fathomless lake which he must cross in Charon's boat and then to "serpents and beasts in thousands", a "mass of mire", and "everlasting dung". Another important literary source is provided by myths put forward by Plato in his dialogues *Gorgias*, *Phaedo*, and *Republic*. The so-called Orphic gold leaves, which date to the 4th century BC, also provide limited information about the imaginary topography of the region. In addition, underworld scenes frequently appear in a series of Apulian amphorae of the later 4th century BC.

Hades' helpers only gradually assumed an identity and always remained somewhat shadowy. The earliest to emerge was Cerberus, the many-headed dog who acted as warder of the dead. Charon, the ferryman of the dead, did not appear until much later. In the Hellenistic period it became customary to place a small coin known as an obol in the mouth of the dead to pay for their fare across the River Styx. Charon is frequently depicted on Attic *lekythoi* (unguent flasks), waiting while the dead approach his boat.

It was a significant feature of Greek belief that the good and the bad led an equally cheerless existence in Hades. In early times very few were accorded a different destiny. They include the "blessed heroes", who, according to Hesiod (*Works and Days*, 166ff.), inhabit the Isles of the Blessed. Deep in the bowels of Hades was a windy region called Tartarus to which were consigned those who had outraged the majesty of the gods. Among its prisoners was Tantalus, who served his son Pelops to the gods to test whether they could distinguish human flesh from animal flesh. Around the mid-5th century BC a more developed belief in a dualistic afterlife emerged, due largely to the popularity of the mystery religions, which offered ill-defined blessedness in the hereafter for initiates. Principal among these was the Eleusinian Mysteries. Greek religion, however, did not promote anything comparable to the Christian notion of "weeping and gnashing of teeth" for those who failed to secure such blessedness.

The quality of life in Hades is well summed up by Achilles' observation to the effect that he would rather work as a day-labourer for a man who had little property than be lord of all the spirits of the dead (*Odyssey*, 11. 489–91). When encountered in the underworld, the dead appear to be frozen in a time warp. Ajax, for instance, is unable to forget the rancour that he feels towards Odysseus for having been beaten in the contest for the arms of Achilles. Equally pathetic is their preoccupation with the welfare of those who have survived them. The dead were believed to remain at the same age and in exactly the same physical condition that they were at the moment of death. Oedipus, for instance, states that the reason why he blinded himself was so that he would not have to look upon the faces of his parents in the underworld (Sophocles, *Oedipus Tyrannus*, 1371–73). Even so, it was infinitely preferable to enter Hades than to pass all eternity between two worlds. Especially to be pitied were the unburied dead. "Bury me as quickly as possible," Patroclus requests of Achilles (*Iliad*,

23. 71ff.), "so that I may enter the gates of Hades." In Sophocles' *Antigone* denial of burial is represented as an offence against the gods.

The Greek notion of Hades was taken up and developed by the Romans, notably by Virgil in *Aeneid* book 6. In the Septuagint Hades is used to translate the Hebrew word "Sheol". In Christianity the term is sometimes used of the place to which Christ descends after the Crucifixion.

ROBERT GARLAND

See also Afterlife, Death

Further Reading

Gantz, Timothy, *Early Greek Myth: A Guide to Literary and Artistic Sources*, 2 vols, Baltimore: Johns Hopkins University Press, 1993
Garland, Robert, *The Greek Way of Death*, London: Duckworth, and Ithaca, New York: Cornell University Press, 1985
Vermeule, Emily, *Aspects of Death in Early Greek Art and Poetry*, Berkeley: University of California Press, 1979

Hadjidakis, Manos 1925–1994

Songwriter and composer

Successfully bridging the worlds of popular and classical music throughout his long career as a songwriter, composer, conductor, and arts administrator, Manos Hadjidakis was a central figure in the musical life of Greece after World War II. He was born in 1925 in the northern Greek town of Xanthi, to a Cretan father and a mother from Adrianople. In Xanthi he received his first musical instruction from an Armenian pianist. After moving to Athens at the age of seven, he developed catholic tastes through exposure to the wide variety of popular and classical music to be heard in the capital. Although his decision to undertake advanced musical studies was frustrated by the onset of World War II, Hadjidakis nevertheless began composing music for the theatre in 1943. Emerging from the German occupation and subsequent civil war an enthusiastic autodidact, he embarked on what he later designated as the first of six creative periods: (1) 1946–50 "Theatre, music, and poetry"; (2) 1951–56 "Eros and a bit of music"; (3) 1957–66, dominated by film scores and popular song; (4) 1967–71 "Abroad"; (5) 1972–89 "Return to Greece and a period of maturity"; and (6) 1990–94.

With the piano suite *For a Small White Seashell* (op. 1, 1947–48), Hadjidakis began to assign opus numbers to what he felt were his most significant works, ultimately setting apart 51 of his 179 major compositions in this way. He regularly transcended the stylistic boundaries observed by such older composers as Yiannis Konstantinidis (1903–84), who wrote popular songs under the pseudonym Kostas Yiannidis. Whereas Konstantinidis, Kalomiris, and the other members of the National School employed Greek folk songs as the basis for classical compositions in the Central European manner, Hadjidakis offered an eclectic synthesis of art music and various types of popular song – including the Westernized cabaret song of the capital's bourgeoisie and the *rebetika* of its underclass – analogous to that created in the United States by his contemporary Leonard Bernstein. Hadjidakis announced his novel creative stance to the Athenian public in 1949 in a controversial lecture entitled "The Interpretation and Role of Popular Song". In this talk, excerpts of which were subsequently published, he scandalized many by placing *rebetika* on a par with folk song as an authentic expression of Greek culture and thereby a legitimate source of compositional inspiration. He further challenged inherited wisdom in 1953 with a series of lectures on modern American composers that were of fundamental importance for the development of Greece's postwar generation of classical musicians.

From the beginning of his career Hadjidakis demonstrated a preference for writing texted or programmatic music. In addition to composing film scores and incidental music for modern and ancient drama, Hadjidakis wrote several ballets, including *Six Popular Pictures* (op. 5, 1949–50) and *The Accursed Snake* (op. 6, 1950). Based on the eponymous karaghiozis shadow play, the latter work, for two solo voices and two pianos, was produced in collaboration with the noted puppeteer Evgenios Spatharis. Each of his first two creative periods also produced an important set of songs for voice and piano assimilating his relatively popular melodic and harmonic idiom to the tradition of the European art song: they are *Two Sailors' Songs* (op. 2, 1947), settings of poems by Miltos Sachtouris; and the *CNS Cycle* (op. 8, 1954), dedicated to Carlos Novi Sanchez, with homoerotic lyrics by the composer.

The advent of Hadjidakis's most prolific and financially profitable third period in 1957 was marked by incidental music for three plays: Iakovos Kampanellis's *Paramyhti Choris Onoma* (Nameless Fable, op. 11); a modern Greek translation by Thrasyboulos Stavrou of Aristophanes' *Lysistrata* (op. 12), including the hit song *Ena Mythos tha sas Po* (Let me Tell You a Story); and Odysseus Elytis's translation of *The Caucasian Chalk Circle* by Berthold Brecht (op. 13). With Nana Mouskouri as his primary interpreter from 1959 to 1963, Hadjidakis became, somewhat to his own surprise, a phenomenally successful composer of popular songs. An Academy Award in 1960 for the music he had written for Jules Dassin's *Never on a Sunday* brought him international recognition for his continuing work in the cinema, which peaked during this period with the composition of an astonishing 41 scores to Greek and foreign films. Typically, Hadjidakis took advantage of his new celebrity to advance the cause of contemporary Greek art music, in 1962 underwriting a competition for composers at the Athens Technological Institute that jointly awarded its first prize to Yiannis Xenakis and Anestis Logothetis. Two years later he founded the Experimental Orchestra of Athens, an ensemble which presented 15 world premieres of modern Greek works under his direction during its brief existence (1964–67). At the same time he continued to write many works for the stage, including an unfinished one-act opera and the musical *Street of Dreams* (op. 20). Successful in rejuvenating the moribund genre of the Athenian revue, the latter was also one of Hadjidakis' first collaborations with the poet and lyricist Nikos Gatsos. Further settings of texts by Gatsos and other noted writers placed Hadjidakis alongside Mikis Theodorakis in the popular imagination as co-creator of the so-called popular art song of the 1960s and 1970s.

In what he described as an attempt to liberate himself from a kind of celebrity he did not want, Hadjidakis moved to New York. He remained abroad for the first five years of the dictatorship (1967–72), which he claims to have met with a policy of non-resistance "without acceptance". After writing only four film scores and some chamber music during his self-imposed exile, he returned to Greece and embarked on an ambitious series of subtly orchestrated vocal works beginning with *O Megalos Erotikos* (The Great Lover, op. 30), for two voices, choir, and 12 instruments on texts by Elytis, Gatsos, Cavafy, Solomos, and others. The fall of the colonels' regime enabled Hadjidakis to recommit himself to the advancement of classical music in his homeland through a series of important posts: deputy director of the National Opera (1974), controller of the Greek Radio's Third Programme, and general director of the State Orchestra of Athens (1975–82). Hadjidakis continued balancing composition, conducting, and arts administration in this way until his death in Athens on 15 June 1994. Particularly significant was his founding of the Orchestra of Colours to promote modern Greek composers through performances, recordings, and publications.

ALEXANDER LINGAS

Biography

Born in 1925 in Xanthi, Hadjidakis's family moved to Athens when he was seven. His studies were interrupted by the outbreak of World War II but he began composing music for the theatre in 1943. He also wrote film scores, ballets, and songs. He lived in New York from 1967 to 1972. Returning to Athens, he was general director of the State Orchestra (1975–82). He died in Athens in 1994.

Further Reading

Foskarines, Thanos (editor), *Anoichtes Epistoles stou Mano Chatzidaki* [Open Letters to Manos Chatzidakis], Athens, 1996

Hadjidakis, Manos, *Ta Scholia tou Tritou* [The Third Commentary], 2nd edition, Athens, 1981

Hadjidakis, Manos, *O Kathrephtis kai to machairi* [The Mirror and the Sword], 4th edition, Athens, 1999

Leotsakos, George S., Hadjidakis entry in *The New Grove Dictionary of Music and Musicians*, edited by Stanley Sadie, vol. 8, London: Macmillan, and Washington, D.C.: Grove, 1980, p. 17

Mitsakis, Kariofilis, *Modern Greek Music and Poetry: An Anthology*, Athens, 1979 (bilingual edition)

Mylonas, Kostas, *Istoria tou Ellinikou Tragoudiou* [History of Greek Song], vols 2–3, Athens, 1985–92

Symeonidou, Aleka, *Lexiko Ellenon Syntheton* [Dictionary of Greek Composers], Athens, 1995, pp. 432–39 (includes a lengthy list of works)

Recording

Hadjidakis, Manos, *Recital*, Compact Disc recording SMH 890005.2, Sirius, 1990

Hadrian AD 76–138

Roman emperor

In an age of Roman philhellenism, Hadrian, the only Roman emperor (reigned AD 117–38) known to have been honoured with a statue in the Parthenon, was himself unusually actively philhellenic. In youth his interest in Greek studies had earned him the nickname "Graeculus". In AD 112 he was archon at Athens, where his friends included Arrian; he may also have met Epictetus at this time. After his accession as emperor in AD 117 he spent considerable periods in the Greek east; among the many instances of the Hellenic emphasis of his life are his wearing a beard (he was the first Roman leader to do so for many generations), his inclusion of a Poecile, a Tempe, and other Greek elements in his villa near Tibur (Tivoli), his initiation into the Mysteries of Eleusis (to which, according to Aurelius Victor, he continued to devote himself, back in Rome in the 130s, "after the manner of the Athenians"), and his "Greek love" relationship with Antinous (whose cult, fostered by Hadrian after Antinous' drowning in the Nile in AD 130, was particularly popular in Greek lands).

Hadrian – like many contemporary and earlier Romans and Greeks – sought to recover the Greek past. He delighted Greeks including Pausanias by restoring the tomb of Epaminondas. He gave back Mantinea its name after 150 years as Antigonea. In taking the name "Olympios" he associated himself not only with Olympian Zeus, whose temple in Athens he completed, but with Pericles, who had also assumed this name. In basing in Athens the Panhellenion, the all-Greek council established in AD 131/32, as in the honour he accorded to such cities as Sparta and Argos, he emphasized past glories, aiming perhaps, as Spawforth and Walker argue, to redress the balance between Achaea and Asia, between "cultural and historical eminence" and "economic and political muscle". (In Asia too, however, he was a benefactor during his visits of AD 123–24 and 129 to cities including Sardis, Smyrna, and Ephesus; Oresta was refounded as Hadrianopolis (Adrianople); at Cyzicus the emperor began the spectacular completion of the temple; Asian foundations included Hadrianutherae (modern Balikesir) in Mysia.)

Hadrian also, of course, sought to Romanize the Greek past or at least to recreate it, as Swain suggests, "in its idealised form" – "making Greece how it should be". In increasing the power of the Areopagus, for instance, he made the Athenian constitution more archaic – but "to the advantage of Rome and the local elite". Tested loyalty to Rome as well as authentic Greekness were conditions for cities wishing to belong to the Panhellenion; as Spawforth and Walker say, the cities' familiar preoccupation with questions of civic origin was transformed "at least indirectly, into a Roman concern ... encouraging a contemporary perception of the Greek past and the Roman present as complementary rather than mutually exclusive". Whatever the exact nature and functions of the Panhellenion – whether it was a new outlet for the social and political aspirations of upper-class Greeks (Spawforth and Walker) or rather "essentially a religious organisation, devoted above all to the cult of Hadrian and later emperors" (Jones) – it clearly involved a relationship between, negotiation between, Greeks and the empire. Hadrian's gate in Athens links and honours old and new with its inscriptions, on one side "This is Athens, once Theseus' city" and on the other "This is Hadrian's city, not Theseus'".

Similarly the buildings of Hadrianic Athens can be seen as "a stylish mixture of Greek and Roman traditions appropriate to the physical setting of a Panhellenic League founded by a Roman emperor" (Spawforth and Jones). Building went on for many years after Hadrian's visits of AD 124–25, 128–29, and 131–32, but among the first works to be begun may have been the temple of Olympian Zeus or Olympieion (in the *temenos* (precinct) of which the Panhellenion may have met), originally begun under Hippias and Hipparchus in the 6th century BC, and dedicated by the emperor in AD 132. The temple was built on a lavish scale, as is still apparent from its remaining columns. It was particularly renowned for its statues, including the ivory and gold cult statue, "worth noticing", according to Pausanias, "as it exceeds all other statues in magnitude except the Rhodian and the Roman colossi". At about the same time, probably, work began on Hadrian's Library or Stoa. This, says Pausanias, boasted 100 columns of Phrygian marble "and pavilions with gilded roofwork and alabaster, decorated with statues and paintings". Hadrian also built the aqueduct from Mount Parnes to the Agora, temples of Zeus Panhellenios and Hera, a gymnasium – 100-columned again, says Pausanias – a Pantheon, and, in the northeast corner of the Agora, a basilica.

Hadrian's cultural investment in Athens helped to transform it, during the course of the 2nd century, from "a provincial backwater by comparison with the great capitals of the eastern provinces at Antioch, Ephesus, or even at Corinth" (Shear) to a major and increasingly cosmopolitan centre. It became also, perhaps more directly as a result of Hadrian's personal initiatives, what Spawforth and Walker argue was "the agonistic centre of the Greek world": between AD 128 and 132 he founded the Panhellenia, the Hadrianeia, and the Olympieia and made the Panathenaia of equal status with these games. Perhaps even more helpfully, he provided the city with an annual grain supply. Already by AD 124–25 he had done enough for Athens for the city to reciprocate by doing him the unusual honour (last conferred on Attalus I of Pergamum in 200 BC) of creating the new *phyle* (tribe) Hadrianis; although this was possibly prompted in part by Rome or self-interest, it can scarcely have been a controversial decision.

The one area of the empire where Hadrian's Hellenism did not easily achieve the desired results was Judea, where the prohibition of circumcision and the decision to transform the ruins of Jerusalem into the *colonia* of Aelia Capitolina were among the main causes of the rising of AD 132–35 (indicating, for Birley, "that his Hellenism had blinded him to reality"). Elsewhere Greek influence was, increasingly, unopposed; Hadrian made a substantial contribution to this already powerful process, not only within the Greek lands but as the first emperor to "persuade the Greeks of old Greece to enter the Senate" and to appoint Greeks to govern provinces in the Latin west (Birley).

MARTIN GARRETT

Biography

Born in AD 76 in Spain, Hadrian was nicknamed "Graeculus" in youth for his devotion to Greek studies. In 112 he served as archon at Athens. He became emperor in 117 and spent long periods in the east where he sought to recover (and to Romanize) the Greek past, transforming Athens into a great eastern capital. He wore a beard to emphasize his Hellenism; he introduced Greek decor into his villa at Tivoli; he was initiated into the Mysteries of Eleusis; and he enjoyed a "Greek love" relationship with his friend Antinous. He died in 138.

Further Reading

Benjamin, A.S, "The Altars of Hadrian in Athens and Hadrian's Panhellenic Programme", *Hesperia*, 32 (1963): pp. 57–86
Birley, Anthony R., *Hadrian: The Restless Emperor*, London and New York: Routledge, 1997
Jones, C.P., "The Panhellenion", *Chiron*, 26 (1996): pp. 29–56
Pausanias, *Guide to Greece*, edited and translated by Peter Levi, 2 vols, Harmondsworth: Penguin, 1971; New York: Penguin, 1979
Shear, T. Leslie, Jr, "Athens: From City-State to Provincial Town", *Hesperia*, 50 (1981): pp. 356–77
Spawforth, A.J.S. and S. Walker, "The World of the Panhellenion" parts 1–2, *Journal of Roman Studies*, 75 (1985): pp. 78–104; and 76 (1986): pp. 88–105
Swain, Simon, *Hellenism and Empire: Language, Classicism, and Power in the Greek World*, AD 50–250, Oxford: Clarendon Press, and New York: Oxford University Press, 1996
Willers, Dietrich, *Hadrians Panhellenisches Programm: Archaologische Beitrage zur Neugestaltung Athens durch Hadrian*, Basel: Vereinigung der Freunde Antiker Kunst, 1990

Hagia Sophia

Former cathedral of Constantinople

The "great church" or cathedral of Byzantine Constantinople was Hagia Sophia – the church of the Holy Wisdom. This was located in the northeast of the city, within the Constantinian walls, north of the Augusteum and close to the Great Palace. The first church of Hagia Sophia on this site was dedicated in AD 360. Little is known, either from texts or from archaeology, of the 4th-century building, although it has been suggested that the domed two-storey structure usually identified as the sacristy of Hagia Sophia (the *skeuophylakion*) may be 4th or 5th century in date.

This first church was destroyed by fire early in the 5th century, and a new church was constructed on the site. The second (Theodosian) church was dedicated by the emperor Theodosius II in 415. There is more evidence for the form of this structure than for its predecessor, although only the west of the building has been excavated. It was a stone basilica with three doors from a narthex, decorated with a sculptural frieze depicting a flock of sheep, and a single line of columns forming a portico, leading down marble steps to an atrium. This building was also destroyed by fire, during the Nike riots in 532.

The emperor Justinian I (527–65) commissioned a new and larger church, to be constructed by Isidorus of Miletus and Anthemius of Tralles. Using marble and other resources from many parts of the empire, the new church was built on a massive scale. This church, dedicated in 537, was an architecturally novel and impressive structure. In plan it was a three-aisled rectangle, with galleries above the aisles. The nave was separated from the aisles by colonnaded arcades, and roofed by a huge dome surrounded by semi-domes. There was an eastern apse and a western narthex, also with a gallery. The galleries were entered by ramps situated in each corner of the church. To the west was an atrium, with a fountain in its centre, of which part (today known as the exonarthex) survives.

Excellent written descriptions of Justinian's church exist, and even today much of its fabric survives above ground. These enable detailed reconstruction of both the interior and exterior, and some understanding of its surroundings. The eastern apse contained a *synthronon* (shared throne) with semicircular steps for seating. The gold- and silverclad altar, positioned in the apse, had an altar cloth of purple embroi-

Hagia Sophia: symbol of Byzantine Christianity, the Great Church was converted to a mosque by the Ottomans and is a museum today

dered in gold and was covered by a ciborium with pyramidal roof. The altar screen was of silverclad marble. The stone pulpit (ambo), located slightly to east of centre of the church, was also magnificently decorated and partly silverclad.

The elaboration of these furnishings was not matched by complex figural or decorative scenes in mosaic. Although parts of the building were decorated with a simple floral design of gold and blue, the ceilings seem to have been covered with simple gold mosaic rather than figural decoration. This gold mosaic decoration must have been especially impressive since the church had a sophisticated lighting scheme, in addition to glazed windows. Glass lamps were suspended from the ceiling, silver lamps hung by the columns at differing levels, lamps on iron stands were positioned both on the floor and above the level of the column capitals, and there was a ring of lamps around the base of the dome.

This church remained the centre of religious activity in Constantinople throughout the Byzantine period. It was used by both the court and citizens of the city, and the nave space was allotted by rank and gender. The church was also well positioned in relation to both religious and secular administration. The Patriarchate was situated immediately adjacent to the church to the southwest, where a very small portion of it survives, and a private porticoed passageway led from the Great Palace to the church.

Written evidence suggests that the 6th-century baptistery may have been to the north of the church, although the structure today identified as the baptistery is a surviving rectangular structure to the south of the church with an octagonal interior plan. As already mentioned, there was also a sacristy, and immediately north of the church were the hospital of St Samson and the church of Hagia Eirene, outside the complex.

Although this church remained in use throughout the remainder of Byzantine history, it was much restored and altered. As early as 558 the dome partially collapsed. This led to a rebuilding and heightening of the dome, with its diameter reduced, the addition of buttresses to the exterior of the building, and other modifications. A cross design was placed in the centre of the dome. The church was rededicated in 562, but was severely damaged in an earthquake in 989 and again restored.

The middle Byzantine church was very different in appearance from its early Byzantine predecessor, and it is from this building that most of the surviving mosaics in the church come. Unlike the early Byzantine cathedral, the 9th-century and later church had very elaborate figural mosaics. These included

restored many times, notably in the years 1847–49 by the Fossati brothers, when Byzantine mosaics were discovered. After the declaration of the modern Turkish republic the building ceased to be a mosque and was opened as a museum in the 1930s. More mosaics, discovered by Thomas Whittemore in that decade, were placed on display at that time, and these continue to give some impression of the church's middle Byzantine splendour. Today the building remains a museum, and is one of the principal tourist attractions of the city.

Ken Dark

See also Architecture (religious)

Summary

Hagia Sophia, the Church of the Holy Wisdom, was the cathedral of Byzantine Constantinople. The first church, dedicated in 360, was destroyed by fire in the 5th century and a second church was destroyed during the Nike riots in 532. The third, still extant, building was commissioned by Justinian and dedicated in 537. It was the centre of religious activity in the city throughout the Byzantine period. The Ottomans turned it into a mosque in 1453. Today it is a museum.

Further Reading

Cormack, R.S. and E.J.W. Hawkins, "The Mosaics of St. Sophia at Istanbul: The Rooms above the Southwest Vestibule and Ramp", *Dumbarton Oaks Papers*, 31 (1977): pp. 175–251

Kahler, Heinz and Cyril Mango, *Hagia Sophia*, New York: Praeger, 1967

Krautheimer, Richard and Slobodan Ćurčić, *Early Christian and Byzantine Architecture*, 4th edition, New Haven, Connecticut and London: Yale University Press, 1986

Mainstone, Rowland J., *Hagia Sophia: Architecture, Structure, and Liturgy of Justinian's Great Church*, London and New York: Thames and Hudson, 1988

Mango, Cyril, *Materials for the Study of the Mosaics of St. Sophia at Istanbul*, Washington, D.C.: Dumbarton Oaks, 1962

Mango, Cyril and E.W. Hawkins, "The Apse Mosaics of St. Sophia at Istanbul", *Dumbarton Oaks Papers*, 19 (1965): pp. 115–51

Mango, Cyril, *The Art of the Byzantine Empire, 312–1453*, Englewood Cliffs, New Jersey: Prentice Hall, 1972

Mango, Cyril and E.W. Hawkins, "The Mosaics of St. Sophia at Istanbul: The Church Fathers in the North Tympanum", *Dumbarton Oaks Papers*, 26 (1972): pp. 1–41

Mango, Cyril, *Byzantine Architecture*, 2nd edition, London: Faber/Electa, 1986

Mark, Robert and Ahmet Çakmak (editors), *Hagia Sophia from the Age of Justinian to the Present*, Cambridge and New York: Cambridge University Press, 1992

Oikonomedes, N., "Leo VI and the Narthex Mosaic of St. Sophia", *Dumbarton Oaks Papers*, 30 (1976) pp. 151–72

Oikonomedes, N., "The Mosaic Panel of Constantine IX and Zoe in St Sophia", *Revue des Etudes Byzantines*, 36 (1978): pp. 219–32

Rodley, Lyn, *Byzantine Art and Architecture: An Introduction*, Cambridge and New York: Cambridge University Press, 1994

Teteriatnikov, Natalia, "Devotional Crosses in the Columns and Walls of Hagia Sophia", *Byzantion*, 68/2 (1998): pp. 419–45

Underwood, P. and E.J.W. Hawkins, "The Mosaics of St Sophia at Istanbul: The Portrait of the Emperor Alexander", *Dumbarton Oaks Papers*, 5 (1961): pp. 189–215

Van Nice, Robert L., *Saint Sophia in Istanbul: An Architectural Survey*, 2 vols, Washington, D.C.: Dumbarton Oaks, 1965–86

Whittemore, Thomas, *The Mosaics of St [Haghia] Sophia at Istanbul*, Paris and Boston, 1933–52

Hagia Sophia: Byzantine mosaics and other decorative features survive alongside incongruous quotations from the Qur'an

depictions of the Virgin and Child in the apse, an image of Christ Pantocrator in the dome, and a depiction of the Virgin flanked by SS Peter and Paul on the west arch.

In 1204 the church was sacked by western troops, and subsequently used as a Roman Catholic cathedral during the Latin occupation. It was the coronation and burial place of the Latin rulers, and the tombstone of one of their leaders – Enrico Dandolo – can still be seen. There were a few modifications under Latin rule, notably the construction of a belfry. After the recapture of the city in 1261, the church was again restored. However, the building was damaged by earthquakes yet again, notably in 1346 and 1355, when the main dome was rebuilt on the last occasion and provided with another Pantocrator mosaic, perhaps the last Byzantine mosaic on this scale.

Hagia Sophia was in use for Christian services until the very end of the Byzantine empire. Legends surround the final moments of the church, but it was promptly emptied by Turkish troops immediately after their capture of Constantinople in 1453 and turned into a mosque. The building continued to suffer earthquake and other damage, and was

Hagiography

Hagiography denotes written documents of all varieties that are relevant to the cult of saints. The purpose of hagiography is to record information on canonized people, thus providing edifying examples of Christian lives.

Hagiographical documents may be schematically divided into two types: the liturgical and the literary. An example of liturgical hagiography are the *Menaia,* in 12 volumes corresponding to the months of the year which include full information (a notice of the life with canons and tropes) about the saints to be commemorated each day; modern versions of a medieval service book, the Menaia, are the *Megas Synaxaristis tis Orthodoxou Ekklisias* (The Great Lives of the Saints of the Orthodox Church). The *Menologion* (Calendar), which is similarily divided by months, gives only the lives of saints. The Menologion was very widely disseminated in the Byzantine world, often with illustrations; the best-known version is that compiled in the mid-10th century by Symeon Metaphrastes, who standardized at a rather formal linguistic level many of the varied texts inherited from the past. The *Synaxarion* gives short notices on saints to be included in the daily office; the *Synaxarion of Constantinople,* probably also compiled in the 10th century, provides a full and interesting collection of material. *Typika,* that is, liturgical calendars giving instructions for each day's services, include notices on saints to be commemorated; from the 9th century three were in general use: that of the Great Church and two monastic types, the Studite and that of Mar Saba.

Many of the notices found in this liturgical material were constructed on the basis of literary hagiographical documents, that is, on the lives of the saints *(bioi* in Greek, *vitae* in Latin. These literary hagiographical documents are several types. In the 2nd and 3rd centuries the early Church had developed an edifying literature in the form, for example, of apocryphal gospels or accounts of apostles' missionary journeys; the journeys of St Paul and St Thekla are well-known instances with more than a hint of the novel. There also developed accounts of mayrtyrdoms *(martyria* in Greek, *passiones* in Latin, often called passions in English) which dealt not with the entire lives of saints but with the process, often gruesome, by which they met their deaths. Collections of sayings *(Apophthegmata Patrum)* are not strictly lives of saints, for they consist of series of gnomic utterances from groups of ill-defined but holy personalities, usually desert hermits, without a narrative structure. Finally there are narrative lives of a sort which would become conventional. There is often a formulaic quality to these: a pious child exhibits early prodigies of asceticism, overcomes temptations of sundry kinds, and ultimately leads a life whose sanctity is fully recognized only at death.

The genre of saintly life owes something to the traditions of ancient secular biography. Eusebius' *Life of Constantine* (written *c.*337–39) is already an example of a biography in which historicity is subordinated to a polemical and didactic purpose. This trend can be seen much more sharply in Athanasius of Alexandria's *Life of Antony* (*c.*356), often taken as the first example of a hagiographical Life; here the miraculous is accepted as normal and the regular passage of chronological time is immaterial. This is a pattern that is found regularly in subsequent lives, such as that of Theodore of Sykeon (d. 613), in which miracles are part of everyday rural life.

From the 4th to the 7th centuries the main centres for the writing of hagiography were Egypt, Syria, and Palestine. Lives of the monks of the desert monasteries, who had withdrawn from city life (and often from communal life also) were written, for example, by Palladius, whose *Lausiac History* on the monks of Egypt was written *c.*419; by Theodoret of Cyrrhus (d. *c.*466),who wrote a *Religious History* on Syrian monks; and by Cyril of Scythopolis (d. *c.*559) who compiled biographies of monks in Palestine.

Between the 7th and 9th centuries, the Byzantine dark ages, few hagiographical texts were produced. From the 9th to the 11th centuries the genre revived. Saintly heroes of this time were much involved with community life, whether founding monasteries, as did Lazaros of Mount Galesios (d. 1053); being the pious mother of a family, as was Mary the Younger (d. *c.*902/3); or playing an active political role, as did Euthymios, patriarch of Constantinople (907–12). It is at this time that the Menologion of Symeon Metaphrastes was compiled. In the 12th century, when interest in secular literature revived, once again relatively little hagiography was written – though what there was came from prominent literary men such as Theodore Prodromos (*Life of Meletios*) or John Tzetzes (*Life of Lucia*). In the 13th and 14th centuries there were a number of prolific hagiographers, such as Constantine Akropolites (d. before 1324), and a variety of approaches, including encomia of past saints and lives of prominent contemporaries, such as the emperor John III Vatatzes (*c.*1192–1254), or the patriarch Athanasios I (d. *c.*1315).

The saints whose lives have been recorded came from many walks of life: they include monks, desert hermits, holy fools, pillar-sitting stylites, military commanders and humble soldiers, empresses and prostitutes (though women are under-represented). The process of acquiring sainthood in the medieval Greek world was informal (the first official canonization in the Orthodox Church appears to have been that of the Patriarch Arsenios in the late 13th century). It depended on a reputation for sanctity and, usually and preferably, for working miracles. From that would develop a cult which would lead to the painting of an icon and the writing of a life.

Many lives are written by named and known authors, some of whom are mentioned above. Other significant hagiographers include Leontios of Neapolis (7th century), author of lives of John the Almsgiver and Symeon of Emesa; John Moschos (d. *c.*634), author of the *Spiritual Meadow,* a set of anecdotes about the monastic communities encountered during his travels; Ignatios the Deacon (d. *c.*845), author of a life of the patriarch Tarasios; Niketas David Paphlagon (early 10th century), author of about 50 encomia on saints; and Philotheos Kokkinos (patriarch of Constantinople 1353–55), a prolific writer on his contemporaries. Many lives are anonymous, especially the early *martyria*.

The audience and readership for hagiographical material in the Byzantine world would have been extensive, whatever the extent of literacy, over which scholarly uncertainty continues. Liturgical passages were read out during church services and so would have been heard by entire congregations. Longer lives would have been used for devotional reading, whether as part of monastic discipline or in a domestic environment. Anna

Komnene in the mid-12th century refers to her mother reading lives of saints, and such lives are recorded in the private library of Eustathios Boilas (d. 1059), so that it is possible to think of hagiographical narratives as the recreational literature of the medieval world.

Hagiography has continued to serve devotional purposes up to the present and the lives of post-medieval saints appear in service books. It also has value for the historian, providing useful insights into the thought of its producers and consumers. From hagiography much information can be gleaned about medieval religious beliefs and practices, about the artifacts of daily life, and, with careful sifting, many incidental details on historical events. A very significant role in the scholarly study of the genre has been played by the order of Bollandists, active in Belgium from the early years of the 17th century to this day, and their monumental series *Acta Sanctorum*.

ELIZABETH M. JEFFREYS

See also Biography and Autobiography, Canonization

Further Reading

Brown, Peter, "The Rise and Function of the Holy Man in Late Antiquity", *Journal of Roman Studies*, 61 (1971): pp. 80–101
Delehaye, Hippolyte, *L'Ancienne Hagiographie byzantine: les sources, les premiers modèles, la formation des genres*, Brussels: Société des Bollandistes, 1991
Hackel, Sergei (editor), *The Byzantine Saint*, London: Fellowship of St Alban and St Sergius, 1981; San Bernardino, California: Borgo Press, 1984
Halkin, François, *Bibliotheca Hagiographica Graeca*, 3rd edition, 3 vols, Brussels: Société des Bollandistes, 1957, reprinted 1986
Halkin, François, *Novum Auctarium Bibliothecae Hagiographicae Graecae*, Brussels: Société des Bollandistes, 1984
Mango, Cyril, "Saints" in *The Byzantines*, edited by Guglielmo Cavallo, Chicago: University of Chicago Press, 1997
Nesbitt, J., "A Geographical and Chronological Guide to Greek Saints' Lives", *Orientalia Christiana*, 35 (1969): pp. 443–89

Website

A survey of English translations of Byzantine saints' lives, maintained by A.M. Talbot at the Dumbarton Oaks Center for Byzantine Studies, is available on the internet at http://www.doaks.org/translives.html

Halicarnassus

City in southwest Asia Minor

Halicarnassus (modern Bodrum) was a Greek city in Caria in southwest Asia Minor, traditionally founded c.900 BC by the city of Troezen in the Argolid region of mainland Greece. With a superb sheltered position on the Mediterranean coast, the orientation of Halicarnassus was naturally outwards towards the Aegean rather than inwards towards the mountainous areas of inland Caria. The city had close ties with other east Greek cities given its position on shipping routes connecting them. In the Archaic period Halicarnassus was one of the cities of the "Dorian Hexapolis" (a loose federation of six cities of Dorian Greeks, which also comprised Cnidus, Cos, and the three cities of Rhodes, Lindus, Camirus, and Ialysus), but by the Classical period the city was Ionian with strong native Carian elements, although Caria as a whole was ruled by a local dynasty subject to the Great King of Persia. Herodotus, the Greek historian of the 5th-century BC wars between the Greeks and the Persians, was a native of Halicarnassus.

Given Persia's suzerainty in the region, Halicarnassus took part in the Persian Wars on the Persian side. The Carian dynast Artemisia I with five ships accompanied the invasion of Greece by the Great King Xerxes in 480 BC, and played a distinguished part in the sea battle off Salamis (recounted by Herodotus, 8. 88), although the battle was a Greek victory. Later, Halicarnassus became a member of the Delian League under the leadership of Athens, and served as an Athenian naval base at the end of the 5th century.

The 4th century BC was the zenith of Halicarnassus. The dynast Mausolus, who became the Persian satrap after Halicarnassus returned to Persian control in 386 BC, moved his capital there from the inland city Mylasa c.370 BC, synoecized (united into one city) neighbouring non-Greek settlements, and embarked upon an ambitious building programme to transform Halicarnassus into a grand city. He built fortification walls, a palace, harbour installations, a Greek-style theatre, various public buildings, and revealed a considerable familiarity with, and appreciation of, Greek culture. He meddled in 4th-century Greek politics in the Aegean to the detriment of the Second Athenian Confederacy, and extended his influence in Asia Minor and the Aegean.

Halicarnassus was justly famous for the great tomb of Mausolus, known as the Mausoleum, probably begun during his lifetime and completed c.350 BC after his death. This monument was a major achievement of Greek art and was considered one of the seven wonders of the ancient world in Hellenistic and Roman times. Built in a commanding position overlooking the harbour, the tomb would have dominated the city and served as a landmark to seafarers. Information about the Mausoleum is derived from ancient literary descriptions and extensive excavation, and, although it has been variously reconstructed, it essentially consisted of an Ionic colonnade atop a high square podium, surmounted by a pyramidal roof. The building was adorned with quantities of free-standing sculpture and several relief friezes. Mausolus had the money and influence to employ the leading Greek sculptors of his day (among them Scopas of Paros, Leochares of Athens, Bryaxis, and Timotheus). The pyramidal roof was a striking feature, perhaps inspired by eastern prototypes (the pyramids of Egypt have been proposed as among the Mausoleum's forerunners).

The Mausoleum had many imitators. To name but a few: Alexander the Great (who surely saw the Mausoleum when he besieged Halicarnassus – see below) built at Babylon an immense pyramidal tomb composed of six stepped levels for his beloved companion Hephaistion after his death in 324 BC. Moreover, Alexander's proposed "Last Plans" (if genuine) included a pyramidal tomb for his father Philip II (Diodorus Siculus, 18. 4. 5). Finally, the famous Lion Tomb in the independent Greek city Cnidus, which lies at the tip of a peninsula just south of the Bodrum peninsula, was topped by a stepped pyramid supporting a platform for an enormous recumbent lion.

Halicarnassus: marble frieze showing battle between Greeks and Amazons from the Mausoleum, *c.* 350 BC, British Museum, London

The smooth course of Alexander the Great's progress down the east coast of Asia Minor during his invasion of the Persian empire was interrupted when Halicarnassus offered resistance, but the city finally fell in 334 BC after a difficult siege (vividly described in Book 1 of Arrian's *Anabasis*). After Alexander's death, Halicarnassus – like other Greek cities in Asia – could not escape the power struggles of his successors, and it was subject at various times to the new Graeco-Macedonian Hellenistic kingdoms (the Ptolemies of Egypt, the Seleucids of Syria, and the Antigonids of Macedonia) as well as to the independent Greek island of Rhodes. It became part of the Roman province of Asia in 129 BC.

During the Byzantine period, Halicarnassus was the seat of a bishop under the metropolitan of the city of Aphrodisias in northeast Caria. It faced capture by the Turks, the Crusaders, the Hospitaller Knights of St John (who in the 15th century AD built the magnificent Castle of St Peter in the harbour of Bodrum largely from blocks of the Mausoleum, whence much of it was recovered), and finally by the Ottoman Turks in the 16th century. Its last appearance in Greek history was the unsuccessful rebellion of the city against Ottoman rule in AD 1770, supported by the navy of Catherine the Great of Russia. After the upheavals of World War I and the fall of the Ottoman empire, Halicarnassus became part of the modern state of Turkey.

E.E. RICE

See also Mausolus, Persian Wars

Summary

A city in Caria, southwest Asia Minor, Halicarnassus (modern Bodrum) was traditionally founded by colonists from Troezen *c.*900 BC. It was the home of the 5th-century BC historian Herodotus. It reached its peak in the 4th century BC under King Mausolus whose tomb, the Mausoleum, was one of the Seven Wonders of the ancient world. The Castle of St Peter was built by the Knights of St John.

Further Reading

Ashmole, Bernard, *Architect and Sculptor in Classical Greece*, London: Phaidon, and New York: New York University Press, 1972

Bean, George E., *Turkey beyond the Maeander*, 2nd edition, London: Benn, and New York: Norton, 1980

Boardman, John, *Greek Sculpture: The Late Classical Period, and Sculpture in Colonies and Overseas*, London and New York: Thames and Hudson, 1995

Fedak, Janos, *Monumental Tombs of the Hellenistic Age: A Study of Selected Tombs from the Pre-classical to the Early Imperial Era*, Toronto: University of Toronto Press, 1990

Hornblower, Simon, *Mausolus*, Oxford: Clarendon Press, and New York: Oxford University Press, 1982

Isager, Jacob (editor), *Hekatomnid Caria and the Ionian Renaissance*, Odense: Odense University Press, 1994

Linders, Tullia and Pontus Hellström (editors), *Architecture and Society in Hecatomnid Caria*, Uppsala: S. Academiae Upsaliensis, 1989

Ruzicka, Stephen, *Politics of a Persian Dynasty: The Hecatomnids in the Fourth Century* BC, Norman: University of Oklahoma Press, 1992

Waywell, G.B., *The Free-Standing Sculptures of the Mausoleum of Halicarnassus in the British Museum: A Catalogue*, London: British Museum Publications, 1978

Waywell, G.B., "The Mausoleum of Halicarnassus" in *The Seven Wonders of the Ancient World*, edited by Peter A. Clayton and Martin J. Price, London and New York: Routledge, 1988

Harbours

Because the Greeks have been a seafaring people since before recorded history, harbours have always played an important part in their life. Certainly the rocky terrain of mainland Greece, and settlement on the islands of the Aegean, encouraged travel by sea as opposed to travel by land. Yet, as Lionel Casson, the naval historian, points out, it was possible to load and unload ships lying off an open beach without using harbour installations until well into the 19th century AD, so the absence of harbours did not necessarily preclude a city or island from participating in seafaring. In the early days, ships could even be drawn up on to shore, literary evidence of which can already be found in the *Iliad* and *Odyssey*, presumably composed in the 8th century BC. Nevertheless, the importance of harbours even at this early date may be reflected in the fact that Nestor led to Troy 90 ships, the second biggest contingent of the Greeks after Agamemnon's 100, according to the catalogue of ships in book 2 of the *Iliad*. (Indeed, some scholars have argued that the catalogue of ships may reflect an actual Mycenaean order of battle for some historical event underlying the myth of the Trojan War.) According to tradition Nestor was also associated with the magnificent natural harbour at Navarino bay in the western Peloponnese, while archaeological finds have linked him with the Bronze Age palace found near the bay.

The *Odyssey* depicts the mythical Phaeacians as living almost in a fairy-tale land, and, among their many blessings, endows them with an idealized harbour consisting of a protective bay with sheds for the storage of sails and rigging, stone bollards for tying ships to, work space for sailmakers, riggers, and shipwrights, and a shrine to Poseidon, surrounded by a meeting place (*Odyssey*, 6. 263–69). These features may be taken as the desiderata of a Greek harbour of the Archaic period. Actual harbours did not lag far behind this poetic one, and soon surpassed it, as in the harbour at Delos with its 8th-century BC mole, 100 m long, constructed from rough-hewn granite blocks. The Phaeacians depended on nature alone for a protected anchorage. At the end of the 6th century BC the tyrant Polycrates built a harbour at Samos comprising two moles, one 370 m long and the other 180, and included it within the circuit of the city's defence wall (Herodotus, 3. 60). Also at the end of 6th century BC, according to the pseudo-Aristotelian *Constitution of Athens*, the tyrant Hippias began fortifying Munychia in the Piraeus, even though Athens continued to use the open roadstead at Phalerum as a harbour until about 493 BC.

At the beginning of the Classical period the ideal Greek harbour had moles (*chomata*) to provide a safe anchorage (*hormos*). A commercial harbour (*emporion*) had quays, open sheds (*neosoikoi*), and warehouses, whereas a naval base (*neorion*) had boathouses (*neosoikoi*) and gear sheds (*skeuothekai* or *hoplothekai*). Defence towers stood at the seaward end of the moles and, being brought within the circuit of the town wall, made it a protected harbour (*limen kleistos*). In fact, several cities in the Classical period went so far as to join their harbours to their cities with long walls, most famously Athens and the Piraeus, Corinth and Lechaeum, its port on the Corinthian Gulf, and Megara and Nisea, its port on the Saronic Gulf. In the Piraeus, Pashalimani (ancient Zea) and Tourkolimano (ancient Munychia) in the Piraeus were *neoria*, whereas Megas Limin (ancient Cantharus) served as both an *emporion* and as a *neorion*, as indeed it still does today. The presence of the harbours, and their use as commercial and naval centres for Athens beginning in 493 BC with Themistocles' founding of a navy to repel Xerxes' invasion, led to a lot of construction in the Piraeus. In about 450 BC Hippodamus of Miletus imposed an orthogonal city plan on the Piraeus which is still reflected in the layout of the modern streets.

Pashalimani in the Piraeus has the best-preserved boathouses, served by a stone slip *c*.3 m wide and 37 m long. (From these dimensions Morrison and Coates have derived the size for their recent reconstruction of the trireme.) The boathouses' roof was supported by columns each just under 6 m wide; the use of columns instead of a solid wall allowed for ventilation. The boathouses stored ships and wooden gear (masts, yards, poles, ladders, and oars). Oeneiadae in Acarnania had longer boathouses with bevelled slips to fit the ships' bilges, and they are therefore thought to have accommodated quadriremes or quinqueremes, larger than the triremes presumably housed at Pashalimani. The Piraeus also had an elaborate gear shed, built in the 4th century BC and known as the arsenal (*skeuotheke*) of Philon; considered something of an architectural wonder, its details are known to us from an inscription (*IG* 2^2, 1668). By the end of the 5th century BC, the essential elements of the commercial harbour in the Greek world had been worked out, becoming more elaborate and increasing in size in later centuries.

The harbours of the Hellenistic age were of vast size and integrated plan. The premier harbour of the period was of course at Alexandria, the city Alexander the Great founded in 330 BC and named after himself. Its plan was crowned by the famous Pharos, a lighthouse which was one of the seven wonders of the ancient world and the light of which could be seen from about 50 km away. There were two basins at Alexandria, the Great Harbour, which faced east, and the Eunostos, which faced west. The Great Harbour was formed by two stone moles (one of which was 900 m long), the tips of which were 600 m apart, though underwater obstacles reduced this opening to two entrances, 100 and 200 m wide, respectively. Such a plan, dominated by a lighthouse, probably influenced the Roman emperors Claudius and Trajan in developing the facilities at Ostia for the reception of the grain fleet from Egypt, for, when Trajan had finished with it in the early 2nd century AD, Ostia also had two harbours dominated by a lighthouse.

Also in the Hellenistic age, Delos became a commercial centre for trade in the Aegean, as well as continuing to be an

Harbours: Mykonos, the principal harbour for those visiting Delos. The slavers of the ancient world have been replaced by the cruise liners of today.

important shrine to Apollo. Inscriptions show that it was a centre of the slave trade, and the Romans deliberately fostered it as a trading rival to Rhodes, expelling the Delians in 166 BC and replacing them with Athenian settlers. In 146 BC Corinthian importers moved there from their own city which had been sacked by the Romans, and the religious festival in honour of Apollo on Delos practically became a trade fair. Delos, however, never recovered from the depredations of Archelaus, the general of Mithridates of Pontus, and pirates in the 1st century BC, and went into a slow decline thereafter.

Since, as Lionel Casson points out, Byzantine ships were, if anything, smaller than their Classical counterparts, harbour installations were even less necessary for handling cargoes. Nevertheless, the Byzantines continued to use those harbours, such as Alexandria, which they inherited from the Romans, and built new ones, for example on the Golden Horn at Constantinople. It was the presence of a harbour at Ravenna that partly led to the establishment of an exarchate there following the reconquest of parts of the Italian peninsula by emperor Justinian in the early 6th century AD, even though the port was already beginning to silt up. In addition, ports like Nauplia, the best harbour in the Argolid, fell into crusader and then Venetian hands after the Fourth Crusade of 1204, and became the focus of intermittent struggle between their owners and the Turks during the following four centuries or more.

During the Tourkokratia, many harbours fell into relative disuse, owing to a lack of interest in trade on the part of the Ottomans. Piraeus, for example, was virtually uninhabited in 1834, when the capital of newly independent Greece was moved to Athens. Its growth in population, from 4000 in 1840 to 11,000 in 1870, to 75,000 in 1907, is an index to the revival of the city of Athens, and the tripling of its population in 1922 testifies to a massive resettlement of refugees from Asia Minor. The harbour at Navarino bay played an important part in the War of Independence when, on 20 October 1827, a combined British, French, and Russian fleet of 26 ships trapped and defeated a larger Turkish fleet of 82, sinking 53 of them. Furthermore, Greek predominance in shipping in the modern era has been enhanced by its many fine harbours.

ERIC KYLLO

See also Ships, Trade

Further Reading

Blackman, D.J., "Ancient Harbours in the Mediterranean", parts 1 and 2, *International Journal of Nautical Archaeology and Underwater Exploration*, 11/2 and 11/3 (1982), pp. 79–104 and 185–211

Casson, Lionel, *Ships and Seamanship in the Ancient World*, Princeton, New Jersey: Princeton University Press, 1971, reprinted Baltimore: Johns Hopkins University Press, 1995

Morrison, John S., and J.F. Coates, *The Athenian Trireme: The History and Reconstruction of an Ancient Greek Warship*, Cambridge and New York: Cambridge University Press, 1986

Healing Cults

A genuine human desire to turn towards higher, spiritual forces beyond "scientific" medicine in times of illness and distress manifested itself very early in Greek culture. Already Linear B tablets from Knossos are addressed to "Paieion" ("Pa-ya-wo-ne") who receives votives of limbs in Palaikastro about 1600 BC (Middle Minoan) and is the doctor of the gods also in the *Iliad* (5. 401, 899f.); he will later amalgamate with Apollo. Apollo's son Asclepius is still a mortal in the *Iliad*, but already a "doctor without fault" (4. 194); not only his two sons, Machaon and Podalirius, but also other heroes such as Patroclus act as physicians if the need arises. Likewise the seer (and later healing hero) Amphiaraus was originally a battle hero, participating in the war of the "Seven against Thebes"; when his army was routed, Zeus would not let his seer die, but conveyed him into the underworld alive by splitting the earth before him. Afterwards, Amphiaraus was revered as a healing and oracle-giving hero, with musical and sports contests (Amphiareia) being held in his honour.

The overall increase of hero cults in the 7th and 6th centuries BC also led to an intensified worship of healing heroes. Above all in Attica there existed plenty of healing gods and heroes, among them heroified historical persons (e.g. Hesiod in Orchomenus; in Athens, Sophocles became the hero Dexion, after he had received the god Asclepius). Almost every other god and goddess could assume healing functions, too, above all Apollo; Artemis cared especially for pregnant women, newborn babies, and young children, and Athena was already in the 6th century BC worshipped as "Athena Hygieia" on the Acropolis.

This variety of healing cults was very much reduced when from about 420 BC onwards Asclepius became the most prominent healing god. His cult first seems to have existed in Thessaly (Trikka) and Messenia; his most important place in the later 5th century BC was Epidaurus, whence the cult spread to Eleusis, Delphi, Paros, Corinth, Cos, Pergamum, and in 420 BC (during the plague) to Athens; in these transfers, Asclepius' holy snake was brought by ship or cart to its new place. The only other healing cult that continued was that of Amphiaraus; his main sanctuary was the Amphiareion in northeast Attica, with a branch established in Athens itself near the Theseum between 377 and 375 BC. Iconographically Asclepius is often represented as a bearded elderly man wrapped in a garment and carrying a stick (Amphiaraus is similarly depicted from the 4th century BC) and together with his family: his wife Epione, his sons Machaon and Podalirius, his daughters Hygieia, Aegle, Aceso, Iaso, Panaceia, and later also with a dwarf called Telesphorus ("who brings to a good end") who is either his son or his servant.

In Hellenistic and Roman times, healing cults and Asclepieia spread through the whole Aegean and beyond. The increasing popularity of these cults coincided with the rise of scientific medicine, which may seem paradoxical at first sight. The basic attitude of ancient doctors was different from that of today. According to Hippocrates, a physician has to do three things: first, to describe the case; second, to draw conclusions about the kind of illness; and finally to decide either "I will treat this illness" or "I won't treat it". In the latter case the sick needed an alternative to whom they could turn, and at this point healing gods and heroes came in.

The best-preserved healing places – the above-mentioned Amphiareion near Oropus (not far from the Boeotian border) and the Asclepieia in Epidaurus and Cos – all show the same main elements: the sanctuary of the god, an incubation hall (see below), baths, a theatre, and guesthouses for the pilgrims; most of these buildings were constructed in the 4th century BC, when the importance of healing cults reached a first climax. The famous theatre of Epidaurus has space for 15,000 spectators, a measure of the immense popularity of the cult. Such additional amenities created the atmosphere of a "holiday resort" and may have been important for the well-being and curing of the visitors. Certain rules of behaviour had to be observed; dying people or women giving birth were denied access, for they would cause religious impurity.

Healing was mainly sought by the process of "incubation", i.e. sleeping in the sanctuary. The patients first had to make a purificatory offering, sacrificing an animal at the altar in front of the temple. After physical cleansing in the baths, patients laid themselves down to sleep on the skin of the sacrificed animal in the *koimeterion* or "incubation hall", a long columned hall, which could be partitioned into small compartments. The god then approached people in their dreams by touching them either with his own hand or with one of his holy animals, the snake or the dog (both already companions of oriental healing gods), which bit or licked the spot where the patients were suffering. The healed placed votive offerings – imitations of limbs in various materials and reliefs depicting the healing – in front of the temple; when the more precious items (in gold, silver, and bronze) were later melted down, an inscription noted the shape of the votive, its donor, and its weight. Tales of miraculous healings were preserved on wooden or marble tablets; in Epidaurus they were collected and inscribed on big marble stelai (1.70 ¥ 0.75 m) in the second half of the 4th century BC; three of these, containing 130 healing miracles, are still extant. It is difficult to form an adequate judgement of these "miracles"; but as modern medicine has long since acknowledged the importance of psychological factors in healing, one should not talk of "cheating", as scholars did in the 19th century. Frequently mentioned in these tales are eye complaints (in the *Plutus* of Aristophanes, the god of wealth himself is cured of his blindness in the course of a very funny incubation), paralysis, speech disorders (the god often cures muteness by a sudden shock), ulcers, abscesses, old sores (in the case of which the god often performs spectacular surgery), and everything connected with pregnancy and desire for children. Interestingly, Christian tales of miraculous healings by saints (as found in records from their holy places) are very similar to these pagan ones; even in our time, observation (in places such as Lourdes) has shown that religious ecstasy can induce spontaneous healing.

There was a second flourishing of healing cults in the 2nd century AD, with the Asclepieion of Pergamum being one of their foremost places; even leading intellectuals such as Aelius

Healing Cults: the Asclepieum at Pergamum, where the cult of Asclepius was brought from Epidaurus in the 4th century BC

Aristides eagerly sought their help. Healing divinities preserved their appeal well into the mysticism of late antiquity; by the 4th and 5th century AD, however, they were increasingly superseded by Christianity (with Christ himself often acting as healer).

Not all places of pagan healing cults were destroyed in late antiquity, but often they were transformed into places of Christian cult, with Christian saints taking over the duties of their pagan predecessors. In Byzantine times miraculous healing could still be brought about by incubation in churches at a holy place; other cures consisted of kissing the tomb of a saint, anointing oneself with oil from the lamp that was suspended above a saint's tomb, drinking oil or water that had come into contact with the saint's relics. From the 4th century AD onward, such relics (the mortal remains of holy persons or objects sanctified by contact with them) were often transferred to various local churches and developed a significant role in healing. Another source of miraculous healing was provided by icons. The Second Council of Nicaea in AD 787 laid down certain principles of icon veneration and in particular acknowledged the powers of miracle-working icons, which had already a centuries-old tradition behind them; above all, *acheiropoieta* (images "not made by human hand", but mysteriously found) were regarded as miraculous. There was an exemplary case of this even in more recent times: on the island of Tinos (on which already in antiquity a great festival for a Poseidon with healing powers had existed) a miraculous icon of the Virgin Mary was found in the early 19th century and provided important moral support to the Greeks fighting for their independence; the icon was placed in the church of Panagia Evangelistria (finished in 1830) and quickly became the most important centre of pilgrimage for healing in the Orthodox world; the Panagia Tiniotissa is now the patron saint of Greece.

BALBINA BÄBLER

See also Medicine

Further Reading

Edelstein, Emma J. and Ludwig Edelstein, *Asclepius: A Collection and Interpretation of the Testimonies*, 2 vols, Baltimore: Johns Hopkins University Press, 1945, reprinted Salem, New Hampshire: Ayer, 1988

Eijk, P.J. van der, H.F.J. Horstmanshoff, and P.H. Schrijvers, *Ancient Medicine in its Socio-Cultural Context*, vol. 2, Amsterdam: Rodopi, 1995

Forsén, Björn, *Griechische Gliederweihungen: Eine Untersuchung zu ihrer Typologie und ihrer religions- und sozialgeschichtlichen Bedeutung*, Helsinki: Suomen Ateenan-Instituutin Säätiö, 1996

Hackel, Sergei (editor), *The Byzantine Saint*, London: Fellowship of St Alban and St Sergius, 1981; San Bernardino, California: Borgo Press, 1984

Henry, P., "The Formulators of Icon Doctrine" in *Schools of Thought in the Christian Tradition*, edited by Patrick Henry, Philadelphia: Fortress Press, 1984

Krug, Antje, *Heilkunst und Heilkult: Medizin in der Antike*, 2nd edition, Munich: Beck, 1993

Laguros, A.S., *I Istoria tis Tinou* [The History of Tinos], Athens, 1983

Talbot, Alice-Mary M., *Faith Healing in Late Byzantium: The Posthumous Miracles of the Patriarch Athanasios I of Constantinople by Theoktistos the Stoudite*, Brookline, Massachusetts: Hellenic College Press, 1983

Health

The standard Greek words for health (e.g. *hygieia, euexia*) do not appear in Homeric and Hesiodic epic, but "disease" (*nousos/nosos*) is a significant theme ever since the tenth line of the *Iliad*, and freedom from disease is depicted as belonging to a faraway land (*Odyssey*, 15. 407–08) or to a lost golden age (Hesiod, *Works and Days*, 90–126). Once the Greeks developed more fully articulated conceptions of "health" in the Classical and Hellenistic periods, they disagreed vigorously among themselves about how to define it, how to achieve it, and where to rank it among the human goods.

1. *Conceptions and definitions of health.* Balance, harmony, due proportion, equilibrium, regularity, and proper mixture or blending ("temperament") were central to the Greek understanding of health in most epochs, but there was no consensus on exactly what constitutes a "harmony", a healthy blending, etc. Furthermore, a significant minority adopted a very different approach to health. The 5th-century BC philosopher-scientist Alcmaeon of Croton might have been the first to claim that the "equal rights" (*isonomia*) of opposing qualitative powers (moist–dry, cold–hot, bitter–sweet) in the body preserves health, whereas a "monarchy" of any single such power causes disease (but the late 1st-century AD doxographic text that attributes this view to Alcmaeon displays suspect, anachronistic terminology). This conception of health recurs in Greek philosophical and medical texts until the Early Modern period. According to the Presocratic Diogenes of Apollonia, for example, health depends on a proper mixture of blood and air in the body, while the Hippocratic treatise *On the Nature of a Human Being* argues that health exists to the greatest degree whenever four juices or humours "that are in the body" – blood, phlegm, yellow bile, black bile – achieve the right quantitative and qualitative proportions relative to one another. For all their strong disagreements about the basic constituents of the human body, several other Hippocratic texts (e.g. *On Ancient Medicine, On Regimen*) as well as Empedocles, Democritus, Philistion of Locri, Plato, Aristotle, Galen, and most Byzantine physicians and philosophers shared this fundamental theory that good health is due to a right blending (*krasis*) or balance of constitutive elements or qualities or substances, whereas disease is due to a rupture of such a blending or balance, resulting in a separation or disproportion of elements, etc.

The quantitative implications of balance and proportionality sometimes were given mathematical expression, notably by the Pythagoreans. They not only characterized health as a harmony and an "equality of parts" (*isomoiria*) of opposites but also called their "perfect number" – the decadic *tetraktys* (i.e. 10 as the sum of 1, 2, 3, and 4) – "the principle (*arche*) of health" and referred to their mathematical symbol of identity (a pentagram) as "health". Furthermore, they advocated the use of music, which they viewed as a mathematical phenomenon, to maintain or restore harmony in the body. Some of Plato's theories of due proportion and mixture are not unrelated to the Pythagoreans' mathematicizing versions of health, but Plato perhaps elaborated the moral and aesthetic dimensions of such a conception more fully, closely correlating health, the well proportioned, the good, and the beautiful (e.g. *Timaeus*, 87c–d).

"Health of the soul" (*psyche*) was often explained in the same terms as physical health. Indeed, a number of Greeks, early and late, viewed health as a condition or disposition of a unitary psychosomatic entity. Closely related was the popular association of physical and mental health with moral uprightness (and, correspondingly, the attribution of diseases, including mental disorders, to moral failings, a recurrent notion in Greek popular culture of all epochs, especially when accompanied by the ascription of illness to divine intervention). Many physicians, including some Hippocratics, Aretaeus of Cappadocia, Soranus of Ephesus, Galen, and later writers, explained mental health by reference to relations or interactions between material elements or substances in the body. At times, however, philosophers – including those who, unlike Plato, offered a materialist account of the soul – attempted to draw sharp distinctions between physical and mental or "psychic" health. Some Stoics, for example, defined the health of the body as a good blend (*eukrasia*) or due proportion (*symmetria*) of the four elementary qualities (hot, cold, wet, dry) but the health of the psyche as a good blend of the opinions of the soul.

2. *Attaining and maintaining health.* The theories of balance, harmony, and proportionality are closely related to a broader ideology of moderation. Critias, for example, suggested in an elegy that the moderate drinking practised by the Spartans is fitted beautifully to health and to the works of Aphrodite, sleep, and temperance ("the neighbour of piety"), while Xenophon attributed the extraordinary health of the Spartans to their moderate eating habits. Similarly, in a comic fragment of Eubulus, Dionysus limits those who are healthy in mind to three kraters of wine: the first for health, the second for eros, the third for sleep; with the fourth krater, he says, one leaves the realm of Dionysus and enters that of hubris. Several Hippocratic treatises (e.g. *Affections*, 49) similarly claim that smaller quantities of food are better for one's health. The frequent ancient Greek criticisms of the excesses characteristic of athletes' diets and exercises, and so too the clear distinction drawn by some physicians between steady good health and exceptional physical strength, are further manifestations of a wide-ranging cultural valorization of moderation, even if there often were considerable gaps between belief and practice.

Starting in the 5th century BC a sizeable body of Greek literature developed on the preservation and restoration of health by means of regimen (*diaita*), i.e. by a stable mode of living, including diet, exercise, bathing, and other regular habits. Herodicus of Selymbria was widely regarded as being among the founders of this tradition, but the 5th-century BC Hippocratic treatise *On Regimen* is the first extant work offering detailed, comprehensive norms for human regimen with a view to health, while also taking account of individual differences in age, gender, season, constitutional type, location, environment, etc. The fundamental tenets of this Hippocratic text remained a cornerstone of much subsequent work on regimen. Many of its prescriptions entail self-control, also in matters of eating and drinking, and this has suggested to modern scholars that its audience – like that of most ancient and Byzantine treatises on health through regimen – was assumed to have an ample food supply. In reality, food shortages were endemic in the ancient Mediterranean, even if not all food crises were severe. The primary audience of the extensive Greek medical literature on regimen therefore probably was a literate socioeconomic elite. Palaeopathological analyses of skeletal remains confirm that certain nutritional deficiencies were common throughout antiquity. Not all such deficiencies are attributable to catastrophic food crises (nor are all recurrent congenital diseases, rheumatic ailments, cases of dental caries, etc.), but it is nonetheless striking that evidence of deficiency, also in children, is at least as common as evidence of dietary excess, even at times of economic prosperity.

Other Greek writers on achieving health through regimen include Acron of Agrigentum, Philistion of Locri, Diocles, Mnesitheus, Dieuches, Praxagoras of Cos, Herophilus, Erasistratus, members of the Empiricist "school", Galen, and numerous early and late Byzantine authors, e.g. Oribasius (especially books 1 and 4), Hierophilus the Sophist (*On Nutriment according to the Months*, i.e. the months of the Julian calendar, and *On the Faculties of Nutriment*), and Symeon Seth.

None of these works was more influential than Galen's monumental *Health* (*Hygieina*) 1–6 and *On the Faculties of Foods* 1–3. In *Hygieina* Galen assigned the preservation of health to "hygiene" ("the art of health") but the restoration of health to therapeutics. His *Health* is based on the classical theory of a due proportion and blending of four primary qualities (hot, cold, wet, dry) and of four humours. Not every deviation from the normal humoral proportions results in a disease; like several precursors, Galen adopted the notion of relative health. Health can range from an ideal condition to one just short of disease. This latitude leaves room *inter alia* for the different temperaments or humoral blendings characteristic of different humans in a normal healthy state and for the 40 different normal human constitutions accommodated in Galen's physiopathology. Food, drinks, exercise, rest, bathing, massage, the surrounding air, sleeping, being awake, excretions, and emotions are interactive factors that can be regulated quantitatively and qualitatively by "hygiene" to preserve health in different human types and under different conditions.

3. *Health and human values.* While there was a broad consensus in most epochs that health should be classified among the goods (*agatha*) or among the excellences or "virtues" (*aretai*) of the body, there was less agreement about its value relative to other goods. In popular morality health often is given first place. A drinking song, for example, ranked health first, beauty second, and wealth third (Plato, *Gorgias*, 451e1–452d4). Isocrates' hierarchy was health first, then prosperity, then being honoured as a morally good person; and the comedian Philemon (*c*.368–267 BC) ranked health first, prosperity second, pleasure third, and owing no debts fourth. Among the maxims attributed to Menander is also the transculturally recurring claim that "nothing is better in life than health". It is hardly surprising that Hippocratics agree that health is worth the most to human beings (e.g. *Regimen in Health* [in *Nature of a Human Being*]).

A related but logically different valorization of health is the depiction of health as a necessary condition of all other human goods. In a paean to the goddess Hygieia (Health), Ariphon of Sicyon (5th–4th century BC), for example, sang "without you no one is happy", claiming that Health alone makes possible the joys of wealth, children, political power, and eros. This commonplace is found in a variety of genres, including medical treatises. The Hellenistic physician Herophilus, for example, depicted the actualization of all human goods – those of the soul, of the body, and external ones – as dependent upon health.

Not all Greeks agreed, however, that health should be accorded first place among the goods. Philosophers, in particular, challenged this popular view. Crantor (*c*.340–275 BC) envisioned a Panhellenic theatre in which personifications of four traditional goods vied for first prize in an oratorical contest. The audience awarded first prize to Courage, second to Health, third to Pleasure, and fourth to Wealth. And in Plato's *Republic* (9) Socrates argues that a wise person will not make physical health a chief aim but will rather subordinate the interests of the body to those of the soul; harmony in the body should merely be in the service of harmony in the soul. Similarly, in Plato's *Laws* (1. 631b6–d6) the Athenian stranger ranks four "divine" goods – wisdom, moderation, justice, courage – above four "lesser human" goods, viz. health, physical beauty, physical strength, and prudent wealth. Aristotle, too, proposed a hierarchical distinction between goods or virtues of the soul (which in turn are subdivided into intellectual and moral virtues), goods of the body (health here being valued more highly than strength and beauty), and external goods. The Stoics went further, arguing that health, though preferable, is neither a virtue nor a vice but morally indifferent (*adiaphoron*).

4. *Health and religion.* The remarkable popularity of the cult of Asclepius in all parts of the Greek world did not eclipse the many other divinities associated with health. *Hygieia* ("Health"), for example, appears as an epithet of Athena as early as 500 BC and, slightly later, as the personification of an attribute of Aphrodite, as a divine daughter of Asclepius, and as an independent goddess. Sometimes Health also shared cult sites with Dionysus, Tyche, and other deities. The Greeks' relation to Hygieia and to other gods of health expressed itself in sacrifices and prayers that signalled an expectation not only of health but also of the enjoyment of other physical, mental, and material "goods" (including especially eros and "blameless wealth"). Criticism of the use of religious practices to achieve health was occasionally voiced by philosophers (e.g. Democritus and Diogenes of Sinope), and magicians and charlatans were explicitly denounced by Hippocratics. But many representatives of scientific medicine, including several Hippocratics and Galen, explicitly accepted the therapeutic

role of religion, notably of Asclepius and of prayer, much as some Byzantine writers transmitted scientific theories of health, even while worshipping Christ as Healer and while accepting a Christian body–soul dualism that devalued physical health and privileged Christ as physician of the soul. About paganism in the Roman empire it has been remarked that "the chief business of religion...was to make the sick well" (MacMullen, 1981). Early and Byzantine Christianity likewise recognized the pervasive longing for mental and physical well-being and, by addressing this desire both theologically and practically (e.g. through care of the infirm and "hospitals"), it rendered Christ a victorious successor to Asclepius, even as Byzantine Christians transmitted Galen's science of health.

HEINRICH VON STADEN

See also Anatomy and Physiology, Disease, Healing Cults, Medicine

Further Reading

Brock, Nadia van, *Recherches sur le vocabulaire médical du grec ancien: soins et guérison*, Paris: Klincksieck, 1961, especially chapters 12–16 (on words for, and concepts of, "health" and "healthy")

Craik, Elizabeth M., "Diet, Diaeta, and Dietetics" in *The Greek World*, edited by Anton Powell, London and New York: Routledge, 1995

Edelstein, Ludwig, *Ancient Medicine*, edited by Owsei Temkin and C. Lilian Temkin, Baltimore: Johns Hopkins Press, 1967

Galen, *A Translation of Galen's Hygiene (De sanitate tuenda)*, translated by Robert Montraville Green, introduction by Henry E. Sigerist, Springfield, Illinois: Thomas, 1951

Galen, *Selected Works*, translated by P.N. Singer, Oxford and New York: Oxford University Press, 1997 (includes *The Thinning Diet, To Thrasybulus: Is Healthiness a Part of Medicine or of Gymnastics, Good Condition*, etc.)

Garnsey, Peter and C.R. Whitaker (editors), *Trade and Famine in Classical Antiquity*, Cambridge: Cambridge Philological Society, 1983

Garnsey, Peter, *Famine and Food Supply in the Graeco-Roman World: Responses to Risk and Crisis*, Cambridge and New York: Cambridge University Press, 1988

Grmek, Mirko D., *Diseases in the Ancient Greek World*, Baltimore: Johns Hopkins University Press, 1989

Kornexl, Elmar, *Begriff und Einschätzung der Gesundheit des Körpers in der griechischen Literatur von ihren Anfängen bis zum Hellenismus*, Munich: Wagner, 1970

Lonie, Iain M., "A Structural Pattern in Greek Dietetics and the Early History of Greek Medicine", *Medical History*, 21 (1977): pp. 235–60

MacMullen, Ramsay, *Paganism in the Roman Empire*, New Haven and London: Yale University Press, 1981

Miller, Timothy S., *The Birth of the Hospital in the Byzantine Empire*, Baltimore: Johns Hopkins University Press, 1985

Oribasius, *Dieting for an Emperor: A Translation of Books 1 and 4 of Oribasius' Medical Compilations with an Introduction and Commentary*, edited and translated by Mark Grant, Leiden: Brill, 1997

Volk, Robert, *Gesundheitswesen und Wohltätigkeit im Spiegel der byzantinischen Klostertypika*, Munich: Institut für Byzantinistik und Neugriechische Philologie, 1983

von Staden, Heinrich, *Herophilus: The Art of Medicine in Early Alexandria: Edition, Translation, and Essays*, Cambridge and New York: Cambridge University Press, 1989, especially chapters 4 ("The Parts of the Art of Medicine") and 8 ("Regimen and Therapeutics")

Wilkins, John, David Harvey and Mike Dobson (editors), *Food in Antiquity*, Exeter: University of Exeter Press, 1995

Wöhrle, Georg, *Studien zur Theorie der antiken Gesundheitslehre*, Stuttgart: Steiner, 1990

Hecataeus of Miletus

Prose writer of the 6th–5th centuries BC

Hecataeus of Miletus, son of Hegesander, the most important of the early Ionian prose writers, was active in the late 6th and early 5th centuries BC. The little that is known of his life is drawn from Herodotus, in whom may repeatedly be detected a tension between unacknowledged exploitation of and polemic against Hecataeus' work. Herodotus introduces Hecataeus in conversation with the priests of Amnon at Thebes (2. 143), an encounter which strongly suggests a symbolic force as the representative of the Ionian enlightenment confronts the custodians of Egypt's ancient wisdom. Hecataeus reappears in a very different context, playing a prominent part in Herodotus' account (5. 36, 124–26) of the planning of the Ionian Revolt (500–494 BC). His prudent opposition, based on geopolitical considerations, suggests a relatively senior figure; he does not forfeit the confidence of the leaders of the liberation movement by his disapproval of their strategy, and his clear-sighted estimate of their chances demonstrates the value of geographical study for those who want to serve their fellow citizens. There is reason to doubt the historicity of Hecataeus' role in both these episodes; the prominence which Herodotus here affords Hecataeus should perhaps be seen primarily as a tribute to one whom he recognized as his intellectual precursor.

Besides improving Anaximander's map of the world, which he envisaged as a flat disc encircled by the river Oceanus, Hecataeus wrote a pioneering work of systematic geography, the *Periegesis* or *Periodos Ges* ("Journey Round the World"), divided into two books, "Europe" and "Asia" (the latter including Africa). The *Periegesis* provides information about the places and peoples to be encountered on a clockwise coastal voyage round the Mediterranean and the Black Sea, starting at the Straits of Gibraltar and ending on the Atlantic coast of Morocco, with diversions to the islands of the Mediterranean and inland to Scythia, Persia, India, Egypt, and Nubia. In addition to the enumeration of peoples and their territorial boundaries, of rivers, mountains, bays, towns and harbours, Hecataeus on occasion notes other items of interest, such as strange customs (e.g. frr. 154, 284, 287) and legendary history (e.g. frr. 76, 129); but if his geographical work could be adequately accommodated in two rolls without further subdivision, he cannot often have gone into much detail. We owe to Hecataeus the familiar description of Egypt as the gift of the Nile (fr. 301; cf. Herodotus, 2. 5. 1, Arrian, *Anabasis*, 5. 6. 5). It is uncertain how far his information was based on his own first-hand observations and inquiries; Miletus, with its extensive colonial network and overseas trade, would have been an ideal environment in which to gather geographical data. We might wonder, too, whether he was indebted to topographical and ethnographical information assembled by the Persian administration. It is difficult to assess how much Herodotus owed to Hecataeus' work, and, though much subsequent geographical writing probably drew on it, precise debts are hard to identify. Over 300 fragments of the *Periegesis* survive, the two parts of the work being about equally represented; but many are merely citations in Stephanus of Byzantium recording the occurrence of a place name in the *Periegesis*. Callimachus regarded as spurious the text of *Asia* known to him (T 15: Athenaeus 70A, 410E; Arrian, *Anabasis*, 5. 6. 5), presumably the source of citations in later authors; we do not know his reasons, but it is likely enough that a topographical work would be tacitly brought up to date so long as it was felt to have some practical utility, and he may have been troubled by references to places beyond the horizons of a writer active around 500 BC.

We do not know whether Hecataeus' geographical work preceded or followed his mythographic treatise, the *Genealogies* (or *Histories* or *Herologia*). This comprised at least four books, but fewer than 40 fragments survive (and some of those conventionally assigned to the *Genealogies* by reason of their subject matter may belong to foundation legends related in the *Periegesis*). The opening of the *Genealogies* proclaims Hecataeus' intellectual independence, and rather suggests that he was influenced by contact with foreign traditions (fr. 1): "Hecataeus of Miletus speaks thus. I write what seems to me to be true; for the Greeks have many tales which, as it appears to me, are absurd." His subject was the legends of families claiming a divine origin (including, apparently, his own (Herodotus, 2. 143)). It is not clear whether his terminus was the Trojan War, or whether he continued to include material relating to the sons of the Homeric heroes; but it should certainly not be supposed that he regularly attempted to follow genealogical traditions down to his own day. In the *Genealogies* legends of the heroic age are transposed into the sober rationalism appropriate to prose; the methods of Ionian science are applied to the legendary past. As is shown by his treatment of Geryon (fr. 26), who is relocated from the far west to Ambracia, and of Cerberus (fr. 27), identified as a formidable snake, called the hound of Hades because of its lethally poisonous bite, Hecataeus evidently believed that behind the fabulous elaborations of tradition lay historical facts distorted by exaggeration or by literal interpretation of metaphorical expressions. Whether he pioneered this demythologizing approach we cannot tell, but certainly it proved immensely influential; Herodotus' treatment of the foundation of Dodona (2. 54–57) well illustrates its application, and Rudolf Bultmann's work on the New Testament demonstrated that still in the mid-20th century the method retained its attraction not only for journalists but even for serious scholars.

Dissimilar as the subject matter of his works may at first sight appear, both alike serve as intermediaries between Archaic catalogue poetry and the more sophisticated methods of synthesizing information about the *oikoumene* characteristic of the 5th century BC. Here, as with many of the developments associated with Ionian intellectuals, we see the beginning of trends often regarded as characteristic of the sophistic movement. The fragments are too short to give a fair idea of his style; ancient critics regarded it as clear but much less varied and attractive than that of Herodotus.

Heraclitus of Ephesus, the approximate contemporary of Hecataeus, took a severe view of his work, including him with Hesiod, Pythagoras, and Xenophanes in his list of those who showed that much learning did not produce good sense (12B40 Diehls-Krantz).

STEPHANIE WEST

Biography

A native of Miletus, active in the late 6th and early 5th centuries BC, Hecataeus was the most important of the Ionian prose-writers and Herodotus' most significant intellectual precursor. Besides revising Anaximander's map, he wrote a geographical work (*Periegesis*) and a rationalizing mythographic treatise (*Genealogies*), of which only fragments survive.

Writings

Fragmenta, edited by Giuseppe Nenci, Florence: Nuova Italia, 1954

In *Die Fragmente der griechischen Historiker*, edited by Felix Jacoby, 2nd edition, 1, Leiden: Brill, 1957

Further Reading

Drews, Robert, *The Greek Accounts of Eastern History*, Washington, D.C.: Center for Hellenic Studies, 1973

Fritz, Kurt von, *Die griechische Geschichtsschreibung*, vol. 1, Berlin: de Gruyter, 1967

Jacoby, Felix, Hecataeus entry in *Real-Encyclopädie der klassischen Altertumswissenschaft*, edited by August Pauly *et al.*, vol. 7, 2666 ff., reprinted in *Griechische Historiker*, Stuttgart: Druckenmüller, 1956, pp. 185 ff.

Pearson, Lionel, *Early Ionian Historians*, Oxford: Clarendon Press, 1939, reprinted Westport, Connecticut: Greenwood Press, 1975

West, Stephanie, "Herodotus' Portrait of Hecataeus", *Journal of Hellenic Studies*, 111 (1991): pp. 144–60

Helena, St *c.*AD 255–*c.*330

Mother of the emperor Constantine I

Helena was born of humble stock in Drepanon, Bithynia, probably in the 250s. She was an innkeeper when she met Constantius Chlorus, whose wife (or concubine) she became, and to whom she bore the future Constantine I. When Constantius, as a junior member of the Tetrarchy – Caesar to the Augustus Maximian – married Maximian's stepdaughter, Theodora, Helena was excluded from court, and she did not return there until after Constantius' death. As the mother of the emperor Constantine, Helena's influence rivalled that of Constantine's wife, Fausta. Under her son's influence she embraced Christianity (earlier she may have been Jewish). She became Augusta, together with Fausta, around 325, and may have had a hand in the murder of Fausta, after the execution of her favourite, her grandson Crispus, in 326. In that year she embarked on a pilgrimage to the Holy Land, where she discovered several sacred sites, and founded and richly endowed the churches at Bethlehem and on the Mount of Olives in Jerusalem. According to a later legend, it was during this pilgrimage that Helena discovered the True Cross, portions of which were to be found throughout the Mediterranean world, venerated as relics, by the end of the 4th century. Eusebius, in his account of the pilgrimage in his *Life of Constantine*, composed in the late 330s, knew nothing of the discovery of the cross, but in 347 Cyril, bishop of Jerusalem, makes mention of the "holy wood of the cross". He, however, appears to have known nothing of any connection with Helena. The last of the Church Fathers to be ignorant of the legend of Helena's discovery of the True Cross appears to be John Chrysostom, and the first account of the legend occurs in the panegyric preached by Ambrose, bishop of Milan, at the death of the emperor Theodosius in 395. After her return from the Holy Land, Helena lived, not at her son's court in Constantinople, but in Rome.

Helena's influence is manifest in two ways: in connection with her legendary discovery of the True Cross, and in connection with her son, Constantine. Legends grew up around her discovery of the cross. Already by the time of Ambrose, the legend tells how three crosses and two nails were discovered by Helena. Barely a decade later, around 403, we find more developed accounts in which the True Cross is identified by its miraculous powers, healing a sick lady according to Rufinus in the continuation appended to his translation of Eusebius' *Church History*, and raising from the dead the body of a man, recently deceased, the final form of the legend, according to Paulinus of Nola (*Epistles*, 31). These legends, further amplified into a story that stretched from Adam, by way of Solomon and Constantine, to Herakleios, who recovered the True Cross from the Persians in 629, perhaps had greater currency in the West than in Byzantium, where the feast of the Exaltation of the Cross, celebrated on 14 September, has as much to do with the cross as a symbol of the divine protection of the Christian empire as with the legend of the True Cross itself.

It is in connection with her son, Constantine, that Helena is honoured as a saint; the pair are described as "sovereigns equal to the apostles" (*isapostoloi basileis*) in the *Synaxarion* (short notices on saints to be included in the daily office) for 21 May, the date of their commemoration. As early as the 5th century, the imperial couple Marcian and Pulcheria were hailed as the new Constantine and the new Helena at the Council of Chalcedon in 451; another pair similarly honoured were Constantine VI and his mother and co-regent Irene, at the end of the 8th century. Constantine and Helena are mentioned, somewhat incongruously perhaps, in the marriage service of the Byzantine Church, when their prayers are invoked in the prayer of blessing of the newly married couple.

ANDREW LOUTH

Biography

Born *c*.AD 255 at Drepanon in Bithynia to humble, possibly Jewish, parents, Helena became the wife or mistress of Constantius Chlorus and by him the mother of the future emperor Constantine I. She received the title Augusta *c*.325. In legend she is celebrated for finding the True Cross in Jerusalem. As a saint she is revered in association with her son. She died in Rome in the 330s.

Further Reading

Couzard, Remi, *Sainte Hélène d'après l'histoire et la tradition*, Paris, 1911
Drijvers, Jan Willem, *Helena Augusta: The Mother of Constantine the Great and the Legend of Her Finding of the True Cross*, Leiden: Brill, 1992
Hunt, E.D., "Helena: History and Legend" in his *Holy Land Pilgrimage in the Later Roman Empire*, AD 312–460, Oxford: Clarendon Press, and New York: Oxford University Press, 1982

Heliodorus

Novelist of the 4th century AD

Author of the *Aithiopika* (Ethiopian Story), the last and most sophisticated of the ancient Greek novels, Heliodorus stands at the crossroads of Hellenism. Probably written shortly after AD 350, in the twilight of paganism, the novel itself looks resolutely backwards to Classical Greece, apparently ignoring the existence of both Rome and Christianity. By its scale – ten books – technical flamboyance, and appropriation of the canonical texts of Classical Greek literature, it seems almost deliberately set up as the final authentic masterpiece to round off the Classical tradition. The fact that it was arguably exploited by Julian the Apostate in two of his orations seems to confirm that it shares the emperor's militant nostalgia for the pagan past. And yet, according to our earliest biographical testimony, that of the 5th-century ecclesiastical historian Socrates, Heliodorus went on to become a Christian bishop who enforced strict celibacy on his clergy at Trikka in Thessaly. Whatever the truth of this report, it was instrumental in ensuring the novel's survival in Byzantium and thence its transmission to the Renaissance in western Europe, where Heliodorus was ranked alongside Homer and Virgil as a master of epic narrative. Though it is not quite what modern readers expect a novel to be, it is, within its own terms, a masterpiece. Recent work has explored Heliodorus' innovative narrative technique, which shows rather than tells and conscripts the reader into an active interpretive role, from the enigmatic opening tableau onwards.

Heliodorus locates his novel firmly in the Classical mainstream. Although its plot follows the romantic stereotype of a beautiful young and noble couple (Theagenes and Charicleia) falling in love at first sight and enduring numerous adventures, ordeals, and attempts on their chastity before living happily ever after, the *Ethiopian Story* is both more intricate and less episodic than its predecessors. It presents its familiar story in a radically new way, by beginning in the middle and then filling in the earlier episodes by means of a long retrospective narration by one of the characters, which ends about halfway through the whole. This format is clearly modelled on the *Odyssey*, and indeed Heliodorus has also modified the standard story so that, for one of its protagonists at least, it becomes, like the *Odyssey*, a journey home, culminating in marriage and paternal recognition. Specific episodes, such as a necromancy, also recall the Homeric prototype, while the secondary narrator, an Egyptian priest called Calasiris, begins with a quotation from the *Odyssey* and is a figure of Odyssean cunning and duplicity – characteristics that inform his narrative technique as well as his actions. The novel is also permeated by references and allusions to the Athenian theatre (often in abstruse technical detail), partly as a meta-literary commentary on its own theatricality, partly as a device of characterization to distinguish between the "tragic" protagonists and "comic" secondary characters. Some episodes recall specific tragic models; for example, the subplot of his stepmother's infatuation with the Athenian Cnemon, which he narrates in the first book, rewrites the story of Hippolytus, and the events of the final book, when the protagonists face human sacrifice at the end of the earth and a king proposes to sacrifice his own daughter for the sake of his community, play on the reader's acquaintance with Euripides' two Iphigenia plays. For the setting, Heliodorus has ransacked Classical historians and geographers: every detail of his Ethiopia, for example, can be traced to literary sources, occasionally in defiance of known reality.

The heroine of the novel, Charicleia, is an Ethiopian princess, born white to black parents, exposed at birth, and subsequently brought up as a Greek by the priest of Apollo at Delphi. The hero, Theagenes, is a descendant of Achilles and characterized as a true Hellene by his victory at the Pythian games. The couple's adventures lead them through Egypt and an encounter with the corrupt and sensual Persian occupying powers – the story is set in the 6th century BC – to Ethiopia, where the novel ends with their installation as priest and priestess of the Sun and Moon, the Ethiopian national gods. It is difficult not to read this scenario as a coded exploration of the nature of Greek cultural or racial identity and its place in the multicultural world of the Roman empire, especially as Heliodorus, at the end of the novel, reveals himself as non-Greek, a Phoenician from Emesa. Similarly the novel's polemically pagan religious apparatus of divine governance and its basically, but unsystematically, Neoplatonic world view – with an almost abstract pure divinity mediated to humanity by a plurality of lower and often malevolent powers – combined with an untypically ascetic sexual ethic applying equally to male and female, look like a displaced engagement with the issues posed by the rise of Christianity.

If we discount an uncorroborated report by the 14th-century historian Nikephoros Kallistos Xanthopoulos, that the bishop Heliodorus had to renounce his see because he refused to disown his novel, we have no evidence for the reception of the *Ethiopian Story* before the Byzantine period. As early as the 7th century a few of Heliodorus' *sententiae* were included in the *Florilegium* of Maximos the Confessor, and from this and similar anthologies passed into Byzantine paroemiographies. His novel was read and summarized by Photios in the 9th century, discussed from a literary and moral perspective by Psellos in the 11th, and subjected to an allegorizing Christian interpretation by Philippos Philagathos in the 12th. In the same century the basic plot structure of the *Ethiopian Story*, with its beginning *in medias res*, was imitated in the literary Byzantine romances of Theodore Prodromos and Niketas Evgenianos, who also took over details of theme and incident. The *Ethiopian Story* was hugely influential in western Europe after the publication of the *editio princeps* in 1534 and Amyot's French translation in 1547, but much less so in Greece. However, in 1804 Adamantios Korais published a groundbreaking edition with modern Greek commentary, in the introduction to which he claimed the modern novel as a Greek invention.

J.R. MORGAN

See also Novel

Biography

Born at Emesa in Syria and probably writing in the 4th century AD, Heliodorus was the author of the *Ethiopian Story*, last of the surviving ancient Greek novels. According to the 5th-century historian Socrates, he later became a Christian bishop. This has been doubted, but the story no doubt ensured the survival of the text.

Writings

Les Ethiopiques, edited by R.M. Rattenbury and T.W. Lumb, 2nd edition, 3 vols, Paris: Belles Lettres, 1960 (Greek text and French translation)
An Ethiopian Story, translated by J.R. Morgan, in *Collected Ancient Greek Novels*, edited by B.P. Reardon, Berkeley: University of California Press, 1989, pp. 349–588
Ethiopian Story, translated by Walter Lamb, edited by J.R. Morgan, London: Dent, and Rutland, Vermont: Tuttle, 1997

Further Reading

Bartsch, Shadi, *Decoding the Ancient Novel: The Reader and the Role of Description in Heliodorus and Achilles Tatius*, Princeton, New Jersey: Princeton University Press, 1989
Gärtner, H., "Charikleia in Byzanz", *Antike und Abendland*, 15 (1969): pp. 47–69
Morgan, J.R., "Heliodoros" in *The Novel in the Ancient World*, edited by Gareth Schmeling, Leiden: Brill, 1996
Paulsen, Thomas, *Inszenierung des Schicksals: Tragödie und Komödie im Roman des Heliodor*, Trier: Wissenschaftlicher Verlag, 1992
Sandy, Gerald N., *Heliodorus*, Boston: Twayne, 1982
Winkler, J.J., "The Mendacity of Kalasiris and the Narrative Strategy of Heliodoros' *Aithiopika*", *Yale Classical Studies*, 27 (1982): pp. 93–158

Hellenes

Ethnonym for ancient and modern Greeks

Although the Greek language was already employed by the time of the Linear B tablets of the 13th century BC, the term "Hellenes" is so far unattested for the Mycenaean period. Thucydides (1. 3) notes that in the Homeric poems the Greeks who participate in the expedition to Troy are denoted variously as Argives, Achaeans, and Danaans rather than described collectively as Hellenes – a term which is only applied to the Phthian contingent led by Achilles; on these grounds the historian hypothesizes that the name originally denoted a small tribe in Phthia (southeast Thessaly) before being disseminated more widely to describe all the populations of Greece. Aristotle (*Meteorologica*, 1. 14. 352a), on the other hand, derives the name "Hellenes" from the Selloi who were thought to have lived in the Epirote region of Dodona in northwest Greece, while a fragment of a 6th-century poem, erroneously ascribed in antiquity to Hesiod, describes Dodona as lying within the country of Hellopia.

A strictly empirical analysis of the occurrence of the terms "Hellas" and "Hellenes" in the extant literature of the Archaic period has prompted many scholars to accept the Thucydidean interpretation regarding the diffusion of the name, though with some modifications. In the *Iliad* Hellas is envisioned as adjacent though not identical to Phthia (2. 683; 9. 478) while the Panhellenes seem to have included the Locrians to the immediate south of Phthia (2. 530). The term "Hellenes" is not attested in the *Odyssey*, but on several occasions Hellas is opposed to Argos in contexts which should suggest that the former designated mainland Greece north of the Corinthian isthmus while the latter indicated the Peloponnese (1. 344; 4.

76, 816; 15. 80). Similarly, in Hesiod's *Works and Days* (early 7th century), the terms "Hellas" and "Panhellenes" appear to be limited to central and northern Greece (528, 651–53). It is sometimes assumed that the vehicle of diffusion for the name was the Delphic Amphictiony – a league of (largely) central Greek states and tribal federations charged with the administration of the Delphic sanctuary – though the early historical existence of the Amphictiony and its struggles with the Delphians are controversial.

By the mid-7th century the term "Panhellenes" appears to be applied to all the populations of the Greek mainland and islands: the Parian Archilochus (fr. 97) refers to the Panhellenic colonization of the island of Thasos in which he took part, while a pseudo-Hesiodic fragment (fr. 130) employs the term to describe the various Greek suitors who sought the hands of the daughters of Proetus. In this period it was almost certainly the sanctuary of Olympia and in particular the Olympic games that acted as the focus of Hellenic identity. Herodotus (5. 22. 1–2) describes, in the context of Alexander I of Macedon's attempts to compete in the games in the early 5th century, how the contest was restricted to Hellenes alone and that competitors' qualifications were judged by officials named the Hellanodikai (whose existence is already attested in an early 6th-century inscription). In the mid-6th century the Ionian cities of Chios, Teos, Phocaea, and Clazomenae teamed up with the Dorian cities of Rhodes, Cnidus, Halicarnassus, and Phaselis and with Aeolian Mytilene to found the Hellenion sanctuary at Naucratis (Herodotus, 2. 178. 2).

It would appear that in the Archaic period the Hellenes conceived of their common identity in ethnic terms (that is, in terms of kinship between their constituent subgroups): the 6th-century *Catalogue of Women* (frr. 9, 10a) expressed this affiliation in genealogical form by deriving the descent of Aeolus, Dorus, Ion, and Achaeus (the eponymous ancestors of the Aeolians, Dorians, Ionians, and Achaeans respectively) from the eponymous Hellen. Nevertheless, in the Persian invasion of 480 BC the Greeks of the mainland were confronted for the first time by an external enemy whose language, customs, and religion appeared so desperately alien that it instigated the rhetorical construction of a barbarian "other" in opposition to which the Greeks began to define themselves. A similar polarization seems to have occurred at the same time among the Greek colonies of south Italy and Sicily where confrontation with the Phoenicians of Carthage prompted the colonists to promote their common Hellenic identity above the Dorian, Ionian, or Achaean affiliations to which they had previously subscribed.

Typical in this regard is the definition of Greekness (*Hellenikon*) which Herodotus (8. 144.2) places in the mouth of an Athenian envoy prior to the battle of Plataea (479 BC): the Hellenes are those who share common blood, a common tongue, common sanctuaries and sacrifices, and similar customs. In the early books of his *Histories* Herodotus presents a series of ethnographic excurses on the Persians, Egyptians, Libyans, and Scythians which serve to highlight the profound cultural differences between Greeks and barbarians and which reflect a growing conceptualization of Hellenic identity in cultural rather than ethnic terms – a definitional shift paralleled also by Sophistic and Hippocratic emphases on environmental rather than biological determinism. Both Herodotus and Thucydides imply that non-Greeks who learned the Greek language and Greek customs could "become" Hellenes and c.380 BC the Athenian orator Isocrates proclaimed that the Hellenes were defined by their shared culture rather than their common nature (*Panegyricus*, 50). The word that Isocrates uses for "culture" is *paideusis* (cognate with *paideia*) which denotes a cultural system imparted through education, and throughout the 4th century there is a strong sense that Hellenism is a matter of the correct education – preferably at Athens, which Pericles had already described half a century earlier as "the school of Hellas" (Thucydides, 2. 41. 1). It was this common Hellenic culture that was thought to engender a sense of *homonoia* (unanimity) – a term frequently invoked in the 4th century BC as part of a Panhellenic rhetoric which aimed at uniting the various Greek city states in a common crusade against the Persian empire, purportedly in retribution for the Persian invasions of the early 5th century.

Though contemplated by both King Agesilaus of Sparta and Philip II of Macedon, this Panhellenic crusade was ultimately undertaken by Alexander the Great whose conquests in the East planted Macedonian–Greek garrisons among indigenous populations as well as disseminating elements of Greek culture throughout much of the known world. While it is perhaps inaccurate to say that the East was "Hellenized", regular interactions and intermarriage between Greeks, Macedonians, and indigenes precluded any strict ethnic definition of the term "Hellenes" which was applied more on the basis of common cultural and behavioural traits transmitted through the traditional Greek *paideia*: so, for example, in documents from Ptolemaic and Roman Egypt Hellenes are regularly described as "those associated with the gymnasium".

The Greeks continued to call themselves Hellenes under Roman occupation despite the fact that their conquerors divided them between the provinces of Macedonia, Achaea, and Creta et Cyrene (to say nothing of the Greeks in Asia Minor and the Hellespontine areas) and referred to them as "Graeci" (itself a word of Greek derivation). A sense of a historical Hellenic identity was once again resurrected with the emperor Hadrian's foundation in AD 131/32 of the Panhellenion – a league of cities to which admission was dependent upon the ability to adduce origins from the cities of old Greece – and writers of what is known as the Second Sophistic period reinvoked an archaizing identity predicated on the Classical Hellenic past. In general, however, the term "Hellenes" retained its linguistic and cultural rather than ethnic connotations, with the Atticizing dialect considered the purest form of the Greek language.

With the spread of Christianity "Hellenes" increasingly came to designate pagans – particularly in the writings of the Church Fathers – and continuity with the Hellenic heritage was consciously ruptured through the rejection of naturalistic sculpted representations of the human form, the rectilineal architectural plan of the Hellenic temple, Hellenic philosophy (or at least some elements of it), and most importantly Hellenic religion. The equation between Hellenism and paganism was, if anything, strengthened in the 4th century AD by the apostasy and promotion of "Hellenic liturgy" on the part of the emperor Julian, and even as late as the 12th century AD the Hellenes are described as possessing a wisdom at odds with the real knowledge to be gained through the Christian religion

(Anna Komnene, 2. 34. 12). Most Greeks of the Byzantine period referred to themselves as "Romaioi" (indicating their affiliation to the Christianized eastern Roman empire), though the 12th-century historian Niketas Choniates equated "Romaioi" with "Hellenes" (496. 50) and this double nomenclature became more common during the 13th century in the face of increasing threats from Franks, Venetians, and Turks, as well as with the gradual contraction of the Byzantine empire to include mainly Greek-speaking areas.

The sack of Constantinople in 1453 and the incorporation of Greeks into the Ottoman empire stemmed appeals to a Hellenic legacy. The Greeks were assigned to the *millet-i-Rum* ("Roman Community") – a "sub-nation" constituted on the basis of the profession of Christian Orthodoxy. Both in nomenclature (*Rum* from *Romaioi*) and in the construction of an Orthodox Christian identity which Greeks shared with Albanians, Arabs, Bulgarians, Romanians, Serbs, and Vlachs, the Greeks of the Early Modern period came to regard themselves as the dispossessed inheritors of the Christian Byzantine Romaioi. Furthermore, Ottoman rule effectively insulated the Greeks from the intellectual tide of the European Renaissance in which a new interest in the Classical "Hellenic" past of Greece was rekindled (although the contribution to western interest in Classical Greece on the part of 15th-century Greek dissidents known as the "Neo-hellenes" should not be underestimated). Towards the end of the 18th century – largely as a result of the emergence of a mobile, mercantile elite – Greeks came increasingly into contact with European romantic scholars who regarded Classical Hellas as the font of Western culture; the result was the birth of a new national consciousness based on the Hellenic legacy. In 1827 Count Ioannis Kapodistria was elected the first president of Greece by the assembly at Troezen and established a 27-member assembly named the Panhellenion (after the Hadrianic organization), while in 1863, a year after the deposition of Otho (the first king of independent Greece), the Danish prince Christian William Ferdinand Adolphus George assumed the title of "George, King of the Hellenes". The titular use of the ethnic (Hellenes) rather than a territorial designation (Hellas) reflected the central aspiration of the Great Idea (*megali idea*) which sought to unite all the Hellenes of the former Byzantine empire into one state centred on Constantinople, but after the Asia Minor catastrophe of 1922 and the subsequent exchanges of population between Greece and Turkey, the term "Hellenes" has generally been used to designate the nationals of the modern state of Greece (Ellas).

JONATHAN M. HALL

See also Great Idea, Identity

Summary

According to Herodotus, Hellenes shared common blood, a common language, common sanctuaries and sacrifices, and similar customs. For Isocrates they were defined by their shared culture (*paideusis*) rather than common nature. In the Roman period Greeks still called themselves Hellenes, but Christianity equated Hellenes with pagans, and Byzantine Greeks called themselves Romans. Not until 1863 did a Greek monarch describe himself as "King of the Hellenes".

Further Reading

Bengtson, Herman, "Hellenen und Barbaren: Gedanken zum Problem des griechischen Nationalbewusstseins" in *Kleine Schriften zur alten Geschichte*, Munich: Beck, 1974

Bloch, Georges, "Hellènes et Doriens" in *Mélanges Perrot: recueil de mémoires concernant l'archaeologie classique*, Paris: Fontemoing, 1903

Bowersock, G.W., *Hellenism in Late Antiquity*, Ann Arbor: University of Michigan Press, 1990

Cameron, Alan, "Julian and Hellenism", *Ancient World*, 24 (1993): pp. 25–29

Clogg, Richard, *A Short History of Modern Greece*, 2nd edition, Cambridge and New York: Cambridge University Press, 1986

Hall, Edith, *Inventing the Barbarian: Greek Self-Definition through Tragedy*, Oxford: Clarendon Press, and New York: Oxford University Press, 1989

Hall, Jonathan M., *Ethnic Identity in Greek Antiquity*, Cambridge and New York: Cambridge University Press, 1997

Hartog, François, *The Mirror of Herodotus: The Representation of the Other in the Writing of History*, Berkeley: University of California Press, 1988

Saïd, Suzanne (editor), *Hellenismos: quelques jalons pour une histoire de l'identité grecque*, Leiden: Brill, 1991

Toynbee, Arnold, *The Greeks and Their Heritages*, Oxford and New York: Oxford University Press, 1981

Walbank, F.W., "The Problem of Greek Nationality", *Phoenix*, 5 (1951): pp. 41–60

Hellenism and Neohellenism in the Greek tradition

The terms "Hellenism" and "Neohellenism" are first and foremost used to designate specific periods of history. By this definition, "Hellenism" is the designator for the pre-Christian civilization and culture of the Hellenes; "Neohellenism" that for the civilization and culture of the Hellenes of the Early Modern and Modern periods. Such definitions, however, both beg the question and are extremely insubstantial. For what, then, are the "Hellenes"? Are they defined by a shared language, a shared culture, a shared religion, or a shared geographic territory? Which of these unifying factors is to be considered dominant is a topic that has long been debated by historians, by non-Greek observers, and by the so-called Hellenes themselves. Clearly, there are Greeks to be found far beyond the geographic confines of the modern Greek state; there are Greeks who do not speak Greek; there are Greeks who are not Orthodox Christians. Conversely, there are Greek-speakers who do not consider themselves Hellenes, just as there are official citizens of Greece who define themselves as members of other nations. Thus it is that a central component of both Hellenism and Neohellenism has been the attempt to define the parameters of the "Hellenic" people.

In addition to the controversy and debate surrounding even these most basic definitions of "Hellenism" and "Neohellenism", there is the confusion arising from the fact that these terms refer also to intellectual movements, schools of historical interpretation, and genres of political rhetoric. Finally, the connection between the two terms is similarly controversial. The clear etymological implication is that "Neohellenism" is simply that – that is, "new" Hellenism. But whether or not the chronological connection between Hellenism and its modern counterpart is best understood as one of continuity or one of the resurrection, rediscovery, and recreation in the Early Modern and Modern periods of an ancient cultural artefact is hotly debated. And again, this debate is one that concerns not just academics but the Greeks themselves.

Let us first begin with an examination of the most basic definition of the "Hellenic" and "Neohellenic" periods. Roughly speaking, "Hellenism" relates to the pre-Byzantine Greek past, particularly the Classical period, while "Neohellenism" refers to the post-Byzantine period of revived interest in the Hellenic Classical heritage. The Byzantine period, then, is thus regarded in some peculiar way as marking a rupture or discontinuity in the Hellenic tradition. The reasons for this are complex and numerous, but one stands out most clearly: Christianity, whose alliance and blending with Hellenic cultural traditions is the very hallmark of the Byzantine period, was explicit in its rejection of many of the central defining features of Classical Hellenism. First and foremost, Byzantine Christianity regarded Hellenism as a tradition of paganism, barbarism, and heresy. Byzantine Christianity, in short, regarded itself as everything that Hellenism was not. Hellenism was polytheistic; Christianity was the purest form of monotheism. Hellenism condoned and fostered barbaric social customs while Christianity was their enemy. And Hellenism was based on fundamentally heretical philosophical premises, while Christianity understood itself to be the only legitimate philosophical system.

Christianity's hostility towards Hellenism was, during the Byzantine period, explicit and intense. Many of the most famous political, ideological, and religious debates of the Byzantine period found their origins in the conflicting world views of Hellenism and Byzantinism. Church attacks on so-called heresy were in most instances attempts on the part of the Church to do away with the cultural and intellectual remnants of the Classical period.

The official Byzantine hostility to the Classical past, however, was not all-embracing. In fact, in some important regards, the Byzantine Church and political establishments fostered the preservation of the Hellenic cultural heritage. This was most markedly the case with literature of a certain genre – while the religious component of many Classical texts was found to be offensive, others (along with "sanitized" versions of mythological works) came to be regarded as the core curriculum for members of the Byzantine intelligentsia. Part and parcel of this educational curriculum was a reverence for the Classical language, knowledge of which by the 10th century was regarded as essential for advancement through the Byzantine political hierarchy.

The Classical education on which such advancement centred can, in its carefully chosen content, be regarded as a perfect example of Byzantium's ambivalent attitude towards the Classical past. On the one hand, the Classical literary record was revered for the precision, clarity, and complexity of its language, as well as for the well-developed rhetorical tradition that made up a large portion of its contents. On the other, however, the ideologies that this rhetorical and linguistic perfection were used to propagate were viewed as dangerous and heretical religious abominations. The Byzantine love of the Classics, then, should not in any way be misunderstood as being tantamount to a cultural – let alone anthropological – interest in the ancient inhabitants of the Hellenic world. The ancient Hellenes may have been the transmitters of an important linguistic legacy, but they were in all other respects regarded as impure and pagan barbarians. Not until the post-Byzantine period of Turkish rule (or Tourkokratia) did the interest in Classical Greek language and rhetoric expand to include a fascination with the peoples who had first deployed it.

"Neohellenism", then, must inevitably be understood in turn not simply as a benign resurrection of interest in the Hellenic Classical past, but also to some extent as an explicit rejection of many of the most dearly held ideals of Byzantinism. Thus "Neohellenism" is not simply a term used to designate a particular period in Hellenic history, but also indicates a certain polemical stance, an attitude of pro-Classicism, at the expense of Christian Byzantium.

Neohellenism, first, is a term used to designate the Early Modern and Modern phenomenon of revived interest – both "indigenous" and foreign – in the Hellenic Classical past, particularly in contradistinction to the relative Byzantine hostility towards the Classical period. Just when this revived interest began is difficult to pinpoint with any degree of accuracy. Indeed, there are those who would argue that it is misguided to speak of Neohellenism as marking a period of "revived" interest, claiming instead that there has been a continuity of interest in the Classical period throughout all periods of Hellenic history, and thus that the Byzantine period does not in fact mark a point of rupture. While there is some validity in this stance, it is important to note that at the very least the interest in the Classical period characteristic of Byzantinism was a very specific and qualified interest; Neohellenism is best understood as a period of more unqualified and positive regard for Classical Greece. In this latter regard we can safely say that the Neohellenism of the late Turkish period marks a distinctive intellectual trend, a marked departure from the dominant cultural attitudes towards the Classical period that were regnant until the 17th and 18th centuries.

Some historians date the earliest rise of Neohellenism to the final centuries of Byzantium, although the Byzantine interest in the Classical past is perhaps best grouped instead under the designator "Hellenism", so as to distinguish it from Neohellenism, which in its most distinct form is properly dated to the 18th century. The rise of Byzantine Hellenism is attributable to a number of political and cultural factors. The most dominant feature of this period was the unavoidable fact of Byzantine decline – by the early 15th century the city of Constantinople stood isolated, an island of Byzantinism in a vast sea of Ottoman territory. Under such circumstances, visions of Greek geographical, religious, and political dominance were difficult to maintain. In their stead, many scholars began instead to focus on a notion of cultural dominance, a form of dominance linked to linguistic, intellectual, and historical superiority. Quite understandably, faced with a bleak historical present, intellectuals came increasingly to focus on an idealized vision of the Greek past, and gave greater attention to memories not just of Byzantine splendour, but to the cultural forms that had preceded Byzantium.

The dominant thinker in this new attitude towards the past was George Gemistos Plethon, who on the eve of the fall of

Constantinople to the Turks in 1453 argued for the foundation of a new "Hellenic" state, to be situated on the Peloponnesian peninsula and guided by a secularized set of Neoplatonic philosophical principles. This proposal was remarkable on a number of counts. Plethon's suggestion was at heart an anti-ecclesiastical one, proposing as it did that the traditional backbone of society – the Byzantine Church – lacked the philosophical sophistication effectively to shape and rule the polity. Moreover, Plethon's argument that the Peloponnese, rather than the Christian city of Constantinople, should make up the core of the new state, was further indication of his belief that the intellectual and political scope of the Classical period far outstripped that of Byzantium. Just as, symbolically speaking, Constantinople was inextricably linked to Greekness in its Christian form, so too was the Morea (the Peloponnese) connotative of the Hellenic Classical past. Finally, and of greatest symbolic importance, was the fact that Plethon, in his discussion of the new state, was the first to make proud use of the collective designator, "Hellenes", to describe the cultural group of which he considered himself a member.

Hitherto, this term had been regarded as an insult, a designator best eschewed because of its implications of ignorance, barbarism, and heresy. For Plethon (and his fellow *Hellenizontes*) to use it instead as the proud signifier for a group of people whom he regarded as unified not by the Christian tradition but rather by culture, language, and history, was a radical departure from the dominant rhetoric of Byzantium.

Plethon's call for the resurrection of a distinctively "Hellenic" nation was both radical and short-lived. For with the final, official death of Byzantium in 1453, this new intellectual fascination with the pre-Byzantine Classical past was dealt a major blow. Not until some four centuries had passed would Greeks again use such explicitly pro-Classicist rhetoric to frame their self-understanding. It is with this later revival of interest in the Greek people's Classical origins that the term "Neohellenism" is now most commonly associated. It is important to note, however, that it had important predecessors as early as the 15th century.

Just as Plethon's early version of Neohellenism (that is, Hellenism as an intellectual movement) was at heart a response to a state of political and cultural crisis, so too were later 18th- and 19th-century Neohellenist movements. In the case of these latter, however, the impetus was not Byzantine degeneration, but rather the perceived decline of the Ottoman state, which by the close of the 16th century had already passed the zenith of its political, cultural, and economic development.

By the 18th century the imminent demise of the Ottoman empire was widely regarded as an inevitability; the only uncertainly was when the Ottomans might meet their final end. In the face of the impending possibility of liberation from Ottoman rule, Greek intellectuals and revolutionaries became increasingly interested in the question of what form a newly liberated Greek nation might take. The two dominant paradigms were both drawn from the past: some argued that Byzantium should provide the model for modern-day Greek political reconstruction, while others felt that the Greeks should reach still further back into the past, and use a reinterpreted version of the forms and ideals of Periclean Athens as the basis for a new Greek state.

The former was the dominant position within Greece itself, and found strong representation among the general populace, whose experience of "Greekness" during Tourkokratia had been most strongly mediated and propagated by the Greek Orthodox Church. For such Greeks, Orthodoxy and Greekness were inextricably linked: their "national" holidays were one and the same with religious ones; almost without exception, Greeks took their names from those of Orthodox saints; even such distinctive cultural forms as cuisine traced much of their origins to the religious establishment. The latter position, however – that the Greeks should look to the Classical, rather than Byzantine, past in their efforts at national regeneration – came to play the more decisive role in the actual process of Greek liberation from Ottoman rule.

The relationship between this attitude towards the Classical past and the emergence of the modern Greek state was forged in the context of a movement that has been termed the "Neohellenic Enlightenment". This movement, dominant during the Greek revolutionary period (dating roughly from the early 1770s to the mid-1830s), is best understood as a syncretism of, on the one hand, Greek revolutionary aspirations generated from within the territories of the Ottoman empire, and, on the other, the ideals of the western secular intellectual elite. (It is important to note, however, that there was from the start significant overlap between these two categories, for wealthy Ottoman Greeks had for centuries travelled to the universities of Europe to pursue their education, and by the time of the Greek War of Independence there were significant mercantile and intellectual Greek diaspora communities throughout Europe.)

The western intellectual establishment's infatuation with Classical Greece dated at least from the time of the Renaissance, and had by the late 18th century become so widespread that many European intellectuals felt that it was their moral obligation to assist the Greeks in their bid for independence from the Ottomans. At stake, such intellectuals believed, was nothing less than the liberation of the very foundations of Europe's own intellectual, cultural, and political traditions. Thus a heavily political component was injected into the Greek intellectual environment: Greek interest in the Classical past would win a greater chance of European philhellenic support than would an emphasis on the Byzantine past. In the context of plans for armed insurrection – an insurrection that could only hope to succeed with European intervention – the debate between the pro-Classicists and the pro-Byzantinists was no longer merely an academic matter. Political concerns came increasingly to affect the terms and tenor of the debate.

The Neohellenic Enlightenment, with its emphasis on the Classical Greek heritage, had as one of its articles of faith that there was a clear genetic and cultural continuity between the modern Greeks and the Hellenes of the Classical period. By this view, the Turkish and Byzantine periods were to some extent responsible for the "contamination" of the Hellenic race, such that many Hellenes were no longer able to recognize themselves as such. Such revolutionary tracts as the *Hellenike Nomarchia* were explicit in their criticism of the Orthodox Church, an institution that many Greeks regarded as the preserver of Greek cultural identity during Tourkokratia. The Neohellenic programme thus had as one of its central components to "teach" Greeks of their true, Classical origins, and to instil in them a sense of unity, a group identity based on the belief in a cultural continuity stretching back thousands of years. Those familiar with the broad contours of the world-wide nationalist movements of the 18th, 19th, and 20th centuries will recognize that such educative ventures stand at the heart of virtually all of them.

The tension between the pro-Classicist and pro-Byzantinist camps was not resolved with the successful conclusion of the Greek War of Independence. Indeed, there remains to this day in Greece a hybrid nationalist self-definitional stance, one that simultaneously embraces the Byzantine and Classical periods as the twin bases for modern Greek society. While this cohabitation is for the most part harmonious, there has nevertheless been ongoing jockeying to rectify the often paradoxical implications of this bipartite stance. One clear example of this tension can be seen in the language debates of the 19th and 20th centuries, when intellectuals, politicians, and Church representatives argued over whether the pro-Classicist katharevousa or the common demotic form of Greek was to be the official language of the new Greek state. The most prominent politicians and intellectuals of the modern period (Vernardakes, Palamas, Dragoumis, Venizelos – to name but a few) have all grappled with the question of the Greek past and its proper role in the formulation of the modern nation-state.

Because of the myriad connotations of the terminology involved, this discussion of Hellenism and Neohellenism in the Greek tradition is perhaps best concluded on a theoretical note. Clearly, both Hellenism and Neohellenism, as intellectual movements that bore obvious political and otherwise polemical implications, were concerned not simply with "rediscovering" the past, but in "recreating" it, in re-visioning it. That is to say, the "past" was not simply a distant and dead artefact, but something to be constructed and created in the present. The central issue here was not "authenticity" (as if such a thing could ever be successfully arrived at), but rather "usefulness", or social functionality. Students of both the Hellenic and Neohellenic revivals must be aware that the imagined past with which pro-Classicists were concerned was informed as much by their own contemporary circumstances as by the actual "facts" of the Classical past. Even in Plethon's time, the Periclean age of Athens was a good long way in the past, and even the abundant Classical texts still available in the 15th century could provide only the basis for the roughest simulacrum of the Classical era.

Hellenism and Neohellenism were intellectual and social movements inspired not just by the past, but by present circumstances as well. They sought to respond to present needs – in the case of the former, the decline of Byzantium; in that of the latter, the formation of the modern Greek state. The richness and subtlety of these movements are based precisely on this fascinating interaction between past and present, and they are rightly understood in this palimpsestic light, which uses thousands of years of Hellenic history as a lens through which to interpret a changing present.

K.E. FLEMING

Further Reading

Burke, John and Stathis Gauntlett (editors), *Neohellenism*, Canberra: Australian National University, 1992

Campbell, John and Philip Sherrard, *Modern Greece*, London: Benn, and New York: Praeger, 1968

Diamanduros, Nikiforos P. (editor), *Hellenism and the First Greek War of Liberation, 1821–1830*, Thessalonica: Institute for Balkan Studies, 1976

Dimaras, C.T., *La Grèce au temps des Lumières*, Geneva: Droz, 1969

Geanakoplos, Deno John, *Interaction of the "Sibling" Byzantine and Western Cultures in the Middle Ages and Italian Renaissance, 330–1600*, New Haven: Yale University Press, 1976

Herzfeld, Michael, *Ours Once More: Folklore, Ideology, and the Making of Modern Greece*, Austin: University of Texas Press, 1982

Nicol, Donald M., *Church and Society in the Last Centuries of Byzantium*, Cambridge and New York: Cambridge University Press, 1979

Seznec, Jean, *The Survival of the Pagan Gods: The Mythological Tradition and Its Place in Renaissance Humanism and Art*, New York: Pantheon, 1953, reprinted Princeton, New Jersey: Princeton University Press, 1995

Stoneman, Richard, *Land of Lost Gods: The Search for Classical Greece*, Norman: University of Oklahoma Press, 1987

Toynbee, Arnold, *The Greeks and Their Heritages*, Oxford and New York: Oxford University Press, 1981

Vryonis, Speros Jr (editor), *The "Past" in Medieval and Modern Greek Culture*, 2 vols, Malibu, California: Undena, 1978

Woodhouse, C.M., *George Gemistos Plethon: The Last of the Hellenes*, Oxford: Clarendon Press, 1986

Hellenism as viewed by visiting artists

Travellers to Greece have in many different regards played a central role in the development and propagation of notions of Hellenism, both within Greece and, especially, in the western European cultural imagination. Many of these travellers have traditionally been artists of various sorts – poets, novelists, painters, and musicians alike have found inspiration in Greece. Even those artists who did not themselves visit the Greek lands used them freely as the backdrop for their work. Underlying this artistic fascination with Greece was a complex set of intellectual and ideological assumptions.

This symbiosis between western artistry and Greece is predicated on what some scholars have termed the "Hellenic Ideal" – that is, as David Constantine (1984) has put it (p. 6), "the admiration of, the longing for those values which the eighteenth century sited in Ancient Greece". Western European travellers have for more than half a millennium been drawn to Greece in the belief that it was a sort of living museum, in which visitors could see nothing less than the living artefacts of Classical Hellenism. It is important, then, to note that travel to Greece was not merely a matter of geography, but also of chronology. Those Europeans who visited Greece were not merely moving eastward through space, but they also felt as if they were in some way moving backward in time. The students who viewed a visit to Greece as an essential part of their educational curriculum were not primarily interested in modern Greece, or even in its Byzantine predecessor. Rather, they regarded travel to Greece as a sort of anachronistic interactive exhibit in which they could find nothing less than the ongoing vestiges of Periclean speech, religion, and philosophy. Thus the so-called Hellenic ideal was intimately connected to Neohellenism's claim of Hellenic continuity, the belief that there was a direct racial and cultural link between the modern Hellenes and their Classical predecessors. So it is that, while artists did not in number start to visit the Greek lands until well after the Renaissance, they almost all focused in their work not on the contemporary Greek physical and cultural landscape, but rather on the image of Classical Greece. Painters depicted noble, decaying columns and broken statues; poets and novelists alluded to the heroes of Classical mythological tradition; and travel writers patterned their itineraries on the travels of Odysseus, Theseus, and other epic protagonists.

The French and particularly British fascination with Hellenic culture had a long and revered history. This specific, cultural interest in Greece was intimately linked to the Renaissance belief that the Classical civilizations of Rome and, later, Greece in some way provided the foundations – political, aesthetic, and philosophical – of western Europe itself. Indeed, this belief ultimately became so entrenched an ideology in Europe that by the end of the 17th century large numbers of travellers journeyed to Greece for no other reason than the educative benefits that such a trip was thought to offer.

Whereas initially the standard educational trip had Italy as its easternmost destination, by the close of the 18th century Greece came to supplant Italy as the most popular destination of the gentleman traveller. This increased interest in the Classical civilization of Greece was linked both to political concerns (the Napoleonic Wars of 1792–1815, for instance, made travel in France and Italy an impossibility) and to the developing sense that Italian culture was a mere shadow image, a cheap imitation, of the real thing – Greece. As Gustave Flaubert wrote after his first visit to Greece: "The Parthenon spoiled Roman art for me: it seems lumpish and trivial in comparison. Greece is so beautiful."

This belief that travel to Greece had a large educative component both fostered, and was fostered by, philhellenism. On the one hand, the belief in the edifying power of travel propelled students eastward in the quest to see the lands that had given rise to many of their central "canonical texts". On the other hand, travel itself was understood to be a central feature of the lives of the ancient Hellenes whom these scholars studied. Classical tradition glorified travel, and the Hellenes themselves had preserved in their literary record the stories of mythic travellers and the importance of travel for their maturation and education. As Olga Augustinos, a leading scholar of philhellenism and the history of European travel in Greece, writes (p. 57): "[The Philhellene travellers'] greatest heroes, Theseus and Jason among others, as well as their most original thinkers, used the voyage to accomplish their tasks." In undertaking travel to Greece, western travellers were thus engaged in an imitative act. And in most instances, this imitation was both self-conscious and quite literal. Travellers attempted to retrace the steps of Odysseus, locate the mooring place of Theseus' ship on Naxos, find the labyrinth where he had slain the Minotaur. Just as the ancient Hellenes were revered as adventurers and voyagers, such that modern travellers who visited Greece understood themselves to be performing an imitative act that linked them directly to the Classical past, so too was artistic production regarded as an imitative act, an attempt to share in the artistic perfection of the ancient Greeks.

During the course of the 18th century, the visual arts became one of the most important transmitters and propagators of such notions as the Hellenic ideal and the Neohellenic belief in Hellenic continuity. Leading members of the Parisian Academy of Painting and Sculpture argued that the Greeks had, as one French artist put it, "perfect[ed] the Arts, whose object is to please by imitating nature". Thus fledgeling artists were to perfect their craft by making Classical works of art – sculptures, monuments, and architecture – the subject of their own work. Initially, travel to Greece was not considered a prerequisite for such work – artists who stayed at home could rely on the accounts and sketches of others (not to mention the growing numbers of artefacts physically removed from Greece and carried back to Europe) as the basis for their own creations. In the middle of the 18th century, however, influential artists began to go to Greece itself to find material from which to work.

Two European artists in particular found great prominence as a result of the pictures they published following their travels. These were Julien David Leroy and the comte de Choiseul-Gouffier. Leroy travelled to Athens in 1755, with the sole aim of drawing its monuments from an eyewitness perspective. The result was his *Ruins of the Most Beautiful Monuments of Greece*, published in 1758. Choiseul-Gouffier also travelled to Greece, spending a good deal of his time there drawing what he viewed as the living legacy of Classical Greece. In 1782 he published the first of the two-volume *Voyage Pittoresque de la Gréce* (Picturesque Voyage of Greece), which met with instant and immense critical acclaim, wide circulation, and translation into German. Choiseul-Gouffier's was but the most popular of a whole slew of works concerned with the artistic depiction of the Hellenic world. While many of these works, such as those of Leroy and Choiseul-Gouffier, were produced by professional artists, many other books included pictures of Greece drawn by amateurs who jotted down illustrations to accompany their journalistic travelogues.

In their obsessive interest in Greece, these artists were involved in the propagation not just of an ancient aesthetic tradition – a tradition that in their view had reached its consummate expression under the ancient Hellenes – but also in the creation of a new one. Whereas many of the Early Modern and Modern travellers who visited Greece believed that the monuments and historic sites that they saw there were nothing less than the pristine, preserved remnants of noble Hellas, the reality was of course quite different. The images produced by these travellers presented Greece as a land of eerie whiteness, lifelessness, and decay, a landscape littered with colourless statues and columns, the site of beautiful monuments and buildings, but a land apparently bereft of any contemporary vitality and life. Although Leroy, who had as one of his primary interests the interaction between the old and the new, was an exception, many artists clothed what few human figures their images included in the apparel of the Classical past and excised any other markers of modernity from their images.

The unspoken – and largely unconscious – premise on which such modes of representation rested was that the modern, contemporary Greeks, unlike their ancient forebears, were unworthy of careful consideration. The written accounts of the many Europeans who arrived on Greece's shores eager to see the living legacy of the Classical past testify to the disappointment that these travellers felt on confronting real, living Greeks. Many chroniclers relate their horror at the degenerate appearance, boorish behaviour, and colloquial language of the Greeks they encountered while on their travels. But rather than readjust their image of Hellas and the Hellenes so as to accommodate the obvious changes wrought by thousands of years of history, many simply filtered out whatever they found disconsonant with their idealized vision of what proper Greekness was.

In large part because of such artistic interpretations of Greece, the modern Greeks have, to the present day, been both blessed and burdened by the legacy of the past. On the one hand, the past made Greece a unique destination, and granted the modern Greeks a privileged position as the direct descendants and inheritors of Classical Greek tradition. On the other hand, however, the contemporary Greeks were cursed by the fact that, to the critical European eye, they did not measure up to what was expected of the Hellenes. Indeed, to measure up to such expectations was, by definition, an impossibility, for the contemporary Greeks were being compared not to a reality, but to an imagined ideal. Many European travellers were so certain that they understood Hellenism and the Hellenes better than the Greeks themselves that they did not hesitate to criticize them for their "incorrect" speech and for what the Europeans viewed as their contaminated, ethnically diluted, physical characteristics. Many of the European artists who visited Greece during the 17th, 18th, and 19th centuries were so invested in their imagined version of the Hellenes, and in the belief that by travelling to Greece they were gaining direct, immediate access to the Classical past, that rather than acknowledge the discrepancy between their imagined version of Greece and the reality with which they were confronted they simply blocked the reality out. Thus it is that travelogues of the period are littered with references to Pausanias, Pindar, Hesiod, and Homer, with descriptions of ancient sites and artefacts, but are often relatively bereft of descriptions of the people and contemporary towns with which their authors came in contact.

"Hellenism" was thus both the quest and the construct of the numerous visiting Europeans who viewed Greece as uniquely equipped to inspire artistry. By way of conclusion, it should be noted that it is *their* version of Greece that has managed to persist in the western European cultural imagination right down to the present day. One need only look at the latest glossy travel brochures advertising "Ancient Greece" to realize that the predominant vision of Greece is, to this day, one of solitary slender marble pillars, silent statues, and dramatic, empty landscapes.

K.E. FLEMING

See also Tourism, Travel

Further Reading

Augustinos, Olga, *French Odysseys: Greece in French Travel Literature from the Renaissance to the Romantic Era*, Baltimore: Johns Hopkins University Press, 1994

Constantine, David, *Early Greek Travellers and the Hellenic Ideal*, Cambridge and New York: Cambridge University Press, 1984

Leith, James A., *The Idea of Art as Propaganda in France, 1750–1799: A Study in the History of Ideas*, Toronto: University of Toronto Press, 1965

Malakis, Emile, *French Travellers in Greece, 1770–1820: An Early Phase in French Philhellenism*, Philadephia: University of Pennsylvania Press, 1925

Manuel, Frank E., *The Eighteenth Century Confronts the Gods*, Cambridge, Massachusetts: Harvard University Press, 1959, reprinted New York: Atheneum, 1967

Spencer, Terence, *Fair Greece! Sad Relic: Literary Philohellenism from Shakespeare to Byron*, London: Weidenfeld and Nicolson, 1954; St Clair Shores, Michigan: Scholarly Press, 1971

Weiss, Roberto, *The Renaissance Discovery of Classical Antiquity*, 2nd edition, Oxford and New York: Blackwell, 1988

Woodhouse, C.M., *The Philhellenes*, London: Hodder and Stoughton, 1969; Rutherford, New Jersey: Fairleigh Dickinson University Press, 1971

Hellenistic Period 323–31 BC

The Hellenistic age begins with Alexander the Great's conquest of the Persian empire and its incorporation into his vast, Macedonian-controlled state. It ends in more piecemeal fashion with the Roman conquest, one by one, of the various regions, now separate kingdoms, into which his empire had divided after his death, ending with the defeat of Cleopatra VII at the battle of Actium in 31 BC, and her suicide in her palace at Alexandria the following year. Its beginning is marked by a massive change in the fortunes and status of the Greek communities. The end is less marked, since in many ways the Roman empire developed out of the Hellenistic world, and in its system of administration was much influenced by it. There were, however, changes in geographical extent. Only the most powerful of kings could hold intact an empire as vast as Alexander's, and on his premature death in 323 BC, leaving only a halfwit and an unborn infant as his legitimate heirs, the empire had disintegrated into separate kingdoms, each controlled by a new dynasty descended from the Macedonian warlord who had originally seized control of it. It took a Roman emperor to reunite it, and by that time much, in Mesopotamia and further east, had been lost to the Hellenistic world.

Thus the Hellenistic world was never a political unity, though all its constituent parts, and their various rulers, looked back to Alexander as the ultimate source of their existence. Behind this there were often considerable local variations, since it included regions with non-Greek forms of civilization much older than that of the Greek world itself. At the same time, the conversion of all this into Hellenistic shape (the term itself is a 19th-century invention, but accepts the fact of the extension into this wider area of a culture that was essentially Hellenic in origin, in a world that thus became Hellenized) was not merely a matter of military conquest. The defeat of the Persian invader by the Greeks in 480/79 BC, long before the counter-crusade promoted by Philip II and executed by Alexander, had given the Greeks – with their political systems that valued independence, and above all with the military skills of their citizen foot soldier that resulted from this – a prestige that was acknowledged by their non-Greek neighbours, and already used by them for their own purposes.

so-called Macedonians in the armies of the Hellenistic kings, following a policy of necessity already instituted by Alexander himself, were not true Macedonians by origin.

As a period, the Hellenistic age has been looked down on as an inferior descendant of its Classical predecessor. Much of the intellectual and artistic excitement seems to have gone. In the Classical tradition of western European education, based on the study of the great authors of the 5th and 4th centuries BC or earlier, the writings of the Hellenistic authors were regarded as markedly inferior in style and content alike. They were neglected, particularly in the late Roman and Byzantine schools, which were more concerned with what seemed to be the purer forms of the earlier texts. Much Hellenistic poetry, and the bulk of the work of the greatest Hellenistic historian, Polybius, was lost when the manuscripts ceased to be copied in this period. In many ways, judging from what has survived, this is understandable.

Thus the Hellenistic age has suffered from a degree of neglect. Yet it is of crucial importance, a vital link in the continuity of the Greek tradition. If it had not existed, or the continuity had been broken, our understanding and appreciation of Greek civilization would have been weakened irrevocably. The Hellenistic states took the Greek tradition, modified it, and moulded it in many ways to suit the different circumstances of what was still, reckoned in terms of the vast majority of its inhabitants, a non-Greek world, and then handed it on to their equally non-Greek but equally infatuated successors, the Romans. The Greek world transmitted through the Roman empire, it must always be remembered, was the Hellenistic world, not that of the Classical city states.

The achievements of the Hellenistic world are found in different subjects; they often depend on local or regional rather than universal circumstances. Foremost is the Museum – that is, the sanctuary of the Muses – at Alexandria, and its library. This was essentially the creation of royal patronage by the Ptolemies, the dynasty that seized Egypt as a largely self-contained area suitable for an independent kingdom in the struggles of Alexander's successors. Alexandria, which was officially "next to" rather than "in" Egypt, emphasizing its non-native character in an essentially alien land, became the capital, a substantial part of its area designated as royal, containing, in addition to the actual palace residence of the kings, the tombs of Alexander himself and the Ptolemies, as well as shrines and sanctuaries including the Museum. In addition to the actual cult of the Muses, the Museum provided a residence and place of study for scholars who were deliberately attracted to the city and paid a salary from royal resources. This royal patronage of the arts and learning, though it echoes that of the age of the tyrants, is very different from the system that prevailed in the Greek city states. The direct antecedent for it is rather Macedon under Archelaus, and later Philip II and Alexander. The intellectuals brought to Alexandria included poets, such as Callimachus and Theocritus, who often had other functions, as tutor to the royal children, or librarian. Though Alexandria was originally intended as a city for those people of Greek origin who had already settled in Egypt when it was conquered by Alexander, it expanded rapidly through an influx of new settlers from the Greek world and elsewhere, particularly in the time of Ptolemy II. It is noticeable that the intellectuals of the Museum, when we can trace their origins,

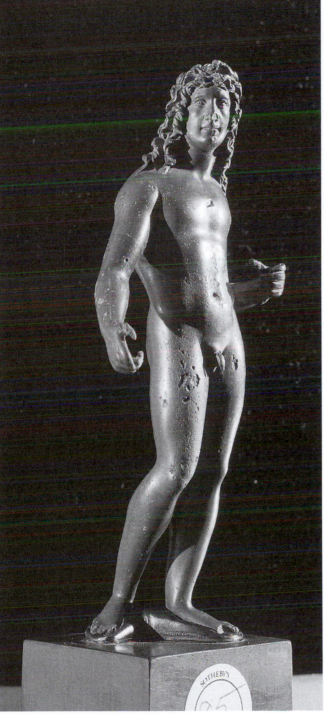

Hellenistic Period: bronze statue of Mithridates VI Eupator, king of Pontus, who mounted a serious challenge to Rome in the 1st century BC, Sotheby's New York

Thus Hellenization was also a state of mind created within the non-Greek. It can be seen clearly at Phoenician Sidon, where the kings (previously influenced by Egyptian customs and form) took over the manners of the Greeks and even, in the case of Strato, Hellenized their names. Greekness was attractive in its own right, not merely through virtue of Macedonian military success, and despite the fact that many invariably came from other parts of the Greek world (Callimachus from Cyrene, Theocritus from Syracuse).

Most members of the Museum were scholars rather than creative artists, and though Alexandria is only one particular and untypical part of the Hellenistic world, it is this aspect that sets a pattern for Hellenistic achievement. The library was not merely a great storehouse of all known Greek literary texts – which the early Ptolemies collected avidly, buying up, for example, the official copies of the texts of Athenian drama, part of that city's state archive – it was also a place where the texts were studied, where necessary codified, and copies manufactured, using the readily available Egyptian papyrus. It was at Alexandria that the definitive text of Homer was established, the two great poems divided into 24 "books", and handed on to posterity. It is through Alexandria that the Classical and earlier texts survived. The commentaries and annotations on them, though generally Byzantine in their surviving form, incorporate and continue the work of Alexandrian scholars.

Even so, the area of greatest strength was in the sciences. The Macedonian kings had a personal interest, and often involvement, in practical engineering, specifically for military purposes, and this continued to be developed in the Hellenistic age, not merely at Alexandria. In other sciences, including astronomy, mathematics, and medicine, scholars based in Alexandria continued work on subjects whose study had originated elsewhere; what was different now was the far greater opportunities available. When Eratosthenes, the polymath from Cyrene, wanted to calculate the size of the earth, he was able to do so – it appears, accurately – by measuring the different angle of shadow cast by the midday sun at Alexandria during the equinox, compared with the overhead sun at Syene (Aswan) which was virtually on the tropic. The distance between the two places was known, and both were of course situated within the kingdom of the Ptolemies. Medicine, too, was briefly in an outstandingly favourable position. Careful (that is, scientific) observation of symptoms, cures, and the progress of diseases had certainly been established by the 5th century BC, by Hippocrates of Cos, and the medical school founded on that island at that time continued to flourish. Doctors trained there and elsewhere were attracted to Alexandria, and one of them, Herophilus, made startling advances in the understanding of the nervous system and optics in particular. The advantage he had was that Ptolemy made available to him the corpses of executed criminals for dissection and even, it is plausibly believed, live criminals for vivisection, forms of research that were unthinkable under the ethics of traditional Greece. Mathematics continued to be hampered by the lack of a simple numerical system; or rather, it transcended this by complex work in geometry, particularly the study of conic sections by Apollonius of Perge, who in his turn had been attracted to Alexandria.

Much of this achievement is difficult to evaluate. Very often the treatises written by these scientists have been lost. Some (particularly, it seems, in medicine) were superseded by later treatises written by those who continued the work in Roman times. Others, particularly where no further advances were made, ceased to be studied and so copied in later times; the Greek was difficult to understand, did not have any literary value, and was of little interest at Constantinople. Yet some of the most important works certainly survived at Alexandria into medieval times, and, if not copied, were translated into Arabic. Thus the Hellenistic tradition continued, not at Constantinople but at Baghdad. It is important to remember this as an instance of the continued survival of the Hellenic tradition in an area that lies outside the world of European civilization.

Alexandria was not the only place where scholars worked. Athens was associated rather with the continuing schools of philosophy, the Academy of Plato and the Lyceum of Aristotle and their successors. This made Athens, rather than Alexandria, the goal of other philosophers, such as the Phoenician Zeno of Citium in Cyprus, who taught in the Painted Stoa of the Agora at Athens, and so instituted the Stoic philosophy; and Epicurus, born on Samos of Athenian parents, whose philosophical school was established in the garden of the house at Athens where he settled towards the end of the 4th century BC. Both these schools of philosophy continued to be of major importance in Roman intellectual life. Pergamum, on the other hand, which became a Hellenistic capital city under its upstart dynasty the Attalids, was developed to emulate Alexandria, particularly in the 2nd century BC when Alexandrian intellectualism seems to have gone into a decline in the face of a lack of interest among the later Ptolemies, culminating in an expulsion of the scholars in 146 BC.

Yet in many ways the greatest importance of Hellenistic civilization lies in the interrelationship of the different cultures, Greek and non-Greek. Throughout, the Greeks maintained a supremacy that was only gradually weakened in the face of military decline. Generally, under their Hellenistic kings they enjoyed a superior position within the community and its political system, and though in the late period vast areas in the east were lost to resurgent oriental states, at the very end the Greeks were able to maintain their social supremacy (at least) through the intervention of the Romans and the takeover of the kingdoms and cities into the Roman empire. Greekness, therefore, was something desirable and to be aimed at, and there was clearly much assimilation into the Greek community by non-Greeks. Important Hellenistic Greek poets, such as Meleager, were of non-Greek origin. In the 1st century AD Juvenal, bemoaning the influence of the Greeks in Rome, has to point out that the corrupting influence comes not from true Greeks but that already, for a long time, it is the Syrian Orontes that has flowed into the Tiber.

The impact of all this can be seen in different ways. The socially superior Greeks lived in cities to which the kings often devoted great expenditure, on architecture or, at times, "shows" of various categories. Architecturally, the Hellenistic cities acquired a magnificence and solidity never found even in the greatest of their Classical predecessors, and this taste for magnificent urbanism was continued and developed by the Romans. Alexandria was a city on an altogether vaster scale, the spaciousness of the royal area contrasting with the densely built tenement blocks of the ordinary inhabitants, a contrast also found at Rome. But perhaps the most significant impact comes within the sphere of religion, expressed through the medium of the common Greek language (Koine) which became a universal second language even among the non-Greeks. Greek religion had been essentially tied to its localities. Greeks uprooted from home in the new Hellenistic settlements began to look to the local religions as apposite to the areas in which they now lived. Sometimes this was deliberately fostered by the kings (Serapis at Alexandria), but more often it was a spontaneous development. It was the Hellenized world that spread the Egyptian Isis cult through the Greek and Roman communities, or the oriental Mithraism taken up by the Roman army. Christianity is an offshoot of the Jewish religion, though its sacred books are in the koine. Even so, it might have remained yet another obscure Jewish sect, had St Paul not seen the light outside the walls of Damascus, and promoted his beliefs in the Greek world; his epistles are a roll-call of the Hellenistic communities. Without the Hellenistic world, the world of Christian Greece would never have existed.

R.A. TOMLINSON

See also Astronomy, Geography, Language, Mathematics, Medicine, Museum of Alexandria, Political History 318–31 BC, Scholarship

Summary

Extending from the death of Alexander the Great to that of Cleopatra VII (323–31 BC), the Hellenistic period is one of political fragmentation but cultural achievement. A major focus of the latter was the Museum and Library in Alexandria where scholars advanced knowledge in fields such as astronomy, mathematics, and geography and librarians assembled and studied the texts of Classical writers. Other centres were at Athens and Pergamum. Greek (Koine) became the universal second language and Greekness the universal fashion.

Further Reading

Austin, M.M., *The Hellenistic World from Alexander to the Roman Conquest: A Selection of Ancient Sources in Translation*, Cambridge and New York: Cambridge University Press, 1981

Boardman, John *et al.* (editors), *The Oxford History of Greece and the Hellenistic World*, Oxford and New York: Oxford University Press, 1991

Cary, Max, *A History of the Greek World from 323 to 146 BC*, 2nd edition, London: Methuen, and New York: Barnes and Noble, 1963

Edelstein, Emma J. and Ludwig Edelstein, *Asclepius: A Collection and Interpretation of the Testimonies*, Baltimore: Johns Hopkins Press, 1945

Forbes, R.J., *Studies in Ancient Technology*, 3rd edition, 3 vols, Leiden and New York: Brill, 1993

Fraser, P.M., *Ptolemaic Alexandria*, Oxford: Clarendon Press, 1972

Heath, Thomas, *A History of Greek Mathematics*, Oxford: Clarendon Press, 1921, reprinted New York: Dover, 1981

Lloyd, G.E.R., *Greek Science after Aristotle*, London: Chatto and Windus, and New York: Norton, 1973

Tarn, W.W., *Hellenistic Civilisation*, London: Arnold, 1927, 3rd edition, revised by Tarn and G.T. Griffiths, London: Arnold, 1962, Cleveland: World, 1961

von Staden, Heinrich, *Herophilus: The Art of Medicine in Early Alexandria: Edition, Translation, and Essays*, Cambridge and New York: Cambridge University Press, 1989

Walbank, F.W. *et al.* (editors), *The Hellenistic World*, Cambridge: Cambridge University Press, 1984 (*The Cambridge Ancient History*, vol. 7, part 1, 2nd edition)

Walbank, F.W., *The Hellenistic World*, revised edition, London: Fontana, and Cambridge, Massachusetts: Harvard University Press, 1992

Hellenization

Hellenization denotes the spread of Hellenic culture in non-Greek, "barbarian" society and the process under which "barbarians" accept, adopt, and incorporate Hellenic culture. The term is closely connected with the Hellenistic period, which runs from the death of Alexander the Great in 323 BC to the death of Cleopatra, queen of Egypt, in 30 BC. Its earliest phase is marked by Alexander's successful invasion of the Persian empire; its termination by the repartition of the Near and Middle East between Rome and the new, Persian-ruled kingdom of Parthia. For much of the intervening three centuries the territory of the former Persian empire was dominated by a series of Macedonian-ruled states wherein Greeks and Greek culture enjoyed a pre-eminent position. Greek scientists formulated ideas and theories that would remain fundamental in a variety of fields until the Renaissance; art and literature flourished; and the foundations of western literary scholarship were laid.

The first modern appearance of the concept of Hellenism and Hellenization occurs in *Geschichte des Hellenismus*, G. Droysen's great three-volume work published between 1833 and 1843. He viewed the Hellenistic period as the time in which, in the territories conquered by Alexander the Great, Greek and Near Eastern cultures were intertwined to create the cultural background from which Christianity emerged. Archaeological excavation also played an important role in the formulation of the concept of Hellenism. The discovery in Europe and Asia of Greek sites of the Hellenistic period has provided information on the physical setting and material culture of the population of these new Macedonian kingdoms and their neighbours; and continues to do so. Archaeology has yielded a wealth of new written evidence – in the form of papyri and inscriptions on stone – which gives scholars a detailed view of the government and society of a major state, Ptolemaic Egypt. The creation in the 19th and 20th centuries of modern European empires in regions once dominated by the Hellenistic kingdoms was a further spur to reassessing the Hellenistic period. These developments encouraged scholars to see Alexander and his Macedonian successors as precursors of contemporary events. In parallel, scholarship was adding new evidence to Droysen's view of Hellenistic civilization as a mixed culture which, although Greek in character, had been enriched by the incorporation of features derived from ancient Near Eastern cultures.

Is Hellenization a term that reflects the reality of an ancient society, or a term and concept created by modern scholars in the course of their studies? Is it a tool, useful shorthand, or a phantom? According to G. Bowersock, "Hellenization is ... a modern idea, reflecting modern forms of cultural domination."

The term "to Hellenize" is first encountered in Thucydides (2. 68), where it is used in not a political but a linguistic context. The acceptance and use of the Greek language by non-Greek societies is known from periods other than the Hellenistic. For example, in the Persian empire of the 5th and 4th centuries BC, whose outlook was anti-Greek, the Greek language was adopted by the Lycian dynasts Pericles of Limyra and Mausolus. At the same time Mausolus avoided the Panhellenic sanctuaries, preferring the local Carian shrines, and denied proxeny (diplomatic representation) to the citizens of Knossos. Greek craftsmen were used widely by local rulers in Anatolia and around the Black Sea to create royal and elite culture long before the Hellenistic period, as is witnessed in the Achaemenid empire or the Thracian kingdom. But this can hardly be described as Hellenization, in which the local melds with and into the Greek. The ideology and everyday life of local rulers remained resolutely untouched; the Greek element extended little beyond a veneer of sophistication, a series of external, material attributes.

In the wake of Alexander the Great's conquests, Greeks moved to the east to populate new regions and establish new cities. Alexandria, Antioch, and other cities were founded. In the Hellenistic period Alexandria, with its library etc., can better be considered the centre of Hellenic culture than mainland Greece; Ai Khanum, Alexandria on the Oxus in northern Afghanistan, with its broad streets, monumental temples, large gymnasium, and theatre, was much more impressive than Athens. Heraclides Creticus warned those travelling from the east not to be disappointed by their first impressions of Athens and other famous cities in metropolitan Greece – the rather run-down houses, the old-fashioned streets, etc. Hellenistic historians themselves considered the new cities in Asia Minor to be melting pots in which Greek and non-Greek cultures and peoples met, mingled, and created a new cosmopolitan civilization.

Greek culture was dominant from the Mediterranean to the borders of India. Everywhere Greek was the language of government. The traditions of Archaic and Classical Greek culture were admired and followed, but not blindly; new features taken from local cultures were introduced. For example, the reliefs on the great altar at Pergamum may seem at first alien to the tranquillity associated with Classical sculpture; in fact, they resemble the sculpture on the pediment of the Parthenon. In the Hellenistic world culture was uniform only on the surface. There were differences between the culture of Aegean Greece and that of the new kingdoms of Asia and Egypt. In the former, writers and artists adhered strictly to centuries of tradition: local dialects and traditional cults and festivals flourished. From a cultural perspective an old Greece of tradition can be identified in the Hellenistic period and beyond; but in the east there was a "new Greece" which admired traditions but was not constrained by them, adding new elements and concepts absorbed from local societies, their practices and cultures. This appears to be more a case of orientalization than Hellenization, a case different from that in Greece at the beginning of the 1st millennium BC. The terminology deployed by modern academics usually fails to penetrate the intrinsic nature of the historical or cultural events in antiquity that it is used to describe. This is as true of the term "orientalization" as it is of "Hellenization". What is being described in both cases is the spread and intermixing of different cultures. In the Hellenistic period different ethnic groups absorbed Hellenic culture and transmitted aspects of their own culture to Greeks. This was a side effect of political developments. If a label has to be attached to this, then "cosmopolitanization" would be more appropriate than either "orientalization" or "Hellenization".

In the Hellenistic period in Greece the polis changed under social and economic pressure. Its political life narrowed and became harsher. New studies suggest that in the Seleucid empire the structure of the polis was less strong than traditionalists seek to depict. There was a continuity with Achaemenid Persian and Babylonian structures. The effects on Jewish culture of Hellenization on the one hand and Seleucid influence on the other remain unclear and disputed.

The Greek polis with its culture survived into the Roman period, and the Romans consolidated their rule in the east through the introduction of the polis. Evidence shows that in the Roman period the only significantly Hellenized part of the population was the elite. Roman culture itself was heavily influenced by the Greek, copying Greek sculpture, for example, and worshipping the same gods though under Roman names. Written Greek was in active use along with Latin and Aramaic. The Byzantine empire inherited not only the Greek language; Christian epigrammatists echo the idioms of their pagan predecessors.

GOCHA R. TSETSKHLADZE

Further Reading

Boardman, John, *The Diffusion of Classical Art in Antiquity*, London: Thames and Hudson, and Princeton, New Jersey: Princeton University Press, 1994

Bowersock, G.W., *Hellenism in Late Antiquity*, Ann Arbor: University of Michigan Press, 1990

Bowman, Alan K., *Egypt after the Pharoahs, 332 BC–AD 642: From Alexander to the Arab Conquest*, 2nd edition, Berkeley: University of California Press, 1996

Burstein, Stanley M., *The Hellenistic Period in World History*, Washington, D.C.: American Historical Association, 1996

Fraser, P.M., *Ptolemaic Alexandria*, 3 vols, Oxford: Clarendon Press, 1972

Green, Peter, *Alexander to Actium: An Essay on the Historical Evolution of the Hellenistic Age*, Berkeley: University of California Press, and London: Thames and Hudson, 1990

Green, Peter (editor), *Hellenistic History and Culture*, Berkeley: University of California Press, 1993

Gruen, Erich S., *Studies in Greek Culture and Roman Policy*, Leiden: Brill, 1990

Hengel, Martin, *Judaism and Hellenism: Studies in Their Encounter in Palestine during the Early Hellenistic Period*, 2 vols, Philadelphia: Fortress Press, 1974

Lewis, Naphtali, *Greeks in Ptolemaic Egypt*, Oxford: Clarendon Press, and New York: Oxford University Press, 1986

Millar, Fergus, *The Roman Near East, 31 BC–AD 337*, Cambridge, Massachusetts: Harvard University Press, 1993

Momigliano, Arnaldo, *Alien Wisdom: The Limits of Hellenization*, Cambridge and New York: Cambridge University Press, 1975

Onians, John, *Art and Thought in the Hellenistic Age: The Greek World View, 350–50 BC*, London: Thames and Hudson, 1979

Rostovtzeff, M.I., *The Social and Economic History of the Hellenistic World*, 3 vols, Oxford: Clarendon Press, 1941; revised 1953

Sherwin-White, Susan and Amélie Kuhrt (editors), *Hellenism in the East: Interaction of Greek and Non-Greek Civilizations from Syria to Central Asia after Alexander*, London: Duckworth, and Berkeley: University of California Press, 1987

Sherwin-White, Susan and Amélie Kuhrt, *From Samarkhand to Sardis: A New Approach to the Seleucid Empire*, London: Duckworth, and Berkeley: University of California Press, 1993

Tarn, W.W., *The Greeks in Bactria and India*, 3rd edition, revised by Frank Lee Holt, Chicago: Ares 1985, with additional bibliography 1997

Walbank, F.W. *et al.* (editors), *The Hellenistic World*, Cambridge: Cambridge University Press, 1984 (*The Cambridge Ancient History*, vol. 7, part 1, 2nd edition)

Heraclitus *fl. c.*500 BC

Philosopher

A citizen of Ephesus, Heraclitus was the first philosopher to approach the study of nature from the standpoint of the human condition. Writing riddling sayings in a dense aphoristic style, which have survived as quotations in later writers, he criticized poets, philosophers, and ordinary people for their failure to see the meaning inherent in the world. There is an order in nature, a *logos* (governing principle), that is always present, but which men miss both when they experience it and when they are told the truth about it, for they move through the world like sleepwalkers. Study of the facts will not teach understanding; what is needed is an understanding of how things fit together. What the *logos* teaches is that all things are one.

Heraclitus inherited from earlier philosophers the view that some one kind of stuff is changed by transformation into all other kinds of stuff. Whereas Thales had said that everything comes from water and Anaximenes that everything comes from air, Heraclitus held that everything comes from fire. Fire turns into water and half of the water generated turns into earth and the other half back into fire, preserving the same proportions of matter through the changes (fr. 31). Unlike his predecessors, who believed that the world came to be from unstructured matter, Heraclitus states that the world order "always was and is and will be everliving fire, kindling by measures and going out by measures" (fr. 30). It is the kindling and quenching of fire that preserves the world. By identifying fire, the most changeable reality, as the basic substance of the universe, Heraclitus seems to be stressing changeability. "Onto those stepping into the same rivers other and other waters flow" (fr. 12): the changing waters constitute the river. Thus change underlies and makes possible the structure of the world and the things in it.

According to Heraclitus, opposites are somehow one: the living and the dead, the waking and the sleeping, the young and the old are the same because they change into one another (fr. 88). The opposing tensions of the bow and the lyre make them work. Day and night are one. "The road up and the road down are one and the same" (fr. 60). What seems to make all things one is their interconnectedness in the series of transformations: there is one road with two-way traffic, one process with two-way changes going on. In the changes of fire there is a constant equivalence of material, something like a conservation of matter, which Heraclitus compares to the exchange of gold for goods and goods for gold (fr. 90). The value of the goods remains constant even though the items exchanged vary. The ultimate reality, then, is not any substance that travels the road, but the process of change itself, the law of transformations symbolized by fire. Overall, Heraclitus seems to have started with a picture of the world much like that of his predecessors, but he moved far beyond them in finding the source of unity in the world not in a single original substance such as water or air, but in a unified order of change. His predecessor Anaximander had seen cyclical changes such as day and night, summer and winter, as embodying acts of strife between opposites to be corrected by a cosmic principle of justice. Heraclitus replies that justice *is* strife, for opposition holds the world together.

Souls arise from the moist and they perish if they return to moisture. It is best for the soul to be fiery, and better souls receive a better lot after death. "Moderation is the greatest virtue and wisdom, to speak and act truly, perceiving according to their nature" (fr. 112). People should rely upon and defend their laws, but above all the one divine law by which all human laws are "nourished", presumably the *logos* (fr. 114). Human nature, then, mirrors nature as a whole, and human society is ultimately governed by the same laws as the cosmos.

In the 4th century BC Plato attributed to Heraclitus the claim that "you can't step into the same river twice" (Cratylus, 402a). The claim, which seems to be an interpretation of fragment 12 (quoted above) – perhaps one Plato got from Cratylus, a Heraclitean – suggests that for Heraclitus nothing stays the same. Plato's own philosophy was heavily influenced by the flux theory he attributed to Heraclitus: he held that the world of sensible objects was always changing. Plato and Aristotle also attributed to Heraclitus the view that opposites are identical (not just the same by virtue of being stages in a single process), which led them to say that he accepted contradictions. Henceforth Heraclitus became known in the doxographical tradition as a philosopher of flux who embraced contradiction and hence had an incoherent philosophy.

In the 3rd century BC the Stoics revived the view that all things come from fire, and also attributed to Heraclitus their view that there are periods of world-conflagration in which all substances turn back into fire, after which the world is regenerated from fire. In the early Christian era intellectuals sometimes saw Heraclitus as a proto-Christian because of his ethical views, his emphasis on *logos*, and his belief (on the Stoic interpretation) in a fiery judgement on the world.

DANIEL W. GRAHAM

See also Philosophy

Biography

Born in Ephesus to an aristocratic family, and active *c.*500 BC, Heraclitus identified fire as the basic substance of the universe. He also posited an order (*logos*) in nature. Only fragments of his writings survive.

Writings

The Cosmic Fragments, edited by G.S. Kirk, Cambridge: Cambridge University Press, 1954 (text and commentary)

Heraclitus: Greek Text with a Short Commentary, edited by M. Marcovich, Mérida, Venezuela: Los Andes University Press, 1967

The Art and Thought of Heraclitus: An Edition of the Fragments with Translation and Commentary, edited and translated by Charles H. Kahn, Cambridge and New York: Cambridge University Press, 1979

Heraclitus Fragments: A Text and Translation with a Commentary, edited and translated by T.M. Robinson, Toronto: University of Toronto Press, 1987

Further Reading

Gigon, Olof, *Untersuchungen zu Heraklit*, Leipzig: Dieterich, 1935

Graham, Daniel W., "Heraclitus' Criticism of Ionian Philosophy", *Oxford Studies in Ancient Philosophy*, 15 (1997): pp. 1–50

Kahn, Charles H., "A New Look at Heraclitus", *American Philosophical Quarterly*, 1 (1964): pp. 189–203

Mourelatos, Alexander P.D., "Heraclitus, Parmenides, and the Naive Metaphysics of Things" in *Exegesis and Argument: Studies in Greek Philosophy Presented to Gregory Vlastos*, edited by E.N. Lee *et al.*, Assen: Van Gorcum, 1973

Nussbaum, Martha Craven, "*Psyche* in Heraclitus", *Phronesis*, 17 (1972): pp. 1–16 and pp. 153–70

Reinhardt, Karl, *Parmenides und die Geschichte der griechischen Philosophie*, Bonn: Cohen, 1916

Vlastos, Gregory, "On Heraclitus", *American Journal of Philology*, 76 (1955): pp. 337–63

Wiggins, David, "Heraclitus' Conceptions of Flux, Fire and Material Persistence" in *Language and Logos: Studies in Greek Philosophy Presented to G.E.L. Owen*, edited by Malcolm Schofield and Martha Craven Nussbaum, Cambridge and New York: Cambridge University Press, 1982

Herakleios *c.*575–641

Emperor

The son of Herakleios and Epiphania, the emperor Herakleios (610–41) was of indeterminate Armenian descent. Between 600 and 610 he lived in Africa with his father, the exarch of Carthage, and his stay there probably made a great impression on him. In 608 he and his father, together with his nephew Niketas, successfully rebelled against the emperor Phokas, initially claiming the title of consuls. Herakleios arrived at Constantinople by sea, executed Phokas, and overcame the resistance of Phokas's brother Komentiolos in Anatolia. His wife Fabia/Eudokia, of African origin, gave birth to a son, Herakleios Constantine, but she died in 612. He tried unsuccessfully to persuade the Sassanian king Khusrau II to desist from his invasion. He also consolidated his control over the armies and eliminated potential rivals such as the general Priscus.

The first two decades of Herakleios's reign were almost entirely taken up with checking and reversing disastrous and embarrassing Persian conquests, which extended over Syria, the Holy Land, including Jerusalem, and, with enormous negative consequences for tax revenues, Egypt. Anatolia was also ravaged. He broke with recent precedent and commanded imperial armies in person, far from Constantinople. In 622 he won initial limited morale-building victories over the Persians in Anatolia. In 624 he set out on an ambitious campaign in the East to break the Persian threat, leaving a regency under his second wife Martina and the *vicarius* (prefect) Bonus, who together with the patriarch Pyrrhus successfully weathered an Avaro-Persian siege and blockade of Constantinople. Herakleios managed to defeat the Sassanian generals Shahin and Shahrbaraz in 625 and 626. After successfully negotiating an alliance with the Kök Turks in the Caucasus, he planned a bold invasion of Mesopotamia from the north; this depended on his alliance with the Kök Turks and on his diplomacy with Shahrbaraz, who broke his allegiance to Khusrau II. In December 627 he defeated the Persians on a plain east of the ruins of ancient Nineveh, then proceeded to occupy and ravage strategic Persian territory, including Khusrau II's residence at Dastagerd. Herakleios's victories in Mesopotamia encouraged the Persians to overthrow Khusrau II in early 628 in favour of Kawad IV/Shiroes, who agreed to peace terms, which included

the restoration of Byzantine territory, property, prisoners, and reparations. Herakleios met Shahrbaraz, who agreed to evacuate Byzantine territory. He personally accompanied fragments believed to be the True Cross to Jerusalem in March 630. Herakleios's power and hopes were at their apogee in 630, at the same time as he was unsuccessfully trying to end strife in the Church by giving his official support to the theological doctrine of Monotheletism or one will in Jesus Christ. In fact, ecclesiastical dissent intensified. His theological policies satisfied very few and aroused the bitter opposition of such prominent ecclesiastics as Maximos the Confessor and patriarch Sophronios of Jerusalem. His ambitious plans for forging a new relationship with Persia foundered with the assassination of his protégés Kawad IV and the ambitious general Shahrbaraz.

Herakleios devised new imperial ceremonies at Constantinople, perhaps to compensate for the violent circumstances surrounding his seizure of power. Many scholars also believe that he created new precedents for the official use of the Greek language by elevating the Greek term *basileus* to be the normal term for emperor, but others dispute the significance of this. He encouraged a thriving Hellenic literature in prose and verse. Prominent authors who wrote in Greek included the historian Theophylactos Simokattes and the poet, panegyrist, and hagiographer George of Pisidia.

Herakleios neglected the defences and prosperity of the Balkans and most of the Greek mainland and islands, giving priority to the security and rehabilitation of endangered or recently recovered territories and cities in western Asia. His policies probably contributed to significant 7th-century Slavic and Avar inroads into the Greek mainland. The evidence for his personal visits to mainland Greece or the islands of the Aegean is insecure, but it is clear that he spent much more time in western Asia than in mainland Greece.

His military victories depended heavily on exploiting divisions within the ranks of his opponents and encouraging them to switch sides; he fostered the breakdown of morale, and exacerbated hatreds and rivalries. His skills in diplomacy, deception, and subversion were at least as important as his military skills, despite the efforts that his propagandists made to celebrate him as a great captain. These skills proved to be of little value to him when he confronted the Muslim invasions that started in the early 630s. He did attempt to devise resistance, but he lived to see Syria, the Holy Land, and upper Mesopotamia fall to the Muslims, and Egypt begin to totter. He attempted in vain to prevent local authorities from reaching separate accords with the Muslims. His tactics and strategy were inadequate to check or repel the Muslims, but he continued unceasingly until the end of his life to devise new defences and techniques to halt their advance in Anatolia and Egypt. The evidence for his skills as an institutional reformer is weak, although it appears that he did order his treasurer (*sakellarios*) Philagrios to take a new census, presumably for fiscal purposes, for the entire empire. It is unclear whether Philagrios managed to implement this census and, if so, to what extent. But even though Herakleios suffered from severe bouts of illness late in his life, it appears that he tried to stiffen morale and military defences against the Muslims.

Herakleios was the last Byzantine emperor to visit an extraordinarily wide range of famous ancient cities and sites and relics. He saw Carthage, Jerusalem, Nineveh (or its vicinity), Antioch, Damascus, and what he believed to be Noah's Ark and the True Cross. No subsequent emperor would ever see such a swathe of lands. He apparently envisioned an empire of vast and diverse scope and never contented himself with purely Greek constituents of it. His controversial second marriage to his niece Martina and the ensuing rivalry for the succession jeopardized and wrecked many of his hopes and plans. He depended heavily on family members to bolster his strength, but their rival passions nearly destroyed the empire at his death. He was an extraordinary and unique figure who experienced supreme victories and defeats. At his death the empire was in an extremely tenuous condition. He reigned in an age of increasing devotion to the cults of saints in almost every corner of his empire. He likewise had to accept a rising tide of apocalypticism with its fears and doubts. He sought to associate such saints as St Theodore of Sykeon and their powers and prestige with himself. But powerful ecclesiastics such as Sophronios and Maximos the Confessor resisted him, and their successors, such as St Anastasios of Sinai, continued to criticize his reputation and that of his dynasty long after his decease.

WALTER E. KAEGI

See also Byzantine Period (Early)

Biography

Born *c.*575 the son of Herakleios, exarch of Carthage, and Epiphania, Herakleios was of indeterminate Armenian descent. From 600 to 610 he lived in Africa, but then seized power for himself. The first 20 years of his reign were spent recovering territory lost to the Persians. Later in his reign he saw much of the same territory lost again, this time to the Arabs. At his death in 641 the empire was in a very weak state.

Further Reading

Haldon, J.F., *Byzantium in the Seventh Century: The Transformation of a Culture*, revised edition, Cambridge and New York: Cambridge University Press, 1997

Kaegi, Walter E., *Byzantium and the Early Islamic Conquests*, revised edition, Cambridge and New York: Cambridge University Press, 1995

Stratos, Andreas N., *Byzantium in the Seventh Century*, Amsterdam: Hakkert, 1968

Heresy

Heresy, in its religious-canonical sense, is more easily defined than historically identified. Simply put, it is the denial of any or all accepted dogma of an orthodox set of beliefs, teachings, or tenets. But what exactly constitutes orthodox dogma has been a very difficult question as is evidenced by the fact that in the 1st century AD Jews accused Christians of being heretics and vice versa. The emperor Julian (361–63) – "the apostate" according to Christians – accused Christians of being heretics, unlike Jews and Hellenes. Further, while most Christians may agree that heretics deny or repudiate biblical doctrine, the teachings of the tradition, or the creeds of the ecumenical councils, there are and always have been extraordinarily diverse views as to what biblical doctrine is or how the creeds

are to be interpreted or the number of creeds to which all Christians must assent. Indeed, on occasion, certain ecumenical creeds themselves have been in or out of favour or had portions rejected, for example, the papal refusal to recognize certain canons of Constantinople I (381) and Chalcedon (451) which they felt jeopardized their primacy.

The word "heresy" originally had no pejorative connotation, meaning, as its etymology reflects (Greek *hairesis* from *haireomai*, "to choose"), simply "choice" in the sense of "assent" to a set of philosophical or religious beliefs. The term was used in Hellenistic times also to refer to the particular philosophical school or sect to which persons gave allegiance by choice, e.g. Phariseeism or Saduceeism, sects, "choices", within Judaism.

In New Testament writings the term lacks the formal and technical designation it acquired after the calling of councils to establish orthodox belief. The neutral Hellenistic sense appears in Acts 5: 17 and 26: 5, where Paul refers to the Pharisees as "the strictest sect [*haeresis*] of our religion".

From the sense of heresy as subdivision there appears the earliest pejorative sense of heresy. In Acts 24: 5 Paul resists the designation of Christians as a sect – "the Nazarene sect" – within Judaism, even though he refers to the Pharisees as a sect of Judaism. "I admit that in serving the God of my forefathers I follow the path which they call a heresy." Paul's objection is not simply resistance to subordinating Christian groups to Judaism; it is also that Paul assumes Christians ideally to be one unified community. And here he employs the pejorative sense of heresy: the practice of introducing, into the Christian community, divisiveness and sectarianism; i.e. sects or groups that, by distinguishing themselves from the rest of the Christian community, dissolve Church unity. Whether the basis for the heretical redivision is doctrinal difference or unique practice is immaterial to Paul. The evil of heresy consists in "dividing the body of Christ" which constitutes the Christian community. The "Judaizers", who required non-Jewish converts to Christianity to observe for a time the requirements of the law, not only introduced new teachings and requirements for salvation but also initiated a new religious practice for Christians, all without authority. Thereby they introduced factions within Christianity and garnered vigorous opposition from Paul. (See also Galatians 5: 20, 1 Corinthians 11: 19, and Titus 3: 10.) Peter also applies the term intramurally, warning Christians of false prophets and false teachers who introduce sectarianism (heresies): "lying teachers who will bring in destructive sects" (2 Peter 2: 1). Both elements of heresy are present in this passage: heterodoxy and disunity.

While combating heresy begins with the New Testament writers (Paul v. Judaizers; John v. Docetists), as early as the late 2nd and early 3rd centuries writers began composing lists of heretical movements and constructing arguments against them. Among the earliest is Justin Martyr's *Syntagma*, a collection of heresies and counter-arguments, often quoted in another early work, Ireneaus of Lyons' *Adversus Haereses* which opposed Gnosticism and Montanism. Hippolytus of Rome also wrote an early and important work, the *Elenchus*, a list of 33 heresies and refutations notable in its strategy of tracing all heresies to false philosophical schools and cultural influences. Among the Fathers, heresy is widely understood as a departure from the faith which is more often a synthetic and syncretistic corruption of orthodoxy than complete repudiation of it. Heretics interpret the teachings of the Church and its tradition by wedding them to some other religious or philosophical system, of which Manicheeism would be an archetype.

Perhaps the most noteworthy works of the late 4th and early 5th centuries are the *Panarion*, by Epiphanius of Salamis (367), and *De Haeresibus* of St Augustine of Hippo (427). The former is a "medicine box" of 80 antidotes to be administered against those infected by heretical poisons. The latter, which relies directly on an edition of the former, was written at the request of one Quodvultdeus who asked for an exhaustive list of heresies from the earliest beginnings of Christianity. In this work, heretical nominations derive usually from the founder of the heresy or the figure of heretical worship, e.g. Simonians, Menandrians, Saturninians, Basilidians, Nicolaites, Gnostics, Adamites, Arians, etc.

St Augustine's work contains an important caveat. Not all error is heretical; nor is every theological interpolation culpable. Catechumens may have been erroneously taught or children may be misled by parents. Such persons are not heretics, having been given no alternatives from which to choose or the understanding to believe otherwise. What is crucial is the disposition of the believer. If one in error readily receives correction and assents to proper teaching, he or she is without blame. The moral failure of heretics is a kind of pride: the audacious presumption that he or she knows better than scripture, the tradition, authority, and the Church. In the east John of Damascus wrote his own *On Heresies* which belongs to the same genre of heretical lists composed in the west, though John lists a number of unique heresies and heretical practices.

In the patristic period a heretic is anyone who introduces into the community disunity as a result of doctrinal or practical difference and refuses all efforts at compromise. But the community from which one dissents needs doctrinal and practical unity to begin with. Much patristic literature is devoted to theological speculation and doctrinal exploration in an effort to clarify Christian doctrine, thus complicating the question of heresy. The distinction becomes clearer, gradually, with the holding of ecumenical councils. During this period Basil the Great distinguishes between heresy and schism, "schism" applying "to those who separate themselves from the religious community due to reasons of church policy or otherwise reconcilable differences" (Migne, *Patrologia Graeca*, 32: 665A). This distinction appears to categorize schismatics according to minor differences of belief as well as the willingness of the dissenting party to seek compromise.

Gnosticism. The term "Gnosticism" has been applied, from Hellenistic times onward, to such diverse beliefs that any characterization risks contradiction. The word derives from the Greek word for "knowledge", *gnosis*, and implies that self-proclaimed Gnostics enjoyed an esoteric enlightenment. This enlightenment included dualist deprecations of materiality, whether personal passions and desires or attachments to the physical world, and cultivation of "spirituality". Gnostics downplayed or denied altogether the incarnation of Christ since, in their view, God's perfection could never stoop to actual association with the physical world; it is impossible to comingle natures. Thus, "Christian" Gnostics were docetists, asserting that perceptions of Christ's body were illusory and Christ's resurrection was metaphorical. Gnosticism was espe-

cially prevalent in North Africa where it allied itself to Middle Platonism. Some have seen Gnostic tendencies in Origen and Clement of Alexandria.

Manicheeism. An extraordinarily prevalent religious sect in the 3rd and early 4th centuries, Manicheeism was a form of dualism positing two ontological principles or powers, good and evil, or light and dark, thus analogous to Zoroastrianism from which it derived. It included elements of Christianity and Gnosticism and so was a theological temptation for many Christians. No less a figure than Augustine was attracted for some years by Manicheeism's emphasis on rational support for belief – however insupportable a system it may have been itself – as well as its powerful explanation of an intractable theological problem: the origin and nature of evil. Manicheeism was vigorously opposed by Christian apologists who used monotheistic and Neoplatonic arguments to show the metaphysical inconsistencies of dualism, particularly its implication that God is neither omnipotent nor the creator of all things.

Pelagianism. Introduced in Rome (*c*.380) by Pelagius, a learned monk from Britain, this doctrine, though vigorously opposed by Augustine, found general tolerance, if not sympathy, outside North Africa. Pelagius emphasized the role of free will in moral action and the contributing role that right moral action plays in salvation, arguing that one could on one's own choose and perform righteous moral acts and thereby deserve a meritorious response from God. Such a view emphasized the vital importance, therefore, of virtuous action throughout one's life as a contributing instrument of salvation. Augustine thought that Pelagius' views jeopardized God's freedom by obliging him to respond to those who performed moral acts. If Pelagius is right, human beings can make a claim upon God. Pelagius also, in Augustine's view, de-emphasized Christ's role as mediator and limited the absolute character of God's grace by introducing other medial instruments in human salvation, relegating the Church and sacraments to a secondary role.

Arianism. The views of Arius (born *c*.250) concerning the nature and status of Christ generated perhaps more controversy than any other theological issue in the first few centuries of Christianity. At least two ecumenical councils dealt directly with his doctrines, Nicea (325) and Constantinople (381). When he began teaching the view for which he is most notable – Christ is not coeternal with the Father – in North Africa, bishop Alexander of Alexandria immediately condemned him and Arius fled to Nicomedia. There he acquired a powerful following including, at one time, the emperor Constantine himself, who recalled Arius from his forced exile after he was condemned in the Nicean council. His doctrine was opposed by Athanasius of Alexandria who was, for a time, himself exiled for his opposition. The anti-Arian party gradually carried the day. Largely as the result of Arianism, much theological speculation focused on the nature of Christ, the Trinity, and the relations among the persons of the Trinity. Among the more noteworthy of the discredited views were Apollonarianism, Monophysitism, and Monothelitism.

Apollonarianism. Apollonarius, bishop of Laodicea, was friend and ally to Athanasius. His opposition to Arius led him to de-emphasize the humanity of Christ, arguing that in place of a human soul, Christ's soul was replaced by the divine *Logos*. He later rescinded his denial of Christ's human soul, but then argued that Christ had a uniquely heavenly intellect (*nous*). Apollinarius was condemned at the Council of Constantinople (381) for views that were labelled in the 7th century as "monophysite".

Monophysitism ("one-naturedness"). Monophysitism sought to explain how a divine personage could become mortal and what such a union of natures means. It was a doctrine denying the dual nature of Christ – divine and human – arguing, in some versions, that Christ was completely divine with no human element – that the divine element overwhelmed or never contacted the human (e.g. Apollinarianism) – or that a new, third nature, a mixed divine–human nature came of the union. Monophysitism, after a particularly violent and destructive history during which some emperors supported it while others fought it vigorously, was condemned at the Council of Chalcedon (451).

Azymes ("without yeast, leaven"). This dispute arose originally between the Byzantines and the Armenians but later (11th century) arose between the Byzantines and the Western Church. The issue was whether the Eucharistic bread should contain yeast. The Armenians and the Latins argued that, because Jesus broke unleavened bread at the last supper, the Eucharistic representation should likewise be unleavened. The Byzantines argued that scripture uses the word for leavened bread, *artos*, and based upon the same precedent, leavened bread should be used. The Byzantines also saw theological symbolism in leavened bread, e.g. resurrection.

Iconoclasm. In the 8th and 9th centuries in the Eastern Church a movement towards radical asceticism argued that the widespread use and veneration of icons constituted worshipping graven images forbidden by the second commandment. Iconoclasts further denigrated all use of icons and denied their sacred character. The basis for their argument, along with the argument from idolatry, seems also to have a basis in apophatic theology, the radical denial of any proper predication of the divine nature, and hence to emphasize the misleading and corrupting character of any representation of God. The 8th-century iconoclastic movement found a champion in Leo III (716–41) who ordered the removal of a famous icon and thereby instigated a riot. He further agitated iconophiles – he had some executed – by forbidding all iconic representations of saints. Constantine V (741–75) continued the iconoclastic movement, condemning icon veneration at a council in Hieria in 754.

Filioque. The *filioque* dispute focuses on the origin and nature of the Holy Spirit. At issue is whether the being of the Holy Spirit emanates from the relation of the Father and the Son ("filioque") or from the Father only. The disagreement arose when the Spanish council at Toledo (589) added material to the resolutions of Nicea I and Constantinople I. The view was attacked rigorously by Photios (866) and originally rejected by John VIII at the Photian council of 879–80. The council forbad all additions, subtractions, or modifications of the creeds. The Council of Lyons (1274) affirmed the *filioque* doctrine, which still is rejected in the East.

In 1054 the doctrinal and jurisdictional disputes between the papacy and the Eastern Church led to mutual excommunications, with cardinal Humbert excommunicating patriarch Michael I Keroularios, who, in turn, excommunicated cardinal Humbert. Though each side accused the other of heresy, the split was viewed as a schism and there have been numerous attempts at reunion, such as the mutual retraction of excommunications in 1965.

Palamism. In 1344 John XIV Kalekas, for reasons that seem as much political as doctrinal – he had previously endorsed Palamas's doctrinal fidelity – excommunicated Gregory Palamas. The doctrinal dispute focused on the knowability of God's essence and the approachability of creature to Creator. Palamas's opponents, particularly Barlaam of Calabria, felt that he elevated the created human soul to the Creator's divine level and diminished God's transcendence. Palamas argued that, while God is in essence unknowable and unapproachable, his energies or powers are not, and one can encounter God directly through these powers by employing the discipline of monastic prayer. Furthermore, through the incarnation, one can establish an immediate relationship to God, i.e. participate in God. Such a participation leads to a direct knowledge of God and makes possible deification. Palamas's views were endorsed by three local councils (Constantinople 1341, 1347, 1351) and with the last council came complete vindication. Canonical approval of Palamas's doctrine was subsequently added to the *Synodikon* of Orthodoxy.

Protestantism. Patriarch Cyril Lukaris, in the 17th century, had strong sympathies with certain Protestant doctrines, particularly Calvinism, which he sought to infuse into the Orthodox faith. He aroused the suspicions of numerous Orthodox bishops by publishing a "Confession of Faith" (1629) in which he professed iconoclasm, repudiated the traditional view of the priesthood, and asserted certain Calvinist views, e.g. the doctrine of "sola scriptura". He was accused of heresy and dethroned.

Controversies such as that surrounding Palamas illustrate the difficult nature of determining orthodoxy and heresy in the history of the Church. With the doctrinal and ecclesiastical solidification of Christianity over time, the procedure has become more precise and orderly.

JAMES L. SIEBACH

See also Christianity, Schism

Further Reading

Augustine, *De Haeresibus*, translated and edited by Liguori G. Muller, Washington, D.C.: Catholic University Press of America, 1956

Bauer, Walter, *Orthodoxy and Heresy in Earliest Christianity*, London: SCM Press, 1972; Philadelphia: Fortress Press, 1979

Epiphanius of Salamis, *The Panarion*, book 1, translated by Frank Williams, Leiden: Brill, 1987

Garsoin, N.G., "Byza-interpretation", *Dumbarton Oaks Papers*, 25 (1971): pp. 85–113

McClure, J., "Handbooks against Heresy in the West, From the Late Fourth to the Late Sixth Centuries", *Journal of Theological Studies*, 30 (1979): pp. 186–97

Meyendorff, John and Michael A. Fahey, *Trinitarian Theology East and West: St Thomas Aquinas, St Gregory Palamas*, Brookline, Massachusetts: Holy Cross Orthodox Press, 1977

Rahner, Karl, *On Heresy*, Freiburg: Herder, 1964

Schlier, H., Heresy entry in *Theological Dictionary of the New Testament*, edited by Gerhard Kittel, Grand Rapids, Michigan: Eerdmans, 1964

Turner, H.E.W., *The Pattern of Christian Truth: A Study in the Relations between Orthodoxy and Heresy in the Early Church*, London: Mowbray, 1954, reprinted New York: AMS Press, 1978

Herodas

Poet of the 3rd century BC

So little is known about Herodas (or Herondas, as he is sometimes called) from sources besides his own poems that neither when nor where he lived and wrote can be determined with any certainty. Various chronological hints in his first, second, and fourth poems point to composition dates in the 270s and early 260s BC. If the settings of his second poem (the island of Cos) and of his sixth and seventh poems (probably in Asia Minor) may be connected with the dwelling-place(s) of the poet himself, Herodas probably spent some periods of his life in parts of the eastern Aegean. His first poem exhibits a certain amount of knowledge and praise of Ptolemaic Egypt, but this does not necessarily indicate that Herodas lived there for some time as well (if he did, he is most likely to have lived in Alexandria).

It was through the fortunate discovery of a papyrus (British Library Pap. 135, first published in 1891) that scholars gained knowledge of substantial parts of the poems of this early Hellenistic author, which exhibit many features typical of Greek poetry of that age. Seven of Herodas' poems are readable in a more or less complete form (the much more fragmentary nos. 8 and 9 are largely unintelligible); their length ranges from 85 to 129 verses, and they are collectively called mimiambs, an appropriate title for their composite nature, as on the one hand their content has much in common with the form of low-level popular drama called mime, while on the other their metrical form and language are taken from iambus, an archaic form of very personal and often invective Greek poetry whose main proponents were Archilochus and Hipponax. Mimes, too, had already existed for hundreds of years before Herodas and continued to do so until (at least) the end of antiquity; they depicted scenes of everyday life (with frequent and rather explicit inclusion of sexual themes and situations) and down-to-earth or even vulgar characters, and they were performed – depending on their length and plot – either by a single person or by a small troupe of itinerant actors; their texts were mainly in prose, and their language usually in the local dialect (Doric in Sicily and southern Italy, for example). By combining mimic content with the form of ancient iambus, Herodas gave his poems a rather rigid form. His main model being Hipponax of Ephesus (to whom he refers at the end of his eighth poem, though the badly mutilated text does not allow us to glimpse specifics), he took over Hipponax's Ionic dialect and his peculiar metre, the so-called choliambos, or limping iambic, in which the penultimate syllable – which would normally be short – is long; this introduces a rhythmical disturbance which noticeably increases the sense of mocking and ridicule of the poems' content. Even within these rigid formal boundaries the scenes and situations depicted by Herodas at first sight seem completely natural, which is a great compliment to the poet's mastery of his art.

A brief examination of the poems' content gives an idea of their characteristic features and their connections with older and contemporary literature. Remarkably often women are the main characters. In the first mimiamb ("The Matchmaker or Procuress") a woman living alone (her companion has gone to Egypt) is visited by the title-figure, who tries to arouse her interest in another man, but is told in rather plain terms that this is out of the question. The second ("The Brothel Keeper") is a plea spoken by the title-figure before a jury: the brothel keeper (a figure familiar from Greek comedy) accuses a foreign ship's captain of attacking his establishment in order to capture a girl, and he tries to project the image of an honest, law-abiding resident, but the poet lets the meaner sides of his character (most of all greed) peep through his words. In the third ("The Schoolmaster") an angry mother drags her wayward son to his schoolmaster and asks him to give the naughty boy a good beating to set him on the right track again; the son, by feigning repentance, avoids the thrashing. The fourth ("The Women who Offer Thanks and Sacrifice to Asclepius") shows two women offering a cock to Asclepius (for curing an illness) and admiring the artworks in the god's temple precinct; Herodas' contemporary Theocritus treated a similar subject in his fifteenth *Idyll*. The fifth mimiamb ("The Jealous One") depicts the most mimic theme of all these poems, adultery (a mime preserved on another papyrus fragment, P.Oxy. 413 verso, shows many similarities). A mistress accuses her slave, whom she uses as a sexual partner, of having bestowed his favours on another woman as well and gives orders for him to be flogged and tattooed; finally, though, she accedes to a plea for mercy uttered by another (female) slave who is dear to her. In the sixth mimiamb ("The Women who are Friends [*or* In Private]") a lady (Metro) visits her female friend (Koritto) and eagerly inquires who the crafty cobbler is who provided her with that most wonderful dildo which she has recently seen with another friend of Koritto's; Koritto is somewhat annoyed that her delightful secret is already going round, but then proceeds to reveal the cobbler's name, Kerdon, whom Metro then rushes out to find. Metro and Kerdon (now a speaking part himself) appear again in the seventh mimiamb ("The Cobbler"), where Kerdon tries his sales pitch in front of some women whom Metro has brought into his shop, and there ensues some very amusing haggling about shoes and prices (and some hinting at other leatherware as well...). In the badly mutilated eighth mimiamb ("The Dream") the poet himself apparently speaks, relating a dream in which he takes part in a Dionysiac festival and competition; at the end he remarks on his relationship to Hipponax. Of the ninth ("The Breakfasting Women") only fragments of the first 13 lines survive and give no clear idea of the poem's narrative. Scholars disagree as to how these amusing pieces were presented to their contemporary audiences: by one reciter (Herodas himself?) alone or by several actors playing the various roles (ranging from two to four in the single poems)? Their very restricted length (see above) rather points to the former as most likely.

Only very few fragments of two, three, or four other poems by Herodas appear as citations in other literature, but they are very few and their meagreness shows that Herodas was not a much-studied author after Hellenistic times. He was still read, though, in Egypt in the 2nd century AD, as two papyri (Brit. Lib. Pap. 135, mentioned above, and the slightly later P.Oxy.

2326) demonstrate. Ironically, it is not a Greek, but a Roman, Pliny the Younger, who paid Herodas the biggest compliment by putting him on the same level as Callimachus in a letter to a friend (4. 3. 3). Soon after, Herodas almost completely vanished from the literary consciousness of antiquity, only to be reborn from the sands of Egypt at the end of the 19th century.

HEINZ-GÜNTHER NESSELRATH

See also Poetry (Lyric)

Biography
The date and place of his birth are unknown, but Herodas (or Herondas) seems to have flourished in the 270s and 260s BC, and may have lived some of the time in the eastern Aegean. He wrote "mimiambs" depicting scenes of everyday life. Seven poems survive largely intact, and fragments of others.

Writings
The Mimes and Fragments, edited by Walter Headlam, notes by A.D. Knox, Cambridge: Cambridge University Press, 1922, reprinted Salem, New Hampshire: Ayer, 1988

Mimiambi, edited by I.C. Cunningham, Oxford: Clarendon Press, 1971 (Greek text and commentary)

Mimes, translated by I.C. Cunningham, Cambridge, Massachusetts: Harvard University Press, 1993 (Loeb edition; includes works by Theophrastus *et al.*)

Mimiambi (I-IV), edited and translated into Italian by Lamberto Di Gregorio, Milan: Vita e Pensiero, 1997

Further Reading
Arnott, W. Geoffrey, "Herodas 1891–1991" in *Studia classica Iohanni Tarditi oblata*, edited by Luigi Belloni, Guido Milanes and Antonietta Porro, Milan: Vita e Pensiero, 1995

Hunter, R., "The Presentation of Herodas' 'Mimiamboi'", *Antichthon*, 27 (1993): pp. 31–44

Mastromarco, Giuseppe, *The Public of Herondas*, Amsterdam: Gieben 1984

Puchner, W., "Zur Raumkonzeption der Mimiamben des Herondas", *Wiener Studien*, 106 (1993): pp. 9–34

Rist, Anna, "That Herodean Diptych Again", *Classical Quarterly*, 43/2 (1993): pp. 440–44

Rist, Anna, "A Fresh Look at Herodas' Bucolic Masquerade [mim. 8]", *Phoenix*, 51/3 (1997): pp. 354–63

Rosen, Ralph M., "Mixing of Genres and Literary Program in Herodas-8", *Harvard Studies in Classical Philology*, 94 (1992): pp. 205–16

Schmidt, Volkmar, *Sprachliche Untersuchungen zu Herondas*, Berlin: de Gruyter, 1968

Simon, Frank-Joachim, *Ta kyll'aeidein: Interpretationen zu den Mimiamben des Herodas*, Frankfurt: Peter Lang, 1991

Herodes Atticus c.AD 101/03–177

Sophist and patron

The Athenian Herodes Atticus was the most striking example in his time of the native Greek who, although highly successful within the political system of imperial Rome and perfectly integrated into upper-class Roman society, nevertheless remained entirely Greek in his cultural orientation. His full name was Lucius Vibullius Hipparchus Tiberius Claudius Atticus Herodes, and he was the son of a very rich Athenian, Tiberius Claudius Atticus Herodes, and of Vibullia Alcia, a niece of her husband. Like his son after him, the father succeeded in penetrating the highest levels of Roman administration. He was the first Greek from old Greece to reach the suffect consulship, around AD 132, and probably also its first member of the Roman Senate.

Already in his education Herodes combined Greek and Roman elements. In Greek he followed the normal upper-class curriculum of his day. He studied literature with Theagenes of Cnidus and Munatius of Tralles. In rhetoric he numbered among his teachers the Athenian Secundus as well as some of the most famous sophists of his day, Scopelian, Polemo, and the Celtic polymath Favorinus. He rounded out his education with a course in Platonic philosophy under the renowned Calvenus Taurus.

He was, however, also educated in a Roman milieu, in the family of P. Calvisius Tullus Ruso, *consul ordinarius* in AD 109 and the grandfather of the future Roman emperor Marcus Aurelius. This sojourn led not only to a familiarity with upper-class Roman society but, presumably, also to his acquiring a perfect and accent-free Latin, a valuable and uncommon asset for a Greek.

As might be expected from a son of the rich and prominent Atticus, Herodes ascended to high office in Athens. Already in his early twenties he became an *agoranomos*, a supervisor of the market; soon after, in AD 126–27, he held the prestigious post of the eponymous archon, a post that not even Hellenistic kings and Roman emperors had disdained. As an ex-archon he also became a life member of the illustrious council of Areopagus.

After his archonship at Athens, Herodes began his Roman political career. Although not clearly attested, his first office must have been one associated with the vigintivirate, possibly that of a *quinquevir litibus iudicandis*. Next, he was honoured by the emperor by being chosen as *quaestor principis*. After his tribuneship and praetorship he was appointed as a *corrector* of the province of Asia for AD 134–35. His career reached its culmination in AD 143 when, as the first Greek from old Greece, he became a *consul ordinarius*, just as his father Atticus had been the first suffect consul. Herodes was subsequently offered the chance of a proconsulship or, possibly, of a second consulship but he turned down this offer.

In addition to his political posts Herodes was also honoured with other offices of great social prestige. He was chosen to be the *agonothetes* (exhibitor) of the Panathenaic games and of the Panhellenia. He was also the *archiereus ton sebaston* (high priest of the Augusti) and the priest of the *Tobacchoi*, as well as a *sodalis Augustalis* and a *sodalis Hadrianalis*.

Herodes was also possibly the most generous private philanthropist of the Roman empire. His greatest Athenian building projects were the Panathenaic stadium, clad in white marble, and the Odeum, roofed with costly cedar. He also built a roofed theatre at Corinth and rebuilt and enlarged the stadium at Delphi. Another of his major structures was the aqueduct at Olympia to supply drinking water for the spectators at the Olympic Games. Numerous less expensive benefactions are also attested. Herodes dreamed of crowning his benefactions with an even mightier accomplishment, the building of a canal across the isthmus of Corinth, a project attempted but not completed by the emperor Nero. He did not, however, muster the courage to ask the emperor for permission.

Although famous for his philanthropy and very successful in public life, Herodes was probably best known at large as the leading figure in the Greek-language cultural movement known as the Second Sophistic. He was the acknowledged master among his fellow sophists, to wit performers and teachers of display oratory. Their show declamations were perhaps the most popular form of Greek-language artistic entertainment from the second half of the 1st century AD to the first half of the 3rd. In these performances a sophist was often expected to deliver a speech, usually on a topic of Classical Greek history proposed by the audience, with only a brief period of time allowed for preparation. Much was expected of these performers by their knowledgeable audiences. Their grasp of Greek history had to be accurate, and they were also required to be Atticists, i.e. to use a Greek borrowed from Classical Greek writers, a Greek that in vocabulary, morphology, and syntax often departed from contemporary educated speech. Above all, they had to express their subject matter in striking and original diction. In addition, the successful declaimer had to act out convincingly, and in a euphonious voice, the historical character he was impersonating. It is noteworthy that despite his immersion in his Roman *cursus honorum* and his marriage into a patrician Roman family, Herodes entirely avoided cultural Romanization and by preference invested his artistic and intellectual energies in an art form not only entirely Greek in language, form, and content but even associated by some with anti-Roman sentiments.

As a teacher, Herodes educated many of the prominent sophists of the next generation and was honoured by being chosen as the teacher of rhetoric of the future emperors Marcus Aurelius and Lucius Verus.

The most lasting legacy of the Second Sophistic, hence of Herodes Atticus, its most resplendent representative, was to entrench among the educated the use of Koine, a common Greek that had reincorporated into itself many of the linguistic features of Classical Greek that had disappeared in oral and written usage during the Hellenistic and early Roman periods. Because this repristinated Greek was adopted by the state and by the educated in the Byzantine period, it enjoyed an existence of well over a thousand years.

Of the written works of Herodes nearly all have been lost. Philostratus, his biographer, writing in the 3rd century AD, reports as extant very many letters, speeches, and diaries, as well as handbooks and anthologies. Still extant is a speech called *Peri Politeias* (On the Constitution) attributed to Herodes by the Codex Crippsianus. It represents, perhaps, the ultimate triumph of Herodes as the perfect Atticizing sophist. The writer's knowledge of Greek history and his skill at avoiding non-Classical Greek are so remarkable that several modern scholars have deemed this speech to have been written by a Greek of the 5th or 4th century BC.

Herodes was less fortunate in his family life. He married Appia Annia Atilia Regilla Caucidia Tertulla, who came from a patrician Roman family with consuls on both her father's and her mother's side. In fact, her paternal and maternal grandfathers were joint *consules ordinarii* in AD 108. Although this marriage signified Herodes' acceptance as a member of the Roman aristocracy, his life as a husband and as a father was less than happy. Of his several children only the one he liked least, his son Bradua, probably the *consul ordinarius* of AD 185, survived him. When his wife Regilla died in premature labour, due, it was said by many, to a kick administered by one of her husband's freedmen, Herodes had to stand trial for murder on the charge of having ordered this assault. Although he was acquitted, the mere fact that so monstrous a charge could be readily believed implies a less than harmonious married life.

Herodes died at the age of 76, between AD 177 and 179, after a reconciliation with his fellow Athenians with whom he had had stormy relationships for most of his life. He received honorary burial in one of his most splendid gifts to Athens, the Panathenaic stadium.

There is no adequate biography of Herodes Atticus in English, though there is in German (Ameling) and an older one in French (Graindor). Philostratus's life of Herodes is translated in the Loeb edition (W.C. Wright), and is the subject of a detailed commentary by the present author. Albini has produced an (Italian) edition of the speech *Peri Politeias*, though he is unconvinced that it is by Herodes as some scholars believe. Herodes' monumental remains are discussed most fully by Tobin.

IVARS AVOTINS

Biography

Born in Athens c.AD 101, Herodes was the son of a Roman senator and followed his father into a political career, becoming consul in AD 143. Educated by many of the best teachers of Greek and Roman culture, Herodes remained entirely Greek in his cultural outlook. He endowed many buildings in Greek cities and was a major representative of the Second Sophistic movement, though most of his works are lost. He died c.177.

Writings

Peri Politeias [On the Constitution], edited by Umberto Albini, Florence: Le Monnier, 1968

Further Reading

Ameling, Walter, *Herodes Atticus*, 2 vols, Hildesheim: Olms, 1983

Anderson, Graham, *Philostratus: Biography and Belles Lettres in the Third Century AD*, London: Croom Helm, 1986

Anderson, Graham, *The Second Sophistic: A Cultural Phenomenon in the Roman Empire*, London and New York: Routledge, 1993

Avotins, I., "A Commentary to the Life of Herodes in the Lives of the Sophists of Philostratus", dissertation, Cambridge, Massachusetts: Harvard University, 1968

Birley, A.R., "Hadrian and Greek Senators", *Zeitschrift für Papyrologie und Epigraphik*, 116 (1997): pp. 209–45

Bowersock, G.W., *Greek Sophists in the Roman Empire*, Oxford: Clarendon Press, 1969

Bowersock, G.W. (editor), *Approaches to the Second Sophistic*, University Park, Pennsylvania: American Philological Association, 1974

Bowie, Ewen L., "Greek Sophists and Greek Poetry in the Second Sophistic" in *Aufstieg und Niedergang der römischen Welt*, edited by Hildegard Temporini *et al.*, 2. 33. 1, Berlin: de Gruyter 1989, 209–58

Flinterman, Jaap-Jan, *Power, Paideia, and Pythagoreanism: Greek Identity, Conceptions of the Relationship between Philosophers and Monarchs, and Political Ideas in Philostratus' Life of Apollonius*, Amsterdam: Gieben, 1995

Graindor, Paul, *Un Milliardaire antique: Hérode Atticus et sa famille*, Cairo: Société Anonyme Egyptienne, 1930, reprinted New York: Arno Press, 1979

Münscher, K., Herodes entry in *Real-Encyclopädie der klassischen Altertumswissenschaft*, edited by August Pauly *et al.*, vol. 13, 1913, 921–54

Philostratus, *Opera*, edited by C.L. Kayser, vol. 2, Leipzig: Teubner, 1871

Philostratus and Eunapius, *The Lives of the Sophists*, translated by W.C. Wright, London: Heinemann, and Cambridge, Massachusetts: Harvard University Press, 1921 (Loeb edition), pp. 138–81

Schumacher, L., "Eine neue Inschrift für den Sophisten Herodes Atticus aus Olympia", *Berichte über die Ausgrabungen in Olympia*, 11 (1998)

Swain, Simon, *Hellenism and Empire: Language, Classicism, and Power in the Greek World*, AD 50–250, Oxford: Clarendon Press, and New York: Oxford University Press, 1996

Tobin, Jennifer, "The Monuments of Herodes Atticus", dissertation, Philadelphia: University of Pennsylvania, 1991

Tobin, Jennifer, *Herodes Attikos and the City of Athens: Patronage and Conflict under the Antonines*, Amsterdam: Gieben, 1997

Herodotus 484–*c*.425 BC

Historian

Herodotus' name is inseparable from that of his one surviving work, the *Histories*, an account of the Persian Wars (490–479 BC), fought between the Persian kings Darius and Xerxes and the cities of Greece and – very broadly defined – of the background to those wars. Though previous works, now surviving only in fragments, such as the *Genealogies* and *Journey round the Earth* of Hecataeus of Miletus, seem in some respects to have been similar in style and approach to the *Histories*, Herodotus has been recognized since antiquity as the "Father of History".

Our knowledge of Herodotus' own life largely derives from the internal evidence of his work. He was born in Halicarnassus (modern Bodrum on the southwest coast of Turkey) at some point in the first half of the 5th century BC, but left as a consequence of a period of political infighting in which his family was involved. The extent of his travels is hotly disputed. Herodotus claims to have travelled to Egypt, the Levant, and the Black Sea, but some aspects of his accounts of foreign lands – his description of unknown (or his omission of well-known) monuments, his ascription of very Greek-sounding ideas to foreign sources, and a number of fanciful details – have led many to suppose that his knowledge of foreign lands was more second-hand, the product not of personal investigation but of Greek tradition (or, less plausibly, of his imagination). At the very least it seems certain that Herodotus spent time in Samos and in Athens, both cities on which he is well informed; he is reputed to have died in the recently founded Greek colony of Thurii in southern Italy, or in Macedonia. References in his work suggest that he wrote in the early years of the Peloponnesian War (431–404 BC): the tension between Athens and Sparta, the two chief protagonists of that war, is a regular undercurrent in his account of earlier events. Possible allusions to his *Histories* in the comedies of Aristophanes, most notably the *Acharnians* and *Birds*, suggest that the work may have been "published" in a number of instalments.

Herodotus' declared object was to record the "great and marvellous deeds of Greeks and Barbarians" and in particular "the reasons why they went to war with one another". Only the last four of the nine books of his *Histories* describe the events of the Persian Wars; Herodotus' focus is much broader. His *Histories* are the chief source for the early history of Greece (from *c*.650 BC to the Persian Wars). At the same time, while tracing the expansion of the Persian empire into Asia Minor, Europe, and Egypt, Herodotus takes the opportunity to describe the customs of all those peoples in the Persians' path. These accounts are written in the present tense, as if the characters of the different peoples were timeless. They cover religious customs, sexual practices, dress, language, hairstyles, and any other "wonderful but true" stories Herodotus thinks fit to include.

The structure of the *Histories* can at first be bewildering. As he declares at one point, it is his intention to "digress" from the main course of his narrative. One such digression – on the history and customs of Egypt – takes up the whole of the lengthy second book. Nevertheless, as recent work has demonstrated, there are a number of underlying patterns to the work that are not initially evident. The search of the Lydian king Croesus for a Greek ally with whom to counter the Persian Cyrus leads Herodotus in book 1 to investigate the relative strengths of Athens and Sparta: the two cities are repeatedly juxtaposed. The close of the *Histories* used to be thought impossibly inconclusive. A number of echoes of the opening of the work reveal, however, a very polished and final ending – albeit one without any of the explicit historical conclusions that modern readers are led to expect. The last main episode of the *Histories* concerns the execution, on a site overlooking the Hellespont, of a Persian commander, Artacytes, for plundering the shrine of the hero Protesilaus. Protesilaus had been the first Greek to cross to Asia, and to die there, in the course of the Trojan Wars. In Artacytes' view, however, Protesilaus had in turn plundered his wealth from the king of Persia; for the Persians, Herodotus explains – recalling a Persian explanation of the earlier hostilities between Asia and Europe at the opening of the *Histories* – believe all of Asia to belong to their king. At the same time, the barbaric manner of Artacytes' punishment – he was nailed to a plank, his son stoned to death before his eyes – points forward to another dangerously expansionist power: the man responsible, the Athenian commander Xanthippus, was the father of Pericles, the figure most associated with Athens' subsequent empire. It has happened before, Herodotus seems to be saying; it will happen again.

The *Histories* are also a rich source of evidence for Greek attitudes and values. Most markedly, Herodotus' work is characterized by strong religious convictions: by beliefs, for example, in the likelihood of divine retribution for unjust acts or in the value of divination, by a pronounced fatalism, and by a sense – expounded most fully by the Athenian character Solon in book 1 – of the unpredictability of all human fortune. At the same time, by acknowledging the possibility, for example, of others' scepticism over divination, Herodotus frequently reflects, even if he does not follow, more sceptical currents of thought. The language and style of his argumentation also find numerous parallels in contemporary medical writings. Though his accounts of foreign peoples are moulded and structured by Greek attitudes and prejudices, Herodotus consequently provides invaluable evidence for the ways in which the Greeks perceived and understood their "barbarian" neighbours. Egyptian customs, for example, frequently mirror those of the Greeks: Egyptian women urinate in standing position and men sitting down. And the geography of Africa also inverts that of Europe: the course of the Danube provides evidence for that of the Nile.

If the allusions to Herodotus' work in the plays of Aristophanes (or of Sophocles) are accepted, this would suggest that his work quickly became well known to a large audience, at least in Athens. Later, unreliable anecdotes of public readings in Athens and at Olympia give the same impression, though they may simply be the product of a later perception of his work as populist. Thucydides, the Athenian historian of the Peloponnesian War, on a number of occasions takes for granted knowledge of Herodotus' work; by extending his *History* back to the aftermath of the Persian Wars, he may have seen himself as a continuator of Herodotus. In many ways, however – by his exclusion of the divine from history, by his more focused scope on the contemporary political and military affairs of Greece, and by pronouncements of his omission of *to mythodes* or "the fabulous" from his work – he may have meant to distance himself from his predecessor.

Herodotus continued to be read throughout antiquity. His influence can be detected on the 4th-century BC historians Ephorus and Theopompus – who wrote an epitome of the *Histories* – and also on Callisthenes. Nearchus, Alexander's admiral, seems to have travelled and written with Herodotus' stories in mind. In the Hellenistic period also Herodotus was mined for factual information by philosophers and by poets such as Apollonius Rhodius and Callimachus as well as by historians; he was commemorated by statues in Halicarnassus and in the library of the kings of Pergamum. His reputation was double-edged, however. Dionysius of Halicarnassus praised him as a stylist rather than as a historian. Others, from Ctesias – himself notoriously unreliable – in the 4th century BC onwards, denounced him as a liar or story-teller. A number of pamphlets, most famously Plutarch's *On the Malignity of Herodotus*, criticized him for lies, plagiarism, for bias against particular Greek states, or as a "barbarian-lover". Just as the expansion of Greek interest in the Near East that followed the conquests of Alexander the Great seems to have given his reputation fresh impetus, later events also gave Herodotus new prominence. His attempts to come to terms with the customs of foreign peoples became more relevant with the discovery of the New World. In the light of the long struggle of the Byzantine empire against the Ottomans, the confrontation of Greeks and Persians also acquired particular potency, as is reflected in the work of the historian Laonikos Chalkokondyles.

THOMAS HARRISON

See also Historiography

Biography

Born in Halicarnassus, traditionally in 484 BC, Herodotus travelled widely, but perhaps not as widely as he would have his readers believe. He certainly spent time in Samos and Athens, and he is said to have died at Thurii in south Italy *c*.425 BC. His one surviving work, the *Histories*, is primarily concerned with the Persian Wars. But his description of the expansion of the Persian empire into Asia Minor, Europe, and Egypt leads him to describe the habits and customs of the peoples they encountered. Traditionally regarded since antiquity as the "Father of History".

Writings

Herodotus, translated by A.D. Godley, 4 vols, London: Heinemann, and New York: Putnam, 1921–24 (Loeb edition; many reprints)

The History, translated by David Grene, Chicago: University of Chicago Press, 1987

The Histories, translated by Aubrey de Sélincourt, revised edition, with introduction by John Marincola, London and New York: Penguin, 1996

Further Reading

Fehling, Detlev, *Herodotus and His "Sources": Citation, Invention, and Narrative Art*, Leeds: Cairns, 1989

Fornara, Charles W., *Herodotus: An Interpretative Essay*, Oxford: Clarendon Press, 1971

Fowler, R.L., "Herodotos and His Contemporaries", *Journal of Hellenic Studies*, 116 (1996): pp. 62–87

Gould, John, *Herodotus*, London: Weidenfeld and Nicolson, and New York: St Martin's Press, 1989

Harrison, Thomas, "Herodotus and the Certainty of Divine Retribution" in *What Is a God? Studies in the Nature of Greek Divinity*, edited by Alan B. Lloyd, London: Duckworth, 1997

Hartog, François, *The Mirror of Herodotus: The Representation of the Other in the Writing of History*, Berkeley: University of California Press, 1988

Momigliano, Arnaldo, "Erodoto e la Storiografia Moderna", *Aevum*, 31 (1957): pp. 74–84

Momigliano, Arnaldo, "The Place of Herodotus in the History of Historiography" in *Studies in Historiography*, London: Weidenfeld and Nicolson, and New York: Harper and Row, 1966

Momigliano, Arnaldo, *The Classical Foundations of Modern Historiography*, Berkeley: University of California Press, 1990

Murray, Oswyn, "Herodotus and Hellenistic Culture", *Classical Quarterly*, 22 (1972): pp. 200–13

Murray, Oswyn, "Herodotus and Oral History" in *Achaemenid History*, vol. 2: *The Greek Sources*, edited by Heleen Sancisi-Weerdenburg and Amélie Kuhrt, Leiden: Nederlands Instituut voor het Nabije Oosten, 1987

Redfield, J., "Herodotus the Tourist", *Classical Philology*, 80 (1985): pp. 97–118

Riemann, K.A., "Das herodotische Geschichtswerk in der Antike", dissertation, Munich, 1967

Heroes and heroines

In the Homeric poems the word *heros* designates a living warrior or another individual of high social standing. It is clearly a term of respect and attaches to groups of warriors such as the Achaeans and Danaans, as well as to individuals such as Protesilaus and Menelaus in the *Iliad*, and to the poet Demodocus and the young Telemachus in the *Odyssey*. By contrast, in Greek cult the word *heros* (and later *heroine* or *heroissa*) refers to a person whose powers had been so remarkable in life that he or she was honoured in death as attaining a status between god and mortal. These cults of heroes were distinct from the family cult of the dead. The cult of heroes has been taken back to the Bronze Age, but archaeological

Heroes: bronze statuette of Heracles, holding his club and the Nemean lion skin, 5th–4th century BC

evidence for this distinctive cult of the dead begins to appear in the early 8th century BC – the age in which the Homeric poems were taking shape and being performed throughout the Greek world. A connection between the spread of the *Iliad* and *Odyssey* and the emergence of hero cults has often been asserted, as has a connection between hero cult and the rise of the polis. The heroes of the Homeric poems – Achilles, Agamemnon, Menelaus and Helen, Meriones and Diomedes, Odysseus and Alcinous – were recipients of a hero cult both in their native countries and throughout the Greek world. Many, such as Achilles and Agamemnon, were worshipped far from their native lands: Achilles was worshipped in the Troad and Black Sea and Agamemnon in Tarentum

This is remarkable, since it is axiomatic of the cult of heroes that these cults are tightly bound to a single place (usually a grave with its monuments) and are the expression of group identity. Although worship of heroes and heroines can reason-

ably be connected with the rise of the polis, the worship of the heroes of the Homeric epics, like the cult of Homer himself, is Panhellenic.

There was nothing like a cult of heroes in the ancient Near East, although Lycian dynasts adopted the cult in the 4th century BC. In the *Iliad* the descriptions of the cults of Erechtheus and Sarpedon have plausibly been taken as reflections of Homer's awareness of hero cult. But it is only in the myth of the ages in Hesiod's *Works and Days* that the race of heroes emerges as a distinct historical phenomenon. This race is inserted in the succession of metallic ages known from the Book of Daniel (gold, silver, bronze, and iron). Coming after the age of bronze, the heroes and "half-gods" (*hemitheoi*) who fought at Thebes and Troy are recognized as receiving honours from the gods in death by being transported to the Islands of the Blest. But it is the men of the silver age who, dwelling beneath the earth, receive honours in death, even though they neglected the gods.

The archaeological record of a hero cult derives from the deposits at the graves and grave precincts of the dead who were recipients of the cult, and from a variety of representations of the dead as the objects of worship by the living human community. Most of these cults are anonymous. The most striking early example of such a cult is the 7th-century BC *heroon* (hero shrine) of a warrior buried with rich grave offerings in the grave complex at the west gate of Eretria in Euboea. There are later reliefs from Laconia showing the heroized dead (both male and female) seated majestically on thrones, with snakes coiling about to indicate their chthonic character as heroes. More common and dating from the late 6th century BC are the reliefs (known as banquet reliefs) that show a male *heros* reclining on a banquet couch with a *phiale* (libation bowl) or *rhyton* (drinking horn) in hand to receive the libations of the living. Such a figure is associated with a seated figure representing his wife. On the upper register of the relief are the emblems of his life: these include his weapons and sometimes his horse looking in through a window in the "wall". Below the couch is a table holding offerings of bread, fruit, and eggs. These are all aristocratic monuments and dedications in a sanctuary rather than grave monuments. Very occasionally dedications with inscriptions have been excavated in these grave precincts: at Mycenae one vase is dedicated "to the hero", another "to Helen", and a stele "to Menelaus" in Sparta.

Heracles was the archetype of the Greek hero. He was half divine and half human, with Zeus as his father and Alcmene as his mother. Herodotus reports that on the island of Thasos, where he had an important sanctuary, he received sacrifices both as an immortal and as a mortal. The one kind of sacrifice was performed on an altar and included libations, as well as the table companionship of the worshippers; the other kind of sacrifice was a holocaust and was deposited, with libations, in a pit (*bothros, eschara*); it did not involve the table fellowship of the worshippers. In the 5th century BC the worship of *heroinai* came into prominence, especially in Attica. These heroines were anonymous but they are clearly conceived of as the ancestors of the worshippers. Women did not share in what are usually counted as the four main categories of hero cult: that of the statesman, the warrior, the athlete, and the poet. Lycurgus and Chilon had their cult at Sparta; Brasidas, the Spartan general, at Amphipolis; the savage athlete Cleomedes at Astypalaea; and Archilochus had his cult on Paros. The cult of Archilochus on Paros had a history of some 800 years, and the cults of Homer throughout the Greek world were about as durable. Philosophers were also honoured by hero cults. The first cult to a philosopher we know of was Parmenides' dedication of a *heroon* to his teacher, Ameinias, in Velium (south of Naples). Cults are recorded for Pythagoras and Plato, as well as for Epicurus and his associates. These cults helped to create a sense of group identity for the members of these philosophical schools (who were most often foreigners) and gave them a kind of corporate identity.

The rise of the polis and the weakening of the grip of the great families within the Greek city state are reciprocal phenomena. The hero cult became civic and, as it did, the family cult and tending of the dead became less important, although elaborate funerary monuments persisted. Rivalling both cults was the new cult of the ruler. The cult of a living ruler emerged well before the Hellenistic age. In the early 4th century BC the Spartan general Lysander received worship on Samos, as did Antigonus II and Demetrius Poliorcetes in Athens early in the next century. With Alexander of Macedon's arrogation to himself of divine status, the cult of rulers began to rival the cult of the gods, especially in the successor kingdoms of the Ptolemies, Attalids, and Seleucids in Egypt, Asia Minor, and the east. The coinage of these states is eloquent. Where coins once showed the emblem of the city and its most important divinity (in the case of Athens the owl and Athena), the coins of Alexander and his successors displayed the portrait of the dynast as equal to the divinity of the city issuing the coin. Associated with these cults of the living ruler were sacrifices, processions, contests, and priesthoods. These paved the way for the cult of the Roman emperor and Roma in the Roman imperial period, but they were short lived and rarely survived the death of the ruler and the emergence to power of his successor.

Neither the rise of the polis nor the partial eclipse of its autonomy in the Hellenistic age arrested the continuity of the family cult and, as the franchise on heroic status became cheap, a family could declare on a small grave block or stele that this was the resting place of "Sostratos, *heros*". The term *heros*, once honorific, was demoted to the status of the term *makarites* in modern Greek – *heros*, like "blessed", simply came to mean "departed". Some families were wealthy and more ambitious. On the island of Thera in the late 3rd century BC an elaborate inscription describes the development of the cult that Epicteta established for her husband and her two sons who had predeceased her and, looking beyond her own death, herself. This will was ratified by the ephorate of the island and thus the private became public.

In her will Epicteta spoke of the precinct that was the centre of her cult as a *mouseion* (or place sacred to the Muses) and the individual graves as *heroa*, that is, monuments to heroes. The place of worship of heroes was often named after them: there is an Archilocheion on Paros and Homereia are known from Smyrna (where Homer was honoured with a temple and library), Chios, and Alexandria. The architectural remains of such *heroa* range from a grave and precinct to the Mausoleum of Mausolus of Caria (erected by his wife after his death in 353 BC), which was one of the wonders of the ancient world and most probably the centre of a hero cult. The Greek practice of

heroizing the dead also spread to Lycia, where the grave of the local dynast Erbinna is contained in the magnificent 4th-century BC Nereid monument (now in the British Museum). The great altar to Zeus at Pergamum probably also functioned as a *heroon* to the ancestral figure of Telephus. The heroic pretensions of the anonymous *heros* buried in an elaborate temple tomb in Calydon are clear from its iconography and the relief showing the local hero Meleager.

With the spread of Christianity, pagan forms of worship – including hero cult – were gradually suppressed. But some pagan temples were converted into early Christian churches, as the Parthenon was given over to the worship of the Virgin (Panaghia). Christian saints supplanted the heroes who had prepared the way for them and, like the heroes and heroines of the past, they had their own place of cult, the centre of their power, and their days on the calendar of the religious year.

DISKIN CLAY

See also Dead

Further Reading

Antonaccio, Carla M., *An Archaeology of Ancestors: Tomb Cult and Hero Cult in Early Greece*, Latham, Maryland: Rowman and Littlefield, 1995

Berard, Claude, *L'Hérôon à la Porte de l'Ouest*, Bern: Francke, 1970

Boyancé, Pierre, *Le culte des Muses chez les philosophes grecs: Etudes d'histoire et de psychologie religieuses*, Paris: Boccard, 1937, reprinted 1972

Brelich, Angelo, *Gli eroi greci: un problema storico-religioso*, Rome: Ateneo, 1958

Burkert, Walter, *Greek Religion: Archaic and Classical*, Oxford: Blackwell, and Cambridge, Massachusetts: Harvard University Press, 1985

Clay, Diskin, "The Cults of Epicurus", *Cronache Ercolanesi*, 16 (1987): pp. 12–28

Farnell, Lewis Richard, *Greek Hero Cults and Ideas of Immortality*, Oxford: Clarendon Press, 1921, reprinted 1970

Fontenrose, Joseph, "The Hero as Athlete", *Classical Antiquity*, 1 (1968): pp. 73–104

Habicht, Christian, *Gottmenschentum und griechische Städte*, 2nd edition, Munich: Beck, 1970

Kearns, Emily, *The Heroes of Attica*, London: University of London Institute of Classical Studies, 1989

Larson, Jennifer, *Greek Heroine Cults*, Madison: University of Wisconsin Press, 1995

Nagy, Gregory, *The Best of the Achaeans: Concepts of the Hero in Archaic Greek Poetry*, Baltimore: Johns Hopkins University Press, 1979

Nock, A.D., "The Cult of Heroes", *Harvard Theological Review*, 37 (1944): pp. 141–74

Stewart, Zeph (editor), *Essays on Religion and the Ancient World*, Oxford: Clarendon Press, 1972; New York: Oxford University Press, 1986

Heron

Mathematician and astronomer of the 1st or 2nd century AD

Very little is known about Heron of Alexandria, and we cannot even be sure when he lived (dates from the 2nd century BC to the 3rd century AD have been suggested). He does, however, seem to be aware of the Romans, and in one of his works an argument uses as an illustration an eclipse of the moon observable in both Rome and Alexandria ten days before the spring equinox. The only such eclipse that took place in the range of periods in which Heron might have lived was in AD 62 (on 10 March). Since there is also some indication that the astronomer Ptolemy, writing in the 2nd century AD, was familiar with more sophisticated mathematical methods than those of Heron, then a date in the late 1st or early 2nd century AD looks plausible.

Heron is the author of 11 surviving treatises, largely on the practical applications of mathematics and mechanics. As practical handbooks they seem to have been modified and partially rewritten in the course of time to meet the needs of later users, and in some cases there are doubts as to how much really goes back to Heron.

The *Metrica* deals with methods of calculating areas and volumes; the *Definitions* is a collection of geometrical terms, and is probably a Byzantine compilation; the *Catoptrica* (which survives only in a medieval Latin translation) is on the mathematics of mirrors and their practical use; the *Geometrica* is a rather unstructured introduction to geometry; the *Stereometrica* deals with the theory of measuring volumes, and goes on to describe its practical application; the *Belopoieca* and the *Cheiroballistra* describe the construction of different kinds of catapult; the *Dioptra* concerns surveying, and particularly the use of the plane table; the *Mechanica* (which survives only in Arabic translation, though substantial fragments of the Greek text are preserved by Pappus) starts with simple theoretical mechanics, and goes on to describe mechanical devices such as the windlass, the lever, the screw, and the pulley, and shows how they can be used to move heavy weights; the *Automatopoietike* is about the construction of automata (largely for entertainment); and the *Pneumatica* describes devices worked by compressed air, steam, and water. A number of other works are credited to Heron, including a commentary on Euclid's *Elements*, of which a few fragments are preserved in quotations by other authors.

Although some of Heron's works contain mathematical material in the same form, and with the same goals, as traditional Euclidean geometry, what is interesting is that he reveals that Greek mathematics was not restricted to those fields in which they were capable of devising formal proofs. He also shows how Greek mathematics could be adapted to practical use. Many procedures are carried out by the application of formulae, as they are today. He knows the formula for calculating the area of a triangle if the length of the sides is given, and another for approximately calculating a cube root, and his method of solving quadratic equations is very close to the one used today. While mathematics in the Euclidean tradition is interested in producing irrefutable proofs, and absolute precision and certainty, Heron does not hesitate to give approximate results, of a kind perfectly adequate for practical purposes. It is very much the kind of mathematics that had long been practised by the Babylonians and the Egyptians, and shows that this tradition of practical mathematics continued to develop among the Greeks alongside the Euclidean tradition that we think of as more characteristically Greek. Heron often illustrates his procedures by examples drawn from real practical situations, such as calculating the capacity of a theatre, a barrel, a well, or the hold of a ship.

He is, however, best known for his descriptions of machines, gadgets, and automata, which preserve some of the few pieces of evidence we have of the application of Greek science to practical technology. He provides, for example, one of the few instances from antiquity of harnessing the power of the wind by means of a windmill; in the example he gives, it is used to drive a mechanical organ. He describes a crude steam turbine in which steam created by boiling water in a cauldron is piped into a ball through tubes on which the ball is pivoted, and allowed to escape through outlets that drive the ball round; he also gives an account of a force pump for use in a fire engine. Many of the machines he describes are designed to amuse or impress. For example, he tells us how to construct a vessel that will, by the manipulation of air inlets, dispense pure wine, wine mixed with water, or plain water (which Heron thinks might be a good joke to play). He describes two different ways of making a model temple whose doors will open of their own accord when a fire is lit on the altar, and another device makes a trumpet sound when a door is opened. He also describes a vending machine that dispenses water (presumably for purification purposes) when a coin is inserted, and gives an account of how to build toy theatres, where the figures are made to move by the force of millet seed or sand trickling out of a container.

It is hard to say how many of these devices were ever actually built or put into use (though some of Heron's descriptions do seem to bear the marks of practical experience). The argument sometimes put forward that Heron's work demonstrates that industrialization was well within the grasp of Greek engineers, but that they were prevented from progressing by social or ideological considerations, is quite misplaced. In most cases, the technology of the day was not sufficiently advanced to enable the construction of more than very small devices. In the case of the steam turbine, which is often cited in this argument, the form in which Heron describes it could hardly have had a practical application. The weak point of the device is the joint between the steam pipes and the ball, which must be tight enough to prevent steam escaping, but loose enough to allow the unimpeded movement of the ball. It has been calculated that the efficiency of such a machine would be no more than 1 per cent; consequently, the effort required to gather fuel and stoke the boiler would be many times greater than any work produced.

RICHARD WALLACE

See also Technology

Biography

Heron was born in Alexandria but little else is known of his life. He may have lived in the 1st or 2nd century AD. He wrote widely on mathematics and the practical applications of mathematics, notably machines, gadgets, and automata. He drew on Babylonian sources as well as the Euclidian tradition.

Writings

Opera, edited by Wilhelm Schmidt *et al.*, 5 vols, Stuttgart: Teubner, 1899–1914, reprinted 1976 (Greek text and German translation)

Further Reading

Heath, Sir Thomas Little, *A History of Greek Mathematics*, Oxford: Clarendon Press, 1921, reprinted New York: Dover, 1981

Hill, Donald, *A History of Engineering in Classical and Medieval Times*, London: Croom Helm, and La Salle, Illinois: Open Court, 1984, reprinted London and New York: Routledge, 1996

Landels, J.G., *Engineering in the Ancient World*, London: Chatto and Windus, and Berkeley: University of California Press, 1978

Herophilus *c.330–c.260* BC

Physician

Herophilus of Chalcedon, an Alexandrian physician, was one of only two ancient scientists (the other being Erasistratus of Ceos) to perform systematic scientific dissections of human cadavers. According to controversial but plausible ancient evidence, he and Erasistratus also performed vivisections on condemned criminals handed over to them by autocratic Hellenistic rulers. Herophilus' pioneering use of human dissection led to numerous remarkable anatomical discoveries, among them his discovery of the nerves, his distinction between sensory and "voluntary" (i.e. motor) nerves, and his description of the paths and functions of at least seven pairs of cranial nerves, including the optic nerve and the oculomotor nerve. He also identified several ventricles of the brain as well as some fine cerebral and vascular structures. Discovering a cavity in the floor of the fourth ventricle of the brain, he named it *kalamos* ("reed pen") because of its resemblance to the carved-out groove of a writing pen. This is but one of his many contributions to modern anatomical nomenclature (*calamus scriptorius*). The confluence of the four great cranial sinuses still bears the name of its discoverer: *torcular Herophili*. His meticulous dissection of the eye also allowed him to become the first to distinguish between the cornea, retina, iris, and chorioid coat.

Herophilus' anatomical investigations yielded considerable advances in the description and understanding of other organs too. An extant fragment from book 1 of his *Dissections*, for example, preserves the first reasonably accurate and detailed description of the human liver, while fragments of book 3 preserve his anatomical account of the male and female reproductive parts. Using the analogy of the male testicles, he discovered the ovaries or, as he called them, female "twins" (*didymoi*, "twins", being a traditional term for the testicles). His investigation of the uterus and of the ovaries also led to his discovery of the Fallopian tubes, although (as Galen was delighted to emphasize) Herophilus failed to recognize their true course and their function. From book 4 of *Dissections* fragments of his extensive anatomy of the vascular system survive, including some concerning the anatomical distinction between veins and arteries, the heart valves, the chambers of the heart, and various complex vascular structures.

Closely linked to Herophilus' radically new anatomical version of the human body was his physiological model of the body. The aim of his dissections and vivisections of humans and animals apparently was not only to *describe* various internal parts of the body, but also to uncover and explain their *functions*. Although insisting that all causal explanation is "hypothetical" or provisional, he freely offered causal accounts of respiration, pulsation, sensation, reproduction, dreams, and physical as well as mental diseases. Locating the "command centre" (*hegemonikon*) of the body in the fourth cerebral ventricle, i.e. in the cerebellum (which is in fact responsible, *inter alia*, for muscular coordination and for the maintenance of physical equilibrium), Herophilus apparently argued that neural transmissions occur by means of *pneuma*, a breath-like substance that runs from the brain through the nerves. This *pneuma* is ultimately derived from the external air through respiration.

Pneuma is present not only in the nerves, according to Herophilus, but also in the arteries, mixed with blood, whereas the veins carry only blood. This uncanny, though not precise, parallel to the modern recognition that the arteries carry oxygenated blood ("blood with *pneuma*" in Herophilus' model) from the heart, whereas the veins convey deoxygenated blood ("blood without *pneuma*", according to Herophilus) triggered a controversy that lasted many centuries, but in the end it was Herophilus' view that prevailed, not least because the influential Galen accepted it, albeit with certain elaborations.

Herophilus' pioneering treatise *On Pulses* became the foundation of practically all ancient pulse theories, as becomes evident in Galen's voluminous accounts of pulse lore. A "power" or "faculty" (*dynamis*) flowing from the heart through the muscular walls of the arteries causes the regular dilation and contraction of the arteries; the words "diastole" and "systole" are further examples of Herophilus' many enduring contributions to medical terminology. The pulsating arteries continuously "pull" the mixture of blood and *pneuma* from the heart, and distribute it to all parts of the body. Using musical analogies, Herophilus described the changing relations between *diastole* and *systole* at different stages of life as successively displaying pyrrhic, trochaic, spondaic, and iambic rhythms, i.e. in infancy, childhood, adulthood, and old age, respectively. So confident was he in the diagnostic value of the pulse that he constructed a clepsydra, adjustable for the patient's age, to measure his patients' pulse rates.

In his *Midwifery* Herophilus apparently tried to demystify the uterus by asserting that not only is it constituted of the same material elements as the rest of the body but it is also governed by the same "powers" or "faculties". Certain "affections", he said, are of course experienced only by women (conception, parturition, lactation), but there is no disease peculiar to women. His discovery of the broad ligaments, which hold the uterus in place, challenged the traditional Hippocratic theory that hysteria or hysterical suffocation is caused by the "wandering womb". The causes of difficult childbirth, the normal duration of pregnancy, the benefits and disadvantages of menstruation, and whether the foetus is a living being are further subjects treated in this work. Tertullian, who vigorously objected to Herophilus' use of human dissection and vivisection, also charges Herophilus with the possession of an instrument known as "foetus-slayer", implying that he performed abortions.

His semiotic theory of diagnosis, known as a "triple-timed inference from signs", his descriptions of the symptoms and causes of numerous physical and mental disorders, and his classification of dreams are among further achievements that provoked both admiring approval and resistance throughout antiquity.

Herophilus' revolutionary discoveries transformed Greek theoretical medicine, but it is difficult to assess their influence on ancient and Byzantine medical practice. Furthermore, resistance to his innovative methods, notably to human dissection, was immediate and forceful. Moral and religious scruples about dissection found a powerful ally in the methodological and epistemological objections of the Empiricists, a new medical "school" founded in Alexandria by Philinus of Cos, a renegade pupil of Herophilus. Although Herophilus had his followers, too – the history of the "Herophilean school" can be traced in Alexandria, Asia Minor, and elsewhere from the 3rd century BC to the 1st century AD – they never seem to have mounted an effective defence of human dissection against the Empiricists' claim that it is a clinically irrelevant and epistemologically suspect method of investigation. Herophilus' discoveries and theories nevertheless continued to have an impact, in large measure thanks to their transmission by an appreciative though not uncritical Galen, by Soranus of Ephesus, by early Byzantine medical encyclopaedists (Oribasius, Aëtius of Amida, Paul of Aegina), and by Hippocratic and Galenic commentators. When systematic human dissection was resumed in the Renaissance, the superior accuracy of Herophilus' observations was recognized anew. In the 20th century, too, innovative theorists have continued to recognize the value of some of Herophilus' insights, even if, in certain cases, reluctantly. In *The Interpretation of Dreams*, for example, Sigmund Freud comments: "I am far from seeking to maintain that I am the first writer to have the idea of deriving dreams from wishes. Those who attach importance to anticipations of this kind may go back to Classical antiquity and quote Herophilus."

HEINRICH VON STADEN

See also Anatomy and Physiology, Health

Biography

Born in Chalcedon *c*.330 BC, Herophilus was a pupil of Praxagoras of Cos before moving to Alexandria. There he performed systematic dissections of human cadavers (and, according to some sources, vivisections on condemned criminals) which led to many important anatomical discoveries and transformed theoretical medicine. His writings included the treatises *Dissections*, *On Pulses*, and *On Midwifery*. He died *c*.260 BC.

Further Reading

Hankinson, R.J., "Saying the Phenomena", *Phronesis*, 35 (1990): pp. 194–215

Lloyd, G.E.R., *Greek Science after Aristotle*, London: Chatto and Windus, and New York: Norton, 1973

Lloyd, G.E.R., *Science, Folklore and Ideology: Studies in the Life Sciences in Ancient Greece*, Cambridge and New York: Cambridge University Press, 1983

Lloyd, G.E.R., *The Revolutions of Wisdom: Studies in the Claims and Practice of Ancient Greek Science*, Berkeley: University of California Press, 1987

von Staden, Heinrich, *Herophilus: The Art of Medicine in Early Alexandria: Edition, Translation, and Essays*, Cambridge and New York: Cambridge University Press, 1989

Hesiod

Epic poet of the 8th or 7th century BC

The works of Hesiod, like those of Homer, deal with two disparate themes. Unlike the *Iliad* and *Odyssey*, however, which are long narratives composed to entertain, Hesiod's *Theogony* and *Works and Days* are shorter poems, instructive in their purpose. They are best understood within the framework of traditions of cosmogonical and wisdom literature prevalent in the ancient Near East (although not only there).

The *Theogony*, which seems to have been composed first (see below), deals with the creation of the universe and its peopling with gods in their generations and their semidivine offspring. After an opening hymn to the Muses and an invocation, the poet goes through divine genealogies from Chaos to the Olympians, the narrative being underpinned by the separate episodes of the divine succession myth, wherein Uranus gives way to Cronus, and Cronus and the Titans to Zeus. The poem ends – or peters out – with a catalogue of the children of goddesses and mortal men, which is closer to the later catalogue of mortal women who lay with gods than to the genuine poetry of Hesiod. Both the creation and succession myths of the *Theogony* have close parallels in oriental mythology.

After a brief introduction, most of the *Works and Days* is cast in the form of an admonition to the poet's unsatisfactory younger brother Perses. Hesiod then tells a story of Prometheus, whose deception of Zeus (over the allocation of shares in animal sacrifice, and the theft of fire, which he gave to mankind), which earned Prometheus agonizing punishment, is described at length in the *Theogony*. Here the earlier story is briefly alluded to, and its sequel is told: in revenge for the theft of fire, Zeus creates Pandora, whom he gives to Prometheus' late-thinking brother Epimetheus, with disastrous results, namely the release of evils upon mankind. The poet is then reminded of another story that traces in a different way the degradation of the human condition. This is the myth of ages, gold–silver–bronze–iron, with the insertion between the last two of the age of heroes who fought at Thebes and Troy. Hesiod then addresses the *basileis*, the chieftains whom Perses appears to have suborned, and Perses. In the bulk of the rest of the poem he gives Perses – who seems somehow to have lost his fortune and to be in need of practical instruction – advice on the agricultural tasks appropriate to each season of the year. A section on domestic and social matters follows, and the poem concludes with an almanac of the days of the month (the "Days" of the title). The motifs of giving advice to a younger person, and the myth of ages, have parallels with eastern literature, but, as with the traditional elements in the *Theogony*, it is not possible to trace any kind of line of descent. It is to be noted as well that, despite the differences in scope and subject matter, Hesiod and Homer both composed in the same artificial epic dialect, which seems to have originated in Aeolis and Ionia, and clearly belong to the same epic tradition.

Hesiod differs from Homer not only in the nature and scope of his work, but also in the way that he presents himself to his audience. Whereas Homer is self-effacing to the point of anonymity, Hesiod goes to great pains to present and identify himself as a man with a name and occupation of his own, living in a specific milieu and with a specific background. How

Hesiod: carved gemstone showing Prometheus fashioning man in the image of the gods as described in Hesiod's *Theogony*, 3rd–2nd century BC, British Museum, London

much of this is genuine, and how much convention, is difficult to say, but where the details he gives can be checked they seem to confirm his story. For example, he claims to live at Ascra, near Mount Helicon. The site has been identified, and his description of the local microclimate is valid even today. He says that his father came from Cyme in Aeolis to settle at Ascra, understandable enough in that he would have moved from one Aeolic-speaking place to another.

The relative dates of Hesiod and Homer (whether he be poet or redactor) are still unsettled, but it seems to be generally agreed that their lifetimes overlapped, near the turn of the 8th and 7th centuries BC. In the *Works and Days* Hesiod reveals that he once won a tripod for a poem sung at the funeral games for Amphidamas of Chalcis: it is generally agreed that the prize poem was the *Theogony*. In both poems the poet speaks freely of himself and his circumstances. Other poems attributed to Hesiod – the *Shield of Heracles* and the various *Catalogues* – are generally, and probably correctly, held to be creations of various authors of the 6th century BC. Hesiod's position as an author within the genre is obfuscated by the fact that later ancient scholarship lumped together under his name all other catalogue poetry, as it attributed all other military epics to Homer.

The earliest critical edition of Hesiod's text was made by Zenodotus of Ephesus, the first librarian of Alexandria, followed by Aristophanes of Byzantium (3rd–2nd century BC) and Aristarchus (2nd century BC). These and other Alexandrian scholars more or less established the text (and several of its recurrent problems, such as the authenticity of the last part of the *Works and Days*, and of the lesser poems).

Substantial commentaries were written by Plutarch (1st–2nd century AD), Proclus (5th century AD), John Tzetzes (12th century), Planoudes (13th century), Moschopoulos (13th–14th centuries), and Triklinios (14th century).

Understandably, Hesiod has not had as much influence on later literature as Homer. His work was, however, well known in antiquity, both in Greece and in Rome. Closer to our own time, George Chapman translated the *Works and Days* (1618), and Milton drew on the *Theogony* for the Creation portion of *Paradise Lost* (1667). Hesiod's Heliconian Muses have, of course, become a symbol for poetic inspiration, and poets from antiquity to the present have used the authority of Hesiod to speak of themselves and their poetic vocation. In the 20th century Kostis Palamas identified himself with Hesiod in his "Man of Ascra" (1903–04), a poem of 666 lines, in which he extends Hesiod's five ages to include a sixth, an Age of Love (retelling the Pandora myth), and adds a motif of his own, of rebirth after death, a metaphor for the rebirth in modern Greece of its ancient heritage.

ALBERT SCHACHTER

See also Poetry (Epic)

Biography

An approximate contemporary of Homer, Hesiod (*fl. c.*700 BC) lived at Ascra in Boeotia where his father had settled after leaving Asia Minor. He is the author of two surviving epic poems, the *Theogony* (on the descent of the gods) and the *Works and Days* (on agriculture and the just life). Other poems have been falsely attributed to him.

Writings

Hesiod, the Homeric Hymns, and Homerica, translated by Hugh G. Evelyn-White, 2nd edition, London: Heinemann, and Cambridge, Massachusetts: Harvard University Press, 1936 (Loeb edition; several reprints)
Hesiod, translated by Richmond Lattimore, Ann Arbor: University of Michigan Press, 1959
Theogony, edited by M.L. West, Oxford: Clarendon Press, 1966 (text and commentary)
Works and Days, edited by M.L. West, Oxford: Clarendon Press, 1978 (text and commentary)
Theogony, and Works and Days, translated by M.L. West, Oxford and New York: Oxford University Press, 1988

Further Reading

Highet, Gilbert, *The Classical Tradition: Greek and Roman Influences on Western Literature*, Oxford: Clarendon Press, and New York: Oxford University Press, 1949, reprinted 1985
Lamberton, Robert, *Hesiod*, New Haven, Connecticut and London: Yale University Press, 1988
Newman, John Kevin, *The Classical Epic Tradition*, Madison: University of Wisconsin Press, 1986
Stavrou, Theopanis G. and C.A. Trypanis, *Kostis Palamas: A Portrait and an Appreciation*, Minneapolis: Nostos, 1985

Hesychasm

Hesychasm is now generally associated with the theology of St Gregory Palamas, worked out in the course of the 14th-century hesychast controversy. Gregory was, however, working on the basis of a tradition that had experienced a certain renaissance from the late-13th century and which was rooted in the very origins of monasticism.

The word "hesychasm" derives from *hesychia* or stillness, tranquillity. The origin of this word is uncertain, though it has been linked to the verb "to be seated". It occurs in Classical Greek to signify both exterior and inner calm and peace. The Septuagint uses it principally to refer to the tranquillity resulting from freedom from external threats, but also in the sense of keeping silence. This second sense also crops up in the Greek of the New Testament, albeit rarely.

The *Apophthegmata Patrum* (5th–6th centuries) speak of *hesychia* not just in terms of the flight from men but also in terms of inner tranquillity. The term "hesychast" came to designate one seeking inner and outer stillness, not necessarily one who lived in complete solitude, but often one who lived in the kind of semi-eremitic communities found at Scetis or Nitria. Hesychasm, of both kinds, is recommended by many writers of the patristic period.

The most complete development of hesychasm as a distinctive spiritual tradition is found in the Sinaitic tradition, most especially in the work of St John Klimakos (7th century). "Few are those", he writes, "who have excelled in profane philosophy! Fewer still, I might say, are those who truly know that wisdom which is *hesychia*!" *Hesychia*, for Klimakos, is a state of inner silence and watchfulness, intimately linked to the remembrance of Jesus and short, repeated prayers. "The hesychast is one who tries to circumscribe the incorporeal in his body: a paradoxical undertaking!" "*Hesychia* is perpetual adoration before God: may the remembrance of Jesus be united with your breath, and then you will know the worth of *hesychia*." It is easy to see how important Klimakos was to be for the hesychasts of the 14th century in defending their psycho-physical methods of prayer. Klimakos does not expressly refer to the Jesus prayer, though this is clearly recommended by Hesychios of Batos, or Sinai (?8th century), his spiritual successor.

The hesychast tradition has tended to fluctuate in its influence, experiencing regular periods of decline and revival. It broke out spectacularly in 11th-century Byzantium with the mystical teaching of St Symeon the New Theologian. After that it seems to have gone into decline. Theoliptos of Philadelphia (c.1250–1322) is singled out by St Gregory Palamas as one of the leading teachers of hesychasm. Nikephoros the Hesychast, a monk of Athos in the 13th century, gave an account of certain methods by which the thoughts might be restrained and the return into oneself, into the depths of the heart, be effected. His teaching is similar to that given in the *Three Methods of Prayer* falsely attributed to St Symeon the New Theologian. Both may simply be records of practices that had long been traditional on Athos. It was these sorts of methods, particularly as practised by inexperienced monks, that so incensed the Calabrian monk Barlaam.

Notwithstanding the work of such men as Nikephoros, when St Gregory of Sinai arrived on Athos, around 1300, he found the practice of hesychasm virtually dead. Gregory settled at the skete of Magoula, near the monastery of Philotheou. While avoiding all controversy, Gregory's standpoint was very much that of his namesake, St Gregory Palamas. He speaks, for example, of the light of the Transfiguration as uncreated and specifically divine. In the course of the hesychast controversy Palamas provided a theological basis for the hesychast tradition of prayer, defending the participation of the body in the spiritual life and providing an explanation whereby the light witnessed in prayer could be regarded as divine and uncreated without negating the transcendence of God.

The victory of the hesychast party led by Palamas had enormous repercussions. It produced a flourishing of the hesychast tradition in the so-called Byzantine Commonwealth, a phenomenon described by John Meyendorff as the "hesychast international". It tended to confirm the monasticization of the patriarchate and the abandonment of the cathedral rite – both processes that had begun long before the hesychast controversy. The Turkish conquest appears to have severely restricted the hesychast tradition for some centuries. A deliberate attempt to revive it is to be found in the *Philokalia*, compiled in the 18th century by St Nikodemos of the Holy Mountain and St Makarios of Corinth. The influence of the *Philokalia* was initially more palpable in the Slavic world. There was a resurgence of the practice of the Jesus prayer in 19th-century Russia that owed much to the hesychast texts in the *Philokalia*. In the 20th century there has been something of a revival of the hesychast tradition on Mount Athos. This revival began in sketes such as that directed by Elder Joseph the Hesychast, and has since spread to many of the coenobia.

MARCUS PLESTED

Summary

Hesychasm, which derives from *hesychia* (stillness), is an aspect of the Eastern Christian spiritual tradition that goes back to the beginnings of monasticism. It is particularly associated with the thought of the 14th-century theologian St Gregory Palamas. The *Philokalia* includes many hesychast texts and the meditative tradition is currently enjoying a revival on Mount Athos.

Further Reading

Hausherr, Irenée, "L'Hésychasme: étude de spiritualité" in *Hésychasme et prière*, Rome: Pontificium Institutum Studiorum, 1966
Lossky, Vladimir, *The Mystical Theology of the Eastern Church*, London: Clarke, 1957, reprinted Crestwood, New York: St Vladimir's Seminary Press, 1976
Meyendorff, John, *Byzantine Hesychasm: Historical, Theological and Social Problems*, London: Variorum, 1974

Hetairists

Also known as the *Philiki Hetaireia*, the "Friendly Society" was a philhellenic secret society that consisted mostly of Greeks living abroad, with the goal of organizing and helping to finance a Greek uprising against the Turks. It was one of the main contributing factors to Greek nationalism in the second decade of the 19th century, and played an active role in setting the stage for the War of Independence.

Founded in Odessa in 1814 by the expatriate merchants Athanasios Tsakalov, Nikolaos Skoufas, and Emmanouil Xanthos, the *Philiki Hetaireia* was organized along the lines of other revolutionary secret societies such as the Freemasons and Carbonari, but also in the tradition of Greek intellectual and literary clubs such as the Philomuse Society founded in Athens in 1812 for the purpose of the cultural regeneration of the Greek nation. The *Hetaireia* moved its headquarters to Constantinople in 1818, as its membership grew and became more cosmopolitan; by the time of its dissolution it included members from nearly every major Greek community in Europe, as well as most regions in Greece itself. It was dissolved in 1821, at the outbreak of the War of Independence, when its nominally democratic organization was superseded by the more traditional loyalties and values necessitated by warfare. Yet in his analysis of hetairist documents, George D. Frangos notes that even in 1821 the records of some 1000 documented members reveal 53.7 per cent merchants, 13.1 per cent professionals (such as teachers, students, physicians, secretaries, etc.), 9.5 per cent clergymen, 8.7 per cent military men, and only 0.6 per cent peasants, the group representing the largest percentage of population in Ottoman-occupied Greece.

Throughout the *Hetaireia*'s existence, members were sent as messengers to European communities where Greeks lived, and to leaders of the Greeks in the Ottoman empire, seeking financial contributions and new initiates into the society. A number of local cells were set up in Greek territory and the Danubian principalities, and certain Orthodox priests in Greece proper openly assisted them. The *Philiki Hetaireia* was especially attractive to Phanariots and others with western sympathies and education, but members also included leaders of the klephts, such as Theodore Kolokotronis; the ruler of the Maniots, Petrobey Mavromichalis; and even the opportunistic Ali Pasha, who hoped to manipulate the *Hetaireia*, and through it the Russian government, into aiding his own uprising against the Sublime Porte. Membership also included a few prominent non-Greeks such as Kavadjordje Petrovic, who had led a successful revolt against the Porte in Serbia in the years 1804–06.

Initiates were intentionally misled into believing that the society had the backing of Russia through Ioannis Kapodistria, who at that time was serving as the principal minister of tsar Alexander I. Kapodistria had in fact been invited at least twice to become the leader of the *Philiki Hetaireia*, but had refused. Barbara Jelavich suggests that possibly it was he who suggested Alexander Ypsilantis, who became the society's leader in 1820 and led the abortive attempt to begin the revolution in the Danubian principalities of Moldavia and Wallachia (modern Romania) in March 1821. The *Philiki Hetaireia* gained considerable support from both Greeks and Romanians in the form of money, weapons, and recruits who believed that they were acting with the tsar's approval. When word came through that the tsar had denounced the revolt and the *Hetaireia*, the Ottoman army easily defeated the rebels. Ypsilantis escaped across the Austrian frontier, but was captured by Austrian authorities and died in the dungeon of Mugats castle in January 1828. His brother, Demetrios Ypsilantis, was chosen by the *Hetaireia* to lead the revolt in Greece itself. Demetrios arrived at Hydra in June 1821, and enjoyed considerably more success on Greek soil than Alexander had in the principalities.

The *Philiki Hetaireia* combined the traditions of the Greek Orthodox Church and Greece's Classical history with a burgeoning nationalism. The society's initiation rituals were elaborate and arcane, requiring all members to become the blood brother of any other member they might chance to meet.

Initiates learned the hetairist symbols and words, then were sworn into the society in the presence of a priest. After this a number of increasingly binding oaths and confessions were made in a secret place, in the name of justice, truth, and the fatherland, and in the name of the Father, the Son, and the Holy Spirit. New members were told almost nothing about the nature of the society's controlling organization, or about its members or activities at any levels above their own.

There were four civilian grades, with correspondingly simple or complicated oaths and responsibilities. The *vlamis* (from the Albanian *vlameria*, or "brotherhood") and *systimenos* (from the Greek root for "drawing together") levels were at the bottom, and the *ierevs* (priest) and *poimin* (shepherd) levels were reserved for wealthier and better-educated Greeks, who paid a higher subscription. The two military grades were *aphieromenos* (dedicated one) and *archigos ton aphieromenon* (leader of the dedicated). At the very top were the *archi*, the inner circle, whose membership was to be kept a strict secret until after the revolution had actually been put in motion.

Although this last measure was taken to protect the personal safety of the *archigoi* ("leaders"), such secretiveness about the society's actual leadership had the additional effect of raising speculation that various well-known and powerful political figures – including Kapodistria and the patriarch Gregory V of Constantinople, the civil and religious leader of the Greeks – were involved, thus increasing membership and interest in the cause. The patriarch was not a member, and had actually denounced and excommunicated Alexander Ypsilantis after the invasion of the Danubian provinces. Nevertheless, he was executed by the Porte on Easter Sunday, 22 April 1821, for allegedly acting as an accessory to the rebellious activities of the *Philiki Hetaireia*. This event, which horrified all Christendom, resulted in widespread support for the revolution, both within Greece and abroad.

SUSAN SPENCER

See also Political History 1453–1832, Independence (War of)

Summary

The hetairists were members of the *Philiki Hetaireia* (or "Friendly Society") whose object was to foster a Greek uprising against the Turks. It was founded in Odessa in 1814 and moved to Constantinople in 1818. It provided links between Greek communities throughout Europe and the Ottoman empire and played a significant role in instigating the War of Independence. It was dissolved in 1821.

Further Reading

Braddock, Joseph, *The Greek Phoenix*, London: Constable, 1972; New York: Coward McCann, 1973

Clogg, Richard (editor and translator), *The Movement for Greek Independence, 1770–1821: A Collection of Documents*, London: Macmillan, 1976

Dakin, Douglas, *The Unification of Greece, 1770–1923*, London: Benn, and New York: St Martin's Press, 1972

Dakin, Douglas, *The Greek Struggle for Independence, 1821–1833*, London: Batsford, and Berkeley: University of California Press, 1973

Finlay, George, *A History of Greece from Its Conquest by the Romans to the Present Time, BC 146 to AD 1864*, revised by H.F.

Tozer, 7 vols, Oxford: Clarendon Press, 1877, reprinted New York: AMS Press, 1970, vol. 6

Frangos, George D., "The *Philiki Etairia*: A Premature National Coalition" in *The Struggle for Greek Independence: Essays to Mark the 150th Anniversary of the Greek War of Independence*, edited by Richard Clogg, London: Macmillan, and Hamden, Connecticut: Archon, 1973

Jelavich, Barbara, *History of the Balkans*, vol. 1: *Eighteenth and Nineteenth Centuries*, Cambridge and New York: Cambridge University Press, 1983

St Clair, William, *That Greece Might Still Be Free: The Philhellenes in the War of Independence*, London and New York: Oxford University Press, 1972

Skiotis, Dennis N., "The Greek Revolution: Ali Pasha's Last Gamble" in *Hellenism and the First Greek War of Liberation, 1821–1830: Continuity and Change*, edited by Nikoforos P. Diamandouros *et al.*, Thessalonica: Institute for Balkan Studies, 1976

Woodhouse, C.M., *The Greek War of Independence: Its Historical Setting*, London: Hutchinson, 1952, reprinted New York: Russell, 1975

Hieron I

Tyrant of Syracuse *fl.* 478–466 BC

In 480 BC, two years before Hieron I succeeded his brother Gelon as tyrant of Syracuse, the city's position as a major power among the western Greeks was confirmed by the decisive victory of the combined forces of Gelon and Theron of Acragas over the Carthaginians at Himera. The resulting security was one of the major factors that enabled Hieron to extend his power and to establish a court famed – not least because it was the poets' job to praise him and his followers – as a centre of artistic patronage.

Hieron had already exercised authority since 485 BC as governor for his brother of Gela, their ancestral home. In Syracuse he consolidated the alliance with Acragas by marrying Theon's niece. (The link had temporarily been threatened, early in the reign, when his disgruntled brother Polyzalus, now governing Gela, attempted to form an alliance with Theron against him.) Outside Sicily, he soon laid claim to larger Panhellenic power or at least prestige. In 477 BC he was able effectively to order Anaxilas, ruler of Rhegium and Messana, not to attack Locri Epizephyrii. (Anaxilas had already been pressurized after Himera into abandoning relations with Carthage and marrying his daughter to Hieron.) In 474 BC he helped Cumae to defeat an Etruscan fleet, a success that poets were not slow to compare to the battle of Salamis, enhancing the tyrant's image as the defender of the western Greeks against barbarians. (The eastern Greeks had been similarly defended at Salamis.)

Hieron's ability to promote this image was much enhanced by his acquisition of the presence or services of poets from the Greek motherland including Aeschylus, Pindar, and Simonides of Ceos and his nephew Bacchylides. (Xenophanes of Colophon also came to Hieron's court but probably more briefly.) The most widely known celebrations of Hieron were those in the epinician odes of Pindar (*Olympian* 1, *Pythians* 1–3) and Bacchylides (*Odes* 3–5) for the victories of his teams in chariot and horse-and-rider events. The tyrant's building of a new stone theatre in Syracuse (*c.*475–470 BC), replacing a

largely wooden one, also helped to proclaim his glory. Here, probably, was staged the Sicilian production of Aeschylus' *Persians* with its potential comparisons between Salamis and Cumae; possibly also, Tommaso Guardì suggests, Phrynicus' similarly appropriate *Phoenician Women*. (Epicharmus, the Sicilian comic playwright, no doubt also produced work – possibly including more by way of implied criticism of the tyrant – for Hieron's court.)

In 472 BC Syracuse became unequivocally the strongest force within Sicily when Hieron defeated Thrasydaeus of Acragas, Theron's less effective successor. Probably at this point Hieron could have installed his own dependants as tyrants of Acragas and Himera; James F. McGlew argues that his reason for not doing so was the desire to represent himself "as the liberator of the politically oppressed cities of Sicily". The cities he himself had most oppressed were Catana and Naxos, which were destroyed in 476 BC after the removal of their entire population to Leontini. (Hieron's help for Chalcidian Cumae may, as David Asheri says, have been designed to "obscure the memory" of his treatment of these fellow Chalcidian foundations.) Catana was refounded as Aetna and repeopled with 10,000 Dorians (half from Syracuse, half from the Peloponnese). One motive for this action was clearly, as Diodorus says, to obtain "from the recently founded city of 10,000 men ... the honours accorded to heroes"; at his death the tyrant indeed received these honours "as having been the founder of the city". Literature again helped to celebrate the founder and to inaugurate his settlement: Aeschylus wrote his lost *Women of Aetna*, performed in the new city probably in 471 BC, and Pindar saluted Aetna in the first Pythian ode and its governor, the loyal Chromios, in the first and ninth Nemean.

Another motive for founding Aetna was, as Diodorus realized, "to have a substantial help ready at hand for any need that might arise". When the crisis came with the expulsion of Thrasybulus, Hieron's brother and successor, the colonists supported him and were themselves expelled from Aetna, which became Catana once more; transferred to Inessa, they continued, according to Diodorus, to honour Hieron as their founding hero. No doubt they would have approved of Pindar's ideal Hieron, "gentle to citizens, not begrudging to good men, and to guests a wondrous father" (*Pythian* 3); it is less certain where the truth lies between this image and that constructed by Diodorus or his source – Hieron as "avaricious and violent and, generally speaking, an utter stranger to sincerity and nobility of character". (Gelon's rule was milder than Hieron's, says Diodorus; that of Thrasybulus, the last of the Deinomenid tyrants, on the other hand, was distinctly worse – he murdered many citizens, confiscated people's property, and was rapidly overthrown.) Hieron was clearly good at seizing the main chance and at claiming, through his poets as well as his deeds, the attention of posterity. Xenophon, for instance, uses his name if little else for the tyrant who debates with Simonides the advantages and disadvantages of tyranny in his *Hieron*. But, like many other Greek tyrannies, his did not survive into the next generation. It relied largely on force. It was underpinned by no constitutional theory, uncertain of its own position. (Finley finds a "touch of reticence" in the failure of Theron, Gelon, and Hieron to put their names, titles, or symbols of office on their coins – a result perhaps of a desire for Panhellenic acknowledgement at a time when tyranny was no longer fashionable in Greece proper, where "tyrant" was, for the first time, becoming a synonym for "despot".) But Hieron's concern with military matters allowed commerce and agriculture to thrive; Asheri goes so far as to say that (except for the suffering of such unfortunates as the people of Catana) his rule was "a golden age for Syracuse".

MARTIN GARRETT

See also Sicily

Biography

Hieron ruled Gela from 485 to 478 BC as regent for his brother Gelon. On Gelon's death (478) Hieron succeeded him as tyrant of Syracuse. Under Hieron Syracuse became the most powerful state in Sicily and he gained a reputation as defender of the western Greeks. He enhanced his prestige by attracting to his court poets such as Aeschylus, Pindar, Simonides, Bacchylides, and Xenophanes. He died at Aetna in 466 BC.

Further Reading

Asheri, D., "Sicily, 478–431 BC", in *The Fifth Century* BC, edited by D.M. Lewis *et al*., Cambridge: Cambridge University Press, 1992 (*The Cambridge Ancient History*, vol. 5, 2nd edition)

Diodorus Siculus, *Diodorus of Sicily*, vol. 4 (books 9–11), translated by C.H. Oldfather, London: Heinemann, and Cambridge, Massachusetts: Harvard University Press, 1961 (Loeb edition)

Finley, M.I., *Ancient Sicily*, revised edition, London: Chatto and Windus, and Totowa, New Jersey: Rowman and Littlefield, 1979

Guardì, Tommaso, "L'attività teatrale nella Siracusa di Gerone I", *Dionisio: Riviste di Studi sul Teatro Antico*, 51 (1980): pp. 25–47

McGlew, James F., *Tyranny and Political Culture in Ancient Greece*, Ithaca, New York: Cornell University Press, 1993

Pindar, *The Odes*, translated by Richmond Lattimore, Chicago: University of Chicago Press, 1947, 2nd edition 1976

Podlecki, A.A., "Simonides in Sicily", *Parola del Passato*, 34 (1979): pp. 5–16

Hieronymus of Cardia c.364–?260 BC

Administrator and historian

Hieronymus made his name in antiquity mainly as a historical figure – a friend and ambassador of kings, a military man with a remarkable fighting record, a local governor and administrator, someone who managed to survive by switching sides at the right moment, and as a *makrobios* (long-lived person) who, notwithstanding his many wounds and war toils, reached the respectable age of 104 (Jacoby, 1962, no. 154, TT2, 6–8, F8). His merits as a writer and as a historian were less admired in antiquity. His work was never seen as a breakthrough in the development of Hellenistic historiography. The influence of his predecessors can be detected in the scanty remains of his work (of which even the title, or rather its contents, is variously reported). Thucydides and Xenophon might have taught him that serious history must be contemporary and "pragmatic" – that is, eyewitnessed and followed closely by an actively participating historian. His ethnogeographical introductions and digressions remind us of Herodotus. Perhaps Theopompus was his model for a new kind of historywriting in making a king or a great individual the centre of the narrative. Thanks to such

traits, Hieronymus belongs to the large crowd of Alexander historians, most of them his contemporaries. Finally, his easy access to documents and memoirs kept in the chancelleries of his masters (Eumenes, Antigonus Monophthalmus, Demetrius Poliorcetes, Antigonus Gonatas) may have influenced his style.

Ancient references to his work outline to some extent Hieronymus' impact on his successors. The first to show some acquaintance with the early literary reputation of Hieronymus is Moschion (late 3rd–early 2nd century BC), the author of a paper in honour of Hieron II of Syracuse, who states that Hieronymus was much admired for his account of the carriage built to convey the body of Alexander the Great (F2). His description of the Dead Sea and its asphalt was noticed by the Hellenistic Florentine Paradoxographer (F5=10 Stern). These two early examples show what kind of material impressed most of Hieronymus' early readers. In the 2nd century BC Agatharcides of Cnidus was aware of Hieronymus' long career (T2); it is remarkable, however, that Polybius, though a great advocate of "pragmatic" history, does not mention him. In the 1st century BC Diodorus mentions Hieronymus four times as a historical figure and as the author of a history of the Diadochi (TT3–6), but he never quotes him as a source in his books 18–20, covering the same period. Dionysius of Halicarnassus, writing in the time of Augustus, includes Hieronymus in a list of historians that "no one can bear to read to the final flourish" (T12). The same Dionysius nevertheless pays homage to Hieronymus for being the first to touch upon the antiquities of Rome (F13). Dionysius' contemporary, the geographer Strabo, took an interest in Hieronymus' ethno-geographical digressions on Corinth, Thessaly and Magnetis, and Crete (F16–18). In the late 1st century AD Josephus complained that Hieronymus omitted in his book any mention of the Jews, although he served in Syria and lived in their vicinity, and concluded that some "bad feeling" must have dimmed Hieronymus' understanding to see the truth (F6). Plutarch used Hieronymus for his *Lives* of the Diadochi, and quotes him as a source in his *Life of Pyrrhus*, but surprisingly not in his *Lives* of Eumenes and Demetrius. He quotes him together with Dionysius of Halicarnassus on the number of the dead at the battle of Heraclea (F11), while on those at Ausculum he quotes him together with Pyrrhus' *Hypomnemata* (which may have been quoted by Hieronymus himself). He is also quoted, together with Phylarchus, for a marginal detail of Pyrrhus' Spartan campaign (F14).

In the 2nd century AD Appian quotes Hieronymus in his *Mithridatica* as saying that Alexander never came into contact with the peoples of Cappadocia, a view rejected by Appian himself (F3). In all likelihood, Hieronymus was Appian's main source on the life and death of two early Cappadocian rulers Ariarathes and Mithridates. But the most interesting piece of evidence on Hieronymus' reputation in the 2nd century AD comes from Pausanias, who in a section on Lysimachus includes a reference to Hieronymus' reporting that Lysimachus, during his war against Pyrrhus, destroyed the tombs of the Epirote kings. This story seemed "incredible" to Pausanias, considering that Hieronymus "had a reputation generally of being biased against all kings except Antigonus", that "it was malice that made him record that a Macedonian desecrated the tombs of the dead", and that "possibly

Hieronymus had grievances against Lysimachus, especially his destroying the city of the Cardians and founding Lysimachia in its stead" (F9, T11). The charge of partiality is repeated by Pausanias in connection with Pyrrhus' death at Argos, Hieronymus' version being "different" from the one given by the Argives themselves. Pausanias was not surprised, for "a man who associates with royalty cannot help being a partial historian" (F15). He does not bother to tell us what was Hieronymus' version, but it evidently was not a supernatural one like that of the Argives.

The last references to Hieronymus in Roman times come from Athenaeus and from a treatise attributed to Lucian. Athenaeus includes Hieronymus in a list of historians recording the length of Perdiccas' reign (F1). This may show that Hieronymus probably had an introduction, or a digression, on the earlier kings of Macedon. Finally, pseudo-Lucian's *Makrobioi* includes four entries of Hieronymus', giving the ages of Ariarathes, Mithridates, Lysimachus, and Antigonus Monophthalmus at their deaths.

No extant Latin author ever mentions Hieronymus, not even Eumenes' biographer Nepos, nor Quintilian in his brief survey of Greek historians (10. 1. 73–5). In Byzantine times, Stephanus of Byzantium apparently did not find in Hieronymus any toponym worth mentioning, and his history was not among the books left unread by Photios' brother Tarasios. Yet, the concise entry in the *Suda* lexicon (T1) shows that he was not altogether forgotten.

In sum, judging from the named fragments, it must be concluded that Hieronymus did not enjoy great popularity in antiquity. His ethnogeographic digressions attracted readers more than his main political and military narrative, and he was much consulted for his numbers – years of age, numbers of dead in battles, lengths of reigns, and measures. He may have been used by historians extensively, but since they rarely acknowledge their debt to their predecessors, the result was that in antiquity nobody ever suspected that Hieronymus may be hidden in Diodorus' books 18–20, or in Plutarch's biographies of the Diadochi. Only in modern times was Hieronymus elevated to the rank of a great historian. On the basis of the widely accepted hypothesis that Diodorus' books 18–20 are basically taken from Hieronymus, scholars tried to reconstruct his work, to assess its value as a history book, and even to redeem its style (although not one verbal quotation of him is preserved). Thus, he has been eulogized for carefully collecting documents, for being a representative of "scientific historiography", for his "lively and lucid narrative", and for his "most appealing" section on Eumenes (on whom he is never actually quoted). The truth is that the case for finding Hieronymus in Diodorus is rather weak. No argument in favour is truly compelling. Diodorus never mentions him as a source, and the correspondence of some five named fragments to Diodorus is only partial, an argument that may be used not for but against Diodorus' dependence on him. Hieronymus is indeed an excellent example of the modern ability of resurrecting a figure that in the Hellenic and Byzantine tradition was only a marginal one.

DAVID ASHERI

See also Historiography

Biography

Born *c.*364 BC at Cardia in the Thracian Chersonese, Hieronymus served on the staff of his fellow Cardian Eumenes, and then with Antigonus Monophthalmus, Demetrius Poliorcetes, and Antigonus Gonatas. He is the author of a history (lost) spanning the years from the death of Alexander the Great (323 BC) to at least the death of Pyrrhus (272 BC). He is reputed to have lived to the age of 104.

Writings

In *Die Fragmente der griechischen Historiker*, edited by Felix Jacoby, 2b.154, Leiden: Brill, 1962

Further Reading

Bosworth, A.B., Hieronymus (1) entry in *The Oxford Classical Dictionary*, 3rd edition, edited by Simon Hornblower and Antony Spawforth, Oxford and New York: Oxford University Press, 1996

Brown, T.S., "Hieronymus of Cardia", *American Historical Review*, 53 (1947): pp. 684 ff.

Brückner, C.A.F., "De vita et scriptis Hieronymi Cardiani", *Zeitschrift für Altertumswissenschaft*, 1842, pp. 252 ff.

Hornblower, Jane, *Hieronymus of Cardia*, Oxford and New York: Oxford University Press, 1981

Jacoby, Felix, *Griechische Historiker*, Stuttgart: Druckenmüller, 1956, pp. 245 ff.

Jacoby, Felix, *Die Fragmente der griechischen Historiker*, 2, Leiden: Brill, 1962

Reuss, Friedrich, *Hieronymus von Kardia*, Berlin: Weidmann, 1876

Rosen, K., "Political Documents in Hieronymus of Cardia", *Acta Classica*, 10 (1967): pp. 41 ff.

Simpson, R.H., "A Possible Case of Misrepresentation in Hieronymus of Cardia", *Historia*, 6 (1957): pp. 504 ff.

Simpson, R.H., "Abbreviation of Hieronymus in Diodorus", *American Journal of Philology*, 80 (1959): pp. 370 ff.

Stern, Menahem (editor), *Greek and Latin Authors on Jews and Judaism*, vol. 1, Jerusalem: Israel Academy of Science and Humanities, 1974, pp.18 ff.

Treves, P., "Ieronimo di Cardia e la politica di Demetrio Poliorcete", *Rivista di Filologia*, 10 (1932): pp. 194 ff.

Hipparchus

Astronomer, geographer, and mathematician of the 2nd century BC

Hipparchus, the first astronomer to combine observation and trigonometry, was born in Nicaea, Bithynia, and flourished in the middle of the 2nd century BC, the years of his recorded observations being between 147 and 127 BC. Ptolemy gives dates for Hipparchan observations as early as 162 BC, but this date is suspect. Quite unlike other scientists in antiquity, whose biographies tend to be preserved in anecdotal gems, Hipparchus' life is poorly known. The single biographical anecdote, that he once attended the theatre in a cloak because he had predicted rain (Aelian, *De Natura Animalium*, 7. 8), is probably spurious. Hipparchus is said to have observed in Nicaea, and Nicaean coinage of Roman imperial date bears witness to that city's claim to his heritage. There is no good evidence, contrary to some opinions, to associate Hipparchus with Alexandria (see Dicks, 1960, pp. 5–8); however, he often refers to Athens, and frequent references to Rhodes suggest that he spent much of his career there.

Although Hipparchus' writings are almost entirely lost, at least 14 separate treatises are known by title; these cover specialized approaches to issues in astronomy, mathematics, and geography. Only one of his works survives in more than just a handful of disparate fragments. Still, judging by the treatment his opinions receive from subsequent authors, it is clear that Hipparchus' contribution in several areas was significant.

Hipparchus' mathematical and astronomical concepts allowed him to predict both solar and lunar eclipses: presumably he published these, and Pliny (*Naturalis Historia*, 2. 54) says that Hipparchus predicted both types of eclipses for a period of 600 years. Whether these data were actually calculated by Hipparchus or digested by him from Babylonian sources remains unclear; but his combination of Babylonian and Greek intellectual traditions produced astronomical knowledge of crucial importance well beyond Ptolemy's transmission of it. Ptolemy, who wrote in the 2nd century AD, had studied Hipparchus carefully but was more interested in improving upon Hipparchus' data than he was in preserving them. Hipparchus, however, retains the distinction of having turned astronomy into a mathematical, predictive science. Dicks (p. 11) regards him as a scientist who was "patient, painstaking, accurate, unwilling to theorize except on definite data which can be scientifically checked and verified, content if his work makes even a small contribution to the general body of knowledge".

Hipparchus was the first to use trigonometry in a precise method – i.e. not by estimation as Aristarchus and Archimedes had – and was the first to construct a chord table, the first element of trigonometry (see *On Chords in a Circle*). His general solution for trigonometrical problems was "as effective as, if more cumbersome than, those of modern trigonometry" (Toomer, 1978, p. 209). Using this tool, Hipparchus calculated the parallax of celestial objects and accurately calculated both solar and lunar parallax. The latter calculation, 58', differs from the International Astronomical Union's value of 57.02'.688", or by less than 2 per cent. Indeed, most of Hipparchus' figures are of similiar accuracy, e.g. his calculated length of the tropical year (365.2467 days) differs from the modern value by just 0.0042 of one day, or about six minutes. Concerning his measurement of the sun's size and distance from the earth with crude and scanty data, Toomer (p. 215) calls Hipparchus' methods "a tour de force". Hipparchus' solar theory was adopted by Ptolemy unchanged, and others, including Vettius Valens, used it as well. He observed a 2-degree precession of Spica over 154 years, between Timocharis' observation and his own (made in 130 BC), and thus anticipated the precession of the equinoxes, and calculated the time it takes for the equinoctial points to make a complete revolution around the earth's celestial perspective. For tools, Hipparchus seems to have used a diopter and a celestial sphere; he may, in fact, have invented the plane astrolabe.

Hipparchus' *Commentary on the* Phaenomena *of Aratus and Eudoxus* contains less of the scientific calculation and explication than we might expect to find in his works. It is, nevertheless, important as a representative of this writer, since it contains much solid argument and not a little of the urgency that Strabo saw in Hipparchus' dispute with Eratosthenes'

geographical treatise. About a century before Hipparchus' birth, the Alexandrian poet Aratus had written his great didactic poem on the constellations. Drawing freely upon the astronomy of Eudoxus of Cnidus (*fl.*340 BC), Aratus composed the *Phaenomena* (*c.*276 BC). To the astronomer possessed of mathematical and observational skills, the eloquence of Aratus' poetry could not compensate for the poem's factual errors. The addressee of the *Commentary*, the otherwise unknown Aeschrion, had shown interest in the poem's astronomy and thus receives from Hipparchus a detailed criticism of its astronomical fallacies. The *Commentary* consists of three books, which comprise extensive criticism of both Aratus' poem and its fundamental basis provided by Eudoxus, and detailed listings of simultaneous risings and settings of constellations. Additionally, Hipparchus addresses mistaken beliefs of his own contemporaries, specifically those of the mathematician Attalus (*fl.* mid-2nd century BC). Arguing against the entrenched popularity of Eudoxus, Aratus, and Attalus, however, proved unsuccessful. Still, painstaking analysis of the data in the *Commentary* "has revealed, and will reveal, a surprising amount" about ancient misunderstandings of Hipparchus and the importance of his research (Toomer, 1978, p.208).

Hipparchus' other writings include a treatise in which he used mathematical data to contradict Eratosthenes' great *Geographica*, especially the geographical and mathematical details. It is surprising to find in his bibliography a treatise on astrology. He also wrote on the calendar, on optics, on permutations and combinations, and, perhaps, on gravity (*On Objects Carried down by Their Weight*).

ROGER T. MACFARLANE

See also Astronomy, Geography, Mathematics

Biography

Born at Nicaea in the mid-2nd century BC, Hipparchus seems to have spent much of his life in Rhodes. His recorded observations date from between 147 and 127 BC. He was the first observational astronomer to use mathematics. His only surviving work is the *Commentary on the* Phaenomena *of Aratus and Eudoxus*.

Writings

Hipparchi in Arati et Eudoxi phaenomena commentariorum libri tres, edited and translated into German by C.L. Manitius, Leipzig: Teubner, 1894

The Geographical Fragments, edited and translated by D.R. Dicks, London: Athlone Press, 1960

Further Reading

Evans, James, *The History and Practice of Ancient Astronomy*, Oxford and New York: Oxford University Press, 1998

Gundel, Wilhelm and H.G. Gundel, *Astrologumena: Die astrologische Literatur in der Antike und ihre Geschichte*, Wiesbaden: Steiner, 1966

Neugebauer, O., *A History of Ancient Mathematical Astronomy*, New York: Springer, 1975, pp. 274–343

Toomer, G.J., Hipparchus entry in *Dictionary of Scientific Biography*, edited by Charles Coulston Gillispie, vol. 15 (supplement 1), New York: Scribner, 1978, pp. 207–24

Hippocrates *c.460–c.370* BC

Physician

Hippocrates of Cos, a Greek physician already renowned by the time of Plato and Aristotle, remains an elusive historical figure despite his fame as the founder of scientific medicine. The earliest characterizations of Hippocrates – for example, in Plato's *Phaedrus* – do not seem to be fully compatible with any of the more than 60 extant works already attributed to him in antiquity (and known in modern times as the Hippocratic Corpus). Furthermore, not even the extant Hippocratic treatises believed by modern scholars to have been written as early as the 5th century BC (for example, *Airs Waters Places*, *Sacred Disease*, *Prognosis*, *Prorrhetic II*, *Epidemics I* and *III*, *Art*, *Ancient Medicine*, *Nature of Humans*, *Regimen in Acute Diseases*, and *Winds*) can be ascribed with certainty to the historical Hippocrates. Epigraphic and literary evidence renders it likely, however, that Hippocrates was only one of several physicians called "Hippocrates", that he belonged to a famous family of physicians, that he claimed patrilineal descent from Asclepius, that he was born on the island of Cos, and that he later lived in Thessaly.

The doctrinal, methodological, and stylistic heterogeneity displayed within the Hippocratic Corpus suggests that its texts were composed, for the most part, between 430 and 330 BC by a variety of authors, drawing on divergent traditions, and that these texts gradually became collected under the name of Hippocrates, starting in the early Hellenistic period. "Hippocrates" remained a magnet for medical texts in the later Hellenistic and Roman periods: his name became attached to post-Classical works such as *Heart*, *Nutriment*, *Law*, *Precepts*, and *Decorum*. Despite the pluralism of traditions represented in the Hippocratic collection, it displays certain recurrent commitments. Among these is an emphasis on meticulous observation (e.g. *Epidemics*, *Prognostic*, *In the Surgery*, *Diseases II*, *Sacred Disease*), on rational inference from observed signs, and on non-divine causes.

The Hippocratic secularization of explanation, i.e. explicitly substituting "natural", physical causes for divine agency, is visible, for example, in the explanations of the Scythians' impotence in *Airs Waters Places* and of epilepsy in *Sacred Disease* (which also offers the first explicit systematic criticism of magic). Furthermore, *Nature of Humans* distinguishes between general diseases caused by miasmic air (which affects numerous people in similar ways) and particular diseases caused by individual regimen, while *Regimen in Acute Diseases* recognizes that a similar effect may be brought about by different causes, and *Regimen* introduces the distinction between cause and coincidence. In all these cases the traditional attribution of human disorders to divine intervention is usurped by an explanation in terms of the interaction of matter with matter, in accordance with the properties of the constituents of things. Some Hippocratics display little interest in aetiology, however, and others advance a cautious view of causal generalization. The author of *On Ancient Medicine*, for example, criticizes new theorists who, like philosophers, engage in general speculation and put forward reductive causal "hypotheses" (the hot, cold, dry, and wet) to explain diseases.

The proven method of medicine, he claims, is instead to start from past observations of the effects of regimen.

For all their secularizing strategies, the Hippocratics do not deny the existence of the gods or of the divine. The Hippocratic *Oath* begins by invoking Apollo, his son Asclepius, Asclepius' daughters Hygieia and Panaceia, and "all gods as well as goddesses". Traditional gestures of respect for the power of the gods are present in other works too (*Regimen I* and *IV*, *Prognostic*, *Nature of Women*). Furthermore, treatises such as *Diseases of Women* accommodate not only the new Hippocratic "scientific" medicine, but also elements of traditional folk medicine, for example, in pharmacological tests for fertility or pregnancy or for the gender of the foetus.

Contest and warfare are central metaphors of Hippocratic medicine, as of modern biology. Within the body an incessant *agon* (struggle) between rival elements, juices (including humours), and parts determines health and disease. The desired outcome is sometimes depicted as a stalemate or balance between the opposing forces, but more often it is a victory of one over the other(s). Internal contestants also enter into an *agon* with external factors: *Airs Waters Places*, *Epidemics*, *Aphorisms*, *Humours*, and *Diseases of Women* present the environment (seasons, winds, sites, water) as a central determinant of health and disease.

The influential theory of bodily "humours" or liquids, whose excess or deficiency can cause disease, appears in several rival versions in the Corpus. A two-humour model – bile and phlegm – is invoked in *Diseases I* and *Affections*, whereas different four-humour theories appear elsewhere: phlegm, bile, blood, and water (*Generation/Nature of Child*, *Diseases IV*); phlegm, bile, black bile, and water (*Affections 36*, *Remedies*); and, the most famous version, phlegm, yellow bile, black bile, blood (*Nature of Humans*). Many Hippocratic works do not, however, make systematic use of any humoral theory. *Regimen* regards fire (hot and dry, providing motion to the body) and water (cold and wet, providing nourishment) as the constituents of living beings, while *Winds* (*Breaths*) argues that air inside the body is the principal cause of illness. A pluralism of traditions is also visible in Hippocratic theories of reproduction and embryology, in gynaecology, and in therapeutics.

The *Oath* displays unique features but it is not entirely incompatible with deontological emphases in other Hippocratic texts. Responsibility to one's *techne* (i.e. to one's result-oriented professional expertise and to a practice consistent with that expertise) and to its reputation is often depicted as the physician's prime motivation. The concern with reputation, perhaps along with the relative insecurity of Greek physicians within the social and economic order, might be a reason both for the defensive posture of some works (*Art*, *Law*) and for the significant role ascribed to accurate prognosis in others (*Prognostic*, *Prorrhetic I–II*, *Coan Prenotions*, *Airs Waters Places*, *Internal Affections*, *Diseases I–II*, *Regimen in Acute Diseases – Appendix*, *Crises*, *Joints*, *Fractures*, *Instruments of Reductions*). The frequent prognosis of incurability and death, the polemics against charlatans, magicians, and incompetent practitioners, the overt awareness of iatrogenesis, and the emphasis on the avoidance of ostentation and theatricality likewise seem to be motivated by a concern with reputation.

Already in antiquity the impact of the works ascribed to Hippocrates was enormous. As early as the 3rd century BC members of rival medical schools began to write Hippocratic lexica and extensive commentaries on Hippocratic texts, and a commentary of the 1st century BC by Apollonius of Citium on the Hippocratic treatise *On Joints* is extant. This exegetical tradition remained active for centuries. The most influential Hippocratic reader of all time was probably Galen, who used early 2nd-century AD editions of "Hippocrates" by Dioscurides the Younger and Artemidorus Capiton. Early Byzantine medical encyclopaedists (Oribasius, Aëtius of Amida, Paul of Aegina) as well as numerous Church Fathers and philosophers, including the Aristotelian commentators, also gave Hippocrates ample recognition, but Galen's commentaries decisively shaped later Alexandrian and Byzantine commentaries on Hippocrates (e.g. by Palladios, Stephanos of Athens, John of Alexandria) as well as the method of teaching "Hippocrates". The medieval translations of Galen's Hippocratic commentaries into Latin, Syriac, and Arabic ensured that Galen presented posterity, both in the east and in the west, with a version of "Hippocrates" that became a culturally obligatory point of departure for subsequent European medicine until the early modern era.

HEINRICH VON STADEN

See also Anatomy and Physiology, Health, Medicine

Hippocrates' *Oath*, translated by the author

1. i.   I swear
   ii.   by Apollo the Physician and
          by Asclepius and
          by health and Panaceia and
          by all the gods as well as goddesses,
             making them judges [witnesses],
   iii.   to bring the following oath and written covenant to
          fulfilment,
   iv.   in accordance with my power and judgement:
2. i.   to regard him who has taught me this *techne* as equal
          to my parents, and
   ii.   to share, in partnership, my livelihood with him and
             to give him a share when he is in need of necessities,
             and
   iii.   to judge the offspring [coming] from him equal
          to [my] male siblings, and
   iv.   to teach them this *techne*,
             should they desire to learn [it],
          without fee and written covenant, and
   v.   to give a share
             both of rules
             and of lectures,
             and of all the rest of learning,
             to my sons and
             to the [sons] of him who has taught me and
             to the pupils who have
                both made a written contract and
                sworn by a medical convention but by no other.
3. i.   And I will use regimens
             for the benefit of the ill
             in accordance with my ability and my judgement,
   ii.   but from [what is] to their harm or injustice
          I will keep [them].

4. i.   And I will not give a drug that is deadly to anyone
             if asked [for it],
   ii.   nor will I suggest the way to such a counsel.
   iii.   And likewise I will not give a woman a destructive
          pessary.
5. i.   And in a pure and holy way
   ii.   I will guard
   iii.   my life and my *techne*.
6. i.   I will not cut,
             and certainly not those suffering from stone,
   ii.   but I will cede [this]
             to men [who are] practitioners of this activity.
7. i.   Into as many houses as I may enter,
             I will go for the benefit of the ill,
   ii.   while being far from all voluntary and destructive
          injustice,
             especially from sexual acts
             both upon women's bodies
             and upon men's,
                both of the free
                and of the slaves.
8. i.   And about whatever I may see or hear
             in treatment,
             or even without treatment,
          in the life of human beings
             – things that should not ever be blurted out outside –
   ii.   I will remain silent,
             holding such things to be unutterable [sacred, not to
             be divulged].
9. i.a. If I render this oath fulfilled,
             and if I do not blur and confound it [making it to no
             effect],
    b. may it be [granted] to me to enjoy the benefits
             both of life and of *techne*,
    c. being held in good repute
             among all human beings
             for time eternal.
   ii.a. If, however, I transgress
             and perjure myself,
    b. the opposite of these.

(*translation © Heinrich von Staden, reprinted by permission*)

Biography

Born *c*.460 BC in Cos, Hippocrates was the most renowned physician of antiquity, yet detailed knowledge of his life remains elusive. More than 60 extant works were attributed to him in antiquity and are now known as the Hippocratic Corpus. Most probably he was one of several physicians with the name Hippocrates, and he belonged to a family of physicians. Most of the "Hippocratic" texts seem to have been written between 430 and 330 BC.

Writings

Oeuvres complètes, edited by Emile Littré, 10 vols, Paris: Baillière, 1839–61 (with French translation, copious introductions, and indices; the only relatively complete modern edition)

Hippocrates, translated by W.H.S. Jones, E.T. Withington, Paul Potter and Wesley D. Smith, 8 vols, London: Heinemann, New York: Putnam, and Cambridge, Massachusetts: Harvard University Press, 1923–95 (Loeb edition)

Further Reading

Baader, Gerhard and Rolf Winau (editors), *Die hippokratischen Epidemien* (Sudhoffs Archiv, Beiheft 27), Stuttgart: Steiner, 1989 (includes important articles in English)

Edelstein, Ludwig, *Ancient Medicine*, edited by Owsei Temkin and C. Lilian Temkin, Baltimore: Johns Hopkins Press, 1967

Jones, W.H.S., *Philosophy and Medicine in Ancient Greece: Including an Edition of Hippocrates' "Ancient Medicine"*, Baltimore: Johns Hopkins Press, 1946, reprinted Chicago: Ares, 1979

Jouanna, Jacques, *Hippocrates*, Baltimore: Johns Hopkins University Press, 1999

Langholf, Volker, *Medical Theories in Hippocrates: Early Texts and the "Epidemics"*, Berlin and New York: de Gruyter, 1990

Lasserre, François and Philippe Mudry (editors), *Formes de pensée dans la Collection hippocratique: Actes du IV Colloque international hippocratique*, Geneva: Droz, 1983 (includes contributions in English)

Lloyd, G.E.R., *Magic, Reason and Experience: Studies in the Origins and Development of Greek Science*, Cambridge and New York: Cambridge University Press, 1979

Lloyd, G.E.R., *Science, Folklore and Ideology: Studies in the Life Sciences in Ancient Greece*, Cambridge and New York: Cambridge University Press, 1983

Lloyd, G.E.R., *Methods and Problems in Greek Science*, Cambridge and New York: Cambridge University Press, 1991, chapters 3, 9, 17

Lonie, Iain M., *The Hippocratic Treatises "On Generation", "On the Nature of the Child", "Diseases IV": A Commentary*, Berlin and New York: de Gruyter, 1981

López, Férez, J.A. (editor), *Tratados hipocráticos*, Madrid: UNED, 1992 (includes contributions in English)

Pinault, Jody Rubin, *Hippocratic Lives and Legends*, Leiden and New York: Brill, 1992

Smith, Wesley D., *The Hippocratic Tradition*, Ithaca, New York: Cornell University Press, 1979

Temkin, Owsei, *Hippocrates in a World of Pagans and Christians*, Baltimore: Johns Hopkins University Press, 1991

Wittern, Renate and Pierre Pellegrin (editors), *Hippokratische Medizin und antike Philosophie*, Hildesheim: Olms Weidmann, 1996 (includes contributions in English)

Hippodrome

A hippodrome was a horse-racing or chariot-racing arena, similar in layout to a stadium for athletics and foot races, with an elongated U shape and tiers of seats surrounding the track. Hippodromes (or circuses) were widespread in the Roman empire, especially in Rome itself and in North Africa, as at Carthage. However, some hippodromes were built in the eastern Roman empire, for example at Thessalonica in Greece.

By far the most celebrated (and historically significant) hippodrome was that in Constantinople. The city's first hippodrome was constructed under Septimius Severus in the 2nd century AD and was rebuilt during the reign of Constantine I (306–37 AD). Like the hippodrome in Thessalonica, it was adjacent to an imperial palace: the Great Palace of the Byzantine emperors.

The hippodrome in Constantinople was built of brick and stone and to a classic elongated U design, with at least some architectural decoration in stone on its exterior. The whole structure was approximately 480 m long and 117.5 m wide. The southern, curved, end (the *sphendone*), the only substantial part of the building still standing, clearly shows several stories of rooms and vaulted brick-built chambers. There was a row of large columns around the upper part of the exterior of the whole building.

The hippodrome had a complex set of entrance arrangements for both court and public. There was a direct covered stairway (the *kochlias*) from the Great Palace into the imperial box (the *kathisma*) located on its eastern side. Behind the box was a private area which in turn led to the palace through bronze doors. The main public entrance was a monumental structure (*carceres*), probably slightly bowed outward, at the northwestern side. Although its exact form is debatable, this entrance once had large bronze doors opening onto the Augusteum, a stepped entranceway, and elaborate decoration.

Although the emperor's entourage sat on seats within the imperial box, the majority of the population sat on tiered seats, affording them a clear view of both the track and the emperor. The track itself was floored with sand and divided into two by a *spina* or central reservation, marked with free-standing monuments. It was around this reservation that the chariots raced. Notable among these monuments are a 5th-century BC bronze tripod (originally in the form of serpents) from Delphi, a 16th-century BC Egyptian obelisk originally from Thebes in Upper Egypt, and a stone pillar (which an inscription records was covered in bronze by Constantine VII Porphyrogennetos), all of which still survive in some form. The base of the obelisk is a 5th-century AD marble block, elaborately sculpted on all sides with scenes depicting the emperor Theodosius I and his family in the hippodrome.

Races were between light two-wheeled chariots. The hippodrome chariots were divided into four teams – the reds, whites, blues, and greens – which attracted mass popular support. The citizens of Constantinople took a great interest in their favourite charioteers, horses, and teams, and stone monuments were even erected in their memory. Organized fan clubs adopted special dress, formed choirs, and took part in mob violence. These groups – especially the increasingly dominant blues and greens – began to adopt specific views on current controversies, and took on a somewhat "political" character. This led to major outbreaks of violence, notably the Nike riot of 532, which was only ended by the use of military force against the protesters and a massacre in the hippodrome itself.

From the 4th century onwards the hippodrome was used not only for chariot racing but also for other entertainments and for public events. The latter included celebratory ceremonies and the execution of criminals and enemies of the state – and western-style jousts in the 12th century. The hippodrome was also the arena for the public acclamation or disapproval of the emperor's policies and court by the populace, who could in this way have a small degree of direct contact with their ruler.

Chariot racing proved exceptionally popular during the early Byzantine period, but increasing religious and official disapproval led to its decline after the 6th century. Although chariot races were still occasionally held in the middle Byzantine period – in the 9th century the emperor Theophilos himself competed in a race – the hippodrome became more generally used for ceremonies and executions. With the Latin conquest of the city in 1204, the hippodrome fell into disuse.

Following the Ottoman conquest of 1453 the ruinous arena was again used for ceremonies and entertainments of other sorts. Although partially demolished in order to construct the

Hippodrome: relief at the foot of an obelisk in the hippodrome in Constantinople showing the emperor Theodosius I in his box watching the games

Sultan Ahmet mosque in the early 17th century, the site is clearly visible today within the urban fabric of Istanbul and survives as an open square known aptly as At Meydani ("the square of the horses").

KEN DARK

See also Architecture (public), Constantinople, Games and Sports

Further Reading

Cameron, Alan, *Porphyrius the Charioteer*, Oxford: Clarendon Press, 1973

Cameron, Alan, *Circus Factions: Blues and Greens at Rome and Byzantium*, Oxford: Clarendon Press, 1976

Casson, Stanley *et al.*, *Preliminary Report upon the Excavations Carried out in and near the Hippodrome in Constantinople in 1927*, London: Oxford University Press, 1928

Casson, Stanley *et al.*, *Second Report upon the Excavations Carried out in and near the Hippodrome in Constantinople in 1928*, London: Oxford University Press, 1929

Dagron, Gilbert, *Naissance d'une capitale: Constantinople et ses institutions de 330 à 451*, Paris: Presses Universitaires de France, 1974

Dagron, Gilbert, *Constantinople Imaginaire*, Paris: Presses Universitaires de France, 1984

Guberti Bassett, S., "Antiquities in the Hippodrome of Constantinople", *Dumbarton Oaks Papers*, 45 (1991): pp. 87–96

Humphrey. John H., *Roman Circuses: Arenas for Chariot Racing*, Berkeley: University of California Press, 1986

McCormick, Michael, *Eternal Victory: Triumphal Rulership in Late Antiquity, Byzantium, and the Early Medieval West*, Cambridge and New York: Cambridge University Press, 1986

Madden, T., "The Serpent Column of Delphi in Constantinople: Placement, Purposes and Mutilations", *Byzantine and Modern Greek Studies*, 16 (1992): pp. 111–45

Mango, Cyril, *The Art of the Byzantine Empire, 312–1453*, Englewood Cliffs, New Jersey: Prentice Hall, 1972

Müller-Wiener, Wolfgang, *Bildlexikon zur Topographie Istanbuls*, Tübingen: Wasmuth, 1977

Williams, Stephen and Gerard Friell, *Theodosius: The Empire at Bay*, London: Batsford, 1994; New Haven, Connecticut: Yale University Press, 1995

Historiography

Antiquity

Historie (inquiry) is the Ionic form of what in other Greek dialects is *historia*. The term is, however, first used by the Ionian writer Herodotus, who talks about "the presentation of his research", undertaken "to preserve the actions of individuals from fading with time and so that the great and wondrous works of peoples, both Greeks and foreigners, should not lack renown" (1. 1). It quickly becomes apparent that any examination of this undertaking inevitably involves consideration of the various techniques and procedures – and raises several questions. For example, when did people first wish to preserve a record of their achievements, and what sort of achievements, particularly? How did they remember their past? How did they reckon the passage of time? Why does all this, for the Greeks at any rate, seem to have begun in "Ionia"?

Although there is no general agreement over the details, certain broad points can be made. As the term *historiography* implies, literacy is a prerequisite for the production of real history – illiterate peoples may have memorized lists of rulers, memorials of great deeds, and even elaborate sagas, but these productions lack the analytical and comparative approach to evidence that is possible only with writing (although oral tradition always remained an important source in Greek historiography). In the Near East and Egypt there was a long tradition, going back to the 3rd millennium BC, of recording the names of rulers and their deeds; and in the Jewish/Hebrew religious tradition there were certain works that can, by the strictest definition, be called historical. Accordingly, just as "Ionia" absorbed and developed crucial elements of eastern mathematics and astronomy, it is equally possible that the fundamentals of chronography and local and regional history and the recording of the great deeds of individuals came to the Greeks from the same source. It was in "Ionia" that the earliest prose accounts appeared of the shape of the world, the customs of various peoples, and examinations of myth and genealogy, and it was here too that local histories first began to be written: little of this work survives beyond testimonia, but Hecataeus of Miletus (*fl. c.*500 BC), writing on geography and genealogy, was important and influential (369 fragments of his work survive in F. Jacoby's *Die Fragmente der griechischen Historiker* (1923–),where he is the first historian listed). This Ionian tradition persisted to at least the end of the 5th century BC, as can be seen from the career of Hellanicus of Lesbos (*c.*480–after 400 BC; 201 fragments survive), among whose numerous works were the *Priestesses of Hera at Argos* (cited apparently by Thucydides at 2. 2) and the first *Atthis*, or local history of Attica.

The Homeric poems, too, exercised an important influence on Greek historiography, though they are not themselves history. They are concerned with the past, however, and Homer frequently refers to the differences between the past and the present and to the human desire to be remembered: great deeds are commemorated in various ways and human glory is closely connected with prowess in war; genealogies occur frequently, as does the idea of the community as the vital centre for human existence (cf. *Iliad*, 5. 304–05, 6. 145–211, 22. 304–05; *Odyssey*, 1. 2–3). The date of "Homer" remains controversial, but if West's recent suggestion that the *Iliad* was composed in its monumental form between 670 and 640 BC (with a preference for 660–650 BC) is cogent, then we are clearly in the literate period; Greek colonization, both in the Black Sea area and in the west, was in full swing; and the main themes of the Homeric poems and the impulses that led to the early Ionian prose chronicles are not only similar but nearly contemporaneous.

Herodotus of Halicarnassus (dates quite uncertain, but probably writing after 440 BC) is, then, heir not only to the various subjects and techniques of the earlier Ionian prose-writers but also to the Homeric subject matter, war, and to Homeric *mimesis*, the recreation of a scene so vividly that the reader seems almost to be part of it. In examining Herodotus' work we have the advantage, rare in Classical historiography, of studying something that is whole and complete: we can see its entire shape as its author planned it, and we do not have to worry about "incomplete revisions" or "strata of composition", nor must we try to identify second, or even third, thoughts on certain topics, as is the case in Thucydidean studies. The great story of the war between Greeks and non-Greeks, which goes back to mythical times and culminates with the victories at Plataea and Mycale and their immediate aftermath in 479 BC, starts with extended ethnographic accounts of the parts of the Persian empire and follows its growth in a historical sequence; the attempts by Darius and Xerxes to expand the empire by incorporating into it all of mainland Greece lead to the climactic war narrative in books 7 to 9. Underlying all of this are the basic notions of action and reaction: someone does something to another, the latter responds, the first does something else, and so on – this is the basic causative impulse in human affairs.

Any reader of Herodotus quickly realizes that he is, above all, a master story-teller; we also know that he recited "sections" of his work before audiences. Over the years and as a result of frequent retelling, these tales came to take on a smooth, effortless form; their sources, whether oral or written, or the result of personal experience or observation, were blurred and "improved on" for narrative effect (the end result of this process can be seen in Hammond's brilliant analysis of Herodotus' narrative techniques in the account of events leading up to Xerxes' invasion in 480 BC (7. 117–79) – the "Chinese box" construction, with recurring verbal markers to indicate stages going into and coming out of a particular topic, and a succession of separate narrative "strings" with key phrases to signal the move from one theme to another). Accordingly, Herodotus' tales, particularly those pertaining to strange and wondrous sights and remarkable events in far-off lands, should not be pressed too far. He is more likely to be careful (and correspondingly more accurate) in books 7 to 9, which deal with near-contemporary history. Finally, we may assume that, when he decided to commit his "lectures" to written form, the whole process was relatively quick and easy.

With the Athenian Thucydides in the later 5th century BC we come to the most interesting, complex, and, above all, authoritative of ancient historians. From Herodotus he may have derived the idea of writing the history of a war, but in Thucydides' case it was a contemporary war. Furthermore, Thucydides talks directly to us about his sources, his methods of handling evidence, and about the speeches that are so striking a feature of his account (1. 21–22). He was not the first historian to provide speeches, but his are so important to his history as a means of conveying important information and forming impressions in the audience's mind that they would merit the attention lavished on them by scholars and critics even if they had not started a practice almost universal in Greek historiography thereafter. However, there is no agreement about what Thucydides meant in a very difficult sentence about his practice with regard to speeches (1. 22. 1): Wilson's suggestion "as it seemed likely to me – keeping as closely as possible to all the points made in what was actually said – that each party would have appropriately spoken about the various situations, so I have written" is possibly as cogent a translation (for avoiding an apparent but improbable self-contradiction in the Greek) as we are likely to get. This was Thucydides' aim: whether he achieved it (or even stuck to it) is another matter altogether. We shall never know how closely the Funeral Oration in book 2 approximates to the actual words uttered by Pericles in the autumn of 431 BC. As for events, Thucydides claims to have written with "the utmost possible accuracy" (*akribeia*: 1. 22. 2). Finally, he expresses the hope that his history will be "useful": he does not state that it will provide a guide for future conduct or furnish pleasure to the reader. Such ideas about history writing came rather later.

Thucydides has always been regarded as an "objective" historian. Modern literary theory, however, denies the possibility of any such absolute concept: in strict logic this is undeniable and recent studies of Thucydides have tended to emphasize such features as his habit of telling his audience what his characters are thinking and his use of phrases designed to make his audience trust him (this is Thucydides the "artful reporter", in Hunter's memorable phrase). However, "objectivity" is a very slippery term and Thucydides still stands out as a beacon for accuracy among ancient historians.

The Thucydidean narrative breaks off abruptly in the year 411 BC and several later historians seem to have aimed to carry on from the break point – more or less: the Athenian Xenophon wrote, over a considerable period of time, the *Hellenica* in seven books, which extended from 411 to 362 BC; the "Oxyrhynchus historian" (probably the Athenian Cratippus: see Harding), of whose work approximately 20 pages of Greek text survive on papyrus and written in the Thucydidean manner (though with no speeches), was probably a contemporary of the events described and covered the period from 411 to 395 BC; and Theopompus of Chios produced *Hellenica* in 12 books, covering the period from 411 to 394 BC; Theopompus, one of the most important historians of the 4th century BC, also produced a new kind of history, focusing on the career of a single individual: his *Philippicae Historiae* in 58 books represented a "universal history" (involving deeds of Greeks and foreigners alike; see below) on a very broad canvas indeed, with numerous digressions and a highly rhetorical style, but with Philip II of Macedon as the unifying core. This type of history, centred on a single, magnetic personality, was continued in the Alexander-histories of Callisthenes, Aristobulus, Chares, Nearchus, Ptolemy I, and many others, including the much later but extant Arrian of Nicomedia (2nd century AD).

The other major historian of the 4th century BC was Ephorus of Cyme (*c.*405–330 BC), whose work in 30 books, from the return of the Heraclidae to the siege of Perinthus in 340 BC, was probably the earliest "universal history". Though not highly regarded today (perhaps unfairly: for a balanced assessment see Fornara, pp.42–46), Ephorus was widely known and quoted throughout antiquity and was the main source (for Classical Greek history) of Diodorus of Sicily (1st century BC) of whose "universal history", the *Bibliotheca*, 15 from an original 40 books survive.

Among the major trends in historiographic theory in the generations immediately following Thucydides are the notion that history can teach us moral lessons (cf. Xenophon,

Hellenica, 5. 3. 7) and a parallel tendency to pass judgement on, or "award points" to, an individual, an entire career, or the behaviour of a political entity (a self-important fatuity that continues to the present day, but which, again, starts with Xenophon; cf. *Helenica*, 7. 5. 8). Ephorus was particularly prone to these practices, especially with regard to the characters of individuals; and these moralizing appraisals, with particular emphasis on praise and blame, became a characteristic feature of later historiography.

Other, older concerns continued to be addressed, however: Timaeus of Tauromenium in Sicily (*c.*350–260 BC) produced a chronology based on Olympic victors, cross-referenced to Athenian archons, Spartan kings and ephors, and priestesses of Hera at Argos: dating by Olympiads soon became standard practice. In addition, Timaeus wrote an extensive history of Sicily in 38 books, incorporating geography and ethnography as well as political history. Furthermore, he is remembered for his critical analysis of the works of his predecessors, which often degenerated into hostile abuse.

The moralizing tendencies of Ephorus and the critical use of earlier historians by Timaeus were developed by Polybius of Megalopolis (*c.*200–*c.*118 BC), of whose 40-book history of Rome's rise to supremacy in the Mediterranean world substantial portions survive. Polybius also believed that history was useful to politicians and that study of the past could enable reasonable predictions about the future to be made (cf. 3. 31–32), an idea that he may have absorbed during his stay in Rome and which finds its most striking expression in the preface to Livy's history *Ab Urbe Condita*. As for sources, Polybius quotes his predecessors, often at considerable length, which is valuable, but frequently also with hostile analysis (cf. his attack on the credibility of Fabius Pictor at 3. 8. 1–9. 5, or his citation of Callisthenes on the Battle of Issus at 12. 17–22). From his examination of Rome's rapid development of overwhelming power Polybius concluded that the city's governance had been the main contributing factor and from this he developed 5th-century ideas of a "mixed" constitution (in this case a combination of monarchy, oligarchy, and democracy, with a precise combination of these three elements) into his main explanatory concept.

Given the eventual predominance of Rome, it is not surprising that several Greek writers at different periods wrote large-scale histories, most notably the scholarly and perceptive Dionysius of Halicarnassus (late 1st century BC), who wrote 30 books (the first 11 survive), from the pre-foundation legends to 264 BC, and Cassius Dio of Nicaea in Bithynia (*c.*AD 164–after 229), a Greek-speaking senator and imperial *amicus*, who wrote a *Roman History* in 80 books, from the beginning to AD 229, of which nearly 24 survive complete, with excerpts and epitomes of the rest. Dio is an interesting combination of Greek and Roman ideas and culture – and historiography: he writes Classical Attic Greek, is much influenced by Thucydides (though he can be moralizing and rhetorical and, at times, too free in inventing speeches), and provides a perceptive analysis of the implications of the change from republic to principate, along with what is, in reality, a political manifesto suggesting solutions for the problems faced by the empire in the 3rd century AD (cf. Reinhold, pp.219–21).

Emphasis must also be placed on the sheer volume and diversity of the historiography of the Hellenistic period in particular. Obviously, in a brief survey such as this, only a few of the many hundreds of names known to us can be mentioned. For example, there was a vast outpouring of historical works in the 2nd century AD, on which see the sardonic essay "How to Write History" by the contemporary Lucian of Samosata; see also Baldwin's discussion.

CHARLES L. MURISON

See also Archives, Chronicles, Chronology

Further Reading

Baldwin, B., "Historiography in the Second Century: Precursors of Dio Cassius", *Klio*, 68 (1986): pp. 479–86

Fehling, Detlev, *Herodotus and His "Sources": Citation, Invention, and Narrative Art*, Leeds: Cairns, 1989

Fornara, Charles W., *The Nature of History in Ancient Greece and Rome*, Berkeley: University of California Press, 1983

Gould, John, *Herodotus*, London: Weidenfeld and Nicolson, and New York: St Martin's Press, 1989

Hammond, N.G.L., "The Narrative of Herodotus VII and the Decree of Themistocles at Troezen", *Journal of Hellenic Studies*, 102 (1982): pp. 75–93

Harding, P., "The Authorship of the Hellenika Oxyrhynchia", *Ancient History Bulletin*, 1 (1987): pp. 101–104

Hornblower, Simon (editor), *Greek Historiography*, Oxford: Clarendon Press, and New York: Oxford University Press, 1994

Hunter, Virginia J., *Thucydides: The Artful Reporter*, Toronto: Hakkert, 1973

Pearson, Lionel, *The Greek Historians of the West: Timaeus and His Predecessors*, Atlanta: Scholars Press, 1987

Reinhold, M., "In Praise of Cassius Dio", *L'Antiquité Classique*, 55 (1986) pp. 213–22

Shrimpton, Gordon Spencer, *Theopompus the Historian*, Montreal: McGill–Queens University Press, 1991

Verdin, H., G. Schepens and E. de Keyser (editors), *Purposes of History: Studies in Greek Historiography from the 4th to the 2nd Centuries BC*, Louvain: Studia Hellenistica, 1990

West, M.L., "The Date of the *Iliad*", *Museum Helveticum*, 52 (1995): pp. 203–19

Wilson, J., "What Does Thucydides Claim for His Speeches?", *Phoenix*, 36 (1982): pp. 95–103

Byzantium and Tourkokratia

Byzantine historiography took three at first largely distinct forms: traditional histories of the "Classical" type, chronicles, and Church histories (hagiography, which began in 356/57 with the *Vita* of St Antony the Great attributed to Athanasius, may be considered separately since its primary function was spiritual edification; but it did overlap with historiography, both profiting from and contributing to chronicles in particular). The Byzantines themselves used the terms "history" and "chronicle" interchangeably with a growing preference for the latter. Moreover, in recent years most scholars have rejected their predecessors' simplistic and rigid division of historiography into, on the one hand, fairly reliable well-written histories by state officials for a sophisticated elite and, on the other, contemptible monkish chronicles catering for an ill-educated readership. Nevertheless, for early Byzantium it is convenient to treat the three forms individually.

The comparatively more settled conditions of the Greek-speaking East and the transference thither of the Roman court encouraged writers to continue the "Classical" form of history, which was usually geographically and chronologically limited in scope, often covering recent or even contemporary themes, and intended both to inform through content and to delight through style. Political and military subject matter dominated at the expense of the economic, social, and religious, although the last played a growing role in some pagan writings. Historians were interested in causation, ascribing events to either *tyche* (fortune) and, increasingly, divine providence, or to the actions and characters of the principals involved, whom they duly praised or censured (most notoriously in the salacious and vitriolic *Anecdota* or *Secret History* by the 6th-century historian Procopius). The East thus contrasted with the West, where the severe dislocation of society consequent upon barbarian assumption of power entrenched an already existing demand for simple epitomes of Roman history and biographical sketches (it is significant that the only "Classical" history in Latin since the 2nd-century history by Tacitus was written in the 4th century by Ammianus Marcellinus, a native Greek-speaker from Antioch). Even in the East, however, there was a break in the continuity of classicizing historical writing between Dexippus in the late 3rd century and Eunapius in the early 5th. Moreover, a liking for epitomes is indicated by the popularity of Greek translations of the late 4th-century breviary of Roman history by Eutropius.

The classicizing language of these historians became increasingly distinct from the commonly spoken demotic and explains why many were rhetoricians, sophists, or lawyers (e.g. Eunapius, Priscus, Malchus, Agathias). Nevertheless, again unlike in the West, many in the East were participants in or eyewitnesses of the events they described: Olympiodorus, Priscus, Nonnosus, and Peter the Patrician were ambassadors, while Procopius was secretary and legal adviser to the general Belisarius. Adherence to Classical forms, and especially to Thucydides, was variably tried and achieved. It included speeches, both heard and imagined by the writers. Set literary pieces, such as Procopius' descriptions of sieges and the plague in Constantinople in 542, were once subject to extreme scholarly suspicion, but are now generally regarded as true in essential facts despite borrowed Thucydidean details. While a few historians were indeed pagan (e.g. Olympiodorus, Zosimus, and Eunapius, the last so belligerently that according to Photios his work had to be re-edited less offensively), perhaps the most remarkable aspect of the classicizing tendency is an almost total avoidance by even Christian writers of Christian content. This led not only Byzantines to be uncertain about an historian's religious beliefs (Photios famously described Malchus as being "not outside the Christian faith"), but also some modern scholars who, to take one example, have erroneously interpreted Procopius' shunning of theological issues and preference for secular causation as evidence for paganism.

Both the other two forms of history – chronicles and Church histories – were the creations of Eusebius of Caesarea. The full title of *Chronological Canons with an Epitome of Universal History both Greek and Non-Greek* describes the scope of what is commonly called his *Chronicle*. Although lost, it is known through epitomes and redactions, most notably Jerome's partial but updated translation with many Western additions. First published in the late 3rd century and completed soon after its terminus in Constantine's Vicennalia (325), it draws upon a long history of Greek and biblical chronographic writing. Its first part (preserved only in an

Armenian version) comprises traditional lists of rulers and officials with occasional commentaries and summaries about each kingdom. The second part opens with three vertical columns giving respectively the rulers of the Hebrews, Assyrians, and Egyptians, the dates from Abraham being indicated in decades in the extreme left margin. Olympiads are added from 776 BC and the columns increase and decrease in number to accommodate the rise and fall of different nations (it ends with only two columns for Rome and Persia). Between these columns are added respectively to left and right facts of biblical and pagan history. Thus on an immediately intelligible grid Eusebius gave readers a synoptic and synchronistic world history designed as an apologia for the Judaeo-Christian tradition which is shown to predate the Roman empire.

As in the West so in the East Eusebius gave impetus to local annalistic chronicles such as the still extant Syriac *Chronicle of Edessa*; but, whereas Latin writers were usually content to compile continuations of Jerome's work, the Byzantines chose also to rewrite from the beginning. Moreover, in a lost redaction of the early 5th century Panodorus and Annianus pushed back this beginning to Adam, an innovation that is found in the earliest surviving Byzantine universal history, the chronicle of John Malalas which breaks off in 565. This work, though often criticized for its inaccuracies, is notable for much information on Antioch, frequent citing of sources, and use of the vernacular, which last enhanced its popularity (it was later translated into both Georgian and Old Church Slavonic). Malalas's work, which blithely ignores Periclean Athens and the whole period of the Roman republic from 509 to 44 BC, encouraged an increasing tendency in universal histories to emphasize biblical at the expense of Classical Greek and even Roman history, knowledge of which grew ever shakier.

Eusebius' *Ecclesiastical History* is at least in part consequent upon the widespread concept of Christians as constituting a nation that required its own history. First written before the triumph of the faith, it emphasizes the struggles along the preordained path to that triumph the consummation of which is found, in later revisions, in the reign of Constantine I, whose Christianity and piety are grossly exaggerated and whose sins are whitewashed to establish him as God's vicegerent on earth (Eusebius is responsible also for a highly eulogistic *Vita Constantini*). The work was ever after held as of great authority despite criticism of its Arian slant and rejection of the cult of images, which led to a prohibition of quotation from it by the Second Council of Nicaea in 787. Eusebius' most important early followers were the lawyers Socrates and the slightly later Sozomenus, and the bishop Theodoretus, whose works cover respectively the periods 305 to 439, 324 to 425 (Sozomenus' later material is lost), and 323 to 428. They were careful historians, Socrates even publishing a second edition of his history upon discovery that a major source (a Latin history by Rufinus of Aquileia) had serious chronological errors; and all follow Eusebius' important innovation of extensive quoting of documentary evidence, an innovation which encouraged emulation in many subsequent secular histories. Their three histories were influential also in the West, where in Latin translation they constituted the *Historia Tripartita*.

The Eusebian preoccupation with detailing the preservation of the Christian faith against pagan assaults is followed in his successors by their detailing the preservation of true doctrine against the assaults of heretics. With the resolution of fundamental doctrinal problems the raison d'être of ecclesiastical histories disappeared in the later 6th century, the last one of which was written by another lawyer, Evagrius Scholasticus. His account deals with the years 431–594 and is valuable for its extensive use of the archives of the Antiochene patriarchate and for its bibliography. Thereafter there is only the strange revival of the genre in the early 14th century by Nikephoros Kallistos Xanthopoulos before the religious conditions of the Tourkokratia once more justified apologetic histories of the Church. Socrates and Sozomenus had already in the 5th century mingled ecclesiastical and secular history, thus paving the way for the complete absorption of the former by the latter after Evagrius.

The end of the early period of Byzantine (or of late antique) historiography is marked by Theophylaktos Simokattes's account of the reign of Maurice (582–602) and the so-called *Paschal Chronicle* which begins with Adam and breaks off in 628. Already in Simokattes's work, however, it is clear how far Byzantine historians had come in their fusing of the discrete ancient genres of history, biography, and encomium (Plutarch became a more important model than Thucydides). The chronicle is largely derivative, but contains valuable and even documentary evidence for the reigns of Phokas (602–10) and Herakleios (610–41) and is the first surviving historical work to date the Creation to 21 March 5509 BC.

From the 7th century to the early 9th century virtually no historical writings have survived, partly because of the decline of learning and partly, it may be assumed, because of the neglect or destruction of iconoclastic works. Our knowledge of the intervening centuries is largely dependent upon two later writers. Theophanes the Confessor continued to the year 813 the unoriginal compilation of his contemporary George the Synkellos (*Selection from Chronographers*) which covers the period from the Creation to the accession of Diocletian (284); and the patriarch Nikephoros I wrote a popular compendious history of the period 602–709 which was later translated into Latin and various Slavic languages. Theophanes' annalistic history was continued in turn by a work of original composition (conventionally known as *Scriptores post Theophanem* or *Theophanes Continuatus*) originally commissioned and perhaps contributed to by the emperor Constantine VII and arranged as a series of imperial biographies designed to support the Macedonian dynasty. It is thus propagandistic history.

From the intellectual revival in the 9th century until the fall of Constantinople in 1453 Byzantine historiography shows great variety. This is becoming increasingly evident in the comprehensive re-evaluation by modern scholarship which finds new personal approaches in even the seemingly most mechanical collections of excerpts. Works vary from universal surveys through recitals of individual reigns or chronicles of individual cities to descriptions of single climactic events or studies of specific subjects (e.g. the works by Constantine VII on the ceremonies of the court, themes, and diplomacy); from largely unoriginal compilations and epitomes to carefully researched independent analyses; from bare and factual accounts to vivid depictions; from conventional assessments to perceptive psychological portrayals (most notably by Psellos); from simply written narratives (some chronicles even in the vernacular and Leontios Machairas' 15th-century *Narrative of the Sweet Land of Cyprus* in Cypriot dialect) to productions on which has been lavished every resource of rhetorical artistry. Prose was the traditional vehicle, but in the 12th century Constantine Manasses innovatingly wrote a chronicle in 6733 15-syllable lines from Adam to 1081. Thereafter verse was chosen in the early 14th century by Ephraim for his history of the rulers of the Old and New Romes and for various anonymous vernacular chronicles (e.g. the *Chronicle of the Morea* on the Frankish occupation of the Peloponnese to 1292, which is possibly a translation of the French version (it exists also in Italian and Aragonese) or may itself be the original, and the *Chronicle of the Tocco* on the ruling family of Ioannina in the 14th to 15th centuries).

Most historians were participants in or at least eyewitnesses of some of the events which they described. Thus Constantine VII and John VI Kantakouzenos were emperors and Nikephoros Bryennios an unsuccessful usurper; among civil servants and diplomats may be numbered Psellos, Attaleiates, Zonaras, Glykas (later involved in a conspiracy and imprisoned), Kinnamos, Skylitzes, Niketas Choniates, Akropolites, Pachymeres, Machairas (at the Lusignan Cypriot court), Doukas, and Sphrantzes; Leo the Deacon took part in the expedition against Bulgaria in 986; Kaminiates (if the account is truly his) wrote on the Arab siege of Thessalonica in 904, while in the 12th century the city's archbishop and gallant defender Eustathios recounted its capture by the Normans in 1185; the Byzantine princess Anna Komnene was an interested observer and critic of the leaders of the First Crusade; Nikephoros Gregoras was deeply involved in the theological politics of his day; Niketas Choniates witnessed the sack of Constantinople by the Fourth Crusade in 1204, John Kananos its siege by Murad II in 1422, Sphrantzes its fall to Mehmet II in 1453.

Apart from the obvious advantages for an historian, this involvement in affairs encouraged a Byzantine intrusion of author into work rare in Greek antiquity: thus, for instance, Psellos exaggerated his own importance in affairs of state, while Kantakouzenos's principal aim was to convince posterity of the rightness of his actions in the civil war (with seeming ingenuousness he recorded lengthy criticisms of himself, but only with his own rejoinders). Various historians chose their subjects for openly professed reasons: thus Attaleiates wanted to immortalize the exemplary deeds and character of Nikephoros III Botaneiates (as Xenophon had those of the Persian usurper Cyrus), Anna Komnene to do justice to her imperial father's achievements. The 12th-century epitomator Kedrenos rightly saw fit to accuse predecessors of "failing in accuracy" through the wish of "one to praise an emperor, one to blame a patriarch, another to eulogize a friend". Although some historians sought to give posterity disinterested accounts, others saw themselves in moral terms, with a mission to lead their readers into "right thinking", whether political or religious, thereby unashamedly justifying prejudice (George Hamartolos, "the sinner", even allowed himself to indulge in obscenities to vent his hatred of iconoclasm, Islam, and Manichaeanism). Nevertheless, despite distortion, which is often merely the result of biased selection of material, and errors of fact due to ignorance, Byzantine writers did not tell deliberate falsehoods, for, as Pachymeres claimed, "truth is the soul of history" (although he did add that there are certain matters not meet to be known, in which cases "it is better for posterity to be ignorant than misinformed").

Byzantine historiography through most of its chronological span fully validates the claim often made for it as the most interesting genre of secular literature for range of factual information, revelations of values both personal and societal, innovative approaches, and variety of styles and linguistic registers.

Life under foreign rule enabled historians to broaden their vision, and so Machairas' chronicle has the added interest of a genuine admiration for the Lusignan kings combined with patriotism and Orthodox faith. The period immediately after the fall of Constantinople in 1453 had a similar effect. In the 1480s Laonikos Chalkokondyles, in clear imitation of Herodotus' study of the conflict between Persians and Greeks, traced the confrontation from 1298 to 1463 of the Byzantines and Ottoman Turks with pointed emphasis on the latter, for whom he was a valuable witness through his access to documentary sources. Michael Kritoboulos, who was governor of Imbros from 1456 until its fall to the Venetians in 1466, went even further in a history of the period from 1451 to 1467 which is stylistically and linguistically modelled on Thucydides: his hero was his master Mehmet II, whose position as successor to Byzantine emperors is validated by an interest in Classical antiquity.

Thereafter, with the death of the generation educated traditionally before the fall, there was virtually no literature in areas under Turkish rule until the late 16th century. Even after the patriarch Cyril I Lukaris (1620–38) established in Constantinople the first printing press in the Greek world, historical writing remained a hazardous genre to pursue. Elsewhere in the old Byzantine world (mainly Cyprus, Crete, and, from the 17th century, the Ionian islands) historical works continued to be written, but at first almost exclusively in verse and in some variant of the vernacular. Members of the diaspora had initially few historiographic interests, but of crucial importance was the pioneering work of the Corfiote Nikolaos Sophianos and others in the mid-15th century in encouraging a belief in the vernacular as a respectable language for intellectuals to employ even in prose, although many still preferred to write in the high language or even in Italian (Sophianos even wrote a demotic grammar, which was not, however, published until 1870).

In Cyprus Georgios Boustronios usefully but less dramatically continued Machairas' prose chronicle up to 1501, but the island's promise to produce an indigenous literary tradition was stifled by the Turkish seizure in 1570, although this initially inspired several historical poems reminiscent of those lamenting the fall of Constantinople (and an eyewitness account by Ioannes Sozomenos in Italian of the Turkish siege of Nicosia at which he was taken prisoner). Indigenous Cretan historiography lasted longer. The earthquake of 1508 and its devastating consequences are the subject of a vivid poem by Manoles Sklavos, while the struggle over the island between the Venetians and the Turks from 1645 to 1669 is detailed in lengthy poems by Athanasios Skleros (unusually in the high language), Anthimos Diakrouses, and (the most vivid) Marinos Bouniales. Emmanuel Georgillas of Rhodes contributed a short poem describing the plague of 1498–1500, but its style is dry and its purpose religious edification. The most interesting of the products of the Ionian islands is the detailed, vivid, but critical description of the popular uprising of Zakynthos against the Venetians in 1628, by Antzolos Soummakes. Certain other works, such as the poem on the siege of Malta in 1565 by the Cretan Antonios Acheles, are merely adaptations of Italian originals.

Local patriotism was sporadically kept alive by chronicles, of which the most interesting is the vernacular *Chronicle of Galaxeidi* composed in 1703 by the monk Euthymios. This charming medley of historical facts, miracles, and fantastic tales describes the history of a village on the northern shore of the Corinthian Gulf from the Byzantine period. For many years the only source of information on general Greek history was the universal chronicle attributed to the perhaps fictitious Dorotheos of Monemvasia. This is an enormous medley of disparate sources, some now lost, and includes lists of Roman, Christian, and Turkish rulers, an account of the Council of Ferrara-Florence, and a section on Venice. Its earliest redaction ends in 1570. By the early 19th century, however, there had been published, often in Italy, not only numerous compilations, adaptations, and partly original works of varying merit but also translations of several foreign histories of Greece (including that by Oliver Goldsmith), and even one of Byzantine historians rendered into a more modern idiom (by Ioannes Stanos in 1767).

Roughly contemporary with the *Chronicle of Dorotheos* is a vernacular *History of the Patriarchs of Constantinople* (this and a universal chronicle are attributed to a Manuel Malaxos who for the latter may have been only the copyist), which was of sufficient merit to warrant publication in 1584 by the German scholar Martin Crusius. Knowledge of their counterparts in Jerusalem was added in an adversely critical 17th-century account by Païsios Ligarides, a man of shifting and dubious religious loyalties (it was used later by the far more reputable and scholarly Dositheos, himself a patriarch of Jerusalem). Useful material on the negotiations of the ecumenical patriarch Jeremias II is to be found in the verse chronicle of his journey to Jerusalem by archbishop Arsenios, written in 1620. Most notable, however, because it can be truly classed as a work of scholarship, is the *Summary of Religious and Profane History* by one of the pioneers of the Greek intellectual renaissance, the Cretan Nektarios who became patriarch of Jerusalem in 1661. A preliminary section based upon the Old Testament is followed by a lengthy history of the monastery of St Catherine, Sinai, for which Nektarios used Arab sources and monastic manuscripts, before adding sections on the history of Egypt, based upon Herodotus and later sources, and the conquest of Egypt by the Ottoman Selim in 1517. Quite different, and analagous to local chronicles, is a lively 17th-century anonymous history of the Athonite monastery of Vatopedi. Of the numerous later ecclesiastical works the most notable is the *Memoirs of Ecclesiastical History* of Sergios Makraios, professor at the Patriarchal School in Constantinople, which gives valuable information on Orthodox-papal relations in the period 1750–1800.

Greek historical interests naturally extended only exceptionally beyond the Mediterranean world (the early 16th-century Corfiote Jakobos Triboles's poem, *The History of the King of Scotland and the Queen of England*, has nothing to do with any personages of those countries, since it is merely a reworking of a tale in Boccaccio). Of peculiar interest, therefore, is a work in Latin by the mercenary soldier Jakobos Basilikos (who gave himself the surname Heraklides and became prince of Moldavia in 1561): his eyewitness account of the campaign of Charles V at Thérouanne and Renty takes the form of a dialogue between Hercules and Nestor. In the 18th century Chrysanthos Notaras's account in the vernacular of the Tatar conquest of China is indicative of the growing internationalism of the Greeks of the disapora, while various works on Russia indicate that country's involvement in Greek affairs. Histories of Wallachia and Moldavia (notably by Kaisarios Dapontes, the finest Greek historian of the 18th century, and, later, Dionysios Photeinos) reflect Phanariot Greek rule there.

The earliest history of the Ottomans by a Greek (after Chalkokondyles and Kritoboulos) is the anonymous late-16th-century vernacular *Chronicle of the Turkish Sultans*, which is, however, based upon an Italian original. The first work of some independent merit is the history, in Italian, of Theodoros Spandounes who fought at the siege of Vienna in 1532. Probably through Italian influence he not only shows himself aware of Greek faults (e.g. their theological quarrels) but demonstrates an interest in Turkish customs. By far the best Ottoman history written by a Greek was that of the Phanariot Demetrios Kantemir (his father was of Tartar origin), who became Prince of Moldavia in 1710: it was little known, however, to his fellow countrymen since it was written in Latin and published in an English translation. Apart from accounts of and lamentations on Turkish victories already mentioned, the Ottoman and Venetian wars were another topic of interest, as in the anonymous 17th-century *Chronicle of Matesis* and Laonikos Zamires' celebration of a Venetian naval victory in 1651. Of greater interest, however, are the works of Christophoros Angelos. As a teacher of Greek at Oxford and Cambridge, Angelos chose the Classical language for a vivid account of his sufferings at the hands of the Turks (1617) and an analysis of the contemporary situation of the Greeks which includes a history of the Greek Church (1619).

The obviously fading power of the Turks from the late-17th to the early-19th century encouraged a Greek consciousness. Indicative of this is a history of Athens from Cecrops to Dionysius the Areopagite which the learned Georgios Kontares deliberately published in the vernacular (Venice, 1675) to inspire the common people. Even the Cretan Nikolaos Komnenos Papadopoulos's Latin *History of the University of Padua* (1726) emphasizes its Greek students, while the dedication of Alexandros Kankellarios's translation of Charles Rollin's *Ancient History* (1750) is to "the famous nation of the Greeks" who will thereby learn of their "glorious past". Local pride is evident in a continuing series of local histories of Athens, Corfu, Cyprus (a major work of scholarship published in 1788 by the archimandrite Kyprianos Kouriokourineos), and Epirus. Also suggesting the perceived need to emphasize a pre-Ottoman history is the vernacular translation of the surviving 15th-century *Chronicle of Ioannina*, itself an important souce for knowledge of medieval Epirus. Contemporary wars between Greeks and Turks were also at last a source of inspiration: most notable are the *Lament of the Peloponnese*, a poem in 2700 rhymed hendecasyllabics of real literary merit by Petros Katsaïtes on the events of 1715; and the *History of Souli and Parga*, a prose account of the Souliots' struggles with Ali

Pasha published by Christophoros Perraibos in 1803. Finally, the Greek War of Independence proper begat an outstanding work in the *Memoirs* of one of its major figures, General Makriyannis, composed after the war's conclusion when he had taught himself to read and write. Although ignored until its publication in 1907, and then despised for some 30 years, its idiosyncratic nature (replete with bizarre spelling and punctuation), vehement expression, and enthralling narrative offer a fitting culmination of the vernacular tradition of the Tourkokratia and Frankokratia which was now driven underground by the katharevousa ("purified" language) of other historians.

A.R. LITTLEWOOD

See also Archives, Chronicles, Chronology, Hagiography

Further Reading

Croke, Brian and Alanna Emmett (editors), *History and Historians in Late Antiquity*, Oxford and New York: Pergamon Press, 1983

Grant, Robert M., *Eusebius as Church Historian*, Oxford: Clarendon Press, 1980

Hunger, Herbert, *Die hochsprachliche profane Literatur der Byzantiner*, vol. 1, Munich: Beck, 1978, pp. 243–504

Karayannopulos, Johannes and Gunter Weiss, *Quellenkunde zur Geschichte von Byzanz, 324–1453*, 2 vols, Wiesbaden: Harrassowitz, 1982

Knös, Börje, *L'Histoire de la littérature néo-grecque: la période jusqu'en 1821*, Stockholm: Almqvist & Wiksell, 1962

Ljubarskij, Jakov Nikolaević, "Man in Byzantine Historiography From John Malalas to Michael Psellos", *Dumbarton Oaks Papers*, 46 (1992): pp. 177–86

Ljubarskij, Jakov Nikolaević, "New Trends in the Study of Byzantine Historiography", *Dumbarton Oaks Papers*, 47 (1993): pp. 131–38

Ljubarskij, Jakov Nikolaević *et al.*, "*Quellenforschung* and/or Literary Criticism: Narrative Structures in Byzantine Historical Writings", *Symbolae Osloenses*, 73 (1998): pp. 5–73

Momigliano, Arnaldo, *Essays in Ancient and Modern Historiography*, Oxford: Blackwell, and Middletown, Connecticut: Wesleyan University Press, 1977

Mosshammer, Alden A., *The Chronicle of Eusebius and Greek Chronographic Tradition*, Lewisburg, Pennsylvania: Bucknell University Press, 1979

Scott, R., "The Classical Tradition in Byzantine Historiography" in *Byzantium and the Classical Tradition*, edited by Margaret Mullett and Roger Scott, Birmingham: Centre for Byzantine Studies, University of Birmingham, 1981

Modern

In the prerevolutionary period of the so-called Neohellenic Enlightenment (1750–1821) the writing, publishing, and dissemination of historical works, whether originals, adaptations, compilations, or translations, formed a major contribution to the ideological and cultural preparation for the raising of national awareness among the Ottoman-ruled Greeks. With the successful outcome of the Greek ethnogenesis, realized in the form of a truncated but independent nation state, historical writing was to evolve in the context of Greek national ideology, echoing the national assumptions of the Greek state, aspiring to establish a legitimate European profile through a historical past and to carry out its liberating mission in the unredeemed Greek-populated lands of Ottoman Turkey.

The first phase of modern Greek historiography spans the first 90 years of free statehood, to Greece's military defeat in Asia Minor in 1922. Not surprisingly, in the early decades (1830–60) historical works on the late prerevolutionary period and, particularly, on the War of Independence were mostly produced by contemporaries of and participants in the events. These consisted of general histories (A. Frantzis's *History of Reborn Greece*, and the 4-volume histories of the revolution by S. Trikoupis and I. Filimon), the memoirs and reminiscences of participants (Palaion Patron Germanos, N. Kasomoulis, T. Kolokotronis, E. Xanthos, C. Perraivos, F. Chrysanthopoulos-Fotakos, N. Spiliadis, Spyromilios), collections of documents and laws (A. Mamoukas), biographies, and various monographs.

Revolutionary Greece was also recorded by contemporary European writers and historians (G. Finlay, T. Gordon, G. Gervinus, F. Pouqueville, F. Thiersch, J. Zinkeisen, and A. Prokesch-Osten). Otherwise, 19th-century Hellenism attracted contemporary foreign historiographic interest either in connection with the complex diplomatic context of the Eastern Question and Ottoman Turkey's difficulties with reform, or as travel literature. With few exceptions (G. Finlay, K. Mendelson-Bartholdy, G. Hertzberg, P. Bickford-Smith), it was the arrival of the 20th century that produced the first major works on modern Greek history by European historians, such as William Miller and E. Driault and M. l'Héritier, whose classic diplomatic history of Greece from 1821 to their times remains in use. European scholarship paid greater attention to medieval and Frankish-ruled Hellenism, partly by the same historians (G. Finlay, G. Hertzberg) along with the medievalists Karl Hopf and J.A. Buchon, while in 1908 William Miller contributed a history of Frankish Greece (1204–1566).

The main themes of 19th-century Greek historiography were shaped by the dominant questions of modern Hellenism, namely historical continuity as an ingredient of the Greek national identity, and the Great Idea as the foremost vision of national integration in its hallucinating dimensions of creating an eastern empire of the Greeks with a capital at Constantinople. The role of the German historian Jacob Philipp Fallmerayer, however unintended and repugnant to the Greeks, was to be seminal, when in his History of the Morea during the Middle Ages (*Geschichte der Halbinsel Morea wahrend des Mittelalters* 2 vols, 1830 and 1836), he dissociated, on a racial basis, modern Greeks from their esteemed ancient ancestors, in the belief that the latter were entirely replaced by an amalgamation of Slavic tribes – a theory opposed at once by such European contemporaries as J.W. Zinkeisen and B. Kopitar. His thesis was felt as a national affront, and provoked a large number of ad-hoc history books and articles in Greece to oppugn it and, thus, restore national self-esteem and establish credentials of historical legitimacy at home and, especially, in the eyes of the West (e.g. *Refutation of the Theories of Fallmerayer* by F. Zamvaldis, *On the Descent of the Race of the Greeks* by C. Poulios, etc.). On academic historiography, in particular, such ideological assumptions weighed heavily, with the Faculty of Philosophy at Athens University (founded 1837) assuming throughout the century a leading role in the elaborations of Greek nationalism. This is where the official national theory of the historical continuity of

Hellenism was formulated – the Greek variant on the similar theme of European nationalism.

Konstantinos Paparrigopoulos (1815–91), a university history professor, was the intellectual who provided the definitive contemporary answer on behalf of Greek historiography on the question of the historical unity of Greek culture in time and place. This he pursued by expounding the concept of a historical continuum from Homeric Greece to modern times through the rehabilitation in the national consciousness and history writing of the hitherto disparaged (by the classicist Enlightenment) medieval Byzantium. Its full elaboration was formulated in the final version of his monumental *Istoria tou Ellinikou Ethnous* (History of the Greek Nation, 1860–74), a work setting a model for Greek history writing for more than a century, both in terms of methodology as factual historical narrative and, primarily, in conceptualizing and establishing in Greek historiography the genuinely lingering pattern of the history of the Greek nation per se.

The discourse that was generated in Greek scholarship over Hellenism and its relationship with Byzantium confirmed the establishment of the tripartite pattern of Greek history from ancient times through to the formation of the Greek state. In 1852 Spyridon Zampelios gave prominence to the Byzantine period and associated it with the Greek consciousness in the *Historical Study on Medieval Hellenism* which prefaced his collection of Greek demotic songs. Five years later he published his *Byzantine Studies*. That the Byzantine period aspired to and was integrated into the scope of historiography as a legitimate, in fact value-imparting, constituent paved the way for the development of Byzantine studies in Greece, along with the unchallenged Classical studies, accredited from the outset by virtue of the underlying classicist values of the Greek state. The political conditions from the last decades of the century onwards encouraged these studies, as the rise of Slavophobia in Greece found ground for confirmation in the study of Byzantium. This was further strengthened by the sharpening of national feeling and the presence of the spirit of an eastern empire among intellectuals before and around the time of the Balkan Wars – a growing trend illustrated by the immediate translation of Karl Krumbacher's bulky *History of Byzantine Literature* (1897–1900), the four-volume comprehensive publication in Greek of the French Byzantinist Gustave Schlumberger's works under the title *Byzantine Épopée* (1904–08), and K.S. Sokolis's book *Empire* (1916). On the whole, 19th-century political and cultural Romanticism, emphasizing the notion of the nation and its historical lineage, prompted the growth of historical studies and, especially, interest in research and the publication of primary sources. In this, folklore, founded by Nikolaos Politis (1852–1921) as a self-sufficient academic discipline under nationally orientated auspices, provided extra material on Greek popular culture and life.

Throughout the 19th and the early 20th centuries the Paparrigopoulos legacy determined the course of Greek historiography, since the national ideological and cultural underpinnings remained by and large unmodified. In particular, the term Hellenism, denoting the presence of the nation far beyond and irrespective of "the narrow precinct of free Greece" (Paparrigopoulos), was universally espoused by the 1880s, partly in place of the Great Idea, which at times provoked

distrust and a critique. Spyridon Lambros (1851–1919) and Pavlos Karolidis (1849–1930), both history professors at Athens University, continued along the lines of the national historicist school, contributing much to Greek historiography. The former dealt extensively with medieval and modern Hellenism, his rich historiographic output including a history of Greece to 1453, while as editor of the historical journal *Neos Ellinomnimon* he worked for the advance of historical studies, with emphasis on source-material publishing. The latter, Karolidis, whose work ranged from national to world history, wrote *inter alia* a history of Greece from 1453 to 1863, and complemented Paparrigopoulos's *History* with an account of the period from independence to 1930. In the same spirit, Epameinondas Kyriakidis (1861–1939), a Constantinopolitan scholar, published a *History of Contemporary Hellenism* (19th century). In addition, Konstantinos Sathas (1842–1924), a dedicated, albeit non-professional, historian, researched and wrote on Ottoman-ruled Hellenism, leaving behind informative books, notably his voluminous *Medieval Library*, *Turkish-dominated Greece*, and biographies of Greek scholars (1453–1821) in his *Neohellenic Literature*.

Of other noteworthy writers and historians, Antonios Miliarakis (1841–1905) was attracted to the history and geography of medieval Greece, but it was Pavlos Kalligas (1814–96) who was among the first after Paparrigopoulos to examine Byzantine Hellenism. Tryfon Evangelidis (1863–1941) dealt *inter alia* with the Tourkokratia and the education of Ottoman-ruled Greeks, while Manouil Gedeon (1854–1943) centred on the history of the Constantinople patriarchate and ecclesiastical matters. In the field of local and regional historiography, besides Andreas Moustoxydis (1785–1860), the groundbreaking historian who continued the exploratory historical work he had started as early as 1804, Panagiotis Chiotis (1814–96), and Andreas Idromenos (1853–1917) occupied themselves with the history of the Ionian islands; Dionysios Sourmelis and, later, Themistoklis Filadelfevs (1838–1920) and Dimitrios Kampouroglou (1852–1942) looked into medieval and modern Athens; the archaeologist and philologist Stefanos Xanthoudidis (1864–1928) wrote a history of Crete; Ioannis Lampridis (1862–1914) published work on Epirus and the Hellenism of Egypt, while others worked on the Peloponnese (C. Korylos) and Thessaly (N. Georgiadis); and, finally, Alexandros Paspatis (1814–91), another writer from Constantinople, left behind many studies in the history of his birthplace. Other 19th-century writers such as A. Mansolas, I. Nouchakis, and I. Stamatakis showed interest in the historical geography and demography of Greece. As regards economic history, after A. Vernardakis, D. Georgiades, and L. Dosios, who wrote economic monographs, Andreas Andreadis (1876–1935), university professor of political economy and finance, laid the scientific foundations of economic history in Greece by writing a history of Greek loans and public finance.

The year 1922, a watershed in Greek history marking the end of the Great Idea as an irredentist vision, marked the opening of a second period of historiography extending to the 1960s. The trend towards reorientation and revision in the Greek national consciousness in the interwar period, and an ideological divergence in place of the unitary effect of the Great Idea, had some repercussions on historiography. Renewal and challenge were introduced methodologically by the Marxist approach and thematically by a sensitivity towards social issues. These developments were accelerated by the formation of the Communist Party, and the increase in social awareness and tensions after Georgios Skliros wrote *Our Social Question* (1907). Marxist historiography was represented by Gianis Kordatos (1891–1961), the first Communist Party leader and an indefatigable historian, who as early as 1924 attempted a class analysis of the Greek revolution, and produced pioneering work on the history of Greek capitalism and of the Greek agrarian and working-class movements. Another communist writer, Serafeim Maximos (1895–1962), turned to the economic history of Greece. The agricultural question in the country was broad-sightedly discussed by K.D. Karavidas in a remarkable book, *Agricultural Issues* (1931), while D.L. Zografos dealt extensively with the history of Greek agriculture. Conventional history writing was not seriously affected, however, since the rise and establishment of Greek authoritarianism, following the brief republican interlude in the interwar period, prevented new historiography from amending the traditional theoretical framework of Greek history. This annulled, too, an early attempt in Greek history studies to overcome their ethnocentric interests: in 1939 the state abolished the chairs of Balkan, Slav, and Arab history and literature for which provision had been made at the recently established Thessalonica University (founded 1926).

In the field of the traditional historiography of modern Hellenism, the following should be mentioned. Nikolaos Vlachos (1893–1956) and Georgios Aspreas (1875–1952; the political history of modern Greece), Dionysios Kokkinos (1884–1967; the Greek revolution), Giannis Vlachogiannis (1868–1945), Kostas Kairofylas (1878–1961), Fanis Michalopoulos (1895–1960), and many others. Xenophon Zolotas (born 1904) partly continued Andreas Andreadis's work, but orientated towards pure economics, producing books on Greece's industrialization and monetary stabilization. Balkan studies owe a great deal to Michail Laskaris (1903–65), the founder of Balkanology in Greece, and Byzantine studies to Byzantinist professors at Athens University, Konstantinos Amantos (1874–1960), Nikolaos Veis (1887–1958), and, throughout the period since World War II, Dionysios Zakythinos (1905–93). Research into Byzantium and medieval studies were early encouraged by the Society for Byzantine Studies and the Society for Medieval Literature, founded in 1918 and 1926 respectively.

The third period of Greek historiography, representing an apogee of historical studies, traces its origins to around the 1960s and manifested itself clearly from the 1970s onwards. It originated with Greek historians abroad, especially in the United States and France, who because of their position were receptive to major developments in international historiography, to which the prevailing post-Civil War climate of ultra-conservatism in Greece remained obstinately immune. It was with the restoration of democracy in 1974 and the ensuing radicalization that conditions were created for the reassociation of Greek scholarship with European intellectual trends, and for history writing and research in the country to flourish.

On Byzantine Hellenism, besides domestic historiographic production, there was already a longer tradition of study in international scholarship to build upon, respectably established by Gustave Schlumberger, Henri Grégoire, Charles Diehl, and more recently Franz Dölger, Alexander Vasiliev, Georg Ostrogorsky, and Romilly Jenkins (followed by S. Vryonis, S. Runciman, D. Obolensky, A. Kazhdan, P. Lemerle, N. Oikonomides, H. Ahrweiler-Glykatzi, D. Geanakoplos, I. Karagiannopoulos, E. Barker, H. Antoniadis-Bibiacou, H.-G. Beck, H. Hunger, D. Nicol, A. Guillou, P. Charanis, and I. Shevchenko). The difference was made far more evident in the field of modern Hellenism, where several leading historians are numbered among those who initiated from abroad the renewal of Greek historiography, such as Lefteris Stavrianos (*The Balkans since 1453*, 1958), John Petropulos (*Politics and Statecraft in the Kingdom of Greece*, 1968), and John Campbell (*Honour, Family and Patronage*, 1964), to name only three from both sides of the Atlantic. But two figures left an indelible imprint on modern Hellenism not merely by their historiographic production, but particularly by providing instruction and inspiration to an unconventionally minded younger generation of historians, namely Konstantinos T. Dimaras (1904–92) and Nikos Svoronos (1911–90), both intellectually influenced by the academic climate in France. Dimaras explored fresh historical ground by focusing on intellectual history with reference to the Neohellenic Enlightenment, while Svoronos, covering a broad range from Byzantium to modern history, sharpened methodologically the approach to social and economic issues. His *Histoire de la Grèce moderne* (1953), the first Marxist-slanted short history of Greece, became a standard work along with Richard Clogg's *Short History of Modern Greece* (1979).

The true renewal of Greek history writing has manifested itself in four respects: in numbers, since there has been an unprecedented increase in historians, history-related institutions and research centres, and historical publications in recent decades; in methodology, either by the introduction of different approaches, with an emphasis on those of broadly interpreted neo-Marxism and on a belated introduction of the French school of the *Annales*, or by interdisciplinary applications, especially from the field of social anthropology, political science, and historical sociology; in themes, marked by a burgeoning of monographs in long-neglected social and economic history, as well as in intellectual history and the "history of mentalities", the latter echoing a strong association with academic developments in France; and in periods, where the research focus has been set on modern Hellenism, especially on the 19th and 20th centuries, including the turbulent decade of the 1940s.

The historiography of this current period has given rise to the exploration of new phenomena such as underdevelopment and dependence in a European context, nationalism, state-building, the identity-formation process, diaspora, and ethnic groups. The social issue in Greek history has received scholarly attention, and the term "society" increasingly elbowed out in analyses that of the "nation"/*genos* (race). The old question of the identity of Hellenism has been freshly addressed, not in the traditional manner of the moulding of its distinct character, but in its dynamic historical perspective and interaction with the West and East in a scheme of cultural pluralism. Emphasis has been given to the horizontal study of historical periods rather than to the diachronic view of history derived from the Paparrigopoulos framework. Symptomatic of this, too, has been an unorthodox trend in the study of Byzantium, especially abroad (in the works of Cyril Mango, for instance), as a phenomenon unrelated to modern Hellenism. In parallel, traditional history writing has been represented by two multi-volume works: Apostolos Vakalopoulos's *History of Modern Hellenism* (Thessalonica, 1961–74), an updated and informative account of Hellenic continuity on the lines of Paparrigopoulos's work, and Spyridon Markezinis's *Political History of Greece, 1828 to 1975* (Athens, 1966–78). Finally, the *History of the Greek Nation* (1977), a 15-volume collective work, despite the traditional overall concept, reflects the results and pursuits of contemporary Greek historiography, standing out as the best encyclopaedic review of Greek history from ancient times to 1941.

Today Greek historiography exhibits a methodological and thematic pluralism and aspires to open communication with international history, while it continues its efforts to come to grips with the problem of traditional ethnocentrism. An indication of this can be seen in the Greece-related theses of the overwhelming majority of Greek graduates pursuing higher degrees in history in European and American universities.

RENNOS EHALIOTIS

See also Archives, Great Idea

Further Reading

Clogg, Mary Jo and Richard Clogg, *Greece*, Oxford and Santa Barbara, California: Clio Press, 1980 (World Bibliographical series, vol. 17)

Dimaras, K.T., C. Koumarianou, and L. Droulia, *Modern Greek Culture: A Selected Bibliography in English, French, German, Italian*, 4th edition, Athens, National Hellenic Committee of the International Association for South Eastern European Studies, 1974

Dimaras, K.T., *Ellinikos Romantismos* [Greek Romanticism], Athens, 1982

Dimaras, K.T., *Konstantinos Paparrigopoulos*, Athens, 1986

Gooch, G.P., *History and Historians in the Ninenteenth Century*, 2nd edition, London: Longman, 1952

Gounaris, Basil C., "Reassessing Ninety Years of Greek Historiography on the 'Struggle for Macedonia 1904–1908'" in *Ourselves and Others: The Development of a Greek Macedonian Cultural Identity since 1912*, edited by Peter Mackridge and Eleni Yannakakis, Oxford and New York: Berg, 1997

Kitroeff, Alexander, "Continuity and Change in Contemporary Greek Historiography", *European History Quarterly* (special issue: Modern Greece), 19/2 (April 1989): pp. 269–98; reprinted in *Modern Greece: Nationalism and Nationality*, edited by Martin Blinkhorn and Thanos Veremis, Athens: Sage / Eliamep, 1990

Macrakis, Lily A., and Nikiforos P. Diamandouros (editors), *New Trends in Modern Greek Historiography*, Hanover, New Hampshire: Modern Greek Studies Association, 1982

Mango, Cyril, "Byzantinism and Romantic Hellenism", *Journal of the Warburg and Courtauld Institute*, 28 (1965): pp. 29–43

Sakellariou, Michail V., "Neoellinikes istorikes spoudes" [Neohellenic Historical Studies], *Nea Estia*, 33 (1943): pp. 26 ff.

"Sychrona Revmata stin Istoriographia tou Neou Ellinismou" [Contemporary Trends in the Historiography of Modern Hellenism], special issue of *Sychrona Themata*, 35–37 (December 1988)

Topping, Peter, "Greek Historical Writing on the Period 1453–1914", *Journal of Modern History*, 33 (1961): pp. 157–73

Veloudis, Georg, "Jakob Philipp Fallmerayer und die Entstehung des neugriechischen historismus", *Sudostforschungen*, 29 (1970): pp. 43–90

Homer

Epic poet of the 8th or 7th century BC

"Homer" is the name associated since ancient times with the author of the *Iliad* and the *Odyssey*, the two epic poems that form the earliest surviving Greek literature and which are probably the most important and influential works ever written in Greek. The *Iliad* describes the Trojan War, the ten-year struggle by the Greeks to conquer the city of Troy in Asia Minor and to recapture Helen, the queen of Sparta who was abducted by the Trojan prince Paris. The poem covers only a few days in the last year of the war, when Achilles, the greatest of the Greek heroes, is insulted by Agamemnon, his commander in chief, and refuses to fight. The Greeks are badly defeated in his absence and plead for his help, but he gives it only when his close friend Patroclus is killed by Hector, the bravest of the Trojan princes. At that point Achilles returns to the battle and kills Hector, though he knows that he is fated to die if he does so. Hector's family mourns him greatly, and his aged father Priam, the king of Troy, comes to Achilles in secret to ransom his son's body, which Achilles allows him to do. These events are influenced but not entirely controlled by the gods, who take an active interest in the course of the war but are far from united in their aims and often engage in highly undignified bickering. The theme of the poem is the wrath of Achilles; it begins with the actions that caused that anger and ends when Achilles lays aside his anger to share Priam's grief, and the story is amazingly cohesive and unified for a poem of such length. Nevertheless the poet also manages, by means of well-placed digressions, to give the story of the entire war in the course of the poem.

The *Odyssey* takes place after the end of the Trojan War and chronicles the homeward journey of Odysseus, one of the Greek heroes. It begins towards the end of his wanderings, and we learn of many of his adventures only when he narrates them himself in the course of his homecoming; narration from various characters also provides us with the story of the part of the Trojan War between the end of the *Iliad* and the beginning of the *Odyssey*. The poet focuses not only on Odysseus and his adventures, but also on the courage and endurance of his wife Penelope, who waited 20 years for her husband to return, and the coming of age of their son Telemachus, who grew up without knowing his father. Both Penelope and Telemachus suffer from the crowd of suitors who occupy their house for years insisting that Penelope remarry, and the poet carefully alternates scenes describing their plight with ones detailing Odysseus' adventures. Finally the two halves of the poem come together, as Odysseus returns to his family and kills the suitors.

A number of shorter poems about the gods, known as the Homeric Hymns, are also attributed to Homer. Internal linguistic evidence suggests that some of these poems are almost as early as the *Iliad* and *Odyssey*, while others were clearly composed much later.

Nothing is known for certain about Homer himself, and his very existence is now disputed; the *Iliad* and *Odyssey* may have different authors, if either can be said to have an author at all. The epics are certainly the product of a long oral tradition, probably dating back at least to the 12th century BC. The extent to which this tradition can be taken as any sort of

Homer: an 18th-century engraving in the style of an ancient portrait bust

centuries and different areas of Greece; it preserves traces of very archaic features next to relatively recent innovations and is not something that was ever spoken as anyone's natural language. Because of the prestige of the poems, however, the "epic dialect" became a recognized form of literary Greek and was often used, in whole or in part, for later Greek poetry.

Throughout antiquity the Homeric epics were regarded as indisputably the best and most important works of Greek literature, a reputation that they have never really lost. Greek schoolchildren studied them, in preference to all other literature, from the beginning of Greek schooling, and the epics were regularly recited on all kinds of occasions both public and private. Once they had been written down, the poems stopped evolving as oral literature and attained a relatively fixed form; this was necessitated in part by their use as an authority on any matter they mentioned, from territorial claims to religious observances. The poems' depiction of the gods as not free of human vices occasioned some discomfort among later philosophers, but not enough to undermine Homer's authority seriously.

Virtually all of ancient literature is indebted to Homer in one way or another; his influence is particularly notable in poetry, since both the language and the mythological material of much Greek poetry are directly traceable to him, but it can also be seen in historical and philosophical works. Some later Greeks, such as Apollonius Rhodius, wrote epics of their own that were close imitations of the Homeric poems, but most writers tended to feel that Homer could not be equalled and therefore should not be directly imitated. Much of ancient art is also clearly dependent on Homer for inspiration.

Homer was the first Greek author to be the subject of scholarship; legend has it that the 6th-century BC Athenian tyrant Pisistratus first ordered that a proper edition of the Homeric poems be compiled. This legend may be without foundation, but it is certainly true that in the Hellenistic period the great scholars of Alexandria devoted much time and energy to editing and commenting on the text of Homer, and many of their observations are still valuable today. Similarly, the enormous preponderance of Homer papyri (ancient copies of the Homeric poems on papyrus, found primarily in Egypt) over those of any other author shows that ancient scribes spent vast amounts of time copying the *Iliad* and *Odyssey*. Early quotations of Homer by other writers suggest that before the Alexandrian period there were a number of variant texts of Homer. This impression is borne out by the earliest Homeric papyri of the Alexandrian period. During that period, however, the papyri reveal the adoption of a standardized text: from about 150 BC virtually all papyri reflect a text very similar to that of the medieval manuscripts on which our own texts are based. Thus in some way the poems became codified during the Alexandrian period, though it is not clear whether this codification was entirely the work of scholars (many of whose emendations do not appear in the codified text) or whether it was also due to the changing practices of Alexandrian book copyists.

In the Roman and Byzantine periods the Homeric poems continued to be read, copied, quoted, imitated, and prized above other pagan literature, and with the introduction of Christianity their status was only slightly diminished. The popularity and importance of the epics made it impossible for

record of actual events in the Mycenaean period is disputed; archaeologists since Heinrich Schliemann have tended to identify Troy with the site of Hissarlik in Turkey, which could have been destroyed by the Greeks around 1250 BC (one ancient date for the Trojan War), but many of the episodes in the poems are certainly fictional and most are probably so. Only a few place names and descriptions of objects can be traced with certainty to the Mycenaean period, and most of the material in the poems is of much later date.

The oral tradition that produced the epics went on evolving until they were written down, which cannot have been earlier than c.800 BC and may have occurred a century or more after that. Today the name "Homer" is often conventionally applied to the last bard in the series (not necessarily the same person for both epics), who presumably shaped the poems into the form in which they were first committed to writing. It is uncertain how much of the final product can be attributed to his individual genius and how much to that of his predecessors. The result of this long evolution is that the language of the *Iliad* and *Odyssey* is a mixture of dialects from different

the Christians to condemn them, and for the most part the pillars of the Church read and used Homer quite happily, although for some the poems' incompatibility with Christian doctrine remained a problem. Several Byzantine authors, such as Tzetzes (12th century) and Psellos (11th century), solved this problem by writing allegorical interpretations of the poems and giving them Christian meaning; in so doing they joined a long tradition of Homeric allegorization that dates back to the Hellenistic period. School curricula in Byzantine times still contained a large component of instruction in and memorization of Homer, and ability to quote from the poems from memory was considered essential in an educated man. Byzantine scholars also produced numerous works on Homer, including the 12th-century archbishop Eustathios' massive commentaries on both epics, which are still of use today. Homer also influenced many vernacular authors of the Byzantine period.

In less educated circles, however, the enormous difference between the epic dialect and the spoken Greek of later periods made the poems more and more difficult to understand, and over time their plots became less familiar to the populace as a whole. Meanwhile, of course, the Homeric poems had been imitated by Latin poets, who in turn inspired medieval poets in western Europe. One result of this was the *Roman de Troie*, a 12th-century French poem on the Trojan War that adapts the Homeric characters into a framework of medieval Christianity, chivalry, and courtly love to the extent that they and their stories are barely recognizable. This poem was brought to Greece by Frankish occupiers and in the 14th century was translated into vernacular Greek as the "War of Troy". It is now the longest surviving medieval Greek vernacular poem (14,367 lines).

With the fall of Constantinople in 1453 the Greeks' contact with their literary past was greatly diminished, but the Homeric poems continued to be used as school texts in those schools that offered training in Greek (particularly those in the Greek diaspora) and so were as influential as any work of ancient Greek literature during this period. The prestige that they continued to hold is illustrated by the story of the reception of a French general sent by Napoleon to annex Corfu in 1797; after the general had delivered a learned speech sprinkled with references to Classical literature, the Corfiots handed him a copy of the *Odyssey* and replied that although the Greeks were not learned they should still be respected because of Homer. At the liberation of Greece in the 19th century Greek education became more widespread, and with it the Homeric poems, which were still used as school texts. They are in fact still so used to this day, continuing an impressive and unbroken tradition of two and a half millennia of Greek education.

The gap between Homeric Greek and the living language has continued to widen, however, resulting in a need for translations. As early as the 17th century Nikolaos Loukanis produced a paraphrase of the *Iliad* in modern Greek, but the first true modern Greek translations were not completed until Polylas's work in the late 19th century.

Modern Greek literature is almost as heavily influenced by Homer as that of the ancient world. The early poets of modern Greece wrote works clearly shaped by Homer, though not always directly alluding to him (e.g. Kalvos, 1824, and Solomos, 1825). Among more recent writers, Cavafy makes indirect use of Homer, while Seferis quotes and refers to the ancient epics frequently. Because of the location of Troy in Asia Minor, the Homeric poems have sometimes been seen as bearing on the modern struggle between Greece and Turkey; for this reason they had more influence on contemporary poetry before 1922, when the Greek army was defeated in Turkey and the Greeks living in Asia Minor were forced to relocate to mainland Greece, than immediately afterwards. Even today, however, Greek literature remains overshadowed by the Homeric poems and their enormous influence on the Greek language and literary tradition. As the poet Elytis put it (1970): "I was given the Greek language, a poor house on Homer's shores."

ELEANOR DICKEY

See also Historiography, Oral Tradition, Poetry (Epic)

Biography

Homer is traditionally assumed to be the author of the two epic poems which represent the earliest surviving examples of Greek literature, the *Iliad* and the *Odyssey*. Based on a long oral tradition, the poems were not written down before 800 BC (and possibly a century or more later); the name "Homer" is conventionally applied to the last bard in that tradition before the poems were committed to writing. All subsequent Greek literature is indebted to Homer in some way.

Writings

The Iliad of Homer, translated by Richmond Lattimore, Chicago: University of Chicago Press, 1951

The Iliad, translated by Robert Fitzgerald, New York: Doubleday, 1974; London: Collins, 1985

The Iliad, translated by Robert Fagles, New York and London: Viking, 1990

The Odyssey, translated by Robert Fitzgerald, New York: Doubleday, 1961; London: Heinemann, 1962

The Odyssey of Homer, translated by Richmond Lattimore, New York: Harper and Row, 1967

The Odyssey, translated by Robert Fagles, New York: Viking, 1996; London: Penguin, 1997

Further Reading

Bowra, C.M., *Homer*, London: Duckworth, and New York: Scribner, 1972

Finley, M.I., *The World of Odysseus*, 2nd edition, London: Chatto and Windus, 1977; New York: Viking, 1978

Griffin, Jasper, *Homer on Life and Death*, Oxford: Clarendon Press, and New York: Oxford University Press, 1980

Kirk, G.S., *The Songs of Homer*, Cambridge: Cambridge University Press, 1962

Lamberton, Robert and John J. Keaney, *Homer's Ancient Readers: The Hermeneutics of Greek Epic's Earliest Exegetes*, Princeton, New Jersey: Princeton University Press, 1992

Morris, Ian, and Barry B. Powell, *A New Companion to Homer*, Leiden: Brill, 1997

Parry, Adam (editor), *The Making of Homeric Verse: The Collected Papers of Milman Parry*, Oxford: Clarendon Press, 1971

Ricks, David, *The Shade of Homer: A Study in Modern Greek Poetry*, Cambridge and New York: Cambridge University Press, 1989

Trypanis, C.A., *The Homeric Epics*, Warminster: Aris and Phillips, 1977

Wace, A.J.B. and Frank H. Stubbings (editors), *A Companion to Homer*, London: Macmillan, and New York: St Martin's Press, 1962

Homosexuality

Homosexuality and the Hellenic tradition are bedfellows of long standing. The gay man or lesbian is no longer the "woman trapped in a man's body" or "the man trapped in a woman's body"; but we are no nearer agreement on what "homosexuality" is than we are able to accept the diversity it represents. Social constructionists argue that no sexualities exist outside culture – that indeed the very concept of "sexuality" is a product of our modern scientific-rational culture; the essentialists proclaim that there is something that "essentially" makes people homosexual, it is a "natural fact". With these two views unreconciled, it is clear there is no one "homosexuality". First, male and female homosexuality must be recognized as different experiences and expressions. Secondly, "homosexuality" is a category of meaning that shifts through time, and it is simplistic to reduce all male homosexual activity to anal intercourse. Homosexuality embraces the homosocial as well as the homoerotic. David Greenberg's masterful survey of the field has pointed out the variety so glibly united in the term "homosexuality". Greenberg's categories are useful in analysing the three broad periods of homosexuality in the Hellenic tradition: the Classical, the medieval, and the modern.

Classical

Sappho provides some evidence of female homoeroticism if not homosexuality:

> and you were anointed with
> a perfume, scented with blossom
> ... although it was fit for a queen
> and on a bed, soft and tender
> ... you satisfied your desire ...

no. 32 (LP 94) in Sappho, *Poems and Fragments*,
translated by Josephine Balmer

Clearer evidence from the Classical period is largely restricted to male homosexuality. For Greenberg the homosexuality of Classical Athens – subject of a definitive study by Kenneth Dover – was transgenerational (in that the lover was older, the beloved little more than a boy without the first growth of a beard); it was based on a differential of power (the lover was older, richer, more experienced, and took the active role; the beloved was younger, without resources, gaining an education, and took the passive role); it was transitional (both parties filled the roles of beloved and lover at different stages); and it was not exclusive (it was indeed "just a stage they were going through", and the lover would frequently have a wife and children at home and in due course the beloved would become an adult citizen and take a wife). This homosexuality – more accurately pederasty – played an institutionalized role in Greek society in the 5th and 4th centuries BC. Not all aspects of this part of Greek culture are clear, but neither are all aspects occluded under the rubric of the "love that dare not speak its name". This love had its names; what is not always clear is what these names meant. The beloved was the *pais* or *eromenos*; the lover was the *erastes*. This part of human experience was socialized and circumscribed into an ideal of accepted behaviours, with some actions clearly prohibited. The beloved, the *eromenos*, was a boy of between 9 and 16, the son of a citizen, who in time would become a citizen himself. One of the leisured classes, he spent his time frequenting the gymnasia where, if he conformed to the Greek ideals of young male beauty, he would come to the attention of a prospective *erastes*, himself a member of the citizenry. The ideal was presented as a hunt: the *eromenos* was the quarry, the *erastes* the hunter. By his attentions, his presence, his example, his guidance, and more concrete gifts of cockerel, hare, or hound, the *erastes* by this theory would inculcate the "best" things of civilized life in his beloved. For his part, the beloved was expected not to give in readily to the importuning of the *erastes*. The willingness of the *erastes* to continue in the pursuit of the apparently unwilling *eromenos* was a clear indicator of the *erastes*' excellence. At a suitable end-point, however, it was accepted that it was "creditable to grant any favour in any circumstances for the sake of becoming a better person", glossed by Dover (p. 91) as "acceptance of the teacher's thrusting penis between his thighs or in his anus is the fee which the pupil pays for good teaching or alternatively a gift from a younger person to an older person whom he has come to love and admire". Here again the Classical Greeks have a word for it: the physical expression was *diamerizein* ("intercrural intercourse"). But there were social constraints. It was assumed that the *eromenos* would gain no physical pleasure (the examples of 100 years of vase painting from 570 to 470 BC show the *eromenos* with flaccid penis and often an almost abstracted air, while the aroused *erastes* is "up for it"). And the *eromenos* was protected from the unwanted advances of an *erastes* by the laws of hubris: in myth Zeus carried off a protesting Ganymede (followed in turn by Poseidon taking Pelops) but boy citizens were protected from such outrage by the legal threat of the death penalty. However, though 4th-century BC Athens readily accepted this "homosexual" ethos of *eromenos* and *erastes* (with evidence provided by the Attic comedies of Aristophanes, by Plato, and by Aeschines' speech of 346 BC in prosecution of Timarchus), the freedoms were constrained. The *eromenos* who, voluntarily or due to parental pressure, gave his favours for material gain in overt prostitution lost his place among the citizens and could be arraigned for hubris if he subsequently attempted to act as a citizen by speaking in the assembly or holding reserved office. Similarly, the man or boy who took the passive (receptive) role in anal intercourse (who allowed himself to be penetrated) separated himself from the citizens and was numbered with women, foreigners, and prostitutes. The role of the beautiful yet aloof object of a worthy male citizen's desire was allowed the beardless youth; a coeval relationship between men – more especially if anal intercourse was imputed to it – was not. The manner in which the physical expression of a homosexual relationship forms a subverting continuum with homosocial relationships – such as between Achilles and Patroclus – caused problems for Classical Hellenism. Pausanias and Agathon continued in the relationship "too long" according to the norms, but their respective roles were clear; for Achilles and Patroclus the question was "which one is the *eromenos*, which one the *erastes*?" as the relationship had to conform to that paradigm.

Medieval

With the advent of Christianity, the easy, though limited, acceptance of some homosexual practice retreated before the model familiar to all Christian European societies. "Homosexuality" was a series of acts, indulged in at the promptings of demons and devils to the peril of one's immortal soul. Homosexuality was constituted as monstrous, perverse, and evil. Any survey of homosexuality in the Hellenic tradition of the Middle Ages must mention *adelphopoiia*, "the adoption of a brother or a sister", which had much in common with other relationships created by the prayers of a ritual – adoption, godparents or *synteknia*, and marriage. A synthesis of the work of Macrides, Boswell, and Rapp provides the following. *Adelphopoiia* was a social relationship, created by a Church rite that connected two individuals. *Adelphopoiia* was part of a spectrum of Byzantine social relationships "by arrangement" that stretched from blood-kin, through marriage, adoption, godparenthood, and *adelphopoiia* to friendship and acquaintance. Rapp presents the evidence for *adelphopoiia*. Hagiographical texts provide four examples (pp. 291–300): St Theodore of Sykeon and Thomas, patriarch of Constantinople; John the Almsgiver, patriarch of Alexandria, and Niketas, governor of Egypt; Symeon the Fool and John the Syrian; and Nikolaos, patriarch of Constantinople, and Leo VI. The complex *adelphopoiia* relationships of Basil I (867–86) with John the son of Danelis and/or with Nikolaos, caretaker of the church of Diomedes, are followed by a treatment of Basil I's *adelphopoiia* with Symbatios and three others (pp.305–12). Romanos IV Diogenes and Nikephoros Bryennios are followed by John III Doukas Vatatzes and Demetrios Tornikes, and John VI Kantakouzenos and Andronikos III Palaiologos (pp.316–18). This wealth of evidence provided by Rapp shows the "pervasiveness of non-biological 'brotherhood', and especially of *adelphopoiesis*, in Byzantine society". The many prohibitions against *adelphopoiia* stand witness to its continued popularity and also the vague feeling that it was the occasion for "many sins". *Adelphopoiia* was a form of ritual kinship that was common in Byzantium, but which was frowned upon by the Church, though the Church itself provided the ritual by which it was created. *Adelphopoiia* gave formal expression to friendship, or created a situation in which friendship might develop. It was a means whereby members of the opposite sex who were not connected by other ties of kinship could gain access to one another. It could have been used by people who were conducting an illicit sexual relationship – either heterosexual or homosexual – to conceal their relationship under the guise of friendship.

Canonists of the 12th century comment carefully on canons dealing with homosexuality, but without the contemporary examples that illustrate their exegesis of the canons on incest, multiple marriages, or even the practice of magic (Laiou, p. 76). The term most commonly used to signify homosexuality was "man-madness". Laiou remarks that, though the disapproval is marked, a certain "economy" was observed in actually carrying out the punishments (p. 77). A preoccupation in

the sources from the 4th and 5th centuries, homosexuality is subsequently rarely mentioned: Laiou suggests that, for all the zeal in normative prohibition, Byzantine society tolerated homosexuality as long as it was not a cause for scandal; in effect, that Byzantium was the first closet society (p. 78). Furthermore, Arethas's scholion to Clement of Alexandria's *Paidagogos* (3. 3. 21. 3) being "the earliest known attestation of 'Lesbian' for a woman erotically oriented toward other women" (Brooten, p. 5, n. 9) seems to position Byzantium clearly at the "queer" end of the spectrum.

Modern

In the period when the modern Greek state came to occupy its present borders, homosexuality in the Hellenic tradition found one voice in the poetry of Cavafy.

> And yet the love you were looking for, I had to give you;
> the love I was looking for
> – so your tired, knowing eyes implied –
> you had to give me.
> Our bodies sensed and sought each other;
> our blood and skin understood.
> But we both hid ourselves, flustered.

"On the Stairs"

The oblique and occluded nature of the remarks in some poems – such as "He Asked about the Quality" – give way gradually to more overt developments, as in "At the Theatre", with "your strange beauty, your decadent youthfulness". Cavafy, however, is a spokesman for the more closeted homosexuality of the early 20th century. In common with a number of European Union democracies, Greece has a confused and complicated attitude to homosexuality. There are gay groups, such as EOK and the refounded AKOE, in Athens and Thessalonica; Mykonos has long been a destination for gay men, Lesbos for lesbians on holiday. Kaliarda, to Greek what Polari is to English, has been the object of etymological and lexical study. A gay press exists in Greece (*Deon* from Athens and *O Podos* from Thessalonica), though titles have in the past been short-lived (though that is not a peculiarity of the Greek-speaking gay world). Orthodox Christians compose 97 per cent of the population and many so-called Christian attitudes to homosexuality (based on a traditionalist reading of Genesis, Leviticus, and Romans) remain. A differential age of consent exists: 17 for male homosexuals, 15 for heterosexuals and lesbians. A survey conducted for the women's magazine *Gynaika* in 1996 (admittedly on only a small sample of 300 individuals) reported that 20.3 per cent of respondents described homosexuality as an illness, 19.6 per cent as taboo, 48.8 per cent as a "different lifestyle", and 14.4 per cent as "nothing unusual". In the same survey 57.6 per cent thought that the adoption of children by a same-sex couple would be "a scandal"; 27.9 per cent thought that the recognition of same-sex marriages was a sign of social decadence, while 33.1 per cent thought it would be a sign of social equality. Were they to discover that their child was homosexual, 23.1 per cent reported that they would take them to a psychiatrist, 56.1 per cent would talk to them about it, 17.4 per cent would leave them free to make their own decisions, and 3.4 per cent would pretend to be unaware of the fact, "even if they [the parents] suffered". A more substantial survey in 1997 on a wide range of political and social questions, with 1600 interviewees aged between 15 and 29, were asked to indicate agreement, disagreement, or neutrality with the statement: "Homosexual relationships are always wrong." In this survey 28.3 per cent agreed with the statement, 41.7 per cent disagreed, and 23.6 per cent neither agreed nor disagreed. Though anecdotal, the situation in modern Greece – as in many other places – seems to be split between the countryside and the metropolitan centres. The Greek notion of "masculinity" (similar to, though distinct from, the *machismo* of Latin America) is a strong force as one leaves the metropolitan centres. Herzfeld's study of the construction of masculinity in a mountain village of Crete mentions homosexuality only twice, both usages being derogatory, but perhaps with an interesting note of continuity as *poushtis* is reported as meaning the passive partner. "Gay Greece" in the Hellenic tradition may lag behind post-Stonewall North America and Western Europe, but evidence on the World Wide Web suggests a vibrant, if limited, gay scene in modern Greece.

Homosexuality in the Hellenic tradition runs through time not as a constant but as constantly changing: from something uncomfortably close to straight paedophilia, through *adelphopoiia*, to postmodern deconstruction of gender roles and what it is to be a sexual human being.

DION C. SMYTHE

See also Minorities, Prostitution

Further Reading

Boswell, John, *Marriage of Likeness: Same-Sex Unions in Pre-Modern Europe*, London: Harper Collins, 1995

Brooten, Bernadette J., *Love between Women: Early Christian Responses to Female Homoeroticism*, Chicago: University of Chicago Press, 1996

Cantarella, Eva, *Bisexuality in the Ancient World*, New Haven and London: Yale University Press, 1992

Dover, K.J., *Greek Homosexuality*, London: Duckworth, and Cambridge, Massachusetts: Harvard University Press, 1978; updated, 1989

Greenberg, David F., *The Construction of Homosexuality*, Chicago: University of Chicago Press, 1988

Herzfeld, Michael, *The Poetics of Manhood: Contest and Identity in a Cretan Mountain Village*, Princeton, New Jersey: Princeton University Press, 1985

Johansson, Warren and William A. Percy, "Homosexuality", in *Handbook of Medieval Sexuality*, edited by Vern L. Bullough and James A. Brundage, New York: Garland, 1996

Laiou, Angeliki E., *Mariage, amour et parenté à Byzance aux Xie–XIIIe siècles*, Paris: Boccard, 1992

Macrides, Ruth J., *Adelphopoiia*, Adoption, and Godparents entries in *The Oxford Dictionary of Byzantium*, edited by A.P. Kazhdan, 3 vols, New York and Oxford: Oxford University Press, 1991

Murray, Jacqueline, "Twice Marginal and Twice Invisible: Lesbians in the Middle Ages" in *Handbook of Medieval Sexuality*, edited by Vern L. Bullough and James A. Brundage, New York: Garland, 1996

Rapp, Claudia "Ritual Brotherhood in Byzantium", *Traditio: Studies in Ancient and Medieval History, Thought, and Religion*, 52 (1997): pp. 285–326

Sappho, *Poems and Fragments*, translated by Josephine Balmer, Newcastle: Bloodaxe, 1992

Honour and Shame

Ancient

A classic description of the values cherished by the ancient Greeks is offered by the speech delivered by the Athenian statesman Pericles in commemoration of those killed during the first year of the Great or Peloponnesian War between Athens and Sparta (430 BC). In this oration, so often compared to Lincoln's Gettysburg Address because of its affirmation of basic principles, Pericles stresses that the dead have won eternal praise before capping his eulogy with a final, and culminating, claim that love of honour alone never grows old and, when one is in the grip of old age and worn out, it is not the pursuit of money, as is asserted, but being honoured that confers the greater pleasure (Thucydides, 2. 44. 4). This sentiment, the supremacy of *time* or honour, is echoed time and time again, both explicitly and implicitly, throughout antiquity: thus Greek literature begins with Homer's *Iliad*, and the *Iliad* begins with the quarrel between Agamemnon and Achilles as a result of which Achilles withdraws from battle and his compatriots are slaughtered. Why does Achilles retreat to his tent? It is because the woman Briseis has been taken from him and so no honour is paid to "the best of Achaeans" (*Iliad*, 1. 412). The law of reciprocity applies: when insulted or injured the man of honour must retaliate in at least equal measure if his personal prestige is to be upheld, and the man of honour is at his most sensitive when a woman from within the family group is in any way threatened. Athenian law, for example, regarded homicide as justified if a man engaged in illicit sex and was caught in the act with a wife or even with other female dependants, (i.e. mother, sister, or daughter), of the killer.

An excessively protective attitude towards female relatives is only one consequence of an obsession with personal and family honour. Honour depends upon the acknowledgement of others and appearance tends to be more important than the truth. "Reputation" is a kind of divinity, according to the poet Hesiod (*Works and Days*, 763–64) who also illustrates reciprocated action: if the first to be wronged in word or deed, you must never turn the other cheek but hit back as hard as you can (709–11); in other words, two wrongs definitely add up to a "right" if the rules of the honour code are observed. Honour, moreover, is reckoned to be a "commodity" and measurable; it is in short supply; and if someone else has honour, it is at your expense and you resent it and try to cut that person down to size by the application of different ranking criteria: if he is powerful or wealthy, then you attack his family background or accuse him of being morally suspect.

It is significant that the word *philotimia*, literally "love of honour", often means "jealousy". As Aristotle remarks, "those who love honour are more envious than those who do not love honour" (*Rhetoric*, 1387b). Recognition, and therefore success, however achieved, is crucial; "if I had succeeded", says the nurse in Euripides' *Hippolytus*, "I would be counted among the wise, since we possess a reputation for intelligence according to success" (700–01). Poverty is a mark of failure, and the poor man has no honour or, as Euripides put it in his *Electra*, "poverty is a disease and it teaches a man to be evil because of his need" (375–76). But a Greek would prefer to scratch a bare living from the soil rather than work for another, for it was the slave who was at another's beck and call and a slave, again, can lay no claim to honour. Greek society was intensely competitive at every level, whether those engaged in competition were athletes, dramatists, statesmen, or soldiers. And it was the relentless pursuit of honour, often at others' expense, that made society so agonistic and, therefore, unstable.

You undertake action to gain honour; you refrain from action to avoid shame or *aidos*. The Christian virtue of guilt was replaced in antiquity by the concept of shame. Hector refuses to run from Achilles though he knows he cannot prevail: "I feel shame before the Trojans, men and women, in case someone my inferior says 'trusting in his strength Hector has destroyed his people'; it would be far better for me to face up to Achilles" (*Iliad*, 22. 105–09). When the Greeks waver on the field of battle the hero Ajax tells them to be men and place shame in their hearts and to feel shame towards each other. Being typically Greek, Ajax also emphasizes the practical advantage of not fleeing – "when men feel shame more survive than are killed and no glory or safety is to be found in flight" (15. 561–64).

But shame acts as a deterrent far away from battle. The goddess Thetis is ashamed to join the deities because of her misery (*Iliad*, 24. 90–91). Women especially must exhibit shame, keeping well out of the way of men: the great glory of a woman, Pericles claims in the Funeral Speech, is to be least talked about by men whether they are praising or criticizing her (Thucydides, 2. 45. 2). What is required of women is similarly applicable to the young: when the young Telemachus came to Pylos in the *Odyssey* in search of news of his father, he is urged to approach the very much older Nestor without hesitation – "You've no need of shame, none at all" – but replies, "How am I to approach him, how shall I address him? That a young man should question an older man is a matter of shame" (*Odyssey*, 3. 14 and 22. 24). Penelope's suitors are said to have no share of shame, since they behave outrageously in another's house (*Odyssey*, 20. 170–71). In the *Iliad* Apollo comments that Achilles, in maltreating the body of the dead Hector, has destroyed pity and has no shame (24. 44–45). He further adds that shame greatly hinders and helps men (45), and this ambiguous quality associated with *aidos* is also acknowledged by Hesiod (*Works and Days*, 318). Shame is no use if you are destitute, merely inhibiting action; then you need to be bold, to exhibit what is termed *tharsos*. When Telemachus and Nestor actually get down to conversation in the *Odyssey*, the former speaks "having been made bold, for Athene herself placed boldness in his heart" (3. 76–77).

PETER WALCOT

Further Reading

Cairns, Douglas L., *Aidos: Psychology and Ethics of Honour and Shame in Ancient Greek Literature*, Oxford: Clarendon Press, and New York: Oxford University Press, 1993

Dover, K.J., *Greek Popular Morality in the Time of Plato and Aristotle*, Oxford: Blackwell, and Berkeley: University of California Press, 1974, reprinted Indianapolis: Hackett, 1994

Walcot, Peter, *Greek Peasants, Ancient and Modern: A Comparison of Social and Moral Values*, Manchester: Manchester University Press, and New York: Barnes and Noble, 1970

Modern

Since 1950, at the end of the Civil War, demographic changes and economic growth in Greece have been rapid and impressive. Most Greeks no longer live in villages and earn their living as peasant farmers. Due to the rapidity of this urbanization process the majority of the Athenian population were either not born in that city, or are the children of parents who were not born there. The extent of its effects, visible in the anarchic physical growth of the city, the widespread ownership of cars, the variety of consumer goods already possessed or on display in shops, in contrast to the decaying mountain villages emptied of their population, easily suggests profound changes in the values and perception that unsophisticated villagers brought with them from their country origins. Attitudes, undoubtedly, have altered in many respects, but changes in the central personal values of popular culture have not yet been fundamental.

In all the variations of local community in Greece the significance of the family is a constant feature. It is not only a domestic association of individuals with affections based on marriage and blood relationship, and a concern for the care and upbringing of children. It is a religious community with icons and other sacred objects, a channel of grace for fertility and protection. It is a corporate enterprise, most obviously so if its main resources are from the land it cultivates, but also in the small manufacturing and retail businesses that are so numerous in Greece. Even where the members of a family work for a wage or a salary (as is increasingly the case) individuals have moral obligations to the family, defined as those who live and eat together in the same house and are protected by the same icons. Among them there is an identity of interest and responsibility. The critical test for any house, and particularly its head, is the honourable settlement of children in marriages that depend on complex property negotiations between families, even where a courtship has its origin in the discovery of personal attractions. Marriage is the proper destiny of every young person and the reputation of a family cannot be subject simply to the play of personal preferences that might result in an unsatisfactory union, or in none at all. Social competition for marriage partners is intense precisely because acceptance of an individual in marriage, which necessarily extends to an acceptance of his or her family, depends on the demonstration of wealth and influence. This is so in both town and country. In these struggles men tend to think of their local world as one of limited resources. The success of one family is seen as depressing the fortunes of another. Secrecy in one's own affairs, and the surveillance of others, are opposite aspects of the same problem. It encourages, indeed requires, a general attitude of wary and intense distrust of all persons who do not live in the same household.

The central traditional value that underlies these institutions is the notion of honour, *time*. Subjectively it expresses an acute awareness of integrity and independence, of not being touched or humiliated before others through particular kinds of failure; outwardly it is the recognition of worth, grudgingly conceded by others. Two sentiments are closely related to it: *philotimo* which is the "love of honour" that encourages a man to act rightly, and therefore is particularly sensitive to any suggestion that he has not done so; and *dropi* (shame), which is the fear of failure that inhibits wrong actions, or a sense of acute discomfort that follows after them. *Time* is related in various ways to a wider complex of value terms, concepts that express ideas about qualities and states of mind such as manliness, self-regard, envy, cleverness, cunning, greed, respect, and self-interest. *Time* itself is applicable to the individual and to any group to which he or she is morally committed, particularly in Greek rural society to the family, the village, and the nation. *Time* emphasizes the moral identity of the individual with the group, so that all members are diminished if an insult is offered to any one of them, and each is responsible to the others for his behaviour and for the public judgement it attracts. As it is popularly understood, the primary reference of *time* is to the moral division of labour within the family, expressed in two sex-linked and complementary qualities, *andrismos*, the manliness of men, and *dropi*, sexual shame in women.

Manliness is, in part, a self-assertive courage and to have it a man must be *varvatos*, that is well endowed with testicles and the strength that is drawn from them. This power, of course, may be ill employed and lead a man to rape or casual killing. The manliness related to honour requires this physical basis but must discipline animal strength and passions to its own ideal ends.

In a fallen world this nobility of men is threatened by the sexuality of women. Only the quality of *dropi*, sexual shame, which implies an instinctive avoidance of sexually provocative behaviour, indeed in traditional communities, an attempt in dress, movement, and attitude not to employ in public the physical attributes of her sex, is an adequate protection of a woman's *time*, her reputation for virginity in the case of a daughter, for fidelity in the case of a wife, against damaging imputations. In reciprocal fashion *andrismos* enables a man to provide for his family and protect its women against insult or assault. Failure in the behaviour required by these values compromises the *time* of all the members of a family and leads to the collapse of its reputation. Such, in very schematic outline, are the principal features of a general moral order in traditional communities. But age is a further dimension that differentiates these values. It is the unmarried son or brother, the *pallikari* or young hero, as yet unburdened by the principal responsibility for a family, who is expected to reply with physical force when an insult is offered. The married head of a family must discipline his anger, establishing the independence and reputation of his family by his astute cleverness, *exypnada*, even, in the world as it is, by lies and cunning.

It will be objected that this pattern of *time* values has little to do with contemporary Greece, an increasingly urbanized and sophisticated society. Social and sexual conventions among the younger generation in Athens appear to be little different from those in other European capital cities. Even remote villages are undergoing a process of embourgoisement. Yet this pattern of values persists at least in a qualified form.

A number of circumstances have contributed to this. The radical definition and complementarity of roles by sex and age in the Greek family, even in a middle-class urban setting, is an important source of its strength and identity, in particular the opposition of *andrismos* and *dropi*, the assertion of manliness and the disciplined attitudes of shame. What does not change is the intense self-regard of men in their competitive struggle for affluence and social status and particularly for the material display of consumer goods such as cars and household furnishings which are markers in establishing a family's social standing. And for women the unchanging sanction of shame still relates to the exceptional value placed on a mother's devotion to her children. It is exactly in this relationship with their mother that children begin to learn these values and the proper behaviour related to them; they accept them as they grow into their appropriate sex roles within the family. In that sense this aspect of rural Greek culture is an intimately domestic culture, and by its nature less easily changed than more external behaviour in the public domain.

Shame also governs the concern of the young woman before her marriage, whatever the accepted relaxations in the conventions of behaviour with members of the opposite sex, to present herself in a manner that is acceptable to candidate bridegrooms and their families. The obligation in the city to arrange an honourable marriage for a daughter remains imperative. Although the control of a family over an unmarried daughter is less secure than in the past, her obligation to her parents and siblings is certainly no less vital and no less subject to her sense of shame. An important aspect of *time* values, therefore, is that these ideas are not semantically linked to particular unchanging details of social behaviour. What is not honourable in one community or at one time may be acceptable in another.

J.K. CAMPBELL

See also Children, Men, Village Society, Women

Further Reading

Campbell, J.K., *Honour, Family and Patronage: A Study of Institutions and Moral Values in a Greek Mountain Community*, Oxford: Clarendon Press, 1964

Herzfeld, M., "Honour and Shame: Problems in the Comparative Analysis of Moral Systems", *Man*, new series 15 (1980): pp. 339–51

Péristiany, J.G. (editor), *Honour and Shame: The Values of Mediterranean Society*, London: Weidenfeld and Nicolson, and Chicago: University of Chicago Press, 1966

Stewart, C, "Honour and Sanctity: Two Levels of Ideology in Greece", *Social Anthropology*, 11/3 (1994): pp. 205–28

Hospitality

The relationship between host and guest, *xenia* ("guest-friendship"), is one of the most hallowed in Greek culture. *Xenia* may exist between two individuals (usually two males), two groups (such as two towns), or an individual (especially a ruler) and a group. For example, Herodotus describes the relationship of Croesus (king of Lydia in the 6th century BC) with the Ionians (1. 27. 50) and Spartans (1. 69. 3) with the term *xenia*. Guest-friendship also existed on an interfamilial and intergenerational level. For example, if a person's father had formed a guest-friendship with another man, the son could expect hospitality from the same household, even if neither the father nor the original host was still alive. In Homer's *Iliad* (6. 215–31) the Trojan Glaucus and the Greek Diomedes break off their duel when they learn that their fathers were guest-friends. The two warriors even exchange gifts, just as their fathers once had. The Homeric ideal carried over into society as is evidenced in the 4th century BC by Demosthenes' speech *Against Polycles* (50.56), which notes how Pasion's son was able to borrow money because of his father's numerous guest-friends. The example of Pasion's son also shows how guest-friendship might also provide a person with relief in times of financial difficulty. Even people who were fugitives from the law or exiled from their native town could expect hospitable treatment (see Demosthenes, 23. 85 (*Against Aristocrates*); Diodorus, 14. 32. 1).

After contact with a stranger was initiated, the guest-friendship was ritualized through the clasping of hands, the partaking of food, and the giving of gifts, especially those given by the host to the guest. The guest could not "insult his host", "demand or take what is not offered", or "refuse what is offered" (Pitt-Rivers, pp. 27–28). On the other hand, the Greek host could not "insult his guest", fail "to protect his guest" or his guest's honour, or fail to be as hospitable as possible (Pitt-Rivers, p. 28). Greek hosts had the added responsibility of providing for the stranger who might arrive unannounced and at an inopportune time. Even if a Greek was approached by a stranger at an inconvenient moment, turning him away was considered disgraceful. The extremes to which a Greek would go to uphold the custom of guest-friendship are displayed in Euripides' *Alcestis* (438 BC), where Heracles arrives unexpectedly at Admetus' home just as Admetus is preparing to bury his wife Alcestis. Despite Heracles' inconvenient arrival, the over-hospitable Admetus refuses to turn him away and even pretends that he is conducting a funeral not for his wife, but for a maidservant.

Besides having to provide for a complete stranger at an inopportune time, Greek hosts seem to have felt compelled to provide the most lavish hospitality possible, even if it was beyond their financial means. In Homer's *Odyssey* the guests of nobles such as Nestor, Menelaus, and Alcinous not only receive the basic amenities (food, drink, and lodging), but are also bathed, given clothing, offered or given transport to their next destination, and given valuable gifts to take with them. Such hospitality recalls the Acragantine Tellias, who lived in the late 5th century BC. Tellias was so wealthy that he had servants stationed at his gates who would invite all strangers who passed by to be his guests. Tellias was even said to have entertained and clothed 500 cavalry from Gela (Diodorus 13. 83. 2). Likewise, Plutarch (*Demetrius*, 12. 1–2) reports that in the late 4th century BC an Athenian proposed that whenever Demetrius I of Macedonia visited Athens he should be provided with the same hospitable honours (*xenismoi*) granted to the divinities Demeter and Dionysus, and that the citizen who was most lavish in his hospitality towards Demetrius should be granted an offering of dedication at public expense. This is in contrast, though, with *Odyssey* 14, where the disguised Odysseus tests the hospitality of his swineherd Eumaeus. Despite Eumaeus' humble estate, the hospitable swineherd provides his guest with food, lodging, and even the cloak off his own back. Odysseus' stay with the swineherd also illustrates the ideal minimum that a stranger might expect from a Greek host.

Hospitality was taken so seriously by the Greeks because the gods themselves were thought to protect strangers. The supreme god Zeus is most often associated with guest-friendship. Homer's Odysseus warns the Cyclops Polyphemus against injuring guests because Zeus would protect strangers (*Odyssey*, 9. 270–71). In another myth Tantalus, who attempted to feed the gods with the flesh of his son Pelops, was killed for this violation of *xenia* and was condemned by Zeus to hunger and thirst perpetually in the underworld. Zeus' punishment of Tantalus is all the more poignant when we consider that some sources make him Zeus' own son. Apollodorus (3. 8. 1) preserves a similar myth about the Arcadian Lycaon. Zeus, having heard that Lycaon and his sons surpassed everyone in their pride, tested them by appearing at their home in the guise of a peasant worker. When they attempted to feed him with human flesh, he destroyed Lycaon and all of his sons (except one saved through Gaia's intervention). Even after the advent of Christianity one still finds references to Zeus as the patron of strangers in Libanius (4th century; *Declamation*, 4. 2. 9), Nonnus (5th century; *Dionysiaca*, 20. 176), and Constantine VII Porphyrogennetos (10th century; *On Virtues and Vices*, 1. 261. 29), to name a few.

As evidenced by the above-cited examples from the *Odyssey*, the importance of proper relations between host and guest is emphasized from the earliest extant Greek literature. Both of the Homeric epics have guest-friendship at their core, and established for the Greeks the ideals of *xenia*. The Trojan War, the backdrop for the *Iliad*, arises out of a violation of guest-friendship as the Trojan Paris abducts Helen, the wife of the Greek Menelaus. Legend has it that Menelaus had entertained Paris in his home for several days before the abduction. Thus, at the heart of Paris' crime is his violation of the custom of guest-friendship (compare Aeschylus, *Agamemnon*, 399–402, 699–708; Euripides, *Trojan Women*, 865–66; Quintus Smyrnaeus, *Posthomerica*, 13. 412–14).

The *Odyssey* "may be viewed as a study in the laws of hospitality" (Pitt-Rivers, p. 13). Odysseus' son Telemachus, as he searches for his long-lost father, enjoys the hospitality of his father's war comrades Nestor and Menelaus. In contrast to his son, Odysseus, returning from the Trojan War, must overcome ogres like the inhospitable Cyclops Polyphemus, who eats several of his men. Eventually Odysseus, having lost all his ships and crew, is transported to his native land thanks to the hospitality of the Phaeacians. When he finally returns home, disguised as a beggar, he is mistreated by the suitors who hope to wed his wife Penelope and have been consuming his estate during his absence. Ultimately Odysseus sheds his beggar disguise and destroys the suitors who, like Polyphemus earlier in the poem, have clearly violated the custom of *xenia*.

Of course, the example of hospitality established in Greek myth and fiction represents an ideal. Still, sources from Greek society show reverence for the bond between host and guest, as well as a tremendous effort to accommodate strangers. In the 5th century BC the guest-friendship between the Spartan Archidamus and the Athenian Pericles led Pericles to believe that when the Spartans invaded Athenian territory Archidamus would avoid Pericles' estate (Thucydides, 2. 13. 1; Plutarch,

Pericles, 8. 4, 33. 2). In the following century Xenophon (*Anabasis*, 3. 2. 4) complains about the treachery of the Persian satrap Tissaphernes who has violated *xenia* and complains particularly about his lack of reverence for Zeus Xenios, "Zeus, the god of hospitality". Xenophon's *Anabasis* contains several references to various towns supplying the Greek army with oxen, sheep, barley-meal, and wine. The people of Sinope, for example, sent the army 1500 jars of wine (*Anabasis*, 6. 1. 15). From the *Anabasis* it becomes clear that the Greek army could not have accomplished their lengthy march without the hospitality of the various towns who provided them with food, drink, and other necessities. In the same century Aeschines' condemnation of Ctesiphon's arrest, torture, and execution of Anaxinus of Oreus is made all the more shocking to his Athenian audience when it is reported that Ctesiphon had formerly dined with Anaxinus in the latter's home. Accordingly, Aeschines claims that Ctesiphon murdered his host, and even claims that Ctesiphon did not deny this charge (*Against Ctesiphon*, 3. 224).

With the advent and spread of Christianity through the Hellenic world, the ideals of *xenia* established by the Homeric epics merged with the new belief system, since the early Christian writings also embraced the ancient ideal of *xenia*. In the Gospel of Matthew (25: 34–46) Jesus praised those who would (among other things) welcome a "stranger" (*xenos*), saying that "whatever you did for one of these least brothers of mine, you did for me". Jesus goes on to say, though, that those who did not (among other things) give a "stranger" welcome would "go off to eternal punishment". Elsewhere in the New Testament the author of Hebrews urges the audience not to neglect hospitality (*philoxenia*), since "through it some have unwittingly entertained angels" (13: 2), an idea reminiscent of the ancient Greek stories such as that of Zeus and Lycaon mentioned above.

The Christian concern for strangers manifests itself in attempts to provide accommodation for them and the poor. In the 4th century AD Basil of Caesarea saw the value in building places for strangers to lodge (*Epistulae*, 94. 1. 36). Procopius (*Buildings*, 1. 2. 14, 17) notes that in the 6th century the emperor Justinian erected in certain cities such buildings, called *xenones* ("rooms for guests" or "rooms for strangers"), for the poor and strangers. Procopius says that the *xenones* at Byzantium were intended as temporary quarters for strangers to the imperial city who found themselves in need of accommodation (1. 11. 27). Justinian took care that similar provisions were afforded to strangers in Antioch, Ciberis, Mocesus, Jerusalem, and Jericho.

Not only would guest-friendship continue to flourish on a public level, but on a private one as well. In a situation similar to that of Archidamus and Pericles, Procopius (*De Bellis*, 3. 9. 5), writing in the 6th century AD, reports that the guest-friendship between the Vandal king Ilderic and Justinian, who had exchanged substantial monetary gifts, was one factor in dissuading the Goth Theodoric from taking revenge against Ilderic and the Vandals for their execution of a number of Goths. A parallel to Pericles' expectation of Archidamus is also found in an anonymous folk song of the 18th or 19th century entitled "Constantine and Arete" (Trypanis, pp. 465–66), where Arete's brother Constantine advocates marrying his sister to a foreigner. Since Constantine would have to serve as a soldier in foreign lands, he reasons that, with his sister married to a foreigner, he would not be considered a stranger if he were in the country of his sister's husband.

The horror evoked by atrocities such as those committed by the Cyclops Polyphemus is echoed in an anecdote from Procopius (*De Bellis*, 6. 20. 27–30). When Belisarius' siege of Urviventus caused utter destitution in the region, two women who lived near Ariminum killed and ate 17 strangers who lodged with them, until the 18th stranger managed to kill them. Writing in the 12th century, Anna Komnene (*Alexiad*, 3. 8. 3) praised Anna Dalassena for allowing her home to be a refuge for poor relatives as well as strangers (*xenoi*). She also notes (*Alexiad*, 15. 7. 3) the concern that her father, emperor Alexios, showed towards prisoners of war and strangers (*xenoi*). While the previous examples show that women could also engage in guest-friendship, in an anonymous folk-song of the 18th or 19th century entitled "The Bridge of Arta" (Trypanis, p. 471) a prophetic bird tells a group of bridge builders, frustrated by the frequent collapse of their bridge, that only by killing a woman, the wife of the bridge's master builder, would the bridge stand firm. The loquacious bird warns the builders, though, that they should not kill an orphan, a stranger, or one who happens to pass by.

Thus, in a culture interwoven with the Homeric ideal and Christianity, the modern Greeks continue to revere the custom of hospitality, although it is no longer as strictly ritualized as in ancient times. Nevertheless, the extension of hospitality to a stranger gives the Greek the opportunity to demonstrate not only to the guest but also to his own neighbours (perhaps what is more important) an outward and visible sign of his wealth and generosity. Thus, the Greek male in particular will extend hospitality not only out of kindness, but also to impress the stranger, as well as to gain "status and respect within the village itself: after all, the ability to consume grandly and to give freely proved the host's success as a winner of wealth" (McNeill, p. 19). Thus, in modern times, the offering of hospitality allows the Greek male to emulate the heroes of his culture.

JOHN E. THORBURN

Further Reading

Finley, M.I., *The World of Odysseus*, 2nd edition, London: Chatto and Windus, 1977; New York: Viking, 1978

Herman, Gabriel, *Ritualised Friendship and the Greek City*, Cambridge and New York: Cambridge University Press, 1987

McNeill, William H., *The Metamorphosis of Greece since World War II*, Chicago: University of Chicago Press, 1978

Pitt-Rivers, Julian, "The Stranger, the Guest and the Hostile Host" in *Contributions to Mediterranean Sociology*, edited by J. G. Péristiany, The Hague: Mouton, 1968

Reece, Steve, *The Stranger's Welcome: Oral Theory and the Aesthetics of the Homeric Hospitality Scene*, Ann Arbor: University of Michigan Press, 1993

Trypanis, C.A. (editor), *The Penguin Book of Greek Verse*, Harmondsworth: Penguin, 1971

Zakythinos, D.A., *The Making of Modern Greece: From Byzantium to Independence*, Oxford: Blackwell, 1976

Hospitaller Knights of St John: Street of the Knights in Rhodes town, which was the headquarters of the Hospitallers from 1309 to 1523

Hospitaller Knights of St John

With the Knights Templar and the Teutonic Knights, the Knights of the Order of St John of Jerusalem, also known as the Knights Hospitallers or Hospitallers, were one of the three great international military orders. The Knights of St John had an obscure beginning. They may have been connected with the Benedictine abbey of Santa Maria Latina in Jerusalem or with another foundation made by the Amalfitans around 1050. Care for the poor and the sick, together with the provision of hospitality to pilgrims, were the core activities of the order and were to remain so after its militarization.

By the mid-1130s, under the mastership of Raymond of Provence (1120–60), the order took on the responsibility of guarding pilgrims on the road from Jaffa to Jerusalem and thus developed the capability to fulfil other military duties such as service with the field army and castle guard. Quite why the order developed in this way is unclear but it may have been connected with the chronic shortage of fighting men in the kingdom of Jerusalem. The order now developed two types of brother: military brothers (knights and sergeants) and brother infirmarians.

With the loss of Acre in 1291 the order turned its back on crusading in the Holy Land and developed in line with contemporary ideas of new directions for active crusading. In 1301, in furtherance of this modernization and in the interests of establishing some sort of equity within this truly international order, the system of *langues*, or national groupings, was introduced.

The order moved first to Cyprus and soon after that conquered the island of Rhodes (1306–09). From this island it was in a good position to play a prime role in naval crusading, protecting western shipping lanes in the Levant and containing Turkish naval aggression, and in turn attacking the Turks and offering advice to others who might resist the advance of the Ottomans. Apart from Genoese and Venetian flotillas, the order was the sole western military force capable of offering assistance to the shrinking territory of Byzantium.

After 1312 the Hospitallers became the most powerful order in Greece, where they acquired the former Templar lands in Achaea and in Crete. Interestingly, the Templar lands in central Greece passed to Gautier de Châtillon, the guardian of the claimant to the duchy of Athens and Thebes which was then ruled by the Catalans. Under the mastership of Juan Fernández de Heredia (1377–96) the Hospitallers' involvement in Greek lands increased dramatically. The island of Rhodes was limited by its size and economic capacity, while the spearhead of the Turkish advance was moving to the southern Balkans. Remedy appeared to be at hand in a five-year lease of the principality of Achaea negotiated with Joanna of Naples in 1377. In the first instance Achaea would act as a springboard for an attack on the despotate of Arta and thus provide the order with territories to exploit economically and from which to resist the Turk. The scheme fell through, but negotiations continued through the 1380s. In 1399 the Greek governor of Mistra ceded Corinth and Mistra to the order for a year because of the invasion of Yakoub Pasha. The order successfully defended the isthmus of Corinth and less successfully tried to galvanize resistance to the Turks along the northern shore of the Gulf of Corinth. By 1404, largely due to local Greek hostility, the order withdrew from southern Greece. One lasting monument to Heredia and to the involvement of the Knights Hospitallers in Greece is the Aragonese/Castilian version of the *Chronicle of Morea*, which was copied on Heredia's orders in 1377. The *Libro de los fechos et conquistas del principado de la Morea* relates the history of the Latin empire and the principality of Achaea from 1200 to 1377 and incorporates much additional information not contained in the French and Greek versions of the chronicle.

PETER LOCK

Summary

One of the military orders formed in the crusader states, the Knights of St John abandoned the Holy Land in 1291 and moved first to Cyprus and then to Rhodes (1309–1523). From there they wielded considerable power in Greece throughout the 14th century and helped to mount a defence against the Turks.

Further Reading

Lock, Peter, *The Franks in the Aegean, 1204–1500*, London and New York: Longman, 1995

Luttrell, Anthony, *The Hospitallers in Cyprus, Rhodes, Greece and the West, 1291–1440*, London: Variorum, 1978

Luttrell, Anthony, *Latin Greece, the Hospitallers and the Crusades, 1291–1440*, London: Variorum, 1982

Riley-Smith, Jonathan (editor), *The Oxford Illustrated History of the Crusades*, Oxford and New York: Oxford University Press, 1995

Sire, H.J.A., *The Knights of Malta*, New Haven, Connecticut and London: Yale University Press, 1994

Humanism

The label "humanism" has been applied to many different, sometimes incompatible, viewpoints. In relation to Greek cultural history, three attitudes may be characterized as paramount: (1) the humanism of Homer and of "Classical" Greece; (2) the humanism inspired by Byzantium-in-exile during the Italian Renaissance; and (3) the "secular humanism" that is the bête noire of much (though not all) traditional religious piety.

For some scholars, the question raised by the humanism of Homer concerns Homer's religious notions, which seem "more advanced and more civilized" than the superstitious practices of Greeks during some later times. How, they wonder, was it possible for Greek culture to regress from Homer's insights, especially given the centrality of the Homeric texts in Classical Greek education?

While such worries may be easily brushed aside (as presupposing an unrealistically "linear" conception of religious enlightenment), there is a much deeper conception of the humanism of Homer. Moses Hadas presents the Homeric ideal as summarized in the line (*Iliad*, 6.208 and 11.784): "to strive always for excellence and to surpass all others". The humanism of Homer represents, he holds, "the authentic peculiarly Greek view", to be contrasted with the "deviation" of Plato and others.

> The goal of excellence, the means of achieving it, and...the approbation it is to receive are all determined by human judgment. The whole outlook, in other words, is anthropocentric: man is the measure of all things. This

does not imply that there are no gods…The important point is that the sphere of the human and the sphere of the divine are disparate…Other items in our Greek legacy are only trimmings or implications of the central doctrine of man the measure.

Whatever may be the best understanding of Homer and of Classical Greece, it is beyond dispute that during the so-called Renaissance in Italy, beginning in the late 13th and early 14th centuries – even as Thomas Aquinas and Dante Alighieri were summing up medieval thought – and lasting for perhaps three centuries, the effect of texts from the Classical period of Greek history was such as to make Renaissance humanism a vital chapter in the story of the emergence of the modern world. The literature on the Renaissance is vast and controversial (for example, concerning the question of how many "renaissances" there were), so its relevance here must be limited to two aspects. First, there is the fact that the Renaissance conception of life's ideals involved concepts and images derived (albeit in sometimes distorted form) from classical Greece. Second, there is the fact that this enormous effect was mediated, if not entirely caused, by the interventions of a small number of Byzantine émigrés during the latter days of Byzantium.

In 1204 Constantinople fell for the first time, to a sidetracked group of Crusaders. Though the city was reclaimed in 1261, its days were numbered. The Byzantine scholar Manuel Chrysoloras was brought to Florence in 1396–97 to teach Greek. Deno Geanakoplos, a prominent 20th-century historian of the period, judges that "the tremendous impetus given to the study of Greek literature in the Renaissance may be ascribed in great part to his teaching." Four decades later, in 1438–39, the Council of Florence met, with the purpose of trying to reunite the Greek and Roman churches. It did not succeed in that aim, but George Gemistos Plethon, who attended as part of the Byzantine delegation, gave lectures on Plato that raised great interest in Florence and led Cosimo de' Medici to found an academy in Florence for the study and translation of Platonic texts. Johannes Bessarion, a former student of Plethon's who was also in the Byzantine delegation, subsequently became a Roman Catholic ecclesiastic and the foremost patron of Greek émigré scholars. In 1453 Constantinople fell to the Turks, and the Byzantine empire effectively expired, occasioning a further flow of emigration. There is little doubt that these Greek-speaking émigrés, along with the texts that they (as well as Latin travellers) brought west, played a major role in the development of humanist ideas in Italy and subsequently in the rest of Europe, whatever other factors may have contributed.

Reading Greek (and teaching it) was not for these émigrés the accomplishment that it would have been for an Italian, of course, and this has led some scholars to question the intellectual eminence and originality of the émigrés, pointing out the limited, strictly philological character of their accomplishment. To assay the justice of such aspersions is beyond our present task, but it seems safe to agree with Arnold Toynbee's assessment: "The refugee Greek instigators of Greek linguistic and literary studies in the West have played a more important part in Modern Western history than in Modern Greek history." He is thinking, of course, of the direct impact of the Renaissance. Indirectly, the effects may be of enormous consequence, to the extent that the changes encouraged by Renaissance humanism

(including, in the view of some, increased secularism, naturalism, and materialism) can be viewed as determining the overwhelming challenge posed by the West to the rest of the world. As Toynbee observes:

> We are all having to try to make life possible and endurable in the artificial manmade environment that has been substituted for our former natural environment by the astonishing modern advance of technology. The Western peoples are not exempt, though the West was the local workshop in which this modern advance was carried out.

And then he adds, of the Greeks: "No other surviving non-Western people has had to contend with pressure from the West for as long."

The nature of Renaissance humanism has been much debated. Paul Oskar Kristeller, the author of many books on the subject, is "unable to discover in the humanist literature any common philosophical doctrine, except a belief in the value of man and the humanities and in the revival of ancient learning". There is also much debate about the value of the reverence for Classics thus instilled. "The humanist movement in the West began as a Latin revival", Deno Geanakoplos says, "but the restoration of Greek letters served perhaps more than any other single factor to expand its intellectual horizon." Toynbee, to the contrary, credits the "Hellenic paideia" with having "prevented the emergence, in the Byzantine Age, of a cultivated literature in Modern Greek", and believes that it "hypnotized Western men of letters" and "held the Western educated public spellbound" during the Renaissance. Only towards the close of the 17th century, he claims, did westerners find "the courage to think and investigate for themselves". Of course, what they proceeded to think for themselves was precisely that religious and scientific ferment that eventuated in the "modern secularizing rationalizing movement", which in turn has produced the politics and technology through which the West has, for good and for ill, unsettled the world.

In this context, it is easier to understand the remark of the Greek soldier quoted by Patricia Storace in her remarkable book, *Dinner with Persephone*:

> The fault is with humanism, the humanism of the Renaissance, which places man at the center of the Universe where God should be, man in all his arrogance, egoism, and materialism. This is why we are in a world where we destroy the environment and value money above life, this idea of the greatness of humanity.

Storace comments (with uncharacteristic derision) that it is "hard to imagine a more arrogant and uncomprehending dismissal of humanism, whatever its flaws." She has a point, of course. The soldier's diatribe hardly does justice to the intentions or achievements of humanism's pious agnostics, let alone Christian humanists such as Erasmus, or the fideist Montaigne, who imbues his humanism with a spirit of toleration and generous curiosity. And yet the soldier's words carry a challenge not to be lightly evaded.

Greek has been the vehicle of Christianity since the New Testament was first written down, and the Eastern Orthodox Church has viewed itself as preserving in authentic form some of Christianity's oldest ritual and liturgy. Greece today continues to be pervaded by Christian belief specifically and, more broadly, by various forms of religious belief and practice that may strike some as "superstitious" when compared with the humanistic religion of Homer. The central Christian conviction, that God "so loved the world", runs counter to the idea that the worlds of gods and of human beings can go about their separate business, unconcerned with one another's existence. "St Socrates" is a quintessential humanist figure because he questions claims of exclusive knowledge lodged by "humanists", on behalf of the all-sufficiency of the "human", just as energetically as he questions the unthinking piety of Mr Orthodox. Renaissance humanists rejected (some) dogma, not religion, though in the long run, as the case of Erasmus illustrates, this set the stage for the Reformation.

In its long-term impact, humanism is helped by links to notions such as freedom and democracy. The link between humanism and freedom comes through the connection between the concepts of humanity and civilization. As Gilbert Murray notes, humanity (what distinguishes human life from that of other animals) requires a buffer against mere necessity which civilization provides:

> To the Greeks civilization begins when men live in a *polis*...He has leisure, and for the first time can begin to do what he wants to do, and not simply what he must do in order to live. The Greeks were fond of distinguishing between *to anagkaion*, the "necessary", the thing you must do because you are compelled, and *to kalon*, "the beautiful", as we clumsily translate it; the thing that looks good, that you desire for its own sake...Civilization...sets man free to live the life he really desires, to study the things that really interest him, and not merely the things which other people compel him or pay him to do.

The link between humanism and democracy comes through the connection between the concepts of humanity and experience. Walter Pater, in an influential discussion of the Renaissance, describes humanism as centred on a sense of the permanent value of the experience of human beings: "the essence of humanism is that belief...that nothing which has ever interested living men and women can wholly lose its vitality" (Pater, "Pico della Mirandola", 1873). In a similar spirit, Gilbert Murray insists that "a scholar...secures his freedom by keeping hold always of the past. He draws out of the past high thoughts and great emotions." And about the "religion of Democracy", Murray says that "the cardinal doctrine of that religion is the right of every human soul to enter, unhindered except by the limitation of its own powers and desires, into the full spiritual heritage of the [human] race." Strictly speaking, democracy is a step beyond humanism, but if one agrees, in Terence's famous words, *homo sum: humani nihil a me alienum puto* ("I am a man; nothing human is alien to me"), then the step, from the value of all human experiences to the democratic value of all human beings, may seem a small one.

Or it may not. The centrality of competition in ancient Greek culture has been often noted. Hadas, among others, sees competition as part of the humanist heritage, "and perhaps the central and all-subsuming factor in our Greek legacy". How to mediate between the doctrine that man is the measure and the doctrine that nothing human is foreign, how to combine a belief in human excellence with a respect for all human beings, remains humanism's puzzling bequest.

EDWARD JOHNSON

See also Freedom

Further Reading

Bolgar, R.R, *The Classical Heritage and Its Beneficiaries*, Cambridge: Cambridge University Press, and New York: Harper and Row, 1954

Bolgar, R.R., "The Greek Legacy" in *The Legacy of Greece: A New Approach*, edited by M.I. Finley, Oxford: Clarendon Press, and New York: Oxford University Press, 1981

Geanakoplos, Deno John, *Greek Scholars in Venice: Studies in the Dissemination of Greek Learning from Byzantium to Western Europe*, Cambridge, Massachusetts: Harvard University Press, 1962; as *Byzantium and the Renaissance: Greek Scholars in Venice*, Hamden, Connecticut: Archon, 1973

Geanakoplos, Deno John, *Constantinople and the West: Essays on the Late Byzantine (Palaeologan) and Italian Renaissances and the Byzantine and Roman Churches*, Madison: University of Wisconsin Press, 1989

Hadas, Moses, *Humanism: The Greek Ideal and Its Survival*, New York: Harper and Row, 1960; London: Allen and Unwin, 1961

Highet, Gilbert, *The Classical Tradition: Greek and Roman Influences on Western Literature*, Oxford: Clarendon Press, and New York: Oxford University Press, 1949, reprinted 1985

Jardine, Lisa, *Worldly Goods: A New History of the Renaissance*, London: Macmillan, and New York: Talese, 1996

Kelley, Donald R., *Renaissance Humanism*, Boston: Twayne, 1991

Kristeller, Paul Oskar, *Renaissance Concepts of Man and Other Essays*, New York: Harper and Row, 1972

Kristeller, Paul Oskar, *Renaissance Thought and Its Sources*, edited by Michael Mooney, New York: Columbia University Press, 1979

Livingstone, R.W., *Greek Ideals and Modern Life*, Oxford: Clarendon Press, and Cambridge, Massachusetts: Harvard University Press, 1935

Makdisi, George, *The Rise of Humanism in Classical Islam and the Christian West*, Edinburgh: Edinburgh University Press, 1990

Morris, Colin, *The Discovery of the Individual, 1050–1200*, New York: Harper and Row, and London: SPCK, 1972

Murray, Gilbert, "Religio Grammatici: The Religion of a 'Man of Letters'" (1918), in his *Humanist Essays*, London: Allen and Unwin, and New York: Barnes and Noble, 1964

Murray, Gilbert, "Humane Letters and Civilization" (1937), in his *Greek Studies*, Oxford: Clarendon Press, 1946

Pater, Walter, *Studies in the History of the Renaissance*, London: Macmillan, 1873; reprinted as *The Renaissance*, edited by Adam Philips, Oxford and New York: Oxford University Press, 1986 (includes the essay "Pico della Mirandola")

Reynolds, L.D. and N.G. Wilson, *Scribes and Scholars: A Guide to the Transmission of Greek and Latin Literature*, 3rd edition, Oxford: Clarendon Press, and New York: Oxford University Press, 1991

Runciman, Steven, *The Last Byzantine Renaissance*, Cambridge: Cambridge University Press, 1970

Storace, Patricia, *Dinner with Persephone: Travels in Greece*, New York: Pantheon, 1996; London: Granta, 1997

Toynbee, Arnold, *The Greeks and Their Heritages*, Oxford and New York: Oxford University Press, 1981

Wilson, N.G., *Scholars of Byzantium*, revised edition, London: Duckworth, and Cambridge, Massachusetts: Medieval Academy of America, 1996

Hunting

Up to the end of the classical period hunting was pursued mainly to supplement a largely vegetarian diet and to protect flocks and homesteads against predators, chiefly wolves and jackals. Myths abound of heroes such as Heracles, Meleager, and Theseus slaying beasts that ravaged their neighbourhoods. Hunting imagery is common in Homer, who describes Odysseus killing for the pot (*Odyssey*, 9. 154[-58; 10. 156–71). Homer's huntsmen go on foot with bow or spear, accompanied when not abroad by hounds. The quarry was chiefly deer, wild goats, and boars. The last of these must have been plentiful since the tusks of some 30 to 40 boars were required to provide the plates that gave strength to a single example of one type of Mycenaean helmet. The hunting of lions, mentioned by Homer only in similes, is uncertain, although fragments of bones have been found at Tiryns in contexts of *c.*1230 BC and lion hunts are depicted on a few pieces of Mycenaean art, such as a late 16th-century BC bronze dagger inlaid with figures of an archer and spearmen with huge shields fighting a pride. Mycenaean bows were "self" bows (from a single stave of wood), although the composite bow, which was probably introduced in the Dark Age, was clearly known to Homer; spears were generally, if not exclusively, for thrusting rather than throwing. There is pictorial evidence for the use of nets in catching boars (although they are not mentioned in Homer's famous description at *Odyssey*, 19. 428–58), stags, and wild cattle (probably the auroch and possibly the wisent) and also for hunting from chariots (despite the unsuitabilty of the terrain). One fragmentary mid 13th-century fresco from Tiryns uniquely depicts huntresses amid the men.

In the Archaic age Spartans hunted game to supplement the meagre diet of their common messes, while in Attica aristocratic men, as is shown principally in vase-paintings, presented younger males with live and dead game as lovers' gifts and, probably, also as tokens of their own manliness.

The principal source of information for hunting in the Classical period is Xenophon's *Cynegeticus* ("The Hunting Man"), which deals principally with nets, dogs and their training, and the hunting of hares, although deer, boar, and other large mammals are mentioned. He warns against allowing hounds to chase foxes, since this ruins them for hunting hares. Although for Xenophon its primary purpose is still for the pot, he does recommend hunting as excellent training for not only warfare, since it fosters hardiness, discipline, and initiative, but even civic responsibilities, in both of which he is supported by Plato (*Laws*, 822d–824c). Presumably for these reasons there was a law at Athens which permitted hunting through standing crops. There is evidence, however, that the development of democratic ideas, of which both Xenophon and Plato highly disapproved, had engendered an adversely critical reaction against hunting as an unnecessary aristocratic extravagance, and that the growth of population had in Attica reduced the extent of accessible terrain for the activity.

The favourite breed of hound for hunting hares (and even boars because of its superior tracking abilities) was the Laconian, of which there were in Xenophon's day two breeds neither of which is recognizable today. The larger was perhaps 45 cm high at the shoulder with a weight of 13 to 18 kg. All hounds wore leather belts, collars, and, for ease of slipping,

separate leashes. The hunters, sometimes wielding curved throwing-sticks, followed most commonly on foot (for Xenophon horses were used only to get to and from the hunt). The hares, when found by the hounds and started, were caught in nets of flax. Purse nets were set in narrow defiles: the mouth was propped open by sticks which fell when the hare hit the net, whereupon the net-watcher (presumably a slave) drew tight the skirting-line. Larger road nets were stretched across paths and long nets, up to 55 m in width, in level open areas both caught hares and diverted them to the purse nets.

Deer (red, roe, and probably fallow) could be caught in nets and, in summer when they tired easily, run down by hounds before being pierced by the hunters' javelins. In spring fawns left concealed by their mothers were tracked and caught to attract hinds. Hunters also used carefully concealed foot snares. These consisted of a wooden clog attached to a noose which lay on a plaited ring of yew with inward-facing iron and wooden nails placed over a hole. The clog both hampered the deer's flight and left an easily visible trail.

The animal most prized by hunters was the boar, whose slaying without the use of nets was deemed by the Macedonians the token of manhood (the unreliable Hegesander reportedly claimed that even at the age of 35 the future king Cassander had still to sit in a chair by his father like an adolescent for his failure to accomplish the deed). Whether caught by a foot snare or driven out of a covert, the boar was a match for hounds and hunters armed with javelins and a thrusting spear especially designed with projecting teeth on the socket to prevent the beast running up the shaft.

Xenophon mentions also (*Cynegeticus*, 11) that in the Pindus range, Thrace, Mysia, and Syria "lions, leopards, lynxes, panthers, bears, and similar wild beasts" were caught by means of poisoned bait and pitfalls to which they were lured by tethered goats.

Fowling was practised principally by professionals, who were generally despised by the literary elite. Plato considers the art unbecoming to a gentleman (*Laws*, 823e), although Xenopohon is on one occasion kinder (*Cyropaedia*, 1. 6. 39). The trapping of fur-bearing animals such as otters and martens was similarly not deemed an honourable pursuit by the aristocracy, although it was quite common despite a lack of the fashionable modern sartorial relish for furs. The fowlers' main quarry was partridges, pheasants, quails, doves, and various smaller birds. Their favourite aids were purse nets, snares, and the use of glutinous birdlime (often made from mistletoe berries) which was either smeared on the twigs of trees or on rods which could be fitted into each other to attain the desired length. Tamed females of the hunted species were employed for decoys, as were also owls since during daylight these are often mobbed by small birds. Aristotle (*Historia Animalium*, 620a33–b6) and others mention the Thracian technique of depending upon wild hawks to drive back to the ground birds started by the fowlers. A mid 2nd-century AD North African mosaic shows a fowler camouflaged by a goatskin. From close observation knowledge of the nature and habits of the animals and birds frequently hunted was extensive and extended remarkably even to leporine superfoetation (the female hare's ability to become pregnant again before the birth of an earlier set of leverets).

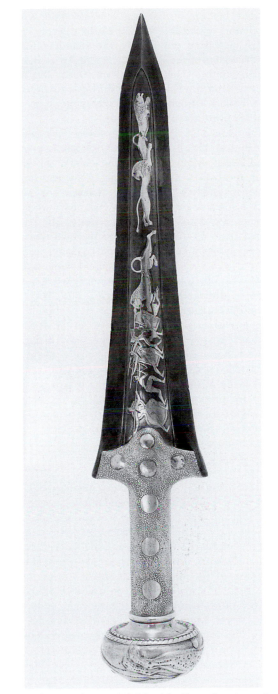

Hunting: bronze dagger inlaid with silver showing a hunting scene on its blade, 1600–1550 BC, from Mycenae, Ashmolean Museum, Oxford

hounds and caught within a single year over 6000 hares, descendants of two introduced from Anaphe some years before.

For the Roman period the main sources are the *Cynegeticus* of Arrian (*c*.AD 86–160), a section (5. 17–86) on hunting in the slightly later thematically arranged dictionary (*Onomasticon*) of Pollux and, in the early 3rd century, an often fanciful hexametric poem in four books (*Cynegetica*) falsely attributed to Oppian which mentions a huge variety of animals from the elephant and rhinoceros to the hedgehog. Arrian, writing under the pseudonym of Xenophon the Younger, is primarily concerned with updating the work of his predecessor by giving information on a Celtic breed of gazehound, probably a type of greyhound unknown to the Classical Greeks, which transformed the hunting of hares. It was now coursing on horseback rather than hunting on foot, the principal aim being the pleasure of the chase rather than the capture of the animal: indeed Arrian proposes that the hare always be given the opportunity to get clear of its form and claims (16. 5–7) to have often himself saved a hare that had run well, a point on which he specifically criticizes Xenophon, who says only (*Cynegeticus*, 5. 14) that "lovers of the chase leave the very young leverets for the goddess (Artemis)". A further innovation in hunting at this period seems to be the use of a cord with brightly coloured feathers to frighten game towards nets. The *venatio* of the amphitheatre so enjoyed by the Romans was not to Greek taste, but hunting became a military duty both to provide wild animals for the games and to protect local livestock.

In Byzantium the rural population continued hunting and fowling for the table, and the former also for protection of livestock, with little change in techniques. The upper class hunted for pleasure and for military training, most enthusiastically in the 12th century when Constantine Manasses and Constantine Pantechnes, among others, wrote *ekphraseis* (descriptions) of the sport. Hunting imagery formed, as in the East, an important element in imperial symbolism. Three emperors (Theodosius I, Basil I, and John II Komnenos) are all reported to have lost their lives in this pursuit; Liutprand (*Antapodosis*, 3. 25) attributes Romanos I Lekapenos's rise to power to his single-handed slaying of a lion; and Andronikos I had himself depicted as a hunter cutting up and cooking venison and wild boar. Aristocrats hunted deer, bear, and boar on horseback both in the wild and, especially from the 10th century, in imperial game parks. The principal weapon was the spear, while dogs and even cheetahs and leopards were trained for the hunt. Most popular among smaller game were hares and quails.

Falconry, although it had been practised from the late Roman period, became an aristocratic enthusiasm chiefly again in the 12th century. Falcons and goshawks, especially from Georgia, were the preferred birds. Various manuals on the subject were produced including the *Hierakosophion*, attributed to the late 14th-century Demetrios Pepagomenos, which deals expertly with breeding, training, and diseases and contains some remarkably precise observations on ocular worms.

During the Tourkokratia, and for a considerable time after, hunting and fowling were perforce entirely utilitarian, the major changes being the addition of the gun to the hunters' weaponry and the greatly reduced use of both hound and horse. In the 20th century hares were still the commonest

Although during the Classical period hunting parties had been small, Alexander's conquests enabled the Greeks of the Hellenistic period to indulge in vast hunts like the Persians, whose game parks were imitated especially in Seleucid Syria. "Hunt clubs" appeared in Macedon for upper-class males and, for the royalty of the Successor Kingdoms – in imitation of oriental predecessors – hunting tropies enhanced prestige. There is evidence too from the 3rd century BC of hunting as a form of pest-control, when, on the advice of the Delphic oracle, the inhabitants of the island of Astypalaia acquired

quarry, while deer and boar were shot in the north of the country. Fowling was completely replaced by shooting, mainly of partridges, woodcock, pigeons, quails, ducks, and geese. Until the mid-1980s laws governing gun-licensing were commonly flouted, headlights illegally used to dazzle game, and closed seasons for hunting poorly enforced. Since then some stocks have improved.

A.R. LITTLEWOOD

See also Animals, Fishing

Further Reading

Anderson, J.K., *Hunting in the Ancient World*, Berkeley: University of California Press, 1985

Hull, Denis Bingham, *Hounds and Hunting in Ancient Greece*, Chicago: University of Chicago Press, 1964 (includes translations of Xenophon and Arrian's *Cynegeticus* and relevant portions of Pollux' *Onomasticon*)

Karpozilos, A., "Basileiou Pediate Ekphrasis Haleoseos Akanthidon" [Basil Pediates's Description of Linnet-Catching], *Epeirotika Chronika*, 23 (1981): pp. 284–98

Koukoules, Phaidon I., "Kynegetika ek tes Epoches ton Komnenon kai ton Palaiologon" [Hunting Manuals from the Times of the Komnenoi and Palaiologoi], *Epeteris Hetaireias Byzantinon Spoudon* [Annual of the Society for Byzantine Studies], 9 (1932): pp. 3–33

Koukoules, Phaidon I., *Byzantinon Bios kai Politismos* [Byzantine Life and Culture], vol. 5, Athens, 1952, pp. 387–423

Lane Fox, Robin, "Ancient Hunting: Homer to Polybios" in *Human Landscapes in Classical Antiquity: Environment and Culture*, edited by Graham Shipley and John Salmon, London and New York: Routledge, 1966

Patlagean, E., "De la Chasse et du sovereign", *Dumbarton Oaks Papers*, 46 (1992): pp. 257–63

Hydra

Aegean island

Hydra is located near the mouth of the gulf of Argos, separated by a 6-km-wide strait from the eastern Peloponnese. It is 20 km long and between 1.5 and 5 km wide. Hydra is mountainous and only a minor part of the land is arable. According to legend, water used to be abundant on the now almost waterless island. Some have even attributed the name of the island to that fabled abundance. In the past Hydra was covered by pine woods, but today they have diminished. The island has several monasteries, but many of them are abandoned. Nowadays the island is a renowned summer resort due to its natural beauty and proximity to Athens.

In ancient times Hydra was an unimportant but inhabited place, as archaeological findings reveal. It is not known exactly when its modern residents settled there. But it is commonly agreed that in 1460 and later many Greek-Orthodox Albanians, under threat of persecution by the Turks, were forced to retreat to the precipitous isle for security reasons. These Albanians were descendants of the Albanians brought by the despots of Mistra, Manuel Kantakouzenos and Theodore Palaiologos, to the Pelopponese in order to supplement the populace decimated by the Turks. The Albanian settlers on Hydra initially attempted to raise cattle and culti-

vate the land, but the surface was so rocky that it scarcely yielded common vegetables. Because of the infertile land and the steadily increasing population, the islanders turned to fishing in the waters of the Peloponnese and Attica in order to support their families. This activity came to an end with the Turkish invasion of the Peloponnese during the 16th century. In fear of Turkish atrocities, many Peloponnesians fled to Hydra and remained there permanently.

Over the years, Hydra became a haven for persecuted Greeks, including rebels from Epirus, Souli, Euboea, Asia Minor, and Attica. Many of them founded family dynasties. More refugees came to the island during the 16th and 17th centuries when raids by pirates and atrocities by Turks, in response to help given by Greeks to Venice in its wars against the Ottomans, devastated many Greek regions. The absence of adequate resources on the island forced the Hydriots to trade with the neighbouring Peloponnese and Cyclades in order to supplement their income. This trade required ships, rather than small boats, and consequently a large number were built. With the signing of the Treaty of Carlovitz (1699) between the Sultan, Venice, Germany, and Poland, Hydriot ships were free to sail not only to nearby waters but also to the open sea, as the immediate fear of Turks had disappeared. Through trade the islanders became first-class navigators and wealthy. Hydriots travelled not only in the seas of the Ottoman empire but also to many western European and Russian ports. Their trade consisted primarily in transporting the produce of the Ottoman empire to other areas of the Mediterranean, and in bringing home cargoes of manufactured articles. The chief export was grain, not only from the plains of the empire but also from abroad. Hydriots and Spetsiotes had a virtual monopoly of the trade in Russian wheat.

During the campaign of the Orloff brothers against the Sublime Porte (1768–74) Hydra refused to take part in the war against the Ottomans and subsequently was bombarded by the Russians. The business of the islanders greatly benefited from the Treaty of Kutchuk Kainardji (1774) that marked the end of the war, and also from the favour shown by the sultan to the island because of its stand against the Russians. Hydriots gained the right to arm their ships in order to defend themselves from pirates, a privilege that turned the island into a great naval power. Moreover, subsequent agreements permitted Hydriot ships to raise the Russian flag, rendering both the ships and their owners immune from any kind of Turkish interference or persecution. During the Napoleonic Wars most Hydriots ignored the continental embargo imposed by Great Britain on France and became very wealthy in the process. They were able to extend their commercial and shipping business all over the Mediterranean, Atlantic Ocean, and even to America. During the war between Russia and the Ottoman empire (1807), empty assurances by the Russians tempted the islanders to revolt against the Turks. The consequent settlement between the two enemies left Hydra defenceless and at the mercy of the Turks. A disaster was avoided by the efforts of Evgenios Voulgaris, the *kodjabashi* (headman) of the island, who actively opposed a revolt against the sultan.

On the eve of the Greek War of Independence (1821) Hydra was the richest region in Greece. It had a population of 26,000 and more than 100 large, armed vessels. However, with the end of the Napoleonic Wars, the islanders' trading operations fell

Hydra: the harbour front is distinguished by a number of rich merchants' houses dating from the late 18th century

into recession. The Society of Friends (*Philiki Hetaireia*) had for several years conscripted volunteers from the island, but by the start of the war the notables were opposed to it, whereupon Captains Antonios Oikonomou and Lazaros Kountouriotis overthrew the authorities and proclaimed a revolution. By public demand, the notables finally took part in the fight for independence. The contribution of Hydra to the War of Independence was huge. Together with Spetsai and Psara, it not only provided a fleet well trained in fighting but also valuable financial assistance. Hydra produced heroes such as Captains Andreas Miaoulis, Iakovos Tompazis, who destroyed the Turkish navy, and Kountouriotis, who committed all of his belongings to the war. Such were the achievements of the island that it was aptly named the Greek Venice and Little England. The acknowledgement of its contributions to the War of Independence came in 1844 when the first National Assembly in Athens granted to Hydra alone the privilege of electing three members of parliament. During the administration of Count Kapodistria, when there were differences over reconstruction and compensation for lost ships, partly due to the authoritarian style of the governor, Hydra became an anti-Kapodistria centre and revolted against him. In the following years the island lost its economic power and Syros became the chief centre of commerce.

Hydra possesses a rich cultural tradition as it is the birthplace of several famous artists including the painters N. Nikolaou and P. Tetsis and the painter-architect-sculptor Nikos Hadjikiriakos-Ghikas (1906–94). Since 1939 the School of Fine Arts of the National Technical University has had a department in Hydra at which many prominent artists have taught. A number of well-known painters have been attracted by the natural beauty of the island and have made it their permanent residence.

DIMITRIOS GKAMAS

Summary

This island near the mouth of the gulf of Argos had an undistinguished history until the Tourkokratia (1453–1821) when it became a haven for persecuted Greeks from elsewhere. The islanders began to trade widely and acquired great wealth and a fleet of fighting ships with well-trained crews. They were therefore well placed to make an important contribution to the War of Independence in the 1820s. The island is now an artists' colony.

Further Reading

Angelomatis-Tsougarakis, Helen, *The Eve of the Greek Revival: British Travellers' Perceptions of Early Nineteenth-Century Greece*, London and New York: Routledge, 1990

Clogg, Richard (editor and translator), *The Movement for Greek Independence, 1770–1821: A Collection of Documents*, London: Macmillan, 1976

Finlay, George, *A History of Greece from Its Conquest by the Romans to the Present Time, BC 146 to AD 1864*, revised by H.F. Tozer, 7 vols, Oxford: Clarendon Press, 1877, reprinted New York: AMS Press, 1970

Michaelides, Constantine E., *Hydra, a Greek Island Town: Its Growth and Form*, Chicago: University of Chicago Press, 1967

Hymnography

The history of Greek hymnography encompasses the devotional and liturgical poetry of paganism and Orthodox Christianity, as well as Byzantine parahymnography. The first examples of hymnography to survive in their entirety are the *Homeric Hymns,* hexameter compositions that were presumably sung by soloists as preludes (*prooimia*) to heroic epic. Pindar and Baccchylides were early composers of two types of choral hymns: paeans, which were sung by soldiers, in private social life and at public festivals; and processionals (*prosodia*), sung as part of the pageantry that could precede a sacrifice. Examples of hymns written to accompany the sacrifices themselves survive in Hellenistic or Roman inscriptions on temple walls. Other complete and fragmentary texts from these later periods, accompanied in exceptional cases by musical notation, have been preserved in manuscripts and papyri. These range from the *Orphic Hymns* (of around the 2nd century AD) – 87 poems from Asia Minor that constitute the only surviving ancient Greek hymnal – to a papyrus fragment of the late-3rd century AD containing the first Christian hymn to have survived with its music.

With the exception of this latter composition in praise of the Holy Trinity and a few other such hymns without musical notation, it is difficult to discern the boundaries between Christian hymnography, psalmody, scripture, and homiletics prior to the 4th century. Although scholars have found abundant hymnic material in the New Testament and deuterocanonical or apocryphal texts, they have generally been unable to identify its provenance or liturgical use. The highly poetic Easter homily of Bishop Melito of Sardis (2nd century), which some have seen as a precursor to the works of Ephraim the Syrian and Romanos the Melodist, may similarly contain echoes of contemporary hymnody. Two hymns by Clement of Alexandria, on the other hand, are probably non-liturgical compositions.

Following the legalization of Christianity, the pressures of pervasive heresy and large numbers of new converts led the Church to regulate its worship by defining a canon of scripture, assigning the performance of chants to ordained specialists, and suppressing all but the most venerable *idiotikous psalmous* ("private psalms"). As a result, only a few ancient hymns – for example, the *Phos Hilaron* for evening prayer – remained in services that were coalescing around presidential prayers and biblical psalmody, the singing of which had recently been popularized by the ascetics of the Egyptian desert. Unlike the monks, who would recite the Psalter as a contemplative exercise, urban Christians chanted select psalms or canticles with newly composed refrains. Those of one

sentence or more were called *troparia,* examples of which include the *Trisagion Hymn* and "Only Begotten Son", a summary of the Nicene Creed attributed to Justinian.

Despite the efforts of Gregory of Nazianzus and Synesius to write extended hymns in quantitative metres, most Christian hymnography in late antiquity employed accentual metres and a relatively popular form of the Greek language. Moreover, the development of hymns more complex than *troparia* in the 5th century appears to have been partially in response to the isosyllabic metrical sermons of such Syriac authors as St Ephraim. Two forms of Byzantine hymns seem especially dependent on Syriac precedents: the isosyllabic *kata stichon* hymns; and the kontakion, which came to maturity in 6th-century Constantinople with the works of St Romanos the Melodist. A kontakion consists of at least one preface (*proimion* or *koukoulion*) introducing the subject of the hymn and its (presumably congregational) refrain, followed by a series of metrically identical strophes (*oikoi*) united by an acrostic that may render the alphabet, the author's name, or the feast commemorated. In keeping with their origins as poetic sermons, kontakia were originally performed paraliturgically between the offices of an all-night cathedral vigil (*pannychis*).

Exchange between the liturgies of the Holy Sepulchre and the monastery of Mar Saba following the destruction of Jerusalem in 614 gave birth to a flourishing school of hymnography represented by such luminaries as Sophronios of Jerusalem, Andrew of Crete, John of Damascus, and Kosmas of Maiouma. Disregarding monasticism's traditional suspicion of hymnody and melodious psalmody, these *melodoi* (hymnographers composing their own melodies) prolifically composed *stichera, kathismata,* and canons to adorn the psalms and canticles of the Palestinian monastic rite on Sundays and the major solemnities of the liturgical year. *Stichera* and *kathismata* are *troparia* that may possess a unique melody (*idiomelon*), or be contrafacta (*prosomoia*) of a standard tune (*automelon*). A comparable system of model melodies is found in canons, long multi-stanza poems consisting of up to nine "odes" of *troparia* farcing (being interpolated into) two or more of the nine canticles of the morning "canon of psalmody". Each ode of a kanon, which is somehow thematically related to its host canticle, features a model stanza (*eirmos*) followed by metrically identical *troparia.*

Sabaïtic hymnography was decisively introduced to Constantinople in 799 when the monastery of Studios adopted the Palestinian Liturgy of the Hours at the behest of its abbot, St Theodore, who was himself a *melodos*. As Studite monasticism spread from southern Italy to Kievan Rus, hymnographers of the Studite school – including Theodore, his brother Joseph of Thessalonica, Theophanes Graptos, Joseph the Hymnographer, Kassia, and many others – systematically filled gaps between the festal propers of the older Sabaïtic collections. The completion in the 11th century of cycles of hymns covering each day of the fixed and movable cycles of the liturgical year established the corpus from which have been extracted the 15 volumes of proper texts currently employed by the Orthodox Church. One result of these developments was a shift towards hymnography as the favoured medium for communicating theology in Orthodox worship, the impact of which was magnified by the growing tendency to read prayers silently and omit the biblical texts that Sabaïtic hymns were written to accompany. Another consequence was the rise of Byzantine parahymnography, that is didactic or satirical poems employing the metres of well-known hymns to enhance their memorability.

From the twilight of Byzantium until the present day, the occasional creation of new feasts has required the composition of hymns in established genres by writers ranging from Theoleptos of Philadelphia and Symeon of Thessalonica to Alexandros Papadiamantis and Metropolitan Nikodemos (Vallendras) of Patras. Hymns composed outside the Sabaïtic mainstream include vivid and presumably non-liturgical poems by Symeon the New Theologian, as well as a wide variety of late and post-Byzantine *troparia* for the festal psalms of the Palestinian all-night vigil (*agrypnia*). Relatively few of the latter – which include short Trinitarian *anoixantaria* (opening) for Psalm 103, the popular *Lamentations* for the singing of Psalm 118 during matins on Holy Saturday, and more substantial compositions in 15-syllable verse – are included in modern service books. Instead, many appear in musical manuscripts or printed chant books in settings by such composers as John Koukouzeles and Manuel Chrysaphes.

ALEXANDER LINGAS

Further Reading

Briere, Elizabeth A., "Scripture in Hymnography: A Study in Some Feasts of the Orthodox Church" (dissertation), Oxford University, 1982

Conomos, Dimitri E., *Byzantine Trisagia and Cheroubika of the Fourteenth and Fifteenth Centuries: A Study of Late Byzantine Liturgical Chant*, Thessalonica: Patriarchal Institute for Patristic Studies, 1974

Conomos, Drimitri E., *Byzantine Hymnography and Byzantine Chant*, Brookline, Massachusetts: Hellenic College Press, 1984

Deiss, Lucien, *Springtime of the Liturgy: Liturgical Texts of the First Four Centuries*, Collegeville, Minnesota: Liturgical Press, 1979

Grosdidier de Matons, José, "Liturgie et hymnographie: kontakion et canon", *Dumbarton Oaks Papers*, 34–35 (1980–81): pp. 31–43

Hadjisolomos, Solomon (Solon) J., *The Modal Structure of the 11 Eothina Anastassima Ascribed to the Emperor Leo (†912)*, Nicosia: Kykko Monastery, 1986

Høeg, Carsten (editor), *The Hymns of the Hirmologium*, vol. 1, Copenhagen: Munksgaard, 1952 (*Monumenta Musicae Byzantinae Transcripta*, 6)

Jeffery, Peter, "The Earliest Christian Chant Repertory Recovered: The Georgian Witnesses to Jerusalem Chant", *Journal of the American Musicological Society*, 47 (1994): pp. 1–39

Lingas, Alexander, "The Liturgical Use of the Kontakion in Constantinople" in *Liturgy, Architecture and Art in the Byzantine World*, edited by Constantin C. Akentiev, St Petersburg, 1995

Lingas, Alexander, *Sunday Matins in the Byzantine Cathedral Rite: Music and Liturgy*, Amsterdam: Harwood, forthcoming

McKinnon, James, *Music in Early Christian Literature*, Cambridge and New York: Cambridge University Press, 1987

Mary, Mother and Kallistos Ware (editors and translators), *The Festal Menaion*, London: Faber, 1969

Mitsakis, Kariofilis, "Byzantine Parahymnography" in *Studies in Eastern Chant*, vol. 5, edited by D. Conomos, Crestwood, New York: St Vladimir's Seminary Press, 1990

Quasten, Johannes, *Music and Worship in Pagan and Christian Antiquity*, Washington, D.C.: National Association of Pastoral Musicians, 1983

Stathis, Gregorios T., *E Dekapentasyllbos Ymnographia en ti Byzantini melopoiia* [Fifteen-Syllable Hymnwriting in Byzantine Musical Composition], Athens, 1977

Strunk, Oliver, *Essays on Music in the Byzantine World*, New York: Norton, 1977

Taft, Robert F., *The Byzantine Rite: A Short History*, Collegeville, Minnesota: Liturgical Press, 1992

Tillyard, H.J.W., "Eothina anastasima: The Morning Hymns of the Emperor Leo", *Annual of the British School at Athens*, 30 (1928–30): pp. 86–108; and 31 (1930–31): pp. 115–47

Tillyard, H.J.W. (editor), *The Hymns of the Octoechus*, 2 vols., Copenhagen, 1940–49 (*Monumenta Musicae Byzantinae Transcripta*, 3 and 6)

Topping, Eva C., *Sacred Songs: Studies in Byzantine Hymnography*, Minneapolis: Light and Life, 1997

Trypanis, C.A. (editor), *The Penguin Book of Greek Verse*, Harmondsworth: Penguin, 1971

Velimirović, Miloš, "The Musical Works of Theoleptos, Metropolitan of Philadelphia", in *Studies in Eastern Chant*, vol. 2, edited by Velimirović and Egon Wellesz, Oxford: Oxford University Press, 1971

Velimirović, Miloš, "The Byzantine Heirmos and Heirmologion" in *Gattungen der Musik in Einzeldarstellungen: Gedenkschrift Leo Schrade*, vol. 1, edited by Wulf Arlt et al., Bern: Francke, 1973

Wellesz, Egon, *A History of Byzantine Music and Hymnography*, 2nd edition, Oxford: Clarendon Press, 1961

West, M.L., *Ancient Greek Music*, Oxford: Clarendon Press, and New York: Oxford University Press, 1992

Williams, Edward V., "A Byzantine *Ars Nova*: The 14th-Century Reforms of John Koukouzeles in the Chanting of Great Vespers" in *Aspects of the Balkans: Continuity and Change*, edited by Henrik Birnbaum and Speros Vryonis, Jr, The Hague: Mouton, 1972

Wybrew, Hugh, *The Orthodox Liturgy: The Development of the Eucharistic Liturgy in the Byzantine Rite*, London: SPCK, 1989; Crestwood, New York: St. Vladimir's Seminary Press, 1990

Hypatia *c.*370–415
Mathematician and philosopher

Among the female mathematicians of antiquity, Hypatia is certainly the best known and, sadly, the only one about whom we have information other than a mere reference. She has attracted enormous attention in modern times and has been exalted to legendary proportions especially by scholars who study the gender difference in scientists. Perhaps much of our idealized image of her has been influenced by the romantic novel *Hypatia, Or New Foes with an Old Face* (1853), by the Classical scholar and historian Charles Kingsley.

There was also a biography written in 1720 by John Toland, a deist. The author uses Hypatia's example in an effort to defame Christianity and especially Cyril, the archbishop of Alexandria, whom he holds responsible for Hypatia's tragic death. In chapter 47 of his influential and widely read *The Decline and Fall of the Roman Empire* (1776–88) Gibbon uses eloquent and emotional language to describe both the beauty and tragic events of Hypatia's death, holding responsible the Christians and their archbishop, Cyril. Whatever the events in relation to Hypatia's murder in AD 415, one thing is certain: they became a chief source of her immortality to the extent that 415 is often considered the seminal date that divides paganism from Christianity. If the closure of the school of Athens by Justinian in 529 is not a suitable conventional date for the end of paganism, then 415 is certainly a good alternative.

There are several primary sources about Hypatia's life. One is a long, but unfortunately in some respects self-contradictory article in the *Suda*. Others are John Malalas's *Chronographia*, Socrates' *Historia Ecclesiastica*, and the letters sent to her by her most famous student and friend Synesius, later bishop of Ptolemais. All these can be found in Migne's *Patrologia Graeca*. Other sources are John of Nikiu's *Chronicle*, the *Historia Ecclesiastica* by Philostorgius, and a brief reference to her in Photios's *Bibliotheca*, in his summary of Damascius' (lost) *Life of Isidorus*. The above-mentioned sources, all Christian and generally favourable to Hypatia, fail to agree on who is to blame for her death.

There is no firm date for Hypatia's birth but it is generally given as around AD 370. This is partly because eclipses described by her father, the astronomer Theon, have been dated to AD 364. Hypatia was a chaste person and a respectful teacher of mathematics and Neoplatonic philosophy in Alexandria. Wearing the cloak of a rough cynic philosopher she taught in public to an audience consisting of both pagans and Christians (Synesius himself was a pagan who later converted to Christianity, to become bishop of Ptolemais). According to the *Suda*, Hypatia wrote commentaries on Diophantus, on the *Astronomical Canon*, and on Apollonius' *Conics*. (The text in the *Suda* has been variously interpreted; it may mean, for example, that there were just two commentaries, the one being Diophantus' *Astronomical Canon*. For various reasons, however, it seems safer to assume that it refers to a separate work of Diophantus, presumably the *Arithmetica*, and then to Ptolemy's *Almagest* or the *Handy Tables*.) Hypatia also collaborated with her father on a commentary on book 3 of Ptolemy's *Almagest* since the text includes the phrase "this book was revised/edited (*paranagnostheisa*) by the philosopher, my daughter Hypatia". A quotation in one of Synesius' letters stating that Hypatia helped him to design an astrolabe shows the breadth of her knowledge. In yet another letter Synesius requested her to construct a hydrometer (*hydroskopeion*) according to his detailed instructions.

There is no doubt that Hypatia was the leading mathematician of her time. However, it seems that no specific original contributions to mathematics or astronomy can be attributed indisputably to her. Whatever her contributions, if any, they are either lost or perhaps diffused in her commentaries. Like her father, she is mostly remembered for her teaching.

The most detailed and reliable account of Hypatia's death was narrated by the historian Socrates some 25 years later. At the time described, there was considerable tension and rivalry between the Jews and the Christians of Alexandria. In those difficult times the prefect of Alexandria, Orestes, and the archbishop, Cyril, known for his harsh way of dealing with the heretic Nestorius, opposed each other. Some 500 monks from the monasteries in Nitria, referred to as savages by the *Suda*, came into town to support Cyril. They accused Orestes (who had been baptized a Christian) of being a pagan and sacrificing to the Greek gods in spite of the emperor Theodosius' ban of all pagan cults. When a monk named Ammonius was tortured to death for hurling a stone at the prefect, Cyril and many moderate Christians found this action intolerable. The pro-Cyril mob turned against Hypatia, Orestes' close associate. Although the prevailing opinion is that Cyril was directly to blame, there is no evidence that he actually gave any such orders or knew of the mob's intention. Indeed, John of Nikiu is even favourable to Cyril, calling Hypatia a pagan magician, and Philostorgius puts the blame on a pro-Arian mob. Be this as it may, Hypatia was stripped and violently dragged to the cathedral where she was killed and subsequently cut to pieces with sharp oyster shells. Her dismembered body was then taken to a location called Dog's Place (Kynarion) and finally burned.

MICHAEL LAMBROU

See also Astronomy, Mathematics

Biography
Hypatia was born in Alexandria about 370. Largely educated by her father Theon, she went on to teach mathematics and Neoplatonic philosophy in Alexandria. She also wrote commentaries on earlier mathematical works. She met a violent end at the hands of a mob in her native city in 415.

Further Reading
Deakin, M.A.B., "Hypatia and Her Mathematics", *American Mathematical Monthly*, 101/3 (1994): pp. 234–43

Hubbard, Elbert, *Little Journeys to the Homes of Great Teachers*, 2 vols, East Aurora, New York: Roycrofters, 1908

Knorr, Wilbur Richard, *Textual Studies in Ancient and Medieval Geometry*, Boston: Birkhäuser, 1989

Mueller, I., Hypatia entry in *Women of Mathematics: A Biobibliographic Sourcebook*, edited by Louise S. Grinstein and Paul J. Campbell, New York: Greenwood Press, 1987

Rist, J.M., "Hypatia", *Phoenix*, 19 (1965): pp. 214–25

I

Icon

The term "icon" is derived from the Greek *eikon*, meaning an image or picture. It is still used in this sense in modern Greek. In a more restricted sense, an icon is a religious image depicting either holy figures or narrative scenes. As a holy image, the icon is the paramount statement of the Orthodox faith, a reflection and statement of the divine.

The holy subject matter can be depicted in a variety of artistic mediums, such as ivory, enamel, mosaic, and fresco. In a narrower sense, an icon is a cult image shown on a wooden panel. Icons in the sense of panel paintings come in a variety of sizes, ranging from small panels no more than 10 × 15 cm to panels ten times larger. The wooden panels may be combined to form diptychs or triptychs. Some icons are painted on both sides (bilateral icons).

The wood chosen for Byzantine icons includes cypress, lime, elder, cedar, and pine. The panel is usually made up of several planks of wood that are held together by strips of wood nailed onto the back, while the front is sometimes hollowed out to create a frame around the outside. Several layers of gesso, consisting in the main of chalk, are applied to the wooden panel to create a smooth surface for the paint. At times, a piece of woven cloth is placed over the wood and beneath the gesso to prevent irregularities in the wood from appearing on the surface of the icon. The next step is the preparation of an outline drawing. Those areas of the icon that are to receive gold leaf are coated in a bole (a layer of clay, usually red). In the early Byzantine period the pigments were suspended in wax encaustic. After iconoclasm the predominant binding medium is egg tempera (the yolk of an egg). Sometimes, a cover consisting of different metal plates is laid over the wooden icon. In some instances the plates cover the entire figure apart from the hands and face; in others it is only the background that is concealed.

Some icons combine painting with relief sculpture. In these, which date in the main from the 12th and 13th centuries and appear to originate in northern Greece, the saint is shown in relief and is surrounded by painted scenes from his or her life. Metal icons were also made in the Byzantine Period, but few survive. The Treasury of San Marco in Venice contains an 11th-century metal icon in high relief of St Michael which is elaborately decorated with enamel. A number of metal icons in low relief survive from Georgia. Another subgroup are steatite icons. In the late Byzantine period, icons were also made in mosaic. Minute tesserae, consisting of glass, semiprecious stones, or gilded copper were added to a bed of wax or resin on a wood support.

The making of icons is considered a spiritual activity. Manuals for the guidance of icon painters survive from the post-Byzantine period, such as the 18th-century *Painter's Guide* of Mount Athos by Dionysios of Phourna. Icons are displayed in churches, homes, and public places – a statement that was probably as true for the Byzantine world as it is for present-day Greece. In an Orthodox church icons are displayed on icon stands (*proskynetaria*) or on the iconostasis, a tall opaque barrier separating the sanctuary from the nave. The iconostasis developed only in the late Byzantine period and found its fullest expression in the Russian and post-Byzantine Greek Orthodox Church. The iconostasis developed out of the templon, a transparent sanctuary partition that consisted of a low barrier and columns supporting a transverse beam. Icons, which often depicted pivotal scenes from the life of Christ, were placed on top of the beam known as the epistyle. It was only at certain points of the liturgy that the altar was concealed from the congregation by curtains being drawn. The templon was transformed into the iconostasis when icons became permanently fixed in the spaces between the columns.

Different types of icons are venerated in the Orthodox Church. They can be classified according to subject matter and their presumed origin. Byzantine and modern icons typically show Christ, the Theotokos (Mother of God), saints, and narrative scenes from the life of Christ or the saints. Among the holiest icons in Orthodox belief are those believed to have come into existence without human agency. These are known as *acheiropoietos* icons ("made without hands") which, for instance, depict the imprint of Christ's face on a cloth. An example are icons showing the Mandylion of Edessa, a relic that in the 10th century was sent to Constantinople where it stayed until the conquest of the city in 1204 by the participants of the Fourth Crusade. Another type of especially holy icon are portraits supposedly painted with the authorization of the person portrayed. The most famous example of this type of portrait is the image of the Theotokos and the Christ Child attributed to St Luke. Although a number of icons attributed to St Luke exist in Italy and elsewhere, only one is recorded for Constantinople: this is the icon of the Theotokos Hodegetria, which was kept in the Hodegon monastery. Even though lost,

Icon: icon painting is a living tradition on Mount Athos

again between 815 and 843 the use of figurative images was banned. Icons were destroyed and icon painters, often monks, persecuted.

Both the opponents of image veneration, the iconoclasts, and the supporters of icons, the iconodules, developed sophisticated theological arguments in support of their views. The iconoclasts argued that images of Christ, who, in his divine form, could not be depicted, undermined the belief about the two natures of Christ. Another iconoclast argument was that the use of images was idolatrous because both the person depicted and the material of which the image was made were venerated. By contrast, iconodule theologians, such as John of Damascus, rebutted iconoclast arguments by arguing that the icon in its materiality was distinct from the person depicted (prototype). It was the prototype, or the reality behind the image, not the icon itself that was venerated. The theology developed in support of image veneration during iconoclasm firmly established the central role of icons in Orthodox belief.

The use of icons proliferated after the end of the iconoclast controversy. Icons survive in increasing numbers from the 12th century onwards. A famous example is the icon of Vladimir, showing the Theotokos holding the Christ Child in a way that emphasizes motherly love. New types of subject matter developed. A late 12th-century icon in the Sinai collection depicts a text written by the Sinaite monk John Klimakos, known as the *Heavenly Ladder*. This icon shows monks ascending a ladder towards spiritual perfection while other monks are pulled off the ladder by black demons. From about 1200 onwards some icons combine the image of the saint with depictions of scenes from his or her life on the border of the icon; these icons are known as *vita* icons. Calendar icons depict the saints venerated during a particular month of the year (menologion icons).

Believers express their veneration of icons by kneeling in front of them, lighting candles, kissing the image, and making the sign of the cross. *Tamata*, offerings frequently in the shape of metal plaques referring to a wish granted or an illness cured, are sometimes attached to the image. In Byzantium the miraculous powers of icons were harnessed by using them as palladia. They were carried in battle or displayed on the walls of a city during a siege. The carrying of icons in religious processions is attested for the Byzantine period and persists in present-day Greece. In Constantinople, for instance, the icon of the Theotokos Hodegetria was displayed publicly every Tuesday, an event that is referred to in several written sources. According to the Spanish traveller Pero Tafur, who visited Constantinople in the early 15th century, the icon was carried by members of a confraternity dressed in red robes. Onlookers were overcome with emotion and handed bits of material, described as cotton wool, to the confraternity members, asking them to bring it in contact with the icon in order to sanctify the material.

BARBARA ZEITLER

numerous copies record the appearance of this cult image: the Christ Child is shown seated on the left arm of the Theotokos who points at him with her right hand. This icon was the most important cult image in Constantinople, probably from about the 11th century onwards, and formed the centre of an elaborate cult (see below).

The icon depicting the portrait of a saint finds its origin in Late Antique funerary portraits painted in encaustic, of which the best-known examples originate from the Fayum in Egypt. The earliest extant icons – a number of 6th- and 7th-century icons kept in the collections of the monastery of St Catherine at Mount Sinai – resemble the Fayum funerary portraits in both format and technique. There are not many icons from the pre-iconoclast period. The early icons at Sinai survive partly because of the area's desert climate, and partly because the Sinai peninsula no longer formed part of Byzantine territory at the time of the iconoclast controversy.

The use of figurative images was a concern to theologians throughout the early Christian period. Central to this debate was the Old Testament prohibition against "graven images" (Exodus 20:4–5). In Byzantium the Old Testament prohibition had particular consequences for depictions of Christ who, according to Orthodox belief, was both human and divine in nature. These concerns, alongside other factors of a political and social nature, led to the iconoclast controversy in the 8th and 9th centuries. From the middle of the 720s to 787 and

Further Reading

Barasch, Moshe, *Icon: The History of an Idea*, New York: New York University Press, 1992

Belting, Hans, *Likeness and Presence: A History of the Image before the Era of Art*, Chicago: University of Chicago Press, 1994

Cormack, Robin, *Painting the Soul: Icons, Death Masks, and Shrouds*, London: Reaktion, 1997

Dubisch, Jill, *In a Different Place: Pilgrimage, Gender, and Politics at a Greek Island Shrine*, Princeton, New Jersey: Princeton University Press, 1995

Maguire, Henry, *Icons of Their Bodies: Saints and Their Images in Byzantium*, Princeton, New Jersey: Princeton University Press, 1996

Weitzmann, Kurt, *The Icon*, London: Chatto and Windus, and New York: Braziller, 1978; reprinted London: Evans, and New York: Knopf, 1982

Iconoclasm

Iconoclasm forbade the making or "veneration" of images, whether of God or of the saints. Condemnation of holy images was nothing new in Christian thinking: it was dominant in the early Church, and the elements that derived from Jewish law were reinforced by Greek philosophy, from the Presocratics to contemporary pagan Neoplatonic thinking. Such expressions as Eusebius' *noera ousia* ("spiritual essence") and Clement of Alexandria's *noete ousia* ("immaterial essence", a term ultimately derived from Plato) represent the Greek side of Christian thinking and helped expand the simple biblical interdiction into a range of theological arguments.

The rise of iconoduly (icon veneration) is poorly documented. Veneration of the icon for itself – a particular image at a particular shrine – had only recently (from the 6th century on) become a major phenomenon and such pro-icon theologians as Leontios of Neapolis of the late 6th century faced considerable opposition. But however strongly felt, the option had remained a matter of personal choice. The public setting up of images by the emperor did not change this, but forbidding of them did.

Icon veneration took very ambiguous forms: prostrations, incense, hymns chanted, prayers addressed to the image itself; the image, not the saint behind it, made godparent of one's child, etc. The emperor Leo III (716–41) reckoned that this was tantamount to idolatry, and by an edict of 730 he forbade it. The iconodule historians nearest to the time whose work survives, Theophanes the Confessor and the patriarch Nikephoros (806–15), say that it was the eruption of Thera in 726 that determined Leo III's decree; he was right, they say, in assuming that God was angry, but his erroneous diagnosis of the reason led to even worse impiety. The evidence suggests that the veneration of images would have remained "impiety", and not become "heresy", if it had not been perceived as having political potential.

Few historians still hold the view that iconoclasm was the most important affair of the period, with every Byzantine deeply involved in it, except for a servile episcopate. In fact the Establishment and the army took it in their stride; most monasteries were in communion with the iconoclast official Church; and even at the time of Constantine V's "war on monks" many, probably most, monks were unquestionably in communion with it. St Theodore of Stoudios, the most redoubtable of the iconodule apologists, notes indignantly that rejecting icons "was not at first recognized for heresy, and still seems to some only moderately wrong" (he himself discovered how wrong it was only when he was looking for an issue over which to fight the patriarch). The iconoclast emperors enjoyed exceptional popularity with the urban masses. Not everyone became iconoclast, they simply accepted the situation; no doubt most people continued to venerate their own icons in their homes.

Besides the bias of the sources the other trap that the subject offers is reducing the question to one of theology and "persecution". Such an issue was bound to become theological, but Leo's concern was with practice; the iconodule opposition turned the question into a purely theological one: could God be represented? The answer was that according to the "new dispensation" (Christianity as against "the Law", i.e. Judaism), God incarnate could be depicted. Iconodule theologians reserved *latreia* ("worship") for God, allowing icons only *proskynesis*, which may be translated as "adoration", addressed, in theory, not to the image but to the person it stood for.

When he decided to forbid the veneration of images, Leo III held public meetings to explain his policy and win support for it: "He summoned all his subjects to a rally, and presiding in their midst like a roaring lion, belched forth from his angry heart, fire and sulphur, like Mount Etna, and pronounced these grievous words: 'The making of icons is a craft of idolatry, they may not be worshipped'" (*Vita Stephani*, chapter 9). Constantine V also sought support from the people:

> The tyrant ... shouted "My good luck has won the day and God has heard my prayer." The crowd cheered and shouted: "When did God ever close His ears to you?" Overjoyed he said with a great laugh: "The Lord has discovered to me the man I was looking for. Shall I show him to you?" The crowd roared back "Punish him! Kill him! Burn him, for disobeying your orders!"

Emperor and people had had similar dialogues in the circus in Rome. Constantine did much to raise living standards for the people in Constantinople.

When Leo initiated iconoclasm by removing an image of Christ from one of the palace gates, "distressed crowds in the capital destroyed a few of the emperor's men who were taking down the image, and many of them were punished for their piety with amputations, exiles, and confiscations". In fact, these were normal legal proceedings after a riot and, according to the historian, no one was condemned to death.

The most famous iconodule "martyr" was St Stephen the Younger (died 764), who was involved in a plot to overthrow the emperor. The punishments or "tortures" inflicted on the "martyrs" and "confessors" were, except for the tattooing of the Graptoi brothers, laid down in the law codes. Iconodule zeal manifested itself through lawbreaking, when it did not involve treason. The iconodule patriarch, Nikephoros, deplored law-abiding under the iconoclast emperors: too many of the clergy, he said, "uphold political laws and recognize civil authorities ... This is not Jacob's heritage, nor are such the ways of those whose dogma and thinking are ordered by piety." The undermining of army morale appears to have been one approved strategy of militant iconoduly: St Theodore of Stoudios, consulted as to whether the canonical condemnation to three years' excommunication of any soldier who killed an enemy on the battlefield should be applied, said that it must: "If they don't want to be excommunicated let them stop killing" (Letter 51). But both attempting to overthrow rulers and inciting the military to disobedience and even desertion in

Iconoclasm: illustration from the Chludov Psalter (c.850–75) drawing a parallel between the whitewashing of an image of Christ (bottom) and the soldier giving Christ bitter vinegar to drink, State Historical Museum, Moscow.

time of war constituted major offences, the penalties for which, recounted with religious horror by the victims' supporters, were those established by the law.

"Iconomachy in action is monachomachy", said Peter Brown. At no time, under iconoclasm, were all the monasteries under attack. For Leo III, the *Ekloge*, the law code he promulgated, is evidence enough that monks as such were not under attack (cf. chapter 7.1: allocating guardianship of orphans whose parents had not named a guardian to religious establishments explicitly including monasteries; chapter 8: conferring freedom on a slave who has become, with the knowledge and consent of his master, a cleric or a monk). Iconoclasm was given dogmatic status by the Council of Hiereia in 754. But icon veneration was restored in 780 and confirmed at the Second Council of Nicaea in 787.

During the second period of iconoclasm (815–43) communion with the patriarch was the test of Orthodoxy, and the operation was made as easy as possible: "All we ask of you is to commune once with Theodotos [the patriarch] ... then you will be free to go out, each to his own monastery, keeping your own belief and opinions" (*Vita Niketa Medikion* 824). It is quite clear from the evidence of his own *Vita* that the austere Ignatios, the future patriarch, was abbot of a monastery in communion with the iconoclast official Church. War was not waged on monasteries so long as they were not out to provoke trouble, except under Constantine V (741–75). He designated monks officially as "the unnamed" (*amnemoneutoi*, a technical term from the *Ekloge* law code for a son disinherited for misbehaving towards his parents), and staged in the Hippodrome a ritual desecration of the monastic habit (after 763: *Vita Stephani* chapter 40). It has been suggested that his aim was to recover potential soldiers, but one might go further: at that time of desperate need, the monks did not supply food, but consumed it; this body of men, several thousand strong and exerting great influence, isolated itself completely from the war effort, and expected to be supported. Nonetheless Constantine did not wage war on monasticism for the first 20 years of his reign, and the apparently sudden change might well be related to the plot referred to above. Whatever the answer, at no point were all the monasteries in difficulties even with him.

Why did iconoduly win in the end? Could it be because of the two female regents, Irene in 780 and Theodora in 842? Not because women were particularly given to veneration, but because these two both loved power. Backed by power groups condemned to remain in the background, such as well-chosen civil servants – eunuchs, ideally – and churchmen, they could hope to enjoy it; the alternative, entrusting their interests to a general, meant surrendering power completely. Neither empress has a dossier that suggests deep personal commitment to icons. Irene ensured for herself the support of safe elements, and once things were well in hand, treated her supporters to tax relief.

Similarly, for Theodora, almost the only fact to emerge clearly from the confusion of the sources on the "Restoration of Orthodoxy" – as the aftermath of Theophilos's death is termed – is the presence of potential male candidates, who might have kept her on as nominal "empress", but without power; and therefore she looked for support from men who could not themselves be emperor. If Irene's case is mainly

deduction, Theodora's hagiographic *Life* states that, so long as her husband lived, she "dared not" allow her iconoduly to be discernible. Naturally, when it became the official policy of the throne, an appropriate image of her was diffused and some of the material has survived.

The victorious iconodules promptly fell out with the new patriarch, Methodios, and his backers ranged against the Stoudites. In due course the row was tidied up, and in successive versions of the *Life* of the great (iconodule) St Joannikios, acid remarks about prominent Stoudites are made "politically acceptable" by simply speaking of unidentified "cantankerous monks".

The measure in itself has been given a weight by modern historians that it certainly did not carry. The "age of iconoclasm" should be termed "the age of iconodule sources": Theophanes and Nikephoros, though militant iconodules, remain historians, giving far more space to foreign or dynastic affairs and natural calamities, but many of our sources are the actual weapons left over from the conflict – letters and pamphlets from the most active proponents, hagiographic accounts written to conceal the fact that the "martyr" had been involved in attempted treason, or, on the contrary, to prove that a convent had not been in communion with the "heretics". These documents come almost exclusively from the winning, iconodule side. The 368 letters of the militant and unscrupulous St Theodore of Stoudios, the accounts of the "martyrdoms" of six iconodule saints, are extremely vivid, and it is only recently that Byzantinists have begun to look at them critically.

Two tangible consequences of the iconoclast affair are recognizable. If the conflict had never arisen, art would have developed differently. If iconoclasm had won, presumably for the time being church decoration would have been very much like that surviving in a few mosques: trees, flowers, and gardens; it is also possible that more profane art would have survived, not necessarily only the Hippodrome scenes that iconoclast emperors are condemned for having commissioned. That the saints would have returned seems likely, but perhaps more willing to share the available space with other images.

Obviously icons had already found a central place in the religion of the Eastern Church, but all except a small minority adapted without any difficulty to official iconoclasm. This suggests that, if the two iconoclast interludes changed the position of icons very little, the "Restoration of Orthodoxy" was a different matter. Leo III had claimed only to enforce well-known divine commandments; converting this to a theological debate, followed by victory for the side that took iconoduly for its emblem, made dogma of a field that was formerly open to individual choice, and gave it an extraordinary new emphasis.

PATRICIA KARLIN-HAYTER

See also Constantine V, Germanos, Icon, Irene, John of Damascus, Leo III, Theodora (d. 867), Theodore of Stoudios

Further Reading

Alexander, Paul Julius, *The Patriarch Nicephorus of Constantinople: Ecclesiastical Policy and Image Worship in the Byzantine Empire*, Oxford: Clarendon Press, 1958

Brown, Peter, "A Dark-Age Crisis: Aspects of the Iconoclastic Controversy", *English Historical Review*, 88 (1973): pp. 1–34

Brubaker, Leslie, "Politics, Patronage and Art in Ninth-Century Byzantium: The Homilies of Gregory Nazianzus in Paris (B.N. gr. 510)", *Dumbarton Oaks Papers*, 39 (1985): pp. 1–13

Bryer, Anthony and Judith Herrin (editors), *Iconoclasm*, Birmingham: Centre for Byzantine Studies, 1977

Bury, J.B., *A History of the Later Roman Empire from Arcadius to Irene, 395 AD to 800 AD*, vol. 2, London and New York: Macmillan, 1889, reprinted Amsterdam: Hakkert, 1966

Bury, J.B., *A History of the Eastern Roman Empire from the Fall of Irene to the Accession of Basil I, AD 802–867*, London and New York: Macmillan, 1912, reprinted New York: Russell, 1965

Charanis, Peter, *Church and State in the Later Roman Empire: The Religious Policy of Anastasius the First, 491–518*, 2nd edition, Thessalonica: Kentron Vyzantinon Erevnon, 1974

Corrigan, Kathleen, *Visual Polemics in the Ninth-Century Byzantine Psalters*, Cambridge and New York: Cambridge University Press, 1992

Devreesse, Robert, *Les Anciens Commentateurs grecs des Psaumes*, Vatican: Biblioteca Apostolica Vaticana, 1970

Frolow, A., "La Fin de la querelle iconoclaste et la date des plus anciens psautiers grecs: illustrations marginales", *Revue de l'Histoire des Religions*, 163 (1963): pp. 201–23

Galavaris, George, *The Icon in the Life of the Church: Doctrine, Liturgy, Devotion*, Leiden: Brill, 1981

Gero, Stephen, *Byzantine Iconoclasm During the Reign of Leo III*, Louvain: Corpus SCO, 1973

Gero, Stephen, *John the Grammarian, the Last Iconoclastic Patriarch of Constantinople: The Man and the Legend*, Uppsala: Nordisk Tidskrift för Byzantinologi, 1974–75, pp. 25–35

Gero, Stephen, *Byzantine Iconoclasm During the Reign of Constantine V*, Louvain: Corpus SCO, 1977

Hennephof, Herman, *Textus byzantinos ad Iconomachiam pertinentes*, Leiden: Brill, 1969

Ladner, G.B., "The Concept of the Image in the Greek Fathers and the Byzantine Iconoclastic Controversy", *Dumbarton Oaks Papers*, 7 (1953): pp. 1–34

Mango, Cyril, *The Brazen House: A Study of the Vestibule of the Imperial Palace of Constantinople*, Copenhagen: Munksgaard, 1959

Nikephoros, Patriarch of Constantinople, *Short History*, translated by Cyril Mango, Washington, D.C.: Dumbarton Oaks, 1990

Theophanes the Confessor, *The Chronicle of Theophanes Confessor: Byzantine and Near Eastern History AD 284–813*, translated by Cyril Mango and Roger Scott, Oxford: Clarendon Press, and New York: Oxford University Press, 1997

Treadgold, Warren, *The Byzantine Revival, 780–842*, Stanford, California: Stanford University Press, 1988

Identity

What it means to belong to a people, the terms used to describe this, and perceptions of distinctiveness in relation to other peoples, will inevitably vary over 40 centuries of history, and all the more so when the sense of Greek identity has at some crucial turning points been the subject of reinterpretation and reconstruction.

The centrality of language is indubitable. Some signs specific to the Linear B syllabary on a circular pebble excavated in a Middle Helladic context indicate that Greek was being written in the Peloponnese around 1650 BC. We do not, however, know what those who then spoke the language called it. The Homeric epics (of the 8th century BC, but incorporating much earlier traditional phraseology) use "Achaioi" as the main generic name with "Danaoi" and "Argeioi" as alterna-

tives. Hittite tablets of the 2nd millennium BC mention "Achiyava" as an important kingdom while Egyptian inscriptions name the "Danaya". None of the three terms was used as an overall self-description by speakers of Greek after Homer. "Argives" and "Achaeans" became confined to subgroups.

The peoples to their east called Greek-speakers by some variant of "Ionians", because Ionians from Euboea, the Aegean islands, and the Asia Minor coast dominated trade there into the 7th century BC. Greek-speakers themselves, however, saw the Ionians rather as one of their main subdivisions. The fragmentary pseudo-Hesiodic *Catalogue of Women* of the 6th century BC presents a genealogy in which they are somewhat closer to the Achaeans, Ion being brother to Achaeus and son to Xuthus, than to Aeolus and Dorus, Hellen's other two sons.

Peoples to the west and the north of the Greek-speakers took the word "Greek" from the Romans. The reason for this choice is uncertain. The *Catalogue of Women* states that Zeus and the daughter of the first man, Deucalion, gave birth to Graecus, and later sources that Hellen, Deucalion's son, gave his name to the people previously called "Graikoi". Since no major subdivision of Greek-speakers called themselves "Graikoi", it is conceivable that what we find here is the echo of an earlier attempt to construct a common genealogy, current when cities of Euboea and the town of Graia (Oropus) opposite were founding the first Greek settlements in Italy.

Neither "Achaean" nor "Ionian" nor "Greek" became the dominant term of self-descriptive identity in Classical antiquity. In Homer "Hellene" referred only to Achilles' kingdom in south Thessaly or Phthiotis (*Iliad*, 2. 680–85). In the 7th century BC, however, Hesiod (*Works and Days*, 1. 653) speaks of all the mainland Greeks as "Hellenes". By the 6th century BC a common shrine of nine cities at Naucratis in Egypt was called the "Hellenion" (Herodotus 2. 178), while "Hellanodikai" was the name of the judges in Olympia.

The Greek-speaking world was composed of a large number of often fiercely competing city states, and, at its periphery, also some more traditional kingdoms. Thus Hellenic identity, in contrast to many others, was not based on a common political loyalty. Herodotus (8. 144) puts in the mouth of the Athenians a catalogue of what made the Hellenes one people – common blood, common language, common temples and sacrifices, and a common way of life. Since the word used for a non-Greek, "barbarian", originally meant "heterophone" (Homer, *Iliad*, 2. 867 uses "barbarophones" to describe the Carians as "of foreign speech"), language was almost certainly the most important of these. The common genealogies already referred to, the common cult centres and sacrifices associated with the Homeric pantheon, and a common way of life were indeed crucial elements in ancient Hellenic identity. Common political institutions and loyalty are not even mentioned.

What constituted the common way of life? For most Hellenes it was life in a city state, which gave citizens their sense of political identity and privilege in relation to slaves or serfs. For all, it was the values instilled by the Homeric epics: on the one hand, a close family at home, as witnessed by the *Odyssey*, a safe haven after long periods of absence, especially at sea; on the other, an agonistic or competitive approach to life in society, whether in war, debate, or athletic games, as witnessed by the *Iliad*. Homer was central to ancient Greek education. The spread of many Homeric values to non-aristocrats helped set off major political experiments and encouraged individual achievement among thinkers, craftsmen, and artists alike.

The word "barbarian" is never used in Homer of non-Greeks as a whole. Nor is moral superiority ascribed to the Achaeans compared with the Trojans. After the Persian Wars, especially in Athenian drama (starting with Aeschylus' *Persae* in 472 BC) and Herodotus, there is a clear sense of superiority based on forms of political organization and military and cultural achievement, the first sure instance in which Hellenic identity is partly defined by opposition. Herodotus (1. 1) states that he wrote so that "the great and marvellous deeds performed, whether by Greeks or by barbarians, should not lose their renown". From the following chapters it is clear that he saw Persians, Phoenicians, Egyptians, and Lydians as cultured and clearly differentiated, yet equally "barbarians".

Although the Persian invasion (480–479 BC), resisted by a voluntary alliance of about 30 city states, proved a defining moment, consensual political unification of all the Hellenes did not follow. In the late 4th century BC Philip and Alexander of Macedon, masters of a kingdom dismissed by Hellenic political opponents as "barbarian", justified the imposition of an alliance as a means to obtain revenge against Persia, but this unity too did not survive Alexander's death.

Alexander's conquests (336–323 BC) formed another defining moment. Hellenes poured eastwards bearing their cultural values such as city life, athletics, philosophy, and art. Large numbers of non-Hellenes began to use Greek as a second language. This brought changes to the language, and loosened the connection of its use with Hellenic identity. Earlier in the 4th century BC Isocrates (*Panegyricus* 50) had already advocated that the name "Hellene" should be applied to those who shared Hellenic culture, rather than ancestry. By contrast, the other two of Herodotus' defining characteristics, a shared way of life and religion, became more important in a cosmopolitan and linguistically united world.

Political fragmentation assisted the Roman conquest, but Roman rule did not diminish the sense of a separate Hellenic identity for several centuries. The Classical revivalists of the 2nd century AD, though content to be part of the empire, were proud to be culturally Hellenes and politically citizens of their particular cities (no longer effectively "states").

Writing to the Corinthians (1 Corinthians 1:18–25) Paul contrasts Jews and Hellenes as two peoples and outlooks from either of which one might come to the Christian faith. What ultimately occurred was more radical. A people noted for its cultural self-confidence and pride in superiority over barbarians came to adopt as its own the empire of one foreign people, the Romans, and the religion, albeit universalized, of another, the Jews. The history of Greek-speakers continued under the mantle of the Romaic empire and as a new Israel.

From the 3rd century AD onwards, the growth in transcendental religion and the gradual decline of cities in an increasingly beleaguered empire led to changes first in the content and then in the self-descriptive aspects of identity. Thus by the 6th century "Hellenes" had come to mean "pagans", actively opposed by Christians. Meanwhile in a significant popular phrase one city alone, Constantinople, came to be known as "the City", mirroring the fact that loyalty was now focused on a single state, the empire of the Romaioi, "Romans" in Greek. Thus two crucial elements of later Greek identity, the Romaic and the Orthodox Christian, enter the scene, not however in their narrower contemporary sense. They were originally, both in principle and in practice, much broader than the Hellenic identity had been, spreading far beyond speakers of a particular language, aspiring indeed to universality.

If the self-descriptive elements of identity changed, there was considerable continuity in content: first, in language, second, in respect for some ancient cultural values, and third, in continued distaste for barbarians. There were several revivals of Attic Greek (as in the 2nd, 4th, and 9th centuries). More important was the influence of the Septuagint translation of the Old Testament and the original Greek text of the New Testament, which, with the hymnody of the Eastern Church they inspired, had a simultaneously conserving and formative effect on Greek, comparable to that of Luther's translation of the Bible on German and the Authorized Version on English. Equally, there was continuing respect for Classical culture among the educated. Quite as important were folk memories (e.g. of Alexander), traditions, and values among the less educated, including the continued insistence on excellence, for example, in craftsmanship. The "barbarians", who were effectively reducing the area of Greek cultural and linguistic influence, were more dangerous than ever. They were now distinguished less by language and more by their uncultured, destructive, and (in the modern sense) barbarous behaviour.

Distaste for the Franks, one of the two specific oppositional aspects of modern Greek identity, probably dates from the 8th century. There was no Frankish kingdom after the 9th century, yet even today Greeks, when seeking a pejorative term, more frequently use "Frank" than "Latin" or "Western", although either of the others would have been more natural at any later period. The Franks introduced the *filioque* into the creed long before Rome, thus challenging the Orthodoxy of Constantinople; they were also the first effectively to challenge the universality of its Christian and Romaic empire. The geographical extension of "Frank" has expanded and contracted at various times from its Franco-German core. The Crusaders' despoliation of Constantinople in 1204 cemented religious and cultural schism. Since they also claimed to be heirs of Rome, first Classicizing intellectuals and then wider circles from the 12th to the 15th centuries began to reuse the word "Hellene" in a positive, self-descriptive sense. Patriarch Gennadios used both "Hellene" and "Romaios", but "Hellene", it seems, more frequently.

The second opposition central to later Greek identity concerns the Turks. This runs even deeper. *Efrangepse* means "he has adopted Western ways" (but has not necessarily therefore ceased to be a Greek), whereas *etourkepse* means "he has become a Muslim and hence a Turk". There is also no parallel to the interchangeable popular phrases *egine thirio* and *egine Tourkos* meaning "he behaved outrageously" (literally "he became a wild animal" and "he became a Turk" respectively). Vitsentzos Kornaros's 16th-century description of a Karamanian, clearly indicating a Turk (*Erotokritos*, 2. 319–64), illustrates this:

He believed in his sword, this is what he worshipped:
wars, hostilities and quarrels ever he was stirring.

During the Frangokratia and Tourkokratia terms of self-description were fluid. For some the only significant identity was that of an Orthodox Christian. Already in the 16th century, however, there are instances of the modern use of "Hellene" with Orthodox Christianity as one of its constituent parts. "Romios" was also used frequently until the War of Independence, and in the areas that remained under Ottoman rule, well beyond. (Modern Turks call Greeks residing in Turkey "Rum"; independent Greece is called "Yunanistan".) Another contender was "Graikos", taken from the Western word. Not until the War of Independence itself was it resolved which would prevail.

In the conscious remoulding of identity that followed the formation of the modern nation state, the choice of "Hellene" reflected Greek, and Western, admiration for the Classical heritage. This encouraged democracy, a high level of education, and competitive achievement, which last has been the most enduring of ancient Hellenic characteristics, rooted as it is in the traditional manner of upbringing. Admiration for Classical Greece also led to an attempt to impose a purified, classicizing language, the katharevousa. This successfully marginalized dialects but ultimately proved unable to resist the "demotic" language, also to some degree a construct, but closer to Greek as it had developed over the centuries.

Two crucial elements of identity, however, were not drawn from antiquity. First, throughout the Romaic period, the Frangokratia, and the Tourkokratia alike, the most fundamental dividing line had been religious rather than linguistic. Some influential Greeks, before and after independence, would have liked to follow current Enlightenment ideals of a linguistically based state. This, however, conflicted with popular attitudes and would have demanded quite as arduous an irredentism as any based on religious allegiance. In practice, Orthodox Christians who spoke Albanian were easily assimilable into the body of modern Hellenes; Muslim speakers of Greek were not. This acceptance of Orthodox Christianity, ranging from the nominal to the fully engaged, remains a more important element of Hellenic identity today than religion in general does in most other European states.

Second, modern Hellenism is a quintessentially political phenomenon, which, until well after Cypriot independence, frowned on the localism central to ancient politics. It drew alike on the western European concept of the nation state; the recollection of united action in antiquity, such as the Persian Wars and Alexander; and the Romaic allegiance to a single supranational empire. Indeed in its first century of independence Athens attempted to reconstitute that empire as a nation state. To this Hieronymous Wolf, the 16th-century German scholar responsible for extending the word "Byzantine" from city to empire (whose subjects had never so used it) made an inadvertent contribution. "Byzantine" history more easily than "Romaic" might be seen as a simple extension of Hellenic antiquity.

Since independence Western influences have flooded into Greece. Despite tensions with individual Western countries, the distaste for the "Franks" has declined over time. There are still, however, points of evident religious and cultural opposition. Events have been less favourable to a diminution of the perception of the Turk as a defining opposite, though human relationships have often been friendly. Positive elements of identity, most obviously close family ties, adherence to the

perceived political and cultural essence of ancient Hellenism, and the combination of humane personalist values and rich liturgical life in Orthodoxy, have suffered erosion by modern mass culture, but continue to enjoy wider support than do traditional values in many European countries. For Greeks their history, if continuously reinterpreted, is more important, and more relevant, than for most.

Costa Carras

See also Hellenes, Language, Orthodox Church

Further Reading

Angold, Michael, *Church and Society in Byzantium under the Comneni: 1081–1261*, Cambridge and New York: Cambridge University Press, 1995, p.512

Bouras, Charalambos, *Nea Moni tis Khiou Istoria kai Arhitektoniki* [History and Architecture of Nea Moni on Chios], Athens, 1981, p.34

Carras, Costa, *3000 Years of Greek Identity: Myth or Reality*, Athens: Domus 1983

Cartledge, Paul, *The Greeks: A Portrait of Self and Others*, Oxford and New York: Oxford University Press, 1993

Hall, Edith, *Inventing the Barbarian: Greek Definition through Tragedy*, Oxford: Clarendon Press, and New York: Oxford University Press, 1989

Hall, Jonathan M., *Ethnic Identity in Greek Antiquity*, Cambridge and New York: Cambridge University Press, 1997

Iakovidis, Speros, *The Mycenaean Inscription from Kafkania*, 1995 (in Greek)

Kitromilides, Paschalis M., "Imagined Communities and the Origins of the National Question in the Balkans" in *Modern Greece: Nationalism and Nationality*, edited by Martin Blinkhorn and Thanos Veremis, Athens: Sage / Eliamep, 1990

Kitromilides, Paschalis M., "Paparrigopoulos, Byzantium and the Great Idea" in *Byzantium and the Modern Greek Identity*, edited by David Ricks and Paul Magdalino, Aldershot, Hampshire: Ashgate, 1998

Mararakis-Ainian, Alexander, *The First Greeks in the West*, Archaeologiki Etairia, 1996 Report (in Greek)

Swain, Simon, *Hellenism and Empire: Language, Classicism, and Power in the Greek World AD 50–250*, Oxford: Clarendon Press, and New York: Oxford University Press, 1996

Veremis, Thanos, "From the National State to the Stateless Nation" in *Modern Greece: Nationalism and Nationality*, edited by Martin Blinkhorn and Thanos Veremis, Athens: Sage / Eliamep, 1990

Vryonis, Spiros, "Byzantine Cultural Self-Consciousness in the Fifteenth Century" in *The Twilight of Byzantium: Aspects of Cultural and Religious History in the Late Byzantine Era*, edited by Slobodan Ćurčić, Princeton, New Jersey: Princeton University Press, 1991

Ignatius, St *c.*AD 30–107

Bishop of Antioch

Ignatius was born in Antioch and was its third bishop (after Peter and Evodius) from around AD 70 until his martyrdom in the Roman Colosseum in the reign of the emperor Trajan (98–117). He therefore belongs to the generation immediately following the Crucifixion. According to tradition, he was converted to Christianity by John the Evangelist and was made bishop by Peter. In fact, we know little about his life before his final journey from Antioch to Rome and martyrdom. In the

4th century, Eusebius *(Historia Ecclesiastica*, 3. 22, 36–38 and 4. 14f.) was unclear about the year of the martyrdom, but is otherwise quite reliable and our chief early source for Ignatius.

Around 107 Ignatius was tried and convicted as a Christian during a local persecution in Antioch – the precise charges are not known. Ten soldiers conducted him to Rome to be fed to wild beasts in the Colosseum. En route, at Smyrna, Ignatius was received with honour by bishop Polycarp and Christians from Ephesus, Magnesia, and Tralles. To these he gave letters thanking their communities for their concern and exhorting them to obey their superiors (bishops or presbyters), who would steer them against the then prevalent Judaizing and Docetic heresies. He also sent ahead a letter to the Christians of Rome urging them not to intervene to prevent his martyrdom, which he earnestly desired.

At Troas he was intercepted by messengers from Antioch who announced that the persecution there had ended. Ignatius wrote two more letters, to the Christians of Philadelphia and Smyrna, again exhorting them to be obedient to their bishop. In the latter he wrote: "Wherever the bishop is, there let the people be, as wherever Jesus Christ is, there is the Catholic Church." This may be the first text that uses the term Catholic Church to mean the body of all Christians. In a last letter to Polycarp, Ignatius asked his friend to support the Antiochene Christians after the recent crisis and to encourage the other churches of Asia to do the same.

A great debate among scholars of the late 19th century settled the question of the authenticity of the epistles. The set of seven accepted epistles written by Ignatius in his last days is usually accompanied by Polycarp's epistle to the Christians of Philippi. The epistles are the principal source for understanding the mind of this martyr, setting forth an orthodoxy that has stood the test of time among Catholic Christians. He was in practice the type of ideal bishop of his epistles.

Ignatius acknowledged the continuity between the Old and New Testaments. Against the Gnostic heresy of Docetism (which taught that Christ was never truly human), Ignatius preached the reality of Jesus' sufferings: "His Birth, Passion and Death were not appearances but realities." He insisted that Christ was both human and divine, did die on the cross for mankind, and is really present in the Eucharist. In discussing the Real Presence, Ignatius was perhaps the first Christian to consider the Eucharist as a *Mysterion* – a Mystery *(Epistle to Tralles*, 2). He is the first writer outside the New Testament to assert the Virgin Birth *(Epistle to Smyrna*, 1. 1) and to describe Christ in the philosophical terms he found in John's gospel: there is only one physician of flesh and spirit, generate and ingenerate, God in man, true life in death, son of Mary, and son of God *(Epistle to Ephesus*, 7). In the face of Docetism and the many other misinterpretations of the Christian faith in his day, from Manichaeism to Arian ideas, Ignatius urged that congregations be guided by a bishop, one trained in orthodoxy and officially appointed as *episkopos* – "overseer" – of his church.

The title of bishop was in use in the eastern Church in the 1st century, though not universally in the west. In Ignatius' century – when all Christians were converts – Antioch had a large Jewish-Christian population but was also the centre of the first and largest gentile Christian congregation. Ignatius thus inherited the effects of Paul's message, which recast Christianity from a sect of Judaism to a religion for all. Teaching and maintaining orthodoxy in such a context was an immense task, requiring strong and clear-headed leadership. Ignatius' work was complicated by the persecutions of Domitian (81–96) and Trajan (98–117) and by the strong presence of Judaizing Christians who still followed the stringent rules and practices of their old religion.

Among the arguments against the authenticity of the letters was their insistence on the importance of the bishop at a time so early in the history of the faith. But in fact, in Asia Minor, Jerusalem, and Syria – the precise places where the epistles place the episcopal office – the episcopacy had existed from apostolic times. And, indeed, Ignatius' use of the word probably applies only to the cities mentioned in the letters, though Irenaeus (c.130–c.202) compiled a list of the bishops of Rome back to the apostles *(Adversus Haereses*, 3. 3. 3). Ignatius does not seem to have written of the doctrine of apostolic succession.

Ignatius' concern was for a leadership system with undoubted authority in matters of doctrine *(Epistle to Philadelphia*, 4). The bishop and priests represent the Lord and the council of the apostles *(Epistle to Magnesia*, 6. 1). Nothing should be done in church – Eucharist, baptism, even the celebration of the Mass – without approval of the bishop *(Epistle to Smyrna*, 8. 1–2).

Ignatius' teaching is strongly Pauline, that is, it is already addressed to a world Christian community. He urged that good Christians live lives of virtue and service to the community. They imitate Christ in his Passion, and most fully by following him to martyrdom.

The once hotly debated question surrounding Ignatius' martyrdom seems resolved by his *Epistle to the Romans* (1. 2; 2. 1; 4. 1). In it he begs the Christians in Rome not to intercede on his behalf to forestall his martyrdom. This presumes that he had already been condemned to death in Antioch by a Roman official other than the emperor and that the Christians in Rome could indeed appeal to Trajan. Ignatius, however, eagerly wished to imitate his Christ even unto death. Furthermore, his martyrdom in Rome is attested by Polycarp. The church of Philippi, having heard Ignatius during his journey, wrote to Polycarp requesting copies of Ignatius' letters written at Smyrna and Troas. Polycarp complied in the epistle we have, which also recalls Ignatius' martyrdom as a revered memory.

Another controversy arose from Ignatius' words in his *Epistle to the Romans*: did he actually acknowledge the primacy of Rome when he said that he knew he could not command Rome's Christians as did "Peter and Paul who were apostles"? Scholars have concluded that he meant only that he could not give them orders concerning his martyrdom. Nowhere, moreover, does he mention a bishop of Rome.

Thus, in a series of seven not overly long epistles, Ignatius of Antioch touched on many points of doctrine and Church administration. He followed in the footsteps of St Paul in insisting upon a solid organization and a strong basis of authority as requirements for an enduring Christian movement.

DANIEL C. SCAVONE

See also Bishops

Biography

Born in Antioch *c.*AD 30, Ignatius was its third bishop from *c.*70 until his martyrdom in Rome *c.*107. Little is known of his life before his final journey from Antioch to Rome via Smyrna, Troas, and Dyrrhachium. During his last days he wrote a series of epistles to Christian communities which are the main source of his teaching on doctrine and Church administration.

Writings

In *The Apostolic Fathers*, translated by Kirsopp Lake, vol. 1, London: Heinemann, and New York: Putnam, 1912 (Greek text and translation of the epistles; Loeb edition, several reprints)
The Epistles of St Clement of Rome and St Ignatius of Antioch, translated by James A. Kleist, London: Longman, and Westminster, Maryland: Newman Press, 1946

Further Reading

Corwin, Virginia, *St Ignatius and Christianity in Antioch*, New Haven, Connecticut: Yale University Press, 1960
Daniélou, Jean, *The Theology of Jewish Christianity*, London: Darton Longman and Todd, and Philadelphia: Westminster Press, 1977
Quasten, Johannes, *Patrology*, vol. 1: *The Beginnings of Patristic Literature*, Utrecht: Spectrum, and Westminster, Maryland: Newman Press, 1950
Richardson, Cyril Charles, *The Christianity of Ignatius of Antioch*, New York: Columbia University Press, 1935
Trevett, Christine, *A Study of Ignatius of Antioch in Syria and Asia*, Lewiston, New York: Mellen, 1992
Wace, Henry, *Dictionary of Christian Biography and Literature*, London: John Murray, and Boston: Little Brown, 1911, reprinted Peabody, Massachusetts: Hendrickson, 1994, pp. 208–22
Zahn, Theodore, *Ignatius von Antiochien*, Gotha: Perthes, 1873

Illyrians

Tribes settled on the northern and eastern shores of the Adriatic

The region where the Illyrians were established is known as Illyria, extending from Epirus in the south to the Danube in the north and as far as the river Morava in the east. The boundaries, however, of the territory of the Illyrians are not clearly defined and little can be learnt from written sources about their origin and culture. Since the Illyrians themselves did not leave any written evidence of their past, information is based on the texts of Greek and Roman authors who referred to these tribes as "barbarian"; the Greeks identified the Illyrians as an *ethnos* (race) different from the Macedonians, Thracians, and themselves. The personal and geographical names appearing in Greek and Latin records and inscriptions contribute to a partial reconstruction of the Illyrian language. It can therefore be deduced that the Illyrians spoke Indo-European dialects. According to a Greek legend, Illyrios was the son of Phoenician Cadmus and Harmonia, who settled in Illyria, and became the ancestor of the Illyrian people. Recent research has demonstrated that the Illyrians comprised a mixture of ethnic groups who did not necessarily have identical origins. Their formation coincides with the beginning of the Iron Age, around 1000 BC.

The Illyrians came in contact with the Greek Aegean at an early date. Excavation finds from the 8th-century BC cemetery at Vergina indicate a temporary Illyrian presence in ancient Macedonia, especially in its northern and western areas. At the same time, Greeks were attracted to Illyrian territory; the silver mines of the region, located inland – e.g. Damastion – increased their interest. Archaeological finds indicate that Greek imported goods, primarily pottery and metalwork, reached the Illyrians who inhabited the Adriatic littoral as early as the 8th and 7th centuries BC. The first Greek cities were established along the Adriatic coast in the late 7th and early 6th centuries BC. By 627 BC a joint expedition from Corinth and Corfu founded the colony at Epidamnus, and around 588 BC another at Apollonia; both became important centres of trade. Thus, the sea crossing to south Italy passed under Greek control and these two ports remained for many centuries the termini of the route across the southern Balkans. Excavations of the early cemeteries of Epidamnus and Apollonia have brought to light numerous examples of Corinthian pottery as well as local Illyrian products. Although Greeks traded in the region north of the river Drin, they did not establish any settlements either on the coast or inland. Three Greek colonies were however founded on the islands of Black Corcyra (Korcula), Issa (Vis), and Pharos (Hvar), by Cnidians, Parians, and Syracusans respectively. The trade which developed between these Greek colonies and the Illyrians contributed significantly to the latter's development and closer contact with Greek culture.

Illyrians made their appearance in Greek affairs in 424 BC. At this time Brasidas and his Spartan army were in Macedonia to assist king Perdiccas and other opponents of Athens to attack the Athenian colonies in Thrace. The Spartans did not at first become involved in Macedon's war with Arrhabaeus, ruler of Lyncus (who was not an ally of Athens but an independent ruler), but following a Macedonian victory they were persuaded to await the arrival of the Illyrian mercenaries who came to join Arrhabaeus. In 423 BC the joint expedition of Macedonians and Spartans ended in retreat because they feared the warlike Illyrians.

The history of the Macedonian kings is marked by a succession of wars against the Illyrian tribes which ended with Roman intervention in the 3rd century BC. The migration of the Celts at the beginning of the 4th century BC disturbed the territory between the Danube and the Adriatic and forced the Illyrians southwards. Consequently, the need for defence united them under Bardylis around 383 BC. The Illyrian attacks on Macedonia brought the latter close to collapse. King Amyntas II and, later, Perdiccas were defeated and the latter was slain (359 BC). It was only in Philip II's reign that the Illyrians were completely crushed and part of their territory was annexed to Macedonia. The Illyrians attacked Macedonia again in Alexander's time, but they were defeated. In the reign of Cassander an Illyrian tribe, the Taulantii, became involved in the struggle between Epirus and Macedonia, offering asylum to the infant Pyrrhus after the expulsion of his father Aeacides from his kingdom among the Molossians. When Pyrrhus became king of Epirus, he strengthened his links with the Illyrian tribes by marriage alliances.

The wars with Macedonia and Epirus brought the Adriatic Illyrians into contact with the Greek world. Major changes in the social and economic life of south Illyria occurred before the end of the 5th century BC, while in the north similar changes appeared a century later. The urbanization which followed the growth of towns – the first fortifications were built in the 5th century BC at Gajtan – altered the tribal structures and created a demand for greater political autonomy. The first public buildings were not constructed however until around the middle of the 3rd century BC at Byllis.

An Illyrian kingdom was established in the 3rd century BC with its capital at Scodra. The dynasty of the Antigonids in Macedonia was often distracted from its attempt to retain power in Greece by Illyrians, especially the Dardani, on the northern frontier. At the same time, a new power, the Ardiaei, who inhabited the south coast of the Adriatic, emerged among the Illyrians. Responding to the request of Demetrius II of Macedonia, the Ardiaei and their king Agron helped Macedon's allies, the Acarnanians, against the Aetolians in the siege of Medion (231 BC). After Agron's death, the command passed to his widow Teuta and the Illyrians engaged in piracy, ravaging the shores of Greece and Italy. The Greeks turned to Rome for help. The two Illyrian wars with Rome (229 and 219 BC) ended with the submission of the Illyrians and the annexation of part of their territory by the Romans.

ELENI ZIMI

See also Macedonia, Philip II

Summary

Around 1000 BC the Illyrians settled the territory north and east of the Adriatic known as Illyria, extending from Epirus in the south to the Danube in the north and the Morava in the east. They left no written records. They were in contact with the Greeks from the 8th century BC and were inevitably caught up in wars between Macedonia and Epirus. They had a reputation for piracy which extended beyond the Roman conquest.

Further Reading

Cabanes, Pierre (editor), *L'Illyrie meridionale et l'Epire dans l'antiquité*, vol. 1, Clermont-Ferrand: Adosa, 1987; vol. 2, Paris: Boccard, 1993

Cabanes, Pierre, *Les Illyriens de Bardylis à Genthios: IVe–IIe siècles avant J.C.*, Paris: SEDES, 1988

Stipčević, Aleksandar, *The Illyrians: History and Culture*, Park Ridge, New Jersey: Noyes Press, 1977

Wilkes, John, *The Illyrians*, Oxford and Cambridge, Massachusetts: Blackwell, 1992

Imperial Cult

The imperial cult almost certainly owes at least part of its acceptance during the Roman empire to the establishment of ruler cults in the late Classical and Hellenistic periods. Although a divine cult for a living person was against Greek tradition, the Spartan commander Lysander had received a cult on Samos after the Peloponnesian War. Only scanty evidence exists for other divine cults to individuals in the 4th century BC before the time of Philip II of Macedon and Alexander the Great. Whether Philip received a cult during his lifetime is debated, but his son certainly did: his personality, conquests, and unlimited power had elevated him to an unprecedented status that demanded special recognition.

Alexander's successors not only bolstered his worship, but were often granted their own ruler cults. The reasons for this were largely due to the community's need to acknowledge the rulers and their families as individuals of immense power and wealth who excelled all others in their benefactions; the cults were an assertion of the rulers' unique abilities to aid their communities. Some rulers, such as the Ptolemies at Alexandria, also established their own dynastic cults to celebrate their families, but these cults rarely lasted very long.

The creation of a Hellenistic ruler cult involved the construction of a temple or shrine only occasionally (about a dozen are known). Far more common were awards of an altar, priest, sacrifices, games, and statues. Statues of the ruler might even be placed in existing temples of traditional deities, where the ruler would "share" the space, honours, and even qualities of that deity.

The purpose of these cults is still debated: were they religious or political in nature? To deny one in favour of the other is difficult, because politics and religion were very closely entwined in antiquity. What is certain is that the people who founded and managed the cults were creating a new reality in which the immense power and influence of the rulers, who now directly affected life in the Hellenistic world, were given prominent recognition.

The imperial cult was not merely a simple continuation of the Hellenistic ruler cult but was, nevertheless, partially inspired by it. A divine cult to a living Roman became part of Italian culture only through contact with Greek cities. Marcus Claudius Marcellus, who sacked Syracuse (212/11 BC), and Titus Quinctius Flamininus, the liberator of Greece (196 BC), both received divine honours. Yet the practice became more common only a century later as other individuals, Greeks and Romans, were given cults in recognition of their benefactions to communities.

The almost simultaneous adoption of the cult of Roma (the power of Rome) in Greek cities from the early 2nd century BC reflected another aspect of the growth of Roman influence in the east. Much more widespread than the earlier ruler cults, the cults associated with Rome mirrored the development and spread of Roman power; they represented an acknowledgement of that power by the Greeks.

The preeminence of deified Julius Caesar and his adopted son Octavian/Augustus altered the practice of these cults in the east. Augustus was praised as the greatest of all benefactors and saviours in the east, because of the peace attributed to him after the defeat of Antony and Cleopatra. So great was his reputation that, before the end of his life, divine cults to non-imperial family members were no longer being created. The omnipotence of the emperor had been recognized by the eastern communities.

In addition to the hundreds of municipal and private household cults established to celebrate the emperors and their families, eastern provincial assemblies were also given permission to create cults. Emperors were always careful to avoid official deification at Rome itself during their lifetimes (with the exception of Caligula and Commodus), officially becoming deities only upon their apotheosis after death. In the provinces, however, they permitted their worship in conjunction with Roma, other imperial family members, and, eventually, among the cult of previously deified emperors and among the established Olympic pantheon. The practice began in 29 BC, when Octavian had given, at the request of the provinces of Asia and Bithynia, permission for temples to be dedicated to Roma and Divus Julius Caesar at Ephesus and Nicaea, and to Roma and Octavian at Pergamum and Nicomedia. Tiberius, the next emperor, refused a request for his cult from Baetica but granted it to Smyrna where the temple was dedicated to him, Livia (his mother and the wife of Augustus), and the Senate. Emperors did have separate temples to themselves, but they commonly shared the honour with others.

Possession of a provincial cult was so prestigious that cities vied with one another for the honour, which, once given, was advertised in the official title of the city. Grants of these cults were quite rare, making them even more desirable considering the economic and political benefits that accrued to them. The members of the provincial elite who managed the cult also benefited: their status within the community and empire increased. Association with these cults was a statement that they and their families accepted the Roman system and hoped to benefit from it.

Imperial cults could be housed in a variety of types of structures, simple to very grand. Existing buildings, such as stoas and gymnasia, were modified to accommodate the cult; others, such as bath buildings, were constructed with special rooms. Unlike the earlier Hellenistic ruler cults, however, many more elaborate complexes were created for imperial ritual. A Caesareum or Sebasteum, the names sometimes used for these special sanctuaries, had no absolute model but might include a temple, altar, and statues among its other features.

The imperial cult was regarded by some in antiquity merely as a form of flattery (Tacitus, *Annals*, 6. 18). Its religious and political importance to the empire is still debated. The ritual probably did help to bring Greek and Roman together, but whether it created any sense of loyalty or instilled devotion among the inhabitants of the empire is difficult to say. Whether the emperor was regarded as a truly divine being is undeterminable; many of the poor and uneducated may have believed so. Yet, since the imperial cult was rarely imposed by the emperor or his court, most will agree that this indicates a willingness on the part of the Greeks to accept the new conditions that accompanied the control of their lands by Rome. The celebration of the imperial cult was an expression of gratitude for the benefactions received or ones that might come in the future. It does not prove or even indicate any real piety towards the emperor. The establishment of Christianity in the 4th century ended the practice.

ANDREW N. SHERWOOD

Further Reading

Benjamin, A.S., "The Altars of Hadrian in Athens and Hadrian's Panhellenic Program", *Hesperia*, 32 (1963): pp. 57–86

Boer, Willem den (editor), *Le Culte des souverains dans l'empire romain*, Geneva: Hardt, 1973

Cannadine, David and Simon Price (editors), *Rituals of Royalty: Power and Ceremonial in Traditional Societies*, Cambridge and New York: Cambridge University Press, 1987

Edson, Charles F., S.R.F. Price, and M. Hammond, "Ruler Cult" in *The Oxford Classical Dictionary*, 3rd edition, edited by Simon Hornblower and Anthony Spawforth, Oxford and New York: Oxford University Press, 1996, pp. 1337–39

Fishwick, Duncan, "The Development of Provincial Ruler Worship in the Western Roman Empire" in *Aufstieg und Niedergang der römischen Welt*, edited by Hildegard Temporini *et al.*, 2.16.2, Berlin: de Gruyter 1978, 1201–53

Fishwick, Duncan, *The Imperial Cult in the Latin West: Studies in the Ruler Cult of the Western Provinces of the Roman Empire*, Leiden and New York: Brill, 1987

Habicht, Christian, *Gottmenschentum und griechische Städte*, 2nd edition, Munich: Beck, 1970

Herz, Peter, "Bibliographie zum römischen Kaiserkult (1955–1975)" in *Aufstieg und Niedergang der römischen Welt*, edited by Hildegard Temporini *et al.*, 2.16.2, Berlin: de Gruyter 1978, 833–910

Mellor, Ronald, *Thea Rhome: The Worship of the Goddess Roma in the Greek World*, Göttingen: Vandenhoeck & Ruprecht, 1975

Mellor, Ronald, "The Goddess Roma" in *Aufstieg und Niedergang der römischen Welt*, edited by Hildegard Temporini *et al.*, 2.17.2, Berlin: de Gruyter 1981, 950–1030

Price, S.R.F., "Gods and Emperors: The Greek Language of the Roman Imperial Cult", *Journal of Hellenic Studies*, 104 (1984): pp. 79–95

Price, S.R.F., *Rituals and Power: The Roman Imperial Cult in Asia Minor*, Cambridge and New York: Cambridge University Press, 1984

Scott, Kenneth, *The Imperial Cult under the Flavians*, Stuttgart and Berlin: Kohlhammer, 1936, reprinted New York: Arno Press, 1975

Taylor, Lily Ross, *The Divinity of the Roman Emperor*, Middletown, Connecticut: American Philological Association, 1931, reprinted Chico, California: Scholar's Press, 1982

Tuchelt, K., "Zum Problem 'Kaisareion-Sebasteion': Eine Frage zu den anfängen des römischen Kaiserkultes", *Mitteilungen des Deutschen Archäologischen Instituts (Abteilung Istanbul)*, 31 (1981): pp. 173–92

Walbank, F.W., "Monarchies and Monarchic Ideas" in *The Hellenistic World*, edited by Walbank *et al.*, Cambridge: Cambridge University Press, 1984 (*The Cambridge Ancient History*, vol. 7, part 1, 2nd edition)

Walbank, F.W., "Könige als Götter: Überlegungen zum Herrscherkult von Alexander bis Augustus", *Chiron*, 17 (1987): pp. 365–82

Weinstock, Stefan, *Divus Julius*, Oxford: Clarendon Press, 1971

Yegül, F., "A Study in Architectural Iconography: Kaisersaal and the Imperial Cult", *Art Bulletin*, 64 (1982): pp. 7–31

Imperialism

Most wars in ancient Greece not fought to gain independence were, as elsewhere, motivated by either the fear or hope of plunder, economic exploitation, or outright annexation. All self-governing Greek states were at all times in some form of military preparedness, if not, as was very frequently the case, actually at war. War, like slavery, which it often facilitated, was so common as rarely to provoke questioning of its morality: whether a Greek was or became free or slave was a quotidian accident of the human condition. The Greeks' love of freedom sprang from a perfervid desire to have complete control over their own destinies, a desire that did not question the right to control the destinies of others; and in confirmation of this, Greek gods of war were deemed far more powerful than any god of peace. As Thucydides makes Athenians inform the Spartans, "it has always been an established rule that the weaker are kept down by the stronger" (1. 76. 2), while Aristotle adds to preservation of one's own liberty and hegemony over one's subjects as legitimate aims of war "the exer-

Imperialism: illustration from the 11th-century chronicle Skylitzes showing the people of Constantinople rising up against the emperor Michael V Kalaphates in 1042. He had foolishly exiled the empress Zoe, and subsequently lost his throne as a result. Biblioteca Nacional, Madrid

cising of the role of master over those who deserve to be slaves" (*Politics*, 1334a2). Thus the continual imperialist bullying by even small states of each other is the very warp of the tapestry of Greek history; and any alliances were inexorably doomed to ephemerality or continuous internal dissension.

The earliest form of Greek imperialism was the *synoikismos* (literally "living together") of the Dark Age, the process by which the polis, or city state, emerged; but the extent to which surrounding communities joined the dominant city voluntarily or under coercion is usually unknown: presumably it varied. In most of these city states equal citizenship was enjoyed by all members. Sparta, however, which became by far the largest city state and had by the end of the 8th century BC conquered Laconia and most of Messenia, was governed by an elite group of Dorians who reduced the mass of the inhabitants (the *perioikoi*, literally "those who live in the surrounding area") to second-class status or collectively owned helotry. Although this policy was not unique to the Spartans, the scale on which they applied it necessitated the reorganization of the elite as a permanent standing army for internal protection (the Lycurgan reforms), which in turn excited further, though often unsuccessful, imperialist adventures in the northern Peloponnese, central and northern Greece, Asia Minor, and even Sicily.

Colonization, which occurred chiefly in the period c.750–c.550 BC, was driven largely through internal pressures rather than imperialist desires, since most colonies were completely self-governing, though retaining religious, cultural, and commercial links with the *metropolis* (mother city). Nevertheless, they were planted, sometimes peaceably and sometimes by force of arms, on the littoral of the Mediterranean from northeastern Spain, southern France, and

southern Italy and Sicily to Libya and what is now southern Turkey and on the eastern and southern shores of the Black Sea. They remained essentially Greek, although there was some acculturization of neighbouring peoples, and many had a long history, some in Asia Minor and Pontus enduring until 1922. In the second half of the 6th century BC the settlers in Asia Minor became the first Greeks to experience foreign imperialism when, having survived the harassment of an expansionist Lydia, they succumbed to the Achaemenid Persian empire, which did, however, practise religious tolerance and generally appointed Greeks as satraps under the watchful eye of officials of the Great King. It was mainland Greek help in the uprising of these cities which led to the Persian Wars of 490–479 BC and the subsequent Athenian attempt at hegemony.

The Delian League (a modern term) was formed in 478 BC to defend Greek states against further Persian reprisals, but its leader, Athens, clearly had imperialist ambitions from the beginning when it forcefully coerced Eion to join. Athens' attempt, despite some federalist elements in the city, to establish for its own economic benefit a rival to the Spartan-led Peloponnesian League is clear from actions such as the reduction of Thasos, which attempted to secede in c.465–462 BC, the transfer of the treasury from Delos to Athens in 454 and the gradual substitution of monetary "tribute" for supplies of ships, the imposition of a huge indemnity on Samos for defiance in 440 BC, and the killing of all adult male citizens and enslavement of the rest of the island's population when Melos refused to join in 416 BC.

The first half of the 4th century BC was marked by various short-lived imperialist attempts by, for instance, Thebes and, in Thessaly, Jason of Pherae; but it was Philip II of Macedon who, having first brought his semi-autonomous barons to obedience and established a standing army, successfully extended his rule over all Greek mainland states except Sparta. Panhellenism, a movement to unite all Greeks against Persian threat, which had been preached by men such as the Athenian Isocrates, played a part in his ambition to invade the Persian empire, but his death in 336 BC left its execution to his son Alexander III. Despite some contemporary propaganda and the romantic view of universal brotherhood held by some modern scholars, the megalomaniacal Alexander was activated by an insatiable lust for conquest which was terminated only by his soldiers' refusal to continue and his own subsequent death. He made little attempt to organize the vast swathe of territory which he had overrun, his policy of forcing Macedonian officers to marry Persian women being driven principally by an infatuation with the charms of Persian imperial trappings and the desire to create an elite neither Macedonian nor Persian with loyalties to himself alone. His conquests did, notwithstanding, have the enormous consequence of spreading a veneer of Greek culture over the Near East and establishing a simplified form of the language as the lingua franca (as evidenced in the New Testament), a legacy which survived the area's incorporation into the Roman empire.

Alexander's failure to nominate an heir ensured the immediate fracturing of his empire, which fell into three main successor states: one (Antigonid) mainly in Macedon and Greece; one (Seleucid) stretching from Anatolia to, initially, Central Asia; and one (Ptolemaic) based upon Alexander's eponymous city in Egypt, which, despite its Macedonian rulers, replaced Athens as the principal centre of Greek culture. Greek imperialism was now exercised by individual rulers attempting to expand their personal empires at their rivals' expense. In the 2nd century BC some small breakaway Greek states invited the Romans to aid them resist reabsorption, but the continuing threats from Macedon and the Seleucids and even quarrels among the smaller states themselves induced the Romans eventually to abandon their policing of Greece and embrace it within their own growing empire. Apart from the destruction of Corinth in 146 BC Roman rule in Greek lands was remarkably lenient. The Roman attitude towards their inhabitants was contempt for their moral laxity, fractiousness, and military inferiority mingled with an admiration for their culture so strong that the poet Horace admitted (*Epistles* 2. 1. 156) that the captive held its captor captive, while upper-class Romans communicated with each other in Greek by preference.

It may be argued that Greeks were involved in the creation of the Roman empire, since its first province, Sicily, was created in 241 BC at least in part to facilitate the Romans' protection of the Greek colonies there against Carthaginian attacks. Moreover, the traditional Roman fetial (priestly) prohibition of the "unjust" war was in theory strengthened (though in practice weakened) by the influence of Greek Stoicism after the Rhodian Panaetius (an intimate of Scipio the Younger and the most important political figure in mid-2nd-century BC Rome) rejected the excesses of Stoic exclusivity and made Stoic philosophy amenable to generals and statesmen. Thus any non-civil Roman war became "just", since it potentially brought the benefits of a superior Roman civilization to the benighted nations of the world and legitimized the elimination of any rulers who opposed conquest. In Virgil's memorable words, Rome's mission became "to spare the down-trodden and vanquish the proud" (*Aeneid*, 6. 853). The process of imperial territorial acquisition and human absorption into the state reached its natural conclusion in an edict of Caracalla (the Antonine Constitution), which gave citizenship (although most of its advantages had by then been abolished) to virtually all free members of the empire probably in AD 212.

The Christianization of the Roman empire initially brought about remarkably little change in the empire's mission and the role of its emperor. Rome was still to spread its civilizing influence over the whole world, albeit now in the name of the Christian God rather than the Stoicized Jupiter. The orb representing the world, which some pagan coins had shown Jupiter handing to the emperor or one emperor passing to another, was now surmounted with a cross to indicate Roman dominion of the world on behalf of God, although it probably remained merely an intangible and mainly numismatic symbol rather than an item of imperial regalia. No longer of divine status himself, the emperor yet became God's vicegerent on earth and remained a quasi-divine figure, whose image was haloed, to whom *proskynesis* (various ceremonial gestures of reverence) was due, and against whom rebellion was sacrilege; and he was also expected, as legal documents proclaim, to exhibit towards his subjects *philanthropia* (love of mankind), which had already been demanded by Hellenistic treatises on kingship but was also the all-important characteristic of God himself.

Despite the empire's proselytizing mandate, the self-righteous bellicosity of the Muslims and western Crusaders was largely unknown in Byzantium, since Christianity engendered an abhorrence of war through the teaching of the New Testament (and its patristic interpretation) and the realization that the killing of a foe was still the killing of something in the image of God. In the 4th century St Basil even ruled that soldiers who had killed in battle should be barred from communion for three years, while in the 10th the petition by Nikephoros II Phokas that his slain soldiers should be made martyrs was denied by the patriarch Polyeuktos. Thus, while imperial expansion was welcomed and military heroes were, with some reservations, applauded, praise was bestowed on emperors who fought with a minimum loss of life on either side and, even more, on those who through diplomacy obtained their objectives bloodlessly. Emperors, with frequently the active support of the Church, strove to build a network of alliances especially in the Balkans, the Caucasus, and the buffer region between Christendom and the Caliphate, which Obolensky, for eastern Europe, so aptly calls "the Byzantine Commonwealth". Byzantine methods of controlling this "client empire", and of playing off its members against each other, are detailed in *De Administrando Imperio*, a manual which was compiled, or at least commissioned, by Constantine VII Porphyrogennetos for the use of his son Romanos II, and which has miraculously survived. Nevertheless, many wars were motivated by irredentism, notably by Justinian I in the west and thereafter principally to recover territory lost in the east to the Arabs and the Turks: this, indeed, was the major consideration of Alexios I in initiating the First Crusade.

The theory that the Roman empire was the sole terrestrial empire and coterminous with Christendom was widely held in both east and west until Charlemagne allowed himself to be crowned emperor of the Romans by Pope Leo III on Christmas Day 800, when the Frankish king, denying the legitimacy of a female ruler, believed that the throne in Constantinople, which was held at that time by Irene, was in fact vacant. Thereafter, despite the implication of the forged "Donation of Constantine" that only emperors created by the popes were valid, westerners increasingly believed in the possibility of rival empires, and Byzantines, while arguing against this, compromised their opposition by adding "of the Romans" to the title of their own emperors. Nevertheless, for some centuries yet the Roman empire, with its capital at Constantinople, had a prestige unmatched in the west and rivals wished not so much to destroy the empire as to take it over. Most notable among these were Symeon of Bulgaria in the early 10th century, the Seljuk Turks (who in anticipation of their desired final conquest named their sultanate Rum) in the 11th to 12th, the briefly successful Latins and the unsuccessful Kalojan of Bulgaria in the 13th, and eventually the victorious Ottoman Turks in the 15th.

Thereafter the Greeks' experience of imperialism was always as subjects. After the fall of Constantinople in 1453, most Greek-speaking areas came under Ottoman rule, although some islands held out for a great many years (as, for example, did Tinos until 1715) while others continued or came to be governed by Venice. Venetian rule was relatively benign, although some Orthodox were more offended by Venetian Catholicism than Ottoman Islam. Under the Turks the Greeks, in accordance with the Muslim use of religion as the defining criterion of nationality, were given a degree of internal self-government as a separate *millet* (community) within the Ottoman empire. A few Phanariots, led by Alexander Mavrokordatos in the late 17th century, rose to the rank of Grand Dragoman (Chief Interpreter) and even Exaporite (Minister of Secrets) at the Sublime Porte and were appointed *hospodars* (governors) in Moldavia and Wallachia. However, as central Ottoman control diminished, the vast majority of rural Greeks became increasingly subject to the often capricious whims of local potentates such as the notorious Ali Pasha of Ioannina (1750–1822).

For a short time following the Treaty of Campo Formio in 1797 the Ionian islands became part of the empire of Napoleon Bonaparte, who declared that for him Corfu, Cephalonia, and Zakynthos were more important than the whole of Italy. The islands were swiftly freed from the French, becoming a Russo-Ottoman condominium and by 1800 a Russian protectorate. They reverted to French rule through the Peace of Tilsit in 1807, but were taken by the British in 1814 and in the following year became "a single, free and independent state under the exclusive protection of His Majesty", a fiction that entailed direct rule by a British Lord High Commissioner until 1864. The Greeks' own imperial ambitions were ended shortly after World War I, when *I Megali Idea* ("The Great Idea") of reestablishing the Byzantine empire with its capital at Constantinople was reduced by the decisions of the victorious allies from a genuine hope to an evanescent dream. Their experience of imperial rule was, however, not quite over. Although Mussolini's occupation of Corfu in 1922 was swiftly termi-

nated, in part through a speech at the League of Nations written by one cricketer (C.B. Fry) and delivered by another (K.S. Ranjitsinhji, Jam Sahib of Nawanagar), Cyprus remained under British control. Though technically under Ottoman sovereignty, the island had been administered by Britain since 1878; it was annexed outright on the outbreak of war in 1914 and became a British colony in 1923. The demand for *enosis* (union with Greece), beginning in the 19th century and culminating in the 1950s with the terrorist activities of EOKA (the National Organization of Cypriot Struggle), resulted in independence for the island in 1959. Since then the sole continuing overt remnant of imperialism for Greeks has been British retention as sovereign areas in Cyprus of the 256 square km constituting the military bases of Dekelia and Akrotiri, although Greek complaints of covert imperialism by the United States have had some justification.

A.R. LITTLEWOOD

See also Commonwealth, Colonization, Delian League, Great Idea, Hellenization, Ottoman Period, Political History 490–318 BC, Political History 318–31 BC, Political History 31 BC–AD 330, Political History AD 330–802, Political History 802–1204, Political History 1204–1261, Political History 1261–1453, Political History 1453–1832, Political History since 1832, Roman Period, Venetokratia

Further Reading

Ahrweiler, Hélène, *L'Idéologie politique de l'empire byzantin*, Paris: Presses Universitaires de France, 1975

Constantine VII Porphyrogennetos, *De Administrando Imperio*, edited by G. Moravcsik, translated by R.J.H. Jenkins, Washington, D.C.: Dumbarton Oaks, 1967

Dvornik, Francis, *Early Christian and Byzantine Political Philosophy: Origins and Background*, 2 vols, Washington, D.C.: Dumbarton Oaks, 1966

Finley, M.I., *Ancient History: Evidence and Models*, London: Chatto and Windus, 1985; New York: Penguin, 1987, pp.67–87

Garnsey, P.D.A. and C.R. Whittaker (editors), *Imperialism in the Ancient World*, Cambridge: Cambridge University Press, 1978

Hunger, Herbert (editor), *Das byzantinische Herrscherbild*, Darmstadt: Wissenschaftliche Buchgesellschaft, 1975

Laiou, A., "On Just War in Byzantium" in *To Hellenikon: Studies in Honor of Speros Vryonis, Jr*, vol. 1, edited by J.S. Langdon *et al.*, New Rochelle, New York: Caratzas, 1993

Laurent, V., "L'Idée de guerre sainte et la tradition byzantine", *Revue historique du sud-est européen*, 23 (1946): pp. 71–98

Lintott, A.W., *Imperium Romanum: Politics and Administration*, London and New York: Routledge, 1993

Obolensky, Dimitri, *The Byzantine Commonwealth: Eastern Europe, 500–1453*, London: Weidenfeld and Nicolson, and New York: Praeger, 1971

Pratt, Michael, *Britain's Greek Empire: Reflections on the History of the Ionian Islands from the Fall of Byzantium*, London: Collings, 1978

Purcell, H.D., *Cyprus*, London: Benn, and New York: Praeger, 1969

Shepard, Jonathan and Simon Franklin (editors), *Byzantine Diplomacy*, Aldershot, Hampshire: Variorum, 1992

Independence, War of 1821–1832

The Greek revolt from the Ottoman empire and the establishment of an independent kingdom of Greece (1821–32) was the

War of Independence: the Battle of Navarino (1827) as depicted by L. Garneray. The Turkish fleet was annihilated in the action and the outcome of the war was finally assured. Hellenic Maritime Museum

first successful challenge to the concert of the "Great Powers" (Britain, Russia, Austria, Prussia, and, after 1818, France, where the Bourbon monarchy was restored after Napoleon's defeat and sought to preserve the status quo in Europe). Differences among the allies had already surfaced before 1821, with Austria, Prussia, and Russia contending that the alliance should suppress revolutions and maintain absolute monarchy, while Britain viewed it as a means to deter further French aggression. Thus Britain opposed intervention in Spain where the Bourbon king Ferdinand VII faced revolt from rebels who insisted that he respect the constitution. Similarly, Britain refused any joint move to restore the king of Naples and Sicily, Ferdinand I, who had broken his promise to respect constitutional reforms when he was restored to his throne in 1815. Nevertheless, in 1821 an Austrian army with Russian backing reinstated Ferdinand I, and the next year a French army restored absolute monarchy in Spain. Thus the Greek revolt was a challenge to the prevailing ideology of European diplomacy after the Napoleonic Wars, while at the same time it opened the delicate "Eastern Question" caused by the Ottoman empire's decline and its waning control of its outlying regions.

Since the fall of Constantinople in 1453, the Greeks had lived under the rule of the Turkish sultan, and what is now modern Greece was a province of an empire with its capital at Constantinople. Turkish rule was arbitrary and treated Christians as inferiors; taxes, although collected by local Greek leaders, were oppressive, and the government could not main-

tain law and order: the klephts (brigands) from their mountain bases practised banditry as a hereditary profession, and some of these klephts such as Theodore Kolokotronis in the Peloponnese, Markos Botsaris in Epirus, and Odysseus Androutsos in central Greece were to become prominent in the revolution. However, the Greeks were permitted their language and their Greek Orthodox faith, and a remarkable degree of cultural continuity persisted both with the Byzantine empire and, among the educated, with the Classical past. Greeks prospered in trade and in the Ottoman administration, and the three cities in the empire with the largest Greek populations were Bucharest, Smyrna, and Constantinople, where the Greek Orthodox patriarch had his seat, and the Greeks of the Phanar (the Greek quarter) were among the sultan's most trusted counsellors. Greek merchant communities were to be found in most of the trading centres of Europe, particularly London, Paris, Geneva, Moscow, and Odessa, and a Russo-Turkish convention of 1783 gave the Greeks the right to trade under the Russian flag. Much of the Greek national revival before the War of Independence took place outside the boundaries of modern Greece.

French and Russian interest in Greece antedated the French Revolution: Catherine the Great played briefly with the idea of reestablishing the Byzantine empire with Constantinople as its capital and her grandson Constantine as emperor, and on the eve of the Revolution, in 1788, France established a consul at Ioannina which had developed into a Greek cultural centre under Ali Pasha, the *veli* (governor) of Epirus who ruled his pashalik with only nominal recognition of Ottoman suzerainty. English aristocrats began to include Greece in their Grand Tour, particularly after the Napoleonic Wars closed Germany and Italy to them, and in 1809 Greece had a famous visitor, Lord Byron, who was already writing the first cantos of *Childe Harold's Pilgrimage*, which was to bring him an international reputation when it was published (1812). In 1814 the British inadvertently gave a strong stimulus to revolution by taking the Ionian islands from Napoleon and making them a protectorate, and in the same year three merchants at Odessa founded the *Philiki Hetaireia* (Friendly Society) which aimed boldly at rebellion.

The rebellion of Ali Pasha in 1820 presented the *Hetaireia* with an opportunity, for it drew off Turkish forces, and the Hetairist conspirators planned a revolt in Greece to coincide with an incursion of Greek expatriates across the Pruth river into Ottoman Wallachia (modern Romania) led by a Phanariot Greek, prince Alexander Hypsilantes, who had been a Russian army officer and aide-de-camp to tsar Alexander I. Hypsilantes advanced on 6 March 1821, but his invasion failed, the tsar disowned him, and he fled to Vienna where he died in exile. But on 25 March Germanos, the metropolitan of Patras, whom a suspicious governor had summoned to Tripolitsa (modern Tripolis) along with other clergy and primates, raised the standard of the cross in the monastery of Hagia Lavra. There followed a general uprising all over Greece, and a massacre of the Turks living in the Peloponnese.

The sultan reacted by hanging the Greek Patriarch Gregory V in Constantinople on Easter Sunday and various other prominent Greeks, and the Greek populations in Constantinople and Smyrna were decimated. On 5 October Tripolitsa in the Peloponnese fell to the Greeks led by Kolokotronis and thousands of Turks were killed or taken as slaves, while early in 1822 the Turks riposted with a massacre of the Greek population on the island of Chios. In July a large Ottoman army led by Mohammed Dramali pushed south through the pass of Thermopylae, took Corinth, and reached Argos where it encountered strong resistance, and when Dramali, running short of supplies, tried to retreat, his army was caught and destroyed (6 August) by Kolokotronis in the Dervenaki pass, which the Turks had neglected to secure. The year 1822 established Greece as an independent state; it began with the proclamation of a constitution with Alexander Mavrokordatos as president, and by the end of the year the Turks had surrendered Nauplia to Kolokotronis, and had withdrawn from all of eastern Greece south of Thermopylae. However Kolokotronis, who now was in control of the Peloponnese, refused to hand over Nauplia to the constitutional government, which had to accept protection from the shipping magnates on Hydra and Spetsai, one of whom, George Kountouriotis, a Hydriot shipowner of Albanian descent, was elected president. But 1823 was still a successful year: the Turkish offensive, hampered by the destruction by fire of the sultan's arsenal in Constantinople, failed in Epirus where Markos Botsaris, the Greek "Leonidas", defeated a Turkish force at Karpenisi, but was killed in the moment of victory, while in the east Kolokotronis abandoned his feud with the national government long enough to crush a new Turkish thrust against the Peloponnese. But sultan Mahmoud

by no means accepted defeat, though circumstances now forced him to turn to the pasha of Egypt for help.

The cause of Greek freedom attracted widespread support in Europe, and a diverse collection of volunteers flocked to Greece: French, Germans, Italians, and Danes, some of them former soldiers in the Napoleonic War, all of them ill informed about local conditions. The first philhellene battalion was almost annihilated in July 1822 at the Battle of Peta near Arta in northwest Greece, and the remnant filtered homewards, disillusioned. A "German Legion" of 120 German and Swiss volunteers recruited by a Greek adventurer, "Baron" Kephalas, landed at Nauplia in 1823, where it was abandoned without supplies, and dispersed. But at the end of the year a group of british Philhellenes arrived in Missolonghi, and they were joined by the most famous philhellene of all, Lord Byron.

Byron, who reached Missolonghi on 5 January 1824 and died on 19 April, was connected with no important victory, but he sparked an enthusiasm for the cause of Greece that served it better than a military success. Byron had been invited by the London Greek Committee to go to Greece as one of three commissioners to administer a loan which was raised in Britain, and after much hesitation he acquiesced. His attempts to get the various Greek factions to cooperate with each other failed, and he had achieved little when he died from the combined effects of malaria and the attentions of his doctors. His death, however, created a deep impression, not all of it favourable. The obituary in *The Times* read "That noblest of enterprises, the deliverance of Greece, employed the whole of Lord Byron's latter days ... It was a cause worthy of a poet and a hero." But the reaction of the British establishment was more correctly expressed by another notice published in *John Bull*, which said that be had died "at a most unfortunate period of his career, and in a most unsatisfactory manner". The factions within Greece reverted to civil war after his death; Kolokotronis was imprisoned and other notables such as Mavrokordatos and Petrobey Mavromichalis, the semifeudal lord of the Mani, retired in disgust. Yet Byron's death awoke the sympathies of Europe and promoted mightily the climate of opinion that demanded liberty for Greece. His statue, beneath which is buried his heart, was erected in 1881 in the "Park of the Heroes" in modern Missolonghi with, on one side, the tomb of Markos Botsaris who died just before before Byron's arrival, and on the other, a tomb for unnamed defenders of Missolonghi.

The London Greek Committee had been formed in 1823, and by the end of the year had 85 members, many of them supporters of political reform in Britain. The committee's success at raising money by voluntary subscription was not impressive, but it was responsible for the Greek loans, the first of which, with a nominal value of 800,000 pounds sterling, discounted at 41 per cent, was floated on the London Stock Exchange in February 1824, followed by a second loan a year later. These loans, exported to Greece as English gold sovereigns and Spanish silver dollars, helped support the authority of the Kountouriotis government, for Kountouriotis was the only Greek included among the three commissioners appointed by the London Greek Committee to administer them, and in order to get a share of the money, Kolokotronis gave up control of Nauplia at last in early summer 1824. But the money soon disappeared to settle the accounts of the Greek shipowners who supplied the fleet, pay political debts, settle the civil wars, and satisfy the avarice of the Greek leaders. Little was done to prepare Greece for the next assault by Mehemet Ali, the pasha of Egypt, who had built up a modern army and fleet trained by former Bonapartist officers. He was the nominal vassal of the sultan, and it was to him that the sultan turned for help against the rebellious Greeks.

In February 1825 an Arab force led by Mehemet Ali's son Ibrahim landed in Greece, laid siege to the fortress of Navarino, and defeated a Greek attempt to relieve it. Then, while Ibrahim devastated the Peloponnese, an Ottoman army launched an offensive in the north. April 1826 brought Missolonghi's long agony to an end, and like the massacre at Chios, its fall was commemorated by a painting by Eugène Delacroix (1799–1863), showing Greece expiring in the ruins of Missolonghi. The Turks followed up the capture by securing most of Roumeli (the region north of the Corinthian gulf) and advancing on Athens. By winter 1826 free Greece had run out of both money and food, and in June of the next year the Acropolis of Athens fell to the Turks.

Deliverance came from outside. In 1825 tsar Alexander I indicated that he would welcome a move from Britain, and in early 1826 the Duke of Wellington went to St Petersburg to sign an Anglo-Russian protocol, one clause of which pledged that neither party would seek any increase in territory, exclusive influence, or commercial advantage for itself. France joined later in the summer; Austria and Prussia remained aloof. The Turks, however, refused mediation and Greece's survival was not assured until the battle of Navarino on 20 October 1827, where combined British, Russian, and French naval squadrons destroyed the Turkish and Egyptian fleets. Even so, Ibrahim did not quit the Peloponnese until the next year, when the French government, with the consent of its allies, landed a force which saw to his withdrawal. But the "Powers" were little disposed to enlarge the new state's territory and a new Russo-Turkish war (April 1828–September 1829) distracted their attention. Meanwhile, a National Assembly of Greece met at Troezen and, passing over the various protagonists of the revolution, on 14 April 1827 chose Count Kapodistria, a Corfiote by birth who had served Tsar Alexander I, as *kyvernitis* (governor) for seven years. Kapodistria attempted both to consolidate his own position, hoping to thwart prince Leopold of Saxe-Coburg, to whom the "Powers" offered the crown in 1830, and to increase the Greek domain: efforts to take Chios and Crete failed, but north of the Corinthian Gulf Missolonghi was taken and Athens blockaded, and the last victory of the war took place between Thebes and Levadia in September 1829. But the authoritarian government of Kapodistria roused resentment, which came to a head in the Mani, where the family of Petrobey Mavromichalis held hereditary dominion. On 9 October 1831 one of Petrobey's sons assassinated Kapodistria in Nauplia as he was on his way to church. Greece slipped into civil war again while the "Powers" turned their attention elsewhere, Russia to a Polish insurrection and Britain and France to the creation of Belgium, whose first king was Leopold of Saxe-Coburg, who had abandoned his ambitions in Greece. On 13 February 1832 the Greek throne was offered to the 17-year-old Otto, second son of the king of Bavaria.

Greece had lapsed into anarchy. To quote George Finlay, whose account of the revolution in his history of Greece from the Roman conquest to AD 1864 was based on personal experience, "the whole substance of the land was devoured by hosts of soldiers, sailors, captains, generals, policemen, government officials, tax-gatherers, secretaries and political adventurers, all living idly at the public expense, while the agricultural population was perishing from starvation." The famine year of 1827 would have claimed thousands more victims except for shipments of food and clothing organized by three American philhellenes, George Jarvis, Jonathan Miller, and Samuel Howe, who managed, with some difficulty, to see to it that most of their relief consignments did not fall into the hands of the various Greek factions that were struggling for power. However, on 21 July 1832 sultan Mahmoud signed a treaty recognizing the kingdom of Greece, with its northern frontier a line from the Gulf of Arta to the Gulf of Volos, and the "Powers" guaranteed a loan for the new government. In January of the next year French troops in Argos suppressed a rebellion by Kolokotronis' faction, and when Otto arrived at Nauplia on 1 February with 3500 Bavarian troops, order had already been restored. To quote Finlay again, "The king landed and mounted his horse under the cyclopean walls of Tiryns, which were covered with spectators...Enthusiasts, who thought of the poetic glories of Homer's Greece, and the historic greatness of the Greece of Thucydides, might be pardoned if they indulged a hope that a third Greece was emerging into life, which would again occupy a brilliant position in the world's annals."

JAMES ALLAN EVANS

See also Ali Pasha, Botsaris, Brigandage, Gregory V, Hetairists, Hydra, Kapodistria, Kolokotronis, Mavrokordatos, Mavromichalis, Philhellenes

Further Reading

Clogg, Richard (editor), *The Struggle for Greek Independence: Essays to Mark the 150th Anniversary of the Greek War of Independence*, London: Macmillan, and Hamden, Connecticut: Archon, 1973

Dakin, Douglas, *The Greek Struggle for Independence, 1821–1833*, London: Batsford, and Berkeley: University of California Press, 1973

Dontas, Domna N., *The Last Phase of the War of Independence in Western Greece (December 1827 to May 1829)*, Thessalonica: Institute for Balkan Studies, 1966, reprinted Amsterdam: Hakkert, 1990

Finlay, George, *History of the Greek Revolution*, 2 vols, Edinburgh: Blackwood, 1861, reprinted London: Zeno, 1971

Makrygiannes, Ioannes, *The Memoirs of General Makriyannis, 1797–1864*, London and New York: Oxford University Press, 1966

Pappas, Paul Constantine, *The United States and the Greek War for Independence, 1821–1828*, Boulder, Colorado: East European Monographs, 1985

St Clair, William, *That Greece Might Still Be Free: The Philhellenes in the War of Independence*, London and New York: Oxford University Press, 1972

Whitcombe, Thomas Douglas, *The Campaign of the Falieri and Piraeus in the Year 1827; or, Journal of a Volunteer*, edited by C.W.J. Eliot, Princeton, New Jersey: American School of Classical Studies at Athens, 1992

Woodhouse, C.M., *The Battle of Navarino*, London: Hodder and Stoughton, and Chester Springs, Pennsylvania: Dufour, 1965

Industry

The early phase of industrialization in Greece can be dated to the 1860s. The first wave of bourgeois social and political activity emerged in the 1860s and 1870s, in a context marked by the prevalence of a liberal party and the establishment in 1875 of parliamentary rule. The 1900s heralded the second wave of bourgeois activity, marked by the 1909 coup and the development of several civil groupings and associations. A short-lived attempt in the direction of an industrial policy was the tariff system introduced in 1917, which for the first time represented a systematic effort to assist domestic industry. But industrial policy remained for the most part patchy and incoherent, the result of an extensive but weak state apparatus being unable to steer through social pressures in order to form a policy line on the desired path of development. In fact, the issue of protectionism was a key issue behind the establishment of an association representing industrial interests. Until the Commercial Association of Athens (ESA) was established in 1902, Greek capitalists involved in manufacturing and other industrial production had no separate association. Although its activities and major concerns shifted in the course of its development, the ESA was established first and foremost as an organizational response on the part of major Athens-based commercial interests to the emerging trade union movement and the spread of strike activity and, more generally, the "new awareness of the social question" after 1900 (Hadziiossif, 1997, p. 15). Several industrialists joined the new organization, although most also expressed an interest in the establishment of a separate industrial association. In 1906 the ESA took a line against tariff protection. Against this background it became increasingly apparent that a separate organization promoting industrial interests was needed. In 1907 the industrialists established their own association, the Federation of Greek Industrialists (SEV), which soon proved an energetic forum.

Between the 1860s and the 1910s a number of new industrial establishments were founded, but the overall growth in industrial activity was very small. Still, the beginning of the century was a turning point for the development of bourgeois and petty bourgeois activity in general. As a share of the national product, combined commercial and industrial activities in the widest sense (including various forms of very small-scale production) amounted to approximately 24 per cent in 1870 and 38 per cent in 1910.

The process of industrialization began in earnest in the 1920s. Industrial development was given a boost in 1922 with the influx of approximately 1.5 million Greek refugees from Asia Minor, following Greece's defeat by the Turks. The year 1922 marked the end of a period during which Greek politics and state policy had been almost completely dominated by irredentist impulses. After the 1920s policy priorities changed, although political developments surrounding the end of the Second Republic (1924–35), combined with the international climate, resulted in unimpressive industrial growth. Although the structure of Greek industry and its patterns of ownership and control changed during these interwar years many elements survived well into the 1960s, affecting the country's profile of industry. The predominance of light consumer goods industries and a relatively low own- to total-capital ratio, indi-

cating companies' large debts, continued to be an important feature. The predominance of very small firms (those employing less than 50 persons) also persisted, with fewer than 1 per cent of manufacturing establishments employing more than 50 persons in 1958. Industry acquired a considerable regional concentration, particularly in Attica and, to a much lesser degree, around Thessalonica and in Volos. The average yearly rate of growth in fixed and variable assets of Greece's industrial enterprises from 1957 to 1960 was approximately 5 per cent. At the same time, in the 1960s the number of new factories rose steadily.

Another continuity with the interwar years was a reluctance to separate ownership and management. The dual role of industrialists as owners and managers of their firms, even as some of these firms grew in size and diversified, was a feature of Greek industry well into the 1960s. Management tended to be highly centralized, and preoccupation with the "commercial" aspects of the enterprises appeared to be more immediately rewarding as well as prone to centralized managerial handling than did measures to improve organizational efficiency. Even as the larger Greek companies evolved, some of their more autocratic features persisted in different forms. The predominance of a small inner circle became a characteristic of large Greek companies, particularly with the adoption early on of the French corporate type of the *société anonyme* (SA). Unlike its US or British counterpart, which is usually characterized by widely dispersed shareholdings, the standard SA has a small core of powerful shareholders and a board which is dominated by the company president or director general.

In the immediate postwar period the state's minimal participation in industrial investments was matched by a system of Marshall Aid allocation which reinforced the lack of coherent industrial policy. Apart from testifying to the structural weaknesses of the Greek state, this tendency echoed the views held by a major strand in the dominant US view regarding the desired development goals of the European semiperiphery. A major aid target was the preservation of social stability. The latter was dependent upon the preservation of the existing political structures and the characteristics of the economic system, and it was intended that an emphasis on specialized agriculture for the world market should become the target for Greek development. Instead of strengthening its industrial base, Greece was expected to specialize in small-scale rural enterprises for processing and marketing labour-intensive crops. The proposition suggested a specific position and clear limits for the country's development within the international division of labour (see Lavdas, 1997). When the Greek government produced a Four Year Plan within the framework of the Marshall Plan in 1948, it soon became clear that funds that were originally earmarked for economic aid were transferred to defence, while economic aid funds originally intended for industrial projects went to agriculture (Kofas, 1990, p.73). To some extent the suggested path derived from a general framework of priorities established in the US-dominated world economy and supported by the Organization for European Economic Cooperation (OEEC). In that framework Greece was expected to specialize in agriculture and light (consumer-goods) industries. In the 1950s, while the first priority of the communist-bloc economic union, Comecon, was the creation of sectors of heavy (producer-goods) industry even in states like Albania, driving ad absurdum the logic of forced industrialization, "the contemporary round of OEEC long-term plans — for plans for dollar viability in 1952–53 were a condition of Marshall Aid — were in revealing contrast: Norway and Greece were rebuked for wanting steel plans" (Kaser, 1965, p.19).

The integration of Greece's industries in the international market was promoted in 1953 with a number of measures which included the liberalization of the tariff system, the devaluation of the drachma, and the adoption of a policy which was explicitly aimed at attracting foreign direct investment. The emphasis on exporting goods, which became the dominant strategy in the late 1950s, went through a series of ups and downs, particularly when it was realized that a strategy relying on agricultural exports would be untenable. The export crisis of 1958–59 manifested the limits of a policy oriented towards agricultural exports and became the background against which the decision was taken to join the EEC as an associate member. From 1960 to the early 1970s the construction boom and foreign direct investments contributed to remarkable growth rates. But from the first (1973) to the second oil shock (1979) the Greek economy lost many of its dynamic characteristics and domestic as well as foreign private investment began to decline. By the time of Greece's accession to the EC as a full member in 1981, Greek industry was in the midst of a period of decline, only worsened by the early policies of the socialist PASOK government of Andreas Papandreou in 1981–85. In 1985 a rigorous but short-lived stabilization effort was undertaken, but the process of relative deindustrialization was only temporarily halted.

On balance, the postwar industrialization process has shown signs of weakening and even reversal since the first oil shock. In contrast to developments in most other countries in the OECD (Organization for Economic Cooperation and Development, which replaced the OEEC in 1961), following the first oil shock profit rates in Greek manufacturing were very slow to reach pre-oil-shock levels. There has been an apparent failure of the manufacturing sector to adjust to international trade and the relaxation of protection and, particularly after the second oil shock in 1979, manufacturing has responded in a defensive manner by retreating to traditional activities such as food and beverages, textiles and clothing (Giannitsis, 1985 and 1993). This has been due to a number of factors, including difficulties in adjusting to rising labour costs following the change of regime in 1974, and the inability to improve productivity (as well as the relatively small margins allowed for a solution that would alleviate the profit squeeze with higher prices), which have led to a deteriorating profit rate since the mid-1970s. In turn, falling profit rates have led firms to rely increasingly on external finance.

In part, the underlying cause of the problem is associated, on the one hand, with the low levels of investment in manufacturing and, on the other hand, with the persistence of the orientation and the structure of production. In the 1950s Greek manufacturing investment per person employed was particularly low in comparison with other European countries. Despite a very high growth rate of manufacturing investment in the 1960s and the 1970s (much higher than the EEC average), manufacturing investment failed to catch up by the mid-1970s, and in the years before EC accession Greek manufacturing investment per person employed was 59 per cent of the EC average. In the late 1980s Greece continued to present a weak industrial gross value-added (the value added to raw materials by production), being at the bottom of the European league with Luxembourg and Ireland (followed by Portugal and Denmark).

The predominance of small firms has persisted. In 1980 more than 70 per cent of the manufacturing labour force was employed in establishments with fewer than 100 persons. The familiar problems of small-scale production are present in the Greek case, although there are also some good sectoral results. While Greek industrial companies (as distinct from their shipping counterparts) have never made it into the top 100 businesses of Europe, industrial small businesses have often been included among the world's top 100 based on a combination of criteria ranging from profitability to foreign market penetration to management efficiency – more recently companies from high technology, construction, and canning (see, for example, *Forbes* magazine, 8 November 1993).

Greece's accession to the European Community in 1981 completed the process of integration in the European economy and at the same time helped to bring into focus various issues of economic policy which had, for the most part, remained vaguely defined or intensely politicized. The Association Agreement of 1961 had reinforced the export-oriented strategy through a new institutional channel, which helped depoliticize and gradually dismantle the remaining areas of protectionism while also focusing on the problems and potential of industrial, not just agricultural, products. However, it must also be remembered that already by the mid-1950s the issue of import-substituting industrialization was dead, and had never been a consistent state policy. Tariff and non-tariff protectionism had been patchy, and no evidence has been found to support the view that economic policy was systematically promoting infant industry. Traditional sectors which were more weighty in political terms were often better protected, albeit with inconsistencies, while modern, capital-intensive, and technologically advanced industries were not granted protection (see Mitsos, 1989).

Despite oscillations, the general trend since the mid-1980s suggests an increase in profitability, raising expectations for increased investment activity. On the other hand, the growth rates of manufacturing production have remained low. Furthermore, import penetration of the Greek market by EU industrial products has grown. Technology flows appear to be declining, indicating the difficulties of Greek industry in absorbing and exploiting technology transfer in production; at the same time, there is an increasing reinforcement of domestic research and development (R&D) activities and higher participation rates of private firms in R&D (Giannitsis, 1993, p. 237). An overall assessment of the impact of EU membership on Greek industry can only be undertaken in a comprehensive context that would take account of the following factors: the effects on political stability; the implications for vertical integration within Greek industry; the creation of collaborative R&D schemes and the effects on domestic technological development as distinct from technology flows; changes in the relationships between public enterprises and the private sector; and the establishment of a level playing field through the implementation of European competition policy combined with the EU-induced development of national competition authorities.

KOSTAS A. LAVDAS

Further Reading

Charalambis, Dimitris, *Stratos kai Politiki Exousia: I Domi tis Exousias stin Metemphyliaki Ellada* [The Military and Political Power: The Structure of Power in Post-Civil War Greece], Athens: Exantas, 1985

Dertilis, George, *Elliniki Viomichania 1830–1910 kai Viomichaniki Epanastasi* [The Greek Economy 1830–1910 and Industrial Revolution], Athens: Sakkoulas, 1984

Freris, Antonis, *The Greek Economy in the Twentieth Century*, London: Croom Helm, and New York: St Martin's Press, 1986

Giannitsis, Tassos, *I Elliniki Viomichania: Anaptyxi kai Krisi* [Greek Industry: Development and Crisis], Athens: Gutenberg, 1985

Giannitsis, Tassos, "World Market Integration: Trade Effects and Implications for Industrial and Technological Change in the Case of Greece" in *Greece, the New Europe, and the Changing International Order*, edited by Harry J. Psomiades and Stavros B. Thomadakis, New York: Pella, 1993

Hadziiossif, Christos, "Apopseis gia tin viosimotita ths Ellados kai to Rolo ths Viomichanias" [Views on the Viability of Greece and the Role of Industry], *Synchrona Themata*, 31 (1987)

Hadziiossif, Christos, "Class Structure and Class Antagonism in Late Nineteenth Century Greece", in *Greek Society in the Making 1863–1913: Realities, Symbols and Visions*, edited by P. Carabott, Aldershot, Hampshire: Ashgate, 1997

Hassid, J., "Industrial Policy" in *Greece and EC Membership Evaluated*, edited by Panos Kazakos and P.C. Ioakimidis, London: Pinter, and New York: St Martin's Press, 1994

Kaser, Michael Charles, *Comecon: Integration Problems of the Planned Economies*, Oxford: Oxford University Press, 1965

Katseli, Louka, "Economic Integration in the Enlarged European Community: Structural Adjustment of the Greek Economy" in *Unity with Diversity in the European Economy: The Community's Southern Frontier*, edited by C. Bliss and J. Braga de Macedo, Cambridge and New York: Cambridge University Press, 1990

Katsoulis, Ilias, Tassos Giannitsis and Panos Kazakos (editors), *I Ellada pros to 2000* [Greece Towards 2000], Athens: Papazisis, 1988

Kofas, Jon, "The Greek Economy" in *Background to Contemporary Greece*, edited by Marion Sarafis and Martin Eve, London: Merlin, and New York: Barnes and Noble, 1990

Kostis, Kostas, *Synergasia kai Antagonismos* [Cooperation and Competition], Athens: Alexandreia, 1997

Lambrinides, M. and T. Pakos, "Fiscal Deficits and the Role of the State in the Greek Economy" in *The Greek Economy: Economic Policy for the 1990s*, edited by Thanos Skouras, London: Macmillan, 1992

Lavdas, Kostas A., *The Europeanization of Greece: Interest Politics and the Crises of Integration*, Basingstoke: Macmillan, and New York: St Martin's Press, 1997

McNeill, William H., *The Metamorphosis of Greece since World War II*, Oxford: Blackwell, and Chicago: University of Chicago Press, 1978

Mazower, Mark, *Greece and the Interwar Economic Crisis*, Oxford: Clarendon Press, and New York: Oxford University Press, 1992

Mitsos, Achilleas, *I Elliniki Viomichania sti Diethni Agora* [Greek Industry in the International Market], Athens: Themelio, 1989

Mouzelis, Nicos P., *Modern Greece: Facets of Underdevelopment*, London: Macmillan, and New York: Holmes and Meier, 1978

Pafilas, P., Viomichania [Industry] entry in *Megali Elliniki Eggyklopedia* [The Great Greek Encyclopedia], vol. 10, Athens: Pirsos, 1934

Pirounakis, Nicholas G., *The Greek Economy: Past, Present and Future*, London: Macmillan, and New York: St Martin's Press, 1997

Skouras, Thanos (editor), *The Greek Economy: Economic Policy for the 1990s*, London: Macmillan, 1992

Tsakalotos, Euclid, *Alternative Economic Strategies: The Case of Greece*, Aldershot, Hampshire: Avebury, 1991

Tsoukalis, Loukas, *The European Community and its Mediterranean Enlargement*, London and Boston: Allen and Unwin, 1981

Vaxevanoglou, Aliki, *Oi Ellines Kephalaioukhoi 1900–1940* [Greek Capitalists 1900–1940], Athens: Themelio, 1994

Inheritance

The transfer of property upon the death of the owner is known as inheritance, and almost every country has special laws that regulate the disposition of private property after the owner's death by naming the relatives or other persons who have first rights of inheritance. It is also permitted to transfer property to persons other than those specified by law by means of a will (the legal instrument that embodies the owner's ability to dispose freely of his or her property posthumously), and rules for making such wills are also set by inheritance law. The person who inherits or who is entitled by law to inherit property after the death of its owner is known as an heir, while the dead owner is called the decedent. Upon the death of a person, the title to all the property, both personal and real, must pass to someone. If there is a valid will, property usually passes to the legatees, i.e. the persons directed by the decedent. In the absence of a valid will, the decedent is said to have died intestate, and the law must then decide who the valid heirs are, and the order and proportion by which they inherit. This is done according to statutes known as intestacy laws. Strictly speaking, an heir is a recipient of money or property left by someone who died intestate, whereas the beneficiary of a will is technically known as a legatee or devisee. But in common usage "heir" refers to anyone awarded an estate, whether or not the deceased person left a will.

In ancient Greece, where our evidence comes chiefly from Athens and the Cretan city of Gortyn, intestate succession was favoured. Wills, which were normally written and witnessed, were allowed only when the testator had no sons. First in order of succession came the dead person's sons and male descendants. Thus, if a deceased man left legitimate sons, they shared the property equally, the eldest getting no more than the others. The western medieval right of primogeniture – according to which land devolved automatically on the eldest legitimate son – had no place in Greek society. If a son died before his father and left sons of his own, then those sons inherited their father's share. If there were no sons or male descendants, the inheritance passed to the decedent's brothers and male descendants, and in the third place to the sons of the decedent's grandfather and their male descendants. Ascendants were excluded if their descendants were alive: the father did not inherit if a brother of the deceased was alive; nor did the grandfather, if an uncle was alive. No distinction was made between natural and adopted sons; but children born out of wedlock were illegitimate, and had no claim on the father's estate. During the Byzantine period, however, all natural persons (i.e. blood descendents, including slaves, minors, and the unborn) could inherit, as also could corporate bodies, communities, the Church, or pious foundations. Christianity, in fact, encouraged donations at death to churches and monasteries as well as the distribution of part of the inheritance among the poor. Moreover, under Byzantine rulers, the state demanded part of the inheritance in the form of voluntary grants or as a mandatory obligation. However, the right of individuals to inherit was diminished or even precluded by a set of punishable offences and other factors: heretics, apostates, and even children of a mixed marriage with a heretic were excluded from succession while manumitted slaves might receive only the so-called *legata* (special legacies). There were also restrictions regarding the inheritance of certain specific types of property: *stratiotika ktemata* (military goods), for example, could be inherited only by those capable of fulfilling military service (perhaps a similar objective was achieved by the Homeric heroes through prizes given at funeral games, cf. *Iliad*, 23). Although slaves could inherit under the Byzantine empire, they were not given the right to transfer property upon death. However, wills of women and monks are known and *paroikoi* (tenants) were entitled to transfer their lands to heirs, though probably only with the approval of their lords.

In Classical Athens the claims of sons and male descendants could not be set aside by testamentary dispositions. Males generally excluded females in the same group of kinship. Only in the absence of sons or male descendants of predeceased sons could a daughter inherit. She was obliged to marry the man to whom her father had destined her either when he was alive or by a will. Failing such disposition, the daughter could be claimed by the next collateral together with her father's fortune. But if a son remained, the daughter had no right to succeed and could demand only a dowry, to be determined at the discretion of her brother. If she was divorced or was childless after marriage, the dowry went back to the heirs, i.e. the male descendants. If the decedent left a daughter but no son, and if the daughter had a son, he would inherit. But as long as she was without a son, she was *epikleros*, i.e. a sort of "heiress", who could be claimed in marriage by her nearest male relative who took charge of the property until their son was old enough to take it over. One must not, however, conclude from this that women in Greek cities could not inherit. Literary and epigraphical sources, from Athens, Gortyn, Naupactus, and Thermus in Aetolia, of the 5th–3rd centuries BC, suggest that women did inherit, in a succession order of varying complexity in different states. In the absence of legitimate children, the inheritance could be claimed by relatives within the *anchisteia* (close kin). It was in effect possible for a man without sons to choose an heir by adoption and thus ensure the continuance of his family and the religious worship connected with it. The adoptee became legally the son of the adopter and so inherited the property, but could not oust an *epikleros*; he might marry her himself (in which case the chief share of the inheritance would fall to this married daughter and her husband, while any other daughters would be given dowries), but anyway her son inherited eventually. If a son had not been adopted, and there were only daughters surviving, the succession passed to them. In such a case the next of kin had a legal right to one of the heiresses, and could claim to marry her

even if she had married someone else before receiving the inheritance. On the other hand, poor heiresses had a legal claim on their nearest of kin either for marriage or for a provision suitable to their circumstance. A man who married an heiress was bound by custom and tradition, if he had sons, to name one as heir to the property that had come with his wife, and thus to restore the house.

According to tradition, it was Solon (*c*.640–560 BC) who introduced wills to Attic law. Previously, the estate of a childless man had gone to his clan. Because it gave one the power to dispose of property after death, the right to make a will was a recognition of the right of private property rather than of family, clan, or tribal ownership. We have surviving accounts of the wills of some well-known personages of antiquity. Aristotle was generous in providing for his family and friends, while Epicurus willed his property to the school hoping "that all those who study philosophy may never be in want ... so far as our power to prevent it may extend" (Diogenes Laertius, 10). According to his first speech *Against Aphobus* (no. 27), Demosthenes' father left in trust for him an estate worth about 14 talents, including two small businesses in cutlery and furniture. The Athenian banker Pasion in his will appointed his former slave Phormio as guardian for his younger son, entrusting him with the management of the bank until the boy should come of age; he also stipulated that Phormio should marry his widow (Demosthenes, 36). Some of the purposes of a will had been achieved by resorting to adoptions, which continued to be common and were treated to some extent like wills. But the will took effect only on the testator's death. No formality was needed for legitimate sons to take possession of the inheritance, and they had no right to refuse it. Other relatives, however, needed an official authorization. If a man died intestate, leaving neither descendants nor adopted sons, the inheritance fell to his nearest relations in the male line and, in default of these, to those in the female line as far as children of first cousins. It was also possible to resort to posthumous adoption by which relatives arranged for one of themselves to become legally the deceased man's son. Disinheriting, however, was possible only in the father's lifetime by solemn declaration. It was not possible to disinherit legitimate children by means of a will or adoption.

At Athens anyone who thought that he had a legal claim to an inheritance made an application to the archon to hand it over to him. This application was displayed in public and read out in the following assembly. The question was then asked whether anyone disputed the claim or raised a counterclaim. If not, the archon assigned the inheritance to the claimant; otherwise the matter was decided by a lawsuit. Even an inheritance once assigned might be disputed in the lifetime of the holder and for five years after his death. The same procedure was followed regarding the claim of the nearest relation to an heiress. The Athenian orator/speech-writer Isaeus (*c*.420–*c*.350 BC) appears to have specialized in cases of inheritance. Of some 50 speeches with which he was credited, the 11 that have survived in entirety all deal with cases of inheritance and are important as illustrations of Athenian testamentary law.

According to the Gortyn law code (12 columns of laws engraved on the interior wall of a former courthouse and attributed to the 5th century BC), the property was shared by the sons and daughters, but a son got twice as much as a daughter, as happens de jure among the Muslims (cf. Qur'an 4: 2 and 34). A daughter without brothers was called *patroiochos* and her rights were generally similar to those of the *epikleros* at Athens, although there were differences of detail.

Both forms of transferring property – through a will and through intestate succession – were recognized in the Byzantine empire. It was also possible to enter into an informal agreement when a dowry was promised for a marriage contract, so that these agreements assume the character of both marriage and inheritance contracts. By the time of the code of Justinian (AD 529), Roman law recognized many types of wills, including oral wills declared in the presence of seven witnesses or before a public official. But for the Byzantines, the will represented only one of many dispositions that a living person could make in view of his death. On the one hand, for a will to be valid, it was not necessary for an heir to have been appointed and, on the other hand, it was possible to make *legata, fideicommissa* (bequests in trust), donations in view of death, to pious foundations, distributions of money for the good of the soul (*psychika*), and similar arrangements independently without being part of a formal will.

The heir entered into the legal position of the deceased and therefore became responsible for the obligations of the testator just as he, in his turn, could put forward the claims of the testator. The heir was also considered a debtor of the legacies bequeathed by the testator. To keep the heir's own property from being liable for the debts of the deceased, it became the practice from the time of Justinian I to establish an inventory documenting the size of the inheritance. A limitation on the responsibility of the heir for paying the bequests made by the testator was guaranteed by the Falcidian Law of 40 BC.

D.P.M. WEERAKKODY

See also Adoption, Children

Further Reading

Cartledge, Paul and F.D. Harvey (editors), *Crux: Essays Presented to G.E.M. de Ste. Croix on His 75th Birthday*, Exeter: Imprint Academic, 1985, pp. 208–32

Chester, Ronald, *Inheritance, Wealth, and Society*, Bloomington: Indiana University Press, 1982

Goody, Jack, Joan Thirsk, and E.P. Thompson, *Family and Inheritance: Rural Society in Western Europe, 1200–1800*, Cambridge and New York: Cambridge University Press, 1976

Hardcastle, M., "Some Non-Legal Arguments in Athenian Inheritance Cases", *Prudentia*, 12 (1980): pp. 11–22

Harrison, A.R.W., *The Law of Athens*, 2nd edition, 2 vols, London: Duckworth, and Indianapolis: Hackett, 1998

Hodkinson, S., "Land Tenure and Inheritance in Classical Sparta", *Classical Quarterly*, 36 (1986): pp. 378–406

Macdowell, Douglas, *The Law in Classical Athens*, London: Thames and Hudson, and Ithaca, New York: Cornell University Press, 1978, pp. 92–108

Schaps, D., "Women in Greek Inheritance Law", *Classical Quarterly*, 25 (1975): pp. 53–57

Thompson, Wesley E., *De Hagniae Hereditate: An Athenian Inheritance Case*, Leiden: Brill, 1976

Todd, S.C., *The Shape of Athenian Law*, Oxford: Clarendon Press, 1993

Inscriptions

Inscriptions can be taken to refer to objects made of different materials – e.g. pottery, clay tablets, metal, and most usually stone – on which letters have been carved, drawn, or painted. The study of inscriptions (epigraphy) usually focuses on inscribed stone or metal objects. In this article some mention will be made of inscriptions on pottery, clay tablets, and coins, but the focus will be on stone and metal inscriptions.

Inscriptions provide the cultural historian of the Hellenic tradition with a wealth of ideas and information about the past and the ways in which the people of the past presented themselves. Inscriptions are more familiar to the historians of the Graeco-Roman world, but inscribed material from the Byzantine, Frankish, and Ottoman eras is also known.

Some students of history still make the mistake of thinking that epigraphic evidence has a greater value than other forms of evidence because of its often more durable nature. Inscriptions, like much historical evidence, have been produced in a temporal and spatial context often with a self-conscious appreciation of meaning and function. The evidence of inscriptions is therefore laden with difficulties of interpretation, in addition to the fact that not all the material that was inscribed has survived or been discovered. Further, not all areas of Greece or Greek communities inscribed; nor did all Greek communities inscribe all the time. These phenomena can be summarized by the term "epigraphic habit". Of all ancient societies, the Greeks were among the most advanced in terms of their epigraphic habit; and of the Greeks, the Athenians provide the most extreme example of display through inscriptions. Greek inscriptions are one index of the diffusion of Greek culture, and their distribution reaches far beyond the shores of the Mediterranean: Greek inscriptions and organized modern collections of ancient material appear in Bulgaria, Romania, and southern Russia; a large body of evidence exists in the Near East, along the African coast, particularly in Egypt and Cyrene. Greek inscriptions appear all over the Graeco-Roman world, thereby illustrating the importance of the Greek language for the development of Western culture.

But in many communities inscriptions were made not only in the Greek alphabet. From some periods and some regions a combination of languages have survived on some inscriptions. The Letoön trilingual is an inscription which provides a parallel text in Aramaic, Greek, and Lycian (Davies, 1983, pp 244–45). In many areas during the Roman period, bilingual Greek–Latin inscriptions were made, the *Res Gestae* of Augustus being perhaps the best-known example (Brunt and Moore, 1967). From the Classical and Hellenistic periods, numerous bilingual inscriptions in Greek and Phoenician have survived, especially on Delos, on Cyprus, and at Athens.

Greek inscriptions first appeared in the Archaic period; the earliest known examples are scratched or painted on pottery and date to the second half of the 8th century BC. Their appearance touches on the related question of the introduction of the Greek alphabet. Modern understanding of the introduction and development of the Greek alphabet is heavily dependent on inscriptions. Of the inscriptions which survive from the archaic period, many examples exhibit a significant difference both in regional dialects and in local letter styles (Jeffrey, 1961).

Although very few of the early inscriptions amount to lengthy texts, the majority are dedications, brief commemorative statements, often in a funerary context. An inscribed bronze helmet dedicated by the Syracusans to Zeus at Olympia is an offering made from the spoils of a victory over the Etruscans by Hieron after a battle at Cumae (Fornara, 1977, no. 64A). According to Diodorus Siculus (11. 51), the successful naval battle was fought in 474 BC. The first lengthy inscriptions survive from the 6th century BC. Among the best known are the legal texts from Crete and in particular the great code from Gortyn which gives vital details about the organization of the Dorian community (Fornara, 1977, no. 88).

By the 5th century BC many areas of the Greek-speaking world were producing inscriptions, often of some length. Athens was the leading producer, exploiting the high-quality marble of the Penteli and Hymettus mountains on which to inscribe decrees. The so-called Athenian tribute lists record the offerings (1/60 of the tribute payment) made to Athena by members of the Delian League. The lists were set up on the Acropolis in Athens and are the largest and probably the most studied series of documents from the 5th century. They provide a lengthy and detailed, if incomplete, list of the payments made by the individual cities who were subject allies of Athens from the middle of the 5th century to the last years of the Peloponnesian War (see Nixon and Price, 1990). In contrast to Athens, its main rival, Sparta, does not offer any detailed epigraphic record for the Classical period. Stone inscriptions were not produced in Sparta in any real quantity until the end of the Hellenistic period.

Inscriptions have many uses in exploring the past. They provide highly specific information, sometimes giving very accurate dates. Ancient chronology is complicated by different regional and civic dating systems. The Parian Marble lists historical events from the early history of Greece down to the 3rd century BC but is riddled with inconsistencies and confusions (Fornara ,1977, no. 1; Harding, 1985, no. 1; Austin, 1981, no. 1). The vast number of inscriptions from Athens provides a well-established body of carefully dated material. The day, month, and year, and the sitting public officials are given in the prescripts of most decrees of the Athenian people.

Inscriptions also offer a huge range of names and form the basis of the study of names (onomastics) and of named individuals (proposopography). The *Lexicon of Greek Personal Names* has collected all known instances of names from different regions of Greece; inscriptions provide the majority of the known evidence.

Inscriptions can also give particularly useful details about events and periods of history. Epigraphic evidence is often the only contemporary documentary information which survives for certain periods of history. The Athenians formed an alliance in 378/7 BC with Thebes and other Greek cities; the founding agreement of the alliance has survived on stone but its existence is omitted, notoriously, from Xenophon's account of this period of 4th-century Greek history (Cargill, 1981; Harding, 1985, no. 35).

Other areas of cultural and social history are illuminated by the evidence of inscriptions. There has been considerable controversy over the extent to which the ancient Greeks practised exposure of infants. Pomeroy (1983) has argued on the basis of an inscription from late 3rd-century Miletus that selec-

tive female infanticide may have been practised among the families of mercenaries. Inscriptions supply enormous amounts of information and details about religious practices in antiquity. Sacred laws were inscribed on stone, as were calendars of religious festivals, dedications to deities, the financial accounts of cults, and decisions of cultic organizations.

The skill and dedication of those who study inscriptions have yielded valuable results. Different regions of the Greek world produced distinctive letter forms. In some areas there are sufficiently large numbers of inscriptions for experts to identify different "hands" of those who inscribed stones. S.V. Tracy has elevated the study and identification of the letter-cutters to such a high degree that many Athenian inscriptions of the 4th to the 1st centuries BC can be dated on the basis of the syle of the carved letters alone (Tracy, 1990, 1995).

Inscriptions were erected by a variety of authorities in antiquity. The state decrees are the most useful source of information for historical events, often concerned with major events or individuals who played some role in them. The most common form of public decree records the community as a whole honouring an individual. Such honorific decrees can be very formulaic in their phrasing and award of thanks. Crowns of olive, ivy, oak, or gold, property ownership rights, seats in the theatre, public acclamation, statues, citizenship rights for an invididual or his family and descendants, and of course erected inscriptions were all different ways in which people were honoured. Many of the honorific decrees from the 4th century onwards reveal important historical details: from Athens in the 270s the decree honouring Callias of Sphettus has revolutionized knowledge of the poorly documented first half of the 3rd century (Shear, 1978).

Public decrees also present important details about the political organization of communities. A collection of Greek public decrees made by Peter Rhodes allows such comparisons to be made among the epigraphically active Greek communities (Rhodes and Lewis, 1997). In the post-Classical period there was a massive increase in the number of communities producing inscriptions, particularly in Asia Minor. The political ideology of a community is often transmitted in its decrees. Decrees were passed by the public assembly, or council, or subgroup of the community (e.g. deme, tribe, etc.). While it is exceptional that fairly detailed descriptions of the Athenian and Spartan constitutions are available from literary sources, the political structures of other Greek communities can sometimes be reconstructed only through the study of inscriptions.

Honorific decrees typically account for the achievements of the honorand, especially from the mid-4th century onwards. But a number of inscriptions self-consciously reframe past events for a contemporary audience. The Themistocles decree from Troezen (Fornara, 1977, no. 55) was inscribed in the 3rd century and provides details of the career of the Athenian general who laid the foundations for the 5th-century empire and commanded the Greek forces against the Persians in 480 BC. From Cyrene a 4th-century inscription erected in the temple of Apollo seems to contain the text of the oath of the settlers who had originally founded the city (Fornara, 1977, no. 18). The founders had travelled from Thera, and established the settlement on the Libyan coast which flourished under the Battiad dynasty in the archaic and early classical periods. The 4th-century text allowed people from Thera to claim property and rights in Cyrene on the basis of the terms of the original 7th-century agreement of the settlers which is here reinscribed. Both the Themistocles decree and the Cyrene inscription illustrate how inscriptions can contain unique documents which not only shed light on history, but also represent how history was shaped for subsequent generations in ancient Greece.

However, it is a mistake to think of inscriptions as simple archives of information. Certainly, decrees and laws served as extensions of a city's authority and legislation. Public records were kept in many Greek cities or temples, but often on perishable materials. The proportion of inscriptions written up on stone was always very small, but did at least represent an authoritative voice in a city's affairs. By the 3rd century BC collections of such decrees were being made, indicating that a far greater awareness of the information that the inscriptions contained was developing: Craterus (c.321–255 BC) published nine volumes of Athenian decrees.

But public decrees are only a small proportion of published inscriptions. A vast array of groups and individuals had inscriptions set up, e.g. groups of soldiers, demes, associations, religious organizations, ambassadors, kings, mothers, fathers, husbands, wives, widows, and children. The largest single type of inscription is the funerary monument; a rough estimate would suggest that of the known inscriptions from Athens between 400 BC and AD 267 perhaps as many as 70 per cent are funerary.

The epigraphic habit of the Greeks was passed down to the Romans. Greek communities continued to inscribe throughout the period of the Roman empire and beyond. The numbers of the later inscriptions are much smaller and their study is less well established than for the Graeco-Roman periods. Inscriptions from the Byzantine period exist but are fewer and the material has not been studied thoroughly: funerary inscriptions are less elaborate and details of donors and benefactors appear painted on pictures.

The Frankish and Ottoman domination of the Greek world imposed different authorities. Few inscriptions survive from this period, and the epigraphic habit virtually died out. However, the study of inscriptions developed in the Middle Ages. Cyriacus of Ancona (1391–c.1455) visited Greece in the 1430s and 1450s and on both occasions recorded inscriptions. The Italian scholars of the Renaissance promoted epigraphy as a subject of value, and although their work concentrated on Italian material, it promoted an interest in inscriptions and enabled the future explosion of interest in Greek epigraphy. Numerous travellers to Greece continued to record inscriptions. In the 17th century, Jacob Spon and George Wheeler recorded texts; the stones themselves became desirable objects. Thomas Arundel collected ancient marbles, including both sculpture and inscriptions. His most famous inscription was the Parian Marble, a catalogue of dates and events drawn up and inscribed in 264/63 BC. The increasing popularity of the Grand Tour in the 18th century ensured that more travellers from western Europe reached Greece. Antony Askew, an English doctor and amateur philologist, recorded over 200 inscriptions at Athens in 1747. The intensifying interest in Greek culture in the late 18th and early 19th centuries resulted in the removal of many antiquities from Greece, most notoriously the Parthenon marbles. Inscriptions were among the

stones removed from Greece, and in the early 19th century the study of epigraphic material reached new heights with the publication by A. Boeckh of the first volume of the *Corpus Inscriptionum Graecarum* (1828).

Inscriptions have become an easily identifiable feature of ancient culture. They offer a remarkable insight into the life and history of the people of antiquity. The legacy of ancient Greek inscriptions for Western culture is quite remarkable: one has only to visit any major 19th-century European cemetery to find imitations of inscribed gravestones from classical Greece. But it is the study of inscriptions and the appreciation of their importance in reaching an understanding of Greek culture that have progressed most rapidly in the last 200 years.

GRAHAM OLIVER

See also Alphabet, Archives, Onomastics

Further Reading

Austin, M.M., *The Hellenistic World from Alexander to the Roman Conquest: A Selection of Ancient Sources in Translation*, Cambridge and New York: Cambridge University Press, 1981

Brunt, P.A. and J.M. Moore (editors), *Res Gestae Divi Augusti: The Achievements of the Divine Augustus*, London: Oxford University Press, 1967

Cargill, Jack L., *The Second Athenian League: Empire or Free Alliance?*, Berkeley: University of California Press, 1981

Cook, B.F., *Greek Inscriptions*, London: British Museum, 1987

Davies, J.K., *Democracy and Classical Greece*, 2nd edition, London: Fontana, and Cambridge, Massachusetts: Harvard University Press, 1993

Fornara, Charles W. (translator and editor), *Archaic Times to the End of the Peloponnesian War*, 2nd edition, Cambridge and New York: Cambridge University Press, 1983 (Translated Documents of Greece and Rome, vol. 1)

Fraser, Peter M. and Elaine Matthews (editors), *A Lexicon of Greek Personal Names*, 3 vols, Oxford: Clarendon Press, and New York: Oxford University Press, 1987–97

Harding, Phillip (translator and editor), *From the End of the Peloponnesian War to the Battle of Ipsus*, Cambridge and New York: Cambridge University Press, 1985 (Translated Documents of Greece and Rome, vol. 2)

Jeffrey, L.H., *The Local Scripts of Archaic Greece: A Study of the Origin of the Greek Alphabet and its Development from the Eighth to the Fifth Centuries BC*, revised edition, edited by A.W. Johnston, Oxford: Clarendon Press, and New York: Oxford University Press, 1990

Millar, Fergus, "Epigraphy" in *Sources for Ancient History*, edited by Michael Crawford, Cambridge and New York: Cambridge University Press, 1983

Nixon, L. and Simon Price, "The Size and Resources of Greek Cities" in *The Greek City from Homer to Alexander*, edited by Oswyn Murray and Simon Price, Oxford: Clarendon Press, and New York: Oxford University Press, 1990

Pomeroy, Sarah B., "Infanticide in Hellenistic Greece" in *Images of Women in Antiquity*, edited by Averil Cameron and Amélie Kuhrt, London: Croom Helm, and Detroit: Wayne State University Press, 1983

Rhodes, Peter J. and David M. Lewis, *The Decrees of the Greek States*, Oxford: Clarendon Press, and New York: Oxford University Press, 1997

Shear, T. Leslie Jr, *Kallias of Sphettos and the Revolt of Athens in 286 BC*, Princeton, New Jersey: American School of Classical Studies at Athens, 1978

Tracy, Stephen V., *Attic Letter-Cutters of 229 to 86 BC*, Berkeley: University of California Press, 1990

Tracy, Stephen V., *Athenian Democracy in Transition: Attic Letter-Cutters of 340 to 290 BC*, Berkeley: University of California Press, 1995

Woodhead, A. Geoffrey, *The Study of Greek Inscriptions*, 2nd edition, London: Bristol Classical Press, and Norman: University of Oklahoma Press, 1992

Instruments, Musical

Musical instruments, many of them borrowed from or shared with neighbouring cultures, have featured prominently in Greek music-making since antiquity. Whether played solo or in ensembles, they have been employed at various times in history for recreation, to accompany songs and dances, and to enhance religious and civic ceremonial. Certain instruments and ensembles have tended to be characteristic of the musical cultures of particular geographic regions or historical periods, with others relegated to special functions or particular classes of people. In both ancient and modern Greece, for example, reedless pipes (*syringes* and *floyeres*) have been associated with shepherds, while rams' horns (*kerata*) and conches have been used as signalling devices.

Since very few specimens have survived even partially intact, scholars studying pre-modern Greek instruments rely heavily on the testimony of literature and art. The number of ancient literary references to instruments is vast and ranges from practical observations to discourses by Plato and Aristotle on their proper role in society. These are all predated by the representations of instruments in Cycladic statuettes of the 3rd millennium BC. Minoan, Mycenaean, and Cypriot art of the 2nd millennium BC depicts the use of lyres, harps, pipes, and other instruments in both cultic and domestic circumstances. For the organology of the Archaic and Classical periods, the many detailed representations of instruments and their players on painted pottery are particularly valuable resources. Much later, illuminated manuscripts and church frescos preserve important information regarding the instruments of the Byzantine and post-Byzantine periods.

Ancient Greek music was dominated by lyres and the wind instruments known as *auloi*. Hellenic lyres, unlike those of their neighbours, were always constructed symmetrically with a soundbox at the base and a pair of arms supporting a crossbar at the top. Suspended between the soundbox and the crossbar were strings of equal length. These were normally made of gut or sinew, passed over a bridge on the soundbox, and tuned at the crossbar by means of thongs or pegs. The instruments were played either by plucking the strings with the left hand or by striking them with a plectrum held in the right hand. Although variants on this basic design appear in ancient literature with overlapping appellations, Greek lyres may conveniently be grouped according to the shape of their soundboxes into box lyres and bowl lyres. Seven- or eight-string specimens of the louder and structurally more complex wooden box lyres, which featured a larger soundbox extending to the arms, appear in Minoan and Mycenaean art. Scholars have identified the smaller and simpler models with a reduced number of strings that appear in later geometric art with the *phorminx* of Homeric epic. With the emergence in the 7th century BC of the *kithara*, a lyre used by professionals in competitions, more elaborate versions again began to be depicted. Timotheos and other innovators of the 5th century BC subsequently extended the harmonic capabilities of the kithara through the addition of up to five additional strings. In addition to a standard square-based concert model, several variants have been identified, including a rectangular "Italiote" kithara and a smaller "cradle" kithara normally played by women. Unlike these kitharas, bowl lyres (such as the *barbitoi*) had a small rounded soundbox made from a tortoise shell or wood covered by hide, and thin arms in the shape of horns, from which they were occasionally fashioned. Small models were employed by amateurs and in education, whereas the larger and therefore deeper *barbitos* was associated with the lyric poetry of Sappho and Alcaeus, as well as with scenes of revelry.

Despite its common mistranslation as a "flute", the aulos was actually a cylindrical reed instrument with finger holes. Early models seem to have featured 3 to 5 holes, while later concert instruments are recorded as possessing up to 24. Although auloi with a single reed like the modern clarinet were probably not unknown, most were fitted with a double reed, thus making them akin to oboes and shawms (e.g. the modern Greek *zournas*). Some players wore a leather strap (*phorbeia*) around their head to support both their cheeks and their instruments, the latter of which came in various sizes and were usually played in pairs. Most artistic representations of paired auloi, the earliest of which is a Cycladic figurine in white marble of the mid-3rd millennium BC (now in the National Archaeological Museum, Athens), show instruments of equal length. Since most ancient art depicts the player's hands in approximately the same position, it is likely that unison playing and heterophony were the norm. Nevertheless, the occasional use of drones and bursts of simple polyphony may be inferred from scattered literary references. Some of these passages, however, may refer specifically to the less common "Phrygian" auloi of unequal length, the larger of which is represented in art with an upturned bell. Credited with the ability to arouse strong emotions, auloi were used publicly in religious rituals, drama, and dance, and domestically at banquets and symposia.

The ancient Greeks employed a variety of other instruments in addition to lyres and auloi, the number of which increased in Hellenistic and Roman times. Harps (e.g. the *trigonon*, *pektis*, and *magadis*) were usually played by women in private during the Classical period, after which larger concert models evolved. Lutes appeared in Cyprus as early as c.1400–1200 BC, but it was not until the 3rd century BC that the three-stringed *pandoura* appeared on the Greek mainland. Other instruments that were adopted from the east in later centuries included the bagpipes and the *psalterion*, a form of zither. The *syrinx* (panpipes), as has already been mentioned, was generally considered a pastoral instrument, as was the later transverse flute (*syrinx monokalamos* or *photinx*). Rattles (e.g. the *seistron*, borrowed from Egypt), cymbals (*kymbala*), clappers (*krotala*), drums (*tympana*), and other percussion instruments were used for apotropaic purposes, for rhythmic accompaniment, or as toys. Early brass instruments such as the trumpet (*salpinx*) were used mainly for signalling, for example to sound the attack in battle or to issue a call to worship. During the Roman period, however, fanfares played by military bands of brass and percussion instruments became a fixture of state ceremonial and remained so until the end of the Byzantine empire.

Also rising to prominence only after the classical era was the *hydraulis*, a hydrostatic organ invented during the 3rd century BC by the Alexandrian engineer Ctesibius. According to Hero, the *hydraulis* supplied a steady flow of pressurized air to its pipes with a piston that expelled water from a chamber (*pnigeus*) lying at the bottom of a sealed cistern. Initially this invention appears to have attracted little attention, but a Delphic inscription of 90 BC records the prize-winning participation of an organist in a competition. Sometime around the 2nd century AD the mechanically complex piston was replaced by bellows, which could be used with or without a cistern. By late Antiquity large organs with multiple ranks had become common in amphitheatres and other public venues, while smaller instruments often graced banquets. The *Book of Ceremonies* of Constantine VII Porphyrogennetos (913–59) and the accounts of foreign visitors to Constantinople testify to the continued use of organs by the imperial court even after the radical contraction of urban life suffered by the Byzantine empire during the 7th and 8th centuries. Tenth-century processions featured portable instruments, and several decorated models were used within the Great Palace alongside such automata as a golden tree with whistling birds. Organs were also sent as gifts to Carolingian rulers, thereby contributing to the revival of the instrument in the West.

The extraordinary continuity with late antiquity observable in the use of certain ceremonial instruments at the Byzantine court was not representative of Hellenic music as a whole, the culture of which had undergone major changes following the advent of Christianity. These partially reflected a puritan reaction to instrumental music that had been building ever since Plato stated that the aulos and other "polyharmonic" instruments should be banned from an ideal state. Continued by pagan thinkers from Aristotle to Lucian, this critique was redoubled by Clement, St John Chrysostom, and other Fathers of the Christian Church who identified musical instruments with the sexual immorality they saw in pagan theatre, banquets, and religion. Vehement criticism was backed up by canonical legislation prohibiting the playing of instruments by clergy and making the baptism of aulos and kithara players dependent on the renunciation of their trade. While these two instruments disappeared along with the theatre of ancient Greece, other string, wind, and percussion instruments continued to be employed in Byzantium for recreation, as domestic entertainment, or to accompany dances. By the 10th century the Hellenic string instrumentarium had undergone significant development and, like contemporary Arab music, had come to include five-stringed bowed fiddles (*lyrai*) as well as psalteries and lutes (*pandourai*). The Orthodox Church, on the other hand, admitted only a very limited number of percussion instruments. Whereas the early monks of the Egyptian desert sounded trumpets to mark the hours of prayer, the Byzantines announced the beginning of services with the striking of wooden planks or metal bands known as *semantra*. After the Latin conquest of Constantinople in 1204, belfries were installed in many Byzantine churches as the practice of bell-ringing was borrowed from the West, only to cease later in areas that fell under Ottoman occupation. Today the ringing of

bells coexists in Greek monasteries with the sounding of small portable and larger stationary semantra, all of which are struck with distinctive rhythms. The only other exceptions to the Church's prohibition of instruments are the small bells affixed to some incense burners and vestments.

Modern Greek folk and popular music employs a heterogeneous body of instruments, many of which have been adapted from or are held in common with the musical cultures of such neighbouring peoples as the Turks, the Arabs, the Slavs, and the Italians. These may be divided into melodic instruments, which play melodies alone or heterophonically in groups, and accompanying instruments, which provide rhythmic or harmonic accompaniment. The identity of the instruments fulfilling these roles has, like the folk-song repertories with which they are associated, traditionally varied from region to region. The leading melodic instrument of Thrace, Crete, and other islands has historically been a pear-shaped bowed fiddle known as the *lyra*, while the Greeks of Pontus and Cappadocia have played bottle-shaped variants (the *kementzes* and *kemanes*, respectively) of this instrument. Their leading role is fulfilled elsewhere by shawms including the *pipiza* and *karamouza* of Rumeli and the Peloponnese, as well as the larger *zournas* of Epirus and Macedonia. All of these double-reed instruments have typically been accompanied by the beating of a cylindrical drum (*daouli*). Native fiddles and shawms, however, have been gradually displaced by western orchestral counterparts, namely the violin, which appeared as early as the 17th century, and the clarinet. The latter was rapidly accepted during the first half of the 20th century alongside such traditional wind instruments as end-blown flutes – e.g. the *souravli* and the shepherd's *floyera*, the side-blown flute and panpipes having died out among the Greeks after the fall of Byzantium – and two types of bagpipes: the mainland *gaida*, with a single chanter and a drone; and the *tsabouna* of the islands, which lacks a drone but features two chanters. Lutes, which may exercise either a melodic or accompanying function depending on the variety of instrument and the musical repertory, remain a mainstay of the Greek instrumentarium. They include the long-necked *taboura* and *sazi*, the Italianate mandolins of the Ionian islands, and the *bouzouki* and smaller *baglamas* popularized by *rebetika* (songs of the urban underclass). Primarily used for accompaniment are the large pear-shaped *laouto* and the *outi* (i.e. the Arabic *'ud*, which was rarely encountered in mainland Greece before the Asia Minor disaster of 1922). In more recent years traditional lutes have been supplemented or replaced by the western guitar and the hybrid *laouto-kitharo*. Three zithers are also encountered in an accompanying role: the plucked *kanonaki* (a descendant of the Byzantine psalterion and Arabic *kanun*), the *santouri* (a trapeziform dulcimer), and its larger cousin the *tsimbalo*.

Urbanization, the relocation of the Greeks of Asia Minor, westernization, and the rise of the mass media have all contributed to the formation of hybrid song repertories in which the regional variations of Hellenic folk music have been rendered progressively meaningless. The instrumentation of popular repertories initially tended to vary markedly by genre (e.g. an Ionian *mantolinata* – mandolin orchestra – for early Athenian song and a bouzouki-led ensemble for *rebetika*). Over the course of the 20th century, however, the spread of western triadic harmonies to nearly all Greek repertories has displaced many traditional instruments. After World War II such syncretism became fully conscious in Greek popular music, the composers of which deliberately placed bouzoukia alongside western orchestral and modern electronic instruments.

ALEXANDER LINGAS

See also Music

Further Reading

Anderson, Warren D., *Music and Musicians in Ancient Greece*, Ithaca, New York: Cornell University Press, 1994

Anoyanakis, Fivos, *Greek Popular Musical Instruments*, Athens: National Bank of Greece, 1979

Bachmann, Werner, "Das byzantinische Musikinstrumentarium" in *Anfänge der slavischen Musik*, edited by Ladislav Mokry, Bratislava: Verlag der Slowakischen Akademie der Wissenschaften, 1966

Barker, Andrew, *Greek Musical Writings*, 2 vols, Cambridge and New York: Cambridge University Press, 1984–89

Baud-Bovy, Samuel, *Essai sur la chanson populaire grecque*, Nauplia: Fondation Ethnographique du Péloponnèse, 1983

Braun, Joachim, "Musical Instruments in Byzantine Illuminated Manuscripts", *Early Music*, 8 (1980): pp. 312–27

Maas, Martha and Jane McIntosh Snyder, *Stringed Instruments of Ancient Greece*, New Haven, Connecticut and London: Yale University Press, 1989

McKinnon, James (editor), *Music in Early Christian Literature*, Cambridge and New York: Cambridge University Press, 1987

McKinnon, James (editor), *Antiquity and the Middle Ages: From Ancient Greece to the 15th Century*, London: Macmillan, and Englewood Cliffs, New Jersey: Prentice Hall, 1990

McKinnon, James, *The Temple, the Church Fathers and Early Western Chant*, Aldershot, Hampshire: Ashgate, 1998

Maliaras, Nikos, *Die Orgel im byzantinischen Hofzeremoniell des 9. und des 10. Jahrhunderts: eine Quellenuntersuchung*, Munich: Institut für Byzantinistik und Neugriechische Philologie der Universität, 1991

Michaelides, Solon, *The Music of Ancient Greece: An Encyclopedia*, London: Faber, 1978

Pennanen, Risto Pekka, *Westernisation and Modernisation in Greek Popular Music*, Tampere: University of Tampere, 1999

Perrot, Jean, *The Organ: From Its Invention in the Hellenistic Period to the End of the Thirteenth Century*, London and New York: Oxford University Press, 1971

Quasten, Johannes, *Music and Worship in Pagan and Christian Antiquity*, Washington, D.C.: National Association of Pastoral Musicians, 1983

Tillyard, H.J.W., "Instrumental Music in the Roman Age", *Journal of Hellenic Studies*, 27 (1907): pp. 160–69

West, M.L., *Ancient Greek Music*, Oxford: Clarendon Press, and New York, Oxford University Press, 1992

Williams, Peter, *A New History of the Organ: From the Greeks to the Present Day*, London: Faber, and Bloomington: Indiana University Press, 1980, pp. 19–33.

Williams, Edward V., *The Bells of Russia: History and Technology*, Princeton, New Jersey: Princeton University Press, 1985, pp. 3–25

Winnington-Ingram, R.P. *et al.*, Greece entry in *The New Grove Dictionary of Music and Musicians*, edited by Stanley Sadie, London: Macmillan, and Washington, D.C.: Grove, 1980, vol.7, pp. 659–82

Ioannina

City in Epirus

Located on the western slopes of Mount Pambotis in the centre of Epirus (the northwesternmost district of Greece), the city of Ioannina has over its long history come under the control of a number of different cultural influences. The site on which Ioannina now stands has been invaded by Alexander the Great, by Byzantines, Romans, Normans, Venetians, Serbs, Turks, Albanians, and, finally, in 1913, by Greeks, who joined Epirus to the modern Greek state in the course of the Balkan Wars. Despite these many external influences, Ioannina has throughout its history been known as a centre of Hellenism.

Much about the city's origins is hotly debated – even its name is of uncertain provenance. Numerous historians (Leake, Hatzedakes, Aravantinos) argue that the name "Ioannina" is taken from the monastery of John the Baptist; others claim that the city was first named after an unidentified Slav called Ioannes; others still that Ioannina was the name of the daughter of one of Justinian I's most valued soldiers.

While it is unclear exactly when the site was established as a city, the historical record indicates that the area has had a sizeable population since the time of Alexander the Great (d. 323 BC). The province of Epirus, of which Ioannina is now capital, was under Roman rule from 168 BC to AD 375. The settlement's growth and establishment as a city of significant proportions was effected under Byzantine rule, which began in AD 375 and continued (with interruptions) until 1430.

Ecclesiastical documents show that Ioannina by the 7th century was important enough to be established as bishopric of the Byzantine Church; this was effected under the metropolitan of Naupactus in AD 674. As Rae Dalven has noted (p. 3), "The presence of a bishop of Ioannina indicates that Ioannina already had a fortress and a permanent population." The Second Council of Nicaea (787) made reference to Ioannina as a city. Such references suggest that already by the 6th century it is appropriate to refer to Ioannina as an area of significant urban concentration.

In 1082 Ioannina was taken from the Byzantines by the Norman Bohemund, but Norman possession of the city was short-lived, and by 1083 Ioannina was back in Byzantine hands. In 1185 the Normans again captured Ioannina, this time virtually destroying it in the process. Ioannina's next period of growth came after the sack of Constantinople during the Fourth Crusade (1204), following which Epirus became a Venetian territory. When in 1210 the Venetians turned Epirus over to the control of Michael Komnenos Doukas, a Venetian vassal, the result was the creation of the so-called "despotate of Epirus", which, Venetian connections notwithstanding, was functionally an independent Greek principality. At the end of the 13th century the despotate of Epirus was once again joined to the Byzantine imperium. It remained under Byzantine control for the next century and a half, until 9 October 1430, when the people of Ioannina peaceably surrendered to the Ottomans.

The period of Ottoman rule of Ioannina was, from a political standpoint, less turbulent than preceding eras in the city's history. Whereas early eras saw numerous invasions, Turkish possession of Ioannina continued uninterrupted for almost 500

Ioannina: view of the city from the island in the lake. The minaret belongs to the mosque of Aslan Pasha which is now a museum of folk art

years. The arrival of Ottoman control did not translate as a diminution of Hellenic cultural norms in Ioannina. If anything, the reverse was the case. If in Anatolia the Ottoman presence led to the gradual dilution of the late-medieval markers of Hellenism (Orthodox Christianity, Greek literary tradition, etc.), in the case of Ioannina the political elite to some extent gradually became assimilated to the dominant Greek cultural forms. Whereas in Anatolia many Greeks converted to Islam and came increasingly to use the Turkish rather than the Greek language, in Ioannina Greek was not just the official language of the Orthodox Church, but it came to be the language of the ruling elite too.

This adoption of Greek for official purposes had a powerful effect on the development of the modern Greek language. Ali Pasha, the Ottoman-appointed Albanian who governed Ioannina during the late 18th and early 19th centuries, used demotic Greek as his official courtly language, and knew very little Ottoman Turkish. The Greek language in Ioannina was thus propagated not just by the Church establishment (which during the Tourkokratia was in most areas the single most important transmitter of the Hellenic linguistic heritage), but also by the state itself.

During the period of Turkish rule Ioannina came to be one of the most important cultural and economic centres of the Greek world. On the trade route linking the port of Salaora (Arta's port) in the west to Thessalonica in the east, Ioannina was the staging post for the exportation of an array of goods. It also had a sizeable trading community of its own, the vast majority of which was made up of Greeks and Hellenized Vlachs. During the 18th and 19th centuries these Greek traders established far-flung links to the Greek diaspora, particularly in the Italian city states, northern Europe, and Russia. As a result of these trade ties, Ioannina was during the later centuries of the Turkish period a very cosmopolitan and wealthy city. The wealth was reflected in a range of arenas, first and foremost of which was Ioannina's renowned educational establishment, which came increasingly to serve as the training ground for the Ottoman pashas' courtiers.

Finally, Ioannina holds a significant place in the history of a very important, although often neglected, strand of Hellenism. Ioannina, until the time of World War II, was a major centre of Greek Judaism. Whereas the sizeable Jewish populations of other Ottoman Greek cultural centres (Thessalonica, for example, or Constantinople) were largely the result of the resettlement of the Sephardim following the persecutions of Spanish and Sicilian Jews at the end of the 15th century, scholars believe that a Romaniote Jewish community had been established in Ioannina as early as the 9th century AD.

Ioannina was an important Jewish as well as Orthodox educational centre during the Tourkokratia. Unlike the

Orthodox community, however, the Jews experienced an increased level of persecution following the Greek War of Independence, and the 19th-century record tells of outbursts of lethal anti-Semitic violence in 1851, 1869, and 1872.

In the early 19th century Ioannina was a centre for Zionism, and with the establishment in the city of the Alliance Israelite Universelle (1904) and the Amale Zion ("Working for Zion", 1905), the city's Jewish community began actively to cultivate economic, intellectual, and religious contacts with the outside world. Virtually half the city's Jewish population emigrated during the next decade, most to the United States. By the mid-1940s some 2000 Jews still lived in Ioannina. Fewer than 200 survived the war – a handful by hiding in the mountains. Only 100 survived Birkenau and Auschwitz. With the destruction of Ioannina's long-flourishing Jewish community, a vital component of Hellenism was effectively extinguished.

K.E. FLEMING

See also Ali Pasha, Epirus, Jews

Summary

Now the capital of the province of Epirus, Ioannina has been occupied at least since the 4th century BC. It largely followed the political fortunes of Epirus, with a long period of stability and prosperity beginning with the onset of Ottoman rule in 1430, but has always been an important centre of Hellenism. It also had a flourishing Jewish community until World War II.

Further Reading

Bowman, Stephen B., *The Jews of Byzantium (1204–1543)*, University: University of Alabama Press, 1984

Dalven, Rae, *The Jews of Ioannina*, Philadelphia: Cadmus Press, 1990

Hobhouse, John Cam (Lord Broughton), *Travels in Albania and Other Provinces of Turkey in 1809 and 1810*, London: John Murray, 1855

Leake, William Martin, *Travels in Northern Greece*, London: Rodwell, 1835, reprinted Amsterdam: Hakkert, 1967

Ionian Islands

Islands off the west coast of mainland Greece

The seven Ionian islands, Corfu, Cephalonia, Zakynthos, Leucas, Ithaca, Cythera, and Paxos, are often referred to as Heptanesus ("seven islands"). They do not, however, form a geographical unit. Even the epithet "Ionian" is of obscure origin, probably stemming from Ionian settlers in ancient times. The political unity of the seven islands is, by contrast, comparatively recent, dating from the establishment of the Septinsular Republic (1800–07).

The first attempt to merge the islands into one political unit was made in the 9th century, when they were formed into a distinct province, the Thema Cephallenia. Although the Ionian islands formed part of the eastern Roman empire ever since its formation, Byzantium's sovereignty over them was frequently challenged. Their exposed offshore geostrategic position made them vulnerable to repeated invasions and conquests. The Normans, led by Robert Guiscard, captured Corfu and Cephalonia in 1081; and the islands were again engulfed by war during the prolonged struggle between Byzantium and western Crusaders in the 12th century. With the establishment of the Latin empire in 1204, the Venetians took possession of Corfu and established their largely uninterrupted predominance in the region. To expedite the process of colonization Venetian aristocratic families were granted fiefdoms on the island. Soon Venice conquered Cephalonia, Zakynthos, and Leucas, and they became tributary to the Venetian republic. The rule of La Serenissima was challenged by corsairs and by Greek and Neapolitan claimants at intervals throughout the later 13th century. By 1386 Corfu had voluntarily submitted to Venetian rule, a move which reflected Venice's rise to the position of leading maritime power in the Mediterranean. In 1485 Venice purchased Zakynthos from the Ottomans, and captured the depopulated island of Cephalonia from them in 1499. Leucas was frequently occupied by Venice but was not finally taken until 1684. Cythera was brought under the republic's control as late as 1717.

The Ionian islands' Venetian period was marked by the payment of heavy tributes which the new rulers exacted from the islanders. Venetian rule rested mainly on the loyalty to the republic of the principal native Ionian families, their adherence being rewarded by the ample bestowal of titles, privileges, and appointments. Venetian political control was cemented by the cultural predominance of this maritime power. The Italian and Greek elements of the population were largely assimilated by intermarriage; the Catholic Church was established; and Greek ceased to be the predominant language, though it was still spoken by the rural population, which also continued to adhere to the Orthodox Church.

With the fall of the Venetian republic in 1797, Venetian rule over the islands came to an end. By the Treaty of Campo Formio, Austria acquired Venice proper, and the Ionian islands were occupied by France, though by the end of the following year, 1798–79, a joint Russo-Turkish expeditionary force had evicted the French occupying troops. By the Russo-Turkish treaty of 1800 the islands became the independent Septinsular Republic. Seven turbulent years followed. There was no internal political stability, and chaos and anarchy prevailed.

In 1807 Russia abrogated its barely concealed protectorate over the islands and, in a secret clause of the Treaty of Tilsit of that year, the islands were ceded to France and recognized as an integral part of the French empire. Now part of the province of Illyria, the Ionian islands remained French territory until the collapse of Napoleonic rule in 1814, though Zakynthos, Cephalonia, Cythera, and Leucas were taken by British forces under General Oswald in 1809–10. Corfu was surrendered to the British in 1814 following the abdication of Napoleon Bonaparte.

In the Treaty of Paris of 1815 the Concert of Europe placed the "United States of the Ionian Islands" under British protection, with Austria enjoying equal commercial rights, an arrangement that had been strongly approved by the Russian foreign minister, the Corfiot Count Ioannis Kapodistria. Although the Treaty of Paris had decreed the Ionian islands to be a "sole free and independent state", its stipulations were not devoid of ambiguities and were certainly open to different interpretations. The islands' constitution of 1817 placed their administration in the hands of a six-man senate controlled by a legislative assembly of 40 members. Real power, however, lay with the British High Commissioner. The first Lord High Commissioner of the Ionian islands, a former governor of Malta, Sir Thomas ("King Tom") Maitland (1815–23), purposefully exploited the ambiguous phrasing of the treaty's stipulations to extend British authority over the islands. British rule was a form of benign authoritarianism. Maitland and his successors used their all-powerful position to effect lasting improvements in the condition of the islands: a major road-construction scheme was carried out, direct taxation was abolished, an impartial justice system established, agricultural reform implemented, and educational institutions created. But public security and material prosperity failed to secure the goodwill of the Ionian population. Already resentful of authoritarian British rule, the administration's preference for Corfu over the other islands and the neglect of the interests of the local peasantry further alienated the Ionian islanders. At the root of this growing disaffection, however, was Greek nationalism, which was steadily gaining strength. Existing opposition was further fomented by Maitland's decision to prevent the islanders from lending assistance to the mainland Greeks in the War of Independence of 1821. Maitland's successors continued his policies, often in a high-handed manner. Sir Howard Douglas (1835–41) was continually faced with intrigues, most prominently led by Andreas Mustoxidi.

The firm policy of Maitland and his successors was replaced by a more lenient approach to the administration of the islands in the 1840s. The European revolutions of 1848–49 provided the spark for local risings against the protectorate and for union with Greece on Cephalonia and elsewhere. The High Commissioner Lord Seaton (1843–49) and his successor Sir Henry Ward (1849–58) tried to appease the unionist movement by offering concessions. It was hoped that a general amnesty of 1 August 1849 would bring an end to the troubles. But renewed violence and an agrarian revolt on Cephalonia at the end of that month dashed such hopes, and the rising was ruthlessly suppressed by military force.

On the restoration of order Ward continued to initiate a series of reforms. A new constitution, granted in November 1849, extended the franchise to all adult males, and offered a wider scope for the activities of the general assembly. In effect, the new constitution marked the end of the ascendancy of the old Venetian one and strengthened Hellenic elements hostile to the British protectorate. The reforms did not prevent the further spread of the Greek nationalist movement on the islands, with the legislative assembly repeatedly using its constitutional liberties of speech and comment to pass resolutions in favour of immediate union with Greece.

Britain's foreign secretary, Lord Palmerston, had always firmly held that continued possession of the Ionian islands, and especially of Corfu, was crucial to the maintenance of Britain's naval position in the Mediterranean. By the late 1850s, however, the islands in this respect had sunk to a position of secondary importance behind Malta. Thus, while the islanders' opposition to British control remained unabated, Britain became decreasingly interested in the continuance of the status quo.

The hopes of the Greek nationalists were raised in 1858 when Palmerston, by now prime minister, found himself in a minority in parliament and resigned. The incoming Conservative administration appointed William Ewart Gladstone as Lord High Commissioner Extraordinary to the Ionian islands. Such a mission by a statesman of Gladstone's stature – a figure well known, moreover, for his Philhellene inclinations – could not but excite unionist hopes. Gladstone, however, was not appointed to bring to a close the protectorate, but to investigate the condition of the islands and to examine their relations with Britain. His brief mission was hampered from the outset by press speculations in London and by a vote of the Ionian assembly declaring union with Greece to be the *thelesis* (absolute and unanimous will) of the islanders. Not surprisingly, Gladstone's mission failed to produce tangible results. The constitutional reform projects with which he had busied himself were buried in a series of reports which were never published. Whatever hopes the Greek nationalist movement may have had of Gladstone's short tenure as High Commissioner were dashed when, after his tour of inspection, he concluded that the majority of the islanders did not wish for the abolition of the British protectorate. Under Gladstone's successor, Sir Henry Storks, who took up his position in February 1859, the contest between the legislative assembly and the protecting power continued. Unionist sentiments remained strong but the British government was slow to realize its precarious position. Indeed, Gladstone himself, by now Chancellor of the Exchequer in Lord Palmerston's last cabinet, declared in 1861 that the cession of the islands to Greece would constitute "a crime against the safety of Europe"; and Storks's reports ignored the discontent of the native population.

While the British government had long realized that the cession of the islands to Greece was not inimical to British interests, it was reluctant to act upon this realization for general strategic reasons. The Greek court under the (Bavarian) King Otho leaned heavily towards Austria's power in the northern Adriatic. Cession of the islands to Greece might therefore conceivably have led to a significant increase in Austrian naval power in the Adriatic and the approaches to the eastern Mediterranean. Barring a complete change in mainland Greek affairs, there was little prospect of any British government consenting to the union of the islands with Greece.

Change, however, did come in October 1862 with the outbreak of the Greek revolution, in the course of which King Otho was forced to abdicate. The Ionian assembly once more reiterated its unionist demands. Now the British government was quick to seize the opportunity of testifying its sympathy with Greek nationalist sentiments and of ridding itself of the Ionian burden in a manner that was not adverse to British interests. The provisional government in Athens was informed that if the Greeks elected to their vacant throne a candidate approved of by queen Victoria, Britain would surrender the islands to the kingdom. The election of the Danish prince Waldemar George of Glücksburg, the brother-in-law of the prince of Wales, as king George I of the Hellenes fulfilled the conditions required by Britain. On 7 October 1863 the Ionian assembly was specifically convened for the purpose and signified its assent to the transfer. On 14 November a protocol was signed by the five great powers of Europe for the formal transfer of the islands to Greece. The final treaty was signed in London on 29 March 1864, declaring Greece, including the Ionian islands, to be a monarchical, independent, and constitutional state under the rule of king George and under the guarantee of Britain, France, and Russia. By treaty stipulation, the fortifications on Corfu and Paxos were demolished, and the two islands, though part of the Hellenic kingdom, were declared perpetually neutral. The British protectorate over the islands had thus come to an end, although they retained their existing system of private law, taxes, and duties.

The final act of British rule came on 28 May 1864, when the last Lord High Commissioner, Sir Henry Storks, delivered the islands to the Greek commissioner. Storks left Corfu on 31 May 1864; in the following month King George received the homage of his new subjects; and in July the Ionian deputies took their seats in the national assembly at Athens. From now on the Ionian islands remained part of Greece, although they were occupied during World War II by Axis forces.

T.G. OTTE

See also Corfu, Cythera, Imperialism

Summary

The seven so-called Ionian islands – Corfu, Cephalonia, Zakynthos, Leucas, Ithaca, Cythera, and Paxos – do not form a geographical unit. All had been ruled by Venice, but they did not form a political unit until 1800–07 as the "Septinsular Republic". Ceded to France in 1807, the islands became a British protectorate in 1815. They were united with Greece in 1864.

Further Reading

Morley, John, *The Life of William Ewart Gladstone*, 3 vols, London and New York: Macmillan, 1903, reprinted New York: Greenwood Press, 1968, vol. 1, pp. 594–620

Dixon, Cyril Willis, *The Colonial Administrations of Sir Thomas Maitland*, London: Longman, 1939, reprinted London: Cass, 1968

Foreign Office (United Kingdom), "The Ionian Islands" in *Accounts and Papers*, vol. 67, 1861

Orkney, George William Hamilton Fitzmaurice, *Four Years in the Ionian Islands*, 2 vols, London: Chapman and Hall, 1864 (vol. 1, contains a chronology of the British protectorate)

Pratt, Michael, *Britain's Greek Empire: Reflections on the History of the Ionian Islands from the Fall of Byzantium*, London: Collings, 1978

Ward, Adolphus William, "Greece and the Ionian Islands, 1832–1864" in *Cambridge History of British Foreign Policy*, vol.3, edited by A.W. Ward and G.P. Gooch, Cambridge: Cambridge University Press, 1922–23, reprinted Westport, Connecticut: Greenwood Press, 1971

Ionians

Ancient Greek ethnic group

The term "Ionian" was employed in two senses in antiquity. In the first place it designated the Greek populations settled in the coastal cities of central Asia Minor and occasionally, by extension, the neighbouring populations in the Troad area in northwest Asia Minor (more properly Aeolians) and in southwest Asia Minor (more properly Dorians). This designation may possibly have originated as a general external appellation for Greeks, who were known throughout the east as Yawani (cf. Old Persian *Yauna*; Old Hebrew *Javan*). However, the term could also be used in a broader sense: in the historical period

Athens, Euboea, the Cycladic islands, parts of Sicily (Naxos, Leontini, Catana, Zancle, Rhegium), Italy (Cumae, Siris) and the western Mediterranean (Massalia, Emporion) as well as the central coastal strip of Asia Minor all claimed a common Ionian identity on the basis of perceived similarities in dialect, rituals, customs, and shared origins. It is entirely possible that the second definition was a historically later extension of the first.

Recent archaeological excavations at Ephesus claim archaeological continuity from the Mycenaean age into the Geometric period. By contrast, although the Homeric epics list "Ionians with their flowing tunics" among the Greek contingents at Troy (*Iliad*, 13. 685), there is no mention of Ionians established on the coast of Asia Minor. Indeed, the earliest extant literary references stress that the Ionian cities of Asia Minor considered themselves to be relatively recent foundations from mainland Greece: the 7th-century elegiac poet Mimnermus (fr. 9) describes how Colophon was founded by Pylos, while 5th-century sources attribute the foundation of Priene to settlers from Thebes (Hellanicus, frag. 101), of Miletus to Neleus, son of the Athenian king Codrus (Herodotus, 9. 97) – dated to 1077 BC by the Parian Marble – and of Ephesus to another son of Codrus named Androclus (Pherecydes, frag. 155). Yet another tradition told how the Ionians had originally occupied the northern part of the Peloponnese but had been expelled by Achaeans fleeing the Dorian onslaught and sought refuge in Athens, from where they had set out to colonize Asia Minor (Herodotus, 1. 145, 7. 94; Pausanias, 7. 1. 2–4). It is no doubt the diversity of these foundation accounts as much as prejudice that caused Herodotus to question the ethnic homogeneity of the Ionians, attributing their origins to an admixture of Abantes from Euboea, Minyans from Boeotian Orchomenus, Cadmeans, Dryopes, Phocians, Molossians, Arcadian Pelasgians, and Dorians from Epidaurus.

Although Athens often plays a central role in many of these 5th-century foundation accounts, there is no explicit testimony that it subscribed to a shared Ionian identity before the early 6th century BC when the Athenian statesman Solon (frag. 4) referred to Attica as "the oldest land of Ionia". The Homeric *Hymn to Apollo* implies that Delos hosted a pan-Ionian festival, possibly by the middle of the 7th century BC, while the Panionium to which Herodotus refers (1. 141–142, 148) was a league of 12 cities (Miletus, Myus, Priene, Ephesus, Colophon, Lebedus, Teus, Clazomenae, Phocaea, Samos, Chios, and Erythrae), centred on the sanctuary of Poseidon Heliconius at Cape Mycale, which was certainly functioning by *c*.600 BC and possibly even earlier.

At the level of dialect, cult, and institutions, Ionian cities shared some undoubted commonalities, though these were not always exclusive or universal. The dialects of the cities of Asia Minor and the Cyclades are the closest and are related to the dialects of Attica and Euboea, but the Ionic dialect also seems to have been spoken in the Dorian city of Halicarnassus by the 5th century BC. A number of festivals (Anthesteria, Apaturia, Boedromia, Lenaea, Plynteria, Pyanopsia, and Thargelia) appear to be characteristic of Athenian and Ionian calendars, although Herodotus (1. 147. 2) says that the Ephesians and Colophonians do not celebrate the Apaturia. Similarly, the citizen bodies of many, though not all, Ionian cities were distributed among the four Ionian "tribes" of the Hopletes, the Aigikoreis, the Geleontes, and the Argadeis.

From the end of the 7th century BC the Ionian cities of Asia Minor were subject to periodic attacks from the neighbouring Lydians, culminating in their conquest by Croesus of Lydia in the mid-6th century and then their incorporation into the Persian empire following Croesus' defeat at the hands of Cyrus the Great c.546 BC. Whether as a result of crippling taxation demands and autocratic abuse or simply the personal ambitions of Greek puppet-tyrants, many of the Ionian cities revolted from Persian rule in 499 BC under the leadership of Aristagoras of Miletus. With the assistance of Athens and Eretria as well as of Carians, Cypriots, and Hellespontines, the Ionians scored some early successes—including the sack of the Lydian capital Sardis—but the revolt was ultimately a failure; following a naval defeat at Lade in 494 BC where the Ionian contingent faced a Phoenician navy almost twice its size, Miletus was sacked and its inhabitants killed or enslaved. The Ionian cities passed back to Persian suzerainty until after the Persian Wars of 480–479 BC.

It may be as a consequence of the Ionians' perceived readiness to endure the rule of barbarians that Athens began to downplay its own Ionian associations: according to Herodotus (1. 143. 3), the Athenians and Euboeans avoided calling themselves Ionians because they were ashamed of the name (since c.506 BC much of Euboea had passed under direct or indirect Athenian control). This new attitude becomes particularly apparent after the Persian Wars when Athens began to stress its own autochthonous origins over its traditional Ionian ties, though this is perhaps prefigured as early as 508 BC when the Athenian statesman Cleisthenes replaced the old four Ionian tribes with ten new tribes named after Attic heroes. It was not, however, politically expedient for Athens to sever all ties with the Ionian cities of the Cyclades and Asia Minor—not least because Ionians constituted a majority of the cities of the Delian League who from 478/77 BC were required to pay tribute to Athens to secure protection against further Persian aggression. The solution that Athens adopted was to make slight but subtle modifications to the vocabulary of its relationship with its tributaries by which the Ionians were no longer placed on an equal footing of kinship but regarded as colonists owing their Athenian metropolis certain obligations. The dependency of this relationship was asserted at the quadrennial Great Panathenaea at which the cities of Ionia were instructed to provide a cow and a panoply to be displayed during the festival. At the same time, Athens sought to bolster a sense of common identity among its Ionian allies by promoting cults to Athena, Ion, and the four eponymous Ionian heroes on Samos and by reorganizing the pan-Ionian festival on Delos (Thucydides, 3. 104. 2). This exploitation of Ionian identity for political purposes became even more marked in the course of the Peloponnesian War, partly in opposition to the claims to shared Dorian origins that Sparta and its allies were proclaiming. Thucydides (3. 86. 3, 6. 6. 1) notes that early Athenian intervention in Sicily in 427 BC and again on the occasion of the later, disastrous Sicilian expedition of 415–413 BC was justified on the specious pretext of shared Ionian kinship.

Appeals to a common Ionian identity began to subside following the Peloponnesian War. Athens was now confident in its autochthonous origins, the Ionian cities of Sicily had begun subscribing to a broader "Siceliot" identity, and the Ionian cities of Asia Minor were effectively distanced from their Ionian kinsmen to the west by their reincorporation within the Persian empire – ratified officially under the terms of the King's Peace of 387/86 BC. The Panionium itself continued to function – at some point in the early years of the Peloponnesian War it had been transferred to Ephesus on the grounds of safety but then restored in the early 4th century to Cape Mycale where it is still attested in the Roman imperial period (Strabo, 14. 20. 1)—and throughout the Hellenistic and Roman periods Panionia festivals were celebrated in many of the cities in Asia Minor.

JONATHAN M. HALL

See also Dialects, Hellenes

Summary

In antiquity two groups of people called themselves Ionians: the Greek populations in the coastal cities of central Asia Minor, and the inhabitants of Athens, Euboea, the Cyclades, parts of Sicily, Italy, and the western Mediterranean as well. The second group may simply represent a later extension of the first. Appeals to a common Ionian identity were frequent until the end of the 5th century BC.

Further Reading

Alty, John, "Dorians and Ionians", *Journal of Hellenic Studies*, 102 (1982): pp. 1–14

Barron, John, "Religious Propaganda of the Delian League", *Journal of Hellenic Studies*, 84 (1964): pp. 35–48

Connor, W.R., "The Ionian Era of Athenian Civic Identity", *Proceedings of the American Philosophical Society*, 137 (1993): pp. 194–206

Cook, J.M., *The Greeks in Ionia and the East*, London: Thames and Hudson, 1962; New York: Praeger, 1963

Emlyn-Jones, C.J., *The Ionians and Hellenism: A Study of the Cultural Achievements of Early Greek Inhabitants of Asia Minor*, London and Boston: Routledge and Kegan Paul, 1980

Georges, Pericles, *Barbarian Asia and the Greek Experience: From the Archaic Period to the Age of Xenophon*, Baltimore: Johns Hopkins University Press, 1994

Graf, Fritz, *Nordionische Kulte: religionsgeschichtliche und epigraphische Untersuchungen zu den Kulten von Chios, Erythrai, Klazomenai und Phokaia*, Rome: Schweizerisches Institut in Rom, 1985

Hall, Jonathan M., *Ethnic Identity in Greek Antiquity*, Cambridge and New York: Cambridge University Press, 1997

Huxley, G.L., *The Early Ionians*, London: Faber, and New York: Humanities Press, 1966, reprinted Shannon: Irish University Press, and New York: Barnes and Noble, 1972

Jones, Nicholas, *Public Organization in Ancient Greece: A Documentary Study*, Philadelphia: American Philosophical Society, 1987

Kleiner, Gerhard *et al.*, *Panionion und Melie*, Berlin: de Gruyter, 1967

Rosivach, Vincent, "Autochthony and the Athenians", *Classical Quarterly*, 37 (1987): pp. 294–306

Sakellariou, Michel B., *La Migration grecque en Ionie*, Athens: Institut Français d'Athènes, 1958

Will, Edouard, *Doriens et ioniens: essai sur la valeur du critère ethnique appliqué à l'étude de l'histoire et de la civilisation grecques*, Paris: Belles Lettres, 1956

Irenaeus *c.*AD 130–*c.*202

Bishop of Lyons and theologian

The birthdate of Irenaeus is unknown, but as bishop of Lyons he wrote to Victor, bishop of Rome, requesting that the Asiatic Christians in that city be allowed to celebrate Easter by their own calendar (Eusebius, *Historia Ecclesiastica*, 5. 24). Here and elsewhere, he appealed to the custom of his friend Polycarp, bishop of Smyrna, who suffered a famous martyrdom in the mid-2nd century. The inference that he himself was an emigrant from Asia is corroborated by his strong adherence to episcopal government at a time when it was not yet fully established in the west. His native tongue was Greek, as was that of his community, to judge by the letter in which they informed the Asiatic churches of the bloody persecution of 177. For all that, his major work *Against the Heresies* is preserved only in Latin, his *Demonstration of the Apostolic Teaching* was unknown before the recovery of an Armenian text in 1904, and his treatise against the heresy of Marcion is still lost.

Irenaeus' main objective in his five books *Against the Heresies* (*c.*180) was to demonstrate that the followers of the Egyptian Valentinus were not Christians. The esoteric doctrine that he professes to be exposing taught that the world was the creation of a harsh and ignorant (if well-meaning) Demiurge, who was himself the offspring of a temporary estrangement between the Father and his Wisdom or Sophia. The matter of this world, having been produced by Wisdom's error, was an evil to be escaped from; and therefore God could never have become incarnate, suffered the pain of martyrdom, or prefigured the resurrection of the body. In his first book Irenaeus rehearses the positions of Valentinus and his followers, comparing them with more notorious heretics such as the Gnostics, Basilides, and Simon Magus. In the next he refutes the Valentinian myth of a division in the Godhead, developing incidentally the first orthodox conception of a consubstantial and coeternal Trinity. In the third he summons the fourfold Gospel and the consensus of the bishops to testify that creation and redemption are the work of a single being, who truly took flesh and died upon the cross. In the fourth he explains that sin originates not with God but with the disobedience of the first human beings, who went astray while still too young to receive the divine perfection. In the fifth he adumbrates the joys of heaven, which cannot be complete without the regenerated flesh.

The *Demonstration* appears to be a later work (*c.*190) and certainly a lesser one. Apologetic rather than polemical, it informs an otherwise unknown Marcianus that the tradition of the Church upholds the divinity of Father, Son and Spirit, and after a brief account of the fall and redemption of humankind, proceeds to demonstrate the majesty of the Son from the theophanies of the Old Testament. It adds little to our understanding of the theology of the treatise *Against the Heresies*. The survival of the latter work in a Latin text of unknown date can be explained by the fact that it appeared to advance a doctrine of papal primacy, at least in the opinion of the translator (*Against the Heresies*, 3. 2). In the absence of the Greek, it is more prudent to construe the passage as saying that the metropolitan see is a perfect mirror to the consensus of the "faithful everywhere", without according any exceptional status to the Roman bishop by virtue of his office. Another misconception, fostered by the liberal revolt against Augustine, is that, since he holds that humans were created free and fallible, he ascribes to them a continuing and unlimited capacity for moral amelioration. It is true that Irenaeus could not accept, as Augustine does, that anyone is condemned for the sin of Adam, but he plainly believes that each of us inherits a liability to sin that would inevitably result in our damnation were it not for the work of Christ. This can be represented in his own words as an atoning sacrifice (5. 17), but his more characteristic doctrine is that Christ defeated Satan by an obedient life that "recapitulated" the disobedient life of Adam. Where Adam was born of virgin earth, Christ was born of Mary; where Adam fell to Satan's wiles in Eden, Christ withstood the temptation in the wilderness; where Adam was condemned to die, thus losing immortality, Christ died of his own free will to live again (*Against the Heresies*, 3. 21–22 etc.). His death unlocked the Spirit, the bond of love among the churches, and it is through the material sacraments of those churches that the faithful can become members of his resurrected body.

Orthodox theologians often trace to Irenaeus a distinction between the image of God, which all possess by nature, and the likeness that remains to be perfected in the Spirit through our individual virtues. While a single passage seems to teach this (5. 6), there are others that imply that both the image and the likeness were conferred at the beginning (5. 1), and others again that intimate that both lie in the future (4. 38. 4). Since the body pertains to both the image and the likeness (5. 6. 1), the image is not equated with our rational capacity, as in Origen and the Cappadocian Fathers. Since the incarnate Christ is the consummation of both the image and the likeness, it seems to be this gratuitous and peculiar act of God, not our inherent properties as a species, that enables us to speak of an affinity between creature and Creator. Orthodox theologians, after some centuries, retrieved Irenaeus' teaching on the sanctity of the body, but the Christocentric and evangelical principles of his thought have often seemed to be more congenial to the reformed tradition of western Christendom.

MARK EDWARDS

Biography

Irenaeus was born in Asia Minor *c.*130 where he was a friend of Polycarp, bishop of Smyrna, but he spent most of his life in Gaul and became bishop of Lyons *c.*178. His native tongue was Greek but his principal work, *Against the Heresies*, survives only in Latin and another work only in Armenian. He died *c.*202.

Writings

The Demonstration of the Apostolic Preaching, translated by J. Armitage Robinson, London: SPCK, and New York: Macmillan, 1920

Against the Heresies, book 1, translated by Dominic J. Unger, revised by John J. Dillon, New York: Paulist Press, 1992

In *The Apostolic Fathers, Justin Martyr, Irenaeus*, vol. 1 of *The Ante-Nicene Fathers*, edited by Alexander Roberts and James Donaldson, reprinted Peabody, Massachusetts: Hendrickson, 1994 (contains *Against Heresies* only)

Further Reading

Grant, Robert M., *Irenaeus of Lyons*, London and New York: Routledge, 1997 (includes translations)

Hick, John, *Evil and the God of Love*, London: Macmillan, 1966

Lawson, John, *The Biblical Theology of St Irenaeus*, London: Epworth Press, 1948

Minns, Denis, *Irenaeus*, London: Geoffrey Chapman, and Washington, D.C.: Georgetown University Press, 1994

Irene *c.752–803*

Byzantine empress

The empress Irene is best known today for summoning the seventh ecumenical council, of Nicaea II (787), which restored the icons at the end of the first half of the iconoclast controversy (726 or 730–84). She is also notorious for having had her son, the emperor Constantine VI, blinded in 797. These two retrospectively fundamental events of her reign, however, mask a more complex and intriguing character who played an important role during a crucial period of Byzantine history. Irene's place in the history of the Greek mainland is also of some importance. Indeed, she appears to have been the first native Greek of either sex to have ruled the Roman empire in her own right and was the first woman to rule by herself – styling herself *basileus* (emperor) rather than its female equivalent, *basilissa*.

In 768 Constantine V chose Irene as a wife for his son and heir, Leo the Khazar (later Leo IV, 775–80). She was crowned during the wedding ceremony, and her name even appears in the regnal dating of one of her father-in-law's edicts. That Irene came from a notable Athenian family may indicate that the Isaurian dynasty's interest in restoring order in the Greek mainland predates her own initiatives as empress.

Irene's activities between her marriage and the death of her husband are unattested. Later stories about her secret iconophile sympathies prior to 780 are probably apocryphal. Initially she appears loyally to have accepted the prevailing iconoclasm, whatever her private feelings may have been. On the death of her husband in 780, she acted as regent for her young son, Constantine VI (780–97), and quickly secured the throne for him by excluding her husband's brothers, the so-called "Caesars", who were exiled to Athens after an unsuccessful revolt in their favour.

Irene originally relied heavily on loyal members of the court and military, including an ambitious general and minister, the eunuch Stavrakios. In 782/83 the latter led a campaign into northern Greece to subdue the Slavs and restore Byzantine administration in the region, thus paving the way for the gradual restoration of Byzantine rule in mainland Greece in the 9th century. Irene and her son took part in a triumphal procession in Thrace in 784 where, accompanied by loyal troops, she refounded the city of Berroia as Irenoupolis (now Stara Zagora) and improved defences in Philippoppolis (now Plovdiv) while generally strengthening Byzantine power in the region. The present church of Hagia Sophia in Thessalonica may date from this time and the iconoclast mosaic cross decoration therein includes medallions bearing the imperial monograms. Macedonia now appears as a *thema*, or province.

Irene: portrait of the empress on a gold coin, *c.*800

In 783/84 there is no indication that Irene was not adhering to the official iconoclast line. Byzantine historians inform us that she began to change her mind after the deathbed repentance of the iconoclast patriarch Paul IV in 784. After having supported or engineered the accession of the noted scholar and administrator Tarasios to the patriarchal throne in 784, Irene announced the convention of a council to restore the icons and unite the Church. Historians have long seen her efforts in this direction as a calculated game played from 780 at the latest, but there is no evidence to back this assertion. It would seem that Irene was genuinely "converted" or at least pushed into open action by the events of 784.

The council finally met in Nicaea in 787 after an attempt to begin proceedings in Constantinople in 786 had been disrupted by troops and a few bishops loyal to the memory of the iconoclast Constantine V. The council proclaimed itself ecumenical (Nicaea II) and acted as a reference point for the final restoration of the icons in 843. Irene regarded Nicaea II as a chance to unite the Church and suppress discord, a goal she seems to have considered more important even than the restoration of the icons itself. She showed her intentions in this respect again during the simoniac controversy of 789/90, when she alienated erstwhile monastic support by insisting that repenting simoniac bishops (those who had given or received money for consecration) should be restored to their sees.

The monks soon forgave her, however, especially those of the Sakkoudion monastery on Mount Olympus in Bithynia, who in 797 were given the dilapidated Stoudios monastery of St John the Forerunner in Constantinople to restore and maintain. Under St Theodore the Stoudite (died 826) this became the most famous of the empire's monasteries, and was to remain so for centuries. Irene's name was, as a consequence, long associated with imperial piety and munificence. It would be wrong, however, to see in her a slave of monastic interests since there was no united monastic front and Irene knew how to play one faction off against the other. Nor was the empress willing to abandon her imperial prerogatives when it came to concessions (or "economies") made on her behalf by the Church. The elevation of Tarasios to the patriarchal throne in 784 and the simoniac controversy are cases in point. However, her generosity to charitable institutions and abolition of the municipal tax and of the customs' duties on the Dardanelles (800/01), although economically unsound by today's standards, were definitely sound by the political standards of a time when popular dissatisfaction could cause problems for an increasingly unstable regime.

Irene's undoing came in her rivalry with her son Constantine VI, who in 790 claimed the throne as his legitimate inheritance. Irene was forced into seclusion that year after the military intervened against her, but was recalled in 792 after Constantine had shown himself singularly incompetent. In 795 she helped to inflame the so-called Moechian controversy (over Constantine's divorce of his wife and "adulterous" marriage to his courtesan). Having undermined her son's position she engineered Constantine's downfall and had him blinded in the purple chamber of the palace in 797.

Irene subsequently ruled alone, styling herself on formal documents as *basileus* (two of these still survive – Dölger *Regesten*, nos. 358, 359 – and involve third marriages and oaths). In 802 she was deposed in a palace coup led by her minister of finance, the *logothete* Nikephoros, ostensibly because the palace eunuch Aetios had become far too powerful and dangerous an independent paragon at court. The empress was exiled to a monastery of hers on Lesbos, where she died a nun the following year. Her remains were, later on in the 9th century, translated to the imperial burial vaults of the church of the Holy Apostles in Constantinople.

Irene has not had a good press in modern histories. Her inability to stem the successes of the Arabs under the caliph Harun al-Rashid, to whom she had to pay tribute on at least two occasions, was criticized even in her own day. During her personal rule the Frankish king Charlemagne was crowned "emperor" in Rome by the pope and the Latins claimed that the imperial throne was vacant in Constantinople because Irene was a woman. But setbacks at the hands of two of the greatest leaders of all time can hardly be blamed on Irene alone. Indeed, her plans to unite the East and West by suggesting that her son marry Charlemagne's daughter, Rotrud (787), showed a shrewd insight that characterized her relations both with the papacy and the Franks. (Charlemagne even offered to marry Irene herself in 801/02, a prospect that alarmed many at court and may have hastened her fall.) Nevertheless, the severe problems faced by iconophile sovereigns between 780 and 813 were held, in 814/15, to justify the restoration of iconoclasm by Leo V. Irene was, perhaps unjustly, seen as initiating this decline.

Her failings have often been attributed – both in her own day and even in modern times – to her sex and the company she "naturally" kept as a woman: monks and eunuchs. In the modern consciousness the blinding of her son remains a notorious event that encapsulates the biased Enlightenment verdict of a Gibbon or Voltaire on Byzantium: it was the epitome of an entire civilization. Both conclusions need substantial qualification if Irene's remarkable reign and powerful character are to be fully appreciated.

DAVID R. TURNER

See also Iconoclasm

Biography

Irene was born in Athens *c*.752. In 768 she was chosen by Constantine V as wife for his son, the future Leo IV. On Leo's death in 780 she acted as regent for her young son, Constantine VI, and reigned as co-empress from 780 to 790. Deposed from 790 to 792, she was restored as co-empress in 792, and reigned as sole empress from 797 to 802. She died on Lesbos in 803.

Further Reading

Anastos, M., "Iconoclasm and Imperial Rule, 717–843" in *The Byzantine Empire*, edited by J.M. Hussey, Cambridge: Cambridge University Press, 1966 (*The Cambridge Medieval History*, vol. 4, part 1, 2nd edition)

Dölger, Franz and Peter Wirth (editors), *Regesten der Kaiserurkunden des oströmischen Reiches*, vol. 1: *565–1025*, Hildesheim: Gerstenberg, 1976; Munich: Bech, 1977 (original edition, 1924)

Speck, P., *Kaiser Konstantin VI*, Munich: Fink, 1978

Treadgold, Warren T., *The Byzantine Revival, 780–842*, Stanford: Stanford University Press, 1988

Iron

Iron differs from other metals used in antiquity in almost every way. The ores are widespread and abundant, but smelting requires much higher temperatures than other metals. Most smelted iron is inferior to bronze, but steel, an alloy of iron and carbon, has properties far in advance of other metals used in antiquity. However, the qualities of steel can only be brought about under carefully controlled conditions of temperature and chemical environment. For these reasons iron replaced bronze very gradually: although the first smelted iron dates from the 3rd millennium BC, iron only came into general use in the Aegean region around 1200 BC. A contributing factor may have been a shortage of tin for making bronze.

Iron is a common element in the earth and rich ores were readily available in antiquity. There were four principal types – metallic iron in meteorites, primary ore in rocks, iron-rich sands, and iron-rich fossil soils (laterites).

Natural metallic iron only occurs in meteorites and very rare terrestrial rocks not found in the Aegean. Meteorites were certainly known in the ancient Greek world: Anaxagoras of Clazomenae examined a meteorite and concluded that heavenly bodies were made of the same material as the earth. They were also venerated at Pessinus (Asia Minor) and possibly elsewhere, but no authenticated meteorites survive from this period. It has been suggested that some early iron objects were made of meteoritic iron on the basis of their chemical composition, primarily their high nickel content. However, such analyses may be suspect as it is only the oxidized surface that is commonly analysed, which is enriched in nickel. In addition, some iron deposits contain substantial quantities of nickel that were sometimes incorporated into the final metal. Finally, most meteoritic iron is difficult to work, unsuitable for making tools, and only available in small quantities.

Many of the primary ores exploited in Greece were precipitated where hot watery fluids released during the crystallization of granite reacted with limestone or marble. Such fluids also carried other metals that were deposited under different conditions. Seriphos was the main source of such ores – the amount of slag from smelting indicates that seven million tonnes of iron were mined here from antiquity onwards. Two different ores were extracted: those at Playa near the centre of the island were deposited at high temperatures (500° to 600°C) and are rich in magnetite. The limonite iron deposits of Mega Livadi were formed at lower temperatures away from the granite. Similar deposits were exploited near Neapolis in the Peloponnese.

One of the largest underground palaeolithic mines in Europe was on Thasos. These deposits were initially exploited for ochre, a red pigment used for cult purposes. From the 9th century BC onwards extraction of iron ore for the production of metal became important from these and other deposits on the island. Sources were limonite/haematite ores associated with silver and gold ores formed in dolomite. Beach sands rich in magnetite and ilmenite (iron-titanium oxide) were also exploited here, and probably elsewhere in the Aegean.

Laterites are ancient "soils" rich in the iron mineral haematite that were formed during Early Cretaceous time (about 90 million years ago) when a tropical climate prevailed in Greece. Intense weathering of the serpentinite bedrock removed most of the chemical elements in solution, leaving behind a layer on the surface up to 10 m thick enriched in iron and nickel. In some areas the laterite was eroded and the sediments transported by rivers to be redeposited on top of Jurassic limestones. At the end of the Cretaceous period the sea invaded the area and limestone was deposited on top of both types of laterite.

Laterites were exploited for iron in Boeotia and Euboea. Pliny mentions an occurrence of iron ore near Hyettos, about 8 km north of Lake Copais. The deposits occur in the mountains northeast of Chalcis, near the Aegean coast (the range that includes Mount Dirphys), and on the adjacent mainland, in northeast Boeotia, between Lake Copais and the north Euboean Gulf. They can be seen as long, thin, meandering lines of dark-red rock between paler limestones or greenish serpentinites. Some of the same deposits have been exploited recently for nickel. Iron produced from these deposits under certain conditions of smelting contained some nickel.

In antiquity iron was used for statues, tools, utensils, and various decorative purposes. It was usually smelted and worked in the solid state, without melting. Iron ore and charcoal were packed into small cylindrical furnaces and fired to over 1000°C. Towards the base of the furnace some of the iron ore was reduced to tiny flakes of metallic iron by the charcoal. Further up in the furnace some of the iron ore combined with silica in the ore or parts of the furnace to form a molten slag dominated by iron silicates that prevented the metallic iron beneath from reoxidizing. The mass of metallic iron thus formed is called a bloom and is very pure. At the end of the firing the bloom was lifted out and the processes started again. The bloom contained much slag that had to be removed by hammering at orange heat (smithing) before the metal could be used. Some slag was always left in the finished product but this did not diminish its properties significantly and enabled pieces to be welded by hammering. Iron produced by this process was a soft metal that needed to be converted to steel by the addition of carbon before the metal could realize its full potential.

To make steel suitable for weapons, smithed iron was packed in charcoal dust and sealed in clay containers to prevent oxidation. It was then heated to red heat for several hours to days. This mass of raw steel was worked to form the desired object. The final step necessary to develop the full strength of the steel was tempering. In this process the finished object was reheated to a special temperature and cooled at a controlled rate. With the precision necessary for all these steps it is no wonder that successful early smiths were so highly regarded.

MICHAEL D. HIGGINS

See also Geography, Geology, Metalwork

Further Reading

Antoniadi, E.M., "On Ancient Meteorites and the Origin of the Crescent and the Star Emblem", *Journal of the Royal Astronomical Society of Canada*, 33 (1939): pp. 177–84

Bakhuizen, S.C., *Chalcis-in-Euboea, Iron and Chalcidians Abroad*, Leiden: Brill, 1976

Bassiakos, Y.E., C.T. Michael and D. Chaikalis, "Ancient Metallurgical and Mining Studies on S.E. Peloponnese (Greece)" in *Archaeometry*, edited by Y. Mariatis, Amsterdam and New York: Elsevier, 1989

Burke, John G., *Cosmic Debris: Meteorites in History*, Berkeley: University of California Press, 1986

Craddock, Paul T., *Early Metal Mining and Production*, Edinburgh: Edinburgh University Press, and Washington, D.C.: Smithsonian Institution Press, 1995

Higgins, Michael Denis and Reynold Higgins, *A Geological Companion to Greece and the Aegean*, London: Duckworth, and Ithaca, New York: Cornell University Press, 1996

Wagner, G.A. and G. Weisgerber, *Antike Edel- und Bunt-Metallgewinnung auf Thasos*, Bochum: Deutsches Bergbau-Museum, 1988

Wertime, Theodore A. and James D. Muhly (editors), *The Coming of the Age of Iron*, New Haven, Connecticut and London: Yale University Press, 1980

Isaac the Syrian, St

Monastic author of the 7th century

Thanks to an early translation into Greek, Isaac the Syrian (Isaac of Nineveh) is the best known, and most influential, of all the monastic writers of the Church of the East. He was born and educated in the region of Qatar in the early 7th century, at a time when this area had a strong Christian presence. Some time in the late 670s he was appointed bishop of Nineveh (modern Mosul), but shortly after he retired to live as a hermit in the mountains of Khuzistan. His writings show him to be a man of considerable education and learning, and he draws on many different earlier Syriac and Greek writers; among the latter (which he read in Syriac translation) are the desert fathers, Gregory the Theologian, Evagrius, the Makarian Homilies, Theodore of Mopsuestia, Mark the Monk, Abba Isaiah, the Dionysian Corpus, and even the non-Christian *Life of Secundus the Silent Philosopher*.

His works have come down to us in their Syriac original in two parts, consisting of 82 and 41 chapters. Of these, the latter has been recovered only recently, while the former has long been most accessible in the Greek translation made by the monks Abramios and Patrikios in the Palestinian monastery of Mar Saba, probably in the late 8th century. The translators must have worked from a Syriac manuscript which, on the one hand, omitted a number of chapters of the full Syriac text (19–21, 23–24, 26, 29, 31, 49, 54, 56, 71, 75, 76), but on the other hand included five texts that are not by Isaac. The first four of these extra texts (chapters 2, 7, 43, and 80 in the printed Greek edition) turn out to be translations of homilies by another monastic writer of the Church of the East, John the Elder, who flourished in the 8th century, while the final letter, addressed to an Abba Symeon, is an abbreviated translation of the letter to Patrikios by the Syrian Orthodox writer Philoxenos of Mabbug (died 523). Since the Symeon in question was for a long time identified as St Symeon the Younger, the 6th-century stylite who lived near Antioch, Isaac of Nineveh was dated to the same century, and it was only when a Syriac biographical notice was published in 1896, which mentioned his consecration as bishop of Nineveh by George, the Catholicos of the Church of the East (c.661–80), that Isaac's true date became apparent.

The Greek translation made at the monastery of Mar Saba has proved extremely influential: not only do a very large number of manuscripts containing it survive, but it also gave rise to many further translations into other languages. The earliest manuscript (fragmentary) belongs to the 9th century (gr. 693 in the Bibliothèque Nationale, Paris), and it must have been in the 9th century that the earliest translations of the Greek text were made into Arabic and Georgian: an Arabic manuscript written in Mar Saba monastery in 885/86 (Strasbourg, Ar. 4226) already contains excerpts, and the same applies to a Georgian manuscript dated 906 (Sinai, Geor. 35), also written in Mar Saba monastery. (Mar Saba remained a centre of great translation activity in the 9th and 10th centuries, well after the sack of the monastery in 813 and the departure of the brothers Graptoi, and other monks, to Constantinople at about that time.) A second, and fuller, Georgian translation was made in the late 10th century on Mount Athos by St Evthymios (died 1028), an indefatigable translator of Greek patristic texts into Georgian.

Excerpts from St Isaac feature in a number of medieval monastic florilegia. Thus, for example, he is well represented in the *Synagoge*, or *Evergetinos*, of Paul (died 1054) of the monastery of the Theotokos Evergetis. Excerpts can also be found in the still unpublished *Eclogae Asceticae* of John V (IV) Oxites, patriarch of Antioch (c.1089–1100), and in the Pandects of Nikon of the Black Mountain (near Antioch), of much the same date. Surprisingly, however, Isaac does not feature in the more famous 18th-century anthology published by Makarios of Corinth and Nikodimos of the Holy Mountain in 1782 under the title *Philokalia*. (Passages from St Isaac, however, were subsequently to be incorporated into the Russian (1884) and Romanian (1981) editions of the *Philokalia*; thus St Isaac features in E. Kadloubovsky's and G. E. H. Palmer's *Early Fathers from the Philokalia* (London, 1954), translated from Russian, but not in the complete English translation of the *Philokalia*, made from Greek.)

In the course of the Middle Ages further translations were made from the Greek text of Isaac into Arabic (and thence, Ethiopic), Slavonic, and Latin. The Slavonic translation belongs to the 14th century, and was probably made in Bulgaria, perhaps by a disciple of St Gregory of Sinai (c.1275–c.1346). The Latin translation (first printed in Venice in 1506) may be the work of Angelo Clareno, the translator of St John of Sinai's *The Ladder*, who died in 1337. It was not until 1770 that the Greek text itself appeared in print, published in Leipzig. The edition was prepared by Nikiphoros Theotokis, at the request of Ephraim, the patriarch of Jerusalem. Unfortunately Theotokis used late manuscripts as the basis for his edition, and at the same time reordered the chapters in order to provide what seemed to him a more logical sequence. As a result, the numeration of chapters differs markedly between the printed Syriac and Greek editions, and thus in all modern translations derived from these (convenient tables can be found, for example, in the English translation of the Greek published by the Holy Transfiguration Monastery, Boston). The current editions of the Greek text reproduce the re-edition by Ioakim Spetsieris (1895) which retained the chapter order (but not the pagination) of the 1770 edition. There is a pressing need for a new edition of the Greek text, based on the several early manuscripts available. A modern Greek translation, by Fr Kallinikos of the Pantocrator monastery on Mount Athos, was first published in 1871, while a demotic Greek rendering of chapters 15, 18, 24, 26, 31, 35, 62, 65, 66, and 68 (of the Greek edition) was made by Photis Kondoglou in his *O Mystikos Kipos* (The Mystical Garden: Athens, 1944; reprinted 1975). In recent times the Greek text has served as the basis for a French translation by J. Touraille (Paris, 1981), and an English translation by Dana Miller (Holy Transfiguration Monastery, Boston, 1984).

From this survey it can be seen that the initial Greek translation made in Palestine by Abramios and Patrikios has proved immensely influential over the centuries, far more so than has been the case with the Syriac original. Often this influence has been through secondary translations made from the Greek. St Isaac's writings today remain widely read, and this is by no means confined to monastic circles, where of course they are particularly appreciated. He described the path to salvation as passing through three stages: repentance, purification, and perfection. The key to his continued popularity over the centuries certainly lies in the profundity of his teaching on the spiritual life in which the mystery of God's unlimited love for creation as a whole and humanity in particular serves as his fundamental starting point.

SEBASTIAN BROCK

Biography

Born near Qatar on the Persian Gulf in the early 7th century, Isaac became a monk of the Church of the East, and in the late 670s bishop of Nineveh. But he soon resigned from his see and went to live as a hermit in southwest Iran. He wrote in Syriac on ascetic and mystical topics but many of his writings were translated into Greek by the monks of Mar Saba and have been most influential.

Writings

Tou osiou patros imon Isaak episkopou Nineve tou Syrou ta evrethenta askitika, translated by Nikiphoros Theotokis, Leipzig 1770; re-edited by I. Spetsieris, 1895, reprinted 1977 (Greek translation of Syriac original)

Oi askitikoi logoi abba Isaak, translated into modern Greek by Fr. Kallinikos of the Holy Mountain, 1871, reprinted Athens, 1966 and Thessalonica, 1976

Mystic Treatises, translated by A.J. Wansinck, Amsterdam, 1923, reprinted Wiesbaden: Sändig, 1969

The Ascetical Homilies, translated by the Holy Transfiguration Monastery, Boston: The Monastery, 1984

On Ascetical Life, translated by Mary Hansbury, Crestwood, New York: St Vladimir's Seminary Press, 1989

The Heart of Compassion, translated by A.M. Allchin, London: Darton Longman and Todd, 1989

Isaac of Nineveh (Isaac the Syrian): The "Second Part", Chapters IV–XLI, translated by Sebastian Brock, Louvain: Peeters, 1995 (Corpus Scriptorum Christianorum Orientalium 555)

The Wisdom of Saint Isaac the Syrian, translated by Sebastian Brock, Oxford: SCG, 1997; Kalamazoo, Michigan: Cistercian Publications, 1998

Further Reading

Alfeyev, H., *The World of Isaac the Syrian,* Kalamazoo: Cistercian Publications, forthcoming

Archimandrite Vasileios, *Abbas Isaak o Syros: Ena Plisiasma ston Kosmo tou* [Abba Isaac the Syrian: An Approach to his World], Athens, 1981

Brock, Sebastian, "Isaac the Syrian" in *La Théologie byzantine,* edited by C. Conticello *et al.,* Turnhout: Brepols, forthcoming

Isocrates *c.*436–338 BC

Orator

Isocrates was an enormously influential Athenian rhetorician. Much is to be gained in understanding his views if it is noted that his life stretched from the time of Pericles to the victory of Philip of Macedon over the free Greeks at Chaeronea; he was first and foremost an ardent patriot of his city, yet he was willing to imagine his polis working as an ally with the newly emerging strongmen of the Greek world. Conservative in outlook, he was also a powerful spokesman for Panhellenism – however, a Panhellenism that always put his native city first. His work, chiefly long epideictic or "display" orations that were not in fact orally delivered (he did not possess a strong voice), was read and cited well into the Byzantine period; his style of writing, itself reflecting the influence of his teacher, the Sophist Gorgias, was widely admired and imitated as a model of Attic prose. He was also an important teacher of composition for orators and historians: many of his "students" were themselves to be significant figures in the field of letters.

His earliest extant works are six speeches that he wrote for others to deliver in courts of law: like his slightly older contemporary Lysias, he was a *logopoios* in his early years, after his family's wealth had been destroyed in the Peloponnesian War. He soon gave up this career, and turned to producing large-scale public orations and other essays. He wrote two encomiastic treatises, the *Helen* and the *Busiris,* much in the tradition of his teacher Gorgias. His *Evagoras,* an oration addressed to that Cypriot king's son and successor Nicocles, is one of the earliest pieces of biography in Greek literature, alongside Xenophon's *Agesilaus.* In a similar vein, he also wrote a number of open letters, primarily to kings in the Greek world.

Isocrates' main achievement, however, lay in his long and elaborate epideictic speeches. The *Panegyricus* (*c.*380 BC) is a Panhellenic speech advocating an all-Greek expedition against Persia, and at the same time defending Athens' imperial past and attacking Sparta. The *De Pace* (On the Peace, 355 BC) represents something of a change in views: it urges Athens to make peace with its rebellious allies of the Second Athenian Confederation (founded 378 BC) and recommends that the Athenians "make lasting peace with all the world", including Persia. A return to the views of the *Panegyricus* is represented by the *Philippus* (346 BC), although now the standard of Panhellenism is to be held by Philip of Macedon, working together with the Athenians at the head of an all-Greek coalition.

Some of his other great orations tell us more about Isocrates' life, political views, and influence. The *Areopagiticus,* written at about the same time as the *De Pace,* is a criticism of moral decay at Athens and a plea for a return to the limited democracy of Solon and Cleisthenes. In *Against the Sophists,* written early in his career (*c.*390 BC), Isocrates tried to differentiate himself from other teachers of rhetoric. The *Panathenaicus* (339 BC) is the last work he wrote and is a summation and defence of his career. Perhaps the most important statement of his views on rhetoric is contained in his *Antidosis,* written in 354/53 BC. It has many points in common with his earlier *Against the Sophists*; further, it contains extracts from his own earlier speeches, and may even allude at points to the famous defence of Socrates. It is in this speech that Isocrates states quite plainly that people can become better and more worthy if they become desirous of speaking well. Isocrates is reputed to have taught the orators Isaeus and Hyperides, and the historians Androtion, Ephorus, and Theopompus, though many today would want to modify this claim, emphasizing Isocrates' influence on others, rather than any actual instruction he may have given.

Isocrates' belief that rhetoric is crucial in the education of leaders became a central tenet of antiquity. For Cicero he was "the father of eloquence" and the "teacher of all orators" (*De Oratore,* 2. 10. 94). It is hardly surprising, then, that his work was influential throughout the Byzantine period. Isocrates was an important model for the Church fathers Basil and Gregory of Nazianzus. Further, he was a central figure for Byzantine educational canons, widely regarded as a model of Attic prose style and a source of moral *dicta.* The *Suda* relies heavily on his work; Manuel II Palaiologos mines him for *sententiae.* Further, his work helped to define the Byzantine ideal of Athens: it is significant that John Malalas groups him (*Chronicle* 214) with Pericles and Thucydides, as opposed to 4th-century BC figures. Despite the lack of interest in the first printed edition of his work (Aldus Manutius, Venice, 1493), he became a central figure in the modern period for defining the educational methods of cultural humanism: Werner Jaeger (*Paideia,* 3. 46) has noted that he is rightfully called the "father of humanistic culture".

JOHN DILLERY

See also Rhetoric

Biography

Born c.436 BC in Athens, Isocrates studied under the sophists Prodicus and Gorgias. In the 390s he wrote speeches for others to deliver in court. But soon he changed to producing large-scale orations and teaching rhetoric to others. His pupils are said to have included the general Timotheus, the orators Isaeus and Hyperides, and the historians Androtion, Ephorus, and Theopompus. His writings were much admired for their purity of style. He starved himself to death in 338 BC.

Writings

Isocrates, translated by George Norlin and La Rue van Hook, 3 vols, London: Heinemann, and New York: Putnam, 1928–45 (Loeb edition)

Further Reading

Baynes, N.H., "Isocrates" in his *Byzantine Studies and Other Essays*, London: Athlone Press, 1955

Bringmann, Klaus, "Studien zu den politischen Ideen des Isokrates", *Hypomnemata*, 14 (1965)

Davidson, J., "Isocrates against Imperialism: An Analysis of the *De Pace*", *Historia*, 39 (1990): pp. 20ff

Eucken, Christoph, *Isokrates: Seine Positionen in der Auseinandersetzung mit den zeitgenössischen Philosophen*, Berlin: de Gruyter, 1983

Jaeger, Werner, *Paideia: The Ideals of Greek Culture*, vol. 3, Oxford: Blackwell, 1961; reprinted Oxford and New York: Oxford University Press, 1986

Mathieu, Georges, *Les Idées politiques d'Isocrate*, Paris: Belles Lettres, 1925, reprinted 1966

Perlman, S., "Isocrates' *Philippus* and Panhellenism", *Historia*, 18 (1969): pp. 370–74

Too, Yun Lee, *The Rhetoric of Identity in Isocrates: Text, Power, Pedagogy*, Cambridge and New York: Cambridge University Press, 1995

Welles, C.B., "Isocrates' View of History" in *The Classical Tradition: Literary and Historical Studies in Honor of Harry Caplan*, edited by Luitpold Wallach, Ithaca, New York: Cornell University Press, 1966

Italos, John

Philosopher of the 11th century

John Italos came to Constantinople in 1049 from south Italy with his father, a Norman, as part of a detachment of westerners who were asked to assist the emperor Constantine IX Monomachos (1042–55) in his campaign against the Pechenegs. His mother was probably a Hellenophone from Sicily or Calabria. He cannot have been very old at the time, although we do not know when he died or at what age so it is impossible to be sure. Of his education, we know only that he eventually became a student and protégé of Michael Psellos and was in time granted the title *hypatos* ("first philosopher"). Italos became most famous as a champion of the dialectic taught by "the ancients", chiefly Aristotle, as is obvious from his extant works. If Anna Komnene is to be believed, he was enormously successful in his role as *hypatos*: "When he took up the chair", she writes (*Alexiad*, 5. 8. 9), "all the young flocked to him, for he opened up to them the teachings [*dogmata*] of Plato ... and Porphyry ... and especially the arts of Aristotle." Anna's portrait of Italos is not wholly

favourable, however. She condemns him (5. 8. 5) as a near-traitor for carrying out a diplomatic mission to the court of Robert Guiscard; notes that he was twice accused of promoting dangerous theological doctrines and was "convicted" the second time, in 1082 (5. 9. 7); and criticizes his style as "rude" and "labyrinthine" (5. 8. 6). However skilful he was at dialectic, "his command of grammar was awkward, and he had not imbibed the nectar of rhetoric" (5. 8. 6).

In 1076/77 Italos was accused anonymously (and evidently without justification) of teachings contrary to Orthodox doctrine and tradition. On this occasion, apparently, the emperor Michael VII Doukas (1071–78) intervened, and Italos was able to retain his position as *hypatos*. It may have been in the period after his first "trial" that Italos composed his *Aporiai*, given confidence, perhaps, by the knowledge that he was under imperial protection. In 1082/83, however, he was not so lucky. Michael had by then abdicated the throne and retired to a monastery. Italos, accordingly, was condemned – on charges that most scholars now think were without foundation – and forced into a monastery.

Among the better-known students of John Italos are Eustratios (who himself was condemned in 1117 for holding that Christ reasoned in an Aristotelian fashion) and Joannes Petric'i (who returned to his native Georgia and produced Georgian versions of Aristotle's *Topica* and *De Interpretatione*). It is not clear whether Theodore of Smyrna, his successor as *hypatos*, was one of his students.

Italos produced several short elementary texts when he was tutor to Andronikos Doukas, Michael's younger brother, including: "To His Royal Highness Andronikos, on His Questions About Dialectic"; a "Synopsis" of the art of rhetoric (wrongly thought by some to have been a synopsis of Aristotle's *Rhetoric*); and a short treatise explicating the dream in *Odyssey*, 19. 560ff. The recently published "Synopsis of the Isagoge from the Lectures of John the Philosopher" (see Further Reading: Romano) might also have been meant for Andronikos.

THOMAS M. CONLEY

Biography

Born in southern Italy c.1025, John Italos moved to Constantinople around 1049 and became a pupil of Michael Psellos. In time he replaced Psellos as *hypatos ton philosophon* ("first of the philosophers"). He became the champion of Aristotelian dialectic but fell foul of the emperor Alexios I Komnenos and in 1082 was banished to a monastery. His date of death is unknown.

Writings

In *Die griechischen Ausleger der aristotelischen Topik*, edited by Max Wallies, Berlin: Gaertner, 1891, p.24–27

Opuscula selecta, edited by G. Cereteli, 2 vols, Tbilisi, 1924–26

Quaestiones Quodlibitales, edited by Perikles Joannou, Ettal: Buch-Kunstverlag, 1956

Opera, edited by N. Ketchakmadze, Tbilisi, 1966

Further Reading

Romano, R., "Un opusculo inedito di Giovanni Italo," *Bollettino dei Classici*, 13 (1992): pp. 14–24

Italy

The Italian peninsula in southern Europe in which the Roman empire later emerged has been exposed to interaction with Greek civilization throughout its recorded history. Many tribes made up the population of the Italian peninsula, which is one of the reasons why the unification under Rome was considered to be a great achievement. Evidence of Minoan and Mycenaean trade has been found in many places, particularly in the southern part of the peninsula and Sicily. There is a history of political, cultural, and religious relations, and intricate reciprocity of influence from one side to the other. Relations with the Greek world were first established by the Etruscans, located mainly in northern Italy. To give one simple example, the Latin alphabet is believed to have been borrowed by the Romans from the Etruscans, who in their turn had taken it from the Greeks c.700 BC. Etruscan art, particularly sculpture and painting, as well as architecture, largely followed the development of Greek art, although it was significantly different. Etruscan culture influenced early Rome in its political organization and religious cults. Whether originating from the East (according to Herodotus, who believed that they came from Lydia), or indigenous Italian (as Dionysius of Halicarnassus thought them to be), their expansion depended much on trade. Through trade they came into contact with many people. Contact with the Greeks was intensified after Greek colonization.

In the period from 800 BC to 500 BC, traders from Greece reached south Italy and Sicily. Mostly for reasons of overpopulation and unfair distribution of land, as well as the need for expansion of trade, Greeks began to colonize places abroad that could offer rich agricultural production and defensible harbours. The use of the terms "colonization" and "colony" for this new kind of settlement is extremely misleading since many of the modern connotations attached to them are not applicable. With the exception of Athens and Thebes, most Greek city states seized every opportunity to expand, particularly in south Italy and Sicily where the climate and agricultural possibilities are very similar to those in mainland Greece. The first Greek settlement (c.750 BC) was at Cyme, mostly known by its Latin name Cumae, founded by the cities of Chalcis, Eretria, and Cyme in Asia Minor. Sparta founded only one colony, Taras, in south Italy in 706. Corinth established Syracuse in Sicily in 733 BC. Naxos founded Naxos in Sicily, Chalcis founded Leontini and Catane, Megara founded Megara Hyblaea. Chalcis later founded Rhegion (modern Reggio) in Calabria. By the 5th century BC, south Italy (but not Sicily) was referred to as "Magna Graecia". Many of the cities that were founded in Archaic and Classical times still bear traces of their Greek past, such as Taras (Latin Tarentum), Syracuse, Poseidonia (Latin Paestum), Tauromenium (Latin Taormina), Acragas (Latin Agrigentum), or Gela. A colony was a separate polis. Although it was independent of the home state, it maintained real links with the mother city. The mother city was often asked to protect the colony when in danger, and the Sicilian expedition in the Peloponnesian War is an example of the kind of relations and tensions that prevailed between mother city and colonies.

The Greeks often came into contention with the people of the Italian peninsula. The Etruscans were defeated by the Greeks at Cumae in 474 BC. Meanwhile, until the 3rd century BC Rome was expanding rapidly in the Italian peninsula. The Latin tribes, the Oscans, and the Samnites soon came under Roman control. There remained only the Greek city states of the south. In the 3rd century the Greeks of Taras, alarmed by Roman expansion, asked for help from Pyrrhus, king of Epirus. He defeated the Romans at Heraclea and Asculum (280 BC and 279 BC) but lost the battle at Beneventum in 275. After that the Romans were kept busy in their wars against the Carthaginians from 264 to 146 BC. They were, however, also drawn into the turbulent affairs of the Hellenistic world – in the Aegean against King Philip V (221–187), and further east against King Antiochus III (223–187). In a series of Macedonian wars enmities among the various Greek city states and leagues also played a significant role. In 197 BC Philip V was defeated and Greece was declared free after the battle of Cynoscephalae. There was now a precedent for Roman intervention in Greek and Hellenistic affairs. King Perseus, the son of Philip V, was no more effective than his father against the Romans. Thus in 146 BC Greece became a Roman province; and in 133 BC Pergamum was bequeathed to Rome by King Eumenes III and also became a province.

Besides action at the military and political levels, it was with the Roman conquest of the Hellenistic world that Hellenic, or rather Hellenistic, culture permeated many aspects of Roman life. An attempt was slowly made to create a Roman literary culture according to the Greek ideal. Already from the time of the Carthaginian wars attempts had been made by Livius Andronicus to translate Homeric epic poetry into Latin. Plautus wrote comedies in the style of Menander. Accius and Pacuvius also wrote comedies and tragedies. Besides the adaptation of many literary genres that had flourished in the Greek world the Romans tried to explore unique Roman ideals in literature and philosophy, that would be canonized later in the Golden Age of Augustus. Cato the Elder reproached the Romans for imitating the Greek way of life. In the realm of religion many cults of the Greek city states entered the Roman pantheon, particularly that of Dionysus. Greek deities had already acquired their position in the Roman pantheon and been given a Latin name. In art and architecture, the meeting of the Greeks and Romans became even more obvious. Many models were copied. Greek educational principles were also transmitted to Rome. Later, both in the republic and in the empire, many Romans went to Athens to pursue their studies, especially in philosophy and rhetoric. In the philosophical works of Cicero it became obvious how Hellenistic philosophy acquired a Roman setting and terminology. Earlier poets, like Lucretius or Catullus, as well as the poets of the Augustan age, drew context and forms from the early Greek literary productions as well as from Hellenistic culture, transforming them into completely new material. Prose writers such as Livy also inherited some elements from their Greek predecessors. On the other hand, there were Greek authors, such as Dionysius of Halicarnassus, Diodorus Siculus, and Polybius, who wrote in Greek about Roman matters. After the unification of Italy under the Roman empire, the meaning and identity of the word Roman was established. But there were still Romans who wrote in Greek, such as the emperor Marcus Aurelius in the 2nd century AD. Many scholars have seen in this period a decline of the Classical ideal, whereas in fact it bears witness to the emergence of new, well-defined tendencies in literature, philosophy, religion, and art.

The spread of Christianity soon reshaped the tensions in the Mediterranean world. The interaction between Greek and Italian was acquiring a new dimension as the Christian religion grew stronger. At first, the new debate of Christian versus pagan appeared in contemporary literary and rhetorical writings, whereas later, once Christianity was established, the debate centred on the Greek versus the Latin rite in ecclesiastical matters. With the establishment of Constantinople as the "new Rome" the polarity between East and West entered a new phase.

In the 8th and 9th centuries, the period of iconoclasm, many educated men sought refuge in peripheral regions of the Byzantine world. Many migrated to south Italy, bringing with them their literary and artistic traditions. The wave of migrations to Italy included many monks and priests. Undoubtedly iconoclasm played an important part in the severing of relations between Byzantium and Italy. Politically, by the 9th century, the republic of Venice had become independent of Byzantine control. In the south, Byzantine influence increased as the emperor Nikephoros Phokas was successful against the Arabs. The number of Greek monasteries and churches also grew. When by the 11th century southern Italy was relatively safe from Arab attacks, the Norman conquests gave a new shape to the history of this region. The Normans steadily advanced into Byzantine Italy. The 12th century marked a "renaissance" in Byzantine literature and art. Due to commercial relations that existed between Italy and Byzantium, many Italian scholars, particularly Venetians and Pisans, who resided in substantial numbers in Constantinople, transmitted Greek learning to the West.

Strained relations developed between Byzantium and Italy in the 12th and 13th centuries and the role of the Crusaders made the issue more complex. Byzantine trade was constantly losing ground to the Italian republics, particularly Venice, Genoa, and Pisa. The schism that divided the Eastern and Western Churches in 1054, for dogmatic reasons, had explosive political repercussions. The Crusades, especially the fourth in 1204, dealt a devastating blow to Byzantium. Despite the tension in political relations in the 13th and 14th centuries, the reciprocal influences in literature and art present one of the most interesting phenomena. Many Greek texts were preserved in Italian libraries such as those of the Vatican, Florence, Venice, and Naples. Around the time of the fall of Constantinople in 1453, many intellectuals fled permanently to Italy. Eminent scholars like Chrysoloras, Janus Laskaris, Argyropoulos, Bessarion, Chalkondyles, Musouros, and others worked extensively in Italy and spread their learning and culture in the West. Venice in particular, and also Florence, became important centres for the study of Greek literature. When typography was invented, the first editions of Greek books were often made by Italian humanists.

In tracing the roots of modern Greek literature to the 10th century AD, relations with Italy and Italian culture can be detected in many places. It was not only Greek texts that survived in manuscripts belonging to Italian libraries, but some entire works have a version in both languages. The *Chronicle of Morea* is preserved in an Italian version as well as in Greek (also in French and Aragonese). Relations with north Italy were more visible in Crete, which remained under Venetian rule from 1204 until 1669, when it became part of the Ottoman empire. Although there was significant political opposition to the Venetians in the beginning, the Cretan renaissance was soon in progress, activated especially by Byzantine scholars who fled to Crete. Authors of the Cretan renaissance like Georgios Chortatsis (*fl.* 1590–1600) or Vitsentzos Kornaros (1553–1613/14) were in close contact with the parallel movement in literature, particularly theatre, in Italy. At approximately the same time, a kind of lyric poetry was developed in Cyprus with evident Italian influence, particularly from Petrarch. They are mostly love poems in Italian hendecasyllables.

The meeting between Greece and Italy becomes more evident in the 17th and 18th centuries in the Ionian islands. They never formed part of the Ottoman empire, and during this period literature flourished there. Dionysios Solomos (1798–1857) became a representative and a "national" poet for Greece. He was educated in Italy and was nourished on Italian literature. It was only natural then that his first writings were in Italian. Although later he reached his full glory with themes deriving from the situation in Greece, he brought a new shape to poetry through his thorough knowledge of Italian forms. Andreas Kalvos (1792–1869), another poet of the Heptanesian school, was also educated in Italy. The poetry of Ugo Foscolo (1778–1827) and other classical Italian poets of the Heptanesian school influenced the direction that Greek literature took. Although scholars, poets, and writers in the late 19th and early 20th centuries absorbed French, German, and English influences, there remained many contacts between Greece and Italy. There are still some areas in south Italy where a Graeco-Italian language is spoken to this day. Its origins (ancient Greek or Byzantine) are hotly disputed.

The two World Wars completely transformed political relations between Greece and Italy but at an intellectual level the traditional affinity continued. The Italian Archaeological School has exerted tremendous influence in archaeology. Nowadays, especially through the European Union, the two countries are in a constant intellectual dialogue that has proved to be effective in all areas of human knowledge, particularly science, literature, and art.

ANDROMACHE KARANIKA-DIMAROGONA

See also Bessarion, Chortatsis, Chrysoloras, Colonization, Etruscans, Genoese, Kalvos, Kornaros, Magna Graecia, Peloponnesian War, Rome, Solomos, Venice

Further Reading

Boardman, John, Jasper Griffin, and Oswyn Murray (editors), *The Oxford History of the Classical World*, Oxford and New York: Oxford University Press, 1986

Cheetham, Nicolas, *Mediaeval Greece*, New Haven, Connecticut and London: Yale University Press, 1981

Fantham, Elaine, *Roman Literary Culture: From Cicero to Apuleius*, Baltimore: Johns Hopkins University Press, 1996

Geanakoplos, Deno John, *Greek Scholars in Venice: Studies in the Dissemination of Greek Learning from Byzantium to Western Europe*, Cambridge, Massachusetts: Harvard University Press, 1962; as *Byzantium and the Renaissance*, Hamden, Connecticut: Archon, 1973

Lindsay, Jack, *Byzantium into Europe*, London: Bodley Head, 1952

Nicol, Donald M., *Byzantium and Venice: A Study in Diplomatic and Cultural Relations*, Cambridge and New York: Cambridge University Press, 1982

Pugliese Carratelli, Giovanni, *The Western Greeks: Classical Civilization in Magna Graecia and Sicily*, New York: Rizzoli, 1996

Spadaro, Giuseppe, *Letteratura cretese e Rinascimento Italiano*, Soveria Mannelli: Rubbettino, 1994

Vitti, Mario, *Historia tes Neoellenikes Logotechnias* [History of Modern Greek Literature], Athens, 1987

Wilson, N.G., *From Byzantium to Italy: Greek Studies in the Italian Renaissance*, London: Duckworth, and Baltimore: Johns Hopkins University Press, 1992

Ivory

Ivory (*elephas*), properly speaking, is the dentine of elephant tusks, and it is from this material that the animal takes its name. The term also commonly denotes material obtained from hippopotamus, sperm whale, and walrus tusks, which, like all tusks, are teeth of continuous growth. There is no evidence that the last two animals supplied any of the ivory employed in the eastern Mediterranean, but elephant and hippopotamus ivory was imported to Greece, directly or indirectly, from the natural habitats of those creatures, i.e. Africa, the Levant, and India. Mammoth ivory, while available to Greeks in small quantities locally as well as from abroad, appears to have been rarely, if ever, used for carving, although a few chance finds may have served as trophies in antiquity, for example, the tusks of the legendary Caledonian boar. Actual boars' tusks adorned the helmets of elite warriors in the Mycenaean period and are mentioned in the Homeric epics.

Whatever its source, ivory was highly prized, serving as a symbol of wealth, status, and prestige from the Bronze Age, through the Classical and Byzantine periods, into the modern era on account of its exotic origins, aesthetic qualities, and reputed magical properties (as in the myths of Pelops and Pygmalion). Its smooth, creamy-white surface, warm lustre, density, and flexibility add to its appeal, and its physical characteristics allow it to be worked by a variety of techniques: it can be carved in the round or relief, cut into veneers or inlays, turned on a lathe, and even moulded. Most ivories were ultimately polished, painted, and gilded. A multipurpose commodity, ivory was employed in all periods in the manufacture of statues, reliefs, furniture components, appliqués, pyxides, handle attachments, pinheads, brooches, bracelets, combs and other toilet articles, seals, game pieces, and amulets.

The beauty and value of ivory are recognized in the earliest Greek texts, as in the Old Testament and earlier Near Eastern documents. The Mycenaean Linear B tablets inventory ivory weapons, chariots, and furniture, and similar objects mentioned in the *Iliad* and *Odyssey* symbolize royal affluence. That ivory-carving flourished in Minoan and Mycenaean society is also evidenced by numerous physical survivals from Bronze Age sites, including raw ivory from Zakros and the Ulu Burun shipwreck, and workshop debris from Knossos, Mycenae, Pylos, and Thebes. Reliefs intended for appliqué are the most common finds, but excavators have also recovered numerous other objects, among the finest of which are the fragments of a 50-cm-tall composite figure of a standing youth excavated at Palaikastro in eastern Crete (Siteia Museum). The exquisite carving of anatomical details of the Palaikastro youth far surpasses that of similar figures in all other media, underscoring not only the superior qualities of dense, fine-grained ivory as a material for sculpture, but also the fact that precious imported tusks were regularly entrusted to the most experienced craftsmen, who, presumably, had been trained in woodcarving, an art now largely lost. Blackened by fire, broken, and much restored, the Palaikastro statuette, like other unequivocally genuine Minoan ivory statuettes excavated at Knossos (Herakleion Museum), originally consisted of numerous individually carved components joined by complex systems of dowels and mortises. The Palaikastro figure also had rock-crystal eyes, stone hair, wooden nipples, and a golden loin cloth and sandals. This statue appears to have been painted, as were ivories in the Classical and Byzantine periods, although such ornamentation is often lost. (Technical, stylistic, and iconographic anomalies indicate that a number of "Minoan" ivory statuettes in collections outside Greece, inevitably said to be from Knossos, are modern forgeries.)

Ivory production in Greece naturally declined sharply during the so-called Dark Age of the late 2nd to early 1st millennium BC, but the material reappears in the Geometric and Orientalizing periods along with motifs and perhaps even craftsmen from the Levant; for 8th-, 7th-, and 6th-century carved ivories recovered from Crete, Athens, Ephesus, Samos, Laconia, Delphi, Perachora, and elsewhere, though sometimes exhibiting local stylistic features, closely parallel items that have been excavated in great quantity in the ancient Near East, particularly at Nimrud.

Like their Bronze Age ancestors, wealthy Greeks of the Archaic, Classical, and Hellenistic periods employed ivory, often combining it with other materials, to furnish their homes and gain the favour of the gods. Luxury furniture is best known from depictions on painted pottery and stone reliefs, but ancient texts, especially the inventories of the temples on the Athenian Acropolis and Delos, fill out the picture. Tombs have yielded fragments of ivory furnishings, but more have been recovered from sanctuaries. Indeed, many surviving ivory statuettes that are often presented as free-standing figures preserve cuttings in their heads or backs that indicate their original function as components of furniture, toilet articles, or even musical instruments. Most renowned in antiquity, however, were free-standing chryselephantine statues, composite works of gold and ivory. Produced at a variety of scales, these were assembled from individually carved ivory faces, hands, and feet attached to wooden armatures that were subsequently sheathed in gold. The hair of such figures, too, was rendered in gold, and these statues, gleaming and glittering in the half-light of temples or treasury buildings, presented stunning images of the gods. Most such works are lost and known only from later literary sources. Pausanias, for example, saw a number of early figures ascribed to pupils of the legendary craftsman Daedalus, as well as the gold, ivory, and cedarwood chest of Cypselus collected in the Heraion at Olympia. These objects do not survive, but a cache of votives from Delphi of the 6th century BC illustrates the technique and provides a notion of the appearance of such images, though they were burned in antiquity and are now much restored.

Ivory: 10th-century ivory triptych. The central panels show the crucifixion with the Archangels Gabriel and Michael, the Virgin, and St John the Evangelist, British Museum, London

Ancient authors explicitly state that the expense of ivory, along with its warm and lustrous colour, so closely approximating unblemished flesh, made it fitting for representations of divinities, and in the Classical period a combination of political and technological developments contributed to the unprecedented use of ivory in colossal statuary. The Athenian decision to erect a monumental statue of Athena (447–438 BC) inside the Parthenon was the result of competitive emulation. Monumental statues had long been erected in stone and bronze, but Phidias combined techniques of furniture-veneering, bronze-casting, and ship-building to create a gigantic composite work in gold and ivory approximately 12.75 m tall. Literary and physical evidence suggests that the Athenian sculptor adapted techniques of unscrolling tusks into thin sheets of ivory that were subsequently softened in acidic baths and then moulded in (or over) clay or wooden forms. This ivory skin, like the hammered gold that formed the drapery (weighing approximately 1137 kg in the case of the *Athena Parthenos*), was then affixed to a massive armature built around a wooden beam, the cutting for which survives in the floor of the temple. The resultant image of the ivory-skinned *Athena Parthenos* robed in golden garments ignited a trend throughout Greece as various city states commissioned similar statues of their own patron deities to demonstrate their piety, wealth, and power. Phidias' second essay in the genre, the *Zeus at Olympia*, came to be ranked among the seven wonders of the ancient world. Praised by numerous ancient authors, it was considered to have added something to traditional religion, and Phidias himself was thought to have travelled to Olympus, so accurately did he capture the essence of the god. This statue, like the *Parthenos*, is lost, known only from ancient descriptions and representations in other media. The workshop in which it was produced, however, was identified by Pausanias, and has been excavated: ivory wasters, bone chisels, terracotta moulds for glass inlays, and even a cup inscribed with Phidias' name are among the finds displayed in the Olympia Museum.

Phidias reputedly made additional chryselephantine statues (and pseudo-chryselephantine ones consisting of marble and gilded wood) at Elis, Plataea, and Pellene, and ancient sources report that similar works were produced at Argos, Megara, Elis, Athens, Calydon, Delos, and Epidaurus in the late 5th and 4th centuries BC by Polyclitus, Theocosmos, Colotes, Alcamenes, Menaechmus and Soidas, and Thrasymedes. Previously reserved for representations of the gods, ivory statues eventually came to be employed by mortal rulers seeking their own glorification, beginning with Philip of Macedon and his son Alexander, who erected a chryselephantine family group by Leochares in the Philippeion at Olympia, not far from Phidias' *Zeus*. Later ivory portraits are also mentioned by ancient authors. Special provisions were made for the maintenance of the largest statues: at Athens and Olympia reflecting pools of water and oil, respectively, were considered beneficial to the ivory, and special "polishers" (or "descendants of Phidias") looked after Phidias' statues.

Meanwhile, ivory continued to be employed for the adornment of the many sumptuous objects mentioned above, as well as for the decoration of the doors and ceilings of temples, and even the panelled rooms of the luxury barges of Hellenistic kings. Best preserved are the composite figurines that decorated couches recovered from Macedonian tombs (Thessalonica Museum). The monetary value of ivory, which was worth approximately one quarter its weight in silver in the 4th century BC according to building inscriptions at Delphi, naturally fluctuated according to its availability. The eastern conquests of Alexander increased supply, and the vast accumulations of the material by his successors are demonstrated by the thousands of tusks recorded to have been displayed in later Roman triumphs. Some Greek ivory statues were eventually carried off to Rome, and the chryselephantine technique continued to be practised under Roman rule: at Athens the emperor Hadrian commissioned another colossal *Zeus* for the Olympieion, and Herodes Atticus dedicated a *Tyche* in that city as well a *Poseidon-Amphitrite* group at Isthmia.

The fate of most of the great Classical ivory statues remains uncertain. Ancient sources record almost 200 such works in Italy, Greece, and the eastern Mediterranean. Not one of these survives, but components of dozens of others have been recovered. Many, depicting pagan gods, were no doubt destroyed by Christian iconoclasts. Phidias' *Zeus Olympios* is said to have been carried off to Constantinople, where it appeared in a Christianizing allegorical programme in the Palace of Lausos, providing a model for the bearded image of Christ Pantokrator before being destroyed by fire in the late 5th century AD. On a considerably smaller scale, ivory continued to be a popular medium for works in diverse genres in the Byzantine period. That its price had fallen considerably from Classical times is clear from the Edict of Diocletian, which lists it at one-fortieth the value of silver.

From the 4th to the 6th centuries statuettes, caskets, plaques, furniture, and other items decorated in classicizing styles with motifs from pagan mythology as well as Christian iconography were produced in Egypt, presumably at Alexandria, as well as Constantinople. Although scholars debate the precise origins of many late Antique and Byzantine ivories, an edict of AD 337 lists ivory workers among artisans exempted from civil obligations so that they might improve their craft and instruct their children, indicating how techniques were transmitted. A slightly later edict restricts all but ordinary consuls from distributing ivory diptychs, suggesting the widespread manufacture of these ceremonial gifts, distributed to celebrate the donor's attainment of the highest magistracy. Many of these socially and politically significant objects survive, having later entered church treasuries on account of their valuable material and the high quality of craftsmanship.

Ivory supplies were apparently disrupted in the late 6th and 7th centuries, and when production resumed after iconoclasm the material was used in the manufacture of fewer types of objects, most bearing religious and/or imperial imagery (such as icons, diptychs and triptychs, reliquaries, and bookcovers), many of which were exported to the west. In the 10th and 11th centuries Constantinople appears to have been the thriving centre for the production of ivory icons, reliquaries, pyxides, and reliefs with Christian as well as pagan imagery, but, as before, the precise origins of many carved ivories of this period cannot be determined. After the fall of the capital in 1453, the Byzantine style continued to be employed in the old provinces for several centuries in the monastic centres of Greece, the Near East, Russia, and even Ethiopia in wood and bone as well as ivory. Following independence, Greece became a consumer of ivory goods along European lines more than a producer, importing billiard balls, handles, bangles, etc. The Treasury of Panayia Evangelistria on Tinos contains raw elephant tusks and others carved in African styles, apparently the dedications of a Greek trader of the 19th century. Since 1990 transport of elephant ivory across international borders has been banned by the Convention on International Trade in Endangered Species (CITES).

KENNETH D.S. LAPATIN

See also Furniture

Further Reading

Andronicos, Manolis, *Vergina: The Royal Tombs and the Ancient City*, Athens: Ekdotike Athenon, 1984

Barnett, Richard D., *Ancient Ivories in the Middle East*, Jerusalem: Hebrew University Institute of Archaeology, 1982

Carter, Jane Burr, *Greek Ivory-Carving in the Orientalizing and Archaic Periods*, New York: Garland, 1985

Carter, Jane Burr, "The Chests of Periander", *American Journal of Archaeology*, 93 (1989): pp. 355–78

Connor, Carolyn L., *The Color of Ivory: Polychromy on Byzantine Ivories*, Princeton, New Jersey: Princeton University Press, 1998

Cutler, Anthony, *The Craft of Ivory: Sources, Techniques, and Uses in the Mediterranean World, AD 200-1400*, Washington, D.C.: Dumbarton Oaks, 1985

Cutler, Anthony, *The Hand of the Master: Craftsmanship, Ivory, and Society in Byzantium, 9th–11th Centuries*, Princeton, New Jersey: Princeton University Press, 1994

Evans, Helen C. and W.D. Wixom (editors), *The Glory of Byzantium: Art and Culture of the Middle Byzantine Era, AD 843–1261*, New York: Metropolitan Museum of Art, 1997 (exhibition catalogue)

Evely, R.D.G., *Minoan Crafts: Tools and Techniques: An Introduction*, vol. 1, Gothenburg: Åström, 1993

Fitton, J. Lesley (editor), *Ivory in Greece and the Eastern Mediterranean from the Bronze Age to the Hellenistic Period*, London: British Museum, 1992

Harris, Diane, *The Treasures of the Parthenon and Erechtheion*, Oxford: Clarendon Press, and New York: Oxford University Press, 1995

Hood, Sinclair, *The Arts in Prehistoric Greece*, Harmondsworth and New York: Penguin, 1978

Krzyszkowska, Olga, *Ivory and Related Materials: An Illustrated Guide*, London: Institute of Classical Studies, 1990

Lapatin, K.D.S., "Pheidias Elephantourgos" [Phidias the Ivory-Worker], *American Journal of Archaeology*, 101 (1997): pp. 663–82

Lapatin, K.D.S., *Chryselephantine Statuary in the Ancient Mediterranean World*, Oxford: Oxford University Press, forthcoming

Leipen, Neda, *Athena Parthenos: A Reconstruction*, Toronto: Royal Ontario Museum, 1971

Poursat, Jean-Claude, *Catalogue des ivoires mycéniens du Musée National d'Athènes*, Athens: École Française d'Athènes, 1977

Randall, Richard H. (editor), *Masterpieces of Ivory from the Walters Art Gallery*, New York: Hudson Hills Press, 1985

Schiering, W., *Die Werkstatt des Pheidias in Olympia*, vol. 2, Berlin: de Gruyter, 1964

Vickers, M. *et al.*, *Ivory: An International History and Illustrated Survey*, New York: Abrams, 1987

J

Janissaries

Elite corps of the Ottoman army

The *yeni ceri*, or "new force", commonly known as the janissaries, were an infantry organized under the rule of Murad I (1360–89), who established Ottoman control in Europe by conquering Bulgaria, Macedonia, Serbia, and Thrace – leaving the Byzantine capital of Constantinople surrounded by a sea of Ottoman-held territory. Over the course of this expansion, Murad became increasingly interested in having a military force which would be under his direct control (the permanent Ottoman army was at the time divided into cavalry and infantry – *musellem* and *yaya* – who were paid largely by fiefs, and who were under the control of their commanders).

To this end, Murad moved to organize a new slave military force, whose members were to be culled in the form of human booty taken from his conquered enemies. The selected individuals, Orthodox Christian boys from the newly taken Balkan territories, were sent to Bursa where they were educated in Turkish, Arabic, and Persian; converted to Islam; given an elite military training; and, if upon the completion of their education they were deemed fit, placed either in the janissary corps or the cavalry (the *sipahis*). This period thus marked a time of transition during which the old Ottoman military elites found themselves subordinated to this new group of fighters who answered directly to the sultan. Thus the new military elite of the Ottoman state had its origins in Balkan Orthodox Christianity.

The process whereby these Orthodox boys were selected for training for the janissary corps came to be known as the *devshirme* (lit.: gathering up, collection). Originally the term referred specifically to the one-fifth portion of the booty allowed as a ruler's right during conquest, a portion which Murad I had taken in the form not of money but rather of young prisoners. The *devshirme* came over time, however, to be a periodic tax levied against Christian subject populations. Again, payment was taken in the form of young men. As part of the tax system, the *devshirme* was instituted by Murad I's successor, Bayezid I (1389–1402), and was most dominant during the 15th century. The *devshirme* was ultimately abandoned in the 17th century. Agents responsible for gathering the *devshirme* tax travelled periodically throughout the Ottoman provinces, gathering up the most promising-looking children on a per-capita basis, and gave the children over to a "driver" (*surucu*) who escorted them to Istanbul or Bursa for their training.

In Greek tradition, the *devshirme* is known as the *paidomazoma* (lit.: gathering of children), and has from the revolutionary period on been widely regarded as having been emblematic of Ottoman cruelty, anti-Christian activity, and exploitation of subject populations. In reality, however, earlier attitudes towards the *devshirme* seem to have been more nuanced. For the undeniable reality is that, for rural boys of the Balkan peasant classes, the *devshirme* was the only available means of upward mobility, and a very dramatic and effective one at that.

The janissary corps, as the elite personal corps of the sultan, was the pinnacle of the Ottoman military hierarchy, and its membership was attainable only to those taken through the *devshirme*. Children of Muslim families were not eligible, nor those of the urban middle classes. This paradox was in part the result of Murad I's desire to have a militia the loyalty of which could be guaranteed. Had the janissary corps' membership been drawn from the ranks of the Ottoman elites, who were theoretically in competition with the sultan's own power, this loyalty could potentially have been undermined. By relying instead on the most peripheral members of society for its membership, the sultan was able to make the janissary corps as free from external influence and interference as possible. So while Greek and Balkan Orthodox folk tradition memorialize the *devshirme* with the vocabulary of mourning and oppression, it must be kept in mind that in reality rural Balkan Orthodox families would have had good reason also to hope that their sons might be selected, in the recognition that the *devshirme*, brutal as it was in psychological terms, might provide their children with an education and wealth undreamed of in the provinces.

The janissary corps and the *sipahis* provided the core foundation of the Ottoman army throughout much of the Tourkokratia. They came also, however, despite the intentions of their original founder, to be in many instances a significant source of opposition to the sultanate. They played an important role, for example, in the deposing of Mustafa I in 1623, and sultans from the late 16th century on were threatened by rival leaders who would attempt to drum up janissary support against the ruler. For this reason the institution was the target of Ottoman-sponsored abolition movements starting in the first half of the 17th century.

It is as yet unclear what percentage of the janissary corps as established and promulgated by Murad and his successors was actually of Greek origin. Ottoman archival documentation suggests that very few Greek children were taken in the *devshirme*, and that the overwhelming majority were of Serbian and Bosnian origin. Some scholars, in fact, argue that the *devshirme* was never undertaken in Greek lands. Nevertheless, the *paidomazoma* and the janissary corps are well-known features of the Greek national cultural/historical imagination right down to the modern era. During the Greek Civil War (1946–49), for instance, when the communists in the north began a programme of evacuating children out of the war zone and into neighbouring communist countries, the Athens government called the programme a "new *paidomazoma*", and argued that the children were being formed into new "janissaries". Thus the cultural significance of such terms is still great, even if the historical reality of the *paidomazoma* and the janissaries has, in the Greek context, perhaps been overstated.

K.E. FLEMING

See also Ottoman Period

Summary

The Janissaries (literally "new force") were an elite cadre of infantry first organized by the Ottomans in the 14th century. Made up of selected Orthodox Christian boys from the newly conquered Balkan territories, the Janissaries and their cavalry counterpart (the Sipahis) were trained to provide the fighting heart of the Ottoman army for much of the period of Tourkokratia.

Further Reading

Gibb, H.A.R. and Harold Bowen, *Islamic Society and the West: A Study of the Impact of Western Civilization on Moslem Culture in the Near East*, London and New York: Oxford University Press, 1950

Inalcik, Halil, *The Ottoman Empire: The Classical Age, 1300–1600*, London: Weidenfeld and Nicolson, and New York: Praeger, 1973

Kafadar, Cemal, *Between Two Worlds: The Construction of the Ottoman State*, Berkeley: University of California Press, 1995

Lewis, Bernard, *The Emergence of Modern Turkey*, London and New York: Oxford University Press, 1961, 2nd edition 1968

Miller, Barnette, *The Palace School of Muhammad the Conqueror*, Cambridge, Massachusetts: Harvard University Press, 1941

Palmer, J.A.B., "The Origins of the Janissaries", *Bulletin of the John Rylands Library*, 25 (1953): pp. 448–81

Shaw, Stanford, *History of the Ottoman Empire and Modern Turkey*, 2 vols, Cambridge and New York: Cambridge University Press, 1976–77

Uzunçarsili, Ismail Hakki, *Osmanli Devletinin Saray Teskilâti* [The Palace Organization of the Ottoman State], Ankara: Türk Tarih Kurumu Basimevi, 1984

Vryonis, Spyros, "Isidore Glabas and the Turkish Devshirme", *Speculum*, 21 (1956): pp. 433–43

Weissmann, Nahoum, *Les Janissaires: étude de l'organisation militaire des Ottomans*, Paris: Librairie Orient, 1964

Jeremias II Tranos c.1530–1595

Patriarch of Constantinople in the late 16th century

Born around 1530 on the coast of the Black Sea at Anchialos (near modern Burgas, Bulgaria), some 200 km northwest of Constantinople, Jeremias was very well educated by leading intellectuals of the day, such as Hierotheos of Monemvasia and Damaskinos the Stoudite, and perhaps at the Patriarchal Academy in the capital. He was elected bishop of Larissa (in Thessaly) in 1565, and, seven years later, through popular demand, ecumenical patriarch. This office he held three times: from 5 May 1572 to 29 November 1579; from August 1580 to late February or early March 1584; and from mid-1587 (officially only from 4 July 1589) to late 1595, when he died. Always retaining the support of his people, he owed his dethronements to jealousies of the Holy Synod dominated by the Phanariots and desire for the *peshkesh* (bribe) payable to the sultan for ratification of each appointment.

During his nearly 20 years as patriarch he proved himself, through competent and energetic administration, possibly the most able figure to hold that position during the Tourkokratia. He was a persistent opponent of simony and was particularly effective in attracting capable figures, most notably perhaps the theologian, poet, and translator Maximos Margounios, as friends or associates. His interest in education never wavered, and through a synod in 1593 he both encouraged metropolitans to establish academies in their cities and gave a new constitution to the Patriarchal Academy, in accordance with which departments of sciences such as chemistry and physiology were established in addition to the recently added philosophy and the traditional theology and literature, each department being overseen by a scholarch appointed by the patriarch. The best known of Jeremias's activities, however, are his correspondence with the Lutherans and his journey to Moscow and the Polish-Lithuanian Commonwealth.

Despite previous failures by the Lutherans (following a similar move by the Hussites as early as 1451) to form a united front with the Orthodox Church against Roman Catholic autocracy and its innovations, a further attempt was initiated in 1574. With the encouragement of the German ambassador in Constantinople, baron David Ungnad von Sonnegk, a group of theologians at the University of Tübingen led by the chancellor Jacob Andreae and the classicist Martin Crusius (Kraus) entered into communication with Jeremias. Copies were sent to Constantinople of a Greek translation of the Confession of Augsburg (Philip Melanchthon's statement of Lutheran views presented to the Diet summoned by the emperor Charles V in 1530), which contained 21 articles of faith followed by a list of "abuses" such as clerical celibacy, monastic vows, and compulsory confession.

Aided by the father and son Ioannes and Theodosios Zygomalas and other researchers, and after consultations with the German ambassadorial chaplain Stephen Gerlach (who had been summoned from Tübingen expressly for this purpose), Jeremias replied in 1576. His courteous but firm response methodically goes through the Confession, and, while accepting all the many points on which the two Churches can agree, it is chiefly a presentation of theological differences, including those of emphasis, and a defence of the Orthodox position which is supported by numerous patristic quotations. The main stumbling blocks he found to any Orthodox rapprochement with the Lutherans were their acceptance of the Roman addition of the *filioque* (the procession of the Holy Ghost from the Son) to the Nicene creed; baptismal practices; the exact meaning of original sin; justification by faith alone without good works, and consequent near-acceptance of predestination; the number of the sacraments; the doctrine of the elements of the Eucharist and the use of unleavened bread; slighting of tradition; denial of spiritual value to many ecclesiastical ceremonies, fasting, monasticism, and celibacy of regular (as opposed to secular) clergy; and denial of the validity of invocations for mediation to the saints.

Replies from Tübingen elicited a more forceful presentation of the Orthodox position from an increasingly reluctant Jeremias in 1579 and, finally, a recapitulation in 1581 in which he begged for a cessation of the fruitless discussion. It is notable, however, that friendly correspondence with Crusius, who greatly admired Jeremias, persisted. This was in spite of a Polish Jesuit, Stanislaus Sokolowski, publishing in 1582 a Latin translation of the patriarch's first response with his own commentary (*Censura Orientalis Ecclesiae, de Praecipuis nostri Saeculi Haereticorum Dogmatibus*) as part of the Roman Church's attack on Lutheranism, which in turn instigated in defence Crusius's publication (1584, in Greek and Latin) of the whole correspondence between the Tübingen theologians and the patriarch. For the Greeks, however, Jeremias's three letters became an important statement of Orthodox belief and were endorsed as authoritative at the Synod of Jerusalem in 1672.

Since the Church in Russia, the only truly independent Orthodox state in the 16th century and, moreover, one considering itself the "Third Rome" and the protector of the true faith, was only a metropolitanate, it had made several demands for promotion to a patriarchate, thus replacing that of the heretical Rome in the pentarchy. In response to a further request, and in order to collect funds for his own beleaguered Church, Jeremias journeyed to Moscow in 1588–89. It appears that Boris Godunov, the chief minister of the feeble-minded tsar Feodor I Ivanovitch, proposed that Jeremias should stay in Russia with a see in Vladimir or in Moscow as ecumenical patriarch or patriarch of Moscow and All Russia. Whatever the exact proposal, Jeremias, with some reluctance since his restoration to the Constantinopolitan throne had not yet been ratified by the Ottomans, rejected it and instead presided over the elevation of the Muscovite metropolitan Job to patriarch on 26 January of the following year. His apparent compliance with Moscow's demand for its ranking immediately after Constantinople and Alexandria in the pentarchy had, however, to await confirmation at a synod in Constantinople attended by the other patriarchs, at which the new patriarchate was placed last after Antioch and Jerusalem. The interpreter on Jeremias's staff in Moscow, Arsenios, archbishop of Elassona (in Thessaly), stayed behind to spend the rest of his life in Russia where he became an influential figure in its spiritual life and wrote a detailed poem on the patriarchal visit.

Having thus, despite his dubious status, cemented a friendship with a powerful protector of Orthodox interests, Jeremias returned to the Polish-Lithuanian Commonwealth, through which he had passed on his way to Moscow and where he had held preliminary talks. Now, with the authorization of Sigismund III to take what action he liked in religious affairs, he deposed and replaced Onesifor Dziewoczka, the incompetent and lax metropolitan of Kiev and chief Ruthenian ecclesiastic. At a subsequent synod at Brest, however, on 6 August 1589, in addition to initiating reforms aimed at raising the moral standard of the clergy, he weakened the powers of the new metropolitan, Michael Rahoza, both by freeing from ecclesiatical jurisdiction and making answerable to himself the influential and largely lay Orthodox Brotherhoods of Vilnius and Lvóv and also by appointing as exarch the bishop of Luck, Cyril Terlecki (Terletskyi), who thus became his personal representative. This attempt at more direct Constantinopolitan control over the Ruthenians was, however, nullified soon after Jeremias's return to Constantinople, when Terlecki himself was involved in discussions with the Catholics which led to the creation at, ironically, the Synod of Brest in 1596 of a uniate Ruthenian Church.

Halecki's cautiously proposed theory that Jeremias was probably at least cognizant of and not opposed to a Roman–Ruthenian rapprochement has been enthusiastically promoted by Tsirpanlis, who asserts that Jeremias was secretly negotiating with the Catholics in order to gain practical Western aid against the Turks even to the extent of initiating a new crusade (as Byzantine emperors such as Michael VIII Palaiologos had done openly). Thus, he claims, Jeremias dismissed Lutheran overtures even at the risk of displeasing the Ottomans (who made mercantile and military alliances with Protestant powers in their struggle against the Habsburgs and the papacy), and was also fully aware of and even encouraged Terlecki's intentions; while any overt opposition by Jeremias to the Catholics was dictated by the necessary prudence of a leader subject to their bitter foes.

Rome unquestionably did make advances to Jeremias: the popes sent ambassadors to Constantinople and in 1583 Gregory XIII personally praised the anti-Protestant stance of his replies to the Tübingen theologians, and after his deposition the following year even contemplated rescuing him from his Turkish prison in Rhodes and, in furtherance of religious reunion, installing him in Russia or, when the Polish king Stefan Batory expressed strong scepticism about the success of such a move, among the Ruthenian Orthodox in the Polish-Lithuanian Commonwealth. It is also beyond question that Jeremias did not rebuff all Roman Catholic approaches, even going so far as to express pleasure at the Greek College (established in Rome in 1577), despite the fact that it sought to convert Orthodox Greeks; and he was himself deposed in 1584 in part on the charge of pro-Roman sympathies, as was his predecessor (and successor) Metrophanes III, and even for being in secret agreement with the pope, although the percipient and sagacious papal envoy Antonio Possevino confessed himself unable to fathom the patriarch's intentions around that time. Jeremias was always conscious of the fact that through the Ottoman *millet* (community) system he was not only spiritual leader but also ethnarch of the Greeks, yet there is no instance of his compromising any article of Orthodox faith for mundane purposes; moreover, he opposed the establishment of the Society of Jesus in Constantinople and even rejected, after some genuine or perhaps politic hesitation, Gregory's repeated request for acceptance of his reformed calendar. Jeremias was a truly ecumenical Ecumenical Patriarch, a highly intelligent and shrewd diplomat courteously polite to Protestants, Catholics, and Turks, but above all a shepherd ever devoted to the best interests of his Orthodox flock, for which he was willing to seek aid from whatever source he could.

A.R. LITTLEWOOD

See also Ecumenism, Protestantism

Biography

Born *c.*1530 at Anchialos on the Black Sea coast of modern Bulgaria, Jeremias received a good education, possibly at the Patriarchal Academy in Constantinople. He was elected bishop of Larissa (Thessaly) in 1565, and ecumenical patriarch three times between 1572 and his death in 1595. He is remembered for his attempts to promote education, his correspondence with the Lutherans, and his journey to Moscow and the Polish-Lithuanian Commonwealth.

Further Reading

Crusius, Martin, *Turcograeciae*, Basel: Leonardus Ostensius, 1584, reprinted Modena: Memor, 1972

Halecki, Oscar, *From Florence to Brest (1439–1596)*, 2nd edition, Hamden, Connecticut: Archon, 1968

Mastrantonis, George (translator), *Augsburg and Constantinople: The Correspondence between the Tübingen Theologians and Patriarch Jeremiah II of Constantinople on the Augsburg Confession*, Brookline, Massachusetts: Holy Cross Orthodox Press, 1982

Petit, L., Jérémie II Tranos entry in *Dictionnaire de Théologie Catholique* vol. 8, Paris: Letouzey & Ané, 1924: coll. 886–894

Runciman, Steven, *The Great Church in Captivity: A Study of the Patriarchate of Constantinople from the Eve of the Turkish Conquest to the Greek War of Independence*, London: Cambridge University Press, 1968

Sathas, Konstantinos N., *Biographiko Schediasma peri tou Patriarchou Hieremiou II (1572–1594)* [Biographical Sketch of Patriarch Jeremias II (1572–1594)], Athens, 1870 (includes Arsenios's poem)

Timiadis, Emilianos, "Trinitarian Economy and Christianity: An Orthodox Approach to the Confessio Augustana with particular reference to Articles I and II" in *The Augsburg Confession in Ecumenical Perspective*, edited by Harding Meyer, Stuttgart: Kreuz, 1979

Tsirpanlis, Constantine N., *The Historical and Ecumenical Significance of Jeremias II's Correspondence with the Lutherans (1573–1581)*, vol. 1, Kingston, New York: EO Press, 1982 (includes English translation of Jeremias's response in 1576)

Jerusalem

The importance of Jerusalem for the Greeks stems first and foremost from its centrality within the Christian tradition. The Greek Orthodox comprise the earliest surviving Christian community in the city, and have always been the largest and most influential Christian community there. All Greek activity in Jerusalem throughout Christian history has been linked to the Greek Orthodox Church, and this is still the case in the present day. This linkage is evidenced in the dramatic change in the status of the city of Jerusalem following the Christianization of the Roman empire during the 4th century AD. A relatively unimportant city before the Christianization of Rome, after the empire's formal adoption of Christianity as a state religion Jerusalem rapidly emerged as a pivotal Christian centre. From AD 324 to 638 Christianity was the dominant cultural feature of the city, and Jerusalem a major religious centre for all Christians.

After his accession in 312, Constantine ordered that the Holy Sepulchre should be uncovered and a church built on the site. From that time on, Jerusalem rapidly began to take on the physical appearance of a Christian city, and came heavily under Greek cultural influences. Dominant among these influences was the Greek language, which was the tongue of the liturgy, and most of the clergy, monks, and nuns were of Greek origin and used the Greek language. This Greek dominance continued to prevail even after other Christian Churches had established bases in the city.

The Greek community was part of the Byzantine imperial Church and adopted the terms of the Council of Chalcedon (451). For the following two centuries the Byzantine imperial authorities made repeated efforts to establish the Church of Jerusalem as a bulwark against competing forms of Christianity within Palestine and Byzantium. These efforts greatly intensified the Greek religious and cultural tone of the city.

Jerusalem played a crucial role in the quarrels between the two important branches of the Eastern Church – the patriarchates of Constantinople and Alexandria – regarding the question of Jesus' nature (Christology). So strong was the city's importance as a centre of Orthodoxy that its last Byzantine patriarch, Sophronios (634–38), severed Jerusalem's relations with the patriarchates of Constantinople and Alexandria at various points when he felt that they had strayed from the doctrines of true Orthodoxy. The patriarchate of Jerusalem had complete control over the Church hierarchy in the region of Palestine, and the bishop of Jerusalem was its highest-ranking ecclesiast.

After the Muslim occupation of the city in 638 the Jerusalem patriarchate lost its control over the other Palestinian churches, but it remained by and large loyal to the leadership in Constantinople. Still under Islam, during the early 10th century, it became once again the head of the (greatly weakened) Christian community throughout Palestine, which was now administered as one diocese. From that time on, the patriarch of Jerusalem became the leader of all Orthodox Christians within the territory. The fact that there was a hazy line between Church and state organization in the Byzantine empire was a perennial source of political problems, stemming from questions regarding the loyalty of the patriarch of Jerusalem to the patriarchate in Constantinople.

Up to the 1970s, most of the higher ranks in the Jerusalem patriarchate were peopled with Greek-born Greeks, and its cultural character has always been Greek. Moreover, the upper stratum of the lay Greek Orthodox population has historically been Greek-speaking. After the Muslim occupation, much of the laity emigrated, or converted to Islam, or became Arabized. From the 8th century on, Greek texts were translated into Arabic, and Arabic emerged as the third language of the Greek Orthodox Church in Jerusalem (after Greek and Syriac). For this reason there has been a longstanding and constant tension between the higher-ranking Greek-speaking clergy and the lower-ranking, native Palestinian and Arabic-speaking clergy during Ottoman, British, Jordanian, and now Israeli rule of

Jerusalem. Nor was there much love lost between the Greek Christians and the Latin crusaders who ruled over the kingdom of Jerusalem from 1100 to 1187.

Because of the historically close connection between Jerusalem and Greece, a connection fostered by the strong Greek Orthodox presence in the city, political events concerning the Greeks in the west have also been felt in Jerusalem. Most notably, when the Greek War of Independence broke out in 1821, all Muslims were ordered to arm themselves in preparation for an anticipated revolt on the part of Jerusalem's Christians. The rumour spread throughout the city that all its Christians were in collusion with the Greeks, and only through the intervention of Muslim officials was the Christian population protected from attack.

With the decline of Ottoman power, the influence of the Greek community in Jerusalem contracted. This contraction was directly tied to the diminution of the formal privileges granted to the Greek Orthodox Church by the Ottomans through the so-called *millet* ("community") system, and was parallel to the similar decline in privilege of the Orthodox Church in Greece following the establishment of the Greek state. Greek presence in Jerusalem, however, continues to be felt. The possessions of the Greek Orthodox patriarchate in Jerusalem include many of the most important sites in Christendom. There are in addition a number of Greek monasteries in Jerusalem and the vicinity. The Greek Church also owns lands outside the walls of the old city of Jerusalem, where it established the colony of Nikophoria, known today as the "Greek Colony". Many of the Greek Church's holdings, however, have in the modern period been sold to Zionist organizations and to the Israeli government.

K.E. FLEMING

See also Crusades

Summary

Previously an unimportant city in the Roman empire, Jerusalem was propelled into international prominence by the Christianization of the empire in the 4th century AD. The Greek Orthodox have always been the largest and most influential of the city's Christian communities, but the number of Christians living in the city today is very small.

Further Reading

Asali, Kamil J. (editor), *Jerusalem in History: 3,000 BC to the Present Day*, revised edition, London: Kegan Paul, and New York: Columbia University Press, 1997

Avigad, Nahman, *Discovering Jerusalem*, Nashville, Tennessee: Nelson, 1983

Gilbert, Martin, *Jerusalem: Rebirth of a City*, London: Chatto and Windus, and New York: Viking, 1985

Peters, F.E., *Jerusalem: The Holy City in the Eyes of Chroniclers, Visitors, Pilgrims and Prophets from the Days of Abraham to the Beginning of Modern Times*, Princeton, New Jersey: Princeton University Press, 1985

Prawer, J., *The Latin Kingdom of Jerusalem: European Colonialism in the Middle Ages*, London: Weidenfeld and Nicolson, 1972; as *The Crusaders' Kingdom*, New York: Praeger, 1972

Jewellery

The art of jewellery making in Greece has a very long and continuous history that provides insight into everyday social and religious life and bears witness to the ingenuity and skill of Greek craftsmen throughout time. The earliest evidence in Greece for jewellery consists of a few small shells pierced with suspension holes that survive from the Palaeolithic period. By the Neolithic period (c.6800–3000 BC), however, jewellery making had begun in earnest. Consisting of valuable objects of personal adornment that may have originally served as protective amulets, jewellery during this early time indicated the wealth and social status of its owners. Common materials for jewellery in the Neolithic period included animal bone, shell, clay, stone, bronze, and gold. Precious stones were virtually unknown at this time, and silver was rare as well. Typical forms included highly stylized anthropomorphic pendants, beads for necklaces, simple finger rings, bracelets, pins, and mouthpieces. The gold and bronze jewellery from the Neolithic period is invariably hammered and cut into sheets. The discovery of precious gold and bronze jewellery in Neolithic cemeteries throughout Greece suggests the early emergence of a stratified society in this region.

During the Bronze Age in Greece the art of jewellery-making flourished under influence from the Near East and from Egypt, while also reflecting the unique ideas and inspiration of local craftsmen. Most pieces from this period were discovered in wealthy tombs, where they symbolized authority and prestige. From the Early Bronze Age (c.3200–2000 BC) several fine examples of bronze and silver jewellery survive from the Cyclades, including an outstanding silver diadem from Amorgos, with the top cut in a zigzag pattern, which is now on display in the National Archaeological Museum in Athens. Pendants and necklaces of bone, shell, and semi-precious or ordinary stone were common in the Cyclades. Some gold and silver diadems, earrings, pendants, and pins are also known from a few sites on the Greek mainland during the Early Bronze Age. Also important is a rich collection of jewellery, known as the "Thyreatis Treasure", in the Staatliche Museen in Berlin, which dates from c.2200 BC and includes an elaborate gold necklace with wedge-shaped pendants. It is thought to come from the Thyreatis in the Peloponnese. The best-known collections of gold jewellery of the Early Bronze Age, however, come from the northeast Aegean, especially from the site of Poliochni on Lemnos and from Troy. The hair spirals, necklaces, pins, and bracelets from these sites are especially impressive for their more advanced techniques, imported from Anatolia, which include filigree and granulation. Spectacular gold jewellery was also being made on Crete in this early period. The most famous examples from the Early Minoan tombs at Mochlos, now on display in the Herakleion Museum, include diadems made of gold sheet with repoussé decoration and fine chains of gold wire, as well as pins, pendants, beads, and bracelets.

During the Middle Bronze Age (c.2000–1600 BC) important advances in the technique of goldsmithing took place on Minoan Crete and resulted in jewellery of great artistic skill and sensitivity. One remarkable example that uses the filigree and granulation techniques with great effect is the famous gold pendant of two conjoined bees or wasps with a honeycomb

Jewellery: gold necklace with miniature pomegranates and amphorae, 4th century BC, Ashmolean Museum, Oxford

(dated *c*.1700 BC) that was discovered in the Khrysolakkos cemetery at Mallia and is now on display in the Herakleion Museum. Other equally elaborate pendants of gold combined with semiprecious stones belong to the well-known "Aegina Treasure", discovered in the form of tomb robbers' loot and now in the British Museum in London. This impressive treasure, dated to the 17th century BC, also includes beads, finger rings, earrings, and diadems of gold as well as gold cutouts in the form of discs with dotted rosettes, which would have been sewn on to garments.

The most remarkable jewellery of the Late Bronze Age (*c*.1600–1100 BC) comes from the royal shaft graves in the two grave circles at Mycenae, a citadel rightly described by Homer as "rich in gold". Dating mainly from the 16th century BC, the abundant gold objects from these tombs betray the powerful influence of the Minoan artistic tradition. Indeed, some of them are pure Minoan imports, while others may have been designed by Minoan craftsmen specifically for the Mycenaean market or by Mycenaean craftsmen working from Minoan models. This incredible jewellery, proudly displayed today in the National Archaeological Museum in Athens, includes fine gold diadems (for both sexes) with repoussé decoration; gold cutouts and roundels with repoussé octopuses, butterflies, spirals, and other natural and curvilinear motifs used to adorn luxurious clothing; as well as elaborate pins, earrings, bracelets, armlets, belts, signet-rings, and necklaces of gold, amber, and semiprecious stones.

During the zenith of the Mycenaean civilization (15th–13th centuries BC) the type of jewellery produced throughout Greece (with the exception of Crete) is different in many important respects from its forerunners in the shaft graves and elsewhere. For example, certain types of jewellery, including diadems, pins, and earrings, were no longer popular. Instead, necklaces with relief beads and pendants are very frequent. These beads and pendants are often in the form of stylized floral and marine motifs known from traditional Minoan iconography. The gold beads and pendants were made from gold sheet hammered into stone moulds, filled with magnetite sand, and often decorated with granulation, enamel (introduced *c*.1425 BC), grooves, and ribs. Moulded glass paste and faience beads were also used with increasing frequency as well as beads of semiprecious stones in a variety of shapes.

After the collapse of the Mycenaean world around 1100 BC, very little jewellery seems to have been produced in Greece for about 200 years. What little has been discovered from this period is of the simplest form, mainly hair spirals, as well as basic rings, bracelets, and pins, generally made of bronze, occasionally of iron, and rarely of gold that was probably acquired by melting down precious metal hoards amassed from Bronze Age tombs. Between 900 and 600 BC, however, Greek contacts with the more prosperous Near East were renewed and the art of jewellery making was revived, initially in Athens, Lefkandi in Euboea, Corinth, and Knossos, and later throughout the entire Greek world. This early Iron Age jewellery exhibits the reintroduction of sophisticated techniques (e.g. repoussé, filigree, granulation, engraving, and inlaying with stone, glass, and amber), as well as the introduction of newer techniques such as the making of chains and the casting of gold. Forms and motifs of Minoan-Mycenaean jewellery were also reintroduced, though the occasional rediscovered object demonstrates the influence of the arts of Phoenicia and Asia Minor. New Eastern motifs appeared as well, including lions, sphinxes, griffins, and the "Mistress of the Animals", who later became identified with the Greek goddess Artemis. Among the most outstanding objects from this period is a pair of elaborate gold earrings with pendant pomegranates (c.850 BC) that were found in a rich woman's grave on the northwest slope of the Areopagus in Athens and are now on display in the Agora Museum. These earrings were probably made by an immigrant Phoenician artisan who set up a workshop in Athens and passed on his skill to local craftsmen.

Very little jewellery of the Archaic period survives from Greece proper, perhaps because of a shortage of gold that led to jewellery making in less durable materials such as bronze and silver. Spectacular gold jewellery does survive, however, from Cyprus, south Russia, and south Italy, suggesting that Greek goldsmiths were working for foreign customers. After the Persian Wars gold was more common in Greece, and although much of this was reserved for religious uses (e.g. chryselephantine statues), impressive jewellery was also produced. Greek jewellery of the Classical period continues Archaic types and decoration but the orientalizing figures and creatures are generally replaced with floral and geometric motifs (e.g. acorn- and vase-shaped pendants), while mythological themes and figures, such as Aphrodite and Eros, also become more popular. Rich decorative techniques such as granulation and filigree begin to decline and the simple sculptural forms of the gold are increasingly emphasized. What results is jewellery that is characterized by a more typically Hellenic sense of balance and restraint. Popular forms include diadems, earrings, necklaces, bracelets, and finger rings. Most impressive, however, are the new gold wreaths, with the leaves and fruit of oak, myrtle, olive, and laurel trees, which were received as prizes; worn in religious ceremonies, processions, and banquets; dedicated in sanctuaries; and buried in private tombs as signs of prestige and victory. Two such golden wreaths, one of oak, the other of myrtle, were found in royal Tomb II at Vergina, which dates from the late 4th century BC.

The Hellenistic period is arguably the greatest age of Greek jewellery. There is much surviving material because, for the first time since the Bronze Age, gold was very plentiful in Greece and Macedonia as a result of Philip II's annexation of the gold mines in the area around Mount Pangaeum in Thrace and the dissemination of captured Persian treasures following the eastern campaigns of Alexander the Great. The popular forms of jewellery in this period remained essentially the same with the addition of animal- or human-headed hoop earrings,

necklaces with chains terminating in lion heads, necklaces formed of straps with pendant buds or spearheads, necklaces with linked rather than threaded beads, and medallions from the tops of ornamental hairnets that are decorated with high-relief heads of various Greek deities. Most remarkable, however, are the elaborate gold diadems discovered in wealthy tombs throughout the Greek world, which are most often decorated with the new central motif of the Heracles knot (a reef or square knot). This motif had an amuletic purpose as well as a decorative one, was associated with marriage and rites of passage in general, and, more specifically, was a symbol of Alexander the Great that evoked the idea of his kinship with the gods. One of the most elaborate examples of this type of diadem, dating from the 2nd century BC, was found in Thessaly and can be seen today in the Benaki Museum in Athens. The centre of this piece is a richly decorated Heracles knot inlaid with garnets. This decorative use of semiprecious stones as well as coloured glass and enamel was also an important innovation of the Hellenistic period that introduced polychromy into the design of Greek jewellery, thereby transforming its appearance.

During the Roman imperial period the main types of Greek jewellery were continued while their often complex designs incorporating naturalistic elements were gradually replaced with simpler compositions, including semiprecious and precious stones as well as stylized, curvilinear motifs. In the early Byzantine period this more abstract style developed into something quite delicate and refined, reflecting the well-attested Byzantine taste for expensive and elaborate jewels. The Byzantines were also well supplied, through domestic sources and trade, with gold, ivory, precious stones, and pearls, which were especially popular. Jewellery, meant to convey wealth and status, was produced for all members of the hierarchical Byzantine society. However, gold jewellery with precious stones was generally restricted to the court and to the Church, while poorer members of society might adorn themselves with plain, undecorated finger rings, bracelets, earrings, and buckles made of bronze, glass, brass, or silver. Rich court officials had beautiful signet rings characteristically decorated with complex monograms as well as elaborately worked sashes of office studded with precious stones.

The most impressive jewellery of the Byzantine period, however, was that which adorned the ears, necks, wrists, fingers, and waists of wealthy Byzantine ladies. In much of this jewellery ancient Graeco-Roman techniques and motifs persisted and were joined by newer techniques such as embossing, engraving highlighted by niello, and cloisonné enamel as well as by new Christian iconography. Popular forms included finger rings in gold, silver, bronze, and glass, which often had bezels adorned with imperial coins, inscriptions, or Christian motifs such as the common scene of Christ uniting the hands of a bride and a groom. Earrings were also very popular during this period and they come in a variety of forms including open-work radiate roses with pendant beads, decorated hemispherical or crescent-shaped discs, and hoops with pendant rods and beads of precious stone. Bracelets of many types are also among the finest jewellery of the Byzantine period. One especially impressive example from the 11th century, which demonstrates the persistence of naturalistic and orientalizing motifs in Greek jewellery, consists of two hinged pieces of gold with a broad band of impressed lions, griffins, and birds highlighted by niello. It can be seen today in the Kanellopoulos Museum in Athens. Also important were the necklaces with protective pendants in the form of pagan amulets, such as coins with the head of Alexander the Great, Christian crosses, and *constantinata*, popular coins with the head of Constantine.

During the difficult times after the fall of Constantinople and the Turkish conquest of Greece the Byzantine practice of wearing coins persisted as a means of transporting and protecting personal wealth, and pendant coins became one of the most common elements of the traditional Greek jewellery of the post-Byzantine era. This traditional jewellery, unlike that of earlier periods in Greek history, was usually made from silver for ordinary people to wear at weddings and other ceremonial events. Wealthy people occasionally did order gold jewellery in a traditional style, but more frequently imported jewellery from Europe as a sign of status. Imported western jewellery or imitations of it were also popular on the Greek islands during this time. But on the mainland traditional jewellery featured a sophisticated combination of metalworking techniques, such as hammering, perforating, casting, filigree, and granulation, as well as enamel working and, to achieve a polychromatic effect, the use of humbler materials including pieces of coloured glass, carnelians, agates, turquoise, rock crystal, and coral beads. Head ornamentation was an important aspect of this traditional jewellery which included elaborate diadems, often decorated with coins, and gold wire caps (*tepelikia*). Long earrings accompanied these headdresses and were often suspended from them. Large pectoral pieces and intricate necklaces (*yiordania*) were also an important feature of traditional jewellery. An impressive silver-gilt example in the Museum of Greek Folk Art in Athens featuring layers of hanging rosettes inlaid with coloured glass, stone, and cameos is typical of Attica, but the specific designs vary by region. Massive belt buckles, however, are the commonest type of traditional jewellery because they formed part of everyday as well as ceremonial dress. Aprons of coins, amulets, bracelets, and rings are also very common. But perhaps the most remarkable feature of traditional Greek jewellery is its continuity with past tradition, evident especially in the decorative motifs, an inexhaustible series of recreations and stylizations from the natural world, as well as in the apotropaic or magical motifs, such as pomegranates, two-headed eagles, crosses, and other Christian imagery.

The development of Greek jewellery in the modern period can be divided into two phases. The first phase begins with the liberation of Greece in 1827 and the abandonment of traditional costumes and their accompanying jewellery. European-style jewellery was widely imported during this time, leading to a decline in the age-old techniques and styles of Hellenic jewellery. In the 1940s and 1950s, however, foreign visitors to Greece began to demand Greek jewellery as souvenirs, leading craftsmen such as Agapitos Poulkouras and Joseph Rousanidis to begin producing silver jewellery featuring the monuments of ancient Greece and copies of ancient coins, which they sold in small shops around the Acropolis. During the 1960s there was remarkable growth in Greek jewellery as the result of increasing and more sophisticated international demand. In this context Efthymios Zolotas, Ilias Lalaounis, and others were instrumental in reviving ancient techniques and breathing new life into the traditional forms of Minoan, Mycenaean,

Classical, and Byzantine jewellery. The success of these pioneers, the continued international demand, and the growth of Athens as a tourist centre, led the Greek Handicraft Organization to promote the entry of artists into the jewellery-making sector, thereby broadening its horizons. Like the traditional craftsmen of the past centuries, these artists, including the self-taught Sophia Thanopoulou "Maroulina", continue to draw on the incredibly rich diachronic heritage of Greek jewellery as well as on the forms and motifs of the natural world. As a result, even in its most contemporary, avant-garde creations, Greek jewellery maintains its unique tradition and is a remarkably eloquent expression of Greek cultural identity.

ANN M. NICGORSKI

See also Enamel, Glass, Gold, Ivory, Metalwork, Silver

Further Reading

Bromberg, Anne R., *Gold of Greece: Jewelry and Ornaments from the Benaki Museum*, Dallas, Texas: Museum of Art, 1990

Delivorrias, Angelos, *Greek Traditional Jewelry*, Athens: Melissa, 1979

Higgins, Reynold, *The Aegina Treasure: An Archaeological Mystery*, London: British Museum Publications, 1979

Higgins, Reynold, *Greek and Roman Jewellery*, 2nd edition, London: Methuen, and Berkeley: University of California Press, 1980

Hoffmann, Herbert and Patricia F. Davidson, *Greek Gold: Jewelry from the Age of Alexander*, Mainz: Von Zabern, 1965 (exhibition catalogue)

Kaplani, Yianoula, *Modern Greek Silverware from the Collections of the Museum of Greek Folk Art*, Athens: Archaeological Receipts Fund, 1997

Kypraiou, Evangelia (editor), *Greek Jewellery: 6000 Years of Tradition*, Athens: Archaeological Receipts Fund, 1997

Ogden, Jack, *Jewellery of the Ancient World*, London: Trefoil, and New York: Rizzoli, 1982

Phillips, Clare, *Jewelry: From Antiquity to the Present*, London and New York: Thames and Hudson, 1996

Tolstikov, Vladimir and Mikhail Treister, *The Gold of Troy: Searching for Homer's Fabled City*, London: Thames and Hudson, and New York: Abrams, 1996 (exhibition catalogue)

Williams, Dyfri and Jack Ogden, *Greek Gold: Jewellery of the Classical World*, London: British Museum Press, and New York: Abrams, 1994

Williams, Dyfri (editor), *The Art of the Greek Goldsmith*, London: British Museum Press, 1998

Zora, Popi, *Embroideries and Jewellery of Greek National Costumes*, 2nd edition, Athens: Museum of Greek Folk Art, 1981

Jews

The Jewish encounter with Hellenic culture has been a continuing phenomenon for the past three millennia. This essay is meant to stimulate new approaches to this encounter from the perspective of Jewish influence on Hellenism. It is with the intellectual fusion of these two unique cultures during the Hellenistic period that the foundations for modern society were firmly laid. This essay will note the main points of the Hellenic–Judaic helix through two major periods (Hellenistic and Byzantine), and residual influence in the modern period. There will be a brief discussion of the origins of the

Hebrew–Hellenic encounter during the biblical period from about 1300 to 300 BC.

The contest between the Aegean migration following the Trojan War and the Israelite survivors of Egyptian bondage lasted throughout the 1st millennium BC: from the period of the Judges (12th–11th centuries) through to the Maccabean period (2nd–1st centuries). During this millennium the fusion had already begun: King David married an Aegean – Ma'akhah (perhaps Maxe/a), the daughter of Talmi (Ptolemaeos), tyrant (*seren*) of Geshur, and perhaps Eglah (better Aigle/a), and his mercenary corps was drawn from Philistines and Cretans. Thus the beginning of mutual influence dates to the first encounters between Hebrew and Hellene in Israel. Compare too the legends in the Book of Judges (compiled late 8th century BC: specifically the parallels between Jephthah's daughter and Iphigeneia, Samson and Heracles, etc.). Greek mythology recalls the Palestinian milieu while archaeology has uncovered the continuity of the Aegean diaspora in Israel throughout the late Judaean monarchy and the period of the Persian empire. The brief expansion of Hellenism in Israel under the influence of the Ptolemaic and Seleucid kingdoms was reversed by the upsurge of Maccabean nationalism and transmuted later by Hellenized Hasmoneans. It was only with the establishment of the Roman hegemony that the Hellenic polytheists reasserted their identity; at the same time the way was prepared for their later adoption of Christianity. The ability of the Aegean diaspora to survive the monotheistic revolution of the Israelites during the 1st millennium BC provided one conduit through which the Hellenic culture of Athens was able to penetrate Israelite society.

The historical and cultural background of the Hellenization of the Jews is fundamental to understanding the necessity for the appearance of the Septuagint. In turn, the Septuagint affected Hellenism and the Hellenes through Egyptian–Jewish polemic (e.g. Manetho) long before its appropriation by the Christians. Post-biblical Jewish influence on Hellenism during the period from the 6th century BC to the 6th century AD, which followed post-biblical influence of Hellenic culture on Jews and Judaism, set the pattern for the subsequent 1500 years of western civilization through the autonomous developments within Latin, Greek, and Slavic Christianity, as well as Islamic and Judaic civilizations, the last dispersed among all the former. It was based on a discussion of man(kind) in social, ethical, psychological (i.e. study of the soul), philosophical (i.e. study of wisdom), rational, scientific, and mystical contexts. Here the Jewish concept developed through the techniques of Greek philosophy and rhetoric to produce an intellectual framework and created the means to "adjust" Hellenism into a monotheistic world view that has sustained western civilization until the present day.

The contacts and mutual influence between the two independent cultures underwent serious change after the conquests of Alexander the Great. The incorporation of the land of Israel and its scattered colonies (henceforth "diaspora") into a Greek-dominated *oikoumene* (world) necessitated a fusion of Hellenic and Israelite culture if the latter was to survive in the newly defined diaspora which offered to anyone the opportunity to *hellenizein* (i.e. to become a Hellene by learning the language and customs of the conquerors). While the autonomous temple-based culture of Jerusalem and the proto-

synagogue Aramaized culture of Babylonia were slow to Hellenize, the Jewish communities of Egypt quickly adapted to the new situation. Widely scattered as part of the administrative and military structure of Persian Egypt, they adjusted to the Macedonian conquest and flocked to the new city of Alexandria. Only fragmentary information is available on the early stages of a parallel process among the Jewish military colonies in Anatolia or the Jewish merchant colonies (metics) in Greece and Macedonia. The widespread Jewish diaspora can be later traced in the Greek translation of Ezekiel (2nd century BC), Philo's report of his embassy to Gaius (1st century AD), and the peregrinations of Paul of Tarsus (1st century AD).

The Jews acculturated rapidly to the new system, in particular through the adoption of the Greek language which replaced the Persian and Aramaic they had used under the previous empire. Within a generation after the establishment of the Ptolemaic kingdom they were Hellenophone, which caused a problem with respect to their sacred scriptures. Since the middle of the 5th century BC Ezra, a priest and royal scribe at the Persian court, had declared that the five books of Moses comprised their Torah, their God-given teaching (Josephus' *nomos*). Earlier prophets, such as Jeremiah, had emphasized the teachings of Moses with a stress on ethical standards and the command to remember their God and Zion. In Ptolemy's Egypt the Jews spoke Greek and so their Torah had become incomprehensible without the mediation of priests and preachers. Hence it was necessary to "interpret" a Greek version for these Jewish Hellenes.

The Septuagint, i.e. the translation of the "Seventy" as retold in the legend of the "Letter of Aristeas" (1st century BC), is one of the seminal phenomena of western civilization. It brought the Torah of Moses and the mythical-legal traditions of the Jews to the wider Greek-speaking world where it became part of the discussion between Hellenes and Jews, both polemically and apologetically, and also provided a means for syncretism as well as fusion of both Hellenic and Hebrew traditions. The Septuagint then was the Jewish claim to the ultimate historical and ethical truth in the Hellenic (i.e. Greek-speaking) *oikoumene*. Since it challenged Hellenic mythical-poetic traditions and philosophic posturings as did no other representation from the conquered peoples, it provided the intellectuals with a challenge to their own systems. Indeed, the first verse of the Septuagint, which allowed for a future doctrine of *creatio ex nihilo* somewhat different from the original Hebrew, would be at the centre of Christianity's polemic against polytheism and its critique of philosophy and science until the 20th century.

The impact of the Septuagint (the Pentateuch was translated in the 280s BC and the remainder by the end of the 1st century) was threefold. The Egyptian priest Manetho wrote an Egyptian history to show the Hellenes the antiquity of Egyptian civilization and its cult. He also denigrated the Jews in response to the Septuagint's rendering of the Exodus story. To his claim that the Jews were lepers banished to Jerusalem by the Pharaohs, later Hellenic rhetoricians from Alexandria and other schools added negative comments and misinterpretations about the Jews and their cult in Jerusalem. These were all gathered and refuted by a Jewish priest, Joseph ben Matityahu (Josephus Flavius), in his classic apologia *Contra Apionem*, written at the end of the 1st century AD. Yet the Septuagint and translations of the former and latter prophets (Joshua to Kings and the classical literary prophets) as well as other scriptures (both those later accepted into the biblical canon and a host of others) added a wealth of historical and ethical material to support the Jewish world view. In the extant Hellenic literature of the Hellenistic and Roman periods there are as many pro-Jewish as anti-Jewish sentiments, attesting to a perceived powerful and magical secret wisdom among the Jews. And there is the phenomenon of Hellenes converting to Judaism or adopting Jewish ethical teachings, even as the evolving Judaism contributed to the multiplicity of syncretic religions and sectarianism that characterized the period.

Three seminal Jewish figures participated in this process, all three of whom were to become virtual if not actual saints in the Greek Orthodox version of Christianity that became the dominant religion of medieval Hellenism: Philo of Alexandria, Paul of Tarsus, and Josephus Flavius. Philo produced an intellectual synthesis of Mosaic teaching and middle Platonic philosophy that successfully allegorized ancient Hebrew legends and laws into the philosophic language of Hellenistic Alexandria. His extensive corpus of commentaries provided the later Church with the tools and materials that would enable it to Christianize this material for its missionary and didactic missions. Paul provided a different synthesis. He successfully reinterpreted the northern Mediterranean fertility myths through the language of Pharisaic Judaism into an expanded conception of the Jewish messiah, the annointed one (*o christos*) who would bring salvation to his followers. So Saul of Tarsus, a former Pharisee (biblical interpreter), used his training in the oral commentary to the Torah, which had been further developed through the adoption and adaptation of Hellenistic rhetorical devices, and became Paul, the teacher to the non-Jewish Hellenes of the new chapter in human salvation initiated by the career of a Palestinian Pharisee who had been crucified by the Romans and later resurrected by the God who made heaven and earth (*cf.* Septuagint, Genesis 1: 1ff). These two near contemporaries, Philo and Paul, thus provided the methodology and ideology for a new synthesis of Hellenistic society and its salvation that was to dominate Hellenism until the present day. Josephus, the third figure, was a priest in Jerusalem who became one of the military leaders in the revolt against Rome (66–73 AD). After his surrender to the Romans, he became tutor to Titus and later a client of the Flavians in Rome where he undertook to write the official story of the Jewish war with Rome (*Jewish War*, 7 books) and to retell the history of the Jews (*Jewish Antiquities*, 20 books). The works of Josephus Flavius were later accepted as a secular (if not divinely inspired) commentary to biblical history by the Christian Church. As such, these works entered the church canon and provided factual and stylistic influence on subsequent theological and historical works among all linguistic varieties of Christianity, in particular Greek Orthodoxy. Indeed, Eusebius of Caesarea is acknowledged by modern scholars to be responsible for the adjustment of Josephus' mention of Jesus of Nazareth into a Jewish acknowledgement of the latter's legitimacy as the Christ, the true Messiah; this was, no doubt, a serious contribution to the "canonization" of Josephus.

Much of the Jewish literature of the Hellenistic and Roman periods was adopted, with appropriate Christianized interpolation, into the library of the new religion. This literature was excerpted by Eusebius of Caesarea and its fragments survive primarily in his massive two-volume apology against polytheism (*Praeparatio Evangelica*) and polemic against Judaism (*Demonstratio Evangelica*). Other works were incorporated into the canon of the Christian Bible in the 4th century AD which comprised works that, with the exception of the Gospel of St Luke and several letters, were written by practising and believing Jews who had accepted Jesus of Nazareth as the expected Messiah. Even more Jewish material survived as Christian apocrypha. Much of this literature contributed to the Hellenic Church's missionary and didactic policies. Martyrdom, for example, which derived from the Books of the Maccabees, became central to Christianity before Constantine the Great, and later became the ideology for the militant among Christians and Muslims to the present day. The survival of non-canonized material also contributed to the growth of heresy and to the ongoing questions of the nature and arrival of the promised redemption. It also contributed to the prevalence of magic and mysticism within Christian and Jewish Hellenic society during the medieval period.

Jewish influence on Hellenism during the Byzantine period affected the areas of proselytism, diplomacy, and intellectual exchange. Proselytism was one of the primary agents in the expansion of medieval Hellenism's power: it was a formal part of Byzantium's political and diplomatic mission on the one hand to save souls, and on the other, to protect and enhance the empire. Here the Jews served as a foil in the argument against polytheism (particularly among the Slavs whom the Byzantines wished to "Hellenize"); Jews too were subject to more aggressive missionizing, including forced baptism, which became part of Byzantine policy under Herakleios, Leo III, Basil I, Romanos Lekapenos, and John III Vatatzes. During the 10th-century persecutions Hasdai ibn Shaprut, vizier to Abdulrahman III, caliph of Islamic Spain, apparently interceded directly and indirectly with Basil's son Leo and Constantine Porphyrogennetos, the former by letter, the latter by negotiation with the kingdom of the Judaized Khazars to which Byzantine Jewish refugees had fled. The Jewish "mission" to the Turkic tribes, though not planned, was part of the competition between Latins and Greeks for the Volga Turks who moved south of the Danube (eventually these Slavicized Bulgars entered the orbit of Byzantium). The 9th-century apostles to the Slavs, Sts Cyril and Methodios, were from Thessalonica; it was perhaps there that they learned the Hebrew letters which they were to add to the Greek alphabet to form the basis for the Cyrillic alphabet still in use among the Slavic Orthodox peoples. Direct and indirect Jewish influence through translated texts and personal contact is pertinent to the understanding of medieval Slavic and Russian Orthodoxy.

Jews continued to be educated through their own traditions (despite Justinian I's prohibition on teaching the *deuterosis*, the "Jewish tradition") based on a growing body of commentary in Hebrew. This commentary was no less than an encyclopaedia of ancient and contemporary wisdom translated into Hebrew and organized around appropriate verses in the Bible or melded into a running commentary on the Mishnah, a 2nd-century code of Jewish law. Thus ancient and medieval physics were discussed within the context of creation in Genesis, etc. Christian scholars came to study with those scholars who were able to explain the original Hebrew as well as ancient and contemporary scholarship which was continually being rendered from Greek and Arabic into Hebrew throughout the Middle Ages (and in Sicily and Spain into Latin). Jerome, for example, had conferred with Palestinian rabbis for his Vulgate translation of the Bible, while in the 14th century Simon Atumano, Archbishop of Thebes, produced a polyglot Bible which included a Hebrew version of the Old Testament with contemporary Jewish comments. Greek scholars discussed astronomy and astrology with their contemporaries, and Jews learned from them as well as teaching each other, e.g. the polymath Shabbetai Donnolo of 10th-century Oria (Byzantine Calabria).

The widespread Jewish diaspora in 12th-century Byzantium can be traced in the unique itinerary of Benjamin of Tudela. There he lists communal leaders and population figures for Jews in some 25 Byzantine communities – e.g. Patras, Thebes (2500), Thessalonica (where he apparently mentions only those in the silk industry), Constantinople; his numbers add up to about 9000 which modern scholars differently extrapolate to a total Jewish population between 12,000 and 100,000: perhaps 75,000 is most useful. Jews were widely settled throughout the empire, mainly along the important commercial routes and the major islands where settlements had existed since Hellenistic times as well as in centres such as Mistra, Andravida, Ioannina, Adrianople, Nicaea, Ephesus, and Philadelphia. Heretics, of course, went to the Jews to learn non-Orthodox readings of ancient literature. Scholars such as George Gemistos Plethon (late 14th–15th century) studied with Jewish scholars (in his case, in Ottoman Edirne/Adrianopolis), as did others who followed in his footsteps in Constantinople shortly after the Ottoman conquest. After the rise of Kabbalah (literally "reception", referring to the new stage in Jewish mysticism) after 1200 as the preferred approach to Jewish mysticism, Jewish scholars used this Judaized Neoplatonic system to explore creation in ways beyond the limited inherited approaches of Plato and Aristotle. Indeed, when combined with traditional Jewish speculation, it was apparent that Greek scholars could in no way compete with them, as Shemarya Ikriti (late 13th–14th century) argued. His comment had a long tradition, for as early as the 2nd century AD Numenius the Pythagorean was often quoted for his remark: "For what is Plato, but Moses speaking in Attic?", i.e. whatever wisdom may be found among the Hellenes was already anticipated by the Jews. This apologetic proposition had been argued more fantastically by Artapanus and other Hellenistic Jewish authors since the 2nd century BC.

In addition to scripture, Hellenic Christianity is indebted to Judaism for the architecture of the church, the structure and content of the liturgy, its music and the hymnal, as well as its calendar. The Hellenistic synagogue, a variation on the Greek model, provided the symbols and architectural structure for the churches, at least those not appropriated directly from the polytheists through the sanctification of their temples by 4th-century monks. The iconostasis was originally set up as a protective barrier for the king and high priest Alexander Yannai who was pelted during Sukkoth (Tabernacles) by the followers of the Pharisees on the grounds of his not being of Davidic descent. The tradition of illustrating Bible scenes in fresco and mosaic is also taken partly from early synagogue

tradition (e.g. Dura Europus). The liturgy is based, like that of the synagogue, on the ritual of the Temple in Jerusalem with the substitution of Christ for the traditional sacrifice. The Orthodox hymnal is replete with the *kantika* of Romanos the hymnographer who, it has been argued, was a convert from Judaism and brought the hymnal traditions of Nisibis to the Hellenic world to produce some of its most stirring prayers. In turn, the Palestinian Jews, during the persecutions of Justinian, developed the *piyyut* (from *poiesis*), that rendered the oral tradition into poeticized liturgical prayer and thus helped preserve Judaism until the Muslim conquest three generations later. The tradition of Temple music, as investigated by Eric Werner and others, fertilized the medieval synagogue and permeates both Western and Eastern church liturgical music. In the adopted biblical calendar, the Orthodox Easter (Pascha) is the most important holy day; it is the Christian reinterpretation of the Hebrew Pesach (Passover) and occurs on the Sunday following the Hebrew dating of that holiday. Indeed, Justinian tried unsuccessfully to sever by law this dependence which appeared to him as a denigration of Christian dominance over Judaism.

Hellenism moved beyond the Hellenic world during the medieval period into the language cultures of Arabic and Latin, both monotheistic offshoots of Hellenistic culture. While Syriac Christians facilitated the translations from Greek via Syriac to Arabic, Jews proficient in Aramaic and Arabic were able to transfer this newly available knowledge to Hebrew and Latin for the edification of the West. Greek-speaking Jews participated in the project of Frederick II Hohenstaufen, king of Sicily (1198–1250), to translate treatises directly from Greek to Latin. It was in Spain that Neoplatonism was Judaized, partially through the splendid poetry of Solomon ibn Gabirol, and was wedded to the language of the Wisdom of Solomon in the Books of Kings and Chronicles to produce the first stages of Kabbalah. Thirteenth-century developments show interesting parallels to the rise of hesychasm, particularly through the career of Abraham Abulafia. The writings of Maimonides (12th century), in particular his *Guide for the Perplexed*, harnessed Aristotle's logical system for monotheism. From Arabic it was translated first to Hebrew and then to Latin where it became the foundation for Thomas Aquinas to build his great *Summa Theologica*. The latter in turn stimulated an Aristotelian rationalist movement in late Byzantine philosophy.

In the modern period the (re)secularization of Hellenism as the foundation for modern physical and social sciences attracted Jewish scholars such as Baruch Spinoza, Karl Marx, Sigmund Freud, Albert Einstein, and Jacques Derrida. These later developments, however, remove us from the world of the Greek-speaking Hellenists where Greek- and Spanish-speaking Jews continued to live scattered in the towns and villages of the Balkans alongside a polyglot society of Hellenic Christians; just as the Hellenic Orthodox world was overshadowed by the Ottoman conquest, so too the Greek-speaking Romaniote Jews sank to a level of survival during the three centuries prior to 1821. Indeed, the structure and content of the Greek Orthodox diaspora under the Ottomans parallels the vicissitudes of the Jewish diaspora under the Christian Romans (4th to 5th centuries). In the 19th century both Christian and Jewish Hellenes awoke to the French clarion of nationalism which stimulated ancestral resonances and led to the rebirth of independent Hellenic and Jewish states. At the same time, the regional diasporas of Hellenes and Jews began to collapse, with the survivors withdrawing to the homeland, under Nazi, communist, and Islamic pressures. Their respective diasporas are today further afield, divorced physically from the Mediterranean and surviving, indeed flourishing, under the auspices of the Hellenistic Jewish idea of a monotheistic socioreligious culture.

STEVEN B. BOWMAN

See also Antisemitism, Septuagint

Further Reading

Bartlett, John R., *Jews in the Hellenistic World: Josephus, Aristeas, the Sybilline Oracles, Eupolemus*, Cambridge and New York: Cambridge University Press, 1985

Bickerman, Elias J., *From Ezra to the Last of the Maccabees: Foundations of Post-Biblical Judaism*, New York: Schocken, 1962

Bickerman, Elias J., *The Jews in the Greek Age*, Cambridge, Massachusetts: Harvard University Press, 1988

Boman, Thorlief, *Hebrew Thought Compared with Greek*, translated by Jules L. Moreau, London: SCM Press, 1960, reprinted New York: Norton, 1970

Feldman, Louis H., *Jew and Gentile in the Ancient World: Attitudes and Interactions from Alexander to Justinian*, Princeton, New Jersey: Princeton University Press, 1993

Gager, John G., *Moses in Greco-Roman Paganism*, Nashville, Tennessee: Abingdon Press, 1972

Gager, John G., *The Origins of Anti-Semitism: Attitudes toward Judaism in Pagan and Christian Antiquity*, Oxford and New York: Oxford University Press, 1983

Goldstein, Jonathan A., "Jewish Acceptance and Rejection of Helenism" in *Jewish and Christian Self-Definition*, vol. 2, edited by E.P. Sanders *et al.*, Philadelphia: Fortress Press, and London: SCM Press, 1981

Goodenough, Erwin Ramsdell, *Jewish Symbols in the Greco-Roman Period*, 13 vols, New York: Pantheon, 1953–68; edited and abridged by Jacob Neusner, Princeton, New Jersey: Princeton University Press, 1988

Gordon, Cyrus H., *Before the Bible: The Common Background of Greek and Hebrew Civilization*, New York: Harper and Row, and London: Collins, 1962

Roth, Norman, "The Theft of Philosophy by the Greeks from the Jews", *Folia*, 31 (1978): pp. 53–67

Schultz, Joseph P. and Lois Spatz, *Sinai and Olympus: A Comparative Study*, Lanham, Maryland: University Press of America, 1995

Shavit, Yaacov, *Athens in Jerusalem: Classical Antiquity and Hellenism in the Making of the Modern Secular Jew*, translated by Chaya Naor and Niki Werner, Portland, Oregon: Littman Library of Jewish Civilization, 1997

Shestov, Lev, *Athens and Jerusalem*, translated by Bernard Martin, Athens, Ohio: Ohio University Press, 1966

Shoham, S. Giora, *Valhalla, Calvary and Auschwitz*, Cincinnati: Bowman and Cody Academic Publishing, 1995

Stern, Menahem (editor), *Greek and Latin Authors on Jews and Judaism*, 3 vols, Jerusalem: Israel Academy of Sciences and Humanities, 1974–84

Stone, Michael E. (editor), *Jewish Writings of the Second Temple Period*, Assen: Van Gorcum, and Philadelphia: Fortress Press, 1984

Werner, Eric, *The Sacred Bridge: The Interdependence of Liturgy and Music in Synagogue and Church during the First Millennium*, London: Dobson, and New York: Columbia University Press, 1959

Wolfson, Harry Austryn, *Philo: Foundations of Religious Philosophy in Judaism, Christianity, and Islam*, revised edition, 2 vols, Cambridge, Massachusetts: Harvard University Press, 1948

John I Tzimiskes *c.*925–976

Emperor

John I Tzimiskes (969–76) was one of the more successful military men who seized the throne and continued the territorial expansion of the Byzantine empire during the 10th century. He was born in Chozana, Armenia, and his name is an Armenian rendering of the Greek word *Mouzakites*, meaning "shorty". John enjoyed some notable military successes during the reigns of Constantine VII Porphyrogennetos (913–59) and Romanos II (959–63). In 958, when he was the *strategos* (supreme commander) of Mesopotamia, he captured the cities of Dara and Samosata, as well as inflicting two defeats on the talented Hamdanid general Sayf al-Dawlah, sending the captives to be paraded through Constantinople. In 962 he commanded a wing of the army led by Nikephoros Phokas into Cilicia. Later he assisted in the capture of Aleppo. After the death of Romanos II (963) John, who was then *strategos* of the Anatolika and the empire's second most famous general, decided to support Nikephoros Phokas in his bid for power. As a reward for his support, Nikephoros made John *domestikos* (commander) of the east. Subsequently John defeated the Arabs near Adana in 964. Later, in 969, Nikephoros would earn John's resentment by transferring the control of eastern operations to Peter the Stratopedarch. John had important dynastic connections of his own: his mother was the sister of Nikephoros Phokas and his first wife Maria was the sister of Bardas Skleros. He was also a grandson of Bardas Phokas and related to John Kourkouas. He eventually came to power as a result of a military coup against the emperor with the cooperation of Nikephoros's wife Theophano, who was also John's lover. Theophano was the former wife of Romanos II and mother and regent of the future emperors Basil II (976–1025) and Constantine VIII (1025–28). Nikephoros was assassinated in 969 while sleeping on the floor of his bedroom in front of his icons. The patriarch Polyeuktos refused to sanction John's coronation unless he did penance for the murder. Among the patriarch's preconditions was that John should send Theophano away. He complied and later married Theodora, the daughter of Constantine VII and aunt of the legitimate emperors Basil II and Constantine VIII.

John waged war successfully on multiple fronts. He won a spectacular victory over Svjatoslav, the Russian prince of Kiev, in Bulgaria. After repulsing Svjatoslav's initial assault, he captured the Bulgarian capital of Preslav, which he renamed Joannopolis after himself, and freed the imprisoned Bulgarian emperor Boris. He later surrounded the main Russian army at Dristra and, after a three-month siege, forced it to capitulate. He renamed the town Theodoropolis after St Theodore Stratelates, who purportedly assisted the Byzantines during the siege. Later he forced Boris to abdicate and annexed most of Bulgaria, organizing it into six new themes. In addition, he demoted the Bulgarian patriarchate to an archbishopric and placed it under the control of Constantinople. John also made an alliance with the German emperor, Otto I, by agreeing to marry his niece Theophano to Otto's son, the future Otto II, in 972. With the conclusion of these arrangements in the west, John was able to focus his attention on extending the eastern frontiers of the empire. In 972 he captured and destroyed Nisibis. In 974 he returned to the east, imposing tributary status upon the emir of Mosul. In 975 John led his forces against the Fatimid Caliphate by campaigning in Syria. He was successful in forcing Damascus to pay tribute and later captured Beirut. He reportedly planned to continue campaigning in the east, hoping eventually to recapture Tripoli and Jerusalem.

In addition to his military achievements, John also passed some legislation concerning the alienation of soldiers' land to the control of the *dynatoi* (notables) and the monasteries. He was pressured to repeal Nikephoros Phokas's legislation, which had not only forbidden future donations of land to the monasteries but also banned the establishment of new ones. John had a standing policy that required local theme officials to investigate the estates of local magnates and monasteries. Any peasants found on these estates who were previously under obligation to the state were to be returned to state control. Like previous emperors, John recognized the need for maintaining the pool of smallholders who formed the basis for military recruiting; however, he also allowed some peasants to remain under the control of the monasteries. In 976 a rumour arose that John was planning to investigate the estates owned by the grand chamberlain Basil Lekapenos in Cilicia, whose property was made up of lands previously belonging to the state. Basil supposedly had the emperor poisoned to prevent this. John died in Constantinople on 10 January 976, most likely a victim of typhoid.

JOHN F. SHEAN

Biography

Born *c*.925 at Chozana in Armenia, John was a most successful general. After the death of Romanos II in 963 he supported Nikephoros Phokas as emperor and in return was made *domestikos* of the east. But in 969 Nikephoros transferred the command and John took his revenge by murdering the emperor. Seizing the throne for himself, John continued to expand the territory of the empire. He died in Constantinople in 976.

Further Reading

Leo the Deacon [Works], edited by C.B. Hase, Bonn: Weber, 1828, (*Corpus Scriptorum Historiae Byzantinae*, vol. 30)

Schlumberger, Gustave, *L'Épopée byzantine à la fin du dixième siècle*, revised edition, 3 vols, Paris: Boccard, 1925

Scylitzes, John, *Synopsis Historiarum*, edited by J. Thurn, Berlin and New York: de Gruyter, 1973 (*Corpus Fontium Historiae Byzantinae*, vol. 5)

John II Komnenos 1087–1143

Emperor

John Komnenos (1118–43) was the eldest son of Alexios I Komnenos (1081–1118). Because of the prejudices of our few extant written sources we know virtually nothing of his activities before 1118, and only slightly more thereafter. He became heir to the throne in 1092 when Alexios's victory over the Pechenegs – a fierce nomadic people who had settled within the northern Balkans – allowed him to disinherit the *porphyrogennetos* ("born to the purple") Constantine Doukas. Doukas had been betrothed to John's sister, Anna Komnene, who had therefore expected to succeed to the throne. John's promotion provoked a bitter rivalry between the siblings, and ultimately led to an attempt by Anna to prevent her brother's accession in 1118. Her coup, in which her mother Irene Doukaina was also involved, failed, and Anna was banished to a nunnery, where she later wrote her *Alexiad*, the history of her father's reign. John is systematically eliminated from her text: Anna mentions her brother only five times, each time with disdain or hostility. Finally she opines: "We enjoyed peace until the end of [Alexios's] life, but with him all the benefits disappeared and his efforts came to nothing through the stupidity of those who inherited the throne."

A fuller, although far from complete, picture of John's reign is painted by the two principal historians of the 12th century, John Kinnamos and Niketas Choniates. From these we learn that John entrusted military commands to relatives, the *sevastoi*, but put civil affairs into the hands of more obscure men, such as John of Poutze, who centralized the administration of the army and navy, commuting service for cash payments in maritime districts. John took personal command of the imperial forces, and campaigned extensively in Anatolia and lands further east, capitalizing on his father's successes. He fought wars against the Danishmendids and captured the strongholds of Kastamon and Gangra after 1134. He restored Byzantine authority in Cilicia in 1137, and in the following year accepted the homage of Raymond of Poitiers, the ruler of Antioch. His subsequent drive into Syria ended with an unsuccessful assault on Aleppo. In the west John was more circumspect, campaigning against northern nomads (probably Cumans) in 1122, and twice against the Hungarians between 1127 and 1129. For most of the 1130s John was allied with the German rulers Lothar III (1125–37) and Conrad III (1138–52). In 1136 Byzantine troops took part in Lothar's campaign, which pressed into Norman-occupied southern Italy as far as Bari. Relations with Conrad were even better, and from 1140 were destined to be cemented by the marriage of John's fourth son, Manuel, to Conrad's sister-in-law, Bertha of Sulzbach. Thus, John was free to concentrate his attention and resources on his eastern campaigns, and it was in Cilicia in 1143 that he was killed in a hunting accident. By then two of his two eldest sons, Alexios and Andronikos, had also died, and the succession was disputed by the two younger sons: Isaac, who had returned to Constantinople, and Manuel, who had been with his father and thus in command of the imperial army. Manuel succeeded.

Although we can extract reliable facts for John's reign from the histories of Kinnamos and Choniates, both authors were more concerned with subsequent events. Both treat John's reign as a mirror that reflects the deeds of his son and heir Manuel I Komnenos, and both have clear and clearly opposed agendas. Kinnamos, Manuel's personal secretary, invites his audience to compare Manuel's actions, his personal valour and achievements, with those of his father; they are expected to recognize the author's innuendo, and conclude with him that the son is greater than the father. Choniates, writing after

John II Komnenos: mosaic (*c.*1118) in Hagia Sophia showing the Virgin and Child standing between the emperor John II Komnenos and his wife, the empress Irene

1204, identifies the roots of the cataclysm in Manuel's reign, highlighting his "Latinophilia", and invites his readers to contrast this with the solid and measured successes achieved by John in the east. Perhaps the best example of the two approaches to John is contained in the contrary accounts of his campaigns against Hungary in the years 1127–29. Although they are fairly insignificant within the context of John's 25-year reign, both authors devote disproportionate space to these exchanges. The reason for this would have been more obvious to contemporaries, who were familiar with Manuel's greatly lauded campaigns against Hungary, than it is to modern readers, who are similarly invited to compare and contrast these with John's limited achievements.

There are a few contemporary accounts of John's activities from which we can glean further information, although they are far from objective: his reign witnessed a flowering of court panegyric, which appears to have complemented the revival of the imperial triumphal procession in 1133. Theodore Prodromos wrote at least 22 verse encomia in honour of John, 11 of which were concerned with the emperor's departure for, or return from, campaign. The glorification of warfare is central to the construction of John's imperial image, and Prodromos celebrates John's qualities as a commander, the spilling of blood and sweat, the vision of the just war of reconquest, and the predicted extension of the emperor's dominion to the ends of the earth. Other striking images of John's imperial style have survived as enduring beacons in the general obscurity. A famous mosaic in Hagia Sophia in Constantinople portrays the emperor with his Hungarian wife, Piroska-Irene (to whom he was married in 1105), flanking the Virgin with infant Christ. To Piroska's left stands the figure of John's eldest son, Alexios, who was to succeed. John and Alexios are also portrayed together in John's illuminated copy of the Gospels, standing beneath the enthroned Christ who bestows their crowns. The faces of the emperor and his son differ from all others in the manuscript, suggesting an attempt by the artist to capture their actual appearance. A third powerful image of John's sovereignty is his roundel, now in the Byzantine collection at Dumbarton Oaks, Washington, D.C. John was buried, with his wife, in the Pantokrator monastery in Constantinople, his own monastic complex, for which the foundation charter (typikon), dated October 1136, survives. The three parallel church buildings stand today, with the Turkish name Zerek Kilise Camii.

PAUL STEPHENSON

See also Komnenos family

Biography

Born in Constantinople in 1087, John succeeded his father Alexios I in 1118, to the dismay of his sister Anna Komnene who had hoped for the accession of her husband. He personally commanded the imperial forces and campaigned vigorously in the east in Anatolia and Syria, and in the west in Hungary and Italy. He died in a hunting accident near Anazarbos in Cilicia in 1143.

Further Reading

Angold, Michael, *The Byzantine Empire, 1025–1204: A Political History*, 2nd edition, London and New York: Longman, 1997

Chalandon, Ferdinand, *Les Comnène: études sur l'empire byzantin au XIe et XIIe siècles*, vol. 2, Paris: Picard, 1912; reprinted New York: Franklin, 1960

Gautier, Paul, "Le Typikon du Christ Sauveur Pantocrator", *Revue des Etudes Byzantines*, 32 (1974): pp. 1–145

Hörandner, Wolfram (editor), *Theodoros Prodromos: historische Gedichte*, Vienna: Akademie der Wissenschaften, 1974

Lilie, Ralph-Johannes, *Byzantium and the Crusader States, 1096–1204*, Oxford: Clarendon Press, and New York: Oxford University Press, 1993

Magdalino, Paul, *The Empire of Manuel I Komnenos, 1143–1180*, Cambridge and New York: Cambridge University Press, 1993

Stephenson, Paul, "John Cinnamus, John II Comnenus and the Hungarian Campaign of 1127–1129", *Byzantion*, 56 (1996): pp. 177–87

John III Vatatzes *c.*1192–1254

Emperor of Nicaea

The emperor John III Doukas Vatatzes (1222–54) consolidated the power of the Byzantine empire in Nicaean exile and laid the groundwork for the reconquest of Constantinople in 1261. He inherited the throne as the son-in-law of the first Laskarid emperor of Nicaea, Theodore I Laskaris (1204–22). John III Vatatzes seized every opportunity to expand the boundaries of the Nicaean state and to tighten the loop around the Latin-held Constantinople. He preferred diplomacy to war, but when necessary he proved to be a talented military commander. In 1224 he defeated the Latins at Poimanenon in Bithynia, depriving them of all their possessions in Asia Minor. His initial advance in the Balkans was impeded by the expansion of the despotate of Epirus. In 1224 the ruler of Epirus, Theodore Komnenos Doukas (*c.*1215–30), seized Thessalonica from the Latins and had himself crowned emperor of the Romans. In the following year he expelled the Nicaean garrison from Adrianople and seemed poised to recapture Constantinople. The ambitions of the Epirot ruler were, however, thwarted by the Bulgarian king Ivan II Asen (1217–41), who defeated him in a pitched battle in 1230 and took him prisoner. Thrace and Macedonia soon fell into Bulgarian hands.

John III Vatatzes managed, however, to benefit from a Nicaean-Bulgarian alliance in 1235 that allowed him to establish a permanent European foothold in southern Thrace. Having stabilized his eastern frontier in the period 1225–31, he launched an attack on Constantinople in 1235/36 together with the Bulgarian forces of Ivan II Asen. The Greek-Bulgarian siege of Constantinople failed, however, since the Bulgarian king withdrew from the alliance at the last moment, realizing that the Nicaean state was a more dangerous enemy that the enfeebled Latin empire. After Ivan II Asen's death, John III Vatatzes took advantage of the preoccupation of Bulgaria with the Mongol threat and conquered Macedonia easily in 1246. In the same year he entered Thessalonica victoriously and put in prison its last ruler Demetrios Komnenos Doukas (1244–46), Theodore Komnenos Doukas's son. He did not manage to subjugate Epirus, which was now under the rule of the energetic despot Michael II (*c.*1237–71), Theodore Komnenos Doukas's nephew. Michael II was forced in 1252 to surrender to John III the cities of Servia in Thessaly and Durazzo in Albania. A marriage alliance between the rulers of Nicaea and Epirus in 1254 failed to cement the unity between the two Greek splinter states. Epirus was to remain an inde-pendent principality until 1340, when it reverted briefly to Byzantine control.

John III Vatatzes maintained friendly relations with various western powers in a diplomatic effort to weaken the Latin empire. In 1237 he concluded an alliance with the Holy Roman emperor Frederick II Barbarossa. After the death of his wife Irene Laskaris, he married, around 1244, Frederick's daughter Constance (Anna). When this alliance failed to bring concrete results, he entered in 1248 into negotiations for union with the Roman Church. He went so far in his concessions as to suggest a recognition of the papal primacy should Rome withdraw its support from the Latin empire.

John III Vatatzes was extremely popular among his subjects and after his death he was honoured as a saint in the churches of Magnesia, where he died, and Nymphaion, where he often resided. In the early 14th century, during the reign of Andronikos II (1282–1328), the inhabitants of Magnesia and other neighbouring cities invoked his name to help them against the advancing Turks in Asia Minor. This posthumous reputation seems to be grounded in the emperor's social policies. He supported the small peasant holders against the landed aristocracy and rebuked the nobility for its luxurious expenditure. He himself encouraged the elimination of luxury items from the imperial court. The historian Nikephoros Gregoras relates the story of how John III Vatatzes used the revenue of his private poultry farm to buy a crown for his wife Irene Laskaris adorned with pearls and precious stones; he called it the "egg-crown". John was one of the few late Byzantine emperors to protect local craftsmanship and manufacturing, cloth production in particular. He issued a special law forbidding the purchase of luxury goods and other articles that were imported from the west. This legislation was directed primarily against the Venetians and the Genoese, who obtained no commercial privileges in Nicaea during his reign. When he died on 4 November 1254, he left Nicaea a vigorous and prosperous state with a territory that had doubled in size since the beginning of his rule. The recapture of Constantinople, however, had to wait until 1261.

John Vatatzes' official canonization by the Orthodox Church took place during the second half of the 17th century. His memory is still observed on 4 November and he is known as St John the Almsgiver. In the last quarter of the 14th century the bishop of Pelagonia George wrote a *Life* of him. A 17th-century vernacular version of the saint's life exists as well.

DIMITER G. ANGELOV

Biography

Born *c.*1192, John married Irene, daughter of the emperor Theodore I Laskaris, and in 1222 inherited the throne from his father-in-law. He defeated the Latins at the battle of Poimanenon in 1224, driving them out of Asia Minor, and advanced into the Balkans. He doubled the size of the Nicaean empire and left it poised to recover Constantinople. He died at Magnesia in 1254 and was canonized in the 17th century.

Further Reading

Angold, Michael, *A Byzantine Government in Exile: Government and Society under the Laskarids of Nicaea, 1204–1261*, Oxford: Oxford University Press, 1975

Constantelos, D., "Emperor John Vatatzes' Social Concern: Basis for Canonization", *Kleronomia*, 4 (1972): pp. 92–103

Gardner, Alice, *The Lascarids of Nicaea: The Story of an Empire in Exile*, London: Methuen, 1912; reprinted Amsterdam: Hakkert, 1964

Langdon, John S., *Byzantium's Last Imperial Offensive in Asia Minor*, New Rochelle, New York: Caratzas, 1992

John VI Kantakouzenos c.1295–1383

Emperor

Descended from an important family of wealthy warrior-nobles, John Kantakouzenos (1341–54) was born in or around 1295, apparently after his father's early death. He was brought up by his mother Theodora, a woman of great ability and character who had family connections with the reigning house of Palaiologos.

By 1320 John was married to Eirene Asenina, an intelligent and spirited woman of Bulgarian and Palaiologan ancestry, whose energy and decisiveness strongly influenced her husband. By this time, too, he was associated with the restless and ambitious prince Andronikos Palaiologos, grandson of the reigning Andronikos II (1282–1328). He used his position and wealth in support of the younger Andronikos's ambitions during the intermittent civil war (1321–27) that replaced the elder emperor with his grandson as Andronikos III (1325/28–1341).

Holding the title of Grand Domestic (*Megas Domestikos*), Kantakouzenos, an able general, became the chief adviser and right-hand man of the new emperor who, at one point of mortal danger, even proposed that he become co-ruler. When Andronikos III died (15 June 1341), leaving behind as heir a 9-year-old son, John V Palaiologos, by his Latin wife Anna of Savoy, Kantakouzenos again resisted suggestions that he assume the imperial title himself, content to be virtual regent for the legitimate dynastic successor. But his erstwhile allies and colleagues – above all the ruthless Alexios Apokavkos – jealously conspired against him while he was out of the capital. Winning the support of the gullible Anna, they seized the government, arrested members of Kantakouzenos's family, and stripped him of office. Reluctant to respond too drastically, Kantakouzenos finally accepted the advice of his wife and advisers and proclaimed himself emperor (26 October 1341), though he scrupulously recognized the legitimate rights of Anna and her son as taking precedence.

Despite his wealth and the support of many other wealthy nobles, Kantakouzenos's position was initially weak, and social tensions prompted violent populist reactions against him as a symbol of the hated elite, particularly bitter ones developing in Thessalonica. In desperation, Kantakouzenos sought help from Stephan Dushan of Serbia and from Turkish princes – first the emir Umur Beg of Aydin, and then the Ottoman emir Orhan. As a result, Kantakouzenos has been condemned for introducing such dangerously ambitious outsiders into the Byzantine scene. In fact, both sides in the conflict cultivated such alliances, which rendered a weakened Byzantium vastly more vulnerable to its neighbours. Kantakouzenos's progress was furthered by the murder of Apokavkos (11 June 1345), who had maintained control of Constantinople. The usurper eventually felt sufficiently strong to stage a formal coronation at Adrianople (21 May 1346), though still affirming his commitment to John V's rights. The following February, Kantakouzenos secured entry into the capital, and arranged a settlement by which his claim to co-sovereignty was accepted and his daughter Helena was married to John V.

Kantakouzenos further solidified his family's position by sending his second son, Manuel, to rule the Byzantine Morea with the title of despot. He managed to suppress the separatist regime in Thessalonica (1350). Above all, he made every effort to restore the empire's frayed boundaries, to stimulate economic recovery (often paying state expenses out of his own wealth), and to bring peace to the Byzantine Church that was torn over the controversial religious doctrines of hesychasm. But the terrible Black Death (1347–48) debilitated the Byzantine world, while the deepened weakness of Byzantium was displayed when Kantakouzenos was caught between the rival powers of Genoa and Venice during their so-called Galata War (1350–52), fought partly in Byzantine waters, at Byzantine cost.

Mounting internal problems, and an inability to cope with increasing Turkish invasions, served to discredit Kantakouzenos's earnest efforts, at a time when John V, increasingly dissatisfied with his status, became restless and threatened new rounds of civil war. Though still reluctant, Kantakouzenos finally retaliated by allowing the coronation (April 1353) of his own eldest son, Matthew Kantakouzenos, as his new co-emperor – a step he had long tried to avoid. Matters came to a head when John V effected entry into Constantinople (November 1354). A series of agreements aimed at accommodating a continued double sovereignty led to Kantakouzenos's decision to abdicate (10 December 1354).

He remained active over the next few years, arranging terms for the dethroned Matthew and for Manuel's continuance in the Morea. Meanwhile Kantakouzenos – and his wife as well – took monastic orders, assuming the name of Joasaph, but still enjoying the honorary title of emperor. While he devoted much of his time to literary activity in semi-retirement, he was nevertheless still active in public life. His daughter remained as John V's empress, his friends were restored to influence at court, and he himself was retained as a trusted adviser by his weak and shallow son-in-law. He was acknowledged as one of the important people at court: some finding him even more powerful now than when he had been emperor on his own. On a number of occasions he wrote or made official appearances, in effect as acting emperor – as in June 1367 when he presided over a discussion with a papal legate over the possibilities of a reunion of the Churches of Rome and Constantinople. John was recurrently involved with this question, which he took very seriously, though insisting upon the rights and integrity of the Orthodox position.

Kantakouzenos was in Constantinople when his grandson Andronikos IV, the selfish eldest son of John V, imprisoned his father and brothers and attempted a government of his own (1376–79). When this regime collapsed, Andronikos fled to his Genoese allies in Galata, taking his grandfather Kantakouzenos and his mother Helena with him as hostages. Upon their release, the weary ex-emperor decided to withdraw from the capital and settle in the family territories of the Morea at Mistra, joining his son Matthew (who had replaced the deceased Manuel). There Kantakouzenos died (15 June 1383) at the age of 88.

Even in its decay, Byzantium could still produce able and dedicated leaders, and Kantakouzenos stands out as one of the last two really great ones, together with his true heir, his grandson Manuel II Palaiologos (emperor 1391–1425). Kantakouzenos's talents certainly qualified him for the throne, but his and his realm's tragedy was that he had to compensate for lack of legitimate claim by recourse to usurpation, at the price of a ruinous civil war that invalidated much of the good work he might do. If his ambition may be condemned, his hesitation must be recognized, the provocations he suffered may be acknowledged, and his scruples should be respected.

Both as patron and as contributor, Kantakouzenos played an important role in Byzantium's late intellectual life. Interested in the thought of western Christendom, he supported Demetrios Kydones and other scholars in their exploration of the works of Thomas Aquinas and other Latin theologians, previously unknown in Byzantium. But he parted company with them in remaining staunchly loyal to the traditions of Orthodoxy, whose rights he upheld without compromise against Latin claims. During his monastic years, he himself composed a number of theological treatises, in which he argued against the beliefs of Islam and of Judaism, as well as on behalf of the ideas of his friend and supporter, the brilliant theologian Gregory Palamas. His literary masterpiece is his *History* of his era, a memoir of apologetics for his usurpation, but a serious and unusually lucid work that is one of the finest examples of Byzantine historical writing.

John Kantakouzenos saw his place as clearly in the tradition of "Roman" sovereignty that extended back some 14 centuries, but as inseparably linked with the spiritual dimension of Greek Orthodox faith. It is thus appropriate that, of the surviving portraits we have of him, the two finest by far show him, respectively, as ruling emperor presiding over a church synod (Paris, Bibliotèque Nationale cod. gr. 1242, f.5), and in a double portrait, on one side as reigning emperor and on the other as the aged monk Joasaph (f.123 of the same manuscript).

JOHN W. BARKER

See also Kantakouzenos family

Biography

Born c.1295, John Kantakouzenos was the (probably posthumous) son of a Peloponnesian aristocrat. He became the friend and chief adviser of the emperor Andronikos III, after whose death in 1341 Kantakouzenos acted as regent for the legitimate emperor John V Palaiologos, becoming co-emperor with him later that year. Crowned in Adrianople in 1346 and in Constantinople in 1347, Kantakouzenos reigned until 1354 when he abdicated and became a monk, though he remained an adviser at court for another 25 years. He died at Mistra in 1383.

Further Reading

Barker, John W., *Manuel II Palaeologus, 1391–1425: A Study in Late Byzantine Statesmanship*, New Brunswick, New Jersey: Rutgers University Press, 1969

Gill, Joseph, "John VI Cantacuzenus and the Turks", *Byzantina*, 13 (1985): pp. 57–76

Kazhdan, A.P., "L'*Histoire* de Cantacuzène en tant qu'oeuvre littéraire", *Byzantion*, 50 (1980): pp. 279–335

Kyrris, Konstantinos P., "John Cantacuzenus and the Genoese, 1321–1348", *Miscellanea Storica Ligure*, 3 (1963): pp. 8–48

Kyrris, Konstantinos P., "John Cantacuzenus, the Genoese, the Venetians, and the Catalans (1348–1354)", *Byzantina*, 4 (1972): pp. 331–56

Loenertz, R.-J., "Ordre et désordre dans les mémoires de Jean Cantacuzène" in his *Byzantina et Franco-Graeca*, vol. 1, Rome: Storia e Litteratura, 1970

Meyendorff, John, *A Study of Gregory Palamas*, London: Faith Press, 1964, 2nd edition 1974

Meyendorff, John, "Projets de concile oecuménique en 1367: un dialogue inédit entre Jean Cantacuzène et le légat Paul" in his *Byzantine Hesychasm: Historical, Theological, and Social Problems: Collected Studies*, London: Variorum, 1974

Miller, Timothy S., "The Plague in John VI Cantacuzenus and Thucydides", *Greek, Roman, and Byzantine Studies*, 18 (1976): pp. 385–95

Nicol, Donald M., *The Byzantine Family of Kantakouzenos (Cantacuzenus), ca.1100–1460: A Genealogical and Prosopographical Study*, Washington, D.C.: Dumbarton Oaks, 1968

Nicol, Donald M., *The Last Centuries of Byzantium, 1261–1453*, 2nd edition, Cambridge and New York: Cambridge University Press, 1993

Nicol, Donald M., *The Reluctant Emperor: A Biography of John Cantacuzene, Byzantine Emperor and Monk, c.1295–1383*, Cambridge and New York: Cambridge University Press, 1996

Ostrogorsky, George, *History of the Byzantine State*, 2nd edition, Oxford: Blackwell, 1968; New Brunswick: Rutgers University Press, 1969

Parisot, Valentin, *Cantacuzène, homme d'état et historien: ou examen critique comparative des Mémoires de l'Empereur Jean Cantacuzène et des sources contemporaines*, Paris: Joubert, 1845

Runciman, Steven, *Mistra: Byzantine Capital of the Peloponnese*, London: Thames and Hudson, 1980

Soulis, George Christos, *The Serbs and Byzantium during the Reign of Tsar Stephen Dusan, 1331–1355 and His Successors*, Washington, D.C.: Dumbarton Oaks, 1984

Weiss, Günther, *Johannes Kantakuzenos: Aristokrat, Staatsmann, Kaiser und Mönch, in der Gesellschaftsentwicklung von Byzanz im 14. Jahrhundert*, Wiesbaden: Harrassowitz, 1969

John VIII Palaiologos 1392–1448

Emperor

Born in mid-December (16, 17, or 18) 1392, John was the first of the surviving six sons of the emperor Manuel II Palaiologos (1391–1425) and the Serbian princess Helena Dragaš. He was groomed from the outset as his father's heir, who addressed to him several literary works of regal admonition. Manuel betrothed him to a princess from Moscow (1411), whom John married in 1414 when he was 22 and she was about 11. John served as regent for his father during Manuel's sojourn in the Morea (1415–16), after which John was sent in his own turn (1416–18) to assist his younger brother, despot Theodore II, in expanding Byzantine control in the Peloponnese at Latin expense, and to gain military experience in the process.

When he returned to Constantinople, John found that his child-bride had died, leaving him available for a second diplomatic marriage. This his father arranged with Sophia of Montferrat, member of a Latin family with which the

John VIII Palaiologos, a bronze medal commemorating the emperor's visit to Italy in 1438–39

Palaiologan dynasty had long-standing contacts. This new marriage was a personal failure: John found Sophia repulsive and avoided her. But their wedding (19 January 1421) also served as the occasion for the ageing Manuel to crown his heir as co-emperor.

By then aged 28, John had become restless and he apparently led a court faction that advocated an activist policy more directly hostile to the Turks than Manuel's careful conciliation had been. Manuel yielded initiative to him and, when the benevolent sultan Mehmet I died later that year, John attempted to intervene in the Turkish succession. This brought down the wrath of the actual heir, sultan Murad II, in the form of sharp military reprisals and a formidable siege of Constantinople in the summer of 1422. The siege was soon abandoned, thanks to the diplomatic machinations of Manuel, who resumed leadership, only to suffer a paralysing stroke (1 October). John assumed direction of the government thereafter. Leaving his younger brother Constantine as his regent, he undertook (November 1422–November 1423) his first journey to the West, in hopes of securing aid from Venice and Sigismund of Hungary. The venture was a failure, however, and in his absence Constantine negotiated a disadvantageous but much-needed peace with the Turks.

The old emperor Manuel died on or around 21 July 1425, leaving John full title to the Byzantine crown. The following year his hapless wife, Sophia of Montferrat, managed (or was allowed, or pressured) to flee westward. Securing a welcome annulment of the marriage, John proceeded (September 1427) to take as his third wife the love of his life, the beautiful princess Maria Komnene, daughter of the Greek emperor of Trebizond. Shortly after, he departed to spend about a year (1427–28) in the Peloponnese, joining his brothers in further

conflicts with the local Latin regime and beginning an arrangement for their sharing of rule in the Byzantine Morea.

The withered Byzantine empire was now completely dependent upon the Turks. Murad II spent most of his reign (1421–51) rounding out territorial conquests generally in the Balkans. In 1423 the Byzantine government had sanctioned the transfer to the Venetian Republic of the important city of Thessalonica, which the Byzantines could no longer defend, and in 1430 Murad's forces took it by storm. Otherwise, Turkish policy bided its time with regard to Constantinople. This relative repose allowed John to renew efforts to seek western aid in order to save what was left of Byzantium from a final onslaught that would be inevitable sooner or later. His father had sought such aid, offering talk of Church union with Rome even while realizing that such a controversial step would be too dangerous to pursue in earnest. By contrast, John seems genuinely to have believed in the cause of union, partly because he had more confidence than his father in its viability, but also because he shared with other Byzantines of his day at least some sense of shame at the mere idea of schism among good Christians.

Accordingly, while doing his best to keep his unruly brothers in line, John began negotiations with the papacy. John would allow no abject submission of Constantinople to Rome, but insisted upon the holding of a full-dress Church Council that the Orthodox could regard as Ecumenical and authoritative, and where issues of difference could be fully debated. For a while, John also conducted parallel negotiations with the Council of Basel, the reformist gathering then attempting to challenge papal authority. But, eventually, John agreed upon terms with pope Eugenius IV and, in November 1437, set out for Italy with his patriarch and a large retinue of Greek clerics, advisers, and courtiers (among them, the philosopher George Gemistos Plethon). The council opened (January–February 1438) in Ferrara, but was transferred (January 1439) to Florence, where the Greek delegation prompted much excitement among artists and intellectuals. Though plagued by ill health, and often distracted by his passion for hunting, John led the Byzantine delegation responsibly, respecting dissident opinions while working for compromises that would achieve union with minimal Byzantine humiliation. The union formula was finally achieved, and the decree, signed by the Greeks on 5 July 1439, was proclaimed in Florence Cathedral the following day.

Certainly aware of the problems in persuading his people to accept the controversial union, John did not return to Constantinople until the following February, where only his respected mother could dare give him the news that his beloved wife, Maria, had died six weeks earlier. The emotional blow is often taken to explain John's failure to pursue actively the official implementation of union at home. But John also faced bitter opposition from clerical and popular circles that made him temporize. At the same time, he had to deal with more squabbling among his younger brothers, and even an outright attack upon him by one of them, Demetrios (1422), who played upon anti-unionist sentiments. Above all, John's hopes for serious western aid which had been promised to Byzantium as the reward for union, were dashed when a formidable crusade army was crushed by the Turks at Varna (10 November 1444), and a supplemental effort under John

Hunyadi of Hungary was smashed soon after (17 October 1448). Worn out and disillusioned, John died on 31 October 1448, not yet 56. The vindictive clergy denied him proper funerary rites at his interment. Childless, he was followed on the throne by his favourite brother, Constantine, who was left to face Byzantium's terminal disaster at the fall of Constantinople (1453).

Though there are suggestions of early intellectual interests, John was neither brilliant in intellect nor clever in statesmanship. Less noble and sophisticated than his father, he was nevertheless earnest and dutiful, perhaps eventually tragic. At a time when "Hellenic" identity was caught between the faded "Roman" tradition of Byzantium and the beleaguered spiritual integrity of Orthodoxy, he tried dutifully if imprudently to serve each and reconcile both. Of slight stature and eventually somewhat crippled, John was highly sensitive to ceremonial and to the prerogatives of his rank. While not handsome, he bore himself well and made a strong impression, as suggested in surviving artistic representations of him, including Byzantine family portraits and, especially, western characterizations. Like his father during the latter's own European journey, John captured the fascination of western artists, who either portrayed him directly (Pisanello, Filarete) or took him as an idealized model for biblical, Roman, or eastern sovereign types (Benozzo Gozzoli, Piero della Francesca).

JOHN W. BARKER

See also Palaiologos Family

Biography

Born in 1392 the eldest son of emperor Manuel II, John was crowned co-emperor with his father in 1421. John had some military success in the Peloponnese but in 1423 Thessalonica was transferred to Venice and in 1430 it fell to the Turks. A keen advocate of church union with Rome, John led the Byzantine delegation to the Council of Ferrara-Florence in 1438–39. The reward for union was to be military aid but the crusading army was defeated by the Turks at Varna in 1444. John died at Constantinople in 1448.

Further Reading

Barker, John W., *Manuel II Palaeologus: A Study in Late Byzantine Statesmanship*, New Brunswick, New Jersey: Rutgers University Press, 1969
Gill, Joseph, *The Council of Florence*, Cambridge: Cambridge University Press, 1959
Gill, Joseph, "John VIII Palaeologus: A Character Study" in his *Personalities of the Council of Florence, and Other Essays*, New York: Barnes and Noble, and Oxford, Blackwell, 1964
Marinesco, Constantin, "Deux Empereurs byzantins: Manuel II et Jean VIII Paléologue, vus par des artistes occidentaux", *Le Flambeau*, 40 (November–December 1957): pp. 759–62
Nicol, Donald M., *The Last Centuries of Byzantium, 1261–1453*, 2nd edition, Cambridge and New York: Cambridge University Press, 1993
Vasiliev, A.A., "Pero Tafur, a Spanish Traveler of the Fifteenth Century, and his Visit to Constantinople, Trebizond, and Italy", *Byzantion*, 7 (1932): pp. 75–122
Walter, C., "A Problem Picture of the Emperor John VIII and the Patriarch Joseph", *Byzantinische Forschungen*, 10 (1985): pp. 295–302
Zakythinos, Denis A., *Le Despotat grec de Morée*, revised by Chryssa Maltézou, 2 vols, London: Variorum, 1975

John Chrysostom, St *c.347–407*
Archbishop of Constantinople

John was the most renowned preacher in the history of the Greek Orthodox Church – hence his posthumous epithet, Chrysostom ("golden mouth"). He was also the most prolific writer among the early Church Fathers, filling 18 volumes of Migne's *Patrologia Graeca*. His approach to exegesis, learned under Diodorus of Tarsus, followed the literalist Antiochene school rather than the allegorical interpretations of Origen and the Alexandrian scholars.

His career in the Church – in Antioch until 398, then as archbishop of Constantinople – was honed by a decade of desert asceticism (c.370–80). Most of John's extant homilies, more than 700, date from his Antioch period. His sermons include the well-known series *On the Statues*, delivered in 387 to calm the fears of the Antiochenes who had destroyed the statues of emperor Theodosius I and his beloved wife during a riot. During this time he also produced significant treatises: in defence of monasticism, *On Virginity*, and his patristic masterpiece *De Sacerdotio*, on the dignity of the priesthood.

In 398 Chrysostom's oratorical reputation made him the choice to succeed Nectarius as archbishop of Constantinople. One of his first acts was to sell Nectarius' rich furnishings, using the revenues to set up hospitals and charities for the poor. As in Antioch, his sermons made him popular among his congregations. But his episcopacy was tragic. In his desire to reform the morals of the capital, he made an enemy of empress Eudoxia, whose lavish lifestyle he castigated from the pulpit. Again, observing the worldliness and laxity of his own clergy, he began a programme of unwelcome reform. Among other things, they were no longer permitted to reside with lay sisters (*subintroductae*) in spiritual, unmarried, and celibate intimacy.

In 401, during a three-month tour of the churches of Asia Minor, John presided over the election of a new bishop of Ephesus and removed six bishops for simony. His actions, however, were of questionable validity in the eyes of his episcopal victims – now enemies – since Heraclea, not Constantinople, was still the seat of the metropolitan of Asia Minor. The door was open to accusations of impropriety against John himself.

When John returned to Constantinople, his relationship with the empress had changed. A tactless reference in a sermon to Eudoxia as Jezebel had proved his undoing. In 403 an occasion for ruining him presented itself: he had sheltered four Egyptian monks exiled for Origenism, and so now he himself underwent trial for alleged Origenist leanings. Urged on by Eudoxia, bishop Theophilus of Alexandria convened the court at Chalcedon (Synod of the Oak), outside John's jurisdiction. The most serious of the charges was his comparing the empress to Jezebel, which was twisted into a charge of inciting the populace to rebellion. John was deposed and sentenced to lifelong exile. However, intimidated by threats of a popular uprising and frightened by an earthquake in the city, Eudoxia urged her husband Arcadius to revoke his sentence. But his triumphal return was temporary: the friendship of Eudoxia did not last.

Later in 403, a monument to Eudoxia was erected near the old Hagia Sophia cathedral. Its boisterous dedication lasted days and disrupted church services. When John called upon the

St John Chrysostom, whose many surviving works have ensured that he is as highly regarded by the western Church as by the eastern

city prefect to disperse the crowds, Eudoxia took it as a personal affront. On the feast of the beheading of John the Baptist, John is reported to have made yet another rash comparison: "Again Herodias dances; again she seeks the head of John." This time John's enemies had a new weapon: two canons of a council of Antioch (341) stating that a deposed bishop reinstated by a secular government should be permanently unseated.

On Holy Saturday in 404 John defied an imperial order of house arrest to baptize personally some 3,000 catechumens he had instructed that year. During the solemn service imperial troops dragged the half-dressed catechumens from the cathedral, injuring many. The capital was as if in a state of siege during Easter week. John's supporters, the Joannites, were imprisoned and tortured. In June John was carried away by boat to exile in Asia, and soon afterwards Hagia Sophia and the neighbouring buildings were destroyed by fire, inaugurating new persecutions of suspected Joannites. John wrote letters to Arcadius' brother Honorius, who was ruling in Ravenna, and to pope Innocent I, and both wrote futile appeals to Arcadius.

John's place of exile was Cucusus in southeastern Turkey, "the most abandoned spot in the world". We have his own report of the difficult journey in his numerous extant letters, all belonging to his period of exile. Chronic fever often nearly finished him, and bandits were a constant threat. When he finally arrived in Cucusus, he found the bishop willing to serve him. Old friends from Antioch visited him, and he corresponded vigorously with them, with supporters in the capital, and with several bishops. His letters dealt with matters of disci-

pline and addressed Arianism and the practices of Jewish converts to Christianity who were still attending synagogue. Meanwhile, he cared for the poor in the region and, in short, performed nearly all of his former episcopal functions. Among the hundred-or-so recipients of his 240 letters, his intimate friend, the deaconess Olympias, received 17, in which John poured forth his deepest self.

Even after the death of Eudoxia in 406, John's enemies sought to harass him to death. Arcadius ordered him moved by forced march to Pityus on the northeastern shore of the Black Sea. On the way, on 14 September 407, John died; he was only 60. In 438 his body was moved to the church of the Holy Apostles in Constantinople by Theodosius II and his sister Pulcheria. Theodoret is the source that this Theodosius, son of Eudoxia, prayed over the body of John Chrysostom to intercede for the sins of his parents. John's biography had already been written by a contemporary, Palladius, and by historians of the 5th century, who first used the surname Chrysostom and exalted his character and life's work.

John's lasting influence over doctrine is subtle. His homilies took a common-sense literal approach to biblical texts and from them drew lessons for practical life and morality. He believed overly in free will; but, he urged, when man freely chooses the good, God provides the grace to carry his intentions through. The relative lack of interest of the Orthodox Church in the issue of grace may therefore be attributed to John.

He taught that Christ was both divine and human, son of Mary perpetually virgin. He was a powerful advocate of the Real Presence in the Eucharist. In his Homily 24 on 1 Corinthians ("The wise men adored Christ in the manger; we see him not in the manger, but on the altar"), John is often credited as a distant source for the Melismos Eucharistic service in which the celebrant cuts the eucharistic bread through a cloth image of the infant Jesus placed over it, visually identifying the child as changing into the crucified victim. The liturgy associated with his name is still in use in the Greek and Russian Churches. Finally, though he seems not to have acknowledged the primacy of Rome, John Chrysostom stood for the moral authority of altar over throne.

DANIEL C. SCAVONE

Biography

Born in Antioch *c.*347, John was a pupil of Libanius and Diodorus of Tarsus. He became a monk and spent a decade as a desert ascetic. Returning to Antioch in 380, he was ordained a deacon and a priest and gained a reputation as a preacher. Some 700 of his sermons survive. In 398 he was chosen to be archbishop of Constantinople. After differences with the empress he was deposed in 403, briefly recalled, and banished in 404. He died in exile in 407. He is the patron saint of preachers.

Writings

In *Patrologia Graeca*, edited by J.-P. Migne, vols 47–64 (no collection of John's entire writings in English translation exists)

Further Reading

Attwater, Donald, *St. John Chrysostom: The Voice of Gold*, Milwaukee: Bruce, 1939
Baur, Chrysostomus, *John Chrysostom and his Time*, translated by M. Gonzaga, 2 vols, Westminster, Maryland: Newman Press, 1959–60

Burger, Douglas, *A Complete Bibliography of the Scholarship on the Life and Works of St. John Chrysostom*, Evanston, Illinois, 1964

Clark, Elizabeth A., *Jerome, Chrysostom, and Friends: Essays and Translations*, New York: Mellen, 1979

Frend, W.H.C., *The Rise of Christianity*, Philadelphia: Fortress Press, and London: Darton, Longman and Todd, 1984

Gibbon, Edward, *The History of the Decline and Fall of the Roman Empire*, 6 vols, 1761–88; edited by J.B. Bury, 7 vols, London: Methuen, 1926–29, chapter 23

Meyer, Robert T. (translator and editor), *Dialogue on the Life of St. John Chrysostom*, New York: Newman Press, 1985

Paverd, Frans van de, *St. John Chrysostom, The Homilies on the Statues: An Introduction*, Rome: Pontificum Institutum Studiorum Orientalium, 1991

Quasten, Johannes, *Patrologia*, vol. 3: *The Golden Age of Patristic Literature*, Utrecht: Spectrum, and Westminster, Maryland: Newman Press, 1950–60,

Stephens, W.R.W., *St. John Chrysostom, His Life and Times: A Sketch of the Church and Empire in the Fourth Century*, London: John Murray, 1872; 3rd edition 1883 (extremely thorough and once considered the most satisfactory biography of John)

Wilken, Robert L., *John Chrysostom and the Jews: Rhetoric and Reality in the Late Fourth Century*, Berkeley: University of California Press, 1983

John of Damascus, St

Monk and theologian of the 7th/8th centuries

There is no clear evidence for the date of John Damascene's birth: estimates range from 650 to 675. He was born in Damascus, to a family that had retained its commanding role in the fiscal administration of the area throughout the political changes of the 7th century. John seems to have succeeded his father, and served under the Umayyad caliph in Damascus. In preparation for this, he received a good Classical education, as is evident from his writings. At some stage, perhaps in the second decade of the 8th century, he left the administrative service and became a monk in the vicinity of Jerusalem, by tradition (only late-attested) at the monastery of Mar Saba, the "Great Lavra". There he devoted himself to his monastic vocation, attained some fame as a preacher, and composed many literary works, both works of theology and liturgical compositions. He died sometime before 754. John is ranked as one of the four great hymnographers of the Orthodox Church.

His importance for the Hellenic tradition lies in his being the greatest representative of the process in which the Byzantine Christian identity was formed. This is at first sight surprising, for John was never a Byzantine subject, and apparently never set foot on territory ruled by the Byzantine emperor (the account in the late *Life* of his visit to Constantinople is certainly legendary). With the collapse of Byzantine rule in the eastern provinces, including Palestine, in the 7th century before the Arab advance, Christians who had supported the Christian orthodoxy of the emperors and the Councils found themselves in a situation, deprived of political support, where many of their neighbours rejected their interpretation of Christianity, or even Christianity at all. So for most of the 7th century they had to define and defend their understanding of orthodoxy against the heresies of Monophysitism and Nestorianism, popular in the east, against Jews and Samaritans, against what the monks

of Palestine in particular regarded as the new imperial heresies of Monenergism and Monothelitism, and eventually against triumphant Islam. This led to a good deal of polemical literature, and attention to matters of logic and the definition of the quite complex terms in which Christological orthodoxy had come to be expressed, as well as to patristic support for their position, for the orthodox had now to convince by the force of their arguments, no longer being able to rely on the secular arm. Hitherto conciliar orthodoxy had had many supporters in Palestine, especially among the monks: it was these whom John joined. John's works thus reflect the fruits of nearly a century of reflection on the nature of orthodoxy, refined in the crucible of political defeat.

John's principal prose work is his *Fount of Knowledge*, which in its final form probably belongs to the last decade of his life, though it is clearly the work of several decades' labour. It is in three parts: *Dialectica*, *On Heresies*, and *On the Orthodox Faith*. The first part is a fruit of the concern for cogent argument, and consists of definitions of logical and metaphysical terms, drawn mostly from 6th-century Alexandrian logical commentaries. The second part, consisting of 100 chapters, reproduces an epitome of Epiphanius of Salamis's *Panarion*, followed by chapters on later heresies drawn from other sources, closing with an account, composed by John himself, on the latest heresy, as he saw it – Islam. The third part, also consisting of 100 chapters, contains brief statements of the fundamental doctrines of the Christian faith (including a long section on the constitution of the human person), drawn almost entirely from the writings of the Fathers. The whole work is, in fact, a huge anthology, compiled by John in accordance with a tradition that can already be traced in the 7th century in, for instance, the works of St Maximos the Confessor. Modern theologians are generally rather rude about John's lack of originality, but John did not, any more than any other Byzantine, seek originality, but truth, a truth he found in the tradition of the Fathers. In his *On the Orthodox Faith* he sought to lay bare the theological synthesis, or theological vision, that his immediate predecessors, not least St Maximos, had discerned in the Fathers. A measure of his success is the popularity of this work from the 9th century onwards: it was translated into Arabic and Old Slavonic by the 10th century, into Georgian by the 11th, into Armenian by the 13th, and into Latin twice in the 12th century, with a revised translation by Robert Grosseteste in the 13th. This Latin translation was Thomas Aquinas's principal recourse for knowledge of the Greek patristic tradition.

A further measure of John's unerring grasp of what the theological vision of Orthodoxy entailed can be seen in his prompt and comprehensive response to the iconoclast policies of the emperor Leo III. By the early 730s he had composed two treatises in defence of the veneration of icons, both flanked by extensive patristic florilegia, and only a little later composed a third, more systematic, treatise, supported by a huge patristic florilegium. These treatises, written with the freedom of one beyond the political reach of the Byzantine emperor, contain perhaps the most broadly based theological defence of the veneration of icons ever written, in which a theology of the image or icon is set out, which reaches from the inner life of the Trinity, through the creation of humans in the image of

God, to the essential role played by the image in human understanding, the critical distinction between worship (*latreia*) and veneration (*proskynesis*), and the fundamental role played by matter in the Christian vision of reality affirmed. For his pains, John was anathematized at the iconoclast council of 754, but acclaimed at the Seventh Ecumenical Council in 787.

It is not clear how much of the considerable amount of liturgical poetry ascribed to John is really his, but his most famous poem, the Easter Canon, is generally acknowledged as genuine, and it is likely that several of the canons that survive under his name for the other great feasts are genuine, too. If this is so, then John would appear to be in himself a complete representative of what Byzantine Orthodoxy inherited from Palestine after the final repudiation of iconoclasm in 843. For it was not simply the theological vision that 9th-century Byzantium received from Palestine, but the whole development of the monastic office as well, which was eventually to replace the cathedral office in the church of Hagia Sophia and wherever Christianity was embraced in its Byzantine form.

ANDREW LOUTH

See also Iconoclasm

Biography

Born in the second half of the 7th century in Damascus, John received a good education and followed his father into the administrative service of the Umayyad caliphate. Later he became a monk near Jerusalem, perhaps at the monastery of Mar Saba, where he devoted himself to preaching and writing. He played a major role in the definition of Byzantine Orthodoxy and is one of the great hymnographers of the Church. He died *c*.750.

Writings

In *Patrologia Graeca*, edited by J.-P. Migne, vols. 94–96
The Fount of Knowledge, translated by Frederic H. Chase, Washington, DC: Catholic University of America Press, 1958
Homelies sur la Nativité et la Dormition, edited and translated by Pierre Voulet, Paris: Cerf, 1961 (Sources Chrétiennes 80)
Die Schriften, edited by Bonifatius Kotter, 5 vols, Berlin: de Gruyter, 1969–88
On the Divine Images, translated by David Anderson, Crestwood, New York: St Vladimir's Seminary Press, 1980 (unreliable)
Philosophische Kapitel, edited by Gerhard Richter, Stuttgart: Hiersemann, 1982 (German translation of *Dialectica*)
Ecrits sur l'Islam, edited by Raymond de Coz, Paris: Cerf, 1992 (Sources Chrétiennes 383)

Further Reading

Rozemond, Keetje, *La Christologie de Saint Jean Damascène*, Ettal: Buch-Kunstverlag, 1959
Sahas, Daniel J., *John of Damascus on Islam: The "Heresy of the Ishmaelites"*, Leiden: Brill, 1972

John Klimakos, St *c*.575–*c*.649

Theologian

John, who now takes his name from his most famous work (*The Ladder of Divine Ascent*), is one of the most important witnesses of the tradition of the Christian desert ascetics. He lived most of his life at St Catherine's, Sinai, and composed perhaps the most influential work of all eastern monastic literature.

He was born sometime around 575 and at the age of 16, *c*.591, he came to Sinai, from an unknown origin, and attached himself to Abba Martyrius, as his neophyte. Daniel of Raithu, his roughly contemporaneous hagiographer, is somewhat obscure about the precise sequence of events; but Abba Martyrius died when John was about 20 years of age, in 595. At this time John must have made his monastic "profession", that is, emerged from his master's cell, no longer a neophyte. Daniel suggests that at this time John went out from Sinai to practise the solitary life, retiring to the Thola region of the desert. He took a cell about 8 km from the main church and here (apart from some journeys to a monastic complex near Alexandria which he speaks of) he lived for 40 years. It was a place of absolute quietude and awesome withdrawal, still pointed out to visitors to Sinai today.

His writings tell of his progress in the monastic life, through what he describes as "standard" stages: his initial tears, his false elations caused by demonic influence, his hatred and disgust for his cell and a desire to flee from the monastic life, his spiritual confirmation in his vocation through perseverance, his beginning of a ministry to others (monks and laity), and finally his acquisition of the gift of "unceasing prayer", and his converse with angels.

After he had pursued the ascetic struggle for many decades, his fame attracted disciples. As more and more began to seek out his cell for spiritual wisdom, the inevitable grumbling began. Monks began to say that he was too garrulous. He silenced criticism by refusing to speak to anyone at all for an entire year, until the community at Sinai finally complained that they had been unfairly deprived of his instruction. It was probably shortly after his year of silence that he was elected as the new superior of the Sinai community, and would have returned to the cenobitic mother-house around 635.

In his final years at Sinai Higumen John of the neighbouring Raithu monastery asked him to compile the work for which he became famous: *The Ladder of Divine Ascent*. It gives practical guidance on the stages of the monastic life and ascetical progress, and probably represents the synoptic form of the numerous spiritual discourses that John had given over the course of a long life. Many parts, therefore, are highly traditional. John's importance lies not so much in his innovative skills, but in his synthesis of an old tradition — a desert master writing in the twilight time, for Arab invasions would soon change the face of Christian Egypt for ever.

After several years as a teacher and leader, John died around 649, according to one tradition appointing his own blood-brother George to be the next abbot, though prophesying that he would rule less than a year. His feast day in the Christian calendar is 30 March and he is also commemorated in the Eastern Church on the Fourth Sunday of Great Lent.

John's book is arranged in 30 sections, the supposed steps of a ladder. The first 23 explain the vices that are dangerous for ascetics; and sections 24–30 interpret the virtues that ought to define a monk. The collation of traditional materials is loosely organized in the work, and some commentators have tried too hard to discern a tight internal structure. Nevertheless, there is a clear sense of breaking with base passions and of ascending to the stages where the disciple can enjoy close spiritual union with God. In placing Love as the highest step in the ascent, John of Sinai was intending to correct the highly intellectual tradition of Evagrius which had enjoyed a strong vogue in earlier periods of Christian desert spirituality. John sees the monastic ideal as the arrival at *hesychia*, or inner and outer quietness. The *logismoi*, the teeming thoughts that arise in a human mind and heart, need to be identified and exposed without guile or resistance. This ascesis is the necessary prerequisite for advancing to the desired state of continuous prayer. To enable the monk to recognize the spirits of wickedness clearly and arrive at self-awareness in the quest for God, John sets out numerous aphoristic definitions. These have the character of much-circulated common monastic wisdom.

John's spiritual tradition simplified (thereby making its dissemination widely successful) the spirituality of the Gaza school, that of Barsanuphius, and Dorotheus his disciple, and was to go on to be the root and foundation of Athonite monasticism and influence the Orthodox East to the present day. The work teaches that the simplification of nature (its quieting down into spiritual hesychasm), which the monk required to advance his prayer, would be assisted by the constant repetition of a sentence concentrating the mind (for example on the name of Jesus, and his saving power): so-called monologistic prayer. The great Christian tradition of the Jesus prayer grew out of this.

Of the book's 30 steps, no fewer than 16 are concerned with the highly practical matters of how a monk ought to proceed when struggling with passions. This is a very sober text that is not interested in esoteric mysticism. Its understanding of ascesis is based on faithful prayer, quiet and enduring discipleship. Its genius lies in the synthesis it makes of many disparate earlier traditions, not least the resolution it effects between the potentially tense relation of eremitical and cenobitic monastic lifestyles, which it sees as intimately related, thus setting an important precedent for the whole of later eastern Christian monasticism. The work also clearly emanates from an author who has had long and magisterial personal experience. The style is highly pragmatic. He frequently uses the term: "I have seen". This appeal to experience, especially when he sets it against common a priori expectations among inexperienced monastics, was one of the reasons that made the book so highly prized among active Christian ascetics both in antiquity and today. It is still prescribed reading in the refectories of Orthodox monasteries in the time of Great Lent.

John also wrote an *Address to the Shepherd*, a small work that lays out the duties of a monastic superior. It takes its lead from Gregory of Nazianzus' highly influential treatise on the priesthood (which in turn had influenced John Chrysostom and the *Regula Pastoralis* of Gregory the Great).

JOHN A. McGUCKIN

Biography

Born *c*.575, John Klimakos (John of the Ladder), also known as Scholastikos or of Sinai, became a monk at the age of 16 on Mount Sinai. For 40 years he lived in the desert as an anchorite and gathered many disciples around him. He returned to the Sinai monastery as abbot *c*.635 where he wrote his best-known work, the *Ladder of Divine Ascent*. He died *c*.649.

Writings

The Ladder of Divine Ascent, translated by Lazarus Moore *et al.*, London: Faber, and New York: Harper, 1959; revised edition Boston: Holy Transfiguration Monastery, 1978, reprinted 1991 (also contains selected letters and the treatise *To the Shepherd*)

The Ladder of Divine Ascent, translated by Colm Luibheid and Norman Russell, London: SPCK, and New York: Paulist Press, 1982

Further Reading

Chitty, Derwas J., *The Desert a City: An Introduction to the Study of Egyptian and Palestinian Monasticism under the Christian Empire*, Oxford: Blackwell, and Crestwood, New York: St Vladimir's Seminary Press, 1966

Couilleau, G., Jean Climaque entry in *Dictionnaire de spiritualité*, edited by Marcel Villar *et al.*, vol. 8, Paris: Beauchesne, 1974, columns 369–89

Hausherr, I., "La Théologie du monachisme chez saint Jean Climaque" in *Théologie de la vie monastique*, Paris: Aubier, 1961

Nau, F., "S. Jean Climaque", *Revue de l'Institut Catholique de Paris*, 7 (1902): pp. 35–37

Nau, F., "Le Texte grec des récits du moine Anastase sur les pères du Sinai", part 1, *Oriens Christianus*, 2 (1902): pp. 58–59 ; part 2, *Oriens Christianus*, 3 (1903): pp. 56–90

Petit, L., S. Jean Climaque entry in *Dictionnaire de Théologie Catholique*, edited by A. Vacant and E. Mangenot, vol. 8, part 1, Paris: Letouzey & Ané, 1924, columns 690–93

Saudrau, A., "La Doctrine spirituelle de S. Jean Climaque", *Vie Spirituelle*, 9 (1924): pp. 352–70

Volker, Walther, *Scala Paradisi: Eine Studie zu Johannes Climacus und zugleich eine Vorstudie zu Symeon dem Neuen Theologen*, Wiesbaden: Steiner, 1968

Yannaras, C., "Eros divin et Eros humain selon S. Jean Climaque", *Contacts*, 21 (1969): pp. 190–204

Joseph the Hymnographer, St

Poet and hymnographer of the 9th century

One of Byzantium's most prolific authors of liturgical poetry, St Joseph the Hymnographer contributed significantly to the cycles of proper hymnodic texts that dominate the modern Byzantine offices. The earliest account of Joseph's life is the late 9th- or early 10th-century *Life* by the monk Theophanes, from which we learn that he was born in Sicily (probably Palermo) between 812 and 818. In or around the year 830 he fled the Arab invasion of his native island with his family. At the age of 15 Joseph left his family in the Peloponnese to continue his studies in Thessalonica, where he entered the monastery of Latomos (known today as Hosios David, but originally dedicated to Christ). Rapid growth in his knowledge and spirituality was followed by his presentation to the city's archbishop for ordination before the canonical age of 30. In Thessalonica Joseph also came into contact with St Gregory the Decapolite, who obtained the permission of his abbot to bring Joseph to Constantinople.

After settling with his new master in the iconophile community of St Antipas, Joseph was sent in 841 by Gregory on a mission to enlist the aid of Pope Gregory IV against the iconoclasts. Captured on the way by pirates and imprisoned on the island of Crete, he was ransomed after the death of the emperor Theophilos in January 842. Theophanes reports that

Joseph miraculously received foreknowledge of his release from St Nicholas, who showed him a book from which he chanted a prayer for deliverance. Upon returning, possibly by way of Thessalonica, to the community of St Antipas in Constantinople, Joseph found that Gregory had recently died. He therefore resumed the monastic life under the direction of John the Ascetic, another follower of the Decapolite. After the latter's death, located by Stiernon around the year 850, Joseph resided for approximately the next five years near a shrine to St John Chrysostom, where he acquired a number of disciples. He then founded a monastery dedicated to St Bartholomew, to which he also translated the bodies of his teachers Gregory and John.

According to Theophanes, Joseph's career as a hymnographer began only after the foundation of his monastery. The story of St Nicholas's appearance and Joseph's authorship of hymns to Cretan saints, however, have led modern scholars to suggest that he began to write soon after his release from captivity. In any case, his productivity probably declined as his friendship with Patriarch Ignatios increasingly involved him in ecclesiastical politics. The deposition of his patron in 858 resulted in Joseph's exile to Cherson until the restoration of Ignatios by Basil I in 867, whereafter he was named *skevophylax* (sacristan) of Hagia Sophia. The eventual reconciliation of Ignatios with his rival Photios allowed Joseph to establish good relations with the latter, who came to hold him in high regard and recommended him as a spiritual father to his clergy. His continuing closeness to the patriarchate is emphasized by Theophanes, who relates how Joseph made a final visit to the patriarchal palace after foreseeing his own death in 886. He died on 3 April, which is observed as his feast day by the Orthodox Church.

The importance of Joseph's contribution to the corpus of Byzantine hymnography is represented in John the Deacon's expanded 11th-century version of his *Life* by the attribution of more than 1000 canons. A more precise assessment is complicated by the difficulty of distinguishing his works from those of Joseph of Thessalonica, the brother of St Theodore of Stoudios. From the preliminary total of 466 pieces assigned to him by E. Tomadakes, it appears that Joseph wrote a vast number of canons while making only minor additions – e.g. 13 *stichera* and nine short kontakia (psalm refrains) – to other repertories. Because his hymns were set to preexisting melodies, Joseph has been honoured as a hymnographer rather than as a *melodos*, a title reserved for poets such as his contemporary Kassia who composed their own melodies.

The work of earlier Sabaïte and Stoudite poets had not left sets of hymnodic propers for every day of the calendar year, and many of Joseph's canons served to fill these gaps in the liturgical cycles of the Palestinian monastic rite. These hymns include poems for the saints of the Byzantine calendar, the commemorations between the eight Sundays of the resurrectional Octoechos, and the movable seasons of Lent and Easter. Although some remain unpublished, a great number of Joseph's canons were included in the liturgical books of the Orthodox Church. Perhaps the most notable of these is the one he wrote to frame the annual Lenten performance of the beloved anonymous (probably 6th-century) *Akathistos* Hymn to the Mother of God. Consisting of 32 stanzas united by an iambic acrostic announcing his authorship, Joseph's hymn is based metrically and melodically on the second canon for the Dormition of the Mother of God (15 August) by John of Damascus. Seven of the Damascene's eight model stanzas are re-used by Joseph with only cosmetic changes to their texts, while the model stanza for the fourth ode is taken from another canon in the same mode. Yet the main inspiration for his text is the *Akathistos* itself, which Joseph uses as a treasury of images for his own song of praise. More densely packed with specific biblical references than the ancient kontakion, Joseph's canon also includes topical references to the Mother of God's role as protectress of Constantinople.

Canonized shortly after his death, Joseph has remained popular as a poet and intercessor. As noted above, his *Life* was expanded in the 11th century, during which John Mavropous also wrote two canons in his honour. A book of rubrics from the same century listing the order of precedence observed in the event of multiple canons for a single saint places the works of Joseph first, followed in descending order of preference by the hymns of Theophanes Graptos, John of Damascus, and Kosmas of Maïouma. Later praised in writing by such late Byzantine authors as Theodore Pediasimos and Nikephoros Kallistos Xanthopoulos, Joseph was also depicted iconographically in the churches of Lagoudera and St Saviour in Chora.

ALEXANDER LINGAS

See also Hymnography, Music

Biography
Born in Palermo between 812 and 818, Joseph and his parents fled from the Arab invasion of Sicily *c*.830. They settled in the Peloponnese; but Joseph went to Thessalonica where he became a monk and then moved to Constantinople where he founded a monastery. As a composer of canons he made an important contribution to Byzantine hymnography. He died in Constantinople *c*.886.

Further Reading
Conomos, Dimitri E., *Byzantine Hymnography and Byzantine Chant*, Brookline, Massachusetts: Hellenic College Press, 1984

Mother Mary and Kallistos Ware (translators), *The Lenten Triodion*, London and Boston: Faber, 1978

Stiernon, Daniel, Joseph L'Hymnographe entry in *Dictionnaire de spiritualité*, vol. 8, Paris: Beauchesne, 1974, columns 1349–54

Tomadakes, Eutychios, *Ioseph ho Hymnographos: Bios kai ergon* [Joseph the Hymnographer: Life and Work], Athens, 1971

Topping, Eva C., "St. Joseph the Hymnographer and St. Mariamne Isapostolos" in her *Sacred Songs: Studies in Byzantine Hymnography*, Minneapolis: Light and Life, 1997

Wellesz, Egon, *A History of Byzantine Music and Hymnography*, 2nd edition, Oxford: Clarendon Press, 1961

Josephus, Flavius AD 37–after AD 93
Jewish historian

Flavius Josephus was an important figure in the Jewish community at the time of the disastrous Jewish rebellion of AD 66–67. Captured by the Romans while commanding part of the revolutionary forces, he was released and treated with honour for the rest of his life after correctly prophesying that Vespasian would become emperor. He then wrote, in Aramaic, a history of the revolt as a warning for Jews in the diaspora. This work, entitled *History of the Jewish War against the Romans*, is lost in the original Aramaic version, but the author later rewrote it in Greek with some help from unnamed Greek assistants, and it became his most influential work and for many centuries the definitive history of the revolt. Josephus then went on to write, this time in Greek, a massive history of Judaism from its origins to his times, entitled *Jewish Antiquities*. This work inevitably covers much of the same ground as the Old Testament, on several versions of which it is largely based, but it also makes use of other traditional Jewish writings and presents the events in a manner influenced by the tradition of Greek historiography. The work also goes substantially beyond the period covered by the Old Testament and in fact overlaps with material covered by the *Jewish War*. In addition, Josephus produced two minor works, an autobiography and a polemic in defence of Judaism known as *Against Apion*.

Josephus' style is not entirely consistent: on the whole his works display a good mastery of the Atticizing Greek used for literary purposes in his day, but occasional semiticisms can also be found. It is unclear how much of Josephus' style is his own and how much is due to the helpers he admits to having employed in rewriting the *Jewish War*, and on whom he may have relied for his other works as well. He tells us that he worked hard to overcome his difficulties with the Greek language and to give himself a solid grounding in Greek literature, but the extent of his acquaintance with the Hellenic tradition has been questioned. The influence of Greek authors such as Thucydides and Polybius can certainly be found in his works, as can a conscious determination to present his story to the educated Greek-speaking world in a manner consistent with, and attractive according to, the rules of the Greek literary tradition. Nevertheless there is reason to believe that the primary influence on Josephus was really the Jewish tradition in which he had been educated.

Despite the occasional infelicity, Josephus' works were praised as stylistic models in the Byzantine period (e.g. by Photios in the 9th century and Theodore Metochites in the 14th century), especially for the vividness and immediacy of his historical narration. They were also imitated by authors such as Niketas Choniates (12th–13th century).

Josephus' main importance for the Greek world, however, is to be found in religious rather than literary history. Thanks to the sanction of Christians such as Origen and Eusebius of Caesarea, in the medieval period Josephus' works became one of the most important historical sources for ancient Palestine. They were copied, epitomized, and excerpted freely and were translated into all the major languages of the medieval Mediterranean. From the 3rd century AD onward Christians saw the *Jewish War* in particular as a sort of continuation of the New Testament, showing the punishment of the Jews for the crucifixion of Christ. Authors such as the chronicler Malalas (6th century), the *Chronicon Paschale* (7th century), and Zonaras (12th century) made use of Josephus, or of works derived from his.

At the end of the Byzantine period Josephus' status as a church historian began to be questioned because of differences between his account of history in the *Jewish Antiquities* and that of the Old Testament, and in the 16th and 17th centuries scholars began to debate the genuineness of a passage known as the "Testimonium Flavianum". This brief section of the *Antiquities* (18. 63–64) mentions Jesus and declares him to have been the Messiah; it seems to have been partly interpolated, perhaps in the 3rd century AD. As this passage was crucial to Josephus' status in the Christian Church (it is probably responsible for the fact that he was the only Jewish historian whose works were entirely preserved by the Byzantines), the debate over its authenticity did considerable damage to his reputation. This debate continued until the 19th century and is to a certain extent still current, though it is no longer crucial to the assessment of Josephus' overall worth as a historian.

For most of the Byzantine period Josephus' works, at least in their Greek form, were essentially the property of the Christian Church and remained basically unknown to the Greek Jewish community. In the 10th century, however, an anonymous historian in southern Italy produced a Hebrew chronicle based primarily on Josephus, and in the 11th century a Judaeo-Arabic version followed. Josephus' works were thus reintroduced to the Jewish community after centuries of use as Christian – and often anti-Semitic – documents.

Josephus remains today an important source of information on Jewish history of the 1st century AD, and his dramatic description of his people's tragic fate is as engrossing to read as ever, but his status as the inspired creator of an almost sacred text has been replaced by that of a fallible and often biased observer. His Greek style is also less highly regarded than it once was, and his current influence on Hellenic culture is minimal.

ELEANOR DICKEY

See also Jews

Biography
Born in AD 37, Josephus was a Jewish priest and a leading figure in Jerusalem at the time of the Jewish rebellion of 66–67. Though captured by the Romans, he was later released and treated well. He wrote in Aramaic a *History of the Jewish War* (of which a Greek version survives) and in Greek a history of Judaism entitled *Jewish Antiquities*. He died after AD 93.

Writings
Works (includes *The Life*, *Against Apion*, *The Jewish War*, *Jewish Antiquities*), translated by H. St J. Thackeray, Ralph Marcus, A.P. Wikgren and L.H. Feldman, 10 vols, London: Heinemann, and New York: Putnam, 1926–81 (Loeb edition)

Further Reading
Bowman, S., "Josephus in Byzantium" in *Josephus, Judaism, and Christianity*, edited by Louis H. Feldman and Gohei Hata, Leiden: Brill, and Detroit: Wayne State University Press, 1987
Rajak, Tessa, *Josephus: The Historian and His Society*, London: Duckworth, 1983; Philadelphia: Fortress Press, 1984

Judicial Procedure

The earliest written Greek laws were believed to be those of Zaleucus of Italian Locri Epizephyrii (c.650 BC). These were noted for their severity, as were the first written laws of Athens, those of Draco (621/20). Solon's laws (594/93) replaced Draco's in all areas except homicide, and the Athenian lawcode was henceforth known as the laws of Solon, regardless of later additions. Under the democracy laws were made in the assembly, and in 410 a revision of the laws was begun. Their inscription on stone led to a distinction between laws (*nomoi*) and decrees (*psephismata*), and from this time decrees of the assembly could not override the written laws, while the framing of new laws was entrusted to groups of "lawmakers" (*nomothetae*).

Athenian laws were essentially procedural rather than substantive. They specified the form of action to be taken against a transgressor without necessarily defining closely the transgression, and sometimes a choice of action was available to the prosecutor. The main categories were public and private actions. In public actions (*dikai demosiai*, but regularly named after the method of initiating the procedure) the offence was thought to affect the whole community, hence in addition to magistrates and officials it was open to "anyone who wishes" (*ho boulomenos*) to raise an action (i.e. any free adult male, except for those who had been disfranchized, and in some cases excluding non-citizens). The fine or penalty in a public action was paid to the state, but rewards were given to those who successfully prosecuted certain actions, especially *apographe* (deposition) and *phasis* (statement). To deter habitual prosecutors (the original use of the term "sycophant"), in most public actions those who initiated but subsequently dropped a case or failed to win at least one-fifth of the jurors' votes had to pay a fine of 1000 drachmas and were debarred from bringing similar actions in future (sycophancy was also an offence, which was prosecuted by *probole* – presentation of a case to the Assembly). Public actions included *graphe*, the regular public action (its name will derive from the fact that originally it was in this kind of action that a written charge was made; by the 4th century BC this had become the norm); *apagoge*, whereby the prosecutor arrested the accused (usually a thief caught in the act or a person caught exercising rights to which he was not entitled) and handed him over to the magistrates (regularly the Eleven); *endeixis*, a similar process to *apagoge*, but where the prosecutor denounced the accused to the magistrates and might then arrest him; *ephegesis*, whereby the prosecutor led the accused to the magistrates and they carried out the arrest; *apographe*, in which the prosecutor listed property allegedly due to the state and being withheld (three-quarters of the property would be given to the successful prosecutor); *phasis*, in which the prosecutor pointed out illegal goods or property (the reward here was one half of the fine imposed or of the confiscated property); *eisangelia*, a denunciation to the council or assembly, which might try the case or refer it to a jury court; *probole*, a denunciation to the assembly, which held a hearing and could, if the prosecutor wished to proceed, send the case to a jury; and cases arising from an official's preliminary examination (*dokimasia*) or his examination after office (*euthynai*).

In private cases (*dikai idiai*, but usually called simply *dikai*) the offence concerned an individual and could only be prosecuted by the person who alleged he had been wronged. If successful, the private prosecutor would be awarded damages or compensation. In *diadikasia* two or more persons disputed a right (especially to an inheritance) or obligation (such as to perform a liturgy) on equal terms. A special form of case was

homicide (*dike phonou*), in which the relatives of the deceased were required to prosecute, but the offence concerned the whole community since killers were polluted. Hence the alleged killer was debarred by a proclamation from sacred and public places, three pre-trial hearings were held instead of the usual one, particularly solemn oaths were sworn, the trial itself was held in the open air in one of the special homicide courts, and the parties were each allowed to make two speeches, again instead of the usual one.

Suits were initiated by the prosecutor submitting his charge to the appropriate magistrate and delivering the summons to the defendant. The eponymous archon presided over cases involving the family and inheritance; the *basileus* (second archon) was in charge of homicide and religious cases; the *polemarchos* (third archon) oversaw cases involving non-citizens; the *thesmothetae* (the six junior archons) managed a wide range of cases in their court, the *eliaia*; the Eleven (police commissioners) were in charge of cases involving theft and similar offences; the generals conducted cases of military offences; and there were some lesser boards of magistrates for specific types of case. In the 4th century most private cases came before the Forty, four judges from each of the ten tribes selected by lot. The magistrate heard statements and evidence at an inquiry (*anakrisis*) and could settle minor cases himself, but otherwise would decide if the case should be sent to trial. In a private suit the accused might object that an incorrect procedure was being employed (*paragraphe*), and this would have to be decided by a separate hearing before the action itself could proceed. A trial in a private case before the Forty might be avoided by resorting to binding arbitration, a procedure that existed from earliest times in many Greek states and became particularly widespread during the Hellenistic period. Private and (in cases involving claims for more than ten drachmas) public arbitrators were used, but their decisions were appellable to the courts.

Trials in the 5th and 4th centuries were conducted in the popular jury courts (*dikasteria*). A panel of 6000 jurors over the age of 30 was selected each year, and Pericles introduced jury pay (two, later three obols per day). The size of the jury varied according to the type of case, but regularly numbered several hundred, and in order to prevent bribery jurors were allocated to the different courts by a lot system which became increasingly complex during the 4th century. The magistrate who had received the charge now presided, but did not act like a modern judge in giving directions or advice. Litigants were expected to represent themselves unless clearly unable to do so, but might call on friends to speak on their behalf (*synegoroi*); women and children were represented by their nearest adult male relative. The prosecutor was followed by the defendant, each making one speech which might have been written for him by a professional speech-writer (*logographos*); in the course of the speech laws and other documents might be read out by the court clerk, when the water-clock which timed the speech was stopped. Witnesses, who tended to act as supporters for the parties rather than as suppliers of information, gave evidence orally until the early 4th century and could only be questioned by the litigant who summoned them, but after this time written evidence was used and witnesses merely acknowledged the text was theirs. The disfranchised, women, and children could not appear as witnesses, and slaves' evidence was only accepted if extracted under torture and by the agreement of both parties (which in practice rarely if ever happened). The jurors had to cast their votes immediately after the speeches, with no summing-up from the magistrate or time to retire for consideration of their verdict. The original system of putting a pebble into one of two urns (one for guilty, one for not guilty) was replaced during the 4th century by a procedure in which each juror had two bronze votes, one of them with a hole to signify guilty, and the votes were cast one into a bronze, "valid" urn, the other into a wooden, "invalid" urn. The verdict was arrived at by a simple majority, with a tie counting as an acquittal (though by the 4th century odd numbers of jurors were used). There was no right of appeal, but the losing party might win compensation from a witness who was proved to have given false evidence, or occasionally have the case reopened. Penalties were either fixed by the law or decided by the jurors, according to the type of suit; in the latter case the two sides made further speeches proposing alternative penalties which the jurors would vote on. Monetary fines were the most common remedy, and other penalties included death, exile, the stocks, full or partial disfranchisement (atimia), and confiscation of property. Unlike in modern penal systems, imprisonment was used sparingly as a punishment.

Athenian law had little or no significance in the development of later legal systems, and reasons for this are not hard to find. The lack of a body of substantive law, in glaring contrast with the extensive Roman system, is the most obvious one, the absence of any doctrine of binding precedent another. But there cannot be precedent when every sitting of every court is the supreme and unaccountable representative of the democracy, and that is the point. The decisions of the dicasts were ephemeral, prone to be swayed by the clever speaker at the expense of truth; but the courts, with their large juries, *were* the people for the litigants appearing before them, and the popular jury system lay at the very heart of the Athenian democracy.

Under Byzantine rule the emperor was the supreme judge, who was empowered to delegate authority to institutions or officials. Government bureaux, called "Sekreta", had some right to condemn and pardon, while other judicial functions were performed by the eparch of the city and the quaestor. The *epi ton deiseon* heard petitions and appeals, and the chief of police (*droungarios tis viglas*) also had judicial duties. The highest court was that of the *velum* or Hippodrome; rarely did the senate act as a court; and bishops' jurisdiction in the ecclesiastical courts might trespass into civil law. In the provinces governors were often called "judge" (*krites*), while local cases might be heard by special magistrates from Constantinople.

MICHAEL J. EDWARDS

See also Law

Further Reading

Bonner, Robert J. and Gertrude Smith, *The Administration of Justice from Homer to Aristotle*, 2 vols, Chicago: University of Chicago Press, 1930–38
Gagarin, Michael, *Drakon and Early Athenian Homicide Law*, New Haven: Yale University Press, 1981
Gagarin, Michael, *Early Greek Law*, Berkeley: University of California Press, 1986
Garner, Richard, *Law and Society in Classical Athens*, London: Croom Helm, and New York: St Martin's Press, 1987
Harrison, A.R.W., *The Law of Athens*, 2 vols, Oxford: Clarendon Press, 1968–71
MacDowell, Douglas M., *The Law in Classical Athens*, London: Thames and Hudson, and Ithaca, New York: Cornell University Press, 1978
Todd, S.C., *The Shape of Athenian Law*, Oxford: Clarendon Press, 1993

Julian the Apostate AD 331/32–363

Last pagan emperor of Rome

Flavius Claudius Julianus, the grandson of the emperor Constantius Chlorus, nephew of Constantine the Great and cousin of Constantius II, was the last ruler of the second Flavian dynasty and also the last Roman emperor to worship the gods of Olympus. In his brief life and even briefer reign, Julian sought to undo the hold that Christianity had acquired over the Roman world in the aftermath of the Edict of Milan in AD 312, which had established official tolerance and quasi-official favour for that religion, and also to renew the traditional religious cults of the Mediterranean basin. In addition, he sought through various reforms to strengthen the empire and counteract some of the failings of the governmental system inaugurated by Diocletian and Constantine from AD 285 on. This project of religious, cultural, and political renewal was cut short by his death in battle during a disastrous campaign against the Persians in Mesopotamia. Since his death, he has continued to exercise a fascination over writers, whether they have been hostile to him, as the Christians of his own and following centuries have been, such as Gregory of Nazianzus, the poet Prudentius, and Augustine, or sympathetic, as not only the pagans of his own and following centuries, but also modern authors from the Renaissance on have been, such as Lorenzo de' Medici, Voltaire, Edward Gibbon, and Gore Vidal.

Julian was born in either AD 331 or 332 to Julius Constantius, the son of Constantius Chlorus, by Flavia Maxima Theodora, daughter of Diocletian's colleague Maximian. Julius Constantius was thus the half-brother of Constantine the Great, who made him consul for the year 335, despite the antipathy of Constantius Chlorus' first wife, and Constantine's mother, Helena. After Constantine's death in 337, however, Julius Constantius was put to death with his eldest son, his brother, his brother's two sons, and four other relatives. It is unclear whether his nephew, Constantius II, ordered the executions. A document allegedly found on Constantine's body excluded Flavia Maxima Theodora's sons and grandsons from power, and the dynastic loyalties of the army were in any case behind Constantius II and his brothers Constans and Constantine II. Julian and his surviving half-brother Gallus were interned first separately and then together. Though Julian was kept in Bithynia away from public scrutiny, he was under the protection of Eusebius, the Arian bishop of Nicomedia. Under the tutelage of Mardonius, a Scythian eunuch who had also taught his mother, Julian learned the elements of the Greek classics that made up the curriculum at that time for all educated men and women, whether pagan or Christian, in the Greek-speaking part of the Roman empire. In later years he was allowed to pursue his studies in Nicomedia, Pergamum, and Ephesus. In 351 Gallus was made Caesar, subordinate under Diocletian's reworking of the governmental structure to the Augustus, or senior emperor, Constantius II, in order to alleviate some of his burdens of rule while the latter dealt with usurpers and uprisings in the west. Both of Constantius' brothers and colleagues had died by this time, victims of political intrigue, so Constantius, in need of a colleague, turned to the older of his only two surviving relatives. Gallus' rule of the east from his headquarters in Antioch became increasingly cruel and irregular, so Constantius removed and executed him in 354, after only three years as Caesar. After a period of time under arrest, Julian was allowed to resume his studies in Athens.

These studies were soon interrupted by a summons to the imperial court at Milan, which resulted in Julian's becoming Caesar in his turn on 6 November 355, and being sent to Gaul, then hard pressed by Germans invading across the Rhine. Though Constantius' dispositions of authority in Gaul seemed designed to leave Julian a mere figurehead who would leave the fighting and governing to others, Julian soon showed aptitudes for both generalship and statecraft remarkable in one who had had no practical experience of either. He took effective control of the Roman armies in Gaul and led them to victories over the Alamannic German invaders, which drove them back across the Rhine and put an end for the time being to their raids. These victories went unacknowledged by Constantius, perhaps partly through the convention of the day that assigned credit to the Augustus for the successes of his Caesar. Julian also encouraged the flourishing of Gaul through resettling and rebuilding cities devastated by the raids of the Alamanni, through reforming tax collection in the lands under his jurisdiction, and through importing grain to make up for shortfalls caused by the depredations of the raiders and by the abandonment of the farmlands by their tillers.

Constantius, perhaps to make up for the loss of six legions in the Persian capture of Amida in August 359, or through concern for his own security caused by Julian's growing prestige, in January 360 send orders to his Caesar to send him his four best legions, plus 300 men each from his other units. The troops, gathered at Julian's winter headquarters at Paris prior to their departure for the emperor's court at Constantinople, were most of them locally recruited and had taken service on the understanding that they would not be called on to cross the Alps. Impelled by this, and perhaps by resentment against Constantius for not acknowledging their victories over the Alamanni, the troops revolted and proclaimed Julian Augustus. It is certainly possible that Julian and his advisers may have induced them to do so, though unclear to what extent. The remainder of that year and much of the next were taken up with fruitless negotiations to settle the situation between Constantius and Julian. When these failed in the face of Constantius' understandable reluctance to surrender power and evident preparations for civil war, Julian began a military campaign against the adherents of Constantius in Italy and the Balkans which was cut short by Constantius' sudden death by illness in November 361.

Julian had hitherto maintained a public persona as a Christian; it was only after his proclamation as Augustus that he openly announced his allegiance to the traditional gods of the Graeco-Roman world. His worship of these gods was shaped by his adherence to the mystery cults of Mithras and of Demeter and Persephone at Eleusis, and by his following of contemporary Neoplatonism, especially of the theurgistic variety practised by Iamblichus and some of his disciples. These tendencies set him apart from the majority of those in the Roman empire who still followed traditional religious practices. Nevertheless, he attempted to undo the work of Constantine in extending tolerance and even favour to Christianity by ending the government subsidies while simultaneously encouraging the maintenance and revival of traditional religious cults. Furthermore, he attempted to sow chaos among Christian congregations by recalling those who had been exiled by Constantius for heresy. A decree forbidding Christians to teach the Greek and Latin classics that made up contemporary education, the indispensable prerequisite to be a gentleman or to pursue a career at the bar or in the civil service, was designed to expose young Christians to pagan propaganda. At the same time he tried to unite pagan cults in a religious hierarchy that could rival the Christian Church by welding them, too, into a centralized organization and especially by imitating Christian philanthropic endeavours to feed the poor. He also sought to reform the imperial court by eliminating many of the servants and functionaries who attended the emperor. In order to strengthen the cities he returned to them the lands and tax revenues to finance their services. In addition, he bolstered the decurions or city councillors, drawn from the local landowning classes and responsible, if need be, for meeting tax assessments and financing city services at their own expense, by cancelling the exemptions from these duties granted to some of these landowners. Plans were also made to reform the tax system as a whole which, however, were not carried out because Julian's reign was cut short.

Julian moved his headquarters to Antioch in the summer of 362 and began to prepare to resume Constantius' war against the Persians by invading their territory. He found himself at odds with the Antiochenes over religious policy, especially after the famous temple of Apollo in the suburb of Daphne was burnt to the ground after he had closed a Christian church in the area. A famine, possibly exacerbated by the concentration of troops in the city for the coming Persian campaign, put the emperor also at odds with the landowning class of Antioch, which he suspected of causing or exploiting the famine for their own gain. Thus, it was possibly with relief that he set out in the spring of 363 on his campaign against the Persians. Though initially successful, he was stymied by a Persian scorched-earth policy and unable to take the Persian capital, Ctesiphon, so he turned his army back towards Roman territory, harried by the Persians on the way. He was mortally wounded in battle, so it was left to his Christian successor Jovian, to extricate the army with a shameful peace that surrendered five Roman provinces to the Persians as the price for the treaty. Rumour persisted in attributing the fatal wound to a Christian Roman, and medieval legend to the supernatural intervention of a saint, though the assailant is unknown and, Roman or Persian, may not have survived the battle.

Julian left three volumes of writings behind, including the fragments of a polemic, *Against the Galileans* [Christians], which have been recovered from a 5th-century rebuttal by Cyril of Alexandria. He also left behind a reputation that was cherished by the dwindling pagans of the Roman empire and execrated by the triumphant Christians. His attempts to discomfit Christianity and promote the traditional cults were of course undone after his death. Indeed the fate of the cause he championed may be summed up in the words (as translated by Algernon Swinburne) that the Delphic Oracle gave his friend Oribasius, who asked on Julian's behalf what could be done to restore the cult of Apollo at Delphi:

> Tell the king, on earth has fallen the glorious dwelling,
> And the water-springs that spake are quenched and dead.
> Not a cell is left the god, no roof, no cover,
> In his hand the prophet laurel flowers no more.

ERIC KYLLO

Biography

Born at Constantinople in AD 331 or 332, Julian was taught in Bithynia by the Arian bishop of Nicomedia and a Scythian eunuch. He later studied in Nicomedia, Pergamum, Ephesus, and Athens. Summoned to Milan by the emperor Constantius II, he was proclaimed Caesar in 355. He won several victories in Gaul and in 361 was acclaimed as Augustus by the army. He sought to restore paganism throughout the empire. He died in battle against the Persians in 363.

Writings

Works, translated by Wilmer Cave Wright, 3 vols, London: Heinemann, and New York: Macmillan, 1913–59 (Loeb edition)

Further Reading

Athanassiadi-Fowden, Polymnia, *Julian and Hellenism: An Intellectual Biography*, Oxford: Clarendon Press, 1981; reprinted London and New York: Routledge, 1992

Bidez, J., *La Vie de l'empereur Julien*, 2nd edition, Paris: Belles Lettres, 1965

Bowersock, G.W., *Julian the Apostate*, Cambridge, Massachusetts: Harvard University Press, and London: Duckworth, 1978

Browning, Robert, *The Emperor Julian*, London: Weidenfeld and Nicolson, 1975; Berkeley: University of California Press, 1976

Gibbon, Edward, *The History of the Decline and Fall of the Roman Empire*, 6 vols, 1761–88; edited by J.B. Bury, 7 vols, London: Methuen, 1926–29, chapter 19

Jones, A.H.M., *The Later Roman Empire, 284–602: A Social, Economic and Administrative Survey*, Oxford: Blackwell, and Norman: University of Oklahoma Press, 1964

Matthews, John, *The Roman Empire of Ammianus*, Baltimore: Johns Hopkins University Press, and London: Duckworth, 1989

Smith, Rowland, *Julian's Gods: Religion and Philosophy in the Thought and Action of Julian the Apostate*, London and New York: Routledge, 1995

Junta 1967–1974

The military coup of 21 April 1967 brought Greece seven years of rule by force, including strict censorship, poll rigging, the banning of political parties and trade unions, involuntary exile, house arrests, imprisonment, and torture. The Colonels' programme for Greece was highly nationalist, irredentist, and Christian, although their efforts ideologically to transform the Greek people never took root. The rule of the military came to a close in July 1974 under its own steam in the midst of growing popular disaffection, a weakening economy, foreign pressures, military mutinies, and a bungled coup on Cyprus. In the intervening years, however, Greece suffered the humiliation of isolation from global affairs and tyrannies at home.

Still a crowned democracy prior to the junta, the Greek state was led by its monarch, who, under the prevailing constitution of 1952, exercised legislative powers. Extremist politics carried their weight, too, as the psychological wounds caused by the internecine and ideological fight of the Civil War (1944–49) had not yet been healed in Greece's political culture. The staunchly rightist leaders of the Junta – colonels George Papadopoulos and Nikolas Makarezos and brigadier Stylianos Pattakos – exploited these phenomena by justifying their actions under the guise of a protectorship against a communist threat, an easy target. A more likely reason for the coup was the predicted electoral victory of Centre Union candidate George Papandreou, who intended to reform the military by purging it of extreme rightists. The colonels eclipsed the May 1967 elections by their swift execution of a NATO manoeuvre, thereby occupying their own country and obliterating political opposition. As the regime scrambled for legitimacy with the monarch, King Constantine attempted his own counter-coup on 13 December 1967, failing miserably and fleeing to Rome. The following year the regime held a referendum on a new constitution. The rigged procedure ensured the constitution's promulgation, which retained the office of the monarch but stripped it of its powers.

As the years passed, the dictatorship reformed its regime by trying to adopt some kind of effective revolutionary government. On 21 March 1972 Papadopoulos was proclaimed regent, merging powers of the head of government with head of state. In 1973 the junta abolished the monarchy by decree, introducing a presidential republic with Papadopoulos as president. He was deposed on 25 November 1973 by a second bloodless coup led by brigadier Demetrios Ioannidis, commander of the military police. Phaedon Gizikis was installed as president with a civilian government. This has been seen as a response to growing civil disobedience, highlighted by the now legendary Polytechnic uprising of 17 November 1973. What began as a peaceful sit-in for free university elections ended with tanks storming the Polytechnic gates and killing unarmed students. This event severely discredited the military regime and attracted greater public opinion against the dictatorship.

Resistance activities, though immediately implemented in April 1967, never gained any radical momentum, although bomb attacks peppered Athens and an attempt on the life of Papadopoulos was made early in his tenure. In addition to gross human rights abuses, restrictions on freedom of expression and a well-documented policy of torture prompted intellectuals both Greek and non-Greek to campaign against the regime, mostly in exile or through underground activities. Artists and writers continued their productivity, publishing abroad or couching their statements in terms understood only by the initiated. Thus began what some scholars consider a new genre in Greek arts, whose impact continues down to the present.

Junta: the Colonels' memorial, Athens – an ugly monument to commemorate an ugly episode in Greek history

The government was buttressed by the implementation of social programmes favourable to those sectors of the population most likely to rebel, including cancellation of agricultural debts, provision of low-cost housing for workers, and the distribution of free textbooks to university students. Meanwhile it brutally carried out its purges of all political opposition, sending dissidents, real or imagined, to prison, exile, and torture. In the infamous words of colonel Papadopoulos, Greece was a patient that had to be tied to the operating table while surgery was performed.

Condemned by most world leaders, and withdrawing in 1969 from the Council of Europe before expulsion, the regime received state visits only from Romania's President Nicolae Ceausescu and US Vice-President Spiro Agnew, whose head of state, Richard M. Nixon, was not entirely free of complicity in the dictatorship. Anti-junta activists, journalists, and Greek political elites campaigned in any venue available, while the latter began to form discreet resistance organizations. Chief among them was the cohort formed around Andreas Papandreou, son of George Papandreou, who would lead the socialists to electoral victory in 1981. Also politically active in exile was the former premier Constantine Karamanlis, later to be hailed as the "restorer" of Greek democracy.

As the junta declined in late 1973 and early 1974, Ioannidis, in an attempt ostensibly to bolster its popularity, tried increasingly to bring Cyprus into the fold of Greece. In July 1974 a coup was launched against Cypriot president archbishop Makarios, which was followed by Turkey's invasion of the island. Three days after the invasion, on 23 July 1974, the dictatorial government surrendered. Under the watchful if not tutelary eye of the United States, Karamanlis the next day was flown in from Paris, like a deus ex machina in Richard Clogg's words, and sworn in as prime minister, in the presence of president Gizikis.

Greece regained its orientation to democratic institutions under the leadership of Karamanlis, who did all the right things – reinstating the Communist Party, putting the monarchy question to referendum, promulgating a new constitution, and making Greece a parliamentary republic. The strong arm of the law also came down hard on the junta leaders and their accomplices, and Papadopoulos remained in jail until his death in 1999. This immediate period of dejuntification clearly enabled Greece to find its footing again both ideologically and psychologically and to start making up for lost time, which it has been doing ever since.

BARBARA SYRRAKOS

See also Modern period, Political History since 1832

Further Reading

Andrews, Kevin, *Greece in the Dark: 1967–1974*, Amsterdam: Hakkert, 1980

Barnstone, Willis (editor), *Eighteen Texts: Writings by Contemporary Greek Authors*, Cambridge, Massachusetts: Harvard University Press, 1972

Clogg, Richard and George Yannopoulos (editors), *Greece under Military Rule*, London: Secker and Warburg, and New York: Basic Books, 1972

Clogg, Richard, *A Concise History of Greece*, Cambridge and New York: Cambridge University Press, 1992

Fleming, Amalia, *A Piece of Truth*, London: Jonathan Cape, 1972

Kutler, Stanley (editor), *Abuse of Power: The New Nixon Tapes*, New York: Free Press, 1997

Mangakis, George, "Letter in a Bottle: From a Greek Prison", *Atlantic*, 228/4 (October 1971): pp. 53–59

Papandreou, Andreas, *Democracy at Gunpoint: The Greek Front*, New York: Doubleday, 1970

Pollis, Adamantia, "Modernity, Civil Society and the Papandreou Legacy", *Journal of the Hellenic Diaspora*, 23/1 (1997): pp. 59–82

Schwab, Peter and George D. Frangos (editors), *Greece under the Junta*, New York: Facts on File, 1973

Stern, Lawrence M., *The Wrong Horse: The Politics of Intervention and the Failure of American Diplomacy*, New York: Times Books, 1977

Theodorakis, Mikis, *Journal of Resistance*, New York: Coward McCann, 1973

Tsoucalas, Constantine, *The Greek Tragedy*, Harmondsworth: Penguin, 1969

Van Dyck, Karen, *Kassandra and the Censors: Greek Poetry since 1967*, Ithaca, New York: Cornell University Press, 1998

Vlachos, Helen, *House Arrest*, Boston: Gambit, and London: Duckworth, 1970

Vlachos, Helen (editor), *Free Greek Voices: A Political Anthology*, London: Doric, 1971

Vryonis, Speros, Jr. (editor), *Greece on the Road to Democracy: From the Junta to PASOK, 1974–1986*, New Rochelle, New York: Caratzas, 1991

Woodhouse, C.M., *Karamanlis: The Restorer of Greek Democracy*, Oxford: Clarendon Press, and New York: Oxford University Press, 1982

Woodhouse, C.M., *The Rise and Fall of the Greek Colonels*, London: Granada, 1985

Justin Martyr, St *c.100–c.165*

Christian apologist

Justin was the outstanding member of the group of Christian writers of the period *c.*120–220 who are collectively known as the "Greek Apologists". He was converted to the faith he was so vigorously to defend about halfway through his life. His family was a pagan one living in Samaria, his birthplace being Floria Neapolis. His education was thorough, in literature, rhetoric, history, and philosophy. It was to the last that Justin devoted most enthusiasm, seeing in philosophical studies a way of arriving at a measure of truth about the nature of reality by which he could shape his conduct. He claims that he followed a course through a succession of philosophies – Stoic, Peripatetic, Pythagorean, and Platonist – before finding the truth for which he was searching in the Christian scriptures, impressed by belief in the prophets as foreshadowing Christ as

the Word and Son of God. He saw no impropriety in continuing to wear his philosopher's cloak as a Christian teacher, as he saw it, of the true philosophy. The period between his conversion and death is sparse in detail. He went to Ephesus and there engaged in a disputation with the Jewish Trypho (*c.*135), before going to Rome to establish a school, though not necessarily a permanent one. He taught there long enough to influence one of his students, Tatian, to follow him in a career of apologetic writing. It was in Rome that Justin wrote his own works in defence of Christianity. The *First Apology* was directed principally to the emperor Antoninus Pius and appeared *c.*155. It was followed by the edition of his *Dialogue with Trypho*. The *Second Apology* has been the subject of debate concerning its relationship with the *First Apology* and its date. It may have followed closely on the *First Apology*, taking up some of its themes, while concentrating its opening attack on a recent specific act of violence against Christians. It has also been dated later, following the accession of the emperor Marcus Aurelius in 161. The vigour of this writing, if indeed it was circulated, may have produced or increased antagonism. Denunciation of Justin and members of his circle is attested, together with an account of their responses. The official report tells how Justin answered the charges against him by offering a digest of the Christian faith, which he concluded was utterly at variance with any demand for sacrifice to the pagan gods. He and his six companions were instantly beheaded.

The demands that Justin made on himself called for a breadth of understanding of contemporary thought and a realistic awareness of the Church's situation within the empire. Before any form of intellectual defence could be offered it was necessary for Justin and his kind to try to dispose of the gossip, whether merely ignorant or knowingly malicious, about the nature of Christian practice. Forays into Platonism, the transcendence of God, or the nature of the divine *Logos* would have little effect on people who accused Christians of incest, cannibalism, or Thyestean feasts, on the basis of garbled reports of Eucharistic worship. Only when this kind of charge had been exposed and that of "atheism" rebutted could debate at a philosophical and religious level begin. Belief in one God inevitably enjoined disbelief in Roman polytheism, but it was claimed that this was not a rejection politically directed against the empire. Justin then felt able to set out the fundamentals of Christian belief in a context that found it unnecessary to abrogate the philosophical background from which he had emerged, particularly its Platonic aspects. The Christian Justin credits with genuine religious insights teachers from the pre-Christian era, including Heraclitus, Socrates, and Plato, alongside Old Testament heroes such as Abraham. This he believes he is able to do because of the very constitution of the human being in the image of God which endows each individual with the possibility of enlightenment, through possession of a share in the divine *Logos*. Human understanding is here based on a much firmer principle than that found in his feeble claim that wisdom among the Greeks is dependent upon their having had access to the writings of Moses. Side by side with this acknowledgement of the status of all humanity goes the unequivocal call for the acceptance of the unique Christian claims on which he has come to base his life and which are to bring him to his death. What emerges is a theology with a strong rooting in

Hebrew prophecy, interpreted, against Philo, as clearly fulfilled in Christ. Whereas this would be a natural line to take with the Jewish thinker, Justin does not shirk from bringing this alien source to the educated Greek readership he seeks in the *First Apology*. However keen he may be to gain a hearing, he does not compromise basic tenets of a distinctively Christian kind, frequently expressing them in a simple credal form, a Trinitarian outline coexisting with a freestanding expression of Christological proclamation. With God the Father presented in transcendent terms, the *Logos* in Justin's thought is vital to any philosophical or religious understanding. He is God's communicator with the world, the sole means by which human beings come to the truth. They are enabled to do this by the very nature of their creation, as within each individual there exists a seed (*sperma*) of the *Logos*, whether the person be Jew, pagan, or Christian. One consequence of Justin's stress on transcendence is a tendency to subordinate the Son. It would, however, be unwise to give too much weight to expressions that take on full significance only later. Again, it is perhaps to be expected that in Justin there should be little more than glancing reference to what was to develop as a theology of the Work of Christ.

Within the Christian community Justin's writing came to be valued not only for the features outlined above, but also for what may be learned in the *First Apology* about the early Church's practice in baptism and the Eucharist. The baptism of those who have come with a knowledge of its significance is administered in the name of the Father, Son, and Holy Spirit, bringing with it remission of sins and spiritual illumination. The liturgy for the newly baptized is described, together with the regular Sunday service, some variants being noted.

Revered as a martyr, respected for his openness to the non-Christian world (his acceptance of Socrates contrasting with his rejection by Theophilus), and as a writer more serviceable than inspiring, Justin, though himself not primarily a theologian, nor yet a philosopher, came to have influence on later theologians, notably Irenaeus and Tertullian and through them on the Christian tradition, as they developed ideas found here in germ.

D.A. SYKES

See also Apologists

Biography

Born *c*.AD 100, Justin was born into a pagan family at Floria Neapolis in Samaria. After a good education he devoted himself to philosophy before becoming converted to Christianity. He went first to Ephesus and then to Rome where he founded a school and wrote two apologias. He was beheaded for his beliefs *c*.165 and is revered as a martyr.

Writings

The Apologies of Justin Martyr, Greek text edited by A.W.F. Blunt, Cambridge: Cambridge University Press, 1911

Works, translated by E.R. Hardie, in *Early Christian Fathers*, edited by Cyril C. Richardson, London: SCM Press, and Philadelphia: Westminster Press, 1953

The First and Second Apologies, translated by Leslie William Barnard, New York: Paulist Press, 1997

Further Reading

Barnard, L.W., *Justin Martyr: His Life and Thought*, London: Cambridge University Press, 1967

Campenhausen, Hans von, *The Fathers of the Greek Church*, New York: Pantheon, 1959; London: A&C Black, 1963, chapter 1

Chadwick, Henry, *Early Christian Thought and the Classical Tradition: Studies in Justinian, Clement, and Origen*, Oxford: Clarendon Press, and New York: Oxford University Press, 1966; reprinted 1984

Chadwick, Henry, "The Beginning of Christian Philosophy: Justin: the Gnostics" in *The Cambridge History of Later Greek and Early Medieval Philosophy*, edited by A.H. Armstrong, London: Cambridge University Press, 1967

Edwards, Mark *et al.*, *Apologetics in the Roman Empire: Pagans, Jews, and Christians*, Oxford: Oxford University Press, 1999

Goodenough, Erwin R., *The Theology of Justin Martyr*, Jena: Verlag Frommansche Buchhandlung, 1923; reprinted Amsterdam: Philo Press, 1968

Grant, Robert M., *Greek Apologists of the Second Century*, Philadelphia: Westminster Press, and London: SCM Press, 1988

Osborn, Eric Francis, *Justin Martyr*, Tübingen: Mohr, 1973

Stead, Christopher, *Philosophy in Christian Antiquity*, Cambridge and New York: Cambridge University Press, 1994

Justinian I *c*.482–565

Emperor

Justinian I (527–65) was the last Latin emperor to rule over a state that encompassed the greater portion of the Mediterranean basin. Procopius of Gaza, the last of the great Classical historians, is our chief source for his reign. Justinian's given name was Flavius Peter Sabbatius and he was born in Bederiana in the province of Dardania around 482. Justinian, originally a member of the imperial bodyguard, was the nephew of the emperor Justin I (518–27) and eventually became co-emperor in 527. He chose as his wife Theodora, who, although known for her unsavoury background, proved to be a great source of strength to him in moments of crisis, especially during the Nika revolt of 532, the most serious challenge to his rule. Justinian was also fortunate in having the able John of Cappadocia as his chief administrator. From the moment he assumed power, Justinian set about achieving the primary goal of his reign, which was the restoration of the empire of Augustus by bringing the lost provinces of the Latin west back under the control of the Roman emperor based in Constantinople. Justinian also felt an obligation to rescue those orthodox Christians in the west who were living under the rule of Arians. To accomplish this goal he launched a series of wars of reconquest under his able generals Belisarius and later Narses against the Vandals in north Africa (533–34) and the Ostrogoths in Italy (535–55). Imperial armies also managed to seize some coastal regions in Spain. However, the renewal of war with Persia forced Justinian to curtail his plans for expansion. Overall, his military endeavours seriously taxed the resources of the Roman state and ultimately proved unsuccessful since many of the newly conquered territories were subsequently lost to the Lombards, who invaded Italy in 568.

In addition to his military achievements, Justinian is famous for his efforts in having all the existing Roman laws, legal text-

Justinian I: mosaic portrait of the emperor in San Vitale, Ravenna, 6th century

books, and legal decisions of famous Roman jurists compiled into a single work known as the *Corpus Iuris Civilis*. Most of this work was supervised by the jurist Tribonian. It was destined to have lasting importance, for it eventually made its way to the Latin west where, in the 11th century, it formed the basis for the revival of the study of Roman law at the newly established universities, such as Bologna, and contributed to the re-establishment of Roman law as the basic rule for continental Europe, a tradition that survives to this day. The emperor also reformed the tax system and sponsored the establishment of a lucrative silk industry in Greece.

Justinian is also renowned for his architectural achievements. He sponsored the building or reconstruction of many new churches and monasteries, the most significant being the monastery of St Catherine on Mount Sinai, which contains one of the most important collections of Byzantine icons dating from the pre-iconoclastic era (8th–9th centuries), and Hagia Sophia in Constantinople. Hagia Sophia is chiefly noted for its spectacular dome and still stands as the third largest church in the world. Upon its completion, it quickly became the most important spiritual centre in the Orthodox world.

Justinian also paid close attention to the spiritual and intellectual lives of his subjects. One of his less commendable acts was to close the Academy in Athens in 529, which was then dominated by pagan Neoplatonists. This act resulted in the emigration of the Academy's scholars to neighbouring Persia, while Neoplatonism continued to attract the interest of Byzantine intellectuals. Justinian also initiated a vigorous campaign of Christianization by ordering the closing of many pagan cult centres and the banning of paganism altogether. How effectively or consistently this policy was carried out is still disputed by scholars since some members of Justinian's administration, such as the jurist Tribonian, were pagans. Another of Justinian's more reprehensible religious policies was his attempt to suppress the Samaritans, a subsect of Judaism, which resulted in a revolt against his rule. In addition, he enacted a series of laws that placed significant legal liabilities on the Jewish community. Other groups singled out for persecution were the Montanists, Manichaeans, and Nestorians. Finally, Justinian tried to resolve the dispute between Monophysite and Chalcedonian Christians over the nature of Christ by convening the Fifth Ecumenical Council at Constantinople in 553. Here he tried to achieve a compromise by condemning the writings of three Nestorian bishops in the Edict of the Three Chapters, even though these writings had been approved by previous ecumenical councils. Justinian also had pope Vigilius brought to Constantinople and held him under house arrest until he agreed to the decisions of the Council. The pope eventually died on his return journey to Italy and was replaced by Pelagius who refused to comply with Justinian's wishes, thus producing a schism that lasted until the 7th century. Ultimately Justinian's efforts to resolve this fundamental division within the Christian community proved a failure and actually served to exacerbate tensions between the Monophysite and Chalcedonian factions.

JOHN F. SHEAN

See also Byzantine Period (Early), Law

Biography

Born near Bederiana in Thrace *c*.482, Justinian inherited the throne from his uncle Justin I in 527. He married Theodora, a former actress who became his staunchest ally. His principal goal was the recovery of the western provinces of the empire in which his success was only shortlived. He also codified the whole of Roman law. He built churches and monasteries; and he tried to resolve the divisions within Christianity by convening an Ecumenical Council in 553. He died in 565.

Further Reading

Agathias of Myrina, *De Imperio et Rebus Gestis Iustiniani*, edited by Rudolf Keydall, Berlin: de Gruyter, 1967 (*Corpus Fontium Historiae Byzantinae*, vol. 2)

Browning, Robert, *Justinian and Theodora*, revised edition, London and New York: Thames and Hudson, 1987

Bury, J.B., *A History of the Later Roman Empire from the Death of Theodosius I to the Death of Justinian*, AD 395 to 565, 2 vols, London: Macmillan, 1923; New York: Dover, 1958

Evans, J.A.S., *The Age of Justinian: The Circumstances of Imperial Power*, London and New York: Routledge, 1996

John Malalas, *Chronographia*, edited by Ludwig Dindorf, Bonn: Weber, 1831 (*Corpus Scriptorum Historiae Byzantinae*, vol. 8)

John of Ephesus, *Ecclesiastical History*, translated into Latin by W.J. Van Douwen and J.P.N. Land, Amsterdam: Müller, 1889

Menander Protector, *The History of Menander the Guardsman*, edited and translated by R.C. Blockley, Liverpool: Cairns, 1985

Moorhead, John, *Justinian*, London and New York: Longman, 1994

Procopius of Caesarea, *Opera omnia*, edited by Jakob Haury, 4 vols, Leipzig: Teubner, 1962–64

Procopius of Caesarea, *History of the Wars, Secret History, and Buildings*, translated by Averil Cameron, New York: Washington Square Press, 1967

Rubin, Berthold, *Das Zeitalter Iustinians*, 2 vols, Berlin: de Gruyter, 1960–95

Stein, Ernst, *Histoire du Bas-Empire*, 2 vols, Paris: Brouwer, 1949–59

K

Kabasilas, Nicholas *c.1319–c.1391*

Statesman and churchman of the 14th century

Nicholas Kabasilas Chamaetos was born in Thessalonica between 1319 and 1323. Of noble birth, he adopted his mother's family name. He first studied in Thessalonica with his uncle Neilos Kabasilas, who succeeded Gregory Palamas as metropolitan of Thessalonica in 1360. (Until recently, Nicholas was often confused with his uncle, whose baptismal name was Nicholas.) While in Thessalonica he began to frequent hesychast circles, founded by monks from nearby Mount Athos. He later continued his studies in Constantinople. In the civil war of the 1340s Nicholas supported John VI Kantakouzenos, and in 1347 became one of his counsellors, together with Demetrios Kydones. In the hesychast controversy Nicholas appears as a friend of St Gregory Palamas and a supporter of hesychasm. His attitude to the growing influence of Latin theology, however, seems to have been more moderate than many of the hesychasts'. After the abdication of John VI Kantakouzenos in 1354, Nicholas retired from public life and we hear no more about him. Letters that survive from Nicholas to Manuel II Palaiologos make it evident that he was still alive in 1391. There has been much dispute as to how he spent the last half of his life: it has been argued that he became a monk or a priest, but many of these arguments rest on confusion with his uncle. It is most probable that he remained a layman, following the prescription of hesychasts such as Gregory of Sinai, who commended a hesychast life, a life of prayer, combined with active charity, lived "in the world".

From his secular career various works survive: panegyrics, treatises against usury and on (and in defence of) philosophy, as well as several letters. Among his religious works are various homilies, including panegyrics of saints (including St Demetrius), and three homilies on feasts of the Mother of God. In many of these works we find the elaborate diction of the highly educated courtier. But his influence rests largely on two works, composed in a much more direct style, his *Commentary on the Divine Liturgy* and his *Life in Christ*. The immediate influence of these works seems to have been slight. Within decades, the Byzantine empire was to fall to the Turks, and it was in monastic circles that the "inner wisdom" of Christianity was most faithfully preserved. Nicholas's two works, unusually for works of Byzantine spirituality, envisage a primarily lay audience; he was not included in the 18th-century hesychast anthology, the *Philokalia*. In recent times, however, they have found recognition as classics of Orthodox sacramental spirituality: the very title of St John of Kronstadt's spiritual autobiography, *My Life in Christ* (1889), pays tribute to Kabasilas.

Both the *Commentary on the Divine Liturgy* and the *Life in Christ* expound a spirituality founded on the sacraments. The *Commentary* explains the actions and prayers of the liturgy from the preparation of the bread and the wine (the *prothesis*) through to communion, with a long theological parenthesis inserted before the final chapter. This parenthesis deals with matters such as the value of the celebration of the liturgy for the departed, the role of the saints, and the nature of the Eucharistic sacrifice. Some have detected the influence of Thomas Aquinas in his parenthesis; earlier on, however, there is a spirited defence of the invocation (*epiklesis*) of the Holy Spirit against Latin objections. The explanation of the liturgical actions it provides is largely an elaboration of traditional explanations that can be traced back to the commentary by Germanos I. The liturgical celebration yields benefits through both intercession and participation. The inspiration of much of Kabasilas's unfolding of the significance of the liturgical action is frequently to be traced to Dionysius the Areopagite. A similar inspiration can be detected in the *Life of Christ*, notably in the choice of the three sacraments, baptism, oil (*myron*), and the Eucharist, that form the subject of the three principal chapters (cf. Dionysius, *Ecclesiasical Hierarchy*, 2–4). This concentration on the sacramental yields a spirituality that neither requires nor advocates monastic seclusion: "the general may remain in command, the farmer may till the soil, the artisan may exercise his craft, and no one will have to desist from his usual employment because of it. One need not betake oneself to a remote spot, nor eat unaccustomed food, nor even dress differently, nor ruin one's health nor venture on any reckless act" (6. 42). Nevertheless prayer is given great importance, and one of the effects of the Eucharist is to create in the communicant a "sanctuary of the heart" (6. 103). Nicholas's two works constitute an unparalleled exposition of the "lay hesychasm", often envisaged in the writings of the hesychast monks.

ANDREW LOUTH

See also Hesychasm

Biography

Born in Thessalonica *c*.1319 into a noble family, Nicholas adopted his mother's name (Kabasilas) instead of his father's (Chamaetos). He studied first in Thessalonica under his uncle Neilos Kabasilas and then in Constantinople. He allied himself with John VI Kantakouzenos in the civil war of the 1340s and with St Gregory Palamas in the hesychast controversy. He wrote on secular as well as religious topics. He died after 1391.

Writings

A Commentary on the Divine Liturgy, translated by J.M. Hussey and P.A. McNulty, London: SPCK, 1966

L'Explication de la divine liturgie, edited by René Bornert, Jean Gouillard and Pierre Périchon, translated into French by Sévérien Salaville, Paris: Cerf, 1967 (*Sources chrétiennes* 4bis)

The Life in Christ, translated by Carmino J. de Catanzaro, Crestwood, New York: St Vladimir's Seminary Press, 1974

La Vie en Christ, edited and translated into French by Marie-Hélène Congourdeau, 2 vols, Paris: Cerf, 1989–90 (*Sources chrétiennes* 355, 361)

Ho Theometor, edited by P. Nellas, 4th edition, Athens, 1995 (edition of three Marian homilies with modern Greek translation)

Further Reading

Angelopoulos, Athanasios A., *Nikolaos Kavasilas Chamaetos: He zoe kai to ergon autou* [Nicholas Kabasilas Chamateos: His Life and Work], Thessalonica, 1970

Lot-Borodine, Myrrha, *Nicolas Cabasilas: un maître de la spiritualité byzantine au XIVe siècle*, Paris: Orante, 1958

Völker, Walther, *Die Sakramentsmystik des Nikolaus Kabasilas*, Wiesbaden: Steiner, 1977

Kafeneion

In the Hellenic world, where there is talk, there is smoke, fire...and caffeine. These elements come together in one of the most omnipresent institutions among Greeks – the coffee shop, or *kafeneion*. Whether the coffee ordered there is prefaced by the modifier "Turkish" or "Greek", it is basically the same article – that heavy muddish potable in a small cup, potent enough to lubricate the wheels of the mind and mysterious enough to ensure a rich fortune-telling in the grounds when the drink nears its end. For Greeks, coffee is both a transient pleasure and a lingering memory fortifying the day until the next cup. Without coffee, and the ritual of its preparation and consumption, Greek life would be a blur of mundane comings and goings. With coffee, less a dietary supplement than a soft narcotic or social stimulant, life comes alive; its busy nature is ensured punctuated respite. And the environment in which it is drunk is the passport to circadian nirvana.

The *kafeneion* can be found wherever more than one person pauses in a public place for a sip. It is not uncommon to find in Greece ad hoc *kafeneia* on street corners, where people spontaneously pull up a chair from a shop and a stool from somewhere else, perhaps a box to serve as table, and pass the time together talking things over. The warm climate encourages these outdoor assemblages. The *kafeneion* as an institution, however, is more uniform. Like any coffee shop round the world, it boasts modest chairs and tables, a pedestrian unadorned atmosphere. The *kafeneion* is well stocked with soft drinks, cocoa, prepackaged ice cream. There its transcendence stops. The Greek coffee shop would not be recognizable without smoke-clouded windows, a counter, perhaps covered in tin, a glass enclosure housing a few small syrup-drenched morsels to complement the bitter coffee on the palate and olives and cheese to complement the aniseed-flavoured ouzo as it eases towards the stomach. Finally there are the coffee-making accoutrements.

The *vriki* is the long-handled lipped copper or sterling pot used for making coffee; quite small in size, and commonly built to hold two, four, and rarely more than six cupfuls at a time. The cups, or *flitzani*, are demitasses, with petite handles and diminutive accompanying saucers. The pulverized coffee is prepared over a direct flame with water and sugar (*sketo*, plain, i.e. without sugar; *metrio*, medium; *glyko*, sweet), raised from the flame as it begins to boil, and set and raised two more times for a full froth before pouring. Some interpreters suggest the thrice-boiled concoction echoes the concept of the Holy Trinity, and hence its practice in the largely Orthodox Greek communities, although secularists lift and set three times merely to maximize the froth (*kaimaki*). The preparatory ritual, in any event, ultimately gives way to consumption, always with a side glass of water. The taste of the *sketo* is bitter and robust.

As a social institution, the *kafeneion* is usually a place reserved for men, as tradition has it. The *kafeneion* is not to be confused with the more variegated coffee houses, cafés, or *zacharoplasteia* (sweet shops), which are more pluralistic in clientele. Women, tourists, students, young professionals frequent these venues, while the *kafeneion* is, in the popular imagination, what it always has been – fairly limited to the discrete, leisurely, and quasi-business activities of a male population. The *kafeneion* is common not only in Greece and Cyprus but in the Hellenic diaspora, in neighbourhoods from Milwaukee to Melbourne. Usually knowing no distinction among class or station, patrons are recognizable to one another by dint of their close spatial proximity – every urban neighbourhood has a *kafeneion*. Hence, there is an implicit, if sometimes superficial, familiar feeling. The *kafeneia*, however, can be political spaces as well, with one *kafeneion* welcoming members only of the rightist party, for example, and the rival *kafeneion* welcoming only the opposition.

The *kafeneion* finds its roots in the early 17th century, where long-distance travellers eastward of the Levant looked to the coffee tent as a country inn of sorts, an outpost between metropolises on the caravan route. Recalling these early roots, in decades prior to the information boom, the more remote, rural areas of Greece and Cyprus, with limited access to newspapers and electronic media, were reliant upon the *kafeneion* as an information-exchange centre. Also the difficulty in obtaining telephone lines in Greece forced face-to-face communal gatherings in the reliable venue of the *kafeneion*, even in the cities. This is still the case in some isolated areas including island villages. As the practice goes, one informant will return to his village from having visited an urban centre and deliver the latest salient development to his cohort. In such rural areas, where village elders, heads of households, and other community or business leaders of the village visit the *kafeneion* regularly, issues of the commonweal might be deliberated and debated until consensus is formed. It is not uncommon for official business to be conducted in this informal environment, and

Kafeneion: traditional *kafeneion* in the port of Karlovasi on Samos

in this respect, the *kafeneion* may serve as an extension of the political realm. Decisions made there may determine how votes are cast in town or village councils.

On the other hand, the *kafeneion* is a place of leisure and male camaraderie, a break from home life, which tends to be the domain of women and children. Gambling might take place, over a game of backgammon, chess, or some manifestation of cards, but rarely for high stakes. In the old days the smoking of hashish brought about a different kind of nirvana, but since the early 20th century the drug has been banned in Greece. If one can speak for a moment about the oral tradition of the Hellenic world, where talk is a pleasure in and of itself, without necessarily consensual ends, the *kafeneion* also occasions demonstrative rhetorical bravado. Not to be outdone by one's companions, participants in the discussion may crescendo and diminuendo with flourishes of thought and speech in both emotive and logical twists and turns before an attentive and critical audience for the sheer joy of performance. In this, *couventa* (conversation) is a key commonality and tacit attraction among *kafeneion* patrons, who claim the *kafeneion* as a place of their own.

BARBARA SYRRAKOS

See also Men

Further Reading

Gumpert, Matthew, "Freedom within the Margin: The Café in the Poetry of Cavafy", *Journal of Modern Greek Studies*, 9/2 (October 1991): pp. 215–35

Heise, Ulla, *Coffee and Coffee-Houses*, West Chester, Pennsylvania: Schiffer, 1987

Herzfeld, Michael, *The Poetics of Manhood: Contest and Identity in a Cretan Mountain Village*, Princeton, New Jersey: Princeton University Press, 1985

Photiadis, John Democritos, "The Coffee House and Its Role in the Village of Stavroupolis, Greece" (dissertation), Ithaca, New York: Cornell University, 1956

Kaftantzoglou, Lysandros 1811–1885

Architect

Lysandros Kaftantzoglou was one of the leading architects of 19th-century Greece. He was born in Thessalonica into an aristocratic Macedonian family, whose name of Spandoni (or Spandouni) was replaced by an honorary one derived from the Ottoman kaftan which certain privileged subjects were allowed to wear. Taken by his mother to France as a refugee from the troubles which followed the start of the War of

Independence in 1821, he was educated initially in Marseilles, and subsequently studied architecture at the Academy of Fine Arts in Rome. In 1834, at the age of 22, he won first prize in an international competition for the design of Milan university. In the same year he graduated and returned to France. He travelled widely in Europe, where his work was highly regarded. He was elected to membership of numerous professional bodies both there and in the United States.

He first returned to Greece in 1838, when he visited Athens to participate in a competition for the design of the university. A show of his work was well received by the public but he was in serious disagreement with the dominant Bavarian and German architects over the town plan for the development of Athens. This reached such a pitch that court action resulted and Kaftantzoglou left Athens, disenchanted, in 1839. He spent the next four years first in Thessalonica, where he studied Byzantine architecture, and then in Constantinople, where he continued his architectural research and designed some houses.

When he returned once more to Athens in 1843, one of the Bavarians who had been removed from office in the anti-Othonian climate which then prevailed was the director of the Techniko Scholeio. The following year Kaftantzoglou became its first Greek director. With the help of Tositsa and Stournari, with whom he had discussed the idea some years earlier, this was now transformed into Athens Polytechnic. With great enthusiasm Kaftantzoglou set about establishing the educational and administrative structures of the institution, as well as teaching. The new polytechnic building (1861–76), in Odos Patission (28 Oktovriou), which he designed, is generally regarded as one of his greatest achievements. The approach is flanked by two single-storey buildings with Doric stoas; the main building, constructed round an open interior court, is approached by a massive Ionic porch at first-floor level.

Kaftantzoglou's architectural style was strongly Neoclassical in character, based on ancient and Renaissance architecture and much influenced by contemporary developments in Europe. He drew also from Byzantine architecture, which at the time was not highly regarded. In his houses, which mostly survive only in drawings, he shows a more varied and lighter touch. His work is often contrasted with that of his contemporary and bitter rival Stamatis Kleanthis (1802–62), whose Romantic style often made use of Gothic elements. The two were professional and personal rivals and conducted highly publicized quarrels in the press. In 1845 Kaftantzoglou succeeded in wresting the commission for the Arsakeion (another of his major works, completed in 1852) from Kleanthis, who had already spent two years on the project.

In addition to the two buildings already mentioned Kaftantzoglou's prolific output included many private houses, very few of which have survived, the Catholic church of St Denis in Panepistimiou (started by Klentze), the Orthodox churches of Hagia Irini and Hagios Konstantinos in Athens, and many other buildings elsewhere in Greece. He was also well known for an ambitiously designed but subsequently unbuilt heroon, designed in 1830 as a monument to the heroes of 1821. His comments on the design show both his attachment to Classical architecture (the Propylaea of Mnesicles) and his interest in the symbolic use of architectural forms and motifs (the Doric and Ionic orders to signify the two tribes of Greece; the circular form, eternity).

His later years were embittered. His leadership of the polytechnic was violently challenged, partly because of the changing political climate. After his resignation (1862) he largely shut himself off from public life and died in Athens in 1885.

ROBIN L.N. BARBER

Biography
Born in Thessalonica in 1811, Kaftantzoglou went with his mother to Paris in 1821. He studied in Marseilles, and then at the Academy of Fine Arts in Rome. In 1834 he won a competition to design Milan University. He returned to Greece in 1838 and in 1844 became director of the Polytechnic, whose new building he designed. He died in Athens in 1885.

Further Reading
Biris, K., *Istoria tou Ethnikou Metsoviou Polytechniou* [History of the Metsovo National Polytechnic], Athens, 1973

Evstathiadis, B., "Lysandros Kaftantzoglou" (in Greek) in *Protoi Ellines Technikoi Epistimones Periodou Apeleutherosis* [The First Greek Technologists of the Liberation], Athens, 1976

Megali Elliniki Enkylopaideia [The Great Greek Encyclopedia], Athens, entry on Kaftantzoglou

Phillippidis, D., *Neoelliniki Architectoniki* [Modern Greek Architecture], Athens, 1984, pp. 84–89

Travlos, J., *Neoclassical Architecture in Greece*, Athens: Commercial Bank of Greece, 1967

Kalamata

Port in the southern Peloponnese

At the head of the Messenian Gulf, sheltered by the huge flanks of the Taygetos mountains, and watered by the river Nedon is Kalamata, the capital of the province of Messenia. With its 44,000 inhabitants Kalamata is one of the larger Greek cities. Harbour, train station, and airport make the city an important commercial centre. Kalamata olives have a high reputation. Tourism is centred in the seaside area of the city. The long boulevard is flanked by numerous hotels and restaurants. On 14 September 1986 a severe earthquake struck the centre of Kalamata. The increased building activities in the city are due to this catastrophe.

Excavations have shown that Kalamata occupies the site of ancient Pherae which is most likely identified with the Pherae of the Homeric poems. In the *Iliad* "sacred Pherae" is one of the seven cities "on the border of sandy Pylos" that Agamemnon offers Achilles, hoping to persuade him to take up arms again (9. 149). According to the *Iliad* (5. 541–53) this Pherae is inhabited by Diocles and his sons, who set out for Troy to gain honour for the Atreids. In the *Odyssey* (3. 488 and 15. 186) Telemachus twice visits Diocles in Pherae on his way from Pylos to Sparta and back.

The status of Pherae in this period is not clear. A Linear B tablet (An 661) from Nestor's palace at Pylos may throw some light on this matter. It says, apparently in a case of emergency, that 30 members of the coast guard are to be sent to the Nedon. This river, and consequently Pherae, seem not to have been part of the area ruled by the palace, because the kingdom's coast was already occupied by guards.

The overall picture seems to indicate that Pherae did not strictly belong to the kingdom of Pylos, nor to Sparta. Situated "on the border of sandy Pylos" here apparently means on the other side of the border, because Nestor did not oppose Agamemnon when the seven cities were offered to Achilles. He would not have been so friendly if Agamemnon had been about to give away seven Pylian cities. The marshes of the Pamisos estuary in the lower Messenian plain could well have formed a natural border between Pylos and Pherae. But Pherae was not a kingdom itself, as stated by Homer, who never calls Diocles and his family kings, but just inhabitants of the city. The participation of Diocles' sons in the Trojan War in the regiments of Menelaus seems to indicate some degree of dependence of Pherae on Sparta.

In the 8th century BC Pherae was annexed by the Spartans, who kept dominion over the city until 371 BC, when the Thebans liberated Messenia. Pherae again fell into Laconian hands after the battle of Actium in 31 BC, when Augustus donated the city to his Spartan allies. Tiberius (AD 14–37) in his turn assigned the cities on the western flank of Mount Taygetos to Messenia. According to Pausanias (4. 30. 3), Pherae was an ancient medical centre. He writes that Diocles' daughter Anticleia married Machaon, the illustrious son of Asclepius. Their descendants remained in Pherae, and with them the power of healing diseases and curing the maimed. Pausanias refers to a sanctuary of Machaon's sons in Pherae and his tomb in Gerenia (modern Kambos).

In Byzantine times the name Pherae changed into Kalamata, perhaps after the monastery of the Panagia of Kalomata. In AD 1208 the Frankish baron Geoffrey I de Villehardouin acquired the barony of Messenia and refortified the Byzantine fortress on the acropolis of ancient Pherae. Here his son William was born in 1218. The Villehardouins kept possession of Kalamata for almost a century. They even retained it after the disastrous battle of Pelagonia in 1259, when they had to give up Mistra and other Laconian possessions to the Byzantine John Palaiologos. William died at Kalamata in 1278, leaving no male heirs. The city passed to Charles d'Anjou and in 1299 to Guy de la Roche. Kalamata was now part of the Duchy of Athens. In 1425 the city passed to the Palaiologoi and in 1460 the Ottomans took control. The Venetians conquered Kalamata during the Morosini campaign of 1685. The German general Dengenfeld took the city with his army of 8000 mercenaries, among who were 1500 Maniots. The Venetians, however, were even less popular than the Turks, and when the vizir Damat Ali appeared in the Peloponnese in 1715, the Venetians were driven out of their fortresses with the help of the people.

During the Orloff campaign of 1770 Kalamata was freed again from the Ottomans. A small division, consisting of 200 Maniots and 12 Russians captured the city. But again the Turks struck back, destroying the churches and the houses.

In 1821 Kalamata is said to have been be the first Greek city to take up arms against the Turks. Indeed, on 23 March Kalamata was liberated from Turkish occupation by the Maniot troops of Petrobey Mavromichalis, Mourtzinos, and Theodore Kolokotronis. Four years later, however, Ibrahim Pasha reconquered the city after heavy bombardments. After the glorious battle of Navarino in 1827 Kalamata was returned to Greek hands for good.

MAARTEN J. GROND

Summary

A city in the southern Peloponnese, Kalamata is the captial of the province of Messenia and an important commercial centre. In antiquity it was known as Pherae and was annexed by Sparta from the 8th to 4th centuries BC. It was an ancient centre of healing cults. Its name was changed to Kalamata in the Byzantine period. It was occupied by Franks in the 13th and 14th centuries and was the first city to take up arms against the Turks in 1821.

Further Reading

Chadwick, John, "The Geography of the Further Province of Pylos", *American Journal of Archaeology*, 77 (1973)

Schmitt-Brandt, R., "Die Oka-tafeln in neuer Sicht", *Studi Micenei ed Egeo-Anatolici*, 7 (1968)

Stamatopoulos, Dimitris, *Kalamata*, Kalamata, 1989

Valmin, Mattias Natan, *Etudes topographiques sur la Messénie ancienne*, Lund: Blom, 1930

Kalvos, Andreas 1792–1869

Poet of the Heptanesian school

With a reputation as the principal renovator of modern Greek lyric expression and the leader of the Neoclassical movement in Greek poetry, Andreas Kalvos is regarded as one of the most important figures in laying the foundations of the modern Greek poetic tradition. At the same time he made an important contribution to the intellectual movement known as the Heptanesian school that flourished in the Ionian islands and signalled a cultural reawakening. However, Kalvos is one of the least prolific poets in the modern Greek literary tradition. His poetic production is confined to a single volume that was published under the general title *Odes* and which comprises two independent collections which appeared under the titles *Lyre* (Geneva, 1824) and *Lyrics* (Paris, 1826). Nevertheless, apart from poetry Kalvos also produced a notable body of literary work of great variety ranging from tragedies, translations, short essays of philosophical, social, and theological content, elementary textbooks of grammar, and other educational material to reports and critical articles of a political nature published in the journals and daily newspapers of his time.

Kalvos composed just 20 poems, all connected with the Greek War of Independence of 1821. However, he loved solitude and throughout his life he remained inaccessible and unknown, and his books of verse were indifferently received and recognized only posthumously. Attached to the idea of nation, as well as to the ancient Greek ideals of morality and justice, he extolled the national revolutionary spirit. His poetry is distinguished for its eye-catching, daring imagery, its impressive mode of expression, and its elegant, extremely personal style.

Kalvos was born and spent his early childhood in Zakynthos in the most transitory period of that island's history. It was the period when the Ionian islands were officially annexed to France. The same period was marked by the endeavour of the petty bourgeoisie to transfer the power of the nobles to its own hands. At the same time, the ideas of the Enlightenment and the Encyclopedists were prevalent and moulded the European intellectual world. Kalvos was prepared to assimilate and evoke the reformist spirit in his verse. His acquaintance with the Italian revolutionary poet Ugo Foscolo had a profound influence on his career and personal style. Thus, influenced by the challenging ideals of the revolutionary age, excited by the national reawakening of his fatherland, and professing his Greekness, he was capable of writing poetry through which all those influences found an expression. His poetry was the melting pot in which French liberalism, Germanic idealism, and idealistic perfectionism in its Romantic or Classical interpretation blended with the Hellenic tradition. As a consequence Kalvos's contribution to the Hellenic tradition is evident from the fact that he never used his poetry as an instrument to express the ideas of Europe but to fertilize them in his own cultural tradition. He was not an imitator of foreign forms and spiritual models but the poet who succeeded in expressing the pulsation of his age and renewing the Hellenic tradition.

The characteristic elements of his poetry are revolutionary patriotism, devotion to his country, and the vital role of justice and virtue in the existence of nations. Through these elements the political character of his poetry becomes evident. In this manner Kalvos had a profound effect on the poetry of the postwar generation of Greek poets who sought the political dimension of poetry (e.g. Ritsos, Vretakos, Seferis).

Turning to the thematic framework of Kalvos's poetry, one could say that nearly all of his poems are connected with and refer directly to the Greek revolution from which he drew his inspiration and to the final success of which he wanted to contribute through his art. However, his aim was a deeper one: to speak up for virtue and justice, the heroic spirit, valour, courage, and ethical integrity, and to oppose injustice, oppression, despotism, and tyranny. His idea of virtue – the clearest theme in his poetry – is a complex but sublime synthesis of many different concepts. For Kalvos virtue is the connecting link that joins the Hellenic tradition from Homer to the contemporary era and to western culture. Kalvos's Aristotelian virtue is perceived as a moral idea with a Christian meaning. It is also perceived in its ancient Greek context as the bravery of Homer's epics or the historical record of Classical Greece. At the same time it is the proud dignity of manliness, a common element in both ancient Greek tradition and popular folksong. And it is identified with the idea of freedom and encapsulates the enduring strength of the Hellenic historical process. A similar idea was presented by Pericles when he thought of virtue as the necessary condition for the existence of freedom. Finally, Kalvos's virtue entailed the idea of social offering and the desire for the fulfilment of human happiness as expressed by Diderot.

An equally significant theme in Kalvos's poems is the idea of religiosity. Kalvos was concerned with religion in its broader context. He often refers to God but categorically refuses to define him. Thus he is thought to have believed in a superhuman controlling power, in a personal god or gods deserving his obedience, respect, and worship. This supernatural power can be seen as the voice of justice and truth, able to punish any abuse. It is the power responsible for the settlement of the moral norm and the ethical order. To this extent, Kalvos's god seems to be identified with Zeus as well as with the ancient punitive and avenging Furies such as are presented in the tragedies of Aeschylus and Sophocles. Nevertheless, Kalvos does not reject the Christian dimension, since he pays respect to an omnipotent monotheistic God, the equivalent of the Byzantine/Orthodox perpetual ruler of the world.

Another distinctive motif of Kalvos's poetry is the idea of love of one's native land. The same feeling of nostalgia overcame Odysseus when he was away from Ithaca and was reminded of home. Meanwhile Kalvos composed a hymn to the natural landscape of Greece. Nature becomes the mother figure, which symbolizes the source of life and the ultimate expression of pure instincts. The same idea runs through the Hellenic literary tradition from Homer to lyric pastoral poetry, and is then transmitted to folk tradition in order to permeate the work of modern Greek poets such as Palamas and Elytis.

With respect to the particular components of Kalvos's poetry one could say that his verse is marked by sublime ideas, dramatic tone, alluring imagery, and sensuous appeal, elements that characterized the verse of Pindar. The plangency of a number of natural images in his poetry owes something to the tone of the Romantics. His correct use of metaphors, his strong similes, and his frequent use of antithesis had an immense influence on the expression, versification, and style of Palamas and Seferis and to an even greater extent on Elytis, who devoted his verse to the description and exaltation of the Greek countryside. Kalvos's strong didactic element and his dense epigrammatic phraseology made an enormous impact on Seferis's verse, where big ideas and ethics are expressed by means of aphorism or axiom. Kalvos did follow a particular metrical norm but was inclined to write in blank verse. In this way he encouraged the next generation to write in blank verse without neglecting the power of the metrical norm which was still the basis for any kind of poetry. Although Kalvos made extensive use of the Neoclassical models, he never escaped the enchanting power of Romanticism, which gives priority to imagination, releases emotions, and liberates poetical expression. His ideal was a Classical one but his expression Romantic. As far as his idiom is concerned, Kalvos's language is an original personal device. It is an admixture of the vernacular spoken language and its inexhaustible archaic form. His idiom contains elements of three different sources: the ancient Greek tradition, the linguistic idiom of Adamantios Korais and Rigas Velestinlis and other Greek intellectuals abroad, and the vernacular language comprising a number of idiomatic expressions and local elements.

Kalvos is not simply a contributor to the Hellenic poetic tradition but, more importantly, he is a genuine representative of his own era as well as a spirited inaugurator of modern Greek poetic expression. In Kalvos's poetry the whole world, nature, and history become a unique omnipotent vision under the patronage and protection of an almighty God.

MARIA ROUMBALOU

Biography

Born in Zakynthos in 1792, Kalvos had little education. But in 1812 he met Ugo Foscolo in Florence and remained his companion in exile until 1820. He wrote only two books of poetry – *Lyre* (1824) and

Lyrics (1826) – each containing ten patriotic odes inspired by the War of Independence. Returning to Greece, he settled in Corfu and taught for a time at the Ionian Academy. In 1852 he moved to England where he married for a second time, and died in 1869.

Further Reading

Dialismas, S., *Andreas Kalvos*, Athens, 1977

Elytis, Odysseus, "I Alithini Fisiognomia ke i Liriki Tolmi tou Andrea Kalvou" [The True Quality and Lyric Power of Andreas Kalvos] in his *Anoichta Chartia* [Open Documents], 2nd edition, Athens, 1982

Keeley, Edmund and Peter Bien, *Modern Greek Writers: Solomos, Calvos, Matesis, Palamas, Cavafy, Kazantzakis, Seferis, Elytis*, Princeton, New Jersey: Princeton University Press, 1972

Sofroniou, A., *Andreas Kalvos: Kritiki Meleti* [Andreas Kalvos: A Critical Study], Athens, 1960

Tsatsos, K., "Kalvos, O Pleetis tis Itheas" [Kalvos, the Poet of Idea], *Aesthetic Studies* (1977)

Kanaris, Constantine 1795–1877

Naval hero of the Greek War of Independence and prime minister of Greece

Kanaris was born on the eastern Aegean island of Psara into a prominent family of mariners. He went to sea at an early age by joining the crew of a veteran captain and family relative as a junior rating. Observers soon noticed the young man's bravery, presence of mind, and seamanship. He was barely 20 when he was given the command of a brig sailing the traditional trade route to and from the Aegean islands and Black Sea ports. It was at the port of Odessa that Kanaris first heard of the *Philiki Hetaireia* (literally, the "Friendly Society"), a clandestine association of prominent members of the Greek diaspora who were planning a rising of the Greeks against Ottoman rule. The young captain declined to join, perhaps uncomfortable with the thought of a secret society, but his dedication to the cause of Greek independence was strong and he maintained close links with *Philiki Hetaireia* members. When he heard of outbreak of the revolution in the spring of 1821, he hastily returned to the Aegean in order to join the battle. Such was his enthusiasm that he turned his ship over to relatives and joined a squadron as commander of a fireship.

So it was, on the night of 6 June 1822, that Kanaris stealthily entered the harbour of Chios island and approached the flagship of the Turkish admiral Kara Ali which was riding at anchor. All hands were merrily observing a Muslim religious holiday. He quickly set the charges and rammed the flagship, causing her to explode and sink within minutes. More than 2000 Turks, including the admiral himself, were trapped inside the ship and went to the bottom. Four months later, Kanaris repeated this feat off the island of Tenedos by ramming and exploding a ship of the line which was escorting the flagship of Mehmet Pasha, Kara Ali's successor. This time the casualties were nearly 1000 men, including many Christians serving under Ottoman colours. As a result of these two actions the Ottoman fleet hastily sought refuge in the Dardanelles. Similar actions in the following years, and always to the grief of his Turkish enemies, made Kanaris the most feared Greek fireship commander in the Aegean. In the summer of 1825 an auda-

cious plan to strike a strategic blow against the Ottoman naval forces brought him to the Egyptian port of Alexandria. He hoisted the Russian flag and entered the harbour pretending to be an innocent arrival. His target was an Ottoman armada comprising 60 ships of the line and nearly 200 transports which was preparing to sail for Greece. Luckily for the unsuspecting Egyptians, a sudden drop in the wind forced Kanaris to abort the attack and escape in the direction of two Greek ships with Ottoman squadrons in hot pursuit.

When the revolution ended with the founding of an independent Greek state in 1829, Kanaris was one of the first officers commissioned in its young navy. He was soon confronted with the vagaries and pains of political instability attending the birth of the new state. An attempt by the first governor of Greece, Ioannis Kapodistria, to establish a centralized administration caused a violent reaction among war veterans, who felt that Kapodistria was attempting to substitute his own version of "Frankish" autocracy for Ottoman rule. Kanaris, who had been promoted to the rank of captain and appointed senator by Kapodistria, was soon ordered to pursue and arrest a prominent Peloponnesian, Petrobey Mavromichalis, whose clan had vowed to fight the governor to the finish and which was to assassinate him soon after Petrobey's arrest. In 1831 Kanaris, now the commanding officer of the Poros naval station, was confronted with a naval mutiny led by his friend, fellow fighter, and admiral from the island of Hydra, Andreas Miaoulis. The mutiny, one of the most dramatic events of the first years of Greek independence, resulted in the scuttling of two precious ships of the line and Miaoulis's escape back to Hydra under fire.

Deeply disillusioned by these fratricidal struggles and by the virulent political infighting, Kanaris retired to his home island of Psara and, later, to the island of Syros. But on the arrival of prince Otto of Bavaria, appointed king of the Hellenes by the Great Powers in 1833, he was recalled to active duty and promoted to vice admiral. In time, however, growing dissatisfaction with king Otho's arrogant rule and his personal cabinet of Bavarian advisers led Kanaris to join a secret political movement that aimed at forcing the king to grant political liberties to his subjects. In September 1843 Otho was confronted by an army ultimatum and, with thousands demonstrating outside his palace, reluctantly agreed to sign a constitution. Despite his involvement with what amounted to a coup d'état, Kanaris was still one of the most respected surviving figures of the War of Independence and was to serve several times as minister and prime minister.

Thirteen years would pass before Kanaris, a man of deeply conservative principles, was ready to side openly with those advocating the overthrow of the king. The catalyst was Otho's refusal in 1862 to appoint to Kanaris's cabinet the ministers the admiral had nominated. In protest, Kanaris rejected the royal mandate to form a government. In May 1863, after Otho's abdication and departure from Greece, Kanaris headed a Greek delegation to Denmark to offer the Hellenic crown to prince George, second son of king Christian. Recognizing Kanaris's revered position among the Greeks, the new king appointed him his prime minister, a post he held for a year. In 1865 the admiral retired to his small house in Athens and there remained as Greece's respected elder statesman until, in May

1877, he was again appointed to head a so-called Ecumenical Government. He died three months later.

Although Kanaris lacked a formal education, his contemporaries spoke of his deep understanding of politics and society and his highly sophisticated sense of leadership. He was described as a fearless, but not a reckless, man. His fellow fighters found him always respectful of the uncertainties of war, but never afraid of the prospect of battle. As a political man, Kanaris conducted himself with a firm sense of balance and a profound respect for political order, a characteristic that often helped him rise above the abysmal enmities and divisions wracking Greek politics. A naturally unassuming man, Kanaris stood out among his fellow war veterans, who often displayed a rather brusque approach to the affairs of state. Those who met him for the first time towards the end of his life expressed surprise at what they saw as a contradiction between a serene, wise old man and the daring young Kanaris who had struck fear in the hearts of his enemies during his many victories at sea.

ANESTIS T. SYMEONIDES

See also Independence (War of)

Biography

Born on the island of Psara in 1795, Kanaris received no formal education and went to sea at an early age. In the War of Independence he served heroically as commander of a fireship. After independence he became a naval officer and in 1831 quelled a mutiny led by Miaoulis. He served several terms as prime minister and in 1863 led the Greek delegation to offer the crown to Prince George of Denmark. He died in Athens in 1877.

Further Reading

Alexandris, Konstandinos, *To Nautikon tou yper Anexartisias Agonos tou 1821–29 kai i Drasis ton Pyrpolikon* [The Naval Aspect of the Struggle for Independence 1821–29 and the Effect of Incendiary Devices], Athens, 1968

Black, William, *Narrative of Cruises in the Mediterranean in HMS "Euryalus" and "Chanticleer" during the Greek War of Independence (1822–1826)*, Edinburgh: Oliver and Boyd, 1900

Clogg, Richard, *The Struggle for Greek Independence: Essays to Mark the 150th Anniversary of the Greek War of Independence*, London: Macmillan, 1973

Henty, George Alfred, *In Greek Waters: A Story of the Grecian War of Independence (1821–1827)*, London: Blackie, 1902; New York: Scribner, 1902

Kokkinos, Dionysios, *Istoria tis Neoteras Hellados* [History of Modern Greece], Athens, 1970

Markezinis, Spyridon, *Politiki Istoria tis Neoteras Hellados* [Political History of Modern Greece], Athens, 1968

Paparigopoulos, Konstandinos, *Istoria tou Ellinikou Ethnous* [History of the Greek Nation], 5 vols, Athens, 1864–75

Phillips, Walter Alison, *The War of Greek Independence, 1821 to 1833*, New York: Scribner, 1897

Kantakouzenos family

The Kantakouzenoi were a noble Byzantine family with a long history reaching back at least to the 11th century. The first recorded Kantakouzenos appears during the reign of Alexios I Komnenos (1081–1118). During the 13th century branches of the family appeared in the Peloponnese and in Nicaea. After the recovery of Constantinople from the Franks in 1261, the family played an important role in the public life of the empire and one member of it, John Kantakouzenos, became emperor. After the fall of Constantinople (1453), some members of the family became governors of the Danubian principalities, while others became prominent as officers in the Russian army and participated in the Greek War of Independence (1821). There are many opinions as to the origin of the name Kantakouzenos. The most probable is that it derives from the local name of a mountain (Kouzenas) near Smyrna. The most prominent members of the family are discussed below.

Kantakouzenos (his first name remains unknown) appears to have been the first member of the family to achieve distinction or rank. He was a general during the reign of Alexios I Komnenos and took part in the defensive campaign against the Cumans in 1094. In 1104 the emperor sent him to Syria against the Genoese fleet where he captured the harbour of Laodicea as well as neighbouring territories. In 1107 he rendered successful and distinguished service in the war against Bohemond in Albania.

John Kantakouzenos was a general with victories against the Serbs, Hungarians, and Pechenegs between 1150 and 1153 and was the military commander of Manuel I Komnenos (1143–80). He was killed in 1176 during the expedition of Manuel against the sultan of Ikonio (Konya). It has been suggested that he was a son or grandson of the above-mentioned Kantakouzenos but there seems to be no evidence to support this hypothesis.

Theodore Kantakouzenos was an opponent of the usurper Andronikos Komnenos (1183–85), who occupied the city of Nicaea. When Andronikos laid siege to it, in 1184, Theodore was captured and beheaded; his head was put on a pole, and displayed triumphantly in Constantinople. After his death the city came into the hands of Andronikos.

John VI Kantakouzenos became emperor of Constantinople (1341–54; see individual entry). His eldest son, Matthew Kantakouzenos, who was born around 1325, followed his father in the civil war against John V Palaiologos (1341/55–91). He was a remarkable soldier whose capabilities were fully understood and appreciated by his father. After the capture of Constantinople by his father in 1347 the army asked for him to be proclaimed heir to the throne. The proposal was not accepted and Matthew left with his supporters for Adrianople where he was given the title of co-emperor in 1353. In 1354 relations between Matthew and John V Palaiologos became strained and John V was forced to leave Constantinople and settle in Tenedos. Matthew was proclaimed emperor but his reign did not last long, because John V took over the city with Genoese support and Matthew retreated to Adrianople. He unsuccessfully fought the Serbs and in 1356 was captured by them. John V paid the ransom for his freedom and Matthew renounced any claim to the throne. In 1380 he became despot of Mistra after the death of his brother Manuel. He died there in 1383.

Irene Kantakouzene was the wife and empress of John VI Katakouzenos. The date of her marriage cannot be accurately determined, but it certainly took place before 1320. She is renowned for her courageous conduct in defence of Constantinople when her husband was abroad as well as for her ability to resolve differences between her eldest son

Matthew and John V Palaiologos. She became a nun after she and John VI Katakouzenos abdicated in 1354.

Helena Kantakouzene was the wife of David, the last emperor of Trebizond. After the fall of Trebizond in 1461 David and his family were shipped to Constantinople, where the whole family was executed apart from Helena. She ignored the sultan's order that the bodies should remain unburied to become the prey of dogs and crows, and secretly dug a trench in which she eventually buried them; a few days later she died.

Serban Kantakouzenos was the ruler of Wallachia (1679–88). The years of his reign are regarded as a landmark in Romanian history. He established institutions of higher education and committees for the translation of the scriptures into Romanian. His great dream was the liberation of the European countries that were occupied by the Turks. He organized a strong army and was recognized by Russia and Germany as the descendant of the imperial Byzantine family, destined to become the emperor of Constantinople after its liberation from the Turks. During the preparations for this he was poisoned by Boyars who were frightened that his plan would damage their country.

Alexander Kantakouzenos left Trieste to fight the Turks during the War of Independence (1821). He followed Demetrios Ypsilantis on his campaign in the Peloponnese and it was proposed that he should become commander of Crete. He refused this position, preferring to stay in the Peloponnese and fight the Turks. After the war he became a minister in the government of Mavrokordatos.

Georgios Kantakouzenos, born in 1837, was a prominent Romanian politician. He became minister of education in 1870. In 1889 he was elected president of the parliament and in 1892 president of the senate. After the leader of the conservatives died in 1899, he was elected president of the party and became prime minister of Romania, a position that he held until 1901. He was forced to resign because of the measures taken to restore the finances of the country. In 1905 he again became prime minister, but resigned because of his opposition to the distribution of land from the nobles to the peasants. He died in 1913.

MARIA ROUMBALOU

Further Reading

Nicol, Donald M., *The Byzantine Family of Kantakouzenos (Cantacuzenus), c.1100–1460*, Washington, D.C.: Dumbarton Oaks, 1968
Nicol, Donald M., *The Last Centuries of Byzantium, 1261–1453*, 2nd edition, Cambridge and New York: Cambridge University Press, 1993
Nicol, Donald M., *The Reluctant Emperor: A Biography of John Cantacuzene, Byzantine Emperor and Monk, c.1295–1383*, Cambridge and New York: Cambridge University Press, 1996

Kapodistria, Count Ioannis 1776–1831

Russian diplomat and first president of the Greek republic

Ioannis Kapodistria was born on 11 February 1776 in Corfu into an ancient aristocratic Corfiote family, which had emigrated there from Istria in 1373. He studied medicine at the university of Padua, but when the Septinsular Republic of the Ionian islands was established in 1800, he became secretary of its legislative council. For the next seven years, in a series of offices, he played an influential role in the affairs of the islands. Early in 1807 he was appointed military governor, in charge of organizing the defence of Leucas against Ali Pasha, the practically independent sovereign of the Turkish province of Ioannina. It was then that Kapodistria first came into contact with Theodore Koloktronis, one of the future leaders in the War of Independence, and through him with early Hellenic nationalism. Throughout this period he was an ardent supporter of a Russophile policy, firmly believing that tsar Alexander I was the most reliable ally of the Greek cause. With the cession of the Ionian islands to France under the Treaty of Tilsit in 1807 such hopes were temporarily dashed.

Kapodistria maintained his connections with the Russian court, and in the same year accepted an offer to enter the Russian diplomatic service. Here his experience of the Near East stood him in good stead. By 1813 he had risen to the rank of councillor of state; he became one of tsar Alexander's most influential advisers. At the Congress of Vienna (1814–15) his influence was particularly conspicuous. Here Kapodistria, who in September 1815 had been promoted joint secretary of state for foreign affairs and governor of Bessarabia, was a vociferous advocate of the cause of the smaller nations in Europe, and he contributed significantly to the formulation of the final treaty of November 1815. Kapodistria's espousal of nationalism, however, raised the suspicions of Europe's leading statesman of the time, the Austrian state chancellor Prince Metternich. The overthrow of this "coryphaeus of liberalism" became vital for the success of Metternich's reactionary policies. Thus, when Kapodistria went on leave to visit Corfu in 1819, he was shadowed by the spies of the apprehensive Austrian.

In Vienna in 1815 Kapodistria had supported the creation of a British protectorate over the Ionian islands, the commercial advantages of which were apparent. Sir Thomas Maitland's robust administration of the islands, however, offended his local patriotism, and he decided to take up the issue with his imperial master in St Petersburg and with the British government. The latter, regarding Kapodistria's initiative as a pretext for Russian interference in what by treaty were wholly British affairs, gave him a cold reception. When he returned to Russia in the autumn of 1819 he found that here, too, his influence was waning. In court circles the "upstart Greek" had always been distrusted, but the murder of the Russian agent August von Kotzebue in 1819 and that of the Duc de Berry in the following year as well as the revolutions in Spain and Naples had shaken the tsar's liberalism, and thus undermined Kapodistria's position in the Russian government. By 1821 it had become untenable.

Alexander Ypsilantis's misguided and abortive raid into the Danubian principalities furnished Metternich with the long-sought opportunity to overthrow Kapodistria. Ypsilantis was the president of the secret revolutionary organization *Philiki Hetaireia*, of which Kapodistria was also a member. Metternich now insinuated that Kapodistria was bending Russian foreign policy to suit Greek ends. Anticipating his dismissal, Kapodistria resigned from his position in the

Russian government on the eve of the Congress of Verona in 1822.

For the next five years he withdrew into private life in Geneva. In April 1827, however, the Greek national assembly at Troezen elected him president of the Greek republic. His election marked a triumph for the Russian faction in the Greek national movement, as indeed Kapodistria had never ceased to regard himself as a Russian official. He accepted the new post but was in no hurry to take up the difficult task. In July he visited tsar Nicholas I; and having obtained the tsar's permission to proceed and being furnished with instructions as to the policy he should pursue in Greece, he went on a tour of the courts of Europe to gain moral and material support. It was only the news of the annihilation of Turkey's Egyptian fleet at the battle of Navarino in 1827, which practically meant the end of the War of Independence, that hastened Kapodistria's return to Greece. He arrived at Nauplia on 19 January 1828 aboard HMS *Warspite*.

The task awaiting Kapodistria was formidable: the finances of the new country were exhausted; it was economically backward; the great powers had placed restrictions on its sovereignty; and, most awkward of all, an undefeated Turkish army under Ibrahim Pasha was still in the southern half of the Morea. Kapodistria was an experienced politician; and he had the support of Russia. His diplomatic efforts to lift some of the restrictions on Greek sovereignty were to some extent successful, but his aristocratic background, his Russian proclivities, his arbitrary government, and his undisguised nepotism antagonized sections of the Greek body politic. Ultimately, his attempt to introduce the centralized Russian administrative system to Greece proved fatal. An open rebellion on some of the islands he was able to squash with Russian naval assistance. But his attempt to coerce the mountain clan of the Mavromichalis under Petros (or Petrobey) Mavromichalis, one of the leaders of the War of Independence, sparked an insurrection in Maina at Easter 1830. Although Petrobey was arrested and the uprising thus quelled, Kapodistria paid dearly for his attempt to enforce his rule on the country. He was murdered on 9 October 1831 on his way to church in a revenge attack for Petrobey's arrest by the latter's son Constantine. Kapodistria's assassination was followed by a state of anarchy which was ended only with the convention of London of May 1832 and the enthronement of prince Otto of Bavaria as king Otho of Greece.

T.G. OTTE

Biography

Born in Corfu in 1776, Kapodistria (also known as Giovanni Capo d'Istria) studied medicine at the University of Padua. In 1800 he became an official of the Septinsular Republic of the Ionian islands. In 1807 he entered the Russian diplomatic service but resigned in 1822 and retired to Geneva. In 1827 he was elected president of the Greek republic. He was assassinated in 1831.

Further Reading

Mendelssohn-Bartholdy, Karl, *Graf Johann Kapodistrias*, Berlin: Mittler, 1864

Phillips, W. Alison, *The War of Greek Independence, 1821 to 1833*, London: Smith Elder, and New York: Scribner, 1897

Karaghiozis

Shadow puppet theatre

Karaghiozis is the Greek term for the shadow puppet theatre known in Turkey as *Karagöz* ("black-eyed"). The figures are usually constructed of thick cardboard on to which paint or coloured transparent paper is applied, or of very thin leather painted in various colours. They are highly ornamented, bearing scalloped edges, sequins, and glitter, so that the various elements that constitute the costume become clearly articulated. The figures are suspended from wooden guiding posts behind a white screen and they are lighted from behind, so that only their shadow touches the screen and creates a coloured illusion. There is a very simple stage set depicted on screen, constituted by the *Seray* (the vizier's mansion, or the sultan's palace), always located on the left side of the screen, and Karaghiozis's shack, always on the right side of the screen. Movement on screen originally occurred in only one direction, clearly demarcating the social space occupied by the various characters. Karaghiozis and the Greek characters exited from the right, whereas the Turkish characters exited from the left. With new techniques in the construction of the figures and the holding of the guiding poles, however, bidirectionality was introduced to the plays around the second half of the 20th century.

The origins of the genre are located in the religious and mystic theatre present in India, Indonesia, and China, although this particular genealogy is all but forgotten in the public discourses on shadow puppet theatre in both Greece and Turkey. The earliest written references to shadow puppet theatre are in the Indian epic *Mahabharata*, while in Java there are literary sources of the 11th century that mention shadow puppet theatre. Around the same time it also appears in Chinese texts. This tradition, however, consisted mainly of highly ritualized, philosophical, and stochastic texts that have little relation to the satirical, teasing, and profane elements that, in different combinations, constitute both the Turkish and the Greek versions of the tradition.

Although there is some debate as to when *Karagöz* first appeared in Turkey, it seems that the most plausible time was the 13th century. The Turkish chronicler Evliya Çelebi, writing in the 17th century, mentions, erroneously, that Karagöz was a messenger of the last Byzantine emperor Constantine XI Palaiologos, while Hacivat (the other main character) was a messenger of sultan Alâeddin. Although the character was known to the Greek inhabitants of Constantinople and other Ottoman urban centres of the Balkans from as early as the 17th century, *Karaghiozis* did not appear in Greece until the early 19th century, in the court of Ali Pasha in Ioannina. There, in 1809, we find the first references to performances of shadow puppet theatre by J.C. Hobhouse. *Karaghiozis* first appeared in Athens after independence, some time in the 1830s. The first specific reference to a performance is in Nauplia in 1841. We next find a reference to the establishment of an "oriental" (*asiatikon*) theatre in Plaka (Athens) in 1852. These performances were still very much Turkish ones, given by either Armenian or Jewish players, using profane language that was abandoned when the plays became "Hellenized". The content of the plays and the adaptation of the supporting characters to Greek personae did not take place until the early 20th century.

The main characters in both traditions are Karagöz / Karaghiozis and Hacivat / Hatziavatis. Karagöz / Karaghiozis is a figure with exaggerated black eyes, of dark complexion, with a short, dark, and bushy beard, bald, stocky, and with a left arm that has one extra joint, making it one-third longer than his right arm. He was either a Turk, or a Greek, or a "Gypsy", and spoke in the vernacular, which he used very well, making extensive uses of linguistic tropes, in order to arrive at doubles entendres, which, when contrasted with his linguistic simplicity, provided the satirical element of the genre. Although perpetually jobless, he was always willing to do minor work and was available for little errands, which he always completed at the expense of Hatziavatis (in the Greek plays) or under the strict supervision and constant terrorization of Hacivat (in the Turkish plays). Karaghiozis was always depicted as being extremely intelligent and cunning and his main preoccupation was feeding his family and himself. He was dressed in rags, shoeless, lived in a shack directly opposite the palace, was married, and, in the Greek plays, had a legion of hungry children in tow, the most famous of which was Kolleteri. Hacivat / Hatziavatis was the sultan's messenger, a character with extensive encyclopaedic knowledge that ranged from the use of learned language in rhymed prose to the names of plants and spices, to music, and to Classical poetry which he could recite by heart. He had excruciatingly good manners and aspirations to high society. His figure was slim and he sported a small pointed beard. His demeanour was quiet and reflective, in stark opposition to the impulsive manners of Karagöz / Karaghiozis. Hadcivat / Hatziavatis was depicted as the keeper of the established order, the benefactor of the underprivileged, credulous and benevolent, whereas Karagöz / Karaghiozis was the innovator, the upsetter, and the trickster. In the Turkish plays Hadcivat was always the one who beat up Karagöz, but in the Greek adaptation the order (and the beatings) were reversed. These two main characters were surrounded by a cast of supporting ones, some of which are almost always present while others make only occasional appearances.

The supporting characters found in the Greek theatre are analogous to those found in the Turkish. The commonest of those are the various women who appear, or are referred to, regularly in the plays (such as Karaghiozis's wife and mother-in-law, the vizier's daughter, the women who come requesting his help); the various regional characters (Morfonios, who is a dwarf with strange manners but a womanizer; Sior Nionios, the Zantean; Stavrakas, the argot-speaking lumpen character from Athens; and, most importantly, Barba-Yiorgos, the mountaineer from western Greece, Karaghiozis's protector, who has no Western manners, sports no Western clothes, but is of the purest heart and intentions, in stark contrast to everyone else who is always trying to take advantage of Karaghiozis). Of the supporting characters only those of the pasha (or the sultan) and the vizier's daughter (E Veziropoula in the Greek plays) have been transferred unchanged, retaining their original titles (names do not appear with reference to these characters), occupying the space of law and authority. The pasha, the vizier, and the sultan rarely speak, whereas the vizier's daughter not only speaks but does so in perfect Greek and with a sweet voice.

Karaghiozis: the figures of Karaghiozis (right) and Hatziavatis are seen next to their respective dwellings, a shack and the sultan's palace

The representatives of authority, those who control it and delegate it, in the Karaghiozis plays are always depicted as mild-mannered and good-hearted, albeit obviously omnipotent, hence awe-inspiring. The characters, however, who draw Karaghiozis's mirth, ridicule, irony, and sarcasm are those who occupy the second tier of authority, those involved in the executive branch of the law, the messengers, such as Hatziavatis, and the policemen and the gendarmes, such as Velighekas and Dervenagas; also those who possess symbolic power by virtue of their profession, such as the doctor, the judge, etc. But if Karaghiozis was verbally, or even physically, abusive to those in power, he reserved and exhibited the utmost respect for the historical characters present in the plays. The Karaghiozis performers engaged in the rewriting of official historical events and characters for the benefit of their audience, in a manner that transcended historical time and space, joining popular lore with the memory of history. It is in this light that one should look at plays such as *Alexander the Great and the Cursed Snake*, *Karaghiozis and Captain Panourgias*, *Karaghiozis and Captain Greece*. The thematic appropriations extended into negotiations with and the subversion of the class structure (with plays such as *Karaghiozis the Millionaire*, *Karaghiozis the Admiral*, *Karaghiozis the Banker*), or, later, the management of the exotic and of change in the experience of everyday realities (such as in the plays *Karaghiozis the Astronaut*, *Karaghiozis the Soccer Player*, *Karaghiozis the Bullfighter*, *Karaghiozis's Divorce*).

Karaghiozis was initially performed within the informal and non-specific space of the *kafeneion* or empty lots (*alanes*). The performances were attended by a mixed audience of children and adults, an audience that, until *Karaghiozis's* exoticism wore off, included members of the upper classes. With de-exoticization *Karaghiozis* was established as a genre of political and social commentary which was allowed to flourish because its criticism always operated under the disguise of comedy. By the middle of the 20th century, however, the genre had lost its political and social edge and had been safely appropriated as children's entertainment and transformed into a folkloristic item of slapstick comedy, prompting Yiorgos Ioannou's comment that the only audience of *Karaghiozis* nowadays are children and intellectuals. *Karaghiozis* lost its edge but retained the jerky, exaggerated movements, the structure of the play, and its musical and dancing form. The performances were eventually moved into open-air enclosures with masonry fences built around them (*mandres*), until they were finally moved spatially and symbolically into the area of tourism. From the beginning of the 20th century, with the introduction of the culturally Greek elements of the play, the shadow puppet theatre was supported by the parallel production of popular publications where the scripts of the various plays were published. With the advent of mass popular culture and the flourishing of a recording industry in Greece 45 rpm disks started being produced and distributed, followed by tape cassettes, and, lately, video recordings of performances, and books with Karaghiozis projects (such as "Build Your Own Shack").

NENI PANOURGIÁ

Summary

Karaghiozis (Turkish *Karagöz*) is the Greek term for the shadow puppet theatre and its eponymous main character. First appearing in Turkey (probably in the 13th century), the genre was not introduced to Greece until the early 19th century at the court of Ali Pasha of Ioannina. The repertory of plays combines folklore with satire and an element of history. By the mid-20th century it had become largely an entertainment for children.

Further Reading

And, Metin, *Karagöz: Turkish Shadow Theatre*, Ankara: Dost, 1975, revised edition 1979

Çelebi, Evliya, *Narrative of Travels in Europe, Asia and Africa in the Seventeenth Century*, translated by Ritter Joseph von Hammer, 2 vols, London: Oriental Translation Fund, 1834–50, reprinted New York: Johnson, 1968

Danforth, Loring, "Humour and Status Reversal in Greek Shadow Theatre", *Byzantine and Modern Greek Studies*, 2 (1976): pp. 99–111

Myrsiades, Linda S. and Kostas Myrsiades, *Karagiozis: Culture and Comedy in Greek Puppet Theatre*, Lexington: University of Kentucky Press, 1992

Mystakidou, Aikaterini, *To Theatro Skion stin Hellada kai stin Tourkia: Eisagogi, hoi komodies, (a) Pharmakeio, (b) Anapodos Gamos* [The Shadow Theatre in Greece and Turkey: Introduction, the Comedies, (a) The Pharmacy, (b) The Cantakerous Marriage], Athens, 1982

Mystakidou, Katerina, *Metamorphoseis tou Karagiozi* [Transformations of the Karaghiozis], Athens, 1998

Stavrakopoulou, Anna, "Variations on the Theme of Marriage in the Karaghiozis Recorded Performances of the Whitman-Rinvolucri Collection" (dissertation), Cambridge, Massachusetts: Harvard University, 1994

Karaiskakis, Georgios 1782–1827

Greek commander in the War of Independence

Georgios Karaiskakis (born Karaiskos), destined to become a hero in the War of Independence, was raised in Epirus among the rugged mountains and valleys of western Greece. G. Finlay describes him as "of middle size, thin, dark complexioned, and haggard, with a bright expressive animal eye". Karaiskakis was accused of playing both sides of the fence in the war, and to some extent he did. One must remember, however, that at the outbreak of the war Greece was not a unified nation, and

Karaiskakis was not the only person to change sides in the course of events. He was employed for a time by Ali Pasha, who ruled from Ioannina; he became a member of Ali's personal bodyguard, and was thus trained by the Turkish forces. When Ali Pasha died, Karaiskakis returned to the mountains and became the leader of a band of fighters and brigands known as *armatoles*. Subsequently he took part in the invasion of the Peloponnese in 1824 in which he fought against those Greeks who were fighting for independence. Ultimately convinced of the need to throw off the Turkish yoke, Karaiskakis therefore changed sides. In subsequent fighting he acquired a reputation for bravery which assuaged the doubts which some had about his loyalty.

Courageous and witty, Karaiskakis went on to fight in some of the most important battles of the war. He was at Krommydi in 1825, and also took part in operations at Messolonghi in August 1825. During the attempt to lift the siege of Messolonghi in April 1826, Karaiskakis was caught in an ambush by Turkish forces who effectively prevented his scheduled arrival. His absence from this operation contributed to the devastating defeat of the Greeks.

In the summer of 1826 Karaiskakis was named commander of the Greek forces by president Zaimis, and he immediately gathered some 2000 troops at Eleusis and marched off with the ultimate goal of lifting the siege of the Acropolis. He planned to do this in a series of battles, but his forces were defeated at the battle of Chaidari, and they withdrew to Boeotia. There he scored some successes, notably the defeat of a group of Turks at Arachova, but he was fighting on the fringe of the war. He returned to Attica, where the British admiral Church was now in control. Karaiskakis had been pushing his plan to cut off the supply lines of the Turks with a series of encircling battles. Church rejected that plan in favour of more direct action. Karaiskakis agreed to take orders from Church, and thus began the attack on the Acropolis.

On 25 April Karaiskakis took his men and marched toward the Acropolis. They met with great success: 13 outposts were captured on that one day. When they came to the monastery of St Spiridion in Munychia, they besieged the 300 Albanians who were holding the place. Attempts were made to negotiate an end to the siege, and it was Karaiskakis who finally persuaded the Albanians to come out. He did so by offering himself as guarantee for their safety. Thus when the gates were opened, the Albanians walked out with him in their midst. In spite of this, an altercation broke out and, disregarding the promise of safe passage, the Greeks slaughtered most of the Albanians. Karaiskakis was horrified, and reportedly called on the Albanians to shoot him, since he was their guarantee, but they were too busy trying to escape the melee. The incident is indicative of his character.

When he and his troops finally reached the Acropolis, the order was given for the battle to begin on 5 May. Accordingly, the troops were in place on the evening of the 4th. One of the Greeks in an outpost, however, fired on the Turks on the night of the 4th, and the battle was launched. Though ill in his tent, Karaiskakis crawled out to attempt to put a stop to the premature fighting. Unfortunately he advanced too far and became cut off from his troops. He was wounded, and died later that night. His death caused great dismay among the Greek troops, but he also became a rallying point for their defeat of the Turks.

Karaiskakis was a fighter of remarkable ferocity. His name was, in fact, proverbial among his enemies. One proverb asked, "Why do you run as though you were being chased by Karaiskakis?" He was clearly a man to be feared, yet he was also said to be a man of great wit. D.A. Zakynthos has written of him that, "In the character of this extraordinary man were present in full measure all those strange and vivid contrasts of light and shade, of baseness and nobility, which give to the actors in the story of the Greek revolt such remarkable dramatic interest".

As a martyr for the cause of freedom, Karaiskakis emerged from the War of Independence a popular figure. His popularity has not abated. In May 1997, to celebrate the anniversary of the storming of the Acropolis, a commemorative statue of Karaiskakis was unveiled on the island of Salamis in the main square of Salamis town.

TIMOTHY F. WINTERS

See also Independence (War of)

Biography

Born in Epirus in 1782 with the name Karaiskos, he joined the staff of Ali Pasha in Ioannina. After Ali's death he became a brigand leader in the mountains and took part in the invasion of the Peloponnese in 1824. He then changed sides and in 1826 was named commander of the Greek forces in the War of Independence. He died in the siege of the Acropolis at Athens in 1827.

Further Reading

Dakin, Douglas, *The Greek Struggle for Independence, 1821–1833*, London: Batsford, and Berkeley: University of California Press, 1973

Eliot, C.W.J. (editor), *The Campaign of the Falieri and Piraeus in the Year 1827; or, Journal of a Volunteer, being the Personal Account of Captain Thomas Douglas Whitcombe*, Princeton, New Jersey: American School of Classical Studies at Athens, 1992

Finlay, George, *A History of Greece from Its Conquest by the Romans to the Present Time, BC 146 to AD 1864*, revised by H.F. Tozer, 7 vols, Oxford: Clarendon Press, 1877, reprinted New York: AMS Press, 1970, vol. 6

Gazis, G., *Dictionary of the Revolution and Other Works*, Ioannina, 1971 (in Greek; Gazis was secretary to Karaiskakis)

Makriyannis, I., *The Memoirs of General Makryannis, 1797–1864*, edited and translated by H.A. Lidderdale, London and New York: Oxford University Press, 1966

Photiades, D., *Karaiskakis*, Athens, 1956 (in Greek)

Phillips, W. Alison, *The War of Greek Independence, 1821–1833*, London: Smith Elder, and New York: Scribner, 1897

Protopsaltis, E. (editor), *Apomnimevmata Agoniston tou '21* [Memoirs of the Fighters of the Greek Revolution], 20 vols, Athens 1955–59

Sakellariou, P.D., *Archeion Karaiskaki* [Karaiskakis Archive], Athens, 1924

Vlachoiannis, G., *Karaiskakis*, Athens, 1943 (in Greek)

Zakythinos, D.A., *The Making of Modern Greece: From Byzantium to Independence*, Oxford: Blackwell, 1976

Karamanlides

The Karamanlides were one of the most interesting, yet poorly understood, groups of Orthodox Christians living under the Ottoman empire. They were Orthodox Christians who were Turkish in speech and constituted a significant portion of the Rum Milleti ("Roman Communities") within the Ottoman empire. They inhabited large areas of Asia Minor and portions of the Crimea as well as parts of Bulgaria and quarters of Constantinople. The Karamanlides were observed by outsiders as far back as the 16th century when the German traveller Hans Dernschwam wrote about the Turkish-speaking "Caramanian" Christians in the Yedikule quarter of Constantinople after his trip to the city in 1553–55. The Karamanlides played an important part after the Greek Revolution of 1821, when efforts were being made by the Greek kingdom to raise its sense of national consciousness. Before the 1923 population exchange as many as 400,000 Karamanlides lived in villages and small towns in Asia Minor in the regions of Nevshehir, Aksaray, Kayseri, Ihlara Vadisi, Peristrama, Ürgüp, Göreme, Derinkuyu, Nigde, Konya, Akshehir, Eregli, Ermenek, Ichel, Antalya, and Fetiye. Today, they make up a small religious community of no more than 80 to 100 people in Istanbul.

The origins of the Karamanlides are still an open matter. According to Greek scholars, the Karamanlides were originally Greek-speakers who adopted the Turkish vernacular either by force from their Muslim overlords or through their isolation from other Greek-speaking Orthodox Christians (who inhabited the coastal regions). The Karamanlides in this view are typically known as "Cappadocian Greeks". Turkish scholars view the Karamanlides as descended from Turks who migrated to Byzantine territories before 1453 and who only adopted the religion of their new rulers, but not the Greek language. The Karamanlides in this thesis are thought to have replaced the Pechenegs as mercenaries in the Byzantine armies and to have settled in the Kayseri and Karaman regions.

Up to 500 works of literature are thought to have been printed in the language of the Karamanlides, *karamanlidika*, by the beginning of the 20th century. These works used a modified Greek alphabet to represent Turkish sounds. For many Karamanlides, access to the Greek language was largely limited to the alphabet. One of the largest distributors of *karamanlidika* texts was the British and Foreign Bible Society, which published numerous editions of the Old and New Testaments. Other translations into *karamanlidika* included works by Aristotle and Confucius and Xavier de Montepin's novels.

There is still some debate as to which language was used for the Divine Liturgy. Some accounts report that Turkish was used throughout the liturgy while others state that Turkish was used only for the reading of the Epistle and Gospel. Preaching, however, was apparently done almost exclusively in Turkish owing to the limited knowledge of spoken Greek in some parts of central Anatolia. Discrepancies in travel accounts over this matter often arose from the traveller's inability to distinguish clearly between liturgical Greek and spoken Turkish, causing some to state that the whole service was performed in Turkish. Despite valid reasons for the existence of a liturgy written in *karamanlidika*, none has been found to date.

A strange example of the interaction between the Karamanlides and the Greek-speaking Orthodox Christians was the case of Papa Eftim (Efthymios Karahisaridis). Papa Eftim, a Karamanli, was ordained priest in 1915 for the town of Keskin in central Anatolia. He was openly hostile to the Ecumenical Patriarchate at the Phanar and had ideas about further Turkifying the Anatolian Orthodox (which were consistent with Kemalist aims). On 15 September 1922 he declared the establishment of the Turkish Orthodox Church at St John's at Zincirdere, Kayseri. His hopes for a viable Turkish Orthodox Church came to a complete stop with the mandatory exchange of populations, but he was able to remain in Turkey by demonstrating his pro-Turkish activities during the war between Greece and Turkey. Papa Eftim then looked towards the Karamanlides in Istanbul (who were not affected by the exchange of populations). This too proved to be useless since the Karamanli community there was firmly attached to the Phanar and the mainstream Greek community of the city. Nevertheless, Papa Eftim travelled to the Phanar on 28 September 1922 where he was very outspoken about the need to elect a Turcophone patriarch who would have a "Turkish heart" and not speak rebelliously against the new Turkish state. On 2 October 1922 Papa Eftim and his Turkish allies stormed the Phanar and caused the deposition of Patriarch Meletios by the Holy Synod. Papa Eftim then made himself the Patriarchal representative in Ankara, only to be dismissed later by the Turkish government on 12 October 1922 on the grounds that religious institutions had no place in the new secular government. Papa Eftim was labeled "mad" by the newspapers at the time.

Karamanlidika inscriptions are found at many cemeteries in Turkey, the largest number being at Balikli (outside the city walls of Istanbul). The inscriptions often talk about the humble origins of unimportant craftsmen from central Anatolia. According to Clogg (1978), they offer a "glimpse of a long past world of Greek and Turkish symbiosis".

MARK A. COUMOUNDUROS

Summary

The Karamanlides were Orthodox Christians who spoke Turkish and lived under the Ottoman empire. They were to be found in many parts of Asia Minor as well as in the Crimea, Bulgaria, and Constantinople. It is uncertain whether they were originally Greek-speakers who adopted the language of their rulers or Turkish-speakers who moved to Byzantine territory before the fall of the empire and adopted the religion, but not the language, of their masters. Today they comprise a tiny religious community in Istanbul.

Further Reading

Alexandris, Alexis, *The Greek Minority of Istanbul and Turkish–Greek Relations, 1918–1974*, Athens: Center for Asia Minor Studies, 1983

Clogg, Richard, "The Publication and Distribution of Karamanli Text by the British and Foreign Bible Society before 1850", *Journal of Ecclesiastical History*, 19/1–2 (1968)

Clogg, Richard, "Some Karamanlidika Inscriptions from the Monastery of the Zoodokhos Pigi, Balikli, Istanbul", *Byzantine and Modern Greek Studies*, 4 (1978)

Clogg, Richard, *A Concise History of Greece*, Cambridge and New York: Cambridge University Press, 1992

Dawkins, R.M., *Modern Greek in Asia Minor: A Study of the Dialects*, Cambridge: Cambridge University Press, 1916

Salaville, Sévérien, Evangelia Balta and Eugène Dallegio, *Karamanlidika: bibliographie analytique d'ouvrages en langue turque imprimés en caractères grecs*, 4 vols, Athens: Center for Asia Minor Studies, 1958–97

Soysü, Hâle, *Kavimler Kapisi*, vol. 1, Istanbul: Kaynak Yayinlari, 1992

Karamanlis, Constantine 1907–1998

Politician

A statesman who listened to the singular voice of politics his whole life, Constantine Karamanlis is best remembered as the man who was chosen to lead Greece out of the darkness of dictatorship in the mid-1970s and as the prime minister who secured Greece's entry into the European Economic Community in 1981. His political career ebbed and flowed for the better part of the 20th century – a time of much institutional upheaval and social duress for Greece – yet despite prolonged retrenchments during some of the worst of times, it lasted into his autumn years. For this he can be called a true political survivor, but one whom history has yet wholly to assess.

Karamanlis was born on 8 March 1907, an Ottoman subject in the Macedonian town of Proti, which was not liberated until the Balkan Wars. As a young boy he worked in his father's tobacco fields. These were formative years, in which he experienced the hardships of farm life and the demands of duty. But he had the privilege of a good education: at the age of 16 he was sent by his father, a schoolteacher, to Athens. Two years later, in 1925, Karamanlis entered Athens University to study law. Though known as rather a loner, and suffering from a developing and socially impeding hearing problem, he nevertheless formed lasting friendships and secured political patronages. After serving for a brief period in the army, Karamanlis set up his own law practice in the town of Serres. With a growing awareness of his own political philosophy, valuing stability over revolution, his political aspirations grew and in the general elections of June 1935 he won election as a deputy under the Popular Party. With the dissolution of parliament under General Metaxas a year later, Karamanlis found himself jobless. He kept a low profile during the dictatorship and rather than publicly oppose the regime, as did some of his contemporaries, he returned to his law practice in Serres. He remained politically inactive through World War II and the German occupation of Athens. It was not until 1946 that he resumed parliamentary activity, under the Popular Party government of Constantine Tsaldaris.

Karamanlis held a number of parliamentary posts, including that of minister of social welfare (1948–50), in which he gained recognition in his handling of the repatriation of war refugees through a welfare-work programme, and later as minister of public works, demonstrating his ability to achieve results and laying the groundwork for the development of Greece's infrastructure. On the death of Marshal Papagos in 1955, Karamanlis, much to the chagrin of his competitors who decried the appointment as favouritism, was made prime minister by king Paul I. The following year, wishing to dissociate himself from the far right and shake off accusations of complicity with the United States, Karamanlis formed the National Radical Union, cleverly adopting the titulary nomenclature of the left.

His transformation of the Greek economy and plans for modernization have left an indelible mark on the Greece of today. His role in the creation of the Republic of Cyprus in 1960, which detractors like to consider problematically derived too, was another of his achievements. Despite Karamanlis's animosity towards the palace and what he considered its meddlesome role in politics, his tenure as prime minister was generally successful. Not suprisingly, procedural ambiguities in the 1952 constitution occasioned ever deepening rifts between Karamanlis and the king, and in 1963, shortly after the assassination of a left-wing deputy by right-wing extremists, and a row between Karamanlis and the king over the latter's impending visit to Britain, Karamanlis left politics and exiled himself in Paris. Karamanlis, though somewhat authoritarian but never quite the strong rightist his critics considered him to be, spent most of his political life trying to distance himself publicly from extremists. He was never implicated in the assassination of the deputy, though some found the coincidence of his self-imposed exile shortly in its wake highly suspicious. For 11 years, mostly during the dark years of the dictatorship of the colonels (1967–74), Karamanlis again withdrew from politics, absorbing, perhaps, the principles of Gaullism, which were to guide him upon his return to Greece in 1974.

Karamanlis made a triumphant return to Greece and to politics. As prime minister under New Democracy, the centre-right party that he founded, he quickly embarked on a programme of dejuntification, reinstated the Communist Party (outlawed since 1947), democratized political institutions including revision of the constitution, put the question of the monarchy to referendum, and returned Greece to the international community. His premiership came to an end with the victory of the Socialists under Andreas Papandreou in 1981, though Karamanlis continued in the role of president. Papandreou's second term, which began in 1985, brought about constitutional amendments and diminished support for Karamanlis to serve a second term as president, despite his impeccable conduct in that post. Papandreou sought to limit the powers of the president, which had been allocated in a constitution of Karamanlis's design. Karamanlis, who so easily in the past had abandoned politics, withdrew again, leaving Papandreou to amend the constitution.

In 1990, and at more than 80 years of age, Karamanlis again rejoined the political fray, serving as president with his own party, New Democracy, in power. He retired from political life at the end of his term five years later. Karamanlis died on 23 April 1998, at the age of 91.

BARBARA SYRRAKOS

Biography

Born in 1907 in the Macedonian town of Proti, Karamanlis studied law at the University of Athens. He first served as a deputy in 1935–36. He re-entered politics in 1946 and became prime minister for the first time in 1955–63. In 1963–74 he went into voluntary exile in Paris. He served again as prime minister in 1974–81 and as president in 1981–85 and 1990–95. He died in 1998.

Further Reading
Featherstone, Kevin and Dimitrios K. Katsoudas (editors), *Political Change in Greece: Before and After the Colonels*, London: Croom Helm, 1987
Woodhouse, C.M., *Karamanlis: The Restorer of Greek Democracy*, Oxford: Clarendon Press, and New York: Oxford University Press, 1982

Kassia
Poet and composer of liturgical music in the 9th century

Popular to the present day for her liturgical poetry and for the legends surrounding her life, the 9th-century nun Kassia is one of a handful of Byzantine women known to have written musical works for liturgical use. She is the only woman whose hymns were transmitted widely in manuscript – where they often appear under such variants of her name as Eikasia, Ikasia, and Kassiane – and were later included in the printed service books of the Orthodox Church. Kassia is also exceptional in that, unlike other Byzantine church musicians of comparable accomplishment, such as Kosmas of Maïouma or Joseph the Hymnographer, she was never canonized.

In the absence of a *vita*, scholars have gleaned information about her from several sources. Letters by St Theodore the Stoudite to a young Kassia reveal her to have been the daugher of a Constantinopolitan courtier, to have received a good literary education, and to have been from her youth a zealous defender of icons. Her early devotion to God and the iconophile cause must have been remarkable, for in one instance the fiery Theodore reproved her for dealing too harshly with an iconoclast, and in another counsel led her to postpone a decision to embrace monasticism. She seems to have followed his advice, for the writings of St Symeon the Logothete (10th century) describe Kassia's participation in a bride-show for the emperor Theophilos. According to Symeon, after a witty reply to a question posed by the emperor lost her the opportunity to become empress, the beautiful Kassia became a nun. Although some scholars have questioned the authenticity of Symeon's account, others have noted that his description of Kassia's character corresponds well with the intolerance she displays in her series of iambic sentences beginning with the phrase "I hate". These contain a denunciation of an illiterate young man of royal blood that may be a reference to Theophilos. She is reported to have founded a monastery on the Constantinopolitan hill of Xerolophos after the final restoration of icons in 843, dying at some point during the reign of Michael III (842–67).

Kassia wrote non-liturgical poetry, of which 261 verses of epigrams and gnomic sentences survive, on a variety of social and ethical themes, including fortune, luck, friendship, women, and social customs. She is, however, primarily remembered for her work as a *melodos*, a hymnographer who composed her own melodies. While only 23 of the 49 hymns attributed to Kassia in manuscripts are regarded by scholars as genuine, there are reasons to suspect that she may have written some of the remaining works of doubtful attribution. Theodore Prodromos (*c.*1100–*c.*1170?), for example, notes that her authorship of a four-ode canon for Holy Saturday was later obscured through reattribution to Kosmas of Maïouma by authorities who thought it unseemly to feature compositions by a woman on such a solemn occasion. This *tetraodion* – which was rewritten at the command of Leo IV, the Wise (886–912) with the addition of the missing odes necessary for a full canon – is the better of her two known canons. The other, a massive 252-verse canon for the dead, is her only genuine work not included in modern service books.

Unlike her prolific contemporary St Joseph the Hymnographer, who wrote mainly canons, Kassia is distinguished by her cultivation of the *sticheron*, a monostrophic genre encompassing all the 47 remaining hymns firmly or doubtfully attributed to her. Written for performance between the verses of the fixed morning and evening psalms of Palestinian monastic matins and vespers, these *stichera* include texts set both to pre-existing tunes (*prosomoia*) and to melodies of her own composition (*idiomela*). It is in the latter that Kassia's genius as a *melodos* is most apparent, for the best of them, as Touliatos has shown, combine expressive texts with finely crafted music. Her *sticheron* for the vespers of Christmas "When Augustus Reigned" emphasizes the parallels drawn in its text between political unification under the Roman empire and the union of all humankind in Christ with a sequence of paired musical phrases employing the same melody for the human and the divine. Kassia's most famous composition is her *sticheron* for the matins of Holy Wednesday on the sinful woman in St Luke's gospel (7: 36–50). In marked contrast to Romanos's treatment of the woman as a stereotypical prostitute, Kassia identifies strongly with her subject. After briefly introducing the sinful woman, she casts the remainder of the *sticheron* as a dramatic monologue of repentance that Topping has likened to a penitential psalm. The hymn's emotional text is reflected by music that comes to rest in a variety of modal areas over an unusually wide vocal range.

From Byzantine times until the present day the musical works of Kassia have been held in high regard. Nikephoros Kallistos Xanthopoulos included her as the only woman in his 14th-century catalogue of hymnographers, and succeeding generations of Byzantine cantors have continuously adapted her works to suit contemporary musical tastes. Kassia's hymn on the sinful woman, which for modern Greeks has become one of the high points of Holy Week, provides the best example of this process. Chant versions of this sticheron still today range from the florid but restrained 18th-century setting of Petros Peloponnesios in the old sticheraric style to virtuoso showpieces by more recent cantors. From the latter half of the 19th century Kassia's hymns have also been set polyphonically by such composers as Themistokles Polykrates, Mikis Theodorakis, Tikey Zes, and John Vergin.

Even though Kassia was never canonized, her life soon entered into the realm of popular legend. Two episodes in particular have captured the imagination of subsequent generations: her participation in the imperial bride-show, the story of which was progressively embroidered; and a presumably apocryphal tale of how Theophilos paid a clandestine visit to her monastery while Kassia was composing her hymn on the sinful woman – with whom she was increas-ingly indentified in the popular imagination – and added several lines to its text after she fled from his presence. Variations on these legends form the basis for modern Greek poems, novels, stories, and plays by D. Bernardakis, A. Stamatiades, A. Papadopoulou, A. Kyriakos, M. Roussos, and others. Paraphrases of her hymn for Holy Wednesday have also been written by poets including Kostis Palamas, whose version was set to music by D. Mitropoulos.

ALEXANDER LINGAS

See also Hymnography

Biography
Born in Constantinople early in the 9th century, Kassia received a good education and was a keen defender of icons. Perhaps rejected in a bride-show for the emperor Theophilos, she became a nun and founded a monastery. She wrote non-liturgical poetry as well as hymns. Her musical works continue to be held in high regard.

Further Reading
Dyck, Andrew R., "On Cassia, Kurie H En Pollais", *Byzantion* 56 (1986): pp. 63–76
Raasted, Jørgen, "Verse and Voice in a Troparion of Cassia" in *Studies in Eastern Chant*, vol. 3, edited by Egon Wellesz and Miloš Velimirović, Oxford: Oxford University Press, 1973
Rochow, Ilse, *Studien zu der Person, den Werken und dem Nachleben der Dichterin Kassia*, Berlin: Akademie, 1967
Tillyard, H.J.W., "A Musical Study of the Hymns of Casia", *Byzantinische Zeitschrift*, 20 (1911): pp. 420–85
Topping, Eva C., *Sacred Songs: Studies in Byzantine Hymnography*, Minneapolis: Light and Life, 1997
Touliatos, Diane, "Women Composers of Medieval Byzantine Chant", *College Music Symposium*, 24 (1984): pp. 62–80
Touliatos, Diane, Kassia entry in *Women Composers*, edited by Martha Furman Schleifer and Sylvia Glickman, vol. 1, New York: G.K. Hall, 1996
Treadgold, Warren, "The Bride-Shows of the Byzantine Emperors", *Byzantion*, 49 (1979): pp. 395–412
Tripolitis, Antonia, *Kassia: The Legend, the Woman, and Her Work*, New York: Garland, 1992
Wellesz, Egon, *A History of Byzantine Music and Hymnography*, 2nd edition, Oxford: Clarendon Press, 1961

Kastoria

City in western Macedonia

Kastoria is unique in that it contains a remarkable number of Byzantine and post-Byzantine monuments which bear witness to the prosperity it knew in the past and the role it played as a cultural centre. Kastoria emerged in the Middle Ages and has had a continuous life up to the present day. The town is built beside Lake Orestias (or the Lake of Kastoria), on the slopes of a hill next to a rocky promontory which juts out into the lake.

Present-day Kastoria probably has its origins in the 9th century AD as is suggested by the dating of its earliest churches, St Stephen and the Taxiarchs, and by the dating of its external walls. The earliest record of the town in a literary source appears in the *History* of John Skylitzes and is related to events of the year 976. The site where Kastoria stands was settled twice before the 9th century. The first settlement was known as

Kastoria: the city viewed from across Lake Orestias. Flat-bottomed fishing boats, built to an ancient pattern, are peculiar to the lake.

Celetrum (Keletron) and is recorded by Livy in connection with events in 199 BC. The same site was resettled in the 6th century AD by order of the emperor Justinian I. According to Procopius, who provides this information, the lake was already known by the name of "Kastoria". There is no other reference to the Justinianic settlement, which may have lain deserted in the 7th and 8th centuries.

The conditions under which the site of Kastoria was resettled in the 9th century are typical of the gradual restoration of Byzantine rule in the Balkans that took place from c.900 onwards. The Byzantine authorities had a special interest in resettling strategic points which could then serve as fortified centres for the provincial administration, and Kastoria occupied an excellent position. The town proved to be strongly defensible by nature, for its access by land was very limited, and it was protected by strong walls. Furthermore, Kastoria lay in a key position for the control of important routes in that part of the Balkans, such as the one which followed the course of the Haliacmon and Devol rivers leading from Macedonia to the port of Avlon on the Adriatic coast. Another axis, in a southerly direction, led from Kastoria to Thessaly. The strategic importance of Kastoria was proved on several occasions, particularly during the wars between Byzantium and the Bulgarians in the years 976–1018, and during the Norman

invasion of 1081–83 when the town was occupied by the Normans and used as a base for launching subsequent operations in western Macedonia and Thessaly.

The development of the medieval town began after the restoration of Byzantine rule, in the year 1018, and culminated during the 12th century, a peaceful period which marked the highest point of prosperity for Kastoria in the Middle Ages. This was the formative period which produced the principal socioeconomic and cultural characteristics of the town lasting into the modern era. The ecclesiastical history of Kastoria is also important. As soon as the Byzantines established the archbishopric of Bulgaria (based in Ohrid) with authority over the areas which they conquered or reoccupied after the wars of 976–1018, the Church of Kastoria was given first place in the hierarchy. The bishop of Kastoria remained the first in rank (*protothronos*) among the subordinates of the archbishop of Bulgaria until the archbishopric was abolished in 1767. After that year, the Church of Kastoria was upgraded to the rank of a metropolitan see and was directly controlled by the Patriarchate of Constantinople.

The development of the town began with the establishment of secular and ecclesiastical authorities and continued with the emergence of a local group of wealthy landowners who held rural estates in the surrounding region. The presence of this group stimulated the development of the town's trade and handicrafts. However, although Kastoria became a centre of commercial and artisanal activity, its economy remained fundamentally rural during the medieval and early modern periods. The population of the surrounding countryside was mainly engaged in cereal cropping, viticulture, and livestock raising, while the practice of keeping vineyards was also common among the townsfolk. Some of Kastoria's inhabitants took advantage of their proximity to the lake and became involved in fishing, which added considerably to the local economy. Information about the town's population and economy is provided by a fiscal register drawn up c.1445, about 60 years after the Ottoman conquest of the town (which took place in 1385 or 1386). According to the register's data, 22.30 per cent of the fiscal revenue that was raised from the town represented commercial taxation, another 22.79 per cent represented fishing, while 24.03 per cent came from the tax on vineyard production and 20.72 per cent from land-usage taxes. At that time Kastoria was inhabited by approximately 4518 people, who were distinguished as 3977 Christians, 431 Jews, and 110 Muslims. In 1519 approximately 4815 people are recorded as resident in the town, 4480 Christians and 335 Muslims. In fact, the Muslims of Kastoria were a minority of the local population and remained so during the five centuries of Ottoman rule, in contrast to other towns of Macedonia, such as Thessalonica, Giannitsa, and Serres, where they made up a large part or even the majority of the population.

Kastoria is renowned for the history and cultural tradition of its Jewish inhabitants. The history of Kastorian Jewry falls into two distinct phases, the Romanite and the Sephardic. The Romanite community of Greek-speaking Jews existed in Kastoria during the Middle Ages until they were transferred to Constantinople in the years after 1453. A Sephardic group of Jews settled in Kastoria sometime during the 16th century, certainly after 1519, for that year's registers contain no reference to them. The modern-day Jews of Kastoria descend from the later settlement; they remained an important element of the town's population until the years of the German occupation of Greece (1941–44), when most of them were driven to concentration camps.

The profession which has been practised in Kastoria for centuries and has made the town famous is fur manufacture and trading (kastor means "beaver" in Greek). The first record of fur manufacture in Kastoria is contained in the aforementioned fiscal register of c.1445, yet it already seems to have been a well-established practice. In later centuries, Kastorian fur traders expanded their business all over the Ottoman empire, to central and western Europe, and finally established their agencies in the USA in the 20th century, bringing great wealth to their town.

The economic development of Kastoria had a profound effect on local artistic production. In fact, there are more than 40 Byzantine and post-Byzantine monuments surviving there, far more than in any other town in Greece, and they provide good evidence for the study of local patronage. The foundation and decoration of these churches were undertaken by local landowners such as Theodoros Lemniotes, who paid for the renovation and redecoration of the church of Sts Anargyroi, and Nikephoros Kasnitzes who founded a church of St Nicholas in the 12th century. Equally, the earliest surviving

mansions, which include the finest examples of secular architecture in Macedonia, date from the 15th and 16th centuries. After the Ottoman conquest and the subsequent collapse of the Greek landowning class, the patronage of culture and the arts fell to the wealthy Kastorian merchants. Most notable among them were Georgios Kyritses and Manolakis Kastorianos (the latter was a prominent fur trader based in Constantinople), who, as part of their various donations, subsidized the establishment of Greek education in the town. The school that was founded in Kastoria in 1614 was the oldest Greek school in Macedonia. Another school was founded in 1705 and a third one in 1715 on the endowment of Georgios Kyritses.

This long-standing cultural tradition resulted in the formation of a strong national sentiment among the population of Kastoria during the years of nationalistic conflict in the late 19th and early 20th centuries. In this respect, Kastoria became the principal centre for the Greek cause in western Macedonia. Most active among the Greeks of Kastoria was the metropolitan Germanos Karavangelis, who organized the first Greek militias, igniting the struggle for Macedonia.

Kastoria was occupied by the Greek army in 1912, during the first Balkan War, and was formally annexed to Greece in 1913. Present-day Kastoria is a small provincial town but a particularly wealthy one due, primarily, to its fur trade and, secondly, to tourism, as the physical attractions of the place and the fame of its surviving medieval monuments attract many visitors.

KONSTANTINOS P. MOUSTAKAS

Summary

Kastoria lies astride important land routes in western Macedonia. According to Livy, a town called Celetrum occupied the site in the 2nd century BC and this was resettled in the 6th century. The present town dates from the 9th century, as do its earliest churches and walls. There was an important Jewish community until the 1940s. The fur trade has been practised since the 15th century.

Further Reading

Drakopoulou, Eugenia, The Town of Kastoria in the Byzantine and Post-Byzantine Era, 12th–16th Centuries, Athens, 1997 (in Greek)

Moutsopoulos, N.C., Ekklesies tes Kastorias 9–11 Aionas [Churches of Kastoria of the 9th–11th Centuries], Thessalonica, 1992

Orlandos, A., "The Byzantine Monuments of Kastoria" (in Greek) in Archeion ton Vyzantion mnemeion tes Hellados [Register of the Byzantine Monuments of Greece], vol. 4, Athens, 1938

Pelekanidis, S. and M. Chatzidakis, Kastoria: Mosaics, Wall Paintings, Athens, 1985

Sokoloski, M., Turski Dokumenti za Istorijata na Makedonskiot Narod. II. Opsirni Popisni Defteri ot XV vek., Skopje, 1973

Tsamises, Panteles, E Kastoria kai ta Mnemeia tes [Kastoria and its Monuments], Athens, 1949

Vacalopoulos, A.E., A History of Macedonia, 1354–1833, Thessalonica: Institute for Balkan Studies, 1973

Kavalla

Port in eastern Macedonia

In contrast to other towns of Macedonia which clearly have a medieval past, collective memory of Kavalla extends only as far back as the period of Ottoman rule. This does not, however, reflect the true situation, since the site was settled in antiquity. The ancient predecessor of Kavalla, Neapolis, was a colony of the Thasians, on the coast opposite their island, and existed at least as early as the 5th century BC, when it was included in the tribute lists of the Delian League. The site combined several geographical and strategic advantages. First, it controlled the narrow pass between the Lekani mountains and the sea which the land route from Macedonia to Thrace (the ancient Via Egnatia) necessarily had to pass through. Second, it provided access to and control of the gold-mines of Mount Pangaeum and the productive plain of Philippi/Drama. And third, it served as an outlet to the sea for the products of those regions. The importance of Neapolis was underlined when it served as the port of Philippi, 15 km to the northwest, throughout its long period of prosperity. Neapolis was renamed Christoupolis, probably in memory of St Paul's disembarking there as he began his tour in Macedonia. By the 9th century the ancient name of Neapolis was probably completely forgotten.

Medieval Christoupolis declined rapidly in the later 14th century and this can be associated with the fighting that accompanied its capture by the Ottomans (c.1382–83), though other reasons, such as the plague, may have played a part. The final blow was dealt when the town was raided and sacked by the Venetians in 1425. The traditional view of a deserted Christoupolis which remained so until it was resettled as Kavalla in the 16th century is mainly based on a description by the Italian Angiollolo who passed by the town in 1470 (Mertzios, 1947, pp. 117, 201–03). Nevertheless, new evidence that comes from the study of Ottoman registers suggests otherwise. Kavalla is first recorded in 1478/79 as forming part of the administrative district of Drama and being inhabited by approximately 475 people (315 Christian, 60 Muslim). By 1519 the Muslims had risen to 110 with the Christians remaining around 355. These figures are not high enough to present Kavalla as a town, but they are not negligible and show clearly that Kavalla was not a deserted place in the 15th and early 16th centuries. The town's Christian inhabitants are described by the French traveller Pierre Belon, who visited the area in the mid-15th century, as Greek (Belon de Mans, 1553, Paris 1553, p. 57). Therefore, Kavalla can be regarded as a continuation of medieval Christoupolis, for the town's site was never fully abandoned during the period of transition. Yet, this is not just a question of continuity in settlement, but one of social, economic, and institutional transformation, for much of what had characterized medieval Christoupolis was absent from early modern Kavalla. Commercial activity was disrupted, the town's church was reduced (there is no longer any record of the medieval bishopric of Christoupolis), and early Ottoman urban institutions were not extensively developed, so Kavalla was partially administered from Drama.

Kavalla's development began during the third decade of the 16th century and has continued to the present. This development was based on the same conditions that allowed for the previous prosperity of Neapolis and Christoupolis, namely its strategic location and also the facilities it offered for the export of the region's products by sea. Kavalla's revival is associated with the efforts of the Grand vizier "Frenk" Ibrahim Pasha

(1523–36) who had shown a particular interest in the town. Those years are marked by significant building activity, most notably by the construction of the town's aqueduct (later known as *kamares*, one of its attractions today) and of several mosques.

The population of Kavalla increased too through the introduction of new settlers, mainly Muslims. The town's Muslim population has a long history starting in the 15th century and continuing until 1923 when they departed in the exchange of populations between Greece and Turkey. A well-known representative of Kavalla's Muslims is Mohammed Ali, an ethnic Albanian, who first became governor of Ottoman Egypt and then independent ruler of the country and founder of the dynasty that reigned there until 1952. Evliya Çelebi provides information on Kavalla for the second half of the 17th century. He describes a town consisting of five neighbourhoods with 500 households in total (this corresponds to a population of at least 2500 people), and with several mosques, religious colleges (*madrasas*), and houses for the poor (*imaret*). The commerce of Kavalla increased further in the 18th century when the town was used as a point of export for the products of eastern Macedonia (grain, cotton, tobacco, etc.). Many European merchants, mainly French but also English, Dutch, Venetians, and Ragusans, were active in Kavalla, where the post of French deputy consul was in operation in the middle years of the century; later on, official representation of France was re-established there by the appointment of an agent of the French consulate of Thessalonica in 1791.

As far as the intellectual and cultural life in the town is concerned, the Muslim community seems to have been in a better position than the Christian one. According to Evliya Çelebi, several mosques and religious colleges were in operation, but there are no records of any significant intellectual activity concerning the local Christians before the 19th century, in contrast to what was usual among the Greek communities in most towns in Macedonia. Greek schools were not founded in Kavalla until the 19th century. Moreover, the town's church was given a low rating until the 19th century, when it was elevated to the rank of a metropolitan see. Like other towns in Macedonia with strong Muslim communities, the Greeks of Kavalla took no action during the Greek War of Independence, unlike those of the nearby island of Thasos who were urged to rebel by some of their compatriots, members of the *Philiki Hetaireia* (Friendly Society). The revolt of the Thasians lasted from June to December 1821 and was terminated without fighting, as they accepted Ottoman terms for surrender.

Kavalla's development in the 19th century is marked by the predominance of tobacco trading which resulted in the industrialization of the town. Several companies engaged in tobacco processing emerged in Kavalla during the 19th and early 20th centuries, due to increased production in the countryside and growing market demands. This made Kavalla one of the few significant industrial centres in the late Ottoman empire. Also in the 19th century the residential quarters expanded towards the harbour, while in previous centuries they were confined to the slopes of the hill below the medieval citadel of the town.

Ottoman rule in Kavalla ended in 1912 as a result of the First Balkan War. The town was first occupied by the

Bulgarians, who were soon driven out by the Greeks, and Kavalla was officially annexed to Greece in 1913 according to the provisions of the Treaty of Bucharest. Nevertheless, the history of Kavalla remained turbulent during the whole first half of the 20th century. One reason for this was Bulgarian irredentism, for Kavalla was regarded as an outlet to the open sea for that country; in fact, the Bulgarian army occupied Kavalla twice, during both world wars, first between 1916 and 1918, and secondly between 1941 and 1944, as a result of Bulgaria's alliance with Germany. Furthermore, between the World Wars, Kavalla was a bed of intense social unrest due to the radicalization of its many tobacco-factory workers. It was also a stronghold of the Greek communist left in those years and still has a reputation for being among the birthplaces of the Greek labour movement.

In the postwar years the tobacco industry has declined in Kavalla. The town still has a considerable amount of industry (fertilizers, food processing, and tobacco processing to some extent) but this cannot be compared to prewar levels. The decline of Kavalla's industry has been counterbalanced by the development of other sectors (e.g. services, tourism), while the population of the town has grown continuously to make it the second largest city in Greek Macedonia, after Thessalonica, and the largest in east Macedonia (56,571 people in 1991). In conclusion, what mainly characterizes the history of Kavalla is its many similarities to Thessalonica as well as its differences from the other towns of Macedonia which retained a traditional economy of medium-scale commerce serving local demands.

KONSTANTINOS P. MOUSTAKAS

Summary

Originally colonized by Thasos and known as Neapolis, the city lies on an important land route (the Via Egnatia) and provides an outlet to the sea for the gold of Mount Pangaeum and the products of the plain of Philippi. Known as Christoupolis in the Middle Ages, the town declined but recovered again in the 16th century. It was an important centre for the tobacco industry.

Further Reading

Chiones, K., *Istoria tis Kavallas* [A History of Kavalla], Kavalla, 1968

Lemerle, Paul, *Philippes et la Macédoine orientale à l'époque chrétienne et byzantine*, Paris: Boccard, 1945

Mertzios, Konstantinos, *Mnemeia Makedonikes Historias* [Records of the History of Macedonia], Thessalonica, 1947

Moschopoulos N., "Greece According to Evliya Çelebi", *Annual of the Society for Byzantine Studies*, 14 (1938): pp. 510–12 (in Greek)

Papazoglou, Fanoula, *Les Villes de Macédoine à l'époque Romaine*, Athens: Ecole Française d'Athènes, 1988

Sakellariou, M.B., *Macedonia: 4000 years of Greek History and Civilization*, Athens: Ekdotike Athenon, 1988

Samsares, Demetrios, *Historike Geographia tes Anatolikes Makedonias kata ten Archaiotita* [A Historical Geography of Eastern Macedonia in Antiquity], Thessalonica, 1976

Skaltsas, K., *Historia tes Kavallas* [A History of Kavalla], Kavalla, 1930

Svoronos, Nikos G., *Salonique et Cavalla*, Paris: Maisonneuve, 1951

Svoronos, Nikos G., *Le Commerce de Salonique au XVIII siècle*, Paris: Presses Universitaires de France, 1956

Vacalopoulos, A.E., *A History of Macedonia, 1354–1833*, Thessalonica: Institute for Balkan Studies, 1973

Vasdravellis, John K., *Klephts, Armatoles, and Pirates in Macedonia during the Rule of the Turks, 1627–1821*, Thessalonica: Hetaireia Makedonikon Spoudon [Society for Macedonian Studies], 1975

Kazantzakis, Nikos 1883–1957

Novelist

Everything about Nikos Kazantzakis has been controversial. During his lifetime, his politics and religiosity were most in question. Now, more than 40 years after his death, one still wonders whether he contributed anything to the Hellenic tradition. Many Greeks considered (and consider) him anti-Hellenic owing to his eager absorption of French and German philosophy (chiefly Bergson and Nietzsche), Eastern religion (chiefly Buddhism), and the literary influences of D'Annunzio, Ibsen, and Dostoevsky, among others. They worry, for example, because his retelling of Homer's *Odyssey* turns Homer inside out in ways they consider quintessentially non-Greek. Yet the opposite view is equally compelling. After all, Kazantzakis chose the Homeric hero to exemplify his own modernist views, changing that hero substantially, it is true, but nevertheless extending one of Hellenism's central myths. In addition, Kazantzakis reworked other ancient Greek materials (e.g. Melissa, Theseus and the Minotaur, Prometheus), Byzantine subjects (e.g. Constantine Palaiologos, Nikiphoros Phokas), revolutionary ones (e.g. Kapodistria), as well as basing novels on Greece's ill-fated expedition into Asia Minor and on its civil war. Like his colleagues George Seferis, Yiannis Ritsos, and Odysseus Elytis, he considered Greek culture a seamless continuity from Homer to the present, and he enhanced that continuity by his conviction that ancient, medieval, and 19th-century Greek literature can speak meaningfully to contemporary audiences.

In addition, Kazantzakis concentrated on Christianity, the other great influence upon Greek civilization. His religiosity was condemned as blasphemous by many Greek Orthodox prelates (very few of whom read the books they were condemning); recently, however, his theology has been greatly appreciated, at least outside Greece, for its pioneering application of "process". As for his politics, he was vilified by right-wingers in Greece as a communist (unjustly) and by Greek communists as an "idealist" (justly). All in all, the various forms of controversy, even though they often made publication difficult and forced him into voluntary exile, seemed not to discourage him but rather to make him more energetic. His basic philosophy placed "struggle" at the centre of the creative life and his circumstances made struggle his ever-present situation. Hence, calamity only prodded him all the more to persevere in creative productivity.

Most people know Kazantzakis through his novels. But he produced these late in life and always considered them secondary. Primary for him were drama, poetry, and religious philosophy. By 1923, at the age of 40, he had formulated his definitive credo – *Askitiki: Salvatores Dei* – based on humanity's obligation to "transubstantiate matter into spirit" by struggling within the material world. His earlier works moved from fin-de-siècle aestheticism to religious pessimism and then to vibrant nationalism. In post-1923 works the credo governs everything as protagonist after protagonist succeeds or fails, wholly or partially, to transubstantiate. The hero who fares best of all is Odysseus in Kazantzakis's gargantuan sequel to Homer's *Odyssey*, written between 1925 and 1938. But figures such as the hero of *The Life and Times of Alexis Zorbas* (composed in the dark days of the German occupation of Greece, 1941–43) and especially priest Fotis in *Christ Recrucified* also progress far along this path.

The plays, many of which are still not translated, show Kazantzakis's eclectic reach beyond Greek subjects. The sardonically entitled *Comedy: A Tragedy* projects his loss of religious faith. *Buddha* examines Western philosophies of action and achievement in relation to Buddhistic resignation. *Christopher Columbus* has its protagonist turn back as soon as his crew sights land, owing to Kazantzakis's conviction that aspiration is holier than achievement.

But Kazantzakis' greatest contribution is perhaps his struggle with the Christianity in which he could no longer believe. Determined none the less to retain Jesus as the exemplar par excellence of the effort to transubstantiate matter into spirit, he treated this hero in a play, a long poem, and finally in the novel *The Last Temptation*, which retells the gospel story in a manner offering happiness as Jesus' (and our) most serious impediment. The book aroused heated opposition both in its own right and in its cinematographic form (Martin Scorsese's *The Last Temptation of Christ*, 1988); yet Kazantzakis's determination to reinvent a Jesus who can speak to, and function in, a world governed by Darwinian process has been welcomed by many religious thinkers of liberal persuasion.

Besides the numerous plays, the huge *Odyssey*, and the well-known novels, Kazantzakis produced a series of very popular travel books, a history of Russian literature, two novels written in French, a dissertation on Nietzsche, an updated Platonic "Symposium", and numerous children's books, besides translations of the *Divine Comedy*, *Faust*, and (with Professor Ioannis Kakridis) Homer's *Iliad* and *Odyssey*. He also left thousands of letters, many of which are now published; indeed, he may be one of the major epistolographers of his period.

Virtually unknown outside Greece until the late 1940s, when *Zorba* won a literary prize in France, Kazantzakis became an international celebrity in the 1950s, his novels translated into all major languages. He and Constantine Cavafy are the best-known modern Greek authors outside Greece. This does not mean, however, that Kazantzakis has always been celebrated inside Greece, although he has always appealed greatly to youth there, as elsewhere. His international vogue subsided in the 1980s. In the late 1990s, however, interest in him – chiefly as a religious thinker, but also as a novelist grappling with political, religious, ethical, and philosophical quandaries – revived. In conclusion, he can perhaps be described as an "acquired taste", somewhat like D.H. Lawrence, whose frenzy, wordiness, and almost pathological intensity he shared. His exuberant, adjective-filled prose is repugnant to readers trained in the laconic restraint of certain modernist writers in Greece and elsewhere. But his engagement with the major carnal and spiritual problems of the mid-20th century is so energetic, prophetic, and (ultimately) optimistic that he still speaks meaningfully to many readers.

PETER BIEN

See also Cavafy, Novel

Biography
Born in Herakleion, Crete, in 1883, Kazantzakis studied in Athens and Paris. He was influenced by the philosophy of Henri Bergson and Nietzsche and was early involved in politics and the language question. He wrote plays, poetry, philosophy, travel books, and, only later in life, novels. He died in 1957.

Writings (in translation)
Fiction
Serpent and Lily, with the manifesto *The Sickness of the Age*, translated by Theodora Vasils, Berkeley: University of California Press, 1980 (Greek edition 1906)
Toda Raba, translated by Amy Mims, New York: Simon and Schuster, 1964 (Greek edition 1934)
The Rock Garden, translated by Richard Howard, New York: Simon and Schuster, 1963 (Greek edition 1939)
Zorba the Greek, translated by Carl Wildman, London: Lehmann, and New York: Simon and Schuster, 1952 (Greek edition 1946)
Freedom or Death, translated by Jonathan Griffin, New York: Simon and Schuster, 1956; as *Freedom and Death*, Oxford: Cassirer, 1956 (Greek edition 1953)
The Greek Passion, translated by Jonathan Griffin, New York: Simon and Schuster, 1953; as *Christ Re-crucified*, Oxford: Cassirer, 1954 (Greek edition 1954)
The Last Temptation of Christ, translated by Peter Bien, New York: Simon and Schuster, 1960; as *The Last Temptation*, Oxford: Cassirer, 1961 (Greek edition 1955)
Saint Francis, translated by Peter Bien, New York: Simon and Schuster, 1962; as *God's Pauper: St. Francis of Assisi*, Oxford: Cassirer, 1962 (Greek edition 1956)
The Fratricides, translated by Athena Gianakas Dallas, New York: Simon and Schuster, 1964; Oxford: Cassirer, 1967 (Greek edition 1963)
At the Palaces of Knossos, translated by Theodora Vasils and Themi Vasils, Athens: Ohio University Press, and London: Peter Owen, 1988 (Greek edition 1981)

Poetry
The Odyssey: A Modern Sequel, translated by Kimon Friar, New York: Simon and Schuster, and London: Secker and Warburg, 1958 (Greek edition 1938)

Plays
Three Plays, translated by Athena Gianakas Dallas, New York: Simon and Schuster, 1969 (contains *Melissa*; *Kouros*; *Christopher Columbus*)
Two Plays, translated by Kimon Friar, St Paul, Minnesota: North Central, 1982 (contains *Sodom and Gomorrah*; *Comedy*)
Buddha, translated by Kimon Friar and Athena Dallis-Damis, San Diego, California: Avant, 1983

Philosophy
The Saviors of God: Spiritual Exercises, translated by Kimon Friar, New York: Simon and Schuster, 1960 (Greek edition 1927, revised 1945)

Further Reading
Bien, Peter, *Kazantzakis and the Linguistic Revolution in Greek Literature*, Princeton, New Jersey: Princeton University Press, 1972
Bien, Peter, *Kazantzakis: Politics of the Spirit*, Princeton, New Jersey: Princeton University Press, 1989

Bien, Peter, *Nikos Kazantzakis: Novelist*, Bristol: Bristol Classical Press, London: Duckworth, and New Rochelle, New York: Caratzas, 1989

Dombroski, Daniel A., *Kazantzakis and God*, Albany: State University of New York Press, 1997

Janiaud-Lust, Colette, *Nikos Kazantzaki: sa vie, son oeuvre, 1883–1957*, Paris: Maspero, 1970

Kazantzakis, Helen, *Nikos Kazantzakis: A Biography Based on His Letters*, translated by Amy Mims, New York: Simon and Schuster, and Oxford: Cassirer, 1968

Lea, James F., *Kazantzakis: The Politics of Salvation*, Tuscaloosa: University of Alabama Press, 1979

Levitt, Morton, *The Cretan Glance: The World and Art of Nikos Kazantzakis*, Columbus: Ohio State University Press, 1980

Middleton, Darren J.N. and Peter Bien (editors), *God's Struggler: Religion in the Writings of Nikos Kazantzakis*, Macon, Georgia: Mercer University Press, 1996

Prevelakis, Pandelis, *Nikos Kazantzakis and His "Odyssey": A Study of the Poet and the Poem*, New York: Simon and Schuster, 1961

Kinship

The Greek words for "kin", *syngeneis*, and for "relationship", *syngeneia*, are compounds of the preposition *syn* and the word *genos*, whose usage is manifold in Greek to denote "genus", "category", "lineage", "family", "generation", "stock", etc. *Syngeneia*, then, means "common stock, generation, or lineage". The term, in its broadest sense, is used to define relationships by consanguinity (*ex aimatos*) or affinity (*ex anchisteias*). Consanguinal relations, however, are considered as closer than those established through the sexual tie of marriage since in consanguinity relatives are thought to share the same substance, that of blood.

Rural and traditional Greek society has often been presented in the anthropological literature as a society overwhelmingly based on kinship. Scholars have singled out the family as Greece's most important social institution and pointed out that kinship pervades all aspects of traditional Greek social life. Kinship constitutes the basis for economic cooperation, political negotiation, and participation in ritual. Its role in the construction of personhood and gender identities is central. Although it can be argued that the urbanization and modernization of Greek society have caused the weakening of kinship ties, kinship still continues to influence social relations on many levels. Nepotism, kinship-based patronage, and formal financial partnerships formed among kin are not uncommon phenomena in the urban context.

The stress on the significance of kinship in the Greek social context is not only confirmed by studies of modern Greece, but also by those of the Classical and Hellenistic periods. The oeuvre of Greek dramatists amply demonstrates the crucial part played by kinship and family in ancient times. There is an observable tendency among Greeks of all periods to define themselves in terms of kinship connections; the ancient Greeks even based political requests and affiliations on real or fictitious kinship ties. Indeed, there is much evidence that shows the immense moral and political importance that the ancient Greeks attached to ancestry. Descent was often traced from a solitary figure, preferably going back to the traditional heroes or deities of Greek mythology. However, it should be pointed out that most of the information available on kinship in antiquity comes from Classical Athens. Generalizations are therefore problematic, and what follows is a synopsis in barest outline.

S.C. Humphreys distinguished four overlapping institutional kinship groupings in ancient Greek society: the official subdivisions of the state (tribe, phratry, deme, and so on), *genos*, kindred, and household. Each of them was characterized by its own structural principles, rules, and patterns of behaviour. Tribes and phratries were the main components or divisions of the citizen body. They functioned as administrative and military units. Membership of them was hereditary and obtained by patrifiliation. Every native-born Athenian male belonged to a phratry, which was a social group over and above the family, responsible mainly for dealing with questions concerning descent, access to citizenship, and inheritance rights. Members of phratries were known as *phrateres*, a word whose meaning is close to that of "brother". Women were usually denied rights of membership to them, but there were cases where women were presented to the phratry of their father or husband. The internal construction of phratries consisted of a variety of subgroups such as the *thiasoi*, responsible for internal political processes of the group, the *genos*, and others. It has been argued that the phratries were themselves subgroups of the Ionian tribes, which were abolished by the new system of Cleisthenes (507 BC). However, this argument rests on a thin base since phratries continued to be functional even after the introduction of the new system, which consisted of tribes and their subdivisions: *trittyes* ("thirdings") and demes. In Athens, each tribe comprised three *trittyes*, one each from the city, shore, and inland regions of Attica, which were divided into ten *trittyes* each. In turn, each *trittys* contained between one and ten demes (in Athens there existed 139 settlements, villages, or town-quarters) and a fixed number of phratries. Hence, Cleisthenes created a ten-tribe structure, each tribe taking the name of a local hero and having a hereditary membership recruited along the male line. Thus, tribes, *trittyes*, demes, and phratries were all patrilineal clans and subclans, which, however, were not genealogically structured as was the case of the Greek patrilineal *genos*.

The *genos* was a kinship institution concerned mainly with aristocratic dominance of the succession to priesthoods. Its earliest use was to denote noble lineage, but in 4th-century BC Athens the term was employed to designate those individual or family groups that had a common plural name, usually derived from that of a genuine or fictive male progenitor. The stress, therefore, was on descent and the *genos* had the structure of a "conical clan". There is evidence suggesting that *gene* were phratry subgroups with a form and function different from phratries and thus not identical to them. Although *gene* were primarily concerned with retaining rights to hereditary priestly office, not all of them were concerned with religious privileges. The larger *gene* showed a variety of other interests relating to common property and admission.

Greek kindred in antiquity was bilateral, extending to second cousins and giving rights to inheritance by the laws governing intestacy. Moreover, marriages between close male kin and *epikleroi* (fatherless heiresses) were encouraged by the Athenian epiclerate. However, marriage in the kindred was restricted, but such impediments varied over time and space.

An Athenian woman could not normally be married to a direct ancestor or descendant, nor to a sibling by the same mother (a practice known in Sparta). Yet, marriage between siblings of the same father or to an uncle or a cousin was allowed. As far as kinship solidarity is concerned, it can be shown that the power of kinship to function as a structural principle of action beyond the bounds of nuclear family was limited in the urban context of the Greek city. Kinship ties did not play an important part in the relationships of Athenian citizens, and political and economic cooperation with kinsfolk was no different from that between friends. In fact, kinship ties were often considered burdensome and dangerous rather than supportive.

The smaller kinship group in ancient Greece was that of the *oikos* (household). The concept of the *oikos* incorporated not only its physical reality, but also designated a group of people who co-resided and were mostly – but not entirely – connected by kin ties (including affines). Finally, it even applied to property, land, and animals as well. Although, from Homeric times onwards, the nuclear family appears to have been the most common residential and economic unit, stem and extended families continued to exist. The circle of kin contained in such units included unmarried female relatives. Labour requirements were often met by the co-residing non-kin household members such as slaves. The emerging picture of the organization of kinship in the household setting is one that exhibits a patrilateral bias since postmarital residence was patrilocal: the bride moved into the groom's house after marriage. Though both matrilocality and patrilocality were a historical reality in Greek society and may have coexisted in the Bronze Age, after Homer the system tended to patrilocal marital residence and partible inheritance of property. In the household unit the man was the *kyrios* (head of household) and acted as such in the public domain. In the Homeric era a man's prestige was completely bound up with his *oikos*. In Classical Athens, however, men became more concerned with public institutions. For this reason, the acquisition of prestige became less *oikos*-centred and more directed towards public contexts.

In Byzantine society the term *syngeneia* was used to denote the family, which by the 8th century was primarily a nuclear one, as well as kinship relations beyond the family unit. From the end of the 11th century we have evidence for the emergence of lineages and for manipulation of ties of kinship in politics. However, unlike the Roman *gens*, Byzantine lineages were not strictly patrilineal and there is no evidence for an organizational structure to lineage and common landownership. The closeness of kinship relations was established by the degree (*vathmos*) of relationship, which was calculated down both collateral lines, beginning with the first births from the original parents and thus arriving at the second degree for two siblings. This reckoning of the degrees of kinship was important for determining marriage prohibitions and rights to inheritance. From the 11th century onwards a restriction of seven degrees appears to have been the prevailing rule adopted by Byzantine law and the Church, which forbade marriage among all blood, adoptive, and spiritual relatives to that degree of relationship and a limit of six degrees for those related by marriage. The rights of kin to inheritance were also determined by the degree of relationship to the deceased. In the case of *ab intestato* succession, from the 6th century onwards the general rule prevailed that all male and female relatives of the same degree of kinship had equal inheritance rights.

The marriage impediments established in Byzantine times are part of Greek Orthodox canon law and are still in force in modern Greece today, though native versions of calculating degrees of kinship are found in many communities. Modern Greece, by most reckonings, is characterized by a bilateral kinship system with a patrilineal skewing or bias that is revealed in various contexts and occasions. In Greece the bilateral form of the kindred is also reflected in terminology. The word for "kindred" is *soi* and refers to one's relatives both through the father and through the mother. Also, we can note the absence of separate terms of address for paternal and maternal relations outside the family.

Yet, it can be argued that modern Greece involves two distinct cultural traditions differing in kinship structure. Such differences are related to distinct modes of organizing postmarital residence, production, transmission of property, names, and reputation. The first cultural tradition is primarily associated with the pastoral and agricultural communities of mainland Greece. Their mode of production dictates an agnatic emphasis in kinship, a bias towards patri-virilocality, and promotes the submissiveness of women. Thus, in such societies brides would join their husbands' households upon marriage, while married sons would either co-reside with their parents or live close to their natal households. Property, names, and reputations are all transferred from father to sons. Yet, it should be pointed out that from the 19th century patrilineal corporate groups were a phenomenon in decline. In Mani the war towers reveal the existence of patrilineal-agnatic clans consisting of all patrilineal descendants of an apical ancestor. Each clan was further subdivided into *genies* (lineages), which branched off to smaller lineages, and these in turn to extended or nuclear families. The Maniot naming system is central to the processes of segmentation, fissioning, and clan formation. Each extended family household of a patriclan takes its surname from the first name of an apical ancestor, while the firstborn sons of male siblings take the first name of their grandfather. Other communities that have a bilateral kinship system with patrilineal overtones are the Sarakatsan shepherds, the Vlachs, and the shepherding communities of Crete. Finally, the agricultural communities of Euboea, Boeotia, and the Ionian islands also practise virilocality. Yet, their kinship system is characterized by a less strongly marked patrilineal bent compared to the societies mentioned above.

The second cultural tradition, which differs in the organization of kinship from the main body of Greece, is that of the Aegean islands. Its main characteristics are matrifocal kinship ties, the uxorilocal residence pattern, where the couple settles in the vicinity of the bride's kin, the rule of house inheritance by women, and the transmission of property and names through both lines, from mother to daughters and from father to sons. Thus, in such communities the kinship structure is characterized by a matrilateral bias, which promotes a comparatively privileged female position and the formation of nuclei of matrilaterally related women (mother and sisters) playing an important role within both the family and the community. This phenomenon should also be linked with the absence of men for long periods of time due to their sea-related occupations. In between these two types of communities there are others that practise neolocality, where each nuclear family resides in its own dwelling and has a fully bilateral kinship system.

In the Greek understanding of kinship there is a clear distinction between blood ties and affinal ones. In the physical world blood relations are considered stronger since they create a natural union among living kin. In the spiritual world, however, blood is substituted by another life-giving substance, that of oil to create a spiritual relationship (*pneumatiki syngeneia*), which is likened to kinship. This relationship is known in Greek as *koumparia* and is established by the sacraments of baptism or marriage. In many areas of Greece it is customary to renew the relationship, which is inherited through the male line. The godfather of the groom, and not of the bride, becomes their wedding sponsor. This may be regarded as a consequence of the patrilineal bias in kinship. Apart from its spiritual function, godparenthood has also acted in the Greek context as a powerful vehicle for strategic alliances, political recruitment, and patronage. Today, however, in the urban context we notice the tendency of selecting godparents from within the circle of close kin or even from within the family itself.

Another form of ritual kinship that existed in the Greek context, but did not endure to the present time, is that of blood brotherhood (*adelphopoiia*). Blood brotherhood appeared in Greek society after the conquests of Alexander the Great. While in the beginning the tie between two people was established through the symbolic exchange of blood, later on, with the spread of Christianity, this symbolic act was replaced by the prayers of a ritual. There were repeated prohibitions against *adelphopoiia* by the Orthodox Church. Nevertheless, the practice remained widespread in many areas of rural Greece up to the civil war. Its social function was to cement friendship, especially in communities where vendettas were common, and carried with it an obligation of mutual help and support. A marriage impediment existed for those belonging to families that were related by blood brotherhood.

Adoption is also regarded as a form of fictive kinship and in Byzantine times became a spiritual relationship, like that of godparenthood, with which it shared similar marriage prohibitions. Adoption was practised when a childless couple or a couple that had no male children desired descendants and heirs. In antiquity we find the institution of the transfer by adoption of one son from a household with several male heirs to the family of a close kin with none. This practice has continued in Greece up until recent times, particularly in communities with agnatic descent, as a means of continuing the family line and perpetuating the family name.

Finally, secular kinship serves as a model for structuring other types of social relations, such as those between superiors and monks or nuns, and between confessor and confessant. In Byzantium kinship terminology was also used to describe the relation of the emperor to his subjects and to foreign Christian rulers.

ELENI SOTIRIU

See also Adoption, Family, Marriage, Patronage

Further Reading

Alexakis, E.P., *Mani: Geni kai Oikogeneia* [Mani: Lineage and Family], Athens, 1998

Beauchamp, J., "To Byzantio kata ton Ilo Aiona: To Paichnidi ton Kanonon kai tis Symperiforas" [Byzantium in the 11th Century: The Game of the Rules and Behaviour] in *Oikogeneia kai Periousia stin Ellada kai stin Kypro* [Family and Property in Greece and Cyprus], edited by C. Piault, Athens, 1994

Brouskou, Aigili, "Anthropologia tis gennisis" [Anthropology of Childbirth], *Archeia Ellinikis Iatrikis* [Archives of Greek Medicine], 8/4 (July–August 1991): pp. 252–56

Caftanzoglou, R., "The Household Formation Pattern of a Vlach Mountain Community of Greece: Syrrako 1898–1929", *Journal of Family History*, 19/1 (1994): pp. 79–98

Caftanzoglou, R., *Syggeneia kai Organosi tou Oikiakou Chorou: Syrrako, 1898–1930* [Kinship and the Organization of Domestic Space: Syrrako, 1898–1930], Athens, 1997

Campbell, J.K., *Honour, Family, and Patronage: A Study of Institutions and Moral Values in a Greek Mountain Community*, Oxford: Clarendon Press, 1964

Casselberry, S.E. and N. Valavanes, "Matrilocal Greek Peasants and a Reconsideration of Residence Terminology", *American Ethnologist*, 3/2 (1976): pp. 215–26

Clark, Gillian, *Women in Late Antiquity: Pagan and Christian Lifestyles*, Oxford: Clarendon Press, and New York: Oxford University Press, 1993

Couroucli, Maria, *Structures économiques et sociales du village Episkepsi a Corfou de 1000 a nos jours* (dissertation), Paris, 1981

Couroucli, Maria, *Les Oliviers du lignage: une Grèce de tradition vénitienne*, Paris: Maisonneuve et Larose, 1985

Couroucli, Maria, "Genia, Proika kai Klironomia: H Periptosi tis Episkepsis stin Kerkyra" [Kinship, Marriage, and Inheritance: The Question of Visits in Corfu] in *Oikogeneia kai Periousia stin Ellada kai stin Kypro* [Family and Property in Greece and Cyprus], edited by C. Piault, Athens, 1994

Davis, J., *People of the Mediterranean: An Essay in Comparative Social Anthropology*, London: Routledge and Kegan Paul, 1977

Dimen, Muriel, and Ernestine Friedl (editors), *Regional Variations in Greece and Cyprus: Toward a Perspective on Ethnography in Greece*, New York: New Academy of Sciences, 1976

Dubisch, Jill (editor), *Gender and Power in Rural Greece*, Princeton, New Jersey: Princeton University Press, 1986

Du Boulay, Juliet, *Portrait of a Greek Mountain Village*, Oxford: Clarendon Press, 1974

Du Boulay, Juliet, "The Meaning of Dowry: Changing Values in Rural Greece", *Journal of Modern Greek Studies*, 1 (1983): pp. 243–70

Du Boulay, Juliet, "The Blood: Symbolic Relationships between Descent, Marriage, Incest Prohibitions and Spiritual Kinship in Greece", *Man*, 19 (1984): pp. 533–56

Friedl, Ernestine, *Vasilika: A Village in Modern Greece*, New York: Holt Rinehart, 1962

Herzfeld, Michael, *The Poetics of Manhood: Contest and Identity in a Cretan Mountain Village*, Princeton, New Jersey: Princeton University Press, 1985

Humphreys, S.C., *Anthropology and the Greeks*, London and Boston: Routledge and Kegan Paul, 1978

Kavadias, Georges B., *Pasteurs-nomades méditerranéens: les Saracatsans de Grèce*, Paris: Gauthier Villars, 1965

Kuriakides, S., Adelphophoiia entry in *Megali Elliniki Enkylopaideia* [The Great Greek Encyclopedia], vol. 1, Athens, no date

Littman, Robert J., *Kinship and Politics in Athens, 600–400 BC*, New York: Peter Lang, 1990

Loizos, Peter and Evthymios Papataxiarchis (editors), *Contested Identities: Gender and Kinship in Modern Greece*, Princeton, New Jersey: Princeton University Press, 1991

Michailides-Nouaros, G., "Peri tis Adelphopoiias en ti Archaia Helladi kai en to Byzantio" [On Blood Brotherhood in Ancient Greece and Byzantium], in *Tomos Konstantinou Harmenopolou* [Festschrift for Constantine Harmenopoulos], Thessalonica, 1952

Nitsiakos, Vassilis, "A Vlach Pastoral Community in Greece: The Effects of its Incorporation into the National Economy and Society" (dissertation), Cambridge University, 1985

Nitsiakos, Vassilis, *Paradosiakes Koinonikes Domes* [Traditional Social Structures], Athens, 1991

Péristiany, J.G. (editor), *Mediterranean Family Structures*, Cambridge and New York: Cambridge University Press, 1976

Sant Cassia, Paul and Constantina Bada, *The Making of the Modern Greek Family: Marriage and Exchange in Nineteenth-Century Athens*, Cambridge and New York: Cambridge University Press, 1992

Seremetakis, C. Nadia, *The Last Word: Women, Death, and Divination in Inner Mani*, Chicago: University of Chicago Press, 1991, pp. 16–43

Klontzas, Georgios c.1535–1608

Painter

Georgios Klontzas was a painter, scholar, and manuscript illuminator of the post-Byzantine period. He was an outstanding figure of the late Cretan renaissance, with an important oeuvre of icons and miniatures. His life and certain aspects of his professional career are to some extent attested by documents discovered in the archives of Venice. A prosperous man, he inherited from his parents houses and the Greek Orthodox church of St Mark in the city of Candia (Herakleion). In 1562 he married Ergina, daughter of the priest Emmanuel Pantaleos, by whom he had three sons, Nicolò, Loukas, and Maneas, who also became painters. He had a fourth son from his second marriage, to Lia Vitzimanopoula.

Klontzas was an independent painter already in 1564, and in 1566 was appointed assessor of an icon by Domenikos Theotokopoulos. In 1586 he executed two paintings (now destroyed), one depicting the healing of the paralytic and another for the Catholic church of the welfare institution of St Anthony in Candia. In 1587 he was commissioned to paint a number of icons by Ioasaph Avouris, bishop of Karpathos. The same year he bought the workshop that he had hitherto rented, which was in the square of St Mark, in the centre of Candia.

Klontzas was certainly associated with cultured circles of the Cretan society of his day. His patrons included Orthodox and Catholic institutions, Venetian noblemen, and Greek bourgeois.

Known works signed by Klontzas (portable icons and triptychs, and two illuminated manuscripts, in Venice and in a private collection in Paris) number barely a dozen. To him or to his close circle are attributed a further 25 icons, an illuminated manuscript of 1577 (Bodleian Library, Oxford), and the surviving folios of two others (Vatican Library, before 1600, and Moscow, State Historical Museum). The book of prophecies that he is said to have given to his son Loukas in 1597 has not been identified or preserved. A few icons bear the forged signature of Georgios Klontzas. This output seems rather limited in terms of quantity, since the painter's career spanned about half a century. Many of his works, however, render multifigural, laborious compositions, and his illuminated manuscripts contain hundreds of complex representations that required many months' work.

Though he was undoubtedly a competent painter of monumental works, he nevertheless preferred miniature scenes on small or large surfaces, on which he unfolded complicated compositions, frequently of an epic spirit. His most important works include his illustration of the hymn "In Thee Rejoiceth" along with other subjects, icons of the Last Judgement, triptychs whose main subject is again the Last Judgement, the a painting of the Seventh Ecumenical Council, a triptych with Christ enthroned and scenes from the *Dodekaorton* (Twelve Great Feasts), an icon with the Transfiguration and scenes of monastic life, an icon with the rare depiction of a sermon in a church, and a painting on panel of the battle of Lepanto. None of these works is dated (the dates on two icons by Klontzas at Sinai are disputed). Stylistic differences between them are related partly to the interval separating the dates at which they were executed, and partly to the fact that other painters worked with Klontzas. No independent works by these other painters have been identified, however. All that has survived is a detailed manuscript map of the city of Candia bearing the signature of his son Maneas.

Klontzas's work as a manuscript illuminator (the idea that he was also a manuscript copyist has been disputed) is of great importance, for both its content and its quality. Two of the manuscripts that he illuminated, containing expanded versions of the prophecies of the Byzantine emperor Leo VI the Wise (Bodleian Library, Oxford, and private collection, Paris) were commissioned from the painter by Francesco Barozzi, an eccentric Venetian nobleman, scholar, mathematician, and occultist, then a resident of Rethymnon, and were intended for Giacomo Foscarini, the Venetian overseer of Crete and collector, who left Crete in 1577. A third, more complex manuscript, of the years 1590–92 (Marciana Library, Venice), includes earlier prophetic and apocalyptic visions, as well as chronicles and historical texts of his time, which Klontzas enlivened with over 400 miniatures. This work by Klontzas continued the great tradition of Byzantine illuminated manuscripts in the spirit of his time, blending elements drawn from the Byzantine legacy with others taken from western European art, the latter derived from foreign engravings and printed books. Another, similar case, though he did not enjoy the same prestige and influence, is that of Klontzas' fellow-Cretan painter Markos Bathas.

Both his miniatures and his independent portable icons betray Klontzas's outstanding ability in the art of miniature painting, of which he was the supreme representative in the post-Byzantine period. With unrivalled skill and facility of drawing he executed ever-moving miniature figures with expressive faces, in a variety of postures. His representations are informed by forceful composition and narrative ability, though *horror vacui* often causes the painted surface to be overburdened.

Though he did not cast off the cloak of the Byzantine tradition, on which his style is based, he made significant strides in the direction of assimilating elements of Western taste, particularly in the matter of perspective rendering of space, architectural features, furniture, and other objects, and he seems to have been particularly attracted by Mannerism. With a freedom unusual in a painter of the Byzantine tradition, he dispensed with the use of the traditional *anthivola* (pricked cartoons used to transfer a motif or even a whole composition to a new icon) and always created new variations, even when repeating the same subject (his depictions of the Last Judgement are characteristic examples). A restless nature with a vivid imagination, he created some original compositions assimilating influences mainly from the art of the Renaissance and Mannerism. The models from which he adapts features include works by Michelangelo, Titian, and other artists, probably known to Klontzas through engravings. As a personality, however, he is closer to Tintoretto. In his paintings, which are also distinguished by their feast of colour and the original use of tones, the traditional gold ground is occasionally replaced by a blue heaven.

Many of the works executed by Klontzas or his workshop were commissioned or purchased by private citizens, noblemen, and bourgeois for purposes of private piety, and some of them even bear coats of arms. The commissions for manuscripts from the nobleman Francesco Barozzi are indicative of Klontzas's fame, and also of his interests, which transcended his accomplishment as an artist. The painter was probably connected in some way with the well-known poet Antonios Achelis, author of the *Siege of Malta* (1571), since there is some correspondence between the visual motifs in Klontzas's works and Achelis's writings.

His works contain some echo of the historical events and social conditions of his time. The striking frequency of representations of the Last Judgement (over 12 examples) reflects the popular fear that the end of the world was nigh at a period when the Turkish threat was steadily advancing in the Mediterranean. With its eschatological meaning, urging people to just deeds, the Last Judgement is given a very evocative treatment in Klontzas's works, and enriched with details drawn from Italian engravings. His painting of a sermon in a church (in Sarajevo) is strongly didactic in character and hints at social criticism with its inscriptions from the speech of Basil the Great urging the rich to acts of charity on pain of eternal damnation. A historical event, the victory of the Christian forces at the battle of Lepanto (1571), was twice depicted by Klontzas, for unknown patrons. With a striking panoramic treatment based on Italian engravings, these paintings, only one of which survives, are further evidence of the extension of Klontzas's work in the direction of the western style of historical panel painting.

Klontzas's departure from the medieval view of the painter is suggested by his adoption of Renaissance styles in signing his works (his signature, sometimes in the form of verse rather than the Byzantine "Hand of ... "), and in this he may be compared with Domenikos Theotokopoulos and Michael Damaskinos. Through his complex, multifaceted work Georgios Klontzas emerged as one of the most important figures in post-Byzantine art. The influence of his work with its distinct character may be noted mainly in the reproduction of his compositions and the imitation of his miniature style (by Frangiskos Kavertzas and Theodoros Poulakis, among others), though none of the later painters possessed his ability or his intellectual interests.

MARIA CONSTANTOUDAKI

See also Renaissance (Veneto-Cretan)

Biography

Born *c*.1535 in Herakleion, the son of Andreas, Klontzas was a prosperous man who associated with the cultured circles of Cretan society. He was a distinguished representative of the late Cretan renaissance and worked for both Catholic and Orthodox patrons. His works include icons, triptychs, and illuminated manuscripts. He drew on elements of Italian Renaissance and Mannerist art as well as the Byzantine tradition. He died in 1608.

Further Reading

After Byzantium: The Survival of Byzantine Sacred Art, London: The Hellenic Centre, 1996 (exhibition catalogue)

Alvarez Lopera, José (editor), *El Greco: Identity and Transformation – Crete, Italy, Spain*, New York: Abbeville, and London: Thames and Hudson, 1999

Chatzidakis, Manolis, *Icānes de Saint-Georges des Grecs et de la collection de l'Institut*, 2nd edition, Venice: Institut Hellénique d'Etudes Byzantines et Post-Byzantines de Venise, 1975

Chatzidakis, Manolis, *Icons of Patmos: Questions of Byzantine and Post-Byzantine Painting*, Athens, 1985

Constantoudaki-Kitromilides, Maria, "La pittura di icone a Creta veneziana (secoli XV e XVI): Questioni di mecenatismo, iconografia e preferenze estetiche" in *Venezia e Creta*, edited by Gherardo Ortalli, Venice: Istituto Veneto di Scienze, Lettere ed Arti, 1998

Constantoudaki-Kitromilides, Maria, "Agnosto triptycho tou Georgiou Klontza kai o Apodektis tou" [An Unpublished Triptych by Georgios Klontzas and its Recipient], *Deltion tis Christianikis Archaiologikis Etaireias* [Bulletin of the Christian Archaeological Society], 4/20 (1998): pp. 335–43

Hadermann-Misguich, L., "Les livres d'oracles illustrés par Georges Klontzas: leur chronologie", *Zograph*, vol.26 (1997): pp. 133–38

Hadermann-Misguich, L. and J. Vereecken, *Les oracles de Léon le Sage illustrés par Georges Klontzas: la version Barozzi dans le codex Bute*, Venice and Herakleion, forthcoming

Holy Image, Holy Space: Icons and Frescoes from Greece, Baltimore: Walters Art Gallery, 1988 (exhibition catalogue)

Hutter, Irmgard, *Corpus der byzantinischen Miniaturenhandschriften*, Stuttgart: Hiersmann, vol.2 (continuing series, six volumes so far, 1977–)

Manafis, X. (editor), *Sinai: The Treasures of the Holy Monastery of Saint Catherine*, Athens, 1990

Paliouras, Athanasios, *Ho zographos Georgios Klontzas, c.1540–1608, kai hai mikrographiai tou kodikos autou* [The Painter Georgios Klontzas and the Miniatures of his Codex], Athens, 1977

Rigo, Antonio, *Oracula Leonis: Tre manoscritti greco-veneziani degli oracoli attribuiti all'imperatore bizantino Leone il Saggio*, Padua: Editoriale Programma, 1988

Vocotopoulos, P., *Eikones tis Kerkyras* [Icons of Corfu], Athens, 1990

Knossos

Urban settlement and palatial centre in Crete

Knossos lies in the centre north of Crete, two hours' walk from the sea: set amongst low hills, on fertile marly soil and well enough watered. This was a combination that attracted the Neolithic settlers, around 7000 BC, and led to their creating over the next three millennia a substantial tell and the largest of their settlements on the island. Knossos occupied a position of importance, even pre-eminence, seldom surrendered throughout its subsequent history.

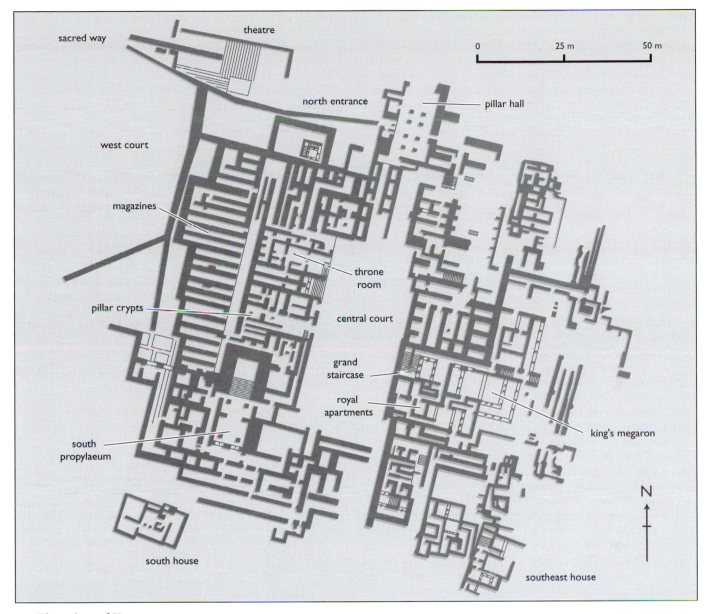

22. The palace of Knossos

Archaeological exploration has revealed that its finest period was as a palatial centre of the Minoans in the Bronze Age (3500–1000 BC), known even then as Knossos. Its rise was gradual, though by 2000 BC (EM III/MM I) the settlement was nearly as extensive as it ever was and already centred on a monumental structure, now replaced by the First Palace. About this extended the town, apparently unfortified, and with cemeteries developed especially to the east and north: it was a "capital" of one of several regional groupings, perhaps jockeying for wider power. Knossos seemingly achieved this c.1700 BC (MM III), when the Second Palace was erected: its prosperity and vigour were shared islandwide; Minoan dominance was evident in the Cyclades and culturally influential in southern Greece. This frenetic burst of activity may have overtaxed the resource base on which it depended: events and reasons are still disputed, but c.1450 BC (LM Ib) much of the island was destroyed in fire and smoke. When this had cleared, power at

Knossos was exercised much as before, but now by an elite with a distinctly Mycenaean flavour: changes were expressed in ceramics, dress, weapons; iconographical themes, stylistic renditions; burial types, customs, and locations; and most significantly by the adaptation of the Minoan administrative system and syllabic script, now utilized to express Greek (Linear B). Their control was maintained at least to 1375 BC (LM IIIA1), when a fire ravaged town and palace. Some scholars see this as the end of the Mycenaeans' control; others prolong their existence well into the 1200s BC (LM IIIB). Either way, the town did survive, at a much-reduced scale, with a simpler, if comfortable, standard of living (LM IIIB) before fading into the very troubled times of the 12th century BC (LM IIIC).

Continuity was somehow maintained in this transitional period: Dorian cultural traits became dominant in this region of Crete. The important early Iron Age cemeteries (11th–7th centuries BC) north of the Bronze Age town indicate this by their use of a Late Bronze Age burial ground, by its rapid expansion, and by the complex burial customs and quite lavish grave goods, with overseas connections visible. Sanctuaries were built over part of the Bronze Age settlement. This flourishing community, with its horse-owning aristocracy, can be traced down to the late 7th century BC, when the evidence dwindles dramatically. The implication is that the polis of Knossos was in decline. Reasons have been sought in military defeat (by Lyttos), plague, and famine. For the Classical period (5th–1st centuries BC) much of the piecemeal evidence comes from literary and epigraphic sources: stasis in the 470s, federal relations with neighbours, migration of ambitious citizens (athletes, architects, and lawgivers) to more progressive milieux. Crete remained peripheral to the Persian and Peloponnesian Wars. By the time of the rise of Macedon, Knossos was populous, to judge from the size of the famine relief donated by Cyrene from 330 to 326 BC. Like much of the Greek world, Knossos was dragged by political manoeuvring into the wider hostilities of the time: internal feuds with Lyttos brought in Phocians and Spartans, and Alexander's campaigns against Darius saw many Cretans dragooned into fighting on the Persian side.

Once released, the genie of military aggression proved to be beyond control. Knossos pursued political domination in the Hellenistic period (4th–3rd centuries BC), more by a network of alliances than outright conquest, though there were exceptions. Knossos' eminence in this struggle is indicated by the island-wide spread of its league, by which it hoped to neutralize more local coalitions. Success was achieved initially: Lykastos, for example, was reportedly razed to the ground; Lyttos fared badly in the war of 221–219 BC; Apollonia and Rhaukos became victims in the early 2nd century BC. But there were setbacks too: a defeat (184 BC) by Gortyn foreshadowed a series of damaging campaigns between these two eminent cities into the 1st century BC; Lyttos grew strong again. Knossian troops were also active abroad as mercenaries, generally staunchly anti-Macedonian.

The Roman incursion (1st century BC) produced one Knossian hero: Lasthenes, who won a sea battle, for which success his house and property were destroyed at the final Roman conquest (69 BC). Gortyn, however, became the premier city, initially in the combined Roman province of Crete and Cyrenaica. After the confusion of the civil wars with Antony, Octavian created the Colonia Julia Nobilis Cnossos in 27 BC. Latin names (settlers from Capua?) feature now in the magistrates and priesthoods. Knossos became a typical Roman provincial city: rebuilt after a series of earthquakes in the early to mid-1st century AD, the colony enjoyed a long spell of prosperity, as well-appointed houses, some rich tombs, and public works (aqueduct) attest. A further major quake in the mid-4th century AD cut this short.

A Christian community was well enough established by the late Roman/early Byzantine times to warrant a bishop's diocese at Knossos (one of 12 in Crete). Remains of three basilicas of 5th- or 6th-century date are reported. Despite all this, the city decayed until finally supplanted by Chandax/Candia after the Arab conquest of the early 9th century. Thereafter a small village of a few hundred souls called Makriteichos marked the locality until the old name was officially restored in the 20th

century, partly as a result of the archaeological discoveries made there by the British in particular.

Not that Knossos was ever exactly forgotten. The town makes regular, if relatively uninformative, appearances in Classical to Roman sources (often in historical or philosophical contexts): Nero was fooled into believing that a cache of tablets (Linear B?) told part of the story of Aeneas' flight to Italy. The Roman ruins were visible for centuries.

Rather the focus of attention has always been more firmly fixed on its Bronze Age past, translated into myth and legend. This process was under way by the 8th century BC, when the island and its peoples played a peripheral part in Homeric epic.

Inevitably, Minos and his court attracted most attention. The positive aspects of his character (as a respected judge in this and the next world; the special relationship with Zeus; and as brother to Rhadamanthys the lawgiver) sit a little at odds with his crueller, imperial side (feuds with Athens, control of the seas, conqueror and dynastic manipulator throughout the Cyclades). His nemesis came upon him in the shameful form of the Minotaur, his downfall at the hands of Theseus, and his death in Sicily from betrayal and an over-hot bath. Daedelus, Icarus, the Labyrinth, Glaucus, Ariadne and Talos are other characters that figure in the same circle of stories. All remain potent icons and symbols, tapped into by today's Greek artists and intelligentsia, and regarded with justifiable pride by modern Cretans.

DON EVELY

See also Minoans

Summary

Knossos was a major city in Crete for four millennia. Founded *c.*7000 BC, it became the most important palatial centre of the Minoans in the 3rd–2nd millennia and remained strong in the Greek period, before being taken into the Roman world, eventually as a colonia, by Octavian. It faded into obscurity in the 5th–6th centuries AD and is now a tourist centre, based on the Minoan palace.

Further Reading

Coldstream, J.N. and G.L. Huxley, "Knossos: The Archaic Gap", *Annual of the British School at Athens*, 94 (1999): pp. 289–307

Evely, Don, Helen Hughes-Brock and Nicoletta Momigliano (editors), *Knossos: A Labyrinth of History*, Oxford: British School at Athens, 1994

Hood, Sinclair and David Smyth, *Archaeological Survey of the Knossos Area*, 2nd edition, London: Thames and Hudson, 1981

Hood, Sinclair and William Taylor, *The Bronze Age Palace at Knossos: Plan and Sections*, London: Thames and Hudson, 1981

Sackett, L. Hugh *et al.*, *Knossos: From Greek City to Roman Colony: Excavations at the Unexplored Mansion*, 2 vols, Athens: British School of Archaeology at Athens, 1992

Sanders, Ian F., *Roman Crete: An Archaeological Survey and Gazetteer of Late Hellenistic, Roman and Early Byzantine Crete*, Warminster: Aris and Phillips, 1982

Kodjabashis

Kodjabashi is a Turkish word meaning "office-holder", from the words *koca* ("big") and *baš* ("head"). In Greek it signified the notable of the village community, while in Turkish this capacity is rendered with the term *ara*. The elevation to community power, term of office, powers, etc. of the *kodjabashis* depended on the system of organization of each individual community. In some regions they were elected to serve for a specific period of time by the adult male inhabitants; elsewhere, they attained their office through the local guilds. Very often, however, their advancement depended on the Turks. Among their various competencies was the allocation of the taxes among the village inhabitants, since under the Ottoman tax system the fiscal units comprised communities and guilds, and not individuals. The allocation of compulsory statute labour imposed by the Turkish authorities was also within their jurisdiction. Moreover, they had military and judicial powers in matters of private law, as well as in minor criminal offences. The transgressions in the exercise of their duties and their despotic behaviour rendered the *kodjabashis*, as a body, detestable to the people and their title synonymous with tyranny. Adamantios Korais compared them to quadrupeds (Sathas, 1962, p. 634), Karl Mendelssohn-Bartholdy called them "Christian Turks" (1873, vol. 1, p. 7), while Chrysanthopoulos-Photakos (1974) has pointed out that they constituted a body which was united on the basis of their common interests, that their high standard of living was similar to that of the Turks, from whom they differed in name only; "instead of calling him Hassan, they called him Yianni and instead of going to a mosque, he went to church. This was the only point in which they differed" (vol. 1, pp. 42–43). The overall system of the community administration of the Greeks under the Ottoman empire changed during the Tanzimat period (1839–76) on the strength of the General (or National) Regulations (1860–62).

DESPINA TSOURKA-PAPASTATHI

Summary

The *kodjabashi* was the headman of a village community under the Ottoman empire. The name *kodjabashi* became synonymous with despotic behaviour and avarice.

Further Reading

Chrysanthopoulos-Photakos, Photios, *Apomnemoneumata peri tes Hellenikes Epanastaseos* [Memoirs of the Greek Revolution], 2 vols, Athens, 1974

Mendelssohn-Bartholdy, Karl, *Geschichte Griechenlands von der Eroberung Konstantinopels durch die Türken im Jahre 1453 bis auf unsere Tage*, 2 vols, Leipzig: Hirzel, 1870

Paschalis, D.P., Kodjabashis entry in *Imerologion tis Megalis Hellados* [Almanac of Great Greece], edited by G. Drosinis, 1935, pp. 301–25

Sathas, Konstantinos, *Tourkokratoumene Hellas, 1453–1821* [Greece under Ottoman Domination, 1453–1821], Athens, 1869, reprinted Athens, 1962

Kolettis, John 1774–1847

Prime Minister of Greece

John Kolettis was Prime Minister of Greece from 1843 to 1847, and one of the 19th century's leading proponents of the irredentist "Great Idea".

In his early political career Kolettis favoured constitutional government and was the leader of the so-called "French" party, which saw France as Greece's natural European ally. This alliance had much to recommend it to irredentist aspirations, as France was less concerned than Britain or Russia with protecting the territorial integrity of the Ottoman empire. The "British" party, under the direction of Alexander Mavrokordatos, looked to Britain's naval superiority in the Mediterranean. The "Russian" party, headed by Count Ioannis and Agostino Kapodistria and Theodore Kolokotronis, emphasized the natural alliance of the Greek and Russian Orthodox Church and opposed the idea of a constitution. These three parties were at odds throughout Kolettis's life.

Kolettis began his career as a physician at the court of Ali Pasha, where he was initiated into the *Philiki Hetaireia*, the secret society in aid of Greek independence. He served as plenipotentiary for Epirus in the First National Assembly of 1821, staying on as minister of war to the provisional national government. His influence with the national government and the Roumeliot chiefs grew as the war proceeded; he was a major force in determining the disposition of funds out of loans from European philhellenes, which meant that large sums went to the Roumeliots and to the shipowners of Hydra and Spetsai, who were the backbone of the Greek navy. It was his strategies that successfully undermined the power and financial base of the swashbuckling but unreliable klepht Odysseus Androutses in eastern Greece.

In October 1824 Kolettis was elected one of five members of the government's executive committee. His knowledge of military strategy was limited – on more than one occasion he was given command of an expedition against the Turks, generally with disastrous results – but his grasp of human psychology and ability to see the big picture made him indispensable.

In 1823–24 two civil wars pitted the leadership of George Kountouriotis against that of Theodore Kolokotronis. Kountouriotis, the elected President of the national government, represented the maritime classes and the Roumeliots. Kolokotronis, the most prominent of the klephtic leaders and commander of the land forces in the Peloponnese, represented the Peloponnesian primates and chieftains, who opposed the idea of centralized government and European-style philhellenism. Kolettis arranged for payment of 50,000 piastres to Kolokotronis and his followers out of the British loan in return for their vacating the capital at Nauplia. When this proved to be only a temporary solution, he organized the Roumeliot troops under Panoutsos Notaras and General Yannis Makriyannis, and drove Kolokotronis's occupying force out. Kolokotronis himself was captured and imprisoned until 1825, when Ibrahim Pasha's attack on the Peloponnese necessitated his release once again to take command of the land forces for the rest of the war. When independence was achieved, both Kolettis and Kolokotronis were awarded positions in president Kapodistria's government.

Upon Kapodistria's assassination in 1831, Kolettis was elected by the Senate to serve with Kolokotronis and Kapodistria's brother, Agostino, on a three-man provisional triumvirate. Civil war again resulted, as Kolokotronis and Agostino Kapodistria tried to establish a new government at Nauplia with the latter as its sole head. In retaliation Kolettis established his own triumvirate, consisting of himself,

Kountouriotis, and the primate Alexander Zaimis, with Alexander Mavrokordatos acting as secretary of state, at Perachora. They were supported in this move by eminent, powerful men such as Petrobey Mavromichalis and Andreas Miaoulis. In April 1832 Kolettis and his Roumeliot troops entered Nauplia once more and forced Kapodistria to resign. Although Kolettis and other Francophiles had initially favoured the son of the duc d'Orléans, the National Assembly met at Pronia in July and approved prince Otto of Bavaria as the new king of Greece.

As a member of the cabinet of prince Otto – now king Otho – Kolettis thrived, despite his position as sole representative of the French party. He was soon appointed minister of the interior, where during the insurrections of 1834 he applied Ali Pasha's technique of using bands of irregulars as peacekeepers. This was an unpopular decision with many non-Greeks at court, who felt such practices might lead to anarchy and "brigandage". He was relieved of office in 1834 and posted as Greek minister to the Paris legation by Otho's most powerful regent, Count Joseph von Armansperg, who leaned towards British allies and the use of European-style police and military.

Even though he would be away for the next nine years, Kolettis' name and policies lived on among his followers. In 1838–40, when it looked as if Mohammed Ali of Egypt might attack the Sublime Porte, and again when the Porte imposed restrictions upon Greek subjects living in Ottoman-occupied lands as retaliation for non-ratification of a Graeco-Turkish commercial treaty, irredentists in Greece and abroad plotted widespread revolt, spreading rumours that Kolettis would return with French funds and military support. The irregular troops he had mobilized, though they were disbanded and ignored by von Armansperg, cherished hopes that they would once again be called into action.

Von Armansperg was dismissed from office and expelled from Greece in 1843, and Kolettis was called back from France. In 1844 he defeated his former ally Alexander Mavrokordatos in an election for the office of prime minister, an outcome that distressed both the British and the Ottoman empires. He continued to work for the Great Idea and strengthened Greece's alliance with the French, though his irredentist zeal overcame his constitutional tendencies: having converted Otho to the Great Idea, Kolettis became an absolutist and supported him utterly. Kolettis's regime, bolstered by his irregular troops and their representatives whom he had brought into office, was widely considered tyrannical. There were accusations of election-fixing and graft; in 1847 he dissolved the Parliament and removed several constitutionalists from public office, then used bribery and "brigands" to elect a government of his liking. Later that year he and his finance minister were accused of falsifying corn averages, which were the basis of taxation. He surrounded himself with a bodyguard of 140 men, maintained at public expense. After his death the government had to confiscate his property to make up for some of the public money he had appropriated for his own purposes. Yet even after his death Otho spoke of Kolettis as his "teacher", and the only minister he had ever fully trusted.

Kolettis died of kidney disease on 6 September 1847. He was succeeded in office by his minister of war, General Tsavellas.

As a politician, Kolettis had an uncanny ability to come out on top in virtually any circumstances. Lord Palmerston complained in a memo to Prince Albert shortly before Kolettis's death that "In the Foreign relations of the Country Mr. Koletti [sic] seems to have had three leading objects in view, aggression towards Turkey, subservience towards France, and insult towards England." The acerbic British historian and philhellene George Finlay, who knew and distrusted Kolettis, describes him as "portly" and "sagacious" in appearance, with a "prudent" and "oracular" demeanour: "Kolettes [sic] wore the wise look well, and had the sense to speak little, but as he was not always silent, his tongue betrayed him." Given Kolettis's success, this last remark might be looked upon as something of an exaggeration.

SUSAN SPENCER

See also Great Idea, Independence (War of)

Biography

Born in 1774 in Syrrakos in northwestern Greece, Kolettis was a Vlach who studied medicine in Pisa. Appointed physician to the court of Ali Pasha, he joined the *Philiki Hetaireia* in 1819. He played a major political and military role in the War of Independence. He became one of the leading proponents of the "Great Idea" and was prime minister of Greece 1843–47. He died in 1847.

Further Reading

Bower, Leonard and Gordon Bolitho, *Otho I, King of Greece: A Biography*, London: Selwyn and Blount, 1939

Braddock, Joseph, *The Greek Phoenix*, London: Constable, and New York: Coward McCann, 1972

Dakin, Douglas, *The Unification of Greece, 1770–1923*, London: Benn, and New York: St Martin's Press, 1972

Dakin, Douglas, *The Greek Struggle for Independence, 1821–1833*, London: Batsford, and Berkeley: University of California Press, 1973

Finlay, George, *A History of Greece from Its Conquest by the Romans to the Present Time, BC 146 to AD 1864*, revised by H.F. Tozer, 7 vols, Oxford: Clarendon Press, 1877, reprinted New York: AMS Press, 1970, vols 6–7

Jelavich, Barbara, *History of the Balkans*, vol. 1: *Eighteenth and Nineteenth Centuries*, Cambridge and New York: Cambridge University Press, 1983

Miller, William, *The Ottoman Empire, 1801–1913*, London: Cambridge University Press, 1913, reprinted with additional material as *The Ottoman Empire and Its Successors, 1801–1927*, 1936

Psomiades, Harry J., "The Character of the New Greek State" in *Hellenism and the First Greek War of Liberation, 1821–1830: Continuity and Change*, edited by Nikoforos P. Diamandouros *et al.*, Thessalonica: Institute for Balkan Studies, 1976

Woodhouse, C.M., *The Greek War of Independence: Its Historical Setting*, London: Hutchinson, 1952, reprinted New York: Russell, 1975

Woodhouse, C.M., *Capodistria: The Founder of Greek Independence*, London and New York: Oxford University Press, 1973

Kollyvades Movement

An Orthodox revival and protest movement of the 18th century

The Kollyvades constituted a significant protest movement that originated on Mount Athos in the second half of the 18th century and played a vital role in the religious and intellectual life of Greece. On the one hand, they initiated a renaissance of patristic spirituality and a return to traditional Orthodox ecclesiastical life; on the other hand, they reacted against strong pro-Western secularizing trends under the influence of the Enlightenment.

The term "Kollyvades" derives from *kollyva*, an oblation of grains of boiled wheat bedecked with sugarplums and distributed to church congregations in remembrance of the dead. "Kollyvades" was in fact a term of opprobrium attributed scornfully to the representatives of the movement by their opponents. The controversy began on Athos in 1754. The monks of St Anne's skete decided for practical reasons to perform memorial sevices on Sundays after the end of the Divine Liturgy instead of on Saturdays, as was the Athonite custom and the canonical tradition. The deacon Neophytos Kavsokalyvitis (1713–84) reacted against this innovation, however, considering that it deviated from ancient Orthodox tradition. The development of the controversy, which divided Athos, later included other matters of dispute, especially that of frequent participation in Holy Communion, as outlined in two relevant books (Venice, 1777 and 1783). The second book was initially condemned by patriarch Gabriel IV in 1785, but this condemnation was later annulled by patriarch Neophytos VII. The leading figures of the Kollyvades movement also included Makarios Notaras (1731–1805), formerly archbishop of Corinth, Nikodimos Agioreitis (1749–1809), and Athanasios Parios (1721–1813). Among the anti-Kollyvades party the monks Theodoritos from Ioannina and Vissarion from Rapsani were particularly notable.

The Kollyvades adduced several arguments from patristic and canonical traditions as well as Orthodox ritual practice to support their views. As may be expected, the whole conflict was not conducted with moderation. It included conspiracies, manipulations, slanders, distortions, banishments, acts of violence, and even the murder of monks. The patriarchate of Constantinople was alerted by these dissensions, and in July 1772 Theodosios II sent a compromise letter, in which, according to the principle of ecclesiastical economy, the opinions of both sides were included. Yet no progress was made, and a second conciliatory letter was sent to the warring factions on 10 June 1773 to restore concord and peace on Athos. After these unsuccessful interventions, the anti-Kollyvades managed through various means to persuade the patriarchate of the justice of their cause. Hence, on 9 June 1776 patriarch Sophronios II issued a condemnation of the Kollyvades, demanding, among other things, that Athanasios Parios be unfrocked. The Kollyvades never accepted this, and remained faithful to their ideas and practices, while Parios worked towards his reinstatement, which finally took place in 1781. The whole conflict was rekindled in 1804 when further accusations were brought against the Kollyvades. In a synod of the Athonite monasteries in Karyes on 19 May 1807 these accusations were thrown out as unfounded, while Agioreitis expounded his *Confession of Faith* on 13 June 1807 before the synod, and his reputation was officially restored. The Kollyvades issue was occasionally raised again in the first half of the 19th century, and several patriarchs took decisions (e.g. Gregory V in August 1819) to settle the whole problem.

The Kollyvades' desire to return to the authentic springs of Orthodox tradition can be understood in the context of the decline of spiritual life even within the Athonite monastic community and from the Western spirit that was growing among the Orthodox faithful. Apart from the immediate cause of the eruption of this conflict, the Kollyvades later incorporated several other issues in their agenda in a holistic attempt to revitalize the traditional Orthodox ethos: frequent participation in the sacraments of the Church and especially Holy Communion; strict adherence to traditional ecclesiastical ceremonial; greater acquaintance with the patristic, hesychast, and ascetic literature and spirituality; and an all-out struggle against the alienation of the Greeks from Orthodoxy because of various Western influences. The Kollyvades' acquaintance with patristic literature is evident from Notaras's and Agioreitis's publication of the *Philokalia*, a florilegium of 1,207 folio pages (Venice, 1782) containing ascetic and mystical texts on the theory and practice of prayer by 38 authors writing between the 4th and the 15th centuries. The Kollyvades also undertook the publication of other patristic writings (e.g. of Symeon the New Theologian), and Agioreitis prepared a complete edition of Gregory Palamas's works (the three-volume manuscript was lost in 1797/78 in Vienna). Moreover, the Kollyvades influenced the Orthodox population in various parts of Greece through their spirituality, preaching, and teaching ministry. They also exerted considerable influence on the Slavic Orthodox world, since the *Philokalia* was translated into Old Church Slavonic by Paisy Velichkovsky and published in Moscow in 1793, and later into Russian, Romanian, and other languages.

Among the Kollyvades, the most bitter opponent of the Enlightenment was Athanasios Parios, who had numerous intense disagreements with his contemporaries (e.g. A. Korais, K. Koumas, D. Proios, Veniamin Lesvios). Parios wrote and published extensively against the Enlightenment and the French Revolution, and his sharp criticism was adopted by the patriarchate of Constantinople for its own defensive policies. Parios also formed an unofficial group of sympathizers (e.g. D. Voulismas) and tried to inhibit the dissemination of Western ideas in Greek schools (e.g. in Chios and in Kydonies). He also made a name for himself by admonishing Orthodox Greeks to keep away from Europe, viz. the West, if they wanted to save their souls.

Though not at all uniform, the Kollyvades occasioned various heated reactions and misunderstandings. A large part of Greek historiography before the 20th century portrayed them in a negative way. They were indiscriminately considered as ignorant, unscrupulous, fanatical, obstinate, manipulative, reactionary, and unaware of Greece's actual needs at the time. But in recent decades the Kollyvades have been reassessed on the basis of a more global view of Greece's religious and intellectual history over the last two centuries. This does not mean that the Kollyvades' exaggerations and erroneous judgements were entirely passed over in silence, but an attempt has been made to consider the whole movement on its own terms and to assess its impact and contributions. From this perspective, it has become obvious that the Kollyvades were instrumental in reorientating the Greek world towards Orthodox ascetic and spiritual sources.

The Kollyvades movement can also be viewed as an antecedent of modern Greek fundamentalism. It started out from private initiative and remained in tension with the official Church and the surrounding culture. It also claimed to represent a more genuine understanding of Orthodoxy and tried to regenerate the fossilized official Church and religious life. The importance that the Orthodox Church now accords to the Kollyvades is apparent in many ways, such as the continuing influence of the *Philokalia*. Most significant perhaps is the fact that three eminent Kollyvades have been canonized: Makarios Notaras soon after his death in 1805, unofficially by the Orthodox flock; Nikodimos Agioreitis in 1955 and Athanasios Parios in 1995, both of them officially.

VASILIOS MAKRIDES

See also Philokalia

Summary

The Kollyvades movement began in the monasteries of Mount Athos in 1754. Originating as a protest against certain religious practices, the Kollyvades became a force for renewal of the authentic Orthodox tradition. They argued for frequent communion, adherence to traditional ceremonial, and familiarity with ascetic and spiritual texts. In 1782 they published the mystical anthology known as the *Philokalia*.

Further Reading

Argyriou, Astérios, *Spirituels néo-grecs: XVe–XXe siècles*, Namur: Editions du Soleil Levant, 1967
Härtel, Hans-Joachim, "Nikodemos Hagioreites: Ein Versuch der Synthese östlicher und westlicher Spiritualität" in *Unser ganzes Leben Christus unserm Gott überantworten: Studien zur ostkirchlichen Spiritualität*, edited by Peter Hauptmann, Göttingen: Vandenhoeck & Ruprecht, 1982
Kavsokalyvitis, Neophytos, *Peri tis sychnis Metalipseos* [On Frequent Repentance], edited by Hieromonk Theodoritos, 2nd edition, Athens, 1992
Le Guillou, M.-J., "La Renaissance spirituelle de XVIIIe siècle", *Istina*, 7 (1960): pp. 95–128
Mastroyannopoulos, Ilias, *Anagennitiko kinima: Paraphyades ton Kollyvadon* [A Revival Movement: Offshoots of the Kollyvades], 2nd edition, Athens, 1987
Metallinos, Georgios, *Athanasios Parios, 1721–1813: Ergographia–Ideologia–Vivliographika* [Athanasios Parios (1721–1813) (Writing–Ideology–Bibliography)], Athens, 1996
Metallinos, Georgios, "I Dynamiki tou Diaphotismou sti Drasi ton Kollyvadon" [The Dynamics of the Enlightenment in the Activities of the Kollyvades], *O Eranistis*, 21 (1997): pp. 189–200
Papaioannou, M.M., *I thriskevtikotita tou Papadiamanti* [Papadiamantis's Piety], Athens, 1948
Papoulides, Konstantinos K., *Makarios Notaras, 1731-1805: Archiepiskopos proen Korinthias* [Makarios Notaras (1731–1805), Former Archbishop of Corinth], Athens, 1974
Papoulides, Konstantinos K., *To kinima ton Kollyvadon* [The Kollyvades Movement], 2nd edition, Athens, 1991
Papoulides, Konstantinos K., *Agioreitika* [Hagoritica], Karyes, 1993, studies 6-11
Parios, Athanasios, *Dilosis tis en to Agio Orei taraxon alitheias* [Discovery of the Truth of the Disturbances on the Holy Mountain], edited by Hieromonk Theodoritos, Athens, 1988
Paschos, Pantelis V., *En Askisei kai Martyrio: Anekdota Philokalika kai Kollyvadika ymnagiologika keimena* [In Self-Discipline and Martyrdom: Unpublished Texts of the Philokalia and of Kollyvadic Hymnography], Athens, 1996
Pirard, M., "Le Starez Paisij Velickovskij, 1722–1794: la Tradition philologico-ascétique en Russie et en Europe orientale", *Messager de l'Exarchat du Patriarchat russe en Europe occidentale*, 21 (1973): pp. 35–57
Podskalsky, Gerhard, *Griechische Theologie in der Zeit der Türkenherrschaft, 1453–1821*, Munich: Beck, 1988, pp. 358–65, 372–74, and 377–82
Rantovits [Radovich], Amphilochios, *I Philokaliki Anagennisi tou XVIII kai XIX aiona kai oi Pnevmatikoi Karpoi tis* [The Philocalic Revival of the 18th and 19th Centuries and its Spiritual Fruits], Athens, 1984
Sotiropoulos, Charalampos G., "Kollyvades / Antikollyvades" in *Antidoron Pnevmatikon: Timitikos Tomos ... tou Kathigitou Gerasimou Io. Konidari* [Spiritual Antidoron: A Volume in Honour of Gerasimos Io. Konidari], Athens, 1981, pp. 461–87
Tachiaos, Antonios-Aimilios, *O Paisios Velichkovsky (1722-1794) kai i Askitikophilologiki Scholi Tou* [Paisy Velichkovsky and his Ascetic-Philological School], Thessalonica, 1964
Tachiaos, Antonios-Aimilios, "De la Philokalia au Dobrotoljubie: la Création d'un 'Sbornik'", *Cyrillomethodianum*, 5 (1981): pp. 208–13
Tzogas, Charilaos S., *I peri Mnimosinon Eris en Agio Orei kata ton 18o Aiona* [The Mnemosynon Controversy in 18th Century Athos], Thessalonica, 1969
Ware, Kallistos, Philocalie entry in *Dictionnaire de spiritualité*, edited by Marcel Viller *et al.*, vol. 12, Paris: Beauchesne, 1984, cols 1336–52
Ware, Kallistos, "The Spirituality of the *Philokalia*", *Sobornost*, 13 (1991): pp. 6–24

Kolokotronis, Theodore 1770–1843

Hero of the War of Independence

Theodore Kolokotronis was the commander-in-chief of the forces in the Morea (Peloponnese) during the War of Independence and its aftermath (1821–33). One of Greece's greatest war heroes and a clever strategist, Kolokotronis was considered the most formidable of the *kapetanoi* (leaders) ranged against the Europeanized "Central Government" represented by Alexander Mavrokordatos, George Kountouriotis, and Demetrios Ypsilantis. Unlike some of the other heroes of the revolution, such as General Makriyannis, Kolokotronis supported the regime of Count Ioannis Kapodistria when he became president of the newly liberated Greece in 1828. When Kapodistria was assassinated in 1831, Kolokotronis was elected by the Senate to serve with Kapodistria's brother, Agostino, and John Kolletis on a three-man provisional triumvirate. The combination was not a happy one; Kolettis favoured the "French" or "Constitutionalist" party and Kolokotronis and Kapodistria favoured the "Russian" or "Kapodistrian". The result was a civil war that raged until prince Otto of Bavaria took the throne as king Otho in 1832.

The Kolokotroni were an old and respected klepht family, in the tradition of the fiercely independent freedom fighter. As a Greek "type", the historian C.M. Woodhouse has compared Kolokotronis with the avenging "outcast" as represented by Antaeus, Sciron, or the Titans. His father, Constantine Kolokotronis, who died fighting at Kastanitza in 1780, was said to have killed at least 700 Turks with his own hands. Kolokotronis himself, at the age of 16, compelled the Sublime Porte to recognize him as chief of the *armatoloi* ("armed men") of Megalopolis. The family became so influential that the Porte ordered extirpation of the entire clan in 1804; 36 of Kolokotronis's brothers, cousins, and relatives, and 150 of their followers, were tortured and killed. Driven from his home, he took refuge on the Ionian islands in 1806.

When the British occupied Zakynthos in 1810, Kolokotronis joined the First Duke of York's Greek Infantry with the rank of captain (later major). He served in the British army under Sir Richard Church for ten years, during which period Kolokotronis was sworn into the *Philiki Hetaireia*, the secret society in aid of Greek independence. With the aid of the hetairists, Kolokotronis slipped back to the Peloponnese shortly before the outbreak of the revolution and, with a growing band of followers, was among the most enthusiastic plunderers of Turkish residents. This activity gave him sufficient funds to maintain the biggest band of armed Greeks in the area, so that by the time Demetrios Ypsilantis arrived in June 1821 to take control on Hydra, Kolokotronis had about 3000 men at his call. He had the biggest contingent at the Tripolitza massacre in October, where several thousand Turkish civilians were slain, and his memoirs grimly describe his triumphal ride over streets carpeted with corpses: "My horse from the walls to the palace never touched the earth." He had another great victory in June 1822 when he annihilated the forces of the Turkish commander Mahmoud Dramali, who was marching from Corinth to attack the new Greek capital at Nauplia.

By the end of 1822 Kolokotronis had allied himself with a few powerful landowners of the Peloponnese, chief of whom was Petrobey Mavromichalis, overlord of the Maniots. The group opposed centralized government and European-style philhellenic nationalism: in December 1822 they prevented the provisional National Assembly from meeting by refusing to allow the members into Nauplia, which Kolokotronis and his son Panos were holding at the time. The central government held the assembly at nearby Astros, and moved that their two major concerns ought to be to send representatives to seek a loan in London and to pass legislation aimed at decreasing Kolokotronis's power. Kolokotronis responded by kidnapping four of the assembly members and removing them under armed guard to Nauplia; the others took refuge on a southern promontory of the Peloponnese where they benefited from the protection of the nearby islands of Hydra and Spetsai. In gratitude for that protection, they elected the Hydriot George Kountouriotis as their new president, but there was no question after this that Kolokotronis was the real power in the Peloponnese.

In 1823 this situation led to the first civil war, which did not come to an end until 1824, when the central government paid Kolokotronis 50,000 piastres out of the first London Greek Committee loan in exchange for his giving up the possession of Nauplia and agreeing to cooperate with them. Shortly afterwards, however, a second civil war broke out over how to spend the remainder of the money. The rebel primates Zaimis and Londos challenged the authority of Kountouriotis's government and Kolokotronis joined them. When Panos was

killed in a skirmish outside Tripolitza, Kolokotronis surrendered and allowed himself to be imprisoned on Hydra.

In 1825, when Ibrahim Pasha was threatening the Peloponnese, public demand forced Kolokotronis's release from prison and reappointment as commander-in-chief of the land forces. In this capacity he made an uneasy alliance with the regular troops of the French philhellene Charles Fabvier, whose tactics were more successful with Ibrahim's European-trained troops than the klephtic guerrilla warfare favoured by Kolokotronis and his followers. In 1827 Kolokotronis invited his old commander, Sir Richard Church, to share the command with him. This partnership lasted the duration of the war.

Though Kolokotronis officially withdrew from politics when King Otho ascended the throne in 1832, the Bavarian regency feared his influence. In September 1832 he was arrested and condemned to death on a trumped-up charge of treason. The sentence was commuted to life imprisonment, but when Otho came of age in 1835, Kolokotronis, along with his brother-in-law and other followers who had been imprisoned with him, was issued a full pardon by the king and restored to favour. Kolokotronis retired to Athens, where he remained a war hero and powerful political voice in favour of Greek nationalism until his death on 4 February 1843.

SUSAN SPENCER

See also Independence (War of)

Biography

Born in 1770 into an old klepht family, Kolokotronis fled from Ottoman persecution to Zakynthos which was occupied by the British from 1810. He served in the British army under Sir Richard Church and also joined the *Philiki Hetaireia*. In the War of Independence he became commander-in-chief of the forces in the Peloponnese and supported the regime of Ioannis Kapodistria. Charged with treason but pardoned, he retired to Athens where he died in 1843.

Writings

Kolokotrones: The Klepht and the Warrior, London: Unwin, and New York: Macmillan, 1892; as *Memoirs from the War of Greek Independence, 1821–1833*, edited by E.M.Edmonds, Chicago: Argonaut, 1969

Further Reading

Braddock, Joseph, *The Greek Phoenix*, London: Constable, and New York: Coward McCann, 1972

Dakin, Douglas, *The Unification of Greece, 1770–1923*, London: Benn, and New York: St Martin's Press, 1972

Dakin, Douglas, "The Formation of the Greek State, 1821–33" in *The Struggle for Greek Independence: Essays to Mark the 150th Anniversary of the Greek War of Independence*, edited by Richard Clogg, London: Macmillan, and Hamden, Connecticut: Archon, 1973

Dakin, Douglas, *The Greek Struggle for Independence, 1821–1833*, London: Batsford, and Berkeley: University of California Press, 1973

Finlay, George, *A History of Greece from Its Conquest by the Romans to the Present Time, BC 146 to AD 1864*, revised by H.F. Tozer, 7 vols, Oxford: Clarendon Press, 1877, reprinted New York: AMS Press, 1970, vols 6–7

Howarth, David, *The Greek Adventure: Lord Byron and Other Eccentrics in the War of Independence*, New York: Atheneum, and London: Collins, 1976

Humphreys, W.H., First "Journal of the Greek War of Independence" (July 1821–February 1822), edited by Sture Linnér, Stockholm: Almqvist & Wiksell, 1967

Jelavich, Barbara, introduction to Russia and Greece during the Regency of King Othon, 1832–1835: Russian Documents on the First Years of Greek Independence, Thessalonica: Institute for Balkan Studies, 1962

Koliopoulos, John S., Brigands with a Cause: Brigandage and Irredentism in Modern Greece, 1821–1912, Oxford: Clarendon Press, and New York: Oxford University Press, 1987

Makriyannis, Yannis, The Memoirs of General Makriyannis, 1797–1864, edited and translated by H.A. Lidderdale, London: Oxford University Press, 1966

Phillips, W. Alison, The War of Greek Independence, 1821 to 1833, London: Smith Elder, and New York: Scribner, 1897

St Clair, William, That Greece Might Still Be Free: The Philhellenes in the War of Independence, London and New York: Oxford University Press, 1972

Woodhouse, C.M., The Greek War of Independence: Its Historical Setting, London: Hutchinson, 1952, reprinted New York: Russell, 1975

Woodhouse, C.M., Capodistria: The Founder of Greek Independence, London and New York: Oxford University Press, 1973

Komnene, Anna 1083–c.1153/54

Historian

Anna Komnene was born on 2 December 1083, the eldest daughter of the emperor Alexios I Komnenos (1081–1118) and his wife Irene Doukaina. In her work the Alexiad Anna herself gives an indication that her life's ambition had been to become empress. A few days after her birth she and the young Constantine Doukas, son of the dethroned emperor Michael VII, had been betrothed; they were associated in her father's reign, and publicly acclaimed. After the birth of a brother, John, her hopes of becoming empress at the side of her future husband were shattered. It was a devastating blow to the woman whom Charles Diehl describes as "très princesse".

Anna received an excellent education, and was further able to perfect her knowledge of Classical literature and mythology without the approval of her parents, who would have considered this a danger to her Christian upbringing. It has been said that her achievements in both the trivium and the quadrivium were well above average. In addition to the standard curriculum of the times, she acquired mastery of geography and medicine.

After the premature death of Constantine Doukas, she married Nikephoros Bryennios, still hoping to gain the throne at the side of her husband. In a famous deathbed scene in the Alexiad she describes how she and her mother desperately tried to persuade the dying emperor to disqualify his son from the throne and designate Bryennios and Anna as his successors. Having failed at this, Anna became involved in an uprising against her brother, and a botched assassination attempt. When this rebellion too had failed, Anna and her mother retired to a convent that the empress had previously founded.

It was during the later years of her life that Anna may have cultivated a circle of scholars. She commissioned Michael of Ephesus to produce a commentary on Aristotle, and seems to have had in mind a more ambitious project, of publishing a whole series of commentaries. After her husband's death (c.1136/37), Anna dedicated the rest of her life to the writing of the history of her father's reign, the Alexiad.

In the preface to the 15 books of the Alexiad Anna writes that she regards her work as a continuation of the historical writings of her husband, Nikephoros Bryennios. Herbert Hunger postulates that, besides Bryennios, the sources of Anna's history included Psellos, Attaleiates, and Skylitzes. In her privileged position she would also have had access to documents and letters in the imperial archives. Her knowledge of the imperial family was based on her intimate personal contacts. Regarding military matters, she would have had many opportunities to question the veterans of her father's campaigns, and she herself had been an eyewitness to the coming of the First Crusade.

Her description of the crusaders, the "Latins" as she generalizes them, is influenced by her distrust of what she, the Byzantine aristocrat, considers to be a barbarian force. She is fascinated by individual participants, such as the Norman prince Bohemond, of whom she gives an admirable picture. In general, however, her prejudices colour her descriptions. Regardless of this, Anna's account of the First Crusade, as seen from the Byzantine perspective, is a very valuable source, and is established as such in modern scholarship.

Her work is also of great importance for the description it gives of various peoples in contact with the empire, especially the Seljuk Turks and other steppe nomads on the empire's northern borders. It contains details as varied as the administration of the empire, military matters, heresies, education, and medicine.

The style of Anna's work is deemed to attest to the conscious efforts made by Byzantine writers of the Komnenian period to return to purer Classical models and Atticism. As such, the Alexiad of Anna stands as the first important work of the literary renaissance of the Komnenian period. Her work is replete with citations from Classical authors – Homer, the tragedians, historians, and the Anthologia Palatina. Regardless of the Classicizing tendencies, however, Anna uses the common language of her time without scruples when she needs to use technical terms.

The Alexiad, Anna's epic account of her father's reign, is the only historical work in Byzantine literature written by a woman; it remains an important creation on both the literary and historical levels.

FRANZISKA E. SHLOSSER

See also Historiography

Biography

Born in Constantinople in 1083, Anna was the eldest daughter of the emperor Alexios I and received a good education. She had early ambitions to become empress but, when her husband died, she retired to a convent. She devoted the rest of her life to writing the history of her father's reign, the Alexiad, the only known Byzantine historical work written by a woman. She died c.1153/4.

Writings

Alexiadis, edited by Ludwig Schopen and August Reifferscheid, 2 vols, Bonn: Weber, 1839–78 (*Corpus scriptorum historiae byzantinae*)

In *Patrologia Graeca*, edited by J. P. Migne, vol. 131, 80–1212

Porphyrogenitae, Alexias, edited by August Reifferscheid, 2 vols, Leipzig: Teubner, 1884

Alexiade, edited and translated into French by Bernard Leib, 4 vols, Paris: Belles Lettres, 1937–76

The Alexiad of Princess Anna Comnena, translated by Elizabeth Dawes, London: Paul Trench Trubner, 1928; New York: Barnes and Noble, 1967

The Alexiad, translated by E.R.A. Sewter, Harmondsworth: Penguin, 1969

Further Reading

Browning, R., "An Unpublished Funeral Oration on Anna Comnena", *Proceedings of the Cambridge Philological Society*, 188 (1962): pp. 1–12

Buckler, Georgina, *Anna Comnena: A Study*, London: Oxford University Press, 1929, reprinted 1968

Diehl, Charles, "Anne Comnène" in his *Figures byzantines*, vol. 2, 8th edition, Paris: Colin, 1927

France, J., "Anna Comnena, the *Alexiad* and the First Crusade", *Reading Medieval Studies*, 10 (1984): pp. 20–38

Hunger, Herbert, "Stilstufen in der byzantinischen Geschichtsschreibung des 12. Jahrhunderts: Anna Komnene und Michael Glykas", *Byzantine Studies / Etudes Byzantines*, 5/1–2 (1978): pp. 139–70

Hunger, Herbert, *Die hochsprachliche profane Literatur der Byzantiner*, vol. 1, Munich: Beck, 1978

Hussey, J.M. (editor), *The Byzantine Empire*, Cambridge: Cambridge University Press, 1966–67 (*The Cambridge Medieval History*, vol. 4, parts 1–2, 2nd edition)

Kambylis, A., "'Zum Program' der byzantinischen Historikerin Anna Komnene", in *Dorema: Festschrift for Hans Diller*, Athens, 1975

Kurtz, E, "Das Testament der Anna Komnene", *Byzantinische Zeitschrift*, 16 (1907): pp. 93–101

Miller, William, "A Byzantine Blue Stocking: Anna Comnena" in his *Essays on the Latin Orient*, Cambridge: Cambridge University Press, 1921, reprinted New York: AMS Press, 1983

Shlosser, F.E., "Byzantine Studies and the History of the Crusades: The *Alexiad* of Anna Comnena as Source for the Crusades", *Byzantinische Forschungen*, 15 (1990): pp. 397–406

Sommerard, L., *Deux Princèsses d'Orient au XIIe siècle: Anna Comnène et Agnès de France*, Paris, 1907

Komnenos family

The Komnenos family was an aristocratic clan that originated presumably from a place called Komne (its location is uncertain, but was probably in the east). By the mid-11th century the family's properties were centred on the fortress of Kastamon, in northern Paphlagonia, which was in Turkish hands intermittently from 1076 and definitively so by the late 12th century. In the early 11th century the Komnenoi became prominent landowners and generals, giving rise to an imperial dynasty that would dominate the Byzantine empire for a century and a name that would retain its imperial lustre until after the Turkish conquest.

Isaac I Komnenos was put forward as emperor (1057–59) by the military aristocracy, who were dissatisfied with the treatment they received from Michael VI (emperor 1056–57).

Komnenos family: woodcut of the Komnenos and Angelos emperors, from left, top row: John II Komnenos, Manuel I Komnenos, Alexios II Komnenos; second row: Andronikos Komnenos, Isaac II Angelos, Alexios III Angelos

Isaac was himself forced to abdicate when his fiscal and religious policies proved widely unpopular. His brother John and John's sons (especially Isaac and Alexios) remained prominent until 1081, when the young Alexios seized Constantinople from Nikephoros III Botaneiates (emperor 1078–81). Alexios, married to Irene Doukaina, united the two most prominent aristocratic clans, the Komnenos and the Doukas, giving him a formidable position in a society where family connections were of increasing importance. His reign brought steady recovery from the disastrous position in which the empire found itself after defeat by the Turks at the battle of Manzikert. Alexios was succeeded by his son John II Komnenos (emperor 1118–43), his grandson Manuel I Komnenos (emperor 1143–80), and his great-grandson Alexios II (emperor 1180–83). All save the last were strong rulers during whose reigns the Byzantine empire regained a measure of stability and economic prosperity, despite continuing Turkish pressure in Asia Minor, constant challenges in Europe, and the disruptive passage of the First and Second Crusades in 1097 and 1147–48 respectively. Alexios II succeeded as a minor and fell victim to civil war in the Komnenos family. He was murdered at the age of 14 by Andronikos I, his father Manuel I's cousin and greatest rival. Both Alexios and Andronikos would fulfil the prophecy that the initial letters of the Komnenoi emperors' names would spell *AIMA* (blood). Andronikos was himself killed in a bloody spectacle in the hippodrome after only three years of rule, and in 1185 power passed to the Angelos family.

Alexios I and his successors consolidated their hold on power by employing in high posts only members of the extended Komnenos family, which was prolific; the word *gambros* (relative by marriage) became a semi-official title. By the mid-12th century virtually every major position, whether in Constantinople or the provinces, was likely to be held by a Komnenos or a close relative. The Komnenos century was once viewed by historians as a period of exploitation of the empire by the imperial family, culminating in the policies of Manuel I, which were condemned as expansionist and ruinously expensive. Trading concessions given to western maritime republics in return for naval aid were regarded as specially dangerous short-term measures. More recently, however, it has been established that the empire was generally prosperous during this period and that concessions offered to westerners were less damaging than had been claimed. Bias in modern scholarship against Manuel has been shown to derive, at least in part, from Niketas Choniates, the dominant historian of Manuel's reign and of the collapse which followed, which led with seeming inevitability to the capture of Constantinople by soldiers of the Fourth Crusade in 1204.

The Komnenos family included several figures important to the development of Byzantine culture. The most prominent was the historian Anna Komnene; her father Alexios I wrote some verse, and an Isaac (probably her brother) essays on Homeric topics. In the 1140s the *sevastokratorissa* (emperor's sister) Irene Komnene (a Komnene by marriage, widow of Manuel I's brother Andronikos) was a significant patron of literature and painting. As well as palaces, members of the family built churches, of which John II's foundation of the monastery and hospital of the Pantokrator in the capital was the most lavish. Several other churches founded by Komnenoi may be found in the southern Balkans. In the history of literature the period of the Komnenoi marks the first appearance in Byzantium of professional littérateurs, of whom Theodore Prodromos is the best-known example. Consequent pressure of the marketplace may be responsible, in part, for two other developments: the first surviving literature in vernacular modern Greek (e.g. the satirical so-called *Ptochoprodromika*, poems by multifaceted Penniless Prodromos, and *Digenis Akritis)*, and the proliferation of court writing dominated by rhetorical praise of the dynasty, which, since the Enlightenment, has given the writing of the time a bad name.

Even after the Komnenos family had lost imperial power, their name continued to exert a resonance, especially in conjunction with others, for example, Angelos or Vatatzes. The Grand Komnenoi, rulers of Trebizond after the Latin conquest of Constantinople in 1204, used the name as a title until finally succumbing to the Turks in 1461.

MICHAEL JEFFREYS

Further Reading

Angold, Michael, *Church and Society in Byzantium under the Comneni, 1081–1261*, Cambridge and New York: Cambridge University Press, 1995

Barzos, K., *I Genealogia ton Komninon* [Genealogy of the Komnenoi], 2 vols, Thessalonica, 1984

Chalandon, Ferdinand, *Les Comnène: études sur l'empire byzantin aux XIe et XIIe siècles*, 2 vols, Paris: Picard, 1900–12, reprinted New York: Franklin, 1960

Magdalino, Paul, *The Empire of Manuel I Komnenos, 1143–1180*, Cambridge and New York: Cambridge University Press, 1993

Trapp, Erich (editor), *Prosopographisches Lexikon der Palaiologenzeit*, Vienna: Akademie der Wissenschaften, 1976–96

Kontoglou, Photis *c.*1895–1965

Painter, iconographer, and writer

Kontoglou's enormous contribution to the cultural life of modern Greece defies simple classification. Chiefly remembered today for having revived the ancient "Byzantine" style of ecclesiastical art, he has left his mark on modern Greek secular art, literature, and religious thought. More than three decades after his death his books are still published, and read by all generations. His two-volume opus, *Ekphrasis tes Orthodoxou Eikonographeias* ("Description of Orthodox Iconography", 1960), still serves as the standard text and guide for icon painters all over the world. Moreover, his forthright and at times childlike simplicity and artlessness characterized qualities held by many Greeks to be quintessentially Hellenic.

Kontoglou was born at Aivali, near the ancient city of Cydoniae in northwest Asia Minor in 1895 or 1896, and was always proud of having been born "in Asia". His childhood surroundings left happy memories that would stay with him all his life, and appear time and again in his work. Indeed, the almost poignant sense of melancholy and nostalgia in much of his secular art and writings seems to have been the result of a constant longing for those happy years.

A relative of Kontoglou's noticed his artistic potential and sent him to Athens to study at the Polytechnic's School of Fine Arts, a highly traditional institution still dominated by artists of the so-called "Munich School" of the 19th century. The outbreak of World War I isolated Kontoglou from Aivali, and being dissatisfied with the School of Fine Arts, he left for Paris where he spent some years working as an illustrator. Here he claims to have met Rodin and Maeterlinck, but his Parisian sojourn hardly left any traces in the painter's work.

Returning to Aivali in 1919, Kontoglou began teaching at the girls' school at Cydoniae. At the same time, he and a group of friends organized an intellectual group called "New People" at Aivali. He also published his first major book, the novel *Pedro Cazas*, which was hailed in Athens and Mytilene as a breath of fresh air in the then stuffy world of Greek letters.

The 1922 catastrophe turned Kontoglou into a refugee, first in Mytilene then in Athens, where he reported feeling like "a caged bird". His love for travel led him in 1923 to visit Mount Athos, where he got his first real taste of the forms and techniques of Byzantine art. This eye-opening experience led to the publication of *Art of Athos: Reproductions and Variations by Photis Kontoglou* (1923) and *Vasanda*, a collection of writings and illustrations inspired by Athos. The same year also saw Kontoglou's first exhibition in Mytilene.

The 1920s and 1930s were productive years for Kontoglou, both as a painter and as a writer. He coordinated the influential but short-lived journal *Philiki Hetaireia* ("Society of Friends"), beginning in 1925, and collaborated with the periodical *Ellinika Grammata* ("Greek Literature"). Kontoglou spent much time travelling in Greece, but his stint at Mistra in the 1930s working on the conservation of the Byzantine murals in the churches there was a decisive influence on his work. He also worked on the murals of the monastery at Kaisariane, near Athens. His house in the Kypriadou district of Athens became a second home for a number of young painters and thinkers including Ioannis Tsarouchis and Nikos

Photis Kontoglou: detail of the fresco *The Kings of Attica*, showing Icarius, king of Attica, on the left, and the invention of a relic of Pelops on the right, Municipal Reading Room, Athens

Engonopoulos. One wall of this house was painted by the group of friends with exotic and fantastic scenes of tropical islands, indigenous peoples of the world, a portrait of Kontoglou's family, and busts of famous men. The mural (now in the National Art Gallery in Athens) is one of the most widely loved of Kontoglou's works.

In addition to more secular commissions and written works (including the *Astrolabe*, 1935), Kontoglou received his first commission to decorate a complete church, at Rio near Patras. In the same year he did restoration work on the murals of the Peribleptos church in Mistra – a task which he found particularly stimulating and inspirational. Work of this calibre had not been used for Byzantine mural conservation till that time.

In 1937–38 Kontoglou undertook an important secular commission in the form of murals for the entrance hall and reading room of the Athens Town Hall. Themes included ancient Greek mythology and a cavalcade of important Greek historical figures up to 1821. This was the first time that a secular work on such a scale employed the Byzantine style, and caused not a little controversy in a country that had been taught to think of that style as "backward" and regressive, in contrast to the naturalism of the Italian Renaissance style, which in the 19th and early 20th centuries was used for both public and religious monuments. Kontoglou was, along with two or three others, instrumental in opening the Greek public's eyes to the sublime spirituality of Byzantine art. His efforts would eventually result in Western "Italianate" art being discouraged and even banned for new or redecorated churches.

The art of portable icon painting also owed its resurgence to Kontoglou and his apprentices, and he invigorated the art of book illustration (chiefly in the woodcut medium) which drew heavily on the Greek folk-art idiom.

The Nazi occupation of Greece during World War II was as hard for Kontoglou and his family as it was for the rest of the nation. He had to sell his beloved home for a little flour and oil, and lived with friends – at one stage in a garage – during the struggle. With his resources limited and commissions few and far between, he put his abundant energy into writing, producing, among other works, *The Mystical Garden* in which he outlined his manifesto for a return to Byzantine art in a 20th-century Orthodox context. For Kontoglou, Byzantine art was not a relic to be revived from the past, but a valid "living" tradition that had to be understood and properly taught.

The postwar period brought one of his most important commissions, the controversial decoration of the Byzantine church of Kapnikarea in central Athens. Despite criticism that no archaeological monument should be interfered with by modern painters, Kontoglou realized one of his most influential and perfect iconographic programmes for a church, which served as a paradigm for his "new" Byzantine style. A host of other church commissions followed, and some designs and cartoons were even dispatched to the United States where they were fitted into new Orthodox churches.

Publishing activity continued apace with widely read contributions to the liberal newspaper *Eleutheria* and the Orthodox periodical *Kivotos*. Here he hailed "the invigoration of

Orthodox convictions, and the heralding of an enlightened return to the essence of tradition". In the newspaper *Orthodoxos Typos* Kontoglou made a name for himself by relentlessly attacking any plans for union with the Roman Catholic Church and defending Orthodoxy from what he saw as the danger of Western materialism. He presided over an informal "school" of painters that included Constantine Georgakopoulos, Petros Odambasis, Ioannis Terzis, Rallis Kopsidis, Petros Vamboulis, and Spyros Papaloukas.

In 1960 *Ekphrasis* appeared in two volumes to universal acclaim, and Kontoglou began to be showered with awards from the state, the Church, and the Athens Academy, including Greece's highest distinction, the Commander of the Phoenix. A complete series of his writings began to appear, published by Astir, and much previously unpublished material has appeared.

Kontoglou died on 13 July 1965 after a protracted illness initiated by wounds from a car crash the previous year. His loss was greatly mourned, and his remains now lie in the grounds of the monastery of Hagia Paraskevi at Nea Makri.

Kontoglou would not have wished to be remembered as a cult figure, but his eccentric bearing, his passion for his Church and traditions, his mistrust of the West and things Western, his contempt for the vanity and socializing of the art world, and his idiosyncratic but charming use of the Greek language made him a revered figure among traditionalist, but also intellectual circles in Greece and in the broader Orthodox community. His unabashed championing of the Byzantine style in secular works greatly influenced younger artists, most notably Tsarouchis. But his signature style ("Through the hand of Photis Kontoglou") underscored the fact that his art was nothing to do with "originality" and "individual expression", but drew on a source as old as the Greek people itself.

DAVID R. TURNER

See also Painting

Biography

Born at Aivali in northwest Asia Minor *c.*1895, Kontoglou studied in Athens and Paris where he worked as an illustrator during World War I. Returning to Aivali in 1919, he taught at a local girls' school and began writing. After the 1922 disaster he moved to Lesbos (where he had his first exhibition of paintings) and then to Athens where he became the centre of a circle of young painters. He found inspiration in Byzantine art and was commissioned to paint many churches. He died in 1965.

Further Reading

Hatziphotis, I.M., *Photios Kontoglou: I Zoi kai to Ergo tou* [Photios Kontoglou: His Life and Works], Athens, 1978

Kontoglou, Photis, *Ekphrasis tes Orthodoxou Eikonographeias* [Description of Orthodox Iconography], 2 vols, Athens, 1960, 2nd edition, revised by P. Vamboulis, 1979

Photis Kontoglou, 1978 (exhibition catalogue: National Art Gallery, Athens; in Greek)

Photis Kontoglou, 1986 (exhibition catalogue: Macedonian Centre for Modern Art, Thessalonica; in Greek)

Zias, N., *Photis Kontoglou: Zographos* [Photis Kontoglou: Painter], Athens, 1993

Korais, Adamantios 1748–1833

Classicist, political theorist, and man of letters

Adamantios Korais was perhaps the foremost representative of the Greek Enlightenment. Born in the cosmopolitan mercantile centre of Smyrna in 1748, he completed his primary education there. Between 1771 and 1777 he was immersed in his family's commercial activities of silk export in Amsterdam. After his return to Smyrna (1778–82) Korais moved back to Western Europe and studied medicine at Montpellier, receiving his doctorate in 1787. In 1788 he moved to Paris where he stayed until his death in 1833. Korais distinguished himself as a critical editor of ancient Greek literature and was highly esteemed by scholarly and political circles, both in France and abroad (e.g. by Thomas Jefferson). Having close contacts with the intellectual and political elite of his day, Korais followed, like a meticulous reporter, all major events in French and international politics (e.g. the French Revolution, Napoleonic wars) and tried to draw useful conclusions for the eventual liberation of his enslaved compatriots.

Korais's concern for Greece remained unwavering throughout his long life. He was particularly concerned with the educational level of his compatriots and the necessary reforms in the school curricula and the teaching methods on the model of "enlightened Europe". Korais realized that the prestige and the international reputation of a nation (e.g. France) depended heavily upon its scholarly and scientific achievements. This was his dream for Greece too. Korais thus proclaimed the notion of *metakenosis*, i.e. the pouring of the acquired wisdom of the West into the Greek vessels of his day. In this way knowledge had been earlier transferred from ancient Greece to the West and had contributed immensely to the achievements there.

Korais was also very critical of the widespread habit of polymathy and stressed the need for more specialized knowledge and expertise that could lead to pathbreaking scholarly achievements. He especially criticized the outdated, arid tradition of teaching grammar and related lessons in Greek schools, which ended up offering nothing useful to the students. His own editorial programme of ancient Greek authors was intended to provide modern Greeks with practical principles and truths that could lead to Greece's regeneration and eventually to its liberation. Korais's final objective was the creation of a well-ordered society, in which happiness, virtue, law, and freedom would reign. He also showed a keen interest in the controversial issue of Greek language, the development of which was absolutely necessary for his compatriots in order to express better their thoughts. Korais tried to find a middle way between the archaizers and the vulgarizers. His own preference for Greek idiom later exerted some influence upon the formation of the simple katharevousa, a largely artificial language that had become the subject of serious debate.

Aside from this, Korais was a vehement opponent of the slavery of thought, especially regarding socially established, old-fashioned perceptions and clerical impact. He was particularly interested in limiting the Church's power and social influence, which were inhibiting Greece's intellectual emancipation and political independence. He also defended his country against accusations about the illiteracy of Greeks made by

Western travellers such as J.L.S. Bartholdy. Among his relevant works, the lecture *Mémoire sur l'état actuel de la civilisation dans la Grèce* at the Société des Observateurs de l'Homme in 1803 must be mentioned here. Yet, when addressing himself to his compatriots, Korais was far more critical and demanding, for he aimed to eradicate all the wrongs that were keeping Greece apart from the civilized nations.

Korais's range of writings and translations is impressive. Apart from his early religious output, Korais wrote on medical issues and published several tracts of patriotic and political content with regard to the Greek cause and the institutions of the new-born Greek state. His greatest achievement was undoubtedly the systematic edition of ancient Greek writers starting in 1799 with Theophrastus's *Characters*. Korais wrote extensive prolegomena and annotations to each volume and discussed burning questions concerning Greek education and language. In addition, there exist several other treatises by Korais (e.g. his Greek translation with notes of Beccaria's *Dei delitti e delle pene* in 1802; 1823) as well as collective volumes containing his numerous shorter texts. Korais also left various other works, which were published posthumously. Finally, his voluminous correspondence, with Greeks and foreigners alike, attests to the wide range of his interests and activities as well as to his total devotion to the Enlightenment and the liberation of the Greek people. Korais had a special interest in coordinating the diaspora Greeks, such as Alexandros Vasileiou in Vienna and Iakovos Rotas in Trieste, with those in the Ottoman empire. He was also concerned to improve the educational status of Chios, the birthplace of his father, and collaborated with many of its residents to that end. The gymnasium of Chios was eventually the sole inheritor of Korais's books and papers. It is also in this island that a rich library exists today bearing his name.

Serious criticism of Korais's opinions, especially on religious matters, was voiced by the patriarchate of Constantinople as well as by other religious circles (e.g. Athanasios Parios). Korais's influence was feared even after the foundation of the Greek state and his opinions were held responsible for the radical changes regarding the Orthodox Church (e.g. the unilateral declaration of the autocephalous Church of Greece in 1833). Orthodox Christians were also occasionally admonished to avoid reading Korais's books. Korais was neither an atheist nor an enemy of Christianity, but he was seriously influenced by the Enlightenment on religious issues. In this respect, his opinions were not in conformity with traditional Byzantine Orthodoxy. Yet, Korais's intention was not to abolish, but to reform and rationalize Orthodoxy. Thus, he put far more emphasis on the social utility of Orthodoxy while criticizing its otherworldly orientations. He supported the translation of the scriptures into modern Greek. He disagreed strongly with the irrational use of religion and its superstitious practices that were hindering social progress. Finally, he exhibited a bitter anticlerical spirit, since he thought that the unworthiness of many Orthodox prelates, priests, and monks was the source of many problems in Greek society.

In short, Korais left an indelible mark upon the intellectual life of Greece not only in his lifetime, but down to the 20th century. It is no wonder therefore that he has had ardent supporters and admirers as well as militant and fanatical opponents. The issues involved in these debates range from religious

Α. ΚΟΡΑΗΣ.

Adamantios Korais, Classical scholar

and linguistic to social and political. The ideological uses of Koraism in the 20th century were multiform and diverse. Korais was turned into the main opponent and enemy of various political, philosophical, philological, and Orthodox theological circles. This phenomenon constitutes further evidence, even if indirectly, of Korais's lasting impact upon and legacy to modern Greece.

VASILIOS MAKRIDES

See also Enlightenment

Biography

Born in Smyrna in 1748, the son of a merchant from Chios, Korais worked for the family business in Amsterdam from 1771 to 1777. From 1782 to 1787 he studied medicine at Montpellier but he was much more interested in Classical scholarship. In 1788 he moved to Paris and lived there for the rest of his life. His aim was to publish a Hellenic Library of Classical texts for Greek readers and to introduce the ideas of the Enlightenment into the Greek curriculum. He died in 1833.

Writings

Allilographia [Correspondence], vols 1–6, edited by K.T. Dimaras *et al.*, Athens, 1964–84

Politika Phylladia (1798-1831) tou Adamantiou Korai [Political Papers (1798–1831) of Adamantios Korais], edited by the Centre

for Neohellenic Research, Athens, 1983 (facsimile reproduction
and edition)

Korais kai Chios: Praktika Synedriou [Korais and Chios: Proceedings
of the Conference], vols 1–2, Athens, 1984

Prolegomena stous Archaious Ellines Syngrapheis [Introduction to
the Writers of Ancient Greece], vols 1–4, Athens, 1986–95

Further Reading

Bartholdy, Jakob L.S., *Bruchstücke zur nähern Kenntniss des heutigen Griechenlands gesammelt auf einer Reise im Jahre
1803–1804*, vol. 1, Berlin: Realschulbuchhandlung, 1805

Centre for Neohellenic Research, *Diimero Korai, 29 kai 30 Aprilou
1983: Prosengiseis sti glossiki theoria, ti skepsi kai to ergo tou
Korai* [Two Days on Korais, 29 and 30 April 1983: Approaches to
Korais's Language Theory, Thought, and Work], Athens, 1984

Chaconas, George, *Adamantios Korais: A Study in Greek
Nationalism*, New York: Columbia University Press, 1942,
reprinted New York: AMS Press, 1968

Clogg, Richard, "The Correspondence of Adhamantios Korais with
the British and Foreign Bible Society (1808)", *Greek Orthodox
Theological Review*, 14 (1969): pp. 65–84

Clogg, Richard (editor and translator), *The Movement for Greek
Independence, 1770–1821: A Collection of Documents*, London:
Macmillan, 1976, pp. 118–31

Daskalakis, Apostolos, *Korais kai Kodrikas: I Megali Philologiki
Diamachi ton Ellinon, 1815–1821* [Korais and Kodrikas: The
Great Greek Philological Dispute 1815–1821], Athens, 1966

Diavazo, 82 (30 November 1983): Korais issue

Dimaras, Konstantinos, *Istorika Phrontismata* [Historical Studies],
vol. 2: *Adamantios Korais*, Athens, 1996

Enepekidis, Polychronis K., *Korais, Koumas, Kalvos*, Athens, 1967

Eranos eis Adamantion Korain [Symposium on Adamantios Korais],
Athens, 1965 (articles by K. Dimaras, P. Iliou, D. Gkinis, A.
Angelou, A. Koumarianou, V. Skouvaras *et al.*)

Gourgouris, Stathis, *Dream Nation: Enlightenment, Colonization,
and the Institution of Modern Greece*, Stanford, California:
Stanford University Press, 1996, pp. 90–112

Gritsopoulos, Tasos, "O antiklirikos Korais ek tis allilographias tou
me ton Protopsaltin Smyrnis Dim. Loton" [Korais the
Anticlericalist as Seen in his Correspondence with the Protopsaltis
of Smyrna Demetrios Lotos], *Theologia*, 56 (1985): pp. 830–77

Iliou, Philippos, "Stin trochia ton Ideologon: Korais–Daunou–
Phournarakis" [On the Track of the Ideologue: Korais–Danou–
Phournarakis], *Chiaka Chronika*, 10 (1978): pp. 36–68

Iliou, Philippos, *Ideologikes Chriseis tou Koraismou ston 200 Aiona*
[Ideological Uses of Korais's Theories in the 20th Century],
Athens, 1989

Jeffreys, Michael, "Adamantios Korais" in *Culture and Nationalism
in Nineteenth-Century Eastern Europe*, edited by Roland Sussex
and J.C. Eade, Columbus, Ohio: Slavica, 1985

Karageorgos, Vasileios, *O Adamantios Korais kai i Evropi*
[Adamantios Korais and Europe], Athens, 1984

Kitromilides, Paschalis M., "Jeremy Bentham and Adamantios
Korais", *Bentham Newsletter*, 9 (June 1985): pp. 34–48

Kitromilides, Paschalis M., *Neoellinikos Diaphotismos: Oi Politikes
kai Koinonikes Idees* [The Modern Greek Enlightenment: Political
and Social Ideas], Athens, 1996, pp. 252–72 and 382–427

Mamoukas, Andreas, *Adamantios Korais: Vios kai Erga* [Adamantios
Korais: Life and Works], Athens, 1989

Metallinos, Georgios, *Paradosi kai Allotriosi* [Tradition and
Alienation], Athens, 1986, pp. 139–90

Nea Estia (Christmas 1983): Korais issue

Papaderos, Alexandros, *Metakenosis: Griechenlands kulturelle
Herausforderung durch die Aufklärung in der Sicht des Korais und
des Oikonomos*, Meisenheim am Glan: Hain, 1970

Petrou, Stamatis, *Grammata apo to Amsterdam* [Letters from
Amsterdam], Athens, 1976

Slot, B.J., "Commercial Activities of Koraïs in Amsterdam", *O
Eranistis*, 16 (1980): pp. 55–139

Thereianos, Dionysios, *Adamantios Korais*, 3 vols, Trieste: Austrian
Loyd, 1889–90, reprinted Athens: Pergamene, 1977

Tomadakis, Nikolaos, "Klassikismos, Diaphotismos kai Adamantios
Korais (Diapistoseis kai provlimata)" [Classicism, Enlightenment,
and Adamantios Korais (Discoveries and Problems)], *Mnimosyni*,
6 (1976/77): pp. 94–116

Vallianatos, E.G., *From Graikos to Hellene: Adamantios Koraes and
the Greek Revolution*, Athens: Akademia Athenon, 1987

Kornaros, Vitsentzos 1553–*c.*1614

Cretan poet

Vitsentzos Kornaros occupies a position of undisputed importance in the history of modern Greek literature and is one of
the major literary figures of the Cretan renaissance. His poetic
romance *Erotokritos* draws on the plot conventions of
medieval romance but tempers the action and characterization
to Renaissance modes of thought, while elevating the Cretan
dialect in which it is written to a sophisticated literary tool of
great expressiveness and musicality. Kornaros is also widely
believed to be the author of the anonymous religious drama
The Sacrifice of Abraham, which exhibits a number of verbal
and stylistic similarities with *Erotokritos*. There is now general
agreement among scholars that Kornaros, who gives brief
autobiographical details at the end of *Erotokritos*, was a
member of the Hellenized Veneto-Cretan noble family of
Cornaro (or Corner), which had been established in Crete since
the 15th century. Vitsentzos (or Vicenzo) was born in the
village of Trapezonta, near Siteia, in 1553. In 1590 he married
Marietta Zeno, in the capital Kastro where he was by then
living, and they had two daughters. His brother Andrea was a
major intellectual figure in the Crete of his time, author of an
unpublished history of Crete and founder of the academy of
the Stravaganti, of which Vitsentzos was also a member.
Vitsentzos occupied various legal and administrative offices,
making the kind of contributions to public life that were
expected of a member of his class. He died in 1613/14.

Erotokritos was completed within the last 20 years or so of
Kornaros's life. It is preserved in an illustrated manuscript,
written in the Ionian islands in 1710 (now in the British
Library), and in printed editions from 1713 onwards. The
poem draws its plot from the French romance *Paris et Vienne*,
by Pierre de la Cypède. The immediate model of the Cretan
poem is an Italian prose version of the romance, first printed
in 1482. Kornaros completely alters the setting and atmosphere of his Italian source, by removing the Christian context
and transferring the story to ancient Athens, but with a deliberately diachronic (or rather anachronistic) perspective. The
heroine, Aretousa, is the daughter of the king and queen of
Athens, while in the tournament which occupies the second of
the five books the participants include a prince of Byzantium
and noblemen from various parts of the east Mediterranean
world: Crete, Cyprus, Naxos, Patras, Mytilene, Methoni,
Koroni, Nauplia, Egripos (Euboea), Macedonia, etc. Many of
these places had (or once had) a particular importance in
Venice's colonial empire. There is also a Karamanite (a Turk),
who challenges the Cretan Charidimos to a duel, a possible
allusion to the battle of Lepanto (1571).

The poem consists of 9982 lines of couplet-rhymed 15-syllable verse, divided into five parts or books. The plot is articulated after the manner of a five-act Neoclassical drama (Alexiou refers to its "daring mixture of genres"); almost half of the poem consists of the direct speech of the characters, although the story is told by an omniscient narrator who is the poet's mouthpiece. The hero Rotokritos (his name appears most commonly in this form) is the son of the king's counsellor; his love for Aretousa and the obstacles he has to overcome in his quest to prove himself a worthy match for the princess constitute the main axes of the plot. Book 1 is about the gradual development of his love (punctuated by the warnings of his friend Polydoros), and the response of Aretousa, first for an unknown admirer who serenades her, and then, with the discovery of Rotokritos' identity, her growing passion for the young man himself, despite the strong disapproval of her nurse Frosyni. In book 2 a tournament organized by the king partly to entertain his daughter and partly to find her a suitable husband of royal birth (the prince of Byzantium is the favoured suitor), provides Rotokritos with the opportunity to prove himself. He is victorious, after overcoming various opponents in the jousts and finally defeating the Cypriot Kypridimos, who has declared himself implacably opposed to Eros. The way is thus open for Rotokritos (in book 3) to persuade his father to approach the king on his behalf. However, the king will not hear of a marriage to a commoner and angrily banishes Rotokritos, who takes his leave of Aretousa with mutual declarations of eternal love. In book 4 Athens is at war with the neighbouring kingdom of Vlachia. Rotokritos, disguised as a Negro, comes to the king's aid in the battle, and saves the kingdom by killing the Vlach champion in singlehanded combat. He is gravely wounded but, in the final part, slowly recovers and is offered a reward. Still in disguise he visits Aretousa in the cell in which her suspicious father has confined her. He tests her fidelity by alleging that her beloved Rotokritos is dead, but finally reveals his true identity. Their union is blessed by the king and the story ends with the celebration of their marriage.

This typical romance plot of separated lovers and eventual reunion derives much of its attraction from its poetic diction. Recurring imagery of fire and organic growth elaborates the love theme. Some scholars have found it long-winded and pedestrian, overlooking the subtlety of the metaphors and similes, the rhetorical construction, and the complex network of allusion and irony. Echoes of Ariosto and the Petrarchistic conceits of Italian Renaissance poetry abound, but the "naturalness" of the poem's language and style has led some scholars to see affinities with Greek folk poetry. It is certainly true that, after it was first printed in Venice in 1713, it circulated widely in the Greek-speaking world and became extremely popular. It is often claimed, probably with some exaggeration, that many Cretans knew the entire poem by heart. What is certain is that particular episodes are still frequently sung to a traditional tune, and the poem is held in great affection by the Cretan people; it also seems to have influenced the popular tradition of improvised couplets (*mantinades*). However, its reception has extended well beyond Crete: Solomos was familiar with it and assimilated its style in his own poetry, particularly in "The Cretan", which contains echoes of the episode featuring the Cretan in book 2. An adaptation into more learned language was published by Dionysios Foteinos in 1818. Angelos Sikelianos, George Seferis, Nikos Kazantzakis, and Yiannis Ritsos are among 20th-century poets who have exploited the poem creatively in their own work (Seferis also wrote an important essay on it). There have also been successful musical settings of *Erotokritos*, as well as theatrical adaptations.

The Sacrifice of Abraham, if it is indeed the work of Kornaros, was written before *Erotokritos*, but after 1586, the date of the first edition of the Italian play *Lo Isach*, by Luigi Grotto, on which it is based. Like most works of Cretan renaissance literature, it is in rhymed 15-syllable verse. The subject matter of the play is the biblical story of God's testing of Abraham's faith by the commandment that he sacrifice his only son Isaac (Genesis 22). The action is spread over at least six days: it begins with the angel's announcement to Abraham of God's command, progresses to the dramatic scene on the mountain, and ends with the return home and the joyful family reunion. The Cretan play improves on the dramatic structure of its model, gives more emphasis to the nature of Abraham's inner struggle, and enhances the roles of the servants. Also notable is the emphasis on family relations, seen in the characterization of Isaac: his mature understanding of his father's dilemma and eventual compliance in the sacrifice, and his concern for his mother. Sarah is depicted with particular tenderness, most notably in her lament for her son, which exhibits a dialogue with popular motifs and themes. The Cretan work represents a sustained attempt to interpret the biblical story for contemporary man. The playwright was clearly interested in theological matters and may have known the work of Origen. The play, which could be classified as a *tragedia di lieto fin*, is not divided into acts and scenes in the extant witnesses (unlike Grotto's play), but none the less has a firm dramatic structure. It is preserved in two manuscripts and in a series of printed editions from 1713 onwards (an edition of 1696 has not survived). As the frequency of these editions shows, it was one of the most successful vernacular literary texts of the 18th and 19th centuries. It was also translated into Turkish in 1783 (printed 1800), for the use of Turkish-speaking Orthodox Christians.

DAVID HOLTON

See also Renaissance (Veneto-Cretan)

Biography

Born in 1553 in the village of Trapezonta, near Siteia in Crete, Kornaros belonged to the Veneto-Cretan family of Cornaro. Both he and his brother Andrea were major figures in the Cretan renaissance of the 16th century. Vitsentzos is the author of the poetic romance *Erotokritos* and possibly also of the religious drama *The Sacrifice of Abraham*. He died c.1614.

Writings

Erotokritos, edited by Stylianos Alexiou, Athens, 1980, shorter version, 1985 (the standard edition)

Erotocritos: circa 1640 AD, translated by Theodore P. Stephanides, Athens: Papazissis, 1984

Erotokritos, edited by Cristina Stevanoni, Verona: Biblioteca Civica, 1995 (facsimile of the 1713 edition)

I Thysia tou Avraam [attributed to Kornaros], edited by W.F. Bakker and A.F. van Gemert, Herakleion, 1996

Further Reading

Bakker, W.F., *The Sacrifice of Abraham: The Cretan Biblical Drama "I Thysia tou Avraam" and Western European and Greek Tradition*, Birmingham: Centre for Byzantine Studies, 1978

Bakker, W.F., "The Sacrifice of Abraham: A First Approach to Its Poetics", *Journal of Modern Greek Studies*, 6 (1988): pp. 81–95

Garland, Linda, "*The Sacrifice of Abraham* Translated from the Medieval Greek with an Introduction", *Modern Greek Studies Yearbook*, 7 (1991): pp. 365–416

Holton, David, "*Erotokritos* and Greek Tradition" in *The Greek Novel AD 1-1985*, edited by Roderick Beaton, London and New York: Croom Helm, 1988

Holton, David (editor), *Literature and Society in Renaissance Crete*, Cambridge and New York: Cambridge University Press, 1991

Holton, David, *Erotokritos*, Bristol: Bristol Classical Press, 1991

Mavromates, Giannes K., *To protypo tou "Erotokritou"* [The Prototype of the *Erotokritos*], Ioannina, 1982

Panagiotakes, Nikolaos M., *O Poiitis tou "Erotokritou" kai alla Venetokritika Meletimata* [The Author of the *Erotokritos*, and Other Essays on the Venetian Domination], Herakleion, 1989

Philippides, Dia M.L., *I Thysia tou Avraam ston ypologisti: The Sacrifice of Abraham on the Computer*, Athens: Hermes, 1986

Philippides, Dia M.L., "Literary Detection in the *Erotokritos* and the *Sacrifice of Abraham*", *Literary and Linguistic Computing*, 3/1 (1988): pp. 1–11

Ricks, David, "The Style of Erotokritos", *Cretan Studies*, 1 (1988): pp. 239–56

Sherrard, Philip, *The Wound of Greece: Studies in Neo-Hellenism*, London: Collings, 1978; New York: St Martin's Press, 1979, especially "The Figure of Aretousa"

Kosmas the Aetolian, St 1714–1779

Orthodox missionary and martyr

St Kosmas the Aetolian is called "equal to the Apostles" and "teacher of the Greek nation" for his contribution to the spiritual and national awakening of the Greek people in the late 18th century. Not officially canonized by the Orthodox Church until 1961, Kosmas has long been venerated in Greece, Albania, and the southern Balkans as one of the "new martyrs of the Turkish yoke". Through his missionary work Kosmas promoted the study of the Orthodox Christian religion and the Greek language. In this way Kosmas helped prepare the Greeks to overthrow the Ottoman Turks and establish their own independent state in the 19th century.

The son of weavers, Kosmas was a native of the Aetolian region of northwestern Greece, in the vicinity of Arta. He pursued an education for himself, eventually enrolling in the Theological Academy on Mount Athos in 1749. Although Kosmas became a hieromonk at the monastery of Philotheou, he sought and was given permission by his fellow monks and patriarch Seraphim II of Constantinople (1757–61) to leave the monastery and become an itinerant preacher. He wanted to bring his knowledge of the gospel, the Church Fathers, and the spiritual life of Mount Athos to the common people.

Attracting huge crowds as he travelled, Kosmas preached using the vernacular Greek language so that everyone could understand his message. But he encouraged the establishment of local schools for the study of the Orthodox Christian faith and the more archaic Greek of the scriptures and the Church. Kosmas is remembered as saying: "My beloved children in Christ, bravely and fearlessly preserve our holy faith and the language of our Fathers, because both of these characterize our most beloved homeland, and without them our nation is destroyed" (Vaporis, 1977, p.146). Kosmas did his best to address the economic, social, and religious pressures which enticed many Orthodox Christians to convert to Islam. He himself lived in apostolic poverty and defended the poor and women against exploitation and abuse. Although his preaching threatened the status quo, Kosmas did manage to attract some wealthy patrons who contributed ecclesiastical items for the benefit of the poor: religious books, prayer ropes, little crosses, baptismal fonts, head coverings, beard combs, candles, bread, and boiled wheat. Kosmas would ask the people to prepare for his visits by confessing their sins, fasting, and holding a vigil service. When he arrived he would typically ask that the sacrament of Holy Unction be performed, then he would preach, and finally the faithful would partake of the *antidoron* (blessed bread) and *kollyva* (boiled wheat consumed at memorial services) forgiving the living and the dead. Because of the crowds, Kosmas often preached outdoors. He would ask the people to set up a wooden cross at the spot where he would preach, and stood on a portable footstool. The cross would remain at the site after he left. According to his disciple and hagiographer Sapphiros Christodoulidis (d. 1856), Kosmas began to effect miracle cures through his preaching. But the power of the holy man could curse as well as bless – Christodoulidis also reports harm coming to those who wanted to hurt the saint or who were disrespectful of his teaching and counsel.

The content of his teaching stressed religious education, repentance, forgiveness, fasting, humility, the dignity of women and marriage, love of God and of one's neighbour. He also brought the Athonite practice of the Jesus prayer to the common people, advising them to pray at all times: "Lord Jesus Christ, Son and *Logos* of the living God, by the intercessions of the Theotokos and all the saints, have mercy on me the sinner and unworthy servant of Thee" (Cavarnos, 1985, p.71). He discouraged Christians from doing business on Sundays, which brought him into conflict with local merchants.

The saint's teachings, prophecies, and martyrdom cannot be understood apart from the political situation of the Greeks under the Tourkokratia in the late 18th century. As much as he preached love, Kosmas fought to promote the continuation of Greek identity by stressing the two things that set the Greeks apart from their neighbours – Roman Catholics, Jews, and Turkish Muslims: the Greek language and the Orthodox Christian religion. He stood firmly within the tradition that saw the rule of the Turks as a chastisement for the sins of the Greeks, but one in which God's mercy was manifest: "And why did God bring the Turks and not some other race? For our good, because the other nations would have caused detriment to our Faith" (Cavarnos, p.23). In fact, Kosmas always asked for permission to preach from both the local bishop and the Turkish authorities as he travelled from town to town. Although his reputation as a holy man earned him admirers across religious lines, it was easy for the authorities to believe that Kosmas and his followers were aligned with the Russian government in an effort to free the Orthodox Christian population of the Balkans from Ottoman rule. He spoke often of Antichrist and the end of the world, and predicted the liberation of Greece within three generations of the one then living. It is no surprise that St Kosmas met his end through martyrdom at the hands of Turkish executioners. While visiting an Albanian town called Kolikontasi or Kalinkontasi he was seized by the agents of the local governor, Kurt Pasha. On 24 August 1779 Kosmas was hanged en route to the governor's residence in Berati (Berat), Albania. "Thus the thrice-blessed Cosmas, that great benefactor of men, became worthy of receiving, at the age of sixty-five, a double crown from the Lord, one as a Peer of the Apostles and the other as a holy Martyr" (Christodoulidis, in Cavarnos, p.45). His body was thrown naked into a river with a stone weighted around his neck. For three days the local Christians searched for the body, until a priest from the monastery of the Presentation of the Most Holy Theotokos near Kolikontasi miraculously discovered it floating upright in the river. His body was then buried at the priest's monastery. A church in his honour was later built at the site, with the encouragement of the vizier Ali Pasha of Tepeleni, whose rise to power the saint had prophesied 30 years earlier.

St Kosmas the Aetolian has made an enormous impact on the national and spiritual consciousness of the Greek people. In the 19th century the Greeks won their national independence and experienced a spiritual revival led by itinerant preachers inspired by the saint's example. He continues to inspire both piety and scholarship – one bibliography published in 1968 lists over 30 books and 600 articles devoted to St Kosmas (Cavarnos, p.27), although works in the English language remain scarce. Thirteen of his letters survive, as well as the sermons recorded by his disciples collectively called "Didachai" ("Teachings"), which were read in churches during his lifetime and after his death. His feast is celebrated on the anniversary of his martyrdom, 24 August.

CONSTANTINA SCOURTIS

See also Neomartyrs

Biography

Born in 1714 near Arta in northwestern Greece, Kosmas was self-taught until he enrolled in the Academy on Mount Athos in 1749. He became a priest monk at the monastery of Philotheou, but left the monastery to become an itinerant preacher. He travelled all over Greece preaching and promoting an awareness of Greek identity. He was hanged by local Turkish authorities in Albania in 1779 and is revered as a martyr.

Further Reading

Cavarnos, Constantine, *St Cosmas Aitolos*, 3rd edition, Belmont, Massachusetts: Institute for Byzantine and Modern Greek Studies, 1985

Christodoulidis, Sapphiros, *Akolouthia kai Bios tou en Hagiois Patros hemon Kosma tou Hieromartyros kai Isapostolou* [Service and Life of our Father among the Saints Kosmas the Martyr, Equal of the Apostles], Venice, 1814; 2nd edition, Patras, 1869

Sardeles, Kostas, *Kosma Aitolou: Analytike Bibliographia, 1765–1973* [Analytical Bibliography of Kosmas the Aetolian 1765–1973], Athens, 1974

Vaporis, Nomikos Michael, *Father Kosmas, the Apostle of the Poor: The Life of St Kosmas Aitolon Together with an English Translation of His Teaching and Letters*, Brookline, Massachusetts: Holy Cross Orthodox Press, 1977

Koukouzeles, St John

Musician of the 13th-14th centuries

St John Koukouzeles is honoured by the Greek Orthodox Church as the "second source" (after St John of Damascus) of its liturgical music. Far from being mere hagiographic hyperbole, this appellation accurately reflects the decisive impact of his labours as a maistor (musical director), composer, hymnographer, scribe, editor, teacher, and theorist during the late 13th and early 14th centuries. Information about his life and career may be derived mainly from two groups of sources: the very large number of musical manuscripts containing his work, the first of which date from the beginning of the 14th century; and the copies of a late and somewhat problematic *Life*, the oldest manuscript of which (Thessalonica, Vlatadon 46) dates from the second half of the 16th century. From the former we learn that his surname was Papadopoulos, that he studied with Xenos Korones under the cantor John Glykes, and that his name was changed to Ioannikios when he became a monk of the Great Schema. The *Life* contains none of these details, but begins by relating how he was born in Dyrrachium to a Slav mother, was taken to study chant in Constantinople, acquired the surname Koukouzeles (supposedly from the words for beans and cabbage), and composed a setting of Psalms 134 and 135 (the "Polyeleos") entitled *Voulgara* on a return visit to his mother. The remainder of his *Life* covers his removal to the monastery of the Great Lavra on Mount Athos, his construction of a chapel dedicated to the Archangels (still extant) outside the monastery walls for the practice of hesychasm, the miracles he experienced, and his death. Modern scholars, however, tend to view the *Life* with mild to extreme scepticism. In addition to containing improbable episodes and dubious etymologies, it is suspiciously similar to that of Gregory the Domestikos, a cantor from the Great Lavra who shares the feast day of 1 October with his contemporary Koukouzeles. Furthermore, Koukouzeles seems never to have written a Polyeleos *Voulgara*, the story being derived from the misattribution of a single Psalm verse by Glykes (Jakovlević, 1982). Nevertheless, most scholars have not followed Erich Trapp (1987) and Simon Karas (1992) in their near total rejection of the *Life*, choosing instead to accept with caution its story of Koukouzeles' monastic vocation.

Regardless of the controversies over his biography, the quality, variety, and wide distribution of Koukouzeles's works are more than sufficient to secure his special place in Byzantine musical history. To Byzantine musical theory he made two substantial contributions: the didactic chant "*Ison, oligon ...*" (known popularly as the *Mega Ison*), a revision of a similar work by Glykes illustrating the standard repertory of melodic figures (*cheironomiai*); and a diagram (the *trochos*, "wheel") illustrating the relations between the modes with a series of concentric rings surrounded by four smaller circles bearing his surname. Koukouzeles also re-edited the entire central repertory of chants for the three Byzantine Eucharistic liturgies and the Palestinian Divine Office of St Sabas into three volumes. To the traditional anonymous melodies of the Eirmologion and the Sticherarion, two venerable collections of hymns (*eirmoi* and *stichera*) for the Sabaïtic offices, he made only relatively minor revisions. Rather, his most distinctive and influential work is to be found in the Akolouthiai or "Orders of Service", a new type of musical manuscript that, for the first time, combined under a single cover all the ordinary chants and psalmodic propers of the Byzantine monastic offices and Eucharistic liturgies. Some copies of the Akolouthiai – of which dozens survive, the earliest being MS Athens 2458 in the National Library of Greece, dated "1336" – begin with a section of theoretical and didactic works. After these one inevitably finds a stylistically broad variety of traditional and newly composed chants, including: anonymous and, for the most part, previously unnotated syllabic, semi-florid, and melismatic melodies, some of which may be supplied with regional (*Agiosophitikon*, *Thessalikon*, etc.) or functional (monastic, cathedral, etc.) variants; and a much larger body of highly individual and often virtuosic chants by Koukouzeles and his late Byzantine colleagues.

It is among the newly composed chants of the Akolouthiai that one finds the melodies on which Koukouzeles' reputation as a composer rests. Encompassing many liturgical genres, these works include verses for the psalms of the all-night vigil, hymns for the eucharistic liturgies, festal hymns – both traditional and new texts, including those from his own pen – for the liturgy of the Hours, and optional codas to traditional hymns and responsories. A great number of these compositions are in the extremely florid "beautified" or "kalophonic" idiom, which is generally characterized by vocal virtuosity, but could also include textual troping, highly melismatic passages, and even textless vocalizations on nonsense syllables ("teretisms"), some of which exist as independent pieces (*kratemata*) bearing evocative names (e.g. *viola*). Although this style of composing antedated him by at least two generations, Koukouzeles brought it to maturity and then succeeded in disseminating it widely through his compilation of the Akolouthiai. The result was what Edward V. Williams has fittingly described as a "Byzantine *ars nova*", whereby Koukouzeles established the stylistic parameters for all subsequent composers of Greek Orthodox chant.

From the 14th to the early 19th century Koukouzeles's works were continuously copied both as originally notated and in florid realizations ("exegeses") by post-Byzantine cantors. His continued popularity is also reflected by the dissemination of his *Life* in multiple recensions and the early adaptation of some of his compositions for performance in Church Slavonic. In the early 19th century a large number of his works were transcribed melismatically into the "New Method" of Byzantine notation by Chourmouzios the Archivist and other exegetes. Perhaps due to their extreme length after being subjected to "exegesis", only a fraction of these were subsequently published, the most prominent of which are his chants for the vesting and entrance of a bishop, the *Mega Ison*, a single Sunday communion verse, and his farced verses for Psalm 103 ("the Great Anoixantaria"). In recent years, however, Greek scholar-performers have begun to explore the unpublished works of Koukouzeles, resulting in an increasing number of recordings and publications.

ALEXANDER LINGAS

See also Hymnography

Biography

According to an anonymous *Life* (of dubious authority), John was born in Dyrrachium to a Slav mother in the second half of the 13th century. Taken to Constantinople to study chant, he acquired the name Koukouzeles. He then moved to the Great Lavra monastery on Mount Athos, where he died. He is regarded as the "second source" (after St John of Damascus) of liturgical music for the Greek Orthodox Church and worked as musical director, composer, hymnographer, scribe, editor, teacher, and theorist.

Recording
Ioannis Koukouzèlis: Le Maïstor byzantin, Greek Byzantine Choir directed by Lycourgas Angelopoulos, Jade compact disc JAD C 129

Further Reading
Conomos, Dimitri E., *The Late Byzantine and Slavonic Communion Cycle: Liturgy and Music*, Washington, D.C.: Dumbarton Oaks, 1985

Devai, Gabor, "The Musical Study of Koukouzeles in a Fourteenth-Century Manuscript", *Acta Antiqua Academiae Scientarum Hungaricae*, 6 (1958): pp. 213–35

Jakovlević, Andrija, "O Megas Maistor Ioannis Koukouzelis Papadopoulos" [The Great Music Director Ioannis Koukouzelis Papadopoulos] (with a summary in English), *Kleronomia*, 14 (1982): pp. 357–74

Lingas, Alexander, "Hesychasm and Psalmody" in *Mount Athos and Byzantine Monasticism*, edited by Anthony Bryer and Mary Cunningham, Aldershot, Hampshire: Variorum, 1996

Touliatos, Diane, "Medieval Balkan Music and Ioannes Koukouzeles", *Kleronomia*, 17 (1985): pp. 377–82

Trapp, Erich, "Critical Notes on the Biography of John Koukouzeles, Byzantine Hymnographer", *Byzantine and Modern Greek Studies*, 11 (1987): pp. 223–29

Troelsgård, C. (editor), *Byzantine Chant: Tradition and Reform*, vol. 2: *1397–1433*, Athens: Danish Institute at Athens, 1997

Williams, Edward V., "John Koukouzeles' Reform of Byzantine Chanting for Great Vespers in the Fourteenth Century" (dissertation), New Haven, Connecticut: Yale University, 1968

Williams, Edward V., "A Byzantine *ars nova*: The Fourteenth-century Reforms of John Koukouzeles in the Chanting of Great Vespers" in *Aspects of the Balkans: Continuity and Change*, edited by Henrik Birnbaum and Spiros Vryonis, Jr, The Hague: Mouton, 1972

Kritoboulos, Michael

Historian of the 15th century

Michael Kritoboulos of Imbros was one of the four 15th-century Byzantine historians (the others are Laonikos Chalkokondyles, George Sphrantzes, and Doukas) who left an account of the fall of Constantinople to the Turks in 1453. His approach of making the rise of the Turks the main theme of his history parallels that of Chalkokondyles. Kritoboulos, however, stands out for his glorification of Mehmet the Conqueror and for his attempt to find an accommodation with the Turks.

Very little is known about Kritoboulos's life, apart from his career in the Ottoman administration after 1453. The original family name of Kritoboulos must have been Kritopoulos, but was later changed in a classicizing fashion to Kritoboulos. It is possible that the historian was identical with the religious writer Michael Kritopoulos, who composed an unpublished homily on the Passion of Christ. The Italian traveller and humanist Cyriac of Ancona, who visited the island of Imbros in 1444, called Kritoboulos a "most learned and noble man". Kritoboulos seems to have belonged to those strata of the Greek political and intellectual elite who readily accepted and were willing to serve the new Ottoman masters. After the Ottoman conquest of Constantinople, Mehmet II the Conqueror (1451–81) appointed Kritoboulos governor of the island of Imbros. In this capacity Kritoboulos negotiated the withdrawal of a papal fleet that had occupied the neighbouring islands of Lemnos and Samothrace in 1457. He was also involved in the expulsion of the Genoese from the island of Lemnos in 1260, which Mehmet then conferred briefly as an appanage on Demetrios Palaiologos, brother of the last Byzantine emperor Constantine XI Palaiologos (1449–53). When the Venetians besieged Imbros in 1466, Kritoboulos withdrew to Constantinople. He survived the plague in the following year, but seems to have lost Mehmet II's favour and to have withdrawn to a monastery on Mount Athos.

Surviving in a single manuscript in Istanbul (Topkapi Sarayi, Cod. G.Ī.3), the history of Kritoboulos covers events in the period 1451–67 and is an important source on the transition of power from the Byzantine to the Ottoman empire. It is dedicated personally to Mehmet the Conqueror and its primary focus is on the Turks. In a way that is analogous to his career in the Ottoman administration, Kritoboulos sought to emphasize elements of continuity with Byzantium. Indeed, he portrayed Mehmet the Conqueror, the main hero of the history, as a Byzantine emperor reborn. In his history Mehmet II bears the Byzantine imperial titles of *basileus* ("king") and *autokrator* ("emperor"), and the historian has ascribed to him patterns of behaviour expected from a Byzantine emperor. In order to make him a worthy successor of the Byzantine rulers, Kritoboulos emphasized Mehmet's interests in Classical antiquity during the sultan's visit to Athens and Troy. The preface to the history compares the Conqueror directly to Alexander the Great and to the emperors of Rome. The characteristics attributed to Mehmet II include centuries-old elements of Byzantine imperial ideology and propaganda, such as the ruler's foresight and care for his subjects, his philanthropy, his piety, his justice, his generosity, etc. Even the vindication of his expansionist wars corresponds to the Byzantine concept of the just war. Kritoboulos emphasized that the enemies of Mehmet II were always first to provoke armed conflicts, while the sultan's role in war was mainly responsive. In his description of the fall of Constantinople Kritoboulos stresses the sultan's mercy towards the inhabitants and praised him for rebuilding and repopulating the capital. If anyone deserved Kritoboulos's critical judgement, it was the Italians and primarily the Venetians. Unlike most of his Greek contemporaries, however, Kritoboulos despised the Latins, not for religious reasons, but because they were the main enemies of the Turks for naval hegemony in the Aegean basin.

Nevertheless, Kritoboulos retained much respect for his fellow Greeks and for Hellenic culture. He found it necessary to apologize to his contemporaries and to future readers for putting the Turks and their sultan in the centre of his history. He admired the last Byzantine emperor Constantine XI Palaiologos and the heroic defence of Constantinople that he led. Furthermore, he took pride in the fact that his work was written in Greek and he pointed out that this was a language widely spoken and studied during his time. For this reason Kritoboulos thought that his history would have a much wider readership than contemporary Ottoman chronicles. He wrote in a classicizing style and imitated Thucydides' *History of the Peloponnesian Wars*. This forced antiquarianism reveals the unceasing importance of the study of Hellenic culture for those Greek thinkers and literati who worked after the fall of Byzantium. Even people like Kritoboulos, who sought accommodation with the Ottomans, drew their literary models and their sense of cultural identity in the distant Hellenic past.

Kritoboulos blamed the demise of Byzantium partly on the bad qualities of its emperors. However, he found the chief explanation, and perhaps even some consolation, in the historical law of the inevitable rise and fall of states. This philosophical consideration not only exonerated Kritoboulos's compatriots who lived through the fall of the Byzantine empire and became adapted to the Ottoman regime, but also held certain, albeit small, hope for the future.

DIMITER G. ANGELOV

See also Historiography

Biography

Little is known of the life of Kritoboulos, who was living on the island of Imbros when Cyriac of Ancona visited him in 1444. After the fall of Constantinople in 1453 he joined the Ottoman administration and Mehmet II made him governor of Imbros in 1456. Ten years later he returned to Constantinople, where he died. His history of the years 1451–67 is written from the Ottoman perspective.

Further Reading

Grecu, V., "Kritobulos aus Imbros", *Byzantinoslavica*, 18 (1957): pp. 1–17

Hunger, Herbert, *Die hochsprachliche profane Literatur der Byzantiner*, vol. 1, Munich: Beck, 1978

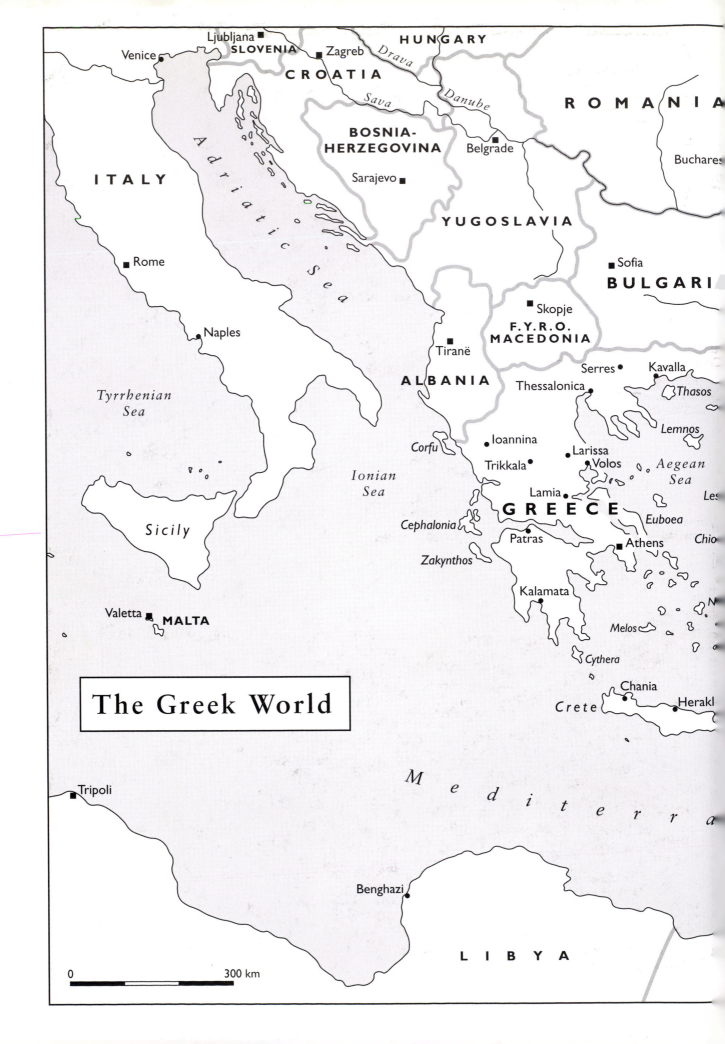

The Greek World